Baseball america®
2011 ALMANAC

BASEBALL AMERICA INC. · DURHAM, N.C.

BaseBall america
2011 ALMANAC

A COMPREHENSIVE REVIEW OF THE 2010 SEASON, FEATURING STATISTICS AND COMMENTARY

Editor
WILL LINGO

Assistant Editors
BEN BADLER, JIM CALLIS, J.J. COOPER, MATT EDDY, CONOR GLASSEY,
AARON FITT, JOSH LEVENTHAL, JOHN MANUEL, NATHAN RODE, JIM SHONERD

Database and Application Development
BRENT LEWIS

Contributing Writer
TOM HAUDRICOURT

Photo Editor
NATHAN RODE

Editorial Assistants
BUBBA BROWN, ALEXIS BRUDNICKI,
TYLER JETT, MICHAEL LEMAIRE

Design & Production
SARA HIATT MCDANIEL, TIFFANY SCHWARZ, LINWOOD WEBB

Cover Photo
TIM LINCECUM BY BILL NICHOLS

BaseBall america
PRESIDENT/PUBLISHER: LEE FOLGER
EDITORS IN CHIEF: WILL LINGO, JOHN MANUEL
EXECUTIVE EDITOR: JIM CALLIS
DESIGN & PRODUCTION DIRECTOR: SARA HIATT MCDANIEL
TECHNOLOGY MANAGER: BRENT LEWIS

DISTRIBUTED BY SIMON & SCHUSTER
ISBN-13: 978-1-932391-33-6

STATISTICS PROVIDED BY MAJOR LEAGUE BASEBALL ADVANCED MEDIA
AND COMPILED BY BASEBALL AMERICA

EDITOR'S NOTE: Major league statistics are based on final, unofficial 2010 averages. >> The organization statistics, which begin on page 43, include all players who participated in at least one game during the 2010 season. >> Pitchers' batting statistics are not included, nor are the pitching statistics of field players who pitched in less than two games. >> For players who played with more than one team in the same league, the player's cumulative statistics appear on the line immediately after the player's statistics with each team. >> Innings pitched have been rounded off to the nearest full inning.

TABLE OF CONTENTS

DIAMOND IMAGES

Stephen Strasburg generated excitement for the Nationals before going down with an injury

MAJOR LEAGUES 6

ORGANIZATION STATISTICS 43

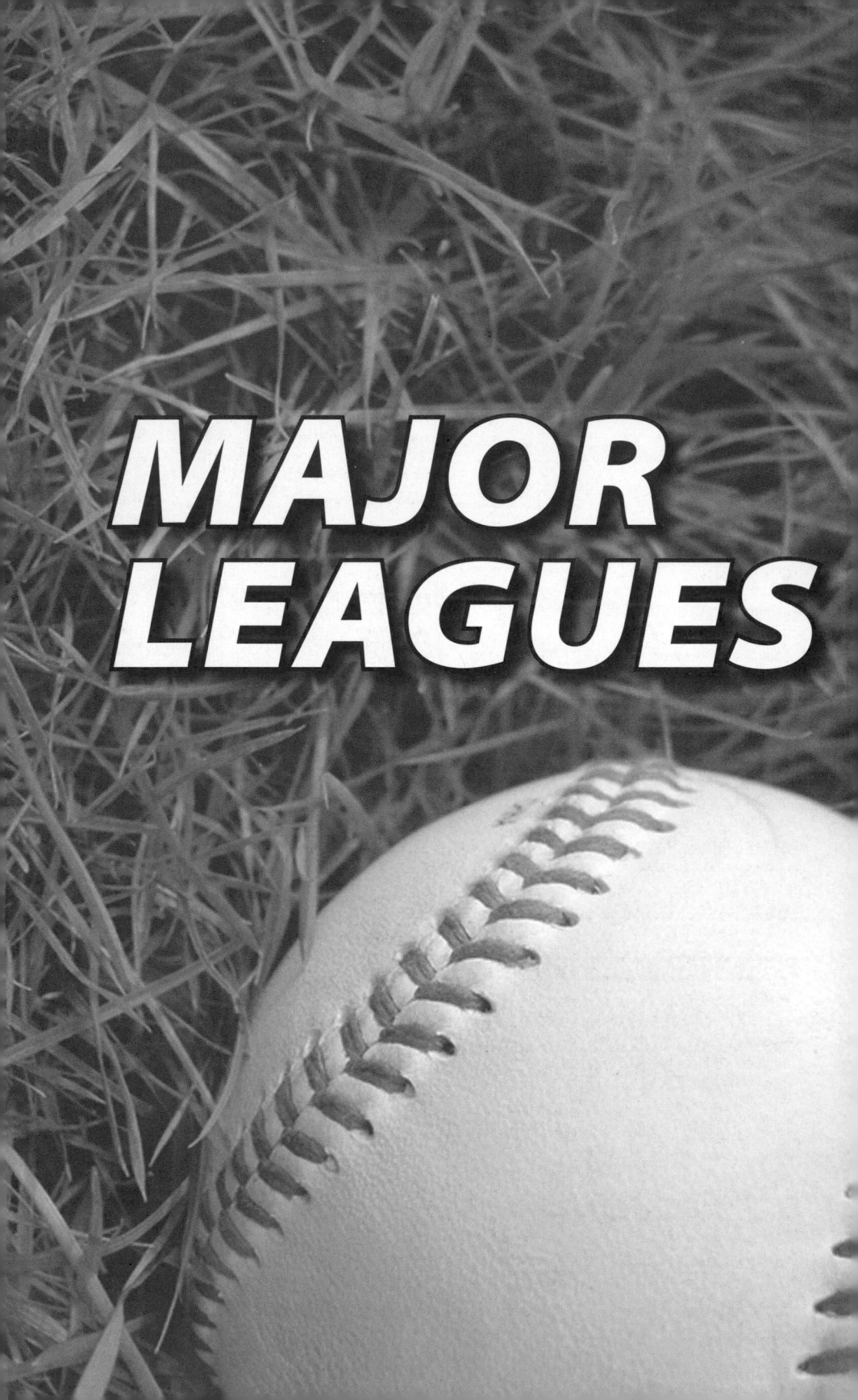

No-hit games reign in 'pitcher perfect' season

BY TOM HAUDRICOURT

In The Year of the Pitcher, it was the perfect game with the imperfect call that dominated the headlines.

Tigers righthander Armando Galarraga, an otherwise obscure pitcher who did not make the club out of spring training, retired the first 26 Indians batters he faced on June 2, leaving him one out shy of the season's third perfect game. Replays showed that Galarraga recorded that out on a close play at first base, but veteran umpire Jim Joyce missed the call, costing the pitcher a spot in the record book.

Galarraga induced a soft groundball from Cleveland's Jason Donald and then raced to first base to take the feed from first baseman Miguel Cabrera. Galarraga barely beat the runner to the bag, but Joyce saw it differently and called Donald safe.

"I just cost that kid a perfect game," a teary-eyed Joyce said after watching the replay later. "It was the biggest call of my career and I blew it."

Beyond creating more cries for expanded replay, the incident became a lesson in humility, grace and class. The next day, with Joyce working the plate at Detroit's Comerica Park, Galarraga brought out the lineup card and the two shook hands and exchanged pats on the back in an emotional scene that drew cheers from the crowd.

Asked after the game about his reaction to Joyce's blown call robbing him of baseball immortality, the remarkably calm Galarraga replied, "Nobody's perfect."

Perhaps not, but Galarraga would have been that night if not for one botched call.

The balance of power shifted back to the mound in 2010. As a collective, big league teams scored 5 percent fewer runs and hit 8.5 percent fewer homers than they had in 2009. Two pitchers even managed to throw perfect games.

On a Mother's Day for the ages in Oakland, lefthander Dallas Braden retired all 27 Tampa Bay batters he faced as the Athletics topped the Rays 4-0. The May 9 contest was an emotional day for Braden, whose mother Jodie died of cancer in 2001. His grandmother, Peggy Lindsey, was there to watch the historic event.

It was the second time in less than a year that the Rays had a perfect game pitched against them.

Armando Galarraga came within one out of tossing the season's third perfect game

White Sox lefty Mark Buehrle victimized them the previous July. Tampa Bay's hitting foibles were especially unlikely in light of their high-powered offense—they finished third in the American League in runs scored in 2010 and fifth in '09.

The second perfect game of the season did not come from an unlikely source like Braden. Roy Halladay, the 2003 AL Cy Young Award winner coveted so highly by Philadelphia that the Phillies jettisoned Cliff Lee to make room, tossed the 20th perfect game in major league history on May 29 in Miami. It marked the first time that two perfect games were authored in the same season, and the total would have been three if not for Joyce's unfortunate lapse in judgment.

Halladay, a 13-year veteran, was not done making history. Not only would he go on to win 21 games for the Phillies, but in the first playoff start of his career, "Doc" pitched a no-hitter in Game One of the National League Division Series against the Reds, the highest-scoring team in the league.

Rockies righthander Ubaldo Jimenez kicked The Year of the Pitcher into gear on April 18 by tossing the first no-hitter in club history in Atlanta.

"It's every pitcher's dream to be out there for nine innings and throw a no-hitter," said Jimenez, who pitched exclusively from the stretch after walking his sixth hitter in the fifth inning. "After the seventh inning, I was like, 'Whoa, there's only two innings left. I have a chance to do this.' "

The same night that Jimenez throttled the Braves, the Cardinals and Mets played 18 scoreless innings in a game New York finally won 2-1 in 20 innings. St. Louis second baseman Felipe Lopez tossed a scoreless inning in that game, though fellow position player Joe Mather didn't fare as well, surrendering both New York runs.

Who says you have to have pinpoint control to toss a no-hitter? Diamondbacks righthander Edwin Jackson walked eight batters, including seven in the first three innings, in his June 25 start against—guess who?—Tampa Bay. Jackson completed his flawed gem in 149 pitches, the highest total in the majors in five years.

After being no-hit for the third time in less than a year, the Rays finally turned the tables on July 26 when flame-throwing righthander Matt Garza held the Tigers hitless in a 5-0 Tampa Bay victory. He faced the minimum 27 batters while allowing only a second-inning walk to Brennan Boesch.

Garza's no-hit gem was the first in Rays history, leaving only the Mets and Padres without no-hitters among major league clubs. The five fine pitching performances by Jimenez, Braden, Halladay, Jackson and Garza represented the most no-hitters since seven were thrown in 1991.

As if three no-nos, two perfect games and one near miss weren't enough, five other pitchers carried no-hitters deep into games.

■ On June 13, Cubs lefthander Ted Lilly took a no-hit bid into the ninth inning of an interleague matchup against the rival White Sox. A leadoff single by Juan Pierre ended that bid in a game the

Ubaldo Jimenez started no-hit season in style with his April 17 gem against Atlanta

Cubs hung on to win 1-0. Incidentally, White Sox starter Gavin Floyd completed six no-hit innings of his own in that game, marking the first time since 1997 that two pitchers had no-nos after six.

■ On July 10, Reds rookie lefty Travis Wood, making his third big league start, took a perfect game into the ninth inning in Philadelphia. Phillies catcher Carlos Ruiz ended that bid with a leadoff double. For hit part, Wood struck out eight and completed nine, one-hit innings, but the Phillies went on to win in 11 innings, notching their third consecutive extra-inning, walk-off victory against the stunned Reds.

■ On Aug. 8, Blue Jays righthander Brandon Morrow turned in perhaps the season's most

NO-NOS AND PERFECTOS

Five pitchers completed no-hitters—two of them perfect games—during the 2010 regular season, more than baseball had seen since 1991. They ranged in quality from Roy Halladay's 11-strikeout perfecto to Edwin Jackson's 149-pitch no-hitter in which eight batters reached via walks, one was hit by a pitch and another reached on an error. Halladay struck again in October, no-hitting the Reds in Game One of the National League Division Series and throwing the first postseason no-hitter since Don Larsen's perfect game in the 1956 World Series.

PITCHER	Date	Opp	IP	H	R	ER	BB	SO	HBP	BF	Pit	Str
Ubaldo Jimenez, Rockies	April 17	@Braves	9	0	0	0	6	7	0	31	128	72
Dallas Braden, A's	May 9	Rays	9	0	0	0	0	6	0	27	109	77
Roy Halladay, Phillies	May 29	@Marlins	9	0	0	0	0	11	0	27	115	72
Edwin Jackson, D-backs	June 25	@Rays	9	0	0	0	8	6	1	36	149	79
Matt Garza, Rays	July 26	Tigers	9	0	0	0	1	6	0	27	120	80
Roy Halladay, Phillies	Oct. 6	Reds	9	0	0	0	1	8	0	28	104	79

dominating pitching performance: a 17-strikeout, complete-game one-hitter. The opponent? The Rays, of course. Morrow just missed recording the sixth no-hitter of the season when, with two outs in the ninth, the Rays' Evan Longoria stroked a single off second baseman Aaron Hill's glove. With the dominating start, Morrow recorded the first complete game of his career.

■ One week later, on Aug. 15, Twins right-hander Kevin Slowey no-hit the A's for seven innings, but he didn't get a chance to finish what he started. Serenaded by a chorus of boos, manager Ron Gardenhire removed Slowey after 106 pitches because he had missed his previous start with elbow tendinitis and was on a 100-pitch limit. Reliever John Rauch surrendered a double to the second batter he faced in what became a three-hitter for the Twins.

"I'd boo me, too," an unapologetic Gardenhire said afterward. "I took a pitcher out with a no-hitter. But I would do it a thousand times the same way."

■ The situation bordered on the ridiculous when Rangers righty Rich Harden came off the disabled list on Aug. 22 after an extended stay and threw 6⅔ no-hit innings against the Twins. Joe Mauer's one-out single in the ninth off closer Neftali Feliz averted a four-pitcher no-no by the Rangers.

Though no-hitters were not involved, two NL pitching staffs stymied their opponents for an extended stretch.

The Mets shut out the Phillies for three games at New York's Citi Field from May 25-28. Starters R.A. Dickey, Hisanori Takahashi and Mike Pelfrey logged 19 of the 27 innings, while ace Johan Santana extended the Mets' shutout streak to 35 innings the next day with eight scoreless frames against the

Brewers. New York lost the scoreless streak—and the game—in the ninth when Corey Hart smacked a two-run homer of reliever Ryota Igarishi.

The Dodgers won consecutive 1-0, extra-inning contests (of 10 and then 14 innings) at home against the Diamondbacks on June 1-2. As was the case with the Mets, Los Angeles rookie right-ies John Ely and Carlos Monasterios seemed like unlikely aces, but they contributed 12 of the 24 shutout innings. In all, the Dodgers aced Arizona for 31 straight frames in the three-game series.

Can't Keep A Good Bat Down

While pitching ruled the roost, hitters occasionally had their say.

Red Sox outfielder Daniel Nava, signed out of the independent Golden League two years before, became an instant legend when he socked a grand slam against Philadelphia's Joe Blanton on the first pitch he saw in the big leagues. That same night, Rays first baseman Carlos Pena homered in his sixth consecutive game, the first player to do so since Oakland's Frank Thomas in September 2006.

Rockies shortstop Troy Tulowitzki went on a record slugging spree in September, totaling 14 home runs over a 15-game span. No player had been so prolific with the long ball since Barry Bonds when he set the all-time record of 73 homers in 2001. Over that stretch, Tulowitzki knocked in an astonishing 33 runs.

Then, there was the Blue Jays' Jose Bautista. With home runs down across the board in both leagues, Bautista thumbed his nose at pitchers with

CONTINUED ON PAGE 11

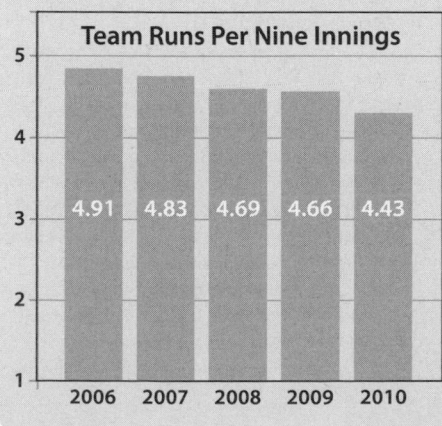

NO OFFENSE: RUN-SCORING LEVELS CONTINUE TO PLUMMET

Team Runs Per Nine Innings

Year	Value
2006	4.91
2007	4.83
2008	4.69
2009	4.66
2010	4.43

While run-scoring decreased markedly in 2010, it did not fall as far as it did in 1968, the real Year of the Pitcher, when major leaguers hit just .237 and teams scored an average of 3.42 per nine innings. Key components of offense—home runs, on-base percentage (OBP) and isolated power (ISO)—have been in free fall since 2006, when run-scoring peaked after the gradual comedown from the high-octane 1994-2004 period. Team rates for runs per nine innings (R/9) and home runs per nine innings (HR/9) in 2010 diminished by 9.8 percent and 14.3 percent, respectively, from 2006 levels.

Yr	R/9	HR/9	OBP	ISO
2006	4.91	1.12	.337	.157
2007	4.83	1.03	.336	.149
2008	4.69	1.01	.333	.147
2009	4.66	1.05	.333	.150
2010	4.43	0.96	.325	.140

Halladay issues 'Doc's' orders

PLAYER OF THE YEAR

ANDREW WOOLLEY

Roy Halladay dazzled in his playoff debut

BY JAYSON STARK

Roy Halladay got our attention with a perfect game in May. He solidified his spot in the record books five months later with just the second no-hitter in postseason history.

But to simply say he made history on Oct. 6 doesn't do this justice. To say he pitched a game that people will talk about for the rest of his life doesn't truly capture the magnitude of it.

So let's look back on the masterpiece that propelled the Phillies to a three-game sweep of the Reds in the National League Division Series and cemented Halladay as the correct choice as the Baseball America Major League Player of the Year.

Halladay headed for the mound that Wednesday afternoon at Citizens Bank Park to do something he'd waited a lifetime for.

He had asked the only team he'd ever pitched for, the Blue Jays, to trade him last winter. He asked specifically to be traded to the Phillies, for a chance to live out this day.

Halladay left millions of dollars on the table to make it happen. He ground his way through 250⅔ grueling innings, launched 3,568 max-effort pitches, all for this.

He did it all, just for a chance to walk to the pitcher's mound on an electrifying afternoon in October and push himself to rise to meet a moment that, for the first 12 seasons of his remarkable career, had seemed to be a part of the life of every pitcher in baseball except his.

Just two other times in postseason history had any pitcher even taken a no-hitter into the eighth inning: Jim Lonborg (7⅔ hitless) in the 1967 World Series, and Bill Bevens (8⅔ hitless) in the 1947 World Series.

Of course, Halladay had already thrown one no-hitter himself this season—a May 29 perfect game in Florida. No pitcher had ever thrown a regular-season no-hitter and a postseason no-hitter in the same season.

On the day he made history, Doc Halladay was so untouchable, the identity of the hitters he steamrollered was almost irrelevant. And once his offense handed him four runs in the first two innings, he was going to win, going to dominate.

Halladay is a strike-throwing machine every day of every year. But this was different. He faced 28 hitters—and threw 25 first-pitch strikes. He went to 0-and-2 on 11 hitters—but went 2-and-0 on none. He never ran a 3-and-0 count or even a 3-and-1 count. It took him 47 pitches before he threw his 10th pitch out of the strike zone.

Halladay's road to this perfect game, and this award, was no ordinary journey. It was 13 years and 169 regular-season wins in the making. One other pitcher in the division-play era (Chuck Finley) won more games before he made his first postseason start. No other pitcher had pitched this many games and had this good a winning percentage (.663) without throwing a single postseason pitch.

So we'll never know now how Roy Halladay would have looked at his career if this day had never come. But we know now, because it did, exactly how we'll look at it for the rest of time.

PREVIOUS 10 WINNERS	
2000	Alex Rodriguez, ss, Mariners
2001	Barry Bonds, of, Giants
2002	Alex Rodriguez, ss, Rangers
2003	Barry Bonds, of, Giants
2004	Barry Bonds, of, Giants
2005	Albert Pujols, 1b, Cardinals
2006	Johan Santana, lhp, Twins
2007	Alex Rodriguez, ss, Yankees
2008	C.C. Sabathia, lhp, Indians/Brewers
2009	Joe Mauer, c, Twins

Full list: BaseballAmerica.com/awards

CONTINUED FROM PAGE 9

a stunning power display.

Bautista, who hit a mere 13 homers the previous year and who never had knocked more than 16 out of the park in one season, clouted his 50th home run on Sept. 23 to beat Mariners ace Felix Hernandez 1-0. In that same game, Seattle's Ichiro Suzuki became the first major leaguer with 10 consecutive 200-hit seasons.

Bautista would finish with 54 home runs, a stunning 15 more than AL runner-up Paul Konerko of the White Sox. In the NL, Cardinals first baseman Albert Pujols (42) was the only player to reach 40 homers for the season.

Alex Rodriguez finished the season with a much more modest total of 30 home runs, but one of them proved historic. On Aug. 4, the Yankees third baseman socked the 600th home run of his career, becoming the seventh player to reach that plateau and the youngest at 35 years, 8 days.

Rodriguez, who admitted to using steroids during the three years he played for the Rangers from 2001-03, reached 600 in 2,267 games. Only Babe Ruth did it faster, getting there in 2,044 games at age 36 years, 196 days.

On July 6, the Tigers' Johnny Damon made the evening in which he collected the 2,500th hit of his career more memorable by later socking a walk-off, two-run homer to beat the Orioles 7-5.

Triple Crown Proves Elusive

Carl Yazstremski won the AL triple crown in 1967 and while no one has done it since, three NL sluggers waged a spirited battle over the final weeks of the 2010 season.

With 42 homers and 118 RBIs, Pujols won two legs of the crown, while Rockies outfielder Carlos Gonzalez won the third, batting .336 to capture the batting title. Reds first baseman Joey Votto hit .324 (to rank second) with 37 homers (third) and 113 RBIs (third). Neither Gonzalez nor Pujols could boast of a top-three finish in all three categories.

Pujols also led the league with 115 runs scored, Gonzalez was tops with 197 hits, and Votto led the way with a .424 on-base percentage and .600 slugging.

Phillies righthander Roy Halladay went 21-10, 2.44 in 33 starts and led the NL with 250⅔ innings, 1.1 walks per nine innings and a 7.3 strikeout-to-walk ratio. His excellence over the course of the long season distinguished him from a strong field of NL pitchers, including the Rockies' Ubaldo Jimenez, the Cardinals' Adam Wainwright and the Marlins' Josh Johnson.

Over in the AL, Tigers first baseman Miguel Cabrera paced all batters with 126 RBIs while hitting .328 (to rank second) with 38 homers (third). Rangers outfielder Josh Hamilton hit .359/.411/.633 to win the batting and slugging titles. His on-base percentage ranked second only to Cabrera.

As usual, Suzuki led the AL with 214 hits, while Yankees first baseman Mark Teixeira led the league with 113 runs scored in an otherwise subpar year.

Yankees lefty C.C. Sabathia continued his successful run with the Yankees, going 21-7, 3.18 in

AMERICAN LEAGUE STANDINGS

EAST	W	L	PCT	GB	Manager	General Manager	Attendance	Average	Last Penn.
Tampa Bay Rays	96	66	.593	—	Joe Maddon	Andrew Friedman	1,864,999	23,025	2008
*New York Yankees	95	67	.586	1	Joe Girardi	Brian Cashman	3,765,807	46,491	2009
Boston Red Sox	89	73	.549	7	Terry Francona	Theo Epstein	3,046,445	37,610	2007
Toronto Blue Jays	85	77	.525	11	Cito Gaston	Alex Anthopoulos	1,625,555	20,069	1993
Baltimore Orioles	66	96	.407	30	D. Trembley/J. Samuel/ B. Showalter	Andy MacPhail	1,733,019	21,663	1983
CENTRAL	W	L	PCT	GB	Manager	General Manager	Attendance	Average	Last Penn.
Minnesota Twins	94	68	.580	—	Ron Gardenhire	Bill Smith	3,223,640	39,798	1991
Chicago White Sox	88	74	.543	6	Ozzie Guillen	Ken Williams	2,194,378	27,091	2005
Detroit Tigers	81	81	.500	13	Jim Leyland	Dave Dombrowski	2,461,237	30,386	2006
Cleveland Indians	69	93	.426	25	Manny Acta	Mark Shapiro	1,391,644	17,396	1997
Kansas City Royals	67	95	.414	27	T. Hillman/N. Yost	Dayton Moore	1,615,327	20,192	1985
WEST	W	L	PCT	GB	Manager	General Manager	Attendance	Average	Last Penn.
Texas Rangers	90	72	.556	—	Ron Washington	Jon Daniels	2,505,171	30,928	2010
Oakland Athletics	81	81	.500	9	Bob Geren	Billy Beane	1,418,391	17,511	1990
Los Angeles Angels	80	82	.494	10	Mike Scioscia	Tony Reagins	3,250,814	40,134	2002
Seattle Mariners	61	101	.377	29	D. Wakamatsu/D. Brown	Jack Zduriencik	2,085,630	25,749	Never

*Wild card

PLAYOFFS—Division Series: Rangers defeated Rays 3-2 and Yankees defeated Twins 3-0 in best-of-five series.
League Championship Series: Rangers defeated Yankees 4-2 in best-of-seven series.

34 starts. Angels righty Jered Weaver struck out an AL-best 233 batters, one more than Mariners righthander Felix Hernandez, whose sensational year was obscured by a 13-12 record. Hernandez led the AL in innings (249⅔), ERA (2.27) and opponent average (.212).

Rookies To The Rescue

The 2010 season also will be remembered for the stunning array of rookies to crash the party, particularly in the NL. The dynamic debuts started on the very first day of the season when Braves right fielder Jason Heyward, who grew up 20 minutes from Atlanta's Turner Field, ripped a three-run homer in his first at-bat off the Cubs' Carlos Zambrano.

Cubs shortstop Starlin Castro had an equally remarkable major league debut a month later. As part of a 14-7 romp of the Reds, Castro—at 20 the youngest shortstop in franchise history—homered in his first at-bat off Homer Bailey and drove in six runs, a record for a debut.

Other rookies made immediate impacts. Right fielder Mike Stanton and first baseman Gaby Sanchez quickly became part of the fabric in Florida. Lefty Jaime Garcia recovered from Tommy John surgery in 2008 to settle in behind Adam Wainwright and Chris Carpenter in the St. Louis rotation. His 2.70 ERA ranked fourth in the NL.

Catcher Buster Posey arrived on the scene in San Francisco two months into the season and energized a previously dormant Giants offense. Pittsburgh seemed to add a contributing newcomer every few weeks with the likes of second baseman Neil Walker, third baseman Pedro Alvarez, righthander Brad Lincoln and outfielder Jose Tabata.

Third baseman Chris Johnson provided power to a flagging Astros offense. John Axford took over for faltering closer Trevor Hoffman in Milwaukee and clicked off saves with regularity. Outfielder Tyler Colvin got better as an otherwise disappointing season progressed for the Cubs, and first baseman Ike Davis settled into the middle of the order for the equally underachieving Mets.

At the end of August, Cuban sensation Aroldis Chapman, a flame-throwing lefthander, arrived to a hero's welcome in Cincinnati. Regularly throwing his fastball at 100 mph and above, Chapman had Reds fans and opponents alike fixated on radar-gun readings.

Three AL rookies made their marks early, and two of them—center fielder Austin Jackson and right fielder Brennan Boesch—helped keep the Tigers in contention during the first half. Rangers closer Neftali Feliz saved 40 games to rank third in the league.

No rookie arrived with more fanfare and expectation than 21-year-old Nationals righthander Stephen Strasburg, the first player taken in the 2009 draft. He breezed through Double-A and Triple-A, going 7-2, 1.30 in 11 starts, and made his carefully-orchestrated big league debut against the Pirates on June 8, one day after Washington made their second consecutive first overall draft selection in outfielder Bryce Harper.

NATIONAL LEAGUE STANDINGS

EAST	W	L	PCT	GB	Manager	General Manager	Attendance	Average	Last Penn.
Philadelphia Phillies	97	65	.599	—	Charlie Manuel	Ruben Amaro Jr.	3,647,249	45,028	2009
*Atlanta Braves	91	71	.562	6	Bobby Cox	Frank Wren	2,510,119	30,989	1999
Florida Marlins	80	82	.494	17	F. Gonzalez/E. Rodriguez	Larry Beinfest	1,524,894	18,826	2003
New York Mets	79	83	.488	18	Jerry Manuel	Omar Minaya	2,559,738	32,402	2000
Washington Nationals	69	93	.426	28	Jim Riggleman	Mike Rizzo	1,828,066	22,569	Never
CENTRAL	W	L	PCT	GB	Manager	General Manager	Attendance	Average	Last Penn.
Cincinnati Reds	91	71	.562	—	Dusty Baker	Walt Jocketty	2,060,551	25,439	1990
St. Louis Cardinals	86	76	.531	5	Tony La Russa	John Mozeliak	3,301,218	40,756	2006
Milwaukee Brewers	77	85	.475	14	Ken Macha	Doug Melvin	2,776,531	34,278	^1982
Houston Astros	76	86	.469	15	Brad Mills	Ed Wade	2,331,490	28,784	2005
Chicago Cubs	75	87	.463	16	Lou Piniella/Mike Quade	Jim Hendry	3,062,973	37,814	1945
Pittsburgh Pirates	57	105	.352	34	John Russell	Neal Huntington	1,613,399	19,919	1979
WEST	W	L	PCT	GB	Manager	General Manager	Attendance	Average	Last Penn.
San Francisco Giants	92	70	.568	—	Bruce Bochy	Brian Sabean	3,037,443	37,499	2010
San Diego Padres	90	72	.556	2	Bud Black	Jed Hoyer	2,131,774	26,318	1998
Colorado Rockies	83	79	.512	9	Jim Tracy	Dan O'Dowd	2,875,245	35,941	2007
Los Angeles Dodgers	80	82	.494	12	Joe Torre	Ned Colletti	3,562,320	43,979	1988
Arizona Diamondbacks	65	97	.401	27	A.J. Hinch/Kirk Gibson	Josh Byrnes	2,056,697	25,391	2001

*Wild card ^American League

PLAYOFFS—Division Series: Phillies defeated Reds 3-0 and Giants defeated Braves 3-1 in best-of-five series.
League Championship Series: Giants defeated Phillies 4-2 in best-of-seven series.

In seven innings, Strasburg allowed just four hits and two runs while striking out 14, a club record. He whiffed the last seven hitters he faced and retired the final 10 in order, much to the delight of a packed house of 40,315 at Nationals Park.

Strasburg quickly became a national phenomenon, boosting attendance both at home and on the road. But alas, his rookie season ended in disappointment and unfulfilled potential. He began experiencing shoulder discomfort in late July and was shut down for a few weeks. Three starts after returning, on Aug. 21, Strasburg felt elbow pain in an outing in Philadelphia and later received the diagnosis that he needed Tommy John surgery.

Needless to say, the news was devastating for Strasburg and the franchise. Aware that he was facing a year of recovery time, he tried to maintain a stiff upper lip.

"It's a new challenge," he said. "I want to be the best at everything. Now, I'm going to be the best at rehabbing."

Twins Stay On Target At Home

Beyond the debuts of those exciting rookies, a new ballpark made the scene in the AL. After 28 seasons in the sterile environment of the Hubert H. Humphrey Metrodome, the Twins moved back into the great outdoors with the opening of Target Field in downtown Minneapolis.

After two exhibition games against the Cardinals, the Twins opened their new baseball palace on April 12 against the Red Sox. Carl Pavano threw the first pitch to Marco Scutaro, Minnesota's Jason Kubel socked the first home run and the day was a complete success when the Twins won 5-2.

Amid concerns over early-season temperatures in the Twin Cities, the game was played under blue skies at a comfortable 65 degrees at first pitch.

"I've been waiting a long time for this," said Twins catcher Joe Mauer, who grew up 10 miles away in St. Paul. "It's definitely a special place, and I'm glad it's here."

Mauer might have changed his mind a bit later when it became evident that Target Field would not match the hitter-friendly conditions of the Metrodome. Mauer's home-run total dropped from 28 in 2009 to a mere nine, with just one at home in 68 games.

The challenging new dimensions did not stop the Twins from forging a home-field advantage in their new digs, however. They went 53-28 at Target Field, the best home record in the AL, and they eventually pulled away from the White Sox to claim the AL Central crown.

With an average attendance of nearly 40,000 per game in the new facility, the Twins eclipsed 3 million fans for the second time in franchise history with an all-time best total of 3,223,640.

AMERICAN LEAGUE BEST TOOLS

A Baseball America survey of American League managers, conducted at midseason 2010, ranked players with the best tools.

BEST HITTER
1. Miguel Cabrera, Tigers
2. Joe Mauer, Twins
3. Josh Hamilton, Rangers

BEST POWER
1 (tie). Miguel Cabrera, Tigers
1 (tie). Josh Hamilton, Rangers
3. Justin Morneau, Twins

BEST BUNTER
1. Ichiro Suzuki, Mariners
2. Juan Pierre, White Sox
3. Erick Aybar, Angels

BEST STRIKE-ZONE JUDGMENT
1. Kevin Youkilis, Red Sox
2. Joe Mauer, Twins
3. Daric Barton, Athletics

BEST HIT-AND-RUN ARTIST
1. Derek Jeter, Yankees
2. Erick Aybar, Angels
3. Ichiro Suzuki, Mariners

BEST BASERUNNER
1. Ichiro Suzuki, Mariners
2. Carl Crawford, Rays
3. Brett Gardner, Yankees

FASTEST BASERUNNER
1. Carl Crawford, Rays
2. Ichiro Suzuki, Mariners
3. Brett Gardner, Yankees

MOST EXCITING PLAYER
1. Carl Crawford, Rays
2. Josh Hamilton, Rangers
3. Ichiro Suzuki, Mariners

BEST PITCHER
1. Cliff Lee, Rangers
2. C.C. Sabathia, Yankees
3. Felix Hernandez, Mariners

BEST FASTBALL
1. Justin Verlander, Tigers
2. Daniel Bard, Red Sox
3. Neftali Feliz, Rangers

BEST CURVEBALL
1. Justin Verlander, Tigers
2. A.J. Burnett, Yankees
3. Josh Beckett, Red Sox

BEST SLIDER
1. Felix Hernandez, Mariners
2. Zack Greinke, Royals
3. C.C. Sabathia, Yankees

BEST CHANGEUP
1. James Shields, Rays
2. Jered Weaver, Angels
3. Mark Buehrle, White Sox

BEST CONTROL
1. Cliff Lee, Rangers
2. Carl Pavano, Twins
3. Mariano Rivera, Yankees

BEST PICKOFF MOVE
1. Mark Buehrle, White Sox
2. Andy Pettitte, Yankees
3. Dallas Braden, Athletics

BEST RELIEVER
1. Mariano Rivera, Yankees
2. Joakim Soria, Royals
3. Rafael Soriano, Rays

BEST DEFENSIVE CATCHER
1. Joe Mauer, Twins
2. Kurt Suzuki, Athletics
3. Jose Molina, Blue Jays

BEST DEFENSIVE 1B
1. Mark Teixeira, Yankees
2. Carlos Pena, Rays
3. Kevin Youkilis, Red Sox

BEST DEFENSIVE 2B
1. Robinson Cano, Yankees
2. Dustin Pedroia, Red Sox
3. Orlando Hudson, Twins

BEST DEFENSIVE 3B
1. Evan Longoria, Rays
2. Adrian Beltre, Red Sox
3. Brandon Inge, Tigers

BEST DEFENSIVE SS
1. Elvis Andrus, Rangers
2. Erick Aybar, Angels
3. Derek Jeter, Yankees

BEST INFIELD ARM
1. Adrian Beltre, Red Sox
2. Elvis Andrus, Rangers
3. Erick Aybar, Angels

BEST DEFENSIVE OF
1. Ichiro Suzuki, Mariners
2. Torii Hunter, Angels
3. Franklin Gutierrez, Mariners

BEST OUTFIELD ARM
1. Ichiro Suzuki, Mariners
2. Nelson Cruz, Rangers
3. Josh Hamilton, Rangers

BEST MANAGER
1. Ron Gardenhire, Twins
2. Mike Scioscia, Angels
3. Jim Leyland, Tigers

CONTINUED ON PAGE 15

Braves' Peach State prize

TONY FARLOW

Jason Heyward narrowly edged fellow Georgian Buster Posey as top rookie

Five years after their teams squared off for the Georgia Class AAAA state championship, Jason Heyward and Buster Posey found themselves on a considerably larger stage.

Heyward's Braves and Posey's Giants met in the National League Division Series, and suddenly a lot of writers from around the country were asking the two Georgia guys about that best-of-three series in 2005.

If you happened to have been at that high school championship series, could you even have imagined you were watching two players who would become the top two major league rookies five years later?

Heyward, who occupied right field for the Braves from Opening Day this season, narrowly edged Posey to win Baseball America Rookie of the Year honors. He's nearly two and a half years younger than Posey, even though he signed one year earlier, and he carried the Braves lineup for most of the season, especially when injuries struck such veterans as Chipper Jones.

Heyward hit .277/.393/.456 with 18 homers, 72 RBIs and 11 stolen bases in 142 games, playing through a thumb injury that diminished his power for about six weeks and eventually required a disabled list stint that kept him out of the All-Star Game after he had been elected as a starter.

Heyward hit a tape-measure homer in his first at-bat on Opening Day, had 10 homers and 38 RBIs in his first two months before the

thumb injury, and led major league rookies with 91 walks and a .393 on-base percentage that was the sixth-highest ever for a player who began a season younger than 21. His OBP and walks both ranked fourth in the NL. His .927 OPS led the team.

Heyward became almost instantly beloved by fans and managers.

"Young kid, 20 years old, full of energy and talent," Braves manager Bobby Cox said early in the season, citing Heyward's positive effect on clubhouse chemistry. "It really is energizing to have somebody like that for the veterans, to have someone come along and help immediately."

Heyward batted .173 with one extra-base hit and one RBI in the Braves' final 14 games. Then he went just 2-for-16 in the Division Series and got dropped to sixth in the lineup for the final game of the series, the first time he had hit lower than third in the order since the beginning of May.

And that alone illustrates how important Heyward was to the Braves all season long. In a team that was often patched together, Heyward was a constant as Atlanta returned to the playoffs for the first time since 2005.

"I would say this season—what a starting point. What a year to build on," Heyward said. "Lot of experiences, lot of fun, a lot to take from. And I enjoyed it and most definitely don't take anything for granted."

PREVIOUS 10 WINNERS

2000	Rafael Furcal, ss/2b, Braves
2001	Albert Pujols, of/3b/1b, Cardinals
2002	Eric Hinske, 3b, Blue Jays
2003	Brandon Webb, rhp, Diamondbacks
2004	Khalil Greene, ss, Padres
2005	Huston Street, rhp, Athletics
2006	Justin Verlander, rhp, Tigers
2007	Ryan Braun, 3b, Brewers
2008	Geovany Soto, c, Cubs
2009	Andrew McCutchen, of, Pirates

Full list: BaseballAmerica.com/awards

ALL-ROOKIE TEAM 2010

POS, PLAYER, TEAM	AGE	AB	AVG	OBP	SLG	2B	HR	RBI	SB	RUNDOWN
C Buster Posey, Giants	23	406	.305	.357	.505	23	18	67	0	Hit like crazy, handled power pitching staff
1B Ike Davis, Mets*	23	523	.264	.351	.440	33	19	71	3	Secured regular play with power, defense
2B Neil Walker, Pirates#	25	426	.296	.349	.462	29	12	66	2	Showed bat that made him '03 first-rounder
3B Danny Valencia, Twins	26	299	.311	.351	.448	18	7	40	2	Held down hot corner, delivered clutch hits
SS Starlin Castro, Cubs	20	463	.300	.347	.408	31	3	41	10	Learning on the job, but hit .300 at a tender age
LF Mike Stanton, Marlins	20	359	.259	.326	.507	21	22	59	5	Slammed 43 HR between Double-A and majors
CF Austin Jackson, Tigers	23	618	.293	.345	.400	34	4	41	27	Flashed five tools in impressive debut
RF Jason Heyward, Braves*	21	520	.277	.393	.456	29	18	72	11	Led rookies in walks, on-base, slugging
DH Gaby Sanchez, Marlins	27	572	.273	.341	.448	37	19	85	5	Oldie but goody: led rookies in doubles, RBIs

POS, PITCHER, TEAM	AGE	W	L	ERA	IP	SO	BB	SV	RUNDOWN
SP Madison Bumgarner, Giants*	21	7	6	3.00	111	86	26	0	Teamed with Posey, went 2-2, 1.18 in last six starts
SP Wade Davis, Rays	25	12	10	4.07	168	113	62	0	Arrived during final 12 starts: 6-1, 3.28, 1.22 WHIP
SP Jaime Garcia, Cardinals*	24	13	8	2.70	163	132	64	0	TJ surgery alumnus finished fourth in NL ERA race
SP Brian Matusz, Orioles*	23	10	12	4.30	176	143	63	0	O's won 10 of his final 11 starts, pointing to '11 breakout
SP Jon Niese, Mets*	23	9	10	4.20	174	148	62	0	Led all rookies in strikeouts, but faltered down stretch
RP John Axford, Brewers	27	8	2	2.48	58	76	27	24	Improved walk rate, supplanted Trevor Hoffman as closer
RP Jonny Venters, Braves*	25	4	4	1.95	83	93	39	1	Equally deadly vs. lefties (.570 OPS) and righties (.543)
CL Neftali Feliz, Rangers	22	4	3	2.73	69	71	18	40	Saved 40 of 43, opponents hit just .176/.246/.269

*Bats/Throws Lefthanded. #Switch-hitter

CONTINUED FROM PAGE 13

Managerial Upheaval

Managers are hired to be fired, or so the saying goes. But in a busy year for managerial firings, four skippers went out on their own terms. Eight others were not as lucky and were fired in-season or just after.

Before play began, the Braves' Bobby Cox and the Blue Jays' Cito Gaston announced they would be retiring after the season.

The Cubs' Lou Piniella eventually would join that farewell party, leaving with six weeks remaining in the season to be with his ailing mother. Instead of continuing their death spiral, the Cubs actually got their act together and played better under interim manager Mike Quade, who began the year as Chicago's third-base coach. For guiding the Cubs to a 24-13 record, Quade received a two-year extension to continue as manager.

Piniella announced his early departure and retirement from baseball in an emotional press conference at Wrigley Field.

"I cried a little bit after the game," Piniella said. "You get emotional. I'm sorry—I'm not trying to be. This will be the last time I put on the uniform."

Dodgers manager Joe Torre (80-82) announced that with the expiration of his contract he would not return to Los Angeles next season. He turned over the reins to anointed successor Don Mattingly, the club's hitting coach.

Cox completed his 30-year managerial career with 2,504 wins, the fourth-highest total of all

time. He helmed the Braves for 25 of those years, including the last 21, during which he won five NL pennants and one World Series in 1995.

By winning on the final day of the regular season to clinch the wild card, the Braves gave the venerable Cox a record 16th trip to the postseason.

"I'm just happy for the guys and the coaching staff that worked so hard," said Cox. "This team is the hardest-working and hardest-trying club we've ever had here. There's no quit in them."

Piniella managed five teams in his 23 years as manager and finished with 1,835 wins to rank 14th all time. His Reds swept the favored A's in the 1990 World Series, providing Piniella's lone pennant, but he also skippered the 2001 Mariners to 116 regular-season wins, the highest total ever.

One by one, other managerial dominoes began to fall. Just six weeks into the season, the Royals dumped manager Trey Hillman (12-23) and replaced him with former Brewers skipper Ned Yost (55-72). Club officials were so impressed with the club's performance under Yost, they later gave him a three-year extension.

On June 4, the Orioles finally stopped Dave Trembley (15-39) from twisting in the wind and replaced him on an interim basis with Juan Samuel (17-34). Baltimore decided a new direction was needed before season's end, however, and brought Buck Showalter out of exile to lead the club. The O's responded to Showalter and went 34-23 from Aug. 2 until the end of the season.

The Marlins' Fredi Gonzalez (34-36) became the third manager to get the ax during the season, getting dismissed on June 23. Triple-A New

Orleans manager Edwin Rodriguez (46-46) took over on an interim basis, but the change did nothing to raise the Marlins from mediocrity. Following the season, the Braves tabbed Gonzalez as Cox's successor in Atlanta.

An unexpected upheaval took place in Arizona on July 2 when general manager Josh Byrnes and manager A.J. Hinch (31-48) were dismissed with no advance warning. Hinch had been on the job little more than a year after replacing Bob Melvin early in the 2009 season. Byrnes had a contract through 2015.

"I appreciate the commitment and dedication that Josh and A.J. demonstrated during their tenures," team owner Ken Kendrick said. "Their dismissal is a significant decision, but one that we find necessary in order to achieve a direction of winning consistently on the field again."

It had been Byrnes who fired Melvin and pulled Hinch out of the front office to direct the Diamondbacks on the field. But when Arizona staggered to 89-123 (.420) under Hinch, Byrnes paid for the decision with his job.

A familiar face in the NL West assumed control of the Diamondbacks at the conclusion of the season. The club selected former Padres GM Kevin Towers to serve in the same role for Arizona.

Towers, in turn, made the decision to keep Kirk Gibson (34-49) on as manager. Gibson had served as bench coach under Hinch and moved into an interim manager position, and Towers liked the way the players responded to the fiery leader.

Considered the right man at the right time the previous season when the Mariners unexpectedly won 85 games, Don Wakamatsu (42-70) received the pink slip on Aug. 9. Seattle promoted Triple-A manager Daren Brown (19-31) to take over the club, but the Mariners finished with 101 losses for the second time in three years.

The casualty list grew at the end of the season. The Mets opted for a complete overhaul of their baseball operation, firing general manager Omar Minaya and manager Jerry Manuel (79-83).

The Brewers also let veteran skipper Ken Macha (77-85) go after two seasons, and the Pirates canned John Russell after a 105-loss season. He compiled a 186-299 (.384) record in three years in Pittsburgh.

A dozen clubs will enter the 2011 season with different managers than they had the previous Opening Day. Half of the NL's 16 clubs—the Braves, Brewers, Cubs, Diamondbacks, Dodgers, Marlins, Mets and Pirates—will be in new hands.

Griffey Bows Out

Managers weren't alone in departing the prem-

ises. On June 2, the same day that Joyce blew Galarraga's no-hitter in Detroit, the Mariners' Ken Griffey Jr. announced his retirement after 22 seasons in the big leagues. A full-time DH in 2010, Griffey batted just .184/.250/.204 in 98 at-bats.

NATIONAL LEAGUE BEST TOOLS

A Baseball America survey of National League managers, conducted at midseason 2010, ranked players with the best tools.

BEST HITTER
1. Albert Pujols, Cardinals
2. Joey Votto, Reds
3. Martin Prado, Braves

BEST POWER
1. Adam Dunn, Nationals
2 (tie). Ryan Howard, Phillies
2 (tie). Albert Pujols, Cardinals

BEST BUNTER
1. Michael Bourn, Astros
2. Nyjer Morgan, Nationals
3. Rafael Furcal, Dodgers

BEST STRIKE-ZONE JUDGMENT
1. Albert Pujols, Cardinals
2. David Eckstein, Padres
3. Adrian Gonzalez, Padres

BEST HIT-AND-RUN ARTIST
1. Placido Polanco, Phillies
2. David Eckstein, Padres
3. Martin Prado, Braves

BEST BASERUNNER
1. Michael Bourn, Astros
2. Andrew McCutchen, Pirates
3. Chris Young, Diamondbacks

FASTEST BASERUNNER
1. Michael Bourn, Astros
2. Nyjer Morgan, Nationals
3. Andrew McCutchen, Pirates

MOST EXCITING PLAYER
1. Albert Pujols, Cardinals
2. Carlos Gonzalez, Rockies
3. Stephen Strasburg, Nationals

BEST PITCHER
1. Josh Johnson, Marlins
2. Roy Halladay, Phillies
3. Ubaldo Jimenez, Rockies

BEST FASTBALL
1. Ubaldo Jimenez, Rockies
2. Stephen Strasburg, Nationals
3. Josh Johnson, Marlins

BEST CURVEBALL
1. Adam Wainwright, Cardinals
2. Jaime Garcia, Cardinals
3. Barry Zito, Giants

BEST SLIDER
1. Roy Halladay, Phillies
2. Josh Johnson, Marlins
3. Ubaldo Jimenez, Rockies

BEST CHANGEUP
1. Johan Santana, Mets
2 (tie). Cole Hamels, Phillies
2 (tie). Tim Lincecum, Giants

BEST CONTROL
1. Roy Halladay, Phillies
2. Josh Johnson, Marlins
3. Adam Wainwright, Cardinals

BEST PICKOFF MOVE
1. Clayton Richard, Padres
2. Chris Capuano, Brewers
3. Clayton Kershaw, Dodgers

BEST RELIEVER
1. Heath Bell, Padres
2. Brian Wilson, Giants
3. Jonathan Broxton, Dodgers

BEST DEFENSIVE C
1. Yadier Molina, Cardinals
2. Brian McCann, Braves
3. Miguel Olivo, Rockies

BEST DEFENSIVE 1B
1. Adrian Gonzalez, Padres
2. Albert Pujols, Cardinals
3. Derrek Lee, Cubs

BEST DEFENSIVE 2B
1. Brandon Phillips, Reds
2. Martin Prado, Braves
3. Chase Utley, Phillies

BEST DEFENSIVE 3B
1. Ryan Zimmerman, Nationals
2 (tie). Scott Rolen, Reds
3 (tie). David Wright, Mets

BEST DEFENSIVE SS
1. Troy Tulowitzki, Rockies
2. Jimmy Rollins, Phillies
3. Jose Reyes, Mets

BEST INFIELD ARM
1. Rafael Furcal, Dodgers
2. Troy Tulowitzki, Rockies
3. Jose Reyes, Mets

BEST DEFENSIVE OF
1. Michael Bourn, Astros
2. Shane Victorino, Phillies
3. Carlos Gomez, Brewers

BEST OUTFIELD ARM
1. Jeff Francoeur, Mets
2 (tie). Jay Bruce, Reds
2 (tie). Carlos Gonzalez, Rockies

BEST MANAGER
1. Bobby Cox, Braves
2. Tony La Russa, Cardinals
3. Bud Black, Padres

Though Junior clearly was nearing the end, the 40-year-old's announcement was no less startling. He batted .284/.370/.538 for his career while collecting 2,781 hits and slugging 630 home runs, fifth-most in major league history. He won the AL MVP award in 1997, when he set career highs with 56 homers and 147 RBIs. He made 13 all-star teams, most recently in 2007.

For his offensive and defensive prowess, Griffey picked up 10 Gold Glove awards and seven Silver Sluggers. The only hole in the center fielder's résumé was never making it to a World Series.

Griffey, who began his career in Seattle in 1989 at the tender age of 19, left town quietly, eschewing a farewell press conference. That understated exit left it to others to define his greatness, particularly as it pertained to the Mariners franchise.

"Ken is both the finest ballplayer I've ever known and one of the finest people I've ever known," Mariners president and COO Chuck Armstrong said. "I consider myself unbelievably fortunate to have had the opportunity to watch a first-ballot Hall of Famer's career unfold in front of me."

Referring to Griffey's role in finally getting the Mariners to the playoffs in 1995, which eventually led to the building of Safeco Field, team CEO

Howard Lincoln said, "Ken's enduring legacy will be as the ballplayer most responsible for keeping major league baseball here in Seattle and the Pacific Northwest. His achievements in baseball are well known and second to none. In the near future, I look forward to seeing Ken inducted into the Hall of Fame in Cooperstown."

While Griffey reached the end of the line, a handful of other veterans kept chugging away, working toward baseball milestones.

In his worst offensive season since his rookie year of 1996, Yankees shortstop Derek Jeter rapped 179 hits to bring his career total to 2,926. At just 36 years old, he's assured of passing 3,000 early in 2011, assuming continued health.

While the Nationals' Ivan Rodriguez has slowed considerably, the 38-year-old catcher worked 102 games behind the plate and collected 106 hits to inch forward to 2,817. If he makes it to 3,000, he'll be the first catcher to do so. Rodriguez already has logged more games behind the plate (2,390) than any catcher in history.

Playing in a part-time DH role for the Twins, Jim Thome smashed 25 homers, giving him 589 for his career. The 40-year-old said he wants to return for another season to take a crack at 600. Albert Pujols (408) and Andruw Jones (407) each hit his 400th home run in 2010.

Baseball Feels Loss Of The Boss

The All-Star Game was played with more than a tinge of sadness after news came earlier in the day that one of the game's icons had died. Yankees owner George Steinbrenner passed away after having a heart attack at age 80.

Just a few days earlier, legendary Yankee Stadium public address announcer Bob Shepard had passed away at age 99. Shepard's baritone voice had been so associated with games in the Bronx that he was dubbed "The Voice of God."

Steinbrenner purchased the Yankees in 1973 from CBS for a mere $10 million, and quickly became known for his passionate and fiery leadership, including a penchant for firing managers. "The Boss" certainly was no stranger to controversy, earning a suspension from the game for authorizing a smear campaign on star outfielder Dave Winfield.

But Steinbrenner evolved to become a hero to Yankees fans for putting his money where his mouth was, turning the franchise into a revenue-generating machine with its own television and radio networks. The free-spending owner thumbed

---

ALL-TIME MANAGER WINS

In a year rife with managerial firings, the Braves' Bobby Cox and the Cubs' Lou Piniella went out on their own terms. Both veteran skippers rank among the 14 winningest managers in history. The top 20, with managers active in 2010 in bold.

No.	Manager	W	L	PCT
1	Connie Mack*	3,731	3,948	.486
2	John McGraw*	2,763	1,948	.586
3	**Tony La Russa**	2,638	2,293	.535
4	**Bobby Cox**	2,504	2,001	.556
5	**Joe Torre**	2,326	1,997	.538
6	Sparky Anderson*	2,194	1,834	.545
7	Bucky Harris*	2,158	2,219	.493
8	Joe McCarthy*	2,125	1,333	.615
9	Walter Alston*	2,040	1,613	.558
10	Leo Durocher*	2,008	1,709	.540
11	Casey Stengel*	1,905	1,842	.508
12	Gene Mauch	1,902	2,037	.483
13	Bill McKechnie*	1,896	1,723	.524
14	**Lou Piniella**	1,835	1,713	.517
15	Ralph Houk	1,619	1,531	.514
16	Fred Clarke*	1,602	1,181	.576
17	Tommy Lasorda*	1,599	1,439	.526
18	Dick Williams*	1,571	1,451	.520
19	**Jim Leyland**	1,493	1,518	.496
20	Clark Griffith*	1,491	1,367	.522

* Hall of Fame.

CONTINUED ON PAGE 19

Giants pick the right pitchers

BY JOHN MANUEL

The Giants have followed the same formula they have used since Brian Sabean took over as general manager in September 1996.

It's a formula that earned them the nod as Organization of the Year after their 11-4 romp through the playoffs that culminated in a World Series win against the Rangers

For 14 seasons, Sabean's philosophy has been to focus on pitching and then supplement the lineup with free agents and trades.

Dick Tidrow, who was Sabean's scouting and farm director from 1997-2007 and now serves as assistant GM, carried out the philosophy and developed a knack for finding power arms and pitching contributors both at the top of the draft and later on, too.

All four playoff starters were drafted by the Giants, with three of them first-rounders taken by Tidrow: Tim Lincecum in 2006, Matt Cain in '02 and Madison Bumgarner in '07.

The Giants staff also has three pitchers selected after the 20th round in lefty starter Jonathan Sanchez, who went from NAIA senior picked in the 27th round to the majors in just over two years; closer Brian Wilson, a 24th-round pick who was paid like a fifth-rounder; and 28th-rounder Sergio Romo, drafted in 2005.

After giving away first-rounders in 2004 and '05, it almost seemed like the organization didn't want to participate in the draft. But once the Giants started to play along, they hit on first-round picks like few others ever have.

When nine teams passed on Lincecum, the Giants pounced, and two Cy Young Awards

Brian Wilson had Tommy John surgery in college but proved to be worth the wait

BILL NICHOLS

later, they have arguably the best player from that draft class.

The Giants picked at No. 10 overall again in 2007 and again went after pitching, snagging Bumgarner. He went 34-6, 2.00 in the minors and then 2-0, 2.18 in four playoff games.

Then the Giants snagged Buster Posey in 2008, and he has stepped in as their best hitter and a fine receiver capable of handling all their talented pitchers as a 23-year-old rookie.

Other offensive standouts include postseason hitting hero (and waiver claim) Cody Ross. Aubrey Huff, Juan Uribe and Pat Burrell were similar bargain-bin buys.

But it's Tidrow's track record with pitchers that separates the Giants from the pack. In the 11 years he oversaw their drafts, the Giants selected 11 pitchers in the first round—mostly hard throwers such as Jason Grilli (1997), Boof Bonser (2000) or David Aardsma (2003)—and only '07 pick Tim Alderson has yet to scratch the big leagues.

"I really think when it comes to pitching," Dodgers assistant general manager Logan White said recently, "there are few guys in the game who know it better than Tidrow."

PREVIOUS 10 WINNERS	
2000	Chicago White Sox
2001	Houston Astros
2002	Minnesota Twins
2003	Florida Marlins
2004	Minnesota Twins
2005	Atlanta Braves
2006	Los Angeles Dodgers
2007	Colorado Rockies
2008	Tampa Bay Rays
2009	Philadelphia Phillies

Full list: BaseballAmerica.com/awards

CONTINUED FROM PAGE 17

his nose at baseball's luxury tax, fielding teams with payrolls far exceeding those of the competition.

In the last few years of Steinbrenner's life, the Yankees fielded teams with payrolls in excess of $200 million.

"Winning is the most important thing in my life, after breathing," Steinbrenner famously said. "Breathing first, winning next."

One of Steinbrenner's last acts as owner was overseeing the construction of new Yankee Stadium at a price of more than $1 billion. Moving from The House that Ruth Built to The House that George Built, the Yankees made sure the mercurial owner would go out on top by claiming their 27th World Series title in 2009.

"He was and always will be as much of a New York Yankee as Babe Ruth, Lou Gehrig, Joe DiMaggio, Mickey Mantle, Yogi Berra, Whitey Ford and all of the other Yankee legends," Commissioner Bud Selig said.

Shepard was so revered in New York that Derek Jeter requested that his voice recording still be used to introduce his at-bats. For the remainder of the season, the Yankees played with patches on their uniforms, commemorating the roles played by Steinbrenner and Shepard in the storied history of the franchise.

The Hawk Enters The Hall

In his ninth try on the ballot, outfielder Andre Dawson finally made it to Cooperstown, garnering 77.9 percent of the vote and serving as the year's sole inductee. As might be expected, the wait was quickly forgotten after "The Hawk" received the news. "If you're a Hall of Famer, eventually you're going to get in, no matter how long it takes," Dawson said.

Don't tell that to righthander Bert Blyleven, who missed election by a mere five votes in his next-to-last try on the writers' ballot. And many were surprised that second baseman Roberto Alomar did not gain first-ballot election, missing by eight votes.

Dawson socked 438 homers and drove in 1,591 runs in a 21-year career spent with the Expos, Cubs, Red Sox and Marlins. He won the NL rookie of the year award in 1977 with the Expos and the NL MVP award 10 years later with the last-place Cubs. Dawson credited that move to Chicago for revitalizing his career.

"It gave me new life, playing on a natural surface after playing in Montreal on an artificial surface for 10 years," said Dawson, who played with constant pain in his knees.

Hall of Fame inductee Andre Dawson amassed 438 homers in a 21-year career

Joining Dawson at the induction ceremonies in Cooperstown were former manager Whitey Herzog and former umpire Doug Harvey, both elected by the veterans committee. Herzog led the Cardinals to the 1982 World Series crown as well as pennants in '85 and '87. Prior to that, he guided the Royals to three division titles in a row from 1976-78.

Harvey umpired in the NL for 31 seasons and worked five World Series and nine NL Championship Series. Because of his strict adherence and focus on baseball rules, Harvey was nicknamed "God" by the players.

Theatre Of The Absurd

The 2010 season also presented plenty of material for the Theatre of the Absurd. In late April, the Brewers stormed through Pittsburgh, sweeping a three-game series by the combined score of 36-1. The sweep included a 20-0 romp that represented the Pirates' worst loss in their 124-year history as well as the most one-sided shutout in the annals of the Brewers.

It only got worse for the Pirates. They lost 105 games and extended their record streak of losing seasons to 18. Despite the years of bad baseball, the franchise typically had avoided crossing the 100-loss plateau, doing so only two other times in the

CONTINUED ON PAGE 21

MAJOR LEAGUE *ALL-STARS* — SELECTED BY BASEBALL AMERICA

Josh Hamilton missed most of September but led all batters in average and slugging

Felix Hernandez won the big league ERA title but narrowly missed the strikeout lead

FIRST TEAM

POS	PLAYER, TEAM	AVG	OBP	SLG	AB	R	H	2B	3B	HR	RBI	SB	CS	BB	SO
C	Joe Mauer*, Twins	.327	.402	.469	510	88	167	43	1	9	75	1	4	65	53
1B	Joey Votto*, Reds	.324	.424	.600	547	106	177	36	2	37	113	16	5	91	125
2B	Robinson Cano*, Yankees	.319	.381	.534	626	103	200	41	3	29	109	3	2	57	77
3B	Ryan Zimmerman, Nationals	.307	.388	.510	525	85	161	32	0	25	85	4	1	69	98
SS	Troy Tulowitzki, Rockies	.315	.381	.568	470	89	148	32	3	27	95	11	2	48	78
LF	Matt Holliday, Cardinals	.312	.390	.532	596	95	186	45	1	28	103	9	5	69	93
CF	Josh Hamilton*, Rangers	.359	.411	.633	518	95	186	40	3	32	100	8	1	43	95
RF	Jose Bautista, Blue Jays	.260	.378	.617	569	109	148	35	3	54	124	9	2	100	116
DH	Miguel Cabrera, Tigers	.328	.420	.622	548	111	180	45	1	38	126	.3	3	89	95

POS	PITCHER, TEAM	W	L	ERA	G	GS	CG	SV	IP	H	R	ER	HR	BB	SO	WHIP
SP	Roy Halladay, Phillies	21	10	2.44	33	33	9	0	251	231	74	68	24	30	219	1.04
SP	Felix Hernandez, Mariners	13	12	2.27	34	34	6	0	250	194	80	63	17	70	232	1.06
SP	Ubaldo Jimenez, Rockies	19	8	2.88	33	33	4	0	222	164	73	71	10	92	214	1.16
SP	Cliff Lee*, Mariners/Rangers	12	9	3.18	28	28	7	0	212	195	84	75	16	18	185	1.00
RP	Brian Wilson, Giants	3	3	1.81	70	0	0	48	75	62	16	15	3	26	93	1.18

SECOND TEAM

POS	PLAYER, TEAM	AVG	OBP	SLG	AB	R	H	2B	3B	HR	RBI	SB	CS	BB	SO
C	Brian McCann*, Braves	.269	.375	.453	479	63	129	25	0	21	77	5	2	74	98
1B	Albert Pujols, Cardinals	.312	.414	.596	587	115	183	39	1	42	118	14	4	103	76
2B	Dan Uggla, Marlins	.287	.369	.508	589	100	169	31	0	33	105	4	1	78	149
3B	Adrian Beltre, Red Sox	.321	.365	.553	589	84	189	49	2	28	102	2	1	40	82
SS	Hanley Ramirez, Marlins	.300	.378	.475	543	92	163	28	2	21	76	32	10	64	93
LF	Carl Crawford*, Rays	.307	.356	.495	600	110	184	30	13	19	90	47	10	46	104
CF	Carlos Gonzalez*, Rockies	.336	.376	.598	587	111	197	34	9	34	117	26	8	40	135
RF	Shin-Soo Choo*, Indians	.300	.401	.484	550	81	165	31	2	22	90	22	7	83	118
DH	Evan Longoria, Rays	.294	.372	.507	574	96	169	46	5	22	104	15	5	72	124

POS	PITCHER, TEAM	W	L	ERA	G	GS	CG	SV	IP	H	R	ER	HR	BB	SO	WHIP
SP	C.C. Sabathia*, Yankees	21	7	3.18	34	34	2	0	238	209	92	84	20	74	197	1.19
SP	Justin Verlander, Tigers	18	9	3.37	33	33	4	0	224	190	89	84	14	71	219	1.16
SP	Adam Wainwright, Cardinals	20	11	2.42	33	33	5	0	230	186	68	62	15	56	213	1.05
SP	Jered Weaver, Angels	13	12	3.01	34	34	0	0	224	187	83	75	23	54	233	1.07
RP	Carlos Marmol, Cubs	2	3	2.55	77	0	0	38	78	40	23	22	1	52	138	1.19

* Bat/Throw lefthanded.

EXECUTIVE OF THE YEAR

LARRY GOREN

Jon Daniels

After a pair of second-place finishes in 2008-09, the Rangers won 90 games and the AL West, making the playoffs for the first time since 1999. They ran out of steam in the World Series, but not before knocking out the Rays and Yankees.

General manager Jon Daniels (and his front office staff) built a contender on the strength of a flurry of near-flawless player acquisitions. At various points, they acquired Josh Hamilton, Cliff Lee, Elvis Andrus, Neftali Feliz, Nelson Cruz and Bengie Molina in trades, while inking free agents like Colby Lewis, Vladimir Guerrero and Darren Oliver last offseason.

PREVIOUS 10 WINNERS

2000: Walt Jocketty, Cardinals
2001: Pat Gillick, Mariners
2002: Billy Beane, Athletics
2003: Brian Sabean, Giants
2004: Terry Ryan, Twins
2005: Mark Shapiro, Indians
2006: Dave Dombrowski, Tigers
2007: Jack Zduriencik, Brewers
2008: Theo Epstein, Red Sox
2009: Dan O'Dowd, Rockies

Full list: BaseballAmerica.com/awards

MANAGER OF THE YEAR

CLIFF WELCH

Bobby Cox

Bobby Cox guided the Braves to one last playoff appearance, the 16th of his career (counting one with the Blue Jays), by winning the NL wild card on the season's final day. A first-round playoff loss to the Giants did nothing to dim a brilliant 30-year career.

• Cox retired with 2,504 wins, the fourth highest total of all time.

• He led the Braves to an unprecedented 14 consecutive division titles from 1991 to 2005.

• In his time in Atlanta, Cox won five NL pennants and one World Series in 1995.

• He shattered John McGraw's mark for career ejections, getting tossed 158 times.

PREVIOUS 10 WINNERS

2000: Dusty Baker, Giants
2001: Lou Piniella, Mariners
2002: Mike Scioscia, Angels
2003: Jack McKeon, Marlins
2004: Bobby Cox, Braves
2005: Ozzie Guillen, White Sox
2006: Jim Leyland, Tigers
2007: Terry Francona, Red Sox
2008: Ron Gardenhire, Twins
2009: Mike Scioscia, Angels

Full list: BaseballAmerica.com/awards

CONTINUED FROM PAGE 19

era of 162-game seasons: in 2001 and 1985.

On May 8, Brewers reserve outfielder Jody Gerut hit for the cycle in Arizona. Never mind that he had only four hits for the season entering that game and was batting .133.

A more stunning cycle came on July 16 in Boston when Rangers catcher Bengie Molina accomplished the feat. Considered by many to be the slowest runner in the game, Molina needed a triple in his final at-bat and, amazingly, came through with one, becoming the first catcher since 1900 to hit for the cycle with a grand slam included.

"For a guy who has been criticized for his speed for 11 years, and may be the slowest guy in the world, it was an unbelievable feeling," Molina said.

Ageless lefty Jamie Moyer, the oldest player in the big leagues at 47, became just the eighth major league pitcher to start a game in four different decades. On May 7, he became the oldest pitcher ever to throw a shutout, blanking Atlanta 7-0 on

two hits for his 10th career shutout.

Moyer later would make news of an unwanted kind when he surrendered the 506th home run of his career, breaking the record of Phillies Hall of Famer Robin Roberts, who retired in 1966.

It's not often a player makes news offensively and defensively in the same night, but Mets center fielder Angel Pagan did exactly that on May 19 in Washington. He socked an inside-the-park homer and started a triple play with a shoestring catch. While New York lost the game, Pagan became the first player to hit that daily double since Phillies shortstop Ted Kazanski against the New York Giants on Sept. 25, 1955.

A walk-off hit became a limp-off hit on May 19 when the Angels' Kendry Morales smacked a game-winning grand slam against Seattle. Morales suffered a broken left leg, and subsequently missed the rest of the season, when mobbed by teammates at the plate. The next day, teammate Howie Kendrick socked a three-run, walk-off homer and was met at home plate by a committee of none.

Angels lefty Scott Kazmir apparently missed the

memo that pitchers ruled in 2010. On July 10, the A's tagged him for 13 runs in five innings in a 15-1 loss in Oakland. Kazmir set a club record for most runs allowed in one game.

Ownerships In Flux

A group headed by Texas icon Nolan Ryan and Pittsburgh sports attorney Chuck Greenberg bought the Rangers from beleaguered owner Tom Hicks in a bankruptcy auction.

That 16-hour process went into the early hours of the morning of Aug. 5 as the Ryan-Greenberg team outlasted Dallas Mavericks owner Mark Cuban. The final sale price of $593 million included $385 million in cash.

"It was a relief just to get it done," said Ryan, who had served as club president under Hicks.

Hoping to expedite the sale process, the Rangers filed for Chapter 11 bankruptcy protection in late May. Instead, that move bogged down the process and led to a court ruling that the team be sold at auction.

The new owners received immediate gratification when the Rangers, already in first place in the AL West, pulled away to win the division and make the playoffs for the first time since 1999.

The situation in Los Angeles involving the Dodgers was much more complicated, not to mention messy. With feuding owners Frank and Jamie McCourt taking their respective positions in divorce court, each laid claim to ownership of the storied franchise.

The tawdry affair degenerated into a case of he-said, she-said. Frank McCourt claimed his estranged wife signed documents that guaranteed he would retain control of the club. Jamie McCourt insisted she did not knowingly agree to that stipulation and sued for 50-50 marital rights.

The Dodgers faded from view in the NL West during the second half of the season.

Rangers Gain Lee-Way

Of all the July 31 trade-deadline maneuvers, none could match the impact of the Rangers' acquisition of lefthander Cliff Lee from the Mariners on July 9. Considering the sale of the team hadn't yet taken place and the finances were basically frozen, it was a stunning move by Texas that beat other contenders to the punch.

Lee made an odd debut for Texas against the Orioles, pitching a complete game but allowing three home runs in a 6-1 loss. Second-year Baltimore starter Chris Tillman out-pitched him, taking a no-hitter into the seventh inning.

Lee pitched effectively for the Mariners in the

Trade acquisition Cliff Lee helped pitch the Rangers to their first World Series

first half, going 8-3, 2.34 in 13 starts, but what really caught the Rangers' eye was the veteran lefty's postseason track record. Lee went 4-0, 1.56 in five postseason starts for the NL pennant-winning Phillies in 2009, a performance that included Philadelphia's only two wins against the Yankees in the World Series.

To get Lee, Texas surrendered young first baseman Justin Smoak as well as three prospects at the Double-A level: righthanders Blake Beavan and Josh Lueke and second baseman Matt Lawson. Eleven months prior to his trade to the Rangers, Lee had been traded by the Indians to the Phillies for a similar package of four young players.

To help replace Lee, the Phillies acquired Roy Oswalt from the Astros on July 31 and paired him with Halladay and Cole Hamels to form a fearsome front three. Houston parted with a second franchise icon that same day when they sent Lance Berkman to the Yankees for a pair of modest talents.

The Angels nabbed Dan Haren from the Diamondbacks on July 25, sacrificing four pitchers, but it was too late to stop Los Angeles' fade from contention in the AL West.

Stopping At 162 Games

The regular season nearly went into overtime for a fourth consecutive year.

CONTINUED ON PAGE 24

NL wins first ASG since '96

ANAHEIM If for no other reason, the 2010 season will be remembered as the year that the National League finally won the All-Star Game. The American League had gone undefeated since 1996, compiling a 12-0-1 record while also claiming home-field advantage in the World Series each year since that prize was attached to the game in 2003.

Just when it appeared the AL would prevail once again in Anaheim, Braves catcher Brian McCann delivered a three-run double in the seventh inning that produced the margin of victory in a tense 3-1 decision. He won game MVP honors for striking the winning blow against hard-throwing White Sox lefty Matt Thornton, who held lefthanded batters, like McCann, to a .175 average on the year.

"Enough was enough," Cardinals righty Adam Wainwright said.

That had been the feeling for years on the NL side. Continuing the theme of the Year of the Pitcher, Rays lefty David Price and Rockies righthander Ubaldo Jimenez set the tone early for another night of frustration for the hitters. Each pitched two scoreless innings.

The victory did not come without drama in the ninth. The Cubs' Marlon Byrd, playing right field, threw out slow-footed David Ortiz at second base after fielding John Buck's bloop single. That heads-up play helped Dodgers closer Jonathan Broxton close out the AL and finally end their long string of dominance.

"It felt great for us to get the win and finally break the streak," Broxton said.

In the seventh inning, Byrd worked a crucial two-out walk and scored on McCann's double.

After four consecutive one-run losses, NL manager Charlie Manuel of Philadelphia tried to impress upon his players the importance of securing home-field advantage for the Fall Classic.

"It's a big deal," said Manuel, whose club overcame that disadvantage in 2008 against Tampa Bay but was unable to do so the following season against the Yankees. "I think teams play better at home. It feels good, it feels real good."

—Tom Haudricourt

ALL-STAR GAME

MORRIS FOSTOFF

The NL won for the first time in 14 years thanks to Brian McCann's double

JULY 13, 2010

National League 3, American League 1

NATIONAL	AB	R	H	BI	AMERICAN	AB	R	H	BI
Ramirez, H, ss	3	0	0	0	Suzuki, I, rf	2	0	0	0
Furcal, ss	0	0	0	0	Hunter, cf	2	0	0	0
Prado, 2b	3	0	0	0	Jeter, ss	2	0	1	0
Phillips, B, 2b	1	0	0	0	j-Andrus, pr-ss	1	0	0	0
Pujols, 1b	2	0	0	0	Cabrera, M, 1b	2	0	1	0
Gonzalez, A, 1b	2	0	0	0	d-Konerko, ph-1b	2	0	0	0
Howard, dh	2	0	0	0	Hamilton, cf-rf	3	0	1	0
b-Votto, ph-dh	2	0	0	0	k-Bautista, J, pr-rf	1	0	0	0
Wright, D, 3b	2	0	2	0	Guerrero, dh	2	0	0	0
Rolen, 3b	2	1	1	0	e-Ortiz, D, ph-dh	2	0	1	0
Braun, lf	2	0	0	0	Longoria, 3b	1	1	1	0
Holliday, lf	1	1	1	0	Wigginton, 3b	0	0	0	0
Bourn, lf	1	0	0	0	f-Swisher, ph	1	0	0	0
Ethier, cf-rf	2	0	1	0	Beltre, 3b	1	0	0	0
c-Young, C, ph-cf	2	0	0	0	Mauer, c	2	0	0	0
Hart, C, rf	2	0	0	0	Buck, J, c	2	0	1	0
Byrd, cf-rf	1	1	0	0	Cano, 2b	1	0	0	1
Molina, Y, c	1	0	1	0	Kinsler, 2b	1	0	0	0
a-McCann, ph-c	2	0	1	3	Crawford, lf	2	0	0	0
					Wells, V, lf	1	0	0	0
Totals	**33**	**3**	**7**	**3**	**Totals**	**31**	**1**	**6**	**1**

National	000	000	300—3
American	000	010	000—1

a-Flied out for Molina in 5th. b-Grounded out for Howard in 7th. c-Popped out for Ethier in 7th. d-Struck out for Cabrera in 6th. e-Struck out for Guerrero in 6th. f-Struck out for Wigginton in 7th. j-Ran for Jeter in the 6th. k-Ran for Hamilton in the 6th.

LOB—National 5, American 7. **2B**—McCann, Longoria, Buck. **SF**—Cano. **GIDP**—Braun, Hamilton. **SB**—Wright, Crawford. **CS**—Andrus. **E**—Kuo. **A**—Byrd.

NATIONAL	IP	H	R	ER	BB	SO	AMERICAN	IP	H	R	ER	BB	SO
Jimenez, U	2.0	2	0	0	1	1	Price	2.0	1	0	0	0	1
Johnson, J	2.0	0	0	0	0	2	Pettitte	1.0	1	0	0	0	2
Kuo	0.2	0	1	0	1	0	Lee, Cl	1.0	0	0	0	0	1
Bell	0.1	0	0	0	0	0	Verlander	1.0	2	0	0	0	2
Halladay	0.2	2	0	0	0	1	Lester	1.0	0	0	0	0	0
Capps (W)	0.1	0	0	0	0	1	Hughes, P (L)	0.1	2	2	2	0	0
Wainwright	1.0	1	0	0	1	2	Thornton	1.0	1	1	1	1	0
Wilson, B	1.0	0	0	0	0	0	Bailey, A	0.1	0	0	0	1	1
Broxton (S)	1.0	1	0	0	0	1	Soriano, R	1.0	0	0	0	0	0
							Valverde	1.0	0	0	0	0	3
Totals	**9.0**	**6**	**1**	**0**	**3**	**8**	**Totals**	**9.0**	**7**	**3**	**3**	**2**	**10**

Umpires: HP—Mike Reilly. **1B**—Mike Winters. **2B**—Brian O'Nora. **3B**—Laz Diaz. **LF**—Bruce Dreckman. **RF**—Jim Wolf. **T**—2:59. **A**—45,408.

CONTINUED FROM PAGE 22

Needing just one victory in their final series of the season, both at home, the Braves and Giants managed to wring every last drop of drama out of the situation. The Braves dropped two in a row to the Phillies, who already had claimed the NL East title, while the Giants lost their first two games to the Padres, who led the NL West for most of the season before fading.

If the Braves and Giants had lost again on the final day of the season, then San Francisco and San Diego would have played one game for the NL West title. The loser would then play Atlanta the next day for the wild card.

That scenario was averted when Atlanta hung on for a tense 8-7 victory against Philadelphia and San Francisco blanked San Diego 3-0, behind the brilliant pitching of lefthander Jonathan Sanchez.

"We nailed it," Giants outfielder Pat Burrell said. "It was looking like it was headed the wrong way. Our guys toughed it out."

The Braves' squeaker allowed Cox to go to the playoffs one last time—and for the first time as a wild-card team. Atlanta's four-year absence from the postseason probably seemed a lot longer to a skipper who led his team to an unprecedented 14 consecutive division titles from 1991 to 2005.

For a team that led the majors with 25 last at-bat victories, the Braves seemed almost destined to play it out until the final inning of the season.

"I knew all along today would be the day," said Chipper Jones, who missed the joyous occasion with a knee injury. "We've waited until the last minute all year. It makes perfect sense to show up on the last day and get it done."

Taking advantage of an uncharacteristic late-season fade by the Cardinals, the Reds pulled away to claim the NL Central by five games. Cincinnati fans had waited since 1995 to see their club return to the playoffs, a stretch that included nine consecutive losing seasons.

The Reds clinched that playoff berth in memorable fashion on Sept. 28 when Jay Bruce's walk-off home run provided a 3-2 victory against the Astros at Great American Ball Park. It was a fitting climax for a club that won 22 games in its final at-bat, second-most in the majors.

"When he hit that one, there was a big sigh of relief and the party was on," Reds manager Dusty Baker said. "This is sweet. This is a special group, special guys and a special feeling."

Over in the AL East, Tampa Bay and New York jockeyed back and forth for the division lead all season, so certainly was no surprise when that

ACTIVE LEADERS

Career leaders among players who more active in 2010. Batters need 1,000 plate appearances and pitchers need 750 innings to qualify for percentage titles.

BATTING			PITCHING		
AVG	Albert Pujols	.331	ERA	Mariano Rivera	2.23
OBP	Albert Pujols	.426	W	Jamie Moyer	267
SLG	Albert Pujols	.624	L	Jamie Moyer	204
OPS	Albert Pujols	1.050	SV	Trevor Hoffman	601
R	Alex Rodriguez	1,757	IP	Jamie Moyer	4,020.1
H	Derek Jeter	2,926	SO	Jamie Moyer	2,405
2B	Ivan Rodriguez	565	BB	Jamie Moyer	1,158
3B	Carl Crawford	105	AVG	Billy Wagner	.187
HR	Ken Griffey Jr.	630	G	Trevor Hoffman	1,035
RBI	Ken Griffey Jr.	1,836	GS	Jamie Moyer	628
BB	Jim Thome	1,679	HR	Jamie Moyer	511
SO	Jim Thome	2,395	SO/9	Billy Wagner	11.92
XBH	Ken Griffey Jr.	1,192	BB/9	Carlos Silva	1.73
SB	Juan Pierre	527	HR/9	Mariano Rivera	0.49

battle came down to the final day of the season. The Rays nipped Kansas City in 12 innings and the Yankees fell to the spoiler Red Sox, allowing the Rays to claim the division by a mere game.

"It would be stupid to say it doesn't matter how you finish," Yankees lefty Andy Pettitte said. "We would have liked to get this thing done, but we didn't. The bottom line is we're the world champs until somebody knocks us off."

It certainly was no novelty that the Yankees made it back to the postseason, along with the Phillies and Twins, but Selig was buoyed by the fact that five of the eight playoff teams were different from the previous season—Atlanta, San Francisco, Cincinnati, Tampa Bay and Texas.

Turnstiles Keep On Turning

With the nation still mired in a slow recovery from the recession, baseball officials worried what that effect might be on the box office. Much to their delight, more than 73 million fans went through the turnstiles, the sixth-highest attendance in major league history. Attendance was down just four-tenths of one percent from the previous season.

It was the seventh consecutive season that baseball surpassed 73 million fans, led by the Yankees, who drew 3.765 million and the Phillies with 3.647 million. For the first time in franchise history, Philadelphia sold out all 81 home games.

Nine clubs surpassed 3 million in attendance and 10 averaged more than 35,000 per game.

"On behalf of Major League Baseball, I am grateful to the fans and proud of the game," Selig said. "Despite the most challenging economic times since the Great Depression, fans once again attended baseball games in extraordinary numbers."

MAJOR LEAGUE DEBUTS

ARIZONA DIAMONDBACKS
Jordan Norberto	April 6
Cole Gillespie	April 21
Daniel Stange	April 29
Cesar Valdez	May 3
Sam Demel	June 16
Barry Enright	June 30
Zach Kroenke	Sept. 10
Konrad Schmidt	Sept. 13

ATLANTA BRAVES
Jason Heyward	April 5
Jonny Venters	April 17
Brandon Hicks	May 5
Craig Kimbrel	May 7
Mike Minor	Aug. 9
Freddie Freeman	Sept. 1
Brandon Beachy	Sept. 20
J.C. Boscan	Oct. 1

BALTIMORE ORIOLES
Rhyne Hughes	April 24
Frank Mata	May 26
Jake Arrieta	June 10
Josh Bell	July 1
Brandon Snyder	Sept. 10

BOSTON RED SOX
Daniel Nava	June 12
Felix Doubront	June 18
Ryan Kalish	July 31
Yamaico Navarro	Aug. 20
Lars Anderson	Sept. 6
Robert Coello	Sept. 6

CHICAGO CUBS
James Russell	April 5
Starlin Castro	May 7
Andrew Cashner	May 31
Brian Schlitter	June 28
Casey Coleman	Aug. 2
Thomas Diamond	Aug. 3
Marcos Mateo	Aug. 9
Welington Castillo	Aug. 11
Darwin Barney	Aug. 12
Scott Maine	Aug. 27
Brad Snyder	Sept. 7

CHICAGO WHITE SOX
Sergio Santos	April 8
Dayan Viciedo	June 20
Jeffrey Marquez	July 9
Lucas Harrell	July 30
Chris Sale	Aug. 6
Gregory Infante	Sept. 7
Brent Morel	Sept. 7

CINCINNATI REDS
Logan Ondrusek	April 5
Mike Leake	April 11
Chris Heisey	May 3
Enerio Del Rosario	May 24
Sam LeCure	May 28
Jordan Smith	June 15
Travis Wood	July 1
Chris Valaika	Aug. 24
Aroldis Chapman	Aug. 31
Yonder Alonso	Sept. 1

CLEVELAND INDIANS
Hector Ambriz	April 30
Jason Donald	May 18
Frank Herrmann	June 4
Carlos Santana	June 11
Jeanmar Gomez	July 18
Josh Tomlin	July 27
Jordan Brown	Aug. 1
Vinnie Pestano	Sept. 23

COLORADO ROCKIES
Chris Nelson	June 19
Matt Reynolds	Aug. 19

Samuel Deduno	Aug. 27
Michael McKenry	Sept. 8
Edgmer Escalona	Sept. 10

DETROIT TIGERS
Austin Jackson	April 5
Scott Sizemore	April 5
Brennan Boesch	April 23
Casper Wells	May 15
Danny Worth	May 16
Jay Sborz	June 22
Andrew Oliver	June 25
Robbie Weinhardt	July 7
Will Rhymes	July 25
Jeff Frazier	July 30
Max St. Pierre	Sept. 4

FLORIDA MARLINS
Bryan Petersen	May 7
Jay Buente	May 27
Mike Stanton	June 8
James Houser	June 24
Alex Sanabia	June 24
Jhan Marinez	July 16
Brad Davis	July 21
Logan Morrison	July 27
Scott Cousins	Sept. 3
Jose Ceda	Sept. 6
Adalberto Mendez	Sept. 6
Brett Sinkbeil	Sept. 15
Chris Hatcher	Sept. 19
Osvaldo Martinez	Sept. 19
Sandy Rosario	Sept. 23
Steve Cishek	Sept. 26

HOUSTON ASTROS
Jason Castro	June 22
Fernando Abad	July 28
Brett Wallace	July 31
Brian Bogusevic	Sept. 1
Henry Villar	Sept. 10

KANSAS CITY ROYALS
Blake Wood	May 12
Greg Holland	Aug. 2
Lucas May	Sept. 4
Jarrod Dyson	Sept. 7

LOS ANGELES ANGELS
Bobby Cassevah	April 9
Francisco Rodriguez	April 15
Michael Kohn	July 26
Peter Bourjos	Aug. 3
Jordan Walden	Aug. 22
Hank Conger	Sept. 11
Mark Trumbo	Sept. 11
Andrew Romine	Sept. 24

LOS ANGELES DODGERS
Carlos Monasterios	April 5
Jon Link	April 20
John Ely	April 28
Kenley Jansen	July 24
John Lindsey	Sept. 8
Russ Mitchell	Sept. 8

MILWAUKEE BREWERS
Jonathan Lucroy	May 21
Zach Braddock	May 23
Lorenzo Cain	July 16
Mike McClendon	Aug. 14
Jeremy Jeffress	Sept. 1
Brandon Kintzler	Sept. 10
Mark Rogers	Sept. 10

MINNESOTA TWINS
Alex Burnett	April 8
Drew Butera	April 9
Luke Hughes	April 28
Wilson Ramos	May 2
Trevor Plouffe	May 21
Danny Valencia	June 3

Anthony Slama	July 21
Matt Fox	Sept. 3
Rob Delaney	Sept. 4
Ben Revere	Sept. 7

NEW YORK METS
Jenrry Mejia	April 7
Hisanori Takahashi	April 7
Ruben Tejada	April 7
Ryota Igarashi	April 8
Raul Valdes	April 11
Ike Davis	April 19
Jesus Feliciano	June 10
Lucas Duda	Sept. 1
Mike Nickeas	Sept. 4
Dillon Gee	Sept. 7

NEW YORK YANKEES
Kevin Russo	May 8
Ivan Nova	May 13
Chad Huffman	June 13
Colin Curtis	June 21
Eduardo Nunez	Aug. 19

OAKLAND ATHLETICS
Tyson Ross	April 7
Steve Tolleson	April 28
Josh Donaldson	April 30
Chris Carter	Aug. 9
Justin James	Sept. 2
Bobby Cramer	Sept. 13
Eric Sogard	Sept. 14

PHILADELPHIA PHILLIES
David Herndon	April 5
Vance Worley	July 24
Domonic Brown	July 28

PITTSBURGH PIRATES
John Raynor	April 8
Argenis Diaz	April 21
Brad Lincoln	June 9
Jose Tabata	June 9
Pedro Alvarez	June 16
Erik Kratz	July 17
Pedro Ciriaco	Sept. 8
Alex Presley	Sept. 8

Mike Stanton hit 21 homers in Double-A
and then 22 more for the Marlins

ST. LOUIS CARDINALS
Allen Craig	April 8
Bryan Anderson	April 15
Jon Jay	April 26
Fernando Salas	May 28
Adam Ottavino	May 29
Evan MacLane	July 7
Steven Hill	Aug. 15
Daniel Descalso	Sept. 18
Mark Hamilton	Sept. 20

SAN DIEGO PADRES
Lance Zawadzki	May 2
Cory Luebke	Sept. 3
Mike Baxter	Sept. 6

SAN FRANCISCO GIANTS
Darren Ford	Sept. 1

SEATTLE MARINERS
Kanekoa Texeira	April 6
Greg Halman	Sept. 23
Matt Mangini	Sept. 23
Dan Cortes	Sept. 24
Anthony Varvaro	Sept. 24

TAMPA BAY RAYS
Jeremy Hellickson	Aug. 2
Desmond Jennings	Sept. 1
Jake McGee	Sept. 14

TEXAS RANGERS
Justin Smoak	April 23
Alexi Ogando	June 15
Omar Beltre	June 30
Mitch Moreland	July 29
Michael Kirkman	Aug. 21

TORONTO BLUE JAYS
Rommie Lewis	April 28
J.P. Arencibia	Aug. 7
Kyle Drabek	Sept. 15

WASHINGTON NATIONALS
Jesse English	April 5
Luis Atilano	April 23
Drew Storen	May 17
Stephen Strasburg	June 8
Danny Espinosa	Sept. 1
Yunesky Maya	Sept. 7

CLUB BATTING

	AVG	G	AB	R	H	2B	3B	HR	RBI	BB	SO	SB	CS	OBP	SLG
Texas	.276	162	5635	787	1556	268	25	162	740	511	986	123	48	.338	.419
Kansas City	.274	162	5604	676	1534	279	31	121	640	471	905	115	50	.331	.399
Minnesota	.273	162	5568	781	1521	318	41	142	749	559	967	68	28	.341	.422
Boston	.268	162	5646	818	1511	358	22	211	782	587	1140	68	17	.339	.451
Chicago	.268	162	5484	752	1467	263	21	177	710	467	922	160	74	.332	.420
Detroit	.268	162	5643	751	1515	308	32	152	717	546	1147	69	30	.335	.415
New York	.267	162	5567	859	1485	275	32	201	823	662	1136	103	30	.350	.436
Baltimore	.259	162	5554	613	1440	264	21	133	577	424	1056	76	34	.316	.386
Oakland	.256	162	5448	663	1396	276	30	109	619	527	1061	156	38	.324	.378
Cleveland	.248	162	5487	646	1362	290	20	128	601	545	1184	91	33	.322	.378
Los Angeles	.248	162	5488	681	1363	276	19	155	656	466	1070	104	52	.311	.390
Toronto	.248	162	5495	755	1364	319	21	257	732	471	1164	58	20	.312	.454
Tampa Bay	.247	162	5439	802	1343	295	37	160	769	672	1292	172	47	.333	.403
Seattle	.236	162	5409	513	1274	227	16	101	485	459	1184	142	39	.298	.339

CLUB PITCHING

	ERA	G	CG	SHO	SV	IP	H	R	ER	HR	BB	SO	AVG
Oakland	3.56	162	7	17	38	1432	1315	626	566	153	512	1070	.245
Tampa Bay	3.78	162	6	12	51	1454	1347	649	611	175	478	1189	.244
Seattle	3.93	162	11	10	38	1438	1402	698	628	157	452	973	.255
Texas	3.93	162	7	8	46	1455	1355	687	636	162	551	1181	.246
Minnesota	3.95	162	9	13	40	1453	1493	671	638	155	383	1048	.266
Los Angeles	4.04	162	10	9	39	1449	1422	702	651	148	565	1130	.256
New York	4.06	162	3	8	39	1442	1349	693	651	179	540	1154	.249
Chicago	4.09	162	6	11	43	1446	1471	704	658	136	490	1149	.264
Boston	4.20	162	3	9	44	1457	1402	744	679	152	580	1207	.253
Toronto	4.22	162	5	11	45	1441	1407	728	676	150	539	1184	.255
Cleveland	4.30	162	10	4	34	1433	1477	752	684	147	572	967	.269
Detroit	4.30	162	6	5	32	1444	1445	743	690	142	537	1056	.262
Baltimore	4.59	162	3	7	35	1436	1508	785	733	186	520	1007	.270
Kansas City	4.97	162	7	3	44	1437	1553	845	794	176	551	1035	.276

CLUB FIELDING

	PCT	PO	A	E	DP		PCT	PO	A	E	DP
New York	.988	4327	1522	69	161	Boston	.982	4370	1588	111	132
Minnesota	.987	4358	1710	78	150	Cleveland	.982	4299	1814	110	179
Tampa Bay	.986	4361	1499	85	134	Detroit	.982	4333	1668	109	171
Toronto	.985	4322	1691	92	172	Seattle	.982	4314	1657	110	145
Oakland	.984	4295	1704	99	147	Texas	.982	4366	1499	105	133
Chicago	.983	4339	1663	103	158	Los Angeles	.981	4348	1562	113	116
Baltimore	.982	4309	1582	105	141	Kansas City	.980	4310	1588	121	138

INDIVIDUAL BATTING LEADERS (MINIMUM 3.1 PA/TEAM GAME)

	AVG	G	AB	R	H	2B	3B	HR	RBI	BB	SO	SB
Josh Hamilton, Texas	.359	133	518	95	186	40	3	32	100	43	95	8
Miguel Cabrera, Detroit	.328	150	548	111	180	45	1	38	126	89	95	3
Joe Mauer, Minnesota	.327	137	510	88	167	43	1	9	75	65	53	1
Adrian Beltre, Boston	.321	154	589	84	189	49	2	28	102	40	82	2
Robinson Cano, New York	.319	160	626	103	200	41	3	29	109	57	77	3
Billy Butler, Kansas City	.318	158	595	77	189	45	0	15	78	69	78	0
Ichiro Suzuki, Seattle	.315	162	680	74	214	30	3	6	43	45	86	42
Paul Konerko, Chicago	.312	149	548	89	171	30	1	39	111	72	110	0
Carl Crawford, Tampa Bay	.307	154	600	110	184	30	13	19	90	46	104	47
Victor Martinez, Boston	.302	127	493	64	149	32	1	20	79	40	52	1

INDIVIDUAL PITCHING LEADERS (MINIMUM 1 IP/TEAM GAME)

	W	L	ERA	G	GS	CG	SHO	SV	IP	H	R	ER	BB	SO
Felix Hernandez, Seattle	13	12	2.28	34	34	6	1	0	250	194	80	63	70	232
Clay Buchholz, Boston	17	7	2.34	28	28	1	0	0	174	142	55	45	67	120
David Price, Tampa Bay	19	6	2.72	32	31	2	1	0	209	170	71	63	79	188
Trevor Cahill, Oakland	18	8	2.98	30	30	1	1	0	197	155	73	65	63	118
Jered Weaver, Los Angeles	13	12	3.01	34	34	0	0	0	224	187	83	75	54	233
C.C. Sabathia, New York	21	7	3.19	34	34	2	0	0	238	209	92	84	74	197
Cliff Lee, Seattle/Texas	12	9	3.19	28	28	7	1	0	212	195	84	75	18	185
Gio Gonzalez, Oakland	15	9	3.24	33	33	1	0	0	201	171	75	72	92	171
Jon Lester, Boston	19	9	3.25	32	32	2	0	0	208	167	81	75	83	225
C.J. Wilson, Texas	15	8	3.35	33	33	3	0	0	204	161	83	76	93	170

AWARD WINNERS

Selected by Baseball Writers Association of America

MOST VALUABLE PLAYER

Player	1st	2nd	3rd	Total
Josh Hamilton, Texas	22	4	—	358
Miguel Cabrera, Detroit	5	11	10	262
Robinson Cano, New York	—	12	12	229
Jose Bautista, Toronto	1	—	4	165
Paul Konerko, Chicago	—	—	—	130
Evan Longoria, Tampa Bay	—	—	—	100
Carl Crawford, Tampa Bay	—	1	—	98
Joe Mauer, Minnesota	—	—	2	97
Adrian Beltre, Boston	—	—	—	83
Delmon Young, Minnesota	—	—	—	44
Vladimir Guerrero, Texas	—	—	—	22
Rafael Soriano, Tampa Bay	—	—	—	21
C.C. Sabathia, New York	—	—	—	13
Shin-Soo Choo, Cleveland	—	—	—	9
Alex Rodriguez, New York	—	—	—	8
Felix Hernandez, Seattle	—	—	—	6
Ichiro Suzuki, Seattle	—	—	—	3
Jim Thome, Minnesota	—	—	—	2
Joakim Soria, Kansas City	—	—	—	1
Mark Teixeira, New York	—	—	—	1

CY YOUNG AWARD

Pitchers	1st	2nd	3rd	Total
Felix Hernandez, Seattle	21	2	3	167
David Price, Tampa Bay	4	15	7	111
C.C. Sabathia, New York	3	10	12	102
Jon Lester, Boston	—	—	1	33
Jered Weaver, Los Angeles	—	1	2	24
Clay Buchholz, Boston	—	—	2	20
Cliff Lee, Seattle/Texas	—	—	1	6
Rafael Soriano, Tampa Bay	—	—	—	5
Trevor Cahill, Oakland	—	—	—	4
Joakim Soria, Kansas City	—	—	—	2
Francisco Liriano, Minnesota	—	—	—	1
Justin Verlander, Detroit	—	—	—	1

ROOKIE OF THE YEAR

Player	1st	2nd	3rd	Total
Neftali Feliz, Texas	20	7	1	122
Austin Jackson, Detroit	8	19	1	98
Danny Valencia, Minnesota	—	1	9	12
Wade Davis, Tampa Bay	—	—	11	11
John Jaso, Tampa Bay	—	1	—	3
Brennan Boesch, Detroit	—	—	3	3
Brian Matusz, Baltimore	—	—	3	3

MANAGER OF THE YEAR

Managers	1st	2nd	3rd	Total
Ron Gardenhire, Minnesota	16	8	4	108
Ron Washington, Texas	10	8	7	81
Joe Maddon, Tampa Bay	1	10	9	44
Terry Francona, Boston	—	2	7	13
Cito Gaston, Toronto	1	—	—	5
Joe Girardi, New York	—	—	1	1

GOLD GLOVE AWARDS

Selected by AL managers

C—Joe Mauer, Minn. **1B**—Mark Teixeira, N.Y. **2B**—Robinson Cano, N.Y. **3B**—Evan Longoria, T.B. **SS**—Derek Jeter, N.Y. **OF**—Carl Crawford, T.B.; Franklin Gutierrez, Sea.; Ichiro Suzuki, Sea. **P**—Mark Buehrle, Chi.

SILVER SLUGGER AWARDS

Selected by AL managers, coaches

C—Joe Mauer, Minn. **1B**—Miguel Cabrera, Det. **2B**—Robinson Cano, N.Y. **3B**—Adrian Beltre, Bos. **SS**—Alexei Ramirez, Chi. **OF**—Jose Bautista, Tor.; Carl Crawford, T.B.; Josh Hamilton, Tex. **DH**—Vladimir Guerrero, Tex..

BATTING

GAMES

Ichiro Suzuki, Mariners	162
Jose Bautista, Blue Jays	161
Chone Figgins, Mariners	161
Robinson Cano, Yankees	160
Nick Markakis, Orioles	160
Juan Pierre, White Sox	160

AT-BATS

Ichiro Suzuki, Mariners	680
Derek Jeter, Yankees	663
Michael Young, Rangers	656
Juan Pierre, White Sox	651
Marco Scutaro, Red Sox	632

PLATE APPEARANCES

Derek Jeter, Yankees	739
Juan Pierre, White Sox	734
Ichiro Suzuki, Mariners	732
Michael Young, Rangers	718
Mark Teixeira, Yankees	712

RUNS

Mark Teixeira, Yankees	113
Miguel Cabrera, Tigers	111
Derek Jeter, Yankees	111
Carl Crawford, Rays	110
Jose Bautista, Blue Jays	109

HITS

Ichiro Suzuki, Mariners	214
Robinson Cano, Yankees	200
Adrian Beltre, Red Sox	189
Billy Butler, Royals	189
Nick Markakis, Orioles	187

TOTAL BASES

Jose Bautista, Blue Jays	351
Miguel Cabrera, Tigers	341
Robinson Cano, Yankees	334
Josh Hamilton, Rangers	328
Adrian Beltre, Red Sox	326

DOUBLES

Adrian Beltre, Red Sox	49
Evan Longoria, Rays	46
Delmon Young, Twins	46
Billy Butler, Royals	45
Miguel Cabrera, Tigers	45
Nick Markakis, Orioles	45

TRIPLES

Carl Crawford, Rays	13
Austin Jackson, Tigers	10
Denard Span, Twins	10
Cliff Pennington, Athletics	8
Brett Gardner, Yankees	7
Curtis Granderson, Yankees	7

EXTRA-BASE HITS

Jose Bautista, Blue Jays	92
Miguel Cabrera, Tigers	84
Adrian Beltre, Red Sox	79
Vernon Wells, Blue Jays	78
Josh Hamilton, Rangers	75

HOME RUNS

Jose Bautista, Blue Jays	54
Paul Konerko, White Sox	39
Miguel Cabrera, Tigers	38
Mark Teixeira, Yankees	33
Josh Hamilton, Rangers	32
David Ortiz, Red Sox	32

RUNS BATTED IN

Miguel Cabrera, Tigers	126
Alex Rodriguez, Yankees	125

Jose Bautista

Jose Bautista, Blue Jays	124
Vladimir Guerrero, Rangers	115
Delmon Young, Twins	112

SACRIFICES

Elvis Andrus, Rangers	17
Chone Figgins, Mariners	17
Juan Pierre, White Sox	15
Daric Barton, Athletics	12
Darnell McDonald, Red Sox	12
Cliff Pennington, Athletics	12

SACRIFICE FLIES

Ben Zobrist, Rays	12
Alex Rodriguez, Yankees	11
Michael Young, Rangers	11
Evan Longoria, Rays	10
Jhonny Peralta, Indians/Tigers	10

HIT BY PITCH

Juan Pierre, White Sox	21

Carlos Quentin, White Sox	20
Adam Jones, Orioles	13
Mark Teixeira, Yankees	13
Travis Hafner, Indians	12
Ichiro Suzuki, Mariners	12
Josh Wilson, Mariners	12

WALKS

Daric Barton, Athletics	110
Jose Bautista, Blue Jays	100
Mark Teixeira, Yankees	93
Ben Zobrist, Rays	92
Miguel Cabrera, Tigers	89

INTENTIONAL WALKS

Miguel Cabrera, Tigers	32
Robinson Cano, Yankees	14
Joe Mauer, Twins	14
David Ortiz, Red Sox	14
Ichiro Suzuki, Mariners	13

STOLEN BASES

Juan Pierre, White Sox	68
Rajai Davis, Athletics	50
Carl Crawford, Rays	47
Brett Gardner, Yankees	47
Chone Figgins, Mariners	42
Ichiro Suzuki, Mariners	42
B.J. Upton, Rays	42

CAUGHT STEALING

Juan Pierre, White Sox	18
Elvis Andrus, Rangers	15
Chone Figgins, Mariners	15
Alex Rios, White Sox	14
Torii Hunter, Angels	12
Scott Podsednik, Royals	12

STOLEN BASE PERCENTAGE

Franklin Gutierrez, Mariners	89%
Ben Zobrist, Rays	89%
Denard Span, Twins	87%
Cliff Pennington, Athletics	85%
Brett Gardner, Yankees	84%

STRIKEOUTS

Austin Jackson, Tigers	170
B.J. Upton, Rays	164
Carlos Pena, Rays	158
David Ortiz, Red Sox	145
Adam Lind, Blue Jays	144

TOUGHEST TO STRIKE OUT
(AT-BATS PER STRIKEOUT)

Juan Pierre, White Sox	13.85
Alberto Callaspo, K.C./L.A.	13.38
A.J. Pierzynski, White Sox	12.15
Kurt Suzuki, Athletics	10.10
Vladimir Guerrero, Rangers	9.88

GROUNDED INTO DOUBLE PLAYS

Billy Butler, Royals	32
Michael Cuddyer, Twins	26
Adrian Beltre, Red Sox	25
Ty Wigginton, Orioles	23
4 tied at	22

MULTI-HIT GAMES

Ichiro Suzuki, Mariners	69
Robinson Cano, Yankees	59
Michael Young, Rangers	55
Billy Butler, Royals	54
3 tied at	53

ON-BASE PERCENTAGE

Miguel Cabrera, Tigers	.420
Josh Hamilton, Rangers	.411
Joe Mauer, Twins	.402
Shin-Soo Choo, Indians	.401
Daric Barton, Athletics	.393

SLUGGING PERCENTAGE

Josh Hamilton, Rangers	.633
Miguel Cabrera, Tigers	.622
Jose Bautista, Blue Jays	.617
Paul Konerko, White Sox	.584
Adrian Beltre, Red Sox	.553

ON-BASE PLUS SLUGGING

Josh Hamilton, Rangers	1.044
Miguel Cabrera, Tigers	1.042
Jose Bautista, Blue Jays	.995
Paul Konerko, White Sox	.977
Adrian Beltre, Red Sox	.919

PITCHING

WINS

C.C. Sabathia, Yankees	21

Miguel Cabrera

LARRY GOREN

DEPARTMENT LEADERS

Jon Lester, Red Sox	19
David Price, Rays	19
Trevor Cahill, Athletics	18
Phil Hughes, Yankees	18
Justin Verlander, Tigers	18

LOSSES

Kevin Millwood, Orioles	16
A.J. Burnett, Yankees	15
Scott Kazmir, Angels	15
James Shields, Rays	15
Dallas Braden, Athletics	14
Fausto Carmona, Indians	14
Doug Fister, Mariners	14
Jeremy Guthrie, Orioles	14
Zack Greinke, Royals	14

GAMES

Randy Choate, Rays	85
Craig Breslow, Athletics	75
Phil Coke, Tigers	74
Matt Guerrier, Twins	74
Daniel Bard, Red Sox	73
Joba Chamberlain, Yankees	73

GAMES STARTED

Felix Hernandez, Mariners	34
C.C. Sabathia, Yankees	34
Jered Weaver, Angels	34
10 tied at	33

GAMES FINISHED

Neftali Feliz, Rangers	59
Kevin Gregg, Blue Jays	56
Joakim Soria, Royals	56
Rafael Soriano, Rays	56
Mariano Rivera, Yankees	55
Jose Valverde, Tigers	55

COMPLETE GAMES

Cliff Lee, Mariners/Rangers	7
Carl Pavano, Twins	7
Felix Hernandez, Mariners	6
Dallas Braden, Athletics	5
Fausto Carmona, Indians	4
Ervin Santana, Angels	4
Justin Verlander, Tigers	4

SHUTOUTS

Dallas Braden, Athletics	2
Carl Pavano, Twins	2
19 tied at	1

SAVES

Rafael Soriano, Rays	45
Joakim Soria, Royals	43

Jered Weaver

LARRY GOREN

Neftali Feliz, Rangers	40
Kevin Gregg, Blue Jays	37
Jonathan Papelbon, Red Sox	37

INNINGS

Felix Hernandez, Mariners	249.2
C.C. Sabathia, Yankees	237.2
Justin Verlander, Tigers	224.1
Jered Weaver, Angels	224.1
Ervin Santana, Angels	222.2

HITS ALLOWED

Mark Buehrle, White Sox	246
James Shields, Rays	246
John Lackey, Red Sox	233
Carl Pavano, Twins	227
Kevin Millwood, Orioles	223

RUNS ALLOWED

James Shields, Rays	128
A.J. Burnett, Yankees	118
Kevin Millwood, Orioles	116
Kyle Davies, Royals	114
Zack Greinke, Royals	114
John Lackey, Red Sox	114

HOME RUNS ALLOWED

James Shields, Rays	34

Javier Vazquez, Yankees	32
Kevin Millwood, Orioles	30
Matt Garza, Rays	28
Ervin Santana, Angels	27

WALKS

C.J. Wilson, Rangers	93
Gio Gonzalez, Athletics	92
Jon Lester, Red Sox	83
Ricky Romero, Blue Jays	82
Kyle Davies, Royals	80

WALKS PER NINE INNINGS

Cliff Lee, Mariners/Rangers	0.76
Carl Pavano, Twins	1.51
Doug Fister, Mariners	1.68
Shaun Marcum, Blue Jays	1.98
Dallas Braden, Athletics	2.01

HIT BATSMEN

A.J. Burnett, Yankees	19
Jeremy Guthrie, Orioles	16
Scott Kazmir, Angels	12
Ervin Santana, Angels	12
Justin Masterson, Indians	11

STRIKEOUTS

Jered Weaver, Angels	233

Felix Hernandez, Mariners	232
Jon Lester, Red Sox	225
Justin Verlander, Tigers	219
Francisco Liriano, Twins	201

STRIKEOUTS PER NINE INNINGS

Jon Lester, Red Sox	9.74
Francisco Liriano, Twins	9.44
Jered Weaver, Angels	9.35
Justin Verlander, Tigers	8.79
Colby Lewis, Rangers	8.78

STRIKEOUTS PER NINE INNINGS (RELIEVERS)

Jonathan Papelbon, Red Sox	10.21
Joakim Soria, Royals	9.73
Joba Chamberlain, Yankees	9.67
Neftali Feliz, Rangers	9.22
Daniel Bard, Red Sox	9.16

DOUBLE PLAYS

Fausto Carmona, Indians	30
Trevor Cahill, Athletics	27
C.C. Sabathia, Yankees	27
5 tied at	25

PICKOFFS

Mark Buehrle, White Sox	11
Dallas Braden, Athletics	8
Bruce Chen, Royals	8
3 tied at	5

WILD PITCHES

Ricky Romero, Blue Jays	18
A.J. Burnett, Yankees	16
Felix Hernandez, Mariners	14
James Shields, Rays	13
2 tied at	12

BALKS

Mark Buehrle, White Sox	5
Jason Vargas, Mariners	4
5 tied at	3

OPPONENT AVERAGE

Felix Hernandez, Mariners	.212
C.J. Wilson, Rangers	.217
Trevor Cahill, Athletics	.220
Jon Lester, Red Sox	.220
David Price, Rays	.221

WORST ERA

Jeremy Bonderman, Tigers	5.53
Kyle Davies, Royals	5.34
A.J. Burnett, Yankees	5.26
James Shields, Rays	5.18
Kevin Millwood, Orioles	5.10

FIELDING

PITCHER

PCT	11 tied at	1.000
PO	Fausto Carmona, Indians	22
	John Lackey, Red Sox	22
	Justin Masterson, Indians	22
A	Trevor Cahill, Athletics	54
E	Colby Lewis, Rangers	5
	Justin Masterson, Indians	5
DP	Fausto Carmona, Indians	6

CATCHER

PCT	Joe Mauer, Twins	.996
PO	A.J. Pierzynski, White Sox	865
A	Jason Kendall, Royals	68
E	Francisco Cervelli, Yankees	13
	Jason Kendall, Royals	13
DP	Jason Kendall, Royals	11
PB	Rob Johnson, Mariners	9

FIRST BASE

PCT	Casey Kotchman, Mariners	.999
PO	Daric Barton, Athletics	1404
A	Lyle Overbay, Blue Jays	101
E	Miguel Cabrera, Tigers	13
DP	Lyle Overbay, Blue Jays	150

SECOND BASE

PCT	Robinson Cano, Yankees	.996
PO	Robinson Cano, Yankees	341
A	Robinson Cano, Yankees	432
E	Chone Figgins, Mariners	19
DP	Robinson Cano, Yankees	114

THIRD BASE

PCT	Brandon Inge, Tigers	.977
PO	Adrian Beltre, Red Sox	138
A	Jose Lopez, Mariners	322
E	Adrian Beltre, Red Sox	19
	Michael Young, Rangers	19
DP	Evan Longoria, Rays	46

SHORTSTOP

PCT	Derek Jeter, Yankees	.989
PO	Yuniesky Betancourt, Royals	256
A	Alexei Ramirez, White Sox	499
E	Cliff Pennington, Athletics	25
DP	Alexei Ramirez, White Sox	109

OUTFIELD

PCT	Franklin Gutierrez, Mariners	1.000
	Vernon Wells, Blue Jays	1.000
	Ben Zobrist, Rays	1.000
PO	Adam Jones, Orioles	422
A	Shin-Soo Choo, Indians	14
E	Brennan Boesch, Tigers	10
DP	Adam Jones, Orioles	6

2010 STATISTICS

CLUB BATTING

	AVG	G	AB	R	H	2B	3B	HR	RBI	BB	SO	SB	CS	OBP	SLG
Cincinnati	.272	162	5579	790	1515	293	30	188	761	522	1218	93	43	.338	.436
Colorado	.263	162	5530	770	1452	270	54	173	741	585	1274	99	42	.336	.425
St. Louis	.263	162	5542	736	1456	285	18	150	689	541	1027	79	41	.332	.402
Milwaukee	.262	162	5606	750	1471	293	33	182	710	546	1216	81	26	.335	.424
Philadelphia	.260	162	5581	772	1451	290	34	166	736	560	1064	108	21	.332	.413
Atlanta	.258	162	5463	738	1411	312	25	139	699	634	1140	63	29	.339	.401
Chicago	.257	162	5512	685	1414	298	27	149	658	479	1236	55	31	.320	.401
San Francisco	.257	162	5488	697	1411	284	30	162	660	487	1099	55	32	.321	.408
Florida	.254	162	5531	719	1440	294	37	152	686	514	1375	92	26	.321	.403
Los Angeles	.252	162	5426	667	1368	270	29	120	621	533	1184	92	50	.322	.379
Arizona	.250	162	5473	713	1366	301	34	180	691	589	1529	86	41	.325	.416
Washington	.250	162	5418	655	1355	250	31	149	634	503	1220	110	41	.318	.390
New York	.249	162	5465	656	1361	266	40	128	625	502	1095	130	44	.314	.383
Houston	.247	162	5452	611	1348	252	25	108	577	415	1025	100	36	.303	.362
San Diego	.246	162	5434	665	1338	236	24	132	630	538	1183	124	50	.317	.371
Pittsburgh	.242	162	5386	587	1303	276	27	126	570	463	1207	87	36	.304	.373

CLUB PITCHING

	ERA	G	CG	SHO	SV	IP	H	R	ER	HR	BB	SO	AVG
San Francisco	3.36	162	6	17	57	1461	1279	583	546	134	578	1331	.236
San Diego	3.39	162	2	20	49	1456	1305	581	549	139	517	1295	.240
Atlanta	3.56	162	2	9	41	1439	1326	629	569	126	505	1241	.246
St. Louis	3.57	162	7	16	32	1454	1412	641	577	133	477	1094	.256
Philadelphia	3.67	162	14	21	40	1456	1402	640	594	168	416	1183	.254
New York	3.70	162	8	19	36	1453	1438	652	597	135	545	1106	.260
Cincinnati	4.01	162	4	9	43	1453	1404	685	648	158	524	1130	.254
Los Angeles	4.01	162	4	16	41	1442	1323	692	643	134	539	1274	.244
Florida	4.08	162	5	17	39	1438	1433	717	652	134	549	1168	.261
Houston	4.09	162	4	11	45	1439	1446	729	654	140	548	1210	.261
Washington	4.13	162	2	5	37	1435	1469	742	658	151	512	1068	.266
Colorado	4.14	162	6	12	35	1442	1405	717	663	139	525	1234	.257
Chicago	4.18	162	1	14	40	1437	1409	767	668	154	605	1268	.255
Milwaukee	4.58	162	3	7	35	1439	1487	804	733	173	582	1258	.267
Arizona	4.81	162	3	3	35	1442	1503	836	765	210	548	1070	.271
Pittsburgh	5.00	162	1	6	31	1412	1567	866	784	167	538	1026	.282

CLUB FIELDING

	PCT	PO	A	E	DP		PCT	PO	A	E	DP
Cincinnati	.988	4359	1608	72	142	Arizona	.983	4296	1572	102	152
San Diego	.988	4369	1621	72	141	Houston	.983	4318	1597	103	135
San Francisco	.988	4383	1485	73	110	Milwaukee	.983	4317	1516	101	142
New York	.986	4359	1665	87	159	Atlanta	.980	4318	1770	126	166
Philadelphia	.986	4369	1687	83	158	Chicago	.979	4310	1550	126	137
Colorado	.984	4326	1707	101	182	Florida	.979	4315	1502	123	130
Los Angeles	.984	4325	1589	98	124	Pittsburgh	.979	4235	1654	127	120
St. Louis	.984	4361	1872	99	172	Washington	.979	4305	1657	127	147

INDIVIDUAL BATTING LEADERS (MINIMUM 3.1 PA/TEAM GAME)

	AVG	G	AB	R	H	2B	3B	HR	RBI	BB	SO	SB
Carlos Gonzalez, Colorado	.336	145	587	111	197	34	9	34	117	40	135	26
Joey Votto, Cincinnati	.324	150	547	106	177	36	2	37	113	91	125	16
Omar Infante, Atlanta	.321	134	471	65	151	15	3	8	47	29	62	7
Troy Tulowitzki, Colorado	.315	122	470	89	148	32	3	27	95	48	78	11
Matt Holliday, St. Louis	.312	158	596	95	186	45	1	28	103	69	93	9
Albert Pujols, St. Louis	.312	159	587	115	183	39	1	42	118	103	76	14
Martin Prado, Atlanta	.307	140	599	100	184	40	3	15	66	40	93	5
Ryan Zimmerman, Washington	.307	142	525	85	161	32	0	25	85	69	98	4
Ryan Braun, Milwaukee	.304	157	619	101	188	45	1	25	103	56	105	14
Starlin Castro, Chicago	.300	125	463	53	139	31	5	3	41	29	71	10

INDIVIDUAL PITCHING LEADERS (MINIMUM 1 IP/TEAM GAME)

	W	L	ERA	G	GS	CG	SHO	SV	IP	H	R	ER	BB	SO
Josh Johnson, Florida	11	6	2.31	28	28	1	0	0	184	155	51	47	48	186
Adam Wainwright, St. Louis	20	11	2.43	33	33	5	2	0	230	186	68	62	56	213
Roy Halladay, Philadelphia	21	10	2.45	33	33	9	4	0	251	231	74	68	30	219
Jaime Garcia, St. Louis	13	8	2.70	28	28	1	1	0	163	151	64	49	64	132
Roy Oswalt, Houston/Phil.	13	13	2.77	33	32	2	2	0	212	162	70	65	55	193
Tim Hudson, Atlanta	17	9	2.84	34	34	1	0	0	229	189	74	72	74	139
R.A. Dickey, New York	11	9	2.84	27	26	2	1	0	174	165	62	55	42	104
Ubaldo Jimenez, Colorado	19	8	2.89	33	33	4	2	0	222	164	73	71	92	214
Clayton Kershaw, Los Angeles	13	10	2.91	32	32	1	1	0	204	160	73	66	81	212
Mat Latos, San Diego	14	10	2.93	31	31	1	1	0	185	150	63	60	50	189

AWARD WINNERS

Selected by Baseball Writers Association of America

MOST VALUABLE PLAYER

Player	1st	2nd	3rd	Total
Joey Votto, Cincinnati	31	1	—	443
Albert Pujols, St. Louis	1	21	8	279
Carlos Gonzalez, Colorado	—	7	13	240
Adrian Gonzalez, San Diego	—	1	3	197
Troy Tulowitzki, Colorado	—	—	2	132
Roy Halladay, Philadelphia	—	1	3	130
Aubrey Huff, San Francisco	—	—	—	70
Jayson Werth, Philadelphia	—	—	—	52
Martin Prado, Atlanta	—	—	—	51
Ryan Howard, Philadelphia	—	1	1	50
Buster Posey, San Francisco	—	—	1	40
Matt Holliday, St. Louis	—	—	—	32
Brian Wilson, San Francisco	—	—	1	28
Scott Rolen, Cincinnati	—	—	—	26
Ryan Braun, Milwaukee	—	—	—	19
Ryan Zimmerman, Washington	—	—	—	18
Carlos Ruiz, Philadelphia	—	—	—	12
Dan Uggla, Florida	—	—	—	12
Adam Wainwright, St. Louis	—	—	—	12
Jason Heyward, Atlanta	—	—	—	11
Brian McCann, Atlanta	—	—	—	9
Adam Dunn, Washington	—	—	—	9
Ubaldo Jimenez, Colorado	—	—	—	7
David Wright, New York	—	—	—	7
Corey Hart, Milwaukee	—	—	—	2
Josh Johnson, Florida	—	—	—	2
Heath Bell, San Diego	—	—	—	2

CY YOUNG AWARD

Pitchers	1st	2nd	3rd	Total
Roy Halladay, Philadelphia	32	—	—	224
Adam Wainwright, St. Louis	—	28	3	122
Ubaldo Jimenez, Colorado	—	4	19	90
Tim Hudson, Atlanta	—	—	3	39
Josh Johnson, Marlins	—	—	5	34
Roy Oswalt, Houston/Phil.	—	—	1	14
Brian Wilson, San Francisco	—	—	—	7
Heath Bell, San Diego	—	—	1	4
Mat Latos, San Diego	—	—	—	4
Brett Myers, Houston	—	—	—	2
Tim Lincecum, San Francisco	—	—	—	2
Bronson Arroyo, Cincinnati	—	—	—	1
Matt Cain, San Francisco	—	—	—	1

ROOKIE OF THE YEAR

Player	1st	2nd	3rd	Total
Buster Posey, San Francisco	20	9	2	129
Jason Heyward, Atlanta	9	20	2	107
Jaime Garcia, St. Louis	1	1	16	24
Gaby Sanchez, Florida	2	1	5	18
Neil Walker, Pittsburgh	—	1	—	3
Starlin Castro, Chicago	—	—	3	3
Ike Davis, New York	—	—	2	2
Jose Tabata, Pittsburgh	—	—	1	1
Jonny Venters, Atlanta	—	—	1	1

MANAGER OF THE YEAR

Managers	1st	2nd	3rd	Total
Bud Black, San Diego	16	7	3	104
Dusty Baker, Cincinnati	13	12	2	103
Bruce Bochy, San Francisco	1	4	13	30
Bobby Cox, Atlanta	1	4	11	28
Charlie Manuel, Philadelphia	1	4	3	20
Brad Mills, Houston	—	1	—	3

GOLD GLOVE AWARDS

Selected by NL managers

C—Yadier Molina, St.L. 1B—Albert Pujols, St.L. 2B—Brandon Phillips, Cin. 3B—Scott Rolen, Cin. SS—Troy Tulowitzki, Col. OF—Michael Bourn, Hou.; Carlos Gonzalez, Col.; Shane Victorino, Phil. P—Bronson Arroyo, Cin.

SILVER SLUGGER AWARDS

Selected by NL managers

C—Brian McCann, Atl. 1B—Albert Pujols, St.L. 2B—Dan Uggla, Fla. 3B—Ryan Zimmerman, Wash. SS—Troy Tulowitzki, Col. OF—Ryan Braun, Mil.; Carlos Gonzalez, Col.; Matt Holliday, St.L. P—Yovani Gallardo, Mil.

BATTING

GAMES
Matt Kemp, Dodgers	162
Prince Fielder, Brewers	161
Chase Headley, Padres	161
James Loney, Dodgers	161
Adrian Gonzalez, Padres	160
Rickie Weeks, Brewers	160

AT-BATS
Rickie Weeks, Brewers	651
Brandon Phillips, Reds	626
Ryan Braun, Brewers	619
Hunter Pence, Astros	614
Chase Headley, Padres	610
Casey McGehee, Brewers	610

PLATE APPEARANCES
Rickie Weeks, Brewers	754
Prince Fielder, Brewers	714
Albert Pujols, Cardinals	700
Adrian Gonzalez, Padres	693
Brandon Phillips, Reds	687

RUNS
Albert Pujols, Cardinals	115
Rickie Weeks, Brewers	112
Carlos Gonzalez, Rockies	111
Joey Votto, Reds	106
Jayson Werth, Phillies	106

HITS
Carlos Gonzalez, Rockies	197
Ryan Braun, Brewers	188
Matt Holliday, Cardinals	186
Martin Prado, Braves	184
Albert Pujols, Cardinals	183

TOTAL BASES
Carlos Gonzalez, Rockies	351
Albert Pujols, Cardinals	350
Joey Votto, Reds	328
Matt Holliday, Cardinals	317
Ryan Braun, Brewers	310

DOUBLES
Jayson Werth, Phillies	46
Ryan Braun, Brewers	45
Matt Holliday, Cardinals	45
Andres Torres, Giants	43
James Loney, Dodgers	41

TRIPLES
Dexter Fowler, Rockies	14
Stephen Drew, D-backs	12
Alcides Escobar, Brewers	10
Jose Reyes, Mets	10
Shane Victorino, Phillies	10

EXTRA-BASE HITS
Albert Pujols, Cardinals	82
Carlos Gonzalez, Rockies	77
Adam Dunn, Nationals	76
Joey Votto, Reds	75
Jayson Werth, Phillies	75

HOME RUNS
Albert Pujols, Cardinals	42
Adam Dunn, Nationals	38
Joey Votto, Reds	37
Carlos Gonzalez, Rockies	34
Dan Uggla, Marlins	33

RUNS BATTED IN
Albert Pujols, Cardinals	118
Carlos Gonzalez, Rockies	117
Joey Votto, Reds	113
Ryan Howard, Phillies	108

Joey Votto

GEORGE GOJKOVICH

Dan Uggla, Marlins	105

SACRIFICES
Clayton Kershaw, Dodgers	18
Ryan Dempster, Cubs	16
Nyjer Morgan, Nationals	15
Barry Zito, Giants	14
Tim Lincecum, Giants	13

SACRIFICE FLIES
David Wright, Mets	12
Jeff Francoeur, Mets	10
Jonny Gomes, Reds	9
Matt Kemp, Dodgers	9
Jayson Werth, Phillies	9

HIT BY PITCH
Rickie Weeks, Brewers	25
Prince Fielder, Brewers	21
Chase Utley, Phillies	18

Carlos Gonzalez

DAVID SCHOFIELD

Marlon Byrd, Cubs	17
Jonny Gomes, Reds	12

WALKS
Prince Fielder, Brewers	114
Albert Pujols, Cardinals	103
Adrian Gonzalez, Padres	93
Jason Heyward, Braves	91
Joey Votto, Reds	91

INTENTIONAL WALKS
Albert Pujols, Cardinals	38
Adrian Gonzalez, Padres	35
Prince Fielder, Brewers	17
Carlos Ruiz, Phillies	13
Hanley Ramirez, Marlins	12
Pablo Sandoval, Giants	12

STOLEN BASES
Michael Bourn, Astros	52
Angel Pagan, Mets	37
Nyjer Morgan, Nationals	34
Shane Victorino, Phillies	34
Andrew McCutchen, Pirates	33

CAUGHT STEALING
Nyjer Morgan, Nationals	17
Matt Kemp, Dodgers	15
Michael Bourn, Astros	12
Brandon Phillips, Reds	12
David Wright, Mets	11

STOLEN BASE PERCENTAGE
Shane Victorino, Phillies	85%
Drew Stubbs, Reds	83%
Michael Bourn, Astros	81%
Angel Pagan, Mets	80%
Chris Young, D-backs	80%

STRIKEOUTS
Mark Reynolds, D-backs	211
Adam Dunn, Nationals	199
Rickie Weeks, Brewers	184
Adam LaRoche, D-backs	172
Matt Kemp, Dodgers	170

TOUGHEST TO STRIKE OUT
(AT-BATS PER STRIKEOUT)
Jeff Keppinger, Astros	14.28
Placido Polanco, Phillies	11.79
Carlos Lee, Astros	10.25
Orlando Cabrera, Reds	9.32
Yadier Molina, Cardinals	9.12

GROUNDED INTO DOUBLE PLAYS
Pablo Sandoval, Giants	26
Ivan Rodriguez, Nationals	25
Derrek Lee, Cubs/Braves	23
Albert Pujols, Cardinals	23
4 tied at	20

MULTI-HIT GAMES
Ryan Braun, Brewers	60
Martin Prado, Braves	58
Carlos Gonzalez, Rockies	57
Marlon Byrd, Cubs	52
Matt Holliday, Cardinals	52

ON-BASE PERCENTAGE
Joey Votto, Reds	.424
Albert Pujols, Cardinals	.414
Prince Fielder, Brewers	.401
Jason Heyward, Braves	.393
Adrian Gonzalez, Padres	.393

SLUGGING PERCENTAGE
Joey Votto, Reds	.600
Carlos Gonzalez, Rockies	.598
Albert Pujols, Cardinals	.596
Troy Tulowitzki, Rockies	.568
Adam Dunn, Nationals	.536

ON-BASE PLUS SLUGGING
Joey Votto, Reds	1.024
Albert Pujols, Cardinals	1.011
Carlos Gonzalez, Rockies	.974
Troy Tulowitzki, Rockies	.949
Matt Holliday, Cardinals	.922

PITCHING

WINS
Roy Halladay, Phillies	21
Adam Wainwright, Cardinals	20
Ubaldo Jimenez, Rockies	19
Bronson Arroyo, Reds	17
Tim Hudson, Braves	17

NATIONAL LEAGUE DEPARTMENT LEADERS

Adam Wainwright

LOSSES

Rodrigo Lopez, D-backs	16
Zach Duke, Pirates	15
Paul Maholm, Pirates	15
Randy Wells, Cubs	14
Barry Zito, Giants	14

GAMES

Pedro Feliciano, Mets	92
Peter Moylan, Braves	85
Nick Masset, Reds	82
Luke Gregerson, Padres	80
Sean Marshall, Cubs	80

GAMES STARTED

Chris Carpenter, Cardinals	35
Ryan Dempster, Cubs	34
Tommy Hanson, Braves	34
Tim Hudson, Braves	34
Randy Wolf, Brewers	34

GAMES FINISHED

Carlos Marmol, Cubs	70
Francisco Cordero, Reds	64
Billy Wagner, Braves	64
Brian Wilson, Giants	59
Heath Bell, Padres	57

COMPLETE GAMES

Roy Halladay, Phillies	9
Adam Wainwright, Cardinals	5
Matt Cain, Giants	4
Ubaldo Jimenez, Rockies	4
Johan Santana, Mets	4

SHUTOUTS

Roy Halladay, Phillies	4
Matt Cain, Giants	2
Yovani Gallardo, Brewers	2
Ubaldo Jimenez, Rockies	2
Roy Oswalt, Astros/Phillies	2
Johan Santana, Mets	2
Adam Waingwright, Cardinals	2

SAVES

Brian Wilson, Giants	48
Heath Bell, Padres	47
Francisco Cordero, Reds	40
Carlos Marmol, Cubs	38
Billy Wagner, Braves	37

INNINGS

Roy Halladay, Phillies	250.2
Chris Carpenter, Cardinals	235
Adam Wainwright, Cards	230.1
Tim Hudson, Braves	228.2
Brett Myers, Astros	223.2

HITS ALLOWED

Roy Halladay, Phillies	231
Paul Maholm, Pirates	228
Rodrigo Lopez, D-backs	227
Livan Hernandez, Nationals	216
Chris Carpenter, Cardinals	214

RUNS ALLOWED

Rodrigo Lopez, D-backs	126
Paul Maholm, Pirates	119
Zach Duke, Pirates	115
Ryan Dempster, Cubs	110
Dave Bush, Brewers	108

HOME RUNS ALLOWED

Rodrigo Lopez, D-backs	37
Ted Lilly, Cubs/Dodgers	32
Bronson Arroyo, Reds	29
Randy Wolf, Brewers	29
Dave Bush, Brewers	28

WALKS

Jonathan Sanchez, Giants	96
Ubaldo Jimenez, Rockies	92

Jon Garland, Padres	87
Randy Wolf, Brewers	87
Ryan Dempster, Cubs	86

WALKS PER NINE INNINGS

Roy Halladay, Phillies	1.08
Ted Lilly, Cubs/Dodgers	2.04
R.A. Dickey, Mets	2.17
Adam Wainwright, Cardinals	2.19
Hiroki Kuroda, Dodgers	2.20

HIT BATSMEN

Tommy Hanson, Braves	14
Chris Carpenter, Cardinals	13
Chad Billingsley, Dodgers	10
Ryan Dempster, Cubs	10
Ian Kennedy, D-backs	10

STRIKEOUTS

Tim Lincecum, Giants	231
Roy Halladay, Phillies	219
Ubaldo Jimenez, Rockies	214
Adam Wainwright, Cardinals	213
Clayton Kershaw, Dodgers	212

STRIKEOUTS PER NINE INNINGS

Tim Lincecum, Giants	9.79
Yovani Gallardo, Brewers	9.73
Jonathan Sanchez, Giants	9.54
Clayton Kershaw, Dodgers	9.34
Mat Latos, Padres	9.21

STRIKEOUTS PER NINE INNINGS (RELIEVERS)

Carlos Marmol, Cubs	15.99
Billy Wagner, Braves	13.50
Joel Hanrahan, Pirates	12.92
Brian Wilson, Giants	11.21
Tyler Clippard, Nationals	11.08

DOUBLE PLAYS

Tim Hudson, Braves	32
Mike Pelfrey, Mets	26
Clayton Richard, Padres	26
5 tied at	25

PICKOFFS

Clayton Kershaw, Dodgers	8
Wade LeBlanc, Padres	8
Clayton Richard, Padres	5
Jonathan Sanchez, Giants	5
7 tied at	3

WILD PITCHES

Ubaldo Jimenez, Rockies	16
Ian Kennedy, D-backs	16
Jonathan Sanchez, Giants	15
Manny Parra, Brewers	14
Jason Hammel, Rockies	13
Edwin Jackson, D-backs	13

BALKS

Zach Duke, Pirates	3
Blake Hawksworth, Cardinals	3
Yunesky Maya, Nationals	3
15 tied at	2

OPPONENT AVERAGE

Jonathan Sanchez, Giants	.204
Ubaldo Jimenez, Rockies	.209
Roy Oswalt, Astros/Phillies	.213
Clayton Kershaw, Dodgers	.214
Mat Latos, Padres	.217

WORST ERA

Paul Maholm, Pirates	5.10
Rodrigo Lopez, D-backs	5.00
Chris Narveson, Brewers	4.99
Joe Blanton, Phillies	4.82
Jason Hammel, Rockies	4.81

FIELDING

PITCHER

PCT	7 tied at	1.000
PO	Chris Carpenter, Cardinals	35
A	Tim Hudson, Braves	57
E	Manny Parra, Brewers	5
	Anibal Sanchez, Marlins	5
	Randy Wells, Cubs	5
DP	Bronson Arroyo, Reds	5
	Adam Wainwright, Cardinals	5

CATCHER

PCT	Yorvit Torrealba, Padres	.996
PO	Brian McCann, Braves	972
A	Yadier Molina, Cardinals	79
E	Brian McCann, Braves	14
DP	Brian McCann, Braves	12
PB	Miguel Olivo, Rockies	10

FIRST BASE

PCT	Albert Pujols, Cardinals	.998
PO	Albert Pujols, Cardinals	1458
A	Albert Pujols, Cardinals	157
E	Ryan Howard, Phillies	14
DP	Albert Pujols, Cardinals	146

SECOND BASE

PCT	David Eckstein, Padres	1.000
PO	Rickie Weeks, Brewers	332
A	Brandon Phillips, Reds	419
E	Dan Uggla, Marlins	18
DP	Kelly Johnson, Diamondbacks	106

THIRD BASE

PCT	Placido Polanco, Phillies	.986
PO	David Wright, Mets	110
A	David Wright, Mets	321

E	David Wright, Mets	20
DP	David Wright, Mets	34

SHORTSTOP

PCT	Troy Tulowitzki, Rockies	.984
PO	Ian Desmond, Nationals	221
A	Brendan Ryan, Cardinals	430
E	Ian Desmond, Nationals	34
DP	Troy Tulowitzki, Rockies	103

OUTFIELD

PCT	Andres Torres, Giants	.997
PO	Chris Young, Diamondbacks	418
A	Jeff Francoeur, Mets	11
	Shane Victorino, Phillies	11
E	Alfonso Soriano, Cubs	7
	Chris Young, Diamondbacks	7
DP	Chris Young, Diamondbacks	6

BILL NICHOLS

The Giants' homegrown World Series rotation of Tim Lincecum (shown here), Matt Cain, Jonathan Sanchez and Madison Bumgarner went 4-1, 2.38 as a group in 34 innings

Giants ride homegrown pitchers to Series title

BY TOM HAUDRICOURT

The last team in was the last team standing.

The Giants, proclaimed by manager Bruce Bochy as a band of "outcasts and misfits," weren't assured of an invitation to the postseason party until they topped the Padres on the final day of the regular season to win the National League West.

That didn't stop San Francisco from going all the way, however. They used superior pitching to dispatch the favored Rangers in five games in the World Series and claim the franchise's first World Series championship since 1954, when the Giants played in the Polo Grounds in New York.

The Giants scrapped all year for runs, playing so many excruciating one-run games that they adopted the theme "torture" to describe their season.

But the Giants proved to have the best and deepest collection of arms from start to finish. They went with an entirely homegrown starting rotation of Tim Lincecum, Matt Cain, Jonathan Sanchez and rookie Madison Bumgarner. Closer Brian

Wilson appeared in 10 postseason games, saving six of them, without surrendering an earned run.

"Everyone knows we're kind of built around pitching and just more pitching on top of that," Lincecum said.

First order of business for the Giants was to ruin the farewell party of Braves' manager Bobby Cox. Just like the Giants, the Braves had to win on the final day of the season to claim the NL wild card berth.

Atlanta was depleted by injuries to regular third baseman Chipper Jones and second baseman Martin Prado, however, making scoring runs even more of a chore than San Francisco's scrappy bunch. It certainly didn't help when fill-in second baseman Brooks Conrad committed three errors in Game Three, allowing the Giants to come from behind for a key 3-2 victory and 2-1 edge in the series.

The Giants eked out another 3-2 decision in Game Four to eliminate the Braves and send Cox into retirement.

Over in the other NLDS, folks were wondering how Philadelphia's Roy Halladay would respond to finally getting a chance to pitch in the postseason after all those fruitless seasons with the Blue Jays. He responded in emphatic fashion by tossing a Game One no-hitter against the Reds, the highest-scoring team in the league.

It was the first no-hitter in postseason play since Don Larsen's perfect game for the Yankees in the 1956 World Series.

The Phillies' rotation of Halladay, Roy Oswalt and Cole Hamels proved too much for the NL Central champs, as they swept the series 3-0. After all that bopping in the regular season, the Reds scored five runs against Philly.

Over in the American League, the Yankees did what they always do in the postseason: thump the Twins. New York swept Minnesota out of the Division Series, ending the Twins' glorious first season in Target Field with a resounding thud.

The other ALDS presented much more intrigue. The Rangers roared into St. Petersburg and took the first two games from Tampa Bay. But the Rays showed that home field meant nothing in the series, going to Texas and winning both games there.

The teams returned to Florida for a winner-take-all Game Five at Tropicana Field. The home-field disadvantage continued as the Rangers pulled away to a 5-1 victory and the first postseason series triumph in franchise history. Lefthander Cliff Lee continued his reputation as the pitching version of Mr. October by tossing a six-hitter to beat Rays ace David Price for the second time in the series.

Never Tell Them The Odds

By the time the ALCS opened in Arlington, Texas, the Rangers still had not won a postseason home game. And when Texas blew a 5-1 lead in the eighth inning of Game One to lose to the Yankees 6-5, one couldn't blame Rangers fans if they decided they'd never see a victory at home.

Undaunted by that opening pratfall, the Rangers pounded the Yankees 7-2 in Game Two and mauled them 8-0 behind Lee when the series shifted to Yankee Stadium for Game Three. The power-packed Rangers lineup thumped the stunned Yankees again in Game Four, winning 10-3 and putting the defending champs on the brink of elimination.

With C.C. Sabathia battling through six innings (11 hits, two runs) in Game Five, the Yankees stayed alive with a 7-2 victory. Perhaps comforted in knowing that Lee was available for a potential Game Seven, the Rangers never let it get that far, pulling away to a 6-1 triumph in Game Six and earning a World Series berth for the first time in

Matt Cain completed 21⅓ innings in the postseason without allowing an earned run

BILL NICHOLS

their 50-year history.

Josh Hamilton led the bludgeoning of the Yankees pitching staff, pounding four homers and driving in seven runs to earn ALCS MVP honors.

Over in the NLCS, folks were buzzing about the Game One pitching matchup of Lincecum vs. Halladay. Lincecum and the Giants spoiled the opener for Philly fans with a 4-3 victory. Emerging postseason hero Cody Ross, an outfielder claimed on waivers from the Marlins just two months earlier, socked two home runs off Halladay.

Oswalt helped the Phillies draw even in Game Two with a pitching gem that produced a 6-1 victory. When the series shifted to San Francisco, Cain out-pitched Hamels in a 3-0 masterpiece, with Ross knocking in another big run.

Desperate for a win in Game Four to even the series, the Phillies battled the Giants to a 5-5 tie entering the ninth inning. At that point, they turned to Oswalt for a rare relief appearance. Veteran infielder Juan Uribe came through again with a sacrifice fly to beat Oswalt and give the Giants a commanding 3-1 lead in the series.

Much as Sabathia did in Game Five of the ALCS, Halladay came through for the Phillies to avoid elimination, beating Lincecum and a shaky San Francisco defense 4-2.

Following the formula of the Rangers, the Giants pulled out a 3-2 squeaker in Game Six on a tie-breaking, eighth-inning homer by Uribe. The blast advanced San Francisco to the Fall Classic for their unlikely matchup against Texas.

Zeroes Produce Giants Heroes

With Lincecum and Lee squaring off in Game One, a tense pitchers duel was expected to open the World Series at San Francisco's AT&T Park. But Lee, who entered the game with a 7-0, 1.26 record in eight career postseason starts, was roughed up for seven runs in 4⅔ innings. The Giants hung on to claim the wild 11-7 slugfest.

It only got worse for the Rangers in Game Two as Cain extended his postseason streak to 21⅓ innings

without allowing an earned run in a 9-0 romp. Before playing its first World Series home game, Texas found itself in an unexpected 0-2 hole.

Home cooking agreed with the Rangers in Game Three as Colby Lewis shackled San Francisco in a 4-2 victory, which offered Texas a glimmering hope of tying the Series. But just like that, the Giants pitching staff turned off the Rangers' offensive faucet.

Looking like anything but a 21-year-old rookie, Bumgarner shut out the Rangers for eight innings

AMERICAN LEAGUE CHAMPIONS, 1901–2010

	PENNANT	PCT		PENNANT	PCT		PENNANT	PCT		PENNANT	PCT
1901	Chicago	.610	1918	Boston	.595	1935	Detroit	.616	1952	New York	.617
1902	Philadelphia	.610	1919	Chicago	.629	1936	New York	.667	1953	New York	.656
1903	Boston	.659	1920	Cleveland	.636	1937	New York	.662	1954	Cleveland	.721
1904	Boston	.617	1921	New York	.641	1938	New York	.651	1955	New York	.623
1905	Philadelphia	.622	1922	New York	.610	1939	New York	.702	1956	New York	.630
1906	Chicago	.616	1923	New York	.645	1940	Detroit	.584	1957	New York	.636
1907	Detroit	.613	1924	Washington	.597	1941	New York	.656	1958	New York	.597
1908	Detroit	.588	1925	Washington	.636	1942	New York	.669	1959	Chicago	.610
1909	Detroit	.645	1926	New York	.591	1943	New York	.636	1960	New York	.630
1910	Philadelphia	.680	1927	New York	.714	1944	St. Louis	.578	1961	New York	.673
1911	Philadelphia	.669	1928	New York	.656	1945	Detroit	.575	1962	New York	.593
1912	Boston	.691	1929	Philadelphia	.693	1946	Boston	.675	1963	New York	.646
1913	Philadelphia	.627	1930	Philadelphia	.662	1947	New York	.630	1964	New York	.611
1914	Philadelphia	.651	1931	Philadelphia	.704	1948	Cleveland	.626	1965	Minnesota	.630
1915	Boston	.669	1932	New York	.695	1949	New York	.630	1966	Baltimore	.606
1916	Boston	.591	1933	Washington	.651	1950	New York	.636	1967	Boston	.568
1917	Chicago	.649	1934	Detroit	.656	1951	New York	.636	1968	Detroit	.636

DIVISION ERA (1969-1993)

*Won pennant. ∧ Won first half; defeated Milwaukee 3-2 in playoff. ∧∧ Won first half, defeated Kansas City 3-0.

	EAST	PCT	WEST	PCT	LCS		EAST	PCT	WEST	PCT	LCS
1969	Baltimore*	.673	Minnesota	.599	3-0						
1970	Baltimore*	.667	Minnesota	.605	3-0						
1971	Baltimore*	.639	Oakland	.627	3-0						
1972	Detroit	.551	Oakland*	.600	3-2	1982	Milwaukee*	.586	California	.574	3-2
1973	Baltimore	.599	Oakland*	.580	3-2	1983	Baltimore*	.605	Chicago	.611	3-1
1974	Baltimore	.562	Oakland*	.556	3-1	1984	Detroit*	.642	Kansas City	.519	3-0
1975	Boston*	.594	Oakland	.605	3-0	1985	Toronto	.615	Kansas City*	.562	4-3
1976	New York*	.610	Kansas City	.556	3-2	1986	Boston*	.590	California	.568	4-3
1977	New York*	.617	Kansas City	.630	3-2	1987	Detroit	.605	Minnesota*	.525	4-1
1978	New York*	.613	Kansas City	.568	3-1	1988	Boston	.549	Oakland*	.642	4-0
1979	Baltimore*	.642	California	.543	3-1	1989	Toronto	.549	Oakland*	.611	4-1
1980	New York	.636	Kansas City*	.599	3-0	1990	Boston	.543	Oakland*	.636	4-0
1981	New York*∧	.607	Oakland∧∧	.587	3-0	1991	Toronto	.562	Minnesota*	.586	4-1
						1992	Toronto*	.593	Oakland	.593	4-2
						1993	Toronto*	.586	Chicago	.580	4-2

WILD CARD ERA (1994-PRESENT)

*Won pennant. † Lost ALCS.

	EAST	PCT	CENTRAL	PCT	WEST	PCT	WILD CARD	PCT	LCS
1994	New York	.619	Chicago	.593	Texas	.456	None		
1995	Boston	.597	Cleveland*	.694	Seattle†	.545	New York (E)	.549	4-2
1996	New York*	.568	Cleveland	.615	Texas	.556	Baltimore (E)†	.543	4-1
1997	Baltimore†	.605	Cleveland*	.534	Seattle	.556	New York (E)	.593	4-2
1998	New York*	.704	Cleveland†	.549	Texas	.543	Boston (E)	.568	4-2
1999	New York*	.605	Cleveland	.599	Texas	.586	Boston (E)†	.580	4-1
2000	New York*	.540	Chicago	.586	Oakland	.565	Seattle (W)†	.562	4-2
2001	New York*	.594	Cleveland	.562	Seattle†	.716	Oakland (W)	.630	4-1
2002	New York	.640	Minnesota†	.584	Oakland	.636	Anaheim (W)*	.611	4-1
2003	New York*	.623	Minnesota	.556	Oakland	.593	Boston (E)†	.586	4-3
2004	New York†	.623	Minnesota	.568	Anaheim	.568	Boston (E)*	.605	4-3
2005	New York	.586	Chicago*	.611	Los Angeles†	.586	Boston (E)	.586	4-1
2006	New York	.599	Minnesota	.593	Oakland†	.574	Detroit (C)*	.586	4-0
2007	Boston*	.593	Cleveland†	.593	Los Angeles	.580	New York (E)	.580	4-3
2008	Tampa Bay*	.599	Chicago	.546	Los Angeles	.617	Boston (E)†	.586	4-3
2009	New York*	.636	Minnesota	.534	Los Angeles†	.599	Boston (E)	.586	4-2
2010	Tampa Bay	.593	Minnesota	.580	Texas*	.556	New York (E)†	.586	4-2

in a 4-0 triumph in Game Five. Lincecum finished off Texas 3-1 in Game Six as the aging shortstop Edgar Renteria slammed a three-run, seventh-inning homer off Lee to snap a scoreless deadlock. Renteria socked a crucial Game Two homer, as well, to nail down World Series MVP honors. He went 7-for-18 (.412) with six RBIs.

In a year dominated by pitching headlines, including six no-hitters (including just the second ever in the postseason), it was only fitting that the team with the most dominating staff took home the hardware. Giants hurlers limited the formerly explosive Rangers lineup to only one run in their final 20 innings. In the process, the Giants became the first team to pitch two shutouts in the World Series since the Orioles blanked the Dodgers three times in 1966.

"It's unbelievable how we pitched," Ross said. "They kept waiting for us to get a big hit, and once we did, they did the rest."

NATIONAL LEAGUE CHAMPIONS, 1901–2010

	PENNANT	PCT		PENNANT	PCT		PENNANT	PCT		PENNANT	PCT
1901	Pittsburgh	.647	1918	Chicago	.651	1935	Chicago	.649	1952	Brooklyn	.627
1902	Pittsburgh	.741	1919	Cincinnati	.686	1936	New York	.597	1953	Brooklyn	.682
1903	Pittsburgh	.650	1920	Brooklyn	.604	1937	New York	.625	1954	New York	.630
1904	New York	.693	1921	New York	.614	1938	Chicago	.586	1955	Brooklyn	.641
1905	New York	.686	1922	New York	.604	1939	Cincinnati	.630	1956	Brooklyn	.604
1906	Chicago	.763	1923	New York	.621	1940	Cincinnati	.654	1957	Milwaukee	.617
1907	Chicago	.704	1924	New York	.608	1941	Brooklyn	.649	1958	Milwaukee	.597
1908	Chicago	.643	1925	Pittsburgh	.621	1942	St. Louis	.688	1959	Los Angeles	.564
1909	Pittsburgh	.724	1926	St. Louis	.578	1943	St. Louis	.682	1960	Pittsburgh	.617
1910	Chicago	.675	1927	Pittsburgh	.610	1944	St. Louis	.682	1961	Cincinnati	.604
1911	New York	.647	1928	St. Louis	.617	1945	Chicago	.636	1962	San Francisco	.624
1912	New York	.682	1929	Chicago	.645	1946	St. Louis	.628	1963	Los Angeles	.611
1913	New York	.664	1930	St. Louis	.597	1947	Brooklyn	.610	1964	St. Louis	.574
1914	Boston	.614	1931	St. Louis	.656	1948	Boston	.595	1965	Los Angeles	.599
1915	Philadelphia	.592	1932	Chicago	.584	1949	Brooklyn	.630	1966	Los Angeles	.586
1916	Brooklyn	.610	1933	New York	.599	1950	Philadelphia	.591	1967	St. Louis	.627
1917	New York	.636	1934	St. Louis	.621	1951	New York	.624	1968	St. Louis	.599

DIVISION ERA (1969-1993)

*Won pennant. ^ Won first half; defeated Milwaukee 3-2 in playoff. ^^ Won first half, defeated Kansas City 3-0.

	EAST	PCT	WEST	PCT	LCS		EAST	PCT	WEST	PCT	LCS
1969	New York*	.617	Atlanta	.574	3-0		Philadelphia	.618	Houston	.623	
1970	Pittsburgh	.549	Cincinnati*	.630	3-0	1982	St. Louis*	.568	Atlanta	.549	3-0
1971	Pittsburgh*	.599	San Francisco	.556	3-1	1983	Philadelphia*	.556	Los Angeles	.562	3-1
1972	Pittsburgh	.619	Cincinnati*	.617	3-2	1984	Chicago	.596	San Diego*	.568	3-2
1973	New York*	.509	Cincinnati	.611	3-2	1985	St. Louis*	.623	Los Angeles	.586	4-2
1974	Pittsburgh	.543	Los Angeles*	.630	3-1	1986	New York*	.667	Houston	.593	4-2
1975	Pittsburgh	.571	Cincinnati*	.667	3-0	1987	St. Louis*	.586	San Francisco	.556	4-3
1976	Philadelphia	.623	Cincinnati*	.630	3-0	1988	New York	.625	Los Angeles*	.584	4-3
1977	Philadelphia	.623	Los Angeles*	.605	3-1	1989	Chicago	.571	San Francisco*	.568	4-1
1978	Philadelphia	.556	Los Angeles*	.586	3-1	1990	Pittsburgh	.586	Cincinnati*	.562	4-2
1979	Pittsburgh*	.605	Cincinnati	.559	3-0	1991	Pittsburgh	.605	Atlanta*	.580	4-3
1980	Philadelphia*	.562	Houston	.571	3-2	1992	Pittsburgh	.593	Atlanta*	.605	4-2
1981	Montreal^	.566	Los Angeles*^^	.632	3-2	1993	Philadelphia*	.599	Atlanta	.642	4-2

WILD CARD ERA (1994-PRESENT)

*Won pennant. † Lost ALCS.

	EAST	PCT	CENTRAL	PCT	WEST	PCT	WILD CARD	PCT	LCS
1994	Montreal	.649	Cincinnati	.593	Los Angeles	.509	None		
1995	Atlanta*	.625	Cincinnati†	.590	Los Angeles	.542	Colorado (W)	.535	4-2
1996	Atlanta*	.593	St. Louis†	.543	San Diego	.562	Los Angeles (W)	.556	4-3
1997	Atlanta†	.623	Houston	.519	San Francisco	.556	Florida (E)*	.568	4-2
1998	Atlanta†	.654	Houston	.630	San Diego*	.605	Chicago (C)	.552	4-2
1999	Atlanta*	.636	Houston	.599	Arizona	.617	New York (E)†	.595	4-2
2000	Atlanta	.586	St. Louis†	.586	San Francisco	.599	New York (E)*	.580	4-1
2001	Atlanta†	.543	Houston	.574	Arizona*	.568	St. Louis (C)	.574	4-1
2002	Atlanta	.631	St. Louis†	.599	Arizona	.605	San Francisco (W)*	.590	4-1
2003	Atlanta	.623	Chicago†	.543	San Francisco	.621	Florida (E)*	.562	4-3
2004	Atlanta	.593	St. Louis*	.648	Los Angeles	.574	Houston (C)†	.568	4-3
2005	Atlanta	.556	St. Louis†	.617	San Diego	.506	Houston (C)*	.549	4-2
2006	New York†	.599	St. Louis*	.516	San Diego	.543	Los Angeles (W)	.543	4-3
2007	Philadelphia	.549	Chicago	.525	Arizona†	.556	Colorado (W)*	.552	4-0
2008	Philadelphia*	.568	Chicago	.602	Los Angeles†	.519	Milwaukee (C)	.556	4-1
2009	Philadelphia*	.574	St. Louis	.562	Los Angeles†	.586	Colorado (W)	.568	4-1
2010	Philadelphia†	.599	Cincinnati	.562	San Francisco*	.568	Atlanta (E)	.562	4-2

Year	Winner	Loser	Result
1903	Boston (AL)	Pittsburgh (NL)	5-3
1904	NO SERIES		
1905	New York (NL)	Philadelphia (AL)	4-1
1906	Chicago (AL)	Chicago (NL)	4-2
1907	Chicago (NL)	Detroit (AL)	4-0
1908	Chicago (NL)	Detroit (AL)	4-1
1909	Pittsburgh (NL)	Detroit (AL)	4-3
1910	Philadelphia (AL)	Chicago (NL)	4-1
1911	Philadelphia (AL)	New York (NL)	4-2
1912	Boston (AL)	New York (NL)	4-3-1
1913	Philadelphia (AL)	New York (NL)	4-1
1914	Boston (NL)	Philadelphia (AL)	4-0
1915	Boston (AL)	Philadelphia (NL)	4-1
1916	Boston (AL)	Brooklyn (NL)	4-1
1917	Chicago (AL)	New York (NL)	4-2
1918	Boston (AL)	Chicago (NL)	4-2
1919	Cincinnati (NL)	Chicago (AL)	5-3
1920	Cleveland (AL)	Brooklyn (NL)	5-2
1921	New York (NL)	New York (AL)	5-3
1922	New York (NL)	New York (AL)	4-0
1923	New York (AL)	New York (NL)	4-2
1924	Washington (AL)	New York (NL)	4-3
1925	Pittsburgh (NL)	Washington (AL)	4-3
1926	St. Louis (NL)	New York (AL)	4-3
1927	New York (AL)	Pittsburgh (NL)	4-0
1928	New York (AL)	St. Louis (NL)	4-0
1929	Philadelphia (AL)	Chicago (NL)	4-1
1930	Philadelphia (AL)	St. Louis (NL)	4-2
1931	St. Louis (NL)	Philadelphia (AL)	4-3
1932	New York (AL)	Chicago (NL)	4-0
1933	New York (NL)	Washington (AL)	4-1
1934	St. Louis (NL)	Detroit (AL)	4-3
1935	Detroit (AL)	Chicago (NL)	4-2
1936	New York (AL)	New York (NL)	4-2
1937	New York (AL)	New York (NL)	4-1
1938	New York (AL)	Chicago (NL)	4-0
1939	New York (AL)	Cincinnati (NL)	4-0
1940	Cincinnati (NL)	Detroit (AL)	4-3
1941	New York (AL)	Brooklyn (NL)	4-1
1942	St. Louis (NL)	New York (AL)	4-1
1943	New York (AL)	St. Louis (NL)	4-1
1944	St. Louis (NL)	St. Louis (AL)	4-2
1945	Detroit (AL)	Chicago (NL)	4-3
1946	St. Louis (NL)	Boston (AL)	4-3
1947	New York (AL)	Brooklyn (NL)	4-3
1948	Cleveland (AL)	Boston (NL)	4-2
1949	New York (AL)	Brooklyn (NL)	4-1
1950	New York (AL)	Philadelphia (NL)	4-0
1951	New York (AL)	New York (NL)	4-2
1952	New York (AL)	Brooklyn (NL)	4-3
1953	New York (AL)	Brooklyn (NL)	4-2
1954	New York (NL)	Cleveland (AL)	4-0
1955	Brooklyn (NL)	New York (AL)	4-3
1956	New York (AL)	Brooklyn (NL)	4-3
1957	Milwaukee (NL)	New York (AL)	4-3
1958	New York (AL)	Milwaukee (NL)	4-3
1959	Los Angeles (NL)	Chicago (AL)	4-2
1960	Pittsburgh (NL)	New York (AL)	4-3
1961	New York (AL)	Cincinnati (NL)	4-1
1962	New York (AL)	San Francisco (NL)	4-3
1963	Los Angeles (NL)	New York (AL)	4-0
1964	St. Louis (NL)	New York (AL)	4-3

TOMASSO DeROSA

World Series MVP Edgar Renteria smashed
the deciding three-run homer in Game Five

Year	Winner	Loser	Result
1965	Los Angeles (NL)	Minnesota (AL)	4-3
1966	Baltimore (AL)	Los Angeles (NL)	4-0
1967	St. Louis (NL)	Boston (AL)	4-3
1968	Detroit (AL)	St. Louis (NL)	4-3
1969	New York (NL)	Baltimore (AL)	4-1
1970	Baltimore (AL)	Cincinnati (NL)	4-1
1971	Pittsburgh (NL)	Baltimore (AL)	4-3
1972	Oakland (AL)	Cincinnati (NL)	4-3
1973	Oakland (AL)	New York (NL)	4-3
1974	Oakland (AL)	Los Angeles (NL)	4-1
1975	Cincinnati (NL)	Boston (AL)	4-3
1976	Cincinnati (NL)	New York (AL)	4-0
1977	New York (AL)	Los Angeles (NL)	4-2
1978	New York (AL)	Los Angeles (NL)	4-2
1979	Pittsburgh (NL)	Baltimore (AL)	4-3
1980	Philadelphia (NL)	Kansas City (AL)	4-2
1981	Los Angeles (NL)	New York (AL)	4-2
1982	St. Louis (NL)	Milwaukee (AL)	4-3
1983	Baltimore (AL)	Philadelphia (NL)	4-1
1984	Detroit (AL)	San Diego (NL)	4-1
1985	Kansas City (AL)	St. Louis (NL)	4-3
1986	New York (NL)	Boston (AL)	4-3
1987	Minnesota (AL)	St. Louis (NL)	4-3
1988	Los Angeles (NL)	Oakland (AL)	4-1
1989	Oakland (AL)	San Francisco (NL)	4-0
1990	Cincinnati (NL)	Oakland (AL)	4-0
1991	Minnesota (AL)	Atlanta (NL)	4-3
1992	Toronto (AL)	Atlanta (NL)	4-2
1993	Toronto (AL)	Philadelphia (NL)	4-2
1994	NO SERIES		
1995	Atlanta (NL)	Cleveland (AL)	4-2
1996	New York (AL)	Atlanta (NL)	4-2
1997	Florida (NL)	Cleveland (AL)	4-3
1998	New York (AL)	San Diego (NL)	4-0
1999	New York (AL)	Atlanta (NL)	4-0
2000	New York (AL)	New York (NL)	4-1
2001	Arizona (NL)	New York (AL)	4-3
2002	Anaheim (AL)	San Francisco (NL)	4-3
2003	Florida (NL)	New York (AL)	4-2
2004	Boston (AL)	St. Louis (NL)	4-0
2005	Chicago (AL)	Houston (NL)	4-0
2006	St. Louis (NL)	Detroit (AL)	4-1
2007	Boston (AL)	Colorado (NL)	4-0
2008	Philadelphia (NL)	Tampa Bay (AL)	4-1
2009	New York (AL)	Philadelphia (NL)	4-2
2010	San Francisco (NL)	Texas (AL)	4-1

WORLD SERIES BOX SCORES

GAME ONE October 27

SAN FRANCISCO 11, TEXAS 7

TEXAS	AB	R	H	BI	BB	SO	SAN FRANCISCO	AB	R	H	BI	BB	SO
Andrus, ss	3	2	1	1	1	1	Torres, cf	4	2	1	0	0	2
Young, M, 3b	4	0	0	0	1	0	Sanchez, F, 2b	5	2	4	3	0	0
Hamilton, cf	4	1	0	0	1	0	Posey, B, c	5	0	1	0	2	0
Guerrero, rf	4	0	1	2	0	1	Burrell, lf	3	1	0	0	1	3
Cruz, N, lf	5	0	1	2	0	1	Schierholtz, rf	1	0	1	1	0	0
Kinsler, 2b	4	1	1	0	1	0	Ross, C, rf-lf	5	1	1	1	0	2
Molina, B, c	4	2	2	1	0	1	Huff, A, 1b	4	1	3	1	0	0
Moreland, 1b	3	0	2	0	0	1	Ramirez, R, p	0	0	0	0	0	0
b-Cantu, ph-1b	1	0	0	0	0	0	Affeldt, p	0	0	0	0	0	0
Lee, Cl, p	2	0	1	0	0	0	Wilson, B, p	0	0	0	0	0	0
O'Day							Uribe, 3b	4	1	1	3	0	3
a-Murphy, Dv, ph	1	0	1	1	0	0	Renteria, ss	3	2	1	0	0	0
Ogando, p	0	0	0	0	0	0	Lincecum, p	3	0	0	0	0	0
Lowe, M, p	0	0	0	0	0	0	Casilla, S, p	0	0	0	0	0	0
Kirkman, p	0	0	0	0	0	0	Romo, p	0	0	0	0	0	0
c-Borbon, ph	1	1	1	0	0	0	Lopez, Ja, p	0	0	0	0	0	0
							1-Ishikawa, ph-1b	1	1	1	0	0	0
TOTALS	36	7	11	7	4	5	TOTALS	38	11	14	11	1	12

Texas	110	002	003—7
San Francisco	002	060	03x—11

a-Singled for O'Day in the 6th. b-Grounded out for Moreland in the 8th. c-Singled for Kirkman in the 9th. 1-Doubled for Lopez in the 8th.

LOB—Texas 8, San Francisco 6. 2B—Lee, Cl (1), Moreland (1), Molina, B (1), Cruz, N (1), Sanchez, F 3 (3), Huff, A (1), Torres (1), Ishikawa (1). HR—Uribe (1). SF—Andrus, Guerrero. CS—Huff, A (1). E—Young, M (1), Andrus (1), Guerrero 2 (2), Huff, A (1), Ishikawa (1).

TEXAS	IP	H	R	ER	BB	SO	SAN FRANCISCO	IP	H	R	ER	BB	SO
Lee, Cl (L)	4.2	8	7	6	1	7	Lincecum (W)	5.2	8	4	4	2	3
O'Day	0.1	1	1	1	0	1	Casilla, S	1.1	0	0	0	0	1
Ogando	0.2	1	0	0	0	4	Romo	0.2	1	0	0	0	1
Lowe, M	0.2	3	3	3	0	0	Lopez, Ja	0.1	0	0	0	0	0
Kirkman	0.1	1	0	0	0	0	Ramirez, R	0.1	1	2	2	1	0
							Affeldt	0.0	0	1	1	1	0
							Wilson, B	0.2	1	0	0	0	0

Affeldt pitched to 1 batter in the 9th.

HBP—Torres (by Lee, Cl), Renteria (by O'Day).

T—3:36. A—43,601.

GAME TWO October 28

SAN FRANCISCO 9, TEXAS 0

TEXAS	AB	R	H	BI	BB	SO	SAN FRANCISCO	AB	R	H	BI	BB	SO
Andrus, ss	3	0	0	0	1	0	Torres, cf	5	0	1	0	1	0
Young, M, 3b	4	0	1	0	0	0	Sanchez, F, 2b	5	0	0	0	0	2
Hamilton, cf	4	0	1	0	0	0	Posey, B, c	4	1	1	0	0	2
Cruz, N, rf	4	0	0	0	0	2	Burrell, lf	2	0	0	1	1	1
Kinsler, 2b	4	0	1	0	0	0	Schierholtz, rf	0	1	0	1	0	0
Murphy, Dv, lf	3	0	0	0	1	0	Ross, C, rf-lf	2	2	1	0	2	0
Treanor, p	3	0	0	0	0	0	Huff, A, 1b	3	1	0	1	1	0
b-Francoeur, ph	1	0	0	0	0	0	Uribe, 3b	3	1	1	2	1	1
Moreland, 1b	2	0	1	0	1	0	Renteria, ss	4	2	2	3	0	1
Wilson, C, p	1	0	0	0	0	0	Cain, p	3	0	1	0	0	1
Oliver	0	0	0	0	0	0	Lopez, Ja, p	0	0	0	0	0	0
a-Borbon, ph	1	0	0	0	0	0	1-Fontenot, p	0	0	0	0	0	0
O'Day, p	0	0	0	0	0	0	2-Rowand, ph	1	1	1	2	0	0
Holland, p	0	0	0	0	0	0	Mota, p	0	0	0	0	0	0
Lowe, M, p	0	0	0	0	0	0							
Kirkman, p	0	0	0	0	0	0							
TOTALS	30	0	4	0	3	2	TOTALS	32	9	8	9	6	9

Texas	000	000	000—0
San Francisco	000	010	17x—9

a-Grounded out for Oliver in the 8th. b-Flied out for Treanor in the 9th. 1-Batted for Lopez in the 8th. 2-Tripled for Fontenot in the 8th.

LOB—Texas 7, San Francisco 5. 2B—Kinsler (1), Ross, C (1), Torres (2). 3B—Rowand (1). HR—Renteria (1). SB—Andrus (1).

TEXAS	IP	H	R	ER	BB	SO	SAN FRANCISCO	IP	H	R	ER	BB	SO
Wilson, C (L)	6.0	3	2	2	2	4	Cain (W)	7.2	4	0	0	2	2
Oliver	1.0	1	0	0	0	2	Lopez, Ja	0.1	0	0	0	0	0
O'Day	0.2	1	1	1	0	2	Mota	1.0	0	0	0	1	0
Holland	0.0	0	3	3	3	0							
Lowe, M	0.0	1	2	2	1	0							
Kirkman	0.1	2	1	1	0	1							

Wilson, pitched to 1 batter in the 7th. Holland pitched to 3 batters in the 8th. Lowe pitched to 2 batters in the 8th.

IBB—Moreland (by Cain).

T—3:17. A—43,622.

GAME THREE October 30

TEXAS 4, SAN FRANCISCO 2

SAN FRANCISCO	AB	R	H	BI	BB	SO	TEXAS	AB	R	H	BI	BB	SO
Torres, cf	4	1	1	1	0	0	Andrus, ss	4	0	2	0	0	1
Sanchez, F, 2b	4	0	1	0	0	0	Young, M, 3b	4	0	2	0	0	0
Huff, A, 1b	3	0	1	0	0	0	Hamilton, cf	4	1	1	0	0	0
Posey, B, c	3	0	1	0	1	1	Guerrero, dh	3	0	0	1	0	0
Burrell, lf	4	0	0	0	0	4	Cruz, N, lf	4	1	1	0	0	0
Ross, C, rf	3	1	1	1	1	0	Kinsler, 2b	4	0	1	0	0	2
Uribe, 3b	4	0	0	0	0	1	Francoeur, rf	2	0	0	1	1	1
Sandoval, P, dh	3	0	0	0	0	1	Molina, B, c	1	1	0	2	0	0
Renteria, ss	3	0	0	0	0	1	Moreland, 1b	3	1	1	3	0	0
TOTALS	31	2	5	2	2	8	TOTALS	29	4	8	4	4	4

San Francisco	000	000	110—2
Texas	030	010	00x—4

LOB—San Francisco 5, Texas 5. 2B—Huff (2), Cruz (2). HR—Ross (1), Torres (1), Moreland (1). CS—Guerrero (1). SB—Kinsler (1). E—Renteria (1).

SAN FRANCISCO	IP	H	R	ER	BB	SO	TEXAS	IP	H	R	ER	BB	SO
Sanchez, J (L)	4.2	6	4	4	3	3	Lewis (W)	7.2	5	2	2	2	6
Mota	1.1	1	0	0	1	0	O'Day	0.1	0	0	0	0	0
Affeldt	1.1	1	0	0	0	1	Feliz, N (S)	1.0	0	0	0	0	2
Ramirez, R	0.2	0	0	0	0	1							

T—2:51. A—52,419.

GAME FOUR October 31

SAN FRANCISCO 4, TEXAS 0

SAN FRANCISCO	AB	R	H	BI	BB	SO	TEXAS	AB	R	H	BI	BB	SO
Torres, cf	5	1	3	1	0	0	Andrus, ss	3	0	0	0	1	0
Sanchez, F, 2b	4	1	1	0	0	0	Young, M, 3b	4	0	1	0	0	2
Huff, A, dh	4	1	1	2	0	1	Hamilton, cf	4	0	0	0	0	1
Posey, B, c	4	1	1	1	0	1	Guerrero, dh	3	0	0	0	0	3
Ross, C, lf	3	0	0	1	1	0	Cruz, N, lf	3	0	1	0	0	0
Uribe, 3b	4	0	0	0	0	0	Kinsler, 2b	2	0	0	0	1	0
Ishikawa, 1b	3	0	0	0	1	1	Francoeur, rf	3	0	0	0	0	0
Renteria, ss	4	1	3	0	0	1	Molina, B, c	3	0	0	0	0	0
Schierholtz, rf	4	0	1	0	0	2	Moreland, 1b	3	0	1	0	0	2
TOTALS	35	4	8	4	2	6	TOTALS	28	0	3	0	2	8

San Francisco	002	000	110—4
Texas	000	000	000—0

LOB—San Francisco 6, Texas 3. 2B—Torres 2 (4). HR—Huff (1), Posey (1). CS—Hamilton (1). SB—Torres (1). E—Uribe (1).

SAN FRANCISCO	IP	H	R	ER	BB	SO	TEXAS	IP	H	R	ER	BB	SO
Bumgarner (W)	8.0	3	0	0	2	6	Hunter, T (L)	4.0	5	2	2	1	1
Wilson, B	1.0	0	0	0	0	2	Ogando	1.2	0	0	0	0	2
							Oliver	1.2	2	1	1	0	2
							O'Day	0.2	1	1	1	0	0
							Holland	1.0	0	0	0	1	1

T—3:09. A—51,920.

GAME FIVE *November 1*
SAN FRANCISCO 3, TEXAS 1

SAN FRANCISCO	AB	R	H	BI	BB	SO	TEXAS	AB	R	H	BI	BB	SO
Torres, rf	4	0	1	0	0	1	Andrus, ss	4	0	0	0	0	1
Sanchez, F, 2b	4	0	1	0	0	0	Young, M, 3b	4	0	1	0	0	0
Posey, B, c	4	0	2	0	0	0	Hamilton, cf	4	0	0	0	0	2
Ross, C, lf	4	1	1	0	0	1	Guerrero, dh	4	0	0	0	0	1
Uribe, 3b	4	1	1	0	0	2	Cruz, N, rf	4	1	1	1	0	2
Huff, A, 1b	3	0	0	0	0	0	Kinsler, 2b	2	0	0	0	1	0
Burrell, dh	4	0	0	0	0	3	Murphy, Dv, lf	3	0	0	0	0	3
Renteria, ss	3	1	1	3	0	0	Molina, B, c	3	0	0	0	0	2
Rowand, cf	3	0	0	0	0	1	Moreland, 1b	2	0	1	0	1	1
TOTALS	**33**	**3**	**7**	**3**	**0**	**8**	**TOTALS**	**30**	**1**	**3**	**1**	**2**	**12**

San Francisco	000	000	300—3
Texas	000	000	100—1

LOB—San Francisco 4, Texas 4. **HR**—Renteria (1), Cruz (1). **E**—Moreland (1).

SAN FRANCISCO	IP	H	R	ER	BB	SO	TEXAS	IP	H	R	ER	BB	SO
Lincecum (W)	8.0	3	1	1	2	10	Lee, Cl (L)	7.0	6	3	3	0	6
Wilson, B	1.0	0	0	0	0	2	Feliz, N	2.0	1	0	0	0	2

T—2:32. **A**—52,045.

2010 WORLD SERIES
TEXAS

PLAYER, POS	AVG	G	AB	R	H	2B	3B	HR	RBI	BB	SO	SB
Elvis Andrus, ss	.176	5	17	2	3	0	0	0	1	3	3	1
Julio Borbon, ph	.500	2	2	1	1	0	0	0	0	0	0	0
Jorge Cantu, 1b	.000	1	1	0	0	0	0	0	0	0	0	0
Nelson Cruz, lf	.200	5	20	2	4	2	0	1	3	0	5	0
Jeff Francoeur, rf	.000	3	6	0	0	0	0	0	0	1	1	0
Vladimir Guerrero, dh	.071	4	14	0	1	0	0	0	2	1	5	0
Josh Hamilton, cf	.100	5	20	2	2	0	0	1	1	1	3	0
Derek Holland, p	—	1	0	0	0	0	0	0	0	0	0	0
Ian Kinsler, 2b	.188	5	16	1	3	1	0	0	0	3	2	1
Michael Kirkman, p	—	2	0	0	0	0	0	0	0	0	0	0
Cliff Lee, p	.500	1	2	0	1	1	0	0	0	0	0	0
Mark Lowe, p	—	2	0	0	0	0	0	0	0	0	0	0
Bengie Molina, c	.182	4	11	3	2	1	0	0	1	2	3	0
Mitch Moreland, 1b	.462	5	13	1	6	1	0	1	3	2	4	0
David Murphy, lf	.143	3	7	0	1	0	0	0	1	1	3	0
Darren O'Day, p	—	2	0	0	0	0	0	0	0	0	0	0
Alexi Ogando, p	—	1	0	0	0	0	0	0	0	0	0	0
Darren Oliver, p	—	1	0	0	0	0	0	0	0	0	0	0
Matt Treanor, c	.000	1	3	0	0	0	0	0	0	0	0	0
C.J. Wilson, p	.000	1	1	0	0	0	0	0	0	0	0	0
Michael Young, 3b	.250	5	20	0	5	0	0	0	0	1	2	0
Totals	**.190**	**5**	**153**	**12**	**29**	**6**	**0**	**3**	**12**	**15**	**31**	**2**

PITCHER	W	L	ERA	G	GS	SV	IP	H	R	ER	BB	SO
Neftali Feliz	0	0	0.00	2	0	1	3.0	1	0	0	0	4
Derek Holland	0	0	27.00	2	0	0	1.0	0	3	3	4	1
Tommy Hunter	0	1	4.50	1	1	0	4.0	5	2	2	1	1
Michael Kirkman	0	0	13.50	2	0	0	0.2	3	1	1	0	1
Cliff Lee	0	2	6.94	2	2	0	11.2	14	10	9	1	13
Colby Lewis	1	0	2.35	1	1	0	7.2	5	2	2	2	6
Mark Lowe	0	0	67.50	2	0	0	0.2	4	5	5	1	0
Darren O'Day	0	0	13.50	4	0	0	2.0	3	3	3	0	3
Alexi Ogando	0	0	0.00	2	0	0	3.2	1	0	0	0	6
Darren Oliver	0	0	3.38	2	0	0	2.2	3	1	1	0	4
C.J. Wilson	0	1	3.00	1	1	0	6.0	3	2	2	4	4
Totals	**1**	**4**	**5.86**	**5**	**5**	**1**	**43.0**	**42**	**29**	**28**	**11**	**43**

SAN FRANCISCO

PLAYER, POS	AVG	G	AB	R	H	2B	3B	HR	RBI	BB	SO	SB
Jeremy Affeldt, p	—	1	0	0	0	0	0	0	0	0	0	0
Pat Burrell, lf	.000	4	13	1	0	0	0	0	0	2	11	0
Matt Cain, p	.333	1	3	0	1	0	0	0	0	0	1	0
Santiago Casilla, p	—	1	0	0	0	0	0	0	0	0	0	0
Mike Fontenot, ph	—	1	0	0	0	0	0	0	0	0	0	0
Aubrey Huff, 1b	.294	5	17	3	5	2	0	1	4	1	1	0
Travis Ishikawa, 1b	.250	2	4	1	1	1	0	0	1	1	1	0
Tim Lincecum, p	.000	1	3	0	0	0	0	0	0	0	0	0
Javier Lopez, p	—	2	0	0	0	0	0	0	0	0	0	0
Guillermo Mota, p	—	1	0	0	0	0	0	0	0	0	0	0
Buster Posey, c	.300	5	20	2	6	0	0	1	2	1	6	0
Ramon Ramirez, p	—	1	0	0	0	0	0	0	0	0	0	0
Edgar Renteria, ss	.412	5	17	6	7	0	0	2	6	0	3	0
Sergio Romo, p	—	1	0	0	0	0	0	0	0	0	0	0
Cody Ross, lf	.235	5	17	5	4	1	0	1	2	4	4	0
Aaron Rowand, cf	.250	2	4	1	1	0	1	0	2	0	1	0
Freddy Sanchez, 2b	.273	5	22	2	6	3	0	0	3	0	2	0
Pablo Sandoval, dh	.000	1	3	0	0	0	0	0	0	0	1	0
Nate Schierholtz, rf	.200	3	5	1	1	0	0	0	1	1	1	0
Andres Torres, cf	.318	5	22	4	7	4	0	1	3	0	4	1
Juan Uribe, 3b	.158	5	19	3	3	0	0	1	5	1	7	0
Brian Wilson, p	—	1	0	0	0	0	0	0	0	0	0	0
Totals	**.249**	**5**	**169**	**29**	**42**	**11**	**1**	**7**	**29**	**11**	**43**	**1**

PITCHER	W	L	ERA	G	GS	SV	IP	H	R	ER	BB	SO
Jeremy Affeldt	0	0	6.75	2	0	0	1.1	1	1	1	1	0
Madison Bumgarner	1	0	0.00	1	1	0	8.0	3	0	0	2	6
Matt Cain	1	0	0.00	1	1	0	7.2	4	0	0	2	2
Santiago Casilla	0	0	0.00	1	0	0	1.1	0	0	0	0	1
Tim Lincecum	2	0	3.29	2	2	0	13.2	11	5	5	4	13
Javier Lopez	0	0	0.00	2	0	0	0.2	0	0	0	0	0
Guillermo Mota	0	0	0.00	2	0	0	2.1	1	0	0	2	0
Ramon Ramirez	0	0	18.00	2	0	0	1.0	1	2	2	1	1
Sergio Romo	0	0	0.00	1	0	0	0.2	1	0	0	1	1
Jonathan Sanchez	0	1	7.71	1	1	0	4.2	6	4	4	3	3
Brian Wilson	0	0	0.00	3	0	1	2.2	1	0	0	0	4
Totals	**4**	**1**	**2.45**	**5**	**5**	**1**	**44.0**	**29**	**12**	**12**	**15**	**31**

E—Young, Andrus, Guerrero 2, Huff, Ishikawa, Renteria, Uribe, Moreland. **DP**—Texas 3, San Francisco 9. **LOB**—Texas 27, San Francisco 26. **SB**—Andrus, Kinsler, Torres. **CS**—Huff, Guerrero, Hamilton. **SH**—Wilson, Huff. **SF**—Andrus, Guerrero. **HBP**—Torres (by Lee), Renteria (by O'Day), Huff (by Lewis). **IBB**—Moreland (by Cain). **WP**—Affeldt, Cain. **PB**—Posey.

SCORE BY INNINGS

Texas	140	012	103—12
San Francisco	004	070	6(12)0—29

AMERICAN LEAGUE DIVISION SERIES

TAMPA BAY VS· TEXAS

TEXAS

PLAYER, POS	AVG	G	AB	R	H	2B	3B	HR	RBI	BB	SO	SB
Elvis Andrus, ss	.333	5	24	2	8	1	0	0	1	0	2	3
Julio Borbon, lf	.000	3	6	1	0	0	0	0	0	0	2	0
Jorge Cantu, 1b	.000	1	4	0	0	0	0	0	0	0	3	0
Nelson Cruz, rf	.400	5	20	5	8	2	0	3	3	0	6	1
Jeff Francoeur, rf	.125	2	8	1	1	1	0	0	1	0	2	0
Vladimir Guerrero, dh	.263	5	19	2	5	1	0	0	1	1	3	0
Josh Hamilton, cf	.111	5	18	1	2	0	0	0	1	2	6	1
Ian Kinsler, 2b	.444	5	18	5	8	0	0	3	6	2	2	0
Bengie Molina, c	.357	4	14	1	5	0	0	1	2	0	1	1
Mitch Moreland, 1b	.200	4	15	1	3	3	0	0	1	0	3	0
David Murphy, lf	.143	2	7	0	1	0	0	0	0	0	1	0
Matt Treanor, c	.000	1	1	1	0	0	0	0	0	1	1	0
Michael Young, 3b	.150	5	20	1	3	0	0	1	3	0	6	0
Totals	**.253**	**5**	**174**	**21**	**44**	**8**	**0**	**8**	**19**	**6**	**38**	**6**

PITCHER	W	L	ERA	G	GS	SV	IP	H	R	ER	BB	SO
Neftali Feliz	0	0	6.75	2	0	0	1.1	2	1	1	3	2
Derek Holland	0	0	5.79	2	0	0	4.2	6	3	3	1	4
Tommy Hunter	0	1	4.50	1	1	0	4.0	6	3	2	0	7
Cliff Lee	2	0	1.13	2	2	0	16.0	11	2	2	0	21
Colby Lewis	0	0	0.00	1	1	0	5.0	2	0	0	5	5
Dustin Nippert	0	0	18.00	1	0	0	1.0	2	2	2	0	0
Darren O'Day	0	0	0.00	4	0	0	2.0	2	0	0	0	4
Alexi Ogando	0	0	0.00	1	0	0	0.1	1	0	0	0	0
Darren Oliver	0	1	4.15	3	0	0	4.1	3	2	2	1	5
C.J. Wilson	1	0	0.00	1	1	0	6.1	2	0	0	2	7
Totals	**3**	**2**	**2.40**	**5**	**5**	**0**	**45.0**	**37**	**13**	**12**	**12**	**55**

TAMPA BAY

PLAYER, POS	AVG	G	AB	R	H	2B	3B	HR	RBI	BB	SO	SB
Willy Aybar, dh	.167	3	6	0	1	1	0	0	0	0	2	0
Rocco Baldelli, dh	.000	1	3	0	0	0	0	0	0	0	2	0
Jason Bartlett, ss	.400	5	15	0	6	1	0	0	0	1	1	0
Reid Brignac, ss	.000	2	3	0	0	0	0	0	0	0	3	0
Carl Crawford, lf	.143	5	21	1	3	0	0	1	1	0	4	1
John Jaso, c	.300	3	10	0	3	0	0	0	1	1	2	0
Desmond Jennings, rf	.000	2	2	1	0	0	0	0	0	0	1	0
Dan Johnson, dh	.222	5	9	1	2	1	0	0	0	3	4	0
Matt Joyce, rf	.222	4	9	0	2	0	0	0	0	0	4	1
Evan Longoria, 3b	.200	5	20	2	4	2	0	1	2	1	4	0
Carlos Pena, 1b	.286	4	14	4	4	1	1	1	4	3	7	0
Sean Rodriguez, 2b	.200	4	10	2	2	0	0	0	0	0	5	0
Kelly Shoppach, c	.000	3	9	0	0	0	0	0	0	1	3	0
B.J. Upton, cf	.190	5	21	0	4	2	0	0	2	0	7	2
Ben Zobrist, 2b	.300	5	20	2	6	2	0	1	2	2	6	0
Totals	**.215**	**5**	**172**	**13**	**37**	**10**	**1**	**4**	**12**	**12**	**55**	**4**

PITCHER	W	L	ERA	G	GS	SV	IP	H	R	ER	BB	SO
Grant Balfour	0	0	0.00	3	0	0	3.2	2	0	0	0	1
Joaquin Benoit	1	0	0.00	3	0	0	3.2	0	0	0	0	3
Randy Choate	0	0	0.00	3	0	0	1.0	0	0	0	0	0
Wade Davis	1	0	3.60	1	1	0	5.0	7	2	2	3	7
Matt Garza	0	0	1.50	1	1	0	6.0	5	2	1	2	4
Jeff Niemann	0	0	0.00	1	0	0	3.0	1	0	0	1	4
David Price	0	2	4.97	2	2	0	12.2	17	8	7	0	14
Chad Qualls	0	0	10.80	2	0	0	1.2	4	2	2	0	0
James Shields	0	1	8.31	1	1	0	4.1	4	4	4	0	2
Rafael Soriano	0	0	9.00	3	0	1	3.0	4	3	3	0	1
Dan Wheeler	0	0	0.00	1	0	0	1.0	0	0	0	0	0
Totals	**2**	**3**	**3.80**	**5**	**5**	**1**	**45.0**	**44**	**21**	**19**	**6**	**38**

E—Andrus 2, Longoria 2, Rodriguez, Kinsler 2, Shields, Kinsler, Hamilton, Shoppach. **DP**—Texas 2, Tampa Bay 7. **LOB**—Texas 26, Tampa Bay 37. **SB**—Hamilton, Crawford, Andrus 3, Joyce, Upton 2, Molina, Cruz. **CS**—Andrus. **HBP**—Bartlett (by Wilson), Treanor 2 (by Shields 2). **PB**—Jaso 2, Molina.

SCORE BY INNINGS

Texas	123 353 103	—21
Tampa Bay	011 221 123	—13

Rays lefty David Price finished on a sour note, going 0-2, 4.97 in two ALDS starts

MINNESOTA VS NEW YORK

NEW YORK

PLAYER, POS	AVG	G	AB	R	H	2B	3B	HR	RBI	BB	SO	SB
Lance Berkman, dh	.500	1	4	2	2	1	0	1	2	0	1	0
Robinson Cano, 2b	.333	3	12	3	4	0	1	0	1	0	0	0
Brett Gardner, lf	.200	3	10	1	2	0	0	0	1	1	3	1
Greg Golson, rf	—	2	0	0	0	0	0	0	0	0	0	0
Curtis Granderson, cf	.455	3	11	2	5	1	1	0	3	1	1	1
Derek Jeter, ss	.286	3	14	0	4	0	0	0	1	0	3	1
Jorge Posada, c	.273	3	11	2	3	0	0	0	2	1	4	0
Alex Rodriguez, 3b	.273	3	11	1	3	0	0	0	1	1	2	1
Nick Swisher, rf	.333	3	12	3	4	2	0	1	1	1	1	0
Mark Teixeira, 1b	.308	3	13	2	4	1	0	1	3	1	2	0
Marcus Thames, dh	.286	2	7	1	2	0	0	1	2	1	1	0
Totals	**.314**	**3**	**105**	**17**	**33**	**5**	**2**	**4**	**17**	**7**	**18**	**4**

PITCHER	W	L	ERA	G	GS	SV	IP	H	R	ER	BB	SO
Phil Hughes	1	0	0.00	1	1	0	7.0	4	0	0	1	6
Boone Logan	0	0	0.00	2	0	0	1.0	1	0	0	0	0
Andy Pettitte	1	0	2.57	1	1	0	7.0	5	2	2	1	4
Mariano Rivera	0	0	0.00	3	0	2	3.1	2	0	0	0	1
David Robertson	0	0	0.00	2	0	0	0.2	0	0	1	1	1
C.C. Sabathia	1	0	4.50	1	1	0	6.0	5	4	3	3	5
Kerry Wood	0	0	4.50	3	0	0	2.0	4	1	1	2	3
Totals	**3**	**0**	**2.00**	**3**	**3**	**2**	**27.0**	**21**	**7**	**6**	**8**	**20**

MINNESOTA

PLAYER, POS	AVG	G	AB	R	H	2B	3B	HR	RBI	BB	SO	SB
Michael Cuddyer, 1b	.182	3	11	1	2	1	0	1	2	0	4	0
J.J. Hardy, ss	.100	3	10	0	1	0	0	0	0	0	2	0
Orlando Hudson, 2b	.333	3	12	2	4	0	0	1	2	0	2	0
Jason Kubel, rf	.000	3	8	0	0	0	0	0	0	0	3	0
Joe Mauer, c	.250	3	12	0	3	0	0	0	0	1	3	0
Jason Repko, rf	—	1	0	0	0	0	0	0	0	0	0	0
Denard Span, cf	.308	3	13	0	4	0	0	0	0	0	0	0
Jim Thome, dh	.100	3	10	2	1	0	0	0	0	2	3	0
Matt Tolbert, 3b	—	1	0	0	0	0	0	0	0	0	0	0
Danny Valencia, 3b	.222	3	9	1	2	1	0	0	0	2	1	0
Delmon Young, lf	.333	3	12	1	4	0	1	0	1	0	1	0
Totals	**.216**	**3**	**97**	**7**	**21**	**3**	**1**	**2**	**6**	**8**	**20**	**0**

PITCHER	W	L	ERA	G	GS	SV	IP	H	R	ER	BB	SO
Scott Baker	0	0	3.86	1	0	0	2.1	3	1	1	0	2
Matt Capps	0	0	9.00	1	0	0	1.0	2	1	1	0	0
Jesse Crain	0	1	54.00	1	0	0	0.1	3	2	2	0	0

CLIFF WELCH

	W	L	ERA	G	GS	SV	IP	H	R	ER	BB	SO
Brian Duensing	0	1	13.50	1	1	0	3.1	7	5	5	1	1
Brian Fuentes	0	0	0.00	2	0	0	2.2	1	0	0	2	2
Matt Guerrier	0	0	0.00	2	0	0	1.2	1	0	0	1	2
Francisco Liriano	0	0	6.35	1	1	0	5.2	6	4	4	3	7
Jose Mijares	0	0	0.00	3	0	0	1.1	0	0	0	1	0
Carl Pavano	0	1	6.00	1	1	0	6.0	10	4	4	1	3
Jon Rauch	0	0	0.00	2	0	0	1.2	0	0	0	0	1
Totals	0	3	5.88	3	3	0	26.0	33	17	17	7	18

E—Mauer. **DP**—NY Yankees 3, Minnesota 3. **LOB**—NY Yankees 20, Minnesota 20. **SB**—Rodriguez, Gardner, Jeter, Granderson. **SH**—Hudson, Granderson. **SF**—Rodriguez, Valencia, Gardner. **HBP**—Thome (by Sabathia). **IBB**—Teixeira (by Mijares). **WP**—Liriano. **PB**—Posada.

SCORE BY INNINGS

New York	011 414 501—17	
Minnesota	031 002 010—7	

NATIONAL LEAGUE DIVISION SERIES

PHILADELPHIA VS. CINCINNATI

CINCINNATI

PLAYER, POS	AVG	G	AB	R	H	2B	3B	HR	RBI	BB	SO	SB
Bronson Arroyo, p	.000	2	2	0	0	0	0	0	0	0	1	0
Homer Bailey, p	—	1	0	0	0	0	0	0	0	0	0	0
Bill Bray, p	—	2	0	0	0	0	0	0	0	0	0	0
Jay Bruce, rf	.250	3	8	1	2	0	0	1	1	2	0	0
Orlando Cabrera, ss	.125	3	8	0	1	0	0	0	0	0	2	0
Miguel Cairo, p	.000	3	3	0	0	0	0	0	0	0	1	0
Aroldis Chapman, p	—	2	0	0	0	0	0	0	0	0	0	0
Johnny Cueto, p	.000	1	1	0	0	0	0	0	0	0	0	0
Juan Francisco, ph	.000	1	1	0	0	0	0	0	0	0	0	0
Jonny Gomes, lf	.000	2	6	0	0	0	0	0	0	0	3	0
Ryan Hanigan, c	.000	2	4	0	0	0	0	0	0	0	0	0
Chris Heisey, lf	.000	1	2	0	0	0	0	0	0	0	1	0
Ramon Hernandez, cf	.143	3	7	0	1	1	0	0	0	0	0	0
Paul Janish, ss	.000	1	1	0	0	0	0	0	0	0	0	0
Nick Masset, p	—	2	0	0	0	0	0	0	0	0	0	0
Laynce Nix, lf	.000	1	3	1	0	0	0	0	0	0	1	0
Logan Ondrusek, p	—	2	0	0	0	0	0	0	0	0	0	0
Brandon Phillips, 2b	.333	3	12	2	4	1	0	1	1	0	1	0
Arthur Rhodes, p	—	1	0	0	0	0	0	0	0	0	0	0
Scott Rolen, 3b	.091	3	11	0	1	0	0	0	0	0	8	0
Drew Stubbs, cf	.111	3	9	0	1	0	0	0	0	2	4	0
Edinson Volquez, p	—	1	0	0	0	0	0	0	0	0	0	0
Joey Votto, 1b	.100	3	10	0	1	0	0	0	1	0	2	0
Travis Wood, p	.000	1	1	0	0	0	0	0	0	0	0	0
Totals	.124	3	89	4	11	2	0	2	3	4	24	0

PITCHER	W	L	ERA	G	GS	SV	IP	H	R	ER	BB	SO
Bronson Arroyo	0	0	1.69	1	1	0	5.1	4	3	1	3	2
Homer Bailey	0	0	0.00	1	0	0	2.0	2	0	0	0	2
Bill Bray	0	0	0.00	2	0	0	1.2	0	0	0	0	2
Aroldis Chapman	0	1	0.00	2	0	0	1.2	3	3	0	0	1
Johnny Cueto	0	1	1.80	1	1	0	5.0	5	2	1	1	2
Nick Masset	0	0	4.50	2	0	0	2.0	2	1	1	2	1
Logan Ondrusek	0	0	0.00	2	0	0	2.0	0	0	0	1	0
Arthur Rhodes	0	0	0.00	1	0	0	0.1	0	0	0	0	1
Edinson Volquez	0	1	21.60	1	1	0	1.2	4	4	4	2	0
Travis Wood	0	0	0.00	1	0	0	3.1	1	0	0	1	3
Totals	0	3	2.52	3	3	0	25.0	21	13	7	10	14

PHILADELPHIA

PLAYER, POS	AVG	G	AB	R	H	2B	3B	HR	RBI	BB	SO	SB
Domonic Brown, ph	.000	1	1	1	0	0	0	0	0	0	0	0
Jose Contreras, p	—	1	0	0	0	0	0	0	0	0	0	0
Chad Durbin, p	—	1	0	0	0	0	0	0	0	0	0	0
Ben Francisco, ph	—	1	0	0	0	0	0	0	0	0	0	0
Roy Halladay, p	.333	1	3	1	1	0	0	0	1	0	0	0
Cole Hamels, p	.000	1	3	0	0	0	0	0	0	0	0	0
Ryan Howard, 1b	.273	3	11	0	3	0	0	0	2	5	0	0
Raul Ibanez, lf	.250	3	12	0	3	1	0	0	0	1	2	0
Brad Lidge, p	—	1	0	0	0	0	0	0	0	0	0	0
Ryan Madson, op	—	1	0	0	0	0	0	0	0	0	0	0
Roy Oswalt, p	.000	1	1	0	0	0	0	0	0	0	0	0
Placido Polanco, 3b	.111	2	9	1	1	0	0	0	0	0	0	0
Jimmy Rollins, ss	.091	3	11	1	1	0	0	0	0	0	0	0
J.C. Romero, p	—	1	0	0	0	0	0	0	0	0	0	0

Jonny Venters pitched in all four Braves NLDS games, fanning eight in 5⅓ innings

GEORGE GOJKOVICH

Carlos Ruiz, c	.250	3	8	1	2	1	0	0	1	3	0	0
Mike Sweeney, ph	1.000	1	1	0	1	0	0	0	0	0	0	0
Chase Utley, 2b	.273	3	11	3	3	0	0	1	4	0	2	1
Wilson Valdez, 3b	.333	1	3	1	1	0	0	0	0	0	0	0
Shane Victorino, cf	.231	3	13	2	3	1	0	0	3	1	0	1
Jayson Werth, rf	.167	3	12	2	2	0	0	0	1	1	5	1
Totals	.212	3	99	13	21	3	0	1	10	10	14	3

PITCHER	W	L	ERA	G	GS	SV	IP	H	R	ER	BB	SO
Jose Contreras	1	0	0.00	1	0	0	1.0	0	0	0	0	1
Chad Durbin	0	0	0.00	1	0	0	0.1	0	0	0	1	0
Roy Halladay	1	0	0.00	1	1	0	9.0	0	0	0	1	8
Cole Hamels	1	0	0.00	1	1	0	9.0	5	0	0	0	9
Brad Lidge	0	0	0.00	1	0	1	1.0	0	0	0	1	0
Ryan Madson	0	0	0.00	1	0	0	1.0	1	0	0	0	1
Roy Oswalt	0	0	5.40	1	1	0	5.0	5	4	3	1	5
J.C. Romero	0	0	0.00	1	0	0	0.2	0	0	0	0	0
Totals	3	0	1.00	3	3	1	27.0	11	4	3	4	24

E—Ondrusek, Phillips 2, Rolen 2, Bruce, Utley 2, Polanco, Cabrera. **DP**—Cincinnati 2, Philadelphia 1. **LOB**—Cincinnati 15, Philadelphia 26. **SB**—Victorino, Werth, Utley. **SH**—Janish, Hamels. **SF**—Utley, Votto. **HBP**—Ruiz (by Rhodes), Francisco (by Ondrusek), Utley (by Chapman). **IBB**—Ruiz (by Wood), Howard (by Masset), Ibanez (by Masset). **WP**—Oswalt, Madson.

SCORE BY INNINGS

Cincinnati	110 110 000—4	
Philadelphia	230 031 310—13	

SAN FRANCISCO VS. ATLANTA

ATLANTA

PLAYER, POS	AVG	G	AB	R	H	2B	3B	HR	RBI	BB	SO	SB
Rick Ankiel, cf	.167	4	12	1	2	0	0	1	1	2	4	0
Melky Cabrera, lf	.000	3	8	1	0	0	0	0	1	0	1	0
Brooks Conrad, 2b	.091	4	11	0	1	0	0	0	0	0	4	0
Matt Diaz, lf	.100	4	10	0	1	0	0	0	0	0	2	0
Michael Dunn, p	—	3	0	0	0	0	0	0	0	0	0	0
Kyle Farnsworth, p	—	2	0	0	0	0	0	0	0	0	0	0
Troy Glaus, 3b	.000	3	4	0	0	0	0	0	0	0	1	0
Alex Gonzalez, ss	.200	4	15	1	3	1	0	0	2	0	5	0
Tommy Hanson, p	.000	1	1	0	0	0	0	0	0	0	1	0
Diory Hernandez, 3b	.000	2	1	0	0	0	0	0	0	0	1	0
Jason Heyward, rf	.125	4	16	0	2	0	0	0	0	1	8	0
Eric Hinske, ph	.333	4	3	1	1	0	0	1	2	1	1	0
Tim Hudson, p	.500	2	2	0	1	0	0	0	0	0	1	0
Omar Infante, 3b	.222	4	18	1	4	1	0	0	0	1	5	0
Craig Kimbrel, p	—	4	0	0	0	0	0	0	0	0	0	0
Derrek Lee, 1b	.125	4	16	2	2	0	0	0	0	1	6	0
Derek Lowe, p	.000	2	4	0	0	0	0	0	0	0	2	0

PLAYER, POS	AVG	G	AB	R	H	2B	3B	HR	RBI	BB	SO	SB
Brian McCann, c	.429	4	14	2	6	1	0	1	3	1	4	0
Nate McLouth, cf	.500	3	2	0	1	0	0	0	0	0	0	0
Peter Moylan, p	—	4	0	0	0	0	0	0	0	0	0	0
David Ross, c			0	0	0	0	0	0	0	0	0	0
Jonny Venters, p	—		0	0	0	0	0	0	0	0	0	0
Billy Wagner, p		1	0	0	0	0	0	0	0	0	0	0
Totals	.175	4	137	9	24	3	0	3	9	7	46	0

PITCHER	W	L	ERA	G	GS	SV	IP	H	R	ER	BB	SO
Michael Dunn	0	0	0.00	3	0	0	1.1	2	0	0	0	2
Kyle Farnsworth	1	0	0.00	2	0	0	2.0	1	0	0	1	1
Tommy Hanson	0	0	9.00	1	1	0	4.0	5	4	4	1	5
Tim Hudson	0	0	0.00	1	1	0	7.0	4	1	0	4	5
Craig Kimbrel	0	1	2.08	4	0	0	4.1	1	2	1	1	7
Derek Lowe	0	2	2.31	2	2	0	11.2	6	4	3	6	14
Peter Moylan	0	0	0.00	4	0	0	1.0	1	0	0	0	1
Jonny Venters	0	0	0.00	4	0	0	5.1	7	0	0	0	8
Billy Wagner	0	0	0.00	1	0	0	0.1	1	0	0	0	0
Totals	1	3	1.95	4	4	0	37.0	28	11	8	13	43

SAN FRANCISCO

PLAYER, POS	AVG	G	AB	R	H	2B	3B	HR	RBI	BB	SO	SB
Madison Bumgarner, p	.000	1	2	0	0	0	0	0	0	0	1	0
Pat Burrell, lf	.200	4	10	1	2	1	0	1	3	2	4	0
Matt Cain, p	.500	1	2	0	1	0	0	0	1	0	1	0
Santiago Casilla, p	—	1	0	0	0	0	0	0	0	0	0	0
Mike Fontenot, 3b	.167	3	6	1	1	0	1	0	0	0	2	0
Aubrey Huff, 1b	.267	4	15	1	4	0	0	0	1	3	6	0
Travis Ishikawa, 1b	.000	3	2	1	0	0	0	0	0	1	0	0
Tim Lincecum, p	.000	1	2	0	0	0	0	0	0	0	2	0
Javier Lopez, p	—	2	0	0	0	0	0	0	0	0	0	0
Buster Posey, c	.375	4	16	3	6	1	0	0	0	2	5	1
Ramon Ramirez, p	—	1	0	0	0	0	0	0	0	0	0	0
Edgar Renteria, ss	1.000	2	2	0	2	0	0	0	0	0	0	0
Sergio Romo, p	—	2	0	0	0	0	0	0	0	0	0	0
Cody Ross, rf	.286	4	14	2	4	1	0	1	3	1	2	0
Aaron Rowand, ph	.500	2	2	0	1	0	0	0	0	0	1	0
Freddy Sanchez, 2b	.125	4	16	2	2	1	0	0	0	1	3	0
Jonathan Sanchez, p	.000	1	3	0	0	0	0	0	0	0	2	0
Pablo Sandoval, 3b	.167	2	6	0	1	0	0	0	0	1	2	0
Nate Schierholtz, rf	.250	4	4	0	1	0	0	0	0	0	1	0
Andres Torres, cf	.125	4	16	0	2	0	0	0	0	1	6	1
Juan Uribe, ss	.071	4	14	0	1	0	0	0	1	1	5	0
Brian Wilson, p	—	3	0	0	0	0	0	0	0	0	0	0
Totals	.212	4	132	11	28	3	1	2	9	13	43	2

PITCHER	W	L	ERA	G	GS	SV	IP	H	R	ER	BB	SO
Madison Bumgarner	1	0	3.00	1	1	0	6.0	6	2	2	1	5
Matt Cain	0	0	0.00	1	1	0	6.2	7	1	0	2	6
Santiago Casilla	0	0	0.00	1	0	0	1.2	1	0	0	0	2
Tim Lincecum	1	0	0.00	1	1	0	9.0	2	0	0	1	14
Javier Lopez	0	0	0.00	2	0	0	0.2	0	0	0	0	2
Ramon Ramirez	0	1	4.50	1	0	0	2.0	1	1	1	0	1
Sergio Romo	1	0	40.50	2	0	0	0.2	3	3	3	0	0
Jonathan Sanchez	0	0	1.23	1	1	0	7.1	2	1	1	1	11
Brian Wilson	0	0	0.00	3	0	2	4.0	2	1	0	2	5
Totals	3	1	1.66	4	4	2	38.0	24	9	7	7	46

E—Conrad 4, Ankiel, Burrell, Sandoval, Fontenot, Gonzalez 2.
DP—Atlanta 7, San Francisco 1. LOB—Atlanta 23, San Francisco 26.
SB—Posey, Torres. CS—Huff, Torres 2. SH—Lincecum, Conrad, Torres.
SF—McCann. HBP—Sanchez (by Farnsworth). IBB—Sandoval (by Lowe).

SCORE BY INNINGS

Atlanta	001 002 050	01—9
San Francisco	320 101 202	00—11

AMERICAN LEAGUE CHAMPIONSHIP SERIES

TEXAS VS. NEW YORK

NEW YORK

PLAYER, POS	AVG	G	AB	R	H	2B	3B	HR	RBI	BB	SO	SB
Lance Berkman, 1b	.250	4	12	1	3	0	1	0	2	2	2	0
Robinson Cano, 2b	.348	6	23	5	8	1	0	4	5	1	3	0
Francisco Cervelli, c	.000	1	2	0	0	0	0	0	0	0	0	0
Brett Gardner, lf	.176	6	17	1	3	0	0	0	1	2	5	1
Greg Golson, rf	—	1	0	0	0	0	0	0	0	0	0	0
Curtis Granderson, cf	.294	6	17	1	5	1	0	1	3	7	4	0
Derek Jeter, ss	.231	6	26	2	6	3	1	0	1	2	7	0
Jorge Posada, c	.263	6	19	1	5	2	0	0	1	1	8	0
Alex Rodriguez, 3b	.190	6	21	4	4	2	0	2	3	4	1	
Nick Swisher, rf	.091	6	22	3	2	1	0	1	1	3	7	0
Mark Teixeira, 1b	.000	4	14	1	0	0	0	0	0	3	4	0
Marcus Thames, dh	.125	6	16	0	2	0	0	0	1	1	7	0
Totals	.201	6	189	19	38	10	2	6	17	25	52	2

PITCHER	W	L	ERA	G	GS	SV	IP	H	R	ER	BB	SO
A.J. Burnett	0	1	7.50	1	1	0	6.0	6	5	5	3	4
Joba Chamberlain	0	0	2.70	3	0	0	3.1	4	1	1	2	3
Phil Hughes	0	2	11.42	2	2	0	8.2	14	11	11	7	6
Boone Logan	0	0	27.00	3	0	0	0.2	2	2	2	1	1
Sergio Mitre	0	0	10.12	3	0	0	2.2	3	3	3	3	1
Dustin Moseley	1	0	0.00	1	0	0	2.0	0	0	0	0	4
Andy Pettitte	0	1	2.57	1	1	0	7.0	5	2	2	0	5
Mariano Rivera	0	0	0.00	3	0	1	3.0	2	0	0	0	1
David Robertson	0	0	20.25	4	0	0	2.2	8	6	6	1	4
C.C. Sabathia	1	0	6.30	2	2	0	10.0	17	7	7	4	10
Kerry Wood	0	0	1.50	4	0	0	6.0	2	1	1	3	4
Totals	2	4	6.58	6	6	1	52.0	63	38	38	24	43

TEXAS

PLAYER, POS	AVG	G	AB	R	H	2B	3B	HR	RBI	BB	SO	SB
Elvis Andrus, ss	.333	6	27	4	9	2	0	0	2	2	3	4
Julio Borbon, ph	.000	3	1	2	0	0	0	0	0	0	1	0
Jorge Cantu, 1b	.000	1	3	0	0	0	0	0	0	0	0	0
Nelson Cruz, rf	.350	6	20	6	7	3	0	2	5	3	6	0
Jeff Francoeur, rf	.200	4	10	0	2	0	0	0	0	0	0	0
Vladimir Guerrero, dh	.269	6	26	2	7	2	0	0	3	0	8	0
Josh Hamilton, cf	.350	6	20	6	7	1	0	4	7	8	4	3
Ian Kinsler, 2b	.250	6	20	1	5	1	1	0	3	3	3	2
Bengie Molina, c	.313	5	16	3	5	1	0	1	5	0	4	0
Mitch Moreland, 1b	.389	6	18	3	7	0	0	0	3	2	2	0
David Murphy, lf	.231	6	13	6	3	1	0	1	2	4	4	0
Matt Treanor, c	.333	2	6	2	2	0	0	0	2	1	1	0
Michael Young, 3b	.333	6	27	3	9	3	0	0	4	1	7	0
Totals	.304	6	207	38	63	14	1	9	36	24	43	9

PITCHER	W	L	ERA	G	GS	SV	IP	H	R	ER	BB	SO
Neftali Feliz	0	0	0.00	3	0	0	3.0	0	0	0	2	5
Derek Holland	1	0	0.00	2	0	0	5.2	3	0	0	2	4
Tommy Hunter	0	0	8.10	1	1	0	3.1	5	3	3	0	5
Michael Kirkman	0	0	0.00	1	0	0	2.0	1	0	0	2	1
Cliff Lee	1	0	0.00	1	1	0	8.0	2	0	0	1	13
Colby Lewis	2	0	1.98	2	2	0	13.2	9	3	3	6	13
Darren O'Day	0	1	13.50	3	0	0	0.2	1	1	1	1	1

Paced by Phil Hughes, Yankees starters gave up 25 runs in 31⅔ ALCS innings

CLIFF WELCHA

	W	L	ERA	G	GS	SV	IP	H	R	ER	BB	SO
Alexi Ogando	0	0	4.50	2	0	0	2.0	3	1	1	1	2
Darren Oliver	0	0	7.71	3	0	1	2.1	1	2	2	3	1
Clay Rapada	0	0	0.00	3	0	0	0.1	1	0	0	1	1
C.J. Wilson	0	1	6.00	2	2	0	12.0	12	9	8	6	6
Totals	**4**	**2**	**3.06**	**6**	**6**	**1**	**53.0**	**38**	**19**	**18**	**25**	**52**

E—Rodriguez, Hamilton, Francoeur. **DP**—NY Yankees 6, Texas 4. **LOB**—NY Yankees 40, Texas 42. **SB**—Hamilton 3, Andrus 4, Gardner, Kinsler 2, Rodriguez. **CS**—Kinsler, Granderson. **SH**—Andrus, Kinsler, Moreland, Gardner. **SF**—Berkman, Kinsler. **HBP**—Granderson (by Lewis), Rodriguez (by Hunter), Molina (by Burnett). **IBB**—Hamilton 5 (by Hughes 3, Mitre, Wood), Murphy 2 (by Robertson, Burnett), Thames (by Wilson), Cruz (by Wood). **WP**—Sabathia, Hughes 2, Lewis 2, Robertson, Mitre, Burnett, Wood. **Balk**—Sabathia, Hunter.

SCORE BY INNINGS

NY Yankees	043 221 160—	19
Texas	724 274 309—	38

NATIONAL LEAGUE CHAMPIONSHIP SERIES

PHILADELPHIA VS SAN FRANCISCO

SAN FRANCISCO

PLAYER, POS	AVG	G	AB	R	H	2B	3B	HR	RBI	BB	SO	SB
Jeremy Affeldt, p	—	3	0	0	0	0	0	0	0	0	0	0
Madison Bumgarner, p	.000	2	1	0	0	0	0	0	0	0	1	0
Pat Burrell, lf	.211	6	19	3	4	2	0	0	1	3	7	0
Matt Cain, p	.000	1	2	0	0	0	0	0	0	0	2	0
Santiago Casilla, p	—	2	0	0	0	0	0	0	0	0	0	0
Mike Fontenot, 3b	.250	4	8	0	2	0	0	0	0	0	1	2	1
Aubrey Huff, 1b	.250	6	24	3	6	0	0	0	3	1	3	0
Travis Ishikawa, 1b	.250	5	4	0	1	0	0	0	0	0	3	0
Tim Lincecum, p	.000	3	5	0	0	0	0	0	0	0	3	0
Javier Lopez, p	—	5	0	0	0	0	0	0	0	0	0	0
Buster Posey, c	.217	6	23	1	5	2	0	0	3	3	7	0
Ramon Ramirez, p	—	2	0	0	0	0	0	0	0	0	0	0
Edgar Renteria, ss	.063	4	16	1	1	0	0	0	0	1	2	0
Sergio Romo, p	—	3	0	0	0	0	0	0	0	0	0	0
Cody Ross, rf	.350	6	20	4	7	3	0	3	5	2	5	0
Aaron Rowand, cf	.200	3	5	1	1	0	0	0	0	0	3	0
Freddy Sanchez, 2b	.360	6	25	1	9	1	0	0	1	0	3	0
Jonathan Sanchez, p	.333	2	3	1	1	0	0	0	0	0	2	0
Pablo Sandoval, 3b	.250	3	8	0	2	1	0	0	2	1	0	0
Nate Schierholtz, rf	.000	4	3	1	0	0	0	0	0	0	3	0
Andres Torres, cf	.350	6	20	2	7	0	0	0	0	2	8	0
Juan Uribe, ss	.214	5	14	1	3	0	0	1	3	0	2	0
Brian Wilson, p	.000	4	1	0	0	0	0	0	0	0	0	0
Totals	**.244**	**6**	**201**	**19**	**49**	**10**	**0**	**4**	**18**	**14**	**56**	**1**

PITCHER	W	L	ERA	G	GS	SV	IP	H	R	ER	BB	SO
Jeremy Affeldt	0	0	3.38	3	0	0	2.2	0	1	1	1	4
Madison Bumgarner	0	0	4.05	2	1	0	6.2	9	3	3	2	7
Matt Cain	1	0	0.00	1	1	0	7.0	2	0	0	3	5
Santiago Casilla	0	0	5.40	2	0	0	1.2	2	1	1	1	2
Tim Lincecum	1	1	3.14	3	2	0	14.1	12	6	5	4	16
Javier Lopez	1	0	2.08	5	0	0	4.1	1	1	1	1	4
Ramon Ramirez	0	0	27.00	2	0	0	1.0	3	3	3	3	1	0
Sergio Romo	0	0	0.00	3	0	0	2.1	2	0	0	1	3
Jonathan Sanchez	0	1	4.50	2	2	0	8.0	8	5	4	5	8
Brian Wilson	1	0	0.00	4	0	3	5.0	2	0	0	2	7
Totals	**4**	**2**	**3.06**	**6**	**6**	**3**	**53.0**	**41**	**20**	**18**	**21**	**56**

PHILADELPHIA

PLAYER, POS	AVG	G	AB	R	H	2B	3B	HR	RBI	BB	SO	SB
Antonio Bastardo, p	—	1	0	0	0	0	0	0	0	0	0	0
Joe Blanton, p	.000	1	1	0	0	0	0	0	0	0	1	0
Domonic Brown, ph	.000	2	2	0	0	0	0	0	0	0	0	0
Jose Contreras, p	—	3	0	0	0	0	0	0	0	0	0	0
Chad Durbin, p	—	1	0	0	0	0	0	0	0	0	0	0
Ben Francisco, lf	.167	6	6	1	1	0	0	0	0	0	3	0
Ross Gload, ph	.000	6	5	0	0	0	0	0	0	1	1	0
Roy Halladay, p	.333	2	3	0	1	0	0	0	0	0	2	0
Cole Hamels, p	.000	1	2	0	0	0	0	0	0	0	1	0
Ryan Howard, b	.318	6	22	1	7	4	0	0	0	3	12	0
Raul Ibanez, lf	.211	5	19	1	4	1	0	0	0	1	6	0
Brad Lidge, p	—	3	0	0	0	0	0	0	0	0	0	0
Ryan Madson, p	—	5	0	0	0	0	0	0	0	0	0	0

Jayson Werth hit two homers in the NLCS, giving him 13 in 44 postseason games

	AVG	G	AB	R	H	2B	3B	HR	RBI	BB	SO	SB
Roy Oswalt, p	.200	3	5	1	1	0	0	0	0	0	0	0
Placido Polanco, 3b	.250	6	20	3	5	2	0	0	5	3	1	1
Jimmy Rollins, ss	.261	6	23	0	6	1	0	0	4	2	7	2
J.C. Romero, p	—	1	0	0	0	0	0	0	0	0	0	0
Carlos Ruiz, c	.167	6	18	2	3	0	0	1	1	1	7	0
Chase Utley, 2b	.182	6	22	5	4	1	0	0	1	4	2	3
Wilson Valdez, pr	—	2	0	0	0	0	0	0	0	0	0	0
Shane Victorino, cf	.208	6	24	3	5	1	0	0	2	2	6	1
Jayson Werth, rf	.222	6	18	3	4	1	0	2	5	4	7	0
Totals	**.216**	**6**	**190**	**20**	**41**	**11**	**0**	**3**	**18**	**21**	**56**	**7**

PITCHER	W	L	ERA	G	GS	SV	IP	H	R	ER	BB	SO
Antonio Bastardo	0	0	0.00	1	0	0	0.1	1	0	0	0	0
Joe Blanton	0	0	5.79	1	1	0	4.2	5	3	3	1	3
Jose Contreras	0	0	0.00	3	0	0	3.0	1	0	0	0	3
Chad Durbin	0	0	18.00	1	0	0	1.0	2	2	2	2	1
Roy Halladay	1	1	4.15	2	2	0	13.0	14	6	6	2	12
Cole Hamels	0	1	4.50	1	1	0	6.0	5	3	3	1	8
Brad Lidge	0	0	0.00	3	0	1	3.0	3	0	0	2	5
Ryan Madson	0	1	1.35	5	0	0	6.2	4	1	1	3	10
Roy Oswalt	1	1	1.84	3	2	0	14.2	14	4	3	3	14
J.C. Romero	0	0	0.00	1	0	0	0.1	0	0	0	0	0
Totals	**2**	**4**	**3.08**	**6**	**6**	**1**	**52.2**	**49**	**19**	**18**	**14**	**56**

E—Fontenot, Rollins, Howard, Huff, A, Sandoval, Polanco. **DP**—San Francisco 4, Philadelphia 5. **LOB**—San Francisco 44, Philadelphia 45. **SB**—Fontenot, Polanco, Utley 3, Victorino, Rollins 2. **CS**—Rollins, Torres. **SH**—Victorino, Sanchez 2, Blanton, Halladay, Ruiz. **SF**—Polanco, Uribe, Werth. **HBP**—Ruiz 3 (by Wilson, Cain, Lincecum), Ishikawa (by Lidge), Victorino (by Cain), Ross (by Blanton), Polanco (by Bumgarner), Werth (by Casilla, S), Utley (by Sanchez), Uribe (by Oswalt). **IBB**—Utley (by Ramirez), Werth 2 (by Affeldt, Bumgarner), Howard (by Casilla), Huff (by Madson), Posey (by Lidge). **WP**—Blanton 2, Casilla, Sanchez. **PB**—Posey.

SCORE BY INNINGS

San Francisco	204 344 011—	19
Philadelphia	304 052 411—	20

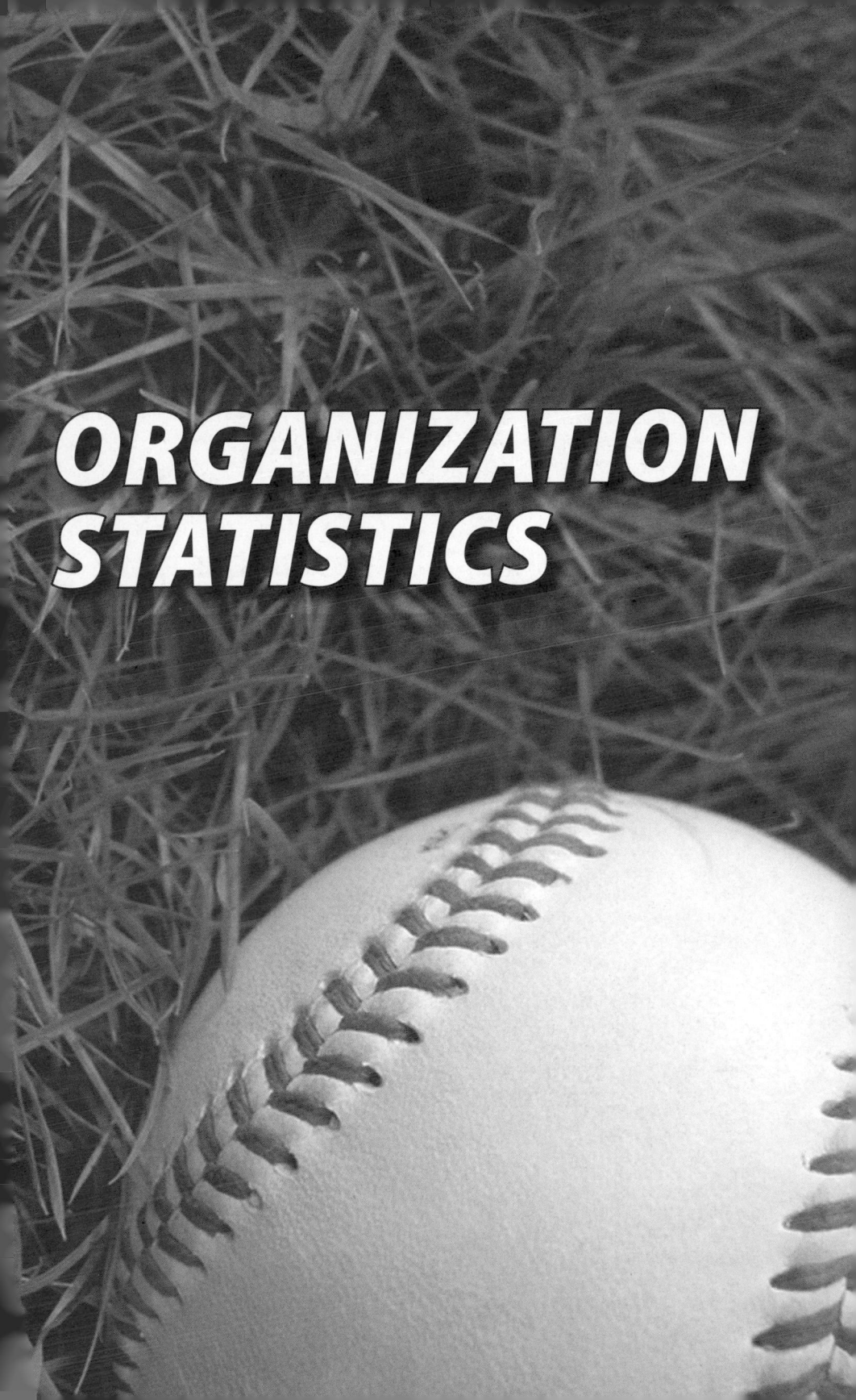

ORGANIZATION STATISTICS

Arizona Diamondbacks

SEASON IN A SENTENCE: After yet another slow start, the Diamondbacks fired general manager Josh Byrnes and manager A.J. Hinch in July, elevating Kirk Gibson from bench coach to the interim managing position to try to right the 31-48 ballclub (his 34-40 record wasn't much better, though he did get the full-time job).

HIGH POINT: It wasn't pretty, but Edwin Jackson threw the second no-hitter in franchise history on June 25. In the 149-pitch effort, he walked eight batters and struck out six as Arizona got the 1-0 win over Tampa Bay. The offensive highlights came from first baseman Adam LaRoche, who hit 25 home runs and led the team in doubles (37) and RBIs (100), and second baseman Kelly Johnson.

LOW POINT: A 10-game losing streak at the end of May into June, nine of them being on the road, solidified a terrible season away from home that saw the Diamondbacks go 25-56. They were a respectable 40-41 at Chase Field.

NOTABLE ROOKIES: First baseman Brandon Allen came up and made an immediate impact, going 2-for-3 with a grand slam in his debut. Daniel Hudson went 7-1, 1.69 in 11 starts after coming from the White Sox when Arizona traded Jackson at midseason.

KEY TRANSACTIONS: Along with making over the front office staff as soon as the season ended, highlighted by the hiring of Kevin Towers as GM, Arizona traded away Dan Haren and Jackson at midseason. Haren brought four pitchers in Patrick Corbin, Rafael Rodriguez, Joe Saunders and Tyler Skaggs. For Jackson, the Diamondbacks received David Holmberg and Hudson, who quickly established himself as a key member of the major league rotation.

DOWN ON THE FARM: The Diamondbacks had five picks in the first 45 selections of the 2009 draft, and the hope was that some of the players would move quickly through the system. First-rounder A.J. Pollock missed the year with an injury, but eighth-rounder Paul Goldschmidt led the system in numerous offensive categories and 12th-rounder Charles Brewer led the system in ERA, strikeouts and opponent average. Top prospect Jarrod Parker missed the season after Tommy John surgery but looked strong in instructional league. Arizona had three of its affiliates finish with winning records, but it is still building back its talent after hits from trades and graduation.

OPENING DAY PAYROLL: $60.7 million (25th)

PLAYERS OF THE YEAR

MAJOR LEAGUE	MINOR LEAGUE
Kelly Johnson	**Paul Goldschmidt**
2b	**1b**
.284/.370/.496	(High Class A)
26 HR, 36 2B	.314/.384/.606
4th in NL in 2B PO	Cal League MVP

ORGANIZATION LEADERS

BATTING   *Minimum 250 at-bats

MAJORS

*AVG	Kelly Johnson	.284
*OPS	Kelly Johnson	.865
HR	Mark Reynolds	32
RBI	Adam LaRoche	100

MINORS

*AVG	Konrad Schmidt, Mobile	.315
*OBP	Ollie Linton, Mobile	.411
*SLG	Paul Goldschmidt, Visalia	.606
R	Marc Krauss, Visalia	107
H	Paul Goldschmidt, Visalia	165
TB	Paul Goldschmidt, Visalia	318
2B	Paul Goldschmidt, Visalia	42
3B	Keon Broxton, South Bend	19
HR	Paul Goldschmidt, Visalia	35
RBI	Paul Goldschmidt, Visalia	108
BB	Brandon Allen, Reno	83
SO	Keon Broxton, South Bend	172
SB	Evan Frey, Mobile	34

PITCHING   †Minimum 75 innings

MAJORS

W	Ian Kennedy	9
†ERA	Daniel Hudson	1.69
SO	Ian Kennedy	168

MINORS

W	Josh Collmenter, Visalia/Reno/Mobile	14
L	Five tied at	10
†ERA	Charles Brewer, South Bend/Visalia	2.45
G	Jason Urquidez, Reno	51
GS	Matt Torra, Mobile/Reno	28
SV	Yonata Ortega, South Bend/Visalia	33
IP	Matt Torra, Mobile/Reno	183
BB	Wade Miley, Visalia/Mobile	65
SO	Charles Brewer, South Bend/Visalia	153
†AVG	Charles Brewer, South Bend/Visalia	.229

2010 PERFORMANCE

General Manager: Josh Byrnes/Jerry DiPoto. **Farm Director:** Mike Berger. **Scouting Director:** Tom Allison.

Class	Team	League	W	L	PCT	Finish*	Manager(s)
Majors	Arizona Diamondbacks	National	65	97	.401	15th (16)	A.J. Hinch/Kirk Gibson
Triple-A	Reno Aces	Pacific Coast	69	74	.483	11th (16)	Brett Butler
Double-A	Mobile BayBears	Southern	75	62	.547	3rd (10)	Rico Brogna
High A	Visalia Rawhide	California	72	68	.514	7th (10)	Audo Vicente
Low A	South Bend Silver Hawks	Midwest	59	78	.431	13th (16)	Mark Haley
Short-season	Yakima Bears	Northwest	43	33	.566	t-2nd (8)	Bob Didier
Rookie	Missoula Osprey	Pioneer	28	47	.373	7th (8)	Hector De La Cruz
Overall 2010 Minor League Record			346	362	.489	22nd (30)	

*Finish in overall standings (No. of teams in league). †League champion.

ORGANIZATION STATISTICS

ARIZONA DIAMONDBACKS
NATIONAL LEAGUE

Batting	B-T	HT	WT	DOB	AVG	vLH	vRH	G	AB	R	H	2B	3B	HR	RBI	BB	HBP	SH	SF	SO	SB	CS	SLG	OBP
Abreu, Tony	B-R	5-9	200	11-13-84	.233	.257	.220	81	193	16	45	11	1	1	13	4	0	0	4	47	2	1	.316	.244
Allen, Brandon	L-R	6-2	235	2-12-86	.267	.143	.289	22	45	5	12	3	0	1	6	10	0	0	1	20	0	0	.400	.393
Church, Ryan	L-L	6-2	215	10-14-78	.265	.000	.310	37	49	9	13	5	0	2	7	4	2	0	0	19	0	0	.490	.345
2-team total (69 Pittsburgh)					.201	—	—	106	219	25	44	16	1	5	25	16	3	0	0	65	1	0	.352	.265
Crosby, Bobby	R-R	6-3	205	1-12-80	.167	.250	.000	9	12	0	2	2	0	0	2	1	0	0	1	5	0	1	.333	.214
2-team total (61 Pittsburgh)					.220	—	—	70	168	9	37	10	0	1	13	17	1	2	1	38	0	3	.298	.294
Drew, Stephen	L-R	6-0	185	3-16-83	.278	.255	.287	151	565	83	157	33	12	15	61	62	3	2	1	108	10	5	.458	.352
Gillespie, Cole	R-R	6-1	205	6-20-84	.231	.204	.255	45	104	11	24	8	0	2	12	7	1	0	1	29	1	1	.365	.283
Hester, John	R-R	6-3	220	9-14-83	.211	.220	.204	38	95	9	20	7	0	2	7	11	0	0	0	32	1	0	.347	.292
Jackson, Conor	R-R	6-2	215	5-7-82	.238	.300	.223	42	151	19	36	11	0	1	11	20	0	0	1	18	4	1	.331	.326
Johnson, Kelly	L-R	6-1	205	2-22-82	.284	.310	.272	154	585	93	166	36	5	26	71	79	2	3	2	148	13	7	.496	.370
LaRoche, Adam	L-L	6-3	205	11-6-79	.261	.264	.259	151	560	75	146	37	2	25	100	48	3	0	4	172	0	1	.468	.320
Montero, Miguel	L-R	5-11	190	7-9-83	.266	.213	.286	85	297	36	79	20	2	9	43	29	2	0	3	71	0	1	.438	.332
Ojeda, Augie	B-R	5-9	175	12-20-74	.190	.258	.146	59	79	6	15	3	0	0	5	8	0	3	2	8	0	1	.228	.258
Parra, Gerardo	L-L	5-11	195	5-6-87	.261	.283	.257	133	364	31	95	19	6	3	30	23	2	3	1	76	1	0	.371	.308
Reynolds, Mark	R-R	6-2	220	8-3-83	.198	.218	.191	145	499	79	99	17	2	32	85	83	9	0	5	211	7	4	.433	.320
Roberts, Ryan	R-R	5-11	195	9-19-80	.197	.143	.292	36	66	8	13	4	0	2	9	3	0	1	1	17	0	0	.348	.229
Ryal, Rusty	R-R	6-2	200	3-16-83	.261	.274	.248	104	207	19	54	7	1	3	11	8	6	1	0	67	0	3	.348	.308
Schmidt, Konrad	R-R	6-0	225	8-2-84	.125	.000	.250	4	8	0	1	0	0	0	1	0	0	0	0	0	0	0	.125	.222
Snyder, Chris	R-R	6-4	245	2-12-81	.231	.200	.241	65	195	22	45	8	0	10	32	36	1	1	1	61	0	0	.426	.352
2-team total (40 Pittsburgh)					.207	—	—	105	319	34	66	9	0	15	48	52	2	1	2	94	0	0	.376	.320
Upton, Justin	R-R	6-2	205	8-25-87	.273	.276	.272	133	495	73	135	27	3	17	69	64	4	1	7	152	18	8	.442	.356
Young, Chris	R-R	6-2	200	9-5-83	.257	.264	.255	156	584	94	150	33	0	27	91	74	2	1	3	145	28	7	.452	.341

Pitching	B-T	HT	WT	DOB	W	L	ERA	G	GS	CG	SV	IP	H	R	ER	HR	BB	SO	AVG	vLH	vRH	K/9	BB/9
Benson, Kris	R-R	6-4	205	11-7-74	1	1	5.14	3	3	0	0	14	18	9	8	2	6	8	.305	.310	.300	5.14	3.86
Boyer, Blaine	R-R	6-3	215	7-11-81	3	2	4.26	54	0	0	0	57	59	32	27	3	29	29	.273	.352	.198	4.58	4.58
Buckner, Billy	R-R	6-2	205	8-27-83	0	3	11.08	3	3	0	0	13	26	17	16	4	5	11	.406	.273	.476	7.62	3.46
Carrasco, D.J.	R-R	6-4	220	4-12-77	1	0	3.18	18	0	0	0	23	18	15	8	1	12	20	.217	.243	.196	7.94	4.76
2-team total (45 Pittsburgh)					3	2	3.68	63	0	0	0	78	68	39	32	5	34	65	—	—	—	7.47	3.91
Demel, Sam	R-R	6-0	215	10-23-85	2	1	5.35	37	0	0	2	37	42	27	22	5	12	33	.278	.237	.304	8.03	2.92
Enright, Barry	R-R	6-3	220	3-30-86	6	7	3.91	17	17	0	0	99	97	43	43	20	29	49	.261	.241	.279	4.45	2.64
Gutierrez, Juan	R-R	6-3	210	7-14-83	0	6	5.08	58	0	0	15	57	55	33	32	13	23	47	.252	.286	.228	7.46	3.65
Hampton, Mike	R-L	5-10	195	9-9-72	0	0	0.00	10	0	0	0	4	3	0	0	0	1	3	.214	.333	.000	6.23	2.08
Haren, Dan	R-R	6-5	215	9-17-80	7	8	4.60	21	21	1	0	141	161	79	72	23	29	141	.285	.286	.284	9.00	1.85
Heilman, Aaron	R-R	6-5	225	11-12-78	5	8	4.50	70	0	0	6	72	73	37	36	9	26	55	.260	.229	.291	6.88	3.25
Howry, Bob	L-R	6-5	220	8-4-73	1	0	10.67	14	0	0	0	14	18	17	17	6	6	6	.300	.333	.273	3.77	3.77
2-team total (24 Chicago)					1	3	7.71	38	0	0	0	35	47	36	30	8	13	14	—	—	—	3.60	3.34
Hudson, Dan	R-R	6-3	225	3-9-87	7	1	1.69	11	11	0	0	80	51	15	15	7	16	70	.183	.174	.190	7.91	1.81
Jackson, Edwin	R-R	6-3	210	9-9-83	6	10	5.16	21	21	1	0	134	141	80	77	13	60	104	.274	.294	.257	6.97	4.02
Kennedy, Ian	R-R	6-0	195	12-19-84	9	10	3.80	32	32	0	0	194	163	87	82	26	70	168	.228	.218	.238	7.79	3.25
Kroenke, Zach	R-L	6-2	210	4-21-84	1	0	6.75	3	1	0	0	7	9	5	5	2	4	2	.333	.143	.400	2.70	5.40
Lopez, Rodrigo	R-R	6-1	185	12-14-75	7	16	5.00	33	33	0	0	200	227	126	111	37	56	116	.286	.293	.280	5.22	2.52
Mulvey, Kevin	R-R	6-2	195	5-26-85	0	0	6.00	2	0	0	0	3	5	2	2	2	2	1	.357	.200	.444	3.00	6.00
Norberto, Jordan	L-L	6-0	195	12-8-86	0	2	5.85	33	0	0	0	20	16	13	13	3	22	15	.225	.235	.216	6.75	9.90
Qualls, Chad	R-R	6-5	220	8-17-78	1	4	8.29	43	0	0	12	38	61	41	35	5	15	34	.363	.380	.348	8.05	3.55
Rivera, Saul	B-R	5-10	180	12-7-77	0	0	22.09	4	0	0	0	4	11	9	9	2	3	1	.550	.500	.571	2.45	7.36
Rodriguez, Rafael	R-R	6-1	175	9-24-84	0	0	6.75	4	0	0	0	3	4	2	2	1	1	2	.333	.250	.375	6.75	3.38
Rosa, Carlos	R-R	6-1	210	9-21-84	0	2	4.50	22	0	0	0	20	20	10	10	1	12	9	.286	.414	.195	4.05	5.40
Rosales, Leo	R-R	6-1	205	5-28-81	2	0	7.16	16	0	0	0	16	25	13	13	2	9	12	.362	.357	.366	6.61	4.96
Saunders, Joe	L-L	6-3	210	6-16-81	3	7	4.25	13	13	1	0	83	97	50	39	11	19	50	.293	.211	.315	5.44	2.07
Stange, Daniel	R-R	6-3	185	12-22-85	0	0	13.50	4	0	0	0	4	4	6	6	1	6	2	.250	.111	.429	4.50	13.50

					W	L	ERA	G	GS	CG	SV	IP	H	R	ER	HR	BB	SO	AVG	vLH	vRH	K/9	BB/9
Valdez, Cesar	R-R	6-2	200	3-17-85	1	2	7.65	9	2	0	0	20	29	19	17	2	10	13	.337	.351	.327	5.85	4.50
Vasquez, Esmerling	R-R	6-1	175	11-7-83	1	6	5.20	57	0	0	0	54	46	32	31	6	38	55	.236	.224	.247	9.22	6.37
Willis, Dontrelle	L-L	6-4	225	1-12-82	1	1	6.85	6	5	0	0	22	24	17	17	3	27	14	.304	.200	.352	5.64	10.88

Fielding

Catcher	PCT	G	PO	A	E	DP	PB
Hester	1.000	33	189	10	0	2	4
Montero	.996	79	484	36	2	1	6
Schmidt	1.000	2	12	0	0	0	0
Snyder	.998	61	411	32	1	1	5

First Base	PCT	G	PO	A	E	DP
Allen	1.000	4	14	0	0	2
Jackson	1.000	3	27	2	0	4
LaRoche	.991	146	1139	122	11	117
Reynolds	1.000	5	7	1	0	1
Ryal	.971	24	127	9	4	16

Second Base	PCT	G	PO	A	E	DP
Abreu	.919	12	16	18	3	3

Catcher	PCT	G	PO	A	E	DP	PB
Crosby	1.000	1	0	1	0	0	
Johnson	.988	149	267	402	8	106	
Ojeda	1.000	15	10	19	0	2	
Roberts	1.000	1	3	4	0	2	

Third Base	PCT	G	PO	A	E	DP
Abreu	.978	20	11	33	1	1
Crosby	.857	2	1	5	1	1
Ojeda	1.000	12	7	1	0	1
Reynolds	.951	142	101	250	18	24
Roberts	1.000	1	1	1	0	0
Ryal	.875	8	2	5	1	2

Shortstop	PCT	G	PO	A	E	DP
Abreu	.891	15	16	33	6	12

Drew		.984	147	206	391	10	86
Ojeda		1.000	9	8	15	0	3

Outfield	PCT	G	PO	A	E	DP
Allen	1.000	14	27	0	0	0
Church	1.000	11	20	0	0	0
Gillespie	.980	36	47	1	1	0
Jackson	.986	36	71	2	1	0
Parra	.983	113	220	9	4	3
Roberts	1.000	15	16	1	0	0
Ryal	.958	36	44	2	2	1
Upton	.985	128	265	1	4	0
Young	.984	156	418	10	7	6

RENO ACES

PACIFIC COAST LEAGUE

TRIPLE-A

Batting	B-T	HT	WT	DOB	AVG	vLH	vRH	G	AB	R	H	2B	3B	HR	RBI	BB	HBP	SH	SF	SO	SB	CS	SLG	OBP
Abreu, Tony	B-R	5-9	200	11-13-84	.351	.321	.364	24	94	17	33	7	1	2	21	4	2	1	1	21	2	0	.511	.386
Allen, Brandon	L-R	6-2	235	2-12-86	.261	.262	.261	107	371	72	97	18	3	25	86	83	10	0	5	95	14	4	.528	.405
Bailey, Jeff	R-R	6-2	200	11-19-78	.289	.312	.279	129	478	88	138	33	7	12	78	63	17	0	6	94	3	1	.462	.387
Ciriaco, Pedro	R-R	6-0	160	9-27-85	.259	.239	.266	87	355	44	92	15	7	6	51	10	1	6	4	53	14	3	.392	.278
Corporan, Carlos	B-R	6-2	220	1-7-84	.290	.342	.271	87	286	38	83	20	4	12	50	24	4	3	5	63	3	2	.514	.356
Coughlin, Sean	L-R	6-1	215	5-14-85	.191	.150	.203	29	89	12	17	4	1	3	9	11	0	0	1	23	1	1	.360	.277
Deeds, Doug	L-L	6-2	195	6-2-81	.302	.276	.310	125	480	86	145	39	8	12	55	64	6	2	4	118	10	10	.492	.388
Easley, Ed	R-R	6-0	200	12-21-85	.188	.111	.205	17	48	4	9	3	0	0	7	3	0	4	0	14	0	0	.250	.235
Gillespie, Cole	R-R	6-1	205	6-20-84	.288	.370	.257	69	264	54	76	14	6	8	49	44	3	0	1	49	8	5	.477	.394
Groff, Eric	R-R	5-11	195	1-25-88	.091	.000	.091	5	11	1	1	0	0	0	0	2	0	0	0	6	0	0	.091	.231
Hallberg, Mark	R-R	5-11	170	12-9-85	.263	.304	.243	121	384	55	101	24	3	1	44	51	3	10	6	47	5	4	.349	.349
Hankerd, Cyle	R-R	6-3	215	1-24-85	.400	.625	.143	7	15	1	6	3	0	0	5	3	0	0	0	1	0	0	.600	.500
Herrnberger, Alex	B-R	6-0	182	7-6-86	1.000	.000	1.000	1	1	1	1	1	0	0	0	0	0	0	0	0	0	0	2.000	1.000
Hester, John	R-R	6-3	220	9-14-83	.370	.400	.352	37	138	34	51	12	4	7	29	16	3	0	2	26	2	4	.667	.440
Jackson, Conor	R-R	6-2	215	5-7-82	.273	.000	.429	3	11	4	3	0	0	1	2	0	1	0	0	2	0	0	.545	.333
2-team total (2 Sacramento)					.158	—		5	19	5	3	0	0	1	2	1	1	1	0	3	0	0	.316	.238
Macias, Drew	L-L	6-3	175	3-7-83	.255	.149	.278	102	274	50	70	11	5	6	28	51	9	3	1	53	10	9	.398	.388
Montero, Miguel	L-R	5-11	190	7-9-83	.333	.333	.333	4	15	1	5	0	0	0	2	1	1	0	0	0	0	0	.333	.412
Parra, Gerardo	L-L	5-11	195	5-6-87	.417	.500	.412	9	36	8	15	4	0	1	7	2	1	1	0	5	3	1	.611	.462
Rahl, Chris	R-R	5-10	185	12-2-83	.291	.367	.242	87	251	44	73	15	2	8	32	20	5	2	3	63	8	7	.462	.351
Roberts, Ryan	R-R	5-11	195	9-19-80	.265	.374	.227	94	347	62	92	25	2	11	55	56	2	1	6	73	16	6	.444	.365
Rogers, Ed	R-R	6-0	190	8-29-78	.282	.333	.262	121	447	65	126	22	7	6	59	36	10	12	6	70	12	5	.403	.345
Sanchez, Yunesky	B-R	6-2	210	5-3-84	.284	.372	.254	105	338	42	96	18	2	7	52	26	0	1	3	45	5	4	.411	.332

Pitching	B-T	HT	WT	DOB	W	L	ERA	G	GS	CG	SV	IP	H	R	ER	HR	BB	SO	AVG	vLH	vRH	K/9	BB/9
Augenstein, Bryan	R-R	6-6	230	7-11-86	6	8	6.26	22	22	0	0	121	162	95	88	12	35	101	.320	.378	.275	7.53	2.61
Ayala, Luis	R-R	6-2	190	1-12-78	0	6	7.86	18	0	0	0	26	38	23	23	1	11	17	.349	.488	.258	5.81	3.76
3-team total (14 Abq., 4 Colorado Springs)					2	10	6.42	36	0	0	4	48	60	35	34	4	18	31	—	—	5.85	3.40
Beam, T.J.	R-R	6-7	215	8-28-80	3	3	6.33	43	0	0	5	54	53	40	38	7	44	34	.269	.270	.269	5.67	7.33
Benson, Kris	R-R	6-4	205	11-7-74	1	2	8.87	7	7	0	0	22	34	26	22	5	11	14	.343	.395	.304	5.64	4.43
Berger, Andrew	R-R	6-3	210	11-24-87	0	1	15.00	1	1	0	0	3	5	5	5	0	5	1	.385	.500	.286	3.00	15.00
Boyer, Blaine	R-R	6-3	215	7-11-81	1	0	1.50	9	0	0	2	6	5	1	1	0	1	9	.227	.125	.286	13.50	1.50
Buckner, Billy	R-R	6-2	205	8-27-83	3	3	3.53	7	7	0	0	43	40	19	17	2	17	27	.255	.222	.282	5.61	3.53
Collmenter, Josh	R-R	6-4	235	2-7-86	4	3	5.77	10	10	0	0	58	64	40	37	8	26	39	.281	.223	.336	6.09	4.06
Cook, Ryan	R-R	6-3	200	6-30-87	0	0	10.80	1	1	0	0	5	7	6	6	1	2	5	.333	.375	.308	9.00	3.60
Ellis, Josh	R-R	6-1	215	8-7-84	0	0	4.26	11	0	0	0	19	25	12	9	0	10	17	.313	.275	.350	8.05	4.74
Hampton, Mike	R-L	5-10	195	9-9-72	1	0	2.70	4	0	0	0	3	3	1	1	0	2	1	.273	.000	.375	2.70	5.40
Kroenke, Zach	R-L	6-2	210	4-21-84	7	3	3.51	40	9	0	2	97	94	41	38	5	39	69	.255	.188	.281	6.38	3.61
Marte, Jose	R-R	6-6	215	9-4-83	3	5	5.67	47	0	0	0	67	64	48	42	10	31	60	.254	.250	.257	8.10	4.18
Moorhouse, Brett	R-R	6-2	190	6-28-87	0	0	0.00	1	0	0	0	1	0	0	0	0	0	0	.000	.000	.000	0.00	.00
Mulvey, Kevin	R-R	6-2	195	5-26-85	7	8	4.65	27	27	0	0	157	161	85	81	11	60	109	.269	.255	.280	6.26	3.45
Norberto, Jordan	L-L	6-0	195	12-8-86	3	0	3.07	21	0	0	4	29	25	12	10	2	19	38	.227	.250	.214	11.66	5.83
Olenberger, Kasey	R-R	6-4	230	3-18-78	1	0	1.93	11	1	0	0	19	13	4	4	2	2	15	.210	.185	.229	7.23	0.96
2-team total (36 New Orleans)					2	3	5.75	47	1	0	6	56	61	36	36	9	17	51	—	—	8.15	2.72
Rivera, Saul	B-R	5-10	180	12-7-77	0	1	7.07	11	0	0	0	14	22	11	11	1	6	6	.361	.333	.375	3.86	3.86
Rodriguez, Rafael	R-R	6-1	175	9-24-84	0	2	9.00	10	0	0	1	13	16	15	13	3	6	7	.286	.409	.206	4.85	4.15
2-team total (37 Salt Lake)					5	5	4.26	47	0	0	11	63	57	34	30	8	21	37	—	—	5.26	2.98
Roemer, Wes	R-R	6-2	205	10-7-86	2	5	7.03	14	12	0	0	72	90	61	56	17	39	57	.310	.345	.287	7.16	4.90
Rosa, Carlos	R-R	6-1	210	9-21-84	0	0	1.63	25	0	0	13	28	20	5	5	2	14	31	.208	.200	.212	10.08	4.55
2-team total (6 Omaha)					2	1	2.25	31	0	0	13	40	33	10	10	4	21	41	—	—	9.23	4.72
Rosales, Leo	R-R	6-1	205	5-28-81	0	0	5.06	6	0	0	0	5	5	3	3	0	1	6	.238	.200	.273	6.75	5.06
Septimo, Leyson	L-L	6-0	150	7-7-85	0	1	11.12	16	0	0	0	17	15	25	21	2	30	20	.231	.100	.289	10.59	15.88

Name	B-T	HT	WT	DOB	W	L	ERA	G	GS	CG	SV	IP	H	R	ER	HR	BB	SO	AVG	vLH	vRH	K/9	BB/9
Spottiswood, Billy	R-R	6-3	208	4-24-85	0	0	18.69	2	0	0	0	4	9	9	9	0	5	2	.500	.429	.545	4.15	10.38
Stange, Daniel	R-R	6-3	185	12-22-85	4	3	6.17	19	0	0	2	23	29	17	16	3	10	16	.309	.318	.300	6.17	3.86
Torra, Matt	R-R	6-3	225	6-29-84	11	7	4.55	27	27	1	0	178	224	97	90	22	34	99	.313	.327	.303	5.01	1.72
Urquidez, Jason	R-R	6-0	175	9-12-82	5	4	4.90	51	0	0	5	72	86	49	39	6	23	71	.296	.308	.285	8.92	2.89
Valdez, Cesar	R-R	6-2	200	3-17-85	6	10	5.90	20	18	0	0	98	110	68	64	12	49	92	.284	.304	.270	8.48	4.52
Vasquez, Esmerling	R-R	6-1	175	11-7-83	0	0	0.00	1	0	0	0	1	1	0	0	0	1	1	.250	.000	.333	9.00	1.00
Wilson, Brad	R-R	6-0	184	5-26-87	0	1	6.75	1	1	0	0	4	3	3	3	1	3	1	.250	.400	.143	2.25	6.75
Zavada, Clay	L-L	6-1	195	6-28-84	0	1	30.00	5	0	0	0	3	6	10	10	0	10	2	.400	.333	.417	6.00	30.00

Fielding

Catcher	PCT	G	PO	A	E	DP	PB
Corporan	.980	78	542	44	12	3	6
Coughlin	.988	25	158	9	2	3	3
Easley	1.000	14	87	5	0	0	5
Hester	.983	30	157	16	3	1	6
Montero	1.000	3	21	0	0	0	0
Roberts	1.000	2	4	0	0	0	0

First Base	PCT	G	PO	A	E	DP
Allen	.990	73	622	42	7	65
Bailey	.991	51	412	37	4	62
Deeds	1.000	1	1	0	0	0
Rogers	.981	29	238	26	5	30

Second Base	PCT	G	PO	A	E	DP
Abreu	1.000	8	23	24	0	6
Ciriaco	.923	3	6	6	1	3

	PCT	G	PO	A	E	DP
Groff	1.000	3	3	6	0	1
Hallberg	.991	74	121	201	3	60
Roberts	.968	50	107	167	9	37
Rogers	1.000	3	2	4	0	0
Sanchez	.976	24	27	53	2	11

Third Base	PCT	G	PO	A	E	DP
Abreu	1.000	3	3	3	0	1
Groff	1.000	1	1	0	0	0
Hallberg	.990	42	27	69	1	7
Roberts	.920	12	6	17	2	3
Rogers	.948	53	29	80	6	11
Sanchez	.967	54	21	98	4	8

Shortstop	PCT	G	PO	A	E	DP
Abreu	.962	11	19	31	2	14
Ciriaco	.964	84	158	276	16	71

	PCT	G	PO	A	E	DP
Hallberg	.923	5	12	12	2	2
Roberts	1.000	6	9	21	0	7
Rogers	.980	32	48	96	3	23
Sanchez	1.000	10	10	29	0	4

Outfield	PCT	G	PO	A	E	DP
Allen	.981	33	48	3	1	1
Bailey	.990	62	97	2	1	1
Deeds	.976	115	201	5	5	0
Gillespie	.978	64	129	3	3	1
Hankerd	.923	7	11	1	1	0
Jackson	1.000	3	8	1	0	0
Macias	.994	92	163	4	1	0
Parra	.935	9	28	1	2	1
Rahl	.990	71	99	3	1	1
Roberts	.946	20	35	0	2	0
Rogers	—	1	0	0	0	0

MOBILE BAYBEARS

DOUBLE-A

SOUTHERN LEAGUE

Batting	B-T	HT	WT	DOB	AVG	vLH	vRH	G	AB	R	H	2B	3B	HR	RBI	BB	HBP	SH	SF	SO	SB	CS	SLG	OBP
Byrne, Bryan	L-R	6-3	200	4-30-84	.279	.320	.264	118	387	55	108	23	0	5	47	81	7	0	5	94	8	6	.377	408
Casto, Kory	L-R	6-0	215	12-8-81	.251	.140	.299	49	167	22	42	6	0	8	30	27	4	1	6	45	1	2	.431	.358
Clifford, Pete	L-R	6-0	190	12-20-83	.182	.364	.136	21	55	5	10	2	0	0	7	11	0	0	1	15	0	0	.218	.313
Coughlin, Sean	L-R	6-1	215	5-14-85	.237	.190	.254	53	156	18	37	6	0	3	21	16	3	0	2	32	0	2	.333	.316
Cowgill, Collin	R-L	5-9	195	5-22-86	.285	.322	.269	131	502	89	143	34	4	16	83	57	8	0	10	73	25	9	.464	.360
Davis, Chris	R-R	6-0	200	9-22-86	.143	.000	.333	2	7	1	1	0	0	1	1	1	0	0	0	2	0	0	.571	.250
Easley, Ed	R-R	6-0	200	12-21-85	.259	.275	.252	55	162	13	42	6	0	1	18	19	0	2	1	36	5	2	.315	.335
Elmore, Jake	R-R	5-10	180	6-15-87	.278	.303	.269	124	388	64	108	16	2	2	31	58	4	7	5	56	25	13	.345	.374
Frey, Evan	L-L	6-0	170	6-7-86	.286	.298	.281	131	517	87	148	23	5	1	49	67	8	2	6	89	34	13	.356	.373
Greene, Kyle	L-R	6-2	200	5-26-86	.111	.167	.083	6	18	1	2	1	0	0	1	1	0	0	0	6	0	0	.167	.158
Hankerd, Cyle	R-R	6-3	215	1-24-85	.245	.313	.208	78	192	21	47	9	0	4	28	24	9	0	1	30	1	1	.354	.354
Harbin, Taylor	R-R	5-9	175	2-13-86	.259	.248	.263	118	433	48	112	27	3	6	45	24	8	3	6	78	10	8	.376	.306
Herrnberger, Alex	R-R	6-0	182	7-6-86	.400	.000	.462	2	5	0	2	0	0	0	1	0	0	0	0	1	0	0	.400	.400
Kaczrowski, Dan	R-R	5-9	170	6-17-87	.250	.500	.176	19	44	2	11	2	1	0	3	1	0	1	2	5	0	1	.341	.255
Linton, Ollie	L-L	5-8	160	4-7-86	.304	.371	.277	125	398	60	121	12	5	3	38	63	11	8	3	100	22	16	.382	.411
Montilla, Gerson	R-R	5-10	168	11-13-89	.180	.231	.162	20	50	6	9	4	0	0	4	5	0	2	0	10	0	0	.260	.255
Rahl, Chris	R-R	5-10	185	12-5-83	.314	.200	.361	20	51	12	16	2	1	1	9	2	0	0	0	9	2	2	.451	.340
Schmidt, Konrad	R-R	6-0	225	8-2-84	.315	.345	.302	107	394	48	124	30	3	11	65	32	8	0	6	63	7	3	.490	.373
Sosa, Ricardo	R-R	6-1	200	5-24-84	.278	.364	.240	16	36	3	10	1	0	1	8	4	1	0	1	8	0	0	.389	.357
Wald, Jake	R-R	6-2	195	2-8-81	.161	.146	.166	72	205	12	33	7	1	1	17	27	2	6	3	88	1	3	.220	.262
Wheeler, Ryan	L-R	6-4	220	7-10-88	.254	.353	.220	19	67	8	17	3	0	3	10	5	1	0	0	16	0	0	.433	.315

Pitching	B-T	HT	WT	DOB	W	L	ERA	G	GS	CG	SV	IP	H	R	ER	HR	BB	SO	AVG	vLH	vRH	K/9	BB/9
Augenstein, Bryan	R-R	6-6	230	7-11-86	0	1	5.40	3	0	0	0	8	10	5	5	1	3	9	.303	.294	.313	9.72	3.24
Collmenter, Josh	R-R	6-4	235	2-7-86	8	3	1.82	12	12	2	0	79	61	18	16	3	22	73	.213	.167	.255	8.28	2.50
Cook, Ryan	R-R	6-3	200	6-30-87	1	1	2.89	3	3	0	0	19	13	7	6	1	10	12	.200	.194	.207	5.79	4.82
Dietz, Jeff	R-R	6-3	215	1-28-86	3	3	4.03	35	0	0	2	51	55	28	23	6	24	48	.274	.281	.268	8.42	4.21
Ellis, Josh	R-R	6-1	215	8-7-84	2	1	2.97	26	0	0	2	36	39	15	12	1	12	44	.281	.343	.222	10.90	2.97
Enright, Barry	R-R	6-3	220	3-30-86	4	1	2.88	14	14	1	0	94	81	34	30	9	15	83	.238	.221	.254	7.98	1.44
Henry, Bryan	R-R	6-3	205	2-15-85	6	4	3.49	32	14	0	0	101	104	40	39	7	26	58	.270	.258	.281	5.19	2.32
Layne, Tom	L-L	6-3	185	11-2-84	12	7	3.74	26	26	3	0	149	146	75	62	9	57	91	.257	.217	.276	5.48	3.44
Mahon, Reid	R-R	6-3	215	6-1-83	4	3	3.06	37	0	0	3	53	53	22	18	3	22	31	.262	.302	.226	5.26	3.74
McAnaney, Pat	R-L	6-3	185	3-11-86	5	10	5.30	22	22	0	0	110	130	79	65	8	53	95	.295	.242	.315	7.75	4.32
Mercedes, Roque	B-R	6-3	185	9-28-86	3	4	4.36	38	0	0	4	54	67	32	26	5	24	45	.306	.272	.336	7.55	4.02
Miley, Wade	L-L	6-2	190	11-13-86	7	3	1.98	13	13	1	0	73	60	26	16	5	28	63	.232	.183	.250	7.80	3.47
Newby, Kyler	R-R	6-4	225	2-22-85	4	3	3.45	31	11	0	0	89	75	35	34	11	28	104	.226	.235	.216	10.56	2.84
Roemer, Wes	R-R	6-0	205	10-7-86	2	1	2.39	8	8	1	0	53	52	15	14	5	11	43	.257	.275	.243	7.35	1.88
Septimo, Leyson	L-L	6-0	150	7-7-85	2	2	4.13	26	0	0	4	28	16	17	13	1	23	37	.176	.154	.192	11.75	7.31
Shaw, Bryan	B-R	6-1	210	11-8-87	4	9	4.26	33	13	0	2	101	102	57	48	4	43	75	.266	.268	.263	6.66	3.82
Stange, Daniel	R-R	6-3	185	12-22-85	4	1	1.69	30	0	0	13	32	14	6	6	1	11	18	.140	.160	.120	5.06	3.09
Torra, Matt	R-R	6-3	225	6-29-84	0	0	0.00	1	1	0	0	5	6	0	0	0	2	4	.300	.364	.222	7.20	3.60
Woodall, Bryan	R-R	6-1	200	10-24-86	1	4	3.70	15	0	0	0	24	30	14	10	2	3	25	.297	.283	.309	9.25	1.11
Woody, Abe	R-R	5-11	200	11-9-82	4	2	3.71	19	0	0	5	27	34	13	11	2	6	14	.315	.245	.382	4.72	2.03
2-team total (3 Carolina)					4	3	4.65	22	0	0	5	31	40	18	16	2	6	17	—	—		4.94	1.74

Fielding

Catcher	PCT	G	PO	A	E	DP	PB
Coughlin	.981	14	96	7	2	0	3
Davis	1.000	2	15	1	0	0	0
Easley	.992	34	227	26	2	3	3
Elmore	1.000	1	1	0	0	0	0
Herrnberger	1.000	2	11	0	0	0	0
Schmidt	.980	89	627	59	14	6	9

First Base	PCT	G	PO	A	E	DP
Byrne	.995	100	784	75	4	65
Coughlin	.965	21	151	14	6	23
Easley	1.000	2	2	1	0	0
Hankerd	.976	26	195	11	5	20
Wheeler	.833	1	5	0	1	0

Second Base	PCT	G	PO	A	E	DP
Casto	1.000	6	12	11	0	3
Elmore	.972	75	150	195	10	40
Harbin	.986	43	90	127	3	34
Kaczrowski	.950	12	18	20	2	4
Montilla	.983	16	26	31	1	9
Rahl	—	2	0	0	0	0

Third Base	PCT	G	PO	A	E	DP
Byrne	.939	20	11	35	3	2
Casto	.934	41	31	68	7	7
Easley	.778	5	2	5	2	1
Elmore	.963	15	7	19	1	4
Greene	1.000	1	0	1	0	0
Harbin	.939	41	23	70	6	4
Sosa	.895	11	7	10	2	0
Wheeler	.968	18	7	23	1	1

Shortstop	PCT	G	PO	A	E	DP
Elmore	.947	38	48	94	8	28
Harbin	.976	38	48	112	4	19
Kaczrowski	.895	5	7	10	2	2
Montilla	.909	3	2	8	1	2
Rahl	—	1	0	0	0	0
Wald	.949	64	106	172	15	35

Outfield	PCT	G	PO	A	E	DP
Clifford	1.000	11	15	4	0	0
Cowgill	.989	128	241	23	3	4
Frey	.977	130	239	11	6	1
Greene	1.000	2	5	0	0	0
Hankerd	.923	19	24	0	2	0
Linton	.987	122	215	5	3	0
Rahl	1.000	12	26	0	0	0

VISALIA RAWHIDE

HIGH CLASS A

CALIFORNIA LEAGUE

Batting	B-T	HT	WT	DOB	AVG	vLH	vRH	G	AB	R	H	2B	3B	HR	RBI	BB	HBP	SH	SF	SO	SB	CS	SLG	OBP
Davidson, Matt	R-R	6-3	225	3-26-91	.169	.100	.180	21	71	6	12	1	0	2	11	12	1	0	0	25	0	0	.268	.298
Davis, Chris	R-R	6-0	200	9-22-86	.208	.133	.237	20	53	5	11	1	0	0	1	14	0	1	0	14	0	1	.226	.373
Diaz, Alberto	R-R	6-0	200	9-3-88	.204	.170	.220	45	147	9	30	6	1	0	8	4	3	3	1	44	1	0	.259	.239
Estevez, Victor	R-R	5-11	193	9-8-88	.194	.214	.190	20	72	2	14	3	0	0	5	3	1	0	0	16	0	1	.236	.237
Ford, Josh	R-R	6-1	225	1-17-83	.273	.227	.290	123	436	72	119	29	0	19	77	36	12	0	5	106	2	0	.470	.342
Gallego, Niko	R-R	6-0	150	12-29-88	.238	.280	.227	39	122	18	29	3	2	1	14	15	5	5	1	28	4	2	.320	.343
Goldschmidt, Paul	R-R	6-4	220	9-10-87	.314	.413	.277	138	525	102	165	42	3	35	108	57	8	0	9	161	5	1	.606	.384
Greene, Kyle	L-R	6-2	200	5-26-86	.255	.207	.275	121	416	49	106	26	1	10	57	60	7	0	3	131	1	1	.394	.356
Greer, Brent	R-R	6-0	185	10-16-87	.215	.171	.230	107	396	43	85	17	1	3	30	36	12	4	3	110	6	5	.285	.298
Herrnberger, Alex	B-R	6-0	182	7-6-86	.250	.000	.333	2	4	0	1	0	0	0	1	0	0	0	0	0	0	0	.250	.250
Kaczrowski, Dan	R-R	5-9	170	6-17-87	.267	.224	.283	98	374	56	100	17	1	3	36	34	2	8	3	49	15	3	.342	.329
Krauss, Marc	L-R	6-3	235	10-5-87	.302	.329	.290	138	530	107	160	27	4	25	87	57	4	0	5	141	1	3	.509	.371
Marte, Alfredo	R-R	6-1	170	3-31-89	.260	.274	.255	130	516	76	134	26	3	9	61	34	8	4	3	107	9	5	.374	.314
Montilla, Gerson	R-R	5-10	168	11-13-89	.247	.340	.211	56	170	20	42	9	0	1	16	13	5	7	1	50	3	0	.318	.317
Navarro, Rey	B-R	5-10	175	12-22-89	.241	.200	.254	19	79	9	19	2	1	1	7	8	0	1	1	18	2	2	.329	.307
Perez, Rossmel	B-R	5-10	180	8-26-89	.259	.228	.273	98	343	42	89	12	0	5	43	33	2	1	5	47	1	4	.338	.324
Sherlock, Tim	L-L	5-11	175	11-30-86	.114	.000	.138	15	35	2	4	1	0	0	0	4	0	0	0	21	1	0	.143	.205
Wheeler, Ryan	L-R	6-4	220	7-10-88	.284	.248	.300	113	465	62	132	25	2	9	57	35	5	0	1	98	3	1	.404	.340
Wiley, Byron	L-L	6-1	200	12-12-86	.278	.154	.348	10	36	9	10	0	0	1	7	7	0	0	0	11	2	1	.361	.395

Pitching	B-T	HT	WT	DOB	W	L	ERA	G	GS	CG	SV	IP	H	R	ER	HR	BB	SO	AVG	vLH	vRH	K/9	BB/9
Anderson, Chase	R-R	6-1	175	11-30-87	5	3	3.60	19	4	0	3	70	58	33	28	7	16	83	.227	.159	.275	10.67	2.06
Beltre, Cristian	R-R	6-1	195	5-10-85	3	2	4.50	31	1	0	3	72	76	37	36	9	23	73	.270	.248	.285	9.13	2.88
Brewer, Charles	R-R	6-4	205	4-7-88	7	3	2.98	14	14	0	0	82	74	29	27	5	15	75	.239	.198	.270	8.27	1.65
Budrow, Brian	R-R	6-3	225	11-12-86	0	0	4.50	2	0	0	0	2	2	1	1	0	0	2	.222	.200	.250	9.00	0.00
Capellan, Victor	R-R	6-2	195	7-24-89	3	5	3.99	36	0	0	2	59	61	33	26	4	30	60	.276	.171	.338	9.20	4.60
Collmenter, Josh	R-R	6-4	235	2-7-86	2	0	2.40	3	3	0	0	15	11	4	4	2	3	21	.204	.308	.107	12.60	1.80
Cook, Ryan	R-R	6-3	200	6-30-87	4	7	4.24	20	20	0	0	108	110	62	51	3	36	100	.263	.293	.241	8.31	2.99
Corbin, Pat	L-L	6-3	165	7-19-89	0	1	1.38	8	8	0	0	26	17	4	4	1	9	30	.189	.280	.154	10.38	3.12
2-team total (11 R. Cucamonga)					5	4	3.13	19	19	0	0	86	74	33	30	8	27	94	—	—	—	9.80	2.81
Eichhorn, Kevin	R-R	6-0	170	2-6-90	0	0	6.35	1	1	0	0	6	9	4	4	0	0	5	.375	.300	.429	7.94	0.00
Gemberling, Brad	R-R	6-1	205	12-9-86	0	2	6.75	4	4	0	0	17	24	16	13	3	9	17	.324	.364	.293	8.83	4.67
Hale, Jake	R-R	6-7	200	12-11-85	0	0	3.38	3	0	0	0	5	11	2	2	0	2	3	.423	.400	.455	5.06	3.38
Hamrick, Randy	R-R	6-2	195	8-27-86	0	0	4.91	1	0	0	0	4	5	3	2	0	2	2	.294	.375	.222	4.91	4.91
Harden, Trevor	B-R	6-2	215	9-1-87	0	2	8.00	2	2	0	0	9	13	9	8	4	1	7	.371	.235	.500	7.00	1.00
Harvil, Will	R-R	6-5	220	6-17-87	0	0	10.80	3	0	0	0	5	6	6	6	1	2	7	.300	.222	.364	12.60	3.60
Hose, T.J.	R-R	5-10	185	4-15-86	1	2	6.41	23	0	0	8	27	33	20	19	1	19	22	.300	.300	.300	7.43	6.41
Mace, Justin	L-R	6-3	205	3-11-86	2	1	6.06	38	0	0	1	65	77	49	44	7	27	57	.293	.402	.229	7.85	3.72
McAnaney, Pat	R-L	6-3	185	3-11-86	4	0	2.48	5	5	0	0	29	25	8	8	1	8	42	.227	.333	.207	13.03	2.48
Miley, Wade	L-L	6-2	190	11-13-86	4	5	3.25	14	14	0	0	80	81	36	29	1	37	50	.266	.272	.263	5.60	4.15
Moorhouse, Brett	R-R	6-2	190	6-28-87	2	2	4.94	21	6	0	0	51	51	29	28	6	37	57	.263	.270	.257	10.06	6.53
Munson, Kevin	R-R	6-2	200	1-3-89	0	0	13.50	1	0	0	0	1	1	1	1	0	2	0	.333	1.000	.000	0.00	27.00
Ortega, Yonata	R-R	6-1	220	11-11-86	1	1	1.42	13	0	0	11	13	7	3	2	1	3	15	.156	.000	.259	10.66	2.13
Robowski, Ryan	L-L	6-0	185	2-3-88	2	4	5.17	35	0	0	2	54	69	34	31	5	16	51	.311	.306	.314	8.50	2.67
Sinclair, Taylor	L-L	6-3	180	12-23-85	8	7	4.74	27	20	1	0	142	149	90	75	8	63	105	.274	.236	.288	6.64	3.98
Smith, Eric	R-R	6-3	220	10-15-88	4	4	4.97	10	10	0	0	51	56	34	28	4	30	36	.284	.366	.238	6.39	5.33
Spottiswood, Billy	R-R	6-3	208	4-24-85	6	6	4.59	35	3	0	4	69	76	37	35	11	24	67	.283	.336	.244	8.78	3.15
Taylor, Dan	L-L	5-11	205	7-25-87	7	6	5.81	19	19	0	0	101	133	75	65	15	23	90	.313	.366	.294	8.05	2.06
Wolcott, Andrew	R-R	6-5	245	9-8-87	2	2	6.14	8	6	0	0	37	54	27	25	0	6	20	.353	.329	.377	4.91	1.47
Woodall, Bryan	R-R	6-1	200	10-24-86	5	3	2.15	29	0	0	9	38	36	12	9	1	10	51	.245	.339	.182	12.19	2.39

Fielding

Catcher	PCT	G	PO	A	E	DP	PB
Davis	.992	16	108	15	1	0	2
Ford	.989	40	334	24	4	1	5
Herrnberger	1.000	1	7	1	0	0	0
Perez	.994	86	685	88	5	7	19

First Base	PCT	G	PO	A	E	DP
Davidson	1.000	1	5	0	0	0
Goldschmidt	.990	128	1162	90	13	88
Greer	—	1	0	0	0	0
Krauss	.946	4	34	1	2	7
Wheeler	1.000	7	68	4	0	12

Second Base	PCT	G	PO	A	E	DP
Estevez	.925	15	20	42	5	5
Gallego	—	1	0	0	0	0

	PCT	G	PO	A	E	DP
Greene	1.000	5	7	10	0	2
Greer	.978	53	89	136	5	27
Kaczrowski	.981	23	37	65	2	9
Montilla	.980	53	114	129	5	37

Third Base	PCT	G	PO	A	E	DP
Davidson	.982	20	9	45	1	2
Greene	.804	16	6	31	9	2
Greer	1.000	1	0	2	0	0
Kaczrowski	—	1	0	0	0	0
Montilla	—	1	0	0	0	0
Wheeler	.947	104	66	203	15	22

Shortstop	PCT	G	PO	A	E	DP
Estevez	1.000	4	4	11	0	2
Gallego	.942	38	38	125	10	14

	PCT	G	PO	A	E	DP
Greer	.952	46	59	141	10	26
Kaczrowski	.951	42	46	108	8	18
Navarro	.936	19	41	62	7	12

Outfield	PCT	G	PO	A	E	DP
Diaz	1.000	45	73	2	0	0
Greene	.967	79	111	5	4	0
Herrnberger	—	1	0	0	0	0
Kaczrowski	.971	39	63	3	2	0
Krauss	.955	127	158	11	8	0
Marte	.983	129	272	9	5	2
Sherlock	.833	14	15	0	3	0
Wheeler	1.000	1	3	0	0	0
Wiley	.800	9	6	2	2	1

SOUTH BEND SILVER HAWKS

MIDWEST LEAGUE

LOW CLASS A

Batting	B-T	HT	WT	DOB	AVG	vLH	vRH	G	AB	R	H	2B	3B	HR	RBI	BB	HBP	SH	SF	SO	SB	CS	SLG	OBP
Babineau, Ryan	R-R	6-2	215	12-13-86	.189	.125	.207	11	37	1	7	2	0	0	3	3	0	0	0	11	0	0	.243	.250
Borchering, Bobby	B-R	6-3	200	10-25-90	.270	.287	.264	135	523	74	141	31	2	15	74	54	5	1	5	128	1	1	.423	.341
Broxton, Keon	R-R	6-3	190	5-7-90	.228	.179	.246	133	531	74	121	17	19	5	32	65	3	4	0	172	21	13	.360	.316
Castillo, Ramon	R-R	5-11	190	9-6-88	.311	.377	.285	65	241	30	75	24	0	7	44	17	11	0	4	35	2	1	.498	.377
Davidson, Matt	R-R	6-3	225	3-26-91	.289	.299	.286	113	415	58	120	35	3	16	79	43	13	0	4	109	0	2	.504	.371
Diaz, Alberto	R-R	6-0	200	9-3-88	.225	.254	.217	75	275	23	62	12	1	2	28	10	3	0	5	71	2	4	.298	.256
Estevez, Victor	R-R	5-11	193	9-8-88	.209	.217	.205	61	211	21	44	7	1	1	16	13	5	4	2	41	4	4	.265	.268
Fie, Andrew	R-R	6-3	205	10-25-87	.202	.183	.209	59	208	23	42	16	1	3	16	15	0	0	1	66	3	2	.332	.254
Helm, Matt	R-R	6-2	197	9-1-90	.210	.169	.224	65	229	18	48	7	1	2	24	18	1	1	0	85	0	1	.275	.270
Hollinger, Errol	R-R	6-3	215	6-14-87	.256	.133	.293	60	195	19	50	4	0	2	25	26	4	0	2	55	0	0	.308	.352
Inciarte, Ender	L-L	5-11	160	10-29-90	.225	.250	.215	66	227	26	51	9	7	1	20	14	3	7	7	35	5	4	.339	.276
Jarrett, Chris	L-L	5-10	175	11-17-88	.305	.227	.333	20	82	11	25	3	5	0	8	7	1	1	1	16	2	4	.463	.363
Kim, Jae Yun	R-T	6-1	185	9-16-90	.125	.000	.167	5	16	0	2	1	0	0	0	2	0	0	0	5	0	0	.188	.222
Narodowski, David	R-R	5-9	193	8-3-88	.223	.243	.216	88	264	27	59	13	0	3	19	35	5	3	2	63	5	5	.307	.324
Nick, David	R-R	6-2	180	2-3-90	.251	.222	.261	128	495	66	124	22	7	7	49	41	10	3	4	97	12	7	.366	.318
Owings, Chris	R-R	5-11	175	8-12-91	.298	.303	.296	62	255	39	76	19	2	5	28	9	2	2	3	50	1	3	.447	.323
Stone, Bobby	L-L	6-2	217	11-14-89	.167	.154	.170	32	120	5	20	4	0	2	7	5	0	0	1	46	0	0	.250	.198
Van Winkle, Tyson	R-R	6-1	190	2-2-88	.214	.217	.213	73	238	23	51	7	1	0	15	28	8	1	2	46	0	0	.252	.315

Pitching	B-T	HT	WT	DOB	W	L	ERA	G	GS	CG	SV	IP	H	R	ER	HR	BB	SO	AVG	vLH	vRH	K/9	BB/9
Allen, Scottie	R-R	6-1	170	7-3-91	4	4	4.73	16	16	0	0	78	88	42	41	5	22	79	.281	.279	.282	9.12	2.54
Anderson, Chase	R-R	6-1	175	11-30-87	2	4	2.82	7	7	1	0	38	36	16	12	1	9	31	.238	.181	.291	7.28	2.11
Belfiore, Mike	R-L	6-2	220	10-3-88	3	10	3.99	25	25	0	0	126	139	75	56	6	42	105	.277	.296	.268	7.48	2.99
Brewer, Charles	R-R	6-4	205	4-7-88	4	5	1.83	13	13	0	0	69	55	20	14	3	20	78	.216	.214	.217	10.17	2.61
Budrow, Brian	R-R	6-3	225	11-12-86	6	2	2.60	40	0	0	4	66	61	19	19	2	15	61	.247	.235	.255	8.36	2.06
Eitel, Derek	R-R	6-4	200	11-21-87	2	0	1.80	4	0	0	1	15	10	3	3	0	6	19	.185	.125	.211	11.40	3.60
Gemberling, Brad	R-R	6-1	205	12-9-86	4	8	6.36	21	11	0	0	81	94	67	57	6	40	74	.289	.331	.254	8.26	4.46
Hagens, Bradin	R-R	6-1	180	5-12-89	3	6	6.56	39	0	0	4	60	90	50	44	2	25	55	.344	.371	.322	8.20	3.73
Munson, Kevin	R-R	6-2	200	1-3-89	2	0	1.10	12	0	0	3	16	8	2	2	1	5	17	.143	.190	.114	9.37	2.76
Odegaard, Chris	R-R	6-3	219	4-17-87	5	3	3.42	38	0	0	1	68	58	33	26	3	33	73	.227	.234	.223	9.61	4.35
Ortega, Yonata	R-R	6-1	220	11-11-86	3	3	4.10	35	0	0	22	42	42	26	19	1	15	41	.259	.247	.272	8.86	3.24
Quezada, Rafael	R-R	6-3	210	11-21-86	1	0	5.77	35	0	0	0	53	72	39	34	6	32	27	.324	.355	.295	4.58	5.43
Rodriguez, Randy	R-R	5-11	183	1-6-88	0	4	6.06	35	3	0	0	71	93	52	48	14	26	47	.325	.373	.288	5.93	3.28
Rosario, Diogenes	R-R	6-2	179	9-1-88	4	10	4.25	31	12	0	0	102	112	58	48	5	40	94	.283	.290	.278	8.32	3.54
Skaggs, Tyler	L-L	6-4	195	7-13-91	1	1	1.69	4	4	0	0	16	13	3	3	1	4	20	.224	.273	.213	11.25	2.25
2-team total (19 Cedar Rapids)					9	5	3.29	23	18	0	0	98	91	38	36	7	25	102	—	—	—	9.34	2.29
Smith, Eric	R-R	6-3	220	10-15-88	5	5	3.53	16	16	1	0	87	85	45	34	4	32	65	.257	.272	.241	6.75	3.32
Sosa, Keny	L-L	6-0	211	3-26-87	1	0	6.45	15	1	0	0	22	25	17	16	1	11	11	.278	.133	.350	4.43	4.43
Taylor, Dan	L-L	5-11	205	7-25-87	2	2	3.69	7	7	0	0	39	43	18	16	2	8	30	.274	.333	.254	6.92	1.85
Wilson, Brad	R-R	6-0	184	5-26-87	0	1	11.05	3	1	0	0	7	14	10	9	0	5	5	.424	.500	.308	6.14	6.14
Wolcott, Andrew	R-R	6-5	245	9-8-87	2	4	5.25	12	12	1	0	62	79	42	36	3	19	49	.306	.333	.285	7.15	2.77
Worthington, Adam	R-R	5-9	190	8-20-87	5	6	5.35	20	9	0	0	66	78	43	39	5	17	64	.290	.288	.291	8.77	2.33

Fielding

Catcher	PCT	G	PO	A	E	DP	PB
Babineau	1.000	10	58	6	0	0	1
Hollinger	.983	53	363	34	7	3	9
Kim	1.000	5	28	2	0	0	0
Van Winkle	.986	73	606	50	9	2	9

First Base	PCT	G	PO	A	E	DP
Castillo	.987	63	509	41	7	32
Estevez	1.000	4	39	1	0	4
Fie	.980	27	229	16	5	13
Helm	.974	12	104	8	3	4
Stone	.980	32	290	9	6	25

Second Base	PCT	G	PO	A	E	DP
Estevez	1.000	1	2	4	0	1
Narodowski	.905	11	15	23	4	6
Nick	.973	126	192	315	14	49

Third Base	PCT	G	PO	A	E	DP
Borchering	.892	84	52	114	20	5
Davidson	.896	52	32	106	16	3
Narodowski	1.000	1	0	4	0	1

Shortstop	PCT	G	PO	A	E	DP
Estevez	.929	47	71	139	16	21

	PCT	G	PO	A	E	DP
Narodowski	.951	31	44	92	7	14
Owings	.962	62	98	184	11	34

Outfield	PCT	G	PO	A	E	DP
Broxton	.976	131	282	5	7	1
Diaz	.951	75	124	11	7	1
Estevez	1.000	9	7	1	0	0
Fie	1.000	26	40	0	0	0
Helm	.988	51	79	0	1	0
Inciarte	.993	66	136	6	1	1
Jarrett	1.000	20	29	2	0	0
Narodowski	.955	38	62	2	3	1

YAKIMA BEARS
SHORT-SEASON

NORTHWEST LEAGUE

Batting	B-T	HT	WT	DOB	AVG	vLH	vRH	G	AB	R	H	2B	3B	HR	RBI	BB	HBP	SH	SF	SO	SB	CS	SLG	OBP
Alegria, Jose	R-R	6-1	200	11-5-90	1.000	.000	1.000	1	1	0	1	0	0	0	0	0	0	0	0	0	0	0	1.000	1.000
Arbelo, Yazy	L-R	6-4	220	4-7-88	.285	.333	.273	68	242	38	69	13	1	14	55	36	1	0	2	62	4	1	.521	.377
Belza, Tom	L-R	6-0	190	7-31-89	.212	.188	.217	43	99	12	21	2	0	0	7	16	0	3	2	18	3	3	.232	.316
Button, Evan	R-L	6-0	195	9-5-86	.194	.000	.197	29	62	2	12	5	0	0	7	5	1	0	0	16	2	3	.274	.265
Comerota, Jimmy	R-R	6-1	175	12-1-86	.202	.152	.250	53	94	13	19	3	0	0	5	14	0	2	0	21	9	1	.234	.306
Emsley-Pai, Kawika	B-R	5-11	195	9-3-88	.167	.059	.192	42	90	10	15	3	0	0	8	10	2	1	0	21	3	0	.200	.265
Freeman, Mike	L-R	6-0	170	8-4-87	.333	.469	.306	53	189	39	63	9	1	1	23	24	0	0	3	29	20	3	.407	.403
Gomez, Raywilly	B-R	5-11	170	1-25-90	.270	.250	.279	56	159	15	43	6	0	3	21	18	1	3	4	13	4	2	.365	.341
Herrnberger, Alex	B-R	6-0	182	7-6-86	.000	.000	.000	3	1	0	0	0	0	0	1	0	0	0	0	0	0	0	.000	.500
Hilt, Justin	R-R	6-1	205	4-29-88	.230	.218	.234	68	230	33	53	12	3	4	24	39	2	1	0	92	17	6	.361	.347
Inciarte, Ender	L-L	5-11	160	10-29-90	.242	.273	.236	19	66	10	16	4	0	0	3	7	0	4	1	17	2	1	.303	.311
Moss, Westley	R-R	6-2	165	7-17-88	.244	.246	.244	67	213	28	52	6	2	0	15	20	11	5	1	57	21	6	.291	.339
Noboa, Michael	R-R	5-8	160	6-21-87	.000	.000	.000	6	2	2	0	0	0	0	0	0	0	0	0	0	0	0	.000	.000
Ortiz, Roberto	R-R	6-1	195	10-28-88	.263	.204	.282	64	205	36	54	14	0	1	20	35	13	1	2	66	23	4	.346	.400
Pimentel, Jhoan	R-R	5-10	195	7-13-89	.186	.182	.188	46	97	6	18	6	0	0	11	9	0	0	1	18	1	0	.247	.252
Torrez, Raoul	R-R	5-10	180	3-16-88	.235	.224	.239	54	187	26	44	6	2	4	24	14	5	1	1	57	13	3	.353	.304
Walters, Zach	B-R	6-3	193	9-5-89	.302	.358	.288	69	275	44	83	18	4	4	43	16	1	1	4	59	14	4	.440	.338
Weber, Michael	L-R	6-0	200	9-6-87	.259	.333	.248	53	174	29	45	7	1	4	21	15	3	2	1	53	10	4	.379	.326
Zabala, Henry	R-R	6-1	175	10-20-89	.261	.288	.250	66	199	27	52	12	3	4	33	19	4	0	2	43	10	9	.412	.335

Pitching	B-T	HT	WT	DOB	W	L	ERA	G	GS	CG	SV	IP	H	R	ER	HR	BB	SO	AVG	vLH	vRH	K/9	BB/9
Albert, Justin	L-L	6-3	235	5-27-87	0	0	4.50	2	0	0	0	2	1	1	0	0	2	.286	.000	.400	9.00	0.00
Andrews, Robbie	R-R	6-3	170	6-8-88	3	1	3.16	19	0	0	0	26	27	14	9	0	18	19	.284	.237	.316	6.66	6.31
Berger, Andrew	R-R	6-3	210	11-24-87	2	5	5.60	13	12	0	0	55	58	35	34	2	18	49	.278	.220	.315	8.07	2.96
Bolsinger, Mike	R-R	6-2	200	1-29-88	1	0	1.69	6	0	0	0	11	6	2	2	0	3	6	.176	.308	.095	5.06	2.53
Burgos, Enrique	R-R	6-4	200	11-23-90	2	1	4.50	15	15	0	0	68	64	41	34	1	54	54	.260	.255	.263	7.15	7.15
Cantwell, Keith	R-R	6-5	215	9-9-87	5	3	2.96	30	0	0	0	46	37	17	15	2	13	48	.218	.274	.175	9.46	2.56
Davisson, Corey	R-R	6-2	215	1-11-88	3	1	3.06	25	0	0	0	35	31	13	12	2	10	41	.238	.277	.217	10.44	2.55
De La Rosa, Eury	L-L	5-9	150	2-24-90	1	1	1.00	27	0	0	9	45	23	10	5	0	14	56	.148	.080	.181	11.20	2.80
Eichhorn, Kevin	R-R	6-0	170	2-6-90	0	1	4.50	1	1	0	0	6	6	3	3	0	5	5	.261	.167	.364	7.50	4.50
Gutierrez, Teo	R-R	6-0	180	5-23-90	2	0	0.47	4	4	0	0	19	12	2	1	0	5	10	.182	.194	.171	4.74	2.37
Hale, Jake	R-R	6-7	200	12-11-85	3	2	0.24	25	0	0	4	38	23	3	1	0	7	44	.172	.207	.145	10.42	1.66
Hogben, Kable	R-R	6-2	176	7-6-90	0	0	0.72	28	0	0	10	37	17	5	3	0	7	43	.137	.143	.133	10.37	1.69
Pena, Miguel	R-R	6-0	160	9-18-90	4	6	3.45	15	15	0	0	76	87	44	29	2	32	47	.292	.298	.289	5.59	3.81
Pizziconi, Andrea	R-R	6-2	190	10-4-91	2	0	1.59	13	6	0	0	40	29	7	7	4	15	22	.206	.214	.200	4.99	3.40
Reagan, Miles	R-R	6-2	200	11-16-90	2	4	5.77	15	8	0	0	44	43	34	28	5	30	31	.269	.243	.289	6.39	6.18
Robinson, Greg	R-R	6-2	230	7-17-87	7	3	4.24	25	0	0	0	40	34	23	19	3	17	46	.230	.156	.262	10.26	3.79
Tucker, Rashad	B-R	6-3	200	9-27-87	1	0	11.57	6	0	0	0	5	7	6	6	1	4	3	.318	.444	.231	5.79	7.71
Upperman, Casey	R-R	6-1	183	11-16-90	1	0	8.10	6	0	0	0	7	8	6	6	0	4	7	.308	.125	.389	9.45	5.40
Wheeler, Cody	L-L	5-11	160	8-19-89	0	1	6.00	3	0	0	0	3	3	3	2	0	4	4	.273	1.000	.000	12.00	12.00
Wilson, Brad	R-R	6-0	184	5-26-87	3	3	4.06	12	12	0	0	64	53	37	29	2	30	45	.221	.217	.224	6.30	4.20
Wolcott, Andrew	R-R	6-5	245	9-8-87	1	1	3.79	3	3	0	0	19	18	8	8	0	8	16	.261	.207	.300	7.58	3.79

Fielding

Catcher	PCT	G	PO	A	E	DP	PB
Emsley-Pai	.996	42	204	34	1	1	8
Gomez	.990	33	179	22	2	1	4
Herrnberger	1.000	1	1	0	0	0	0
Ortiz	—	1	0	0	0	0	0
Pimentel	1.000	37	204	30	0	3	3

First Base	PCT	G	PO	A	E	DP
Arbelo	.982	66	607	32	12	59
Belza	1.000	1	2	0	0	0
Comerota	.987	20	76	1	1	9
Pimentel	1.000	10	31	2	0	6
Weber	1.000	5	18	0	0	2

Second Base	PCT	G	PO	A	E	DP
Belza	.983	16	19	39	1	6
Comerota	.989	25	35	55	1	22
Freeman	.982	49	84	136	4	37
Noboa	—	2	0	0	0	0
Weber	.950	4	7	12	1	4

Third Base	PCT	G	PO	A	E	DP
Belza	.000	1	0	0	1	0
Comerota	1.000	5	6	10	0	2
Gomez	1.000	3	4	1	0	0
Torrez	.947	49	24	102	7	10
Weber	.926	25	19	31	4	6

Shortstop	PCT	G	PO	A	E	DP
Belza	.934	21	28	57	6	17
Comerota	.800	2	1	3	1	0
Freeman	—	1	0	0	0	0
Walters	.928	62	89	206	23	40

Outfield	PCT	G	PO	A	E	DP
Belza	1.000	3	3	0	0	0
Button	1.000	10	5	1	0	0
Comerota	1.000	1	1	0	0	0
Hilt	.983	60	107	7	2	2
Inciarte	.974	18	33	4	1	1
Moss	.991	65	107	1	1	1
Ortiz	.947	51	67	5	4	1
Zabala	.955	50	55	9	3	2

MISSOULA OSPREY
ROOKIE

PIONEER LEAGUE

Batting	B-T	HT	WT	DOB	AVG	vLH	vRH	G	AB	R	H	2B	3B	HR	RBI	BB	HBP	SH	SF	SO	SB	CS	SLG	OBP
Aguila, Roidany	R-R	5-10	175	10-22-90	.234	.308	.206	29	94	9	22	5	0	0	6	8	2	0	1	20	3	2	.287	.305
Canelo, Adonys	B-R	5-11	165	1-23-89	.248	.310	.230	42	129	25	32	7	0	3	11	13	0	2	0	30	2	1	.372	.317
Cardullo, Stephen	R-R	6-0	212	8-31-87	.172	.214	.159	20	58	4	10	0	0	0	5	6	1	0	1	19	0	1	.172	.258
Eaton, Adam	L-L	5-9	180	12-6-88	.385	.305	.413	68	226	48	87	14	4	7	37	35	19	0	2	44	20	8	.575	.500
Groff, Eric	R-R	5-11	195	1-25-88	.281	.367	.254	63	249	31	70	15	3	8	40	11	0	1	3	63	3	0	.462	.308
Helm, Matt	R-R	6-1	197	9-1-90	.230	.222	.233	32	113	11	26	7	0	5	14	9	3	0	1	50	1	3	.425	.302
Jarrett, Chris	L-L	5-10	175	11-17-88	.228	.263	.217	46	158	22	36	12	3	2	20	17	6	0	0	35	5	2	.380	.326
Kim, Jae Yun	R-R	6-1	185	9-16-90	.208	.222	.205	47	168	21	35	7	0	4	12	5	9	1	0	51	0	1	.321	.269

ARIZONA DIAMONDBACKS

	B-T	HT	WT	DOB	AVG	vLH	vRH	G	AB	R	H	2B	3B	HR	RBI	BB	HBP	SH	SF	SO	SB	CS	SLG	OBP
Linton, Tyler	R-R	6-3	195	1-17-91	—	.000	.000	1	0	0	0	0	0	0	0	0	1	0	0	0	0	0	—	1.000
Navarro, Raul	R-R	5-11	160	2-5-92	.305	.339	.294	63	243	39	74	11	5	2	28	18	2	2	0	41	2	3	.416	.357
Pena, Fidel	R-R	5-11	165	7-19-91	.272	.333	.250	33	103	12	28	2	2	1	16	9	1	2	0	15	1	2	.359	.336
Rodriguez, Roberto	L-L	6-0	156	3-22-89	.309	.309	.310	69	278	57	86	16	6	7	31	19	4	1	1	70	13	3	.486	.361
Rowland, Richie	B-R	6-3	205	8-18-88	.291	.367	.270	67	227	19	66	11	0	5	34	20	1	0	5	47	0	2	.405	.344
Sepulveda, Antonio	B-R	5-9	150	12-31-91	.243	.077	.279	31	74	11	18	1	1	1	7	6	0	0	1	26	3	0	.324	.296
Soriano, Domingo	R-R	6-1	165	10-29-89	.106	.111	.103	36	85	6	9	1	0	0	6	2	0	0	0	35	0	0	.118	.126
Stone, Bobby	L-L	6-2	217	11-14-89	.280	.347	.254	73	268	41	75	15	1	10	52	40	2	0	3	69	3	4	.455	.374
Varnell, Zach	R-R	6-1	200	6-25-86	.000	.000	.000	4	5	0	0	0	0	0	0	0	0	0	0	4	0	0	.000	.000
Williams, Javan	R-R	5-11	185	10-18-89	.274	.333	.260	35	95	13	26	2	0	1	10	7	1	1	0	21	7	2	.326	.330

Pitching	B-T	HT	WT	DOB	W	L	ERA	G	GS	CG	SV	IP	H	R	ER	HR	BB	SO	AVG	vLH	vRH	K/9	BB/9
Acosta, Victor	R-R	5-11	175	3-10-90	0	0	10.80	15	0	0	0	20	28	28	24	2	18	22	.322	.395	.265	9.90	8.10
Albert, Justin	L-L	6-3	235	5-27-87	2	1	3.31	19	1	0	5	35	31	17	13	3	10	29	.237	.303	.214	7.39	2.55
Bradley, J.R.	R-R	6-4	185	6-9-92	1	7	5.93	14	14	0	0	55	66	48	36	7	24	40	.301	.359	.260	6.59	3.95
Cooper, Blake	R-R	5-10	188	3-30-88	1	0	3.38	8	0	0	1	8	8	3	3	1	3	8	.250	.200	.273	9.00	3.38
De Los Santos, Sammy	R-R	6-1	185	12-9-89	1	2	5.02	15	0	0	1	38	46	26	21	5	11	37	.286	.259	.299	8.84	2.63
Eichhorn, Kevin	R-R	6-0	170	2-6-90	5	5	4.94	13	13	0	0	75	80	49	41	12	15	71	.271	.279	.265	8.56	1.81
Eitel, Derek	R-R	6-4	200	11-21-87	2	2	5.11	11	8	0	0	49	61	35	28	3	22	32	.307	.238	.357	5.84	4.01
Erben, Jeremy	R-R	5-10	190	9-15-87	1	3	4.24	13	0	0	3	17	11	11	8	3	6	27	.175	.200	.163	14.29	3.18
Gutierrez, Teo	R-R	6-0	180	5-23-90	0	0	6.97	11	0	0	0	21	24	18	16	2	17	15	.304	.226	.354	6.53	7.40
Hamrick, Randy	R-R	6-2	195	8-27-86	2	3	4.29	19	1	0	1	50	58	30	24	5	17	45	.293	.300	.289	8.05	3.04
Harvil, Will	R-R	6-5	220	6-17-87	0	0	2.70	6	0	0	3	10	9	5	3	1	5	17	.237	.250	.231	15.30	4.50
Holmberg, David	R-L	6-4	220	7-19-91	1	4	3.86	7	7	0	0	37	47	26	16	2	7	47	.294	.257	.304	11.33	1.69
2-team total (8 Great Falls)					2	5	4.17	15	15	0	0	78	99	49	36	4	16	76	—	—		8.81	1.85
Lara, Victor	R-R	5-10	205	12-3-88	1	5	8.02	17	0	0	1	21	27	20	19	5	17	22	.307	.282	.327	9.28	7.17
Perry, Blake	R-R	6-5	190	2-3-92	0	0	0.00	1	1	0	0	1	1	0	0	0	0	1	.250	1.000	.000	0.00	0.00
Pizzicconi, Andrea	R-R	6-2	190	10-4-91	0	1	6.75	4	0	0	0	9	12	7	7	1	4	5	.324	.500	.217	4.82	3.86
Rowland, Robby	B-R	6-6	205	12-15-91	4	6	5.67	14	14	0	0	54	62	42	34	7	21	40	.291	.349	.254	6.67	3.50
Schuster, Patrick	R-L	6-2	165	10-30-90	5	4	3.76	15	15	0	0	77	76	50	32	3	34	60	.261	.226	.271	7.04	3.99
Shields, Jeff	R-R	6-3	205	2-22-90	1	1	3.78	12	0	0	0	17	13	10	7	0	11	14	.220	.292	.171	7.56	5.94
Taylor, Dan	L-L	5-11	205	7-25-87	0	1	1.13	1	1	1	0	8	4	1	1	0	0	11	.148	.000	.222	12.38	0.00
Tucker, Rashad	B-R	6-3	200	9-27-87	0	0	14.40	5	0	0	0	5	10	8	8	1	3	3	.400	.250	.538	5.40	5.40
Upperman, Casey	R-R	6-1	183	11-16-90	1	0	5.21	11	0	0	0	19	16	15	11	2	15	16	.225	.136	.265	7.58	7.11
Watt, Trey	R-R	6-0	230	2-26-88	0	2	7.17	19	0	0	0	21	33	24	17	0	10	17	.327	.395	.286	7.17	4.22

Fielding

Catcher	PCT	G	PO	A	E	DP	PB
Aguila	.968	28	186	28	7	1	5
Kim	.985	45	355	42	6	2	8
Pena	1.000	5	14	0	0	0	0
Rowland	.944	3	16	1	1	0	0

First Base	PCT	G	PO	A	E	DP
Rowland	.882	5	30	0	4	2
Stone	.986	72	613	36	9	65

Second Base	PCT	G	PO	A	E	DP
Canelo	.942	28	42	72	7	17
Groff	.973	23	41	66	3	19

	PCT	G	PO	A	E	DP
Pena	.920	20	36	44	7	7
Sepulveda	.909	10	12	18	3	2

Third Base	PCT	G	PO	A	E	DP
Canelo	1.000	3	1	0	0	0
Cardullo	1.000	4	4	4	0	0
Groff	.943	40	30	85	7	5
Helm	.817	31	11	47	13	5

Shortstop	PCT	G	PO	A	E	DP
Canelo	.846	3	4	7	2	2
Cardullo	.872	11	17	24	6	4
Navarro	.918	63	115	176	26	46

	PCT	G	PO	A	E	DP
Pena	1.000	1	1	0	0	0
Sepulveda	.750	2	1	2	1	0

Outfield	PCT	G	PO	A	E	DP
Canelo	—	1	0	0	0	0
Eaton	.964	66	128	4	5	1
Jarrett	.977	44	81	4	2	1
Rodriguez	.947	68	99	9	6	1
Sepulveda	.789	12	15	0	4	0
Soriano	.931	30	27	0	2	0
Varnell	—	2	0	0	0	0
Williams	.952	33	39	1	2	0

DSL DIAMONDBACKS   ROOKIE
DOMINICAN SUMMER LEAGUE

Batting	B-T	HT	WT	DOB	AVG	vLH	vRH	G	AB	R	H	2B	3B	HR	RBI	BB	HBP	SH	SF	SO	SB	CS	SLG	OBP
Abreu, Jesus	R-R	5-10	155	4-14-92	.265	.600	.228	45	151	26	40	4	2	0	23	26	4	4	2	10	8	4	.318	.383
Alegria, Jose	R-R	6-1	200	11-5-90	.286	.333	.280	11	28	4	8	0	1	0	7	8	4	0	0	11	0	0	.357	.500
Arena, Harry	L-L	6-2	170	4-30-91	.244	.000	.278	18	41	4	10	1	0	0	0	2	1	0	0	8	0	0	.268	.295
Betemit, Felipe	B-R	5-11	182	7-6-91	.175	.000	.194	33	103	13	18	1	1	0	3	13	2	1	1	31	4	1	.204	.277
Bolivar, Anderson	B-R	5-11	165	9-9-92	.125	.000	.150	8	24	3	3	0	0	0	2	0	1	0	0	4	0	1	.125	.160
Brito, Socrates	L-L	6-2	197	9-6-92	.293	.375	.284	22	82	11	24	4	1	0	8	9	0	0	0	15	0	4	.366	.363
Castillo, William	R-R	5-10	158	7-11-92	.284	.368	.274	53	183	36	52	4	3	0	16	29	1	6	2	26	11	3	.339	.381
Delgado, Elvin	R-R	5-11	177	8-17-90	.189	.111	.198	32	90	11	17	3	0	0	7	10	12	2	0	20	0	2	.222	.348
Dicent, Jose	R-R	6-2	176	10-1-90	.133	.143	.132	15	45	7	6	2	0	0	4	9	1	0	0	14	1	0	.178	.291
Gomez, Jeremia	R-R	6-3	185	2-10-91	.243	.429	.224	22	74	15	18	4	1	2	10	12	0	0	0	17	2	1	.405	.349
Gonzalez, Michael	R-R	5-11	170	3-12-92	.259	.143	.260	29	81	12	21	2	2	1	12	16	0	0	0	20	2	0	.370	.381
Gutierrez, Yosbel	R-R	5-10	170	1-20-93	.232	.375	.222	31	99	10	23	4	3	0	17	9	8	0	0	24	1	1	.333	.345
Javier, Kelvin	R-R	6-2	200	10-7-90	.176	.200	.174	24	51	5	9	3	0	0	3	20	5	0	0	23	0	0	.235	.447
Mateo, Wagner	L-L	6-2	190	3-30-93	.257	.111	.274	67	237	45	61	14	4	4	45	35	3	0	1	83	16	10	.401	.359
Ortiz, Roberto	R-R	6-1	195	10-28-88	.231	.333	.217	8	26	9	6	2	1	0	3	4	2	0	0	2	0	0	.385	.375
Perez, Jonathan	R-R	6-0	205	9-14-90	.221	.077	.236	49	136	26	30	7	1	1	23	37	7	1	2	41	5	1	.309	.407
Ruiz, Pedro	B-R	5-11	165	8-30-91	.190	.286	.174	58	168	40	32	2	4	0	24	46	5	3	1	42	8	5	.250	.377
Santana, Wilmer	L-L	6-0	170	2-19-92	.225	.238	.226	53	182	20	41	5	0	2	23	19	4	0	1	35	1	3	.286	.322
Santiago, Alan	L-R	6-1	170	7-24-90	.225	.500	.188	35	111	14	25	3	5	0	12	23	0	1	1	21	1	1	.342	.356
Sosa, Maximo	R-R	6-2	191	3-10-92	.248	.222	.253	52	165	36	41	7	0	3	30	36	11	0	3	50	2	1	.327	.409
Valdez, Samuel	R-R	6-2	206	4-2-91	.188	.263	.177	52	160	32	30	12	0	0	23	36	10	0	1	44	2	0	.263	.335

Pitching	B-T	HT	WT	DOB	W	L	ERA	G	GS	CG	SV	IP	H	R	ER	HR	BB	SO	AVG	vLH	vRH	K/9	BB/9
Acosta, Victor	R-R	5-11	175	3-10-90	0	0	0.00	1	0	0	0	2	2	2	0	0	0	3	.200	.000	.250	13.50	0.00
Camacho, Yiomar	R-R	6-1	172	2-24-90	3	5	3.89	12	12	0	0	69	65	41	30	3	22	51	.249	.275	.233	6.62	2.86
Collado, Juan	R-R	6-1	175	4-4-90	0	0	5.40	3	0	0	0	7	11	5	4	1	1	8	.379	.308	.438	10.80	1.35
Cruz, Berling	R-R	6-1	183	6-3-91	2	3	4.34	9	8	0	0	46	55	34	22	1	9	34	.297	.250	.318	6.70	1.77
De Jesus, Cesse	R-R	5-11	155	5-16-90	1	0	2.77	8	1	0	1	13	11	5	4	0	11	11	.239	.316	.185	7.62	7.62
Escanio, Bryan	R-R	6-1	185	12-17-91	0	0	8.44	3	0	0	1	5	6	5	5	0	2	4	.286	.200	.313	6.75	3.38
Falcon, Juan	R-R	6-3	200	3-7-92	0	0	5.25	14	0	0	0	24	20	23	14	0	21	14	.230	.250	.220	5.25	7.88
Garcia, Manuel	B-R	5-11	170	3-8-89	0	0	6.75	1	0	0	0	3	3	2	2	1	3	5	.273	.167	.400	16.88	10.13
Guzman, Francisco	L-L	6-5	190	7-2-89	1	5	2.77	15	14	2	0	65	50	31	20	0	33	47	.216	.192	.218	6.51	4.57
Hernandez, Luis	R-R	6-2	187	6-22-92	4	2	4.45	13	2	0	0	30	30	25	15	0	23	15	.248	.200	.276	4.45	6.82
Jaime, Johan	L-L	5-11	185	12-7-89	6	3	3.10	14	14	1	0	70	50	32	24	0	36	77	.200	.125	.211	9.95	4.65
Leon, Danny	R-R	6-5	180	9-16-89	3	1	7.20	7	0	0	1	10	10	9	8	0	8	14	.263	.200	.304	12.60	7.20
Matos, Joel	R-R	6-5	200	9-17-92	0	3	4.26	4	2	0	0	6	6	9	3	0	9	2	.261	.300	.231	2.84	12.79
Perdomo, Leonardo	R-R	6-5	180	3-1-93	0	3	16.62	3	3	0	0	9	12	17	16	1	7	5	.333	.286	.364	5.19	7.27
Santana, Diony	L-L	6-0	150	1-15-91	3	4	2.17	12	7	1	0	54	51	29	13	0	18	37	.249	.214	.251	6.17	3.00
Santana, Frank	R-R	6-2	200	2-21-89	4	0	1.97	18	0	0	7	32	17	7	7	1	8	29	.157	.143	.163	8.16	2.25
Solis, Jency	R-R	6-1	180	2-22-93	2	2	3.89	17	2	0	1	37	34	22	16	2	15	24	.239	.233	.244	5.84	3.65
Valdez, Juan	R-R	6-1	160	3-23-92	2	1	2.45	12	1	0	1	29	19	12	8	1	8	22	.188	.125	.217	6.75	2.45
Vizcaino, Eduardo	L-L	5-11	165	1-23-88	1	4	3.60	13	4	1	1	40	42	25	16	1	14	26	.263	.429	.247	5.85	3.15

Fielding

Catcher	PCT	G	PO	A	E	DP	PB
Alegria	.977	10	71	13	2	0	1
Bolivar	.981	8	43	10	1	0	3
Delgado	.971	32	213	25	7	1	4
Gutierrez	.944	29	149	37	11	0	6

First Base	PCT	G	PO	A	E	DP
Javier	1.000	1	6	1	0	0
Perez	.987	9	69	6	1	8
Santana	.966	38	243	11	9	22
Valdez	.976	35	266	18	7	28

Second Base	PCT	G	PO	A	E	DP
Abreu	.956	19	42	44	4	16
Betemit	.909	29	51	49	10	9

Castillo	.971	17	30	37	2	8
Ruiz	.981	13	29	24	1	5

Third Base	PCT	G	PO	A	E	DP
Abreu	.945	24	28	58	5	2
Dicent	.650	12	10	16	14	0
Perez	.871	39	30	78	16	2
Ruiz	1.000	2	1	4	0	1
Valdez	.400	2	0	2	3	0

Shortstop	PCT	G	PO	A	E	DP
Abreu	1.000	1	1	2	0	0
Betemit	.667	2	1	3	2	0
Castillo	.910	35	55	87	14	24
Ruiz	.872	39	66	104	25	21

Outfield	PCT	G	PO	A	E	DP
Arena	1.000	8	6	0	0	0
Brito	.939	21	30	1	2	0
Gomez	.970	19	30	2	1	0
Gonzalez	.939	27	31	0	2	0
Javier	1.000	7	7	0	0	0
Mateo	.950	63	104	11	6	1
Ortiz	1.000	8	17	2	0	0
Perez	1.000	1	2	0	0	0
Santana	.944	14	17	0	1	0
Santiago	.884	25	35	3	5	0
Sosa	.934	44	53	4	4	0

Atlanta Braves

SEASON IN A SENTENCE: The Braves went on a tear going into the all-star break, and held things together through a rash of injuries in the second half to give manager Bobby Cox one more trip to the playoffs before he retired.

HIGH POINT: Atlanta came back from a nine-game losing streak at the end of April with a 39-18 run in the two months heading into the all-star break and had the best record in the National League in July. But the high point came on the last day of the regular season when they finally claimed the wild card, returning to the playoffs for the first time since 2005.

LOW POINT: The Braves battled injuries all season, none more significant than Chipper Jones tearing the ACL in his left knee on Aug. 10. And when Martin Prado tore his left oblique muscle and suffered a hip pointer while making an acrobatic catch with only six days left in the regular season, the team proved punchless in the playoffs.

NOTABLE ROOKIES: Jason Heyward started in right field on Opening Day and hit a three-run home run with the first swing of his career. His legend only grew from there, as he batted .277/.393/.456 with 18 home runs and was Baseball America's Rookie of the Year. Not to be overlooked was lefthander Jonny Venters, who arrived at big league camp as an unknown but made 79 appearances and compiled a 1.95 ERA.

KEY TRANSACTIONS: Shortstop Yunel Escobar was one of the Braves' best young players, but he was having a down year at the plate so they dealt him to the Blue Jays for veteran Alex Gonzalez to try to shore up the lineup at the trade deadline. Atlanta also sent Tim Collins, Gregor Blanco and Jesse Chavez to the Royals for Rick Ankiel and Kyle Farnsworth. And in August, the Braves picked up Derek Lee from the Cubs to try to offset the loss of Jones.

DOWN ON THE FARM: Only one of Atlanta's affiliates finished 2010 with a record above .500, and Triple-A Gwinnett was 72-71. But there were plenty of good development stories. Freddie Freeman hit a career-high .319 with 18 home runs and led the International League in hits (147) and total bases (240). Righthander Brandon Beachy opened the year in the Double-A bullpen and finished it making three major league starts during Atlanta's playoff drive, posting a 3.00 ERA and striking out 15 over 15 innings. He went 5-1, 1.73 in the minors.

OPENING DAY PAYROLL: $84.4 million (15th)

PLAYERS OF THE YEAR

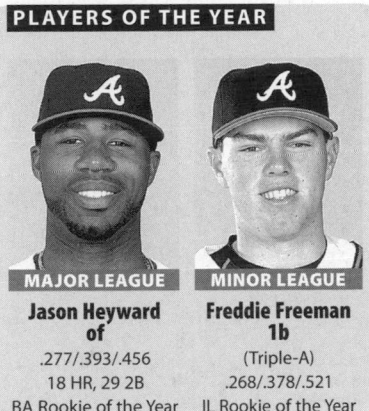

MAJOR LEAGUE	MINOR LEAGUE
Jason Heyward	**Freddie Freeman**
of	1b
.277/.393/.456	(Triple-A)
18 HR, 29 2B	.268/.378/.521
BA Rookie of the Year	IL Rookie of the Year

ORGANIZATION LEADERS

BATTING		*Minimum 250 at-bats
MAJORS		
*AVG	Omar Infante	.321
*OPS	Jason Heyward	.849
HR	Brian McCann	21
RBI	Brian McCann	77
MINORS		
*AVG	Barbaro Canizares, Gwinnett	.341
*OBP	Barbaro Canizares, Gwinnett	.403
*SLG	Freddie Freeman, Gwinnett	.521
R	Matt Young, Gwinnett	88
H	Freddie Freeman, Gwinnett	147
TB	Freddie Freeman, Gwinnett	240
2B	Mauro Gomez, Mississippi	42
3B	Cole Miles, Myrtle Beach/Mississippi	10
HR	Freddie Freeman, Gwinnett	18
	Cody Johnson, GCL/Mississippi/Myrtle Beach	18
	Mitch Jones, Gwinnett	18
RBI	Freddie Freeman, Gwinnett	87
BB	Wes Timmons, Gwinnett	60
SO	Cody Johnson, GCL/Mississippi/Myrtle Beach	151
SB	Matt Young, Gwinnett	39

PITCHING		†Minimum 75 innings
MAJORS		
W	Tim Hudson	17
†ERA	Jonny Venters	1.95
SO	Tommy Hanson	173
MINORS		
W	J.J. Hoover, Myrtle Beach/Mississippi	14
L	Jose Ortegano, Myrtle Beach/Gwinnett	15
†ERA	Brandon Beachy, Mississippi/Gwinnett	1.73
G	Stephen Marek, Mississippi/Gwinnett	60
GS	Three players tied at	28
SV	Craig Kimbrel, Gwinnett	23
IP	Todd Redmond, Gwinnett	162.7
BB	Erik Cordier, Mississippi/Gwinnett	76
SO	Randall Delgado, Myrtle Beach/Mississippi	162
†AVG	Julio Teheran, Rome/Myrtle Beach/Miss.	.208

2010 PERFORMANCE

General Manager: Frank Wren. **Farm Director:** Kurt Kemp. **Scouting Director:** Tony DeMacio.

Class	Team	League	W	L	PCT	Finish*	Manager(s)
Majors	Atlanta Braves	National	91	71	.562	t-3rd (16)	Bobby Cox
Triple-A	Gwinnett Braves	International	72	71	.503	7th (14)	Dave Brundage
Double-A	Mississippi Braves	Southern	63	74	.460	8th (10)	Phillip Wellman
High A	Myrtle Beach Pelicans	Carolina	58	82	.414	8th (8)	Rocket Wheeler
Low A	Rome Braves	South Atlantic	59	80	.424	13th (14)	Randy Ingle
Rookie	Danville Braves	Appalachian	34	34	.500	t-4th (10)	Paul Runge
Rookie	GCL Braves	Gulf Coast	27	31	.466	11th (15)	Luis Ortiz
Overall 2010 Minor League Record			313	372	.457	28th (30)	

*Finish in overall standings (No. of teams in league). †League champion.

ORGANIZATION STATISTICS

ATLANTA BRAVES
NATIONAL LEAGUE

Batting	B-T	HT	WT	DOB	AVG	vLH	vRH	G	AB	R	H	2B	3B	HR	RBI	BB	HBP	SH	SF	SO	SB	CS	SLG	OBP
Ankiel, Rick	L-L	6-2	205	7-19-79	.210	.154	.226	47	119	17	25	6	1	2	9	19	1	0	0	42	2	1	.328	.324
Blanco, Gregor	L-L	5-11	170	12-24-83	.310	.333	.306	36	58	9	18	1	1	0	3	8	0	0	0	15	1	2	.362	.394
Boscan, J.C.	R-R	6-2	215	12-26-79	—	.000	.000	1	0	1	0	0	0	0	0	0	0	0	0	0	0	0	—	1.000
Cabrera, Melky	B-L	6-0	200	8-11-84	.255	.233	.266	147	458	50	117	27	3	4	42	42	1	5	3	64	7	1	.354	.317
Clevlen, Brent	R-R	6-1	205	10-27-83	.250	.000	1.000	4	4	2	1	1	0	0	0	0	0	0	0	1	0	0	.500	.250
Conrad, Brooks	B-R	5-11	190	1-16-80	.250	.278	.242	103	156	31	39	11	1	8	33	16	1	4	0	45	5	1	.487	.324
Diaz, Matt	R-R	6-1	215	3-3-78	.250	.273	.223	84	224	27	56	17	2	7	31	13	4	2	1	44	3	1	.438	.302
Escobar, Yunel	R-R	6-2	200	11-2-82	.238	.273	.226	75	261	28	62	12	0	0	19	37	1	2	0	31	5	1	.284	.334
Freeman, Freddie	L-R	6-5	225	9-12-89	.167	.667	.095	20	24	3	4	1	0	1	1	0	0	0	0	8	0	0	.333	.167
Glaus, Troy	R-R	6-5	240	8-3-76	.240	.234	.243	128	412	52	99	18	0	16	71	63	4	0	4	100	0	0	.400	.344
Gonzalez, Alex	R-R	5-11	215	2-15-77	.240	.234	.242	72	267	27	64	17	2	6	38	14	6	3	2	53	0	2	.386	.291
Hernandez, Diory	R-R	6-0	185	4-8-84	.111	.200	.000	20	9	5	1	0	0	0	1	0	0	1	0	4	0	0	.444	.111
Heyward, Jason	L-L	6-5	240	8-9-89	.277	.249	.291	142	520	83	144	29	5	18	72	91	10	0	2	128	11	6	.456	.393
Hicks, Brandon	R-R	6-2	200	9-14-85	.000	.000	.000	16	5	7	0	0	0	0	0	1	0	0	0	2	0	0	.000	.167
Hinske, Eric	L-R	6-2	235	8-5-77	.256	.381	.246	131	281	38	72	21	1	11	51	33	3	0	3	75	0	0	.456	.338
Infante, Omar	R-R	6-0	180	12-26-81	.321	.276	.342	134	471	65	151	15	3	8	47	29	0	4	2	62	7	6	.416	.359
Jones, Chipper	B-R	6-4	210	4-24-72	.265	.245	.275	95	317	47	84	21	0	10	46	61	0	3	4	47	5	0	.426	.381
Lee, Derrek	R-R	6-5	245	9-6-75	.287	.382	.253	39	129	17	37	14	0	3	24	21	0	0	1	33	0	0	.465	.384
2-team total (109 Chicago)					.260	—	—	148	547	80	142	35	0	19	80	73	2	0	4	134	1	3	.428	.347
McCann, Brian	L-R	6-3	230	2-20-84	.269	.263	.272	143	479	63	129	25	0	21	77	74	9	0	4	98	5	2	.453	.375
McLouth, Nate	L-R	5-11	180	10-28-81	.190	.135	.205	85	242	30	46	12	1	6	24	33	5	6	2	57	7	2	.322	.298
Prado, Martin	R-R	6-1	190	10-27-83	.307	.275	.320	140	599	100	184	40	3	15	66	40	3	3	6	86	5	3	.459	.350
Ross, David	R-R	6-2	205	3-19-77	.289	.308	.256	59	121	15	35	13	2	2	28	20	1	2	1	28	0	1	.479	.392

Pitching	B-T	HT	WT	DOB	W	L	ERA	G	GS	CG	SV	IP	H	R	ER	HR	BB	SO	AVG	vLH	vRH	K/9	BB/9
Beachy, Brandon	R-R	6-3	215	9-3-86	0	2	3.00	3	3	0	0	15	16	9	5	0	7	15	.267	.273	.259	9.00	4.20
Chavez, Jesse	R-R	6-2	170	8-21-83	3	2	5.89	28	0	0	0	37	40	24	24	6	12	29	.278	.255	.290	7.12	2.95
Dunn, Mike	L-L	6-1	195	5-23-85	2	0	1.89	25	0	0	0	19	15	4	4	1	17	21	.211	.211	.212	12.79	8.05
Farnsworth, Kyle	R-R	6-4	230	4-14-76	0	2	5.40	23	0	0	0	20	15	12	12	2	7	25	.208	.281	.150	11.25	3.15
Hanson, Tommy	R-R	6-6	220	8-28-86	10	11	3.33	34	34	1	0	203	182	86	75	14	56	173	.239	.226	.251	7.68	2.49
Hudson, Tim	R-R	6-1	175	7-14-75	17	9	2.83	34	34	1	0	229	189	74	72	20	74	139	.229	.233	.225	5.47	2.91
Jurrjens, Jair	R-R	6-1	200	1-29-86	7	6	4.64	20	20	0	0	116	120	63	60	13	42	86	.270	.294	.250	6.65	3.25
Kawakami, Kenshin	R-R	5-11	200	6-22-75	1	10	5.15	18	16	0	0	87	98	57	50	10	32	59	.284	.299	.271	6.08	3.30
Kimbrel, Craig	R-R	5-11	205	5-28-88	4	0	0.44	21	0	0	1	21	9	2	1	0	16	40	.125	.176	.079	17.42	6.97
Lowe, Derek	R-R	6-6	230	6-1-73	16	12	4.00	33	33	0	0	194	204	88	86	18	61	136	.273	.287	.259	6.32	2.83
Martinez, Cristhian	R-R	6-1	185	3-6-82	0	0	4.85	18	0	0	0	26	28	14	14	3	6	22	.272	.326	.228	7.62	2.08
Medlen, Kris	B-R	5-10	190	10-7-85	6	2	3.68	31	14	0	0	108	108	48	44	13	21	83	.267	.281	.257	6.94	1.76
Minor, Mike	R-L	6-3	210	12-26-87	3	2	5.98	9	8	0	0	41	53	28	27	6	11	43	.314	.293	.320	9.52	2.43
Moylan, Peter	R-R	6-2	200	12-2-78	6	2	2.97	85	0	0	1	64	53	24	21	5	37	52	.236	.308	.214	7.35	5.23
O'Flaherty, Eric	L-L	6-2	220	2-5-85	3	2	2.45	56	0	0	0	44	37	14	12	2	18	36	.230	.231	.229	7.36	3.68
Proctor, Scott	R-R	6-1	195	1-2-77	0	0	6.35	9	0	0	0	6	4	4	4	1	4	6	.200	.182	.222	9.53	6.35
Resop, Chris	R-R	6-3	220	11-4-82	0	0	22.50	1	0	0	0	2	5	5	5	0	3	2	.455	.571	.250	9.00	13.50
2-team total (22 Pittsburgh)					0	0	3.86	23	0	0	0	21	15	9	9	1	13	26	—	—	—	11.14	5.57
Reyes, Jo-Jo	L-L	6-2	230	11-20-84	0	1	24.30	1	0	0	0	3	10	9	9	2	3	2	.500	.333	.571	5.40	8.10
Saito, Takashi	L-R	6-2	200	2-14-70	2	3	2.83	56	0	0	1	54	41	20	17	4	17	69	.203	.244	.172	11.50	2.83
Venters, Jonny	L-L	6-3	195	3-20-85	4	4	1.95	79	0	0	1	83	61	30	18	1	39	93	.204	.198	.207	10.08	4.23
Wagner, Billy	L-L	5-10	180	7-25-71	7	2	1.43	71	0	0	37	69	38	14	11	5	22	104	.159	.071	.186	13.50	2.86

Fielding

Catcher	PCT	G	PO	A	E	DP	PB
Boscan	1.000	1	2	0	0	0	0
McCann	.987	136	972	64	14	12	5
Ross	.987	57	276	22	4	0	1

First Base	PCT	G	PO	A	E	DP
Freeman	1.000	12	36	5	0	1
Glaus	.991	114	977	46	9	110
Hinske	.995	32	179	10	1	15
Lee	.997	39	283	24	1	26

Prado	1.000	5	7	0	0	0

Second Base	PCT	G	PO	A	E	DP
Conrad	.938	9	2	13	1	0
Hernandez	—	1	0	0	0	0
Hicks	—	1	0	0	0	0

Infante	.978	65	110	195	7	43
Prado	.987	98	184	285	6	66
Third Base	**PCT**	**G**	**PO**	**A**	**E**	**DP**
Conrad	.903	37	17	48	7	5
Glaus	1.000	1	0	1	0	0
Hicks	1.000	3	0	3	0	0
Hinske	1.000	1	0	2	0	0
Infante	.925	29	7	30	3	1
Jones	.952	89	40	159	10	10

Prado	.958	43	29	84	5	12
Shortstop	**PCT**	**G**	**PO**	**A**	**E**	**DP**
Escobar	.975	74	99	250	9	62
Gonzalez	.974	72	91	214	8	49
Hernandez	1.000	4	3	1	0	1
Hicks	—	2	0	0	0	0
Infante	.951	19	29	69	5	13
Outfield	**PCT**	**G**	**PO**	**A**	**E**	**DP**
Ankiel	.975	45	73	4	2	1

Blanco	.977	33	42	1	1	1
Cabrera	.982	136	213	8	4	2
Clevlen	1.000	2	5	0	0	0
Diaz	.979	63	93	1	2	0
Heyward	.976	140	235	5	6	1
Hinske	.985	50	65	0	1	0
Infante	.960	21	23	1	1	0
McLouth	.986	77	145	1	2	1

GWINNETT BRAVES   TRIPLE-A
INTERNATIONAL LEAGUE

Batting	B-T	HT	WT	DOB	AVG	vLH	vRH	G	AB	R	H	2B	3B	HR	RBI	BB	HBP	SH	SF	SO	SB	CS	SLG	OBP
Anderson, Josh	R-R	6-2	195	8-10-82	.189	.000	.208	19	53	8	10	1	0	0	1	2	1	3	0	11	3	1	.208	.232
2-team total (17 Louisville)					.161	—	—	36	93	10	15	3	0	0	1	2	1	4	0	17	8	1	.194	.188
Blanco, Gregor	L-L	5-11	170	12-24-83	.286	.206	.308	44	154	26	44	8	0	1	11	23	1	9	0	28	9	1	.357	.382
Bolivar, Luis	R-R	6-0	192	2-15-81	.217	.200	.224	58	184	19	40	6	2	2	13	8	4	1	1	46	9	0	.304	.264
Boscan, J.C.	R-R	6-2	215	12-26-79	.250	.213	.260	66	220	20	55	11	0	5	21	22	2	4	0	51	1	0	.368	.324
Cabrera, Willie	R-R	5-11	185	8-3-86	.192	.250	.143	8	26	1	5	1	0	0	2	1	0	0	0	6	0	1	.231	.222
Canizares, Barbaro	R-R	6-3	240	11-21-79	.341	.326	.345	126	425	58	145	28	1	13	77	40	7	0	4	54	2	0	.504	.403
Clevlen, Brent	R-R	6-1	205	10-27-83	.257	.233	.264	53	191	19	49	8	0	3	29	22	0	0	1	62	3	0	.346	.332
Diaz, Matt	R-R	6-1	215	3-3-78	.250	.000	.273	3	12	2	3	1	0	0	3	0	0	0	0	3	0	0	.333	.250
Escobar, Yunel	R-R	6-2	200	11-2-82	.667	.667	.000	1	3	1	2	0	0	0	1	0	0	0	0	1	0	0	.667	.750
Freeman, Freddie	L-R	6-5	225	9-12-89	.319	.268	.337	124	461	73	147	35	2	18	87	43	6	0	9	84	6	2	.521	.378
Glaus, Troy	R-R	6-5	240	8-3-76	.333	.182	.421	8	30	10	10	2	0	2	8	4	1	0	0	10	0	0	.600	.429
Hernandez, Diory	R-R	6-0	185	4-8-84	.319	.241	.345	30	116	13	37	7	2	0	17	4	1	0	1	21	3	1	.414	.344
Hicks, Brandon	R-R	6-2	200	9-14-85	.211	.210	.211	77	261	27	55	9	1	7	22	20	5	1	0	74	10	6	.333	.280
Holt, J.C.	L-R	5-9	175	12-8-82	.167	.000	.176	15	36	4	6	0	0	0	3	3	0	0	0	6	1	1	.167	.231
Jones, Mitch	R-R	6-2	215	10-15-77	.250	.338	.221	89	324	42	81	23	1	18	45	19	2	0	4	83	2	5	.494	.292
2-team total (30 Indianapolis)					.247	—	—	119	417	57	103	31	1	19	54	26	5	0	6	105	6	6	.463	.795
McLouth, Nate	L-R	5-11	180	10-28-81	.234	.244	.229	34	128	18	30	1	0	8	18	19	2	0	2	21	7	0	.383	.338
Mercado, Orlando	R-R	5-9	220	3-13-85	.069	.200	.042	9	29	4	2	0	0	1	5	3	0	0	1	10	0	0	.172	.152
Nelson, Dan	B-R	5-11	180	2-12-84	.429	.200	.500	5	21	3	9	2	0	1	6	0	0	0	0	2	0	0	.667	.429
Prado, Martin	R-R	6-1	190	10-27-83	.250	.000	.250	1	4	0	1	0	0	0	0	0	0	0	0	0	0	0	.250	.250
Ramirez, Wilkin	R-R	6-2	190	10-25-85	.253	.267	.250	24	83	16	21	3	1	4	14	10	3	0	1	22	2	0	.458	.351
2-team total (41 Toledo)					.229	—	—	65	236	31	54	7	3	8	28	20	5	0	1	82	9	2	.386	.302
Richardson, Antoan	R-R	5-8	165	10-8-83	.280	.167	.316	7	25	1	7	0	0	0	2	5	1	0	1	9	3	0	.280	.406
Romero, Alex	L-R	6-0	198	9-9-83	.190	.211	.179	18	58	2	11	1	0	1	2	3	1	1	0	10	1	0	.259	.242
Sammons, Clint	R-R	6-1	210	5-15-83	.162	.134	.172	84	271	24	44	7	0	5	24	30	4	2	3	59	2	4	.244	.253
Schafer, Jordan	L-L	6-1	190	9-4-86	.201	.188	.206	52	189	16	38	5	1	1	8	14	0	5	1	47	9	8	.254	.255
Taveras, Willy	R-R	6-0	180	12-25-81	.119	.222	.091	17	42	6	5	1	0	0	1	4	1	0	0	6	4	1	.143	.213
2-team total (23 Lehigh Valley)					.181	—	—	40	138	16	25	5	1	0	4	8	3	2	0	24	13	1	.232	.242
Thurston, Joe	L-R	5-11	210	9-29-79	.273	.198	.295	131	465	53	127	18	4	13	67	32	4	7	4	64	7	7	.413	.323
Timmons, Wes	R-R	6-0	190	7-12-79	.293	.327	.281	114	386	67	113	23	1	6	43	60	11	5	3	33	19	8	.404	.400
Young, Matt	L-R	5-8	175	10-3-82	.300	.268	.308	134	487	88	146	33	5	3	35	57	7	2	2	53	39	7	.407	.380

Pitching	B-T	HT	WT	DOB	W	L	ERA	G	GS	CG	SV	IP	H	R	ER	HR	BB	SO	AVG	vLH	vRH	K/9	BB/9
Beachy, Brandon	R-R	6-3	215	9-3-86	2	0	2.17	8	7	0	1	46	40	17	11	2	6	48	.229	.231	.227	9.46	1.18
Broadway, Mike	R-R	6-5	225	3-30-87	4	0	5.73	17	0	0	0	22	21	17	14	1	9	19	.256	.226	.275	7.77	3.68
Cordier, Erik	R-R	6-4	230	2-25-86	1	1	5.63	2	2	0	0	8	7	5	5	0	7	4	.233	.250	.200	4.50	7.88
Diamond, Scott	L-L	6-3	215	7-30-86	4	1	3.36	10	10	1	0	56	53	25	21	2	15	33	.260	.247	.267	5.27	2.40
Dunn, Mike	L-L	6-1	195	5-23-85	2	0	1.52	38	0	0	7	47	31	12	8	1	25	64	.183	.132	.218	12.17	4.75
Gearrin, Cory	R-R	6-3	200	4-14-86	3	5	3.36	52	0	0	0	80	72	32	30	6	32	66	.246	.273	.224	7.39	3.59
Gomez, Mariano	L-L	6-6	240	9-12-82	3	2	2.89	30	0	0	1	47	41	18	15	2	18	28	.247	.234	.258	5.40	3.47
Gustafson, Tim	R-R	6-3	185	12-29-84	7	6	5.70	14	13	0	0	66	82	44	42	6	39	36	.313	.323	.303	4.88	5.29
Hyde, Lee	R-L	6-2	205	2-14-85	2	3	4.29	22	0	0	0	21	24	12	10	2	12	17	.308	.389	.238	7.29	5.14
Jurrjens, Jair	R-R	6-1	200	1-29-86	1	1	5.54	3	3	0	0	13	20	8	8	2	6	9	.357	.429	.286	6.23	4.15
Kawakami, Kenshin	R-R	5-11	200	6-22-75	0	1	4.29	5	5	0	0	21	26	12	10	5	5	22	.302	.268	.333	9.43	2.14
Kimbrel, Craig	R-R	5-11	205	5-28-88	3	2	1.62	48	0	0	23	56	28	13	10	3	35	83	.148	.179	.124	13.42	5.66
Lyman, Jeff	R-R	6-3	225	1-14-87	0	0	4.72	21	0	0	0	34	32	24	18	2	23	26	.250	.145	.329	6.82	6.03
Marek, Stephen	L-R	6-2	230	9-3-83	2	2	1.43	49	0	0	9	50	38	13	8	4	19	56	.207	.159	.245	10.01	3.40
Martinez, Cristhian	R-R	6-1	185	3-6-82	5	1	3.08	23	2	0	0	53	45	22	18	3	8	49	.225	.111	.318	8.37	1.37
Minor, Mike	R-L	6-3	210	12-26-87	4	1	1.89	6	6	0	0	33	19	7	7	1	12	37	.171	.175	.169	9.99	3.24
Nunez, Vladimir	R-R	6-4	240	3-15-75	1	4	4.50	31	0	0	1	52	61	30	26	4	25	41	.299	.350	.250	7.10	4.33
O'Flaherty, Eric	L-L	6-2	220	2-5-85	0	0	0.00	3	0	0	0	4	1	0	0	0	1	5	.077	.000	.125	11.25	2.25
Ortegano, Jose	L-L	6-1	175	8-5-87	3	11	6.20	21	20	0	0	103	122	77	71	13	44	85	.295	.264	.310	7.43	3.84
Parr, James	R-R	6-1	205	2-27-86	2	5	5.16	9	9	0	0	45	54	26	26	3	17	28	.305	.330	.273	5.56	3.38
Proctor, Scott	R-R	6-1	195	1-2-77	4	3	7.08	31	0	0	0	34	45	29	27	6	15	29	.321	.375	.286	7.60	3.93
Redmond, Todd	R-R	6-3	215	5-17-85	9	10	4.26	28	28	1	0	163	156	86	77	21	44	142	.250	.255	.246	7.86	2.43
Resop, Chris	R-R	6-3	220	11-4-82	6	3	2.09	15	15	1	0	82	53	20	19	6	32	90	.187	.204	.170	9.99	3.51
Reyes, Jo-Jo	L-L	6-2	230	11-20-84	1	5	5.70	12	10	0	0	47	57	33	30	8	15	50	.295	.279	.304	9.51	2.85
Reynoso, Ryne	L-R	6-2	215	3-15-85	2	2	5.40	14	0	0	0	57	76	41	34	3	26	40	.329	.348	.311	6.35	4.13
Saito, Takashi	R-R	6-2	200	2-14-70	0	0	0.00	1	1	0	0	1	1	0	0	0	1	1	.333	.500	.000	9.00	9.00
Venters, Jonny	L-L	6-3	195	3-20-85	1	0	1.35	2	1	0	0	7	4	1	1	0	1	6	.167	.125	.188	8.10	1.35

Fielding

Catcher	PCT	G	PO	A	E	DP	PB
Boscan	.997	66	536	37	2	2	5
Mercado	1.000	3	20	1	0	0	1
Sammons	.998	75	559	56	1	3	7

First Base	PCT	G	PO	A	E	DP
Canizares	.993	34	256	34	2	22
Freeman	.994	111	907	74	6	93
Jones	1.000	1	8	0	0	2
Timmons	—	1	0	0	0	0

Second Base	PCT	G	PO	A	E	DP
Bolivar	.982	17	23	33	1	7
Hernandez	1.000	6	9	18	0	3
Holt	1.000	10	13	26	0	5
Prado	1.000	1	1	4	0	1
Thurston	.978	97	144	254	9	62
Timmons	.933	5	3	11	1	1
Young	.981	27	44	61	2	14

Third Base	PCT	G	PO	A	E	DP
Bolivar	.900	3	2	7	1	0
Glaus	.882	8	3	12	2	2
Hernandez	.667	3	0	2	1	0
Mercado	—	2	0	0	0	0
Nelson	1.000	5	2	12	0	3
Prado	—	1	0	0	0	0
Sammons	1.000	4	1	4	0	1
Thurston	.886	22	12	19	4	4
Timmons	.966	109	68	156	8	12

Shortstop	PCT	G	PO	A	E	DP
Bolivar	.921	36	42	75	10	20
Escobar	.909	1	3	7	1	2
Hernandez	.964	21	34	46	3	9
Hicks	.942	76	113	209	20	47
Thurston	.921	19	17	41	5	8

Outfield	PCT	G	PO	A	E	DP
Anderson	1.000	17	27	0	0	0
Blanco	1.000	41	78	8	0	0
Bolivar	1.000	2	4	0	0	0
Cabrera	.875	7	7	0	1	0
Clevlen	.960	51	93	4	4	2
Diaz	1.000	2	2	0	0	0
Holt	1.000	1	1	0	0	0
Jones	.976	80	119	5	3	1
McLouth	.988	33	82	1	1	0
Ramirez	.957	24	45	0	2	0
Richardson	.950	7	19	0	1	0
Romero	1.000	16	24	2	0	0
Schafer	.985	52	129	5	2	1
Taveras	1.000	15	23	1	0	0
Thurston	1.000	2	4	0	0	0
Young	.985	104	187	4	3	1

MISSISSIPPI BRAVES   DOUBLE-A

SOUTHERN LEAGUE

Batting	B-T	HT	WT	DOB	AVG	vLH	vRH	G	AB	R	H	2B	3B	HR	RBI	BB	HBP	SH	SF	SO	SB	CS	SLG	OBP
Anderson, Chris	R-R	6-0	210	10-27-85	.286	.167	.333	7	21	1	6	0	0	0	2	5	0	0	0	8	0	1	.286	.423
Bolivar, Luis	R-R	6-0	192	2-15-81	.277	.226	.289	47	159	22	44	6	2	3	17	13	2	1	0	41	5	4	.396	.339
Cabrera, Willie	R-R	5-11	185	8-3-86	.306	.283	.315	99	366	48	112	37	1	5	56	29	9	0	3	36	13	6	.454	.369
Colonel, Christian	R-R	6-2	210	12-25-81	.324	.455	.261	11	34	10	11	3	1	1	4	3	1	0	0	8	1	0	.559	.395
Daniel, Mike	L-R	6-3	180	8-17-84	.244	.309	.219	77	246	24	60	10	1	3	25	24	4	0	5	47	14	4	.329	.313
Duncan, Eric	L-R	6-3	210	12-7-84	.267	.214	.282	119	439	56	117	23	5	8	64	35	4	0	5	108	6	4	.396	.323
Gomez, Mauro	R-R	6-2	230	9-7-84	.281	.291	.277	133	495	67	139	42	2	16	80	46	10	0	8	122	1	2	.471	.349
Gomez, Yasser	L-L	5-9	170	4-1-80	.323	.406	.295	38	127	9	41	3	0	0	9	19	0	0	0	9	1	3	.346	.411
Gonzalez, Juan	B-R	6-0	210	2-23-82	.206	.286	.164	34	102	7	21	4	0	0	12	14	4	1	1	26	0	0	.245	.322
Gress, Randy	R-R	6-3	180	12-6-84	.250	.217	.260	39	96	13	24	4	0	2	6	11	2	3	0	26	0	1	.354	.339
Johnson, Cody	L-R	6-4	240	8-18-88	.189	.078	.220	75	233	26	44	6	0	10	31	25	1	0	1	114	9	5	.343	.269
Johnson, Benji	R-R	6-1	210	7-17-86	.079	.000	.111	13	38	4	3	1	0	0	1	7	2	0	0	15	0	0	.105	.255
Jones, Mycal	R-R	5-10	165	5-30-87	.200	.333	.143	7	30	5	6	0	1	2	5	1	0	2	0	9	1	0	.467	.226
Jones, Travis	R-R	5-9	190	11-10-85	.225	.316	.192	33	71	13	16	2	0	1	5	6	2	0	0	19	3	1	.296	.304
Linares, Donell	R-R	6-1	210	10-28-83	.240	.317	.214	109	417	48	100	19	1	11	47	14	10	3	3	41	2	1	.369	.279
Machado, Alejandro	B-R	6-0	185	4-26-82	.275	.391	.217	49	138	24	38	7	0	2	19	24	2	5	2	21	2	2	.370	.386
McGill, Shawn	R-R	6-4	195	2-29-84	.313	.400	.273	13	48	5	15	5	0	1	12	2	0	1	0	8	3	0	.479	.340
Mercado, Orlando	R-R	5-9	220	3-13-85	.286	.250	.295	84	262	30	75	9	0	0	20	39	1	0	3	38	3	2	.321	.377
Miles, Cole	B-R	5-8	165	3-24-87	.176	.250	.154	5	17	1	3	0	1	0	3	0	1	0	0	6	0	1	.294	.300
Nelson, Dan	B-R	5-11	180	2-12-84	.196	.273	.175	18	51	9	10	2	0	1	6	11	0	1	1	9	1	1	.294	.333
Pastornicky, Tyler	R-R	5-11	170	12-13-89	.254	.242	.257	38	134	22	34	5	2	2	15	16	1	7	2	22	11	2	.366	.333
Richardson, Antoan	R-R	5-8	165	10-8-83	.279	.269	.283	74	272	60	76	8	1	0	20	41	12	3	3	47	24	3	.316	.393
Rodriguez, Concepcion	R-R	6-2	205	9-19-86	.220	.208	.224	14	77	17	38	7	2	0	24	20	3	1	3	36	3	2	.283	.307
Romero, Alex	L-R	6-0	198	9-9-83	.279	.303	.273	43	165	25	46	8	1	1	19	20	1	2	2	14	1	2	.358	.356
Schafer, Jordan	L-L	6-1	200	9-4-86	.175	.118	.196	18	63	7	11	3	0	0	5	8	0	1	1	12	1	1	.222	.264
Sucre, Jesus	R-R	6-0	200	4-30-88	.297	.372	.265	38	145	20	43	11	1	2	12	10	1	1	1	29	0	0	.428	.301
Ware, L.V.	R-R	5-10	185	3-18-87	.360	.375	.353	7	25	5	9	2	1	0	3	2	2	0	0	3	0	0	.520	.448
Zazueta, Amadeo	B-R	5-10	160	1-31-86	.000	.000	.000	2	4	0	0	0	0	0	0	0	0	1	0	1	0	0	.000	.000

Pitching	B-T	HT	WT	DOB	W	L	ERA	G	GS	CG	SV	IP	H	R	ER	HR	BB	SO	AVG	vLH	vRH	K/9	BB/9
Abreu, Juan	R-R	6-0	180	4-8-85	4	2	3.02	39	0	0	11	45	41	18	15	2	22	47	.243	.256	.228	9.47	4.43
Beachy, Brandon	R-R	6-0	215	9-3-86	3	1	1.47	27	6	0	1	74	53	17	12	3	22	100	.200	.211	.190	12.22	2.69
Broadway, Mike	R-R	6-5	225	3-30-87	1	1	3.45	23	0	0	1	31	30	12	12	2	16	38	.252	.385	.149	10.91	4.60
Butts, Brett	R-R	6-1	205	4-24-86	0	1	1.52	15	0	0	3	24	18	5	4	0	6	28	.212	.194	.222	10.65	2.28
Castro, Yeliar	R-R	6-3	180	12-3-87	2	2	8.27	10	0	0	0	16	15	15	5	3	18	13	.254	.286	.208	7.16	9.92
Chapman, Jaye	R-R	6-0	180	5-22-87	1	4	5.19	36	1	0	0	50	60	35	29	1	25	53	.291	.350	.236	9.48	4.47
Cofield, Kyle	R-R	6-5	230	1-23-87	1	3	4.39	18	10	0	0	55	58	30	27	4	23	38	.264	.303	.231	6.18	3.74
Collins, Tim	L-L	5-7	155	8-21-89	0	0	1.13	6	0	0	2	8	4	1	1	1	3	14	.154	.143	.167	15.75	3.38
Cordier, Erik	R-R	6-4	230	2-25-86	11	7	3.71	25	21	0	0	136	116	61	56	3	69	113	.236	.241	.230	7.50	4.58
Delgado, Randall	R-R	6-3	165	2-9-90	3	5	4.74	8	8	0	0	44	36	26	23	2	20	42	.222	.221	.224	8.66	4.12
Diamond, Scott	L-L	6-3	215	7-30-86	4	3	3.52	17	17	0	0	102	113	45	40	4	39	90	.288	.237	.314	7.92	3.43
Gustafson, Tim	R-R	6-3	185	12-29-84	4	3	4.63	16	9	0	0	58	54	36	30	5	26	36	.249	.254	.242	5.55	4.01
Harris, Ty'Relle	R-R	6-4	235	12-12-86	0	0	1.46	4	1	0	1	12	6	3	2	0	6	11	.140	.167	.105	8.03	4.38
2-team total (4 Tennessee)					1	1	3.38	8	3	0	1	24	19	10	9	1	9	19	—	—		7.13	3.38
Hoover, J.J.	R-R	6-3	215	8-13-87	3	1	3.48	4	4	0	0	21	15	8	8	1	5	34	.203	.289	.111	14.81	6.53
Huber, Jon	R-R	6-2	195	7-7-81	0	0	3.38	3	0	0	0	3	1	1	1	0	2	1	.143	.200	.000	3.38	6.75
2-team total (36 Chattanooga)					3	3	2.30	39	0	0	0	47	37	15	12	2	13	49	—	—		9.38	2.49
Hyde, Lee	R-L	6-2	205	2-14-85	2	3	2.95	29	0	0	8	40	42	20	13	2	12	35	.271	.230	.298	7.94	2.72
Lyman, Jeff	R-R	6-3	225	1-14-87	0	0	9.00	1	0	0	0	2	1	1	0	0	1	0	.400	.000	.667	9.00	9.00
Marek, Stephen	L-R	6-2	230	9-3-83	4	0	0.00	11	0	0	4	13	7	0	0	0	1	18	.163	.176	.154	12.46	0.69
Minor, Mike	R-L	6-3	210	12-26-87	2	6	4.03	15	15	0	0	87	74	48	39	8	34	109	.233	.200	.247	11.28	3.52

	B-T	HT	WT	DOB	W	L	ERA	G	GS	CG	SV	IP	H	R	ER	HR	BB	SO	AVG	vLH	vRH	K/9	BB/9
Palica, Tommy	L-L	6-3	215	7-21-87	3	1	7.31	25	0	0	1	32	39	27	26	2	16	45	.298	.308	.293	12.66	4.50
Pruneda, Benino	R-R	5-9	170	8-8-88	0	4	3.63	25	0	0	0	35	30	16	14	2	23	49	.236	.227	.246	12.72	5.97
Resop, Chris	R-R	6-3	220	11-4-82	0	0	4.15	2	2	0	0	4	5	2	2	0	1	2	.294	.200	.429	4.15	2.08
Reynoso, Ryne	L-R	6-2	215	3-15-85	0	1	5.68	6	0	0	0	13	11	8	8	2	4	14	.224	.167	.258	9.95	2.84
Sullivan, Richard	L-L	6-3	235	4-14-87	4	11	5.09	36	13	0	2	120	140	81	68	10	40	91	.294	.263	.312	6.81	2.99
Teheran, Julio	R-R	6-2	150	1-27-91	3	2	3.38	7	7	0	0	40	29	15	15	2	17	38	.204	.205	.203	8.55	3.83
Thompson, Jacob	R-R	6-6	235	11-19-86	8	10	4.72	27	23	0	0	132	163	85	69	12	45	87	.301	.329	.272	5.95	3.08

Fielding

Catcher

	PCT	G	PO	A	E	DP	PB
Anderson	1.000	7	53	4	0	1	0
Johnson	1.000	13	109	11	0	2	1
McGill	.991	13	108	7	1	1	2
Mercado	.990	72	584	81	7	6	12
Sucre	.968	35	271	34	10	5	6
Machado	.990	23	45	53	1	14	
Nelson	.938	3	4	11	1	3	

First Base

	PCT	G	PO	A	E	DP
Duncan	.982	13	100	10	2	4
Gomez	.988	125	1038	69	13	90
Gress	1.000	1	2	0	0	0
Mercado	1.000	1	7	2	0	0

Second Base

	PCT	G	PO	A	E	DP
Bolivar	1.000	5	10	19	0	5
Duncan	.977	84	144	240	9	53
Gonzalez	.949	9	14	23	2	5
Gress	1.000	1	1	1	0	0
Jones	.984	19	28	35	1	7

Third Base

	PCT	G	PO	A	E	DP
Bolivar	.750	4	2	1	1	0
Colonel	1.000	10	12	8	0	2
Duncan	.950	10	4	15	1	1
Gonzalez	1.000	2	0	2	0	0
Gress	1.000	1	2	1	0	0
Linares	.946	104	63	183	14	14
Machado	—	1	0	0	0	0
Mercado	1.000	2	2	1	0	0
Nelson	1.000	9	11	21	0	2
Sucre	1.000	1	0	1	0	0

Shortstop

	PCT	G	PO	A	E	DP
Bolivar	.921	34	52	99	13	23
Gonzalez	.879	17	22	36	8	11
Gress	.917	28	33	67	9	13
Jones	.889	7	11	13	3	4
Machado	.931	16	16	38	4	6
Nelson	1.000	3	3	4	0	0
Pastornicky	.964	37	44	91	5	24
Zazueta	.778	1	5	2	2	0

Outfield

	PCT	G	PO	A	E	DP
Cabrera	.976	92	157	8	4	2
Daniel	.971	62	98	3	3	1
Duncan	1.000	3	2	0	0	0
Gomez	.963	33	49	3	2	0
Johnson	.933	57	94	4	7	1
Richardson	1.000	73	161	2	0	1
Rodriguez	.965	37	52	3	2	0
Romero	.966	41	56	0	2	0
Schafer	1.000	17	27	3	0	0
Ware	1.000	7	13	1	0	1

MYRTLE BEACH PELICANS
CAROLINA LEAGUE

HIGH CLASS A

Batting	B-T	HT	WT	DOB	AVG	vLH	vRH	G	AB	R	H	2B	3B	HR	RBI	BB	HBP	SH	SF	SO	SB	CS	SLG	OBP
Anderson, Chris	R-R	6-0	210	10-27-85	.154	.000	.182	4	13	1	2	0	0	0	1	4	0	0	0	6	0	0	.154	.353
Avila, Gerardo	L-L	6-2	185	7-15-86	.230	.240	.225	41	152	20	35	6	1	7	22	17	0	1	0	49	1	2	.421	.308
Barba, Ryan	R-R	6-0	190	12-6-84	.170	.163	.174	36	112	5	19	7	0	0	5	4	3	1	1	17	3	0	.232	.217
Campusano, Yoel	R-R	5-11	200	12-14-86	.192	.289	.141	36	130	14	25	5	0	3	11	19	0	0	1	27	2	1	.300	.293
Culver, Calvin	R-R	6-0	220	10-7-88	.217	.196	.232	39	138	8	30	3	0	0	10	7	1	1	3	22	0	2	.239	.255
Curley, Chris	R-R	6-0	185	8-25-87	.357	.200	.444	4	14	1	5	1	1	0	0	1	0	0	0	3	0	1	.571	.400
Daniel, Mike	L-R	6-3	180	8-17-84	.143	.176	.125	11	49	1	7	2	0	0	2	2	0	1	0	10	0	1	.184	.176
Gosselin, Phil	R-R	6-1	190	10-3-88	.154	.111	.176	6	26	2	4	1	1	0	0	0	0	0	0	7	0	0	.269	.154
Gress, Randy	R-R	6-3	180	12-6-84	.167	.000	.333	3	6	1	1	0	0	0	0	2	0	0	0	3	0	0	.167	.375
Harrilchak, Cory	L-L	5-10	175	10-27-87	.269	.224	.281	58	234	29	63	16	5	2	25	21	1	1	2	45	4	4	.406	.329
Johnson, Cody	L-R	6-4	240	8-18-88	.264	.091	.362	25	91	12	24	4	0	6	25	10	0	0	1	29	2	2	.505	.333
Jones, Michael	L-R	6-2	195	6-14-85	.282	.245	.298	97	372	40	105	20	0	5	47	34	2	0	4	80	1	7	.376	.342
Jones, Mycal	R-R	5-10	165	5-30-87	.269	.329	.249	69	275	51	74	19	1	7	22	31	7	2	3	66	15	4	.422	.354
Jones, Travis	R-R	5-9	190	11-10-85	.225	.196	.240	43	151	25	34	8	0	6	23	23	2	1	3	39	3	1	.397	.330
Kennelly, Matt	R-R	6-1	180	3-21-89	.226	.233	.215	76	261	26	59	11	1	7	26	27	0	2	1	42	1	4	.356	.298
Kreke, Jordan	R-R	6-1	205	5-21-87	.226	.348	.178	48	164	22	37	7	1	2	15	27	2	2	1	36	1	3	.317	.323
Marval, Osman	B-R	6-1	185	11-26-86	.286	.214	.310	20	56	6	16	4	0	1	7	1	0	1	0	9	0	0	.411	.298
McGill, Shawn	R-R	6-4	195	2-29-84	.154	.500	.091	6	13	2	2	0	0	0	1	1	1	0	0	6	0	0	.154	.267
Miles, Cole	B-R	5-8	165	3-24-87	.251	.279	.240	108	374	52	94	7	9	0	26	35	5	14	1	75	27	11	.318	.323
Milligan, Adam	L-R	6-3	210	3-14-88	.200	.033	.291	21	85	13	17	3	0	4	8	9	0	0	0	35	2	0	.376	.277
Moody, Shayne	R-R	6-0	200	10-24-84	.241	.148	.283	23	87	15	21	2	0	1	9	11	1	1	0	12	0	1	.299	.298
Nelson, Dan	R-R	6-0	180	2-12-84	.281	.259	.291	72	270	47	76	18	0	9	46	31	1	2	3	42	4	4	.448	.354
2-team total (17 Potomac)					.278	—	—	89	331	59	92	20	0	11	56	40	3	2	4	55	6	4	.438	.357
Rodriguez, Geraldo	R-R	6-1	195	10-25-87	.253	.242	.258	85	320	50	81	15	4	13	53	26	4	0	6	110	5	5	.447	.312
Santamaria, Jahdiel	R-R	6-3	170	4-5-87	.100	.083	.111	9	30	2	3	0	0	1	2	1	0	0	0	7	0	0	.200	.129
Schlehuber, Braeden	R-R	6-2	205	1-7-88	.115	.105	.118	27	87	9	10	1	1	2	6	3	4	2	2	0	12	0	.218	.172
Shehan, Chris	R-R	6-0	205	5-5-87	.181	.200	.170	22	72	5	13	1	2	0	3	9	1	3	1	17	3	0	.250	.277
Sime, Samuel	R-R	6-2	180	4-20-87	.258	.289	.243	98	357	33	92	13	1	7	42	21	0	2	1	83	10	3	.359	.298
Sucre, Jesus	R-R	6-0	200	4-30-88	.220	.229	.215	48	191	14	42	9	0	5	22	7	1	1	0	26	1	0	.346	.251
Sumoza, Luis	R-R	6-0	170	7-15-88	.219	.235	.213	81	278	23	61	11	4	2	24	22	2	2	2	82	6	3	.309	.280
Ware, L.V.	R-R	5-10	185	3-18-87	.253	.288	.240	76	233	36	59	9	4	3	21	17	7	7	3	62	11	8	.365	.319
Zazueta, Amadeo	B-R	5-10	160	1-31-86	.163	.138	.175	23	92	7	15	4	0	2	7	12	2	1	2	11	2	0	.272	.189

Pitching	B-T	HT	WT	DOB	W	L	ERA	G	GS	CG	SV	IP	H	R	ER	HR	BB	SO	AVG	vLH	vRH	K/9	BB/9
Abreu, Juan	R-R	6-0	180	4-8-85	0	0	8.22	8	0	0	1	15	14	14	14	5	8	15	.241	.278	.182	8.80	4.70
Avilan, Luis	L-L	6-2	165	7-19-89	4	3	3.94	31	0	0	9	48	42	25	21	5	18	37	.240	.226	.246	6.94	3.38
Berryhill, Thomas	R-R	5-10	185	12-9-87	2	2	7.71	10	0	0	0	14	19	12	12	1	7	14	.339	.444	.289	9.00	4.50
Castro, Yeliar	R-R	6-3	180	12-3-87	5	2	3.49	29	2	0	0	59	45	30	23	0	36	60	.211	.213	.210	9.10	5.46
Chapman, Jaye	R-R	6-0	180	5-22-87	0	1	5.68	10	0	0	2	13	10	8	8	1	7	21	.208	.077	.364	14.92	4.97
Clemens, Paul	R-R	6-4	170	2-14-88	0	4	3.69	27	8	0	2	76	83	46	31	5	28	65	.275	.218	.315	7.73	3.33
Crim, Matt	L-L	6-0	195	8-14-87	7	11	4.87	29	23	1	0	150	180	101	81	15	59	86	.300	.252	.314	5.17	3.55
Delgado, Randall	R-R	6-3	165	2-9-90	4	7	2.76	20	20	0	0	117	89	46	36	7	32	120	.210	.228	.195	9.20	2.45
Francis, David	R-R	6-1	200	2-8-88	2	3	4.31	21	0	0	0	40	49	22	19	2	14	29	.304	.242	.347	6.58	4.99
Harris, Ty'Relle	R-R	6-4	235	12-12-86	1	2	3.71	17	0	0	1	27	23	11	11	0	12	37	.232	.231	.233	12.49	4.05

Player	B-T	HT	WT	DOB	W	L	ERA	G	GS	CG	SV	IP	H	R	ER	HR	BB	SO	AVG	vLH	vRH	K/9	BB/9
Hoover, J.J.	R-R	6-3	215	8-13-87	11	6	3.26	24	24	0	0	133	126	56	48	7	35	118	.245	.251	.238	8.01	2.37
Lorick, Jeff	L-L	6-0	195	12-18-87	0	0	0.00	1	0	0	0	2	1	0	0	0	0	2	.143	.333	.000	9.00	0.00
Lowey, Jason	R-R	5-11	180	12-26-84	1	0	0.00	6	0	0	0	8	5	0	0	0	0	16	.167	.167	.167	18.00	0.00
Oberholtzer, Brett	L-L	6-2	190	7-1-89	6	6	4.15	22	18	0	2	113	123	59	52	7	18	107	.279	.269	.282	8.55	1.44
Ortegano, Jose	L-L	6-1	175	8-5-87	2	4	5.14	7	7	0	0	28	41	20	16	3	7	14	.342	.308	.351	4.50	2.25
Palica, Tommy	L-L	6-3	215	7-21-87	0	0	2.28	16	0	0	1	28	24	8	7	3	9	26	.235	.259	.227	8.46	2.93
Paulino, Angelo	R-R	6-4	190	12-15-86	3	5	2.66	41	0	0	3	74	73	26	22	2	28	65	.261	.236	.280	7.87	3.39
Pope, Van	R-R	6-0	200	2-26-84	0	2	6.35	9	0	0	0	11	8	9	8	3	16	5	.190	.227	.150	3.97	12.71
Proctor, Scott	R-R	6-1	195	1-2-77	1	0	6.14	6	0	0	0	7	8	5	5	0	2	5	.267	.333	.200	6.14	2.45
Pruneda, Benino	R-R	5-9	170	8-8-88	1	1	2.70	20	0	0	5	30	25	14	9	0	14	44	.223	.262	.176	13.20	4.20
Rasmus, Cory	R-R	6-1	220	11-6-87	0	3	3.27	8	8	0	0	41	38	19	15	3	18	30	.247	.263	.237	6.53	3.92
Rodgers, Chad	L-L	6-3	185	11-23-87	1	8	4.73	33	0	0	2	46	45	31	24	0	27	37	.260	.314	.238	7.29	5.32
Rohrbough, Cole	L-L	6-3	205	5-23-87	0	3	10.80	7	4	0	0	27	21	20		4	11	16	.370	.500	.331	6.84	5.94
Spruill, Zeke	B-R	6-4	184	9-11-89	3	5	5.54	14	13	1	0	65	83	44	40	4	13	41	.310	.276	.338	5.68	1.80
Teheran, Julio	R-R	6-2	150	1-27-91	4	4	2.98	10	10	0	0	63	56	22	21	6	13	76	.233	.216	.246	10.80	1.85
Vizcaino, Arodys	R-R	6-0	189	11-13-90	0	0	4.61	3	3	0	0	14	16	9	7	1	3	11	.296	.333	.238	7.24	1.98
Wilson, Andrew	R-R	6-2	180	7-30-87	0	0	4.09	6	0	0	0	11	8	6	5	1	6	7	.235	.333	.200	5.73	4.91

Fielding

Catcher

Catcher	PCT	G	PO	A	E	DP	PB
Anderson	.973	4	34	2	1	1	1
Kennelly	.993	69	507	46	4	4	8
Marval	1.000	7	39	7	0	1	2
McGill	.973	4	34	2	1	1	0
Schlehuber	.986	27	186	18	3	1	0
Sucre	.979	35	288	38	7	2	4

First Base

First Base	PCT	G	PO	A	E	DP
Avila	.985	38	369	21	6	28
Jones	.991	86	718	46	7	68
Marval	1.000	6	16	3	0	2
Nelson	1.000	3	9	0	0	0
Rodriguez	.991	13	105	9	1	10

Second Base

Second Base	PCT	G	PO	A	E	DP
Barba	1.000	8	9	20	0	5
Campusano	.984	35	60	119	3	19
Gosselin	.900	5	9	18	3	5
Jones	.972	41	52	120	5	14
Kreke	.940	39	65	106	11	25
Miles	1.000	5	12	13	0	4
Nelson	.965	11	26	29	2	6
Sime	1.000	3	3	2	0	1

Third Base

Third Base	PCT	G	PO	A	E	DP
Curley	1.000	4	2	11	0	1
Gress	1.000	1	0	1	0	0
Kreke	1.000	2	2	5	0	1
Marval	1.000	2	0	1	0	0
Moody	.891	23	9	40	6	3
Nelson	.901	44	16	66	9	7
Sime	.911	73	43	141	18	8
Zazueta	1.000	2	0	4	0	1

Shortstop

Shortstop	PCT	G	PO	A	E	DP
Barba	.957	29	37	75	5	11
Gress	1.000	1	3	1	0	0
Jones	.940	67	114	169	18	47
Kreke	.968	7	7	23	1	3
Sime	.948	20	26	47	4	6
Zazueta	.961	22	33	66	4	16

Outfield

Outfield	PCT	G	PO	A	E	DP
Culver	.955	31	58	5	3	1
Daniel	.923	9	23	1	2	0
Harrilchak	.992	53	118	3	1	0
Johnson	.938	10	14	1	1	0
Miles	.974	86	144	6	4	1
Milligan	1.000	18	22	0	0	0
Nelson	1.000	4	4	0	0	0
Rodriguez	.990	50	92	8	1	1
Santamaria	.938	9	14	1	1	1
Shehan	.977	20	42	1	1	1
Sumoza	.970	75	157	7	5	2
Ware	.994	72	147	7	1	4

ROME BRAVES   LOW CLASS A

SOUTH ATLANTIC LEAGUE

Batting	B-T	HT	WT	DOB	AVG	vLH	vRH	G	AB	R	H	2B	3B	HR	RBI	BB	HBP	SH	SF	SO	SB	CS	SLG	OBP
Anderson, Chris	R-R	6-0	210	10-27-85	.143	.200	.125	8	21	3	3	0	0	0	0	1	1	1	0	12	1	0	.143	.217
Barba, Ryan	R-R	6-0	190	12-6-84	.667	.000	.667	1	3	0	2	0	0	0	0	0	0	0	0	0	0	1	.667	.667
Bethancourt, Christian	R-R	6-2	175	9-2-91	.251	.233	.257	108	399	31	100	19	2	3	34	14	2	0	5	62	11	3	.331	.276
Clevlen, Brent	R-R	6-1	205	10-27-83	.750	1.000	.667	1	4	1	3	0	0	0	0	0	0	0	0	0	0	0	.750	.750
Cunningham, Todd	B-B	6-0	200	3-20-89	.260	.253	.263	65	231	32	60	9	3	1	20	14	15	2	1	30	7	4	.338	.341
Curley, Chris	R-R	6-0	185	8-25-87	.214	.180	.228	61	206	23	44	5	4	3	23	9	4	2	1	38	0	1	.320	.259
Flores, Juan	R-R	6-2	190	10-2-86	.217	.344	.179	39	138	14	30	6	4	1	13	3	2	2	1	24	4	2	.341	.243
Gosselin, Phil	R-R	6-1	190	10-3-88	.294	.314	.285	57	214	26	63	9	3	2	24	25	3	1	1	51	7	3	.393	.374
Hanson, Jake	R-R	6-0	180	11-20-89	.208	.169	.223	85	279	27	58	15	3	3	28	19	6	2	2	111	9	4	.315	.271
Harrilchak, Cory	L-L	5-10	175	10-27-87	.306	.320	.302	60	219	31	67	10	3	1	22	24	4	1	3	24	18	11	.393	.380
Hefflinger, Robby	R-R	6-5	225	1-3-90	.245	.310	.223	77	282	28	69	19	0	6	53	25	0	0	4	85	2	5	.376	.302
Jones, Mycal	R-R	5-10	165	5-30-87	.261	.265	.260	53	199	27	52	12	0	6	34	11	2	3	4	48	6	3	.412	.301
Kleinknecht, Barrett	R-R	6-0	200	7-30-88	.158	.143	.167	6	19	2	3	2	0	0	0	1	1	0	0	1	3	0	.263	.238
Kramer, Matt	R-R	6-3	215	5-7-86	.178	.375	.135	12	45	0	8	3	0	0	2	0	0	1	0	15	0	1	.244	.174
Kreke, Jordan	R-R	6-1	205	5-21-87	.248	.233	.254	75	282	35	70	14	1	0	32	24	8	0	2	50	7	5	.305	.323
Leonard, Joe	R-R	6-5	215	8-26-88	.268	.314	.247	29	112	11	30	7	2	3	19	6	0	1	1	22	0	0	.446	.303
Lovett, Chris	R-R	6-0	180	12-21-88	.239	.250	.233	30	92	11	22	5	1	0	2	9	0	1	0	13	0	3	.315	.307
Marval, Osman	B-R	6-1	185	11-26-86	.234	.240	.232	34	107	10	25	5	0	1	10	8	1	1	1	18	0	0	.308	.291
Odreman, Alberto	R-R	6-3	210	3-12-89	.111	.000	.143	9	27	1	3	1	0	0	0	1	0	0	0	11	0	0	.148	.143
Query, Ryan	R-R	5-11	190	8-24-87	.111	.000	.200	3	9	0	1	0	0	0	0	0	0	0	0	2	0	0	.111	.111
Rauh, Bobby	R-R	6-0	172	11-25-87	.193	.190	.194	32	83	13	16	3	0	0	3	11	1	3	1	24	5	3	.229	.292
Rose, Kyle	R-R	6-0	165	5-24-89	.259	.216	.275	87	321	52	83	7	3	0	21	28	7	5	1	69	26	23	.299	.331
Salcedo, Edward	B-R	6-3	195	7-30-91	.197	.292	.166	54	193	23	38	5	4	2	16	11	0	4	1	56	6	5	.295	.239
Schafer, Jordan	L-L	6-1	200	9-4-86	.273	.429	.200	6	22	4	6	2	0	0	1	4	0	0	0	5	2	1	.364	.385
Schlehuber, Braeden	R-R	6-2	205	1-7-88	.221	.233	.216	48	154	17	34	6	0	1	15	6	8	3	2	20	2	2	.279	.282
Spanjer-Furstenburg, Riaan	R-R	6-2	235	2-8-88	.266	.293	.253	62	229	26	61	13	1	2	22	19	4	0	1	41	0	2	.358	.332
Terdoslavich, Joey	R-R	6-2	190	9-9-88	.316	.300	.322	21	79	7	25	9	0	0	10	5	1	0	0	18	0	0	.430	.365
Ware, L.V.	R-R	5-10	185	3-18-87	.222	.231	.218	38	126	20	28	4	1	1	8	6	6	1	1	27	16	4	.294	.298
Weaver, Matt	R-R	6-0	175	1-27-90	.267	.309	.250	100	345	27	92	20	3	2	37	19	4	8	2	86	4	9	.359	.311
Whitmer, Jace	R-R	6-4	225	12-18-87	.273	.235	.284	43	150	16	41	10	1	2	17	5	4	1	0	23	1	0	.393	.314
Wiley, Derek	R-R	6-4	217	4-9-87	.250	.308	.200	8	28	2	7	1	0	0	2	1	0	0	0	8	0	1	.286	.276

Pitching	B-T	HT	WT	DOB	W	L	ERA	G	GS	CG	SV	IP	H	R	ER	HR	BB	SO	AVG	vLH	vRH	K/9	BB/9
Acord, Dalton	R-R	6-3	210	3-10-90	0	0	5.09	11	0	0	2	18	15	10	10	2	6	17	.224	.242	.206	8.66	3.06
Avilan, Luis	L-L	6-2	165	7-19-89	2	1	2.61	10	0	0	0	21	15	8	6	1	9	21	.203	.208	.200	9.15	3.92
Berryhill, Thomas	R-R	5-10	185	12-9-87	3	1	3.80	31	0	0	5	45	51	29	19	0	15	30	.276	.308	.252	6.00	3.00
Brewer, Caleb	R-R	6-3	205	2-2-89	3	2	4.65	9	9	0	0	41	42	24	21	4	26	24	.273	.229	.310	5.31	5.75
Clemens, Paul	R-R	6-4	170	2-14-88	2	0	1.42	8	0	0	1	19	11	5	3	1	8	16	.164	.167	.162	7.58	3.79
DeVall, Brett	R-L	6-3	215	1-8-90	7	9	4.39	19	19	1	0	107	134	74	52	5	28	71	.309	.306	.310	5.99	2.36
Estevez, Wilton	R-R	6-1	175	5-30-87	1	2	6.87	27	0	0	0	37	50	37	28	1	37	29	.342	.316	.360	7.12	9.08
Figueroa, Steven	R-R	6-0	215	5-1-88	0	2	6.52	5	0	0	0	10	10	10	7	1	3	5	.238	.231	.241	4.66	2.79
Fouch, Matt	L-L	6-1	185	11-22-87	0	0	0.00	4	0	0	1	5	3	0	0	0	0	3	.167	.167	.167	5.40	0.00
Francis, David	R-R	6-1	200	2-8-88	0	2	2.83	17	0	0	4	29	23	14	9	1	10	21	.228	.286	.197	6.59	3.14
Hale, David	R-R	6-2	200	9-27-87	5	8	4.13	28	7	0	5	94	97	52	43	1	44	69	.268	.250	.280	6.63	4.23
Harris, Ty'Relle	R-R	6-4	235	12-12-86	0	0	2.53	9	0	0	4	11	9	3	3	0	4	12	.231	.250	.222	10.13	3.38
Jurik, Dan	R-R	6-3	200	6-18-87	1	1	2.12	3	3	0	0	17	12	7	4	2	4	11	.190	.227	.171	5.82	2.12
Kempf, Willie	R-R	6-0	195	9-30-87	4	2	2.06	7	4	0	1	35	30	9	8	1	6	31	.229	.190	.260	7.97	1.54
Kent, Steve	L-L	6-0	200	5-8-89	2	0	0.69	19	3	0	1	39	27	4	3	1	8	54	.180	.171	.183	12.36	1.83
Lopez, Robinson	R-R	6-2	190	3-2-91	3	8	4.37	24	16	0	0	93	84	51	45	5	43	70	.241	.252	.232	6.80	4.18
Lorick, Jeff	L-L	6-0	195	12-18-87	3	6	2.32	26	4	0	4	50	42	25	13	2	21	41	.227	.128	.261	7.33	3.75
Masters, Chris	L-L	6-0	225	10-1-87	3	11	4.30	27	26	0	0	136	134	80	65	14	52	123	.256	.231	.263	8.14	3.44
Mertins, Kyle	R-R	6-2	220	2-4-88	0	2	4.82	9	0	0	0	19	20	12	10	3	6	16	.270	.257	.282	7.71	2.89
Northcraft, Aaron	R-R	6-4	225	5-28-90	1	3	8.16	4	3	0	0	14	21	18	13	1	15	8	.328	.345	.314	5.02	9.42
Oberholtzer, Brett	L-L	6-2	190	7-1-89	0	2	1.96	4	4	0	0	23	22	7	5	1	5	19	.262	.333	.222	7.43	1.96
Perez, Carlos	L-L	6-2	195	11-20-91	0	1	3.86	2	2	0	0	7	8	9	3	1	3	4	.267	.444	.190	5.14	3.86
Rasmus, Cory	R-R	6-1	220	11-6-87	6	6	3.14	20	12	0	1	83	77	39	29	6	29	72	.242	.283	.215	7.81	3.14
Stovall, Tyler	L-L	6-1	180	12-27-89	0	0	9.00	6	0	0	0	8	8	9	8	0	8	5	.286	.556	.158	5.63	9.00
Surinach, Julio	R-R	6-1	157	7-29-88	0	2	3.53	24	0	0	2	43	37	22	17	3	26	34	.234	.242	.229	7.06	5.40
Teheran, Julio	R-R	6-2	150	1-27-91	2	2	1.14	7	7	0	0	39	23	8	5	1	10	45	.168	.125	.191	10.30	2.29
Vizcaino, Arodys	R-R	6-0	189	11-13-90	9	4	2.39	14	14	0	0	72	63	25	19	1	9	68	.229	.208	.243	8.54	1.13
Weber, Ryan	R-R	6-0	170	8-12-90	2	5	5.13	18	0	0	0	60	74	45	34	5	14	39	.312	.345	.282	5.88	2.11
Wilson, Andrew	R-R	6-2	180	7-30-87	0	0	2.61	24	0	0	1	41	33	12	12	1	16	29	.223	.169	.258	6.31	3.48

Fielding

Catcher	PCT	G	PO	A	E	DP	PB
Anderson	.974	8	32	5	1	0	0
Bethancourt	.981	80	536	77	12	6	15
Kramer	1.000	2	19	1	0	0	0
Marval	.987	10	69	9	1	0	0
Query	1.000	3	15	1	0	0	1
Schlehuber	.976	38	252	34	7	2	1
Whitmer	.985	10	61	3	1	0	1

First Base	PCT	G	PO	A	E	DP
Hanson	.889	1	8	0	1	1
Hefflinger	.992	14	123	3	1	13
Kramer	1.000	9	83	1	0	4
Marval	.980	18	141	8	3	12
Odreman	1.000	8	61	2	0	8
Spanjer-Furstenburg	.979	53	436	26	10	37
Terdoslavich	.955	3	19	2	1	0
Weaver	1.000	3	21	3	0	1
Whitmer	.977	31	250	10	6	18

Second Base	PCT	G	PO	A	E	DP
Wiley	.959	8	68	2	3	4
Barba	1.000	1	1	5	0	0
Curley	.977	16	30	55	2	8
Gosselin	.976	53	101	141	6	30
Kleinknecht	.941	6	6	10	1	0
Lovett	.898	11	21	23	5	6
Weaver	.953	57	91	152	12	34

Third Base	PCT	G	PO	A	E	DP
Curley	.932	35	27	69	7	8
Hanson	1.000	1	1	0	0	0
Kreke	.927	53	39	100	11	9
Leonard	.871	12	9	18	4	3
Lovett	.851	13	11	29	7	0
Marval	1.000	3	2	7	0	0
Terdoslavich	.872	18	11	23	5	3
Weaver	.889	7	2	6	1	0

Shortstop	PCT	G	PO	A	E	DP
Curley	.913	4	9	12	2	0
Jones	.901	51	73	128	22	24
Kreke	.947	20	29	60	5	13
Salcedo	.896	52	73	167	28	27
Weaver	.908	12	19	40	6	11

Outfield	PCT	G	PO	A	E	DP
Clevlen	.500	1	1	0	1	0
Cunningham	.980	62	140	7	3	0
Flores	.913	35	76	8	8	1
Hanson	.954	76	122	3	6	0
Harrilchak	.960	54	112	7	5	2
Hefflinger	.984	40	61	0	1	0
Rauh	.984	31	60	1	1	0
Rose	.953	81	162	1	8	0
Schafer	1.000	6	14	0	0	0
Ware	1.000	35	56	0	0	0
Weaver	.970	20	31	1	1	1

DANVILLE BRAVES   ROOKIE
APPALACHIAN LEAGUE

Batting	B-T	HT	WT	DOB	AVG	vLH	vRH	G	AB	R	H	2B	3B	HR	RBI	BB	HBP	SH	SF	SO	SB	CS	SLG	OBP
Brooks, Robert	R-R	6-1	180	5-29-88	.077	.000	.111	4	13	0	1	0	1	0	2	0	1	0	0	3	0	0	.231	.143
Brownsten, Cory	R-R	6-0	210	6-3-88	.750	.000	.750	1	4	3	3	2	0	0	5	0	0	0	0	0	0	0	1.250	.750
Curley, Chris	R-R	6-0	185	8-25-87	.250	.400	.000	3	8	2	2	0	1	0	0	0	0	0	0	2	0	0	.500	.250
Dalfonso, Jakob	L-R	6-3	200	1-25-90	.301	.161	.336	50	153	24	46	6	2	1	16	11	13	0	0	19	4	2	.386	.395
De Los Santos, Fernando	R-R	6-1	180	1-18-90	.000	.000	.000	1	3	0	0	0	0	0	0	1	0	0	0	0	0	0	.000	.250
Delgado, Ryan	R-R	5-11	215	1-11-90	.301	.217	.336	45	153	26	46	14	0	6	24	9	3	0	1	28	0	0	.510	.349
Falcon, Daniel	R-R	6-1	220	12-27-88	.206	.348	.133	21	68	7	14	3	1	3	11	1	2	0	0	15	1	0	.412	.239
Fleming, Kenny	L-L	6-1	185	9-14-89	.226	.243	.221	53	168	19	38	5	5	0	19	7	3	1	2	37	7	4	.315	.267
Fleming, Kurt	B-R	5-11	193	8-30-91	.333	.000	.500	4	9	2	3	1	0	0	0	0	0	1	0	1	0	0	.444	.333
Flores, Juan	R-R	6-2	190	10-2-86	.333	.250	.400	8	36	6	12	2	0	0	4	1	0	0	0	8	1	0	.389	.351
Frierson, Jarred	B-R	5-11	185	3-23-87	.291	.250	.320	33	86	15	25	3	3	1	8	10	1	0	0	20	2	2	.430	.351
Gattis, Evan	R-R	6-4	230	8-18-86	.288	.406	.241	60	222	33	64	10	0	4	29	6	12	0	2	44	0	0	.387	.339
Kleinknecht, Barrett	R-R	6-0	200	7-30-88	.301	.351	.276	53	219	33	66	17	0	5	35	5	3	0	2	25	6	3	.447	.323
Leonard, Joe	R-R	6-5	215	8-26-88	.278	.167	.300	10	36	6	10	2	0	1	5	3	0	0	0	7	0	0	.417	.333
Linger, Jim	R-R	5-11	195	9-6-90	.200	.000	.250	3	10	1	2	0	0	1	1	0	0	0	0	0	0	0	.200	.273
Lipka, Matt	R-R	6-1	180	4-15-92	.125	.000	.143	4	16	1	2	0	0	0	1	2	0	1	0	1	1	0	.125	.176
Mowry, Jason	L-L	5-11	180	10-16-89	.223	.233	.218	55	193	20	43	8	2	2	20	18	0	1	3	29	3	6	.316	.285
Odreman, Alberto	R-R	6-3	210	3-12-89	.225	.191	.262	33	89	10	20	6	1	2	12	9	0	0	0	25	1	0	.382	.296
Query, Ryan	R-R	5-11	190	8-24-87	.250	.167	.500	2	8	0	2	1	0	0	0	0	0	0	0	4	1	0	.375	.250

Batting	B-T	HT	WT	DOB	AVG	vLH	vRH	G	AB	R	H	2B	3B	HR	RBI	BB	HBP	SH	SF	SO	SB	CS	SLG	OBP
Rauh, Bobby	R-R	6-0	172	11-25-87	.321	.294	.333	20	56	15	18	3	0	2	8	8	0	2	0	13	3	1	.482	.406
Reyes, Elmer	R-R	5-11	150	11-26-90	.294	.242	.318	53	194	27	57	15	2	5	24	7	10	0	2	36	2	3	.469	.347
Rohm, David	R-R	6-3	215	1-22-90	.319	.375	.289	17	69	10	22	6	0	0	9	3	1	0	2	9	2	0	.406	.347
Simmons, Andrelton	R-R	6-2	170	9-4-89	.276	.233	.301	62	239	36	66	11	1	2	26	16	9	1	4	14	18	4	.356	.340
Terdoslavich, Joey	B-R	6-1	200	9-9-88	.296	.228	.326	49	189	27	56	10	2	2	24	15	1	0	0	27	3	3	.402	.351
Whitmer, Jace	R-R	6-4	225	12-18-87	.278	.333	.250	22	72	7	20	4	0	1	11	6	5	1	2	9	0	1	.375	.365
Wiley, Keenan	L-L	6-0	175	4-27-87	.328	.333	.327	20	67	7	22	4	0	0	7	4	2	1	0	9	3	3	.388	.384

Pitching	B-T	HT	WT	DOB	W	L	ERA	G	GS	CG	SV	IP	H	R	ER	HR	BB	SO	AVG	vLH	vRH	K/9	BB/9
Acord, Dalton	R-R	6-3	210	3-10-90	2	1	2.79	11	0	0	3	19	15	6	6	0	15	32	.208	.235	.184	14.90	6.98
Alvarez, Danilo	R-R	6-0	210	1-14-90	0	0	16.88	2	0	0	0	3	5	5	5	0	3	4	.417	.500	.375	13.50	10.13
Farrell, Kyle	R-R	6-4	210	5-6-89	5	3	4.04	14	10	0	1	65	67	32	29	6	7	47	.265	.217	.292	6.54	0.97
Filak, Dave	R-R	6-4	220	11-24-89	0	2	2.42	10	8	0	0	26	18	7	7	1	11	27	.198	.222	.188	9.35	3.81
Foster, Stephen	L-L	6-0	170	3-4-87	0	0	0.00	1	0	0	0	2	1	0	0	0	1	2	.143	.000	.143	9.00	4.50
Fouch, Matt	L-L	6-1	185	11-22-87	0	0	0.00	2	0	0	0	4	0	0	0	0	1	7	.000	.000	.000	15.75	2.25
Hayes, Jamie	R-R	6-0	195	10-21-86	0	0	6.38	10	0	0	0	18	23	13	13	2	8	18	.303	.344	.273	8.84	3.93
Hess, Tyler	R-R	6-5	240	8-29-88	0	1	1.13	1	0	0	0	8	11	3	1	0	5	8	.324	.167	.357	9.00	5.63
Jurik, Dan	R-R	6-3	200	6-18-87	0	2	5.09	4	4	0	0	23	21	13	13	3	6	14	.247	.138	.304	5.48	2.35
Kempf, Willie	R-R	6-0	195	9-30-87	2	0	1.91	5	4	0	0	28	17	6	6	1	2	28	.177	.184	.172	8.89	0.64
LaPoint, Lucas	R-R	6-3	215	3-30-91	4	3	4.47	11	5	0	0	56	59	33	28	7	9	41	.272	.247	.285	6.55	1.44
Lewis, Matt	R-R	6-3	220	9-25-88	0	3	13.25	12	0	0	0	18	28	35	26	3	25	13	.359	.400	.333	6.62	12.74
Marshall, Ian	R-R	6-3	172	3-3-87	1	1	2.70	3	2	0	0	13	8	5	4	1	4	13	.178	.182	.176	8.78	2.70
Mertins, Kyle	R-R	6-2	220	2-4-88	0	1	3.86	7	0	0	0	12	7	6	5	0	5	5	.189	.067	.273	3.86	3.86
Mora, Edigson	R-R	6-1	195	10-20-87	0	2	4.55	12	0	0	2	28	28	16	14	3	14	25	.267	.250	.279	8.13	4.55
Northcraft, Aaron	R-R	6-5	225	5-28-90	6	1	2.73	10	9	0	0	53	44	18	16	1	9	38	.228	.215	.237	6.49	1.54
Pacheco, Ronan	L-L	6-6	170	7-29-88	4	6	5.62	14	11	0	2	58	72	42	36	0	18	59	.308	.310	.307	9.21	2.81
Perez, Carlos	L-L	6-2	195	11-20-91	2	0	1.13	6	0	0	0	32	20	8	4	0	14	27	.185	.227	.174	7.59	3.94
Russ, Nate	R-R	5-11	180	8-30-86	0	0	1.13	6	0	0	2	8	3	1	1	0	3	5	.120	.000	.188	5.63	3.38
Shreve, Chase	L-L	6-3	180	7-12-90	2	0	2.25	8	0	0	1	16	16	5	4	1	3	20	.267	.167	.278	11.25	1.69
Sims, Blaine	L-L	6-0	185	3-10-89	0	3	4.19	5	2	0	0	19	23	9	9	2	4	10	.303	.182	.323	4.66	1.86
Stovall, Tyler	L-L	6-1	180	12-27-89	1	0	2.70	12	0	0	0	23	17	13	7	1	19	22	.210	.200	.213	8.49	7.33
Suschak, Matt	R-R	6-4	205	12-27-88	2	3	6.07	16	0	0	4	30	33	25	20	0	19	30	.282	.326	.257	9.10	5.76
Weber, Ryan	R-R	6-0	170	8-12-90	3	2	2.81	8	6	0	0	42	32	14	13	4	3	36	.212	.237	.196	7.78	0.65
Winnie, Dan	R-R	6-4	225	3-28-90	0	0	0.00	1	0	0	0	2	1	0	0	0	0	1	.143	.333	.000	4.50	0.00

Fielding

Catcher	PCT	G	PO	A	E	DP	PB
Brownsten	1.000	1	10	2	0	0	0
Delgado	1.000	17	104	24	0	3	4
Gattis	.986	35	253	34	4	0	7
Query	.923	2	12	0	1	0	0
Whitmer	1.000	19	118	20	0	0	7

First Base	PCT	G	PO	A	E	DP
Dalfonso	.986	24	196	10	3	26
Odreman	.992	24	227	12	2	19
Terdoslavich	.967	30	285	12	10	25

Second Base	PCT	G	PO	A	E	DP
Brooks	.917	3	3	8	1	3
Curley	1.000	1	1	3	0	1

	PCT	G	PO	A	E	DP
De Los Santos	1.000	1	1	4	0	0
Frierson	.977	12	14	28	1	5
Kleinknecht	.971	8	11	23	1	10
Linger	.947	3	6	12	1	1
Reyes	.983	48	81	154	4	29

Third Base	PCT	G	PO	A	E	DP
Dalfonso	1.000	4	0	1	0	0
Kleinknecht	.942	41	33	81	7	10
Leonard	.889	10	7	17	3	1
Terdoslavich	.900	18	7	38	5	3

Shortstop	PCT	G	PO	A	E	DP
Kleinknecht	.917	3	3	8	1	3
Lipka	1.000	1	1	6	0	0

	PCT	G	PO	A	E	DP
Reyes	1.000	8	4	18	0	5
Simmons	.974	62	101	231	9	47

Outfield	PCT	G	PO	A	E	DP
Dalfonso	1.000	14	27	1	0	0
Falcon	.897	21	23	3	3	1
Fleming	1.000	51	58	5	0	0
Fleming	1.000	2	2	0	0	0
Flores	.917	8	10	1	1	0
Frierson	.969	20	30	1	1	0
Mowry	1.000	52	82	6	0	1
Rauh	1.000	20	27	0	0	0
Rohm	1.000	17	20	1	0	1
Terdoslavich	—	1	0	0	0	0
Wiley	.974	20	36	1	1	0

GCL BRAVES — ROOKIE

GULF COAST LEAGUE

Batting	B-T	HT	WT	DOB	AVG	vLH	vRH	G	AB	R	H	2B	3B	HR	RBI	BB	HBP	SH	SF	SO	SB	CS	SLG	OBP
Beckwith, William	R-L	6-2	220	8-19-90	.243	.286	.224	21	70	8	17	4	0	2	18	12	2	0	1	13	4	0	.386	.365
Brownsten, Cory	R-R	6-0	210	6-3-88	.287	.200	.311	34	94	17	27	3	2	2	14	16	3	1	0	11	1	1	.426	.407
Cadette, Victor	R-R	6-0	180	12-6-90	.225	.214	.228	48	151	18	34	5	1	2	16	16	1	1	0	34	7	2	.311	.304
Contreras, Luis	L-L	6-0	170	3-31-91	.273	.000	.375	5	11	4	3	0	1	0	3	1	0	0	1	2	0	0	.455	.308
De Los Santos, Fernando	R-R	6-1	180	1-18-90	.250	.321	.232	49	140	20	35	7	2	0	8	10	3	1	0	35	2	3	.329	.314
De Los Santos, Ramon	R-R	6-0	190	12-26-89	.157	.316	.098	26	70	9	11	3	0	2	6	3	2	0	0	16	1	1	.286	.213
Drury, Brandon	R-R	6-2	190	8-21-92	.198	.205	.196	52	192	20	38	7	1	3	17	9	4	1	1	50	2	2	.292	.248
Falcon, Daniel	R-R	6-1	220	12-27-88	.271	.222	.283	34	133	18	36	9	0	3	18	6	0	0	0	28	9	0	.406	.302
Fleming, Kurt	B-R	5-11	193	8-30-91	.262	.306	.250	44	164	23	43	4	2	4	15	9	3	0	0	20	8	4	.384	.313
Franco, Carlos	R-R	6-2	170	12-20-91	.123	.091	.130	23	65	9	8	1	0	2	5	8	4	0	1	24	1	0	.231	.256
Johnson, Cody	L-R	6-4	240	8-18-88	.250	.000	.278	6	20	5	5	0	0	2	4	2	0	0	0	8	1	1	.550	.318
Lipka, Matt	R-R	6-1	188	4-15-92	.302	.283	.308	48	192	33	58	8	4	1	24	14	3	0	1	22	20	3	.401	.357
Marin, Ivan	R-R	5-9	140	12-21-88	.297	.222	.326	32	64	13	19	2	0	1	9	7	1	0	0	15	3	2	.375	.375
Pigott, Jonathan	R-R	6-2	200	10-25-87	.333	.556	.250	14	33	3	11	3	0	0	3	2	1	1	0	7	0	0	.424	.389
Query, Ryan	R-R	5-11	190	8-24-87	.246	.227	.250	28	82	11	20	3	1	5	16	1	1	0	0	18	0	1	.488	.262
Reyes, Elmer	R-R	5-11	150	11-26-90	.364	.444	.308	6	22	8	8	0	0	1	5	2	3	0	0	5	3	0	.500	.481
Rivera, Wilson	R-R	6-1	195	10-30-89	.219	.211	.221	51	151	15	33	7	3	1	17	15	6	0	0	37	6	4	.325	.310
Rohm, David	R-R	6-3	215	1-22-90	.320	.269	.347	19	75	10	24	3	1	1	15	8	0	0	0	7	1	1	.427	.386
Rose, Kyle	R-R	6-0	165	5-24-89	.500	.000	.600	4	12	2	6	1	0	0	1	2	6	0	0	0	1	3	.583	.538
Rowland, Brendan	R-R	6-3	185	4-7-88	.154	1.000	.120	9	26	2	4	1	0	0	2	3	1	0	2	6	0	0	.192	.250

	B-T	HT	WT	DOB	AVG	vLH	vRH	G	AB	R	H	2B	3B	HR	RBI	BB	HBP	SH	SF	SO	SB	CS	SLG	OBP
Sanchez, Alejandro	R-R	6-0	183	6-15-92	.174	.250	.133	13	23	5	4	0	1	0	2	2	0	0	0	4	2	0	.261	.240
Sanchez, Edison	R-R	6-4	195	11-1-90	.236	.227	.239	30	89	9	21	6	0	1	11	17	3	0	0	28	0	1	.337	.376
Spanjer-Furstenburg, Riaan	R-R	6-2	235	2-8-88	.286	.000	.667	2	7	0	2	1	0	0	1	0	0	0	0	1	0	0	.429	.286
Tsai, Meng	R-R	6-0	190	5-13-90	.000	.000	.000	3	4	0	0	0	0	0	0	0	0	0	0	2	0	0	.000	.000

Pitching

Pitching	B-T	HT	WT	DOB	W	L	ERA	G	GS	CG	SV	IP	H	R	ER	HR	BB	SO	AVG	vLH	vRH	K/9	BB/9
Alvarez, Danilo	R-R	6-0	210	1-14-90	1	1	2.21	14	0	0	0	20	12	5	5	0	5	19	.169	.136	.184	8.41	2.21
Burns, Jonathan	R-R	6-1	190	6-9-88	1	3	3.86	17	0	0	2	23	27	10	10	2	5	24	.290	.400	.224	9.26	1.93
Castillo, Eduardo	R-R	6-2	170	7-27-90	1	3	4.95	8	7	0	0	36	41	21	20	3	12	20	.297	.250	.338	4.95	2.97
Cofield, Kyle	R-R	6-5	230	1-23-87	0	1	6.00	2	2	0	0	3	4	2	2	0	1	3	.333	.000	.400	9.00	3.00
de Luna, Luis	R-R	6-4	200	6-18-90	2	0	3.30	9	4	0	1	30	34	13	11	1	9	21	.281	.263	.297	6.30	2.70
Foster, Stephen	L-L	6-0	170	3-4-87	2	1	3.65	15	0	0	0	25	24	10	10	2	10	17	.258	.207	.281	6.20	3.65
Gaxiola, Amilcar	L-L	6-2	170	10-27-90	2	3	3.95	16	0	0	0	27	24	15	12	3	7	26	.238	.267	.225	8.56	2.30
Hess, Tyler	R-R	6-5	240	8-29-88	2	3	5.92	9	3	0	1	24	19	17	16	2	11	23	.213	.184	.235	8.51	4.07
Jurik, Dan	R-R	6-3	200	6-18-87	3	0	2.20	7	5	0	0	29	23	10	7	0	5	27	.219	.244	.203	8.48	1.57
Kempf, Willie	R-R	6-0	195	9-30-87	2	0	0.00	3	1	0	0	11	6	0	0	3	12	.158	.000	.231	9.82	2.45
LaFreniere, Frank	R-R	6-5	185	6-2-90	0	0	1.93	5	0	0	0	9	8	3	2	0	1	5	.235	.000	.286	4.82	0.96
Lucas, Joe	R-R	6-5	190	4-23-89	0	1	0.00	3	0	0	0	5	1	0	0	2	3	.000	.000	.000	5.40	3.60
Marshall, Ian	R-R	6-3	172	3-3-87	3	2	5.03	10	7	0	0	39	50	27	22	5	8	26	.314	.297	.326	5.95	1.83
Mertins, Kyle	R-R	6-2	220	2-4-88	0	0	3.00	4	0	0	2	6	4	2	2	0	1	5	.182	.250	.143	7.50	1.50
Perez, Williams	R-R	6-0	183	5-21-91	0	6	5.63	12	11	0	0	54	66	36	34	3	8	43	.304	.295	.309	7.12	1.33
Pinto, Alexis	L-L	6-0	170	1-21-90	0	1	7.94	10	0	0	0	11	21	13	10	3	5	12	.404	.250	.472	9.53	3.97
Rohrbough, Cole	L-L	6-3	205	5-23-87	0	0	1.50	3	3	0	0	6	4	1	1	0	0	9	.182	.273	.091	13.50	0.00
Russ, Nate	R-R	5-11	180	8-30-86	0	0	4.22	10	0	0	3	11	12	7	5	1	4	10	.279	.400	.174	8.44	3.38
Sekiguchi, Shohei	L-L	6-6	225	4-14-89	1	1	3.77	8	0	0	0	14	17	8	6	1	3	10	.304	.316	.297	6.28	1.88
Silva, Ernesto	R-R	6-4	180	2-5-92	2	1	4.57	8	2	0	0	22	30	15	11	0	8	14	.337	.405	.288	5.82	3.32
Spruill, Zeke	B-R	6-4	184	9-11-89	0	0	3.00	2	2	0	0	3	4	1	1	0	1	1	.333	.333	.333	3.00	3.00
Tate, Richie	R-R	6-6	225	4-11-92	1	0	5.19	5	0	0	0	9	7	5	5	2	6	4	.233	.235	.231	4.15	6.23
Winnie, Dan	R-R	6-4	225	3-28-90	4	2	5.79	14	10	0	0	42	52	32	27	4	15	35	.306	.291	.319	7.50	3.21
Yamarin, Yoshinori	R-R	6-2	190	4-15-90	2	2	5.65	15	1	0	0	29	35	19	18	0	13	27	.307	.407	.217	8.48	4.08

Fielding

Catcher	PCT	G	PO	A	E	DP	PB
Brownsten	.983	34	196	31	4	4	1
De Los Santos	.981	19	92	9	2	0	4
Query	.991	20	105	6	1	0	2
Rowland	1.000	1	3	0	0	0	0
Tsai	1.000	2	2	3	0	0	0

First Base	PCT	G	PO	A	E	DP
Beckwith	.966	14	105	7	4	5
De Los Santos	1.000	6	48	1	0	4
Falcon	.978	22	161	19	4	10
Rohm	1.000	3	27	0	0	2
Sanchez	1.000	1	2	0	0	0
Sanchez	.986	21	138	5	2	9
Spanjer-Furstenburg	1.000	2	11	3	0	0

Second Base	PCT	G	PO	A	E	DP
Cadette	1.000	1	0	2	0	0
De Los Santos	.966	35	67	74	5	23
Marin	1.000	26	36	61	0	4
Pigott	1.000	1	1	0	0	0
Reyes	1.000	4	8	6	0	0
Sanchez	.895	8	9	8	2	1

Third Base	PCT	G	PO	A	E	DP
De Los Santos	1.000	6	1	6	0	0
Drury	.947	37	28	61	5	5
Franco	.939	15	8	23	2	1
Marin	—	1	0	0	0	0
Sanchez	.857	7	5	13	3	1

Shortstop	PCT	G	PO	A	E	DP
De Los Santos	.938	9	3	12	1	1

	PCT	G	PO	A	E	DP
Drury	1.000	9	14	28	0	4
Lipka	.934	41	48	108	11	11
Marin	1.000	3	3	8	0	1
Reyes	1.000	3	6	8	0	3

Outfield	PCT	G	PO	A	E	DP
Cadette	.963	43	75	3	3	1
Contreras	1.000	5	4	1	0	0
De Los Santos	—	1	0	0	0	0
Falcon	1.000	13	13	1	0	1
Fleming	.943	42	79	3	5	1
Johnson	1.000	6	10	1	0	0
Pigott	1.000	11	15	2	0	0
Query	1.000	4	2	1	0	0
Rivera	.988	49	78	2	1	1
Rohm	1.000	17	24	2	0	0
Rose	1.000	4	7	0	0	0

DSL BRAVES   ROOKIE
DOMINICAN SUMMER LEAGUE

Batting	B-T	HT	WT	DOB	AVG	vLH	vRH	G	AB	R	H	2B	3B	HR	RBI	BB	HBP	SH	SF	SO	SB	CS	SLG	OBP
Alcantara, Aris	R-R	6-2	170	5-5-90	.282	.268	.287	61	213	29	60	17	4	1	38	31	6	2	2	42	5	4	.413	.385
Caballero, Luis	R-R	6-2	165	7-8-92	.212	.273	.182	9	33	5	7	1	1	0	2	6	0	0	0	9	1	0	.303	.235
Castro, Daniel	R-R	5-11	170	11-14-92	.176	.105	.219	19	51	7	9	2	0	0	1	8	2	0	0	5	2	1	.216	.311
Daniel, Emmanuel	R-R	6-1	165	12-25-91	.138	.098	.153	45	159	14	22	4	0	1	15	11	6	5	3	37	2	1	.182	.218
Franco, Carlos	R-R	6-2	170	12-20-91	.218	.325	.176	37	142	8	31	4	1	2	19	18	1	0	1	31	3	0	.303	.309
Galvan, Deion	L-L	5-9	150	11-8-92	.128	.067	.156	29	47	5	6	1	0	0	2	8	0	1	0	12	3	4	.149	.255
Garcia, Hector	B-R	6-2	170	6-19-92	.260	.224	.273	59	192	28	50	4	2	1	11	23	2	4	0	57	16	6	.318	.346
Gimenez, Carlos	R-R	5-11	195	5-14-90	.170	.071	.205	20	53	7	9	1	0	1	4	6	2	4	1	13	1	0	.245	.274
Herrera, Elisaul	R-R	5-11	160	7-17-91	.229	.417	.167	16	48	6	11	0	0	1	5	2	3	0	0	6	0	0	.292	.302
Luna, Ronald	R-R	6-0	145	8-18-82	.315	.333	.307	54	213	32	67	5	0	0	20	17	5	4	2	24	7	3	.338	.376
Machado, Roberto	R-R	5-8	175	9-6-92	.000	.000	.000	1	1	0	0	0	0	0	0	1	0	0	0	0	0	0	.000	.500
Madrid, Luis	R-R	6-0	165	3-11-93	.175	.154	.185	13	40	3	7	0	0	3	3	3	0	0	0	10	2	1	.175	.283
Maldonado, Erick	R-R	6-1	170	6-17-93	.222	.182	.250	10	27	3	6	0	0	0	1	1	0	0	0	12	0	1	.222	.276
Marte, Felix	R-R	6-1	180	11-14-90	.269	.259	.273	58	208	25	56	17	3	6	24	26	3	1	1	74	3	3	.466	.357
Noboa, Michael	R-R	5-8	160	6-21-91	.143	.200	.125	13	42	3	6	1	0	0	1	4	1	1	0	9	4	1	.167	.234
Nunez, Anthony	R-R	6-3	205	2-2-90	.193	.091	.227	34	88	10	17	4	0	0	6	13	1	0	0	21	0	1	.239	.304
Peguero, Juan	R-R	6-2	215	10-17-91	.184	.200	.177	47	158	9	29	6	0	1	12	13	9	0	2	58	1	2	.241	.280
Ramirez, Luis	R-R	6-0	180	6-15-88	.111	.000	.135	14	45	4	5	2	0	0	4	5	0	0	0	9	0	0	.156	.184
Reyes, Gerardo	R-R	5-10	170	2-2-91	.301	.172	.351	59	206	36	62	13	0	0	27	15	13	7	2	32	20	9	.364	.381
Rijkhof, Ruben	R-R	6-1	215	4-25-92	.083	.000	.111	4	12	3	1	0	0	0	1	4	0	0	0	8	2	0	.083	.313
Salcedo, Edward	R-R	6-3	195	7-30-91	.297	.261	.314	23	74	16	22	5	1	1	11	18	3	0	0	19	8	1	.432	.453
Tovar, Bruno	R-R	6-1	165	5 4-91	.180	.167	.184	18	50	4	9	1	0	0	2	2	1	1	0	19	0	1	.200	.226
Velazquez, Victor	R-R	5-11	165	8-26-92	.048	.091	.000	7	21	0	1	0	0	0	1	3	0	0	0	8	0	0	.048	.167

Pitching

Pitching	B-T	HT	WT	DOB	W	L	ERA	G	GS	CG	SV	IP	H	R	ER	HR	BB	SO	AVG	vLH	vRH	K/9	BB/9
Briceno, Rafael	R-R	6-2	175	10-29-90	7	4	2.91	17	12	0	1	74	62	28	24	2	19	66	.229	.268	.215	7.99	2.30
Caicedo, Oriel	R-R	6-1	185	3-25-91	1	2	4.15	15	1	0	0	22	13	12	10	1	25	21	.173	.200	.164	8.72	10.38
Castillo, Eduardo	R-R	6-2	170	7-27-90	1	2	1.69	8	6	0	0	37	24	12	7	0	4	21	.179	.286	.118	5.06	0.96
Espinosa, Abraham	R-R	6-1	175	6-3-93	5	3	1.41	14	12	1	0	70	60	21	11	3	11	54	.234	.232	.236	6.94	1.41
Garcia, Elvin	L-L	5-11	175	5-14-90	5	1	1.34	23	4	0	2	61	57	11	9	1	5	27	.251	.333	.245	4.01	0.74
Geronimo, Ignacio	R-R	6-1	170	6-1-91	3	0	0.72	22	0	0	7	38	20	7	3	0	10	36	.155	.195	.136	8.60	2.39
Gil, Jean Carlos	R-R	6-2	155	10-12-90	3	2	1.89	17	11	0	0	67	56	14	14	1	7	66	.233	.253	.221	8.91	0.95
Medina, Enrique	L-L	5-11	180	3-5-92	2	2	2.57	9	1	0	0	21	11	9	6	0	6	14	.162	.500	.152	6.00	2.57
Mendez, Henry	R-R	6-3	195	4-12-89	1	2	2.76	25	0	0	3	29	28	9	9	0	15	26	.250	.281	.238	7.98	4.60
Morales, Javier	R-R	6-2	180	11-24-92	1	0	7.71	4	1	0	0	7	9	6	6	0	5	3	.300	.273	.316	3.86	6.43
Moreno, Ramy	L-L	6-6	200	6-23-91	0	1	10.29	5	1	0	0	7	7	8	8	0	6	0	.280	.000	.280	0.00	7.71
Nin, Amable	R-R	6-2	190	6-2-90	1	4	4.54	21	4	0	3	42	38	23	21	0	11	38	.242	.378	.188	8.21	2.38
Saldeno, Jesus	R-R	6-0	170	10-28-92	4	3	2.67	14	10	1	0	61	47	20	18	2	13	57	.217	.157	.245	8.46	1.93
Sauceda, Ramon	R-R	6-1	185	8-19-92	0	0	2.03	5	2	0	0	13	5	4	3	0	7	4	.119	.111	.121	2.70	4.72
Torres, Carlos	R-R	6-2	205	5-13-90	1	0	4.35	8	0	0	0	10	13	6	5	0	2	10	.325	.200	.367	8.71	1.74
Valdez, Elias	L-L	6-3	165	9-4-92	1	2	6.32	11	0	0	0	16	17	17	11	1	6	13	.254	.400	.242	7.47	3.45
Zavala, Alexander	L-L	6-3	210	7-8-89	0	1	18.00	1	0	0	0	1	2	3	2	0	1	1	.400	.000	.500	9.00	9.00

Fielding

Catcher	PCT	G	PO	A	E	DP	PB
Gimenez	1.000	20	100	22	0	1	3
Herrera	.991	16	100	10	1	0	3
Machado	.833	1	4	1	1	0	0
Nunez	.988	34	208	30	3	4	1
Velazquez	.983	7	49	8	1	0	0

First Base	PCT	G	PO	A	E	DP
Alcantara	.992	60	587	29	5	45
Peguero	.988	9	77	4	1	6

Second Base	PCT	G	PO	A	E	DP
Castro	1.000	7	13	11	0	3
Luna	1.000	1	1	3	0	1
Madrid	.957	11	18	26	2	5

	PCT	G	PO	A	E	DP
Reyes	.989	55	124	137	3	23

Third Base	PCT	G	PO	A	E	DP
Franco	.914	36	25	81	10	11
Luna	.961	16	9	40	2	3
Noboa	.750	4	1	5	2	0
Salcedo	—	1	0	0	0	0
Tovar	.889	11	6	24	4	1

Shortstop	PCT	G	PO	A	E	DP
Caballero	.879	8	8	21	4	1
Castro	.952	6	6	14	1	2
Franco	1.000	1	1	1	0	0
Luna	.933	20	21	62	6	7
Ramirez	.929	12	13	39	4	4

	PCT	G	PO	A	E	DP
Reyes	1.000	3	2	1	0	0
Salcedo	.918	20	26	52	7	4
Tovar	1.000	2	2	5	0	0

Outfield	PCT	G	PO	A	E	DP
Daniel	.946	24	32	3	2	0
Galvan	.963	23	25	1	1	1
Garcia	.990	59	93	7	1	1
Maldonado	1.000	7	9	0	0	0
Marte	.989	57	81	6	1	3
Noboa	1.000	9	14	0	0	0
Peguero	.909	32	29	1	3	0
Rijkhof	1.000	1	1	0	0	0

Baltimore Orioles

SEASON IN A SENTENCE: The Orioles became the first team in major league history to have three different managers for at least 50 games in what was their 13th consecutive losing season, but Baltimore finished respectably under new manager Buck Showalter, with their first winning August in the same span.

HIGH POINT: Baltimore's season turned around with the addition of Showalter, who succeeded Dave Trembley and Juan Samuel. The Orioles put together a decent finish, going 34-23 under Showalter. Luke Scott hit a career-high 27 home runs and carried the offense in the last part of the season, after getting off to a slow start. The young Orioles rotation also started to come around, particularly Brad Bergesen, Brian Matusz and Jake Arrieta, highlighted by Bergesen's complete games against Cleveland and Toronto, and Matusz's seven scoreless innings against Tampa Bay on Sept. 27.

LOW POINT: Baltimore played sloppy and was hurt by injuries in the first half of the season, most notably losing Brian Roberts to a back injury in the home opener. Felix Pie, Koji Uehara, Jim Johnson and Michael Gonzalez also missed significant time. The lowest point came when the Yankees completed a sweep on June 3 to push the Orioles to 15-39, prompting Trembley's ouster.

NOTABLE ROOKIES: Expectations were high for Matusz, and he had his ups and downs, but he seemed to respond to Showalter and went 7-1, 2.17 in his final 11 starts. Arrieta also started to come around, lowering his ERA from 5.47 to 4.66 in his final eight starts. Third baseman Josh Bell also made his major league debut but looked like he needed more polish, batting .214/.224/.302.

KEY TRANSACTIONS: The Orioles didn't make any blockbusters, but did flip Miguel Tejada to the Padres for pitching prospect Wynn Pelzer at the trade deadline. They also traded Will Ohman to the Marlines for Rick Vanden Hurk. The biggest deal was signing shortstop Manny Machado, the third overall pick in the 2010 draft, for $5.25 million.

DOWN ON THE FARM: Orioles' affiliates were 27th in the majors with a .463 winning percentage. The organization also left its longtime Rookie-level outpost in Bluefield to go down to a more conventional six domestic affiliates. The best hope for quick big league help is lefthander Zach Britton, who led the organization in ERA (2.70) and was second in strikeouts (124).

OPENING DAY PAYROLL: $81.6 million (17th)

ORGANIZATION LEADERS

BATTING	*Minimum 250 at-bats	
MAJORS		
*AVG	Nick Markakis	.297
*OPS	Luke Scott	.902
HR	Luke Scott	27
RBI	Ty Wigginton	76
MINORS		
*AVG	Joe Mahoney, Bowie/Frederick	.307
*OBP	Brian Conley, Delmarva/Frederick	.381
*SLG	Joel Guzman, Bowie	.519
R	Joel Guzman, Bowie	87
H	Ryan Adams, Bowie	158
TB	Joel Guzman, Bowie	264
2B	Ryan Adams, Bowie	43
3B	Steven Bumbry, Delmarva	9
HR	Joel Guzman, Bowie	33
RBI	Joel Guzman, Bowie	98
BB	Brian Conley, Delmarva/Frederick	74
SO	Brandon Waring, Bowie	179
SB	Kyle Hudson, Frederick	40

PITCHING	†Minimum 75 innings	
MAJORS		
W	Jeremy Guthrie	11
†ERA	Jeremy Guthrie	3.83
SO	Brian Matusz	143
MINORS		
W	Chris Tillman, Norfolk	11
L	Nathan Nery, Bowie/Frederick	13
†ERA	Zach Britton, Bowie/Norfolk	2.70
G	Brandon Cooney, Frederick/Bowie	49
	Pat Egan, Bowie/Norfolk	49
GS	Three tied at	28
SV	Dennis Sarfate, Norfolk	20
IP	Rick Zagone, Frederick/Rowie	155.3
BB	Chorye Spoone, Bowie	79
SO	Steve Johnson, Bowie	128
†AVG	Zach Britton, Bowie/Norfolk	.237

2010 PERFORMANCE

General Manager: Andy MacPhail. **Farm Director:** John Stockstill. **Scouting Director:** Joe Jordan.

Class	Team	League	W	L	PCT	Finish*	Manager(s)
Majors	Baltimore Orioles	American	66	96	.407	13th (14)	D.Trembley/J.Samuel/B.Showalter
Triple-A	Norfolk Tides	International	67	77	.465	t-10th (14)	Gary Allenson/Bobby Dickerson
Double-A	Bowie Baysox	Eastern	75	67	.528	5th (12)	Brad Komminsk
High A	Frederick Keys	Carolina	72	68	.514	4th (8)	Orlando Gomez
Low A	Delmarva Shorebirds	South Atlantic	59	81	.421	14th (14)	Ryan Minor
Short-season	Aberdeen Ironbirds	New York-Penn	34	40	.459	t-10th (14)	Gary Kendall
Rookie	Bluefield Orioles	Appalachian	23	45	.338	10th (10)	Einar Diaz
Rookie	GCL Orioles	Gulf Coast	25	34	.424	14th (15)	Ramon Sambo
Overall 2010 Minor League Record			355	412	.463	27th (30)	

*Finish in overall standings (No. of teams in league). †League champion.

ORGANIZATION STATISTICS

BALTIMORE ORIOLES

AMERICAN LEAGUE

Batting	B-T	HT	WT	DOB	AVG	vLH	vRH	G	AB	R	H	2B	3B	HR	RBI	BB	HBP	SH	SF	SO	SB	CS	SLG	OBP
Andino, Robert	R-R	6-0	195	4-25-84	.295	.300	.293	16	61	6	18	4	0	2	6	3	1	0	1	13	1	1	.459	.333
Atkins, Garrett	R-R	6-3	215	12-12-79	.214	.204	.220	44	140	5	30	7	0	1	9	12	0	0	0	30	0	0	.286	.276
Bell, Josh	B-R	6-3	220	11-13-86	.214	.217	.212	53	159	15	34	5	0	3	12	2	0	0	0	53	0	1	.302	.224
Fox, Jake	R-R	6-0	220	7-20-82	.220	.167	.269	38	100	10	22	5	1	5	10	3	2	0	0	23	0	0	.440	.257
2-team total (39 Oakland)					.217	—	—	77	198	21	43	10	1	7	22	8	4	0	1	49	0	0	.384	.261
Hughes, Rhyne	L-L	6-2	215	9-9-83	.213	.250	.209	14	47	3	10	2	0	0	4	4	0	0	0	19	0	0	.255	.275
Izturis, Cesar	B-R	5-9	180	2-10-80	.230	.205	.240	150	473	42	109	13	1	1	28	25	6	7	2	53	11	5	.268	.277
Jones, Adam	R-R	6-2	215	8-1-85	.284	.259	.293	149	581	76	165	25	5	19	69	23	13	2	2	119	7	7	.442	.325
Lugo, Julio	R-R	6-1	175	11-16-75	.249	.306	.210	93	241	26	60	4	2	0	20	15	2	6	0	50	5	7	.282	.298
Markakis, Nick	L-L	6-1	200	11-17-83	.297	.361	.260	160	629	79	187	45	3	12	60	73	2	0	5	93	7	2	.436	.370
Montanez, Lou	R-R	6-1	195	12-15-81	.140	.053	.184	26	57	2	8	0	0	3	1	0	0	0	9	1	0	.140	.155
Moore, Scott	L-R	6-2	195	11-17-83	.209	.000	.222	41	86	8	18	2	0	3	10	8	0	1	1	19	3	0	.337	.274
Patterson, Corey	L-R	5-10	180	8-13-79	.269	.207	.292	90	308	43	83	16	1	8	32	20	1	10	1	75	21	4	.406	.315
Pie, Felix	L-L	6-2	185	2-8-85	.274	.230	.286	82	288	39	79	15	5	5	31	13	1	3	3	52	5	2	.413	.305
Reimold, Nolan	R-R	6-4	205	10-12-83	.207	.265	.164	39	116	9	24	5	0	3	14	12	1	0	2	26	0	0	.328	.282
Roberts, Brian	B-R	5-9	175	10-9-77	.278	.288	.275	59	230	28	64	14	0	4	15	26	2	1	2	40	12	2	.391	.354
Scott, Luke	L-R	6-0	205	6-25-78	.284	.240	.297	131	447	70	127	29	1	27	72	59	4	0	7	98	2	0	.535	.368
Snyder, Brandon	R-R	6-2	215	11-23-86	.300	.400	.200	10	20	1	6	2	0	0	3	0	0	0	0	3	0	1	.400	.300
Tatum, Craig	R-R	6-1	225	3-18-83	.281	.214	.319	43	114	11	32	4	0	0	9	12	0	0	0	21	1	0	.316	.349
Tejada, Miguel	R-R	5-9	210	5-25-74	.269	.239	.281	97	401	40	108	16	0	7	39	15	9	0	3	39	0	0	.362	.308
Turner, Justin	R-R	5-11	200	11-23-84	.000	.000	.000	5	9	0	0	0	0	0	0	0	0	0	0	3	0	0	.000	.000
Wieters, Matt	B-R	6-5	225	5-21-86	.249	.210	.263	130	446	37	111	22	1	11	55	47	2	0	7	94	0	1	.377	.319
Wigginton, Ty	R-R	6-0	230	10-11-77	.248	.237	.252	154	581	63	144	29	1	22	76	50	8	1	9	116	0	1	.415	.312

Pitching	B-T	HT	WT	DOB	W	L	ERA	G	GS	CG	SV	IP	H	R	ER	HR	BB	SO	AVG	vLH	vRH	K/9	BB/9
Albers, Matt	L-R	6-0	205	1-20-83	5	3	4.52	62	0	0	0	76	78	41	38	6	34	49	.269	.297	.250	5.83	4.04
Arrieta, Jake	R-R	6-4	225	3-6-86	6	6	4.66	18	18	0	0	100	106	57	52	9	48	52	.271	.315	.213	4.66	4.31
Bergesen, Brad	L-R	6-2	210	9-25-85	8	12	4.98	30	28	2	0	170	193	104	94	26	51	81	.285	.303	.266	4.29	2.70
Berken, Jason	R-R	6-0	205	11-27-83	3	3	3.03	41	0	0	0	62	64	24	21	5	19	45	.270	.253	.279	6.50	2.74
Castillo, Alberto	L-L	6-3	220	7-5-75	1	0	10.13	14	0	0	0	11	16	12	12	5	6	6	.356	.391	.318	9.28	5.06
Gabino, Armando	R-R	6-3	210	8-31-83	0	0	13.50	5	0	0	0	5	9	7	7	3	2	2	.391	.571	.313	3.86	5.79
Gonzalez, Mike	R-L	6-2	215	5-23-78	1	3	4.01	29	0	0	1	25	18	11	11	1	14	31	.205	.324	.130	11.31	5.11
Guthrie, Jeremy	R-R	6-1	205	4-8-79	11	14	3.83	32	32	0	0	209	193	93	89	25	50	119	.243	.253	.234	5.12	2.15
Hendrickson, Mark	L-L	6-9	240	6-23-74	1	6	5.26	52	1	0	0	75	97	47	44	9	20	55	.313	.317	.311	6.57	2.39
Hernandez, David	R-R	6-2	230	5-13-85	8	8	4.31	41	8	0	2	79	72	40	38	9	42	72	.242	.198	.271	8.17	4.76
Johnson, Jim	R-R	6-5	231	6-27-83	1	1	3.42	26	0	0	1	26	32	11	10	2	5	22	.296	.264	.327	7.52	1.71
Mata, Frank	R-R	6-1	235	3-11-84	0	0	7.79	15	0	0	0	17	24	16	15	2	8	14	.324	.346	.313	4.67	4.15
Matusz, Brian	L-L	6-4	190	2-11-87	10	12	4.30	32	32	0	0	176	173	88	84	19	63	143	.255	.218	.266	7.33	3.23
Meredith, Cla	R-R	6-0	190	6-4-83	0	2	5.40	21	0	0	1	15	18	9	9	4	4	7	.300	.333	.286	4.20	2.40
Mickolio, Kam	R-R	6-9	255	5-10-84	0	0	7.36	3	0	0	0	4	5	3	3	1	3	4	.313	.250	.375	9.82	7.36
Millwood, Kevin	R-R	6-4	230	12-24-74	4	16	5.10	31	31	1	0	191	223	116	108	30	65	132	.297	.307	.276	6.23	3.07
Ohman, Will	L-L	6-2	190	8-13-77	0	0	3.30	51	0	0	0	30	30	12	11	3	18	29	.270	.226	.327	8.70	5.40
Patton, Troy	B-L	6-1	185	9-3-85	0	0	0.00	1	0	0	0	1	1	0	0	0	1	1	.333	.333	.000	13.50	13.50
Simon, Alfredo	R-R	6-4	230	5-8-81	4	2	4.93	49	0	0	17	49	54	30	27	10	22	37	.277	.269	.284	6.75	4.01
Tillman, Chris	R-R	6-5	200	4-15-88	2	5	5.87	11	11	0	0	54	51	37	35	9	31	31	.255	.274	.238	5.20	5.20
Uehara, Koji	R-R	6-1	190	4-3-75	1	2	2.86	43	0	0	13	44	37	15	14	5	5	55	.220	.263	.185	11.25	1.02
VandenHurk, Rick	R-R	6-5	215	5-22-85	0	1	4.96	7	1	0	0	16	13	10	9	2	7	17	.228	.333	.167	9.37	3.86
Viola, Pedro	L-L	6-1	185	6-29-83	0	0	13.50	2	0	0	0	1	1	2	2	1	1	3	.200	.000	1.000	20.25	6.75

Fielding

Catcher	PCT	G	PO	A	E	DP	PB
Fox	1.000	11	49	6	0	0	0
Tatum	.988	42	222	17	3	1	1

Wieters	.994	126	775	51	5	10	2

First Base	PCT	G	PO	A	E	DP
Atkins	.996	30	242	16	1	24

	PCT	G	PO	A	E	DP
Fox	.984	10	58	4	1	5
Hughes	.990	11	98	3	1	6
Moore	1.000	10	19	3	0	0

	PCT	G	PO	A	E	DP
Scott	.982	19	153	11	3	17
Snyder	.958	10	44	2	2	2
Wigginton	.988	98	748	73	10	75

Second Base	PCT	G	PO	A	E	DP
Andino	1.000	8	6	10	0	1
Lugo	.996	59	93	131	1	26
Moore	.978	22	36	52	2	9
Roberts	.987	59	86	146	3	38
Turner	1.000	3	4	4	0	1
Wigginton	.964	40	66	97	6	13

Third Base	PCT	G	PO	A	E	DP
Andino	1.000	6	6	4	0	1
Bell	.963	50	27	77	4	8
Fox	—	1	0	0	0	0
Lugo	1.000	7	0	1	0	0
Moore	.500	4	0	1	1	0
Tejada	.946	93	68	197	15	22
Wigginton	.902	22	13	33	5	3

Shortstop	PCT	G	PO	A	E	DP
Andino	.950	7	5	14	1	3
Izturis	.985	150	212	382	9	78
Lugo	.986	26	25	48	1	11

	PCT	G	PO	A	E	DP
Turner	1.000	1	1	0	0	0

Outfield	PCT	G	PO	A	E	DP
Fox	1.000	4	4	0	0	0
Jones	.984	149	422	12	7	6
Lugo	1.000	1	1	0	0	0
Markakis	.991	159	332	7	3	1
Montanez	.968	20	28	2	1	0
Patterson	.966	64	138	4	5	1
Pie	.994	77	167	9	1	4
Reimold	.977	23	42	1	1	0
Scott	1.000	14	22	0	0	0

NORFOLK TIDES
TRIPLE-A
INTERNATIONAL LEAGUE

Batting	B-T	HT	WT	DOB	AVG	vLH	vRH	G	AB	R	H	2B	3B	HR	RBI	BB	HBP	SH	SF	SO	SB	CS	SLG	OBP
Abreu, Miguel	R-R	5-10	190	11-14-84	.269	.333	.250	6	26	1	7	3	0	0	3	0	1	0	0	3	0	0	.385	.296
Andino, Robert	R-R	6-0	195	4-25-84	.264	.336	.240	132	546	72	144	30	4	13	76	29	4	2	7	110	16	3	.405	.302
Angle, Matt	L-R	5-10	175	9-10-85	.260	.320	.235	87	350	55	91	4	4	1	24	41	1	5	2	54	24	4	.303	.338
Aubrey, Michael	L-L	6-0	190	4-15-82	.235	.183	.250	102	366	52	86	25	2	22	68	37	7	0	9	60	2	3	.495	.310
Bell, Josh	B-R	6-3	220	11-13-86	.278	.250	.288	81	316	43	88	25	0	13	50	23	2	0	3	78	2	4	.481	.328
Britton, Buck	L-R	6-1	163	5-16-86	.111	.000	.143	5	18	1	2	0	0	0	1	0	0	0	0	3	1	0	.111	.158
Britton, Phillip	R-R	6-0	205	9-25-84	.333	.333	.000	1	3	0	1	0	0	0	0	0	0	0	0	0	0	0	.333	.333
Davis, Blake	L-R	5-11	170	12-22-83	.246	.245	.246	75	244	32	60	14	2	4	23	17	0	6	1	43	3	4	.369	.294
Donachie, Adam	R-R	6-1	215	3-3-84	.201	.241	.188	78	249	23	50	8	0	4	21	26	2	7	5	62	0	2	.281	.277
Figueroa, Danny	R-R	5-11	182	2-19-83	.143	.333	.000	2	7	1	1	0	0	1	2	0	0	0	0	3	0	0	.571	.143
Figueroa, Paco	R-R	5-11	180	2-19-83	.266	.239	.278	90	297	32	79	16	1	2	26	21	3	10	1	40	8	6	.347	.320
Gathright, Joey	L-L	5-10	175	4-27-81	.185	.209	.179	61	216	25	40	4	2	0	7	21	0	5	2	40	12	6	.222	.255
Hernandez, Michel	R-R	6-0	215	8-12-78	.263	.211	.286	58	190	25	50	4	0	3	22	22	1	2	2	24	2	1	.332	.340
Hughes, Rhyne	L-L	6-2	215	9-9-83	.258	.222	.271	104	388	44	100	25	2	10	39	29	4	1	3	121	8	3	.410	.314
Lerud, Steve	L-R	6-1	215	10-13-84	.095	.000	.095	9	21	2	2	1	0	0	2	7	0	0	0	6	0	0	.143	.321
Montanez, Lou	R-R	6-1	195	12-15-81	.289	.263	.295	74	97	14	28	5	2	2	24		0	0	0	12	2	1	.443	.317
Moore, Scott	L-R	5-11		11-17-83	.280	.196	.305	61	225	34	63	9	1	11	45	21	3	1	3	47	2	3	.476	.345
Patterson, Corey	L-R	5-10	180	8-13-79	.368	.250	.400	14	57	6	21	5	1	0	2	5	0	0	0	8	3	3	.491	.419
Reimold, Nolan	R-R	6-4	205	10-12-83	.249	.272	.241	94	337	52	84	12	0	10	37	54	8	0	2	61	9	2	.384	.364
Salazar, Jeff	L-L	6-0	195	11-24-80	.252	.217	.266	117	436	59	110	14	1	16	55	48	2	0	6	82	26	3	.399	.325
Snyder, Brandon	R-R	6-2	215	11-23-86	.257	.353	.224	98	339	36	87	22	1	9	43	28	7	0	2	101	4	1	.407	.324
Tatum, Craig	R-R	6-1	225	3-18-83	.095	.200	.063	6	21	1	2	0	1	0	3	3	0	1	0	5	0	1	.190	.208
Tucker, Jonathan	R-R	5-8	180	7-2-83	.226	.353	.178	21	62	8	14	5	0	1	6	8	0	0	0	13	3	1	.306	.314
Turner, Justin	R-R	5-11	200	11-23-84	.250	.160	.288	23	84	11	21	8	0	1	8	9	0	1	1	13	2	0	.381	.319
2-team total (78 Buffalo)					.316	—	—	101	396	69	125	30	1	12	43	33	6	5	3	51	7	3	.487	.374

Pitching	B-T	HT	WT	DOB	W	L	ERA	G	GS	CG	SV	IP	H	R	ER	HR	BB	SO	AVG	vLH	vRH	K/9	BB/9
Arrieta, Jake	R-R	6-4	225	3-6-86	6	2	1.85	12	11	0	0	73	48	18	15	3	34	64	.189	.186	.191	7.89	4.19
Bascom, Tim	R-R	6-1	205	1-4-85	4	7	6.94	17	17	0	0	84	116	67	65	17	32	44	.328	.324	.332	4.70	3.42
Bergesen, Brad	L-R	6-2	210	9-25-85	1	0	4.30	3	3	0	0	15	17	7	7	3	3	10	.274	.278	.273	6.14	1.84
Britton, Zach	L-L	6-3	195	12-22-87	3	4	2.98	12	12	0	0	66	63	31	22	3	23	56	.245	.259	.238	7.60	3.12
Castillo, Alberto	L-L	6-3	220	7-5-75	1	2	4.54	39	0	0	4	46	46	20	20	4	15	43	.284	.167	.378	9.76	3.40
Clark, Zach	R-R	6-0	195	7-11-83	0	5	4.13	6	4	0	0	28	32	15	13	3	10	16	.286	.333	.241	5.08	3.18
Egan, Pat	R-R	6-8	225	10-25-84	1	1	5.11	27	0	0	0	37	54	26	21	2	9	17	.351	.481	.280	4.14	2.19
Erbe, Brandon	R-R	6-4	190	12-25-87	0	10	5.73	14	14	0	0	71	86	48	45	11	22	50	.294	.295	.293	6.37	2.80
Gabino, Armando	R-R	6-3	210	8-31-83	7	0	2.37	30	8	0	2	84	62	29	22	7	23	75	.204	.259	.155	8.07	2.47
George, Chris	L-L	6-2	200	9-16-79	5	7	4.20	26	20	0	0	124	129	66	58	16	36	101	.264	.235	.278	7.31	2.61
Gonzalez, Mike	R-L	6-2	215	5-23-78	0	0	10.80	2	1	0	0	2	3	2	2	0	2	4	.375	.667	.200	21.60	10.80
Hinckley, Mike	R-L	6-3	195	10-5-82	1	4	4.19	24	1	0	0	39	41	20	18	2	15	29	.299	.286	.276	6.75	3.49
Hoey, Jim	R-R	6-6	210	12-30-82	4	0	3.38	18	0	0	0	21	11	8	8	0	17	32	.151	.143	.158	13.50	7.17
Johnson, Jim	R-R	6-5	231	6-27-83	0	0	0.00	1	0	0	0	1	1	0	0	0	0	0	.250	.500	.000	0.00	0.00
Mata, Frank	R-R	6-1	235	3-11-84	5	3	3.16	36	0	0	0	43	34	17	15	2	20	30	.219	.242	.204	6.33	4.22
Meredith, Cla	R-R	6-0	190	6-4-83	1	2	6.00	20	0	0	0	27	32	18	18	2	12	17	.291	.375	.243	5.67	4.00
Mickolio, Kam	R-R	6-9	255	5-10-84	4	3	6.37	30	0	0	0	35	44	25	25	4	17	48	.297	.243	.346	12.23	4.33
Miller, Jim	R-R	6-1	200	4-28-82	1	0	4.84	33	0	0	0	58	60	33	31	9	18	53	.271	.269	.273	8.27	2.81
Mitchell, Andy	R-R	6-3	205	9-10-78	0	1	6.89	16	1	0	0	33	43	32	25	0	7	17	.394	.409	.383	4.68	1.93
Patton, Troy	B-L	6-1	185	9-3-85	8	11	4.43	25	25	0	0	136	144	79	67	15	43	89	.271	.231	.290	5.89	2.85
Sarfate, Dennis	R-R	6-4	225	4-9-81	2	2	2.73	47	0	0	20	56	32	18	17	4	27	72	.166	.216	.124	11.57	4.34
Simon, Alfredo	R-R	6-4	230	5-8-81	1	1	1.59	4	3	0	0	17	15	4	3	1	5	14	.238	.265	.207	7.41	2.65
Tillman, Chris	R-R	6-5	200	4-15-88	11	7	3.34	21	21	2	0	121	120	50	45	10	30	94	.258	.263	.253	6.97	2.23
Uehara, Koji	R-R	6-1	190	4-3-75	0	0	0.00	2	0	0	0	2	2	0	0	0	0	1	.250	.500	.167	4.50	0.00
VandenHurk, Rick	R-R	6-5	215	5-22-85	1	1	2.18	3	3	0	0	21	15	7	5	0	4	7	.205	.171	.250	3.05	1.74
Viola, Pedro	R-L	6-1	185	6-29-83	0	2	17.65	11	0	0	0	9	19	18	17	1	10	8	.432	.368	.480	8.31	10.38
2-team total (1 Louisville)					0	2	15.83	12	0	0	0	10	19	18	17	1	10	9	—	—	—	8.38	9.31
Wolf, Ross	R-R	6-0	180	10-18-82	0	2	1.88	25	0	0	0	38	29	12	8	1	15	26	.207	.213	.203	6.10	3.52

Fielding

Catcher	PCT	G	PO	A	E	DP	PB
Donachie	.990	77	534	43	6	6	4
Hernandez	.993	57	381	16	3	1	3
Lerud	1.000	9	54	7	0	0	2
Tatum	.979	6	45	2	1	0	1

First Base	PCT	G	PO	A	E	DP
Aubrey	.996	32	260	16	1	34
Hughes	.992	16	116	11	1	15
Reimold	.974	29	246	17	7	29
Snyder	.985	76	594	53	10	64

Second Base	PCT	G	PO	A	E	DP
Abreu	1.000	1	1	4	0	2
Andino	.975	21	29	49	2	10
Davis	.957	18	41	47	4	15
Figueroa	.985	77	142	245	6	63

	PCT	G	PO	A	E	DP
Moore	.937	14	26	33	4	7
Tucker	.909	4	3	7	1	3
Turner	.967	16	31	56	3	15

Third Base	PCT	G	PO	A	E	DP
Bell	.930	73	60	126	14	16
Britton	1.000	2	0	3	0	0
Davis	.931	22	15	39	4	5
Figueroa	.833	5	1	4	1	0
Moore	.920	34	23	46	6	4
Snyder	.941	9	7	9	1	2
Tucker	1.000	3	1	2	0	0
Turner	1.000	2	0	4	0	0

Shortstop	PCT	G	PO	A	E	DP
Andino	.946	111	167	341	29	79
Davis	.946	22	36	70	6	17

	PCT	G	PO	A	E	DP
Figueroa	.957	6	12	10	1	6
Moore	.909	5	11	9	2	4
Turner	1.000	1	5	4	0	0

Outfield	PCT	G	PO	A	E	DP
Abreu	.900	5	9	0	1	0
Angle	1.000	87	215	5	0	3
Aubrey	.966	15	26	2	1	1
Davis	1.000	11	24	2	0	0
Figueroa	1.000	2	3	1	0	0
Gathright	.985	58	125	3	2	1
Hughes	.938	61	120	1	8	0
Montanez	.959	23	44	3	2	1
Patterson	.972	14	34	1	1	1
Reimold	.969	50	88	5	3	2
Salazar	.995	106	188	4	1	1
Tucker	1.000	13	34	1	0	1

BOWIE BAYSOX — DOUBLE-A

EASTERN LEAGUE

Batting	B-T	HT	WT	DOB	AVG	vLH	vRH	G	AB	R	H	2B	3B	HR	RBI	BB	HBP	SH	SF	SO	SB	CS	SLG	OBP
Abreu, Miguel	R-R	5-10	190	11-14-84	.198	.163	.217	33	126	12	25	2	0	3	15	2	2	0	1	25	4	5	.286	.221
Adams, Ryan	R-R	5-11	195	4-21-87	.298	.350	.271	134	530	81	158	43	0	15	68	47	12	0	5	121	2	3	.464	.365
Angle, Matt	L-R	5-10	175	9-10-85	.383	.429	.359	14	60	11	23	2	0	1	9	6	0	3	1	5	5	2	.467	.433
Avery, Xavier	L-L	5-11	180	1-1-90	.234	.105	.304	27	107	10	25	6	0	3	18	7	2	2	2	34	10	0	.374	.288
Booker, Zach	R-R	6-0	220	4-24-85	.000	.000	.000	1	3	0	0	0	0	0	0	0	0	0	0	1	0	0	.000	.000
Britton, Phillip	R-R	6-0	205	9-25-84	.167	.077	.217	10	36	2	6	3	0	0	2	2	1	0	0	9	0	0	.250	.231
Davis, Blake	L-R	5-11	170	12-22-83	.190	.000	.222	7	21	1	4	1	0	0	2	3	0	0	1	2	0	0	.238	.280
Donachie, Adam	R-R	6-1	215	3-3-84	.150	.000	.176	5	20	1	3	1	0	0	2	3	0	0	0	6	0	0	.200	.261
Figueroa, Danny	R-R	5-11	182	2-19-83	.210	.228	.200	80	257	33	54	7	2	0	19	44	12	8	1	52	10	3	.253	.350
Figueroa, Paco	R-R	5-11	180	2-19-83	.306	.261	.339	28	108	14	33	4	2	1	10	7	2	2	3	25	2	2	.407	.350
Florimon, Pedro	B-R	6-2	180	12-10-86	.183	.178	.187	37	120	16	22	3	0	1	12	10	0	2	1	31	4	1	.233	.250
Guzman, Joel	R-R	6-5	245	11-24-84	.279	.273	.282	130	509	87	142	21	1	33	98	45	6	2	1	121	4	4	.519	.344
Henson, Tyler	R-R	6-1	190	12-15-87	.278	.258	.288	124	486	69	135	37	3	12	60	38	1	4	4	156	7	5	.440	.329
Hoes, L.J.	R-R	6-1	181	3-5-90	.222	.000	.250	3	9	1	2	0	0	0	1	0	0	0	0	1	0	0	.222	.222
Joseph, Caleb	R-R	6-3	180	6-18-86	.235	.263	.220	106	378	43	89	15	1	11	51	33	4	2	3	63	1	6	.368	.301
Lerud, Steve	L-R	6-1	215	10-13-84	.203	.093	.245	49	153	18	31	7	1	6	14	18	7	1	0	47	0	0	.379	.315
Mahoney, Joe	L-L	6-7	255	2-1-87	.319	.305	.326	52	191	30	61	12	2	9	29	17	1	0	0	39	8	1	.545	.378
Miclat, Greg	R-R	5-9	180	7-23-87	.246	.313	.220	62	228	35	56	9	2	1	16	24	0	3	0	52	4	6	.316	.317
Montanez, Lou	R-R	6-1	195	12-15-81	.444	1.000	.375	2	9	2	4	1	0	0	0	0	0	0	1	0	0	0	.556	.444
Pie, Felix	L-L	6-2	180	2-8-85	.348	.286	.444	6	23	2	8	2	1	0	1	3	1	0	0	4	1	0	.522	.444
Roberts, Brian	B-R	5-9	175	10-9-77	.429	.286	.571	3	14	3	6	2	0	0	3	0	0	0	0	2	0	0	.571	.429
Rojas, Carlos	R-R	6-1	186	1-11-84	.239	.244	.236	93	306	35	73	12	2	1	40	30	3	1	6	58	1	3	.301	.307
Tucker, Jonathan	R-R	5-8	180	7-2-83	.221	.198	.232	83	285	39	63	12	1	2	27	36	2	1	1	36	22	4	.291	.312
Tucker, Matt	B-R	6-1	185	6-5-83	.196	.188	.200	16	56	4	11	1	0	0	2	4	1	0	0	13	0	0	.214	.262
Waring, Brandon	R-R	6-4	195	1-2-86	.242	.254	.236	129	472	70	114	32	2	22	70	59	11	2	2	179	0	1	.458	.338
Widlansky, Robbie	L-R	6-2	210	11-6-84	.269	.245	.281	113	424	56	114	27	1	8	61	32	5	2	2	50	0	0	.380	.327

Pitching	B-T	HT	WT	DOB	W	L	ERA	G	GS	CG	SV	IP	H	R	ER	HR	BB	SO	AVG	vLH	vRH	K/9	BB/9
Bascom, Tim	R R	6-1	205	1-4-85	3	4	3.43	11	11	0	0	63	71	32	24	6	10	41	.275	.252	.295	5.86	1.43
Beato, Pedro	R-R	6-6	230	10-27-86	4	0	2.11	43	0	0	16	60	49	14	14	4	19	50	.225	.214	.236	7.54	2.87
Britton, Zach	L-L	6-3	195	12-22-87	7	3	2.48	15	14	0	0	87	76	33	24	4	28	68	.231	.253	.223	7.03	2.90
Clark, Zach	R-R	6-0	195	7-11-83	1	1	3.41	14	2	0	1	37	38	18	14	2	6	19	.275	.315	.231	4.62	1.46
Cooney, Brandon	R-R	6-6	240	8-2-85	3	2	3.40	35	0	0	2	45	36	22	17	1	21	37	.221	.250	.190	7.40	4.20
Diaz, Jose	R-R	6-4	300	2-27-84	1	0	2.16	19	0	0	4	25	19	7	6	1	11	25	.213	.240	.179	9.00	3.96
Egan, Pat	R-R	6-8	225	10-25-84	6	1	2.12	22	0	0	5	47	29	12	11	1	7	25	.177	.190	.163	4.82	1.35
Gabino, Armando	R-R	6-3	210	8-31-83	0	0	4.15	2	0	0	1	4	6	4	2	0	2	3	.300	.222	.364	4.15	4.15
Gamboa, Eddie	R-R	6-2	195	12-21-84	7	5	3.75	36	11	0	2	98	97	45	41	10	27	83	.261	.245	.280	7.60	2.47
Gleason, Sean	L-R	6-0	190	8-21-85	2	1	3.00	16	0	0	0	24	27	10	8	1	6	17	.278	.250	.306	6.38	2.25
Gonzalez, Mike	R-L	6-2	215	5-23-78	1	0	2.25	4	0	0	0	4	2	1	1	1	1	4	.143	.167	.125	9.00	2.25
Hernandez, David	R-R	6-2	230	5-13-85	0	0	0.00	2	0	0	0	2	1	0	0	0	1	3	.143	.000	.333	13.50	4.50
Hinckley, Mike	R-L	6-3	195	10-5-82	0	1	2.25	6	0	0	0	8	5	2	2	0	4	6	.179	.182	.176	6.75	4.50
Hoey, Jim	R-R	6-6	210	12-30-82	2	0	3.16	24	0	0	0	31	26	11	11	1	17	38	.224	.250	.200	10.91	4.88
Johnson, Jim	R-R	6-5	231	6-27-83	0	0	1.80	4	1	0	0	5	2	1	1	1	0	6	.118	.000	.333	10.80	0.00
Johnson, Steve	R-R	6-1	200	8-31-87	7	8	5.09	28	28	0	0	145	144	87	82	24	78	128	.259	.265	.250	7.94	4.84
McCrory, Bob	R-R	6-1	205	5-3-82	3	4	4.88	19	0	0	2	28	25	19	15	1	12	23	.231	.246	.213	7.48	5.53
Nery, Nate	R-L	6-4	210	8-25-85	0	4	10.24	4	4	0	0	19	43	30	22	6	3	16	.413	.543	.348	6.05	1.40
Ouellette, Ryan	R-R	5-11	185	10-4-85	1	0	3.38	9	0	0	0	13	14	5	5	0	11	7	.269	.321	.208	4.72	7.43
Pelzer, Wynn	R-R	6-1	205	6-23-86	1	0	4.50	10	1	0	0	20	24	10	10	2	7	20	.296	.341	.250	9.00	3.15
Perez, Wilfrido	L-L	6-0	145	8-12-84	0	0	10.80	5	0	0	3	5	8	6	6	0	5	6	.364	.455	.273	9.00	9.00
Perrault, Josh	R-R	5-11	215	6-11-82	0	2	6.75	10	1	0	0	17	21	14	13	5	10	10	.304	.333	.278	5.19	2.60
Rivero, Raul	R-R	6-0	165	5-6-86	1	2	2.66	15	0	0	0	24	15	9	7	1	9	11	.273	.278	.267	4.18	3.42
Spoone, Chorye	R-R	6-1	215	9-16-85	7	6	4.02	24	24	0	0	132	132	71	59	12	79	88	.267	.301	.222	6.00	5.39

Name	B-T	HT	WT	DOB	W	L	ERA	G	GS	CG	SV	IP	H	R	ER	HR	BB	SO	AVG	vLH	vRH	K/9	BB/9
Tanaka, Ryohei	R-R	6-0	169	11-18-82	8	12	5.64	29	22	0	0	129	162	89	81	22	25	64	.307	.299	.317	4.45	1.74
Thall, Chad	L-L	6-4	220	8-2-85	2	1	3.79	39	0	0	1	40	39	18	17	6	16	39	.257	.222	.288	8.70	3.57
Uehara, Koji	R-R	6-1	190	4-3-75	0	0	0.00	2	2	0	0	2	1	0	0	0	1	1	.167	.500	.000	4.50	4.50
Viola, Pedro	L-L	6-1	185	6-29-83	3	4	3.59	23	10	0	0	63	61	26	25	2	19	64	.256	.217	.288	9.19	2.73
Zagone, Rick	L-L	6-4	215	9-30-86	5	5	4.34	13	11	0	0	77	81	41	37	8	23	40	.274	.264	.280	4.70	2.70

Fielding

Catcher	PCT	G	PO	A	E	DP	PB
Britton	1.000	10	52	5	0	0	2
Donachie	.978	5	41	3	1	0	1
Joseph	.988	93	621	64	8	3	11
Lerud	.975	38	212	25	6	2	2

First Base	PCT	G	PO	A	E	DP
Guzman	.990	31	271	22	3	28
Joseph	1.000	4	27	3	0	0
Lerud	1.000	1	9	1	0	0
Mahoney	.984	42	348	26	6	40
Waring	.995	20	170	16	1	12
Widlansky	.992	50	436	33	4	33

Second Base	PCT	G	PO	A	E	DP
Abreu	.778	2	4	3	2	0
Adams	.959	94	172	295	20	48
Davis	—	1	0	0	0	0
Figueroa	.933	2	7	7	1	1
Roberts	1.000	2	5	5	0	2

	PCT	G	PO	A	E	DP
Rojas	.987	44	83	139	3	31
Tucker	.667	1	2	0	1	0

Third Base	PCT	G	PO	A	E	DP
Adams	.938	32	17	58	5	9
Davis	1.000	1	0	3	0	0
Figueroa	.923	4	1	11	1	2
Guzman	.833	3	0	5	1	0
Henson	.800	7	4	8	3	0
Lerud	1.000	1	0	1	0	0
Tucker	—	1	0	0	0	0
Waring	.950	96	58	168	12	17

Shortstop	PCT	G	PO	A	E	DP
Davis	1.000	2	2	7	0	1
Florimon	.927	37	65	101	13	23
Miclat	.968	55	84	160	8	34
Rojas	.964	45	69	148	8	27
Tucker	1.000	5	8	9	0	1

Outfield	PCT	G	PO	A	E	DP
Abreu	1.000	29	72	3	0	0
Angle	1.000	14	40	1	0	0
Avery	.973	27	70	2	2	1
Davis	1.000	3	6	0	0	0
Figueroa	.974	78	181	5	5	2
Figueroa	1.000	12	21	0	0	0
Guzman	.937	38	57	2	4	0
Henson	.964	114	204	10	8	1
Joseph	1.000	4	8	0	0	0
Mahoney	.947	10	18	0	1	0
Montanez	—	1	0	0	0	0
Pie	1.000	6	14	0	0	0
Rojas	1.000	1	1	0	0	0
Tucker	.989	83	174	9	2	3
Tucker	1.000	9	12	1	0	0
Waring	.895	8	14	3	2	0
Widlansky	1.000	3	7	0	0	0

FREDERICK KEYS

HIGH CLASS A

CAROLINA LEAGUE

Batting	B-T	HT	WT	DOB	AVG	vLH	vRH	G	AB	R	H	2B	3B	HR	RBI	BB	HBP	SH	SF	SO	SB	CS	SLG	OBP
Abreu, Miguel	R-R	5-10	190	11-14-84	.273	.327	.249	82	311	42	85	16	2	7	49	13	5	3	3	39	9	2	.405	.310
Avery, Xavier	L-L	5-11	180	1-1-90	.280	.217	.309	109	447	73	125	25	6	4	48	42	6	2	1	96	28	14	.389	.349
Bernardo, Luis	R-R	6-0	185	1-16-88	.167	.220	.139	37	120	9	20	4	0	2	8	8	1	4	1	32	2	0	.250	.223
Britton, Buck	L-R	6-1	163	5-16-86	.260	.310	.244	99	334	35	87	16	2	5	48	22	5	3	2	54	2	4	.365	.314
Britton, Phillip	R-R	6-0	205	9-25-84	.229	.280	.207	26	83	7	19	5	0	1	11	2	0	2	1	12	1	0	.325	.244
Conley, Brian	L-R	6-2	195	5-7-86	.222	.364	.176	16	45	2	10	0	1	1	4	4	0	1	1	8	1	1	.333	.280
Crancer, Wally	L R	6-0	215	7-7-84	.225	.333	.206	12	40	7	9	3	0	0	5	4	1	0	0	6	0	0	.300	.311
Florimon, Pedro	B-R	6-2	180	12-10-86	.288	.271	.296	62	222	32	64	10	4	4	33	20	7	0	3	52	8	5	.423	.361
Givens, Mychal	R-R	6-1	190	5-13-90	.500	.000	.500	1	4	2	2	0	0	0	1	0	1	0	0	0	0	1	.500	.600
Hoes, L.J.	R-R	6-1	181	3-5-90	.278	.292	.270	97	353	52	98	19	2	3	44	53	3	2	2	70	10	8	.368	.375
Hudson, Kyle	L-L	5-11	175	1-7-87	.260	.238	.272	136	516	83	134	17	3	0	28	62	8	11	1	129	40	15	.304	.348
Julius, Jacob	L-L	6-5	210	3-13-86	.285	.226	.308	65	221	38	63	15	0	12	50	23	7	2	1	67	6	2	.516	.369
Mahoney, Joe	L-L	6-7	255	2-1-87	.299	.287	.305	72	271	37	81	18	0	9	49	22	4	0	2	56	5	3	.465	.358
Miclat, Greg	B-R	5-9	180	7-23-87	.311	.294	.319	48	164	30	51	12	0	1	19	20	6	3	1	27	8	2	.402	.403
Mooney, Mike	B-R	5-8	160	6-12-88	.122	.214	.074	16	41	4	5	0	0	0	3	5	1	2	0	9	1	0	.122	.234
Moore, Kyle	R-R	6-0	190	3-4-86	.000	.000	.000	1	2	0	0	0	0	0	0	0	0	0	0	1	0	0	.000	.000
Pie, Felix	L-L	6-2	185	2-8-85	.417	.333	.444	3	12	3	5	0	0	0	2	2	0	0	2	0	0	0	.417	.500
Rowell, Bill	L-R	6-5	205	9-10-88	.275	.287	.269	117	436	62	120	25	0	11	61	43	6	0	1	153	9	4	.408	.348
Schoop, Jon	R-R	6-1	187	10-6-91	.238	.125	.308	6	21	5	5	3	0	0	3	1	0	0	0	4	0	0	.381	.273
Stevens, Bobby	R-R	6-0	190	3-30-87	.256	.339	.197	95	266	46	68	9	2	4	39	29	12	6	1	67	11	2	.350	.354
Townsend, Tyler	L-R	6-3	215	5-14-88	.284	.304	.273	19	67	6	19	5	2	3	14	10	1	0	0	15	1	0	.552	.385
Ward, Brian	R-R	5-11	200	10-17-85	.199	.220	.188	83	236	28	47	7	0	2	30	39	5	6	3	58	2	2	.254	.322
Welty, Ronnie	R-R	6-2	180	1-19-88	.282	.247	.299	130	504	86	142	32	3	18	82	47	8	0	5	159	11	4	.464	.349
White, Jason	L-R	6-1	175	6-7-84	.308	.750	.111	6	13	2	4	1	0	0	3	1	0	1	0	4	1	0	.385	.500

Pitching	B-T	HT	WT	DOB	W	L	ERA	G	GS	CG	SV	IP	H	R	ER	HR	BB	SO	AVG	vLH	vRH	K/9	BB/9
Berry, Ryan	R-R	6-1	195	8-3-88	2	2	3.04	17	12	0	2	71	57	30	24	5	25	63	.218	.236	.205	7.99	3.17
Bordes, Brett	L-L	5-10	175	11-30-83	4	3	3.40	43	0	0	2	45	31	20	17	2	29	42	.203	.185	.212	8.40	5.80
Clark, Zach	R-R	6-0	195	7-11-83	2	3	5.25	9	9	0	0	48	58	31	28	4	12	38	.309	.367	.266	7.13	2.25
Cooney, Brandon	R-R	6-6	240	8-2-85	2	2	0.55	14	0	0	6	16	12	2	1	0	7	19	.211	.263	.184	10.47	3.86
Diaz, Jose	R-R	6-4	300	2-27-84	3	0	1.69	26	0	0	12	27	21	5	5	1	9	33	.216	.300	.158	11.14	3.04
Dowdy, Josh	R-R	6-0	200	1-18-87	1	0	9.20	14	0	0	3	15	24	15	15	3	9	16	.358	.333	.367	9.82	5.52
Drake, Oliver	R-R	6-4	210	1-13-87	6	6	4.36	24	21	0	0	128	135	70	62	19	37	100	.272	.266	.277	7.03	2.60
Duran, Jose	R-R	6-1	205	5-1-85	5	3	3.73	28	0	0	1	63	57	29	26	3	36	57	.252	.224	.270	8.19	5.17
Gleason, Sean	L-R	6-0	190	8-21-85	1	4	3.02	24	0	0	3	42	43	20	14	1	10	48	.257	.219	.282	10.37	2.16
Jacobson, Brett	R-R	6-6	205	11-9-86	8	1	2.79	34	0	0	1	71	67	37	22	7	24	67	.246	.267	.234	8.49	3.04
Johnson, Jim	R-R	6-5	231	6-27-83	0	0	3.00	2	0	0	0	3	6	1	1	0	1	6	.429	.429	.429	3.00	0.00
Mariotti, John	L-R	6-0	225	8-19-84	3	6	4.08	41	0	0	3	75	77	42	34	0	46	34	.263	.323	.219	4.08	5.52
McCurry, Cole	L-L	6-2	180	9-25-85	5	6	4.23	30	12	0	2	96	90	60	45	10	46	101	.246	.278	.236	9.50	4.33
Moreau, Nathan	L-L	6-4	222	9-15-86	4	5	5.29	10	10	1	0	49	43	29	29	9	22	39	.223	.207	.226	7.11	4.01
Moreland, Kenny	R-R	5-11	200	4-2-86	2	3	5.80	12	9	0	0	50	59	37	32	7	12	37	.303	.260	.343	6.70	2.17
Nery, Nate	R-L	6-4	210	8-25-85	5	9	5.04	25	14	0	0	105	128	67	59	15	30	59	.301	.263	.313	5.04	2.56
Noel, Luis	R-R	6-1	175	9-29-87	3	2	6.18	11	10	0	0	51	57	37	35	8	23	46	.284	.274	.291	8.12	4.06
O'Shea, Ryan	L-R	6-1	200	5-29-86	7	8	3.84	28	28	0	0	141	148	73	60	17	64	105	.272	.264	.277	6.72	4.09

Rivero, Raul	R-R	6-0	165	5-6-86	3	1	3.27	22	0	0	0	44	40	21	16	4	16	49	.237	.173	.287	10.02	3.27
Startup, Will	L-L	6-0	195	8-4-84	1	0	0.00	3	0	0	0	7	4	0	0	0	3	1	.200	.333	.143	1.35	4.05
Zagone, Rick	L-L	6-4	215	9-30-86	5	6	3.20	15	15	1	0	79	79	42	28	7	22	54	.261	.257	.262	6.18	2.52

Fielding

Catcher	PCT	G	PO	A	E	DP	PB
Bernardo	.978	33	235	34	6	0	3
Britton	.994	26	152	16	1	0	2
Crancer	1.000	7	47	5	0	0	4
Ward	.982	82	571	68	12	8	6

First Base	PCT	G	PO	A	E	DP
Abreu	1.000	1	1	1	0	0
Bernardo	.714	2	5	0	2	0
Britton	.986	32	269	21	4	37
Julius	.974	28	239	20	7	25
Mahoney	.991	69	595	40	6	48
Townsend	.983	19	171	7	3	18

Second Base	PCT	G	PO	A	E	DP
Abreu	.951	42	70	123	10	26

	PCT	G	PO	A	E	DP
Britton	.941	18	19	45	4	13
Hoes	.971	79	164	232	12	53
Mooney	1.000	4	8	12	0	1
Stevens	.973	9	14	22	1	7
Third Base	PCT	G	PO	A	E	DP
Abreu	.949	14	7	30	2	5
Britton	.901	31	11	62	8	5
Rowell	.878	84	29	165	27	16
Stevens	.861	18	4	27	5	4
White	1.000	4	1	11	0	0
Shortstop	PCT	G	PO	A	E	DP
Abreu	1.000	1	1	0	0	0
Florimon	.954	62	92	196	14	43
Miclat	.946	47	75	153	13	33

	PCT	G	PO	A	E	DP
Mooney	.918	11	11	34	4	8
Schoop	1.000	1	3	4	0	1
Stevens	.966	22	29	56	3	9
White	1.000	2	3	4	0	2
Outfield	PCT	G	PO	A	E	DP
Abreu	1.000	5	10	0	0	0
Avery	.964	108	181	7	7	2
Conley	1.000	16	29	1	0	1
Hudson	.972	133	241	4	7	1
Julius	.968	20	30	0	1	0
Mahoney	1.000	4	4	0	0	0
Pie	1.000	1	2	0	0	0
Schoop	—	1	0	0	0	0
Stevens	.970	26	32	1	0	0
Welty	.981	127	243	9	5	2

DELMARVA SHOREBIRDS
SOUTH ATLANTIC LEAGUE

LOW CLASS A

Batting	B-T	HT	WT	DOB	AVG	vLH	vRH	G	AB	R	H	2B	3B	HR	RBI	BB	HBP	SH	SF	SO	SB	CS	SLG	OBP
Baxter, T.J.	L-R	6-1	208	12-13-85	.243	.245	.242	106	404	64	98	16	4	8	34	41	5	6	3	118	34	13	.361	.318
Bernardo, Luis	R-R	6-0	185	1-16-88	.198	.200	.198	32	111	10	22	5	1	0	9	7	0	1	1	25	0	0	.261	.244
Bumbry, Steve	L-L	5-11	185	4-4-88	.263	.253	.267	105	372	42	98	23	9	4	34	38	5	3	3	131	9	11	.406	.337
Carolus, Levi	R-R	6-0	160	9-22-87	.222	.244	.211	64	239	24	53	14	2	6	27	13	3	0	2	68	2	4	.372	.268
Casamayor, Omar	R-R	5-11	170	11-3-86	.279	.450	.248	35	129	11	36	6	0	0	12	11	1	2	0	19	1	2	.326	.340
Conley, Brian	L-R	6-2	195	5-7-86	.270	.306	.255	98	337	52	91	16	5	6	29	70	1	2	4	70	20	3	.401	.393
Dalles, Justin	R-R	6-2	205	12-30-88	.208	.200	.211	48	168	19	35	4	0	4	14	12	3	2	1	45	0	0	.304	.272
Flacco, Mike	R-R	6-5	220	1-17-87	.324	.304	.329	29	102	8	33	7	0	0	13	3	0	1	0	17	0	1	.392	.412
Givens, Mychal	R-R	6-1	190	5-13-90	.222	.333	.200	7	18	2	4	0	0	0	4	5	3	0	1	4	1	1	.222	.444
Helmick, Gary	R-R	5-11	185	8-29-87	.219	.208	.226	83	283	46	62	15	0	4	26	32	8	5	3	55	15	4	.314	.313
Kelly, Ty	L-R	6-0	185	7-20-88	.259	.200	.281	129	487	68	126	30	6	4	58	68	3	11	2	81	5	4	.370	.352
Kolodny, Tyler	R-R	6-2	210	3-9-88	.260	.189	.297	41	154	29	40	9	3	10	29	16	8	1	1	45	5	0	.552	.358
Mooney, Mike	B-R	5-8	160	6-12-88	.196	.154	.212	25	92	11	18	1	0	0	6	3	3	2	13	0	2	.207	.262
Moore, Kyle	R-R	6-0	190	3-4-86	.213	.300	.189	16	47	2	10	2	0	0	3	2	0	0	0	8	0	0	.255	.245
Mummey, Trent	L-L	5-10	185	1-5-89	.167	.200	.147	13	54	7	9	0	3	0	5	3	1	0	0	8	2	2	.278	.224
Ohlman, Michael	R-R	6-4	205	12-14-90	.174	.250	.148	34	109	14	19	6	0	2	17	16	2	2	3	34	1	0	.284	.285
Planeta, Mike	R-R	6-3	195	10-17-89	.226	.245	.217	117	438	36	99	18	3	0	33	18	6	7	4	123	14	8	.281	.264
Pope, Kieron	R-R	6-1	195	10-3-86	.250	.324	.224	75	284	23	71	17	2	6	44	20	10	6	2	94	2	1	.387	.316
Rauch, Austin	R-R	6-3	210	3-30-88	.233	.286	.217	8	30	5	7	2	0	1	6	4	0	0	0	6	0	0	.400	.324
Rosa, Garabez	R-R	6-2	166	10-12-89	.251	.275	.240	124	459	57	115	32	2	5	44	7	6	5	1	114	3	3	.362	.271
Stampone, Tyler	R-R	6-2	220	5-21-87	.247	.261	.238	67	239	27	59	12	0	0	30	25	11	3	1	46	4	0	.297	.344
Stifler, Jason	R-R	6-0	215	8-12-86	.129	.143	.107	24	70	5	9	2	0	0	5	3	0	1	0	22	0	0	.157	.164
Townsend, Tyler	L-R	6-3	215	5-14-88	.342	.273	.358	30	117	16	40	12	2	3	26	9	2	0	0	18	0	1	.556	.398

Pitching	B-T	HT	WT	DOB	W	L	ERA	G	GS	CG	SV	IP	H	R	ER	HR	BB	SO	AVG	vLH	vRH	K/9	BB/9
Allar, Brent	R-R	6-3	230	3-1-85	2	4	5.00	29	10	0	2	76	76	51	42	4	47	71	.259	.256	.262	8.44	5.59
Beal, Jesse	B-R	6-6	210	7-12-90	7	6	3.86	19	19	0	0	114	122	56	49	8	23	64	.268	.263	.271	5.04	1.81
Berry, Ryan	R-R	6-1	195	8-3-88	0	3	3.50	8	8	0	0	46	49	23	18	4	11	43	.268	.324	.232	8.35	2.14
Brandhorst, James	R-R	6-4	240	8-26-87	1	8	3.39	46	0	0	5	61	50	27	23	3	28	65	.224	.237	.215	9.59	4.13
Bundy, Bobby	R-R	6-2	215	1-13-90	4	6	3.65	28	18	1	0	116	100	60	47	12	42	91	.238	.234	.241	7.06	3.26
Butler, Tony	L-L	6-7	220	11-18-87	1	4	7.66	12	8	0	0	45	60	51	38	7	35	39	.326	.349	.319	7.86	7.05
Clark, Zach	R-R	6-0	195	7-11-83	0	0	0.00	1	0	0	0	2	1	0	0	0	0	1	.143	.000	.250	4.50	0.00
Copeland, Scott	R-R	6-3	200	12-15-87	1	0	0.00	1	1	0	0	6	5	0	0	0	2	4	.238	.286	.214	6.00	3.00
Cowan, Jake	L-R	6-3	165	6-30-88	3	1	3.51	7	7	0	0	41	40	18	16	3	18	40	.261	.268	.258	8.78	3.95
Dowdy, Josh	R-R	6-0	200	1-18-87	0	2	1.23	25	0	0	15	29	24	6	4	0	10	38	.220	.317	.162	11.66	3.07
Haughian, Nick	L-L	6-0	205	1-7-88	4	3	3.97	35	5	0	0	93	110	52	41	5	33	90	.293	.226	.312	8.71	3.19
Henry, Randy	R-R	6-3	190	5-10-90	1	1	5.64	10	0	0	0	22	28	17	14	1	5	30	.289	.286	.290	12.09	2.01
Hobgood, Matt	R-R	6-4	245	8-3-90	3	7	4.40	21	21	0	0	94	90	56	46	6	38	59	.257	.255	.259	5.65	3.64
Kantakevich, Pat	R-R	6-2	215	8-11-86	0	0	6.24	19	11	0	0	66	88	53	46	7	27	49	.308	.361	.275	6.65	3.66
Keating, Travis	R-R	6-2	205	9-16-85	2	2	5.57	7	0	0	0	14	16	9	9	4	1	7	.208	.111	.257	4.50	0.64
Landry, Kevin	R-R	6-7	220	5-9-88	2	1	2.88	16	0	0	0	25	27	12	8	2	7	21	.273	.256	.286	7.56	2.52
McCurry, Cole	L-L	6-2	180	9-25-85	0	1	10.80	1	1	0	0	2	3	2	2	1	3	0	4	.286	.000	.286	21.60	16.20
Moreau, Nathan	L-L	6-4	222	9-15-86	2	3	2.98	16	7	0	0	60	45	22	20	3	23	70	.209	.191	.214	10.44	3.43
Moreland, Kenny	R-R	5-11	200	4-2-86	7	7	4.26	16	16	0	0	101	101	54	47	6	10	69	.263	.268	.258	6.26	0.89
Noel, Luis	R-R	6-1	175	9-29-87	4	2	2.59	8	8	0	0	42	37	19	12	1	16	40	.247	.311	.202	8.64	3.46
Palsha, Ryan	R-R	6-1	180	5-17-90	1	1	4.00	5	0	0	0	9	8	5	4	1	4	9	.229	.143	.286	9.00	4.00
Parker, Blair	R-R	6-4	195	8-21-85	2	1	2.36	20	0	0	2	53	45	14	14	4	9	41	.233	.253	.220	6.92	1.52
Phelps, Thomas	R-R	6-2	215	10-12-87	3	2	5.72	15	0	0	0	28	33	21	18	2	12	18	.292	.216	.355	5.72	3.81
Rasner, Jesse	R-R	6-3	200	12-4-86	0	0	4.00	5	0	0	0	9	7	5	4	1	6	6	.226	.333	.125	6.00	6.00
Schrader, Clay	L-R	6-0	200	4-28-90	0	1	6.75	3	0	0	0	4	5	4	3	0	3	6	.250	.571	.000	13.50	4.50

Name	B-T	HT	WT	DOB	W	L	ERA	G	GS	CG	SV	IP	H	R	ER	HR	BB	SO	AVG	vLH	vRH	K/9	BB/9
Smith, Jake	L-L	6-4	210	10-1-85	3	2	4.54	18	0	0	0	34	43	19	17	3	10	22	.316	.240	.333	5.88	2.67
Startup, Will	L-L	6-0	195	8-4-84	1	0	1.98	7	0	0	1	14	9	3	3	1	1	16	.184	.250	.162	10.54	0.66
Swenson, Aaron	R-R	5-11	200	3-25-87	1	1	6.75	7	0	0	0	15	24	16	11	1	5	14	.400	.450	.375	8.59	3.07
Walters, David	R-R	6-3	190	8-13-87	2	1	4.91	22	0	0	4	26	24	15	14	2	10	15	.250	.214	.278	5.26	3.51

Fielding

Catcher	PCT	G	PO	A	E	DP	PB
Bernardo	.980	31	235	59	6	3	5
Dalles	.992	47	331	43	3	6	5
Moore	.989	15	84	5	1	0	0
Ohlman	.991	29	204	18	2	2	6
Rauch	.967	7	49	10	2	0	2
Stifler	.986	20	126	14	2	1	7

First Base	PCT	G	PO	A	E	DP
Baxter	.974	25	210	17	6	18
Flacco	.990	29	276	19	3	24
Kolodny	.983	12	105	8	2	10
Stampone	.990	51	444	37	5	47
Townsend	.992	27	231	15	2	25

Second Base	PCT	G	PO	A	E	DP
Casamayor	.986	25	64	80	2	22
Helmick	.962	57	99	156	10	36
Kelly	.960	37	60	110	7	15
Mooney	.988	21	30	49	1	8
Stampone	1.000	1	2	2	0	0

Third Base	PCT	G	PO	A	E	DP
Carolus	.800	7	5	15	5	2
Casamayor	1.000	2	1	5	0	1
Helmick	1.000	2	2	2	0	0
Kelly	.962	86	72	158	9	8
Kolodny	.844	25	17	48	12	4
Rosa	1.000	5	6	4	0	0
Stampone	.920	14	12	34	4	4

Shortstop	PCT	G	PO	A	E	DP
Givens	.857	5	8	16	4	2
Helmick	.955	17	20	44	3	9
Mooney	1.000	2	3	4	0	2
Rosa	.925	119	202	364	46	80

Outfield	PCT	G	PO	A	E	DP
Baxter	.953	44	55	6	3	0
Bumbry	.956	98	188	9	9	3
Carolus	.936	31	40	4	3	1
Conley	.949	91	158	10	9	1
Mummey	.880	13	22	0	3	0
Planeta	.977	116	234	17	6	3
Pope	.944	39	66	2	4	1

ABERDEEN IRONBIRDS   SHORT-SEASON

NEW YORK-PENN LEAGUE

Batting	B-T	HT	WT	DOB	AVG	vLH	vRH	G	AB	R	H	2B	3B	HR	RBI	BB	HBP	SH	SF	SO	SB	CS	SLG	OBP
Anderson, David	R-R	6-6	240	9-1-87	.274	.241	.287	60	190	22	52	11	1	12	35	39	2	0	2	74	0	1	.532	.399
Casamayor, Omar	B-R	5-11	170	11-3-86	.309	.182	.356	24	81	13	25	5	2	0	10	5	1	5	0	9	0	1	.420	.356
Donaldson, Auburn	B-R	5-11	175	4-9-88	.105	.000	.118	9	19	4	2	0	0	0	3	2	1	0	0	9	0	0	.105	.227
Dunlap, Blair	R-R	5-10	180	7-2-87	.276	.179	.314	29	98	11	27	6	0	0	6	15	1	5	1	18	3	1	.337	.374
Flacco, Mike	R-R	6-5	220	1-17-87	.250	.231	.257	30	100	12	25	2	1	0	16	13	4	3	1	29	0	1	.290	.356
Florimon, Pedro	B-R	6-2	180	12-10-86	.158	.167	.154	5	19	1	3	0	0	0	1	0	0	0	0	6	0	1	.158	.200
Gaylord, Adam	R-R	6-3	210	5-12-88	.273	.232	.287	68	264	25	72	13	1	2	26	7	5	1	3	42	1	2	.352	.301
Givens, Mychal	R-R	6-1	190	5-13-90	.364	.200	.393	8	33	8	12	3	0	3	5	6	2	0	0	2	1	1	.727	.488
Goolsby, Austin	R-R	6-2	185	4-28-88	.146	.154	.143	14	41	2	6	2	0	0	4	7	1	1	0	19	0	0	.195	.286
Hoes, L.J.	R-R	6-1	181	3-5-90	.464	.375	.500	8	28	8	13	5	1	1	5	2	2	0	0	1	1	1	.821	.531
Knight, Austin	D-R	5-11	195	2-13-90	.225	.203	.234	54	187	15	42	4	1	0	17	12	1	3	1	35	3	5	.257	.274
Kolodny, Tyler	R-R	6-2	210	3-9-88	.207	.167	.217	10	29	8	6	2	0	1	4	7	3	0	1	12	4	0	.379	.400
Machado, Manny	R-R	6-3	185	7-6-92	.345	.571	.273	7	29	2	10	1	1	0	3	3	0	0	0	2	0	0	.448	.406
Moore, Zach	L-R	6-4	205	8-6-88	.185	.286	.170	25	54	9	10	1	0	1	5	3	0	1	0	15	3	2	.259	.228
Mummey, Trent	L-L	5-10	185	1-5-89	.266	.340	.240	49	207	30	55	16	2	3	24	23	1	0	0	28	6	2	.406	.342
Narron, Connor	B-R	6-3	195	11-12-91	.121	.000	.143	8	33	1	4	1	0	0	3	1	0	0	0	13	0	0	.152	.216
Nowak, Jeremy	B-R	6-0	205	3-17-88	.179	.067	.225	52	156	15	28	10	3	1	17	17	0	2	2	56	0	0	.301	.257
Oliveira, Joe	R-R	6-0	195	9-30-87	.204	.217	.200	36	108	19	22	4	1	0	7	14	4	2	1	21	1	1	.259	.315
Polanco, Joel	R-R	6-2	190	9-27-85	.194	.192	.195	23	67	5	13	2	0	2	5	2	0	2	0	14	0	0	.313	.217
Rauch, Austin	R-R	6-3	210	3-30-88	.197	.150	.214	29	76	7	15	3	0	1	9	13	1	0	5	19	0	0	.276	.305
Ricardo, Dashenko	R-R	6-0	160	3-1-90	.122	.133	.118	16	49	2	6	1	0	0	2	4	1	2	0	19	0	0	.143	.204
Rooney, Michael	R-R	5-11	170	8-7-88	.234	.250	.230	58	175	27	41	5	1	0	11	25	3	5	1	37	6	3	.274	.338
Schutz, Kipp	L-L	6-4	170	3-21-88	.313	.375	.297	68	265	32	83	11	5	4	42	18	0	5	3	50	1	4	.438	.353
Snyder, Brandon	R-R	6-2	215	11-23-86	.231	.000	.333	3	13	2	3	1	0	1	4	0	0	0	0	2	0	0	.538	.231
Stampone, Tyler	R-R	6-2	220	5-21-87	.351	.333	.360	12	37	4	13	2	2	0	4	9	3	0	0	9	2	0	.514	.510
Starr, Sammie	R-R	5-8	165	5-31-88	.242	.225	.250	35	132	17	32	4	1	0	6	14	3	2	1	16	4	0	.288	.327

Pitching	B-T	HT	WT	DOB	W	L	ERA	G	GS	CG	SV	IP	H	R	ER	HR	BB	SO	AVG	vLH	vRH	K/9	BB/9
Adleman, Tim	R-R	6-5	198	11-13-87	2	4	3.44	13	13	0	0	68	52	31	26	6	25	62	.215	.255	.182	8.21	3.31
Anderson, Justin	L-L	6-4	195	10-21-87	4	5	6.10	12	11	0	0	52	61	39	35	3	20	27	.290	.348	.264	4.70	3.48
Barajas, Jose	R-R	6-4	190	2-25-88	1	2	5.94	19	0	0	1	33	46	25	22	1	14	43	.324	.400	.268	11.61	3.78
Bridwell, Parker	R-R	6-4	190	8-2-91	0	0	0.00	2	0	0	0	4	3	0	0	0	1	2	.214	.286	.143	4.50	2.25
Copeland, Scott	R-R	6-3	200	12-15-87	2	5	2.91	12	12	0	0	65	45	22	21	1	23	49	.197	.236	.160	6.78	3.18
Deain, Andy	R-R	6-0	195	10-23-86	0	0	0.00	3	0	0	0	3	0	0	0	0	1	3	.000	.000	.000	9.00	3.00
Erbe, Brandon	R-R	6-4	190	12-25-87	0	0	6.00	1	1	0	0	3	1	2	2	0	2	1	.111	.000	.250	3.00	6.00
Gonzalez, Mike	R-L	6-2	215	5-23-78	0	1	5.40	4	1	0	0	5	7	3	3	2	0	5	.333	.333	.333	9.00	0.00
Gurka, Jason	L-L	6-0	170	1-10-88	2	2	4.93	22	0	0	0	38	27	22	21	4	19	46	.200	.100	.242	10.80	4.46
Henry, Randy	R-R	6-3	190	5-10-90	0	1	13.50	1	0	0	0	1	2	1	1	0	1	0	.667	.000	.667	0.00	13.50
Holloway, Brandon	L-L	6-3	245	4-26-86	1	1	0.00	3	0	0	0	6	3	2	0	0	2	6	.136	.000	.231	6.00	3.00
Keating, Travis	R-R	6-6	205	9-16-85	3	3	3.42	19	0	0	3	26	27	13	10	1	7	26	.265	.235	.279	8.89	2.39
Klein, Dan	R-R	6-3	190	7-27-88	1	0	0.00	5	0	0	1	6	1	0	0	0	1	10	.048	.000	.067	14.21	1.42
Mazur, Steven	R-R	6-0	195	1-29-88	1	1	1.64	15	0	0	6	22	22	5	4	3	9	29	.272	.314	.239	11.86	3.68
Mechaw, Blake	L-L	6-2	200	8-19-88	1	0	4.97	15	2	0	0	29	28	19	16	0	23	23	.267	.265	.268	7.14	7.14
Mickolio, Kam	R-R	6-9	255	5-10-84	1	0	1.80	4	0	0	0	5	1	1	1	1	1	7	.063	.111	.000	12.60	1.80
Moore, Justin	R-R	6-3	190	7-26-89	3	2	2.57	11	11	0	0	56	56	19	16	0	19	28	.273	.310	.248	4.50	3.05
Parker, Brian	R-R	6-4	195	8-21-85	1	0	6.35	4	0	0	0	6	9	5	4	0	1	4	.391	.444	.357	6.35	1.59
Pettit, Jacob	L-L	6-1	185	10-28-86	0	0	1.80	1	0	0	0	5	2	1	1	0	1	5	.118	.111	.125	9.00	1.80
Rasner, Jesse	R-R	6-3	200	12-4-86	2	0	0.87	7	0	0	0	10	13	1	1	0	3	11	.325	.438	.250	9.58	2.61
Sanchez, Bruno	R-R	6-6	170	11-8-86	3	4	4.07	15	10	0	0	60	64	32	27	1	19	42	.275	.321	.236	6.34	2.87
Schmarzo, Alex	R-R	6-3	185	2-28-89	0	1	4.91	4	0	0	0	5	3	2	0	3	.333	.333	.333	7.36	7.36	

	B-T	HT	WT	DOB	W	L	ERA	G	GS	CG	SV	IP	H	R	ER	HR	BB	SO	AVG	vLH	vRH	K/9	BB/9
Schrader, Clay	L-R	6-0	200	4-28-90	1	0	0.00	7	0	0	1	8	4	2	0	0	4	10	.148	.154	.143	11.25	4.50
Sexton, Tyler	L-L	6-4	205	7-24-85	2	6	6.04	13	12	0	0	67	71	49	45	8	23	55	.281	.236	.298	7.39	3.09
Startup, Will	L-L	6-0	195	8-4-84	1	0	2.13	14	0	0	0	25	16	7	6	2	5	21	.186	.167	.196	7.46	1.78
Tolliver, Ashur	L-L	6-0	170	1-24-88	0	1	5.77	20	0	0	0	39	40	26	25	2	16	29	.268	.308	.247	6.69	3.69
Walters, David	R-R	6-3	190	8-13-87	2	0	0.00	9	0	0	3	10	2	0	0	0	0	4	.063	.000	.133	3.60	0.00
Wirsch, Aaron	R-L	6-6	200	11-15-90	0	1	3.00	1	1	0	0	3	3	1	1	0	2	4	.333	.667	.167	12.00	6.00

Fielding

Catcher	PCT	G	PO	A	E	DP	PB
Goolsby	.991	14	95	13	1	0	7
Oliveira	.989	34	246	21	3	1	8
Polanco	1.000	6	19	2	0	0	
Rauch	.981	15	91	14	2	0	5
Ricardo	.983	16	97	20	2	2	3

First Base	PCT	G	PO	A	E	DP
Anderson	.985	48	431	33	7	35
Flacco	.994	17	150	11	1	15
Gaylord	1.000	2	20	2	0	0
Kolodny	1.000	2	32	2	0	0
Rauch	.952	4	37	3	2	5
Rooney	1.000	1	1	0	0	0
Snyder	1.000	2	25	1	0	0
Stampone	1.000	3	29	1	0	1

Second Base	PCT	G	PO	A	E	DP
Casamayor	.962	21	30	46	3	13
Donaldson	1.000	6	5	11	0	2
Givens	.889	6	9	15	3	2
Hoes	.909	5	6	14	2	1
Knight	.980	19	43	55	2	14
Starr	.992	23	43	80	1	13

Third Base	PCT	G	PO	A	E	DP
Casamayor	1.000	2	1	3	0	0
Flacco	1.000	1	2	2	0	0
Gaylord	.970	64	27	164	6	10
Narron	.875	5	4	10	2	0
Stampone	.857	2	1	5	1	1
Starr	1.000	2	2	4	0	1

Shortstop	PCT	G	PO	A	E	DP
Casamayor	—	1	0	0	0	0
Donaldson	.700	2	2	5	3	1
Florimon	1.000	4	5	14	0	1
Knight	1.000	2	1	3	0	0
Machado	.955	5	7	14	1	2
Rooney	.967	57	92	170	9	34
Starr	.930	9	21	19	3	5

Outfield	PCT	G	PO	A	E	DP
Dunlap	.931	29	52	2	4	0
Knight	.973	26	35	1	1	0
Kolodny	1.000	7	13	2	0	0
Moore	1.000	1	1	0	0	0
Moore	.909	10	10	0	1	0
Mummey	.990	48	94	4	1	2
Nowak	.940	45	59	4	4	0
Schutz	.978	63	84	3	2	0
Stampone	1.000	2	4	0	0	0

BLUEFIELD ORIOLES   ROOKIE

APPALACHIAN LEAGUE

Batting	B-T	HT	WT	DOB	AVG	vLH	vRH	G	AB	R	H	2B	3B	HR	RBI	BB	HBP	SH	SF	SO	SB	CS	SLG	OBP
Childers, Anderson	L-R	6-1	187	8-21-86	.053	.000	.067	10	19	2	1	0	0	0	1	5	0	0	1	5	1	1	.053	.240
Cintron, Edwin	B-R	5-11	175	6-29-90	.148	.125	.156	26	61	8	9	0	1	0	3	1	1	1	1	23	3	1	.180	.172
Ciriaco, Moises	R-R	5-11	185	8-31-88	.267	.306	.252	51	180	27	48	6	1	2	18	14	2	4	0	22	2	5	.344	.327
Clinton, Chris	R-R	6-1	185	7-24-89	.192	.143	.211	27	78	9	15	5	0	1	10	7	2	1	0	19	0	0	.295	.276
Decater, Brad	R-R	6-1	185	12-28-88	.213	.229	.206	45	155	17	33	10	0	0	11	11	4	0	2	53	0	0	.277	.279
Goolsby, Austin	R-R	6-2	185	4-28-88	.148	.125	.158	10	27	2	4	2	0	0	1	1	0	1	1	12	0	0	.222	.172
Guerrero, Janesni	R-R	6-0	170	5-21-89	.115	.091	.133	9	26	2	3	1	1	0	4	1	0	0	0	7	1	0	.231	.148
Hoppy, Kyle	L-L	6-0	195	5-8-91	.171	.151	.180	44	175	16	30	2	1	0	9	21	1	1	0	42	0	1	.194	.264
Hornback, Riley	R-R	6-0	185	10-21-89	.340	.444	.317	20	50	9	17	2	1	0	7	8	1	0	0	14	1	0	.420	.441
Leonora, Dudley	R-R	6-1	154	12-15-91	.245	.280	.226	38	143	22	35	3	1	0	15	5	3	3	0	17	1	1	.280	.285
Mosby, Michael	R-R	6-0	195	10-30-89	.167	.250	.136	11	30	4	5	3	0	1	2	6	0	0	0	14	0	0	.367	.306
Ohlman, Michael	R-R	6-4	205	12-14-90	.233	.386	.170	50	150	11	35	8	1	0	20	17	1	1	0	52	0	0	.300	.315
Perez, Dennis	B-R	5-11	185	7-30-88	.273	.500	.222	5	11	0	3	0	0	0	1	0	0	0	0	1	0	0	.273	.273
Ramirez, Luis	L-L	6-3	170	4-24-88	.280	.195	.307	47	168	25	47	13	5	2	18	3	4	0	1	37	3	2	.452	.307
Ricardo, Dashenko	R-R	6-0	160	3-1-90	.241	.368	.179	16	58	6	14	2	1	1	4	1	0	0	0	14	0	1	.362	.254
Santana, Javier	B-R	6-1	160	7-31-87	.195	.200	.193	30	77	8	15	2	1	1	5	12	1	1	0	19	0	1	.312	.311
Schoop, Jon	R-R	6-1	187	10-6-91	.316	.298	.326	39	133	16	42	11	1	2	16	12	0	3	0	14	1	1	.459	.372
Schram, Greyson	R-R	6-1	195	4-15-88	.172	.133	.214	11	29	3	5	1	0	2	4	2	1	0	0	14	0	0	.414	.250
Shelby, Jeremy	R-R	6-1	170	8-14-87	.228	.229	.228	38	127	16	29	3	3	2	14	12	1	0	1	41	4	3	.346	.295
Thomas, Corey	R-R	6-2	201	9-23-88	.242	.254	.237	59	219	30	53	8	2	4	28	11	5	1	1	81	5	5	.352	.292
Velleggia, Joe	R-R	6-6	215	7-23-88	.210	.115	.255	31	81	8	17	4	0	1	9	9	2	0	2	34	0	0	.296	.298
Webb, Brenden	L-L	6-3	190	2-24-90	.227	.228	.226	61	194	25	44	5	8	5	25	32	4	1	0	58	5	2	.412	.348
Young, Cody	R-R	6-4	200	1-5-88	.130	.133	.129	22	46	6	6	2	1	0	1	3	2	0	0	24	0	0	.217	.216
Zazueta, Vinny	R-R	6-0	150	11-28-90	.167	.333	.083	11	36	4	6	0	0	0	1	0	0	0	0	12	1	0	.167	.167

Pitching	B-T	HT	WT	DOB	W	L	ERA	G	GS	CG	SV	IP	H	R	ER	HR	BB	SO	AVG	vLH	vRH	K/9	BB/9
Ast, Cory	L-L	6-3	180	9-29-87	1	0	3.75	11	0	0	0	12	9	5	5	1	4	17	.260	.308	.243	12.75	3.00
Baker, David	R-R	6-4	195	4-17-91	0	2	7.90	4	4	0	0	14	14	15	12	1	11	12	.250	.217	.273	7.90	7.24
Carder, Dustin	R-R	6-5	220	2-2-87	1	3	4.28	22	0	0	2	27	25	15	13	1	8	18	.245	.167	.288	5.93	2.63
Cespedes, Angel	R-R	6-2	170	8-27-89	3	6	3.42	13	13	0	0	71	84	40	27	3	9	31	.287	.362	.245	3.93	1.14
De La Cruz, Jairo	R-R	6-3	183	7-15-87	0	1	7.91	11	0	0	0	19	26	16	17	6	19	7	.321	.333	.314	3.26	8.84
Deain, Andy	R-R	6-0	195	10-23-86	0	1	3.96	16	0	0	3	25	28	18	11	0	7	24	.286	.310	.275	8.64	2.52
Gross, Billy	R-R	6-2	195	9-3-87	1	2	5.48	9	0	0	0	21	26	13	13	5	2	25	.299	.353	.286	10.55	0.84
Huebner, Andrew	R-R	6-2	200	11-5-86	1	1	3.77	16	0	0	1	29	29	13	12	1	8	21	.269	.250	.275	6.59	2.51
Martin, Jarret	L-L	6-3	200	8-14-89	3	5	4.07	13	13	0	0	60	43	38	27	3	46	68	.204	.188	.207	10.26	6.94
Mazur, Steven	R-R	6-0	195	1-29-88	0	0	0.00	8	0	0	0	8	3	1	0	0	0	9	.107	.091	.118	10.13	0.00
McCrory, Pat	R-R	5-9	175	12-9-88	0	0	7.36	4	0	0	0	4	8	3	3	0	3	5	.421	.429	.417	12.27	7.36
Petersime, Zach	R-R	6-3	175	1-19-89	1	4	5.09	16	7	0	0	53	56	33	30	2	13	26	.277	.338	.228	4.42	2.21
Petrini, Chris	R-L	6-0	235	2-11-87	3	1	2.22	15	0	0	0	24	19	8	6	1	11	29	.216	.263	.203	10.73	4.07
Pettit, Jacob	L-L	6-1	185	10-28-86	3	5	2.68	11	11	0	0	57	57	26	17	4	4	50	.257	.172	.269	7.89	0.63
Ramirez, Eiris	R-R	6-0	173	8-2-88	1	2	9.18	8	2	0	0	17	26	19	17	9	4	36	.365	.385	.354	2.16	4.86
Roth, Cameron	L-L	6-1	202	4-5-89	2	4	4.23	12	0	0	0	55	48	32	26	5	21	47	.233	.324	.215	7.64	3.42
Strong, Travis	R-R	6-6	210	8-13-88	0	2	4.05	20	0	0	0	27	23	16	12	3	16	22	.225	.222	.227	7.43	5.40
Tavarez, Daurin	R-R	6-6	160	2-8-89	0	5	7.57	6	6	0	0	27	42	29	23	2	12	19	.353	.348	.356	6.26	3.95
Taveras, Sam	R-R	6-3	180	1-4-88	3	1	4.01	23	0	0	0	34	31	18	15	0	17	30	.244	.217	.259	8.02	4.54

Fielding

Catcher	PCT	G	PO	A	E	DP	PB
Goolsby	1.000	9	61	10	0	2	4
Guerrero	1.000	9	36	5	0	0	5
Hornback	1.000	7	37	2	0	0	5
Ohlman	1.000	31	193	28	0	3	9
Perez	1.000	5	19	1	0	0	1
Ricardo	.982	16	97	14	2	0	2
Schram	1.000	4	18	2	0	0	2

First Base	PCT	G	PO	A	E	DP
Decater	1.000	1	8	0	0	1
Thomas	.979	59	510	45	12	52
Velleggia	.959	13	91	2	4	12

Second Base	PCT	G	PO	A	E	DP
Childers	.952	8	18	22	2	8
Ciriaco	.950	49	101	126	12	34
Leonora	.969	12	26	37	2	16
Santana	.895	6	6	11	2	2

Third Base	PCT	G	PO	A	E	DP
Decater	.879	37	24	70	13	10
Leonora	.910	28	17	54	7	9
Mosby	.909	11	6	24	3	1

Shortstop	PCT	G	PO	A	E	DP
Santana	.868	24	26	73	15	14

	PCT	G	PO	A	E	DP
Schoop	.913	38	65	114	17	25
Young	1.000	1	0	1	0	0
Zazueta	.865	11	10	35	7	6

Outfield	PCT	G	PO	A	E	DP
Cintron	.970	20	31	1	1	0
Clinton	1.000	20	34	2	0	0
Hoppy	.899	42	58	4	7	2
Ramirez	.941	40	71	9	5	4
Shelby	.948	35	51	4	3	0
Webb	.958	56	89	3	4	0
Young	.958	16	21	2	1	1

GCL ORIOLES   ROOKIE
GULF COAST LEAGUE

Batting	B-T	HT	WT	DOB	AVG	vLH	vRH	G	AB	R	H	2B	3B	HR	RBI	BB	HBP	SH	SF	SO	SB	CS	SLG	OBP
Cleofa, Rojean	R-R	5-11	176	9-11-90	.224	.256	.206	35	107	21	24	7	0	1	13	9	4	2	0	20	6	2	.318	.308
Dalles, Justin	R-R	6-2	205	12-30-88	.200	.250	.167	5	10	2	2	1	0	0	1	5	0	0	0	1	0	0	.300	.467
Donaldson, Auburn	B-R	5-11	175	4-9-88	.194	.125	.250	14	36	4	7	0	0	0	3	7	0	1	0	14	3	1	.194	.326
Givens, Mychal	R-R	6-1	190	5-13-90	.207	.250	.190	7	29	2	6	2	0	0	2	0	0	0	0	4	0	0	.276	.207
Gonzalez, Grolmann	B-R	6-1	180	10-12-88	.294	.298	.290	35	109	18	32	6	2	2	7	13	1	2	0	26	2	3	.440	.374
Guerrero, Janensi	R-R	6-0	170	5-21-89	.238	.182	.300	8	21	0	5	1	0	0	2	2	0	0	0	6	0	0	.286	.304
Hale, Preston	L-L	5-10	195	3-7-88	.269	.268	.269	53	201	19	54	14	3	1	29	12	9	0	4	32	1	1	.383	.332
Hornback, Riley	R-R	6-0	185	10-21-89	.176	.150	.194	16	51	8	9	2	0	0	2	9	0	2	1	7	1	0	.216	.295
Jones, Marcus	L-R	6-4	220	11-24-85	.227	.000	.263	7	22	3	5	4	0	0	1	2	1	0	0	9	0	0	.409	.320
Leonora, Dudley	R-R	6-1	154	12-15-91	.288	.375	.263	20	73	12	21	2	2	0	12	7	2	5	3	6	0	1	.370	.353
Lopez, Xavier	R-R	6-2	180	1-18-90	.180	.222	.156	21	50	5	9	1	0	0	10	6	2	1	1	13	3	0	.200	.288
Machado, Manny	R-R	6-3	185	7-6-92	.143	.000	.200	2	7	1	1	0	0	1	0	0	0	0	0	1	0	0	.571	.143
Melenciano, Jaynnertt	R-R	6-1	170	11-13-87	.257	.234	.268	41	144	14	37	9	0	1	14	11	1	2	0	25	5	6	.340	.314
Montanez, Lou	R-R	6-1	195	12-15-81	.200	.167	.222	4	15	1	3	0	0	0	1	0	0	0	0	2	0	0	.200	.200
Moranci, Gino	L-L	6-4	188	1-27-90	.275	.241	.219	33	102	8	23	4	0	0	7	7	0	1	0	26	0	0	.265	.275
Mosby, Michael	R-R	6-0	195	10-30-89	.207	.277	.156	34	111	8	23	4	1	0	9	8	8	0	1	26	1	1	.261	.305
Murphy, Tanner	L-R	6-1	190	7-4-92	.200	.154	.219	16	45	2	9	0	0	0	4	4	0	1	0	10	0	0	.200	.265
Narron, Connor	R-R	6-3	195	11-12-91	.206	.267	.158	11	34	0	7	0	0	0	4	2	1	1	1	11	1	0	.206	.282
Nivar, Jose	B-R	6-1	170	2-28-89	.167	.118	.186	19	60	8	10	2	2	0	8	10	1	0	0	14	0	1	.267	.296
Parra, Freuny	R-R	5-11	195	11-2-87	.000	.000	.000	3	3	0	0	0	0	0	0	0	0	0	0	0	0	0	.000	.000
Petit, Rolando	B-R	6-2	205	4-27-90	.203	.333	.146	18	59	4	12	2	0	1	5	4	0	0	0	16	0	0	.288	.254
Pie, Felix	L-L	6-2	185	2-8-85	.125	.000	.167	2	8	1	1	0	0	0	0	0	0	0	0	2	1	1	.125	.125
Rivera, David	L-R	6-0	190	3-20-91	.219	.250	.204	23	73	6	16	0	1	1	9	6	2	1	24	1	1		.288	.275
Roberts, Brian	B-R	5-9	175	10-9-77	.533	.000	.615	5	15	1	8	1	0	0	2	2	0	0	0	3	0	0	.600	.588
Rodriguez, Pedro	R-R	5-11	145	4-20-90	.272	.242	.286	33	103	21	28	6	0	0	8	6	4	0	14	8	2		.330	.312
Sawyer, Wynston	R-R	6-3	190	11-14-91	.231	.111	.294	9	26	1	6	0	0	1	1	0	1	0	0	4	0	0	.346	.259
Schoop, Jon	R-R	6-1	187	10-6-91	.250	.118	.302	17	60	11	15	4	0	3	16	7	1	0	2	7	0	0	.467	.329
Scott, Luke	L-R	6-0	205	6-25-78	.222	.000	.333	3	9	1	2	0	0	0	2	2	0	0	0	1	0	0	.222	.364
Serrata, Martin	R-R	6-1	170	11-3-88	.295	.291	.297	42	156	19	46	5	1	0	10	10	2	4	2	24	7	3	.340	.341
Stampone, Tyler	R-R	6-2	220	5-21-87	.091	.000	.200	3	11	1	1	1	0	0	1	0	0	0	1	2	0	0	.182	.083
Tejeda, Anyi	R-R	6-3	173	1-19-89	.220	.200	.231	40	123	14	27	2	0	0	7	4	4	3	1	29	2	1	.236	.265
Townsend, Tyler	L-R	6-3	215	5-14-88	.385	.250	.444	3	13	3	5	4	0	0	5	1	0	0	0	2	0	0	.692	.429
Zazueta, Vinny	R-R	6-0	150	11-28-90	.185	.233	.157	23	81	6	15	5	1	0	2	2	1	2	1	26	2	2	.198	.230

Pitching	B-T	HT	WT	DOB	W	L	ERA	G	GS	CG	SV	IP	H	R	ER	HR	BB	SO	AVG	vLH	vRH	K/9	BB/9
Adrian, Yancorix	L-L	6-5	185	7-7-89	3	2	2.14	12	7	0	0	59	44	25	14	3	21	52	.207	.265	.189	7.93	3.20
Alfonso, Orlando	R-R	6-5	230	8-15-89	6	1	1.57	12	8	0	0	52	48	13	9	0	11	34	.242	.229	.255	5.92	1.92
Ast, Cory	L-L	6-3	180	9-29-87	1	0	2.31	5	0	0	0	12	8	4	3	1	2	13	.190	.167	.200	10.03	1.54
Batista, Luiyi	R-R	6-1	170	4-22-88	1	7	4.40	12	12	0	0	61	65	38	30	3	20	46	.269	.267	.270	6.75	2.93
Berry, Tim	L-L	6-3	180	3-18-91	0	1	1.35	14	0	0	0	20	13	9	3	0	14	23	.181	.125	.188	10.35	6.30
Bridwell, Parker	R-R	6-4	190	8-2-91	0	0	5.40	2	2	0	0	2	1	1	1	0	3	4	.167	.333	.000	21.60	16.20
Coffey, Cameron	L-L	6-5	215	9-20-90	0	1	5.73	7	0	0	0	11	19	8	7	1	2	8	.373	.286	.405	6.55	1.64
Deain, Andy	R-R	6-0	195	10-23-86	0	1	2.61	7	0	0	1	10	7	3	3	0	3	14	.194	.350	.000	12.19	2.61
Drummond, Matt	L-L	6-1	170	4-5-88	2	1	1.76	8	0	0	0	15	5	4	3	1	11	21	.096	.167	.075	12.33	6.46
Ferguson, D.J.	R-R	6-1	190	11-27-87	4	3	1.09	12	8	0	1	58	40	13	7	2	14	44	.196	.232	.152	6.83	2.17
Gonzalez, Mike	L-L	6-2	215	5-23-78	0	0	0.00	2	2	0	0	2	1	0	0	0	3	3	.143	.000	.250	13.50	13.50
Goodin, Josh	R-R	6-1	200	8-17-86	1	0	6.48	4	0	0	0	8	11	6	6	0	3	7	.344	.412	.267	7.56	3.24
Hanks, D.D.	R-R	5-11	240	1-9-87	0	2	3.48	5	2	0	0	10	16	5	4	0	5	9	.356	.458	.238	7.84	4.35
Hervey, Chris	R-R	6-2	190	12-10-86	0	2	3.68	4	0	0	0	7	7	5	3	1	4	7	.241	.333	.143	8.59	4.91
Jimenez, Enrico	R-L	6-3	195	2-7-89	2	2	2.68	12	8	0	0	57	45	24	17	1	25	72	.208	.261	.194	11.37	3.95
Johnson, Jim	R-R	6-5	231	6-27-83	0	0	6.75	4	4	0	0	4	5	3	3	1	1	5	.313	.300	.333	11.25	2.75
Lamb, Chris	L-L	6-1	175	9-6-90	1	2	9.20	14	0	0	0	15	23	23	15	2	14	14	.359	.412	.340	8.59	8.59
Mota, Jose	R-R	5-11	180	8-18-88	1	2	2.32	20	0	0	6	31	20	9	8	1	5	32	.189	.200	.176	9.29	1.45
Petrini, Chris	R-L	6-0	235	2-11-87	0	1	1.53	6	0	0	2	18	10	3	3	0	7	23	.172	.273	.149	11.72	3.57
Rasner, Jesse	R-R	6-3	200	12-4-86	1	0	4.15	3	0	0	0	4	5	2	2	0	0	6	.278	.300	.250	12.46	0.00
Richardson, David	R-R	5-11	170	1-31-91	0	2	10.80	13	0	0	1	12	12	15	14	0	20	14	.267	.304	.227	10.80	15.43

Name	B-T	HT	WT	DOB	W	L	ERA	G	GS	CG	SV	IP	H	R	ER	HR	BB	SO	AVG	vLH	vRH	K/9	BB/9
Schmitt, Chris	R-R	6-0	190	12-31-86	0	0	1.08	3	0	0	0	8	5	2	1	0	3	7	.179	.200	.154	7.56	3.24
Swenson, Aaron	R-R	5-11	200	3-25-87	1	2	2.03	6	2	0	0	13	8	5	3	0	4	10	.160	.185	.130	6.75	2.70
Vader, Sebastian	R-R	6-4	175	6-3-92	1	0	7.30	9	0	0	0	12	8	10	10	2	9	16	.182	.158	.200	11.68	6.57
Wirsch, Aaron	R-L	6-6	200	11-15-90	0	2	8.64	5	4	0	0	8	12	9	8	0	6	9	.353	.222	.400	9.72	6.48

Fielding

Catcher	PCT	G	PO	A	E	DP	PB
Dalles	1.000	4	23	3	0	0	1
Guerrero	.951	8	50	8	3	0	4
Hornback	1.000	11	95	9	0	1	1
Lopez	.966	16	101	12	4	0	2
Murphy	.935	11	55	3	4	0	2
Parra	1.000	2	4	0	0	0	0
Petit	.985	17	121	8	2	3	6
Sawyer	1.000	8	45	7	0	1	1

First Base	PCT	G	PO	A	E	DP
Hale	.983	32	264	28	5	21
Moranci	.955	24	179	14	9	13
Petit	1.000	1	3	0	0	0
Stampone	1.000	2	18	1	0	3
Townsend	1.000	3	21	0	0	1

Second Base	PCT	G	PO	A	E	DP
Donaldson	.930	13	12	28	3	2
Leonora	1.000	3	4	9	0	3
Lopez	.750	2	3	3	2	1
Roberts	1.000	3	2	4	0	2
Rodriguez	.977	32	57	69	3	10
Tejeda	.983	15	26	33	1	10
Zazueta	1.000	1	2	4	0	0

Third Base	PCT	G	PO	A	E	DP
Leonora	.962	18	14	36	2	6
Mosby	.905	33	24	62	9	3
Tejeda	.821	13	7	16	5	2

Shortstop	PCT	G	PO	A	E	DP
Givens	.818	4	5	4	2	1
Mosby	1.000	1	0	1	0	0
Narron	.966	8	8	20	1	0
Schoop	.981	16	17	34	1	7
Tejeda	.922	12	17	30	4	4
Zazueta	.968	22	29	61	3	13

Outfield	PCT	G	PO	A	E	DP
Cleofa	.981	30	50	1	1	0
Gonzalez	.974	25	38	0	1	0
Hale	1.000	10	14	0	0	0
Jones	1.000	3	3	0	0	0
Melenciano	.961	40	68	5	3	1
Montanez	—	2	0	0	0	0
Nivar	.975	17	37	2	1	1
Rivera	.960	17	22	2	1	0
Scott	1.000	1	1	0	0	0
Serrata	.961	41	72	1	3	0

DSL ORIOLES 1   *ROOKIE*

DOMINICAN SUMMER LEAGUE

Batting	B-T	HT	WT	DOB	AVG	vLH	vRH	G	AB	R	H	2B	3B	HR	RBI	BB	HBP	SH	SF	SO	SB	CS	SLG	OBP
Aguirre, Wilder	R-R	6-0	160	4-16-92	.267	.000	.320	19	30	3	8	2	0	0	2	3	1	0	0	6	0	0	.333	.353
Araujo, Cristian	R-R	5-11	170	4-22-92	.189	.226	.181	55	180	21	34	4	1	1	18	22	8	3	1	29	5	3	.239	.303
Beltre, Moises	R-R	5-11	190	11-15-90	.182	.100	.206	21	44	3	8	2	1	1	10	4	4	0	0	11	0	0	.341	.308
Bernadina, Roderick	R-R	6-1	162	8-10-92	.242	.191	.256	70	223	37	54	13	1	1	26	30	7	4	2	38	13	8	.341	.347
Boni, Junior	R-R	6-0	175	2-5-91	.239	.269	.233	49	142	22	34	7	2	0	21	16	9	4	1	39	11	5	.317	.351
Cueva, Daceilin	R-R	6-0	170	6-22-91	.190	.250	.176	23	21	6	4	0	0	0	3	1	0	0	4	1	0	.190	.320
Gonzalez, Henry	L-L	6-4	210	3-31-92	.182	.222	.171	56	165	14	30	6	0	4	24	30	5	0	1	47	2	0	.291	.323
Hernandez, Manuel	R-R	6-1	190	8-19-92	.127	.080	.138	47	134	15	17	2	1	0	5	23	8	0	1	39	4	3	.157	.289
Justo, Moises	R-R	6-3	200	6-7-92	.146	.100	.158	46	96	10	14	6	0	0	10	15	9	2	2	42	2	5	.208	.311
Ledesma, Ronarsy	R-R	5-11	170	4-19-93	.265	.400	.254	24	68	8	18	3	1	3	13	6	3	0	0	14	3	0	.471	.351
Lorenzo, Gregory	R-R	6-0	160	5-31-91	.252	.289	.243	69	226	41	57	4	5	0	15	34	4	7	0	49	27	6	.314	.360
Martinez, Rockny	B-R	6-2	175	7-14-92	.123	.100	.127	29	65	7	8	0	1	0	6	3	3	1	22	0	1	.154	.237
Mercedes, Alexander	R-R	6-0	160	3-20-92	.195	.063	.226	54	169	33	33	5	1	0	9	19	1	4	1	14	7	5	.237	.279
Parra, Gustavo	R-R	5-11	172	8-4-90	.256	.235	.262	30	82	6	21	3	3	1	6	12	2	2	0	25	1	3	.402	.365
Perez, Pedro	R-R	5-11	170	5-8-91	.177	.214	.167	55	130	8	23	0	0	8	10	1	6	0	8	0	3	.200	.241
Ramirez, Freidderyx	R-R	6-3	175	4-20-92	.165	.091	.184	37	109	7	18	3	1	0	6	8	0	1	0	27	0	4	.211	.222
Taveras, Junior	R-R	5-10	187	12-28-92	.257	.250	.259	16	35	5	9	0	1	0	3	5	2	0	0	6	0	0	.314	.381
Zorrilla, Alexander	R-R	6-1	169	5-16-91	.259	.154	.282	69	220	34	57	10	1	0	24	22	10	16	2	46	29	12	.314	.350

Pitching	B-T	HT	WT	DOB	W	L	ERA	G	GS	CG	SV	IP	H	R	ER	HR	BB	SO	AVG	vLH	vRH	K/9	BB/9
Alba, Victor	R-R	6-2	165	2-11-92	1	1	6.47	27	0	0	4	32	32	28	23	0	37	34	.281	.302	.268	9.56	10.41
Aquino, Wilmer	L-L	5-9	170	12-5-91	0	1	6.23	11	3	0	1	17	11	13	12	0	24	25	.183	.000	.212	12.98	12.46
Beltre, Franyer	R-R	6-0	180	4-14-93	0	4	10.62	21	1	0	2	20	21	28	24	0	24	17	.247	.267	.236	7.52	10.62
Bolivar, Miguel	R-R	6-0	180	1-24-92	0	1	10.80	3	2	0	0	5	2	7	6	0	8	2	.111	.000	.182	3.60	14.40
Castillo, Yancarlos	R-R	6-2	175	1-7-91	0	2	3.86	7	1	0	2	12	14	5	5	0	2	11	.318	.267	.345	8.49	1.54
Garcia, Rafael	R-R	6-3	170	9-15-89	4	4	2.07	24	2	1	2	65	63	36	15	0	18	45	.246	.210	.269	6.20	2.48
Guzman, Juan	R-R	6-0	190	2-25-91	3	6	2.60	14	13	1	0	69	43	31	20	2	31	58	.182	.150	.206	7.53	4.02
Mejias, Jesus	L-L	6-0	190	6-20-90	1	2	6.62	16	6	0	0	34	35	34	25	1	39	31	.278	.467	.252	8.21	10.32
Mercedes, Daniel	R-R	6-4	180	5-12-92	3	1	5.82	21	0	0	0	39	42	30	25	1	28	24	.261	.338	.223	5.59	6.52
Perez, Julio	R-R	6-2	175	1-16-92	0	2	15.15	12	1	0	0	14	24	25	23	1	22	13	.407	.462	.364	8.56	14.49
Princivil, William	R-R	6-2	180	4-12-90	7	5	2.71	14	14	1	0	83	81	37	25	2	23	61	.252	.306	.209	6.61	2.49
Rodriguez, Eduardo	L-L	6-2	175	4-7-93	3	4	2.33	12	12	1	0	89	49	26	17	0	28	62	.213	.207	.214	8.50	3.84
Rojas, Yancarlos	R-R	6-4	185	5-4-91	0	5	6.03	17	3	0	1	34	27	28	23	0	21	34	.261	.183	.361	9.81	5.50
Salas, Domingo	R-R	5-11	175	5-11-91	3	5	3.13	13	13	0	0	69	66	34	24	0	23	43	.256	.240	.265	5.61	3.00
Santana, Juan	R-R	6-4	165	5-3-92	0	2	9.21	19	1	0	1	28	33	33	29	1	31	16	.295	.304	.288	5.08	9.85
Soto, Luis	R-R	6-0	190	8-22-89	0	1	18.00	3	0	0	0	2	2	4	4	0	4	2	.250	.500	.167	9.00	18.00

Fielding

Catcher	PCT	G	PO	A	E	DP	PB
Aguirre	.959	17	66	4	3	0	7
Beltre	1.000	3	21	4	0	0	1
Boni	1.000	1	1	0	0	0	0
Ledesma	.950	6	31	7	2	0	6
Parra	1.000	10	50	8	0	1	3
Perez	.980	54	280	57	7	2	5
Taveras	.952	13	49	10	3	2	4

First Base	PCT	G	PO	A	E	DP
Aguirre	.900	2	7	2	1	0
Araujo	1.000	1	3	0	0	0
Beltre	.333	1	0	1	2	0
Gonzalez	.966	45	314	24	12	28
Hernandez	.963	6	26	0	1	2
Justo	.973	31	171	11	5	13
Ledesma	—	1	0	1	0	0
Parra	1.000	4	23	3	0	1

Second Base	PCT	G	PO	A	E	DP
Araujo	.962	5	10	15	1	3
Cueva	.769	3	4	6	3	1
Mercedes	1.000	1	3	5	0	1
Zorrilla	.933	67	148	172	23	28

Third Base	PCT	G	PO	A	E	DP
Araujo	.900	48	25	74	11	6
Cueva	.750	1	2	1	1	1
Hernandez	.721	16	18	13	12	1
Justo	1.000	1	2	1	0	0
Mercedes	.714	8	10	15	10	0
Parra	1.000	2	0	4	0	0
Ramirez	1.000	3	2	3	0	0

Shortstop	PCT	G	PO	A	E	DP
Araujo	.895	4	8	9	2	2
Cueva	.700	5	4	3	3	0

Mercedes	.912	40	68	87	15	9
Ramirez	.857	34	54	78	22	16
Zorrilla	—	1	0	0	0	0

Outfield	PCT	G	PO	A	E	DP
Bernadina	.973	70	136	9	4	2
Boni	.943	31	32	1	2	0
Hernandez	1.000	2	2	0	0	0

Hernandez	.938	22	28	2	2	0
Justo	1.000	14	17	1	0	0
Lorenzo	.952	69	93	7	5	1
Martinez	.909	27	27	3	3	0

DSL ORIOLES 2   ROOKIE

DOMINICAN SUMMER LEAGUE

Batting	B-T	HT	WT	DOB	AVG	vLH	vRH	G	AB	R	H	2B	3B	HR	RBI	BB	HBP	SH	SF	SO	SB	CS	SLG	OBP
Aguida, Nelson	R-R	6-1	180	4-22-92	.150	.250	.139	26	40	2	6	0	0	0	4	2	0	1	3	3	0	0	.150	.178
Aguilar, Andrew	R-R	6-2	177	4-16-91	.250	.500	.219	16	36	2	9	1	0	0	1	4	0	1	0	17	1	0	.278	.325
Antigua, Erik	R-R	6-4	220	11-4-91	.100	.091	.103	20	50	0	5	1	0	0	2	2	4	0	0	17	0	0	.120	.196
Avila, Eliecer	R-R	6-2	175	1-30-90	.223	.296	.202	50	121	9	27	6	0	1	11	18	1	4	2	23	3	4	.298	.324
Bido, Felix	R-R	6-2	170	8-7-91	.208	.116	.228	67	240	20	50	9	0	1	20	7	7	1	1	55	12	3	.258	.251
Capellan, Byron	R-R	5-11	150	8-9-93	.204	.344	.168	55	157	18	32	4	0	0	5	14	4	6	0	30	4	3	.229	.286
Cleofa, Rojean	R-R	5-11	176	9-11-90	.295	.500	.255	17	61	13	18	5	1	1	5	12	3	1	0	11	2	2	.459	.434
Conde, Jhason	R-R	5-11	165	11-20-90	.257	.267	.255	54	183	23	47	7	5	0	14	19	3	7	1	33	8	6	.350	.335
Dominguez, Dioni	B-R	6-1	175	10-20-90	.210	.176	.217	66	200	31	42	3	8	0	13	33	3	7	0	41	6	7	.305	.331
Familia, Elvis	B-R	6-1	190	5-2-91	.243	.333	.227	57	181	14	44	12	3	0	21	25	3	8	0	47	0	3	.343	.344
Hanley, Cesar	B-R	5-11	170	4-4-91	.201	.217	.198	61	149	12	30	3	1	0	7	17	3	3	0	34	11	12	.235	.296
Lartiguez, Oswill	R-R	6-1	179	8-11-92	.179	.152	.185	55	184	26	33	4	2	0	19	21	4	3	0	31	4	8	.223	.278
Lino, Gabriel	R-R	6-3	195	5-17-93	.200	.217	.197	54	140	15	28	10	0	0	19	28	9	2	4	21	4	0	.271	.359
Paez, Carlos	R-R	6-0	180	6-18-91	.151	.000	.178	44	106	7	16	1	0	0	9	10	1	5	1	41	0	1	.160	.229
Pimentel, Jerfry	R-R	6-0	170	12-4-91	.227	.286	.221	35	75	10	17	2	1	0	4	6	4	2	0	25	7	1	.280	.318
Portes, Wilmer	R-R	6-1	193	3-25-91	—	.000	.000	1	0	1	0	0	0	0	0	0	0	0	0	0	0	0	—	—
Santana, Alexander	B-R	5-11	170	8-26-91	.217	.208	.219	41	120	15	26	2	3	0	6	5	3	2	1	31	1	2	.283	.264
Santana, Yigui	R-R	6-2	180	3-2-92	.146	.000	.158	34	41	8	6	1	0	0	3	5	1	0	0	21	3	1	.171	.255
Zambrano, Alfredo	R-R	5-10	150	8-20-93	.140	.000	.167	18	50	5	7	1	0	0	3	6	0	3	0	5	1	3	.160	.232

Pitching	B-T	HT	WT	DOB	W	L	ERA	G	GS	CG	SV	IP	H	R	ER	HR	BB	SO	AVG	vLH	vRH	K/9	BB/9
Alcantara, Saulo	R-R	6-0	195	3-15-91	1	2	2.77	11	0	0	0	26	15	11	8	1	15	25	.169	.231	.143	8.65	5.19
Chalas, Miguel	R-R	6-0	170	6-27-92	5	1	1.72	14	13	2	0	78	56	21	15	1	16	64	.196	.211	.191	7.35	1.84
Espiritu, Alexander	R-R	6-0	190	3-30-91	0	0	14.40	4	0	0	0	5	5	10	8	1	17	1	.278	.500	.214	1.80	21.60
Figuereo, Jose	R-R	6-1	150	3-23-92	0	0	5.95	8	0	0	0	20	24	18	13	1	15	14	.296	.476	.233	6.41	6.86
Florentino, Angel	R-R	6-2	160	9-29-89	3	3	4.80	16	0	0	3	30	38	20	16	0	7	23	.306	.290	.312	6.90	2.10
Hernandez, Ivan	R-R	6-2	195	7-28-91	0	8	5.37	11	10	1	0	55	69	44	33	1	26	17	.304	.322	.298	2.77	4.23
Jean, Samuel	L-L	6-1	175	6-22-89	7	2	1.79	14	14	1	0	86	84	27	17	0	22	53	.264	.220	.271	5.57	2.31
Jimenez, Gabriel	R-R	6-4	190	1-1-90	0	3	5.87	15	2	0	0	31	20	22	20	2	29	22	.189	.148	.203	6.46	8.51
Jimenez, Joan	R-R	6-2	179	6-27-90	0	2	3.42	8	2	0	1	24	17	10	9	1	11	20	.202	.148	.228	7.61	4.18
Medina, Jhondaniel	R-R	5-11	158	2-8-93	3	3	2.32	10	10	0	0	50	39	19	13	0	17	49	.211	.194	.220	8.76	3.04
Pina, Edgar	R-R	6-0	172	3-5-93	1	0	7.45	6	0	0	0	10	12	11	8	2	6	8	.316	.500	.267	7.45	5.59
Ramirez, Cesar	R-R	6-4	190	8-3-92	0	1	12.96	6	1	0	0	8	10	13	12	0	18	10	.323	1.000	.300	10.80	19.44
Rivera, Jorge	L-L	6-0	200	10-30-90	3	4	1.21	20	0	0	8	52	44	16	7	0	23	56	.234	.360	.215	9.69	3.98
Severino, Janser	R-R	6-2	140	9-16-91	2	8	4.19	15	12	0	1	62	66	43	29	3	21	56	.262	.247	.269	8.09	3.03
Sosa, Israel	L-L	6-2	180	6-6-89	3	5	2.83	14	6	0	0	48	41	25	15	1	28	45	.228	.263	.224	8.50	5.29

Fielding

Catcher	PCT	G	PO	A	E	DP	PB
Aguida	.906	20	48	10	6	0	3
Avila	.968	36	185	26	7	0	3
Lino	.984	37	223	27	4	2	5
Paez	.917	4	11	0	1	0	0
Santana	1.000	3	8	1	0	0	1

First Base	PCT	G	PO	A	E	DP
Antigua	.978	17	124	7	3	11
Avila	.959	10	65	6	3	6
Bido	.965	13	53	2	2	5
Lino	1.000	7	56	0	0	3
Paez	.980	38	235	13	5	21
Santana	1.000	1	1	0	0	0
Santana	.962	12	47	3	2	7

Second Base	PCT	G	PO	A	E	DP
Conde	.953	43	88	95	9	25
Hanley	.990	25	53	50	1	12
Santana	.800	3	3	1	1	0
Zambrano	.950	7	16	22	2	6

Third Base	PCT	G	PO	A	E	DP
Antigua	1.000	1	1	0	0	0
Bido	.921	61	61	115	15	9
Capellan	1.000	2	0	1	0	0
Conde	1.000	1	0	1	0	0
Hanley	.897	12	10	25	4	1
Santana	.900	8	4	5	1	0

Shortstop	PCT	G	PO	A	E	DP
Capellan	.929	50	79	143	17	31
Conde	.889	9	18	22	5	4
Pimentel	.773	10	11	23	10	4
Zambrano	.857	8	7	17	4	2

Outfield	PCT	G	PO	A	E	DP
Aguilar	1.000	13	16	1	0	0
Cleofa	.893	17	23	2	3	1
Dominguez	.942	65	122	7	8	1
Familia	.977	33	37	5	1	2
Hanley	1.000	3	2	1	0	0
Lartiguez	.895	51	63	5	8	1
Pimentel	.895	18	16	1	2	0
Santana	.934	29	56	1	4	0

BALTIMORE ORIOLES

Boston Red Sox

SEASON IN A SENTENCE: With the highest payroll they've ever had, the Red Sox failed to make the playoffs after battling injuries all season as well as inconsistent pitching and defense.

HIGH POINT: Boston was never in first all season, and spent just 12 days even in second place—coming within a half-game of first at the beginning of July—so the highlight of the season may have come at the end, when the Red Sox closed with two victories against the Yankees. They tied the season series at 9-9 and kept New York from winning the American League East division in the process, relegating them to the wild card.

LOW POINT: After winning nine of their first 12 meetings against the Blue Jays in 2010, the Red Sox suffered their worst loss in three years against Toronto, a 16-2 pounding on Aug. 19. In the worst outing of his career, Jon Lester gave up nine runs in two innings. The loss came only hours after the announcement that Dustin Pedroia would likely be out for the remainder of the season, just one of the many significant injuries the team dealt with. The loss of Pedroia and Kevin Youkilis sank a team that had 19 players spend time on the disabled list.

NOTABLE ROOKIES: Outfielder Daniel Nava made news when he hit a grand slam in his first major league plate appearance at Fenway, capping an amazing run from independent league find to major leaguer. Outfielder Ryan Kalish struggled in his start with the big league club, but improved as the season wore on and ended up batting .294/.356/.476. Righthander Michael Bowden went 6-4, 3.66 in 106 innings between the rotation and bullpen.

KEY TRANSACTIONS: The Red Sox were quiet in the trade market, making minor deals like sending Ramon Ramirez to the Giants for Daniel Turpen and Manny Delcarmen to the Rockies for Chris Balcom-Miller in August. They spent big on the draft again, shelling out $10.7 million in bonuses.

DOWN ON THE FARM: Felix Doubront was the organization pitcher of the year in the minors, going 8-3, 2.81 between Double-A and Triple-A before getting called up. First baseman Anthony Rizzo and catcher Ryan Lavarnway were the offensive standouts, as Rizzo hit .260 with 25 home runs, 42 doubles, 100 RBIs and 61 walks, and Lavarnway hit .288 with 22 homers, 27 doubles and 70 walks.

OPENING DAY PAYROLL: $162.4 million (2nd)

PLAYERS OF THE YEAR

MAJOR LEAGUE	MINOR LEAGUE
Jon Lester	**Anthony Rizzo**
lhp	**1b**
19-9, 3.25	(High A/Double-A)
225 SO/208 IP	.260/.334/.480
Led AL in SO/9	25 HR, 42 2B

ORGANIZATION LEADERS

BATTING		*Minimum 250 at-bats
MAJORS		
*AVG	Adrian Beltre	.321
*OPS	Kevin Youkilis	.975
HR	David Ortiz	32
RBI	David Ortiz/Adrian Beltre	102
MINORS		
*AVG	Daniel Butler, Salem/Greenville/Pawtucket	.310
*OBP	Daniel Butler, Salem/Greenville/Pawtucket	.411
*SLG	Ryan Lavarnway, Salem/Portland	.489
R	Nate Spears, Portland	104
H	Oscar Tejeda, Salem	156
TB	Anthony Rizzo, Salem/Portland	255
2B	Anthony Rizzo, Salem/Portland	42
3B	Jeremy Hazelbaker, Greenville	9
HR	Anthony Rizzo, Salem/Portland	25
RBI	Ryan Lavarnway, Salem/Portland	102
BB	Nate Spears, Portland	84
SO	Jeremy Hazelbaker, Greenville	135
SB	Jeremy Hazelbaker, Greenville	63

PITCHING		†Minimum 75 innings
MAJORS		
W	Jon Lester	19
†ERA	Clay Buchholz	2.33
SO	Jon Lester	225
MINORS		
W	Blake Maxwell, Salem/Pawtucket/Portland	11
L	Caleb Clay, Salem	13
	Kris Johnson, Pawtucket	13
†ERA	Kendal Volz, Greenville	3.71
G	Fernando Cabrera, Pawtucket	54
	Chad Paronto, Pawtucket	54
GS	Alex Wilson, Salem/Portland	27
SV	Fernando Cabrera, Pawtucket	22
IP	Jeremy Kehrt, Salem/Portland	142.7
BB	Ryne Miller, Lowell/Portland	57
SO	Robert Coello, Portland/Pawtucket	130
†AVG	Kyle Weiland, Portland	.236

2010 PERFORMANCE

General Manager: Theo Epstein. **Farm Director:** Mike Hazen. **Scouting Director:** Amiel Sawdaye.

Class	Team	League	W	L	PCT	Finish*	Manager(s)
Majors	Boston Red Sox	American	89	73	.549	5th (14)	Terry Francona
Triple-A	Pawtucket Red Sox	International	66	78	.458	12th (14)	Torey Lovullo
Double-A	Portland Sea Dogs	Eastern	70	71	.496	7th (12)	Arnie Beyeler
High A	Salem Red Sox	Carolina	73	65	.529	3rd (8)	Kevin Boles
Low A	Greenville Drive	South Atlantic	77	62	.554	3rd (14)	Billy McMillon
Short-season	Lowell Spinners	New York-Penn	24	50	.324	14th (14)	Bruce Crabbe
Rookie	GCL Red Sox	Gulf Coast	31	28	.525	t-5th (15)	Dave Tomlin
Overall 2010 Minor League Record			341	354	.491	19th (30)	

*Finish in overall standings (No. of teams in league). †League champion.

ORGANIZATION STATISTICS

BOSTON RED SOX

AMERICAN LEAGUE

Batting	B-T	HT	WT	DOB	AVG	vLH	vRH	G	AB	R	H	2B	3B	HR	RBI	BB	HBP	SH	SF	SO	SB	CS	SLG	OBP
Anderson, Lars	L-L	6-4	215	9-25-87	.200	.000	.219	18	35	4	7	1	0	0	4	7	0	0	1	8	0	0	.229	.326
Beltre, Adrian	R-R	5-11	220	4-7-79	.321	.328	.318	154	589	84	189	49	2	28	102	40	5	0	7	82	2	1	.553	.365
Brown, Dusty	R-R	6-0	180	6-19-82	.250	.143	.400	7	12	0	3	1	0	0	2	0	0	0	0	2	0	0	.333	.250
Cameron, Mike	R-R	6-2	215	1-8-73	.259	.357	.225	48	162	24	42	11	0	4	15	14	3	0	1	44	0	1	.401	.328
Cash, Kevin	R-R	6-0	200	12-6-77	.133	.267	.089	29	60	1	8	1	0	0	1	6	1	1	0	16	0	0	.150	.224
Drew, J.D.	L-R	6-1	200	11-20-75	.255	.208	.277	139	478	69	122	24	2	22	68	60	4	0	4	105	3	1	.452	.341
Ellsbury, Jacoby	L-L	6-1	185	9-11-83	.192	.235	.180	18	78	10	15	4	0	0	5	4	1	0	0	9	7	1	.244	.241
Hall, Bill	R-R	6-0	210	12-28-79	.247	.199	.283	119	344	44	85	16	1	18	46	34	1	2	1	104	9	1	.456	.316
Hermida, Jeremy	L-R	6-3	220	1-30-84	.203	.136	.213	52	158	14	32	8	0	5	27	12	0	1	0	45	1	0	.348	.257
2-team total (21 Oakland)					.216	—	—	73	222	19	48	12	0	6	29	16	0	0	1	58	1	0	.351	.268
Kalish, Ryan	L-L	6-1	205	3-28-88	.252	.233	.258	53	163	26	41	11	1	4	24	12	1	2	1	38	10	1	.405	.305
Lopez, Felipe	B-R	6-0	205	5-12-80	.267	.333	.250	4	15	2	4	0	0	1	1	1	0	0	0	4	0	0	.467	.313
Lowell, Mike	R-R	6-3	210	2-24-74	.239	.224	.250	73	218	23	52	13	0	5	26	23	0	0	3	34	0	0	.367	.307
Lowrie, Jed	B-R	6-0	180	4-17-84	.287	.338	.250	55	171	31	49	14	0	9	24	25	1	0	0	25	1	1	.526	.381
Martinez, Victor	B-R	6-2	210	12-23-78	.302	.400	.257	127	493	64	149	32	1	20	79	40	0	0	5	52	1	0	.493	.351
McDonald, Darnell	R-R	5-11	205	11-17-78	.270	.294	.247	117	319	40	86	18	3	9	34	30	2	12	0	85	9	1	.429	.336
Molina, Gustavo	R-R	6-1	245	2-24-82	.143	.000	.250	4	7	1	1	0	0	0	0	0	0	0	0	2	0	0	.143	.143
Nava, Daniel	B-L	5-10	200	2-22-83	.242	.207	.250	60	161	23	39	14	1	1	26	19	8	0	0	46	1	1	.360	.351
Navarro, Yamaico	R-R	5-11	170	10-31-87	.143	.200	.111	20	42	4	6	0	0	0	5	2	0	0	2	17	0	0	.143	.174
Ortiz, David	L-L	6-4	230	11-18-75	.270	.222	.297	145	518	86	140	36	1	32	102	82	2	0	4	145	0	1	.529	.370
Patterson, Eric	L-R	6-0	170	4-8-83	.226	.500	.189	45	84	13	19	3	3	2	7	7	1	1	0	31	5	1	.405	.293
2-team total (45 Oakland)					.214	—	—	90	187	26	40	8	5	6	16	14	1	2	0	62	11	1	.406	.272
Pedroia, Dustin	R-R	5-9	180	8-17-83	.288	.236	.304	75	302	53	87	24	1	12	41	37	4	2	6	38	9	1	.493	.367
Reddick, Josh	L-R	6-2	180	2-19-87	.194	.400	.175	29	62	5	12	3	1	1	5	1	0	0	0	15	1	0	.323	.206
Romero, Niuman	B-R	6-1	190	1-24-85	.000	.000	.000	2	4	1	0	0	0	0	0	0	0	0	0	0	0	0	.000	.000
Saltalamacchia, Jarrod	B-R	6-4	235	5-2-85	.158	.143	.200	10	19	2	3	3	0	0	1	6	0	0	0	4	0	0	.316	.360
2-team total (2 Texas)					.167	—	—	12	24	2	4	3	0	0	2	6	0	0	0	5	0	0	.292	.333
Sanchez, Angel	R-R	6-2	205	9-20-83	.000	.000	.000	1	3	0	0	0	0	0	0	0	0	0	0	0	0	0	.000	.000
Scutaro, Marco	R-R	5-10	185	10-30-75	.275	.282	.273	150	632	92	174	38	0	11	56	53	3	4	3	71	5	4	.388	.333
Shealy, Ryan	R-R	6-5	240	8-29-79	.000	.000	.000	5	7	0	0	0	0	0	0	0	0	0	0	2	0	0	.000	.000
Van Every, Jonathan	L-L	6-1	200	11-27-79	.211	.000	.267	21	19	6	4	1	0	1	1	2	0	0	0	9	0	0	.421	.286
Varitek, Jason	B-R	6-2	230	4-11-72	.232	.222	.235	39	112	18	26	6	0	7	16	10	0	0	1	35	0	0	.473	.293
Youkilis, Kevin	R-R	6-1	220	3-15-79	.307	.404	.275	102	362	77	111	26	5	19	62	58	10	0	5	67	4	1	.564	.411

Pitching	B-T	HT	WT	DOB	W	L	ERA	G	GS	CG	SV	IP	H	R	ER	HR	BB	SO	AVG	vLH	vRH	K/9	BB/9
Atchison, Scott	R-R	6-2	200	3-29-76	2	3	4.50	43	1	0	0	60	58	37	30	9	19	41	.252	.290	.220	6.15	2.85
Bard, Daniel	R-R	6-4	200	6-25-85	1	2	1.93	73	0	0	3	75	45	18	16	6	30	76	.176	.141	.215	9.16	3.62
Beckett, Josh	R-R	6-5	225	5-15-80	6	6	5.78	21	21	0	0	128	151	89	82	20	45	116	.292	.310	.267	8.18	3.17
Bonser, Boof	R-R	6-4	245	10-14-81	0	0	18.00	2	0	0	0	2	6	4	4	0	2	0	.545	.600	.500	0.00	9.00
2-team total (13 Oakland)					1	0	6.12	15	0	0	0	25	33	17	17	2	8	17	—	—	—	6.12	2.88
Bowden, Michael	R-R	6-3	215	9-9-86	0	1	4.70	14	0	0	0	15	20	8	8	2	4	13	.323	.379	.273	7.63	2.35
Buchholz, Clay	L-R	6-3	190	8-14-84	17	7	2.33	28	28	1	0	174	142	55	45	9	67	120	.226	.230	.221	6.22	3.47
Cabrera, Fernando	R-R	6-4	225	11-16-81	0	0	20.25	1	0	0	0	1	2	3	3	1	2	0	.400	.000	.500	0.00	13.50
Coello, Robert	R-R	6-5	250	11-23-84	0	0	4.76	6	0	0	0	6	4	3	3	0	5	5	.190	.444	.000	7.94	7.94
Delcarmen, Manny	R-R	6-2	205	2-16-82	3	2	4.70	48	0	0	0	44	33	24	23	7	28	32	.204	.165	.241	6.55	5.73
Doubront, Felix	L-L	6-2	165	10-23-87	2	2	4.32	12	3	0	0	25	27	16	12	3	10	23	.270	.189	.317	8.28	3.60
Fox, Matt	R-R	6-2	195	12-4-82	0	0	10.80	3	0	0	0	2	4	2	2	0	1	0	.500	.000	.800	0.00	5.40
2-team total (1 Minnesota)					0	0	4.91	4	1	0	0	7	8	4	4	0	2	0	—	—	—	0.00	2.45
Hill, Rich	L-L	6-4	185	3-11-80	1	0	0.00	6	0	0	0	4	5	0	0	0	1	3	.294	.125	.444	6.75	2.25
Lackey, John	R-R	6-6	245	10-23-78	14	11	4.40	33	33	0	0	215	233	114	105	18	72	156	.277	.298	.251	6.53	3.01
Lester, Jon	L-L	6-4	240	1-7-84	19	9	3.25	32	32	2	0	208	167	81	75	14	83	225	.220	.226	.219	9.74	3.59
Manuel, Robert	R-R	6-3	205	7-9-83	1	0	4.26	10	0	0	0	13	10	6	6	5	7	5	.213	.150	.259	3.55	4.97
Matsuzaka, Daisuke	R-R	6-0	185	9-13-80	9	6	4.69	25	25	0	0	154	137	84	80	13	74	133	.240	.265	.211	7.79	4.33
Nelson, Joe	R-R	6-1	205	10-25-74	0	0	9.72	8	0	0	0	8	14	9	9	2	6	9	.359	.440	.214	9.72	6.48

Name	B-T	HT	WT	DOB	W	L	ERA	G	GS	CG	SV	IP	H	R	ER	HR	BB	SO	AVG	vLH	vRH	K/9	BB/9
Okajima, Hideki	L-L	6-1	195	12-25-75	4	4	4.50	56	0	0	0	46	59	24	23	6	20	33	.314	.284	.340	6.46	3.91
Papelbon, Jonathan	R-R	6-4	225	11-23-80	5	7	3.90	65	0	0	37	67	57	34	29	7	28	76	.226	.255	.189	10.21	3.76
Ramirez, Ramon	R-R	5-11	190	8-31-81	0	3	4.46	44	0	0	2	42	39	21	21	6	16	31	.250	.265	.239	6.59	3.40
Richardson, Dustin	L-L	6-6	220	1-9-84	0	0	4.15	26	0	0	0	13	15	6	6	2	14	12	.300	.360	.240	8.31	9.69
Schoeneweis, Scott	L-L	6-0	190	10-2-73	1	0	7.90	15	0	0	0	14	19	12	12	2	10	13	.333	.346	.323	8.56	6.59
Wakefield, Tim	R-R	6-2	210	8-2-66	4	10	5.34	32	19	0	0	140	153	92	83	19	36	84	.272	.273	.271	5.40	2.31

Fielding

Catcher	PCT	G	PO	A	E	DP	PB
Brown	1.000	7	26	4	0	2	2
Cash	.994	29	148	14	1	0	6
Martinez	.993	110	778	44	6	2	4
Molina	1.000	4	15	1	0	0	1
Saltalamacchia	.976	6	38	2	1	0	0
Varitek	1.000	39	242	13	0	2	1

First Base	PCT	G	PO	A	E	DP
Anderson	1.000	18	96	9	0	9
Lowell	.994	43	310	24	2	35
Lowrie	.923	7	10	2	1	2
Martinez	.982	14	95	14	2	10
Ortiz	1.000	4	23	1	0	1
Romero	1.000	1	4	1	0	0
Saltalamacchia	—	1	0	0	0	0
Shealy	1.000	1	5	0	0	1
Youkilis	.997	101	809	72	3	66

Second Base	PCT	G	PO	A	E	DP
Hall	.966	51	72	100	6	19
Lopez	1.000	3	4	6	0	0
Lowrie	.976	28	44	77	3	14
Navarro	1.000	3	4	5	0	1
Patterson	.969	9	16	15	1	3
Pedroia	.991	75	137	212	3	50
Romero	—	1	0	0	0	0
Scutaro	.969	16	17	46	2	8

Third Base	PCT	G	PO	A	E	DP
Beltre	.957	154	138	285	19	31
Hall	.909	5	4	6	1	1
Lopez	.500	2	1	0	1	0
Lowell	1.000	4	2	6	0	1
Lowrie	1.000	1	0	1	0	0
Navarro	.909	4	3	7	1	0
Youkilis	1.000	2	3	5	0	0

Shortstop	PCT	G	PO	A	E	DP
Hall	.917	6	3	8	1	3
Lopez	1.000	1	2	0	0	0
Lowrie	.986	23	26	46	1	17
Navarro	.969	15	14	17	1	4
Sanchez	1.000	1	0	4	0	2
Scutaro	.965	132	152	344	18	57

Outfield	PCT	G	PO	A	E	DP
Cameron	.983	46	111	3	2	1
Drew	.996	133	234	1	1	1
Ellsbury	1.000	18	44	0	0	0
Hall	.964	65	104	3	4	0
Hermida	.957	49	86	3	4	0
Kalish	.982	51	105	3	2	1
McDonald	.990	114	187	9	2	1
Nava	1.000	54	65	2	0	0
Patterson	.973	35	33	3	1	0
Reddick	1.000	25	37	1	0	0
Van Every	1.000	21	15	0	0	0

PAWTUCKET RED SOX   TRIPLE-A

INTERNATIONAL LEAGUE

Batting	B-T	HT	WT	DOB	AVG	vLH	vRH	G	AB	R	H	2B	3B	HR	RBI	BB	HBP	SH	SF	SO	SB	CS	SLG	OBP
Anderson, Lars	L-L	6-4	215	9-25-87	.262	.215	.278	113	409	49	107	32	3	10	53	44	6	0	3	109	2	2	.428	.340
Apodaca, Juan	R-R	5-11	180	7-15-86	.209	.083	.258	14	43	3	9	3	0	1	6	6	0	0	0	15	0	0	.349	.306
Bates, Aaron	R-R	6-4	230	3-10-84	.240	.200	.256	122	429	49	103	15	2	12	54	59	6	0	3	119	0	1	.368	.338
Bell, Bubba	L-R	6-0	195	10-9-82	.293	.302	.290	104	351	46	103	17	1	6	49	41	1	0	3	62	13	7	.399	.366
Brown, Dusty	R-R	6-0	180	4-19-82	.218	.262	.202	71	238	32	52	19	0	7	29	27	3	1	2	66	1	0	.387	.304
Butler, Daniel	R-R	5-10	190	10-17-86	.000	.000	.000	2	5	0	0	0	0	0	0	0	0	0	0	1	0	0	.000	.000
Cameron, Mike	R-R	6-2	205	1-8-73	.286	1.000	.167	5	14	3	4	1	0	1	3	4	0	0	1	4	0	0	.571	.421
Cash, Kevin	R-R	6-0	200	12-6-77	.250	.333	.000	1	4	1	1	0	0	0	1	0	0	0	0	1	0	0	.250	.250
Delgado, Carlos	L-R	6-3	245	6-25-72	.231	.143	.333	5	13	0	3	0	0	0	2	0	1	0	1	6	0	0	.231	.267
Ellsbury, Jacoby	L-L	6-1	185	9-11-83	.471	.333	.545	4	17	5	8	1	0	0	2	1	0	0	0	0	0	0	.529	.500
Frandsen, Kevin	R-R	6-0	185	5-24-82	.258	.308	.222	17	62	9	16	3	0	2	4	5	3	1	0	3	2	0	.403	.343
Hannahan, Jack	L-R	6-2	210	3-4-80	.255	.290	.241	33	110	15	28	8	0	4	12	17	1	0	0	27	2	0	.436	.359
Hassan, Alex	R-R	6-3	195	4-1-88	.000	.000	.000	3	3	0	0	0	0	0	0	0	1	0	0	0	0	0	.000	.000
Hermida, Jeremy	L-R	6-3	220	1-30-84	.288	.172	.378	19	66	7	19	1	0	2	12	4	1	0	2	16	0	0	.394	.329
Hulett, Tug	L-R	5-10	185	2-28-83	.201	.182	.208	86	284	38	57	21	2	4	29	53	2	2	2	63	6	3	.331	.328
Jimenez, Jorge	L-R	6-1	215	9-12-84	.217	.218	.216	95	337	37	73	10	1	3	33	32	4	0	3	43	1	3	.279	.290
Kalish, Ryan	L-L	6-1	205	3-28-88	.294	.389	.236	37	143	22	42	9	1	5	18	14	1	0	2	32	12	2	.476	.356
Kang, James	R-R	5-9	175	10-19-87	.222	.000	.250	4	9	2	2	2	0	0	1	0	0	1	0	3	0	0	.444	.222
Khoury, Ryan	R-R	5-10	180	3-19-84	.244	.231	.250	17	45	3	11	2	1	0	2	1	0	0	0	12	0	0	.333	.261
Lowell, Mike	R-R	6-3	210	2-24-74	.500	.714	.125	5	22	5	11	4	0	4	10	0	0	0	0	3	0	0	1.227	.500
Lowrie, Jed	B-R	6-0	180	4-17-84	.333	.000	.455	4	15	3	5	3	0	1	4	1	0	0	1	4	1	0	.733	.353
McDonald, Darnell	R-R	5-11	205	11-17-78	.341	.429	.296	10	41	6	14	6	1	2	8	2	0	0	0	7	1	0	.683	.372
Molina, Gustavo	R-R	6-1	245	2-24-82	.241	.276	.229	35	112	12	27	5	0	8	18	7	0	0	0	23	0	0	.500	.286
Nava, Daniel	B-L	5-10	200	2-22-83	.289	.276	.294	77	284	41	82	16	1	10	48	28	11	0	2	64	4	2	.458	.372
Navarro, Yamaico	R-R	5-11	170	10-31-87	.283	.300	.279	16	53	8	15	4	0	3	6	5	0	0	1	6	2	1	.528	.339
Patterson, Eric	L-R	6-0	170	4-8-83	.235	.000	.267	4	17	4	4	2	0	1	0	0	0	0	0	7	3	0	.471	.278
Pedroia, Dustin	R-R	5-9	180	8-17-83	.167	.200	.000	2	6	1	1	0	0	0	1	0	0	0	0	0	0	0	.167	.286
Reddick, Josh	L-R	6-2	180	2-19-87	.266	.274	.263	114	451	59	120	28	4	18	65	25	0	0	5	73	4	7	.466	.301
Reyes, Argenis	B-R	5-10	180	9-25-82	.256	.333	.214	14	43	3	11	0	0	1	5	2	0	0	6	1	1		.279	.333
2-team total (16 Columbus)					.302	—		30	96	8	29	3	0	5		6	1	2	0	11	1	1	.333	.333
Romero, Niuman	R-R	6-1	190	1-24-85	.246	.253	.243	99	350	42	86	14	0	3	20	32	3	0	0	57	14	6	.311	.314
Saltalamacchia, Jarrod	B-R	6-4	235	5-2-85	.278	.200	.290	9	36	5	10	5	0	1	6	4	0	0	0	9	0	0	.500	.350
Sanchez, Angel	R-R	6-2	205	9-20-83	.274	.310	.261	62	223	26	61	10	1	0	17	17	2	2	1	30	6	1	.327	.348
Shealy, Ryan	R-R	6-5	240	8-29-79	.219	.304	.198	32	114	14	25	7	0	5	17	17	2	0	0	34	0	0	.412	.331
2-team total (48 Durham)					.231	—		80	286	41	66	22	1	15	55	46	5	0	2	82	0	0	.472	.345
Sheely, Matt	R-R	5-9	160	8-30-86	.222	.200	.231	7	18	2	4	0	0	0	1	0	0	1	1	3	1	0	.222	.211
Varitek, Jason	B-R	6-2	230	4-11-72	.400	.000	.400	2	5	0	2	0	0	0	1	0	0	0	1	0	0	0	.400	.333
Velazquez, Gil	R-R	6-2	170	10-17-79	.249	.319	.219	72	241	24	60	15	2	1	18	17	2	3	0	54	4	1	.340	.304
Wagner, Mark	R-R	6-1	205	6-11-84	.205	.333	.148	36	127	12	26	5	0	3	16	10	0	2	4	25	0	0	.315	.255

Pitching	B-T	HT	WT	DOB	W	L	ERA	G	GS	CG	SV	IP	H	R	ER	HR	BB	SO	AVG	vLH	vRH	K/9	BB/9
Atchison, Scott	R-R	6-2	200	3-29-76	1	0	4.05	11	0	0	0	13	13	6	6	0	5	17	.241	.250	.233	11.48	3.38
Beckett, Josh	R-R	6-5	225	5-15-80	0	0	4.50	2	2	0	0	8	7	4	4	2	1	7	.226	.200	.273	7.88	1.13

Bierd, Randor	R-R	6-4	190	3-14-84	2	4	5.59	15	9	0	0	48	61	35	30	5	21	30	.314	.311	.317	5.59	3.91
Bonser, Boof	R-R	6-4	245	10-14-81	0	2	6.34	9	8	0	0	33	37	23	23	3	14	25	.294	.298	.290	6.89	3.86
Bowden, Michael	R-R	6-3	215	9-9-86	6	4	3.66	31	16	0	1	106	84	43	43	13	37	77	.222	.252	.200	6.56	3.15
Buchholz, Clay	L-R	6-3	190	8-14-84	0	0	4.91	1	1	0	0	4	4	2	2	1	1	2	.286	.125	.500	4.91	2.45
Cabrera, Fernando	R-R	6-4	225	11-16-81	2	5	3.86	54	0	0	22	61	64	29	26	5	24	76	.277	.340	.229	11.27	3.56
Castro, Fabio	L-L	5-7	185	1-20-85	7	9	4.93	31	15	0	0	104	113	60	57	9	50	102	.277	.263	.284	8.83	4.33
Coello, Robert	R-R	6-5	250	11-23-84	3	5	4.22	18	9	0	0	64	44	33	30	10	30	79	.192	.245	.153	11.11	4.22
Doubront, Felix	L-L	6-2	165	10-23-87	4	3	3.16	9	8	0	0	37	36	13	13	1	16	34	.261	.259	.261	8.27	3.89
Embree, Alan	L-L	6-2	200	1-23-70	0	0	3.68	8	0	0	0	7	2	3	3	0	5	6	.083	.000	.182	7.36	6.14
2-team total (6 Charlotte)					0	1	6.00	14	0	0	0	15	13	12	10	0	10	16	—	—	—	9.60	6.00
Gabbard, Kason	L-L	6-3	200	4-8-82	0	2	5.65	11	1	0	0	14	17	12	9	2	15	10	.293	.154	.333	6.28	9.42
Hill, Rich	L-L	6-4	185	3-11-80	3	1	3.74	19	6	0	0	53	45	22	22	3	29	55	.233	.170	.257	9.34	4.92
Holliman, Mark	R-R	6-0	195	9-19-83	0	3	9.24	3	3	0	0	13	14	13	13	2	10	17	.275	.348	.214	12.08	7.11
Hottovy, Tommy	L-L	6-1	195	7-9-81	0	1	4.54	26	0	0	0	36	37	19	18	5	23	22	.264	.222	.284	5.55	5.80
Johnson, Kris	L-L	6-4	170	10-14-84	6	13	4.88	28	24	0	0	133	152	81	72	15	52	79	.290	.312	.280	5.36	3.53
Large, T.J.	R-R	6-4	185	5-28-83	4	1	7.64	21	1	0	0	35	37	31	30	5	24	20	.270	.190	.329	5.09	6.11
Luis, Santo	R-R	6-4	200	1-27-84	0	1	7.36	13	0	0	0	18	19	15	15	1	14	16	.268	.316	.250	7.85	6.87
Manuel, Robert	R-R	6-3	205	7-9-83	8	2	1.68	45	0	0	13	64	46	14	12	4	13	48	.200	.239	.176	6.72	1.82
Matsuzaka, Daisuke	R-R	6-0	185	9-13-80	2	0	1.62	3	3	0	0	17	11	4	3	1	1	13	.186	.242	.115	7.02	0.54
Maxwell, Blake	R-R	6-5	255	8-1-84	0	0	6.43	3	0	0	0	7	8	5	5	1	3	3	.267	.267	.267	3.86	3.86
Mills, Adam	R-R	5-11	190	11-19-84	4	10	5.47	25	25	1	0	132	175	87	80	17	25	58	.318	.344	.297	3.96	1.71
Nelson, Joe	R-R	6-1	205	10-25-74	3	2	2.49	16	0	0	1	22	18	7	6	1	14	21	.234	.143	.286	8.72	5.82
Okajima, Hideki	L-L	6-1	195	12-25-75	0	0	19.29	3	0	0	0	2	6	5	5	1	0	4	.500	.333	.556	0.00	0.00
Paronto, Chad	R-R	6-5	255	7-28-75	3	5	4.22	54	0	0	2	75	80	36	35	9	30	47	.281	.330	.249	5.67	3.62
Ramirez, Ramon A.	R-R	6-0	190	9-16-82	5	5	4.92	28	13	1	0	97	105	60	53	16	36	80	.276	.237	.298	7.42	3.34
Richardson, Dustin	L-L	6-6	220	1-9-84	3	0	2.66	32	0	0	2	44	27	14	13	4	31	56	.181	.237	.144	11.45	6.34

Fielding

Catcher	PCT	G	PO	A	E	DP	PB
Apodaca	1.000	14	106	3	0	0	
Brown	.987	65	425	34	6	6	5
Butler	1.000	1	8	1	0	0	0
Cash	1.000	1	12	0	0	0	0
Molina	.995	30	185	14	1	2	1
Saltalamacchia	1.000	6	52	2	0	0	0
Varitek	1.000	1	6	1	0	0	0
Wagner	.996	32	231	14	1	2	0

First Base	PCT	G	PO	A	E	DP
Anderson	.989	105	778	58	9	75
Bates	.995	26	186	11	1	27
Delgado	1.000	2	6	0	0	1
Hannahan	—	1	0	0	0	0
Jimenez	1.000	11	67	6	0	6
Lowell	1.000	1	7	1	0	0
Romero	1.000	4	13	1	0	2
Saltalamacchia	1.000	1	8	0	0	1
Shealy	1.000	3	12	5	0	2

Second Base	PCT	G	PO	A	E	DP
Frandsen	1.000	4	9	9	0	3
Hannahan	.923	3	5	7	1	1
Hulett	.987	53	115	112	3	41

Second Base (cont.)	PCT	G	PO	A	E	DP
Kang	1.000	4	3	8	0	2
Khoury	.970	7	12	20	1	2
Lowrie	1.000	1	0	1	0	0
Navarro	1.000	2	3	4	0	1
Patterson	.889	2	4	4	1	2
Pedroia	1.000	1	2	2	0	0
Reyes	.979	11	13	33	1	6
Romero	.989	45	76	100	2	23
Sanchez	1.000	5	5	5	1	0
Velazquez	.985	13	36	28	1	9

Third Base	PCT	G	PO	A	E	DP
Frandsen	.857	1	1	5	1	2
Hannahan	.970	27	25	71	3	12
Hulett	1.000	9	3	9	0	1
Jimenez	.952	85	69	149	11	18
Khoury	.800	6	4	8	3	1
Lowell	1.000	1	0	1	0	0
Lowrie	1.000	1	1	0	0	0
Navarro	1.000	2	3	1	0	0
Reyes	1.000	1	2	2	0	0
Sanchez	1.000	1	1	2	0	1
Velazquez	1.000	17	18	31	0	4

Shortstop	PCT	G	PO	A	E	DP
Frandsen	.977	10	17	26	1	6
Hulett	1.000	1	1	0		1
Khoury	1.000	2	5	1	0	0
Lowrie	1.000	1	0	1	0	0
Navarro	.875	11	11	17	4	3
Romero	.980	40	40	104	3	16
Sanchez	.955	47	60	88	7	29
Velazquez	.955	41	45	82	6	14

Outfield	PCT	G	PO	A	E	DP
Bates	.980	79	139	6	3	0
Bell	.987	100	212	8	3	3
Brown	—	1	0	0	0	0
Cameron	1.000	3	5	1	0	1
Ellsbury	1.000	2	4	0	0	0
Hassan	1.000	3	5	0	0	0
Hermida	1.000	16	32	0	0	0
Kalish	.981	34	100	1	2	0
McDonald	1.000	9	22	1	0	0
Nava	.994	72	164	5	1	0
Patterson	1.000	1	4	0	0	0
Reddick	.971	108	259	9	8	2
Romero	.964	14	27	0	1	0
Shealy	1.000	7	12	0	0	0

PORTLAND SEA DOGS   DOUBLE-A

EASTERN LEAGUE

Batting	B-T	HT	WT	DOB	AVG	vLH	vRH	G	AB	R	H	2B	3B	HR	RBI	BB	HBP	SH	SF	SO	SB	CS	SLG	OBP
Anderson, Lars	L-L	6-4	215	9-25-87	.355	.350	.357	17	62	13	22	5	0	5	16	7	0	0	2	16	1	1	.677	.408
Apodaca, Juan	R-R	5-11	180	7-15-86	.248	.265	.242	41	133	12	33	6	0	2	6	20	3	0	0	32	1	0	.338	.359
2-team total (23 Akron)					.242	—	—	64	207	24	50	6	0	4	13	32	4	0	1	52	1	0	.329	.352
Cameron, Mike	R-R	6-2	205	1-8-73	.385	.000	.385	3	13	4	5	2	0	2	3	0	0	0	0	4	0	0	1.000	.385
Chang, Ray	R-R	5-11	205	8-24-83	.298	.302	.296	116	440	57	131	30	2	9	55	51	12	2	2	64	0	1	.436	.384
Chiang, Chih-Hsien	L-R	6-2	170	2-21-88	.260	.288	.249	121	438	54	114	35	1	11	65	31	4	1	4	64	2	0	.420	.312
Ellsbury, Jacoby	L-L	6-1	185	9-11-83	.429	.000	.429	2	7	2	3	1	0	0	1	0	0	0	0	1	0	0	.571	.500
Exposito, Luis	R-R	6-3	210	1-20-87	.260	.344	.229	125	473	65	123	39	1	11	94	55	6	0	8	92	1	2	.416	.339
Hermida, Jeremy	L-R	6-3	220	1-30-84	.273	.333	.250	3	11	1	3	2	0	0	3	1	0	0	0	0	0	0	.455	.333
Iglesias, Jose	R-R	5-11	175	1-5-90	.285	.250	.296	57	221	29	63	10	3	0	13	8	3	3	3	49	5	2	.357	.315
Kalish, Ryan	L-L	6-1	205	3-28-88	.293	.289	.295	41	150	35	44	9	1	8	29	28	2	0	3	21	13	1	.527	.404
Khoury, Ryan	R-R	5-10	180	3-19-84	.246	.271	.236	69	244	31	60	16	4	2	19	24	5	1	2	41	4	2	.369	.324
Lavarnway, Ryan	R-R	6-4	225	8-7-87	.285	.302	.276	44	158	25	45	9	0	8	39	26	4	0	2	42	0	0	.494	.395
Lin, Che-Hsuan	R-R	6-0	180	9-21-88	.275	.242	.288	119	458	88	126	17	4	2	34	72	11	1	1	63	26	12	.343	.386
Linares, Juan Carlos	R-R	5-11	190	9-7-84	.239	.300	.222	13	46	3	11	4	0	1	4	0	2	0	0	13	1	1	.391	.271
Navarro, Yamaico	R-R	5-11	170	10-31-87	.274	.383	.238	88	329	49	90	19	3	8	55	47	3	1	3	53	16	5	.422	.358
Padron, Jorge	L-L	6-1	200	7-20-86	.286	.333	.264	47	182	15	52	10	0	0	19	10	1	1	2	23	2	0	.341	.323

Batting	B-T	HT	WT	DOB	AVG	vLH	vRH	G	AB	R	H	2B	3B	HR	RBI	BB	HBP	SH	SF	SO	SB	CS	SLG	OBP
Peley, Josue	R-R	6-0	177	12-24-87	.000	.000	.000	6	21	0	0	0	0	0	0	0	1	0	0	0	6	0	0	.000	.045
Peterson, Bryan	L-R	6-3	190	3-21-90	.200	.000	.250	3	5	0	1	0	0	0	0	0	0	0	0	0	3	0	0	.200	.200
Place, Jason	R-R	6-3	205	5-8-88	.127	.192	.094	25	79	5	10	2	2	1	8	13	0	0	0	29	0	1	.241	.250
Rizzo, Anthony	L-L	6-3	220	8-8-89	.263	.207	.287	107	414	66	109	30	0	20	80	45	2	0	6	100	7	1	.481	.334
Segovia, Luis	B-R	5-10	150	7-19-86	.273	.500	.188	8	22	4	6	2	0	0	2	2	0	1	0	4	1	1	.364	.333
Sheely, Matt	R-R	5-9	160	8-30-86	.238	.306	.213	74	231	28	55	8	4	1	22	18	4	9	1	77	9	7	.320	.303
Spears, Nate	L-R	5-11	165	5-3-85	.272	.301	.261	136	514	104	140	30	4	20	82	84	11	1	10	93	13	1	.463	.380
Vazquez, Will	R-R	6-2	190	2-22-85	.160	.156	.163	45	131	16	21	2	0	1	8	15	4	1	1	42	0	1	.198	.265

Pitching	B-T	HT	WT	DOB	W	L	ERA	G	GS	CG	SV	IP	H	R	ER	HR	BB	SO	AVG	vLH	vRH	K/9	BB/9
Coello, Robert	R-R	6-5	250	11-23-84	4	1	3.32	14	4	0	1	43	38	16	16	4	14	51	.233	.231	.235	10.59	2.91
Cox, Bryce	R-R	6-4	205	8-10-84	1	6	4.89	42	0	0	12	53	53	31	29	3	28	39	.257	.290	.226	6.58	4.72
Delcarmen, Manny	R-R	6-2	205	2-16-82	0	0	0.00	1	1	0	0	1	0	0	0	0	0	0	.000	.000	.000	0.00	0.00
Dobies, Andrew	L-L	6-1	180	4-20-83	0	0	1.80	3	0	0	0	5	5	1	1	0	1	8	.263	.250	.273	14.40	1.80
Doubront, Felix	L-L	6-2	165	10-23-87	4	0	2.51	8	8	0	0	43	39	13	12	0	17	38	.250	.269	.240	7.95	3.56
Fernandes, Kyle	L-L	6-0	190	9-12-85	0	0	0.00	1	0	0	0	3	2	0	0	0	0	2	.222	.250	.200	6.75	0.00
Fife, Stephen	R-R	6-3	210	10-4-86	8	6	4.75	26	26	0	0	136	144	84	72	11	46	82	.272	.248	.298	5.41	3.04
Herold, Mitch	L-L	6-0	200	10-8-86	3	4	5.29	26	0	0	0	51	57	30	30	2	13	43	.288	.289	.287	7.59	2.29
Hottovy, Tommy	L-L	6-1	195	7-9-81	3	2	5.22	15	0	0	0	40	49	25	23	6	20	34	.302	.328	.287	7.71	4.54
Kehrt, Jeremy	R-R	6-2	190	12-21-85	3	11	5.20	20	19	0	0	106	123	69	61	11	36	58	.293	.330	.259	4.94	3.07
Kelly, Casey	R-R	6-3	195	10-4-89	3	5	5.31	21	21	0	0	95	118	60	56	10	35	81	.307	.326	.280	7.67	3.32
Large, T.J.	R-R	6-4	185	5-28-83	1	0	4.26	3	0	0	0	6	2	3	3	1	2	5	.095	.100	.091	7.11	2.84
Lawson, Ryne	L-R	6-2	180	6-21-85	6	5	3.78	33	1	0	2	79	81	36	33	5	40	38	.276	.255	.293	4.33	4.58
Luis, Santo	R-R	6-4	200	1-27-84	5	1	2.72	23	0	0	1	46	39	15	14	0	21	45	.225	.253	.195	8.74	4.08
Maxwell, Blake	R-R	6-5	255	8-1-84	7	0	2.61	11	7	0	0	48	48	15	14	4	10	32	.259	.268	.252	5.96	1.86
Miller, Ryne	R-R	6-4	230	9-25-85	2	6	6.43	27	12	0	0	84	89	63	60	20	56	73	.274	.293	.248	7.82	6.00
Portice, Eammon	R-R	6-2	185	6-18-85	3	7	4.65	40	1	0	0	93	102	57	48	9	25	96	.279	.290	.268	9.29	2.42
Reynoso, Ryne	L-R	6-2	215	3-15-85	3	0	3.54	9	0	0	0	20	17	8	8	1	5	17	.224	.190	.265	7.52	2.21
Rice, Jason	R-R	6-0	190	5-13-86	3	2	2.85	48	0	0	13	60	45	20	19	6	30	71	.211	.208	.214	10.65	4.50
Turpen, Dan	R-R	6-4	230	8-17-86	2	1	4.91	12	0	0	3	18	18	11	10	0	9	18	.261	.294	.229	8.84	4.42
2-team total (37 Richmond)					7	6	4.30	49	0	0	4	69	73	35	33	4	28	60	—	—		7.83	3.65
Weiland, Kyle	L-R	6-4	195	9-12-86	5	9	4.42	25	25	0	0	128	112	70	63	13	49	120	.236	.213	.264	8.42	3.44
Wilson, Alex	R-R	6-1	205	11-3-86	4	5	6.66	16	16	0	0	78	95	59	58	15	34	56	.302	.277	.327	6.43	3.91

Fielding

Catcher	PCT	G	PO	A	E	DP	PB
Apodaca	.994	24	163	10	1	1	1
Exposito	.990	85	607	95	7	7	14
Lavarnway	1.000	16	95	10	0	3	4
Vazquez	1.000	22	118	19	0	2	1

First Base	PCT	G	PO	A	E	DP
Anderson	.993	17	139	7	1	7
Chang	1.000	6	54	3	0	1
Padron	1.000	2	18	2	0	2
Rizzo	.985	107	933	86	15	95
Vazquez	.988	12	71	11	1	13

Second Base	PCT	G	PO	A	E	DP
Chang	1.000	2	5	8	0	2
Chiang	1.000	1	1	0	0	0

Khoury	1.000	9	16	26	0	6
Segovia	.889	3	3	5	1	1
Spears	.982	130	201	389	11	96

Third Base	PCT	G	PO	A	E	DP
Chang	.986	86	65	145	3	14
Khoury	.935	35	26	74	7	11
Navarro	.952	22	18	42	3	4
Segovia	1.000	1	0	4	0	0
Vazquez	1.000	3	0	3	0	1

Shortstop	PCT	G	PO	A	E	DP
Chang	.964	19	36	45	3	11
Iglesias	.966	55	67	129	7	25
Navarro	.971	66	108	162	8	41
Spears	.933	5	8	20	2	3

Outfield	PCT	G	PO	A	E	DP
Cameron	1.000	3	7	1	0	0
Chiang	.963	104	169	14	7	3
Ellsbury	1.000	2	6	0	0	0
Hermida	—	1	0	0	0	0
Kalish	.946	36	68	2	4	0
Khoury	.964	22	27	0	1	0
Lin	.991	118	320	15	3	4
Linares	1.000	13	26	0	0	0
Padron	.989	43	85	3	1	0
Peterson	1.000	2	2	0	0	0
Place	1.000	20	31	3	0	1
Sheely	.963	70	126	3	5	0
Vazquez	1.000	2	3	0	0	0

SALEM RED SOX   HIGH CLASS A

CAROLINA LEAGUE

Batting	B-T	HT	WT	DOB	AVG	vLH	vRH	G	AB	R	H	2B	3B	HR	RBI	BB	HBP	SH	SF	SO	SB	CS	SLG	OBP
Bermudez, Ronald	R-R	6-1	165	6-6-88	.239	.208	.255	24	71	7	17	6	0	0	6	6	1	2	0	13	0	0	.324	.308
Butler, Daniel	R-R	5-10	190	10-17-86	.292	.229	.321	35	113	16	33	12	0	1	17	23	6	0	1	21	1	0	.425	.434
Dening, Mitch	L-R	6-1	165	8-17-88	.274	.264	.278	116	446	69	122	19	6	3	45	47	4	4	4	84	14	9	.363	.345
Dent, Ryan	R-R	6-0	190	3-15-89	.225	.264	.206	112	382	44	86	17	3	6	37	30	6	5	4	86	9	11	.332	.289
Dominguez, Drew	R-R	5-11	195	12-27-86	.129	.100	.143	13	31	0	4	0	0	0	2	2	0	0	0	9	0	0	.129	.182
Escobar, Leonel	R-R	5-10	175	9-4-90	.500	.000	.571	3	8	2	4	0	0	1	1	0	0	0	2	0	0	0	.500	.556
Federowicz, Tim	R-R	5-10	213	5-5-87	.253	.260	.250	109	407	47	103	34	1	6	61	43	2	0	5	86	1	1	.371	.324
Hassan, Alex	R-R	6-3	195	4-1-88	.287	.305	.278	104	342	46	98	28	3	8	48	57	8	0	4	69	6	1	.456	.397
Hedman, Drew	L-L	6-2	200	7-20-86	.230	.287	.204	93	326	31	75	15	2	3	34	23	3	0	1	87	3	1	.316	.286
Hee, Jonathan	B-R	6-0	180	8-11-85	.242	.326	.200	88	277	33	67	13	1	0	20	29	14	2	2	50	0	3	.307	.342
Hissey, Pete	L-L	6-1	180	1-17-90	.234	.254	.225	112	444	63	104	22	6	1	37	42	7	9	3	127	25	9	.318	.308
Ibarra, Adalberto	L-R	5-10	205	4-3-87	.244	.364	.200	14	41	7	10	1	0	0	3	5	2	0	0	12	2	0	.268	.400
Lavarnway, Ryan	R-R	6-4	225	8-7-87	.289	.238	.315	82	304	66	88	18	0	14	63	44	9	0	3	62	1	0	.487	.392
Mailman, David	L-L	6-2	180	10-7-88	.130	.063	.148	23	77	7	10	2	3	1	10	13	1	0	0	25	1	2	.273	.264
Middlebrooks, Will	R-R	6-4	200	9-9-88	.276	.235	.294	114	435	69	120	31	2	12	70	35	4	0	7	121	5	3	.439	.331
Padron, Jorge	L-L	6-1	200	7-20-86	.270	.208	.311	31	122	14	33	10	0	1	17	10	0	0	3	17	0	0	.377	.323
Peterson, Bryan	L-R	6-3	190	3-21-90	.231	.333	.200	4	13	1	3	0	0	0	0	0	0	0	0	4	0	0	.231	.286
Place, Jason	R-R	6-3	205	5-8-88	.214	.000	.231	4	14	3	3	0	0	0	2	3	0	1	0	7	0	0	.643	.267
Rizzo, Anthony	L-L	6-3	220	8-8-89	.248	.244	.250	29	117	26	29	5	2	20	16	0	0	2	32	3	0	.479	.333	
Segovia, Luis	B-R	5-10	150	7-19-86	.205	.172	.220	35	88	10	18	4	0	2	9	2	2	2	0	29	0	1	.318	.239

Batting	B-T	HT	WT	DOB	AVG	vLH	vRH	G	AB	R	H	2B	3B	HR	RBI	BB	HBP	SH	SF	SO	SB	CS	SLG	OBP
Tejeda, Oscar	R-R	6-1	177	12-26-89	.307	.331	.296	126	508	76	156	32	5	11	69	32	2	0	10	96	17	7	.455	.344
Vazquez, Will	R-R	6-2	190	2-22-85	.357	.500	.167	4	14	1	5	1	0	0	4	0	2	0	0	1	1	0	.429	.438

Pitching	B-T	HT	WT	DOB	W	L	ERA	G	GS	CG	SV	IP	H	R	ER	HR	BB	SO	AVG	vLH	vRH	K/9	BB/9
Cabral, Cesar	L-L	6-3	175	2-11-89	2	0	5.81	28	0	0	4	48	60	31	31	1	14	45	.314	.229	.343	8.44	2.63
Clay, Caleb	R-R	6-2	180	2-15-88	4	13	4.57	26	25	0	1	132	138	79	67	9	27	67	.273	.284	.263	4.57	1.84
Court, Chris	R-R	6-0	180	5-19-87	0	0	0.00	1	0	0	0	2	1	0	0	0	0	3	.143	.000	.250	13.50	0.00
Fernandes, Kyle	L-L	6-0	190	9-12-85	4	3	3.68	44	0	0	11	66	53	31	27	4	26	63	.213	.150	.243	8.59	3.55
Fox, Stephen	R-R	6-5	210	11-10-85	0	0	0.00	1	0	0	0	1	1	0	0	0	0	2	.250	.000	.333	18.00	0.00
Garrison, Seth	B-R	6-5	220	8-13-85	1	1	4.28	13	1	0	0	27	31	13	13	1	13	24	.292	.267	.311	7.90	4.28
Gonzalez, Miguel	R-R	6-1	170	5-27-84	6	4	4.54	17	16	0	0	73	82	42	37	5	18	47	.287	.271	.301	5.77	2.21
Hammes, Zach	R-R	6-6	240	5-15-84	3	3	4.63	26	0	0	0	45	39	34	23	0	36	34	.234	.282	.191	6.85	7.25
Herold, Mitch	L-L	6-0	200	6-18-86	2	0	1.05	11	0	0	1	26	12	3	3	0	4	17	.141	.194	.111	5.96	1.40
Holliman, Mark	R-R	6-0	195	9-19-83	4	0	2.81	9	7	1	1	48	38	16	15	2	11	39	.217	.208	.224	7.31	2.06
Huntzinger, Brock	R-R	6-3	200	7-2-88	7	8	4.14	25	25	1	0	135	135	69	62	14	35	69	.268	.223	.311	4.61	2.34
Kehrt, Jeremy	R-R	6-2	190	12-21-85	3	1	3.65	11	2	0	3	37	40	23	15	3	13	32	.272	.232	.308	7.78	3.16
Latimer, Will	L-L	6-3	190	12-4-85	5	6	3.48	38	0	0	2	78	87	43	30	4	21	68	.283	.253	.294	7.88	2.43
Lee, Michael	R-R	6-7	220	11-18-86	9	7	4.42	32	11	0	2	112	109	61	55	7	30	93	.252	.234	.265	7.47	2.41
Marin, Leandro	R-R	5-11	165	11-9-88	0	0	1.50	3	0	0	0	6	6	1	1	0	6	6	.240	.100	.333	9.00	1.50
Maxwell, Blake	R-R	6-5	255	8-1-84	4	1	2.66	24	0	0	3	44	48	13	13	3	9	30	.281	.214	.327	6.14	1.84
McClain, Lance	R-L	6-1	175	3-26-87	2	2	4.50	29	0	0	2	50	62	28	25	3	21	35	.312	.327	.306	6.30	3.78
Pimentel, Stolmy	R-R	6-3	186	2-1-90	9	11	4.06	26	26	0	0	129	120	65	58	11	42	102	.248	.290	.206	7.13	2.94
Ryan, Patrick	R-R	6-0	200	5-31-83	2	1	0.70	18	0	0	4	26	14	5	2	0	7	27	.159	.077	.224	9.47	2.45
Williamson, Fabian	R-L	6-2	175	10-20-88	4	3	3.72	14	14	0	0	65	58	30	27	3	34	40	.242	.304	.223	5.51	4.68
Wilson, Alex	R-R	6-1	205	11-3-86	2	1	3.40	11	11	0	0	56	43	24	21	4	15	50	.212	.235	.188	8.08	2.43

Fielding

Catcher	PCT	G	PO	A	E	DP	PB
Butler	.994	24	143	17	1	5	0
Escobar	1.000	3	13	2	0	0	0
Federowicz	.989	75	474	68	6	2	4
Lavarnway	.989	37	243	35	3	1	7
Vazquez	1.000	2	7	2	0	0	0

First Base	PCT	G	PO	A	E	DP
Hassan	1.000	2	14	2	0	3
Hedman	.992	52	479	31	4	34
Hee	1.000	42	402	20	0	33
Padron	.970	21	179	18	6	25
Rizzo	.996	24	252	16	1	19

Second Base	PCT	G	PO	A	E	DP
Dominguez	.974	12	11	26	1	3
Hee	1.000	2	3	5	0	0
Segovia	1.000	7	9	18	0	2
Tejeda	.961	119	234	352	24	74
Vazquez	.909	2	3	7	1	0

Third Base	PCT	G	PO	A	E	DP
Hee	.971	26	19	49	2	4
Middlebrooks	.945	106	73	253	19	29
Segovia	.893	10	4	21	3	1

Shortstop	PCT	G	PO	A	E	DP
Dent	.965	110	165	331	18	61

	PCT	G	PO	A	E	DP
Hee	.968	18	17	43	2	6
Segovia	.938	13	18	43	4	10
Outfield	PCT	G	PO	A	E	DP
Bermudez	.983	23	57	2	1	0
Dening	.987	114	223	11	3	4
Hassan	.986	96	136	7	2	0
Hedman	.963	40	49	3	2	0
Hissey	.993	112	269	9	2	1
Mailman	.931	23	27	0	2	0
Padron	.875	7	6	1	1	0
Peterson	1.000	4	5	0	0	0

GREENVILLE DRIVE

SOUTH ATLANTIC LEAGUE

LOW CLASS A

Batting	B-T	HT	WT	DOB	AVG	vLH	vRH	G	AB	R	H	2B	3B	HR	RBI	BB	HBP	SH	SF	SO	SB	CS	SLG	OBP
Almanzar, Michael	R-R	6-3	190	12-2-90	.246	.238	.249	127	487	56	120	27	3	10	55	30	6	0	8	114	4	1	.376	.294
Bermudez, Ronald	R-R	6-1	165	6-6-88	.281	.213	.299	95	363	55	102	28	3	10	54	30	6	0	4	81	4	3	.457	.342
Butler, Daniel	R-R	5-10	190	10-17-86	.327	.302	.335	61	214	37	70	18	3	6	31	20	9	0	1	44	0	0	.523	.406
Frias, Vladimir	B-R	6-2	170	9-6-86	.201	.188	.206	91	313	35	63	11	2	4	29	15	5	4	2	61	19	5	.288	.248
Fuentes, Reymond	L-L	6-0	160	2-12-91	.270	.276	.268	104	374	59	101	15	5	5	41	25	8	5	2	87	42	5	.377	.328
Garcia, Joantoni	R-R	5-11	165	9-9-90	.200	.182	.205	18	55	7	11	2	0	0	5	6	1	1	0	17	0	1	.236	.290
Garcia, Jose	R-R	5-11	165	4-23-91	.000	.000	.000	1	3	0	0	0	0	0	0	1	0	0	0	1	0	0	.000	.000
Gentile, Zach	L-R	5-8	165	11-1-86	.233	.141	.259	98	330	40	77	13	2	0	25	47	1	6	5	37	5	2	.285	.326
Gibson, Derrik	R-R	6-1	170	12-5-89	.230	.214	.234	122	487	77	112	22	3	2	40	61	6	7	4	101	39	7	.300	.321
Hazelbaker, Jeremy	L-R	6-3	190	8-14-87	.267	.324	.250	116	442	78	118	29	9	12	62	59	6	0	1	135	63	17	.455	.360
Killeen, Sean	R-R	6-0	205	3-2-87	.326	.429	.281	18	46	4	15	5	0	0	13	11	2	0	1	18	0	0	.435	.467
McGuiness, Chris	L-L	6-1	210	4-8-88	.298	.286	.302	78	282	41	84	20	1	12	46	53	5	0	1	59	2	3	.504	.416
Pichardo, Wilfred	B-R	5-9	146	10-21-89	.237	.219	.241	50	169	28	40	7	1	0	13	22	2	3	0	49	29	7	.290	.332
Rodriguez, Reynaldo	R-R	6-0	195	2-7-86	.281	.321	.270	85	278	44	78	20	2	14	59	39	12	1	4	57	12	4	.518	.387
Roque, Kenneth	L-R	5-11	162	9-20-89	.184	.217	.177	43	136	10	25	6	1	1	11	6	3	0	1	41	3	2	.265	.233
Sanchez, Felix	B-R	6-0	165	6-2-90	.000	.000	.000	1	3	0	0	0	0	0	0	1	0	0	1	0	0	0	.000	.250
Segovia, Luis	B-R	5-10	150	7-19-86	.316	.000	.333	6	19	5	6	2	0	1	2	1	1	1	0	3	0	0	.579	.381
Thomas, Michael	R-R	6-4	220	12-5-88	.156	.105	.169	31	90	9	14	2	1	2	6	12	2	0	0	42	1	1	.267	.269
Vazquez, Christian	R-R	5-9	195	8-21-90	.283	.189	.275	79	270	34	71	11	0	3	32	23	4	0	2	62	3	1	.337	.328
Vitek, Kolbrin	R-R	6-2	195	4-1-89	.275	.125	.313	12	40	7	11	3	1	0	3	7	0	0	0	13	4	1	.400	.383
Wilkerson, Shannon	R-R	6-0	198	7-20-88	.245	.271	.236	73	269	26	66	13	4	0	36	17	5	2	5	57	11	6	.323	.297

Pitching	B-T	HT	WT	DOB	W	L	ERA	G	GS	CG	SV	IP	H	R	ER	HR	BB	SO	AVG	vLH	vRH	K/9	BB/9
Balcom-Miller, Chris	R-R	6-2	210	3-3-89	1	0	3.00	1	1	0	0	6	5	2	2	1	0	3	.217	.182	.250	4.50	0.00
2-team total (19 Asheville)					7	7	3.30	20	20	1	0	115	91	44	42	4	19	120	—	—	—	9.42	1.49
Batista, Anatanaer	R-R	5-10	150	2-2-89	6	5	4.04	38	0	0	5	69	81	36	31	4	18	72	.288	.278	.295	9.39	2.35
Bayer, Jeremiah	R-R	6-2	200	12-26-85	7	2	3.39	32	0	0	10	98	101	42	37	7	29	86	.258	.235	.275	7.87	2.65
Britton, Drake	L-L	6-2	200	5-22-89	2	3	2.97	21	21	0	0	76	69	32	25	5	23	78	.240	.203	.252	9.28	2.74
Cabral, Cesar	L-L	6-3	175	2-11-89	2	0	0.29	17	0	0	5	31	16	1	1	0	7	35	.158	.125	.165	10.05	2.01
Castillo, Yeiper	R-R	6-3	158	9-6-88	4	5	3.58	15	15	1	0	75	75	36	30	4	23	69	.265	.257	.271	8.24	2.75
Court, Chris	R-R	6-0	180	5-19-87	5	0	3.56	18	0	0	0	43	45	17	17	4	15	35	.273	.275	.271	7.33	3.14

	B-T	HT	WT	DOB	W	L	ERA	G	GS	CG	SV	IP	H	R	ER	HR	BB	SO	AVG	vLH	vRH	K/9	BB/9
Ebert, Tom	R-R	6-6	245	10-31-87	10	4	2.87	23	1	0	1	94	76	37	30	4	30	92	.226	.178	.263	8.81	2.87
Flasher, Jordan	R-R	5-11	165	10-14-87	5	2	4.57	27	0	0	3	45	45	24	23	5	21	51	.257	.224	.278	10.13	4.17
Fox, Stephen	R-R	6-5	210	11-10-85	0	0	16.20	1	0	0	0	2	5	4	3	0	0	2	.417	.250	.500	10.80	0.00
Mendez, Roman	R-R	6-2	180	7-25-90	0	2	11.40	6	6	0	0	15	29	24	19	5	10	18	.392	.417	.380	10.80	6.00
Neuman, Dennis	R-R	5-11	185	10-18-89	0	3	2.95	43	0	0	14	64	54	24	21	4	20	65	.228	.269	.201	9.14	2.81
Perez, Pedro	R-R	6-4	170	5-3-88	8	5	3.94	28	2	0	0	94	100	48	41	5	36	75	.273	.308	.251	7.21	3.46
Pressly, Ryan	R-R	6-3	175	12-15-88	5	7	3.72	26	24	0	0	114	110	55	47	9	43	96	.256	.239	.269	7.60	3.40
Rivera, Manuel	L-L	6-0	170	9-1-89	5	9	4.10	27	26	0	0	130	140	72	59	12	21	107	.271	.314	.260	7.43	1.46
Ruiz, Pete	R-R	6-3	205	8-21-87	10	8	4.19	26	20	1	0	125	136	73	58	11	23	109	.280	.320	.259	7.87	1.66
Volz, Kendal	R-R	6-5	225	12-2-87	6	5	3.71	26	24	0	0	116	127	53	48	10	14	94	.275	.257	.286	7.27	1.08
Zerpa, Armando	L-L	5-11	175	2-13-87	1	2	2.76	15	0	0	2	29	31	12	9	1	13	33	.277	.286	.273	10.13	3.99

Fielding

Catcher	PCT	G	PO	A	E	DP	PB
Butler	.980	52	399	44	9	4	2
Killeen	.979	11	84	11	2	0	1
Thomas	.970	23	141	23	5	2	2
Vazquez	.991	60	465	72	5	3	9

First Base	PCT	G	PO	A	E	DP
Almanzar	.966	3	27	1	1	2
Gentile	.991	12	101	6	1	8
Killeen	1.000	3	19	0	0	1
McGuiness	.992	66	545	41	5	41
Rodriguez	.983	58	497	34	9	46
Segovia	1.000	1	9	0	0	1
Vazquez	.944	3	32	2	2	1

Second Base	PCT	G	PO	A	E	DP
Frias	.978	30	65	68	3	14
Garcia	.967	16	29	29	2	10
Gentile	.976	63	105	135	6	30
Roque	.948	42	66	97	9	25
Vazquez	1.000	1	2	1	0	0

Third Base	PCT	G	PO	A	E	DP
Almanzar	.904	118	79	261	36	23
Frias	.906	11	6	23	3	4
Gentile	.889	7	6	10	2	2
Segovia	1.000	2	1	6	0	0
Vitek	.889	5	1	7	1	1

Shortstop	PCT	G	PO	A	E	DP
Frias	.903	16	22	34	6	6

	PCT	G	PO	A	E	DP
Garcia	1.000	1	3	2	0	0
Garcia	1.000	1	5	3	0	2
Gibson	.960	121	159	364	22	56
Segovia	1.000	3	6	13	0	1

Outfield	PCT	G	PO	A	E	DP
Bermudez	.972	89	131	7	4	0
Frias	.945	29	50	2	3	1
Fuentes	.980	96	194	4	4	1
Gentile	1.000	16	20	0	0	0
Hazelbaker	.965	110	186	7	7	2
Pichardo	.953	17	40	1	2	0
Rodriguez	1.000	6	10	0	0	0
Sanchez	.500	1	1	0	1	0
Wilkerson	.981	67	101	5	2	1

LOWELL SPINNERS   SHORT-SEASON
NEW YORK-PENN LEAGUE

Batting	B-T	HT	WT	DOB	AVG	vLH	vRH	G	AB	R	H	2B	3B	HR	RBI	BB	HBP	SH	SF	SO	SB	CS	SLG	OBP
Blair, Carson	R-R	6-1	190	10-18-89	.167	.000	.250	4	12	0	2	0	0	0	1	1	0	0	0	5	0	0	.167	.231
Brentz, Bryce	R-R	6-1	180	12-30-88	.198	.263	.170	69	262	28	52	14	4	5	39	21	1	0	2	76	5	4	.340	.259
Brown, Dusty	R-R	6-0	180	6-19-82	.500	.400	.667	2	8	1	4	1	0	1	1	0	0	0	0	1	0	0	1.000	.500
Cash, Kevin	R-R	6-0	200	12-6-77	.250	.000	.500	1	4	0	1	1	0	0	0	0	0	0	0	0	0	0	.500	.250
Chen, Chia-Chu	L-R	5-10	175	4-7-89	.171	.050	.210	23	82	3	14	1	0	1	6	3	0	0	0	15	0	0	.220	.200
Dominguez, Drew	R-R	5-11	195	12-27-86	.143	.000	.250	2	7	0	1	0	0	0	1	0	0	0	0	3	0	0	.143	.250
Garcia, Joantoni	R-R	5-11	165	9-9-90	.217	.222	.216	57	161	13	35	8	0	0	15	6	1	3	3	35	0	0	.267	.246
Garcia, Jose	R-R	5-11	165	4-23-91	.242	.302	.214	51	194	22	47	13	0	2	15	14	3	2	1	47	7	4	.340	.302
Head, Miles	R-R	6-0	215	5-2-91	.240	.328	.206	65	229	21	55	16	2	1	35	30	4	1	8	36	1	1	.341	.328
Hernandez, Jayson	R-R	5-10	200	9-2-88	.207	.250	.190	21	58	4	12	0	0	0	4	7	2	2	1	9	1	0	.207	.309
Iglesias, Jose	R-R	5-11	175	1-5-90	.350	.250	.375	13	40	8	14	2	2	0	7	7	1	0	0	8	2	1	.500	.458
Jacobs, Brandon	R-R	6-1	225	12-8-90	.242	.243	.241	64	236	30	57	18	2	6	31	21	3	0	3	59	4	1	.411	.308
Kang, James	R-R	5-9	175	10-19-87	.202	.225	.188	33	104	15	21	6	0	0	8	21	3	2	2	30	4	4	.260	.341
Killeen, Sean	R-R	6-0	205	3-2-87	.179	.050	.250	17	56	9	10	1	0	5	11	7	1	0	0	17	0	0	.464	.281
Lowrie, Jed	B-R	6-0	180	4-17-84	.400	.571	.250	6	15	2	6	1	0	0	5	5	0	0	1	1	0	0	.467	.524
Peley, Josue	R-R	6-0	177	12-24-87	.291	.391	.264	31	110	10	32	6	3	0	9	4	2	0	1	16	3	1	.400	.325
Peterson, Bryan	L-R	6-3	190	3-21-90	.189	.125	.207	14	37	3	7	1	0	0	1	4	0	1	0	11	0	0	.216	.302
Ramos, Henry	B-R	6-2	187	4-15-92	.125	.000	.150	7	24	1	3	0	0	0	2	1	0	0	0	8	0	0	.125	.160
Robinson, Nick	L-R	6-1	195	3-5-88	.211	.375	.184	20	57	6	12	2	0	0	4	13	0	0	0	12	2	0	.246	.357
Sanchez, Felix	B-R	6 0	165	6-2-90	.323	.230	.358	57	220	45	71	6	2	0	9	26	2	3	0	59	38	11	.368	.399
Schwindenhammer, Seth	L-R	6-2	205	7-1-91	.192	.273	.155	33	104	11	20	3	0	1	9	14	1	0	1	48	0	2	.250	.292
Vitek, Kolbrin	R-R	6-2	195	4-1-89	.270	.276	.267	56	204	30	55	13	3	4	30	26	5	0	4	61	13	2	.422	.360
Wagner, Mark	R-R	6-1	205	6-11-84	.500	.000	1.000	1	2	1	1	0	0	0	0	1	0	0	0	0	0	0	.500	.667

Pitching	B-T	HT	WT	DOB	W	L	ERA	G	GS	CG	SV	IP	H	R	ER	HR	BB	SO	AVG	vLH	vRH	K/9	BB/9
Angeloni, Chez	R-R	6-2	190	1-23-87	1	3	4.21	17	0	0	2	36	42	24	17	5	17	28	.280	.308	.265	6.94	4.21
Broughton, Jay	R-R	6-1	185	11-10-86	0	3	9.33	11	0	0	0	18	17	23	19	1	19	14	.236	.300	.190	6.87	9.33
Celestino, Miguel	R-R	6-6	205	10-10-89	2	2	2.62	9	9	0	0	45	39	16	13	0	17	28	.245	.250	.243	5.64	3.43
Cervenka, Hunter	L-L	6-1	215	1-3-90	2	4	3.59	14	13	0	0	63	53	35	25	2	42	55	.226	.239	.223	7.90	6.03
Consuegra, Randy	R-R	6-2	211	10-14-89	0	2	270.00	2	2	0	0	0	10	10	10	0	10	0	.000	.000	.000	0.00	270.00
Couch, Keith	L-R	6-2	210	11-5-89	1	6	4.39	14	11	0	0	55	64	31	27	3	9	43	.282	.260	.299	6.99	1.46
Fox, Stephen	R-R	6-5	210	11-10-85	4	2	4.96	16	0	0	1	45	41	27	25	6	17	43	.229	.213	.237	8.54	3.38
Garrison, Seth	R-R	6-5	220	8-13-85	0	0	0.00	2	2	0	0	5	1	0	0	0	1	6	.059	.000	.111	10.80	1.80
Hacker, Mike	L-L	5-9	175	11-6-85	0	1	6.10	8	0	0	4	16	18	8	7	0	3	12	.269	.267	.300	10.45	2.61
Hernandez, Chris	L-L	6-1	185	12-14-88	0	0	4.50	1	1	0	0	2	3	1	1	0	0	2	.375	.333	.400	9.00	0.00
Lavigne, Tyler	R-R	6-0	190	7-30-88	1	3	7.33	10	0	0	0	23	28	19	19	1	11	26	.292	.256	.321	10.03	4.24
Matos, Wilson	R-R	6-2	180	4-10-88	1	5	4.39	19	0	0	2	27	24	19	13	2	19	24	.242	.325	.186	8.10	6.41
Mendez, Roman	R-R	6-2	180	7-25-90	2	3	4.36	8	8	0	0	33	31	21	16	5	19	35	.240	.396	.148	9.55	5.18
Miller, Ryne	R-R	6-4	230	9-25-85	1	0	0.00	1	0	0	0	2	1	0	0	0	1	3	.167	.000	.200	13.50	4.50
Ramirez, Ramon A.	R-R	6-0	190	9-16-82	0	0	0.00	1	0	0	0	2	1	0	0	1	0	2	.167	.000	.250	13.50	4.50
Rau, Garrett	R-R	6-0	185	12-22-88	0	4	3.53	15	0	0	0	51	52	25	20	2	12	22	.277	.307	.257	5.65	2.12
Rosario, Charle	R-R	5-10	158	7-23-88	1	0	4.07	17	0	0	2	55	60	31	25	5	18	50	.273	.277	.269	8.13	2.93
Rutter, Kyle	R-R	6-3	175	7-12-86	0	0	6.75	10	0	0	0	11	10	14	8	0	12	9	.227	.368	.120	7.59	10.13

	B-T	HT	WT	DOB	W	L	ERA	G	GS	CG	SV	IP	H	R	ER	HR	BB	SO	AVG	vLH	vRH	K/9	BB/9
Wilson, Tyler	R-R	6-5	192	12-24-89	3	4	4.20	14	14	0	0	64	69	37	30	5	19	41	.275	.333	.226	5.74	2.66
Younginer, Madison	R-R	6-4	195	11-3-90	3	7	4.79	14	14	0	0	62	56	40	33	2	31	40	.247	.294	.208	5.81	4.50
Zerpa, Armando	L-L	5-11	175	2-13-87	1	1	9.82	4	0	0	0	4	5	4	4	0	3	5	.385	.200	.500	12.27	7.36

Fielding

Catcher	PCT	G	PO	A	E	DP	PB
Blair	1.000	3	14	1	0	0	2
Brown	.929	2	11	2	1	0	0
Cash	1.000	1	6	0	0	0	0
Chen	.982	21	154	11	3	0	1
Hernandez	.975	21	133	20	4	1	5
Killeen	1.000	5	36	2	0	0	2
Peley	.979	24	158	28	4	1	4
Wagner	1.000	1	4	1	0	0	0

First Base	PCT	G	PO	A	E	DP
Head	.987	64	564	38	8	47
Killeen	1.000	7	54	0	0	7

Peley	1.000	5	37	4	0	8

Second Base	PCT	G	PO	A	E	DP
Dominguez	.857	2	4	2	1	1
Garcia	.977	31	55	75	3	22
Kang	.963	30	52	77	5	17
Robinson	.975	20	36	41	2	6

Third Base	PCT	G	PO	A	E	DP
Kang	.400	2	0	2	3	1
Renfroe	.891	44	39	83	15	9
Vitek	.837	29	21	51	14	7

Shortstop	PCT	G	PO	A	E	DP
Garcia	.962	28	31	70	4	13

Garcia	.895	47	54	133	22	25
Iglesias	1.000	2	3	9	0	0
Kang	.900	3	5	4	1	0
Lowrie	1.000	3	1	5	0	1

Outfield	PCT	G	PO	A	E	DP
Brentz	.971	64	125	7	4	5
Jacobs	.963	58	100	4	4	2
Peterson	.875	13	13	1	2	1
Ramos	.882	7	15	0	2	0
Sanchez	.976	57	119	2	3	0
Schwindenhammer	.981	31	46	5	1	0

GCL RED SOX

GULF COAST LEAGUE

Batting	B-T	HT	WT	DOB	AVG	vLH	vRH	G	AB	R	H	2B	3B	HR	RBI	BB	HBP	SH	SF	SO	SB	CS	SLG	OBP
Blair, Carson	R-R	6-1	190	10-18-89	.269	.200	.286	8	26	7	7	1	0	1	3	4	0	0	0	10	0	0	.423	.367
Brown, Dusty	R-R	6-0	180	6-19-82	.500	.000	.500	1	2	0	1	0	0	0	0	0	0	0	0	1	0	0	.500	.500
Coyle, Sean	R-R	5-8	175	1-17-92	.200	1.000	.111	3	10	5	2	1	0	0	1	1	0	0	0	3	0	0	.300	.333
De La Cruz, Keury	L-L	5-11	170	11-28-91	.263	.282	.248	51	198	35	52	10	7	6	31	17	1	0	3	50	8	6	.475	.320
Ellsbury, Jacoby	L-L	6-1	185	9-11-83	.250	.250	.250	3	8	3	2	0	0	0	2	1	0	0	0	1	0	0	.250	.455
Escobar, Leonel	R-R	5-10	175	9-4-90	.259	.238	.273	27	54	5	14	0	0	0	6	8	4	1	1	9	1	0	.259	.388
Holmes, Willie	R-R	5-11	215	8-20-87	.234	.240	.230	36	124	21	29	8	0	6	27	14	5	0	2	37	0	0	.444	.331
Ibarra, Adalberto	L-R	5-10	205	4-3-87	.188	.286	.111	5	16	4	3	1	0	0	6	4	0	0	1	3	0	0	.250	.333
Kang, James	R-R	5-9	175	10-19-87	.235	.200	.250	9	34	9	8	1	0	1	2	1	2	0	0	2	0	0	.353	.297
Kapstein, Zach	R-R	6-2	195	5-28-92	.000	.000	.000	8	5	0	0	0	0	0	0	2	1	0	0	2	0	0	.000	.375
Larsson-Danforth, Trygg	L-R	6-6	235	2-9-87	.255	.200	.300	42	145	20	37	10	0	2	15	23	1	1	3	39	1	1	.366	.359
Linares, Juan Carlos	R-R	5-11	190	9-7-84	.267	.200	.300	4	15	2	4	1	0	0	1	1	0	0	0	2	0	0	.333	.313
Lucas, Trey	R-R	6-0	200	9-25-87	.000	.000	.000	4	2	0	0	0	0	0	1	1	0	1	0	0	0	0	.000	.333
Menses, Heiker	R-R	5-9	160	7-1-91	.250	.247	.252	56	208	27	52	8	3	3	24	12	4	2	0	47	17	6	.361	.304
Moanaroa, Boss	L-R	6-1	200	7-12-91	.268	.259	.276	18	56	8	15	3	0	2	9	9	1	0	1	14	0	0	.429	.373
Moanaroa, Moko	L-L	6-0	215	12-22-89	.296	.302	.292	31	108	13	32	7	0	0	15	8	6	0	1	18	1	0	.361	.374
Perez, Oscar	R-R	6-1	185	11-9-91	.250	.308	.200	30	84	7	21	1	0	0	6	6	0	0	2	23	2	0	.262	.300
Perkins, Kendrick	L-R	6-2	225	9-12-91	.000	.000	.000	3	7	1	0	0	0	0	1	1	0	0	1	7	0	0	.000	.111
Pichardo, Wilfred	B-R	5-9	146	10-21-89	.239	.381	.120	13	46	5	11	1	0	1	5	1	0	0	0	15	4	0	.326	.255
Place, Jason	R-R	6-3	205	5-8-88	.115	.000	.214	9	26	3	3	2	0	1	3	0	0	0	0	12	0	0	.308	.115
Ramos, Henry	B-R	6-2	187	4-15-92	.309	.262	.347	43	136	18	42	8	1	3	26	12	3	2	3	28	12	6	.449	.370
Ramos, Roberto	B-R	5-10	160	9-4-88	.225	.300	.150	13	40	3	9	0	1	0	4	2	0	1	0	7	2	2	.275	.262
Reyes, Roberto	R-R	6-3	240	8-1-90	.263	.500	.154	9	19	2	5	1	0	1	3	0	0	0	0	8	0	1	.474	.364
Roque, Kenneth	L-R	5-11	162	9-20-89	.231	.083	.296	12	39	6	9	1	0	1	3	2	0	0	1	9	2	0	.333	.262
Sallis, Jordan	B-R	5-8	165	7-2-88	.294	.429	.200	8	17	3	5	1	0	0	2	3	0	0	0	4	1	1	.353	.400
Sanchez, Maykol	R-R	5-11	176	5-30-88	.304	.364	.250	12	23	3	7	3	0	0	1	4	1	1	0	3	0	0	.435	.429
Thompson, Jason	B-R	6-1	180	7-30-90	.227	.276	.188	50	172	18	39	10	1	5	23	13	2	2	3	50	9	1	.384	.284
Vinicio, Jose	B-R	5-11	150	7-10-93	.253	.265	.244	43	158	23	40	4	6	1	22	7	2	1	2	26	13	1	.373	.290
Wagner, Mark	R-R	6-1	205	6-11-84	.600	1.000	.333	3	5	1	3	0	0	0	5	0	0	0	0	1	0	0	.600	.800
Yoder, Luke	R-R	5-11	195	7-14-87	.256	.220	.278	50	156	43	40	9	5	4	14	28	12	1	1	45	13	2	.455	.406

Pitching	B-T	HT	WT	DOB	W	L	ERA	G	GS	CG	SV	IP	H	R	ER	HR	BB	SO	AVG	vLH	vRH	K/9	BB/9
Bastardo, Luis	R-R	6-1	165	5-14-90	3	2	3.43	16	0	0	1	45	43	22	17	3	12	39	.257	.225	.287	7.86	2.42
Castillo, Yeiper	R-R	6-3	158	9-6-88	0	0	2.45	2	2	0	0	4	3	1	1	1	4	2	.214	.000	.375	9.82	2.45
Celestino, Miguel	R-R	6-6	205	10-10-89	2	0	0.90	4	3	0	0	20	18	6	2	0	3	14	.228	.267	.176	6.30	1.35
Curtis, Eric	R-R	6-2	220	7-22-89	0	1	3.78	9	8	0	0	33	30	17	14	3	12	26	.236	.257	.211	7.02	3.24
Dahlstrand, Jacob	R-R	6-5	205	3-26-92	0	1	6.00	2	2	0	0	3	4	2	2	1	2	3	.333	.500	.167	9.00	6.00
Erasmus, Justin	R-R	5-10	175	1-22-90	1	3	2.12	21	0	0	10	30	26	13	7	0	9	33	.236	.192	.276	10.01	2.73
Garcia, Jason	R-R	6-0	185	11-21-92	1	3	3.03	9	0	0	0	30	31	16	10	0	6	17	.267	.246	.288	5.16	1.82
Garrison, Seth	B-R	6-5	220	8-13-85	0	0	0.00	1	1	0	0	2	1	0	0	0	5	.125	.200	.000	22.50	0.00
Gleason, Mike	R-R	6-1	195	3-12-88	1	2	4.28	14	0	0	2	40	47	28	19	1	8	30	.299	.366	.244	6.75	1.80
Gomez, Sergio	R-R	6-3	155	8-24-93	0	0	6.37	13	12	0	0	30	32	26	21	2	14	29	.271	.273	.269	8.80	4.25
Hacker, Mike	L-L	5-9	175	11-6-85	0	0	0.00	2	0	0	1	3	1	0	0	0	3	.100	.000	.100	9.00	0.00
Huijer, Swen	R-R	6-9	205	11-7-90	5	2	3.78	16	0	0	0	33	40	22	14	4	10	26	.291	.272	.317	7.02	2.70
Killen, John	L-L	6-7	185	8-20-90	0	1	13.50	4	1	0	0	2	4	3	3	0	7	3	.000	.000	.000	13.50	31.50
Large, T.J.	R-R	6-4	185	5-28-83	0	0	2.40	9	0	0	1	15	10	4	4	0	2	12	.192	.071	.333	7.20	1.20
Phillips, Matt	L-L	6-3	215	2-7-88	3	0	0.78	12	0	0	1	23	14	4	2	0	7	19	.171	.136	.183	7.43	2.74
Reynoso, Ryne	L-R	6-2	215	3-15-85	0	1	10.13	3	1	0	0	3	4	3	3	0	1	2	.308	.286	.333	6.75	3.38
Rodriguez, Juan	R-R	6-5	165	12-12-88	5	1	3.51	12	9	0	0	49	41	22	19	2	13	51	.222	.220	.223	9.43	2.42
Swinson, Scott	R-R	6-2	190	3-11-88	2	1	3.33	15	1	0	3	49	52	30	18	3	9	36	.265	.255	.276	6.66	1.66
Taveras, Francisco	L-L	6-0	180	5-23-91	2	3	4.98	12	9	0	0	43	52	30	24	0	17	37	.306	.405	.278	7.68	3.53
Vellette, Raynel	R-R	6-2	165	6-10-91	5	2	2.54	12	2	0	1	50	34	21	14	3	11	45	.190	.213	.173	8.15	1.99
Wasielewski, Richie	L-L	6-4	240	9-23-89	1	0	0.00	1	0	0	0	2	1	0	0	0	0	2	.143	.333	.000	9.00	0.00

Fielding

Catcher	PCT	G	PO	A	E	DP	PB
Blair	.977	7	41	1	1	0	4
Brown	1.000	1	7	1	0	0	0
Escobar	.979	23	121	19	3	1	5
Kapstein	1.000	8	13	0	0	0	0
Lucas	1.000	4	10	0	0	0	1
Perez	.976	30	175	31	5	5	6
Reyes	1.000	1	2	0	0	0	0
Sanchez	.985	12	61	4	1	1	1
Wagner	1.000	2	8	1	0	0	1

First Base	PCT	G	PO	A	E	DP
Larsson-Danforth	.981	40	323	30	7	31
Moanaroa	.978	15	123	9	3	8
Moanaroa	1.000	5	34	5	0	2
Reyes	1.000	2	2	0	0	1

Second Base	PCT	G	PO	A	E	DP
Coyle	1.000	1	3	0	0	1
Menses	1.000	3	3	11	0	0
Roque	.923	10	9	27	3	5
Sallis	.958	7	8	15	1	3
Thompson	.938	47	69	114	12	25

Third Base	PCT	G	PO	A	E	DP
Escobar	1.000	4	3	3	0	0
Holmes	.813	6	5	8	3	0
Kang	.917	7	6	16	2	1
Menses	.949	40	39	73	6	4
Ramos	.842	5	3	13	3	1
Reyes	.600	3	1	2	2	0

Shortstop	PCT	G	PO	A	E	DP
Kang	.750	1	2	1	1	0

	PCT	G	PO	A	E	DP
Menses	.967	16	31	27	2	10
Ramos	1.000	1	1	0	0	0
Roque	.929	4	10	3	1	1
Vinicio	.880	43	65	103	23	20

Outfield	PCT	G	PO	A	E	DP
De La Cruz	.972	47	102	2	3	1
Ellsbury	1.000	2	3	0	0	0
Holmes	.935	15	28	1	2	0
Linares	1.000	4	2	2	0	1
Moanaroa	.968	23	30	0	1	0
Place	.750	2	3	0	1	0
Ramos	.943	42	64	2	4	1
Ramos	.786	8	11	0	3	0
Yoder	1.000	45	71	5	0	1

DSL RED SOX   ROOKIE
DOMINICAN SUMMER LEAGUE

Batting	B-T	HT	WT	DOB	AVG	vLH	vRH	G	AB	R	H	2B	3B	HR	RBI	BB	HBP	SH	SF	SO	SB	CS	SLG	OBP
Bogaerts, Jair	R-R	6-2	230	10-1-92	.170	.194	.164	46	165	12	28	6	0	2	20	18	1	0	2	53	0	0	.242	.253
Bogaerts, Xander	R-R	6-3	175	10-1-92	.314	.288	.324	63	239	39	75	7	5	3	42	30	6	0	5	37	4	5	.423	.396
Doran, Curtney	R-R	6-0	180	4-30-92	.225	.317	.202	67	209	34	47	12	2	2	29	68	6	0	2	52	8	10	.330	.425
Duncan, Roberto	R-R	6-3	175	2-18-93	.212	.167	.225	50	165	19	35	6	0	0	18	25	7	0	1	44	5	0	.248	.338
Gonzalez, Aly	R-R	6-1	185	2-9-91	.211	.316	.184	40	95	14	20	0	0	0	11	21	3	1	1	17	0	0	.211	.367
Guerrero, Dreily	B-R	5-11	162	10-12-90	.247	.200	.263	71	263	50	65	13	5	1	38	38	4	2	5	66	23	5	.346	.345
Gutierrez, Javier	R-R	6-1	200	8-26-90	.268	.083	.330	40	142	22	38	10	0	2	16	27	4	0	1	30	3	1	.380	.397
Kortstam, Racell	R-R	6-3	180	1-20-92	.143	.077	.167	20	49	9	7	1	0	0	4	6	4	0	0	27	1	3	.163	.288
Loya, Jesus	L-R	6-0	170	6-15-92	.266	.261	.267	69	256	34	68	8	6	0	27	41	2	1	4	45	15	6	.344	.366
Ruiz, Derward	L-R	5-9	190	11-11-91	.203	.194	.205	53	182	17	37	1	2	0	17	31	4	0	1	30	8	3	.231	.330
Sopilka, David	R-R	6-0	170	8-30-93	.156	.125	.163	38	122	11	19	2	1	0	11	20	2	1	2	23	0	0	.189	.281
Ugas, Juan	R-R	6-0	160	3-21-80	.208	.132	.231	55	168	25	35	7	0	0	20	42	8	0	1	36	7	1	.250	.388
Urena, Lewis	R-R	5-8	145	5-6-91	.195	.185	.199	67	241	44	47	8	1	0	14	46	7	8	0	42	12	4	.237	.340

Pitching	B-T	HT	WT	DOB	W	L	ERA	G	GS	CG	SV	IP	H	R	ER	HR	BB	SO	AVG	vLH	vRH	K/9	BB/9
Alcantara, Mario	R-R	6-2	170	12-27-92	1	7	4.55	14	14	0	0	55	62	39	28	0	21	30	.277	.333	.255	4.88	3.42
Alcantara, Raul	R-R	6-3	180	12-4-92	5	3	3.28	13	13	1	0	60	61	31	22	1	8	34	.260	.258	.260	5.07	1.19
Bastardo, Luis	R-R	6-1	165	5-14-90	1	0	1.54	4	0	0	1	12	8	4	2	1	1	18	.182	.091	.212	13.89	0.77
Betancourt, Ricardo	L-L	6-2	175	9-9-92	1	1	4.88	13	0	0	4	24	25	15	13	1	7	15	.266	.250	.267	5.63	2.63
Bonnelly, Sully	R-R	6-2	215	10-14-92	3	3	2.49	14	2	0	3	43	29	19	12	2	19	25	.188	.175	.193	5.19	3.95
Cabral, Cesar	R-R	6-1	190	1-2-91	0	0	18.69	5	0	0	0	4	3	9	9	0	11	2	.214	.000	.300	4.15	22.85
Cuevas, William	R-R	6-0	160	10-14-90	2	4	3.11	14	6	0	1	55	54	22	19	0	12	38	.258	.122	.300	6.22	1.96
Diaz, Luis	R-R	6-3	210	4-9-92	3	1	3.11	13	12	0	0	55	51	21	19	1	14	31	.249	.149	.278	5.07	2.29
Gil, Kiler	L-L	6-1	175	3-23-93	4	1	3.54	12	0	0	0	41	36	19	16	0	11	24	.235	.000	.240	5.31	2.43
Januario, Iago	R-R	6-6	205	1-20-93	1	1	6.30	8	0	0	2	10	14	7	7	0	8	8	.341	.364	.333	7.20	7.20
Jimenez, Ellis	R-R	6-2	175	6-26-92	1	3	3.92	16	0	0	4	41	41	21	18	2	12	22	.266	.244	.274	4.79	2.61
Mateo, Alexander	R-R	5-11	165	4-10-91	5	2	2.60	15	0	0	2	35	27	15	10	0	8	24	.225	.125	.250	6.23	2.08
Montas, Francellis	R-R	6-2	185	3-21-93	0	3	9.55	12	4	0	0	22	28	30	23	2	18	18	.322	.300	.328	7.48	7.48
Ogando, Nefi	R-R	6-2	185	0-0-00	3	1	2.91	11	4	0	0	34	33	15	11	1	15	31	.248	.219	.257	8.21	3.97
Ortega, Yunior	R-R	5-11	170	8-10-91	5	1	1.91	14	14	0	0	71	60	21	15	1	21	42	.238	.258	.231	5.35	2.67
Perez, Israel	L-L	6-1	175	1-13-91	0	0	3.86	3	0	0	0	2	1	1	1	0	4	5	.125	.000	.143	19.29	15.43
Pinales, Carlos	R-R	6-1	180	4-5-92	1	3	1.46	11	3	0	1	37	37	12	6	2	7	18	.262	.316	.243	4.38	1.70
Reyes, Pedro	L-L	6-0	155	5-28-93	1	1	4.38	8	0	0	0	12	9	9	6	0	13	8	.209	.000	.214	5.84	9.49

Fielding

Catcher	PCT	G	PO	A	E	DP	PB
Bogaerts	1.000	17	92	12	0	1	9
Gonzalez	.984	27	108	13	2	2	3
Sopilka	.983	37	203	26	4	0	12

First Base	PCT	G	PO	A	E	DP
Bogaerts	.983	14	110	9	2	9
Gonzalez	.986	8	64	4	1	1
Ugas	.996	54	451	37	2	42

Second Base	PCT	G	PO	A	E	DP
Diaz	1.000	1	1	2	0	0

	PCT	G	PO	A	E	
Guerrero	1.000	1	3	5	0	0
Ruiz	.958	17	29	39	3	9
Urena	.975	55	127	149	7	31

Third Base	PCT	G	PO	A	E	DP
Duncan	.855	48	41	89	22	4
Gonzalez	—	1	0	0	0	0
Guerrero	.861	19	12	50	10	4
Ruiz	.800	6	3	13	4	1
Ugas	.833	3	3	2	1	1
Urena	.857	1	3	3	1	1

Shortstop	PCT	G	PO	A	E	DP
Bogaerts	.929	59	110	164	21	29
Guerrero	.962	14	28	48	3	13

Outfield	PCT	G	PO	A	E	DP
Doran	.975	67	108	9	3	6
Guerrero	1.000	32	51	1	0	0
Gutierrez	.967	34	58	1	2	1
Kortstam	1.000	16	21	2	0	0
Loya	.994	69	147	8	1	5
Urena	.909	8	9	1	1	0

Chicago Cubs

SEASON IN A SENTENCE: The Cubs expected to contend for the playoffs but finished with the 13th-best record in the National League, leading manager Lou Piniella to retire before season's end.

HIGH POINT: Closer Carlos Marmol's dominance in the last month of the regular season capped off a year that saw him break a Cubs record and a major league record. In September, Marmol recorded a save in each of his 13 opportunities without allowing a run. He ended with 138 strikeouts on the season, passing Bruce Sutter for the Cubs' single-season record for a closer, and he established a major league record with an average of 15.99 strikeouts per nine innings.

LOW POINT: On June 26, the Cubs suspended Carlos Zambrano indefinitely for a tantrum and an altercation with teammate Derrek Lee. They placed Zambrano on the restricted list and sent him to anger management therapy. On the positive side, Zambrano returned to action at the end of July and worked his way back into the rotation, getting wins in eight of his last 10 starts.

NOTABLE ROOKIES: Tyler Colvin had such a great spring that he forced his way into the big league lineup. Unfortunately his year ended early with a freak accident, when a broken bat punctured his chest on Sept. 19. Starlin Castro finished his rookie season batting .300/.347/.408 after finishing 2009 in Double-A. He hit a three-run home run in his first major league at-bat on May 7.

KEY TRANSACTIONS: The Cubs unloaded several veterans in July and August, sending Ted Lilly and Ryan Theriot to the Dodgers for Blake DeWitt, Kyle Smit and Brett Wallach; Mike Fontenot to the Giants for Evan Crawford; and finally Derrek Lee to the Braves for Robinson Lopez, Tyrelle Harris and Jeffrey Lorick. None is expected to be a star, but it gave the farm system needed depth.

DOWN ON THE FARM: All the changes in the big leagues created opportunity for younger players. In September, Brad Snyder made the major league roster for the first time in his eight-year professional baseball career after notching 25 home runs and 106 RBIs on the farm. Justin Berg was with Chicago three separate times over the season, and went 4-1, 3.64 in the Iowa bullpen. But the breakout player in the farm system was righthander Chris Archer, who went 15-3, 2.34 and then pitched well for Team USA in the Pan Am qualifying tournament after the season.

OPENING DAY PAYROLL: $146.6 million (3rd)

PLAYERS OF THE YEAR

MAJOR LEAGUE

Carlos Marmol
rhp

2-3, 2.55, 38 SV
138 SO/78 IP
Led NL with 70 GF

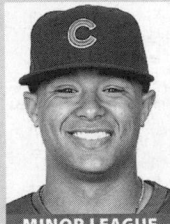

MINOR LEAGUE

Chris Archer
rhp

(High A/Double-A)
15-3, 2.34
149 SO/142 IP

ORGANIZATION LEADERS

BATTING — *Minimum 250 at-bats

MAJORS

*AVG	Starlin Castro	.300
*OPS	Geovany Soto	.890
HR	Aramis Ramirez	25
RBI	Aramis Ramirez	83

MINORS

*AVG	Brandon Guyer, Tennessee	.344
*OBP	Robinson Chirinos, Iowa/Tennessee	.416
*SLG	Brandon Guyer, Tennessee	.588
R	Brett Jackson, Daytona/Tennessee	103
H	D.J. LeMahieu, Daytona	174
TB	Brad Snyder, Iowa	271
2B	Brandon Guyer, Tennessee	39
3B	Brett Jackson, Daytona/Tennessee	14
HR	Bryan LaHair, Iowa	25
	Brad Snyder, Iowa	25
RBI	Brad Snyder, Iowa	106
BB	Brett Jackson, Daytona/Tennessee	73
SO	Kyler Burke, Daytona	131
SB	Tony Campana, Tennessee	48

PITCHING — †Minimum 75 innings

MAJORS

W	Ryan Dempster	15
†ERA	Carlos Marmol	2.55
SO	Ryan Dempster	208

MINORS

W	Chris Archer, Daytona/Tennessee	15
L	Dae-Eun Rhee, Daytona	13
†ERA	Chris Archer, Daytona/Tennessee	2.34
G	Luke Sommer, Daytona/Tennessee/Iowa	58
GS	Three tied at	27
SV	Luke Sommer, Daytona/Tennessee/Iowa	14
IP	Jay Jackson, Iowa	157.3
BB	Jeff Samardzija, Iowa	67
SO	Chris Archer, Daytona/Tennessee	149
†AVG	Chris Archer, Daytona/Tennessee	.200

2010 PERFORMANCE

General Manager: Jim Hendry. **Farm Director:** Oneri Fleita. **Scouting Director:** Tim Wilken.

Class	Team	League	W	L	PCT	Finish*	Manager(s)
Majors	Chicago Cubs	National	75	87	.463	13th (16)	Lou Piniella/Mike Quade
Triple-A	Iowa Cubs	Pacific Coast	82	62	.569	t-1st (16)	Ryne Sandberg
Double-A	Tennessee Smokies	Southern	86	53	.619	1st (10)	Bill Dancy
High A	Daytona Cubs	Florida State	75	64	.540	4th (12)	Buddy Bailey
Low A	Peoria Chiefs	Midwest	71	66	.518	8th (16)	Casey Kopitzke
Short-season	Boise Hawks	Northwest	34	42	.447	5th (8)	Jody Davis
Rookie	AZL Cubs	Arizona	26	29	.473	8th (12)	Juan Cabreja
Overall 2010 Minor League Record			374	316	.542	2nd (30)	

*Finish in overall standings (No. of teams in league). †League champion.

ORGANIZATION STATISTICS

CHICAGO CUBS

NATIONAL LEAGUE

Batting	B-T	HT	WT	DOB	AVG	vLH	vRH	G	AB	R	H	2B	3B	HR	RBI	BB	HBP	SH	SF	SO	SB	CS	SLG	OBP
Baker, Jeff	R-R	6-2	210	6-21-81	.272	.350	.106	79	206	29	56	13	2	4	21	16	1	0	1	50	1	0	.413	.326
Barney, Darwin	R-R	5-10	180	11-8-85	.241	.280	.222	30	79	12	19	4	0	0	2	6	0	0	0	12	0	0	.291	.294
Byrd, Marlon	R-R	6-0	245	8-30-77	.293	.357	.267	152	580	84	170	39	2	12	66	31	17	0	2	98	5	1	.429	.346
Castillo, Welington	R-R	5-10	200	4-24-87	.300	.250	.333	7	20	3	6	4	0	1	5	1	0	0	0	7	0	0	.650	.333
Castro, Starlin	R-R	6-0	190	3-24-90	.300	.339	.286	125	463	53	139	31	5	3	41	29	6	4	4	71	10	8	.408	.347
Colvin, Tyler	L-L	6-3	210	9-5-85	.254	.250	.256	135	358	60	91	18	5	20	56	30	3	1	2	100	6	1	.500	.316
DeWitt, Blake	L-R	5-11	190	8-20-85	.250	.294	.240	53	184	18	46	9	1	4	22	17	1	0	2	37	1	0	.375	.314
2-team total (82 Los Angeles)					.261	—	—	135	440	47	115	24	5	5	52	47	4	2	3	86	3	2	.373	.336
Fontenot, Mike	L-R	5-8	170	6-9-80	.284	.286	.284	75	169	14	48	11	3	1	20	10	3	1	2	28	1	2	.402	.332
2-team total (28 San Francisco)					.283	—	—	103	240	24	68	13	3	1	25	15	3	1	4	41	1	4	.375	.331
Fukudome, Kosuke	L-R	6-0	200	4-26-77	.263	.262	.263	130	358	45	94	20	2	13	44	64	0	3	4	67	7	8	.439	.371
Fuld, Sam	L-L	5-10	180	11-20-81	.143	.333	.120	19	28	3	4	1	0	0	3	3	0	0	0	5	0	0	.179	.226
Hill, Koyie	B-R	6-1	210	3-9-79	.214	.297	.197	77	215	18	46	13	1	1	17	12	0	3	1	61	1	0	.298	.254
Hoffpauir, Micah	L-L	6-3	215	3-1-80	.173	.286	.156	24	52	5	9	3	0	0	5	5	0	0	0	15	0	0	.231	.246
Lee, Derrek	R-R	6-5	245	9-6-75	.251	.237	.257	109	418	63	105	21	0	16	56	52	2	0	3	101	1	3	.416	.335
2-team total (39 Atlanta)					.260	—	—	148	547	80	142	35	0	19	80	73	2	0	4	134	1	3	.428	.347
Nady, Xavier	R-R	6-2	215	11-14-78	.256	.242	.265	119	317	33	81	13	0	6	33	17	8	1	4	85	0	0	.353	.306
Ramirez, Aramis	R-R	6-1	215	6-25-78	.241	.259	.235	124	465	61	112	21	1	25	83	34	3	0	5	90	0	0	.452	.294
Scales, Bobby	B-R	6-0	185	10-4-77	.308	1.000	.250	10	13	4	4	0	0	0	2	7	0	0	0	5	1	0	.308	.550
Snyder, Brad	L-L	6-3	200	5-25-82	.185	.000	.217	12	27	1	5	1	0	0	5	1	0	0	0	12	0	0	.222	.214
Soriano, Alfonso	R-R	6-1	195	1-7-76	.258	.295	.243	147	496	67	128	40	3	24	79	45	3	1	3	123	5	1	.496	.322
Soto, Geovany	R-R	6-1	220	1-20-83	.280	.367	.235	105	322	47	90	19	0	17	53	62	0	0	3	83	0	1	.497	.393
Theriot, Ryan	R-R	5-11	180	12-7-79	.284	.278	.286	96	388	45	110	10	2	1	21	19	2	2	1	46	16	6	.327	.320
2-team total (54 Los Angeles)					.270	—	—	150	586	72	158	15	2	2	29	41	4	7	2	74	20	9	.312	.321
Tracy, Chad	L-R	6-2	215	5-22-80	.250	.000	.262	28	44	6	11	2	0	0	5	5	0	0	0	15	0	0	.295	.327
2-team total (41 Florida)					.247	—	—	69	146	11	36	8	0	1	15	11	2	0	1	36	0	0	.322	.306

Pitching	B-T	HT	WT	DOB	W	L	ERA	G	GS	CG	SV	IP	H	R	ER	HR	BB	SO	AVG	vLH	vRH	K/9	BB/9
Atkins, Mitch	R-R	6-3	230	10-1-85	0	0	6.30	5	0	0	0	10	12	8	7	2	6	10	.286	.375	.231	9.00	5.40
Berg, Justin	R-R	6-3	230	6-7-84	0	1	5.18	41	0	0	0	40	45	27	23	3	20	14	.280	.235	.300	3.15	4.50
Caridad, Esmailin	R-R	5-10	195	10-28-83	0	1	11.25	8	0	0	0	4	4	7	5	1	5	4	.235	.400	.167	9.00	11.25
Cashner, Andrew	R-R	6-6	210	9-11-86	2	6	4.80	53	0	0	0	54	55	31	29	8	30	50	.267	.300	.246	8.28	4.97
Coleman, Casey	L-R	6-0	180	7-3-87	4	2	4.11	12	8	0	0	57	56	27	26	3	25	27	.260	.278	.250	4.26	3.95
Dempster, Ryan	R-R	6-2	215	5-3-77	15	12	3.85	34	34	1	0	215	198	110	92	25	86	208	.244	.234	.252	8.69	3.59
Diamond, Thomas	R-R	6-3	240	4-6-83	1	3	6.83	16	3	0	0	29	33	23	22	5	18	36	.295	.268	.310	11.17	5.59
Gorzelanny, Tom	L-L	6-2	205	7-12-82	7	9	4.09	29	23	0	1	136	136	70	62	11	68	119	.260	.286	.251	7.86	4.49
Grabow, John	L-L	6-2	205	11-4-78	1	3	7.36	28	0	0	0	26	35	24	21	5	13	20	.321	.294	.333	7.01	4.56
Gray, Jeff	R-R	6-3	195	11-19-81	1	0	6.75	7	0	0	0	9	12	9	7	1	5	4	.316	.455	.259	3.86	4.82
Howry, Bob	L-R	6-5	220	8-4-73	0	3	5.66	24	0	0	0	21	29	19	13	2	7	8	.319	.259	.344	3.48	3.05
2-team total (14 Arizona)					1	3	7.71	38	0	0	0	35	47	36	30	8	13	14	—	—	—	3.60	3.34
Lilly, Ted	L-L	6-1	195	1-4-76	3	8	3.69	18	18	0	0	117	104	53	48	19	29	89	.236	.284	.224	6.85	2.23
2-team total (12 Los Angeles)					10	12	3.62	30	30	1	0	194	165	83	78	32	44	166	—	—	—	7.71	2.04
Maine, Scott	L-L	6-3	210	2-2-85	0	0	2.08	13	0	0	0	13	9	4	3	1	5	11	.188	.300	.158	7.62	3.46
Marmol, Carlos	R-R	6-2	215	10-14-82	2	3	2.55	77	0	0	38	78	40	23	22	1	52	138	.147	.130	.161	15.99	6.03
Marshall, Sean	L-L	6-7	220	8-30-82	7	5	2.65	80	0	0	1	75	58	25	22	3	25	90	.210	.196	.218	10.85	3.01
Mateo, Marcos	R-R	6-1	160	4-18-84	0	1	5.82	21	0	0	0	22	20	15	14	6	9	26	.247	.273	.229	10.80	3.74
Russell, James	L-L	6-4	205	1-8-86	1	1	4.96	57	0	0	0	49	55	37	27	11	11	42	.279	.238	.308	7.71	2.02
Samardzija, Jeff	R-R	6-5	225	1-23-85	2	2	8.38	7	3	0	0	19	21	22	18	4	20	9	.269	.103	.367	4.19	9.31
Schlitter, Brian	R-R	6-5	235	12-21-85	0	1	12.38	7	0	0	0	8	18	11	11	2	5	7	.429	.579	.304	7.88	5.63
Silva, Carlos	R-R	6-4	250	4-23-79	10	6	4.22	21	21	0	0	113	120	55	53	11	24	80	.273	.259	.282	6.37	1.91
Stevens, Jeff	R-R	6-2	205	9-5-83	0	0	6.11	18	0	0	0	18	21	15	12	4	10	16	.288	.385	.261	7.64	5.09
Wells, Randy	R-R	6-5	230	8-28-82	8	14	4.26	32	32	0	0	194	209	97	92	19	63	144	.273	.261	.280	6.67	2.92
Zambrano, Carlos	B-R	6-5	260	6-1-81	11	6	3.33	36	20	0	0	130	119	55	48	7	69	117	.246	.279	.221	8.12	4.79

Fielding

Catcher	PCT	G	PO	A	E	DP	PB
Castillo	1.000	5	33	3	0	0	0
Hill	.992	72	493	29	4	4	4
Soto	.995	104	762	45	4	7	2

First Base	PCT	G	PO	A	E	DP
Baker	1.000	4	19	1	0	0
Hoffpauir	.985	12	61	6	1	9
Lee	.993	105	784	92	6	73
Nady	.998	52	389	36	1	47
Tracy	1.000	2	4	0	0	0

Second Base	PCT	G	PO	A	E	DP
Baker	1.000	26	52	54	0	13
Barney	.938	10	13	17	2	4
DeWitt	.976	48	88	119	5	30

	PCT	G	PO	A	E	DP	PB
Fontenot	.969	33	62	64	4	16	
Theriot	.978	66	117	150	6	31	

Third Base	PCT	G	PO	A	E	DP
Baker	.903	33	9	56	7	2
Barney	1.000	6	1	11	0	1
DeWitt	.500	1	0	2	2	0
Fontenot	.909	13	3	17	2	1
Hill	—	1	0	0	0	0
Ramirez	.939	118	56	190	16	9
Scales	.813	7	7	6	3	1
Tracy	.947	10	6	12	1	2

Shortstop	PCT	G	PO	A	E	DP
Barney	1.000	11	10	30	0	9
Castro	.950	123	183	334	27	74

	PCT	G	PO	A	E	DP
Fontenot	1.000	4	7	9	0	2
Theriot	.974	29	38	74	3	13

Outfield	PCT	G	PO	A	E	DP
Baker	1.000	4	5	0	0	0
Byrd	.992	151	371	6	3	2
Colvin	.967	111	174	4	6	0
Fukudome	.995	110	190	4	1	1
Fuld	1.000	14	23	0	0	0
Hoffpauir	1.000	5	5	0	0	0
Nady	.970	28	30	2	1	0
Snyder	1.000	7	12	0	0	0
Soriano	.968	134	204	6	7	0

IOWA CUBS
PACIFIC COAST LEAGUE

TRIPLE-A

Batting	B-T	HT	WT	DOB	AVG	vLH	vRH	G	AB	R	H	2B	3B	HR	RBI	BB	HBP	SH	SF	SO	SB	CS	SLG	OBP
Adduci, Jim	L-L	6-2	210	5-15-85	.248	.214	.261	114	367	60	91	9	1	3	33	27	3	6	4	80	23	9	.302	.302
Barney, Darwin	R-R	5-10	180	11-8-85	.299	.287	.304	114	479	72	143	24	4	2	49	23	3	2	5	52	11	3	.378	.333
Camp, Matt	L-R	6-0	200	5-29-84	.264	.294	.254	130	436	49	115	16	2	2	40	43	6	6	4	41	13	5	.323	.335
Castillo, Welington	R-R	5-10	200	4-24-87	.255	.221	.269	69	239	35	61	17	1	13	59	19	6	1	7	58	0	2	.498	.317
Chirinos, Robinson	R-R	6-1	195	6-5-84	.364	.650	.200	15	55	10	20	4	3	1	10	2	5	0	0	8	0	0	.600	.435
Dubois, Jason	R-R	6-5	220	3-26-79	.300	.369	.259	72	223	47	67	12	1	20	59	28	4	0	2	62	0	0	.632	.385
Fuld, Sam	L-L	5-10	180	11-20-81	.272	.250	.279	112	368	69	100	15	9	4	27	66	2	1	3	37	21	9	.394	.383
Hoffpauir, Micah	L-L	6-3	215	3-1-80	.283	.252	.296	118	427	81	121	35	2	22	95	56	5	0	6	74	1	0	.529	.368
Johnson, Mark	L-R	6-0	200	9-12-75	.500	1.000	.000	2	2	1	1	0	0	0	0	0	0	0	0	1	0	0	.500	.500
LaHair, Bryan	L-R	6-5	240	11-5-82	.308	.227	.337	125	422	71	130	30	0	25	81	51	3	0	2	94	3	1	.557	.385
Mota, Jonathan	R-R	6-0	180	6-1-87	.267	.333	.250	11	30	2	8	0	1	3	3	0	0	0	7	0	0	.367	.333
Robinson, Chris	R-R	6-0	220	5-12-84	.248	.267	.241	67	230	15	57	10	1	2	26	17	1	6	2	34	1	0	.326	.300
Scales, Bobby	B-R	6-0	185	10-4-77	.268	.233	.284	119	373	68	100	33	3	10	53	72	10	3	4	77	7	3	.453	.397
Smith, Marquez	R-R	5-10	210	3-20-85	.314	.357	.297	91	303	60	95	26	1	17	53	31	5	1	2	70	2	0	.574	.384
Snyder, Brad	L-L	6-3	200	5-25-82	.308	.326	.301	132	477	97	147	37	6	25	106	56	4	0	6	125	19	4	.568	.381
Tracy, Chad	L-R	6-2	215	5-22-80	.396	.333	.422	26	91	21	36	8	0	5	18	5	0	0	0	9	0	1	.648	.427
Wright, Ty	R-R	6-0	200	2-26-85	.240	.170	.270	58	175	22	42	7	1	1	16	7	5	1	3	24	3	0	.309	.284

Pitching	B-T	HT	WT	DOB	W	L	ERA	G	GS	CG	SV	IP	H	R	ER	HR	BB	SO	AVG	vLH	vRH	K/9	BB/9
Atkins, Mitch	R-R	6-3	230	10-1-85	8	3	3.63	28	15	0	1	107	98	49	43	14	42	76	.241	.258	.226	6.41	3.54
Berg, Justin	R-R	6-3	230	6-7-84	4	1	3.64	21	0	0	0	30	24	14	12	2	12	16	.238	.267	.214	4.85	3.64
Bibens-Dirkx, Austin	R-R	6-2	190	4-29-85	5	4	4.61	13	8	0	0	53	55	34	27	9	21	34	.264	.304	.233	5.81	3.59
Cales, David	R-R	5-11	200	7-27-87	0	1	6.67	22	0	0	3	27	31	21	20	2	12	21	.282	.273	.286	7.00	4.00
Caridad, Esmailin	R-R	5-10	195	10-28-83	0	1	3.00	2	0	0	0	3	2	1	1	1	2	2	.182	.000	.333	6.00	3.00
Carpenter, Chris	R-R	6-4	215	12-26-85	0	0	5.40	3	3	0	0	15	19	9	9	3	9	12	.317	.280	.343	7.20	5.40
Carrillo, Marco	R-R	5-11	215	2-1-87	0	0	2.45	4	0	0	0	7	6	2	2	2	1	5	.222	.273	.188	6.14	1.23
Cashner, Andrew	R-R	6-6	210	9-11-86	3	0	0.86	5	3	0	0	21	17	3	2	0	2	17	.221	.241	.208	7.29	0.86
Chen, Hung-Wen	R-R	5-11	210	2-3-86	3	4	5.98	16	5	0	0	50	57	35	33	12	12	38	.279	.281	.278	6.89	2.17
Coleman, Casey	L-R	6-0	180	7-3-87	10	7	4.07	20	20	2	0	117	106	58	53	10	35	59	.243	.298	.200	4.53	2.68
Diamond, Thomas	R-R	6-3	240	4-6-83	5	4	3.16	21	21	0	0	108	86	40	38	9	46	104	.218	.232	.204	8.64	3.82
Gaub, John	R-L	6-2	210	4-28-85	3	4	6.52	30	0	0	3	29	27	21	21	1	25	38	.248	.350	.188	11.79	7.76
Gonzalez, Yohan	R-R	6-4	210	4-15-90	0	0	0.00	1	0	0	0	0	0	0	0	0	1	0	.000	.000	.000	27.00	0.00
Grabow, John	L-L	6-2	205	11-4-78	0	0	6.75	4	0	0	0	4	6	3	3	0	1	2	.400	.250	.455	4.50	2.25
Gray, Jeff	R-R	6-3	195	11-19-81	3	1	5.66	25	0	0	1	35	45	27	22	2	15	25	.315	.267	.349	6.43	3.86
Jackson, Jay	R-R	6-1	195	10-27-87	11	8	4.63	32	25	0	0	157	153	86	81	20	48	119	.256	.260	.253	6.81	2.75
Lilly, Ted	L-L	6-1	195	1-4-76	0	0	2.25	1	1	0	0	4	1	1	1	1	1	4	.077	.000	.167	9.00	2.25
Maine, Scott	L-L	6-3	210	2-2-85	3	1	3.51	33	0	0	5	41	33	17	16	4	21	47	.213	.213	.213	10.32	4.61
Martin, Corey	R-R	6-3	195	5-14-87	0	0	10.80	1	0	0	0	2	3	2	2	0	3	2	.375	.500	.250	16.20	0.00
Mateo, Marcos	R-R	6-1	160	4-18-84	0	1	4.97	8	0	0	0	13	12	8	7	0	4	15	.235	.190	.267	10.66	2.84
Mathes, J.R.	L-L	6-3	210	11-9-81	9	8	5.44	23	23	0	0	129	158	85	78	18	28	64	.298	.234	.315	4.47	1.95
Muyco, Jake	R-R	6-0	190	9-16-84	0	0	5.59	14	0	0	0	19	18	12	12	2	6	9	.247	.269	.234	4.19	2.79
Parisi, Mike	R-R	6-3	215	4-18-83	0	3	8.50	5	5	0	0	18	24	20	17	2	9	13	.329	.310	.355	6.50	4.50
Parker, Blake	R-R	6-3	225	6-19-85	1	4	4.74	35	0	0	2	49	52	30	26	9	28	42	.280	.342	.236	7.66	5.11
Russell, James	L-L	6-4	205	1-8-86	0	0	5.73	5	0	0	0	11	11	7	7	5	4	10	.262	.353	.200	8.18	3.27
Samardzija, Jeff	R-R	6-5	225	1-23-85	11	3	4.37	35	15	0	0	111	98	64	54	9	67	102	.186	.231	.135	8.25	5.42
Schlitter, Brian	R-R	6-5	235	12-21-85	2	1	3.15	37	0	0	13	46	44	18	16	3	21	42	.250	.282	.229	8.28	4.14
Sommer, Luke	L-L	6-3	190	6-22-85	1	0	4.05	7	0	0	0	7	9	3	3	1	2	3	.321	.154	.467	4.05	2.70
Stevens, Jeff	R-R	6-2	205	9-5-83	0	2	3.16	36	0	0	10	43	31	16	15	3	26	43	.201	.293	.114	9.07	5.48
Zambrano, Carlos	B-R	6-5	260	6-1-81	0	0	6.75	3	0	0	0	4	6	3	3	0	1	4	.333	.143	.455	9.00	2.25

Fielding

Catcher	PCT	G	PO	A	E	DP	PB
Castillo	.986	68	460	37	7	5	9
Chirinos	.990	15	89	11	1	1	0

	PCT	G	PO	A	E	DP	PB
Johnson	1.000	1	4	0	0	0	0
Robinson	.996	66	435	41	2	4	1

First Base	PCT	G	PO	A	E	DP
Dubois	.917	1	11	0	1	2
Hoffpauir	.993	100	796	66	6	61

CHICAGO CUBS

LaHair	.991	47	424	29	4	35
Scales	1.000	1	8	0	0	0

Second Base	PCT	G	PO	A	E	DP
Barney	1.000	2	5	0	0	0
Camp	.973	55	90	160	7	31
Mota	1.000	7	15	11	0	3
Scales	.990	89	168	211	4	47
Smith	1.000	2	3	1	0	0

Third Base	PCT	G	PO	A	E	DP
Camp	.956	41	24	84	5	7

Mota	.000	1	0	0	1	0
Scales	.905	17	9	29	4	3
Smith	.938	77	41	124	11	7
Tracy	.949	19	14	42	3	1

Shortstop	PCT	G	PO	A	E	DP
Barney	.970	111	158	301	14	58
Camp	.971	33	49	87	4	17
Mota	1.000	1	2	2	0	0

Outfield	PCT	G	PO	A	E	DP
Adduci	1.000	97	194	4	0	0

Camp	1.000	2	1	0	0	0
Dubois	.983	39	58	0	1	0
Fuld	.996	106	267	7	1	2
Hoffpauir	.957	12	22	0	1	0
LaHair	.987	50	73	2	1	0
Scales	1.000	2	5	1	0	0
Snyder	.981	121	199	7	4	3
Wright	.955	45	83	2	4	0

TENNESSEE SMOKIES
DOUBLE-A

SOUTHERN LEAGUE

Batting	B-T	HT	WT	DOB	AVG	vLH	vRH	G	AB	R	H	2B	3B	HR	RBI	BB	HBP	SH	SF	SO	SB	CS	SLG	OBP
Campana, Tony	L-L	5-8	160	5-30-86	.319	.331	.315	131	489	76	156	22	5	0	39	44	5	8	4	82	48	20	.384	.378
Canzler, Russ	R-R	6-2	215	4-11-86	.287	.320	.270	112	355	68	102	28	4	21	66	46	5	0	5	95	5	4	.566	.372
Castro, Starlin	R-R	6-0	190	3-24-90	.376	.432	.347	26	109	20	41	8	5	1	20	9	1	0	2	11	4	5	.569	.421
Chirinos, Robinson	R-R	6-1	195	6-5-84	.318	.388	.285	77	264	53	84	24	0	15	64	42	5	0	7	35	1	5	.580	.412
Clevenger, Steve	L-R	6-0	195	4-5-86	.317	.173	.372	88	271	37	86	24	0	5	47	20	2	0	1	28	0	6	.461	.367
Flaherty, Ryan	L-R	6-3	220	7-27-86	.183	.150	.196	23	71	10	13	2	0	1	9	10	1	0	2	12	1	0	.254	.286
Gonzalez, Marwin	B-R	6-1	186	3-14-89	.246	.246	.246	86	305	24	75	11	3	4	41	17	1	3	4	40	6	4	.341	.284
Guyer, Brandon	R-R	6-1	210	1-28-86	.344	.356	.339	102	369	76	127	39	6	13	58	27	7	5	2	51	30	3	.588	.398
Jackson, Brett	L-R	6-2	210	8-2-88	.276	.270	.279	61	228	47	63	13	6	6	28	30	4	3	3	63	18	4	.465	.366
Lalli, Blake	L-R	6-1	205	5-12-83	.311	.311	.311	130	453	63	141	23	0	4	52	68	2	0	1	53	0	2	.389	.403
Macias, David	B-R	5-9	175	3-9-87	.240	.333	.211	13	25	4	6	1	0	0	2	0	0	0	0	2	0	0	.280	.296
Mercedes, Mario	R-R	5-10	160	11-22-86	.200	.250	.182	5	15	1	3	0	0	0	1	0	0	0	0	2	0	0	.200	.200
Mota, Jonathan	R-R	6-0	180	6-1-87	.217	.333	.176	10	23	2	5	2	0	0	1	0	0	0	0	6	0	0	.304	.217
Opitz, Jake	R-R	6-0	180	7-28-86	.220	.125	.242	23	41	10	9	3	0	1	10	10	1	0	1	8	1	0	.366	.377
Reed, Mark	L-R	5-11	175	4-13-86	.438	.667	.385	6	16	1	7	1	0	0	3	3	0	1	0	4	1	0	.500	.526
Samson, Nate	R-R	6-0	170	8-19-87	.262	.294	.243	84	233	25	61	6	1	1	21	14	3	3	4	36	1	4	.309	.307
Smith, Marquez	R-R	5-10	210	3-20-85	.182	.222	.171	16	44	8	8	2	0	3	5	5	1	0	0	13	0	0	.432	.280
Spencer, Matt	L-L	6-4	230	1-27-86	.268	.237	.278	112	377	62	101	19	2	17	65	35	4	0	4	86	10	2	.454	.333
Thomas, Tony	R-R	5-10	180	7-10-86	.276	.267	.280	116	402	67	111	29	11	11	73	33	7	2	5	100	15	2	.485	.338
Vitters, Josh	R-R	6-2	200	8-27-89	.223	.259	.209	63	206	28	46	12	0	7	26	13	7	2	0	41	2	0	.383	.292
Wright, Ty	R-R	6-0	200	2-26-85	.298	.333	.284	73	289	50	86	21	0	10	51	14	5	1	2	35	4	2	.474	.339

Pitching	B-T	HT	WT	DOB	W	L	ERA	G	GS	CG	SV	IP	H	R	ER	HR	BB	SO	AVG	vLH	vRH	K/9	BB/9
Archer, Chris	R-R	6-3	190	9-26-88	8	2	1.80	13	13	0	0	70	48	19	14	2	39	67	.198	.210	.182	8.61	5.01
Bibens-Dirkx, Austin	R-R	6-2	190	4-29-85	5	3	3.27	16	16	0	0	85	59	34	31	6	27	68	.196	.185	.206	7.17	2.85
Buchter, Ryan	L-L	6-3	185	2-13-87	7	2	4.65	47	1	0	0	60	61	37	31	6	47	71	.268	.259	.272	10.65	7.05
Cabrera, Alberto	R-R	6-4	170	10-25-88	0	4	6.33	10	9	0	0	43	57	39	30	1	24	35	.315	.358	.289	7.38	5.06
Cales, David	R-R	5-11	195	7-27-87	4	1	2.51	35	0	0	10	47	40	13	13	2	12	37	.238	.240	.237	7.14	2.31
Caridad, Esmailin	R-R	5-10	195	10-28-83	0	1	5.19	7	0	0	1	9	12	5	5	1	3	8	.324	.467	.227	8.31	3.12
Carpenter, Chris	R-R	6-4	215	12-26-85	8	6	3.16	23	23	0	0	120	118	56	42	5	48	100	.262	.239	.282	7.52	3.61
Carrillo, Marco	R-R	5-11	215	2-1-87	5	0	4.47	25	1	0	2	46	52	28	23	3	18	44	.286	.344	.225	8.55	3.50
Cashner, Andrew	R-R	6-6	210	9-11-86	3	1	2.75	6	6	0	0	36	22	12	11	1	13	26	.176	.161	.190	10.50	3.25
Chen, Hung-Wen	R-R	5-11	210	2-3-86	8	7	2.96	16	16	0	0	97	96	38	32	9	23	58	.259	.228	.284	5.36	2.13
Dolis, Rafael	R-R	6-4	215	1-10-88	5	4	4.07	12	10	0	0	55	65	32	25	3	27	45	.295	.307	.283	7.32	4.39
Harris, Ty'Relle	R-R	6-4	235	12-12-86	1	1	5.40	4	2	0	0	12	13	7	7	1	3	8	.283	.391	.174	6.17	2.31
2-team total (4 Mississippi)					1	1	3.38	8	3	0	1	24	19	10	9	1	9	19	—	—	—	7.13	3.38
Leverton, James	R-L	6-2	185	5-13-86	1	0	3.18	4	0	0	0	6	5	2	2	0	3	4	.250	.125	.333	6.35	4.76
Maestri, Alex	R-R	5-11	175	6-5-85	2	3	6.25	28	0	0	2	40	43	31	28	3	21	32	.269	.258	.277	7.14	4.69
Maine, Scott	L-L	6-3	210	2-2-85	1	1	2.20	12	0	0	5	16	12	8	4	1	4	15	.200	.227	.184	8.27	2.20
Martin, Corey	R-R	6-3	195	5-1-87	0	0	3.00	1	0	0	0	3	1	1	1	1	1	2	.111	.000	.125	6.00	3.00
Martinez, Oswaldo	R-R	6-0	180	9-25-88	2	1	5.40	9	0	0	0	17	24	15	10	2	4	10	.338	.242	.421	5.40	2.16
Mateo, Marcos	R-R	6-1	160	4-18-84	0	0	2.18	17	1	0	4	21	21	8	5	2	3	29	.258	.405	.154	12.63	1.31
McNutt, Trey	R-R	6-4	205	8-2-89	0	1	5.74	3	3	0	0	16	21	12	10	2	4	13	.333	.250	.419	7.47	2.30
Muschko, Craig	R-R	6-2	192	8-17-85	9	3	3.77	26	23	0	1	143	141	67	60	17	27	103	.261	.266	.257	6.47	1.70
Muyco, Jake	R-R	6-0	190	9-16-84	4	2	3.67	40	0	0	5	56	70	26	23	3	12	23	.310	.360	.277	3.67	1.92
Papelbon, Jeremy	R-L	6-1	205	6-24-83	1	2	5.54	31	8	0	1	76	102	48	47	8	16	59	.326	.200	.377	6.96	1.89
Parisi, Mike	R-R	6-3	215	4-18-83	0	0	3.38	1	1	0	0	3	3	1	1	1	1	0	.333	.500	.286	0.00	3.38
Parker, Blake	R-R	6-3	225	6-19-85	0	1	2.65	13	0	0	5	17	11	5	5	0	6	25	.183	.111	.242	13.24	3.18
Rusin, Chris	L-L	6-2	185	10-22-86	2	1	1.89	4	4	0	0	19	21	8	4	0	4	16	.284	.348	.255	7.11	1.89
Sasser, Dustin	L-L	6-0	200	9-13-85	2	3	4.61	23	0	0	2	27	35	17	14	2	18	18	.318	.405	.274	5.93	5.93
Shafer, Aaron	L-R	6-5	185	12-2-86	2	5	5.03	25	0	0	2	34	34	20	19	3	10	30	.262	.281	.242	7.94	2.65
Smit, Kyle	R-R	6-3	165	10-14-87	5	1	1.96	12	0	0	1	18	23	5	4	0	4	16	.311	.333	.286	7.85	1.96
2-team total (3 Chattanooga)					5	1	1.69	15	0	0	1	21	25	6	4	0	4	17	—	—	—	7.17	1.69
Sommer, Luke	L-L	6-3	190	6-22-85	1	1	2.02	30	0	0	8	36	39	11	8	1	10	19	.281	.197	.346	4.79	2.52

Fielding

Catcher	PCT	G	PO	A	E	DP	PB
Chirinos	.988	70	509	52	7	6	5
Clevenger	.994	63	422	53	3	7	3
Lalli	—	1	0	0	0	0	0

Mercedes	1.000	5	31	4	0	0	1
Reed	.974	5	36	1	1	0	0

First Base	PCT	G	PO	A	E	DP
Canzler	.984	27	175	14	3	19
Lalli	.992	110	858	68	7	95
Spencer	.980	20	131	16	3	19

Second Base	PCT	G	PO	A	E	DP
Flaherty	1.000	18	31	36	0	10
Macias	1.000	6	7	11	0	1
Opitz	1.000	2	1	3	0	0
Samson	.970	18	33	32	2	9
Smith	.968	7	13	17	1	4
Thomas	.973	105	210	301	14	85

Third Base	PCT	G	PO	A	E	DP
Canzler	.878	56	30	92	17	6
Clevenger	.500	1	0	1	1	1
Flaherty	1.000	3	0	3	0	0

	PCT	G	PO	A	E	DP
Macias	1.000	2	1	0	0	1
Mota	1.000	4	0	5	0	1
Opitz	.840	17	5	16	4	1
Samson	.969	20	8	23	1	1
Smith	1.000	5	4	5	0	1
Vitters	.902	58	32	88	13	10

Shortstop	PCT	G	PO	A	E	DP
Castro	.953	26	40	62	5	8
Gonzalez	.935	81	108	235	24	61
Macias	1.000	1	1	3	0	1
Mota	.941	5	7	9	1	3

	PCT	G	PO	A	E	DP
Samson	.941	41	75	116	12	33

Outfield	PCT	G	PO	A	E	DP
Campana	.978	125	268	5	6	3
Canzler	1.000	10	12	0	0	0
Gonzalez	—	2	0	0	0	0
Guyer	.986	97	202	12	3	3
Jackson	.990	55	93	3	1	1
Spencer	.978	77	128	6	3	0
Thomas	.857	8	11	1	2	0
Wright	.971	72	125	11	4	5

DAYTONA CUBS

FLORIDA STATE LEAGUE

Batting	B-T	HT	WT	DOB	AVG	vLH	vRH	G	AB	R	H	2B	3B	HR	RBI	BB	HBP	SH	SF	SO	SB	CS	SLG	OBP
Borges, Smaily	R-R	6-3	210	1-28-84	.227	.263	.189	74	225	36	51	14	2	6	26	8	3	1	2	55	1	3	.387	.261
Brenly, Michael	R-R	6-3	210	10-14-86	.270	.305	.256	102	367	48	99	16	0	5	35	29	6	1	1	57	3	1	.354	.333
Burke, Kyler	L-L	6-3	205	4-20-88	.212	.222	.207	135	515	61	109	29	5	7	60	43	6	1	2	131	6	3	.328	.279
Crawford, Evan	R-R	6-2	165	8-5-88	.278	.214	.300	18	54	7	15	1	2	0	3	1	0	1	1	16	3	0	.370	.286
Flaherty, Ryan	L-R	6-3	220	7-27-86	.286	.227	.306	108	420	65	120	34	3	9	63	41	4	1	9	74	6	3	.445	.348
Flores, Luis	R-R	5-10	195	11-2-86	.304	.188	.571	10	23	3	7	3	1	0	1	1	0	0	0	2	0	0	.522	.333
Gonzalez, Marwin	B-R	6-1	186	3-14-89	.271	.241	.286	23	85	7	23	3	0	0	5	7	1	2	1	13	7	1	.306	.330
Jackson, Brett	L-R	6-2	210	8-2-88	.316	.344	.299	67	263	56	83	19	8	6	38	43	5	0	1	63	12	7	.517	.420
Lake, Junior	R-R	6-2	200	3-27-90	.264	.308	.247	120	394	56	104	18	4	9	46	35	7	8	3	99	13	9	.398	.333
Lemahieu, D.J.	R-R	6-4	185	7-13-88	.314	.411	.275	135	554	63	174	24	5	2	73	29	1	10	6	61	17	7	.386	.346
Macias, David	B-R	5-9	175	3-7-86	.223	.232	.219	93	332	36	74	8	3	2	34	21	4	11	3	53	4	1	.283	.275
Mercedes, Mario	R-R	5-10	160	11-22-86	.286	.000	.286	2	7	0	2	0	0	0	0	0	0	0	0	0	0	0	.786	.286
Mota, Jonathan	R-R	6-0	180	6-1-87	.000	.000	.000	1	6	0	0	0	0	0	0	0	0	0	0	5	0	0	.000	.000
Opitz, Jake	L-R	6-0	180	7-28-86	.239	.326	.217	74	230	19	55	11	2	1	19	20	3	3	2	39	1	2	.317	.306
Perez, Nelson	L-R	6-3	215	11-16-87	.163	.286	.151	27	80	10	13	5	1	1	7	5	1	0	1	29	0	1	.288	.218
Reed, Mark	L-R	5-11	175	4-13-86	.245	.222	.251	65	212	20	52	7	7	2	20	10	3	4	1	54	4	1	.325	.288
Ridling, Rebel	R-R	6-4	230	5-27-86	.267	.266	.266	121	469	50	125	34	1	13	76	50	3	0	6	93	3	6	.426	.312
Rohan, Greg	R-R	6-0	205	5-11-86	.250	.333	.224	41	140	17	35	8	0	1	15	9	0	1	0	27	0	1	.329	.295
Spencer, Matt	L-L	6-4	230	1-27-86	.286	.556	.192	9	35	3	10	2	0	2	4	0	0	0	0	5	0	0	.514	.286
Valdez, Jose	B-R	6-1	170	9-5-87	.254	.333	.213	63	185	29	47	3	1	0	6	17	6	2	1	43	16	6	.281	.335
Vitters, Josh	R-R	6-2	200	8-27-89	.291	.290	.291	28	110	16	32	8	0	3	13	8	2	0	0	2	4	1	.445	.350
White, Ryne	L-L	5-11	205	10-17-86	.182	.125	.200	11	33	5	6	1	0	0	1	8	0	0	0	5	0	0	.212	.341

Pitching	B-T	HT	WT	DOB	W	L	ERA	G	GS	CG	SV	IP	H	R	ER	HR	BB	SO	AVG	vLH	vRH	K/9	BB/9
Archer, Chris	R-R	6-3	180	9-26-88	7	1	2.86	15	14	0	0	72	54	27	23	4	26	82	.202	.185	.216	10.20	3.24
Beliveau, Jeff	L-L	6-1	197	1-17-87	4	2	2.89	40	0	0	2	53	41	20	17	4	23	74	.208	.131	.243	12.57	3.91
Cabrera, Alberto	R-R	6-4	170	10-25-88	7	5	3.28	18	17	1	0	93	92	44	34	6	26	90	.253	.268	.239	8.68	2.51
Carrillo, Marco	R-R	5-11	215	2-1-87	2	0	1.67	17	0	0	3	32	22	7	6	1	7	30	.195	.159	.217	8.35	1.95
Dolis, Rafael	R-R	6-4	215	1-10-88	4	5	2.92	14	13	0	0	71	63	31	23	3	30	48	.242	.279	.215	6.08	3.80
Huseby, Chris	R-R	6-7	220	1-11-88	0	0	16.88	3	0	0	0	3	5	5	5	0	6	2	.417	.000	.625	6.75	20.25
Lambert, Casey	L-L	5-11	175	12-11-85	1	0	2.95	14	0	0	0	21	16	7	7	1	11	20	.219	.316	.185	8.44	4.64
Leverton, James	R-L	6-2	185	5-13-86	4	0	2.80	26	0	0	5	35	36	12	11	3	11	28	.259	.158	.297	7.13	2.80
Maestri, Alex	R-R	5-11	175	6-1-85	3	2	3.79	22	0	0	1	36	27	19	15	4	15	38	.218	.200	.228	9.59	3.79
Martinez, Oswaldo	R-R	6-0	180	9-25-88	3	7	4.94	34	1	0	5	58	54	34	32	3	30	46	.241	.255	.231	7.10	4.63
McNutt, Trey	R-R	6-4	205	8-2-89	4	0	2.63	9	9	0	0	41	29	16	12	3	9	49	.191	.141	.243	10.76	1.98
Patton, David	R-R	6-3	205	5-18-84	2	5	5.03	39	0	0	3	59	60	37	33	3	42	35	.265	.224	.297	5.34	6.41
Perconte, Mike	R-R	6-4	170	3-18-86	5	2	3.71	48	1	0	7	87	88	45	36	6	36	97	.262	.292	.245	10.00	3.71
Raley, Brooks	L-R	6-3	185	6-29-88	8	6	3.50	27	27	0	0	136	151	62	53	9	43	97	.284	.283	.284	6.40	2.84
Rhee, Dae-Eun	L-R	6-2	190	3-23-89	5	13	5.27	26	25	0	0	114	125	74	67	11	40	70	.279	.305	.263	5.51	3.15
Rusin, Chris	L-L	6-2	185	10-22-86	4	3	3.36	20	17	0	0	91	79	43	34	6	15	84	.232	.153	.252	8.31	1.48
Searle, Ryan	R-R	6-0	190	6-22-89	1	1	4.60	4	2	0	0	16	15	8	8	1	5	11	.273	.323	.208	6.32	2.87
Shafer, Aaron	L-R	6-5	185	12-2-86	2	1	0.96	24	0	0	5	47	29	7	5	1	10	47	.170	.167	.171	9.06	1.93
Siegfried, Chris	L-L	6-5	195	12-12-85	3	7	4.26	46	4	0	1	82	74	41	39	4	34	77	.239	.174	.265	8.42	3.72
Sommer, Luke	L-L	6-3	190	6-22-87	1	1	2.52	21	0	0	6	25	28	11	7	0	4	20	.286	.250	.297	7.20	1.44
Struck, Nick	R-R	5-11	185	10-7-89	3	2	5.14	3	2	0	0	14	15	8	8	3	6	12	.263	.300	.243	7.71	3.86
Whitenack, Robert	R-R	6-5	185	11-20-88	3	1	2.04	7	7	0	0	40	32	10	9	2	10	28	.218	.339	.136	6.35	2.27

Fielding

Catcher	PCT	G	PO	A	E	DP	PB
Brenly	.995	84	618	37	3	3	11
Flores	1.000	9	38	6	0	2	1
Mercedes	.950	2	18	1	1	0	0
Reed	.993	55	422	35	3	3	6

First Base	PCT	G	PO	A	E	DP
Gonzalez	1.000	11	104	5	0	8
Opitz	.990	30	269	20	3	19
Reed	—	1	0	0	0	0
Ridling	.993	90	777	66	6	64
Rohan	1.000	1	0	0	0	0

	PCT	G	PO	A	E	DP
Spencer	1.000	4	38	4	0	1
White	1.000	8	72	5	0	3

Second Base	PCT	G	PO	A	E	DP
Flaherty	.955	39	69	124	9	22
Gonzalez	1.000	2	6	8	0	1
Lemahieu	.990	65	114	191	3	36
Macias	.970	28	46	82	4	15
Opitz	1.000	11	15	19	0	2

Third Base	PCT	G	PO	A	E	DP
Flaherty	.902	52	16	103	13	10

	PCT	G	PO	A	E	DP
Gonzalez	1.000	3	0	10	0	0
Lake	.850	12	6	28	6	4
Lemahieu	.954	39	18	86	5	5
Macias	1.000	5	4	9	0	1
Opitz	.810	10	3	14	4	1
Rohan	.000	2	0	0	1	0
Vitters	.912	21	17	35	5	0

Shortstop	PCT	G	PO	A	E	DP
Flaherty	.926	5	7	18	2	3
Gonzalez	1.000	3	1	12	0	1
Lake	.925	107	120	310	35	47

Lemahieu	.957	25	34	76	5	15
Macias	.929	4	5	8	1	2
Outfield	**PCT**	**G**	**PO**	**A**	**E**	**DP**
Borges	.971	52	63	3	2	0

Burke	.972	131	239	8	7	2
Crawford	.967	18	29	0	1	0
Gonzalez	1.000	4	4	0	0	0
Jackson	.987	62	146	4	2	2
Macias	.968	54	85	5	3	3

Opitz	.857	5	6	0	1	0
Perez	.962	19	25	0	1	0
Rohan	.980	38	49	0	1	0
Spencer	1.000	1	1	0	0	0
Valdez	.967	59	140	5	5	1

PEORIA CHIEFS — LOW CLASS A

MIDWEST LEAGUE

Batting	B-T	HT	WT	DOB	AVG	vLH	vRH	G	AB	R	H	2B	3B	HR	RBI	BB	HBP	SH	SF	SO	SB	CS	SLG	OBP
Bour, Justin	L-R	6-4	250	5-28-88	.291	.277	.296	127	475	59	138	31	1	12	87	58	9	0	5	100	1	0	.436	.375
Cerda, Matt	L-R	5-9	165	6-20-90	.271	.220	.290	124	451	79	122	21	6	5	80	68	3	3	7	68	4	1	.377	.365
Fitzgerald, D.J.	R-R	6-0	190	12-20-88	.283	.339	.259	99	378	56	107	17	7	6	46	39	1	0	1	89	10	6	.413	.351
Flores, Luis	R-R	5-10	195	11-2-86	.216	.256	.198	40	134	14	29	7	0	4	18	14	2	1	2	26	0	0	.358	.296
Giansanti, Anthony	R-R	5-10	190	9-28-88	.296	.174	.333	30	98	9	29	10	0	0	13	11	3	0	2	19	2	1	.398	.377
Guevara, Jose	R-R	6-1	180	3-17-88	.167	.167	.167	9	30	2	5	1	0	0	2	2	1	0	0	11	0	0	.200	.242
Guzman, Francisco	L-L	6-1	160	4-12-88	.243	.270	.236	56	177	23	43	5	1	0	12	20	1	8	2	34	7	6	.282	.320
Ha, Jae-Hoon	R-R	6-1	185	10-29-90	.317	.345	.306	77	293	36	93	15	4	7	46	10	0	1	5	45	9	4	.468	.334
Jones, Richard	L-R	6-0	215	1-31-88	.216	.167	.231	37	134	10	29	8	1	2	17	1	1	1	1	35	0	0	.336	.226
Lee, Hak-Ju	R-L	6-2	170	11-4-90	.282	.285	.282	122	485	85	137	22	4	1	40	49	5	11	1	86	32	7	.351	.354
Matheus, George	R-R	6-0	170	7-21-88	.164	.106	.203	40	116	14	19	8	0	0	6	9	1	1	1	25	0	1	.233	.228
May, Brandon	R-R	6-1	205	1-7-88	.229	.250	.217	10	35	4	8	2	0	1	3	4	1	1	0	13	0	0	.371	.325
Mercedes, Mario	R-R	5-10	160	11-22-86	.269	.277	.266	51	175	21	47	4	0	0	20	13	1	2		18	1	0	.291	.319
Morelli, Jesus	R-R	6-3	180	4-25-90	.276	.364	.222	10	29	5	8	0	0	0	1	2	2	0	0	5	0	0	.276	.364
Mota, Jonathan	R-R	6-0	180	6-1-87	.281	.326	.265	44	160	20	45	8	0	2	24	10	4	1	2	21	0	0	.369	.335
Perez, Nelson	L-R	6-3	215	11-16-87	.289	.171	.323	82	305	43	88	16	2	11	48	17	2	0	1	92	2	1	.462	.329
Ramirez, Alvaro	L-L	5-9	160	4-5-86	.200	.375	.128	16	55	5	11	0	0	0	2	2	0	0	0	13	1	2	.218	.228
Ramirez, Aramis	R-R	6-1	215	6-25-78	.167	.000	.167	2	6	1	1	0	0	0	1	2	0	0	0	2	0	0	.167	.375
Rohan, Greg	R-R	6-0	205	5-11-86	.298	.295	.299	75	292	40	87	17	3	5	53	23	4	1	3	51	1	2	.428	.354
Rosa, Jovan	R-R	6-2	180	10-26-87	.103	.182	.071	10	39	3	4	1	0	0	2	3	0	0	0	13	0	0	.128	.167
Soto, Elliot	R-R	5-9	160	8-21-89	.111	.167	.000	3	9	1	1	0	0	0	0	1	0	0		1	0	0	.111	.273
Szczur, Matt	R-R	6-1	190	7-20-89	.192	.308	.077	6	26	6	5	1	0	2	3	1	0	0		5	0	0	.308	.300
Thomas, Charles	R-R	6-4	225	7-2-88	.176	.121	.191	43	148	13	26	3	0	4	16	12	0	2	2	44	1	0	.277	.235
Valdez, Jose	B-R	6-1	170	9-5-87	.226	.297	.192	33	115	17	26	1	1	0	5	4	3	0	2	27	17	6	.252	.288
Watkins, Logan	L-R	5-11	170	8-29-89	.261	.248	.266	118	440	69	115	15	8	1	30	58	3	18	1	97	19	10	.339	.351

Pitching	B-T	HT	WT	DOB	W	L	ERA	G	GS	CG	SV	IP	H	R	ER	HR	BB	SO	AVG	vLH	vRH	K/9	BB/9
Antigua, Jeffry	R-L	6-1	170	6-23-90	4	5	4.16	21	17	0	0	93	88	47	43	11	33	88	.251	.276	.244	8.52	3.19
Batista, Frank	R-R	5-10	170	6-26-89	2	1	4.46	22	11	0	2	73	74	37	36	13	24	67	.268	.276	.261	8.30	2.97
Beliveau, Jeff	L-L	6-1	197	1-17-87	0	0	1.59	6	0	0	0	11	6	2	2	1	6	23	.162	.222	.143	18.26	4.76
Clubb, Tim	R-R	6-3	195	9-4-86	0	1	19.64	3	0	0	0	4	8	8	2	4	4	8	.476	.375	.538	9.82	9.82
de Leon, Manolin	R-R	6-0	175	11-23-86	1	1	3.98	21	0	0	0	32	30	15	14	2	12	30	.248	.295	.200	8.53	3.41
Gonzalez, Yohan	R-R	6-4	210	4-15-90	2	2	2.89	34	0	0	4	56	56	22	18	1	16	40	.260	.244	.244	6.43	2.57
Grife, Steve	R-R	6-0	177	11-4-86	3	3	4.06	38	0	0	3	58	46	30	26	8	29	63	.219	.231	.210	9.83	4.53
Hatley, Marcus	R-R	6-5	190	3-26-88	0	0	3.38	7	7	0	0	13	14	6	5	0	7	13	.188	.448	.067	8.78	4.72
Jung, Su-Min	R-R	6-2	190	4-1-90	7	4	3.94	22	14	0	0	89	85	50	39	7	39	79	.256	.248	.261	7.99	3.94
Keefe, Danny	R-R	6-4	185	8-15-87	2	1	1.50	16	0	0	1	30	23	7	5	1	12	24	.232	.222	.241	7.20	3.60
Kirk, Austin	L-L	6-1	200	5-22-90	1	1	3.55	3	0	0	0	13	8	5	5	1	9	17	.174	.150	.192	12.08	6.39
Latham, Jordan	R-R	6-1	180	9-25-86	1	3	4.81	35	0	0	11	39	37	33	21	4	28	43	.237	.283	.208	9.84	6.41
Leverton, James	R-L	6-2	185	5-13-86	5	1	2.60	19	0	0	4	28	23	11	8	1	9	25	.228	.243	.219	8.13	2.93
Lilly, Ted	L-L	6-1	195	1-4-76	1	0	1.29	1	1	0	0	7	3	1	1	0	1	9	.125	.000	.150	11.57	1.29
Liria, Luis	B-R	6-2	170	1-19-90	1	0	10.29	3	0	0	0	7	8	9	8	0	10	6	.296	.143	.350	7.71	12.86
Lopez, Robinson	R-R	6-2	190	3-2-91	0	0	2.61	4	2	0	0	10	10	3	3	1	9	6	.256	.176	.318	5.23	7.84
Lorick, Jeff	L-L	6-0	195	12-18-87	0	0	4.82	4	2	0	0	9	6	5	5	0	0	12	.265	.273	.261	11.57	8.68
Martin, Corey	R-R	6-3	195	5-1-87	4	2	6.11	22	0	0	6	28	40	22	19	4	8	23	.333	.317	.339	7.39	2.57
McNutt, Trey	R-R	6-4	205	8-2-89	6	1	1.51	13	13	0	0	60	43	14	10	0	24	70	.202	.198	.205	10.56	3.62
Morla, Ronny	R-R	6-3	190	5-19-88	4	3	4.00	43	0	0	3	79	76	39	35	7	20	86	.247	.231	.261	9.84	2.29
Nagel, Jon	R-R	6-4	230	1-18-87	1	2	4.34	7	4	0	0	29	17	11	9	0	7	20	.233	.222	.239	9.64	3.33
Quezada, Andres	B-R	5-11	170	3-15-86	0	1	5.40	10	0	0	0	15	17	11	9	1	10	18	.288	.250	.308	7.80	6.00
Searle, Ryan	R-R	6-0	190	6-23-88	4	9	4.38	22	19	0	0	109	115	60	53	7	37	90	.274	.259	.285	7.43	3.06
Silva, Carlos	R-R	6-4	250	4-23-79	0	1	6.14	2	2	0	0	7	8	5	5	1	2	5	.276	.429	.133	6.14	2.45
Struck, Nick	R-R	5-11	185	10-7-89	8	8	3.22	25	18	1	0	115	93	50	41	7	40	84	.225	.230	.220	6.59	3.14
Suarez, Larry	R-R	6-4	245	12-20-89	1	3	4.98	27	0	0	1	47	51	35	26	5	22	51	.276	.224	.305	9.77	4.21
Wallach, Brett	R-R	6-5	205	12-2-88	0	4	5.76	7	7	0	0	30	28	26	19	2	18	20	.257	.254	.262	7.28	5.46
2-team total (17 Great Lakes)					6	4	4.25	24	24	0	0	104	101	65	54	9	61	116	—	—		9.13	4.80
Whitenack, Robert	R-R	6-5	185	11-20-88	8	7	4.96	21	20	0	1	103	102	64	57	5	30	63	.262	.244	.275	5.49	2.61

Fielding

Catcher	PCT	G	PO	A	E	DP	PB
Flores	.989	38	311	41	4	3	2
Guevara	.988	9	76	5	1	1	4
Mercedes	.995	51	361	48	2	5	6
Mota	.996	31	242	27	1	2	6
Rosa	1.000	10	83	10	0	1	2

First Base	PCT	G	PO	A	E	DP
Bour	.986	118	970	83	15	89
Jones	.956	4	42	1	2	7
Matheus	1.000	1	2	0	0	1
May	.917	2	9	2	1	1
Rohan	1.000	13	130	2	0	7

Second Base	PCT	G	PO	A	E	DP
Cerda	.991	49	95	122	2	32
Matheus	.974	17	30	44	2	8
Watkins	.972	74	96	185	8	48

Third Base	PCT	G	PO	A	E	DP
Cerda	.916	62	38	103	13	6
Matheus	.925	17	17	20	3	1

CHICAGO CUBS

	PCT	G	PO	A	E	DP
Mota	1.000	10	10	13	0	1
Ramirez	1.000	1	0	1	0	0
Rohan	.900	21	14	22	4	2
Thomas	.872	29	18	57	11	4
Shortstop	**PCT**	**G**	**PO**	**A**	**E**	**DP**
Lee	.939	118	178	349	34	73
Matheus	1.000	2	1	0	0	0

	PCT	G	PO	A	E	DP
Soto	1.000	2	6	5	0	3
Watkins	.926	19	25	50	6	10
Outfield	**PCT**	**G**	**PO**	**A**	**E**	**DP**
Fitzgerald	.956	59	79	8	4	1
Giansanti	.972	29	65	5	2	2
Guzman	.966	55	135	7	5	2
Ha	.982	74	105	5	2	0

	PCT	G	PO	A	E	DP
Jones	.921	25	33	2	3	0
Morelli	1.000	9	9	0	0	0
Perez	.950	72	128	6	7	0
Ramirez	.963	16	26	0	1	0
Rohan	.946	23	34	1	2	0
Szczur	.962	6	25	0	1	0
Valdez	.924	32	71	2	6	1
Watkins	.944	23	31	3	2	1

BOISE HAWKS · SHORT-SEASON
NORTHWEST LEAGUE

Batting	B-T	HT	WT	DOB	AVG	vLH	vRH	G	AB	R	H	2B	3B	HR	RBI	BB	HBP	SH	SF	SO	SB	CS	SLG	OBP
Alcantara, Arismendy	B-R	5-10	160	10-29-91	.283	.216	.304	59	219	29	62	5	6	3	24	10	1	3	2	53	7	3	.402	.315
Chen, Pin-Chieh	L-R	6-1	170	7-23-91	.318	.000	.333	6	22	1	7	0	0	0	2	3	0	0	0	2	0	1	.318	.400
Cuneo, Ryan	L-R	6-3	205	10-10-88	.200	.067	.236	20	70	8	14	5	1	2	10	8	0	1	0	22	0	0	.386	.282
Darvill, Wes	L-R	6-2	175	9-10-91	.143	.067	.158	31	91	9	13	1	0	0	6	13	1	1	0	18	3	2	.154	.257
Davis, Runey	R-R	6-0	185	1-2-89	.174	.200	.171	14	46	3	8	2	1	2	3	1	0	1	0	19	2	1	.391	.191
Gibbs, Micah	B-R	5-11	223	7-27-88	.203	.381	.132	42	148	18	30	7	0	0	13	13	2	1	1	33	0	1	.250	.274
Guevara, Jose	R-R	6-1	180	3-17-88	.083	.000	.108	17	48	3	4	0	0	0	3	2	0	0		16	0	1	.083	.170
Harrington, Dustin	R-R	5-11	180	11-14-88	.250	.229	.258	35	124	16	31	7	1	0	12	3	3	3	2	25	2	1	.323	.280
Jones, Richard	L-R	6-0	215	1-31-88	.287	.275	.290	68	258	25	74	16	2	5	42	12	6	0	2	69	2	2	.422	.331
LePage, Pierre	R-R	5-8	168	2-23-89	.331	.375	.318	65	254	39	84	20	4	1	38	11	6	2	4	26	9	6	.453	.367
Matheus, George	R-R	6-0	170	7-21-88	.237	.333	.207	16	38	7	9	1	0	0	2	11	2	0	1	6	1	1	.263	.423
May, Brandon	R-R	6-1	205	1-7-88	.262	.273	.260	17	61	5	16	5	0	3	14	6	0	0	0	15	0	0	.492	.328
Morelli, Jesus	R-R	6-3	180	4-25-90	.248	.254	.246	69	270	27	67	13	0	1	24	17	4	1	3	39	2	5	.307	.299
Na, Kyung-Min	L-L	5-10	170	12-12-91	.208	.250	.196	66	178	23	37	4	1	0	11	21	2	7	0	49	6	5	.242	.299
Noble, Chad	R-R	6-1	195	11-18-87	.400	1.000	.333	3	10	1	4	1	0	0	2	0	0	0		2	0	0	.500	.400
Ramirez, Alvaro	L-L	5-9	160	4-5-86	.350	.274	.375	62	246	40	86	11	4	4	29	8	4	0	2	35	10	9	.476	.377
Shields, Cody	R-R	6-4	190	8-3-87	.296	.200	.318	7	27	2	8	3	0	0	3	1	0	0	0	5	0	1	.407	.321
Soto, Elliot	R-R	5-9	160	8-21-89	.271	.261	.274	48	181	24	49	10	1	0	21	9	3	2	1	31	5	0	.337	.314
Szczur, Matt	R-R	6-1	190	7-20-89	.397	.294	.429	18	73	17	29	9	0	0	8	6	1	0	2	11	1	0	.521	.439
Vigurs, Jeff	L-R	6-0	190	3-10-88	.165	.000	.177	32	103	5	17	4	0	1	10	10	0	0	2	23	1	0	.233	.235

Pitching	B-T	HT	WT	DOB	W	L	ERA	G	GS	CG	SV	IP	H	R	ER	HR	BB	SO	AVG	vLH	vRH	K/9	BB/9
Beeler, Dallas	R-R	6-5	205	6-12-89	0	0	0.00	1	0	0	0	2	2	0	0	0	0	2	.250	.333	.200	9.00	0.00
Carmona, Rogelino	R-R	6-3	210	8-30-91	1	0	7.80	11	0	0	0	15	21	16	13	3	10	10	.328	.364	.310	6.00	6.00
Ebinger, Brent	R-L	6-0	190	6-30-88	3	2	3.60	11	7	0	0	45	42	20	18	2	5	48	.251	.191	.275	9.60	1.00
Figueroa, Eduardo	R-R	6-1	185	11-30-88	2	3	4.17	10	5	0	0	41	43	26	19	4	20	24	.276	.410	.231	5.27	4.39
Fitzgerald, Dustin	R-R	6-4	210	12-6-89	2	4	5.22	11	6	0	0	40	44	30	23	3	14	22	.280	.298	.270	4.99	3.18
Ginley, Jesse	R-R	6-5	180	1-7-90	0	0	6.00	2	0	0	0	3	7	6	2	0	1	0	.438	.500	.429	0.00	3.00
Greathouse, Cam	L-L	6-1	190	7-29-90	3	2	2.75	10	7	0	0	39	32	16	12	1	11	44	.221	.219	.221	10.07	2.52
Grife, Steve	L-R	6-0	177	11-4-86	1	0	1.80	5	0	0	2	5	5	1	1	0	1	8	.278	.333	.250	14.40	1.80
Hatley, Marcus	R-R	6-5	190	3-26-88	0	0	2.45	2	2	0	0	4	2	1	1	0	2	4	.154	.143	.167	9.82	4.91
Huseby, Chris	R-R	6-7	220	1-11-88	0	0	0.00	3	0	0	0	3	4	1	0	0	3	3	.364	.333	.375	9.00	9.00
Jokisch, Eric	R-L	6-3	180	7-29-89	2	3	7.08	14	7	0	0	34	46	29	27	6	23	28	.329	.378	.311	7.34	6.03
Keefe, Danny	R-R	6-4	185	8-15-87	0	1	3.94	10	0	0	1	16	14	7	7	0	6	10	.237	.318	.189	5.63	3.38
Kirk, Austin	L-L	6-1	200	5-22-90	4	5	3.31	12	10	0	0	52	51	19	19	6	12	48	.262	.293	.253	8.36	2.09
Kurcz, Aaron	R-R	6-0	175	8-8-90	2	1	2.05	25	0	0	9	26	15	7	6	2	11	46	.161	.128	.185	15.72	3.76
Latham, Jordan	R-R	6-1	180	9-25-86	1	1	3.38	12	0	0	1	11	7	9	4	1	6	9	.179	.000	.259	7.59	5.06
Loosen, Matt	R-R	6-2	205	4-10-89	1	3	4.54	11	6	0	0	38	39	22	19	4	8	32	.267	.269	.266	7.65	1.91
Martin, Corey	R-R	6-3	195	5-1-87	0	0	1.00	8	0	0	7	9	5	1	1	1	0	9	.156	.167	.143	9.00	0.00
Mincone, John	L-L	6-1	215	7-23-89	0	3	4.18	6	4	0	0	24	34	18	11	0	8	16	.321	.273	.333	6.08	3.04
Mitchell, Tarlandas	R-R	5-8	195	3-9-90	1	0	5.68	5	3	0	0	13	13	9	8	0	15	6	.260	.261	.259	4.26	10.66
Perez, Marcos	L-R	6-1	175	1-1-90	2	2	5.93	9	2	0	0	30	46	23	20	3	6	25	.346	.270	.375	7.42	1.78
Quezada, Andres	B-R	5-11	170	3-15-86	1	1	3.11	22	0	0	1	38	28	14	13	1	3	19	.204	.275	.163	6.93	4.54
Rice, Eric	R-R	5-11	180	9-21-89	1	1	4.05	13	0	0	0	13	9	6	6	0	5	17	.180	.176	.182	11.48	3.38
Rojas, Carlos	R-R	6-1	170	5-22-90	3	2	4.89	13	0	0	0	46	52	28	25	3	17	33	.291	.369	.246	6.46	3.33
Serrano, Juan Yasser	R-R	5-10	220	3-3-88	5	4	5.48	15	12	0	0	64	64	41	39	7	20	45	.259	.250	.267	6.33	2.81
Suarez, Larry	R-R	6-4	245	12-20-89	0	0	5.30	7	0	0	0	19	22	13	11	3	9	20	.297	.158	.345	9.64	4.34
Wang, Yao-Lin	R-R	6-0	180	2-5-91	0	2	6.43	4	3	0	0	14	19	11	10	0	7	10	.352	.381	.333	6.43	4.50
Zeller, Joe	R-R	5-10	190	10-17-87	0	1	6.14	4	1	0	0	7	13	10	5	1	2	6	.361	.353	.368	7.36	2.45

Fielding

Catcher	PCT	G	PO	A	E	DP	PB
Gibbs	.987	33	272	25	4	3	5
Guevara	.966	13	73	11	3	0	1
Noble	1.000	3	17	1	0	0	1
Vigurs	.987	28	220	10	3	2	7

First Base	PCT	G	PO	A	E	DP
Cuneo	1.000	14	122	9	0	12
Gibbs	.889	1	8	0	1	1
Guevara	1.000	3	20	1	0	1
Jones	.988	54	466	25	6	55
Matheus	1.000	1	5	0	0	0
May	1.000	5	58	0	0	1
Vigurs	.889	1	8	0	1	0

Second Base	PCT	G	PO	A	E	DP
Alcantara	.942	11	20	29	3	15
Chen	1.000	5	9	20	0	2
Darvill	.985	11	23	41	1	8
LePage	.971	50	104	163	8	36
Matheus	1.000	1	2	2	0	0

Third Base	PCT	G	PO	A	E	DP
Alcantara	.733	20	5	28	12	2
Cuneo	.750	2	0	6	2	0
Darvill	.870	8	7	13	3	0
Guevara	.000	1	0	0	1	0
Harrington	.949	30	13	61	4	3
Matheus	.889	12	4	20	3	0
May	.927	10	9	29	3	0

Shortstop	PCT	G	PO	A	E	DP
Alcantara	.913	19	23	50	7	9
Darvill	.966	9	3	25	1	3
Harrington	.923	3	2	10	1	3
Matheus	1.000	2	4	7	0	3
Soto	.955	45	69	144	10	40

Outfield	PCT	G	PO	A	E	DP
Cuneo	1.000	3	5	0	0	0
Davis	1.000	14	22	0	0	0
Huseby	.947	15	14	4	1	1
LePage	1.000	3	5	0	0	0
Morelli	.957	64	84	5	4	0
Na	.992	66	118	6	1	1
Ramirez	.938	61	111	9	8	1
Shields	.923	7	12	0	1	0
Szczur	.955	11	20	1	1	0

AZL CUBS — ROOKIE

ARIZONA LEAGUE

Batting	B-T	HT	WT	DOB	AVG	vLH	vRH	G	AB	R	H	2B	3B	HR	RBI	BB	HBP	SH	SF	SO	SB	CS	SLG	OBP
Batista, Xavier	R-R	6-3	190	1-18-92	.212	.194	.216	45	170	16	36	5	2	2	25	13	0	0	3	63	1	1	.300	.263
Bieneme, Vismeldy	B-R	5-10	160	3-19-90	.282	.342	.264	46	163	35	46	2	4	0	12	18	2	2	0	47	17	7	.344	.361
Burruel, Sergio	L-R	5-11	210	7-22-91	.273	.235	.283	25	77	5	21	2	1	1	14	13	1	0	1	26	0	2	.364	.380
Camarena, Melvin	R-R	6-4	210	10-12-89	.185	.222	.167	9	27	4	5	1	0	0	1	1	3	0	0	12	3	0	.222	.290
Chen, Pin-Chieh	L-R	6-1	170	7-23-91	.292	.333	.278	42	168	25	49	4	1	0	17	20	2	0	1	19	10	7	.327	.372
Cherry, Doug	R-R	5-10	175	6-9-88	.000	.000	.000	3	8	1	0	0	0	0	0	1	0	0	0	1	0	0	.000	.111
Cuneo, Ryan	L-R	6-3	205	10-10-88	.358	.423	.337	28	109	17	39	9	3	2	21	10	0	2	2	33	2	2	.550	.415
Darvill, Wes	L-R	6-2	175	9-10-91	.301	.273	.309	26	103	19	31	3	0	0	7	14	1	0	1	21	12	1	.330	.387
Giansanti, Anthony	R-R	5-10	190	9-28-88	.337	.304	.346	27	101	17	34	2	3	2	19	9	1	1	4	13	3	2	.475	.383
Gibbs, Micah	B-R	5-11	223	7-27-88	.000	.000	.000	1	4	0	0	0	0	0	0	0	0	0	0	0	0	0	.000	.000
Golden, Reggie	R-R	5-10	210	10-10-91	.333	1.000	.286	4	15	3	5	1	0	0	1	1	0	0	0	7	1	0	.400	.412
Harrington, Dustin	R-R	5-11	180	11-14-88	.245	.179	.271	26	98	7	24	7	1	1	17	1	1	0	1	19	0	1	.367	.257
Hernandez, Albert	R-R	6-1	170	2-25-89	.261	.333	.245	33	115	18	30	3	0	1	11	11	0	0	0	28	1	0	.313	.325
LePage, Pierre	R-R	5-8	168	2-23-89	.700	.000	.700	2	10	2	7	0	0	0	0	0	0	0	0	2	1	0	.700	.700
May, Brandon	R-R	6-1	205	1-7-88	.286	.000	.286	2	7	1	2	2	0	0	1	1	0	0	0	2	0	0	.571	.375
McAloose, Jake	R-R	5-11	195	10-24-87	.242	.229	.246	45	157	27	38	9	0	2	20	23	5	0	3	46	5	1	.338	.351
Noble, Chad	R-R	6-1	195	11-18-87	.206	.148	.227	28	102	14	21	7	0	1	16	12	0	0	1	21	1	0	.304	.287
Romero, Carlos	R-R	6-1	180	5-28-90	.276	.300	.271	17	58	8	16	2	0	0	8	2	2	1	0	9	1	0	.310	.317
Shields, Cody	R-R	6-4	190	8-3-87	.280	.306	.273	48	175	28	49	5	3	0	25	10	3	2	2	33	20	5	.343	.326
Soto, Elliot	R-R	5-9	160	8-21-89	.375	.571	.222	4	16	3	6	0	0	0	1	0	0	1	0	2	2	0	.375	.375
Springfield, Blair	R-R	5-11	190	2-18-91	.169	.176	.167	25	83	9	14	2	1	1	4	15	0	0	0	24	2	2	.253	.296
Szczur, Matt	R-R	6-1	190	7-20-89	.500	1.000	.000	1	2	1	1	0	0	0	0	1	0	0	0	0	1	0	.500	.750
Wagner, Bobby	L-R	6-3	205	7-9-86	.000	.000	.000	2	6	1	0	0	0	0	0	1	0	0	1	2	0	0	.000	.125

Pitching	B-T	HT	WT	DOB	W	L	ERA	G	GS	CG	SV	IP	H	R	ER	HR	BB	SO	AVG	vLH	vRH	K/9	BB/9
Ackerman, Hunter	L-L	6-1	190	10-24-90	0	2	8.22	10	0	0	0	15	19	16	14	0	12	16	.311	.417	.286	9.39	7.04
Beeler, Dallas	R-R	6-5	205	6-12-89	0	3	3.31	8	2	0	0	16	20	9	6	0	2	16	.303	.375	.262	8.82	1.10
Bristow, Justin	R-R	6-4	220	3-6-87	0	0	0.00	2	0	0	0	2	0	1	0	0	0	3	.000	.000	.000	13.50	0.00
Caridad, Esmailin	R-R	5-10	195	10-28-83	0	0	13.50	1	1	0	0	1	3	1	1	0	0	1	.600	.667	.500	13.50	0.00
de Leon, Manolin	R-R	6-0	175	11-23-86	0	1	40.50	1	1	0	0	1	2	3	3	0	0	0	.500	.500	.500	0.00	0.00
Ebinger, Brent	R-L	6-0	190	6-30-88	0	0	0.00	3	2	0	0	7	4	0	0	0	1	9	.167	.333	.111	11.57	1.29
Figueroa, Eduardo	R-R	6-1	185	11-30-88	0	0	2.25	4	1	0	0	16	11	5	4	0	3	19	.190	.316	.128	10.69	1.69
Fitzgerald, Dustin	R-R	6-4	210	12-6-89	1	1	0.00	1	0	0	0	10	5	3	0	0	0	12	.152	.077	.200	11.17	0.00
Gaub, John	R-L	6-2	210	4-28-85	0	1	81.00	1	1	0	0	1	4	9	9	0	6	3	.333	.000	.333	27.00	54.00
Ginley, Jesse	R-R	6-5	180	1-7-90	1	1	11.12	6	0	0	0	11	20	14	14	0	7	11	.392	.474	.344	8.74	5.56
Gray, Jeff	R-R	6-3	195	11-19-81	0	0	2.25	3	2	0	0	4	3	1	1	0	0	3	.214	.222	.200	6.75	0.00
Greathouse, Cam	L-L	6-1	190	7-29-90	1	0	0.00	3	1	0	0	5	2	0	0	0	0	6	.118	.000	.133	10.80	0.00
Hams, Cody	L-L	6-5	200	11-23-89	1	1	3.24	14	0	0	2	25	26	12	9	1	9	21	.263	.333	.240	7.56	3.24
Hartman, Ryan	R-R	6-3	180	5-10-92	0	1	3.77	8	2	0	0	14	10	7	6	0	5	15	.208	.133	.242	9.42	3.14
Hatley, Marcus	R-R	6-5	190	3-26-88	0	0	0.00	2	2	0	0	3	2	0	0	0	0	3	.182	.000	.333	9.00	0.00
Jimenez, Alvido	R-R	6-1	160	11-22-91	0	2	4.40	14	0	0	1	29	34	20	14	3	9	33	.286	.298	.278	10.36	2.83
Jokisch, Eric	R-L	6-3	180	7-29-89	0	0	0.00	1	0	0	0	1	0	0	0	0	0	3	.000	.000	.000	27.00	0.00
Kurcz, Aaron	R-R	6-0	175	8-8-90	0	0	0.00	1	0	0	0	1	0	0	0	0	0	2	.000	.000	.000	18.00	0.00
Lambert, Casey	L-L	5-11	175	12-11-85	0	1	5.19	5	3	0	0	9	12	5	5	0	0	10	.333	.286	.345	10.38	0.00
Liria, Luis	B-R	6-2	170	1-15-90	2	2	2.40	12	7	0	0	45	36	16	12	0	12	46	.216	.203	.226	9.20	2.40
Loosen, Matt	R-R	6-2	205	4-10-89	1	0	0.00	3	3	0	0	7	4	0	0	0	1	8	.174	.000	.235	10.80	1.35
Mateo, Marcos	R-R	6-1	160	4-18-84	0	0	0.00	1	0	0	0	1	0	0	0	0	0	1	.000	.000	.000	9.00	0.00
Mayora, Hector	R-R	6-1	178	6-22-89	1	1	4.32	10	4	0	1	25	27	15	12	1	6	27	.267	.273	.265	9.72	2.16
Mendez, Jadel	R-R	6-2	170	11-21-88	2	1	9.97	14	0	0	1	22	38	24	24	6	7	18	.384	.467	.348	7.48	2.91
Mitchell, Tarlandas	R-R	5-8	195	3-9-90	0	0	0.00	3	3	0	0	6	1	0	0	0	7	3	.071	.000	.167	4.76	11.12
Nagel, Jon	R-R	6-4	230	1-18-87	0	0	0.00	2	2	0	0	2	3	0	0	0	1	2	.375	.250	.500	9.00	4.50
Perez, Marcos	L-R	6-1	175	1-1-90	3	1	1.45	6	1	0	1	19	16	6	3	2	1	19	.222	.118	.255	9.16	0.48
Reed, Austin	R-R	6-3	200	10-31-91	3	2	2.94	12	5	0	0	34	24	12	11	0	11	34	.205	.167	.227	9.09	2.94
Rice, Eric	R-R	5-11	180	9-21-89	0	0	5.87	7	0	0	0	8	9	5	5	2	2	8	.290	.167	.368	9.39	2.35
Richardson, Colin	R-R	6-1	180	8-13-91	1	1	4.35	13	0	0	0	21	26	10	10	1	2	23	.317	.313	.320	10.02	0.87
Rodriguez, Jhon	R-R	6-0	185	7-18-90	0	0	1.80	5	0	0	0	10	8	4	2	0	1	9	.205	.167	.222	8.10	0.90
Rosario, Jose	R-R	6-1	170	8-29-90	1	2	7.57	11	1	0	0	27	31	26	23	2	14	33	.277	.270	.280	10.87	4.61
Rundle, Drew	L-L	6-4	180	11-5-87	0	0	0.00	1	0	0	0	2	3	0	0	0	5	2	.333	.000	.333	20.25	13.50
Serrano, Juan Yasser	R-R	5-10	220	3-3-88	0	0	0.00	1	0	0	0	3	4	0	0	0	1	3	.333	.429	.200	9.00	0.00
Shafer, Bryce	R-R	6-0	180	11-14-88	0	0	1.80	6	0	0	0	10	5	3	2	0	5	4	.139	.200	.095	3.60	4.50
Wang, Tzu-An	R-R	6-6	210	11-9-90	0	2	7.32	16	0	0	2	20	23	16	16	0	10	19	.303	.379	.255	8.69	4.58
Wang, Yao-Lin	R-R	6-0	180	2-5-91	1	1	2.12	8	2	0	0	17	22	14	4	0	6	19	.301	.250	.333	10.06	3.18
Zambrano, Carlos	B-R	6-5	260	6-1-81	0	0	0.00	1	0	0	0	1	0	0	0	0	1	0	.000	.000	.000	9.00	0.00
Zeller, Joe	R-R	5-10	190	10-17-87	3	2	7.04	11	1	0	0	31	44	29	24	2	7	28	.333	.417	.286	8.22	2.05

CHICAGO CUBS

Fielding

Catcher	PCT	G	PO	A	E	DP	PB
Burruel	.974	19	168	16	5	1	3
Gibbs	.917	1	9	2	1	0	0
Noble	.985	21	174	19	3	1	3
Romero	.973	16	133	13	4	1	3
Shields	1.000	1	9	1	0	1	1

First Base	PCT	G	PO	A	E	DP
Burruel	1.000	2	3	0	0	0
Cuneo	.992	27	218	18	2	16
Geiger	1.000	1	4	0	0	0
May	1.000	1	8	2	0	1
McAloose	.983	24	217	18	4	17
Noble	1.000	4	32	2	0	5
Romero	1.000	1	5	0	0	0

Second Base	PCT	G	PO	A	E	DP
Bieneme	.959	22	39	55	4	12
Chen	.987	29	54	93	2	17
Cherry	1.000	3	5	7	0	0
Harrington	1.000	1	2	3	0	1
McAloose	1.000	1	4	2	0	1

Third Base	PCT	G	PO	A	E	DP
Bieneme	.833	3	1	4	1	0
Cuneo	1.000	1	0	1	0	0
Geiger	.911	34	16	76	9	10
Giansanti	.500	2	1	0	1	0
Harrington	1.000	2	2	2	0	0
McAloose	.878	17	12	24	5	5
Wagner	1.000	1	1	0	0	0

Shortstop	PCT	G	PO	A	E	DP
Bieneme	.786	4	2	9	3	3
Darvill	.921	26	29	76	9	10
Harrington	.928	22	36	67	8	11
LePage	1.000	2	1	6	0	0
Soto	.941	4	3	13	1	2

Outfield	PCT	G	PO	A	E	DP
Batista	.955	44	60	3	3	1
Bieneme	1.000	2	1	0	0	0
Burruel	1.000	1	1	0	0	0
Camarena	.909	6	9	1	1	0
Giansanti	.926	25	45	5	4	1
Hernandez	.962	28	25	0	1	0
McAloose	1.000	4	2	0	0	0
Shields	.988	45	80	2	1	1
Springfield	.967	20	27	2	1	1

DSL CUBS 1 · ROOKIE

DOMINICAN SUMMER LEAGUE

Batting	B-T	HT	WT	DOB	AVG	vLH	vRH	G	AB	R	H	2B	3B	HR	RBI	BB	HBP	SH	SF	SO	SB	CS	SLG	OBP
Amaya, Gioskar	R-R	5-11	175	12-13-92	.282	.244	.289	69	238	33	67	8	3	1	29	28	10	5	4	33	18	8	.353	.375
Arcila, Delbis	L-	6-3	190	4-30-93	.254	.250	.255	43	134	22	34	4	2	1	22	29	3	0	3	38	2	3	.336	.391
Barrios, Manuel	L-L	5-11	160	6-1-93	.194	.125	.214	13	36	4	7	0	0	0	1	4	1	2	0	6	4	2	.194	.293
Casilla, Jose	R-R	6-2	205	1-10-92	.211	.000	.255	21	57	9	12	0	0	1	6	8	2	0	1	26	7	1	.263	.324
Encarnacion, Kelvin	B-R	6-0	175	11-23-91	.233	.250	.229	63	176	27	41	9	1	0	15	36	2	6	2	32	15	13	.295	.366
Gonzalez, Eduardo	L-L	5-10	170	2-9-92	.258	.000	.276	9	31	6	8	0	0	0	2	3	0	0	0	5	1	0	.258	.324
Gonzalez, Jasly	R-R	6-3	190	1 28-91	.205	.150	.217	46	112	13	23	4	1	3	15	8	4	0	1	34	3	3	.339	.280
Hernandez, Marco	L-R	6-0	170	9-6-92	.294	.265	.302	46	163	21	48	13	1	1	14	15	4	1	2	21	16	7	.405	.364
Jimenez, Gabriel	L-L	6-0	188	9-26-93	.218	.300	.208	28	87	9	19	5	0	0	9	11	1	1	1	36	3	1	.276	.310
Liria, Yamel	R-R	5-11	190	11-5-89	.204	.091	.233	30	54	13	11	5	0	0	3	3	11	1	0	14	1	1	.296	.368
Lugo, Antoni	R-R	6-1	195	6-16-88	.301	.304	.300	37	113	25	34	8	0	6	17	14	6	0	1	23	1	1	.531	.403
Montecino, Jose	B-R	5-11	175	7-31-90	.231	.231	.231	48	160	24	37	4	1	0	18	22	5	2	0	22	15	5	.288	.389
Montero, Carlos	R-R	6-0	175	7-6-91	.277	.163	.300	72	253	37	70	15	0	1	36	24	2	1	3	39	10	10	.348	.340
Rodriguez, Jesus	B-R	6-0	170	9-5-91	.298	.200	.319	21	57	15	17	2	0	0	5	15	3	1	0	10	6	4	.333	.467
Santana, Engel	B-R	6-0	180	7-26-89	.260	.190	.276	67	223	35	58	7	6	1	35	27	7	0	1	23	10	9	.359	.357
Suarez, Hector	B-R	6-1	170	5-5-92	.228	.167	.243	48	127	21	29	4	0	1	12	28	6	1	0	45	0	1	.283	.391
Zapata, Oliver	B-R	5-9	180	9-13-92	.241	.167	.258	71	261	45	63	8	2	4	33	33	2	2	3	46	19	9	.333	.328

Pitching	B-T	HT	WT	DOB	W	L	ERA	G	GS	CG	SV	IP	H	R	ER	HR	BB	SO	AVG	vLH	vRH	K/9	BB/9
Cabreja, Enger	R-R	6-2	180	1-28-92	1	0	1.35	5	3	0	0	13	3	2	2	0	10	8	.075	.077	.074	5.40	6.75
Castro, Javier	R-R	6-0	160	2-10-92	1	2	1.59	7	0	0	1	11	5	4	2	0	11	8	.139	.222	.111	6.35	8.74
Colinas, Augusto	L-L	6-0	178	12-20-92	5	1	1.93	21	0	0	4	42	38	14	9	1	10	37	.238	.188	.250	7.93	2.14
Cruz, Willengton	R-L	6-2	170	8-8-90	4	0	1.90	13	13	0	0	52	25	15	11	1	32	59	.152	.333	.126	10.21	5.54
Diplan, Rafael	R-R	6-1	190	10-27-91	6	0	1.49	19	2	0	1	42	24	11	7	0	15	26	.161	.151	.167	5.53	3.19
Estrada, Denis	L-L	6-1	176	6-16-89	1	1	4.50	12	0	0	2	18	16	10	9	0	7	11	.232	.000	.246	5.50	3.50
Galvez, Carlos	L-L	6-1	170	4-26-90	4	3	2.57	18	6	0	1	42	43	19	12	0	21	26	.277	.412	.261	5.57	4.50
Garcia, Ramon	R-R	6-2	170	8-2-91	6	1	0.97	12	7	0	0	46	31	10	5	0	7	30	.188	.212	.177	5.83	1.36
Martinez, Eric	R-R	6-2	185	1-25-90	1	1	6.00	8	0	0	0	12	15	8	8	1	5	5	.313	.500	.235	3.75	3.75
Padron, Loiger	R-R	6-0	180	1-31-91	1	2	5.06	17	0	0	1	27	26	16	15	0	14	32	.250	.286	.232	10.80	4.72
Paulino, Amaury	R-R	6-1	175	8-31-91	2	0	3.32	5	4	0	0	19	16	7	7	1	8	18	.242	.316	.213	8.53	3.79
Pena, Felix	R-R	6-2	186	2-25-90	1	2	1.17	20	1	0	2	46	36	11	6	1	9	38	.216	.132	.254	7.38	1.75
Peralta, Starlin	R-R	6-4	180	11-11-90	1	2	4.82	7	7	1	0	28	26	17	15	1	7	30	.246	.286	.218	9.64	2.25
Pichardo, Roderick	R-R	5-10	180	9-24-90	6	0	1.13	25	0	0	10	40	17	7	5	1	16	43	.186	.233	.167	9.68	3.60
Rodriguez, Santo	L-R	6-1	185	9-26-89	0	0	1.80	2	0	0	0	5	5	4	1	0	5	2	.278	.500	.167	3.60	9.00
Salazar, Victor	—	0-0	0	1-21-93	3	0	5.74	10	0	0	0	16	22	16	10	0	8	6	.306	.286	.310	3.45	4.60
Sanchez, Yilver	R-R	6-2	198	7-31-90	3	1	1.13	13	10	0	0	48	39	19	6	2	8	27	.214	.213	.215	5.06	1.50
Sandoval, Jean	R-R	6-1	190	7-28-88	1	1	0.84	8	7	0	0	32	29	10	3	0	7	26	.228	.295	.193	7.31	1.97
Tineo, Jose	R-R	5-10	170	8-29-90	2	0	1.42	8	0	0	0	13	11	2	2	0	7	11	.239	.400	.194	7.82	4.97
Villalba, Luis	L-L	6-2	182	10-28-92	2	4	3.12	13	12	0	0	52	49	25	18	2	34	34	.253	.200	.259	5.88	3.81

Fielding

Catcher	PCT	G	PO	A	E	DP	PB
Liria	.971	24	92	8	3	0	1
Montecino	1.000	1	1	0	0	0	0
Santana	.988	34	214	36	3	1	2
Suarez	.990	31	176	13	2	1	7

First Base	PCT	G	PO	A	E	DP
Gonzalez	.955	9	36	6	2	1
Jimenez	.976	28	226	15	6	16
Liria	1.000	3	1	0	0	0
Lugo	.987	37	288	18	4	15
Montecino	1.000	9	41	7	0	4

Rodriguez	.923	2	11	1	1	0
Santana	1.000	2	5	1	0	0
Suarez	1.000	1	7	0	0	2

Second Base	PCT	G	PO	A	E	DP
Amaya	.963	27	45	58	4	12
Arcila	1.000	1	5	3	0	0
Hernandez	.982	13	33	21	1	1
Montecino	1.000	26	36	45	0	8
Rodriguez	.965	17	35	47	3	7
Zapata	1.000	3	3	2	0	1

Third Base	PCT	G	PO	A	E	DP
Amaya	1.000	4	3	10	0	0
Montecino	1.000	1	2	0	0	0
Montero	.907	72	45	178	23	10

Shortstop	PCT	G	PO	A	E	DP
Amaya	.914	42	59	110	16	18
Hernandez	.965	32	50	89	5	8
Montecino	—	2	0	0	0	0
Rodriguez	.941	3	5	11	1	1

Outfield	PCT	G	PO	A	E	DP
Arcila	.962	39	48	2	2	0

Barrios	1.000	8	10	1	0	0		Gonzalez	1.000	7	8	1	0	0		Montecino	—	6	0	0	0	0
Casilla	.889	18	24	0	3	0		Gonzalez	.944	30	33	1	2	0		Santana	.750	4	3	0	1	0
Encarnacion	.978	62	85	5	2	1		Hernandez	.667	1	2	0	1	0		Zapata	.978	68	132	3	3	0

DSL CUBS 2   ROOKIE

DOMINICAN SUMMER LEAGUE

Batting	B-T	HT	WT	DOB	AVG	vLH	vRH	G	AB	R	H	2B	3B	HR	RBI	BB	HBP	SH	SF	SO	SB	CS	SLG	OBP
Altagracia, Joel	R-R	6-2	180	9-1-91	.110	.056	.122	42	100	6	11	3	0	0	7	11	0	1	1	44	2	0	.140	.196
Arcila, Delbis	L-L	6-3	190	4-30-93	.286	.143	.304	19	63	7	18	5	0	0	6	12	1	2	0	14	2	0	.365	.408
2-team total (43 Cubs 1)					.264	—	—	62	197	29	52	9	2	1	28	41	4	2	3	52	4	3	.345	.396
Cabrera, Frammi	R-R	6-3	170	1-11-90	.263	.250	.266	70	224	29	59	6	2	0	19	18	5	4	2	33	9	9	.308	.329
Casilla, Jose	R-R	6-2	205	1-10-92	.269	.350	.247	31	93	14	25	3	2	3	9	11	2	0	0	36	5	6	.441	.358
2-team total (21 Cubs 1)					.247	—	—	52	150	23	37	3	2	4	15	19	4	0	1	62	12	7	.373	.345
Contreras, Willson	R-R	6-1	175	5-13-92	.313	.214	.340	17	64	11	20	2	1	0	9	8	2	0	0	6	2	0	.375	.405
De Jesus, Johan	R-R	5-11	180	8-24-88	.255	.294	.247	63	212	20	54	11	0	1	23	9	4	1	5	19	5	3	.321	.291
Disla, Rafael	B-R	5-10	160	3-27-91	.179	.182	.179	31	67	12	12	5	1	0	13	0	0	0	0	15	15	1	.284	.313
Figueroa, Darlyn	R-R	6-3	190	12-21-89	.251	.259	.250	62	187	33	47	6	1	1	20	29	3	1	4	51	12	3	.310	.354
Gonzalez, Eduardo	L-L	5-10	170	2-9-92	.240	.222	.243	49	154	23	37	7	3	0	17	24	2	3	2	26	7	2	.325	.346
2-team total (9 Cubs 1)					.243	—	—	58	185	29	45	7	3	0	19	27	2	3	2	31	8	2	.314	.343
Gonzalez, Gregori	R-R	5-9	170	7-11-89	.290	.258	.296	61	210	36	61	8	5	0	25	12	9	0	4	23	16	8	.376	.349
Hernandez, Marco	L-R	6-0	170	9-6-92	.272	.143	.295	23	92	10	25	8	0	0	7	6	0	0	0	6	6	5	.359	.316
2-team total (46 Cubs 1)					.286	—	—	69	255	31	73	21	1	1	21	21	4	1	2	27	22	12	.388	.348
Inoa, Brain	B-R	5-10	170	2-21-91	.279	.242	.288	60	179	22	50	7	3	1	19	17	5	1	1	56	3	4	.369	.356
Jimenez, Gabriel	L-L	6-0	188	9-26-93	.229	.412	.193	31	105	5	24	0	0	1	9	7	2	0	0	29	1	1	.276	.289
2-team total (28 Cubs 1)					.224	—	—	59	192	14	43	5	1	1	18	18	3	1	1	65	4	2	.276	.299
Liria, Yamel	R-R	5-11	190	11-5-89	.000	.000	.000	1	1	0	0	0	0	0	0	0	0	0	0	0	0	0	.000	.000
2-team total (30 Cubs 1)					.200	—	—	31	55	13	11	5	0	0	3	3	11	1	0	14	0	1	.291	.362
Lugo, Antoni	R-R	6-1	195	6-16-88	.284	.154	.315	21	67	4	19	3	0	1	6	9	0	0	1	7	1	0	.373	.342
2-team total (37 Cubs 1)					.294	—	—	58	180	29	53	11	0	1	26	20	6	1	3	30	2	1	.472	.382
Montecino, Jose	R-R	5-11	175	7-31-90	.212	.250	.207	12	33	6	7	1	0	0	3	7	0	0	0	9	5	1	.242	.350
2-team total (48 Cubs 1)					.226	—	—	60	137	33	31	5	1	0	21	29	5	2	0	31	20	6	.277	.380
Perez, Felix	R-R	5-10	170	5-24-92	.129	.000	.148	12	31	1	4	1	0	0	2	1	0	1	0	4	0	0	.161	.156
Perez, Melido	L-R	5-10	160	10-22-90	.217	.000	.227	13	23	2	5	0	0	0	1	0	0	0	0	8	1	0	.217	.217
Petit, Wilfredo	B-R	5-11	165	2-9-93	.065	.000	.073	20	46	2	3	0	0	0	1	5	0	0	1	10	0	0	.065	.157
Puente, Jeffry	R-R	6-4	170	4-21-92	.162	.143	.165	58	154	20	25	3	1	0	12	24	3	1	0	45	7	2	.195	.287
Rodriguez, Jesus	B-R	6-0	170	9-5-91	.223	.286	.213	31	103	11	23	3	0	0	8	1	0	0	4	24	5	2	.252	.286
2-team total (21 Cubs 1)					.250	—	—	52	160	26	40	5	0	0	17	23	4	1	0	34	11	6	.281	.358
Valdez, Rander	R-R	6-2	180	9-28-91	.125	.091	.129	40	96	4	12	1	1	3	4	6	2	0	2	40	1	0	.250	.200

Pitching	B-T	HT	WT	DOB	W	L	ERA	G	GS	CG	SV	IP	H	R	ER	HR	BB	SO	AVG	vLH	vRH	K/9	BB/9
Abreu, Gilberto	R-R	6-2	180	8-8-93	0	3	4.33	12	5	0	0	27	21	21	13	0	28	14	.221	.045	.274	4.67	9.33
Arias, Jose	R-R	6-5	220	1-17-91	1	2	6.00	10	9	0	0	36	42	27	24	1	17	33	.290	.259	.297	8.25	4.25
Bremon, Jane	R-R	6-3	180	10-27-90	0	1	14.40	6	0	0	0	5	6	10	8	0	8	3	.261	.000	.300	5.40	14.40
Castro, Javier	R-R	6-0	160	2-10-92	0	0	3.18	6	0	0	0	17	15	10	6	0	10	11	.246	.300	.220	5.82	5.29
2-team total (7 Cubs 1)					1	2	2.54	13	6	0	1	28	20	14	8	0	21	19	—	—	—	6.04	6.67
Diaz, Alberto	L-L	5-9	157	6-12-91	1	1	4.18	11	1	0	0	32	34	23	15	2	15	23	.270	.300	.267	6.40	4.18
Encarnacion, Antonio	R-R	6-1	170	11-6-91	0	2	8.72	11	1	0	0	22	27	26	21	2	19	10	.318	.231	.356	4.15	7.89
Estrada, Denis	L-L	6-1	176	6-16-89	2	1	1.63	12	0	0	4	28	20	6	5	0	12	31	.196	.400	.174	10.08	3.90
2-team total (12 Cubs 1)					3	2	2.76	24	0	0	6	46	36	16	14	0	19	42	—	—	—	8.28	3.74
Garcia, Victor	L-L	6-2	175	4-1-92	0	3	6.60	12	1	0	0	30	34	26	22	2	20	29	.291	.111	.306	8.70	6.00
Gomez, Guido	L-L	5-10	160	3-7-91	0	3	9.28	4	3	0	0	11	17	13	11	2	5	11	.378	.333	.385	4.22	4.22
Gonzalez, Enyel	R-R	6-2	195	9-4-91	0	2	4.91	10	2	0	0	22	31	23	12	0	13	11	.333	.438	.279	4.50	5.32
Leyba, Richard	L-L	6-4	210	10-25-91	2	3	5.74	14	1	0	2	27	25	26	17	1	29	21	.240	.083	.261	7.09	9.79
Paulino, Amaury	R-R	6-1	175	8-31-91	1	3	2.14	9	9	0	0	42	32	15	10	1	11	38	.208	.159	.227	8.14	2.36
2-team total (5 Cubs 1)					3	3	2.51	14	13	0	0	61	48	22	17	2	19	56	—	—	—	8.26	2.80
Pena, Enyelberth	R-R	6-2	175	9-8-90	3	4	3.35	15	1	0	0	43	43	24	16	0	26	19	.274	.333	.254	3.98	5.44
Peralta, Starlin	R-R	6-4	180	11-11-90	0	2	3.00	8	8	0	0	39	34	17	13	1	12	37	.239	.211	.250	8.54	2.77
2-team total (7 Cubs 1)					1	4	3.76	15	15	1	0	67	60	34	28	2	19	67	—	—	—	9.00	2.55
Reyes, Ramon	B-R	6-3	185	1-2-89	2	5	3.33	10	8	3	0	54	45	24	20	1	14	42	.228	.318	.203	7.00	2.33
Rodriguez, Santo	L-R	6-1	185	9-26-89	1	0	0.53	9	2	0	3	17	13	7	1	0	7	13	.217	.167	.229	6.88	3.71
2-team total (2 Cubs 1)					1	0	0.82	11	2	0	2	22	18	11	2	0	12	15	—	—	—	6.14	4.91
Salazar, Victor	—	0-0	0	1-21-93	0	3	9.00	6	4	0	0	19	29	19	19	0	17	9	.354	.182	.380	4.74	4.26
2-team total (10 Cubs 1)					3	3	7.53	16	4	0	0	35	51	37	29	0	17	16	—	—	—	4.15	4.41
Severino, Deuris	R-R	6-1	170	8-26-90	2	4	4.71	12	0	0	1	50	43	39	26	2	40	40	.238	.189	.258	7.25	6.52
Telles, Wladimir	R-R	6-1	200	2-5-93	0	5	6.64	20	3	0	0	46	57	48	31	5	24	29	.315	.392	.285	6.21	5.14
Turbi, Francisco	R-R	6-4	210	12-19-88	4	5	5.96	20	1	0	0	45	54	39	30	1	22	23	.302	.294	.305	4.57	4.37

Fielding

Catcher	PCT	G	PO	A	E	DP	PB		First Base	PCT	G	PO	A	E	DP							
De Jesus	.985	46	262	66	5	1	4		Altagracia	1.000	16	89	6	0	4		Figueroa	.955	11	59	4	3	6
Inoa	.933	26	124	30	11	2	10		Cabrera	.923	3	11	1	1	1		Inoa	1.000	1	1	0	0	0
Perez	1.000	3	7	2	0	0	0		De Jesus	.978	13	82	5	2	5		Jimenez	.979	27	216	13	5	19
Petit	.982	11	47	7	1	0	3		Disla	1.000	1	2	0	0	1		Lugo	.958	6	45	1	2	6
																	Montecino	1.000	2	8	0	0	1

	PCT	G	PO	A	E	DP
Perez	.971	4	30	3	1	3
Puente	1.000	6	41	1	0	0
Rodriguez	1.000	1	5	0	0	0

Second Base	PCT	G	PO	A	E	DP
Altagracia	.875	3	1	6	1	0
Disla	.911	11	21	20	4	6
Gonzalez	.938	20	44	32	5	6
Montecino	.944	4	9	8	1	1
Perez	.750	2	3	0	1	0
Perez	.917	4	5	6	1	2
Puente	.950	24	54	60	6	13
Rodriguez	.954	18	42	41	4	8

Third Base	PCT	G	PO	A	E	DP
Altagracia	.888	24	24	47	9	9
Contreras	.839	17	23	50	14	5

	PCT	G	PO	A	E	DP
De Jesus	.875	2	3	4	1	0
Disla	.850	7	7	10	3	0
Figueroa	1.000	1	1	1	0	0
Gonzalez	.857	9	5	19	4	0
Inoa	.500	1	1	1	2	0
Lugo	.875	16	11	38	7	6
Montecino	.600	1	1	2	2	1
Puente	.778	5	3	11	4	0

Shortstop	PCT	G	PO	A	E	DP
Disla	.846	6	14	19	6	3
Gonzalez	.907	23	44	44	9	9
Hernandez	.921	22	38	67	9	7
Montecino	.923	4	5	7	1	1
Puente	.971	19	32	34	2	6
Rodriguez	.771	7	7	20	8	4

Outfield	PCT	G	PO	A	E	DP
Arcila	.889	14	22	2	3	1
Cabrera	.974	63	106	6	3	2
Casilla	.925	28	33	4	3	0
Figueroa	.952	39	54	6	3	3
Gonzalez	.990	46	91	7	1	3
Gonzalez	.967	10	26	3	1	1
Inoa	—	1	0	0	0	0
Jimenez	1.000	4	4	0	0	0
Liria	1.000	1	1	0	0	0
Puente	1.000	1	4	0	0	0
Robles	—	1	0	0	0	0
Valdez	.909	33	30	0	3	0

Chicago White Sox

SEASON IN A SENTENCE: The White Sox surged to the American League Central lead at the all-star break, but could not hold off the Twins and gave up the lead by mid-August, sinking further back as the season dragged on.

HIGH POINT: In June, Omar Vizquel became the everyday third baseman, after an injury to Mark Teahen. With his .276 average and exceptional defense, he spurred the White Sox into first place. After a 24-33 start to the season, the White Sox went on a 28-8 run to make up 13 games on the Twins and move into first place, with a high-water mark of 3½ games up on July 20. The offense was driven all season by Paul Konerko, who had the best season of his career by batting .312/.393/.584.

LOW POINT: Chicago's rotation, projected to be a strength after the addition of Jake Peavy in 2009, went on a streak from Sept. 4 in Boston to Sept. 25 in Anaheim without a win, over a franchise-record 18 starts. During that time, starters posted a combined ERA of just over 6.00 and an opponent average of .320. The Twins officially finished off the Sox on Sept. 16 when they completed a three-game sweep, part of an eight-game losing streak.

NOTABLE ROOKIES: Chris Sale came onto the scene just two months after being selected in the first round of the 2010 draft and was closing for the White Sox by the end of the season. The White Sox will give him a chance to compete for a rotation spot in 2011. Reclamation project Sergio Santos was a revelation in the bullpen, compiling a 2.96 ERA in 56 appearances.

KEY TRANSACTIONS: The best deal of the season was made in June when the White Sox quickly signed Sale and he got on the fast track to the big leagues. They called him up at the beginning of August and he had a 1.93 ERA in 21 appearances. At the trade deadline, Chicago acquired Edwin Jackson from the Diamondbacks for Daniel Hudson and David Holmberg, and while he went 4-2, 3.24 in 11 starts it wasn't enough to stabilize the rotation. On Aug. 30, the White Sox picked Manny Ramirez up off waivers from the Dodgers, but he contributed next to nothing.

DOWN ON THE FARM: In an overall down year for White Sox affiliates, high Class A Winston-Salem stood out with the best record in the Carolina League (81-58). The organization's top prospect, outfielder Jared Mitchell, injured his ankle in spring training and missed the season.

OPENING DAY PAYROLL: $105.5 million (7th)

PLAYERS OF THE YEAR

MAJOR LEAGUE	MINOR LEAGUE
Paul Konerko	**Brent Morel**
1b	**3b**
.312/.393/.584	(Double-A/Triple-A)
39 HR, 2nd in AL	.322/.359/.480
4th in AL in OPS	10 HR, 37 2B

ORGANIZATION LEADERS

BATTING		*Minimum 250 at-bats
MAJORS		
*AVG	Paul Konerko	.312
*OPS	Paul Konerko	.977
HR	Paul Konerko	39
RBI	Paul Konerko	111
MINORS		
*AVG	Brent Morel, Birmingham/Charlotte	.322
*OBP	Jim Gallagher, Birmingham	.392
*SLG	Seth Loman, Winston-Salem	.514
R	Seth Loman, Winston-Salem	88
H	Jon Gilmore, Winston-Salem	177
TB	Seth Loman, Winston-Salem	264
2B	Brent Morel, Birmingham/Charlotte	37
3B	Justin Greene, Winston-Salem/Birmingham	12
HR	Stefan Gartrell, Charlotte	27
RBI	Ian Gac, Kannapolis	91
BB	Jim Gallagher, Birmingham	74
SO	Stefan Gartrell, Charlotte	152
SB	Daniel Wagner, Kannapolis	37

PITCHING		†Minimum 75 innings
MAJORS		
W	John Danks	15
†ERA	Edwin Jackson	3.24
SO	John Danks	162
MINORS		
W	Charles Leesman, Winston-Salem/Birmingham	14
L	Justin Collop, Kannapolis	12
	Justin Edwards, Winston-Salem/Birmingham	12
†ERA	Terry Doyle, Kannapolis/Winston-Salem	2.94
G	Kyle Bellamy, Kannapolis/W-S/Birmingham	55
G	Gregory Infante, Winston-Salem/Birmingham	55
GS	Three tied at	28
SV	Anthony Carter, Birmingham	22
IP	Terry Doyle, Kannapolis/Winston-Salem	168.3
BB	Carlos Torres, Charlotte	71
SO	Terry Doyle, Kannapolis/Winston-Salem	157
†AVG	Carlos Torres, Charlotte	.217

2010 PERFORMANCE

General Manager: Ken Williams. **Farm Director:** Buddy Bell. **Scouting Director:** Doug Laumann.

Class	Team	League	W	L	PCT	Finish*	Manager(s)
Majors	Chicago White Sox	American	88	74	.543	6th (14)	Ozzie Guillen
Triple-A	Charlotte Knights	International	67	77	.465	t-10th (14)	Chris Chambliss
Double-A	Birmingham Barons	Southern	53	87	.379	10th (10)	Ever Magallanes
High A	Winston-Salem Dash	Carolina	81	58	.583	1st (8)	Joe McEwing
Low A	Kannapolis Intimidators	South Atlantic	65	74	.468	t-9th (14)	Ernie Young
Rookie	Bristol White Sox	Appalachian	32	36	.471	7th (10)	Ryan Newman
Rookie	Great Falls Voyagers	Pioneer	47	28	.627	1st (8)	Chris Cron
Overall 2010 Minor League Record			345	360	.489	21st(30)	

*Finish in overall standings (No. of teams in league). †League champion.

ORGANIZATION STATISTICS

CHICAGO WHITE SOX

AMERICAN LEAGUE

Batting	B-T	HT	WT	DOB	AVG	vLH	vRH	G	AB	R	H	2B	3B	HR	RBI	BB	HBP	SH	SF	SO	SB	CS	SLG	OBP
Beckham, Gordon	R-R	6-0	185	9-16-86	.252	.224	.261	131	444	58	112	25	2	9	49	37	7	6	4	92	4	6	.378	.317
Castro, Ramon	R-R	6-3	240	3-1-76	.278	.286	.275	37	115	18	32	2	0	8	21	9	0	3	1	26	1	0	.504	.328
De Aza, Alejandro	L-L	6-0	175	4-11-84	.300	.250	.308	19	30	7	9	3	0	0	2	1	0	1	0	4	2	1	.400	.323
Flowers, Tyler	R-R	6-4	245	1-24-86	.091	.000	.125	8	11	2	1	0	0	0	4	0	0	0	5	0	0	.091	.333
Jones, Andruw	R-R	6-1	230	4-23-77	.230	.256	.219	107	278	41	64	12	1	19	48	45	3	0	2	73	9	2	.486	.341
Konerko, Paul	R-R	6-2	220	3-5-76	.312	.339	.304	149	548	89	171	30	1	39	111	72	5	0	6	110	0	1	.584	.393
Kotsay, Mark	L-L	6-0	210	12-2-75	.239	.000	.258	107	327	30	78	17	2	8	31	32	0	0	3	36	1	3	.376	.306
Lillibridge, Brent	R-R	5-11	185	9-18-83	.224	.303	.185	64	98	19	22	5	2	2	16	3	0	0	0	36	5	3	.378	.248
Lucy, Donny	R-R	6-2	205	8-8-82	.333	.400	.200	7	15	2	5	3	0	1	2	2	1	0	0	3	1	0	.733	.444
Morel, Brent	R-R	6-2	220	4-21-87	.231	.375	.184	21	65	9	15	3	0	3	7	4	0	0	1	17	2	0	.415	.271
Nix, Jayson	R-R	5-11	195	8-26-82	.163	.071	.286	24	49	3	8	1	0	1	5	7	0	1	0	12	0	0	.245	.268
2-team total (78 Cleveland)					.224			102	331	32	74	15	0	14	34	20	7	3	2	87	1	2	.396	.281
Pierre, Juan	L-L	5-11	185	8-14-77	.275	.297	.268	160	651	96	179	18	3	1	47	45	21	15	2	47	68	18	.316	.341
Pierzynski, A.J.	L-R	6-3	230	12-30-76	.270	.250	.276	128	474	43	128	29	0	9	56	15	6	6	2	39	3	4	.388	.300
Quentin, Carlos	R-R	6-2	235	8-28-82	.243	.211	.253	131	453	73	110	25	2	26	87	50	20	0	4	83	2	2	.479	.342
Ramirez, Alexei	R-R	6-2	175	9-22-81	.282	.278	.283	156	585	83	165	29	2	18	70	27	2	7	5	82	13	8	.431	.313
Ramirez, Manny	R-R	6-0	200	5-30-72	.261	.231	.268	24	69	6	18	1	0	1	2	14	5	0	0	23	0	0	.319	.420
Rios, Alex	R-R	6-5	205	2-18-81	.284	.259	.292	147	567	89	161	29	3	21	88	38	7	0	5	93	34	14	.457	.334
Teahen, Mark	L-R	6-3	210	9-6-81	.258	.162	.276	77	233	31	60	13	2	4	25	25	0	2	2	61	3	5	.382	.327
Viciedo, Dayan	R-R	5-11	240	3-10-89	.308	.340	.278	38	104	17	32	7	0	5	13	2	0	0	0	25	1	0	.519	.321
Vizquel, Omar	B-R	5-9	175	4-24-67	.276	.207	.290	108	344	36	95	11	1	2	30	34	2	7	4	45	11	7	.331	.341

Pitching	B-T	HT	WT	DOB	W	L	ERA	G	GS	CG	SV	IP	H	R	ER	HR	BB	SO	AVG	vLH	vRH	K/9	BB/9
Buehrle, Mark	L-L	6-2	235	3-23-79	13	13	4.28	33	33	3	0	210	246	105	100	17	49	99	.295	.275	.303	4.24	2.10
Danks, John	L-L	6-2	210	4-15-85	15	11	3.72	32	32	1	0	213	189	93	88	18	70	162	.237	.221	6.85	2.96
Floyd, Gavin	R-R	6-6	235	1-27-83	10	13	4.08	31	31	1	0	187	199	92	85	14	58	151	.274	.259	.292	7.25	2.79
Garcia, Freddy	R-R	6-4	250	10-6-76	12	6	4.64	28	28	0	0	157	171	85	81	23	45	89	.279	.271	.287	5.10	2.58
Harrell, Lucas	B-R	6-2	200	6-3-85	1	0	4.88	8	3	0	0	24	34	18	13	2	17	15	.337	.396	.271	5.63	6.38
Hudson, Dan	R-R	6-3	225	3-9-87	1	1	6.32	3	3	0	0	16	17	11	11	1	11	14	.293	.313	.269	8.04	6.32
Infante, Gregory	R-R	6-2	185	7-10-87	0	0	0.00	5	0	0	0	5	2	0	0	0	4	5	.133	.286	.000	9.64	7.71
Jackson, Edwin	R-R	6-3	210	9-9-83	4	2	3.24	11	11	0	0	75	73	31	27	8	18	77	.248	.243	.261	9.24	2.16
Jenks, Bobby	R-R	6-4	275	3-14-81	1	3	4.44	55	0	0	27	53	54	28	26	3	18	61	.260	.243	.277	10.42	3.08
Linebrink, Scott	R-R	6-3	220	8-4-76	3	2	4.40	52	0	0	0	57	59	31	28	11	17	52	.262	.288	.234	8.16	2.67
Marquez, Jeff	R-R	6-2	190	8-10-84	0	0	18.00	1	0	0	0	1	2	2	2	1	0	0	.400	.500	.333	0.00	0.00
Peavy, Jake	R-R	6-1	195	5-31-81	7	6	4.63	17	17	1	0	107	98	55	55	13	34	93	.242	.275	.209	7.82	2.82
Pena, Tony	R-R	6-2	230	1-9-82	5	3	5.10	52	3	0	0	101	108	63	57	10	45	56	.278	.244	.308	5.01	4.02
Putz, J.J.	R-R	6-5	250	2-22-77	7	5	2.83	60	0	0	3	54	41	18	17	4	15	65	.204	.253	.164	10.83	2.50
Sale, Chris	L-L	6-5	170	3-30-89	2	1	1.93	21	0	0	4	23	15	5	5	2	10	32	.185	.290	.120	12.34	3.86
Santos, Sergio	R-R	6-3	240	7-4-83	2	2	2.96	56	0	0	1	52	53	18	17	2	26	56	.261	.207	.298	9.75	4.53
Thornton, Matt	L-L	6-6	235	9-15-76	5	4	2.67	61	0	0	8	61	41	18	18	3	20	81	.191	.175	.203	12.02	2.97
Threets, Erick	L-L	6-5	240	11-4-81	0	0	0.00	11	0	0	0	12	9	1	0	0	3	6	.220	.286	.185	4.38	2.19
Torres, Carlos	R-R	6-1	190	10-22-82	0	1	8.56	5	1	0	0	14	23	13	13	2	9	13	.377	.400	.355	8.56	5.93
Williams, Randy	L-L	6-4	200	9-18-75	0	1	5.40	27	0	0	0	25	37	17	15	2	21	22	.346	.327	.362	7.92	7.56

Fielding

Catcher	PCT	G	PO	A	E	DP	PB
Castro	.996	34	214	14	1	0	1
Flowers	1.000	7	30	1	0	0	0
Lucy	1.000	7	43	0	0	0	0
Pierzynski	.995	127	865	61	5	5	3

First Base	PCT	G	PO	A	E	DP
Konerko	.994	125	1069	83	7	124
Kotsay	.997	38	298	20	1	23

Teahen	1.000	3	5	0	0	0
Viciedo	1.000	7	30	0	0	2

Second Base	PCT	G	PO	A	E	DP
Beckham	.981	126	245	375	12	100
Lillibridge	.957	25	34	56	4	12
Nix	1.000	3	5	2	0	0
Vizquel	1.000	19	22	41	0	9

Third Base	PCT	G	PO	A	E	DP
Lillibridge	1.000	3	1	1	0	0
Morel	.974	20	5	32	1	2
Nix	.833	16	8	17	5	2
Teahen	.919	52	32	82	10	6
Viciedo	.897	23	8	27	4	5
Vizquel	.979	83	31	110	3	15

Shortstop	PCT	G	PO	A	E	DP
Lillibridge	1.000	4	1	0	0	0
Nix	1.000	2	2	1	0	0
Ramirez	.974	156	249	499	20	109
Vizquel	1.000	9	13	15	0	6

Outfield	PCT	G	PO	A	E	DP
De Aza	1.000	12	17	0	0	0
Jones	.980	89	136	8	3	2
Kotsay	1.000	8	9	2	0	0
Lillibridge	1.000	8	8	0	0	0
Nix	1.000	1	3	0	0	0
Pierre	.997	149	307	4	1	1
Quentin	.959	104	183	4	8	1
Rios	.987	144	388	6	5	3
Teahen	1.000	10	12	0	0	0

CHARLOTTE KNIGHTS

INTERNATIONAL LEAGUE **TRIPLE-A**

CHICAGO WHITE SOX

Batting	B-T	HT	WT	DOB	AVG	vLH	vRH	G	AB	R	H	2B	3B	HR	RBI	BB	HBP	SH	SF	SO	SB	CS	SLG	OBP
Castillo, Javier	R-R	6-3	210	8-29-83	.200	.167	.209	15	55	1	11	3	0	0	3	6	0	0	0	8	1	0	.255	.279
Castro, Ramon	R-R	6-3	240	3-1-76	.154	.000	.182	4	13	1	2	0	0	1	2	3	0	0	0	5	0	0	.385	.313
Coats, Buck	L-R	6-3	200	6-9-82	.284	.297	.276	80	320	41	91	15	2	5	38	28	2	4	4	53	6	1	.391	.342
Colina, Javier	R-R	6-1	200	2-15-79	.189	.241	.175	40	132	9	25	9	0	4	15	5	1	6	3	27	0	1	.348	.220
Cortez, Fernando	L-R	6-1	175	8-10-81	.276	.246	.294	48	170	23	47	6	2	1	15	14	0	3	1	18	1	3	.353	.330
Danks, Jordan	L-R	6-4	210	8-7-86	.245	.271	.234	119	445	62	109	27	3	8	42	41	4	9	3	151	15	6	.373	.312
De Aza, Alejandro	L-L	6-0	175	4-11-84	.302	.212	.342	79	318	53	96	21	4	5	49	29	5	3	3	60	16	3	.440	.366
Flowers, Tyler	R-R	6-4	245	1-24-86	.220	.234	.214	100	346	43	76	22	2	16	53	55	6	2	3	121	2	1	.434	.334
Gartrell, Stefan	R-R	6-3	230	1-14-84	.255	.268	.249	139	534	74	136	20	1	27	80	41	8	4	2	152	4	2	.448	.316
Hudson, Robert	R-R	6-0	170	8-31-83	.227	.198	.240	88	308	45	70	17	1	7	28	9	2	7	1	55	3	1	.357	.253
Kroeger, Josh	L-L	6-3	230	8-31-82	.204	.199	.206	119	442	52	90	22	2	15	54	44	7	1	2	83	16	7	.364	.285
Lillibridge, Brent	R-R	5-11	185	9-18-83	.270	.209	.289	48	185	26	50	8	0	4	16	17	1	0	3	46	19	3	.378	.330
Lucy, Donny	R-R	6-2	205	8-8-82	.225	.257	.208	59	204	24	46	10	2	2	11	10	3	7	1	52	3	2	.324	.271
Morel, Brent	R-R	6-2	220	4-21-87	.320	.323	.319	81	306	40	98	24	4	8	34	13	0	5	0	50	3	0	.503	.348
Reed, Jeremy	L-L	6-0	195	6-15-81	.286	.227	.324	44	168	24	48	8	2	6	22	10	1	1	1	28	0	1	.464	.328
Retherford, C.J.	R-R	5-10	195	8-14-85	.201	.094	.228	44	159	10	32	7	0	4	13	8	2	2	0	30	0	1	.321	.249
Ricks, Adam	B-R	5-10	190	9-24-82	.067	.000	.087	10	30	0	2	1	0	0	1	1	0	0	1	4	0	0	.100	.094
Rodriguez, Luis	R-S	5-9	190	6-27-80	.293	.261	.308	94	345	50	101	17	2	16	56	42	1	4	8	35	3	5	.493	.364
Teahen, Mark	L-R	6-3	210	9-6-81	.364	.308	.400	11	33	7	12	2	0	0	4	10	1	0	2	7	0	0	.424	.500
Viciedo, Dayan	R-R	5-11	240	3-10-89	.274	.356	.245	86	343	42	94	15	0	20	47	11	6	3	0	78	1	1	.493	.308

Pitching	B-T	HT	WT	DOB	W	L	ERA	G	GS	CG	SV	IP	H	R	ER	HR	BB	SO	AVG	vLH	vRH	K/9	BB/9
Adkins, Jon	L-R	6-1	205	8-30-77	1	2	4.15	14	1	0	0	22	29	14	10	2	9	6	.337	.333	.340	2.49	3.74
2-team total (34 Louisville)					2	6	4.92	48	1	0	10	53	68	35	29	3	17	19	—	—		3.23	2.89
Aquino, Greg	R-R	6-1	190	1-11-78	1	6	5.66	40	0	0	0	49	45	31	31	11	23	48	.245	.301	.198	8.76	4.20
Braun, Ryan	R-R	6-1	220	7-29-80	1	3	2.20	52	0	0	18	57	45	14	14	4	34	61	.213	.262	.167	9.58	5.34
Cassel, Justin	R-R	6-2	215	9-25-84	0	0	3.00	2	0	0	0	3	1	1	1	0	3	2	.111	.167	.000	6.00	9.00
Corley, Tyson	R-R	6-6	200	1-26-86	0	0	3.00	1	0	0	0	3	2	1	1	0	0	5	.200	.250	.167	15.00	0.00
Dobies, Andrew	L-L	6-1	180	4-20-83	0	0	6.23	4	0	0	0	4	5	3	3	1	3	4	.278	.222	.333	8.31	6.23
Dolsi, Freddy	R-R	6-0	160	1-9-83	3	7	4.91	46	8	0	0	92	93	65	50	15	45	71	.262	.288	.241	6.97	4.42
Elarton, Scott	R-R	6-8	240	2-23-76	1	2	8.24	16	0	0	0	20	26	21	18	7	8	13	.310	.311	.308	5.95	3.66
Embree, Alan	L-L	6-2	200	1-23-70	0	1	8.22	6	0	0	0	8	7	7	7	0	6	4	.314	.316	.313	11.74	5.87
2-team total (8 Pawtucket)					0	1	6.00	14	0	0	0	15	13	12	10	0	10	16	—	—		9.60	6.00
Garcia, Angel	R-R	6-7	230	10-28-83	0	0	12.00	2	0	0	0	3	6	5	4	1		5	.400	.300	.600	15.00	3.00
Harrell, Lucas	B-R	6-2	200	6-3-85	10	10	4.58	26	26	0	0	138	141	79	70	11	61	84	.268	.284	.251	5.49	3.99
Hudson, Dan	R-R	6-3	225	3-9-87	11	4	3.47	17	17	1	0	93	81	41	36	11	31	108	.228	.242	.209	10.41	2.99
Hynick, Brandon	R-R	6-3	205	3-7-85	1	4	6.22	11	11	0	0	59	79	42	41	13	21	44	.319	.351	.282	6.67	3.19
Johnson, Garrett	L-L	6-10	205	9-2-87	0	1	7.27	3	0	0	0	11	7	7	7	2	5		.355	.273	.400	5.19	7.27
Marquez, Jeff	R-R	6-2	190	8-10-84	8	9	4.48	27	26	0	0	145	160	79	72	14	49	89	.282	.307	.258	5.54	3.05
McCulloch, Kyle	R-R	6-2	190	3-20-85	3	4	5.94	24	4	0	0	47	60	38	31	8	15	16	.316	.269	.361	3.06	2.87
Nunez, Jhonny	L-R	6-3	215	11-26-85	5	2	5.48	32	0	0	1	44	46	34	27	6	19	45	.274	.304	.247	9.14	3.86
Sale, Chris	L-L	6-5	170	3-30-89	0	0	2.84	7	0	0	0	6	3	2	2	2	4	15	.136	.167	.100	21.32	5.68
Santeliz, Clevelan	R-R	6-0	180	9-1-86	1	4	4.67	38	0	0	2	54	40	28	28	9	34	50	.213	.239	.188	8.33	5.67
Shirek, Charlie	R-R	6-3	205	10-25-85	0	0	11.12	1	1	0	0	6	6	7	7	1	4	3	.273	.333	.143	4.76	6.35
Socolovich, Miguel	R-R	6-1	155	7-24-86	3	1	3.12	18	0	0	0	26	22	10	9	2	18	30	.218	.196	.240	10.38	6.23
Threets, Erick	L-L	6-5	240	11-4-81	1	0	0.86	17	0	0	2	21	12	2	2	0	5	10	.169	.147	.189	4.29	2.14
Torres, Carlos	R-R	6-1	190	10-22-82	9	9	3.42	27	25	0	0	160	125	65	61	13	71	140	.217	.232	.202	7.86	3.99
Whisler, Wes	L-L	6-5	240	4-7-83	0	0	5.02	19	0	0	0	29	30	22	16	3	16	19	.259	.250	.265	5.97	5.02
Williams, Randy	L-L	6-4	200	9-18-75	1	0	2.53	21	1	0	2	32	26	10	9	1	9	22	.218	.208	.225	6.19	2.53
Zaleski, Matt	R-R	6-1	190	12-2-81	7	8	5.17	28	24	0	1	139	138	82	80	23	46	85	.260	.278	.241	5.49	2.97

Fielding

Catcher	PCT	G	PO	A	E	DP	PB
Castro	.947	4	17	1	1	0	0
Flowers	.993	93	665	51	5	8	7
Lucy	.983	42	286	12	5	0	4
Ricks	1.000	8	44	2	0	0	0

First Base	PCT	G	PO	A	E	DP
Castillo	1.000	3	33	0	0	2
Colina	1.000	5	43	2	0	7
Cortez	.947	2	17	1	1	1
Kroeger	.987	57	490	52	7	58
Reed	.988	19	140	26	2	16
Teahen	1.000	1	6	0	0	1
Viciedo	.986	59	525	34	8	56

Second Base	PCT	G	PO	A	E	DP
Colina	.968	12	30	31	2	5
Cortez	.939	37	67	86	10	21
Danks	.750	1	1	2	1	0
Hudson	.994	29	52	115	1	31
Lillibridge	.980	9	18	32	1	7
Retherford	.984	27	52	73	2	21
Rodriguez	.985	31	44	91	2	22

Third Base	PCT	G	PO	A	E	DP
Castillo	1.000	6	5	10	0	0
Colina	.974	12	17	20	1	2
Cortez	.500	1	1	1	0	0
Hudson	1.000	9	5	11	0	1

	PCT	G	PO	A	E	DP
Morel	.981	63	45	114	3	11
Retherford	.941	13	11	21	2	6
Ricks	1.000	1	2	1	0	0
Rodriguez	.917	10	8	25	3	2
Teahen	1.000	4	5	5	0	1
Viciedo	.961	26	20	54	3	7

Shortstop	PCT	G	PO	A	E	DP
Cortez	.857	2	4	2	1	0
Hudson	.962	47	69	134	8	37
Lillibridge	.927	36	54	99	12	25
Morel	1.000	17	28	46	0	9
Rodriguez	.971	44	68	130	6	38

Outfield	PCT	G	PO	A	E	DP
Coats	.993	67	135	3	1	0
Quilla	1.000	2	2	0	0	0
Cortez	1.000	1	1	0	0	0

Danks	.992	112	233	4	2	3
De Aza	.978	70	132	3	3	1
Gartrell	.986	122	209	5	3	1
Kroeger	1.000	39	76	4	0	2

Lillibridge	1.000	3	7	0	0	0
Reed	1.000	18	21	1	0	0
Teahen	1.000	2	7	0	0	0

BIRMINGHAM BARONS

DOUBLE-A

SOUTHERN LEAGUE

Batting	B-T	HT	WT	DOB	AVG	vLH	vRH	G	AB	R	H	2B	3B	HR	RBI	BB	HBP	SH	SF	SO	SB	CS	SLG	OBP
Armstrong, Cole	L-R	6-3	210	8-24-83	.276	.274	.277	97	315	33	87	16	0	8	43	49	0	0	4	56	0	0	.403	.370
Blackwood, Chase	R-R	5-10	205	11-24-87	.000	.000	.000	3	0	0	0	0	0	0	0	0	0	1	0	2	0	0	.000	.000
Bour, Jason	R-R	6-3	215	7-2-86	.237	.370	.125	18	59	7	14	2	0	2	2	2	0	1	0	16	0	0	.271	.262
Coats, Buck	L-R	6-3	200	6-9-82	.338	.185	.439	18	68	12	23	4	0	2	8	9	0	1	0	12	1	0	.485	.416
Cortez, Fernando	L-R	6-1	175	8-10-81	.380	.333	.403	23	92	7	35	9	0	0	11	5	0	1	0	4	5	2	.478	.412
Cruz, Lee	R-R	6-2	190	6-13-83	.197	.167	.204	21	66	5	13	3	0	1	6	3	0	1	0	20	0	0	.288	.229
Escobar, Eduardo	B-R	5-10	150	1-5-89	.262	.321	.242	49	202	22	53	8	3	3	22	9	0	5	0	35	3	0	.376	.294
Fuller, Justin	L-R	6-1	190	7-10-83	.188	.211	.180	25	80	8	15	0	2	0	5	10	1	5	1	21	2	0	.238	.283
Gallagher, Jimmy	L-L	6-1	195	9-3-85	.294	.262	.307	136	503	71	148	35	1	10	53	74	9	1	3	89	4	3	.427	.392
Greene, Justin	R-R	6-0	185	10-10-85	.232	.140	.264	47	168	20	39	7	3	3	22	8	1	2	0	54	6	4	.363	.271
Hudson, Robert	R-R	6-0	170	8-31-83	.214	1.000	.154	4	14	3	3	1	0	0	2	3	0	0	0	3	1	0	.286	.353
Kuhn, Tyler	L-R	5-10	185	9-9-86	.279	.266	.283	109	384	52	107	17	6	5	50	36	4	9	2	75	6	5	.393	.345
Marrero, Christian	L-L	6-1	185	7-30-86	.270	.328	.249	137	488	55	132	28	3	7	67	72	4	3	9	85	12	5	.383	.363
Mollenhauer, Dale	L-R	5-10	170	6-26-86	.262	.216	.275	101	343	33	90	17	1	1	27	31	2	8	4	55	17	4	.327	.324
Morel, Brent	R-R	6-2	220	4-21-87	.326	.429	.296	49	184	25	60	13	1	2	30	14	2	1	2	36	5	5	.440	.376
Negron, Miguel	L-L	6-1	190	8-22-82	.241	.250	.238	35	145	27	35	5	0	3	16	18	0	1	0	13	7	3	.338	.325
Paiml, Greg	R-R	6-0	185	8-3-84	.237	.333	.182	70	232	29	55	9	1	2	21	11	3	7	1	54	5	1	.310	.279
Phegley, Josh	R-R	5-10	215	2-12-88	.292	.389	.259	18	72	7	21	4	0	2	13	2	1	3	1	22	0	0	.431	.316
Price, Jared	R-R	6-1	230	3-18-82	.196	.250	.167	35	102	9	20	4	0	3	5	9	1	4	0	39	0	0	.324	.268
Retherford, C.J.	R-R	5-10	195	8-14-85	.200	.213	.196	79	305	34	61	14	0	3	28	20	3	4	2	67	0	0	.275	.255
Richard, Michael	R-R	5-11	180	8-20-84	.214	.000	.273	6	14	1	3	0	0	0	2	1	0	0	0	5	1	0	.214	.353
Ricks, Adam	B-R	5-10	190	9-24-82	.000	.000	.000	1	3	0	0	0	0	0	1	0	0	0	1	0	0	0	.000	.000
Sanchez, Salvador	R-R	6-6	195	9-13-85	.240	.175	.262	109	391	47	94	19	4	11	53	24	3	3	1	99	9	2	.394	.289
Shelby III, John	R-R	5-10	185	8-6-85	.249	.315	.219	111	398	63	99	18	7	11	43	24	3	10	5	111	15	9	.412	.293

Pitching	B-T	HT	WT	DOB	W	L	ERA	G	GS	CG	SV	IP	H	R	ER	HR	BB	SO	AVG	vLH	vRH	K/9	BB/9
Axelrod, Dylan	R-R	6-0	195	7-30-85	0	1	2.70	2	2	0	0	10	8	3	3	0	3	8	.216	.222	.211	7.20	2.70
Bellamy, Kyle	R-R	6-5	220	10-25-87	2	2	6.31	20	0	0	0	26	31	19	18	1	22	19	.304	.333	.288	6.66	7.71
Brooks, Ricky	R-R	6-3	180	7-18-84	1	3	4.54	24	2	0	1	42	54	29	21	3	10	38	.314	.444	.220	8.21	2.16
Burdie, Charlis	R-R	6-1	185	9-8-85	0	0	0.00	2	0	0	0	2	2	0	0	0	2	2	.286	.000	.400	9.00	9.00
Carter, Anthony	L-R	6-3	180	4-4-86	1	4	3.92	46	2	0	22	57	47	25	25	6	22	58	.226	.154	.282	9.10	3.45
Cassel, Justin	R-R	6-2	215	9-25-84	0	3	2.90	5	5	0	0	31	25	13	10	1	9	15	.225	.216	.230	4.35	2.61
Corley, Tyson	R-R	6-6	200	1-26-86	0	3	7.20	15	0	0	1	15	24	15	12	0	12	12	.381	.409	.366	7.20	6.00
Dobies, Andrew	L-L	6-1	180	4-20-83	3	4	6.43	14	0	0	0	21	25	18	15	1	10	23	.291	.294	.288	9.86	4.29
Edwards, Justin	L-L	6-0	180	9-7-87	3	10	5.99	20	20	0	0	107	140	80	71	20	34	47	.326	.297	.342	3.97	2.87
Garcia, Angel	R-R	6-7	230	10-28-83	1	5	6.11	18	5	0	0	56	62	39	38	8	22	31	.292	.267	.311	4.98	3.54
Heath, Deunte	R-R	6-4	215	8-8-85	2	4	3.12	39	0	0	2	58	49	22	20	4	32	84	.231	.236	.228	13.11	4.99
Hynick, Brandon	R-R	6-3	205	3-7-85	3	1	2.36	10	10	1	0	53	51	15	14	3	13	37	.254	.172	.324	6.24	2.19
Infante, Gregory	R-R	6-2	185	7-10-87	2	2	3.42	24	0	0	3	26	23	11	10	0	12	34	.235	.167	.286	11.62	4.10
Leesman, Charlie	L-L	6-4	210	3-10-87	5	2	2.69	11	11	0	0	64	47	20	19	5	11	51	.210	.192	.219	7.21	2.83
Long, Matt	R-R	6-5	220	2-23-84	7	9	4.89	22	21	1	0	114	122	69	62	15	24	79	.275	.240	.304	6.24	1.89
Lowe, Johnnie	R-R	6-5	220	3-21-85	6	5	3.96	25	24	0	0	120	122	56	53	5	48	74	.272	.288	.257	5.53	3.59
Luis, Santo	R-R	6-4	200	1-27-84	1	0	3.00	2	0	0	0	3	2	1	1	0	2	3	.222	.200	.250	9.00	6.00
Mabee, Henry	R-R	6-4	230	7-10-85	4	6	3.65	49	0	0	2	86	76	40	35	5	42	62	.242	.190	.282	6.46	4.38
McCulloch, Kyle	R-R	6-3	190	3-20-85	2	1	5.59	12	7	0	0	47	59	33	29	3	12	23	.311	.306	.314	4.44	2.31
Nunez, Jhonny	L-R	6-3	215	11-26-85	1	4	3.71	10	10	0	0	51	53	24	21	3	17	38	.265	.333	.216	6.71	3.00
Omogrosso, Brian	R-R	6-4	230	4-26-84	0	1	3.00	3	0	0	0	3	2	1	1	0	1	3	.182	.167	.200	9.00	3.00
Ouellette, Ryan	R-R	5-11	185	10-4-85	1	1	3.06	12	0	0	0	18	18	7	6	2	3	8	.269	.346	.220	4.08	1.53
Rasner, Jake	R-R	6-4	210	12-4-86	1	6	5.02	22	8	0	0	61	72	44	34	7	32	52	.300	.355	.265	7.67	4.72
Shirek, Charlie	R-R	6-3	205	10-25-85	2	3	3.69	14	13	0	0	68	83	31	28	1	17	37	.303	.322	.289	4.87	2.24
Socolovich, Miguel	R-R	6-1	155	7-24-86	4	5	3.44	33	0	0	2	52	34	28	20	2	27	47	.177	.188	.171	8.08	4.64
Sues, Jeff	R-R	6-4	225	6-8-83	0	1	4.76	4	0	0	0	6	4	4	3	0	5	6	.211	.300	.111	9.53	7.94
Torres, Joe	L-L	6-2	195	9-3-82	1	1	4.50	16	0	0	0	14	14	11	7	2	11	14	.259	.389	.194	9.00	7.07

Fielding

Catcher	PCT	G	PO	A	E	DP	PB
Armstrong	.992	83	539	45	5	5	10
Blackwood	1.000	2	8	0	0	0	0
Bour	.979	18	89	6	2	2	2
Phegley	.989	10	80	10	1	1	1
Price	.991	35	202	13	2	0	5
Ricks	1.000	1	7	0	0	0	0

First Base	PCT	G	PO	A	E	DP
Gallagher	.988	80	743	51	10	73
Marrero	.991	61	511	45	5	48
Retherford	1.000	1	1	0	0	0

Second Base	PCT	G	PO	A	E	DP
Fuller	1.000	9	7	25	0	4
Kuhn	.988	35	65	98	2	23
Mollenhauer	.981	51	106	152	5	37
Retherford	.978	49	99	125	5	28
Richard	.867	3	7	6	2	1

Third Base	PCT	G	PO	A	E	DP
Cortez	.958	10	7	16	1	2
Fuller	1.000	5	5	16	0	1
Mollenhauer	.956	47	35	96	6	7
Morel	.939	48	38	85	8	8

Paiml	.867	4	4	9	2	0
Retherford	.936	31	19	54	5	2

Shortstop	PCT	G	PO	A	E	DP
Cortez	.952	13	20	40	3	10
Escobar	.954	49	52	157	10	27
Fuller	.857	12	17	37	9	11
Hudson	.929	3	2	11	1	2
Paiml	.960	65	98	193	12	47
Richard	1.000	3	4	4	0	2

Outfield	PCT	G	PO	A	E	DP
Coats	1.000	14	25	0	0	0

Cruz	1.000	2	3	1	0	0
Gallagher	1.000	40	75	10	0	1
Greene	.975	42	74	3	2	1

Kuhn	1.000	45	69	3	0	0
Marrero	.974	61	112	1	3	0
Negron	.986	31	68	0	1	0

Sanchez	.979	92	179	7	4	0
Shelby III	.975	98	182	10	5	0

WINSTON-SALEM DASH   HIGH CLASS A

CAROLINA LEAGUE

Batting	B-T	HT	WT	DOB	AVG	vLH	vRH	G	AB	R	H	2B	3B	HR	RBI	BB	HBP	SH	SF	SO	SB	CS	SLG	OBP
Blackwood, Chase	R-R	5-10	205	11-24-87	.111	.000	.111	1	9	0	1	0	0	0	1	0	0	0		6	0	0	.111	.111
Bour, Jason	R-R	6-3	215	7-2-86	.302	.265	.320	41	149	34	45	14	4	6	26	16	3	0	2	39	0	0	.570	.376
Cheatham, Jordan	L-L	5-10	185	11-2-87	.250	.333	.234	38	128	20	32	10	3	1	16	17	0	1	1	23	2	3	.398	.336
Ciolli, Nick	L-R	6-2	215	12-6-87	.375	.250	.406	10	40	10	15	6	0	1	5	1	0	1	0	9	0	0	.600	.390
Escobar, Eduardo	B-R	5-10	150	1-5-89	.285	.326	.271	87	368	57	105	18	8	3	39	23	2	11	4	76	8	5	.402	.327
Garcia, Drew	B-R	6-1	175	4-22-86	.253	.223	.265	119	438	61	111	29	0	9	70	35	9	5	5	101	5	1	.381	.318
Gilmore, Jon	R-R	6-3	195	8-23-88	.312	.396	.282	135	568	79	177	24	4	5	80	34	2	1	6	89	1	3	.394	.349
Greene, Justin	R-R	6-0	185	10-10-85	.309	.317	.306	74	249	50	77	15	9	10	45	28	6	6	2	73	17	7	.562	.389
Johnson, Logan	L-R	5-9	175	11-22-83	.281	.235	.294	52	160	20	45	11	0	6	29	24	10	4	1	39	0	1	.463	.405
Kayne, Zach	B-R	5-10	185	11-22-85	.000	.000	.000	2	3	0	0	0	0	0	0	0	0	0	0	2	0	0	.000	.250
Lewis, Ozzie	R-R	6-4	193	3-21-86	.300	.374	.271	108	414	62	124	26	1	10	56	33	5	2	1	92	2	3	.440	.358
Loman, Seth	L-R	6-4	225	12-16-85	.292	.325	.278	133	514	88	150	33	3	25	88	43	30	0	1	127	0	2	.514	.379
Martinez, Jose	R-R	6-5	170	7-25-88	.242	.172	.264	61	236	28	57	8	1	5	24	17	2	3	3	42	4	1	.347	.295
Paiml, Greg	R-R	6-0	185	8-3-84	.272	.259	.277	29	92	10	25	8	1	0	10	8	3	3	0	24	2	0	.380	.350
Phegley, Josh	R-R	5-10	215	2-12-88	.292	.379	.250	25	89	16	26	3	0	3	12	7	0	1	2	22	0	0	.427	.337
Richard, Michael	R-R	5-11	180	8-20-84	.254	.261	.250	21	63	9	16	0	0	0	3	11	2	2	1	9	4	1	.254	.377
Ricks, Adam	B-R	5-10	190	9-24-82	.333	.000	.333	1	3	0	1	0	0	0	0	1	0	0	0	1	0	0	.333	.500
Shelton, Kyle	R-R	6-0	184	5-15-86	.301	.369	.274	68	229	36	69	12	2	4	31	21	3	2	2	43	2	0	.424	.365
Short, Brandon	R-R	6-1	175	9-9-88	.316	.373	.296	116	491	77	155	31	5	15	79	28	14	4	7	107	7	10	.491	.365
Sierra, Luis	L-R	5-11	150	7-23-87	.293	.275	.297	79	287	48	84	17	2	5	41	22	2	3	4	45	0	1	.418	.343
Williams Jr., Kenny	B-R	6-0	180	5-22-86	.252	.281	.238	74	274	33	69	17	1	4	33	17	5	4	1	57	0	3	.365	.306

Pitching	B-T	HT	WT	DOB	W	L	ERA	G	GS	CG	SV	IP	H	R	ER	HR	BB	SO	AVG	vLH	vRH	K/9	BB/9
Axelrod, Dylan	R-R	6-0	195	7-30-85	8	3	1.99	23	13	1	0	99	95	30	22	2	12	84	.252	.289	.223	7.61	1.09
Bellamy, Kyle	R-R	6-5	220	10-25-87	5	0	1.52	31	0	0	5	47	38	15	8	1	14	59	.216	.282	.163	11.22	2.66
Burdie, Charlis	R-R	6-1	185	9-8-85	4	2	5.01	37	0	0	1	56	44	40	31	2	32	48	.214	.214	.213	7.76	5.17
Corley, Tyson	R-R	6-6	200	1-26-86	0	0	1.79	30	0	0	10	40	28	10	8	0	13	37	.200	.242	.167	8.26	2.90
Doyle, Terry	R-R	6-4	225	11-2-85	8	8	3.71	20	20	0	0	121	115	60	50	13	34	99	.249	.256	.244	7.34	2.52
Edwards, Justin	L-L	6-0	180	9-7-87	5	2	2.37	8	8	0	0	49	44	15	13	1	15	29	.238	.255	.231	5.29	2.74
Griffith, Nevin	R-R	6-3	210	3-23-89	4	2	3.11	12	12	0	0	64	61	34	22	2	27	41	.251	.268	.237	5.80	3.82
Hunt, Leroy	R-R	6-6	240	11-28-87	0	4	8.66	26	1	0	0	35	49	35	34	2	39	25	.348	.406	.299	6.37	9.93
Infante, Gregory	R-R	6-2	185	7-10-87	1	2	3.48	31	0	0	9	34	32	15	13	0	15	35	.250	.310	.200	9.36	4.01
Johnson, Garrett	L-L	6-10	205	9-2-87	2	0	4.15	10	0	0	0	17	15	8	8	2	9	7	.246	.071	.298	3.63	4.67
Jones, Nathan	R-R	6-5	190	1-28-86	11	6	4.08	28	28	1	0	152	176	77	69	10	56	109	.296	.298	.295	6.44	3.31
Kloess, Brandon	R-R	6-2	195	12-9-84	1	2	5.82	13	0	0	1	17	21	14	11	2	5	24	.309	.286	.319	12.71	2.65
Kussmaul, Ryan	R-R	6-4	185	9-19-86	1	0	4.15	5	0	0	1	9	6	4	4	0	4	9	.200	.400	.100	9.35	4.15
Leesman, Charlie	L-L	6-4	210	3-10-87	9	4	5.10	17	17	0	0	85	98	51	48	6	44	39	.294	.299	.293	4.15	4.68
O'Neil, Drew	R-R	6-3	200	11-8-85	0	1	14.40	4	0	0	0	5	11	10	8	0	11	2	.458	.600	.421	3.60	19.80
Rasner, Jake	R-R	6-4	210	12-4-86	1	2	5.79	12	2	0	0	33	32	22	21	1	17	26	.254	.385	.162	7.16	4.68
Remenowsky, Dan	R-R	6-5	245	4-7-86	2	1	2.75	25	0	0	5	39	34	12	12	3	13	60	.236	.250	.225	13.73	2.97
Rodriguez, Santos	L-L	6-5	180	1-2-88	2	0	3.57	32	0	0	0	40	27	18	16	0	32	59	.193	.225	.180	13.17	7.14
Sale, Chris	L-L	6-5	170	3-30-89	0	0	2.25	4	0	0	0	4	3	2	1	0	2	4	.200	.333	.167	9.00	4.50
Santiago, Hector	R-L	6-0	210	12-16-87	4	5	4.15	37	1	0	2	61	63	29	28	4	19	61	.267	.279	.262	9.05	2.82
Sauer, Stephen	R-R	6-2	185	8-13-86	8	10	4.89	26	26	0	0	151	193	90	82	7	41	80	.321	.336	.308	4.77	2.44
Serafin, Joe	L-L	5-10	185	2-27-86	3	4	5.63	11	11	0	0	56	71	41	35	5	27	28	.313	.326	.310	4.50	4.34
Sues, Jeff	R-R	6-4	225	6-8-83	0	0	6.75	1	0	0	0	1	2	1	1	2	1	1	.333	.333	.333	6.75	13.50
Thompson, Taylor	R-R	6-5	225	6-18-87	1	0	1.80	3	0	0	0	5	5	1	1	0	4	5	.278	.400	.231	9.00	7.20
Wickswat, Matt	L-L	6-2	210	8-4-86	0	0	18.00	2	0	0	0	2	7	6	4	0	1	3	.500	.333	.545	13.50	4.50

Fielding

Catcher	PCT	G	PO	A	E	DP	PB
Blackwood	.962	1	23	2	1	0	0
Bour	.990	41	274	33	3	4	6
Johnson	.990	30	175	22	2	0	4
Phegley	.989	20	150	23	2	0	6
Ricks	1.000	1	7	1	0	0	0
Sierra	.990	52	361	33	4	4	15

First Base	PCT	G	PO	A	E	DP
Johnson	.933	2	13	1	1	2
Loman	.992	110	1061	58	9	118
Shelton	.987	17	140	15	2	15
Sierra	.990	14	98	6	1	9

Second Base	PCT	G	PO	A	E	DP
Garcia	.981	117	254	377	12	97
Shelton	.991	20	46	61	1	18
Sierra	1.000	5	11	12	0	5
Paiml	.964	29	41	93	5	21
Richard	.928	21	25	65	7	21

Third Base	PCT	G	PO	A	E	DP
Gilmore	.893	126	69	248	38	25
Shelton	.909	6	2	8	1	2
Sierra	.957	8	4	18	1	0

Shortstop	PCT	G	PO	A	E	DP
Escobar	.964	87	114	290	15	59
Garcia	.938	3	5	10	1	5
Kayne	—	1	0	0	0	0

Outfield	PCT	G	PO	A	E	DP
Cheatham	.938	38	56	4	4	0
Ciolli	1.000	10	31	1	0	0
Greene	.986	74	132	8	2	1
Lewis	.917	35	52	3	5	0
Martinez	.983	61	111	6	2	0
Shelton	1.000	23	26	2	0	0
Short	.976	115	196	8	5	1
Williams Jr.	.984	72	119	4	2	1

KANNAPOLIS INTIMIDATORS LOW CLASS A

SOUTH ATLANTIC LEAGUE

Batting	B-T	HT	WT	DOB	AVG	vLH	vRH	G	AB	R	H	2B	3B	HR	RBI	BB	HBP	SH	SF	SO	SB	CS	SLG	OBP
Castillo, Jorge	L-R	6-2	225	9-26-86	.244	.500	.233	12	45	2	11	2	0	0	3	0	0	1	1	6	1	0	.289	.239
Cheatham, Jordan	L-L	5-10	185	11-2-87	.274	.185	.302	66	226	21	62	14	2	3	23	17	1	3	3	50	11	3	.394	.324
Ciolli, Nick	L-R	6-2	215	12-6-87	.296	.291	.298	115	439	57	130	22	5	12	73	17	2	2	7	123	13	7	.451	.320
Colligan, Kyle	R-R	6-2	210	4-23-87	.284	.316	.272	93	348	57	99	21	4	9	42	26	10	3	4	71	18	4	.445	.348
Davis, Kyle	R-R	5-11	160	1-8-87	.150	.133	.156	18	60	4	9	1	0	0	3	7	1	1	0	12	0	0	.167	.250
Dubler, Kevin	L-R	6-1	200	2-18-87	.197	.303	.169	51	157	27	31	4	0	2	13	27	2	2	0	25	2	1	.261	.323
Gac, Ian	R-R	6-3	240	8-10-85	.276	.262	.280	134	504	65	139	34	0	20	91	45	5	0	7	124	3	1	.462	.337
Gonzalez, Miguel	R-R	5-11	180	12-3-90	.218	.253	.206	92	326	35	71	9	2	2	19	16	4	4	4	63	2	1	.276	.260
Hamme, Ryan	L-R	6-3	210	3-13-87	.300	.200	.327	22	70	8	21	3	0	2	7	3	0	1	1	15	1	1	.429	.324
Kayne, Zach	B-R	5-10	185	11-22-86	.175	.353	.127	24	80	8	14	2	1	0	7	7	2	2	0	17	1	0	.225	.258
Lee, Ryan	R-R	6-0	185	2-11-86	.208	.500	.150	6	24	3	5	0	0	0	1	2	0	0	0	8	2	0	.208	.269
Oester, Jake	R-R	6-1	190	7-22-86	.207	.241	.196	72	237	27	49	13	3	2	21	16	5	4	3	69	0	1	.312	.268
Richard, Michael	R-R	5-11	180	8-20-84	.283	.333	.258	13	46	7	13	2	1	0	6	4	3	0	0	7	4	1	.370	.377
Saladino, Tyler	R-R	5-11	180	7-20-89	.309	.400	.275	47	165	40	51	14	1	2	18	22	4	4	3	44	4	2	.442	.397
Shoemaker, Brady	R-R	6-0	200	5-10-87	.293	.274	.299	96	338	61	99	23	1	12	55	39	10	0	1	98	3	2	.473	.381
Silverio, Juan	R-R	6-1	175	4-18-91	.200	.278	.175	63	220	20	44	12	3	4	24	6	5	4	1	57	3	4	.336	.237
Spatola, John	L-L	6-0	190	4-2-87	.212	.000	.216	17	52	7	11	1	3	1	6	2	1	0	0	14	0	0	.404	.255
Tezak, Jeff	R-R	5-10	180	2-23-86	.231	.000	.300	6	13	3	3	0	0	2	5	0	0	0	5	0	0	.231	.444
Thompson, Trayce	R-R	6-3	195	3-15-91	.229	.183	.247	58	210	28	48	13	3	8	31	21	2	0	2	69	6	4	.433	.302
Vargas, Jose	R-R	6-2	225	12-15-87	.254	.247	.256	98	343	40	87	20	2	9	43	22	4	1	2	90	2	0	.402	.305
Vera, Rafael	R-R	6-1	180	11-21-87	.279	.233	.291	34	140	14	39	13	0	0	13	8	1	3	0	35	1	0	.414	.322
Villegas, Jesus	R-R	5-10	180	9-21-86	.265	.257	.269	26	102	13	27	5	0	0	11	6	0	1	1	21	2	1	.314	.303
Wagner, Daniel	L-R	6-0	185	7-12-88	.272	.259	.275	128	515	70	140	19	3	2	47	36	3	9	4	66	37	13	.332	.321

Pitching	B-T	HT	WT	DOB	W	L	ERA	G	GS	CG	SV	IP	H	R	ER	HR	BB	SO	AVG	vLH	vRH	K/9	BB/9
Ballinger, J.R.	R-R	6-1	190	4-2-88	0	5	3.13	35	0	0	1	46	43	24	16	4	22	35	.240	.193	.262	6.85	4.30
Bayne, Cameron	R-R	6-2	195	2-14-88	12	9	3.60	27	26	2	0	165	174	87	66	9	35	101	.269	.270	.269	5.51	1.91
Bellamy, Kyle	R-R	6-5	220	10-25-87	0	0	1.80	4	0	0	0	5	2	1	1	0	3	6	.125	.000	.167	10.80	5.40
Buch, Ryan	R-R	6-3	205	11-8-87	5	3	3.13	24	10	0	1	72	61	33	25	1	26	61	.230	.176	.264	7.63	3.25
Collop, Justin	R-R	6-1	185	5-30-88	9	12	4.26	26	26	3	0	154	170	84	73	10	31	130	.284	.271	.292	7.58	1.81
Cooney, Chase	R-R	6-8	245	12-18-87	0	1	4.08	14	0	0	0	18	20	8	8	1	7	13	.294	.276	.308	6.62	3.57
Doyle, Terry	R-R	6-4	225	11-2-85	4	2	0.96	7	7	0	0	47	31	5	5	2	12	58	.187	.096	.228	11.11	2.30
Garcia, Angel	R-R	6-7	230	10-28-83	0	0	0.00	4	0	0	0	7	3	0	0	0	4	3	.130	.000	.200	3.68	4.91
Heidenreich, Matt	L-R	6-5	185	1-17-91	0	0	18.00	1	0	0	0	1	3	2	2	0	0	2	.600	.500	.667	18.00	0.00
Hollis, Jamaal	R-R	6-2	195	12-3-87	0	0	0.00	3	0	0	0	3	1	0	0	0	3	5	.100	.000	.200	15.00	9.00
Hopps, Matt	R-R	6-5	235	10-8-85	2	10	6.58	28	19	0	0	107	150	92	78	7	49	55	.346	.420	.301	4.64	4.13
Hunt, Leroy	R-R	6-6	240	11-28-87	0	0	9.00	2	0	0	0	3	6	3	3	0	2	1	.429	.333	.500	3.00	6.00
Johnson, Garrett	L-L	6-10	205	9-2-87	4	4	3.68	29	0	0	0	44	35	20	18	2	17	39	.219	.171	.232	7.98	3.48
Kloess, Brandon	R-R	6-2	195	12-9-84	1	1	1.18	25	0	0	9	38	32	5	5	1	9	47	.224	.200	.235	11.13	2.13
Kussmaul, Ryan	R-R	6-5	185	9-19-86	0	0	1.20	9	0	0	1	15	5	2	2	0	3	17	.104	.200	.061	10.20	1.80
Marin, Terance	R-R	6-1	170	8-21-89	0	0	0.00	1	0	0	0	1	0	0	0	0	1	0	.000	.000	.000	9.00	0.00
Moran, Kevin	R-R	6-4	195	7-7-89	1	0	3.52	5	0	0	0	5	3	3	0	0	5	6	.172	.250	.118	7.04	5.87
Negus, Phil	R-R	6-2	205	11-10-87	0	0	2.45	4	0	0	0	4	3	1	1	3	5	2	.222	.600	.077	12.27	7.36
O'Neil, Drew	R-R	6-3	200	11-8-85	2	2	4.06	22	0	0	1	31	32	17	14	0	19	28	.271	.292	.266	8.13	5.52
Petricka, Jacob	R-R	6-5	170	6-5-88	0	1	3.72	9	0	0	0	10	13	11	4	0	8	10	.295	.350	.250	9.31	7.45
Piccola, Zach	R-L	6-3	225	3-27-85	2	5	7.88	21	1	0	0	32	46	31	28	2	18	33	.357	.409	.346	9.28	5.06
Rienzo, Andre	R-R	6-3	160	7-5-88	8	4	3.65	20	18	2	0	101	95	45	41	5	32	125	.242	.273	.222	11.14	2.85
Santos, Orlando	R-R	6-0	187	12-10-86	1	1	3.38	39	0	0	15	51	40	20	19	3	11	59	.219	.292	.178	10.48	1.95
Schatz, Pat	R-R	6-0	185	8-16-87	0	1	7.71	2	0	0	0	2	4	2	2	1	0	3	.400	.333	.429	11.57	0.00
Serafin, Joe	L-L	5-10	185	2-27-86	7	5	3.47	16	16	0	0	96	104	55	37	9	28	59	.280	.311	.272	5.53	2.63
Thompson, Taylor	R-R	6-5	225	6-18-87	0	1	2.20	18	0	0	6	29	24	9	7	0	10	32	.224	.200	.239	10.05	3.14
Wickswat, Matt	L-L	6-2	210	8-4-86	7	7	3.93	30	16	0	1	119	117	57	52	6	40	113	.261	.233	.268	8.55	3.03

Fielding

Catcher	PCT	G	PO	A	E	DP	PB
Dubler	.990	51	374	42	4	4	3
Gonzalez	.984	92	646	110	12	4	12

First Base	PCT	G	PO	A	E	DP
Castillo	1.000	4	39	3	0	1
Gac	.991	120	1085	81	10	104
Vargas	1.000	15	128	7	0	12
Vera	1.000	1	5	1	0	0

Second Base	PCT	G	PO	A	E	DP
Kayne	.909	6	16	14	3	6
Oester	1.000	7	15	16	0	3
Tezak	1.000	1	3	3	0	2
Vera	.842	3	5	11	3	2
Villegas	1.000	1	3	5	0	2

Wagner	.973	124	233	354	16	79

Third Base	PCT	G	PO	A	E	DP
Gac	.500	1	1	0	1	0
Oester	.903	65	41	127	18	14
Silverio	.927	44	32	120	12	11
Tezak	.500	1	0	1	1	0
Vargas	.833	17	3	42	9	4
Vera	.875	14	6	43	7	9

Shortstop	PCT	G	PO	A	E	DP
Davis	.948	17	37	54	5	14
Kayne	.911	17	28	44	7	7
Richard	.918	12	21	35	5	12
Saladino	.970	46	49	110	5	18
Silverio	.925	12	26	36	5	7

	PCT	G	PO	A	E	DP
Vera	.841	13	10	48	11	9
Villegas	.919	25	40	62	9	20

Outfield	PCT	G	PO	A	E	DP
Cheatham	.972	62	104	1	3	0
Ciolli	.964	114	199	14	8	5
Colligan	.983	85	113	2	2	1
Hamme	.947	21	34	2	2	0
Lee	1.000	5	5	0	0	0
Oester	—	1	0	0	0	0
Shoemaker	.990	57	92	3	1	0
Spatola	1.000	15	12	1	0	0
Thompson	.962	57	121	5	5	2
Vargas	1.000	13	19	0	0	0
Vera	.750	4	3	0	1	0

BRISTOL SOX

ROOKIE

APPALACHIAN LEAGUE

Batting	B-T	HT	WT	DOB	AVG	vLH	vRH	G	AB	R	H	2B	3B	HR	RBI	BB	HBP	SH	SF	SO	SB	CS	SLG	OBP
Ashbrook, J.D.	R-R	5-10	167	1-7-88	.218	.184	.243	37	119	14	26	7	0	2	12	11	5	0	0	24	2	2	.328	.311
Black, Dan	L-R	6-5	240	7-2-87	.288	.217	.324	57	208	23	60	15	2	6	33	23	3	0	2	47	1	0	.466	.364
Blackwood, Chase	R-R	5-10	205	11-24-87	.192	.244	.168	48	146	16	28	8	1	4	12	6	11	5	1	47	0	0	.342	.274
Cummings, Robby	R-R	6-2	195	8-14-87	.258	.276	.243	21	66	8	17	4	0	1	7	7	1	1	1	22	0	0	.364	.333
Keegan, Jordan	R-R	6-0	175	12-23-89	.249	.208	.269	62	237	36	59	12	1	2	18	20	5	3	0	59	3	2	.333	.321
Lee, Drew	R-R	5-11	185	3-22-88	.282	.253	.295	62	255	32	72	24	0	5	39	10	0	2	1	49	5	4	.435	.308
Martinez, Jose	R-R	6-5	170	7-25-88	.409	.300	.500	6	22	5	9	1	0	1	5	2	0	0	0	3	1	0	.591	.458
Mercedes, Daurys	R-R	6-1	165	2-26-90	.167	.000	.200	2	6	2	1	0	0	0	0	2	0	0	0	4	1	1	.167	.375
Millender, Qualon	B-R	5-10	170	3-31-87	.240	.234	.242	55	196	28	47	5	1	0	5	11	4	8	1	46	12	6	.276	.292
O'Connell, Sean	L-R	6-4	181	12-12-91	.132	.143	.128	20	53	1	7	1	0	0	1	4	1	1	0	22	0	0	.151	.207
Patino, Jeffer	R-R	5-10	163	10-8-88	.316	.171	.367	35	133	14	42	7	0	1	9	4	2	3	0	21	1	0	.391	.345
Phegley, Josh	R-R	5-10	215	2-12-88	.200	.000	.300	5	15	1	3	1	0	0	1	2	1	0	0	4	0	0	.267	.333
Ravelo, Rangel	R-R	6-2	207	4-24-92	.254	.273	.246	48	173	17	44	9	1	1	21	9	0	5	0	25	0	2	.335	.291
Saladino, Tyler	R-R	5-11	180	7-20-89	.292	.222	.333	13	48	7	14	3	0	1	6	5	1	1	1	12	1	2	.417	.364
Salgado, Brad	R-R	6-1	185	7-15-91	.188	.195	.183	31	101	6	19	5	0	1	11	11	2	0	0	29	2	1	.267	.281
Schwartz, Mike	L-R	6-0	220	5-4-87	.241	.316	.203	38	112	12	27	8	0	1	19	26	7	1	0	33	0	2	.339	.414
Spatola, John	L-L	6-0	190	4-2-87	.264	.319	.241	42	159	18	42	9	0	7	21	7	1	2	1	39	1	1	.453	.298
Spencer, Marcus	R-R	6-1	205	4-14-86	.215	.063	.265	25	65	7	14	4	0	2	4	5	0	1	0	28	2	2	.369	.271
Tonneson, Dylan	R-R	6-3	220	9-5-87	.000	.000	.000	1	1	1	0	0	0	0	0	1	0	0	0	0	0	0	.000	.500
Wilson, Ethan	R-R	6-0	190	3-9-89	.142	.143	.141	32	106	8	15	0	3	0	1	8	2	2	0	35	3	0	.198	.216

Pitching	B-T	HT	WT	DOB	W	L	ERA	G	GS	CG	SV	IP	H	R	ER	HR	BB	SO	AVG	vLH	vRH	K/9	BB/9
Arroyo, Spencer	L-L	6-2	166	8-9-88	7	2	2.49	13	13	1	0	76	57	22	21	7	14	75	.206	.208	.205	8.88	1.66
Billeaud, Josh	R-R	6-3	210	3-22-87	0	0	4.82	16	3	0	0	28	29	21	15	0	16	23	.266	.243	.278	7.39	5.14
Buch, Ryan	R-R	6-3	205	11-8-87	2	1	2.45	4	4	0	0	22	14	6	6	3	3	20	.182	.313	.148	8.18	1.23
Casey, Jarrett	R-L	6-0	185	10-27-87	1	7	4.33	15	9	0	3	54	55	35	26	5	13	32	.261	.194	.272	5.33	2.17
Cooney, Chase	R-R	6-8	245	12-18-87	0	0	0.00	3	0	0	1	5	1	0	0	0	2	3	.063	.125	.000	5.40	3.60
Copenhaver, Raymond	R-R	6-5	235	11-22-87	0	0	4.91	2	0	0	0	4	4	2	2	0	0	4	.267	.000	.308	9.82	0.00
Evans, Austin	R-R	6-3	220	11-5-87	2	2	5.19	16	0	0	0	26	24	16	15	1	12	22	.253	.190	.270	7.62	4.15
Heidenreich, Matt	L-R	6-5	185	1-17-91	6	2	2.49	13	11	0	0	76	73	30	21	2	11	58	.253	.259	.250	6.87	1.30
Hollis, Jamaal	R-R	6-2	195	12-3-87	3	0	2.12	17	0	0	0	30	24	8	7	2	13	32	.222	.205	.234	9.71	3.94
Icard, Ethan	R-R	6-2	180	8-28-90	1	2	6.95	16	2	0	0	22	29	24	17	1	17	10	.322	.607	.194	4.09	6.95
Long, Matt	R-R	6-5	220	2-23-84	0	1	1.50	2	2	0	0	6	3	2	1	0	3	1	.150	.182	.111	4.50	0.00
Marin, Terance	R-R	6-1	170	8-21-89	0	1	3.46	8	0	0	1	13	13	6	5	0	13	.250	.250	.276	9.00	0.00
Marshall, Ricky	R-R	6-2	215	7-20-88	1	1	5.03	13	0	0	0	20	17	15	11	5	17	.253	.250	.255	7.78	2.29
Matos, Darwin	R-R	6-0	170	8-4-90	1	1	4.76	6	1	0	0	11	13	9	6	1	4	11	.271	.273	.269	8.74	3.18
Moran, Kevin	R-R	6-4	195	7-7-89	0	2	2.37	16	0	0	9	19	14	7	5	0	6	22	.197	.045	.265	10.42	2.84
Omogrosso, Brian	R-R	6-4	230	4-26-84	0	0	0.00	2	0	0	0	2	1	0	0	0	2	2	.167	.000	.200	9.00	9.00
Petricka, Jacob	R-R	6-5	170	6-5-88	2	4	2.86	8	8	0	0	35	25	12	11	1	7	38	.197	.205	.193	9.87	1.82
Phippen, Sam	R-R	6-9	210	9-15-87	0	0	1.50	5	0	0	1	6	2	1	1	0	5	9	.105	.286	.000	13.50	7.50
Rath, Kevin	L-L	6-5	220	8-18-89	0	5	5.46	18	0	0	2	28	25	21	17	1	14	37	.240	.222	.247	11.89	4.50
Schatz, Pat	R-R	6-0	185	8-16-87	1	1	1.50	8	1	0	0	18	12	4	3	0	2	16	.188	.238	.163	8.00	1.00
Shelton, Spencer	R-R	6-3	195	9-24-87	2	1	3.57	10	2	0	0	23	21	11	9	1	7	22	.233	.333	.190	8.74	2.78
Young, Robert	L-L	6-3	230	6-20-88	4	3	2.78	14	12	0	0	65	53	28	20	1	14	44	.224	.174	.236	6.12	1.95
Zagyi, Chris	R-R	6-5	215	8-5-89	0	0	9.00	1	0	0	0	1	1	1	1	0	1	1	.250	.000	.333	9.00	9.00

Fielding

Catcher	PCT	G	PO	A	E	DP	PB
Black	.979	11	84	10	2	0	2
Blackwood	.984	48	331	42	6	1	8
O'Connell	.966	12	50	6	2	1	2
Phegley	1.000	3	24	1	0	0	1
Tonneson	1.000	1	1	0	0	0	1

First Base	PCT	G	PO	A	E	DP
Black	.995	40	404	22	2	41
Cummings	1.000	1	6	0	0	1
Schwartz	.986	23	214	5	3	17
Spatola	1.000	6	45	3	0	5

Second Base	PCT	G	PO	A	E	DP
Lee	.978	37	63	115	4	26
Mercedes	1.000	2	1	9	0	1
Patino	.955	13	23	41	3	7
Salgado	1.000	4	8	12	0	2
Wilson	.982	12	20	34	1	10

Third Base	PCT	G	PO	A	E	DP
Cummings	.875	5	3	11	2	1
Patino	.954	21	18	44	3	1
Ravelo	.887	42	25	108	17	7
Wilson	1.000	1	0	1	0	0

Shortstop	PCT	G	PO	A	E	DP
Lee	.950	15	22	54	4	15
Saladino	.931	12	19	35	4	7
Salgado	.888	23	29	58	11	18
Wilson	.902	19	32	60	10	15

Outfield	PCT	G	PO	A	E	DP
Ashbrook	.966	37	57	0	2	0
Keegan	.959	61	86	7	4	1
Martinez	1.000	6	7	2	0	0
Millender	.942	54	96	2	6	1
Spatola	.956	31	41	2	2	1
Spencer	.970	20	32	0	1	0

GREAT FALLS VOYAGERS

ROOKIE

PIONEER LEAGUE

Batting	B-T	HT	WT	DOB	AVG	vLH	vRH	G	AB	R	H	2B	3B	HR	RBI	BB	HBP	SH	SF	SO	SB	CS	SLG	OBP
Blanke, Mike	R-R	6-4	220	10-17-88	.329	.392	.312	62	240	35	79	20	1	7	43	23	6	1	1	33	0	0	.508	.400
Cummings, Robby	R-R	6-2	195	8-14-87	.154	.200	.167	6	13	4	2	0	0	0	1	4	0	0	0	3	0	0	.154	.353
Davis, Kyle	R-L	5-11	160	1-8-87	.235	.186	.246	68	230	40	54	5	4	2	22	35	6	5	2	69	6	3	.317	.348
Earley, Michael	R-R	6-0	192	3-15-88	.263	.340	.242	61	228	42	60	12	1	5	37	21	13	3	2	33	13	6	.390	.356
Hamme, Ryan	L-R	6-3	210	3-13-87	.279	.500	.246	38	140	26	39	11	1	2	24	19	1	0	3	23	2	0	.414	.362
Harvard, Dusty	R-R	6-3	196	10-28-87	.242	.250	.240	66	240	37	58	8	3	2	28	34	0	0	1	72	12	6	.325	.335
Lee, Ryan	R-R	6-0	185	2-11-86	.331	.351	.326	49	169	32	56	8	2	1	25	9	2	8	3	35	15	2	.420	.366

Name	B-T	HT	WT	DOB	AVG	vLH	vRH	G	AB	R	H	2B	3B	HR	RBI	BB	HBP	SH	SF	SO	SB	CS	SLG	OBP
McDonald, Jared	L-R	6-1	180	3-1-88	.248	.167	.258	37	101	22	25	5	1	2	13	13	2	2	2	16	0	0	.376	.339
Pangilinan, Leighton	L-R	6-3	230	3-6-91	.289	.067	.323	29	114	16	33	7	0	3	16	7	2	2	2	30	0	1	.430	.336
Ramos, Jose	R-R	5-11	190	7-19-87	.219	.182	.238	17	32	5	7	1	0	1	3	1	0	1	0	7	0	0	.344	.242
Silverio, Juan	R-R	6-1	175	4-18-91	.299	.143	.313	20	87	11	26	9	0	3	16	6	0	0	1	20	3	1	.506	.340
Tezak, Jeff	B-R	5-10	180	2-23-86	.318	.083	.384	40	110	19	35	6	0	1	19	16	2	1	2	14	0	1	.400	.408
Thorpe, Randall	R-R	6-1	175	4-2-89	.226	.268	.215	59	199	32	45	16	1	1	25	39	4	6	5	68	5	7	.332	.356
Vaughn, Rob	R-R	5-10	190	7-7-87	.277	.300	.270	19	47	4	13	0	0	0	5	6	0	0	1	10	0	1	.277	.352
Vera, Rafael	R-R	6-1	180	11-21-87	.286	.174	.320	54	196	28	56	15	0	5	32	14	2	2	5	54	2	0	.439	.332
Wilkins, Andy	L-R	6-2	225	9-13-88	.307	.317	.305	53	218	37	67	14	1	6	40	33	1	1	3	31	7	2	.463	.396
Wilson, Ross	R-R	5-11	185	11-9-88	.289	.333	.277	65	256	61	74	14	4	2	34	32	9	5	3	45	6	1	.398	.383

Pitching	B-T	HT	WT	DOB	W	L	ERA	G	GS	CG	SV	IP	H	R	ER	HR	BB	SO	AVG	vLH	vRH	K/9	BB/9
Arroyo, Spencer	L-L	6-2	166	8-9-88	0	0	0.82	2	2	0	0	11	4	2	1	0	6	11	.121	.000	.154	9.00	4.91
Burnside, Paul	R-R	6-4	225	11-20-86	7	3	4.14	17	13	0	1	72	69	42	33	6	20	77	.246	.248	.243	9.67	2.51
Copenhaver, Raymond	R-R	6-5	235	11-22-87	0	0	27.00	4	0	0	0	4	14	11	11	0	1	2	.583	.600	.571	4.91	2.45
Curry, Nelson	R-R	6-0	190	1-14-87	3	4	5.75	21	0	0	1	36	45	29	23	6	18	33	.308	.344	.282	8.25	4.50
Delk, Trey	R-R	6-2	190	12-17-85	7	3	5.08	16	16	0	0	78	107	57	44	9	17	81	.320	.331	.311	9.35	1.96
Garcia, Rene	R-R	6-2	200	6-15-86	2	0	3.82	15	0	0	2	33	38	16	14	5	7	26	.292	.358	.247	7.09	1.91
Gehle, Pete	L-L	6-4	240	1-15-88	3	3	3.91	19	0	0	1	46	61	21	20	2	14	42	.326	.284	.354	8.22	2.74
Holmberg, David	R-L	6-4	220	7-19-91	1	1	4.46	8	8	0	0	40	52	23	20	2	9	29	.315	.319	.314	6.47	2.01
2-team total (7 Missoula)					2	5	4.17	15	15	0	0	78	99	49	36	4	16	76	—	—	—	8.81	1.85
Huff, Stephen	L-L	6-0	200	4-5-88	1	1	4.63	14	0	0	1	23	22	13	12	1	17	22	.247	.250	.245	8.49	6.56
McCray, Stephen	L-R	6-3	230	10-6-87	6	2	2.48	18	6	0	2	54	52	23	15	5	15	45	.245	.306	.205	7.45	2.48
Murray, Doug	R-R	6-2	195	9-26-88	2	4	1.91	20	0	0	2	47	35	11	10	3	20	31	.220	.290	.167	5.94	3.83
Reed, Addison	L-R	6-4	215	12-27-88	1	0	1.80	13	2	0	1	30	17	7	6	1	6	44	.162	.180	.145	13.20	1.80
Royse, Thomas	R-R	6-5	210	9-7-88	1	1	3.41	10	8	0	0	34	28	18	13	2	6	28	.217	.230	.206	7.34	1.57
Schatz, Pat	R-R	6-0	185	8-16-87	0	2	7.78	5	5	0	0	20	28	17	17	6	6	11	.354	.320	.414	5.03	2.75
Simmons, Goldy	R-R	6-4	210	10-29-88	3	0	4.50	16	0	0	0	28	26	17	14	0	25	27	.250	.326	.190	8.68	8.04
Thompson, Taylor	R-R	6-5	225	6-18-87	0	0	0.00	1	0	0	0	2	0	0	0	0	0	2	.000	.000	.000	9.00	0.00
Upchurch, Steven	R-R	6-4	180	9-14-89	4	2	3.78	15	15	0	0	86	82	48	36	6	18	47	.245	.301	.206	4.94	1.89
Wilson, Jake	R-R	6-0	195	8-12-87	6	2	3.62	23	0	0	5	32	24	14	13	3	11	50	.203	.244	.182	13.92	3.06

Fielding

Catcher	PCT	G	PO	A	E	DP	PB
Blanke	.977	48	380	38	10	0	4
Ramos	.985	14	59	8	1	0	5
Vaughn	.990	18	91	7	1	1	1
Vera	.975	11	69	9	2	0	7

First Base	PCT	G	PO	A	E	DP
Hamme	.993	16	129	12	1	5
McDonald	.986	19	134	8	2	11
Pangilinan	.974	22	209	12	6	10
Vera	.984	21	181	8	3	18
Wilkins	.983	9	47	10	1	5

Second Base	PCT	G	PO	A	E	DP
McDonald	1.000	1	0	3	0	0
Tezak	.959	35	59	103	7	13
Vera	.667	1	0	2	1	0
Wilson	.966	47	75	126	7	22

Third Base	PCT	G	PO	A	E	DP
Cummings	1.000	2	2	0	0	0
McDonald	1.000	3	3	6	0	0
Silverio	.918	19	14	42	5	3
Vera	1.000	4	2	7	0	1
Wilkins	.942	43	24	89	7	11
Wilson	—	1	0	0	0	0

	PCT	G	PO	A	E	DP
Wilson	.952	11	3	17	1	1

Shortstop	PCT	G	PO	A	E	DP
Davis	.948	68	115	193	17	32
Wilson	.967	10	8	21	1	1

Outfield	PCT	G	PO	A	E	DP
Earley	.986	55	70	2	1	0
Hamme	1.000	19	18	2	0	0
Harvard	.983	58	112	4	2	1
Lee	.955	44	61	3	3	1
McDonald	—	2	0	0	0	0
Thorpe	.976	59	122	2	3	0

DSL WHITE SOX — ROOKIE
DOMINICAN SUMMER LEAGUE

Batting	B-T	HT	WT	DOB	AVG	vLH	vRH	G	AB	R	H	2B	3B	HR	RBI	BB	HBP	SH	SF	SO	SB	CS	SLG	OBP
Acuna, Hector	B-R	6-2	200	8-26-88	.204	.214	.196	43	137	18	28	6	0	3	21	11	4	0	3	31	3	1	.314	.277
Alcala, Julio	R-R	6-0	165	12-24-90	.261	.216	.280	64	203	37	53	15	1	0	30	33	5	1	0	24	6	0	.345	.378
Becerra, Ifran	L-R	5-10	155	6-13-91	.244	.192	.273	37	82	17	20	3	1	0	11	16	2	3	1	16	3	4	.305	.376
Buda, Maurizo	R-R	6-1	175	1-7-92	.159	.391	.101	43	113	15	18	5	0	0	5	17	4	0	0	34	0	4	.204	.291
Del Valle, Jaime	B-R	6-1	170	1-3-90	.246	.000	.289	43	114	17	28	3	3	0	14	25	5	4	0	11	4	5	.325	.403
Dorantes, Jose	B-R	5-11	180	10-5-92	.093	.091	.097	17	43	2	4	1	0	0	2	3	1	0	0	11	0	0	.116	.170
Fernandez, Andelson	R-R	6-2	170	2-22-91	.233	.238	.228	55	172	16	40	7	1	0	21	23	7	1	2	45	6	4	.285	.343
Garcia, Miguel	R-R	6-1	150	5-16-90	.159	.273	.100	31	44	4	7	0	0	0	1	5	1	1	0	12	0	1	.159	.260
Mercedes, Daurys	R-R	6-1	165	2-26-90	.256	.250	.257	39	129	30	33	3	2	0	7	30	4	2	1	40	5	5	.310	.409
Pascual, Oliver	R-R	5-10	170	11-13-89	.253	.308	.236	30	99	11	25	3	0	1	7	13	0	3	1	20	1	0	.343	.312
Polanco, Luis	R-R	6-3	190	9-30-91	.206	.188	.206	48	131	12	27	3	2	0	17	10	10	0	0	30	1	2	.260	.311
Puentes, Jerry	R-R	6-1	170	7-18-91	.330	.324	.329	56	188	31	62	6	1	0	22	18	3	2	2	31	8	8	.372	.393
Ramirez, Juan	R-R	6-4	196	8-28-90	.162	.222	.136	10	31	4	5	1	0	0	3	1	1	0	0	12	0	0	.290	.212
Sanchez, Carlos	R-R	5-11	165	6-29-92	.269	.242	.279	52	156	26	42	5	2	1	18	41	4	1	1	26	7	3	.346	.431
Trujillo, Rather	R-R	6-0	185	2-23-89	.264	.278	.260	58	159	27	42	12	3	0	14	26	5	0	1	14	6	4	.377	.382
Ubri, Carlos	R-R	5-11	175	11-28-91	.291	.231	.304	67	223	42	65	10	5	5	37	19	8	2	2	48	14	6	.448	.365
Yepez, Daniel	R-R	6-1	170	5-6-91	.230	.333	.209	44	139	14	32	7	1	0	13	17	4	2	1	43	3	3	.309	.287

Pitching	B-T	HT	WT	DOB	W	L	ERA	G	GS	CG	SV	IP	H	R	ER	HR	BB	SO	AVG	vLH	vRH	K/9	BB/9
Bautista, Jose	L-L	6-1	175	3-31-92	3	2	1.30	9	5	0	0	35	18	7	5	0	16	33	.154	.214	.146	8.57	4.15
Brito, Jose	R-R	6-0	175	10-10-90	3	1	5.35	11	8	0	0	37	33	24	22	0	29	28	.241	.333	.204	6.81	7.05
Cabrera, Raldy	R-R	6-0	180	9-25-89	1	2	5.40	18	1	0	2	20	18	13	12	0	25	16	.257	.231	.273	7.20	11.25
Calixto, Tiago	R-R	6-0	180	5-6-89	1	0	5.02	8	2	0	0	14	12	8	8	0	14	9	.261	.100	.306	5.65	8.79
Chevalier, Mariano	R-R	6-2	180	8-30-90	3	1	4.36	9	4	0	0	33	30	18	16	2	21	21	.248	.256	.244	5.73	5.73
Cueva, Jorge	R-R	6-3	205	3-24-89	2	4	3.86	22	0	0	3	35	37	21	15	0	16	36	.282	.255	.303	9.26	4.11

Duque, Jean	R-R	6-3	190	7-17-89	5	3	1.21	14	13	1	0	74	50	23	10	1	27	82	.192	.185	.196	9.93	3.27
Echezuria, Luis	R-R	6-0	179	5-10-91	1	0	6.26	18	0	0	0	23	23	18	16	0	21	21	.264	.233	.281	8.22	8.22
Jean, Dominque	R-R	6-2	170	11-24-88	2	1	1.88	20	0	0	4	38	28	14	8	2	24	30	.201	.155	.235	7.04	5.63
Leyer, Euclides	R-R	6-2	172	12-28-92	5	5	2.65	12	11	0	0	58	52	25	17	4	20	51	.254	.292	.236	7.96	3.12
Magallanes, Yensi	L-L	6-0	185	2-2-93	0	0	27.00	3	2	0	0	2	5	5	5	0	3	0	.556	.000	.556	0.00	16.20
Morillo, Scarly	R-R	6-1	175	6-17-89	1	5	4.46	17	1	0	0	34	34	22	17	0	25	34	.256	.245	.263	8.91	6.55
Nieves, Wilce	R-R	6-0	175	5-12-92	2	1	3.51	13	6	0	0	33	26	15	13	2	23	16	.226	.261	.203	4.32	6.21
Ortega, Yorvix	R-R	5-11	175	8-1-89	7	4	2.35	13	13	0	0	65	55	24	17	2	35	35	.255	.215	.285	4.85	4.85
Rosario, Carlos	L-L	5-10	160	3-13-88	3	0	1.52	16	0	0	5	30	20	9	5	0	7	26	.190	.211	.186	7.89	2.12

Fielding

Catcher	PCT	G	PO	A	E	DP	PB
Del Valle	.963	22	136	21	6	1	6
Dorantes	.981	16	85	18	2	1	3
Pascual	.970	26	165	29	6	3	5
Polanco	.500	1	1	0	1	0	1
Yepez	.982	15	98	14	2	0	4

First Base	PCT	G	PO	A	E	DP
Acuna	.968	23	167	15	6	16
Del Valle	1.000	6	44	6	0	3
Polanco	.992	31	240	11	2	20
Yepez	.978	18	122	10	3	16

Second Base	PCT	G	PO	A	E	DP
Becerra	.973	21	27	46	2	7
Garcia	1.000	2	1	1	0	0

	PCT	G	PO	A	E	DP
Mercedes	.949	27	60	69	7	15
Puentes	.988	27	44	40	1	8
Sanchez	1.000	4	3	6	0	2
Ubri	1.000	2	2	7	0	0

Third Base	PCT	G	PO	A	E	DP
Acuna	—	1	0	0	0	0
Garcia	.857	4	1	5	1	0
Polanco	.889	11	4	12	2	2
Puentes	.938	14	15	30	3	4
Sanchez	.943	46	46	87	8	8
Ubri	.556	4	1	4	4	0

Shortstop	PCT	G	PO	A	E	DP
Fernandez	.945	54	103	136	14	25
Mercedes	.920	12	18	28	4	7

	PCT	G	PO	A	E	DP
Puentes	.944	8	17	17	2	0
Sanchez	1.000	3	6	5	0	1

Outfield	PCT	G	PO	A	E	DP
Acuna	1.000	2	1	0	0	0
Alcala	.943	58	75	8	5	0
Becerra	—	1	0	0	0	0
Buda	.946	40	31	4	2	0
Del Valle	—	1	0	0	0	0
Garcia	1.000	20	10	0	0	0
Ramirez	1.000	10	6	3	0	1
Trujillo	.988	57	76	6	1	1
Ubri	.963	60	97	7	4	2

Cincinnati Reds

SEASON IN A SENTENCE: Cincinnati made the playoffs for the first time since 1995, winning the National League Central with outstanding defense (three Gold Glove winners) and an incredible offensive season from Joey Votto.

HIGH POINT: Outside of Jay Bruce's division-clinching walk-off home run in the bottom of the ninth inning against the Astros on Sept. 28, which returned the Reds to the playoffs, Votto's accomplishments highlighted the season. He was named the National League's winner of the Hank Aaron award, giving recognition to the most outstanding offensive performer, after he was originally left off the NL all-star roster. The first baseman finished at or near the top of just about every offensive category in the NL.

LOW POINT: There were 19 lead changes for the top two spots in the NL Central between the Reds and the Cardinals. The rivals met for a series at Great American Ball Park from Aug. 9-11 that began with some provocative comments about St. Louis from Brandon Phillips and resulted with a bench-clearing brawl. The series ended with an embarrassing sweep for the Reds, though they quickly bounced back from it. A Division Series sweep at the hands of the Phillies was a downer but did not take the shine off a strong season.

NOTABLE ROOKIES: Aroldis Chapman made his much-anticipated debut for the Reds in August, hitting the 103 mph mark in his first appearance. On Sept. 24 at San Diego, Chapman registered the fastest pitch ever recorded at 105.1 mph. Though he faded a bit in the second half of the season, 2009 first-round pick Mike Leake was a big factor in bolstering the Reds rotation. He was the first starting pitcher to go straight from the draft to the majors since Jim Abbott in 1989, and ended up with an 8-4, 3.78 mark. Chris Heisey also proved to be a useful option in the outfield, hitting eight home runs in 201 at-bats.

KEY TRANSACTIONS: The only trade the Reds made during the season was on Aug. 10 when they sent Chris Dickerson to Milwaukee for Jim Edmonds. Signing Chapman in January was the biggest move of the year.

DOWN ON THE FARM: The Reds had just two affiliates reach the playoffs, and their farm system has thinned with so many young players contributing in Cincinnati. Yonder Alonso made his major league debut as a September callup after hitting 15 home runs between Double-A and Triple-A.

OPENING DAY PAYROLL: $71.8 million (20th)

PLAYERS OF THE YEAR

RODGER WOOD

MAJOR LEAGUE

Joey Votto
1b
.324/.424/.600
Led NL in OBP, SLG
2nd in AVG

MINOR LEAGUE

Devin Mesoraco
c
(High A/AA/AAA)
.302/.377/.587
25 2B, 26 HR

ORGANIZATION LEADERS

BATTING		*Minimum 250 at-bats
MAJORS		
*AVG	Joey Votto	.324
*OPS	Joey Votto	1.024
HR	Joey Votto	37
RBI	Joey Votto	113
MINORS		
*AVG	Dave Sappelt, Lynch./Carolina/Louisville	.342
*OBP	Dave Sappelt, Lynch./Carolina/Louisville	.395
*SLG	Devin Mesoraco, Lynch./Carolina/Louisville	.587
R	Zack Cozart, Louisville	91
H	Dave Sappelt, Lynch./Carolina/Louisville	174
TB	Dave Sappelt, Lynch./Carolina/Louisville	258
2B	Cody Puckett, Lynchburg/Carolina	42
3B	Ronald Torreyes, VSL/AZL/Dayton	12
HR	Devin Mesoraco, Lynch./Carolina/Louisville	26
RBI	Henry Rodriguez, Dayton/Lynchburg	82
BB	Yonder Alonso, Carolina/Louisville	56
SO	Todd Frazier, Louisville	127
SB	Billy Hamilton, Billings	48

PITCHING		†Minimum 75 innings
MAJORS		
W	Bronson Arroyo	17
†ERA	Nick Masset	3.40
SO	Johnny Cueto	138
MINORS		
W	Matt Klinker, Carolina/Louisville	11
L	Curtis Partch, Carolina/Lynchburg	12
	Justin Walker, Dayton/Lynchburg	12
†ERA	Jordan Hotchkiss, Lynchburg/Carolina	2.43
G	Donnie Joseph, Dayton/Lynchburg/Carolina	57
GS	Matt Klinker, Carolina/Louisville	27
	Travis Webb, Lynchburg/Carolina	27
SV	Donnie Joseph, Dayton/Lynchburg/Carolina	24
IP	Matt Klinker, Carolina/Louisville	163.7
BB	Travis Webb, Lynchburg/Carolina	74
SO	Matt Klinker, Carolina/Louisville	138
†AVG	Jordan Hotchkiss, Lynchburg/Carolina	.216

2010 PERFORMANCE

General Manager: Walt Jocketty. **Farm Director:** Terry Reynolds. **Scouting Director:** Chris Buckley.

Class	Team	League	W	L	PCT	Finish*	Manager(s)
Majors	Cincinnati Reds	National	91	71	.562	t-3rd (16)	Dusty Baker
Triple-A	Louisville Bats	International	79	64	.552	3rd (14)	Rick Sweet
Double-A	Carolina Mudcats	Southern	58	79	.423	9th (10)	David Bell
High A	Lynchburg Hillcats	Carolina	61	77	.442	7th (8)	Pat Kelly
Low A	Dayton Dragons	Midwest	53	85	.384	15th (16)	Todd Benzinger
Rookie	Billings Mustangs	Pioneer	38	37	.507	5th (8)	Delino DeShields
Rookie	AZL Reds	Arizona	31	24	.564	t-3rd (12)	Julio Garcia
Overall 2010 Minor League Record			320	366	.466	26th (30)	

*Finish in overall standings (No. of teams in league). †League champion.

ORGANIZATION STATISTICS

CINCINNATI REDS

NATIONAL LEAGUE

Batting	B-T	HT	WT	DOB	AVG	vLH	vRH	G	AB	R	H	2B	3B	HR	RBI	BB	HBP	SH	SF	SO	SB	CS	SLG	OBP
Alonso, Yonder	L-R	6-2	210	4-8-87	.207	.111	.250	22	29	2	6	2	0	0	3	0	0	0	0	10	0	0	.276	.207
Bloomquist, Willie	R-R	5-11	195	11-27-77	.294	.100	.571	11	17	0	5	0	0	0	0	1	0	0	0	3	0	0	.294	.333
Bruce, Jay	L-L	6-3	225	4-3-87	.281	.277	.283	148	509	80	143	23	5	25	70	58	1	0	5	136	5	4	.493	.353
Cabrera, Orlando	R-R	5-10	195	11-2-74	.263	.326	.240	123	494	64	130	33	0	4	42	28	3	5	7	53	11	4	.354	.303
Cairo, Miguel	R-R	6-1	225	5-4-74	.290	.262	.304	91	200	30	58	12	0	4	28	17	4	2	3	30	4	0	.410	.353
Dickerson, Chris	L-L	6-3	230	4-10-82	.205	.000	.231	20	44	9	9	1	1	0	0	1	0	0	0	19	3	0	.273	.222
2-team total (25 Milwaukee)					.206	—	—	45	97	11	20	2	2	0	5	6	0	2	1	34	4	0	.268	.250
Edmonds, Jim	L-L	6-1	210	6-27-70	.207	.000	.231	13	29	6	6	2	0	3	3	3	0	0	0	7	0	0	.586	.281
2-team total (73 Milwaukee)					.276	—	—	86	246	44	68	23	0	11	23	24	1	0	1	60	2	0	.504	.342
Francisco, Juan	L-R	6-2	180	6-24-87	.273	.222	.283	36	55	3	15	3	0	1	7	4	0	0	0	20	0	1	.382	.322
Gomes, Jonny	R-R	6-1	225	11-22-80	.266	.285	.257	148	511	77	136	24	3	18	86	39	12	0	9	123	5	3	.431	.327
Hanigan, Ryan	R-R	6-0	200	8-16-80	.300	.291	.304	70	203	25	61	11	0	5	40	33	4	1	2	21	0	0	.429	.405
Heisey, Chris	R-R	6-0	215	12-14-84	.254	.169	.321	97	201	33	51	10	1	8	21	16	6	1	2	57	1	2	.433	.324
Hernandez, Ramon	R-R	6-0	225	5-20-76	.297	.303	.295	97	313	30	93	18	1	7	48	29	5	3	2	49	0	0	.428	.364
Janish, Paul	R-R	6-2	195	10-12-82	.260	.308	.237	82	200	23	52	10	0	5	25	22	2	3	1	30	1	3	.385	.338
Miller, Corky	R-R	6-1	245	3-18-76	.243	.179	.283	32	74	5	18	5	0	2	9	2	2	1	0	16	0	0	.392	.282
Nix, Laynce	L-L	6-1	220	10-30-80	.291	.313	.289	97	165	16	48	11	2	4	18	15	0	2	0	39	0	1	.455	.350
Phillips, Brandon	R-R	6-0	200	6-28-81	.275	.291	.268	155	626	100	172	33	5	18	59	46	8	6	1	83	16	12	.430	.332
Rolen, Scott	R-R	6-4	250	4-4-75	.285	.260	.295	133	471	66	134	34	3	20	83	50	8	0	8	82	1	2	.497	.358
Stubbs, Drew	R-R	6-4	205	10-4-84	.255	.240	.262	150	514	91	131	19	6	22	77	55	5	3	6	168	30	6	.444	.329
Sutton, Drew	B-R	6-3	200	6-30-83	.667	1.000	.500	2	3	1	2	0	0	0	1	4	0	0	0	1	0	0	1.667	.667
Valaika, Chris	R-R	6-0	215	8-14-85	.263	.400	.174	19	38	3	10	1	0	1	2	1	0	1	0	9	0	0	.368	.282
Votto, Joey	L-R	6-3	230	9-10-83	.324	.283	.347	150	547	106	177	36	2	37	113	91	7	0	3	125	16	5	.600	.424

Pitching	B-T	HT	WT	DOB	W	L	ERA	G	GS	CG	SV	IP	H	R	ER	HR	BB	SO	AVG	vLH	vRH	K/9	BB/9
Arroyo, Bronson	R-R	6-4	195	2-24-77	17	10	3.88	33	33	2	0	216	188	95	93	29	59	121	.234	.285	.185	5.05	2.46
Bailey, Homer	R-R	6-3	210	5-3-86	4	3	4.46	19	19	1	0	109	109	55	54	11	40	100	.260	.238	.272	8.26	3.30
Bray, Bill	L-L	6-3	220	6-5-83	0	2	4.13	35	0	0	0	28	21	13	13	4	10	30	.198	.106	.271	9.53	3.18
Burton, Jared	R-R	6-5	230	6-2-81	0	0	0.00	4	0	0	0	3	0	0	0	0	0	1	.000	.000	.000	2.70	0.00
Chapman, Aroldis	L-L	6-4	185	2-28-88	2	2	2.03	15	0	0	0	13	9	4	3	0	5	19	.196	.154	.212	12.83	3.38
Cordero, Francisco	R-R	6-5	235	5-11-75	6	5	3.84	75	0	0	40	72	68	32	31	5	36	59	.246	.274	.226	7.31	4.46
Cueto, Johnny	R-R	5-10	210	2-15-86	12	7	3.64	31	31	1	0	186	181	79	75	19	56	138	.257	.234	.276	6.69	2.71
Del Rosario, Enerio	R-R	6-2	165	10-16-85	1	1	2.08	9	0	0	0	9	13	4	2	0	4	3	.382	.385	.381	3.12	4.15
2-team total (2 Houston)					1	1	4.50	11	0	0	0	10	17	7	5	0	4	4	—	—	—	3.60	3.60
Fisher, Carlos	R-R	6-4	225	2-22-83	1	1	5.64	18	0	0	0	22	22	14	14	1	13	21	.256	.286	.235	8.46	5.24
Harang, Aaron	R-R	6-7	260	5-9-78	6	7	5.32	22	20	0	0	112	139	71	66	16	38	82	.305	.283	.323	6.61	3.06
Herrera, Daniel Ray	L-L	5-6	165	10-21-84	1	3	3.91	36	0	0	0	23	31	10	10	2	6	14	.323	.316	.328	5.48	2.35
Leake, Mike	R-R	6-1	190	11-12-87	8	4	4.23	24	22	0	0	138	158	77	65	19	49	91	.292	.292	.291	5.92	3.19
LeCure, Sam	R-R	6-1	205	5-4-84	2	5	4.50	15	6	0	0	48	50	24	24	6	25	37	.272	.304	.252	6.94	4.69
Lincoln, Mike	R-R	6-2	210	4-10-75	1	0	7.32	19	0	0	0	20	25	16	16	1	10	12	.309	.222	.352	5.49	4.58
Maloney, Matt	L-L	6-4	220	1-16-84	2	2	3.05	7	2	0	0	21	20	7	7	2	5	13	.256	.148	.314	5.66	2.18
Masset, Nick	R-R	6-4	235	5-17-82	4	4	3.40	82	0	0	2	77	64	31	29	7	33	85	.226	.196	.242	9.98	3.87
Ondrusek, Logan	R-R	6-8	225	2-13-85	5	0	3.68	60	0	0	0	59	49	25	24	7	20	39	.225	.205	.236	5.98	3.07
Owings, Micah	R-R	6-5	231	9-28-82	3	2	5.40	22	0	0	0	33	28	20	20	3	25	35	.230	.357	.163	9.45	6.75
Rhodes, Arthur	L-L	6-2	220	10-24-69	4	4	2.29	69	0	0	0	55	38	14	14	4	18	50	.196	.214	.182	8.18	2.95
Smith, Jordan	R-R	6-4	220	2-4-86	3	2	3.86	37	0	0	1	42	45	18	18	7	11	26	.273	.333	.241	5.57	2.36
Springer, Russ	R-R	6-4	225	11-7-68	0	0	5.40	2	0	0	0	2	2	1	1	0	0	1	.286	1.000	.167	5.40	0.00
Volquez, Edinson	R-R	6-0	210	7-3-83	4	3	4.31	12	12	0	0	63	59	30	30	6	35	67	.253	.229	.273	9.62	5.03
Wood, Travis	R-L	5-11	165	2-6-87	5	4	3.51	17	17	0	0	103	85	45	40	9	26	86	.222	.136	.240	7.54	2.28

Fielding

Catcher	PCT	G	PO	A	E	DP	PB
Hanigan	.991	68	436	21	4	4	2
Hernandez	.994	91	594	49	4	4	2
Miller	1.000	32	126	10	0	1	0

First Base	PCT	G	PO	A	E	DP
Alonso	.933	6	24	4	2	5

Cairo	.990	14	97	4	1	14
Edmonds	1.000	3	17	0	0	2
Hernandez	1.000	5	19	0	0	2
Votto	.996	148	1132	128	5	101

Second Base	PCT	G	PO	A	E	DP
Bloomquist	—	2	0	0	0	0
Cairo	1.000	6	3	8	0	1
Janish	1.000	7	7	0		1
Phillips	.996	152	281	419	3	95
Sutton	1.000	1	0	1	0	0
Valaika	1.000	13	19	24	0	7

Third Base	PCT	G	PO	A	E	DP
Cairo	.958	37	17	29	2	4
Francisco	.917	12	3	8	1	3
Janish	1.000	11	5	16	0	2
Rolen	.977	130	83	259	8	28
Sutton	—	1	0	0	0	0

Shortstop	PCT	G	PO	A	E	DP
Cabrera	.977	121	165	300	11	60
Cairo	—	1	0	0	0	0
Janish	.981	62	88	119	4	33
Sutton	1.000	1	0	1	0	0

Valaika	1.000	1	0	2	0	1

Outfield	PCT	G	PO	A	E	DP
Bloomquist	1.000	8	6	0	0	0
Bruce	.992	146	343	7	3	1
Cairo	1.000	1	1	0	0	0
Dickerson	1.000	13	20	0	0	0
Edmonds	1.000	7	8	0	0	0
Gomes	.981	129	197	6	4	1
Heisey	.982	77	106	2	2	0
Nix	1.000	55	61	3	0	2
Stubbs	.987	147	380	7	5	2

LOUISVILLE BATS

TRIPLE-A

INTERNATIONAL LEAGUE

Batting	B-T	HT	WT	DOB	AVG	vLH	vRH	G	AB	R	H	2B	3B	HR	RBI	BB	HBP	SH	SF	SO	SB	CS	SLG	OBP
Alonso, Yonder	L-R	6-2	210	4-8-87	.296	.269	.307	101	406	50	120	31	2	12	56	37	1	0	1	76	9	1	.470	.355
Anderson, Josh	L-R	6-2	195	8-10-82	.125	.000	.152	17	40	2	5	2	0	0	0	0	0	1	0	6	5	0	.175	.125
2-team total (19 Gwinnett)					.161	—	—	36	93	10	15	3	0	0	1	2	1	4	0	17	8	1	.194	.188
Balentien, Wladimir	R-R	6-2	220	7-2-84	.282	.360	.251	116	401	71	113	23	2	25	78	37	2	1	11	85	12	1	.536	.337
Burke, Chris	R-R	5-11	195	3-11-80	.238	.299	.211	66	248	38	59	6	4	5	26	26	5	2	3	39	14	4	.355	.319
Castillo, Wilkin	B-R	6-0	200	6-1-84	.256	.301	.242	92	317	45	81	16	3	9	35	12	2	6	0	50	11	3	.410	.287
Costanzo, Mike	L-R	6-3	215	9-9-83	.167	.500	.100	6	12	2	2	1	0	1	3	0	0	0	5	0	0	.250	.333
Cozart, Zack	R-R	6-0	195	8-12-85	.255	.258	.254	136	553	91	141	30	4	17	67	40	6	6	5	107	30	4	.416	.310
Denove, Chris	R-R	6-1	215	12-9-82	.262	.250	.265	33	107	16	28	3	0	1	9	11	3	1	0	20	1	0	.318	.347
Dickerson, Chris	L-L	6-3	230	4-10-82	.442	.300	.485	13	43	12	19	5	0	3	7	9	0	2	1	13	6	1	.767	.528
Dorn, Danny	L-L	6-2	205	7-20-84	.302	.259	.313	84	275	50	83	24	2	13	46	38	6	0	0	81	0	0	.545	.398
Eymann, Eric	R-R	6-2	191	2-9-84	.294	.333	.267	18	51	7	15	4	1	1	6	1	0	0	1	11	0	1	.471	.302
Francisco, Juan	L-R	6-2	180	6-24-87	.286	.215	.316	77	308	46	88	24	4	18	59	16	3	0	2	81	1	0	.565	.325
Frazier, Todd	R-R	6-3	220	2-12-86	.258	.277	.251	130	480	71	124	32	4	17	66	45	10	1	2	127	14	4	.448	.333
Griffin, Michael	R-R	5-9	200	10-1-83	.258	.235	.267	72	186	23	48	17	1	7	22	5	1	4	2	35	1	4	.473	.278
Hanigan, Ryan	R-R	6-0	200	8-16-80	.239	.133	.290	13	46	6	11	3	0	0	2	4	2	0	0	6	0	0	.304	.327
Heisey, Chris	R-R	6-0	215	12-14-84	.241	.188	.254	20	79	6	19	3	0	4	13	7	1	1	1	23	2	0	.430	.307
Henry, Sean	R-R	5-10	185	8-18-85	.500	.333	.600	4	8	3	4	1	0	0	3	0	0	0	0	0	0	0	.625	.500
Long, Jacob	R-R	6-1	180	4-17-86	.375	1.000	.167	7	8	1	3	0	0	0	1	0	0	0	1	0	0	0	.375	.444
Matthews Jr., Gary	B-R	6-3	225	8-25-74	.317	.407	.284	23	101	16	32	7	1	3	6	7	0	0	0	26	3	2	.495	.361
Mesoraco, Devin	R-R	6-1	220	6-19-88	.231	.200	.250	14	52	5	12	3	0	3	13	6	0	0	0	14	1	0	.462	.310
Miller, Corky	R-R	6-1	245	3-18-76	.276	.317	.264	54	181	29	50	13	0	6	35	19	5	3	1	31	0	1	.448	.359
Negron, Kris	R-R	6-0	180	2-1-86	.190	.000	.267	7	21	1	4	1	0	0	0	0	0	0	0	5	0	1	.238	.190
Sappelt, David	R-R	5-9	193	1-2-87	.324	.429	.274	25	108	12	35	8	3	1	8	6	1	0	0	14	1	4	.481	.365
Sutton, Drew	B-R	6-3	200	6-30-83	.262	.273	.259	84	263	35	69	16	1	3	27	43	3	5	5	71	5	3	.365	.366
2-team total (29 Columbus)					.273	—	—	113	359	45	98	24	1	5	42	61	4	8	6	92	9	3	.387	.379
Terrero, Luis	R-R	6-3	205	5-18-80	.302	.314	.295	30	96	15	29	6	0	8	25	2	1	0	0	26	2	1	.615	.323
Valaika, Chris	R-R	6-0	215	8-14-85	.304	.358	.286	118	424	49	129	28	2	4	53	19	2	4	10	72	3	3	.408	.330

Pitching	B-T	HT	WT	DOB	W	L	ERA	G	GS	CG	SV	IP	H	R	ER	HR	BB	SO	AVG	vLH	vRH	K/9	BB/9
Adkins, Jon	L-R	6-1	205	8-30-77	1	4	5.46	34	0	0	10	31	39	21	19	1	8	13	.307	.302	.311	3.73	2.30
2-team total (14 Charlotte)					2	6	4.92	48	1	0	10	53	68	35	29	3	17	19	—	—	—	3.23	2.89
Avery, James	R-R	6-0	209	6-10-84	0	0	4.50	1	1	0	0	6	7	3	3	1	0	4	.280	.364	.214	6.00	0.00
Baez, Federico	R-R	6-2	190	8-4-81	1	1	3.21	18	0	0	0	28	25	14	10	4	19	12	.238	.327	.161	3.86	6.11
Bailey, Homer	R-R	6-3	210	5-3-86	2	0	2.37	4	3	0	0	19	15	5	5	0	5	15	.221	.259	.195	7.11	2.37
Bray, Bill	L-L	6-3	220	6-5-83	0	0	0.00	6	0	0	1	6	2	0	0	0	1	5	.105	.000	.286	11.12	1.59
Burton, Jared	R-R	6-5	230	6-2-81	3	2	2.61	33	0	0	4	38	29	14	11	4	16	34	.204	.224	.187	8.05	3.79
Chapman, Aroldis	L-L	6-4	185	2-28-88	9	6	3.57	39	13	1	8	96	77	46	38	7	52	125	.218	.195	.230	11.76	4.89
Cochran, Tom	L-L	6-2	195	10-16-82	0	0	6.75	1	1	0	0	4	8	3	3	0	2	5	.400	.500	.333	11.25	4.50
Del Rosario, Enerio	R-R	6-2	165	10-16-85	4	4	3.09	50	0	0	4	64	61	22	22	7	17	34	.252	.248	.254	4.78	2.39
Delgado, Jesus	R-R	6-0	225	4-19-84	2	2	3.54	30	3	0	1	56	64	22	22	2	21	39	.292	.265	.314	6.27	3.38
Fisher, Carlos	R-R	6-4	225	2-22-83	1	1	2.23	30	0	0	4	36	23	10	9	4	8	38	.178	.259	.120	9.41	1.98
Gil, Jerry	R-R	6-3	200	10-14-82	2	0	5.87	7	0	0	0	8	9	6	5	0	6	4	.273	.118	.438	7.04	5.87
Harang, Aaron	R-R	6-7	260	5-9-78	0	2	9.00	2	2	0	0	11	14	11	11	1	2	10	.311	.370	.222	8.18	1.64
Herrera, Daniel Ray	L-L	5-6	165	10-21-84	2	2	4.30	26	1	0	5	38	31	18	18	2	5	34	.226	.197	.254	8.12	1.19
Horst, Jeremy	L-L	6-4	220	10-1-85	1	0	2.51	6	2	0	0	17	17	5	4	0	5	12	.309	.217	.375	7.53	3.14
Isringhausen, Jason	R-R	6-3	230	9-7-72	1	0	9.53	7	0	0	0	4	6	5	4	0	2	5	.316	.250	.100	7.94	11.12
Jukich, Ben	L-L	6-5	205	10-17-82	7	4	3.90	29	18	0	1	115	108	52	50	8	46	103	.249	.287	.226	8.04	3.59
Klinker, Matt	R-R	6-5	220	10-8-84	1	5	5.85	10	9	0	1	52	61	35	34	9	21	41	.300	.345	.241	7.05	3.61
Krebs, Joseph	L-L	6-0	200	9-14-84	0	0	0.61	11	0	0	0	15	5	1	1	0	7	8	.111	.043	.182	4.91	4.30
LeCure, Sam	R-R	6-1	205	5-4-84	3	7	3.67	15	15	1	0	98	98	40	40	8	23	87	.262	.285	.234	7.99	2.11
Lehr, Justin	R-R	6-2	204	8-3-77	1	3	6.57	7	7	0	0	37	59	29	27	2	12	15	.371	.373	.368	3.65	2.92
Maloney, Matt	L-L	6-4	220	1-16-84	10	7	3.34	24	23	0	0	135	132	65	50	9	28	104	.250	.250	.263	6.95	1.87
Ondrusek, Logan	R-R	6-8	225	2-13-85	0	1	4.12	14	0	0	1	20	21	9	9	0	3	14	.269	.231	.319	6.41	1.37
Owings, Micah	R-R	6-5	231	9-28-82	0	0	2.21	8	5	0	0	20	20	5	5	1	10	12	.270	.237	.306	5.75	4.43
Reineke, Chad	R-R	6-6	230	4-9-82	9	9	3.91	32	19	0	1	131	136	60	57	17	36	83	.271	.284	.257	5.69	2.47
Serrano, Mark	L-R	6-1	185	9-14-85	0	1	12.60	1	1	0	0	5	7	7	7	3	3	3	.350	.400	.200	5.40	5.40
Smith, Jordan	R-R	6-4	220	2-4-86	0	0	8.10	3	0	0	0	3	5	3	3	1	1	0	.333	.375	.286	0.00	2.70

					W	L	ERA	G	GS	CG	SV	IP	H	R	ER	HR	BB	SO	AVG	vLH	vRH	K/9	BB/9
Springer, Russ	R-R	6-4	225	11-7-68	0	0	0.00	7	0	0	0	6	2	0	0	0	2	5	.100	.000	.154	7.11	2.84
Tabor, Lee	L-L	6-2	175	12-17-84	1	1	4.26	8	0	0	0	13	13	6	6	1	5	13	.271	.333	.222	9.24	3.55
Valiquette, Philippe	L-L	6-1	205	2-14-87	2	1	4.29	29	0	0	1	36	34	19	17	2	14	31	.250	.217	.276	7.82	3.53
Viola, Pedro	L-L	6-1	185	6-29-83	0	0	0.00	1	0	0	0	1	0	0	0	0	0	1	.000	.000	.000	9.00	0.00
2-team total (11 Norfolk)					0	2	15.83	12	0	0	0	10	19	18	17	1	10	9	—	—	—	8.38	9.31
Volquez, Edinson	R-R	6-0	210	7-3-83	0	3	1.96	4	4	0	0	23	11	5	5	1	8	21	.143	.111	.171	8.22	3.13
Wood, Travis	R-L	5-11	165	2-6-87	5	6	3.06	16	16	0	0	100	86	40	34	9	24	99	.233	.197	.253	8.91	2.16

Fielding

Catcher	PCT	G	PO	A	E	DP	PB
Castillo	.987	45	361	25	5	3	4
Denove	.989	29	167	16	2	0	4
Hanigan	1.000	8	56	6	0	0	1
Long	1.000	2	2	0	0	0	0
Mesoraco	.991	13	103	10	1	0	0
Miller	1.000	51	365	38	0	3	6

First Base	PCT	G	PO	A	E	DP
Alonso	.997	82	707	56	2	82
Castillo	1.000	1	7	0	0	0
Dorn	.996	30	222	19	1	24
Eymann	1.000	1	1	0	0	0
Francisco	.967	3	27	2	1	1
Frazier	1.000	17	140	12	0	17
Sutton	1.000	19	151	17	0	18

Second Base	PCT	G	PO	A	E	DP
Burke	1.000	2	4	5	0	1
Castillo	.920	13	16	30	4	8

Eymann	1.000	2	0	3	0	0
Griffin	1.000	12	22	35	0	9
Negron	1.000	6	7	8	0	3
Sutton	1.000	20	25	36	0	5
Valaika	.984	104	173	269	7	61

Third Base	PCT	G	PO	A	E	DP
Castillo	.886	18	10	21	4	1
Costanzo	1.000	4	1	7	0	1
Eymann	1.000	12	12	24	0	2
Francisco	.927	62	42	98	11	5
Frazier	.968	35	28	64	3	8
Griffin	1.000	4	2	5	0	0
Sutton	.824	10	5	9	3	1
Valaika	.625	3	0	5	3	0

Shortstop	PCT	G	PO	A	E	DP
Cozart	.977	136	228	411	15	109
Negron	1.000	1	3	2	0	0
Sutton	1.000	1	0	2	0	1

Valaika	.951	9	14	25	2	6

Outfield	PCT	G	PO	A	E	DP
Alonso	1.000	17	22	2	0	0
Anderson	1.000	12	20	0	0	0
Balentien	.966	94	164	9	6	1
Burke	1.000	57	116	2	0	0
Castillo	1.000	4	1	0	0	0
Dickerson	.960	13	24	0	1	0
Dorn	.981	32	51	1	1	0
Francisco	.917	5	10	1	1	0
Frazier	.987	75	147	7	2	2
Griffin	.986	45	69	3	1	2
Heisey	.974	20	34	3	1	1
Henry	1.000	3	1	0	0	0
Matthews Jr.	.981	23	49	2	1	0
Sappelt	1.000	25	64	1	0	0
Sutton	1.000	25	31	1	0	0
Terrero	.971	19	29	5	1	1

CAROLINA MUDCATS   DOUBLE-A
SOUTHERN LEAGUE

Batting	B-T	HT	WT	DOB	AVG	vLH	vRH	G	AB	R	H	2B	3B	HR	RBI	BB	HBP	SH	SF	SO	SB	CS	SLG	OBP
Alonso, Yonder	L-R	6-2	210	4-8-87	.267	.273	.266	31	101	19	27	5	0	3	13	19	1	0	0	16	4	2	.406	.388
Carlson, Shane	R-R	6-0	185	4-7-87	.250	.500	.200	4	12	1	3	1	0	1	2	0	1	0	0	1	0	0	.583	.308
Castro, Jose	B-R	5-11	172	11-5-86	.235	.240	.234	113	357	24	84	13	0	0	32	14	7	11	4	39	1	0	.272	.275
Costanzo, Mike	L-R	6-3	215	9-9-83	.270	.253	.276	88	307	47	83	21	2	11	50	33	6	1	4	84	7	0	.459	.349
Danielson, Sean	B-R	5-8	165	8-6-82	.258	.289	.250	79	194	20	50	5	0	1	8	20	2	0	0	38	9	7	.299	.333
Day, Kyle	L-R	5-11	200	7-13-86	.333	.333	.333	4	9	1	3	2	0	0	2	4	0	0	0	2	0	0	.556	.538
Denove, Chris	R-R	6-1	215	12-9-82	.313	.318	.311	48	150	22	47	11	0	4	26	16	1	0	0	24	3	0	.467	.383
Eymann, Eric	R-R	6-2	191	2-9-84	.259	.253	.261	90	328	37	85	18	2	5	38	21	2	1	4	56	7	3	.372	.304
Griffin, Michael	R-R	5-9	200	10-1-83	.250	.111	.324	18	52	3	13	4	0	1	9	2	0	1	2	7	0	0	.385	.268
Henry, Sean	R-R	5-10	180	8-18-85	.298	.291	.305	121	406	50	121	23	3	5	56	27	8	4	1	64	15	8	.406	.353
Kahaulelio, Jake	R-R	5-10	182	6-7-85	.257	.296	.245	113	408	61	105	26	1	13	52	43	7	4	1	77	5	3	.422	.338
Kainer, Carson	R-R	6-1	210	10-27-84	.000	.000	.000	1	4	0	0	0	0	0	0	0	0	0	0	1	0	0	.000	.000
McMurray, Chris	R-R	6-1	195	10-12-86	.241	.222	.246	30	83	9	20	5	0	1	8	1	0	3	0	24	0	0	.337	.276
Mendez, Carlos	R-R	6-0	195	9-15-86	.231	.385	.192	42	130	16	30	4	1	0	6	4	0	0	0	19	0	1	.277	.281
Mesoraco, Devin	R-R	6-1	220	6-19-88	.294	.365	.267	56	187	42	55	11	3	13	31	18	4	0	3	37	1	0	.594	.363
Negron, Kris	R-R	6-0	180	2-1-86	.272	.301	.263	120	470	79	128	19	6	11	41	51	16	7	3	97	34	9	.409	.361
Parker, Logan	L-L	6-3	215	7-18-84	.111	.000	.111	5	18	1	2	0	0	0	1	0	0	1	1	4	2	0	.111	.105
Perez, Felix	L-L	6-2	190	11-14-84	.266	.242	.274	35	139	11	37	5	1	2	11	5	7	1	0	31	8	4	.360	.325
Phipps, Denis	R-R	6-2	177	7-22-85	.228	.212	.233	104	372	44	85	22	3	4	35	32	4	1	2	86	8	9	.336	.295
Puckett, Cody	R-R	5-10	175	4-3-87	.500	.750	.375	4	12	3	6	2	0	0	1	0	0	0	0	1	1	0	.667	.500
Rojas, Miguel	R-R	5-9	175	2-24-89	.222	.167	.238	7	27	1	6	0	0	0	4	2	0	0	0	4	1	1	.222	.276
Sappelt, David	R-R	5-9	193	1-2-87	.361	.425	.337	89	330	53	119	19	8	9	62	31	3	4	4	46	15	13	.548	.416
Terrero, Luis	R-R	6-3	205	5-18-80	.270	.324	.250	46	141	22	38	13	0	4	23	17	3	1	4	40	6	0	.447	.352
Yarbrough, Brandon	L-R	6-2	180	11-9-84	.253	.045	.275	82	233	24	59	15	0	3	22	20	0	1	3	84	1	3	.356	.309

Pitching	B-T	HT	WT	DOB	W	L	ERA	G	GS	CG	SV	IP	H	R	ER	HR	BB	SO	AVG	vLH	vRH	K/9	BB/9
Avery, James	R-R	6-0	209	6-10-84	2	3	5.63	7	7	0	0	40	52	26	25	7	16	21	.321	.325	.317	4.72	3.60
Baez, Federico	R-R	6-2	190	8-4-81	0	1	2.86	20	0	0	5	28	25	9	9	0	19	25	.245	.233	.254	6.04	2.86
Boxberger, Brad	R-R	6-2	200	5-27-88	1	4	8.49	22	0	0	0	30	35	28	28	4	22	40	.289	.279	.302	12.13	6.67
Buck, Dallas	R-R	6-2	195	11-11-84	3	4	6.41	9	9	0	0	39	56	30	28	3	14	21	.339	.354	.325	4.81	3.20
Carroll, Scott	R-R	6-5	210	9-24-84	3	9	3.68	20	20	2	0	117	120	58	48	6	30	66	.268	.249	.288	5.06	2.30
Christiani, Nick	R-R	5-10	180	7-17-87	0	0	4.50	2	0	0	0	2	4	1	1	0	0	1	.500	.667	.400	4.50	0.00
Cochran, Tom	L-L	6-2	195	10-16-82	8	5	2.69	25	25	0	0	137	117	52	41	11	53	99	.237	.266	.228	6.50	3.48
De La Vara, Gilbert	L-L	5-10	190	10-4-84	0	0	14.40	4	0	0	0	5	10	8	8	1	3	5	.417	.417	.417	9.00	5.40
Delgado, Jesus	R-R	6-0	225	4-19-84	1	0	5.19	6	0	0	0	9	10	5	5	1	4	5	.303	.313	.294	5.19	4.15
Fairel, Matt	L-L	6-3	203	7-8-87	5	3	3.98	10	10	1	0	61	51	30	27	11	24	44	.228	.167	.250	6.49	3.54
Freeman, Justin	R-R	6-1	170	10-22-86	0	0	2.45	9	0	0	0	11	8	3	3	0	2	5	.205	.238	.167	4.09	1.64
Gil, Jerry	R-R	6-3	200	10-14-82	3	1	4.66	40	0	0	7	56	54	29	29	4	53	46	.263	.235	.283	7.39	8.52
Harang, Daryl	L-L	6-2	225	11-19-82	1	2	7.36	14	0	0	0	26	27	23	21	3	13	9	.270	.111	.329	3.16	4.56
Horst, Jeremy	L-L	6-4	220	10-1-85	3	2	2.09	27	0	0	0	43	35	13	10	1	9	46	.217	.304	.183	9.63	1.88
Hotchkiss, Jordan	R-R	6-4	220	4-6-87	0	1	3.38	3	3	0	0	16	15	11	6	3	6	11	.250	.220	.316	6.19	3.38
Joseph, Donnie	L-L	6-3	180	11-1-87	1	0	5.14	7	0	0	1	7	7	6	4	0	2	7	.250	.333	.188	9.00	2.57
Klinker, Matt	R-R	6-5	220	10-8-84	7	6	2.83	18	18	0	0	111	97	43	35	9	24	97	.233	.274	.198	7.84	1.94

	B-T	HT	WT	DOB	W	L	ERA	G	GS	CG	SV	IP	H	R	ER	HR	BB	SO	AVG	vLH	vRH	K/9	BB/9
Krebs, Joseph	L-L	6-0	200	9-14-84	3	2	4.29	43	0	0	1	57	60	27	27	2	23	51	.283	.264	.293	8.10	3.65
Medina, Ruben	R-R	5-11	157	7-29-86	4	2	2.87	45	0	0	2	69	60	26	22	3	41	38	.244	.265	.229	4.96	5.35
Partch, Curtis	R-R	6-5	200	2-13-87	0	1	21.00	1	1	0	0	3	7	7	7	2	2	1	.467	.000	.538	3.00	6.00
Smit, Alexander	L-L	6-3	215	10-2-85	1	5	9.14	10	9	0	0	43	55	45	44	6	29	39	.311	.263	.324	8.10	6.02
Smith, Jordan	R-R	6-4	220	2-4-86	1	3	5.08	27	0	0	9	28	38	20	16	3	8	14	.319	.302	.333	4.45	2.54
Tabor, Lee	L-L	6-2	175	12-17-84	3	3	4.88	33	0	0	1	55	62	36	30	4	22	51	.295	.253	.319	8.30	3.58
Thompson, Daryl	R-R	6-0	185	11-2-85	0	5	3.71	12	12	0	0	51	38	25	21	3	11	52	.211	.221	.200	9.18	1.94
Valiquette, Philippe	L-L	6-1	205	2-14-87	2	0	3.99	25	0	0	4	29	34	14	13	0	16	21	.309	.167	.378	6.44	4.91
Watson, Sean	R-R	6-2	215	7-24-85	0	1	14.54	9	0	0	0	9	17	16	14	1	9	9	.425	.313	.500	9.35	9.35
Webb, Travis	R-R	6-5	205	8-2-84	6	10	4.93	23	23	0	0	119	126	65	65	14	63	94	.281	.234	.299	7.13	4.78
Woody, Abe	R-R	5-11	200	11-9-82	0	1	10.38	3	0	0	0	4	6	5	5	0	0	3	.316	.364	.250	6.23	0.00
2-team total (19 Mobile)					4	3	4.65	22	0	0	5	31	40	18	16	2	6	17	—	—	—	4.94	1.74

Fielding

Catcher

	PCT	G	PO	A	E	DP	PB
Denove	.993	37	267	28	2	2	3
McMurray	1.000	26	152	20	0	4	1
Mesoraco	.978	49	323	35	8	1	6
Yarbrough	.982	32	200	15	4	0	5

First Base

	PCT	G	PO	A	E	DP
Alonso	.991	14	100	6	1	12
Costanzo	.986	34	257	17	4	32
Denove	—	1	0	0	0	0
Eymann	.993	63	528	43	4	49
Kahaulelio	1.000	2	17	3	0	2
Mendez	.982	31	262	17	5	24
Parker	1.000	4	30	1	0	1

Second Base

	PCT	G	PO	A	E	DP
Castro	.987	53	101	129	3	33
Eymann	.964	5	10	17	1	3
Griffin	1.000	4	6	7	0	1
Henry	—	1	0	0	0	0
Kahaulelio	.981	87	185	239	8	61
Puckett	.933	4	4	10	1	3

Third Base

	PCT	G	PO	A	E	DP
Carlson	.667	3	2	2	2	0
Castro	.933	45	22	89	8	17
Costanzo	.933	56	39	100	10	9
Eymann	1.000	22	17	36	0	9
Griffin	.875	5	1	6	1	0
Kahaulelio	.918	26	15	52	6	4
Mendez	1.000	4	1	5	0	2

Shortstop

	PCT	G	PO	A	E	DP
Carlson	1.000	1	0	1	0	0
Castro	.958	14	15	31	2	7
Eymann	1.000	2	0	4	0	0
Negron	.965	120	185	346	19	66
Rojas	.976	7	16	24	1	6

Outfield

	PCT	G	PO	A	E	DP
Alonso	.952	13	18	2	1	0
Danielson	.974	48	68	7	2	1
Day	1.000	3	4	0	0	0
Griffin	1.000	8	16	1	0	0
Henry	.973	96	167	16	5	0
Kainer	1.000	1	2	0	0	0
Mendez	—	1	0	0	0	0
Perez	.989	33	82	4	1	1
Phipps	.949	99	179	9	10	1
Sappelt	.995	86	205	10	1	3
Terrero	.907	32	38	1	4	1
Yarbrough	.900	22	26	1	3	1

LYNCHBURG HILLCATS   HIGH CLASS A

CAROLINA LEAGUE

Batting	B-T	HT	WT	DOB	AVG	vLH	vRH	G	AB	R	H	2B	3B	HR	RBI	BB	HBP	SH	SF	SO	SB	CS	SLG	OBP
Buchholz, Alex	R-R	6-0	182	9-30-87	.271	.195	.307	65	240	19	65	17	0	6	36	18	4	2	3	32	6	4	.417	.328
Carlson, Shane	R-R	6-0	185	4-7-87	.286	.303	.272	42	147	20	42	11	0	3	17	5	4	1	1	27	2	0	.422	.325
Coddington, Kevin	R-R	6-4	205	7-21-87	.240	.200	.256	62	221	12	53	10	1	0	12	16	4	1	0	41	0	4	.294	.303
Contreras, Efrain	R-R	6-1	165	2-6-87	.199	.255	.172	62	171	16	34	8	0	4	17	15	2	4	1	51	3	2	.316	.270
Day, Kyle	L-R	5-11	200	7-13-86	.276	.203	.296	95	322	38	89	24	2	7	45	33	3	2	1	85	5	3	.429	.348
Feiner, Kevyn	R-R	6-1	170	6-11-87	.222	.286	.164	38	117	9	26	1	0	2	10	5	2	2	3	31	4	2	.282	.262
Fellhauer, Josh	L-L	5-11	180	3-24-88	.240	.223	.249	129	496	50	119	25	1	6	42	36	6	9	4	82	8	7	.331	.297
Greene, Brodie	R-R	6-1	195	9-25-87	.269	.256	.275	70	264	38	71	11	1	1	20	22	3	3	5	50	8	3	.330	.327
Gregorius, Didi	L-R	6-1	175	2-18-90	.240	.125	.294	7	25	4	6	0	0	0	2	1	1	0	6	0	0	.240	.321
Gualdron, Jose	R-R	5-11	185	7-18-87	.254	.123	.293	81	280	25	71	16	0	2	19	9	2	4	0	49	3	4	.332	.282
LaMarre, Ryan	R-L	6-2	185	11-21-88	.222	.375	.158	8	27	2	6	2	0	1	3	2	0	0	0	4	1	1	.407	.276
McMurray, Chris	R-R	6-1	195	10-14-86	.188	.286	.111	10	32	6	6	2	0	0	1	2	1	0	0	8	0	1	.250	.257
Means, Andrew	R-R	6-1	215	9-11-86	.667	.667	.000	1	3	3	2	1	0	0	0	0	0	0	0	1	1	0	1.000	.667
Mendez, Carlos	R-R	6-0	195	9-15-86	.295	.337	.276	72	288	35	85	21	0	0	23	12	1	0	1	29	2	2	.368	.325
Mesoraco, Devin	R-R	6-1	220	6-19-88	.335	.271	.364	43	158	24	53	11	2	10	31	19	3	0	1	29	2	2	.620	.414
Perez, Felix	L-L	6-2	190	11-14-84	.338	.333	.341	16	65	8	22	4	2	0	9	4	3	0	1	10	1	1	.462	.397
Phipps, Denis	R-R	6-2	177	7-22-85	.333	.333	.333	25	93	23	31	10	1	8	21	10	0	0	0	19	9	1	.720	.398
Puckett, Cody	R-R	5-10	175	4-3-87	.277	.329	.255	125	473	72	131	40	4	18	54	45	11	8	5	124	17	4	.493	.350
Reed, Justin	L-R	5-11	185	11-29-87	.158	.083	.192	25	76	9	12	3	0	2	5	9	1	0	0	33	3	3	.276	.256
Richburg, Chris	R-R	6-2	210	12-29-85	.291	.400	.245	37	134	20	39	10	1	5	26	6	4	0	3	39	0	0	.493	.333
Rodriguez, Henry	B-R	5-10	150	2-9-90	.250	.200	.286	6	24	2	6	0	0	0	4	0	0	0	0	5	0	0	.250	.250
Rojas, Miguel	R-R	5-9	175	2-24-89	.230	.266	.212	74	244	28	56	3	2	1	14	11	3	0	3	38	12	4	.270	.271
Sappelt, David	R-R	5-9	193	1-2-87	.282	.333	.255	19	71	7	20	5	0	4	5	1	0	0	6	15	6	4	.352	.338
Satterwhite, Cameron	R-R	6-2	185	12-13-86	.250	.200	.286	3	12	0	3	1	0	0	1	0	0	0	0	5	0	0	.333	.250
Soto, Neftali	R-R	6-2	180	2-28-89	.268	.247	.277	134	522	73	140	33	2	21	73	32	8	0	3	105	0	0	.460	.319
Wideman, Jordan	R-R	5-11	200	3-14-89	.210	.171	.229	33	105	10	22	5	0	0	6	6	2	2	1	20	0	0	.257	.263
Wiley, Byron	L-L	6-1	200	12-12-86	.205	.167	.219	13	44	3	9	0	0	1	2	5	0	0	0	20	0	0	.273	.286

Pitching	B-T	HT	WT	DOB	W	L	ERA	G	GS	CG	SV	IP	H	R	ER	HR	BB	SO	AVG	vLH	vRH	K/9	BB/9
Avery, James	R-R	6-0	209	6-10-84	6	3	3.31	12	12	0	0	65	58	31	24	3	20	42	.241	.267	.215	5.79	2.76
Bowman, Drew	R-L	6-4	190	11-8-85	1	3	5.16	45	0	0	0	66	64	40	38	2	46	51	.259	.301	.234	6.92	6.24
Boxberger, Brad	R-R	6-2	200	5-27-88	4	6	3.19	14	13	0	0	62	57	30	22	3	20	70	.249	.312	.173	10.16	2.90
Bray, Bill	L-L	6-3	220	6-5-83	0	0	0.00	4	0	0	0	5	1	0	0	0	2	9	.063	.167	.000	17.36	3.86
Carroll, Scott	R-R	6-5	210	9-24-84	1	2	2.10	5	4	0	0	30	24	8	7	4	7	13	.220	.246	.192	3.90	2.10
Carson, Blair	R-R	6-2	200	10-3-87	1	0	2.41	9	1	0	0	19	18	5	5	2	7	12	.257	.303	.216	5.79	3.38
Christiani, Nick	R-R	5-10	180	7-17-87	1	3	3.44	38	0	0	4	52	56	25	20	6	11	37	.276	.295	.261	6.36	1.89
Fairel, Matt	L-L	6-3	203	7-8-87	5	1	3.04	10	10	0	0	56	44	23	19	4	13	36	.216	.172	.233	5.75	2.08
Freeman, Justin	R-R	6-1	170	10-22-86	1	2	2.91	45	0	0	7	56	49	19	18	4	7	53	.232	.281	.191	8.57	1.13
Gaffney, Scott	R-R	6-3	190	3-13-86	0	1	12.38	8	0	0	0	8	10	11	11	1	7	4	.303	.235	.375	4.50	7.88

Name	T	HT	WT	DOB	W	L	ERA	G	GS	CG	SV	IP	H	R	ER	HR	BB	SO	AVG	vLH	vRH	K/9	BB/9
Gonzalez, Aguido	L-L	5-10	185	9-19-86	0	1	40.50	2	0	0	0	1	6	6	6	0	1	0	.600	.600	.600	0.00	6.75
Guerrero, Daniel	R-R	6-1	190	7-21-85	2	2	4.46	15	2	0	0	36	34	20	18	3	6	29	.248	.255	.244	7.18	1.49
Harang, Daryl	L-L	6-2	225	11-19-82	0	1	12.46	5	0	0	0	9	19	15	12	4	3	4	.442	.467	.429	4.15	3.12
Horst, Jeremy	L-L	6-4	220	10-1-85	0	2	4.30	11	0	0	0	15	17	8	7	1	4	17	.283	.381	.231	10.43	2.45
Hotchkiss, Jordan	R-R	6-4	220	4-3-86	10	4	2.30	31	15	0	0	114	86	33	29	9	31	90	.211	.183	.235	7.13	2.45
Infante, Ezequiel	L-L	5-10	185	8-31-88	0	1	5.09	8	1	0	0	18	23	11	10	3	5	13	.324	.263	.346	6.62	2.55
Janke, Lance	R-R	6-2	190	10-8-86	3	9	6.44	24	12	0	0	88	105	71	63	11	26	53	.300	.272	.331	5.42	2.66
Jeffords, Jeff	R-R	6-0	205	11-4-84	3	1	3.84	39	0	0	0	59	52	27	25	1	22	59	.236	.275	.203	9.05	3.38
Joseph, Donnie	L-L	6-3	180	11-1-87	0	4	2.31	31	0	0	17	35	23	11	9	2	16	56	.181	.256	.143	14.40	4.11
Medina, Ruben	R-R	5-11	157	7-29-86	1	0	6.14	5	0	0	0	7	8	5	5	1	0	8	.286	.250	.313	9.82	0.00
Partch, Curtis	R-R	6-5	200	2-13-87	7	11	4.98	28	24	0	0	132	165	93	73	11	45	96	.308	.346	.271	6.55	3.07
Ravin, Josh	R-R	6-4	220	1-21-88	2	1	2.08	5	5	0	0	26	19	9	6	2	12	25	.198	.190	.204	8.65	4.15
Salinas, Doug	R-R	6-4	195	12-5-88	0	1	5.40	4	0	0	0	5	4	4	3	0	1	3	.222	.143	.273	5.40	1.80
Serrano, Mark	L-R	6-1	185	9-14-85	3	6	4.54	15	15	0	0	77	83	48	39	9	20	72	.281	.275	.288	8.38	2.33
Thurman, Mace	L-L	6-1	180	4-5-87	0	0	6.35	5	0	0	3	6	7	4	4	0	5	5	.304	.400	.231	7.94	7.94
Villarreal, Pedro	R-R	6-1	215	12-9-87	0	3	6.86	6	5	0	0	26	26	17	15	3	8	16	.321	.361	.289	7.32	3.66
Volquez, Edinson	R-R	6-0	210	7-3-83	1	0	0.00	2	2	0	0	8	3	0	0	0		7	.111	.214	.000	7.88	0.00
Walker, Justin	L-L	6-5	200	11-3-86	4	2	6.59	6	6	0	0	27	37	20	20	7	3	28	.314	.167	.351	9.22	0.99
Ware, Chase	R-R	6-6	200	7-16-87	1	3	4.25	18	7	0	0	49	48	26	23	2	20	33	.258	.262	.255	6.10	3.70
Watson, Sean	R-R	6-2	215	7-24-85	2	3	3.70	19	0	0	0	24	25	15	10	2	11	22	.266	.244	.286	8.14	4.07
Webb, Travis	L-L	6-4	205	8-2-84	0	1	2.79	4	4	0	0	19	18	7	6	2	11	19	.243	.407	.149	8.84	5.12
Woody, Abe	R-R	5-11	200	11-9-82	2	0	2.08	4	0	0	0	4	5	1	1	0	4	4	.294	.250	.333	8.31	8.31

Fielding

Catcher	PCT	G	PO	A	E	DP	PB
Coddington	.982	58	448	33	9	1	3
McMurray	.961	9	68	5	3	1	0
Mesoraco	.991	31	199	20	2	3	7
Soto	.971	10	60	6	2	2	2
Wideman	.989	32	227	34	3	2	2

First Base	PCT	G	PO	A	E	DP
Gualdron	1.000	1	5	0	0	0
Mendez	.987	41	368	24	5	33
Richburg	1.000	8	70	3	0	8
Soto	.991	91	765	51	7	71

Second Base	PCT	G	PO	A	E	DP
Buchholz	1.000	11	14	37	0	8
Carlson	.974	7	22	16	1	6
Greene	1.000	8	15	27	0	9
Gualdron	.940	20	30	48	5	11

(Second Base cont.)	PCT	G	PO	A	E	DP
Puckett	.975	89	172	259	11	52
Rodriguez	.900	4	8	10	2	1

Third Base	PCT	G	PO	A	E	DP
Buchholz	.927	46	31	96	10	6
Carlson	.905	23	14	53	7	10
Gualdron	.939	40	28	79	7	5
Mendez	.917	23	9	46	5	4
Rodriguez	—	1	0	0	0	0
Soto	.889	7	6	10	2	1

Shortstop	PCT	G	PO	A	E	DP
Buchholz	.974	7	12	25	1	2
Carlson	.931	7	12	15	2	4
Greene	.940	46	71	116	12	21
Gregorius	.971	7	12	21	1	7
Rojas	.958	72	129	237	16	43

Outfield	PCT	G	PO	A	E	DP
Carlson	1.000	1	1	0	0	0
Contreras	.971	60	96	3	3	0
Day	.973	67	103	5	3	2
Feiner	1.000	36	66	2	0	1
Fellhauer	.965	128	207	13	8	3
Greene	.957	12	22	0	1	0
LaMarre	1.000	8	19	1	0	0
Means	—	1	0	0	0	0
Perez	1.000	16	37	0	0	0
Phipps	1.000	24	56	4	0	2
Puckett	1.000	32	49	6	0	0
Reed	.976	25	38	3	1	0
Rojas	—	1	0	0	0	0
Sappelt	.974	19	36	2	1	1
Wiley	.909	9	10	0	1	0

DAYTON DRAGONS   LOW CLASS A

MIDWEST LEAGUE

Batting	B-T	HT	WT	DOB	AVG	vLH	vRH	G	AB	R	H	2B	3B	HR	RBI	BB	HBP	SH	SF	SO	SB	CS	SLG	OBP
Cabrera, Orlando	R-R	5-10	195	11-2-74	.000	.000	.000	1	3	0	0	0	0	0	0	0	0	0	0	0	0	0	.000	.000
Carlson, Shane	R-R	6-0	185	4-7-87	.275	.232	.302	38	142	20	39	9	2	1	25	9	1	0	3	11	3	1	.387	.316
Coddington, Kevin	R-R	6-4	205	7-21-87	.239	.400	.167	31	113	12	27	2	1	3	10	8	2	2	1	16	2	4	.354	.298
Conner, Sean	L-R	6-2	196	7-28-87	.167	.000	.167	2	6	0	1	0	1	0	2	0	0	0	0	3	0	0	.500	.167
Contreras, Efrain	R-R	6-1	165	2-6-87	.203	.115	.245	24	79	10	16	1	0	0	6	5	1	4	2	17	1	0	.215	.253
D'Anna, Dominic	L-R	6-1	215	12-23-88	.155	.182	.149	17	58	6	9	3	0	0	7	7	1	0	2	15	0	0	.207	.250
Diaz, Samuel	B-R	5-11	170	2-28-91	.118	.333	.071	6	17	0	2	1	0	0	1	1	0	0	0	5	0	0	.176	.211
Feiner, Kevyn	R-R	6-1	170	6-11-87	.200	.241	.176	50	160	16	32	4	1	3	17	6	4	3	2	41	1	3	.294	.244
Fleury, Mark	L-R	6-0	189	5-4-88	.255	.215	.266	104	365	50	93	26	3	11	48	50	7	1	4	95	4	1	.433	.352
Garton, Josh	L-R	6-2	215	4-27-88	.243	.214	.251	89	313	44	76	20	3	10	37	27	5	2	3	104	6	3	.422	.310
Gregorius, Didi	L-R	6-1	175	2-18-90	.273	.190	.299	120	501	65	137	16	11	5	41	33	7	6	1	62	16	7	.379	.327
Kaskow, Jonathan	B-R	6-4	220	10-6-88	.079	.000	.107	10	38	4	3	0	0	1	3	1	3	0	0	14	0	0	.158	.167
LaMarre, Ryan	R-L	6-2	185	11-21-88	.282	.269	.286	60	227	44	64	11	0	5	29	21	12	1	2	53	18	7	.396	.370
Means, Andrew	R-R	6-1	215	9-11-86	.253	.242	.256	74	312	33	79	11	1	2	22	10	6	3	2	74	21	4	.314	.288
Nurre, Tommy	R-R	6-3	235	2-11-87	.223	.180	.239	59	224	21	50	9	0	4	27	9	6	0	2	50	4	0	.317	.270
Oliveras, Alex	L-R	6-0	180	3-29-89	.233	.226	.235	90	317	34	74	15	3	5	29	12	1	3	1	103	11	5	.347	.263
Pfister, Frank	R-R	6-1	205	8-25-86	.266	.336	.239	119	440	41	117	26	1	8	50	11	12	5	3	68	5	4	.384	.300
Reed, Justin	L-R	5-11	185	11-29-87	.247	.148	.293	21	85	14	21	2	3	2	8	7	0	3	0	24	0	0	.412	.304
Richburg, Chris	R-R	6-2	210	12-29-85	.251	.286	.240	72	271	37	68	17	1	14	51	19	12	0	6	61	2	0	.476	.328
Rodriguez, Cristobal	R-R	5-11	165	11-1-89	.111	.000	.111	3	9	0	1	0	0	0	1	0	0	0	0	4	0	0	.111	.100
Rodriguez, Henry	B-R	5-10	150	2-9-90	.307	.270	.321	124	514	76	158	37	3	14	78	22	4	1	6	70	33	13	.473	.337
Satterwhite, Cameron	R-R	6-0	185	12-13-86	.253	.260	.250	77	285	38	72	19	1	8	43	24	3	0	5	82	6	4	.411	.312
Torreyes, Ronald	R-R	5-10	150	9-2-92	.240	.250	.235	6	25	3	6	1	0	0	2	0	0	0	0	3	0	0	.400	.240
Vidal, David	R-R	5-11	185	10-23-89	.154	.000	.222	4	13	2	2	1	0	0	2	2	1	0	0	4	0	0	.231	.313
Weems, Chase	L-R	6-2	189	1-17-89	.220	.242	.213	43	141	17	31	5	0	0	5	17	1	0	0	44	0	0	.255	.308
Wideman, Jordan	R-R	5-11	200	3-14-89	.176	.000	.231	14	34	7	6	1	0	1	2	5	4	0	0	2	0	0	.294	.349
Wiley, Byron	L-L	6-1	200	12-12-86	.209	.313	.176	19	67	11	14	2	0	4	9	15	2	1	0	22	2	0	.418	.369

Pitching	B-T	HT	WT	DOB	W	L	ERA	G	GS	CG	SV	IP	H	R	ER	HR	BB	SO	AVG	vLH	vRH	K/9	BB/9
Arico, Kevin	R-R	6-5	195	8-30-88	0	3	6.43	15	0	0	2	21	35	20	15	2	7	9	.376	.500	.265	3.86	3.00
Bailey, Homer	R-R	6-3	210	5-3-86	0	1	6.75	1	1	0	0	4	4	3	3	0	1	5	.250	.400	.182	11.25	2.25
Bowen, Ricky	R-R	6-3	178	8-6-87	5	8	5.38	19	15	0	0	82	106	55	49	11	21	68	.316	.272	.343	7.46	2.30
Braun, Jason	R-R	6-5	190	11-24-86	2	2	5.26	35	0	0	0	53	54	38	31	4	28	48	.263	.322	.217	8.15	4.75
Carson, Blair	R-R	6-2	200	10-3-87	3	5	3.78	27	4	0	0	64	68	32	27	3	18	36	.269	.297	.244	5.04	2.52
Chiu, Tzu-Kai	L-L	6-0	220	9-14-87	1	0	2.05	15	0	0	0	22	23	7	5	1	3	19	.256	.226	.271	7.77	1.23
Christiani, Nick	R-R	5-10	180	7-17-87	1	0	3.86	7	0	0	1	14	12	6	6	1	2	12	.235	.105	.313	7.71	1.29
Corcino, Daniel	R-R	5-11	165	8-26-90	1	1	4.31	6	6	0	0	31	31	16	15	1	15	29	.254	.271	.243	8.33	4.31
Crabbe, Tim	R-R	6-4	195	2-20-88	3	7	4.26	18	16	0	0	82	79	50	39	7	55	76	.261	.256	.265	8.31	6.01
Howell, Blaine	L-L	5-11	210	10-2-88	0	2	2.08	13	0	0	5	17	13	7	4	1	4	10	.200	.222	.191	5.19	2.08
Infante, Ezequiel	L-L	5-10	185	8-31-88	1	2	3.04	28	0	0	1	56	54	21	19	3	27	36	.255	.236	.264	5.75	4.31
James, Mark	R-R	6-0	188	7-24-87	0	0	0.00	3	0	0	2	2	2	0	0	0	2	0	.222	.200	.250	0.00	23.14
Johnson, Jacob	R-R	6-4	215	9-12-90	8	7	4.47	25	25	0	0	129	134	77	64	8	42	82	.264	.278	.254	5.72	2.93
Joseph, Donnie	L-L	6-3	180	11-1-87	2	1	0.78	19	0	0	6	23	13	3	2	0	7	40	.160	.115	.182	15.65	2.74
Konstanty, Mike	R-R	6-4	220	4-17-86	0	4	6.46	9	0	0	0	15	24	14	11	2	12	9	.364	.393	.342	5.28	7.04
Martinez, Junior	R-R	6-0	240	4-30-86	1	4	5.28	47	0	0	1	61	61	47	36	4	54	50	.258	.247	.265	7.34	7.92
Pearl, Brian	L-R	6-1	190	5-17-88	1	1	4.50	5	5	0	0	22	21	12	11	1	6	13	.256	.278	.239	5.32	2.45
Ravin, Josh	R-R	6-4	220	1-21-88	2	6	4.79	12	12	0	0	56	68	39	30	4	28	43	.308	.327	.291	6.87	4.47
Renken, Daniel	R-R	6-3	190	7-5-89	0	0	3.00	5	0	0	0	6	4	2	2	0	8	4	.200	.000	.267	6.00	12.00
Salinas, Doug	R-R	6-4	195	12-5-88	3	3	2.38	23	0	0	7	42	35	14	11	1	11	50	.223	.313	.183	10.80	2.38
Shunick, Clayton	R-R	6-1	175	9-10-86	3	2	3.92	7	7	0	0	41	40	19	18	3	13	19	.256	.284	.236	4.14	2.83
Smith, Josh	R-R	6-2	220	8-7-87	1	1	2.13	7	0	0	1	13	8	4	3	1	6	15	.174	.214	.156	10.66	4.26
Sulbaran, Juan Carlos	R-R	6-2	220	11-9-89	4	6	4.99	16	15	0	0	79	78	55	44	6	49	83	.252	.282	.224	9.42	5.56
Villarreal, Pedro	R-R	6-1	215	12-9-87	4	7	3.84	26	14	0	2	96	89	52	41	7	29	77	.241	.224	.253	7.22	2.72
Volquez, Edinson	R-R	6-0	210	7-3-83	0	0	1.38	2	2	0	0	13	11	4	2	2	4	19	.224	.263	.200	13.15	2.77
Walczak, Jamie	R-R	6-2	195	5-4-87	1	3	6.14	18	0	0	0	37	43	32	25	2	26	30	.303	.228	.353	7.36	6.38
Walker, Justin	L-L	6-5	200	11-3-86	3	10	5.88	20	16	0	0	101	122	75	66	16	16	84	.300	.285	.307	7.49	1.43
Ware, Chase	R-R	6-6	200	7-16-87	3	1	1.84	21	0	0	7	49	40	12	10	1	9	49	.229	.193	.261	9.00	1.65

Fielding

Catcher	PCT	G	PO	A	E	DP	PB
Coddington	.995	22	174	25	1	1	2
Fleury	.977	69	503	50	13	4	13
Weems	.966	39	257	26	10	3	9
Wideman	.990	14	92	11	1	1	2

First Base	PCT	G	PO	A	E	DP
D'Anna	.994	15	147	7	1	10
Kaskow	.990	10	94	7	1	8
Nurre	.976	47	423	26	11	45
Pfister	.964	10	72	8	3	7
Richburg	.992	59	476	31	4	44

Second Base	PCT	G	PO	A	E	DP
Carlson	.867	4	9	4	2	1
Feiner	1.000	15	28	31	0	9
Rodriguez	1.000	1	4	0	1	

Rodriguez	.975	118	219	319	14	77
Torreyes	1.000	6	14	27	0	5

Third Base	PCT	G	PO	A	E	DP
Carlson	.905	17	11	27	4	3
Feiner	.756	15	7	24	10	3
Nurre	1.000	1	0	1	0	
Pfister	.912	102	79	241	31	19
Rodriguez	.667	1	0	2	1	0
Vidal	.800	4	1	7	2	1

Shortstop	PCT	G	PO	A	E	DP
Cabrera	1.000	1	1	3	0	1
Carlson	.952	6	9	11	1	5
Diaz	.950	6	7	12	1	3
Gregorius	.945	119	194	339	31	68
Rodriguez	1.000	1	0	4	0	1

Rodriguez	.971	6	12	22	1	5

Outfield	PCT	G	PO	A	E	DP
Carlson	.800	3	4	0	1	0
Conner	1.000	2	4	0	0	0
Contreras	.981	24	48	5	1	2
Feiner	1.000	18	18	4	0	1
Fleury	.667	2	2	0	1	1
Garton	.960	83	142	3	6	1
LaMarre	1.000	55	127	7	0	0
Means	.991	72	210	3	2	0
Oliveras	.941	74	107	4	7	2
Reed	.970	19	30	2	1	0
Satterwhite	.979	60	89	3	2	0
Wiley	.957	17	21	1	1	0

BILLINGS MUSTANGS

ROOKIE

PIONEER LEAGUE

Batting	B-T	HT	WT	DOB	AVG	vLH	vRH	G	AB	R	H	2B	3B	HR	RBI	BB	HBP	SH	SF	SO	SB	CS	SLG	OBP
Barnhart, Tucker	B-R	5-8	175	1-7-91	.306	.278	.312	35	111	17	34	9	0	0	12	18	2	0	0	25	4	1	.387	.412
Berset, Chris	B-R	6-0	190	1-27-88	.244	.000	.300	31	86	9	21	5	0	1	9	15	4	1	0	16	2	3	.337	.381
Bowe, Theo	L-R	5-9	160	8-5-90	.300	.308	.299	44	130	21	39	3	1	1	9	17	2	1	2	24	12	9	.362	.384
Conner, Sean	L-R	6-2	196	7-28-87	.194	.167	.200	8	31	3	6	3	0	0	6	1	0	0	0	8	0	0	.290	.219
D'Anna, Dominic	L-R	6-1	215	12-23-88	.254	.154	.280	18	63	8	16	1	1	0	9	8	1	0	1	7	0	0	.302	.342
Duran, Juan	R-R	6-5	190	9-2-91	.244	.188	.254	54	201	23	49	10	1	6	25	19	0	1	0	71	2	3	.393	.309
Hamilton, Billy	B-R	6-1	160	9-9-90	.318	.362	.309	69	283	61	90	13	10	2	24	28	3	0	2	56	48	9	.456	.383
Hernandez, Danny	R-R	6-0	200	10-9-88	.184	.167	.188	11	38	3	7	2	0	1	4	2	0	0	1	15	0	0	.316	.220
Hunt, Stephen	L-L	6-0	190	1-11-89	.170	.125	.179	14	47	6	8	3	0	2	5	7	0	0	1	16	2	0	.362	.273
Kaskow, Jonathan	L-R	6-0	190	10-6-88	.224	.231	.222	35	116	16	26	3	1	3	20	23	5	0	2	29	1	0	.345	.370
Lohman, Devin	R-R	6-1	185	4-14-89	.239	.256	.235	64	230	33	55	12	2	1	31	24	6	8	2	47	2	5	.322	.324
Lutz, Donald	L-R	6-4	230	2-6-89	.286	.233	.295	55	203	36	58	10	4	5	28	21	4	0	5	45	6	2	.478	.356
Maddox, Robert	L-L	6-2	195	10-8-89	.071	.333	.000	4	14	1	1	0	0	0	0	2	0	0	0	3	0	0	.071	.188
Manz, Trey	L-R	6-1	185	9-1-87	.241	.364	.217	36	137	11	33	6	1	3	16	9	1	0	0	40	0	0	.365	.293
Read, Dayne	R-R	5-11	190	12-31-88	.257	.258	.257	44	167	34	43	9	2	3	21	17	2	2	3	53	10	5	.389	.328
Rodriguez, Cristobal	R-R	5-11	165	11-1-89	.189	.091	.214	17	53	7	10	2	0	0	9	7	1	0	0	21	2	1	.226	.295
Rodriguez, Yorman	R-R	6-3	180	8-15-92	.339	.172	.373	43	171	25	58	8	3	2	39	8	0	1	4	30	12	2	.456	.361
Santos, Oliver	R-R	6-0	190	2-5-87	.274	.265	.276	62	219	32	60	10	3	0	29	13	5	1	2	29	10	3	.347	.326
Sierra, Jefry	R-R	5-10	165	4-16-90	.247	.233	.249	58	215	26	53	8	2	0	24	9	3	4	3	59	22	4	.302	.283
Vidal, David	R-R	5-11	185	10-23-89	.172	.000	.217	8	29	2	5	0	0	0	2	2	0	0	0	8	0	1	.172	.273

Pitching	B-T	HT	WT	DOB	W	L	ERA	G	GS	CG	SV	IP	H	R	ER	HR	BB	SO	AVG	vLH	vRH	K/9	BB/9
Adames, Jesus	R-R	6-4	195	1-25-91	1	3	6.80	17	3	0	0	41	57	39	31	4	22	22	.328	.313	.336	4.83	4.83
Arico, Kevin	R-R	6-5	195	8-30-88	0	2	7.50	7	0	0	1	12	16	10	10	1	4	10	.340	.364	.320	7.50	3.00

Name	B-T	HT	WT	DOB	W	L	ERA	G	GS	CG	SV	IP	H	R	ER	HR	BB	SO	AVG	vLH	vRH	K/9	BB/9
Chiu, Tzu-Kai	L-L	6-0	220	9-14-87	1	0	1.04	6	0	0	0	17	17	5	2	1	0	9	.262	.333	.227	4.67	0.00
Cline, Tyler	R-R	6-2	205	6-24-90	2	1	2.17	8	3	0	0	29	27	9	7	0	10	21	.252	.298	.217	6.52	3.10
Corcino, Daniel	R-R	5-11	165	8-26-90	1	3	3.40	9	9	0	0	40	38	18	15	2	17	31	.255	.224	.280	7.03	3.86
Correa, Jonathan	R-R	6-1	168	9-13-90	2	2	5.00	6	6	0	0	27	25	15	15	3	10	34	.248	.250	.243	11.33	3.33
Doyle, Pat	R-R	6-2	205	5-12-88	4	0	2.84	18	0	0	3	32	26	11	10	1	9	39	.222	.262	.200	11.08	2.56
Gerson, Starlin	R-R	6-4	175	8-26-88	3	4	4.88	15	15	0	0	76	89	46	41	9	18	52	.298	.306	.290	6.19	2.14
Guerrero, Daniel	R-R	6-1	190	7-21-85	0	0	12.60	2	0	0	1	5	6	7	7	1	2	3	.286	.500	.091	5.40	3.60
Hayes, Drew	R-R	6-1	190	9-3-87	1	3	2.42	14	0	0	0	22	13	10	6	1	16	25	.173	.071	.234	10.07	6.45
Henry, Mike	R-R	6-3	205	9-1-89	0	0	6.57	9	0	0	0	12	11	11	9	0	15	14	.239	.227	.250	10.22	10.95
Howell, Blaine	L-L	5-11	210	10-2-88	0	2	1.53	9	0	0	0	18	13	5	3	0	6	18	.213	.125	.244	9.17	3.06
Leonard, Matt	L-L	6-0	190	9-2-88	0	1	3.80	10	0	0	1	24	29	11	10	1	5	14	.302	.297	.305	5.32	1.90
Lotzkar, Kyle	R-R	6-2	205	10-24-89	2	0	0.45	4	4	0	0	20	8	1	1	1	2	33	.119	.114	.125	14.85	0.90
Martinez, Porfirio	R-R	5-10	175	11-29-89	3	2	1.67	20	0	0	6	27	24	7	5	1	12	29	.231	.231	.231	9.67	4.00
Muhammad, El'Hajj	R-R	6-2	200	7-7-91	0	0	4.91	2	1	0	0	7	9	5	4	1	4	5	.310	.273	.333	6.14	4.91
Panerati, Luca	L-L	6-2	167	12-2-89	0	1	3.38	7	0	0	0	13	14	5	5	0	5	15	.275	.200	.346	10.13	3.38
Quinn, Pat	R-R	6-4	200	3-6-90	0	1	4.15	2	0	0	0	4	7	3	2	0	4	3	.389	.364	.429	6.23	8.31
Robles, Tanner	L-L	6-4	205	2-24-89	3	2	2.98	14	14	1	0	60	39	27	20	3	32	66	.179	.174	.180	9.85	4.77
Shunick, Clayton	R-R	6-1	175	9-10-86	3	1	4.00	7	7	0	0	36	36	23	16	2	6	23	.259	.288	.241	5.75	1.50
Smith, Josh	R-R	6-2	220	8-7-87	1	2	2.14	12	0	0	0	21	16	5	5	1	10	28	.216	.185	.234	12.00	4.29
Smith, Ryan	R-R	6-3	205	11-4-89	4	1	5.33	14	0	0	1	25	25	17	15	4	10	24	.260	.361	.200	8.53	3.55
Tuttle, Daniel	R-R	6-1	175	8-21-90	5	3	4.32	13	13	0	0	58	58	32	28	6	29	52	.258	.283	.241	8.02	4.47
Walczak, Jamie	R-R	6-2	195	5-4-87	0	3	3.18	4	0	0	0	6	4	2	2	0	4	4	.190	.200	.182	6.35	6.35
Wolford, Dan	R-R	6-2	210	8-19-88	2	2	4.85	16	0	0	4	30	29	17	16	3	16	42	.252	.222	.266	12.74	4.85

Fielding

Catcher	PCT	G	PO	A	E	DP	PB
Barnhart	.994	35	262	56	2	4	8
Berset	.992	31	231	27	2	1	3
Manz	1.000	14	125	13	0	4	1

First Base	PCT	G	PO	A	E	DP
D'Anna	.976	14	116	6	3	5
Hernandez	1.000	1	1	0	0	0
Kaskow	.977	33	285	17	7	27
Lutz	.976	28	231	14	6	24
Maddox	1.000	2	13	3	0	2

Second Base	PCT	G	PO	A	E	DP
Hamilton	.979	55	106	175	6	43

Rodriguez	.905	10	13	25	4	9
Santos	.889	2	3	5	1	0
Sierra	.957	9	24	21	2	2
Vidal	1.000	3	6	5	0	1

Third Base	PCT	G	PO	A	E	DP
Hernandez	.941	7	3	13	1	0
Rodriguez	.944	7	6	11	1	2
Santos	.960	60	41	104	6	11
Vidal	.909	5	3	7	1	1

Shortstop	PCT	G	PO	A	E	DP
Hamilton	.935	13	25	33	4	7
Lohman	.920	63	90	173	23	34

Rodriguez	1.000	1	5	2	0	0

Outfield	PCT	G	PO	A	E	DP
Bowe	.967	34	51	7	2	3
Conner	.800	3	3	1	1	0
Duran	.877	45	53	4	8	0
Hunt	1.000	12	17	1	0	0
Lutz	.667	8	2	2	2	0
Read	.960	43	72	0	3	0
Rodriguez	.942	38	61	4	4	1
Sierra	.950	49	108	5	6	0

AZL REDS — ROOKIE

ARIZONA LEAGUE

Batting	B-T	HT	WT	DOB	AVG	vLH	vRH	G	AB	R	H	2B	3B	HR	RBI	BB	HBP	SH	SF	SO	SB	CS	SLG	OBP
Arias, Junior	R-R	6-2	178	1-9-92	.287	.357	.275	47	195	44	56	10	5	6	25	12	3	1	1	58	4	3	.482	.336
Conner, Sean	L-R	6-2	196	7-28-87	.278	1.000	.188	5	18	4	5	1	0	0	4	1	0	0	0	6	0	0	.333	.316
D'Anna, Dominic	L-R	6-1	215	12-23-88	.406	.400	.407	19	69	17	28	10	1	0	13	14	0	0	0	11	0	0	.580	.529
Diaz, Samuel	B-R	5-11	170	2-28-91	.307	.346	.295	31	114	17	35	4	1	0	11	4	1	0	1	11	4	0	.360	.333
Felipe, Ayeudi	R-R	6-0	175	3-12-90	.250	.000	.250	2	8	0	2	0	0	0	1	0	0	0	0	0	0	0	.250	.250
Gonzalez, Yovan	R-R	5-10	186	11-11-89	.240	.227	.244	30	104	14	25	5	0	0	9	5	4	2	1	12	0	0	.288	.298
Grandal, Yasmani	B-R	6-2	215	11-8-88	.286	.167	.318	8	28	4	8	1	0	0	4	1	0	0	4	0	1	.321	.394
Harford, Will	R-R	6-1	195	12-31-86	.200	.222	.194	14	40	7	8	2	0	0	7	2	0	0	0	10	0	0	.250	.238
Hernandez, Danny	R-R	6-0	200	10-9-88	.304	.571	.265	15	56	11	17	2	1	2	14	2	2	0	4	18	0	0	.482	.328
Hunt, Stephen	L-L	6-0	190	1-11-91	.338	.385	.328	22	77	12	26	6	0	0	10	10	0	0	1	22	0	2	.416	.409
Maddox, Robert	L-L	6-2	195	10-18-88	.283	.255	.291	48	198	38	56	15	6	7	46	13	2	1	2	30	1	0	.525	.330
Matthews, Jaren	L-L	6-2	210	2-20-89	.290	.292	.289	29	100	22	29	5	2	7	22	20	4	1	0	38	3	0	.590	.427
Morrison, Carter	L-L	6-4	195	6-23-90	.333	.000	.333	1	3	0	1	0	0	0	0	0	0	0	0	2	0	0	.333	.333
Muenster, Adam	B-R	5-10	189	4-23-87	.214	.261	.200	31	98	10	21	2	0	0	12	15	2	2	2	21	4	3	.235	.325
Muller, Kurt	R-R	5-10	170	7-7-89	.317	.487	.273	49	189	28	60	6	2	0	22	16	9	1	4	24	7	0	.370	.390
Poulk, Drew	R-R	6-0	190	3-14-88	.300	.400	.262	21	90	9	27	3	1	0	10	4	1	0	1	20	0	0	.422	.333
Rodriguez, Cristobal	R-R	5-11	165	11-1-89	.304	.000	.333	5	23	5	7	3	1	0	2	0	0	0	0	5	0	0	.522	.304
Rojas, Miguel	R-R	5-9	175	2-24-89	.750	1.000	.500	1	4	1	3	0	0	0	0	0	0	0	0	0	1	0	.750	.750
Silva, Juan	L-L	6-0	190	1-8-91	.230	.176	.243	44	178	26	41	6	5	3	24	23	1	2	0	48	4	1	.371	.322
Taylor, Jeff	R-R	6-0	195	6-14-88	.206	.100	.250	18	34	7	7	1	1	1	3	6	0	1	0	9	2	1	.382	.325
Torreyes, Ronald	R-R	5-10	150	9-2-92	.349	.421	.328	18	83	13	29	7	1	1	11	3	2	0	5	2	2	.494	.379
Vicioso, Danny	R-R	6-0	190	10-27-88	.292	.250	.304	27	89	11	26	3	0	1	10	1	0	0	13	0	1	.360	.308
Vidal, David	R-R	5-11	185	10-23-89	.297	.448	.259	36	145	30	43	13	2	6	34	14	0	1	2	30	0	0	.538	.354
Waldrop, Kyle	L-L	6-3	190	11-26-91	.214	.286	.190	7	28	1	6	1	0	0	1	0	0	0	0	9	0	0	.250	.241

Pitching	B-T	HT	WT	DOB	W	L	ERA	G	GS	CG	SV	IP	H	R	ER	HR	BB	SO	AVG	vLH	vRH	K/9	BB/9
Amezcua, Tony	R-R	6-0	175	5-27-91	1	0	3.65	5	1	0	1	12	12	6	5	0	5	10	.261	.235	.276	7.30	3.65
Chi, Po-Cheng	R-R	6-2	185	10-31-90	1	0	5.02	12	0	0	0	14	13	13	8	0	17	5	.255	.467	.167	3.14	10.67
Clarke, Mitchell	R-L	6-2	220	8-29-90	3	1	2.08	12	6	0	2	39	38	20	9	0	8	46	.242	.281	.232	9.46	1.85
Contreras, Carlos	R-R	6-0	165	1-8-91	2	4	6.45	10	6	0	2	38	44	29	27	8	16	30	.288	.306	.275	7.17	3.82
Correa, Jonathan	R-R	6-1	168	9-13-90	4	2	2.06	8	8	0	0	39	36	16	9	1	9	49	.243	.340	.194	11.21	2.06
Driessen, Nathan	L-L	6-2	190	6-28-91	1	2	3.42	13	0	0	1	24	31	16	9	1	4	28	.301	.185	.342	10.65	1.52

	B-T	HT	WT	DOB	W	L	ERA	G	GS	CG	SV	IP	H	R	ER	HR	BB	SO	AVG	vLH	vRH	K/9	BB/9
Ernst, Joel	R-R	6-4	208	1-10-87	1	1	2.08	11	0	0	3	17	19	7	4	0	1	18	.264	.500	.160	9.35	0.52
Guillon, Ismael	L-L	6-3	185	2-13-92	3	3	3.32	12	10	0	0	57	39	26	21	1	23	73	.193	.200	.191	11.53	3.63
Henry, Mike	R-R	6-3	205	9-1-89	2	2	7.62	8	0	0	0	13	13	13	11	3	6	14	.260	.313	.235	9.69	4.15
Hildenbrandt, Evan	L-R	6-2	190	2-13-89	0	0	7.82	4	3	0	0	13	11	12	11	3	13	9	.256	.357	.207	6.39	9.24
Leonard, Matt	L-L	6-0	190	9-2-88	1	1	3.75	6	0	0	1	12	9	6	5	0	2	12	.200	.000	.250	9.00	1.50
Lotzkar, Kyle	L-R	6-4	200	10-24-89	1	1	3.33	8	6	0	0	24	20	9	9	1	12	27	.230	.294	.189	9.99	4.44
Lowery, Derrick	L-L	6-1	215	5-3-88	0	2	15.19	4	0	0	0	5	12	9	9	0	2	7	.462	.400	.476	11.81	3.38
Marizan, Jose	L-L	6-1	170	2-7-88	2	0	3.57	16	0	0	1	23	17	9	9	1	7	18	.205	.190	.210	7.15	2.78
Mugarian, Wes	R-R	6-0	185	9-18-91	1	1	4.03	7	5	0	0	22	17	14	10	0	11	31	.200	.231	.174	12.49	4.43
Muhammad, El'Hajj	R-R	6-2	200	7-7-91	1	0	1.38	14	0	0	0	33	24	9	5	1	16	44	.205	.163	.230	12.12	4.41
O'Rear, Lucas	L-R	6-7	240	11-24-88	1	1	4.38	8	0	0	0	12	11	6	6	0	13	12	.239	.308	.212	8.76	9.49
Panerati, Luca	R-R	6-2	167	12-2-89	1	0	0.00	3	0	0	0	2	0	0	0	0	0	6	.125	.250	.083	10.80	0.00
Quezada, Radhames	R-R	6-2	175	7-6-90	2	2	4.82	6	5	0	0	28	25	19	15	2	12	34	.231	.382	.162	10.93	3.86
Quinn, Pat	R-R	6-4	200	3-6-90	0	1	1.42	8	0	0	0	13	11	5	2	0	4	12	.229	.176	.258	8.53	2.84
Ravin, Josh	R-R	6-4	220	1-21-88	1	0	3.38	2	2	0	0	8	5	3	3	0	4	7	.179	.200	.154	7.88	4.50
Rodriguez, Raul	R-R	6-3	190	10-16-90	1	0	5.73	6	0	0	0	11	15	9	7	0	4	11	.313	.462	.257	9.00	3.27
Salinas, Doug	R-R	6-4	195	12-5-88	0	0	0.00	4	0	0	0	5	3	0	0	0	0	10	.167	.000	.250	18.00	0.00
Smith, Ryan	R-R	6-3	205	11-4-89	0	0	1.29	4	0	0	1	7	6	1	1	0	1	10	.231	.375	.167	12.86	1.29
Thompson, Daryl	R-R	6-0	185	11-2-85	1	0	2.45	3	3	0	0	11	10	3	3	1	2	17	.238	.176	.280	13.91	1.64

Fielding

Catcher	PCT	G	PO	A	E	DP	PB
Gonzalez	.985	30	272	50	5	1	4
Grandal	1.000	4	34	3	0	0	0
Harford	1.000	6	24	2	0	0	5
Vicioso	.976	26	189	18	5	1	5

First Base	PCT	G	PO	A	E	DP
D'Anna	.993	16	128	8	1	7
Maddox	.957	27	214	8	10	14
Matthews	.971	12	98	2	3	6

Second Base	PCT	G	PO	A	E	DP
Diaz	.958	14	36	33	3	5
Muenster	.959	21	38	55	4	8
Rodriguez	.929	3	9	4	1	0

Torreyes	1.000	18	40	52	0	13

Third Base	PCT	G	PO	A	E	DP
Diaz	.900	2	4	5	1	0
Hernandez	.868	13	14	19	5	1
Muenster	.842	6	3	13	3	1
Rodriguez	1.000	3	1	5	0	1
Vidal	.911	33	20	62	8	9

Shortstop	PCT	G	PO	A	E	DP
Arias	.861	43	56	99	25	15
Diaz	.894	15	13	29	5	2
Muenster	1.000	1	0	1	0	1
Rojas	1.000	1	1	0	0	0

Outfield	PCT	G	PO	A	E	DP
Conner	1.000	3	2	1	0	0
Felipe	1.000	2	5	0	0	0
Harford	1.000	1	1	0	0	0
Hunt	.941	22	31	1	2	0
Maddox	1.000	1	1	0	0	0
Matthews	.900	13	17	1	2	0
Morrison	1.000	1	1	0	0	0
Muller	1.000	49	88	7	0	4
Poulk	1.000	21	40	1	0	0
Silva	.909	44	58	2	6	0
Taylor	1.000	8	6	1	0	0
Waldrop	1.000	4	5	0	0	0

DSL REDS   ROOKIE

DOMINICAN SUMMER LEAGUE

Batting	B-T	HT	WT	DOB	AVG	vLH	vRH	G	AB	R	H	2B	3B	HR	RBI	BB	HBP	SH	SF	SO	SB	CS	SLG	OBP
Arias, Brayan	R-R	6-2	180	11-27-91	.292	.188	.311	34	106	19	31	3	2	0	10	19	2	0	0	32	5	2	.358	.409
Baez, Ariel	R-R	6-0	183	1-22-91	.271	.364	.259	56	170	30	46	8	3	3	24	31	6	3	0	35	4	4	.406	.401
Bens, Edward	R-R	6-1	189	1-15-89	.212	.200	.214	29	52	6	11	2	0	0	6	9	2	0	3	8	0	1	.250	.333
Bueno, Ronald	B-R	5-10	154	10-4-92	.290	.300	.287	67	224	37	65	7	4	0	21	41	5	5	3	35	12	9	.357	.407
Estevez, Wilfrel	R-R	6-0	177	8-11-90	.258	.310	.243	64	213	30	55	9	5	2	31	26	1	0	4	31	5	3	.376	.336
Galindez, Ronald	R-R	6-0	170	7-29-90	.267	.240	.272	53	161	22	43	8	1	1	16	22	5	4	1	23	8	11	.348	.370
Gomez, Wagner	B-R	6-1	180	12-2-91	.224	.167	.236	36	107	15	24	6	0	2	14	9	5	0	0	27	4	2	.336	.314
Ortuno, Jose	R-R	6-1	185	12-23-90	.167	.071	.200	22	60	6	10	1	0	0	1	6	1	3	0	16	1	1	.183	.254
Perez, Felix	L-L	6-2	190	11-14-84	.429	.000	.466	16	63	11	27	5	1	1	14	7	0	0	0	8	2	3	.587	.486
Perez, Moises	L-R	6-1	189	12-24-92	.241	.250	.239	20	54	8	13	2	1	1	7	7	1	0	0	10	0	1	.370	.339
Pineda, Lorgi	R-R	6-1	173	10-31-91	.000	.000	.000	7	11	4	0	0	0	0	0	1	0	1	0	4	1	0	.000	.083
Quintero, Jose	L-R	6-1	175	12-6-90	.231	.250	.231	39	108	26	25	4	2	1	13	25	1	4	2	24	9	3	.333	.375
Ramirez, Robert	L-R	6-1	170	7-19-92	.198	.212	.195	56	202	29	40	8	4	2	19	25	1	4	1	34	0	4	.307	.288
Rivas, Jefry	R-R	6-1	175	9-6-92	.118	.133	.115	42	93	15	11	2	0	1	10	16	1	2	0	24	3	2	.172	.255
Sanchez, Carlos	L-L	5-10	175	4-4-91	.348	.306	.354	71	244	40	85	13	4	3	44	35	6	0	5	21	14	9	.471	.434
Soto, Junior	R-R	5-11	188	9-27-91	.137	.167	.128	24	51	4	7	0	0	0	4	4	6	0	0	10	1	1	.137	.279
Suero, Jonathan	B-R	6-0	170	2-28-93	.147	.133	.149	41	102	20	15	3	0	0	11	12	8	2	1	39	6	2	.176	.285
Victor, Jose	R-R	6-2	170	5-25-90	.255	.118	.286	49	102	25	26	7	2	2	10	18	6	2	0	22	7	2	.422	.397

Pitching	B-T	HT	WT	DOB	W	L	ERA	G	GS	CG	SV	IP	H	R	ER	HR	BB	SO	AVG	vLH	vRH	K/9	BB/9
Beard, Eliezer	R-R	6-4	202	4-23-91	7	2	1.81	13	12	0	0	70	50	18	14	1	20	34	.202	.180	.215	4.39	2.58
Caceres, Cesar	R-R	6-3	180	8-28-88	4	3	3.00	12	12	0	0	60	52	36	20	1	21	62	.226	.215	.230	9.30	3.15
Cantalizo, Eury	R-R	6-2	185	9-24-91	3	4	4.32	19	1	1	4	42	25	26	20	1	20	44	.179	.167	.183	9.50	4.32
Cortes, Waldo	R-R	6-4	221	10-3-91	0	0	15.95	9	0	0	0	7	16	13		0	16	2	.087	.000	.143	2.45	19.64
De Los Santos, Abel	R-R	6-1	215	5-17-92	1	1	1.85	14	14	2	0	78	48	24	16	1	34	63	.185	.207	.169	7.30	3.94
Guzman, Jose	R-R	6-3	175	9-18-91	5	4	2.03	21	3	0	1	49	24	17	11	0	32	50	.145	.130	.156	9.25	5.92
Lora, Luis	R-R	6-4	193	12-28-89	3	4	5.26	14	10	0	0	53	50	36	31	4	37	38	.250	.286	.238	6.45	6.28
Marizan, Jose	L-L	6-1	170	2-7-88	1	0	1.23	3	0	0	1	7	2	1	1	0	4	6	.091	.000	.091	7.36	4.91
Munoz, Jose	R-R	6-1	180	4-4-92	2	1	4.56	12	3	0	0	24	19	14	12	1	18	18	.218	.146	.283	6.85	6.85
Peralta, Wandy	L-L	6-1	205	7-27-91	3	3	2.24	15	7	0	0	52	38	21	13	1	21	40	.205	.148	.215	6.88	3.61
Polanco, Miguel	R-R	6-4	195	2-26-91	0	0	9.28	12	0	0	0	11	13	15	11	2	10	5	.302	.143	.379	4.22	8.44
Quezada, Radhames	R-R	6-2	175	7-6-90	2	1	2.09	7	7	2	0	43	32	17	10	1	17	29	.213	.286	.185	6.07	3.56
Ramirez, Harold	R-R	6-0	197	9-19-92	1	0	8.79	12	0	0	0	14	20	16	14	2	15	15	.339	.333	.341	9.42	9.42
Ramos, Carlos	R-R	6-0	176	11-4-90	3	0	0.55	24	0	9	9	33	19	3	2	0	13	36	.165	.189	.154	9.82	3.55
Rosario, Jose	L-L	6-4	209	3-19-91	1	2	6.10	18	0	0	1	21	23	19	14	2	15	18	.277	.000	.311	7.84	6.53
Tineo, Carlos	R-R	6-5	195	3-12-91	1	1	5.46	14	3	0	0	28	30	23	17	0	18	29	.263	.150	.287	9.32	5.79

Fielding

Catcher	PCT	G	PO	A	E	DP	PB
Bens	.994	27	131	22	1	0	6
Gomez	.932	28	182	25	15	1	18
Ortuno	.981	18	90	11	2	1	4
Soto	.968	21	109	13	4	0	6

First Base	PCT	G	PO	A	E	DP
Baez	1.000	2	14	0	0	0
Bens	1.000	1	1	0	0	0
Estevez	1.000	2	3	1	0	0
Perez	.982	16	102	5	2	6
Sanchez	.985	60	497	38	8	41
Soto	1.000	1	2	0	0	0
Victor	1.000	1	1	0	0	1

Second Base	PCT	G	PO	A	E	DP
Bueno	.993	30	55	78	1	13
Ramirez	.955	18	25	38	3	7
Rivas	.985	19	28	38	1	5
Soto	1.000	1	2	1	0	0
Suero	.930	18	24	42	5	7

Third Base	PCT	G	PO	A	E	DP
Baez	.899	36	28	70	11	7
Gomez	1.000	1	0	1	0	0
Pineda	—	1	0	0	0	0
Ramirez	.924	38	28	81	9	6
Rivas	—	1	0	0	0	0
Suero	.778	6	0	7	2	0

Shortstop	PCT	G	PO	A	E	DP
Bueno	.938	35	49	88	9	15
Pineda	.909	4	4	6	1	2
Ramirez	1.000	2	3	3	0	1
Rivas	.905	20	30	37	7	9
Suero	.866	17	21	37	9	2

Outfield	PCT	G	PO	A	E	DP
Arias	.862	19	24	1	4	1
Estevez	.958	48	66	2	3	0
Galindez	.986	44	66	4	1	0
Perez	1.000	15	27	1	0	1
Quintero	.956	34	41	2	2	2
Reynoso	.897	28	46	6	6	0
Victor	.985	38	65	0	1	0

VSL REDS   ROOKIE
VENEZUELAN SUMMER LEAGUE

Batting	B-T	HT	WT	DOB	AVG	vLH	vRH	G	AB	R	H	2B	3B	HR	RBI	BB	HBP	SH	SF	SO	SB	CS	SLG	OBP
Aldazoro, Argenis	L-L	6-2	160	9-17-92	.212	.059	.240	43	113	23	24	7	5	0	13	14	3	2	1	31	4	0	.363	.313
Benedetto, Nick	R-R	6-0	150	2-27-93	.245	.188	.271	33	102	21	25	5	0	0	6	8	2	4	0	36	7	1	.294	.313
Diaz, Samuel	B-R	5-11	170	2-28-91	.344	.368	.333	37	131	18	45	8	0	2	20	18	3	3	0	7	10	5	.450	.434
Duque, Andres	R-R	6-3	176	2-9-92	.230	.273	.218	35	100	13	23	5	0	0	14	7	1	2	1	25	1	3	.280	.284
Farinez, Rusbel	R-R	5-9	160	4-27-92	.286	.233	.306	42	154	25	44	8	2	0	19	18	2	6	1	20	5	3	.364	.366
Flores, Ponceano	R-R	6-1	182	4-6-90	.290	.333	.276	33	100	16	29	7	2	0	14	4	6	0	1	15	3	3	.400	.351
Lopez, Frederman	L-L	6-1	185	1-11-90	.238	.226	.241	54	164	23	39	8	0	4	28	27	4	0	0	40	3	3	.360	.359
Lopez, Yimmy	R-R	6-0	216	8-19-92	.264	.313	.246	51	174	15	46	6	2	2	26	11	5	1	1	48	1	1	.356	.325
Moreno, William	R-R	5-11	170	1-17-92	.230	.154	.250	40	126	19	29	5	1	0	15	13	5	6	2	18	4	1	.286	.322
Morillo, Julio	R-R	5-11	176	12-27-92	.254	.333	.225	42	138	14	35	7	1	0	17	20	0	3	3	17	1	4	.319	.342
Peraza, Juan Carlos	R-R	6-2	197	3-12-93	.219	.000	.232	27	73	14	16	5	0	1	7	6	3	1	0	25	1	1	.329	.305
Rivero, Kleyber	R-R	5-10	215	9-13-92	.181	.174	.183	34	83	14	15	3	3	0	8	14	4	1	0	33	6	1	.289	.327
Rodriguez, Adrian	R-R	5-11	176	4-24-92	.236	.242	.233	48	123	25	29	4	3	0	17	21	4	1	0	35	9	3	.317	.365
Santoni, Andres	R-R	5-11	170	6-6-91	.243	.394	.196	43	140	17	34	9	0	1	16	11	8	3	1	46	4	3	.329	.331
Torreyes, Ronald	R-R	5-10	150	9-2-92	.390	.407	.385	67	241	56	94	20	10	4	33	23	16	1	4	11	23	15	.606	.468
Valor, Humberto	R-R	6-1	186	9-9-92	.264	.314	.247	57	197	28	52	10	1	3	30	16	10	6	2	19	3	5	.371	.347

Pitching	B-T	HT	WT	DOB	W	L	ERA	G	GS	CG	SV	IP	H	R	ER	HR	BB	SO	AVG	vLH	vRH	K/9	BB/9
Bastardo, Alexis	R-R	6-0	160	5-8-87	2	2	4.62	15	1	0	0	37	39	25	19	3	17	26	.260	.237	.268	6.32	4.14
Bier, Deivis	R-R	6-1	180	5-6-87	2	2	6.07	17	1	0	3	30	35	24	20	3	12	17	.302	.281	.310	5.16	3.64
Carreno, Josmar	R-R	5-11	202	8-13-87	1	1	17.36	4	0	0	0	5	13	12	9	0	5	1	.520	.571	.500	1.93	9.64
Castellano, Josue	L-L	6-0	190	1-13-92	2	2	6.51	14	3	0	0	28	33	26	20	0	14	15	.311	.267	.319	4.88	4.55
Chacin, Alejandro	R-R	6-0	200	6-24-93	3	3	1.53	24	0	0	7	35	20	9	6	0	14	29	.167	.208	.156	7.39	3.57
Chiquiin, Jose	R-R	6-1	164	4-24-90	4	0	1.42	13	0	0	0	38	27	11	6	0	16	13	.199	.147	.216	3.08	3.79
Farias, Rafael	R-R	6-3	160	9-27-89	1	1	4.26	6	3	0	0	19	17	10	9	0	5	12	.246	.158	.280	5.68	2.37
Gonzalez, Luis	L-L	6-1	170	3-25-93	3	2	2.49	12	12	1	0	65	49	23	18	1	14	44	.210	.192	.213	6.09	1.94
Hernandez, Joyce	R-R	6-2	170	10-28-92	1	1	5.97	15	1	0	2	29	29	27	19	2	20	12	.259	.423	.209	3.77	6.28
Lopez, Jean	R-R	6-2	175	3-31-88	2	1	2.50	13	5	1	1	36	32	13	10	0	11	25	.242	.276	.233	6.25	2.75
Martinez, Daniel	L-L	6-2	170	6-4-90	0	0	4.32	8	2	0	0	17	15	10	8	0	18	16	.242	.250	.241	8.64	9.72
Mieres, Oswaldo	R-R	6-3	178	5-14-92	7	2	3.84	14	14	0	0	73	60	37	31	2	23	61	.227	.154	.251	7.56	2.85
Moreno, Robert	R-R	5-11	169	9-20-89	2	5	3.16	23	0	0	9	31	35	19	11	0	9	13	.285	.158	.308	3.73	2.59
Morillo, JR	L-L	5-11	167	10-30-91	2	5	4.19	12	12	0	0	54	62	35	25	3	20	39	.290	.261	.293	6.54	3.35
Navarro, Victor	R-R	6-3	180	11-7-89	0	1	12.00	2	0	0	0	3	6	4	4	0	2	0	.400	.800	.200	0.00	6.00
Romero, Franderlin	R-R	6-1	190	2-21-91	3	6	2.65	13	12	1	0	68	68	40	20	2	23	43	.256	.210	.276	5.69	3.04

Fielding

Catcher	PCT	G	PO	A	E	DP	PB
Flores	.972	31	145	28	5	0	10
Lopez	1.000	1	3	0	0	0	1
Morillo	.971	42	232	33	8	0	5
Santoni	—	1	0	0	0	0	0

First Base	PCT	G	PO	A	E	DP
Benedetto	—	1	0	0	0	0
Flores	1.000	1	6	0	0	1
Lopez	.984	30	231	16	4	20
Lopez	.972	18	128	9	4	9
Moreno	1.000	2	3	0	0	0
Peraza	.979	12	90	4	2	7
Santoni	.985	18	128	3	2	13

Second Base	PCT	G	PO	A	E	DP
Diaz	.955	13	28	35	3	11
Farinez	.951	38	88	88	9	16
Peraza	—	1	0	0	0	0
Torreyes	1.000	2	2	5	0	0
Valor	.936	15	30	43	5	11

Third Base	PCT	G	PO	A	E	DP
Diaz	.929	16	16	36	4	6
Peraza	.826	13	7	31	8	2
Santoni	.849	16	14	31	8	4
Torreyes	.899	29	24	74	11	12
Valor	.909	3	4	6	1	1

Shortstop	PCT	G	PO	A	E	DP
Diaz	.864	5	9	10	3	2
Farinez	—	1	0	0	0	0
Torreyes	.959	27	65	76	6	12
Valor	.931	40	51	98	11	14

Outfield	PCT	G	PO	A	E	DP
Aldazoro	.896	42	53	7	7	0
Benedetto	.989	31	84	2	1	0
Duque	1.000	33	30	2	0	0
Lopez	1.000	10	11	0	0	0
Moreno	.988	40	77	8	1	2
Rivero	.907	31	47	2	5	0
Rodriguez	.943	45	47	3	3	0
Torreyes	1.000	5	6	1	0	0

Cleveland Indians

SEASON IN A SENTENCE: Cleveland had the lowest attendance in the big leagues this year, and those who did come out didn't have much to watch, after injuries to the players that hadn't been traded away essentially ended the season by August and a 69-93 finish left the Indians fourth in the American League Central.

HIGH POINT: In the ninth inning of a blowout loss on July 29 against the Yankees, Andy Marte at least provided a light moment. The third baseman took the mound and retired the side in order, striking out Nick Swisher in the process. Acquired in the 2006 Coco Crisp deal, Marte's relief appearance was unfortunately one of his best moments, and the team cut ties with him after the season.

LOW POINT: Whatever chance the Indians had was undone by injuries. A knee injury requiring surgery took Grady Sizemore out for most of the season, Asdrubal Cabrera missed about a third of the year with a broken left forearm, and Carlos Santana's promising major league debut was cut short by knee damage caused by a home-plate collision. Cleveland also released veterans Mark Grudzielanek and Mike Redmond, and traded away Jake Westbrook, Jhonny Peralta, Kerry Wood and Austin Kearns, giving the team a younger look as the year went on.

NOTABLE ROOKIES: Mitch Talbot got off to a great start and notched eight consecutive victories prior to the all-star break, and he finished the season 10-13, 4.41. Santana played 46 games before his injury and had a .260 average with six home runs. Outfielder Michael Brantley showed signs in the second half that he could be a good leadoff hitter for the Indians in years to come.

KEY TRANSACTIONS: Cleveland continued its recent trend of trading away big names for minor league help, sending Russell Branyan to Seattle for Ezequiel Carrera and Juan Diaz, Peralta to Detroit for Giovanny Soto, Kearns to the Yankees for Zach McAllister, Wood to the Yankees for Matt Cusick and Andrew Shive, and Westbrook to the Cardinals for Corey Kluber.

DOWN ON THE FARM: The farm system finished with a .505 winning percentage, with Triple-A Columbus winning the Triple-A National Championship. The organization felt good about its depth of prospects, including Jason Kipnis, who played at three levels and hit a combined .307/.386/.492, and Matt Packer, whose 2.04 ERA was second in all of the minor leagues.

OPENING DAY PAYROLL: $61.2 million (24th)

PLAYERS OF THE YEAR

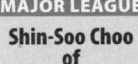

MAJOR LEAGUE	MINOR LEAGUE
Shin-Soo Choo	**Jason Kipnis**
of	2b
.300/.401/.484	(High A/Double-A)
22 HR, 22 SB	.307/.386/.492
4th in AL in OBP	16 HR, 32 2B

ORGANIZATION LEADERS

BATTING		*Minimum 250 at-bats
MAJORS		
*AVG	Shin-Soo Choo	.300
*OPS	Shin-Soo Choo	.885
HR	Shin-Soo Choo	22
RBI	Shin-Soo Choo	90
MINORS		
*AVG	Jose Constanza, Columbus	.319
*OBP	Jordan Henry, Akron/Kinston	.411
*SLG	Jared Goedert, Akron/Columbus	.532
R	Jason Kipnis, Kinston/Akron	96
H	Jason Kipnis, Kinston/Akron	159
TB	Jared Goedert, Akron/Columbus	256
2B	Chun-Hsiu Chen, Lake County/Kinston	38
3B	Luigi Rodriguez, DSL Indians	10
HR	Jared Goedert, Akron/Columbus	27
RBI	Lonnie Chisenhall, Akron	84
BB	Roberto Perez, Lake County	80
SO	Delvi Cid, Lake County	132
SB	Delvi Cid, Lake County	71

PITCHING		†Minimum 75 innings
MAJORS		
W	Fausto Carmona	13
†ERA	Fausto Carmona	3.77
SO	Justin Masterson	140
MINORS		
W	Joseph Gardner, Lake County/Kinston	13
L	Scott Barnes, Akron	11
	Trey Haley, Lake County	11
†ERA	Matt Packer, Lake County/Akron	2.04
G	Vinnie Pestano, Akron/Columbus	57
GS	Joseph Gardner, Lake County/Kinston	28
SV	Cory Burns, Lake County/Kinston	42
IP	Alex White, Kinston/Akron	150.7
BB	Trey Haley, Lake County	86
SO	Joseph Gardner, Lake County/Kinston	142
†AVG	Joseph Gardner, Lake County/Kinston	.197

2010 PERFORMANCE

General Manager: Chris Antonetti. **Farm Director:** Ross Atkins. **Scouting Director:** Brad Grant.

Class	Team	League	W	L	PCT	Finish*	Manager(s)
Majors	Cleveland Indians	American	69	93	.426	11th (14)	Manny Acta
Triple-A	Columbus Clippers	International	79	65	.549	†4th (14)	Mike Sarbaugh
Double-A	Akron Aeros	Eastern	71	71	.500	6th (12)	Joel Skinner
High A	Kinston Indians	Carolina	73	67	.521	2nd (8)	Aaron Holbert
Low A	Lake County Captains	Midwest	77	62	.554	†4th (16)	Ted Kubiak
Short-season	Mahoning Valley Scrappers	New York-Penn	30	46	.395	13th (14)	Travis Fryman
Rookie	AZL Indians	Arizona	21	35	.375	10th (12)	Chris Tremie
Overall 2010 Minor League Record			351	346	.504	15th (30)	

*Finish in overall standings (No. of teams in league). †League champion.

ORGANIZATION STATISTICS

CLEVELAND INDIANS

AMERICAN LEAGUE

Batting	B-T	HT	WT	DOB	AVG	vLH	vRH	G	AB	R	H	2B	3B	HR	RBI	BB	HBP	SH	SF	SO	SB	CS	SLG	OBP
Brantley, Michael	L-L	6-2	200	5-15-87	.246	.172	.266	72	297	38	73	9	3	3	22	22	0	4	2	38	10	2	.327	.296
Branyan, Russell	L-R	6-3	230	12-19-75	.263	.205	.280	52	171	24	45	9	0	10	24	16	1	1	1	49	0	0	.491	.328
2-team total (57 Seattle)					.237	—	—	109	376	47	89	19	0	25	57	46	3	1	2	131	1	0	.487	.323
Brown, Jordan	L-L	6-0	205	12-18-83	.230	.300	.221	26	87	9	20	7	0	0	2	4	1	0	0	10	0	0	.310	.272
Cabrera, Asdrubal	B-R	6-0	180	11-13-85	.276	.264	.281	97	381	39	105	16	1	3	29	25	5	11	3	60	6	4	.346	.326
Carlin, Luke	B-R	5-10	195	12-20-80	.357	.500	.300	6	14	4	5	0	0	2	3	2	0	0	0	5	0	0	.786	.438
Choo, Shin-Soo	L-L	5-11	200	7-13-82	.300	.264	.319	144	550	81	165	31	2	22	90	83	11	0	2	118	22	7	.484	.401
Crowe, Trevor	B-R	6-0	190	11-17-83	.251	.202	.266	122	442	48	111	24	3	2	36	29	3	5	0	73	20	7	.333	.302
Donald, Jason	R-R	6-1	195	9-4-84	.253	.286	.243	88	296	39	75	19	3	4	24	22	3	4	0	70	5	1	.378	.312
Duncan, Shelley	R-R	6-5	225	9-29-79	.231	.264	.211	85	229	29	53	10	0	11	36	26	3	0	1	76	1	0	.419	.317
Gimenez, Chris	R-R	6-2	215	12-27-82	.190	.250	.158	28	58	6	11	5	0	1	8	8	0	1	0	22	0	0	.328	.288
Grudzielanek, Mark	R-R	6-1	195	6-30-70	.273	.286	.265	30	110	10	30	0	0	0	11	8	1	0	0	10	2	0	.273	.328
Hafner, Travis	L-R	6-3	240	6-3-77	.278	.273	.279	118	396	46	110	29	0	13	50	51	12	0	3	94	2	1	.449	.374
Hernandez, Anderson	B-R	5-9	185	10-30-82	.246	.133	.283	22	61	6	15	3	0	0	2	2	0	0	0	9	1	0	.295	.270
Kearns, Austin	R-R	6-3	240	5-20-80	.272	.250	.284	84	301	42	82	18	1	8	42	34	5	0	2	78	4	1	.419	.354
2-team total (36 New York)					.263	—	—	120	403	55	106	21	1	10	49	46	10	0	2	116	4	1	.395	.351
LaPorta, Matt	R-R	6-2	210	1-8-85	.221	.216	.223	110	376	41	83	15	1	12	41	46	1	0	2	82	0	0	.362	.306
Marson, Lou	R-R	6-1	200	6-26-86	.195	.286	.161	81	262	29	51	15	0	3	22	26	3	2	1	55	8	1	.286	.274
Marte, Andy	R-R	6-1	205	10-21-83	.229	.290	.194	80	170	18	39	7	2	5	19	17	0	0	1	35	0	3	.382	.298
Nix, Jayson	R-R	5-11	195	8-26-82	.234	.306	.214	78	282	29	66	14	0	13	39	13	7	2	2	75	1	2	.422	.283
2-team total (24 Chicago)					.224	—	—	102	331	32	74	15	0	14	34	20	7	3	2	87	1	2	.396	.281
Peralta, Jhonny	R-R	6-2	215	5-28-82	.246	.239	.248	91	334	37	82	23	2	7	43	32	1	0	6	69	1	0	.389	.308
2-team total (57 Detroit)					.249	—	—	148	551	60	137	30	2	15	81	53	1	0	10	103	1	0	.392	.311
Redmond, Mike	R-R	5-11	200	5-5-71	.206	.250	.196	22	63	7	13	4	0	0	5	2	1	2	0	10	0	0	.270	.242
Santana, Carlos	B-R	5-11	190	4-8-86	.260	.146	.314	46	150	23	39	13	0	6	22	37	1	0	4	29	3	0	.467	.401
Sizemore, Grady	L-L	6-2	200	8-2-82	.211	.122	.266	33	128	15	27	6	2	0	13	9	2	0	1	35	4	2	.289	.271
Sutton, Drew	B-R	6-3	200	6-30-83	.222	.333	.200	11	36	4	8	1	0	1	4	3	0	0	0	12	0	0	.333	.282
Valbuena, Luis	L-R	5-10	195	11-30-85	.193	.318	.169	91	275	22	53	12	0	2	24	28	3	2	2	61	1	2	.258	.273

Pitching	B-T	HT	WT	DOB	W	L	ERA	G	GS	CG	SV	IP	H	R	ER	HR	BB	SO	AVG	vLH	vRH	K/9	BB/9
Ambriz, Hector	L-R	6-2	235	5-24-84	0	2	5.59	34	0	0	0	48	68	31	30	10	17	37	.338	.324	.354	6.89	3.17
Carmona, Fausto	R-R	6-4	230	12-7-83	13	14	3.77	33	33	4	0	210	203	98	88	17	72	124	.258	.269	.244	5.31	3.08
Carrasco, Carlos	R-R	6-3	220	3-21-87	2	2	3.83	7	7	1	0	45	47	20	19	6	14	38	.276	.193	.356	7.66	2.82
Germano, Justin	R-R	6-3	205	8-6-82	0	3	3.31	23	1	0	0	35	27	15	13	6	8	29	.206	.213	.200	7.39	2.04
Gomez, Jeanmar	R-R	6-3	170	2-10-88	4	5	4.68	11	11	0	0	58	73	36	30	7	22	34	.307	.268	.360	5.31	3.43
Herrmann, Frank	L-R	6-4	220	5-30-84	0	1	4.03	40	0	0	1	45	48	22	20	6	9	24	.276	.310	.241	4.84	1.81
Huff, David	L-L	6-2	215	8-22-84	2	11	6.21	15	15	1	0	80	101	61	55	14	34	37	.310	.342	.300	4.18	3.84
Laffey, Aaron	L-L	6-0	200	4-15-85	2	3	4.53	79	5	0	0	56	62	30	28	1	28	28	.283	.308	.261	4.53	4.53
Lewis, Jensen	R-R	6-3	205	5-16-84	4	2	2.97	37	0	0	0	36	28	12	12	1	19	29	.215	.264	.182	7.18	4.71
Masterson, Justin	R-R	6-6	250	3-22-85	6	13	4.70	34	29	1	0	180	197	107	94	14	73	140	.278	.290	.263	7.00	3.65
Perez, Chris	R-R	6-4	230	7-1-85	2	2	1.71	63	0	0	23	63	40	15	12	4	28	61	.182	.216	.154	8.71	4.00
Perez, Rafael	L-L	6-3	195	5-15-82	6	1	3.25	70	0	0	0	61	72	23	22	3	25	36	.300	.306	.295	5.31	3.69
Pestano, Vinnie	R-R	6-1	205	2-20-85	0	0	3.60	5	0	0	1	5	4	2	2	0	5	8	.222	.375	.100	14.40	9.00
Sipp, Tony	L-L	6-0	190	7-12-83	2	2	4.14	70	0	0	1	63	48	30	29	12	39	69	.218	.212	.223	9.86	5.57
Smith, Joe	R-R	6-2	205	3-22-84	2	2	3.83	53	0	0	0	40	30	18	17	4	24	32	.208	.342	.160	7.20	5.40
Talbot, Mitch	R-R	6-2	200	10-17-83	10	13	4.41	28	28	1	0	159	169	88	78	13	69	88	.276	.255	.295	4.97	3.90
Todd, Jess	R-R	5-11	210	4-20-86	0	0	7.50	5	0	0	0	6	9	5	5	0	3	9	.333	.333	.333	13.50	4.50
Tomlin, Josh	R-R	6-1	195	10-19-84	6	4	4.56	12	12	1	0	73	72	38	37	10	19	43	.264	.236	.296	5.30	2.34
Westbrook, Jake	R-R	6-3	215	9-29-77	6	7	4.65	21	21	1	0	128	133	68	66	15	44	73	.273	.260	.285	5.15	3.10
Wood, Kerry	R-R	6-5	210	6-16-77	1	4	6.30	23	0	0	8	20	21	15	14	3	11	19	.263	.231	.293	8.10	4.95
2-team total (24 New York)					3	4	3.13	47	0	0	8	46	35	17	16	4	29	49	—	—	—	9.59	5.67
Wright, Jamey	R-R	6-6	230	12-24-74	1	2	5.48	18	0	0	0	21	25	18	13	1	9	9	.294	.342	.255	3.80	3.80
2-team total (28 Seattle)					1	3	4.17	46	0	0	0	58	55	33	27	3	25	28	—	—	—	4.32	3.86

Fielding

Catcher	PCT	G	PO	A	E	DP	PB
Carlin	1.000	6	34	4	0	1	0
Gimenez	.992	24	109	14	1	2	1
Marson	.993	87	504	44	4	1	5
Redmond	.990	22	87	11	1	1	1
Santana	.989	40	245	22	3	2	4

First Base	PCT	G	PO	A	E	DP
Branyan	.989	47	426	44	5	64
Brown	1.000	10	70	2	0	5
Duncan	1.000	4	15	0	0	1
LaPorta	.997	93	815	58	3	80
Marte	.990	32	186	11	2	17

Second Base	PCT	G	PO	A	E	DP
Donald	.984	41	61	128	3	18
Grudzielanek	.986	27	54	86	2	22
Hernandez	.900	3	3	6	1	2
Nix	1.000	25	53	80	0	21
Sutton	1.000	4	5	17	0	4
Valbuena	.989	71	127	232	4	59

Third Base	PCT	G	PO	A	E	DP
Hernandez	1.000	1	0	2	0	0
Marte	.894	45	21	55	9	6
Nix	.899	40	34	64	11	4
Peralta	.981	91	61	194	5	24
Valbuena	.882	9	3	12	2	0

Shortstop	PCT	G	PO	A	E	DP
Cabrera	.972	95	148	271	12	73
Donald	.956	47	58	138	9	34
Hernandez	1.000	16	25	43	0	12
Sutton	1.000	7	11	16	0	2
Valbuena	.862	5	8	17	4	5

Outfield	PCT	G	PO	A	E	DP
Brantley	.988	72	161	0	2	0
Brown	1.000	7	17	1	0	0
Choo	.986	142	267	14	4	3
Crowe	.983	116	274	9	5	1
Duncan	1.000	48	75	7	0	1
Gimenez	1.000	2	1	0	0	0
Hernandez	—	1	0	0	0	0
Kearns	.978	84	173	1	4	0
LaPorta	1.000	7	5	0	0	0
Nix	1.000	2	2	1	0	0
Sizemore	.985	32	64	0	1	0
Valbuena	—	1	0	0	0	0

COLUMBUS CLIPPERS — TRIPLE-A
INTERNATIONAL LEAGUE

Batting	B-T	HT	WT	DOB	AVG	vLH	vRH	G	AB	R	H	2B	3B	HR	RBI	BB	HBP	SH	SF	SO	SB	CS	SLG	OBP
Bixler, Brian	R-R	6-1	195	10-22-82	.278	.328	.260	64	230	32	64	13	1	3	27	20	5	1	3	46	9	4	.383	.345
3-team total (11 Indianapolis, 27 Syracuse)					.285	—	—	102	368	45	105	18	4	4	47	30	7	2	4	82	18	7	.389	.347
Brantley, Michael	L-L	6-2	200	5-15-87	.319	.263	.342	67	273	54	87	13	2	4	29	34	2	5	2	28	13	5	.425	.395
Branyan, Russell	L-R	6-3	230	12-19-75	.286	.125	.500	4	14	1	4	2	0	0	1	1	0	0	0	2	0	0	.429	.333
Brown, Jordan	L-L	6-0	205	12-18-83	.298	.324	.285	83	326	31	97	28	1	8	67	21	3	0	5	48	2	0	.463	.341
Buscher, Brian	L-R	6-0	220	4-18-81	.265	.355	.244	47	162	19	43	9	2	4	26	17	1	2	5	10	0	0	.420	.330
Carlin, Luke	B-R	5-10	195	12-20-80	.231	.250	.226	13	39	9	9	2	0	2	6	7	0	1	1	11	0	0	.436	.340
2-team total (63 Indianapolis)					.238	—	—	76	244	32	58	10	1	4	29	34	2	1	3	60	5	2	.336	.332
Carrera, Ezequiel	L-L	5-10	185	6-11-87	.286	.327	.264	41	161	19	46	7	3	1	16	12	1	8	1	34	11	3	.385	.337
Constanza, Jose	B-L	5-9	150	9-1-83	.319	.357	.307	113	404	69	129	11	8	1	32	35	0	8	1	54	34	6	.394	.373
Crowe, Trevor	B-R	6-0	190	11-17-83	.244	.233	.247	29	119	21	29	4	1	1	13	7	0	0	2	19	6	1	.319	.281
Donald, Jason	R-R	6-1	195	9-4-84	.277	.222	.297	37	137	27	38	10	2	2	17	21	6	1	0	33	10	2	.423	.396
Duncan, Shelley	R-R	6-5	225	9-29-79	.301	.250	.321	38	146	21	44	11	0	6	34	17	2	0	1	28	0	0	.500	.380
Espino, Damaso	R-R	6-1	210	5-8-83	.250	.208	.268	26	80	7	20	2	0	0	11	10	0	1	2	10	0	0	.275	.326
Gimenez, Chris	R-R	6-2	215	12-27-82	.276	.234	.295	55	196	32	54	10	0	9	30	32	0	2	1	38	1	1	.464	.341
Goedert, Jared	R-R	6-2	200	5-25-85	.261	.266	.259	81	318	54	83	23	1	20	51	37	5	0	2	77	2	0	.528	.345
Head, Jerad	R-R	6-1	205	11-15-82	.257	.212	.293	21	74	12	19	9	0	2	15	5	3	0	1	20	0	0	.459	.325
Hernandez, Anderson	B-R	5-9	185	10-30-82	.234	.152	.264	47	171	13	40	4	0	1	17	12	0	1	3	23	2	4	.275	.280
Hodges, Wes	R-R	6-2	205	9-14-84	.270	.267	.271	125	493	65	133	28	3	15	60	30	0	2	6	96	2	0	.430	.308
Horwitz, Brian	R-R	6-1	185	11-7-82	.267	.250	.273	6	15	1	4	2	0	0	2	1	1	0	1	0	0	0	.400	.333
LaPorta, Matt	R-R	6-2	210	1-8-85	.362	.444	.333	18	69	7	25	6	0	5	16	12	0	0	0	10	0	1	.638	.457
Marson, Lou	R-R	6-1	200	6-26-86	.202	.190	.207	37	124	19	25	7	1	4	14	22	1	0	0	24	5	0	.371	.327
Martinez, Richard	R-R	6-0	185	6-19-87	.353	.429	.300	5	17	1	6	3	0	0	6	3	0	0	0	4	0	0	.529	.450
McBride, Matt	R-R	6-2	215	5-23-85	.269	.209	.303	31	119	16	32	6	0	4	11	5	0	2	1	17	0	0	.420	.296
Phelps, Josh	R-R	6-3	225	5-12-78	.190	.429	.071	6	21	1	4	3	0	0	2	0	0	0	0	7	0	0	.333	.190
Phelps, Cord	B-R	6-2	200	1-23-87	.317	.316	.317	66	243	41	77	20	4	6	31	24	4	1	1	39	3	2	.506	.386
Reyes, Argenis	B-R	5-10	180	9-25-82	.340	.357	.333	16	53	5	18	2	0	0	4	5	1	0	0	5	0	2	.377	.364
2-team total (14 Pawtucket)					.302	—	—	30	96	8	29	3	0	0	5	6	1	2	0	11	1	1	.333	.350
Rodriguez, Josh	R-R	6-0	185	12-18-84	.293	.264	.308	86	317	49	93	23	1	12	46	40	1	4	2	75	6	2	.486	.372
Santana, Carlos	B-R	5-11	190	4-8-86	.316	.237	.350	57	196	39	62	14	1	13	51	45	3	0	2	39	6	0	.597	.447
Smith, Kyle	R-R	6-1	190	12-25-87	.300	.000	.375	6	10	4	3	0	0	1	2	0	0	0	0	3	0	0	.300	.462
Sutton, Drew	B-R	6-3	200	6-30-83	.302	.303	.302	29	96	10	29	8	0	2	15	18	1	3	1	21	4	0	.448	.414
2-team total (84 Louisville)					.273	—	—	113	359	45	98	24	1	5	42	61	4	8	6	92	9	3	.387	.379
Toole, Justin	R-R	6-0	180	9-10-86	.000	.000	.000	1	1	0	0	0	0	0	0	0	0	0	0	1	0	0	.000	.000
Toregas, Wyatt	R-R	5-11	210	12-2-82	.200	.125	.235	14	50	3	10	1	0	2	6	1	1	0	1	9	0	0	.340	.226
Valbuena, Luis	L-R	5-10	195	11-30-85	.313	.333	.300	25	96	23	30	8	1	6	20	19	1	2	1	21	2	0	.604	.427
Weglarz, Nick	L-L	6-3	240	12-16-87	.286	.319	.273	50	175	30	50	17	1	6	20	28	4	0	2	43	2	2	.497	.392

Pitching	B-T	HT	WT	DOB	W	L	ERA	G	GS	CG	SV	IP	H	R	ER	HR	BB	SO	AVG	vLH	vRH	K/9	BB/9
Ambriz, Hector	L-R	6-2	235	5-24-84	0	0	1.13	7	0	0	0	8	9	1	1	0	1	15	.273	.250	.294	16.88	1.13
Berger, Eric	L-L	6-2	205	4-22-86	0	1	5.84	5	5	0	0	25	31	18	16	2	20	17	.304	.276	.315	6.20	7.30
Carrasco, Carlos	R-R	6-3	220	3-21-87	10	6	3.65	25	25	0	0	150	139	69	61	16	46	133	.250	.233	.265	7.96	2.75
Espino, Paolo	R-R	5-10	190	1-10-87	3	3	5.62	7	7	0	0	42	43	26	26	7	12	32	.259	.275	.247	6.91	2.59
Germano, Justin	R-R	6-3	205	8-6-82	3	2	3.38	17	6	1	1	53	49	23	20	8	10	37	.241	.284	.198	6.24	1.69
Gomez, Jeanmar	R-R	6-3	170	2-10-88	8	8	5.20	20	20	1	0	116	129	74	67	16	42	78	.284	.300	.267	6.05	3.26
Gosling, Mike	L-L	6-2	210	9-23-80	3	0	2.96	13	2	0	0	22	10	9	7	2	8	23	.214	.184	.231	7.90	2.96
Herrmann, Frank	L-R	6-4	220	5-30-84	3	0	0.31	19	0	0	2	29	15	1	1	0	8	22	.171	.148		6.91	2.51
Huff, David	L-L	6-2	215	8-22-84	2	2	4.36	12	12	0	0	74	84	37	36	8	21	52	.288	.324	.268	6.30	2.54
Jimenez, Francisco	L-L	5-11	164	10-2-88	0	0	27.00	1	0	0	0	1	8	6	5	0	2	0	.667	.500	.700	0.00	5.40
Judy, Josh	R-R	6-4	200	2-9-86	3	0	2.68	38	0	0	7	47	48	18	14	5	14	55	.262	.302	.227	10.53	2.69
Kluber, Corey	R-R	6-4	215	4-10-86	1	3	3.27	2	2	0	0	11	10	4	4	1	6	8	.263	.208	.357	6.55	4.91
Laffey, Aaron	L-L	6-0	200	4-15-85	0	1	3.67	10	4	0	0	27	29	11	11	1	16	12	.279	.263	.288	4.00	5.33
Lewis, Jensen	R-R	6-3	220	5-16-84	2	1	2.67	24	0	0	2	30	29	9	9	3	8	30	.252	.286	.220	8.90	2.37

Name	B-T	HT	WT	DOB	W	L	ERA	G	GS	CG	SV	IP	H	R	ER	HR	BB	SO	AVG	vLH	vRH	K/9	BB/9
Lewis, Scott	B-L	6-0	185	9-26-83	2	0	2.12	3	3	0	0	17	12	6	4	1	4	18	.194	.385	.143	9.53	2.12
Lindsay, Shane	R-R	6-1	205	1-25-85	0	1	8.18	7	0	0	0	11	13	11	10	1	16	12	.295	.389	.231	9.82	13.09
McAllister, Zach	R-R	6-5	230	12-8-87	1	2	6.88	3	3	0	0	17	20	13	13	1	7	11	.303	.342	.250	5.82	3.71
2-team total (24 Scranton/W-B)					9	12	5.29	27	27	1	0	150	185	95	88	21	45	99	—	—	—	5.95	2.71
Pestano, Vinnie	R-R	6-1	205	2-20-85	1	2	1.55	43	0	0	14	46	35	10	8	1	14	59	.202	.244	.161	11.46	2.72
Pino, Yohan	R-R	6-2	190	12-26-83	10	9	5.75	26	26	1	0	146	175	101	93	25	47	114	.294	.292	.296	7.04	2.90
Popham, Marty	R-R	6-6	235	8-4-87	0	1	13.50	1	1	0	0	4	9	6	6	1	3	2	.474	.500	.444	4.50	6.75
Putnam, Zach	R-R	6-2	225	7-3-87	0	1	3.33	17	0	0	0	24	20	10	9	2	7	24	.222	.191	.256	8.88	2.59
Rivera, Saul	B-R	5-10	180	12-7-77	2	1	1.50	21	0	0	5	24	13	5	4	0	12	14	.160	.100	.220	5.25	4.50
Rondon, Hector	R-R	6-3	180	2-26-88	1	3	8.53	7	7	0	0	32	48	32	30	12	10	33	.343	.373	.315	9.38	2.84
Smith, Carlton	L-R	6-2	205	1-23-86	1	5	6.38	37	0	0	1	48	66	36	34	7	20	30	.325	.376	.282	5.63	3.75
Smith, Joe	R-R	6-2	205	3-22-84	2	1	1.96	20	0	0	2	23	17	8	5	0	10	19	.207	.267	.173	7.43	3.91
Sowers, Jeremy	L-L	6-1	180	5-17-83	2	6	5.85	27	4	0	0	52	55	38	34	2	18	29	.270	.282	.263	4.99	3.10
Stowell, Bryce	R-R	6-2	205	9-23-86	1	1	5.49	17	0	0	0	20	11	12	12	2	17	28	.167	.200	.139	12.81	7.78
Todd, Jess	R-R	5-11	210	4-20-86	4	2	3.31	44	0	0	4	49	46	20	18	6	18	53	.241	.225	.255	9.73	3.31
Tomlin, Josh	R-R	6-1	195	10-19-84	8	4	2.68	20	17	1	0	107	83	34	32	11	33	80	.212	.246	.184	6.71	2.77
Wright, Steve	R-R	6-1	200	8-30-84	0	1	7.59	9	0	0	0	11	13	9	9	2	5	10	.295	.143	.435	8.44	4.22

Fielding

Catcher	PCT	G	PO	A	E	DP	PB
Carlin	.990	13	90	6	1	3	3
Espino	1.000	26	182	12	0	3	2
Gimenez	1.000	18	109	6	0	1	2
Marson	.989	36	264	17	3	5	2
Martinez	1.000	5	31	1	0	0	1
Santana	.992	45	348	20	3	2	1
Toregas	1.000	7	55	1	0	0	0

First Base	PCT	G	PO	A	E	DP
Branyan	1.000	2	5	1	0	1
Brown	.986	17	127	10	2	8
Duncan	1.000	5	33	3	0	1
Gimenez	1.000	3	23	1	0	3
Hodges	.987	98	803	53	11	79
LaPorta	1.000	7	63	7	0	5
McBride	.980	11	94	6	2	11
Phelps	.917	2	10	1	1	2
Sutton	1.000	3	15	2	0	1

Second Base	PCT	G	PO	A	E	DP
Bixler	.968	13	25	35	2	10
Donald	.985	28	44	85	2	21
Hernandez	1.000	8	8	24	0	2

Catcher	PCT	G	PO	A	E	DP
Phelps	.975	57	79	154	6	31
Reyes	.968	6	12	18	1	8
Rodriguez	.953	19	33	49	4	7
Sutton	.976	10	19	22	1	6
Valbuena	1.000	6	15	17	0	5

Third Base	PCT	G	PO	A	E	DP
Bixler	.977	15	23	19	1	1
Buscher	.952	42	29	70	5	4
Gimenez	—	1	0	0	0	0
Goedert	.912	68	57	130	18	19
Head	1.000	3	1	7	0	1
Reyes	1.000	7	1	18	0	4
Rodriguez	.667	1	1	1	1	1
Sutton	.500	1	0	1	1	1
Valbuena	1.000	7	6	8	0	0

Shortstop	PCT	G	PO	A	E	DP
Bixler	.985	29	56	77	2	19
Donald	1.000	9	12	22	0	4
Hernandez	.969	39	55	101	5	25
Reyes	1.000	1	0	2	0	0
Rodriguez	.959	54	78	158	10	33
Smith	1.000	1	1	2	0	0

	PCT	G	PO	A	E	DP
Sutton	1.000	3	0	4	0	0
Valbuena	.950	10	11	27	2	4

Outfield	PCT	G	PO	A	E	DP
Bixler	1.000	4	8	0	0	0
Brantley	1.000	67	168	5	0	0
Brown	.988	43	75	4	1	0
Carrera	1.000	40	118	4	0	2
Constanza	.991	110	211	7	2	2
Crowe	1.000	29	68	4	0	1
Duncan	.889	14	16	0	2	0
Gimenez	.984	34	59	2	1	1
Head	1.000	18	34	1	0	1
Horwitz	1.000	6	5	0	0	0
LaPorta	1.000	10	12	0	0	0
McBride	.950	16	37	1	2	0
Phelps	1.000	2	3	0	0	0
Reyes	1.000	1	3	0	0	0
Rodriguez	1.000	5	9	0	0	0
Sutton	.897	13	26	0	3	0
Weglarz	.959	41	66	4	3	0

AKRON AEROS
DOUBLE-A

EASTERN LEAGUE

Batting	B-T	HT	WT	DOB	AVG	vLH	vRH	G	AB	R	H	2B	3B	HR	RBI	BB	HBP	SH	SF	SO	SB	CS	SLG	OBP
Apodaca, Juan	R-R	5-11	180	7-15-86	.230	.053	.291	23	74	12	17	0	0	2	7	12	1	0	1	20	0	0	.311	.341
2-team total (41 Portland)					.242	—		64	207	24	50	6	0	4	13	32	4	0	1	52	1	0	.329	.352
Arnal, Cristo	R-R	6-0	175	9-17-85	.222	.170	.240	54	176	30	39	3	1	1	11	17	2	3	1	28	7	0	.267	.296
Baker, Trent	R-L	6-0	175	6-14-90	.154	.250	.111	4	13	2	2	2	0	0	0	0	0	1	0	3	0	0	.308	.154
Branyan, Russell	L-R	6-3	230	12-19-75	.250	.333	.200	2	8	1	2	0	0	0	0	0	0	0	0	2	0	0	.250	.250
Cabrera, Asdrubal	B-R	6-0	180	11-13-85	.357	.429	.286	4	14	4	5	2	0	1	3	0	0	0	3	2	0	1	.714	.471
Castillo, Alex	R-R	6-2	195	11-29-85	.083	.000	.105	8	24	3	2	2	0	0	0	2	0	1	0	8	0	0	.167	.154
Chisenhall, Lonnie	L-R	6-1	200	10-4-88	.278	.234	.301	117	460	81	128	22	3	17	84	46	10	0	8	77	3	0	.450	.351
Choo, Shin-Soo	L-L	5-11	200	7-13-82	.091	.143	.000	3	11	1	1	0	0	0	0	0	0	0	0	3	1	0	.091	.091
Davis, Adam	R-R	5-9	190	10-15-84	.176	.400	.083	5	17	2	3	1	0	0	1	0	0	0	0	4	0	0	.235	.263
DeGeorge, Dan	R-R	5-10	180	2-19-87	.000	.000	.000	3	9	1	0	0	0	0	0	1	0	0	0	2	0	0	.000	.100
Drennen, John	L-L	5-11	195	8-26-86	.300	.313	.295	119	440	44	132	26	6	7	58	33	7	1	5	56	2	3	.434	.355
Espino, Damaso	R-R	6-1	210	5-8-83	.250	.313	.217	59	196	22	49	4	0	2	20	19	0	2	0	24	0	0	.301	.316
Fedroff, Tim	L-R	5-11	220	2-4-87	.274	.232	.294	118	445	65	122	19	5	4	36	48	4	2	2	90	7	5	.366	.349
Goedert, Jared	R-R	6-2	200	5-25-85	.325	.339	.317	44	163	26	53	14	0	7	32	16	2	0	5	35	2	0	.540	.382
Head, Jerad	R-R	6-1	210	11-15-82	.312	.329	.304	65	237	47	74	18	0	15	51	18	4	1	3	46	2	1	.578	.366
Henry, Jordan	L-R	6-3	175	6-13-88	.300	.295	.302	74	287	45	86	4	4	0	16	46	0	4	0	59	15	4	.355	.396
Kipnis, Jason	L-R	5-10	175	4-3-87	.311	.324	.304	79	315	63	98	20	5	10	43	31	7	2	0	61	7	1	.502	.385
McBride, Matt	R-R	6-2	215	5-23-85	.283	.333	.252	96	361	54	102	25	1	17	64	30	8	0	5	62	0	2	.499	.347
Mills, Beau	L-R	6-3	220	8-15-86	.241	.223	.251	113	427	55	103	26	1	10	72	42	4	0	4	71	2	1	.397	.312
Montero, Lucas	B-R	5-11	180	10-18-84	.241	.182	.278	17	58	4	14	1	1	0	3	6	0	0	0	14	1	0	.293	.313
Perez, Miguel	R-R	6-3	235	9-25-83	.280	.250	.292	44	157	18	44	12	0	0	14	6	0	1	0	27	0	0	.357	.329
Phelps, Cord	B-R	6-2	200	1-23-87	.296	.284	.303	53	199	25	59	8	3	2	23	15	1	1	2	39	1	4	.397	.346
Rivas, Ronald	R-R	6-2	184	1-16-88	.200	.111	.273	5	20	1	4	0	0	1	3	0	0	0	0	4	0	0	.300	.200
Rivero, Carlos	R-R	6-3	200	5-20-88	.232	.256	.221	110	406	39	94	16	2	6	43	28	1	2	7	81	0	3	.325	.278
Rodriguez, Josh	R-R	6-0	185	12-18-84	.317	.360	.289	21	63	11	20	7	0	1	11	11	1	0	4	10	0	2	.476	.453
Toole, Justin	R-R	5-11			.143	.000	.143	3	7	1	1	0	0	0	0	0	0	0	0	2	0	0	.143	.143
Toregas, Wyatt	R-R	5-11	210	12-2-82	.203	.154	.217	17	59	3	12	3	0	1	6	6	1	0	2	8	0	0	.305	.279
Weglarz, Nick	L-L	6-3	240	12-16-87	.285	.260	.299	37	123	21	39	10	0	7	27	22	2	0	2	26	1	0	.511	.387

Pitching	B-T	HT	WT	DOB	W	L	ERA	G	GS	CG	SV	IP	H	R	ER	HR	BB	SO	AVG	vLH	vRH	K/9	BB/9
Aguilar, Omar	R-R	5-11	220	3-31-85	2	7	3.77	47	0	0	7	62	57	33	26	2	30	72	.236	.232	.239	10.45	4.35
Barnes, Scott	L-L	6-4	185	9-5-87	6	11	5.22	26	26	0	0	138	126	90	80	15	58	127	.241	.232	.245	8.28	3.78
Berger, Eric	L-L	6-2	205	4-22-86	5	5	4.64	18	17	1	0	87	78	46	45	9	52	73	.239	.181	.258	7.52	5.36
Bryson, Rob	R-R	6-1	200	12-11-87	1	1	1.80	12	3	0	0	20	11	5	4	1	11	21	.162	.107	.200	9.45	4.95
De La Cruz, Kelvin	L-L	6-5	190	8-1-88	5	6	5.77	20	20	0	0	94	98	68	60	12	64	77	.274	.273	.274	7.40	6.15
Edell, Ryan	L-L	6-1	215	7-6-83	1	1	6.85	5	5	0	0	22	30	18	17	2	4	18	.316	.429	.296	7.25	1.61
Espino, Paolo	R-R	5-10	190	1-10-87	9	4	4.00	21	15	0	0	101	95	49	45	13	35	92	.245	.225	.263	8.17	3.11
Germano, Justin	R-R	6-3	205	8-6-82	2	1	2.79	7	1	0	0	19	17	6	6	0	4	16	.239	.265	.216	7.45	1.86
Graham, Connor	R-R	6-6	235	12-30-85	3	6	3.43	43	4	0	2	79	74	44	30	5	50	65	.245	.239	.249	7.44	5.72
Grening, Brian	R-R	5-11	200	6-10-85	0	0	4.86	15	0	0	0	17	14	9	9	3	12	16	.226	.185	.257	8.64	6.48
Hagadone, Nick	L-L	6-5	230	1-1-86	2	2	4.50	19	7	0	1	48	44	27	24	5	34	44	.242	.192	.262	8.25	6.38
Judy, Josh	R-R	6-4	200	2-9-86	0	0	9.00	2	0	0	0	2	6	2	2	0	0	2	.545	.500	.571	9.00	0.00
Kaminsky, Alex	R-R	6-1	190	2-25-88	1	0	0.00	1	0	0	0	3	2	0	0	0	2	2	.200	.000	.286	6.00	6.00
Kluber, Corey	R-R	6-4	215	4-10-86	2	2	3.76	5	5	0	0	26	38	12	11	0	10	21	.345	.417	.290	7.18	3.42
Laffey, Aaron	L-L	6-0	200	4-15-85	0	0	0.00	1	0	0	0	1	1	0	0	0	0	0	.333	.000	.333	0.00	0.00
Lee, Chen	R-R	5-11	175	10-21-86	5	4	3.22	44	0	0	0	73	59	30	26	6	22	82	.219	.179	.247	10.16	2.72
Lindsay, Shane	R-R	6-1	205	1-25-85	1	0	3.45	12	1	0	1	16	7	8	6	0	17	23	.127	.143	.111	13.21	9.77
McFarland, T.J.	L-L	6-3	190	6-8-89	0	0	11.25	1	1	0	0	4	9	6	5	1	2	5	.429	.400	.438	11.25	4.50
Packer, Matt	L-L	6-0	200	8-28-87	1	2	3.16	6	5	0	0	37	35	14	13	3	9	31	.267	.103	.314	7.54	2.19
Pestano, Vinnie	R-R	6-1	205	2-20-85	1	1	2.70	14	0	0	3	13	12	6	4	1	2	18	.235	.286	.200	12.15	1.35
Popham, Marty	R-R	6-6	235	8-4-87	0	0	1.50	1	1	0	0	6	5	1	1	0	0	6	.227	.214	.250	9.00	0.00
Price, Bryan	R-R	6-4	210	11-13-86	6	3	3.25	40	0	0	1	69	75	32	25	7	22	69	.273	.281	.266	8.96	2.86
Putnam, Zach	R-R	6-2	225	7-3-87	4	1	3.86	20	7	0	3	51	58	25	22	2	9	41	.286	.329	.260	7.19	1.58
Reyes, Anthony	R-R	6-2	230	10-16-81	0	2	25.41	3	3	0	0	6	8	16	16	0	11	3	.348	.333	.364	4.76	17.47
Smith, Carlton	L-R	6-2	205	1-23-86	1	1	0.87	9	0	0	2	10	6	3	1	0	3	8	.176	.091	.217	6.97	2.61
Stiller, Erik	R-R	6-5	210	7-10-84	1	0	3.86	8	0	0	0	14	11	6	6	1	3	12	.216	.158	.250	7.71	1.93
Stowell, Bryce	R-R	6-2	205	9-23-86	1	0	0.00	14	1	0	7	22	15	0	0	0	11	33	.192	.143	.233	13.30	4.43
Wagner, Neil	R-R	6-0	195	1-1-84	1	1	6.28	13	0	0	4	14	17	12	10	0	7	15	.283	.381	.231	9.42	4.40
White, Alex	R-R	6-3	200	8-29-88	8	7	2.28	18	17	0	0	107	91	45	27	8	27	76	.226	.231	.222	6.41	2.25
Wood, Kerry	R-R	6-5	210	6-16-77	0	1	20.25	3	1	0	0	3	4	6	6	0	3	2	.364	.250	.429	6.75	10.13
Wright, Steve	R-R	6-1	200	8-30-84	2	2	4.31	39	2	0	5	65	73	33	31	4	21	48	.286	.297	.278	6.68	2.92

Fielding

Catcher	PCT	G	PO	A	E	DP	PB
Apodaca	.995	23	183	12	1	1	0
Castillo	1.000	8	47	5	0	0	3
Espino	.996	59	448	40	2	2	7
Perez	.994	37	295	13	2	3	4
Toregas	.987	17	138	12	2	2	4

First Base	PCT	G	PO	A	E	DP
Arnal	1.000	5	42	3	0	4
Branyan	1.000	2	17	0	0	0
McBride	.990	33	271	22	3	27
Mills	.992	97	810	64	7	82
Perez	.965	6	51	4	2	2

Second Base	PCT	G	PO	A	E	DP
Arnal	.961	9	20	29	2	6
DeGeorge	1.000	1	2	2	0	0
Head	1.000	1	3	2	0	1

	PCT	G	PO	A	E	DP
Kipnis	.964	75	127	226	13	58
Phelps	.959	52	101	135	10	33
Rodriguez	1.000	4	3	7	0	1
Toole	.929	3	7	6	1	4

Third Base	PCT	G	PO	A	E	DP
Arnal	.960	9	10	14	1	3
Chisenhall	.929	96	55	168	17	18
Davis	.800	2	2	2	1	0
DeGeorge	1.000	1	0	3	0	0
Goedert	.957	26	16	50	3	3
Rodriguez	.944	8	4	13	1	2

Shortstop	PCT	G	PO	A	E	DP
Arnal	.960	24	26	71	4	16
Cabrera	1.000	3	3	8	0	2
Rivas	.789	5	3	12	4	2
Rivero	.943	107	140	321	28	63

	PCT	G	PO	A	E	DP
Rodriguez	.885	5	7	16	3	3
Outfield	PCT	G	PO	A	E	DP
Arnal	.800	3	4	0	1	0
Baker	.800	4	4	0	1	0
Choo	1.000	1	4	0	0	0
Davis	1.000	3	12	0	0	0
Drennen	.990	113	195	2	2	1
Fedroff	.990	108	194	6	2	1
Goedert	.800	4	4	0	1	0
Head	.957	41	64	2	3	0
Henry	.982	73	156	7	3	2
McBride	.971	34	65	2	2	0
Montero	.857	15	17	1	3	0
Rodriguez	1.000	2	4	0	0	0
Weglarz	.952	30	58	2	3	0

KINSTON INDIANS

HIGH CLASS A

CAROLINA LEAGUE

Batting	B-T	HT	WT	DOB	AVG	vLH	vRH	G	AB	R	H	2B	3B	HR	RBI	BB	HBP	SH	SF	SO	SB	CS	SLG	OBP
Abreu, Abner	R-R	6-3	170	10-24-89	.252	.241	.257	106	409	44	103	21	6	4	58	20	2	2	2	130	11	2	.362	.289
Arnal, Cristo	R-R	6-0	175	9-17-85	.194	.182	.205	22	72	5	14	1	0	0	1	7	1	2	0	12	4	1	.208	.275
Baker, Trent	R-L	6-4	175	6-14-90	.136	.000	.250	7	22	4	3	1	0	0	1	0	0	0	0	5	1	0	.182	.136
Bellows, Kyle	R-R	6-3	210	8-19-88	.253	.189	.282	124	462	48	117	21	5	10	66	39	6	2	3	91	4	3	.385	.318
Castillo, Alex	R-R	6-1	195	11-29-85	.212	.333	.159	36	99	5	21	5	0	0	8	12	0	3	0	31	2	1	.263	.297
Chen, Chun	R-R	6-1	200	11-1-88	.320	.360	.303	52	172	31	55	17	0	6	30	38	3	0	4	36	4	1	.523	.442
Davis, Adam	B-R	5-9	190	10-15-84	.225	.179	.250	26	80	9	18	3	0	3	8	12	1	1	0	21	2	1	.375	.333
Diaz, Juan	B-R	6-3	180	12-12-88	.271	.345	.245	61	218	17	59	7	1	1	19	15	0	5	0	51	2	2	.326	.318
Greenwell, Bo	L-L	6-0	185	10-15-88	.292	.294	.291	65	240	31	70	9	1	2	21	25	3	3	1	51	10	5	.363	.364
Henry, Jordan	L-R	6-3	175	6-13-88	.333	.393	.302	42	162	32	54	4	0	0	13	30	0	1	0	27	14	2	.358	.438
Kersten, Chris	R-R	6-4	225	12-28-85	.167	.231	.143	26	96	10	16	2	0	3	7	3	2	0	0	42	0	1	.281	.208
Kipnis, Jason	L-R	5-10	175	4-3-87	.300	.235	.333	54	203	33	61	12	3	6	31	24	6	2	2	46	2	3	.478	.387
Martinez, Richard	R-R	6-0	185	6-19-87	.130	.111	.138	47	161	9	21	4	0	0	15	18	0	1	0	48	1	1	.155	.218
Montero, Lucas	B-R	5-11	180	10-18-84	.265	.260	.267	94	321	45	85	12	5	3	29	47	2	5	0	80	24	5	.361	.362
Palincsar, Tim	L-L	6-3	190	4-4-87	.156	.077	.188	12	45	4	7	0	1	0	2	3	0	0	0	12	0	1	.200	.208
Pena, Roman	L-L	6-0	175	9-2-86	.148	.188	.133	21	61	9	9	1	2	1	9	11	0	1	1	19	2	2	.328	.274
Pickens, Doug	R-R	6-0	190	6-19-85	.248	.233	.254	96	322	28	80	12	0	6	38	29	6	2	4	62	5	2	.342	.319
Recknagel, Nate	R-R	6-2	220	4-29-86	.213	.232	.202	53	188	27	40	11	0	5	22	19	1	1	0	54	1	2	.351	.288
Rivas, Ronald	R-R	6-2	184	1-16-88	.243	.253	.239	82	259	30	63	13	1	2	28	29	5	5	2	48	1	3	.324	.329

Name	B-T	HT	WT	DOB	AVG	vLH	vRH	G	AB	R	H	2B	3B	HR	RBI	BB	HBP	SH	SF	SO	SB	CS	SLG	OBP
Sanchez, Karexon	B-R	5-11	175	8-22-87	.257	.261	.255	126	452	68	116	23	4	10	51	75	14	10	1	114	9	7	.392	.378
Tice, Jeremie	R-R	6-1	225	9-25-86	.283	.281	.284	51	191	26	54	15	2	5	28	12	4	1	1	47	0	0	.461	.337
Toole, Justin	R-R	6-0	180	9-10-86	.212	.188	.220	28	66	9	14	0	0	0	5	9	2	4	0	9	1	1	.212	.325
Webb, Donnie	B-R	5-11	190	4-30-86	.267	.236	.284	77	258	44	69	14	1	5	34	29	12	3	3	67	12	4	.388	.364

Pitching	B-T	HT	WT	DOB	W	L	ERA	G	GS	CG	SV	IP	H	R	ER	HR	BB	SO	AVG	vLH	vRH	K/9	BB/9
Adams, Austin	R-R	5-11	185	8-19-86	6	1	1.53	13	12	0	0	59	50	14	10	5	15	51	.228	.156	.285	7.82	2.30
Brach, Brett	R-R	6-3	185	3-29-88	0	1	3.38	2	0	0	0	3	4	2	1	0	1	2	.364	.571	.000	6.75	3.38
Bryson, Rob	R-R	6-1	200	12-11-87	2	1	2.25	13	0	0	1	20	7	5	5	2	8	38	.108	.111	.105	17.10	3.60
Burns, Cory	R-R	6-1	180	10-9-87	1	2	1.83	40	0	0	30	39	30	13	8	2	13	56	.210	.263	.174	12.81	2.97
De La Cruz, Kelvin	L-L	6-5	190	8-1-88	2	2	2.91	6	6	0	0	34	22	14	11	3	8	28	.183	.091	.218	7.41	2.12
Frias, Santo	R-R	6-3	189	12-8-87	0	1	2.45	5	0	0	0	7	5	5	2	1	3	9	.179	.273	.118	11.05	3.68
Gardner, Joe	R-R	6-4	220	3-18-88	12	6	2.65	22	22	0	0	122	85	44	36	4	51	104	.199	.222	.182	7.65	3.75
Grening, Brian	R-R	5-11	200	6-10-85	4	3	3.74	29	0	0	0	53	41	26	22	7	28	67	.214	.179	.237	11.38	4.75
Hagadone, Nick	L-L	6-5	230	1-1-86	1	3	2.39	10	10	0	0	38	28	11	10	2	29	45	.206	.159	.228	10.75	6.93
House, T.J.	R-L	6-2	215	9-29-89	6	10	3.91	27	26	0	0	136	135	74	59	7	61	106	.264	.317	.248	7.03	4.05
Jones, Chris	L-L	6-2	165	9-19-88	4	3	2.39	31	0	0	4	68	60	20	18	2	27	65	.234	.203	.247	8.65	3.59
Langwell, Matt	R-R	6-3	220	5-6-86	4	2	2.41	45	0	0	5	56	44	16	15	4	14	58	.219	.227	.212	9.32	2.25
Mahalic, Joey	R-R	6-3	205	11-28-88	5	8	4.16	25	20	0	0	110	117	61	51	5	58	68	.280	.317	.252	5.55	4.73
McFarland, T.J.	L-L	6-3	190	6-8-89	11	5	3.13	24	19	1	0	127	121	50	44	9	40	92	.246	.227	.253	6.54	2.84
Perez, Alexander	R-R	6-2	156	7-24-89	0	1	2.70	2	2	0	0	7	5	2	2	0	2	8	.200	.250	.176	10.80	2.70
Popham, Marty	R-R	6-6	235	8-4-87	4	4	3.92	17	13	0	3	83	82	41	36	10	20	77	.260	.279	.242	8.38	2.18
Roberts, David	L-R	6-2	215	10-29-86	1	3	6.03	41	2	0	0	75	98	53	50	11	22	66	.314	.383	.257	7.96	2.65
Smith, Steve	R-R	6-0	195	10-27-85	0	3	8.22	9	0	0	5	8	5	7	7	2	11	6	.192	.000	.385	7.04	12.91
Stowell, Bryce	R-R	6-2	205	9-23-86	1	0	1.42	11	0	0	0	25	16	6	4	2	8	41	.186	.119	.250	14.57	2.84
Sturdevant, Tyler	R-L	6-1	170	12-20-85	3	2	3.72	15	0	0	0	29	28	12	12	3	11	35	.248	.344	.210	10.86	3.41
Turek, Travis	R-R	6-1	170	9-2-87	4	3	3.73	41	0	0	2	80	82	41	33	6	30	45	.269	.293	.253	5.08	3.39
White, Alex	R-R	6-3	200	8-29-88	2	3	2.86	8	8	0	0	44	32	18	14	4	19	41	.204	.157	.241	8.39	3.89

Fielding

Catcher	PCT	G	PO	A	E	DP	PB
Castillo	.992	27	218	27	2	1	3
Chen	.993	35	264	25	2	3	13
Martinez	.995	45	364	37	2	4	6
Pickens	.977	38	275	19	7	1	6

First Base	PCT	G	PO	A	E	DP
Arnal	1.000	4	27	6	0	3
Davis	1.000	1	2	0	0	1
Kersten	1.000	26	209	23	0	20
Martinez	.900	2	8	1	1	1
Pena	.976	6	39	2	1	5
Pickens	.984	20	169	12	3	2
Recknagel	.988	45	402	17	5	38
Tice	.982	39	311	22	6	28
Toole	1.000	8	46	3	0	2

Second Base	PCT	G	PO	A	E	DP
Arnal	1.000	5	5	13	0	2
Castillo	1.000	1	2	0	0	0
Kipnis	.959	46	104	131	10	39
Rivas	.925	9	18	19	3	6
Sanchez	.976	75	151	213	9	52
Toole	1.000	9	10	25	0	3

Third Base	PCT	G	PO	A	E	DP
Bellows	.978	119	77	286	8	30
Castillo	—	1	0	0	0	0
Davis	1.000	1	0	4	0	1
Rivas	.000	1	0	0	1	0
Sanchez	.930	19	16	37	4	3
Toole	1.000	3	0	2	0	0

Shortstop	PCT	G	PO	A	E	DP
Arnal	1.000	7	11	25	0	3
Diaz	.960	60	66	172	10	33
Rivas	.920	66	92	209	26	36
Sanchez	.969	7	10	21	1	5
Toole	1.000	2	0	1	0	0

Outfield	PCT	G	PO	A	E	DP
Abreu	.946	88	135	6	8	0
Arnal	1.000	4	4	0	0	0
Baker	1.000	7	9	0	0	0
Castillo	1.000	3	3	0	0	0
Davis	.971	25	32	1	1	0
Greenwell	1.000	65	129	3	0	0
Henry	.973	42	69	3	2	2
Moncrief	1.000	3	5	0	0	0
Montero	.993	87	142	6	1	1
Palincsar	1.000	10	10	2	0	2
Pena	1.000	12	11	1	0	0
Pickens	1.000	9	8	0	0	0
Rivas	—	2	0	0	0	0
Toole	1.000	8	10	0	0	0
Webb	.970	76	124	5	4	0

LAKE COUNTY CAPTAINS   LOW CLASS A

MIDWEST LEAGUE

Batting	B-T	HT	WT	DOB	AVG	vLH	vRH	G	AB	R	H	2B	3B	HR	RBI	BB	HBP	SH	SF	SO	SB	CS	SLG	OBP
Abraham, Adam	R-R	6-0	210	3-27-87	.264	—	—	114	402	50	106	26	1	13	61	34	6	0	1	75	6	2	.430	.330
Baker, Trent	R-L	6-0	175	6-14-90	.165	—	—	28	91	9	15	3	0	0	3	13	1	1	0	28	2	3	.198	.276
Burnette, Chase	L-L	6-2	195	5-20-88	.185	—	—	8	27	2	5	2	0	1	2	1	0	0	0	9	0	0	.370	.214
Carlson, Ben	L-L	6-3	230	10-8-87	.171	—	—	73	240	19	41	8	2	2	20	10	6	6	1	65	1	2	.246	.222
Chen, Chun	R-R	6-1	200	11-1-88	.312	—	—	58	218	27	68	21	3	6	39	17	3	1	1	38	1	1	.518	.368
Childs, Dwight	R-R	6-2	175	7-23-88	.103	—	—	16	39	3	4	0	0	0	5	3	0	3	1	15	0	0	.103	.163
Cid, Delvi	R-R	6-2	170	7-19-89	.253	—	—	132	513	83	130	16	2	2	33	36	10	9	2	132	71	16	.304	.314
Folgia, Greg	B-R	5-11	195	3-31-88	.230	—	—	104	343	41	79	15	3	6	38	35	5	1	5	88	6	4	.344	.307
Frawley, Casey	R-R	5-11	190	9-17-87	.262	—	—	129	488	81	128	25	9	13	74	44	9	1	4	97	8	4	.430	.332
Greenwell, Bo	L-L	6-0	185	10-15-88	.310	—	—	66	248	47	77	13	2	4	36	32	4	2	2	34	15	6	.427	.395
Holt, Tyler	R-R	5-11	190	3-10-89	.286	—	—	22	70	12	20	8	2	0	8	15	1	1	2	12	5	3	.457	.409
Kersten, Chris	R-R	6-4	225	12-28-85	.240	—	—	68	242	30	58	11	1	13	39	15	11	1	1	75	1	3	.455	.312
Marte, Andy	R-R	6-1	205	10-21-83	.500	—	—	1	4	2	2	0	0	0	1	0	0	0	0	0	0	0	.500	.600
Martinez, Argenis	B-R	5-11	160	4-8-90	.219	—	—	100	319	48	70	4	3	0	23	48	3	15	3	79	22	9	.251	.324
Palincsar, Tim	L-L	6-3	190	4-4-87	.200	—	—	9	35	2	7	0	0	1	3	1	1	0	0	7	2	0	.286	.243
Perez, Roberto	R-R	6-0	200	12-23-88	.217	—	—	118	378	54	82	22	3	6	38	80	5	2	1	88	1	2	.339	.360
Smit, Jason	R-R	6-0	165	10-27-89	.262	—	—	86	313	39	82	20	1	8	41	12	7	4	3	92	8	1	.409	.301
Smith, Kyle	R-R	6-1	190	12-25-87	.246	—	—	103	353	31	87	13	3	3	24	26	8	2	0	98	4	1	.326	.313
Tice, Jeremie	R-R	6-1	225	9-25-86	.282	—	—	66	245	31	69	19	1	9	51	19	5	2	3	59	1	0	.478	.342

Pitching	B-T	HT	WT	DOB	W	L	ERA	G	GS	CG	SV	IP	H	R	ER	HR	BB	SO	AVG	vLH	vRH	K/9	BB/9
Adams, Austin	R-R	5-11	185	8-19-86	2	4	3.54	13	8	0	1	53	40	22	21	7	21	61	—	—	—	10.29	3.54
Brach, Brett	R-R	6-3	185	3-29-88	5	8	3.46	22	22	1	0	120	115	49	46	9	28	90	—	—	—	6.77	2.11

Name	B-T	HT	WT	DOB	W	L	ERA	G	GS	CG	SV	IP	H	R	ER	HR	BB	SO	AVG	vLH	vRH	K/9	BB/9
Bryson, Rob	R-R	6-1	200	12-11-87	4	0	4.05	8	0	0	0	13	13	7	6	2	2	21	—	—	—	14.18	1.35
Burns, Cory	R-R	6-1	180	10-9-87	0	0	2.30	14	0	0	12	16	13	4	4	0	1	25	—	—	—	14.36	0.57
Cespedes, Ramon	R-R	6-2	174	11-1-90	1	0	5.40	8	0	0	1	13	15	8	8	2	8	15	—	—	—	10.13	5.40
Cook, Clayton	R-R	6-3	175	7-23-90	6	7	3.35	23	23	0	0	118	109	49	44	7	37	83	—	—	—	6.31	2.81
Dew, Owen	R-R	6-2	180	9-26-88	1	2	4.50	7	0	0	0	16	15	8	8	2	4	13	—	—	—	7.31	2.25
Flores, Jose	R-R	6-3	185	6-4-89	1	1	2.14	28	0	0	6	42	35	10	10	1	7	51	—	—	—	10.93	1.50
Gardner, Joe	R-R	6-4	220	3-18-88	1	0	3.24	6	6	0	0	25	17	13	9	2	11	38	—	—	—	13.68	3.96
Guilmet, Preston	R-R	6-2	200	7-27-87	4	1	2.25	30	0	0	11	52	35	13	13	3	10	79	—	—	—	13.67	1.73
Haley, Trey	R-R	6-3	180	6-21-90	5	11	5.97	27	26	0	0	116	122	95	77	13	86	97	—	—	—	7.53	6.67
Hubbard, Antwonie	R-R	6-3	250	7-30-88	2	0	3.05	22	0	0	2	44	39	16	15	0	16	43	—	—	—	8.73	3.25
Jimenez, Francisco	L-L	5-10	164	10-2-88	8	1	3.59	35	2	0	1	80	79	34	32	7	21	72	—	—	—	8.07	2.35
Johnson, Jeremy	R-R	5-10	165	1-7-87	3	2	5.00	25	0	0	1	45	48	28	25	2	13	43	—	—	—	8.60	2.60
Jones, Chris	L-L	6-2	165	9-19-88	2	2	2.86	7	1	0	1	22	16	8	7	2	2	20	—	—	—	8.18	0.82
Kirk, Nick	L-L	6-0	195	12-16-86	0	0	5.79	9	0	0	1	14	13	9	9	1	9	15	—	—	—	9.64	5.79
Knapp, Jason	R-R	6-5	235	8-31-90	1	0	3.94	4	4	0	0	16	12	8	7	0	8	29	—	—	—	16.31	4.50
Laffey, Aaron	L-L	6-0	200	4-15-85	0	0	4.50	2	1	0	0	2	2	1	1	1	0	3	—	—	—	13.50	0.00
Morris, Ryan	L-L	6-3	175	1-10-88	0	2	12.71	5	0	0	1	6	5	8	8	1	6	4	—	—	—	6.35	9.53
Nakamura, Takafumi	R-R	6-5	195	1-3-88	1	1	6.23	3	0	0	1	4	9	3	3	1	1	1	—	—	—	2.08	2.08
Nuno, Vidal	L-L	5-11	195	7-26-87	6	8	4.96	21	16	0	0	94	104	54	52	13	14	94	—	—	—	8.97	1.34
Packer, Matt	L-L	6-0	200	8-28-87	8	5	1.60	24	13	1	1	96	77	23	17	4	13	92	—	—	—	8.66	1.22
Popham, Marty	R-R	6-6	235	8-4-87	3	1	3.71	8	4	0	0	34	36	16	14	4	7	28	—	—	—	7.41	1.85
Rayl, Mike	L-L	6-5	180	11-1-88	0	0	10.80	1	0	0	0	3	5	4	4	0	4	4	—	—	—	10.80	10.80
Salazar, Danny	R-R	6-0	180	1-11-90	1	1	4.45	7	7	0	0	32	34	16	16	7	13	23	—	—	—	6.40	3.62
Sarianides, Nick	R-R	6-1	200	8-29-89	6	3	4.59	34	0	0	1	69	69	40	35	5	21	45	—	—	—	5.90	2.75
Soto, Giovanni	L-L	6-3	155	5-18-91	3	2	3.77	6	6	0	0	31	22	13	13	5	11	31	—	—	—	9.00	3.19
Sturdevant, Tyler	R-L	6-1	170	12-20-85	3	0	0.76	16	0	0	2	36	17	5	3	1	8	56	—	—	—	14.13	2.02

Fielding

Catcher	PCT	G	PO	A	E	DP	PB
Chen	.991	25	211	21	2	1	5
Childs	.982	16	96	14	2	1	1
Perez	.997	104	850	109	3	5	15

First Base	PCT	G	PO	A	E	DP
Abraham	1.000	31	252	14	0	29
Burnette	1.000	3	28	0	0	2
Carlson	.988	69	570	22	7	50
Kersten	1.000	10	74	4	0	12
Smit	.989	28	245	14	3	20
Tice	1.000	3	20	2	0	1

Second Base	PCT	G	PO	A	E	DP
Frawley	1.000	8	14	17	0	7

Catcher (cont.)	PCT	G	PO	A	E	DP
Martinez	.973	87	153	250	11	69
Smith	.981	48	82	126	4	29

Third Base	PCT	G	PO	A	E	DP
Abraham	.946	71	51	140	11	14
Frawley	1.000	6	2	5	0	1
Marte	1.000	1	0	3	0	0
Martinez	.875	2	3	4	1	1
Smith	.875	9	5	16	3	0
Tice	.887	55	32	78	14	10

Shortstop	PCT	G	PO	A	E	DP
Frawley	.959	98	116	254	16	55
Martinez	.950	10	13	25	2	4
Smit	.750	1	1	2	1	0

Outfield	PCT	G	PO	A	E	DP
Smith	.962	36	49	101	6	26
Baker	.942	27	48	1	3	0
Burnette	1.000	5	4	0	0	0
Cid	.985	131	256	6	4	0
Folgia	.994	101	169	7	1	1
Frawley	1.000	11	15	2	0	1
Greenwell	.982	66	104	7	2	0
Holt	1.000	16	31	1	0	0
Kersten	.333	9	1	0	2	0
Palincsar	1.000	8	11	0	0	0
Smit	.976	56	77	3	2	2

MAHONING VALLEY SCRAPPERS — SHORT-SEASON

NEW YORK-PENN LEAGUE

Batting	B-T	HT	WT	DOB	AVG	vLH	vRH	G	AB	R	H	2B	3B	HR	RBI	BB	HBP	SH	SF	SO	SB	CS	SLG	OBP
Aguilar, Jesus	R-R	6-3	241	6-30-90	.244	.308	.227	32	123	8	30	9	0	2	17	11	0	0	2	28	2	0	.366	.301
Aponte, Juan	R-R	6-0	185	3-2-88	.125	.000	.167	2	8	1	1	0	0	0	1	1	0	0	0	5	0	0	.125	.222
Baker, Trent	R-L	6-0	175	6-14-90	.184	.154	.194	15	49	4	9	3	0	0	2	5	1	0	0	14	3	0	.245	.273
Bartolone, Nick	R-R	5-11	170	10-22-90	.255	.368	.227	24	94	7	24	3	0	0	7	7	2	2	0	18	8	3	.287	.323
Burnette, Chase	L-L	6-2	195	5-20-88	.274	.197	.305	64	248	29	68	15	3	8	28	13	1	0	1	55	1	0	.456	.312
Cabrera, Asdrubal	B-R	6-0	180	11-13-85	.333	.500	.250	2	6	0	2	1	0	0	2	1	0	0	0	1	0	0	.500	.429
Cannon, Tyler	B-R	6-1	185	8-30-87	.201	.275	.172	40	139	20	28	9	2	0	17	15	1	4	1	29	1	1	.295	.282
Casas, Jordan	L-R	5-11	180	3-17-88	.236	.306	.207	31	123	13	29	6	3	0	10	14	6	2	1	14	4	1	.333	.340
DeGeorge, Dan	R-R	5-10	180	2-19-87	.252	.256	.250	43	139	14	35	5	0	0	7	8	2	3	0	31	6	3	.288	.302
Fields, Aaron	R-R	6-0	190	6-20-88	.190	.214	.176	28	79	10	15	2	1	0	8	6	1	2	1	14	4	1	.241	.253
Fontanez, Kevin	R-R	5-11	170	6-20-90	.199	.232	.188	62	226	22	45	12	2	1	13	18	4	3	2	43	7	2	.283	.268
Gallas, Anthony	R-R	6-2	210	12-14-87	.235	.000	.267	4	17	2	4	1	0	1	3	0	0	0	0	6	0	0	.471	.235
Heere, Brian	L-R	5-11	170	8-6-87	.255	.208	.272	66	204	24	52	5	2	1	18	49	2	5	3	39	3	2	.314	.399
Kinney, Andrew	L-R	6-3	190	1-6-88	.181	.304	.146	29	105	13	19	3	0	0	2	7	0	1	0	34	0	0	.210	.232
Martinez, Richard	R-R	6-0	185	6-19-87	.103	.143	.080	13	39	1	4	1	0	0	2	5	0	0	0	10	0	0	.128	.205
Montero, Moises	R-R	6-0	210	11-4-89	.171	.125	.185	32	105	8	18	3	0	1	10	7	2	1	0	30	0	0	.229	.237
Rucker, Kevin	R-R	6-1	185	9-14-89	.230	.270	.216	47	148	18	34	3	1	2	11	14	3	1	2	46	1	2	.304	.305
Seastrunk, Diego	B-R	5-9	190	1-11-88	.192	.214	.184	48	156	19	30	7	0	4	19	22	1	0	4	33	0	1	.314	.290
Toole, Justin	R-R	6-0	180	9-10-86	.083	.250	.000	5	12	1	1	0	0	0	1	0	2	1	0	1	0	0	.083	.214
Toregas, Wyatt	R-R	5-11	210	12-2-82	.368	.333	.385	7	19	9	7	1	0	2	2	8	0	0	0	3	0	0	.737	.556
Urshela, Giovanny	R-R	6-0	185	10-11-91	.290	.186	.327	58	221	22	64	8	0	3	35	12	3	1	6	32	5	3	.367	.326

Pitching	B-T	HT	WT	DOB	W	L	ERA	G	GS	CG	SV	IP	H	R	ER	HR	BB	SO	AVG	vLH	vRH	K/9	BB/9
Cook, Cole	R-R	6-6	200	10-18-88	0	3	5.40	4	4	0	0	15	14	12	9	3	6	14	.226	.222	.229	8.40	4.81
Cooper, Jordan	R-R	6-2	190	5-10-89	5	5	4.94	14	13	0	0	62	79	39	34	9	18	41	.309	.250	.351	5.95	2.61
Dew, Owen	R-R	6-2	180	9-26-88	1	2	2.64	9	9	0	0	48	36	14	14	4	4	25	.206	.221	.194	4.72	0.76
Dickerson, Dale	R-R	6-2	210	9-11-86	2	1	5.06	23	0	0	0	32	31	25	18	0	28	21	.263	.186	.307	5.91	7.88
Dischler, Tony	R-R	6-3	190	3-6-89	0	0	0.00	2	2	0	0	5	3	1	0	0	1	5	.176	.143	.200	9.00	1.80

Name	B-T	HT	WT	DOB	W	L	ERA	G	GS	CG	SV	IP	H	R	ER	HR	BB	SO	AVG	vLH	vRH	K/9	BB/9
Ehlert, Clayton	R-R	6-1	195	11-2-87	0	2	3.27	22	0	0	9	33	31	15	12	2	11	42	.244	.196	.276	11.45	3.00
Gardner, Ryan	R-R	5-10	175	11-7-88	0	1	9.00	2	0	0	0	3	7	5	3	0	2	2	.438	.500	.400	6.00	6.00
Gaynor, Casey	R-R	6-2	205	4-10-87	5	2	4.04	16	5	0	0	49	52	25	22	3	19	37	.275	.256	.290	6.80	3.49
Goodnight, Michael	R-R	6-4	215	6-10-89	0	2	4.05	4	4	0	0	13	10	8	6	0	10	12	.217	.188	.233	8.10	6.75
Goryl, J.D.	R-R	6-0	205	5-29-86	1	4	5.17	24	0	0	0	38	50	32	22	2	16	20	.314	.361	.286	4.70	3.76
Kaminsky, Alex	R-R	6-1	190	2-25-88	6	5	2.48	14	14	0	0	69	55	20	19	4	18	58	.222	.205	.238	7.57	2.35
Kirk, Nick	L-L	6-0	195	12-16-86	0	0	2.53	16	0	0	6	21	18	8	6	0	6	32	.217	.231	.211	13.50	2.53
Nakamura, Takafumi	R-R	6-5	195	1-3-88	3	2	3.86	18	0	0	0	37	35	16	16	2	7	31	.257	.235	.271	7.47	1.69
Ramirez, Julio	R-R	6-2	187	10-30-84	1	2	6.55	13	0	0	0	22	23	16	16	4	18	23	.271	.278	.265	9.41	7.36
Rayl, Mike	L-L	6-5	180	11-1-88	2	4	2.81	14	14	0	0	67	57	26	21	1	21	56	.234	.270	.221	7.49	2.81
Reichenbach, J.D.	L-L	6-2	165	8-29-87	1	3	3.38	20	0	0	3	37	32	16	14	3	18	29	.232	.279	.211	6.99	4.34
Rosario, Gregorio	R-R	6-4	180	8-26-88	1	1	5.16	14	0	0	0	23	25	14	13	3	17	9	.287	.235	.321	3.57	6.75
Smith, Kyle C.	R-R	6-6	220	9-5-87	0	0	6.54	19	0	0	0	32	24	29	23	3	26	46	.202	.282	.163	13.07	7.39
Striz, Nate	R-R	6-2	220	10-15-88	0	0	0.00	2	0	0	0	2	0	0	0	0	1	2	.000	.000	.000	9.00	4.50
Talbot, Mitch	R-R	6-2	200	10-17-83	0	0	3.00	1	1	0	0	3	2	1	1	0	1	0	.222	.200	.250	0.00	3.00
Wetmore, Kirk	L-L	6-2	205	3-17-89	2	7	6.26	15	10	0	0	55	60	41	38	6	31	44	.284	.347	.265	7.24	5.10

Fielding

Catcher	PCT	G	PO	A	E	DP	PB
Aponte	1.000	1	3	0	0	0	0
Martinez	1.000	4	26	3	0	0	0
Montero	.973	31	197	20	6	1	10
Seastrunk	.994	41	283	40	2	1	12
Toregas	1.000	5	25	1	0	0	0

First Base	PCT	G	PO	A	E	DP
Aguilar	.976	24	227	21	6	23
Aponte	1.000	2	19	1	0	3
Burnette	.980	27	224	22	5	24
Kinney	.976	23	192	12	5	15
Martinez	1.000	2	16	5	0	0
Toole	1.000	1	7	0	0	0

Second Base	PCT	G	PO	A	E	DP
Bartolone	.750	1	1	2	1	0
Cannon	.958	5	12	11	1	0
DeGeorge	.947	29	56	88	8	25
Fields	.954	21	34	49	4	8
Fontanez	.938	25	42	64	7	14

Third Base	PCT	G	PO	A	E	DP
Cannon	.968	10	6	24	1	4
DeGeorge	.957	12	2	20	1	0
Toole	1.000	3	5	3	0	1
Urshela	.957	55	52	124	8	11

Shortstop	PCT	G	PO	A	E	DP
Bartolone	.960	24	29	68	4	12

	PCT	G	PO	A	E	DP
Cabrera	1.000	1	1	3	0	1
Cannon	.937	20	29	60	6	12
DeGeorge	1.000	1	3	3	0	0
Fontanez	.947	34	44	98	8	19

Outfield	PCT	G	PO	A	E	DP
Baker	1.000	15	25	0	0	0
Burnette	.957	19	22	0	1	0
Casas	.982	27	55	0	1	0
Gallas	.875	4	7	0	1	0
Heere	.952	62	109	11	6	1
Moncrief	.979	66	135	6	3	0
Rucker	.959	41	67	4	3	0

AZL INDIANS

ARIZONA LEAGUE

ROOKIE

Batting	B-T	HT	WT	DOB	AVG	vLH	vRH	G	AB	R	H	2B	3B	HR	RBI	BB	HBP	SH	SF	SB	CS	SLG	OBP
Aguilar, Jesus	R-R	6-3	241	6-30-90	.259	.281	.250	29	112	15	29	2	1	7	22	5	2	0	4	33	1	1	.482	.293
Aponte, Juan	R-R	6-3	185	3-2-88	.274	.294	.270	35	106	12	29	3	0	0	11	6	2	0	4	25	0	0	.302	.314
Bartolone, Nick	R-R	5-11	170	10-22-90	.303	.371	.278	32	132	25	40	3	0	0	9	9	3	0	0	18	15	4	.326	.361
Bradley, Marcus	L-L	5-9	160	8-30-90	.200	.200	.200	11	35	4	7	1	0	0	1	4	0	0	1	3	1	0	.229	.282
Brown, Mark	L-L	5-9	160	9-11-91	.158	.200	.143	6	19	0	3	1	0	0	2	1	0	0	1	8	1	0	.211	.273
Carrera, Ezequiel	L-L	5-10	185	6-11-87	.429	.500	.417	4	14	2	6	1	0	0	4	1	0	0	0	2	0	0	.500	.467
Childs, Dwight	R-R	6-2	175	7-23-88	.333	.000	.333	2	3	1	1	0	0	0	0	2	0	0	0	0	0	0	.333	.600
Dunn, Henry	R-R	5-7	185	3-26-89	.176	.154	.182	39	125	17	22	7	3	2	16	12	0	1	0	23	4	2	.328	.248
Fuentes, Miguel	R-R	5-11	178	4-5-90	.095	.000	.105	9	21	1	2	0	1	0	1	0	0	0	1	8	0	0	.190	.091
Gallas, Anthony	R-R	6-2	210	12-14-87	.276	.186	.303	50	185	19	51	10	3	2	23	11	4	0	1	40	2	1	.395	.328
Garcia, Robel	B-R	6-0	168	3-28-93	.164	.188	.157	43	140	18	23	6	4	1	20	32	2	1	0	41	6	3	.286	.328
Jones, Hunter	R-R	6-2	185	8-17-91	.190	.333	.152	11	42	4	8	0	0	0	1	5	1	0	0	13	5	0	.190	.292
Kinney, Andrew	L-R	6-3	190	6-8-88	.260	.273	.256	15	50	3	13	2	0	0	4	6	1	0	0	11	0	1	.300	.351
Lavisky, Alex	R-R	6-1	200	1-13-91	.200	.250	.182	5	15	0	3	0	0	0	0	0	0	0	0	7	0	0	.200	.200
Martinez, Jorge	B-R	6-2	170	3-29-93	.216	.212	.217	46	190	23	41	5	0	2	21	10	1	2	2	41	3	4	.274	.256
Monsalve, Alex	R-R	6-2	185	4-22-92	.220	.186	.230	43	182	18	40	8	3	1	18	4	2	0	1	52	0	0	.313	.243
Recknagel, Nate	R-R	6-2	220	4-29-86	.364	.375	.357	9	22	6	8	3	0	0	7	2	0	0	0	7	1	0	.500	.548
Romero, Juan	R-R	6-1	175	6-16-93	.241	.308	.227	40	145	21	35	10	2	7	14	16	1	0	0	67	2	1	.483	.321
Siliga, Aaron	L-L	5-10	180	8-24-92	.250	.108	.294	42	156	17	39	7	2	2	12	9	3	3	2	37	8	5	.359	.300
Thompson, Logan	R-R	6-0	150	8-4-89	.227	.429	.189	25	88	12	20	4	0	0	4	7	0	2	0	20	1	1	.273	.284
Torres, Joel	R-R	6-0	185	7-4-89	.184	.286	.151	38	114	10	21	5	3	1	14	12	0	0	1	55	2	4	.307	.260
Washington, LeVon	L-R	5-11	170	7-26-91	.444	.333	.500	3	9	4	4	0	0	0	3	3	0	0	0	1	1	0	.444	.583
Webb, Donnie	B-R	5-11	190	4-30-86	.125	.000	.167	8	24	3	3	0	1	0	3	3	0	0	1	6	2	0	.208	.214
Wolters, Tony	L-R	5-10	165	6-9-92	.211	.100	.118	5	19	2	4	0	0	0	2	5	0	0	0	2	0	0	.211	.286

Pitching	B-T	HT	WT	DOB	W	L	ERA	G	GS	CG	SV	IP	H	R	ER	HR	BB	SO	AVG	vLH	vRH	K/9	BB/9
Cespedes, Ramon	R-R	6-2	174	11-1-90	2	0	0.39	11	0	0	3	23	9	2	1	0	3	28	.117	.125	.111	10.96	1.17
Encarnacion, Luis	R-R	6-3	170	10-25-91	0	4	5.15	14	11	0	0	44	36	33	25	2	22	43	.220	.200	.231	8.86	4.53
Flores, Fernando	R-R	6-3	230	11-11-90	1	1	4.88	19	0	0	1	31	31	21	17	1	12	32	.248	.313	.208	9.19	3.45
Gardner, Ryan	R-R	5-10	175	11-7-88	4	3	2.17	22	0	0	5	29	18	10	7	0	8	37	.173	.125	.203	11.48	2.48
Guerrero, Harold	L-L	6-3	215	5-21-90	2	2	4.21	11	2	0	0	26	14	14	12	1	12	33	.156	.083	.182	11.57	4.21
Homblert, Rafael	R-R	6-5	178	9-4-91	0	1	5.93	18	0	0	0	27	33	22	18	0	17	30	.303	.267	.328	9.88	5.60
Jimenez, Danny	L-L	6-2	205	9-23-89	3	3	3.42	12	8	0	0	55	62	28	21	4	44	28	.281	.185	.311	7.16	1.14
Knapp, Jason	R-R	6-5	235	8-31-90	0	2	1.46	5	5	0	0	12	5	4	2	0	4	18	.119	.059	.160	13.14	2.92
Lopez, Jose	R-R	6-2	185	3-20-91	2	1	4.28	18	0	0	0	27	14	15	13	2	23	27	.231	.179	.262	8.89	7.57
Morales, Alexander	R-R	6-0	161	7-26-89	0	8	6.11	13	13	0	0	53	70	45	36	2	21	54	.317	.300	.328	9.17	3.57
Morel, Luis	R-R	6-0	170	11-19-92	0	1	5.40	5	4	0	0	18	17	15	11	1	7	21	.230	.125	.280	10.31	3.44
Morris, Ryan	L-L	6-3	193	1-10-88	0	1	1.26	6	0	0	0	14	15	3	2	0	3	8	.283	.200	.302	5.02	1.88
Pacheco, Enriquez	R-R	6-3	165	12-10-89	0	1	4.82	7	0	0	0	9	6	5	5	0	5	5	.257	.286	.238	4.82	4.82

Player	B-T	HT	WT	DOB	W	L	ERA	G	GS	CG	SV	IP	H	R	ER	HR	BB	SO	AVG	vLH	vRH	K/9	BB/9
Pereira, Orlando	R-R	6-5	180	9-10-91	3	1	5.64	17	0	0	0	30	28	27	19	1	18	29	.243	.271	.224	8.60	5.34
Petter, Kyle	L-L	6-0	180	4-5-90	0	1	3.51	14	0	0	1	26	29	13	10	1	9	28	.290	.333	.276	9.82	3.16
Reyes, Anthony	R-R	6-2	230	10-16-81	0	1	4.15	2	2	0	0	4	3	3	2	0	2	6	.188	.167	.200	12.46	4.15
Speake, Matt	R-R	6-0	200	8-19-86	2	1	7.40	17	0	0	1	24	30	25	20	0	7	32	.291	.158	.369	11.84	2.59
Sterling, Felix	R-R	6-3	200	3-15-93	2	3	3.16	12	11	0	0	51	40	21	18	2	20	57	.222	.246	.207	9.99	3.51

Fielding

Catcher	PCT	G	PO	A	E	DP	PB
Aponte	.990	12	92	12	1	1	5
Childs	1.000	1	6	1	0	0	0
Fuentes	.923	5	22	2	2	0	2
Lavisky	1.000	4	24	1	0	0	1
Monsalve	.972	40	363	49	12	3	11

First Base	PCT	G	PO	A	E	DP
Aguilar	.982	24	187	27	4	14
Aponte	.991	21	107	9	1	10
Childs	1.000	1	1	0	0	0
Kinney	.992	15	124	7	1	13
Recknagel	.974	6	32	6	1	3

Second Base	PCT	G	PO	A	E	DP
Garcia	.930	27	48	84	10	15
Martinez	.952	13	23	37	3	9
Thompson	.885	18	25	52	10	9

Third Base	PCT	G	PO	A	E	DP
Bartolone	.958	11	1	22	1	3
Garcia	.778	10	5	16	6	1
Jones	.905	7	9	10	2	0
Romero	.878	28	17	48	9	6

Shortstop	PCT	G	PO	A	E	DP
Bartolone	.918	18	34	55	8	15
Garcia	.889	5	12	4	2	2

	PCT	G	PO	A	E	DP
Jones	1.000	1	1	4	0	1
Martinez	.891	29	47	75	15	13
Wolters	.920	5	7	16	2	4

Outfield	PCT	G	PO	A	E	DP
Bradley	1.000	9	20	1	0	0
Brown	1.000	6	10	0	0	0
Carrera	1.000	3	5	1	0	0
Dunn	.971	36	66	1	2	0
Gallas	.987	43	71	4	1	0
Siliga	.950	40	53	4	3	0
Thompson	1.000	4	4	1	0	1
Torres	.958	36	64	5	3	0
Webb	1.000	7	7	0	0	0

DSL INDIANS   ROOKIE

DOMINICAN SUMMER LEAGUE

Batting	B-T	HT	WT	DOB	AVG	vLH	vRH	G	AB	R	H	2B	3B	HR	RBI	BB	HBP	SH	SF	SO	SB	CS	SLG	OBP
Avila, Jack	B-R	6-1	165	5-30-92	.167	.000	.250	5	12	2	2	1	0	0	2	1	0	0	0	2	0	0	.250	.231
Boscan, Manuel	B-R	6-0	160	3-10-93	.233	.143	.262	21	86	13	20	4	0	0	4	2	0	0	1	9	1	0	.279	.247
Castillo, Leonardo	R-R	6-2	190	3-7-93	.269	.205	.288	59	197	18	53	10	2	0	16	16	2	4	2	29	1	5	.340	.327
De Jesus, Victor	R-R	6-2	170	1-13-93	.214	.370	.181	56	154	16	33	11	0	1	11	17	2	5	0	56	6	1	.305	.301
De La Cruz, Juan	B-R	6-1	195	8-5-93	.154	.167	.148	30	78	9	12	0	0	0	8	14	3	0	1	12	0	1	.154	.302
De Los Santos, Xavier	R-R	6-0	180	10-13-88	.173	.250	.144	44	133	12	23	5	0	1	7	9	3	2	2	26	0	1	.233	.238
Delgado, Richard	R-R	5-10	165	9-10-92	.264	.000	.295	41	106	17	28	2	0	7	10	1	2	1	10	6	8	.283	.331
Figueroa, Starling	R-R	6-0	160	11-5-91	.177	.130	.196	29	79	9	14	3	0	0	11	8	6	0	0	27	0	3	.215	.301
Fledi, Joel	R-R	6-2	180	2-17-93	.132	.077	.160	16	38	3	5	1	0	0	1	6	0	0	0	23	0	0	.158	.250
Galvez, Fermin	L-L	6-3	225	1-25-93	.206	.154	.218	26	68	5	14	2	0	0	8	11	0	0	0	17	0	0	.235	.316
Gonzalez, Erik	R-R	6-1	165	8-31-91	.346	.346	.346	64	240	38	83	18	1	1	27	14	2	0	2	19	9	4	.442	.384
Hernandez, Angel	R-R	6-1	180	9-24-92	.256	.571	.188	14	39	4	10	1	0	0	8	5	0	0	0	6	0	0	.282	.341
Kelly, Jairo	B-R	6-0	170	9-20-92	.250	.170	.277	61	212	35	53	8	2	0	26	30	2	2	2	47	14	7	.363	.346
Marte, Juan	R-R	6-0	180	11-17-90	.185	.250	.167	32	54	6	10	2	0	0	3	4	1	0	0	24	3	0	.222	.254
Mejia, Joel	R-R	5-11	157	4-7-93	.165	.125	.177	37	103	14	17	1	4	0	6	20	2	2	0	34	4	2	.252	.312
Moreno, Franklin	R-R	6-1	180	3-25-93	.189	.167	.194	15	37	1	7	0	0	0	4	4	1	0	1	9	0	0	.189	.279
Ramirez, Luis	B-R	6-3	200	7-12-92	.259	.280	.253	36	116	16	30	6	0	0	18	9	1	0	4	22	0	1	.310	.308
Rodriguez, Luigi	B-R	5-11	160	11-13-92	.301	.333	.292	63	206	43	62	7	10	2	27	36	2	1	4	35	31	9	.461	.403
Rojas, Gustavo	B-R	6-2	190	11-12-91	.167	.222	.156	23	54	4	9	2	0	0	6	4	1	0	1	15	1	0	.204	.233
Tejeda, Aderlin	R-R	6-2	175	11-23-91	.240	.500	.217	11	25	2	6	2	0	0	3	5	1	0	0	5	1	1	.320	.387
Valerio, Charlie	B-R	6-0	204	11-7-90	.276	.292	.271	65	214	32	59	9	1	4	37	37	5	1	5	34	3	3	.383	.387

Pitching	B-T	HT	WT	DOB	W	L	ERA	G	GS	CG	SV	IP	H	R	ER	HR	BB	SO	AVG	vLH	vRH	K/9	BB/9
Abad, Che Yeyne	L-L	5-11	162	6-30-90	1	1	7.59	4	0	0	0	11	12	12	9	0	9	6	.267	.000	.273	5.06	7.59
Cabrera, Luis	R-R	6-4	175	7-27-92	0	0	5.91	7	1	0	0	11	13	12	7	0	10	6	.283	.375	.263	5.06	8.44
Caripa, Yan	R-R	6-2	180	1-13-93	2	0	2.19	8	0	0	0	12	8	3	3	0	2	10	.200	.000	.258	7.30	1.46
Carmona, Manuel	R-R	6-0	190	6-21-92	1	2	2.57	8	5	0	0	28	16	18	8	2	18	28	.158	.115	.173	9.00	5.79
Cleto, Jeffry	R-R	6-3	190	6-14-91	0	1	6.75	3	2	0	0	8	9	6	6	0	5	6	.281	.250	.292	6.75	5.63
Colon, Frangy	R-R	6-2	170	1-18-93	0	1	5.11	7	2	0	0	12	14	10	7	1	3	6	.286	.375	.242	4.38	2.19
Damaso, Juan	L-L	6-0	170	1-22-91	5	2	3.76	9	9	0	0	41	41	25	17	1	11	41	.247	.000	.253	9.07	2.43
Del Carmen, Carlos	R-R	6-0	170	5-12-90	3	1	3.73	14	1	0	0	31	24	16	13	2	19	16	.216	.207	.220	4.60	5.46
Encarnacion, Isaias	L-L	6-4	200	7-10-91	1	1	6.57	8	2	0	0	12	13	11	9	0	19	14	.277	1.000	.261	10.22	13.86
Homblert, Rafael	R-R	6-5	178	9-4-91	0	1	2.84	3	2	0	0	13	13	9	4	0	5	9	.255	.263	.250	6.39	3.55
Leon, Ernesto	R-R	6-0	175	4-22-93	2	0	1.96	8	1	0	0	18	13	6	4	0	9	10	.220	.176	.238	4.91	4.42
Machiz, Arleski	R-R	6-4	170	11-4-90	0	0	10.50	5	0	0	0	6	2	8	7	0	14	6	.118	.250	.077	9.00	21.00
Morel, Luis	R-R	6-0	170	11-19-92	1	1	2.08	3	3	0	0	13	5	3	3	0	10	13	.125	.143	.115	9.00	6.92
Munoz, Oswell	R-R	6-5	179	11-22-90	3	2	1.86	14	9	1	0	73	55	16	15	3	6	73	.210	.167	.228	9.04	0.74
Paredes, Alexis	R-R	6-3	175	1-24-92	4	4	2.55	18	7	0	0	49	38	23	14	0	27	42	.213	.182	.224	7.66	4.93
Polanco, Jose	R-R	6-5	171	1-29-91	0	0	7.50	10	1	0	0	12	18	13	10	0	13	9	.346	.294	.371	6.75	9.75
Ramirez, Julio	R-R	6-2	187	10-30-84	0	0	1.29	9	0	0	0	14	10	3	2	0	7	21	.196	.250	.186	13.50	4.50
Ramirez, Moisses	R-R	5-11	170	3-8-90	2	4	1.26	26	0	0	14	36	27	7	5	1	8	35	.201	.194	.204	8.83	2.02
Rivas, Alejandro	R-R	6-1	200	8-21-91	2	4	2.83	22	0	0	3	41	37	20	13	0	21	40	.245	.222	.258	8.71	4.57
Robles, Jefry	R-R	6-4	205	7-7-90	0	2	5.23	4	0	0	0	10	10	6	6	5	10	.233	.300	.212	8.71	4.35
Sanchez, Eliezer	R-R	6-4	227	1-11-92	1	0	4.28	11	8	0	0	34	38	23	16	1	18	28	.275	.243	.287	7.49	4.83
Santana, Amiro	R-R	6-2	170	3-22-93	0	2	17.65	6	2	0	0	9	15	17	17	1	6	8	.375	.556	.323	6.23	8.31
Santana, Juan	R-R	6-2	170	7-2-93	0	0	16.20	2	1	0	0	2	3	3	3	0	1	1	.375	.333	.400	5.40	5.40
Tejeda, Enosil	R-R	6-0	185	6-21-89	7	3	1.76	12	12	0	0	72	62	23	14	2	15	78	.238	.262	.230	9.80	1.88
Valdez, Phillip	R-R	6-2	160	11-16-91	0	0	8.40	10	0	0	0	15	16	14	14	1	11	14	.271	.412	.214	8.40	6.60
Villa, Alejandro	R-R	6-2	160	5-29-92	2	1	1.34	17	0	0	0	34	29	6	5	1	6	26	.248	.333	.241	6.95	1.60

Fielding

Catcher	PCT	G	PO	A	E	DP	PB
Avila	1.000	2	12	0	0	0	0
De La Cruz	.978	10	77	14	2	0	0
De Los Santos	.983	43	293	49	6	2	4
Moreno	1.000	8	28	3	0	0	0
Rojas	1.000	8	27	2	0	0	2
Valerio	.965	17	116	22	5	1	2

First Base	PCT	G	PO	A	E	DP
De La Cruz	.922	8	43	4	4	3
Galvez	.988	24	158	9	2	10
Gonzalez	1.000	5	10	5	0	0
Moreno	1.000	1	7	0	0	0
Valerio	.987	48	353	29	5	29

Second Base	PCT	G	PO	A	E	DP
Boscan	.918	10	23	22	4	3
Delgado	.927	31	59	56	9	10
Gonzalez	.987	21	39	36	1	4
Kelly	1.000	1	0	2	0	0
Rodriguez	.947	21	32	39	4	10

Third Base	PCT	G	PO	A	E	DP
Boscan	.800	3	1	3	1	0
Castillo	.887	58	47	102	19	8
Delgado	1.000	1	3	4	0	1
Gonzalez	.880	20	15	29	6	2

Shortstop	PCT	G	PO	A	E	DP
Boscan	.906	8	9	20	3	3

	PCT	G	PO	A	E	DP
Gonzalez	.891	12	20	21	5	1
Kelly	.929	58	97	150	19	30

Outfield	PCT	G	PO	A	E	DP
De Jesus	.904	56	80	5	9	1
Figueroa	1.000	17	16	0	0	0
Fledi	.889	13	14	2	2	0
Gonzalez	.909	18	19	1	2	0
Hernandez	—	1	0	0	0	0
Lebron	1.000	17	13	1	0	0
Marte	1.000	25	20	2	0	0
Mejia	.980	30	44	4	1	0
Ramirez	.889	31	37	3	5	0
Rodriguez	.945	42	67	2	4	0
Tejeda	1.000	10	12	2	0	1

Colorado Rockies

SEASON IN A SENTENCE: After a trip to the World Series in 2007 and a trip to the playoffs in 2009, expectations for the Rockies were high in 2010, and finishing third in the National League West thanks to a suspect pitching staff didn't quite meet them.

HIGH POINT: Ubaldo Jimenez threw the franchise's first no-hitter on April 17. He started the year 13-1, 1.15 and became Colorado's first pitcher to start the All-Star Game. Carlos Gonzalez also had an outstanding season, winning his first Gold Glove and first Silver Slugger awards. Gonzalez led the league in batting, and challenged for the home run and RBI titles as well.

LOW POINT: Absences from the roster did damage in Colorado. Closer Huston Street and starter Jorge de la Rosa each missed more than 60 games with injuries, and both had been expected to be key parts of the pitching staff. Troy Tulowitzki missed 33 games at midseason and couldn't take part in the All-Star Game because of a broken wrist. The true lowest moment of the year, however, came when club president Keli McGregor died April 20 at age 47 during a business trip. An autopsy revealed that his heart had been damaged by a rare virus.

NOTABLE ROOKIES: The Rockies farm system provided several young players who could be contributors in coming seasons. Jhoulys Chacin went 9-11, 3.28 in 137 innings and should find a spot in the rotation going forward. Esmil Rogers could also be a contributor, as could infielders Jonathan Herrera, Eric Young Jr. and Chris Nelson.

KEY TRANSACTIONS: Colorado didn't make any headline trades in 2010, with the only notable deal coming in August when it sent minor leaguer Chris Balcom-Miller to the Red Sox for Manny Delcarmen. In the draft, the Rockies picked up two Atlantic Coast Conference quarterbacks and invested in their baseball futures. First-rounder Kyle Parker of Clemson signed for $1.4 million, while four-rounder Russell Wilson of North Carolina State signed for $200,000.

DOWN ON THE FARM: Among Colorado's minor league affiliates, only high Class A Modesto finished with a winning record. But several of the organization's top prospects performed well, including Tyler Matzek, the 2009 first-round pick. Though he had trouble with his command at times and missed time with biceps tendinitis, he went 5-1, 2.92 in 18 starts for low Class A Asheville.

OPENING DAY PAYROLL: $84.2 million (16th)

PLAYERS OF THE YEAR

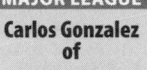

MAJOR LEAGUE	MINOR LEAGUE
Carlos Gonzalez	**Juan Nicasio**
of	rhp
.336/.376/.598	(High Class A)
Led NL in AVG, H, TB	12-10, 3.91
2nd in SLG, 3rd in OPS	171 SO/177 IP

ORGANIZATION LEADERS

BATTING		*Minimum 250 at-bats
MAJORS		
*AVG	Carlos Gonzalez	.336
*OPS	Carlos Gonzalez	.974
HR	Carlos Gonzalez	34
RBI	Carlos Gonzalez	117
MINORS		
*AVG	Matt Miller, Colorado Springs	.325
*OBP	Jared Clark, Asheville	.412
*SLG	Brad Eldred, Colorado Springs	.566
R	Matt Miller, Colorado Springs	90
H	Matt Miller, Colorado Springs	165
TB	Ben Paulsen, Modesto	236
2B	Nolan Arenado, Asheville	41
3B	James Cesario, Modesto	10
	Cole Garner, Colorado Springs	10
HR	Brad Eldred, Colorado Springs	30
RBI	Jordan Pacheco, Modesto/Tulsa	89
BB	Jared Clark, Asheville	76
SO	David Christensen, Modesto	132
SB	Juan Ciriaco, DSL Rockies	34

PITCHING		†Minimum 75 innings
MAJORS		
W	Ubaldo Jimenez	19
†ERA	Ubaldo Jimenez	2.88
SO	Ubaldo Jimenez	214
MINORS		
W	Ethan Hollingsworth, Tulsa/Modesto	12
	Juan Nicasio, Modesto	12
L	Brandon Durden, Colorado Springs/Tulsa	14
†ERA	Ethan Hollingsworth, Tulsa/Modesto	3.69
G	Two tied at	58
GS	Juan Nicasio, Modesto	28
SV	Adam Jorgenson, Modesto/Tulsa	24
IP	Juan Nicasio, Modesto	177.3
BB	Tyler Matzek, Asheville	62
SO	Juan Nicasio, Modesto	171
†AVG	Wes Musick, Asheville	.265

2010 PERFORMANCE

General Manager: Dan O'Dowd. **Farm Director:** Marc Gustafson. **Scouting Director:** Bill Schmidt.

Class	Team	League	W	L	PCT	Finish*	Manager(s)
Majors	Colorado Rockies	National	83	79	.512	7th (16)	Jim Tracy
Triple-A	Colorado Springs Sky Sox	Pacific Coast	64	79	.448	14th (16)	Stu Cole
Double-A	Tulsa Drillers	Texas	69	70	.496	5th (8)	Ron Gideon
High A	Modesto Nuts	California	73	67	.521	6th (10)	Jerry Weinstein
Low A	Asheville Tourists	South Atlantic	69	70	.496	7th (14)	Joe Mikulik
Short-season	Tri-City Dust Devils	Northwest	30	46	.395	8th (8)	Fred Ocasio
Rookie	Casper Ghosts	Pioneer	37	39	.487	6th (8)	Tony Diaz
Overall 2010 Minor League Record			342	371	.480	25th (30)	

*Finish in overall standings (No. of teams in league). †League champion.

ORGANIZATION STATISTICS

COLORADO ROCKIES

NATIONAL LEAGUE

Batting	B-T	HT	WT	DOB	AVG	vLH	vRH	G	AB	R	H	2B	3B	HR	RBI	BB	HBP	SH	SF	SO	SB	CS	SLG	OBP
Barmes, Clint	R-R	6-1	205	3-6-79	.235	.280	.214	133	387	43	91	21	0	8	50	35	5	2	3	66	3	2	.351	.305
Eldred, Brad	R-R	6-5	290	7-12-80	.250	.333	.167	11	24	4	6	1	0	1	3	2	1	0	0	10	0	0	.417	.333
Fowler, Dexter	B-R	6-4	190	3-22-86	.260	.260	.260	132	439	73	114	20	14	6	36	57	2	7	0	104	13	8	.410	.347
Giambi, Jason	L-R	6-3	240	1-8-71	.244	.277	.233	87	176	17	43	9	0	6	35	35	6	0	5	47	2	0	.398	.378
Gonzalez, Carlos	L-L	6-1	210	10-17-85	.336	.320	.345	145	587	111	197	34	9	34	117	40	2	0	7	135	26	8	.598	.376
Hawpe, Brad	L-L	6-3	210	6-22-79	.255	.256	.254	88	259	24	66	21	2	7	37	36	1	0	4	68	2	1	.432	.343
Helton, Todd	L-L	6-2	215	8-20-73	.256	.272	.248	118	398	48	102	18	1	8	37	67	2	0	6	90	0	0	.367	.362
Herrera, Jonathan	B-R	5-9	150	11-3-84	.284	.292	.280	76	222	34	63	6	2	1	21	25	0	7	3	36	2	2	.342	.352
Iannetta, Chris	R-R	6-0	230	4-8-83	.197	.222	.184	61	188	20	37	6	1	9	27	30	4	0	1	48	1	0	.383	.318
McKenry, Michael	R-R	5-10	200	3-4-85	.000	.000	.000	6	8	0	0	0	0	0	0	0	0	0	0	5	0	0	.000	.111
Mora, Melvin	R-R	5-11	200	2-7-72	.285	.296	.276	113	316	39	90	12	5	7	45	31	5	2	0	53	2	1	.421	.358
Nelson, Chris	R-R	5-11	175	9-3-85	.280	.444	.188	17	25	7	7	1	0	0	0	1	0	1	0	4	1	0	.320	.308
Olivo, Miguel	R-R	6-0	230	7-15-78	.269	.295	.259	112	394	55	106	17	6	14	58	27	1	2	3	117	7	4	.449	.315
Payton, Jay	R-R	5-10	205	11-22-72	.343	.200	.450	20	35	3	12	4	1	0	1	1	0	0	0	4	1	0	.514	.361
Phillips, Paul	R-R	5-11	200	4-15-77	.217	.167	.235	12	23	4	5	0	0	0	1	2	0	0	0	7	0	0	.217	.280
Smith, Seth	L-L	6-3	210	9-30-82	.246	.154	.261	133	358	55	88	19	5	17	52	35	2	0	3	67	2	1	.469	.314
Spilborghs, Ryan	R-R	6-1	200	9-5-79	.279	.257	.296	134	341	41	95	20	2	10	39	39	5	2	1	83	4	5	.437	.360
Stewart, Ian	L-R	6-3	215	4-5-85	.256	.231	.264	121	386	54	99	14	2	18	61	45	5	0	5	110	5	2	.443	.338
Tulowitzki, Troy	R-R	6-3	215	10-10-84	.315	.342	.302	122	470	89	148	32	3	27	95	48	5	1	5	78	11	2	.568	.381
Young Jr., Eric	B-R	5-10	180	5-25-85	.244	.238	.248	51	172	26	42	5	1	0	8	17	0	0	0	32	17	6	.285	.312

Pitching	B-T	HT	WT	DOB	W	L	ERA	G	GS	CG	SV	IP	H	R	ER	HR	BB	SO	AVG	vLH	vRH	K/9	BB/9
Beimel, Joe	L-L	6-3	215	4-19-77	1	2	3.40	71	0	0	0	45	46	18	17	5	15	21	.269	.221	.329	4.20	3.00
Belisle, Matt	R-R	6-4	225	6-6-80	7	5	2.93	76	0	0	1	92	84	34	30	7	16	91	.246	.232	.253	8.90	1.57
Betancourt, Rafael	R-R	6-2	215	4-29-75	5	1	3.61	72	0	0	1	62	52	25	25	9	8	89	.220	.279	.187	12.85	1.16
Buchholz, Taylor	R-R	6-4	220	10-13-81	1	0	4.50	7	0	0	0	10	5	5	5	2	6	9	.278	.278	.278	8.10	5.40
Chacin, Jhoulys	R-R	6-3	215	1-7-88	9	11	3.28	28	21	0	0	137	114	64	50	10	61	138	.227	.266	.201	9.04	4.00
Cook, Aaron	R-R	6-3	215	2-8-79	6	8	5.08	23	23	2	0	128	147	77	72	11	52	62	.290	.337	.258	4.37	3.67
Corpas, Manuel	R-R	6-3	210	12-3-82	3	5	4.62	56	0	0	10	62	66	33	32	7	22	47	.269	.326	.239	6.79	3.18
Daley, Matt	R-R	6-2	180	6-23-82	0	1	4.24	28	0	0	0	23	27	11	11	2	10	18	.293	.345	.270	6.94	3.86
De La Rosa, Jorge	L-L	6-1	215	4-5-81	8	7	4.22	20	20	0	0	122	105	62	57	15	55	113	.235	.206	.244	8.36	4.07
Deduno, Samuel	R-R	6-3	190	7-2-83	0	0	3.38	4	0	0	0	3	3	1	1	1	3	.273	.200	.333	10.13	3.38
Delcarmen, Manny	R-R	6-2	205	2-16-82	0	2	6.48	9	0	0	0	8	12	6	6	1	4	6	.324	.357	.304	6.48	4.32
Dotel, Octavio	R-R	6-0	220	11-25-73	0	1	5.06	8	0	0	0	5	6	4	3	1	4	6	.250	.286	.235	10.13	6.75
3-team total (19 Los Angeles, 41 Pittsburgh)					3	4	4.08	68	0	0	22	64	52	32	29	9	32	75	—	—	—	10.55	4.50
Escalona, Edgmer	R-R	6-4	215	10-6-86	0	0	1.50	5	0	0	0	6	4	1	1	0	4	2	.190	.400	.125	3.00	6.00
Flores, Randy	L-L	6-0	190	7-31-75	2	0	2.96	47	0	0	0	27	22	10	9	4	13	18	.224	.220	.229	5.93	4.28
Francis, Jeff	L-L	6-5	220	1-8-81	4	6	5.00	20	19	0	0	104	119	61	58	11	23	67	.293	.309	.290	5.78	1.98
Hammel, Jason	R-R	6-6	215	9-2-82	10	9	4.81	30	30	0	0	178	201	97	95	18	47	141	.287	.282	.291	7.14	2.38
Jimenez, Ubaldo	R-R	6-4	210	1-22-84	19	8	2.88	33	33	4	0	222	164	73	71	10	92	214	.209	.191	.227	8.69	3.74
Morales, Franklin	L-L	6-0	210	1-24-86	0	4	6.28	35	0	0	3	29	28	22	20	5	24	27	.255	.171	.293	8.48	7.53
Reynolds, Matt	L-L	6-5	240	10-2-84	1	0	2.00	11	0	0	0	18	10	4	4	2	5	17	.164	.152	.179	8.50	2.50
Rincon, Juan	R-R	5-11	210	1-23-79	0	0	4.50	2	0	0	0	2	3	1	1	0	2	3	.333	.250	.400	13.50	9.00
Rogers, Esmil	R-R	6-1	190	8-14-85	2	3	6.13	28	8	0	0	72	94	59	49	5	26	66	.318	.370	.278	8.25	3.25
Smith, Greg	L-L	6-1	190	12-22-83	1	2	6.23	8	0	0	0	39	49	28	27	8	24	31	.322	.179	.355	7.15	5.54
Street, Huston	R-R	6-0	190	8-2-83	4	4	3.61	44	0	0	20	47	39	21	19	5	11	45	.225	.208	.238	8.56	2.09

Fielding

Catcher	PCT	G	PO	A	E	DP	PB
Iannetta	.985	52	373	32	6	2	5
McKenry	1.000	2	5	1	0	0	0
Olivo	.990	111	821	62	9	9	10
Phillips	.978	10	43	2	1	0	0

First Base	PCT	G	PO	A	E	DP
Eldred	1.000	6	52	3	0	5
Giambi	.986	37	267	8	4	25
Hawpe	1.000	6	42	4	0	6
Helton	.992	115	932	77	8	116
Iannetta	1.000	3	10	1	0	2

	PCT	G	PO	A	E	DP
Mora	.983	25	109	8	2	10
Phillips	1.000	1	0	1	0	0

Second Base	PCT	G	PO	A	E	DP
Barmes	.986	88	163	198	5	59
Herrera	.984	57	91	149	4	32
Mora	.970	19	26	38	2	6

	PCT	G	PO	A	E	DP
Nelson	.882	4	8	7	2	0
Young Jr.	.958	35	44	94	6	23
Third Base	**PCT**	**G**	**PO**	**A**	**E**	**DP**
Barmes	—	1	0	0	0	0
Herrera	1.000	16	3	10	0	3
Iannetta	—	1	0	0	0	0
Mora	.957	63	26	84	5	7
Nelson	1.000	4	2	2	0	0

	PCT	G	PO	A	E	DP
Stewart	.964	115	59	212	10	17
Shortstop	**PCT**	**G**	**PO**	**A**	**E**	**DP**
Barmes	.974	47	50	141	5	33
Herrera	1.000	7	1	1	0	0
Tulowitzki	.984	122	211	388	10	103
Outfield	**PCT**	**G**	**PO**	**A**	**E**	**DP**
Fowler	.996	120	239	2	1	0

Gonzalez	.996	142	259	8	1	1
Hawpe	.990	63	97	1	1	0
Mora	1.000	4	4	1	0	0
Payton	1.000	10	12	0	0	0
Smith	.981	101	155	4	3	2
Spilborghs	.964	107	131	2	5	1
Young Jr.	.917	10	11	0	1	0

COLORADO SPRINGS SKY SOX

TRIPLE-A

PACIFIC COAST LEAGUE

Batting	B-T	HT	WT	DOB	AVG	vLH	vRH	G	AB	R	H	2B	3B	HR	RBI	BB	HBP	SH	SF	SO	SB	CS	SLG	OBP
Bowden, Johnny	R-R	6-3	205	8-15-84	.333	.000	.333	1	3	0	1	1	0	0	0	0	0	0	0	2	0	0	.667	.333
Eldred, Brad	R-R	6-5	200	7-12-80	.264	.231	.278	106	394	67	104	27	1	30	84	33	5	0	2	119	6	0	.566	.327
Fowler, Dexter	B-R	6-4	190	3-22-86	.340	.324	.347	27	106	23	36	10	4	2	13	17	1	0	0	27	1	0	.566	.435
Frey, Chris	L-L	6-1	180	8-11-83	.288	.258	.296	101	288	39	83	20	4	1	25	25	4	9	2	52	8	4	.396	.351
Garner, Cole	R-R	6-2	210	12-15-84	.304	.310	.301	111	415	81	126	31	10	13	61	39	8	6	1	89	8	5	.520	.374
Hawpe, Brad	L-L	6-3	210	6-22-79	.222	.250	.200	2	9	2	2	1	0	0	0	1	0	0	0	3	0	0	.333	.300
Herrera, Jonathan	B-R	5-9	150	11-3-84	.261	.230	.273	58	222	30	58	6	1	2	17	27	1	7	3	29	3	3	.324	.340
Iannetta, Chris	R-R	6-0	230	4-8-83	.349	.467	.313	17	63	17	22	7	0	5	21	10	2	0	1	10	0	0	.698	.447
Lo Duca, Paul	R-R	5-9	215	4-12-72	.233	.556	.147	14	43	5	10	0	0	1	7	3	1	0	1	5	0	0	.302	.292
Matsui, Kazuo	B-R	5-10	185	10-23-75	.262	.195	.288	82	301	54	79	12	4	2	29	31	1	3	2	50	7	0	.349	.331
McKenry, Michael	R-R	5-10	200	3-4-85	.265	.277	.261	99	347	44	92	23	1	10	49	32	2	0	3	77	1	1	.424	.328
Metcalf, Travis	R-R	6-3	215	8-17-82	.296	.352	.276	120	416	64	123	34	4	10	67	47	0	4	4	86	3	2	.469	.364
Miller, Matt	R-R	6-2	210	12-26-82	.325	.336	.321	136	507	90	165	22	2	10	81	66	6	0	7	93	2	0	.436	.404
Nelson, Chris	R-R	5-11	175	9-3-85	.313	.271	.325	85	319	60	100	15	3	12	55	29	4	2	2	57	3	3	.492	.376
Paulk, Mike	L-L	6-2	195	4-23-84	.262	.192	.280	107	366	59	96	20	8	8	59	39	1	2	2	69	4	3	.426	.333
Payton, Jay	R-R	5-10	205	11-22-72	.323	.311	.328	116	439	62	142	36	5	6	74	25	4	1	1	47	13	3	.469	.365
Phillips, Paul	R-R	5-11	200	4-15-77	.238	.226	.242	34	122	15	29	8	1	0	10	13	1	0	0	12	1	1	.320	.316
Quintanilla, Omar	L-R	5-9	190	10-24-81	.252	.300	.242	34	119	14	30	7	1	1	15	11	1	2	2	25	1	1	.353	.316
Schaeffer, Warren	R-R	6-0	180	1-28-85	.252	.289	.231	33	103	16	26	5	2	2	19	5	3	5	0	19	0	1	.398	.306
Scott, Joe	R-R	6-0	185	8-22-86	.143	.000	.143	3	7	0	1	0	0	0	0	0	1	0	1	0	4	0	0	.143	.250
Torres, Eider	B-R	5-8	165	1-16-83	.323	.278	.340	17	65	8	21	4	0	0	10	3	0	1	4	8	1	2	.385	.333
Tulowitzki, Troy	R-R	6-3	215	10-10-84	.250	.000	.250	2	4	1	1	0	0	0	0	0	0	0	0	0	0	0	.250	.250
Young Jr., Eric	B-R	5-10	180	5-25-85	.252	.438	.187	33	123	20	31	5	1	1	9	15	2	1	1	32	10	0	.333	.340

Pitching	B-T	HT	WT	DOB	W	L	ERA	G	GS	CG	SV	IP	H	R	ER	HR	BB	SO	AVG	vLH	vRH	K/9	BB/9
Aristil, Jonnathan	R-R	6-1	160	11-30-86	0	0	0.00	1	0	0	0	2	0	0	0	0	0	0	.000	.000	.000	0.00	0.00
Ayala, Luis	R-R	6-2	190	1-12-78	1	1	4.91	4	0	0	0	7	8	4	4	2	0	4	.308	.400	.000	4.91	0.00
3-team total (14 Albuquerque, 18 Reno)					2	10	6.42	36	0	0	4	48	60	35	34	4	18	31	—	—		5.85	3.40
Beimel, Joe	L-L	6-3	215	4-19-77	0	0	0.00	2	0	0	0	3	2	0	0	0	2	0	.200	.333	.143	6.75	0.00
Bierbrodt, Nick	L-L	6-5	215	5-16-78	1	0	10.02	21	0	0	0	21	35	26	23	7	18	19	.372	.243	.456	8.27	7.84
Birkins, Kurt	L-L	6-2	190	8-11-80	5	8	5.71	23	15	1	0	80	101	58	51	9	22	58	.305	.295	.308	6.50	2.46
Buchholz, Taylor	R-R	6-4	220	10-13-81	0	1	5.89	18	0	0	0	18	22	12	12	3	9	12	.301	.324	.282	5.89	4.42
Chacin, Jhoulys	R-R	6-3	215	1-7-88	3	2	1.51	7	7	0	0	36	27	10	6	1	17	34	.214	.154	.257	8.58	4.29
Daley, Matt	R-R	6-2	180	6-23-82	0	0	13.50	6	0	0	0	5	10	8	8	2	3	7	.417	.600	.286	11.81	5.06
De La Rosa, Jorge	L-L	6-1	215	4-5-81	1	2	5.52	3	3	0	0	15	17	10	9	1	4	15	.293	.143	.341	9.20	2.45
Deduno, Samuel	R-R	6-3	190	7-2-83	3	1	2.93	6	6	0	0	31	20	12	10	3	18	29	.190	.170	.207	8.51	5.28
Durden, Brandon	R-L	6-3	215	7-20-84	0	3	8.40	3	0	0	0	15	20	14	14	0	8	7	.333	.391	.297	4.20	4.80
Escalona, Edgmer	R-R	6-4	215	10-6-86	3	5	6.00	57	0	0	1	69	66	47	46	17	32	74	.253	.245	.258	9.65	4.17
Francis, Jeff	L-L	6-5	220	1-8-81	0	0	0.00	1	1	0	0	3	1	0	0	0	1	3	.111	.250	.000	9.00	3.00
Gobble, Jimmy	L-L	6-3	210	7-19-81	0	0	4.50	2	0	0	0	2	3	1	1	0	0	6	.375	.667	.200	0.00	0.00
Graham, Andy	R-R	6-4	210	6-29-84	0	0	5.40	9	0	0	1	15	15	12	9	2	10	9	.263	.381	.194	5.40	6.00
Hammel, Jason	R-R	6-6	215	9-2-82	1	0	5.14	1	1	0	0	7	9	4	4	1	1	6	.333	.375	.273	7.71	1.29
Johnson, Alan	R-R	6-1	180	8-24-83	10	8	5.91	28	25	1	0	142	189	106	93	14	43	100	.326	.332	.322	6.35	2.73
Johnston, Andrew	R-R	5-11	205	4-20-84	3	3	4.85	55	0	0	1	56	66	33	30	5	18	35	.306	.256	.333	5.66	2.91
Lindsay, Shane	R-R	6-1	205	1-25-85	0	1	6.59	14	0	0	0	14	15	10	10	0	17	19	.288	.176	.343	12.51	11.20
Lo, Ching-Lung	R-R	6-0	190	8-20-85	1	0	1.80	2	1	0	0	5	5	3	1	0	5	1	.250	.231	.286	1.80	9.00
Morales, Franklin	L-L	6-0	210	1-24-86	3	0	2.67	24	0	0	1	30	20	9	9	3	19	34	.192	.147	.214	10.09	5.64
Moss, Damian	R-L	6-0	183	11-24-76	2	2	7.93	25	0	0	0	36	47	35	32	1	27	27	.320	.243	.345	6.69	6.69
Muecke, Josh	L-L	6-3	195	1-9-82	6	9	5.94	25	22	0	0	120	150	81	79	13	43	81	.315	.338	.306	6.09	3.23
Redding, Tim	R-R	5-11	230	2-12-78	1	1	4.32	5	5	0	0	25	34	12	12	2	5	21	.337	.417	.264	7.56	1.80
Reynolds, Matt	L-L	6-5	240	10-2-84	1	3	2.62	50	0	0	7	55	49	18	16	2	16	67	.236	.192	.262	10.96	2.62
Rice, Scott	L-L	6-6	217	9-21-81	0	1	6.75	23	0	0	3	23	27	17	17	0	15	15	.303	.233	.339	5.96	5.96
Rincon, Juan	R-R	5-11	210	1-23-79	4	4	7.88	47	0	0	8	46	58	43	40	4	37	42	.312	.380	.270	8.28	7.29
Roe, Chaz	R-R	6-1	190	10-9-86	9	13	5.98	27	27	2	0	158	210	115	105	18	53	115	.325	.322	.327	6.55	3.02
Rogers, Esmil	R-R	6-1	190	8-14-85	3	3	5.75	12	11	0	0	61	62	41	39	6	19	53	.261	.333	.203	7.82	2.80
Smith, Greg	L-L	6-1	190	12-22-83	2	5	6.12	15	15	0	0	75	88	59	51	14	30	49	.288	.318	.275	5.88	3.60
Street, Huston	R-R	6-0	190	8-2-83	1	1	10.29	7	1	0	0	7	11	8	8	1	2	9	.344	.545	.238	11.57	2.57
Wilhite, Matt	R-R	5-11	185	7-3-81	1	1	6.75	40	0	0	0	59	80	45	44	10	23	44	.333	.371	.308	6.75	3.53

Fielding

Catcher	PCT	G	PO	A	E	DP	PB
Bowden	.833	1	5	0	1	0	0
Iannetta	.991	15	101	11	1	1	0
Lo Duca	1.000	2	17	0	0	0	0
McKenry	.990	94	624	60	7	7	2
Phillips	.989	33	251	25	3	6	1

First Base	PCT	G	PO	A	E	DP
Eldred	.993	83	679	46	5	78
Iannetta	1.000	1	2	0	0	0
Lo Duca	1.000	4	38	0	0	5
Metcalf	1.000	8	42	3	0	6
Paulk	.986	57	463	27	7	54

Second Base	PCT	G	PO	A	E	DP
Herrera	1.000	10	20	22	0	9
Lo Duca	.923	2	7	5	1	1
Matsui	.986	69	154	195	5	61
Metcalf	.935	7	11	18	2	2
Nelson	.981	23	43	59	2	19
Quintanilla	.941	5	13	19	2	6
Schaeffer	.988	19	35	48	1	6
Scott	1.000	2	2	2	0	1

Young Jr.	.979	20	43	50	2	13

Third Base	PCT	G	PO	A	E	DP
Eldred	.920	12	1	22	2	4
Herrera	1.000	3	2	5	0	1
Lo Duca	.667	2	1	1	1	0
Metcalf	.956	107	53	208	12	25
Nelson	.864	11	5	14	3	5
Quintanilla	.917	12	8	25	3	7
Schaeffer	1.000	6	2	3	0	0

Shortstop	PCT	G	PO	A	E	DP
Herrera	.987	46	66	156	3	32
Matsui	.980	10	18	31	1	7
Metcalf	1.000	1	1	2	0	0
Nelson	.938	52	70	142	14	36
Quintanilla	.985	14	15	51	1	8

Schaeffer	.964	7	10	17	1	4
Torres	.984	15	18	43	1	9
Tulowitzki	1.000	2	5	7	0	5

Outfield	PCT	G	PO	A	E	DP
Eldred	—	1	0	0	0	0
Fowler	1.000	24	60	0	0	0
Frey	.989	90	173	6	2	2
Garner	.968	98	176	8	6	4
Hawpe	1.000	1	1	0	0	0
Miller	.991	122	220	9	2	2
Nelson	—	1	0	0	0	0
Paulk	.969	26	31	0	1	0
Payton	.979	88	141	1	3	1
Young Jr.	.833	10	15	0	3	0

TULSA DRILLERS
DOUBLE-A
TEXAS LEAGUE

Batting	B-T	HT	WT	DOB	AVG	vLH	vRH	G	AB	R	H	2B	3B	HR	RBI	BB	HBP	SH	SF	SO	SB	CS	SLG	OBP
Beerer, Scott	R-R	6-1	200	7-4-82	.258	.293	.237	112	391	40	101	10	0	4	40	20	2	7	4	63	5	4	.315	.295
Blackmon, Charlie	L-L	6-3	200	7-1-86	.297	.303	.293	86	337	53	100	22	4	11	55	32	4	3	5	43	19	7	.484	.360
Bowden, Johnny	R-R	6-3	205	8-15-84	.250	.333	.200	7	16	3	4	1	0	0	1	1	1	1	0	6	1	0	.313	.333
Buller, Dayton	R-R	6-0	190	6-22-81	.227	.250	.219	13	44	5	10	4	0	0	5	7	1	0	0	10	0	1	.318	.346
Davis, Lars	L-R	6-3	205	11-7-85	.289	.351	.264	40	128	22	37	5	0	2	11	19	7	1	0	31	0	2	.375	.409
Gomez, Hector	R-R	6-2	180	3-5-88	.314	.091	.417	9	35	6	11	4	0	0	3	0	0	0	0	8	0	0	.429	.314
Jackson, Anthony	B-R	5-8	175	6-17-84	.251	.252	.251	122	434	67	109	12	7	2	40	60	9	8	4	73	33	12	.325	.351
Kindel, Jeff	L-L	6-3	205	1-9-83	.242	.256	.235	75	256	26	62	14	1	5	32	33	1	2	4	43	2	2	.363	.327
Mayora, Daniel	R-R	5-11	145	7-27-85	.286	.333	.264	66	234	27	67	21	3	3	30	21	4	2	2	35	4	6	.440	.352
Mitchell, Mike	R-R	6-1	200	8-24-85	.230	.317	.174	48	152	18	35	4	3	2	11	17	3	4	2	36	10	1	.336	.316
Nazario, Radames	R-R	6-0	166	6-14-87	.245	.230	.252	62	192	16	47	9	0	2	21	25	5	2	0	42	1	1	.323	.347
Pacheco, Jordan	R-R	6-1	190	1-30-86	.333	.378	.293	21	78	11	26	5	0	1	19	6	4	0	3	6	1	1	.436	.396
Perez, Kenny	B-R	6-2	190	9-28-81	.228	.261	.206	32	114	11	26	3	1	0	7	6	0	0	0	17	0	0	.281	.290
Repec, Matt	R-R	6-1	190	8-30-83	.196	.211	.187	84	240	24	47	16	1	1	22	28	1	5	2	54	0	1	.283	.280
Roling, Kiel	R-R	6-3	240	1-23-87	.225	.223	.226	93	329	44	74	17	0	12	46	28	2	1	2	100	0	1	.386	.288
Rosario, Wilin	R-R	5-11	190	2-23-89	.285	.357	.244	73	270	42	77	13	1	19	52	21	3	2	1	57	1	0	.552	.342
Sardinha, Bronson	L-R	6-1	220	4-6-83	.299	.217	.322	81	268	48	80	25	3	10	50	35	2	1	0	50	8	4	.526	.415
Schaeffer, Warren	R-R	6-0	180	1-28-85	.238	.324	.201	69	240	29	57	11	0	1	24	12	6	5	1	57	0	1	.296	.290
Torres, Eider	B-R	5-8	165	1-16-83	.272	.235	.290	26	103	8	28	4	1	0	4	6	0	2	0	11	4	1	.330	.312
Tulowitzki, Troy	R-R	6-3	215	10-10-84	.143	.333	.000	2	7	1	1	1	0	0	0	0	1	0	0	6	0	0	.286	.125
Van Kooten, Jason	R-R	6-0	170	9-1-84	.271	.319	.244	112	398	70	108	31	4	17	58	35	7	5	2	102	11	7	.497	.339
Young Jr., Eric	B-R	5-10	180	5-25-85	.231	.250	.222	4	13	3	3	0	0	0	0	1	0	0	0	2	0	0	.231	.286

Pitching	B-T	HT	WT	DOB	W	L	ERA	G	GS	CG	SV	IP	H	R	ER	HR	BB	SO	AVG	vLH	vRH	K/9	BB/9
Alburquerque, Al	R-R	6-0	195	6-10-86	2	4	4.98	25	0	0	3	34	32	23	19	1	19	32	.258	.226	.290	8.39	4.98
Aristil, Jonnathan	R-R	6-1	160	11-30-86	1	1	4.39	11	3	0	0	27	20	17	13	6	19	24	.208	.176	.244	8.10	6.41
Baker, Craig	R-R	6-2	210	1-31-85	1	1	9.16	20	0	0	5	19	28	21	19	1	12	13	.346	.243	.432	6.27	5.79
Bennigson, Craig	R-L	6-2	215	3-21-87	0	0	3.00	5	0	0	0	6	3	2	2	1	2	5	.130	.200	.111	7.50	3.00
Bierbrodt, Nick	L-L	6-5	215	5-16-78	0	1	2.20	14	0	0	1	16	13	4	4	0	7	13	.193	.185	.200	7.16	3.86
Billings, Bruce	R-R	6-0	200	11-18-85	11	6	3.28	34	14	0	1	110	86	40	40	6	44	101	.217	.225	.206	8.29	3.61
Brothers, Rex	L-L	6-0	205	12-18-87	2	1	3.91	24	0	0	4	23	14	13	10	2	18	27	.177	.098	.263	10.57	7.04
Cook, Aaron	R-R	6-3	215	2-8-79	1	1	2.53	2	2	0	0	11	8	3	3	1	3	10	.211	.188	.227	8.44	2.53
Daley, Matt	R-R	6-2	180	6-23-82	0	0	3.00	3	0	0	0	3	1	1	1	1	1	0	.000	.000	.000	0.00	0.00
Durden, Brandon	R-L	6-2	215	7-20-84	5	11	4.61	23	22	1	0	135	161	73	69	23	26	72	.298	.299	.298	4.81	1.74
Francis, Jeff	L-L	6-5	220	1-8-81	0	0	1.54	2	2	0	0	12	11	2	2	1	2	5	.256	.231	.267	3.86	1.54
Friedrich, Christian	R-L	6-4	215	7-8-87	3	6	5.05	18	18	0	0	87	100	54	49	10	35	78	.293	.348	.265	8.04	3.61
Graham, Andy	R-R	6-4	210	6-29-84	4	3	4.64	36	0	0	0	54	55	29	28	6	18	44	.263	.255	.271	7.29	2.98
Hollingsworth, Ethan	R-R	6-2	200	5-4-87	0	0	9.58	2	2	0	0	10	15	13	11	2	4	9	.341	.375	.300	7.84	3.48
Jarrett, Sean	R-R	6-5	210	4-26-83	3	1	1.80	18	0	0	0	30	29	6	6	2	8	18	.259	.255	.262	5.40	2.40
Jorgenson, Adam	R-R	6-0	185	9-10-85	2	0	5.40	12	0	0	0	12	13	9	7	2	5	14	.277	.286	.269	10.80	3.86
Lo, Ching-Lung	R-R	6-6	190	8-20-85	3	4	3.82	31	8	0	0	73	68	38	31	8	22	45	.247	.250	.245	5.30	2.71
Malone, Chris	R-R	6-4	215	6-28-83	3	5	4.10	44	0	0	5	59	56	29	27	9	27	45	.253	.266	.224	6.83	4.10
Pomeranz, Stuart	R-R	6-7	220	12-17-84	1	6	3.67	51	0	0	8	49	57	24	20	5	20	53	.285	.261	.304	9.73	3.67
Reynolds, Greg	R-R	6-7	225	7-3-85	7	12	5.22	17	17	0	0	90	105	55	52	10	15	45	.290	.277	.304	4.52	1.51
Rice, Scott	L-L	6-6	217	9-21-81	2	0	0.96	35	0	0	4	47	23	8	5	0	18	33	.145	.145	.144	6.36	3.47
Riordan, Cory	R-R	6-4	200	5-25-86	11	9	4.01	27	24	0	0	162	168	75	72	20	38	135	.270	.292	.245	7.52	2.12
Street, Huston	R-R	6-0	190	8-2-83	0	0	0.00	2	1	0	0	1	1	0	0	0	1	2	.200	.250	.000	13.50	6.75
Weiser, Keith	R-L	6-2	190	9-21-84	0	0	4.18	26	26	1	0	157	182	88	73	17	33	84	.296	.300	.294	4.82	1.89

Fielding

Catcher	PCT	G	PO	A	E	DP	PB
Bowden	1.000	5	29	7	0	0	0
Buller	.988	12	71	10	1	0	0
Davis	.988	38	235	15	3	1	4
Pacheco	.994	20	165	8	1	0	1

Rosario	.977	67	403	55	11	7	11

First Base	PCT	G	PO	A	E	DP
Kindel	.986	39	325	39	5	32
Perez	1.000	2	17	1	0	1

Repec	1.000	10	88	5	0	12
Roling	.994	83	771	47	5	65
Schaeffer	.989	10	76	10	1	6

Second Base	PCT	G	PO	A	E	DP
Jackson	.929	25	36	69	8	14
Mayora	1.000	10	14	24	0	7
Nazario	.938	2	3	12	1	2
Schaeffer	1.000	4	12	18	0	7
Van Kooten	.977	103	214	307	12	72
Young Jr.	.941	4	9	7	1	0

Third Base	PCT	G	PO	A	E	DP
Mayora	.928	35	29	61	7	8
Nazario	1.000	1	0	2	0	0

	PCT	G	PO	A	E	DP
Perez	.908	24	18	51	7	6
Repec	.933	61	46	107	11	5
Schaeffer	.976	29	18	64	2	12

Shortstop	PCT	G	PO	A	E	DP
Gomez	.878	9	10	26	5	9
Jackson	.750	1	2	1	1	1
Mayora	.962	25	36	92	5	18
Nazario	.979	59	67	164	5	24
Perez	.929	4	5	8	1	1
Schaeffer	.984	31	32	90	2	14

	PCT	G	PO	A	E	DP
Torres	.991	26	43	73	1	12
Tulowitzki	1.000	2	1	5	0	1

Outfield	PCT	G	PO	A	E	DP
Beerer	.982	84	158	7	3	0
Blackmon	.960	75	160	7	7	1
Harvey	.974	57	101	12	3	3
Jackson	1.000	90	186	9	0	0
Kindel	1.000	21	32	1	0	0
Mitchell	1.000	42	85	4	0	0
Sardinha	.991	64	107	4	1	1

MODESTO NUTS   HIGH CLASS A

CALIFORNIA LEAGUE

Batting	B-T	HT	WT	DOB	AVG	vLH	vRH	G	AB	R	H	2B	3B	HR	RBI	BB	HBP	SH	SF	SO	SB	CS	SLG	OBP
Bowden, Johnny	R-R	6-3	205	8-15-84	.200	.222	.190	12	30	4	6	1	0	1	4	4	3	2	1	12	0	0	.333	.342
Cesario, Jimmy	L-R	5-11	200	10-15-85	.316	.341	.306	128	475	78	150	30	10	6	71	29	14	3	6	76	16	6	.459	.368
Christensen, David	R-R	6-1	195	2-11-88	.192	.222	.176	101	312	44	60	9	3	8	36	39	4	5	2	132	21	2	.317	.289
Field, Thomas	R-R	5-9	175	2-22-87	.284	.305	.276	124	440	84	125	21	7	15	72	66	21	9	7	114	16	5	.466	.397
Garneau, Dustin	R-R	6-1	200	8-13-87	.310	.278	.333	12	42	5	13	2	2	1	13	2	0	0	0	9	0	1	.524	.341
Gonzalez, Maikol	R-R	5-10	175	3-25-86	.268	.368	.234	50	149	28	40	8	5	0	11	21	4	7	0	36	10	5	.389	.374
Hawpe, Brad	L-L	6-3	210	6-22-79	.250	.000	.333	1	4	0	1	1	0	0	1	0	0	0	0	2	0	0	.500	.250
Laurent, Chandler	R-R	5-10	180	10-17-87	.259	.273	.250	9	27	7	7	2	0	0	2	0	0	0	0	8	2	0	.333	.310
Mitchell, Mike	R-R	6-1	200	8-24-85	.292	.346	.256	17	65	13	19	3	0	6	9	6	0	2	2	13	9	1	.338	.368
Nazario, Radames	R-R	6-0	166	6-14-87	.220	.200	.240	17	50	7	11	3	0	1	1	5	0	0	0	15	0	0	.340	.291
Pacheco, Jordan	R-R	6-1	190	1-30-86	.321	.308	.326	104	390	59	125	27	3	5	70	54	8	1	7	36	5	6	.444	.407
Paulsen, Ben	L-R	6-4	205	10-27-87	.311	.278	.326	130	498	65	155	29	8	12	83	33	3	0	7	113	5	4	.474	.353
Peisel, Ryan	R-R	6-3	200	6-14-86	.264	.240	.279	83	269	29	71	18	3	4	39	14	1	5	2	60	5	1	.398	.301
Rike, Brian	I-L	6-2	200	12-13-85	.257	.194	.282	69	241	37	62	24	1	6	42	22	6	2	4	76	6	4	.440	.330
Robinson, Scott	R-R	6-0	185	7-6-88	.228	.194	.245	105	386	50	88	22	6	2	38	11	4	5	4	95	27	9	.332	.254
Sanders, Joseph	R-R	6-0	195	4-24-88	.221	.190	.236	48	181	26	40	9	2	8	21	12	0	0	3	43	2	1	.425	.265
Scott, Joe	R-R	6-0	185	8-22-86	.105	.154	.000	8	19	2	2	0	0	0	4	0	0	0	6	2	0	2	.105	.261
Seabury, Beau	R-R	6-1	190	6-13-85	.215	.204	.220	59	181	11	39	9	0	0	18	12	4	9	1	52	1	2	.265	.278
Wetzel, Erik	R-R	6-1	180	12-25-86	.277	.252	.290	97	328	47	91	11	0	0	36	34	1	8	2	54	19	12	.311	.345
Wheeler, Tim	L-R	6-4	205	1-21-88	.249	.206	.266	129	510	88	127	21	6	12	63	60	13	5	4	114	22	8	.384	.341
Zuanich, Mike	R-L	6-4	225	7-10-86	.325	.310	.336	59	197	30	64	16	0	3	26	18	0	0	4	46	4	0	.452	.412

Pitching	B-T	HT	WT	DOB	W	L	ERA	G	GS	CG	SV	IP	H	R	ER	HR	BB	SO	AVG	vLH	vRH	K/9	BB/9
Aristil, Jonnathan	R-R	6-1	160	11-30-86	1	4	7.12	21	1	0	0	43	56	35	34	7	22	47	.316	.316	.316	9.84	4.60
Ballard, Rhett	R-R	6-5	235	11-13-85	0	1	6.10	8	0	0	0	10	12	8	7	1	10	10	.293	.412	.208	8.71	8.71
Brothers, Rex	L-L	6-0	205	12-18-87	0	2	2.68	33	0	0	3	37	20	14	11	0	19	43	.165	.189	.155	10.46	4.62
Buchholz, Taylor	R-R	6-4	220	10-13-81	0	0	0.00	3	1	0	0	3	0	0	0	0	0	4	.000	.000	.000	12.00	0.00
DeRatt, Alan	R-R	6-5	225	11-6-85	3	1	4.76	19	0	0	0	28	26	17	15	4	12	34	.236	.231	.239	10.80	3.81
Dodson, Stephen	R-R	6-5	200	8-29-85	3	2	4.69	46	1	0	0	71	71	45	37	5	27	55	.258	.222	.289	6.97	3.42
Durst, Kenny	B-L	6-0	195	10-11-85	9	6	5.36	27	18	0	0	124	154	82	74	19	48	74	.310	.293	.317	5.36	3.47
Frazier, Parker	R-R	6-5	159	11-11-88	2	2	4.70	9	0	0	0	46	49	27	24	1	11	38	.269	.329	.229	7.43	2.15
Froneberger, Isaiah	L-L	5-8	200	6-23-89	2	3	4.52	45	0	0	1	70	63	36	35	8	43	70	.242	.244	.242	9.04	5.56
Hollingsworth, Ethan	R-R	6-2	200	5-4-87	12	8	3.31	25	25	0	0	160	161	79	59	14	34	153	.260	.247	.269	8.59	1.91
Houston, Dan	R-R	6-3	205	10-24-86	5	7	5.92	21	20	0	0	114	157	84	75	9	43	80	.333	.339	.328	6.32	3.39
Jorgenson, Adam	R-R	6-0	185	9-10-85	0	2	1.60	41	0	0	24	39	31	10	7	1	13	47	.208	.217	.200	10.75	2.97
Malone, Chris	R-R	6-4	215	6-28-83	0	2	4.91	3	0	0	1	4	6	3	2	0	1	0	.333	.143	.455	0.00	2.45
Marbry, Michael	R-R	6-3	185	9-3-84	3	1	4.28	23	0	0	0	34	38	16	16	3	7	39	.279	.295	.267	10.43	1.87
Nicasio, Juan	R-R	6-3	200	8-31-86	12	10	3.91	28	28	1	0	177	186	91	77	14	31	171	.266	.259	.271	8.68	1.57
Reynolds, Greg	R-R	6-7	225	7-3-85	1	0	0.82	2	2	0	0	11	13	4	1	1	2	6	.260	.286	.241	4.91	1.64
Scahill, Rob	R-R	6-2	205	2-15-87	10	7	4.73	27	27	1	0	156	173	91	82	9	59	140	.284	.265	.297	8.08	3.40
Sullivan, Josh	R-R	6-4	215	7-5-84	3	3	5.86	19	4	0	0	28	29	27	18	2	18	23	.274	.222	.300	7.48	5.86
Trice, Tyler	R-R	6-4	205	5-16-86	0	0	243.00	1	0	0	0	0	8	9	9	2	1	1	.889	.667	1.000	27.00	27.00
Weathers, Casey	R-R	6-1	200	6-10-85	0	1	6.75	20	0	0	4	19	18	14	14	2	17	25	.250	.240	.255	12.05	8.20
Yacko, Kurt	R-R	5-11	180	8-22-87	6	5	3.50	49	0	0	5	64	58	28	25	6	18	70	.242	.227	.252	9.79	2.52

Fielding

Catcher	PCT	G	PO	A	E	DP	PB
Bowden	.979	12	83	10	2	0	1
Cesario	1.000	1	1	0	0	0	0
Garneau	.973	12	99	9	3	2	6
Pacheco	.993	71	540	42	4	2	13
Seabury	.994	58	411	53	3	4	11

First Base	PCT	G	PO	A	E	DP
Cesario	.982	7	53	1	1	8
Paulsen	.990	124	960	76	10	86
Peisel	1.000	3	7	1	0	2
Sanders	1.000	4	32	2	0	2
Zuanich	.990	13	92	9	1	9

Second Base	PCT	G	PO	A	E	DP
Cesario	1.000	24	47	45	0	12
Gonzalez	.978	28	44	88	3	14
Nazario	1.000	6	12	15	0	5
Sanders	.976	10	16	24	1	6
Scott	1.000	4	8	12	0	1
Wetzel	.969	84	150	228	12	43

Third Base	PCT	G	PO	A	E	DP
Cesario	.865	24	11	34	7	1
Gonzalez	.960	20	10	14	1	0
Nazario	.600	6	1	5	4	1
Paulsen	1.000	1	1	0	0	0
Peisel	.894	76	53	107	19	12
Sanders	.917	36	31	57	8	12

Shortstop	PCT	G	PO	A	E	DP
Field	.947	121	154	324	27	62
Gonzalez	.947	8	6	12	1	5
Nazario	1.000	6	12	17	0	4
Scott	.750	3	1	2	1	0
Wetzel	.976	10	16	25	1	5

Outfield	PCT	G	PO	A	E	DP
Cesario	1.000	14	24	1	0	0
Christensen	.994	97	167	5	1	0
Gonzalez	1.000	1	1	0	0	0
Hawpe	—	1	0	0	0	0
Laurent	.933	8	12	2	1	0
Mitchell	1.000	17	25	0	0	0
Rike	.964	68	102	6	4	2

COLORADO ROCKIES

Robinson .970 95 160 2 5 1   Wheeler .970 127 292 4 9 2   Zuanich 1.000 18 20 1 0 0

ASHEVILLE TOURISTS
LOW CLASS A

SOUTH ATLANTIC LEAGUE

Batting	B-T	HT	WT	DOB	AVG	vLH	vRH	G	AB	R	H	2B	3B	HR	RBI	BB	HBP	SH	SF	SO	SB	CS	SLG	OBP
Aguilera, Anthony	R-R	6-0	215	10-30-86	.232	.250	.227	18	56	7	13	0	0	1	5	5	1	0	0	9	0	1	.286	.306
Arenado, Nolan	R-R	6-1	205	4-16-91	.308	.302	.311	92	373	45	115	41	1	12	65	19	1	0	7	52	1	3	.520	.338
Barnes, Avery	R-L	6-1	170	9-17-86	.296	.291	.299	100	388	56	115	14	8	4	35	21	5	2	2	87	32	11	.405	.339
Clark, Jared	R-R	6-4	215	5-9-86	.299	.248	.318	110	381	62	114	20	0	24	82	76	4	0	10	113	10	4	.541	.412
Cleary, Delta	B-R	6-3	180	8-14-89	.246	.275	.232	76	313	54	77	13	2	5	33	22	1	5	2	75	18	5	.348	.296
Gonzalez, Jose	R-R	6-1	165	6-23-87	.228	.177	.252	53	193	22	44	11	0	1	15	11	2	2	2	49	3	3	.301	.274
Hines, Nathan	L-R	5-10	180	12-9-85	.269	.333	.241	22	78	14	21	5	0	1	14	5	1	3	1	12	4	1	.372	.312
Martinez, Carlos	R-R	5-11	182	9-22-88	.274	.340	.248	44	164	23	45	9	1	3	19	19	4	0	1	54	11	5	.396	.362
Massey, Tyler	L-L	6-0	205	7-21-89	.209	.206	.210	100	354	31	74	15	6	3	26	25	5	2	1	90	6	7	.311	.270
Matthes, Kent	R-R	6-2	215	1-8-87	.185	.269	.145	21	81	9	15	7	1	1	11	5	4	0	2	32	0	0	.333	.261
Mesa, Eliezer	R-R	5-11	180	11-24-88	.302	.316	.295	117	483	83	146	33	9	2	42	39	2	5	0	91	29	11	.420	.357
Nina, Angelys	R-R	5-11	165	11-16-88	.272	.246	.281	103	416	57	113	16	3	4	51	15	3	2	4	57	24	7	.353	.299
Sanders, Joseph	R-R	6-0	195	4-24-88	.267	.263	.270	66	258	28	69	16	1	9	40	13	0	0	6	58	3	3	.442	.296
Sandoval, Orlando	R-R	6-0	185	1-22-88	.279	.311	.266	97	344	48	96	22	4	5	42	30	12	2	0	103	12	13	.410	.358
Scott, Joe	R-R	6-0	185	8-22-86	.222	.143	.250	10	27	5	6	4	0	0	4	6	0	0	0	11	1	1	.370	.364
Tarleton, Dallas	L-R	5-11	200	8-5-87	.251	.217	.263	72	235	35	59	14	0	3	29	44	3	1	3	91	2	4	.349	.372
Velazquez, Helder	R-R	6-3	165	10-14-88	.223	.216	.226	82	273	26	61	13	0	2	25	14	4	2	2	75	6	4	.293	.270
Wong, Joey	L-R	5-10	175	8-22-88	.223	.256	.210	84	273	33	61	15	0	3	32	27	3	12	4	57	4	3	.311	.296
Zuanich, Mike	R-L	6-4	225	7-10-86	.382	.778	.240	9	34	2	13	4	0	1	10	3	1	0	0	11	1	1	.588	.447

Pitching	B-T	HT	WT	DOB	W	L	ERA	G	GS	CG	SV	IP	H	R	ER	HR	BB	SO	AVG	vLH	vRH	K/9	BB/9
Balcom-Miller, Chris	R-R	6-2	210	3-3-89	6	7	3.31	19	19	1	0	109	86	42	40	3	19	117	.214	.268	.176	9.69	1.57
2-team total (1 Greenville)					7	7	3.30	20	20	1	0	115	91	44	42	4	19	120	—	—	—	9.42	1.49
Ballard, Rhett	R-R	6-5	235	11-13-85	1	3	4.67	44	0	0	2	52	53	29	27	2	24	46	.275	.313	.254	7.96	4.15
Bargas, Paul	L-L	6-1	205	10-13-88	5	4	3.59	58	0	0	5	68	57	31	27	3	19	64	.227	.159	.250	8.51	2.53
Bettis, Chad	R-R	6-1	193	4-26-89	2	0	0.96	3	3	0	0	19	14	2	2	1	3	17	.209	.200	.219	8.20	1.45
DeRatt, Alan	R-R	6-5	225	11-6-85	3	1	2.28	19	2	0	3	43	32	11	11	4	9	37	.206	.185	.218	7.68	1.87
Duarte, Marco	R-R	6-2	185	8-19-86	1	0	9.49	9	0	0	0	12	24	16	13	1	9	10	.387	.297	.520	7.30	6.57
Gomez, Leuris	R-R	6-0	170	10-20-86	6	5	4.62	48	0	0	1	78	91	45	40	3	20	75	.292	.252	.312	8.65	2.31
Gonzalez, Juan	R-R	6-2	206	4-5-90	3	8	4.54	22	22	0	0	115	133	65	58	7	31	69	.298	.280	.309	5.40	2.43
Hungerman, Josh	L-L	6-3	195	9-8-86	0	0	6.00	11	0	0	0	12	10	10	10	0	11	23	.231	.286	.222	6.00	6.00
Kuo, Sheng-An	L-L	6-2	190	1-1-86	3	1	4.87	55	0	0	20	61	60	40	33	9	22	60	.261	.247	.270	8.85	3.25
Matzek, Tyler	L-L	6-3	210	10-19-90	5	1	2.92	18	18	0	0	89	62	31	29	6	62	88	.204	.176	.213	8.87	6.25
Musick, Wes	L-L	6-0	190	12-30-86	8	7	4.05	23	23	0	0	122	127	68	55	7	26	109	.265	.198	.283	8.02	1.91
Perkins, Dan	R-R	6-4	200	3-5-86	6	6	4.90	38	10	0	1	90	103	60	49	12	45	76	.289	.284	.293	7.60	4.50
Rose, Chad	R-R	6-2	200	2-17-88	8	6	3.63	48	0	0	1	87	83	39	35	8	31	94	.251	.205	.278	9.76	3.22
Ruiz, Charlie	R-R	6-1	180	10-10-88	0	1	5.23	11	0	0	5	10	8	6	6	0	4	11	.211	.100	.250	9.58	3.48
Schnaitmann, Nick	R-R	6-6	190	11-16-89	8	10	5.32	25	24	0	0	132	163	90	78	12	38	59	.312	.327	.304	4.02	2.59
Vargas, Jonathan	L-L	6-2	150	5-29-89	4	9	6.53	22	18	0	0	94	113	75	68	12	54	55	.310	.264	.321	5.28	5.19
Woods, Coty	R-R	6-2	190	3-14-88	0	1	2.70	16	0	0	1	27	28	9	8	3	2	32	.269	.306	.250	10.80	0.68

Fielding

Catcher	PCT	G	PO	A	E	DP	PB
Aguilera	.987	18	139	12	2	1	4
Gonzalez	.980	51	382	56	9	9	11
Tarleton	.990	72	517	59	6	8	4

First Base	PCT	G	PO	A	E	DP
Clark	.989	102	896	61	11	74
Martinez	1.000	1	10	1	0	0
Sanders	.990	10	94	8	1	16
Velazquez	.994	20	145	12	1	16
Wong	1.000	3	15	4	0	1
Zuanich	1.000	4	40	1	0	4

Second Base	PCT	G	PO	A	E	DP
Barnes	.939	15	22	40	4	7

	PCT	G	PO	A	E	DP	PB
Martinez	.962	6	15	10	1	3	
Nina	.962	87	161	239	16	55	
Sanders		1	0	0	0	0	
Scott	1.000	3	1	7	0	0	
Velazquez	.969	20	31	62	3	13	
Wong	1.000	10	17	22	0	8	

Third Base	PCT	G	PO	A	E	DP
Arenado	.936	81	86	134	15	17
Clark	1.000	2	3	5	0	0
Martinez	.850	4	6	11	3	2
Sanders	.950	45	36	96	7	7
Velazquez	.900	10	2	16	2	3

Shortstop	PCT	G	PO	A	E	DP
Martinez	.934	27	46	68	8	14
Nina	.949	8	15	22	2	6
Scott	.941	7	8	24	2	4
Velazquez	.910	29	33	68	10	12
Wong	.975	72	121	233	9	53

Outfield	PCT	G	PO	A	E	DP
Barnes	.967	64	108	10	4	3
Cleary	.987	73	150	7	2	2
Hines	1.000	19	19	1	0	0
Massey	.955	86	134	13	7	3
Matthes	.947	13	15	3	1	0
Mesa	.971	95	195	9	6	5
Sandoval	.971	77	132	4	4	0

TRI-CITY DUST DEVILS
SHORT-SEASON

NORTHWEST LEAGUE

Batting	B-T	HT	WT	DOB	AVG	vLH	vRH	G	AB	R	H	2B	3B	HR	RBI	BB	HBP	SH	SF	SO	SB	CS	SLG	OBP
Altobelli, Dom	R-R	6-1	195	3-7-87	.244	.391	.214	39	135	20	33	10	0	2	16	14	3	1	0	36	8	2	.363	.329
Garneau, Dustin	R-R	6-1	200	8-13-87	.224	.125	.236	42	143	20	32	11	2	2	21	21	7	1	2	30	3	2	.371	.347
Gomez, Hector	R-R	6-2	180	3-5-88	.246	.235	.250	18	69	8	17	2	1	2	7	5	0	0	1	15	0	3	.391	.293
Hernandez, David	R-R	6-2	165	2-1-88	.265	.556	.200	18	49	5	13	0	0	3	5	0	0	0	8	1	1	.265	.333
Hines, Nathan	L-R	5-10	180	12-9-85	.276	.259	.279	51	192	22	53	9	4	0	16	21	0	3	1	34	6	8	.365	.346
Jacobsen, Chad	R-R	6-1	210	4-3-86	.149	.238	.130	33	121	6	18	5	0	2	13	8	1	0	1	43	0	1	.240	.206
Langfels, Jayson	R-R	6-2	205	8-17-88	.166	.269	.143	44	145	11	24	4	2	4	11	10	0	1	0	61	2	3	.303	.219

Batting	B-T	HT	WT	DOB	AVG	vLH	vRH	G	AB	R	H	2B	3B	HR	RBI	BB	HBP	SH	SF	SO	SB	CS	SLG	OBP
Laurent, Chandler	R-R	5-10	180	10-17-87	.263	.259	.264	59	232	44	61	14	4	11	36	17	7	2	4	71	14	5	.500	.327
Martinez, Carlos	R-R	5-11	182	9-22-88	.286	.167	.306	10	42	7	12	3	0	1	3	2	0	0	0	12	0	2	.429	.318
Massanari, Bryce	R-R	6-2	215	4-29-86	.242	.319	.222	61	227	23	55	12	0	6	23	24	4	2	1	46	1	1	.374	.324
Powers, Josh	R-R	6-2	185	8-18-88	.250	.000	.267	6	16	2	4	0	0	0	2	3	2	0	0	3	0	0	.250	.429
Reyes, Leonardo	R-R	6-0	165	8-2-88	.268	.296	.260	70	254	34	68	9	0	3	29	25	5	2	1	48	8	2	.339	.344
Rutledge, Josh	R-R	6-1	190	4-21-89	.128	.000	.179	11	39	6	5	0	0	0	4	4	1	1	0	10	1	0	.128	.227
Sammy, Jeremiah	L-R	6-2	190	7-13-87	.240	.214	.247	53	192	25	46	12	0	1	13	22	0	2	2	47	7	3	.318	.315
Sanders, Matt	R-R		180	5-10-87	.182	.000	.200	4	11	0	2	0	0	0	2	3	0	0	0	4	1	1	.182	.357
Scott, Joe	R-R	6-0	185	8-22-86	.160	.050	.197	26	81	5	13	2	0	1	3	9	2	1	0	39	0	1	.222	.261
Simon, Jared	R-R	6-1	210	3-3-89	.226	.227	.226	62	234	16	53	6	3	1	19	18	8	1	0	68	6	2	.291	.304
Tracy, Mark	R-R	6-4	220	1-1-88	.209	.162	.220	58	201	18	42	6	1	4	22	15	7	3	1	67	2	2	.308	.286
Wilson, Russell	R-R	6-0	192	11-29-88	.230	.273	.220	32	122	18	28	4	4	2	11	16	4	0	1	36	4	6	.377	.336

Pitching

Pitching	B-T	HT	WT	DOB	W	L	ERA	G	GS	CG	SV	IP	H	R	ER	HR	BB	SO	AVG	vLH	vRH	K/9	BB/9
Baker, Craig	R-R	6-2	210	1-31-85	0	0	2.25	4	0	0	0	4	3	1	1	0	0	6	.200	.167	.222	13.50	0.00
Bennigson, Craig	R-L	6-2	215	3-21-87	0	2	2.51	15	0	0	7	14	16	4	4	0	5	8	.276	.294	.268	5.02	3.14
Bettis, Chad	R-R	6-1	193	4-26-89	4	1	1.12	10	9	0	0	48	44	11	6	0	10	39	.227	.229	.225	7.26	1.86
Cabrera, Edward	L-L	6-0	160	10-20-87	1	8	3.07	14	14	0	0	73	71	34	25	2	24	87	.251	.242	.253	10.68	2.95
Deduno, Samuel	R-R	6-3	190	7-2-83	0	2	5.51	4	4	0	0	16	18	11	10	0	5	20	.290	.321	.265	11.02	2.76
Federico, Eric	R-R	5-11	175	9-4-87	2	2	4.30	18	0	0	0	23	23	13	11	2	3	20	.250	.419	.164	7.83	1.17
Frazier, Parker	R-R	6-5	159	11-11-88	1	3	7.52	5	5	0	0	20	28	21	17	1	8	15	.318	.243	.373	6.64	3.54
Hungerman, Josh	L-L	6-3	195	9-8-86	5	4	2.18	14	11	0	0	66	47	20	16	0	22	77	.203	.203	.203	10.50	3.00
Jarrett, Sean	R-R	6-5	210	4-26-83	1	1	2.25	4	0	0	0	4	4	1	1	0	0	6	.286	.375	.167	13.50	0.00
McAtee, Brad	R-R	6-5	215	3-15-87	1	1	1.63	29	0	0	5	39	28	12	7	1	16	33	.201	.228	.183	7.68	3.72
Mueller, Josh	R-R	6-4	215	1-18-89	2	3	4.69	14	9	0	0	48	51	30	25	2	17	36	.271	.307	.248	6.75	3.19
Ruiz, Charlie	R-R	6-1	180	10-10-88	0	0	3.00	3	0	0	0	3	2	1	1	0	5	4	.182	.333	.125	12.00	15.00
Sitton, Kraig	L-L	6-5	190	7-13-88	1	0	2.86	20	0	0	1	28	21	9	9	1	10	35	.210	.267	.186	11.12	3.18
Slaats, Josh	R-R	6-5	225	12-22-88	1	3	1.95	8	5	0	0	32	20	10	7	2	10	42	.174	.174	.174	11.69	2.78
Stavert, Erik	R-R	6-3	185	11-20-87	3	4	2.90	13	13	0	0	68	57	28	22	1	26	61	.224	.185	.247	8.03	3.42
Sullivan, Josh	R-R	6-4	215	7-5-84	1	2	6.23	5	5	0	0	22	25	16	15	2	9	15	.275	.289	.264	6.23	3.74
Testa, Ricky	R-R	6-3	205	4-8-87	2	2	2.40	29	0	0	0	49	45	19	13	2	6	51	.236	.225	.242	9.43	1.11
Tilford, Clint	R-R	6-3	195	4-2-88	3	3	5.45	23	0	0	0	40	42	29	24	5	11	45	.263	.221	.293	10.21	2.32
Trice, Tyler	R-R	6-4	205	5-16-86	1	3	5.91	18	1	0	0	32	40	26	21	8	17	32	.299	.314	.289	9.00	4.78
Vopinek, Billy	R-R	6-3	200	11-16-85	1	2	5.34	28	0	0	3	29	36	22	17	2	12	18	.303	.273	.320	5.65	3.77
Weathers, Casey	R-R	6-1	200	6-10-85	0	0	0.00	10	0	0	1	11.2	1	0	0	0	5	21	.056	.000	.077	16.20	3.86

Fielding

Catcher	PCT	G	PO	A	E	DP	PB
Garneau	.985	41	355	39	6	1	8
Massanari	.977	30	277	17	7	2	3
Powers	.976	4	38	2	1	0	3
Tracy	1.000	1	6	0	0	0	0

First Base	PCT	G	PO	A	E	DP
Jacobsen	.989	18	168	5	2	11
Massanari	.971	4	33	0	1	2
Tracy	.988	54	480	34	6	34

Second Base	PCT	G	PO	A	E	DP
Altobelli	.925	12	20	29	4	5
Hernandez	.941	15	24	40	4	7
Sammy	1.000	3	4	8	0	1
Sanders	1.000	3	2	3	0	1
Scott	.915	16	30	35	6	6
Wilson	.993	31	51	90	1	14

Third Base	PCT	G	PO	A	E	DP
Altobelli	.902	26	11	44	6	0
Langfels	.891	43	26	80	13	6
Sammy	.944	9	1	16	1	0
Sanders	1.000	1	1	5	0	0

Shortstop	PCT	G	PO	A	E	DP
Gomez	.943	11	14	36	3	7
Hernandez	1.000	2	2	5	0	1
Martinez	.905	10	12	26	4	3
Rutledge	.902	9	10	27	4	5
Sammy	.926	39	43	131	14	23
Scott	.896	10	14	29	5	4

Outfield	PCT	G	PO	A	E	DP
Altobelli	—	1	0	0	0	0
Hines	.977	48	77	7	2	2
Laurent	.975	58	110	6	3	1
Reyes	.957	64	88	1	4	0
Sammy	1.000	4	12	1	0	1
Simon	.972	55	68	2	2	0

CASPER GHOSTS   *ROOKIE*

PIONEER LEAGUE

Batting	B-T	HT	WT	DOB	AVG	vLH	vRH	G	AB	R	H	2B	3B	HR	RBI	BB	HBP	SH	SF	SO	SB	CS	SLG	OBP
Adames, Cristhian	B-R	6-0	160	7-26-91	.290	.273	.297	37	145	30	42	9	0	1	15	14	1	5	0	24	4	5	.372	.356
Aguilera, Anthony	R-R	6-0	215	10-30-86	.324	.267	.368	9	34	6	11	1	0	1	4	4	1	0	0	9	0	0	.441	.410
Ballard, Jordan	R-R	6-3	210	11-9-87	.244	.244	.244	36	135	16	33	4	0	4	20	8	1	0	1	36	0	0	.363	.290
Casteel, Ryan	R-R	6-1	205	6-6-91	.305	.231	.326	43	177	21	54	8	1	3	22	10	0	0	0	35	2	0	.412	.342
Crousset, Juan	L-L	5-11	193	4-30-90	.271	.267	.271	52	207	24	56	8	1	5	28	10	0	2	1	66	7	5	.391	.303
De La Cruz, Robert	R-R	5-11	189	10-10-89	.237	.268	.222	47	173	21	41	4	2	3	22	7	2	1	1	53	3	2	.335	.273
Dickerson, Corey	L-R	6-2	210	5-22-89	.348	.299	.364	69	276	54	96	22	9	13	61	28	3	0	1	51	12	6	.634	.412
DiNatale, David	R-R	6-1	202	2-9-87	.148	.167	.133	7	27	2	4	3	0	0	2	1	0	0	0	10	0	0	.259	.179
Helton, Todd	L-L	6-2	215	8-20-73	.500	.400	.600	3	10	1	5	1	0	0	5	2	0	0	1	1	0	0	.600	.538
Hernandez, David	R-R	6-2	165	2-1-88	.111	.167	.083	5	18	3	2	0	1	0	1	2	0	0	0	6	2	0	.222	.200
Kandilas, David	R-R	6-2	185	9-14-90	.262	.185	.288	28	107	16	28	3	2	2	15	5	0	2	1	24	5	2	.383	.292
McDade, Blake	L-L	6-1	208	7-1-87	.327	.289	.335	58	220	36	72	14	1	3	40	22	3	0	3	31	1	3	.441	.391
Ortega, Rafael	L-R	5-11	150	5-15-91	.358	.300	.376	71	288	69	103	17	3	7	45	28	2	2	2	42	23	9	.510	.416
Powers, Josh	R-R	6-2	185	8-18-88	.318	.125	.429	7	22	1	7	1	0	0	3	0	0	0	0	2	0	0	.364	.318
Ramirez, Michael	R-R	5-10	165	4-27-90	.229	.167	.239	24	83	7	19	0	0	0	3	4	1	0	0	21	1	6	.229	.264
Rivera, Jose	R-R	5-10	170	4-18-90	.200	.282	.171	47	150	18	30	5	0	0	18	10	0	0	0	23	4	0	.233	.250
Roja, Yafistel	B-R	5-11	150	10-26-91	.210	.190	.215	30	100	9	21	0	0	0	8	4	1	0	1	31	3	0	.210	.245
Sosa, Francisco	R-R	6-4	180	2-27-90	.176	.000	.250	5	17	3	3	0	0	0	1	0	1	0	0	5	0	1	.176	.222
Squier, Jeff	R-R	6-3	190	3-3-87	.256	.250	.258	53	172	32	44	8	3	6	14	13	3	5	1	43	11	4	.442	.317
Swanner, Will	R-R	5-9	195	9-10-91	.303	.467	.262	18	76	14	23	4	0	7	13	0	2	0	0	33	1	0	.632	.321
Tanos, Brett	R-R	5-11	175	10-6-88	.270	.339	.249	65	241	40	65	20	2	1	29	31	5	2	2	59	5	4	.382	.362

Pitching	B-T	HT	WT	DOB	W	L	ERA	G	GS	CG	SV	IP	H	R	ER	HR	BB	SO	AVG	vLH	vRH	K/9	BB/9
Barraza, Alejandro	R-R	6-1	205	10-25-90	1	7	6.79	14	14	0	0	58	82	52	44	8	19	51	.329	.280	.359	7.87	2.93
Bergman, Christian	R-R	6-1	180	5-4-88	1	4	5.96	14	5	0	0	48	62	39	32	5	11	37	.304	.280	.320	6.89	2.05
Brewer, Russell	R-R	6-0	200	2-25-88	0	0	9.00	1	0	0	0	1	2	1	1	0	0	1	.400	.500	.333	9.00	0.00
Campos, Albert	R-R	6-4	222	2-4-91	4	4	2.05	15	15	1	0	88	80	29	20	5	17	68	.244	.230	.256	6.95	1.74
Crocker, Matt	R-L	6-3	190	5-24-89	2	0	5.63	13	0	0	0	16	22	15	10	0	8	15	.324	.300	.342	8.44	4.50
Ferrer, Ricardo	R-R	6-2	174	10-11-89	1	3	6.25	11	4	0	2	32	38	27	22	5	21	16	.304	.340	.282	4.55	5.97
Gagnon, Tyler	R-R	6-2	175	3-22-89	5	3	3.89	15	15	0	0	76	94	41	33	6	17	63	.305	.256	.343	7.43	2.00
Gibson, Trevor	R-R	6-3	225	9-6-86	0	0	13.50	4	0	0	0	4	8	6	6	2	4	3	.400	.400	.400	6.75	9.00
Gonzalez, Nelson	R-R	6-1	168	2-15-90	2	2	4.18	20	0	0	0	32	33	18	15	5	10	34	.252	.286	.232	9.46	2.78
Hancock, Kyle	R-R	6-3	185	8-20-87	1	1	4.86	8	2	0	0	17	18	11	9	3	11	13	.273	.259	.282	7.02	5.94
Junker, Steve	L-L	6-5	180	9-18-86	0	0	14.29	6	0	0	0	6	12	10	9	0	3	5	.414	.364	.444	7.94	4.76
Keitzman, Blake	B-L	5-11	185	1-9-88	3	1	3.03	17	0	0	0	33	43	18	11	2	13	38	.305	.226	.367	10.47	3.58
Kern, Bruce	R-R	6-1	175	4-24-88	0	3	4.68	14	4	0	1	33	51	26	17	4	9	24	.357	.340	.367	6.61	2.48
Mayo, Vianney	R-R	6-2	200	4-6-90	1	0	3.80	11	0	0	0	21	22	12	9	0	13	22	.265	.294	.245	9.28	5.48
McKinney, Clint	R-R	6-1	200	11-17-86	2	1	1.15	11	0	0	0	16	14	4	2	1	4	15	.246	.200	.270	8.62	2.30
Mejias, Alving	R-R	6-1	185	12-26-91	6	5	6.81	15	15	0	0	75	107	66	57	5	14	50	.331	.368	.305	5.97	1.67
Perez, Juan	R-R	6-0	190	5-30-89	3	1	2.60	21	0	0	10	28	18	10	8	2	11	23	.186	.174	.196	7.48	3.58
Reid, Taylor	R-R	6-3	215	6-8-89	0	1	3.78	16	0	0	1	17	20	17	7	1	11	13	.299	.217	.341	7.02	5.94
Roberts, Kenny	L-L	6-1	200	3-9-88	3	1	3.22	16	2	0	0	36	39	17	13	0	6	21	.260	.278	.250	5.20	1.49
Suarez, Rafael	R-R	6-0	200	5-14-89	1	2	3.13	18	0	0	1	23	27	15	8	3	6	21	.281	.265	.290	8.22	2.35
Woods, Coty	R-R	6-2	190	3-14-88	1	0	2.19	8	0	0	3	12	7	4	3	1	4	14	.171	.267	.115	10.22	2.92

Fielding

Catcher	PCT	G	PO	A	E	DP	PB
Aguilera	1.000	9	75	8	0	0	0
Casteel	.986	33	259	32	4	4	9
Powers	.971	7	34	0	1	0	3
Ramirez	.955	24	133	15	7	3	10
Swanner	.971	8	65	3	2	0	4

First Base	PCT	G	PO	A	E	DP
Ballard	.989	21	162	13	2	12
Helton	1.000	1	9	0	0	1
McDade	.984	58	489	64	9	37

Second Base	PCT	G	PO	A	E	DP
Hernandez	1.000	3	5	3	0	1

	PCT	G	PO	A	E	DP
Rivera	.968	44	85	130	7	22
Roja	.914	15	20	33	5	6
Squier	.949	12	22	34	3	5
Tanos	.889	9	6	26	4	3

Third Base	PCT	G	PO	A	E	DP
Ballard	.887	16	14	33	6	2
Hernandez	1.000	1	2	2	0	0
Rivera	1.000	1	0	1	0	0
Squier	.938	5	6	9	1	0
Tanos	.909	57	40	90	13	8

Shortstop	PCT	G	PO	A	E	DP
Adames	.969	37	55	131	6	21

	PCT	G	PO	A	E	DP
Hernandez	.778	1	4	3	2	0
Rivera	.923	2	6	6	1	2
Roja	.786	7	10	23	9	4
Squier	.883	30	49	79	17	11

Outfield	PCT	G	PO	A	E	DP
Crousset	.899	46	67	4	8	1
De La Cruz	.962	22	23	2	1	1
Dickerson	.945	57	80	6	5	0
DiNatale	1.000	5	10	0	0	0
Kandilas	.979	26	45	1	1	0
Ortega	.976	68	160	6	4	2
Sosa	1.000	1	2	0	0	0
Squier	1.000	4	7	0	0	0

DSL ROCKIES

ROOKIE

DOMINICAN SUMMER LEAGUE

Batting	B-T	HT	WT	DOB	AVG	vLH	vRH	G	AB	R	H	2B	3B	HR	RBI	BB	HBP	SH	SF	SO	SB	CS	SLG	OBP
Bacilio, Jesus	R-R	6-0	180	4-7-93	.223	.290	.208	59	175	19	39	5	0	1	25	23	8	5	3	36	10	7	.269	.335
Briceno, Jose	R-R	6-0	195	9-19-92	.205	.304	.188	52	151	12	31	6	0	0	17	17	3	2	2	28	9	5	.245	.295
Bustamante, Daniel	L-R	6-2	160	4-13-91	.188	.091	.203	36	85	9	16	6	0	0	6	11	4	1	2	18	7	2	.188	.304
Ciriaco, Juan	R-R	5-9	155	7-6-90	.233	.257	.227	59	176	35	41	5	1	0	13	20	7	6	3	25	34	11	.273	.330
De Leon, Miguel	R-R	6-2	195	8-5-91	.283	.444	.260	44	145	18	41	4	1	1	10	11	9	1	1	40	3	1	.345	.367
Galvez, Cesar	R-R	5-9	145	7-24-91	.199	.257	.183	55	166	17	33	5	1	0	12	16	2	9	1	21	13	5	.241	.276
Herrera, Rosell	R-B	6-3	180	10-16-92	.237	.214	.242	67	232	27	55	6	1	1	26	24	6	3	1	24	17	8	.284	.323
Morales, Juan	R-R	6-0	180	7-17-92	.238	.250	.236	40	130	11	31	3	0	1	12	6	1	0	0	22	4	3	.285	.277
Morrobel, Eddy	R-R	5-11	185	3-26-93	.161	.294	.129	30	87	6	14	2	0	0	4	6	0	1	0	19	2	4	.184	.215
Pena, Franmy	R-R	5-10	175	6-8-92	.179	.050	.207	42	112	15	20	2	1	0	15	20	4	4	2	25	6	6	.214	.319
Reyes, Angel	R-R	6-2	195	10-23-90	.242	.194	.752	57	190	21	46	4	2	0	19	18	7	6	2	18	8	3	.284	.327
Reyes, Gabriel	R-R	6-0	166	4-28-91	.268	.292	.263	53	138	15	37	2	1	0	15	22	6	9	1	21	8	8	.297	.389
Soriano, Wilson	R-R	5-9	140	12-31-91	.213	.125	.233	43	89	14	19	0	1	0	3	16	0	4	0	4	9	6	.236	.333
Sosa, Francisco	R-B	6-4	180	2-27-92	.148	.364	.100	23	61	8	9	3	0	0	1	9	3	1	0	21	4	5	.197	.288
Yan, Julian	R-R	6-2	180	11-27-91	.201	.194	.202	64	209	26	42	3	1	0	16	25	16	9	4	59	15	11	.311	.285

Pitching	B-T	HT	WT	DOB	W	L	ERA	G	GS	CG	SV	IP	H	R	ER	HR	BB	SO	AVG	vLH	vRH	K/9	BB/9
Acosta, Amin	L-L	6-1	170	9-25-91	2	1	3.20	11	3	0	0	20	21	11	7	0	13	21	.288	.375	.277	9.61	5.95
Aquino, Jayson	L-L	6-1	170	11-22-92	4	3	1.02	12	12	2	0	62	35	10	7	0	9	59	.161	.320	.140	8.61	1.31
Bernal, Luiding	R-R	6-1	180	11-5-90	0	0	4.50	5	0	0	0	6	3	3	3	0	9	7	.273	.000	.429	10.50	13.50
Brazoban, Gustavo	R-R	6-3	159	8-13-91	4	3	1.64	12	11	2	0	66	48	22	12	1	31	41	.199	.223	.184	5.59	4.23
Fernandez, Raul	R-R	6-2	180	6-22-90	4	3	1.52	12	11	0	0	65	55	15	11	0	21	46	.232	.216	.244	6.37	2.91
Franco, Jose	R-R	6-2	180	9-11-90	5	1	2.17	24	1	0	2	46	34	14	11	1	13	38	.207	.204	.209	7.49	2.56
Hernandez, Jefri	R-R	6-1	170	4-27-91	3	2	1.39	13	7	0	0	45	39	11	7	2	10	25	.239	.205	.250	4.96	1.99
Hernandez, Raul	R-R	6-0	175	10-2-92	2	5	3.32	16	7	0	1	57	54	26	21	1	9	62	.244	.234	.248	9.79	1.42
Jiminian, Johendi	R-R	6-3	165	10-14-92	3	5	4.40	12	11	0	0	47	46	31	23	1	17	31	.256	.238	.265	5.94	3.26
Leon, Carlos	R-R	6-2	195	4-10-92	3	1	3.09	12	1	0	0	23		9	8	1	10	15	.261	.212	.291	5.79	3.86
Mayo, Vianney	R-R	6-2	200	4-6-90	4	2	1.39	12	2	0	0	32	15	7	5	1	9	25	.142	.195	.108	6.96	2.51
Medina, Jose	R-R	6-2	195	9-24-92	0	0	1.64	10	0	0	0	11	10	6	2	0	7	12	.222	.154	.250	9.82	5.73
Montilla, Manuel	R-R	6-4	205	9-7-91	0	2	6.00	12	2	0	1	21	26	16	14	0	9	13	.302	.343	.275	5.57	3.86
Ortiz, Elvin	L-L	6-3	180	11-8-91	0	0	6.75	3	0	0	0	3	2	3	2	0	5	0	.200	.333	.143	0.00	16.88
Pacheco, Anthony	R-R	6-1	160	10-6-89	0	0	0.00	1	0	0	0	1	1	0	0	0	1	0	.250	.333	.000	9.00	9.00
Pena, Raul	L-L	6-0	195	2-16-87	2	2	2.53	33	0	0	20	32	31	12	9	3	15	22	.246	.263	.243	6.19	4.22

Sanchez, Julio	R-R	6-0	160	9-28-91	1	0	5.25	11	0	0	0	12	8	8	7	1	13	12	.200	.167 .214 9.00 9.75
Sanchez, Miguel	R-R	6-2	190	6-12-90	1	4	0.95	14	0	0	0	19	15	9	2	0	11	11	.234	.238 .233 5.21 5.21
Toribio, Israel	R-R	6-4	180	9-24-91	0	0	1.29	5	0	0	0	7	4	5	1	0	7	7	.160	.200 .133 9.00 9.00
Valerio, Radhames	L-L	6-2	200	10-17-92	0	0	1.69	10	2	0	0	16	11	5	3	0	12	6	.186	.091 .208 3.38 6.75

Fielding

Catcher	PCT	G	PO	A	E	DP	PB
Briceno	.977	42	252	44	7	1	8
Morales	1.000	1	7	0	0	0	0
Pena	1.000	2	10	2	0	0	1
Reyes	.995	24	156	25	1	0	6
Reyes	.981	6	45	7	1	0	3

First Base	PCT	G	PO	A	E	DP
Bacilio	1.000	1	10	0	0	0
Briceno	1.000	4	32	1	0	2
De Leon	.993	20	142	6	1	13
Morales	—	1	0	0	0	0
Pena	.984	16	111	9	2	8
Reyes	.976	20	162	3	4	18
Reyes	.994	23	167	13	1	8

Second Base	PCT	G	PO	A	E	DP
Ciriaco	.958	37	61	99	7	16
Galvez	.942	21	39	42	5	10
Morrobel	.956	18	40	46	4	10
Soriano	1.000	5	6	10	0	1

Third Base	PCT	G	PO	A	E	DP
De Leon	1.000	1	1	0	0	0
Galvez	.891	27	21	61	10	4
Herrera	.923	3	4	8	1	0
Morrobel	.636	8	5	9	8	0
Pena	.884	21	17	44	8	5
Reyes	—	2	0	0	0	0
Soriano	.825	21	10	42	11	1

Shortstop	PCT	G	PO	A	E	DP
Ciriaco	.860	12	15	34	8	3

	PCT	G	PO	A	E	DP
Galvez	.958	7	10	13	1	1
Herrera	.947	58	109	158	15	28
Morrobel	—	1	0	0	0	0
Soriano	1.000	1	2	0	0	0

Outfield	PCT	G	PO	A	E	DP
Bacilio	.962	57	69	7	3	2
Bustamante	1.000	27	28	1	0	0
Galvez	—	1	0	0	0	0
Morales	.978	33	43	2	1	0
Pena	—	1	0	0	0	0
Reyes	.875	2	7	0	1	0
Reyes	.974	26	36	1	1	0
Soriano	1.000	8	12	0	0	0
Sosa	.938	21	29	1	2	0
Yan	.927	62	110	4	9	1

Detroit Tigers

SEASON IN A SENTENCE: After clawing their way to the American League Central division lead at the end of June, the Tigers fell fast and hard, falling out of first by the all-star break and sinking into third by season's end, as injuries and inconsistent performance took a toll.

HIGH POINT: What could have been a low moment turned into a good one, as all concerned reacted well when umpire Jim Joyce blew a call at first base that cost Armando Galarraga a perfect game, calling Cleveland's Jason Donald safe when he was clearly out in what would have been the final out of the game. After the game, Joyce emphatically said he was wrong and later, in tears, hugged Galarraga and apologized, and Galarraga and the rest of the team accepted with grace. Beyond that game, Miguel Cabrera had another standout season and led the AL in on-base percentage.

LOW POINT: On July 24 against the Blue Jays, Magglio Ordonez slid into home and not only was out but also was done for the season with a broken ankle. After also losing Brandon Inge and Carlos Guillen, the injury to Ordonez was too much for the Tigers to handle. Detroit lost 15 of its next 19 and fell to 10 games back in the division.

NOTABLE ROOKIES: Austin Jackson posted 100 runs, 170 hits, 30 doubles, 10 triples and 20 stolen bases, becoming just the third rookie in the last 25 years to do so. He also showed strong defense in center field. Will Rhymes was called up twice during the season as a fill-in for Guillen and was the biggest surprise of the team, providing speed and timely hits, often from No. 2 in the order.

KEY TRANSACTIONS: Signing Johnny Damon in February gave the lineup another veteran presence. During the season, the Tigers made several minor deals, most notably trading Dontrelle Willis to the Diamondbacks for Billy Buckner, and Giovanny Soto to the Indians for Jhonny Peralta.

DOWN ON THE FARM: Triple-A Toledo and Double-A Erie both finished last in their divisions, but high Class A Lakeland, short-season Connecticut and the Rookie-level Gulf Coast League team all finished with winning records. Jeff Frazier led the International League with 61 extra-base hits and ranked among the top four in home runs and doubles for Toledo. Andy Dirks set career highs in runs, doubles, triples, home runs, RBIs and steals at Erie, and after being promoted to Triple-A, he batted .375 with 10 doubles and four homers in 22 games.

OPENING DAY PAYROLL: $122.9 million (6th)

PLAYERS OF THE YEAR

MAJOR LEAGUE	MINOR LEAGUE
Miguel Cabrera of	**Jacob Turner** rhp
.328/.420/.622	(Low A/High A)
Led AL in OPB	6-5, 3.28
2nd in AVG, SLG, OPS	1.12 WHIP

ORGANIZATION LEADERS

BATTING	*Minimum 250 at-bats	
MAJORS		
*AVG	Miguel Cabrera	.328
*OPS	Miguel Cabrera	1.042
HR	Miguel Cabrera	38
RBI	Miguel Cabrera	126
MINORS		
*AVG	Alden Carrithers, Erie/Lakeland	.312
*OBP	Alden Carrithers, Erie/Lakeland	.422
*SLG	Jeff Frazier, Toledo	.493
R	Wade Gaynor, West Michigan	91
H	Wade Gaynor, West Michigan	147
TB	Jeff Frazier, Toledo	235
2B	Wade Gaynor, West Michigan	39
3B	Two tied at	8
HR	Jeff Frazier, Toledo	25
RBI	Rawley Bishop, Lakeland/Erie	87
BB	Jamie Johnson, West Michigan	98
SO	Cale Iorg, Erie/Toledo	159
SB	Gustavo Nunez, Lakeland	33

PITCHING	†Minimum 75 innings	
MAJORS		
W	Justin Verlander	18
†ERA	Justin Verlander	3.37
SO	Justin Verlander	219
MINORS		
W	Brooks Brown, Erie	12
	Trevor Feeney, West Michigan	12
L	Two tied at	13
†ERA	Adam Wilk, Lakeland/Erie	2.74
G	Kenny Faulk, West Michigan	49
	Josh Rainwater, Erie/Toledo	49
GS	Trevor Feeney, West Michigan	29
SV	Lester Oliveros, Lakeland/Erie	23
IP	Thad Weber, Erie/Toledo	189.7
BB	Ramon Lebron, W. Mich./GCL/Connecticut	58
SO	Charles Furbush, Lakeland/Erie/Toledo	183
†AVG	Brayan Villarreal, Lakeland/Erie	.232

General Manager: Dave Dombrowski. **Farm Director:** Dan Lunetta. **Scouting Director:** David Chadd.

Class	Team	League	W	L	PCT	Finish*	Manager(s)
Majors	Detroit Tigers	American	81	81	.500	t-8th (14)	Jim Leyland
Triple-A	Toledo Mud Hens	International	70	73	.490	9th (14)	Larry Parrish
Double-A	Erie SeaWolves	Eastern	66	76	.465	t-10th (12)	Phil Nevin
High A	Lakeland Flying Tigers	Florida State	71	67	.514	7th (12)	Andy Barkett
Low A	West Michigan Whitecaps	Midwest	62	77	.446	11th (16)	Joe DePastino
Short-season	Connecticut Tigers	New York-Penn	38	37	.507	7th (14)	Howie Bushong
Rookie	GCL Tigers	Gulf Coast	30	28	.517	7th (15)	Basilio Cabrera

Overall 2010 Minor League Record   337   358   .485   t-23rd (30)

*Finish in overall standings (No. of teams in league). †League champion.

ORGANIZATION STATISTICS

DETROIT TIGERS

AMERICAN LEAGUE

Batting	B-T	HT	WT	DOB	AVG	vLH	vRH	G	AB	R	H	2B	3B	HR	RBI	BB	HBP	SH	SF	SO	SB	CS	SLG	OBP
Avila, Alex	L-R	5-11	210	1-29-87	.228	.182	.234	104	294	28	67	12	0	7	31	36	2	1	0	71	2	2	.340	.316
Boesch, Brennan	L-L	6-4	235	4-12-85	.256	.337	.233	133	464	49	119	26	3	14	67	40	5	0	3	99	7	1	.416	.320
Cabrera, Miguel	R-R	6-4	240	4-18-83	.328	.313	.333	150	548	111	180	45	1	38	126	89	3	0	8	95	3	3	.622	.420
Damon, Johnny	L-L	6-2	205	11-5-73	.271	.275	.270	145	539	81	146	36	5	8	51	69	2	2	1	90	11	1	.401	.355
Everett, Adam	R-R	6-0	180	2-5-77	.185	.231	.164	31	81	6	15	5	0	0	4	4	0	3	1	18	2	1	.247	.221
Frazier, Jeff	R-R	6-3	195	8-10-82	.217	.167	.273	9	23	3	5	1	0	0	1	1	0	0	0	6	0	0	.261	.250
Guillen, Carlos	B-R	6-1	215	9-30-75	.273	.234	.286	68	253	26	69	17	1	6	34	21	0	0	1	41	1	2	.419	.327
Inge, Brandon	R-R	5-11	190	5-19-77	.247	.254	.245	144	514	47	127	28	5	13	70	54	5	0	7	134	4	3	.397	.321
Jackson, Austin	R-R	6-1	185	2-1-87	.293	.226	.317	151	618	103	181	34	10	4	41	47	4	3	3	170	27	6	.400	.345
Kelly, Don	L-R	6-4	190	2-15-80	.244	.217	.247	119	238	30	58	4	0	9	27	8	2	1	2	42	3	0	.374	.272
Laird, Gerald	R R	6-1	225	11-13-79	.207	.183	.224	89	270	22	56	11	0	5	25	18	3	6	2	57	3	1	.304	.263
Larish, Jeff	L-R	6-2	210	10-11-82	.200	.250	.167	3	10	0	2	0	0	0	1	0	0	0	0	4	0	0	.200	.200
2-team total (24 Oakland)					.179	—	—	27	67	5	12	3	0	2	9	7	1	0	0	24	1	0	.313	.267
Ordonez, Magglio	R-R	6-0	215	1-28-74	.303	.371	.285	84	323	56	98	17	1	12	59	40	0	0	2	38	1	0	.474	.378
Peralta, Jhonny	R-R	6-2	215	5-28-82	.253	.245	.256	57	217	23	55	7	0	8	38	21	0	0	4	34	0	0	.396	.314
2-team total (91 Cleveland)					.249	—	—	148	551	60	137	30	2	15	81	53	1	0	10	103	1	0	.392	.311
Raburn, Ryan	R-R	6-0	185	4-17-81	.280	.295	.273	113	371	54	104	25	1	15	62	27	8	1	3	92	2	2	.474	.340
Rhymes, Will	L-R	5-9	155	4-1-83	.304	.351	.292	54	191	30	58	12	3	1	19	14	0	7	1	16	0	3	.414	.350
Santiago, Ramon	B-R	5-11	185	8-31-79	.263	.313	.249	112	320	38	84	9	1	3	22	30	7	8	2	56	2	2	.325	.337
Sizemore, Scott	R-R	6-0	185	1-4-85	.224	.224	.223	48	143	19	32	7	0	3	14	15	0	4	1	40	0	0	.336	.296
St. Pierre, Max	R-R	6-0	175	4-17-80	.222	.333	.000	6	9	1	2	1	0	0	0	0	0	0	0	2	0	0	.333	.222
Wells, Casper	R-R	6-2	210	11-23-84	.323	.265	.386	36	93	14	30	6	1	4	17	6	0	0	0	19	0	1	.538	.364
Worth, Danny	R-R	6-1	185	9-30-85	.255	.283	.233	39	106	10	27	5	0	2	8	6	0	3	0	13	1	2	.358	.295

Pitching	B-T	HT	WT	DOB	W	L	ERA	G	GS	CG	SV	IP	H	R	ER	HR	BB	SO	AVG	vLH	vRH	K/9	BB/9
Bonderman, Jeremy	R-R	6-2	220	10-28-82	8	10	5.53	30	29	0	0	171	187	113	105	25	60	112	.277	.303	.250	5.89	3.16
Bonine, Eddie	R-R	6-5	220	6-6-81	4	1	4.63	47	1	0	0	68	84	37	35	7	22	26	.305	.275	.329	3.44	2.91
Coke, Phil	L-L	6-1	210	7-19-82	7	5	3.76	74	1	0	2	65	67	29	27	2	26	53	.275	.273	.276	7.38	3.62
Fien, Casey	R-R	6-2	195	10-21-83	0	0	10.13	2	0	0	0	3	4	3	3	2	0	0	.364	.400	.333	0.00	0.00
Figaro, Alfredo	R-R	6-0	175	7-7-84	0	2	6.75	8	1	0	0	15	18	12	11	1	8	5	.310	.304	.314	3.07	4.91
Galarraga, Armando	R-R	6-4	180	1-15-82	4	9	4.49	25	24	2	0	144	143	75	72	21	51	74	.258	.241	.276	4.61	3.18
Gonzalez, Enrique	R-R	5-10	225	7-14-82	0	1	3.81	18	0	0	0	26	21	11	11	4	17	13	.236	.214	.255	4.50	5.88
Ni, Fu-Te	L-L	6-0	170	11-14-82	0	1	6.65	22	0	0	0	23	27	19	17	2	19	22	.290	.306	.281	8.61	7.43
Oliver, Andy	L-L	6-3	210	12-3-87	0	4	7.36	5	5	0	0	22	26	22	18	3	13	18	.310	.269	.328	7.36	5.32
Perry, Ryan	R-R	6-4	200	2-13-87	3	5	3.59	60	0	0	2	63	55	26	25	6	23	45	.243	.167	.284	6.46	3.30
Porcello, Rick	R-R	6-5	200	12-27-88	10	12	4.92	27	27	0	0	163	188	96	89	18	38	84	.288	.303	.272	4.65	2.10
Sborz, Jay	R-R	6-4	210	1-24-85	0	0	67.50	1	0	0	0	1	3	5	5	0	0	1	.600	.667	.500	13.50	0.00
Scherzer, Max	R-R	6-3	220	7-27-84	12	11	3.50	31	31	0	0	196	174	84	76	20	70	184	.244	.239	.250	8.46	3.22
Schlereth, Daniel	L-L	6-0	210	5-9-86	2	0	2.89	18	0	0	1	19	20	7	6	2	10	19	.270	.310	.244	9.16	4.82
Thomas, Brad	L-L	6-4	235	10-12-77	6	2	3.89	49	2	0	0	69	77	31	30	4	29	30	.292	.252	.322	3.89	3.76
Valverde, Jose	R-R	6-4	255	3-24-78	2	4	3.00	60	0	0	26	63	41	24	21	5	32	63	.184	.165	.204	9.00	4.57
Verlander, Justin	R-R	6-5	225	2-20-83	18	9	3.37	33	33	4	0	224	190	89	84	14	71	219	.228	.230	.225	8.79	2.85
Weinhardt, Robbie	R-R	6-2	205	12-8-85	2	2	6.14	28	0	0	0	29	40	23	20	2	8	21	.328	.214	.388	6.44	2.45
Willis, Dontrelle	L-L	6-4	225	1-12-82	1	2	4.98	9	8	0	0	43	48	24	24	3	29	33	.284	.224	.308	6.85	6.02
Zumaya, Joel	R-R	6-3	210	11-9-84	2	1	2.58	31	0	0	1	38	32	13	11	1	11	34	.229	.215	.240	7.98	2.58

Fielding

Catcher	PCT	G	PO	A	E	DP	PB
Avila	.993	98	556	34	4	5	6
Laird	.991	87	516	52	5	5	5
St. Pierre	1.000	4	12	1	0	0	

First Base	PCT	G	PO	A	E	DP
Cabrera	.990	148	1218	96	13	133

	PCT	G	PO	A	E	DP	PB
Kelly	.987	28	146	10	2	24	
Larish	1.000	1	5	0	0	0	
Peralta	1.000	2	7	1	0	0	
Raburn	1.000	1	6	1	0	1	

Second Base	PCT	G	PO	A	E	DP
Guillen	.987	47	86	138	3	32

	PCT	G	PO	A	E	DP
Raburn	.986	18	27	43	1	11
Rhymes	.984	53	89	150	4	37
Santiago	.986	25	24	44	1	11
Sizemore	.955	40	59	90	7	24
Worth	1.000	12	14	31	0	9

DETROIT TIGERS

Third Base	PCT	G	PO	A	E	DP
Inge	.977	144	119	267	9	24
Kelly	.927	15	5	33	3	5
Peralta	1.000	9	7	9	0	3
Raburn	1.000	2	1	1	0	0
Sizemore	.933	6	7	7	1	1
Worth	1.000	3	0	2	0	0

Shortstop	PCT	G	PO	A	E	DP
Everett	.992	31	48	74	1	24
Peralta	.984	46	70	118	3	26
Santiago	.979	85	106	227	7	53
Worth	1.000	24	41	56	0	14

Outfield	PCT	G	PO	A	E	DP
Boesch	.957	118	216	9	10	2
Damon	.967	36	57	2	2	1

	PCT	G	PO	A	E	DP
Frazier	1.000	4	11	1	0	1
Guillen	.857	4	6	0	1	0
Jackson	.985	149	383	9	6	2
Kelly	1.000	74	90	4	0	0
Ordonez	.979	71	135	7	3	3
Raburn	.969	91	150	4	5	0
Wells	1.000	36	35	4	0	0

TOLEDO MUD HENS   TRIPLE-A

INTERNATIONAL LEAGUE

Batting	B-T	HT	WT	DOB	AVG	vLH	vRH	G	AB	R	H	2B	3B	HR	RBI	BB	HBP	SH	SF	SO	SB	CS	SLG	OBP
Bertram, Michael	R-R	6-2	220	2-25-84	.231	.240	.228	28	104	15	24	5	1	3	17	8	2	0	2	28	2	0	.385	.293
Boesch, Brennan	L-L	6-4	235	4-12-85	.379	.294	.415	15	58	6	22	3	1	3	17	4	4	0	0	17	2	1	.621	.455
Bouchie, Andy	R-R	6-1	205	8-6-85	.143	.000	.200	2	7	0	1	1	0	0	3	1	0	0	0	0	0	0	.286	.250
Ciriaco, Audy	R-R	6-3	195	6-16-87	.000	.000	.000	1	3	0	0	0	0	0	0	0	0	0	0	0	0	0	.000	.000
Diaz, Robinzon	R-R	5-11	215	9-19-83	.255	.323	.233	71	251	29	64	17	2	1	21	5	1	2	3	13	0	0	.351	.269
Dirks, Andy	L-L	6-0	195	1-24-86	.375	.304	.400	22	88	14	33	10	1	4	17	3	1	0	1	12	3	0	.648	.398
Dlugach, Brent	R-R	6-4	200	3-3-83	.258	.259	.257	117	450	52	116	22	3	6	41	25	5	2	2	149	12	4	.360	.303
Flores, Angel	R-R	6-0	200	8-16-86	.375	.333	.400	2	8	0	3	0	0	0	2	1	0	0	0	2	0	0	.375	.444
Frazier, Jeff	R-R	6-3	195	8-10-82	.256	.267	.251	123	477	72	122	34	2	25	73	32	4	0	3	89	7	1	.493	.306
Guez, Ben	R-R	5-10	170	1-24-87	.251	.274	.240	68	223	32	56	9	3	9	32	24	7	2	3	63	5	6	.439	.339
Guillen, Carlos	B-R	6-1	215	9-30-75	.333	.455	.143	5	18	5	6	3	0	1	2	2	0	0	0	4	0	0	.667	.400
Henry, Justin	L-R	6-3	180	4-30-85	.269	.325	.250	44	156	18	42	8	1	0	14	18	1	2	2	25	9	4	.333	.345
Iorg, Cale	R-R	6-2	180	9-6-85	.242	.176	.265	16	66	7	16	6	1	1	9	2	1	0	1	20	0	1	.409	.271
Kunkel, Jeff	B-R	5-11	200	3-11-83	.239	.303	.200	25	88	8	21	4	1	0	8	4	0	2	1	22	0	0	.307	.269
Larish, Jeff	L-R	6-2	200	10-11-82	.275	.211	.303	84	298	43	82	21	0	15	55	45	4	1	4	84	1	0	.497	.373
Leon, Max	B-R	5-11	190	6-27-84	.238	.222	.246	89	298	37	71	10	6	3	27	24	5	2	4	59	2	1	.342	.302
Rabelo, Mike	B-R	6-1	200	1-17-80	.143	.250	.111	10	35	4	5	2	0	1	8	1	0	0	0	8	0	0	.286	.167
Raburn, Ryan	R-R	6-0	185	4-17-81	.444	.222	.556	7	27	5	12	6	0	0	2	2	0	0	0	3	1	1	.667	.483
Ramirez, Wilkin	R-R	6-2	190	10-25-85	.216	.180	.233	41	153	15	33	4	2	4	14	10	2	0	0	60	7	2	.346	.273
2-team total (24 Gwinnett)					.229	—		65	236	31	54	7	3	8	28	20	5	0	1	82	9	2	.386	.302
Rhymes, Will	L-R	5-9	155	4-1-83	.305	.309	.303	95	364	59	111	20	7	2	35	36	4	13	4	35	22	5	.415	.370
Roof, Shawn	R-R	5-10	175	8-3-84	.354	.316	.367	25	79	12	28	3	1	0	8	11	2	1	1	14	4	4	.418	.441
Scram, Deik	L-R	6-2	180	2-1-84	.208	.154	.217	31	96	12	20	6	2	0	9	15	1	0	1	34	2	1	.313	.319
Sizemore, Scott	R-R	6-0	185	1-4-85	.298	.314	.291	76	299	49	89	23	1	9	37	31	9	1	2	77	2	2	.472	.378
St. Pierre, Max	R-R	6-0	175	4-17-80	.300	.350	.278	39	130	16	39	7	0	5	22	11	2	1	3	21	1	1	.469	.356
Strieby, Ryan	R-R	6-5	235	4-15-86	.245	.253	.242	76	290	29	71	15	0	10	49	33	1	0	1	85	1	1	.400	.323
Thomas, Clete	L-R	5-11	195	11-14-83	.183	.200	.174	21	71	14	13	2	1	4	13	12	0	0	2	32	9	0	.408	.318
2-team total (47 Scranton/W-B)					.257	—		68	241	27	62	13	2	1	16	24	1	0	1	42	5	2	.340	.326
Weber, Jon	L-L	5-10	190	1-20-78	.256	.056	.317	21	78	9	20	6	0	1	5	6	0	0	0	17	5	0	.372	.310
Wells, Casper	R-R	6-2	210	11-23-84	.233	.248	.227	103	387	56	90	22	6	21	46	34	9	0	0	111	7	8	.483	.309
White, Chris	B-R	5-11	170	11-12-87	.284	.278	.286	23	81	9	23	5	0	1	5	3	0	3	0	17	6	0	.383	.310
Worth, Danny	R-R	6-1	185	9-30-85	.287	.381	.254	45	164	18	47	5	0	2	18	10	2	0	1	29	12	2	.354	.333

Pitching	B-T	HT	WT	DOB	W	L	ERA	G	GS	CG	SV	IP	H	R	ER	HR	BB	SO	AVG	vLH	vRH	K/9	BB/9
Buckner, Billy	R-R	6-2	205	8-27-83	3	5	9.40	8	8	1	0	37	60	44	39	8	16	21	.359	.368	.352	5.06	3.86
De La Vara, Gilbert	L-L	5-10	190	10-4-84	2	2	4.94	8	2	0	0	24	39	15	13	1	3	25	.382	.370	.393	9.51	1.14
Drucker, Scot	R-R	6-1	192	5-30-82	4	5	5.61	42	5	0	1	87	107	58	54	10	29	69	.310	.353	.269	7.17	3.01
Dumatrait, Phil	R-L	6-2	205	7-12-81	4	1	3.16	8	8	0	0	43	40	19	15	3	18	17	.248	.163	.286	3.59	3.80
Fien, Casey	R-R	6-2	195	10-21-83	3	3	2.60	44	0	0	8	52	54	21	18	8	13	44	.235	.257	.217	6.35	1.88
Figaro, Alfredo	R-R	6-0	175	7-7-84	10	6	4.14	23	23	0	0	124	142	60	57	11	39	112	.290	.272	.311	8.13	2.83
Furbush, Charlie	L-L	6-5	215	4-11-86	3	4	6.29	9	9	0	0	49	59	37	34	9	16	37	.311	.190	.364	6.84	2.96
Gagnier, L.J.	R-R	6-2	210	2-28-85	7	7	3.51	21	20	1	0	121	111	60	47	15	44	94	.239	.283	.197	7.01	3.28
Galarraga, Armando	R-R	6-4	180	1-15-82	4	2	3.65	8	7	0	0	44	40	18	18	4	14	40	.235	.289	.191	8.12	2.84
Garcia, Ramon	L-L	6-2	165	10-30-84	1	0	9.00	3	0	0	0	3	6	3	3	1	0	2	.500	.600	.429	6.00	0.00
Gonzalez, Enrique	R-R	5-10	225	7-14-82	4	5	3.41	12	11	1	0	66	69	29	25	9	16	54	.263	.241	.287	7.36	2.18
Hoffman, Matt	L-L	6-2	195	11-18-88	0	0	10.38	3	0	0	0	4	9	5	5	1	4	4	.474	.429	.500	8.31	8.31
Ketchner, Ryan	L-L	6-1	190	4-19-82	6	5	4.00	28	22	0	1	124	122	66	55	20	39	95	.258	.302	.235	6.91	2.84
Lugo, Ruddy	B-R	6-0	210	5-22-80	2	4	8.16	11	0	0	1	43	63	43	39	10	19	18	.348	.333	.363	3.77	3.98
Marte, Luis	R-R	5-11	170	8-26-86	0	0	0.00	1	0	0	0	1	1	0	0	1	1	1	.250	.500	.000	9.00	9.00
Ni, Fu-Te	L-L	6-0	170	11-14-82	0	0	7.50	12	0	0	0	6	10	5	5	0	3	16	.346	.250	.429	12.00	6.00
Oliver, Andy	L-L	6-3	210	12-3-87	3	6	3.23	9	9	0	0	53	43	23	19	6	25	49	.226	.143	.261	8.32	4.25
Perry, Ryan	R-R	6-4	200	2-13-87	0	0	0.00	3	0	0	0	4	1	1	0	0	0	4	.077	.000	.250	9.82	9.82
Porcello, Rick	R-R	6-5	200	12-27-88	1	2	3.21	4	4	0	0	28	24	11	10	0	10	10	.245	.255	.233	6.11	3.21
Rainwater, Josh	R-R	6-2	220	4-9-85	2	4	4.64	45	0	0	1	76	91	40	39	8	20	54	.301	.288	.311	6.42	2.38
Sborz, Jay	R-R	6-4	210	1-24-85	1	6	4.74	43	0	0	19	44	38	24	23	8	24	42	.232	.277	.185	8.66	4.95
Scherzer, Max	R-R	6-3	220	7-27-84	0	0	0.60	2	2	0	0	15	4	1	1	0	2	17	.083	.120	.043	10.20	1.20
Schlereth, Daniel	L-L	6-0	210	5-9-86	1	3	2.37	38	0	0	0	49	40	17	13	6	44	35	.235	.208	.225	10.95	6.20
Simons, Zach	L-R	6-2	200	5-23-85	0	0	3.78	10	0	0	0	17	18	7	7	1	7	18	.281	.083	.400	9.72	3.78
Waddell, Jason	R-L	6-2	190	6-11-81	0	1	5.40	10	0	0	0	10	7	6	6	1	9	10	.206	.188	.222	8.10	8.10
Weber, Thad	R-R	6-2	200	9-28-84	2	1	1.64	3	3	0	0	22	14	4	4	2	3	7	.187	.200	.171	6.95	1.23
Weinhardt, Robbie	R-R	6-2	205	12-8-85	1	1	1.57	24	0	0	0	34	26	7	6	0	7	25	.211	.283	.143	6.55	1.85
Wise, Brendan	L-R	6-2	190	1-9-86	4	2	2.08	28	0	0	2	52	53	14	12	0	12	23	.279	.333	.239	3.98	2.08

Fielding

Catcher	PCT	G	PO	A	E	DP	PB
Bouchie	1.000	2	9	1	0	0	0
Diaz	.991	71	475	53	5	8	10
Flores	1.000	2	19	4	0	0	3
Kunkel	.983	25	148	23	3	3	4
Rabelo	1.000	9	62	5	0	0	0
St. Pierre	.986	38	263	20	4	3	1

First Base	PCT	G	PO	A	E	DP
Bertram	1.000	25	186	12	0	23
Frazier	.987	48	410	36	6	43
Henry	1.000	1	8	0	0	0
Larish	.997	36	292	20	1	29
Leon	.992	16	120	7	1	10
Strieby	.994	21	161	18	1	19

Second Base	PCT	G	PO	A	E	DP
Dlugach	.833	2	2	3	1	2
Guillen	1.000	5	8	11	0	3
Henry	1.000	19	37	39	0	15
Leon	.914	12	10	22	3	6

	PCT	G	PO	A	E	DP
Rhymes	.996	65	105	171	1	41
Roof	1.000	2	3	4	0	3
Sizemore	.974	41	81	104	5	32
Worth	1.000	5	12	15	0	5

Third Base	PCT	G	PO	A	E	DP
Ciriaco	1.000	1	0	2	0	0
Dlugach	.967	14	3	26	1	6
Guez	—	1	0	0	0	0
Henry	.972	10	9	26	1	5
Larish	.973	46	33	77	3	8
Leon	.885	9	13	10	3	2
Rhymes	.889	13	7	17	3	2
Roof	.922	18	13	34	4	6
Sizemore	1.000	11	8	23	0	2
Worth	.966	24	11	46	2	3

Shortstop	PCT	G	PO	A	E	DP
Dlugach	.947	100	159	251	23	57
Iorg	.987	16	27	50	1	11
Leon	.500	1	0	1	1	0

	PCT	G	PO	A	E	DP
Rhymes	1.000	7	9	16	0	6
Roof	.947	5	10	8	1	1
Sizemore	.714	2	1	4	2	1
Worth	.976	17	44	37	2	14

Outfield	PCT	G	PO	A	E	DP
Boesch	1.000	13	22	1	0	0
Dirks	.985	22	63	3	1	0
Frazier	.992	54	118	5	1	1
Guez	.983	61	115	1	2	0
Henry	1.000	8	10	0	0	0
Leon	1.000	4	5	0	0	0
Raburn	1.000	7	21	3	0	3
Ramirez	.978	38	87	3	2	2
Rhymes	1.000	3	3	0	0	0
Scram	.981	26	53	0	1	0
Strieby	.987	51	71	5	1	1
Thomas	.965	20	55	0	2	0
Weber	.947	10	17	1	1	0
Wells	.981	101	243	12	5	6
White	.970	22	30	2	1	1

ERIE SEAWOLVES
DOUBLE-A
EASTERN LEAGUE

Batting	B-T	HT	WT	DOB	AVG	vLH	vRH	G	AB	R	H	2B	3B	HR	RBI	BB	HBP	SH	SF	SO	SB	CS	SLG	OBP
Bertram, Michael	L-R	6-2	220	2-25-84	.256	.215	.273	94	363	44	93	24	2	10	50	25	4	0	0	97	3	1	.416	.311
Bishop, Rawley	R-R	6-3	205	11-19-85	.252	.260	.249	67	246	42	62	11	0	9	45	28	6	1	5	65	6	0	.407	.337
Bouchie, Andy	R-R	6-1	205	8-6-85	.205	.224	.195	59	200	24	41	10	0	8	26	10	1	3	3	42	0	1	.375	.243
Bourquin, Ron	L-R	6-3	205	4-29-85	.238	.500	.211	6	21	4	5	0	0	2	2	3	0	0	0	9	0	1	.524	.333
Burrus, Josh	R-R	5-11	190	8-20-83	.207	.127	.243	59	203	27	42	5	2	7	28	20	5	1	1	60	8	5	.355	.293
Carrithers, Alden	L-R	5-9	165	11-14-84	.262	.309	.245	59	210	28	55	7	0	1	12	35	4	2	0	29	7	4	.310	.378
Ciriaco, Audy	R-R	6-3	195	6-16-87	.241	.232	.244	61	241	28	58	4	0	9	36	8	0	1	1	49	6	0	.419	.264
De Leon, Santo	R-R	6-2	175	11-1-83	.207	.167	.217	10	29	3	6	1	0	1	2	1	0	0	8	0	0	.345	.281
Dirks, Andy	L-L	6-0	195	1-24-86	.278	.238	.297	98	388	64	108	20	2	11	46	35	5	1	5	59	19	4	.425	.342
Douglas, Brandon	R-R	6-0	185	8-27-85	.359	.230	.402	35	145	27	52	17	2	0	15	11	1	1	1	17	6	2	.503	.405
Flores, Angel	R-R	6-0	200	8-16-86	.229	.364	.167	13	35	3	8	2	0	1	3	2	0	0	0	10	0	0	.371	.270
Guez, Ben	R-R	5-10	170	1-24-87	.357	.250	.500	9	28	2	10	3	0	0	3	3	0	1	0	5	3	2	.464	.419
Henry, Justin	L-R	6-3	180	4-30-85	.260	.179	.280	67	200	28	52	12	2	1	15	36	0	4	1	40	9	6	.355	.371
Iorg, Cale	R-R	6-2	180	9-6-85	.211	.228	.204	110	427	50	90	22	1	10	33	17	4	6	0	139	12	5	.337	.248
Jaime, Carmelo	B-R	5-9	170	7-16-85	.000	.000	.000	1	2	1	0	0	0	0	0	1	0	0	0	1	0	0	.000	.333
Johnson, Ben	R-R	6-1	230	6-18-81	.167	.250	.158	12	42	7	7	2	0	1	7	6	1	0	0	12	0	0	.286	.286
Jones, Brandon	L-L	6-1	215	12-10-83	.258	.526	.192	29	97	10	25	8	0	0	8	27	0	0	0	37	1	1	.340	.419
2-team total (31 Altoona)					.251	—	—	60	207	20	52	13	0	1	15	40	0	0	0	37	1	1	.329	.372
Kaiser, Kody	B-R	5-9	185	4-6-85	.247	.273	.233	49	182	20	45	8	2	4	20	17	0	2	3	57	7	4	.379	.307
Kendrick, Tyson	R-R	6-1	195	2-8-88	.000	.000	.000	1	4	0	0	0	0	0	0	0	0	0	0	2	0	0	.000	.000
Kunkel, Jeff	B-R	5-11	200	3-11-83	.261	.281	.255	44	142	19	37	2	2	4	17	15	3	2	1	27	1	1	.387	.342
Mansilla, Matt	R-R	6-0	185	5-25-86	.250	.333	.227	12	28	3	7	0	0	0	2	0	0	0	0	11	0	0	.250	.300
Murrian, John	R-R	6-2	215	6-15-88	.217	.077	.255	17	60	4	13	4	1	0	8	1	0	1	1	15	0	0	.367	.226
Nicolas, Cesar	R-R	6-4	230	4-17-82	.279	.280	.278	70	244	28	68	19	0	7	38	33	8	0	4	50	1	0	.443	.377
Nowlin, Billy	R-R	6-1	210	12-16-86	.268	.342	.240	40	142	18	38	11	1	5	26	3	6	1	0	40	0	0	.465	.309
Peter, Kyle	L-R	6-2	185	2-4-86	.185	.167	.200	10	27	3	5	1	0	0	3	2	1	1	0	10	1	0	.222	.267
Pounds, Bryan	R-R	6-0	195	10-4-85	.281	.206	.320	53	185	24	52	9	1	6	29	21	2	1	1	52	1	2	.438	.359
Ramirez, Wilkin	R-R	6-2	190	10-25-85	.241	.292	.218	56	212	34	51	10	4	15	42	22	0	0	1	84	5	6	.538	.311
Roof, Shawn	R-R	5-10	175	8-3-84	.223	.299	.160	64	193	27	43	7	2	0	15	10	5	3	0	46	7	3	.280	.279
Scram, Deik	L-R	6-2	180	2-1-84	.221	.191	.231	80	263	32	58	18	3	7	34	38	6	1	1	84	14	4	.392	.331
St. Pierre, Max	R-R	6-0	175	4-17-80	.217	.211	.220	20	60	13	13	0	1	5	14	11	1	2	0	12	5	2	.500	.347
White, Chris	B-R	5-11	170	11-12-87	.211	.290	.150	27	71	7	15	4	0	2	7	13	4	3	0	18	4	3	.352	.282
Wyatt, Brent	B-R	5-10	185	1-25-85	.228	.250	.220	16	57	6	13	2	1	2	7	4	3	0	0	12	1	1	.404	.313

Pitching	B-T	HT	WT	DOB	W	L	ERA	G	GS	CG	SV	IP	H	R	ER	HR	BB	SO	AVG	vLH	vRH	K/9	BB/9
Below, Duane	L-L	6-2	205	11-15-85	7	12	4.93	28	28	0	0	126	137	78	69	17	37	103	.275	.264	.279	7.36	2.64
Brown, Brooks	L-R	6-3	210	6-20-85	12	9	4.15	28	18	4	2	128	120	61	59	8	39	85	.247	.224	.265	5.98	2.74
Crichton, Erik	R-R	5-10	190	6-6-85	0	0	18.00	2	0	0	0	3	9	7	6	1	1	1	.529	.667	.375	3.00	3.00
Furbush, Charlie	L-L	6-5	215	4-11-86	1	0	3.24	5	5	0	0	33	31	12	12	5	10	37	.248	.255	.244	9.99	2.70
Gagnier, L.J.	R-R	6-2	210	2-28-85	3	0	2.83	6	6	0	0	35	35	13	11	5	8	28	.255	.328	.197	7.20	2.06
Garcia, Ramon	L-L	6-2	165	10-30-84	0	5	5.25	27	7	0	1	74	89	51	43	15	15	49	.303	.343	.280	5.99	1.83
Gayhart, Jared	L-R	6-3	195	10-29-86	0	4	6.06	22	0	0	1	33	30	23	22	3	20	28	.250	.250	.250	7.71	5.51
Hamilton, Cory	R-R	6-1	195	4-15-88	4	1	4.62	26	0	0	0	37	34	23	19	2	31	26	.248	.255	.244	6.32	7.54
Hoffman, Matt	L-L	6-2	195	11-18-88	1	2	7.43	26	0	0	0	27	36	26	22	3	20	22	.308	.280	.328	7.43	6.75
Ketchner, Ryan	L-L	6-1	190	4-19-82	1	1	3.86	5	0	0	1	14	15	6	6	1	2	6	.273	.286	.268	3.86	1.29
Kibler, Jon	L-L	6-4	215	8-10-86	4	7	6.44	15	15	0	0	80	94	61	57	11	31	39	.297	.374	.261	4.41	3.50
Marte, Luis	R-R	5-11	170	8-26-86	2	2	5.06	38	0	0	7	48	44	31	27	5	26	53	.244	.221	.259	9.94	4.88
Oliver, Andy	L-L	6-3	210	12-3-87	6	4	3.61	14	14	0	0	77	74	35	31	7	25	70	.253	.242	.258	8.15	2.91

	B-T	HT	WT	DOB	W	L	ERA	G	GS	CG	SV	IP	H	R	ER	HR	BB	SO	AVG	vLH	vRH	K/9	BB/9
Oliveros, Lester	R-R	5-11	178	5-28-88	1	2	4.97	24	0	0	14	25	20	14	14	3	21	36	.217	.231	.208	12.79	7.46
Ortega, Jose	R-R	5-11	165	10-12-88	1	0	3.04	15	1	0	0	24	22	8	8	2	7	19	.242	.167	.306	7.23	2.66
Rainwater, Josh	R-R	6-2	220	4-9-85	0	0	10.80	4	0	0	0	5	12	6	6	0	4	4	.462	.429	.500	7.20	7.20
Shawler, Anthony	R-R	6-3	188	5-16-87	5	4	4.75	28	12	0	0	102	109	62	54	15	22	83	.274	.323	.230	7.30	1.93
Simons, Zach	L-R	6-3	200	5-23-85	3	4	2.36	34	0	0	3	53	36	14	14	5	21	54	.193	.208	.183	9.11	3.54
Villareal, Brayan	R-R	6-0	170	5-10-87	0	4	3.71	8	8	0	0	44	37	21	18	6	16	46	.231	.173	.282	9.48	3.30
Voss, Jay	L-L	6-4	195	4-22-87	2	3	5.81	33	0	0	1	48	61	39	31	6	25	33	.319	.211	.391	6.19	4.69
Waite, Rob	R-R	6-3	210	1-9-87	0	0	2.66	12	0	0	0	20	16	14	6	1	7	14	.208	.257	.167	6.20	3.10
Weber, Thad	R-R	6-2	200	9-28-84	9	12	4.08	25	25	2	0	168	176	87	76	17	41	113	.273	.260	.285	6.07	2.20
Wilk, Adam	L-L	6-2	175	12-9-87	2	0	1.14	3	3	0	0	24	10	3	3	1	5	14	.128	.152	.111	5.32	1.90
Wise, Brendan	R-R	6-2	190	1-9-86	2	0	1.44	15	0	0	4	25	14	6	4	0	11	17	.157	.152	.161	6.12	3.96

Fielding

Catcher	PCT	G	PO	A	E	DP	PB
Bouchie	.993	58	389	29	3	5	4
Flores	1.000	13	67	3	0	1	0
Kendrick	1.000	1	3	1	0	0	0
Kunkel	.994	44	293	27	2	2	0
Murrian	.991	15	103	6	1	0	1
St. Pierre	.993	20	117	22	1	3	0

First Base	PCT	G	PO	A	E	DP
Bertram	.989	69	588	40	7	71
Bishop	.995	61	530	42	3	71
Bourquin	.875	1	7	0	1	1
Nicolas	1.000	9	84	7	0	5
Nowlin	.964	3	26	1	1	2
Roof	—	1	0	0	0	0
Wyatt	1.000	1	3	0	0	1

Second Base	PCT	G	PO	A	E	DP
Carrithers	.969	38	48	106	5	37
Douglas	1.000	17	23	55	0	14
Henry	.976	54	129	152	7	41
Roof	.970	31	47	82	4	16
Wyatt	.978	10	14	30	1	6

Third Base	PCT	G	PO	A	E	DP
Bertram	.786	3	2	9	3	0
Ciriaco	.925	56	39	110	12	10
De Leon	.864	10	5	14	3	1
Henry	1.000	1	0	3	0	0
Nicolas	.833	14	12	18	6	5
Pounds	.942	50	35	110	9	4
Roof	.882	16	7	23	4	4

Shortstop	PCT	G	PO	A	E	DP
Ciriaco	.895	5	6	11	2	4
Douglas	.905	18	40	55	10	16
Henry	1.000	1	0	2	0	1
Iorg	.953	109	171	319	24	84
Jaime	.500	1	2	0	2	0
Roof	.954	13	20	42	3	11

Outfield	PCT	G	PO	A	E	DP
Bertram	1.000	6	7	1	0	0
Bouchie	—	1	0	0	0	0
Burrus	.958	48	106	9	5	3
Carrithers	1.000	23	45	1	0	1
Dirks	.979	95	175	16	4	5
Guez	.929	8	13	0	1	0
Henry	1.000	9	19	0	0	0
Johnson	.963	10	26	0	1	0
Jones	.976	22	40	0	1	0
Kaiser	.972	48	101	4	3	2
Mansilla	.962	12	22	3	1	0
Nowlin	1.000	8	7	0	0	0
Peter	.941	10	16	0	1	0
Ramirez	.985	53	125	5	2	2
Scram	.985	70	123	7	2	1
White	1.000	21	40	0	0	0
Wyatt	1.000	7	10	0	0	0

LAKELAND FLYING TIGERS   HIGH CLASS A

FLORIDA STATE LEAGUE

Batting	B-T	HT	WT	DOB	AVG	vLH	vRH	G	AB	R	H	2B	3B	HR	RBI	BB	HBP	SH	SF	SO	SB	CS	SLG	OBP
Aguasvivas, Juaner	R-R	6-3	225	9-15-89	.125	.000	.286	4	16	0	2	0	0	0	1	1	0	0	0	6	0	0	.125	.176
Alvino, Billy	R-R	5-11	200	9-2-87	.161	.111	.182	11	31	2	5	0	0	0	1	2	1	1	0	2	1	0	.161	.235
Bishop, Rawley	R-R	6-3	205	11-19-86	.301	.455	.254	66	236	39	71	18	1	6	42	26	8	1	3	65	7	0	.462	.385
Bouchie, Andy	R-R	6-1	205	8-6-85	.135	.158	.121	16	52	5	7	0	0	2	4	4	0	0	1	10	0	0	.250	.193
Carrithers, Alden	L-R	5-9	165	11-14-84	.359	.458	.331	60	220	42	79	11	0	1	20	43	1	2	1	29	10	4	.423	.464
Castillo, Luis	R-R	5-11	160	5-15-89	.167	.235	.135	16	54	2	9	0	0	0	3	3	0	4	1	9	0	1	.167	.207
Douglas, Brandon	R-R	6-0	185	8-27-85	.331	.273	.350	37	136	20	45	7	3	0	8	13	2	3	1	16	3	1	.426	.395
Fields, Daniel	L-R	6-1	201	1-23-91	.240	.219	.245	109	375	33	90	13	6	8	47	55	5	1	2	119	8	9	.371	.343
Flores, Angel	R-R	6-0	200	8-16-86	.208	.429	.118	6	24	2	5	1	0	0	3	1	1	1	0	7	0	0	.250	.269
Gomez, Gilbert	R-R	6-0	165	4-30-90	.250	.000	.250	2	4	1	1	0	0	0	1	0	0	0	0	1	0	0	.250	.250
Guez, Ben	R-R	5-10	170	1-24-87	.207	.115	.246	28	87	9	18	7	0	1	8	10	5	0	0	23	6	2	.322	.324
Holaday, Bryan	R-R	6-0	205	11-19-87	.220	.308	.192	44	159	14	35	8	0	3	12	21	7	0	1	43	0	0	.327	.335
Jaime, Carmelo	R-R	5-9	170	7-16-85	.209	.200	.213	18	67	6	14	0	1	0	7	4	0	1	0	12	1	1	.239	.254
Kaiser, Kody	B-R	5-9	185	4-6-85	.325	.328	.325	63	252	32	82	15	6	5	40	20	1	1	2	52	13	2	.492	.375
Lennerton, Jordan	L-L	6-2	217	2-16-86	.301	.286	.305	57	206	25	62	15	0	9	33	30	2	0	1	54	1	0	.505	.393
Mansilla, Matt	R-R	6-0	185	5-25-86	.164	.125	.170	19	55	6	9	1	0	0	5	5	1	2	0	22	1	0	.182	.246
Martinez, Francisco	R-R	6-1	180	9-1-90	.271	.303	.261	89	340	47	92	17	1	3	29	28	3	1	2	71	12	5	.353	.330
McKenna, Pat	R-R	5-10	170	6-24-87	.245	.310	.222	36	110	22	27	5	0	1	5	20	1	3	0	43	9	3	.318	.366
Moreno, Alexander	R-R	6-4	185	4-1-90	.213	.176	.233	15	47	3	10	0	0	0	6	4	0	1	0	17	2	0	.213	.275
Murrian, John	R-R	6-0	205	6-15-88	.264	.263	.264	62	216	27	57	14	0	4	21	25	2	2	2	55	4	2	.384	.343
Nowlin, Billy	R-R	6-1	210	12-16-86	.262	.237	.268	83	298	28	78	9	1	9	45	32	6	0	1	59	1	2	.389	.344
Nunez, Gustavo	B-R	5-10	170	2-8-88	.222	.235	.218	128	523	66	116	13	6	2	33	21	9	16	3	93	33	8	.281	.263
Peter, Kyle	L-R	6-2	185	2-4-86	.267	.000	.267	4	15	0	4	1	0	0	1	0	0	0	0	4	0	0	.333	.267
Pounds, Bryan	R-R	6-0	195	10-4-85	.269	.267	.269	48	175	20	47	3	1	2	24	20	5	0	3	46	0	0	.331	.355
Purroy, Gabriel	R-R	5-9	160	4-16-92	.167	.600	.000	6	18	0	3	1	0	0	1	0	0	0	0	4	0	0	.222	.211
Rijo, Samir	B-R	6-2	205	6-26-90	.222	.233	.218	39	117	7	26	5	0	1	12	10	1	2	1	31	0	2	.291	.287
Rodriguez, Julio	R-R	6-2	200	8-3-89	.208	.261	.192	28	101	9	21	4	0	2	13	2	1	3	2	11	0	0	.307	.226
Sanz, Luis	R-R	5-10	165	2-23-91	.250	1.000	.143	4	8	0	2	0	0	0	0	0	0	0	0	2	0	0	.250	.250
Sedon, Chris	R-R	5-10	175	11-6-87	.178	.000	.222	30	90	7	16	1	0	2	6	13	0	3	1	35	4	1	.256	.279
Tang, Chao-Ting	L-R	5-11	176	10-12-87	.209	.200	.212	16	43	1	9	1	0	0	4	3	0	1	1	14	0	2	.233	.255
White, Chris	B-R	5-11	170	11-12-87	.187	.148	.196	42	134	15	25	2	3	2	11	9	3	0	2	29	4	2	.291	.252
Workman, Josh	L-R	6-1	200	11-4-85	.191	.273	.167	18	47	3	9	0	0	0	1	8	1	0	0	13	2	1	.191	.321
Wyatt, Brent	B-R	5-10	185	1-25-85	.258	.298	.247	109	372	50	96	18	3	5	43	53	12	7	2	75	16	5	.363	.367

Pitching	B-T	HT	WT	DOB	W	L	ERA	G	GS	CG	SV	IP	H	R	ER	HR	BB	SO	AVG	vLH	vRH	K/9	BB/9
Barfield, Jeff	R-R	6-0	205	2-11-88	1	2	6.07	3	3	0	0	13	10	10	9	1	9	5	.200	.200	.200	3.38	6.07
Conn, Tyler	L-L	6-1	180	11-9-85	1	4	3.53	26	0	0	2	36	50	15	14	0	13	22	.347	.413	.316	5.55	3.28
Crichton, Erik	R-R	5-10	190	6-6-85	4	5	5.02	41	0	0	5	57	67	39	32	5	22	30	.296	.280	.306	4.71	3.45
Furbush, Charlie	L-L	6-5	215	4-11-86	4	5	3.39	13	13	0	0	77	68	35	29	7	14	109	.229	.247	.221	12.74	1.64

Player	B-T	HT	WT	DOB	W	L	ERA	G	GS	CG	SV	IP	H	R	ER	HR	BB	SO	AVG	vLH	vRH	K/9	BB/9
Garcia, Ramon	L-L	6-2	165	10-30-84	2	0	1.26	8	0	0	0	14	11	2	2	2	3	14	.208	.294	.167	8.79	1.88
Gayhart, Jared	L-R	6-3	195	10-29-86	4	4	2.51	23	0	0	9	32	26	9	9	1	11	33	.230	.238	.225	9.19	3.06
Gentzler, Dan	R-R	6-0	185	10-9-87	2	0	4.00	15	0	0	1	18	22	8	8	1	6	11	.306	.400	.238	5.50	3.00
Hamilton, Cory	R-R	6-1	195	4-15-88	0	0	0.57	10	0	0	2	16	10	1	1	1	3	6	.185	.200	.172	3.45	1.72
Hoffman, Matt	L-L	6-2	195	11-18-88	0	1	1.59	16	0	0	3	23	17	5	4	1	2	18	.215	.214	.216	7.15	0.79
Kibler, Jon	L-L	6-4	215	8-10-86	4	4	3.58	12	12	0	0	70	73	28	28	4	22	53	.279	.213	.293	6.78	2.82
Little, Matt	R-R	5-11	180	3-19-88	1	1	1.80	7	0	0	0	10	2	2	2	0	6	10	.069	.143	.045	9.00	5.40
Mejia, Miguel	R-R	6-2	210	1-19-88	2	1	4.91	15	0	0	1	22	19	15	12	4	9	20	.224	.161	.259	8.18	3.68
Morrison, Michael	R-R	6-1	210	12-17-87	0	0	0.00	3	0	0	0	5	2	0	0	0	0	6	.118	.125	.111	10.80	0.00
Nelson, Cole	L-L	6-7	233	7-14-89	0	0	0.75	2	2	0	0	12	1	1	1	0	6	9	.028	.000	.032	6.75	4.50
Oliveros, Lester	R-R	5-11	178	5-28-88	0	1	1.89	20	0	0	9	19	13	5	4	0	6	24	.194	.182	.206	11.37	2.84
Ortega, Jose	R-R	5-11	165	10-12-88	2	1	0.95	10	0	0	0	19	14	2	2	0	7	20	.212	.261	.186	9.47	3.32
Palacios, Wilson	R-R	6-3	180	12-15-89	0	0	3.86	1	0	0	0	2	1	1	1	0	2	0	.143	.000	.200	0.00	7.71
Putkonen, Luke	R-R	6-6	200	5-10-86	9	7	3.18	27	26	1	0	153	144	55	54	8	44	87	.257	.278	.240	5.13	2.59
Ramirez, Wilfredo	L-L	6-4	210	11-24-87	0	2	4.94	28	3	0	1	51	58	32	28	4	5	37	.279	.346	.256	6.53	0.88
Rondon, Bruce	R-R	6-2	190	12-9-90	0	0	1.35	4	0	0	2	7	2	1	1	1	2	7	.095	.111	.083	9.45	2.70
Shawler, Anthony	R-R	6-3	188	5-16-87	1	0	0.96	11	0	0	2	19	15	2	2	0	1	15	.224	.267	.189	7.23	0.48
Sorensen, Mark	R-R	6-3	205	2-21-86	10	12	4.03	27	25	1	0	147	160	76	66	11	29	113	.276	.307	.254	6.90	1.77
Stohr, Tyler	L-R	6-2	210	9-19-86	1	0	0.00	3	0	0	0	5	3	0	0	0	4	2	.188	.167	.200	3.60	7.20
Teufel, Shawn	L-L	6-3	215	7-16-86	0	2	2.45	9	1	0	0	15	12	5	4	1	5	19	.222	.286	.200	11.66	3.07
Torrealba, Michael	R-R	5-11	150	11-19-89	1	2	5.32	12	0	0	0	22	24	15	13	1	4	20	.276	.229	.308	8.18	1.64
Turner, Jacob	R-R	6-5	210	5-21-91	4	2	2.93	13	13	0	0	61	53	22	20	3	14	51	.231	.296	.183	7.48	2.05
Villareal, Brayan	R-R	6-0	170	5-10-87	7	4	3.47	16	16	1	0	86	73	37	33	8	23	90	.232	.264	.212	9.46	2.42
Voss, Jay	L-L	6-4	195	4-22-87	0	1	1.40	11	0	0	2	19	16	5	3	2	2	16	.229	.214	.232	7.45	0.93
Waite, Rob	R-R	6-3	210	1-9-87	2	2	3.64	25	0	0	0	42	35	22	17	2	13	39	.222	.273	.185	8.36	2.79
Wilk, Adam	L-L	6-2	175	12-9-87	9	5	3.01	24	24	1	0	144	139	58	48	8	19	100	.250	.267	.245	6.26	1.19
Wood, Austin	L-L	6-2	195	11-2-86	0	0	0.00	2	0	0	0	1	0	0	0	0	0	3	.000	.000	.000	20.25	0.00

Fielding

Catcher	PCT	G	PO	A	E	DP	PB
Alvino	1.000	9	45	3	0	1	2
Bouchie	.993	15	126	12	1	0	1
Flores	1.000	6	42	5	0	0	0
Holaday	.996	33	248	13	1	1	5
Murrian	.990	45	281	19	3	1	6
Purroy	1.000	5	26	2	0	0	1
Rodriguez	.979	28	216	17	5	2	4
Sanz	1.000	4	16	0	0	1	0

First Base	PCT	G	PO	A	E	DP
Aguasvivas	.969	3	30	1	1	1
Bishop	.996	52	460	31	2	36
Lennerton	.990	52	444	42	5	51
Nowlin	.990	33	271	22	3	31
Pounds	1.000	3	22	0	0	6

Second Base	PCT	G	PO	A	E	DP
Carrithers	.967	57	81	155	8	30
Douglas	.991	26	53	58	1	23
Jaime	.952	12	20	40	3	7
McKenna	.985	25	42	86	2	20
Sedon	.956	22	33	53	4	14
Wyatt	1.000	2	1	2	0	1

Third Base	PCT	G	PO	A	E	DP
Bishop	1.000	3	1	3	0	0
Douglas	1.000	4	1	4	0	0
Martinez	.936	86	55	193	17	21
McKenna	.833	2	1	4	1	0
Pounds	.927	41	20	81	8	7
Wyatt	.947	7	4	14	1	3

Shortstop	PCT	G	PO	A	E	DP
Douglas	1.000	5	8	16	0	2
Jaime	.867	5	6	7	2	2
McKenna	1.000	6	8	9	0	3
Nunez	.959	123	214	388	26	76

Outfield	PCT	G	PO	A	E	DP
Castillo	1.000	16	30	1	0	0
Fields	.996	102	216	7	1	4
Guez	1.000	26	39	3	0	1
Jaime	1.000	1	2	0	0	0
Kaiser	.984	56	113	7	2	1
Mansilla	.957	18	21	1	1	1
Moreno	1.000	13	18	0	0	0
Peter	1.000	2	5	0	0	0
Pounds	.750	4	3	0	1	0
Rijo	.933	38	77	6	6	2
Tang	1.000	14	17	1	0	0
White	.986	38	67	3	1	0
Workman	1.000	12	10	0	0	0
Wyatt	.990	98	183	20	2	5

WEST MICHIGAN WHITECAPS

LOW CLASS A

MIDWEST LEAGUE

Batting	B-T	HT	WT	DOB	AVG	vLH	vRH	G	AB	R	H	2B	3B	HR	RBI	BB	HBP	SH	SF	SO	SB	CS	SLG	OBP
Alvino, Billy	R-R	5-11	200	9-2-87	.262	.167	.288	30	84	8	22	3	0	0	1	15	4	2	0	6	1	0	.298	.398
Bourquin, Ron	L-R	6-3	205	4-29-85	.237	.333	.219	11	38	3	9	3	0	0	3	8	1	0	0	11	1	0	.316	.383
Brantly, Rob	R-L	6-3	205	7-14-89	.255	.122	.293	52	188	26	48	10	1	1	21	23	5	1	0	22	2	2	.335	.352
Espinoza, Alexis	R-R	6-1	180	12-20-88	.241	.266	.230	67	253	34	61	8	6	6	28	6	8	0	1	88	4	3	.391	.280
Garcia, Avisail	R-R	6-3	190	6-12-91	.281	.301	.275	125	494	58	139	17	4	4	63	20	5	0	5	113	20	4	.356	.313
Gaynor, Wade	R-R	6-3	225	4-19-88	.286	.331	.271	131	514	91	147	39	4	10	80	46	10	0	4	111	13	5	.436	.354
Gosse, Mike	L-R	5-7	165	5-30-86	.226	.217	.228	37	137	13	31	9	3	0	13	11	1	2	0	17	1	0	.336	.289
Guillen, Carlos	B-R	6-1	215	9-30-75	.333	.000	.400	2	6	0	2	0	0	0	1	0	0	0	0	0	0	0	.333	.429
Gulliver, Jimmy	R-L	5-11	175	6-6-86	.255	.217	.262	42	145	16	37	6	1	2	18	12	0	0	3	42	3	4	.352	.306
Inge, Brandon	R-R	5-11	190	5-19-77	.400	.667	.000	1	5	0	2	0	0	0	0	0	0	0	0	2	0	0	.800	.400
Johnson, Jamie	L-R	5-9	180	4-26-87	.284	.260	.292	122	443	76	126	21	8	3	41	98	3	6	5	76	11	7	.388	.413
Jones, Clay	R-R	6-2	205	11-11-87	.270	.161	.316	50	189	22	51	10	0	2	24	17	6	0	2	31	1	0	.354	.346
Jones, Corey	L-R	6-0	190	5-4-86	.304	.360	.304	48	189	27	68	19	0		30	17	15	4	1	27	1	0	.460	.450
Lennerton, Jordan	L-L	6-2	217	2-16-86	.290	.275	.294	59	214	21	62	15	0	3	23	31	3	0	1	65	0	0	.402	.386
Palacios, Luis	R-R	5-10	162	7-7-89	.191	.129	.222	27	94	11	18	3	1	0	5	8	0	0	0	28	2	0	.245	.255
Perez, Hernan	R-R	6-0	160	3-26-91	.235	.182	.255	124	473	45	111	15	0	5	50	25	2	2	5	98	5	1	.298	.273
Plagman, Tony	L-L	6-2	211	8-14-87	.272	.170	.296	63	243	33	66	19	3	5	35	22	4	0	4	47	1	0	.436	.337
Rockett, Michael	R-R	6-1	180	7-26-87	.235	.270	.222	99	379	53	89	20	5	7	43	12	5	3	3	81	5	7	.369	.266
Rodriguez, Julio	R-R	6-2	200	8-3-89	.250	1.000	.000	2	8	0	2	0	0	0	1	0	0	0	0	1	0	0	.250	.250
Roof, Eric	R-L	6-5	185	11-15-86	.233	.216	.241	50	129	9	28	5	1	0	14	14	2	0	0	40	0	2	.292	.324
Rowland, Jeff	L-L	5-10	185	4-1-88	.281	.214	.305	57	210	42	59	9	3	1	24	34	2	4	2	51	5	3	.367	.383
Salas, Luis	R-R	6-1	220	1-2-89	.146	.156	.141	31	103	6	15	6	0	0	8	5	1	1	1	32	1	0	.204	.191
Sanz, Luis	R-R	5-10	165	2-23-91	.254	.240	.262	21	67	5	17	1	0	3	7	2	2	1	10	3	1	.269	.338

	B-T	HT	WT	DOB	AVG	vLH	vRH	G	AB	R	H	2B	3B	HR	RBI	BB	HBP	SH	SF	SO	SB	CS	SLG	OBP
Sedon, Chris	R-R	5-10	175	11-6-87	.250	.412	.203	24	76	6	19	1	0	3	7	3	2	0	1	32	1	2	.382	.293
Soto, Elvin	L-R	6-2	190	5-6-89	.130	.111	.135	16	46	4	6	2	1	1	4	9	0	1	0	18	0	3	.283	.273

Pitching	B-T	HT	WT	DOB	W	L	ERA	G	GS	CG	SV	IP	H	R	ER	HR	BB	SO	AVG	vLH	vRH	K/9	BB/9
Cain, Nolan	R-R	6-3	235	1-2-86	0	0	3.38	9	0	0	0	11	11	6	4	2	6	10	.244	.133	.300	8.44	5.06
Cooper, Patrick	R-R	6-3	204	8-25-89	2	1	5.72	8	8	0	0	39	42	26	25	4	23	26	.280	.268	.291	5.95	5.26
Cruz, Antonio	L-L	5-11	160	10-7-91	2	0	2.79	10	0	0	0	19	19	6	6	0	10	13	.253	.273	.245	6.05	4.66
Faulk, Kenny	L-L	6-0	210	5-27-87	5	4	2.16	49	0	0	12	58	52	17	14	0	30	78	.235	.226	.239	12.03	4.63
Feeney, Trevor	R-R	6-1	185	6-4-86	12	13	3.46	29	29	1	0	185	216	85	71	12	22	123	.293	.304	.287	5.99	1.07
Hamilton, Cory	R-R	6-1	195	4-15-88	0	0	0.84	4	0	0	2	11	9	1	1	0	4	9	.243	.385	.167	7.59	3.38
Hess, Kevan	R-R	6-2	190	3-30-88	0	1	8.00	10	0	0	1	18	17	17	16	1	17	15	.243	.192	.273	7.50	8.50
Larez, Victor	R-R	6-3	160	5-28-87	8	11	4.27	33	17	0	2	131	150	73	62	13	35	59	.289	.282	.295	4.06	2.41
Lebron, Ramon	R-R	6-1	180	2-1-89	4	5	6.85	13	13	0	0	47	50	38	36	5	39	55	.267	.230	.292	10.46	7.42
Little, Matt	R-R	5-11	180	3-19-88	1	0	4.71	15	0	0	0	21	17	11	11	0	14	25	.213	.161	.245	10.71	6.00
Mejia, Miguel	R-R	6-2	160	11-19-88	1	0	4.05	7	0	0	0	13	13	6	6	1	6	13	.260	.214	.278	8.78	4.05
Mercedes, Melvin	R-R	6-2	190	11-2-90	1	2	5.03	15	0	0	3	20	16	11	11	0	19	12	.225	.286	.186	5.49	8.69
Moody, Nolan	L-R	6-1	200	9-23-85	0	0	4.82	10	0	0	0	19	24	11	10	3	6	18	.320	.103	.457	8.68	2.89
Newman, Nate	R-R	6-3	210	12-17-86	0	5	4.46	28	4	0	0	69	69	39	34	3	34	45	.261	.314	.228	5.90	4.46
Ortega, Jose	R-R	5-11	165	10-12-88	0	3	4.56	18	0	0	1	26	28	14	13	1	17	22	.275	.250	.288	7.71	5.96
Pratt, Jordan	R-R	6-3	215	9-25-89	1	2	2.63	19	0	0	4	27	26	8	8	0	9	26	.255	.300	.226	8.56	2.96
Samuels, Zach	L-R	6-2	180	10-8-86	4	1	2.98	30	0	0	3	66	63	27	22	3	25	53	.255	.270	.245	7.19	3.39
Sanz, Luis	R-R	6-1	173	11-19-87	4	7	5.38	25	12	0	0	87	93	59	52	8	43	62	.284	.290	.277	6.41	4.45
Soto, Giovanni	L-L	6-3	155	5-18-91	6	6	2.61	16	16	2	0	83	75	29	24	2	25	76	.248	.375	.213	8.27	2.72
Teufel, Shawn	L-L	6-3	215	7-16-86	1	1	2.60	9	0	0	0	17	11	6	5	1	8	14	.180	.333	.143	7.27	4.15
Todd, Jade	R-R	6-3	190	3-22-90	0	8	5.11	14	14	1	0	69	78	43	39	6	24	56	.287	.230	.303	7.34	3.15
Turner, Jacob	R-R	6-5	210	5-21-91	3	3	3.67	11	10	0	0	54	53	26	22	4	9	51	.245	.186	.294	8.50	1.50
Wesson, Jared	L-L	6-5	190	1-30-86	7	2	3.44	19	15	0	0	81	74	35	31	1	41	85	.243	.257	.239	9.44	4.56
Zumaya, Richard	R-R	6-0	180	11-10-89	1	2	5.05	27	1	0	0	46	55	31	26	4	18	28	.297	.312	.287	5.44	3.50

Fielding

Catcher	PCT	G	PO	A	E	DP	PB
Alvino	1.000	30	209	17	0	2	2
Brantly	.995	52	353	39	2	2	7
Rodriguez	1.000	2	13	1	0	0	0
Roof	.980	36	265	25	6	2	3
Sanz	.994	21	153	13	1	1	1

First Base	PCT	G	PO	A	E	DP
Bourquin	.984	6	58	5	1	3
Jones	.981	23	190	20	4	16
Lennerton	.993	46	399	27	3	30
Plagman	.985	51	422	29	7	41
Soto	1.000	14	99	11	0	8

Second Base	PCT	G	PO	A	E	DP
Gosse	.992	30	50	69	1	17
Guillen	.800	2	2	2	1	1
Gulliver	.990	24	38	59	1	12
Jones	.974	46	82	107	5	26
Palacios	.987	18	29	45	1	10
Sedon	.972	24	53	51	3	9

Third Base	PCT	G	PO	A	E	DP
Gaynor	.927	127	82	237	25	16
Gulliver	.857	12	3	15	3	2
Inge	1.000	1	0	2	0	0
Palacios	.944	4	5	12	1	0

Shortstop	PCT	G	PO	A	E	DP
Gulliver	.957	10	19	26	2	9
Palacios	.895	5	5	12	2	1
Perez	.943	124	200	380	35	68

Outfield	PCT	G	PO	A	E	DP
Espinoza	.941	17	30	2	2	1
Garcia	.976	117	233	12	6	0
Johnson	.978	116	252	15	6	2
Rockett	.979	90	178	13	4	1
Rowland	.992	55	112	6	1	0
Salas	.964	29	50	3	2	1

CONNECTICUT TIGERS SHORT-SEASON
NEW YORK-PENN LEAGUE

Batting	B-T	HT	WT	DOB	AVG	vLH	vRH	G	AB	R	H	2B	3B	HR	RBI	BB	HBP	SH	SF	SO	SB	CS	SLG	OBP
Anderson, Brett	R-R	6-3	185	9-3-90	.199	.211	.195	45	151	12	30	8	0	2	13	11	4	0	2	42	1	2	.291	.268
Ashenbrenner, Josh	L-R	6-0	190	8-29-87	.260	.346	.234	63	227	28	59	12	3	0	18	18	6	1	3	19	2	1	.339	.327
Enos, Ryan	L-L	5-10	185	12-19-87	.265	.250	.268	63	238	37	63	9	3	4	31	21	0	6	1	42	16	5	.378	.323
Kendrick, Tyson	R-R	6-1	195	2-8-88	.250	.000	.333	12	20	1	5	0	0	0	3	0	0	0	3	0	1	.250	.348
Machado, Dixon	R-R	6-0	140	2-22-92	.292	.333	.267	7	24	4	7	1	0	0	1	3	1	2	0	5	1	2	.333	.393
Mansilla, Matt	R-R	6-0	185	5-25-86	.130	.235	.081	17	54	5	7	0	0	2	9	3	0	1	1	21	1	0	.241	.172
Nunez, Alexander	R-R	5-11	172	5-4-90	.223	.262	.210	68	265	29	59	14	4	2	27	14	2	4	2	76	14	6	.328	.265
Perry, Matt	L-R	6-2	190	7-17-87	.259	.265	.256	51	174	13	45	6	0	0	19	21	0	2	1	36	2	2	.293	.337
Polk, P.J.	R-R	5-9	170	12-12-88	.267	.298	.257	64	236	35	63	13	1	2	15	24	4	5	1	52	29	6	.356	.343
Robbins, James	L-L	6-0	225	9-26-90	.251	.161	.279	69	259	26	65	11	3	3	37	12	4	0	1	91	2	2	.351	.293
Rodriguez, Julio	R-R	6-2	200	8-3-89	.270	.302	.257	52	189	19	51	10	2	1	14	10	4	0	2	32	2	0	.360	.317
Roof, Eric	R-L	6-5	185	11-15-86	.232	.200	.240	39	125	9	29	9	1	2	16	8	2	2	3	31	0	0	.368	.283
Rowland, Jeff	L-L	5-10	185	4-1-88	.341	.444	.314	11	44	9	15	1	0	0	7	7	1	1	0	11	4	3	.364	.442
Sedon, Chris	R-R	5-10	175	11-6-87	.333	.500	.222	6	15	2	5	1	0	1	3	3	0	0	0	5	0	0	.600	.444
Smith, Les	L-R	6-1	190	12-24-89	.185	.261	.155	27	81	4	15	4	1	0	2	6	0	1	1	31	1	0	.259	.239
Soares, Ryan	R-R	6-1	195	7-10-87	.220	.184	.236	38	127	14	28	5	0	1	8	5	0	1	1	23	3	2	.283	.248
Tang, Chao-Ting	L-R	5-11	176	10-12-87	.197	.194	.198	42	127	15	25	3	2	0	11	7	1	2	2	15	7	5	.252	.241
Taylor, Londell	R-R	6-2	200	9-13-88	.128	.241	.077	32	94	9	12	3	1	3	7	9	2	0	3	44	3	2	.277	.213

Pitching	B-T	HT	WT	DOB	W	L	ERA	G	GS	CG	SV	IP	H	R	ER	HR	BB	SO	AVG	vLH	vRH	K/9	BB/9
Barrow, Brandon	L-L	6-4	195	4-18-89	0	0	4.50	1	0	0	0	2	1	1	1	0	1	0	.143	.000	.250	0.00	4.50
Baxter, Lance	L-L	6-1	194	9-8-87	0	2	10.50	2	2	0	0	6	11	7	7	0	3	6	.423	.000	.500	9.00	4.50
Carreno, Josue	R-R	6-1	170	6-26-91	5	6	4.76	14	14	0	0	64	64	44	34	5	33	59	.254	.296	.227	8.25	4.62
Clark, Tyler	B-R	6-2	185	1-4-89	3	1	2.05	21	0	0	3	44	39	15	10	1	20	43	.234	.235	.232	8.80	4.09
Cooper, Patrick	R-R	6-3	204	8-25-89	2	1	3.91	5	4	0	0	23	15	11	10	1	7	24	.181	.235	.143	9.39	2.74
Cruz, Antonio	L-L	5-11	160	10-7-91	0	1	2.08	9	0	0	0	13	10	5	3	0	6	12	.233	.214	.241	8.31	4.15
Ferrell, Jeff	R-R	6-3	185	11-23-90	0	0	4.26	2	0	0	0	6	7	3	3	0	3	7	.318	.167	.375	9.95	4.26
Finefrock, Sean	R-R	6-5	200	2-11-87	0	0	7.71	4	0	0	0	3	4	4	0	2	3	.429	.500	.385	5.79	3.86

Name	B-T	HT	WT	DOB	W	L	ERA	G	GS	CG	SV	IP	H	R	ER	HR	BB	SO	AVG	vLH	vRH	K/9	BB/9
Gagnier, Drew	R-R	6-4	225	9-21-88	1	0	2.95	19	0	0	0	37	35	17	12	2	24	38	.250	.212	.273	9.33	5.89
Guichardo, Rayni	L-L	6-1	165	8-13-91	4	5	3.86	14	14	0	0	63	70	33	27	3	37	38	.279	.268	.281	5.43	5.29
Hess, Kevan	R-R	6-2	190	3-30-88	2	0	2.87	12	0	0	1	16	16	7	5	1	5	16	.276	.190	.324	9.19	2.87
Hoch, Logan	L-L	6-2	185	5-5-87	1	1	5.64	22	0	0	4	30	30	21	19	1	19	32	.261	.348	.239	9.49	5.64
Lawson, Patrick	R-R	6-2	190	5-20-88	3	3	2.93	16	9	0	0	58	47	21	19	1	30	38	.229	.233	.226	5.86	4.63
Lebron, Ramon	R-R	6-1	180	2-1-89	1	1	8.44	7	0	0	1	11	12	11	10	1	10	20	.267	.222	.296	16.88	8.44
Little, Matt	R-R	5-11	180	3-19-88	0	0	1.50	4	0	0	1	6	6	2	1	1	1	7	.240	.500	.158	10.50	1.50
Mejia, Miguel	R-R	6-2	210	1-19-88	3	2	1.02	13	2	0	4	35	21	4	4	1	11	33	.174	.308	.110	8.41	2.80
Mendoza, Clemente	R-R	6-0	170	7-24-90	6	5	4.61	15	15	1	0	84	86	48	43	8	25	56	.261	.209	.290	6.00	2.68
Mowry, Tim	R-R	6-5	215	9-28-87	2	0	3.60	11	0	0	1	20	20	10	8	2	8	15	.260	.276	.250	6.75	3.60
Palacios, Wilsen	R-R	6-3	180	12-15-89	0	0	0.00	2	0	0	0	10	4	0	0	0	0	9	.114	.077	.136	7.84	0.00
Sanz, Luis	R-R	6-1	173	11-19-87	3	0	0.56	3	3	0	0	16	11	2	1	0	7	15	.212	.154	.231	8.44	3.94
Smith, Brennan	R-R	6-3	200	8-4-89	1	7	3.38	15	12	1	1	69	70	28	26	7	22	58	.265	.233	.286	7.53	2.86
Teufel, Shawn	L-L	6-3	215	7-16-86	0	0	3.00	2	0	0	0	3	3	1	1	0	2	6	.250	.000	.300	18.00	6.00
Torrealba, Michael	R-R	5-11	150	11-19-89	0	2	1.83	9	0	0	2	20	12	4	4	1	7	24	.182	.105	.213	10.98	3.20
Weinhardt, Robbie	R-R	6-2	205	12-8-85	1	0	2.25	3	0	0	0	4	2	1	1	0	2	5	.133	.000	.167	11.25	4.50
White, Tyler	R-R	6-3	205	8-8-89	0	0	8.00	11	0	0	3	9	10	15	8	1	13	11	.250	.316	.190	11.00	13.00

Fielding

Catcher	PCT	G	PO	A	E	DP	PB
Kendrick	.950	6	18	1	1	0	1
Rodriguez	.989	50	391	53	5	2	5
Roof	.984	27	166	20	3	2	8

First Base	PCT	G	PO	A	E	DP
Perry	1.000	10	65	7	0	5
Robbins	.989	67	527	35	6	42

Second Base	PCT	G	PO	A	E	DP
Nunez	.965	67	118	158	10	32

Sedon	1.000	2	4	3	0	0
Soares	1.000	7	13	10	0	3

Third Base	PCT	G	PO	A	E	DP
Ashenbrenner	.954	62	48	117	8	7
Perry	.907	14	9	30	4	2

Shortstop	PCT	G	PO	A	E	DP
Anderson	.875	38	64	97	23	25
Machado	.938	7	13	17	2	1
Soares	.952	30	31	89	6	14

Outfield	PCT	G	PO	A	E	DP
Enos	.973	51	102	5	3	1
Mansilla	1.000	15	33	0	0	0
Polk	.980	62	143	2	3	0
Rowland	1.000	11	24	1	0	0
Smith	.968	21	29	1	1	0
Tang	1.000	39	77	1	0	1
Taylor	.963	32	49	3	2	1

GCL TIGERS
ROOKIE
GULF COAST LEAGUE

Batting	B-T	HT	WT	DOB	AVG	vLH	vRH	G	AB	R	H	2B	3B	HR	RBI	BB	HBP	SH	SF	SO	SB	CS	SLG	OBP
Aguasvivas, Juaner	R-R	6-3	225	9-15-89	.226	.233	.224	52	186	19	42	14	0	5	27	8	3	0	1	66	1	0	.382	.268
Aird, Byron	R-R	6-0	192	5 8-91	.182	.333	.125	14	33	4	6	1	0	0	2	4	0	3	0	12	0	0	.212	.270
Azcona, Javier	R-R	6-1	185	9-28-91	.256	.222	.264	52	176	21	45	9	4	3	14	7	3	3	0	51	9	2	.403	.296
Castellanos, Nick	R-R	6-4	195	3-4-92	.333	.500	.318	7	24	5	8	2	0	0	3	4	0	0	1	5	0	1	.417	.414
Castillo, Luis	R-R	5-11	160	5-15-90	.323	.250	.347	19	65	5	21	3	0	0	6	2	0	1	0	9	3	2	.369	.343
Corcino, Edgar	B-R	6-2	190	6-7-92	.218	.250	.206	27	87	8	19	3	0	0	9	8	0	1	0	27	2	1	.253	.284
Gomez, Edwin	B-R	6-3	175	8-26-91	.226	.150	.250	46	168	11	38	2	2	0	19	11	1	0	3	49	5	1	.262	.273
Gomez, Gilbert	R-R	6-0	165	4-30-90	.243	.313	.231	36	107	13	26	5	1	2	8	4	1	3	1	39	1	2	.364	.274
Jones, Corey	L-R	6-0	190	9-14-87	.000	.000	.000	3	5	0	0	0	0	0	1	0	2	0	1	0	0	0	.000	.250
Leyland, Patrick	R-R	6-2	198	10-11-91	.219	.189	.229	41	146	10	32	3	0	0	12	6	3	2	3	17	0	1	.240	.259
Machado, Dixon	R-R	6-0	140	2-22-92	.261	.410	.214	43	165	22	43	4	3	0	11	14	0	2	2	27	12	3	.321	.315
McClendon, Bo	R-R	5-10	215	10-4-87	.179	.300	.138	15	39	5	7	0	0	0	3	9	1	0	0	10	1	1	.179	.347
McKenna, Pat	R-R	5-10	170	6-24-87	.326	.250	.353	15	46	8	15	4	1	2	5	7	0	2	0	15	2	3	.587	.415
Meador, James	R-R	6-0	200	12-9-87	.240	.182	.250	25	75	7	18	5	0	0	6	4	5	3	0	12	3	1	.307	.321
Miller, Pete	R-R	5-11	180	3-10-87	.287	.286	.287	40	115	18	33	5	1	0	6	20	4	2	0	34	2	2	.348	.410
Moreno, Alexander	R-R	6-4	185	4-1-90	.236	.333	.189	19	55	5	13	2	1	0	6	4	2	0	1	14	2	1	.309	.306
Moya, Steven	L-R	6-6	220	9-8-91	.190	.147	.204	40	137	12	26	5	2	2	11	6	1	0	0	64	0	0	.299	.229
Peter, Kyle	L-R	6-2	185	2-4-86	.298	.429	.280	16	57	8	17	4	0	0	5	5	1	1	1	11	3	2	.368	.359
Pounds, Bryan	R-R	6-0	195	10-4-85	.000	.000	.000	2	5	0	0	0	0	0	0	1	0	0	0	0	0	0	.000	.167
Purroy, Gabriel	R-R	5-9	160	4-16-92	.258	.192	.284	26	93	7	24	2	1	2	15	2	1	0	0	17	0	1	.366	.281
Rijo, Samir	B-R	6-2	205	6-26-91	.231	.250	.225	15	52	4	12	3	1	0	1	5	0	0	0	16	0	1	.327	.298
Smith, Les	L-R	6-1	190	12-24-89	.368	.333	.385	5	19	5	7	2	0	1	7	0	0	0	1	2	0	0	.632	.350
Soto, Elvin	L-R	6-2	190	5-6-89	.000	.000	.000	1	3	0	0	0	0	0	0	0	1	0	0	0	0	0	.000	.250

Pitching	B-T	HT	WT	DOB	W	L	ERA	G	GS	CG	SV	IP	H	R	ER	HR	BB	SO	AVG	vLH	vRH	K/9	BB/9
Barfield, Jeff	R-R	6-0	205	2-11-88	1	4	5.30	10	4	0	0	36	39	21	21	2	3	30	.285	.360	.241	7.57	0.76
Burgos, Alex	L-L	5-11	170	12-1-90	0	0	1.54	8	0	0	1	12	10	5	2	1	3	15	.227	.125	.286	11.57	2.31
Celis, Fernando	R-R	6-1	165	3-27-89	2	3	2.61	19	0	0	1	41	36	15	12	4	5	33	.238	.224	.247	7.19	1.09
Crnkovich, Steve	R-R	6-4	192	10-8-87	5	3	1.58	10	8	0	0	46	26	9	8	1	7	51	.166	.171	.164	10.05	1.38
Crosby, Casey	R-L	6-5	200	9-17-88	0	1	8.76	3	3	0	0	12	21	15	12	1	4	10	.382	.364	.386	7.30	2.92
Cruz, Antonio	L-L	5-11	160	10-7-91	0	0	7.20	5	0	0	0	5	5	4	4	0	4	3	.278	.400	.231	5.40	7.20
Duffey, Jack	L-L	6-2	190	4-18-92	1	0	0.00	4	0	0	0	13	4	0	0	0	5	14	.100	.053	.143	9.95	3.55
Ferrell, Jeff	R-R	6-3	185	11-23-90	5	5	3.14	11	11	2	0	57	52	26	20	2	12	57	.242	.296	.187	8.95	1.88
Finefrock, Sean	R-R	6-5	200	2-11-87	1	1	1.69	4	0	0	1	5	3	1	1	0	2	2	.176	.111	.250	3.38	3.38
Gentzler, Dan	R-R	6-0	185	10-9-87	2	2	1.88	10	0	0	0	14	11	4	3	1	2	11	.208	.300	.152	6.91	1.26
Green, Scott	R-R	6-7	240	8-10-85	0	0	0.00	1	0	0	0	1	0	0	0	0	2	5	.071	.333	.000	11.25	4.50
Lebron, Ramon	R-R	6-1	180	2-1-89	1	0	2.28	11	2	0	0	28	16	8	7	0	9	43	.167	.150	.179	13.93	2.92
Medina, Kelvin	L-L	6-4	147	7-30-90	0	0	5.40	11	1	0	0	18	13	12	11	0	21	18	.197	.105	.234	8.84	10.31
Mowry, Tim	R-R	6-5	215	9-28-87	1	1	3.86	9	0	0	0	18	8	8	5	2	4	9	.195	.000	.258	6.94	3.09
Nelson, Cole	L-L	6-7	233	7-14-89	1	0	0.59	7	1	0	1	15	11	5	1	0	7	27	.186	.077	.217	15.85	4.11
Palacios, Wilsen	R-R	6-3	180	12-15-89	4	4	2.79	11	11	1	0	61	52	20	19	1	11	58	.221	.242	.207	8.51	1.61
Polanco, Yadiel	L-L	6-2	185	3-21-91	2	0	8.79	13	0	0	0	14	23	15	14	0	5	5	.383	.417	.361	3.14	3.14

DETROIT TIGERS

	B-T	HT	WT	DOB	W	L	ERA	G	GS	CG	SV	IP	H	R	ER	HR	BB	SO	AVG	vLH	vRH	K/9	BB/9
Rondon, Bruce	R-R	6-2	190	12-9-90	0	0	0.70	24	0	0	15	26	11	2	2	1	14	26	.133	.105	.156	9.12	4.91
Ryan, Kyle	L-L	6-5	180	9-25-91	2	4	4.17	12	12	0	0	54	58	30	25	2	13	46	.267	.241	.277	7.67	2.17
Todd, Jade	R-L	6-2	190	3-22-90	2	0	2.25	5	5	0	0	24	19	6	6	1	5	22	.216	.128	.286	8.25	1.88
White, Tyler	R-R	6-3	205	8-8-89	0	0	16.20	2	0	0	0	2	3	3	3	0	2	2	.375	.500	.333	10.80	10.80

Fielding

Catcher	PCT	G	PO	A	E	DP	PB
Aird	1.000	5	19	1	0	0	3
Leyland	.984	38	293	17	5	1	5
Purroy	.984	21	178	10	3	0	3

First Base	PCT	G	PO	A	E	DP
Aguasvivas	.983	51	387	24	7	26
Gomez	.983	9	52	5	1	4
Meador	.957	4	19	3	1	3
Soto	1.000	1	9	1	0	1

Second Base	PCT	G	PO	A	E	DP
Azcona	.981	13	20	33	1	7
Jones	1.000	2	5	6	0	2

McKenna	1.000	14	24	40	0	8
Miller	.951	31	40	58	5	8

Third Base	PCT	G	PO	A	E	DP
Azcona	.946	27	15	55	4	2
Castellanos	.667	3	0	4	2	1
Corcino	.841	25	18	35	10	3
Gomez	1.000	2	1	2	0	1
Miller	.909	4	2	8	1	0
Pounds	1.000	1	0	6	0	0

Shortstop	PCT	G	PO	A	E	DP
Azcona	.898	13	17	36	6	3
Machado	.967	43	71	105	6	19

Miller	1.000	4	5	10	0	1

Outfield	PCT	G	PO	A	E	DP
Castillo	1.000	19	42	1	0	0
Gomez	.975	43	76	3	2	0
Gomez	.967	21	27	2	1	0
McClendon	1.000	11	15	0	0	0
Meador	1.000	16	28	1	0	0
Moreno	.929	13	11	2	1	1
Moya	.941	40	62	2	4	0
Peter	1.000	7	11	1	0	0
Rijo	1.000	14	22	1	0	0
Smith	1.000	4	5	1	0	0

DSL TIGERS — ROOKIE

DOMINICAN SUMMER LEAGUE

Batting	B-T	HT	WT	DOB	AVG	vLH	vRH	G	AB	R	H	2B	3B	HR	RBI	BB	HBP	SH	SF	SO	SB	CS	SLG	OBP
Acevedo, Sandy	L-L	6-0	170	12-25-92	.236	.333	.216	48	123	15	29	5	6	0	16	15	4	1	0	32	6	3	.374	.338
Carranza, Daniel	R-R	6-1	182	1-25-93	.108	.000	.130	21	65	6	7	1	0	0	2	2	1	0	2	24	0	2	.123	.159
Contreras, Francisco	R-R	6-1	180	12-3-92	.242	.300	.227	57	194	21	47	5	1	0	15	12	1	0	1	33	2	2	.278	.288
Crafort, Samuel	B-R	6-0	147	7-31-93	.157	.140	.162	57	198	27	31	5	3	1	7	36	5	3	1	86	6	6	.227	.300
De Los Santos, Carlos	B-R	6-0	177	11-1-90	.261	.259	.261	39	115	9	30	0	2	0	11	9	1	1	4	18	7	5	.296	.310
Delgado, Alwin	R-R	6-3	175	11-3-92	.204	.271	.182	61	240	12	49	7	0	1	18	10	2	3	2	46	0	1	.246	.240
Figueroa, Robinson	R-R	6-0	160	3-11-90	.212	.091	.273	12	33	4	7	1	0	0	4	2	1	1	0	9	0	0	.242	.278
Guzman, Raynolds	R-R	6-0	185	3-16-90	.261	.367	.231	41	134	8	35	4	0	1	12	5	5	3	0	12	2	0	.313	.313
Lara, Confesor	R-R	6-2	170	8-7-90	.198	.160	.211	57	197	16	39	6	1	0	12	11	11	0	0	59	9	4	.239	.279
Leiva, Raul	B-R	6-2	185	1-3-90	.253	.200	.273	27	75	7	19	2	0	0	6	10	1	0	1	12	1	0	.280	.345
Marte, Ernesto	R-R	6-2	190	9-11-89	.125	.083	.139	18	48	4	6	1	0	1	2	2	4	0	0	16	0	1	.208	.222
Navia, Aldo	R-R	6-0	180	11-30-89	.193	.087	.231	34	88	9	17	0	1	0	3	6	4	1	0	20	4	4	.216	.276
Olivo, Ricardo	R-R	6-0	179	11-5-90	.161	.143	.167	12	31	4	5	1	0	0	5	4	2	0	1	7	0	0	.194	.289
Ortiz, Samuel	R-R	5-11	155	6-12-91	.273	.308	.260	45	139	18	38	6	3	0	10	15	2	3	0	24	2	0	.360	.353
Oses, Omar	R-R	5-11	159	5-25-93	.286	.313	.275	18	56	4	16	1	0	0	4	4	0	0	0	8	0	0	.304	.333
Ovalles, Victor	R-R	6-4	165	6-23-93	.107	.000	.130	11	28	1	3	1	0	0	3	1	0	1	0	6	2	3	.143	.219
Romero, Javier	R-R	6-2	190	2-13-91	.207	.170	.219	57	193	17	40	7	3	1	11	19	2	2	2	46	2	3	.290	.282
Santana, Arturo	R-R	6-2	200	2-1-90	.125	.100	.133	18	40	3	5	0	0	1	2	4	0	0	0	20	0	1	.200	.205
Turiano, Franklin	B-R	5-11	175	1-16-89	.161	.000	.185	12	31	2	5	0	0	0	3	0	0	0	0	5	0	0	.161	.235

Pitching	B-T	HT	WT	DOB	W	L	ERA	G	GS	CG	SV	IP	H	R	ER	HR	BB	SO	AVG	vLH	vRH	K/9	BB/9
Acosta, Alvin	R-R	6-2	170	6-12-90	0	3	9.93	15	2	0	0	23	36	28	25	0	21	26	.356	.462	.320	10.32	8.34
Alvarado, Carlos	R-R	6-4	175	10-22-89	1	1	0.95	13	0	0	3	19	21	5	2	0	6	19	.269	.308	.250	9.00	2.84
Burgos, Cesar	R-R	6-2	185	3-1-93	1	0	5.79	10	0	0	0	9	10	6	6	0	5	10	.278	.333	.267	9.64	4.82
Calderon, Yinio	R-R	6-4	170	11-16-90	2	3	2.89	22	3	0	0	53	43	28	17	1	35	46	.223	.163	.243	7.81	5.94
Castillo, Alejandro	L-L	5-10	170	3-2-90	1	0	1.93	7	2	0	0	23	13	5	5	0	5	38	.163	.000	.169	14.66	1.93
De La Rosa, Edgar	R-R	6-6	215	11-20-90	2	9	4.43	20	11	0	2	65	76	47	32	2	25	64	.295	.311	.288	8.86	3.46
Del Orbe, Emmanuel	R-R	6-3	188	12-20-90	0	0	1.13	5	5	0	0	8	6	4	1	0	4	9	.200	.000	.240	10.13	4.50
Diaz, Robert	L-L	6-2	180	2-12-89	0	0	9.64	6	0	0	0	5	8	8	5	0	5	3	.333	.000	.381	5.79	9.64
Dionicio, Victor	L-L	6-1	180	2-10-90	0	0	—	1	0	0	0	0	0	2	2	0	3	0	.000	.000	.000	—	—
Duran, Darlin	L-L	6-0	160	3-3-89	3	5	2.88	24	2	0	0	69	54	26	22	1	17	87	.219	.063	.229	11.40	2.23
Hidalgo, Luis	R-R	6-1	170	1-18-91	3	7	2.81	19	1	0	0	67	72	37	21	2	17	70	.274	.318	.253	9.36	2.27
Lachapel, Walter	R-R	6-0	180	8-16-91	1	4	4.60	23	2	0	0	43	42	25	22	1	33	45	.264	.327	.234	9.42	6.91
Medina, Jorge	L-L	6-1	185	12-21-89	4	2	1.96	20	7	1	0	64	40	19	14	0	26	65	.176	.385	.164	9.09	3.64
Mejia, Henry	R-R	6-1	185	4-2-89	0	3	3.24	8	0	0	0	8	6	5	3	0	7	6	.200	.100	.250	6.48	7.56
Morillo, Gregory	R-R	6-2	180	3-4-92	0	2	26.04	12	1	0	0	9	19	30	27	3	24	6	.413	.353	.448	5.79	23.14
Paulino, Brenny	R-R	6-4	170	2-21-93	1	8	3.88	16	15	0	0	46	34	31	20	0	45	55	.205	.159	.221	10.68	8.74
Solano, Gregorio	R-R	6-3	180	7-9-92	0	2	4.61	6	3	0	0	14	13	9	7	0	7	14	.236	.238	.235	9.22	4.61
Valdez, Jose	R-R	6-1	167	3-1-90	1	1	2.18	17	0	0	11	21	11	6	5	0	13	21	.159	.063	.189	9.15	5.66

Fielding

Catcher	PCT	G	PO	A	E	DP	PB
Guzman	.976	27	252	30	7	4	3
Leiva	.960	14	104	17	5	2	5
Olivo	.942	12	100	14	7	1	6
Oses	.981	17	138	20	3	1	8
Santana	1.000	1	2	0	0	0	0
Turiano	1.000	1	12	2	0	1	0

First Base	PCT	G	PO	A	E	DP
Contreras	1.000	5	31	4	0	4
Guzman	.976	17	119	2	3	11
Leiva	.989	15	85	6	1	9

Marte	.973	17	104	5	3	12
Ortiz	1.000	1	5	1	0	0
Oses	1.000	1	2	0	0	1
Santana	.982	17	102	6	2	9
Turiano	.966	9	54	3	2	9

Second Base	PCT	G	PO	A	E	DP
Crafort	.971	9	17	16	1	2
De Los Santos	.942	30	64	65	8	18
Delgado	.961	13	28	46	3	10
Ortiz	.922	15	32	27	5	9
Turiano	1.000	2	1	2	0	1

Third Base	PCT	G	PO	A	E	DP
Contreras	.901	52	48	88	15	12
Ortiz	.828	14	8	16	5	3
Ovalles	.895	8	9	8	2	2

Shortstop	PCT	G	PO	A	E	DP
Crafort	.823	30	37	56	20	12
De Los Santos	1.000	1	1	1	0	0
Delgado	.898	34	43	89	15	16

Outfield	PCT	G	PO	A	E	DP
Acevedo	.889	45	36	4	5	1
Carranza	.800	21	19	1	5	0
Figueroa	.905	11	18	1	2	0
Lara	.918	49	51	5	5	0
Navia	.824	31	23	5	6	2
Ortiz	1.000	2	5	0	0	0
Romero	.950	53	57	0	3	0

VSL TIGERS   ROOKIE

VENEZUELAN SUMMER LEAGUE

Batting	B-T	HT	WT	DOB	AVG	vLH	vRH	G	AB	R	H	2B	3B	HR	RBI	BB	HBP	SH	SF	SO	SB	CS	SLG	OBP
Alvarado, Jesus	R-R	6-1	160	11-25-91	.222	.320	.189	60	198	27	44	4	0	2	14	24	6	6	0	46	6	9	.273	.325
Carranza, Daniel	R-R	6-1	182	1-25-93	.252	.231	.258	36	115	11	29	4	0	4	18	7	0	2	1	43	3	1	.391	.293
Cortez, Luis	R-R	6-0	155	1-8-92	.267	.176	.297	58	206	28	55	12	0	4	19	19	5	7	1	52	2	4	.383	.342
Gomez, Oscar	R-R	5-11	155	3-25-91	.187	.143	.198	54	166	15	31	8	0	3	22	12	3	0	2	54	5	0	.289	.251
Hoyer, Wilfredo	R-R	6-1	180	5-14-91	.225	.107	.261	40	120	11	27	1	0	0	7	4	3	1	1	26	1	0	.233	.266
Leiva, Raul	B-R	6-2	185	1-3-90	.250	.133	.279	23	76	9	19	5	1	0	5	13	3	0	0	15	1	1	.342	.380
Lizardo, David	R-R	6-1	168	10-22-92	.241	.167	.261	26	87	11	21	3	0	0	10	15	1	2	0	14	3	0	.276	.359
Oses, Omar	R-R	5-11	159	5-25-93	.170	.100	.191	29	88	5	15	3	1	1	8	5	4	3	0	16	1	1	.261	.247
Petit, Jesus	R-R	6-0	180	12-26-91	.259	.364	.234	16	58	6	15	3	0	1	3	5	2	2	0	15	1	0	.362	.338
Soledad, Jose	R-R	5-11	165	7-22-92	.295	.321	.287	57	210	26	62	9	1	1	25	9	7	1	1	26	1	5	.362	.344
Soto, Erick	R-R	5-11	186	9-21-92	.231	.222	.233	62	234	22	54	18	0	1	25	24	3	5	1	37	4	0	.321	.309
Suarez, Eugenio	B-R	5-11	155	7-18-91	.311	.233	.339	61	225	32	70	12	2	1	18	23	7	4	2	44	8	6	.396	.389
Tenia, Gabriel	R-R	6-0	203	1-18-93	.202	.260	.182	56	198	26	40	8	0	2	18	6	2	7	1	61	1	2	.333	.284
Ustariz, Jesus	R-R	6-1	192	4-26-93	.281	.326	.266	48	171	23	48	8	0	2	18	23	2	0	0	1	3		.363	.372

Pitching	B-T	HT	WT	DOB	W	L	ERA	G	GS	CG	SV	IP	H	R	ER	HR	BB	SO	AVG	vLH	vRH	K/9	BB/9
Aguirre, Gino	R-R	6-2	155	9-12-90	0	2	2.45	4	4	0	0	4	2	4	1	0	5	1	.167	.000	.286	2.45	12.27
Belisario, Johan	R-R	5-11	155	8-13-93	1	6	7.04	14	9	0	2	38	42	36	30	5	24	28	.278	.310	.270	6.57	5.63
Briceno, Endrys	R-R	6-4	150	2-7-92	2	5	5.63	14	9	0	0	46	56	32	29	2	16	33	.303	.314	.299	6.41	3.11
Carreno, Angel	L-L	6-3	203	9-17-90	4	2	3.24	13	4	0	0	42	56	16	15	7	15	30	.339	.238	.354	6.48	3.24
Espinoza, Juan	L-L	5-11	155	10-20-91	1	3	4.03	15	9	0	1	51	68	25	23	3	13	23	.329	.250	.335	4.03	2.28
Guilarte, Julio	R-R	6-3	170	5-17-92	3	1	3.59	18	4	0	1	48	47	26	19	2	21	27	.264	.137	.315	5.10	3.97
Hernandez, Daniel	R-R	6-2	160	2-11-92	2	2	6.00	13	2	0	0	27	37	24	18	1	18	19	.343	.231	.378	6.33	6.00
Lopez, Yorfrank	R-R	6-3	170	12-1-90	2	3	4.97	14	3	0	0	42	46	26	23	5	16	24	.293	.211	.319	5.18	3.46
Mendoza, Jose	R-R	6-1	158	4-1-93	0	4	4.41	13	5	0	0	35	41	34	17	1	18	14	.287	.405	.238	3.63	4.67
Morandi, Manuel	R-R	6-4	180	8-2-91	0	3	5.35	17	1	0	0	35	40	26	21	2	20	22	.282	.222	.302	5.60	5.09
Musquera, Yonny	R-R	5-10	170	1-16-91	1	4	4.10	20	5	0	1	37	46	26	17	0	26	24	.317	.278	.330	5.79	6.27
Nesbitt, Angel	R-R	6-1	175	12-4-90	1	2	1.34	20	1	0	4	34	26	7	5	0	18	19	.217	.333	.188	5.08	4.81
Rodriguez, Jose	R-R	5-11	180	12-30-92	1	2	4.91	15	3	0	1	37	47	28	20	1	10	17	.307	.389	.282	4.17	2.45
Rodriguez, Luis	R-R	6-1	160	5-11-92	0	1	11.25	7	0	0	0	8	6	11	10	0	14	5	.207	.000	.240	5.63	15.75
Sanchez, Jairo	R-R	5-11	204	8-11-92	1	1	4.66	6	0	0	1	10	4	5	5	0	6	6	.138	.300	.053	5.59	5.59
Tablante, Jose	L-L	5-10	135	1-18-92	1	2	3.58	15	4	0	0	38	30	29	15	0	24	33	.214	.143	.222	7.88	5.73
Vasquez, Leonel	R-R	6-0	150	2-10-91	0	3	2.88	15	3	0	0	34	22	15	11	1	30	30	.190	.212	.181	7.86	7.86

Fielding

Catcher	PCT	G	PO	A	E	DP	PB
Gomez	1.000	3	3	2	0	0	0
Hoyer	.974	20	93	20	3	5	1
Leiva	.926	7	41	9	4	1	2
Oses	.986	12	62	7	1	1	5
Tenia	.978	31	180	38	5	2	6
Ustariz	—	1	0	0	0	0	0

First Base	PCT	G	PO	A	E	DP
Gomez	.925	5	34	3	3	8
Hoyer	.973	18	136	10	4	16
Leiva	.992	14	122	6	1	16
Soledad	.989	21	171	7	2	15
Ustariz	.981	13	100	6	2	7

Second Base	PCT	G	PO	A	E	DP
Cortez	.944	33	65	69	8	20
Gomez	1.000	2	5	2	0	0
Soto	.943	32	63	69	8	22
Suarez	1.000	3	8	4	0	1

Third Base	PCT	G	PO	A	E	DP
Alvarado	.000	1	0	0	1	0
Cortez	.900	2	5	4	1	0
Soledad	.841	32	24	66	17	6
Suarez	.926	8	7	18	2	1
Ustariz	.870	27	25	69	14	6

Shortstop	PCT	G	PO	A	E	DP
Cortez	.936	18	31	57	6	13
Lizardo	.884	19	37	47	11	8
Petit	—	1	0	0	0	0
Soto	.761	12	20	34	17	4
Suarez	.933	22	47	64	8	20

Outfield	PCT	G	PO	A	E	DP
Alvarado	.967	59	156	19	6	8
Carranza	.982	35	52	2	1	0
Gomez	.924	44	57	4	5	1
Hoyer	1.000	1	1	0	0	0
Leiva	1.000	2	2	0	0	0
Oses	.963	18	26	0	1	0
Petit	.971	16	31	3	1	0
Suarez	.968	30	54	6	2	1
Ustariz	.700	6	7	0	3	0

DETROIT TIGERS

Florida Marlins

SEASON IN A SENTENCE: The Marlins quickly fell back in the National League East, costing manager Fredi Gonzalez his job at the end of June, and new manager Edwin Rodriguez kept them right about where they had been all season, around .500.

HIGH POINT: Other than the continuing construction of a new retractable-roof stadium, the biggest moment for the Marlins probably came when Mike Stanton came up to the big leagues on June 8. In his short time in the big leagues Stanton showed the potential to be a star, batting .259/.326/.507 with 22 home runs.

LOW POINT: Though they nearly reached .500, the Marlins were never further behind than they were at the end of the season, 18 games out on Oct. 2. But the low moment came in May, when star shortstop Hanley Ramirez publicly criticized Gonzalez for benching him when he didn't run out a ground ball. Ramirez apologized a few days later to Gonzalez and to his teammates, though the Marlins tacitly endorsed Ramirez by firing Gonzalez a month later.

NOTABLE ROOKIES: In any other year, Stanton's strong four months in the big leagues might have generated rookie of the year talk, but players like Buster Posey and Jason Heyward got in the way. Still, Stanton's 22 home runs led all rookies. As usual, the Marlins continued to provide ample opportunity for unproven talent, with 16 players making their major league debuts. The most notable behind Stanton is outfielder Logan Morrison, who batted .283/.390/.447 in 244 at-bats.

KEY TRANSACTIONS: The Marlins didn't make any blockbuster deals, most notably dealing Jorge Cantu to the Rangers for Evan Reed and Omar Poveda at the trade deadline, but went into the offseason looking at possible deals for Ramirez or Dan Uggla. They also cut bait on two young players acquired from the Tigers in the December 2007 deal for Miguel Cabrera and Dontrelle Willis, shipping out Andrew Miller to the Red Sox and Cameron Maybin to the Padres.

DOWN ON THE FARM: Double-A Jacksonville finished with the second-best record in the Southern League and charged to the league title in the playoffs. The Marlins squad in the Rookie-level Gulf Coast League had the best record in that league. High Class A Jupiter, on the other hand, was one of the worst teams in the minors, finishing 46-92.

OPENING DAY PAYROLL: $57.0 million (26th)

PLAYERS OF THE YEAR

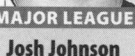

MAJOR LEAGUE	MINOR LEAGUE
Josh Johnson	**Mike Stanton**
rhp	of
11-6, 2.30	(Double-A)
Led NL in ERA	.313/.442/.729
186 SO/48 BB	21 HR, 2nd in SL

ORGANIZATION LEADERS

BATTING   *Minimum 250 at-bats

MAJORS

*AVG	Hanley Ramirez	.300
*OPS	Dan Uggla	.877
HR	Dan Uggla	33
RBI	Dan Uggla	105

MINORS

*AVG	Danny Richar, New Orleans	.315
*OBP	Vinny Rottino, Jacksonville/New Orleans	.390
*SLG	Hector Luna, New Orleans	.477
R	Osvaldo Martinez, Jacksonville	90
H	Osvaldo Martinez, Jacksonville	156
TB	Kyle Jensen, Greensboro	210
2B	Brandon Tripp, Jacksonville	35
3B	Ryan Fisher, Jamestown	9
HR	Marcell Ozuna, Greensboro/Jamestown	22
RBI	Kyle Jensen, Greensboro	86
BB	Tim Torres, New Orleans/Jacksonville	64
SO	Kyle Skipworth, Greensboro/Jacksonville	135
SB	Kevin Mattison, N.O./Jupiter/Jacksonville	49

PITCHING   †Minimum 75 innings

MAJORS

W	Ricky Nolasco	14
†ERA	Clay Hensley	2.16
SO	Josh Johnson	186

MINORS

W	Tom Koehler, Jacksonville	16
L	Robert Bono, Jacksonville/Jupiter	13
†ERA	Elih Villanueva, Jacksonville	2.26
G	Brett Sinkbeil, New Orleans	58
GS	Tom Koehler, Jacksonville	28
	Elih Villanueva, Jacksonville	28
SV	Alejandro Ramos, Greensboro	28
IP	Elih Villanueva, Jacksonville	179
BB	Andrew Miller, Jupiter/Jacksonville	76
SO	Tom Koehler, Jacksonville	145
†AVG	Elih Villanueva, Jacksonville	.212

2010 PERFORMANCE

General Manager: Larry Beinfest. **Farm Director:** Jim Fleming. **Scouting Director:** Stan Meek.

Class	Team	League	W	L	PCT	Finish*	Manager(s)
Majors	Florida Marlins	National	80	82	.494	t-8th (16)	Fredi Gonzalez/Edwin Rodriguez
Triple-A	New Orleans Zephyrs	Pacific Coast	66	77	.462	13th (16)	Edwin Rodriguez/Greg Norton
Double-A	Jacksonville Suns	Southern	81	59	.579	†2nd (10)	Tim Leiper
High A	Jupiter Hammerheads	Florida State	46	92	.333	12th (12)	Ron Hassey
Low A	Greensboro Grasshoppers	South Atlantic	66	74	.471	8th (14)	Andy Haines
Short-season	Jamestown Jammers	New York-Penn	43	32	.573	3rd (14)	Dave Berg
Rookie	GCL Marlins	Gulf Coast	37	19	.661	1st (15)	Jorge Hernandez
Overall 2010 Minor League Record			339	353	.490	20th (30)	

*Finish in overall standings (No. of teams in league). †League champion.

ORGANIZATION STATISTICS

FLORIDA MARLINS
NATIONAL LEAGUE

Batting	B-T	HT	WT	DOB	AVG	vLH	vRH	G	AB	R	H	2B	3B	HR	RBI	BB	HBP	SH	SF	SO	SB	CS	SLG	OBP
Baker, John	L-R	6-1	220	1-20-81	.218	.125	.229	23	78	7	17	3	1	0	6	9	1	0	0	18	0	0	.282	.307
Barden, Brian	R-R	5-11	200	4-2-81	.179	.200	.167	35	28	2	5	0	0	0	3	3	1	0	0	12	0	2	.179	.281
Bonifacio, Emilio	B-R	5-11	200	4-23-85	.261	.348	.231	73	180	30	47	6	3	0	10	17	0	1	3	42	12	0	.328	.320
Cantu, Jorge	R-R	6-3	210	1-30-82	.262	.256	.264	97	374	41	98	25	0	10	54	23	6	0	7	76	0	0	.409	.310
Carroll, Brett	R-R	6-0	210	10-3-82	.197	.154	.220	32	76	13	15	4	0	2	7	6	7	0	1	29	2	1	.329	.311
Coghlan, Chris	L-R	6-0	205	6-18-85	.268	.261	.270	91	358	60	96	20	3	5	28	33	4	3	2	84	10	3	.383	.335
Cousins, Scott	L-L	6-1	195	1-22-85	.297	.500	.273	27	37	2	11	2	2	0	2	1	0	0	0	13	0	0	.459	.316
Davis, Brad	R-R	6-1	190	12-29-82	.211	.160	.226	33	109	8	23	7	1	3	16	9	1	1	3	37	2	0	.376	.270
Hatcher, Chris	R-R	6-2	205	1-12-85	.000	.000	.000	5	6	0	0	0	0	0	2	0	0	0	0	6	0	0	.000	.250
Hayes, Brett	R-R	6-1	205	2-13-84	.208	.143	.222	26	77	6	16	6	1	2	6	6	0	0	0	26	0	0	.390	.265
Helms, Wes	R-R	6-4	230	5-12-76	.220	.324	.180	127	254	25	56	12	4	4	39	26	4	0	3	76	0	2	.346	.300
Lamb, Mike	L-R	6-1	205	8-9-75	.184	.000	.184	39	38	2	7	1	1	0	4	2	0	0	0	6	0	0	.263	.225
Luna, Hector	R-R	6-1	225	2-1-80	.138	.167	.118	27	29	2	4	1	0	2	4	0	0	0	1	13	0	1	.379	.133
Martinez, Ozzie	R-R	5-10	190	5-7-88	.326	.250	.370	14	43	8	14	4	1	0	2	4	0	1	0	6	1	0	.465	.383
Maybin, Cameron	R-R	6-3	210	4-4-87	.234	.222	.238	82	291	46	68	7	3	8	28	24	5	1	1	92	9	2	.361	.302
Morrison, Logan	L-L	6-3	235	8-25-87	.283	.342	.257	62	244	43	69	20	7	2	18	41	2	0	0	51	0	1	.447	.390
Murphy, Donnie	R-R	5-10	195	3-10-83	.318	.500	.250	29	44	9	14	6	1	3	16	2	0	1	0	19	0	0	.705	.348
Paulino, Ronny	R-R	6-3	250	4-21-81	.259	.358	.217	91	316	31	82	18	0	4	37	25	0	0	3	51	1	0	.354	.311
Petersen, Bryan	L-R	6-0	195	4-9-86	.083	.000	.087	23	24	1	2	0	0	0	2	1	0	0	0	6	0	0	.083	.120
Ramirez, Hanley	R-R	6-3	230	12-23-83	.300	.286	.305	142	543	92	163	28	2	21	76	64	7	0	5	93	32	10	.475	.378
Rivera, Mike	R-R	6-1	235	9-8-76	.000	.000	.000	7	14	0	0	0	0	0	0	0	2	1	0	3	0	0	.000	.176
Ross, Cody	R-L	5-10	195	12-23-80	.265	.280	.261	120	452	60	120	24	3	11	58	30	4	0	1	100	9	1	.405	.316
2-team total (33 San Francisco)					.269	—	—	153	525	71	141	28	3	14	65	37	5	0	2	121	9	2	.413	.322
Sanchez, Gaby	R-R	6-1	225	9-2-83	.273	.324	.256	151	572	72	156	37	3	19	85	57	5	3	6	101	5	0	.448	.341
Stanton, Mike	R-R	6-5	235	11-8-89	.259	.218	.272	100	359	45	93	21	1	22	59	34	2	0	1	123	5	2	.507	.326
Tracy, Chad	L-R	6-2	215	5-22-80	.245	.333	.242	41	102	5	25	6	0	1	10	6	2	0	1	21	0	0	.333	.297
2-team total (28 Chicago)					.247	—	—	69	146	11	36	8	0	1	15	11	2	0	1	36	0	0	.322	.306
Uggla, Dan	R-R	5-11	205	3-11-80	.287	.306	.281	159	589	100	169	31	0	33	105	78	2	0	5	149	4	1	.508	.369

Pitching	B-T	HT	WT	DOB	W	L	ERA	G	GS	CG	SV	IP	H	R	ER	HR	BB	SO	AVG	vLH	vRH	K/9	BB/9
Badenhop, Burke	R-R	6-5	220	2-8-83	2	5	3.99	53	0	0	1	68	62	33	30	5	21	47	.246	.238	.252	6.25	2.79
Buente, Jay	R-R	6-2	185	9-28-83	0	0	6.55	8	0	0	0	11	16	8	8	0	11	9	.340	.227	.440	7.36	9.00
Ceda, Jose	R-R	6-4	275	1-28-87	0	0	5.19	8	0	0	0	9	8	5	5	1	11	9	.242	.333	.133	9.35	11.42
Cishek, Steven	R-R	6-6	200	6-18-86	0	0	0.00	3	0	0	0	4	1	0	0	0	1	3	.071	.000	.111	6.23	2.08
Hensley, Clay	R-R	5-11	190	8-31-79	3	4	2.16	68	0	0	7	75	54	20	18	3	29	77	.200	.216	.184	9.24	3.48
Houser, James	L-L	6-4	205	12-15-84	0	0	20.25	1	0	0	0	1	3	3	3	1	1	1	.500	1.000	.400	6.75	6.75
Johnson, Josh	L-R	6-7	250	1-31-84	11	6	2.30	28	28	1	0	184	155	51	47	7	48	186	.229	.223	.235	9.11	2.35
Jones, Hunter	L-L	6-4	250	1-10-84	0	0	0.00	3	0	0	0	2	0	0	0	1	3	.000	.000	16.20	5.40		
Leroux, Chris	L-R	6-6	225	4-14-84	0	0	7.00	17	0	0	0	18	24	15	14	1	11	18	.343	.321	.357	9.00	5.50
2-team total (6 Pittsburgh)					0	1	6.75	23	0	0	0	23	28	18	17	1	14	22	—	—	—	8.74	5.56
Marinez, Jhan	R-R	6-1	165	8-12-88	1	1	6.75	4	0	0	0	3	3	3	2	1	3	3	.273	.333	.000	10.13	10.13
Mendez, Adalberto	R-R	6-2	160	2-22-82	1	3	5.11	5	5	0	0	25	28	14	14	7	12	11	.295	.315	.268	4.01	4.38
Meyer, Dan	R-L	6-2	225	7-3-81	0	1	9.64	13	0	0	0	9	15	10	10	1	12	4	.366	.400	.346	3.86	11.57
Miller, Andrew	L-L	6-7	210	5-21-85	1	5	8.54	9	7	0	0	33	51	34	31	6	26	28	.372	.405	.360	7.71	7.16
Nolasco, Ricky	R-R	6-2	230	12-13-82	14	9	4.51	26	26	1	0	158	169	82	79	24	33	147	.273	.283	.263	8.39	1.88
Nunez, Leo	R-R	6-2	190	8-14-83	4	3	3.46	68	0	0	30	65	62	27	25	5	21	71	.250	.214	.291	9.83	2.91
Ohman, Will	L-L	6-2	190	8-13-77	0	2	3.00	17	0	0	0	12	10	6	4	1	5	14	.222	.238	.208	10.50	3.75
Pinto, Renyel	L-L	6-4	280	7-8-82	0	0	2.70	20	0	0	0	17	16	5	5	1	9	16	.250	.364	.190	8.64	4.86
Robertson, Nate	R-L	6-2	225	9-3-77	6	8	5.47	19	18	0	0	100	110	70	61	11	40	61	.283	.269	.286	5.47	3.59
2-team total (2 Philadelphia)					6	8	5.95	21	18	0	0	101	115	76	67	12	42	63	—	—	—	5.60	3.73
Rosario, Sandy	R-R	6-1	170	8-22-85	0	0	54.00	2	0	0	0	1	9	6	6	2	1	0	.818	.800	.833	0.00	9.00
Sanabia, Alex	R-R	6-2	165	9-8-88	5	3	3.73	15	12	0	0	72	74	32	30	6	16	47	.261	.204	.313	5.85	1.99

FLORIDA MARLINS

Pitching	B-T	HT	WT	DOB	W	L	ERA	G	GS	CG	SV	IP	H	R	ER	HR	BB	SO	AVG	vLH	vRH	K/9	BB/9
Sanches, Brian	R-R	6-0	190	8-8-78	2	2	2.26	61	0	0	0	64	43	20	16	7	27	54	.194	.192	.195	7.63	3.82
Sanchez, Anibal	R-R	6-0	205	2-27-84	13	12	3.55	32	32	1	0	195	192	89	77	10	70	157	.257	.262	.252	7.25	3.23
Sinkbeil, Brett	R-R	6-2	210	12-26-84	0	0	13.50	3	0	0	0	2	2	3	3	0	1	0	.250	.333	.200	4.50	22.50
Sosa, Jorge	R-R	6-2	220	4-28-77	2	3	4.66	22	2	0	0	37	39	22	19	4	18	19	.271	.286	.261	4.66	4.42
Strickland, Scott	R-R	5-11	225	4-26-76	0	0	9.00	3	0	0	0	2	5	2	2	0	1	0	.500	.200	.800	0.00	4.50
Tankersley, Taylor	L-L	6-0	215	3-7-83	0	0	7.50	27	0	0	0	12	12	11	10	4	7	7	.250	.200	.333	5.25	5.25
VandenHurk, Rick	R-R	6-5	215	5-22-85	0	0	6.75	2	0	0	0	1	3	4	1	0	1	1	.375	.400	.333	6.75	6.75
Veras, Jose	R-R	6-6	235	10-20-80	3	3	3.75	48	0	0	0	48	32	20	20	5	29	54	.188	.155	.221	10.13	5.44
Volstad, Chris	R-R	6-8	230	9-23-86	12	9	4.58	30	30	2	0	175	187	94	89	17	60	102	.277	.292	.263	5.25	3.09
West, Sean	L-L	6-8	260	6-15-86	0	2	7.71	2	2	0	0	9	15	9	8	2	4	8	.375	.500	.353	7.71	3.86
Wood, Tim	R-R	6-0	180	11-16-82	0	1	5.53	26	0	0	1	28	33	19	17	2	15	10	.306	.261	.339	3.25	4.88

Fielding

Catcher	PCT	G	PO	A	E	DP	PB
Baker	.988	21	152	9	2	1	1
Davis	.983	32	215	16	4	0	1
Hatcher	1.000	4	20	2	0	0	0
Hayes	1.000	24	142	13	0	2	1
Paulino	.991	85	644	47	6	4	6
Rivera	.968	5	28	2	1	0	2

First Base	PCT	G	PO	A	E	DP
Cantu	1.000	40	109	10	0	15
Helms	1.000	2	17	2	0	0
Lamb	1.000	1	11	0	0	1
Sanchez	.991	149	1115	70	11	97
Tracy	1.000	5	46	3	0	4

Second Base	PCT	G	PO	A	E	DP
Barden	.900	2	1	8	1	0
Bonifacio	.941	5	2	14	1	3
Luna	1.000	1	1	1	0	0
Murphy	1.000	1	2	1	0	0
Uggla	.976	158	312	415	18	84

Third Base	PCT	G	PO	A	E	DP
Barden	1.000	16	3	10	0	3
Bonifacio	1.000	6	3	10	0	1
Cantu	.909	81	42	118	16	11
Helms	.952	90	39	101	7	8
Luna	1.000	4	2	5	0	1
Murphy	1.000	4	1	7	0	0
Tracy	.948	24	13	42	3	5

Shortstop	PCT	G	PO	A	E	DP
Barden	1.000	7	6	7	0	1
Bonifacio	1.000	9	11	11	0	1
Martinez	1.000	11	10	22	0	3
Murphy	1.000	4	1	6	0	1
Ramirez	.971	140	200	342	16	78

Outfield	PCT	G	PO	A	E	DP
Bonifacio	.983	29	55	3	1	0
Carroll	.972	25	33	2	1	0
Coghlan	.994	90	160	7	1	0
Cousins	1.000	11	18	0	0	0
Maybin	.982	77	215	4	4	3
Morrison	.976	62	116	4	3	0
Petersen	1.000	6	2	0	0	0
Ross	.986	118	268	6	4	2
Stanton	.983	98	219	10	4	1

NEW ORLEANS ZEPHYRS TRIPLE-A

PACIFIC COAST LEAGUE

Batting	B-T	HT	WT	DOB	AVG	vLH	vRH	G	AB	R	H	2B	3B	HR	RBI	BB	HBP	SH	SF	SO	SB	CS	SLG	OBP
Aguila, Chris	R-R	5-11	200	2-23-79	.269	.556	.118	10	26	5	7	1	0	2	5	1	0	0	1	3	0	0	.538	.286
2-team total (44 Las Vegas)					.274	—	—	54	186	35	51	14	2	6	26	19	1	0	4	41	3	1	.468	.338
Barden, Brian	R-R	5-11	200	4-2-81	.353	.420	.328	49	184	30	65	14	1	3	23	18	0	0	2	38	3	3	.489	.407
Bonifacio, Emilio	B-R	5-11	200	4-23-85	.274	.271	.276	40	164	19	45	8	3	0	11	16	0	2	0	33	8	4	.360	.339
Burns, Greg	L-L	6-2	185	11-7-86	.400	.000	.500	2	5	1	2	0	0	0	1	0	0	0	0	1	0	0	.400	.500
Carroll, Brett	R-R	6-0	210	10-3-82	.221	.278	.205	70	244	32	54	16	0	8	30	22	6	3	2	54	4	2	.385	.299
Corsaletti, Jeff	L-R	6-0	190	2-22-83	.500	.667	.400	5	8	2	4	0	0	0	0	0	0	0	0	1	0	1	.500	.500
Cousins, Scott	L-L	6-1	195	1-22-85	.285	.310	.279	118	410	74	117	20	5	14	49	32	2	1	6	78	12	4	.461	.336
Davis, Brad	R-R	6-1	190	12-29-82	.287	.286	.287	73	244	35	70	14	0	9	34	24	2	1	1	53	1	2	.455	.354
Dawkins, Gookie	R-R	6-1	180	5-12-79	.268	.290	.260	76	261	33	70	23	1	10	39	25	1	1	2	89	1	1	.479	.332
Fermin, Miguel	R-R	5-11	175	2-11-85	.250	.250	.000	1	4	1	1	0	0	0	0	0	0	0	0	2	0	0	.250	.250
Fortenberry, Seth	L-L	6-2	175	9-1-83	1.000	.000	1.000	3	2	1	2	0	0	0	1	0	0	0	0	0	0	0	1.000	1.000
Guzman, Javier	B-R	6-0	170	5-4-82	.364	.500	.286	12	33	3	12	0	0	0	3	3	0	2	0	2	0	1	.455	.417
Hatcher, Chris	R-R	6-2	205	1-12-85	.167	.400	.140	17	48	10	8	1	0	2	10	9	3	1	0	19	0	0	.313	.333
Hayes, Brett	R-R	6-1	205	12-3-84	.220	.158	.250	16	59	7	13	3	0	1	5	2	0	0	0	9	0	0	.322	.254
Klosterman, Ryan	R-R	5-11	190	5-28-82	.215	.136	.256	28	65	8	14	2	1	2	7	12	0	0	0	18	4	0	.369	.338
Lamb, Mike	L-R	6-1	205	8-9-75	.319	.357	.306	60	213	36	68	7	0	7	42	31	3	0	2	17	1	0	.451	.385
Lane, Jason	R-L	6-2	225	12-22-76	.229	.196	.244	47	170	22	39	6	0	3	14	10	1	0	1	40	1	1	.318	.302
2-team total (42 Las Vegas)					.275	—	—	89	334	50	92	21	0	9	49	44	3	0	3	66	4	3	.419	.362
Luna, Hector	R-R	6-1	225	2-1-80	.294	.266	.302	97	354	55	104	17	0	16	71	42	5	0	10	64	7	1	.477	.367
Machado, Alejandro	B-R	6-0	185	4-26-82	.209	.235	.192	24	43	2	9	0	0	2	2	2	0	2	0	7	0	0	.209	.244
Mattison, Kevin	L-L	6-0	180	9-20-85	.207	.111	.250	7	29	4	6	0	0	0	1	0	1	0	1	7	1	1	.207	.233
Maybin, Cameron	R-R	6-3	210	4-4-87	.338	.303	.351	33	130	21	44	6	2	4	23	13	2	2	0	24	5	1	.508	.407
Mense, Hunter	L-L	5-11	185	8-30-84	.185	.000	.227	12	27	0	5	1	0	0	1	1	0	0	0	8	0	0	.222	.214
Mientkiewicz, Doug	L-R	6-2	210	6-19-74	.250	.250	.250	4	16	1	4	1	0	0	1	0	0	0	0	3	0	0	.313	.333
Mitchell, Lee	R-R	6-1	200	4-21-82	.216	.244	.200	35	116	11	25	9	1	0	8	5	1	0	1	29	2	0	.310	.252
Morrison, Logan	L-L	6-3	235	8-25-87	.307	.314	.304	68	238	36	73	17	4	6	45	48	4	0	3	35	1	2	.487	.427
Murphy, Donnie	R-R	5-10	195	3-10-83	.277	.281	.275	57	206	31	57	12	1	12	35	16	2	0	0	41	0	0	.519	.335
Petersen, Bryan	L-R	6-0	205	4-9-86	.255	.244	.259	91	322	47	82	13	2	5	27	34	5	4	3	63	5	4	.354	.332
Raynor, John	R-R	6-1	205	1-4-84	.284	.375	.233	41	134	21	38	6	0	2	13	13	1	2	1	27	3	0	.373	.349
Richar, Danny	L-R	6-1	205	10-8-83	.277	.221	.342	128	467	57	147	29	0	7	50	19	1	8	3	74	7	4	.422	.341
Rivera, Mike	R-R	6-1	235	9-8-76	.111	.000	.200	3	9	1	1	0	0	0	1	0	0	1	0	0	0	0	.111	.200
2-team total (14 Albuquerque)					.123	—	—	17	57	5	7	2	0	2	2	2	1	0	0	20	0	0	.263	.180
Rottino, Vinny	R-R	6-0	215	4-7-80	.375	1.000	.286	5	8	1	3	0	0	1	5	0	0	0	0	3	1	0	.875	.615
Saccomanno, Mark	R-R	6-3	225	4-30-80	.261	.240	.270	56	176	24	46	9	0	7	29	5	2	0	1	42	0	1	.438	.325
Scott, Lorenzo	L-L	6-3	210	3-1-82	.290	.125	.348	9	31	5	9	1	0	2	4	1	0	2	0	13	1	0	.516	.313
Synan, Jeremy	L-R	6-0	193	7-14-86	.000	.000	.000	2	1	0	0	0	0	0	0	0	0	0	0	0	0	0	.000	.500
Torres, Tim	B-R	6-2	180	11-12-83	.265	.286	.259	14	34	5	9	2	0	0	2	2	0	0	0	11	1	1	.324	.390
Wilson, Neil	R-R	6-1	190	12-7-83	.222	.303	.196	40	135	15	30	7	0	6	20	12	2	1	1	34	0	0	.400	.312

Pitching	B-T	HT	WT	DOB	W	L	ERA	G	GS	CG	SV	IP	H	R	ER	HR	BB	SO	AVG	vLH	vRH	K/9	BB/9
Badenhop, Burke	R-R	6-5	220	2-8-83	0	1	2.81	12	1	0	0	16	16	6	5	0	7	9	.267	.333	.212	5.06	3.94

Name	B-T	HT	WT	DOB	W	L	ERA	G	GS	CG	SV	IP	H	R	ER	HR	BB	SO	AVG	vLH	vRH	K/9	BB/9
Battisto, A.J.	R-R	6-0	193	9-30-83	0	0	6.00	5	0	0	0	9	11	7	6	2	5	7	.297	.500	.143	7.00	5.00
Benitez, Armando	R-R	6-4	260	11-3-72	0	1	2.70	8	0	0	4	7	6	6	2	2	5	5	.240	.333	.188	6.75	6.75
Buente, Jay	R-R	6-2	185	9-28-83	0	1	2.67	20	0	0	0	30	22	13	9	3	18	38	.200	.180	.217	11.27	5.34
DeSalvo, Matt	R-R	6-0	180	9-11-80	0	2	10.38	4	3	0	0	13	16	17	15	1	14	14	.286	.273	.294	9.69	9.69
Doolittle, Todd	R-R	5-10	175	11-1-82	0	0	2.08	6	0	0	0	9	6	3	2	0	4	6	.194	.176	.214	6.23	4.15
Gogal, Jeff	R-L	6-2	195	6-10-82	0	0	0.00	3	0	0	0	4	2	0	0	0	2	2	.182	.000	.286	4.91	4.91
Gunderson, Kyle	R-R	6-3	215	1-31-85	1	0	3.38	2	0	0	0	3	3	1	1	0	0	3	.300	.333	.250	10.13	0.00
Houser, James	L-L	6-4	205	12-15-84	1	2	3.67	24	4	0	1	49	53	22	20	6	20	41	.270	.310	.248	7.53	3.67
Jones, Hunter	L-L	6-4	250	1-10-84	0	5	4.17	10	7	0	0	45	47	28	21	3	22	31	.263	.282	.257	6.15	4.37
Korpi, Wade	R-L	5-11	185	3-10-86	0	0	0.00	1	0	0	0	3	0	0	0	0	0	0	.000	.000	.000	5.40	0.00
Lawrence, Brian	R-R	6-0	195	5-14-76	11	8	4.42	26	25	1	0	143	167	80	70	19	39	115	.292	.328	.259	7.25	2.46
Leroux, Chris	L-R	6-6	225	4-14-84	0	3	6.95	21	0	0	1	22	26	17	17	2	7	20	.295	.263	.320	8.18	2.86
Mastny, Tom	R-R	6-6	225	2-4-81	4	5	4.27	18	14	0	0	86	89	42	41	9	34	60	.261	.293	.237	6.25	3.54
Mendez, Adalberto	R-R	6-2	160	2-22-82	5	4	4.14	28	9	0	1	72	64	35	33	7	29	73	.238	.228	.247	9.17	3.64
Meyer, Dan	R-L	6-2	195	7-3-81	1	2	3.38	32	0	0	2	40	32	17	15	4	16	27	.227	.246	.214	6.08	3.60
Olenberger, Kasey	R-R	6-4	230	3-18-78	1	3	7.65	36	0	0	6	38	48	32	32	7	15	36	.312	.355	.269	8.60	3.58
2-team total (11 Reno)					2	3	5.75	47	1	0	6	56	61	36	36	9	17	51	—	—		8.15	2.72
Peterson, Matt	R-R	6-5	230	2-11-82	3	3	4.50	19	0	0	0	32	37	20	16	4	18	20	.287	.268	.301	5.63	5.06
Rosario, Jose	R-R	6-0	170	2-16-86	0	1	23.14	1	1	0	0	2	10	7	6	1	2	1	.588	.778	.375	3.86	7.71
Sanabia, Alex	R-R	6-2	165	9-8-88	1	0	1.29	2	2	0	0	14	9	2	2	0	3	5	.184	.192	.174	3.21	1.93
Schroder, Chris	R-R	6-3	210	8-20-78	1	0	8.83	10	0	0	0	17	28	17	17	2	9	9	.384	.290	.452	4.67	4.67
Sinkbeil, Brett	R-R	6-2	210	12-26-84	3	3	5.71	58	0	0	0	63	76	44	40	4	31	56	.296	.327	.271	8.00	4.43
Sosa, Jorge	R-R	6-2	220	4-28-77	5	4	4.73	23	9	0	1	59	74	31	31	5	15	45	.314	.283	.341	6.86	2.29
Stone, Brad	R-R	6-3	190	5-20-84	3	1	4.29	7	6	0	0	36	40	18	17	1	14	16	.272	.271	.274	4.04	3.53
Strickland, Scott	R-R	5-11	225	4-26-76	4	3	3.45	31	0	0	14	32	39	17	16	3	16	22	.300	.309	.293	6.12	4.45
Tankersley, Taylor	L-L	6-0	215	3-7-83	4	2	3.42	27	0	0	1	26	20	12	10	3	8	22	.206	.118	.254	7.52	2.73
Tucker, Ryan	R-R	6-1	200	12-6-86	0	5	6.15	7	7	0	0	34	41	26	23	3	17	19	.295	.265	.324	5.08	4.54
Ungs, Nic	R-R	6-1	220	9-3-79	1	2	6.68	7	7	0	0	34	40	28	25	6	13	18	.296	.339	.266	4.81	3.48
VandenHurk, Rick	R-R	6-5	215	5-22-85	8	4	4.68	19	19	2	0	98	100	54	51	11	40	87	.260	.286	.233	7.99	3.67
Veras, Jose	R-R	6-6	235	10-20-80	1	1	4.60	24	0	0	2	29	34	15	15	2	15	37	.283	.313	.264	11.35	4.60
Volstad, Chris	R-R	6-8	230	9-23-86	1	0	3.18	3	3	0	0	17	13	6	6	1	9	13	.271	.200	.240	6.88	4.76
West, Sean	L-L	6-8	260	6-15-86	4	3	3.12	11	11	2	0	58	60	28	20	4	19	46	.271	.125	.342	7.18	2.97
Whisler, Wes	L-L	6-5	240	4-7-83	3	7	6.25	16	15	0	0	76	96	62	53	12	52	37	.315	.270	.333	4.36	6.13
Wood, Tim	R-R	6-0	180	11-16-82	0	1	6.43	14	0	0	0	14	19	12	10	4	4	12	.311	.321	.303	7.71	2.57

Fielding

Catcher	PCT	G	PO	A	E	DP	PB
Davis	.983	70	488	30	9	5	2
Fermin	1.000	1	8	0	0	1	0
Hatcher	.961	16	114	9	5	0	7
Hayes	.992	16	120	10	1	0	1
Rivera	.958	3	22	1	1	0	0
Wilson	.992	40	231	14	2	0	7

First Base	PCT	G	PO	A	E	DP
Carroll	1.000	5	28	2	0	3
Davis	1.000	1	2	0	0	0
Lamb	.991	16	106	6	1	11
Lane	.977	5	37	5	1	2
Luna	1.000	8	47	2	0	6
Mientkiewicz	1.000	3	24	2	0	3
Mitchell	.987	20	141	8	2	11
Morrison	.991	49	387	35	4	37
Saccomanno	.988	46	306	22	4	17

Second Base	PCT	G	PO	A	E	DP
Barden	1.000	12	20	26	0	6
Bonifacio	.939	10	17	14	2	6
Dawkins	1.000	13	26	25	0	6
Guzman	.950	4	8	11	1	3

(Second Base cont.)	PCT	G	PO	A	E	DP
Klosterman	1.000	8	12	15	0	5
Machado	1.000	4	2	4	0	0
Mitchell	1.000	3	3	6	0	0
Richar	.985	97	173	222	6	47
Torres	1.000	4	9	15	0	3

Third Base	PCT	G	PO	A	E	DP
Barden	.961	19	22	27	2	3
Dawkins	1.000	2	3	5	0	1
Guzman	1.000	1	0	1	0	0
Lamb	.932	30	27	41	5	4
Luna	.943	83	50	131	11	11
Machado	1.000	5	1	1	0	0
Mitchell	.857	3	1	5	1	0
Richar	.882	9	3	12	2	1

Shortstop	PCT	G	PO	A	E	DP
Barden	.967	17	26	33	2	4
Bonifacio	.935	8	11	18	2	5
Dawkins	.941	56	87	119	13	19
Guzman	.895	4	6	11	2	2
Klosterman	.930	14	17	36	4	7
Murphy	.969	51	60	129	6	32
Torres	1.000	1	1	1	0	1

Outfield	PCT	G	PO	A	E	DP
Aguila	1.000	7	25	1	0	1
Barden	—	1	0	0	0	0
Bonifacio	.925	25	34	3	3	0
Burns	1.000	2	6	0	0	0
Carroll	.992	62	122	8	1	2
Corsaletti	1.000	1	2	0	0	0
Cousins	.992	106	232	7	2	1
Fortenberry	—	1	0	0	0	0
Lane	.974	40	74	1	2	0
Mattison	1.000	7	29	0	0	0
Maybin	.989	30	90	0	1	0
Mense	1.000	11	15	0	0	0
Mientkiewicz	1.000	1	3	0	0	0
Mitchell	1.000	7	7	0	0	0
Morrison	1.000	19	38	0	0	0
Petersen	.986	81	196	9	3	4
Raynor	.971	33	67	0	2	0
Richar	.667	5	4	0	2	0
Rottino	1.000	3	5	0	0	0
Scott	1.000	9	23	0	0	0
Torres	1.000	3	8	0	0	0

JACKSONVILLE SUNS   DOUBLE-A

SOUTHERN LEAGUE

Batting	B-T	HT	WT	DOB	AVG	vLH	vRH	G	AB	R	H	2B	3B	HR	RBI	BB	HBP	SH	SF	SO	SB	CS	SLG	OBP
Burns, Greg	L-L	6-2	185	11-7-86	.156	.146	.159	77	186	27	29	6	3	1	9	39	0	2	0	82	6	4	.237	.302
Corsaletti, Jeff	L-R	6-0	190	2-22-83	.250	.188	.278	16	52	9	13	0	0	0	6	12	0	1	0	9	1	0	.250	.391
Curry, Ryan	R-R	5-10	185	4-18-85	.251	.264	.241	118	387	45	97	21	1	6	37	17	5	12	4	36	5	4	.357	.288
Delaney, Jason	R-R	6-3	215	11-9-82	.197	.157	.211	78	193	24	38	11	0	3	22	30	2	1	1	54	1	0	.301	.310
Dominguez, Matt	R-R	6-1	205	8-28-89	.252	.222	.266	138	504	61	127	34	2	14	81	56	9	1	7	96	0	2	.411	.333
Fortenberry, Seth	L-L	6-2	175	9-1-83	.000	.000	.000	2	2	0	0	0	0	0	0	0	0	0	0	0	0	0	.000	.000
Gran, Paul	R-R	5-11	182	4-7-86	.250	.222	.273	9	20	1	5	1	0	0	1	0	0	0	0	7	0	0	.300	.286
Guzman, Javier	B-R	6-0	170	5-4-82	.208	.211	.207	31	48	2	10	4	0	0	5	3	1	0	2	10	1	1	.292	.259
Hatcher, Chris	R-R	6-2	205	1-12-85	.202	.266	.176	84	267	23	54	9	1	3	26	20	2	2	2	92	1	2	.277	.261
Martinez, Ozzie	R-R	5-10	190	5-7-88	.302	.329	.290	130	516	90	156	28	4	5	54	49	9	11	2	64	13	9	.401	.372
Mattison, Kevin	L-L	6-0	180	9-20-85	.222	.167	.259	16	45	10	10	4	1	0	1	4	0	2	0	10	4	0	.356	.286

FLORIDA MARLINS

Batting	B-T	HT	WT	DOB	AVG	vLH	vRH	G	AB	R	H	2B	3B	HR	RBI	BB	HBP	SH	SF	SO	SB	CS	SLG	OBP
Mense, Hunter	L-L	5-11	185	8-30-84	.385	.500	.364	10	13	2	5	2	0	0	0	2	0	0	0	0	0	0	.538	.467
Mitchell, Lee	R-R	6-1	200	4-21-82	.310	.380	.281	67	242	29	75	16	6	8	53	23	3	1	2	68	5	1	.525	.374
Otness, John	R-R	5-11	200	9-15-81	.233	.286	.210	37	116	11	27	6	0	1	17	11	6	2	3	12	0	1	.310	.324
Rottino, Vinny	R-R	6-0	215	4-7-80	.307	.323	.300	116	433	67	133	27	1	8	69	53	3	1	3	51	22	2	.430	.384
Saccomanno, Mark	R-R	6-3	225	4-30-80	.244	.203	.260	70	275	30	67	13	2	6	38	13	2	0	3	63	0	3	.371	.280
Scott, Lorenzo	L-L	6-3	210	5-1-86	.265	.267	.263	73	272	62	72	12	5	6	33	42	4	4	2	103	7	3	.412	.369
Skipworth, Kyle	L-R	6-4	205	3-1-90	.000	.000	.000	2	7	1	0	0	0	0	0	1	0	0	0	3	0	0	.000	.125
Stanton, Mike	R-R	6-5	235	11-8-89	.313	.346	.300	53	192	42	60	13	2	21	52	44	2	0	2	53	1	0	.729	.442
Torres, Tim	B-R	6-2	180	11-15-81	.275	.243	.289	109	335	55	92	16	5	14	46	57	1	5	1	88	12	2	.478	.381
Tripp, Brandon	L-R	6-2	200	4-2-85	.289	.280	.292	118	394	52	114	35	2	8	46	34	18	0	4	111	5	3	.449	.369
Wilson, Neil	R-R	6-1	190	12-7-83	.333	.500	.000	2	3	0	1	0	0	0	0	0	0	0	0	0	0	0	.333	.333

Pitching	B-T	HT	WT	DOB	W	L	ERA	G	GS	CG	SV	IP	H	R	ER	HR	BB	SO	AVG	vLH	vRH	K/9	BB/9
Allison, Jeff	R-R	6-2	195	11-7-84	6	11	5.04	29	20	0	0	111	132	73	62	16	33	56	.308	.340	.278	4.55	2.68
Andrelczyk, Pete	R-R	6-1	185	11-10-85	0	0	7.20	3	0	0	0	5	7	4	4	2	0	3	.304	.357	.222	5.40	0.00
Battisto, A.J.	R-R	6-0	193	9-30-83	0	0	12.15	5	0	0	0	5	7	6	6	2	2	1	.345	.545	.222	4.05	10.80
Bono, Robert	R-R	6-2	175	12-12-88	0	0	3.60	1	1	0	0	5	6	2	2	1	1	0	.333	.417	.167	0.90	1.80
Buente, Jay	R-R	6-2	185	9-28-83	1	0	4.05	10	1	0	1	13	13	6	6	1	5	12	.260	.222	.304	8.10	3.38
Ceda, Jose	R-R	6-4	275	1-28-87	4	1	1.39	27	0	0	6	32	18	5	5	2	20	45	.168	.216	.125	12.53	5.57
Cishek, Steven	R-R	6-6	200	6-18-86	3	1	4.31	22	0	0	2	31	30	16	15	0	10	34	.250	.296	.212	9.77	2.87
Doolittle, Todd	R-R	5-10	175	11-1-82	4	4	2.91	44	0	0	2	68	59	25	22	6	22	73	.236	.228	.243	9.66	2.91
Evans, Bryan	R-R	6-3	205	2-25-87	0	0	0.00	1	0	0	0	1	2	0	0	0	0	0	.500	.500	.500	0.00	0.00
Fulton, Jon	R-R	6-4	200	12-1-83	0	1	10.80	2	0	0	0	3	2	2	2	0	2	0	.500	.000	.600	0.00	10.80
Gogal, Jeff	R-L	6-2	195	6-10-82	1	1	4.26	12	0	0	0	13	9	6	6	1	2	10	.205	.200	.207	7.11	1.42
Gunderson, Kyle	R-R	6-3	215	1-31-85	1	0	3.28	14	0	0	0	25	23	9	9	3	7	17	.247	.250	.245	6.20	2.55
Hand, Brad	L-L	6-2	185	3-20-90	1	0	3.00	1	1	0	0	6	3	2	2	0	3	4	.143	.182	.100	6.00	4.50
Harvey, Kris	R-R	6-2	200	1-5-84	1	0	5.40	22	1	0	0	32	30	19	19	4	16	25	.248	.263	.234	7.11	4.55
Houser, James	L-L	6-4	205	12-15-84	0	2	14.09	4	2	0	0	8	16	12	12	1	4	7	.432	.357	.478	8.22	4.70
Jennings, Dan	L-L	6-3	190	4-17-87	4	2	2.56	37	0	0	0	53	49	18	15	0	26	44	.257	.257	.256	7.52	4.44
Koehler, Tom	R-R	6-3	235	6-29-86	16	2	2.61	28	28	0	0	159	140	57	46	11	46	145	.241	.263	.221	8.22	2.61
Korpi, Wade	R-L	5-11	185	3-10-86	0	3	5.12	37	1	0	0	39	44	24	22	3	24	35	.303	.271	.326	8.15	5.59
Loomis, Andy	L-L	5-10	175	11-25-85	0	0	4.50	5	0	0	0	4	4	3	2	0	1	3	.250	.333	.200	6.75	2.25
Marinez, Jhan	R-R	6-1	165	8-12-88	1	0	2.16	15	0	0	6	17	9	5	4	1	7	20	.164	.200	.120	10.80	3.78
Mendez, Adalberto	R-R	6-2	160	2-22-82	0	1	3.14	12	0	0	0	14	15	8	5	1	12	15	.259	.250	.263	9.42	7.53
Meyer, Dan	R-L	6-2	225	7-3-81	0	0	0.00	1	0	0	0	2	1	0	0	0	2	1	.143	1.000	.000	4.50	9.00
Miller, Andrew	L-L	6-7	210	5-21-85	1	8	6.01	18	18	0	0	85	98	63	57	6	61	66	.294	.287	.297	6.96	6.43
Parcell, Garrett	R-R	6-5	220	7-12-84	5	7	3.36	53	0	0	0	75	71	39	28	4	32	61	.257	.319	.213	7.32	3.84
Peterson, Matt	R-R	6-5	230	2-11-82	3	3	1.47	37	0	0	18	37	28	13	6	1	15	26	.215	.237	.197	6.38	3.68
Reed, Evan	R-R	6-4	225	12-31-85	0	0	0.00	1	0	0	0	2	1	0	0	0	1	1	.200	.000	.250	5.40	5.40
Rosario, Jose	R-R	6-0	170	2-16-86	5	4	3.24	17	17	0	0	83	79	36	30	7	38	68	.249	.271	.232	7.34	4.10
Rosario, Sandy	R-R	6-1	170	8-22-85	0	0	0.00	1	0	0	0	0	0	0	0	0	0	3	.000	.000	.000	13.50	0.00
Sanabia, Alex	R-R	6-2	165	9-8-88	5	1	2.03	14	14	0	0	84	59	22	19	2	16	65	.194	.197	.191	6.94	1.71
Stone, Brad	R-R	6-3	190	5-20-84	3	3	3.95	11	8	0	0	41	37	23	18	5	8	26	.239	.229	.247	5.71	3.29
Villanueva, Elih	R-R	6-2	235	7-26-86	14	4	2.26	28	28	4	0	179	137	56	45	15	34	115	.212	.182	.238	5.78	1.71

Fielding

Catcher	PCT	G	PO	A	E	DP	PB
Hatcher	.988	81	508	81	7	8	9
Otness	.992	33	245	16	2	0	1
Rottino	.988	32	215	23	3	1	4
Skipworth	1.000	1	10	0	0	0	0
Wilson	1.000	2	9	1	0	0	0

First Base	PCT	G	PO	A	E	DP
Delaney	.984	28	167	16	3	13
Mitchell	.994	37	304	17	2	27
Otness	1.000	1	4	1	0	1
Rottino	.989	13	86	3	1	7
Saccomanno	.983	65	528	37	10	45
Torres	1.000	9	58	7	0	5

Second Base	PCT	G	PO	A	E	DP
Curry	.970	102	184	236	13	47
Gran	1.000	1	2	5	0	1
Guzman	1.000	1	2	2	0	1
Mitchell	1.000	5	7	9	0	4
Torres	.969	46	85	104	6	23

Third Base	PCT	G	PO	A	E	DP
Dominguez	.955	137	119	246	17	30
Gran	1.000	1	2	2	0	0
Mitchell	.818	2	4	5	2	0
Torres	1.000	2	0	1	0	0

Shortstop	PCT	G	PO	A	E	DP
Gran	.750	2	1	1	1	
Guzman	.800	2	1	3	1	1
Martinez	.953	128	166	299	23	61
Torres	.909	11	10	20	3	3

Outfield	PCT	G	PO	A	E	DP
Burns	.991	64	113	2	1	1
Corsaletti	1.000	15	40	2	0	0
Curry	1.000	1	2	0	0	0
Delaney	1.000	11	24	2	0	0
Guzman	—	2	0	0	0	0
Mattison	1.000	15	32	2	0	0
Mense	1.000	5	2	0	0	0
Mitchell	.967	13	28	1	1	0
Rottino	.987	69	148	2	2	0
Scott	.982	69	162	5	3	1
Stanton	1.000	51	108	6	0	0
Torres	.991	46	99	9	1	2
Tripp	.989	99	173	8	2	3

JUPITER HAMMERHEADS   HIGH CLASS A

FLORIDA STATE LEAGUE

Batting	B-T	HT	WT	DOB	AVG	vLH	vRH	G	AB	R	H	2B	3B	HR	RBI	BB	HBP	SH	SF	SO	SB	CS	SLG	OBP
Baker, John	L-R	6-1	220	1-20-81	.333	.000	.667	3	6	2	2	0	0	0	0	2	0	0	0	1	0	0	.333	.500
Carroll, Brett	R-R	6-0	210	10-3-82	.294	.333	.286	5	17	4	5	1	0	0	3	5	0	0		5	2	1	.353	.520
Ceballos, Jose	R-R	6-0	190	12-27-89	.213	.100	.243	76	235	18	50	10	0	3	23	5	4	7	4	57	0	2	.294	.238
Cooper, Marquise	R-S	5-9	175	10-16-91	.130	.125	.133	7	23	1	3	0	0	0	1	4	1	0	0	7	2	0	.130	.286
Corsaletti, Jeff	L-R	6-0	190	2-22-83	.000	.000	.000	1	4	0	0	0	0	0	0	0	0	0	0	0	0	0	.000	.000
Dayleg, Terrence	R-R	6-0	170	9-19-87	.214	.000	.273	10	28	3	6	1	0	0	1	1	2	1		5	0	0	.250	.258
Dunn, Chris	R-R	5-10	180	3-8-84	.194	.258	.161	27	93	5	18	4	0	1	6	2	0	0	1	19	2	2	.269	.208
Fermin, Miguel	R-R	5-11	175	2-11-85	.227	.200	.236	39	119	7	27	7	0	0	12	6	3	3	3	24	5	3	.286	.280
Fortenberry, Seth	L-L	6-2	175	11-8-83	.213	.095	.247	28	94	6	20	4	0	0	8	9	0	2	0	32	1	2	.340	.282

Name	B-T	HT	WT	DOB	AVG	vLH	vRH	G	AB	R	H	2B	3B	HR	RBI	BB	HBP	SH	SF	SO	SB	CS	OBP	SLG
Galloway, Isaac	R-R	6-2	190	10-10-89	.200	.222	.195	30	100	9	20	3	3	0	6	5	3	0	0	21	4	3	.290	.259
Gran, Paul	R-R	5-11	182	4-7-86	.267	.259	.270	94	352	45	94	22	2	8	30	24	10	5	3	101	7	5	.409	.329
Guzman, Javier	B-R	6-0	170	5-4-82	.229	.320	.209	38	140	15	32	4	1	3	11	13	1	5	2	10	3	6	.336	.295
Hayes, Brett	R-R	6-1	205	2-13-84	.217	.250	.211	7	23	6	5	1	0	2	7	4	0	0	0	7	0	0	.522	.333
Hickman, Tom	L-L	6-1	180	4-18-88	.233	.189	.243	67	210	23	49	11	0	7	38	30	5	2	6	53	0	2	.386	.335
Hord, Dallas	R-R	6-0	175	11-25-87	.333	.333	.333	2	6	0	2	0	0	0	0	0	0	0	0	1	0	0	.333	.333
Keedy, Ryan	L-R	6-3	220	8-15-85	.223	.167	.226	39	121	18	27	10	1	0	11	16	4	2	3	34	1	0	.322	.326
Klosterman, Ryan	R-R	5-11	190	5-28-82	.167	.000	.211	8	24	2	4	2	0	0	2	4	0	1	1	10	0	1	.250	.276
Lasater, Ben	R-R	6-3	195	5-25-84	.246	.200	.260	124	452	44	111	24	1	6	48	26	6	7	3	101	2	1	.343	.294
Lopez, Alfredo	R-R	5-10	160	10-7-89	.438	1.000	.400	7	16	2	7	0	0	0	2	2	1	0	0	2	0	1	.438	.526
Manzanillo, Ernesto	R-R	5-11	165	12-24-88	.252	.190	.274	64	226	26	57	9	3	2	19	16	3	1	4	60	7	1	.345	.305
Mattison, Kevin	L-L	6-0	180	9-20-85	.218	.183	.227	90	362	46	79	13	4	3	29	22	7	3	3	87	44	10	.301	.274
Mense, Hunter	L-L	5-11	185	8-30-84	.199	.190	.219	43	156	11	31	8	1	0	12	8	2	0	1	31	3	4	.263	.246
Morrison, Logan	L-L	6-3	235	8-25-87	.381	.300	.455	5	21	3	8	2	2	0	2	0	0	0	0	3	0	0	.667	.381
Muecklisch, Todd	R-R	5-10	175	7-9-88	.250	.100	.318	12	32	3	8	3	1	0	2	4	0	0	0	10	0	0	.406	.333
Ontiveros, Emilio	R-R	5-11	170	1-2-85	.193	.241	.179	80	249	15	48	8	1	0	12	16	11	5	1	49	2	2	.233	.271
Paulino, Carlos	R-R	6-0	167	9-24-89	.125	.000	.125	3	8	1	1	0	0	1	0	0	0	0	0	1	0	0	.250	.125
Pertusati, Danny	R-R	6-1	185	4-27-90	.207	.263	.189	110	376	37	78	10	0	2	26	41	6	1	4	76	14	2	.250	.293
Rodriguez, Eddie	R-R	6-1	215	7-29-88	.200	.500	.143	8	25	2	5	2	0	1	4	1	0	0	0	3	0	0	.400	.231
Smolinski, Jake	R-R	5-11	185	2-9-89	.264	.271	.263	109	405	45	107	27	3	5	51	31	3	0	4	62	8	5	.383	.318
Stonecipher, Sequoyah	R-R	6-0	195	11-6-89	.156	.222	.130	13	32	2	5	0	0	0	2	4	1	0	0	6			.156	.270
Synan, Jeremy	L-R	6-0	193	7-14-86	.236	.207	.244	119	428	51	101	24	4	7	47	37	4	4	1	111	5	4	.360	.302
Taylor, Robert	R-R	6-2	210	10-10-85	.208	.222	.205	18	48	4	10	2	0	0	6	4	2	0	1	17	1	0	.250	.291
Wade, Chris	R-R	6-0	170	9-25-87	.164	.167	.163	19	61	9	10	1	1	0	9	10	0	0		8			.262	.257

Pitching	B-T	HT	WT	DOB	W	L	ERA	G	GS	CG	SV	IP	H	R	ER	HR	BB	SO	AVG	vLH	vRH	K/9	BB/9
Andrelczyk, Pete	R-R	6-1	185	11-10-85	3	4	3.04	43	0	0	2	68	48	26	23	4	30	72	.203	.170	.220	9.53	3.97
Bono, Robert	R-R	6-2	175	12-12-88	5	13	5.74	25	22	1	0	129	187	89	82	12	28	69	.344	.321	.362	4.83	1.96
Cishek, Steven	R-R	6-6	200	6-18-86	0	6	2.83	26	0	0	4	35	29	15	11	0	19	28	.223	.216	.228	7.20	4.89
Dilone, Natividad	R-R	6-0	160	9-8-82	0	1	6.62	13	0	0	0	18	26	15	13	0	16	16	.333	.444	.300	8.15	8.15
Dorn, Johnny	R-R	6-3	210	8-4-85	4	12	4.75	28	27	1	0	153	177	88	81	13	43	100	.288	.276	.296	5.87	2.52
Evans, Bryan	R-R	6-3	205	2-25-87	3	6	3.45	18	15	0	0	89	94	44	34	3	15	67	.263	.217	.299	6.80	1.52
Fulton, Jon	R-R	6-4	200	12-1-83	1	1	4.43	10	0	0	0	22	24	12	11	1	9	16	.282	.143	.351	6.45	3.63
Gogal, Jeff	R-L	6-2	195	6-10-82	1	0	1.46	22	0	0	1	25	19	4	4	0	7	26	.200	.171	.217	9.49	2.55
Gunderson, Kyle	R-R	6-3	215	1-31-85	1	3	2.76	9	0	0	0	16	19	5	5	1	3	18	.279	.231	.310	9.92	1.65
Hand, Brad	L-L	6-2	185	3-20-90	8	8	3.33	26	26	2	0	141	153	68	52	10	49	134	.278	.282	.277	8.57	3.14
Harvey, Kris	R-R	6-2	200	1-5-84	1	0	0.00	4	0	0	0	7	4	0	0	1	6		.160	.125	.176	7.71	1.29
Hensley, Clay	R-R	5-11	190	8-31-79	0	0	0.00	2	0	0	0	3	1	0	0	1	2		.111	.000	.250	6.75	3.38
Johnson, Graham	R-R	6-6	215	10-13-89	2	12	6.18	26	15	1	1	95	114	72	65	4	52	60	.298	.324	.278	5.70	4.94
Kaminska, Kyle	L-R	6-4	180	10-5-88	1	4	3.51	10	7	0	0	49	46	22	19	3	8	33	.242	.213	.267	6.10	1.48
Korpi, Wade	R-L	5-11	185	3-10-86	2	1	1.17	9	0	0	0	15	6	2	2	0	7	12	.128	.083	.143	7.04	4.11
Leroux, Chris	L-R	6-6	225	4-14-84	0	0	3.38	2	0	0	0	3	2	1	1	0	0	3	.200	.000	.333	0.00	3.38
Loomis, Andy	L-L	5-10	175	11-25-85	2	2	3.50	36	1	0	0	62	56	27	24	0	16	59	.247	.247	.247	8.61	2.34
Madden, Corey	R-R	6-1	195	3-30-84	1	5	3.86	40	0	0	0	49	40	26	21	0	22	62	.220	.237	.208	11.39	4.04
Mahoney, Dan	R-R	6-3	195	2-17-88	0	0	0.00	1	1	0	0	3	0	1	0	0	4		.000	.000	.000	0.00	12.00
Marinez, Jhan	R-R	6-1	165	8-12-88	1	1	1.42	21	0	0	4	25	12	4	4	1	14	44	.148	.161	.140	15.63	4.97
Meyer, Dan	R-L	6-2	225	7-3-81	0	0	0.00	3	0	0	0	4	1	0	0	1	8		.067	.000	.071	18.00	2.25
Miller, Andrew	L-L	6-7	210	5-21-85	1	1	1.72	3	3	0	0	16	8	3	3	0	15	23	.145	.133	.150	13.21	8.62
Morales, Isaac	L-L	6-0	188	5-4-87	1	1	1.69	5	0	0	0	11	8	2	2	2	6	8	.211	.300	.179	6.75	5.06
O'Gara, Joey	R-R	6-7	205	4-20-88	7	6	3.84	18	16	1	0	96	113	45	41	3	19	42	.301	.301	.300	3.94	1.78
Pinto, Renyel	L-L	6-4	280	7-8-82	0	1	1.80	3	3	0	0	5	2	1	1	0	6	9	.125	.091	.200	16.20	10.80
Rembisz, Scott	R-R	6-1	205	9-26-88	0	0	4.50	2	0	0	0	4	4	2	2	1	1	3	.267	.000	.333	6.75	2.25
Robertson, Zach	R-L	6-1	205	7-27-88	0	0	45.00	1	0	0	0	1	4	5	5	0	2	0	.667	.000	.667	0.00	18.00
Sanches, Brian	R-R	6-0	190	8-8-78	0	1	2.25	3	1	0	0	4	2	1	1	0	0	6	.143	.000	.222	13.50	0.00
Sprague, Holden	R-R	6-2	210	7-24-87	0	0	10.80	2	0	0	0	2	6	2	2	0	4	6	.545	.400	.667	16.20	0.00
Squires, Chris	R-R	6-2	195	3-29-88	1	1	1.08	8	0	0	0	17	21	5	2	0	5	20	.296	.286	.300	10.80	2.70
Tucker, Ryan	R-R	6-1	200	12-6-86	1	3	6.00	23	0	0	6	30	35	20	20	0	24	18	.318	.271	.355	5.40	7.20
Veres, Adam	R-R	6-4	230	3-19-88	0	0	10.80	3	0	0	0	2	2	2	2	0	2	1	.250	.500	.167	5.40	10.80

Fielding

Catcher	PCT	G	PO	A	E	DP	PB
Baker	—	1	0	0	0	0	0
Ceballos	.988	76	532	59	7	5	9
Fermin	.981	38	237	27	5	4	8
Hayes	1.000	5	21	3	0	0	0
Hord	1.000	2	15	1	0	0	0
Paulino	.882	3	14	1	2	0	0
Rodriguez	.962	7	49	1	2	0	0
Taylor	1.000	16	105	6	0	1	2

First Base	PCT	G	PO	A	E	DP
Fortenberry	.956	4	37	6	2	6
Gran	.982	10	51	4	1	4
Keedy	.985	14	120	10	2	14
Lasater	.990	109	896	61	10	95
Mense	1.000	3	20	1	0	2
Morrison	.978	5	43	1	1	5

Second Base	PCT	G	PO	A	E	DP
Gran	.957	19	39	49	4	9
Guzman	1.000	1	2	3	0	0
Klosterman	1.000	2	6	6	0	1
Lopez	1.000	3	7	7	0	2
Manzanillo	.966	14	25	31	2	7
Ontiveros	1.000	4	6	9	0	2
Pertusati	.954	102	194	278	23	75

Third Base	PCT	G	PO	A	E	DP
Dayleg	.800	2	2	6	2	2
Gran	.985	45	33	97	2	11
Lopez	.889	4	1	7	1	1
Manzanillo	.714	3	2	8	4	0
Muecklisch	.875	3	2	5	1	1
Smolinski	.932	86	59	159	16	14

Shortstop	PCT	G	PO	A	E	DP
Dayleg	.939	6	14	17	2	6
Gran	.929	11	10	29	3	5
Guzman	.938	15	21	39	4	5
Klosterman	.893	6	5	20	3	6
Manzanillo	.960	5	8	16	1	3
Muecklisch	.919	8	7	27	3	3
Ontiveros	.970	75	113	215	10	50
Wade	.933	19	18	52	5	9

Outfield	PCT	G	PO	A	E	DP
Carroll	1.000	4	4	1	0	1
Cooper	1.000	7	10	1	0	0
Dunn	.982	26	55	1	1	1
Fortenberry	.973	19	35	1	1	1

Galloway	.970	30	64	1	2	1	Mattison	.991	89	220	10 2 4
Guzman	.967	15	27	2	1	0	Mense	.974	31	35	3 1 0
Hickman	.992	62	121	2	1	0	Smolinski	.917	11	11	0 1 0
Manzanillo	.969	34	57	5	2	0	Stonecipher	.909	9	10	0 1 0

Synan	.975	90	152 4 4 1
Taylor	1.000	1	2 0 0 0

GREENSBORO GRASSHOPPERS — LOW CLASS A

SOUTH ATLANTIC LEAGUE

Batting	B-T	HT	WT	DOB	AVG	vLH	vRH	G	AB	R	H	2B	3B	HR	RBI	BB	HBP	SH	SF	SO	SB	CS	SLG	OBP
Austin, Chase	R-R	6-2	185	12-4-87	.268	.238	.277	106	380	55	102	25	0	14	52	42	8	5	4	74	8	6	.445	.350
Bass, Justin	R-R	6-0	205	12-12-85	.240	.221	.245	103	388	59	93	21	2	19	50	27	15	0	3	98	9	3	.451	.312
Corsaletti, Jeff	L-R	6-0	190	2-22-83	.301	.320	.293	23	83	13	25	3	1	3	12	18	0	0	0	13	4	0	.470	.426
Cregar, Chad	L-R	6-4	221	10-30-86	.220	.256	.210	108	391	48	86	16	1	17	57	23	4	2	2	108	5	6	.396	.269
Dayleg, Terrence	R-R	6-0	170	9-19-87	.242	.278	.231	50	153	15	37	10	0	3	18	10	2	2	1	26	5	2	.386	.295
Duarte, Jose	R-R	5-10	165	3-7-85	.300	.324	.293	74	300	58	90	20	1	7	40	28	3	4	0	54	15	4	.443	.366
Hickman, Tom	L-L	6-1	180	4-18-88	.230	.250	.224	17	61	6	14	2	0	5	12	4	2	1	1	22	0	1	.508	.294
Jensen, Kyle	R-L	6-4	230	5-20-88	.272	.303	.261	125	470	61	128	26	1	18	86	45	8	0	6	119	5	1	.447	.342
Keedy, Ryan	L-R	6-3	220	8-15-85	.218	.077	.246	21	78	9	17	1	0	2	8	7	3	0	1	14	0	1	.308	.303
Krick, Taylor	R-R	6-1	200	3-31-88	.223	.267	.207	40	112	12	25	2	0	2	10	22	3	1	2	28	2	1	.295	.360
Long, Wes	R-R	5-11	195	6-12-82	.203	.118	.238	15	59	5	12	4	1	0	6	2	1	1	1	14	1	2	.305	.238
Markel, Austin	L-R	6-1	195	9-12-86	.198	.150	.209	30	106	15	21	3	0	5	9	11	3	0	2	34	1	0	.368	.287
Ozuna, Marcell	R-R	6-2	190	11-12-90	.160	.200	.150	6	25	3	4	0	0	1	2	2	0	0	0	10	0	0	.280	.222
Pasek, Mike	R-R	5-9	160	9-8-89	.199	.308	.164	77	211	26	42	6	2	2	23	31	5	4	2	57	10	4	.275	.313
Paulino, Carlos	R-R	6-0	167	9-24-89	.184	.120	.205	64	201	17	37	10	0	0	10	6	2	6	1	49	0	0	.234	.214
Poulk, Dallas	L-R	5-11	175	5-16-88	.121	.000	.154	10	33	2	4	1	0	0	4	0	0	0	0	7	0	0	.152	.216
Skipworth, Kyle	L-R	6-4	205	3-1-90	.249	.185	.266	107	397	55	99	17	1	17	59	32	5	0	2	132	1	2	.426	.312
Smith, Rand	R-R	6-0	190	6-11-87	.223	.209	.227	117	417	66	93	11	3	5	37	53	4	6	4	94	25	6	.300	.314
Stonecipher, Sequoyah	R-R	6-0	195	11-6-89	.213	.256	.190	33	122	12	26	4	1	1	10	5	2	1	0	18	3	1	.287	.256
Torres, Jose	R-R	6-0	170	10-22-90	.251	.187	.270	101	327	40	82	11	0	0	24	35	5	12	2	40	4	5	.284	.331
Wade, Chris	R-R	6-0	170	9-25-87	.233	.163	.250	62	223	17	52	19	0	1	17	11	0	9	1	32	10	4	.332	.268
Weaver, Brent	R-R	6-1	175	3-2-85	.162	.091	.192	23	74	4	12	6	0	1	5	11	0	0	0	25	1	0	.284	.271
Yelich, Christian	L-R	6-4	189	12-5-91	.348	.000	.381	6	23	2	8	2	0	0	1	0	0	0	0	6	0	0	.435	.375

Pitching	B-T	HT	WT	DOB	W	L	ERA	G	GS	CG	SV	IP	H	R	ER	HR	BB	SO	AVG	vLH	vRH	K/9	BB/9
Alvarez, Jose	L-L	5-11	150	5-6-89	10	3	3.58	26	13	0	0	108	114	52	43	9	32	113	.273	.173	.297	9.42	2.67
Benjamin, Ramon	R-L	6-2	180	6-14-87	3	3	3.46	43	0	0	1	68	57	41	26	6	34	71	.218	.194	.226	9.44	4.52
Caminero, Arquimedes	R-R	6-4	185	6-16-87	5	2	3.01	48	0	0	3	75	55	34	25	4	34	97	.200	.190	.206	11.69	4.10
Carrillo, Erick	R-R	6-1	185	1-3-87	6	7	4.36	32	15	0	1	118	124	60	57	11	35	90	.273	.312	.248	6.88	2.68
Ceda, Jose	R-R	6-4	275	1-28-87	0	0	4.50	7	0	0	0	8	7	4	4	2	1	5	.226	.500	.095	5.63	1.13
Chirinos, Luis	R-R	6-2	170	4-22-90	0	0	1.69	3	0	0	0	5	5	2	1	0	3	3	.250	.250	.250	5.06	5.06
Conley, Jordan	R-R	6-1	180	7-19-86	0	0	21.60	1	0	0	0	2	4	5	4	0	2	2	.400	.500	.375	10.80	10.80
Dilone, Natividad	R-R	6-0	160	9-8-82	2	4	3.83	21	2	0	0	56	52	27	24	1	25	50	.259	.302	.239	7.99	3.99
Evans, Bryan	R-R	6-3	205	2-25-87	4	3	5.27	11	6	0	0	43	54	27	25	3	6	36	.312	.308	.314	7.59	1.27
James, Chad	L-L	6-3	185	1-23-91	5	10	5.12	24	24	0	0	114	116	70	65	3	65	105	.269	.310	.259	8.27	5.12
Martinez, Anillins	L-L	6-2	176	4-6-87	1	0	5.33	17	0	0	1	27	32	17	16	2	16	21	.308	.375	.295	7.00	5.33
Montgomery, Matt	R-R	6-4	210	7-21-87	11	12	3.23	28	27	0	0	159	162	68	57	8	28	135	.258	.295	.237	7.64	1.58
Morales, Isaac	L-L	6-0	188	5-4-87	1	0	4.70	7	0	0	1	15	14	8	8	1	6	16	.241	.182	.278	9.39	3.52
Morey, Robert	R-R	6-1	185	11-27-88	1	3	3.65	12	12	0	0	44	45	18	18	6	12	41	.257	.303	.209	8.32	2.44
Olmos, Edgar	L-L	6-5	180	4-12-90	3	9	4.37	25	25	0	0	117	122	68	57	9	59	108	.271	.248	.277	8.28	4.53
Petersen, Curtis	R-R	6-3	180	8-28-89	4	8	6.32	28	15	0	0	98	103	82	69	11	65	53	.273	.229	.304	4.85	5.95
Ramos, A.J.	R-R	5-10	210	9-20-86	3	7	3.70	49	0	0	28	58	40	26	24	3	32	78	.198	.280	.150	12.03	4.94
Rasmussen, Rob	R-L	5-10	155	4-2-89	0	0	1.35	5	0	0	0	7	1	1	1	0	2	4	.040	.000	.333	5.40	2.70
Robertson, Zach	R-L	6-1	205	7-27-88	0	0	2.45	1	0	0	0	4	5	1	1	0	2	3	.333	.250	.364	7.36	4.91
Rosario, Sandy	R-R	6-1	170	8-22-85	7	2	3.60	43	0	0	3	90	92	47	36	9	17	122	.263	.264	.262	12.20	1.70
Shafer, Chris	R-R	6-2	245	5-16-89	0	1	1.59	6	1	0	0	11	3	2	2	1	2	10	.086	.071	.095	7.94	1.59

Fielding

Catcher	PCT	G	PO	A	E	DP	PB
Krick	1.000	10	54	9	0	4	3
Paulino	.982	60	428	55	9	7	2
Skipworth	.985	81	672	94	12	3	18

First Base	PCT	G	PO	A	E	DP
Bass	.954	8	62	0	3	10
Cregar	.988	89	752	40	10	55
Keedy	.984	21	183	7	3	15
Krick	.987	7	68	6	1	4
Weaver	.994	18	159	10	1	6

Second Base	PCT	G	PO	A	E	DP
Dayleg	.967	21	44	45	3	10
Long	.963	13	16	36	2	7
Pasek	.979	66	121	163	6	32

Catcher (cont.)	PCT	G	PO	A	E	DP	PB
Poulk	.951	7	13	26	2	8	
Torres	.964	24	42	65	4	14	
Wade	.966	20	35	50	3	3	

Third Base	PCT	G	PO	A	E	DP
Austin	.926	101	56	205	21	11
Dayleg	.882	9	3	27	4	0
Krick	.875	21	8	34	6	2
Pasek	.857	8	6	6	2	0
Smith	.000	1	0	0	1	0
Weaver	.833	4	1	9	2	1

Shortstop	PCT	G	PO	A	E	DP
Dayleg	.925	18	26	48	6	5
Long	.833	2	3	2	1	1
Pasek	.750	2	1	2	1	0

	PCT	G	PO	A	E	DP
Poulk	1.000	3	6	7	0	2
Torres	.951	78	118	235	18	50
Wade	.931	45	57	104	12	22

Outfield	PCT	G	PO	A	E	DP
Bass	.988	87	151	7	2	2
Corsaletti	1.000	15	24	1	0	0
Cregar	1.000	11	18	1	0	1
Duarte	.993	70	133	9	1	2
Hickman	.955	12	20	1	1	1
Jensen	.917	73	95	4	9	1
Markel	.917	9	10	1	1	1
Ozuna	.923	6	11	1	1	1
Smith	.990	112	185	13	2	3
Stonecipher	.944	26	34	0	2	0
Yelich	1.000	5	9	0	0	0

JAMESTOWN JAMMERS

NEW YORK-PENN LEAGUE

Batting	B-T	HT	WT	DOB	AVG	vLH	vRH	G	AB	R	H	2B	3B	HR	RBI	BB	HBP	SH	SF	SO	SB	CS	SLG	OBP
Black, Danny	L-R	6-2	170	8-19-88	.271	.317	.257	43	181	32	49	8	8	0	15	17	1	1	0	45	8	1	.403	.337
Brantley, Harold	L-R	5-10	180	5-19-88	.302	.444	.269	27	96	16	29	8	2	1	15	11	0	0	2	18	2	3	.458	.367
Bryan, Luis	R-R	6-2	165	11-26-90	.150	.200	.133	7	20	0	3	0	0	0	1	0	1	1	1	8	0	0	.150	.182
Canha, Mark	R-R	6-2	195	2-15-89	.264	.278	.257	14	53	7	14	3	1	4	9	6	0	0	0	13	0	0	.585	.339
Diaz, Aury	R-R	6-1	155	5-29-90	.245	.375	.167	33	106	19	26	2	1	0	17	16	1	0	1	23	6	0	.283	.347
Dudley, Aaron	L-R	6-3	193	2-17-88	.262	.267	.261	38	122	14	32	8	0	2	18	13	1	2	2	23	1	1	.377	.333
Fisher, Ryan	L-R	6-3	195	4-24-88	.274	.258	.280	67	252	47	69	24	9	8	49	22	7	0	2	77	1	1	.536	.346
Gimenez, Wilfredo	R-R	6-0	180	12-18-90	.226	.333	.195	32	106	11	24	3	0	2	11	8	1	0	1	21	0	1	.311	.284
Hord, Dallas	R-R	6-0	175	11-25-87	.235	.361	.188	41	132	21	31	4	3	0	16	15	0	2	1	37	4	0	.311	.311
Keys, Brent	L-R	6-1	210	7-14-89	.267	.296	.258	65	217	39	58	8	1	0	25	31	2	8	3	36	11	4	.313	.360
Lopez, Alfredo	R-R	5-10	160	10-7-89	.250	.400	.100	6	20	3	5	0	0	0	3	2	0	0	1	1	0	.250	.400
Mendoza, Pedro	R-R	6-0	148	5-11-91	.316	.500	.267	4	19	3	6	3	0	0	5	0	0	0	0	1	0	0	.474	.316
Muecklisch, Todd	R-R	5-10	175	7-9-88	.140	.125	.146	18	57	19	8	2	1	1	5	17	6	0	0	20	4	0	.263	.388
Ozuna, Marcell	R-R	6-2	190	11-12-90	.267	.247	.275	68	270	53	72	11	2	21	60	17	3	0	3	94	3	1	.556	.314
Perio, Noah	L-R	6-0	170	11-14-91	.258	.238	.265	59	225	30	58	10	0	0	31	17	2	0	2	25	7	0	.302	.313
Poulk, Dallas	L-R	5-11	175	5-16-88	.280	.250	.292	45	157	21	44	8	1	1	21	17	1	1	3	36	4	1	.363	.348
Senne, Aaron	L-L	6-2	180	11-5-87	.296	.304	.293	60	213	33	63	14	0	1	29	27	4	1	3	39	2	1	.376	.381
Stonecipher, Sequoyah	R-R	6-0	195	11-6-89	.325	.462	.259	22	80	15	26	7	2	2	15	9	1	0	1	18	2	0	.538	.396
Wooster, James	L-L	6-1	200	6-19-89	.251	.205	.265	48	175	19	44	11	4	2	23	14	2	0	1	44	2	1	.394	.313

Pitching	B-T	HT	WT	DOB	W	L	ERA	G	GS	CG	SV	IP	H	R	ER	HR	BB	SO	AVG	vLH	vRH	K/9	BB/9
Chirinos, Luis	R-R	6-2	170	4-22-90	4	4	4.08	15	8	0	0	46	50	26	21	1	20	34	.284	.329	.255	6.60	3.88
Conley, Jordan	R-R	6-1	180	7-19-86	1	2	1.52	30	0	0	16	30	14	7	5	2	11	37	.136	.133	.138	11.22	3.34
Cravey, Kevin	R-R	6-1	180	8-15-87	1	0	0.00	3	0	0	0	7	2	0	0	0	3	.087	.000	.167	3.86	0.00
Cunniff, Brandon	R-R	6-0	185	10-7-88	0	0	3.38	1	0	0	0	3	3	1	1	0	1	4	.273	.333	.250	13.50	3.38
Dayton, Grant	L-L	6-2	200	11-25-87	1	1	1.26	17	0	0	1	29	18	6	4	0	15	23	.186	.226	.167	7.22	4.71
Estevez, Alvaro	R-R	6-2	180	3-15-89	1	2	10.57	4	2	0	0	8	11	10	9	2	9	3	.314	.375	.263	3.52	10.57
Gonzalez, Saul	R-R	6-1	182	9-19-88	3	1	3.14	12	6	0	1	43	41	15	15	2	9	29	.256	.203	.292	6.07	1.88
Heatley, Jeremy	R-R	6-2	215	12-17-87	3	2	3.23	16	0	0	0	31	32	15	11	1	16	30	.262	.205	.317	8.80	4.70
Hodges, Josh	R-R	6-7	235	6-21-91	3	3	6.04	12	12	0	0	54	57	42	36	4	23	38	.270	.202	.320	6.37	3.86
Holmes, Bobby	R-R	6-2	230	5-23-88	0	0	6.75	5	0	0	0	5	1	4	4	0	12	1	.056	.143	.000	1.69	20.25
Kainer, Andy	L-L	6-1	215	8-22-86	1	0	3.68	18	0	0	0	22	19	10	9	1	15	14	.238	.154	.278	5.73	6.14
Lambert, John	L-L	6-7	210	10-11-87	0	0	11.25	3	0	0	0	4	7	5	5	0	4	4	.389	.143	.545	9.00	9.00
Morales, Isaac	L-L	6-0	188	5-4-87	4	2	3.20	11	0	0	0	25	24	10	9	0	10	29	.247	.133	.299	10.30	3.55
Neal, Zach	R-R	6-3	220	11-9-88	1	1	1.74	4	0	0	0	21	19	10	4	1	2	21	.235	.083	.356	9.15	0.87
Oaks, Alan	R-R	6-3	225	4-4-88	1	2	1.50	5	4	0	0	18	10	6	3	0	6	17	.147	.143	.152	8.50	3.00
Ojala, Mike	R-R	6-3	195	8-24-88	0	0	3.86	11	5	0	0	26	25	15	11	1	12	36	.255	.262	.250	12.62	4.21
Robertson, Zach	R-L	6-1	205	7-27-88	1	1	4.50	8	0	0	0	16	18	12	8	1	4	12	.273	.200	.304	6.75	2.25
Rogers, Jared	R-R	6-6	180	5-9-88	0	0	0.00	1	0	0	0	4	3	1	0	0	1	.188	.500	.083	2.25	0.00
Sprague, Holden	R-R	6-2	210	7-24-87	5	4	2.97	18	9	0	0	64	55	30	21	6	29	34	.228	.231	.226	4.81	4.10
Squires, Chris	R-R	6-2	195	3-29-88	0	0	9.00	1	0	0	0	1	1	1	1	0	1	3	.250	.333	.000	27.00	9.00
Toves, Ken	R-L	6-3	180	7-31-89	4	2	3.61	24	0	0	2	42	34	18	17	4	18	39	.221	.122	.257	8.29	3.83
Varner, Rett	R-R	6-4	185	2-3-88	4	1	2.14	10	10	0	0	46	40	19	11	1	14	33	.230	.235	.226	6.41	2.72
Veres, Adam	R-R	6-4	230	3-19-88	4	3	4.14	15	15	0	0	72	75	43	33	5	22	41	.267	.303	.241	5.15	2.76

Fielding

Catcher	PCT	G	PO	A	E	DP	PB
Dudley	.989	13	84	7	1	0	4
Gimenez	.980	29	174	18	4	1	8
Hord	.996	41	244	37	1	4	11

First Base	PCT	G	PO	A	E	DP
Dudley	.974	14	144	6	4	11
Fisher	.957	7	65	2	3	2
Senne	.981	54	485	33	10	45

Second Base	PCT	G	PO	A	E	DP
Black	.970	34	44	116	5	22
Diaz	.889	2	5	3	1	1
Lopez	.875	3	6	8	2	1
Perio	.957	16	27	61	4	10

	PCT	G	PO	A	E	DP	PB
Poulk	.950	20	37	58	5	8	

Third Base	PCT	G	PO	A	E	DP
Black	1.000	1	1	3	0	1
Diaz	.899	30	19	61	9	5
Fisher	.879	32	19	68	12	4
Muecklisch	1.000	1	1	0	0	0
Poulk	.970	11	9	23	1	3

Shortstop	PCT	G	PO	A	E	DP
Black	.952	5	7	13	1	2
Bryan	.920	7	1	10	13	2
Diaz	—	1	0	0	0	0
Lopez	.800	2	0	4	1	0
Mendoza	.955	4	7	14	1	4

	PCT	G	PO	A	E	DP
Muecklisch	.886	17	20	50	9	5
Perio	.917	33	59	95	14	20
Poulk	.951	9	17	22	2	7

Outfield	PCT	G	PO	A	E	DP
Brantley	.957	11	21	1	1	0
Canha	.913	13	19	2	2	0
Fisher	.941	26	48	0	3	0
Keys	.969	65	116	9	4	4
Ozuna	.975	57	111	7	3	2
Senne	1.000	2	5	0	0	0
Stonecipher	.912	18	30	1	3	0
Wooster	.935	32	52	6	4	0

GCL MARLINS

GULF COAST LEAGUE

Batting	B-T	HT	WT	DOB	AVG	vLH	vRH	G	AB	R	H	2B	3B	HR	RBI	BB	HBP	SH	SF	SO	SB	CS	SLG	OBP
Bryan, Luis	R-R	6-2	165	11-26-90	.237	.304	.214	28	93	14	22	4	2	0	13	2	5	0	1	26	0	2	.323	.287
Canha, Mark	R-R	6-2	195	2-15-89	.176	.333	.143	6	17	3	3	0	0	0	1	2	1	0	1	1	1	1	.176	.286
Castillo, Nestor	B-R	6-2	176	10-24-89	.346	.308	.361	38	133	18	47	8	1	2	23	3	1	0	2	21	1	2	.436	.359
Cooper, Marquise	R-R	5-9	175	10-16-91	.236	.216	.243	43	148	29	35	2	2	1	15	25	6	1	1	45	13	5	.297	.367
Corsaletti, Jeff	L-R	6-0	190	2-22-83	.313	.300	.316	14	48	12	15	1	1	2	13	10	0	0	0	10	1	1	.500	.431
Dewitt, Kentrell	L-R	5-11	180	3-20-91	.183	.038	.239	36	93	15	17	3	1	2	10	11	3	1	1	32	8	3	.301	.287

Name	B-T	HT	WT	DOB	AVG	vLH	vRH	G	AB	R	H	2B	3B	HR	RBI	BB	HBP	SH	SF	SO	SB	CS	OBP	SLG
Glime, Gregg	B-R	5-11	200	10-29-87	.289	.286	.290	23	38	8	11	2	0	0	4	8	2	1	0	5	0	0	.342	.438
Lopez, Alfredo	R-R	5-10	160	10-7-89	.222	.000	.240	11	27	3	6	0	0	0	2	2	1	0	0	4	0	0	.222	.300
Martinez, Juancito	R-R	6-1	170	6-10-89	.237	.176	.262	26	59	10	14	2	1	0	4	1	1	2	0	11	2	3	.305	.262
Maybin, Cameron	R-R	6-3	210	4-4-87	.364	.500	.333	3	11	4	4	1	0	1	5	2	1	0	0	1	0	0	.727	.500
McConkey, Brian	L-R	6-2	210	12-17-88	.304	.349	.290	53	181	24	55	14	2	1	30	21	6	0	2	25	1	0	.420	.390
Mendoza, Pedro	R-R	6-0	148	5-11-91	.254	.188	.276	53	193	28	49	10	1	0	22	15	0	7	2	17	2	1	.316	.305
Morales, Jobduan	B-R	5-10	180	6-7-91	.310	.343	.296	38	116	21	36	7	1	0	13	15	0	2	2	20	0	0	.388	.383
Muecklisch, Todd	R-R	5-10	175	7-9-88	.000	.000	.000	5	11	1	0	0	0	0	1	2	1	0	0	3	0	0	.000	.214
Peralta, Rony	L-R	6-0	160	8-19-90	.262	.265	.261	47	126	19	33	9	2	0	14	11	3	4	2	22	3	2	.365	.331
Perez, Yefri	R-R	5-11	162	2-24-91	.290	.280	.294	30	93	12	27	2	0	0	8	7	0	2	2	18	8	2	.312	.333
Peters, David	R-R	6-0	195	1-26-91	.129	.125	.130	14	31	3	4	0	0	1	2	6	1	0	0	10	0	0	.226	.289
Ramirez, Marc	R-R	6-2	185	7-17-91	.134	.158	.125	30	67	10	9	2	0	1	6	1	0	0	1	19	1	0	.209	.145
Raynor, John	R-R	6-1	205	1-4-84	.000	.000	.000	2	3	0	0	0	0	0	1	2	0	0	1	0	0	0	.000	.333
Realmuto, J.T.	R-R	6-1	190	3-18-91	.175	.250	.156	12	40	2	7	0	0	0	4	7	0	0	0	11	0	1	.175	.298
Rodriguez, Eddie	R-R	6-1	215	7-29-88	.194	.200	.192	14	36	1	7	0	0	0	5	0	0	0	0	4	0	0	.194	.194
Rosa, Viosergy	L-L	6-3	185	6-16-90	.202	.350	.159	32	89	15	18	7	0	1	12	15	3	0	0	26	0	1	.315	.336
Scott, Lorenzo	L-L	6-3	210	3-1-82	.333	.000	.357	5	15	1	5	0	1	0	3	1	0	0	1	6	0	0	.467	.353
Soto, Mayobanez	R-R	6-3	185	5-5-91	.192	.160	.208	28	73	8	14	4	0	2	13	9	2	0	2	22	1	0	.329	.291
Yelich, Christian	L-R	6-4	189	12-5-91	.375	.333	.389	6	24	3	9	1	1	0	3	2	0	0	0	7	1	0	.500	.423

Pitching	B-T	HT	WT	DOB	W	L	ERA	G	GS	CG	SV	IP	H	R	ER	HR	BB	SO	AVG	vLH	vRH	K/9	BB/9
Brewer, Blake	R-R	6-5	177	3-2-90	1	0	10.13	9	0	0	0	5	4	6	6	0	16	8	.211	.250	.200	13.50	27.00
Brice, Austin	R-R	6-3	190	6-19-92	0	1	4.32	6	0	0	0	8	7	6	4	0	7	8	.219	.333	.174	8.64	7.56
Buente, Jay	R-R	6-2	185	9-28-83	1	0	3.60	4	0	0	0	5	5	2	2	0	1	4	.278	.200	.308	7.20	1.80
Buret, Alfredo	R-R	6-1	160	8-22-87	4	3	1.45	18	0	0	2	31	27	6	5	2	2	20	.233	.219	.238	5.81	0.58
Cravey, Kevin	R-R	6-1	180	8-15-87	3	2	0.76	11	6	0	0	36	30	12	3	0	4	35	.222	.250	.215	8.83	1.01
Cunniff, Brandon	R-R	6-0	185	10-7-88	2	0	2.25	17	0	0	5	32	26	10	8	1	5	32	.222	.063	.248	9.00	1.41
Dayton, Grant	L-L	6-2	200	11-25-87	0	0	0.00	1	0	0	0	1	0	0	0	0	0	1	.000	.000	.000	9.00	0.00
Estevez, Alvaro	R-R	6-2	180	3-15-89	0	1	1.06	5	2	0	0	17	10	5	2	0	4	9	.159	.200	.140	4.76	2.12
Ferreira, Kelvin	L-L	6-0	156	10-31-90	1	0	0.00	3	0	0	0	4	4	0	0	0	3	2	.250	1.000	.200	4.50	6.75
Heatley, Jeremy	R-R	6-2	215	12-17-87	0	0	0.00	1	0	0	0	2	0	0	0	0	0	0	.000	.000	.000	0.00	0.00
Holmes, Bobby	R-R	6-2	230	5-23-88	0	1	40.50	2	0	0	0	1	1	3	3	0	3	1	.333	.000	.333	13.50	40.50
Jorge, Eduardo	R-R	6-0	194	12-19-91	0	0	7.71	5	0	0	0	7	8	6	6	0	6	7	.296	.500	.280	9.00	7.71
Kaminska, Kyle	L-R	6-4	180	10-5-88	1	0	4.50	2	2	0	0	8	13	6	4	0	1	1	.371	1.000	.333	1.13	1.13
Lambert, John	L-L	6-7	210	10-11-87	1	0	0.00	1	0	0	0	2	0	0	0	1	2	.400	.000	.500	18.00	9.00
Leroux, Chris	L-R	6-6	225	4-14-84	1	0	4.50	3	0	0	0	4	4	2	2	0	0	3	.267	.200	.300	6.75	0.00
Mahoney, Dan	R-R	6-3	195	2-17-88	1	2	6.49	11	0	0	0	35	33	28	25	0	21	22	.252	.440	.208	5.71	5.45
Manzueta, Jheyson	R-R	6-2	162	12-5-89	3	0	1.93	12	9	0	0	47	27	12	10	0	23	50	.167	.148	.170	9.64	4.44
Neal, Zach	R-R	6-3	220	11-9-88	1	0	0.84	3	2	0	0	11	8	2	1	0	1	16	.195	.556	.094	13.50	0.84
Oaks, Alan	R-R	6-3	225	4-4-88	0	0	3.00	2	0	0	0	3	4	3	1	0	1	3	.333	.000	.333	9.00	3.00
Ojala, Mike	R-R	6-3	195	8-24-87	1	0	0.00	2	0	0	0	3	0	0	0	0	1	2	.000	.000	.000	6.00	3.00
Rembisz, Scott	R-R	6-1	230	9-26-88	2	0	1.96	12	6	0	0	41	39	14	9	1	5	43	.239	.275	.228	9.36	1.09
Robertson, Zach	R-L	6-1	205	7-27-88	0	1	3.18	8	1	0	1	11	12	5	4	0	7	9	.279	.250	.282	7.15	5.56
Rodriguez, Jose	R-R	6-1	195	9-24-90	2	2	2.50	8	0	0	0	40	28	11	11	0	10	31	.200	.214	.196	7.03	2.27
Rogers, Jared	R-R	6-6	180	5-9-88	6	1	1.21	12	5	2	1	45	32	6	6	0	2	38	.201	.154	.205	7.66	0.40
Rosario, Jose	R-R	6-0	170	2-16-86	0	0	1.80	2	1	0	1	5	3	1	1	0	5	.176	.000	.231	9.00	0.00
Shafer, Chris	R-R	6-2	245	5-16-89	0	0	1.80	4	0	0	1	5	3	1	1	0	2	4	.176	.000	.231	7.20	3.60
Solano, Aneurys	R-R	6-1	180	11-18-88	1	2	5.14	9	0	0	0	14	13	9	8	0	10	7	.260	.200	.267	4.50	6.43
Squires, Chris	R-R	6-2	195	3-29-88	1	1	0.00	5	0	0	0	6	4	2	0	0	2	5	.190	1.000	.150	7.94	3.18
Stein, Steven	R-R	6-0	170	12-25-88	2	1	2.53	16	0	0	3	21	17	7	6	0	13	21	.224	.222	.224	8.86	5.48
Stone, Brad	R-R	6-3	190	5-20-84	1	0	2.57	3	2	0	0	7	7	3	2	0	4	5	.233	.143	.261	6.43	5.14
Tucker, Ryan	R-R	6-1	200	12-6-86	1	0	0.00	2	1	0	0	4	5	0	0	0	7	.333	.500	.273	15.75	0.00
Ungs, Nic	R-R	6-1	220	9-3-79	0	1	0.00	7	0	0	0	5	3	2	0	0	0	3	.176	.000	.273	5.40	0.00
Varner, Rett	R-R	6-4	185	2-3-88	0	0	0.00	2	0	0	0	4	1	0	0	0	2	4	.071	.000	.071	9.00	4.50
Weber, Jeremy	R-R	6-5	185	5-21-90	1	0	2.35	6	0	0	0	8	6	2	2	0	5	6	.214	.500	.167	7.04	5.87

Fielding

Catcher	PCT	G	PO	A	E	DP	PB
Glime	.992	23	113	12	1	0	1
Morales	.975	34	210	24	6	2	6
Peters	1.000	5	20	1	0	0	0
Realmuto	1.000	5	16	4	0	1	4
Rodriguez	.984	10	56	4	1	0	1

First Base	PCT	G	PO	A	E	DP
McConkey	.991	37	309	13	3	19
Rosa	.982	23	210	6	4	18
Soto	1.000	1	1	0	0	0

Second Base	PCT	G	PO	A	E	DP
Lopez	1.000	7	11	15	0	3
Mendoza	.946	17	34	54	5	13
Peralta	.970	8	12	20	1	1
Perez	.943	29	38	62	6	14

Third Base	PCT	G	PO	A	E	DP
Bryan	.920	10	7	16	2	1
McConkey	.000	1	0	0	1	0
Muecklisch	.900	5	0	9	1	0
Peralta	.866	36	9	62	11	6
Realmuto	1.000	1	0	1	0	0
Soto	.829	16	7	27	7	1

Shortstop	PCT	G	PO	A	E	DP
Bryan	.940	18	23	56	5	9
Lopez	.923	3	4	8	1	0
Mendoza	.987	37	40	116	2	16
Peralta	1.000	4	7	9	0	3
Perez	1.000	1	1	1	0	0

Outfield	PCT	G	PO	A	E	DP
Canha	1.000	6	15	0	0	0
Castillo	1.000	37	59	3	0	0
Cooper	1.000	42	65	4	0	3
Corsaletti	1.000	14	9	1	0	1
Dewitt	.973	30	35	1	1	0
Martinez	1.000	21	33	5	0	1
Maybin	1.000	3	3	0	0	0
Ramirez	1.000	27	41	0	0	0
Raynor	1.000	2	1	0	0	0
Scott	1.000	4	9	0	0	0
Yelich	1.000	6	9	1	0	1

DSL MARLINS ROOKIE

DOMINICAN SUMMER LEAGUE

Batting	B-T	HT	WT	DOB	AVG	vLH	vRH	G	AB	R	H	2B	3B	HR	RBI	BB	HBP	SH	SF	SO	SB	CS	SLG	OBP
Acosta, Pedro	R-R	6-2	213	7-11-90	.288	.231	.306	33	111	9	32	6	3	0	14	9	4	0	0	12	0	0	.396	.363
Astacio, Juan	R-R	6-1	180	9-29-92	.148	.118	.159	28	88	8	13	2	1	0	3	8	0	0	0	40	1	3	.193	.219
Bautista, Juan	B-R	5-10	170	1-25-90	.259	.261	.258	41	116	3	30	2	1	0	14	16	1	1	2	12	1	0	.293	.348
Castillo, Felix	R-R	5-11	191	7-16-91	.238	.300	.229	32	105	10	25	4	0	1	15	12	2	0	4	12	2	0	.305	.317
Castro, Victor	R-R	6-1	198	1-10-92	.176	.192	.173	44	136	23	24	4	1	4	15	24	10	0	1	41	6	2	.309	.339
Cuevas, Carlos	R-R	6-1	170	11-26-91	.248	.063	.277	44	137	16	34	6	1	2	11	31	3	0	0	42	1	1	.350	.398
Diaz, Carlos	R-R	6-2	146	9-20-91	.174	.000	.174	9	23	2	4	0	0	0	2	3	0	0	0	13	2	0	.174	.269
Duran, Carlos	L-R	6-1	192	5-24-92	.179	.107	.195	60	184	10	33	7	1	0	7	23	9	1	1	18	0	2	.228	.300
Eusebio, Johan	R-R	6-0	197	1-26-91	.161	.167	.160	35	112	8	18	4	1	0	10	16	2	0	0	44	2	3	.214	.277
Garcia, Fraiquelin	B-R	6-2	165	8-15-91	.205	.000	.231	23	44	13	9	0	0	0	5	9	1	0	0	19	6	1	.205	.352
Gomez, Jose	R-R	6-2	185	12-1-91	.139	.167	.133	24	72	9	10	1	0	0	4	15	1	2	0	18	0	2	.153	.295
Hernandez, Yeison	R-R	5-10	150	6-29-92	.235	.174	.257	64	200	28	47	5	3	0	14	38	1	7	2	34	7	3	.290	.357
Jimenez, Joel	R-R	5-11	189	4-30-92	.048	.000	.053	7	21	2	1	0	0	0	0	4	1	0	0	8	0	0	.048	.231
Lorenzo, Raffi	B-R	5-10	161	11-2-91	.107	.000	.143	32	56	8	6	2	0	0	6	6	1	0	0	23	5	4	.143	.206
Morales, Oswaldo	R-R	6-1	155	7-8-91	.138	.118	.146	35	65	8	9	1	0	0	2	7	10	0	1	11	7	4	.154	.313
Mota, Juan	R-R	6-1	167	9-17-92	.187	.241	.167	33	107	11	20	3	1	0	8	23	1	1	0	21	2	0	.234	.336
Munoz, Felix	L-L	6-1	193	4-7-92	.250	.310	.240	44	156	18	39	6	1	2	15	23	2	0	0	17	2	0	.340	.354
Ortiz, Luis	R-R	5-10	161	3-14-92	.257	.292	.250	49	171	24	44	5	0	0	12	26	2	0	0	24	31	10	.287	.362
Solorzano, Jesus	R-R	6-0	190	8-8-90	.286	.225	.301	51	175	22	50	7	2	0	13	11	11	3	0	47	12	3	.349	.365
Vigil, Rodrigo	R-R	6-0	164	1-3-93	.134	.071	.147	30	82	7	11	1	2	0	7	8	5	2	1	14	1	1	.195	.250

Pitching	B-T	HT	WT	DOB	W	L	ERA	G	GS	CG	SV	IP	H	R	ER	HR	BB	SO	AVG	vLH	vRH	K/9	BB/9
Beltre, Andy	R-R	6-4	195	7-6-93	0	0	8.38	7	0	0	0	10	12	9	9	1	8	10	.300	.222	.323	9.31	7.45
Caracas, Jhondervisth	R-R	6-1	165	1-10-92	0	0	10.80	2	0	0	0	3	1	4	4	0	4	3	.077	.000	.200	8.10	10.80
De La Rosa, Esmerling	R-R	6-2	199	5-15-91	0	1	2.92	8	0	0	0	12	8	4	4	0	10	11	.200	.167	.227	8.03	7.30
Del Orbe, Ramon	R-R	5-11	177	2-17-92	4	4	3.77	13	11	0	0	72	70	40	30	1	27	53	.264	.255	.269	6.66	3.39
Delgadillo, Yonalis	R-R	6-2	170	1-26-91	3	8	3.90	15	11	1	1	67	60	38	29	2	35	45	.248	.321	.226	6.04	4.70
Fermin, Yeraldo	R-R	5-11	136	10-2-91	2	2	2.35	6	5	0	0	38	31	13	10	0	7	26	.220	.234	.213	6.10	1.64
German, Domingo	R-R	6-2	172	8-4-92	2	3	3.69	18	0	0	6	46	29	22	19	1	27	43	.184	.103	.210	8.35	5.24
Holguin, Cristian	R-R	6-1	145	2-15-93	1	2	3.67	9	3	0	0	27	37	13	11	1	7	8	.339	.636	.264	2.67	2.33
Jorge, Eduardo	R-R	6-0	194	12-19-91	0	2	0.41	4	4	1	0	22	16	3	1	0	4	24	.195	.292	.155	9.82	1.64
Liriano, German	R-R	6-0	180	6-29-93	3	2	2.13	8	2	0	1	25	22	12	6	0	5	9	.247	.259	.242	3.20	1.78
Lopez, Cesar	R-R	6-2	176	3-14-92	1	0	2.31	6	0	0	1	12	10	4	3	1	6	12	.233	.182	.250	9.26	4.43
Mendoza, Yeims	R-R	6-2	155	2-27-93	0	1	6.35	7	0	0	0	6	4	5	4	0	5	2	.174	.429	.063	3.18	7.94
Palin, Nelson	R-R	6-3	182	9-22-92	0	2	3.00	12	1	0	1	24	18	11	8	0	10	20	.209	.190	.215	7.50	3.75
Parra, Andy	R-R	6-1	175	8-15-92	0	0	4.26	4	1	0	0	6	3	5	3	1	4	4	.136	.125	.143	5.68	5.68
Reyes, Helpi	R-R	5-11	175	7-27-92	4	4	2.17	12	12	2	0	75	65	28	18	1	24	62	.241	.250	.238	7.47	2.89
Tamares, Joel	R-R	6-2	155	8-13-90	2	2	2.45	4	4	1	0	22	21	10	6	0	5	16	.241	.250	.237	6.55	2.05
Urena, Jose	R-R	6-3	172	9-12-91	5	6	2.61	13	13	3	0	83	76	32	24	2	7	66	.241	.250	.236	7.19	0.76

Fielding

Catcher	PCT	G	PO	A	E	DP	PB
Acosta	.980	14	81	17	2	0	4
Bautista	.987	36	191	45	3	4	4
Castillo	.981	25	129	24	3	1	3
Jimenez	1.000	6	41	8	0	0	0

First Base	PCT	G	PO	A	E	DP
Acosta	.981	6	50	1	1	8
Cuevas	1.000	2	2	1	0	0
Duran	.993	41	374	24	3	34
Munoz	.988	24	224	17	3	16

Second Base	PCT	G	PO	A	E	DP
Diaz	.857	1	2	4	1	0

	PCT	G	PO	A	E	DP
Lorenzo	.945	20	26	43	4	6
Mota	.964	6	11	16	1	2
Ortiz	.948	46	98	101	11	22
Vigil	1.000	13	15	21	0	3

Third Base	PCT	G	PO	A	E	DP
Cuevas	.823	44	28	74	22	4
Mota	.892	25	24	50	9	4
Ortiz	.750	7	1	5	2	0
Vigil	1.000	2	0	1	0	0

Shortstop	PCT	G	PO	A	E	DP
Diaz	.880	8	6	16	3	3
Hernandez	.935	63	86	188	19	35

	PCT	G	PO	A	E	DP
Mota	.750	3	2	4	2	1
Vigil	1.000	3	3	9	0	3

Outfield	PCT	G	PO	A	E	DP
Astacio	.925	27	33	4	3	0
Castro	.965	43	53	2	2	0
Duran	1.000	1	2	0	0	0
Eusebio	.897	29	33	2	4	0
Garcia	.960	19	23	1	1	0
Gomez	1.000	22	27	0	0	0
Morales	1.000	30	41	2	0	0
Munoz	1.000	10	10	1	0	0
Solorzano	.990	51	92	4	1	0

FLORIDA MARLINS

Houston Astros

SEASON IN A SENTENCE: It couldn't exactly be called a successful season, but when the Astros traded franchise cornerstones Roy Oswalt and Lance Berkman and committed themselves to a youth movement, the team responded to manager Brad Mills and played much better in the second half.

HIGH POINT: After a disastrous first half of the season, the Astros put together a couple of modest winning streaks in the second half. The highlight came when they completed a four-game series sweep from the Phillies on Aug. 26, moving to 11 games under .500. Hunter Pence and Carlos Lee provided reliable power, combining for 49 home runs, while Brett Myers established himself as the pitching staff's new ace.

LOW POINT: The Astros got off to a 0-8 start and continued sinking, but the lowest point came on July 24, when they lost 7-0 to the Reds in Oswalt's final start for the team before he was traded to the Phillies. That moved Houston's record to 39-58, and Berkman headed off to the Yankees four days later.

NOTABLE ROOKIES: Third baseman Chris Johnson was arguably the team's best player, batting .308/.337/.481 after coming into the season ranked as the organization's No. 16 prospect. Jason Castro was not as strong in his debut but is still being counted on as the Astros' catcher of the future. Brett Wallace, who was obtained from the Blue Jays in the machinations from the Oswalt deal, will be expected to fill Berkman's place at first base and in the lineup.

KEY TRANSACTIONS: Obviously the departures of Berkman and Oswalt turned the page on one era of Astros baseball and started another. Oswalt left first, bringing Anthony Gose, J.A. Happ and Jonathan Villar from the Phillies (Gose was immediately flipped to the Jays for Wallace), while Berkman brought Jimmy Paredes and Mark Melancon from the Yankees. Houston also dealt Pedro Feliz to the Cardinals for David Carpenter in August.

DOWN ON THE FARM: The Astros have a thin farm system in terms of prospect talent, and it played out on the field in 2010 as well, with the 29th-best composite record in the game. Short-season Tri-City did fight to the New York-Penn League title, the first in franchise history after the team became the first Astros affiliate to reach the postseason in two years.

OPENING DAY PAYROLL: $92.4 million (13th)

PLAYERS OF THE YEAR

MAJOR LEAGUE	MINOR LEAGUE
Brett Myers	**Jordan Lyles**
rhp	**rhp**
14-8, 3.14	(Double-A/Triple-A)
5th in NL in IP	7-12, 3.57
180 SO/66 BB	137 SO/46 BB

ORGANIZATION LEADERS

BATTING	*Minimum 250 at-bats	
MAJORS		
*AVG	Chris Johnson	.308
*OPS	Chris Johnson	.818
HR	Hunter Pence	25
RBI	Hunter Pence	91
MINORS		
*AVG	J.D. Martinez, Lexington/Corpus Christi	.341
*OBP	J.D. Martinez, Lexington/Corpus Christi	.407
*SLG	J.D. Martinez, Lexington/Corpus Christi	.531
R	J.D. Martinez, Lexington/Corpus Christi	107
H	J.D. Martinez, Lexington/Corpus Christi	183
TB	J.D. Martinez, Lexington/Corpus Christi	285
2B	Jacob Goebbert, Lexington	48
3B	Albert Cartwright, Lancaster/Corpus Christi	14
HR	Brandon Barnes, Lancaster/Round Rock	28
RBI	Jacob Goebbert, Lexington	98
BB	Koby Clemens, Corpus Christi	69
	Kody Hinze, Lexington	69
SO	Koby Clemens, Corpus Christi	143
SB	Jay Austin, Lancaster	54

PITCHING	†Minimum 75 innings	
MAJORS		
W	Brett Myers	14
†ERA	Brandon Lyon	3.12
SO	Brett Myers	180
MINORS		
W	Josh Banks, Round Rock	9
W	Robert Donovan, Lexington/Lancaster	9
L	Dallas Keuchel, Lancaster/Corpus Christi	14
†ERA	Douglas Arguello, Corpus Christi	2.55
G	Kirk Clark, Lexington	52
GS	Ross Seaton, Lancaster	28
SV	Kirk Clark, Lexington	29
IP	Andy Van Hekken, Round Rock	177.3
BB	Juan Minaya, Lexington	73
SO	Jordan Lyles, Corpus Christi/Round Rock	137
†AVG	Jose Cisnero, Lexington	.221

General Manager: Ed Wade. **Farm Director:** Fred Nelson. **Scouting Director:** Bobby Heck.

Class	Team	League	W	L	PCT	Finish*	Manager(s)
Majors	Houston Astros	National	76	86	.469	12th (16)	Brad Mills
Triple-A	Round Rock Express	Pacific Coast	57	87	.396	16th (16)	Marc Bombard
Double-A	Corpus Christi Hooks	Texas	63	77	.450	7th (8)	Wes Clements
High A	Lancaster JetHawks	California	54	86	.386	9th (10)	Tom Lawless
Low A	Lexington Legends	South Atlantic	71	68	.511	6th (14)	Rodney Linares
Short-season	Tri-City Dust Devils	New York-Penn	38	36	.514	†6th (14)	Jim Pankovits
Rookie	Greeneville Astros	Appalachian	31	35	.470	8th (10)	Ed Romero
Rookie	GCL Astros	Gulf Coast	20	36	.357	15th (15)	Omar Lopez

Overall 2010 Minor League Record   334   432   .436   29th (30)
*Finish in overall standings (No. of teams in league). †League champion.

ORGANIZATION STATISTICS

HOUSTON ASTROS

NATIONAL LEAGUE

Batting	B-T	HT	WT	DOB	AVG	vLH	vRH	G	AB	R	H	2B	3B	HR	RBI	BB	HBP	SH	SF	SO	SB	CS	SLG	OBP
Berkman, Lance	B-L	6-1	230	2-10-76	.245	.188	.261	85	298	39	73	16	1	13	49	60	0	0	0	70	3	2	.436	.372
Blum, Geoff	B-R	6-3	220	4-26-73	.267	.138	.289	93	202	22	54	10	1	2	22	15	1	0	0	33	0	0	.356	.321
Bogusevic, Brian	L-L	6-3	210	2-18-84	.179	.000	.192	19	28	5	5	3	0	0	3	3	0	0	0	12	1	1	.286	.258
Bourgeois, Jason	R-R	5-9	190	1-4-82	.220	.250	.190	69	123	16	27	4	1	0	3	13	0	0	0	16	12	4	.268	.294
Bourn, Michael	L-R	5-11	180	12-27-82	.265	.229	.276	141	535	84	142	25	6	2	38	59	3	6	2	109	52	12	.346	.341
Cash, Kevin	R-R	6-0	200	12-6-77	.204	.231	.195	20	54	3	11	1	0	2	4	5	0	2	0	13	0	0	.333	.271
Castro, Jason	L-R	6-3	210	6-18-87	.205	.070	.243	67	195	26	40	8	1	2	8	22	0	0	4	41	0	0	.287	.286
Downs, Matt	R-R	6-2	190	3-19-84	.105	.167	.077	11	19	2	2	0	0	0	1	1	0	0	2	0	0	.105	.190
2-team total (29 San Francisco)					.216	—	—	40	97	8	21	7	0	1	7	9	2	0	1	20	0	0	.320	.294
Esposito, Brian	R-R	6-1	205	2-24-79	.000	.000	.000	7	3	0	0	0	0	0	0	0	0	0	0	1	0	0	.000	.000
Feliz, Pedro	R-R	6-1	210	4-27-75	.221	.270	.205	97	289	22	64	12	1	4	31	9	1	0	5	31	1	1	.311	.243
2-team total (40 St. Louis)					.218	—	—	137	409	36	89	12	2	5	40	13	1	0	6	41	1	1	.293	.240
Hernandez, Anderson	B-R	5-9	185	10-30-82	.188	.167	.190	32	48	7	9	2	0	0	1	8	0	0	0	10	2	0	.229	.304
Johnson, Chris	R-R	6-3	220	10-1-84	.308	.386	.316	94	341	40	105	22	2	11	52	15	2	0	4	91	3	0	.481	.337
Keppinger, Jeff	R-R	6-0	185	4-21-80	.288	.304	.282	137	514	62	148	34	1	6	59	51	1	5	4	36	4	1	.393	.351
Lee, Carlos	R-R	6-2	265	6-20-76	.246	.274	.238	157	605	67	149	29	1	24	89	37	3	0	4	59	3	3	.417	.291
Manzella, Tommy	R-R	6-2	200	4-16-83	.225	.290	.201	83	258	17	58	7	0	1	21	13	3	5	3	71	0	1	.264	.267
Matsui, Kazuo	B-R	5-10	185	10-23-75	.141	.000	.147	27	71	4	10	1	0	0	1	4	1	2	0	10	1	1	.155	.197
Michaels, Jason	R-R	6-0	210	5-4-76	.253	.275	.232	106	186	23	47	14	1	8	26	12	4	0	1	29	0	0	.468	.310
Navarro, Oswaldo	R-R	6-0	155	10-2-84	.050	.000	.077	14	20	2	1	0	0	0	0	5	0	0	0	4	0	0	.050	.240
Pence, Hunter	R-R	6-4	220	4-13-83	.282	.292	.279	156	614	93	173	29	3	25	91	41	0	0	3	105	18	9	.461	.325
Quintero, Humberto	R-R	5-9	220	8-2-79	.234	.165	.263	88	265	13	62	10	0	4	20	8	2	1	0	59	0	0	.317	.262
Sanchez, Angel	R-R	6-2	205	9-20-83	.280	.292	.275	65	250	30	70	9	4	0	25	11	2	6	0	45	0	1	.348	.316
Sullivan, Cory	L-L	6-0	200	8-20-79	.188	.000	.197	57	64	6	12	1	1	0	4	6	0	1	0	18	0	0	.234	.257
Towles, J.R.	R-R	6-2	190	2-11-84	.191	.111	.211	17	47	3	9	3	0	1	8	2	1	0	1	12	0	0	.319	.235
Wallace, Brett	L-R	6-2	245	8-26-86	.222	.240	.218	51	144	14	32	6	1	2	13	8	7	0	0	50	0	0	.319	.296

Pitching	B-T	HT	WT	DOB	W	L	ERA	G	GS	CG	SV	IP	H	R	ER	HR	BB	SO	AVG	vLH	vRH	K/9	BB/9
Abad, Fernando	L-L	6-2	205	12-17-85	0	1	2.84	22	0	0	0	19	14	6	6	3	5	12	.200	.179	.214	5.68	2.37
Banks, Josh	R-R	6-3	215	7-18-82	0	1	13.50	1	1	0	0	4	8	6	6	1	4	1	.400	.200	.467	2.25	9.00
Byrdak, Tim	L-L	5-11	195	10-31-73	2	2	3.49	64	0	0	0	39	40	15	15	4	20	29	.272	.213	.333	6.75	4.66
Chacin, Gustavo	L-L	5-11	205	11-4-80	2	2	4.70	44	0	0	1	38	51	22	20	3	20	31	.315	.323	.310	7.28	4.70
Daigle, Casey	R-R	6-5	230	4-4-81	1	1	11.32	13	0	0	0	10	25	13	13	3	6	6	.439	.632	.342	5.23	5.23
Del Rosario, Enerio	R-R	6-2	165	10-16-85	0	0	20.25	2	0	0	0	1	4	3	3	0	0	1	.500	1.000	.200	6.75	0.00
2-team total (9 Cincinnati)					1	1	4.50	11	0	0	0	10	17	7	5	0	4	4	—	—	—	3.60	3.60
Figueroa, Nelson	R-R	6-1	180	5-18-74	5	3	3.22	18	10	0	0	67	64	28	24	9	25	58	.251	.301	.217	7.79	3.36
2-team total (13 Philadelphia)					7	4	3.29	31	11	0	1	93	84	38	34	10	34	73	—	—	—	7.06	3.29
Fulchino, Jeff	R-R	6-5	285	11-26-79	2	1	5.51	50	0	0	0	47	53	30	29	7	22	46	.279	.257	.292	8.75	4.18
Gervacio, Sammy	R-R	6-0	175	1-10-85	0	1	12.27	6	0	0	0	4	4	6	5	1	5	3	.267	.143	.375	7.36	12.27
Happ, J.A.	L-L	6-6	200	10-19-82	5	4	3.75	13	13	1	0	72	60	33	30	7	35	61	.230	.137	.252	7.63	4.38
2-team total (3 Philadelphia)					6	4	3.40	16	16	1	0	87	73	37	33	8	47	70	—	—	—	7.21	4.84
Lindstrom, Matt	R-R	6-3	220	2-11-80	2	5	4.39	58	0	0	23	53	68	26	26	5	20	43	.306	.268	.336	7.26	3.38
Lopez, Wilton	R-R	6-0	190	7-19-83	5	2	2.96	68	0	0	1	67	66	23	22	4	5	50	.261	.284	.245	6.72	0.67
Lyon, Brandon	R-R	6-1	195	8-10-79	6	6	3.12	79	0	0	20	78	68	28	27	2	31	54	.231	.195	.257	6.23	3.58
Majewski, Gary	R-R	6-2	215	2-26-80	0	0	22.50	2	0	0	0	2	5	5	5	1	1	1	.417	1.000	.364	4.50	4.50
Melancon, Mark	R-R	6-2	215	3-28-85	2	0	3.12	20	0	0	0	17	12	8	6	1	8	19	.194	.130	.231	9.87	4.15
Moehler, Brian	R-R	6-3	220	12-31-71	1	4	4.92	20	8	0	0	57	66	32	31	5	26	28	.299	.282	.314	4.45	4.13
Myers, Brett	R-R	6-4	240	8-17-80	14	8	3.14	33	33	2	0	224	212	88	78	20	66	180	.248	.240	.254	7.24	2.66
Norris, Bud	R-R	6-2	215	3-2-85	9	10	4.92	27	27	0	0	154	151	94	84	18	77	158	.256	.241	.269	9.25	4.51
Oswalt, Roy	R-R	6-0	190	8-29-77	6	12	3.42	20	20	1	0	129	109	52	49	13	34	120	.229	.249	.211	8.37	2.37
2-team total (13 Philadelphia)					13	13	2.76	33	32	2	0	212	162	70	65	19	55	193	—	—	—	8.21	2.34
Paulino, Felipe	R-R	6-2	270	10-5-83	1	9	5.11	19	14	0	0	92	95	63	52	4	46	83	.270	.306	.248	8.15	4.52

Name	B-T	HT	WT	DOB	W	L	ERA	G	GS	CG	SV	IP	H	R	ER	HR	BB	SO	AVG	vLH	vRH	K/9	BB/9
Rodriguez, Wandy	R-L	5-11	195	1-18-79	11	12	3.60	32	32	0	0	195	183	95	78	16	68	178	.250	.247	.250	8.22	3.14
Sampson, Chris	R-R	6-1	195	5-23-78	1	0	5.93	35	0	0	0	30	43	22	20	7	8	16	.336	.306	.354	4.75	2.37
Villar, Henry	R-R	5-11	170	5-24-87	0	0	4.50	8	0	0	0	6	5	3	3	0	3	3	.227	.000	.294	4.50	4.50
Wright, Wesley	R-L	5-11	175	1-28-85	1	2	5.73	14	4	0	0	33	37	27	21	6	13	29	.287	.206	.316	7.91	3.55

Fielding

Catcher	PCT	G	PO	A	E	DP	PB
Cash	1.000	19	131	9	0	2	1
Castro	.996	67	449	34	2	6	7
Esposito	1.000	2	2	0	0	0	0
Quintero	.992	87	561	49	5	5	4
Towles	.990	15	92	7	1	0	0

First Base	PCT	G	PO	A	E	DP
Berkman	.999	85	696	72	1	60
Blum	.989	14	90	4	1	16
Feliz	.968	15	83	9	3	11
Lee	.992	20	115	12	1	6
Wallace	.992	48	327	32	3	31

Second Base	PCT	G	PO	A	E	DP
Blum	1.000	8	9	21	0	1

	PCT	G	PO	A	E	DP
Bourgeois	1.000	2	2	2	0	1
Downs	1.000	2	2	0	0	0
Hernandez	.967	8	14	15	1	5
Keppinger	.990	126	217	351	6	66
Matsui	.990	21	42	56	1	12
Sanchez	1.000	8	14	19	0	5

Third Base	PCT	G	PO	A	E	DP
Blum	.976	14	8	32	1	1
Downs	1.000	2	0	3	0	1
Feliz	.942	63	28	103	8	13
Johnson	.908	90	42	135	18	13

Shortstop	PCT	G	PO	A	E	DP
Blum	.937	18	23	36	4	5
Downs	1.000	2	2	2	0	1

	PCT	G	PO	A	E	DP
Hernandez	1.000	2	2	10	0	3
Keppinger	.971	12	14	19	1	9
Manzella	.973	82	121	207	9	41
Navarro	.967	10	8	21	1	3
Sanchez	.976	57	79	128	5	29

Outfield	PCT	G	PO	A	E	DP
Bogusevic	1.000	11	18	0	0	0
Bourgeois	1.000	48	65	0	0	0
Bourn	.992	138	359	8	3	2
Lee	.969	133	183	6	6	1
Michaels	1.000	55	56	1	0	0
Pence	.983	155	340	9	6	2
Sullivan	1.000	17	14	0	0	0

ROUND ROCK EXPRESS
PACIFIC COAST LEAGUE
TRIPLE-A

Batting	B-T	HT	WT	DOB	AVG	vLH	vRH	G	AB	R	H	2B	3B	HR	RBI	BB	HBP	SH	SF	SO	SB	CS	SLG	OBP
Barnes, Brandon	R-R	6-2	210	5-15-86	.286	.000	.353	6	21	2	6	1	0	1	1	1	0	0	0	6	1	0	.476	.318
Bellorin, Edwin	R-R	5-10	240	2-21-82	.233	.125	.273	36	120	9	28	5	0	1	8	10	0	3	1	21	0	0	.300	.290
2-team total (38 Omaha)					.196	—	—	74	250	15	49	8	0	1	12	20	2	6	2	44	0	0	.240	.259
Berkman, Lance	B-L	6-2	230	2-10-76	.500	.000	.500	2	6	3	3	2	0	0	3	0	0	0	1	2	0	0	1.333	.429
Bogusevic, Brian	L-L	6-3	210	2-18-84	.277	.319	.262	131	502	91	139	26	2	13	57	67	3	1	2	108	23	1	.414	.364
Bourgeois, Jason	R-R	5-9	190	1-4-82	.345	.394	.325	65	235	37	81	10	3	5	28	21	3	2	0	28	18	6	.477	.405
Cabral, Marcos	R-R	5-11	185	4-4-84	.241	.231	.244	18	58	2	14	1	0	1	4	3	0	1	0	13	0	0	.310	.279
Cash, Kevin	R-R	6-0	200	12-6-77	.235	.143	.300	10	34	3	8	0	0	0	4	3	0	0	0	10	0	0	.235	.297
Castro, Jason	L-R	6-3	210	6-18-87	.265	.269	.264	57	211	31	56	7	0	4	26	32	1	0	0	34	1	1	.355	.365
Cook, David	R-R	5-11	205	7-21-81	.280	.286	.278	9	25	3	7	3	0	1	6	4	0	0	1	10	1	0	.520	.367
Cruz, Lee	R-R	6-2	190	6-13-83	1.000	.000	1.000	1	1	0	1	1	0	0	0	0	0	0	0	0	0	0	2.000	1.000
Curtis, John	L-R	6-2	210	11-22-84	.333	.000	.375	3	9	1	3	1	0	0	0	2	0	0	0	3	0	0	.444	.455
DeLome, Collin	L-R	6-2	195	12-18-85	.224	.226	.224	95	343	49	77	15	6	17	56	17	5	1	2	113	11	3	.452	.270
Downs, Matt	R-R	6-2	190	3-19-84	.105	.167	.077	6	19	0	2	1	0	0	2	1	0	0	2	1	1	1	.158	.190
2-team total (56 Fresno)					.241	—	—	62	216	37	52	10	1	7	30	26	5	1	1	37	4	5	.394	.335
Duran, German	R-R	5-10	185	8-3-84	.238	.250	.234	33	84	8	20	5	0	1	8	2	2	1	0	11	2	0	.333	.273
Esposito, Brian	R-R	6-1	205	2-24-79	.225	.324	.197	45	151	11	34	5	0	2	18	5	3	3	1	31	0	0	.298	.263
Everidge, Tommy	R-R	6-0	275	4-16-83	.297	.371	.263	30	111	17	33	3	0	5	14	11	2	0	1	26	0	0	.459	.368
3-team total (7 Sacramento, 65 Tacoma)					.249	—	—	102	390	48	97	22	0	13	57	40	3	0	4	95	0	0	.405	.320
Garciaparra, Michael	R-R	6-1	165	4-2-83	.366	.538	.286	20	41	8	15	5	0	0	8	2	1	0	0	12	0	0	.488	.409
Hernandez, Anderson	B-R	5-9	185	10-30-82	.241	.500	.174	7	29	5	7	1	0	0	1	1	0	0	0	6	2	0	.276	.267
Johnson, Chris	R-R	6-3	220	10-1-84	.329	.375	.312	38	149	26	49	10	1	8	33	9	1	0	4	23	0	0	.570	.362
Kata, Matt	B-R	6-1	185	3-14-78	.270	.290	.262	132	485	63	131	25	2	6	47	26	11	3	5	50	4	0	.367	.319
Locke, Drew	R-R	6-1	205	2-28-83	.279	.260	.286	135	477	71	133	36	4	17	74	43	1	0	3	92	6	1	.478	.338
Manzella, Tommy	R-R	6-2	200	4-16-83	.333	.250	.400	6	27	4	9	2	0	1	4	2	0	0	0	6	0	0	.519	.379
Maysonet, Edwin	R-R	6-1	195	10-17-81	.252	.263	.248	86	302	29	76	14	2	2	36	25	3	5	3	63	2	2	.331	.312
Maza, Luis	R-R	5-8	195	6-22-80	.258	.500	.200	15	31	4	8	2	0	1	4	5	0	1	0	4	0	0	.419	.361
Meyer, Drew	L-R	5-10	205	8-29-81	.241	.257	.236	46	145	15	35	6	2	2	13	22	0	1	1	26	3	0	.352	.339
2-team total (32 Salt Lake)					.257	—	—	78	261	30	67	13	3	3	26	34	0	2	1	50	4	1	.364	.341
Navarro, Oswaldo	R-R	6-0	155	10-2-84	.271	.229	.284	88	288	41	78	24	1	6	37	34	8	1	2	67	2	3	.424	.361
Santangelo, Lou	R-R	6-1	200	3-16-83	.000	.000	.000	1	4	0	0	0	0	0	0	0	0	0	0	0	0	0	.000	.000
Shelton, Chris	R-R	6-0	235	6-26-80	.294	.354	.269	82	285	26	71	11	0	10	42	29	3	0	5	77	0	0	.393	.320
Shuck, J.B.	L-L	5-11	185	6-18-87	.273	.235	.286	36	139	15	38	2	0	2	7	16	0	1	0	15	7	3	.317	.348
Sutil, Wladimir	R-R	5-10	155	10-31-84	.237	.364	.188	45	156	28	37	6	0	1	12	19	3	4	2	20	8	2	.295	.328
Vazquez, Ramon	L-R	5-11	195	8-21-76	.352	.263	.400	16	54	6	19	6	0	0	7	9	0	0	1	8	0	0	.463	.438
2-team total (35 Tacoma)					.257	—	—	51	179	19	46	14	1	1	17	18	2	2	1	32	0	0	.363	.330

Pitching	B-T	HT	WT	DOB	W	L	ERA	G	GS	CG	SV	IP	H	R	ER	HR	BB	SO	AVG	vLH	vRH	K/9	BB/9
Abad, Fernando	L-L	6-2	205	12-17-85	0	1	1.42	5	0	0	0	6	5	1	1	1	3	9	.208	.231	.182	12.79	2.84
Abreu, Erick	R-R	6-1	170	8-9-83	0	1	2.77	5	1	0	0	13	15	6	4	1	3	11	.283	.296	.269	7.62	2.08
Banks, Josh	R-R	6-3	215	7-18-82	9	12	4.04	27	27	3	0	172	177	88	77	25	37	72	.270	.262	.278	3.77	1.94
Bayliss, Jonah	R-R	6-0	205	8-13-80	1	4	3.58	43	0	0	0	65	65	27	26	7	21	61	.261	.240	.276	8.40	2.89
Bazardo, Yorman	R-R	6-2	230	7-11-84	4	5	3.87	34	5	0	1	88	97	43	38	12	26	58	.281	.295	.270	5.91	2.65
Burton, T.J.	L-R	6-3	185	7-30-83	2	3	5.52	18	1	0	1	29	31	18	18	4	14	17	.265	.321	.219	5.22	4.30
Byrdak, Tim	L-L	5-11	195	10-31-73	0	0	4.50	2	1	0	0	2	1	1	1	0	2	1	.167	.000	.167	4.50	9.00
Cespedes, Leandro	R-R	5-11	160	4-19-87	0	0	7.50	1	0	0	0	6	8	5	5	2	3	1	.333	.231	.455	1.50	4.50
Chacin, Gustavo	L-L	5-11	205	11-4-80	1	1	3.60	6	5	0	0	25	24	10	10	5	6	14	.255	.212	.279	5.04	2.16
Corcoran, Roy	R-R	5-10	190	5-11-80	2	10	4.60	47	3	0	9	72	76	39	37	6	23	50	.270	.276	.266	6.22	2.86
Daigle, Casey	R-R	6-5	230	4-4-81	2	3	4.91	35	0	0	8	44	54	27	24	6	13	35	.298	.349	.255	7.16	2.66

Name	B-T	HT	WT	DOB	W	L	ERA	G	GS	CG	SV	IP	H	R	ER	HR	BB	SO	AVG	vLH	vRH	K/9	BB/9
Englebrook, Evan	R-R	6-8	255	4-28-82	0	1	5.97	19	0	0	0	29	33	23	19	3	16	27	.289	.383	.224	8.48	5.02
Fulchino, Jeff	R-R	6-5	285	11-26-79	0	0	0.00	4	0	0	0	4	3	0	0	0	1	2	.214	.167	.250	4.50	2.25
Gervacio, Sammy	R-R	6-0	175	1-10-85	0	0	3.48	2	0	0	0	10	6	4	4	0	5	10	.171	.000	.333	8.71	4.35
Lopez, Wilton	R-R	6-0	190	7-19-83	2	1	5.40	3	0	0	0	5	8	3	3	0	0	2	.364	.667	.154	3.60	0.00
Loux, Shane	R-R	6-2	235	8-31-79	6	12	5.25	20	19	1	0	108	134	72	63	11	16	62	.300	.351	.249	5.17	1.33
Lyles, Jordan	R-R	6-4	185	10-19-90	0	3	5.40	6	6	1	0	32	48	21	19	2	11	22	.348	.383	.321	6.25	3.13
Majewski, Gary	R-R	6-2	215	2-26-80	4	5	6.24	40	0	0	2	53	69	42	37	7	18	40	.321	.366	.287	6.75	3.04
Melancon, Mark	R-R	6-2	215	3-28-85	1	0	0.00	3	0	0	1	4	5	0	0	0	1	2	.278	.250	.286	4.15	2.08
Meszaros, Danny	R-R	6-0	170	9-6-85	2	1	5.40	7	0	0	0	8	6	5	5	1	6	5	.207	.143	.227	5.40	6.48
Moehler, Brian	R-R	6-3	220	12-31-71	0	0	0.00	1	1	0	0	3	1	0	0	0	0	1	.091	.000	.111	3.00	0.00
Norris, Bud	R-R	6-0	225	3-2-85	1	0	3.07	3	3	0	0	15	16	5	5	1	6	14	.281	.300	.259	8.59	3.68
Perez, Sergio	R-R	6-3	230	12-5-84	3	4	5.40	14	10	0	0	63	72	45	38	9	31	38	.290	.300	.283	5.40	4.41
Sampson, Chris	R-R	6-1	195	5-23-78	1	2	2.35	13	0	0	0	15	17	5	4	1	4	11	.298	.304	.294	6.46	2.35
Thompson, Brad	R-R	6-1	190	1-31-82	1	1	8.87	15	0	0	0	23	41	27	23	3	4	12	.373	.373	.373	4.63	1.54
2-team total (3 Omaha)					1	2	7.71	18	3	0	0	35	57	35	30	4	5	15	—	—	—	3.86	1.29
Trinidad, Polin	L-L	6-3	195	11-19-84	3	8	5.02	23	20	0	0	118	144	85	66	13	32	74	.298	.306	.295	5.63	2.43
Van Hekken, Andy	R-L	6-3	185	7-31-79	8	8	4.36	29	27	2	0	177	184	92	86	14	50	114	.272	.288	.267	5.79	2.54
Wells, Jared	R-R	6-4	200	10-31-81	0	1	22.09	4	0	0	0	4	11	9	9	0	1	6	.500	.625	.429	14.73	2.45
Wright, Wesley	R-L	5-11	175	1-28-85	4	1	4.65	15	14	0	0	70	76	39	36	8	33	41	.281	.274	.285	5.30	4.26

Fielding

Catcher	PCT	G	PO	A	E	DP	PB
Bellorin	.992	35	223	16	2	1	8
Cash	.963	9	47	5	2	0	1
Castro	.994	54	319	32	2	4	4
Curtis	1.000	3	27	0	0	0	0
Esposito	.992	43	224	21	2	3	3
Santangelo	.900	1	9	0	1	0	0

First Base	PCT	G	PO	A	E	DP
Berkman	.917	2	9	2	1	0
Bogusevic	.991	32	305	10	3	37
Cash	1.000	1	1	0	0	0
Everidge	.991	22	190	19	2	18
Garciaparra	.985	8	61	5	1	2
Kata	.995	20	170	17	1	18
Locke	1.000	7	49	7	0	3
Shelton	.993	60	499	42	4	53

Second Base	PCT	G	PO	A	E	DP
Cabral	.971	9	13	21	1	7
Downs	.923	6	13	11	2	3
Duran	1.000	20	38	67	0	12

(Second Base cont.)	PCT	G	PO	A	E	DP
Hernandez	.857	3	5	7	2	3
Kata	.987	34	66	83	2	19
Maysonet	1.000	3	10	6	0	3
Maza	1.000	7	11	13	0	4
Meyer	.986	29	52	85	2	13
Navarro	.966	34	59	110	6	27
Sutil	.933	11	24	18	3	4
Vazquez	.950	5	9	10	1	4

Third Base	PCT	G	PO	A	E	DP
Cabral	1.000	2	1	2	0	0
Duran	1.000	2	3	3	0	1
Garciaparra	.667	2	0	2	1	0
Hernandez	.857	3	1	5	1	0
Johnson	.905	37	28	67	10	5
Kata	.940	58	46	112	10	11
Maysonet	1.000	15	12	36	0	8
Maza	1.000	4	1	0	0	0
Meyer	.947	12	11	25	2	2
Navarro	.976	16	7	34	1	1
Vazquez	1.000	6	3	12	0	2

Shortstop	PCT	G	PO	A	E	DP
Cabral	.931	6	11	16	2	6
Garciaparra	.833	1	1	4	1	2
Hernandez	.833	1	1	4	1	1
Manzella	1.000	6	8	16	0	4
Maysonet	.986	67	98	183	4	29
Meyer	1.000	3	1	5	0	0
Navarro	.973	35	37	71	3	14
Sutil	.986	35	37	100	2	23
Vazquez	.950	5	3	16	1	2

Outfield	PCT	G	PO	A	E	DP
Barnes	.944	6	17	0	1	0
Bogusevic	1.000	95	214	7	0	2
Bourgeois	.974	48	110	1	3	1
Cook	.833	8	10	0	2	0
DeLome	.969	80	154	4	5	0
Kata	.941	17	30	2	2	0
Locke	.975	105	221	9	6	2
Meyer	1.000	1	1	0	0	0
Ramirez	.974	58	143	9	4	3
Shuck	1.000	35	66	4	0	0

CORPUS CHRISTI HOOKS   DOUBLE-A

TEXAS LEAGUE

Batting	B-T	HT	WT	DOB	AVG	vLH	vRH	G	AB	R	H	2B	3B	HR	RBI	BB	HBP	SH	SF	SO	SB	CS	SLG	OBP
Affronti, Mike	R-R	6-2	195	2-13-84	.279	.267	.286	62	219	22	61	5	3	3	29	13	2	1	2	40	5	5	.370	.322
2-team total (4 Midland)					.276	—	—	66	232	22	64	5	3	3	29	13	3	1	2	45	5	6	.362	.320
Blum, Geoff	B-R	6-3	220	4-26-73	.222	.167	.333	3	9	0	2	2	0	0	1	1	0	0	0	0	0	0	.444	.300
Butera, Barry	L-R	5-11	175	6-5-87	.176	.375	.086	22	51	3	9	0	1	0	1	2	0	1	0	11	0	0	.216	.208
Cabral, Marcos	R-R	5-11	185	4-4-84	.265	.301	.241	52	185	19	49	8	0	4	20	15	0	1	0	22	2	3	.373	.320
Cartwright, Albert	R-R	5-10	180	10-31-87	.229	.196	.250	35	140	15	32	4	1	0	11	11	2	0	1	39	7	4	.271	.289
Clemens, Koby	R-R	5-11	193	12-4-86	.241	.243	.240	127	452	75	109	22	3	26	85	69	9	0	5	143	9	3	.476	.350
Cook, David	R-R	5-11	205	7-21-81	.245	.287	.210	109	310	50	76	13	2	11	36	40	4	1	2	84	7	2	.406	.337
Curtis, John	L-R	6-2	210	11-22-84	.000	.000	.000	1	1	0	0	0	0	0	0	0	0	0	0	0	0	0	.000	.000
Duran, German	R-R	5-10	185	8-3-84	.254	.284	.330	124	422	24	63	10	0	4	28	20	0	0	5	29	1	2	.383	.336
Esposito, Brian	R-R	6-0	205	2-24-79	.130	.125	.136	14	46	2	6	2	1	0	0	2	0	0	0	9	0	0	.217	.130
Fixler, Jon	R-R	6-1	205	6-13-86	.265	.222	.290	33	98	12	26	4	2	5	14	13	2	2	0	33	1	2	.500	.363
Florentino, Jhon	R-R	6-0	155	8-22-83	.256	.267	.250	95	316	30	81	17	3	4	36	27	0	4	1	55	2	2	.367	.314
Garciaparra, Michael	R-R	6-1	165	4-2-83	.233	.357	.125	11	30	3	7	1	0	0	2	4	0	0	1	5	0	0	.267	.314
Gaston, Jon	L-R	6-0	210	10-13-86	.245	.234	.252	132	461	64	113	16	8	13	51	47	6	2	4	105	13	5	.399	.320
Heath, Ben	R-R	6-2	220	10-7-88	.500	1.000	.333	4	12	0	6	1	0	0	4	1	0	1	0	3	0	0	.583	.538
Hernandez, Federico	B-R	6-0	170	2-9-88	.304	.381	.250	19	56	8	17	5	0	1	5	4	0	0	0	11	0	0	.446	.350
Keppinger, Jeff	R-R	6-0	185	4-21-80	.400	.500	.000	2	5	0	2	0	0	0	1	1	0	0	0	0	0	0	.400	.500
Kirkland, Kody	R-R	6-4	200	6-9-83	.286	.231	.333	19	56	12	16	6	0	2	8	7	1	1	0	16	3	0	.500	.375
Manzella, Tommy	R-R	6-2	200	4-16-83	.429	.250	.667	5	14	4	6	1	0	0	1	0	0	0	0	0	2	0	.500	.429
Martinez, J.D.	R-R	6-3	175	8-21-87	.302	.253	.336	50	189	24	57	9	1	3	25	15	2	0	1	42	2	2	.407	.357
Parejo, Freddy	R-R	6-2	193	10-16-84	.300	.303	.298	48	170	19	51	7	1	0	17	7	4	0	0	31	7	1	.353	.343
Santangelo, Lou	R-R	6-1	200	3-16-83	.234	.275	.211	84	252	22	59	11	0	6	20	35	0	4	0	64	0	1	.349	.328
Shuck, J.B.	L-L	5-11	185	6-1-87	.298	.389	.296	101	389	52	116	14	2	2	28	46	0	0	6	59	9	4	.360	.372
Steele, T.J.	R-R	6-3	185	9-21-86	.228	.260	.207	67	241	25	55	9	3	2	18	10	1	0	1	67	9	4	.315	.259
Sutil, Wladimir	R-R	5-10	155	10-31-84	.277	.314	.253	74	264	29	73	7	0	0	17	19	1	5	3	23	15	4	.303	.324
Towles, J.R.	R-R	6-2	190	2-11-84	.143	.333	.091	5	14	3	2	1	0	0	3	4	2	0	0	4	2	0	.214	.400

	B-T	HT	WT	DOB	AVG	vLH	vRH	G	AB	R	H	2B	3B	HR	RBI	BB	HBP	SH	SF	SO	SB	CS	SLG	OBP
Vallejo, Jose	B-R	6-0	200	9-11-86	.111	.108	.113	34	99	6	11	0	0	0	2	7	0	1	0	37	1	1	.111	.170
Van Ostrand, Jimmy	B-T	6-4	210	8-7-84	.244	.292	.202	105	312	22	76	17	0	3	44	18	1	1	3	62	1	3	.327	.284

Pitching	B-T	HT	WT	DOB	W	L	ERA	G	GS	CG	SV	IP	H	R	ER	HR	BB	SO	AVG	vLH	vRH	K/9	BB/9
Abad, Fernando	L-L	6-2	205	12-17-85	4	3	2.50	14	4	0	0	40	48	16	11	3	6	33	.306	.277	.318	7.49	1.36
Abreu, Erick	R-R	6-1	170	8-9-83	4	5	3.34	31	9	0	0	86	80	35	32	11	21	77	.244	.205	.289	8.03	2.19
Arguello, Doug	L-L	6-3	190	11-21-84	7	5	2.55	22	22	2	0	127	120	50	36	4	47	100	.254	.259	.252	7.09	3.33
Burton, T.J.	R-R	6-3	185	7-30-83	3	0	10.00	7	0	0	0	9	17	12	10	2	3	3	.395	.520	.222	3.00	3.00
Buzachero, Bubbie	R-R	5-11	180	6-13-81	1	1	4.23	8	3	0	0	28	25	13	13	0	7	15	.240	.219	.275	4.88	2.28
Englebrook, Evan	R-R	6-8	255	4-28-82	0	2	2.96	23	0	0	4	27	25	10	9	3	7	22	.243	.298	.174	7.24	2.30
Johnson, Jeremy	R-R	6-3	170	7-19-82	5	10	4.30	22	22	1	0	111	128	61	53	13	42	72	.290	.311	.261	5.84	3.41
Keuchel, Dallas	L-L	6-3	200	1-1-88	2	6	4.70	9	9	0	0	54	59	32	28	2	11	36	.285	.259	.302	6.04	1.84
Leon, Arcenio	R-R	6-1	162	9-22-86	0	2	7.83	18	0	0	0	23	29	20	20	3	22	23	.312	.308	.317	9.00	8.61
Lindstrom, Matt	R-R	6-3	220	2-11-80	0	0	0.00	1	1	0	0	1	0	0	0	0	0	1	.000	.000	.000	9.00	0.00
Lo, Chia-Jen	R-R	5-11	185	4-7-86	0	1	1.80	7	0	0	0	15	9	3	3	0	10	13	.176	.000	.220	7.80	6.00
Lumsden, Tyler	L-L	6-4	215	5-9-83	4	8	4.04	20	16	1	0	91	92	47	41	4	34	33	.266	.240	.281	3.25	3.35
2-team total (9 San Antonio)					5	13	4.51	29	25	1	0	142	151	87	71	7	55	61	—	—	—	3.88	3.49
Lyles, Jordan	R-R	6-4	185	10-19-90	7	9	3.12	21	20	1	0	127	133	54	44	10	35	115	.267	.259	.279	8.15	2.48
Meszaros, Danny	R-R	6-0	170	9-6-85	3	1	3.09	26	0	0	10	32	28	13	11	1	16	42	.231	.212	.246	11.81	4.50
Nevarez, Matt	R-R	6-4	220	2-26-87	2	1	3.76	36	0	0	1	38	30	17	16	1	46	41	.224	.267	.169	9.63	10.80
Paulino, Felipe	R-R	6-2	270	10-5-83	0	0	0.00	1	1	0	0	4	2	0	0	0	1	3	.154	.250	.000	6.75	2.25
Payano, Nelson	L-L	6-1	190	11-13-82	1	1	5.83	26	0	0	1	29	31	19	19	2	23	36	.279	.278	.281	11.05	7.06
Peguero, Jailen	R-R	6-0	185	1-4-81	3	4	1.70	32	0	0	3	53	38	11	10	1	22	56	.201	.208	.194	9.51	3.74
Perez, Sergio	R-R	6-3	230	12-5-84	2	3	3.09	8	8	0	0	44	49	22	15	0	19	20	.287	.237	.326	4.12	3.92
Sampson, Chris	R-R	6-1	195	5-23-78	0	0	0.00	1	1	0	0	2	0	0	0	0	1	1	.000	.000	.000	9.00	9.00
Stiller, Erik	R-R	6-5	210	7-10-84	0	0	4.81	15	0	0	0	24	24	13	13	7	5	17	.258	.409	.122	6.29	1.85
Trinidad, Polin	L-L	6-3	195	11-19-84	1	3	4.02	5	4	0	0	31	42	19	14	2	8	19	.313	.264	.346	5.46	2.30
Urckfitz, Pat	L-L	6-3	190	7-21-88	0	0	3.60	1	1	0	0	5	8	2	2	0	1	4	.364	.250	.429	7.20	1.80
Valdez, Jose	R-R	6-4	185	1-22-83	0	0	1.46	9	0	0	0	12	5	2	2	0	4	10	.119	.100	.136	8.03	2.92
Villar, Henry	R-R	5-11	170	5-24-87	4	7	4.15	36	11	0	5	102	95	49	47	11	42	68	.242	.229	.259	6.00	3.71
Wabick, Brian	R-R	6-0	180	8-3-87	1	0	7.84	6	0	0	0	10	20	10	9	1	4	2	.426	.370	.500	1.74	3.48
Walker, Edwin	R-L	6-3	205	10-26-83	4	1	2.84	19	0	0	0	25	23	9	8	0	14	21	.250	.260	.238	7.46	4.97
Wells, Jared	R-R	6-4	200	10-31-81	5	4	3.81	31	8	0	3	78	73	39	33	8	46	60	.258	.256	.261	6.92	5.31
Wolf, Shane	L-L	6-3	225	9-10-86	0	0	3.18	4	0	0	0	6	5	3	2	0	1	5	.208	.111	.267	7.94	1.59

Fielding

Catcher	PCT	G	PO	A	E	DP	PB
Esposito	.981	14	92	10	2	0	3
Fixler	.982	33	210	10	4	2	6
Heath	1.000	4	21	2	0	0	1
Hernandez	.983	18	104	13	2	1	1
Santangelo	.989	78	504	33	6	7	3
Towles	1.000	5	34	2	0	1	0

First Base	PCT	G	PO	A	E	DP
Cabral	1.000	1	11	0	0	1
Clemens	.991	111	972	61	9	113
Kirkland	1.000	1	1	0	0	1
Santangelo	1.000	4	26	4	0	0
Van Ostrand	.996	29	225	17	1	28

Second Base	PCT	G	PO	A	E	DP
Affronti	1.000	5	7	9	0	2
Butera	.952	12	10	30	2	8
Cabral	1.000	12	20	24	0	3
Cartwright	.948	34	53	112	9	31

	PCT	G	PO	A	E	DP
Duran	.979	57	110	165	6	49
Garciaparra	1.000	5	14	14	0	2
Keppinger	1.000	2	4	7	0	0
Kirkland	1.000	3	8	9	0	1
Vallejo	.969	22	38	56	3	12

Third Base	PCT	G	PO	A	E	DP
Affronti	.944	28	15	53	4	4
Butera	.833	3	1	4	1	0
Cabral	.765	10	1	12	4	1
Clemens	1.000	3	0	3	0	1
Duran	1.000	1	0	1	0	0
Florentino	.937	91	52	155	14	18
Garciaparra	.857	3	1	5	1	0
Kirkland	.939	14	12	19	2	0
Vallejo	.900	7	1	8	1	1

Shortstop	PCT	G	PO	A	E	DP
Affronti	.984	34	48	75	2	17
Blum	1.000	3	6	3	0	2

	PCT	G	PO	A	E	DP
Butera	1.000	3	1	7	0	0
Cabral	.943	31	39	93	8	18
Duran	.800	1	1	3	1	0
Florentino	1.000	1	2	1	0	0
Garciaparra	.947	3	10	8	1	2
Manzella	1.000	5	4	5	0	2
Sutil	.943	72	128	201	20	66

Outfield	PCT	G	PO	A	E	DP
Affronti	—	1	0	0	0	0
Cook	.962	64	125	2	5	0
Gaston	.993	123	261	16	2	5
Hernandez	—	1	0	0	0	0
Martinez	.949	42	72	3	4	0
Parejo	.962	36	73	2	3	1
Shuck	.982	95	157	5	3	2
Steele	1.000	61	145	3	0	0
Van Ostrand	1.000	25	29	3	0	0

LANCASTER JETHAWKS   HIGH CLASS A
CALIFORNIA LEAGUE

Batting	B-T	HT	WT	DOB	AVG	vLH	vRH	G	AB	R	H	2B	3B	HR	RBI	BB	HBP	SH	SF	SO	SB	CS	SLG	OBP
Altuve, Jose	R-R	5-5	148	5-6-90	.276	.308	.267	31	116	18	32	5	2	4	22	9	1	1	0	17	3	4	.457	.333
Austin, Jay	L-L	5-11	170	8-10-90	.261	.220	.277	131	532	83	139	25	13	10	59	39	5	4	4	122	54	20	.414	.314
Barnes, Brandon	R-R	6-2	210	5-15-86	.269	.272	.268	126	491	81	132	31	5	27	80	37	5	4	1	122	14	3	.517	.326
Butera, Barry	L-R	5-11	175	6-5-87	.264	.290	.253	32	110	8	29	4	2	2	20	4	0	2	2	27	0	5	.391	.284
Cartwright, Albert	R-R	5-10	180	10-31-87	.319	.283	.335	92	354	72	113	26	13	10	48	33	3	2	1	80	24	12	.551	.381
Comadena, Jordan	R-R	5-10	210	11-16-85	.209	.333	.143	20	43	8	9	2	0	0	5	7	5	2	1	11	2	1	.256	.375
Contreras, Rayner	R-R	6-0	150	9-21-86	.277	.256	.290	28	101	12	28	3	0	0	9	4	0	0	0	25	1	2	.307	.305
Cruz, Lee	R-R	6-2	190	6-13-83	.354	.371	.348	67	274	49	97	21	2	15	58	10	4	0	4	44	5	4	.609	.380
Curtis, John	L-R	6-2	210	11-22-84	.262	.250	.265	51	183	18	48	8	0	2	18	17	1	0	0	42	0	1	.339	.328
Florentino, Jhon	R-R	6-0	155	8-22-83	.235	.000	.286	4	17	1	4	0	0	1	3	0	0	0	0	6	0	0	.412	.235
Flores, David	R-R	6-2	220	10-13-86	.269	.243	.278	115	424	67	114	24	1	14	57	22	15	0	6	66	3	2	.429	.323
Flores, Josh	R-R	6-0	200	11-18-85	.220	.167	.239	35	91	18	20	3	0	1	2	12	0	0	0	23	8	1	.286	.311
Garcia, Rene	R-R	6-1	172	3-21-90	.053	.000	.067	5	19	2	1	1	0	0	1	0	0	0	0	4	0	0	.105	.053
Hernandez, Federico	B-R	6-0	170	2-9-88	.267	.218	.292	85	296	34	79	15	4	8	46	11	2	1	4	54	1	3	.426	.294
Lane, Bryce	R-R	6-0	190	8-24-89	.356	.429	.342	15	45	6	16	4	1	1	10	8	1	2	0	8	0	3	.556	.463

	B-T	HT	WT	DOB	AVG	vLH	vRH	G	AB	R	H	2B	3B	HR	RBI	BB	HBP	SH	SF	SO	SB	CS	SLG	OBP
Ori, Mark	L-R	6-4	225	12-16-83	.284	.216	.305	113	412	47	117	26	2	4	52	29	6	1	0	69	2	2	.386	.340
Parejo, Freddy	R-R	6-2	193	10-16-84	.308	.258	.332	75	286	38	88	12	2	3	32	19	3	2	4	52	6	4	.395	.353
Pellegrini, Brian	R-R	6-1	240	10-3-84	.283	.273	.286	53	205	40	58	10	0	16	45	27	5	0	2	45	1	1	.566	.377
Rosario, Ebert	R-R	6-3	165	5-27-87	.246	.299	.210	48	167	16	41	12	0	1	17	5	1	0	2	31	0	0	.335	.269
Simunic, Andy	R-R	6-0	170	8-7-85	.318	.322	.316	59	214	45	68	17	3	2	33	27	3	1	1	56	6	0	.453	.400
Villar, Jonathan	B-R	6-0	180	5-2-91	.225	.259	.216	32	129	18	29	6	2	3	19	12	1	0	1	50	7	2	.372	.294
Wikoff, Brandon	L-R	5-9	170	4-5-88	.257	.282	.246	113	374	40	96	3	0	0	27	31	2	17	2	42	1	3	.265	.315

Pitching	B-T	HT	WT	DOB	W	L	ERA	G	GS	CG	SV	IP	H	R	ER	HR	BB	SO	AVG	vLH	vRH	K/9	BB/9
Berner, David	L-L	6-2	205	8-16-87	5	5	2.96	50	0	0	12	67	68	27	22	4	22	62	.265	.190	.316	8.33	2.96
Carpenter, David	R-R	6-2	200	7-15-85	1	1	3.52	6	0	0	0	8	8	4	3	0	4	8	.267	.308	.235	9.39	4.70
Cespedes, Leandro	R-R	5-11	160	4-19-87	2	7	6.94	32	14	0	0	96	122	83	74	15	45	89	.309	.296	.320	8.34	4.22
Donovan, Robby	R-R	6-5	230	4-24-88	2	2	5.73	8	0	0	0	38	46	24	24	5	23	33	.309	.400	.263	7.88	5.50
Duncan, David	L-L	6-9	230	6-1-86	0	3	7.84	7	4	0	0	21	27	19	18	4	7	16	.318	.267	.345	6.97	3.05
Dydalewicz, Brad	L-L	6-1	180	3-24-90	1	6	11.39	11	11	0	0	36	52	50	46	6	26	22	.347	.393	.315	5.45	6.44
Godfrey, Kyle	R-R	6-4	200	2-6-86	3	5	3.36	48	0	0	1	67	59	37	25	3	43	43	.238	.208	.261	5.78	5.78
Greenwalt, Kyle	R-R	6-0	200	9-29-88	8	7	5.93	27	27	1	0	137	191	111	90	14	42	90	.332	.321	.341	5.93	2.77
Keuchel, Dallas	L-L	6-3	200	1-1-88	5	8	3.36	19	18	3	0	121	129	58	45	10	25	97	.273	.318	.247	7.23	1.86
Modica, Mike	L-L	6-0	175	12-16-86	4	5	5.10	37	2	0	2	60	79	42	34	7	21	32	.317	.346	.304	4.80	3.15
Mowdy, Ashton	R-R	6-0	185	6-21-86	2	3	4.91	38	0	0	0	73	81	51	40	9	41	57	.278	.282	.275	7.00	5.03
Schurz, Mike	R-R	6-2	205	9-12-86	0	1	10.69	12	0	0	0	16	22	20	19	3	15	15	.314	.324	.303	8.44	8.44
Seaton, Ross	L-R	6-4	213	9-18-89	6	13	6.64	28	28	0	0	146	198	126	108	22	45	85	.327	.328	.326	5.23	2.77
Trinidad, Jose	R-R	5-11	150	7-13-87	0	1	6.97	13	0	0	1	21	28	17	16	1	10	12	.329	.314	.340	5.23	4.35
Urckfitz, Pat	L-L	6-1	190	7-21-88	5	9	4.13	35	12	0	0	105	115	55	48	9	32	103	.290	.336	.272	8.86	2.75
Wabick, Brian	R-R	6-0	180	8-3-87	3	5	5.18	43	0	0	3	64	73	38	37	10	24	43	.289	.279	.296	6.02	3.36
Walker, Edwin	R-L	6-3	205	10-26-83	0	1	4.63	26	1	0	2	47	40	27	24	5	24	50	.237	.138	.288	9.64	4.63
Wolf, Shane	L-L	6-3	225	9-10-86	7	4	4.72	30	15	0	0	109	137	64	57	14	26	71	.308	.277	.325	5.88	2.15

Fielding

Catcher	PCT	G	PO	A	E	DP	PB
Comadena	.991	20	98	7	1	0	1
Curtis	.985	47	343	40	6	6	4
Garcia	.951	5	34	5	2	0	1
Hernandez	.989	77	455	63	6	4	15

First Base	PCT	G	PO	A	E	DP
Cruz	1.000	3	25	4	0	3
Flores	.990	20	189	13	2	12
Hernandez	1.000	2	2	0	0	1
Ori	.989	102	908	61	11	96
Pellegrini	.990	22	190	15	2	13

Second Base	PCT	G	PO	A	E	DP
Altuve	.985	26	49	83	2	20

	PCT	G	PO	A	E	DP
Butera	.981	19	40	64	2	14
Cartwright	.954	82	165	254	20	63
Contreras	.944	3	6	11	1	0
Simunic	1.000	5	6	9	0	0
Wikoff	.952	10	18	22	2	5

Third Base	PCT	G	PO	A	E	DP
Altuve	1.000	1	3	2	0	0
Florentino	.857	4	1	5	1	0
Flores	.938	88	59	182	16	13
Rosario	.904	29	10	56	7	2
Simunic	.931	22	12	69	6	9

Shortstop	PCT	G	PO	A	E	DP
Butera	.894	11	17	25	5	4

	PCT	G	PO	A	E	DP
Rosario	—	1	0	0	0	
Simunic	.750	1	3	0	1	0
Villar	.913	31	49	97	14	22
Wikoff	.979	100	163	313	10	67

Outfield	PCT	G	PO	A	E	DP
Austin	.983	128	270	12	5	3
Barnes	.969	122	234	19	8	4
Cruz	1.000	33	38	1	0	0
Flores	1.000	24	29	4	0	0
Lane	.885	15	20	3	3	0
Parejo	.960	66	115	6	5	0
Pellegrini	1.000	12	15	3	0	0
Simunic	1.000	32	45	4	0	0

LEXINGTON LEGENDS   LOW CLASS A
SOUTH ATLANTIC LEAGUE

Batting	B-T	HT	WT	DOB	AVG	vLH	vRH	G	AB	R	H	2B	3B	HR	RBI	BB	HBP	SH	SF	SO	SB	CS	SLG	OBP
Altuve, Jose	R-R	5-5	148	5-6-90	.308	.311	.307	94	393	75	121	15	3	11	45	33	2	5	1	49	39	14	.445	.364
Arrendell, Miguel	L-R	6-0	165	3-26-88	.228	.234	.227	78	241	30	55	9	1	3	25	34	2	3	2	56	13	4	.311	.326
Bray, Aaron	R-L	6-0	180	7-4-87	.245	.273	.237	94	319	32	78	12	5	0	41	34	3	2	2	74	3	3	.313	.321
Butera, Barry	L-R	5-11	175	6-5-87	.171	.400	.080	12	35	4	6	3	0	0	2	5	2	1	0	12	1	0	.257	.310
Comadena, Jordan	R-R	5-10	210	11-16-85	.113	.231	.075	20	53	5	6	1	1	1	5	2	2	1	0	8	0	0	.226	.175
Fixler, Jon	R-R	6-1	205	6-13-86	.203	.143	.222	20	59	6	12	3	0	1	8	8	2	0	1	16	0	0	.305	.314
Garcia, Rene	R-R	6-1	172	3-21-90	.262	.233	.271	84	309	20	81	10	1	2	35	16	3	1	4	35	5	2	.320	.301
Goebbert, Jake	L-L	6-0	200	9-24-87	.291	.258	.301	135	519	91	151	48	1	10	98	52	11	2	7	78	14	4	.445	.363
Heath, Ben	R-R	6-2	220	10-7-88	.290	.167	.316	20	69	9	20	2	2	4	13	11	3	0	1	17	0	1	.551	.405
Hinze, Kody	R-R	6-0	225	7-29-87	.277	.228	.296	124	458	69	127	29	0	19	97	66	6	3		128	1	4	.455	.385
Hogue, Grant	R-R	6-1	190	6-26-86	.285	.255	.295	117	400	65	114	10	3	0	34	26	18	9	1	58	29	16	.325	.355
Kemp, Brian	R-R	5-9	180	9-2-88	.226	.234	.224	61	190	21	43	8	0	0	14	19	8	2	0	22	8	2	.268	.323
Martinez, J.D.	R-R	6-3	175	8-21-87	.362	.341	.369	88	348	83	126	31	3	15	64	33	11	0	1	55	3	0	.598	.433
Meyer, Jonathan	R-R	6-1	195	11-1-90	.245	.310	.220	121	461	36	113	25	1	2	49	37	3	4	2	108	4	7	.317	.304
Mier, Jiovanni	R-R	6-2	175	8-26-90	.235	.238	.235	131	493	83	116	31	1	2	53	63	5	3	9	107	15	7	.314	.323
Paredes, Jimmy	B-R	6-1	178	11-25-88	.299	.306	.297	34	147	24	44	10	1	3	17	7	0	0	0	25	14	1	.442	.331
2-team total (99 Charleston, SC)					.287	—	—	133	551	83	158	34	7	8	65	25	2	5	5	107	50	11	.417	.317
Pena, Roberto	R-R	6-0	180	6-8-92	.188	.250	.125	4	16	1	3	1	0	0	1	0	0	0	0	4	0	1	.250	.188
Simunic, Andy	R-R	6-0	170	8-7-85	.246	.171	.288	39	114	23	28	4	0	1	10	18	1	1	0	21	11	1	.307	.353
Tello, Renzo	R-R	6-1	155	6-30-87	.244	.250	.242	34	123	13	30	11	0	1	15	2	3	1	2	32	1	2	.358	.269
Williams, Bubby	R-R	6-0	190	3-13-89	.147	.250	.115	12	34	1	5	2	0	0	4	0	0	0	0	8	0	0	.206	.147

Pitching	B-T	HT	WT	DOB	W	L	ERA	G	GS	CG	SV	IP	H	R	ER	HR	BB	SO	AVG	vLH	vRH	K/9	BB/9
Alvino, Wander	R-R	5-11	159	2-10-87	5	4	3.00	46	0	0	1	87	85	33	29	7	27	73	.258	.248	.263	7.55	2.79
Bushue, Tanner	R-R	6-4	180	6-20-91	7	8	4.11	25	25	0	0	134	129	72	61	18	48	114	.256	.264	.252	7.68	3.23
Cisnero, Jose	R-R	6-3	185	4-11-89	8	6	3.65	26	26	0	0	133	106	69	54	11	65	121	.221	.199	.235	8.53	4.40
Clark, Kirk	R-R	6-2	202	7-19-88	5	2	4.07	52	0	0	29	55	53	26	25	6	22	55	.266	.292	.252	8.95	3.58
Cruz, Luis	L-L	5-9	170	9-10-90	8	5	3.61	20	16	1	0	100	96	49	40	5	26	88	.253	.250	.254	7.95	2.35

Name	B-T	HT	WT	DOB	W	L	ERA	G	GS	CG	SV	IP	H	R	ER	HR	BB	SO	AVG	vLH	vRH	K/9	BB/9
Donovan, Robby	R-R	6-5	230	4-24-88	7	6	3.61	18	18	0	0	92	94	46	37	7	37	59	.269	.292	.256	5.75	3.61
Duncan, David	L-L	6-9	230	6-1-86	3	2	6.35	5	5	0	0	23	23	16	16	8	3	13	.261	.474	.203	5.16	1.19
Dydalewicz, Brad	L-L	6-1	180	3-24-90	1	4	6.46	18	6	0	0	47	51	42	34	6	34	32	.288	.167	.313	6.08	6.46
Grimmett, Zach	R-R	6-3	185	2-5-90	5	3	4.61	29	9	0	2	98	89	53	50	11	32	84	.243	.270	.227	7.74	2.95
Leon, Arcenio	R-R	6-1	162	9-22-86	2	2	2.33	26	0	0	4	54	40	22	14	0	23	60	.201	.273	.165	10.00	3.83
Minaya, Juan	R-R	6-4	185	9-18-90	4	12	4.79	26	26	0	0	128	111	80	68	7	73	96	.236	.220	.244	6.77	5.15
Modica, Mike	L-L	6-0	175	12-16-86	0	1	3.00	3	0	0	0	6	5	2	2	0	1	3	.250	.143	.308	4.50	1.50
Pettus, Nate	R-R	6-1	200	10-9-88	1	0	6.75	2	0	0	0	4	4	3	3	0	1	5	.250	.143	.333	11.25	2.25
Pitkin, Colton	R-L	6-3	210	8-10-89	3	4	5.05	39	2	0	1	73	93	49	41	4	27	46	.307	.291	.313	5.67	3.33
Ramirez, Yordany	R-R	6-1	190	7-31-84	0	0	4.76	5	0	0	0	6	6	3	3	0	5	7	.261	.444	.143	11.12	7.94
Sarisky, Dan	R-R	6-1	175	5-25-88	3	0	4.62	21	0	0	0	25	39	16	13	2	10	20	.364	.400	.339	7.11	3.55
Schurz, Mike	R-R	6-2	205	9-12-86	1	4	6.65	26	0	0	2	45	54	34	33	10	24	46	.300	.455	.211	9.27	4.84
Stines, Brenden	R-R	6-2	190	1-12-87	2	0	3.08	14	0	0	2	26	21	13	9	4	15	19	.223	.281	.194	6.49	5.13
Trinidad, Jose	R-R	5-11	150	7-13-87	5	2	2.57	30	0	0	0	63	53	25	18	3	13	48	.227	.275	.203	6.86	1.86
Walker, Brandt	R-R	6-1	190	11-9-87	1	3	10.25	8	6	0	0	26	31	33	30	3	20	16	.290	.378	.226	5.47	6.84

Fielding

Catcher	PCT	G	PO	A	E	DP	PB
Comadena	1.000	20	106	7	0	0	3
Fixler	.980	18	132	16	3	0	3
Garcia	.979	84	604	80	15	5	7
Heath	.972	16	95	11	3	2	2
Pena	1.000	4	27	6	0	0	1
Williams	.986	10	61	7	1	0	2

First Base	PCT	G	PO	A	E	DP
Bray	.989	59	494	29	6	61
Hinze	.992	80	689	53	6	60
Simunic	1.000	4	29	2	0	3

Second Base	PCT	G	PO	A	E	DP
Altuve	.973	91	167	232	11	57

	PCT	G	PO	A	E	DP
Arrendell	.944	18	27	41	4	12
Paredes	.947	34	61	99	9	20
Simunic	1.000	1	1	0	0	0

Third Base	PCT	G	PO	A	E	DP
Altuve	—	1	0	0	0	0
Arrendell	.765	10	3	10	4	0
Bray	.882	5	4	11	2	1
Butera	1.000	2	0	4	0	0
Meyer	.914	119	89	220	29	21
Simunic	.964	8	5	22	1	0

Shortstop	PCT	G	PO	A	E	DP
Arrendell	.917	13	16	28	4	10
Butera	—	1	0	0	0	0

	PCT	G	PO	A	E	DP
Mier	.943	129	199	359	34	80
Simunic	1.000	3	3	5	0	0

Outfield	PCT	G	PO	A	E	DP
Arrendell	1.000	1	1	0	0	0
Bray	1.000	2	5	1	0	1
Goebbert	.983	129	226	10	4	2
Hogue	.972	116	273	9	8	4
Kemp	.988	60	72	13	1	1
Martinez	.976	65	114	9	3	0
Simunic	1.000	24	40	1	0	0
Tello	.983	34	58	1	1	0

TRI-CITY VALLEYCATS   SHORT-SEASON

NEW YORK-PENN LEAGUE

Batting	B-T	HT	WT	DOB	AVG	vLH	vRH	G	AB	R	H	2B	3B	HR	RBI	BB	HBP	SH	SF	SO	SB	CS	SLG	OBP
Adamson, Daniel	R-R	5-11	210	9-15-87	.262	.214	.276	69	252	33	66	11	4	9	35	27	8	0	1	79	11	4	.444	.351
Afenir, Buck	R-R	6-1	205	5-3-87	.247	.188	.283	28	85	6	21	4	0	0	10	4	2	1	1	22	0	0	.294	.293
Almonte, Frank	R-R	6-2	190	1-24-89	.188	.278	.152	21	64	10	12	3	0	2	7	4	1	1	2	23	0	0	.328	.239
Bailey, Adam	L-L	6-1	195	3-6-88	.235	.250	.232	66	234	20	55	15	1	4	33	13	0	2	2	51	3	2	.359	.273
Burnett, Tyler	L-R	6-0	205	5-9-89	.250	.228	.256	71	260	39	65	17	1	6	31	45	3	1	3	56	6	6	.392	.363
Figueroa, Oscar	R-R	5-11	154	1-10-88	.200	.167	.211	40	120	11	24	2	0	1	10	14	1	6	1	21	1	1	.242	.287
Healey, Jacke	R-R	6-2	180	6-26-88	.170	.179	.167	44	141	15	24	4	2	5	21	7	1	2	3	44	0	1	.333	.211
Heath, Ben	R-R	6-2	220	10-7-88	.248	.258	.245	37	129	20	32	9	0	6	21	20	5	0	2	36	1	0	.457	.365
Hernandez, Enrique	R-R	5-11	170	8-24-91	.280	.267	.285	60	246	31	69	18	1	3	33	14	2	1	2	35	3	0	.398	.322
Infante, Wilton	R-R	6-1	175	8-11-87	.230	.174	.248	54	183	24	42	5	3	1	10	15	1	5	1	41	9	4	.306	.290
Kvasnicka, Mike	R-R	6-2	200	1-13-87	.234	.206	.244	68	261	31	61	10	1	5	36	27	1	0	3	48	2	1	.337	.305
McCurdy, Ryan	R-R	5-10	175	12-28-87	.150	.400	.067	12	20	3	3	2	0	1	2	3	2	0	0	2	0	0	.250	.320
Nash, Telvin	R-R	6-1	230	2-20-91	.308	.500	.222	4	13	2	4	1	1	1	1	0	0	0	0	7	0	1	.769	.308
Nidiffer, Marcus	R-R	6-2	200	1-13-87	.250	.263	.246	21	80	13	20	1	1	3	12	5	4	1	0	11	3	0	.425	.326
Orloff, Ben	R-R	5-11	170	4-26-87	.307	.340	.297	63	238	52	73	4	0	0	16	34	6	6	1	19	23	5	.324	.405
Stanley, Nick	L-R	6-2	195	5-12-87	.164	.222	.155	24	67	4	11	1	0	0	3	7	0	0	0	10	1	0	.179	.253
Tello, Renzo	R-R	6-1	155	6-30-87	.213	.154	.235	13	47	5	10	2	0	1	5	5	0	0	0	10	1	1	.319	.288
Wallace, Chris	R-R	6-0	205	4-27-88	.250	.385	.218	20	68	10	17	2	0	2	8	7	1	2	0	12	1	0	.368	.329
Wates, Austin	R-R	6-1	175	9-2-88	.316	.250	.333	12	38	11	12	2	1	3	6	4	0	0	0	9	6	0	.500	.447

Pitching	B-T	HT	WT	DOB	W	L	ERA	G	GS	CG	SV	IP	H	R	ER	HR	BB	SO	AVG	vLH	vRH	K/9	BB/9
Belliard, Joan	R-R	6-2	185	3-3-89	3	3	3.72	22	0	0	0	36	32	16	15	5	11	36	.232	.204	.247	8.92	2.72
Blankenship, Travis	L-L	6-1	185	10-16-87	2	1	2.35	24	0	0	0	31	24	12	8	2	18	23	.224	.157	.286	6.75	5.28
Blazek, Chris	L-L	6-0	195	3-2-84	2	1	2.77	11	1	0	0	13	10	4	4	0	8	20	.213	.294	.167	13.85	5.54
Buchanan, Jake	R-R	6-0	200	9-24-89	4	5	4.28	14	14	0	0	61	69	32	29	3	11	42	.286	.287	.287	6.20	1.62
Castillo, Jeiler	R-R	6-0	155	10-26-87	0	0	3.18	3	0	0	0	6	7	3	2	1	3	6	.292	.333	.267	9.53	4.76
Champion, Adam	L-L	6-7	230	9-22-87	0	2	4.26	24	0	0	0	25	27	14	12	2	13	21	.273	.278	.270	7.46	4.62
Chowning, Jason	R-R	6-2	178	10-17-87	2	2	3.22	16	0	0	0	22	18	8	8	2	9	23	.220	.229	.213	9.27	3.63
Doran, Bobby	R-R	6-6	235	3-21-89	4	5	4.67	15	15	0	0	71	85	42	37	4	9	50	.297	.256	.333	6.31	1.14
Frawley, John	R-R	6-2	185	11-29-85	0	0	3.12	7	0	0	0	9	8	4	3	1	2	8	.235	.231	.238	8.31	2.08
Gouvea, Murillo	R-R	6-2	200	9-15-88	1	3	6.30	18	4	0	0	40	42	28	28	5	21	56	.278	.300	.267	12.60	4.72
Martinez, David	R-R	6-2	180	8-4-87	5	2	3.02	17	10	0	0	66	72	29	22	5	11	57	.282	.287	.287	7.81	1.51
Ness, Michael	R-R	6-4	210	10-20-87	2	2	3.23	24	0	0	0	31	30	13	11	3	9	28	.250	.319	.205	8.22	2.64
Quevedo, Carlos	R-R	6-1	222	9-30-89	7	3	3.06	15	15	0	0	85	76	35	29	7	8	55	.245	.262	.231	5.80	0.84
Robinson, Andrew	R-R	6-1	185	2-13-88	3	2	2.83	20	0	0	0	54	50	20	17	2	10	46	.254	.320	.213	7.67	1.67
Shirley, Tommy	R-L	6-5	220	11-11-88	0	0	0.00	5	5	0	0	17	9	1	0	0	10	16	.158	.182	.152	14.82	5.29
Sogard, Alex	L-L	6-3	215	7-25-87	1	2	3.51	22	3	0	0	41	40	20	16	4	12	36	.263	.224	.282	7.90	2.63
Stines, Brenden	R-R	6-2	190	1-12-87	0	1	4.91	5	0	0	0	7	12	4	4	1	7	7	.444	.400	.471	8.59	8.59
Streilein, Brian	R-R	6-4	205	11-3-88	0	0	0.00	1	0	0	0	1	0	0	0	0	1	1	.000	.000	.000	9.00	9.00
Walker, Brandt	R-R	6-1	190	11-9-87	2	2	2.86	21	0	0	0	28	28	10	9	2	23	32	.275	.243	.292	10.16	7.31

Fielding

Catcher	PCT	G	PO	A	E	DP	PB
Afenir	.969	19	142	16	5	1	1
Heath	.992	30	224	25	2	2	8
Kvasnicka	1.000	5	41	7	0	0	4
McCurdy	.965	14	51	4	2	0	3
Wallace	.994	18	137	26	1	3	5

First Base	PCT	G	PO	A	E	DP
Burnett	.994	36	336	17	2	33
Figueroa	1.000	5	34	3	0	3
Nidiffer	.990	20	186	10	2	20
Stanley	.993	18	125	18	1	14

Second Base	PCT	G	PO	A	E	DP
Figueroa	1.000	1	0	1	0	0
Hernandez	.973	52	111	144	7	33
Orloff	.977	23	55	70	3	18

Third Base	PCT	G	PO	A	E	DP
Burnett	.929	29	12	57	6	7
Figueroa	.850	6	3	14	3	0
Kvasnicka	.866	25	13	45	9	3
Orloff	.953	15	13	28	2	4

Shortstop	PCT	G	PO	A	E	DP
Figueroa	.955	26	37	68	5	14

	PCT	G	PO	A	E	DP
Healey	.964	37	57	106	6	26
Orloff	.959	16	21	50	3	12
Outfield						
Adamson	.969	65	121	6	4	2
Almonte	1.000	11	12	0	0	0
Bailey	1.000	60	76	7	0	1
Infante	.980	51	94	3	2	2
Kvasnicka	.977	30	39	4	1	2
Nash	1.000	1	1	0	0	0
Tello	1.000	12	20	3	0	0
Wates	1.000	4	6	0	0	0

GREENEVILLE ASTROS — ROOKIE
APPALACHIAN LEAGUE

Batting	B-T	HT	WT	DOB	AVG	vLH	vRH	G	AB	R	H	2B	3B	HR	RBI	BB	HBP	SH	SF	SO	SB	CS	SLG	OBP
DeShields, Delino	R-R	5-9	188	8-16-92	.313	.344	.286	16	67	11	21	6	1	0	8	5	0	0	1	18	5	1	.433	.356
Feliz, Pedro	B-R	6-0	150	12-5-90	.200	.167	.220	28	95	6	19	3	1	0	3	9	0	2	1	30	3	1	.253	.267
Garcia, Ricardo	R-R	5-9	142	1-20-89	.246	.254	.241	52	175	17	43	8	1	0	18	17	2	5	1	31	10	3	.303	.318
Heredia, Ricardo	R-R	6-2	170	3-1-89	.155	.121	.172	37	97	6	15	1	1	0	8	2	1	2	1	21	0	1	.186	.178
Humphrey, Ryan	R-R	6-0	190	9-19-88	.210	.176	.227	36	100	10	21	1	1	1	7	4	1	2	0	32	4	1	.270	.248
King, Emilio	R-R	6-1	180	8-17-89	.210	.208	.211	63	205	27	43	13	1	1	10	16	6	2	1	65	1	3	.298	.285
Lane, Bryce	R-R	6-0	190	8-24-89	.202	.182	.214	37	89	8	18	1	0	0	7	4	0	2	2	22	4	2	.213	.232
Lovett, Chris	R-R	6-0	180	12-21-88	.157	.192	.120	21	51	9	8	3	0	1	5	5	1	1	1	12	1	2	.275	.241
McCurdy, Ryan	R-R	5-10	175	12-28-87	.143	.333	.000	6	7	1	1	0	0	0	0	1	1	1	0	1	0	0	.143	.333
Medrano, Jhonny	R-R	6-1	156	9-12-87	.295	.265	.314	44	173	29	51	13	2	7	24	11	2	0	1	49	8	1	.514	.342
Merritt, Jonathan	R-R	5-8	160	1-13-88	.248	.207	.275	58	202	34	50	9	7	4	22	31	9	1	3	56	12	5	.421	.367
Mojica, Carlos	R-R	6-0	190	6-7-88	.184	.250	.162	19	49	2	9	3	0	0	3	2	1	1	0	19	0	0	.245	.231
Nash, Telvin	R-R	6-1	230	2-20-91	.265	.300	.242	57	200	30	53	12	1	12	39	25	1	0	1	64	1	1	.515	.348
Nidiffer, Marcus	R-R	6-2	200	1-13-87	.303	.267	.324	48	165	27	50	10	2	11	24	13	14	0	4	48	6	2	.580	.393
Pena, Roberto	B-R	6-0	180	6-8-92	.191	.185	.200	12	47	4	9	1	0	0	5	1	1	0	0	10	0	0	.213	.224
Rodriguez, Hector	R-R	5-11	150	8-8-89	.303	.362	.264	43	119	15	36	6	1	0	9	1	1	2	0	25	2	3	.370	.314
Valenzuela, Rafael	L-R	6-1	175	10-20-87	.293	.245	.329	34	123	18	36	12	1	3	16	6	0	0	2	24	2	0	.480	.321
Wallace, Chris	R-R	6-0	190	4-27-88	.310	.361	.282	47	171	29	53	6	3	8	32	17	6	0	1	44	3	2	.520	.390
Williams, Bubby	R-R	6-0	190	3-13-89	.244	.143	.281	25	78	14	19	3	0	5	12	1	2	0	0	18	0	0	.474	.272

Pitching	B-T	HT	WT	DOB	W	L	ERA	G	GS	CG	SV	IP	H	R	ER	HR	BB	SO	AVG	vLH	vRH	K/9	BB/9
Alaniz, R.J.	R-R	6-4	175	6-14-91	6	4	4.21	12	12	0	0	58	65	32	27	5	10	42	.280	.303	.263	6.55	1.56
Batista, Ricardo	L-L	6-2	170	8-19-91	0	5	6.29	12	12	0	0	49	64	46	34	5	23	35	.318	.298	.325	6.47	4.25
Bullock, Garrett	L-L	6-3	195	6-9-86	3	1	1.26	21	0	0	2	43	39	10	6	0	14	40	.245	.238	.250	8.37	2.93
Castillo, Jeiler	R-R	6-0	155	10-26-87	3	3	4.21	18	2	0	1	36	40	19	17	3	9	21	.280	.256	.288	5.20	2.23
Cole, Ryan	R-R	5-11	205	12-12-87	3	3	2.83	22	0	0	2	35	30	15	11	2	8	28	.222	.292	.184	7.20	2.06
Cotton, Jamaine	R-R	6-2	185	9-27-90	0	1	8.36	13	0	0	0	14	28	21	13	3	7	15	.412	.483	.359	9.64	4.50
Foltynewicz, Mike	R-R	6-4	200	10-7-91	0	3	4.03	12	12	0	0	45	46	24	20	3	15	39	.272	.323	.240	7.86	3.02
Frawley, John	R-R	6-2	185	11-29-85	1	0	2.61	5	0	0	0	10	13	3	3	0	1	17	.302	.278	.320	14.81	0.87
Garcia, Gabriel	L-L	5-11	140	5-11-89	0	1	3.86	6	4	0	0	16	19	7	7	2	3	17	.284	.294	.280	9.37	1.65
Gerrish, Paul	R-R	6-4	215	7-11-86	2	2	4.56	14	0	0	1	24	32	19	12	0	4	17	.340	.240	.377	6.46	1.52
Gonzalez, Angel	L-L	6-0	160	8-12-88	1	3	7.22	8	5	0	0	29	32	24	23	3	12	22	.286	.278	.287	6.91	3.77
Hagen, B.J.	R-R	6-3	230	5-28-86	1	0	9.90	7	0	0	0	10	19	11	11	1	0	5	.388	.333	.412	4.50	0.00
Harper, Justin	R-R	6-4	185	6-10-88	0	0	5.00	11	0	0	0	18	19	15	10	0	13	16	.268	.346	.222	8.00	6.50
Lucati, Andrea	R-R	6-3	247	1-17-90	0	0	3.00	2	0	0	0	3	5	2	1	0	2	1	.417	.400	.429	3.00	6.00
Quezada, Euris	R-R	6-6	210	4-6-89	3	3	5.83	12	12	0	0	63	81	44	41	8	12	38	.313	.391	.250	5.40	1.71
Quintero, Rodney	R-R	6-2	215	11-8-90	0	0	2.45	3	0	0	0	4	1	1	0	1	5	6	.375	.500	.333	14.73	12.27
Rorabaugh, Phil	R-R	6-0	185	10-5-86	1	1	4.91	21	0	0	1	29	38	20	16	6	7	12	.314	.333	.307	3.68	2.15
Smink, Travis	L-L	6-2	200	4-10-87	3	2	3.34	19	1	0	6	30	31	11	11	2	4	28	.272	.270	.273	8.49	1.21
Streilein, Brian	R-R	6-4	205	11-3-88	2	1	5.06	20	0	0	5	32	39	26	18	1	8	35	.293	.370	.253	9.84	2.25
Velasquez, Vincent	B-R	6-3	185	6-7-92	2	2	3.07	8	6	0	0	29	24	12	10	4	5	25	.216	.278	.187	7.67	1.53

Fielding

Catcher	PCT	G	PO	A	E	DP	PB
McCurdy	1.000	6	23	2	0	0	1
Mojica	.961	14	88	11	4	1	5
Pena	.990	12	81	15	1	2	4
Wallace	.987	30	210	19	3	2	1
Williams	.947	13	68	3	4	0	0

First Base	PCT	G	PO	A	E	DP
Garcia	1.000	1	3	0	0	0
Medrano	.945	11	49	3	3	5
Nidiffer	.990	47	395	22	4	34
Valenzuela	.988	22	154	7	2	23

Second Base	PCT	G	PO	A	E	DP
Feliz	.952	27	53	66	6	15
Garcia	.953	41	78	125	10	27
Lovett	.818	3	5	4	2	0

Third Base	PCT	G	PO	A	E	DP
Garcia	1.000	3	1	1	0	0
Lovett	1.000	12	5	5	0	0
Medrano	.930	21	12	54	5	3
Rodriguez	.923	29	21	39	5	3
Valenzuela	.961	17	13	36	2	1

Shortstop	PCT	G	PO	A	E	DP
Lovett	1.000	1	0	1	0	1

	PCT	G	PO	A	E	DP
Merritt	.924	56	77	178	21	29
Rodriguez	.983	13	19	39	1	13
Outfield						
DeShields	.935	15	28	1	2	0
Garcia	—	1	0	0	0	0
Heredia	1.000	31	27	1	0	0
Humphrey	1.000	33	53	2	0	2
King	.986	63	132	14	2	5
Lane	.964	34	53	1	2	0
Nash	.891	51	55	2	7	0
Rodriguez	—	1	0	0	0	0

GULF COAST LEAGUE

HOUSTON ASTROS

Batting	B-T	HT	WT	DOB	AVG	vLH	vRH	G	AB	R	H	2B	3B	HR	RBI	BB	HBP	SH	SF	SO	SB	CS	SLG	OBP
DeLome, Collin	L-R	6-2	195	12-18-85	.286	.500	.250	4	14	2	4	1	0	0	1	1	1	0	0	3	0	0	.357	.375
DeShields, Delino	R-R	5-9	188	8-16-92	.111	.000	.143	2	9	3	1	0	0	0	0	1	0	0	0	2	0	0	.111	.200
Ditthardt, Ryan	R-R	6-3	205	8-3-88	.274	.324	.257	42	135	18	37	6	1	1	12	9	10	0	0	23	0	1	.356	.364
Fernandez, Jose	R-R	6-1	170	5-20-93	.232	.250	.228	48	177	16	41	7	6	1	22	9	0	1	1	49	4	3	.356	.267
Genoves, Ernesto	R-R	5-11	203	6-4-91	.278	.357	.259	23	72	7	20	4	0	0	10	7	3	1	0	11	0	0	.333	.366
Lane, Bryce	R-R	6-0	190	8-24-89	.333	.286	.348	8	30	3	10	1	0	0	3	5	0	0	0	7	0	1	.367	.429
Magee, Josh	R-R	5-10	160	10-1-91	.227	.214	.231	46	176	21	40	4	2	1	18	13	2	4	1	35	7	4	.290	.286
Martone, Luca	B-R	5-8	150	10-21-92	.173	.154	.179	20	52	4	9	0	0	0	3	4	1	0	0	14	0	0	.173	.246
Maysonet, Edwin	R-R	6-1	195	10-17-81	.176	.200	.167	4	17	2	3	2	0	0	4	1	0	0	0	0	0	0	.294	.222
Monzon, Jose	R-R	6-0	170	12-30-91	.250	.280	.243	35	128	24	32	6	0	3	11	14	3	1	0	32	9	5	.367	.338
Moon, Chan	L-R	6-0	160	3-23-91	.215	.167	.232	33	93	15	20	2	0	0	6	19	0	0	0	36	6	5	.237	.348
Parra, Wilder	R-R	6-0	175	3-2-91	.127	.000	.167	18	55	4	7	2	0	1	4	0	2	1	0	16	0	0	.218	.158
Pellegrini, Brian	R-R	6-1	240	10-3-84	.333	.000	.333	3	9	1	3	1	0	0	1	2	0	0	0	2	0	0	.444	.455
Pena, Roberto	B-R	6-0	180	6-8-92	.256	.353	.230	23	78	5	20	4	1	0	11	5	0	1	2	10	0	0	.333	.294
Redinger, Kyle	R-R	6-3	205	12-19-91	.219	.294	.198	47	155	16	34	4	2	0	13	15	3	1	2	41	2	1	.271	.297
Sanchez, Ronald	L-R	5-10	180	8-9-91	.132	.105	.138	31	106	1	14	3	0	0	4	7	1	0	1	31	0	0	.160	.191
Scott, Jordan	L-R	6-2	180	9-22-91	.301	.387	.278	42	146	19	44	6	2	0	10	14	3	1	1	33	6	4	.370	.372
Shelton, Chris	R-R	6-0	215	6-26-80	.333	1.000	.250	3	9	1	3	0	0	0	2	2	0	0	0	2	0	0	.333	.455
Suniaga, Geber	R-R	5-11	160	6-17-91	.200	.200	.200	23	65	9	13	2	1	0	8	3	4	0	2	17	4	0	.262	.270
Valenzuela, Rafael	L-R	6-1	175	10-20-87	.275	.500	.233	16	51	10	14	5	2	1	7	6	1	1	0	6	2	1	.510	.362
Vallejo, Jose	B-R	6-0	200	9-11-86	.167	.000	.200	2	6	0	1	0	1	0	0	1	0	0	0	1	0	0	.500	.286
Vargas, Jose	R-R	6-0	200	4-30-91	.225	.289	.205	41	160	16	36	12	2	2	23	10	1	0	1	33	1	1	.363	.273
Wates, Austin	R-R	6-1	179	9-2-88	.000	.000	.000	1	3	1	0	0	0	0	0	1	0	0	0	2	0	0	.000	.250
Wright, Garen	R-R	6-3	230	12-25-90	.231	.207	.238	40	130	18	30	2	0	1	15	14	2	0	1	31	14	6	.269	.313

Pitching	B-T	HT	WT	DOB	W	L	ERA	G	GS	CG	SV	IP	H	R	ER	HR	BB	SO	AVG	vLH	vRH	K/9	BB/9
Bueno, Kristian	L-L	6-2	195	12-10-88	0	0	2.87	11	0	0	3	16	17	7	5	0	8	14	.298	.667	.278	8.04	4.60
Cedano, Enmanuel	R-R	6-2	194	12-28-88	1	0	4.50	14	0	0	0	18	7	11	9	1	13	18	.117	.364	.061	9.00	6.50
Del Rio, Danilo	R-R	5-11	179	9-28-90	1	7	5.65	11	11	2	0	57	72	46	36	4	13	37	.310	.393	.284	5.81	2.04
Diaz, Dayan	R-R	5-10	156	2-10-89	0	1	13.50	2	0	0	1	4	2	2	0	2	1		.500	.500	.500	6.75	13.50
Feliz, Rafael	R-R	6-0	180	9-21-89	0	0	9.82	13	0	0	0	15	17	19	16	1	20	6	.304	.385	.279	3.68	12.27
Gomez, Pedro	R-R	6-3	204	5-20-91	4	4	7.76	21	0	0	2	31	34	41	27	1	8	23	.362	.393	.355	6.61	2.30
Gonzalez, Angel	L-L	6-0	160	8-12-88	0	2	4.38	3	0	0	0	12	14	11	6	1	2	11	.269	.500	.260	8.03	1.46
Grills, Evan	L-L	6-4	205	6-13-92	0	2	8.76	6	4	0	0	12	20	14	12	0	7	15	.345	.600	.321	10.95	5.11
Hagen, B.J.	R-R	6-3	230	5-28-86	0	3	1.86	5	1	0	1	10	12	5	2	0	5	4	.316	.286	.333	3.72	4.66
Holley, Krishawn	R-R	6-0	195	2-8-92	0	0	0.00	1	0	0	0	1	1	0	0	0	0	1	.250	.000	.500	9.00	0.00
Jones, Mark	R-R	6-7	205	8-29-90	2	2	3.91	11	10	0	0	48	53	29	21	1	29	31	.290	.186	.321	5.77	5.40
Lucas, Austin	R-R	6-5	200	12-5-87	0	1	3.52	6	0	0	0	8	11	5	3	0	2	11	.333	.600	.286	12.91	2.35
Lucati, Andrea	R-R	6-3	247	1-17-90	1	1	8.44	5	0	0	0	5	8	5	5	0	5	1	.421	.667	.375	1.69	8.44
Meiners, Jeremiah	L-L	6-0	200	8-16-88	1	2	6.95	16	0	0	0	22	28	21	17	1	8	19	.295	.375	.287	7.77	3.27
Mojica, Juan	R-R	6-4	190	2-13-89	1	0	3.38	7	0	0	0	11	10	4	4	0	3	12	.238	.444	.182	10.13	2.53
Ordosgoitti, Luis	R-R	6-4	180	9-22-92	0	1	3.09	5	5	0	0	23	30	10	8	1	5	18	.309	.250	.318	6.94	1.93
Paul, Dieudone	L-L	6-2	187	9-28-87	2	0	1.60	13	0	0	2	34	29	11	6	1	15	39	.221	.438	.191	10.43	4.01
Pena, Kilby	L-L	6-0	170	11-25-92	0	1	18.90	6	0	0	0	3	3	8	7	0	7	3	.231	.000	.250	8.10	18.90
Perdomo, Jose	R-R	6-0	180	10-24-91	4	3	1.67	11	11	0	0	59	38	19	11	1	20	69	.172	.230	.150	10.47	3.03
Perez, Juri	R-R	5-11	148	8-8-90	1	0	5.40	6	0	0	0	8	8	5	5	2	4	4	.258	.000	.276	4.32	4.32
Pettus, Nate	R-R	6-0	200	10-9-88	0	0	0.00	5	0	0	0	1	0	0	0	0	2	4	.136	.300	.000	6.35	3.18
Ramirez, Francis	R-R	6-5	205	1-12-92	1	1	4.54	10	10	0	0	40	40	25	20	1	18	36	.256	.254	.254	8.17	4.08
Rivera, Raul	R-R	6-3	185	2-5-91	0	0	21.60	2	0	0	0	2	5	4	4	1	0	1	.500	.500	.500	5.40	0.00
Smith, Matison	R-R	6-0	185	6-26-88	1	3	1.59	19	1	0	4	34	32	10	6	0	6	21	.244	.271	.229	5.56	1.59
Valdez, Jose	R-R	6-4	185	1-22-83	0	0	0.00	4	0	0	0	4	2	0	0	0	0	4	.154	.000	.154	9.00	0.00

Fielding

Catcher	PCT	G	PO	A	E	DP	PB
Genoves	.972	23	150	22	5	3	6
Parra	.960	16	103	16	5	4	3
Pena	.984	22	156	25	3	1	5

First Base	PCT	G	PO	A	E	DP
Ditthardt	.968	28	203	9	7	13
Pellegrini	1.000	1	5	0	0	0
Redinger	1.000	1	16	2	0	2
Sanchez	.984	26	233	17	4	23
Shelton	1.000	3	16	1	0	1
Valenzuela	.975	4	39	0	1	3

Second Base	PCT	G	PO	A	E	DP
Magee	.944	42	89	98	11	24
Martone	.947	15	20	34	3	6
Maysonet	1.000	2	3	4	0	2
Vallejo	1.000	2	3	4	0	1

Third Base	PCT	G	PO	A	E	DP
Martone	.500	1	0	1	1	0
Moon	.855	19	12	41	9	1
Redinger	.906	35	27	69	10	4
Valenzuela	.815	9	5	17	5	2

Shortstop	PCT	G	PO	A	E	DP
Fernandez	.879	46	87	146	32	28

	PCT	G	PO	A	E	DP
Maysonet	1.000	2	5	11	0	3
Moon	.796	14	7	32	10	5

Outfield	PCT	G	PO	A	E	DP
DeLome	1.000	2	2	0	0	0
Ditthardt	.857	6	5	1	1	0
Lane	.913	8	21	0	2	1
Magee	—	1	0	0	0	0
Monzon	.961	35	72	2	3	0
Scott	1.000	38	60	3	0	1
Suniaga	1.000	11	8	0	0	0
Vargas	.877	41	66	5	10	0
Wright	.956	35	40	3	2	0

DSL ASTROS   ROOKIE

DOMINICAN SUMMER LEAGUE

Batting	B-T	HT	WT	DOB	AVG	vLH	vRH	G	AB	R	H	2B	3B	HR	RBI	BB	HBP	SH	SF	SO	SB	CS	SLG	OBP
Alcantara, Carlos	R-R	6-4	210	2-16-90	.250	.467	.212	38	100	7	25	4	0	0	5	19	4	0	2	39	2	3	.290	.384

	B-T	HT	WT	DOB	AVG	vLH	vRH	G	AB	R	H	2B	3B	HR	RBI	BB	HBP	SH	SF	SO	SB	CS	OBP	SLG
Angulo, Yoiner	R-R	6-1	175	10-7-91	.129	.000	.143	31	62	9	8	2	0	0	2	1	3	0	0	18	2	3	.161	.182
Ayarza, Max	B-R	6-0	160	3-11-92	.260	.200	.275	46	150	18	39	6	0	1	13	9	2	1	0	24	4	2	.320	.311
Campusano, Fredwin	R-R	5-11	170	10-8-91	.326	.545	.295	31	89	23	29	4	4	0	13	13	3	0	1	15	14	5	.461	.425
De La Rosa, Luis	B-R	6-1	162	1-2-92	.270	.262	.272	64	226	33	61	15	5	2	30	21	6	0	2	48	12	5	.407	.345
Diaz, Kenny	R-R	5-9	175	5-9-92	.198	.176	.202	40	116	11	23	3	0	0	7	16	2	1	1	17	2	1	.224	.304
Gonzalez, Mario	L-R	6-1	195	12-25-91	.262	.219	.273	60	164	17	43	5	1	0	17	27	4	0	3	30	2	3	.305	.374
Laguna, Mesac	R-R	6-2	185	1-12-92	.243	.222	.247	40	115	9	28	6	1	0	15	4	1	2	4	24	4	2	.313	.266
Lopez, Raymer	R-R	5-10	145	3-31-91	.250	.167	.270	57	156	26	39	4	1	1	12	24	4	3	3	28	13	4	.308	.358
Marte, Ydarqui	R-R	6-1	188	10-10-92	.240	.234	.241	61	217	31	52	10	1	2	26	16	3	0	0	28	9	5	.323	.301
Mejia, Yonathan	B-R	6-2	175	9-19-92	.235	.326	.213	59	221	20	52	12	3	2	27	12	3	0	1	43	4	2	.344	.283
Moronta, Cristian	R-R	5-10	185	12-5-89	.364	.200	.412	8	22	5	8	0	0	1	3	2	0	0	1	5	1	0	.500	.400
Perez, Rainier	R-R	6-1	185	8-19-90	.194	.125	.204	25	62	6	12	0	1	0	4	4	3	0	1	18	2	2	.226	.271
Polanco, Franny	R-R	6-1	185	12-20-91	.248	.211	.255	43	129	8	32	5	0	0	16	8	2	0	1	18	4	3	.287	.300
Rivera, Darwin	R-R	5-11	180	10-27-91	—	.000	.000	1	0	0	0	0	0	0	0	0	0	0	0	0	0	0	—	—
Sierra, Andru	B-R	5-9	168	11-13-91	.294	.364	.281	28	68	16	20	3	3	0	12	3	2	0	1	12	5	1	.426	.338
Solano, Jose	R-R	6-2	175	3-15-92	.276	.333	.266	56	181	23	50	11	1	2	20	10	5	0	2	30	9	3	.381	.338
Vizcaino, Kelvin	R-R	6-0	175	9-30-92	.191	.229	.180	47	157	22	30	9	2	3	15	18	0	0	2	37	7	1	.331	.271

Pitching	B-T	HT	WT	DOB	W	L	ERA	G	GS	CG	SV	IP	H	R	ER	HR	BB	SO	AVG	vLH	vRH	K/9	BB/9
Alayon, Leonardo	R-R	6-2	187	4-29-92	4	4	3.24	15	12	0	0	75	74	33	27	1	13	58	.256	.268	.251	6.96	1.56
Arias, Johan	R-R	6-0	170	1-1-92	0	2	5.68	14	0	0	1	19	16	16	12	0	14	7	.232	.167	.255	3.32	6.63
Baso, Xavier	R-R	6-0	190	1-12-91	7	3	1.33	16	0	0	3	41	34	9	6	0	15	34	.230	.279	.210	7.52	3.32
De Leon, Ambiorix	L-L	6-3	185	8-7-91	0	0	6.23	10	0	0	0	13	13	10	9	1	12	6	.255	.000	.265	4.15	8.31
De Leon, Elias	L-L	5-11	185	7-8-90	4	3	3.88	17	1	0	1	49	46	22	21	1	20	45	.258	.500	.253	8.32	3.70
Feliz, Andres	L-L	6-2	170	10-30-90	1	1	9.32	14	0	0	0	28	32	34	29	4	27	18	.283	.111	.298	5.79	8.68
Feliz, Michael	R-R	6-4	210	9-28-93	0	1	4.26	3	3	0	0	13	9	7	6	1	3	13	.196	.182	.200	9.24	2.13
Ferreira, Edgar	L-L	6-3	180	10-15-92	0	0	2.70	10	3	0	0	17	9	8	5	0	25	14	.167	.000	.170	7.56	13.50
Franco, Enderson	R-R	6-2	170	12-29-92	1	3	3.67	9	7	0	0	34	39	20	14	4	7	21	.285	.212	.308	5.50	1.83
Guduan, Reymin	L-L	6-4	185	3-16-92	1	2	11.95	15	4	0	0	20	38	34	27	0	31	19	.384	.250	.396	8.41	13.72
Gustave, Jandel	R-R	6-2	160	10-12-92	0	5	8.20	14	5	0	0	26	24	30	24	0	33	27	.245	.200	.270	9.23	11.28
Gutierrez, Rochi	R-R	6-2	187	4-9-92	0	0	2.41	13	0	0	1	19	11	7	5	0	10	16	.157	.200	.140	7.71	4.82
Iturralde, Roliner	R-R	5-11	167	11-23-90	2	3	4.14	15	5	0	3	50	55	27	23	2	13	36	.272	.290	.264	6.48	2.34
Martinez, Alexander	R-R	6-2	160	3-11-93	0	1	8.53	8	0	0	0	13	13	16	12	1	17	5	.289	.273	.294	3.55	12.08
Montero, Jose	R-R	6-4	190	1-22-93	1	3	2.59	13	13	0	0	56	47	22	16	0	24	48	.227	.140	.260	7.76	3.88
Perdomo, Yeudy	L-R	6-1	155	12-19-91	0	0	4.15	6	0	0	0	4	5	2	2	0	3	2	.313	.000	.357	4.15	6.23
Ramirez, Felix	R-R	6-5	150	7-12-90	1	2	8.18	15	2	0	0	11	15	12	10	1	10	10	.349	.231	.400	8.18	8.18
Rodriguez, Richard	R-R	6-4	185	3-4-90	2	1	2.00	5	5	0	0	18	14	5	4	0	5	16	.241	.500	.174	8.00	2.50
Tiburcio, Frederick	R-R	6-3	192	11-1-90	0	7	6.37	13	9	0	0	35	39	28	25	2	24	38	.275	.341	.248	9.68	6.11

Fielding

Catcher	PCT	G	PO	A	E	DP	PB
Diaz	.975	35	200	33	6	2	5
Moronta	1.000	6	42	12	0	0	1
Polanco	.978	38	224	40	6	2	10

First Base	PCT	G	PO	A	E	DP
Alcantara	.964	27	180	6	7	11
Gonzalez	.993	52	410	15	3	34
Laguna	1.000	2	3	2	0	0
Mejia	1.000	1	1	0	0	1
Perez	—	1	0	0	0	0
Polanco	.917	5	10	1	1	1

Second Base	PCT	G	PO	A	E	DP
Ayarza	—	1	0	0	0	0
Campusano	1.000	9	18	22	0	5
De La Rosa	1.000	2	4	3	0	0
Lopez	.958	8	11	12	1	2
Mejia	.921	23	37	45	7	10
Sierra	1.000	9	14	26	0	4
Solano	.936	30	49	54	7	12

Third Base	PCT	G	PO	A	E	DP
Campusano	.923	16	14	34	4	2
Diaz	.941	5	4	12	1	0
Gonzalez	1.000	7	6	9	0	0
Lopez	.925	20	17	32	4	3
Mejia	.902	29	30	62	10	6
Sierra	.667	1	1	3	2	0
Solano	.895	4	4	13	2	2

Shortstop	PCT	G	PO	A	E	DP
Ayarza	.933	40	49	91	10	7
Lopez	.988	25	27	57	1	10
Solano	.804	14	11	26	9	4

Outfield	PCT	G	PO	A	E	DP
Angulo	.906	22	27	2	3	0
Campusano	1.000	3	4	0	0	0
De La Rosa	.950	57	69	7	4	2
Gonzalez	—	1	0	0	0	0
Laguna	.974	27	35	2	1	0
Lopez	.917	5	10	1	1	1
Marte	.984	61	115	9	2	2
Moronta	—	1	0	0	0	0
Perez	.964	17	26	1	1	0
Sierra	1.000	4	4	1	0	0
Vizcaino	.982	29	52	4	1	1

Kansas City Royals

SEASON IN A SENTENCE: Another year, another last-place finish for the Royals, who have now finished last in the American League Central in five of the past seven seasons.

HIGH POINT: In a season that never had a winning streak of more than three games, it's hard to find a lot to get giddy about. When the Royals fired manager Trey Hillman after a 12-23 start and replaced him with Ned Yost, it didn't make a big difference in team's record but it did seem to restore some lost credibility to the post.

LOW POINT: Conversely, in a 95-loss season it's not hard to find a few down times. The team was never at .500 and fell as many as 29 games under at the end of September—and nearly 30 games out of the division lead—but the lowest moment had to be a 19-1 loss to the Twins on July 26. Ace Zack Greinke gave up eight runs in four innings of work, and the bullpen just threw fuel on the fire, while Francisco Liriano and two relievers held the Royals to five hits in front of 19,306 fans at Kauffman Stadium.

NOTABLE ROOKIES: The Royals had just four players make their major league debuts in 2010, and first baseman Kila Ka'aihue was the only notable prospect to get significant major league time, batting .217/.307/.294 in 180 at-bats.

KEY TRANSACTIONS: Kansas City jettisoned some of its veterans in July and August to add more talent to its minor league system and clear the way for younger players. Rick Ankiel and Kyle Farnsworth went to the Braves for three players, Scott Podsednik went to the Dodgers for two players, and Jose Guillen went to the Giants for Kevin Pucetas. Getting rid of Guillen not only added an arm to the organization but also rid the Royals of a headache in Guillen, who was implicated in an HGH scandal in October and left off the Giants playoff roster. The Royals also continued to invest heavily in the draft, which is starting to pay dividends . . .

DOWN ON THE FARM: If Royals fans are looking for hope, this is where they'll find it. Double-A Northwest Arkansas was Baseball America's Minor League Team of the Year after going 86-54 and winning the Texas League playoffs. The farm system is loaded with talent that should be able to contribute in the major leagues soon, highlighted by third baseman Mike Moustakas and first baseman Eric Hosmer. Right behind them is catcher Wil Myers.

OPENING DAY PAYROLL: $71.4 million (21st)

PLAYERS OF THE YEAR

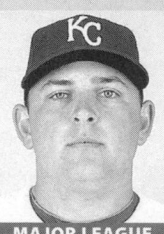

MAJOR LEAGUE	MINOR LEAGUE
Billy Butler	**Mike Moustakas**
1b	**3b**
.318/.388/.469	(Double-A/Triple-A)
189 H, 3rd in AL	.322/.369/.630
15 HR, 45 2B	36 HR, 124 RBI

ORGANIZATION LEADERS

BATTING		*Minimum 250 at-bats
MAJORS		
*AVG	Billy Butler	.318
*OPS	Wilson Betemit	.889
HR	Jose Guillen/Yuniesky Betancourt	16
RBI	Yuniesky Betancourt/Billy Butler	78
MINORS		
*AVG	Eric Hosmer, Wilmington/NW Arkansas	.338
*OBP	Kila Ka'aihue, Omaha	.463
*SLG	Mike Moustakas, NW Arkansas/Omaha	.630
R	Mike Moustakas, NW Arkansas/Omaha	94
H	Eric Hosmer, Wilmington/NW Arkansas	176
TB	Mike Moustakas, NW Arkansas/Omaha	305
2B	Eric Hosmer, Wilmington/NW Arkansas	43
3B	Carlo Testa, Burlington	14
HR	Mike Moustakas, NW Arkansas/Omaha	36
RBI	Mike Moustakas, NW Arkansas/Omaha	124
BB	Kila Ka'aihue, Omaha	88
SO	Ernesto Mejia, NW Arkansas/Wilmington	127
SB	Carlos Garcia, DSL Royals	50
	Derrick Robinson, NW Arkansas	50

PITCHING		†Minimum 75 innings
MAJORS		
W	Bruce Chen	12
†ERA	Zack Greinke	4.17
SO	Zack Greinke	181
MINORS		
W	Everett Teaford, Omaha/NW Arkansas	14
L	Timothy Melville, AZL Royals/Wilmington	13
†ERA	John Lamb, Burl./Wilm./NW Arkansas	2.38
G	Mitch Hodge Nielsen, Burlington	46
GS	Aaron Crow, NW Arkansas/Wilmington	29
SV	Patrick Keating, Wilmington/NW Arkansas	15
IP	Aaron Crow, NW Arkansas/Wilmington	163.3
BB	Tyler Sample, Burlington	95
SO	John Lamb, Burl./Wilm./NW Arkansas	159
†AVG	John Lamb, Burl./Wilm./NW Arkansas	.226

2010 PERFORMANCE

General Manager: Dayton Moore. **Farm/Scouting Director:** J.J. Picollo.

Class	Team	League	W	L	PCT	Finish*	Manager(s)
Majors	Kansas City Royals	American	67	95	.414	12th (14)	Trey Hillman/Ned Yost
Triple-A	Omaha Royals	Pacific Coast	81	63	.563	3rd (16)	Mike Jirschele
Double-A	Northwest Arkansas Naturals	Texas	86	54	.614	†1st (8)	Brian Poldberg
High A	Wilmington Blue Rocks	Carolina	68	70	.493	6th (8)	Brian Rupp
Low A	Burlington Bees	Midwest	46	90	.338	16th (16)	Jim Gabella
Rookie	Idaho Falls Chukars	Pioneer	27	49	.355	8th (8)	Brian Buchanan
Rookie	Burlington Royals	Appalachian	34	34	.500	t-4th (10)	Nelson Liriano
Rookie	AZL Royals	Arizona	31	25	.554	5th (12)	Darryl Kennedy
Overall 2010 Minor League Record			373	385	.492	18th (30)	

*Finish in overall standings (No. of teams in league). †League champion.

ORGANIZATION STATISTICS

KANSAS CITY ROYALS

AMERICAN LEAGUE

Batting	B-T	HT	WT	DOB	AVG	vLH	vRH	G	AB	R	H	2B	3B	HR	RBI	BB	HBP	SH	SF	SO	SB	CS	SLG	OBP
Ankiel, Rick	L-L	6-2	205	7-19-79	.261	.172	.302	27	92	14	24	7	0	4	15	7	1	0	1	29	1	0	.467	.317
Aviles, Mike	R-R	5-10	205	3-13-81	.304	.263	.319	110	424	63	129	16	3	8	32	20	1	0	3	49	14	5	.413	.335
Betancourt, Yuniesky	R-R	5-11	210	1-31-82	.259	.289	.250	151	556	60	144	29	2	16	78	23	1	4	4	64	2	3	.405	.288
Betemit, Wilson	B-R	6-2	220	11-2-81	.297	.312	.291	84	276	36	82	20	0	13	43	36	1	0	2	74	0	0	.511	.378
Blanco, Gregor	L-L	5-11	170	12-24-83	.274	.149	.318	49	179	22	49	8	3	1	11	21	0	2	1	35	10	2	.369	.348
Bloomquist, Willie	R-R	5-11	195	11-27-77	.265	.315	.227	72	170	31	45	10	1	3	17	8	0	2	1	25	8	5	.388	.296
Butler, Billy	R-R	6-1	240	4-18-86	.318	.267	.330	158	595	77	189	45	0	15	78	69	5	0	9	78	0	0	.469	.388
Callaspo, Alberto	B-R	5-8	200	4-19-83	.275	.250	.282	88	349	40	96	19	2	8	43	19	0	0	5	29	3	1	.410	.300
2-team total (58 Los Angeles)					.265	—	—	146	562	61	149	27	2	10	56	31	1	1	6	42	5	3	.374	.302
DeJesus, David	L-L	5-11	190	12-20-79	.318	.258	.340	91	352	46	112	23	3	5	37	34	4	3	1	47	3	3	.443	.384
Dyson, Jarrod	L-R	5-9	160	8-15-84	.211	.091	.239	18	57	11	12	4	2	1	5	6	0	2	0	16	9	1	.404	.286
Fields, Josh	R-R	6-1	240	12-14-82	.306	.364	.259	13	49	5	15	0	0	3	6	1	0	0	0	9	0	0	.490	.320
Getz, Chris	L-R	5-11	180	8-30-83	.237	.304	.219	72	224	23	53	9	0	0	18	19	2	3	0	28	15	2	.277	.302
Gordon, Alex	L-R	6-2	220	2-10-84	.215	.200	.220	74	242	34	52	10	0	8	20	34	2	2	1	62	1	5	.355	.315
Guillen, Jose	R-R	6-0	215	5-17-76	.255	.217	.265	106	396	46	101	17	2	16	62	27	9	0	5	84	1	0	.429	.314
Ka'aihue, Kila	L-R	6-4	235	3-29-84	.217	.250	.206	52	180	22	39	6	1	8	25	24	0	1	1	39	0	1	.394	.307
Kendall, Jason	R-R	6-0	190	6-26-74	.256	.323	.237	118	434	39	111	18	0	0	37	37	6	6	7	45	12	7	.297	.318
Maier, Mitch	L-R	6-2	215	6-30-82	.263	.221	.274	117	373	41	98	15	6	5	39	41	0	4	3	68	3	2	.375	.333
May, Lucas	R-R	5-11	195	10-24-84	.189	.100	.222	12	37	3	7	1	0	0	6	1	0	1	0	10	0	1	.216	.205
Miller, Jai	R-R	6-3	205	1-17-85	.236	.292	.194	20	55	5	13	3	0	1	4	4	1	0	0	23	1	0	.345	.300
Pena, Brayan	B-R	5-11	235	1-7-82	.253	.204	.275	60	158	11	40	10	0	1	19	12	1	1	2	27	2	0	.335	.306
Podsednik, Scott	L-L	6-0	185	3-18-76	.310	.318	.307	95	390	46	121	18	6	5	44	29	1	0	6	57	30	12	.400	.353

Pitching	B-T	HT	WT	DOB	W	L	ERA	G	GS	CG	SV	IP	H	R	ER	HR	BB	SO	AVG	vLH	vRH	K/9	BB/9
Bannister, Brian	R-R	6-1	215	2-28-81	7	12	6.34	24	23	0	0	128	158	92	90	23	50	77	.302	.273	.330	5.43	3.52
Bullington, Bryan	R-R	6-4	210	9-30-80	1	4	6.12	13	3	0	0	43	51	29	29	6	17	29	.297	.330	.256	6.12	3.59
Chavez, Jesse	R-R	6-2	170	8-21-83	2	3	5.88	23	0	0	0	26	29	20	17	5	11	16	.279	.264	.294	5.54	3.81
Chen, Bruce	L-L	6-2	215	6-19-77	12	7	4.17	33	23	1	1	140	136	68	65	17	57	98	.254	.259	.253	6.29	3.66
Colon, Roman	R-R	6-5	245	8-13-79	0	0	18.00	5	0	0	0	2	5	4	4	0	1	.455	.250	.571	4.50	9.00
Cruz, Juan	R-R	6-1	165	10-15-78	0	0	3.38	5	0	0	0	5	9	2	2	0	4	7	.391	.333	.429	11.81	6.75
Davies, Kyle	R-R	6-1	210	9-9-83	8	12	5.34	32	32	1	0	184	206	114	109	20	80	126	.283	.279	.288	6.17	3.92
Farnsworth, Kyle	R-R	6-4	230	4-14-76	3	0	2.42	37	0	0	0	45	40	13	12	2	12	36	.240	.256	.225	7.25	2.42
Greinke, Zack	R-R	6-2	190	10-21-83	10	14	4.17	33	33	3	0	220	219	114	102	18	55	181	.260	.280	.235	7.40	2.25
Hochevar, Luke	R-R	6-5	220	9-15-83	6	6	4.81	18	17	1	0	103	110	61	55	9	37	76	.272	.288	.255	6.64	3.23
Holland, Greg	R-R	5-11	190	11-20-85	0	1	6.75	15	0	0	0	19	23	15	14	3	8	23	.295	.278	.310	11.09	3.86
Hughes, Dusty	L-L	5-10	185	6-29-82	1	3	3.83	57	0	0	0	56	59	28	24	3	24	34	.273	.260	.283	5.43	3.83
Humber, Philip	R-R	6-3	210	12-21-82	2	1	4.15	8	1	0	0	22	22	10	10	1	7	16	.259	.275	.244	6.65	2.91
Lerew, Anthony	L-R	6-4	225	10-28-82	1	4	8.54	6	6	0	0	26	34	25	25	9	18	18	.321	.277	.356	6.15	3.08
Marte, Victor	R-R	6-2	255	11-8-80	3	0	9.76	22	0	0	0	28	38	30	30	8	15	19	.319	.292	.338	6.18	4.88
Meche, Gil	R-R	6-3	220	9-8-78	0	5	5.69	20	9	1	0	62	65	42	39	9	38	41	.273	.273	.274	5.98	5.55
Mendoza, Luis	R-R	6-3	235	10-31-83	0	1	22.50	4	0	0	0	4	10	10	10	4	3	1	.455	.429	.467	2.25	6.75
O'Sullivan, Sean	R-R	6-2	230	9-1-87	3	6	6.11	14	13	0	0	71	83	56	48	14	27	37	.288	.261	.330	4.71	3.44
2-team total (5 Los Angeles)					4	6	5.49	19	14	0	0	84	90	53	51	15	31	43	—	—	—	4.63	3.33
Parrish, John	L-L	5-11	200	11-26-77	1	1	3.00	9	0	0	0	6	4	2	2	2	5	4	.190	.300	.091	6.00	7.50
Rupe, Josh	R-R	6-2	215	8-18-82	1	1	5.59	11	0	0	0	10	14	6	6	1	7	8	.341	.278	.391	7.45	6.52
Soria, Joakim	R-R	6-3	200	5-18-84	1	2	1.78	66	0	0	43	66	53	13	13	4	16	71	.216	.231	.196	9.73	2.19
Tejeda, Robinson	R-R	6-2	245	3-24-82	3	5	3.54	54	0	0	0	61	55	28	24	5	26	56	.242	.252	.234	8.26	3.84
Texeira, Kanekoa	R-R	6-2	190	2-6-86	1	0	4.64	27	0	0	0	43	51	24	22	3	15	19	.309	.315	.304	4.01	3.16
2-team total (16 Seattle)					1	1	4.84	43	0	0	0	61	73	36	33	3	25	33	—	—	—	4.84	3.67
Thompson, Brad	R-R	6-1	190	1-31-82	0	4	6.41	16	0	0	0	20	25	16	14	4	4	10	.305	.382	.250	4.58	1.83
Wood, Blake	R-R	6-5	230	8-8-85	1	3	5.07	51	0	0	0	50	54	29	28	6	22	31	.286	.286	.286	5.62	3.99

Fielding

Catcher	PCT	G	PO	A	E	DP	PB
Kendall	.984	118	721	68	13	11	6
May	1.000	10	60	3	0	0	4
Pena	.990	47	269	24	3	3	1

First Base	PCT	G	PO	A	E	DP
Betemit	.971	5	33	0	1	1
Bloomquist	1.000	3	4	1	0	0
Butler	.995	127	1002	96	6	101
Gordon	1.000	1	1	0	0	0
Ka'aihue	.993	34	277	21	2	18
Maier	1.000	1	1	1	0	0

Second Base	PCT	G	PO	A	E	DP
Aviles	.976	87	183	258	11	40
Betemit	.833	2	1	4	1	0

Catcher	PCT	G	PO	A	E	DP	PB
Bloomquist	.947	4	9	9	1	2	
Callaspo	.980	11	19	30	1	9	
Getz	.989	64	113	164	3	43	

Third Base	PCT	G	PO	A	E	DP
Aviles	.750	5	2	1	1	0
Betemit	.929	53	30	75	8	9
Bloomquist	.852	11	5	18	4	4
Callaspo	.968	76	45	139	6	13
Fields	.848	12	9	19	5	0
Getz	.000	2	0	0	1	0
Gordon	.765	10	3	10	4	0

Shortstop	PCT	G	PO	A	E	DP
Aviles	.959	13	18	29	2	5
Betancourt	.974	151	256	418	18	84

Bloomquist	—	1	0	0	0	0

Outfield	PCT	G	PO	A	E	DP
Ankiel	.972	25	68	1	2	1
Betemit	1.000	2	3	0	0	0
Blanco	1.000	44	99	3	0	1
Bloomquist	1.000	35	58	3	0	0
DeJesus	1.000	88	183	5	0	1
Dyson	.962	15	48	2	2	2
Gordon	.979	58	137	2	3	1
Guillen	.977	22	41	1	1	0
Maier	.981	114	259	4	5	1
Miller	.971	19	34	0	1	0
Podsednik	.986	92	205	0	3	0

OMAHA ROYALS   TRIPLE-A
PACIFIC COAST LEAGUE

Batting	B-T	HT	WT	DOB	AVG	vLH	vRH	G	AB	R	H	2B	3B	HR	RBI	BB	HBP	SH	SF	SO	SB	CS	SLG	OBP
Ankiel, Rick	L-L	6-2	205	7-19-79	.254	.256	.250	18	67	8	17	6	0	4	9	1	0	0	0	19	0	0	.522	.265
Aviles, Mike	R-R	5-10	205	3-13-81	.271	.273	.271	17	70	8	19	3	1	1	8	4	1	0	0	10	0	0	.386	.320
Bellorin, Edwin	R-R	5-10	240	2-21-82	.162	.114	.179	38	130	6	21	3	0	0	4	10	2	3	1	23	0	0	.185	.231
2-team total (36 Round Rock)					.196	—	—	74	250	15	49	8	0	1	12	20	2	6	2	44	0	0	.240	.259
Betemit, Wilson	B-R	6-2	220	11-2-81	.265	.238	.282	29	113	9	30	6	2	2	17	17	1	1	2	23	1	1	.407	.358
Bonilla, Jose	R-R	5-10	188	8-4-88	1.000	.000	1.000	1	1	1	1	0	0	0	0	0	0	0	0	0	0	0	1.000	1.000
Clark, Cody	R-R	6-3	195	9-14-81	.255	.346	.226	72	220	27	56	13	2	4	25	22	1	11	3	35	1	1	.386	.321
Coats, Buck	L-R	6-3	200	6-9-82	.315	.250	.342	15	54	5	17	4	0	0	2	5	1	1	1	9	1	0	.389	.377
Duarte, Jose	R-R	5-10	165	3-7-85	.231	.000	.300	6	13	1	3	1	0	0	3	0	0	0	0	4	0	0	.308	.231
Dyson, Jarrod	L-R	5-9	160	8-15-84	.272	.203	.301	46	195	33	53	10	1	1	19	16	1	5	2	32	13	3	.349	.327
Falu, Irving	B-R	5-11	180	6-6-83	.272	.282	.268	119	503	75	137	14	6	1	46	42	0	5	2	39	15	4	.330	.327
Getz, Chris	L-R	5-11	180	8-30-83	.333	1.000	.200	2	6	3	2	0	0	0	0	2	0	0	0	1	0	0	.333	.500
Gordon, Alex	L-R	6-2	220	2-10-84	.315	.326	.310	68	260	59	82	20	3	14	44	51	8	2	0	72	7	2	.577	.442
Howell, Jeff	R-R	6-0	205	4-1-83	.235	.333	.182	4	17	1	4	1	0	0	2	0	0	0	0	4	0	0	.294	.235
Ka'aihue, Kila	L-R	6-4	235	3-29-84	.319	.308	.326	94	323	46	67	103	16	1	24	78	88	1	1	3	69	2	0	.598	.463
Lough, David	L-L	5-11	180	1-20-86	.280	.265	.288	120	460	65	129	15	12	11	58	40	8	19	4	72	14	5	.437	.346
Lucas, Ed	R-R	6-3	205	5-24-82	.307	.376	.279	99	352	52	108	20	1	13	50	52	3	5	3	68	7	1	.480	.398
Maddox, Marc	R-R	5-11	185	9-16-83	.263	.258	.265	102	361	53	95	19	3	2	39	35	6	8	3	56	4	2	.349	.336
May, Lucas	R-R	5-11	195	10-24-84	.275	.407	.219	24	91	14	25	7	0	5	13	12	1	0	1	19	0	0	.516	.362
2-team total (73 Albuquerque)					.291	—	—	97	351	61	102	20	3	16	58	34	2	1	2	79	4	2	.501	.355
Mertins, Kurt	R-R	6-0	175	4-22-86	.233	.284	.209	70	253	35	59	12	3	4	27	16	4	6	0	50	4	0	.352	.289
Miller, Jai	R-R	6-3	205	1-17-85	.267	.275	.263	84	311	45	83	24	2	18	56	35	1	0	3	113	2	3	.531	.340
2-team total (10 Sacramento)					.252	—	—	94	345	47	87	24	2	18	57	38	1	0	3	132	5	3	.490	.326
Moustakas, Mike	L-R	5-11	230	9-11-88	.293	.218	.333	52	225	36	66	16	0	15	48	8	0	0	3	25	2	0	.564	.314
Parraz, Jordan	R-R	6-3	215	10-8-84	.266	.291	.255	123	432	58	115	27	1	11	61	39	19	7	4	78	8	5	.410	.350
Pina, Manny	R-R	6-0	230	6-5-87	.218	.261	.188	17	55	5	12	2	0	2	5	3	1	0	1	7	0	0	.364	.267
Thorman, Scott	L-R	6-3	225	1-6-82	.280	.212	.305	125	479	78	134	31	2	22	85	48	3	1	1	75	6	4	.491	.348

Pitching	B-T	HT	WT	DOB	W	L	ERA	G	GS	CG	SV	IP	H	R	ER	HR	BB	SO	AVG	vLH	vRH	K/9	BB/9
Anderson, Brian	R-R	6-2	220	3-11-82	0	0	2.57	6	0	0	0	7	4	2	2	0	1	6	.160	.100	.200	7.71	1.29
Baez, Manauris	B-R	5-11	182	8-16-85	2	2	7.09	8	6	0	0	33	43	26	26	4	18	17	.316	.350	.289	4.64	4.91
Bannister, Brian	R-R	6-1	215	2-28-81	0	1	3.68	3	3	0	0	7	10	3	3	1	0	3	.333	.250	.389	3.68	0.00
Bowden, Barry	R-R	6-1	205	11-9-84	0	0	13.50	2	0	0	0	2	2	3	3	2	2	0	.286	.250	.333	0.00	9.00
Bullington, Bryan	R-R	6-4	210	9-30-80	8	2	2.82	20	15	1	0	102	86	35	32	8	28	73	.231	.232	.230	6.44	2.47
Campillo, Jorge	R-R	6-0	230	8-10-78	0	0	3.18	4	2	0	0	11	8	4	4	2	0	8	.190	.111	.250	6.35	0.00
Castaneda, Federico	R-R	6-3	187	1-26-84	4	2	3.69	31	4	0	0	76	58	34	31	13	30	54	.212	.240	.188	6.42	3.57
Chen, Bruce	L-L	6-2	220	6-19-77	0	1	1.31	3	3	0	0	21	13	3	3	0	5	20	.186	.211	.176	8.71	2.18
Coleman, Louis	R-R	6-4	195	4-4-86	5	2	2.23	21	0	0	1	40	31	11	10	2	11	48	.215	.254	.185	10.71	2.45
Collins, Tim	L-L	5-7	155	8-21-89	2	1	1.33	15	0	0	4	20	9	3	3	1	8	21	.127	.185	.091	9.30	3.54
Colon, Roman	R-R	6-5	245	8-13-79	0	0	0.00	2	0	0	0	2	1	0	0	0	1	1	.143	.333	.000	4.50	4.50
Hardy, Blaine	L-L	6-2	195	3-14-87	3	4	3.49	28	8	0	3	67	65	30	26	9	21	48	.255	.244	.260	6.45	2.82
Hayes, Chris	R-R	6-1	195	2-5-83	0	0	3.95	19	0	0	2	27	36	20	12	5	10	10	.319	.340	.302	3.29	1.65
Herges, Matt	L-R	5-11	205	4-1-70	9	4	4.63	43	5	0	0	89	102	49	46	10	36	49	.291	.287	.296	4.94	3.63
Hernandez, Gaby	R-R	6-3	215	5-21-86	10	6	4.91	31	22	0	0	145	139	81	79	31	56	114	.253	.268	.240	7.09	3.48
Hochevar, Luke	R-R	6-5	220	9-15-83	0	0	1.80	2	2	0	0	5	3	1	1	0	1	4	.167	.125	.200	7.20	1.80
Holland, Greg	R-R	5-11	190	11-20-85	3	3	3.81	36	0	0	3	57	40	26	24	3	30	60	.199	.222	.180	9.53	4.76
Humber, Philip	R-R	6-3	210	12-21-82	5	6	4.47	21	20	1	0	119	131	68	59	17	20	80	.278	.305	.257	6.07	1.52
Johnson, Blake	R-R	6-5	200	6-14-85	0	1	9.72	6	1	0	0	8	11	9	9	1	3	3	.371	.353	.389	3.24	3.24
Lerew, Anthony	L-R	6-4	225	10-28-82	9	4	2.55	22	19	1	0	124	121	43	35	4	44	74	.257	.274	.243	5.39	3.20
Lowery, Devon	L-R	6-1	215	3-24-83	0	1	4.80	11	0	0	0	15	18	8	8	2	6	12	.300	.318	.289	7.20	3.60
Marte, Victor	R-R	6-2	255	11-8-80	4	1	3.32	25	0	0	3	41	40	17	15	3	15	29	.258	.227	.281	6.42	3.32
Meche, Gil	R-R	6-3	220	9-8-78	0	1	8.31	4	1	0	0	9	10	8	8	2	4	4	.294	.263	.333	6.23	4.15
Mendoza, Luis	R-R	6-3	235	10-31-83	10	9	4.10	24	22	0	0	132	145	66	60	13	32	59	.282	.270	.291	4.03	2.19
Osuna, Edgar	L-L	6-1	185	11-25-87	1	3	9.62	7	5	0	0	29	43	35	31	12	16	19	.341	.395	.318	5.90	4.97

Pitching	B-T	HT	WT	DOB	W	L	ERA	G	GS	CG	SV	IP	H	R	ER	HR	BB	SO	AVG	vLH	vRH	K/9	BB/9
Parrish, John	L-L	5-11	200	11-26-77	0	1	9.00	3	2	0	0	2	1	2	2	0	2	2	.143	.000	.200	9.00	9.00
Rosa, Carlos	R-R	6-1	210	9-21-84	2	1	3.65	6	0	0	0	12	13	5	5	2	7	10	.289	.389	.222	7.30	5.11
2-team total (25 Reno)					2	1	2.25	31	0	0	13	40	33	10	10	4	21	41	—	—	—	9.23	4.72
Rupe, Josh	R-R	6-2	215	8-18-82	2	4	2.92	40	0	0	10	52	49	19	17	5	23	49	.245	.191	.288	8.43	3.96
Teaford, Everett	L-L	6-0	155	5-15-84	0	1	13.50	1	1	0	0	5	8	7	7	2	1	4	.364	.333	.375	7.71	1.93
Thompson, Brad	R-R	6-1	190	1-31-82	0	1	5.40	3	3	0	0	12	16	8	7	1	1	3	.333	.500	.136	2.31	0.77
2-team total (15 Round Rock)					1	2	7.71	18	3	0	0	35	57	35	30	4	5	15	—	—	—	3.86	1.29
Wood, Blake	R-R	6-5	230	8-8-85	2	1	2.16	12	0	0	5	17	12	5	4	0	7	12	.207	.194	.222	6.48	3.78

Fielding

Catcher	PCT	G	PO	A	E	DP	PB
Bellorin	.980	38	224	20	5	6	1
Bonilla	—	1	0	0	0	0	0
Clark	.996	72	418	36	2	5	5
Howell	1.000	4	22	6	0	0	0
May	.994	22	146	10	1	2	5
Pina	.975	17	111	6	3	2	0

First Base	PCT	G	PO	A	E	DP
Betemit	1.000	8	72	11	0	11
Ka'aihue	.997	75	664	60	2	70
Maddox	1.000	1	1	0	0	1
Thorman	.997	62	553	32	2	57

Second Base	PCT	G	PO	A	E	DP
Aviles	1.000	1	2	3	0	1
Falu	.976	37	67	95	4	22

	PCT	G	PO	A	E	DP
Getz	1.000	2	0	3	0	0
Lucas	.957	22	33	57	4	16
Maddox	.990	44	66	138	2	28
Mertins	.983	44	88	146	4	36

Third Base	PCT	G	PO	A	E	DP
Betemit	.933	6	2	12	1	2
Falu	—	1	0	0	0	0
Lucas	.955	23	17	47	3	4
Maddox	.947	43	30	78	6	12
Mertins	.941	5	3	13	1	0
Moustakas	.945	52	36	102	8	11
Thorman	.963	20	16	36	2	5

Shortstop	PCT	G	PO	A	E	DP
Aviles	.941	15	25	39	4	11
Betemit	1.000	12	14	31	0	7

	PCT	G	PO	A	E	DP
Falu	.951	81	104	265	19	61
Lucas	.970	36	40	88	4	17
Mertins	.947	5	7	11	1	3

Outfield	PCT	G	PO	A	E	DP
Ankiel	1.000	13	21	0	0	0
Coats	.967	15	29	0	1	0
Duarte	1.000	4	12	0	0	0
Dyson	.987	46	146	5	2	1
Gordon	.964	63	128	6	5	1
Lough	.985	113	263	6	4	1
Lucas	.962	16	24	1	1	1
Miller	.993	56	149	1	1	0
Parraz	.977	114	242	10	6	5
Thorman	.857	5	6	0	1	0

NORTHWEST ARKANSAS NATURALS   DOUBLE-A

TEXAS LEAGUE

Batting	B-T	HT	WT	DOB	AVG	vLH	vRH	G	AB	R	H	2B	3B	HR	RBI	BB	HBP	SH	SF	SO	SB	CS	SLG	OBP
Costa, Shane	L-R	6-0	205	12-12-81	.000	.000	.000	1	3	0	0	0	0	0	0	0	0	0	0	0	0	0	.000	.000
Dyson, Jarrod	L-R	5-9	160	8-15-84	.240	.250	.231	7	25	6	6	0	0	0	6	5	1	0	1	2	3	3	.240	.375
Eigsti, Ryan	R-R	6-2	195	8-24-85	.161	.333	.091	13	31	3	5	0	0	0	2	3	1	1	0	6	0	0	.161	.257
Fields, Josh	R-R	6-1	240	12-14-82	.436	.467	.417	11	39	10	17	8	0	0	9	1	0	0	1	4	1	0	.641	.439
Giavotella, Johnny	R-R	5-8	185	7-10-87	.322	.322	.322	134	522	92	168	35	5	9	65	61	4	7	3	67	13	7	.460	.395
Hosmer, Eric	L-L	6-4	215	10-24-89	.313	.338	.298	50	195	39	61	14	3	13	35	15	1	0	0	27	3	1	.615	.365
Howell, Jeff	R-R	6-0	205	4-1-83	.242	.262	.229	46	157	20	38	12	0	4	25	13	2	1	2	38	0	2	.395	.305
McConnell, Chris	R-R	5-11	175	12-18-85	.231	.233	.230	122	359	44	83	19	5	3	39	49	8	10	4	76	11	7	.337	.333
Mejia, Ernesto	R-R	6-5	245	12-2-85	.268	.344	.226	71	261	36	70	18	0	11	48	22	6	0	4	86	1	0	.464	.334
Mertins, Kurt	R-R	6-0	175	4-22-86	.311	.438	.276	22	74	12	23	3	1	0	9	8	2	0	2	7	3	0	.378	.384
Moustakas, Mike	L-R	5-11	230	9-11-88	.347	.348	.347	66	259	58	90	25	0	21	76	26	7	0	6	42	0	1	.687	.413
Orlando, Paulo	R-R	6-3	185	11-1-85	.305	.316	.300	121	419	84	128	22	6	13	64	24	18	5	3	62	25	10	.480	.366
Pina, Manny	R-R	6-0	230	6-5-87	.259	.274	.253	74	266	39	69	16	0	7	44	24	2	4	6	37	0	0	.398	.319
Robinson, Clint	L-L	6-4	225	2-16-85	.335	.326	.341	129	477	90	160	41	5	29	98	58	6	2	5	86	4	3	.625	.410
Robinson, Derrick	B-L	5-11	180	9-28-87	.286	.245	.303	127	511	74	146	26	8	2	48	45	4	5	5	86	50	17	.380	.345
Romak, Jamie	R-R	6-2	220	9-30-85	.278	.326	.253	45	133	23	37	6	0	6	16	19	5	3	0	30	0	3	.459	.389
Seratelli, Anthony	B-R	6-0	205	2-27-83	.254	.213	.273	101	299	41	76	9	3	3	39	49	2	2	2	65	15	6	.334	.361
Smith, Tim	L-L	6-3	225	6-14-86	.306	.297	.309	95	307	52	94	18	0	9	50	33	1	6	3	42	15	5	.453	.372
Theriot, Ben	L-R	6-1	190	12-8-87	.310	.083	.370	19	58	6	18	1	1	0	5	3	0	1	0	13	0	0	.362	.344
Van Stratten, Nick	R-R	6-1	185	5-22-85	.262	.319	.226	86	302	41	79	18	0	2	34	28	6	5	1	41	8	5	.341	.335

Pitching	B-T	HT	WT	DOB	W	L	ERA	G	GS	CG	SV	IP	H	R	ER	HR	BB	SO	AVG	vLH	vRH	K/9	BB/9
Barrera, Henry	R-R	6-0	195	11-25-85	3	1	1.80	16	0	0	1	25	17	6	5	1	7	25	.193	.333	.109	9.00	2.52
Bowden, Barry	R-R	6-1	205	11-9-84	1	1	5.73	7	0	0	0	11	13	7	7	1	3	11	.295	.333	.261	9.00	2.45
Caldera, Alex	R-R	6-3	200	10-1-85	3	2	5.12	8	7	0	0	39	38	22	22	8	18	28	.268	.273	.262	6.52	4.19
Castaneda, Federico	R-R	6-3	187	1-26-84	0	0	0.00	3	0	0	2	10	4	0	0	0	1	11	.121	.182	.091	10.24	0.93
Chavez, Chris	L-R	6-3	195	9-11-84	2	0	7.31	20	0	0	0	32	40	32	26	5	21	21	.296	.291	.300	5.91	5.91
Coleman, Louis	R-R	6-4	195	4-4-86	2	1	2.09	21	1	0	6	52	31	13	12	5	14	55	.171	.247	.115	9.58	2.44
Crow, Aaron	R-R	6-3	190	11-11-86	7	7	5.66	22	22	0	0	119	130	86	75	13	59	90	.279	.326	.237	6.79	4.45
Duffy, Danny	L-L	6-3	195	12-21-88	5	2	2.95	7	7	1	0	40	38	17	13	3	9	41	.255	.154	.309	9.30	2.04
Dwyer, Chris	R-L	6-3	210	4-10-88	2	1	3.06	4	4	0	0	18	11	8	6	2	10	20	.175	.200	.167	10.19	5.09
Hardy, Blaine	L-L	6-2	195	3-14-87	1	0	0.69	12	0	0	4	26	11	2	2	0	8	16	.128	.143	.121	5.54	2.77
Hardy, Rowdy	L-L	6-4	170	10-26-82	4	3	3.44	36	0	0	3	81	88	32	31	4	18	57	.285	.214	.325	6.33	2.00
Johnson, Blake	R-R	6-5	200	6-14-85	5	3	3.81	23	10	0	1	80	90	39	34	3	23	51	.293	.274	.322	5.71	2.58
Keating, Patrick	R-R	6-2	215	6-9-87	1	1	3.10	27	0	0	10	41	33	14	14	3	19	60	.221	.224	.220	13.28	4.20
Lamb, John	L-L	6-3	195	7-10-90	2	1	5.45	7	7	0	0	33	37	24	20	2	13	26	.280	.240	.305	7.09	3.55
Meche, Gil	R-R	6-3	220	9-8-78	0	0	0.00	1	1	0	0	4	2	0	0	0	3	3	.154	.125	.200	6.75	6.75
Montgomery, Mike	L-L	6-5	180	7-1-89	5	4	3.47	13	13	0	0	60	56	31	23	4	26	48	.255	.256	.254	7.24	3.92
Osuna, Edgar	L-L	6-1	185	11-25-87	6	2	2.95	17	17	0	0	95	99	48	31	11	11	64	.268	.356	.226	6.08	1.05
Paulino, Eduardo	R-R	5-11	176	9-29-85	8	5	4.04	28	21	0	0	114	118	62	51	7	63	85	.268	.312	.218	6.73	4.99
Santiago, Mario	R-R	6-2	210	12-16-84	6	6	3.56	18	17	1	0	94	97	43	37	6	25	60	.272	.291	.254	5.77	2.40
Sisk, Brandon	L-L	6-3	210	7-13-85	4	6	4.46	40	0	0	9	69	73	38	34	7	28	63	.275	.279	.273	8.26	3.67
Swaggerty, Ben	L-L	6-1	180	8-8-82	4	5	3.81	36	1	0	1	59	56	32	25	3	33	58	.245	.194	.279	8.85	5.03
Teaford, Everett	L-L	6-0	155	5-15-84	14	3	3.36	27	12	0	0	99	91	39	37	7	32	113	.243	.259	.234	10.27	2.91
Villa, Kelvin	L-L	5-10	170	12-14-85	1	0	7.80	9	0	0	0	15	22	14	13	2	8	11	.328	.360	.310	6.60	4.80

Fielding

Catcher	PCT	G	PO	A	E	DP	PB
Eigsti	.987	12	73	4	1	2	0
Howell	.991	45	306	26	3	2	2
Pina	.979	74	502	63	12	8	2
Theriot	.987	19	138	14	2	0	1

First Base	PCT	G	PO	A	E	DP
Hosmer	.994	43	331	27	2	43
Mejia	.978	9	81	7	2	9
Robinson	.983	83	744	52	14	72
Seratelli	.988	10	79	4	1	5

Second Base	PCT	G	PO	A	E	DP
Giavotella	.978	130	203	364	13	81
Mertins	.900	4	3	6	1	0
Seratelli	.980	10	16	34	1	8

Third Base	PCT	G	PO	A	E	DP
Fields	.909	9	1	9	1	1
Howell	1.000	1	0	1	0	0
Mertins	.947	14	12	24	2	2
Moustakas	.929	61	40	130	13	21
Romak	.967	41	19	39	2	5
Seratelli	.929	31	14	38	4	4

Shortstop	PCT	G	PO	A	E	DP
McConnell	.973	122	171	362	15	81
Mertins	1.000	3	2	9	0	1
Seratelli	.934	27	35	64	7	11

Outfield	PCT	G	PO	A	E	DP
Dyson	1.000	7	19	2	0	0
Orlando	.945	116	217	8	13	0
Robinson	.667	1	2	0	1	0
Robinson	.969	125	274	6	9	3
Seratelli	.976	28	38	3	1	1
Smith	.956	78	106	3	5	0
Van Stratten	.982	83	151	13	3	6

WILMINGTON BLUE ROCKS

HIGH CLASS A

CAROLINA LEAGUE

Batting	B-T	HT	WT	DOB	AVG	vLH	vRH	G	AB	R	H	2B	3B	HR	RBI	BB	HBP	SH	SF	SO	SB	CS	SLG	OBP
Alfaro, J.D.	R-R	5-9	170	4-28-88	.183	.125	.213	22	71	4	13	3	1	0	9	1	0	2	0	13	0	0	.254	.194
Colon, Christian	R-R	6-1	180	5-14-89	.278	.242	.291	60	245	38	68	12	2	3	30	13	6	4	3	33	2	4	.380	.326
Costa, Shane	L-R	6-0	205	12-12-81	.111	.000	.167	2	9	1	1	0	0	1	2	0	0	0	0	2	0	0	.444	.111
Dyson, Jarrod	L-R	5-9	160	8-15-84	.327	.200	.359	12	49	7	16	6	2	0	9	1	0	0	2	9	5	1	.531	.327
Francis, Nick	R-R	6-3	195	3-5-86	.284	.282	.284	84	335	55	95	24	3	16	61	19	4	1	2	85	8	4	.516	.328
Frost, Adam	R-R	5-11	165	10-13-86	.245	.159	.284	43	139	19	34	7	2	4	16	8	1	1	0	28	14	4	.410	.291
Garcia, Fernando	B-R	6-0	160	7-28-86	.186	.118	.215	60	172	20	32	4	2	0	11	14	4	13	2	37	8	6	.233	.260
Gordon, Alex	L-R	6-2	220	2-10-84	.235	.429	.100	7	17	7	4	3	0	0	2	9	4	0	1	3	1	0	.412	.548
Graterol, Juan	R-R	6-1	170	2-14-89	.000	.000	.000	3	6	0	0	0	0	0	2	1	0	0	1	1	0	0	.000	.125
Hosmer, Eric	L-L	6-4	215	10-24-89	.354	.376	.344	87	325	48	115	29	6	7	51	44	2	0	4	39	11	1	.545	.429
Jones, Travis	R-R	6-2	200	5-23-89	.000	.000	.000	4	13	0	0	0	0	0	0	0	0	0	0	2	0	0	.000	.000
Lewis, Joey	R-R	6-4	220	10-13-87	.206	.118	.239	18	63	4	13	2	0	2	4	2	1	0	0	20	0	0	.333	.242
Mejia, Ernesto	R-R	6-5	245	12-2-85	.288	.385	.246	43	170	25	49	13	2	5	21	14	1	0	3	41	0	0	.476	.340
Myers, Wil	R-R	6-3	190	12-10-90	.346	.286	.365	58	205	28	71	18	2	4	38	37	4	0	1	39	2	3	.512	.453
Navarro, Rey	B-R	5-10	175	12-22-89	.237	.250	.231	107	393	43	93	12	5	5	38	11	3	9	5	44	5	5	.331	.260
Norris, Patrick	B-R	6-2	190	3-17-86	.244	.256	.238	122	442	69	108	20	7	1	42	41	3	13	3	102	30	17	.328	.311
Oriental, Rene	R-R	6-3	225	5-4-84	.212	.250	.193	23	85	12	18	4	0	1	8	5	1	0	1	17	1	0	.294	.261
Ortiz, Adrian	L-R	6-0	172	1-14-87	.289	.287	.290	106	436	59	126	17	8	2	34	22	0	20	2	71	32	15	.378	.322
Perez, Salvador	R-R	6-3	175	5-10-90	.290	.299	.286	99	365	35	106	21	1	7	53	18	3	1	9	38	1	1	.411	.322
Prasch, Eddie	L-R	6-0	190	1-25-86	.210	.200	.214	47	162	16	34	12	1	2	18	20	1	1	2	45	0	1	.333	.297
Rivera, Juan	B-R	6-0	150	3-17-87	.146	.114	.167	36	89	17	13	1	0	0	3	12	0	4	1	21	0	3	.157	.245
Romak, Jamie	R-R	6-2	220	9-30-85	.304	.333	.292	82	299	44	91	23	1	7	48	34	8	0	2	60	4	2	.458	.388
Seratelli, Anthony	B-R	6-0	205	2-27-83	.277	.222	.310	13	47	7	13	5	1	0	5	4	1	0	0	16	0	1	.426	.346
Stovall, Ryan	R-R	5-11	190	12-16-86	.300	.000	.375	3	10	0	3	0	1	0	0	0	0	0	0	2	0	0	.500	.300
Taylor, Jason	R-R	6-1	210	1-14-88	.173	.167	.176	30	110	11	19	4	1	2	9	6	1	1	2	23	2	3	.282	.218
Theriot, Ben	L-R	6-1	190	12-8-87	.269	.167	.291	20	67	8	18	3	1	0	6	4	1	0	0	11	0	0	.343	.319
Walton, Jamar	L-R	6-4	195	1-5-86	.200	.207	.197	59	215	22	43	5	3	3	24	8	4	1	3	58	4	4	.293	.239
2-team total (16 Potomac)					.220	—	—	75	268	28	59	8	4	4	35	9	4	1	4	72	4	4	.325	.253
Wood, Ryan	R-R	6-4	185	5-5-87	.136	.143	.132	20	66	6	9	2	1	2	6	13	0	0	0	24	0	1	.288	.278

Pitching	B-T	HT	WT	DOB	W	L	ERA	G	GS	CG	SV	IP	H	R	ER	HR	BB	SO	AVG	vLH	vRH	K/9	BB/9
Baez, Manauris	B-R	5-11	182	8-16-85	2	4	4.13	25	5	0	4	70	84	34	32	3	24	42	.304	.255	.337	5.43	3.10
Barrera, Henry	R-R	6-0	195	11-25-85	0	0	4.50	6	0	0	1	8	9	4	4	0	3	10	.281	.154	.368	11.25	3.38
Basurto, Eric	R-R	6-3	200	4-17-86	3	1	3.46	22	0	0	4	26	20	13	10	0	17	31	.222	.200	.236	10.73	5.88
Baumann, Buddy	L-L	5-10	175	12-9-87	4	2	2.24	31	14	0	4	100	76	29	25	3	36	113	.212	.189	.220	10.14	3.23
Bowden, Barry	R-R	6-1	205	11-9-84	2	5	1.56	34	0	0	11	40	32	9	7	2	14	40	.218	.230	.205	8.93	3.12
Caldera, Alex	L-R	6-3	200	10-1-85	6	4	3.25	13	12	0	0	75	75	31	27	5	20	71	.262	.264	.260	8.56	2.41
Chapman, Kevin	L-L	6-4	210	12-9-87	1	1	5.50	14	0	0	1	18	20	13	11	1	8	20	.267	.222	.281	10.00	4.00
Crow, Aaron	R-R	6-3	190	11-11-86	2	3	5.93	7	7	0	0	44	51	32	29	6	6	53	.290	.338	.261	10.84	1.23
Cuevas, Jairo	R-R	6-2	215	1-24-84	4	9	5.85	18	16	0	0	68	87	54	44	12	14	44	.309	.344	.281	5.85	1.86
De La Rosa, Starling	L-L	6-5	160	9-19-87	0	0	9.00	4	0	0	0	5	6	7	5	1	4	7	.261	.286	.250	12.60	7.20
Dennick, Ryan	L-L	6-0	185	1-10-87	2	0	4.97	8	0	0	0	13	17	8	7	0	7	8	.321	.250	.341	5.68	4.97
Duffy, Danny	L-L	6-3	195	12-21-88	0	0	2.57	3	3	0	0	14	8	6	4	2	7	18	.170	.167	.171	11.57	4.50
Dwyer, Chris	R-L	6-3	210	4-10-88	3	3	2.99	15	15	1	0	84	79	36	28	3	33	93	.246	.196	.266	9.92	3.52
Hodgson, Ivor	B-L	6-2	190	4-25-86	6	9	4.22	26	17	0	0	111	124	60	52	6	35	88	.288	.278	.292	6.49	2.84
Keating, Patrick	R-R	6-2	215	6-9-87	2	0	1.19	13	0	0	5	30	18	5	4	2	10	41	.171	.200	.150	12.16	2.97
Lafferty, Brendan	L-L	6-3	180	5-27-86	4	1	3.15	28	0	0	1	66	55	28	23	4	18	57	.235	.258	.227	7.81	2.47
Lamb, John	L-L	6-3	195	7-10-90	6	3	1.45	13	13	0	0	75	59	18	12	1	15	90	.219	.215	.220	10.85	1.81
Lowery, Devon	L-R	6-1	215	3-24-83	0	0	0.00	2	0	0	0	3	1	0	0	0	4	4	.100	.000	.000	12.00	12.00
Melville, Tim	R-R	6-5	210	10-9-89	2	12	4.97	22	22	0	0	112	101	72	62	10	54	90	.240	.253	.230	7.21	4.33
Montgomery, Mike	L-L	6-5	180	7-1-89	2	0	1.09	4	4	0	0	25	14	5	3	0	4	33	.165	.067	.186	12.04	1.46
Mozingo, Harold	R-R	6-1	175	3-29-85	5	2	4.22	25	0	0	3	53	53	29	25	8	15	53	.255	.231	.274	8.94	2.53
Paukovits, Bryan	R-R	6-7	240	6-29-87	3	5	5.88	14	12	0	0	67	83	50	44	5	23	49	.302	.328	.282	6.55	3.07
Pena, Riquy	R-R	6-2	160	6-17-85	0	1	13.50	5	0	0	0	9	21	15	15	2	7	6	.420	.370	.478	5.40	6.30
Smith, Will	R-L	6-5	235	7-10-89	4	1	2.80	8	8	0	0	45	48	20	17	6	4	51	.283	.209	.239	8.40	0.66
Thompson, James	R-R	6-3	195	8-15-87	2	4	8.24	24	0	0	0	39	47	50	36	4	32	38	.290	.258	.313	8.69	7.32
Worrell, Josh	R-R	6-5	215	11-17-86	0	0	0.00	2	0	0	0	3	3	0	0	0	0	3	.250	.500	.125	9.00	0.00

Fielding

Catcher	PCT	G	PO	A	E	DP	PB
Graterol	1.000	2	13	1	0	0	0
Jones	1.000	4	29	2	0	0	3
Lewis	.900	2	9	0	1	0	1
Myers	.995	28	185	23	1	0	3
Perez	.993	85	732	77	6	6	11
Theriot	.968	20	164	15	6	0	3

First Base	PCT	G	PO	A	E	DP
Frost	—	1	0	0	0	0
Hosmer	.988	80	619	45	8	58
Lewis	1.000	3	24	2	0	4
Mejia	.992	42	370	25	3	24
Prasch	1.000	2	10	1	0	2
Romak	1.000	10	44	4	0	3
Seratelli	1.000	1	11	0	0	2
Stovall	1.000	3	20	2	0	3
Taylor	1.000	1	5	0	0	0

Second Base	PCT	G	PO	A	E	DP
Alfaro	1.000	11	21	30	0	6
Frost	1.000	5	8	12	0	5
Garcia	.975	54	97	141	6	40
Navarro	.965	55	109	140	9	25
Rivera	.925	13	13	24	3	1
Seratelli	.929	3	4	9	1	1

Third Base	PCT	G	PO	A	E	DP
Alfaro	.750	7	0	6	2	0
Frost	.949	38	32	61	5	4
Gordon	1.000	6	3	8	0	1
Prasch	1.000	19	5	29	0	2
Rivera	.857	10	4	14	3	1
Romak	.927	44	30	59	7	7
Taylor	.837	18	13	28	8	3
Wood	.889	4	4	4	1	0

Shortstop	PCT	G	PO	A	E	DP
Alfaro	.950	4	6	13	1	2

	PCT	G	PO	A	E	DP
Colon	.936	60	74	173	17	33
Navarro	.950	53	83	144	12	30
Rivera	1.000	6	6	18	0	5
Seratelli	1.000	1	0	4	0	0
Wood	.902	15	18	28	5	9

Outfield	PCT	G	PO	A	E	DP
Costa	1.000	2	1	0	0	0
Dyson	.974	12	36	2	1	0
Francis	.965	83	162	3	6	0
Norris	.968	121	262	11	9	2
Oriental	.953	23	38	3	2	1
Ortiz	1.000	106	220	13	0	1
Rivera	1.000	2	1	0	0	0
Romak	.970	22	31	1	1	1
Seratelli	1.000	7	13	0	0	0
Taylor	—	1	0	0	0	0
Walton	.986	37	67	1	1	1

BURLINGTON BEES

LOW CLASS A

MIDWEST LEAGUE

Batting	B-T	HT	WT	DOB	AVG	vLH	vRH	G	AB	R	H	2B	3B	HR	RBI	BB	HBP	SH	SF	SO	SB	CS	SLG	OBP
Alfaro, J.D.	R-R	5-9	170	4-28-88	.193	.174	.198	28	109	11	21	6	1	3	13	4	0	3	0	34	2	4	.349	.221
Aparicio, Julio	R-R	6-2	175	1-4-90	.188	.184	.191	30	85	6	16	4	0	0	7	4	1	0	1	33	2	1	.235	.231
Batista, Deivy	R-R	5-11	150	5-7-88	.236	.256	.228	108	398	55	94	14	4	6	32	34	1	2	7	100	18	5	.337	.293
Bonilla, Jose	R-R	5-10	188	8-4-88	.239	.275	.225	88	284	35	68	8	4	4	38	38	8	1	1	70	3	3	.338	.344
Caldwell, Keven	L-L	5-11	170	3-29-88	.176	.238	.151	23	74	9	13	5	0	0	8	10	1	0	2	16	0	3	.243	.276
Cruz, Fernando	B-R	6-2	205	3-28-90	.221	.183	.235	106	376	33	83	15	2	0	23	21	2	7	1	59	2	3	.271	.265
Del Rosario, Luis	R-R	6-2	181	5-21-90	.176	.174	.178	27	68	5	12	2	0	0	4	9	1	1	0	22	0	1	.206	.282
Ferguson, Tim	R-R	6-1	190	10-25-88	.172	.333	.130	7	29	5	5	0	0	0	3	4	0	0	0	7	1	1	.172	.273
Frost, Adam	R-R	5-11	165	10-13-86	.258	.154	.302	25	89	8	23	6	2	1	15	6	1	2	1	20	7	1	.404	.309
Graterol, Juan	R-R	6-1	170	2-14-89	.292	.310	.286	31	113	9	33	4	0	0	9	6	1	0	0	9	0	0	.327	.333
Hall, Gerard	B-R	5-9	170	7-9-88	.224	.203	.233	120	433	67	97	25	3	3	41	55	1	6	4	109	19	8	.316	.310
Kuebler, Alex	R-R	6-5	200	9-3-89	.265	.281	.255	45	166	17	44	7	0	2	21	18	2	1	3	35	0	0	.343	.339
Lewis, Joey	R-R	6-4	220	10-13-87	.243	.189	.255	82	300	36	73	21	1	6	45	44	0	1	1	93	1	2	.380	.339
Liberto, Michael	R-R	5-7	170	6-21-88	.118	.143	.100	10	34	2	4	0	0	0	3	3	1	0	0	8	1	0	.118	.211
McClure, Alex	B-R	6-0	185	6-16-89	.225	.161	.250	27	111	17	25	6	0	1	14	8	0	1	1	28	5	2	.306	.275
Merrifield, Whit	R-R		175	1-24-89	.253	.297	.230	47	186	24	47	8	3	5	26	15	3	4	1	42	5	3	.409	.317
Myers, Wil	R-R	6-3	190	12-10-90	.289	.288	.290	68	242	42	70	19	1	10	45	48	2	0	2	55	10	3	.500	.408
Oriental, Rene	R-R	6-3	225	5-4-84	.254	.301	.239	81	299	40	76	13	2	6	41	21	3	2	5	71	7	5	.371	.305
Richardson, Hilton	L-L	6-3	200	1-10-89	.204	.172	.215	107	367	50	75	14	6	5	38	33	1	6	0	79	33	7	.316	.272
Robertson, Drew	R-R	6-3	185	12-22-87	.194	.000	.240	10	31	0	6	0	0	0	3	1	1	3	0	4	0	0	.194	.242
Stovall, Ryan	R-R	5-11	190	12-16-86	.179	.313	.137	17	67	5	12	6	1	0	8	2	0	0	1	21	1	0	.299	.203
Testa, Carlo	L-L	6-3	218	12-16-86	.275	.258	.282	128	461	83	127	24	14	12	50	60	7	3	4	125	28	9	.466	.365
Theriot, Ben	L-R	6-1	190	12-8-87	.300	.333	.277	30	110	13	33	13	0	1	20	11	0	1	2	25	0	0	.445	.358
Wood, Ryan	R-R	6-4	185	5-5-87	.211	.333	.178	18	57	5	12	0	1	0	7	10	1	1	0	12	0	0	.246	.338

Pitching	B-T	HT	WT	DOB	W	L	ERA	G	GS	CG	SV	IP	H	R	ER	HR	BB	SO	AVG	vLH	vRH	K/9	BB/9
Anderson, Brian	R-R	6-2	220	3-11-82	0	0	3.38	4	0	0	0	5	4	3	2	0	4	5	.211	.308	.000	8.44	6.75
Barrow, Brandon	L-L	6-4	195	4-18-89	1	0	4.35	8	0	0	0	10	7	5	5	2	5	4	.212	.364	.136	3.48	4.35
Byrne, Chas	B-R	6-3	185	1-26-89	0	1	7.71	5	0	0	0	7	12	7	6		5	10	.400	.474	.273	12.86	6.43
De La Rosa, Starling	L-L	6-5	160	9-19-87	1	1	5.09	12	0	0	0	23	19	16	13	1	26	24	.221	.138	.263	9.39	10.17
Dennick, Ryan	L-L	6-0	185	1-10-87	3	4	4.33	27	0	0	6	44	44	22	21	2	15	41	.260	.255	.263	8.45	3.09
Encarnacion, Rodolfo	R-R	5-11	180	5-8-86	1	2	8.03	36	0	0	3	49	53	54	44	6	45	45	.285	.333	.233	8.21	8.21
Hayenga, Keaton	R-R	6-4	190	7-10-88	3	12	6.13	21	19	1	0	106	130	90	72	12	47	43	.307	.294	.323	3.66	4.00
Herrera, Kelvin	R-R	5-10	162	12-31-89	2	3	4.35	8	8	0	0	41	38	20	20	1	15	40	.253	.237	.264	8.71	3.27
Hodge, Mitch	R-R	6-2	210	6-15-89	0	2	6.35	46	0	0	2	67	72	52	47	2	45	44	.279	.281	.277	5.94	6.07
Kelley, Scott	R-R	6-0	190	10-2-86	1	3	3.84	42	0	0	3	68	54	42	29	6	45	50	.220	.235	.208	6.62	5.96
Lafferty, Brendan	L-L	6-3	180	5-27-86	1	2	3.12	6	0	0	1	17	14	7	6	1	7	19	.219	.267	.204	9.87	3.63
Lamb, John	L-L	6-3	195	7-10-90	2	3	1.58	8	8	0	0	40	26	12	7	2	17	43	.188	.200	.183	9.68	3.83
Lehmann, Mike	B-R	6-2	185	5-3-89	1	4	6.82	15	1	0	1	32	43	27	24	6	17	21	.331	.283	.364	5.97	4.83
Marimon, Sugar Ray	R-R	6-1	168	9-30-88	2	6	5.91	14	14	0	0	70	73	48	46	4	27	50	.270	.274	.265	6.43	3.47
Mitchell, Matt	R-R	6-2	205	3-31-89	1	9	5.60	27	19	0	0	98	109	71	61	12	49	82	.280	.262	.296	7.53	4.50
Mozingo, Harold	R-R	6-1	175	3-29-85	1	0	6.23	6	0	0	1	9	9	6	6	3	5	10	.265	.111	.320	11.42	5.19
Odenbach, Dusty	R-R	6-3	225	9-3-87	8	10	5.21	31	15	0	0	102	114	66	59	6	56	92	.289	.263	.315	8.12	4.94
Paukovits, Bryan	R-R	6-7	240	6-29-87	3	3	3.32	13	9	0	1	62	43	30	23	5	16	65	.189	.183	.195	9.39	2.31
Pimentel, Elisaul	R-R	6-2	170	7-10-88	1	3	5.76	5	5	0	0	25	29	16	16	1	16	19	.299	.262	.375	6.84	5.76
2-team total (17 Great Lakes)					10	6	3.98	22	21	0	0	115	100	53	51	7	51	116	—	.—		9.05	3.98
Runion, Sam	R-R	6-4	220	11-9-88	0	2	6.45	23	0	0	1	38	51	34	27	3	14	24	.325	.349	.297	5.73	3.35
Sample, Tyler	L-R	6-7	245	6-27-88	6	10	4.69	26	26	1	0	121	105	75	63	8	95	115	.231	.258	.212	8.55	7.07
Sirrett, Onassis	R-R	5-11	180	12-15-88	1	1	8.31	21	0	0	1	30	41	30	28	5	23	35	.315	.303	.328	10.38	6.53
Wooley, Nick	R-R	6-2	160	4-18-88	2	6	6.75	17	12	0	0	75	87	58	56	6	44	54	.299	.284	.313	6.51	5.30
Worrell, Josh	R-R	6-5	215	11-17-86	0	0	1.50	3	0	0	0	6	4	2	1	0	2	5	.182	.143	.250	7.50	3.00

KANSAS CITY ROYALS

Fielding

Catcher	PCT	G	PO	A	E	DP	PB
Bonilla	.986	56	361	47	6	7	8
Cruz	.952	4	20	0	1	0	3
Graterol	1.000	7	52	9	0	1	1
Myers	.989	47	318	43	4	2	17
Robertson	.989	10	78	10	1	1	1
Theriot	.994	20	149	24	1	3	3

First Base	PCT	G	PO	A	E	DP
Cruz	.990	14	99	3	1	9
Frost	1.000	1	3	0	0	0
Graterol	.982	18	154	9	3	16
Kuebler	.989	42	349	21	4	34
Lewis	.982	66	540	58	11	60

Second Base	PCT	G	PO	A	E	DP
Batista	.971	73	118	217	10	45

	PCT	G	PO	A	E	DP
Frost	.944	8	14	20	2	4
Hall	.968	50	86	126	7	28
Liberto	.950	9	15	23	2	6
Wood	1.000	3	2	4	0	0

Third Base	PCT	G	PO	A	E	DP
Batista	.889	25	17	31	6	3
Cruz	.914	91	65	137	19	17
Frost	1.000	8	3	22	0	0
Hall	—	1	0	0	0	0
Stovall	.826	8	8	11	4	0
Wood	.850	11	2	15	3	1

Shortstop	PCT	G	PO	A	E	DP
Alfaro	.945	27	34	70	6	10
Batista	.846	11	15	29	8	6
Hall	.936	68	123	184	21	45

	PCT	G	PO	A	E	DP
Liberto	1.000	1	1	1	0	1
McClure	.961	27	48	75	5	19
Wood	.920	7	9	14	2	3

Outfield	PCT	G	PO	A	E	DP
Aparicio	.938	13	13	2	1	0
Caldwell	.955	23	40	2	2	2
Del Rosario	.964	13	24	3	1	1
Ferguson	1.000	7	15	0	0	0
Frost	1.000	7	12	0	0	0
Merrifield	.991	47	106	9	1	1
Oriental	.970	81	156	3	5	1
Richardson	.956	106	189	7	9	3
Testa	.978	124	211	16	5	6

BURLINGTON ROYALS   ROOKIE
APPALACHIAN LEAGUE

Batting	B-T	HT	WT	DOB	AVG	vLH	vRH	G	AB	R	H	2B	3B	HR	RBI	BB	HBP	SH	SF	SO	SB	CS	SLG	OBP
Baldwin, Geoff	L-L	6-4	195	11-8-90	.184	.078	.228	50	174	16	32	5	0	0	14	13	2	0	1	73	1	2	.213	.247
Escobar, Edul	R-R	5-11	185	9-2-90	.230	.225	.232	38	122	6	28	5	1	2	15	3	2	3	0	25	0	0	.336	.260
Figueroa, Yunior	B-R	6-0	170	8-8-90	.251	.265	.246	54	179	14	45	6	0	3	22	2	1	4	0	26	0	3	.335	.264
Fletcher, Brian	R-R	6-0	190	10-26-88	.313	.000	.313	4	16	4	5	0	0	2	4	1	0	0	0	5	2	0	.688	.353
Furmanek, Seth	R-R	6-1	200	12-31-87	.308	.125	.389	9	26	5	8	1	0	3	3	4	2	0	0	7	0	1	.692	.438
Howard, Anthony	L-L	6-1	180	11-9-90	.220	.220	.220	43	141	14	31	5	2	3	12	14	3	2	0	46	4	2	.348	.304
Jenkins, Ryan	R-R	6-2	215	1-26-87	.273	.255	.282	47	165	21	45	14	0	3	23	15	0	0	0	30	3	3	.412	.333
Liberto, Michael	R-R	5-7	170	6-21-88	.222	.118	.261	19	63	7	14	1	2	0	6	6	3	2	0	14	1	3	.302	.319
Llanos, Alex	R-R	6-1	160	9-21-90	.259	.228	.275	60	232	32	60	15	3	1	26	16	1	2	1	60	17	8	.362	.308
MacDougall, Gabe	R-R	6-1	190	4-13-87	.201	.238	.184	57	199	21	40	8	2	3	15	10	15	3	2	58	5	5	.307	.288
Martinez, Adrian	R-R	6-1	158	1-12-91	.205	.234	.187	36	122	13	25	3	0	0	9	7	3	2	0	28	2	3	.230	.265
McClure, Alex	B-R	6-0	185	6-16-89	.236	.204	.255	40	148	15	35	5	0	0	15	9	6	1	1	35	6	3	.270	.305
Piterson, Luis	R-R	5-11	155	6-10-90	.263	.225	.281	60	240	37	63	15	0	6	27	9	5	4	1	36	13	9	.400	.302
Robertson, Drew	R-R	6-3	185	12-22-87	.111	.000	.133	12	36	3	4	1	0	0	3	4	0	0	0	10	0	0	.139	.200
Rodriguez, Derek	R-R	5-9	160	2-13-89	.195	.222	.179	53	149	21	29	5	1	1	9	16	2	8	1	30	18	6	.262	.280
Stovall, Ryan	R-R	5-11	190	12-16-86	.303	.298	.306	61	241	33	73	15	5	4	24	20	1	0	0	41	12	8	.456	.374
Taylor, Reggie	R-R	6-1	200	9-28-86	.136	.333	.063	7	22	3	3	0	0	0	1	1	0	0	0	8	1	1	.136	.174

Pitching	B-T	HT	WT	DOB	W	L	ERA	G	GS	CG	SV	IP	H	R	ER	HR	BB	SO	AVG	vLH	vRH	K/9	BB/9
Avinazar, Willian	R-R	6-4	195	2-27-89	6	3	2.63	13	13	0	0	72	67	27	21	4	11	67	.246	.240	.250	8.38	1.38
Bavera, Claudio	L-L	5-10	200	6-30-87	2	4	4.50	21	0	0	2	32	36	17	16	2	6	25	.281	.241	.293	7.03	1.69
Byrne, Chas	B-R	6-3	185	1-26-89	1	0	0.80	15	0	0	6	34	19	3	3	1	5	38	.165	.149	.176	10.16	1.34
Dooley, Gates	R-R	6-0	205	8-22-88	4	6	4.37	14	12	0	0	60	66	35	29	5	12	40	.281	.283	.279	6.03	1.81
Giovenco, Mike	R-R	6-6	235	1-4-88	0	5	6.39	16	7	0	2	44	49	36	31	2	23	47	.283	.297	.275	9.69	4.74
Hernandez, Danny	R-R	6-1	180	4-14-89	2	0	2.19	8	1	0	1	12	8	3	3	0	3	13	.174	.083	.206	9.49	2.19
Keck, Jonathon	L-L	6-6	215	6-18-88	3	3	4.68	15	6	0	0	42	40	27	22	4	27	37	.244	.175	.266	7.87	5.74
Leaper, J.J.	R-R	6-1	160	3-12-87	0	0	3.00	14	0	0	2	21	22	10	7	3	8	13	.268	.154	.321	5.57	3.43
Lohden, Cole	R-R	6-4	220	6-13-88	1	4	3.74	17	0	0	1	34	30	19	14	6	19	32	.234	.317	.195	8.55	5.08
Mazur, Justin	R-R	6-2	195	4-20-88	0	2	5.34	17	0	0	0	32	38	23	19	5	9	26	.295	.333	.272	7.31	2.53
Penny, Robbie	L-R	6-3	215	11-8-88	1	1	1.75	19	1	0	5	46	37	13	9	1	12	36	.220	.233	.213	6.99	2.33
Ramsey, Jake	R-R	6-2	195	6-21-88	1	0	6.75	6	0	0	0	8	12	9	6	1	3	6	.333	.500	.227	6.75	3.38
Santiago, Leonel	R-R	6-0	178	12-23-89	6	3	2.78	14	14	0	0	81	73	29	25	5	17	66	.239	.202	.262	7.33	1.89
Simmons, Crawford	R-L	6-2	185	6-10-91	6	2	2.77	14	14	0	0	78	62	27	24	7	19	70	.220	.230	.217	8.08	2.19
Worrell, Josh	R-R	6-5	215	11-17-86	1	1	2.57	11	0	0	0	14	14	4	4	1	6	12	.264	.368	.206	7.71	3.86

Fielding

Catcher	PCT	G	PO	A	E	DP	PB
Escobar	.978	33	230	35	6	1	8
Furmanek	1.000	2	11	1	0	0	0
Jenkins	.983	28	201	28	4	1	4
Robertson	.975	11	65	12	2	1	5

First Base	PCT	G	PO	A	E	DP
Baldwin	.964	46	410	21	16	46
Furmanek	1.000	2	16	1	0	2
Stovall	.996	27	227	10	1	17

Second Base	PCT	G	PO	A	E	DP
Liberto	1.000	2	4	2	0	1

	PCT	G	PO	A	E	DP
Martinez	.958	6	4	19	1	2
Piterson	.970	59	140	179	10	43
Stovall	.933	5	9	5	1	3

Third Base	PCT	G	PO	A	E	DP
Figueroa	.847	46	26	85	20	11
Liberto	—	1	0	0	0	0
Martinez	.895	7	4	13	2	1
Stovall	.916	24	23	53	7	5

Shortstop	PCT	G	PO	A	E	DP
Liberto	.976	17	20	60	2	11
Martinez	.964	14	15	39	2	6

	PCT	G	PO	A	E	DP
McClure	.966	39	46	123	6	23
Stovall	1.000	1	3	4	0	2

Outfield	PCT	G	PO	A	E	DP
Fletcher	.833	4	5	0	1	0
Howard	1.000	43	66	2	0	0
Llanos	.962	59	119	6	5	2
MacDougall	.976	56	78	3	2	1
Rodriguez	1.000	45	91	2	0	0
Taylor	1.000	7	9	0	0	0

AZL ROYALS   ROOKIE
ARIZONA LEAGUE

Batting	B-T	HT	WT	DOB	AVG	vLH	vRH	G	AB	R	H	2B	3B	HR	RBI	BB	HBP	SH	SF	SO	SB	CS	SLG	OBP
Alcantara, Ysmelin	R-R	6-2	180	5-13-90	.262	.150	.303	44	149	14	39	8	3	5	22	10	3	2	0	49	4	2	.456	.321

Name	B-T	HT	WT	DOB	AVG	vLH	vRH	G	AB	R	H	2B	3B	HR	RBI	BB	HBP	SH	SF	SO	SB	CS	SLG	OBP
Antonio, Mike	R-R	6-2	190	10-26-91	.264	.171	.289	40	163	19	43	14	5	1	12	8	0	0	1	31	7	4	.429	.297
Beltre, Geulin	B-R	6-0	185	10-27-90	.273	.000	.300	3	11	4	3	1	0	0	2	1	1	0	0	4	0	0	.364	.385
Blanco, Jerico	R-R	6-1	160	5-25-92	.165	.056	.186	33	115	9	19	4	0	0	8	3	2	3	1	36	2	1	.200	.198
Bonifacio, Jorge	R-R	6-1	192	6-4-93	.211	.333	.188	21	76	9	16	0	5	0	6	6	1	1	2	31	1	2	.342	.271
Conner, Cameron	L-L	6-2	185	1-16-88	.213	.265	.198	42	150	15	32	4	6	1	16	14	3	2	0	58	11	3	.340	.293
Costa, Shane	L-R	6-0	205	12-12-81	.361	.571	.310	11	36	8	13	3	0	1	6	3	0	0	2	5	1	0	.528	.390
Cuthbert, Cheslor	R-R	6-1	190	11-16-92	.265	.077	.309	18	68	14	18	3	2	1	5	6	2	0	0	19	1	1	.412	.342
Dyson, Jarrod	L-R	5-9	160	8-15-84	.520	.667	.500	6	25	4	13	1	1	0	6	0	0	0	0	3	3	1	.640	.520
Eigsti, Ryan	R-R	6-2	195	8-24-85	.280	.400	.250	8	25	2	7	1	0	0	2	3	1	0	0	3	1	0	.320	.379
Fields, Josh	R-R	6-1	240	12-14-82	.400	.250	.500	3	10	2	4	1	1	0	4	3	0	0	0	2	0	0	.700	.538
Furmanek, Seth	R-R	6-1	200	12-31-87	.250	.200	.267	7	20	4	5	2	0	0	1	3	0	0	0	5	0	0	.350	.348
Liberto, Michael	R-R	5-7	170	6-21-88	.111	.000	.115	8	27	3	3	1	0	0	0	2	1	1	0	2	1	0	.148	.200
Marquez, Alexander	R-R	5-11	190	12-10-92	.141	.286	.100	26	64	7	9	0	0	0	3	16	1	3	0	17	1	1	.141	.321
Mateo, Daniel	B-R	6-1	178	8-10-91	.218	.261	.206	52	206	19	45	11	5	2	25	10	1	3	2	48	7	1	.350	.256
Moreno, Henry	R-R	6-2	162	6-6-89	.327	.182	.364	45	162	32	53	22	5	4	32	16	3	0	1	39	0	1	.599	.396
Polonia, Juan	B-R	6-1	173	12-16-89	.093	.000	.133	17	43	4	4	0	0	0	2	6	1	0	0	17	4	2	.093	.220
Prasch, Eddie	L-R	6-0	190	1-25-86	.182	.000	.333	4	11	2	2	0	0	0	2	3	0	0	2	3	0	0	.182	.313
Rodriguez, Jose	B-R	5-8	165	11-25-87	.266	.323	.250	39	143	22	38	2	4	0	17	7	4	2	1	29	13	6	.336	.316
Sandford, Darian	B-R	5-9	170	4-28-87	.279	.385	.250	38	122	28	34	4	3	0	9	16	1	0	1	36	30	6	.361	.364
Shin, Jin-Ho	R-R	6-2	200	10-20-91	.152	.154	.152	39	125	16	19	3	0	1	11	21	2	0	2	49	1	1	.200	.280
Soto, Victor	R-R	5-11	175	10-16-88	.252	.200	.268	34	107	12	27	4	2	0	20	6	1	2	2	26	8	1	.327	.293
Van Stratten, Nick	R-R	6-1	185	5-22-85	.333	.500	.250	4	12	4	4	3	0	0	1	2	1	0	0	2	0	0	.583	.467

Pitching	B-T	HT	WT	DOB	W	L	ERA	G	GS	CG	SV	IP	H	R	ER	HR	BB	SO	AVG	vLH	vRH	K/9	BB/9
Anderson, Brian	R-R	6-2	220	3-11-82	0	0	0.00	4	4	0	0	5	2	0	0	0	6	.118	.000	.167	10.80	0.00
Baez, Angel	R-R	6-3	196	2-14-91	0	2	5.40	7	4	0	0	15	9	15	9	1	10	14	.167	.136	.188	8.40	6.00
Bangs, Parker	R-R	6-4	210	12-22-87	0	0	18.00	4	0	0	0	3	10	6	6	0	5	1	.667	.000	.769	3.00	15.00
Blanco, Nicolas	R-R	6-2	190	3-23-87	0	0	4.50	4	0	0	0	4	6	3	2	0	2	7	.353	.125	.556	15.75	4.50
Boruff, Chase	L-R	6-2	195	7-27-88	0	1	1.80	6	0	0	3	10	6	5	2	0	4	11	.176	.263	.067	9.90	3.60
Brown, Rudy	L-L	6-4	225	6-16-88	2	1	2.52	15	1	0	0	39	40	14	11	1	10	40	.261	.138	.290	9.15	2.29
Cuevas, Gary	R-R	6-2	200	5-23-88	1	1	12.91	7	4	0	0	8	12	11	11	1	3	8	.364	.364	.364	9.39	3.52
Diaz, Eric	L-L	6-2	184	10-4-88	1	1	5.29	12	6	0	0	17	11	15	10	2	7	20	.167	.143	.173	10.59	3.71
Duffy, Danny	L-L	6-3	195	12-21-88	0	0	3.38	2	2	0	0	3	2	1	1	0	1	4	.222	.333	.167	13.50	3.38
Gatrell, Tyler	R-R	6-1	190	8-27-87	1	0	1.29	20	0	0	12	21	16	5	3	0	11	40	.205	.389	.150	17.14	4.71
Kriech, Kyle	L-L	6-3	220	10-27-87	2	2	7.25	16	0	0	0	22	41	22	18	2	5	15	.423	.333	.447	6.04	2.01
Lindsay, Dylan	R-R	6-2	185	9-9-91	1	1	4.61	10	0	0	0	14	15	11	7	1	2	6	.263	.333	.238	3.95	1.32
Lowery, Devon	L-R	6-1	215	3-24-83	0	0	0.00	1	0	0	0	1	3	0	0	0	2	.429	.333	.500	13.50	0.00
Martin, Brennon	L-L	6-3	195	5-5-87	3	2	2.57	6	3	0	0	28	20	9	8	0	4	29	.196	.323	.141	9.32	1.29
Melville, Tim	R-R	6-5	210	10-9-89	0	1	3.86	2	2	0	0	5	4	2	2	0	2	6	.222	.000	.308	11.57	3.86
Mitchell, Jason	R-R	6-2	185	3-13-88	0	0	0.00	2	0	0	0	2	1	0	0	1	1	.143	.000	.250	9.00	4.50
Montgomery, Mike	L-L	6-5	180	7-1-89	0	1	1.04	3	3	0	0	9	6	1	1	0	1	7	.207	.125	.238	7.27	1.04
Osuna, Edgar	L-L	6-1	185	11-25-87	0	0	0.00	1	0	0	0	3	3	0	0	0	4	.250	.250	.250	12.00	0.00
Peacock, Brian	L-L	6-3	190	5-7-90	0	0	0.00	2	1	0	0	3	1	1	0	0	4	.100	.000	.125	12.00	0.00
Pimentel, Julio	R-R	6-1	195	12-14-85	0	0	4.00	7	0	0	0	9	6	7	4	0	9	9	.171	.154	.182	9.00	9.00
Rodriguez, Jonathan	R-R	6-1	165	12-13-88	5	3	3.33	13	1	0	0	54	55	28	20	3	9	48	.261	.221	.284	8.00	1.50
Rogers, Nick	R-R	6-2	225	10-2-87	0	1	3.26	16	0	0	0	19	18	12	7	0	9	30	.231	.194	.255	13.97	4.19
Roualdes, Jordan	L-L	6-2	225	9-4-87	0	0	0.71	7	0	0	1	13	9	1	1	0	3	11	.184	.300	.154	7.82	2.13
Sanchez, Jose	L-L	5-10	160	4-20-89	1	1	3.60	15	0	0	0	20	21	10	8	0	8	24	.269	.318	.250	10.80	3.60
Soto, Jorge	R-R	6-3	180	11-1-91	0	2	4.74	7	2	0	1	25	30	16	13	3	2	27	.300	.345	.282	9.85	0.73
Ventura, Yordano	R-R	5-11	140	6-3-91	4	2	3.25	14	6	0	0	53	49	28	19	3	17	58	.236	.274	.210	9.91	2.91
White, Cole	R-R	6-2	195	1-22-88	0	0	0.00	6	1	0	3	7	2	0	0	0	3	.087	.000	.125	11.05	3.68
Wooley, Nick	R-R	6-2	160	4-18-88	0	0	0.00	4	0	0	1	6	1	0	0	0	2	5	.056	.000	.083	7.50	3.00
Yambati, Robinson	R-R	6-3	185	1-15-91	8	2	2.71	14	6	0	0	66	65	28	20	0	12	64	.252	.237	.261	8.68	1.63

Fielding

Catcher	PCT	G	PO	A	E	DP	PB
Eigsti	1.000	6	39	4	0	2	2
Furmanek	.833	1	4	1	1	0	1
Marquez	.991	25	204	19	2	0	16
Shin	.977	32	276	23	7	2	7

First Base	PCT	G	PO	A	E	DP
Furmanek	.963	3	26	0	1	1
Moreno	.977	45	396	32	10	29
Soto	.964	9	75	5	3	2

Second Base	PCT	G	PO	A	E	DP
Liberto	1.000	4	5	14	0	3
Mateo	.867	6	11	15	4	6
Rodriguez	.935	36	48	96	10	12

Sandford	—	1	0	0	0	0
Soto	.898	11	18	26	5	3

Third Base	PCT	G	PO	A	E	DP
Cuthbert	.854	17	12	23	6	1
Liberto	1.000	1	1	1	0	0
Mateo	.881	28	11	41	7	4
Prasch	1.000	3	4	3	0	0
Sandford	.600	2	0	3	2	0
Soto	.826	8	6	13	4	1

Shortstop	PCT	G	PO	A	E	DP
Antonio	.896	35	30	99	15	12
Liberto	1.000	3	3	8	0	2
Mateo	.873	17	27	42	10	9

	PCT	G	PO	A	E	DP
Soto	.750	2	2	4	2	0
Outfield	PCT	G	PO	A	E	DP
Alcantara	.950	36	54	3	3	0
Beltre	1.000	3	3	0	0	0
Blanco	.978	33	42	3	1	2
Bonifacio	.964	17	22	5	1	2
Conner	.979	31	45	1	1	0
Costa	1.000	7	11	0	0	0
Dyson	1.000	5	7	2	0	0
Polonia	.964	17	25	2	1	1
Rodriguez	—	1	0	0	0	0
Sandford	.983	29	53	6	1	0
Van Stratten	1.000	4	12	0	0	0

IDAHO FALLS CHUKARS

ROOKIE

PIONEER LEAGUE

Batting	B-T	HT	WT	DOB	AVG	vLH	vRH	G	AB	R	H	2B	3B	HR	RBI	BB	HBP	SH	SF	SO	SB	CS	SLG	OBP
Adams, Lane	R-R	6-4	190	11-13-89	.282	.259	.287	41	170	31	48	8	3	2	18	18	0	3	2	38	8	0	.400	.347
Aparicio, Julio	R-R	6-2	175	1-4-90	.286	.000	.333	4	14	3	4	0	1	0	1	1	1	0	0	4	0	0	.429	.375

Batting	B-T	HT	WT	DOB	AVG	vLH	vRH	G	AB	R	H	2B	3B	HR	RBI	BB	HBP	SH	SF	SO	SB	CS	SLG	OBP
Beltre, Geulin	B-R	6-0	185	10-27-90	.236	.097	.259	57	220	31	52	7	2	4	29	21	2	1	1	50	6	6	.341	.307
Conner, Cameron	L-L	6-2	185	1-16-88	.175	.000	.184	9	40	5	7	2	1	0	3	5	0	0	0	13	4	0	.275	.267
Cornstubble, Dale	R-R	5-11	175	3-4-88	.265	.133	.302	19	68	8	18	2	0	0	8	6	0	0	1	16	0	0	.294	.320
Culver, Malcom	R-R	6-2	190	2-9-90	.217	.222	.216	66	230	36	50	8	1	4	22	28	2	3	2	61	8	7	.313	.305
Cuthbert, Cheslor	R-R	6-1	190	11-16-92	.233	.333	.222	14	60	10	14	4	1	2	10	3	1	0	0	16	1	0	.433	.281
David, Kevin	R-R	6-1	205	4-10-88	.277	.400	.261	37	130	14	36	12	0	2	16	10	5	0	4	29	2	1	.415	.342
Espinal, Yowill	R-R	6-0	170	4-1-91	.252	.378	.227	58	218	33	55	6	2	1	27	26	3	7	1	61	16	6	.312	.339
Ferguson, Tim	R-R	6-0	190	10-25-88	.296	.500	.264	40	162	25	48	7	1	1	12	10	0	1	1	43	4	1	.370	.335
Figueroa, Correy	L-R	6-0	180	6-30-87	.209	.286	.202	30	91	10	19	0	0	0	3	10	1	0	0	16	1	1	.209	.294
Howard, Anthony	L-L	6-1	180	11-9-90	.105	.000	.118	6	19	1	2	1	0	0	0	1	2	0	0	4	1	1	.158	.227
Jones, Travis	R-R	6-2	200	5-23-89	.284	.217	.297	37	141	12	40	7	0	3	18	10	2	1	0	35	0	1	.397	.340
Kuebler, Jake	R-R	6-5	200	9-3-89	.330	.353	.325	23	94	16	31	9	0	3	18	6	0	0	1	26	3	2	.521	.366
Liberto, Michael	R-R	5-7	170	6-21-88	.400	.000	.444	5	20	5	8	2	0	0	4	2	0	0	0	4	2	0	.500	.455
Monger, Cameron	R-R	6-2	210	8-5-88	.288	.538	.205	14	52	12	15	4	1	0	8	2	1	1	0	12	6	0	.404	.327
Pickett, Jovan	L-L	5-8	160	11-11-87	.387	.000	.444	9	31	8	12	0	1	0	3	4	0	0	0	7	4	1	.452	.457
Polonia, Juan	B-R	6-1	173	12-16-89	.218	.111	.239	30	110	10	24	4	1	0	8	10	1	0	2	43	10	5	.273	.289
Taylor, Reggie	R-R	6-1	200	9-28-86	.242	.267	.238	32	95	15	23	5	3	1	9	15	2	0	1	27	4	0	.389	.354
Trapp, Justin	R-R	6-1	175	10-7-90	.269	.205	.281	67	260	39	70	14	0	0	21	26	5	13	1	71	21	6	.323	.346
Watts, Murray	L-R	6-7	270	10-8-87	.279	.243	.285	69	251	37	70	13	1	14	57	45	2	0	3	75	2	0	.506	.389
Zebroski, Tom	R-R	5-10	188	9-8-88	.243	.423	.200	40	136	15	33	8	1	1	18	7	0	2	0	26	3	2	.338	.280

Pitching	B-T	HT	WT	DOB	W	L	ERA	G	GS	CG	SV	IP	H	R	ER	HR	BB	SO	AVG	vLH	vRH	K/9	BB/9
Alexander, Scott	L-L	6-2	190	7-10-89	1	6	5.73	12	11	0	0	55	73	47	35	6	22	41	.320	.306	.325	6.71	3.60
Billo, Greg	R-R	6-4	220	7-15-90	4	8	5.17	17	13	0	0	78	92	56	45	11	23	79	.291	.320	.266	9.08	2.64
Blauer, Chad	R-R	6-3	215	12-21-87	2	1	6.14	18	5	0	0	51	69	41	35	1	9	47	.315	.337	.298	8.24	1.58
Cantrell, Eric	R-R	6-4	210	7-25-89	0	0	9.00	1	0	0	0	3	2	3	2	0	0	2	.375	.500	.250	9.00	0.00
Carl, Edwin	R-R	6-0	210	8-31-88	1	1	7.02	10	0	0	2	17	17	13	13	4	6	28	.250	.261	.244	15.12	3.24
De La Rosa, Starling	L-L	6-5	160	9-19-87	0	3	6.10	6	2	0	0	21	25	16	14	1	5	22	.287	.297	.280	9.58	2.18
Duffy, Danny	L-L	6-3	195	12-21-88	0	1	1.50	2	2	0	0	6	4	1	1	0	0	6	.182	.222	.154	9.00	0.00
Garrido, Santiago	R-R	6-1	195	10-4-89	2	3	6.06	12	10	0	0	49	70	40	33	5	17	33	.335	.335	.333	6.06	3.12
Graffeo, Nick	R-R	6-2	190	12-14-87	0	1	4.05	18	0	1	0	33	36	23	15	1	14	46	.271	.340	.225	12.42	3.78
Graham, Tyler	R-R	6-4	250	10-5-87	1	1	5.58	18	0	0	1	31	40	22	19	2	20	27	.323	.370	.295	7.92	5.87
Lohden, Cole	R-R	6-4	220	6-13-88	1	0	7.20	2	0	0	0	5	4	4	4	0	5	3	.250	.250	.250	5.40	9.00
Lowery, Devon	L-R	6-1	215	3-24-83	0	0	1.50	3	0	0	1	6	2	1	1	0	1	10	.105	.200	.000	15.00	1.50
Mariot, Michael	R-R	6-0	190	10-20-88	2	2	3.54	15	7	0	0	56	50	29	22	4	16	64	.237	.260	.216	10.29	2.57
Martin, Brennon	L-L	6-3	195	5-5-87	4	3	4.36	12	5	0	0	43	58	29	21	8	5	45	.310	.226	.352	9.35	1.04
Mitchell, Jason	R-R	6-2	185	3-13-88	1	2	5.48	14	0	0	0	23	29	18	14	0	13	19	.302	.333	.290	7.43	5.09
Peacock, Brian	L-L	6-3	190	5-7-90	0	5	6.86	13	7	0	0	39	58	41	30	3	18	30	.352	.360	.348	6.86	4.12
Penny, Robbie	L-R	6-3	215	11-8-88	1	0	3.00	2	0	0	0	6	4	2	2	0	2	8	.200	.222	.182	12.00	3.00
Perez, Leondy	R-R	6-1	190	8-19-89	3	6	5.70	14	14	0	0	66	76	45	42	7	28	75	.289	.318	.268	10.18	3.80
Rivers, Alex	R-R	5-10	170	8-13-88	1	2	5.34	21	0	0	6	29	39	21	17	1	7	38	.312	.345	.286	11.93	2.20
Roualdes, Jordan	L-L	6-2	225	9-4-87	1	1	5.96	11	0	0	0	23	29	17	15	2	8	13	.326	.290	.345	5.16	3.18

Fielding

Catcher	PCT	G	PO	A	E	DP	PB
Cornstubble	.968	19	171	40	7	1	4
David	.984	29	209	42	4	3	5
Jones	.980	30	258	32	6	3	10

First Base	PCT	G	PO	A	E	DP
Culver	.986	24	200	9	3	17
Kuebler	.985	19	186	14	3	15
Watts	.991	34	308	16	3	22

Second Base	PCT	G	PO	A	E	DP
Espinal	.915	46	90	146	22	29
Figueroa	.950	21	31	64	5	11
Zebroski	.986	12	21	49	1	9

Third Base	PCT	G	PO	A	E	DP
Culver	.901	38	40	69	12	6
Cuthbert	.957	11	5	17	1	0
Figueroa	.818	7	0	9	2	1
Liberto	.867	5	5	8	2	1
Zebroski	.844	17	11	27	7	3

Shortstop	PCT	G	PO	A	E	DP
Espinal	.900	5	5	13	2	3
Figueroa	1.000	1	0	3	0	1
Trapp	.891	67	86	183	33	35
Zebroski	1.000	4	7	9	0	2

Outfield	PCT	G	PO	A	E	DP
Adams	.985	38	62	5	1	1
Aparicio	1.000	4	5	2	0	1
Beltre	.917	53	82	6	8	2
Conner	1.000	9	10	0	0	0
Culver	1.000	4	6	0	0	0
Ferguson	.970	39	59	5	2	1
Figueroa	—	1	0	0	0	0
Howard	1.000	6	6	0	0	0
Monger	.950	10	18	1	1	0
Pickett	1.000	9	11	0	0	0
Polonia	.942	29	48	1	3	0
Taylor	.850	30	30	4	6	0

DSL ROYALS   ROOKIE

DOMINICAN SUMMER LEAGUE

Batting	B-T	HT	WT	DOB	AVG	vLH	vRH	G	AB	R	H	2B	3B	HR	RBI	BB	HBP	SH	SF	SO	SB	CS	SLG	OBP
Bello, Rainier	B-R	5-10	165	6-1-92	.159	.091	.183	27	82	6	13	1	0	0	9	5	4	0	1	8	1	0	.171	.239
Bonifacio, Jorge	R-R	6-1	192	6-4-93	.335	.395	.314	48	164	22	55	16	2	1	28	26	3	0	3	27	13	5	.476	.429
Caxito, Orlando	R-R	5-11	160	2-3-92	.227	.250	.220	20	66	10	15	6	0	0	12	13	0	0	1	13	3	1	.318	.350
Cordova, Jesus	B-R	5-11	155	1-29-91	.214	.242	.202	48	117	14	25	1	2	0	3	17	2	5	0	40	11	3	.256	.324
Garcia, Carlos	R-R	6-0	176	3-18-92	.255	.246	.258	70	235	36	60	11	0	0	26	42	7	6	2	27	50	12	.302	.381
Giron, Jose	R-R	5-11	155	6-27-93	.236	.191	.250	65	199	28	47	4	1	0	9	28	2	10	2	44	18	14	.266	.333
Gomez, Moises	R-R	5-11	180	1-20-92	.169	.160	.173	31	77	6	13	0	0	0	10	14	1	2	1	14	1	0	.169	.301
Gonzalez, Pedro	R-R	6-2	162	1-28-92	.252	.139	.287	52	151	13	38	7	0	0	20	19	4	5	3	26	2	1	.298	.345
Nivar, Pedro	R-R	5-10	170	1-13-92	.253	.250	.254	53	150	19	38	12	2	0	8	11	4	8	5	40	8	5	.400	.369
Patino, Alfredo	R-R	6-1	175	5-18-93	.236	.233	.237	45	123	19	29	0	0	1	16	7	3	0	2	22	9	4	.236	.356
Santos, Ramon	R-R	6-3	193	11-5-91	.251	.204	.268	64	187	24	47	8	2	3	25	12	5	4	6	36	7	3	.364	.305
Suriel, Joelfi	R-R	6-0	185	12-27-91	.176	.138	.188	45	125	11	22	3	1	2	16	13	1	2	0	42	1	0	.264	.259
Torres, Ramon	B-R	5-10	155	1-22-93	.229	.414	.193	56	179	30	41	6	1	1	20	22	3	11	3	26	15	7	.291	.319

	B-T	HT	WT	DOB																								
Vasquez, Jhorman	R-R	6-4	205	3-30-91	.206	.083	.244	35	102	12	21	7	0	0	10	2	8	1	2	33	0	1	.275	.272				
Villegas, Luis	R-R	5-10	170	12-2-92	.218	.296	.193	42	110	16	24	3	2	1	8	18	6	2	1	22	0	0	.309	.356				

Pitching	B-T	HT	WT	DOB	W	L	ERA	G	GS	CG	SV	IP	H	R	ER	HR	BB	SO	AVG	vLH	vRH	K/9	BB/9
Baez, Angel	R-R	6-3	196	2-14-91	0	1	2.93	8	7	0	0	31	29	12	10	1	14	25	.257	.161	.293	7.34	4.11
Bravo, Oswaldo	L-L	5-9	152	4-23-93	1	0	3.68	12	0	0	2	15	11	7	6	0	7	10	.208	.333	.200	6.14	4.30
Brazoban, Jose	R-R	5-9	165	5-28-93	4	1	1.30	14	14	0	0	69	45	15	10	2	26	49	.191	.190	.191	6.39	3.39
Diaz, Frankelis	R-R	6-0	190	9-25-91	4	2	3.20	12	7	0	0	51	50	27	18	0	11	26	.258	.212	.275	4.62	1.95
Garcia, Dilson	R-R	6-2	184	9-9-91	2	4	3.17	14	9	1	0	48	50	23	17	1	10	41	.266	.250	.271	7.63	1.86
Guete, Elkin	R-R	6-1	170	12-24-91	0	0	22.09	6	0	0	0	7	20	22	18	0	11	7	.513	.600	.483	8.59	13.50
Guzman, Luis	R-R	6-3	222	7-21-91	0	0	24.30	8	0	0	0	7	15	19	18	1	12	2	.429	.375	.444	2.70	16.20
Martinez, Jossiel	L-L	5-10	160	11-9-91	2	3	4.45	14	1	0	5	30	31	15	15	1	10	26	.261	.400	.254	7.71	2.97
Melgar, Luis	R-R	6-3	153	2-5-92	1	2	3.34	12	3	0	0	30	19	16	11	0	12	19	.184	.226	.167	5.76	3.64
Nina, Aroni	R-R	6-4	160	4-9-90	3	3	3.38	12	0	0	1	24	20	12	9	0	15	12	.230	.192	.246	4.50	5.63
Ortiz, Jesus	R-R	5-10	170	1-6-91	0	1	10.13	9	1	0	0	11	16	12	12	2	5	10	.327	.273	.342	8.44	4.22
Penalo, Victor	R-R	5-10	154	7-12-91	3	2	3.51	17	0	0	6	33	39	22	13	0	15	29	.289	.387	.260	7.83	4.05
Rodriguez, Freddy	R-R	6-3	188	12-1-90	1	0	0.79	5	0	0	0	11	9	1	1	0	0	4	.220	.300	.194	3.18	0.00
Rosario, Sergio	R-R	5-11	184	8-20-90	3	3	2.04	14	12	1	0	62	45	19	14	0	20	61	.207	.277	.178	8.90	2.92
Santos, Erlin	R-R	6-1	185	1-22-91	1	2	8.10	7	0	0	2	13	15	13	12	0	10	11	.288	.263	.301	7.43	6.75
Soto, Jorge	R-R	6-3	180	11-1-91	2	4	3.29	8	7	0	0	38	32	17	14	0	7	38	.219	.188	.235	8.92	1.64
Velasquez, Angelo	R-R	6-0	160	9-19-91	4	4	2.96	16	4	0	3	46	41	17	15	2	16	31	.241	.250	.237	6.11	3.15
Ventura, Yordano	R-R	5-11	140	6-3-91	0	1	2.31	3	3	0	0	12	9	5	3	0	1	13	.209	.125	.259	10.03	0.77

Fielding

Catcher	PCT	G	PO	A	E	DP	PB
Bello	1.000	10	48	6	0	0	2
Gomez	.939	9	38	8	3	0	0
Gonzalez	.983	47	228	55	5	1	6
Villegas	.992	20	95	22	1	0	4

First Base	PCT	G	PO	A	E	DP
Suriel	.987	33	299	6	4	18
Vasquez	.978	34	254	15	6	26
Villegas	.964	11	77	4	3	7

Second Base	PCT	G	PO	A	E	DP
Cordova	.971	36	60	73	4	13

	PCT	G	PO	A	E	DP
Garcia	.951	23	39	59	5	17
Nivar	.667	1	2	0	1	0
Patino	1.000	3	0	2	0	0
Torres	1.000	18	32	41	0	10

Third Base	PCT	G	PO	A	E	DP
Cordova	.880	7	7	15	3	2
Garcia	.903	26	15	50	7	3
Nivar	—	1	0	0	0	0
Patino	.885	35	27	81	14	6
Suriel	.833	11	5	10	3	0

Shortstop	PCT	G	PO	A	E	DP
Caxito	.967	15	18	40	2	7
Garcia	.901	27	28	45	8	5
Torres	.963	39	56	100	6	25

Outfield	PCT	G	PO	A	E	DP
Bonifacio	.944	46	79	5	5	1
Giron	.975	65	112	5	3	2
Nivar	.936	42	42	2	3	0
Patino	.875	7	7	0	1	0
Santos	.991	64	99	6	1	2

KANSAS CITY ROYALS

Los Angeles Angels

SEASON IN A SENTENCE: After three straight American League West titles, the Angels fell back to third in 2010 thanks to injuries and a sputtering offense.

HIGH POINT: The Angels spent all of one day alone in first place in 2010, going up by a half-game on June 7 after a 4-2 win over the Athletics, capping a six-game winning streak. The lineup produced plenty of power, with four players hitting at least 20 home runs, but not enough runs.

LOW POINT: The Angels should have known they were in for a long year when they went on a seven-game swing through Detroit and Boston at the beginning of May and lost all seven games, salvaging the trip only by taking two of three in Seattle. But the low point had to come on May 29, when Kendry Morales hit a walkoff grand slam in a 5-1 win over the Mariners, then broke his leg in the celebration at home plate, knocking him out for the rest of the season

NOTABLE ROOKIES: Though not technically a rookie, former top prospect Brandon Wood still is not established and failed yet again in his effort to break through in the major leagues, batting .146 in 226 at-bats. Outfielder Peter Bourjos showed flashes but batted just .204 himself. The most promising rookie was righthander Jordan Walden, who had a 2.35 in 15 late-season innings and should be an important member of the major league bullpen in 2011.

KEY TRANSACTIONS: The Angels were buyers at the trade deadline, bringing in Dan Haren from the Diamondbacks and Alberto Callaspo from the Royals at the cost of six players, including lefthander Joe Saunders. By the time August rolled around, they were selling, unloading closer Brian Fuentes to the Twins for marginal prospect Loek van Mil. The most significant transaction occurred after that, however, when the organization fired scouting director Eddie Bane, who had been in the position since 2004. They promoted national crosschecker Ric Wilson to take his place.

DOWN ON THE FARM: Outfielder Mike Trout emerged as one of the top prospects in the game, finishing as the top prospect in both the low Class A Midwest and high Class A California leagues. Four of the Angels' six affiliates had winning records, though Double-A Arkansas was the worst team in the Texas League and several prospects like lefthander Trevor Reckling took steps back in their development.

OPENING DAY PAYROLL: $104.9 million (8th)

PLAYERS OF THE YEAR

MAJOR LEAGUE	MINOR LEAGUE
Jered Weaver	**Mike Trout**
rhp	of
13-12, 3.01	(High A/Low A)
Led AL with 233 SO,	.341/.428/.490
3rd in WHIP, IP	Midwest League MVP

ORGANIZATION LEADERS

BATTING		*Minimum 250 at-bats
MAJORS		
*AVG	Torii Hunter	.281
*OPS	Hideki Matsui	.820
HR	Mike Napoli	26
RBI	Torii Hunter	90
MINORS		
*AVG	Mike Trout, Cedar Rapids/Rancho Cuca.	.341
*OBP	Mike Trout, Cedar Rapids/Rancho Cuca.	.428
*SLG	Mark Trumbo, Salt Lake	.577
R	Mike Trout, Cedar Rapids/Rancho Cuca.	106
H	Mike Trout, Cedar Rapids/Rancho Cuca.	173
TB	Mark Trumbo, Salt Lake	307
2B	Luis Jimenez, Cedar Rapids/Rancho Cuca.	46
3B	Four tied at	12
HR	Mark Trumbo, Salt Lake	36
RBI	Mark Trumbo, Salt Lake	122
BB	Mike Trout, Cedar Rapids/Rancho Cuca.	73
SO	Angel Castillo, Rancho Cucamonga	140
SB	Mike Trout, Cedar Rapids/Rancho Cuca.	56

PITCHING		†Minimum 75 innings
MAJORS		
W	Ervin Santana	17
†ERA	Dan Haren	2.87
SO	Jered Weaver	233
MINORS		
W	Tyler Chatwood, Rancho/Arkansas/Salt Lake	13
	Patrick Corbin, Cedar Rapids/Rancho Cuca.	13
L	Manuel Flores, Rancho Cucamonga/Arkansas	14
†ERA	Tyler Chatwood, Rancho/Arkansas/Salt Lake	2.84
G	Eddie McKiernan, Salt Lake/Rancho Cuca.	56
GS	Tim Kiely, Salt Lake/Arkansas	28
	Trevor Reckling, Salt Lake/Arkansas	28
SV	Eddie McKiernan, Salt Lake/Rancho Cuca.	28
IP	Tim Kiely, Salt Lake/Arkansas	163
BB	Trevor Reckling, Salt Lake/Arkansas	85
SO	Garrett Richards, Cedar Rapids/Rancho Cuca.	149
†AVG	Orangel Arenas, Cedar Rapids/Rancho Cuca.	.241

General Manager: Tony Reagins. **Farm Director:** Abe Flores. **Scouting Director:** Eddie Bane.

Class	Team	League	W	L	PCT	Finish*	Manager(s)
Majors	Los Angeles Angels	American	80	82	.494	10th (14)	Mike Scioscia
Triple-A	Salt Lake Bees	Pacific Coast	73	71	.507	9th (16)	Bobby Mitchell
Double-A	Arkansas Travelers	Texas	55	85	.393	8th (8)	Bobby Magallanes
High A	Rancho Cucamonga Quakes	California	78	62	.557	2nd (10)	Keith Johnson
Low A	Cedar Rapids Kernels	Midwest	82	56	.594	3rd (16)	Bill Mosiello
Rookie	Orem Owlz	Pioneer	39	36	.520	4th (8)	Tom Kotchman
Rookie	AZL Angels	Arizona	24	31	.436	9th (12)	Tyrone Boykin
Overall 2010 Minor League Record			351	341	.507	13th (30)	

*Finish in overall standings (No. of teams in league). †League champion.

ORGANIZATION STATISTICS

LOS ANGELES ANGELS

AMERICAN LEAGUE

Batting	B-T	HT	WT	DOB	AVG	vLH	vRH	G	AB	R	H	2B	3B	HR	RBI	BB	HBP	SH	SF	SO	SB	CS	SLG	OBP
Abreu, Bobby	L-R	6-0	210	3-11-74	.255	.228	.267	154	573	88	146	41	1	20	78	87	2	0	5	132	24	10	.435	.352
Aldridge, Cory	L-R	6-1	225	6-13-79	.077	.000	.111	5	13	0	1	0	1	0	1	0	0	0	0	5	0	0	.231	.077
Aybar, Erick	B-R	5-10	170	1-14-84	.253	.252	.253	138	534	69	135	18	4	5	29	35	7	11	2	81	22	8	.330	.306
Bourjos, Peter	R-R	6-1	180	3-31-87	.204	.182	.214	51	181	19	37	6	4	6	15	6	2	3	1	40	10	3	.381	.237
Budde, Ryan	R-R	5-11	210	8-15-79	.400	1.000	.143	6	10	2	4	1	0	1	3	1	0	0	0	5	0	0	.800	.455
Callaspo, Alberto	B-R	5-8	200	4-19-83	.249	.200	.260	58	213	21	53	8	0	2	13	12	1	1	1	13	2	2	.315	.291
2-team total (88 Kansas City)					.265	—	—	146	562	61	149	27	2	10	56	31	1	1	6	42	5	3	.374	.302
Conger, Hank	B-R	6-1	220	1-29-88	.172	.000	.185	13	29	2	5	1	1	0	5	5	0	0	0	9	0	0	.276	.294
Evans, Terry	R-R	6-3	205	1-19-82	.000	.000	.000	1	1	0	0	0	0	0	0	0	0	0	0	1	0	0	.000	.000
Frandsen, Kevin	R-R	6-0	185	5-24-82	.250	.226	.262	54	160	24	40	11	0	0	14	9	1	3	0	10	2	0	.319	.294
Hunter, Torii	R-R	6-2	225	7-18-75	.281	.257	.292	152	573	76	161	36	0	23	90	61	7	0	5	106	9	12	.464	.354
Izturis, Maicer	B-R	5-8	170	9-12-80	.250	.280	.241	61	212	27	53	13	1	3	27	21	2	1	2	27	7	3	.363	.321
Kendrick, Howard	R-R	5-10	215	7-12-83	.279	.264	.286	158	616	67	172	41	4	10	75	28	5	4	5	94	14	4	.407	.313
Mathis, Jeff	R-R	6-0	200	3-31-83	.195	.204	.192	68	205	19	40	6	1	3	18	6	1	3	3	59	3	0	.278	.219
Matsui, Hideki	L-R	6-2	210	6-12-74	.274	.236	.289	145	482	55	132	24	1	21	84	67	1	0	4	98	0	1	.459	.361
McAnulty, Paul	L-R	5-11	225	2-24-81	.136	.000	.136	9	22	2	3	0	0	1	2	2	0	0	0	11	0	0	.273	.208
Morales, Kendry	B-R	6-1	225	6-20-83	.290	.208	.339	51	193	29	56	5	0	11	39	12	5	0	1	31	0	1	.487	.346
Napoli, Mike	R-R	6-0	215	10-31-81	.238	.305	.208	140	453	60	108	24	1	26	68	42	11	0	4	137	4	2	.468	.316
Quinlan, Robb	R-R	6-1	215	3-17-77	.121	.250	.048	23	33	4	4	2	0	0	2	2	0	1	0	6	2	0	.182	.171
Rivera, Juan	R-R	6-2	230	7-3-78	.252	.264	.246	124	416	53	105	20	0	15	52	33	4	0	2	58	2	2	.409	.312
Romine, Andrew	B-R	6-1	190	12-24-85	.091	.000	.100	5	11	0	1	0	0	0	0	0	0	1	0	4	0	0	.091	.091
Ryan, Michael	L-R	5-11	220	7-6-77	.205	.100	.211	22	39	3	8	4	0	0	2	1	0	0	1	5	0	0	.308	.220
Trumbo, Mark	R-R	6-4	220	1-16-86	.067	.000	.100	8	15	2	1	0	0	0	2	1	0	0	0	8	0	0	.067	.125
Willits, Reggie	B-R	5-11	185	5-30-81	.258	.255	.259	97	159	23	41	7	0	0	8	19	1	3	0	26	2	4	.302	.341
Wilson, Bobby	R-R	6-0	220	4-8-83	.229	.250	.222	40	96	12	22	6	0	4	15	8	0	2	0	23	0	0	.417	.288
Wood, Brandon	R-R	6-3	210	3-2-85	.146	.169	.134	81	226	20	33	2	0	4	14	6	2	8	1	71	1	0	.208	.174

Pitching	B-T	HT	WT	DOB	W	L	ERA	G	GS	CG	SV	IP	H	R	ER	HR	BB	SO	AVG	vLH	vRH	K/9	BB/9
Bell, Trevor	L-R	6-2	185	10-12-86	2	5	4.72	25	7	0	0	61	77	35	32	2	21	45	.312	.308	.316	6.64	3.10
Bulger, Jason	R-R	6-4	210	12-6-78	0	0	4.88	25	0	0	0	24	25	14	13	3	15	25	.269	.250	.283	9.38	5.63
Cassevah, Bobby	R-R	6-3	195	9-11-85	1	2	3.15	16	0	0	0	20	23	11	7	0	8	8	.277	.386	.154	3.60	3.60
Fuentes, Brian	L-L	6-4	230	8-9-75	4	1	3.52	39	0	0	23	38	28	17	15	5	18	39	.201	.132	.228	9.16	4.23
2-team total (9 Minnesota)					4	1	2.81	48	0	0	24	48	31	17	15	5	20	47	—	—	—	8.81	3.75
Haren, Dan	R-R	6-5	215	9-17-80	5	4	2.87	14	14	1	0	94	84	31	30	8	25	75	.237	.220	.256	7.18	2.39
Jepsen, Kevin	R-R	6-3	215	7-26-84	2	4	3.97	68	0	0	0	59	54	26	26	2	29	61	.250	.239	.263	9.31	4.42
Kazmir, Scott	L-L	6-0	175	1-24-84	9	15	5.94	28	28	0	0	150	158	103	99	25	79	93	.271	.274	.271	5.58	4.74
Kohn, Michael	R-R	6-0	200	6-26-86	2	0	2.11	24	0	0	1	21	17	5	5	0	16	20	.227	.325	.114	8.44	6.75
O'Sullivan, Sean	R-R	6-2	230	9-1-87	1	0	2.08	5	1	0	0	13	7	3	3	1	4	6	.156	.111	.185	4.15	2.77
2-team total (14 Kansas City)					4	6	5.49	19	14	0	0	84	90	53	51	15	31	43	—	—	—	4.63	3.33
Palmer, Matt	R-R	6-2	225	3-21-79	1	2	4.54	14	1	0	0	34	38	20	17	1	20	17	.281	.268	.291	4.54	5.35
Pineiro, Joel	R-R	6-1	200	9-25-78	10	7	3.84	23	23	3	0	152	155	66	65	15	34	92	.261	.239	.284	5.44	2.01
Rodney, Fernando	R-R	5-11	215	3-18-77	4	3	4.24	72	0	0	14	68	70	33	32	4	35	53	.263	.273	.254	7.01	4.63
Rodriguez, Francisco	R-R	6-1	195	2-26-83	1	3	4.37	43	0	0	0	47	46	23	23	5	26	36	.254	.338	.192	6.85	4.94
Rodriguez, Rafael	R-R	6-1	175	9-24-84	0	0	4.50	1	0	0	0	2	1	1	1	0	2	1	.143	.250	.000	4.50	9.00
Santana, Ervin	R-R	6-2	185	12-12-82	17	10	3.92	33	33	4	0	223	221	104	97	27	73	169	.259	.271	.246	6.83	2.95
Saunders, Joe	L-L	6-3	210	6-16-81	6	10	4.62	20	20	2	0	121	135	70	62	14	45	64	.290	.287	.291	4.77	3.36
Shields, Scot	R-R	6-1	180	7-22-75	0	3	5.28	43	1	0	0	46	45	31	27	6	34	39	.254	.172	.333	7.63	6.65
Stokes, Brian	R-R	6-1	210	9-7-79	0	0	8.10	16	0	0	0	17	26	18	15	4	16	16	.361	.382	.342	8.64	8.64
Thompson, Rich	R-R	6-1	180	7-1-84	2	0	1.37	13	0	0	0	20	12	4	3	2	4	15	.171	.100	.225	6.86	1.83
Walden, Jordan	R-R	6-5	240	11-16-87	0	1	2.35	16	0	0	1	15	13	4	4	1	7	23	.224	.214	.233	13.50	4.11
Weaver, Jered	R-R	6-7	205	10-4-82	13	12	3.01	34	34	0	0	224	187	83	75	23	54	233	.222	.223	.220	9.35	2.17

Fielding

Catcher	PCT	G	PO	A	E	DP	PB
Budde	1.000	6	35	2	0	1	2
Conger	.957	10	63	3	3	0	0
Mathis	.985	67	433	36	7	2	6
Napoli	.986	66	405	32	6	4	5
Wilson	.996	38	217	12	1	2	3

First Base	PCT	G	PO	A	E	DP
Frandsen	1.000	4	35	3	0	4
Kendrick	.990	15	98	4	1	5
McAnulty	.978	5	45	0	1	3
Morales	.996	51	435	25	2	35
Napoli	.989	70	502	44	6	33
Quinlan	.986	13	71	1	1	7
Rivera	.991	13	98	12	1	8
Ryan	1.000	4	28	2	0	3
Trumbo	1.000	6	38	4	0	5
Wilson	1.000	1	4	0	0	0

Wood	1.000	2	11	0	0	1

Second Base	PCT	G	PO	A	E	DP
Callaspo	—	1	0	0	0	0
Frandsen	.900	4	3	6	1	2
Izturis	.988	22	30	52	1	6
Kendrick	.986	143	259	366	9	74

Third Base	PCT	G	PO	A	E	DP
Callaspo	.972	54	38	100	4	12
Frandsen	.953	43	28	73	5	3
Izturis	.984	28	14	47	1	7
Quinlan	—	1	0	0	0	0
Wood	.956	56	33	76	5	6

Shortstop	PCT	G	PO	A	E	DP
Aybar	.963	135	198	344	21	59
Izturis	1.000	7	5	24	0	3
Romine	.900	4	9	9	2	3

Wood	.940	22	22	56	5	7

Outfield	PCT	G	PO	A	E	DP
Abreu	.976	134	242	7	6	2
Aldridge	1.000	5	5	0	0	0
Bourjos	.994	51	149	10	1	1
Callaspo	—	1	0	0	0	0
Evans	1.000	1	1	0	0	0
Frandsen	.000	1	0	0	1	0
Hunter	.992	143	358	4	3	0
Kendrick	—	1	0	0	0	0
Matsui	1.000	18	16	1	0	0
Quinlan	1.000	4	1	0	0	0
Rivera	.978	105	214	8	5	1
Ryan	1.000	11	11	0	0	0
Trumbo	.667	1	1	1	1	0
Willits	.991	76	109	5	1	0

SALT LAKE BEES   TRIPLE-A
PACIFIC COAST LEAGUE

Batting	B-T	HT	WT	DOB	AVG	vLH	vRH	G	AB	R	H	2B	3B	HR	RBI	BB	HBP	SH	SF	SO	SB	CS	SLG	OBP
Aldridge, Cory	L-R	6-1	225	6-13-79	.318	.281	.328	83	299	53	95	24	1	13	59	35	1	0	3	83	2	1	.535	.388
Amarista, Alexi	L-R	5-8	150	4-6-89	.400	.350	.422	15	65	13	26	6	3	0	9	1	1	2	1	4	4	2	.585	.412
Auer, Tyson	R-R	6-0	188	10-24-85	.255	.200	.281	14	47	8	12	2	3	0	4	3	2	1	0	9	1	1	.426	.327
Bailey, Dwayne	R-R	6-2	185	8-11-86	.167	.400	.077	9	18	1	3	0	0	0	2	0	0	2	0	6	0	0	.167	.167
Bourjos, Peter	R-R	6-1	180	3-31-87	.314	.366	.290	102	414	85	130	13	12	13	52	24	10	4	3	78	27	5	.498	.364
Brooks, Beau	L-R	6-1	200	8-3-87	.154	.200	.125	4	13	4	2	1	0	0	1	2	0	0	0	3	0	0	.231	.267
Budde, Ryan	R-R	5-11	210	8-15-79	.244	.250	.241	53	172	24	42	7	0	1	13	21	1	2	3	58	1	1	.302	.325
Campos, Jesus	R-R	5-10	175	3-6-88	.182	.000	.222	8	22	1	4	1	0	0	2	0	1	0	0	7	0	0	.227	.250
Colmenares, Carlos	B-R	6-0	175	2-11-86	.302	.414	.246	25	86	8	26	2	1	0	8	5	0	0	1	16	1	0	.349	.337
Conger, Hank	B-R	6-0	210	1-29-88	.300	.193	.344	108	387	56	116	26	2	11	49	55	1	5	4	58	0	2	.463	.385
Coon, Brad	L-L	6-0	175	12-11-82	.353	.800	.167	5	17	1	6	0	1	0	2	0	1	0	0	2	2	0	.471	.333
Evans, Terry	R-R	6-3	205	1-19-82	.283	.257	.296	122	466	80	132	27	4	15	72	28	2	1	5	100	19	8	.455	.323
Figueroa, Luis	R-R	5-9	165	2-16-74	.312	.272	.336	53	218	25	68	12	1	3	36	13	2	3	4	12	2	1	.417	.350
2-team total (62 Las Vegas)					.319	—	—	115	492	51	146	27	4	5	71	25	2	5	5	19	3	2	.429	.354
Frandsen, Kevin	R-R	6-0	185	5-24-82	.277	.326	.255	36	137	25	38	9	1	1	12	7	9	2	0	19	2	1	.380	.353
Gorneault, Nick	R-R	6-3	220	4-19-79	.228	.169	.257	89	272	41	62	14	3	9	43	28	1	3	2	69	3	2	.401	.300
Izturis, Maicer	R-R	5-8	170	9-12-80	.286	.000	.286	2	7	1	2	0	0	1	0	0	0	0	0	0	1	0	.286	.286
Mathis, Jeff	R-R	6-0	200	3-31-83	.242	.333	.190	9	33	6	8	1	1	1	5	4	0	0	0	10	0	0	.424	.324
McAnulty, Paul	L-R	5-11	225	2-24-81	.302	.337	.286	73	275	43	83	18	1	10	54	27	0	0	3	39	0	1	.484	.361
Meyer, Drew	L-R	5-10	205	8-29-81	.276	.370	.214	32	116	15	32	7	1	1	13	12	0	1	0	24	1	1	.379	.344
2-team total (46 Round Rock)					.257	—	—	78	261	30	67	13	3	3	26	34	0	2	1	50	4	1	.364	.341
Nieves, Abel	R-R	5-11	175	8-14-85	.188	.111	.286	7	16	1	3	0	0	0	3	1	0	0	0	6	0	0	.188	.350
Patchett, Gary	R-R	6-2	180	9-25-78	.255	.169	.292	60	196	18	50	4	1	1	25	14	6	6	4	51	0	2	.301	.318
Perez, Darwin	B-R	5-10	160	7-27-89	.191	.045	.320	13	47	4	9	0	1	1	7	2	1	3	0	13	0	0	.298	.240
Quinlan, Robb	R-R	6-1	215	3-17-77	.258	.233	.271	34	128	13	33	6	0	0	15	8	0	1	0	23	1	0	.305	.336
Ryan, Michael	L-R	5-11	220	7-6-77	.277	.229	.295	81	307	48	85	22	4	4	37	24	0	2	5	46	2	0	.414	.324
Sandoval, Freddy	B-R	6-1	200	8-16-82	.210	.200	.216	22	81	13	17	1	1	0	10	2	0	0	0	12	0	0	.247	.252
Statia, Hainley	B-R	5-10	160	1-19-86	.260	.296	.246	30	96	10	25	4	1	0	13	10	0	1	0	14	1	1	.323	.349
Sutton, Nate	L-R	6-0	195	9-1-82	.259	.248	.264	113	397	63	103	19	7	2	38	46	4	3	2	72	13	7	.358	.341
Trumbo, Mark	R-R	6-4	220	1-16-86	.301	.325	.290	139	532	103	160	29	5	36	122	58	1	0	4	126	3	4	.577	.368
Walker, Brian	L-R	6-0	215	7-16-85	.300	.400	.267	6	20	1	6	1	0	0	6	1	0	1	0	3	0	0	.350	.333
Wilson, Bobby	R-R	6-0	200	4-8-83	.500	.000	.750	3	6	3	3	0	0	1	3	4	0	1	1	1	0	0	1.000	.636
Wood, Brandon	R-R	6-3	210	3-2-85	.196	.286	.162	13	51	4	10	0	0	1	2	3	0	0	0	17	0	0	.255	.241

Pitching	B-T	HT	WT	DOB	W	L	ERA	G	GS	CG	SV	IP	H	R	ER	HR	BB	SO	AVG	vLH	vRH	K/9	BB/9
Albano, Marco	R-R	5-11	215	8-26-83	3	6	6.52	15	10	0	0	59	67	43	43	3	43	31	.298	.318	.280	4.70	6.52
Aldridge, Ryan	R-R	6-2	210	9-10-83	0	0	6.00	3	0	0	1	3	7	2	2	0	0	4	.467	.500	.444	12.00	0.00
Bell, Trevor	R-R	6-2	185	10-12-86	2	0	3.00	6	0	0	0	12	10	3	6	1	9	8	.256	.286	.235	5.70	1.80
Browning, Barret	L-L	6-2	205	12-28-84	2	1	6.54	26	1	0	0	43	61	33	31	4	22	41	.351	.339	.356	8.65	4.64
Bulger, Jason	R-R	6-4	210	12-6-78	0	0	0.96	10	0	0	0	9	3	1	1	0	9	12	.103	.067	.143	11.57	8.68
Cabrera, Daniel	R-R	6-9	260	5-28-81	0	2	11.70	3	3	0	0	10	14	13	13	1	7	8	.318	.643	.167	7.20	6.30
Carmona, Ysmael	R-R	6-1	190	2-12-85	1	1	3.18	6	0	0	0	6	5	2	2	0	6	7	.227	.000	.357	11.12	9.53
Cassevah, Bobby	R-R	6-3	195	9-11-85	3	4	4.27	45	0	0	5	59	69	32	28	7	25	38	.290	.287	.292	5.80	3.81
Chatwood, Tyler	R-R	6-0	185	12-16-89	1	0	6.35	1	1	0	0	6	9	4	4	1	0	3	.346	.556	.235	4.76	0.00
Davidson, Daniel	L-L	6-4	210	1-8-81	8	2	5.17	16	16	0	0	87	98	51	50	14	28	63	.282	.282	.282	6.52	2.90
DeHoyos, Gabe	R-R	5-11	260	4-14-80	5	1	3.06	38	0	0	1	82	72	31	28	4	33	80	.235	.311	.186	8.74	3.61
Diaz, Amalio	R-R	6-2	170	9-10-86	5	6	5.68	28	12	0	1	90	111	61	57	4	40	69	.312	.343	.292	6.87	3.99
Hill, Jeremy	R-R	5-11	200	8-8-77	1	0	3.78	17	0	0	3	17	17	9	7	3	4	13	.246	.276	.225	7.02	2.16
Houston, Ryan	R-R	6-4	230	9-22-79	0	1	6.64	14	0	0	1	20	28	17	15	1	11	12	.333	.316	.348	5.31	4.87
Junge, Eric	R-R	6-5	215	1-5-77	5	3	5.15	14	12	0	0	80	92	49	46	10	23	60	.294	.346	.258	6.72	2.58
Kiely, Tim	R-R	6-1	190	8-26-85	3	2	9.00	7	7	0	0	39	61	42	39	7	11	18	.361	.347	.371	4.15	2.54

Kohn, Michael	R-R	6-0	200	6-26-86	3	2	1.95	26	0	0	8	28	16	7	6	3	17	32	.170	.125	.194	10.41	5.53
McKiernan, Eddie	R-R	5-11	160	3-21-89	0	0	20.25	1	0	0	1	3	3	3	0	1	2		.429	.667	.250	13.50	6.75
Mendoza, Tommy	R-R	6-2	195	8-18-87	0	4	8.89	6	5	0	0	27	45	30	27	12	7	13	.375	.383	.370	4.28	2.30
Mosebach, Bobby	R-R	6-4	195	9-14-84	2	1	7.00	13	0	0	4	18	25	15	14	3	4	8	.347	.360	.340	4.00	2.00
Nabors, Kevin	R-R	6-3	220	8-12-85	0	0	1.69	4	0	0	0	5	6	1	1	0	3	4	.316	.273	.375	6.75	5.06
O'Sullivan, Sean	R-R	6-2	230	9-1-87	5	5	4.76	15	15	1	0	85	95	50	45	8	31	58	.289	.255	.320	6.14	3.28
Oye, Matt	R-R	6-5	230	2-25-86	0	0	16.20	1	0	0	0	2	4	3	3	1	1	1	.444	1.000	.286	5.40	5.40
Palmer, Matt	R-R	6-2	225	3-21-79	2	3	2.72	13	7	0	2	46	32	17	14	4	19	36	.198	.167	.219	6.99	3.69
Reckling, Trevor	L-L	6-2	205	5-22-89	4	7	8.53	14	14	0	0	70	99	69	66	11	50	46	.339	.269	.364	5.94	6.46
Rodriguez, Fernando	R-R	6-3	215	6-18-84	4	6	5.92	31	17	0	0	97	134	78	64	12	42	84	.329	.323	.333	7.77	3.88
Rodriguez, Francisco	R-R	6-1	195	2-26-83	2	1	3.63	13	0	0	0	22	19	9	9	0	6	19	.229	.290	.192	7.66	2.42
Rodriguez, Rafael	R-R	6-1	175	9-24-84	5	3	3.04	37	0	0	10	50	41	19	17	5	15	30	.219	.210	.226	5.36	2.68
2-team total (10 Reno)					5	5	4.26	47	0	0	11	63	57	34	30	8	21	37	—	—	—	5.26	2.98
Shoemaker, Matt	R-R	6-2	225	9-27-86	1	5	5.87	3	2	0	0	15	20	10	10	0	8	9	.328	.259	.382	5.28	4.70
Smith, Will	R-L	6-5	235	7-10-89	2	4	5.60	9	9	0	0	53	65	39	33	6	20	40	.305	.246	.327	6.79	3.40
Stokes, Brian	R-R	6-1	210	9-7-79	1	1	3.78	13	0	0	0	17	21	9	7	1	6	13	.318	.313	.324	7.02	3.24
Thompson, Rich	R-R	6-1	180	7-1-84	1	1	0.61	19	0	0	2	30	17	2	2	0	10	30	.177	.139	.200	9.10	3.03
Vogelsong, Ryan	R-R	6-3	215	7-22-77	1	3	4.66	8	7	0	0	37	47	23	19	2	22	37	.315	.345	.297	9.08	5.40
Walden, Jordan	R-R	6-5	240	11-16-87	0	0	4.05	6	0	0	0	7	8	3	3	0	2	3	.296	.333	.278	4.05	2.70

Fielding

Catcher	PCT	G	PO	A	E	DP	PB
Brooks	.944	4	15	2	1	0	0
Budde	.988	48	310	25	4	2	1
Conger	.979	81	554	47	13	9	0
Mathis	1.000	7	50	5	0	1	1
Walker	1.000	6	34	6	0	1	0
Wilson	1.000	2	13	1	0	0	0

First Base	PCT	G	PO	A	E	DP
Budde	1.000	2	14	2	0	0
Colmenares	1.000	1	3	0	0	0
Frandsen	1.000	2	15	0	0	2
McAnulty	.990	24	179	10	2	22
Quinlan	.986	15	135	9	2	12
Ryan	1.000	6	38	5	0	5
Trumbo	.986	97	811	64	12	91
Wilson	1.000	1	7	0	0	0
Wood	1.000	1	9	2	0	1

Second Base	PCT	G	PO	A	E	DP
Amarista	1.000	15	25	40	0	10
Bailey	1.000	7	6	17	0	7
Colmenares	1.000	7	11	26	0	1
Frandsen	1.000	9	22	23	0	10
Meyer	1.000	31	62	88	0	31
Nieves	1.000	4	7	6	0	2
Ryan	1.000	1	2	0	0	0
Statia	.992	24	44	73	1	16
Sutton	.987	57	87	145	3	34

Third Base	PCT	G	PO	A	E	DP
Budde	.818	2	0	9	2	0
Campos	.941	8	5	11	1	1
Colmenares	.893	13	4	21	3	2
Frandsen	.926	18	12	38	4	1
Izturis	—	1	0	0	0	0
McAnulty	.913	13	5	16	2	2
Nieves	.900	3	5	4	1	1
Quinlan	.900	13	5	13	2	0
Sandoval	1.000	21	26	39	0	7
Sutton	.935	50	30	100	9	8
Wood	.968	11	11	19	1	2

Shortstop	PCT	G	PO	A	E	DP
Amarista	—	1	0	0	0	0
Colmenares	.833	6	4	11	3	2
Figueroa	.969	51	85	161	8	45
Frandsen	1.000	8	16	18	0	4
Izturis	1.000	1	0	3	0	0
Patchett	.971	60	99	168	8	46
Perez	.982	13	23	31	1	6
Statia	.968	6	14	16	1	2
Sutton	1.000	2	0	2	0	0
Wood	.750	1	2	1	1	1

Outfield	PCT	G	PO	A	E	DP
Aldridge	.986	53	70	3	1	0
Auer	.964	14	26	1	1	0
Bourjos	.992	101	258	6	2	1
Coon	1.000	5	6	0	0	0
Evans	.975	115	219	13	6	4
Gorneault	.976	85	156	7	4	1
McAnulty	1.000	1	4	0	0	0
Quinlan	1.000	2	4	0	0	0
Ryan	.989	52	86	2	1	0
Sutton	1.000	6	6	3	0	0
Trumbo	1.000	23	58	1	0	0

ARKANSAS TRAVELERS   DOUBLE-A

TEXAS LEAGUE

Batting	B-T	HT	WT	DOB	AVG	vLH	vRH	G	AB	R	H	2B	3B	HR	RBI	BB	HBP	SH	SF	SO	SB	CS	SLG	OBP
Alvarez, Ricky	R-R	5-11	217	2-7-89	.130	.077	.200	7	23	0	3	0	0	0	3	1	1	0	0	6	1	0	.130	.200
Amarista, Alexi	L-R	5-8	150	4-6-89	.288	.368	.235	48	191	25	55	2	1	1	20	13	2	2	5	15	4	1	.325	.332
Auer, Tyson	R-R	6-0	188	10-24-85	.308	.333	.290	44	185	30	57	8	1	2	8	14	1	2	0	31	13	7	.395	.360
Bailey, Dwayne	B-R	6-2	185	8-11-86	.143	.000	.200	3	7	0	1	0	0	0	0	0	0	1	0	3	0	0	.143	.143
Blackburn, Mitch	L-R	5-8	175	12-21-87	.056	.000	.083	7	18	0	1	0	0	0	1	0	0	0	0	7	0	0	.056	.105
Brannon, Nolan	L-R	6-0	185	7-5-85	.083	.000	.111	4	12	1	1	0	0	0	0	0	0	0	0	2	0	0	.167	.083
Brooks, Beau	L-R	6-1	200	8-3-87	.157	.120	.172	30	83	4	13	1	0	0	4	10	1	1	0	35	0	1	.169	.255
Brossman, Jay	R-R	6-1	210	1-17-85	.149	.119	.173	26	94	8	14	4	0	1	8	5	1	0	1	22	0	1	.223	.198
Campos, Jesus	R-R	5-10	175	3-6-88	.238	.222	.250	8	21	1	5	0	0	1	1	1	0	1	0	8	0	0	.238	.273
Cates, Rich	R-L	5-11	180	12-11-86	.175	.143	.186	22	57	5	10	4	0	0	2	5	0	2	0	13	1	1	.246	.242
Colmenares, Carlos	B-R	6-0	175	2-11-86	.275	.308	.258	54	189	29	52	4	2	0	8	26	1	2	0	41	8	6	.317	.366
Contreras, Ivan	B-R	5-9	155	1-3-87	.272	.275	.269	31	92	10	25	4	3	0	3	4	0	1	0	19	1	3	.380	.302
De Los Santos, Anel	R-R	6-3	210	6-19-88	.225	.333	.146	20	71	4	16	1	0	1	5	1	0	0	1	14	1	2	.324	.233
Demperio, Michael	R-R	5-10	170	2-17-88	.217	.667	.150	7	23	1	5	0	0	0	1	4	0	0	0	11	0	0	.217	.333
Fuller, Clay	B-R	6-2	190	6-17-87	.168	.168	.168	63	208	18	35	3	0	4	22	17	4	7	1	59	6	4	.240	.243
Gorneault, Nick	R-R	6-3	220	4-19-79	.422	.294	.500	11	45	9	19	2	0	3	11	4	0	0	0	8	2	2	.667	.469
Jimenez, Jose	L-R	5-10	240	1-2-87	.071	.000	.100	5	14	0	1	0	0	0	0	1	0	0	1	3	0	0	.143	.067
Jimerson, Charlton	R-R	6-3	215	9-22-79	.229	.259	.213	43	166	27	38	9	2	7	25	7	2	0	1	41	9	3	.434	.267
Kiniry, Rian	L-R	5-10	160	12-12-86	.147	.190	.130	25	75	3	11	3	1	0	3	4	0	4	0	14	0	2	.213	.190
Lopez, Roberto	R-R	6-0	195	10-1-85	.239	.291	.208	85	276	35	66	13	1	7	41	29	9	4	7	53	0	5	.370	.324
McAnulty, Paul	L-R	5-11	225	2-24-81	.331	.329	.333	44	148	31	49	3	1	14	27	24	2	0	2	36	1	2	.649	.426
Moore, Jeremy	L-R	6-1	195	6-29-87	.303	.262	.325	128	456	72	138	14	10	13	61	39	3	5	5	122	24	10	.463	.358
Mount, Ryan	L-R	6-0	190	8-17-86	.231	.183	.256	85	308	36	71	13	3	10	41	17	4	0	1	80	8	4	.390	.279
Navarro, Efren	L-L	6-0	200	5-14-86	.267	.242	.280	128	453	46	121	24	2	6	50	31	3	4	3	47	6	4	.369	.316
Nieves, Abel	R-R	5-11	175	8-14-85	.232	.228	.236	93	310	30	72	6	4	3	23	40	2	7	3	58	2	2	.306	.321
Perez, Darwin	B-R	5-10	160	7-27-89	.161	.231	.111	10	31	3	5	0	0	0	1	6	0	0	0	7	0	0	.161	.297
Perez, Julio	R-R	6-2	160	9-28-85	.227	.239	.220	64	233	24	53	14	1	5	34	24	3	0	1	55	6	5	.361	.307

	B-T	HT	WT	DOB	AVG	vLH	vRH	G	AB	R	H	2B	3B	HR	RBI	BB	HBP	SH	SF	SO	SB	CS	SLG	OBP
Ramos, Kevin	R-R	5-11	170	6-6-86	.211	.194	.222	23	76	5	16	5	0	0	5	6	0	3	1	18	2	2	.276	.265
Romine, Andrew	B-R	6-1	190	12-24-85	.282	.314	.261	106	383	55	108	15	4	3	34	50	5	13	2	66	21	9	.366	.370
Rosario, Alberto	R-R	5-10	190	1-10-87	.193	.176	.207	51	166	11	32	3	0	0	8	/	0	5	1	31	2	2	.211	.224
Statia, Hainley	B-R	5-10	160	1-19-86	.417	.333	.500	4	12	2	5	1	0	0	2	3	0	0	0	1	1	2	.500	.533
Walker, Brian	L-R	6-0	215	7-16-85	.250	.174	.273	29	100	9	25	6	0	4	23	5	1	0	1	22	4	1	.430	.290
Younger, Adam	R-R	6-2	207	8-25-85	.125	.000	.167	3	8	1	1	0	0	0	0	1	0	0	0	4	0	0	.125	.222

Pitching	B-T	HT	WT	DOB	W	L	ERA	G	GS	CG	SV	IP	H	R	ER	HR	BB	SO	AVG	vLH	vRH	K/9	BB/9
Aldridge, Ryan	R-R	6-2	210	9-10-83	0	0	0.75	9	0	0	0	12	5	1	1	0	6	15	.125	.211	.048	11.25	4.50
Anton, Michael	L-L	6-3	195	4-3-85	5	12	5.01	27	24	0	0	138	141	82	77	22	63	108	.271	.315	.257	7.03	4.10
Berg, Jeremy	R-R	6-0	180	7-17-86	1	0	1.50	20	0	0	1	24	15	5	4	0	5	16	.174	.138	.193	9.75	1.88
Brasier, Ryan	R-R	6-0	200	8-26-87	7	12	5.07	28	23	1	0	142	127	89	80	28	68	94	.242	.278	.211	5.96	4.31
Browning, Barret	L-L	6-2	205	12-28-84	5	4	3.91	25	1	0	0	46	38	22	20	3	22	44	.225	.180	.244	8.61	4.30
Cabrera, Daniel	R-R	6-9	260	5-28-81	0	1	4.32	8	2	0	1	17	10	8	8	2	9	12	.172	.152	.200	6.48	4.86
Carmona, Ysmael	R-R	6-1	190	2-12-85	4	2	2.60	38	0	0	12	55	35	21	16	2	34	52	.188	.182	.193	8.46	5.53
Chatwood, Tyler	R-R	6-0	185	12-16-89	4	6	3.82	12	12	1	0	68	72	38	29	3	27	36	.273	.295	.248	4.74	3.56
Diaz, Amalio	R-R	6-2	170	9-10-86	0	0	2.29	10	0	0	2	20	11	6	5	2	1	16	.155	.190	.140	7.32	0.46
Fish, Robert	L-L	6-3	225	1-19-88	3	5	8.93	39	0	0	2	42	69	50	42	9	18	48	.356	.352	.358	10.20	3.83
Flores, Manuel	L-L	6-2	170	6-1-87	1	5	5.81	9	9	1	0	48	63	36	31	2	13	26	.323	.356	.313	4.88	2.44
Geltz, Steve	R-R	5-10	170	11-1-87	1	0	2.41	16	0	0	0	19	9	5	5	0	16	36	.145	.091	.175	17.36	7.71
Haynes, Jeremy	R-R	6-2	180	5-28-86	3	0	6.14	30	0	0	0	48	45	34	33	1	53	40	.259	.311	.220	7.45	9.87
Kiely, Tim	R-R	6-1	190	8-26-85	7	10	5.08	21	21	2	0	124	155	83	70	15	28	66	.308	.290	.327	4.79	2.03
Kohn, Michael	R-R	6-0	200	6-26-86	2	2	2.45	15	0	0	3	18	12	5	5	0	8	25	.194	.261	.154	12.27	3.93
Mendoza, Tommy	R-R	6-2	195	8-18-87	1	1	3.44	4	4	0	0	18	13	9	7	2	14	13	.197	.194	.200	6.38	6.87
Miller, Jayson	L-L	5-11	180	11-25-85	0	4	6.42	12	7	0	0	41	56	39	29	4	15	25	.322	.333	.319	5.53	3.32
Ortega, Anthony	R-R	6-0	185	8-24-85	0	1	8.04	10	0	0	0	16	21	18	14	4	14	12	.328	.360	.308	6.89	8.04
Oye, Matt	R-R	6-5	230	2-25-86	0	0	7.71	2	0	0	0	2	6	6	2	0	2	2	.429	.444	.400	7.71	7.71
Pugliese, Nick	R-R	6-1	205	9-18-85	0	0	1.80	3	0	0	0	5	6	1	1	0	4	8	.300	.250	.333	14.40	7.20
Reckling, Trevor	L-L	6-2	205	5-22-89	3	6	4.56	14	14	1	0	79	74	49	40	4	35	62	.254	.164	.281	7.06	3.99
Rembisz, Bryan	R-R	5-8	165	8-16-85	0	0	4.50	4	0	0	0	4	3	3	2	1	3	3	.188	.250	.125	6.75	6.75
Smith, Will	R-L	6-5	235	7-10-89	1	2	7.23	4	4	0	0	19	33	16	15	3	9	8	.398	.444	.342	3.86	4.34
Taylor, Drew	R-L	6-1	190	8-18-86	1	3	4.70	15	4	0	0	38	38	21	20	2	18	21	.264	.170	.319	4.93	4.23
Thorne, Jeremy	R-R	6-4	260	10-4-85	2	4	5.68	14	12	0	0	65	67	44	41	7	48	30	.272	.256	.287	4.15	6.65
Van Mil, Loek	R-R	7-1	220	9-15-84	0	0	0.00	1	0	0	0	1	0	0	0	0	1	0	.000	.000	.000	0.00	9.00
Walden, Jordan	R-R	6-5	240	11-16-87	1	1	3.35	38	0	0	8	43	44	18	16	2	22	38	.277	.278	.276	7.95	4.60
Wilding, Taylor	R-R	6-1	190	10-22-84	3	4	6.00	25	3	0	0	54	67	39	36	5	25	42	.310	.278	.333	7.00	4.17

Fielding

Catcher	PCT	G	PO	A	E	DP	PB
Brannon	.955	4	21	0	1	0	0
Brooks	.995	30	188	16	1	0	3
De Los Santos	1.000	18	100	12	0	2	0
Jimenez	.976	5	38	2	1	0	0
Lopez	.981	24	146	12	3	0	7
Rosario	.984	49	323	55	6	5	10
Walker	1.000	19	109	6	0	0	4

First Base	PCT	G	PO	A	E	DP
Colmenares	1.000	1	8	0	0	0
Contreras	.833	1	4	1	1	0
Lopez	.986	10	67	1	1	3
McAnulty	.833	1	5	0	1	0
Navarro	.995	119	1007	96	6	101
Nieves	.980	11	92	4	2	8

Second Base	PCT	G	PO	A	E	DP
Amarista	.973	45	91	126	6	28
Blackburn	1.000	4	9	8	0	1
Campos	1.000	4	8	8	0	3
Colmenares	1.000	1	5	5	0	1
Contreras	.963	13	22	30	2	6
Mount	.942	37	60	87	9	11
Nieves	.959	30	41	76	5	19
Ramos	1.000	9	20	27	0	6
Statia	1.000	2	5	7	0	4

Third Base	PCT	G	PO	A	E	DP
Alvarez	.929	7	4	9	1	1
Bailey	1.000	1	1	0	0	0
Blackburn	.857	2	2	4	1	2
Brossman	.929	22	16	49	5	7
Campos	1.000	2	0	1	0	0
Colmenares	.966	27	17	40	2	2
Contreras	.950	6	7	12	1	1
Demperio	1.000	6	4	17	0	1
Mount	.938	30	13	62	5	2
Nieves	.941	39	22	74	6	6
Ramos	.913	8	11	10	2	1
Statia	1.000	1	0	2	0	0

Shortstop	PCT	G	PO	A	E	DP
Bailey	—	1	0	0	0	0
Blackburn	—	1	0	0	0	0
Campos	.667	1	1	1	1	0
Colmenares	.893	9	11	14	3	3
Contreras	.957	6	6	16	1	3
Demperio	—	1	0	0	0	0
Nieves	1.000	5	6	10	0	3
Perez	.960	10	17	31	2	8
Ramos	.808	6	9	12	5	5
Romine	.974	104	159	323	13	58
Statia	.667	1	0	2	1	0
Younger	1.000	3	3	5	0	0

Outfield	PCT	G	PO	A	E	DP
Auer	.981	42	93	9	2	3
Bailey	1.000	1	1	0	0	0
Cates	1.000	11	25	1	0	0
Colmenares	1.000	17	28	4	0	0
Contreras	.750	4	5	1	2	0
Fuller	.992	63	126	4	1	1
Gorneault	1.000	6	12	0	0	0
Jimerson	.987	32	72	2	1	0
Kiniry	.980	24	49	0	1	0
Lopez	.983	29	55	2	1	1
McAnulty	.950	8	18	1	1	0
Moore	.952	124	247	9	13	2
Mount	.970	14	31	1	1	1
Perez	.975	57	116	2	3	0

RANCHO CUCAMONGA QUAKES   HIGH CLASS A

CALIFORNIA LEAGUE

Batting	B-T	HT	WT	DOB	AVG	vLH	vRH	G	AB	R	H	2B	3B	HR	RBI	BB	HBP	SH	SF	SO	SB	CS	SLG	OBP
Alvarez, Ricky	R-R	5-11	217	2-7-89	.357	.400	.333	4	14	1	5	1	0	1	5	0	2	0	0	1	1	0	.643	.438
Amarista, Alexi	L-R	5-8	150	4-6-89	.303	.281	.313	72	297	39	90	19	6	4	39	19	3	2	2	42	17	10	.448	.349
Auer, Tyson	R-R	6-0	188	10-24-85	.332	.345	.326	65	256	57	85	6	8	3	27	23	2	12	3	42	40	12	.453	.387
Bailey, Dwayne	B-R	6-2	185	8-11-86	.239	.174	.273	20	67	9	16	2	1	0	10	4	1	2	1	6	5	1	.299	.288
Baird, Dillon	L-R	6-3	190	1-13-88	.270	.213	.294	85	322	45	87	24	0	13	58	23	4	0	4	86	3	3	.466	.323
Brooks, Beau	L-R	6-1	200	8-3-87	.158	.073	.200	54	165	22	26	8	0	3	17	24	1	3	3	65	1	0	.261	.264
Campos, Jesus	R-R	5-10	175	3-6-88	.230	.182	.256	17	61	10	14	1	1	1	10	2	1	3	0	14	0	1	.328	.266
Castillo, Angel	R-R	6-3	190	6-7-89	.259	.273	.252	127	467	72	121	22	3	21	70	41	7	2	5	140	12	6	.454	.325
Cates, Rich	R-L	5-11	180	12-11-86	.277	.167	.340	23	83	7	23	2	1	0	12	4	0	2	1	17	0	1	.325	.307

Batting	B-T	HT	WT	DOB	AVG	vLH	vRH	G	AB	R	H	2B	3B	HR	RBI	BB	HBP	SH	SF	SO	SB	CS	SLG	OBP
Colmenares, Carlos	B-R	6-0	175	2-11-86	.321	.167	.364	7	28	4	9	2	1	0	8	0	1	0	0	6	3	0	.464	.345
Contreras, Ivan	B-R	5-9	155	1-3-87	.244	.294	.214	14	45	6	11	3	1	0	3	4	0	3	0	8	1	0	.356	.306
De Los Santos, Anel	R-R	6-3	210	6-19-88	.000	.000	.000	3	8	0	0	0	0	0	0	1	1	1	0	2	0	0	.000	.200
Fuller, Clay	B-R	6-2	190	6-17-87	.331	.244	.363	44	154	39	51	10	4	6	25	21	7	2	0	45	12	3	.565	.434
Gomez, Rolando	L-R	5-7	145	6-18-89	.000	.000	.000	1	3	0	0	0	0	0	0	0	0	1	0	1	1	0	.000	.000
Jacobo, Gabe	R-R	6-2	190	4-14-87	.296	.333	.279	133	541	82	160	26	7	22	107	24	9	3	6	94	6	9	.492	.333
Jimenez, Luis	R-R	6-1	205	1-18-88	.286	.367	.250	81	318	52	91	31	4	12	43	13	6	4	3	43	15	8	.522	.324
Kiniry, Rian	L-R	5-10	160	12-12-86	.270	.198	.303	88	307	48	83	9	3	4	33	16	3	8	5	72	26	13	.358	.308
Lopez, Roberto	R-R	6-0	195	10-1-85	.346	.444	.294	46	182	33	63	19	1	5	42	13	10	0	6	35	5	2	.544	.408
Oliver, Eric	R-R	6-1	215	1-29-87	.271	.338	.233	54	181	26	49	14	0	4	30	19	1	0	2	32	1	1	.414	.340
Perez, Darwin	B-R	5-10	160	7-27-89	.282	.340	.259	97	326	60	92	6	7	2	36	32	4	13	2	76	15	8	.362	.352
Ramos, Kevin	R-R	5-11	170	6-6-86	.238	.244	.235	36	122	14	29	8	0	0	7	6	3	3	0	21	3	0	.303	.290
Rife, Jake	L-L	5-11	206	6-7-87	.233	.222	.238	9	30	2	7	1	0	0	2	0	0	0	1	11	1	0	.267	.281
Rosario, Alberto	R-R	5-10	190	1-10-87	.304	.269	.318	48	181	34	55	9	1	4	24	11	5	10	3	25	8	1	.431	.355
Sumi, Ikko	R-R	5-9	200	10-20-87	.238	.194	.257	35	101	6	24	3	0	0	4	7	2	3	0	31	0	0	.267	.300
Townsend, Jon	R-R	6-0	190	9-24-84	.243	.190	.266	83	268	28	65	12	0	6	24	29	5	10	1	89	7	5	.354	.327
Trout, Mike	R-R	6-1	217	8-7-91	.306	.237	.336	50	196	30	60	9	2	4	19	27	1	5	3	33	11	6	.434	.388
Willits, Reggie	B-R	5-11	185	5-30-81	.267	.600	.100	5	15	3	4	1	0	0	1	4	1	0	1	2	2	0	.333	.429
Wilson, Bobby	R-R	6-0	220	4-8-83	.333	.333	.333	2	6	0	2	0	0	0	0	0	0	0	0	0	2	0	.333	.333
Younger, Adam	R-R	6-2	207	8-25-85	.262	.200	.293	21	61	9	16	4	3	2	8	3	3	0	0	24	1	2	.525	.375

Pitching	B-T	HT	WT	DOB	W	L	ERA	G	GS	CG	SV	IP	H	R	ER	HR	BB	SO	AVG	vLH	vRH	K/9	BB/9
Arenas, Orangel	R-R	6-0	200	3-31-89	7	3	4.55	17	17	0	0	97	93	54	49	9	45	71	.255	.298	.210	6.59	4.18
Berg, Jeremy	R-R	6-0	180	7-17-86	1	0	1.45	10	0	0	0	19	16	3	3	1	2	27	.232	.243	.219	13.02	0.96
Bulger, Jason	R-R	6-4	210	12-6-78	0	0	27.00	1	0	0	0	1	2	2	2	0	1	0	.500	.000	1.000	13.50	0.00
Chaffee, Ryan	R-R	6-2	190	5-18-88	7	6	6.36	20	20	0	0	105	126	82	74	13	46	83	.301	.294	.307	7.14	3.96
Chatwood, Tyler	R-R	6-0	185	12-16-89	8	3	1.77	14	13	0	0	81	71	18	16	6	36	70	.241	.237	.245	7.75	3.98
Corbin, Pat	L-L	6-3	165	7-19-89	5	3	3.88	11	11	0	0	60	57	29	26	7	18	64	.247	.267	.241	9.55	2.69
2-team total (8 Visalia)					5	4	3.13	19	19	0	0	86	74	33	30	8	27	94	—	—		9.80	2.81
Correa, Manuarys	R-R	6-3	170	1-5-89	1	11	7.83	19	14	0	0	79	123	74	69	20	12	33	.357	.354	.359	3.74	1.36
Fish, Robert	L-L	6-3	225	1-19-88	2	0	1.13	10	0	0	0	16	7	2	2	0	8	25	.132	.208	.069	14.06	4.50
Flores, Manuel	L-L	6-2	170	6-1-87	5	9	4.23	17	17	0	0	104	120	56	49	8	22	46	.289	.232	.314	3.97	1.90
Fuentes, Brian	L-L	6-4	230	8-9-75	0	0	0.00	1	0	0	0	1	0	0	0	0	0	1	.000	.000	.000	9.00	0.00
Geltz, Steve	R-R	5-10	170	11-1-87	3	1	3.44	22	0	0	2	34	20	14	13	4	10	51	.167	.159	.175	13.50	2.65
Haynes, Jeremy	R-R	6-2	180	5-28-86	1	0	2.45	11	0	0	1	18	15	8	5	1	8	16	.224	.265	.182	7.85	3.93
Hurst, Kyle	R-R	6-4	230	8-23-85	5	3	5.31	24	7	0	1	59	60	38	35	7	17	44	.261	.226	.290	6.67	2.58
Jang, Pill Joon	R-R	6-3	190	4-8-88	1	0	2.70	2	2	0	0	10	10	4	3	1	1	9	.256	.261	.250	8.10	0.90
Kazmir, Scott	L-L	6-0	175	1-24-84	0	0	4.26	1	1	0	0	6	8	3	3	0	0	6	.296	.111	.389	8.53	0.00
Kenney, Mike	R-R	6-4	212	8-16-86	0	0	1.93	4	0	0	0	5	5	1	1	0	7	1	.263	.167	.308	1.93	13.50
Lopez, Baudilio	R-R	6-1	190	11-20-90	1	0	2.25	13	0	0	0	20	14	8	5	2	10	14	.192	.231	.170	6.30	4.50
McKiernan, Eddie	R-R	5-11	160	3-21-89	3	2	3.40	55	0	0	28	56	47	23	21	5	20	57	.227	.261	.200	9.22	3.23
Meyer, Matt	L-L	6-4	220	1-17-85	1	0	4.32	7	0	0	0	8	10	4	4	0	0	12	.278	.182	.320	12.96	0.00
Nabors, Kevin	R-R	6-3	220	8-12-85	1	0	0.00	7	0	0	1	4	0	0	0	2	7	.125	.100	.167	6.52	1.86
Oye, Matt	R-R	6-5	230	2-25-86	1	0	0.00	5	0	0	0	5	2	0	0	0	1	6	.118	.000	.200	10.80	1.80
Pena, Ariel	R-R	6-3	186	5-20-89	0	1	8.71	3	3	0	0	10	10	10	10	0	13	8	.270	.214	.444	6.97	11.32
Perez, Jose	R-R	6-2	180	9-14-87	1	2	4.16	36	0	0	1	71	67	35	33	10	29	73	.247	.200	.288	9.21	3.66
Piazza, Mike	R-R	6-4	205	11-24-86	1	1	1.40	10	1	0	0	19	11	3	3	0	6	10	.164	.214	.128	12.57	2.79
Pugliese, Nick	R-R	6-1	205	9-18-85	4	1	5.31	36	0	0	0	58	62	34	34	5	18	51	.274	.311	.242	7.96	2.81
Richards, Garrett	R-R	6-3	210	5-27-88	4	1	3.89	7	7	0	0	35	38	17	15	4	9	41	.281	.232	.316	10.64	2.34
Scholl, Chris	R-R	5-11	195	10-27-87	2	1	3.41	38	0	0	1	69	64	27	26	2	20	82	.252	.252	.248	10.75	2.62
Shoemaker, Matt	R-R	6-2	225	9-27-86	7	8	4.93	20	20	2	0	122	138	75	67	14	39	119	.283	.279	.287	8.75	2.87
Smith, Will	R-L	6-5	235	7-10-89	2	2	4.58	6	6	0	0	37	36	23	19	4	13	31	.259	.208	.286	7.47	3.13
Stokes, Brian	R-R	6-1	210	9-7-79	0	0	9.00	1	0	0	0	1	2	1	1	0	0	1	.400	.000	.667	9.00	0.00
Taylor, Drew	R-L	6-1	190	8-18-86	4	1	2.06	20	0	0	0	35	24	9	8	1	14	39	.186	.167	.203	10.03	3.60

Fielding

Catcher	PCT	G	PO	A	E	DP	PB
Brooks	.986	51	381	47	6	3	10
Cisterna	1.000	1	5	1	0	0	0
De Los Santos	1.000	3	24	1	0	0	0
Lopez	1.000	11	81	15	0	1	2
Rosario	.995	48	371	47	2	6	9
Sumi	.992	32	230	31	2	1	2
Wilson	1.000	2	6	5	0	0	0

First Base	PCT	G	PO	A	E	DP
Baird	.917	1	10	1	1	2
Colmenares	1.000	1	9	0	0	1
Jacobo	.998	118	1073	76	2	90
Lopez	.984	11	119	6	2	14
Oliver	1.000	10	89	6	0	3

Second Base	PCT	G	PO	A	E	DP
Amarista	.997	68	120	224	1	51
Bailey	.949	12	30	36	3	7
Colmenares	1.000	1	2	4	0	1
Contreras	.950	3	7	12	1	2
Ramos	.972	21	42	61	3	14
Townsend	.972	35	49	92	4	13
Younger	1.000	3	4	13	0	2

Third Base	PCT	G	PO	A	E	DP
Alvarez	1.000	3	3	4	0	0
Bailey	1.000	3	0	4	0	0
Baird	.906	56	31	124	16	10
Jimenez	.928	47	28	88	9	5
Townsend	.986	28	22	49	1	3
Younger	.938	6	4	11	1	2

Shortstop	PCT	G	PO	A	E	DP
Campos	1.000	17	21	39	0	9
Castillo	1.000	1	1	0	0	0
Colmenares	1.000	3	7	7	0	2
Contreras	.846	3	6	5	2	2
Gomez	1.000	1	1	0	1	0
Perez	.970	90	127	265	12	56
Ramos	.955	15	22	41	3	7
Townsend	.667	2	2	0	1	0

Outfield	PCT	G	PO	A	E	DP
Auer	.980	63	141	3	3	1
Bailey	1.000	2	2	0	0	0
Castillo	.977	123	203	7	5	2
Cates	.949	23	36	1	2	0
Colmenares	1.000	1	1	0	0	0
Contreras	1.000	6	8	0	0	0
Fuller	.985	38	64	0	1	0
Kiniry	.974	84	145	7	4	1
Lopez	.846	9	11	0	2	0
Oliver	.920	21	22	1	2	0
Rife	.800	5	8	0	2	0
Townsend	1.000	5	6	0	0	0
Trout	.990	50	93	3	1	0
Willits	.900	5	9	0	1	0

Younger (Outfield) | 1.000 | 11 | 18 | 27 | 0 | 8

CEDAR RAPIDS KERNELS

MIDWEST LEAGUE

LOS ANGELES ANGELS

Batting	B-T	HT	WT	DOB	AVG	vLH	vRH	G	AB	R	H	2B	3B	HR	RBI	BB	HBP	SH	SF	SO	SB	CS	SLG	OBP
Alliman, Terrell	R-R	6-3	185	10-15-88	.244	.227	.253	47	135	28	33	5	0	4	23	10	3	1	1	33	2	2	.370	.309
Alvarez, Ricky	R-R	5-11	217	2-7-89	.294	.400	.250	6	17	2	5	2	0	0	3	1	1	0	5	0	0		.412	.368
Bailey, Dwayne	B-R	6-2	185	8-11-86	.130	.000	.158	23	46	6	6	1	0	0	3	5	0	2	0	17	2	1	.152	.216
Bass, Justin	R-R	5-11	190	4-6-89	.251	.218	.262	110	399	61	100	12	6	3	42	29	3	3	4	47	14	6	.333	.303
Beuerlein, Drew	B-R	6-0	205	1-13-88	.368	.500	.333	5	19	5	7	1	0	2	4	0	0	1	0	6	0	0	.737	.368
Blackburn, Mitch	L-R	5-8	175	12-21-87	.444	.500	.333	2	9	1	4	0	0	0	1	1	0	0	0	1	0	0	.444	.500
Brannon, Nolan	L-R	6-0	185	7-5-85	.278	.000	.333	7	18	3	5	1	0	0	3	2	0	1	0	2	0	0	.333	.350
Cates, Rich	R-L	5-11	180	11-21-86	.270	.273	.270	19	74	10	20	3	0	0	11	7	0	0	1	12	1	1	.311	.329
Contreras, Ivan	B-R	5-9	155	1-3-87	.233	.333	.190	8	30	9	7	4	1	0	3	7	0	0	0	9	4	0	.433	.378
Cruz, Jeremy	R-R	6-1	225	4-19-87	.289	.273	.294	69	270	44	78	16	4	7	41	18	2	0	2	63	4	5	.456	.336
Demperio, Michael	R-R	5-10	170	2-17-88	.031	.000	.045	18	32	3	1	0	0	0	0	4	3	2	0	15	1	1	.031	.205
Grichuk, Randal	R-R	6-1	195	8-13-91	.292	.373	.259	52	202	41	59	19	4	7	36	9	2	0	1	50	4	0	.530	.327
Haerther, Casey	R-R	6-2	210	10-5-87	.307	.315	.305	113	433	54	133	26	2	8	74	29	3	2	4	72	10	4	.432	.352
Jimenez, Jose	L-R	5-10	240	1-2-87	.245	.200	.254	88	294	35	72	15	1	7	42	40	3	2	5	56	2	0	.374	.336
Jimenez, Luis	R-R	6-1	205	1-18-88	.292	.196	.339	43	168	32	49	15	5	2	38	11	1	0	4	27	6	2	.476	.332
Karcich, Jon	R-R	6-2	195	9-10-87	.273	.342	.248	93	297	56	81	21	4	6	29	44	7	5	3	63	7	7	.431	.376
Long, Matt	L-R	5-11	180	4-30-87	.305	.348	.291	125	466	87	142	30	12	4	74	59	5	14	9	67	23	9	.446	.382
Mann, Tyler	L-R	6-2	195	7-21-89	.174	.000	.222	10	23	4	4	1	0	0	3	3	1	1	0	7	0	0	.217	.231
Oliver, Ira	R-R	6-1	215	1-29-87	.245	.192	.272	47	155	26	38	9	0	3	23	11	2	0	2	26	0	0	.381	.374
Ramirez, Carlos	R-R	5-11	205	3-19-88	.226	.346	.173	77	257	39	58	9	2	9	34	35	9	0	2	72	3	2	.381	.337
Ramos, Kevin	R-R	5-11	170	6-6-86	.164	.238	.130	25	67	9	11	1	0	0	5	7	1	4	1	17	1	2	.179	.259
Segura, Jean	R-R	5-11	155	3-17-90	.313	.275	.324	130	515	89	161	24	12	10	79	45	2	11	8	72	50	10	.464	.365
Tignor, Hampton	R-R	6-0	205	8-31-87	.000	.000	.000	1	2	0	0	0	0	0	0	0	0	1	0	0	0	0	.000	.000
Trout, Mike	R-R	6-1	217	8-7-91	.362	.324	.373	81	312	76	113	19	7	6	39	46	7	2	1	52	45	9	.526	.454
Wing, Michael	R-R	6-1	180	10-25-88	.287	.312	.279	90	296	33	85	16	4	8	48	28	5	6	5	56	2	8	.449	.353
Younger, Adam	R-R	6-2	207	8-25-85	.156	.083	.189	23	77	10	12	2	0	3	11	8	0	0	0	24	0	1	.299	.235

Pitching	B-T	HT	WT	DOB	W	L	ERA	G	GS	CG	SV	IP	H	R	ER	HR	BB	SO	AVG	vLH	vRH	K/9	BB/9
Almeida, Yeison	R-R	5-11	150	3-30-90	2	0	5.50	9	0	0	0	18	18	11	11	0	10	13	.247	.190	.323	6.50	5.00
Andrew, Carson	R-R	6-2	205	10-7-87	1	2	3.38	13	1	0	0	27	32	17	10	2	9	20	.302	.305	.298	6.75	3.04
Arenas, Orangel	R-R	6-0	200	3-31-89	4	5	2.01	9	0	0	0	54	41	17	12	2	15	36	.212	.268	.156	6.04	2.52
Bachanov, Jon	R-R	6-4	230	1-30-89	2	0	5.47	18	0	0	2	26	31	17	16	1	14	23	.304	.293	.311	7.86	4.78
Baez, Suammy	R-R	6-4	200	9-28-88	0	0	2.79	3	1	0	0	10	8	3	3	0	8	11	.229	.200	.267	10.24	7.45
Berg, Jeremy	R-R	6-0	180	7-17-86	0	0	1.17	16	0	0	4	23	17	4	3	0	4	20	.200	.286	.140	7.83	1.57
Boshers, Buddy	L-L	6-3	205	5-9-88	3	0	4.31	36	7	1	0	77	84	44	37	5	20	75	.270	.234	.300	8.73	2.33
Bressoud, C.J.	R-R	6-2	205	5-12-85	0	1	8.53	5	0	0	0	6	8	6	6	0	6	10	.370	.273	.438	14.21	8.53
Carpenter, David	R-R	6-3	185	9-1-87	2	4	2.58	37	0	0	8	45	36	19	13	2	19	52	.225	.274	.184	10.32	3.77
Corbin, Pat	L-L	6-3	165	7-19-89	8	0	3.86	9	9	0	0	58	52	28	25	2	10	42	.245	.275	.231	6.48	1.54
Correa, Manuarys	R-R	6-3	170	1-5-89	1	1	2.45	11	1	0	0	22	16	9	6	1	2	11	.198	.219	.184	4.50	0.82
George, Bryant	R-R	5-10	178	7-17-88	1	1	13.50	3	0	0	0	3	3	4	4	1	3	4	.250	.143	.400	13.50	10.13
Hellweg, Johnny	R-R	6-9	210	10-29-88	2	4	4.33	41	0	0	16	44	20	21	21	2	45	66	.133	.103	.159	13.60	9.27
Hurst, Kyle	R-R	6-4	230	8-23-85	4	2	2.84	9	0	0	0	19	14	10	6	1	7	20	.203	.258	.158	9.47	3.32
Jung, Youngil	R-R	6-2	190	11-16-88	2	1	4.37	19	0	0	0	23	12	12	11	1	22	23	.156	.128	.184	9.13	8.74
Kehrer, Tyler	L-L	6-3	210	3-23-88	6	5	4.56	27	14	0	4	116	106	72	59	7	70	108	.245	.224	.255	8.36	5.42
Kenney, Mike	R-R	6-4	212	8-16-86	4	3	3.51	34	0	0	5	51	41	21	20	4	15	44	.219	.256	.188	7.71	2.63
Locke, Stephen	L-L	6-1	188	5-6-86	8	7	4.37	19	18	1	0	117	136	63	57	9	31	77	.294	.296	.292	5.91	2.38
Martinez, Fabio	R-R	6-3	190	10-29-89	7	3	3.92	20	19	0	0	103	80	49	45	6	76	141	.216	.217	.216	12.28	6.62
Oye, Matt	R-R	6-5	230	2-25-86	0	1	1.85	15	0	0	0	24	21	5	5	0	7	22	.231	.204	.270	8.14	2.59
Pena, Ariel	R-R	6-3	186	5-20-89	7	5	3.76	18	18	1	0	103	93	51	43	7	60	88	.242	.260	.222	7.69	5.24
Richards, Garrett	R-R	6-3	210	5-27-88	8	4	3.41	19	19	2	0	108	92	48	41	6	34	108	.229	.276	.181	8.97	2.82
Russell, Max	L-L	6-2	190	9-21-88	2	3	5.31	8	0	0	0	42	55	26	25	10	8	30	.322	.329	.315	6.38	1.70
Skaggs, Tyler	L-L	6-4	195	7-13-91	8	4	3.61	19	14	0	0	82	78	35	33	6	21	82	.252	.303	.229	8.96	2.30
2-team total (4 South Bend)					9	5	3.29	23	18	0	0	98	91	38	36	7	25	102	—	—	—	9.34	2.29

Fielding

Catcher	PCT	G	PO	A	E	DP	PB
Beuerlein	.973	5	32	4	1	0	1
Brannon	1.000	1	3	0	0	0	0
Jimenez	.990	57	442	31	5	3	7
Ramirez	.992	77	640	75	6	11	3
Tignor	1.000	1	9	3	0	0	0

First Base	PCT	G	PO	A	E	DP
Bailey	1.000	4	11	1	0	1
Cruz	.991	13	102	11	1	12
Haerther	.990	92	794	60	9	72
Jimenez	.988	20	156	7	2	12
Mann	1.000	4	26	1	0	1
Oliver	.979	19	125	16	3	12
Ramos	1.000	1	1	0	0	0
Wing	1.000	5	21	5	0	1

Second Base	PCT	G	PO	A	E	DP
Bailey	1.000	5	6	8	0	1
Blackburn	1.000	1	2	3	0	0
Contreras	.889	2	2	6	1	0
Demperio	.933	3	5	9	1	1
Ramos	.929	5	3	10	1	3
Segura	.979	125	210	396	13	77
Wing	1.000	6	6	16	0	5

Third Base	PCT	G	PO	A	E	DP
Alvarez	1.000	4	3	4	0	1
Bailey	.947	9	7	11	1	2
Blackburn	1.000	1	0	1	0	0
Brannon	1.000	1	1	0	0	0
Contreras	1.000	2	3	5	0	2
Cruz	.855	25	13	46	10	3
Demperio	.733	11	5	6	4	0

	PCT	G	PO	A	E	DP
Jimenez	1.000	1	0	1	0	0
Jimenez	.920	30	11	70	7	12
Ramos	1.000	6	4	8	0	1
Wing	.952	64	48	111	8	12

Shortstop	PCT	G	PO	A	E	DP
Bailey	1.000	1	1	1	0	0
Demperio	1.000	1	5	2	0	1
Karcich	.930	92	134	224	27	50
Ramos	.964	12	26	28	2	4
Wing	.934	15	24	33	4	9
Younger	.953	22	29	53	4	10

Outfield	PCT	G	PO	A	E	DP
Alliman	1.000	44	62	0	0	0
Bailey	1.000	3	3	0	0	0
Bass	.952	77	117	3	6	1
Cates	1.000	6	12	0	0	0

Contreras	1.000	4	3	0	0	0
Cruz	.974	28	35	3	1	0
Grichuk	.976	51	78	4	2	2

Long	.974	121	173	14	5	6
Mann	1.000	2	3	0	0	0
Oliver	1.000	15	13	1	0	0

Ramos	1.000	1	1	0	0	0
Trout	1.000	80	134	7	0	1
Wing	—	1	0	0	0	0

OREM OWLZ
ROOKIE
PIONEER LEAGUE

Batting	B-T	HT	WT	DOB	AVG	vLH	vRH	G	AB	R	H	2B	3B	HR	RBI	BB	HBP	SH	SF	SO	SB	CS	SLG	OBP
Alliman, Terrell	R-R	6-3	185	10-15-88	.282	.417	.222	9	39	5	11	1	0	0	3	3	0	0	0	13	0	3	.308	.333
Alvarez, Ricky	R-R	5-11	217	2-7-89	.211	.280	.185	25	90	10	19	7	0	2	12	0	2	0	1	29	0	0	.356	.226
Arendse, Kevin	R-R	6-3	240	11-7-87	.111	.000	.143	4	9	0	1	0	0	0	0	0	1	0	0	1	0	0	.111	.200
Beuerlein, Drew	B-R	6-0	205	1-13-88	.225	.455	.138	15	40	8	9	3	0	0	8	4	1	1	1	10	0	0	.300	.304
Broussard, Ryan	R-R	5-11	181	9-15-89	.203	.286	.179	43	123	19	25	6	0	1	11	11	2	6	1	23	2	3	.276	.277
Calhoun, Kole	L-L	5-10	200	10-14-87	.292	.265	.301	56	202	43	59	14	4	7	42	39	3	1	2	45	3	1	.505	.411
Campos, Jesus	R-R	5-10	175	3-6-88	.190	.250	.154	6	21	1	4	0	0	0	2	1	0	1	0	5	0	1	.238	.227
Cates, Rich	R-L	5-11	180	12-11-86	.400	.000	.400	1	5	0	2	0	0	0	2	0	0	0	0	1	0	0	.400	.400
Cowart, Kaleb	B-R	6-3	190	6-2-92	.400	.000	.400	1	5	1	2	0	0	1	3	1	0	0	0	2	0	0	1.000	.500
Decker, Brandon	L-R	6-3	235	3-22-88	.341	.200	.371	52	173	33	59	15	0	13	47	16	12	0	2	44	0	0	.653	.429
Eichelberger, Dan	R-R	6-0	175	12-30-87	.252	.115	.292	42	115	19	29	2	5	3	15	5	2	2	1	25	2	2	.435	.293
Farnsworth, Nick	L-L	6-2	210	6-17-89	.260	.154	.286	60	200	33	52	11	1	8	34	29	2	0	2	73	1	1	.445	.356
Gomez, Rolando	L-R	5-7	145	6-18-89	.250	.258	.248	55	192	27	48	8	5	4	20	13	0	1	0	55	7	4	.406	.298
Hatton, Wes	R-R	5-10	165	12-28-90	.301	.472	.254	66	246	37	74	9	7	4	37	15	1	6	5	71	5	2	.443	.337
Heid, Drew	L-R	5-10	175	12-14-87	.362	.360	.363	68	287	62	104	12	1	9	34	35	4	4	3	40	9	6	.505	.435
Nichols, Thomas	L-R	6-2	190	2-9-89	.239	.263	.233	61	218	35	52	16	0	9	36	13	11	4	3	64	1	0	.436	.310
Oldfield, Drew	B-R	5-10	190	11-17-87	.136	.105	.145	32	81	12	11	3	0	1	3	6	4	4	1	34	0	1	.210	.228
Pardo, Braulio	B-R	5-11	180	10-10-86	.000	.000	.000	1	4	0	0	0	0	0	0	0	0	0	0	2	0	0	.000	.000
Rife, Jake	L-L	5-11	206	6-7-87	.343	.188	.371	29	105	21	36	1	3	4	19	11	2	2	2	20	7	2	.524	.408
Sodders, Mike	R-R	6-2	185	1-8-88	.253	.440	.189	33	99	18	25	5	0	5	17	8	1	1	0	31	0	0	.455	.315
Tignor, Hampton	R-R	6-0	205	8-31-87	.192	.360	.147	42	120	12	23	2	0	0	7	8	5	4	1	30	0	0	.208	.269
Witherspoon, Travis	R-R	6-2	190	4-16-89	.309	.298	.312	71	288	57	89	11	3	10	45	24	2	8	1	73	20	0	.472	.365

Pitching	B-T	HT	WT	DOB	W	L	ERA	G	GS	CG	SV	IP	H	R	ER	HR	BB	SO	AVG	vLH	vRH	K/9	BB/9
Almeida, Yeison	R-R	5-11	150	3-30-90	2	0	4.76	10	0	0	0	17	19	9	9	3	5	13	.284	.429	.217	6.88	2.65
Andrew, Carson	R-R	6-2	205	10-7-87	0	1	3.45	6	0	0	0	16	12	7	6	1	2	14	.194	.250	.167	8.04	1.15
Blanco, Josh	L-L	6-2	190	11-16-89	1	4	5.87	14	6	0	0	38	37	31	25	3	30	42	.264	.275	.260	9.86	7.04
Cendejas, Eric	R-R	6-0	175	1-28-88	1	0	5.79	3	0	0	0	5	5	4	3	0	5	4	.278	.600	.154	7.71	9.64
Diemer, Brian	R-R	6-5	240	3-25-88	2	1	5.48	20	4	0	0	44	40	30	27	1	30	45	.235	.266	.217	9.14	6.09
Fowler, Seth	R-R	6-3	225	3-31-87	0	0	8.50	11	1	0	0	18	27	21	17	3	11	10	.338	.556	.226	5.00	5.50
George, Bryant	R-R	5-10	178	7-17-88	4	1	1.98	20	0	0	1	41	37	11	9	1	15	44	.243	.302	.202	9.66	3.29
Giardina, Carmine	L-L	6-3	210	2-20-88	3	3	5.51	14	6	0	0	33	58	23	20	2	11	31	.400	.333	.430	8.54	3.03
Graham, Caleb	R-R	6-2	201	1-18-87	2	1	3.45	19	0	0	1	29	33	16	11	1	16	30	.284	.405	.216	9.42	5.02
Gregersen, Erik	R-R	6-5	225	9-19-86	0	0	7.71	2	0	0	0	2	2	2	2	0	4	5	.000	.000	.000	19.29	15.43
Jang, Pill Joon	R-R	6-3	190	4-8-88	2	3	3.96	15	15	0	0	75	88	49	33	7	16	39	.290	.328	.260	4.68	1.92
Johnson, Kevin	L-R	6-5	240	8-19-88	1	4	4.75	18	9	0	0	61	71	37	32	3	24	44	.293	.311	.286	6.53	3.56
Kinzer, Taylor	R-R	6-3	213	1-7-88	1	1	4.85	16	0	0	0	26	34	16	14	1	9	24	.333	.425	.274	8.31	3.12
LaTempa, Justin	R-R	6-5	205	11-21-86	1	2	2.84	5	0	0	0	6	4	5	2	0	2	5	.190	.500	.067	7.11	2.84
Meade, Aaron	B-L	6-2	185	5-2-88	0	2	5.87	7	6	0	0	15	14	13	10	1	13	9	.233	.278	.214	5.28	7.63
Melioris, Joe	R-R	6-10	240	5-29-90	0	0	14.40	3	0	0	0	5	12	8	8	3	0	3	.462	.455	.467	5.40	0.00
Nichols, Heath	R-R	6-2	180	11-23-88	4	2	3.57	7	7	1	0	35	30	17	14	2	13	26	.226	.154	.272	6.62	3.31
Oye, Matt	R-R	6-5	230	2-25-86	0	0	1.69	3	0	0	1	5	5	1	1	0	1	6	.227	.200	.235	10.13	1.69
Piazza, Mike	R-R	6-4	205	11-24-86	0	0	5.84	8	0	0	1	12	16	9	8	3	7	17	.320	.429	.241	12.41	5.11
Reynolds, Danny	R-R	6-0	170	5-2-91	0	0	0.00	4	0	0	0	5	2	0	0	0	1	4	.125	.333	.000	7.20	1.80
Roach, Donn	R-R	6-2	190	12-14-89	4	1	6.04	16	10	0	0	54	64	39	36	6	16	59	.294	.314	.274	9.89	2.68
Robinson, Dakota	L-L	6-3	190	6-5-88	1	5	5.21	21	0	0	0	38	45	25	22	3	12	28	.306	.380	.268	6.63	2.84
Russell, Max	L-L	6-2	190	9-21-88	4	0	3.41	7	6	0	0	32	27	12	12	4	3	31	.229	.222	.233	8.81	0.85
Schugel, A.J.	R-R	6-0	180	6-27-89	2	2	8.59	6	0	0	1	7	8	7	7	0	6	9	.267	.333	.222	11.05	7.36
Tillman, Daniel	R-R	6-1	185	3-14-89	2	2	1.95	22	0	0	10	32	23	8	7	0	10	50	.195	.111	.232	13.92	2.78
Tullo, Aaron	R-R	6-3	195	3-9-88	2	1	2.05	7	5	0	0	22	16	6	5	0	8	21	.205	.321	.140	8.59	3.27

Fielding

Catcher	PCT	G	PO	A	E	DP	PB
Arendse	1.000	4	13	2	0	0	3
Beuerlein	1.000	12	75	10	0	4	3
Cisterna	.931	6	27	0	2	0	2
Oldfield	.984	32	212	31	4	3	4
Pardo	.750	1	9	0	3	0	0
Tignor	.980	40	255	45	6	4	9

First Base	PCT	G	PO	A	E	DP
Decker	.993	32	275	18	2	27
Farnsworth	.980	44	375	25	8	39
Sodders	.988	11	78	2	1	7

Second Base	PCT	G	PO	A	E	DP
Broussard	.967	10	10	19	1	3

	PCT	G	PO	A	E	DP
Campos	1.000	1	1	3	0	0
Hatton	.939	66	91	203	19	41
Sodders	.786	5	4	7	3	2

Third Base	PCT	G	PO	A	E	DP
Alvarez	.957	20	9	36	2	6
Broussard	.800	3	2	2	1	0
Cowart	.667	1	0	2	1	0
Nichols	.923	56	33	111	12	10
Sodders	1.000	4	1	0	0	0

Shortstop	PCT	G	PO	A	E	DP
Broussard	.952	25	41	77	6	20
Campos	.955	5	10	11	1	4
Gomez	.930	52	73	139	16	20

Outfield	PCT	G	PO	A	E
Alliman	.769	6	9	1	3
Alvarez	1.000	1	2	1	0
Broussard	—	2	0	0	0
Calhoun	.981	55	93	9	2
Cates	1.000	1	1	0	0
Decker	1.000	1	1	0	0
Eichelberger	1.000	27	27	0	0
Heid	.967	68	104	12	4
Nichols	—	1	0	0	0
Rife	1.000	8	2	0	0
Witherspoon	.969	71	149	6	5

ARIZONA LEAGUE

Batting	B-T	HT	WT	DOB	AVG	vLH	vRH	G	AB	R	H	2B	3B	HR	RBI	BB	HBP	SH	SF	SO	SB	CS	SLG	OBP
Arendse, Kevin	R-R	6-3	240	11-7-87	.222	.000	.273	8	27	3	6	1	0	0	1	2	1	0	0	8	0	0	.259	.300
Baird, Dillon	L-R	6-3	190	1-13-88	.231	.000	.273	4	13	4	3	1	0	0	0	2	1	0	0	2	0	0	.308	.333
Barber, George	R-R	6-0	180	8-8-89	.235	.667	.143	7	17	4	4	1	0	0	1	2	2	1	0	7	1	0	.294	.381
Beuerlein, Drew	B-R	6-0	205	1-13-88	.250	.273	.240	9	36	5	9	1	0	0	3	2	1	0	0	16	1	0	.278	.308
Blackburn, Mitch	L-R	5-8	175	12-21-87	.204	.286	.171	14	49	3	10	1	0	0	5	3	1	1	2	11	0	1	.224	.255
Bolaski, Michael	R-R	6-3	185	2-5-92	.230	.239	.227	43	165	15	38	6	0	0	14	11	3	0	0	45	2	4	.267	.291
Bolden, Ryan	R-L	6-2	195	9-17-91	.187	.186	.187	44	150	17	28	1	5	0	16	14	5	0	0	68	11	7	.260	.278
Brossman, Jay	R-R	6-1	210	1-17-85	.000	.000	.000	2	3	0	0	0	0	0	0	1	0	0	0	0	0	0	.000	.250
Campos, Jesus	R-R	5-10	175	3-6-88	.429	.500	.400	2	7	0	3	1	0	0	1	0	0	0	0	1	0	1	.571	.500
Clarke, Chevez	B-R	5-11	185	1-9-92	.216	.150	.238	38	162	26	35	5	7	3	16	14	4	0	0	55	9	2	.389	.294
Cowart, Kaleb	B-R	6-3	190	6-2-92	.143	.143	.143	6	21	0	3	0	0	0	4	0	0	0	1	6	0	0	.143	.136
De Los Santos, Anel	R-R	6-3	210	6-19-88	.167	.000	.200	2	6	0	1	0	0	0	2	0	0	0	1	1	0	0	.167	.143
Grichuk, Randal	R-R	6-1	195	8-13-91	.327	.333	.324	12	49	7	16	3	2	4	10	3	0	0	0	9	0	0	.714	.365
Irvine, Steven	R-R	5-10	185	9-7-87	.266	.300	.254	25	79	17	21	6	1	0	11	17	1	2	1	17	1	0	.367	.398
Lindsey, Taylor	L-R	6-0	195	12-2-91	.284	.327	.269	45	194	26	55	12	6	0	18	12	1	2	2	33	8	3	.407	.325
Mallard, Jamie	R-R	6-0	265	8-23-90	.250	.250	.250	4	16	1	4	2	0	0	3	2	0	0	0	9	0	0	.375	.333
Mitchell, Gary	L-R	6-4	235	4-3-89	.231	.281	.216	40	134	20	31	4	4	0	13	17	2	1	1	59	7	1	.321	.325
Pardo, Braulio	B-R	5-11	180	10-10-86	1.000	.000	1.000	1	1	0	1	0	0	0	0	1	0	0	0	0	0	0	1.000	1.000
Rife, Jake	L-L	5-11	206	6-7-87	.276	.270	.279	27	105	15	29	4	6	0	12	11	1	0	0	22	2	3	.429	.350
Rivers, Ryan	R-R	6-5	230	1-7-89	.174	.250	.151	20	69	7	12	2	0	0	5	4	2	0	0	28	0	0	.203	.240
Rodriguez, Jean	R-R	5-10	204	3-27-89	.242	.306	.217	33	128	19	31	3	3	7	20	11	2	0	3	42	1	0	.477	.306
Sanford, Tyler	R-R	6-0	190	6-10-87	.247	.286	.226	23	81	11	20	2	0	1	9	7	0	0	3	30	0	2	.309	.307
Sneed, James	L-L	5-10	170	2-21-92	.000	.000	.000	3	6	0	0	0	0	0	0	0	0	0	0	1	0	0	.000	.000
Soto, Eduardo	R-R	6-0	165	4-25-91	.125	.000	.171	17	48	3	6	1	1	0	2	4	0	1	0	22	1	0	.188	.192
Soto, Wendell	B-R	5-8	150	5-11-92	.260	.296	.250	32	127	14	33	2	2	0	16	10	1	1	0	36	13	4	.307	.319
Turner, Mike	R-R	6-1	210	5-1-90	.118	.067	.139	16	51	4	6	3	0	0	4	2	0	2	3	1	1	.118	.182
Yakubik, Jerod	L-L	6-2	200	11-30-87	.307	.313	.305	41	153	26	47	10	3	0	22	17	4	0	1	27	2	2	.412	.389

Pitching	B-T	HT	WT	DOB	W	L	ERA	G	GS	CG	SV	IP	H	R	ER	HR	BB	SO	AVG	vLH	vRH	K/9	BB/9
Andrew, Carson	R-R	6-2	205	10-7-87	0	0	3.38	2	0	0	0	3	4	1	1	0	0	6	.364	.750	.143	20.25	0.00
Baez, Suammy	R-R	6-4	200	9-28-88	4	4	2.68	13	13	0	0	74	78	31	22	7	17	70	.266	.252	.274	8.51	2.07
Bedrosian, Cam	R-R	6-0	204	10-2-91	0	2	4.50	5	4	0	0	12	13	11	6	0	7	10	.283	.250	.300	7.50	5.25
Burkard, Alex	L-L	6-8	215	1-4-89	1	2	5.91	15	1	0	0	21	30	18	14	0	18	28	.323	.360	.309	11.81	7.59
Cendejas, Eric	R-R	6-0	175	1-28-88	3	1	1.96	15	0	1	0	23	18	5	5	0	4	25	.209	.207	.211	9.78	1.57
Clerici, Adam	L-R	6-5	215	10-4-85	0	0	13.50	4	0	0	0	3	10	5	5	0	1	4	.526	.714	.417	10.80	2.70
Fowler, Seth	R-R	6-3	225	3-31-87	0	0	3.60	5	0	0	1	5	6	2	2	0	2	7	.300	.625	.083	12.60	3.60
Gregersen, Erik	R-R	6-5	225	9-19-86	0	0	0.87	17	0	0	2	21	13	4	2	0	5	27	.181	.226	.146	11.76	2.18
Kelley, Ty	R-R	6-4	196	8-18-88	1	1	14.29	6	0	0	0	6	9	9	9	0	3	9	.375	.167	.583	14.29	4.76
Kinzer, Taylor	R-R	6-3	213	1-7-88	0	0	3.00	3	0	0	0	3	2	1	1	1	0	4	.200	.000	.250	12.00	0.00
Lopez, Baudilio	R-R	6-1	190	11-20-90	1	1	6.00	7	1	0	1	15	18	11	10	0	3	16	.281	.100	.364	9.60	1.80
Marshall, Kris	L-L	5-9	160	11-13-87	3	2	3.55	18	0	0	0	25	24	12	10	1	5	26	.253	.400	.225	9.24	1.78
Meade, Aaron	B-L	6-2	185	5-2-88	1	1	2.25	2	2	0	0	8	9	3	2	0	6	6	.281	.556	.174	6.75	6.75
Melioris, Joe	R-R	6-10	240	5-29-90	3	3	3.44	12	7	0	0	50	58	28	19	1	5	48	.291	.266	.304	8.70	0.91
Mistric, Chance	R-R	6-4	245	5-9-84	3	4	4.50	12	10	0	0	52	57	30	26	3	15	44	.292	.329	.269	7.62	2.60
Mosebach, Bobby	R-R	6-4	195	9-14-84	0	0	3.86	5	0	0	0	7	8	5	3	0	0	6	.286	.143	.333	7.71	0.00
Nichols, Heath	R-R	6-2	180	11-23-88	2	3	4.20	8	5	0	1	45	47	25	21	3	10	44	.269	.241	.292	8.80	2.00
Ortega, Anthony	R-R	6-0	185	8-24-85	0	0	8.00	5	3	0	0	9	11	8	8	1	5	11	.297	.273	.308	11.00	5.00
Palmer, Matt	R-R	6-2	225	3-21-79	0	0	0.00	2	1	0	0	4	2	0	0	0	1	2	.182	.000	.286	4.50	2.25
Schugel, A.J.	R-R	6-0	180	6-27-89	0	0	1.72	11	0	0	0	5	12	16	15	5	3	0	5	12	.259	.200	.279	6.89	2.87
Sookee, Aaron	R-R	6-3	172	6-5-91	1	2	4.60	14	2	0	0	31	28	21	16	3	12	27	.235	.174	.274	7.76	3.45
St. John, Vinnie	R-R	6-1	200	3-24-89	0	0	9.00	4	0	0	0	7	11	7	7	0	4	8	.393	.333	.438	10.29	5.14
Wiedenbauer, John	L-L	6-3	185	1-16-88	0	3	6.46	14	6	0	2	39	54	31	28	3	16	28	.318	.205	.351	6.46	3.69
Yinger, Chad	R-R	6-8	225	7-16-88	1	2	1.74	16	0	0	3	21	18	8	4	0	8	16	.228	.281	.191	6.97	3.48

Fielding

Catcher	PCT	G	PO	A	E	DP	PB
Arendse	1.000	8	63	6	0	1	5
Beuerlein	1.000	7	65	7	0	0	0
Pardo	1.000	1	2	1	0	0	0
Rodriguez	.970	21	170	21	6	0	9
Sanford	.994	20	150	21	1	0	3

First Base	PCT	G	PO	A	E	DP
Bolaski	1.000	4	49	0	0	1
Mallard	1.000	2	22	3	0	0
Rivers	.974	15	145	5	4	13
Yakubik	.988	36	305	35	4	29

Second Base	PCT	G	PO	A	E	DP
Bolaski	1.000	2	4	8	0	4

	PCT	G	PO	A	E	DP
Irvine	1.000	6	9	15	0	0
Lindsey	.971	45	68	136	6	27
Soto	.800	2	3	5	2	1

Third Base	PCT	G	PO	A	E	DP
Baird	1.000	3	2	8	0	1
Bolaski	.842	36	24	56	15	2
Brossman	.750	2	3	0	1	0
Campos	1.000	1	3	3	0	0
Cowart	.500	2	0	1	1	0
Irvine	.914	12	7	25	3	1
Soto	.857	4	1	5	1	0

Shortstop	PCT	G	PO	A	E	DP
Blackburn	.957	14	26	41	3	7
Campos	1.000	1	0	3	0	0

	PCT	G	PO	A	E	DP
Soto	.905	10	14	24	4	2
Soto	.920	30	54	108	14	25

Outfield	PCT	G	PO	A	E	DP
Barber	1.000	7	13	0	0	0
Bolden	.921	44	65	5	6	1
Clarke	.918	37	52	4	5	0
Grichuk	1.000	8	11	0	0	0
Irvine	1.000	5	8	2	0	0
Mitchell	.938	39	67	8	5	1
Rife	.833	16	20	0	4	0
Sneed	.667	2	2	0	1	0
Turner	.833	12	8	2	2	0
Yakubik	1.000	3	2	1	0	0

DOMINICAN SUMMER LEAGUE

Batting	B-T	HT	WT	DOB	AVG	vLH	vRH	G	AB	R	H	2B	3B	HR	RBI	BB	HBP	SH	SF	SO	SB	CS	SLG	OBP
Adames, Waskal	R-R	5-11	195	2-28-89	.296	.306	.294	54	179	28	53	11	5	3	26	22	7	1	3	44	19	5	.464	.389
Alamanzar, Michael	R-R	5-10	185	2-16-91	.167	.000	.182	12	24	0	4	0	0	0	0	1	0	0	0	10	0	0	.167	.200
Beltran, Glenn	R-R	6-2	220	12-23-91	.286	.233	.296	52	182	22	52	11	2	0	25	12	4	1	1	35	7	4	.368	.342
De La Cruz, Ercilio	B-R	5-11	160	10-28-92	.218	.190	.228	30	78	7	17	2	1	0	6	18	0	2	0	31	5	1	.269	.365
Dionicio, Ismael	B-R	5-10	165	7-19-91	.277	.103	.315	50	159	20	44	2	1	0	17	11	1	3	1	28	10	9	.302	.326
Encarnacion, David	R-R	5-10	165	11-2-90	.192	.250	.186	25	78	8	15	2	0	0	4	5	0	1	1	29	5	0	.218	.238
Grance, Moises	R-R	5-11	160	12-1-91	.220	.222	.220	48	159	18	35	11	3	1	13	22	3	3	0	36	5	3	.346	.326
Hernandez, Jonattan	B-R	5-11	175	7-11-90	.198	.200	.197	27	81	9	16	3	0	2	14	6	1	0	0	18	0	0	.309	.261
Jolly, Luis	R-R	6-2	180	3-21-93	.168	.200	.163	30	95	8	16	4	4	0	2	10	6	0	0	47	6	1	.295	.288
Linares, Raul	B-R	5-11	160	10-4-90	.245	.216	.252	59	188	40	46	9	3	1	26	30	9	13	1	32	23	7	.340	.373
Lugo, Carlos	R-R	6-0	190	11-20-89	.207	.233	.198	51	116	30	24	2	1	1	15	35	7	4	1	32	2	4	.267	.415
Martinez, Sandy	B-R	5-11	180	7-18-92	.000	.000	.000	2	3	0	0	0	0	0	1	2	0	0	0	0	0	0	.000	.400
Mateo, Steven	R-R	6-2	188	8-19-92	.229	.130	.256	33	105	8	24	5	0	0	12	10	1	0	2	31	0	2	.276	.297
Piron, Lorenzo	R-R	6-0	200	8-25-90	.228	.240	.224	40	123	10	28	2	0	0	17	9	4	2	2	21	3	3	.244	.297
Rodriguez, Angel	R-R	5-10	170	4-28-92	.210	.267	.191	40	124	20	26	1	1	0	14	8	9	2	2	21	10	2	.234	.301
Ruiz, Reynaldo	R-R	6-2	185	4-21-93	.125	.000	.143	15	32	3	4	1	0	0	6	1	2	0	1	4	1	2	.156	.282
Salcedo, Erick	B-R	5-10	155	6-28-93	.226	.222	.226	29	62	14	14	3	2	0	5	8	0	2	1	17	1	0	.339	.310
Suriel, Alexander	B-L	6-2	190	9-27-90	.216	.222	.215	36	102	7	22	2	1	0	15	9	1	1	0	27	0	1	.255	.286
Toribio, Pedro	R-R	5-10	158	7-21-90	.303	.270	.318	39	122	27	37	1	3	0	15	14	3	0	1	18	15	3	.361	.386
Vivas, Enyelber	R-R	6-1	175	8-26-92	.107	.500	.077	13	28	3	3	1	0	0	3	5	1	0	1	4	0	0	.143	.257

Pitching	B-T	HT	WT	DOB	W	L	ERA	G	GS	CG	SV	IP	H	R	ER	HR	BB	SO	AVG	vLH	vRH	K/9	BB/9
Araujo, Joan	R-L	6-3	170	4-22-91	0	1	3.60	8	0	0	1	10	6	6	4	1	11	13	.171	.500	.152	11.70	9.90
Batista, Lay	R-R	6-2	180	8-4-89	3	2	1.74	14	0	0	1	31	18	8	6	0	19	25	.168	.087	.190	7.26	5.52
Cruz, Junior	R-R	6-1	180	4-5-90	4	3	2.94	12	12	0	0	70	64	32	23	0	26	46	.244	.311	.224	5.89	3.33
Garcia, Franklin	R-R	6-3	195	3-23-90	3	3	4.44	12	2	0	0	24	25	15	12	0	17	15	.275	.300	.268	5.55	6.29
Gomez, Jordany	R-R	6-3	180	9-1-90	3	0	2.35	14	0	0	3	23	24	8	6	0	8	18	.282	.385	.237	7.04	3.13
Hurtado, Daniel	R-R	6-3	180	7-25-92	4	0	2.23	9	9	0	0	44	31	13	11	4	10	36	.207	.122	.248	7.31	2.03
Jimenez, Eswarlin	L-L	6-1	187	11-27-91	4	5	2.50	13	13	2	0	83	72	29	23	0	20	85	.238	.600	.229	9.25	2.18
Perez, Gabriel	R-R	6-0	185	6-3-91	5	4	2.85	12	12	1	0	66	55	27	21	1	18	67	.225	.175	.243	9.09	2.44
Ramirez, Orlando	R-R	6-1	170	5-4-92	1	1	1.57	12	0	0	1	23	21	6	4	0	2	19	.250	.095	.302	7.43	0.78
Reyes, Jose	R-R	6-2	160	2-3-93	0	1	5.40	8	1	0	0	10	9	9	6	3	8	8	.231	.250	.226	7.20	7.20
Santiago, Yancarlos	L-L	6-0	180	1-23-91	4	2	2.19	12	12	1	0	74	58	28	18	3	19	71	.212	.308	.207	8.64	2.31
Santos, Edward	R-R	6-2	220	10-22-89	1	2	2.08	14	0	0	7	22	22	6	5	0	10	18	.275	.222	.290	7.48	4.15
Toribio, Roberto	R-R	6-0	180	11-2-89	0	1	0.00	2	0	0	0	5	3	2	0	0	0	8	.167	.000	.188	14.40	0.00

Fielding

Catcher	PCT	G	PO	A	E	DP	PB
Alamanzar	.941	5	13	3	1	0	1
Hernandez	.941	14	87	8	6	0	4
Lugo	.994	50	317	34	2	2	6
Martinez	1.000	1	5	2	0	0	0
Vivas	.989	11	83	5	1	1	3

First Base	PCT	G	PO	A	E	DP
Piron	.981	16	148	6	3	16
Rodriguez	.995	24	176	7	1	21
Suriel	.986	35	268	10	4	31

Second Base	PCT	G	PO	A	E	DP
Dionicio	.981	22	50	52	2	17

	PCT	G	PO	A	E	DP
Grance	.970	26	68	61	4	22
Linares	.973	7	12	24	1	6
Rodriguez	.934	11	28	29	4	8
Salcedo	1.000	1	1	0	0	0

Third Base	PCT	G	PO	A	E	DP
Linares	.939	47	40	129	11	18
Mateo	.741	9	5	15	7	1
Piron	.773	7	8	9	5	1
Rodriguez	.818	5	2	7	2	0

Shortstop	PCT	G	PO	A	E	DP
Grance	.946	21	35	70	6	11
Salcedo	.951	19	24	54	4	10

	PCT	G	PO	A	E	DP
Toribio	.910	30	40	91	13	17

Outfield	PCT	G	PO	A	E	DP
Adames	.946	48	83	4	5	2
Beltran	.955	50	53	10	3	2
De La Cruz	.926	30	47	3	4	0
Dionicio	.892	19	29	4	4	0
Encarnacion	.906	24	28	1	3	0
Jolly	.900	25	25	2	3	0
Ruiz	.800	15	8	0	2	0

Los Angeles Dodgers

SEASON IN A SENTENCE: The Dodgers made more news off the field than on it in 2010, and most of the news was bad, with the divorce of owners Frank and Jamie McCourt taking center stage and the Manny Ramirez show leaving town.

HIGH POINT: A year after winning the National League West with the best record in the league, the Dodgers got off to a good start and were in first place in mid-June, with Clayton Kershaw winning his seventh game on June 16 in a 6-2 win over the Reds. The offense was led all season by outfielder Andre Ethier, who batted .292/.364/.493 with 23 home runs.

LOW POINT: If you don't include the numerous revelations that the McCourts had been using the franchise as their personal piggybank over the years, the lowest moments on the field occurred after the all-star break, as the team stumbled to two six-game losing streaks in quick succession. When the archrival Giants swept the Dodgers out of San Francisco on Aug. 1, the season was essentially over. Ramirez was dumped on the White Sox in a waiver claim at the end of August. By mid-September, Joe Torre had seen enough to announce that he wouldn't be back for 2011. He'll be replaced by Don Mattingly.

NOTABLE ROOKIES: Righthander John Ely made 18 starts, going 4-10, 5.49, but the Dodgers didn't have any other significant rookie contributors. One of the season's few feel-good stories, however, came when minor league veteran John Lindsey made his big league debut in his 16th professional season. He had one hit in 12 at-bats.

KEY TRANSACTIONS: The Dodgers made several deadline deals to try to rejuvenate the team, though none made a significant difference. They brought in Scott Podsednik from the Royals, Ted Lilly and Ryan Theriot from the Cubs, and Octavio Dotel from the Pirates, in deals that cost them seven prospects. The most notable deal, however, may have been signing first-round pick Zach Lee away from a Louisiana State football scholarship.

DOWN ON THE FARM: The Great Lakes Loons were one of the best teams in the minors, going 90-49 in the low Class A Midwest League, though they faltered in the playoffs. The team had several players who should be Dodgers contributors in future years, led by outfielder Jerry Sands, who jumped to Double-A Chattanooga at midseason, joining top prospect Dee Gordon.

OPENING DAY PAYROLL: $95.4 million (11th)

PLAYERS OF THE YEAR

MAJOR LEAGUE	MINOR LEAGUE
Clayton Kershaw rhp	**Jerry Sands** of
13-10, 2.91	(Low A/Double-A)
212 SO/204 IP	.301/.395/.586
4th in NL in H/9, SO/9	35 HR, 93 RBI

ORGANIZATION LEADERS

BATTING		*Minimum 250 at-bats
MAJORS		
*AVG	Rafael Furcal	.300
*OPS	Andre Ethier	.857
HR	Matt Kemp	28
RBI	Matt Kemp	89
MINORS		
*AVG	John Lindsey, Albuquerque	.353
*OBP	Chris Gutierrez, Inland Empire	.416
*SLG	John Lindsey, Albuquerque	.657
R	Jerry Sands, Great Lakes/Chattanooga	102
H	Jamie Hoffmann, Albuquerque	169
TB	Jerry Sands, Great Lakes/Chattanooga	294
2B	Brian Cavazos-Galvez, Great Lakes	43
3B	Dee Gordon, Chattanooga	10
HR	Jerry Sands, Great Lakes/Chattanooga	35
RBI	John Lindsey, AZL Dodgers/Albuquerque	97
BB	Chris Gutierrez, Inland Empire	74
SO	Kyle Russell, Inland Empire/Chattanooga	177
SB	Dee Gordon, Chattanooga	53

PITCHING		†Minimum 75 innings
MAJORS		
W	Clayton Kershaw	13
†ERA	Clayton Kershaw	2.91
SO	Clayton Kershaw	212
MINORS		
W	Alberto Bastardo, Albuquerque/Chattanooga	12
	Allen Webster, Great Lakes	12
L	Jesus A. Castillo, Albuquerque/Chattanooga	15
†ERA	Allen Webster, Great Lakes	2.88
G	Scott Dohmann, Albuquerque	47
	Juan Perez, AZL Dodgers/Albuquerque	47
GS	Two tied at	27
SV	Luis Vasquez, Great Lakes	20
IP	Josh Wall, Great Lakes	153
BB	Ethan Martin, Inland Empire	81
SO	Josh Wall, Great Lakes	151
†AVG	Matt Magill, Great Lakes	.194

General Manager: Ned Colletti. **Farm Director:** DeJon Watson. **Scouting Director:** Logan White.

Class	Team	League	W	L	PCT	Finish*	Manager(s)
Majors	Los Angeles Dodgers	National	80	82	.494	t-8th (16)	Joe Torre
Triple-A	Albuquerque Isotopes	Pacific Coast	72	71	.503	10th (16)	Tim Wallach
Double-A	Chattanooga Lookouts	Southern	65	74	.468	7th (10)	Carlos Subero
High A	Inland Empire 66ers	California	50	90	.357	10th (10)	Jeff Carter
Low A	Great Lakes Loons	Midwest	90	49	.647	1st (16)	Juan Bustabad
Rookie	Ogden Raptors	Pioneer	44	31	.587	2nd (8)	Damon Berryhill
Rookie	AZL Dodgers	Arizona	30	25	.545	7th (12)	Lorenzo Bundy
Overall 2010 Minor League Record			351	340	.508	11th (30)	

*Finish in overall standings (No. of teams in league). †League champion.

ORGANIZATION STATISTICS

LOS ANGELES DODGERS

NATIONAL LEAGUE

Batting	B-T	HT	WT	DOB	AVG	vLH	vRH	G	AB	R	H	2B	3B	HR	RBI	BB	HBP	SH	SF	SO	SB	CS	SLG	OBP
Anderson, Garret	L-L	6-3	225	6-30-72	.181	.133	.192	80	155	8	28	6	1	2	12	5	0	1	2	34	1	0	.271	.204
Ausmus, Brad	R-R	5-11	190	4-14-69	.222	.154	.240	21	63	4	14	2	0	0	2	7	1	0	0	15	0	0	.254	.310
Barajas, Rod	R-R	6-1	245	9-5-75	.297	.250	.318	25	64	9	19	3	0	5	13	5	2	0	1	15	0	0	.578	.361
2-team total (74 New York)					.240	—		99	313	39	75	14	0	17	47	13	8	1	4	54	0	0	.447	.284
Belliard, Ron	R-R	5-10	210	4-7-75	.216	.167	.250	82	162	24	35	10	1	2	19	18	1	2	2	35	2	2	.327	.295
Blake, Casey	R-R	6-2	205	8-23-73	.248	.314	.222	146	509	56	126	28	1	17	64	48	8	3	3	138	0	4	.407	.320
Carroll, Jamey	R-R	5-9	170	2-18-74	.291	.295	.289	133	351	48	102	15	1	0	23	51	2	5	5	64	12	4	.339	.379
Castro, Juan	R-R	5-11	190	6-20-72	.000	.000	.000	1	3	0	0	0	0	0	0	1	0	0	0	2	0	0	.000	.250
2-team total (54 Philadelphia)					.194	—		55	129	7	25	5	0	0	13	8	0	1	2	25	0	1	.233	.237
DeWitt, Blake	L-R	5-11	190	8-20-85	.270	.222	.280	82	256	29	69	15	4	1	30	30	3	2	1	49	2	2	.371	.352
2-team total (53 Chicago)					.261	—		135	440	47	115	24	5	5	52	47	4	2	3	86	3	2	.373	.336
Ellis, A.J.	R-R	6-2	225	4-9-81	.278	.250	.284	44	108	6	30	5	0	0	16	14	1	4	1	18	0	0	.324	.363
Ethier, Andre	L-L	6-2	210	4-10-82	.292	.233	.318	139	517	71	151	33	1	23	82	59	3	0	6	102	2	1	.493	.364
Furcal, Rafael	B-R	5-8	195	10-24-77	.300	.277	.310	97	383	66	115	23	7	8	43	40	1	2	2	60	22	4	.460	.366
Gibbons, Jay	L-L	5-11	190	3-2-77	.280	.333	.267	37	75	11	21	2	0	5	17	4	0	0	1	14	0	1	.507	.313
Green, Nick	R-R	6-0	180	9-10-78	.125	.143	.000	5	8	0	1	0	0	0	0	1	0	0	0	2	0	0	.125	.222
Hu, Chin-Lung	R-R	5-11	190	2-2-84	.130	.286	.063	14	23	2	3	1	0	0	1	0	1	0	1	5	1	0	.174	.160
Johnson, Reed	R-R	5-10	180	12-8-76	.262	.301	.222	102	202	24	53	11	2	2	15	5	4	2	2	50	2	2	.366	.291
Kemp, Matt	R-R	6-3	225	9-23-84	.249	.295	.233	162	602	82	150	25	6	28	89	53	4	0	9	170	19	15	.450	.310
Lindsey, John	R-R	6-1	245	1-30-77	.083	.000	.143	11	12	0	1	0	0	0	0	1	0	0	1	3	0	0	.083	.154
Loney, James	L-L	6-3	220	5-7-84	.267	.222	.286	161	588	67	157	41	2	10	88	52	4	0	4	95	10	5	.395	.329
Martin, Russell	R-R	5-10	230	2-15-83	.248	.235	.252	97	331	45	82	13	0	5	26	48	4	1	3	61	6	2	.332	.347
Mitchell, Russ	R-R	5-11	205	2-15-85	.143	.188	.115	15	42	3	6	0	0	2	4	0	0	0	1	8	0	0	.286	.140
Oeltjen, Trent	L-L	6-0	190	2-28-83	.217	.000	.227	14	23	5	5	1	1	0	1	4	1	2	0	8	0	0	.348	.357
Paul, Xavier	L-R	6-0	195	2-25-85	.231	.238	.230	44	121	16	28	8	1	0	11	8	0	3	1	24	3	1	.314	.277
Podsednik, Scott	L-L	6-0	185	3-18-76	.262	.200	.281	39	149	17	39	6	1	1	7	11	0	0	0	26	5	3	.336	.313
Ramirez, Manny	R-R	6-0	200	5-30-72	.311	.270	.321	66	196	32	61	15	0	8	40	32	1	0	3	38	1	1	.510	.405
Theriot, Ryan	R-R	5-11	180	12-7-79	.242	.302	.221	54	198	27	48	5	0	1	8	22	2	5	1	28	4	3	.283	.323
2-team total (96 Chicago)					.270	—		150	586	72	158	15	2	2	29	41	4	7	2	74	20	9	.312	.321

Pitching	B-T	HT	WT	DOB	W	L	ERA	G	GS	CG	SV	IP	H	R	ER	HR	BB	SO	AVG	vLH	vRH	K/9	BB/9
Belisario, Ronald	R-R	6-3	235	12-31-82	3	1	5.04	59	0	0	2	55	52	31	31	6	19	38	.250	.257	.246	6.18	3.09
Billingsley, Chad	R-R	6-1	245	7-29-84	12	11	3.57	31	31	1	0	192	176	82	76	8	69	171	.244	.252	.236	8.03	3.24
Broxton, Jonathan	R-R	6-4	295	6-16-84	5	6	4.04	64	0	0	22	62	64	30	28	4	28	73	.270	.243	.292	10.54	4.04
Dotel, Octavio	R-R	6-0	220	11-25-73	1	1	3.38	19	0	0	1	19	11	7	7	3	11	21	.167	.261	.116	10.13	5.30
3-team total (8 Colorado, 41 Pittsburgh)					3	4	4.08	68	0	0	22	64	52	32	29	9	32	75	—			10.55	4.50
Elbert, Scott	L-L	6-1	215	8-13-85	0	0	13.50	1	0	0	0	1	1	1	1	0	3	0	.333	1.000	.000	0.00	40.50
Ely, John	R-R	6-2	200	5-13-86	4	10	5.49	18	18	0	0	100	105	63	61	12	40	76	.276	.240	.299	6.84	3.60
Haeger, Charlie	R-R	6-1	210	9-19-83	0	4	8.40	9	6	0	0	30	36	32	28	4	26	30	.295	.354	.257	9.00	7.80
Jansen, Kenley	B-R	6-0	220	9-30-87	1	0	0.67	25	0	0	4	27	12	2	2	0	15	41	.130	.205	.063	13.67	5.00
Kershaw, Clayton	L-L	6-3	225	3-19-88	13	10	2.91	32	32	1	0	204	160	73	66	13	81	212	.214	.200	.218	9.34	3.57
Kuo, Hong-Chih	L-L	6-1	240	7-23-81	3	2	1.20	56	0	0	12	60	29	8	8	1	18	73	.139	.095	.159	10.95	2.70
Kuroda, Hiroki	R-R	6-1	190	2-10-75	11	13	3.39	31	31	0	0	196	180	87	74	15	48	159	.243	.245	.241	7.29	2.20
Lilly, Ted	L-L	6-1	195	1-4-76	7	4	3.52	12	12	1	0	77	61	30	30	13	15	77	.218	.333	.196	9.04	1.76
2-team total (18 Chicago)					10	12	3.62	30	30	1	0	194	165	83	78	32	44	166	—			7.71	2.04
Link, Jon	R-R	6-1	190	3-23-84	0	0	4.15	9	0	0	0	9	12	7	4	0	4	4	.333	.385	.304	4.15	4.15
McDonald, James	L-R	6-5	195	10-19-84	0	1	8.22	4	1	0	0	8	11	7	7	1	5	7	.344	.412	.267	8.22	5.87
2-team total (11 Pittsburgh)					4	6	4.02	15	12	0	0	72	70	32	32	4	29	68	—			8.54	3.64
Miller, Justin	R-R	6-2	200	8-27-77	0	0	4.44	19	0	0	0	24	22	12	12	4	8	30	.244	.286	.226	11.10	2.96
Monasterios, Carlos	R-R	6-2	175	3-21-86	3	5	4.38	32	13	0	0	88	99	48	43	15	29	52	.286	.242	.313	5.30	2.95
Ortiz, Ramon	R-R	6-0	175	5-23-73	1	0	6.30	16	2	0	0	30	33	22	21	5	16	21	.287	.357	.220	6.30	4.80
Ortiz, Russ	R-R	6-1	220	6-5-74	0	1	10.29	6	0	0	0	7	10	8	8	0	5	6	.345	.308	.375	7.71	6.43

	B-T	HT	WT	DOB			ERA	G	GS	CG	SV	IP	H	R	ER	HR	BB	SO	AVG	vLH	vRH	K/9	BB/9
Padilla, Vicente	R-R	6-2	220	9-27-77	6	5	4.07	16	16	1	0	95	79	46	43	14	24	84	.226	.167	.267	7.96	2.27
Schlichting, Travis	R-R	6-4	190	10-19-84	1	0	3.57	14	0	0	0	23	20	9	9	0	10	14	.233	.171	.275	5.56	3.97
Sherrill, George	L-L	6-0	230	4-19-77	2	2	6.69	65	0	0	0	36	46	28	27	4	24	25	.311	.192	.427	6.19	5.94
Taschner, Jack	L-L	6-3	205	4-21-78	0	0	27.00	3	0	0	0	1	1	1	1	0	3	0	.333	.000	.333	0.00	81.00
2-team total (17 Pittsburgh)					1	0	6.41	20	0	0	0	20	23	14	14	3	11	17	—	—	—	7.78	5.03
Troncoso, Ramon	R-R	6-1	220	2-16-83	2	3	4.33	52	0	0	0	54	55	28	26	7	18	34	.262	.244	.274	5.67	3.00
Weaver, Jeff	R-R	6-5	200	8-22-76	5	1	6.09	43	0	0	0	44	48	30	30	5	20	26	.291	.321	.275	5.28	4.06

Fielding

Catcher	PCT	G	PO	A	E	DP	PB
Ausmus	.994	21	168	5	1	0	0
Barajas	1.000	23	165	6	0	0	0
Ellis	.996	43	263	21	1	4	1
Martin	.987	93	681	59	10	2	5

First Base	PCT	G	PO	A	E	DP
Belliard	.981	10	46	6	1	6
Blake	1.000	1	1	0	0	0
Ethier	—	1	0	0	0	0
Gibbons	1.000	3	16	2	0	1
Lindsey	1.000	2	8	1	0	2
Loney	.997	160	1286	78	4	103
Mitchell	.958	3	22	1	1	1

Second Base	PCT	G	PO	A	E	DP
Belliard	.987	20	38	37	1	9
Carroll	1.000	48	48	78	0	12
DeWitt	.980	78	169	182	7	41
Green	1.000	3	4	9	0	2
Theriot	.996	53	103	125	1	25

Third Base	PCT	G	PO	A	E	DP
Belliard	.917	16	10	23	3	3
Blake	.957	139	80	257	15	17
Carroll	.905	11	5	14	2	1
Mitchell	.895	6	4	13	2	3

Shortstop	PCT	G	PO	A	E	DP
Carroll	.986	69	80	195	4	32
Castro	1.000	1	1	1	0	1

Furcal	.955	93	127	275	19	47
Green	—	1	0	0	0	0
Hu	.958	10	13	10	1	4

Outfield	PCT	G	PO	A	E	DP
Anderson	.952	34	38	2	2	0
Carroll	1.000	5	13	0	0	0
Ethier	.996	132	223	6	1	2
Gibbons	.963	16	25	1	1	0
Johnson	1.000	84	100	0	0	0
Kemp	.985	158	330	3	5	2
Mitchell	1.000	3	2	0	0	0
Oeltjen	1.000	8	9	0	0	0
Paul	.963	38	49	3	2	1
Podsednik	.972	38	70	0	2	0
Ramirez	.959	46	68	2	3	0

ALBUQUERQUE ISOTOPES
PACIFIC COAST LEAGUE

TRIPLE-A

Batting	B-T	HT	WT	DOB	AVG	vLH	vRH	G	AB	R	H	2B	3B	HR	RBI	BB	HBP	SH	SF	SO	SB	CS	SLG	OBP
Ausmus, Brad	R-R	5-11	190	4-14-69	.125	.333	.000	4	8	0	1	0	0	0	0	0	0	0	0	2	0	0	.125	.125
Castro, Juan	R-R	5-11	190	6-20-72	.286	.000	.308	5	14	2	4	0	0	1	2	0	0	0	2	0	0	0	.286	.375
Closser, J.D.	B-R	5-10	180	1-15-80	.268	.250	.274	92	254	34	68	9	0	3	27	24	1	4	1	48	3	1	.339	.332
Collado, Keyter	R-R	5-9	182	6-8-86	.400	.000	.400	1	5	1	2	0	0	0	0	0	0	0	0	1	0	0	.400	.400
De Jesus Jr., Ivan	R-R	5-11	190	5-1-87	.296	.284	.301	130	533	89	158	33	2	7	70	32	2	7	6	81	6	1	.405	.335
Denker, Travis	R-R	5-9	205	8-5-85	.243	.400	.219	13	37	4	9	1	1	6	2	1	0	0	7	1	0	.405	.300
2-team total (7 Tacoma)					.222	—		20	54	5	12	3	1	6	5	1	0	0	10	1	1	.370	.300
Ellis, A.J.	R-R	6-2	225	4-9-81	.262	.313	.244	18	61	11	16	5	1	0	7	13	1	1	0	12	1	0	.377	.400
Ethier, Andre	L-L	6-2	210	4-10-82	.600	.500	.667	2	5	4	3	0	0	0	2	1	0	1	0	0	0	0	.600	.667
Furcal, Rafael	B-R	5-8	195	10-24-77	.600	.000	.600	2	5	3	3	1	1	1	4	1	0	0	0	0	0	0	01.800	.667
Gibbons, Jay	L-L	5-11	190	3-2-77	.347	.528	.300	95	352	60	122	28	1	19	83	19	0	0	5	30	0	0	.594	.375
Green, Nick	R-R	6-0	180	9-10-78	.204	.167	.216	29	98	15	20	9	2	2	10	3	1	2	0	19	1	0	.398	.235
2-team total (40 Portland)					.240	—		69	242	32	58	18	3	4	31	16	1	4	0	52	1	4	.388	.290
Guerrero, Pedro	R-R	6-3	185	12-3-88	.500	.000	.500	2	2	0	1	0	0	0	0	0	0	0	0	0	0	0	.500	.500
Herrera, Elian	B-R	5-11	190	2-1-85	.229	.250	.222	25	48	8	11	0	1	0	8	10	0	0	1	9	1	1	.271	.356
Hoffman, Jamie	R-R	6-3	235	8-20-84	.310	.335	.300	139	545	91	169	36	3	8	74	43	11	4	5	98	17	7	.431	.369
Hu, Chin-Lung	R-R	5-11	190	2-2-84	.317	.435	.259	58	208	37	66	11	1	4	25	8	0	5	2	16	8	1	.438	.339
Lindsey, John	R-R	6-1	245	1-30-77	.353	.410	.329	107	408	74	144	41	4	25	97	19	16	0	4	78	0	0	.657	.400
Lopez, Esteban	R-R	6-1	210	6-20-84	.333	.500	.300	7	12	0	4	2	0	0	5	0	0	0	0	5	0	0	.500	.333
May, Lucas	R-R	5-11	195	10-24-84	.296	.309	.291	73	260	47	77	13	3	11	45	22	1	1	1	60	4	2	.496	.352
2-team total (24 Omaha)					.291	—		97	351	61	102	20	3	16	58	34	2	1	2	79	4	2	.501	.355
Mitchell, Russ	R-R	5-11	205	2-15-85	.315	.381	.290	127	505	97	159	38	2	23	87	38	4	4	6	78	1	3	.535	.363
Nivar, Ramon	R-R	5-10	185	2-22-80	.271	.367	.200	24	70	11	19	6	1	1	8	2	0	1	0	7	0	0	.429	.292
Oeltjen, Trent	L-L	6-1	190	2-28-83	.347	.288	.371	49	199	40	69	18	5	5	33	23	2	0	2	43	14	5	.563	.416
2-team total (70 Nashville)					.320	—		119	465	87	149	42	7	13	71	44	5	4	5	102	27	7	.525	.382
Paul, Xavier	L-R	6-0	195	2-25-85	.325	.311	.331	57	228	46	74	20	1	12	38	18	4	0	0	41	7	3	.579	.384
Perez, Timo	L-L	5-9	180	4-8-75	.296	.200	.305	41	115	19	34	7	1	2	10	6	1	1	0	10	3	0	.426	.336
Redman, Prentice	R-R	6-3	185	8-23-79	.332	.413	.288	61	214	43	71	13	2	10	41	25	1	0	1	42	7	2	.551	.402
Restovich, Michael	R-R	6-6	240	1-3-79	.305	.353	.283	111	321	52	98	22	4	12	50	33	1	0	1	76	1	1	.511	.371
Rivera, Mike	R-R	6-1	235	9-8-76	.125	.000	.158	14	48	4	6	2	0	2	2	2	1	1	0	19	0	0	.292	.176
2-team total (3 New Orleans)					.123	—		17	57	5	7	2	0	2	2	2	1	1	0	20	0	0	.263	.180
Sellers, Justin	R-R	5-10	160	2-1-86	.285	.316	.273	90	288	51	82	17	1	14	56	40	3	7	6	49	5	3	.497	.391
Van Slyke, Scott	R-R	6-5	195	7-24-86	.289	.250	.300	12	38	5	11	4	0	1	5	0	0	0	0	7	0	0	.474	.289

Pitching	B-T	HT	WT	DOB	W	L	ERA	G	GS	CG	SV	IP	H	R	ER	HR	BB	SO	AVG	vLH	vRH	K/9	BB/9
Adkins, James	L-L	6-6	200	11-26-85	0	1	18.00	5	0	0	0	4	13	9	8	0	2	4	.542	.727	.385	9.00	4.50
Ayala, Luis	R-R	6-2	190	1-12-78	1	3	4.50	14	0	0	4	14	14	8	7	1	7	10	.259	.267	.250	6.43	4.50
3-team total (4 Colorado Springs, 18 Reno)					2	10	6.42	36	0	0	4	48	60	35	34	4	18	31	—	—	—	5.85	3.40
Bastardo, Alberto	L-L	6-0	160	4-6-84	5	4	6.99	12	12	0	0	57	81	57	44	9	19	39	.332	.316	.339	6.19	3.02
Blevins, Jerry	R-R	6-0	200	11-6-85	1	1	4.5	5	2	0	0	17	23	8	8	5	5	12	.354	.385	.308	2.62	2.60
Calero, Kiko	R-R	6-1	210	1-9-75	0	0	3.00	15	0	0	1	15	15	5	5	1	7	11	.268	.345	.185	6.60	4.20
Castillo, Jesus	R-R	6-0	195	5-31-84	1	5	10.27	4	4	0	0	24	34	27	27	4	15	13	.354	.365	.341	4.94	5.70
Choi, Hyang-Nam	R-R	6-2	190	3-28-71	1	2	5.84	12	0	0	0	25	37	19	16	0	7	17	.359	.286	.426	6.20	2.55
Colome, Jesus	R-R	6-2	240	12-23-77	0	0	33.75	3	0	0	0	1	4	5	5	0	2	1	.500	.571	.000	6.75	13.50
2-team total (4 Oklahoma City)					0	0	15.43	7	0	0	0	5	7	10	8	0	3	3	—	—	—	5.79	5.79
Corcoran, Tim	R-R	6-2	205	4-15-78	9	8	6.31	25	18	0	0	107	140	78	75	10	33	92	.324	.362	.292	7.74	2.78

Dohmann, Scott	R-R	6-1	200	2-13-78	1	2	5.82	47	0	0	16	51	64	33	33	8	20	42	.309	.318	.300	7.41	3.53
Elbert, Scott	L-L	6-1	215	8-13-85	1	1	4.98	9	9	0	0	43	46	26	24	4	34	45	.277	.217	.300	9.35	7.06
Ely, John	R-R	6-2	200	5-13-86	5	4	6.22	13	13	1	0	68	70	48	47	10	29	56	.269	.306	.242	7.41	3.84
Etherton, Seth	R-R	6-1	195	10-17-76	5	7	5.33	19	17	0	0	103	120	66	61	16	23	95	.288	.313	.265	8.30	2.01
Felix, Francisco	R-R	5-11	205	7-28-83	2	0	4.26	2	2	0	0	13	11	6	6	3	3	11	.250	.389	.154	7.82	2.13
Geary, Geoff	R-R	6-0	180	8-26-76	0	1	5.06	8	0	0	0	11	13	6	6	0	4	16	.302	.429	.182	13.50	3.38
2-team total (23 Oklahoma City)					4	6	5.32	31	6	0	0	69	96	49	41	7	25	48	—	—	—	6.23	3.25
Gonzalez, Edgar	R-R	6-2	210	2-23-83	1	1	4.81	4	4	0	0	24	29	15	13	3	6	29	.296	.216	.344	10.73	2.22
Haeger, Charlie	R-R	6-2	210	9-19-83	4	3	5.70	11	10	0	0	54	45	38	34	4	42	41	.231	.208	.255	6.88	7.04
Koronka, John	L-L	6-0	200	7-3-80	1	0	54.00	1	1	0	0	1	7	8	8	2	1	0	.636	.750	.571	0.00	6.75
Leach, Brent	L-L	6-5	215	11-18-82	3	2	6.35	26	3	0	0	40	49	28	28	2	24	37	.299	.302	.297	8.39	5.45
Lindblom, Josh	R-R	6-5	240	6-15-87	3	2	6.54	40	10	0	0	95	143	79	69	12	32	84	.340	.358	.325	7.96	3.03
Link, Jon	R-R	6-1	190	3-23-84	3	2	3.71	45	1	0	4	61	65	33	25	5	21	55	.274	.299	.260	8.16	3.12
Livingston, Bobby	L-L	6-3	205	9-3-82	0	1	14.85	3	1	0	0	7	16	11	11	1	1	3	.444	.467	.429	4.05	1.35
McDonald, James	L-R	6-5	195	10-19-84	6	1	4.41	12	12	0	0	63	64	31	31	4	24	57	.262	.243	.279	8.10	3.41
Miller, Justin	R-R	6-2	200	8-27-77	0	1	1.95	32	0	0	0	37	29	9	8	2	16	37	.213	.269	.179	9.00	3.89
Monasterios, Carlos	R-R	6-2	175	3-21-86	0	0	5.40	2	2	0	0	7	7	5	4	1	3	5	.269	.200	.364	6.75	4.05
Padilla, Vicente	R-R	6-2	220	9-27-77	0	1	6.35	1	1	0	0	6	8	6	4	2	0	5	.320	.250	.353	7.94	0.00
Perez, Juan	R-L	6-0	180	9-3-78	4	3	2.96	45	0	0	1	46	38	19	15	4	20	53	.224	.203	.242	10.45	3.94
Pratt, Jordan	R-R	6-3	212	5-17-85	0	0	18.00	1	0	0	0	1	2	2	2	1	1	1	.400	.000	.500	9.00	9.00
Rodriguez, Jesus	R-R	6-0	180	9-13-85	3	1	5.82	27	0	0	0	39	44	27	25	6	18	18	.278	.231	.325	4.19	4.19
Schlichting, Travis	R-R	6-4	190	10-19-84	3	0	4.75	27	0	0	1	47	55	27	25	5	13	29	.294	.316	.278	5.51	2.47
Sherrill, George	L-L	6-0	230	4-19-77	0	0	0.00	2	1	0	0	2	2	0	0	0	0	3	.286	.500	.000	16.20	0.00
Taschner, Jack	L-L	6-3	205	4-21-78	0	0	3.60	10	0	0	2	10	7	4	4	4	0	4	.184	.217	.133	3.60	0.00
Thompson, Eric	R-R	6-6	210	4-4-88	0	0	22.09	2	0	0	0	4	8	9	9	2	4	2	.421	.200	.667	4.91	9.82
Towers, Josh	R-R	6-1	185	2-26-77	2	5	8.05	8	8	0	0	38	62	42	34	9	6	18	.358	.344	.373	4.26	1.42
Troncoso, Ramon	R-R	6-1	220	2-16-83	0	2	5.73	15	0	0	1	22	23	14	14	5	19	19	.277	.306	.255	7.77	4.50
Vargas, Claudio	R-R	6-4	235	6-19-78	2	6	5.89	10	10	0	0	47	52	34	31	6	20	45	.277	.330	.223	8.56	3.80
Wade, Cory	R-R	6-2	190	5-28-83	3	0	4.91	21	0	0	2	29	35	16	16	4	3	20	.292	.264	.313	6.14	0.92
White, Cody	L-L	6-3	185	2-27-85	3	0	7.33	8	2	0	0	23	34	21	19	3	17	15	.343	.355	.338	5.79	6.56

Fielding

Catcher	PCT	G	PO	A	E	DP	PB
Ausmus	1.000	4	8	0	0	0	0
Closser	.992	46	349	24	3	5	1
Collado	1.000	1	10	0	0	0	0
Ellis	.992	18	118	14	1	0	1
Lopez	1.000	4	23	0	0	0	0
May	.994	69	455	27	3	1	9
Rivera	1.000	13	98	8	0	0	2

First Base	PCT	G	PO	A	E	DP
Closser	.980	31	138	10	3	14
Gibbons	.992	28	220	20	2	18
Lindsey	.989	87	666	44	8	64
Mitchell	.990	13	90	7	1	10
Restovich	.990	15	87	13	1	11

Second Base	PCT	G	PO	A	E	DP
Castro	.500	2	1	0	1	0
De Jesus Jr.	.974	114	212	303	14	64
Denker	1.000	3	4	7	0	2

	PCT	G	PO	A	E	DP
Green	.955	5	10	11	1	1
Herrera	.931	9	10	17	2	4
Hu	.985	15	29	36	1	8
Mitchell	1.000	5	7	8	0	3
Nivar	.972	9	13	22	1	6

Third Base	PCT	G	PO	A	E	DP
Castro	1.000	1	1	3	0	0
Closser	.944	11	2	15	1	2
Denker	.846	8	5	6	2	1
Green	.972	16	8	27	1	2
Herrera	1.000	1	0	1	0	0
Mitchell	.958	103	61	190	11	22
Nivar	.964	9	9	18	1	1
Sellers	.917	3	1	8	1	1

Shortstop	PCT	G	PO	A	E	DP
Castro	1.000	2	2	5	0	1
De Jesus Jr.	.931	20	18	36	4	5
Furcal	1.000	2	2	5	0	2

	PCT	G	PO	A	E	DP
Green	.926	8	10	15	2	3
Hu	.953	45	58	104	8	22
Sellers	.955	83	143	218	17	50

Outfield	PCT	G	PO	A	E	DP
Closser	1.000	3	4	0	0	0
Ethier	1.000	2	2	0	0	0
Gibbons	.982	40	52	4	1	0
Green	1.000	1	2	0	0	0
Herrera	1.000	13	18	0	0	0
Hoffmann	.997	137	297	6	1	2
Mitchell	1.000	13	22	0	0	0
Oeltjen	.987	48	74	0	1	0
Paul	.974	54	105	7	3	2
Perez	1.000	30	58	3	0	1
Redman	.964	51	79	2	3	1
Restovich	.955	66	83	2	4	0
Van Slyke	1.000	9	19	0	0	0

CHATTANOOGA LOOKOUTS DOUBLE-A

SOUTHERN LEAGUE

Batting	B-T	HT	WT	DOB	AVG	vLH	vRH	G	AB	R	H	2B	3B	HR	RBI	BB	HBP	SH	SF	SO	SB	CS	SLG	OBP
Amezaga, Alfredo	B-R	5-10	180	1-16-78	1.000	1.000	1.000	1	2	1	2	0	0	0	1	1	0	0	0	0	0	0	1.000	1.000
Baez, Pedro	R-R	6-2	195	3-11-88	.385	.429	.368	7	26	2	10	1	0	0	2	2	1	0	0	8	1	0	.423	.448
Collado, Keyter	R-R	5-9	182	6-8-86	.300	.400	.280	9	30	4	9	1	0	0	1	0	0	0	0	5	2	0	.333	.323
Denker, Travis	R-R	5-9	205	8-5-85	.229	.263	.207	16	48	2	11	2	0	0	2	3	1	0	1	8	0	1	.271	.283
Garabedian, Alex	R-R	6-2	210	8-26-85	.239	.143	.281	19	46	9	11	3	0	2	7	6	0	0	0	16	0	0	.435	.327
Giles, Tommy	L-L	6-0	190	8-28-83	.236	.147	.270	46	123	15	29	3	2	3	12	13	4	1	0	23	1	0	.366	.329
Gordon, Dee	L-R	5-11	150	4-22-88	.277	.237	.296	133	555	86	154	17	10	2	39	40	7	9	3	89	53	20	.355	.332
Hatch, Anthony	L-R	6-3	200	8-30-83	.205	.167	.217	31	78	10	16	5	0	2	10	9	0	0	1	18	0	1	.346	.284
Herrera, Elian	B-R	5-11	190	2-1-85	.258	.279	.246	97	299	44	77	11	4	2	38	47	4	12	3	71	31	10	.341	.363
Lambo, Andrew	L-L	6-3	190	8-11-88	.271	.381	.237	47	181	26	49	11	2	4	25	15	0	1	1	39	1	1	.420	.325
May, Lucas	R-R	5-11	195	10-24-84	.167	.000	.211	7	24	2	4	1	0	0	1	2	1	0	0	7	0	0	.208	.259
Mier, Jessie	R-R	6-1	215	3-5-85	.269	.179	.302	46	145	16	39	6	1	1	14	13	3	1	0	24	3	1	.345	.342
Nivar, Ramon	R-R	5-10	185	2-22-80	.306	.405	.242	32	108	17	33	10	1	0	16	3	1	1	1	9	5	4	.417	.327
Pedroza, Jaime	B-R	5-8	167	9-12-86	.280	.341	.251	130	411	53	115	21	4	7	37	62	4	8	2	101	11	8	.401	.378
Perez, Eduardo	B-R	6-1	175	8-30-84	.271	.319	.248	130	432	47	117	33	0	4	58	36	2	2	4	93	12	2	.375	.327
Rivera, Mike	R-R	6-1	235	9-8-76	.257	.246	.262	58	183	20	47	16	0	2	22	35	4	0	2	48	2	2	.388	.367
Robinson, Trayvon	B-R	5-11	195	9-1-87	.300	.319	.291	120	434	80	130	23	5	9	57	73	5	8	3	125	38	15	.438	.404
Russell, Kyle	L-L	6-5	195	6-27-86	.245	.225	.254	76	273	36	67	23	3	10	28	29	2	1	3	113	3	2	.462	.319
Sands, Jerry	R-R	6-4	225	9-28-87	.270	.221	.291	68	259	54	70	12	2	17	47	33	6	0	5	62	4	0	.529	.360

Batting	B-T	HT	WT	DOB	AVG	vLH	vRH	G	AB	R	H	2B	3B	HR	RBI	BB	HBP	SH	SF	SO	SB	CS	SLG	OBP
Silverio, Alfredo	R-R	6-0	205	5-6-87	.063	.167	.000	4	16	1	1	0	0	0	0	0	0	0	0	3	0	0	.063	.063
Smith, Corey	R-R	6-1	200	4-15-82	.275	.219	.305	115	403	58	111	34	2	13	86	38	7	0	7	74	6	2	.467	.343
Van Slyke, Scott	R-R	6-5	195	7-24-86	.235	.211	.247	65	217	28	51	7	3	4	29	18	3	1	2	37	4	2	.350	.300
Wallach, Matt	L-R	6-1	205	2-17-86	.265	.357	.241	24	68	13	18	3	0	3	11	13	1	0	2	10	1	0	.441	.381
Yount, Dustin	L-R	6-1	198	10-27-82	.229	.125	.250	34	48	5	11	1	0	1	5	7	0	0	0	16	0	0	.313	.327

Pitching	B-T	HT	WT	DOB	W	L	ERA	G	GS	CG	SV	IP	H	R	ER	HR	BB	SO	AVG	vLH	vRH	K/9	BB/9
Adkins, James	L-L	6-6	230	11-26-85	3	1	4.76	40	0	0	1	45	40	24	24	6	23	50	.238	.185	.272	9.93	4.57
Alvarez, Mario	R-R	6-0	205	3-26-84	6	6	4.94	33	19	1	2	120	156	75	66	8	52	79	.319	.280	.348	5.91	3.89
Bastardo, Alberto	L-L	6-0	160	4-6-84	7	4	4.79	15	15	0	0	83	92	46	44	5	28	76	.282	.241	.297	8.27	3.05
Blevins, Bobby	R-R	6-0	200	1-16-85	1	1	5.31	8	2	0	0	20	21	14	12	0	7	14	.269	.359	.179	6.20	3.10
Castillo, Jesus	R-R	6-0	195	5-31-84	4	10	3.83	19	19	0	0	103	126	58	44	9	35	66	.302	.308	.297	5.75	3.05
De La Rosa, Rubby	R-R	6-1	170	3-4-89	3	1	1.41	8	8	0	0	51	38	12	8	1	21	39	.215	.163	.271	6.88	3.71
Garcia, Harvey	R-R	6-2	220	3-16-84	1	1	8.02	15	0	0	1	21	25	25	19	4	16	25	.291	.323	.273	10.55	6.75
Guerra, Javy	R-R	6-0	205	10-31-85	2	0	2.33	28	0	0	5	27	24	12	7	1	22	27	.240	.250	.233	9.00	7.33
Huber, Jon	R-R	6-2	195	7-7-81	3	3	2.23	36	0	0	18	44	36	14	11	2	11	48	.220	.243	.202	9.74	2.23
2-team total (3 Mississippi)					3	3	2.30	39	0	0	18	47	37	15	12	2	13	49	—	—	—	9.38	2.49
Jansen, Kenley	B-R	6-6	220	9-30-87	4	0	1.67	22	0	0	8	27	14	6	5	0	17	50	.151	.209	.103	16.67	5.67
Koronka, John	L-L	6-0	200	7-3-80	0	3	4.95	7	7	0	0	36	38	25	20	2	20	29	.271	.343	.248	7.18	4.95
Krebs, Eric	R-R	6-3	210	5-16-85	0	2	3.89	30	0	0	1	39	35	19	17	2	29	42	.238	.167	.280	9.61	6.64
Leach, Brent	L-L	6-5	215	11-18-82	7	3	4.57	13	13	0	0	65	64	36	33	5	29	52	.260	.261	.260	7.20	4.02
Miller, Aaron	L-L	6-3	200	9-18-87	1	4	7.04	6	6	0	0	23	28	22	18	3	18	22	.304	.207	.349	8.61	7.04
Miller, Justin	R-R	6-2	190	8-2-87	2	2	2.76	28	0	0	1	42	39	16	13	3	24	18	.255	.300	.205	3.83	5.10
Pfeiffer, David	L-L	6-3	190	8-17-85	7	5	4.06	36	3	0	0	82	84	40	37	10	22	62	.278	.302	.263	6.80	2.41
Pratt, Jordan	R-R	6-3	212	5-17-85	1	0	6.00	8	1	0	0	9	8	8	6	0	16	8	.242	.375	.118	8.00	16.00
Rodriguez, Jesus	R-R	6-0	180	9-13-85	1	1	5.01	15	0	0	0	23	26	17	13	2	9	17	.286	.278	.291	6.56	3.47
Sartor, Matt	R-R	6-6	250	8-18-84	1	3	7.50	14	0	0	0	18	28	17	15	1	7	20	.354	.407	.327	10.00	3.50
Savage, Will	R-R	6-4	215	8-25-84	0	1	10.80	4	0	0	0	17	34	23	20	2	5	10	.436	.417	.467	5.40	2.70
Sexton, Tim	R-R	6-6	185	6-10-87	3	12	5.06	25	14	1	0	101	128	67	57	8	33	79	.309	.298	.317	7.02	2.93
Smit, Kyle	R-R	6-3	165	10-14-87	0	0	0.00	3	0	0	0	3	1	0	0	0	1	4	.100	.200	.000	3.00	0.00
2-team total (12 Tennessee)					5	1	1.69	15	0	0	1	21	24	5	4	0	4	17	—	—	—	7.17	1.69
Solano, Javier	R-R	6-0	177	3-31-90	2	0	2.29	13	0	0	0	20	16	5	5	2	4	23	.219	.222	.216	10.53	1.83
St. Clair, Cole	L-L	6-5	225	7-30-86	1	2	4.60	36	0	0	1	61	63	32	31	3	30	59	.267	.294	.252	8.75	4.45
Thompson, Eric	R-R	6-6	210	4-4-88	0	0	6.00	1	1	0	0	3	3	2	2	1	2	3	.250	.200	.286	9.00	6.00
Withrow, Chris	R-R	6-3	195	4-1-89	4	9	5.97	27	27	1	0	130	146	92	86	13	69	120	.285	.286	.285	8.33	4.79

Fielding

Catcher	PCT	G	PO	A	E	DP	PB
Collado	1.000	8	69	6	0	0	0
Garabedian	.962	12	70	6	0	0	0
May	.943	7	49	1	3	0	1
Mier	.989	43	321	41	4	3	4
Rivera	.987	56	407	51	6	10	6
Wallach	.982	20	138	22	3	1	1

First Base	PCT	G	PO	A	E	DP
Garabedian	1.000	1	8	1	0	1
Hatch	1.000	2	9	0	0	1
Perez	.993	104	766	72	6	77
Sands	.981	21	144	9	3	13
Smith	.995	25	177	9	1	12
Yount	1.000	6	30	1	0	1

Second Base	PCT	G	PO	A	E	DP
Denker	.818	2	3	6	2	3

(Second Base cont.)	PCT	G	PO	A	E	DP
Hatch	1.000	1	3	2	0	1
Herrera	.987	24	33	41	1	9
Nivar	.976	8	15	25	1	3
Pedroza	.967	122	197	296	17	63

Third Base	PCT	G	PO	A	E	DP
Baez	.857	6	5	7	2	1
Denker	.897	11	4	22	3	2
Hatch	.934	24	16	41	4	2
Herrera	.950	22	15	23	2	1
Nivar	.952	10	6	14	1	2
Perez	.750	4	1	2	1	1
Sands	1.000	1	0	1	0	0
Smith	.919	83	57	135	17	15
Wallach	—	1	0	0	0	0

Shortstop	PCT	G	PO	A	E	DP
Amezaga	1.000	1	0	2	0	0
Gordon	.936	133	199	345	37	73
Herrera	.800	6	6	10	4	2
Nivar	.900	2	2	7	1	2

Outfield	PCT	G	PO	A	E	DP
Giles	1.000	32	46	1	0	1
Herrera	.980	55	95	3	2	2
Lambo	.962	43	72	3	3	0
Nivar	1.000	10	18	1	0	0
Robinson	.985	120	256	12	4	2
Russell	.986	72	133	6	2	2
Sands	.990	48	87	8	1	2
Silverio	1.000	4	5	1	0	0
Smith	.000	1	0	0	1	0
Van Slyke	.975	62	114	3	3	1
Wallach	—	1	0	0	0	0
Yount	1.000	4	3	0	0	0

INLAND EMPIRE 66ERS   HIGH CLASS A
CALIFORNIA LEAGUE

Batting	B-T	HT	WT	DOB	AVG	vLH	vRH	G	AB	R	H	2B	3B	HR	RBI	BB	HBP	SH	SF	SO	SB	CS	SLG	OBP
Ausmus, Brad	R-R	5-11	190	4-14-69	.500	.500	.500	4	12	1	6	0	0	0	2	2	0	0	0	1	0	0	.500	.571
Baez, Pedro	R-R	6-2	195	3-11-88	.259	.348	.221	75	309	41	80	10	0	6	42	17	5	1	2	68	4	1	.350	.306
Buss, Nick	L-R	6-2	195	12-15-86	.243	.147	.285	65	247	32	60	10	6	0	25	13	1	7	3	33	6	3	.332	.280
Calfee, Clay	L-R	6-6	220	6-2-86	.233	.200	.242	36	116	12	27	7	0	2	11	9	1	1	1	44	1	0	.345	.291
Caseres, Steven	L-R	6-4	220	3-26-87	.256	.269	.251	87	324	35	83	12	1	9	57	37	6	2	3	93	0	3	.383	.341
Delmonico, Tony	R-R	6-0	194	4-27-87	.284	.279	.286	60	194	25	55	3	0	3	16	36	9	4	0	35	4	1	.345	.418
Denker, Travis	R-R	5-9	205	8-5-85	.332	.360	.314	74	286	45	95	21	3	7	44	30	7	0	2	49	5	1	.500	.406
Furcal, Rafael	R-B	5-8	195	10-24-77	.000	.000	.000	2	4	0	0	0	0	0	0	0	0	0	2	0	0	0	.000	.333
Gallagher, Austin	L-R	6-5	210	11-16-88	.291	.309	.284	111	422	47	123	26	2	6	64	38	2	0	4	78	0	2	.405	.350
Garabedian, Alex	R-R	6-2	210	8-26-85	.321	.300	.341	23	84	6	27	6	0	1	14	8	0	0	1	15	0	1	.429	.376
Garcia, Johan	R-R	6-0	170	9-6-86	.256	.200	.280	78	250	27	64	14	2	2	26	11	0	5	2	46	9	3	.352	.285
Giles, Tommy	L-L	6-0	190	8-28-83	.203	.238	.184	19	59	9	12	5	2	0	11	6	1	0	1	18	0	1	.390	.288
Gutierrez, Chris	R-R	5-9	185	3-12-84	.312	.360	.293	121	446	73	139	24	4	1	35	74	6	5	1	101	16	5	.390	.416
Gutierrez, Gabriel	R-R	5-11	190	11-24-83	.368	.000	.389	5	19	2	7	1	0	0	2	1	1	0	0	2	0	0	.421	.429
Hatch, Anthony	L-R	6-3	200	8-30-83	.258	.366	.209	34	132	11	34	9	0	2	14	10	0	1	0	16	1	0	.371	.310
Hernandez, Bryant	R-R	5-8	170	3-5-88	.224	.286	.214	15	49	10	11	2	0	1	3	3	0	0		16	0	0	.327	.309

Batting	B-T	HT	WT	DOB	AVG	vLH	vRH	G	AB	R	H	2B	3B	HR	RBI	BB	HBP	SH	SF	SO	SB	CS	SLG	OBP
Hunt, Bridger	R-R	5-11	162	7-24-85	.170	.189	.158	27	94	12	16	1	0	0	7	11	0	2	1	12	3	1	.181	.255
Ishibashi, Fumimasa	R-R	6-0	190	9-11-83	.250	.500	.000	1	4	0	1	0	0	0	0	0	0	0	0	2	0	0	.250	.250
Jean, Ramon	R-R	6-0	160	10-10-87	.271	.213	.297	80	291	28	79	14	2	1	30	11	3	5	3	45	13	9	.344	.302
Johnson, Reed	R-R	5-10	180	12-8-76	.500	.000	.500	2	6	2	3	1	0	0	0	0	0	0	0	0	0	0	.667	.500
Mattingly, Preston	R-R	6-2	209	8-28-87	.194	.222	.178	24	72	7	14	1	0	2	8	0	0	0	2	24	0	0	.292	.189
Perez, Andres	R-R	6-0	200	5-23-84	.285	.281	.286	41	144	17	41	14	2	2	20	7	1	0	3	36	1	1	.451	.316
Ramirez, Manny	R-R	6-0	200	5-30-72	.105	.000	.154	8	19	1	2	0	0	0	1	3	0	0	0	11	0	0	.105	.227
Russell, Kyle	L-L	6-5	195	6-27-86	.354	.350	.355	53	198	42	70	11	4	16	53	32	5	0	4	64	8	3	.692	.448
Sellers, Justin	R-R	5-10	160	2-1-86	.260	.294	.242	24	96	15	25	7	0	0	12	9	1	1	2	16	2	0	.333	.324
Silverio, Alfredo	R-R	6-0	205	5-6-87	.292	.260	.307	95	387	66	113	27	6	12	43	18	2	6	4	63	17	7	.486	.324
Suarez, Cesar	R-R	6-0	180	8-17-83	.202	.148	.228	21	84	11	17	4	1	0	6	3	3	0	0	7	5	0	.274	.256
Van Slyke, Scott	R-R	6-5	195	7-24-86	.307	.327	.299	48	189	34	58	12	2	9	35	17	2	0	1	39	3	1	.534	.368
Wallach, Matt	L-R	6-1	205	11-28-86	.263	.197	.288	67	243	40	64	12	4	8	31	15	4	1	3	38	0	3	.444	.313
Yount, Austin	L-R	6-0	185	10-9-86	.204	.286	.190	13	49	4	10	1	0	0	5	1	0	0	2	14	0	0	.224	.241
Yount, Dustin	L-R	6-1	198	10-27-82	.302	.182	.327	20	63	10	19	5	1	3	10	10	0	1	0	19	0	1	.556	.397

Pitching	B-T	HT	WT	DOB	W	L	ERA	G	GS	CG	SV	IP	H	R	ER	HR	BB	SO	AVG	vLH	vRH	K/9	BB/9
Aguasviva, Geison	L-L	6-2	166	8-3-87	4	4	3.75	31	5	0	0	72	70	46	30	2	33	57	.254	.157	.310	7.13	4.13
Belisario, Ronald	R-R	6-3	235	12-31-82	0	0	4.50	2	2	0	0	2	1	1	1	0	2	2	.200	.000	.200	4.50	9.00
Blevins, Bobby	R-R	6-0	200	1-16-85	2	8	6.09	20	7	0	1	68	97	53	46	10	14	40	.334	.374	.298	5.29	1.85
Boothe, Robert	R-R	6-2	190	1-30-86	1	2	6.89	29	0	0	0	48	57	44	37	8	36	45	.298	.280	.312	8.38	6.70
Contreras, Edwin	R-R	6-2	165	9-17-88	0	1	11.37	4	0	0	0	6	10	10	8	0	7	5	.357	.471	.182	7.11	9.95
Eovaldi, Nate	R-R	6-3	195	2-13-90	3	5	4.45	16	14	2	0	85	99	46	42	3	33	58	.302	.289	.315	6.14	3.49
Haeger, Charlie	R-R	6-1	210	9-19-83	2	3	5.14	5	5	0	0	21	21	14	12	2	12	17	.263	.275	.250	7.29	5.14
Jansen, Kenley	B-R	6-6	220	9-30-87	1	1	1.50	11	0	0	0	18	15	3	3	0	6	28	.231	.250	.212	14.00	3.00
Koss, Paul	R-R	6-4	215	6-17-85	1	5	5.93	22	0	0	2	30	42	24	20	4	18	22	.331	.323	.339	6.53	5.34
Krebs, Eric	R-R	6-3	210	5-16-85	0	2	6.75	15	0	0	5	17	23	15	13	2	12	27	.311	.348	.294	14.02	6.23
Kuo, Hong-Chih	L-L	6-1	240	7-23-81	0	0	0.00	2	1	0	0	2	0	0	0	0	2	3	.000	.000	.000	13.50	0.00
Mann, Brandon	L-L	6-2	200	5-16-84	3	0	4.13	37	0	0	1	48	63	32	22	4	25	48	.317	.369	.278	9.00	4.69
Martin, Ethan	R-R	6-2	195	6-6-89	9	14	6.35	25	22	1	0	113	120	84	80	10	81	105	.279	.302	.260	8.34	6.43
Melgarejo, Thomas	L-L	6-1	216	1-10-87	0	0	8.10	2	0	0	0	3	3	3	3	1	0	5	.231	.200	.250	13.50	0.00
Miller, Aaron	L-L	6-3	200	9-18-87	6	4	2.92	19	17	0	0	102	76	43	33	6	48	99	.207	.216	.204	8.76	4.25
Padilla, Vicente	R-R	6-2	220	9-27-77	0	0	0.84	3	3	0	0	11	6	1	1	0	1	10	.162	.217	.071	8.44	0.84
Redding, JonMichael	R-R	6-1	195	11-16-87	4	10	5.56	27	23	0	0	144	177	100	89	10	53	86	.313	.300	.324	5.38	3.31
Sanfler, Miguel	L-L	5-11	165	10-5-84	0	3	5.40	36	1	0	0	70	81	45	42	3	34	48	.281	.258	.291	6.17	4.37
Sartor, Matt	R-R	6-6	250	8-18-84	3	6	2.88	32	0	0	8	41	36	13	13	0	21	51	.240	.344	.169	11.29	4.65
Savage, Will	R-R	6-4	215	8-25-84	4	2	4.70	8	8	0	0	52	55	28	27	7	10	34	.278	.344	.216	5.92	1.74
Sexton, Tim	R-R	6-6	185	6-10-87	0	1	7.07	5	3	0	0	28	33	24	22	6	8	31	.295	.250	.339	9.96	2.57
Sherrill, George	L-L	6-0	230	4-19-77	0	0	4.50	2	1	0	0	2	3	1	1	0	0	2	.429	.333	.500	9.00	0.00
Smit, Kyle	R-R	6-3	165	10-14-87	5	3	2.49	34	1	0	6	51	51	17	14	4	10	46	.262	.242	.280	8.17	1.78
Solano, Javier	R-R	6-0	177	3-31-90	1	1	3.22	22	0	0	0	45	42	19	16	2	9	49	.243	.267	.224	9.87	1.81
St. Clair, Cole	L-L	6-5	225	7-30-86	0	1	2.25	8	0	0	2	12	7	3	3	0	4	15	.167	.188	.154	11.25	3.00
Thompson, Eric	R-R	6-6	210	4-4-88	0	1	8.10	1	0	0	0	20	31	20	18	3	8	18	.341	.263	.396	8.10	3.60
Wade, Cory	R-R	6-2	190	5-28-83	0	0	9.00	2	2	0	0	5	5	2	2	1	0	5	.455	.200	.667	9.00	4.50
Walter, Josh	R-R	6-4	250	4-5-85	1	10	6.59	24	18	0	0	96	111	78	70	13	64	85	.291	.309	.277	8.00	6.02
Weaver, Jeff	R-R	6-5	200	8-22-76	0	0	0.00	1	1	0	0	3	2	0	0	0	1	3	.200	.143	.333	9.00	3.00
White, Cody	L-L	6-3	185	2-27-85	0	3	8.56	8	5	0	0	27	35	26	26	4	13	17	.318	.324	.316	5.60	4.28

Fielding

Catcher	PCT	G	PO	A	E	DP	PB
Ausmus	1.000	2	3	1	0	0	0
Delmonico	.984	47	330	50	6	1	19
Garabedian	.993	16	113	20	1	5	0
Gutierrez	.980	5	46	4	1	0	0
Ishibashi	.917	1	11	0	1	0	0
Wallach	.992	62	467	54	4	8	2
Yount	.990	13	96	6	1	0	5

First Base	PCT	G	PO	A	E	DP
Calfee	.932	5	39	2	3	4
Caseres	.996	57	485	34	2	50
Gallagher	.982	75	598	59	12	59
Hatch	1.000	2	26	3	0	3
Perez	1.000	3	19	0	0	3
Wallach	1.000	3	11	0	0	0
Yount	1.000	1	1	0	0	0

Second Base	PCT	G	PO	A	E	DP
Denker	.989	66	147	214	4	45

	PCT	G	PO	A	E	DP
Garcia	.964	26	48	59	4	21
Gutierrez	.982	22	51	58	2	10
Hernandez	1.000	2	3	2	0	1
Hunt	.966	5	18	10	1	4
Jean	.951	10	16	42	3	7
Suarez	1.000	15	22	34	0	4

Third Base	PCT	G	PO	A	E	DP
Baez	.903	73	49	147	21	14
Denker	1.000	6	7	10	0	3
Garcia	.934	33	28	57	6	7
Hatch	.973	29	24	49	2	7
Suarez	1.000	2	1	2	0	0
Wallach	1.000	2	6	1	0	0

Shortstop	PCT	G	PO	A	E	DP
Furcal	1.000	2	2	2	0	0
Garcia	.965	13	20	35	2	10
Gutierrez	.950	93	154	246	21	57
Hernandez	.946	12	19	34	3	8

Jean	1.000	1	0	3	0	1
Sellers	.972	23	46	60	3	15

Outfield	PCT	G	PO	A	E	DP
Buss	.991	61	104	6	1	4
Calfee	.956	23	39	4	2	1
Giles	1.000	17	30	2	0	1
Hunt	1.000	19	34	0	0	0
Jean	.941	72	124	4	8	1
Johnson	1.000	1	2	1	0	0
Mattingly	.933	19	28	0	2	0
Perez	.952	25	38	2	2	0
Ramirez	1.000	3	4	0	0	0
Russell	.960	52	96	0	4	0
Silverio	.972	92	161	11	5	2
Van Slyke	1.000	43	70	4	0	0
Yount	1.000	14	13	0	0	0

GREAT LAKES LOONS
LOW CLASS A

MIDWEST LEAGUE

Batting	B-T	HT	WT	DOB	AVG	vLH	vRH	G	AB	R	H	2B	3B	HR	RBI	BB	HBP	SH	SF	SO	SB	CS	SLG	OBP
Banks, Stetson	R-R	6-0	185	1-14-88	.283	.313	.267	20	46	8	13	1	1	0	3	1	0	0	0	11	0	3	.348	.298
Becker, Joe	R-R	5-11	175	11-8-85	.255	.333	.207	14	47	5	12	2	1	0	5	2	0	0	1	9	1	0	.340	.280

Batting	B-T	HT	WT	DOB	AVG	vLH	vRH	G	AB	R	H	2B	3B	HR	RBI	BB	HBP	SH	SF	SO	SB	CS	SLG	OBP
Buss, Nick	L-R	6-2	195	12-15-86	.285	.360	.266	61	242	42	69	9	2	1	23	24	5	4	3	30	20	5	.351	.358
Cavazos-Galvez, Brian	R-R	6-0	215	5-17-87	.318	.313	.320	121	490	76	156	43	4	16	77	12	8	0	3	60	43	13	.520	.343
Erickson, Gorman	B-R	6-4	220	3-11-88	.215	.239	.206	82	261	32	56	13	3	2	27	34	2	1	1	45	3	0	.310	.309
Garcia, Johan	R-R	6-0	170	9-6-86	.185	.143	.200	16	54	9	10	3	0	1	7	0	0	3	0	10	0	0	.296	.185
Guerrero, Pedro	R-R	6-3	185	12-3-88	.167	.200	.156	13	42	4	7	3	0	0	3	1	0	1	0	13	0	0	.238	.186
Hernandez, Bryant	R-R	5-8	170	3-5-88	.164	.205	.150	50	146	17	24	6	3	1	17	7	3	4	0	53	1	1	.267	.218
Jacobs, Chris	R-R	6-5	257	11-25-88	.215	.167	.234	42	149	21	32	8	0	7	25	10	0	1	0	50	0	0	.409	.263
Lara, Christian	B-R	5-11	185	4-11-85	.290	.325	.281	108	435	66	126	25	8	10	49	49	0	6	3	99	17	9	.453	.359
McGee, Lenell	R-R	6-1	185	8-10-88	.235	.222	.238	27	81	7	19	5	0	2	8	11	2	3	0	20	3	3	.370	.340
Ortiz, Jaime	L-L	6-1	220	7-14-88	.270	.295	.264	85	311	38	84	18	3	8	41	19	3	0	1	53	2	1	.424	.317
Ruggiano, Brian	R-R	6-0	180	6-9-86	.255	.186	.271	108	373	50	95	24	5	6	48	34	7	3	6	89	15	12	.394	.324
Sands, Jerry	R-R	6-4	225	9-28-87	.333	.283	.370	69	243	48	81	16	3	18	46	40	3	0	1	61	14	2	.646	.432
Smith, Blake	L-R	6-2	225	12-9-87	.281	.303	.276	115	430	77	121	28	2	19	76	49	8	3	3	135	2	3	.488	.363
Songco, Angelo	L-R	6-0	195	9-9-88	.274	.250	.280	135	507	87	139	30	6	15	71	51	6	1	5	91	6	1	.446	.344
Wise, J.T.	R-R	6-0	210	6-2-86	.309	.362	.293	86	301	44	93	23	0	12	62	26	4	0	8	61	0	0	.505	.363
Ynoa, Rafael	B-R	6-0	180	8-7-87	.286	.305	.280	124	441	67	126	19	5	1	31	51	1	14	3	55	40	14	.395	.340
Yount, Austin	L-R	6-0	185	10-9-86	.118	.000	.125	24	76	7	9	1	1	0	3	5	2	0	0	12	1	0	.158	.193

Pitching	B-T	HT	WT	DOB	W	L	ERA	G	GS	CG	SV	IP	H	R	ER	HR	BB	SO	AVG	vLH	vRH	K/9	BB/9
Ames, Steven	R-R	6-1	205	3-15-88	0	2	2.54	23	0	0	16	28	21	9	8	0	3	44	.196	.152	.230	13.98	0.95
Christenson, Ryan	L-L	6-1	185	1-11-89	3	1	6.75	8	7	0	0	36	50	27	27	1	13	26	.331	.341	.327	6.50	3.25
Contreras, Edwin	R-R	6-2	165	9-17-88	3	2	4.83	18	5	0	0	67	67	30	27	5	25	30	.327	.372	.299	5.36	4.47
De La Rosa, Rubby	R-R	6-1	170	3-4-89	4	1	3.19	14	5	0	6	59	49	23	21	3	17	55	.223	.213	.229	8.34	2.58
Gaudi, Nick	R-R	6-5	215	8-2-86	0	1	7.94	6	0	0	0	11	13	10	10	0	5	12	.289	.333	.250	9.53	3.97
Lee, Ji-Mo	R-R	6-1	188	10-30-86	1	0	2.57	5	0	0	0	7	6	2	2	0	4	3	.261	.375	.200	3.86	5.14
Magill, Matt	R-R	6-3	190	11-10-89	7	4	3.28	24	20	1	2	126	87	50	46	13	52	135	.194	.191	.197	9.62	3.70
Miller, Justin	R-R	6-2	190	8-2-87	4	0	1.30	16	0	0	3	35	27	6	5	0	14	29	.208	.216	.203	7.53	3.63
Paxson, J.B.	R-R	6-3	240	7-28-86	5	2	3.02	34	0	0	1	54	45	23	18	0	31	54	.232	.279	.206	9.06	5.20
Pimentel, Elisaul	R-R	6-1	170	7-10-88	3	7	3.49	17	16	0	0	90	71	37	35	6	35	97	.215	.189	.235	9.66	3.49
2-team total (5 Burlington)					10	6	3.98	22	21	0	0	115	100	53	51	7	51	116	—	—	—	9.05	3.98
Roberts, Jordan	L-L	6-2	200	1-5-86	6	4	2.95	31	0	0	3	64	53	24	21	4	16	47	.232	.238	.230	6.61	2.25
Savage, Will	R-R	6-4	215	8-25-84	6	2	2.80	13	13	1	0	84	.85	36	26	3	14	58	.267	.269	.266	6.24	1.51
Smith, Steve	R-R	6-2	215	5-15-86	4	5	2.69	42	0	0	6	74	60	26	22	5	19	66	.223	.230	.218	8.06	2.32
Suiter, Andy	L-L	6-3	215	6-10-87	4	2	3.91	30	0	0	1	53	39	26	23	3	46	76	.202	.260	.182	12.91	7.81
Vasquez, Luis	R-R	6-4	192	4-3-86	3	2	2.68	37	0	0	20	40	24	12	12	2	26	39	.173	.170	.174	8.70	5.80
Wall, Josh	R-R	6-6	218	1-21-87	9	7	4.24	26	26	1	0	153	144	80	72	11	68	151	.248	.285	.222	8.88	4.00
Wallach, Brett	R-R	6-5	205	12-2-88	6	0	3.72	17	17	0	0	85	73	35	35	7	43	92	.230	.262	.209	9.78	4.57
2-team total (7 Peoria)					6	4	4.25	24	24	0	0	114	101	65	54	9	61	116	—	—	—	9.13	4.80
Webster, Allen	R-R	6-3	185	2-10-90	12	9	2.88	26	23	0	0	131	119	55	42	6	53	114	.239	.258	.227	7.81	3.63
Wilborn, Greg	L-L	6-2	175	6-3-87	4	2	3.26	7	7	0	0	39	35	16	14	1	16	49	.243	.167	.275	11.41	3.72

Fielding

Catcher	PCT	G	PO	A	E	DP	PB
Erickson	.991	80	624	57	6	10	8
Wise	.990	63	563	52	6	3	7
Yount	1.000	3	12	0	0	0	0

First Base	PCT	G	PO	A	E	DP
Jacobs	.991	27	205	22	2	18
Lara	—	1	0	0	0	0
Ortiz	.987	73	565	37	8	45
Sands	.994	41	320	29	2	30
Wise	1.000	2	1	7	0	0
Yount	1.000	1	5	0	0	1

Second Base	PCT	G	PO	A	E	DP
Banks	1.000	2	3	6	0	0
Becker	.986	12	24	45	1	8

Garcia	1.000	1	4	3	0	2
Guerrero	.971	9	16	18	1	6
Hernandez	1.000	4	6	5	0	3
Ynoa	.988	113	199	284	6	52

Third Base	PCT	G	PO	A	E	DP
Garcia	.912	13	6	25	3	2
Guerrero	.875	2	3	4	1	0
Hernandez	—	2	0	0	0	0
Lara	.868	18	10	23	5	2
Ruggiano	.911	104	57	167	22	11
Yount	.700	7	1	6	3	2

Shortstop	PCT	G	PO	A	E	DP
Guerrero	1.000	1	2	3	0	1
Hernandez	.981	41	48	104	3	20

Lara	.951	91	137	234	19	46
Ynoa	.964	11	22	31	2	6

Outfield	PCT	G	PO	A	E	DP
Banks	1.000	14	27	1	0	1
Buss	.985	60	132	3	2	0
Cavazos-Galvez	.976	89	158	8	4	3
McGee	.976	25	40	0	1	0
Ruggiano	1.000	1	2	0	0	0
Sands	.985	27	64	2	1	1
Smith	.975	97	181	11	5	1
Songco	.981	112	150	4	3	0

OGDEN RAPTORS

PIONEER LEAGUE

ROOKIE

Batting	B-T	HT	WT	DOB	AVG	vLH	vRH	G	AB	R	H	2B	3B	HR	RBI	BB	HBP	SH	SF	SO	SB	CS	SLG	OBP
Akins, Nick	R-R	6-1	220	12-25-87	.316	.368	.302	47	177	39	56	10	2	15	46	24	5	0	1	53	1	1	.650	.411
Bosnik, Jesse	L-R	6-0	215	7-23-88	.253	.213	.265	55	194	33	49	11	1	4	31	27	4	1	2	44	2	0	.381	.352
Coyle, Bobby	L-L	6-1	215	3-6-89	.316	.292	.323	54	237	38	75	16	1	4	52	10	1	0	1	29	7	1	.443	.345
Dean, Blake	L-L	6-1	175	2-25-88	.302	.310	.300	59	232	37	70	16	1	5	35	28	0	0	1	15	2	3	.444	.375
Domecus, Steve	R-R	6-3	220	6-29-87	.252	.385	.219	34	131	19	33	8	2	4	23	6	6	1	1	19	2	0	.435	.313
Garcia, Jonathan	R-R	5-11	175	11-11-91	.305	.288	.310	61	239	45	73	19	2	10	40	19	5	0	3	59	4	1	.527	.365
Gilmore, Chance	L-L	5-11	187	4-1-87	.234	.125	.256	14	47	11	11	1	1	5	6	1	0	0	18	3	1	.362	.333
Grider, Casio	R-R	6-1	165	8-17-87	.281	.304	.275	62	253	36	71	14	3	4	33	10	6	5	2	68	22	6	.407	.321
Guerrero, Pedro	R-R	6-3	185	12-3-88	.230	.235	.228	31	113	20	26	9	3	1	17	7	2	1	4	29	2	3	.398	.278
Henderson, Chris	R-L	5-11	190	6-23-88	.341	.371	.333	47	176	36	60	12	1	1	24	21	7	0	1	22	2	3	.438	.429
King, Austin	R-R	6-2	200	12-1-88	.241	.250	.238	35	108	23	26	6	0	3	13	9	1	1	1	30	15	2	.380	.303
Landry, Leon	L-R	5-11	185	9-20-89	.341	.413	.326	57	249	46	87	20	4	4	38	20	2	1	2	36	13	9	.510	.399
Lemmerman, Jake	R-R	6-1	192	5-4-89	.363	.276	.388	66	259	69	94	24	2	12	47	31	6	1	6	56	5	4	.610	.434
Lincoln, Joe	R-R	6-4	210	9-16-88	.179	.143	.188	15	39	4	7	0	0	0	4	5	2	0	0	10	0	0	.179	.304

Batting	B-T	HT	WT	DOB	AVG	vLH	vRH	G	AB	R	H	2B	3B	HR	RBI	BB	HBP	SH	SF	SO	SB	CS	SLG	OBP
Pericht, Mike	R-R	6-5	235	5-23-88	.278	.286	.276	54	205	35	57	13	0	9	38	14	13	0	2	66	2	1	.473	.359
Tavarez, Pedro	R-R	6-0	215	6-28-87	.222	.214	.227	12	36	3	8	0	0	0	0	0	1	0	0	8	0	0	.222	.243

Pitching	B-T	HT	WT	DOB	W	L	ERA	G	GS	CG	SV	IP	H	R	ER	HR	BB	SO	AVG	vLH	vRH	K/9	BB/9
Bawcom, Logan	R-R	6-2	200	11-2-88	3	1	4.28	16	0	0	2	27	32	16	13	4	7	29	.294	.388	.217	9.55	2.30
Budkevics, Pete	R-R	6-2	165	10-14-87	4	1	3.38	12	5	0	0	40	45	18	15	6	10	44	.283	.257	.303	9.90	2.25
Burgos, Raul	B-R	6-1	210	8-18-87	1	1	4.74	17	0	0	0	25	34	17	13	1	8	25	.330	.435	.246	9.12	2.92
Cash, Ralston	R-R	6-2	197	8-20-91	0	0	12.00	2	2	0	0	6	11	10	8	2	3	5	.367	.500	.250	7.50	4.50
Castillo, Antonio	L-L	5-11	185	3-5-88	3	6	8.32	14	11	0	0	49	76	48	45	3	12	42	.362	.381	.354	7.77	2.22
Cone, Derek	R-R	6-5	210	6-20-90	0	0	0.00	3	0	0	0	4	4	1	0	0	1	1	.235	.375	.111	2.08	2.08
Eovaldi, Nate	R-R	6-3	195	2-13-90	1	0	1.80	1	1	0	0	5	3	2	1	0	0	4	.167	.182	.143	7.20	0.00
Ferreras, Luis	R-R	5-9	150	12-28-89	1	1	5.55	16	0	0	0	24	39	18	15	1	8	18	.364	.392	.339	6.66	2.96
Frias, Carlos	R-R	6-4	170	11-13-89	2	6	7.78	13	8	0	0	39	45	38	34	7	21	43	.278	.321	.238	9.84	4.81
Fructuoso, Beyker	R-R	6-4	205	4-8-90	0	0	14.73	2	0	0	0	4	8	8	6	0	3	3	.400	.556	.273	7.36	7.36
Gaudi, Nick	R-R	6-5	215	8-2-86	1	0	3.00	13	0	0	3	18	19	6	6	1	9	23	.271	.219	.316	11.50	4.50
Gomez, Gustavo	R-R	6-1	150	5-24-91	1	1	3.52	2	1	0	0	8	5	4	3	1	3	9	.185	.267	.083	10.57	3.52
Gould, Garrett	R-R	6-4	190	7-19-91	1	4	4.06	13	13	0	0	58	68	41	26	4	20	52	.292	.322	.273	8.12	3.12
Lee, Ji-Mo	R-R	6-1	188	10-30-86	2	0	1.35	9	0	0	1	13	8	5	2	1	4	6	.178	.143	.208	4.05	2.70
McCarter, Jake	R-R	6-2	200	8-31-84	0	2	3.38	19	0	0	1	37	30	18	14	4	9	46	.217	.218	.217	11.09	2.17
Medina, Bolivar	L-L	6-2	175	8-11-88	0	1	11.25	2	0	0	0	4	8	5	5	0	3	4	.421	.000	.571	9.00	6.75
Montgomery, Bret	R-R	6-6	250	8-6-85	4	3	4.99	14	6	0	0	52	58	44	29	3	10	54	.272	.313	.248	9.29	1.72
Ozoria, Arismendy	R-R	6-0	195	8-7-90	4	1	4.55	7	6	0	0	32	27	18	16	4	18	24	.235	.280	.200	6.82	5.12
Patterson, Red	R-R	6-3	210	5-11-87	6	1	3.33	14	14	0	0	68	70	37	25	6	17	66	.264	.314	.224	8.78	2.26
Pevsner, Andrew	L-L	6-3	205	10-15-88	3	0	1.91	18	0	0	0	28	25	6	6	3	14	30	.245	.250	.241	9.53	4.45
Rivas, Rick	R-R	6-1	180	2-12-84	2	1	10.29	14	0	0	0	21	32	28	24	2	10	17	.352	.406	.322	7.29	4.29
Tolleson, Shawn	R-R	6-2	215	1-19-88	1	1	0.63	26	0	0	17	29	17	2	2	1	5	39	.175	.190	.164	12.24	1.57
Whetsel, J.J.	R-R	6-1	190	10-31-84	0	0	7.75	17	0	0	2	34	50	32	29	7	15	27	.340	.333	.345	7.22	4.01
Wilborn, Greg	L-L	6-2	175	6-3-87	4	0	2.06	8	8	0	0	44	38	14	10	2	8	58	.236	.292	.212	11.95	1.65

Fielding

Catcher	PCT	G	PO	A	E	DP	PB
Domecus	.963	26	219	17	9	1	9
Lincoln	1.000	7	54	7	0	2	2
Pericht	.977	41	353	34	9	1	14
Tavarez	.971	5	30	3	1	0	0

First Base	PCT	G	PO	A	E	DP
Dean	.991	57	501	41	5	43
Henderson	.995	18	165	16	1	16

Second Base	PCT	G	PO	A	E	DP
Bosnik	1.000	1	2	0	0	1

	PCT	G	PO	A	E	DP
Grider	.931	49	75	140	16	27
Guerrero	.960	25	58	86	6	22

Third Base	PCT	G	PO	A	E	DP
Bosnik	.887	54	25	101	16	11
Guerrero	.909	3	1	9	1	2
Henderson	.867	19	10	29	6	4

Shortstop	PCT	G	PO	A	E	DP
Grider	.889	11	20	36	7	7
Guerrero	.714	3	2	3	2	0
Lemmerman	.943	64	104	163	16	41

Outfield	PCT	G	PO	A	E	DP
Akins	.946	38	51	2	3	1
Coyle	.973	31	35	1	1	0
Domecus	1.000	5	4	0	0	0
Garcia	.918	60	89	12	9	1
Gilmore	1.000	12	18	1	0	1
King	.982	30	50	4	1	0
Landry	.990	56	94	2	1	0

AZL DODGERS

ARIZONA LEAGUE

ROOKIE

Batting	B-T	HT	WT	DOB	AVG	vLH	vRH	G	AB	R	H	2B	3B	HR	RBI	BB	HBP	SH	SF	SO	SB	CS	SLG	OBP
Aguilar, Alexis	R-R	5-11	162	6-17-91	.253	.333	.239	25	83	11	21	2	1	0	9	8	0	2	3	16	2	2	.301	.309
Akins, Nick	R-R	6-1	220	12-25-87	.400	.611	.333	20	75	19	30	10	1	6	24	10	2	0	1	19	1	2	.800	.477
Baez, Pedro	R-R	6-2	195	3-11-88	.000	.000	.000	2	7	0	0	0	0	0	1	1	0	0	1	1	0	0	.000	.111
Baldwin III, James	L-R	6-3	190	10-10-91	.274	.057	.326	46	179	25	49	6	2	2	22	9	2	3	2	60	17	3	.363	.313
Becker, Joe	R-R	5-11	175	11-8-85	.435	.250	.474	6	23	2	10	1	2	0	2	0	0	0	1	0	0	0	.652	.435
Brett, Beau	L-L	6-3	185	7-14-89	.239	.222	.243	28	92	11	22	3	1	0	6	11	1	0	1	28	0	1	.293	.324
Cilladi, Steve	R-R	5-9	182	3-15-87	.292	.667	.238	11	24	3	7	0	0	1	3	3	1	0	1	7	0	0	.417	.379
Cuevas, Noel	R-R	6-2	187	10-2-91	.333	.000	.500	3	6	0	2	1	0	0	0	0	0	0	0	2	0	0	.500	.333
Delmonico, Tony	R-R	6-0	194	4-27-87	.250	.667	.190	7	24	2	6	2	1	0	2	2	1	0	0	5	2	0	.417	.333
Drowne, Mike	R-L	5-10	175	7-28-88	.143	.000	.143	4	7	1	1	0	0	0	1	1	0	0	0	2	0	2	.143	.250
Edge, Andrew	R-R	6-2	230	12-31-87	.259	.261	.259	21	81	13	21	6	1	4	15	6	1	0	0	27	1	0	.506	.318
Ethier, Devon	R-R	6-0	165	6-4-90	.200	.000	.250	2	5	0	1	0	0	0	2	0	0	0	1	1	0	0	.200	.200
Franco, Bladimir	R-R	6-1	172	2-4-91	.224	.250	.218	35	125	13	28	3	2	2	20	7	2	1	2	49	3	2	.328	.272
Gilmore, Chance	L-L	5-11	187	4-1-87	.267	.308	.261	27	101	16	27	7	5	2	16	11	1	0	1	38	6	1	.495	.342
Hunt, Jeff	L-R	6-2	190	2-13-91	.240	.300	.225	18	50	9	12	1	0	2	7	4	0	0	2	11	0	1	.380	.286
Iden, David	R-R	5-9	160	3-4-87	.267	.296	.254	30	90	15	24	3	0	1	14	6	4	1	3	14	5	0	.333	.330
Kirkland, Matt	R-R	6-2	210	3-13-91	.239	.111	.270	16	46	10	11	2	0	0	6	11	0	0	2	14	0	0	.283	.373
Lara, Christian	B-R	5-11	185	4-11-85	.167	.000	.333	2	6	1	1	1	0	0	0	1	1	0	0	2	0	0	.333	.286
LaRosa, B.J.	R-R	6-2	200	4-28-88	.280	.333	.250	10	25	2	7	1	0	0	2	9	0	1	0	4	0	0	.320	.471
Lindsey, John	R-R	6-1	245	1-30-77	.000	.000	.000	1	3	0	0	0	0	0	0	0	0	0	0	1	0	0	.000	.000
Mattingly, Preston	R-R	6-2	209	8-24-87	.237	.136	.268	25	93	17	22	5	0	0	9	6	1	1	0	27	8	2	.290	.290
Mirabal, Charlie	R-L	5-11	164	4-2-87	.295	.125	.351	36	129	26	38	5	0	0	21	17	2	0	1	21	8	5	.333	.383
Morales, Enlly	R-R	5-11	168	9-13-89	.273	.200	.286	35	139	18	38	6	0	0	13	7	1	2	3	21	2	1	.317	.307
Moses, Tony	R-R	6-4	210	7-22-87	.145	.188	.134	31	83	10	12	2	0	1	11	7	5	3	1	34	2	1	.205	.250
Nam, Tae-Hyeok	R-R	6-0	209	3-13-91	.243	.300	.229	40	148	22	36	6	2	3	24	21	1	0	0	40	1	1	.372	.341
Orr, Kyle	L-R	6-5	205	9-29-88	.000	.000	.000	1	2	0	0	0	0	0	0	0	0	0	0	1	0	0	.000	.000
Pederson, Joc	L-L	6-1	185	4-21-92	.000	.000	.000	3	7	1	0	0	0	0	0	4	1	0	0	5	0	0	.000	.417
Ponte, Angelo	R-R	5-11	215	12-16-86	.152	.200	.143	11	33	3	5	0	0	0	3	4	1	1	0	12	0	0	.152	.263
Ray, Melvin	R-R	6-4	205	4-23-89	.269	.176	.300	20	67	11	18	3	3	0	6	4	1	1	0	26	5	2	.403	.319

	B-T	HT	WT	DOB	AVG	vLH	vRH	G	AB	R	H	2B	3B	HR	RBI	BB	HBP	SH	SF	SO	SB	CS	SLG	OBP
Schebler, Scott	L-R	6-1	208	10-6-90	.294	.000	.357	5	17	3	5	0	2	0	1	1	0	0	0	5	1	0	.529	.333
Vazquez, Jan	B-R	5-10	165	4-29-91	.226	.167	.240	28	93	14	21	6	1	0	6	11	5	1	1	27	1	1	.312	.336

Pitching

	B-T	HT	WT	DOB	W	L	ERA	G	GS	CG	SV	IP	H	R	ER	HR	BB	SO	AVG	vLH	vRH	K/9	BB/9
Ames, Steven	R-R	6-1	205	3-15-88	0	0	0.00	3	0	0	0	3	2	0	0	0	0	4	.182	.000	.286	12.00	0.00
Cash, Ralston	R-R	6-1	197	8-20-91	2	2	3.60	9	8	0	0	30	29	13	12	0	11	25	.248	.286	.221	7.50	3.30
Christenson, Ryan	L-L	6-1	185	1-11-89	0	0	0.61	5	4	0	0	15	10	1	1	0	3	16	.192	.143	.200	9.82	1.84
Corcoran, Tim	R-R	6-2	205	4-15-78	0	0	0.00	2	2	0	0	3	0	0	0	0	1	4	.000	.000	.000	12.00	3.00
De Aza, Carlos	R-R	6-3	178	5-4-90	3	4	7.13	14	2	0	0	24	34	22	19	2	11	17	.337	.468	.222	6.38	4.13
Dedeaux, Adam	L-L	6-0	200	7-1-86	0	0	4.22	10	0	0	1	11	11	6	5	0	7	17	.262	.333	.233	14.34	5.91
Eovaldi, Nate	R-R	6-3	195	2-13-90	0	1	4.32	3	3	0	0	8	6	4	4	0	4	10	.214	.100	.278	10.80	4.32
Feliciano, Roberto	L-L	6-0	214	8-16-90	1	0	6.28	9	0	0	0	14	21	12	10	0	5	16	.323	.318	.326	10.05	3.14
Fructuoso, Beyker	R-R	6-4	205	4-8-90	0	0	3.04	15	0	0	0	27	20	12	9	1	9	31	.202	.250	.175	10.46	3.04
Garcia, Yimi	R-R	6-1	175	8-18-90	1	2	7.04	13	4	0	1	31	47	26	24	1	8	22	.356	.313	.381	6.46	2.35
Gomez, Gustavo	R-R	6-1	150	5-24-91	3	2	3.68	12	7	0	0	44	46	25	18	0	13	38	.261	.278	.250	7.77	2.66
Guerra, Javy	R-R	6-0	205	10-31-85	0	1	4.50	2	0	0	0	2	2	1	1	0	3		.250	.000	.400	13.50	0.00
Haeger, Charlie	R-R	6-1	210	9-19-83	0	0	0.00	1	0	0	0	1	0	0	0	0	0	4	.000	.000	.000	18.00	0.00
Handke, Chris	R-R	6-10	235	3-19-88	1	0	4.03	15	1	0	0	22	20	14	10	1	18	20	.247	.357	.189	8.06	7.25
Lee, Ji-Mo	R-L	6-1	188	10-30-86	0	0	0.00	1	0	0	0	1	0	0	0	0	0	0	.000	.000	.000	0.00	0.00
Lima, Joel	R-R	6-0	165	8-7-89	2	1	2.04	16	0	0	3	18	16	7	4	0	7	16	.242	.375	.167	8.15	3.57
Marshall, Jimmy	R-R	6-6	195	4-13-87	2	1	1.93	12	0	0	1	14	10	4	3	1	8	12	.200	.263	.161	7.71	5.14
Martinez, Brandon	R-R	6-4	150	11-25-90	3	2	5.25	12	5	0	0	36	48	26	21	2	9	32	.312	.321	.306	8.00	2.25
Matre, Steve	R-R	6-2	185	5-21-88	0	0	4.50	2	0	0	0	4	4	1	1	0	2	1	.444	.500	.400	4.50	9.00
McDonald, James	L-R	6-5	195	10-19-84	0	0	1.59	2	2	0	0	6	3	3	1	0	3	8	.158	.333	.077	12.71	4.76
McRee, Alex	L-L	6-7	235	6-18-88	0	0	18.00	1	0	0	0	1	3	2	2	0	0	1	.500	1.000	.250	9.00	0.00
Medina, Bolivar	L-L	6-2	175	8-11-88	1	2	5.88	12	5	0	0	34	44	30	22	3	17	35	.303	.302	.304	9.36	4.54
Montgomery, Bret	R-R	6-6	250	8-6-85	0	0	0.00	1	0	0	0	1	0	0	0	0	0	1	.000	.000	.000	9.00	0.00
Ozoria, Arismendy	R-R	6-0	195	8-7-90	4	1	2.78	8	6	0	0	36	34	14	11	2	9	37	.250	.281	.228	9.34	2.27
Perez, Juan	R-L	6-0	180	9-3-78	0	0	0.00	2	0	0	0	2	0	0	0	0	5	0	.000	.000	.000	22.50	0.00
Rodriguez, Yimy	R-R	6-2	215	9-1-87	2	0	3.92	16	0	0	1	21	20	9	9	2	3	11	.270	.440	.184	4.79	1.31
Santiago, Andres	R-R	6-2	200	10-26-89	2	0	2.18	6	3	0	0	21	20	7	5	1	3	17	.247	.231	.255	7.40	1.31
Tavarez, Gari	R-R	6-0	170	10-26-88	1	0	4.94	18	0	0	3	24	27	17	13	1	7	18	.278	.289	.271	6.85	2.66
Urriola, Marlon	R-R	6-2	165	7-1-88	2	4	3.18	14	0	0	0	28	30	27	10	3	9	23	.261	.319	.221	7.31	2.86
Wade, Cory	R-R	6-2	190	5-28-83	0	1	9.00	2	2	0	0	2	2	2	2	0	0	2	.250	.400	.000	9.00	0.00
White, Cody	L-L	6-3	185	2-27-85	0	1	1.50	4	0	0	0	6	7	3	1	0	2	6	.259	.000	.350	9.00	3.00

Fielding

Catcher	PCT	G	PO	A	E	DP	PB
Cilladi	.972	11	62	7	2	0	0
Delmonico	.955	6	38	4	2	0	3
Edge	.962	10	89	12	4	0	1
LaRosa	.906	6	23	6	3	0	2
Ponte	.974	5	35	3	1	0	2
Vazquez	.961	25	184	36	9	3	6

First Base	PCT	G	PO	A	E	DP
Brett	.981	26	194	11	4	15
Mattingly	1.000	1	3	0	0	0
Nam	.972	33	283	27	9	22
Orr	1.000	1	5	2	0	1
Ponte	.667	1	2	0	1	0

Second Base	PCT	G	PO	A	E	DP
Becker	.971	6	22	11	1	2
Iden	.945	22	51	69	7	19
Morales	.956	29	54	76	6	10

Third Base	PCT	G	PO	A	E	DP
Aguilar	.625	1	1	4	3	1
Baez	1.000	2	0	6	0	0
Franco	.884	30	18	66	11	9
Hunt	.926	13	4	21	2	1
Kirkland	.840	10	3	18	4	1
Nam	.667	1	1	3	2	0

Shortstop	PCT	G	PO	A	E	DP
Aguilar	.928	18	23	54	6	8
Iden	.800	1	1	3	1	2
Lara	1.000	2	2	8	0	0
Mirabal	.964	35	53	108	6	15

Outfield	PCT	G	PO	A	E	DP
Aguilar	1.000	4	3	0	0	0
Akins	.923	19	34	2	3	0
Baldwin III	.969	45	92	3	3	0
Cuevas	1.000	3	2	0	0	0
Drowne	—	3	0	0	0	0
Ethier	1.000	2	1	0	0	0
Gilmore	.960	27	47	1	2	0
Mattingly	.969	25	29	2	1	1
Moses	.971	30	31	2	1	0
Pederson	1.000	2	2	0	0	0
Ray	.882	19	30	0	4	0

DSL DODGERS   ROOKIE
DOMINICAN SUMMER LEAGUE

Batting	B-T	HT	WT	DOB	AVG	vLH	vRH	G	AB	R	H	2B	3B	HR	RBI	BB	HBP	SH	SF	SO	SB	CS	SLG	OBP
Aguilar, Alexis	R-R	5-11	162	6-17-91	.293	.467	.250	21	75	13	22	1	0	1	14	8	1	0	1	9	10	1	.347	.365
Capellan, Jose	R-R	6-0	190	10-10-90	.326	.167	.350	16	46	4	15	1	0	1	8	6	1	2	0	8	1	0	.413	.415
Cordero, Josmar	R-R	5-10	175	9-16-91	.255	.241	.259	51	145	17	37	7	0	4	20	11	3	2	1	22	1	4	.386	.319
De Jesus, Frank	B-R	6-1	192	6-4-88	.205	.429	.162	17	44	8	9	2	0	0	3	9	0	0	0	8	0	1	.250	.340
De La Rosa, Ricardo	R-R	6-0	184	4-19-91	.163	.000	.182	35	49	10	8	0	0	0	4	14	1	0	1	11	2	2	.163	.354
Feliz, Railing	R-R	5-11	184	7-17-91	.182	.250	.172	14	33	5	6	1	0	0	1	3	1	1	0	8	0	0	.212	.270
Infante, Jorky	B-R	6-0	155	2-24-91	.270	.333	.259	57	174	32	47	2	1	2	14	28	0	7	1	27	13	2	.328	.369
Lugo, Jose	R-R	6-1	200	5-9-90	.176	.400	.152	25	51	5	9	1	0	0	7	8	1	0	1	9	0	1	.196	.283
Lugo, Ronny	R-R	6-2	170	2-18-90	.231	.375	.203	46	147	18	34	5	4	2	18	10	3	3	0	24	6	0	.361	.294
Martinez, Vladimir	B-R	6-2	173	6-26-92	.241	.333	.214	16	54	7	13	0	0	0	10	4	0	1	1	10	2	1	.241	.288
Mercedes, Carlos	R-R	6-2	190	7-26-91	.253	.059	.306	33	79	7	20	7	0	2	9	12	2	0	1	38	0	1	.418	.362
Morales, Delvis	B-R	6-1	146	8-29-90	.220	.261	.211	65	236	41	52	5	1	0	15	37	3	4	0	33	18	8	.250	.333
Nieto, Abdul	R-R	6-3	180	12-9-91	.176	.125	.187	27	91	11	16	3	0	0	8	11	4	0	0	24	1	3	.242	.292
Oguisten, Faustino	R-R	6-2	165	1-17-91	.253	.333	.231	31	83	14	21	5	0	0	7	12	3	1	0	18	5	2	.325	.367
Pena, Gregory	B-R	6-0	175	12-16-91	.212	.184	.220	58	179	28	38	5	0	0	12	25	8	6	0	39	14	5	.240	.333
Ramirez, Jose	R-R	6-2	200	9-24-88	.279	.244	.287	62	208	32	58	6	0	5	33	26	10	1	1	38	14	10	.380	.384
Rivas, Webster	R-R	6-0	195	8-8-90	.246	.244	.247	59	211	23	52	16	2	1	34	12	9	1	6	12	3	2	.355	.307
Rodriguez, Arce	R-R	6-0	191	12-10-92	.222	.219	.223	45	144	7	32	6	0	0	13	3	3	2	2	32	2	2	.264	.250
Rodriguez, Leo	R-R	5-11	160	12-11-91	.277	.367	.252	49	137	19	38	4	0	0	12	17	5	1	1	21	5	0	.307	.375

Pitching	B-T	HT	WT	DOB	W	L	ERA	G	GS	CG	SV	IP	H	R	ER	HR	BB	SO	AVG	vLH	vRH	K/9	BB/9
Angeles, Aris	R-R	6-0	179	9-9-89	1	0	6.07	10	0	0	0	13	20	14	9	1	16	16	.345	.357	.341	10.80	10.80
Araujo, Victor	R-R	5-11	171	11-9-89	2	0	2.45	8	0	0	1	15	9	4	4	0	6	19	.180	.133	.200	11.66	3.68
Beras, Leonel	L-L	5-11	143	5-7-91	8	3	2.26	15	15	0	0	72	45	25	18	1	33	71	.178	.000	.190	8.92	4.14
Botello, Ariel	R-R	6-2	217	11-15-89	2	1	3.66	18	0	0	4	32	28	14	13	2	14	24	.237	.200	.247	6.75	3.94
Chavez, Giordanny	R-R	6-3	185	4-19-91	4	2	1.85	17	12	0	0	68	57	23	14	1	29	47	.230	.300	.207	6.22	3.84
Colmenarez, Wilmer	R-R	6-4	165	4-16-90	1	0	10.80	1	0	0	0	2	3	2	2	0	0	1	.375	.333	.400	5.40	0.00
De Dios, Leandro	R-R	5-11	184	6-20-89	2	3	2.66	17	1	0	3	41	32	19	12	0	27	36	.212	.244	.198	7.97	5.98
Dominguez, Jose	R-R	6-0	160	8-7-90	1	1	1.13	5	4	0	1	24	17	4	3	1	6	21	.191	.080	.234	7.88	2.25
Eugenia, Ivan	R-R	6-1	185	9-17-91	0	0	9.00	1	0	0	0	1	1	1	1	0	2	0	.333	.000	.500	0.00	18.00
Mateo, Jackson	R-R	6-0	193	8-22-92	2	1	1.23	17	0	0	7	22	14	7	3	0	8	18	.169	.200	.159	7.36	3.27
Mendez, Irvit	R-R	6-6	225	4-11-90	1	1	3.31	16	1	0	1	33	31	14	12	1	27	36	.256	.286	.247	9.92	7.44
Mesa, Luis	R-R	6-4	170	7-13-90	4	4	3.02	12	11	0	0	57	47	23	19	1	22	46	.227	.209	.232	7.31	3.49
Oviedo, Grabiel	R-R	6-4	187	10-30-89	0	0	0.00	1	0	0	0	0	0	0	0	0	2	1	.000	.000	.000	27.00	54.00
Pena, Ariel	R-R	6-4	208	1-8-92	0	1	5.29	12	0	0	0	17	27	16	10	2	16	8	.355	.350	.357	4.24	8.47
Rosano, Luis	R-R	6-2	190	4-25-91	1	4	6.37	11	6	0	0	30	44	29	21	5	15	15	.352	.270	.386	4.55	4.55
Ruiz, Adner	L-L	6-1	180	4-1-89	1	2	2.06	15	1	0	4	39	38	16	9	1	18	33	.255	.000	.262	7.55	4.12
Tamares, Daniel	R-R	6-3	170	12-20-89	5	3	1.41	10	9	1	0	57	27	13	9	0	17	46	.141	.143	.140	7.22	2.67
Tamarez, Moises	R-R	6-3	195	3-6-93	3	4	4.06	9	8	0	0	44	47	24	20	1	16	28	.285	.278	.287	5.68	3.25
Velasquez, Abdiel	R-R	6-3	184	3-4-93	2	1	2.53	12	3	0	1	32	16	12	9	1	20	28	.150	.167	.145	7.88	5.63

Fielding

Catcher	PCT	G	PO	A	E	DP	PB
Capellan	.968	15	107	13	4	0	3
Cordero	.983	29	150	22	3	3	5
De Jesus	.962	7	46	4	2	1	3
Feliz	.955	6	20	1	1	0	0
Lugo	.982	23	98	13	2	0	1
Mercedes	1.000	1	1	0	0	0	0
Rivas	.989	14	73	14	1	0	1

First Base	PCT	G	PO	A	E	DP
De Jesus	.917	3	11	0	1	0
Mercedes	.952	20	114	6	6	8
Nieto	.967	10	86	3	3	8
Rivas	.993	49	385	30	3	31

Second Base	PCT	G	PO	A	E	DP
Aguilar	.944	3	7	10	1	3

	PCT	G	PO	A	E	DP
Infante	1.000	1	1	3	0	0
Morales	.961	24	56	42	4	11
Oguisten	.983	11	27	31	1	7
Rodriguez	.980	37	79	66	3	18

Third Base	PCT	G	PO	A	E	DP
Aguilar	.955	7	6	15	1	1
Infante	.919	49	32	115	13	4
Martinez	1.000	2	1	0	0	0
Oguisten	.902	12	7	30	4	2
Rivas	1.000	2	1	4	0	0
Rodriguez	.923	3	3	9	1	1

Shortstop	PCT	G	PO	A	E	DP
Aguilar	.923	5	5	19	2	3
Martinez	.900	12	18	27	5	3
Morales	.937	44	73	120	13	24
Oguisten	.846	7	10	12	4	1
Rodriguez	.975	9	17	22	1	7

Outfield	PCT	G	PO	A	E	DP
Aguilar	1.000	7	10	0	0	0
De La Rosa	.976	30	35	5	1	2
Infante	—	1	0	0	0	0
Lugo	.968	46	53	8	2	3
Martinez	1.000	4	3	1	0	0
Mercedes	1.000	3	2	1	0	0
Pena	1.000	1	2	0	0	0
Pena	.955	54	80	4	4	1
Ramirez	1.000	61	95	6	0	2
Rodriguez	.951	31	35	4	2	1

Milwaukee Brewers

SEASON IN A SENTENCE: The Brewers posted their second straight losing season at 77-85 thanks in large part to their pitching, with a team 4.59 ERA that ranked 14th in the National League.

HIGH POINT: Trevor Hoffman stumbled early in the season and wound up with a career-worst 5.89 ERA, but the all-time saves leader reached the 600 saves milestone in September. Hoffman also tutored former nondrafted free agent John Axford, who emerged as the team's most reliable reliever. Axford went 8-2, 2.48 and averaged 11.8 strikeouts per nine innings while picking up 24 saves.

LOW POINT: Milwaukee got off to a 15-16 start, then fell out of contention with a nine-game losing streak. Starting pitchers absorbed seven of the losses, the Brewers scored more than five runs only once in the stretch, and Milwaukee never came within five games of the .500 mark for the rest of the season.

NOTABLE ROOKIES: Axford, 27, gives the Brewers a low-cost power arm for the back of the bullpen, as does 22-year-old lefthander Zach Braddock (2.94 ERA in 46 games). Shortstop Alcides Escobar, 23, didn't quite defend up to expectations, and his .235/.288/.326 offensive line was less than hoped for. Jonathan Lucroy, 24, earned the starting catching spot after a May callup and threw out 31 percent of basestealers while batting a modest .253/.300/.329.

KEY TRANSACTIONS: The Brewers fired manager Ned Yost late in their 2008 playoff run, and eventually replaced him with Ken Macha. The 60-year-old Macha had two losing seasons in Milwaukee before being fired at the end of the 2010 campaign. The club made few trades during the season, with the biggest coming when they got outfielder Chris Dickerson from the Reds for 40-year-old veteran Jim Edmonds.

DOWN ON THE FARM: The Brewers finally got 2004 first-rounder Mark Rogers to the majors, after he went 6-8, 3.65 with 114 strikeouts in 116 innings. Righty Jake Odorizzi was the organization's pitcher of the year, and the 2008 supplemental first-rounder established himself as the organization's top starting pitching prospect. But 2009 first-rounder Eric Arnett (3-9, 6.79) had a hideous first season, including a demotion to the Rookie-level Arizona League, while outfielder Logan Schafer, the organization's player of the year in 2009, missed the entire season with two injuries.

OPENING DAY PAYROLL: $81.1 million (18th)

PLAYERS OF THE YEAR

MAJOR LEAGUE	MINOR LEAGUE
Ryan Braun	**Brett Lawrie**
of	2b
.304/.365/.501	(Double-A)
25 HR, 45 2B, 103 RBI	.285/.346/.451
2nd in NL with 188 H	36 2B, 16 3B, 30 SB

ORGANIZATION LEADERS

BATTING		*Minimum 250 at-bats
MAJORS		
*AVG	Ryan Braun	.304
*OPS	Prince Fielder	.871
HR	Prince Fielder	32
RBI	Casey McGehee	104
MINORS		
*AVG	Erik Komatsu, Brevard County	.323
*OBP	Cutter Dykstra, Wisconsin	.416
*SLG	Brendan Katin, Nashville	.580
R	Erik Komatsu, Brevard County	90
	Brett Lawrie, Huntsville	90
H	Brett Lawrie, Huntsville	158
TB	Brett Lawrie, Huntsville	250
2B	Ryan Gennett, Wisconsin	39
3B	Brett Lawrie, Huntsville	16
HR	Brendan Katin, Nashville	26
	Joe Koshansky, Nashville	26
RBI	Sean Halton, Wisconsin/Brevard County	88
BB	Khristopher Davis, Wisconsin	77
SO	Brock Kjeldgaard, Brevard County	175
SB	Josh Prince, Brevard County	44

PITCHING		†Minimum 75 innings
MAJORS		
W	Yovani Gallardo	14
†ERA	Yovani Gallardo	3.84
SO	Yovani Gallardo	200
MINORS		
W	Amaury Rivas, Huntsville	11
L	Michael Bowman, Huntsville	13
†ERA	Kyle Heckathorn, Wisconsin/Brevard County	2.98
G	Two tied at	50
GS	Two tied at	27
SV	Chris Smith, Nashville	26
IP	Chase Wright, Nashville	151
BB	Evan Frederickson, Brevard County/Helena	76
SO	Dan Merklinger, Huntsville/Brevard/Nashville	148
†AVG	Mark Rogers, Nashville/Huntsville	.209

2010 PERFORMANCE

General Manager: Doug Melvin. **Farm Director:** Reid Nichols. **Scouting Director:** Bruce Seid.

Class	Team	League	W	L	PCT	Finish*	Manager(s)
Majors	Milwaukee Brewers	National	77	85	.475	11th (16)	Ken Macha
Triple-A	Nashville Sounds	Pacific Coast	77	67	.535	5th (16)	Don Money
Double-A	Huntsville Stars	Southern	67	73	.479	6th (10)	Mike Guerrero
High A	Brevard County Manatees	Florida State	64	75	.460	9th (12)	Bob Miscik
Low A	Wisconsin Timber Rattlers	Midwest	58	80	.420	14th (16)	Jeff Isom
Rookie	Helena Brewers	Pioneer	41	34	.547	†3rd (8)	Joe Ayrault
Rookie	AZL Brewers	Arizona	34	22	.607	†2nd (12)	Tony Diggs
Overall 2010 Minor League Record			341	351	.493	17th (30)	

*Finish in overall standings (No. of teams in league). †League champion.

ORGANIZATION STATISTICS

MILWAUKEE BREWERS

NATIONAL LEAGUE

Batting	B-T	HT	WT	DOB	AVG	vLH	vRH	G	AB	R	H	2B	3B	HR	RBI	BB	HBP	SH	SF	SO	SB	CS	SLG	OBP
Braun, Ryan	R-R	6-1	200	11-17-83	.304	.271	.315	157	619	101	188	45	1	25	103	56	6	0	3	105	14	3	.501	.365
Cain, Lorenzo	R-R	6-2	200	4-13-86	.306	.289	.314	43	147	17	45	11	1	1	13	9	1	0	1	28	7	1	.415	.348
Counsell, Craig	L-R	6-0	180	8-21-70	.250	.206	.259	102	204	16	51	8	0	2	21	21	1	3	1	29	1	1	.319	.322
Cruz, Luis	R-R	6-1	210	2-10-84	.235	.091	.500	7	17	2	4	0	1	0	1	0	0	0	0	2	0	0	.353	.235
Dickerson, Chris	L-L	6-3	230	4-10-82	.208	.000	.220	25	53	2	11	1	1	0	5	5	0	2	1	15	1	0	.264	.271
2-team total (20 Cincinnati)					.206	—	—	45	97	11	20	2	2	0	5	6	0	2	1	34	4	0	.268	.250
Edmonds, Jim	L-L	6-1	210	6-27-70	.286	.256	.293	73	217	38	62	21	0	8	20	21	1	0	1	53	2	0	.493	.350
2-team total (13 Cincinnati)					.276	—	—	86	246	44	68	23	0	11	23	24	1	0	1	60	2	0	.504	.342
Escobar, Alcides	R-R	6-1	180	12-16-86	.235	.236	.235	145	506	57	119	14	10	4	41	36	3	4	3	70	10	4	.326	.288
Fielder, Prince	L-R	5-11	270	5-9-84	.261	.226	.280	161	578	94	151	25	0	32	83	114	21	0	1	138	1	0	.471	.401
Gamel, Mat	L-R	6-0	200	7-26-85	.200	.500	.154	12	15	1	3	1	0	0	1	1	0	0	0	8	0	0	.267	.294
Gerut, Jody	L-L	6-0	190	9-18-77	.197	.350	.137	32	71	7	14	4	1	2	8	3	0	0	0	17	0	1	.366	.230
Gomez, Carlos	R-R	6-4	215	12-4-85	.247	.196	.273	97	291	38	72	11	3	5	24	17	4	6	0	72	18	3	.357	.298
Hart, Corey	R-R	6-6	230	3-24-82	.283	.318	.271	145	558	91	158	34	4	31	102	45	6	0	5	140	7	6	.525	.340
Inglett, Joe	L-R	5-9	175	6-29-78	.254	.105	.276	102	142	15	36	8	5	1	8	15	2	0	1	34	1	0	.401	.331
Kottaras, George	L-R	6-0	185	5-10-83	.203	.200	.204	67	212	24	43	12	1	9	26	33	0	1	4	44	2	0	.396	.305
Lucroy, Jonathan	R-R	6-0	195	6-13-86	.253	.284	.241	75	277	24	70	9	0	4	26	18	1	0	1	44	4	2	.329	.300
McGehee, Casey	R-R	6-1	195	10-12-82	.285	.316	.274	157	610	70	174	38	1	23	104	50	2	0	8	102	1	1	.464	.337
Stern, Adam	L-R	5-11	190	2-12-80	.000	.000	.000	6	8	0	0	0	0	0	1	0	0	0	0	2	0	0	.000	.000
Weeks, Rickie	R-R	5-10	215	9-13-82	.269	.329	.251	160	651	112	175	32	4	29	83	76	25	0	2	184	11	4	.464	.366
Zaun, Gregg	B-R	5-10	170	4-14-71	.265	.161	.310	28	102	11	27	7	0	2	14	11	3	0	1	12	0	0	.392	.350

Pitching	B-T	HT	WT	DOB	W	L	ERA	G	GS	CG	SV	IP	H	R	ER	HR	BB	SO	AVG	vLH	vRH	K/9	BB/9
Axford, John	R-R	6-5	195	4-1-83	8	2	2.48	50	0	0	24	58	42	17	16	1	27	76	.204	.225	.183	11.79	4.19
Braddock, Zach	L-L	6-2	235	8-23-87	1	2	2.94	46	0	0	0	34	29	11	11	1	19	41	.228	.151	.284	10.96	5.08
Bush, Dave	R-R	6-2	205	11-9-79	8	13	4.54	32	31	0	0	174	198	108	88	28	65	107	.286	.277	.293	5.52	3.36
Capuano, Chris	L-L	6-2	225	8-19-78	4	4	3.95	24	9	0	0	66	65	29	29	9	21	54	.259	.224	.272	7.36	2.86
Coffey, Todd	R-R	6-4	240	9-9-80	2	4	4.76	69	0	0	0	62	65	40	33	8	23	56	.270	.275	.267	8.09	3.32
Davis, Doug	R-L	6-4	215	9-21-75	1	4	7.51	8	8	0	0	38	55	36	32	6	21	34	.333	.265	.351	7.98	4.93
Estrada, Marco	R-R	6-0	180	7-5-83	0	0	9.53	7	1	0	0	11	14	13	12	3	6	13	.280	.429	.172	10.32	4.76
Gallardo, Yovani	R-R	6-2	220	2-27-86	14	7	3.84	31	31	2	0	185	178	89	79	12	75	200	.251	.280	.228	9.73	3.65
Hawkins, LaTroy	R-R	6-5	215	12-21-72	0	3	8.44	18	0	0	0	16	21	15	15	2	6	18	.323	.269	.359	10.13	3.38
Hoffman, Trevor	R-R	6-0	220	10-13-67	2	7	5.89	50	0	0	10	47	49	31	31	8	19	30	.268	.298	.242	5.70	3.61
Jeffress, Jeremy	R-R	6-0	195	9-21-87	1	0	2.70	10	0	0	0	10	8	4	3	0	6	8	.229	.273	.208	7.20	5.40
Kintzler, Brandon	R-R	6-1	185	8-1-84	0	1	7.36	7	0	0	0	7	10	6	6	2	4	9	.357	.300	.389	11.05	4.91
Loe, Kameron	R-R	6-8	230	9-10-81	3	5	2.78	53	0	0	0	58	54	23	18	6	15	46	.245	.274	.228	7.10	2.31
McClendon, Mike	R-R	6-5	215	4-3-85	2	0	3.00	17	0	0	0	21	15	7	7	2	7	21	.195	.194	.196	9.00	3.00
Narveson, Chris	L-L	6-3	205	12-20-81	12	9	4.99	37	28	0	0	168	172	96	93	21	59	137	.266	.226	.280	7.35	3.17
Parra, Manny	L-L	6-3	215	10-30-82	3	10	5.02	42	16	0	0	122	135	76	68	18	63	129	.281	.326	.264	9.52	4.65
Riske, David	R-R	6-2	190	10-23-76	0	0	5.01	23	0	0	0	23	25	14	13	2	8	16	.269	.133	.333	6.17	3.09
Rogers, Mark	R-R	6-3	220	1-30-86	0	0	1.80	4	2	0	0	10	2	2	2	0	3	11	.067	.000	.091	9.90	2.70
Smith, Chris	R-R	6-0	190	4-9-81	0	0	5.40	3	0	0	0	3	4	2	2	0	1	4	.308	.667	.200	10.80	2.70
Stetter, Mitch	L-L	6-4	210	1-16-81	0	0	14.73	9	0	0	0	4	7	6	6	1	3	3	.389	.357	.500	7.36	7.36
Suppan, Jeff	R-R	6-2	230	1-2-75	0	2	7.84	15	2	0	0	31	50	29	27	4	12	18	.388	.418	.365	5.23	3.48
2-team total (15 St. Louis)					3	8	5.06	30	15	0	0	101	130	61	57	13	37	51	—	—	—	4.53	3.29
Vargas, Claudio	R-R	6-4	235	6-19-78	1	0	7.32	17	0	0	0	20	28	16	16	3	10	18	.337	.250	.404	8.24	4.58
Villanueva, Carlos	R-R	6-2	230	11-28-83	2	0	4.61	50	0	0	1	53	48	27	27	7	22	67	.238	.232	.243	11.45	3.76
Wolf, Randy	L-L	6-0	200	8-22-76	13	12	4.17	34	34	1	0	216	213	107	100	29	87	142	.258	.286	.250	5.93	3.63

Fielding

Catcher	PCT	G	PO	A	E	DP	PB
Kottaras	.991	61	434	20	4	4	4
Lucroy	.992	75	614	44	5	6	1
Zaun	.992	28	221	13	2	4	0

First Base	PCT	G	PO	A	E	DP
Edmonds	1.000	3	12	1	0	3
Fielder	.997	160	1251	86	4	116
Kottaras	1.000	2	1	0	0	0
McGehee	1.000	3	12	0	0	1

Second Base	PCT	G	PO	A	E	DP
Counsell	.909	3	3	7	1	2
Inglett	.941	8	6	10	1	4
Weeks	.980	159	332	389	15	102

Third Base	PCT	G	PO	A	E	DP
Counsell	.900	20	7	20	3	5
Gamel	—	3	0	0	0	0
McGehee	.954	153	81	268	17	31

Shortstop	PCT	G	PO	A	E	DP
Counsell	.982	42	30	79	2	17
Cruz	1.000	5	7	7	0	1
Escobar	.964	138	174	358	20	71

Outfield	PCT	G	PO	A	E	DP
Braun	.990	153	279	6	3	1
Cain	.981	39	101	3	2	2
Dickerson	1.000	17	28	0	0	0
Edmonds	.993	55	146	6	1	3

	PCT	G	PO	A	E	DP
Escobar	1.000	5	8	0	0	0
Gamel	1.000	1	1	0	0	0
Gerut	1.000	18	32	3	0	1
Gomez	.970	81	157	2	5	0
Hart	.993	141	272	7	2	1
Inglett	.970	24	30	2	1	0
Kottaras	—	1	0	0	0	0
Stern	1.000	2	3	0	0	0

NASHVILLE SOUNDS

TRIPLE-A

PACIFIC COAST LEAGUE

Batting	B-T	HT	WT	DOB	AVG	vLH	vRH	G	AB	R	H	2B	3B	HR	RBI	BB	HBP	SH	SF	SO	SB	CS	SLG	OBP
Almonte, Erick	R-R	6-2	180	2-1-78	.320	.330	.316	110	325	40	104	21	2	2	38	28	2	0	0	63	4	0	.415	.377
Anderson, Drew T.	R-R	6-2	200	6-9-81	.333	.286	.345	13	36	7	12	2	0	2	4	6	1	0	0	9	0	0	.556	.442
Anderson, Josh	L-R	6-2	195	8-10-82	.245	.000	.255	17	49	9	12	2	0	0	2	3	0	3	0	9	4	1	.286	.288
Arlis, Patrick	R-R	6-0	215	12-18-80	.180	.333	.132	19	50	5	9	2	0	0	2	10	1	2	0	11	0	0	.220	.328
Cain, Lorenzo	R-R	6-2	200	4-13-86	.299	.455	.276	22	87	13	26	5	3	0	9	11	1	1	0	17	5	1	.425	.384
Caufield, Chuck	R-R	6-1	205	7-6-83	.000	.000	.000	4	2	4	0	0	0	0	0	2	0	0	0	1	0	0	.000	.500
Cruz, Luis	R-R	6-1	210	2-10-84	.281	.312	.270	129	488	54	137	29	3	10	68	15	7	4	4	56	0	0	.414	.309
De La Rosa, Anderson	R-R	6-0	190	8-31-82	.263	.500	.200	12	38	6	10	5	0	0	4	3	1	1	1	7	0	0	.395	.326
Dowdy, Brett	R-R	6-0	190	2-22-82	.143	.500	.000	3	7	1	1	0	0	0	0	0	0	0	0	0	0	0	.143	.143
Farris, Eric	R-R	5-10	170	3-3-86	.274	.246	.283	60	230	28	63	9	1	2	15	9	4	5	1	25	14	2	.348	.311
Gamel, Mat	L-R	6-0	200	7-26-85	.309	.234	.333	82	311	54	96	24	0	13	67	38	5	0	5	64	3	1	.511	.387
Gomez, Carlos	R-R	6-4	215	12-4-85	.286	.333	.273	8	28	7	8	0	0	0	2	5	1	0	0	9	2	1	.286	.412
Heether, Adam	R-R	6-0	195	1-14-82	.245	.351	.197	50	184	30	45	7	1	9	28	23	6	0	3	35	2	1	.440	.343
2-team total (49 Sacramento)					.237	—	—	99	329	57	78	15	1	10	41	54	10	0	5	68	7	3	.380	.357
Hopper, Norris	R-R	5-11	205	3-24-79	.286	.271	.292	119	458	51	131	14	0	0	38	37	0	10	4	43	22	9	.317	.337
Johnson, Ben	R-R	6-0	220	10-17-81	.179	.182	.179	42	145	13	26	5	0	4	14	1	2	2	45	0	0	.255	.204
Katin, Brendan	R-R	6-1	235	1-28-83	.286	.289	.285	94	336	65	96	19	1	26	76	39	15	0	3	91	1	0	.580	.382
Koshansky, Joe	L-L	6-4	230	5-26-82	.264	.325	.249	131	425	67	112	21	0	26	79	62	11	2	2	152	3	2	.496	.370
Lucroy, Jonathan	R-R	6-0	195	6-13-86	.238	.174	.263	21	80	8	19	4	0	2	11	3	0	0	0	14	0	0	.363	.265
Maldonado, Martin	R-R	6-1	210	8-16-86	.253	.241	.255	52	174	19	44	9	0	7	26	14	2	7	4	45	0	1	.425	.309
Oeltjen, Trent	L-L	6-1	190	2-28-83	.301	.296	.303	70	266	47	80	24	2	8	38	21	3	4	3	59	13	2	.496	.355
2-team total (49 Albuquerque)					.320	—	—	119	465	87	149	42	7	13	71	44	5	4	5	102	27	7	.525	.382
Olmedo, Ray	B-R	5-11	175	5-31-81	.284	.254	.295	114	416	65	118	21	5	4	55	25	5	13	3	69	10	6	.387	.330
Raburn, Johnny	B-R	6-0	165	2-16-79	.264	.279	.256	77	197	25	52	8	3	3	28	34	0	6	5	33	4	1	.381	.364
Salome, Angel	R-R	5-7	200	6-8-86	.333	.333	.333	5	12	3	4	0	0	1	3	2	0	0	0	1	0	1	.583	.429
Stern, Adam	L-R	5-11	190	2-12-80	.325	.208	.352	86	286	48	93	18	3	5	29	35	0	1	0	47	7	4	.462	.399

Pitching	B-T	HT	WT	DOB	W	L	ERA	G	GS	CG	SV	IP	H	R	ER	HR	BB	SO	AVG	vLH	vRH	K/9	BB/9
Axford, John	R-R	6-5	195	4-1-83	3	2	2.03	12	0	0	2	13	14	7	3	0	5	19	.264	.300	.242	12.83	3.38
Bennett, Jeff	R-R	6-3	200	6-10-80	0	1	11.32	12	0	0	1	10	14	13	13	3	11	8	.359	.294	.409	6.97	9.58
Braddock, Zach	L-L	6-2	235	8-23-87	0	0	4.50	11	0	0	1	16	10	8	8	1	9	28	.182	.143	.206	15.75	5.06
Bruney, Brian	R-R	6-3	235	2-17-82	0	0	0.00	2	0	0	0	3	4	0	0	0	1	2	.308	.286	.333	5.40	2.70
Butler, Josh	R-R	6-5	200	12-11-84	5	1	4.53	8	8	0	0	46	43	25	23	2	20	27	.251	.233	.265	5.32	3.94
Capuano, Chris	L-L	6-2	225	8-19-78	1	1	1.80	4	4	0	0	25	21	6	5	0	4	16	.221	.172	.242	5.76	1.44
Coffey, Todd	R-R	6-4	240	9-9-80	0	0	0.00	1	0	0	0	1	0	0	0	0	0	1	.000	.000	.000	9.00	0.00
Davis, Doug	R-L	6-4	215	9-21-75	1	0	1.13	2	2	0	0	8	5	1	1	0	2	12	.192	.250	.118	13.50	2.25
Dillard, Tim	R-R	6-4	225	7-19-83	5	7	4.12	41	8	0	1	109	98	53	50	6	32	82	.247	.274	.229	6.75	2.63
Estrada, Marco	R-R	6-0	180	7-5-83	1	2	3.15	7	7	0	0	40	30	15	14	1	11	33	.208	.143	.284	7.43	2.48
Hand, Donovan	R-R	6-4	210	4-20-86	2	0	4.62	21	0	0	0	25	29	16	13	1	5	11	.287	.273	.294	3.91	1.78
Hawkins, LaTroy	R-R	6-5	195	12-21-72	0	0	0.00	4	0	0	1	6	4	0	0	0	1	6	.182	.167	.188	1.42	0.00
Hinton, Robert	R-R	6-2	210	8-13-84	0	0	4.50	2	0	0	0	2	2	1	1	0	3	2	.250	.500	.167	9.00	13.50
Johnson, David	R-R	6-5	205	8-25-82	2	2	4.43	48	0	0	0	65	63	33	32	10	29	66	.249	.226	.268	9.14	4.02
Jones, Mike	R-R	6-4	235	4-23-83	0	0	0.71	8	0	0	0	13	8	2	1	0	3	6	.178	.118	.214	4.26	9.24
Kintzler, Brandon	R-R	6-1	185	8-1-84	3	0	2.36	22	0	0	6	27	19	7	7	1	6	21	.196	.194	.197	7.09	2.03
Loe, Kameron	R-R	6-8	230	9-10-81	4	3	3.16	10	10	0	0	63	57	28	22	6	19	39	.242	.272	.200	5.60	2.73
Lofgren, Chuck	L-L	6-3	190	11-24-86	7	8	5.19	28	23	0	0	132	143	85	76	24	75	91	.284	.212	.314	6.22	5.13
McClendon, Mike	R-R	6-5	215	4-3-85	4	3	2.44	25	3	0	2	55	53	16	15	1	14	44	.259	.250	.264	7.16	2.28
McLeary, Marty	R-R	6-4	225	10-26-74	7	4	5.15	14	14	1	0	79	104	52	45	11	27	56	.328	.358	.301	6.41	3.09
2-team total (9 Las Vegas)					7	9	7.00	23	19	1	0	107	165	101	83	20	45	79	—	—	—	6.67	3.80
Merklinger, Daniel	L-L	6-1	195	11-19-85	1	0	7.20	1	1	0	0	5	6	4	4	1	3	2	.316	.333	.308	3.60	5.40
Murray, A.J.	B-L	6-3	220	3-17-82	0	2	4.44	23	0	0	0	26	25	15	13	1	13	22	.258	.233	.278	7.52	4.44
Narron, Sam	L-L	6-7	200	7-12-81	9	7	4.14	17	16	1	0	104	125	53	48	7	21	54	.306	.279	.319	4.66	1.81
Riske, David	R-R	6-2	190	10-23-76	2	0	4.00	9	0	0	0	9	6	4	4	1	4	8	.258	.231	.278	8.00	4.00
Rogers, Mark	R-R	6-3	220	1-30-86	0	0	2.08	1	1	0	0	4	3	1	1	0	3	3	.188	.000	.231	6.23	6.23
Smith, Chris	R-R	6-0	190	4-9-81	4	3	3.56	47	0	0	26	48	47	23	19	7	21	62	.257	.329	.209	11.63	3.94
Stetter, Mitch	L-L	6-4	210	1-16-81	3	2	6.86	41	0	0	0	42	46	32	32	5	18	52	.272	.200	.337	11.14	3.86
Villanueva, Carlos	R-R	6-2	230	11-28-83	0	0	3.77	11	0	0	1	14	13	6	6	2	4	22	.228	.227	.229	8.79	4.40
Waters, Chris	L-L	6-0	170	8-17-80	5	10	4.44	21	20	0	0	105	101	61	52	18	56	61	.248	.238	.253	5.21	4.78
Wright, Chase	L-L	6-2	205	2-8-83	8	9	5.13	28	27	1	1	151	169	93	86	20	55	93	.287	.268	.296	5.54	3.23

Fielding

Catcher	PCT	G	PO	A	E	DP	PB
Arlis	.982	18	106	5	2	1	1
De La Rosa	.974	12	68	6	2	1	3
Johnson	.982	40	250	21	5	3	3
Lucroy	.988	21	152	12	2	1	2
Maldonado	.995	52	346	42	2	5	6
Salome	1.000	4	28	2	0	0	0

First Base	PCT	G	PO	A	E	DP
Almonte	.987	30	269	25	4	28
Gamel	.944	2	17	0	1	1
Koshansky	.991	114	1019	90	10	125

Second Base	PCT	G	PO	A	E	DP
Cruz	1.000	2	0	3	0	0
Farris	.986	59	113	179	4	44

	PCT	G	PO	A	E	DP
Olmedo	.975	61	116	196	8	42
Raburn	.960	31	59	85	6	29
Third Base	PCT	G	PO	A	E	DP
Almonte	.833	3	1	4	1	1
Cruz	1.000	4	1	7	0	1
Gamel	.920	72	39	134	15	21
Heether	.951	50	24	92	6	11
Olmedo	.964	14	4	23	1	2
Raburn	1.000	2	0	3	0	0
Shortstop	PCT	G	PO	A	E	DP
Cruz	.967	124	214	405	21	104
Olmedo	.979	24	31	62	2	14
Outfield	PCT	G	PO	A	E	DP
Almonte	1.000	3	4	0	0	0

	PCT	G	PO	A	E	DP
Anderson	.923	11	12	0	1	0
Anderson	.957	11	22	0	1	0
Cain	.985	22	62	2	1	0
Dowdy	1.000	1	2	0	0	0
Gamel	1.000	5	7	2	0	0
Gomez	1.000	8	17	0	0	0
Hopper	.992	114	241	5	2	3
Johnson	—	1	0	0	0	0
Katin	.987	89	142	6	2	0
Oeltjen	.971	68	129	4	4	2
Olmedo	.875	11	13	1	2	0
Raburn	1.000	30	46	1	0	1
Stern	.992	72	113	7	1	1

HUNTSVILLE STARS
DOUBLE-A
SOUTHERN LEAGUE

Batting	B-T	HT	WT	DOB	AVG	vLH	vRH	G	AB	R	H	2B	3B	HR	RBI	BB	HBP	SH	SF	SO	SB	CS	SLG	OBP
Anderson, Drew T.	L-R	6-2	200	6-9-81	.273	.275	.273	74	256	46	70	23	2	6	44	34	4	0	2	66	2	2	.449	.365
Arlis, Patrick	R-R	6-0	215	12-18-80	.115	.000	.150	14	26	2	3	0	0	0	0	2	0	1	0	8	0	0	.115	.179
Brewer, Brent	R-R	6-2	198	12-19-87	.275	.125	.313	17	40	9	11	3	0	0	3	2	0	1	0	18	0	1	.350	.310
Buller, Dayton	R-R	6-0	190	6-22-81	.222	.277	.200	50	167	17	37	5	3	2	16	19	1	0	1	57	0	1	.323	.303
Cain, Lorenzo	R-R	6-2	205	4-13-86	.324	.284	.341	62	244	45	79	6	6	3	18	34	1	1	0	52	21	2	.434	.409
Caufield, Chuck	R-R	6-1	205	7-6-83	.283	.306	.268	85	184	21	52	10	1	4	25	21	4	5	1	52	2	0	.413	.367
De La Rosa, Anderson	R-R	6-0	190	8-1-84	.211	.303	.161	28	95	7	20	5	0	1	6	2	2	3	1	21	0	0	.295	.240
Dowdy, Brett	R-R	6-0	190	2-22-82	.111	.000	.125	3	9	1	1	0	0	0	0	0	0	1	0	2	0	0	.111	.111
Errecart, Chris	R-L	6-1	210	2-11-85	.226	.244	.218	45	155	17	35	10	2	5	19	4	4	0	2	37	1	0	.413	.261
Gamel, Mat	L-R	6-2	210	7-26-85	.393	.222	.474	8	28	6	11	2	0	1	5	4	0	0	0	9	0	0	.571	.469
Gindl, Caleb	L-L	5-9	185	8-31-88	.272	.302	.260	128	463	61	126	33	1	9	60	55	5	6	5	78	10	5	.406	.352
Green, Taylor	L-R	5-11	198	11-2-86	.260	.188	.283	113	393	51	102	29	1	13	81	45	4	1	8	67	0	2	.438	.336
Haydel, Lee	L-L	5-11	170	7-15-87	.285	.300	.281	127	452	61	129	18	7	0	36	35	2	5	3	97	22	6	.356	.337
Krieger, Scott	R-R	6-0	215	1-30-87	.176	.000	.300	8	17	2	3	1	0	1	1	0	0	1	0	5	0	0	.412	.176
Lawrie, Brett	R-R	6-0	213	1-18-90	.285	.336	.266	135	554	90	158	36	16	8	63	47	5	2	1	118	30	13	.451	.346
Lucroy, Jonathan	R-R	6-0	195	6-13-86	.452	.400	.469	10	42	8	19	3	0	0	5	4	0	1	0	3	0	0	.524	.500
Machado, Anderson	B-R	6-0	185	1-25-81	.265	.312	.237	99	249	23	66	20	1	1	30	38	1	5	2	67	0	1	.365	.362
Maldonado, Martin	R-R	6-1	210	8-16-86	.252	.043	.313	34	103	9	26	6	0	3	9	7	2	2	2	24	0	2	.369	.347
McCraw, Sean	L-R	6-0	185	3-11-86	.177	.294	.133	21	62	6	11	2	0	0	7	4	1	2	0	18	0	1	.210	.239
Nowak, Chris	R-R	6-5	225	2-21-83	.236	.236	.236	49	182	27	43	8	1	5	28	19	3	0	3	48	4	1	.374	.314
2-team total (64 Montgomery)					.243	—		113	404	60	98	17	2	12	61	59	4	0	6	99	12	2	.384	.340
Salome, Angel	R-R	5-7	200	6-8-86	.000	.000	.000	2	2	0	0	0	0	0	0	0	0	0	0	1	0	0	.000	.000
Sanchez, Juan	R-R	5-11	167	1-16-87	.040	.000	.050	15	25	1	1	0	0	0	1	2	1	3	0	4	0	0	.040	.143
Wheeler, Zelous	R-R	5-10	215	1-16-87	.275	.299	.266	135	480	76	132	21	2	11	65	70	15	1	3	77	8	4	.396	.382
Wilson, Steffan	R-R	6-1	220	5-24-86	.201	.132	.224	60	209	22	42	11	0	6	31	19	2	0	3	65	3	1	.340	.270

Pitching	B-T	HT	WT	DOB	W	L	ERA	G	GS	CG	SV	IP	H	R	ER	HR	BB	SO	AVG	vLH	vRH	K/9	BB/9
Baron, Casey	L-L	6-1	220	11-29-84	1	0	6.62	13	0	0	0	18	20	14	13	1	10	14	.294	.214	.350	7.13	5.09
Bowman, Michael	R-R	6-2	195	5-2-87	9	13	5.62	26	26	1	0	131	149	89	82	14	52	94	.287	.299	.275	6.44	3.56
Butler, Josh	R-R	6-5	200	12-11-84	3	5	4.56	10	10	0	0	53	56	31	27	5	26	36	.271	.313	.231	6.07	4.39
Cody, Chris	L-L	6-0	190	1-7-84	7	8	4.19	26	19	1	1	110	121	57	51	16	33	80	.284	.331	.262	6.57	2.71
Fiers, Michael	R-R	6-3	205	6-15-85	1	1	3.69	10	4	0	1	32	28	13	13	3	9	36	.231	.175	.293	10.23	2.56
Green, Nick	R-R	6-4	200	8-20-84	0	2	5.25	32	0	0	1	48	54	33	28	4	12	45	.274	.281	.269	8.44	2.25
Hand, Donovan	R-R	6-4	210	4-20-86	2	1	2.86	27	1	0	2	50	57	25	16	3	8	38	.285	.265	.306	6.79	1.43
Henderson, Jim	L-R	6-5	190	10-21-82	4	5	5.46	45	0	0	7	61	49	44	37	8	35	60	.219	.222	.216	8.85	5.16
Hinton, Robert	R-R	6-2	210	8-13-84	4	4	4.15	48	0	0	4	65	59	38	30	7	25	81	.238	.252	.225	11.22	3.46
Jeffress, Jeremy	R-R	6-0	195	9-21-87	1	1	1.26	11	0	0	3	14	8	3	2	0	2	15	.160	.158	.161	9.42	1.26
Jones, Mike	R-R	6-4	220	4-23-83	1	1	3.95	11	2	0	0	27	25	16	12	0	16	19	.243	.250	.236	6.26	5.27
Kintzler, Brandon	R-R	6-1	185	8-1-84	1	0	0.40	20	0	0	10	22	11	2	1	0	1	23	.141	.125	.158	9.27	0.40
Lamontagne, Andre	B-R	6-5	210	3-24-86	4	3	3.63	13	7	0	1	45	35	27	18	4	24	39	.217	.171	.253	7.86	4.84
Luetge, Lucas	L-L	6-3	180	3-24-87	3	2	3.48	23	2	0	0	44	52	25	17	4	17	47	.286	.158	.344	9.61	3.48
McClendon, Mike	R-R	6-5	215	4-3-85	1	1	0.61	7	0	0	0	15	7	1	1	0	1	15	.143	.091	.185	9.20	0.61
Merklinger, Daniel	L-L	6-1	195	11-19-85	0	1	0.00	1	1	0	0	4	5	4	0	0	1	4	.294	.333	.273	8.31	2.08
Morlan, Eduardo	R-R	6-2	220	3-1-86	2	2	2.74	32	0	0	3	49	46	17	15	3	12	44	.241	.213	.261	8.03	2.19
2-team total (12 Montgomery)					3	2	3.52	44	0	0	3	72	78	30	28	7	21	60	—			7.53	2.64
Peralta, Wily	R-R	6-2	225	5-8-89	2	3	3.61	8	8	0	0	42	43	22	17	5	24	29	.269	.343	.215	6.17	5.10
Periard, Alex	L-R	6-1	215	6-15-87	2	2	4.71	11	11	0	0	63	78	38	33	6	18	24	.308	.305	.311	3.43	2.57
Rivas, Amaury	R-R	6-2	210	12-20-85	11	6	3.37	25	25	2	0	142	130	59	53	7	55	114	.253	.233	.272	7.24	3.49
Rogers, Mark	R-R	6-3	220	1-30-86	6	8	3.71	24	24	0	0	112	86	60	46	3	69	111	.210	.226	.198	8.95	5.56
Willinsky, Mark	R-R	6-4	215	3-14-87	2	2	6.36	24	0	0	0	47	66	42	33	7	24	42	.327	.330	.324	8.10	4.63

Fielding

Catcher	PCT	G	PO	A	E	DP	PB
Arlis	1.000	6	29	3	0	2	0
Buller	.992	49	348	38	3	2	8
De La Rosa	.989	28	241	30	3	4	3
Lucroy	.989	10	78	8	1	2	0
Maldonado	.983	34	211	22	4	1	5

	PCT	G	PO	A	E	DP
McCraw	.985	20	122	12	2	1	3

First Base	PCT	G	PO	A	E	DP
Anderson	.969	8	59	4	2	7
Arlis	1.000	2	8	1	0	1
Errecart	.986	38	325	24	5	43
Green	.895	3	16	1	2	0
Krieger	1.000	1	3	0	0	0
Machado	.971	7	33	1	1	3
Nowak	.985	48	431	19	7	44
Wilson	.989	45	348	20	4	38

Second Base	PCT	G	PO	A	E	DP
Green	1.000	1	1	6	0	2
Lawrie	.961	131	226	385	25	89
Machado	.966	7	15	13	1	1

Sanchez	—	1	0	0	0	0
Wheeler	.952	4	4	16	1	5

Third Base	PCT	G	PO	A	E	DP
Gamel	.875	6	1	6	1	0
Green	.935	102	63	198	18	19
Machado	1.000	1	1	0	0	0
Nowak	1.000	2	1	3	0	0
Wheeler	.961	36	22	76	4	5
Wilson	1.000	1	3	4	0	3

Shortstop	PCT	G	PO	A	E	DP
Machado	.935	51	68	147	15	38
Sanchez	.800	4	0	4	1	0
Wheeler	.923	93	129	257	32	63

Outfield	PCT	G	PO	A	E	DP
Anderson	.988	56	83	0	1	0
Brewer	1.000	9	12	1	0	0
Cain	.966	59	140	2	5	1
Caufield	.986	56	68	2	1	0
Dowdy	1.000	2	4	0	0	0
Errecart	—	1	0	0	0	0
Gindl	.974	123	214	8	6	2
Haydel	.991	122	206	5	2	2
Krieger	1.000	4	5	0	0	0
Machado	1.000	1	2	0	0	0
Sanchez	1.000	8	8	1	0	1
Wheeler	1.000	1	3	0	0	0
Wilson	1.000	10	10	1	0	0

BREVARD COUNTY MANATEES   HIGH CLASS A

FLORIDA STATE LEAGUE

Batting	B-T	HT	WT	DOB	AVG	vLH	vRH	G	AB	R	H	2B	3B	HR	RBI	BB	HBP	SH	SF	SO	SB	CS	SLG	OBP
Braun, Steve	R-R	6-0	185	5-17-85	.140	.161	.132	48	107	10	15	4	0	0	2	14	2	4	0	32	3	2	.178	.252
Brewer, Brent	R-R	6-2	198	12-19-87	.154	.111	.167	11	39	4	6	0	0	0	2	2	0	1	1	11	1	3	.154	.190
Cline, Matt	R-R	5-10	180	10-18-85	.298	.333	.285	112	406	61	121	19	2	0	39	50	20	2	4	53	14	15	.355	.398
Davis, Kentrail	L-R	5-9	195	6-29-88	.244	.263	.235	33	123	20	30	3	2	5	0	17	17	10	0	0	28	8	2	.341	.380
De La Rosa, Anderson	R-R	6-0	190	8-1-84	.203	.275	.184	53	187	21	38	8	1	1	21	14	3	2	1	44	2	0	.273	.268
Dhanani, Kyle	R-R	6-3	195	9-6-87	.167	.000	.167	2	6	0	1	0	0	0	1	0	1	0	1	0	0	0	.167	.250
Fatse, Peter	R-L	5-10	170	8-3-87	.250	.333	.239	42	132	16	33	7	0	0	13	13	2	0	2	32	6	1	.303	.322
Gamel, Mat	L-R	6-0	200	7-26-85	.100	.091	.111	6	20	3	2	1	0	0	2	6	0	0	0	8	0	0	.150	.308
Halton, Sean	R-R	6-5	240	6-7-87	.292	.227	.320	104	397	42	116	17	1	10	77	28	9	2	9	88	2	2	.416	.345
Kjeldgaard, Brock	R-R	6-5	215	1-22-86	.245	.266	.238	132	490	60	120	29	2	17	75	36	10	0	3	175	3	2	.416	.308
Komatsu, Erik	L-L	5-10	190	10-1-87	.323	.295	.333	130	486	90	157	31	6	5	63	68	9	5	4	61	28	9	.442	.413
Krieger, Scott	R-R	6-0	215	1-30-87	.239	.296	.215	69	234	27	56	8	2	10	31	16	4	1	1	85	4	0	.419	.298
Maldonado, Martin	R-R	6-1	210	8-16-86	.121	.250	.048	10	33	1	4	0	0	0	3	1	2	0	1	8	1	0	.121	.189
McCraw, Sean	L-R	6-0	185	3-11-86	.255	.167	.273	31	106	11	27	5	0	1	13	16	1	2	0	21	1	0	.330	.358
Miller, Erik	R-R	6-3	200	8-23-87	.206	.125	.220	28	107	6	22	8	1	0	8	4	3	0	2	29	4	2	.299	.250
Miranda, Sergio	B-R	5-9	180	3-5-87	.294	.326	.283	126	486	52	143	18	3	3	71	28	4	12	14	45	14	4	.362	.329
Prince, Josh	R-R	6-0	180	1-26-88	.233	.239	.230	106	408	62	95	13	2	1	19	32	0	7	2	80	44	11	.282	.287
Roberts, Michael	R-R	6-2	185	8-28-87	.202	.179	.214	23	84	10	17	2	1	0	9	6	0	1	0	30	2	1	.250	.266
Romero, Franklin	R-R	5-11	180	6-24-88	.286	.143	.429	6	14	0	4	0	0	0	2	1	0	0	0	4	0	0	.286	.333
Salome, Angel	R-R	5-7	200	6-8-86	.286	.259	.294	66	245	28	70	18	0	6	40	23	2	0	2	45	0	1	.433	.349
Sanchez, Juan	R-R	5-11	160	6-24-86	.245	.185	.265	97	330	35	81	12	3	2	23	16	9	3	2	68	4	5	.318	.297
Schafer, Logan	L-L	6-1	180	9-8-86	.174	.300	.077	7	23	7	4	2	0	0	1	4	0	0	1	6	0	0	.261	.286
Zarraga, Shawn	R-R	6-2	215	1-21-89	.281	.292	.277	74	249	31	70	13	0	3	28	31	10	0	2	61	4	0	.369	.380

Pitching	B-T	HT	WT	DOB	W	L	ERA	G	GS	CG	SV	IP	H	R	ER	HR	BB	SO	AVG	vLH	vRH	K/9	BB/9
Anundsen, Evan	R-R	6-3	215	5-17-88	0	1	6.00	1	1	0	0	3	4	2	2	0	0	1	.308	.500	.143	3.00	0.00
Bobo, Dexter	L-L	6-0	195	11-10-87	0	2	32.40	2	0	0	0	2	7	6	6	0	2	2	.583	.800	.429	10.80	10.80
Butler, Josh	R-R	6-5	200	12-11-84	0	0	10.80	3	0	0	0	7	11	8	8	1	5	3	.344	.308	.368	4.05	6.75
Byrd, Darren	R-R	6-3	170	10-24-86	2	4	4.18	13	11	0	0	60	65	32	28	4	16	41	.274	.309	.252	6.12	2.39
Capuano, Chris	L-L	6-2	225	8-19-78	2	0	1.23	3	3	0	0	15	12	2	2	1	0	17	.214	.250	.188	10.43	0.00
Costello, Matt	L-L	6-1	190	12-17-86	0	0	4.50	1	0	0	0	2	5	1	1	0	0	5	.500	.250	.667	4.50	0.00
Fiers, Michael	R-R	6-3	205	6-15-85	4	8	3.47	17	15	0	0	93	78	37	36	6	23	94	.229	.221	.237	9.06	2.22
Flores, Ruben	R-R	6-4	170	5-19-84	1	3	4.74	32	0	0	2	44	43	25	23	2	35	42	.270	.253	.292	8.66	7.21
Frederickson, Evan	L-L	6-6	240	9-23-86	0	1	8.22	12	0	0	0	15	21	15	14	0	28	15	.333	.409	.293	8.80	16.43
Frerichs, Corey	R-R	5-11	200	5-7-86	3	5	3.05	50	0	0	12	86	59	29	29	3	34	79	.197	.213	.183	8.30	3.57
Green, Nick	R-R	6-4	200	8-20-84	0	1	1.80	13	0	0	5	15	11	4	3	0	8	14	.212	.214	.208	8.40	4.80
Heckathorn, Kyle	R-R	6-6	225	6-17-88	4	0	3.00	8	8	1	0	39	40	15	13	1	10	23	.265	.262	.269	5.31	2.31
Jeffress, Jeremy	R-R	6-0	195	9-21-87	0	0	5.40	8	0	0	1	10	10	8	6	0	7	14	.244	.174	.333	12.60	6.30
Lamontagne, Andre	B-R	6-5	210	3-24-86	1	1	2.35	11	0	0	0	15	10	4	4	1	6	14	.185	.227	.156	8.22	3.52
Luetge, Lucas	L-L	6-3	180	3-24-87	1	1	2.29	16	1	0	0	35	36	10	9	1	10	21	.273	.224	.311	5.35	2.55
Meadows, Dan	L-L	6-5	235	11-3-87	6	5	2.86	42	0	0	2	91	77	36	29	8	26	92	.228	.192	.243	9.07	2.56
Merklinger, Daniel	L-L	6-1	195	11-19-85	7	6	3.64	25	21	0	1	134	124	61	54	9	41	142	.245	.240	.246	9.56	2.76
Peralta, Wily	R-R	6-2	225	5-8-89	6	3	3.86	19	17	0	0	105	102	50	45	5	40	75	.253	.252	.254	6.43	3.43
Ramlow, Mike	L-R	6-6	185	3-2-86	4	2	3.13	23	3	0	0	55	49	20	19	4	17	59	.239	.344	.194	9.71	2.80
Riske, David	R-R	6-2	190	10-23-76	0	1	9.00	3	3	0	0	4	7	5	4	0	2	3	.389	.000	.412	6.75	4.50
Ritchie, Brandon	L-L	6-4	230	12-10-86	3	6	6.17	39	2	0	0	70	100	60	48	5	49	38	.352	.308	.373	4.89	6.30
Scarpetta, Cody	R-R	6-3	240	8-25-88	7	12	3.87	27	27	1	0	128	120	61	55	4	67	142	.247	.201	.282	9.98	4.71
Seidel, R.J.	R-R	6-5	200	9-3-87	4	2	3.70	22	14	0	0	66	60	32	27	0	27	30	.246	.198	.293	4.11	3.70
Tyson, Nick	R-R	6-3	185	1-13-88	0	1	6.75	5	0	0	0	7	10	5	5	2	1	6	.345	.214	.467	8.10	1.35
Watten, Trey	R-R	6-3	180	12-16-86	4	8	3.96	15	10	0	0	105	105	55	46	6	39	63	.262	.282	.247	5.42	3.35
Willinsky, Mark	R-R	6-4	215	3-14-87	0	2	4.13	15	0	0	4	24	29	13	11	1	7	15	.299	.368	.254	5.63	2.63

Fielding

Catcher	PCT	G	PO	A	E	DP	PB
De La Rosa	.982	44	334	50	7	3	9
McCraw	.992	31	239	25	2	5	0
Maldonado	1.000	10	72	11	0	1	2
Roberts	.969	12	87	8	3	1	3
Zarraga	.994	44	300	36	2	6	4

First Base	PCT	G	PO	A	E	DP
De La Rosa	1.000	2	17	2	0	2
Halton	.992	104	894	69	8	77
Kjeldgaard	.996	25	225	11	1	18
Miranda	1.000	12	94	7	0	9

Second Base	PCT	G	PO	A	E	DP
Braun	.988	37	59	99	2	23
Cline	.959	55	103	153	11	30
Miranda	.968	55	85	154	8	31
Sanchez	1.000	5	9	20	0	3

Third Base	PCT	G	PO	A	E	DP
Cline	.978	54	37	97	3	3

De La Rosa	—	1	0	0	0	0
Dhanani	1.000	2	1	1	0	0
Fatse	.964	11	9	18	1	3
Gamel	.929	5	7	6	1	2
Miranda	.961	61	50	121	7	17
Sanchez	.833	15	10	35	9	2

Shortstop	PCT	G	PO	A	E	DP
Brewer	.864	6	9	10	3	1
Cline	1.000	4	3	7	0	2
Miranda	—	1	0	0	0	0
Prince	.947	100	129	265	22	55
Sanchez	.961	34	34	89	5	15

Outfield	PCT	G	PO	A	E	DP
Braun	1.000	1	1	0	0	0
Davis	.973	32	69	2	2	1
Fatse	.967	18	26	3	1	0
Kjeldgaard	.966	106	192	7	7	0
Komatsu	.985	125	255	4	4	1
Krieger	.979	59	88	4	2	2
Miller	1.000	28	64	6	0	2
Romero	1.000	6	11	0	0	0
Salome	1.000	4	9	0	0	0
Sanchez	.979	47	87	7	2	0
Schafer	1.000	5	11	0	0	0

WISCONSIN TIMBER RATTLERS

LOW CLASS A

MIDWEST LEAGUE

Batting	B-T	HT	WT	DOB	AVG	vLH	vRH	G	AB	R	H	2B	3B	HR	RBI	BB	HBP	SH	SF	SO	SB	CS	SLG	OBP
Davis, Kentrail	L-R	5-9	195	6-29-88	.335	.373	.323	64	245	44	82	26	5	3	46	31	9	0	5	36	3	1	.518	.421
Davis, Khris	R-R	6-0	195	12-21-87	.280	.303	.273	128	457	86	128	26	4	22	72	77	15	2	4	120	17	10	.499	.398
Dennis, Chris	L-R	6-1	205	9-15-88	.270	.304	.259	128	455	72	123	35	7	18	87	61	5	0	1	143	11	3	.497	.362
Dhanani, Kyle	R-R	6-3	195	9-6-87	.132	.133	.132	17	53	3	7	2	0	0	2	6	0	2	1	19	0	2	.170	.217
Dykstra, Cutter	R-R	5-11	180	6-29-89	.312	.297	.315	100	353	66	110	10	5	5	39	55	8	4	0	72	27	8	.411	.416
Fatse, Peter	R-L	5-10	170	8-3-87	.212	.195	.217	56	179	27	38	9	6	3	31	26	4	2	7	48	8	2	.380	.315
Garfield, Cameron	R-R	6-1	195	5-23-91	.245	.174	.267	102	384	41	94	19	0	3	46	22	3	3	6	74	2	4	.318	.287
Gennett, Scooter	L-L	5-9	164	5-1-90	.309	.330	.303	118	482	87	149	39	4	9	55	31	5	3	4	91	14	4	.463	.354
George, Carlos	R-R	6-2	165	2-6-89	.217	.143	.239	19	60	8	13	2	2	0	10	3	0	3	1	11	2	2	.317	.250
Gomez, Carlos	R-R	6-4	215	12-4-85	.286	.000	.286	2	7	0	2	0	0	0	1	0	0	0	0	2	1	.286	.375
Halton, Sean	R-R	6-5	240	6-7-87	.221	.280	.197	23	86	11	19	4	0	1	15	5	1	0	1	14	0	1	.267	.269
Lind, Connor	R-R	5-11	170	6-10-87	.154	.273	.067	9	26	2	4	0	0	0	5	0	0	0	5	1	1	.154	.290
Marseco, Michael	R-R	5-9	145	1-7-87	.221	.214	.223	126	417	47	92	17	8	0	44	29	2	21	3	83	10	9	.300	.273
Miller, Erik	R-R	6-3	200	8-23-87	.189	.275	.163	58	169	17	32	4	0	0	9	10	5	4	2	35	3	10	.213	.253
Morris, Hunter	L-R	6-2	200	10-7-88	.251	.214	.262	71	291	38	73	19	4	9	44	20	3	0	0	58	7	2	.436	.306
Paciorek, Joey	R-R	6-2	225	9-20-88	.212	.167	.228	46	137	14	29	6	1	0	12	24	2	2	0	40	4	3	.270	.337
Richardson, D'Vontrey	R-R	6-1	200	7-30-88	.243	.264	.237	132	522	78	127	28	8	7	51	58	11	1	1	164	17	15	.368	.331
Romero, Franklin	R-R	5-11	180	6-24-88	.164	.172	.161	35	116	12	19	4	4	1	13	4	2	0	0	49	2	1	.293	.205
Stockfisch, Austin	B-R	6-2	205	4-26-86	.206	.217	.204	38	126	10	26	6	0	1	19	7	3	0	2	20	0	1	.278	.261

Pitching	B-T	HT	WT	DOB	W	L	ERA	G	GS	CG	SV	IP	H	R	ER	HR	BB	SO	AVG	vLH	vRH	K/9	BB/9
Almonte, Rigoberto	R-R	6-2	172	1-4-87	2	0	3.97	7	0	0	0	11	9	5	5	0	3	10	.220	.105	.318	7.94	2.38
Arnett, Eric	R-R	6-5	230	1-25-88	1	9	6.70	20	16	0	1	85	98	75	63	14	39	60	.282	.265	.294	6.38	4.15
Bucci, Nick	R-R	6-1	210	7-16-90	6	7	3.51	26	20	0	1	121	96	58	47	12	68	100	.220	.239	.206	7.46	5.07
Burgos, Hiram	R-R	6-1	210	8-4-87	5	7	4.48	19	8	0	0	74	77	40	37	5	21	62	.271	.248	.293	7.51	2.54
Butler, Tony	L-L	6-7	220	11-18-87	0	0	72.00	2	0	0	0	1	4	8	8	1	4	0	.571	1.000	.500	0.00	36.00
Costello, Matt	L-L	6-1	190	12-17-86	3	4	3.66	29	0	0	1	47	39	21	19	4	17	37	.229	.222	.233	7.14	3.28
Davis, Doug	R-L	6-4	215	9-21-75	1	0	1.29	1	1	0	0	7	6	1	1	0	3	4	.240	.200	.267	5.14	3.86
Heckathorn, Kyle	R-R	6-6	225	6-17-88	6	6	2.96	17	13	1	0	85	82	41	28	2	23	67	.246	.237	.252	7.09	2.44
Howell, Del	L-L	6-3	185	9-6-87	3	7	4.68	24	16	0	1	100	110	61	52	8	61	66	.284	.257	.294	5.94	5.49
Jeffress, Jeremy	R-R	6-0	195	9-21-87	0	0	0.00	5	0	0	0	8	0	0	0	0	3	14	.000	.000	.000	15.75	3.38
Jones, Alex	R-R	6-6	190	3-3-87	0	1	40.50	2	0	0	0	1	4	6	6	0	4	2	.500	1.000	.429	13.50	27.00
Krestalude, Damon	R-R	6-4	185	6-5-89	2	10	7.00	21	19	0	1	90	112	76	70	8	41	65	.307	.346	.276	6.50	4.10
Lamontagne, Andre	B-R	6-5	210	3-24-86	2	2	2.36	16	0	0	5	27	21	8	7	0	14	26	.219	.250	.200	8.78	4.72
Lasker, Maverick	R-R	6-2	190	2-17-90	7	4	4.61	23	17	0	0	105	106	62	54	3	35	70	.259	.286	.235	5.98	2.99
Manzanillo, Santo	R-R	6-0	190	12-20-88	1	1	5.77	26	0	0	0	53	58	36	34	3	30	40	.279	.250	.304	6.79	5.09
Nieves, Efrain	L-L	6-0	169	11-15-89	4	5	5.56	23	7	0	1	70	83	52	43	4	41	53	.295	.256	.312	6.85	5.30
Odorizzi, Jake	R-R	6-2	175	3-27-90	7	3	3.43	23	20	0	1	121	99	52	46	7	40	135	.220	.245	.202	10.07	2.98
Pokorny, Jon	R-L	6-2	225	4-4-88	4	6	3.43	46	0	0	17	60	47	26	23	5	26	87	.216	.190	.226	12.98	3.88
Robinson, Chad	R-R	6-5	210	11-3-87	0	2	5.84	10	0	0	1	12	9	9	8	4	5	7	.196	.125	.233	5.84	10.22
Rosario, Adrian	R-R	6-4	180	9-30-89	4	0	4.50	14	0	0	2	32	28	19	16	0	15	44	.230	.250	.204	12.38	4.22
Sanchez, Jose	R-R	6-1	180	10-4-88	0	0	43.20	2	0	0	0	2	7	8	8	0	2	1	.538	.500	.556	5.40	10.80
Sauter, Andrew	L-R	6-1	190	7-15-86	0	3	7.58	22	0	0	0	30	45	26	25	1	12	23	.352	.377	.322	6.98	3.64
Suppan, Jeff	R-R	6-2	230	1-2-75	0	0	2.08	1	1	0	0	4	7	1	1	0	3	4	.389	.333	.417	8.31	6.23
Thielbar, Caleb	L-L	6-0	200	1-31-87	0	2	5.60	30	0	0	3	53	65	41	33	6	14	43	.294	.297	.293	7.30	2.38

Fielding

Catcher	PCT	G	PO	A	E	DP	PB
Garfield	.989	101	758	76	9	6	10
Stockfisch	.980	38	269	18	6	1	7

First Base	PCT	G	PO	A	E	DP
Dennis	.987	66	582	21	8	48
Dhanani	1.000	4	32	0	0	2
Dykstra	1.000	1	11	0	0	0
Halton	.979	11	87	7	2	7
Morris	.984	58	478	27	8	41
Paciorek	1.000	1	2	0	0	0

Second Base	PCT	G	PO	A	E	DP
Dhanani	.889	2	5	3	1	1
Dykstra	.667	1	1	1	1	0
Fatse	.947	8	7	11	1	0
Gennett	.959	107	201	296	21	69
George	.929	5	13	13	2	5
Lind	.892	9	13	20	4	3
Marseco	1.000	3	7	10	0	2
Paciorek	1.000	9	10	30	0	2

Third Base	PCT	G	PO	A	E	DP
Dhanani	.844	9	11	16	5	4
Dykstra	.894	79	32	145	21	18
Fatse	.808	13	5	16	5	1
Marseco	.974	11	12	26	1	3
Paciorek	.886	34	17	53	9	3

Shortstop	PCT	G	PO	A	E	DP
Dhanani	1.000	2	3	3	0	0
Gennett	.923	13	15	33	4	5
George	.793	13	14	32	12	5

Marseco	.978	112	158	333	11	60
Paciorek	1.000	2	1	0	0	0

Outfield	PCT	G	PO	A	E	DP
Davis	.975	61	117	1	3	0

Davis	.981	87	159	0	3	1
Dennis	1.000	6	19	0	0	0
Fatse	.979	35	44	2	1	0
Gomez	1.000	2	3	0	0	0

Miller	.979	55	90	4	2	0
Morris	.941	13	13	3	1	0
Richardson	.946	131	281	18	17	4
Romero	.972	35	68	1	2	1

AZL BREWERS
ROOKIE

ARIZONA LEAGUE

MILWAUKEE BREWERS

Batting	B-T	HT	WT	DOB	AVG	vLH	vRH	G	AB	R	H	2B	3B	HR	RBI	BB	HBP	SH	SF	SO	SB	CS	SLG	OBP
Allison, Kenny	R-R	6-3	185	2-21-90	.296	.321	.287	51	203	39	60	11	1	2	28	9	7	5	1	46	16	4	.389	.345
Berard, Kevin	R-R	5-10	160	12-3-91	.212	.333	.200	10	33	3	7	0	0	0	3	1	0	0	2	11	1	0	.212	.222
Bivens, John	L-R	6-2	215	1-28-88	.187	.278	.158	22	75	9	14	3	0	1	9	6	4	0	2	21	4	0	.267	.276
Dhanani, Kyle	R-R	6-3	195	9-6-87	.250	.200	.263	13	48	6	12	2	0	0	8	2	0	2	0	15	3	1	.292	.280
Farris, Eric	R-R	5-10	170	3-3-86	.250	.250	.250	10	32	5	8	5	0	1	9	1	0	0	2	3	1	0	.500	.257
Felix, Steve	L-R	6-1	215	4-21-88	.171	.286	.143	11	35	5	6	2	1	0	4	2	1	0	0	6	1	1	.286	.237
Garvey, Robbie	L-L	5-8	165	4-26-89	.356	.316	.370	18	73	17	26	2	4	0	13	5	0	1	0	11	6	2	.493	.397
Gerut, Jody	L-L	6-0	190	9-18-77	.347	.444	.325	14	49	11	17	5	0	2	11	9	0	0	0	3	0	0	.571	.448
Javier, Jhonatan	R-R	6-1	197	9-16-87	.254	.130	.313	19	71	10	18	2	2	0	11	3	3	0	1	16	6	1	.338	.308
Johnson, Ben	B-R	6-0	220	10-17-81	.000	.000	.000	1	3	0	0	0	0	0	0	0	0	0	0	2	0	0	.000	.000
McKelvie, Demetrius	R-L	6-3	210	10-27-90	.174	.194	.167	30	115	17	20	4	3	1	8	6	2	1	1	60	1	0	.287	.226
Mittelstaedt, T.J.	L-R	5-10	185	2-13-88	.282	.231	.300	45	149	28	42	10	3	1	17	23	2	2	1	39	10	3	.409	.383
Neda, Rafael	R-R	6-1	215	10-12-88	.143	.000	.250	2	7	0	1	0	0	0	1	0	0	0	0	2	0	0	.143	.143
Ogrinc, Gerard	R-R	6-3	230	2-5-88	.000	.000	.000	1	4	0	0	0	0	0	0	0	0	0	0	1	0	0	.000	.000
Paciorek, Joey	R-R	6-2	225	9-20-88	.308	.176	.371	14	52	12	16	3	1	0	8	5	3	0	0	16	4	0	.404	.400
Parker, Justin	R-R	6-1	205	3-14-88	.242	.238	.244	18	62	10	15	5	1	0	12	5	5	0	1	18	2	0	.355	.342
Rivera, Yadiel	R-R	6-2	175	5-2-92	.209	.229	.203	49	206	22	43	8	1	0	23	9	1	0	2	72	6	2	.257	.243
Roberts, Tyler	R-R	6-0	226	10-25-90	.288	.344	.274	42	156	30	45	17	0	6	23	15	2	0	0	30	0	0	.513	.354
Rogers, James	R-R	6-2	250	3-13-88	.281	.267	.285	42	160	31	45	7	1	3	32	20	3	0	2	32	5	2	.394	.368
Shaw, Derrick	R-R	6-0	190	12-13-88	.269	.136	.310	30	93	12	25	4	2	1	15	9	1	1	5	18	8	3	.387	.324
Shaw, Nick	R-R	5-11	160	8-25-88	.339	.298	.356	48	165	34	56	13	5	0	19	37	4	1	0	31	14	1	.479	.471
Walla, Max	L-L	5-11	195	4-12-91	.252	.345	.228	38	143	27	36	8	1	2	21	15	4	1	2	59	6	3	.364	.335

Pitching	B-T	HT	WT	DOB	W	L	ERA	G	GS	CG	SV	IP	H	R	ER	HR	BB	SO	AVG	vLH	vRH	K/9	BB/9
Amedee, Dane	L-L	6-1	190	8-5-90	2	4	4.87	13	6	0	0	41	39	25	22	2	16	43	.248	.333	.228	9.52	3.54
Arnett, Eric	R-R	6-5	230	1-25-88	2	0	7.31	5	1	0	1	16	20	13	13	1	7	19	.313	.360	.282	10.69	3.94
Bashara, Charly	L-L	6-1	190	5-31-87	5	2	2.37	13	2	0	0	57	45	17	15	2	15	64	.218	.258	.201	10.11	2.37
Billings, Blake	R-R	6-5	200	1-8-90	0	0	9.00	1	1	0	0	1	1	1	1	0	1	1	.333	.000	.333	9.00	9.00
Bobo, Dexter	L-L	6-0	195	11-10-87	2	0	2.37	16	0	0	1	30	25	8	8	1	11	45	.217	.333	.187	13.35	3.26
Bramhall, Bobby	L-L	5-10	181	7-13-85	0	0	3.38	3	2	0	0	5	3	3	1	0	3	0	.385	.500	.333	0.00	10.13
Britt, Dan	R-R	6-4	180	3-13-88	2	1	3.33	9	7	0	0	24	29	9	9	1	7	19	.309	.282	.327	7.03	2.59
Bueno, Kristian	L-L	6-2	195	12-10-88	0	0	9.00	1	1	0	0	1	3	2	1	0	0	1	.500	.500	.500	9.00	0.00
Butler, Tony	L-L	6-7	220	11-18-87	0	0	9.00	1	0	0	0	2	2	2	2	1	0	3	.250	.500	.167	13.50	0.00
Crawford, Skyler	R-R	6-1	175	4-20-88	4	1	1.80	7	1	0	0	15	11	3	3	0	6	15	.208	.278	.171	9.00	3.60
Hall, Brooks	R-R	6-5	200	6-26-90	3	4	5.44	14	9	0	0	46	55	33	28	5	16	43	.294	.288	.298	8.35	3.11
Harvey, Seth	R-R	6-2	205	1-20-88	0	2	2.45	16	0	0	6	22	20	8	6	0	8	32	.241	.212	.260	13.09	3.27
Hawkins, LaTroy	R-R	6-5	195	12-21-72	0	0	2.45	2	2	0	0	4	4	1	1	0	0	5	.267	.143	.375	12.27	0.00
Holle, Greg	R-R	6-8	240	11-16-88	3	1	0.79	8	1	0	0	23	16	3	2	0	9	16	.200	.189	.209	6.35	3.57
Johnson, R.J.	R-R	6-3	185	3-23-92	0	0	7.23	9	5	0	0	24	20	20	19	4	19	14	.235	.297	.188	5.32	7.23
Kyles, Marques	L-L	6-9	220	9-24-85	1	0	7.11	12	0	0	1	27	27	21	20	0	17	23	.287	.300	.284	6.13	6.04
Marzec, Eric	R-R	6-0	190	1-13-88	0	0	4.15	3	0	0	0	4	5	3	2	0	1	7	.263	.182	.375	14.54	2.08
Oviedo, Jose	R-R	6-2	165	11-30-88	3	1	2.10	6	1	0	0	26	14	9	6	1	9	29	.157	.192	.143	10.17	3.16
Periard, Alex	L-R	6-1	215	6-15-87	0	1	19.29	2	2	0	0	2	6	6	5	1	4	4	.462	.429	.500	15.43	15.43
Rivero, Francisco	R-R	6-2	204	3-11-91	3	1	4.70	6	4	0	0	23	28	17	12	2	5	20	.308	.329	.283	7.83	1.96
Sanchez, Jose	R-R	6-1	180	10-4-88	0	1	2.05	17	0	0	7	26	21	11	6	0	4	33	.212	.316	.148	11.28	1.37
Schaub, Michael	R-R	6-2	180	5-31-92	1	1	4.88	10	7	0	0	24	18	14	13	1	12	21	.222	.282	.167	7.88	4.50
Shackelford, Kevin	R-R	6-5	215	4-7-89	1	2	5.40	13	6	1	0	40	33	25	24	6	16	25	.220	.171	.270	5.63	3.60
Stortz, Travis	L-L	6-0	175	9-27-88	2	0	4.58	12	0	0	0	20	24	12	10	0	8	19	.296	.158	.339	8.69	3.66

Fielding

Catcher	PCT	G	PO	A	E	DP	PB
Berard	1.000	1	7	0	0	0	2
Felix	1.000	5	22	2	0	1	1
Javier	.957	14	118	14	6	1	7
Johnson	1.000	1	4	1	0	0	1
Neda	1.000	1	6	1	0	0	0
Ogrinc	1.000	1	6	0	0	0	0
Roberts	.986	39	326	30	5	3	15

First Base	PCT	G	PO	A	E	DP
McKelvie	.982	17	156	5	3	14
Paciorek	.976	5	38	2	1	5
Rogers	.982	37	311	20	6	30

Second Base	PCT	G	PO	A	E	DP
Berard	.833	2	2	3	1	0
Farris	1.000	7	7	16	0	3
Mittelstaedt	1.000	8	6	19	0	2
Paciorek	1.000	3	3	3	0	0
Shaw	.975	42	65	130	5	28

Third Base	PCT	G	PO	A	E	DP
Dhanani	.875	12	6	22	4	4
Mittelstaedt	.970	27	17	47	2	4
Paciorek	.909	8	2	8	1	0
Parker	1.000	16	8	19	0	0
Rogers	—	1	0	0	0	0

Shortstop	PCT	G	PO	A	E	DP
Dhanani	1.000	1	2	1	0	0
Rivera	.954	49	83	164	12	40
Shaw	.913	6	3	18	2	0

Outfield	PCT	G	PO	A	E	DP
Allison	1.000	50	86	4	0	2
Bivens	.957	20	20	2	1	1
Garvey	1.000	18	26	1	0	1
Gerut	1.000	12	27	0	0	0
McKelvie	1.000	1	3	0	0	0
Mittelstaedt	1.000	10	15	0	0	0
Shaw	.972	27	33	2	1	0
Walla	1.000	36	66	7	0	2

HELENA BREWERS

ROOKIE

PIONEER LEAGUE

Batting	B-T	HT	WT	DOB	AVG	vLH	vRH	G	AB	R	H	2B	3B	HR	RBI	BB	HBP	SH	SF	SO	SB	CS	SLG	OBP
Allison, Kenny	R-R	6-3	185	2-21-90	.333	.500	.286	6	18	2	6	1	0	1	4	1	1	0	0	5	0	0	.556	.400
Bivens, John	L-R	6-2	215	1-28-88	.143	.050	.175	22	77	5	11	0	0	1	6	15	1	2	0	22	3	5	.182	.290
Dean, Brent	R-R	6-1	210	7-26-86	.272	.421	.225	44	158	27	43	12	0	4	30	9	7	0	2	26	0	2	.424	.335
Dishon, Johnny	R-R	5-11	193	3-21-89	.267	.290	.259	71	255	45	68	13	5	5	28	32	8	2	0	105	13	5	.416	.366
Garvey, Robbie	L-L	5-8	165	4-26-89	.291	.152	.324	43	172	28	50	8	3	4	20	13	0	1	0	31	7	6	.442	.341
George, Carlos	R-R	6-2	165	2-6-89	.324	.439	.280	59	241	34	78	9	2	1	25	6	3	2	1	38	8	7	.390	.347
Hawn, Cody	L-L	6-1	195	8-11-88	.308	.200	.335	65	253	36	78	20	0	13	61	35	7	0	0	58	0	0	.542	.407
Hopkins, Greg	R-R	6-1	200	11-22-88	.285	.393	.255	67	277	44	79	17	0	6	48	21	4	1	2	36	4	3	.412	.342
Keen, Reggie	R-R	5-10	180	12-2-87	.348	.316	.362	17	66	20	23	7	0	1	8	5	4	1	1	7	4	0	.500	.421
Lind, Connor	R-R	5-11	170	6-10-87	.136	.333	.086	15	44	6	6	1	0	0	2	3	0	2	0	9	0	1	.159	.191
Neda, Rafael	R-R	6-1	215	10-12-88	.250	.231	.259	11	40	1	10	0	0	2	4	2	0	0	6	0	1	.250	.348
Ogrinc, Gerard	R-R	6-3	230	2-5-88	.208	.125	.230	20	77	5	16	3	0	0	3	3	1	0	0	21	0	0	.247	.247
Pechek, Tony	B-R	6-2	195	10-12-86	.245	.400	.176	16	49	5	12	1	0	2	8	5	1	1	0	16	2	0	.388	.327
Roberts, Tyler	R-R	6-0	226	10-25-90	.000	.000	.000	1	3	0	0	0	0	0	0	0	1	0	0	1	0	0	.000	.250
Romero, Franklin	R-R	5-11	180	6-24-88	.291	.250	.303	48	196	34	57	7	3	5	25	4	5	7	0	53	7	4	.434	.322
Shaw, Nick	R-R	5-11	160	8-25-88	.235	.000	.235	5	17	3	4	1	0	0	1	1	0	0	0	5	0	0	.294	.316
Sizemore, Brandon	R-R	6-0	205	12-10-86	.255	.326	.235	50	196	31	50	12	0	7	32	14	2	0	3	42	2	2	.423	.307
Vucinich, Shea	R-R	6-1	185	12-1-88	.265	.304	.252	72	275	51	73	14	3	5	29	32	17	3	5	77	4	1	.393	.371
Walker, Mike	L-R	6-3	215	6-12-88	.277	.305	.269	74	267	41	74	14	2	8	41	60	2	0	0	78	1	1	.434	.413

Pitching	B-T	HT	WT	DOB	W	L	ERA	G	GS	CG	SV	IP	H	R	ER	HR	BB	SO	AVG	vLH	vRH	K/9	BB/9
Bashara, Charly	L-L	6-1	190	5-31-87	0	0	2.25	1	0	0	0	4	4	1	1	0	1	3	.286	.400	.222	6.75	2.25
Bernal, Ryan	R-R	6-4	220	10-21-87	1	2	6.86	14	0	0	1	21	27	17	16	3	11	13	.321	.394	.275	5.57	4.71
Burgos, Hiram	R-R	6-1	210	8-4-87	3	0	2.37	6	6	0	0	38	31	11	10	1	5	48	.215	.167	.264	11.37	1.18
Butler, Tony	L-L	6-7	220	11-18-87	1	1	3.86	8	0	0	0	12	8	5	5	0	10	8	.200	.250	.179	6.17	7.71
Cravy, Tyler	R-R	6-3	180	7-13-89	6	6	5.87	15	12	0	0	77	81	58	50	7	28	70	.269	.256	.279	8.22	3.29
Currie, Rob	R-R	6-6	230	4-29-87	2	2	3.61	24	0	0	2	42	33	19	17	3	11	38	.219	.250	.195	8.08	2.34
Frederickson, Evan	L-L	6-6	240	9-23-86	3	4	5.30	14	10	0	0	53	38	33	31	1	48	56	.204	.250	.185	9.57	8.20
Garman, Brian	L-L	5-10	180	7-19-88	3	1	0.90	22	0	0	9	30	20	7	3	1	18	42	.189	.200	.183	12.60	5.40
Jones, Alex	R-R	6-1	190	3-3-87	1	0	1.61	21	0	0	1	22	13	11	4	1	16	35	.165	.188	.149	14.10	6.45
Keeling, Thomas	L-L	6-3	185	3-30-88	0	0	21.13	9	0	0	0	8	8	18	18	1	23	7	.276	.273	.278	8.22	27.00
Lintz, Seth	R-R	6-1	170	2-7-90	1	3	10.07	15	4	0	0	39	61	45	44	6	25	27	.353	.446	.296	6.18	5.72
Marzec, Eric	R-R	6-0	190	1-13-88	4	4	1.53	20	0	0	0	29	21	10	5	1	8	39	.202	.200	.203	11.97	2.45
Miller, Matt	R-R	6-6	220	1-30-89	7	2	4.06	14	14	0	0	71	63	35	32	7	28	53	.244	.274	.216	6.72	3.55
Nelson, Jimmy	R-R	6-6	245	6-5-89	2	0	3.71	12	0	0	3	27	30	21	11	2	13	33	.268	.269	.267	11.14	4.39
Oviedo, Jose	R-R	6-2	165	11-30-88	1	3	8.90	9	6	0	0	29	46	31	29	3	15	18	.365	.245	.452	5.52	4.60
Periard, Alex	L-R	6-1	215	6-15-87	0	0	0.00	2	0	0	0	2	3	0	0	0	2	3	.333	.200	.500	9.00	0.00
Robinson, Chad	R-R	6-5	200	11-13-87	0	1	4.91	14	0	0	1	18	15	11	10	4	12	11	.221	.267	.184	5.40	5.89
Rosario, Adrian	R-R	6-4	180	9-30-89	1	0	1.26	5	0	0	1	14	11	2	2	0	3	15	.224	.120	.333	9.42	1.88
Ross, Austin	R-R	6-2	200	8-12-88	2	1	2.70	10	5	0	0	47	43	16	14	1	6	52	.246	.244	.247	10.03	1.16
Sanchez, Jose	R-R	6-1	180	10-4-88	0	0	0.00	1	0	0	0	1	0	0	0	0	0	2	.000	.000	.000	18.00	0.00
Thielbar, Caleb	L-L	6-0	200	1-31-87	0	0	3.68	9	0	0	0	15	16	7	6	2	0	9	.286	.278	.289	5.52	0.00
Thornburg, Tyler	R-R	5-11	185	9-29-88	1	0	1.93	9	0	0	1	23	15	6	5	2	11	38	.179	.143	.204	14.66	4.24
Wawrzasek, Stosh	R-R	6-0	225	8-30-90	2	4	4.98	14	12	0	0	60	65	34	33	5	18	58	.281	.263	.294	8.75	2.72

Fielding

Catcher	PCT	G	PO	A	E	DP	PB
Dean	.971	39	297	37	10	4	8
Neda	.988	8	77	8	1	0	0
Ogrinc	.985	19	172	24	3	1	2
Pechek	.992	16	110	15	1	1	4
Roberts	1.000	1	8	1	0	0	0

First Base	PCT	G	PO	A	E	DP
Hawn	.998	47	401	29	1	22
Hopkins	1.000	1	7	0	0	0
Sizemore	.990	11	94	9	1	5
Walker	.985	21	180	16	3	13

Second Base	PCT	G	PO	A	E	DP
Hopkins	.983	13	17	41	1	5
Lind	.952	13	23	36	3	9
Shaw	1.000	4	6	14	0	2
Vucinich	.981	47	79	125	4	16

Third Base	PCT	G	PO	A	E	DP
Hawn	.667	1	2	0	1	0
Hopkins	.946	46	25	98	7	2
Vucinich	.875	4	1	6	1	0
Walker	.847	26	21	40	11	2

Shortstop	PCT	G	PO	A	E	DP
Bivens	—	1	0	0	0	0

George	.909	58	111	148	26	22
Lind	1.000	1	2	2	0	1
Vucinich	.988	17	27	52	1	8

Outfield	PCT	G	PO	A	E	DP
Allison	.833	5	4	1	1	0
Bivens	.963	21	23	3	1	1
Dishon	.980	69	94	5	2	2
Garvey	.963	42	74	3	3	1
Keen	.963	15	25	1	1	0
Romero	.955	48	78	6	4	2
Sizemore	.932	34	51	4	4	0

DSL BREWERS

ROOKIE

DOMINICAN SUMMER LEAGUE

Batting	B-T	HT	WT	DOB	AVG	vLH	vRH	G	AB	R	H	2B	3B	HR	RBI	BB	HBP	SH	SF	SO	SB	CS	SLG	OBP
Abreu, Joan	R-R	5-11	180	7-15-90	.212	.250	.200	41	99	15	21	1	0	0	14	9	2	2	2	19	1	3	.222	.286
Arias, Hitaniel	R-R	6-6	202	9-20-90	.225	.196	.235	64	200	23	45	12	2	2	25	29	13	0	2	58	1	5	.335	.357
Cequea, Wilson	R-R	6-1	175	6-16-90	.283	.250	.293	38	120	16	34	5	0	2	22	13	2	3	2	15	3	2	.375	.358
De La Cruz, Jorge	R-R	6-1	180	9-9-92	.250	.375	.179	24	44	9	11	0	0	1	7	14	2	0	1	13	0	2	.318	.443
De Leon, Juan	R-R	6-4	217	2-27-92	.201	.159	.219	51	149	10	30	8	0	0	14	22	5	0	0	51	0	1	.255	.324
Diaz, Jhonatan	R-R	5-11	170	6-5-93	.080	.000	.105	11	25	3	2	1	0	0	2	0	1	0	0	11	0	0	.120	.115
Garcia, Jose	B-R	6-3	195	3-5-91	.205	.208	.204	59	200	25	41	9	2	3	17	16	12	0	2	64	13	4	.315	.268
Hernandez, Yonki	B-R	5-10	160	10-5-90	.207	.070	.254	57	169	26	35	2	1	2	15	40	10	2	3	53	14	5	.266	.383

Name	B-T	HT	WT	DOB	AVG	vLH	vRH	G	AB	R	H	2B	3B	HR	RBI	BB	SO	SB	CS	OBP	SLG
Hinojosa, Dionis	R-R	6-1	180	8-14-90	.071	.000	.071	8	14	2	1	0	1	0	1	1	1	0	0	5	0	2	.214	.188
Martinez, Andres	R-R	6-2	188	1-26-92	.245	.150	.270	64	188	21	46	4	2	1	13	22	2	4	1	70	16	7	.303	.329
Mejia, Deyvi	R-R	6-0	195	11-3-89	.161	.167	.160	14	31	4	5	1	0	0	3	7	0	0	0	6	0	1	.194	.316
Mendoza, Alejandro	R-R	5-11	156	2-12-92	.243	.444	.179	17	37	9	9	2	0	0	5	10	1	0	0	8	1	0	.297	.417
Mondesi, Raul	R-R	5-10	182	8-23-92	.233	.273	.218	36	120	18	28	6	1	2	18	8	5	0	1	34	4	2	.350	.306
Pena, Carlos	R-R	5-11	190	9-28-92	.236	.185	.253	42	110	13	26	4	2	2	13	16	3	2	1	29	0	1	.364	.346
Pena, Jose	R-R	6-2	192	3-3-93	.204	.204	.204	58	186	28	38	9	5	2	25	33	2	3	3	56	4	3	.339	.326
Puello, Ronny	R-R	6-6	200	10-23-89	.288	.391	.248	47	163	23	47	13	1	4	28	12	4	0	0	44	2	2	.454	.352
Rodriguez, Orton	R-R	6-2	187	9-15-89	.308	.353	.286	26	52	9	16	2	0	1	12	7	0	1	0	7	4	2	.404	.390
Salaya, Erickson	R-R	6-1	168	5-9-92	.275	.364	.250	28	51	13	14	1	0	0	7	5	1	5	0	13	6	3	.294	.351
Sanchez, Ruben	L-L	6-2	180	8-20-91	.301	.349	.283	54	163	37	49	7	2	0	18	21	14	1	1	19	19	13	.368	.422
Sotelo, Julio	R-R	5-11	182	4-1-91	.256	.200	.276	21	39	8	10	1	0	0	2	10	2	0	0	5	0	0	.282	.431

Pitching	B-T	HT	WT	DOB	W	L	ERA	G	GS	CG	SV	IP	H	R	ER	HR	BB	SO	AVG	vLH	vRH	K/9	BB/9
Almonte, Rigoberto	R-R	6-2	172	1-4-87	5	1	1.98	19	0	0	9	36	26	8	8	2	11	41	.213	.160	.227	10.16	2.72
Belen, Javier	R-R	6-4	190	10-19-91	0	2	5.82	10	0	0	0	17	17	12	11	0	16	12	.274	.167	.318	6.35	8.47
Capellan, Jean	R-R	6-2	190	10-8-91	0	0	6.10	10	0	0	0	10	9	8	7	0	13	9	.231	.182	.250	7.84	11.32
Cepeda, Jose	R-R	6-0	182	3-27-90	3	4	3.04	14	6	0	0	53	42	25	18	0	24	35	.227	.133	.245	5.91	4.05
Dicent, Joel	R-R	6-3	176	8-4-91	0	3	5.48	9	4	0	0	21	14	22	13	0	20	20	.165	.143	.169	8.44	8.44
Francisco, Juan	R-R	6-5	180	12-15-90	0	6	3.90	9	6	0	0	28	25	15	12	0	20	22	.250	.389	.220	7.16	6.51
Garcia, Jose	L-L	5-11	185	4-20-91	0	0	7.71	8	0	0	0	9	3	9	8	0	19	8	.130	.000	.130	7.71	18.32
Lambertus, Pedro	R-R	5-10	190	6-4-88	0	0	3.60	5	0	0	0	5	1	2	2	0	3	2	.059	.000	.083	3.60	5.40
Lorenzo, Leonard	R-R	6-0	190	7-16-91	3	1	4.26	8	7	1	0	38	28	25	18	6	30	34	.209	.129	.233	8.05	7.11
Mejia, Jairo	R-R	6-6	184	8-20-90	1	0	3.38	11	0	0	1	11	6	6	4	0	12	5	.171	.333	.138	4.22	10.13
Montano, Eliezer	L-L	6-7	170	10-21-91	2	5	4.41	12	9	0	0	51	58	40	25	3	25	31	.291	.222	.295	5.47	4.41
Mora, Elvis	R-R	6-1	170	2-7-92	3	0	6.63	15	0	0	0	19	18	14	14	2	14	15	.261	.333	.241	7.11	6.63
Pascual, Rolando	B-R	6-6	245	2-8-89	2	6	4.67	13	11	0	0	52	39	38	27	1	41	43	.211	.244	.201	7.44	7.10
Perez, Osmel	R-R	6-3	196	7-28-93	1	1	2.51	12	3	0	0	29	28	13	8	0	10	27	.237	.261	.232	8.48	3.14
Reyes, Eduard	R-R	6-0	174	8-23-90	1	3	2.50	9	7	0	1	40	31	16	11	1	16	42	.217	.250	.210	9.53	3.63
Roman, Christopher	L-L	6-0	190	6-18-92	0	1	12.79	11	0	0	0	13	18	24	18	1	22	13	.346	.500	.340	9.24	15.63
Ruiz, Manuel	L-L	6-5	175	12-12-88	2	1	2.88	11	4	0	1	34	21	15	11	2	33	52	.181	.143	.183	13.63	8.65
Saba, Jeffrey	R-R	6-2	152	9-7-91	3	5	3.90	12	12	3	0	62	57	41	27	4	21	37	.241	.263	.236	5.34	3.03
Santiago, Juan	L-L	5-11	176	12-23-90	0	0	3.81	12	2	0	0	26	19	16	11	0	27	34	.202	.000	.218	11.77	9.35
Sosa, Carlos	R-R	6-6	236	9-6-91	2	4	2.92	17	0	0	2	25	19	10	8	2	11	24	.221	.263	.209	8.76	4.01

Fielding

Catcher	PCT	G	PO	A	E	DP	PB
Cequea	.714	2	5	0	2	0	0
Diaz	.973	11	69	4	2	1	2
Mejia	.943	14	73	10	5	0	5
Pena	.971	39	258	41	9	2	8
Pena	1.000	1	8	2	0	0	1
Rodriguez	1.000	6	25	5	0	0	0
Sotelo	.980	20	85	14	2	2	3

First Base	PCT	G	PO	A	E	DP
Arias	.976	61	425	24	11	37
De Leon	1.000	11	56	2	0	5
Puello	.981	5	51	0	1	2
Rodriguez	1.000	2	8	1	0	1

Second Base	PCT	G	PO	A	E	DP
Abreu	.937	19	32	27	4	8
Cequea	.882	4	8	7	2	3
De La Cruz	.947	5	11	7	1	3
Hernandez	.949	50	84	66	8	15
Mendoza	1.000	4	2	4	0	0

Third Base	PCT	G	PO	A	E	DP
Abreu	1.000	7	2	6	0	0
Arias	—	1	0	0	0	0
Cequea	.923	21	18	54	6	9
De La Cruz	.697	17	2	21	10	0
De Leon	.848	31	24	71	17	5
Hernandez	—	1	0	0	0	0
Mendoza	.875	8	8	13	3	2
Pena	1.000	1	1	4	0	0

Shortstop	PCT	G	PO	A	E	DP
Abreu	.902	14	11	26	4	2
Martinez	.904	64	93	152	26	25
Mendoza	.824	7	4	10	3	2

Outfield	PCT	G	PO	A	E	DP
Abreu	—	1	0	0	0	0
Arias	1.000	1	2	0	0	0
Garcia	.987	50	69	5	1	1
Hinojosa	1.000	6	4	1	0	1
Mondesi	.917	33	51	4	5	0
Pena	1.000	2	3	0	0	0
Pena	1.000	49	71	7	0	3
Puello	.833	22	25	5	6	0
Salaya	.958	20	23	0	1	1
Sanchez	.971	48	96	4	3	2

Minnesota Twins

SEASON IN A SENTENCE: The Twins opened open-air Target Field by winning the American League Central for the sixth time since 2002, running away with it and clinching the division on Sept. 21, but in the playoffs they ran out of steam and into their nemesis, the Yankees, who swept them for the second straight season.

HIGH POINT: The Twins put the White Sox away with a four-game sweep in September, but Jim Thome's Aug. 17 walkoff, two-run homer against the White Sox, in a 7-6 victory at first-year Target Field, may have been the highlight of the year. A sellout crowd of 40,714 was on hand as the Twins were en route to drawing more than 3.2 million fans, and Thome was a smash hit, hitting a team-high 25 homers in just 276 at-bats and filling in admirably for Justin Morneau, who didn't play after suffering a concussion on July 7.

LOW POINT: With more than 42,000 fans on hand for two home playoff games, the Twins blew a pair of early leads against the Yankees, then were blown out 6-1 in the final game of the Division Series. Minnesota managed just 21 hits in three games. The Twins have just two victories in their last five Division Series (2-15) since losing in the 2002 AL Championship Series.

NOTABLE ROOKIES: Danny Valencia may prove to be the long-term answer at third base that the Twins have sought since Corey Koskie's heyday. He was the short-term answer in 2010 as he hit .311/.351/.448, played fine defense and held his own in the playoffs.

KEY TRANSACTIONS: Signing Thome in the offseason for just $1.5 million was the best move general manager Bill Smith made all season, even ahead of locking up Joe Mauer to an eight-year contract. Smith also added to the bullpen with solid results, trading blocked catcher Wilson Ramos to the Nationals for closer Matt Capps (2-0, 2.00, 16 SV) and giving up 7-foot-1 Dutch righty Loek Van Mil for lefty reliever Brian Fuentes.

DOWN ON THE FARM: Minnesota's six farm clubs had the worst winning percentage in the game at .434, dragged down by its top two affiliates. Double-A New Britain (.310, worst in baseball) and Triple-A Rochester (.340) were among the minors' worst teams, even though both had some prospects. Righthander Kyle Gibson, the 2009 first-round pick, cruised to Triple-A in his first full season, giong 11-6, 2.96 overall and proving his durability by pitching 152 innings.

OPENING DAY PAYROLL: $97.6 million (10th)

PLAYERS OF THE YEAR

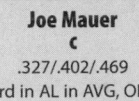

MAJOR LEAGUE	MINOR LEAGUE
Joe Mauer	**Kyle Gibson**
c	rhp
.327/.402/.469	(High A/AA/AAA)
3rd in AL in AVG, OBP	11-6, 2.96
3rd Gold Glove	126 SO/39 BB/152 IP

ORGANIZATION LEADERS

BATTING		*Minimum 250 at-bats
MAJORS		
*AVG	Justin Morneau	.345
*OPS	Justin Morneau	1.055
HR	Jim Thome	25
RBI	Delmon Young	112
MINORS		
*AVG	Ben Revere, New Britain	.305
*OBP	Aaron Hicks, Beloit	.401
*SLG	Joe Benson, Fort Myers/New Britain	.538
R	Aaron Hicks, Beloit	86
H	James Beresford, Beloit	146
TB	Joe Benson, Fort Myers/New Britain	247
2B	Steve Singleton, New Britain	43
3B	Angel Morales, Beloit/Fort Myers	10
HR	Joe Benson, Fort Myers/New Britain	27
RBI	Erik Lis, New Britain/Rochester	71
BB	Aaron Hicks, Beloit	88
SO	Daniel Rams, New Britain/Beloit	154
SB	Ben Revere, New Britain	36

PITCHING		†Minimum 75 innings
MAJORS		
W	Carl Pavano	17
†ERA	Brian Duensing	2.62
SO	Francisco Liriano	201
MINORS		
W	Miguel Munoz, Beloit	12
L	Tyler Robertson, Rochester/New Britain	14
†ERA	Daniel Osterbrock, Beloit/Fort Myers	2.65
G	Rob Delaney, Rochester	61
GS	Tyler Robertson, Rochester/New Britain	28
SV	Billy Bullock, Fort Myers/New Britain	27
IP	Kyle Gibson, Fort Myers/N.B./Rochester	152
BB	Shooter Hunt, Fort Myers	84
SO	Kyle Gibson, Fort Myers/N.B./Rochester	126
†AVG	Daniel Osterbrock, Beloit/Fort Myers	.236

General Manager: Bill Smith. **Farm Director:** Jim Rantz. **Scouting Director:** Deron Johnson.

Class	Team	League	W	L	PCT	Finish*	Manager(s)
Majors	Minnesota Twins	American	94	68	.580	3rd (14)	Ron Gardenhire
Triple-A	Rochester Red Wings	International	49	95	.340	14th (14)	Tom Nieto
Double-A	New Britain Rock Cats	Eastern	44	98	.310	12th (12)	Jeff Smith
High A	Fort Myers Miracle	Florida State	64	74	.464	10th (12)	Jake Mauer
Low A	Beloit Snappers	Midwest	71	65	.522	7th (16)	Nelson Prada
Rookie	Elizabethton Twins	Appalachian	41	25	.621	2nd (10)	Ray Smith
Rookie	GCL Twins	Gulf Coast	29	31	.483	10th (15)	Chris Heintz/Ramon Borrego

Overall 2010 Minor League Record 298 388 .434 30th (30)
*Finish in overall standings (No. of teams in league). †League champion.

ORGANIZATION STATISTICS

MINNESOTA TWINS

AMERICAN LEAGUE

Batting	B-T	HT	WT	DOB	AVG	vLH	vRH	G	AB	R	H	2B	3B	HR	RBI	BB	HBP	SH	SF	SO	SB	CS	SLG	OBP
Butera, Drew	R-R	6-1	205	8-9-83	.197	.183	.207	49	142	12	28	6	1	2	13	4	4	3	2	25	0	0	.296	.237
Casilla, Alexi	B-R	5-9	185	7-20-84	.276	.364	.252	69	152	26	42	7	4	1	20	13	0	4	1	17	6	1	.395	.331
Cuddyer, Michael	R-R	6-2	225	3-27-79	.271	.285	.265	157	609	93	165	37	5	14	81	58	4	0	4	93	7	3	.417	.336
Hardy, J.J.	R-R	6-2	200	8-19-82	.268	.210	.294	101	340	44	91	19	3	6	38	28	0	3	4	54	1	1	.394	.320
Harris, Brendan	R-R	6-1	205	8-26-80	.157	.178	.143	43	108	11	17	3	0	1	4	9	2	0	1	23	0	0	.213	.233
Hudson, Orlando	B-R	6-0	190	12-12-77	.268	.261	.272	126	497	80	133	24	5	6	37	50	4	5	3	87	10	3	.372	.338
Hughes, Luke	R-R	5-11	205	8-2-84	.286	.250	.333	2	7	1	2	0	0	1	1	0	0	0	0	3	0	1	.714	.286
Kubel, Jason	L-R	6-0	210	5-25-82	.249	.225	.260	143	518	68	129	23	3	21	92	56	3	0	5	116	0	1	.427	.323
Mauer, Joe	L-R	6-5	230	4-19-83	.327	.272	.365	137	510	88	167	43	1	9	75	65	3	0	6	53	1	4	.469	.402
Morales, Jose	B-R	5-11	200	2-24-83	.194	.250	.188	19	36	4	7	2	0	0	7	6	0	0	2	14	0	0	.250	.295
Morneau, Justin	L-R	6-4	235	5-15-81	.345	.325	.358	81	296	53	102	25	1	18	56	50	0	0	2	62	0	0	.618	.437
Plouffe, Trevor	R-R	6-2	200	6-15-86	.146	.200	.139	22	41	7	6	1	0	2	6	0	0	2	1	14	0	0	.317	.143
Punto, Nick	B-R	5-9	190	11-8-77	.238	.253	.231	88	252	24	60	11	1	1	20	28	1	4	3	50	6	2	.302	.313
Ramos, Wilson	R-R	6-0	220	8-10-87	.296	.556	.167	7	27	2	8	3	0	0	1	0	1	0	0	3	0	0	.407	.321
Repko, Jason	R-R	5-11	190	12-27-80	.228	.196	.250	58	127	19	29	6	0	3	9	13	5	1	0	38	3	2	.346	.324
Revere, Ben	L-R	5-9	175	5-3-88	.179	.154	.200	13	28	1	5	0	0	0	2	2	0	0	0	5	0	1	.179	.233
Span, Denard	L-L	6-0	205	2-27-84	.264	.279	.256	153	629	85	166	24	10	3	58	60	4	10	2	74	26	4	.348	.331
Thome, Jim	L-R	6-3	250	8-27-70	.283	.241	.302	108	276	48	78	16	2	25	59	60	2	0	2	82	0	0	.627	.412
Tolbert, Matt	B-R	6-0	185	5-4-82	.230	.056	.275	48	87	8	20	4	3	1	18	9	0	1	3	18	1	1	.379	.293
Valencia, Danny	R-R	6-2	210	9-19-84	.311	.374	.280	85	299	30	93	18	1	7	40	20	0	0	3	46	2	0	.448	.351
Young, Delmon	R-R	6-3	200	9-14-85	.298	.312	.292	153	570	77	170	46	1	21	112	28	6	0	9	81	5	4	.493	.333

Pitching	B-T	HT	WT	DOB	W	L	ERA	G	GS	CG	SV	IP	H	R	ER	HR	BB	SO	AVG	vLH	vRH	K/9	BB/9
Baker, Scott	R-R	6-4	220	9-19-81	12	9	4.49	29	29	0	0	170	186	87	85	23	43	148	.277	.277	.277	7.82	2.27
Blackburn, Nick	R-R	6-4	225	2-24-82	10	12	5.42	28	26	1	0	161	194	101	97	25	40	68	.302	.285	.318	3.80	2.24
Burnett, Alex	R-R	6-0	210	7-26-87	2	2	5.29	41	0	0	0	48	52	28	28	6	23	37	.287	.351	.258	6.99	4.34
Capps, Matt	R-R	6-2	245	9-3-83	2	0	2.00	27	0	0	16	27	24	7	6	1	8	21	.247	.255	.240	7.00	2.67
Crain, Jesse	R-R	6-1	215	7-5-81	1	1	3.04	71	0	0	1	68	53	27	23	5	27	62	.215	.196	.228	8.21	3.57
Delaney, Rob	L-R	6-3	230	9-8-84	0	0	9.00	1	0	0	0	1	2	1	1	1	1	0	.500	.000	.667	0.00	9.00
Duensing, Brian	L-L	5-11	195	2-22-83	10	3	2.62	53	13	1	0	131	122	42	38	11	35	78	.247	.162	.282	5.37	2.41
Flores, Randy	L-L	6-0	190	7-31-75	0	0	4.91	11	0	0	0	4	10	2	2	2	2	2	.500	.636	.333	4.91	4.91
Fox, Matt	R-R	6-2	195	12-4-82	1	1	3.18	1	1	0	0	6	4	2	2	0	1	0	.211	.286	.167	0.00	1.59
2-team total (3 Boston)					0	0	4.91	4	1	0	0	7	8	4	4	0	2	0	—	—	—	0.00	2.45
Fuentes, Brian	L-L	6-4	230	8-9-75	0	0	0.00	9	0	0	1	10	3	0	0	0	2	8	.094	.111	.087	7.45	1.86
2-team total (39 Los Angeles)					4	1	2.81	48	0	0	24	48	31	17	15	5	20	47	—	—	—	8.81	3.75
Guerrier, Matt	R-R	6-3	195	8-2-78	5	7	3.17	74	0	0	1	71	56	28	25	7	22	42	.219	.236	.210	5.32	2.79
Liriano, Francisco	L-L	6-2	220	10-26-83	14	10	3.62	31	31	0	0	192	184	77	77	9	58	201	.252	.218	.262	9.44	2.72
Mahay, Ron	L-L	6-2	195	6-28-71	1	1	3.44	41	0	0	0	34	33	15	13	5	8	25	.252	.219	.284	6.62	2.12
Manship, Jeff	R-R	6-2	210	1-16-85	2	1	5.28	13	1	0	0	29	34	20	17	3	6	21	.293	.236	.344	6.52	1.86
Mijares, Jose	L-L	6-0	230	10-29-84	1	1	3.31	47	0	0	0	33	34	14	12	4	9	28	.268	.268	.268	7.71	2.48
Neshek, Pat	B-R	6-3	210	9-4-80	1	0	5.00	11	0	0	0	9	7	5	5	1	8	9	.206	.286	.185	9.00	8.00
Pavano, Carl	R-R	6-5	250	1-8-76	17	11	3.75	32	32	7	0	221	227	95	92	24	37	117	.266	.292	.242	4.76	1.51
Perkins, Glen	L-L	6-0	205	3-2-83	1	1	5.82	13	1	0	0	22	29	16	14	3	5	14	.337	.241	.386	5.82	2.08
Rauch, Jon	R-R	6-11	290	9-27-78	3	1	3.12	59	0	0	21	58	61	20	20	3	14	46	.268	.288	.248	7.18	2.18
Slama, Anthony	R-R	6-3	205	1-6-84	0	1	7.71	5	0	0	0	5	6	4	4	1	5	5	.300	.333	.273	9.64	9.64
Slowey, Kevin	R-R	6-3	205	5-4-84	13	6	4.45	30	28	0	0	156	172	80	77	21	29	116	.280	.275	.284	6.71	1.68

Fielding

Catcher	PCT	G	PO	A	E	DP	PB
Butera	.985	47	301	26	5	3	4
Mauer	.996	112	696	34	3	3	4
Morales	1.000	11	43	1	0	0	0
Ramos	1.000	7	41	1	0	0	0

First Base	PCT	G	PO	A	E	DP
Cuddyer	.996	84	760	39	3	70
Harris	1.000	3	14	0	0	1
Morales	1.000	2	19	2	0	2
Morneau	.999	77	674	59	1	64

Tolbert	1.000	4	5	0	0	0

Second Base	PCT	G	PO	A	E	DP
Casilla	.988	24	34	51	1	11
Cuddyer	1.000	1	3	3	0	0
Harris	—	1	0	0	0	0

Hudson	.987	123	255	374	8	78
Plouffe	1.000	2	2	4	0	1
Punto	.936	12	15	29	3	5
Tolbert	.984	20	21	41	1	7

Third Base	PCT	G	PO	A	E	DP
Casilla	1.000	6	1	2	0	0
Cuddyer	.960	14	3	21	1	1
Harris	1.000	27	11	40	0	3
Hughes	1.000	2	0	4	0	1
Punto	1.000	48	29	93	0	6

Tolbert	.967	14	8	21	1	1
Valencia	.973	81	46	171	6	14

Shortstop	PCT	G	PO	A	E	DP
Casilla	.961	30	30	69	4	15
Hardy	.976	100	150	289	11	62
Harris	1.000	11	9	21	0	5
Plouffe	.971	9	13	20	1	5
Punto	.962	31	48	80	5	16
Tolbert	1.000	3	2	2	0	1

Outfield	PCT	G	PO	A	E	DP
Casilla	1.000	1	1	0	0	0
Cuddyer	.984	67	118	5	2	0
Kubel	.972	98	169	7	5	3
Repko	1.000	48	87	5	0	1
Revere	.947	11	18	0	1	0
Span	.990	153	407	5	4	3
Tolbert	—	1	0	0	0	0
Young	.984	149	239	12	4	2

ROCHESTER RED WINGS
TRIPLE-A

INTERNATIONAL LEAGUE

Batting	B-T	HT	WT	DOB	AVG	vLH	vRH	G	AB	R	H	2B	3B	HR	RBI	BB	HBP	SH	SF	SO	SB	CS	SLG	OBP
De San Miguel, Allan	R-R	5-9	200	2-1-88	.074	.111	.060	22	68	5	5	0	0	1	3	6	0	2	0	28	0	0	.118	.149
Dinkelman, Brian	L-R	5-11	195	11-10-83	.265	.312	.247	137	525	58	139	32	2	8	54	52	6	6	3	99	9	4	.379	.336
Fernandez, Jair	R-R	6-1	170	12-10-86	.176	.167	.179	12	34	2	6	1	0	0	1	6	0	0	0	8	0	0	.206	.300
Gardenhire, Toby	B-R	6-0	190	9-11-82	.188	.212	.176	50	154	14	29	1	0	1	15	11	3	4	1	16	1	1	.214	.254
Harris, Brendan	R-R	6-1	205	8-26-80	.233	.310	.199	62	232	31	54	14	1	4	29	14	7	1	4	41	0	1	.353	.292
Hughes, Luke	R-R	5-11	205	8-2-84	.257	.143	.326	22	74	12	19	8	0	1	7	5	1	1	0	18	2	0	.405	.313
Jimenez, D'Angelo	B-R	6-0	190	12-21-77	.225	.192	.241	67	231	20	52	12	3	6	43	27	0	2	5	48	0	1	.381	.300
Jones, Jacque	L-L	5-10	205	4-25-75	.280	.288	.278	96	339	36	95	24	0	4	31	18	2	0	1	84	4	0	.386	.319
Lehmann, Danny	R-R	5-11	185	9-5-85	.263	.321	.229	25	76	9	20	7	0	0	5	7	2	3	0	6	0	0	.355	.341
Lis, Erik	L-L	6-1	220	3-8-84	.205	.156	.223	51	166	15	34	7	0	6	23	10	2	1	2	46	0	1	.355	.256
Macri, Matt	R-R	6-2	215	5-29-82	.251	.291	.232	97	338	46	85	23	1	9	36	33	4	2	4	91	2	5	.405	.322
Martin, Dustin	L-L	6-2	215	4-4-84	.257	.247	.261	132	483	70	124	24	7	11	67	52	0	2	0	138	12	7	.404	.329
Morales, Jose	B-R	5-11	200	2-20-83	.264	.279	.259	73	258	30	68	19	1	3	25	34	1	1	1	63	0	0	.380	.350
Ortiz, Yancarlos	B-R	5-9	150	9-15-84	.241	.000	.269	7	29	5	7	1	1	1	6	2	0	0	2	5	0	0	.448	.273
Peterson, Brock	R-R	6-3	215	11-20-83	.245	.252	.242	128	437	63	107	21	3	19	57	51	9	1	4	131	0	2	.437	.333
Plouffe, Trevor	R-R	6-2	205	6-15-86	.244	.246	.243	102	402	53	98	22	4	15	49	27	6	8	2	90	5	5	.430	.300
Ramos, Wilson	R-R	6-0	220	8-10-87	.241	.296	.218	71	278	25	67	14	0	5	30	12	3	2	0	49	1	2	.345	.280
2-team total (20 Syracuse)					.258	—		91	357	39	92	17	1	8	38	15	3	2	0	61	1	2	.378	.293
Repko, Jason	R-R	5-11	190	12-27-80	.281	.232	.297	60	228	38	64	8	2	6	28	30	2	2	1	49	10	3	.412	.368
Roberts, Brandon	L-R	6-0	185	11-9-84	.333	.367	.317	38	153	19	51	7	2	1	15	10	5	0	3	20	9	3	.425	.386
Tolbert, Matt	B-R	6-0	185	5-4-82	.283	.289	.281	42	173	19	49	9	3	1	11	13	0	1	1	30	6	1	.387	.332
Valencia, Danny	R-R	6-2	210	9-19-84	.292	.254	.311	49	185	22	54	15	0	4	24	14	2	0	1	34	2	0	.373	.347

Pitching	B-T	HT	WT	DOB	W	L	ERA	G	GS	CG	SV	IP	H	R	ER	HR	BB	SO	AVG	vLH	vRH	K/9	BB/9
Blackburn, Nick	R-R	6-4	225	2-24-82	1	0	2.49	4	4	0	0	22	19	7	6	2	6	13	.229	.216	.250	5.40	2.49
Bromberg, David	L-R	6-5	241	9-14-87	1	4	3.98	9	9	0	0	52	47	30	23	9	13	47	.234	.216	.253	8.13	2.25
Burnett, Alex	R-R	6-0	210	7-26-87	0	2	5.49	14	0	0	2	20	26	12	12	1	8	18	.329	.385	.275	8.24	3.66
Condrey, Clay	R-R	6-3	225	11-19-75	0	0	18.00	1	0	0	0	1	3	2	2	0	0	0	.500	1.000	.400	0.00	0.00
Delaney, Rob	L-R	6-3	230	9-8-84	7	9	4.72	61	0	0	4	80	82	48	42	12	23	92	.264	.220	.304	10.35	2.59
DeVries, Cole	R-R	6-2	185	2-12-85	0	3	5.79	9	3	0	0	23	26	17	15	2	14	24	.277	.241	.325	9.26	5.40
Fox, Matt	R-R	6-2	195	12-4-82	6	9	3.95	35	21	0	0	123	124	61	54	17	51	104	.264	.296	.234	7.61	3.73
Gibson, Kyle	R-R	6-6	210	10-23-87	0	0	1.72	3	3	0	0	16	12	5	3	0	5	9	.214	.200	.226	5.17	2.87
Guerra, Deolis	R-R	6-5	250	4-17-89	0	3	6.84	5	4	0	0	25	35	21	19	5	8	18	.337	.397	.261	6.48	2.88
Gutierrez, Carlos	R-R	6-3	205	9-22-86	0	0	2.25	2	0	0	0	4	5	1	1	0	2	6	.333	.333	.333	13.50	4.50
Hennessey, Brad	R-R	6-2	195	2-7-80	1	3	7.76	14	1	0	0	27	46	25	23	5	8	13	.377	.412	.352	4.39	2.70
Herrera, Yoslan	R-R	6-2	200	4-28-81	0	3	6.07	6	6	0	0	27	33	19	18	3	15	14	.306	.315	.296	4.72	5.06
Hirschfeld, Steve	R-R	6-5	226	9-8-85	0	0	4.50	1	1	0	0	6	6	3	3	2	1	2	.250	.375	.188	3.00	1.50
Lahey, Tim	R-R	6-6	250	2-7-82	5	3	5.08	45	1	0	0	80	72	48	45	8	43	57	.247	.293	.208	6.44	4.86
Lugo, Jose	L-L	6-1	180	4-10-84	0	6	6.72	56	2	0	0	86	106	68	64	16	44	84	.298	.305	.293	8.82	4.62
Manship, Jeff	R-R	6-2	210	1-16-85	3	8	5.13	19	18	1	0	98	134	60	56	13	22	83	.329	.348	.314	7.60	2.01
Maroth, Mike	L-L	6-0	190	8-17-77	0	2	1.64	3	3	0	0	11	12	8	2	2	3	11	.261	.211	.296	9.00	2.45
Mijares, Jose	L-L	6-0	230	10-29-84	0	0	27.00	2	0	0	0	2	6	5	5	1	1	2	.545	.000	.750	10.80	5.40
Mullins, Ryan	L-L	6-6	180	11-13-83	4	7	4.60	19	16	0	0	90	106	49	46	14	26	58	.291	.235	.313	5.80	2.60
Neshek, Pat	B-R	6-3	210	9-4-80	5	3	3.89	30	0	0	1	39	40	21	17	4	13	25	.270	.343	.210	5.72	2.97
Perkins, Glen	L-L	6-0	205	3-2-83	4	9	5.81	26	24	0	0	124	160	91	80	14	36	98	.309	.326	.301	7.11	2.61
Province, Chris	R-R	6-3	220	1-20-85	0	2	6.06	2	0	0	0	16	15	13	11	1	7	16	.238	.265	.207	8.82	3.86
Robertson, Tyler	L-L	6-5	220	12-23-87	0	1	5.40	1	1	0	0	5	6	3	3	0	2	6	.273	.364	.182	10.80	3.60
Slama, Anthony	R-R	6-3	205	1-6-84	2	2	2.20	54	0	0	17	65	41	16	16	5	32	74	.178	.242	.130	10.19	4.41
Swarzak, Anthony	R-R	6-4	225	9-10-85	5	12	6.21	22	22	0	0	112	143	87	77	14	38	69	.312	.277	.345	5.56	3.06
Waldrop, Kyle	R-R	6-4	205	10-27-85	5	3	2.57	59	0	0	2	88	89	38	25	5	20	60	.262	.277	.247	6.16	2.05
Zink, Charlie	R-R	6-1	190	8-26-79	0	2	12.75	3	3	0	0	12	15	18	17	2	19	3	.306	.280	.333	2.25	14.25

Fielding

Catcher	PCT	G	PO	A	E	DP	PB
De San Miguel	.975	22	144	11	4	3	3
Fernandez	1.000	10	50	3	0	0	2
Gardenhire	1.000	1	2	0	0	0	0
Lehmann	.985	25	183	15	3	1	2
Morales	.986	35	268	13	4	3	7
Ramos	.988	54	384	29	5	5	2

First Base	PCT	G	PO	A	E	DP
Jimenez	1.000	2	17	0	0	2
Lis	1.000	12	104	12	0	8
Macri	.979	6	45	2	1	3
Peterson	.990	127	1000	86	11	99

Second Base	PCT	G	PO	A	E	DP
Dinkelman	.983	25	45	73	2	10

Gardenhire	.963	36	64	94	6	24
Harris	.976	13	13	27	1	5
Hughes	.985	16	26	39	1	4
Jimenez	.968	16	30	31	2	5
Macri	.969	34	46	78	4	18
Plouffe	1.000	2	3	5	0	3
Tolbert	.989	19	40	49	1	23

Third Base	PCT	G	PO	A	E	DP
Gardenhire	1.000	2	2	6	0	0
Harris	.923	23	11	37	4	5
Hughes	1.000	4	3	6	0	2
Jimenez	.950	32	22	54	4	4
Macri	.916	34	16	60	7	3
Plouffe	.941	7	4	12	1	1
Tolbert	.833	3	0	5	1	1
Valencia	.963	46	25	78	4	8

Shortstop	PCT	G	PO	A	E	DP
Gardenhire	.960	12	15	33	2	9
Harris	.986	21	27	44	1	8
Macri	.909	2	4	6	1	2
Ortiz	.933	7	10	18	2	2
Plouffe	.971	92	138	225	11	62
Tolbert	.919	14	17	40	5	7
Outfield	**PCT**	**G**	**PO**	**A**	**E**	**DP**
Dinkelman	.979	107	178	7	4	3

	PCT	G	PO	A	E	DP
Gardenhire	—	1	0	0	0	0
Jones	.981	79	150	2	3	0
Macri	.980	23	49	1	1	0
Martin	.970	127	288	4	9	2
Repko	1.000	60	148	2	0	0
Roberts	.968	38	88	4	3	0
Tolbert	.941	8	16	0	1	0

NEW BRITAIN ROCK CATS

DOUBLE-A

EASTERN LEAGUE

Batting	B-T	HT	WT	DOB	AVG	vLH	vRH	G	AB	R	H	2B	3B	HR	RBI	BB	HBP	SH	SF	SO	SB	CS	SLG	OBP
Benson, Joe	R-R	6-2	211	3-5-88	.251	.283	.240	102	374	65	94	20	7	23	49	39	9	0	1	115	14	9	.527	.336
Bigley, Evan	R-R	6-1	200	3-9-87	.336	.444	.302	27	113	17	38	9	1	4	15	3	1	0	1	22	0	2	.540	.356
Casilla, Alexi	B-R	5-9	185	7-20-84	.350	.286	.385	6	20	1	7	0	0	0	3	0	0	0	1	1	0		.350	.435
Cates, Chris	R-R	5-3	145	4-15-85	.197	.172	.204	90	290	25	57	5	0	0	13	17	2	5	0	20	4	1	.214	.246
De Los Santos, Estarlin	B-R	5-10	185	1-20-87	.177	.247	.144	64	237	21	42	11	1	1	17	21	2	4	1	60	6	8	.245	.249
De San Miguel, Allan	R-R	5-9	200	2-1-88	.217	.125	.237	16	46	7	10	3	0	0	8	10	1	1	1	18	0	0	.283	.362
Dolenc, Mark	R-R	6-3	218	11-8-84	.259	.297	.244	117	382	45	99	17	3	7	50	28	2	2	2	129	15	5	.374	.312
Fernandez, Jair	R-R	6-0	170	12-10-86	.267	.362	.233	55	176	21	47	11	1	4	23	15	1	3	1	30	0	0	.409	.326
Gardenhire, Toby	B-R	6-0	190	9-11-82	.225	.412	.087	15	40	2	9	1	0	0	3	3	1	1	0	6	0	1	.250	.295
Howell, Jeff	R-R	6-0	205	4-1-83	.209	.375	.149	25	91	9	19	8	0	2	12	3	0	0	2	24	0	0	.363	.229
Lehmann, Danny	R-R	5-11	185	9-5-85	.236	.321	.205	34	106	10	25	1	1	1	8	9	2	3	1	18	0	0	.292	.305
Lis, Erik	L-L	6-1	220	3-8-84	.233	.183	.247	76	283	28	66	12	0	10	48	24	3	0	2	71	0	0	.382	.298
Ortiz, Yancarlos	B-R	5-9	150	9-15-84	.171	.086	.189	77	199	14	34	3	0	1	13	16	0	1	0	46	2	0	.201	.233
Parmelee, Chris	L-L	6-1	220	2-24-88	.275	.226	.292	111	411	51	113	25	2	6	44	43	2	0	7	70	3	2	.389	.341
Portes, Juan	R-R	5-11	200	11-26-85	.213	.230	.207	127	441	48	94	17	4	9	55	43	5	2	5	96	0	1	.331	.287
Rams, Danny	R-R	6-2	221	12-19-88	.071	.167	.000	4	14	0	1	1	0	0	1	0	0	0	0	9	0	0	.143	.071
Revere, Ben	L-R	5-9	175	5-3-88	.305	.319	.300	94	361	44	110	10	4	1	23	32	8	2	3	41	36	13	.363	.371
Robbins, Whit	L-R	6-0	205	9-25-84	.146	.333	.083	16	48	3	7	1	0	0	4	5	3	0	0	5	0	1	.167	.268
Roberts, Brandon	L-R	6-0	185	11-9-84	.316	.138	.376	35	114	26	36	5	1	1	15	20	7	3	2	18	7	0	.404	.441
Singleton, Steve	L-R	6-0	185	9-12-85	.267	.248	.273	138	502	68	134	43	4	7	50	39	9	4	10	57	2	5	.410	.325
Solarte, Yangervis	B-R	5-11	176	7-7-87	.276	.273	.277	32	127	14	35	9	0	3	19	8	3	0	1	18	1	1	.417	.290
Soto, Alexander	R-R	5-11	205	11-8-86	.245	.250	.244	29	98	11	24	6	0	2	7	7	0	0	0	20	0	1	.367	.295
Streich, Tobias	R-R	6-0	218	4-5-88	.143	.250	.087	12	35	1	5	0	0	0	2	1	1	2	0	15	0	0	.143	.189
Tosoni, Rene	L-R	6-0	195	7-2-86	.270	.237	.286	52	185	22	50	8	4	4	24	25	5	2	2	52	3	1	.422	.369

Pitching	B-T	HT	WT	DOB	W	L	ERA	G	GS	CG	SV	IP	H	R	ER	HR	BB	SO	AVG	vLH	vRH	K/9	BB/9
Allen, Michael	R-R	6-3	220	5-27-87	1	1	7.84	16	0	0	0	21	31	27	18	2	10	14	.330	.372	.294	6.10	4.35
Arias, Henry	R-R	6-2	201	1-6-85	0	1	11.42	6	0	0	0	9	18	11	11	1	6	4	.462	.444	.476	4.15	6.23
Arias, Santos	R-R	5-11	162	3-17-87	0	7	4.82	23	2	0	0	37	41	24	20	5	20	25	.281	.286	.275	6.03	4.82
Blevins, Steve	R-R	6-2	215	11-17-86	0	0	4.35	4	0	0	1	10	9	6	5	0	2	7	.225	.263	.190	6.10	1.74
Bromberg, David	L-R	6-5	241	9-14-87	5	5	3.62	17	17	0	0	99	105	43	40	4	35	65	.273	.236	.311	5.89	3.17
Bullock, Billy	R-R	6-6	225	2-27-88	2	4	3.44	30	0	0	13	37	34	18	14	3	24	60	.239	.235	.243	14.73	5.89
Davis, Tony	B-L	5-11	185	1-16-88	1	2	2.68	25	0	0	1	37	26	16	11	0	28	26	.203	.214	.194	6.32	6.81
DeVries, Cole	R-R	6-2	185	2-12-85	1	5	5.80	39	2	0	1	68	87	53	44	10	25	63	.309	.315	.302	8.30	3.29
Gibson, Kyle	R-R	6-6	210	10-23-87	7	5	3.68	16	16	1	0	93	91	39	38	5	22	77	.259	.275	.241	7.45	2.13
Guerra, Deolis	R-R	6-5	250	4-17-89	2	10	6.24	19	19	1	0	102	127	83	71	14	37	67	.308	.322	.293	5.89	3.25
Gutierrez, Carlos	R-R	6-3	205	9-22-86	5	8	4.57	32	16	0	2	122	136	71	62	7	50	81	.291	.313	.273	5.98	3.69
Hirschfeld, Steve	R-R	6-5	226	9-8-85	0	0	5.32	11	3	0	0	22	22	14	13	4	13	21	.265	.268	.262	8.59	5.32
Holbrooks, Kane	R-R	6-3	230	6-8-87	0	0	5.40	1	1	0	0	5	6	3	3	1	1	3	.316	.400	.222	5.40	1.80
Lanigan, Bobby	R-R	6-4	220	5-5-87	2	3	5.23	9	8	0	0	41	54	25	24	5	12	17	.314	.366	.267	3.70	2.61
Martin, Blake	L-L	6-2	182	6-19-86	0	1	8.10	8	0	0	0	13	18	14	12	3	6	10	.316	.235	.350	6.75	4.05
McCardell, Mike	R-R	6-5	220	4-13-85	3	13	5.28	31	23	2	0	150	178	95	88	23	46	81	.299	.327	.271	4.86	2.76
Province, Chris	R-R	6-3	220	1-20-85	6	6	5.58	45	4	0	5	81	101	51	50	6	32	46	.305	.331	.281	5.13	3.57
Pugh, Bruce	R-R	6-3	180	7-18-88	0	2	15.43	2	2	0	0	7	15	16	12	2	8	4	.429	.467	.400	5.14	10.29
Robertson, Tyler	L-L	6-5	220	12-23-87	4	13	5.41	27	27	0	0	145	181	100	87	17	57	91	.308	.275	.323	5.66	3.55
Steedley, Spencer	L-L	6-2	194	5-31-85	1	3	3.00	10	0	0	0	18	15	8	6	3	7	7	.221	.200	.273	9.50	3.50
Testa, Joe	L-L	5-10	175	12-18-85	1	1	8.25	21	0	0	0	24	28	25	22	3	16	21	.301	.200	.377	7.88	6.00
Van Mil, Loek	R-R	7-1	220	9-15-84	1	2	6.37	23	0	0	0	30	40	24	21	1	22	21	.315	.407	.247	6.37	6.67
Watts, Dakota	R-R	6-5	201	11-16-87	0	0	12.27	2	0	0	0	4	4	5	5	0	2	5	.267	.375	.143	12.27	4.91
Williams, Matt	R-R	6-1	180	2-28-87	2	3	5.23	28	2	0	3	43	48	33	25	6	19	28	.274	.277	.272	5.86	3.98

Fielding

Catcher	PCT	G	PO	A	E	DP	PB
De San Miguel	1.000	16	99	9	0	2	0
Fernandez	.991	40	197	21	2	1	3
Gardenhire	1.000	1	9	0	0	0	0
Howell	.989	23	162	11	2	1	6
Lehmann	.986	33	193	20	3	1	3
Rams	1.000	4	27	3	0	1	0
Soto	1.000	23	139	16	0	5	2
Streich	1.000	8	48	3	0	0	2

First Base	PCT	G	PO	A	E	DP
Gardenhire	1.000	3	34	2	0	4
Lis	.982	55	488	47	10	56
Parmelee	.987	72	588	76	9	65
Robbins	1.000	14	110	6	0	7
Soto	—	1	0	0	0	0
Tosoni	1.000	1	8	1	0	0

Second Base	PCT	G	PO	A	E	DP
Casilla	1.000	2	5	7	0	2
Cates	.961	14	21	53	3	11
De Los Santos		5	12	14	0	5
Gardenhire	.947	5	5	13	1	2
Ortiz	1.000	8	12	16	0	2
Portes	—	1	0	0	0	0
Singleton	.976	112	200	337	13	87
Solarte	1.000	2	1	4	0	0

Third Base	PCT	G	PO	A	E	DP
Casilla	1.000	2	1	3	0	0
Cates	1.000	12	4	19	0	1
Fernandez	.500	3	0	1	1	0
Gardenhire	.813	6	6	7	3	1
Ortiz	.947	35	23	67	5	6
Portes	.880	58	27	98	17	9
Singleton	.927	16	11	27	3	3
Solarte	.986	29	15	53	1	4

Shortstop	PCT	G	PO	A	E	DP
Casilla	1.000	2	2	9	0	1
Cates	.977	64	91	207	7	47
De Los Santos	.923	58	88	177	22	39
Ortiz	.959	29	46	70	5	21
Singleton	.667	3	0	2	1	0
Outfield	PCT	G	PO	A	E	DP
Benson	.978	96	206	13	5	3
Bigley	.980	22	40	8	1	1
Dolenc	.966	109	191	7	7	2
Lis	—	1	0	0	0	0
Ortiz	—	2	0	0	0	0
Parmelee	.974	36	69	6	2	1
Portes	.966	43	55	1	2	0
Revere	.982	91	216	7	4	0
Roberts	.986	34	72	0	1	0
Solarte	1.000	4	4	0	0	0
Tosoni	1.000	7	11	4	0	1

FORT MYERS MIRACLE — HIGH CLASS A

FLORIDA STATE LEAGUE

Batting	B-T	HT	WT	DOB	AVG	vLH	vRH	G	AB	R	H	2B	3B	HR	RBI	BB	HBP	SH	SF	SO	SB	CS	SLG	OBP
Benson, Joe	R-R	6-2	211	3-5-88	.294	.316	.288	21	85	16	25	11	1	4	13	8	3	0	0	21	5	0	.588	.375
Bigley, Evan	R-R	6-1	200	3-9-87	.262	.274	.258	97	374	41	98	24	1	2	28	15	3	4	3	80	2	1	.348	.294
Casilla, Alexi	B-R	5-9	185	7-20-84	.167	.000	.200	3	12	0	2	0	0	0	1	2	0	0	0	2	1	1	.167	.286
Cates, Chris	R-R	5-3	145	4-15-85	.202	.250	.190	33	104	12	21	1	0	0	7	9	0	2	2	7	3	0	.212	.261
De Los Santos, Estarlin	B-R	5-10	185	1-20-87	.274	.228	.288	59	234	25	64	11	3	0	23	22	2	3	1	55	13	2	.346	.340
De San Miguel, Allan	R-R	5-9	200	2-1-88	.194	.179	.200	49	139	17	27	6	0	5	24	31	4	4	2	53	1	0	.345	.352
Dozier, Brian	R-R	6-0	185	5-15-87	.274	.301	.266	93	350	44	96	11	1	5	42	44	1	9	6	41	10	4	.354	.352
Fernandez, Jair	R-R	6-1	170	12-10-86	.203	.067	.245	21	64	8	13	3	0	0	9	14	2	0	0	18	0	0	.250	.363
Goncalves, Jonathan	R-R	5-11	159	5-13-89	.240	.240	.240	97	325	37	78	9	0	2	24	38	8	4	2	96	6	6	.286	.332
Hanson, Nate	R-R	6-0	195	2-8-87	.254	.316	.235	110	405	47	103	18	1	11	49	37	7	1	5	70	2	1	.385	.324
Harrington, Michael	L-R	5-11	200	10-6-85	.153	.111	.157	36	111	5	17	3	0	0	5	8	1	1	0	31	0	0	.180	.217
Herrmann, Chris	L-R	6-0	200	11-24-87	.219	.188	.226	107	356	34	78	17	3	2	30	41	7	2	2	74	3	2	.301	.310
Kelly, Paul	R-R	6-0	185	10-19-86	.286	.286	.286	12	42	4	12	1	0	0	4	4	0	0	0	11	0	0	.310	.348
Morales, Angel	R-R	6-1	180	11-24-89	.272	.266	.274	73	261	35	71	11	3	1	19	28	3	7	2	75	11	5	.349	.347
Parmelee, Chris	L-L	6-1	220	2-24-88	.338	.389	.323	22	80	9	27	2	1	2	17	13	0	0	0	11	0	1	.463	.430
Roberts, Brandon	L-R	6-0	185	11-9-84	.333	.200	.347	14	54	8	18	2	0	1	8	2	1	0	0	6	6	0	.426	.368
Rohlfing, Dan	R-R	6-0	185	2-12-89	.242	.185	.257	41	132	13	32	13	0	1	13	15	3	2	0	36	0	1	.364	.333
Romero, Deibinson	R-R	6-1	200	9-24-86	.252	.250	.252	111	397	52	100	16	5	6	54	53	8	0	4	91	1	1	.363	.348
Romero, Nick	B-R	6-1	200	7-15-87	.251	.247	.252	110	394	39	99	27	5	3	44	43	4	2	7	85	4	2	.368	.326
Santana, Ramon	R-R	5-9	152	6-20-86	.199	.132	.220	45	156	15	31	10	2	1	12	11	5	1	0	51	1	1	.308	.273
Solarte, Yangervis	B-R	5-11	176	7-7-87	.320	.350	.311	45	172	19	55	9	1	2	15	13	1	2	0	13	3	0	.419	.371
Streich, Tobias	R-R	6-0	218	4-5-88	.292	.000	.368	7	24	4	7	1	1	0	4	2	1	0	0	7	0	0	.417	.308
Thompson, Drew	L-R	6-1	160	11-7-86	.203	.208	.202	78	261	33	53	13	1	4	22	31	1	2	4	76	4	1	.307	.286

Pitching	B-T	HT	WT	DOB	W	L	ERA	G	GS	CG	SV	IP	H	R	ER	HR	BB	SO	AVG	vLH	vRH	K/9	BB/9
Allen, Michael	R-R	6-3	220	5-27-87	0	2	6.00	21	0	0	3	30	31	23	20	3	14	35	.261	.308	.224	10.50	4.20
Alloway, Nick	R-R	6-4	225	1-6-89	0	1	24.00	2	1	0	0	3	10	8	8	0	4	3	.526	.667	.400	9.00	12.00
Arias, Henry	R-R	6-3	201	1-6-85	0	0	21.00	2	0	0	0	3	7	10	7	1	3	4	.412	.500	.400	12.00	9.00
Arias, Santos	R-R	5-11	162	3-17-87	4	5	4.17	12	12	1	0	69	76	37	32	4	15	28	.277	.248	.301	3.65	1.96
Blevins, Steve	R-R	6-2	215	11-17-86	3	4	4.34	33	1	0	3	58	77	33	28	1	21	38	.324	.310	.333	5.90	3.26
Bullock, Billy	R-R	6-6	225	2-27-88	0	4	3.62	28	0	0	14	37	39	15	15	2	19	45	.281	.306	.267	10.85	4.58
Carroll, Brett	R-L	6-1	210	8-10-87	1	0	3.38	3	0	0	0	8	10	4	3	0	0	7	.294	.125	.346	7.88	0.00
Carter, Bart	L-L	6-1	208	7-8-87	0	0	20.25	1	0	0	0	1	4	3	3	0	0	1	.500	.000	.500	6.75	0.00
Condrey, Clay	R-R	6-3	225	11-19-75	0	0	0.00	1	0	0	0	3	3	0	0	0	0	1	.273	.429	.000	3.00	0.00
Davis, Tony	B-L	5-11	185	1-16-88	0	0	2.87	17	0	0	1	31	32	13	10	1	18	19	.267	.216	.289	5.46	5.17
Deminsky, David	L-L	6-3	205	6-12-87	0	0	6.55	2	2	0	0	11	15	8	8	2	6	8	.366	.200	.389	6.55	4.91
Garcia, Jhon	R-R	6-1	216	5-19-87	2	1	2.08	11	0	0	3	26	18	8	6	1	6	20	.202	.139	.245	6.92	2.08
Gibson, Kyle	R-R	6-6	210	10-23-87	4	1	1.87	7	7	1	0	43	33	11	9	2	12	40	.213	.197	.226	8.31	2.49
Gonzalez, Jose	L-L	5-9	166	2-3-90	0	0	1.17	8	0	0	1	15	12	4	2	0	1	10	.207	.267	.186	5.87	0.59
Hendriks, Liam	R-R	6-1	190	2-10-89	6	3	1.93	13	12	1	0	75	63	20	16	2	8	66	.225	.233	.220	7.96	0.96
Hirschfeld, Steve	R-R	6-5	226	9-8-85	0	0	13.50	1	0	0	0	2	3	3	3	0	1	1	.333	.333	.333	4.50	4.50
Holbrooks, Kane	R-R	6-3	230	6-8-87	4	3	2.27	8	7	1	0	44	37	12	11	2	15	36	.226	.284	.169	7.42	3.09
Hunt, Shooter	R-R	6-3	200	8-16-86	1	5	7.35	40	7	0	3	67	54	62	55	5	84	79	.224	.163	.260	10.56	11.23
Lanigan, Bobby	R-R	6-4	220	5-5-87	3	1	2.15	11	10	0	0	54	43	19	13	2	7	41	.212	.209	.214	6.79	1.16
Lobanov, Andrei	L-L	6-3	171	1-25-90	2	0	2.03	14	0	0	0	27	26	7	6	1	5	22	.255	.133	.306	7.43	1.69
Mahay, Ron	L-L	6-2	195	6-28-71	0	1	1.93	4	0	0	0	5	5	1	1	0	1	4	.278	.000	.333	7.71	1.93
Martin, Blake	L-L	6-2	182	6-19-86	4	3	4.79	28	3	0	0	56	70	43	30	6	28	47	.310	.323	.304	7.51	4.47
Neshek, Pat	B-R	6-3	210	9-4-80	0	0	13.50	2	0	0	0	2	3	3	3	0	2	2	.333	.500	.200	9.00	9.00
Osterbrock, Dan	R-L	6-3	190	1-27-87	7	8	2.73	20	18	0	0	112	103	43	34	6	23	79	.243	.305	.228	6.35	1.85
Pugh, Bruce	R-R	6-3	180	7-18-88	7	10	4.03	20	19	0	0	103	81	52	46	10	48	106	.215	.263	.182	9.29	4.21
Salcedo, Adrian	R-R	6-4	175	4-24-91	1	3	6.26	6	6	0	0	27	42	21	19	3	8	16	.378	.390	.371	5.27	2.63
Schuld, Matt	R-R	6-3	210	12-7-87	0	1	3.78	6	0	0	2	17	17	10	7	0	4	11	.270	.261	.275	5.94	2.16
See, Zach	R-R	6-2	185	11-23-88	0	0	2.25	1	0	0	1	4	3	1	1	0	0	3	.231	.333	.143	0.00	0.00
Tarsi, Mike	R-L	6-8	202	8-11-86	5	10	5.02	24	18	0	0	99	110	70	55	6	36	70	.279	.267	.283	6.39	3.28
Testa, Joe	L-L	5-10	175	12-18-85	1	1	3.30	15	0	0	1	30	39	13	11	1	12	29	.312	.185	.347	8.70	3.60
Tippett, Brad	R-R	6-2	185	2-11-88	0	0	6.28	10	5	0	0	29	39	24	20	3	9	21	.315	.360	.284	7.22	2.83
Van Mil, Loek	R-R	7-1	220	9-15-84	0	1	4.50	3	0	0	0	4	4	2	2	0	0	6	.267	.222	.333	13.50	0.00
Watts, Dakota	R-R	6-5	201	11-16-87	4	2	3.19	17	0	0	6	31	26	11	11	2	12	29	.228	.277	.194	8.42	3.48
Williams, Matt	R-R	6-1	180	2-28-87	3	2	3.88	17	6	0	1	58	56	26	25	4	16	45	.248	.242	.252	6.98	2.48
Wimmers, Alex	L-R	6-2	195	11-1-88	0	0	0.57	4	4	0	0	16	6	1	1	0	5	23	.113	.143	.103	13.21	2.87

Fielding

Catcher	PCT	G	PO	A	E	DP	PB
De San Miguel	.983	48	323	27	6	4	4
Fernandez	.977	21	150	23	4	1	2
Herrmann	.988	42	301	26	4	2	3
Rohlfing	.978	28	196	22	5	1	6
Streich	1.000	7	29	3	0	1	2

First Base	PCT	G	PO	A	E	DP
Hanson	.993	101	789	78	6	72
Harrington	.975	10	73	5	2	9
Parmelee	.992	13	115	13	1	15
Romero	1.000	14	104	3	0	9
Romero	1.000	4	29	3	0	4

Second Base	PCT	G	PO	A	E	DP
Casilla	1.000	2	0	7	0	2
Cates	.857	4	6	6	2	2
De Los Santos	.969	22	38	56	3	16
Dozier	.979	12	22	24	1	5

(Second Base cont.)	PCT	G	PO	A	E	DP
Romero	.955	29	46	81	6	19
Santana	1.000	5	5	15	0	0
Solarte	.914	7	14	18	3	6
Thompson	.948	62	108	164	15	38

Third Base	PCT	G	PO	A	E	DP
Cates	—	1	0	0	0	0
Dozier	1.000	14	15	20	0	0
Hanson	.962	10	3	22	1	3
Romero	.888	43	23	96	15	9
Romero	.896	40	24	62	10	9
Santana	.857	7	4	8	2	0
Solarte	.934	29	16	55	5	4

Shortstop	PCT	G	PO	A	E	DP
Casilla	1.000	1	1	2	0	0
Cates	.913	26	33	51	8	13
De Los Santos	.907	35	59	87	15	20
Dozier	.948	66	92	165	14	34

(Shortstop cont.)	PCT	G	PO	A	E	DP
Kelly	.970	11	18	47	2	16
Solarte	.857	3	3	3	1	1

Outfield	PCT	G	PO	A	E	DP
Benson	.980	21	47	1	1	0
Bigley	1.000	88	161	12	0	1
Cates	1.000	3	1	0	0	0
Goncalves	.983	97	223	5	4	1
Harrington	1.000	24	34	1	0	0
Herrmann	.992	61	115	5	1	3
Morales	.986	72	201	6	3	4
Parmelee	1.000	2	4	0	0	0
Roberts	1.000	14	24	0	0	0
Rohlfing	.875	6	7	0	1	0
Romero	.923	18	23	1	2	0
Santana	1.000	20	28	4	0	0
Solarte	1.000	4	6	0	0	0

BELOIT SNAPPERS

LOW CLASS A

MIDWEST LEAGUE

Batting	B-T	HT	WT	DOB	AVG	vLH	vRH	G	AB	R	H	2B	3B	HR	RBI	BB	HBP	SH	SF	SO	SB	CS	SLG	OBP
Beresford, James	L-R	6-1	162	1-19-89	.297	.271	.307	126	491	70	146	19	5	1	59	34	6	7	2	56	14	14	.363	.349
Dozier, Brian	R-R	6-0	185	5-15-87	.278	.275	.279	39	151	24	42	7	1	0	17	16	0	3	0	16	6	1	.338	.347
Gonzales, Mike	L-R	6-6	270	6-16-88	.236	.187	.251	94	326	47	77	27	0	13	52	36	6	0	2	107	0	0	.439	.322
Hardy, J.J.	R-R	6-2	200	8-19-82	.000	.000	.286	3	10	0	2	0	0	0	0	1	0	0	2	0	0	0	.200	.333
Harrington, Michael	L-R	5-11	200	10-6-85	.275	.000	.304	16	51	8	14	4	0	1	9	6	1	0	1	11	0	0	.412	.356
Hicks, Aaron	B-R	6-2	185	10-2-89	.279	.362	.248	115	423	86	118	27	6	8	49	88	0	4	3	112	21	11	.428	.401
Hidalgo, Anderson	R-S	5-9	192	9-5-88	.316	.357	.298	81	282	38	89	25	1	3	28	24	4	3	2	50	3	9	.443	.375
Liddle, Steven	L-L	6-1	205	11-24-87	.253	.257	.252	116	435	63	110	18	0	15	70	50	3	2	3	80	14	4	.398	.332
Lin, Wang-Wei	L-R	6-0	191	6-28-88	.236	.241	.234	99	280	49	66	7	1	1	27	39	6	10	0	57	11	3	.279	.342
Martinez, Yorby	B-R	6-0	170	1-12-89	.191	.273	.176	49	141	23	27	5	0	0	11	20	1	7	1	41	1	1	.227	.294
McCallum, Derek	L-R	5-11	181	3-22-88	.228	.100	.270	47	162	15	37	11	0	0	15	19	4	3	1	42	3	4	.296	.323
Morales, Angel	R-R	6-1	180	11-24-89	.289	.333	.270	60	211	34	61	13	7	4	36	24	8	3	1	65	18	7	.474	.381
Pinto, Josmil	R-R	5-11	232	3-31-89	.225	.237	.220	100	347	60	78	21	1	10	54	32	5	2	6	67	2	3	.378	.295
Rams, Danny	R-R	6-2	221	12-19-88	.243	.238	.245	110	407	52	99	28	4	16	68	31	9	1	2	145	1	0	.450	.310
Ray, Lance	L-R	6-1	194	9-2-89	.279	.250	.285	47	165	30	46	14	0	3	28	28	1	0	5	28	4	4	.418	.377
Santana, Daniel	B-R	5-11	173	11-7-90	.238	.261	.234	40	130	14	31	4	3	0	11	7	2	2	2	40	10	4	.315	.289
Streich, Tobias	R-R	6-0	218	4-5-88	.124	.194	.100	40	121	10	15	4	1	0	4	18	2	0	1	44	1	1	.174	.246
Williams, Reggie	L-R	6-2	180	11-5-88	.236	.218	.242	106	360	39	85	19	4	6	53	31	4	9	3	76	7	14	.361	.302

Pitching	B-T	HT	WT	DOB	W	L	ERA	G	GS	CG	SV	IP	H	R	ER	HR	BB	SO	AVG	vLH	vRH	K/9	BB/9
Armstrong, Chris	L-L	5-10	184	2-10-88	0	1	18.00	10	0	0	0	10	25	23	20	1	11	10	.463	.421	.486	9.00	9.90
Blevins, Steve	R-R	6-2	215	11-17-86	2	0	3.86	12	0	0	6	12	13	6	5	2	8	9	.283	.250	.300	6.94	6.17
Cardenas, Eliecer	R-R	6-2	218	1-30-88	5	1	3.69	38	0	0	8	63	57	36	26	6	44	53	.245	.265	.229	7.53	6.25
Dempster, Clint	L-L	6-0	180	8-29-89	3	2	3.60	10	6	0	1	40	43	23	16	3	20	32	.267	.270	.265	7.20	4.50
Fuentes, Nelvin	L-L	6-0	196	4-7-89	1	1	4.60	15	0	0	1	29	26	20	15	4	11	41	.230	.205	.243	12.58	3.38
Garcia, Jhon	R-R	6-1	216	5-19-87	0	2	3.35	22	3	0	0	43	45	19	16	1	17	22	.273	.190	.318	4.60	3.56
Garcia, Martire	L-L	5-11	150	3-1-90	2	1	6.00	6	6	0	0	27	27	19	18	2	23	30	.252	.143	.291	10.00	7.67
Guerra, Pedro	R-R	6-0	180	1-9-90	2	1	3.54	8	5	0	0	28	28	13	11	0	23	20	.264	.250	.278	6.43	7.39
Hauser, Matt	R-R	6-2	195	3-30-88	1	0	0.00	4	0	0	1	7	5	0	0	1	4		.238	.333	.167	5.40	1.35
Hendriks, Liam	R-R	6-1	190	2-10-89	2	1	1.32	6	6	0	0	34	16	6	5	0	4	39	.138	.125	.150	10.32	1.06
Hermsen, B.J.	R-R	6-5	235	12-1-89	4	6	5.00	12	12	1	0	72	85	46	40	6	15	46	.295	.275	.310	5.75	1.88
Holbrooks, Kane	R-R	6-3	230	6-8-87	5	3	1.67	33	2	0	9	54	47	16	10	2	13	71	.227	.247	.213	11.83	2.17
Ibarra, Edgar	L-L	6-0	189	5-31-89	6	11	4.81	33	17	0	1	112	112	71	60	6	60	122	.259	.321	.237	9.77	4.81
Kennelly, Peter	R-R	6-2	217	11-15-87	0	3	7.14	32	2	0	1	47	51	43	37	4	38	40	.280	.272	.287	7.71	7.33
Lobanov, Andrei	L-L	6-3	171	1-25-90	1	2	3.44	21	0	0	2	34	37	18	13	1	9	30	.274	.381	.226	7.94	2.38
Munoz, Miguel	R-R	6-2	182	8-4-88	12	7	4.37	34	21	1	1	132	134	68	64	9	48	121	.266	.265	.267	8.27	3.28
Osterbrock, Dan	R-L	6-3	190	1-27-87	2	1	2.30	5	5	1	0	27	21	8	7	1	5	27	.208	.231	.200	8.89	1.65
See, Zach	R-R	6-2	185	11-23-88	1	0	7.04	10	0	0	0	15	16	15	12	2	11	9	.254	.280	.237	5.28	6.46
Spangler, Sam	L-L	6-2	195	9-24-87	0	2	9.16	12	3	0	0	19	22	20	19	4	12	20	.310	.364	.286	9.64	5.79
Stillings, Brad	L-R	6-4	208	1-20-88	8	4	3.40	22	19	0	0	98	102	48	37	3	40	75	.269	.216	.309	6.89	3.67
Stuifbergen, Tom	R-R	6-3	261	9-26-88	6	4	2.98	19	17	0	0	94	99	36	31	5	23	88	.273	.256	.289	8.46	2.21
Tone, Matt	L-L	6-1	219	2-17-88	3	5	5.09	11	0	0	2	69	71	43	39	4	44	76	.265	.244	.275	9.91	5.74
Tonkin, Mike	R-R	6-7	220	11-19-89	3	6	4.29	13	12	0	0	65	76	43	31	7	8	40	.287	.286	.287	5.54	2.49
Tootle, Ben	R-R	6-2	185	1-9-88	0	1	7.64	13	0	0	0	18	22	17	15	1	12	14	.286	.357	.245	7.13	6.11
Watts, Dakota	R-R	6-5	201	11-16-87	2	1	2.31	30	0	0	2	47	31	13	12	2	30	55	.193	.214	.181	10.61	5.79

Fielding

Catcher	PCT	G	PO	A	E	DP	PB
Pinto	.982	66	517	39	10	2	10
Rams	.992	46	339	41	3	4	12
Streich	.978	35	245	28	6	3	10

First Base	PCT	G	PO	A	E	DP
Gonzales	.982	77	564	37	11	51
Hidalgo	.800	1	4	0	1	0
Liddle	.971	15	94	7	3	9

	PCT	G	PO	A	E	DP
Rams	.981	45	342	28	7	25
Ray	.982	8	52	2	1	4

Second Base	PCT	G	PO	A	E	DP
Beresford	.985	28	62	72	2	21

Dozier	1.000	3	4	7	0	1
Martinez	.943	12	14	19	2	5
McCallum	.943	38	60	73	8	12
Santana	.965	25	38	73	4	5
Williams	.917	37	50	82	12	19

Third Base	PCT	G	PO	A	E	DP
Beresford	1.000	4	1	6	0	0
Dozier	.778	3	2	5	2	0
Hidalgo	.938	79	44	107	10	8
Martinez	.902	21	16	39	6	0

Pinto	1.000	1	1	0	0	0
Santana	1.000	1	0	1	0	1
Williams	.886	34	27	51	10	5

Shortstop	PCT	G	PO	A	E	DP
Beresford	.959	91	132	243	16	47
Dozier	.967	32	48	97	5	23
Hardy	.929	3	5	8	1	1
Martinez	.941	7	6	10	1	3
Santana	.800	12	14	18	8	3
Williams	.833	1	2	3	1	0

Outfield	PCT	G	PO	A	E	DP
Gonzales	.750	2	3	0	1	0
Harrington	.905	11	18	1	2	1
Hicks	.977	103	246	5	6	5
Liddle	.954	93	173	15	9	2
Lin	.969	89	181	7	6	1
Martinez	1.000	7	14	1	0	0
Morales	.971	58	94	6	3	0
Ray	.985	37	61	3	1	1
Santana	—	2	0	0	0	0
Williams	.979	28	45	2	1	0

ELIZABETHTON TWINS — ROOKIE
APPALACHIAN LEAGUE

Batting	B-T	HT	WT	DOB	AVG	vLH	vRH	G	AB	R	H	2B	3B	HR	RBI	BB	HBP	SH	SF	SO	SB	CS	SLG	OBP
Arcia, Oswaldo	L-R	6-0	210	5-9-91	.375	.330	.398	64	259	47	97	21	7	14	51	19	4	0	1	67	4	4	.672	.424
Arias, Jhonatan	R-R	5-10	180	2-18-89	.242	.233	.246	32	99	10	24	9	0	3	15	8	0	2	1	20	0	0	.424	.296
Burke, Brian	R-R	6-2	225	7-28-86	.286	.366	.250	60	231	37	66	15	1	6	26	14	6	0	0	63	0	0	.437	.343
Choi, Hyeong-rok	R-R	5-11	189	8-23-89	.237	.273	.222	11	38	5	9	1	0	1	4	4	0	0	2	14	0	0	.342	.295
Glad, Gunner	R-R	6-0	190	8-14-86	.241	.179	.275	44	158	14	38	9	0	2	15	7	7	1	3	32	2	0	.335	.297
Hawkins, Jamaal	R-R	5-9	180	10-27-88	.209	.148	.231	53	201	29	42	12	0	1	20	24	4	1	2	53	8	2	.284	.303
Henderson, Brandon	R-R	6-2	180	4-18-89	.243	.333	.215	35	103	13	25	6	0	0	11	7	5	0	1	35	3	0	.301	.319
Knudson, Kyle	R-R	6-3	210	9-12-87	.261	.237	.273	47	180	20	47	9	0	2	27	9	4	1	1	43	0	1	.344	.309
Leer, Andy	R-R	6-2	200	1-3-88	.266	.243	.276	63	248	35	66	17	1	5	36	16	2	0	3	63	2	2	.403	.312
Lockwood, Nick	R-R	6-1	175	1-7-91	.180	.133	.200	30	100	13	18	1	0	1	8	5	0	0	1	19	1	0	.220	.217
Munroe, Buddy	R-R	5-11	185	8-28-87	.145	.143	.145	24	83	7	12	3	0	3	5	4	2	3	0	34	0	0	.289	.202
Ortiz, Danny	L-L	5-11	166	1-5-90	.259	.224	.273	62	239	35	62	16	4	11	43	14	2	0	6	60	1	0	.498	.299
Phillips, Derrick	R-R	6-3	220	9-21-90	.125	.000	.158	8	24	5	3	2	0	1	2	3	0	0	1	11	0	0	.333	.214
Ray, Lance	L-R	6-1	194	9-2-87	.314	.286	.327	17	70	11	22	5	1	0	5	3	2	1	0	20	0	0	.414	.360
Roberts, Nate	L-L	6-2	200	2-25-89	.336	.343	.333	35	128	30	43	10	1	5	17	21	4	0	0	29	5	2	.547	.444
Santana, Daniel	B-R	5-11	173	11-7-90	.264	.184	.308	30	140	23	37	8	1	4	16	3	1	0	30	5	4	.421	.285

Pitching	B-T	HT	WT	DOB	W	L	ERA	G	GS	CG	SV	IP	H	R	ER	HR	BB	SO	AVG	vLH	vRH	K/9	BB/9
Achter, A.J.	R-R	6-5	205	8-27-88	1	0	4.91	4	0	0	0	7	7	4	4	0	3	8	.250	.250	.250	9.82	3.68
Darnell, Logan	L-L	6-2	210	2-2-89	2	3	2.08	11	5	0	0	35	28	16	8	2	6	32	.220	.250	.214	8.31	1.56
Dean, Pat	L-L	6-1	180	5-25-89	2	2	2.59	5	5	0	0	24	17	10	7	3	1	32	.198	.000	.221	11.84	0.37
Dempster, Clint	L-L	6-0	180	8-29-89	1	1	2.35	4	0	0	0	8	9	2	2	1	2	7	.273	.267	.278	8.22	2.35
Fuentes, Nelvin	L-L	6-0	196	4-7-89	0	0	0.61	9	0	0	2	15	6	1	1	0	6	20	.125	.000	.105	12.27	3.68
Gallant, Dallas	R-R	6-3	195	1-25-89	2	0	1.98	6	0	0	0	14	9	3	3	2	5	15	.184	.231	.167	9.88	3.29
Garcia, Martire	L-L	5-11	150	3-1-90	6	0	1.75	8	8	0	0	46	42	13	9	2	15	63	.243	.250	.241	12.24	2.91
Gonzalez, Jose	L-L	5-9	166	2-3-91	1	1	0.41	18	0	0	6	22	8	1	1	1	6	33	.110	.176	.089	13.50	2.45
Gutierrez, David	R-R	6-0	150	9-29-87	2	1	2.51	15	0	0	3	29	23	8	8	1	8	25	.217	.156	.243	7.85	2.51
Hauser, Matt	R-R	6-2	195	3-30-88	0	0	1.00	8	0	0	3	9	7	1	1	0	2	13	.206	.167	.227	13.00	2.00
Hermsen, B.J.	R-R	6-5	235	12-1-89	2	2	3.32	8	6	0	0	38	39	15	14	2	4	39	.257	.281	.242	9.24	0.95
Lobanov, Andrei	L-L	6-3	171	1-25-90	0	0	0.00	2	0	0	1	4	3	0	0	0	4	4	.214	.000	.214	9.00	0.00
Mijares, Jean	L-L	5-11	149	1-10-88	2	1	2.67	15	2	0	1	34	24	13	10	4	17	45	.195	.212	.189	12.03	4.54
Necke, Kyle	R-R	6-2	240	3-20-87	0	0	9.00	2	0	0	0	2	4	2	2	1	1	3	.400	.500	.333	13.50	4.50
O'Rourke, Ryan	R-L	6-3	217	4-30-88	1	3	5.10	13	5	0	0	42	52	26	24	2	7	39	.306	.091	.358	8.29	1.49
Salcedo, Adrian	R-R	6-4	175	4-24-91	4	3	3.27	16	8	0	1	66	55	27	24	3	10	65	.230	.250	.217	8.86	1.36
See, Zach	R-R	6-2	185	11-23-88	5	0	1.37	12	0	0	0	20	17	3	3	1	5	25	.230	.179	.261	11.44	2.29
Soliman, Manuel	R-R	6-2	185	8-11-89	5	2	3.48	12	12	0	0	65	47	28	25	5	21	74	.201	.160	.222	10.30	2.92
Spangler, Sam	L-L	6-2	195	9-24-87	1	0	3.15	9	2	0	0	20	23	7	7	3	6	21	.303	.200	.328	9.45	2.70
Tonkin, Mike	R-R	6-7	220	11-19-89	1	0	1.08	10	0	0	1	25	18	6	3	1	4	26	.196	.261	.174	9.36	1.44
Weller, Blayne	R-R	6-5	220	1-30-90	3	6	4.57	13	13	0	0	65	82	41	33	4	16	55	.307	.298	.315	7.62	2.22

Fielding

Catcher	PCT	G	PO	A	E	DP	PB
Arias	.983	27	242	39	5	0	5
Knudson	.991	21	194	20	2	3	3
Munroe	.990	22	189	18	2	1	6

First Base	PCT	G	PO	A	E	DP
Burke	.994	59	512	19	3	36
Glad	1.000	1	4	0	0	0
Knudson	.967	3	26	3	1	1
Ray	.972	5	32	3	1	4

Second Base	PCT	G	PO	A	E	DP
Choi	.976	10	19	21	1	6

Glad	.982	12	30	26	1	6
Hawkins	.927	15	25	26	4	7
Lockwood	.965	28	43	66	4	12
Santana	1.000	3	4	11	0	1

Third Base	PCT	G	PO	A	E	DP
Burke	.750	1	1	2	1	0
Glad	.889	9	10	22	4	2
Leer	.937	57	41	123	11	8

Shortstop	PCT	G	PO	A	E	DP
Hawkins	.899	33	33	83	13	17
Leer	.938	6	8	22	2	6

Santana	.925	27	34	64	8	10

Outfield	PCT	G	PO	A	E	DP
Arcia	1.000	63	97	2	0	1
Arias	—	1	0	0	0	0
Glad	.969	22	30	1	1	1
Henderson	.962	34	49	2	2	1
Ortiz	.958	58	80	11	4	2
Phillips	1.000	1	2	0	0	0
Ray	1.000	10	15	0	0	0
Roberts	1.000	16	20	1	0	0

GCL TWINS — ROOKIE
GULF COAST LEAGUE

Batting	B-T	HT	WT	DOB	AVG	vLH	vRH	G	AB	R	H	2B	3B	HR	RBI	BB	HBP	SH	SF	SO	SB	CS	SLG	OBP
Casilla, Alexi	B-R	5-9	185	7-20-84	.143	.333	.091	5	14	1	2	1	0	0	0	3	0	0	0	0	0	0	.214	.294

MINNESOTA TWINS

Player	B-T	HT	WT	DOB	AVG	vLH	vRH	G	AB	R	H	2B	3B	HR	RBI	BB	HBP	SH	SF	SO	SB	CS	OBP	SLG
Cross, Kelly	B-R	6-3	205	3-21-92	.250	.200	.333	3	8	2	2	1	0	0	2	3	0	1	0	3	0	1	.375	.455
Goodrum, Niko	B-R	6-3	167	2-28-92	.161	.125	.174	36	118	10	19	4	0	0	5	9	0	0	1	34	4	2	.195	.219
Guillen, Wander	R-R	5-11	170	8-24-92	.172	.154	.178	34	99	6	17	3	0	0	9	6	2	0	2	27	1	2	.202	.229
Hanvi, Frederic	R-R	6-2	180	5-2-89	.131	.200	.118	23	61	5	8	2	0	0	5	3	3	1	3	26	0	2	.164	.200
Hejma, Matej	R-R	6-6	215	5-4-90	.306	.389	.273	21	62	12	19	6	0	1	7	5	2	0	1	11	1	1	.452	.371
Hendricks, Joshua	R-R	6-3	217	11-9-91	.091	.000	.138	13	44	2	4	1	0	0	2	0	0	0	1	17	0	0	.114	.089
Kang, In Kyun	L-R	6-1	200	4-21-89	.250	.217	.267	21	68	2	17	2	1	0	5	5	0	0	1	14	0	1	.309	.297
Kepler, Max	L-L	6-4	180	2-10-93	.286	.341	.263	37	140	15	40	6	1	0	11	13	0	0	0	27	6	1	.343	.346
Lockwood, Nick	R-R	6-1	175	1-7-91	.323	.250	.333	8	31	4	10	2	0	0	4	2	0	0	0		1	1	.387	.364
Martinez, Yorby	B-R	6-0	170	1-12-89	.207	.000	.250	8	29	2	6	0	0	0	2	1	3	1	0	5	1	2	.207	.303
Mention, Kelvin	L-L	5-11	198	2-18-92	.167	.143	.182	6	18	2	3	0	0	0	1	3	1	1	0	3	3	0	.167	.318
Parker, Matt	R-R	6-1	210	2-9-88	.225	.200	.232	23	71	8	16	1	0	0	6	8	1	2	1	12	0	0	.239	.309
Pimentel, Candido	B-R	5-11	160	7-19-90	.265	.257	.267	46	155	27	41	7	1	0	12	21	0	1	0	33	13	5	.323	.352
Polanco, Jorge	B-R	5-11	165	7-5-93	.223	.310	.189	34	103	12	23	5	0	1	12	12	0	2	2	9	2	4	.301	.299
Quesada, Michael	R-R	6-0	180	2-1-90	.100	.000	.111	3	10	1	1	0	0	0	1	1	0	0	0	5	0	0	.100	.182
Rhodes, Rory	R-R	6-2	200	7-28-91	.319	.240	.348	27	91	13	29	6	1	0	13	11	3	0	0	17	3	1	.407	.410
Rodriguez, Jairo	R-R	5-11	180	8-24-88	.209	.286	.186	25	91	10	19	7	0	0	10	3	0	2	0	10	0	0	.286	.234
Rosario, Eddie	L-R	6-0	170	9-28-91	.294	.255	.308	51	194	34	57	9	2	5	26	16	0	0	3	28	22	5	.438	.343
Sano, Miguel	R-R	6-3	195	5-11-93	.291	.302	.284	41	148	23	43	14	0	4	19	10	1	1	1	43	2	2	.466	.338
Santana, Ramon	R-R	5-9	152	6-20-86	.571	.000	.800	2	7	2	4	2	0	0	0	0	0	0	0	0	0	0	.857	.571
Silvania, Kelvin	L-L	6-1	185	10-3-90	.273	.261	.276	28	99	13	27	5	1	2	12	4	1	0	0	18	0	2	.404	.308
Solarte, Yangervis	R-R	5-11	176	7-7-87	.174	.000	.235	7	23	3	4	0	0	0	0	1	0	0	0	4	0	0	.174	.208
Tindall, Nick	R-R	6-4	190	8-23-91	.152	.000	.200	12	33	3	5	3	0	0	2	7	1	0	0	9	1	1	.242	.317
Tolbert, Matt	B-R	6-0	185	5-4-82	.333	.333	.333	4	12	4	4	2	0	0	3	0	0	0	3	1	1		.500	.467
Vargas, Kennys	B-R	6-5	215	8-1-90	.324	.208	.383	39	142	24	46	15	1	3	26	13	3	0	2	40	1	0	.507	.388
Williams, J.D.	B-R	5-11	183	11-20-90	.214	.148	.235	37	112	8	24	4	1	1	9	10	0	2	0	43	5	1	.295	.279

Pitching

Player	B-T	HT	WT	DOB	W	L	ERA	G	GS	CG	SV	IP	H	R	ER	HR	BB	SO	AVG	vLH	vRH	K/9	BB/9
Ahorrio, Eddie	R-R	5-11	165	10-28-90	0	2	2.38	15	1	0	4	23	14	6	6	2	13	24	.177	.188	.170	9.53	5.16
Alloway, Nick	R-R	6-4	225	1-6-89	2	1	3.99	14	3	0	2	29	23	13	13	3	14	41	.223	.224	.222	12.58	4.30
Arevalo, Ricardo	R-R	6-3	210	2-28-91	0	7	4.97	12	11	0	0	51	47	36	28	3	26	40	.249	.263	.239	7.11	4.62
Calcano, Richard	R-R	6-1	204	1-15-91	0	0	9.00	1	0	0	0	1	1	1	1	0	1	0	.250	.000	.500	9.00	0.00
Carroll, Brett	R-L	6-1	210	8-10-87	3	2	3.26	15	0	0	2	30	29	14	11	1	8	22	.252	.235	.255	6.53	2.37
Carter, Bart	L-L	6-1	208	7-8-87	2	0	2.12	16	0	0	0	30	26	10	7	1	5	34	.228	.231	.227	10.31	1.52
Christensen, Derek	R-R	6-1	180	6-19-89	3	0	0.66	7	1	0	0	14	7	3	1	0	5	9	.140	.125	.154	5.93	3.29
Ciurcina, Cesar	R-R	5-11	192	10-23-90	5	4	2.91	12	11	2	0	65	60	29	21	3	8	53	.240	.270	.211	7.34	1.11
Condrey, Clay	R-R	6-3	225	11-19-75	0	0	6.75	3	3	0	0	5	8	4	4	1	2	7	.364	.538	.111	11.81	3.38
Dean, Pat	L-L	6-1	180	5-25-89	0	0	0.00	4	0	0	0	5	3	0	0	0	0	5	.176	.250	.154	9.00	0.00
Deminsky, David	L-L	6-3	205	6-12-87	3	3	2.70	10	8	1	0	53	45	19	16	1	8	51	.226	.273	.213	8.61	1.35
Fawbush, Nathan	R-R	6-7	193	7-3-90	0	2	13.50	3	0	0	0	3	5	6	5	0	3	4	.313	.250	.375	10.80	8.10
Guerra, Pedro	R-R	6-0	180	1-9-90	2	2	2.84	12	0	0	0	38	26	14	12	0	15	27	.200	.241	.167	6.39	3.55
Herr, Tyler	R-R	6-8	220	10-8-90	0	1	5.82	14	2	0	1	22	21	20	14	1	15	23	.256	.293	.220	9.55	6.23
Hirschfeld, Steve	R-R	6-5	226	9-8-85	0	0	4.50	2	0	0	0	2	3	1	1	0	1	2	.333	.500	.200	9.00	4.50
Johnson, Trayvone	R-R	6-1	220	7-25-87	0	0	4.50	6	0	0	0	8	9	4	4	0	7	7	.300	.444	.083	7.88	7.88
Maroth, Mike	L-L	6-0	190	8-17-77	0	0	0.00	1	0	0	0	2	1	0	0	0	0	2	.167	.000	.200	10.80	0.00
Nunez, Luis	L-L	5-11	160	9-26-91	1	3	3.10	19	1	0	1	29	30	14	10	1	15	30	.263	.227	.272	9.31	4.66
Parker, Justin	L-L	6-4	195	4-21-90	6	2	2.23	12	12	0	0	61	63	19	15	2	16	42	.272	.263	.273	6.23	2.37
Robb, Hein	L-L	6-4	185	5-12-92	0	1	12.54	9	0	0	0	9	18	13	13	2	7	3	.439	.385	.464	2.89	6.75
Schuld, Matt	R-R	6-3	210	12-7-87	2	0	2.57	11	0	0	1	21	21	6	6	1	3	17	.266	.235	.289	7.29	1.29
Tippett, Brad	R-R	6-2	185	2-11-88	0	0	0.00	2	0	0	0	3	3	3	0	0	1	3	.214	.111	.400	8.10	2.70
Trau, Mark	R-R	6-5	176	6-27-91	0	1	5.56	11	0	0	0	11	9	10	7	2	7	15	.220	.250	.200	7.15	7.15

Fielding

Catcher	PCT	G	PO	A	E	DP	PB
Cross	1.000	2	18	1	0	0	0
Hanvi	1.000	1	1	0	0	0	
Hendricks	1.000	3	14	2	0	0	2
Parker	.982	22	148	19	3	1	1
Quesada	.900	2	15	3	2	0	0
Rodriguez	.990	25	181	19	2	0	5
Tindall	.988	10	75	7	1	0	1

First Base	PCT	G	PO	A	E	DP
Guillen	—	2	0	0	0	0
Hendricks	.800	1	8	0	2	1
Kang	.981	5	46	5	1	2
Rhodes	.990	13	91	5	1	10
Silvania	.972	18	132	9	4	12
Vargas	.988	28	234	16	3	23

Second Base	PCT	G	PO	A	E	DP
Casilla	.947	5	10	8	1	4
Goodrum	.919	10	14	20	3	7
Guillen	1.000	7	9	12	0	3
Lockwood	1.000	4	5	20	0	3
Martinez	.750	2	2	1	1	1
Polanco	.974	13	18	19	1	6
Solarte	1.000	3	1	5	0	1
Tolbert	1.000	3	1	2	1	0
Williams	.987	28	28	50	1	11

Third Base	PCT	G	PO	A	E	DP
Goodrum	.875	6	3	4	1	0
Guillen	.925	25	14	48	5	2
Hanvi	—	1	0	0	0	0
Kang	.600	5	2	4	4	0
Martinez	.857	3	0	6	1	0
Rhodes	.900	5	1	8	1	0
Sano	.818	21	11	34	10	2
Santana	1.000	1	0	1	0	0
Solarte	—	1	0	0	0	0
Tolbert	1.000	1	0	1	0	0

Shortstop	PCT	G	PO	A	E	DP
Goodrum	.928	16	22	42	5	11
Lockwood	.900	3	6	12	2	2
Martinez	.800	4	5	11	4	0
Polanco	.929	24	28	50	6	12
Sano	.951	16	31	47	4	11
Tolbert	1.000	2	4	10	0	3

Outfield	PCT	G	PO	A	E	DP
Goodrum	1.000	4	7	3	0	0
Hanvi	1.000	19	20	1	0	0
Hejma	.972	21	35	0	1	0
Kepler	.973	37	69	3	2	0
Mention	1.000	6	14	1	0	0
Pimentel	.987	45	72	4	1	1
Rosario	.970	51	97	1	3	0
Santana	1.000	1	2	0	0	0
Silvania	1.000	2	4	0	0	0
Williams	1.000	8	14	1	0	0

DOMINICAN SUMMER LEAGUE

Batting	B-T	HT	WT	DOB	AVG	vLH	vRH	G	AB	R	H	2B	3B	HR	RBI	BB	HBP	SH	SF	SO	SB	CS	SLG	OBP
Arias, Victor	B-R	5-11	170	3-26-91	.165	.167	.156	40	115	13	19	3	0	0	4	12	3	0	0	25	7	2	.191	.262
Baez, Dubal	R-R	6-0	175	6-14-93	.250	.400	.229	14	40	9	10	0	0	0	7	8	2	1	0	9	1	0	.250	.400
Blanco, Juan	R-R	5-10	152	4-24-89	.319	.424	.282	50	166	27	53	11	1	0	15	10	6	1	0	17	18	11	.398	.379
Ciprian, Ernesto	R-R	6-2	175	2-9-91	.250	.235	.259	25	76	4	19	6	0	0	6	10	1	1	0	13	4	0	.329	.345
De Oliveira, Alexandre	L-R	6-1	185	7-15-92	.187	.242	.160	41	134	10	25	3	1	0	19	19	2	0	3	37	3	1	.224	.291
Estaba, Pedro	B-R	5-10	165	8-4-92	.205	.278	.191	38	112	18	23	3	2	0	18	13	1	0	1	23	2	4	.268	.291
Gallardo, Felix	R-R	6-1	178	6-25-91	.169	.136	.183	36	83	11	14	3	0	0	5	16	7	0	0	19	2	3	.205	.349
Gonzalez, Erick	R-R	6-1	184	5-4-91	.210	.211	.202	44	143	22	30	5	1	0	11	19	0	0	1	34	4	4	.259	.301
Martinez, Felix	R-R	6-2	190	12-6-88	.088	.100	.086	35	91	8	8	0	1	0	6	11	7	0	0	38	1	2	.110	.239
Mejia, Aderlin	B-R	5-11	170	5-12-92	.224	.241	.219	42	125	11	28	2	0	0	10	15	3	2	1	26	8	7	.240	.319
Ortiz, Kelvin	R-R	5-11	178	10-19-91	.264	.158	.287	38	106	14	28	7	1	1	11	15	5	0	1	45	12	5	.377	.378
Pacheco, Adonis	L-L	5-11	175	7-14-91	.214	.192	.220	53	154	14	33	4	2	0	16	22	1	1	3	32	7	9	.266	.311
Pina, Randy	R-R	6-0	189	5-1-91	.085	.080	.088	35	94	6	8	1	0	0	6	12	5	0	1	32	3	1	.096	.223
Polanco, Jorge	R-R	5-11	165	7-5-93	.250	.357	.227	18	60	5	15	2	0	0	7	6	0	0	2	9	1	3	.283	.309
Ramirez, Jose	B-R	5-10	165	9-6-91	.218	.160	.235	34	110	15	24	3	1	0	7	21	2	1	1	19	11	6	.264	.351
Sano, Miguel	R-R	6-3	195	5-11-93	.344	.429	.327	20	64	11	22	2	1	3	10	14	1	0	1	17	2	1	.547	.463
Sepulveda, Emilio	R-R	6-2	170	8-27-91	.152	.120	.163	42	105	18	16	2	0	0	4	22	1	1	0	32	6	2	.171	.305
Silva, Jhon	B-R	5-11	160	6-5-93	.230	.250	.225	38	87	18	20	3	0	0	6	24	1	2	0	39	5	6	.264	.402
Trinidad, Romy	R-R	6-2	170	5-14-91	.301	.324	.294	36	123	19	37	7	2	1	17	11	4	1	2	20	9	5	.415	.371
Ynojoso, Jonatan	R-R	5-11	150	10-23-92	.147	.000	.186	33	95	11	14	2	0	0	3	15	2	1	1	27	5	2	.168	.274

Pitching	B-T	HT	WT	DOB	W	L	ERA	G	GS	CG	SV	IP	H	R	ER	HR	BB	SO	AVG	vLH	vRH	K/9	BB/9
Bonilla, Sterling	R-R	6-0	165	2-26-92	4	2	1.36	14	13	2	0	66	43	19	10	2	14	40	.181	.130	.206	5.45	1.91
Calcano, Richard	R-R	6-1	204	1-15-91	1	0	4.50	15	0	0	0	24	11	15	12	0	31	21	.138	.080	.164	7.88	11.63
Florentino, Yeison	R-R	6-3	180	1-16-92	1	2	2.70	12	1	0	0	17	9	9	5	0	22	11	.164	.063	.205	5.94	11.88
Frias, Frank	R-R	6-3	170	8-15-89	0	2	5.17	9	1	0	0	16	14	17	9	0	11	12	.219	.348	.146	6.89	6.32
Jimenez, Jose	R-R	6-3	215	12-12-91	1	5	3.45	14	13	0	0	60	50	28	23	2	15	33	.728	.250	.219	4.95	2.25
Martinez, Edgar	R-R	6-0	145	9-1-90	6	2	3.10	26	0	0	4	41	37	20	14	1	9	38	.240	.189	.267	8.41	1.99
Mata, Angel	R R	6-2	190	12-3-92	1	5	2.12	13	10	1	0	59	50	17	14	0	15	54	.230	.230	.231	8.19	2.28
Nunez, Francisco	R-R	6-3	180	12-28-91	0	2	3.93	5	3	0	0	18	22	9	8	1	1	14	.297	.182	.317	6.87	0.49
Suarez, Carlos	R-R	6-1	182	11-24-92	0	2	9.26	11	0	0	2	12	19	20	12	1	15	9	.373	.417	.333	6.94	11.57
Subero, Junior	R-R	6-0	180	3-14-92	1	4	2.91	21	4	0	2	46	39	21	15	3	14	32	.228	.215	.239	6.22	2.72
Vargas, Javier	R-R	6-1	185	1-28-93	1	1	8.31	12	0	0	2	13	20	13	12	1	8	10	.345	.261	.400	6.92	5.54
Vasquez, Jose	R-R	6-0	170	3-27-91	0	3	8.04	8	0	0	1	16	21	16	14	3	11	9	.318	.259	.359	5.17	6.32
Veras, Luis	R-R	6-3	185	12-9-90	0	1	5.04	21	0	0	1	30	32	21	17	3	23	21	.267	.237	.280	2.97	6.82
Villaroel, Orlando	R-R	6-0	190	3-18-90	4	4	3.47	13	12	0	0	57	42	30	22	1	21	43	.208	.231	.197	6.79	3.32
Villasana, Elias	R-R	6-1	190	3-22-93	1	4	2.08	21	3	0	0	43	46	20	10	0	28	27	.266	.310	.235	5.61	5.82
Zarzuela, Ezequiel	R-R	6-1	170	11-18-90	7	3	2.68	12	11	0	0	54	50	23	16	0	20	36	.250	.264	.245	6.04	3.35

Fielding

Catcher	PCT	G	PO	A	E	DP	PB
Gallardo	.994	28	154	24	1	0	5
Martinez	.994	23	134	24	1	0	1
Pina	.970	31	139	25	5	0	7

First Base	PCT	G	PO	A	E	DP
Blanco	1.000	16	96	12	0	6
De Oliveira	.974	27	205	19	6	15
Gallardo	1.000	6	36	2	0	2
Gonzalez	.971	24	190	14	6	19
Martinez	.967	9	57	2	2	8

Second Base	PCT	G	PO	A	E	DP
Arias	.923	13	24	36	5	8
Baez	.926	7	14	11	2	2
Blanco	.982	11	17	37	1	5
Estaba	.971	7	12	22	1	6
Gonzalez	1.000	2	2	6	0	2
Mejia	.909	6	10	10	2	0

Third Base	PCT	G	PO	A	E	DP
Polanco	.789	3	9	6	4	1
Ramirez	.951	19	28	49	4	7
Ynojoso	.952	10	16	24	2	2
Arias	.891	17	16	25	5	4
Baez	.000	1	0	0	1	0
Blanco	.943	16	6	27	2	3
Estaba	.896	13	12	31	5	2
Gonzalez	.867	13	9	17	4	1
Mejia	.500	2	0	2	2	0
Ramirez	1.000	5	8	8	0	2
Sano	.854	15	14	27	7	1

Shortstop	PCT	G	PO	A	E	DP
Arias	.929	5	11	15	2	3
Baez	.923	4	5	7	1	3
Blanco	1.000	2	4	5	0	0
Gonzalez	.750	3	7	5	4	2

	PCT	G	PO	A	E	DP
Mejia	.899	26	47	60	12	10
Polanco	.837	11	18	23	8	6
Ramirez	.941	6	15	17	2	4
Sano	.833	2	2	3	1	1
Ynojoso	.859	15	24	37	10	7

Outfield	PCT	G	PO	A	E	DP
Blanco	1.000	10	19	2	0	1
Ciprian	.889	17	22	2	3	0
De Oliveira	.947	9	18	0	1	0
Estaba	1.000	2	1	0	0	0
Gonzalez	—	1	0	0	0	0
Ortiz	.957	33	41	4	2	0
Pacheco	.919	50	62	6	6	1
Ramirez	1.000	2	4	0	0	0
Sepulveda	.913	40	59	4	6	1
Silva	.968	35	58	3	2	1
Trinidad	.971	35	67	0	2	0

New York Mets

SEASON IN A SENTENCE: The Mets had their second straight losing season, one that cost general manager Omar Minaya and manager Jerry Manuel their jobs as New York's injury-plagued, anemic offense ranked 13th in the National League in scoring.

HIGH POINT: New York had two eight-game winning streaks, one of them coming in June and ending during an interleague series loss to the Yankees. That streak also helped push the Mets to their high-water point, which they reached June 27 with a 6-0 victory against the Twins. Rookie lefthander Jonathon Niese tossed six scoreless innings to lead the way, and the Mets were 11 games over .500 at 43-32, a half-game back of Atlanta in the NL East.

LOW POINT: The Mets' highest-priced pitchers ended the season as non-factors. Closer Francisco Rodriguez imploded in August, injuring his hand and getting arrested after an incident involving his child's grandfather. In September, ace lefthander Johan Santana added injury to insult when he came down with a torn capsule in his throwing shoulder. He could miss part of 2011 as well.

NOTABLE ROOKIES: Niese slumped in the second half but went 9-10, 4.20 overall and made 30 starts. First baseman Ike Davis was called up in April, and the 2008 first-rounder lived up to his advance billing during an uneven but at times brilliant debut season. He finished second on the club to David Wright in homers and RBIs. Ruben Tejada, 20, flashed a fine glove in the middle infield, while unheralded Josh Thole hit a respectable .277/.357/.366 while shouldering much of the catcher load after veteran Rod Barajas was traded.

KEY TRANSACTIONS: Minaya's tenure ended with a thud after six seasons, and Manuel finished with a 204-213 mark in just under three years with the Mets. One move the Mets didn't make stands out, though. They kept Oliver Perez and never persuaded him to go to the minors. Instead, Perez went 0-5, 6.80 in just 17 games, $12 million worth of dead weight.

DOWN ON THE FARM: The Mets didn't have a ton of great news in the minors, as 2008 first-rounders Reese Havens (injury) and Brad Holt (poor performance) went backward, as did top prospect Jenrry Mejia after he was rushed to the majors. Mejia went 0-4, 4.62 in 33 appearances, including three starts.

OPENING DAY PAYROLL: $134.4 million (5th)

PLAYERS OF THE YEAR

MAJOR LEAGUE

David Wright
3b
.283/.354/.503
29 HR, 103 RBI; 5th
straight All-Star Game

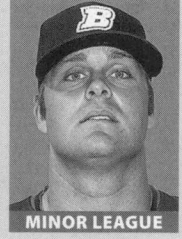

MINOR LEAGUE

Lucas Duda
of/1b
(Double-A/Triple-A)
.304/.398/.569
40 2B, 23 HR

ORGANIZATION LEADERS

BATTING		*Minimum 250 at-bats
MAJORS		
*AVG	Angel Pagan	.290
*OPS	David Wright	.856
HR	David Wright	29
RBI	David Wright	103
MINORS		
*AVG	Joshua Satin, St. Lucie/Binghamton	.311
*OBP	Joshua Satin, St. Lucie/Binghamton	.399
*SLG	Lucas Duda, Binghamton/Buffalo	.569
R	Kirk Nieuwenhuis, Binghamton/Buffalo	91
H	Wilmer Flores, Savannah/St. Lucie	160
TB	Nick Evans, Binghamton/Buffalo	261
2B	Nick Evans, Binghamton/Buffalo	44
3B	Darrell Ceciliani, Brooklyn	12
HR	Lucas Duda, Binghamton/Buffalo	23
	Nick Evans, Binghamton/Buffalo	23
RBI	Lucas Duda, Binghamton/Buffalo	87
BB	Joshua Satin, St. Lucie/Binghamton	66
SO	Richard Lucas, St. Lucie	149
SB	Cesar Puello, Savannah	45

PITCHING		†Minimum 75 innings
MAJORS		
W	Mike Pelfrey	15
†ERA	R.A. Dickey	2.84
SO	Jonathon Niese	148
MINORS		
W	Dillon Gee, Buffalo	13
L	Bradley Holt, Binghamton/St. Lucie	14
†ERA	James Fuller, Savannah/St. Lucie	2.19
G	Roy Merritt, Buffalo/Binghamton	64
GS	Michael Antonini, Binghamton/Buffalo	29
SV	Manuel Alvarez, St. Lucie/Bing./Buffalo	17
IP	Michael Antonini, Binghamton/Buffalo	168.3
BB	Bradley Holt, Binghamton/St. Lucie	79
SO	Dillon Gee, Buffalo	165
	Brandon Moore, Savannah/St. Lucie/Bing.	165
†AVG	Armando Rodriguez, Savannah	.214

2010 PERFORMANCE

General Manager: Omar Minaya. **Farm Director:** Adam Wogan. **Scouting Director:** Rudy Terrasas.

Class	Team	League	W	L	PCT	Finish*	Manager(s)
Majors	New York Mets	National	79	83	.488	10th (16)	Jerry Manuel
Triple-A	Buffalo Bisons	International	76	68	.528	5th (14)	Ken Oberkfell
Double-A	Binghamton Mets	Eastern	66	76	.465	t-10th (12)	Tim Teufel
High A	St. Lucie Mets	Florida State	62	76	.449	11th (12)	Edgar Alfonzo
Low A	Savannah Sand Gnats	South Atlantic	75	64	.540	t-4th (14)	Pedro Lopez
Short-season	Brooklyn Cyclones	New York-Penn	51	24	.680	1st (14)	Wally Backman
Rookie	Kingsport Mets	Appalachian	28	39	.418	9th (10)	Mike DiFelice
Rookie	GCL Mets	Gulf Coast	31	25	.554	4th (15)	Sandy Alomar
Overall 2010 Minor League Record			389	372	.511	9th (30)	

*Finish in overall standings (No. of teams in league). †League champion.

ORGANIZATION STATISTICS

NEW YORK METS

NATIONAL LEAGUE

Batting	B-T	HT	WT	DOB	AVG	vLH	vRH	G	AB	R	H	2B	3B	HR	RBI	BB	HBP	SH	SF	SO	SB	CS	SLG	OBP
Arias, Joaquin	R-R	6-1	170	9-21-84	.200	.375	.136	22	30	5	6	1	0	0	4	2	0	1	0	6	0	0	.233	.250
Barajas, Rod	R-R	6-1	245	9-5-75	.225	.169	.242	74	249	30	56	11	0	12	34	8	6	1	3	39	0	0	.414	.263
2-team total (25 Los Angeles)					.240	—	—	99	313	39	75	14	0	17	47	13	8	1	4	54	0	0	.447	.284
Bay, Jason	R-R	6-2	205	9-20-78	.259	.259	.258	95	348	48	90	20	6	6	47	44	5	0	4	91	10	0	.402	.347
Beltran, Carlos	B-R	6-1	200	4-24-77	.255	.292	.244	64	220	21	56	11	3	7	27	30	1	0	4	39	3	1	.427	.341
Blanco, Henry	R-R	5-11	220	8-29-71	.215	.167	.239	50	130	10	28	5	0	2	8	11	0	0	3	26	1	0	.300	.271
Carter, Chris	L-L	6-0	230	9-16-82	.263	.143	.269	100	167	15	44	9	0	4	24	12	1	0	0	17	1	2	.389	.317
Castillo, Luis	B-R	5-11	195	9-12-75	.235	.243	.232	86	247	28	58	4	2	0	17	39	0	11	2	25	8	3	.267	.337
Catalanotto, Frank	L-R	6-0	195	4-27-74	.160	.000	.167	25	25	2	4	1	0	0	1	1	0	0	0	5	0	0	.200	.192
Cora, Alex	L-R	6-0	200	10-18-75	.207	.160	.215	62	169	14	35	6	3	0	20	10	4	2	2	16	4	1	.278	.265
Davis, Ike	L-L	6-4	215	3-22-87	.264	.295	.254	147	523	73	138	33	1	19	71	72	1	0	5	138	3	2	.440	.351
Duda, Lucas	L-R	6-5	240	2-3-86	.202	.158	.215	29	84	11	17	6	0	4	13	6	1	0	1	22	0	0	.417	.261
Evans, Nick	R-R	6-2	220	1-30-86	.306	.333	.267	20	36	5	11	3	0	1	5	1	0	0	0	10	0	0	.472	.324
Feliciano, Jesus	L-L	5-10	190	6-6-79	.231	.200	.237	54	108	12	25	4	1	0	3	6	1	3	1	12	1	0	.287	.276
Francoeur, Jeff	R-R	6-5	220	1-8-84	.237	.280	.223	124	401	43	95	16	2	11	54	29	7	0	10	76	8	2	.369	.293
Hernandez, Luis	B-R	5-10	180	6-26-84	.250	.500	.211	17	44	4	11	1	0	2	6	2	1	0	0	7	1	0	.409	.298
Hessman, Mike	R-R	6-5	215	3-5-78	.127	.185	.071	32	55	6	7	2	1	1	6	8	2	0	0	23	0	0	.255	.262
Jacobs, Mike	L-R	6-3	215	10-30-80	.208	.000	.217	7	24	1	5	1	0	1	2	3	0	1	0	7	0	0	.375	.296
Martinez, Fernando	L-R	6-1	200	10-10-88	.167	.000	.167	7	18	1	3	0	0	0	2	1	2	0	1	5	0	1	.167	.273
Matthews Jr., Gary	B-R	6-3	225	8-25-74	.190	.143	.205	36	58	9	11	3	0	0	1	6	0	1	0	24	1	0	.241	.266
Nickeas, Mike	R-R	6-0	210	2-13-83	.200	.000	.286	5	10	0	2	0	0	0	0	0	0	0	0	5	0	0	.200	.200
Pagan, Angel	B-R	6-2	195	7-2-81	.290	.261	.300	151	579	80	168	31	7	11	69	44	1	6	3	97	37	9	.425	.340
Reyes, Jose	B-R	6-1	200	6-11-83	.282	.309	.274	133	563	83	159	29	10	11	54	31	2	4	3	63	30	10	.428	.321
Tatis, Fernando	R-R	5-11	185	1-1-75	.185	.250	.048	41	65	6	12	4	0	2	6	6	0	1	0	19	0	0	.338	.254
Tejada, Ruben	R-R	5-11	160	10-27-89	.213	.296	.185	78	216	28	46	12	0	1	15	22	8	6	3	38	2	2	.282	.305
Thole, Josh	L-R	6-1	205	10-28-86	.277	.143	.299	73	202	17	56	7	1	3	17	24	1	0	0	25	1	0	.366	.357
Turner, Justin	R-R	5-11	200	11-23-84	.125	.000	.250	4	8	1	1	1	0	0	0	1	0	0	0	0	0	0	.250	.222
Wright, David	R-R	6-0	210	12-20-82	.283	.339	.267	157	587	87	166	36	3	29	103	69	2	0	12	161	19	11	.503	.354

Pitching	B-T	HT	WT	DOB	W	L	ERA	G	GS	CG	SV	IP	H	R	ER	HR	BB	SO	AVG	vLH	vRH	K/9	BB/9
Acosta, Manny	B-R	6-4	170	5-1-81	3	2	2.95	41	0	0	1	40	30	13	13	4	18	42	.219	.163	.245	9.53	4.08
Dessens, Elmer	R-R	5-11	200	1-13-71	4	2	2.30	53	0	0	0	47	41	14	12	4	16	16	.240	.232	.243	3.06	3.06
Dickey, R.A.	R-R	6-2	215	10-29-74	11	9	2.84	27	26	2	0	174	165	62	55	13	42	104	.251	.226	.269	5.37	2.17
Feliciano, Pedro	L-L	5-10	190	8-25-76	3	6	3.30	92	0	0	0	63	66	24	23	1	30	56	.273	.211	.336	8.04	4.31
Gee, Dillon	R-R	6-1	200	4-28-86	2	2	2.18	5	5	0	0	33	25	10	8	2	15	17	.212	.170	.239	4.64	4.09
Green, Sean	R-R	6-6	225	4-20-79	0	0	3.86	11	0	0	0	9	7	6	4	1	8	12	.200	.333	.172	11.57	7.71
Igarashi, Ryota	R-R	5-11	200	5-28-79	1	1	7.12	34	0	0	0	30	29	24	24	4	18	25	.254	.279	.239	7.42	5.34
Maine, John	R-R	6-4	200	5-8-81	1	3	6.13	9	9	0	0	40	47	29	27	8	25	39	.297	.200	.357	8.85	5.67
Mejia, Jenrry	R-R	6-0	160	10-11-89	0	4	4.62	33	3	0	0	39	46	21	20	3	20	22	.289	.203	.340	5.08	4.62
Misch, Pat	R-L	6-2	195	8-18-81	0	4	3.82	12	6	0	0	38	43	20	16	4	4	23	.283	.294	.280	5.50	0.96
Niese, Jon	L-L	6-4	215	10-27-86	9	10	4.20	30	30	2	0	174	192	97	81	20	62	148	.280	.266	.283	7.67	3.21
Nieve, Fernando	R-R	6-0	215	7-15-82	2	4	6.00	40	1	0	0	42	37	28	28	10	22	38	.234	.240	.231	8.14	4.71
Parnell, Bobby	R-R	6-4	200	9-8-84	0	1	2.83	41	0	0	0	35	41	13	11	1	8	33	.295	.327	.276	8.49	2.06
Pelfrey, Mike	R-R	6-7	230	1-14-84	15	9	3.66	34	33	0	1	204	213	88	83	12	68	113	.275	.279	.272	4.99	3.00
Perez, Oliver	L-L	6-3	205	8-15-81	0	5	6.80	17	7	0	0	46	54	37	35	9	42	37	.293	.214	.317	7.19	8.16
Rodriguez, Francisco	R-R	6-0	195	1-7-82	4	2	2.20	53	0	0	25	57	45	14	14	3	21	67	.213	.245	.188	10.52	3.30
Santana, Johan	L-L	6-0	210	3-13-79	11	9	2.98	29	29	4	0	199	179	67	66	16	55	144	.240	.273	.229	6.51	2.49
Stoner, Tobi	R-R	6-2	215	12-3-84	0	1	3.86	1	0	0	0	2	3	1	1	0	1	0	.300	.000	.375	0.00	3.86
Takahashi, Hisanori	L-L	5-10	170	4-2-75	10	6	3.61	53	12	0	8	122	116	51	49	13	43	114	.252	.217	.264	8.41	3.17
Valdes, Raul	L-L	5-11	190	11-27-77	3	3	4.91	38	1	0	1	59	59	33	32	7	27	56	.260	.330	.216	8.59	4.14

Fielding

Catcher	PCT	G	PO	A	E	DP	PB
Barajas	.994	73	516	21	3	5	3
Blanco	.997	46	284	27	1	4	3
Nickeas	.938	4	14	1	1	0	0
Thole	.992	61	341	29	3	2	4

First Base	PCT	G	PO	A	E	DP
Catalanotto	—	1	0	0	0	0
Cora	1.000	2	1	0	0	0
Davis	.993	146	1239	105	9	133
Hessman	1.000	6	50	1	0	4
Jacobs	.981	7	50	1	1	3
Tatis	1.000	14	67	5	0	6

Second Base	PCT	G	PO	A	E	DP
Arias	.970	13	19	13	1	4
Castillo	.993	74	122	176	2	38
Cora	.994	47	86	81	1	29
Hernandez	1.000	10	17	32	0	7
Tatis	—	3	0	0	0	0
Tejada	.972	50	79	126	6	31
Turner	1.000	3	4	3	0	2

Third Base	PCT	G	PO	A	E	DP
Hernandez	—	2	0	0	0	0
Hessman	1.000	8	4	13	0	3
Tatis	1.000	4	2	1	0	1
Turner	1.000	1	0	2	0	1
Wright	.956	155	110	321	20	34

Shortstop	PCT	G	PO	A	E	DP
Arias	.500	2	1	0	1	0
Cora	.947	6	7	11	1	4
Hernandez	1.000	4	4	8	0	2
Reyes	.973	133	179	362	15	77
Tejada	.982	28	33	75	2	15

Outfield	PCT	G	PO	A	E	DP
Arias	—	1	0	0	0	0
Bay	.993	93	141	6	1	1
Beltran	1.000	61	146	4	0	1
Carter	1.000	30	30	0	0	0
Catalanotto	—	1	0	0	0	0
Duda	1.000	24	32	1	0	1
Evans	1.000	10	13	0	0	0
Feliciano	1.000	35	52	1	0	0
Francoeur	.987	118	221	11	3	5
Martinez	1.000	6	7	0	0	0
Matthews Jr.	1.000	19	31	1	0	0
Pagan	.987	145	368	10	5	2

BUFFALO BISONS   TRIPLE-A
INTERNATIONAL LEAGUE

Batting	B-T	HT	WT	DOB	AVG	vLH	vRH	G	AB	R	H	2B	3B	HR	RBI	BB	HBP	SH	SF	SO	SB	CS	SLG	OBP
Adams, Russ	L-R	6-0	200	8-30-80	.264	.095	.304	108	383	58	101	28	2	16	58	37	4	2	3	68	4	2	.473	.333
Barrett, Michael	R-R	6-0	225	10-22-76	.185	.250	.147	16	54	1	10	2	0	0	6	1	0	0	2	12	0	0	.222	.193
Blaquiere, Jean Luc	R-R	6-0	196	2-27-86	.318	.667	.188	6	22	3	7	3	0	2	5	1	1	1	0	6	0	0	.727	.375
Carter, Chris	L-L	6-0	230	9-16-82	.336	.370	.326	29	113	17	38	9	2	6	22	8	2	0	0	8	0	0	.611	.390
Cervenak, Mike	R-R	5-11	195	8-17-76	.249	.250	.249	111	433	48	108	24	0	8	40	11	7	0	3	56	2	1	.360	.278
Cintron, Alex	B-R	6-2	210	12-17-78	.228	.385	.182	20	57	5	13	1	0	1	3	4	0	0	0	12	0	1	.298	.279
Davis, Ike	L-L	6-4	215	3-22-87	.364	.286	.385	10	33	8	12	3	0	2	4	9	0	0	0	5	0	0	.636	.500
Duda, Lucas	L-R	6-5	240	2-3-86	.314	.244	.348	70	264	44	83	23	2	17	53	31	2	0	1	57	0	0	.610	.389
Evans, Nick	R-R	6-2	220	1-30-86	.314	.310	.316	37	140	26	44	14	1	6	25	15	1	1	0	23	0	0	.557	.385
Feliciano, Jesus	L-L	5-10	190	6-6-79	.339	.326	.344	89	336	55	114	18	1	1	28	21	6	3	3	35	6	5	.408	.385
Garcia, Emmanuel	L-R	6-2	185	3-4-86	.160	.063	.206	17	50	5	8	2	0	0	1	0	0	3	0	14	0	0	.200	.160
Green, Andy	R-R	5-10	180	7-7-77	.239	.250	.233	78	218	35	52	15	1	5	24	22	3	5	2	45	3	1	.385	.314
Hernandez, Luis	B-R	5-10	180	6-26-84	.280	.271	.285	47	189	25	53	10	4	0	12	10	2	4	3	31	2	1	.376	.319
Hessman, Mike	R-R	6-5	215	3-5-78	.274	.286	.271	64	248	43	68	20	0	18	58	27	4	0	3	60	0	0	.573	.351
House, J.R.	R-R	6-0	215	11-11-79	.253	.303	.233	67	225	20	57	14	0	4	29	13	2	2	1	31	0	0	.369	.299
Hubbard, Marshall	L-R	6-3	215	4-16-82	.059	.000	.077	5	17	0	1	1	0	0	1	0	0	0	0	7	0	0	.118	.111
Jacobs, Mike	L-R	6-3	215	10-30-80	.260	.231	.273	86	339	53	88	23	3	15	57	28	0	0	4	65	1	0	.478	.313
Lutz, Zach	R-R	6-1	220	6-3-86	.300	.000	.429	5	20	3	6	4	0	1	9	2	0	0	0	3	0	0	.650	.364
Maccani, Tony	R-R	6-3	191	9-24-84	.400	.000	.400	3	5	1	2	1	0	0	0	0	0	0	0	0	0	0	.600	.400
Malo, Jonathan	R-R	6-2	180	9-29-83	.238	.300	.182	11	21	3	5	2	1	0	1	3	0	0	0	5	0	0	.429	.333
Manriquez, Salomon	R-R	6-1	200	9-15-82	.167	.200	.000	3	6	0	1	1	0	0	0	1	0	0	0	2	0	0	.333	.286
Martinez, Fernando	L-R	6-1	200	10-10-88	.253	.242	.257	71	257	39	65	16	0	12	33	17	8	3	2	65	1	0	.455	.317
Murphy, Daniel	L-R	6-2	215	4-1-85	.294	.125	.346	8	34	4	10	3	0	1	8	1	0	0	0	2	1	0	.471	.314
Nickeas, Mike	R-R	6-0	210	2-13-83	.214	.250	.208	7	28	1	6	1	0	0	0	1	0	0	0	7	0	0	.250	.241
Nieuwenhuis, Kirk	L-R	6-3	210	8-7-87	.225	.125	.261	30	120	10	27	8	1	2	17	11	1	1	0	39	0	0	.358	.295
Padilla, Jorge	R-R	6-2	205	8-11-79	.313	.386	.272	48	160	26	50	10	0	2	22	14	2	2	5	26	6	2	.413	.365
Pascucci, Valentino	R-R	6-6	270	11-17-78	.258	.303	.234	72	190	40	49	10	0	17	38	44	1	0	1	65	0	0	.579	.398
Pridie, Jason	L-R	6-1	205	10-9-83	.280	.220	.301	40	164	17	46	6	1	3	19	12	0	1	0	36	9	3	.384	.330
Riggans, Shawn	R-R	6-2	200	7-25-80	.200	.000	.200	2	5	0	1	0	0	0	0	0	0	0	0	0	0	0	.200	.200
Santos, Omir	R-R	6-0	215	4-29-81	.194	.455	.080	16	36	2	7	4	0	0	1	1	0	0	0	8	0	0	.306	.216
Tejada, Ruben	R-R	5-11	160	10-27-89	.280	.276	.281	65	218	25	61	11	0	1	16	14	3	7	2	36	1	3	.344	.329
Thole, Josh	L-R	6-1	205	10-28-86	.267	.233	.274	48	165	20	44	19	1	2	17	22	1	1	2	25	0	0	.430	.353
Turner, Justin	R-R	5-11	200	11-23-84	.333	.374	.315	78	312	58	104	22	1	11	35	24	6	4	2	38	5	3	.516	.390
2-team total (23 Norfolk)					.316	—	—	101	396	69	125	30	1	12	43	33	6	5	3	51	7	3	.487	.374
Wabick, D.J.	L-R	6-2	185	5-30-84	.333	.333	.333	5	12	0	4	1	0	0	1	1	0	0	1	0	1	0	.417	.429

Pitching	B-T	HT	WT	DOB	W	L	ERA	G	GS	CG	SV	IP	H	R	ER	HR	BB	SO	AVG	vLH	vRH	K/9	BB/9
Acosta, Manny	B-R	6-4	170	5-1-81	2	3	3.47	28	0	0	5	36	28	14	14	4	15	36	.220	.273	.181	8.92	3.72
Alvarez, Manuel	R-R	5-11	200	12-18-85	0	2	6.00	4	0	0	0	6	8	4	4	1	2	3	.333	.444	.267	4.50	3.00
Antonini, Mike	R-L	6-2	200	8-6-85	2	3	5.11	6	6	0	0	37	45	23	21	6	5	25	.306	.316	.300	6.08	1.22
Blackley, Travis	L-L	6-3	205	11-4-82	0	0	8.53	4	0	0	0	6	6	6	6	2	7	4	.250	.222	.267	5.68	9.95
Brazoban, Yhency	R-R	6-1	250	11-6-80	0	0	6.10	10	0	0	1	10	11	7	7	1	5	10	.282	.320	.214	8.71	4.35
Bruney, Brian	R-R	6-3	235	2-17-82	0	1	4.50	8	0	0	0	8	9	7	4	0	7	7	.273	.182	.318	7.88	7.88
Calero, Kiko	R-R	6-1	210	1-9-75	0	0	10.59	10	0	0	0	17	24	20	20	4	9	16	.324	.379	.289	8.47	4.76
Cordero, Chad	R-R	6-0	220	3-18-82	1	1	1.69	17	0	0	0	16	15	4	3	0	5	14	.254	.296	.219	7.88	2.81
De La Torre, Jose	R-R	5-9	175	10-17-85	3	2	2.98	36	0	0	1	48	36	21	16	5	22	58	.203	.103	.266	10.80	4.10
Dessens, Elmer	R-R	5-11	200	1-13-71	0	0	2.12	13	0	0	6	17	20	4	4	0	3	18	.299	.323	.278	9.53	1.59
Dickey, R.A.	R-R	6-2	215	10-29-74	4	2	2.23	8	8	2	0	61	55	21	15	3	8	37	.239	.258	.226	5.49	1.19
Gee, Dillon	R-R	6-1	200	4-28-86	13	8	4.96	28	28	0	0	161	174	96	89	23	41	165	.275	.270	.279	9.20	2.29
Green, Sean	R-R	6-4	225	4-20-79	1	1	4.64	17	0	0	0	21	23	11	11	1	8	20	.288	.208	.344	8.44	3.38
Igarashi, Ryota	R-R	5-11	200	5-28-79	2	1	3.31	15	0	0	1	16	18	8	6	2	6	16	.277	.350	.244	8.82	3.31
Livingston, Bobby	L-L	6-3	205	9-3-82	3	8	5.34	22	15	0	0	93	108	64	55	8	39	58	.297	.264	.310	5.63	3.79
2-team total (5 Durham)					3	8	5.31	27	20	0	0	120	142	81	71	12	44	73	—	—	—	5.46	3.29

	B-T	HT	WT	DOB	W	L	ERA	G	GS	CG	SV	IP	H	R	ER	HR	BB	SO	AVG	vLH	vRH	K/9	BB/9
Lujan, John	R-R	6-1	200	5-10-84	2	3	5.79	31	0	0	4	37	48	24	24	5	12	45	.318	.282	.350	10.85	2.89
Maine, John	R-R	6-4	200	5-8-81	0	0	0.00	1	1	0	0	4	1	1	0	0	3	4	.067	.091	.000	8.31	6.23
Mejia, Jenrry	R-R	6-0	160	10-11-89	0	0	1.13	1	1	0	0	8	5	1	1	1	1	9	.200	.176	.250	10.13	1.13
Merritt, Roy	L-L	6-0	170	9-22-85	0	1	14.54	4	0	0	0	4	9	8	7	0	1	3	.429	.333	.500	6.23	2.08
Misch, Pat	R-L	6-2	195	8-18-81	11	4	3.23	23	23	2	0	151	150	61	54	11	24	99	.259	.297	.243	5.91	1.43
Niese, Jon	L-L	6-4	215	10-27-86	0	0	3.00	1	1	0	0	6	8	2	2	1	0	3	.333	.167	.500	4.50	0.00
Nieve, Fernando	R-R	6-0	215	7-15-82	2	1	5.63	8	8	0	0	40	49	25	25	3	13	31	.304	.337	.267	6.98	2.93
O'Connor, Mike	L-L	6-3	185	8-17-80	5	2	2.67	51	0	0	6	71	65	25	21	5	17	70	.246	.269	.231	8.92	2.17
Ortiz, Ramon	R-R	6-0	175	5-23-73	2	3	3.94	8	8	1	0	48	43	22	21	1	8	32	.239	.272	.212	6.00	1.50
2-team total (4 Durham)					2	4	4.57	12	12	1	0	65	66	35	33	3	14	44	—	—	—	6.09	1.94
Owen, Dylan	R-R	5-11	185	7-12-86	3	4	7.11	10	7	0	0	44	59	36	35	6	14	41	.319	.320	.318	8.32	2.84
Parnell, Bobby	R-R	6-4	200	9-8-84	1	1	4.14	24	0	0	4	41	36	22	19	3	17	42	.231	.242	.223	9.15	3.70
Perez, Oliver	L-L	6-3	205	8-15-81	0	0	2.31	2	2	0	0	12	10	4	3	2	7	10	.233	.250	.222	7.71	5.40
Pettyjohn, Adam	R-L	6-3	200	6-11-77	2	4	4.94	44	3	0	2	62	66	38	34	6	34	47	.274	.178	.343	6.82	4.94
Stinson, Josh	R-R	6-4	210	3-14-88	2	2	2.57	4	4	1	0	28	22	10	8	5	8	21	.212	.254	.156	6.75	2.57
Stoner, Tobi	B-R	6-2	215	12-3-84	6	10	5.97	23	22	0	0	121	158	88	80	18	43	83	.317	.333	.303	6.19	3.21
Valdes, Raul	L-L	5-11	190	11-27-77	2	1	3.00	9	7	0	0	36	34	12	12	3	9	36	.250	.226	.265	9.00	2.25

Fielding

Catcher	PCT	G	PO	A	E	DP	PB
Barrett	.991	15	100	6	1	2	3
Blaquiere	1.000	6	56	0	0	0	0
House	.994	59	458	34	3	4	10
Maccani	1.000	2	5	0	0	0	0
Nickeas	1.000	7	67	6	0	3	0
Riggans	.900	1	9	0	1	0	0
Santos	1.000	10	56	5	0	2	0
Thole	.989	48	343	19	4	8	6

First Base	PCT	G	PO	A	E	DP
Carter	1.000	5	24	4	0	3
Cervenak	1.000	1	5	1	0	0
Davis	.989	10	86	7	1	10
Duda	1.000	5	28	6	0	2
Evans	.993	34	266	19	2	25
Hessman	1.000	7	65	3	0	6
Hubbard	1.000	2	15	1	0	1
Jacobs	.982	63	567	50	11	50
Manriquez	.938	2	14	1	1	2
Murphy	.980	5	44	4	1	3
Pascucci	.992	15	110	14	1	13

Second Base	PCT	G	PO	A	E	DP
Adams	.973	57	100	150	7	34
Cintron	.974	10	20	17	1	4
Green	.990	24	36	60	1	11
Hernandez	.978	6	18	26	1	6
Malo	1.000	2	2	6	0	2
Murphy	1.000	2	4	6	0	0
Tejada	.950	7	19	19	2	3
Turner	.986	49	81	132	3	25

Third Base	PCT	G	PO	A	E	DP
Adams	1.000	2	1	2	0	0
Cervenak	.932	79	55	136	14	13
Evans	.917	4	7	4	1	1
Green	.818	4	2	7	2	0
Hessman	.984	47	22	105	2	14
Lutz	.875	4	3	4	1	1
Turner	.895	8	3	14	2	2

Shortstop	PCT	G	PO	A	E	DP
Adams	1.000	10	13	20	0	5
Cintron	1.000	3	3	2	0	1
Green	.957	15	20	25	2	7

Hernandez	.966	41	57	111	6	25
Tejada	.968	58	61	179	8	27
Turner	.946	21	42	46	5	15

Outfield	PCT	G	PO	A	E	DP
Adams	.967	23	28	1	1	0
Carter	1.000	14	22	0	0	0
Cervenak	.975	25	39	0	1	0
Cintron	—	1	0	0	0	0
Duda	.969	60	88	5	3	1
Feliciano	1.000	86	183	11	0	2
Garcia	1.000	15	40	0	0	0
Green	1.000	19	17	0	0	0
House	—	1	0	0	0	0
Hubbard	1.000	3	6	1	0	0
Malo	1.000	7	9	0	0	0
Martinez	.985	68	127	8	2	1
Nieuwenhuis	.967	30	52	6	2	2
Padilla	.977	46	82	3	2	0
Pascucci	1.000	21	29	1	0	0
Pridie	.990	39	99	3	1	1
Wabick	.667	3	2	0	1	0

BINGHAMTON METS
DOUBLE-A
EASTERN LEAGUE

Batting	B-T	HT	WT	DOB	AVG	vLH	vRH	G	AB	R	H	2B	3B	HR	RBI	BB	HBP	SH	SF	SO	SB	CS	SLG	OBP
Campbell, Eric	R-R	6-3	220	4-9-87	.279	.314	.271	50	179	26	50	11	0	6	30	12	2	4	2	32	1	0	.441	.328
Centeno, Juan	L-R	5-9	172	11-16-89	.000	.000	.000	1	1	0	0	0	0	0	0	0	0	0	0	0	0	0	.000	.000
Coronado, Jose	B-R	6-1	190	4-13-86	.254	.338	.234	122	414	66	105	24	1	6	50	40	5	6	4	80	2	4	.360	.324
Duda, Lucas	L-R	6-5	240	2-3-86	.286	.143	.325	45	161	30	46	17	0	6	34	29	6	0	1	27	1	0	.503	.411
Evans, Nick	R-R	6-2	220	1-30-86	.294	.384	.270	88	347	62	102	30	0	17	55	40	1	0	3	65	0	1	.527	.366
Fisher, Michael	B-R	6-2	188	3-22-85	.298	.333	.294	18	57	7	17	1	0	3	5	1	0	1	0	16	1	0	.474	.310
Guzman, Carlos	L-R	6-3	195	5-24-86	.259	.194	.279	47	158	19	41	5	0	0	10	20	3	1	1	36	0	2	.291	.352
Havens, Reese	L-R	6-1	195	10-20-86	.338	.308	.345	18	68	12	23	2	1	6	12	6	1	0	0	15	0	2	.662	.400
Hernandez, Luis	B-R	5-10	180	6-26-84	.298	.333	.286	57	225	28	67	12	4	3	32	16	2	1	5	30	4	4	.427	.343
Hubbard, Marshall	L-R	6-2	215	4-16-82	.247	.125	.276	104	332	53	82	19	0	9	51	43	6	0	4	62	1	0	.386	.340
Lutz, Zach	R-R	6-1	220	6-3-86	.289	.226	.308	61	225	42	65	14	0	17	42	33	4	1	0	63	0	2	.578	.389
Maldonado, Brahiam	R-R	5-11	205	9-18-85	.284	.250	.296	75	250	40	71	19	4	14	38	19	6	3	1	84	7	2	.560	.348
Malo, Jonathan	R-R	6-2	180	9-29-83	.215	.209	.218	86	246	35	53	13	3	2	22	30	4	3	1	57	6	5	.321	.310
Manriquez, Salomon	R-R	6-1	200	9-15-82	.289	.211	.310	34	90	11	26	5	0	4	15	3	1	2	0	22	0	0	.478	.319
Montz, Luke	R-R	6-2	225	7-7-83	.182	.219	.167	33	110	10	20	3	0	2	15	12	0	0	3	32	0	2	.264	.256
Moras, Michael	R-R	6-1	200	9-11-85	.182	.000	.286	3	11	0	2	0	0	0	2	1	0	0	0	4	0	0	.182	.250
Nickeas, Mike	R-R	6-0	210	2-13-83	.283	.145	.319	82	265	27	75	15	0	5	33	49	4	0	0	43	1	1	.396	.403
Nieuwenhuis, Kirk	L-R	6-3	210	8-7-87	.289	.291	.289	94	394	81	114	35	2	16	60	30	1	3	5	93	13	7	.510	.337
Pellot, Hector	R-R	5-11	184	2-8-87	.127	.214	.105	7	8	9	3	1	0	5	4	2	2	1	31	1	0	.197	.192
Ratliff, Sean	L-L	6-3	185	2-24-87	.317	.333	.312	73	281	48	89	21	0	16	50	23	3	1	3	72	1	2	.562	.371
Reyes, Raul	L-L	6-0	195	12-30-86	.232	.256	.227	59	211	24	49	8	2	0	26	9	4	0	0	63	2	0	.403	.277
Riggans, Shawn	R-R	6-2	200	7-25-80	.400	.000	.400	2	5	0	2	0	0	0	2	0	0	0	0	1	0	0	.800	.400
Santos, Omir	R-R	6-0	215	4-29-81	.138	.083	.152	17	58	5	8	3	0	1	8	4	1	0	1	7	0	0	.241	.203
Satin, Josh	R-R	6-2	200	12-23-84	.308	.288	.312	79	286	49	88	24	1	7	39	36	7	0	3	71	1	0	.472	.395
Valdespin, Jordany	L-R	6-0	174	12-23-87	.232	.240	.230	28	112	8	26	8	0	0	8	2	0	2	1	23	4	2	.429	.249
Wabick, D.J.	L-R	6-2	215	5-30-84	.304	.333	.299	50	168	21	51	16	1	1	22	8	1	0	2	32	2	2	.429	.335

Pitching	B-T	HT	WT	DOB	W	L	ERA	G	GS	CG	SV	IP	H	R	ER	HR	BB	SO	AVG	vLH	vRH	K/9	BB/9
Alvarez, Manuel	R-R	5-11	200	12-18-85	3	1	2.87	34	0	0	8	47	35	17	15	5	6	57	.203	.250	.163	10.91	1.15
Antonini, Mike	R-L	6-2	200	8-6-85	6	9	4.32	73	23	1	0	131	132	64	63	17	26	106	.261	.278	.252	7.26	1.78

Pitching	B-T	HT	WT	DOB	W	L	ERA	G	GS	CG	SV	IP	H	R	ER	HR	BB	SO	AVG	vLH	vRH	K/9	BB/9
Beaulac, Eric	R-R	6-5	190	11-13-86	0	2	9.00	2	2	0	0	6	8	6	6	1	7	3	.364	.455	.273	4.50	10.50
Carson, Robert	L-L	6-3	220	1-23-89	1	6	8.32	10	10	0	0	49	68	46	45	7	23	30	.343	.280	.365	5.55	4.25
Cohoon, Mark	L-L	6-2	195	9-15-87	5	4	4.18	13	13	1	0	71	74	41	33	5	15	56	.272	.269	.273	7.10	1.90
De La Torre, Jose	R-R	5-9	175	10-17-85	0	0	2.05	15	0	0	2	22	16	5	5	0	12	22	.211	.222	.200	9.00	4.91
Ellison, Derrick	L-L	6-2	195	9-6-78	1	2	3.41	29	0	0	2	37	21	14	14	2	17	29	.167	.158	.174	7.05	4.14
Everts, Clint	B-R	6-2	195	8-10-84	3	1	6.94	26	0	0	2	35	46	28	27	3	21	37	.317	.308	.325	9.51	5.40
2-team total (15 New Hampshire)					4	1	5.59	41	3	0	2	74	82	47	46	6	48	67	—	—	—	8.15	5.84
Frederick, Emary	R-R	6-0	190	1-17-84	1	1	4.71	18	0	0	0	21	23	16	11	0	11	18	.271	.351	.208	7.71	4.71
Holt, Brad	R-R	6-4	194	10-13-86	1	5	10.20	10	9	0	0	30	43	35	34	2	23	25	.336	.340	.333	7.50	6.90
Kunz, Eddie	R-R	6-6	260	4-8-86	7	8	5.34	42	12	0	3	111	116	73	66	8	68	63	.278	.314	.252	5.09	5.50
Lujan, John	R-R	6-1	200	5-10-84	0	1	2.55	20	0	0	3	25	23	11	7	0	13	26	.250	.350	.173	9.49	4.74
Maine, John	R-R	6-4	200	5-8-81	0	0	0.00	1	1	0	0	4	1	0	0	0	2	5	.077	.250	.000	11.25	4.50
Mejia, Jenrry	R-R	6-0	160	10-11-89	2	0	1.32	6	6	1	0	27	19	5	4	0	14	26	.200	.167	.234	8.56	4.61
Merritt, Roy	L-L	6-0	170	9-22-85	4	5	3.86	60	0	0	9	82	75	41	35	7	27	65	.246	.228	.257	7.16	2.98
Moore, Brandon	R-R	6-3	190	1-24-86	0	1	24.30	1	1	0	0	3	8	9	9	4	4	6	.421	.333	.571	16.20	10.80
Muniz, Carlos	R-R	6-1	190	3-12-81	0	1	8.38	9	0	0	0	10	14	9	9	0	6	8	.341	.400	.308	7.45	5.59
Niesen, Eric	L-L	6-0	185	9-4-85	4	6	5.14	33	13	0	0	77	80	52	44	8	60	59	.270	.241	.287	6.90	7.01
Owen, Dylan	R-R	5-11	185	7-12-86	4	4	3.94	26	10	0	0	82	72	44	36	10	38	67	.235	.274	.203	7.32	4.15
Ramirez, Edgar	R-R	6-4	250	11-30-83	6	1	4.93	41	1	0	1	77	84	48	42	10	29	63	.275	.296	.257	7.40	3.40
Ramirez, Elvin	R-R	6-3	208	10-10-87	0	1	4.05	3	0	0	0	7	5	3	3	2	6	7	.208	.231	.182	9.45	8.10
Schwinden, Chris	R-R	6-3	215	9-22-86	4	7	5.56	17	14	1	0	79	100	53	49	8	19	69	.306	.296	.315	7.83	2.16
Shaw, Scott	R-R	6-5	230	3-8-86	4	7	8.42	22	13	0	0	73	96	71	68	16	39	45	.318	.310	.325	5.57	4.83
Stinson, Josh	R-R	6-4	210	3-14-88	9	3	4.24	32	14	0	1	110	108	57	52	7	50	68	.260	.243	.276	5.55	4.08
Turgeon, Erik	R-R	6-0	170	3-25-87	1	0	3.86	6	0	0	0	9	11	4	4	0	6	10	.306	.240	.389	9.64	5.79

Fielding

Catcher	PCT	G	PO	A	E	DP	PB
Manriquez	1.000	21	134	13	0	1	2
Montz	.977	31	196	18	5	3	1
Moras	1.000	3	17	0	0	1	0
Nickeas	.986	77	533	44	8	2	4
Riggans	1.000	2	12	0	0	0	0
Santos	.990	15	93	3	1	2	1

First Base	PCT	G	PO	A	E	DP
Duda	1.000	9	65	4	0	8
Evans	1.000	74	577	48	0	56
Hubbard	.985	27	182	17	3	21
Manriquez	1.000	4	15	2	0	1
Montz	1.000	1	1	1	0	0
Nickeas	.952	3	19	1	1	4
Santos	1.000	1	1	0	0	0
Satin	.996	34	236	17	1	27

Second Base	PCT	G	PO	A	E	DP
Coronado	.966	28	46	67	4	17
Fisher	1.000	8	12	15	0	4
Havens	.965	16	24	58	3	6
Malo	.952	22	28	32	3	7
Pellot	.976	18	33	47	2	10
Satin	.982	37	76	90	3	22
Valdespin	.932	28	58	66	9	18

Third Base	PCT	G	PO	A	E	DP
Campbell	.931	35	23	58	6	9
Coronado	.938	35	18	58	5	2
Evans	1.000	12	6	24	0	5
Fisher	.889	3	1	7	1	1
Lutz	.936	57	25	78	7	6
Pellot	1.000	6	2	6	0	0
Satin	1.000	5	2	7	0	1

Shortstop	PCT	G	PO	A	E	DP
Coronado	.976	55	85	164	6	30
Fisher	.857	2	1	5	1	2
Hernandez	.979	56	91	142	5	34
Malo	.974	36	53	98	4	20

Outfield	PCT	G	PO	A	E	DP
Campbell	1.000	15	21	3	0	0
Duda	.971	35	65	3	2	0
Evans	1.000	2	3	1	0	1
Guzman	.970	46	97	1	3	0
Hubbard	1.000	9	11	0	0	0
Maldonado	.993	67	135	1	1	0
Malo	.971	25	63	3	2	1
Nieuwenhuis	.978	91	260	7	6	2
Ratliff	.967	73	147	1	5	0
Reyes	.975	57	113	4	3	0
Wabick	1.000	26	39	0	0	0

ST. LUCIE METS

HIGH CLASS A

FLORIDA STATE LEAGUE

Batting	B-T	HT	WT	DOB	AVG	vLH	vRH	G	AB	R	H	2B	3B	HR	RBI	BB	HBP	SH	SF	SO	SB	CS	SLG	OBP
Abruzzo, Jordan	B-R	6-3	230	8-2-84	.250	.000	.333	1	4	0	1	0	0	0	0	0	0	0	0	2	0	0	.250	.250
August, Joey	L-L	6-1	190	9-23-86	.262	.233	.268	72	237	25	62	16	0	3	22	20	4	2	0	29	7	2	.367	.330
Barajas, Rod	R-R	6-1	245	9-5-75	.235	.250	.231	4	17	1	4	0	0	0	2	0	0	0	0	2	0	0	.235	.235
Barrett, Michael	R-R	6-0	225	10-22-76	.220	.263	.194	15	50	3	11	1	0	0	3	4	0	0	0	8	0	0	.240	.278
Beltran, Carlos	B-R	6-0		4-24-77	.367	.250	.405	14	49	5	18	5	0	0	5	7	0	0	1	6	0	0	.469	.439
Blaquiere, Jean Luc	R-R	6-0	196	2-27-86	.186	.205	.180	52	172	10	32	3	1	1	16	6	0	3	0	53	0	3	.233	.213
Bouchard, Matt	R-R	6-0	185	12-12-86	.192	.000	.208	9	26	2	5	0	0	0	4	1	0	0	0	6	0	1	.192	.222
Campbell, Eric	R-R	6-3	220	4-9-87	.335	.386	.317	46	170	37	57	14	1	4	20	21	3	1	1	22	2	5	.500	.415
Castillo, Luis	B-R	5-11	195	9-12-75	.154	.500	.000	4	13	3	2	1	0	0	0	3	0	0	0	2	0	0	.231	.313
Centeno, Juan	L-R	5-9	172	11-16-89	.200	.125	.222	11	35	1	7	0	0	0	1	3	0	2	1	7	1	0	.200	.256
Cherry, Will	R-R	6-1	200	1-29-87	.000	.000	.000	1	1	0	0	0	0	0	0	0	0	0	0	1	0	0	.000	.000
Fernandez, Rafael	L-L	6-1	171	8-3-88	.300	.283	.305	59	200	26	60	11	4	3	22	14	0	3	3	46	2	1	.440	.341
Fisher, Michael	B-R	6-2	188	3-22-85	.277	.250	.287	41	148	23	41	13	0	3	19	12	1	2	3	31	5	0	.426	.329
Flores, Wilmer	R-R	6-3	175	8-6-91	.300	.508	.238	67	277	32	83	18	1	4	40	9	2	0	2	40	2	4	.415	.324
Freeman, Taylor	L-R	6-0	190	8-24-87	.333	.333	.333	2	6	1	2	0	1	0	2	2	0	0	0	1	0	0	.667	.500
Garcia, Emmanuel	L-R	6-2	185	3-4-86	.241	.212	.250	34	133	18	32	6	0	0	9	16	0	0	0	37	18	3	.286	.322
Green, Andy	R-R	5-10	180	7-7-77	.333	.000	.333	2	6	1	2	0	0	1	3	2	1	0	0	2	0	0	.833	.556
Gronauer, Kai	R-R	6-1	205	11-28-86	.324	.324	.324	38	139	18	45	5	0	2	20	10	2	0	1	26	1	0	.403	.375
Havens, Reese	L-R	6-1	195	10-20-86	.281	.333	.242	14	57	9	16	2	1	3	7	8	0	0	0	18	1	0	.509	.369
Holliday, Cody	L-L	6-3	215	9-30-87	.250	.000	.250	1	4	1	1	0	0	0	0	0	0	0	0	2	0	0	.250	.250
Lagares, Juan	R-R	6-1	175	3-17-89	.233	.225	.237	33	133	16	31	5	0	2	16	2	1	0	1	18	7	3	.316	.248
Lucas, Richard	R-R	6-1	205	11-2-88	.212	.207	.207	129	434	55	92	18	2	11	52	34	12	1	5	149	5	3	.339	.285
Lutz, Zach	R-R	6-1	220	6-3-86	.000	.000	.000	1	4	0	0	0	0	0	0	0	0	0	0	2	0	0	.000	.000
Maccani, Tony	R-R	6-3	191	9-24-84	.235	.250	.231	11	34	3	8	1	0	1	3	1	0	1	1	9	0	0	.353	.250
Maldonado, Braham	R-R	5-11	205	9-18-85	.276	.350	.262	31	123	18	34	6	0	7	18	10	1	0	2	48	2	2	.496	.331
Martinez, Fernando	L-R	6-1	200	10-10-88	.267	.125	.429	4	15	1	4	1	0	0	1	0	0	0	0	2	0	0	.333	.313

Name	B-T	HT	WT	DOB	AVG	vLH	vRH	G	AB	R	H	2B	3B	HR	RBI	BB	HBP	SH	SF	SO	SB	CS	SLG	OBP
Mollica, Ryan	R-L	6-0	185	2-25-86	.277	.429	.250	31	94	11	26	5	1	1	13	5	0	0	0	26	1	2	.383	.313
Montz, Luke	R-R	6-2	225	7-7-83	.250	.143	.333	6	16	3	4	0	0	1	2	5	0	0	0	4	0	0	.438	.429
Moras, Michael	R-R	6-1	200	9-11-85	.186	.000	.228	27	70	9	13	0	0	1	7	9	1	1	0	23	0	1	.229	.288
Murphy, Daniel	L-R	6-2	215	4-1-85	.727	.500	.778	3	11	2	8	1	0	1	6	2	0	0	0	0	0	0	1.091	.769
Nieves, Luis	R-R	5-11	160	12-15-88	.132	.158	.105	17	38	3	5	0	1	0	1	2	0	0	0	8	1	0	.184	.175
Pellot, Hector	R-R	5-11	184	2-8-87	.253	.327	.220	54	170	25	43	6	1	3	14	13	3	4	1	46	1	3	.353	.316
Pena, Francisco	R-R	6-2	230	10-12-89	.270	.571	.200	10	37	3	10	2	0	0	7	2	0	0	1	12	0	0	.324	.300
Ratliff, Sean	L-L	6-3	185	2-24-87	.275	.310	.262	57	222	35	61	14	3	5	30	17	2	0	1	66	9	2	.432	.331
Reyes, Jose	B-R	6-2		6-11-83	.000	.000	.000	1	4	0	0	0	0	0	0	0	0	0	0	0	0	0	.000	.000
Reyes, Raul	L-L	6-0	195	12-30-86	.218	.189	.226	52	174	19	38	12	0	4	11	9	1	3	0	44	3	0	.356	.261
Sandoval, Rylan	R-R	5-10	185	8-10-87	.217	.125	.267	10	23	4	5	0	0	0	3	5	0	0	0	11	1	0	.217	.419
Satin, Josh	R-R	6-2	200	12-23-84	.316	.286	.294	58	209	27	66	15	0	5	35	30	3	1	2	50	1	5	.459	.406
Semel, John	R-R	6-0	182	3-31-88	.158	.000	.231	5	19	0	3	0	0	0	1	0	0	0	0	5	0	0	.158	.158
Shields, Robbie	R-R	6-1	195	12-7-87	.286	.667	.000	2	7	0	2	0	0	0	1	1	0	0	0	1	0	0	.286	.375
Torres, Juan	R-R	6-1	180	10-7-88	.333	.143	.429	6	21	2	7	2	0	0	6	0	0	0	0	6	1	0	.429	.333
Tovar, Wilfredo	R-R	5-10	160	8-11-91	.246	.250	.244	30	118	14	29	5	1	0	6	3	2	1	0	22	4	3	.305	.276
Valdespin, Jordany	L-R	6-0	174	12-23-87	.289	.246	.300	65	270	40	78	16	3	6	33	8	6	3	1	45	13	10	.437	.323
Welch, Stefan	R-R	6-3	175	8-12-88	.256	.239	.262	133	496	64	127	29	8	8	68	37	16	2	4	126	2	1	.395	.325
Williams, Seth	R-R	6-2	205	11-21-85	.077	.000	.111	5	13	0	1	0	0	0	0	0	0	0	0	6	0	0	.077	.077
Zapata, Pedro	R-R	6-4	185	10-3-87	.246	.225	.252	40	167	20	41	2	4	0	6	5	0	4	1	48	9	7	.305	.266

Pitching	B-T	HT	WT	DOB	W	L	ERA	G	GS	CG	SV	IP	H	R	ER	HR	BB	SO	AVG	vLH	vRH	K/9	BB/9
Allen, Kyle	R-R	6-3	195	2-12-90	6	8	5.24	21	19	0	0	101	106	67	59	6	54	53	.273	.267	.278	4.71	4.80
Alvarez, Manuel	R-R	5-11	200	12-18-85	3	1	0.00	18	0	0	9	26	12	2	0	0	4	24	.148	.207	.115	8.42	1.40
Beaulac, Eric	R-R	6-5	190	11-13-86	5	5	3.68	21	19	0	0	103	93	61	42	3	55	76	.237	.265	.219	6.66	4.82
Bierd, Jose	R-R	6-2	155	5-8-85	3	3	4.63	32	0	0	8	45	52	30	23	2	22	41	.294	.309	.287	8.26	4.43
Calero, Angel	L-L	6-1	210	9-25-86	1	2	5.40	11	0	0	1	18	25	12	11	2	10	21	.313	.200	.338	10.31	4.91
Carr, Nick	R-R	6-1	195	4-19-87	1	1	5.40	16	0	0	0	23	25	15	14	2	16	26	.275	.286	.268	10.03	6.17
Carson, Robert	L-L	6-3	220	1-23-89	7	5	4.17	17	16	0	0	86	98	42	40	5	33	69	.287	.247	.299	7.19	3.44
Clyne, Stephen	B-R	6-2	215	9-22-84	1	1	3.86	10	0	0	0	14	16	8	6	0	9	11	.291	.348	.250	7.07	5.79
Cruz, Rhiner	R-R	6-2	205	11-1-86	0	5	3.46	51	0	0	6	75	62	34	29	6	53	66	.232	.270	.205	7.88	6.33
Cuan, Angel	L-L	5-11	150	5-29-89	0	0	0.00	3	0	0	0	4	4	0	0	0	1	2	.200	.125	.286	4.15	2.08
Familia, Jeurys	R-R	6-3	185	10-10-89	6	9	5.58	24	24	0	0	121	117	87	75	7	74	137	.257	.262	.254	10.19	5.50
Frederick, Emary	R-R	6-0	190	1-17-84	0	0	2.35	17	0	0	3	23	18	6	6	1	4	25	.214	.258	.189	9.78	1.57
Fuller, Jimmy	L-L	5-10	180	6-1-87	3	2	3.38	5	5	0	0	24	26	10	9	2	9	25	.274	.125	.287	9.38	3.38
Green, Sean	R-R	6-6	225	4-20-79	0	0	4.50	4	0	0	0	4	6	2	2	0	1	6	.333	.250	.400	13.50	2.25
Holt, Brad	R-R	6-4	194	10-13-86	14	14	7.48	14	14	0	0	65	68	57	54	4	56	62	.276	.229	.312	8.58	7.75
Igarashi, Ryota	R-R	5-11	200	5-28-79	1	0	2.35	5	2	0	0	8	10	2	2	0	1	11	.313	.118	.533	12.91	1.17
Johnson, Jimmy	L-L	6-0	195	11-24-85	4	3	4.93	28	1	0	0	38	41	23	21	4	10	33	.266	.261	.269	7.75	2.35
Martinez, Pedro P.	R-R	6-4	191	7-8-85	0	0	2.70	4	0	0	0	7	6	2	2	0	5	5	.261	.125	.333	6.75	6.75
Martinez, Samuel	R-R	5-11	175	7-6-87	0	0	2.84	3	0	0	0	6	2	2	2	0	3	6	.105	.250	.000	8.53	4.26
Mejia, Jenrry	R-R	6-0	160	10-11-89	0	0	0.00	1	1	0	0	4	1	0	0	0	0	7	.077	.000	.125	15.75	0.00
Moore, Brandon	R-R	6-3	190	1-24-86	2	4	3.82	12	12	0	0	66	69	35	28	4	26	61	.270	.295	.252	8.32	3.55
Moviel, Scott	R-R	6-11	235	5-7-88	3	7	5.56	26	16	0	2	110	126	78	68	7	55	90	.294	.283	.303	7.36	4.50
Muniz, Carlos	R-R	6-1	190	3-12-81	1	0	1.13	7	0	0	0	8	3	1	1	1	3	8	.115	.091	.133	9.00	3.38
Needham, Brian	R-R	6-7	195	9-21-86	0	0	0.00	2	0	0	0	3	4	6	2	0	3	0	.308	.500	.143	0.00	9.00
Perez, Oliver	L-L	6-3	205	8-15-81	1	1	4.63	2	0	0	0	12	7	6	6	2	4	14	.167	.118	.200	10.80	3.09
Powers, Michael	R-R	6-3	180	4-7-86	2	1	5.29	10	0	0	0	17	21	10	10	1	12	12	.313	.227	.356	6.35	6.35
Ramirez, Elvin	R-R	6-3	208	10-10-87	4	3	4.17	49	0	0	0	73	56	37	34	0	43	65	.212	.234	.196	7.98	5.28
Rustich, Brant	R-R	6-6	230	1-23-85	0	1	3.38	5	0	0	0	5	9	3	2	0	6	7	.391	.444	.357	11.81	10.13
Schwinden, Chris	R-R	6-3	215	9-22-86	3	0	1.83	7	2	0	0	34	34	8	7	2	5	23	.258	.283	.241	6.03	1.31
Shaw, Scott	R-R	6-5	230	8-3-86	0	0	5.54	7	1	0	0	13	12	9	8	5	6	12	.231	.278	.206	8.31	4.15
Tabata, Marcos	R-R	6-0	180	6-12-86	0	2	3.48	10	0	0	0	21	19	12	8	2	10	24	.244	.229	.256	10.45	4.35
Tovar, Orlando	L-L	6-3	213	3-26-88	0	1	37.80	1	1	0	0	2	8	9	7	1	0	0	.615	.000	.667	0.00	5.40
Turgeon, Erik	R-R	6-0	170	3-25-87	2	2	3.56	22	0	0	4	30	29	13	12	2	13	32	.259	.217	.288	9.49	3.86
Wrenn, Wes	R-R	5-11	185	4-17-86	1	0	1.80	2	2	0	0	10	10	2	2	0	1	4	.270	.375	.190	3.60	0.90

Fielding

Catcher	PCT	G	PO	A	E	DP	PB
Abruzzo	1.000	1	7	0	0	0	
Barajas	.977	4	39	4	1	0	0
Barrett	.963	7	52	0	2	0	3
Blaquiere	.985	49	340	51	6	3	13
Centeno	1.000	9	56	10	0	0	1
Freeman	1.000	2	13	0	0	0	0
Gronauer	.993	29	250	26	2	5	5
Maccani	1.000	10	53	4	0	0	2
Montz	.981	5	44	7	1	0	0
Moras	.992	20	115	16	1	1	3
Pena	1.000	5	46	4	0	1	0
Torres	1.000	6	43	5	0	0	1

First Base	PCT	G	PO	A	E	DP
Campbell	.987	8	69	6	1	6
Fisher	.979	7	45	1	1	3
Lucas	.960	3	21	3	1	2
Murphy	1.000	3	29	3	0	8
Satin	1.000	1	1	0	0	1
Welch	.992	118	960	68	8	91

Second Base	PCT	G	PO	A	E	DP
Bouchard	1.000	1	3	3	0	0
Castillo	1.000	4	1	7	0	1
Fisher	.950	23	42	54	5	12
Green	.917	2	4	7	1	2
Havens	1.000	32	132	41	0	10
Mollica	.945	16	24	28	3	4
Nieves	.818	2	6	3	2	2
Pellot	.941	5	5	11	1	1
Sandoval	.750	2	1	2	1	2
Satin	.977	39	68	104	4	25
Tovar	1.000	3	7	8	0	4
Valdespin	.983	36	79	95	3	27

Third Base	PCT	G	PO	A	E	DP
Campbell	.944	11	8	26	2	3
Fisher	1.000	3	2	4	0	1
Lucas	.931	123	60	225	21	16
Lutz	1.000	1	1	1	0	0
Mollica	1.000	2	0	4	0	0
Nieves	.600	2	1	2	2	0
Pellot	.500	1	1	0	1	0
Sandoval	1.000	1	1	2	0	0

Shortstop	PCT	G	PO	A	E	DP
Bouchard	.920	5	5	18	2	3
Fisher	.933	4	5	9	1	1
Flores	.945	67	84	157	14	39
Nieves	.957	12	19	26	2	7
Reyes	1.000	1	1	2	0	1
Sandoval	.950	5	11	8	1	3
Tovar	.957	27	53	81	6	22

	PCT	G	PO	A	E	DP
Valdespin	.889	23	35	53	11	9
Outfield	**PCT**	**G**	**PO**	**A**	**E**	**DP**
August	.990	64	95	1	1	1
Beltran	1.000	10	22	0	0	0
Campbell	.973	22	33	3	1	0
Cherry	—	1	0	0	0	0
Fernandez	.956	58	108	1	5	0
Garcia	.986	32	65	6	1	0
Holliday	1.000	1	2	0	0	0
Lagares	.974	33	69	5	2	2
Maldonado	.947	28	53	1	3	0
Martinez	1.000	3	6	1	0	0
Moras	.000	1	0	0	1	0
Pellot	.957	36	65	1	3	0
Ratliff	.974	54	113	1	3	0
Reyes	.986	45	67	1	1	0
Semel	1.000	5	12	0	0	0
Williams	1.000	3	6	0	0	0
Zapata	.989	38	83	3	1	0

SAVANNAH SAND GNATS   LOW CLASS A

SOUTH ATLANTIC LEAGUE

NEW YORK METS

Batting	B-T	HT	WT	DOB	AVG	vLH	vRH	G	AB	R	H	2B	3B	HR	RBI	BB	HBP	SH	SF	SO	SB	CS	SLG	OBP
Abruzzo, Jordan	B-R	6-3	230	8-2-84	.196	.083	.231	14	51	2	10	1	0	0	5	2	3	0	0	15	0	1	.216	.268
Butler, Jet	B-R	6-2	200	10-6-87	.218	.265	.202	40	133	15	29	5	0	3	14	10	5	1	2	32	2	2	.323	.293
Cordero, Albert	R-R	5-11	175	1-14-90	.667	.000	.667	1	3	0	2	0	0	0	1	0	0	0	0	0	0	0	.667	.667
den Dekker, Matt	L-L	6-1	205	8-10-87	.346	.250	.382	27	104	21	36	13	0	0	15	9	1	0	0	28	3	0	.471	.404
Doyle, Dock	L-R	6-0	200	3-24-86	.230	.213	.237	55	178	20	41	4	0	0	14	27	2	0	0	21	1	2	.253	.338
Farrell, Patrick	R-R	6-3	210	12-29-86	.174	.000	.211	6	23	0	4	0	0	0	1	0	0	0	0	14	0	0	.174	.174
Fernandez, Rafael	L-L	6-1	171	8-3-88	.253	.156	.274	45	178	19	45	7	3	2	14	14	1	3	1	52	6	3	.360	.309
Fisher, Michael	B-R	6-2	188	3-22-85	.354	.368	.348	17	65	9	23	4	2	3	14	6	0	1	1	12	0	1	.615	.403
Flagg, Jeff	R-R	6-6	246	11-7-85	.162	.105	.174	27	105	8	17	2	2	1	6	11	1	0	1	40	0	0	.248	.246
Flores, Wilmer	R-R	6-3	175	8-6-91	.278	.264	.281	66	277	30	77	18	2	7	44	23	5	0	2	37	2	1	.433	.342
Gregory, Alex	R-R	6-0	210	11-7-86	.241	.207	.253	68	212	23	51	9	0	0	21	20	4	3	2	51	2	2	.283	.315
Gronauer, Kai	R-R	6-1	205	11-28-86	.267	.226	.275	50	191	23	51	10	1	2	23	18	7	3	2	32	3	1	.361	.349
Harris, Alonzo	R-R	5-11	165	11-16-89	.224	.244	.218	105	380	51	85	18	6	5	42	20	6	6	5	90	18	7	.342	.270
Harris, R.J.	L-L	6-2	205	2-19-87	.191	.179	.197	67	251	30	48	7	2	6	32	24	3	1	2	90	4	2	.307	.268
Harrison, Brian	R-R	6-2	180	12-15-88	.250	.000	.286	5	16	2	4	2	0	0	0	0	0	0	0	3	0	0	.375	.250
Holliday, Cody	L-L	6-3	215	9-30-87	.241	.182	.278	9	29	8	7	2	0	0	4	7	1	0	0	12	1	0	.310	.405
Honeck, Sam	L-L	6-2	210	6-19-87	.091	.000	.105	6	22	5	2	1	0	0	0	6	0	0	4	0	0	.136	.286
Lagares, Juan	R-R	6-1	175	3-17-89	.300	.267	.309	67	290	42	87	13	9	5	39	7	3	2	5	44	18	2	.459	.318
Marte, Jefry	R-R	6-1	187	6-21-91	.264	.253	.268	82	329	40	87	19	4	6	44	30	5	0	2	65	4	5	.401	.333
Mollica, Ryan	R-L	6-0	185	2-25-86	.000	.000	.000	2	3	0	0	0	0	0	0	0	0	0	0	1	0	0	.000	.000
Moras, Michael	R-R	6-1	200	9-11-85	.000	.000	.000	2	9	1	0	0	0	0	0	1	1	0	0	3	0	0	.000	.182
Nieves, Luis	R-R	5-11	160	12-15-88	.339	.389	.316	16	56	10	19	4	0	1	7	5	0	0	0	9	2	0	.464	.393
Ozga, Travis	B-R	6-2	210	12-7-86	.265	.233	.278	55	204	30	54	8	0	4	31	17	1	1	2	33	6	0	.363	.321
Puello, Cesar	R-R	6-2	195	4-1-91	.292	.312	.286	109	404	80	118	22	1	1	34	32	22	10	1	82	45	10	.359	.375
Rivera, Luis	R-R	6-1	187	1-25-84	.217	.167	.229	21	60	9	13	1	0	0	7	1	2	4	1	8	2	0	.233	.250
Rodriguez, Aderlin	R-R	6-3	210	11-18-91	.200	.267	.133	8	30	3	6	1	0	1	11	6	1	0	2	10	0	0	.333	.333
Sandoval, Rylan	R-R	5-10	185	8-10-87	.115	.000	.130	9	26	3	3	0	0	0	1	5	4	0	0	9	0	0	.115	.343
Santomauro, Nick	R-L	6-3	205	6-13-88	.191	.160	.202	81	299	27	57	13	0	0	13	20	2	0	4	63	2	2	.234	.243
Schroeder, James	R-R	6-0	210	12-13-86	.229	.333	.207	11	35	7	8	1	0	1	3	3	1	1	1	3	2	0	.343	.300
Shields, Robbie	R-R	6-1	195	12-7-87	.290	.340	.270	39	162	26	47	10	1	5	26	10	0	1	0	34	4	0	.457	.331
Torres, Juan	R-R	6-1	180	10-7-88	.234	.279	.216	42	145	19	34	9	0	3	19	5	6	3	4	23	0	1	.359	.281
Tovar, Wilfredo	R-R	5-10	160	8-11-91	.281	.267	.287	44	160	12	45	10	0	0	17	8	3	2	0	12	4	5	.344	.327
Van Gurp, Ray	R-R	5-11	165	1-2-89	.333	1.000	.000	1	3	1	1	0	0	0	1	0	0	0	0	0	0	0	.333	.500
Zapata, Pedro	R-R	6-4	185	10-3-87	.288	.238	.302	84	365	53	105	15	7	2	45	29	2	3	1	88	27	6	.384	.343

Pitching	B-T	HT	WT	DOB	W	L	ERA	G	GS	CG	SV	IP	H	R	ER	HR	BB	SO	AVG	vLH	vRH	K/9	BB/9
Church, John	R-R	6-3	235	11-4-86	7	2	2.64	36	10	1	1	92	76	32	27	2	36	76	.228	.208	.237	7.43	3.52
Cohoon, Mark	L-L	6-2	195	9-15-87	7	1	1.30	13	13	3	0	90	68	15	13	2	17	75	.213	.281	.198	7.47	1.69
Edgin, Josh	L-L	6-1	225	12-17-86	0	0	0.00	2	0	0	0	3	3	0	0	0	0	5	.273	.250	.286	15.00	0.00
Figuereo, Johan	R-R	6-2	195	3-2-86	0	0	10.80	2	0	0	0	2	2	2	2	1	1	1	.286	.500	.200	5.40	5.40
Fuller, Jimmy	L-L	5-10	180	6-1-87	8	3	1.93	19	19	0	0	107	92	36	23	1	29	99	.229	.241	.228	8.30	2.43
Germen, Gonzalez	R-R	6-1	175	9-23-87	1	0	2.77	2	2	1	0	13	11	4	4	1	1	10	.220	.179	.273	6.92	0.69
Gorski, Darin	L-L	6-4	210	10-6-87	6	8	4.58	25	18	0	3	114	125	/0	58	12	43	109	.280	.293	.276	8.61	3.39
Hebert, Mike	R-R	6-3	180	8-11-90	0	0	1.42	2	0	0	1	6	3	1	1	1	2	4	.150	.000	.188	5.68	2.84
Hilliard, Chris	L-L	6-0	175	10-26-87	1	1	1.69	9	0	0	0	5	3	1	1	0	2	3	.167	.000	.176	5.06	3.38
Hoge, Lance	L-L	5-10	185	5-6-87	2	0	3.75	18	0	0	1	36	40	21	15	3	6	33	.265	.227	.271	8.25	1.50
Leduc, Guillaume	R-R	6-4	192	7-28-87	1	2	4.32	18	0	0	0	33	34	19	16	3	14	33	.240	.219	.291	8.91	3.78
Martinez, Pedro P.	R-R	6-4	191	7-8-85	0	1	3.18	6	0	0	0	11	15	9	4	1	2	6	.313	.333	.292	4.76	1.59
Martinez, Samuel	R-R	5-11	175	7-6-87	0	1	5.95	14	0	0	0	20	19	13	13	1	10	18	.250	.367	.174	8.24	4.58
McHugh, Collin	R-R	6-2	195	6-19-87	7	8	3.33	28	20	0	1	132	139	65	49	7	38	129	.268	.312	.239	8.77	2.58
Moore, Brandon	R-R	6-3	190	1-24-86	3	4	2.49	14	12	0	2	80	62	28	22	5	11	98	.215	.330	.159	11.07	1.24
Peralta, Ramiro	R-R	6-3	180	9-8-89	0	0	0.00	2	0	0	0	2	3	0	0	0	2	0	.300	.667	.143	0.00	7.71
Powers, Michael	R-R	6-3	180	4-7-86	3	4	2.28	41	0	0	15	51	39	16	13	4	23	52	.210	.286	.171	9.12	4.03
Rodriguez, Armando	R-R	6-2	185	1-28-88	8	9	3.08	27	27	0	0	146	116	61	50	5	46	152	.214	.232	.204	9.37	2.84
Rojas, Luis	R-R	5-10	185	7-29-89	2	0	3.58	23	0	0	1	38	37	18	15	2	21	21	.268	.230	.299	5.02	5.02
Sage, Brandon	L-L	6-2	210	10-3-86	3	6	3.07	40	0	0	7	59	51	26	20	2	12	49	.227	.220	.229	7.52	1.84
Tabata, Marcos	R-R	6-0	180	6-12-86	4	1	4.25	21	0	0	1	36	40	17	17	0	13	33	.288	.288	.287	8.25	3.25
Turgeon, Erik	R-R	6-0	170	3-25-87	3	2	1.46	25	0	0	1	37	31	9	6	0	7	30	.220	.310	.182	7.30	1.70
Whitenton, Taylor	R-R	6-3	190	2-20-88	8	9	4.57	26	18	0	1	108	110	60	55	6	68	113	.264	.235	.283	9.39	5.65
Zavala, Gabriel	R-R	6-3	180	5-14-87	1	1	1.56	20	0	0	0	35	22	11	6	1	10	38	.173	.170	.175	9.87	2.60

Fielding

Catcher	PCT	G	PO	A	E	DP	PB
Cordero	1.000	1	8	2	0	0	0
Doyle	.993	51	393	27	3	1	4
Farrell	1.000	1	8	1	0	0	0
Gronauer	.994	49	460	38	3	8	7
Torres	.989	40	330	37	4	5	5

First Base	PCT	G	PO	A	E	DP
Butler	1.000	4	26	2	0	2
Fisher	.987	10	70	7	1	11
Flagg	.995	25	210	7	1	19
Gregory	.986	52	405	22	6	26
Honeck	1.000	3	30	4	0	0
Ozga	.986	45	337	12	5	34
Rivera	1.000	7	55	2	0	4

Second Base	PCT	G	PO	A	E	DP
Butler	1.000	18	25	32	0	9
Fisher	.933	4	7	7	1	2
Harris	.956	105	192	262	21	56

	PCT	G	PO	A	E	DP
Mollica	1.000	1	2	3	0	1
Nieves	1.000	5	9	11	0	5
Rivera	.938	4	8	7	1	1
Tovar	1.000	7	16	13	0	5
Van Gurp	1.000	1	2	5	0	0

Third Base	PCT	G	PO	A	E	DP
Butler	.759	12	5	17	7	0
Harrison	.800	5	6	6	3	1
Marte	.892	80	51	155	25	13
Nieves	1.000	4	7	3	0	1
Ozga	.850	8	5	12	3	0
Rivera	1.000	7	9	9	0	0
Rodriguez	.944	8	19	15	2	4
Sandoval	.957	8	7	15	1	0
Schroeder	.862	11	3	22	4	3

Shortstop	PCT	G	PO	A	E	DP
Butler	.667	2	1	3	2	0
Fisher	1.000	2	6	7	0	4

	PCT	G	PO	A	E	DP
Flores	.957	65	85	185	12	35
Nieves	.933	8	9	19	2	3
Rivera	1.000	2	2	3	0	1
Sandoval	1.000	1	0	2	0	0
Shields	.902	23	37	46	9	11
Tovar	.950	37	55	115	9	19

Outfield	PCT	G	PO	A	E	DP
Butler	—	1	0	0	0	0
den Dekker	.968	26	58	3	2	1
Fernandez	.949	32	53	3	3	0
Gregory	—	3	0	0	0	0
Harris	.977	64	118	8	3	1
Holliday	1.000	9	11	1	0	1
Lagares	.978	61	128	6	3	2
Ozga	1.000	3	1	0	0	0
Puello	.966	102	217	8	8	2
Santomauro	.942	58	91	6	6	1
Zapata	1.000	66	151	4	0	3

BROOKLYN CYCLONES — SHORT-SEASON

NEW YORK-PENN LEAGUE

Batting	B-T	HT	WT	DOB	AVG	vLH	vRH	G	AB	R	H	2B	3B	HR	RBI	BB	HBP	SH	SF	SO	SB	CS	SLG	OBP
Bonfe, Joe	R-R	6-4	220	12-28-87	.326	.288	.336	72	270	41	88	13	1	4	28	26	2	6	1	56	8	2	.426	.388
Brown, J.B.	L-R	6-1	220	4-30-89	.308	.296	.310	57	201	28	62	12	4	3	29	13	0	8	2	29	2	1	.453	.347
Butler, Jet	B-R	6-2	200	10-6-87	.250	.667	.176	6	20	3	5	1	0	0	2	3	0	0	0	3	0	0	.300	.348
Ceciliani, Darrell	L-L	6-1	205	6-22-90	.351	.344	.353	68	271	56	95	19	12	2	35	24	4	3	1	56	21	14	.531	.410
Centeno, Juan	L-R	5-9	172	11-16-89	.371	.353	.375	32	89	17	33	8	1	1	10	6	1	8	0	8	1	0	.517	.417
Cherry, Will	R-R	6-1	200	1-29-87	.234	.240	.242	56	197	26	46	8	3	5	34	17	0	9	3	55	5	8	.381	.290
Farrell, Patrick	R-R	6-3	210	12-29-86	.133	.000	.167	7	15	1	2	0	0	1	3	0	0	0	0	6	1	0	.333	.133
Flagg, Jeff	R-R	6-6	246	11-7-85	.252	.295	.239	73	270	39	68	17	5	9	52	27	7	3	8	79	9	2	.452	.327
Forsythe, Blake	R-R	6-2	220	7-31-89	.238	.476	.175	30	101	14	24	5	1	3	8	11	1	1	3	41	1	1	.396	.310
Freeman, Taylor	L-R	6-0	190	8-24-87	.170	.214	.154	17	53	6	9	2	0	1	6	4	0	2	1	16	0	1	.264	.224
Hall, ZeErika	R-R	6-0	175	6-29-88	.167	.000	.231	6	18	2	3	0	0	0	2	2	0	0	0	3	1	0	.167	.250
Harris, R.J.	L-L	6-2	205	2-19-87	.300	.000	.333	3	10	1	3	2	0	0	0	0	0	0	0	1	0	0	.500	.300
Harrison, Brian	R-R	6-2	180	12-15-88	.286	.385	.260	35	126	24	36	10	1	7	22	10	4	3	2	18	2	0	.548	.352
Holliday, Cody	L-L	6-3	215	9-30-87	.200	.083	.219	35	65	15	17	4	1	0	8	12	1	2	0	22	2	2	.271	.306
Nieves, Luis	R-R	5-11	160	12-15-88	.267	.308	.255	23	60	11	16	1	2	2	10	3	0	2	1	7	5	0	.450	.297
Sandoval, Rylan	R-R	5-10	185	8-10-87	.330	.341	.326	47	185	34	61	13	0	9	29	16	7	2	0	35	8	5	.546	.404
Schafer, Justin	R-R	6-1	190	6-12-87	.227	.294	.185	14	44	4	10	2	0	0	6	3	0	1	1	5	0	0	.273	.271
Schroeder, James	R-R	6-0	210	12-13-86	.258	.194	.288	36	97	18	25	9	0	1	9	10	1	6	0	23	1	1	.381	.333
Steinhauer, Kurt	R-R	6-1	205	3-29-86	.141	.091	.163	29	71	8	10	1	0	2	8	4	1	1	3	25	0	1	.239	.190
Tovar, Wilfredo	R-R	5-10	160	8-11-91	.265	.188	.288	18	68	11	18	2	1	0	6	2	3	3	1	9	4	3	.324	.311
Valdez, Amauris	R-R	5-11	194	8-24-88	.143	.333	.000	2	7	1	1	0	0	0	0	0	0	1	0	2	0	0	.286	.143
Vaughn, Cory	R-R	6-3	225	5-1-89	.307	.379	.286	72	264	45	81	14	5	14	56	34	9	0	6	63	12	5	.557	.396

Pitching	B-T	HT	WT	DOB	W	L	ERA	G	GS	CG	SV	IP	H	R	ER	HR	BB	SO	AVG	vLH	vRH	K/9	BB/9
Almonte, Yohan	R-R	6-1	150	11-9-89	8	4	1.91	15	15	1	0	90	68	28	19	1	15	60	.207	.232	.181	6.02	1.51
Bennett, Hamilton	R-L	6-1	180	6-26-88	2	2	3.49	19	0	0	0	28	27	13	11	1	9	24	.257	.289	.233	7.62	2.86
Carela, Daniel	R-R	6-3	225	9-18-87	2	1	1.82	19	0	0	2	25	16	5	5	2	15	25	.188	.086	.260	9.12	5.47
Carnevale, Hunter	R-R	5-11	200	8-27-88	0	0	18.00	5	0	0	0	5	11	11	10	0	5	8	.393	.417	.375	14.40	9.00
Carr, Nick	R-R	6-1	195	4-19-87	0	0	0.00	3	0	0	0	2	1	0	0	0	3	3	.125	.000	.250	11.57	11.57
Chism, T.J.	L-L	5-10	190	8-9-88	0	0	1.59	5	0	0	0	6	4	1	1	0	3	12	.192	.143	.214	19.06	4.76
Cuan, Angel	L-L	5-11	150	5-29-89	5	1	2.03	14	14	0	0	80	68	26	18	2	17	64	.230	.227	.231	7.23	1.92
Figuereo, Johan	R-R	6-2	195	3-2-86	5	1	2.40	24	0	0	8	30	24	10	8	1	15	35	.216	.200	.225	10.50	4.50
Fraser, Ryan	R-R	6-3	190	8-27-88	3	3	1.44	26	0	0	12	31	16	7	5	0	20	39	.155	.238	.098	11.20	5.74
Hilliard, Chris	L-L	6-0	175	10-26-87	5	1	3.74	14	14	0	0	79	79	40	33	2	14	50	.259	.302	.239	5.67	1.59
Houck, Mitch	L-L	6-1	200	5-26-87	4	1	3.73	10	9	0	0	51	53	28	21	3	17	41	.270	.339	.241	7.28	3.02
Kolarek, Adam	L-L	6-3	215	1-14-89	2	1	2.89	17	0	0	1	28	16	11	9	3	14	30	.168	.172	.167	9.64	4.50
Kountis, Jonathan	R-R	6-3	220	3-15-88	1	1	5.95	9	4	0	0	20	23	14	13	2	14	23	.303	.250	.350	10.53	6.41
Leduc, Guillaume	R-R	6-4	192	7-28-87	0	0	0.00	1	0	0	0	1	0	0	0	0	1	0	.000	.000	.000	9.00	9.00
Martinez, Pedro P.	R-R	6-4	191	7-8-85	0	0	9.00	2	0	0	0	2	1	2	2	1	2	2	.143	.200	.000	9.00	9.00
Needham, Brian	R-R	6-7	195	9-21-86	0	0	5.63	14	0	0	1	16	20	11	10	3	11	12	.308	.167	.390	6.75	6.19
Pereira, Nelson	L-L	5-11	180	2-12-89	1	0	3.28	16	2	0	1	36	30	15	13	1	12	38	.219	.316	.150	9.59	3.03
Pinera, A.J.	R-R	6-3	185	7-2-87	2	3	2.44	16	11	0	0	63	62	24	17	3	12	54	.256	.303	.224	7.76	1.72
Taveras, Samuel	R-R	6-2	190	4-14-89	2	0	3.86	12	0	0	0	14	15	6	6	1	6	10	.283	.211	.324	6.43	3.86
Weldon, Todd	R-R	6-4	215	7-21-87	0	0	4.15	2	0	0	0	4	5	3	2	0	4	2	.357	.600	.222	4.15	8.31
Wrenn, Wes	R-R	5-11	185	4-17-86	5	5	3.61	20	0	0	0	62	65	34	25	4	12	46	.259	.284	.242	6.64	1.73

Fielding

Catcher	PCT	G	PO	A	E	DP	PB
Centeno	.986	31	187	32	3	0	3
Farrell	1.000	6	25	2	0	1	1

	PCT	G	PO	A	E	DP	PB
Forsythe	.996	28	225	16	1	0	8
Freeman	.984	16	115	7	2	1	3
Valdez	1.000	2	16	1	0	0	0

First Base	PCT	G	PO	A	E	DP
Bonfe	.977	5	40	2	1	3
Flagg	.997	71	659	36	2	56

Second Base	PCT	G	PO	A	E	DP
Brown	.968	53	93	149	8	34
Nieves	1.000	2	2	1	0	0
Sandoval	1.000	4	2	9	0	1
Schafer	.975	9	12	27	1	4
Schroeder	.980	11	18	30	1	5

Third Base	PCT	G	PO	A	E	DP
Bonfe	.857	24	15	39	9	3
Butler	.833	5	3	7	2	0

Harrison	.840	29	20	43	12	5
Schafer	1.000	1	2	2	0	0
Schroeder	.911	21	8	33	4	1

Shortstop	PCT	G	PO	A	E	DP
Nieves	.952	20	30	49	4	10
Sandoval	.943	43	52	131	11	25
Schafer	1.000	2	1	1	0	0
Tovar	.960	18	26	46	3	11

Outfield	PCT	G	PO	A	E	DP
Ceciliani	.969	63	154	2	5	1
Cherry	.952	51	74	5	4	1
Hall	1.000	6	7	0	0	0
Harris	1.000	2	2	0	0	0
Holliday	.977	31	40	2	1	0
Schroeder	1.000	1	1	0	0	0
Steinhauer	.974	24	36	1	1	0
Vaughn	.977	70	123	6	3	2

KINGSPORT METS   ROOKIE

APPALACHIAN LEAGUE

Batting	B-T	HT	WT	DOB	AVG	vLH	vRH	G	AB	R	H	2B	3B	HR	RBI	BB	HBP	SH	SF	SO	SB	CS	SLG	OBP
Brown, Brandon	R-R	6-1	180	7-28-87	.209	.179	.227	47	153	12	32	12	0	0	14	9	2	2	0	24	9	4	.288	.262
Cordero, Albert	R-R	5-11	175	1-14-90	.277	.305	.258	54	206	32	57	11	2	8	32	8	2	1	3	24	2	1	.466	.306
Farrell, Patrick	R-R	6-3	210	12-29-86	.263	.167	.429	5	19	2	5	0	0	1	5	0	0	0	0	8	0	0	.421	.263
Freeman, Taylor	L-R	6-0	190	8-24-87	.174	.375	.067	10	23	0	4	0	0	0	2	0	0	0	0	11	0	0	.174	.240
Greene, Chase	R-R	5-11	180	4-22-90	.228	.215	.238	37	145	18	33	6	0	1	9	14	1	1	1	23	5	5	.290	.298
Hall, ZeErika	R-R	6-0	175	6-29-88	.264	.281	.255	61	254	42	67	14	0	2	20	16	5	1	4	63	14	4	.343	.315
Hinojosa, Charlie	R-R	6-3	190	6-16-89	.153	.154	.153	31	98	12	15	0	1	2	4	6	1	2	0	29	1	0	.235	.210
Lora, Eddie	B-L	6-2	215	3-21-89	.088	.000	.136	12	34	2	3	2	0	1	6	6	0	3	0	20	0	0	.235	.209
Ozga, Travis	B-R	6-2	210	12-7-86	.500	.500	.000	1	4	2	2	1	0	1	2	0	0	0	0	0	0	0	1.500	.500
Rodriguez, Aderlin	R-R	6-3	210	11-18-91	.312	.341	.297	61	250	44	78	22	0	13	48	15	1	0	1	43	3	1	.556	.352
Rodriguez, Javier	R-R	6-2	165	4-4-90	.319	.302	.327	41	160	29	51	15	2	4	24	6	3	0	1	28	1	2	.513	.353
Schafer, Justin	R-R	6-1	190	6-12-88	.333	.367	.312	30	126	17	42	9	1	1	16	12	1	2	1	19	5	5	.444	.393
Semel, John	R-R	6-0	182	3-31-88	.301	.193	.358	45	163	21	49	6	4	0	14	13	0	3	1	33	2	6	.387	.350
Stewart, Luke	L-R	6-4	205	2-29-88	.255	.224	.271	58	216	38	55	12	1	8	31	23	11	0	2	68	1	0	.431	.353
Tijerina, Ismael	R-R	6-0	165	8-19-89	.259	.208	.294	40	116	15	30	5	0	0	10	12	1	3	1	21	5	0	.302	.331
Valdez, Amauris	R-R	5-11	194	8-24-88	.278	.429	.182	14	18	1	5	0	0	0	3	0	1	1	0	3	0	0	.278	.316
Van Gurp, Ray	R-R	5-11	165	1-2-89	.271	.281	.264	47	170	22	46	9	3	1	28	16	3	0	2	28	5	4	.376	.340
Zapata, Nelfi	R-R	6-0	203	12-13-90	.247	.273	.237	53	186	17	46	6	0	2	20	17	5	0	0	27	1	0	.312	.327

Pitching	B-T	HT	WT	DOB	W	L	ERA	G	GS	CG	SV	IP	H	R	ER	HR	BB	SO	AVG	vLH	vRH	K/9	BB/9
Aldama, Eduardo	R-R	6-1	175	12-23-89	2	3	4.95	8	8	0	0	36	35	22	20	3	9	30	.252	.237	.263	7.43	2.23
Birdwell, Peter	R-R	6-4	225	2-3-87	2	1	3.94	16	1	0	0	32	32	22	14	6	21	28	.264	.233	.282	7.88	5.91
Carnevale, Hunter	R-R	5-11	200	8-27-88	3	1	3.86	12	0	0	1	23	26	13	10	1	7	27	.283	.231	.321	10.41	2.70
Chism, T.J.	L-L	5-10	190	8-9-88	4	0	0.45	18	0	0	0	20	15	2	1	0	6	17	.203	.227	.192	7.65	2.70
deGrom, Jacob	L-R	6-4	185	6-19-88	1	1	5.19	6	6	0	0	26	35	15	15	2	6	22	.324	.300	.345	7.62	2.08
Edgin, Josh	L-L	6-1	225	12-17-86	0	1	2.84	18	0	0	3	32	28	15	10	2	12	41	.231	.310	.190	11.65	3.41
Feliz, Tony	R-R	6-1	205	11-3-85	0	0	4.50	5	0	0	0	6	7	3	3	0	3	5	.304	.286	.313	7.50	4.50
Germen, Gonzalez	R-R	6-1	175	9-23-87	2	5	3.69	10	10	0	0	61	64	33	25	3	11	54	.274	.291	.264	7.97	1.62
Hebert, Mike	R-R	6-3	180	8-11-90	3	7	4.47	11	11	0	0	56	64	44	28	2	29	53	.282	.302	.270	8.47	4.63
Hodge, Lachlan	L-L	6-2	185	2-3-89	0	3	11.05	6	4	0	0	15	22	22	18	3	14	13	.361	.294	.386	7.98	8.59
Holdzkom, John	R-R	6-7	225	10-19-87	0	0	11.25	5	0	0	0	4	4	7	5	0	8	8	.235	.250	.231	18.00	18.00
Kolarek, Adam	L-L	6-3	215	1-14-89	0	0	3.86	5	0	0	0	9	3	4	4	1	3	15	.100	.250	.077	14.46	2.89
Kountis, Jonathan	R-R	6-3	220	3-15-88	0	1	4.35	5	5	0	0	21	21	13	10	3	10	16	.276	.333	.255	6.97	4.35
Mitchell, Bret	R-R	6-2	190	12-10-88	2	2	5.94	8	8	0	0	36	39	26	24	4	13	42	.271	.417	.198	10.40	3.22
Taveras, Samuel	R-R	6-2	190	4-14-89	2	1	1.93	6	0	0	0	14	11	5	3	1	2	18	.204	.167	.214	11.57	1.29
Torres, Jhonathan	L-L	5-11	170	3-20-90	1	1	5.29	15	2	0	0	34	42	20	20	5	10	47	.302	.226	.324	12.44	2.65
Tovar, Orlando	L-L	6-3	213	3-26-88	4	0	3.43	13	4	0	0	45	51	26	17	3	9	40	.288	.297	.286	8.06	1.81
Vasquez, Carlos	L-L	5-11	180	9-3-91	0	1	2.25	2	2	0	0	12	6	3	3	1	3	7	.154	.222	.133	5.25	2.25
Von Tersch, Zach	R-R	6-4	195	4-22-88	0	2	9.28	4	2	0	0	11	18	12	11	7	5	11	.346	.375	.321	9.28	4.22
Walters, Jeff	R-R	6-3	170	11-6-87	0	2	8.10	3	2	0	0	10	13	11	9	2	6	9	.310	.250	.364	8.10	5.40
Weldon, Todd	R-R	6-4	215	7-21-87	1	3	3.96	19	0	0	6	25	16	15	11	2	14	30	.174	.129	.197	10.80	5.04
Winnick, Steve	R-R	6-1	195	9-16-87	1	2	4.57	13	0	0	2	22	26	18	11	0	7	12	.299	.455	.204	4.98	2.91

Fielding

Catcher	PCT	G	PO	A	E	DP	PB
Cordero	.980	31	244	51	6	2	8
Farrell	1.000	2	8	2	0	0	0
Freeman	1.000	4	18	3	0	1	0
Valdez	1.000	8	18	0	0	0	0
Zapata	.983	33	263	25	5	5	16

First Base	PCT	G	PO	A	E	DP
Brown	.957	3	20	2	1	2
Lora	1.000	9	67	4	0	6
Ozga	1.000	1	12	0	0	0
Stewart	.987	56	508	20	7	56

Second Base	PCT	G	PO	A	E	DP
Hinojosa	1.000	3	6	7	0	4
Schafer	.929	9	13	26	3	7
Tijerina	.950	16	25	32	3	7
Van Gurp	.966	46	103	123	8	36

Third Base	PCT	G	PO	A	E	DP
Brown	1.000	4	2	10	0	1
Rodriguez	.891	58	47	116	20	15
Stewart	1.000	1	0	1	0	0
Tijerina	1.000	8	3	9	0	0

Shortstop	PCT	G	PO	A	E	DP
Brown	.877	34	36	92	18	17
Schafer	.966	20	35	78	4	19
Tijerina	.955	16	17	47	3	7

Outfield	PCT	G	PO	A	E	DP
Brown	1.000	3	4	0	0	0
Greene	.981	37	52	1	1	1
Hall	.967	61	112	6	4	1
Hinojosa	.973	24	34	2	1	1
Rodriguez	.983	40	53	5	1	1
Semel	.984	44	51	9	1	2

GULF COAST LEAGUE

Batting	B-T	HT	WT	DOB	AVG	vLH	vRH	G	AB	R	H	2B	3B	HR	RBI	BB	HBP	SH	SF	SO	SB	CS	SLG	OBP
Abruzzo, Jordan	B-R	6-3	230	8-2-84	.279	.167	.297	11	43	4	12	3	0	2	11	1	1	0	1	5	0	0	.488	.304
Barajas, Rod	R-R	6-1	245	9-5-75	.250	.000	.250	1	4	1	1	0	0	1	3	0	0	0	0	1	0	0	1.000	.250
Brown, Dylan	R-R	6-3	210	10-21-87	.173	.138	.182	45	139	17	24	2	2	4	9	16	7	2	0	55	3	2	.302	.290
Campbell, Eric	R-R	6-3	220	4-9-87	.273	.250	.286	3	11	1	3	1	0	0	1	0	0	0	0	1	1	0	.364	.273
Concepcion, Julio	R-R	6-4	194	9-5-89	.282	.350	.261	50	174	21	49	10	5	4	28	7	6	1	3	34	2	2	.466	.326
De La Cruz, Yucarybert	R-R	6-0	160	10-23-90	.210	.160	.221	40	138	16	29	2	0	2	9	10	0	4	2	28	5	4	.268	.260
De Leon, Jeyckol	R-R	6-2	185	7-25-90	.204	.188	.211	17	54	8	11	0	0	1	6	1	2	2	1	12	0	0	.259	.241
den Dekker, Matt	L-L	6-1	205	8-10-87	.278	.333	.267	5	18	2	5	2	0	0	5	2	0	1	0	5	0	0	.389	.350
Dunn, Josh	R-R	6-3	198	12-9-90	.250	.200	.258	11	36	4	9	1	0	0	5	2	2	0	0	12	0	0	.278	.325
Forsythe, Blake	R-R	6-2	220	7-31-89	.200	.333	.143	3	10	0	2	0	0	0	1	0	0	1	0	2	0	0	.200	.273
Glenn, Jeff	R-R	6-3	185	9-22-91	.231	.357	.203	24	78	7	18	4	0	1	4	6	1	0	0	19	1	0	.321	.294
Gomez, Gilbert	R-R	6-3	190	3-8-92	.229	.222	.231	45	157	25	36	11	2	1	15	9	5	1	2	31	7	2	.344	.289
Harrison, Brian	R-R	6-2	180	12-15-88	.296	.500	.261	8	27	3	8	3	1	1	3	2	1	0	0	5	0	0	.593	.367
Hessman, Mike	R-R	6-5	215	3-5-78	.500	1.000	.000	1	4	1	2	0	0	0	2	0	0	0	0	0	0	0	.500	.500
Lutz, Zach	R-R	6-1	220	6-3-86	.316	.500	.231	5	19	2	6	1	0	1	4	1	0	0	0	4	0	0	.526	.350
Maron, Cam	L-R	6-1	175	1-20-91	.313	.500	.286	20	48	8	15	1	1	1	7	7	1	3	0	8	0	0	.438	.411
Montz, Luke	R-R	6-2	225	7-7-83	.294	.000	.385	5	17	2	5	0	0	1	2	3	0	0	0	3	1	0	.471	.400
Moreno, Nestor	B-R	5-11	195	6-21-88	.314	.278	.327	22	70	8	22	5	1	0	9	11	0	0	0	10	1	1	.414	.407
Pena, Francisco	R-R	6-2	230	10-12-89	.313	.600	.259	10	32	4	10	1	0	0	2	1	0	0	0	6	0	0	.344	.436
Pridie, Jason	L-R	6-1	205	10-9-83	.364	.000	.364	4	11	3	4	1	0	0	0	3	0	0	0	5	0	0	.455	.500
Pugh, Tillman	R-R	6-0	190	2-19-89	.230	.400	.174	23	61	11	14	4	1	0	5	15	2	4	0	16	6	3	.328	.397
Sanchez, Alexander	R-R	6-3	200	11-28-90	.269	.438	.231	47	175	23	47	16	1	2	23	6	8	0	2	23	2	0	.406	.319
Santana, Randoll	R-R	6-0	165	11-12-90	.252	.308	.240	44	155	23	39	6	2	0	13	10	9	1	1	29	14	5	.316	.331
Shields, Robbie	R-R	6-1	195	12-7-87	.244	.250	.243	23	82	11	20	5	0	1	7	11	0	0	1	15	0	0	.341	.330
Soto, Breiner	R-R	6-2	147	2-23-90	.333	.400	.313	10	21	8	7	0	0	0	2	1	0	0	0	8	1	1	.333	.417
Tabb, Donnie	R-R	5-10	185	12-8-90	.217	.133	.241	23	69	13	15	3	1	0	6	5	3	0	1	12	2	1	.290	.295
Tejada, Miguel	R-R	6-1	175	11-11-90	.230	.105	.265	32	87	11	20	8	0	2	9	7	2	6	0	35	1	0	.391	.302
Vernouij, Marinus	R-R	6-3	215	1-30-89	.214	.353	.170	26	70	11	15	4	0	0	9	7	1	0	0	21	1	1	.271	.295

Pitching	B-T	HT	WT	DOB	W	L	ERA	G	GS	CG	SV	IP	H	R	ER	HR	BB	SO	AVG	vLH	vRH	K/9	BB/9
Aldama, Eduardo	R-R	6-1	175	12-23-89	1	1	9.00	5	0	0	0	6	8	7	6	1	4	7	.320	.333	.316	10.50	6.00
Birdwell, Peter	R-R	6-4	225	2-3-87	0	0	0.00	1	0	0	0	1	0	0	0	0	2	1	.000	.000	.000	9.00	18.00
Camarena, Marcos	R-R	6-3	202	9-8-90	3	3	2.68	10	5	1	1	44	40	14	13	0	7	24	.244	.229	.250	4.95	1.44
Carela, Daniel	R-R	6-3	225	9-18-87	0	0	0.00	3	0	0	2	3	2	0	0	0	1	3	.182	.250	.143	9.00	3.00
Carr, Nick	R-R	6-1	195	4-19-87	1	1	3.60	5	0	0	0	5	5	2	2	0	4	7	.294	.250	.308	12.60	7.20
Dotson, Zach	L-L	6-1	180	10-30-90	0	1	3.31	4	4	0	0	16	12	6	6	0	9	18	.207	.333	.184	9.92	4.96
Feliz, Tony	R-R	6-4	205	11-3-85	0	1	4.50	9	0	0	2	10	6	5	5	0	2	7	.176	.455	.043	6.30	1.80
Frias, Darwin	R-R	6-0	192	2-18-92	2	0	2.84	15	0	0	1	25	21	10	8	0	10	21	.223	.138	.262	7.46	3.55
Goeddel, Erik	R-R	6-3	185	12-20-88	0	0	0.00	1	0	0	0	1	1	0	0	0	0	1	.250	.000	.333	9.00	0.00
Gould, Jeremy	R-L	6-4	205	6-6-88	1	2	3.12	13	0	0	1	17	14	7	6	1	7	11	.233	.000	.264	5.71	3.63
Green, Sean	R-R	6-6	225	4-20-79	1	0	3.00	3	0	0	0	3	1	1	1	0	2	5	.100	.000	.167	15.00	6.00
Holdzkom, John	R-R	6-7	225	10-19-87	0	0	0.00	1	0	0	0	1	0	0	0	0	2	2	.000	.000	.000	18.00	18.00
Kaplan, Jeff	R-R	6-0	190	7-9-85	0	0	0.00	1	0	0	0	3	0	0	0	0	0	1	.000	.000	.333	9.00	0.00
Mejia, Jenrry	R-R	6-0	160	10-11-89	0	0	3.00	1	1	0	0	3	4	1	1	0	1	3	.333	.667	.250	9.00	3.00
Morel, Estarlin	R-R	6-0	185	10-2-89	2	1	1.40	13	0	0	1	19	23	5	3	0	3	12	.291	.318	.281	5.59	1.40
Morris, Akeel	R-R	6-1	170	11-14-92	1	1	2.19	8	6	0	0	25	13	11	6	0	17	28	.148	.200	.132	10.22	6.20
Muniz, Carlos	R-R	6-1	190	3-12-81	1	0	9.35	7	0	0	0	9	12	9	9	1	3	7	.324	.333	.321	7.27	3.12
O'Neill, Adam	R-R	6-1	180	5-22-90	1	0	3.52	11	0	0	0	15	13	6	6	0	7	12	.213	.235	.205	7.04	4.11
Peralta, Ramiro	R-R	6-3	180	9-8-89	1	0	1.69	15	0	0	6	21	11	5	4	1	9	27	.157	.190	.143	11.39	3.80
Rustich, Brant	R-R	6-6	230	1-23-85	0	0	5.79	8	0	0	0	9	8	7	6	0	5	6	.216	.100	.259	5.79	4.82
Tapia, Domingo	R-R	6-4	186	12-16-91	4	3	3.45	10	10	0	0	47	49	25	18	0	10	29	.269	.279	.266	5.55	1.91
Urbina, Juan	L-L	6-2	170	5-31-93	5	3	5.03	11	11	0	0	48	54	32	27	5	14	38	.284	.286	.284	7.08	2.61
Vasquez, Carlos	L-L	5-11	180	9-3-91	4	2	4.72	11	5	0	3	48	53	29	25	3	8	43	.282	.333	.276	8.12	1.51
Villasmil, Edioglis	R-R	6-2	164	4-10-92	2	3	3.11	11	11	0	0	55	56	30	19	2	27	26	.271	.288	.265	4.25	4.42
Von Tersch, Zach	R-R	6-4	195	4-22-88	0	1	1.80	3	0	0	0	5	3	2	1	0	3	2	.167	.200	.154	3.60	5.40
Winnick, Steve	R-R	6-1	195	9-16-87	0	0	0.00	4	0	0	1	6	3	1	0	0	1	1	.227	.500	.200	1.50	1.50
Yanez, Ernesto	R-R	6-0	162	1-22-90	1	2	3.86	17	3	0	1	33	28	22	14	1	11	18	.230	.195	.247	4.96	3.03

Fielding

Catcher	PCT	G	PO	A	E	DP	PB
De Leon	.946	12	64	6	4	0	4
Forsythe	1.000	2	8	0	0	0	0
Glenn	.978	24	164	17	4	3	2
Maron	.979	18	83	12	2	2	6
Montz	1.000	3	18	1	0	1	0
Moreno	1.000	3	10	0	0	0	0
Pena	.964	4	27	0	1	0	1

First Base	PCT	G	PO	A	E	DP
De Leon	1.000	1	10	0	0	0
Moreno	.968	12	85	7	3	7
Sanchez	.995	41	339	25	2	33

Vernouij	1.000	4	27	0	0	2

Second Base	PCT	G	PO	A	E	DP
De La Cruz	.969	26	37	57	3	13
Santana	.987	14	40	36	1	8
Tabb	.938	16	29	32	4	9
Tejada	1.000	6	8	12	0	2

Third Base	PCT	G	PO	A	E	DP
Campbell	1.000	3	2	4	0	1
De Leon	1.000	3	2	6	0	0
Dunn	.840	9	3	18	4	2
Harrison	.917	7	8	14	2	0
Lutz	1.000	3	1	8	0	0

Sanchez	.769	7	2	8	3	0
Tejada	.889	14	2	22	3	1
Vernouij	.940	22	15	48	4	2

Shortstop	PCT	G	PO	A	E	DP
De La Cruz	.877	16	23	34	8	9
Santana	.952	30	54	85	7	16
Shields	.897	11	15	37	6	7
Tejada	.870	7	7	13	3	1

Outfield	PCT	G	PO	A	E	DP
Brown	1.000	41	76	3	0	1
Concepcion	.967	49	57	1	2	0
den Dekker	1.000	5	14	1	0	0

Gomez	.991	45	112	4	1	2		Pugh	.951	21	39	0	2	0		Tabb	1.000	4	7	0	0	0
Pridie	1.000	3	4	0	0	0		Soto	1.000	3	3	1	0	0		Tejada	.929	9	12	1	1	0

DSL METS 1 — ROOKIE
DOMINICAN SUMMER LEAGUE

Batting	B-T	HT	WT	DOB	AVG	vLH	vRH	G	AB	R	H	2B	3B	HR	RBI	BB	HBP	SH	SF	SO	SB	CS	SLG	OBP
Avila, Wandel	R-R	6-2	190	4-10-91	.238	.214	.244	50	147	17	35	3	3	2	13	16	4	3	0	36	7	0	.340	.329
Barrera, Edwin	L-L	6-2	200	9-15-90	.206	.268	.191	62	214	25	44	9	2	0	24	15	3	0	2	39	8	1	.266	.265
Cessa, Luis	R-R	6-3	190	4-25-92	.162	.059	.196	23	68	2	11	2	0	0	3	4	2	0	0	19	1	0	.191	.230
De Leon, Daniel	R-R	6-2	174	5-29-92	.208	.227	.201	60	183	15	38	7	0	1	14	18	7	2	2	26	5	4	.262	.300
Diaz, David	R-R	6-2	205	9-24-90	.232	.333	.204	29	69	5	16	3	0	0	5	5	1	0	0	17	1	1	.275	.293
Gamboa, Juan Carlos	L-R	5-7	152	4-18-91	.294	.233	.309	61	221	38	65	11	4	0	21	34	0	1	0	31	16	7	.380	.388
Leal, Miguel	R-R	6-0	184	7-4-91	.223	.280	.207	42	112	13	25	5	1	0	9	12	1	3	1	16	5	0	.286	.302
Mercedes, Ariel	B-R	6-1	190	10-15-91	.261	.232	.270	69	234	32	61	9	2	3	39	36	6	3	0	60	15	7	.355	.373
Natera, Luis	R-R	6-1	195	9-20-90	.191	.240	.174	60	199	21	38	8	2	0	25	19	4	1	1	44	5	2	.251	.274
Pina, Eudy	R-R	6-3	188	4-12-91	.310	.396	.287	69	248	42	77	14	4	3	45	19	15	2	5	48	29	7	.435	.387
Rivero, Nohisglin	R-R	6-0	180	1-26-91	.185	.250	.169	23	81	8	15	1	3	0	1	4	2	2	0	22	1	3	.272	.241
Rondon, Pedro	R-R	6-1	180	4-30-92	.245	.250	.244	64	216	42	53	6	2	0	15	41	5	3	0	39	26	6	.292	.378
Ruiz, Yeixon	B-R	6-0	155	3-19-91	.282	.220	.297	41	142	26	40	5	4	1	24	26	3	4	2	17	16	5	.394	.399
Weijgertse, Kevin	R-R	6-4	176	2-22-91	.125	.129	.124	51	136	20	17	2	0	0	6	25	3	6	1	32	2	3	.140	.273

Pitching	B-T	HT	WT	DOB	W	L	ERA	G	GS	CG	SV	IP	H	R	ER	HR	BB	SO	AVG	vLH	vRH	K/9	BB/9
Acosta, Octavio	R-R	6-0	165	3-20-90	2	2	4.83	17	0	0	0	32	40	17	17	4	15	31	.320	.270	.341	8.81	4.26
Arias, Martires	R-R	6-7	207	11-10-90	6	5	3.15	16	15	0	0	69	52	33	24	0	22	35	.208	.162	.227	4.59	2.88
Baez, Carlos	L-L	6-6	200	5-26-91	0	0	7.71	11	0	0	1	14	10	13	12	0	19	8	.204	.400	.182	5.14	12.21
Baldonado, Alberto	L-L	6-2	160	2-1-93	3	1	1.41	13	8	1	1	45	29	11	7	0	19	50	.188	.176	.190	10.07	3.83
Cabrera, Reynaldo	R-R	6-6	205	2-1-90	0	2	4.91	11	0	0	0	18	27	19	10	1	9	6	.338	.385	.315	2.95	4.42
Cordoba, Tony	R-R	5-11	154	9-16-91	1	0	2.00	2	1	0	1	9	5	2	2	0	2	3	.161	.000	.263	3.00	2.00
Estevez, Ramon	R-R	6-0	165	10-27-90	2	0	4.33	15	1	0	0	27	28	17	13	0	14	25	.272	.273	.271	8.33	4.67
Feliz, Gabriel	L-L	5-11	160	11-12-92	1	3	6.39	10	0	0	1	13	15	10	9	0	5	7	.300	.250	.304	4.97	3.55
Gomez, Carlos	R-R	6-1	160	3-30-91	7	2	1.47	15	13	0	0	73	62	21	12	0	21	46	.229	.200	.240	5.65	2.58
Hilario, Julian	R-R	6-1	190	8-17-90	3	2	3.51	13	7	0	1	49	50	21	19	0	16	28	.269	.293	.258	5.18	2.96
Marinez, John	R-R	6-5	185	9-23-92	0	1	5.14	4	0	0	0	7	6	5	4	1	2	6	.240	.143	.278	7.71	2.57
Ortega, Flabio	R-R	6-1	170	8-19-90	2	4	2.04	18	1	0	0	35	29	10	8	1	14	30	.232	.244	.225	7.64	3.57
Peralta, Victor	L-L	5-11	178	7-2-89	3	0	2.64	24	0	0	9	31	26	12	9	1	15	43	.228	.125	.236	12.62	4.40
Ramos, Eduard	R-R	6-2	195	2-22-92	0	0	2.25	4	0	0	0	4	2	3	1	0	4	9	.182	.333	.125	9.00	9.00
Robles, Hansel	R-R	5-11	185	8-13-90	3	3	3.09	14	12	0	1	67	64	27	23	1	13	51	.257	.260	.256	6.85	1.75
Romero, Johel	R-R	6-3	220	4-16-91	1	0	3.66	9	0	0	0	20	20	11	8	1	14	10	.260	.474	.190	4.58	6.41
Rosario, Lenny	L-L	6-1	162	5-15-91	3	2	2.50	15	5	0	0	40	12	15	11	0	38	53	.094	.000	.101	12.03	8.62
Ruane, Luis	R-R	6-1	195	0-0-00	1	2	3.13	11	2	0	0	23	20	16	8	0	15	21	.233	.182	.250	8.22	5.87
Sanchez, Erigson	R-R	6-1	180	11-3-90	0	1	2.25	1	1	0	0	4	4	2	1	0	0	4	.250	.167	.300	9.00	0.00
Santiago, Paul	R-R	5-11	165	1-12-92	1	1	4.91	11	2	0	0	18	15	18	10	0	18	10	.224	.261	.205	4.91	8.84
Tapia, Domingo	R-R	6-4	186	12-16-91	0	1	3.09	3	3	0	0	12	8	4	4	0	5	5	.195	.273	.167	3.86	3.86
Velasquez, Gustavo	R-R	6-2	191	10-3-91	0	0	0.00	1	0	0	0	1	1	0	0	0	1	0	.250	.000	.500	0.00	9.00

Fielding

Catcher	PCT	G	PO	A	E	DP	PB
Avila	.955	28	172	20	9	1	4
Diaz	.927	23	103	12	9	1	5
Leal	.984	29	165	22	3	1	3
Rivero	.981	8	45	8	1	0	3

First Base	PCT	G	PO	A	E	DP
Avila	.991	17	105	6	1	12
Barrera	.988	19	157	11	2	7
Weijgertse	.972	49	399	22	12	34

Second Base	PCT	G	PO	A	E	DP
Cessa	.962	10	21	30	2	6

	PCT	G	PO	A	E	DP
Gamboa	1.000	2	2	5	0	2
Natera	.970	20	47	49	3	12
Rondon	.957	4	5	17	1	3
Ruiz	.956	37	61	111	8	16
Weijgertse	—	1	0	0	0	0

Third Base	PCT	G	PO	A	E	DP
Cessa	.966	10	7	21	1	4
De Leon	.908	31	21	58	8	7
Natera	.943	35	30	70	6	7
Ruiz	1.000	1	0	2	0	1
Weijgertse	1.000	4	3	5	0	0

Shortstop	PCT	G	PO	A	E	DP
De Leon	.907	21	25	43	7	10
Gamboa	.943	59	80	183	16	28
Natera	.750	1	2	1	1	0
Ruiz	1.000	2	0	1	0	0

Outfield	PCT	G	PO	A	E	DP
Barrera	.906	31	44	4	5	1
De Leon	.889	8	8	0	1	0
Mercedes	.930	57	62	4	5	1
Pina	.978	65	122	12	3	7
Rivero	1.000	6	8	1	0	1
Rondon	.971	59	94	5	3	1

DSL METS 2 — ROOKIE
DOMINICAN SUMMER LEAGUE

Batting	B-T	HT	WT	DOB	AVG	vLH	vRH	G	AB	R	H	2B	3B	HR	RBI	BB	HBP	SH	SF	SO	SB	CS	SLG	OBP
Abreu, Adrian	R-R	6-0	185	6-14-91	.228	.182	.239	20	57	9	13	5	0	0	7	6	1	0	1	8	4	0	.316	.308
Alvarez, Hector	R-R	5-11	170	2-14-91	.249	.225	.255	62	201	31	50	19	0	1	28	17	10	1	3	25	7	3	.358	.333
Batista, Sneider	R-R	5-11	182	9-13-90	.277	.271	.278	63	235	38	65	8	2	0	21	16	5	4	1	22	23	6	.328	.335
Bernal, Michael	R-R	6-1	195	12-27-91	.176	.385	.048	18	34	4	6	0	1	3	5	1	0	0	14	1	2	.324	.300
Caba, Arickson	R-R	6-3	190	2-23-89	.238	.268	.228	67	227	26	54	17	2	1	22	20	4	3	3	33	9	2	.344	.307
Chavez, Anthony	R-R	6-2	185	11-8-92	.228	.146	.251	64	215	29	49	7	1	0	31	36	5	1	2	59	7	0	.270	.349
De Wolf, Thomas	L-R	6-3	198	12-22-89	.250	.250	.250	69	204	31	51	11	4	3	25	43	12	1	1	75	4	6	.387	.408
Decena, Joan	R-R	6-3	195	9-9-91	.256	.231	.269	11	39	5	10	2	0	1	8	1	2	0	0	4	0	1	.385	.310
Guillen, Marcus	B-R	5-11	175	5-29-90	.185	.196	.182	72	232	39	43	4	6	1	23	41	8	4	2	72	15	9	.267	.325
Hato, Bjorn	R-R	6-1	160	6-26-91	.208	.263	.190	39	77	16	16	1	0	0	8	20	1	1	0	13	5	4	.221	.378

	B-T	HT	WT	DOB				G	AB	R	H	2B	3B	HR	RBI	BB	HBP	SH	SF	SO	SB	CS		
Liriano, Victor	R-R	6-4	193	5-23-93	.177	.171	.179	54	175	17	31	3	2	0	14	9	8	2	0	55	2	3	.217	.250
Machillanada, Alex	R-R	5-11	177	10-1-91	.145	.154	.143	38	69	1	10	2	0	0	6	6	4	0	1	13	1	0	.174	.250
Moreno, Nestor	B-R	5-11	195	6-21-88	.228	.200	.238	19	57	13	13	4	1	1	6	12	0	0	0	10	2	0	.386	.362
Ponce, Dimas	R-R	5-11	140	1-22-91	.251	.292	.240	67	227	21	57	10	2	1	33	27	5	2	6	45	7	3	.326	.336
Rivero, Nohisglin	R-R	6-0	180	1-26-90	.254	.226	.261	40	142	19	36	5	1	0	10	10	0	1	1	32	10	4	.303	.301
2-team total (23 Mets1)					.229	—	—	63	223	27	51	6	4	0	11	14	2	3	1	54	11	7	.291	.279
Ruiz, Yeixon	B-R	6-0	155	3-19-91	.171	.143	.179	17	35	2	6	0	0	0	2	3	2	1	0	3	3	0	.171	.275
2-team total (41 Mets1)					.260	—	—	58	177	28	46	5	4	1	26	29	5	5	2	20	19	5	.350	.376

Pitching	B-T	HT	WT	DOB	W	L	ERA	G	GS	CG	SV	IP	H	R	ER	HR	BB	SO	AVG	vLH	vRH	K/9	BB/9
Acosta, Jose	R-R	6-2	205	1-20-90	4	1	1.98	7	0	0	1	14	8	3	3	0	8	7	.174	.154	.182	4.61	5.27
Celas, Jose	R-R	6-1	180	1-12-91	3	1	5.40	9	3	0	0	27	26	18	16	1	13	24	.265	.296	.254	8.10	4.39
Coronado, Carlos	R-R	5-11	176	9-26-91	0	2	5.82	11	0	0	0	17	19	12	11	0	15	13	.288	.294	.286	6.88	7.94
Diaz, Miller	R-R	6-1	209	6-22-92	4	4	2.05	14	9	0	1	48	36	18	11	0	14	42	.208	.227	.202	7.82	2.61
Fana, Jose	R-R	6-2	193	10-19-90	3	1	3.05	12	0	0	2	21	16	11	7	0	12	22	.213	.143	.241	9.58	5.23
Febrillet, Lefty	R-R	6-3	175	11-16-89	1	2	2.31	10	2	0	1	23	14	7	6	0	14	17	.175	.273	.138	6.56	5.40
Garcia, Hugo	R-R	6-2	172	7-26-92	0	0	7.04	8	0	0	0	8	10	10	6	1	5	8	.333	.500	.292	9.39	5.87
Gonzalez, Marcos	R-R	6-0	175	10-22-92	3	1	2.18	17	0	0	4	45	50	13	11	2	5	25	.286	.333	.272	4.96	0.99
Javier, Yancarlos	L-L	6-3	170	4-7-91	1	1	2.05	9	9	0	0	26	16	6	6	0	15	28	.170	.100	.179	9.57	5.13
Lara, Rainy	R-R	6-4	180	3-14-91	4	2	1.97	14	12	0	1	64	48	14	14	2	13	51	.209	.197	.213	7.17	1.83
Lebron, Hector	L-L	6-4	190	4-19-92	1	0	0.00	6	0	0	0	6	2	0	0	0	7	6	.100	.000	.111	8.53	9.95
Monroe, Isaac	L-L	5-10	155	10-9-90	4	2	1.08	13	3	0	3	42	27	9	5	1	13	41	.185	.077	.195	8.86	2.81
Nuez, Yoryi	R-R	6-1	153	2-13-93	0	0	2.45	8	0	0	2	7	6	2	2	0	4	10	.240	.500	.158	12.27	4.91
Perez, Andres E.	R-R	6-2	184	2-8-91	3	1	4.15	12	0	0	0	30	31	14	14	1	18	22	.284	.217	.302	6.53	5.34
Rengel, Luis	R-R	6-2	165	3-19-90	1	2	1.69	10	8	0	0	37	22	9	7	0	16	37	.176	.147	.187	8.92	3.86
Reyes, Persio	R-R	6-2	151	3-17-93	2	3	4.39	11	9	0	0	41	40	23	20	0	20	26	.255	.286	.246	5.71	4.39
Reyes, Ruben	R-R	6-4	178	9-22-90	3	2	3.07	15	3	0	0	41	26	21	14	0	21	35	.177	.216	.164	7.68	4.61
Soriano, Cristian	L-L	6-3	184	9-5-91	1	1	4.39	11	2	0	0	27	32	14	13	0	18	22	.311	.500	.295	7.43	6.07
Uceta, Rolando	R-R	6-2	190	12-4-90	0	0	4.70	7	0	0	0	8	8	5	4	0	3	2	.250	.200	.273	2.35	3.52
Ynoa, Gabriel	R-R	6-2	158	5-26-93	5	3	1.99	14	12	1	0	72	63	22	16	1	8	35	.243	.205	.261	4.35	1.00

Fielding

Catcher	PCT	G	PO	A	E	DP	PB
Abreu	.931	4	24	3	2	0	0
Alvarez	.987	42	253	41	4	1	2
Bernal	—	1	0	0	0	0	0
Machillanada	.989	20	74	14	1	0	3
Moreno	.980	6	45	3	1	0	0
Rivero	.954	16	90	13	5	0	1

First Base	PCT	G	PO	A	E	DP
Alvarez	.982	20	157	5	3	18
Caba	.995	42	348	14	2	24
Machillanada	.980	11	43	5	1	4
Moreno	1.000	11	80	8	0	6
Rivero	—	1	0	0	0	0

Second Base	PCT	G	PO	A	E	DP
Batista	.966	47	108	93	7	23
Hato	.977	25	40	46	2	11
Machillanada	—	1	0	0	0	0
Ruiz	.875	10	16	19	5	7
Hato	—	1	0	0	0	0
Ponce	.958	18	25	43	3	5

Third Base	PCT	G	PO	A	E	DP
Batista	.905	17	10	28	4	2
Chavez	.906	9	7	22	3	3
Ponce	.913	49	32	115	14	9
Ruiz	1.000	3	0	1	0	0

Shortstop	PCT	G	PO	A	E	DP
Chavez	.961	55	72	174	10	21

Outfield	PCT	G	PO	A	E	DP
Abreu	—	1	0	0	0	0
Batista	—	2	0	0	0	0
Bernal	1.000	12	11	0	0	0
Caba	.933	28	40	2	3	0
De Wolf	.972	69	98	8	3	2
Decena	.917	11	10	1	1	0
Guillen	.970	72	151	8	5	1
Liriano	.944	19	15	2	1	0
Rivero	1.000	23	33	2	0	0

New York Yankees

SEASON IN A SENTENCE: The Yankees won 95 games and earned a playoff spot for the 15th time in 16 seasons, this time as the American League wild card, but after sweeping the Twins in the Division Series they faltered and lost to the Rangers in the AL Championship Series.

HIGH POINT: The Yankees' regular season was a grind, and the team was just 39-35 after the All-Star Game. The highlights included Alex Rodriguez's 600th career home run on Aug. 4 in a victory against the Blue Jays and an eight-game winning streak from Aug. 28-Sept. 4. It was the team's longest of the season and all but clinched a playoff spot for the Bronx Bombers.

LOW POINT: The Yankees finished the season with three memorials on their uniforms. A black band on the right sleeve commemorated 1960s manager Ralph Houk, who died July 21. On July 11, former Yankee Stadium announcer Bob Sheppard died at age 99; the club honored him with a patch, featuring a microphone, on the left sleeve. And on the chest, the Yankees honored owner George Steinbrenner, who died July 13 after a massive heart attack in Tampa.

NOTABLE ROOKIES: Francisco Cervelli broke in as the Yankees' backup catcher and actually played more innings behind the plate than 38-year-old Jorge Posada. The light-hitting Cervelli tailed off after a fast start and had just 14 extra-base hits. Righthander Ivan Nova made seven starts in the second half but didn't exhaust his rookie eligibility.

KEY TRANSACTIONS: New York's biggest off-season acquisition, righthander Javier Vazquez, backfired, going just 10-10, 5.32 and getting left off the playoff roster. General manager Brian Cashman improved the team's bench by picking up Lance Berkman from the Astros, then added Kerry Wood to the bullpen, and he proved to be the team's top set-up man. Neither deal cost the organization a top prospect.

DOWN ON THE FARM: New York's top three full-season teams all made the playoffs, while high Class A Tampa won the Florida State League championship. Triple-A Scranton/Wilkes-Barre won its fourth straight division championship led by top prospect Jesus Montero, while starting pitching—including bounce-back seasons by highly touted righthanders Dellin Betances and Andrew Brackman—carried Tampa and Double-A Trenton to the postseason.

OPENING DAY PAYROLL: $206.3 million (1st)

PLAYERS OF THE YEAR

MAJOR LEAGUE

Robinson Cano
2b
.319/.381/.534
6th in AL in OPS
Won first Gold Glove

MINOR LEAGUE

Jesus Montero
c
(Triple-A)
.289/.353/.517
21 HR, 34 2B

ORGANIZATION LEADERS

BATTING		*Minimum 250 at-bats
MAJORS		
*AVG	Robinson Cano	.319
*OPS	Robinson Cano	.914
HR	Mark Teixeira	33
RBI	Alex Rodriguez	125
MINORS		
*AVG	Robert Lyerly, Charleston	.312
*OBP	Justin Christian, Scranton/Trenton	.366
*SLG	Jesus Montero, Scranton	.517
R	Brandon Laird, Trenton/Scranton	86
H	Robert Lyerly, Charleston	157
TB	Brandon Laird, Trenton/Scranton	256
2B	Robert Lyerly, Charleston	36
3B	Jose Pirela, Tampa	13
HR	Brandon Laird, Trenton/Scranton	25
RBI	Brandon Laird, Trenton/Scranton	102
BB	Austin Krum, Trenton	64
SO	Neil Medchill, Tampa/Charleston	154
SB	Raymond Kruml, Charleston/Tampa	42

PITCHING		†Minimum 75 innings
MAJORS		
W	C.C. Sabathia	21
†ERA	C.C. Sabathia	3.18
SO	C.C. Sabathia	197
MINORS		
W	Hector Noesi, Tampa/Trenton/Scranton	14
L	Andrew Brackman, Tampa/Trenton	11
†ERA	Graham Stoneburner, Charleston/Tampa	2.41
G	Jonathan Albaladejo, Scranton	57
	Wilkins Arias, Trenton	57
GS	Hector Noesi, Tampa/Trenton/Scranton	27
	Lance Pendleton, Trenton/Scranton	27
SV	Jonathan Albaladejo, Scranton	43
IP	Hector Noesi, Tampa/Trenton/Scranton	160.3
BB	D.J. Mitchell, Trenton/Scranton	64
SO	Hector Noesi, Tampa/Trenton/Scranton	153
†AVG	Graham Stoneburner, Charleston/Tampa	.209

2010 PERFORMANCE

General Manager: Brian Cashman. **Farm Director:** Pat Roessler. **Scouting Director:** Damon Oppenheimer.

Class	Team	League	W	L	PCT	Finish*	Manager(s)
Majors	New York Yankees	American	95	67	.586	2nd (14)	Joe Girardi
Triple-A	Scranton/W-B Yankees	International	87	56	.608	2nd (14)	Dave Miley
Double-A	Trenton Thunder	Eastern	83	59	.585	1st (12)	Tony Franklin
High A	Tampa Yankees	Florida State	78	57	.578	†1st (12)	Torre Tyson
Low A	Charleston RiverDogs	South Atlantic	65	74	.468	t-9th (14)	Greg Colbrunn
Short-season	Staten Island Yankees	New York-Penn	34	40	.459	t-10th (14)	Jody Reed/Josh Paul
Rookie	GCL Yankees	Gulf Coast	24	32	.429	t-12th (15)	Tom Slater
Overall 2010 Minor League Record			371	318	.538	3rd (30)	

*Finish in overall standings (No. of teams in league). †League champion.

ORGANIZATION STATISTICS

NEW YORK YANKEES

AMERICAN LEAGUE

Batting	B-T	HT	WT	DOB	AVG	vLH	vRH	G	AB	R	H	2B	3B	HR	RBI	BB	HBP	SH	SF	SO	SB	CS	SLG	OBP
Berkman, Lance	B-L	6-1	230	2-10-76	.255	.111	.284	37	106	9	27	7	0	1	9	17	0	0	0	15	0	0	.349	.358
Cano, Robinson	L-R	6-0	205	10-22-82	.319	.285	.337	160	626	103	200	41	3	29	109	57	8	0	5	77	3	2	.534	.381
Cervelli, Francisco	R-R	6-1	210	3-6-86	.271	.322	.246	93	266	27	72	11	3	0	38	33	6	8	4	42	1	1	.335	.359
Curtis, Colin	L-L	6-1	200	2-1-85	.186	.222	.180	31	59	7	11	3	0	1	8	4	1	0	0	15	0	0	.288	.250
Gardner, Brett	L-L	5-10	185	8-24-83	.277	.252	.287	150	477	97	132	20	7	5	47	79	5	5	3	101	47	9	.379	.383
Golson, Greg	R-R	6-0	190	9-17-85	.261	.353	.000	24	23	3	6	2	0	0	2	0	0	0	0	3	0	2	.348	.261
Granderson, Curtis	L-L	185	3-16-81	.247	.234	.253	136	466	76	115	17	7	24	67	53	2	4	3	116	12	2	.468	.324
Huffman, Chad	R-R	6-1	215	4-29-85	.167	.091	.286	9	18	1	3	0	0	0	2	2	1	0	0	5	0	0	.167	.286
Jeter, Derek	R-R	6-3	195	6-26-74	.270	.321	.246	157	663	111	179	30	3	10	67	63	9	1	3	106	18	5	.370	.340
Johnson, Nick	L-L	6-3	235	9-19-78	.167	.190	.157	24	72	12	12	4	0	2	8	24	2	0	0	23	0	1	.306	.388
Kearns, Austin	R-R	6-3	240	5-20-80	.235	.255	.218	36	102	13	24	3	0	2	7	12	5	0	0	38	0	0	.324	.345
2-team total (84 Cleveland)					.263	—	—	120	403	55	106	21	1	10	49	46	10	0	2	116	4	1	.395	.351
Miranda, Juan	L-L	6-0	220	4-25-83	.219	.167	.224	33	64	7	14	2	1	3	10	7	0	0	0	12	0	0	.422	.296
Moeller, Chad	R-R	6-3	210	2-18-75	.214	.400	.111	9	14	2	3	3	0	0	1	0	0	0	0	4	0	0	.429	.267
Nunez, Eduardo	R-R	6-0	155	6-15-87	.280	.269	.292	30	50	12	14	1	0	1	7	3	0	0	2	5	0	0	.360	.321
Pena, Ramiro	B-R	5-11	165	7-18-85	.227	.161	.244	85	154	18	35	1	1	0	18	6	1	4	2	27	7	1	.247	.258
Posada, Jorge	B-R	6-2	215	8-17-71	.248	.257	.243	120	383	49	95	23	1	18	57	59	7	0	2	99	3	1	.454	.357
Rodriguez, Alex	R-R	6-3	230	7-27-75	.270	.217	.290	137	522	74	141	29	2	30	125	59	3	0	11	98	4	3	.506	.341
Russo, Kevin	R-R	5-11	190	7-8-84	.184	.222	.136	31	49	5	9	2	0	0	4	3	1	1	0	9	1	0	.224	.245
Swisher, Nick	B-L	5-11	210	11-25-80	.288	.294	.285	150	566	91	163	33	3	29	89	58	6	3	2	139	1	2	.511	.359
Teixeira, Mark	B-R	6-3	220	4-11-80	.256	.278	.247	158	601	113	154	36	0	33	108	93	13	0	5	122	0	1	.481	.365
Thames, Marcus	R-R	6-2	220	3-6-77	.288	.300	.268	82	212	22	61	7	0	12	33	19	3	0	3	61	0	0	.491	.350
Winn, Randy	B-R	6-2	195	6-9-74	.213	.000	.260	29	61	7	13	0	1	1	8	8	0	1	1	15	1	0	.295	.300

Pitching	B-T	HT	WT	DOB	W	L	ERA	G	GS	CG	SV	IP	H	R	ER	HR	BB	SO	AVG	vLH	vRH	K/9	BB/9
Aceves, Alfredo	R-R	6-3	220	12-8-82	3	0	3.00	10	0	0	1	12	10	5	4	1	4	2	.208	.235	.194	1.50	3.00
Albaladejo, Jonathan	R-R	6-5	260	10-30-82	0	0	3.97	10	0	0	0	11	9	5	5	1	8	8	.231	.222	.238	6.35	6.35
Burnett, A.J.	R-R	6-4	230	1-3-77	10	15	5.26	33	33	1	0	187	204	118	109	25	78	145	.285	.286	.285	6.99	3.76
Chamberlain, Joba	R-R	6-2	230	9-23-85	3	4	4.40	73	0	0	3	72	71	37	35	6	22	77	.253	.246	.258	9.67	2.76
Gaudin, Chad	R-R	5-10	190	3-24-83	1	2	4.50	30	0	0	0	48	46	27	24	11	20	33	.254	.265	.241	6.19	3.75
2-team total (12 Oakland)					1	4	5.65	42	0	0	0	65	73	45	41	16	25	53	—	—	—	7.30	3.44
Hughes, Phil	R-R	6-5	240	6-24-86	18	8	4.19	31	29	0	0	176	162	83	82	25	58	146	.244	.235	.253	7.45	2.96
Logan, Boone	R-L	6-5	215	8-13-84	2	0	2.93	51	0	0	0	40	34	13	13	3	20	38	.231	.190	.279	8.55	4.50
Marte, Damaso	L-L	6-2	215	2-14-75	0	0	4.08	30	0	0	0	18	10	8	8	2	11	12	.161	.146	.190	6.11	5.60
Melancon, Mark	R-R	6-2	215	3-28-85	0	0	9.00	2	0	0	0	4	7	5	4	1	2	3	.389	.286	.455	6.75	0.00
Mitre, Sergio	R-R	6-3	225	2-16-81	0	3	3.33	27	3	0	1	54	43	23	20	7	16	29	.223	.226	.218	4.83	2.67
Moseley, Dustin	R-R	6-4	215	12-26-81	4	4	4.96	16	9	0	0	65	66	36	36	13	27	33	.269	.281	.256	4.55	3.72
Nova, Ivan	R-R	6-4	210	1-12-87	1	2	4.50	10	7	0	0	42	44	22	21	4	17	26	.268	.268	.269	5.57	3.64
Park, Chan Ho	R-R	6-2	210	6-30-73	2	1	5.60	27	0	0	0	35	40	25	22	7	12	29	.280	.328	.237	7.39	3.06
Pettitte, Andy	L-L	6-5	225	6-15-72	11	3	3.28	21	21	0	0	129	123	52	47	13	41	101	.257	.186	.283	7.05	2.86
Ring, Royce	L-L	6-0	220	12-21-80	0	0	15.43	5	0	0	0	2	3	4	4	0	2	2	.300	.375	.000	7.71	7.71
Rivera, Mariano	R-R	6-2	185	11-29-69	3	3	1.80	61	0	0	33	60	39	14	12	2	11	45	.183	.214	.155	6.75	1.65
Robertson, David	R-R	5-11	190	4-9-85	4	5	3.82	64	0	0	1	61	59	26	26	5	33	71	.258	.268	.250	10.42	4.84
Sabathia, C.C.	L-L	6-7	290	7-21-80	21	7	3.18	34	34	2	0	238	209	92	84	20	74	197	.239	.261	.232	7.46	2.80
Sanchez, Romulo	R-R	6-5	260	4-28-84	0	0	0.00	2	0	0	0	4	1	0	0	0	5	.071	.143	.000	10.38	6.23
Vazquez, Javier	R-R	6-2	210	7-25-76	10	10	5.32	31	26	0	0	157	155	96	93	32	65	121	.257	.275	.240	6.92	3.72
Wood, Kerry	R-R	6-5	210	6-16-77	2	0	0.69	24	0	0	0	26	14	2	2	1	18	31	.161	.189	.140	10.73	6.23
2-team total (23 Cleveland)					3	4	3.13	47	0	0	8	46	35	17	16	4	29	49	—	—	—	9.59	5.67

Fielding

Catcher	PCT	G	PO	A	E	DP	PB
Cervelli	.980	90	579	45	13	2	2
Moeller	1.000	9	33	6	0	0	2
Posada	.986	83	562	22	8	2	8

First Base	PCT	G	PO	A	E	DP
Berkman	.982	8	54	2	1	8
Huffman	—	1	0	0	0	0
Johnson	1.000	2	18	0	0	1

	PCT	G	PO	A	E	DP
Miranda	1.000	13	53	5	0	5
Posada	—	1	0	0	0	0
Swisher	1.000	6	19	2	0	2
Teixeira	.998	149	1227	80	3	137

Second Base / Infield Fielding

Second Base	PCT	G	PO	A	E	DP
Cano	.996	158	341	432	3	114
Nunez	—	1	0	0	0	0
Pena	.967	8	12	17	1	6
Russo	1.000	2	2	1	0	0
Third Base	**PCT**	**G**	**PO**	**A**	**E**	**DP**
Cervelli	1.000	2	1	0	0	0
Nunez	.944	15	3	14	1	1
Pena	.966	48	17	67	3	5

	PCT	G	PO	A	E	DP
Rodriguez	.976	124	61	224	7	25
Russo	1.000	16	4	6	0	1
Thames	.000	1	0	0	1	0
Shortstop	**PCT**	**G**	**PO**	**A**	**E**	**DP**
Jeter	.989	151	182	365	6	94
Nunez	1.000	11	7	16	0	4
Pena	.979	23	22	24	1	7
Outfield	**PCT**	**G**	**PO**	**A**	**E**	**DP**
Curtis	1.000	23	22	0	0	0

	PCT	G	PO	A	E	DP
Gardner	.997	146	287	12	1	2
Golson	1.000	23	25	1	0	1
Granderson	.994	134	316	5	2	2
Huffman	1.000	7	14	0	0	0
Kearns	1.000	34	55	1	0	1
Pena	1.000	2	1	0	0	0
Russo	.933	11	14	0	1	0
Swisher	.986	134	265	10	4	1
Thames	.947	32	34	2	2	1
Winn	1.000	27	31	1	0	0

SCRANTON/WILKES-BARRE YANKEES TRIPLE-A

INTERNATIONAL LEAGUE

Batting	B-T	HT	WT	DOB	AVG	vLH	vRH	G	AB	R	H	2B	3B	HR	RBI	BB	HBP	SH	SF	SO	SB	CS	SLG	OBP
Bruntlett, Eric	R-R	6-2	200	3-29-78	.265	.242	.273	70	253	35	67	14	0	9	38	16	4	0	2	59	4	0	.427	.316
2-team total (44 Syracuse)					.243	—	—	114	415	61	101	24	1	10	49	37	6	2	2	94	8	2	.378	.313
Christian, Justin	R-R	6-1	190	4-3-80	.242	.333	.216	16	66	9	16	0	0	0	4	8	0	0	0	9	2	0	.242	.324
Corona, Reegie	B-R	5-11	160	11-7-86	.238	.302	.214	105	387	46	92	20	5	5	31	36	2	3	0	58	14	1	.354	.306
Curtis, Colin	L-L	6-1	200	2-1-85	.289	.293	.287	66	239	28	69	24	0	5	27	21	6	1	2	38	1	2	.452	.358
Cusick, Matt	L-R	5-10	190	5-5-86	.265	.118	.303	29	83	11	22	6	0	0	9	10	0	1	2	7	0	0	.337	.337
Golson, Greg	R-R	6-0	190	9-17-85	.263	.272	.259	116	415	51	109	23	5	10	40	25	6	2	2	99	17	4	.414	.313
Gonzalez, Edwar	R-R	5-10	200	1-1-83	.154	.250	.111	4	13	1	2	0	0	0	0	1	0	0	0	5	0	0	.154	.214
Gorecki, Reid	R-R	6-1	175	12-22-80	.253	.338	.222	78	281	45	71	18	5	3	30	32	2	2	1	67	12	3	.384	.332
Granderson, Curtis	L-R	6-1	185	3-16-81	.250	.500	.167	5	16	0	4	0	0	0	2	2	0	0	0	2	0	0	.250	.333
Hammock, Robby	R-R	5-10	185	5-13-77	.180	.263	.143	22	61	6	11	2	0	0	4	11	0	0	0	13	0	1	.213	.306
Huffman, Chad	R-R	6-1	215	4-29-85	.274	.280	.272	104	368	48	101	20	0	10	45	40	1	1	1	81	0	2	.410	.353
Laird, Brandon	R-R	6-1	215	9-11-87	.246	.257	.241	31	122	13	30	6	2	4	21	4	0	0	1	27	0	0	.344	.268
Miranda, Juan	L-L	6-0	220	4-25-83	.285	.233	.306	80	295	52	84	15	1	15	43	33	9	0	3	71	1	0	.495	.371
Moeller, Chad	R-R	6-3	210	2-18-75	.230	.348	.188	28	87	8	20	6	0	1	9	6	3	0	0	15	0	0	.333	.302
Montero, Jesus	R-R	6-4	225	11-28-89	.289	.284	.292	123	453	66	131	34	3	21	75	46	1	0	4	91	0	0	.517	.353
Natale, Jeff	R-R	5-9	180	8-24-82	.182	.100	.250	14	22	3	4	1	0	0	6	3	1	0	2	1	0	0	.227	.286
Nunez, Eduardo	R-R	6-0	155	6-15-87	.289	.260	.300	118	464	55	134	25	3	4	50	32	5	3	2	60	23	5	.381	.340
Pilittere, P.J.	R-R	5-10	215	11-23-81	.357	.167	.409	22	56	6	20	4	0	1	5	1	0	0	3	6	0	0	.482	.419
Rivera, Rene	R-R	5-10	215	7-31-83	.250	.240	.256	19	68	3	17	3	0	2	11	1	0	0	1	17	0	0	.382	.257
Russo, Kevin	R-R	5-11	190	7-8-84	.259	.287	.246	81	332	41	86	16	2	1	24	28	9	1	0	65	9	4	.328	.333
Snyder, Justin	L-R	5-9	190	4-8-86	.333	.333	.333	2	6	0	2	0	0	0	0	0	0	0	0	0	0	0	.333	.333
Thames, Marcus	R-R	6-2	220	3-6-77	.200	.333	.000	4	15	0	3	0	0	0	1	0	0	0	0	6	0	0	.200	.200
Tracy, Chad	L-R	6-2	215	5-22-80	.324	.400	.279	18	68	14	22	5	0	6	18	4	0	0	1	6	0	0	.662	.356
Vazquez, Jorge	R-R	6-0	225	3-15-82	.270	.264	.272	76	293	47	79	21	0	18	62	17	3	0	3	95	0	1	.526	.313
Weber, Jon	L-L	5-10	190	1-20-78	.258	.231	.266	47	163	18	42	7	2	0	11	18	1	0	1	25	0	2	.325	.333
2-team total (21 Toledo)					.257	—	—	68	241	27	62	13	2	1	16	24	1	0	1	42	5	2	.340	.326
Winfree, David	R-R	6-3	230	8-5-85	.264	.352	.231	52	201	24	53	16	0	5	33	9	3	0	3	32	0	0	.418	.301

Pitching	B-T	HT	WT	DOB	W	L	ERA	G	GS	CG	SV	IP	H	R	ER	HR	BB	SO	AVG	vLH	vRH	K/9	BB/9
Aceves, Alfredo	R-R	6-3	220	12-8-82	0	0	7.36	3	2	0	0	4	4	4	3	0	5	4	.267	.364	.000	9.82	12.27
Albaladejo, Jonathan	R-R	6-5	260	10-30-82	4	2	1.42	57	0	0	43	63	38	10	10	3	18	82	.170	.224	.111	11.65	2.56
Duff, Grant	R-R	6-6	210	12-19-82	0	0	6.00	4	0	0	0	6	8	4	4	0	2	6	.333	.071	.700	9.00	3.00
Hirsh, Jason	R-R	6-8	250	2-20-82	9	7	3.90	26	19	0	0	122	102	55	53	17	39	95	.224	.207	.243	6.99	2.87
Igawa, Kei	L-L	6-1	210	7-13-79	3	4	4.32	22	10	0	0	77	81	37	37	9	23	68	.267	.250	.277	7.95	2.69
Kontos, George	R-R	6-3	215	6-12-85	0	1	10.13	2	0	0	0	3	5	3	3	1	1	2	.385	.750	.222	6.75	3.38
Logan, Boone	R-L	6-5	215	8-13-84	0	1	2.11	14	0	0	0	21	18	5	5	1	4	23	.228	.162	.286	9.70	1.69
McAllister, Zach	R-R	6-5	230	12-8-87	8	10	5.09	24	24	1	0	133	165	82	75	20	38	88	.308	.279	.337	5.97	2.58
2-team total (3 Columbus)					9	12	5.29	27	27	1	0	150	185	95	88	21	45	99	—	—	—	5.95	2.71
Melancon, Mark	R-R	6-2	215	3-28-85	6	1	3.67	40	0	0	6	56	63	24	23	5	31	58	.285	.274	.296	9.27	4.95
Mitchell, D.J.	R-R	6-2	165	5-13-87	2	0	3.57	3	3	0	0	18	19	7	7	0	7	16	.271	.317	.207	8.15	3.57
Mitre, Sergio	R-R	6-3	225	2-16-81	0	1	7.04	2	2	0	0	8	9	6	6	1	2	7	.300	.273	.316	8.22	2.35
Moseley, Dustin	R-R	6-4	215	12-26-81	4	4	4.21	12	12	0	0	73	83	40	34	6	18	55	.285	.287	.284	6.81	2.23
Noesi, Hector	R-R	6-2	175	1-26-87	1	1	4.82	3	3	1	0	19	23	10	10	1	4	14	.311	.233	.364	6.75	1.93
Norton, Tim	R-R	6-5	230	5-23-83	0	0	0.00	1	0	0	0	1	1	0	0	0	1	1	.250	.333	.000	9.00	9.00
Nova, Ivan	R-R	6-4	210	1-12-87	12	9	2.86	23	23	0	0	145	135	50	46	10	48	115	.250	.266	.232	7.14	2.98
Park, Chan Ho	R-R	6-2	210	6-30-73	0	0	0.00	1	1	0	0	1	1	0	0	0	0	2	.250	1.000	.000	18.00	0.00
Pendleton, Lance	L-R	6-2	205	9-10-83	2	1	4.24	6	4	0	0	34	29	17	16	6	12	22	.225	.283	.174	5.82	3.18
Phelps, David	R-R	6-3	190	10-9-86	4	2	3.07	12	11	0	0	70	76	31	24	4	13	57	.274	.265	.286	7.29	1.66
Redding, Tim	R-R	5-11	230	2-12-78	7	4	2.46	13	12	1	0	84	68	24	23	2	17	62	.221	.257	.189	6.64	1.82
Ring, Royce	L-L	6-0	220	12-21-80	2	1	1.93	52	0	0	2	42	35	12	9	2	11	39	.222	.202	.246	8.36	2.36
Sanchez, Romulo	R-R	6-5	260	4-28-84	10	3	3.97	31	14	0	0	104	88	50	46	8	59	96	.232	.223	.241	8.28	5.09
Sanit, Amaury	R-R	5-8	205	7-4-79	3	2	7.75	21	1	0	0	34	47	29	29	7	13	22	.333	.316	.354	5.88	4.01
Schmidt, Josh	R-R	6-4	175	11-14-81	1	0	7.20	2	0	0	0	5	8	4	4	0	2	3	.286	.385	.125	5.40	3.60
Segovia, Zack	R-R	6-2	245	4-11-83	2	2	4.19	44	0	0	4	62	68	32	29	6	14	51	.269	.325	.213	7.36	2.02
Van Benschoten, John	R-R	6-4	215	4-14-80	2	0	2.31	6	1	0	1	12	13	3	3	1	6	8	.283	.333	.250	6.17	4.63
Whelan, Kevin	R-R	6-0	200	1-8-84	2	1	6.30	17	0	0	1	20	19	15	14	2	10	22	.244	.214	.278	9.90	4.50
Wordekemper, Eric	R-R	6-1	190	8-8-83	2	0	3.13	24	0	0	1	32	31	11	11	2	9	29	.258	.269	.250	8.24	2.56

NEW YORK YANKEES

Fielding

Catcher	PCT	G	PO	A	E	DP	PB
Hammock	1.000	4	19	1	0	0	0
Moeller	.995	26	187	9	1	4	1
Montero	.992	105	703	76	6	6	15
Pilittere	1.000	8	41	1	0	0	1
Rivera	1.000	9	72	3	0	0	0

First Base	PCT	G	PO	A	E	DP
Hammock	1.000	1	3	0	0	0
Huffman	.993	16	138	10	1	18
Laird	1.000	2	15	0	0	1
Miranda	.992	61	461	43	4	45
Natale	1.000	3	2	1	0	0
Pilittere	.976	8	37	3	1	2
Tracy	1.000	2	21	0	0	2
Vazquez	.988	38	291	34	4	28
Winfree	.995	21	182	8	1	12

Second Base	PCT	G	PO	A	E	DP
Bruntlett	.962	12	13	38	2	4
Corona	.998	91	166	282	1	51
Hammock	.929	4	8	5	1	3
Huffman	—	1	0	0	0	0
Natale	.960	6	10	14	1	3
Nunez	.889	5	4	12	2	4
Russo	.992	29	47	80	1	16

Third Base	PCT	G	PO	A	E	DP
Bruntlett	.975	18	15	24	1	1
Corona	.895	9	4	13	2	4
Cusick	.921	28	13	45	5	1
Hammock	1.000	10	5	10	0	1
Laird	.969	29	21	42	2	5
Nunez	.917	11	12	10	2	1
Russo	.906	23	20	38	6	6
Tracy	.943	14	11	22	2	2
Vazquez	.857	8	2	10	2	0

Shortstop	PCT	G	PO	A	E	DP
Bruntlett	.971	27	39	61	3	20
Corona	.909	8	9	21	3	5
Nunez	.976	101	146	254	10	57
Russo	.963	10	13	13	1	5

Outfield	PCT	G	PO	A	E	DP
Bruntlett	.973	13	34	2	1	1
Christian	1.000	15	24	1	0	0
Curtis	1.000	61	125	4	0	1
Golson	.983	114	278	7	5	1
Gonzalez	1.000	4	7	0	0	0
Gorecki	.974	74	175	11	5	3
Granderson	1.000	3	8	0	0	0
Huffman	.987	84	147	8	2	2
Moeller	—	1	0	0	0	0
Russo	.973	21	34	2	1	0
Snyder	1.000	2	3	0	0	0
Thames	1.000	3	5	0	0	0
Weber	.929	20	26	0	2	0
Winfree	.962	25	49	1	2	2

TRENTON THUNDER   DOUBLE-A
EASTERN LEAGUE

Batting	B-T	HT	WT	DOB	AVG	vLH	vRH	G	AB	R	H	2B	3B	HR	RBI	BB	HBP	SH	SF	SO	SB	CS	SLG	OBP
Adams, David	R-R	6-2	190	5-15-87	.309	.400	.277	39	152	31	47	15	3	3	32	18	3	0	0	31	5	2	.507	.393
Baker, Ryan	R-R	5-9	205	11-9-84	.000	.000	.000	3	3	0	0	0	0	0	0	0	0	0	0	1	0	0	.000	.000
Berkman, Lance	B-L	6-1	230	2-10-76	.250	.500	.000	2	8	1	2	0	0	0	1	0	0	0	0	0	0	0	.250	.333
Brewer, Dan	R-R	6-0	185	7-19-87	.270	.244	.279	136	508	83	137	34	3	10	84	53	10	2	7	117	29	10	.407	.346
Christian, Justin	R-R	6-1	190	4-3-80	.297	.329	.287	87	343	65	102	21	6	9	51	40	5	1	5	47	20	5	.472	.374
Cusick, Matt	L-R	5-10	190	5-5-86	.234	.114	.268	59	201	17	47	7	3	3	26	22	1	1	2	31	3	1	.343	.310
Gil, Jose	R-R	6-0	170	9-4-86	.236	.387	.173	31	106	19	25	6	1	5	25	9	2	1	1	23	0	0	.453	.305
Gonzalez, Edwar	R-R	5-10	200	1-1-83	.235	.274	.214	74	243	37	57	8	4	6	35	20	8	0	0	59	4	2	.374	.333
Gorecki, Reid	R-R	6-1	175	12-22-80	.257	.258	.257	29	105	10	27	7	0	2	15	13	2	0	1	20	8	3	.381	.347
Grote, Taylor	L-R	6-2	195	12-5-88	.000	.000	.000	1	1	0	0	0	0	0	0	0	0	0	0	1	0	0	.000	.500
Joseph, Corban	L-R	6-0	168	10-28-88	.216	.119	.275	31	111	11	24	6	4	0	13	15	0	2	2	33	1	0	.342	.305
Krum, Austin	L-L	6-0	190	1-19-86	.229	.206	.238	120	459	77	105	17	1	5	44	64	4	6	0	86	16	7	.303	.328
Laird, Brandon	R-R	6-1	215	9-11-87	.291	.330	.277	107	409	73	119	22	2	23	90	38	4	0	3	84	2	2	.523	.355
Mahoney, Kevin	L-R	6-1	205	5-11-87	.267	.000	.286	6	15	2	4	1	0	0	1	5	1	0	0	6	0	0	.333	.476
Nunez, Luis	R-R	5-11	160	11-21-86	.241	.279	.226	131	449	60	108	24	5	8	44	25	4	9	5	70	7	10	.370	.284
Rivera, Rene	R-R	5-10	230	7-31-83	.319	.289	.339	25	94	13	30	10	0	5	17	7	1	0	1	17	0	0	.585	.369
Romine, Austin	R-R	6-1	195	11-22-88	.268	.319	.251	115	455	61	122	31	0	10	69	37	2	0	3	94	2	0	.402	.324
Rye, Jack	L-L	6-1	200	3-8-86	.212	.313	.167	15	52	5	11	3	1	1	7	6	0	0	0	9	1	0	.365	.293
Smith, Kevin	L-R	6-1	215	1-15-84	.168	.048	.191	41	131	9	22	6	0	0	5	17	2	0	0	49	0	0	.214	.273
Snyder, Justin	L-R	5-9	190	4-8-86	.245	.162	.275	90	261	56	64	13	2	3	27	49	2	4	3	44	2	1	.345	.365
Sublett, Damon	L-R	6-1	190	9-22-85	.214	.125	.239	35	112	14	24	4	1	2	14	22	0	0	0	37	1	1	.321	.343
Vazquez, Jorge	R-R	6-0	225	3-15-82	.390	.444	.375	10	41	4	16	4	0	2	6	1	0	0	0	8	0	0	.488	.405
Vechionacci, Marcos	B-R	6-2	170	8-7-86	.283	.290	.280	114	406	56	115	17	3	11	55	40	2	2	1	111	6	2	.421	.350

Pitching	B-T	HT	WT	DOB	W	L	ERA	G	GS	CG	SV	IP	H	R	ER	HR	BB	SO	AVG	vLH	vRH	K/9	BB/9
Aceves, Alfredo	R-R	6-3	220	12-8-82	0	0	5.63	4	3	0	0	8	10	5	5	1	1	7	.313	.357	.278	7.88	1.13
Arbiso, Cory	R-R	6-3	210	4-21-86	5	5	4.38	32	11	0	0	84	100	46	41	9	22	49	.299	.291	.307	5.23	2.35
Arias, Wilkins	L-L	6-1	150	11-4-80	4	3	3.65	57	0	0	0	62	61	27	25	5	30	70	.264	.214	.311	10.22	4.38
Banuelos, Manuel	L-L	5-10	155	3-13-91	0	1	3.52	3	3	0	0	15	15	8	6	2	8	17	.273	.318	.242	9.98	4.70
Betances, Dellin	R-R	6-8	245	3-23-88	0	0	3.77	3	3	0	0	14	10	7	6	3	3	20	.200	.241	.143	12.56	1.88
Bleich, Jeremy	L-L	6-2	185	6-18-87	3	2	4.79	8	8	0	0	41	35	22	22	2	28	26	.236	.255	.226	5.66	6.10
Brackman, Andrew	R-R	6-10	240	12-4-85	5	7	3.01	15	14	0	0	81	77	38	27	3	30	70	.252	.267	.239	7.81	3.35
Bush, Paul	R-R	6-1	195	10-5-79	0	2	15.00	3	0	0	0	3	3	5	5	1	4	4	.250	.200	.286	12.00	12.00
Castillo, Noel	R-R	6-1	160	10-5-83	3	2	6.27	17	0	0	0	19	12	15	13	4	16	20	.182	.129	.229	9.64	7.71
Cox, J.B.	L-R	6-3	205	5-13-84	3	0	4.28	26	0	0	2	34	34	18	16	1	12	23	.254	.127	.366	6.15	3.21
De La Rosa, Wilkin	L-L	6-0	185	2-21-85	2	4	5.33	36	8	0	0	73	82	51	43	7	41	56	.286	.263	.297	6.94	5.08
Duff, Grant	R-R	6-6	210	12-19-82	1	4	2.84	28	0	0	8	32	30	16	10	4	16	38	.244	.241	.246	10.80	4.55
Garcia, Christian	R-R	6-5	215	8-24-85	1	0	0.00	1	1	0	0	6	2	0	0	0		3	.111	.125	.100	4.76	1.59
Kontos, George	R-R	6-3	215	6-12-85	0	2	3.38	17	0	0	0	32	30	13	12	2	11	28	.254	.278	.234	7.88	3.09
Mitchell, D.J.	R-R	6-2	165	5-13-87	11	4	4.06	23	22	0	0	133	128	69	60	11	57	96	.254	.263	.250	6.50	3.86
Noesi, Hector	R-R	6-2	175	1-26-87	8	1	3.10	17	16	2	0	99	90	37	34	7	18	86	.243	.250	.236	7.84	1.64
Norton, Tim	R-R	6-5	230	5-23-83	1	0	0.90	6	0	0	1	10	4	1	1	0	3	15	.129	.000	.190	13.50	2.70
Olbrychowski, Adam	R-R	6-3	205	9-7-86	0	2	2.08	2	0	0	0	4	4	1	1	0	1	4	.235	.000	.364	8.31	2.08
Pendleton, Lance	L-R	6-3	205	9-10-83	10	4	3.43	23	22	0	0	121	95	50	46	9	45	111	.215	.238	.194	8.28	3.36
Phelps, David	R-R	6-3	190	10-9-86	6	0	2.04	14	14	0	0	88	63	21	20	2	23	84	.199	.219	.182	8.56	2.34
Pope, Ryan	R-R	6-3	190	5-21-86	4	6	4.20	46	7	0	17	94	88	48	44	10	31	85	.246	.202	.284	8.11	2.96
Schmidt, Josh	R-R	6-4	175	11-14-82	3	3	2.67	47	0	0	2	61	41	18	18	3	28	71	.189	.180	.195	10.53	4.15
Van Benschoten, John	R-R	6-4	215	4-14-80	2	0	0.00	2	0	0	0	6	4	1	0	0	4	6	.182	.083	.300	6.00	6.00
Vendette, Pat	R-B	6-1	180	6-30-85	1	1	9.00	2	0	0	0	2	4	2	2	0	1	4	.400	.200	.600	18.00	4.50
Warren, Adam	R-R	6-1	200	8-25-87	4	2	3.15	10	10	0	0	54	49	26	19	2	16	59	.232	.281	.191	9.77	2.65

	B-T	HT	WT	DOB	W	L	ERA	G	GS	CG	SV	IP	H	R	ER	HR	BB	SO	AVG	vLH	vRH	K/9	BB/9
Whelan, Kevin	R-R	6-0	200	1-8-84	3	3	5.83	24	0	0	3	29	20	19	19	1	21	40	.194	.224	.167	12.27	6.44
Wordekemper, Eric	R-R	6-1	200	8-8-83	3	0	2.88	23	0	0	8	34	26	12	11	5	8	35	.208	.207	.209	9.17	2.10

Fielding

Catcher	PCT	G	PO	A	E	DP	PB
Baker	1.000	3	4	1	0	0	0
Gil	.986	26	196	18	3	2	6
Rivera	.994	18	139	14	1	3	4
Romine	.994	99	787	61	5	0	6

First Base	PCT	G	PO	A	E	DP
Laird	1.000	4	36	4	0	0
Smith	.990	35	292	19	3	35
Snyder	1.000	4	21	2	0	1
Vazquez	.955	3	21	0	1	2
Vechionacci	.991	100	795	64	8	83

Second Base	PCT	G	PO	A	E	DP
Adams	1.000	36	56	112	0	24
Cusick	.988	23	31	52	1	12
Joseph	.954	31	53	92	7	22
Mahoney	.900	6	8	10	2	4
Snyder	.981	48	71	131	4	26

Third Base	PCT	G	PO	A	E	DP
Cusick	1.000	24	12	24	0	0
Laird	.922	99	50	186	20	17
Snyder	.938	20	11	34	3	2
Vazquez	1.000	3	1	5	0	0
Vechionacci	1.000	2	1	4	0	0

Shortstop	PCT	G	PO	A	E	DP
Nunez	.974	131	204	324	14	92
Snyder	.896	12	14	29	5	7

Outfield	PCT	G	PO	A	E	DP
Brewer	.992	129	234	14	2	3
Christian	.993	70	138	4	1	0
Gonzalez	.990	54	90	5	1	2
Gorecki	1.000	21	38	3	0	0
Grote	—	1	0	0	0	0
Krum	.990	116	285	9	3	2
Rye	.926	13	24	1	2	0
Snyder	1.000	6	7	0	0	0
Sublett	.929	21	23	3	2	1

TAMPA YANKEES HIGH CLASS A
FLORIDA STATE LEAGUE

Batting	B-T	HT	WT	DOB	AVG	vLH	vRH	G	AB	R	H	2B	3B	HR	RBI	BB	HBP	SH	SF	SO	SB	CS	SLG	OBP
Abeita, Mitch	R-R	6-0	185	4-7-86	.273	.291	.266	77	256	33	70	15	1	1	26	42	0	0	1	60	0	0	.352	.375
Almonte, Abraham	R-R	5-9	205	6-27-89	.263	.200	.286	15	57	9	15	3	1	0	3	6	0	0	0	16	5	3	.351	.333
Almonte, Zoilo	B-R	5-11	165	6-10-89	.261	.188	.287	63	238	26	62	10	3	3	26	23	0	0	3	65	8	1	.366	.322
Baker, Ryan	R-R	5-9	205	11-9-84	.086	.182	.042	15	35	6	3	0	0	0	2	7	1	0	1	15	0	0	.086	.250
Felix, Anderson	B-R	6-0	155	5-11-92	.280	.200	.333	10	25	6	7	1	0	1	4	3	0	0	0	9	2	0	.440	.357
Flores, Ramon	L-L	5-10	150	3-26-92	.250	.000	.318	8	28	0	7	0	0	0	2	0	0	0	0	5	0	0	.250	.250
Gil, Jose	R-R	6-0	170	9-4-86	.255	.345	.232	40	141	17	36	4	0	5	19	11	2	1	1	31	4	0	.390	.316
Ibarra, Walter	B-R	5-11	180	11-1-87	.301	.317	.293	72	246	28	74	12	1	1	14	15	5	4	4	46	15	7	.370	.348
Joseph, Corban	L-R	6-0	168	10-28-88	.302	.287	.308	98	381	52	115	27	3	6	52	43	7	1	5	74	5	8	.436	.378
Kruml, Ray	L-R	5-11	175	8-5-85	.271	.227	.287	66	291	44	79	14	2	1	21	21	2	0	0	63	30	6	.344	.325
Leslie, Myron	B-R	6-3	220	5-2-82	.262	.238	.277	80	260	40	68	14	1	6	39	30	2	0	3	53	8	0	.392	.339
Lockwood, Trent	L-L	6-4	235	5-5-86	.257	.278	.252	86	292	37	75	17	0	4	37	35	0	0	2	67	2	0	.356	.334
Mahoney, Kevin	L-R	6-1	205	5-11-87	.400	.500	.333	3	5	0	2	2	0	0	1	1	0	0	0	2	0	0	.800	.500
Maruszak, Addison	R-R	6-1	195	12-21-86	.284	.240	.304	68	243	32	69	16	0	1	34	11	2	1	7	40	3	2	.362	.312
Medchill, Neil	L-R	6-4	220	6-25-87	.178	.170	.180	51	180	17	32	5	1	3	21	18	2	0	0	70	3	2	.267	.260
Mesa, Melky	L-R	6-1	165	1-31-87	.260	.231	.272	121	446	81	116	21	9	19	74	44	11	1	5	129	31	9	.475	.338
Pena, Henry	L-R	6-0	180	10-26-90	.000	.000	.000	1	3	0	0	0	0	0	0	0	0	0	0	2	0	0	.000	.000
Pirela, Jose	B-R	5-10	191	11-21-89	.252	.267	.246	130	497	68	125	15	13	5	61	57	4	8	7	87	30	7	.364	.329
Rye, Jack	L-L	6-1	200	3-8-86	.274	.245	.288	92	332	49	91	22	3	6	45	34	3	3	5	41	7	1	.413	.342
Santana, Francisco	L-L	5-10	170	6-18-88	.135	.091	.154	23	74	3	10	4	1	0	8	1	0	4	1	23	1	0	.216	.145
Suttle, Bradley	B-R	6-2	215	1-24-86	.272	.265	.275	133	514	61	140	33	4	10	80	53	4	0	8	136	12	2	.411	.340

Pitching	B-T	HT	WT	DOB	W	L	ERA	G	GS	CG	SV	IP	H	R	ER	HR	BB	SO	AVG	vLH	vRH	K/9	BB/9
Banuelos, Manuel	L-L	5-10	155	3-13-91	0	3	2.23	10	10	0	0	44	38	16	11	1	14	62	.230	.216	.234	12.59	2.84
Bartleski, Philip	R-R	6-7	240	4-22-83	3	3	4.54	37	0	0	3	69	82	41	35	8	17	57	.296	.388	.224	7.40	2.21
Betances, Dellin	R-R	6-8	245	3-23-88	8	1	1.77	14	14	0	0	71	43	18	14	1	19	88	.169	.217	.129	11.15	2.41
Black, Sean	R-R	6-3	185	4-23-88	1	0	1.59	2	2	0	0	11	9	2	2	0	1	12	.225	.188	.250	9.53	0.79
Braboy, Brandon	R-R	6-0	195	10-31-85	0	0	3.57	11	2	0	1	23	31	11	9	0	4	17	.323	.277	.367	6.75	1.59
Brackman, Andrew	R-R	6-10	240	12-4-85	5	4	5.10	12	12	0	0	60	67	38	34	5	9	56	.278	.347	.233	8.40	1.35
Castillo, Noel	R-R	6-1	160	10-5-83	2	2	2.28	16	0	0	0	28	18	8	7	2	13	36	.188	.176	.194	11.71	4.23
Claiborne, Preston	R-R	6-2	215	1-21-88	0	1	3.68	5	0	0	0	7	7	3	3	1	4	6	.269	.333	.235	7.36	4.91
Cox, J.B.	R-R	6-3	205	5-13-84	0	1	8.59	5	0	0	0	7	14	11	7	1	2	4	.400	.375	.421	4.91	2.45
Flannery, Ryan	R-R	6-4	245	1-6-86	1	0	2.25	2	0	0	0	4	2	1	1	0	0	6	.143	.200	.111	13.50	0.00
Forer, Nathan	R-R	6-1	172	6-6-88	0	0	9.39	6	0	0	0	8	16	8	8	0	4	5	.432	.500	.391	5.87	4.70
Hall, Shaeffer	R-L	6-1	205	10-2-87	9	5	3.91	15	14	0	0	69	81	38	30	7	10	57	.293	.246	.308	7.43	1.30
Heredia, Jairo	R-R	6-1	190	10-8-89	0	6	6.93	6	6	0	0	25	37	28	19	2	11	14	.359	.364	.354	5.11	4.01
Heyer, Craig	R-R	6-3	205	11-15-85	4	3	3.52	26	12	1	0	92	92	42	36	1	6	66	.257	.288	.233	6.46	0.59
Kapala, Dan	R-R	6-5	220	9-6-85	1	6	4.53	12	11	0	0	58	61	33	29	2	30	26	.275	.328	.217	4.06	4.68
Kontos, George	R-R	6-3	215	6-12-85	0	1	2.61	5	2	0	0	10	7	3	3	0	3	8	.194	.188	.200	6.97	2.61
Lare, Trenton	L-L	6-4	195	8-25-84	1	2	4.00	42	1	0	0	74	95	46	33	6	19	73	.308	.314	.306	8.84	2.30
Marcano, Juan	L-L	6-1	165	8-24-90	1	0	0.00	3	0	0	0	5	1	0	0	0	3	8	.067	.000	.077	14.40	5.40
Marshall, Brett	R-R	6-0	195	3-22-90	0	0	4.50	1	1	0	0	4	5	3	2	0	0	6	.294	.400	.250	13.50	0.00
Marte, Ronny	R-R	6-1	173	2-25-86	1	0	2.93	9	0	0	0	15	16	9	5	0	8	11	.262	.042	.405	6.46	4.70
Mitre, Sergio	R-R	6-3	225	2-16-81	0	0	0.00	1	0	0	0	1	0	0	0	0	0	1	.000	.000	.000	9.00	0.00
Noesi, Hector	R-R	6-2	175	1-26-87	5	2	2.72	8	8	0	0	43	35	14	13	3	6	53	.212	.173	.250	11.09	1.26
Norton, Tim	R-R	6-5	230	5-23-83	0	0	1.69	12	0	0	2	21	16	7	4	2	3	32	.195	.200	.191	13.50	1.27
Olbrychowski, Adam	R-R	6-3	205	9-7-86	3	2	4.02	30	1	0	1	63	59	33	28	1	27	52	.252	.256	.250	7.47	3.88
Ortiz, Jonathan	R-R	5-10	170	10-29-85	7	1	2.47	46	0	0	21	55	41	17	15	4	11	62	.202	.264	.155	10.21	1.81
Romanski, Josh	L-L	6-0	185	10-18-86	0	1	4.50	3	3	0	0	15	6	6	6	0	4	12	.300	.400	.289	9.00	3.00
Rulon, Brad	L-R	5-11	185	6-22-86	1	0	2.50	11	0	0	0	18	18	8	5	1	6	16	.243	.257	.231	8.00	3.00
Sanit, Amaury	R-R	5-8	205	7-4-79	0	0	1.80	3	0	0	0	5	0	1	1	0	2	6	.000	.000	.000	10.80	3.60
Stoneburner, Graham	R-R	6-1	190	9-29-87	8	5	2.53	19	19	1	0	103	80	35	29	4	24	93	.214	.216	.212	8.13	2.10
Van Benschoten, John	R-R	6-4	215	4-14-80	2	1	4.50	12	2	0	0	26	30	14	13	4	8	24	.303	.333	.286	8.31	2.77

Name	B-T	HT	WT	DOB	W	L	ERA	G	GS	CG	SV	IP	H	R	ER	HR	BB	SO	AVG	vLH	vRH	K/9	BB/9
Venditte, Pat	R-B	6-1	180	6-30-85	4	1	1.73	41	0	0	6	73	49	17	14	2	14	85	.187	.158	.209	10.53	1.73
Warren, Adam	R-R	6-1	200	8-25-87	7	5	2.22	15	15	1	0	81	72	23	20	2	17	67	.235	.235	.236	7.44	1.89
Whitley, Chase	R-R	6-4	220	6-14-89	0	0	3.00	2	0	0	0	3	1	1	1	1	0	6	.100	.000	.167	18.00	0.00

Fielding

Catcher	PCT	G	PO	A	E	DP	PB
Abeita	.991	75	620	39	6	5	9
Baker	1.000	15	78	6	0	0	1
Gil	.997	39	323	24	1	2	3
Leslie	.983	16	99	17	2	0	7

First Base	PCT	G	PO	A	E	DP
Gil	1.000	1	4	1	0	0
Leslie	.989	64	493	39	6	44
Lockwood	.979	45	350	30	8	38
Maruszak	1.000	28	221	14	0	21
Suttle	.978	10	83	5	2	3

Second Base	PCT	G	PO	A	E	DP
Felix	1.000	6	8	10	0	3

	PCT	G	PO	A	E
Ibarra	.964	24	36	70	4	17
Joseph	.972	85	128	224	10	52
Leslie	1.000	2	2	2	0	1
Pirela	.957	23	27	62	4	11

Third Base	PCT	G	PO	A	E	DP
Felix	—	1	0	0	0	0
Ibarra	.917	19	12	32	4	2
Joseph	.864	6	3	16	3	0
Mahoney	1.000	3	0	2	0	1
Maruszak	1.000	15	5	27	0	3
Suttle	.951	96	64	186	13	20

Shortstop	PCT	G	PO	A	E	DP
Felix	.833	1	2	3	1	0

	PCT	G	PO	A	E	DP
Ibarra	.971	15	17	51	2	8
Maruszak	.904	24	31	63	10	16
Pirela	.938	99	129	262	26	50

Outfield	PCT	G	PO	A	E	DP
Almonte	.958	15	22	1	1	0
Almonte	.991	58	108	3	1	0
Flores	1.000	8	14	0	0	0
Ibarra	1.000	7	6	0	0	0
Kruml	.975	62	113	3	3	0
Medchill	1.000	44	50	1	0	0
Mesa	.985	112	255	6	4	3
Pena	1.000	1	2	0	0	0
Rye	.982	81	158	4	3	1
Santana	1.000	22	31	0	0	0

CHARLESTON RIVERDOGS

LOW CLASS A

SOUTH ATLANTIC LEAGUE

Batting	B-T	HT	WT	DOB	AVG	vLH	vRH	G	AB	R	H	2B	3B	HR	RBI	BB	HBP	SH	SF	SO	SB	CS	SLG	OBP
Almonte, Zoilo	B-R	5-11	165	6-10-89	.278	.333	.257	58	227	33	63	13	2	10	35	21	2	3	2	65	7	6	.485	.341
Arcia, Francisco	B-R	6-0	155	9-14-89	.314	.125	.349	17	51	2	16	4	0	0	3	7	0	0	0	8	1	0	.392	.397
Castro, Kelvin	R-R	6-3	164	12-14-87	.224	.274	.207	123	437	55	98	20	5	2	39	30	2	3	5	96	15	11	.307	.274
Flores, Ramon	L-L	5-10	150	3-26-92	.250	.267	.242	14	48	3	12	3	0	0	2	3	0	0	0	15	1	0	.313	.294
Grote, Taylor	L-R	6-2	195	12-5-88	.278	.417	.256	28	90	11	25	7	0	2	9	16	0	1	1	30	1	2	.422	.383
Heathcott, Slade	L-L	6-1	190	9-28-90	.258	.250	.262	76	298	48	77	16	3	2	30	42	6	3	2	101	15	10	.352	.359
Higashioka, Kyle	R-R	6-1	190	4-20-90	.225	.253	.215	90	320	35	72	18	0	6	24	31	5	2	1	64	0	2	.338	.303
Kruml, Ray	L-R	5-11	175	8-5-85	.261	.255	.263	51	184	21	48	9	1	0	11	7	3	2	1	35	12	2	.321	.297
Landoni, Emerson	B-R	5-10	146	2-18-89	.280	.321	.262	84	261	39	73	13	1	3	32	21	1	6	5	44	13	8	.372	.330
Lassiter, Garrison	L-R	6-1	185	12-22-89	.107	.059	.113	27	28	2	9	1	0	0	4	14	0	0	1	36	1	1	.114	.223
Liccien, Jhorge	R-R	6-0	165	10-10-90	.200	.250	.000	2	5	0	1	0	0	0	1	0	0	0	2	0	0	.200	.333
Lyerly, Rob	R-L	6-2	200	7-23-87	.312	.278	.324	131	503	72	157	36	0	7	71	34	0	0	5	129	9	7	.425	.352
Mack, DeAngelo	R-L	5-10	190	11-19-86	.252	.179	.279	116	424	52	107	20	5	12	56	46	5	1	0	99	5	7	.408	.333
Mahoney, Kevin	L-R	6-1	205	5-11-87	.298	.438	.265	26	84	15	25	8	0	2	7	13	2	0	0	25	1	1	.464	.404
Medchill, Neil	L-R	6-4	220	6-25-87	.215	.169	.230	65	237	29	51	10	1	9	32	23	4	0	0	84	5	4	.380	.295
Milo, Justin	L-R	5-8	180	2-23-87	.231	.167	.250	16	52	8	12	0	0	0	4	11	0	1	1	15	3	1	.231	.359
Murphy, J.R.	B-R	6-0	190	5-13-91	.255	.298	.240	87	330	46	84	15	2	7	54	36	2	1	5	64	4	5	.376	.327
Murton, Luke	R-R	6-4	222	5-21-86	.282	.350	.259	106	397	48	112	32	2	12	55	39	12	0	3	71	2	0	.463	.361
Paredes, Jimmy	B-R	6-1	178	11-25-88	.282	.333	.267	99	404	59	114	24	6	5	48	18	2	5	5	82	36	10	.408	.312
2-team total (34 Lexington)					.287	—	—	133	551	83	158	34	7	8	65	25	2	5	5	107	50	11	.417	.317
Rabago, Hector	R-R	5-10	185	8-24-88	.160	.235	.129	40	119	7	19	3	0	3	16	9	4	5	2	29	0	0	.261	.293
Santana, Francisco	L-L	5-10	170	6-18-88	.257	.192	.280	34	101	16	26	5	2	2	15	5	0	2	0	22	2	1	.406	.292
Toussen, Jose	L-L	6-1	155	11-13-89	.000	.000	.000	2	3	1	0	0	0	0	0	0	0	0	0	0	0	0	.000	.000

Pitching	B-T	HT	WT	DOB	W	L	ERA	G	GS	CG	SV	IP	H	R	ER	HR	BB	SO	AVG	vLH	vRH	K/9	BB/9
Acosta, Ryan	R-R	6-2	170	11-4-88	5	4	3.50	42	0	0	1	62	61	31	24	0	23	46	.255	.224	.273	6.71	3.36
Barreda, Manuel	R-R	5-11	165	10-8-88	1	0	0.00	6	0	0	0	7	8	0	0	0	5	7	.296	.286	.300	8.59	6.14
Black, Sean	R-R	6-3	185	4-23-88	7	8	3.88	23	22	1	0	116	118	75	50	6	40	92	.259	.211	.280	7.14	3.10
Flannery, Ryan	R-R	6-4	245	1-6-86	7	6	2.26	45	0	0	14	80	61	25	20	2	14	70	.207	.262	.176	7.91	1.58
Gil, Daniel	R-R	6-3	187	4-24-89	1	3	1.25	28	0	0	9	36	32	10	5	0	12	27	.232	.213	.242	6.75	3.00
Gipson, Mike	R-R	6-1	195	9-15-88	0	2	7.88	3	2	0	0	8	11	7	7	1	3	6	.314	.263	.375	6.75	3.38
Greene, Shane	R-R	6-4	210	11-17-88	0	2	4.58	4	4	0	0	20	14	10	10	1	8	22	.206	.286	.150	10.07	3.66
Hall, Shaeffer	R-L	6-1	205	10-2-87	2	2	1.85	10	10	0	0	68	52	19	14	1	11	46	.208	.150	.219	6.09	1.46
Heredia, Jairo	R-R	6-1	190	10-8-89	4	2	3.45	20	9	0	0	70	74	34	27	4	19	65	.266	.287	.254	8.32	2.43
Marquez, Dickson	R-R	6-2	170	4-19-86	0	1	10.62	15	0	0	1	20	30	25	24	1	12	10	.349	.333	.356	4.43	5.31
Marshall, Brett	R-R	6-0	195	3-22-90	4	2	2.50	13	13	1	0	72	52	26	20	2	22	56	.199	.203	.196	7.00	2.75
Marte, Ronny	R-R	6-1	173	2-26-86	2	3	3.13	35	2	0	4	55	67	30	19	4	15	36	.306	.307	.305	5.93	2.47
Martinez, Richard	R-R	6-1	194	7-19-88	1	0	3.60	1	1	0	0	5	5	2	2	0	4	8	.250	1.000	.167	7.20	3.60
Perez, Kelvin	R-R	6-1	140	10-10-85	5	5	3.18	30	13	0	0	105	93	53	37	6	36	80	.239	.186	.265	6.88	3.10
Quintana, Jose	L-L	6-0	170	1-24-89	0	1	4.70	5	3	0	0	15	11	10	8	1	10	12	.193	.000	.244	7.04	5.87
Ramirez, Jose	R-R	6-1	155	1-21-90	6	5	3.60	22	21	0	0	115	106	56	46	3	42	105	.239	.232	.232	8.22	3.29
Rodriguez, Wilton	R-R	6-3	195	11-6-90	0	1	7.71	1	1	0	0	5	4	4	4	0	4	3	.222	.250	.200	5.79	7.71
Romanski, Josh	L-L	6-0	185	10-18-86	8	4	3.16	15	15	0	0	88	84	39	31	8	17	73	.248	.261	.246	7.44	1.73
Rondon, Francisco	L-L	6-1	160	4-19-88	1	2	7.71	10	0	0	1	12	12	10	10	3	7	16	.255	.286	.250	12.34	5.40
Shive, Andy	R-R	6-6	260	11-5-85	1	1	3.38	6	0	0	0	4	7	3	0	0	4	6	.148	.182	.125	4.50	9.00
Solbach, Michael	R-R	6-3	185	7-31-85	4	6	3.90	30	15	0	0	99	109	47	43	4	23	95	.276	.314	.255	8.61	2.08
Stoneburner, Graham	R-R	6-1	190	9-29-87	1	3	2.08	7	7	0	0	39	27	11	9	2	10	44	.194	.229	.176	10.15	2.31
Tatis, Gabriel	R-R	6-0	180	5-18-85	2	3	4.14	37	0	0	0	59	56	38	27	2	18	49	.240	.241	.240	7.52	2.76
Watkins, Ben	R-R	6-3	225	3-11-87	3	4	3.88	35	1	0	0	58	59	28	25	3	16	34	.263	.222	.287	5.28	2.48

Fielding

Catcher

	PCT	G	PO	A	E	DP	PB
Arcia	.981	16	90	12	2	0	1
Higashioka	.987	59	423	50	6	0	4
Liccien	1.000	2	17	3	0	0	
Murphy	.973	53	347	45	11	4	13
Rabago	.979	17	125	14	3	0	3

First Base

	PCT	G	PO	A	E	DP
Flores	1.000	1	1	0	0	0
Landoni	.980	6	45	5	1	2
Lyerly	.987	47	437	31	6	25
Mahoney	1.000	2	16	0	0	0
Murton	.995	88	813	57	4	63

Second Base

	PCT	G	PO	A	E	DP
Castro	.977	10	13	30	1	5
Landoni	.964	44	79	106	7	23
Mahoney	1.000	12	13	34	0	6
Paredes	.935	71	131	201	23	37
Rabago	.870	5	11	9	3	2
Toussen	1.000	1	1	3	0	0

Third Base

	PCT	G	PO	A	E	DP
Landoni	.881	14	15	22	5	3
Lassiter	.889	15	9	31	5	4
Lyerly	.873	76	45	141	27	7
Mahoney	.974	14	4	34	1	1
Paredes	.792	7	3	16	5	0
Rabago	.879	17	9	42	7	1

Shortstop

	PCT	G	PO	A	E	DP
Castro	.938	110	166	378	36	67
Landoni	.927	15	16	35	4	4
Paredes	.897	16	23	47	8	10

Outfield

	PCT	G	PO	A	E	DP
Almonte	.974	55	110	3	3	0
Flores	1.000	1	15	0	0	0
Grote	1.000	20	39	2	0	0
Heathcott	.953	75	135	8	7	0
Kruml	1.000	50	102	3	0	0
Landoni	1.000	2	1	0	0	0
Mack	.955	106	161	7	8	2
Medchill	.979	61	92	1	2	0
Milo	.952	16	20	0	1	0
Santana	.982	29	53	3	1	1

STATEN ISLAND YANKEES — SHORT-SEASON

NEW YORK-PENN LEAGUE

Batting

	B-T	HT	WT	DOB	AVG	vLH	vRH	G	AB	R	H	2B	3B	HR	RBI	BB	HBP	SH	SF	SO	SB	CS	SLG	OBP
Arcia, Francisco	B-R	6-0	155	9-14-89	.224	.154	.250	25	98	13	22	4	0	2	14	5	1	1	1	13	1	0	.327	.267
Brown, Isaiah	R-R	6-0	160	10-16-89	.218	.188	.239	24	78	7	17	5	1	1	5	10	0	0	0	26	4	1	.346	.307
Brown, Shane	R-R	5-11	197	1-11-88	.234	.265	.220	60	209	30	49	7	0	2	25	37	11	2	2	28	2	4	.297	.375
Culver, Cito	B-R	6-0	185	8-26-92	.186	.444	.118	15	43	2	8	1	0	0	8	2	1	0	10	1	1		.209	.340
De Leon, Kelvin	R-R	6-2	180	10-29-90	.236	.164	.263	69	259	33	61	12	1	6	37	17	2	0	0	80	5	1	.359	.288
Duran, Kelvin	L-L	5-11	165	11-10-90	.172	.211	.154	18	58	4	10	3	0	0	4	2	1	1	0	31	2	2	.224	.213
Farnham, Jeff	R-R	6-1	195	8-30-87	.227	.171	.253	36	110	15	25	5	0	0	11	13	4	2	0	19	4	1	.273	.331
Ferraro, Mike	L-L	6-2	200	5-31-88	.204	.128	.230	43	152	14	31	10	0	1	13	5	5	2	1	47	1	1	.289	.252
Lassiter, Garrison	L-R	6-1	185	12-22-89	.285	.235	.303	39	123	10	35	3	1	0	10	19	2	3	0	29	1	3	.325	.389
Mahoney, Kevin	L-R	6-1	205	5-11-87	.276	.167	.337	38	134	18	37	5	2	6	22	18	6	0	1	35	4	1	.478	.384
McCoy, Nick	R-R	5-10	180	3-2-87	.237	.286	.222	20	59	5	14	4	0	0	7	9	3	0	0	16	1	0	.305	.366
Mojica, Jose	R-R	6-0	145	12-26-88	.241	.219	.252	53	187	16	45	10	0	0	12	11	1	2	2	20	2	1	.294	.284
Parache, Luis	L-R	5-8	175	11-25-88	.235	.325	.202	45	149	17	35	9	1	3	20	10	1	5	2	20	4	2	.369	.284
Roller, Kyle	L-R	6-1	235	3-27-88	.272	.268	.274	67	246	36	67	11	3	5	31	31	6	0	0	65	3	2	.402	.367
Sanchez, Gary	R-R	6-2	195	12-2-92	.278	.231	.293	16	54	8	15	2	0	2	7	3	2	0	1	16	1	1	.426	.333
Segedin, Rob	R-R	6-3	220	11-10-88	.243	.304	.213	20	70	13	17	6	1	1	7	7	1	0	0	7	0	1	.400	.321
Sosa, Eduardo	L-L	5-11	155	3-14-91	.256	.259	.254	47	180	31	46	13	3	2	15	24	3	1	0	48	15	6	.394	.353
Stevenson, Casey	R-R	6-3	200	5-18-88	.217	.119	.267	50	198	18	43	8	0	2	23	10	4	1	2	35	0	2	.348	.266
Urena, Carlos	R-R	6-1	183	11-17-89	.182	.182	.182	6	22	1	4	2	0	0	3	0	0	0	0	5	0	0	.273	.182

Pitching

	B-T	HT	WT	DOB	W	L	ERA	G	GS	CG	SV	IP	H	R	ER	HR	BB	SO	AVG	vLH	vRH	K/9	BB/9
Barreda, Manuel	R-R	5-11	165	10-8-88	0	0	4.76	7	0	0	0	17	14	9	9	0	11	18	.222	.217	.225	9.53	5.82
Brooks, Gavin	L-L	6-3	220	10-27-87	0	0	0.00	1	0	0	0	1	0	0	0	0	0	0	.500	1.000	.000	0.00	0.00
Burawa, Daniel	R-R	6-3	190	12-30-88	0	0	7.71	6	0	0	0	7	8	7	6	0	7	10	.286	.333	.263	12.86	9.00
Claiborne, Preston	R-R	6-2	215	1-21-88	1	2	2.28	19	0	0	0	24	20	9	6	0	8	30	.241	.333	.180	11.41	3.04
Cotton, Bryant	R-R	6-2	190	2-15-88	1	1	6.20	14	0	0	0	20	24	15	14	1	6	23	.293	.423	.232	10.18	2.66
Elam, Sam	L-L	6-3	220	6-16-87	0	1	8.68	4	2	0	0	9	9	13	9	2	15	9	.273	.143	.308	8.68	14.46
Forer, Nathan	R-R	6-1	172	6-6-88	0	1	1.99	16	0	0	0	23	19	7	5	2	7	14	.229	.133	.283	5.56	2.78
Gipson, Mike	R-R	6-1	195	9-15-88	3	1	4.42	12	6	0	0	39	37	21	19	4	11	50	.240	.295	.204	11.64	2.56
Greene, Shane	R-R	6-4	210	11-17-88	2	6	4.59	10	10	0	0	49	57	28	25	1	21	44	.289	.298	.283	8.08	3.86
Hobbs, Dustin	R-R	6-2	200	8-18-89	0	2	9.00	2	2	0	0	9	11	10	9	0	7	5	.324	.300	.333	5.00	7.00
Jernstad, Matt	L-L	6-2	240	6-10-88	2	2	3.32	14	3	0	0	43	38	18	16	3	11	44	.238	.371	.200	9.14	2.28
Kahnle, Tommy	R-R	6-1	220	8-7-89	0	0	0.56	11	0	0	3	16	3	1	1	0	5	25	.061	.063	.061	14.06	2.81
Lewis, Freddy	L-L	6-2	210	12-16-86	1	0	2.45	5	0	0	0	4	3	2	1	0	5	3	.250	.000	.333	7.36	12.27
Martinez, Richard	R-R	6-1	194	7-19-88	4	1	1.69	16	2	0	0	32	22	9	6	1	16	34	.191	.250	.160	9.56	4.50
Mitchell, Bryan	L-R	6-2	175	4-19-91	0	1	6.75	1	1	0	0	4	7	4	3	0	1	3	.368	.222	.500	6.75	2.25
O'Brien, Mikey	R-R	5-11	185	3-3-90	6	2	2.08	11	11	0	0	61	49	19	14	1	18	38	.228	.239	.216	5.64	2.67
Oliver, Will	R-R	6-2	185	7-4-87	0	0	5.06	4	0	0	0	5	7	4	3	0	1	7	.273	.400	.235	11.81	6.75
Recchia, Mike	R-R	6-1	210	4-2-89	0	1	4.93	22	0	0	0	35	30	22	19	1	12	30	.231	.214	.243	7.79	3.12
Rodriguez, Wilton	R-R	6-3	195	11-6-90	1	3	4.39	4	0	0	0	27	38	22	13	0	17	34	.322	.423	.242	5.74	2.36
Shive, Andy	R-R	6-6	260	11-5-85	0	1	5.17	10	0	0	0	16	17	10	9	1	6	14	.293	.300	.292	5.74	6.89
Sneed, Kramer	L-L	6-3	185	10-7-88	1	3	4.09	8	7	0	0	33	35	20	15	3	7	42	.263	.321	.248	11.45	1.91
Turley, Nik	L-L	6-7	195	9-11-89	4	4	4.38	12	12	1	0	62	57	36	30	2	29	47	.259	.289	.251	6.86	4.23
Varce, Zach	R-R	6-0	195	12-14-88	4	6	4.54	15	14	0	0	71	75	42	36	4	17	74	.269	.304	.246	9.34	2.14
Whitley, Chase	R-R	6-4	220	1-24-89	4	2	1.31	28	0	0	15	34	18	8	5	0	15	44	.157	.174	.145	11.53	3.93

Fielding

Catcher

	PCT	G	PO	A	E	DP	PB
Arcia	.976	23	174	33	5	1	3
Farnham	.981	24	188	16	4	0	3
McCoy	.988	19	148	16	2	0	11
Sanchez	.991	12	95	10	1	0	2

First Base

	PCT	G	PO	A	E	DP
Brown	1.000	2	16	1	0	0
Farnham	.986	10	62	10	1	9
Lassiter	1.000	1	3	0	0	0
Mahoney	.986	16	13	105	10	2
Roller	.987	44	358	23	5	38
Urena	.974	4	35	2	1	2

Second Base

	PCT	G	PO	A	E	DP
Mahoney	1.000	5	10	17	0	2
Parache	.975	27	43	72	3	11
Stevenson	.970	43	57	106	5	26

Third Base

	PCT	G	PO	A	E	DP
Brown	.818	3	6	3	2	0
Lassiter	.958	31	16	53	3	4
Mahoney	.955	16	8	34	2	1
Parache	.933	5	3	11	1	0

	PCT	G	PO	A	E	DP
Segedin	.940	19	15	32	3	7
Urena	1.000	1	1	1	0	0
Shortstop	**PCT**	**G**	**PO**	**A**	**E**	**DP**
Culver	.897	14	21	31	6	10

	PCT	G	PO	A	E	DP
Mojica	.914	53	76	127	19	29
Parache	.900	11	22	23	5	5
Outfield	**PCT**	**G**	**PO**	**A**	**E**	**DP**
Brown	.921	17	31	4	3	1

	PCT	G	PO	A	E	DP
Brown	.949	50	73	2	4	0
De Leon	.953	67	115	8	6	1
Duran	.964	18	27	0	1	0
Ferraro	.909	31	38	2	4	1
Sosa	.983	47	111	6	2	0

GCL YANKEES — ROOKIE

GULF COAST LEAGUE

Batting	B-T	HT	WT	DOB	AVG	vLH	vRH	G	AB	R	H	2B	3B	HR	RBI	BB	HBP	SH	SF	SO	SB	CS	SLG	OBP
Alcantara, Jorge	R-R	6-1	195	8-9-91	.229	.455	.125	10	35	2	8	3	0	0	2	0	0	0	10	0	1		.314	.229
Aron, Nathan	R-R	6-1	185	5-15-91	.240	.300	.200	9	25	5	6	1	0	0	2	5	2	0	1	8	0	0	.280	.394
Austin, Tyler	R-R	6-2	200	9-6-91	.000	.000	.000	2	2	0	0	0	0	0	0	0	2	0	0	1	0	0	.000	.500
Culver, Cito	B-R	6-0	185	8-26-92	.269	.205	.293	40	160	21	43	7	1	2	18	13	0	4	2	41	6	3	.363	.320
Duran, Kelvin	L-L	5-11	165	11-10-90	.221	.184	.235	35	136	18	30	5	0	2	10	17	0	0	2	35	10	4	.301	.303
Felix, Anderson	B-R	6-0	155	5-11-92	.273	.316	.255	47	198	33	54	9	6	4	27	15	0	0	0	44	11	7	.439	.324
Flores, Ramon	L-L	5-10	150	3-26-92	.329	.381	.310	43	158	33	52	10	4	2	22	28	2	1	0	22	4	1	.481	.436
Gamel, Ben	L-L	5-10	156	5-17-92	.280	.364	.214	7	25	3	7	1	0	0	3	0	0	0	0	8	1	2	.320	.357
Golsan, Judd	L-R	6-1	180	12-6-90	.188	.250	.173	35	101	9	19	4	0	0	9	8	2	1	0	35	9	3	.228	.261
Gumbs, Angelo	R-R	6-0	175	10-13-92	.192	.091	.267	7	26	1	5	1	0	0	0	1	0	0	0	3	3	0	.231	.222
Hammock, Robby	R-R	5-10	185	5-13-77	.500	.000	.545	4	12	4	6	2	0	2	4	1	0	0	0	1	1	0	1.167	.538
Kuo, Fu-Lin	R-R	6-0	185	1-7-91	.243	.346	.218	42	136	21	33	4	0	4	23	15	4	1	3	34	0	0	.360	.329
Liccien, Jhorge	R-R	6-0	165	10-10-90	.215	.211	.217	27	79	9	17	5	1	1	14	7	0	2	0	22	0	1	.342	.279
Maruszak, Addison	R-R	6-1	195	12-21-86	.375	1.000	.167	3	8	1	3	1	0	0	2	0	0	0	0	0	0	0	.500	.375
Moronta, Eladio	R-R	5-11	175	12-16-88	.107	.111	.105	9	28	1	3	0	0	3	1	0	0	1	0	1	0	1	.107	.188
Nunez, Reymond	R-R	6-4	210	9-25-90	.222	.208	.226	27	108	10	24	4	1	3	20	5	1	0	0	30	1	0	.361	.263
Pena, Henry	L-R	6-0	180	10-26-90	.302	.250	.323	26	86	12	26	7	1	3	7	14	1	1	0	25	3	0	.512	.406
Perkins, Kyle	R-R	6-1	175	6-20-91	.083	.000	.105	13	24	1	2	0	0	1	0	6	0	0	1	9	0	0	.083	.258
Rosario, Jose	R-R	5-11	160	11-29-91	.245	.333	.208	36	110	22	27	4	1	2	7	8	5	0	2	22	6	0	.355	.320
Sanchez, Gary	R-R	6-2	195	12-2-92	.353	.394	.337	31	119	25	42	11	0	6	36	11	4	0	2	28	1	1	.597	.419
Segedin, Rob	R-R	6-3	220	11-10-88	.250	.500	.167	2	8	3	2	0	0	0	3	0	0	0	0	1	0	0	.625	.333
Sublett, Damon	L-R	6-1	190	9-9-85	.158	.250	.133	5	19	3	3	0	0	1	3	0	0	0	3	0	0	1	.316	.273
Taveras, Damian	R-R	6-1	205	11 28 89	.252	.281	.240	31	107	14	27	5	0	2	14	10	5	0	3	30	2	0	.355	.336
Toussen, Jose	L-L	6-1	155	11-13-89	.277	.333	.259	45	148	24	41	4	0	1	15	11	3	3	3	20	9	1	.324	.333
Williams, Mason	L-R	6-0	150	8-21-91	.222	.300	.125	5	18	0	4	0	0	0	0	0	0	0	0	1	1	2	.222	.263

Pitching	B-T	HT	WT	DOB	W	L	ERA	G	GS	CG	SV	IP	H	R	ER	HR	BB	SO	AVG	vLH	vRH	K/9	BB/9
Arias, Justo	R-R	6-2	145	10-29-88	2	2	5.40	14	0	0	0	27	37	19	16	2	4	27	.322	.325	.320	9.11	1.35
Banuelos, Manuel	L-L	5-10	155	3-13-91	0	0	1.80	2	2	0	0	5	1	1	1	0	3	6	.063	.000	.100	10.80	5.40
Checo, Mariel	R-R	6-3	190	10-16-89	0	1	5.92	10	2	0	0	24	26	21	16	4	11	24	.263	.167	.304	8.88	4.07
DeLuca, Evan	L-L	6-1	195	3-9-91	1	3	9.35	9	6	0	0	26	37	36	27	4	24	30	.330	.293	.352	10.38	8.31
Elam, Sam	L-L	6-3	220	6-16-87	0	0	4.26	10	0	0	0	13	6	6	0	0	15	15	.182	.100	.206	10.66	10.66
Garce, Harold	R-R	6-4	205	11-28-85	2	0	2.79	12	0	0	1	19	13	7	6	0	13	9	.181	.156	.200	4.19	6.05
Garcia, Charlyn	R-R	6-1	165	6-9-86	0	0	10.29	7	0	0	0	7	15	8	8	0	1	4	.441	.467	.421	5.14	1.29
Gerritse, Brett	R-R	6-4	220	3-4-91	2	2	3.82	9	2	0	1	35	39	20	15	3	12	27	.285	.233	.311	6.88	3.06
Hobbs, Dustin	R-R	6-2	200	8-18-89	3	1	2.30	7	7	0	0	27	23	10	7	0	7	33	.221	.176	.243	10.87	2.30
Ibabel, George	R-R	6-6	230	9-9-89	0	0	18.00	2	0	0	0	2	5	4	4	1	0	3	.455	.667	.375	13.50	4.50
Johnson, Trevor	L-L	6-3	190	7-29-88	0	2	9.00	7	0	0	0	7	9	9	7	1	5	2	.310	.200	.333	2.57	6.43
Lewis, Freddy	L-L	6-2	210	12-16-86	0	1	2.25	9	0	0	0	8	5	2	2	0	11	15	.225	.143	.242	11.25	8.25
Marcano, Juan	L-L	6-1	165	8-24-90	1	1	1.05	6	3	0	1	26	15	3	3	0	2	21	.161	.133	.167	7.36	0.70
Marshall, Brett	R-R	6-0	195	3-22-90	0	0	2.25	2	0	0	0	8	5	2	2	0	4	8	.194	.125	.267	9.00	4.50
Marte, Joel	R-R	5-11	195	1-18-88	0	2	3.43	18	0	0	2	21	25	13	8	0	7	25	.281	.233	.305	10.71	3.00
Mitchell, Bryan	L-R	6-2	175	4-19-91	2	1	3.67	10	9	0	0	42	28	24	17	2	22	36	.190	.188	.191	7.78	4.75
Mitre, Sergio	R-R	6-3	225	2-16-81	0	1	1.80	2	2	0	0	5	2	1	1	0	0	8	.118	.000	.182	14.40	0.00
Mullee, Conor	R-R	6-3	185	2-25-88	2	1	1.64	14	0	0	0	22	19	9	4	0	6	20	.235	.250	.228	8.18	2.45
Nuding, Zach	R-R	6-4	250	3-29-90	0	1	4.50	1	1	0	0	2	4	1	1	0	2	2	.400	.000	.400	9.00	4.50
Oliver, Will	R-R	6-2	185	7-4-87	2	0	4.38	8	0	0	1	12	12	9	6	2	4	10	.267	.235	.286	7.30	2.92
Quintana, Jose	L-L	6-0	170	1-24-89	3	1	2.31	15	0	0	0	23	14	11	6	0	8	32	.169	.050	.206	12.34	3.09
Reyes, Yobanny	R-R	6-0	165	11-29-88	0	1	21.21	4	0	0	0	5	9	11	11	0	3	4	.625	.375	.771	5.79	
Richardson, Matt	R-R	6-1	175	5-28-90	1	1	4.00	11	9	0	0	45	38	36	25	1	29	36	.224	.226	.222	7.20	5.80
Rodriguez, Wilton	R-R	6-3	195	11-6-90	0	3	4.05	6	4	0	0	20	16	13	9	2	9	21	.205	.265	.159	9.45	4.05
Rutckyj, Evan	R-L	6-5	213	1-31-92	0	0	0.00	1	0	0	0	1	0	0	0	0	0	0	.000	.000	.000	0.00	0.00
Sanit, Amaury	R-R	5-8	205	7-4-79	0	0	2.70	3	3	0	0	7	4	2	2	0	0	10	.174	.000	.222	13.50	0.00
Sneed, Kramer	L-L	6-3	185	10-7-88	0	0	2.70	4	0	0	0	7	3	2	2	0	3	9	.136	.000	.200	12.15	4.05
Tapia, Eric	L-L	6-1	193	9-6-87	2	1	1.15	9	0	0	0	16	7	3	2	1	5	14	.130	.143	.128	8.04	2.87
Triplett, David	R-R	5-11	185	2-28-87	0	0	2.00	2	0	0	0	2	0	0	0	0	0	0	.000	.000	.000	9.00	0.00
Turley, Nik	L-L	6-7	195	9-11-89	0	2	0.84	9	2	0	0	11	11	7	1	0	5	9	.239	.100	.278	7.59	1.69
Van Benschoten, John	R-R	6-4	215	4-14-80	1	1	1.29	4	3	0	0	7	5	1	1	1	2	8	.192	.222	.176	10.29	2.57

Fielding

Catcher	PCT	G	PO	A	E	DP	PB
Hammock	1.000	3	15	0	0	0	0
Liccien	.967	25	185	21	7	3	7
Perkins	.958	9	44	2	2	0	1
Sanchez	.959	18	152	12	7	0	14
Taveras	.944	10	76	8	5	0	7

First Base	PCT	G	PO	A	E	DP
Austin	1.000	1	3	0	0	0
Flores	.948	21	137	9	8	13
Kuo	1.000	1	7	0	0	1

	PCT	G	PO	A	E	DP
Maruszak	1.000	1	6	0	0	0
Nunez	.976	26	228	21	6	18
Taveras	.977	9	83	2	2	7
Second Base	**PCT**	**G**	**PO**	**A**	**E**	**DP**
Alcantara	.909	1	5	5	1	1

Felix	.946	37	55	102	9	18
Rosario	.898	10	17	27	5	5
Toussen	.921	10	16	19	3	2

Third Base	PCT	G	PO	A	E	DP
Flores	1.000	1	0	2	0	0
Kuo	.853	36	28	65	16	9
Rosario	.886	15	9	22	4	1
Segedin	.833	2	3	2	1	0
Toussen	.909	5	4	6	1	1

Shortstop	PCT	G	PO	A	E	DP
Culver	.918	36	56	90	13	14
Felix	.927	7	14	24	3	4
Gumbs	.880	6	8	14	3	1
Rosario	.839	7	11	15	5	1
Toussen	.800	2	4	4	2	2

Outfield	PCT	G	PO	A	E	DP
Alcantara	.625	7	4	1	3	0
Aron	1.000	9	8	0	0	0

Duran	.970	35	61	3	2	1
Flores	.978	23	42	2	1	0
Gamel	.875	6	7	0	1	0
Golsan	.965	35	53	2	2	0
Moronta	.917	9	11	0	1	0
Pena	.972	25	35	0	1	0
Rosario	—	1	0	0	0	0
Sublett	1.000	3	7	1	0	0
Toussen	.912	24	30	1	3	0
Williams	1.000	4	7	0	0	0

DSL YANKEES 1 ROOKIE

DOMINICAN SUMMER LEAGUE

Batting	B-T	HT	WT	DOB	AVG	vLH	vRH	G	AB	R	H	2B	3B	HR	RBI	BB	HBP	SH	SF	SO	SB	CS	SLG	OBP
Alcantara, Jorge	R-R	6-1	195	8-9-91	.331	.100	.362	44	148	38	49	8	5	4	23	25	4	0	3	32	9	3	.534	.433
Arias, Gian	B-R	5-11	179	10-6-91	.385	.333	.333	4	13	3	5	1	0	1	2	1	0	0	0	3	0	0	.692	.429
Beard, Edwin	R-R	6-3	188	8-31-89	.250	.263	.242	36	116	20	29	7	0	1	11	15	2	3	0	26	6	2	.336	.346
Calderon, Yeicok	L-L	6-2	185	12-23-91	.339	.320	.349	69	245	40	83	16	6	8	44	43	4	2	4	56	5	4	.551	.439
Castillo, Ali	R-R	5-10	165	6-19-89	.342	.231	.367	31	73	18	25	3	4	0	16	13	2	2	1	7	5	4	.493	.449
Custodio, Claudio	R-R	5-10	155	10-30-90	.217	.152	.242	61	203	46	44	9	3	5	36	30	5	2	3	38	14	3	.365	.328
De La Rosa, Elio	R-R	6-0	185	4-18-91	.264	.259	.260	30	106	9	28	7	1	2	19	7	1	1	3	28	0	1	.406	.308
Fulgencio, Edwin	R-R	6-2	190	7-22-91	.152	.333	.108	16	46	8	7	2	0	2	5	7	2	0	0	17	0	0	.326	.291
Gonzalez, Maldueno	R-R	5-11	215	3-7-91	.077	.000	.143	12	13	2	1	0	0	0	0	2	3	0	0	10	0	0	.077	.333
Guzman, Miguel	R-R	5-11	157	7-18-90	.185	.083	.195	32	54	9	10	0	0	0	2	10	2	4	0	13	3	1	.185	.333
Leonora, Ericson	R-R	5-11	174	8-25-92	.272	.429	.234	68	246	37	67	8	2	2	27	31	3	5	1	46	14	5	.346	.359
Lopez, Daniel	R-R	6-2	175	1-17-92	.293	.294	.287	70	270	48	79	10	6	1	33	28	14	1	5	57	17	10	.385	.382
Lopez, Jerison	R-R	5-11	177	8-24-91	.243	.217	.242	45	115	25	28	8	0	0	16	5	3	1	1	17	2	2	.313	.348
Moronta, Eladio	R-R	5-11	175	12-16-88	.301	.300	.294	19	73	14	22	4	0	2	11	6	4	2	4	16	4	6	.438	.368
Orozco, Jamiel	R-R	5-11	160	1-29-93	.267	.268	.265	61	206	28	55	9	2	0	15	25	7	3	2	38	4	4	.350	.363
Palomo, Jesus	R-R	5-11	170	12-15-89	.250	.200	.258	32	72	10	18	3	0	0	8	5	2	1	3	20	1	0	.292	.305
Taveras, Damian	R-R	6-1	205	11-28-89	.270	.091	.346	9	37	4	10	0	0	1	4	0	2	0	0	3	1	2	.351	.308
Tejeda, Isaias	R-R	6-0	195	10-28-91	.255	.261	.244	58	220	29	56	16	0	3	33	15	3	0	2	30	0	0	.368	.308
Valera, Jackson	R-R	6-1	175	4-8-92	.269	.077	.314	22	67	10	18	4	0	0	14	9	1	1	4	4	2	1	.328	.346

Pitching	B-T	HT	WT	DOB	W	L	ERA	G	GS	CG	SV	IP	H	R	ER	HR	BB	SO	AVG	vLH	vRH	K/9	BB/9
Agramonte, Kenedy	R-R	5-10	150	12-4-90	1	1	2.61	13	12	0	0	62	32	22	18	2	30	80	.152	.189	.131	11.61	4.35
Alvarez, Isaias	R-R	6-2	175	12-9-89	3	0	4.38	11	0	0	1	12	11	6	6	0	7	5	.239	.208	.273	3.65	5.11
Bautista, Rony	L-L	6-7	200	9-17-91	0	2	11.57	4	4	0	0	7	13	9	9	0	13	9	.259	.000	.318	11.57	16.71
Bello, Yoely	L-L	6-2	150	12-16-90	1	1	3.25	15	0	0	1	36	31	16	13	0	16	42	.231	.182	.241	10.50	4.00
Beriguete, Victor	R-R	6-1	185	11-6-88	2	0	1.49	13	3	0	2	42	33	13	7	0	22	23	.220	.238	.213	4.89	4.68
Bravo, Wilfi	R-R	6-2	180	2-26-89	4	1	1.37	20	0	0	2	26	23	10	4	2	7	21	.230	.143	.264	7.18	2.39
Cabrera, Cristofer	R-R	6-0	180	12-25-92	3	1	0.51	8	8	0	0	35	15	4	2	0	12	32	.129	.156	.113	8.23	3.09
Camilo, Gustavo	R-R	5-10	156	1-2-92	2	0	4.58	11	0	0	1	18	22	14	9	0	17	12	.293	.267	.311	6.11	8.66
Croussett, Melvin	L-L	6-1	168	12-28-88	2	2	2.91	19	0	0	7	22	12	9	7	1	16	24	.152	.429	.125	9.97	6.65
Cruz, Dawerd	R-R	6-1	170	12-7-88	4	2	2.69	14	12	0	0	60	60	33	18	2	25	40	.268	.268	.268	5.97	3.73
De La Cruz, Joel	B-R	6-1	190	6-9-89	1	0	0.00	2	0	0	0	1	1	0	0	0	2	2	.250	.000	.250	18.00	18.00
Ibabel, George	R-R	6-6	230	9-9-89	2	2	1.38	6	0	0	0	13	10	6	2	0	6	16	.200	.125	.235	11.08	4.15
Jimenez, Warlin	R-R	6-0	165	9-14-89	1	0	3.38	4	2	0	0	8	10	7	3	1	5	6	.303	.400	.300	6.75	5.63
Mejia, Edison	R-R	6-1	185	7-2-90	3	2	2.96	12	4	0	1	46	38	24	15	1	11	41	.217	.200	.225	8.08	2.17
Mojica, Deivi	R-R	6-1	185	3-19-91	8	2	2.00	13	2	0	0	54	36	18	12	1	11	18	.193	.119	.227	3.00	1.83
Olivo, Heri	R-R	6-3	190	7-6-90	0	1	6.75	3	3	0	0	9	10	9	7	0	8	8	.286	.083	.391	7.71	7.71
Pena, Jose	R-R	6-0	190	3-22-91	6	2	2.64	14	13	0	0	61	48	25	18	3	14	63	.213	.183	.227	9.24	2.05
Perez, Elvin	R-R	6-4	193	8-3-90	0	4	1.91	14	6	0	0	33	20	11	7	0	19	24	.180	.175	.183	6.55	5.18
Ramirez, Jose	R-R	6-1	160	10-29-88	1	1	4.07	19	0	0	2	24	21	15	11	2	15	19	.239	.345	.186	7.03	5.55
Rincon, Angel	R-R	6-1	180	9-26-92	0	0	4.50	2	1	0	1	6	3	3	3	1	1	6	.143	.667	.056	9.00	1.50
Santana, Gabriel	R-R	6-2	170	11-9-89	0	1	8.31	9	0	0	0	9	7	10	8	0	11	5	.233	.333	.190	5.19	11.42
Soto, Dubeny	R-R	5-11	185	10-30-88	0	1	3.60	7	2	0	0	15	18	7	6	1	4	13	.277	.158	.326	7.80	2.40
Tolentino, Israel	R-R	6-4	190	1-11-88	0	0	8.00	3	0	0	0	9	11	11	8	0	7	7	.314	.429	.238	7.00	7.00

Fielding

Catcher	PCT	G	PO	A	E	DP	PB
Gonzalez	.938	7	15	0	1	0	0
Lopez	1.000	1	4	0	0	0	0
Palomo	.971	24	117	18	4	0	3
Taveras	.938	5	39	6	3	1	1
Tejeda	.974	45	309	60	10	1	14
Valera	.964	7	47	6	2	1	1

First Base	PCT	G	PO	A	E	DP
Beard	.981	35	284	22	6	32
Castillo	1.000	4	25	2	0	2
De La Rosa	.947	15	135	9	8	8
Gonzalez	1.000	3	19	0	0	2
Lopez	1.000	1	1	0	0	0
Lopez	1.000	2	13	1	0	0

Palomo	.963	6	24	2	1	0
Tejeda	.980	5	46	2	1	4
Valera	.967	9	53	6	2	4

Second Base	PCT	G	PO	A	E	DP
Alcantara	.780	11	19	13	9	5
Custodio	.968	35	65	88	5	20
Guzman	1.000	5	6	8	0	3
Lopez	.959	26	53	63	5	12
Orozco	1.000	5	5	13	0	0
Palomo	.500	1	0	1	1	0

Third Base	PCT	G	PO	A	E	DP
Alcantara	.845	30	19	52	13	7
Arias	.833	4	1	4	1	0

Castillo	.882	7	4	11	2	1
Custodio	1.000	4	7	9	0	1
De La Rosa	.824	12	13	15	6	3
Guzman	.829	12	10	19	6	1
Lopez	.933	8	3	11	1	0
Orozco	.950	6	7	12	1	2
Tejeda	1.000	1	1	0	0	0

Shortstop	PCT	G	PO	A	E	DP
Alcantara	.667	1	1	1	1	0
Custodio	.951	20	36	42	4	9
Guzman	.970	12	10	22	1	3
Orozco	.935	49	80	123	14	25

Outfield	PCT	G	PO	A	E	DP												
Calderon	.953	62	57	4	3	0	Guzman	1.000	2	1	0	0	0	Moronta	.871	19	25	2	4	0
Castillo	1.000	14	13	4	0	0	Leonora	.942	49	63	2	4	0	Palomo	1.000	4	6	1	0	0
Fulgencio	1.000	11	8	0	0	0	Lopez	.952	64	136	3	7	3	Tejeda	1.000	1	2	0	0	0
							Lopez	.667	2	2	0	1	0							

DSL YANKEES 2
ROOKIE

DOMINICAN SUMMER LEAGUE

Batting	B-T	HT	WT	DOB	AVG	vLH	vRH	G	AB	R	H	2B	3B	HR	RBI	BB	HBP	SH	SF	SO	SB	CS	SLG	OBP
Acenor, Bien Benil	R-R	6-0	184	6-19-92	.500	.000	.500	1	2	0	1	0	0	0	0	0	0	0	0	0	1	0	.500	.500
Aquino, Melvin	R-R	5-11	160	7-14-92	.263	.182	.296	49	152	27	40	8	0	5	27	22	10	1	0	43	5	4	.414	.391
Arias, Gian	B-R	5-11	179	10-6-91	.256	.273	.250	58	207	37	53	9	1	2	26	34	3	3	3	40	10	5	.338	.364
2-team total (4 Yankees 1)					.264	—	—	62	220	40	58	10	1	3	28	35	3	3	4	43	10	5	.359	.368
Brito, Sandy	R-R	6-3	170	6-9-93	.199	.152	.215	57	176	36	35	8	6	3	22	40	4	3	1	71	3	1	.364	.357
Castellon, Alfredo	L-R	6-2	166	6-4-92	.232	.211	.240	22	69	11	16	5	0	0	10	9	2	0	1	14	0	1	.304	.333
Castillo, Ali	R-R	5-10	165	6-19-89	.324	.263	.346	25	71	17	23	4	1	1	12	8	1	1	3	4	4	1	.451	.386
2-team total (31 Yankees 1)					.333	—	—	56	144	35	48	7	5	1	28	21	3	3	4	10	9	5	.472	.419
Coa, Rainiero	R-R	5-10	170	1-3-93	.255	.279	.245	49	153	16	39	7	0	0	18	20	4	0	4	23	2	1	.301	.348
De La Rosa, Elio	R-R	6-0	185	4-18-91	.262	.316	.239	36	126	16	33	7	1	4	27	13	0	0	3	28	1	1	.429	.324
2-team total (30 Yankees 1)					.263	—	—	66	232	25	61	14	2	6	46	20	1	1	6	56	1	2	.418	.317
Duran, Francisco	R-R	6-2	185	10-3-91	.221	.317	.173	48	122	20	27	9	1	1	15	12	2	0	2	43	3	0	.336	.297
Fulgencio, Edwin	R-R	6-2	190	7-22-91	.222	.286	.200	9	27	3	6	1	0	1	3	1	1	0	0	9	0	0	.370	.276
2-team total (16 Yankees 1)					.178	—	—	25	73	11	13	3	0	3	8	8	3	0	0	26	0	0	.342	.286
Javier, Jose	R-R	5-10	160	9-16-92	.181	.250	.155	55	160	18	29	4	2	0	12	19	6	1	1	35	4	5	.231	.290
Lopez, Jose	R-R	5-10	178	8-13-91	.214	.200	.217	16	28	1	6	1	0	0	1	3	0	0	0	10	0	0	.250	.290
Matos, Guillermo	R-R	6-2	210	10-26-91	.143	.148	.141	31	98	12	14	5	0	2	6	18	2	0	0	29	2	1	.255	.288
Morillo, Ronald	R-R	5-11	155	1-15-90	.283	.263	.294	22	53	7	15	3	0	0	7	8	1	0	0	9	2	1	.340	.387
Moronta, Eladio	R-R	5-11	175	12-16-88	.286	.192	.323	26	91	13	26	5	2	1	5	7	4	0	0	19	9	5	.418	.363
2-team total (19 Yankees 1)					.293	—	—	45	164	27	48	9	2	3	16	13	8	2	4	35	13	11	.427	.365
Oliberto, Mikeson	R-R	5-10	164	8-23-90	.287	.237	.304	41	150	21	43	8	2	6	31	7	0	0	1	34	3	2	.487	.316
Perez, Fernando	B-R	6-2	160	12-9-90	.216	.143	.239	26	88	14	19	1	1	0	9	18	1	2	0	27	6	3	.250	.355
Polo, Rafael	R-R	6-2	165	4-2-93	.323	.304	.330	63	248	43	80	17	9	1	30	12	5	3	1	29	6	5	.476	.365
Ramos, Abraham	R-R	5-10	150	8-3-92	.267	.412	.209	21	60	8	16	4	0	0	8	5	1	1	0	7	2	0	.333	.333
Santana, Ravel	R-R	6-2	160	5-1-92	.322	.255	.342	63	199	46	64	10	1	10	38	35	8	1	1	38	22	5	.533	.440

Pitching	B-T	HT	WT	DOB	W	L	ERA	G	GS	CG	SV	IP	H	R	ER	HR	BB	SO	AVG	vLH	vRH	K/9	BB/9
Aquino, Daury	R-R	6-1	179	4-4-91	1	0	6.75	1	0	0	0	1	2	1	1	0	3	1	.333	.500	.250	6.75	20.25
Batista, Jean	R-R	6-4	174	10-27-91	1	0	3.45	11	0	0	0	16	16	10	6	0	14	11	.258	.222	.273	6.32	8.04
Bello, Hector	L-L	6-1	175	5-19-91	0	2	13.06	12	0	0	0	10	14	17	15	0	13	7	.326	1.000	.310	6.10	11.32
De La Cruz, Joel	B-R	6-1	190	6-9-89	1	0	7.11	7	0	0	2	6	10	5	5	0	1	5	.345	.200	.375	7.11	1.42
2-team total (2 Yankees 1)					1	1	6.14	9	0	0	2	7	11	6	5	0	3	7	—	—	—	8.59	3.68
De La Rosa, Maikel	L-L	6-2	190	11-25-90	1	1	6.75	11	0	0	0	16	18	14	12	0	23	18	.290	.714	.236	10.13	12.94
de Leon, Nestor	R-R	6-2	200	6-22-89	1	1	3.18	8	0	0	2	11	8	5	4	0	9	7	.205	.444	.133	5.56	7.15
De Los Santos, Alexander	R-R	6-2	180	8-16-90	0	0	8.10	3	0	0	0	7	11	11	6	0	7	6	.324	.182	.391	8.10	9.45
Delgado, Johansel	R-R	5-11	155	12-3-90	3	1	3.86	19	0	0	1	28	35	22	12	1	15	14	.299	.278	.309	4.50	4.82
Eusebio, Wilkinson	R-R	6-2	178	9-26-90	2	1	4.32	6	0	0	1	8	7	5	4	0	6	9	.250	.250	.250	9.72	6.48
Garcia, Samuel	R-R	6-0	180	3-4-93	0	5	7.66	8	7	0	0	22	27	25	19	1	22	26	.297	.407	.250	10.48	8.87
Gonzalez, Felipe	R-R	6-2	165	8-15-91	4	2	3.38	13	13	0	0	56	55	27	21	0	12	49	.257	.267	.252	7.88	1.93
Heredia, Juan	L-L	6-3	160	1-20-89	0	2	5.40	6	5	0	0	17	16	10	10	1	4	13	.239	.143	.250	7.02	2.16
Jimenez, Antonio	R-R	6-0	175	3-1-91	0	0	4.66	8	1	0	0	10	7	6	5	0	12	3	.219	.308	.158	2.79	11.17
Mateo, Andres	R-R	5-11	200	4-24-91	1	1	15.88	7	0	0	0	6	7	12	10	1	13	5	.304	.333	.286	7.94	20.65
Mercedes, Melvin	R-R	6-3	170	8-28-89	1	5	3.05	15	11	0	1	56	56	33	19	2	21	43	.259	.290	.247	6.91	3.38
Peroza, Yunior	R-R	6-2	155	8-9-91	2	2	2.26	13	7	0	0	52	46	18	13	2	9	41	.235	.211	.245	7.14	1.57
Polanco, Reynaldo	R-R	6-2	178	5-20-93	0	6	7.67	11	10	0	0	32	33	35	27	4	20	25	.262	.293	.247	7.11	5.68
Reyes, Derbin	R-R	6-1	175	3-12-87	2	2	7.71	13	1	0	0	19	23	19	16	0	14	15	.303	.286	.309	7.23	6.75
Rodino, Manuel	R-R	6-2	190	3-7-90	1	0	1.59	12	0	0	5	17	14	7	3	0	8	10	.233	.267	.222	5.29	4.24
Rodriguez, Edwin	R-R	6-0	150	5-16-90	2	4	3.48	16	6	0	1	52	53	34	20	1	17	53	.266	.236	.278	9.23	2.96
Rodriguez, Johel	R-R	6-0	193	1-13-91	0	4	4.82	11	0	0	0	19	20	14	10	1	11	14	.263	.235	.271	6.75	5.30
Rodriguez, Ramon	R-R	6-1	170	7-23-91	0	3	9.22	5	5	0	0	14	18	17	14	1	14	8	.327	.214	.366	5.27	9.22
Saavedra, Jhon	R-R	6-2	180	2-2-89	2	1	4.36	14	3	0	0	33	38	19	16	1	17	38	.288	.341	.264	10.36	4.64
Sanchez, Anthony	R-R	6-4	185	7-3-91	0	0	27.00	2	0	0	0	2	4	7	5	0	3	1	.364	.500	.286	5.40	16.20
Santana, Gabriel	R-R	6-2	170	11-9-89	0	0	6.75	6	0	0	0	11	13	9	8	1	7	10	.289	.400	.257	8.44	5.91
2-team total (9 Yankees 1)					0	1	7.45	15	0	0	0	19	20	19	16	1	18	15	—	—	—	6.98	8.38
Soto, Dubeny	R-R	5-11	185	10-30-88	1	2	4.15	11	1	0	1	26	21	14	12	0	14	26	.214	.160	.233	9.00	4.85
2-team total (7 Yankees 1)					1	3	3.95	19	3	0	1	41	39	21	18	1	18	39	—	—	—	8.56	3.95
Vargas, Cesar	R-R	6-1	160	12-30-91	2	2	2.06	14	2	0	2	39	37	12	9	0	10	34	.248	.277	.235	7.78	2.29

Fielding

Catcher	PCT	G	PO	A	E	DP	PB
Arias	.964	7	47	6	2	0	5
Castellon	1.000	10	52	5	0	0	4
Coa	.979	28	162	28	4	1	10
Duran	.977	33	182	30	5	2	10
Lopez	1.000	11	43	6	0	0	0

First Base	PCT	G	PO	A	E	DP
Arias	.987	28	225	11	3	9
Castellon	1.000	1	5	0	0	0
De La Rosa	1.000	17	119	5	0	4
Duran	.778	2	7	0	2	0
Matos	.978	27	207	13	5	15
Morillo	1.000	1	6	0	0	0

Second Base	PCT	G	PO	A	E	DP
Aquino	.727	6	9	7	6	0
Castillo	.875	4	2	5	1	2
Javier	.969	52	86	104	6	15
Morillo	.875	4	5	2	1	0
Polo	.923	5	12	12	2	2
Ramos	.885	7	12	11	3	2

Third Base	PCT	G	PO	A	E	DP
Aquino	.900	17	9	27	4	3
Arias	.960	5	8	16	1	1
Castillo	1.000	7	4	9	0	1
De La Rosa	.875	17	15	27	6	2
Morillo	.944	10	6	11	1	1
Polo	.843	14	17	26	8	2
Ramos	.950	10	5	14	1	1

Shortstop	PCT	G	PO	A	E	DP
Aquino	.875	7	9	19	4	3

	PCT	G	PO	A	E	DP
Castillo	.889	7	11	13	3	3
Javier	1.000	1	0	1	0	1
Perez	.842	21	32	48	15	5
Polo	.903	38	56	75	14	8
Ramos	1.000	1	1	3	0	0

Outfield	PCT	G	PO	A	E	DP
Acenor	1.000	1	1	0	0	0
Aquino	.840	18	18	3	4	0
Brito	.924	55	70	3	6	0
Castillo	1.000	9	14	1	0	0

	PCT	G	PO	A	E	DP
Duran	1.000	11	12	0	0	0
Fulgencio	1.000	9	14	1	0	0
Lopez	1.000	2	1	0	0	0
Morillo	.900	8	8	1	1	0
Moronta	.932	23	40	1	3	0
Oliberto	.943	41	76	6	5	1
Ramos	.500	3	1	0	1	0
Santana	.929	61	110	7	9	2

Oakland Athletics

SEASON IN A SENTENCE: While the Athletics had their first winning season since 2006, thanks to the league's best ERA at 3.58, they never really threatened the Rangers for American League West supremacy, finishing second while ranking 11th in the league in runs and 13th in homers.

HIGH POINT: Dallas Braden became a celebrity, first by challenging Alex Rodriguez for running over the pitcher's mound on his way back to the dugout in an April game, then for pitching a perfect game on Mother's Day, May 9 against the Rays. Braden's gem, which he movingly dedicated to his grandmother, who raised him after his mother died and was at the game. The team's ace was 22-year-old righty Trevor Cahill, who ranked fourth in the league in wins and ERA. Only an injury to Brett Anderson, limiting him to 19 starts, dampened Oakland's long-term mound outlook.

LOW POINT: Injuries contributed to the A's demise, as back problems once again sidelined Eric Chavez, while the likes of Justin Duchscherer and Ben Sheets, Ryan Sweeney and Coco Crisp, Mark Ellis and Landon Powell all saw significant time on the disabled list. Oakland had 23 players on the DL, second-most in franchise history.

NOTABLE ROOKIES: Despite a young roster, Oakland broke in few new players in 2010. Last year's top prospect, Chris Carter, got off to a slow start in the minors and wasn't ready when he got his big league callup, going 0-for-19 with 13 strikeouts before breaking through. Righthander Tyson Ross reached the majors and made two starts before an August elbow injury, after he had been sent to Triple-A to get stretched out for a return to the rotation, sidelined him.

KEY TRANSACTIONS: The A's gambled on Sheets and lost. Sheets didn't stay healthy enough either to contribute on the mound or to get traded at the deadline. They also hoped Conor Jackson, a Bay Area product out of Cal who was acquired from the Diamondbacks, could infuse some offense into the lineup, but he never got healthy enough to help either.

DOWN ON THE FARM: Many of Oakland's top prospects failed to come through, from Carter to outfielder Michael Taylor (acquired in the offseason three-team deal that sent Roy Halladay to Philadelphia) to injured lefthander Pedro Figueroa. While their top prospects, in general, didn't perform well, the A's still posted a .527 winning percentage with their domestic affiliates.

OPENING DAY PAYROLL: $51.7 million (28th)

PLAYERS OF THE YEAR

MAJOR LEAGUE	MINOR LEAGUE
Trevor Cahill	**Grant Green**
rhp	ss
18-8, 2.97	(High Class A)
118 SO/63 BB/197 IP	.318/.363/.520
4th in AL in ERA, WHIP	20 HR, 39 2B

ORGANIZATION LEADERS

BATTING		*Minimum 250 at-bats
MAJORS		
*AVG	Ryan Sweeney	.294
*OPS	Jack Cust	.834
HR	Kevin Kouzmanoff	16
RBI	Kevin Kouzmanoff/Kurt Suzuki	17
MINORS		
*AVG	Grant Green, Stockton	.318
*OBP	Conner Crumbliss, Kane County	.421
*SLG	Chris Carter, Sacramento	.529
R	Grant Green, Stockton	107
H	Grant Green, Stockton	174
TB	Grant Green, Stockton	285
2B	Grant Green, Stockton	39
3B	Corey Brown, Midland/Sacramento	11
HR	Chris Carter, Sacramento	31
RBI	Stephen Parker, Stockton	98
BB	Conner Crumbliss, Kane County	126
SO	Michael Spina, Stockton	142
SB	Corey Wimberly, Sacramento	56

PITCHING		†Minimum 75 innings
MAJORS		
W	Trevor Cahill	18
†ERA	Brett Anderson	2.80
SO	Gio Gonzalez	171
MINORS		
W	Clay Mortensen, Sacramento	13
L	Three tied at	13
†ERA	Ian Krol, Kane County/Stockton	2.80
G	Trey Barham, Stockton	59
GS	Three tied at	28
SV	Paul Smyth, Stockton	28
IP	Clay Mortensen, Sacramento	165.3
BB	Anthony Capra, Midland	89
SO	Shawn Haviland, Sacramento/Stockton	169
†AVG	Ian Krol, Kane County/Stockton	.226

General Manager: Billy Beane. **Farm Director:** Keith Lieppman. **Scouting Director:** Eric Kubota.

Class	Team	League	W	L	PCT	Finish*	Manager(s)
Majors	Oakland Athletics	American	81	81	.500	t-8th (14)	Bob Geren
Triple-A	Sacramento River Cats	Pacific Coast	79	65	.549	4th (16)	Tony DeFrancesco
Double-A	Midland RockHounds	Texas	70	70	.500	4th (8)	Darren Bush
High A	Stockton Ports	California	74	66	.529	5th (10)	Steve Scarsone
Low A	Kane County Cougars	Midwest	71	67	.514	9th (16)	Aaron Nieckula
Short-season	Vancouver Canadians	Northwest	42	34	.553	4th (8)	Rick Magnante
Rookie	AZL Athletics	Arizona	30	26	.536	6th (12)	Marcus Jensen
Overall 2010 Minor League Record			366	328	.527	6th (30)	

*Finish in overall standings (No. of teams in league). †League champion.

ORGANIZATION STATISTICS

OAKLAND ATHLETICS

AMERICAN LEAGUE

Batting	B-T	HT	WT	DOB	AVG	vLH	vRH	G	AB	R	H	2B	3B	HR	RBI	BB	HBP	SH	SF	SO	SB	CS	SLG	OBP
Barton, Daric	L-R	6-0	215	8-16-85	.273	.310	.259	159	556	79	152	33	5	10	57	110	3	12	5	102	7	3	.405	.393
Buck, Travis	L-R	6-2	230	11-18-83	.167	.200	.156	14	42	6	7	2	0	1	2	4	1	1	0	14	1	0	.286	.255
Carson, Matt	R-R	6-2	200	7-1-81	.177	.167	.211	36	79	7	14	2	0	4	9	2	0	0	2	23	4	0	.354	.193
Carter, Chris	R-R	6-5	230	12-18-86	.186	.200	.180	24	70	8	13	1	0	3	7	7	0	0	1	21	1	0	.329	.256
Chavez, Eric	L-R	6-1	215	12-7-77	.234	.111	.245	33	111	10	26	8	0	1	10	8	0	0	4	31	0	0	.333	.276
Crisp, Coco	B-R	6-0	180	11-1-79	.279	.329	.261	75	290	51	81	14	4	8	38	30	0	3	5	49	32	3	.438	.342
Cust, Jack	L-R	6-1	235	1-7-79	.272	.221	.285	112	349	50	95	16	0	13	52	68	5	0	3	127	2	2	.438	.395
Davis, Rajai	R-R	5-10	195	10-19-80	.284	.304	.276	143	525	66	149	28	3	5	52	26	4	1	5	78	50	11	.377	.320
Donaldson, Josh	R-R	6-0	215	12-8-85	.156	.250	.000	14	32	1	5	1	0	1	4	2	0	0	0	12	0	0	.281	.206
Ellis, Mark	R-R	5-11	195	6-6-77	.291	.330	.279	124	436	45	127	24	0	5	49	40	8	3	5	56	7	6	.381	.358
Fox, Jake	R-R	6-0	220	7-20-82	.214	.242	.167	39	98	11	21	5	0	2	12	5	2	0	1	26	0	0	.327	.264
2-team total (38 Baltimore)					.217	—	—	77	198	21	43	10	1	7	22	8	4	0	1	49	0	0	.384	.261
Gross, Gabe	L-R	6-3	220	10-21-79	.239	.167	.253	105	222	27	53	11	1	1	25	17	0	2	2	39	5	1	.311	.290
Hermida, Jeremy	L-R	6-3	220	1-30-84	.250	.250	.250	21	64	5	16	4	0	1	2	4	0	0	0	13	0	0	.359	.294
2-team total (52 Boston)					.216	—	—	73	222	19	48	12	0	6	29	16	0	0	1	58	1	0	.351	.268
Iwamura, Akinori	L-R	5-9	200	2-9-79	.129	.143	.125	10	31	3	4	1	0	0	4	5	0	0	0	10	0	0	.161	.250
Jackson, Conor	R-R	6-2	215	5-7-82	.228	.000	.260	18	57	6	13	2	0	1	5	11	1	0	0	9	2	0	.316	.362
Kouzmanoff, Kevin	R-R	6-1	210	7-25-81	.247	.261	.242	143	551	59	136	32	1	16	71	24	6	0	5	96	2	1	.396	.283
Larish, Jeff	L-R	6-2	200	10-11-82	.175	.000	.200	24	57	5	10	3	0	2	8	7	1	0	0	20	1	0	.333	.277
2-team total (3 Detroit)					.179	—	—	27	67	5	12	3	0	2	9	7	1	0	0	24	1	0	.313	.267
Patterson, Eric	L-R	6-0	170	4-8-83	.204	.091	.235	45	103	13	21	5	2	4	9	7	0	1	0	31	6	0	.408	.255
2-team total (45 Boston)					.214	—	—	90	187	26	40	8	5	6	16	14	1	2	0	62	11	1	.406	.272
Pennington, Cliff	B-R	5-11	200	6-15-84	.250	.258	.247	156	508	64	127	26	8	6	46	50	3	12	3	96	29	5	.368	.319
Powell, Landon	B-R	6-3	255	3-19-82	.214	.167	.232	41	112	13	24	4	0	2	11	15	0	1	1	29	1	0	.304	.305
Rosales, Adam	R-R	6-2	195	5-20-83	.271	.289	.261	80	255	31	69	8	2	7	31	19	1	2	2	65	2	2	.400	.321
Sogard, Eric	L-R	5-10	185	5-22-86	.429	1.000	.200	4	7	0	3	0	0	0	0	2	0	0	0	1	0	1	.429	.556
Suzuki, Kurt	R-R	5-11	210	10-4-83	.242	.213	.253	131	495	55	120	18	2	13	71	33	12	0	4	49	3	2	.366	.303
Sweeney, Ryan	L-L	6-4	225	2-20-85	.294	.246	.307	82	303	41	89	20	2	1	36	24	0	1	3	41	1	1	.383	.342
Tolleson, Steve	R-R	5-11	185	11-1-83	.286	.375	.200	25	49	5	14	3	0	1	4	4	4	0	0	9	0	0	.408	.340
Watson, Matt	L-R	5-11	205	9-5-78	.200	.000	.200	12	30	2	6	2	0	1	4	3	0	0	0	5	0	0	.367	.273

Pitching	B-T	HT	WT	DOB	W	L	ERA	G	GS	CG	SV	IP	H	R	ER	HR	BB	SO	AVG	vLH	vRH	K/9	BB/9
Anderson, Brett	L-L	6-4	235	2-1-88	7	6	2.80	19	19	0	0	112	112	41	35	6	22	75	.257	.299	.243	6.01	1.76
Bailey, Andrew	R-R	6-3	245	5-31-84	1	3	1.47	47	0	0	25	49	34	8	8	3	13	42	.199	.195	.202	7.71	2.39
Blevins, Jerry	L-L	6-6	180	9-6-83	2	1	3.70	63	0	0	1	49	54	20	20	7	18	46	.274	.231	.311	8.51	3.33
Bunser, Bonf	R-R	6-4	245	10-14-81	1	0	5.09	13	0	0	0	23	27	13	13	2	6	17	.300	.319	.279	6.65	2.35
2-team total (2 Boston)					1	0	6.12	15	0	0	0	25	31	17	17	2	8	17	—	—	—	6.12	2.88
Bowers, Cedrick	B-L	6-2	220	2-10-78	0	1	4.50	14	0	0	0	14	12	9	7	4	6	18	.218	.333	.162	11.57	3.86
Braden, Dallas	L-L	6-1	190	8-13-83	11	14	3.50	30	30	5	0	193	180	83	75	17	43	113	.249	.271	.242	5.28	2.01
Breslow, Craig	L-L	6-1	180	8-8-80	4	4	3.01	75	0	0	5	75	53	26	25	9	29	71	.194	.181	.201	8.56	3.50
Cahill, Trevor	R-R	6-4	220	3-1-88	18	8	2.97	30	30	1	0	197	155	73	65	19	63	118	.220	.237	.198	5.40	2.88
Cramer, Bobby	L-L	6-1	210	10-28-79	2	1	3.04	4	4	0	0	24	20	8	8	5	6	13	.233	.313	.214	4.94	2.28
Duchscherer, Justin	R-R	6-3	200	11-19-77	2	1	2.89	5	5	0	0	28	26	11	9	3	12	18	.255	.192	.320	5.79	3.86
Gaudin, Chad	R-R	5-10	190	3-24-83	0	2	8.83	12	0	0	0	17	27	18	17	5	5	20	.360	.345	.370	10.38	2.60
2-team total (30 New York)					1	4	5.65	42	0	0	0	65	73	45	41	16	25	53	—	—	—	7.30	3.44
Gonzalez, Gio	R-L	5-11	205	9-19-85	15	9	3.23	33	33	1	0	201	171	75	72	15	92	171	.229	.209	.235	7.67	4.13
James, Justin	R-R	6-3	215	9-13-81	0	0	4.50	5	0	0	0	4	7	2	2	0	4	5	.389	.333	.444	11.25	9.00
Kilby, Brad	L-L	6-0	240	2-19-83	0	0	2.16	5	0	0	0	8	7	2	2	2	0	8	.219	.154	.263	8.64	0.00
Mazzaro, Vin	R-R	6-2	210	9-27-86	6	8	4.27	24	18	0	0	122	127	70	58	19	50	79	.267	.289	.246	5.81	3.68
Mortensen, Clay	R-R	6-4	180	4-10-85	0	0	4.50	1	1	0	0	6	6	4	3	1	2	7	.250	.125	.313	10.50	3.00
Ramirez, Edwar	R-R	6-3	165	3-28-81	0	0	4.91	7	0	0	0	11	9	7	6	1	10	10	.220	.267	.192	8.18	8.18
Rodriguez, Henry	R-R	6-0	220	2-25-87	1	0	4.55	29	0	0	0	28	25	16	14	2	13	33	.240	.283	.207	10.73	4.23

	B-T	HT	WT	DOB	W	L	ERA	G	GS	CG	SV	IP	H	R	ER	HR	BB	SO	AVG	vLH	vRH	K/9	BB/9
Ross, Tyson	R-R	6-6	225	4-22-87	1	4	5.49	26	2	0	1	39	39	24	24	4	20	32	.271	.258	.282	7.32	4.58
Sheets, Ben	R-R	6-1	220	7-18-78	4	9	4.53	20	20	0	0	119	123	65	60	18	43	84	.267	.255	.278	6.34	3.24
Wolf, Ross	R-R	6-0	180	10-18-82	0	0	4.26	11	0	0	0	13	12	6	6	1	6	9	.250	.318	.192	6.39	4.26
Wuertz, Michael	R-R	6-3	225	12-15-78	2	3	4.31	48	0	0	6	40	35	21	19	6	21	40	.240	.265	.227	9.08	4.76
Ziegler, Brad	R-R	6-4	210	10-10-79	3	7	3.26	64	0	0	0	61	54	24	22	4	28	41	.241	.317	.213	6.08	4.15

Fielding

Catcher	PCT	G	PO	A	E	DP	PB
Donaldson	.979	7	44	3	1	0	1
Fox	.975	8	37	2	1	0	0
Powell	.972	38	198	8	6	1	0
Suzuki	.991	123	825	35	8	5	7

First Base	PCT	G	PO	A	E	DP
Barton	.993	157	1404	78	10	121
Chavez	1.000	1	7	0	0	0
Donaldson	.667	2	2	0	1	1
Larish	1.000	10	41	5	0	8
Powell	1.000	1	4	0	0	1
Rosales	1.000	7	34	1	0	4

Second Base	PCT	G	PO	A	E	DP
Ellis	.995	116	218	328	3	77
Patterson	1.000	5	6	4	0	0
Rosales	1.000	47	72	126	0	30

	PCT	G	PO	A	E	DP
Sogard	1.000	3	4	5	0	4
Tolleson	.900	4	5	4	1	2

Third Base	PCT	G	PO	A	E	DP
Fox	1.000	3	0	1	0	0
Iwamura	.957	10	11	11	1	1
Kouzmanoff	.968	142	90	278	12	29
Larish	.800	5	3	5	2	0
Rosales	1.000	5	4	12	0	1
Tolleson	1.000	6	3	7	0	0

Shortstop	PCT	G	PO	A	E	DP
Pennington	.966	156	218	496	25	100
Rosales	.943	14	7	26	2	3
Tolleson	1.000	11	9	9	0	4

Outfield	PCT	G	PO	A	E	DP
Buck	1.000	13	16	0	0	0

	PCT	G	PO	A	E	DP
Carson	1.000	33	45	2	0	0
Carter	.926	22	25	0	2	0
Crisp	.989	73	182	2	2	0
Cust	.970	16	29	3	1	0
Davis	.987	140	294	5	4	2
Fox	1.000	9	12	1	0	0
Gross	.992	95	112	6	1	0
Hermida	1.000	21	31	1	0	0
Jackson	1.000	16	24	1	0	0
Larish	1.000	7	3	0	0	0
Patterson	.982	30	54	1	1	0
Rosales	1.000	5	4	0	0	0
Sweeney	1.000	81	149	4	0	1
Tolleson	1.000	1	1	0	0	0
Watson	1.000	12	6	0	0	0

SACRAMENTO RIVER CATS

TRIPLE-A

PACIFIC COAST LEAGUE

Batting	B-T	HT	WT	DOB	AVG	vLH	vRH	G	AB	R	H	2B	3B	HR	RBI	BB	HBP	SH	SF	SO	SB	CS	SLG	OBP
Affronti, Mike	R-R	6-2	195	2-13-84	.214	.231	.208	46	145	18	31	6	1	1	14	5	1	3	0	23	1	0	.290	.245
Baisley, Jeff	R-R	6-3	220	12-19-82	.274	.318	.259	49	179	26	49	14	0	6	32	17	7	0	1	39	1	0	.453	.358
Brown, Corey	L-L	6-1	205	11-26-85	.193	.212	.186	41	135	21	26	4	3	5	20	11	0	2	0	36	3	1	.378	.253
Buck, Travis	L-R	6-2	230	11-18-83	.298	.295	.299	32	121	22	36	7	2	3	17	11	4	1	4	28	3	2	.463	.364
Cardenas, Adrian	L-R	6-0	205	10-10-87	.267	.240	.275	58	210	30	56	8	1	1	21	17	0	3	1	28	2	2	.329	.320
Carson, Matt	R-R	6-2	200	7-1-81	.303	.359	.283	64	244	53	74	18	2	13	36	24	6	0	2	58	13	4	.553	.377
Carter, Chris	R-R	6-5	230	12-18-86	.258	.294	.245	125	465	92	120	29	2	31	94	73	8	0	5	138	1	1	.529	.365
Crisp, Coco	B-R	6-0	180	11-1-79	.591	.500	.611	6	22	7	13	2	1	0	5	2	0	0	0	3	2	1	.773	.625
Cust, Jack	L-R	6-1	235	1-7-79	.273	.235	.289	33	110	21	30	6	0	4	19	33	1	0	0	33	0	0	.436	.444
Donaldson, Josh	R-R	6-0	215	12-8-85	.238	.235	.239	86	294	52	70	14	1	18	67	45	2	0	7	79	3	1	.476	.336
Ellis, Mark	R-R	5-11	195	6-6-77	.250	.333	.000	1	4	0	1	0	0	0	0	0	0	0	0	1	0	0	.250	.250
Fveridge, Tommy	R-R	6-0	275	4-20-83	.233	.250	.231	7	30	3	7	1	0	1	2	0	0	1	7	0	0	.367	.273
3-team total (30 Round Rock, 65 Tacoma)					.249	—	—	102	390	48	97	22	0	13	57	40	3	0	4	95	0	0	.405	.320
Harper, Brett	L-R	6-2	245	7-31-81	.231	.077	.282	14	52	4	12	3	0	1	2	2	0	0	0	12	0	0	.346	.286
Heether, Adam	R-R	6-0	195	1-14-82	.228	.109	.283	49	145	27	33	8	0	1	13	31	4	0	2	33	5	2	.303	.374
2-team total (50 Nashville)					.237	—	—	99	329	57	78	15	1	10	41	54	10	0	5	68	7	3	.380	.357
Hermida, Jeremy	L-R	6-3	220	1-30-84	.308	1.000	.250	3	13	3	4	2	0	0	3	1	0	0	0	3	0	0	.462	.357
Jackson, Conor	R-R	6-2	215	5-7-82	.000	.000	.000	2	8	1	0	0	0	0	0	1	0	0	0	1	0	0	.000	.111
2-team total (3 Reno)					.158	—	—	5	19	5	3	0	0	1	2	1	1	0	0	3	0	0	.316	.238
Jernigan, Ryne	R-R	5-10	175	6-27-85	—	.000	.000	1	0	0	0	0	0	0	0	0	0	0	0	0	0	0	—	—
Ladendorf, Tyler	R-R	6-0	210	3-7-88	.100	.000	.143	4	10	0	1	1	0	0	1	0	0	0	0	3	0	0	.200	.182
Larish, Jeff	L-R	6-2	200	10-11-82	.361	.182	.440	8	36	8	13	2	0	5	19	3	0	0	0	9	0	1	.833	.410
McPherson, Dallas	L-R	6-4	235	7-23-80	.267	.273	.265	84	318	49	85	17	2	22	75	31	4	0	1	101	1	0	.541	.339
Miller, Jai	R-R	6-3	205	1-17-85	.118	.000	.133	10	34	2	4	0	0	1	3	0	0	0	0	19	3	0	.118	.189
2-team total (84 Omaha)					.252	—	—	94	345	47	87	24	2	18	57	38	1	0	3	132	5	3	.490	.326
Mitchell, Jermaine	L-L	6-0	205	11-2-84	.182	.250	.000	3	11	1	2	1	0	0	2	1	0	0	0	3	1	0	.273	.250
Napoleon, Dusty	L-R	6-2	208	5-21-86	.231	.250	.222	5	13	2	3	1	0	1	1	5	0	0	0	4	0	0	.538	.444
Powell, Landon	B-R	6-3	255	3-19-82	.200	.143	.226	14	45	6	9	2	0	1	2	10	0	0	0	9	0	0	.311	.345
Price, Jared	R-R	6-1	230	3-18-82	.167	.133	.179	20	54	3	9	2	0	2	7	3	1	2	2	19	0	0	.315	.217
Recker, Anthony	R-R	6-1	205	8-29-83	.288	.361	.265	80	250	36	72	18	2	10	42	22	0	0	4	62	0	1	.496	.341
Sogard, Eric	L-R	5-10	185	5-22-86	.300	.291	.303	137	514	82	154	28	6	5	65	75	4	1	3	68	14	9	.407	.391
Suzuki, Kurt	R-R	5-11	210	10-4-83	.375	.667	.200	3	8	4	3	2	0	0	1	5	2	0	0	1	0	0	1.000	.500
Taylor, Michael	R-R	6-6	260	12-19-85	.272	.261	.275	127	464	79	126	26	6	6	78	51	5	0	3	92	16	5	.392	.348
Tolleson, Steve	R-R	5-11	185	11-1-83	.332	.386	.311	80	292	52	97	17	3	9	43	37	4	4	2	50	8	2	.503	.412
Watson, Matt	L-R	5-11	205	9-5-78	.288	.220	.313	37	153	25	44	12	0	9	26	11	1	0	0	24	0	0	.542	.339
Wimberly, Corey	B-R	5-8	174	10-26-83	.284	.275	.288	135	531	97	151	14	7	3	57	58	18	14	2	64	56	18	.354	.373

Pitching	B-T	HT	WT	DOB	W	L	ERA	G	GS	CG	SV	IP	H	R	ER	HR	BB	SO	AVG	vLH	vRH	K/9	BB/9
Anderson, Brett	L-L	6-4	235	2-1-88	1	0	4.05	3	3	0	0	13	19	6	6	0	3	12	.333	.333	.333	8.10	2.03
Bailey, Andrew	R-R	6-3	245	5-31-84	0	0	27.00	1	1	0	0	1	3	2	2	0	0	1	.750	.667	1.000	13.50	0.00
Banwart, Travis	R-R	6-4	205	2-14-86	4	2	4.81	15	11	0	0	73	78	40	39	9	29	71	.270	.276	.265	8.75	3.58
Benacka, Mike	R-R	6-2	210	8-2-82	6	2	4.08	40	0	0	5	46	30	22	21	5	39	61	.189	.117	.256	11.85	7.58
Blackley, Travis	L-L	6-3	205	11-4-82	2	1	2.52	15	4	0	0	36	31	10	10	2	22	35	.230	.279	.189	8.83	5.55
Bonser, Boof	R-R	6-4	245	10-14-81	2	1	4.56	5	5	0	0	24	20	14	12	2	11	17	.233	.256	.209	6.46	4.18
Bowers, Cedrick	B-L	6-2	220	2-10-78	2	1	3.66	29	0	0	0	32	24	14	13	1	26	50	.203	.273	.162	14.06	7.31
Cahill, Trevor	R-R	6-4	220	3-1-88	1	0	1.04	2	2	0	0	9	7	3	1	0	5	8	.226	.200	.238	8.31	5.19

Name	B-T	HT	WT	DOB	W	L	ERA	G	GS	CG	SV	IP	H	R	ER	HR	BB	SO	AVG	vLH	vRH	K/9	BB/9
Cramer, Bobby	L-L	6-1	210	10-28-79	2	2	1.94	7	7	0	0	42	41	10	9	0	11	35	.252	.333	.226	7.56	2.38
Demel, Sam	R-R	6-0	215	10-23-85	2	0	1.26	22	0	0	6	29	22	6	4	1	9	28	.212	.167	.250	8.79	2.83
DiNardo, Lenny	L-L	6-2	220	9-19-79	2	5	3.40	10	9	1	0	48	57	27	18	5	15	28	.302	.257	.312	5.29	2.83
Giese, Dan	R-R	6-2	200	5-19-77	0	0	1.74	8	0	0	0	10	9	2	2	2	2	4	.225	.050	.400	3.48	1.74
Godfrey, Graham	R-R	6-3	205	8-9-84	4	7	5.59	24	16	0	0	106	108	76	66	9	53	87	.266	.296	.237	7.36	4.49
Halama, John	L-L	6-5	215	2-22-72	6	2	5.44	18	14	0	0	88	106	59	53	12	27	40	.308	.280	.320	4.11	2.77
Haviland, Shawn	R-R	6-2	200	11-10-85	0	0	5.40	1	1	0	0	3	6	5	2	0	2	3	.353	.364	.333	8.10	5.40
Hernandez, Fernando	R-R	5-11	210	7-31-84	5	6	4.77	45	4	0	4	77	82	52	41	8	26	65	.266	.269	.264	7.56	3.03
Hunton, Jon	R-R	6-9	250	11-30-82	6	6	3.57	51	0	0	6	63	72	35	25	5	25	40	.283	.260	.299	5.71	3.57
James, Justin	R-R	6-3	215	9-13-81	1	1	1.37	16	0	0	4	20	14	3	3	0	9	28	.194	.179	.205	12.81	4.12
Jennings, Jason	L-R	6-2	235	7-17-78	0	0	6.23	3	3	0	0	13	16	9	9	1	4	9	.296	.292	.300	6.23	2.77
Kilby, Brad	L-L	6-0	240	2-19-83	0	0	5.54	12	0	0	0	13	18	8	8	0	6	18	.327	.263	.361	12.46	4.15
Lansford, Jared	R-R	6-0	190	10-22-86	1	2	7.94	16	0	0	0	17	22	16	15	1	8	15	.310	.286	.326	7.94	4.24
Mazzaro, Vin	R-R	6-2	205	9-27-86	3	1	3.13	7	6	0	0	37	35	16	13	2	17	38	.245	.204	.270	9.16	4.10
McBeth, Marcus	R-R	6-2	185	8-23-80	1	0	6.46	14	0	0	0	15	18	14	11	2	16	14	.290	.280	.297	8.22	9.39
Middleton, Kyle	R-R	6-4	225	6-13-80	6	8	3.77	23	14	0	1	103	97	56	43	10	48	69	.255	.245	.262	6.05	4.21
Mortensen, Clay	R-R	6-4	180	4-10-85	13	6	4.25	26	26	0	0	165	161	91	78	20	53	112	.258	.225	.290	6.10	2.89
Ramirez, Edwar	R-R	6-3	165	3-28-81	3	4	3.62	36	0	0	9	50	48	24	20	5	23	35	.257	.253	.260	6.34	4.17
Rodriguez, Henry	R-R	6-0	220	2-25-87	0	2	1.69	20	0	0	11	21	10	8	4	1	9	31	.133	.179	.106	13.08	3.80
Ross, Tyson	R-R	6-6	225	4-22-87	2	1	3.55	6	6	0	0	25	22	10	10	1	13	30	.253	.273	.241	10.66	4.62
Sanchez, Jesus	L-L	5-10	165	10-11-74	0	1	12.00	3	3	0	0	12	16	16	16	3	12	8	.348	.250	.382	6.00	9.00
Souza, Justin	R-R	6-1	185	10-22-85	0	0	8.00	5	0	0	0	9	8	11	8	2	6	7	.242	.208	.333	7.00	6.00
Storey, Mickey	R-R	6-2	185	3-16-86	1	1	5.54	11	0	0	1	13	15	10	8	3	5	14	.278	.300	.250	9.69	3.46
Tomko, Brett	R-R	6-4	220	4-7-73	1	7	7.16	6	6	0	0	28	42	22	22	2	9	14	.356	.340	.369	4.55	2.93
Vaughan, Beau	B-R	6-4	230	6-4-81	1	0	7.04	6	0	0	0	8	6	6	6	1	6	7	.323	.308	.333	8.22	7.04
Wolf, Ross	R-R	6-0	180	10-18-82	0	1	5.59	10	0	0	3	10	13	8	6	1	3	11	.289	.250	.310	10.24	2.79
Wright, Jamey	R-R	6-6	230	12-24-74	1	0	9.00	10	0	1	0	14	23	14	14	2	9	16	.371	.400	.351	10.29	5.79
Wuertz, Michael	R-R	6-3	225	12-15-78	0	0	0.00	4	3	0	0	5	4	0	0		3	3	.235	.200	.250	5.79	5.79

Fielding

Catcher	PCT	G	PO	A	E	DP	PB
Donaldson	.985	64	457	59	8	1	3
Napoleon	1.000	4	17	1	0	0	0
Powell	1.000	7	47	3	0	0	0
Price	.992	16	124	8	1	0	0
Recker	.981	67	415	50	9	3	10
Suzuki	1.000	3	15	0	0	0	0

First Base	PCT	G	PO	A	E	DP
Baisley	1.000	13	129	6	0	11
Carter	.988	96	770	43	10	76
Donaldson	1.000	3	12	0	0	0
Everidge	.984	7	58	3	1	8
Harper	.964	4	25	2	1	1
Larish	1.000	2	10	0	0	0
McPherson	.991	25	200	17	2	18
Powell	.900	2	9	0	1	2
Recker	1.000	1	10	1	0	0

Second Base	PCT	G	PO	A	E	DP
Affronti	1.000	1	0	2	0	0

	PCT	G	PO	A	E	DP
Cardenas	.957	36	68	88	7	16
Ellis	1.000	1	1	4	0	0
Ladendorf	1.000	1	1	5	0	0
Sogard	.979	95	202	268	10	56
Tolleson	1.000	5	6	14	0	2
Wimberly	.935	11	18	25	3	6

Third Base	PCT	G	PO	A	E	DP
Baisley	.978	35	24	65	2	3
Cardenas	.894	19	14	28	5	3
Donaldson	.944	8	6	11	1	2
Heether	.976	18	9	31	1	1
Ladendorf	1.000	3	0	11	0	0
Larish	.944	7	2	15	1	1
McPherson	.927	19	12	26	3	3
Sogard	1.000	14	8	19	0	0
Tolleson	.912	13	8	23	3	1
Wimberly	.806	17	6	23	7	2

Shortstop	PCT	G	PO	A	E	DP
Affronti	.957	43	59	118	8	31

	PCT	G	PO	A	E	DP
Sogard	.968	25	42	80	4	16
Tolleson	.925	54	64	122	15	26
Wimberly	.964	31	44	64	4	19

Outfield	PCT	G	PO	A	E	DP
Brown	.970	40	95	2	3	1
Buck	1.000	23	48	1	0	1
Carson	.987	63	146	2	2	0
Carter	.964	28	50	3	2	0
Crisp	1.000	6	9	0	0	0
Cust	.969	13	31	0	1	0
Donaldson	1.000	1	1	0	0	0
Heether	1.000	30	41	0	0	0
Hermida	1.000	2	3	0	0	0
Jackson	1.000	2	4	0	0	0
Miller	1.000	10	14	0	0	0
Mitchell	1.000	3	13	1	0	1
Taylor	.961	120	212	12	9	5
Tolleson	1.000	6	14	1	0	0
Watson	.957	24	43	2	2	1
Wimberly	.981	87	152	5	3	1

MIDLAND ROCKHOUNDS — DOUBLE-A

TEXAS LEAGUE

Batting	B-T	HT	WT	DOB	AVG	vLH	vRH	G	AB	R	H	2B	3B	HR	RBI	BB	HBP	SH	SF	SO	SB	CS	SLG	OBP
Affronti, Mike	R-R	6-2	195	2-13-84	.231	.000	.250	4	13	0	3	0	0	0	0	1	0	0		5	0	1	.231	.286
2-team total (62 Corpus Christi)					.276	—		66	232	22	64	5	3	3	29	13	3	1	2	45	5	6	.362	.320
Baisley, Jeff	R-R	6-3	220	12-19-82	.325	.323	.326	51	197	23	64	19	1	4	34	19	3	0	5	53	3	2	.492	.384
Brown, Corey	L-L	6-1	205	11-26-85	.320	.264	.354	90	331	63	106	14	8	10	49	52	2	0	1	93	19	1	.502	.415
Cardenas, Adrian	L-R	6-0	205	10-10-87	.345	.359	.382	51	194	36	67	15	0	3	32	33	3	0	6	23	4	6	.469	.436
Carter, Yusuf	R-R	6-2	205	2-6-85	.206	.282	.174	41	131	13	27	5	1	1	8	12	0	0	1	37	4	0	.282	.271
Chen, Yung Chi	R-R	5-11	170	7-13-83	.168	.115	.187	28	101	11	17	5	2	0	9	7	0	1	2	14	0	0	.257	.218
Gilbert, Archie	R-R	5-8	184	7-8-83	.247	.272	.235	116	445	65	110	31	1	11	54	51	8	1	4	69	28	11	.396	.333
Holt, J.C.	L-R	5-9	175	12-8-82	.229	.241	.221	51	210	27	48	13	1	2	19	11	1	3	2	45	10	1	.288	.268
Horton, Josh	L-R	6-1	195	2-19-86	.286	.294	.281	108	420	60	120	18	3	3	51	41	5	0	4	50	4	3	.364	.353
Kleen, Steve	R-R	6-4	200	5-21-83	.197	.125	.228	39	132	13	26	6	0	4	20	14	4	0	2	33	1	1	.333	.289
Majewski, Val	L-L	6-2	220	6-19-81	.262	.224	.282	81	302	36	79	18	0	9	56	37	1	0	3	69	5	2	.411	.341
Mitchell, Jermaine	L-L	6-0	205	11-2-84	.223	.200	.235	37	121	16	27	3	3	0	11	19	1	1	1	41	2	6	.298	.331
Napoleon, Dusty	L-R	6-2	208	5-21-86	.200	.000	.286	4	10	0	2	1	0	0	3	0	0	0	0	0	0	0	.300	.385
Ortiz, Gabriel	R-R	6-1	215	11-7-85	.226	.278	.203	34	115	11	26	6	0	1	12	5	1	0	1	31	1	1	.304	.262
Paramore, Petey	B-R	6-2	195	10-30-86	.263	.346	.213	65	205	20	54	8	0	3	19	33	2	0	6	54	0	0	.346	.371
Peterson, Shane	L-L	6-0	195	2-11-88	.265	.253	.272	128	460	61	122	24	4	5	59	57	11	0	8	108	11	2	.367	.354
Price, Jared	R-R	6-1	230	3-18-82	.250	.000	.250	1	4	0	1	0	0	0	0	0	0	0	0	1	0	0	.250	.250
Recker, Anthony	R-R	6-1	245	8-29-83	.211	.167	.231	11	38	8	8	1	0	1	3	7	2	0	0	12	1	0	.316	.362

Name	B-T	HT	WT	DOB	AVG	vLH	vRH	G	AB	R	H	2B	3B	HR	RBI	BB	HBP	SH	SF	SO	SB	CS	SLG	OBP
Richard, Michael	R-R	5-11	180	8-20-84	.185	.100	.235	9	27	1	5	0	0	0	2	4	0	0	0	6	1	0	.185	.290
Sulentic, Matt	L-R	5-10	170	10-6-87	.275	.272	.276	123	440	55	121	18	3	1	45	49	2	3	3	109	11	5	.336	.348
Thomas, David	R-R	5-11	180	7-29-86	.333	.500	.000	1	3	1	1	0	0	0	2	0	0	0	0	1	0	0	.667	.333
Valdez, Alex	B-R	6-1	160	9-2-84	.262	.250	.269	134	526	82	138	29	8	13	74	39	5	1	3	123	10	1	.422	.318
Weeks, Jemile	B-R	5-9	170	1-26-87	.267	.287	.257	67	273	43	73	14	7	3	33	28	3	2	6	37	11	6	.403	.335
Whitney, Matt	R-R	6-3	215	2-13-84	.095	.143	.071	6	21	1	2	0	0	0	1	4	0	0	0	8	0	0	.095	.231

Pitching	B-T	HT	WT	DOB	W	L	ERA	G	GS	CG	SV	IP	H	R	ER	HR	BB	SO	AVG	vLH	vRH	K/9	BB/9
Banwart, Travis	R-R	6-4	205	2-14-86	5	5	2.92	14	14	0	0	83	71	36	27	7	31	59	.231	.259	.200	6.37	3.35
Capra, Anthony	L-L	6-1	200	4-3-87	6	13	4.27	28	28	0	0	131	120	72	62	9	89	118	.249	.258	.245	8.13	6.13
Daley, Gary	R-R	6-3	200	11-1-85	0	0	19.29	2	0	0	0	2	5	5	5	0	5	1	.500	.500	.500	3.86	19.29
2-team total (20 Springfield, MO)					3	11	7.02	22	18	0	0	91	122	86	71	10	58	63	—	—	—	6.23	5.74
De Los Santos, Fautino	R-R	6-2	220	2-15-86	1	5	6.54	25	0	0	0	32	31	26	23	1	16	51	.250	.286	.221	14.49	4.55
Edell, Ryan	L-L	6-1	215	7-6-83	10	4	3.17	21	20	0	0	125	136	47	44	6	20	92	.277	.333	.259	6.62	1.44
Figueroa, Pedro	L-L	6-1	205	11-23-85	1	6	5.30	13	13	0	0	71	84	45	42	6	29	57	.295	.196	.342	7.19	3.66
Friend, Justin	R-R	6-1	200	6-21-86	3	3	3.70	36	1	0	0	56	63	29	23	1	38	50	.292	.305	.284	8.04	6.11
Godfrey, Graham	R-R	6-3	205	8-9-84	0	1	3.86	5	4	0	0	19	22	9	8	0	9	16	.301	.276	.318	7.71	4.34
Gordon, Derrick	L-L	5-9	185	10-16-83	2	2	5.43	40	1	0	1	71	69	48	43	7	35	63	.256	.234	.267	7.95	4.42
Hernandez, Carlos	L-L	5-11	155	3-4-87	9	3	4.37	26	25	0	0	130	145	66	63	6	48	96	.286	.265	.294	6.66	3.33
Hornbeck, Ben	R-L	6-5	180	7-22-87	2	3	5.87	8	7	0	1	38	43	27	25	3	19	26	.289	.326	.274	6.10	4.46
James, Justin	R-R	6-3	215	9-13-81	1	0	2.29	12	0	0	1	20	11	5	5	1	7	21	.157	.229	.086	9.61	3.20
Lansford, Jared	R-R	6-0	190	10-22-86	4	1	2.43	30	0	0	12	37	31	11	10	0	19	29	.242	.254	.231	7.05	4.62
Leon, Arnold	R-R	6-1	205	9-6-88	0	0	6.23	3	0	0	0	4	6	3	3	1	3	1	.333	.333	.333	2.08	6.23
Lyman, Jeff	R-R	6-4	225	1-14-87	0	0	8.58	10	8	0	0	28	40	28	27	5	15	25	.331	.364	.303	7.94	4.76
Murray, Justin	R-R	6-4	200	5-11-87	0	1	4.32	4	3	0	0	17	21	10	8	0	11	7	.313	.314	.313	3.78	5.94
Ray, Jason	R-R	5-11	195	7-14-84	3	3	4.41	24	0	0	0	35	37	22	17	4	21	17	.272	.328	.227	4.41	5.45
Sattler, Dan	R-R	6-3	190	11-11-83	1	2	4.17	33	0	0	1	45	45	22	21	4	24	38	.260	.281	.248	7.54	4.76
Sewell, Lance	L-L	6-3	195	6-17-86	0	0	3.94	13	0	0	0	16	18	10	7	0	3	10	.281	.400	.245	5.63	1.69
Souza, Justin	R-R	6-1	185	10-22-85	2	2	3.38	28	0	0	6	40	35	17	15	1	20	38	.230	.302	.188	8.55	4.50
Storey, Mickey	R-R	6-2	185	3-16-86	5	4	3.30	43	1	0	8	71	58	31	26	5	22	63	.222	.192	.242	7.99	2.79
Vaughan, Beau	B-R	6-4	230	6-4-81	1	3	1.95	24	0	0	6	32	30	12	7	0	6	29	.238	.292	.205	8.07	1.67
Wagner, Neil	R-R	6-0	195	1-1-84	6	2	3.70	33	0	0	1	49	55	25	20	1	27	45	.282	.185	.351	8.32	4.99
Wright, Matt	R-R	6-4	270	3-13-82	7	3	3.20	15	15	0	0	79	88	35	28	8	12	44	.278	.285	.272	5.03	1.37

Fielding

Catcher	PCT	G	PO	A	E	DP	PB
Carter	.988	34	224	28	3	0	11
Napoleon	.962	4	25	0	1	0	0
Ortiz	.984	34	223	22	4	2	4
Paramore	.994	65	470	28	3	2	5
Price	1.000	1	4	1	0	0	0
Recker	1.000	9	59	6	0	1	2

First Base	PCT	G	PO	A	E	DP
Baisley	.988	27	235	15	3	24
Carter	.969	4	30	1	1	4
Kleen	.991	34	289	29	3	24
Majewski	1.000	7	54	2	0	5
Ortiz	1.000	1	2	0	0	0
Peterson	.998	64	541	46	1	54
Recker	1.000	1	7	1	0	0
Whitney	.983	6	54	3	1	3

Second Base	PCT	G	PO	A	E	DP
Cardenas	.962	16	25	50	3	7
Chen	.955	4	11	10	1	3
Holt	.964	34	67	119	7	30
Richard	.889	4	10	6	2	1
Valdez	.917	21	38	62	9	16
Weeks	.972	64	129	178	9	31

Third Base	PCT	G	PO	A	E	DP
Baisley	1.000	19	12	44	0	5
Cardenas	.864	26	15	36	8	2
Chen	1.000	1	1	1	0	1
Holt	1.000	1	0	3	0	0
Kleen	—	1	0	0	0	0
Valdez	.964	95	74	195	10	11

Shortstop	PCT	G	PO	A	E	DP
Affronti	1.000	4	4	14	0	2

	PCT	G	PO	A	E	DP
Chen	.971	21	36	66	3	12
Horton	.971	106	169	307	14	75
Richard	.875	3	4	3	1	0
Valdez	.963	6	14	12	1	3

Outfield	PCT	G	PO	A	E	DP
Brown	.978	79	178	4	4	1
Carter	1.000	1	1	0	0	0
Gilbert	.984	104	179	4	3	0
Holt	.917	5	10	1	1	0
Kleen	—	1	0	0	0	0
Majewski	1.000	59	111	10	0	1
Mitchell	.948	27	55	0	3	0
Peterson	.978	51	84	4	2	1
Sulentic	.980	95	190	8	4	2
Thomas	1.000	1	0	0	0	0

STOCKTON PORTS

HIGH CLASS A

CALIFORNIA LEAGUE

Batting	B-T	HT	WT	DOB	AVG	vLH	vRH	G	AB	R	H	2B	3B	HR	RBI	BB	HBP	SH	SF	SO	SB	CS	SLG	OBP
Barfield, Jeremy	R-L	6-5	240	7-12-88	.272	.294	.265	135	508	72	138	21	1	17	92	52	6	1	11	93	1	1	.417	.340
Carter, Yusuf	R-R	6-2	205	2-6-85	.278	.176	.301	48	180	32	50	14	0	13	42	12	1	0	1	51	1	0	.572	.325
Castillo, Gernaldo	R-R	5-11	145	7-17-89	.176	.000	.231	5	17	1	3	0	0	0	0	2	0	0	0	3	0	0	.176	.263
Christian, Jason	L-R	6-3	170	6-16-87	.162	.000	.240	12	37	5	6	0	0	0	2	7	0	0	0	10	1	1	.162	.295
Crisotomo, Jose	L-R	6-1	181	4-20-89	.192	.250	.182	9	26	1	5	0	0	0	2	1	0	0	0	4	0	1	.192	.222
Crisp, Coco	B-R	6-0	180	11-1-79	.833	.000	.833	2	6	2	5	0	1	1	3	1	0	0	0	0	0	0	1.667	.857
Ellis, Mark	R-R	5-11	195	6-6-77	.200	.000	.200	2	5	0	1	0	0	0	1	0	0	0	0	0	0	0	.200	.286
Galarraga, Joel	R-R	5-11	185	3-20-82	.235	.286	.200	5	17	2	4	0	0	0	1	0	0	0	0	3	0	0	.235	.278
Green, Grant	R-R	6-3	180	9-27-87	.318	.373	.298	131	548	107	174	39	6	20	87	38	7	3	10	117	9	5	.520	.363
Horton, Josh	L-R	6-1	195	2-19-86	.467	.333	.524	8	30	5	14	5	1	2	6	1	0	0	0	5	0	1	.900	.484
Jackson, Conor	R-R	6-2	215	5-7-82	.286	.500	.200	2	7	1	2	1	0	0	2	0	0	0	1	1	0	0	.429	.250
Johnson, Toddric	L-L	6-1	202	12-17-84	.205	.196	.207	82	307	39	63	13	3	6	38	25	2	0	3	66	6	5	.326	.267
Ka'aihue, Kala	R-R	6-2	230	3-29-85	.167	.120	.195	23	66	11	11	4	0	3	12	20	2	0	1	19	2	0	.364	.371
Keough, Shane	B-R	6-3	196	9-11-86	.223	.206	.229	67	251	31	56	12	2	2	27	21	4	2	2	78	8	7	.331	.291
Ladendorf, Tyler	R-R	6-0	210	3-7-88	.274	.288	.269	126	478	60	131	30	4	5	41	35	3	5	3	110	20	4	.385	.326
Lopez, Diomes	R-R	6-2	195	1-30-89	.667	1.000	.500	1	3	0	2	0	0	0	1	0	0	0	0	1	0	0	.667	.750
Mitchell, Jermaine	L-L	6-0	205	11-2-84	.309	.409	.265	78	304	68	94	21	7	10	32	51	3	1	0	86	21	9	.523	.413
Napoleon, Dusty	L-R	6-2	208	5-21-86	.143	.125	.150	11	28	3	4	0	0	0	1	12	1	0	0	9	0	0	.143	.415

Name	B-T	HT	WT	DOB	AVG	vLH	vRH	G	AB	R	H	2B	3B	HR	RBI	BB	HBP	SH	SF	SO	SB	CS	SLG	OBP
Ortiz, Ryan	R-R	6-3	195	9-29-87	.277	.319	.262	58	188	35	52	12	1	8	35	36	1	1	1	47	1	0	.479	.394
Paramore, Petey	B-R	6-2	195	10-30-86	.255	.258	.254	46	149	18	38	7	0	3	23	34	0	0	1	37	0	1	.362	.391
Parker, Steve	L-R	6-2	200	9-3-87	.296	.268	.306	139	524	102	155	38	5	21	98	84	7	0	12	105	3	1	.508	.392
Pinckney, Brandon	R-R	5-10	165	4-12-82	.320	.235	.345	24	75	8	24	6	1	1	9	11	0	3	2	12	0	0	.467	.398
Richard, Michael	R-R	5-11	180	8-20-84	.214	.179	.229	33	98	13	21	3	0	0	5	11	2	1	1	21	2	5	.245	.304
Soto, Ramon	R-R	6-2	190	11-3-87	.231	.000	.250	4	13	1	3	1	0	0	1	0	1	0	0	5	0	1	.308	.286
Spina, Mike	R-R	6-1	220	12-17-86	.253	.187	.274	135	514	74	130	27	1	23	88	64	13	0	3	142	1	0	.444	.348
Thomas, David	B-R	5-11	180	7-29-86	.233	.255	.227	65	223	40	52	14	4	2	30	22	10	5	1	41	6	5	.359	.328
Walton, Kent	R-R	6-1	185	12-11-86	.257	.278	.250	41	140	18	36	7	0	3	17	14	0	1	1	35	4	1	.371	.323
Whitney, Matt	R-R	6-3	215	2-13-84	.279	.111	.324	12	43	6	12	2	1	3	7	5	2	0	0	7	0	0	.581	.380

Pitching

Name	B-T	HT	WT	DOB	W	L	ERA	G	GS	CG	SV	IP	H	R	ER	HR	BB	SO	AVG	vLH	vRH	K/9	BB/9
Barham, Trey	L-L	6-0	215	11-7-85	3	2	2.77	59	0	0	1	68	67	30	21	5	19	56	.257	.282	.236	7.38	2.50
Blackley, Travis	L-L	6-3	205	11-4-82	0	0	1.80	2	2	0	0	5	3	1	1	0	0	2	.167	.000	.231	3.60	0.00
Braden, Dallas	L-L	6-1	190	8-13-83	0	0	6.75	1	1	0	0	4	7	3	3	2	1	4	.333	.600	.250	9.00	2.25
Carignan, Andrew	R-R	5-11	205	7-23-86	3	3	6.27	30	0	0	0	33	28	31	23	2	34	44	.228	.245	.214	12.00	9.27
De Los Santos, Fautino	R-R	6-2	220	2-15-86	1	0	2.30	12	0	0	1	16	13	4	4	0	3	22	.224	.217	.229	12.64	1.72
Deal, Scott	R-R	6-3	195	12-11-86	3	4	3.15	39	1	0	1	69	61	29	24	6	23	44	.237	.298	.202	5.77	3.01
Hart, Michael	R-R	6-1	210	2-9-87	2	0	2.77	9	0	0	1	13	12	7	4	0	7	12	.240	.176	.273	8.31	4.85
Haviland, Shawn	R-R	6-2	200	11-10-85	9	6	3.65	27	27	0	0	150	156	77	61	15	40	166	.266	.282	.256	9.94	2.39
Hodsdon, Scott	R-R	6-1	185	5-31-85	2	3	6.18	45	0	0	4	71	88	68	49	3	33	54	.300	.302	.299	6.81	4.16
Hornbeck, Ben	R-L	6-5	190	7-22-87	2	3	4.44	18	18	0	0	93	113	62	46	18	41	112	.300	.230	.321	10.80	3.95
Hunter, Brett	R-R	6-4	215	6-27-87	2	1	6.51	25	0	0	0	28	32	21	20	4	25	44	.294	.278	.301	14.31	8.13
Huttenlocker, A.J.	L-L	6-3	190	8-5-86	1	0	5.79	6	0	0	1	9	12	8	6	1	1	8	.300	.100	.367	7.71	0.96
Krol, Ian	L-L	6-1	180	5-9-91	1	0	3.66	4	4	0	0	20	18	9	8	3	9	20	.247	.235	.250	9.15	4.12
Madsen, Michael	R-R	6-0	160	11-29-82	1	4	5.00	6	6	0	0	27	30	19	15	2	8	32	.275	.333	.224	10.67	2.67
Marks, Justin	L-L	6-2	170	1-12-88	3	1	4.58	5	4	0	0	20	17	13	10	4	8	17	.239	.267	.232	7.78	3.66
McDaniel, Dan	R-R	6-3	220	4-18-88	0	0	10.38	4	0	0	0	4	5	5	5	1	6	6	.235	.286	.200	12.46	12.46
Murray, Justin	R-R	6-4	200	5-11-87	10	4	3.67	26	18	1	1	118	133	59	48	11	54	83	.284	.271	.293	6.35	4.13
Oseguera, Paul	L-L	6-0	180	1-6-84	2	4	6.16	7	7	0	0	38	49	29	26	2	16	37	.316	.270	.331	8.76	3.79
Pina, Jose	R-R	6-2	150	11-2-85	2	4	6.66	31	1	0	1	49	57	39	36	11	19	45	.298	.360	.259	8.32	3.51
Ramirez, Anvioris	L-L	6-1	165	3-10-88	0	6	7.94	8	8	0	0	40	54	35	35	6	14	17	.329	.359	.310	3.86	3.18
Sattler, Dan	R-R	6-3	190	11-11-83	0	1	2.35	8	0	0	2	8	5	2	2	0	3	8	.192	.143	.250	9.39	3.52
Sewell, Lance	L-L	6-2	195	6-17-86	7	0	1.76	33	0	0	0	46	30	12	9	5	11	41	.181	.206	.163	8.02	2.15
Smalley, Ken	R-R	6-2	195	7-25-87	3	6	6.46	18	12	0	0	77	85	57	55	13	41	64	.282	.279	.286	7.51	4.81
Smith, Murphy	R-R	6-3	210	8-25-87	3	5	6.19	10	9	0	0	48	72	38	33	4	12	34	.350	.348	.351	6.38	2.25
Smyth, Paul	R-R	5-11	210	4-1-87	3	6	3.01	58	0	0	28	78	68	35	26	4	21	94	.231	.236	.227	10.89	2.43
Thomas, Dan	R-R	6-2	200	2-10-86	0	0	8.71	9	0	0	1	7	11	10	10	0	13	13	.189	.167	.200	11.32	11.32
Thomson, Matt	R-R	6-4	195	3-22-88	1	0	0.00	1	1	0	0	5	2	0	0	0	2	10	.125	.222	.000	18.00	3.60
Tomko, Brett	R-R	6-4	220	4-7-73	0	1	7.52	6	6	0	0	26	37	22	22	11	7	22	.322	.311	.329	7.52	2.39
Williamson, Fabian	R-L	6-2	175	10-20-88	5	2	4.57	13	13	0	0	63	67	35	32	6	45	49	.288	.368	.261	7.00	6.43
Wuertz, Michael	R-R	6-3	225	12-15-78	0	0	0.00	2	2	0	0	3	3	0	0	0	0	3	.250	.400	.143	9.00	0.00

Fielding

Catcher	PCT	G	PO	A	E	DP	PB
Carter	.994	37	300	42	2	1	21
Galarraga	1.000	5	46	2	0	0	2
Lopez	.917	1	11	0	1	0	2
Napoleon	1.000	5	32	1	0	1	0
Ortiz	.985	54	466	52	8	3	11
Paramore	.993	36	258	30	2	1	4
Soto	.950	4	34	4	2	1	1

First Base	PCT	G	PO	A	E	DP
Carter	1.000	2	7	1	0	1
Ka'aihue	1.000	8	69	6	0	5
Napoleon	.967	5	25	4	1	2
Ortiz	1.000	2	19	1	0	1
Paramore	1.000	1	4	0	0	0
Parker	1.000	3	25	3	0	5
Spina	.984	119	949	68	17	94
Whitney	.950	6	53	4	3	4

Second Base	PCT	G	PO	A	E	DP
Castillo	.963	5	10	16	1	4
Christian	.980	10	14	34	1	7
Ellis	1.000	2	3	5	0	3
Green	—	1	0	0	0	0
Horton	1.000	4	10	13	0	3
Ladendorf	.963	97	184	254	17	65
Parker	1.000	1	1	1	0	0
Pinckney	.979	12	18	28	1	6
Richard	.948	18	22	33	3	10
Spina	1.000	2	2	2	0	0

Third Base	PCT	G	PO	A	E	DP
Ladendorf	1.000	1	1	1	0	0
Parker	.909	129	94	234	33	35
Pinckney	.917	5	3	8	1	3
Spina	1.000	5	4	11	0	2
Whitney	1.000	2	0	1	0	0

Shortstop	PCT	G	PO	A	E	DP
Green	.920	114	155	272	37	56
Horton	1.000	1	2	4	0	2
Ladendorf	.969	21	40	55	3	12
Pinckney	1.000	3	3	11	0	1
Richard	.880	5	11	11	3	0

Outfield	PCT	G	PO	A	E	DP
Barfield	.960	133	238	24	11	5
Carter	—	1	0	0	0	0
Crisotomo	1.000	8	14	0	0	0
Crisp	1.000	2	2	0	0	0
Jackson	1.000	2	1	1	0	0
Johnson	.991	62	108	4	1	1
Ka'aihue	.933	6	11	3	1	1
Keough	.955	58	100	6	5	1
Ladendorf	1.000	8	11	0	0	0
Mitchell	.958	73	132	4	6	1
Thomas	.976	58	123	1	3	0
Walton	1.000	23	32	0	0	0

KANE COUNTY COUGARS
MIDWEST LEAGUE

LOW CLASS A

Batting	B-T	HT	WT	DOB	AVG	vLH	vRH	G	AB	R	H	2B	3B	HR	RBI	BB	HBP	SH	SF	SO	SB	CS	SLG	OBP
Affinito, Chris	R-R	6-3	230	2-10-87	.167	.087	.188	32	108	11	18	4	0	3	14	12	1	1	2	51	0	0	.287	.252
Aliotti, Anthony	L-L	6-0	204	7-16-87	.278	.282	.277	133	478	75	133	29	2	5	77	92	7	3	7	132	14	4	.379	.397
Christian, Jason	L-R	6-3	170	6-16-87	.277	.220	.299	58	213	31	59	13	2	4	32	17	1	1	3	56	11	2	.413	.329
Crisotomo, Jose	L-R	6-1	181	4-20-89	.260	.196	.283	49	173	23	45	4	2	0	25	10	0	9	0	17	6	4	.306	.301
Crumbliss, Conner	R-L	5-8	175	4-19-87	.271	.301	.259	134	491	95	133	20	2	5	56	126	6	5	6	92	24	8	.371	.421
Dixon, Rashun	R-R	6-2	210	8-27-90	.275	.293	.268	119	444	69	122	18	3	8	54	58	11	0	2	135	9	7	.383	.371
Gil, Leonardo	R-R	6-1	160	8-18-87	.252	.267	.246	117	437	63	110	26	6	13	72	26	6	2	10	107	4	2	.428	.296

Name	B-T	HT	WT	DOB	AVG	vLH	vRH	G	AB	R	H	2B	3B	HR	RBI	BB	HBP	SH	SF	SO	SB	CS	SLG	OBP
Gilmartin, Michael	R-R	6-0	180	7-14-87	.245	.137	.276	119	421	41	103	30	4	5	53	46	7	7	4	118	15	5	.371	.326
Hernandez, Franklin	R-R	6-3	165	4-19-87	.193	.138	.213	33	109	9	21	5	0	1	13	5	1	1	0	26	1	1	.266	.235
House, Tyreace	R-R	5-10	175	3-1-88	.245	.218	.256	121	424	83	104	10	3	1	32	96	12	7	4	88	37	13	.290	.396
LeVier, Mitch	L-L	5-11	185	1-12-88	.313	.385	.286	25	96	17	30	6	1	3	21	9	0	0	0	23	1	0	.490	.371
Leyja, Nino	R-R	5-10	170	10-2-90	.224	.143	.240	37	125	13	28	2	0	0	11	8	0	2	0	38	4	2	.240	.271
Napoleon, Dusty	L-R	6-2	208	5-21-86	.400	.000	.400	2	5	0	2	1	0	0	0	4	0	0	0	2	0	0	.600	.667
Nunez, Juan	R-R	6-2	191	8-27-87	.171	.256	.142	44	152	12	26	4	0	1	16	6	1	2	1	51	0	1	.217	.206
Richard, Myrio	R-R	6-1	190	8-27-88	.281	.277	.283	98	359	48	101	27	2	2	34	38	6	2	1	58	11	7	.384	.359
Stassi, Max	R-R	5-10	190	3-15-91	.229	.239	.225	110	411	54	94	21	1	13	51	45	5	1	3	141	3	3	.380	.310
Walton, Kent	R-L	6-1	185	12-11-86	.270	.227	.281	52	204	25	55	18	2	2	32	14	6	0	3	49	4	2	.407	.330

Pitching	B-T	HT	WT	DOB	W	L	ERA	G	GS	CG	SV	IP	H	R	ER	HR	BB	SO	AVG	vLH	vRH	K/9	BB/9
Christensen, Kyle	R-R	6-3	225	9-18-88	0	2	6.92	5	2	0	0	13	13	10	10	0	6	4	.265	.280	.250	2.77	4.15
Doolittle, Ryan	R-R	6-3	185	3-25-88	0	0	4.07	18	0	0	2	24	34	11	11	3	1	19	.330	.295	.356	7.03	0.37
Garcia, Hector	R-R	6-3	160	10-22-85	0	1	4.34	12	0	0	0	19	17	13	9	1	15	18	.233	.192	.255	8.68	7.23
Gilliam, Rob	R-R	6-1	195	11-29-87	7	6	3.89	24	18	0	0	111	105	53	48	7	35	101	.253	.292	.220	8.19	2.84
Guzman, Jose	R-R	5-11	185	11-5-87	4	2	3.40	45	0	0	18	50	46	23	19	3	15	49	.241	.231	.246	8.76	2.68
Hoehn, Connor	R-R	6-1	205	7-5-89	7	4	3.80	44	0	0	1	88	69	40	37	6	39	101	.216	.222	.211	10.37	4.00
Huttenlocker, A.J.	L-L	6-3	190	8-5-86	1	2	3.02	28	0	0	1	45	39	15	15	1	13	46	.238	.214	.250	9.27	2.62
Joseph, Jonathan	R-R	6-1	180	5-17-88	2	5	3.33	14	9	0	0	54	49	27	20	2	26	55	.241	.205	.267	9.17	4.33
Krol, Ian	L-L	6-1	180	5-9-91	9	4	2.65	24	23	0	0	119	98	42	35	5	19	91	.223	.216	.226	6.90	1.44
Lansford, Josh	R-R	6-2	215	7-31-84	1	2	4.11	40	0	0	1	50	53	29	23	5	16	58	.268	.226	.305	10.37	2.86
Larsen, Aaron	R-L	6-1	190	3-1-87	0	1	7.94	2	2	0	0	6	10	10	5	3	3	5	.357	.429	.286	7.94	4.76
Macias, Jose	R-R	6-2	180	7-18-89	0	1	6.43	2	2	0	0	7	10	5	5	0	3	4	.345	.278	.455	5.14	3.86
Marks, Justin	L-L	6-3	170	1-12-88	3	12	4.92	20	20	0	0	110	109	66	60	11	41	119	.261	.197	.287	9.77	3.36
Mederos, Chris	R-R	6-3	175	5-17-87	7	5	3.01	15	13	0	0	72	60	32	24	4	22	57	.224	.203	.240	7.16	2.76
Peterson, Max	L-L	6-2	210	6-27-88	4	5	3.76	34	0	0	2	53	40	23	22	4	30	70	.214	.209	.217	11.96	5.13
Pina, Jose	R-R	6-2	150	11-2-85	2	1	3.74	13	0	0	1	22	27	15	9	3	6	29	.307	.343	.283	12.05	2.49
Quigley, Ryan	L-L	6-4	220	9-11-87	0	0	6.62	11	0	0	0	18	22	16	13	3	10	17	.310	.227	.347	8.66	5.09
Ramirez, Anvioris	L-L	6-1	165	3-10-88	0	1	5.89	6	2	0	1	18	23	14	12	1	7	10	.315	.235	.339	4.91	3.44
Schultz, Patrick	R-R	6-3	215	9-25-85	6	1	2.87	41	0	0	0	75	57	31	24	2	34	65	.208	.254	.173	7.77	4.06
Smalley, Ken	R-R	6-2	195	7-25-87	0	2	5.88	13	3	0	0	26	27	17	17	3	15	23	.273	.275	.271	7.96	5.19
Smith, Murphy	R-R	6-3	210	8-25-87	8	2	3.64	17	16	0	0	96	91	50	39	1	25	70	.251	.217	.283	6.54	2.34
Straily, Dan	R-R	6-2	220	12-1-88	10	7	4.32	28	28	0	0	148	138	75	71	13	61	149	.254	.240	.265	9.06	3.71

Fielding

Catcher	PCT	G	PO	A	E	DP	PB
Affinito	.964	6	50	3	2	0	2
Nunez	.974	43	340	32	10	2	6
Stassi	.984	77	732	82	14	9	10

First Base	PCT	G	PO	A	E	DP
Affinito	.875	3	20	1	3	1
Aliotti	.991	126	1055	96	11	91
Gil	1.000	2	21	2	0	3
Hernandez	.967	11	85	4	3	7

Second Base	PCT	G	PO	A	E	DP
Christian	.857	3	2	4	1	2

	PCT	G	PO	A	E	DP
Crumbliss	.982	120	190	309	9	59
Leyja	.974	18	26	49	2	3

Third Base	PCT	G	PO	A	E	DP
Christian	.925	26	10	39	4	3
Gil	.951	100	71	203	14	20
Leyja	1.000	15	6	34	0	2

Shortstop	PCT	G	PO	A	E	DP
Christian	.959	17	28	42	3	10
Gil	.893	6	11	14	3	6
Gilmartin	.946	117	155	299	26	55

Outfield	PCT	G	PO	A	E	DP
Crisotomo	.975	45	76	1	2	0
Crumbliss	.905	13	18	1	2	0
Dixon	.981	109	201	10	4	1
Hernandez	.857	16	18	0	3	0
House	.961	110	190	8	8	2
LeVier	.893	13	25	0	3	0
Napoleon	1.000	1	5	0	0	0
Richard	.961	82	141	5	6	2
Walton	.966	35	53	3	2	0

VANCOUVER CANADIANS

SHORT-SEASON

NORTHWEST LEAGUE

Batting	B-T	HT	WT	DOB	AVG	vLH	vRH	G	AB	R	H	2B	3B	HR	RBI	BB	HBP	SH	SF	SO	SB	CS	SLG	OBP
Affinito, Chris	R-R	6-3	230	2-10-87	.320	.200	.333	16	50	5	16	3	0	1	7	15	3	0	1	17	0	0	.440	.493
Bercume, Jeff	L-R	5-8	175	6-15-87	.280	.171	.300	65	254	31	71	10	3	0	24	22	5	7	3	38	10	4	.343	.345
Castillo, Gernaldo	R-R	5-11	145	7-17-89	.125	.000	.146	18	48	3	6	1	0	0	2	7	0	2	0	10	1	0	.146	.236
Choice, Michael	R-R	6-1	215	11-10-89	.284	.148	.333	27	102	20	29	10	2	7	26	15	3	0	1	43	6	1	.627	.388
Crisotomo, Jose	L-R	6-1	181	4-20-89	.267	.200	.275	13	45	4	12	0	0	0	4	1	0	1	0	9	1	2	.267	.283
Fabiaschi, Michael	R-R	5-11	185	8-17-88	.234	.250	.230	31	94	13	22	6	1	0	4	17	4	3	0	25	2	2	.319	.374
Hurley, Zach	L-L	6-0	200	5-27-87	.271	.000	.281	19	59	9	16	4	1	0	5	2	0	1	0	12	0	0	.373	.295
Kirby-Jones, A.J.	R-R	5-10	215	10-2-88	.259	.245	.263	75	247	41	64	10	0	14	42	61	8	0	3	82	1	1	.470	.417
Kirkland, Wade	R-R	5-10	180	4-4-89	.271	.190	.293	68	280	34	76	18	2	0	27	9	2	3	3	59	4	2	.350	.296
Landaeta, Douglas	R-R	6-1	170	11-25-88	.293	.356	.276	71	280	28	82	15	1	2	32	18	1	2	3	36	5	9	.375	.334
LeVier, Mitch	L-L	5-11	185	1-12-88	.318	.286	.333	5	22	3	7	2	0	1	3	0	0	2	0	8	0	0	.545	.318
Leyja, Nino	R-R	5-10	170	10-2-90	.220	.208	.222	43	141	19	31	3	1	1	13	22	3	5	3	22	5	0	.277	.289
Lipkin, Ryan	R-R	6-1	200	10-8-87	.272	.225	.285	52	184	21	50	12	0	1	33	13	3	3	1	32	1	1	.353	.328
Luis, Marcos	R-R	5-11	180	11-27-85	.205	.200	.208	15	39	1	8	0	0	0	2	1	0			6	0	0	.205	.244
Nester, John	R-R	6-1	210	5-28-89	.182	.056	.220	22	77	7	14	3	0	0	7	8	0	1	3	26	0	1	.221	.256
Petitti, Daniel	R-R	6-1	190	5-12-88	.123	.188	.105	26	73	3	9	1	1	0	6	2	4	1	0	20	0	0	.164	.207
Pineda, Ryan	R-R	5-11	180	4-17-89	.221	.320	.186	26	95	16	21	9	0	0	8	17	0	1	1	20	1	0	.316	.336
Thompson, Tony	R-R	6-4	219	12-19-88	.246	.182	.260	62	236	30	58	11	0	3	21	23	3	0	0	43	1	1	.331	.321
Tripp, Jordan	R-R	6-1	215	10-27-89	.125	.154	.116	18	56	9	7	1	0	0	2	7	2	2	0	21	0	3	.143	.246
Wells, Jeremy	R-R	5-11	175	8-9-86	.231	.250	.222	6	13	1	3	0	0	0	1	3	1	0	0	4	1	0	.231	.412
Whitaker, Josh	R-R	6-3	235	2-8-89	.232	.150	.265	43	142	19	33	5	0	4	22	16	1	3	3	40	6	2	.352	.309

Pitching	B-T	HT	WT	DOB	W	L	ERA	G	GS	CG	SV	IP	H	R	ER	HR	BB	SO	AVG	vLH	vRH	K/9	BB/9
Bowman, Josh	R-R	6-2	195	9-9-88	0	2	3.74	14	0	0	0	22	29	16	9	2	5	23	.302	.211	.362	9.55	2.08
Brown, Jake	R-L	6-2	220	12-28-86	2	3	1.82	19	0	0	0	30	24	9	6	0	5	31	.218	.200	.229	9.40	1.52
Chitwood, Logan	R-R	6-1	185	3-28-89	1	1	4.66	9	0	0	1	10	12	5	5	1	4	6	.308	.375	.261	5.59	3.72
Christensen, Kyle	R-R	6-3	225	9-18-88	0	2	4.32	13	9	0	0	42	39	21	20	3	19	23	.250	.246	.253	4.97	4.10
Doolittle, Ryan	R-R	6-3	185	3-25-88	2	0	0.00	6	0	0	0	16	7	3	0	0	1	18	.127	.037	.214	10.13	0.56
Frankoff, Seth	R-R	6-5	200	8-27-88	3	2	3.30	7	7	0	0	30	31	13	11	0	13	31	.263	.240	.279	9.30	3.90
Griffin, A.J.	R-R	6-5	215	1-28-88	1	1	2.95	20	0	0	15	21	14	9	7	0	7	27	.184	.154	.200	11.39	2.95
Hart, Michael	R-R	6-1	210	2-9-87	1	1	1.06	13	0	0	6	17	21	4	2	0	5	27	.304	.313	.297	14.29	2.65
Hassebrock, Blake	R-R	6-5	205	7-15-89	0	1	5.12	14	0	0	0	19	25	11	11	0	8	18	.329	.302	.364	8.38	3.72
Jimenez, Deivi	R-R	6-3	205	12-30-89	4	4	3.54	12	12	0	0	61	61	28	24	5	13	48	.264	.283	.250	7.08	1.92
Joseph, Jonathan	R-R	6-1	180	5-17-88	1	1	2.68	8	0	0	0	40	37	17	12	0	14	35	.240	.274	.217	7.81	3.12
Long, Nathan	R-R	6-2	210	2-9-86	8	2	3.10	15	15	0	0	87	95	34	30	4	19	47	.284	.290	.280	4.86	1.97
McDaniel, Dan	R-R	6-3	220	4-18-88	1	1	3.64	20	1	0	0	30	22	20	12	1	16	32	.208	.132	.250	9.71	4.85
Quigley, Ryan	L-L	6-4	220	9-11-87	3	3	7.39	20	1	0	0	35	56	32	29	1	20	25	.361	.314	.385	6.37	5.09
Ramirez, Anvioris	L-L	6-1	165	3-10-88	2	6	3.41	14	14	0	0	63	63	31	24	6	17	55	.255	.250	.257	7.82	2.42
Tenholder, Daniel	R-R	6-2	198	7-6-88	4	0	1.86	24	0	0	2	39	26	12	8	0	11	38	.188	.193	.185	8.84	2.56
Thomson, Matt	R-R	6-4	195	3-22-88	3	2	2.15	12	9	0	0	46	35	13	11	0	8	61	.202	.273	.146	11.93	1.57
Thornton, Zack	R-R	6-6	220	5-19-88	2	2	4.39	15	0	0	0	27	33	21	13	2	8	29	.314	.295	.328	9.79	2.70
Tyson, Drew	R-R	6-5	195	8-11-89	0	0	1.00	6	0	0	0	9	10	1	1	0	4	8	.294	.400	.211	8.00	4.00
Vidal, Pedro	R-R	6-3	194	7-31-87	4	0	2.92	24	0	0	0	37	46	16	12	0	10	31	.303	.302	.303	7.54	2.43

Fielding

Catcher	PCT	G	PO	A	E	DP	PB
Affinito	1.000	1	5	3	0	0	0
Lipkin	.984	39	282	21	5	1	3
Nester	.993	14	131	9	1	2	1
Petitti	.991	26	206	25	2	3	2

First Base	PCT	G	PO	A	E	DP
Affinito	.982	5	50	5	1	7
Kirby-Jones	.981	67	572	37	12	54
Luis	.970	7	29	3	1	5

Second Base	PCT	G	PO	A	E	DP
Castillo	.923	10	21	27	4	3
Fabiaschi	1.000	16	21	33	0	10

Leyja	.949	25	44	85	7	13
Pineda	.985	25	57	75	2	14
Wells	1.000	3	8	14	0	6

Third Base	PCT	G	PO	A	E	DP
Castillo	.857	4	3	9	2	1
Fabiaschi	.500	1	0	1	1	0
Leyja	.853	11	7	22	5	1
Luis	.846	4	3	8	2	3
Thompson	.879	59	35	118	21	8

Shortstop	PCT	G	PO	A	E	DP
Castillo	.733	3	4	7	4	2
Fabiaschi	.962	7	14	11	1	5

Kirkland	.923	68	111	177	24	46

Outfield	PCT	G	PO	A	E	DP
Bercume	.991	53	105	9	1	3
Choice	.967	27	57	1	2	0
Crisotomo	1.000	12	13	1	0	0
Hurley	.955	13	19	2	1	0
Landaeta	.974	69	104	9	3	1
LeVier	1.000	5	16	0	0	0
Tripp	.977	16	42	0	1	0
Whitaker	.980	36	44	4	1	0

AZL ATHLETICS

ROOKIE

ARIZONA LEAGUE

Batting	B-T	HT	WT	DOB	AVG	vLH	vRH	G	AB	R	H	2B	3B	HR	RBI	BB	HBP	SH	SF	SO	SB	CS	SLG	OBP
Affinito, Chris	R-R	6-3	230	2-10-87	.286	.167	.318	9	28	9	8	1	0	3	10	10	0	0	0	12	0	0	.643	.474
Brazoban, Yeudy	R-R	6-1	185	9-9-88	.204	.318	.171	28	98	8	20	6	1	2	9	4	0	0	1	25	4	0	.347	.233
Buck, Travis	L-R	6-2	230	11-18-83	.188	.333	.154	6	16	3	3	1	0	0	4	5	0	0	0	4	0	0	.250	.381
Cabrera, Yordy	R-R	6-1	205	9-3-90	.188	.000	.214	5	16	3	3	1	0	0	0	4	0	0	0	5	0	0	.250	.350
Carter, Yusuf	R-R	6-2	205	2-6-85	.333	.500	.286	3	9	1	3	1	0	0	4	1	0	0	1	1	0	0	.444	.364
Chavez, Eric	L-R	6-1	215	12-7-77	.333	.000	.333	1	3	0	1	0	0	0	0	0	0	0	0	0	0	0	.333	.333
Choice, Michael	R-R	6-1	215	11-10-89	.000	.000	.000	3	7	1	0	0	0	0	2	0	0	0	0	2	0	0	.000	.222
Christian, Jason	L-R	6-3	170	6-16-87	.167	.500	.100	3	12	2	2	0	0	0	2	0	0	0	0	5	2	0	.167	.286
Clime, Neudy	R-R	5-11	185	2-1-89	.278	.231	.290	35	133	22	37	6	2	1	19	9	1	2	0	33	9	1	.376	.329
Consigli, Royce	L-R	6-2	205	9-7-91	.340	.290	.352	41	156	25	53	12	4	1	31	20	0	0	4	33	4	3	.487	.406
De La Cruz, Jonatan	R-R	6-0	160	5-28-88	.228	.185	.238	45	149	18	34	7	1	0	17	11	4	3	1	40	2	0	.289	.297
Galarraga, Joel	R-R	5-11	185	3-20-82	.197	.231	.188	19	61	8	12	2	0	0	5	7	1	0	1	18	3	0	.230	.286
Garcia, Elvis	R-R	6-2	178	11-8-89	.197	.160	.206	45	132	21	26	3	2	1	9	12	4	3	2	28	4	3	.273	.275
Jackson, Conor	R-R	6-2	215	5-7-82	.000	.000	.000	3	7	0	0	0	0	0	1	0	0	0	1	2	0	0	.000	.000
LeVier, Mitch	L-L	5-11	185	1-12-88	.200	.333	.188	10	35	6	7	3	1	0	4	3	0	0	0	11	0	0	.343	.263
Lewis, Chad	R-R	6-3	200	12-10-91	.231	.500	.182	4	13	5	3	0	0	0	3	3	0	0	0	5	0	0	.231	.375
Lopez, Diomes	R-R	6-2	195	11-30-88	.266	.318	.253	36	109	11	29	11	0	1	12	12	4	1	0	39	0	1	.394	.360
Marte, Miguel	R-R	6-3	230	8-29-89	.230	.214	.235	52	204	21	47	9	0	4	27	4	6	1	1	73	1	0	.333	.265
Martinez, Hiram	B-R	6-1	143	9-30-92	.188	.389	.109	26	64	6	12	2	0	0	4	8	0	1	0	17	1	0	.219	.278
Pan, Zhi Fang	B-R	6-1	170	11-12-90	.331	.387	.317	43	157	31	52	9	4	0	11	13	1	1	0	24	3	4	.439	.386
Peralta, Jensi	R-R	6-2	180	7-2-91	.223	.190	.232	32	103	11	23	5	1	0	8	4	0	0	0	38	0	1	.291	.252
Pineda, Ryan	R-R	5-11	180	4-17-89	.143	.000	.182	4	14	2	2	0	0	0	0	1	0	0	0	6	0	0	.143	.333
Ramsey, Rashad	L-L	6-0	175	5-10-92	.152	.143	.154	25	66	11	10	0	1	0	4	4	0	0	1	20	6	0	.182	.197
Rojas, Kelvin	R-R	6-2	188	8-7-89	.216	.214	.216	16	51	5	11	2	0	0	8	6	0	1	0	11	1	0	.255	.298
Shaw, Anthione	R-R	6-1	187	8-22-87	.167	.071	.206	25	48	6	8	1	0	0	2	9	0	0	0	21	3	0	.229	.298
Shipman, Aaron	L-L	6-0	175	1-27-92	.118	.250	.077	4	17	2	2	0	0	0	2	0	0	0	0	6	3	0	.118	.118
Soto, Ramon	R-R	6-2	190	11-3-87	.275	.278	.274	28	102	13	28	7	1	2	14	7	3	0	2	27	1	0	.422	.339
Thomas, David	B-R	5-11	180	7-29-86	.357	.000	.385	3	14	4	5	1	0	0	4	1	0	0	0	7	1	0	.571	.400
Tripp, Jordan	R-R	6-4	215	10-27-89	.261	.429	.231	13	46	8	12	3	1	1	7	4	2	0	0	16	0	0	.435	.346
Weeks, Jemile	B-R	5-9	170	1-26-87	.306	.778	.148	10	36	9	11	2	1	0	1	7	1	0	0	4	5	1	.417	.432
Whitaker, Josh	R-R	6-3	235	2-8-89	.333	.500	.290	10	39	4	13	6	0	0	4	2	0	0	0	7	1	0	.487	.366

Pitching	B-T	HT	WT	DOB	W	L	ERA	G	GS	CG	SV	IP	H	R	ER	HR	BB	SO	AVG	vLH	vRH	K/9	BB/9
Adames, Joselito	R-R	6-3	175	10-26-88	2	4	5.26	15	11	0	0	53	56	37	31	0	18	59	.257	.274	.246	10.02	3.06
Anderson, Brett	L-L	6-4	235	2-1-88	0	0	3.00	2	2	0	0	6	11	2	2	0	0	6	.458	.857	.294	9.00	0.00

Name	B-T	HT	WT	DOB	W	L	ERA	G	GS	CG	SV	IP	H	R	ER	HR	BB	SO	AVG	vLH	vRH	K/9	BB/9
Avila, Andres	R-R	6-0	185	6-20-90	0	2	5.65	12	0	0	2	14	13	12	9	1	6	16	.232	.053	.324	10.05	3.77
Bailey, Andrew	R-R	6-5	215	3-30-89	0	0	4.38	7	0	0	0	12	9	11	6	0	11	11	.196	.294	.138	8.03	8.03
Bowman, Josh	R-R	6-2	195	9-9-88	0	0	0.00	1	0	0	0	1	0	0	0	0	0	0	.000	.000	.000	18.00	0.00
Chitwood, Logan	R-R	6-1	185	3-28-89	0	0	2.84	6	0	0	1	6	3	3	2	0	3	10	.136	.182	.091	14.21	4.26
DiNardo, Lenny	L-L	6-2	220	9-19-79	0	0	5.40	2	2	0	0	3	3	2	2	1	5	2	.231	.000	.273	5.40	13.50
Duran, Omar	L-L	6-3	209	2-26-90	3	1	2.01	14	2	0	0	40	33	20	9	0	17	54	.221	.269	.196	12.05	3.79
Frankoff, Seth	R-R	6-5	200	8-27-88	2	3	2.28	8	4	0	0	28	14	8	7	0	14	35	.146	.114	.164	11.39	4.55
Griffin, A.J.	R-R	6-5	215	1-28-88	0	0	0.00	4	0	0	0	5	1	0	0	0	0	6	.063	.000	.111	10.80	0.00
Hassebrock, Blake	R-R	6-5	205	7-15-89	0	0	10.80	3	1	0	0	3	6	6	4	0	1	7	.353	.167	.455	18.90	2.70
Hughes, Ryan	L-L	6-6	220	5-20-88	2	0	4.72	9	0	0	1	13	13	7	7	0	4	13	.265	.300	.256	8.78	2.70
Jennings, Jason	L-R	6-2	235	7-17-78	0	0	1.00	3	3	0	0	9	3	2	1	0	3	10	.097	.063	.133	10.00	3.00
Larsen, Aaron	R-L	6-1	190	3-1-87	5	2	2.89	14	4	0	0	37	25	18	12	3	10	31	.177	.262	.113	7.47	2.41
Macias, Jose	R-R	6-2	180	7-18-89	3	0	1.29	7	0	0	0	14	9	3	2	1	3	11	.188	.167	.208	7.07	1.93
Mederos, Chris	R-R	6-3	175	5-17-87	0	1	13.50	2	1	0	0	3	3	4	4	0	0	6	.273	.200	.333	20.25	0.00
Menna, J.C.	R-R	6-2	175	12-24-88	1	2	5.79	13	1	0	0	23	25	24	15	0	13	15	.263	.250	.270	5.79	5.01
Murphy, Sean	B-R	6-6	215	8-23-88	2	0	2.57	14	0	0	2	21	15	9	6	0	8	32	.190	.250	.164	13.71	3.43
Mye, Chaz	L-L	6-3	200	4-27-88	1	4	3.52	16	0	0	1	23	25	12	9	3	11	23	.263	.393	.209	9.00	4.30
Paez, Argenis	R-R	6-3	180	10-20-90	6	3	3.15	14	10	0	0	66	69	29	23	3	17	53	.268	.311	.251	7.26	2.33
Skaalen, Chris	R-R	6-4	190	3-9-88	0	0	8.68	9	0	0	0	9	20	13	9	0	5	8	.417	.500	.367	7.71	4.82
Thornton, Zack	R-R	6-6	220	5-19-88	0	0	0.00	3	0	0	0	3	2	0	0	0	2	2	.182	.333	.125	5.40	0.00
Tomko, Brett	R-R	6-4	220	4-7-73	0	1	6.23	2	2	0	0	9	13	8	6	4	0	14	.333	.227	.471	14.54	0.00
Tyson, Drew	R-R	6-5	195	8-11-89	1	0	1.33	13	0	0	1	27	21	4	4	0	3	41	.214	.297	.164	13.67	1.00
Urlaub, Jeff	L-L	6-2	160	4-24-87	1	0	2.39	15	0	0	2	26	23	10	7	0	3	26	.235	.231	.236	8.89	1.03
Vail, Tyler	R-R	6-1	187	11-3-91	0	2	3.13	13	10	0	0	32	26	14	11	1	8	29	.218	.236	.203	8.24	2.27
Ynoa, Michael	R-R	6-7	210	9-24-91	0	1	5.00	3	3	0	0	9	6	5	5	1	4	11	.188	.167	.214	11.00	4.00

Fielding

Catcher	PCT	G	PO	A	E	DP	PB
Affinito	1.000	2	11	0	0	0	0
Carter	1.000	2	6	3	0	0	1
Galarraga	.984	13	115	7	2	0	1
Lopez	.990	35	280	31	3	2	3
Marte	.917	2	11	0	1	0	2
Soto	.982	12	98	14	2	0	3

First Base	PCT	G	PO	A	E	DP
Affinito	1.000	4	37	2	0	6
De La Cruz	1.000	11	51	1	0	2
Marte	.985	49	421	34	7	31

Second Base	PCT	G	PO	A	E	DP
Clime	.927	29	60	79	11	14
De La Cruz	.909	8	8	12	2	2
Martinez	.727	3	4	4	3	1
Pan	.918	12	12	33	4	6

	PCT	G	PO	A	E	DP
Peralta	.800	1	1	3	1	1
Pineda	.864	4	10	9	3	2
Weeks	.958	8	6	17	1	4

Third Base	PCT	G	PO	A	E	DP
Christian	.875	3	2	5	1	0
Clime	.700	4	2	5	3	0
De La Cruz	.965	32	20	62	3	4
Lewis	.667	4	2	4	3	0
Pan	1.000	1	0	2	0	0
Peralta	.789	17	4	26	8	2

Shortstop	PCT	G	PO	A	E	DP
Brazoban	—	1	0	0	0	0
Cabrera	1.000	5	4	15	0	2
Martinez	.859	21	20	47	11	7
Pan	.905	27	27	87	12	8
Peralta	.867	13	15	24	6	6

Outfield	PCT	G	PO	A	E	DP
Brazoban	.864	18	19	0	3	0
Buck	1.000	5	4	1	0	0
Choice	1.000	2	3	0	0	0
Consigli	.955	40	59	4	3	2
Garcia	1.000	43	56	6	0	1
Jackson	1.000	2	1	0	0	0
LeVier	1.000	10	14	0	0	0
Ramsey	.957	19	21	1	1	1
Rojas	1.000	13	16	0	0	0
Shaw	.944	21	15	2	1	1
Shipman	1.000	4	5	0	0	0
Thomas	1.000	3	3	0	0	0
Tripp	1.000	13	13	0	0	0
Whitaker	1.000	7	7	0	0	0

DSL ATHLETICS   ROOKIE
DOMINICAN SUMMER LEAGUE

Batting	B-T	HT	WT	DOB	AVG	vLH	vRH	G	AB	R	H	2B	3B	HR	RBI	BB	HBP	SH	SF	SO	SB	CS	SLG	OBP
Baez, Luis	R-R	6-3	165	5-24-91	.282	.303	.277	52	170	24	48	15	1	4	23	8	4	3	1	30	10	5	.453	.328
Blanco, Charli	R-R	6-0	155	2-23-91	.211	.059	.244	37	95	13	20	6	1	1	10	8	5	3	3	36	5	2	.326	.297
Contreras, Franklin	R-R	6-2	165	6-10-90	.284	.182	.304	25	67	10	19	3	1	2	11	13	0	0	0	10	4	1	.448	.400
De La Rosa, Anderson	R-R	6-1	180	8-12-91	.182	.158	.189	61	181	18	33	4	1	2	17	23	4	3	3	47	7	7	.249	.284
De Leon, Abraham	R-R	6-0	194	2-20-89	.209	.357	.170	26	67	8	14	4	0	0	7	10	3	1	0	12	0	1	.269	.338
Ledezma, Diego	R-R	6-5	170	8-14-90	.164	.188	.154	20	55	4	9	1	0	1	3	1	1	1	0	9	0	2	.236	.193
Marte, Miguel	R-R	6-3	230	8-29-91	.270	.167	.290	11	37	7	10	2	0	2	12	5	3	0	0	10	1	0	.486	.400
Martinez, Wilman	R-R	5-11	204	1-13-93	.152	.200	.141	33	79	6	12	1	0	0	3	18	3	2	0	22	3	3	.165	.330
Mateo, Reynaldo	R-R	5-9	209	7-16-89	.236	.258	.230	56	157	19	37	9	0	1	14	32	8	0	3	36	6	1	.312	.385
Osorio, Luis	B-R	6-1	155	4-5-91	.227	.273	.211	57	172	29	39	12	1	1	16	31	3	0	3	40	15	4	.326	.349
Penalo, Rodolfo	B-R	5-7	130	8-27-92	.243	.200	.256	46	103	12	25	2	1	0	8	18	3	2	0	18	12	8	.282	.371
Rojas, Kelvin	R-R	6-2	188	8-7-89	.273	.000	.273	3	11	1	3	0	0	1	2	1	0	1	0	0	0	0	.545	.333
Rosario, Jose	R-R	6-5	219	9-2-90	.241	.333	.219	51	158	16	38	7	0	1	16	20	4	2	4	23	5	2	.304	.333
Santana, Gabriel	R-R	6-0	165	8-23-92	.234	.114	.275	45	137	24	32	3	0	0	5	13	9	1	2	25	2	5	.255	.335
Sayegh, Jose	R-R	6-2	180	12-7-91	.183	.320	.154	54	142	20	26	8	1	0	11	25	5	3	1	51	2	2	.254	.324
Solano, Wilfredo	R-R	6-2	185	1-15-93	.179	.296	.155	45	156	22	28	2	0	0	10	30	1	1	1	30	6	2	.192	.314
Sosa, Alfredo	R-R	5-10	189	1-18-93	.192	.158	.204	33	73	8	14	1	0	1	6	11	0	4	2	20	4	2	.247	.291
Soto, Michael	R-R	6-3	195	11-17-91	.238	.186	.251	64	210	25	50	8	1	5	36	35	3	0	6	63	2	4	.357	.346
Trinidad, Victor	R-R	6-0	173	12-23-90	—	.000	.000	5	0	1	0	0	0	0	0	0	0	0	0	0	0	0	—	—
Zarraga, Jonesy	R-R	6-1	170	6-3-92	.233	.143	.261	10	30	6	7	0	1	0	2	4	2	1	0	7	3	0	.300	.361

Pitching	B-T	HT	WT	DOB	W	L	ERA	G	GS	CG	SV	IP	H	R	ER	HR	BB	SO	AVG	vLH	vRH	K/9	BB/9
Astacio, Andres	R-R	6-3	180	8-20-90	1	2	3.69	10	6	0	0	39	39	19	16	0	6	28	.262	.222	.270	6.46	1.38
Azor, Jose	R-R	6-2	185	10-12-88	0	1	0.95	6	4	0	1	19	20	6	2	0	5	12	.274	.105	.333	5.68	2.37
Bautista, William	L-L	6-4	173	8-20-91	1	3	7.64	17	1	0	1	35	50	32	30	2	21	15	.340	.400	.336	3.82	5.35
Benzant, Leonel	R-R	6-6	213	12-20-91	1	2	7.11	7	3	0	0	19	17	15	15	1	24	11	.250	.385	.218	5.21	11.37

Name	T-B	Ht	Wt	DOB	W	L	ERA	G													AVG	vL	vR		
Castillo, Jose	R-R	6-2	185	2-22-91	2	2	4.28	9	6	0	0	27	20	20	13	1	25	27	.208	.174	.219	8.89	8.23
De Los Santos, Robinson	R-R	6-3	170	2-21-90	4	2	1.73	14	12	0	0	62	36	13	12	0	22	77	.162	.167	.161	11.12	3.18
Fortuna, Anderson	R-R	6-4	200	10-20-89	1	2	2.82	11	5	0	0	38	29	15	12	0	19	26	.209	.167	.215	6.10	4.46
Jose, Luis	R-R	6-4	195	9-26-87	5	2	2.76	19	0	0	4	42	34	17	13	1	14	44	.221	.200	.227	9.35	2.98
Juma, Alexis	R-R	6-1	180	5-23-88	1	1	2.25	4	4	0	0	20	14	6	5	0	4	19	.206	.000	.275	8.55	1.80
Merestil, Rene	L-L	6-3	185	12-30-86	3	6	9.17	13	9	0	0	36	41	45	37	0	33	46	.291	.250	.292	11.39	8.17
Navas, Carlos	R-R	6-1	170	8-13-92	2	2	1.66	13	5	0	0	43	30	9	8	0	15	30	.201	.250	.186	6.23	3.12
Nolasco, Alex	L-L	6-4	190	9-11-90	2	0	3.38	12	0	0	0	19	9	9	7	0	28	15	.141	.250	.133	7.23	13.50
Perez, Cristhian	R-R	6-2	180	9-13-91	2	2	5.68	18	0	0	2	32	38	25	20	3	15	29	.295	.226	.316	8.24	4.26
Ramirez, Benito	R-R	6-5	180	9-23-88	0	0	21.94	5	0	0	0	5	9	13	13	0	10	2	.429	.429	.429	3.38	16.88
Rodriguez, Kevin	L-L	6-4	190	6-26-91	0	2	6.75	6	4	0	0	11	10	10	8	2	5	10	.263	.286	.258	8.44	4.22
Zapata, Roberto	R-R	6-4	171	6-28-89	0	1	13.50	3	0	0	0	3	8	5	5	0	3	3	.444	.333	.467	8.10	8.10

Fielding

Catcher	PCT	G	PO	A	E	DP	PB
De Leon	.959	22	120	22	6	0	5
Ledezma	1.000	12	51	5	0	0	1
Mateo	.976	45	270	56	8	3	9
Ramirez	1.000	12	31	2	0	1	7

First Base	PCT	G	PO	A	E	DP
Contreras	—	1	0	0	0	0
Marte	1.000	10	69	8	0	11
Martinez	—	1	0	0	0	0
Osorio	1.000	3	1	0	0	0
Rosario	.991	48	411	18	4	35
Soto	.992	18	123	5	1	4

Second Base	PCT	G	PO	A	E	DP
Baez	1.000	5	8	5	0	1

	PCT	G	PO	A	E	DP	PB
Blanco	—	1	0	0	0	0	
Contreras	.918	18	27	29	5	7	
Osorio	1.000	15	27	26	0	7	
Penalo	.951	40	62	55	6	14	
Santana	1.000	14	31	26	0	6	
Solano	1.000	1	0	1	0	0	

Third Base	PCT	G	PO	A	E	DP
Baez	.946	14	12	23	2	4
Martinez	.872	27	22	60	12	2
Santana	1.000	8	9	25	0	1
Soto	.917	24	26	62	8	8

Shortstop	PCT	G	PO	A	E	DP
Baez	.923	2	5	7	1	2

	PCT	G	PO	A	E	DP
Contreras	1.000	2	3	2	0	1
Osorio	.925	12	13	24	3	3
Santana	.978	25	28	62	2	11
Solano	.945	43	51	103	9	18

Outfield	PCT	G	PO	A	E	DP
Baez	.912	22	26	5	3	1
Blanco	1.000	35	49	4	0	1
De La Rosa	.956	60	82	4	4	1
De Leon	—	1	0	0	0	0
Osorio	.931	20	23	4	2	0
Rojas	1.000	3	5	0	0	0
Sayegh	.960	54	85	11	4	2
Sosa	1.000	30	48	1	0	0
Zarraga	1.000	10	18	1	0	0

Philadelphia Phillies

SEASON IN A SENTENCE: The Phillies started slowly and had plenty of injuries, as one would expect for a team with one regular under the age of 30, but went 50-25 in the second half to sprint to the majors' best record—a first for the franchise—before losing in six games to the Giants in the National League Championship Series.

HIGH POINT: The offseason centered around acquiring Roy Halladay—to the point of dealing Cliff Lee away, theoretically to replenish the farm system. Halladay performed as hoped, earning BA's Major League Player of the Year Award while pitching a perfect game on May 29 at Florida. He provided another highlight with a no-hitter against the Reds in the Division Series opener—the first postseason no-hitter since Don Larsen's 1956 World Series perfect game.

LOW POINT: Injuries to Jimmy Rollins, Chase Utley and Ryan Howard, among others, upset the Phillies' offense all season. Philadelphia had enough firepower to rank second in the NL in scoring but the offense was inconsistent, and the Giants' superior starting pitching shut down the Phillies' bats in October. Philly hit .216 in the NLCS, with Ryan Howard striking out looking to end the series. He struck out 12 times in 22 at-bats, though his .900 OPS in the series was bested only by Jayson Werth.

NOTABLE ROOKIES: Righthander David Herndon, a Rule 5 draft pickup from the Angels, was the only player to exhaust his eligibility this season. He was a long reliever who rarely was used in high-leverage situations. Top prospect Domonic Brown came up in late July and had two hits in his debut but got just four starts after Aug. 11.

KEY TRANSACTIONS: The two trades involving Lee and Halladay began an eventful year in Philadelphia. The Phillies acquired a third ace to join Halladay and Cole Hamels when they acquired Roy Oswalt from Houston in late July, giving up top 2009 rookie J.A. Happ and minor leaguers Jonathan Villar and Anthony Gose.

DOWN ON THE FARM: Despite all their trades in the last two years, the Phillies still showed talent on the farm, including Brown. Most of their talent is at the lower levels, though, including a strong Lakewood club that went 84-55 and won its second straight low Class A South Atlantic League championship. Triple-A Lehigh Valley struggled again, posting its second sub-60-win season in the last three.

OPENING DAY PAYROLL: $141.9 million (4th)

PLAYERS OF THE YEAR

MAJOR LEAGUE	MINOR LEAGUE
Roy Halladay rhp	**Domonic Brown** of
21-10, 2.44	(Double-A/Triple-A)
Threw perfect game,	.327/.391/.589
2nd playoff no-hitter	22 2B, 20 HR, 17 SB

ORGANIZATION LEADERS

BATTING		*Minimum 250 at-bats
MAJORS		
*AVG	Carlos Ruiz	.302
*OPS	Jayson Werth	.921
HR	Ryan Howard	31
RBI	Ryan Howard	108
MINORS		
*AVG	Matt Rizzotti, Reading/Clearwater/L.V.	.343
*OBP	Matt Rizzotti, Reading/Clearwater/L.V.	.430
*SLG	Tagg Bozied, Reading	.631
R	Jiwan James, Lakewood	85
H	Jiwan James, Lakewood	150
TB	Cody Overbeck, Clearwater/Reading	240
2B	Darin Ruf, Lakewood/Clearwater	41
3B	Anthony Gose, Clearwater	11
HR	Tagg Bozied, Reading	27
RBI	Tagg Bozied, Reading	92
BB	Andy Tracy, Lehigh Valley	68
SO	Anthony Hewitt, Lakewood	158
SB	Rich Thompson, Reading/Lehigh Valley	41

PITCHING		†Minimum 75 innings
MAJORS		
W	Roy Halladay	21
†ERA	Roy Oswalt	1.74
SO	Roy Halladay	219
MINORS		
W	Three tied at	12
L	Heitor Correa, Clearwater	14
†ERA	Jesus Sanchez, Clearwater	2.99
G	Scott Mathieson, Lehigh Valley	54
GS	Brian Mazone, Lehigh Valley	28
SV	Scott Mathieson, Lehigh Valley	26
IP	Drew Naylor, Reading	167
BB	Trevor May, Clearwater/Lakewood	81
SO	Trevor May, Clearwater/Lakewood	182
†AVG	Trevor May, Clearwater/Lakewood	.213

General Manager: Ruben Amaro. **Farm Director:** Steve Noworyta. **Scouting Director:** Marti Wolever.

Class	Team	League	W	L	PCT	Finish*	Manager(s)
Majors	Philadelphia Phillies	National	97	65	.599	1st (16)	Charlie Manuel
Triple-A	Lehigh Valley IronPigs	International	58	86	.403	13th (14)	Dave Huppert
Double-A	Reading Phillies	Eastern	69	72	.489	8th (12)	Steve Roadcap
High A	Clearwater Threshers	Florida State	67	72	.482	8th (12)	Dusty Wathan
Low A	Lakewood BlueClaws	South Atlantic	84	55	.604	†1st (14)	Mark Parent
Short-season	Williamsport Crosscutters	New York-Penn	43	33	.566	4th (14)	Chris Truby
Rookie	GCL Phillies	Gulf Coast	32	24	.571	†3rd (15)	Rolando de Armas
Overall 2010 Minor League Record			353	342	.508	12th (30)	

*Finish in overall standings (No. of teams in league). †League champion.

ORGANIZATION STATISTICS

PHILADELPHIA PHILLIES

NATIONAL LEAGUE

Batting	B-T	HT	WT	DOB	AVG	vLH	vRH	G	AB	R	H	2B	3B	HR	RBI	BB	HBP	SH	SF	SO	SB	CS	SLG	OBP
Bocock, Brian	R-R	5-11	185	3-9-85	.000	.000	.000	6	5	2	0	0	0	0	0	0	0	0	0	3	0	0	.000	.000
Brown, Domonic	L-L	6-5	200	9-3-87	.210	.077	.245	35	62	8	13	3	0	2	13	5	0	0	3	24	2	1	.355	.257
Castro, Juan	R-R	5-11	190	6-20-72	.198	.233	.188	54	126	7	25	5	0	0	13	7	0	1	2	23	0	1	.238	.237
2-team total (1 Los Angeles)					.194	—	—	55	129	7	25	5	0	0	13	8	0	1	2	25	0	1	.233	.237
Dobbs, Greg	L-R	6-1	205	7-2-78	.196	.188	.197	88	163	13	32	7	0	5	15	12	0	1	0	39	1	1	.331	.251
Francisco, Ben	R-R	6-1	190	10-24-81	.268	.284	.253	88	179	24	48	13	0	6	28	14	2	1	1	35	8	0	.441	.327
Gload, Ross	L-L	6-1	190	4-5-76	.281	.273	.282	94	128	16	36	8	0	6	22	8	1	1	0	15	1	0	.484	.328
Hoover, Paul	R-R	6-1	220	4-14-76	.227	.300	.167	9	22	6	5	2	0	0	2	3	0	0	0	5	0	0	.318	.320
Howard, Ryan	L-L	6-4	255	11-19-79	.276	.264	.283	143	550	87	152	23	5	31	108	59	8	0	3	157	1	1	.505	.353
Ibanez, Raul	L-R	6-2	225	6-2-72	.275	.268	.277	155	561	75	154	37	5	16	83	68	0	0	7	108	4	3	.444	.349
Mayberry Jr., John	R-R	6-6	235	12-21-83	.333	.500	.167	11	12	4	4	0	0	2	6	1	0	0	0	4	0	1	.833	.385
Polanco, Placido	R-R	5-10	190	10-10-75	.298	.280	.305	132	554	76	165	27	2	6	52	32	7	1	8	47	5	0	.386	.339
Ransom, Cody	R-R	6-2	190	2-17-76	.190	.194	.182	22	42	6	8	0	0	2	5	3	0	1	0	11	1	0	.333	.244
Rollins, Jimmy	B-R	5-8	170	11-27-78	.243	.297	.218	88	350	48	85	16	3	8	41	40	1	0	3	32	17	1	.374	.320
Ruiz, Carlos	R-R	5-10	215	1-22-79	.302	.327	.291	121	371	43	112	28	1	8	53	55	6	1	0	54	0	1	.447	.400
Sardinha, Dane	R-R	6-0	215	4-8-79	.205	.222	.200	13	39	5	8	2	0	3	8	1	0	0	0	13	0	0	.487	.225
Schneider, Brian	L-R	6-1	210	11-26-76	.240	.056	.271	47	125	17	30	4	1	4	15	19	1	2	0	25	0	0	.384	.345
Sweeney, Mike	R-R	6-3	225	7-22-73	.231	.219	.250	26	52	10	12	2	0	2	8	5	1	0	0	7	1	0	.385	.310
Utley, Chase	L-R	6-1	190	12-17-78	.275	.294	.266	115	425	75	117	20	2	16	65	63	18	0	5	63	13	2	.445	.387
Valdez, Wilson	R-R	5-11	170	5-20-78	.258	.242	.265	111	333	37	86	16	3	4	35	21	2	7	0	43	7	0	.360	.306
Victorino, Shane	B-R	5-9	190	11-30-80	.259	.321	.235	147	587	84	152	26	10	18	69	53	7	0	1	79	34	6	.429	.327
Werth, Jayson	R-R	6-5	220	5-20-79	.296	.287	.300	156	554	106	164	46	2	27	85	82	5	1	0	9	147	13	3	.532	.388

Pitching	B-T	HT	WT	DOB	W	L	ERA	G	GS	CG	SV	IP	H	R	ER	HR	BB	SO	AVG	vLH	vRH	K/9	BB/9
Baez, Danys	R-R	6-3	225	9-10-77	3	4	5.48	51	0	0	0	48	55	31	29	6	23	28	.301	.306	.297	5.29	4.34
Bastardo, Antonio	L-L	5-11	195	9-21-85	2	0	4.34	25	0	0	0	19	19	9	9	1	9	26	.253	.200	.300	12.54	4.34
Blanton, Joe	R-R	6-3	245	12-11-80	9	6	4.82	29	28	0	0	176	206	104	94	27	43	134	.291	.266	.314	6.87	2.20
Carpenter, Drew	R-R	6-3	240	5-18-85	0	0	9.00	1	0	0	0	3	5	3	3	1	0	2	.385	.600	.250	6.00	0.00
Contreras, Jose	R-R	6-4	255	12-6-71	6	4	3.34	67	0	0	4	57	53	22	21	5	16	57	.255	.253	.256	9.05	2.54
Durbin, Chad	R-R	6-2	225	12-3-77	4	1	3.80	64	0	0	0	69	63	29	29	7	27	63	.246	.324	.195	8.26	3.54
Figueroa, Nelson	R-R	6-1	180	5-18-74	2	1	3.46	13	1	0	1	26	20	10	10	1	9	15	.220	.225	.216	5.19	3.12
2-team total (18 Houston)					7	4	3.29	31	11	0	1	93	84	38	34	10	34	73	—	—	—	7.06	3.29
Halladay, Roy	R-R	6-6	230	5-14-77	21	10	2.44	33	33	9	0	251	231	74	68	24	30	219	.245	.259	.231	7.86	1.08
Hamels, Cole	L-L	6-3	190	12-27-83	12	11	3.06	33	33	1	0	209	185	74	71	26	61	211	.237	.196	.240	9.10	2.63
Happ, J.A.	L-L	6-6	200	10-19-82	1	0	1.76	3	3	0	0	15	13	4	3	1	12	9	.232	.313	.200	5.28	7.04
2-team total (13 Houston)					6	4	3.40	16	16	1	0	87	73	37	33	8	47	70	—	—	—	7.21	4.84
Herndon, David	R-R	6-5	230	9-4-85	1	3	4.30	47	0	0	0	52	67	27	25	2	17	39	.321	.328	.317	4.99	2.92
Kendrick, Kyle	R-R	6-3	215	8-26-84	11	10	4.73	33	31	1	0	181	199	103	95	26	49	84	.283	.312	.254	4.18	2.44
Lidge, Brad	R-R	6-5	210	12-23-76	1	1	2.96	50	0	0	27	46	32	16	15	5	24	52	.194	.214	.173	10.25	4.73
Madson, Ryan	L-R	6-6	200	8-28-80	6	2	2.55	55	0	0	5	53	42	16	15	4	13	64	.212	.217	.208	10.87	2.21
Mathieson, Scott	R-R	6-3	190	2-27-84	0	0	10.80	2	0	0	0	2	5	3	2	0	2	2	.556	.500	.600	10.80	10.80
Moyer, Jamie	L-L	6-0	185	11-18-62	9	9	4.84	19	19	2	0	112	103	64	60	20	20	63	.240	.194	.249	5.08	1.61
Oswalt, Roy	R-R	6-0	190	8-29-77	7	1	1.74	13	12	1	0	83	53	18	16	6	21	73	.186	.205	.170	7.95	2.29
2-team total (20 Houston)					13	13	2.76	33	32	2	0	212	162	70	65	19	55	193	—	—	—	8.21	2.34
Robertson, Nate	R-L	6-2	225	9-3-77	0	0	54.00	2	0	0	0	1	5	6	6	1	2	2	.625	.000	.625	18.00	18.00
2-team total (19 Florida)					6	8	5.95	21	18	0	0	101	115	76	67	12	42	63	—	—	—	5.60	3.73
Romero, J.C.	B-L	5-11	215	6-4-76	1	0	3.68	60	0	0	3	37	30	17	15	3	29	28	.222	.217	.231	6.87	7.12
Worley, Vance	R-R	6-2	230	9-25-87	1	1	1.38	5	2	0	0	13	8	2	2	1	4	12	.178	.100	.240	8.31	2.77
Zagurski, Mike	L-L	6-0	220	1-27-83	0	0	10.29	8	0	0	0	7	8	8	8	1	5	11	.320	.308	.333	14.14	6.43

Fielding																
Catcher	PCT	G	PO	A	E	DP	PB	Ruiz		.993	118	814	60	6	7	4		Schneider		.993	46	257	17	2	4	1
Hoover	.957	9	42	2	2	0	0	Sardinha		1.000	12	84	4	0	0	1

First Base	PCT	G	PO	A	E	DP
Dobbs	1.000	2	14	1	0	0
Gload	1.000	18	92	6	0	9
Howard	.990	139	1266	59	14	117
Ibanez	1.000	1	3	0	0	0
Ransom	1.000	3	15	1	0	2
Sweeney	.982	14	104	6	2	8

Second Base	PCT	G	PO	A	E	DP
Castro	.926	7	12	13	2	5
Polanco	1.000	12	15	37	0	7
Ransom	1.000		6	5	0	3
Utley	.981	114	228	347	11	86
Valdez	.993	42	57	91	1	20

Third Base	PCT	G	PO	A	E	DP
Castro	.917	11	1	10	1	1
Dobbs	.898	36	16	37	6	3
Polanco	.986	123	88	258	5	32
Ransom	.938	9	6	9	1	2
Valdez	1.000	7	3	12	0	0

Shortstop	PCT	G	PO	A	E	DP
Bocock	1.000	6	3	2	0	1
Castro	.973	32	31	78	3	15
Rollins	.982	87	102	227	6	53
Valdez	.991	59	83	148	2	35

Outfield	PCT	G	PO	A	E	DP
Brown	.967	15	28	1	1	0
Dobbs	—	1	0	0	0	0
Francisco	1.000	45	60	3	0	0
Gload	.909	8	10	0	1	0
Ibanez	.991	145	212	4	2	1
Mayberry Jr.	1.000	4	2	0	0	0
Oswalt	1.000	1	1	0	0	0
Victorino	.995	143	360	11	2	4
Werth	.987	153	293	8	4	2

LEHIGH VALLEY IRONPIGS   TRIPLE-A
INTERNATIONAL LEAGUE

Batting	B-T	HT	WT	DOB	AVG	vLH	vRH	G	AB	R	H	2B	3B	HR	RBI	BB	HBP	SH	SF	SO	SB	CS	SLG	OBP
Aguila, Chris	R-R	5-11	200	2-23-79	.199	.222	.189	48	151	10	30	9	0	3	11	9	0	0	1	43	0	1	.318	.242
Bocock, Brian	R-R	5-11	185	3-9-85	.226	.277	.212	120	380	37	86	11	3	4	31	49	1	4	5	88	13	6	.303	.313
Brown, Domonic	L-L	6-5	200	9-3-87	.346	.311	.371	28	107	15	37	6	1	5	21	8	1	0	2	25	1	1	.561	.390
Chavez, Ozzie	B-R	6-1	175	7-13-83	.219	.188	.234	55	201	21	44	5	0	4	14	12	1	4	3	38	3	0	.303	.263
DeRenne, Keoni	B-R	5-7	170	4-30-79	.250	.000	.300	6	12	0	3	0	0	0	2	0	0	0	1	0	0		.250	.357
Dobbs, Greg	L-R	6-0	205	7-2-78	.210	.278	.182	16	62	10	13	3	1	2	9	7	0	0	1	12	2	0	.387	.286
Dorta, Melvin	R-R	5-11	160	1-15-82	.287	.321	.275	98	331	40	95	14	1	4	29	19	1	6	5	29	7	5	.372	.323
Duffy, Chris	L-L	5-9	185	4-20-80	.243	.253	.240	91	346	47	84	18	4	5	34	25	8	0	3	99	12	4	.361	.306
Hoover, Paul	R-R	6-1	220	4-14-76	.247	.300	.231	77	255	23	63	13	3	2	21	26	4	1	0	65	0	0	.345	.326
Mayberry Jr., John	R-R	6-6	235	12-21-83	.267	.350	.239	128	495	75	132	25	1	15	65	39	8	1	4	111	20	3	.412	.328
Maza, Luis	R-R	5-8	195	6-22-80	.220	.270	.206	51	168	18	37	5	1	0	10	16	1	2	2	25	1	0	.262	.289
Ransom, Cody	R-R	6-2	190	2-17-76	.261	.221	.271	110	394	58	103	25	1	18	63	40	4	1	4	108	5	2	.467	.333
Rizzotti, Matt	L-L	6-5	235	12-24-85	.200	.222	.185	17	45	0	9	3	0	0	4	6	1	0	0	14	0	0	.267	.308
Ruiz, Carlos	R-R	5-10	215	1-22-79	.000	.000	.000	1	2	0	0	0	0	0	0	0	1	0	0	1	0	0	.000	.333
Sardinha, Dane	R-R	6-0	215	4-8-79	.207	.146	.224	67	222	24	46	8	0	5	24	13	4	1	2	68	0	0	.311	.261
Schneider, Brian	L-R	6-1	210	11-26-76	.000	.000	.000	3	8	0	0	0	0	0	0	1	0	0	0	0	0	0	.000	.111
Sellers, Neil	R-R	6-0	195	4-3-82	.236	.262	.229	122	394	32	93	25	1	6	39	37	4	1	4	81	0	3	.350	.305
Suomi, John	L-R	5-11	200	10-5-80	.245	.125	.268	18	49	2	12	0	0	1	5	2	1	1	0	7	1	1	.306	.288
Taveras, Willy	L-R	6-0	180	12-25-81	.208	.158	.221	39	86	16	20	5	1	0	3	4	2	2	0	18	9	0	.271	.255
2-team total (17 Gwinnett)					.181	—	—	40	138	16	25	5	1	0	4	8	3	2	0	24	13	1	.232	.242
Thompson, Rich	L-R	6-3	185	4-23-79	.279	.150	.317	99	348	47	97	14	4	4	31	24	5	8	3	55	28	4	.376	.332
Tracy, Andy	L-R	6-3	230	12-11-73	.275	.286	.272	125	425	64	117	23	3	21	80	68	2	0	6	114	2	1	.492	.373
Valdez, Wilson	R-R	5-11	170	5-24-78	.455	.429	.467	5	22	2	10	0	0	3	5	3	0	1	0	3	2	2	.455	.520
Victorino, Shane	B-R	5-9	190	11-30-80	.667	.667	.000	2	6	1	4	0	1	0	3	0	0	0	0	0	0	0	1.500	.667
Wise, Dewayne	L-L	5-11	195	2-24-78	.270	.103	.315	37	137	17	37	11	5	4	18	8	1	0	0	27	2	2	.511	.315

Pitching	B-T	HT	WT	DOB	W	L	ERA	G	GS	CG	SV	IP	H	R	ER	HR	BB	SO	AVG	vLH	vRH	K/9	BB/9
Anderson, Jason	L-R	6-0	188	6-9-79	0	3	4.35	9	0	0	1	10	13	6	5	0	4	5	.302	.200	.391	4.35	3.48
Baez, Danys	R-R	6-3	225	9-10-77	0	0	9.00	1	0	0	0	2	1	1	1	0	0	0	.400	.000	.400	0.00	0.00
Bastardo, Antonio	L-L	5-11	195	9-21-85	1	1	2.08	20	0	0	3	17	12	4	4	0	6	27	.190	.212	.167	14.02	3.12
Bump, Nate	R-R	6-2	195	7-24-76	8	4	3.35	20	20	0	0	107	123	47	40	7	25	54	.293	.326	.264	4.53	2.10
Carpenter, Drew	R-R	6-3	240	5-18-85	8	11	4.05	27	27	0	0	151	152	75	68	18	54	116	.263	.230	.290	6.91	3.22
Cisco, Mike	R-R	5-11	190	5-23-87	0	0	7.11	1	1	0	0	6	8	5	5	2	1	5	.308	.292	.500	7.11	1.42
Concepcion, Alexander	R-R	6-1	180	9-27-84	2	2	6.00	23	1	0	0	30	26	21	20	5	18	18	.226	.302	.161	5.40	5.40
Duckworth, Brandon	R-R	6-1	210	1-23-76	5	4	3.32	25	16	0	0	106	94	44	39	5	45	102	.242	.275	.217	8.69	3.83
Ennis, John	R-R	6-5	220	10-17-79	0	0	9.00	1	0	0	0	1	2	1	1	0	1	1	.400		.500	9.00	9.00
Figueroa, Nelson	R-R	6-1	180	5-18-74	3	0	0.95	3	3	0	0	19	10	2	2	1	3	18	.149	.080	.190	8.53	1.42
Gordon, Brian	L-R	6-0	190	8-16-78	1	3	3.46	40	0	0	0	78	73	33	30	2	19	86	.247	.289	.208	9.92	2.19
Happ, J.A.	L-L	6-6	200	10-19-82	0	1	4.84	5	4	0	0	22	26	12	12	3	15	22	.295	.297	.294	8.87	6.04
Lidge, Brad	R-R	6-5	210	12-23-76	0	0	0.00	1	0	0	0	1	0	0	0	0	0	1	.000	.000	.000	9.00	9.00
Loop, Derrick	R-L	6-3	210	12-11-83	1	0	0.00	1	0	0	0	3	1	0	0	0	0	4	.100		.125	12.00	9.00
Madson, Ryan	L-R	6-6	200	8-28-80	0	0	5.40	2	0	0	0	2	1	1	1	0	2	2	.200	.000	.250	10.80	10.80
Mathieson, Scott	R-R	6-3	190	2-27-84	3	6	2.80	54	0	0	26	64	49	21	20	8	24	83	.212	.261	.167	11.61	3.36
Mazone, Brian	L-L	6-2	200	7-26-76	7	13	3.82	28	28	0	0	165	174	85	70	19	30	104	.269	.304	.256	5.67	1.64
Robertson, Nate	R-L	6-2	225	9-3-77	1	1	3.38	2	2	0	0	11	10	5	4	0	2	6	.244	.400	.194	5.06	1.69
Romero, J.C.	B-L	5-11	215	6-4-76	0	1	0.00	3	1	0	0	2	1	0	0	0		4	.222	.333	.167	15.43	15.43
Savery, Joe	L-L	6-3	215	11-4-85	1	12	4.66	28	19	0	0	127	154	78	66	13	51	67	.303	.261	.323	4.74	3.60
Schwimer, Michael	R-R	6-8	246	2-19-86	2	2	1.35	16	0	0	0	20	16	6	3	1	7	18	.213	.229	.200	8.10	3.15
Stutes, Mike	R-R	6-1	185	9-4-86	3	1	3.10	28	0	0	0	41	29	15	14	5	23	42	.200	.210	.193	9.30	5.09
Taubenheim, Ty	R-R	6-5	228	11-17-82	2	4	4.26	8	7	1	0	38	37	19	18	4	17	28	.259	.260	.256	6.63	4.03
Villarreal, Oscar	L-R	6-0	190	11-22-81	4	3	4.40	49	0	0	1	57	54	33	28	7	26	42	.254	.318	.211	6.59	4.08
Vogelsong, Ryan	R-R	6-3	215	7-22-77	2	5	4.91	25	7	0	1	59	60	38	32	6	40	73	.264	.260	.268	11.20	6.14
Wassermann, Ehren	B-R	6-0	190	12-6-80	0	3	6.23	18	0	0	0	26	29	18	18	5	13	13	.296	.302	.291	4.15	4.50
Woods, Jake	L-L	6-0	200	9-3-81	0	0	3.60	3	0	0	0	5	3	2	2	0	2	2	.316	.375	.273	9.00	3.60
Worley, Vance	R-R	6-2	230	9-25-87	1	3	3.77	8	8	0	0	45	46	19	19	3	10	36	.264	.280	.243	7.15	1.99
Zagurski, Mike	L-L	6-0	220	1-27-83	2	3	3.27	52	0	0	3	52	44	26	19	3	27	71	.228	.274	.193	12.21	4.64

Fielding

Catcher	PCT	G	PO	A	E	DP	PB
Hoover	.986	67	470	38	7	4	6
Ruiz	1.000	1	6	0	0	0	0
Sardinha	.996	65	470	35	2	2	10
Schneider	1.000	3	16	1	0	0	0
Suomi	.991	15	107	5	1	0	0

First Base	PCT	G	PO	A	E	DP
Dorta	1.000	6	45	5	0	4
Hoover	.981	8	48	3	1	7
Rizzotti	.988	12	78	7	1	12
Sellers	.997	38	307	21	1	23
Tracy	.992	87	657	72	6	60

Second Base	PCT	G	PO	A	E	DP
Chavez	.961	47	80	139	9	40
DeRenne	1.000	4	5	11	0	3
Dorta	.967	52	91	114	7	18

Maza	.976	47	82	122	5	23
Ransom	1.000	1	1	2	0	0
Valdez	.938	4	8	7	1	2

Third Base	PCT	G	PO	A	E	DP
Dobbs	1.000	4	2	8	0	0
Dorta	.500	1	0	1	1	0
Ransom	.899	81	52	118	19	10
Sellers	.959	64	27	115	6	11
Tracy	1.000	1	1	1	0	1

Shortstop	PCT	G	PO	A	E	DP
Bocock	.977	119	194	309	12	71
Chavez	1.000	6	11	17	0	4
Dorta	.959	16	18	29	2	6
Ransom	.923	10	6	18	2	2
Valdez	1.000	2	2	4	0	1

Outfield	PCT	G	PO	A	E	DP
Aguila	1.000	29	48	0	0	0
Brown	1.000	28	49	3	0	1
Dobbs	.950	11	18	1	1	1
Dorta	.973	19	35	1	1	0
Duffy	.988	86	160	3	2	1
Gordon	—	1	0	0	0	0
Mayberry Jr.	.996	125	257	4	1	1
Ransom	.714	4	5	0	2	0
Sellers	—	1	0	0	0	0
Taveras	1.000	22	63	0	0	0
Thompson	.986	86	209	6	3	1
Tracy	—	1	0	0	0	0
Victorino	1.000	2	6	0	0	0
Wise	1.000	32	76	3	0	0

READING PHILLIES
DOUBLE-A
EASTERN LEAGUE

Batting	B-T	HT	WT	DOB	AVG	vLH	vRH	G	AB	R	H	2B	3B	HR	RBI	BB	HBP	SH	SF	SO	SB	CS	SLG	OBP
Berry, Quintin	L-L	6-0	175	11-21-84	.210	.262	.199	66	238	35	50	10	2	2	25	33	3	9	2	50	23	6	.294	.312
Bozied, Tagg	R-R	6-3	215	7-24-79	.315	.327	.311	104	355	65	112	29	1	27	92	47	6	0	2	85	1	3	.631	.402
Brown, Domonic	L-L	6-5	200	9-3-87	.318	.321	.317	65	236	50	75	16	3	15	47	29	2	0	4	51	12	6	.602	.391
Chavez, Ozzie	B-R	6-1	175	7-13-83	.218	.152	.232	67	188	25	41	10	0	1	18	26	1	2	0	33	3	4	.287	.316
DeRenne, Keoni	B-R	5-7	170	4-30-79	.207	.125	.250	34	92	11	19	3	0	0	8	16	1	0	1	10	0	0	.239	.327
Dorta, Melvin	R-R	5-11	160	1-15-82	.176	.000	.250	5	17	3	3	0	0	0	2	0	1	0	1	1	0	.176	.263
Galvis, Freddy	B-R	5-10	170	11-14-89	.233	.207	.241	138	502	58	117	16	4	5	48	30	1	8	4	89	15	4	.311	.276
Garcia, Harold	R-R	5-11	164	10-25-86	.281	.282	.281	55	231	27	65	9	2	5	32	15	6	5	1	57	12	5	.403	.340
Gillies, Tyson	L-R	6-2	195	10-31-88	.238	.174	.256	26	105	15	25	2	1	2	6	5	2	1	0	24	2	2	.333	.286
Gosewisch, Tuffy	R-R	5-11	180	8-17-83	.241	.250	.238	97	311	46	75	22	1	9	32	49	5	5	0	67	0	0	.405	.353
Hernandez, Fidel	R-R	5-11	190	1-18-86	.467	.000	.467	4	15	3	7	0	0	1	0	1	0	0	0	3	0	0	.467	.500
Langley, Torre	R-R	5-9	175	10-9-87	.167	.000	.200	2	6	1	1	0	0	0	0	0	0	0	0	2	0	0	.167	.286
Mahar, Kevin	R-R	6-5	220	6-8-81	.261	.272	.257	116	364	50	95	16	2	13	53	43	3	3	2	90	6	4	.423	.342
Nelson, Kevin	R-R	6-3	215	4-8-81	.241	.260	.234	54	174	15	42	8	0	2	19	12	3	1	3	38	0	1	.322	.297
Overbeck, Cody	R-R	6-1	200	6-5-86	.255	.305	.233	78	275	48	70	10	1	13	41	25	8	0	1	83	0	1	.440	.333
Perez, Timo	L-L	5-9	180	4-8-75	.255	.190	.291	43	161	19	41	7	1	4	25	17	0	1	3	21	4	1	.385	.320
Pinckney, Brandon	R-R	5-10	165	4-12-82	.221	.114	.252	51	154	13	34	10	0	2	16	5	1	4	1	29	0	1	.325	.271
Rizzotti, Matt	L-L	6-5	235	12-24-85	.361	.375	.357	77	266	48	96	25	0	16	62	40	4	0	6	56	1	1	.635	.452
Sellers, Neil	R-R	6-1	195	4-3-82	.125	.000	.167	4	16	3	2	1	0	1	3	1	0	0	0	4	0	0	.375	.176
Spidale, Mike	R-R	6-1	190	3-12-82	.303	.296	.305	131	479	74	145	21	3	3	50	35	5	4	3	64	31	11	.378	.354
Stavisky, Brian	L-R	6-3	230	7-6-80	.276	.300	.271	39	105	14	29	4	0	3	11	10	1	0	0	25	1	1	.400	.345
Suarez, Gabe	R-R	6-0	170	12-14-84	.278	.250	.286	5	18	2	5	1	0	0	1	1	0	0	0	2	1	0	.333	.316
Suomi, John	L-R	5-11	200	10-5-80	.262	.344	.239	46	145	21	38	5	0	3	18	10	1	0	3	33	1	2	.359	.299
Thompson, Rich	L-R	6-3	185	4-23-79	.297	.333	.288	33	128	23	38	4	3	1	14	9	4	4	1	20	13	0	.398	.359

Pitching	B-T	HT	WT	DOB	W	L	ERA	G	GS	CG	SV	IP	H	R	ER	HR	BB	SO	AVG	vLH	vRH	K/9	BB/9
Anderson, Jason	L-R	6-0	188	6-9-79	2	5	4.50	33	6	0	3	66	75	36	33	5	15	51	.292	.284	.297	6.95	2.05
Aumont, Phillippe	L-R	6-7	255	1-7-89	1	6	7.43	11	11	0	0	50	55	45	41	4	38	38	.284	.278	.291	6.89	6.89
Blanton, Joe	R-R	6-3	245	12-11-80	0	1	5.63	2	2	0	0	8	9	5	5	2	2	5	.273	.286	.250	5.63	2.25
Brummett, Tyson	R-R	6-0	180	8-15-84	1	2	5.01	28	2	0	1	56	66	34	31	2	15	34	.292	.240	.336	5.50	2.43
Chapman, Chance	R-R	6-4	210	2-27-84	2	3	5.36	29	3	0	0	50	51	30	30	3	22	37	.270	.272	.268	6.62	3.93
Cisco, Mike	R-R	5-11	190	5-23-87	4	11	4.73	16	16	1	0	91	100	51	48	10	20	62	.272	.263	.281	6.11	1.97
Cloyd, Tyler	R-R	6-3	190	5-16-87	1	1	4.00	2	1	0	0	9	5	4	4	3	1	6	.152	.429	.077	6.00	1.00
De Fratus, Justin	B-R	6-4	215	10-21-87	1	0	2.19	20	0	0	6	25	17	6	6	2	5	28	.195	.140	.250	10.22	1.82
Ennis, John	R-R	6-5	220	10-17-79	2	0	4.09	18	1	0	2	33	34	15	15	6	9	28	.260	.281	.243	7.64	2.45
Escalona, Sergio	L-L	6-0	210	8-3-84	4	8	3.81	50	0	0	10	54	46	25	23	6	22	53	.227	.188	.262	8.78	3.64
Flande, Yohan	L-L	6-2	180	1-27-86	10	8	4.38	27	27	1	0	158	178	84	77	10	44	84	.286	.271	.294	4.77	2.50
Fogg, Josh	R-R	6-0	205	12-13-76	0	2	11.32	3	3	0	0	10	21	16	13	3	5	4	.429	.385	.478	3.48	4.35
German, Matt	L-L	6-0	190	6-27-84	1	2	5.87	43	0	0	0	46	46	31	30	5	23	38	.260	.237	.286	7.43	4.50
Happ, J.A.	L-L	6-6	200	10-19-82	1	0	8.03	3	3	0	0	12	18	11	11	3	4	10	.333	.375	.326	7.30	2.92
Hyatt, Austin	R-R	6-2	180	5-23-86	1	0	4.91	4	4	0	0	22	21	14	12	4	9	25	.247	.164	.400	10.23	3.68
Kissock, Chris	R-R	6-4	195	5-2-85	1	0	3.86	11	0	0	0	23	20	10	10	1	4	14	.247	.316	.186	5.40	1.54
Lidge, Brad	R-R	6-5	210	12-23-76	0	0	0.00	2	0	0	0	3	1	0	0	1	4	.091	.111	.000	12.00	3.00
Madson, Ryan	L-R	6-6	200	8-28-80	0	0	0.00	1	0	0	0	2	2	0	0	0	1	.286	.667	.000	4.50	0.00
Naylor, Drew	R-R	6-4	235	5-31-86	12	10	4.63	27	26	3	0	167	173	93	86	12	44	113	.267	.220	.309	6.09	2.37
Ramirez, J.C.	R-R	6-3	225	8-16-88	13	13	5.45	13	13	1	0	78	89	51	47	11	24	60	.291	.321	.255	6.95	2.78
Rosenberg, B.J.	R-R	6-2	215	9-17-85	1	0	9.22	11	0	0	0	14	15	14	14	6	5	15	.278	.286	.269	9.88	3.29
Schwimer, Michael	R-R	6-8	246	2-19-86	5	3	3.60	32	0	0	11	40	34	16	16	5	14	58	.225	.259	.206	13.05	3.15
Stephens, Jay	R-R	6-5	200	10-10-84	0	0	0.00	4	0	0	0	13	7	0	0	0	4	7	.156	.174	.136	4.72	2.70
Stutes, Mike	R-R	6-1	185	9-4-86	3	0	3.79	25	0	0	2	36	28	15	15	2	21	37	.217	.191	.246	9.34	5.30
Taubenheim, Ty	R-R	6-5	228	11-17-82	4	2	4.80	13	4	0	1	45	51	27	24	6	13	26	.291	.351	.222	6.00	2.60
Worley, Vance	R-R	6-2	230	9-25-87	9	4	3.20	19	19	1	0	113	114	48	40	9	36	83	.264	.245	.280	6.63	2.88

Fielding

Catcher	PCT	G	PO	A	E	DP	PB
Gosewisch	.997	94	626	46	2	4	2
Langley	1.000	2	12	0	0	0	1
Nelson	.988	36	227	15	3	2	2
Suomi	.980	15	91	6	2	2	2

First Base	PCT	G	PO	A	E	DP
Bozied	.991	48	305	26	3	28
Mahar	.990	37	256	30	3	23
Nelson	.947	5	32	4	2	3
Overbeck	1.000	1	8	1	0	0
Rizzotti	.995	52	406	32	2	27
Stavisky	.976	17	115	6	3	12

Second Base	PCT	G	PO	A	E	DP
Chavez	.987	62	100	127	3	27
DeRenne	1.000	14	20	32	0	6
Dorta	1.000	5	8	17	0	2

	PCT	G	PO	A	E	DP
Garcia	.987	53	76	149	3	24
Hernandez	1.000	4	6	12	0	2
Mahar	1.000	1	1	1	0	0
Pinckney	1.000	14	27	27	0	8
Sellers	1.000	3	5	4	0	0

Third Base	PCT	G	PO	A	E	DP
Bozied	.906	33	26	51	8	5
Chavez	.875	4	3	4	1	0
DeRenne	.600	2	1	2	2	1
Garcia	1.000	2	1	3	0	0
Mahar	—	1	0	0	0	0
Overbeck	.908	76	53	114	17	6
Pinckney	.975	39	21	56	2	6
Sellers	1.000	2	0	2	0	0

Shortstop	PCT	G	PO	A	E	DP
Chavez	1.000	4	4	5	0	1

DeRenne	1.000	4	7	14	0	6
Galvis	.982	138	220	393	11	72

Outfield	PCT	G	PO	A	E	DP
Berry	.981	64	147	5	3	1
Bozied	1.000	7	10	0	0	0
Brown	.971	61	134	2	4	0
DeRenne	.958	11	22	1	1	0
Gillies	.986	26	67	3	1	0
Gosewisch	1.000	2	1	0	0	0
Mahar	.992	72	122	7	1	0
Perez	.974	39	73	3	2	2
Spidale	.983	122	229	3	4	0
Stavisky	1.000	1	1	0	0	0
Suarez	1.000	5	12	0	0	0
Suomi	.960	14	24	0	1	0
Thompson	.987	31	76	1	1	0

CLEARWATER THRESHERS

HIGH CLASS A

FLORIDA STATE LEAGUE

Batting	B-T	HT	WT	DOB	AVG	vLH	vRH	G	AB	R	H	2B	3B	HR	RBI	BB	HBP	SH	SF	SO	SB	CS	SLG	OBP
DeRenne, Keoni	B-R	5-7	170	4-30-79	.400	.286	.462	7	20	5	8	2	0	0	3	3	1	0	0	2	0	0	.500	.500
Garcia, Harold	B-R	5-11	164	10-25-86	.335	.264	.365	46	179	27	60	13	3	3	32	12	9	0	4	37	17	6	.492	.397
Gload, Ross	L-L	6-1	190	4-5-76	.125	.000	.167	2	8	1	1	0	0	1	0	0	0	0	0	1	0	0	.500	.125
Gose, Anthony	L-L	6-1	190	8-10-90	.263	.252	.268	103	418	67	110	17	11	4	21	32	6	5	0	103	36	27	.385	.325
2-team total (27 Dunedin)					.262	—		130	512	88	134	20	13	7	27	45	9	7	1	132	45	32	.393	.332
Gump, Brian	L-L	6-2	195	6-16-87	.183	.105	.212	22	71	5	13	2	1	0	7	7	1	0	3	27	1	0	.239	.256
Hanzawa, Troy	R-R	5-9	155	9-12-85	.224	.246	.214	122	397	39	89	15	0	0	36	23	6	9	2	75	2	3	.262	.276
Hernandez, Fidel	R-R	5-11	190	1-18-86	.279	.309	.266	69	265	27	74	7	1	1	22	13	1	1	3	24	4	3	.325	.312
Kennelly, Tim	R-R	6-0	180	12-5-86	.274	.275	.274	115	416	50	114	18	1	5	59	35	8	2	2	53	2	2	.358	.341
Langley, Torre	R-R	5-9	175	10-9-87	.203	.100	.250	20	64	7	13	1	0	0	4	6	0	1	0	16	1	1	.219	.271
Lanning, Jeff	R-R	6-0	210	1-1-87	.143	.000	.143	4	14	2	2	0	0	0	0	0	0	0	0	4	0	0	.286	.143
Mintken, Korby	L-R	6-0	180	3-12-86	.203	.087	.244	61	177	24	36	5	1	0	12	22	1	3	0	57	13	1	.243	.295
Mitchell, Derrick	R-R	6-2	170	1-5-87	.264	.310	.245	116	398	69	105	28	3	13	51	31	6	3	4	90	28	6	.447	.323
Murphy, Jim	R-R	6-4	240	9-16-85	.239	.198	.257	115	397	46	95	29	1	6	43	32	14	0	3	123	2	0	.363	.316
Myers, D'Arby	R-R	6-3	175	12-9-88	.268	.263	.270	66	239	28	64	9	2	3	28	15	3	1	1	64	14	3	.360	.318
Naughton, Joel	L-R	6-1	180	8-27-86	.308	.316	.304	51	182	24	56	7	0	5	31	14	0	2	2	37	0	1	.429	.354
Overbeck, Cody	R-R	6-1	200	6-5-86	.302	.333	.290	58	215	31	65	19	1	11	41	27	0	0	5	51	0	0	.553	.380
Owen, Cale	B-R	5-9	165	3-26-87	.333	.000	.333	1	3	0	1	0	0	0	0	0	0	0	0	0	0	0	.333	.333
Perdomo, Carlos	R-R	5-10	168	4-25-90	.237	.345	.191	30	97	13	23	0	0	0	10	7	1	3	0	7	0	1	.237	.295
Polanco, Placido	R-R	5-10	190	10-10-75	.250	.000	.250	1	4	1	1	0	0	0	0	0	0	0	0	0	0	0	.250	.250
Rizzotti, Matt	L-L	6-5	235	12-24-85	.358	.326	.379	31	109	18	39	8	1	1	10	13	0	0	0	22	0	0	.477	.426
Rollins, Jimmy	B-R	5-8	170	11-27-78	.143	.333	.091	5	14	2	2	0	0	0	2	1	0	0	2	1	0	0	.143	.176
Ruf, Darin	R-R	6-3	220	7-28-86	.277	.270	.280	97	368	45	102	34	2	5	50	26	8	0	4	87	2	2	.421	.335
Stumpo, Bob	B-R	6-4	220	7-17-87	.120	.063	.147	18	50	3	6	1	0	0	1	6	0	1	0	21	0	0	.140	.214
Suarez, Gabe	R-R	6-0	170	12-14-84	.263	.429	.167	7	19	5	5	2	0	0	3	3	1	0	0	4	1	0	.368	.391
Suomi, John	L-R	5-11	200	10-5-80	.333	.125	.500	6	18	2	6	2	0	1	4	1	0	0	0	5	0	2	.611	.368
Susdorf, Steve	L-L	6-1	195	3-28-86	.278	.264	.284	128	489	60	136	28	2	11	77	46	4	0	4	109	6	4	.411	.343
Utley, Chase	L-R	6-1	190	12-17-78	.250	.250	.250	4	12	1	3	0	2	0	1	1	0	0	0	2	0	0	.583	.308

Pitching	B-T	HT	WT	DOB	W	L	ERA	G	GS	CG	SV	IP	H	R	ER	HR	BB	SO	AVG	vLH	vRH	K/9	BB/9
Aumont, Phillippe	L-R	6-7	255	1-7-89	2	5	4.48	16	10	1	1	72	74	41	36	6	42	77	.270	.287	.255	9.58	5.23
Bastardo, Antonio	L-L	5-11	195	9-21-85	0	0	0.00	3	0	0	0	3	3	0	0	0	0	6	.250	.000	.429	18.00	0.00
Brummett, Tyson	R-R	6-0	180	8-15-84	0	0	0.59	11	0	0	2	15	7	1	1	0	4	11	.130	.125	.133	6.46	2.35
Chapman, Chance	R-R	6-4	210	2-27-84	0	0	0.00	1	0	0	0	2	0	0	0	0	0	2	.000	.000	.000	9.00	0.00
Cisco, Mike	R-R	5-11	190	5-23-87	0	0	1.93	2	2	0	0	9	9	2	2	0	4	3	.250	.280	.182	2.89	3.86
Cloyd, Tyler	R-R	6-3	190	5-16-87	4	3	5.32	35	4	0	0	69	85	45	41	8	16	67	.299	.274	.317	8.70	2.08
Correa, Heitor	R-R	6-3	200	8-25-89	8	14	6.62	27	25	0	0	137	176	116	101	18	60	85	.315	.256	.365	5.57	3.93
De Fratus, Justin	B-R	6-4	215	10-21-87	2	0	1.79	29	0	0	15	40	31	9	8	1	11	43	.215	.271	.176	9.60	2.45
Diekman, Jacob	L-L	6-4	190	1-21-87	0	2	3.66	24	0	0	0	32	22	20	13	2	23	26	.195	.240	.182	7.31	6.47
Durbin, Chad	R-R	6-2	225	12-3-77	1	0	0.00	2	0	0	0	3	0	0	0	0	1	1	.000	.000	.000	3.00	0.00
Ellis, Jordan	R-R	6-2	198	9-11-85	1	3	2.25	20	0	0	4	32	27	15	8	1	19	34	.229	.348	.153	9.56	5.34
Esposito, Joe	L-R	5-11	220	5-15-85	1	1	2.20	5	5	0	0	29	19	7	7	3	15	32	.184	.163	.200	10.05	4.71
Garcia, Edgar	R-R	6-2	190	9-20-87	3	4	4.16	34	10	1	0	93	93	48	43	10	33	83	.257	.292	.234	8.03	3.19
Happ, J.A.	L-L	6-6	200	10-19-82	0	1	6.00	1	1	0	0	3	3	2	2	0	2	2	.231	.500	.182	6.00	6.00
Hutchison, Matt	R-R	6-4	215	7-19-88	0	0	9.72	2	1	0	0	8	13	9	9	1	3	2	.361	.438	.300	2.16	3.24
Hyatt, Austin	R-R	6-2	180	5-23-86	11	5	3.04	23	21	0	0	124	100	47	42	5	35	156	.220	.205	.232	11.29	2.53
Kissock, Chris	R-R	6-4	195	5-2-85	6	3	2.17	36	0	0	4	54	49	14	13	4	8	36	.241	.205	.267	6.00	1.33
Lidge, Brad	R-R	6-5	210	12-23-76	0	1	7.94	6	3	0	0	6	5	5	5	0	2	5	.250	.167	.375	7.94	3.18
Loop, Derrick	R-L	6-3	220	12-11-83	4	1	0.36	15	0	0	0	25	14	3	1	1	9	9	.173	.160	.179	10.08	3.24
Madson, Ryan	L-R	6-6	200	8-28-80	0	1	4.50	2	0	0	0	2	1	1	1	0	1	3	.125	.000	.250	13.50	0.00
May, Trevor	R-R	6-3	195	9-23-89	5	5	5.01	16	14	0	0	70	53	41	39	7	61	90	.212	.200	.221	11.57	7.84
Noles, Korey	L-L	5-11	185	7-18-85	1	1	3.72	21	0	0	0	29	37	18	12	2	12	16	.303	.244	.333	4.97	3.72

Name	B-T	HT	WT	DOB	W	L	ERA	G	GS	CG	SV	IP	H	R	ER	HR	BB	SO	AVG	vLH	vRH	K/9	BB/9
Ramirez, J.C.	R-R	6-3	225	8-16-88	4	3	4.06	11	11	0	0	64	63	34	29	2	17	50	.259	.310	.224	7.69	2.38
Romero, J.C.	B-L	5-11	215	6-4-76	0	0	2.25	3	3	0	0	4	3	1	1	1	1	5	.214	.000	.273	11.25	2.25
Rosenberg, B.J.	R-R	6-2	215	9-17-85	1	0	1.38	8	0	0	1	13	9	2	2	2	4	17	.191	.167	.207	11.77	2.77
Sanchez, Jesus	R-R	5-11	160	9-24-87	9	7	2.99	23	22	1	0	129	109	47	43	9	33	84	.230	.239	.223	5.85	2.30
Sandoval, Juan	R-R	6-2	170	1-13-81	1	1	6.68	21	0	0	0	34	46	27	25	4	15	21	.343	.311	.370	5.61	4.01
Schuler, Marshall	R-R	6-0	170	1-19-88	0	1	4.50	1	0	0	0	2	1	1	1	1	1	1	.167	.000	.250	4.50	4.50
Sterner, Zack	R-R	6-2	170	11-7-85	0	0	40.50	3	0	0	0	2	9	9	9	0	2	1	.643	.571	.714	4.50	9.00
Velasquez, Jon	R-R	6-0	169	10-15-85	3	9	3.19	45	5	0	6	87	68	39	31	9	35	77	.217	.215	.219	7.94	3.61
Way, Matt	L-L	6-1	195	1-25-87	0	1	7.50	2	2	0	0	6	8	5	5	0	4	4	.333	.333	.333	6.00	6.00
Whatcott, Jordan	R-R	6-0	198	6-10-85	0	0	16.71	4	0	0	0	7	14	13	13	1	6	8	.389	.353	.421	10.29	7.71

Fielding

Catcher	PCT	G	PO	A	E	DP	PB
Kennelly	.982	52	402	35	8	2	5
Langley	.994	20	140	25	1	0	2
Lanning	.933	4	26	2	2	0	1
Naughton	.982	47	350	23	7	0	4
Stumpo	.979	17	127	13	3	1	3
Suomi	.946	4	35	0	2	0	0

First Base	PCT	G	PO	A	E	DP
Gload	1.000	1	8	1	0	0
Murphy	.997	75	582	46	2	53
Rizzotti	1.000	8	73	3	0	2
Ruf	.987	57	437	30	6	35
Susdorf	1.000	3	12	1	0	2

Second Base	PCT	G	PO	A	E	DP
DeRenne	1.000	5	9	16	0	4
Garcia	.994	38	63	96	1	25
Hernandez	.970	68	122	173	9	32

	PCT	G	PO	A	E	DP
Mintken	.953	25	27	54	4	9
Perdomo	1.000	8	14	14	0	2
Utley	.800	3	3	5	2	1

Third Base	PCT	G	PO	A	E	DP
Garcia	.875	7	5	9	2	1
Hernandez	1.000	1	0	3	0	0
Kennelly	.941	31	25	39	4	5
Mintken	.951	18	12	27	2	5
Murphy	.912	13	10	21	3	0
Overbeck	.949	53	44	106	8	8
Owen	1.000	1	1	2	0	0
Perdomo	.882	21	12	33	6	1
Polanco	.800	1	2	2	1	0

Shortstop	PCT	G	PO	A	E	DP
DeRenne	.889	2	2	6	1	1
Hanzawa	.960	122	152	300	19	56
Mintken	.923	14	18	30	4	6

	PCT	G	PO	A	E	DP
Rollins	.933	5	4	10	1	1
Suarez	1.000	3	2	9	0	2

Outfield	PCT	G	PO	A	E	DP
Gose	.982	103	252	15	5	1
Gump	1.000	21	42	1	0	1
Kennelly	.986	34	66	4	1	1
Mintken	—	1	0	0	0	0
Mitchell	.986	11	195	17	3	4
Murphy	—	1	0	0	0	0
Myers	.979	65	137	4	3	0
Ruf	1.000	4	7	0	0	0
Rundle	1.000	2	9	0	0	0
Stumpo	1.000	1	2	0	0	0
Suarez	1.000	4	5	0	0	0
Susdorf	1.000	88	129	3	0	0

LAKEWOOD BLUECLAWS
SOUTH ATLANTIC LEAGUE

LOW CLASS A

Batting	B-T	HT	WT	DOB	AVG	vLH	vRH	G	AB	R	H	2B	3B	HR	RBI	BB	HBP	SH	SF	SO	SB	CS	SLG	OBP
Barnes, Jeremy	R-R	5-10	190	4-13-87	.292	.319	.281	109	390	55	114	38	4	4	51	58	4	2	7	86	10	9	.441	.383
Batts, Stephen	R-R	6-0	200	2-14-86	.278	.200	.303	86	316	53	88	21	3	5	36	25	4	2	2	99	7	3	.411	.337
Buschini, Adam	R-R	6-2	205	5-6-87	.219	.291	.190	83	302	49	66	19	4	2	28	37	3	5	0	54	16	6	.328	.310
Castro, Leandro	R-R	5-11	175	6-15-89	.257	.250	.260	124	502	78	129	27	9	10	81	34	5	6	9	92	22	13	.406	.305
Dabbs, Mike	L-R	6-0	185	3-29-87	.297	.240	.310	37	138	19	41	6	2	1	14	9	7	1	2	27	9	6	.391	.365
DeRenne, Keoni	R-S	5-7	170	4-30-79	.333	.400	.320	10	30	5	10	5	0	0	4	4	1	0	0	4	0	1	.500	.429
Doss, David	R-R	6-2	190	4-28-87	.222	.000	.222	9	9	0	2	0	0	0	0	0	0	0	0	2	0	1	.222	.222
Gump, Brian	L-L	6-2	195	6-16-87	.255	.188	.282	17	55	5	14	3	2	0	5	1	0	0	0	14	2	2	.382	.328
Hewitt, Anthony	R-R	6-1	190	4-27-88	.202	.203	.202	116	440	47	89	16	3	11	49	13	11	0	1	158	10	6	.327	.243
Howard, Ryan	L-L	6-4	255	11-19-79	.500	.500	.000	1	2	0	1	1	0	0	1	0	0	0	0	0	0	0	1.000	.667
James, Jiwan	B-R	6-4	180	4-11-89	.270	.238	.281	133	556	85	150	26	6	5	64	35	11	6	9	132	33	20	.365	.321
Klocke, Jim	L-R	6-0	195	7-6-88	.600	.333	1.000	1	5	3	3	0	0	0	1	0	0	0	0	1	0	0	.600	.600
Lafrenz, Bronco	R-R	6-1	190	2-6-87	.241	.194	.259	39	112	8	27	7	0	1	11	1	1	1	2	39	2	0	.330	.250
Langley, Torre	R-R	5-9	175	10-9-87	.293	.308	.286	16	41	3	12	2	0	0	5	3	0	0	1	10	1	1	.341	.333
Lanning, Jeff	R-R	6-0	210	1-1-87	—	.000	.000	1	0	0	0	0	0	0	0	0	0	0	0	0	0	0	—	—
McConnell, Matt	L-R	5-10	185	9-6-86	.000	.000	.000	1	1	0	0	0	0	0	0	0	1	0	0	0	0	0	.000	.000
Mintken, Korby	L-R	6-0	180	3-12-86	.214	.167	.250	9	28	3	6	0	0	0	3	6	0	0	0	9	3	1	.214	.389
Perdomo, Carlos	R-R	5-10	168	4-25-90	.200	.000	.200	5	10	1	2	0	0	0	1	0	0	0	0	1	0	0	.200	.200
Ruf, Darin	R-R	6-3	220	7-28-86	.330	.474	.260	32	115	25	38	7	3	4	17	21	3	1	1	23	3	2	.548	.443
Ruiz, Carlos	R-R	5-10	215	1-22-79	.500	1.000	.429	2	8	1	4	2	0	0	1	0	0	0	0	2	0	0	.750	.500
Ruth, Keoni	R-R	5-11	200	3-21-85	.248	.220	.266	28	105	8	26	9	0	0	13	5	4	1	3	8	3	2	.333	.299
Santana, Domingo	R-R	6-5	200	8-5-92	.182	.180	.183	49	165	27	30	10	0	3	16	29	6	0	2	76	5	6	.297	.324
Schoenberger, Alan	B-L	5-10	160	1-19-89	.253	.273	.247	96	285	42	72	15	3	5	35	29	2	8	2	78	7	8	.379	.324
Singleton, Jonathan	L-L	6-2	215	9-18-91	.290	.290	.290	104	376	64	109	25	2	14	77	62	6	0	6	74	9	7	.479	.393
Suarez, Gabe	R-R	6-0	170	12-14-84	.125	.333	.000	9	8	1	1	0	0	0	0	0	0	0	2	0	0	.125	.125
Valle, Sebastian	R-R	6-1	170	7-24-90	.255	.248	.257	117	447	51	114	28	1	16	74	27	3	2	6	101	3	2	.430	.298
Villar, Jonathan	B-R	6-1	180	5-2-91	.272	.278	.270	100	371	61	101	14	3	2	38	32	3	2	103	38	13	.358	.332

Pitching	B-T	HT	WT	DOB	W	L	ERA	G	GS	CG	SV	IP	H	R	ER	HR	BB	SO	AVG	vLH	vRH	K/9	BB/9
Beal, Justin	R-R	6-2	205	5-21-86	2	3	2.88	20	0	0	0	34	38	12	11	1	14	23	.297	.333	.270	6.03	3.67
Blanton, Joe	R-R	6-3	245	12-11-80	0	0	0.00	1	1	0	0	2	0	0	0	0	0	2	.000	.000	.000	9.00	0.00
Bolsenbroek, Mike	R-R	6-8	210	3-11-87	0	1	3.38	18	2	0	0	32	35	13	12	2	18	23	.285	.315	.261	6.47	5.06
Carr, Kyle	R-L	6-5	200	11-11-86	0	0	0.68	19	0	0	0	26	18	3	2	0	16	19	.205	.185	.213	6.49	5.47
Colvin, Brody	R-R	6-3	195	8-14-90	6	8	3.39	27	27	0	0	138	138	73	52	7	42	120	.258	.242	.270	7.83	2.74
Cosart, Jarred	R-R	6-3	180	5-25-90	7	3	3.79	14	14	1	0	71	60	34	30	3	16	77	.224	.234	.218	9.71	2.02
Diekman, Jacob	L-L	6-4	190	1-21-87	2	0	1.90	21	0	0	0	24	16	11	5	0	20	18	.178	.174	.179	11.41	5.70
Ellis, Jordan	R-R	6-2	198	9-11-85	3	3	2.47	33	0	0	11	44	31	15	12	1	17	55	.200	.200		11.34	3.50
Esposito, Joe	L-R	5-11	220	5-15-85	1	1	3.77	9	0	0	0	14	24	10	6	2	5	18	.387	.250	.474	11.30	3.14
Hernandez, Nick	L-L	6-4	216	7-30-88	3	1	1.61	8	0	0	0	56	38	16	10	4	8	52	.192	.075	.222	8.36	1.29
Lebron, Siulman	R-R	6-1	170	6-11-87	1	2	6.68	14	1	0	0	32	47	32	24	4	7	35	.333	.354	.323	9.74	1.95
Lugo, Ebelin	R-R	6-2	190	4-23-90	3	5	1.91	43	0	0	6	66	52	15	14	4	21	58	.217	.184	.235	7.91	2.86

Name	B-T	HT	WT	DOB	W	L	ERA	G	GS	CG	SV	IP	H	R	ER	HR	BB	SO	AVG	vLH	vRH	K/9	BB/9
Massingham, Eric	R-R	6-2	205	11-19-86	5	2	3.43	34	1	0	3	63	51	26	24	1	15	50	.219	.194	.237	7.14	2.14
May, Trevor	R-R	6-5	215	9-23-89	7	3	2.91	11	11	0	0	65	51	22	21	3	20	92	.214	.206	.221	12.74	2.77
McGuire, Mike	R-R	6-7	240	6-29-86	1	1	2.67	18	1	0	6	30	27	10	9	2	7	35	.233	.190	.257	10.38	2.08
Pettibone, Jon	L-R	6-5	200	7-19-90	8	6	3.49	24	23	1	0	131	114	63	51	10	41	84	.237	.207	.256	5.76	2.81
Poe, Chad	R-R	6-2	185	11-14-87	1	0	6.75	12	0	0	0	17	21	17	13	2	12	13	.318	.391	.279	6.75	6.23
Rodriguez, Julio	R-R	6-4	195	8-29-90	5	1	1.44	13	7	0	0	56	32	12	9	2	22	90	.160	.181	.145	14.38	3.51
Shreve, Colby	R-R	6-5	210	1-5-88	7	5	3.95	23	18	0	0	109	95	58	48	11	30	76	.234	.224	.242	6.26	2.47
Way, Matt	L-L	6-1	195	1-25-87	7	4	3.65	15	14	0	0	86	80	43	35	5	26	81	.252	.200	.259	8.44	2.71
Wertz, Luke	R-R	6-1	175	9-20-85	4	4	1.27	39	0	0	3	71	49	13	10	1	15	63	.192	.158	.214	7.99	1.90
Zeid, Josh	R-R	6-5	210	3-24-87	8	4	2.93	43	12	0	8	107	95	41	35	7	27	111	.238	.224	.247	9.31	2.26

Fielding

Catcher	PCT	G	PO	A	E	DP	PB
Doss	1.000	7	22	4	0	0	0
Klocke	1.000	1	10	0	0	0	0
Lafrenz	.980	37	270	25	6	1	5
Langley	.990	13	78	18	1	0	2
Lanning	1.000	1	1	0	0	0	0
Ruiz	1.000	1	8	1	0	0	0
Valle	.990	101	823	106	9	9	12

First Base	PCT	G	PO	A	E	DP
Batts	.993	18	139	8	1	16
Howard	.750	1	3	0	1	0
Ruf	.990	30	283	21	3	17
Singleton	.995	95	816	65	4	63

Second Base	PCT	G	PO	A	E	DP
Barnes	.963	68	97	191	11	26

DeRenne	1.000	6	8	12	0	2
McConnell	1.000	1	1	0	0	0
Perdomo	.875	1	3	4	1	1
Ruth	.991	26	43	70	1	15
Schoenberger	.980	44	85	113	4	31

Third Base	PCT	G	PO	A	E	DP
Barnes	.921	22	12	46	5	2
Batts	.933	33	21	62	6	3
Buschini	.912	82	50	147	19	6
Perdomo	1.000	2	0	1	0	1
Schoenberger	1.000	4	2	8	0	0

Shortstop	PCT	G	PO	A	E	DP
Barnes	—	1	0	0	0	0
DeRenne	.867	3	6	7	2	0
Mintken	1.000	6	8	22	0	7

Perdomo	1.000	2	1	1	0	0
Schoenberger	.928	36	52	76	10	12
Suarez	.800	2	0	8	2	1
Villar	.913	99	169	272	42	56

Outfield	PCT	G	PO	A	E	DP
Batts	1.000	11	19	0	0	0
Castro	.981	114	188	14	4	3
Dabbs	.985	31	59	5	1	1
Gump	1.000	15	24	3	0	0
Hewitt	.952	81	134	6	7	2
James	.992	130	243	10	2	0
Mintken	1.000	2	7	0	0	0
Santana	.972	41	68	1	2	0
Schoenberger	1.000	2	2	0	0	0

WILLIAMSPORT CROSSCUTTERS   SHORT-SEASON
NEW YORK-PENN LEAGUE

Batting	B-T	HT	WT	DOB	AVG	vLH	vRH	G	AB	R	H	2B	3B	HR	RBI	BB	HBP	SH	SF	SO	SB	CS	SLG	OBP
Alonso, Carlos	R-R	5-11	205	7-15-88	.265	.364	.237	45	147	27	39	13	0	3	14	15	4	1	1	22	2	1	.415	.347
Altherr, Aaron	R-R	6-5	190	1-14-91	.287	.240	.304	28	94	11	27	7	3	0	10	8	1	1	0	22	3	3	.426	.350
Alvarez, Miguel	R-R	6-1	172	8-27-89	.329	.264	.355	68	258	42	85	21	4	1	34	11	3	5	2	48	13	7	.453	.361
Cusick, Jeff	R-R	6-2	205	5-20-88	.233	.215	.241	58	210	20	49	12	0	1	12	9	2	3	0	18	1	2	.305	.271
Dabbs, Mike	L-R	6-0	185	3-29-87	.298	.278	.303	24	84	12	25	6	0	1	7	3	1	2	0	16	4	3	.405	.330
Doss, David	R-R	6-2	190	4-28-87	.250	.500	.214	7	16	2	4	2	0	0	2	1	0	0	1	3	0	1	.375	.278
Dugan, Kelly	B-R	6-3	195	9-18-90	.250	.111	.275	19	60	6	15	6	0	0	4	5	4	1	1	17	0	0	.350	.343
Duran, Edgar	R-R	5-11	154	2-10-91	.235	.224	.239	71	251	28	59	12	2	0	24	13	0	5	4	47	8	5	.299	.269
Hernandez, Cesar	B-R	5-10	166	5-23-90	.325	.391	.301	65	255	36	83	13	2	0	23	26	3	0	3	27	32	6	.392	.390
Hudson, Kyrell	R-R	6-1	185	12-6-90	.173	.107	.188	49	156	13	27	5	0	0	15	5	2	4	3	45	11	3	.205	.205
Klocke, Jim	L-R	6-0	195	7-6-88	.274	.143	.296	29	95	8	26	5	2	1	16	6	0	1	0	7	1	0	.400	.317
Lanning, Jeff	R-R	6-0	210	1-1-87	.264	.182	.306	48	163	30	43	10	1	8	30	16	3	0	3	40	1	1	.485	.335
McConnell, Matt	L-R	5-10	185	9-6-86	.248	.179	.267	42	129	16	32	5	0	0	12	19	2	3	2	26	3	2	.287	.349
Mendez, Geancarlo	R-R	6-2	170	11-17-89	.125	.167	.000	2	8	0	1	0	0	0	0	0	0	0	0	1	1	0	.125	.125
Rupp, Cameron	R-R	6-1	240	9-28-88	.218	.189	.229	55	193	20	42	16	0	5	28	25	4	0	1	51	0	0	.378	.318
Santana, Domingo	R-R	6-5	200	8-5-92	.237	.311	.213	54	186	28	44	9	0	5	20	23	5	0	0	73	4	4	.366	.336
Smith, Jake	R-R	6-2	190	9-25-87	.132	.133	.131	27	91	6	12	4	1	0	6	2	2	1	2	34	0	0	.198	.165
White, Ryne	L-L	5-11	205	10-17-86	.219	.556	.164	19	64	8	14	3	1	2	14	6	0	0	0	11	0	0	.391	.286

Pitching	B-T	HT	WT	DOB	W	L	ERA	G	GS	CG	SV	IP	H	R	ER	HR	BB	SO	AVG	vLH	vRH	K/9	BB/9
Angelle, Kevin	L-L	6-2	195	2-27-88	3	1	1.36	8	8	0	0	46	30	10	7	2	10	43	.186	.103	.205	8.35	1.94
Beal, Justin	R-R	6-2	205	5-21-86	1	0	1.93	4	0	0	0	5	6	6	1	0	1	5	.353	.444	.250	1.93	1.93
Biddle, Jesse	L-L	6-4	225	10-22-91	1	0	2.61	3	3	0	0	10	5	4	3	0	11	9	.152	.071	.211	7.84	9.58
Blanks, Bradley	R-R	6-4	185	3-17-85	4	1	2.73	16	0	0	0	33	25	11	10	1	15	25	.214	.264	.172	6.82	4.09
Bonilla, Lisalverto	R-R	6-1	164	6-6-90	1	3	6.49	10	3	0	0	26	33	22	19	5	12	18	.308	.300	.313	6.15	4.10
Borup, Jake	R-R	6-5	210	5-6-87	2	1	2.68	16	4	0	2	47	37	14	14	2	13	34	.215	.192	.232	6.51	2.49
Buchanan, David	R-R	6-3	190	5-11-89	3	1	4.21	13	13	0	0	62	61	32	29	1	23	30	.254	.243	.264	4.35	3.34
Carr, Kyle	R-L	6-5	200	11-11-86	0	1	3.72	8	0	0	0	10	5	4	4	0	7	9	.152	.200	.130	8.38	6.52
Claypool, Garett	R-R	6-2	170	8-21-88	3	3	3.18	12	4	0	0	34	28	13	12	1	16	45	.231	.270	.190	11.91	4.24
Fritsch, Craig	R-R	6-4	180	12-29-87	2	0	4.38	16	7	1	0	37	31	21	18	0	33	35	.223	.237	.206	8.51	8.03
Garner, Perci	R-R	6-3	225	12-13-88	0	2	18.00	2	2	0	0	4	8	8	8	1	1	1	.400	.462	.286	2.25	2.25
Gomez, Juary	R-R	6-2	205	5-23-90	0	0	0.00	1	0	0	0	3	0	0	0	0	0	0	.000	.000	.000	0.00	0.00
Hollands, Mario	L-L	6-5	205	8-26-88	4	4	4.57	14	14	0	0	65	63	35	33	6	16	63	.252	.284	.237	8.72	2.22
Johnson, Chase	R-R	6-5	245	4-29-88	1	2	2.79	26	0	0	15	29	22	12	9	2	16	32	.212	.179	.231	9.93	4.97
Knigge, Tyler	R-R	6-4	215	10-27-88	0	1	27.00	1	0	0	0	1	1	3	3	0	1	1	.500	1.000	1.000	9.00	9.00
Lebron, Siulman	R-R	6-1	170	6-11-87	0	1	1.69	5	0	0	0	11	7	3	2	1	3	8	.189	.286	.063	6.75	2.53
Manzanillo, Ervis	L-L	6-2	160	8-25-91	1	2	6.29	6	6	0	0	24	19	14	13	8	23	22	.202	.200	.203	8.51	6.66
Morgado, Bryan	L-L	6-3	205	12-8-88	1	2	7.71	14	0	0	0	16	11	15	14	0	22	21	.190	.250	.167	11.57	12.12
Pettis, Eric	R-R	6-2	200	6-9-88	8	0	1.37	20	5	0	7	59	43	9	9	0	7	67	.204	.232	.181	10.22	1.07
Pirela, Jesus	R-R	6-0	152	3-13-89	1	1	7.59	7	0	0	0	11	8	9	9	1	12	15	.205	.077	.269	12.66	10.13
Poe, Chad	R-R	6-2	185	11-14-87	0	0	7.11	3	0	0	0	6	9	5	5	1	4	8	.333	.316	.375	11.37	5.68
Rodriguez, Julio	R-R	6-4	195	8-29-90	2	2	2.65	7	5	0	0	34	25	14	10	2	15	36	.200	.215	.183	9.53	3.97

	B-T	HT	WT	DOB	W	L	ERA	G	GS	CG	SV	IP	H	R	ER	HR	BB	SO	AVG	vLH	vRH	K/9	BB/9
Sampson, Julian	R-R	6-5	210	1-21-89	2	2	4.97	21	1	0	1	38	49	25	21	3	9	41	.314	.324	.307	9.71	2.13
Sosa, Juan	R R	6-2	165	10-11-89	3	2	2.08	24	0	0	6	48	37	15	11	0	17	41	.213	.234	.196	7.74	3.21
Whatcott, Jordan	R-R	6-0	198	6-10-85	0	0	15.00	2	0	0	0	3	8	5	5	0	3	3	.533	.500	.545	9.00	9.00

Fielding

Catcher	PCT	G	PO	A	E	DP	PB
Doss	1.000	2	23	2	0	0	0
Klocke	.982	21	150	17	3	0	5
Lanning	.984	28	224	18	4	1	7
Rupp	.970	28	206	18	7	1	8

First Base	PCT	G	PO	A	E	DP
Cusick	.989	58	483	35	6	37
Dabbs	.909	1	8	2	1	1
Smith	1.000	2	24	3	0	3
White	.985	15	125	4	2	11

Second Base	PCT	G	PO	A	E	DP
Hernandez	.978	65	135	179	7	40
McConnell	.962	13	11	39	2	3

Third Base	PCT	G	PO	A	E	DP
Alonso	.969	41	28	67	3	2
McConnell	.917	13	10	23	3	1
Smith	.898	24	11	42	6	4

Shortstop	PCT	G	PO	A	E	DP
Duran	.948	71	93	181	15	36
Klocke	1.000	1	0	1	0	0

McConnell	1.000	9	6	20	0	4

Outfield	PCT	G	PO	A	E	DP
Altherr	1.000	26	53	1	0	0
Alvarez	.964	65	105	3	4	1
Dabbs	.958	17	23	0	1	0
Dugan	1.000	17	21	2	0	1
Hudson	.965	49	109	2	4	1
McConnell	1.000	8	9	0	0	0
Mendez	1.000	2	3	0	0	0
Rundle	1.000	8	9	0	0	0
Santana	.959	45	91	2	4	0

GCL PHILLIES   ROOKIE
GULF COAST LEAGUE

Batting	B-T	HT	WT	DOB	AVG	vLH	vRH	G	AB	R	H	2B	3B	HR	RBI	BB	HBP	SH	SF	SO	SB	CS	SLG	OBP
Altherr, Aaron	R-R	6-5	190	1-14-91	.304	.211	.351	27	115	12	35	6	1	1	15	3	2	0	1	22	10	3	.400	.331
Beltre, Luis	R-R	6-1	190	2-1-92	.189	.158	.200	24	74	8	14	5	1	1	6	2	1	0	1	26	0	0	.324	.218
Chavarin, Angel	L-R	6-0	176	11-22-90	.192	.000	.238	11	26	2	5	2	0	0	1	1	0	0	0	10	0	0	.269	.222
Diaz, Francisco	B-R	5-10	158	3-21-90	.307	.474	.250	29	75	14	23	6	0	0	11	9	0	1	1	9	1	0	.387	.376
Duffy, Chris	L-R	6-2	200	12-17-87	.272	.241	.287	47	169	29	46	12	0	6	32	29	3	0	2	40	0	0	.450	.384
Dugan, Kelly	B-R	6-3	195	9-18-90	.576	.250	.621	9	33	12	19	4	1	1	4	4	3	2	0	4	2	2	.848	.650
Franco, Maikel	R-R	6-1	180	8-26-92	.222	.143	.254	51	194	23	43	11	2	2	29	16	4	1	2	46	0	0	.330	.292
Gillies, Tyson	L-R	6-2	195	10-31-88	.500	.000	.500	2	2	3	1	0	0	0	1	2	0	0	0	0	0	0	.500	.750
Gump, Brian	L-L	6-2	195	6-16-87	.238	.556	.000	5	21	2	5	1	1	0	2	1	0	0	0	6	2	0	.381	.273
Malcolm, Stephen	R-R	6-0	170	4-9-90	.253	.208	.270	27	87	10	22	3	0	0	10	8	4	1	0	25	7	2	.287	.343
Mendez, Geancarlo	R-R	6-2	170	11-17-89	.264	.241	.274	52	193	35	51	15	4	6	40	15	5	3	3	25	7	2	.477	.329
Mitchell, Marlon	L-R	6-1	180	9-30-90	.273	.300	.261	26	66	10	18	4	0	0	6	6	6	0	0	17	1	1	.333	.385
Murray, Pat	R-R	6-2	220	12-24-86	.313	.390	.278	52	192	27	60	15	0	2	26	17	7	0	2	33	4	1	.422	.385
Numata, Chace	B-R	6-0	175	8-14-92	.222	.067	.300	31	45	8	10	1	0	0	6	8	0	0	0	12	1	1	.244	.340
Owen, Cale	B-R	5-9	165	3-26-87	.208	.308	.175	21	53	8	11	0	0	0	3	6	0	1	0	17	1	0	.208	.288
Payton, Matt	L-R	5-9	185	2-3-88	.228	.171	.244	42	158	24	36	6	3	0	10	14	4	1	0	35	9	0	.304	.307
Perdomo, Carlos	R-R	5-10	168	4-25-90	.255	.357	.212	15	47	4	12	1	1	1	5	3	0	1	2	4	1	.383	.357
Pointer, Brian	L-L	6-0	190	1-28-92	.143	.000	.200	5	7	0	1	0	0	0	0	0	0	0	0	4	0	0	.143	.143
Polanco, Placido	R-R	5-10	190	10-10-75	1.000	.000	1.000	1	3	1	3	1	0	0	2	0	0	0	0	0	0	0	1.333	1.000
Rice, Bill	L-R	5-11	185	9-7-88	.230	.389	.163	22	61	10	14	1	1	3	9	10	1	1	1	7	3	1	.426	.342
Rios, Nerio	B-R	6-0	150	10-5-91	.248	.360	.211	30	101	6	25	6	0	0	9	6	1	2	0	15	3	0	.307	.296
Stumpo, Bob	B-R	6-4	220	7-17-87	.333	.000	.400	4	6	2	2	1	0	0	2	2	1	0	0	1	0	0	.500	.556
Torres, Winder	R-R	5-11	160	8-2-90	—	.000	.000	1	0	1	0	0	0	0	0	0	0	0	0	0	0	0	—	—
Unda, Luis	L-L	6-1	155	1-28-90	.245	.196	.266	44	155	18	38	9	2	0	16	8	2	0	2	17	2	4	.329	.287

Pitching	B-T	HT	WT	DOB	W	L	ERA	G	GS	CG	SV	IP	H	R	ER	HR	BB	SO	AVG	vLH	vRH	K/9	BB/9
Biddle, Jesse	L-L	6-4	225	10-22-91	3	1	4.32	9	9	1	0	33	35	23	16	2	9	41	.263	.257	.265	11.07	2.43
Bonilla, Lisalverto	R-R	6-1	164	6-6-90	2	1	1.95	6	6	0	0	32	32	15	7	3	5	38	.246	.208	.268	10.58	1.39
Brown, Tim	L-R	6-3	205	3-20-87	0	0	1.50	7	2	0	1	24	22	5	4	1	3	18	.250	.273	.236	6.75	1.13
Davis, Neal	L-L	6-5	195	2-3-88	0	0	9.00	3	0	0	0	4	6	4	4	0	3	4	.353	.167	.455	9.00	6.75
Erwin, Drew	R-R	6-1	195	2-9-89	1	0	2.00	6	0	0	0	9	6	2	2	1	2	4	.188	.231	.158	4.00	2.00
Garces, Orlando	L-L	5-11	181	8-24-90	3	2	4.13	15	0	0	0	28	30	16	13	2	20	28	.263	.314	.241	8.89	6.35
Gomez, Juary	R-R	6-2	200	5-23-90	0	0	0.66	20	0	0	9	27	17	2	2	0	7	30	.181	.286	.151	9.88	2.30
Hernandez, Nick	L-L	6-4	216	7-30-88	0	1	7.88	4	0	0	8	10	8	7	0	5	7	.345	.444	.300	7.88	5.63
Hutchison, Matt	R-R	6-4	215	7-19-88	4	0	2.36	13	1	0	1	34	29	11	9	1	11	18	.240	.152	.273	4.72	2.88
Kleven, Colin	R-R	6-5	200	4-15-91	0	5	7.04	9	7	1	0	31	37	26	24	3	11	22	.291	.222	.329	6.46	3.23
Knigge, Tyler	R-R	6-4	215	10-27-88	0	3	5.04	10	4	0	0	30	27	17	17	4	14	27	.237	.182	.271	8.01	4.15
Manzanillo, Ervis	L L	6-0	160	8-25-91	3	0	2.16	7	7	0	0	33	21	10	8	1	11	33	.183	.143	.195	8.91	2.97
Martinez, Lino	L-L	6-0	160	9-17-91	2	2	4.93	11	3	0	0	35	42	23	19	1	9	30	.294	.226	.313	7.79	2.34
Nunez, Miguel	R-R	6-6	215	10-27-92	1	4	5.20	8	5	0	0	28	31	16	16	1	15	21	.287	.270	.296	6.83	4.88
Pirela, Jesus	R-R	6-0	152	3-13-89	3	1	4.30	10	2	0	0	29	27	14	14	0	13	23	.241	.182	.266	7.06	3.99
Rosenberg, B.J.	R-R	6-2	215	9-17-85	0	0	0.00	1	0	0	0	1	1	0	0	0	0	1	.250	.000	.500	9.00	0.00
Schuler, Marshall	R-R	6-0	170	1-19-88	4	2	2.95	19	0	0	3	21	21	8	7	0	11	21	.266	.259	.269	8.86	4.64
Snowdon, Andrew	R-R	6-3	225	3-13-86	0	1	0.93	7	0	0	0	10	7	1	1	0	1	10	.200	.250	.174	9.31	0.93
Walter, Kevin	R-R	6-5	215	5-1-92	0	0	4.50	1	0	0	0	2	1	1	1	0	0	0	.143	.000	.200	0.00	0.00
Whatcott, Jordan	R-R	6-0	198	6-10-85	2	0	1.08	12	0	0	2	17	10	2	2	0	3	13	.164	.200	.146	7.02	1.62

Fielding

Catcher	PCT	G	PO	A	E	DP	PB
Chavarin	.948	10	47	8	3	0	3
Diaz	.991	29	181	31	2	4	2
Mitchell	.982	26	148	18	3	2	6
Numata	1.000	18	52	5	0	0	6
Stumpo	.938	3	15	0	1	0	0

First Base	PCT	G	PO	A	E	DP
Duffy	1.000	23	192	13	0	23
Mendez	1.000	4	31	3	0	1
Murray	.983	29	223	11	4	10
Payton	1.000	1	6	0	0	0
Perdomo	.941	3	15	1	1	1

Second Base	PCT	G	PO	A	E	DP
Mendez	1.000	3	2	5	0	0
Owen	.964	9	11	16	1	5
Payton	.977	41	62	111	4	18
Perdomo	.976	8	11	30	1	6

Third Base	PCT	G	PO	A	E	DP
Franco	.937	50	50	98	10	6
Owen	.933	6	5	9	1	0
Perdomo	1.000	2	1	4	0	0
Polanco	1.000	1	0	1	0	0
Shortstop	**PCT**	**G**	**PO**	**A**	**E**	**DP**
Malcolm	.922	27	43	64	9	13

	PCT	G	PO	A	E	DP
Owen	.714	3	1	4	2	0
Perdomo	1.000	2	2	5	0	0
Rios	.936	30	53	79	9	13
Outfield	**PCT**	**G**	**PO**	**A**	**E**	**DP**
Altherr	.981	27	51	1	1	0
Beltre	.971	23	29	4	1	1
Dugan	1.000	9	18	0	0	0

	PCT	G	PO	A	E	DP
Gillies	—	2	0	0	0	0
Gump	1.000	5	6	0	0	0
Mendez	1.000	48	65	5	0	0
Owen	1.000	3	1	0	0	0
Pointer	1.000	5	3	1	0	0
Rice	1.000	22	44	2	0	1
Unda	.982	43	55	1	1	0

DSL PHILLIES   ROOKIE
DOMINICAN SUMMER LEAGUE

Batting	B-T	HT	WT	DOB	AVG	vLH	vRH	G	AB	R	H	2B	3B	HR	RBI	BB	HBP	SH	SF	SO	SB	CS	SLG	OBP
Balentien, Rudney	R-R	6-0	160	11-3-89	.196	.357	.181	49	158	14	31	6	1	2	11	24	2	2	0	41	9	9	.285	.310
Berroa, Eladio	B-R	5-8	155	2-2-91	.226	.286	.221	30	84	11	19	5	1	0	11	8	0	0	2	10	4	4	.310	.287
Castillo, Jorge	R-R	5-10	170	10-19-90	.253	.318	.246	67	229	21	58	14	4	6	37	21	2	2	5	57	7	9	.428	.315
De La Cruz, Rafael	R-R	6-2	200	7-29-91	.256	.563	.182	37	82	9	21	3	0	2	9	8	6	6	0	22	2	3	.366	.365
Dicen, Francisco	R-R	6-3	180	9-9-90	.192	.143	.200	24	52	4	10	0	0	0	3	7	4	3	1	11	3	1	.192	.328
Esquea, Edwin	R-R	6-0	200	9-11-91	.208	.000	.219	55	144	12	30	6	0	1	15	22	6	1	2	40	2	0	.271	.333
Francisco, Delvi	R-R	6-1	190	8-24-92	.238	.208	.241	66	227	31	54	12	1	3	23	13	9	3	2	35	11	4	.339	.303
Jimenez, Witer	B-R	6-1	180	4-12-89	.272	.148	.286	71	265	36	72	9	4	0	17	22	2	2	3	31	20	18	.336	.329
Marine, Felix	R-R	6-0	180	5-25-90	.206	.150	.213	55	175	20	36	9	2	1	16	16	9	5	0	52	8	5	.297	.305
Mejia, Lissander	R-R	6-1	185	10-9-91	.152	.000	.171	30	46	5	7	0	0	0	2	5	1	3	1	14	2	1	.152	.245
Morales, Yeisson	R-R	6-3	195	4-28-92	.268	.273	.267	54	168	23	45	12	3	1	19	17	4	0	4	40	6	2	.393	.342
Olmo, Yan	R-R	6-3	200	12-15-90	.237	.118	.257	42	118	16	28	3	0	1	8	8	4	3	1	26	5	1	.288	.305
Ramirez, Riswish	B-T	5-11	170	11-1-91	.107	.000	.136	21	28	2	3	0	0	1	3	0	0	0	2	1	0	.107	.194
Torres, Robinson	R-R	5-10	160	2-12-92	.238	.267	.235	50	147	24	35	10	1	0	12	22	6	1	1	24	9	5	.320	.358
Valenzuela, Carlos	R-R	5-11	170	9-18-90	.269	.231	.274	71	245	32	66	9	0	1	22	15	7	6	8	29	28	16	.318	.320
Ventura, Nelson	R-R	5-11	174	5-14-90	.222	.000	.244	21	45	9	10	3	0	0	4	8	5	1	1	11	1	1	.289	.390

Pitching	B-T	HT	WT	DOB	W	L	ERA	G	GS	CG	SV	IP	H	R	ER	HR	BB	SO	AVG	vLH	vRH	K/9	BB/9
Arias, Gabirel	R-R	6-2	185	12-6-89	4	2	1.22	14	10	2	0	74	62	19	10	1	6	67	.228	.261	.217	8.19	0.73
Astacio, Anthony	R-R	6-2	185	9-10-91	0	0	4.50	1	0	0	0	2	1	1	1	0	2	1	.143	.000	.200	4.50	9.00
Basil, Alvaro	R-R	6-3	170	10-28-90	2	1	2.70	11	0	0	2	23	20	10	7	0	9	20	.222	.143	.246	7.71	3.47
Bautista, Erinzon	R-R	6-4	180	11-26-89	0	0	3.86	5	0	0	0	7	6	4	3	0	0	8	.222	.500	.059	10.29	0.00
Best, Carlos	R-R	6-2	170	1-13-91	5	2	1.55	16	11	1	0	76	58	22	13	1	17	66	.217	.184	.230	7.85	2.02
Charles, Francique	R-R	6-0	178	2-28-89	0	1	2.70	5	0	0	0	10	12	5	3	0	8	9	.300	.273	.310	8.10	7.20
De La Cruz, Daniel	R-R	6-3	175	8-10-90	5	0	1.11	17	0	0	6	41	26	7	5	1	11	32	.181	.122	.211	7.08	2.43
Gonzalez, Luis	L-L	6-2	170	1-17-92	3	3	4.14	10	9	1	0	37	28	23	17	0	36	29	.217	.333	.205	7.05	8.76
Guzman, Marlon	R-R	6-4	200	12-3-90	0	0	2.45	2	0	0	0	4	0	1	1	0	3	3	.000	.000	.000	7.36	7.36
Lora, Pedro	L-L	6-1	190	8-11-88	3	4	2.58	9	7	0	1	38	30	15	11	1	10	37	.224	.000	.288	8.69	2.35
Lorenzo, Jorge	R-R	6-2	175	9-29-90	2	1	5.40	8	0	0	0	12	10	8	7	0	5	11	.233	.235	.231	8.49	3.86
Neris, Hector	R-R	6-2	175	6-14-89	1	1	3.24	16	1	0	5	42	30	18	15	1	13	34	.199	.195	.200	7.34	2.81
Nunez, Miguel	R-R	6-6	215	10-27-92	0	3	10.13	3	3	0	0	13	15	16	15	1	6	13	.268	.316	.243	8.78	4.05
Oviedo, Ramon	R-R	6-4	160	7-24-90	4	1	1.57	13	3	0	1	34	27	14	6	0	14	26	.216	.361	.157	6.82	3.67
Reyes, Julio	R-R	6-3	200	4-19-91	2	0	1.89	8	4	1	0	33	22	7	7	0	21	26	.212	.294	.171	7.02	5.67
Sierra, Adrian	L-L	5-11	155	1-10-91	3	4	1.23	15	13	1	0	88	65	16	12	0	25	66	.214	.143	.223	6.78	2.57
Solano, San Lazaro	R-R	5-11	170	12-17-90	4	3	2.57	12	8	1	0	49	52	23	14	1	23	27	.278	.314	.256	4.96	4.22
Sosa, Yari	R-R	6-0	180	9-30-90	4	1	2.05	12	0	0	4	22	21	8	5	0	6	14	.241	.111	.300	5.73	2.45
Vasquez, Jose	L-L	5-11	200	12-11-89	0	0	0.00	1	0	0	0	1	0	0	0	0	0	0	.000	.000	.000	0.00	0.00

Fielding

Catcher	PCT	G	PO	A	E	DP	PB
De La Cruz	.988	28	150	13	2	3	3
Esquea	.972	36	213	34	7	2	8
Marine	1.000	5	25	5	0	0	1
Ventura	.976	20	114	9	3	0	4

First Base	PCT	G	PO	A	E	DP
Berroa	1.000	1	2	0	0	0
De La Cruz	.932	9	38	3	3	3
Dicen	1.000	1	5	0	0	0
Esquea	1.000	4	32	1	0	5
Jimenez	.980	9	90	7	2	5
Marine	.983	49	449	24	8	26
Morales	1.000	12	97	8	0	9
Valenzuela	1.000	1	11	1	0	1

Second Base	PCT	G	PO	A	E	DP
Berroa	.972	7	12	23	1	3
Castillo	.889	4	6	10	2	3
De La Cruz	—	1	0	0	0	0
Ramirez	1.000	9	12	7	0	1
Torres	.955	46	72	99	8	17
Valenzuela	.950	15	20	37	3	7

Third Base	PCT	G	PO	A	E	DP
Berroa	.833	3	1	4	1	0
De La Cruz	1.000	1	0	3	0	0
Morales	.875	33	14	63	11	1
Ramirez	.750	1	0	3	1	0
Valenzuela	.870	47	26	115	21	8

Shortstop	PCT	G	PO	A	E	DP
Berroa	.930	20	31	49	6	8

	PCT	G	PO	A	E	DP
Jimenez	.922	49	95	130	19	28
Ramirez	1.000	2	1	2	0	0
Torres	1.000	1	0	1	0	0
Valenzuela	.960	16	20	52	3	7
Outfield	**PCT**	**G**	**PO**	**A**	**E**	**DP**
Balentien	.955	49	78	6	4	1
Castillo	.977	38	36	6	1	3
De La Cruz	—	1	0	0	0	0
Dicen	1.000	16	22	3	0	2
Francisco	.945	62	95	8	6	1
Jimenez	1.000	16	11	0	0	0
Marine	1.000	3	1	0	0	0
Mejia	1.000	20	18	0	0	0
Olmo	.905	36	37	1	4	0

VSL PHILLIES   ROOKIE
VENEZUELAN SUMMER LEAGUE

Batting	B-T	HT	WT	DOB	AVG	vLH	vRH	G	AB	R	H	2B	3B	HR	RBI	BB	HBP	SH	SF	SO	SB	CS	SLG	OBP
Astudillo, Williams	R-R	5-9	182	10-14-91	.312	.286	.318	56	186	24	58	14	1	0	24	13	10	6	4	4	9	1	.398	.380
Briceno, Jesus	L-R	6-0	160	4-12-92	.237	.286	.222	22	59	3	14	2	0	1	9	5	0	0	2	6	2	1	.322	.288
Chavez, Albertin	R-R	5-10	172	1-21-92	.256	.226	.266	40	125	18	32	4	0	0	13	8	3	3	2	9	7	5	.288	.312

	B-T	HT	WT	DOB	AVG	vLH	vRH	G	AB	R	H	2B	3B	HR	RBI	BB	HBP	SH	SF	SO	SB	CS	OBP	SLG
Davalillo, Marco	R-R	6-1	210	11-5-90	.260	.333	.241	25	73	10	19	3	0	1	12	7	0	0	1	5	4	0	.342	.321
Fajardo, Rosmel	R-R	6-2	177	7-19-92	.286	.250	.295	43	133	29	38	6	1	1	17	12	2	3	2	36	10	1	.368	.349
Fernandez, Rafael	R-R	5-10	168	5-13-92	.213	.243	.202	47	141	13	30	4	0	1	17	14	4	1	3	18	4	3	.262	.296
Machado, Gregorio	B-R	6-1	184	10-28-91	.234	.184	.248	58	175	29	41	11	1	2	19	18	2	3	1	52	9	2	.343	.311
Martinez, Luis	R-R	6-5	183	12-22-89	.317	.167	.348	46	139	25	44	10	1	2	22	11	3	1	4	23	9	5	.446	.369
Mayorga, Jose	R-R	5-10	175	8-20-92	.192	.200	.190	33	73	5	14	0	0	0	5	10	1	1	0	18	1	0	.192	.298
Miranda, Jorge	R-R	6-0	164	5-26-91	.223	.212	.226	52	148	24	33	6	0	2	27	17	4	2	3	28	2	1	.304	.314
Nunez, Rosmer	R-R	5-10	165	6-12-92	.253	.265	.250	60	174	17	44	7	0	0	16	12	7	8	1	31	1	5	.293	.325
Oberto, Wilmer	L-L	5-11	188	11-2-92	.298	.429	.242	36	94	10	28	6	0	0	5	12	1	2	0	17	1	4	.362	.383
Oliveros, Jose	R-R	5-10	195	5-24-92	.263	.300	.250	33	80	11	21	2	1	0	10	11	0	0	0	11	3	0	.313	.352
Salazar, Alexis	R-R	5-11	184	1-26-91	.285	.154	.320	59	186	28	53	6	0	0	17	20	3	2	0	13	7	5	.317	.364
Tolo, Eduards	R-S	5-9	140	10-7-90	.253	.365	.221	65	233	35	59	8	0	0	23	31	3	7	1	14	11	9	.288	.347
Villalobos, Alejandro	R-R	5-11	170	8-20-91	.154	1.000	.083	5	13	1	2	1	0	1	3	1	0	0	0	3	0	1	.462	.214
Villegas, Enderson	R-R	5-10	168	1-31-92	.228	.269	.212	36	92	15	21	4	0	2	15	12	1	2	1	16	3	2	.337	.321

Pitching	B-T	HT	WT	DOB	W	L	ERA	G	GS	CG	SV	IP	H	R	ER	HR	BB	SO	AVG	vLH	vRH	K/9	BB/9
Bastidas, Leonel	R-R	6-3	184	6-26-89	4	4	3.82	14	9	0	0	66	69	40	28	1	16	45	.266	.310	.258	6.14	2.18
Calanche, Jean	R-R	6-1	150	12-31-92	3	1	5.25	14	1	0	0	24	21	15	14	0	19	13	.244	.148	.288	4.88	7.13
Campo, Kirlian	B-L	6-0	180	5-17-90	1	4	6.33	13	0	0	1	27	23	20	19	1	24	25	.235	.385	.212	8.33	8.00
Diaz, Manuel	R-R	6-0	188	9-29-91	2	2	4.76	11	0	0	0	17	25	12	9	0	7	11	.352	.357	.351	5.82	3.71
Escaray, Atilio	R-R	6-2	153	12-29-89	1	1	4.06	15	0	0	2	31	30	16	14	3	12	24	.256	.200	.280	6.97	3.48
Gonzalez, Jorge	L-L	5-11	175	3-30-90	1	1	2.03	4	2	0	0	13	10	5	3	1	2	15	.200	.000	.204	10.13	1.35
Guzman, Jorge	R-R	6-1	201	8-14-91	0	1	3.78	10	10	0	0	50	44	24	21	5	17	32	.229	.259	.217	5.76	3.06
Hernandez, Jose	R-R	6-2	170	1-21-88	1	2	3.50	18	2	0	8	36	35	18	14	1	13	47	.248	.250	.248	11.75	3.25
Honora, Zael	R-R	6-2	199	3-15-90	3	5	3.91	12	12	0	0	51	47	30	22	1	33	36	.250	.226	.262	6.39	5.86
Izurriaga, Ely	L-L	5-11	188	6-29-90	2	5	2.68	15	2	0	4	40	33	14	12	0	24	48	.229	.200	.233	10.71	5.36
Leon, Luis	R-R	6-2	166	11-24-89	1	5	3.63	10	0	0	0	17	20	14	7	0	12	10	.299	.217	.341	5.19	6.23
Martinez, Jose	R-R	6-2	209	2-14-89	7	1	2.31	12	7	0	0	51	33	17	13	0	18	42	.184	.263	.163	7.46	3.20
Mendez, Ronald	R-R	6-5	211	2-27-93	0	0	4.58	12	9	0	0	39	40	23	20	1	16	13	.263	.375	.223	2.97	3.66
Mora, Audrys	L-L	5-11	170	6-14-93	0	0	8.44	12	0	0	1	16	27	18	15	2	12	7	.375	.235	.418	3.94	6.75
Morales, Luis	R-R	6-3	195	3-16-93	1	1	6.75	11	1	0	0	19	20	18	14	1	10	3	.290	.346	.256	1.45	4.82
Rivas, Moises	R-R	6-1	169	10-15-90	3	0	2.78	10	2	0	0	23	20	11	7	1	10	21	.244	.261	.237	8.34	3.97
Silva, Yovan	R-R	6-0	209	2-6-90	2	3	5.05	12	11	0	0	46	49	28	26	1	28	30	.282	.375	.246	5.83	5.44

Fielding

Catcher	PCT	G	PO	A	E	DP	PB
Astudillo	.959	13	83	11	4	0	7
Briceno	1.000	8	42	6	0	0	2
Davalillo	.943	14	67	16	5	3	1
Fernandez	.993	22	126	16	1	3	4
Mayorga	.972	10	32	3	1	1	1
Oliveros	.984	13	50	10	1	0	1
Villegas	.894	10	36	6	5	0	0

First Base	PCT	G	PO	A	E	DP
Davalillo	.976	10	76	4	2	4
Fernandez	.990	12	91	7	1	10
Martinez	.975	27	216	16	6	10
Oberto	1.000	9	56	2	0	6
Oliveros	1.000	14	82	7	0	7

	PCT	G	PO	A	E	DP
Salazar	—	1	0	0	0	0
Villegas	.988	13	75	9	1	2

Second Base	PCT	G	PO	A	E	DP
Astudillo	1.000	7	8	21	0	5
Chavez	.967	18	36	23	2	6
Mayorga	1.000	2	3	7	0	0
Nunez	.962	49	74	103	7	16
Villalobos	1.000	4	8	5	0	1

Third Base	PCT	G	PO	A	E	DP
Astudillo	.904	39	40	92	14	6
Chavez	.921	25	15	55	6	5
Davalillo	.667	1	0	4	2	2
Nunez	1.000	3	1	6	0	0

	PCT	G	PO	A	E	DP
Salazar	—	1	0	0	0	0
Tolo	1.000	6	5	15	0	0

Shortstop	PCT	G	PO	A	E	DP
Nunez	.918	10	16	29	4	6
Tolo	.961	59	93	179	11	20
Villalobos	1.000	1	2	1	0	0

Outfield	PCT	G	PO	A	E	DP
Fajardo	.924	41	67	6	6	0
Machado	.928	52	72	5	6	3
Martinez	1.000	19	27	3	0	0
Miranda	.939	48	43	3	3	0
Oberto	.944	25	31	3	2	0
Salazar	.961	51	93	5	4	1

Pittsburgh Pirates

SEASON IN A SENTENCE: The Pirates extended the worst stretch in American professional sports history with their 18th consecutive losing season. This one wasn't close at 57-105, their first 100-loss season since 2001 and the second-worst in modern franchise history.

HIGH POINT: The Pirates were competitive at home, going 40-41 at PNC Park, where attendance actually increased from 2009. The walk-off, three-run home run from Pedro Alvarez in an Aug. 8 victory against Colorado—in front of a capacity crowd of 38,147—was a happy convergence of the fan support, the team's better play at home and some of its future hope. Outfielder Andrew McCutchen built on his strong rookie season with a .286/.365/.449 sophomore effort.

LOW POINT: A 105-loss season obviously has too many candidates. The 17-63 road mark included 17-game and 14-game losing streaks, and the team had the worst run differential of any major league team since 1900 at minus-276 runs. That extended to a ridiculous number on April 22, when the Brewers pounded the Pirates 20-0. The pitching staff was the worst in baseball, with a 5.00 team ERA, and no one on the staff reached double digits in wins.

NOTABLE ROOKIES: The bright spots for 2010 were on offense. Pittsburgh area native Neil Walker hit 12 homers and surprisingly showed he could play some second base. Alvarez, the 2008 first-round pick, tied for second on the team with 16 homers. And outfielder Jose Tabata hit .299 with 19 stolen bases, second on the club.

KEY TRANSACTIONS: The Pirates were in sell mode and managed to get prospects James McDonald and Andrew Lambo from the Dodgers for Octavio Dotel. McDonald may have been the team's best pitcher after the trade, going 4-5, 3.52 in 11 starts. They also traded Javier Lopez to San Francisco, where the veteran emerged as a postseason hero. The team spent a record $11.9 million in the draft, highlighted by No. 2 overall pick Jameson Taillon. Finally, Pittsburgh fired manager John Russell after the season.

DOWN ON THE FARM: Matt Walbeck managed Altoona to the Double-A Eastern League championship, then was fired after the season. Pirates affiliates ranked 10th in baseball with a cumulative .511 winning percentage, but the system provided little help for the beleaguered major league pitching staff.

OPENING DAY PAYROLL: $34.9 million (30th)

PLAYERS OF THE YEAR

 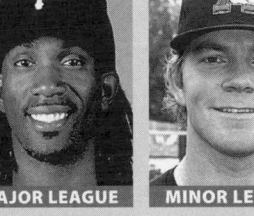

MAJOR LEAGUE	MINOR LEAGUE
Andrew McCutchen	**Rudy Owens**
of	lhp
.286/.365/.449	(Double-A)
16 HR, 9 3B	12-6, 2.46
33 SB, 5th in NL	Led EL in ERA

ORGANIZATION LEADERS

BATTING	*Minimum 250 at-bats	
MAJORS		
*AVG	Jose Tabata	.299
*OPS	Andrew McCutchen	.814
HR	Garrett Jones	21
RBI	Garrett Jones	86
MINORS		
*AVG	Alex Presley, Altoona/Indianapolis	.320
*OBP	Evan Chambers, West Virginia	.384
*SLG	Hector Gimenez, Altoona	.533
R	Chase D'Arnaud, Altoona	91
H	Alex Presley, Altoona/Indianapolis	166
TB	Alex Presley, Altoona/Indianapolis	256
2B	Jarek Cunningham, West Virginia	37
	David Rubinstein, West Virginia	37
3B	Alex Presley, Altoona/Indianapolis	13
HR	Brandon Moss, Indianapolis	22
RBI	Quincy Latimore, Bradenton	100
BB	Evan Chambers, West Virginia	92
SO	Rogelios Noris, West Virginia	144
SB	Evan Chambers, West Virginia	35

PITCHING	†Minimum 75 innings	
MAJORS		
W	Paul Maholm	9
†ERA	Evan Meek	2.14
SO	Paul Maholm	102
MINORS		
W	Three tied at	12
L	Michael Crotta, Altoona/Indianapolis	10
†ERA	Rudy Owens, Altoona	2.46
G	Noah Krol, Bradenton	63
GS	Michael Crotta, Altoona/Indianapolis	28
SV	Noah Krol, Bradenton	34
IP	Michael Crotta, Altoona/Indianapolis	156.7
BB	Justin Wilson, Altoona	71
SO	Jeff Locke, Bradenton/Altoona	139
†AVG	Kyle McPherson, West Virginia/Bradenton	.213

2010 PERFORMANCE

General Manager: Neal Huntington. **Farm Director:** Kyle Stark. **Scouting Director:** Greg Smith.

Class	Team	League	W	L	PCT	Finish*	Manager(s)
Majors	Pittsburgh Pirates	National	57	105	.352	16th (16)	John Russell
Triple-A	Indianapolis Indians	International	71	73	.493	8th (14)	Frank Kremblas
Double-A	Altoona Curve	Eastern	82	60	.577	†2nd (12)	Matt Walbeck
High A	Bradenton Marauders	Florida State	76	62	.551	3rd (12)	P.J. Forbes
Low A	West Virginia Power	South Atlantic	65	74	.468	t-9th (14)	Gary Green
Short-season	State College Spikes	New York-Penn	33	42	.440	12th (14)	Gary Robinson
Rookie	GCL Pirates	Gulf Coast	29	30	.492	9th (15)	Tom Prince
Overall 2010 Minor League Record			356	341	.511	10th (30)	

*Finish in overall standings (No. of teams in league). †League champion.

ORGANIZATION STATISTICS

PITTSBURGH PIRATES

NATIONAL LEAGUE

Batting	B-T	HT	WT	DOB	AVG	vLH	vRH	G	AB	R	H	2B	3B	HR	RBI	BB	HBP	SH	SF	SO	SB	CS	SLG	OBP
Alvarez, Pedro	L-R	6-3	225	2-6-87	.256	.228	.270	95	347	42	89	21	1	16	64	37	0	0	2	119	0	0	.461	.326
Bowker, John	L-L	6-2	200	7-8-83	.232	.286	.226	26	69	7	16	5	0	2	13	8	0	0	0	10	0	1	.391	.312
2-team total (41 San Francisco)					.219	—	—	67	151	16	33	8	0	5	21	14	0	0	2	33	0	1	.371	.281
Cedeno, Ronny	R-R	6-0	190	2-2-83	.256	.291	.246	139	468	42	120	29	3	8	38	23	2	7	2	106	12	3	.382	.293
Church, Ryan	L-L	6-2	215	10-14-78	.182	.147	.191	69	170	16	31	11	1	3	18	12	1	0	0	46	1	0	.312	.240
2-team total (37 Arizona)					.201	—	—	106	219	25	44	16	1	5	25	16	3	0	0	65	1	0	.352	.265
Ciriaco, Pedro	R-R	6-0	160	9-27-85	.500	.000	.500	8	6	3	3	1	1	0	1	0	0	0	0	3	0	0	1.000	.500
Clement, Jeff	L-R	6-1	225	8-21-83	.201	.257	.183	54	144	11	29	3	0	7	12	6	1	1	1	37	0	0	.368	.237
Crosby, Bobby	R-R	6-3	205	1-12-80	.224	.213	.232	61	156	9	35	8	0	1	11	16	1	2	0	33	0	2	.295	.301
2-team total (9 Arizona)					.220	—	—	70	168	9	37	10	0	1	13	17	1	2	1	38	0	3	.298	.294
Diaz, Argenis	R-R	6-0	190	2-12-87	.242	.000	.276	22	33	0	8	1	0	0	2	3	0	0	0	10	0	1	.273	.306
Doumit, Ryan	B-R	6-1	210	4-3-81	.251	.186	.282	124	406	42	102	22	1	13	45	41	8	0	1	87	1	0	.406	.331
Iwamura, Akinori	L-R	5-9	200	2-9-79	.182	.091	.205	54	165	18	30	6	1	2	9	26	0	1	1	31	3	1	.267	.292
Jaramillo, Jason	B-R	6-0	210	10-9-82	.149	.238	.121	33	87	2	13	2	0	1	6	8	1	0	1	14	0	0	.207	.227
Jones, Garrett	L-L	6-4	230	6-21-81	.247	.220	.262	158	592	64	146	34	1	21	86	53	1	0	8	123	7	3	.414	.306
Kratz, Erik	R-R	6-4	255	6-15-80	.118	.143	.111	9	34	2	4	0	0	0	1	2	0	0	0	9	0	0	.118	.167
LaRoche, Andy	R-R	6-1	195	9-13-83	.206	.256	.180	102	247	26	51	8	0	4	16	19	2	2	1	43	1	1	.287	.268
McCutchen, Andrew	R-R	5-10	175	10-10-86	.286	.324	.273	154	570	94	163	35	5	16	56	70	5	1	7	89	33	10	.449	.365
Milledge, Lastings	R-R	5-11	200	4-5-85	.277	.320	.256	113	379	38	105	21	3	4	34	28	3	2	0	62	5	3	.380	.332
Moss, Brandon	L-R	6-0	210	9-16-83	.154	.000	.160	17	26	2	4	1	0	0	2	1	0	0	0	6	0	0	.192	.185
Pearce, Steve	R-R	5-11	190	4-13-83	.276	.294	.250	15	29	4	8	2	1	0	5	7	0	0	2	6	0	0	.414	.395
Presley, Alex	L-L	5-9	180	7-25-85	.261	.500	.238	19	23	2	6	1	0	0	0	1	0	1	0	8	1	1	.304	.292
Raynor, John	R-R	6-1	205	1-4-84	.200	.143	.333	11	10	1	2	0	0	0	1	0	0	0	0	3	0	0	.200	.273
Snyder, Chris	R-R	6-4	245	2-12-81	.169	.179	.167	40	124	12	21	1	0	5	16	16	1	0	1	33	0	0	.298	.268
2-team total (65 Arizona)					.207	—	—	105	319	34	66	9	0	15	48	52	2	1	2	94	0	0	.376	.320
Tabata, Jose	R-R	5-11	210	8-12-88	.299	.247	.315	102	405	61	121	21	4	4	35	28	2	5	1	57	19	7	.400	.346
Walker, Neil	B-R	6-3	210	9-10-85	.296	.295	.296	110	426	57	126	29	3	12	66	34	3	2	4	83	2	3	.462	.349
Young, Delwyn	B-R	5-10	190	6-30-82	.236	.333	.224	110	191	22	45	11	1	2	18	13	1	1	1	52	1	0	.414	.286

Pitching	B-T	HT	WT	DOB	W	L	ERA	G	GS	CG	SV	IP	H	R	ER	HR	BB	SO	AVG	vLH	vRH	K/9	BB/9
Bass, Brian	R-R	6-2	215	1-6-82	0	0	12.27	4	0	0	0	7	9	11	10	0	10	5	.310	.429	.273	6.14	12.27
Burres, Brian	L-L	6-2	190	4-8-81	4	5	4.99	20	13	0	0	79	87	48	44	9	34	45	.275	.308	.265	5.11	3.86
Carrasco, D.J.	R-R	6-4	220	4-12-77	2	2	3.88	45	0	0	0	56	50	24	24	4	22	45	.248	.269	.237	7.28	3.56
2-team total (18 Arizona)					3	2	3.68	63	0	0	0	78	68	39	32	5	34	65	—	—	—	7.47	3.91
Donnelly, Brendan	R-R	6-3	240	7-4-71	3	1	5.58	38	0	0	0	31	26	21	19	6	25	26	.234	.389	.160	7.63	7.34
Dotel, Octavio	R-R	6-0	210	11-25-73	2	2	4.28	41	0	0	21	40	35	21	19	5	17	48	.236	.317	.176	10.80	3.83
3-team total (8 Colorado, 19 Los Angeles)					3	4	4.08	68	0	0	22	64	52	32	29	9	32	75	—	—	—	10.55	4.50
Duke, Zach	L-L	6-2	205	4-19-83	8	15	5.72	29	29	0	0	159	212	115	101	25	51	96	.321	.328	.319	5.43	2.89
Eveland, Dana	L-L	6-1	235	10-29-83	0	1	8.38	3	1	0	0	10	15	9	9	0	5	3	.375	.333	.382	2.79	4.66
Gallagher, Sean	R-R	6-2	235	12-30-85	2	1	6.03	31	0	0	0	34	38	26	23	2	22	22	.277	.230	.316	5.77	5.77
2-team total (15 San Diego)					2	1	5.77	46	0	0	0	58	62	40	37	7	41	43	—	—	—	6.71	6.40
Hanrahan, Joel	R-R	6-4	245	10-6-81	4	1	3.62	72	0	0	6	70	58	28	28	6	26	100	.221	.219	.222	12.92	3.36
Jackson, Steven	R-R	6-5	230	3-15-82	0	1	8.74	11	0	0	0	11	17	11	11	4	6	7	.362	.273	.440	5.56	4.76
Jakubauskas, Chris	R-R	6-2	215	12-22-78	0	1	27.00	1	1	0	0	1	2	2	2	0	0	0	.500	1.000	.000	0.00	0.00
Karstens, Jeff	R-R	6-3	185	9-24-82	3	10	4.92	26	19	0	0	123	146	72	67	21	27	72	.300	.364	.249	5.28	1.98
Ledezma, Wil	L-L	6-4	225	1-21-81	0	3	6.86	27	0	0	0	20	25	16	15	2	6	22	.294	.367	.255	10.07	2.75
Leroux, Chris	L-R	6-6	225	4-14-84	0	1	5.79	6	0	0	0	5	4	3	3	0	4	3	.222	.100	.375	7.71	5.79
2-team total (17 Florida)					0	1	6.75	23	0	0	0	23	28	18	17	1	14	22	—	—	—	8.74	5.56
Lincoln, Brad	L-R	6-0	210	5-25-85	1	4	6.66	11	9	0	0	53	66	42	39	9	15	25	.310	.299	.319	4.27	2.56
Lopez, Javier	L-R	6-4	210	7-11-77	2	2	2.79	50	0	0	0	39	39	14	12	1	18	22	.273	.204	.315	5.12	4.19
2-team total (27 San Francisco)					4	2	2.34	77	0	0	0	58	50	17	15	2	20	38	—	—	—	5.93	3.12
Maholm, Paul	L-L	6-2	220	6-25-82	9	15	5.10	32	32	1	0	185	228	119	105	15	62	102	.303	.231	.316	4.95	3.01
Martinez, Joe	L-R	6-2	195	2-26-83	0	0	3.12	5	0	0	0	9	11	5	3	0	3	6	.297	.316	.278	6.23	3.12

	B-T	HT	WT	DOB	W	L	ERA	G	GS	CG	SV	IP	H	R	ER	HR	BB	SO	AVG	vLH	vRH	K/9	BB/9
2-team total (4 San Francisco)					0	1	4.12	9	1	0	0	20	26	11	9	1	9	9	—	—	—	4.12	4.12
McCutchen, Daniel	R-R	6-2	215	9-26-82	2	5	6.12	28	9	0	0	68	83	48	46	13	28	38	.299	.315	.286	5.05	3.72
McDonald, James	L-R	6-5	195	10-19-84	4	5	3.52	11	11	0	0	64	59	25	25	3	24	61	.249	.228	.272	8.58	3.38
2-team total (4 Los Angeles)					4	6	4.02	15	12	0	0	72	70	32	32	4	29	68	—	—	—	8.54	3.64
Meek, Evan	R-R	6-0	225	5-12-83	5	4	2.14	70	0	0	4	80	53	25	19	5	31	70	.185	.168	.199	7.88	3.49
Morton, Charlie	R-R	6-5	230	11-12-83	2	12	7.57	17	17	0	0	80	112	79	67	15	26	59	.332	.329	.335	6.67	2.94
Ohlendorf, Ross	R-R	6-4	245	8-8-82	1	11	4.07	21	21	0	0	108	106	54	49	12	44	79	.260	.273	.250	6.56	3.66
Park, Chan Ho	R-R	6-2	210	6-30-73	2	2	3.49	26	0	0	0	28	25	14	11	2	7	23	.227	.182	.258	7.31	2.22
Penn, Hayden	R-R	6-3	200	10-13-84	0	0	30.86	3	0	0	0	2	8	8	8	0	3	0	.615	.833	.429	0.00	11.57
Resop, Chris	R-R	6-3	220	11-4-82	0	0	1.89	22	0	0	0	19	10	4	4	1	10	24	.156	.200	.128	11.37	4.74
2-team total (1 Atlanta)					0	0	3.86	23	0	0	0	21	15	9	9	1	13	26	—	—	—	11.14	5.57
Taschner, Jack	L-L	6-3	205	4-21-78	1	1	6.05	17	0	0	0	19	22	13	13	3	8	17	.275	.286	.269	7.91	3.72
2-team total (3 Los Angeles)					1	0	6.41	20	0	0	0	20	23	14	14	3	11	17	—	—	—	7.78	5.03
Thomas, Justin	L-L	6-3	220	1-18-84	0	1	6.23	12	0	0	0	13	21	9	9	3	5	5	.375	.533	.317	3.46	3.46

Fielding

Catcher	PCT	G	PO	A	E	DP	PB
Doumit	.990	100	533	55	6	3	9
Jaramillo	.984	31	170	12	3	2	1
Kratz	1.000	9	56	9	0	0	0
Snyder	.990	40	268	26	3	1	1

First Base	PCT	G	PO	A	E	DP
Bowker	.970	5	29	3	1	1
Clement	.994	38	295	18	2	20
Crosby	1.000	7	47	3	0	6
Doumit	.962	3	23	2	1	1
Jones	.991	112	893	88	9	70
LaRoche	1.000	2	15	0	0	2
Pearce	.988	11	78	7	1	8

Second Base	PCT	G	PO	A	E	DP
Crosby	1.000	15	18	21	0	2
Iwamura	.983	40	75	94	3	26
LaRoche	.950	6	8	11	1	1
Walker	.985	105	222	234	7	62
Young	1.000	5	1	11	0	2

Third Base	PCT	G	PO	A	E	DP
Alvarez	.938	94	61	198	17	17
Crosby	1.000	8	1	11	0	0
LaRoche	.938	54	33	119	10	8
Walker	.933	6	4	10	1	0
Young	.842	8	6	10	3	1

Shortstop	PCT	G	PO	A	E	DP
Cedeno	.969	136	183	382	18	68
Ciriaco	1.000	1	1	2	0	1
Crosby	.922	22	33	62	8	9
Diaz	.923	15	5	19	2	3

Outfield	PCT	G	PO	A	E	DP
Bowker	.968	16	30	0	1	0
Church	1.000	45	76	5	0	1
Doumit	.929	18	38	1	3	0
Jones	.972	49	101	4	3	0
McCutchen	.987	152	373	8	5	2
Milledge	.995	105	190	6	1	2
Moss	1.000	7	5	0	0	0
Presley	1.000	14	3	0	0	0
Raynor	1.000	3	2	0	0	0
Tabata	.995	102	211	5	1	1
Young	.969	21	29	2	1	0

INDIANAPOLIS INDIANS   TRIPLE-A

INTERNATIONAL LEAGUE

Batting	B-T	HT	WT	DOB	AVG	vLH	vRH	G	AB	R	H	2B	3B	HR	RBI	BB	HBP	SH	SF	SO	SB	CS	SLG	OBP
Alvarez, Pedro	L-R	6-3	225	2-6-87	.277	.323	.261	66	242	42	67	15	4	13	53	32	2	0	2	68	4	4	.533	.363
Bernier, Doug	R-R	6-0	185	6-24-80	.240	.301	.205	69	200	24	48	14	0	1	15	17	1	7	1	48	6	1	.325	.301
Bixler, Brian	R-R	6-1	195	10-22-82	.171	.143	.214	11	35	1	6	0	1	0	1	6	0	0	0	11	3	0	.229	.194
3-team total (64 Columbus, 27 Syracuse)					.285	—	—	102	368	45	105	18	4	4	47	30	7	2	4	82	18	7	.389	.347
Bowker, John	L-L	6-2	200	7-8-83	.319	.207	.371	25	91	10	29	7	2	4	10	6	1	0	0	20	0	0	.571	.367
Carlin, Luke	R-R	5-10	195	12-20-80	.239	.327	.209	63	205	23	49	8	1	2	23	27	2	0	2	49	5	2	.317	.331
2-team total (13 Columbus)					.238	—	—	76	244	32	58	10	1	4	29	34	2	1	3	60	5	2	.336	.332
Ciriaco, Pedro	R-R	6-0	160	9-27-85	.281	.390	.225	32	121	19	34	9	1	0	6	2	0	1	2	21	5	1	.372	.288
Clement, Jeff	L-R	6-1	225	8-21-83	.304	.341	.290	42	168	23	51	15	1	8	33	9	0	0	1	48	1	4	.548	.337
Diaz, Argenis	R-R	6-0	190	2-12-87	.248	.293	.236	80	274	28	68	8	1	0	22	19	2	9	0	61	5	1	.285	.302
Doumit, Ryan	B-R	6-1	210	4-3-81	.167	.000	.167	4	12	2	2	1	0	1	2	1	0	0	0	2	0	0	.500	.231
Friday, Brian	R-R	5-11	190	12-16-85	.257	.234	.265	93	288	41	74	19	5	2	28	39	2	6	2	69	10	7	.378	.347
Iwamura, Akinori	L-R	5-9	200	2-9-79	.264	.262	.264	50	163	26	43	10	1	3	16	38	1	0	1	32	0	2	.393	.404
Jaramillo, Jason	B-R	6-0	210	10-9-82	.239	.192	.258	25	88	3	21	3	0	1	13	5	1	0	2	16	0	0	.307	.281
Jones, Brandon	L-R	6-1	215	12-10-83	.205	.178	.216	48	156	15	32	7	1	3	14	16	0	3	1	38	2	3	.321	.277
Jones, Mitch	R-R	6-2	215	10-15-77	.237	.211	.255	30	93	15	22	8	0	5	17	9	3	0	2	22	4	1	.355	.305
2-team total (89 Gwinnett)					.247	—	—	119	417	57	103	31	1	19	54	26	5	0	6	105	6	6	.463	.295
Kratz, Erik	R-R	6-4	255	6-15-80	.274	.309	.259	70	230	30	63	22	1	9	41	32	9	0	3	54	1	2	.496	.380
Melillo, Kevin	L-R	5-11	185	5-14-82	.276	.218	.294	98	352	54	97	24	5	10	44	44	1	2	6	53	9	5	.457	.352
Moss, Brandon	L-R	6-0	210	9-16-83	.266	.248	.274	136	500	73	133	32	2	22	96	42	7	4	3	118	12	7	.450	.330
Myrow, Brian	L-R	5-11	215	9-4-76	.223	.269	.209	94	301	42	67	12	1	7	43	55	6	2	2	72	4	1	.339	.352
Negrych, Jim	L-R	5-10	180	3-2-85	.295	.400	.262	48	166	26	49	7	2	3	19	21	0	3	1	34	8	2	.416	.372
Pearce, Steve	R-R	5-11	190	4-13-83	.326	.269	.340	35	129	25	42	14	2	3	15	24	1	0	4	27	7	2	.535	.424
Presley, Alex	L-L	5-9	180	7-25-85	.294	.310	.286	69	272	44	80	15	6	3	20	17	1	0	4	42	8	7	.460	.349
Tabata, Jose	R-R	5-11	210	8-12-88	.308	.235	.329	53	224	42	69	13	2	3	19	23	2	0	3	35	25	6	.424	.373
Van Every, Jonathan	L-L	6-1	200	11-27-79	.214	.204	.218	74	210	32	45	9	0	10	29	37	2	1	2	85	3	4	.400	.335
Walker, Neil	B-R	6-3	210	9-10-85	.321	.152	.385	43	168	25	54	18	2	6	29	13	1	0	1	31	10	1	.560	.392

Pitching	B-T	HT	WT	DOB	W	L	ERA	G	GS	CG	SV	IP	H	R	ER	HR	BB	SO	AVG	vLH	vRH	K/9	BB/9
Bass, Brian	R-R	6-2	215	1-6-82	4	4	3.26	41	1	0	2	69	74	26	25	3	23	53	.280	.317	.246	6.91	3.00
Burres, Brian	L-L	6-2	190	4-8-81	5	4	4.50	15	14	0	0	82	75	42	41	10	34	61	.245	.172	.277	6.70	3.73
Chick, Travis	R-R	6-3	220	6-10-84	0	0	27.00	1	0	0	0	1	4	3	3	0	1	0	.667	1.000	.333	0.00	9.00
Chulk, Vinnie	R-R	6-2	200	12-19-78	1	0	4.96	28	0	0	0	33	39	18	18	3	12	38	.293	.278	.278	10.47	3.31
Claggett, Anthony	B-R	6-3	195	7-15-84	3	1	6.26	35	0	0	1	55	55	39	38	7	22	44	.270	.263	.274	7.24	3.62
Crotta, Mike	R-R	6-6	210	9-24-84	5	10	4.93	24	24	0	0	131	160	76	72	10	37	89	.305	.287	.324	6.10	2.54
Dubee, Michael	R-R	6-3	185	1-12-86	0	0	0.00	1	0	0	0	1	0	0	0	0	0	0	.000	.000	.000	0.00	18.00
Eveland, Dana	L-L	6-1	235	10-29-83	0	2	7.96	11	5	0	0	26	41	25	23	5	6	25	.353	.267	.384	9.00	2.08
Hamman, Corey	L-L	6-2	200	4-12-80	1	1	3.74	29	0	0	0	43	39	18	18	7	18	36	.242	.167	.280	7.48	3.74
Hankins, Derek	R-R	6-4	192	7-1-83	1	0	16.20	3	0	0	0	2	4	3	3	1	2	1	.400	.429	.333	5.40	10.80

	B-T	HT	WT	DOB	W	L	ERA	G	GS	CG	SV	IP	H	R	ER	HR	BB	SO	AVG	vLH	vRH	K/9	BB/9
Hart, Kevin	R-R	6-4	230	12-29-82	1	0	6.75	5	4	0	1	17	18	14	13	1	11	19	.257	.343	.171	9.87	5.71
Jackson, Steven	K-K	6-5	230	3-15-82	4	0	3.51	41	0	0	0	56	59	24	22	6	19	37	.267	.309	.234	5.91	3.04
Jakubauskas, Chris	R-R	6-2	215	12-22-78	1	4	4.45	8	5	0	0	30	35	15	15	2	10	24	.287	.309	.269	7.12	2.97
Karstens, Jeff	R-R	6-3	185	9-24-82	1	2	7.31	5	1	0	0	16	21	14	13	3	2	12	.304	.357	.268	6.75	1.13
Ledezma, Wil	L-L	6-4	225	1-21-81	0	1	0.94	35	0	0	8	38	20	6	4	1	19	50	.156	.146	.161	11.74	4.46
Lincoln, Brad	L-R	6-0	210	5-25-85	7	5	4.12	17	17	0	0	94	83	47	43	9	24	84	.235	.257	.214	8.04	2.30
Machi, Jean	R-R	6-0	250	2-1-82	5	5	3.92	58	0	0	23	60	51	29	26	6	32	58	.231	.269	.203	8.75	4.83
Martinez, Joe	L-R	6-2	195	2-26-83	1	2	5.72	7	4	0	1	28	46	22	18	6	7	18	.365	.375	.357	5.72	2.22
McCutchen, Daniel	R-R	6-2	215	9-26-82	4	8	3.99	13	13	0	0	79	71	35	35	12	19	39	.243	.233	.253	4.44	2.16
Morton, Charlie	R-R	6-5	230	11-12-83	4	4	3.83	14	14	1	0	80	83	46	34	6	30	53	.265	.284	.248	5.96	3.38
Moskos, Danny	R-L	6-1	210	4-28-86	0	5	10.38	19	0	0	1	17	26	20	20	3	20	18	.351	.353	.350	9.35	10.38
Penn, Hayden	R-R	6-3	200	10-13-84	4	4	4.68	12	12	0	0	65	76	37	34	3	23	56	.299	.230	.355	7.71	3.17
Powell, Jeremy	R-R	6-5	240	6-18-76	11	9	4.62	31	21	0	0	134	139	75	69	15	39	87	.267	.250	.282	5.83	2.61
Thomas, Justin	L-L	6-3	220	1-18-84	5	0	2.48	40	0	0	4	54	33	16	15	4	10	51	.176	.118	.216	8.45	1.66
Veal, Donald	L-L	6-4	235	9-18-84	3	2	4.35	9	9	0	0	50	42	26	24	3	23	41	.232	.227	.234	7.43	4.17

Fielding

Catcher	PCT	G	PO	A	E	DP	PB
Carlin	.988	60	373	37	5	0	3
Clement	1.000	1	4	0	0	0	0
Doumit	1.000	1	5	0	0	0	1
Jaramillo	.990	24	180	23	2	3	1
Kratz	.986	63	435	46	7	5	4

First Base	PCT	G	PO	A	E	DP
Bernier	.981	4	46	5	1	6
Bowker	.986	14	126	10	2	15
Clement	.990	30	260	26	3	22
Jones	1.000	12	95	5	0	16
Kratz	1.000	3	10	3	0	2
Myrow	.994	47	425	40	3	36
Pearce	.995	24	208	13	1	25
Van Every	.981	11	94	8	2	13
Walker	1.000	7	60	6	0	8

Second Base	PCT	G	PO	A	E	DP
Bernier	.979	13	15	32	1	5
Bixler	1.000	4	3	5	0	0
Diaz	1.000	4	4	6	0	2
Friday	.981	69	118	189	6	58
Iwamura	.971	9	10	24	1	6
Melillo	1.000	3	5	8	0	3
Negrych	.979	32	53	89	3	23
Walker	.990	21	36	62	1	12

Third Base	PCT	G	PO	A	E	DP
Alvarez	.936	62	28	134	11	8
Bernier	.938	21	12	48	4	8
Bixler	.929	4	2	11	1	1
Iwamura	.958	38	21	70	4	9
Jones	1.000	4	0	10	0	2
Melillo	1.000	1	1	2	0	0
Myrow	1.000	7	5	11	0	1
Negrych	.938	9	1	14	1	0
Pearce	.895	5	4	13	2	1
Walker	1.000	1	0	4	0	0

Shortstop	PCT	G	PO	A	E	DP
Bernier	.970	21	32	66	3	17
Bixler	1.000	1	0	4	0	0
Ciriaco	.931	31	42	92	10	24
Diaz	.978	75	107	207	7	52
Friday	.989	20	32	61	1	17

Outfield	PCT	G	PO	A	E	DP
Bernier	1.000	3	4	0	0	0
Bixler	1.000	2	4	0	0	0
Bowker	1.000	12	15	1	0	0
Carlin	1.000	1	1	0	0	0
Doumit	—	1	0	0	0	0
Jones	.938	31	44	1	3	0
Jones	1.000	11	18	0	0	0
Melillo	.973	86	137	6	4	0
Moss	.989	105	168	7	2	0
Myrow	1.000	9	17	0	0	0
Negrych	1.000	3	7	0	0	0
Pearce	1.000	5	12	0	0	0
Powell	1.000	1	1	0	0	0
Presley	.987	67	147	5	2	1
Tabata	1.000	53	122	2	0	1
Van Every	.991	50	107	1	1	0
Walker	1.000	14	29	1	0	0

ALTOONA CURVE   DOUBLE-A
EASTERN LEAGUE

Batting	B-T	HT	WT	DOB	AVG	vLH	vRH	G	AB	R	H	2B	3B	HR	RBI	BB	HBP	SH	SF	SO	SB	CS	SLG	OBP
Chen, Yung Chi	R-R	5-11	170	7-13-83	.238	.314	.200	32	105	11	25	5	1	1	14	8	1	1	1	17	2	0	.333	.296
d'Arnaud, Chase	R-R	6-1	175	1-21-87	.247	.270	.238	132	530	91	131	33	9	6	48	56	12	5	4	102	33	7	.377	.331
De Los Santos, Jose L.	R-R	5-11	160	2-17-85	.200	.212	.194	54	150	15	30	4	0	0	12	5	2	10	4	35	9	3	.227	.230
Durham, Miles	R-R	6-4	205	3-21-83	.259	.245	.265	136	483	64	125	27	6	10	69	52	6	0	5	139	9	9	.402	.335
Ford, Shelby	B-R	6-3	185	12-15-84	.245	.278	.227	56	151	16	37	8	1	4	16	6	3	0	3	39	4	0	.391	.288
Gimenez, Hector	B-R	5-10	225	9-28-82	.305	.331	.289	94	338	49	103	29	0	16	72	46	1	1	6	72	6	1	.533	.384
Hague, Matt	R-R	6-3	225	8-20-85	.295	.286	.298	135	509	90	150	30	0	15	86	61	7	0	4	62	3	6	.442	.375
Harrison, Josh	R-R	5-8	175	7-8-87	.300	.285	.306	135	520	74	156	33	3	4	75	32	9	14	10	52	19	7	.398	.345
Hernandez, Gorkys	R-R	6-0	185	9-7-87	.266	.250	.274	92	368	45	98	11	4	2	26	33	5	6	2	95	17	3	.334	.333
Jones, Brandon	L-R	6-1	215	12-10-83	.245	.182	.261	31	110	10	27	5	0	1	7	13	0	0	0	17	0	0	.318	.325
2-team total (29 Erie)					.251	—	—	60	207	20	52	13	0	1	15	40	0	0	0	37	1	1	.329	.372
Lambo, Andrew	L-L	6-3	190	8-11-88	.275	.194	.317	26	91	12	25	1	0	2	10	9	2	0	0	30	0	0	.352	.353
Mercer, Jordy	R-R	6-3	191	8-27-86	.282	.287	.281	126	485	67	137	31	2	3	65	31	7	6	9	69	7	1	.373	.329
Negrych, Jim	L-R	5-10	180	3-2-85	.274	.290	.268	75	230	33	63	11	3	1	35	31	3	1	1	45	2	5	.361	.366
Norman, Anthony	R-R	6-0	185	10-20-84	.220	.109	.255	71	191	28	42	8	2	4	20	28	7	2	3	49	4	2	.346	.336
Presley, Alex	L-L	5-9	180	7-25-85	.350	.358	.345	67	246	42	86	13	7	6	47	19	2	1	1	33	5	1	.533	.399
Skelton, James	L-R	5-11	165	10-28-85	.250	.000	.250	4	4	1	1	0	0	0	0	0	0	0	0	2	0	0	.250	.250
Watts, Kris	L-R	6-1	209	7-15-84	.266	.147	.295	56	173	26	46	13	0	4	19	31	5	3	1	22	0	0	.410	.390

Pitching	B-T	HT	WT	DOB	W	L	ERA	G	GS	CG	SV	IP	H	R	ER	HR	BB	SO	AVG	vLH	vRH	K/9	BB/9
Aguero, Ramon	R-R	6-4	195	12-21-84	2	5	8.68	17	0	0	2	19	27	18	18	1	14	17	.333	.333	.333	8.20	6.75
Alderson, Tim	R-R	6-6	217	11-3-88	7	6	5.62	18	18	0	0	90	112	60	56	10	27	59	.313	.317	.307	5.92	2.71
Barthmaier, Jimmy	R-R	6-5	205	1-6-84	0	0	12.00	5	0	0	0	3	6	5	4	0	5	2	.462	.571	.333	6.00	15.00
Boleska, Tom	R-R	6-0	190	7-30-86	1	1	2.73	12	0	0	3	26	25	10	8	2	8	18	.250	.213	.283	6.15	2.73
Claggett, Anthony	B-R	6-3	195	7-15-84	0	0	3.00	12	0	0	0	15	15	5	5	0	5	13	.268	.310	.222	7.80	3.00
Colla, Mike	R-R	6-2	220	12-23-86	2	0	3.10	13	0	0	1	29	27	11	10	5	8	23	.245	.244	.246	7.14	2.48
Crotta, Mike	R-R	6-6	210	9-24-84	2	0	1.78	4	4	0	0	25	14	5	5	0	3	16	.250	.200	.100	5.68	1.07
Dubee, Michael	R-R	6-3	185	1-12-86	6	2	2.24	45	0	0	5	76	62	23	19	4	19	68	.219	.216	.222	8.02	2.24
Duke, Zach	L-L	6-2	205	4-19-83	0	0	2.57	2	2	0	0	7	5	2	2	1	1	1	.217	.182	.250	1.29	1.29
Hamman, Corey	L-L	6-2	200	4-12-80	0	0	18.00	5	0	0	0	9	15	18	18	4	9	6	.366	.222	.406	6.00	9.00
Hankins, Derek	R-R	6-4	192	7-1-83	5	5	2.83	34	7	1	1	102	88	36	32	7	30	68	.239	.192	.283	6.02	2.66
Hansen, Craig	R-R	6-6	230	11-15-83	0	0	0.00	1	0	0	0	2	0	0	0	0	2	0	.000	.000	.000	9.00	9.00
Hughes, Jared	R-R	6-7	220	7-4-85	12	8	4.42	30	23	0	0	151	166	93	74	15	41	120	.280	.311	.242	7.17	2.45

Name	B-T	HT	WT	DOB	W	L	ERA	G	GS	CG	SV	IP	H	R	ER	HR	BB	SO	AVG	vLH	vRH	K/9	BB/9
Locke, Jeff	L-L	6-2	180	11-20-87	3	2	3.59	10	10	0	0	58	57	24	23	5	12	56	.257	.300	.237	8.74	1.87
Molleken, Dustin	L-R	6-4	228	8-21-84	4	4	4.15	31	0	0	0	61	55	30	28	3	21	62	.237	.250	.226	9.20	3.12
Moreno, Diego	R-R	6-1	177	7-21-86	0	0	7.04	7	0	0	2	8	10	6	6	1	3	12	.313	.353	.267	14.09	3.52
Morris, Bryan	L-R	6-3	210	3-28-87	6	4	4.25	19	16	0	0	89	87	45	42	9	31	84	.258	.238	.279	8.49	3.13
Moskos, Danny	R-L	6-1	210	4-28-86	3	1	1.52	37	0	0	21	41	26	10	7	0	16	43	.179	.170	.185	9.34	3.43
Ohlendorf, Ross	R-R	6-4	245	8-8-82	0	0	0.00	1	1	0	0	4	3	0	0	0	1	6	.200	.167	.333	13.50	2.25
Owens, Rudy	L-L	6-3	215	12-18-87	12	6	2.46	26	26	0	0	150	124	46	41	11	23	132	.226	.204	.239	7.92	1.38
Sues, Jeff	R-R	6-4	225	6-8-83	0	2	3.86	19	0	0	4	26	28	12	11	3	12	19	.269	.259	.283	6.66	4.21
Taschner, Jack	L-L	6-3	205	4-21-78	0	0	4.50	2	0	0	0	2	2	1	1	0	1	2	.250	.000	.500	9.00	4.50
Uviedo, Ronald	R-R	6-1	160	10-7-86	0	2	3.22	16	0	0	0	22	13	8	8	3	12	28	.165	.194	.140	11.28	4.84
2-team total (25 New Hampshire)					5	5	4.72	41	5	0	1	80	69	49	42	15	39	93	—	—	—	10.46	4.39
Watson, Tony	L-L	6-4	223	5-30-85	6	4	2.67	34	9	0	2	111	82	33	33	11	24	105	.203	.131	.248	8.49	1.94
Wilson, Justin	L-L	6-2	233	8-18-87	11	8	3.09	27	26	0	0	143	109	59	49	4	71	134	.215	.243	.201	8.45	4.48

Fielding

Catcher	PCT	G	PO	A	E	DP	PB
Gimenez	.987	92	701	64	10	1	10
Skelton	1.000	2	2	0	0	0	0
Watts	.998	53	400	23	1	3	7

First Base	PCT	G	PO	A	E	DP
Durham	1.000	8	40	3	0	6
Ford	1.000	7	29	6	0	4
Gimenez	1.000	2	12	1	0	1
Hague	.992	134	1211	74	10	106
Mercer	1.000	1	1	2	0	0

Second Base	PCT	G	PO	A	E	DP
Chen	.833	3	3	7	2	1
d'Arnaud	1.000	17	41	46	0	6
De Los Santos	1.000	5	9	18	0	5
Ford	.984	15	27	35	1	11
Harrison	.971	48	90	145	7	29
Mercer	.985	49	84	179	4	40
Negrych	.962	13	23	28	2	3

Third Base	PCT	G	PO	A	E	DP
De Los Santos	.800	4	2	2	1	0
Ford	1.000	2	1	0	0	0
Hague	.000	1	0	1	0	0
Harrison	.939	86	70	146	14	18
Mercer	.943	54	34	99	8	10
Negrych	1.000	1	1	2	0	0

Shortstop	PCT	G	PO	A	E	DP
Chen	.933	3	3	11	1	2
d'Arnaud	.943	115	158	309	28	72
De Los Santos	.957	7	7	15	1	2
Ford	.778	4	2	5	2	1
Mercer	.962	20	28	48	3	11

Outfield	PCT	G	PO	A	E	DP
Chen	.800	15	10	2	3	0
De Los Santos	.956	32	42	1	2	0
Durham	.980	133	236	11	5	0
Ford	1.000	6	4	2	0	0
Hernandez	.975	92	190	6	5	0
Jones	.956	24	42	1	2	0
Lambo	1.000	15	22	1	0	1
Negrych	.909	12	10	0	1	0
Norman	.978	59	90	0	2	0
Presley	.991	66	113	2	1	1

BRADENTON MARAUDERS HIGH CLASS A

FLORIDA STATE LEAGUE

Batting	B-T	HT	WT	DOB	AVG	vLH	vRH	G	AB	R	H	2B	3B	HR	RBI	BB	HBP	SH	SF	SO	SB	CS	SLG	OBP
Anderson, Calvin	R-R	6-7	240	5-8-87	.259	.314	.243	125	464	57	120	29	0	11	73	37	14	0	6	141	2	2	.392	.328
Bishop, Jorge	R-R	5-10	152	3-12-91	.250	.000	.333	4	12	2	3	1	1	0	0	1	0	0	0	3	1	0	.500	.308
Cardona, Rodolfo	R-R	5-10	155	11-27-86	.250	.308	.222	12	40	9	10	2	0	1	5	7	0	0	0	11	0	1	.375	.362
Chourio, Adenson	B-R	5-9	160	7-22-86	.224	.146	.263	49	147	25	33	2	2	0	14	12	0	5	1	37	9	0	.265	.281
Davis, Adam	B-R	5-9	190	10-15-84	.272	.250	.277	69	239	30	65	8	1	0	20	27	2	1	1	51	5	3	.314	.349
De Los Santos, Jose L.	R-R	5-11	160	2-17-85	.216	.214	.216	29	116	14	25	5	0	0	9	6	1	2	1	16	8	4	.259	.258
Farrell, Jeremy	R-R	6-3	200	11-11-86	.298	.417	.265	75	275	39	82	25	0	9	43	23	8	0	0	57	6	2	.487	.369
Ford, Shelby	B-R	6-3	185	12-15-84	.244	.241	.245	36	135	20	33	5	1	2	17	13	2	1	2	35	1	3	.341	.316
Friday, Brian	R-R	5-11	190	12-16-85	.238	1.000	.200	5	21	4	5	1	0	0	1	3	0	0	0	9	1	0	.286	.333
Fryer, Eric	R-R	6-2	215	8-26-85	.300	.312	.293	83	287	53	86	16	5	8	48	37	8	2	3	64	10	1	.474	.391
Gourley, Walker	R-R	6-0	185	6-28-91	.125	.000	.125	3	8	0	1	0	0	0	0	2	0	0	0	2	0	0	.125	.300
Grossman, Robbie	B-L	6-1	190	9-16-89	.245	.279	.233	125	470	84	115	29	3	4	50	66	8	12	6	118	15	8	.345	.344
Holt, Brock	L-R	5-10	165	6-11-88	.351	.449	.317	49	194	31	68	12	1	1	27	19	2	1	2	30	6	3	.438	.410
Huber, Erik	R-R	6-6	230	3-6-85	.220	.302	.188	61	191	15	42	8	0	0	20	16	2	3	0	33	2	0	.262	.287
Latimore, Quincy	R-R	5-10	175	2-3-89	.266	.277	.263	134	518	84	138	31	2	19	100	30	17	1	7	136	11	1	.444	.323
Marte, Starling	R-R	6-1	170	10-9-88	.315	.262	.328	60	222	41	70	16	5	0	33	12	15	2	2	59	22	8	.432	.386
McClune, Austin	R-R	6-2	175	11-15-87	.222	.161	.243	99	338	46	75	13	1	1	30	33	2	4	2	58	9	5	.275	.293
Newton, Jordan	R-R	5-10	195	8-29-85	.331	.394	.309	39	130	17	43	7	0	1	16	16	1	0	1	29	2	0	.408	.405
Ngoepe, Gift	B-R	5-10	165	1-18-90	.250	.333	.000	2	4	0	1	0	0	0	0	1	0	0	0	2	0	0	.250	.400
Norman, Anthony	R-R	6-0	185	10-20-84	.200	.000	.250	4	5	3	1	0	0	0	0	3	0	0	0	1	0	0	.200	.556
Pearce, Steve	R-R	5-11	190	4-13-83	.429	.000	.500	2	7	3	3	2	0	0	2	1	0	0	0	1	0	0	.714	.500
Picart, Greg	B-R	5-11	175	9-25-85	.245	.203	.257	77	282	41	69	5	2	0	25	22	2	5	2	26	14	3	.277	.302
Reyes, Milver	R-R	5-11	200	9-3-82	.091	.333	.000	4	11	0	1	0	0	0	0	1	0	0	0	2	0	0	.091	.167
Sanchez, Tony	R-R	6-0	213	5-20-88	.314	.278	.327	59	207	31	65	17	0	4	35	28	11	0	4	41	2	1	.454	.416
Skelton, James	L-R	5-11	165	10-28-85	.280	.179	.318	69	207	27	58	14	0	3	35	44	2	4	3	45	7	1	.391	.406
Walker, Andrew	R-R	6-0	212	1-22-86	.091	.050	.109	22	66	6	6	0	0	1	3	11	0	1	0	24	0	0	.136	.221

Pitching	B-T	HT	WT	DOB	W	L	ERA	G	GS	CG	SV	IP	H	R	ER	HR	BB	SO	AVG	vLH	vRH	K/9	BB/9
Adcock, Nathan	R-R	6-5	190	2-25-88	11	7	3.37	27	26	0	0	141	131	66	53	8	38	113	.243	.225	.257	7.20	2.42
Aguero, Ramon	R-R	6-4	195	12-21-84	0	0	1.69	8	0	0	1	11	10	2	2	0	3	8	.256	.250	.259	6.75	2.53
Alderson, Tim	R-R	6-6	217	11-3-88	4	3	6.98	9	7	0	0	39	47	32	30	5	13	25	.297	.375	.233	5.82	3.03
Ascanio, Jose	R-R	5-11	190	5-2-85	0	0	0.00	1	1	0	0	2	2	0	0	0	0	4	.250	.000	.333	18.00	0.00
Baker, Nate	L-L	6-3	190	12-27-87	2	3	3.02	9	9	0	0	45	42	17	15	7	31	.258	.281	.252	6.25	3.43
Barthmaier, Jimmy	R-R	6-5	205	1-6-84	0	0	3.00	2	0	0	0	3	1	1	1	0	1	.111	.000	.500	3.00	0.00
Boleska, Tom	R-R	6-0	190	7-30-86	2	3	3.67	30	0	0	2	49	50	26	20	3	9	42	.260	.287	.238	7.71	1.65
Colla, Mike	R-R	6-2	220	12-23-86	0	5	3.42	33	0	0	1	53	46	23	20	4	10	49	.235	.247	.227	8.37	1.71
Cox, Tyler	R-L	6-3	200	4-19-86	5	2	3.32	44	0	0	1	62	46	32	23	8	33	70	.199	.184	.206	10.11	4.76
Erickson, Casey	R-R	6-3	187	8-28-85	6	2	3.38	36	6	0	0	80	79	35	30	3	23	65	.256	.323	.205	7.31	2.59
Felix, Mike	L-L	5-11	206	8-13-85	0	2	6.75	13	0	0	0	16	17	16	12	3	15	12	.270	.313	.255	6.75	8.44
Hanrahan, Joel	R-R	6-4	245	10-6-81	0	0	0.00	2	0	0	2	2	0	0	0	0	0	3	.000	.000	.000	13.50	0.00

	B-T	HT	WT	DOB	W	L	ERA	G	GS	CG	SV	IP	H	R	ER	HR	BB	SO	AVG	vLH	vRH	K/9	BB/9
Hansen, Craig	R-R	6-6	230	11-15-83	1	3	3.86	11	0	0	0	14	13	10	6	0	11	15	.250	.294	.229	9.64	7.07
Jakubauskas, Chris	R-R	6-2	215	12-22-78	0	0	6.23	1	1	0	0	4	7	3	3	0	2	3	.368	.400	.357	6.23	4.15
Krol, Noah	B-R	6-2	185	6-6-84	5	6	3.08	63	0	0	34	64	50	26	22	6	28	48	.212	.211	.212	6.72	3.92
Laureano, Melkin	R-R	6-3	205	8-26-85	3	1	3.82	11	3	0	0	33	28	16	14	4	15	40	.226	.215	.237	10.91	4.09
Leach, Brian	R-R	6-3	195	4-14-86	9	9	3.85	27	25	0	0	138	144	70	59	6	44	98	.268	.226	.298	6.39	2.87
Locke, Jeff	L-L	6-2	180	11-20-87	9	3	3.54	17	17	0	0	86	82	42	34	6	14	83	.248	.337	.218	8.65	1.46
McPherson, Kyle	B-R	6-3	205	11-11-87	0	0	0.00	2	0	0	0	4	2	0	0	0	0	7	.133	.000	.250	15.75	0.00
McSwain, Matt	R-R	6-2	185	8-15-85	2	3	3.64	19	6	0	0	59	70	26	24	2	10	27	.302	.263	.331	4.10	1.52
Moreno, Diego	R-R	6-1	177	7-21-86	4	1	1.17	28	0	0	1	38	14	6	5	3	5	57	.105	.132	.088	13.38	1.17
Morris, Bryan	L-R	6-3	210	3-28-87	3	0	0.60	8	8	0	0	45	37	8	3	0	7	40	.220	.267	.183	8.06	1.41
Pribanic, Aaron	R-R	6-4	200	9-1-86	7	6	3.33	27	27	0	0	154	157	74	57	9	33	71	.263	.285	.245	4.15	1.93
Strickland, Hunter	R-R	6-5	200	9-24-88	2	1	4.50	4	2	0	0	14	16	11	7	1	6	10	.291	.360	.233	6.43	3.86
Taveras, Yerfi	R-R	6-2	160	11-7-88	0	1	6.75	3	0	0	0	4	5	5	3	1	3	1	.333	.000	.417	2.25	6.75
Welker, Duke	L-R	6-7	220	2-10-86	0	1	3.70	20	0	0	0	24	16	12	10	2	23	20	.182	.313	.107	7.40	8.51

Fielding

Catcher	PCT	G	PO	A	E	DP	PB
Fryer	.985	52	363	31	6	2	12
Newton	.958	10	64	4	3	0	0
Reyes	1.000	2	8	2	0	0	0
Sanchez	.976	40	305	14	8	2	4
Skelton	1.000	31	167	22	0	3	6
Walker	.986	12	64	9	1	0	2

First Base	PCT	G	PO	A	E	DP
Anderson	.979	113	1023	69	23	83
Davis	1.000	1	7	0	0	2
Huber	.996	26	198	26	1	19
Pearce	1.000	1	8	2	0	0

Second Base	PCT	G	PO	A	E	DP
Bishop	.938	4	7	8	1	1
Cardona	.941	10	14	18	2	4
Chourio	.970	17	25	40	2	9
Davis	.962	13	28	23	2	7

De Los Santos	1.000	25	42	75	0	16
Ford	.990	22	41	62	1	15
Friday	1.000	2	3	7	0	0
Gourley	1.000	1	0	3	0	0
Ngoepe	.875	2	2	5	1	1
Picart	.974	23	41	70	3	13
Skelton	.960	32	43	101	6	17

Third Base	PCT	G	PO	A	E	DP
Cardona	.889	2	0	8	1	0
Chourio	.727	5	1	7	3	0
Davis	.932	59	35	129	12	12
De Los Santos	.933	4	4	10	1	3
Farrell	.910	72	40	162	20	12
Gourley	1.000	1	0	1	0	0
Huber	—	3	0	0	0	0
Picart	—	1	0	0	0	0

Shortstop	PCT	G	PO	A	E	DP
Chourio	.929	28	27	77	8	14
Ford	.920	16	13	33	4	12
Friday	.933	2	3	11	1	2
Gourley	1.000	1	2	2	0	1
Holt	.927	47	57	120	14	20
Picart	.961	54	73	171	10	23

Outfield	PCT	G	PO	A	E	DP
Chourio	—	1	0	0	0	0
De Los Santos	1.000	1	1	0	0	0
Grossman	.978	124	218	7	5	1
Huber	.941	15	15	1	1	0
Latimore	.970	130	218	6	7	1
Marte	.950	52	105	9	6	2
McClune	.986	96	191	17	3	6
Newton	1.000	5	6	0	0	0
Norman	1.000	3	4	0	0	0

WEST VIRGINIA POWER   LOW CLASS A

SOUTH ATLANTIC LEAGUE

Batting	B-T	HT	WT	DOB	AVG	vLH	vRH	G	AB	R	H	2B	3B	HR	RBI	BB	HBP	SH	SF	SO	SB	CS	SLG	OBP
Baker, Aaron	L-R	6-2	220	9-10-87	.253	.252	.253	125	459	64	116	34	2	18	79	52	11	4	5	115	3	6	.453	.340
Brito, Jesus	R-R	6-1	160	12-25-87	.197	.196	.197	108	366	61	72	16	5	11	49	48	3	7	8	123	5	3	.358	.289
Cabrera, Ramon	B-R	5-7	202	11-5-89	.269	.224	.282	90	342	49	92	14	4	1	40	22	1	3	4	42	3	4	.342	.312
Chambers, Evan	R-R	5-11	210	3-24-89	.239	.247	.236	116	415	71	99	21	2	12	52	92	8	2	3	116	35	17	.386	.384
Chourio, Adenson	B-R	5-9	160	7-22-86	.217	.385	.152	15	46	2	10	0	0	0	4	2	0	2	1	9	5	1	.217	.245
Cunningham, Jarek	R-R	6-1	195	12-25-89	.258	.265	.256	121	488	72	126	37	7	12	49	30	8	2	5	132	11	7	.436	.309
Freeman, Wes	R-R	6-4	215	1-29-90	.155	.103	.182	24	84	3	13	5	1	0	6	6	2	0	2	44	1	4	.238	.223
Gonzalez, Benji	R-R	5-11	160	1-16-90	.236	.235	.237	122	406	40	96	12	1	1	35	35	3	14	2	71	18	14	.278	.300
Gonzalez, Elevys	B-R	5-11	175	10-23-89	.275	.233	.290	67	236	30	65	9	4	6	31	31	0	5	4	48	8	11	.424	.354
Hernandez, Jose	L-R	5-11	195	3-19-86	.271	.170	.305	107	369	51	100	21	2	12	57	51	11	1	5	81	2	4	.436	.372
Irvine, Pat	R-L	6-0	197	1-27-86	.212	.333	.167	10	33	2	7	1	0	0	2	4	0	0	0	7	1	0	.242	.297
Marquez, Jairo	R-R	6-0	170	4-7-88	.303	.278	.310	21	76	11	23	7	1	2	9	1	1	1	0	10	0	0	.500	.321
Morgan, Kyle	L-L	6-1	215	8-8-86	.203	.175	.211	87	295	38	60	16	5	11	36	21	11	0	1	102	3	1	.403	.280
Noris, Rogelios	R-R	6-2	192	3-12-89	.236	.218	.242	111	407	61	96	20	3	15	57	15	12	1	3	144	9	2	.410	.281
Peley, Josue	R-R	6-0	177	12-24-87	.179	.227	.156	19	67	5	12	4	0	0	6	3	1	0	1	14	0	0	.239	.222
Rubinstein, David	R-R	6-2	190	5-18-87	.289	.347	.266	113	433	54	125	37	3	5	30	31	10	1	5	95	23	9	.409	.347
Vasquez, Andy	L-R	6-1	168	10-8-87	.300	.182	.333	13	50	10	15	1	3	1	8	2	0	0	0	20	3	1	.500	.327

Pitching	B-T	HT	WT	DOB	W	L	ERA	G	GS	CG	SV	IP	H	R	ER	HR	BB	SO	AVG	vLH	vRH	K/9	BB/9
Alvarado, Gabriel	R-R	6-2	175	5-19-87	3	5	4.21	40	4	0	5	83	86	44	39	8	26	60	.266	.349	.213	6.48	2.81
Baca, Marc	R-R	5-11	190	10-11-86	5	3	5.26	39	0	0	4	65	75	47	38	4	31	51	.285	.276	.291	7.06	4.29
Baker, Nate	L-L	6-3	190	12-27-87	6	5	3.29	16	16	0	0	87	68	36	29	3	20	63	.210	.213	.209	6.49	2.06
Bankston, Maurice	R-R	6-4	205	6-17-87	7	4	4.68	38	2	0	3	83	85	47	43	7	29	58	.265	.264	.266	6.31	3.16
Black, Victor	R-R	6-3	185	5-23-88	0	0	9.64	2	2	0	0	5	3	5	5	1	5	8	.176	.286	.100	15.43	9.64
Ennis, Justin	L-L	6-1	210	4-20-88	1	1	6.35	3	0	0	0	6	10	4	4	0	3	5	.400	.500	.368	7.94	4.76
Erickson, Jason	R-R	6-1	175	2-3-87	8	6	4.27	31	20	1	0	129	137	68	61	9	24	86	.272	.220	.306	6.02	1.68
Foster, Zach	R-R	6-6	220	5-24-87	5	4	4.28	37	0	0	6	61	63	38	29	8	21	45	.260	.288	.237	6.64	3.10
Holden, Brandon	R-R	6-4	185	1-1-88	1	9	7.25	16	10	0	0	58	77	47	47	10	19	39	.326	.392	.281	6.02	2.93
Irwin, Phillip	R-R	6-3	220	2-25-87	6	3	3.35	23	20	0	0	113	99	46	42	9	20	111	.235	.171	.278	8.84	1.59
Kelly, Ryan	R-R	6-2	170	10-30-87	2	3	4.20	38	1	0	4	75	75	47	35	9	14	75	.253	.254	.253	9.00	1.68
Laureano, Melkin	R-R	6-3	205	8-26-85	2	3	4.15	14	8	0	0	52	53	25	24	6	20	39	.264	.290	.241	6.75	3.46
Lorin, Brett	L-R	6-7	245	3-31-87	2	5	5.18	12	9	0	0	42	50	32	24	5	9	29	.288	.314	.286	6.91	1.94
McPherson, Kyle	B-R	6-3	205	11-11-87	9	7	3.59	26	21	0	0	118	96	58	47	14	31	124	.216	.225	.210	9.48	2.37
Miller, Quinton	R-R	6-1	185	11-28-89	3	6	5.13	10	10	0	0	47	59	32	27	1	15	30	.309	.322	.298	5.70	2.85
Navarro, Eliecer	L-L	5-9	177	10-26-87	1	2	3.49	16	6	0	1	49	46	20	19	6	12	42	.247	.231	.252	7.71	2.20
Ramos, Jhonatan	L-L	5-8	156	8-7-89	1	1	6.63	9	2	0	0	19	29	15	14	2	2	18	.345	.500	.319	8.53	0.95

	B-T	HT	WT	DOB	W	L	ERA	G	GS	CG	SV	IP	H	R	ER	HR	BB	SO	AVG	vLH	vRH	K/9	BB/9
Strickland, Hunter	R-R	6-5	200	9-24-88	0	4	5.86	8	8	0	0	43	58	30	28	6	8	15	.345	.400	.311	3.14	1.67
Welker, Duke	L-R	6-7	220	2-10-86	1	1	3.63	20	0	0	5	22	16	14	9	0	24	25	.198	.200	.196	10.07	9.67
Williams, Mike	L-L	6-5	235	8-11-86	2	2	4.75	26	0	0	2	55	64	38	29	5	13	29	.279	.340	.264	4.75	2.13

Fielding

Catcher	PCT	G	PO	A	E	DP	PB
Cabrera	.990	90	654	72	7	5	12
Irvine	.955	9	59	4	3	0	3
Marquez	1.000	21	134	22	0	0	4
Peley	.992	19	114	16	1	2	3

First Base	PCT	G	PO	A	E	DP
Baker	.982	111	984	62	19	76
Morgan	.975	28	262	14	7	28

Second Base	PCT	G	PO	A	E	DP
Chourio	1.000	8	11	13	0	8

	PCT	G	PO	A	E	DP
Cunningham	.965	119	193	335	19	71
Gonzalez	.977	16	36	49	2	10

Third Base	PCT	G	PO	A	E	DP
Brito	.905	107	62	214	29	20
Chourio	1.000	3	0	7	0	1
Gonzalez	.909	30	27	63	9	9
Vasquez	.875	2	3	4	1	2

Shortstop	PCT	G	PO	A	E	DP
Chourio	.800	4	5	11	4	2
Gonzalez	.940	122	159	340	32	60

	PCT	G	PO	A	E	DP
Gonzalez	.942	15	19	46	4	7

Outfield	PCT	G	PO	A	E	DP
Chambers	.983	115	270	12	5	2
Freeman	1.000	24	59	4	0	0
Hernandez	.971	72	131	5	4	2
Morgan	1.000	5	8	1	0	0
Noris	.985	108	184	13	3	4
Rubinstein	.974	92	176	8	5	1
Vasquez	1.000	6	9	0	0	0

STATE COLLEGE SPIKES

SHORT-SEASON

NEW YORK-PENN LEAGUE

Batting	B-T	HT	WT	DOB	AVG	vLH	vRH	G	AB	R	H	2B	3B	HR	RBI	BB	HBP	SH	SF	SO	SB	CS	SLG	OBP
Acevedo, Andury	R-R	6-4	200	8-23-90	.129	.000	.160	13	31	0	4	0	0	0	0	1	0	0	0	20	0	1	.129	.156
Bencsko, Justin	L-L	6-1	185	8-13-87	.188	.158	.200	19	69	10	13	2	2	0	3	10	0	1	0	15	6	2	.275	.291
Brown, Kelson	R-R	6-3	170	11-7-87	.293	.295	.293	62	225	34	66	12	3	0	26	18	2	1	2	31	3	1	.373	.348
Curry, Matt	L-R	6-1	225	7-27-88	.299	.333	.289	58	197	36	59	14	0	7	29	39	3	0	1	47	7	5	.477	.421
De La Cruz, Melbin	R-R	5-11	180	3-5-90	.167	.250	.000	3	6	0	1	0	0	0	0	0	0	0	0	3	0	0	.167	.167
Gourley, Walker	R-R	6-0	185	6-28-91	.168	.143	.178	61	232	20	39	8	1	1	23	12	4	6	1	76	7	6	.224	.221
Irvine, Pat	R-L	6-0	197	1-27-86	.221	.038	.267	39	131	17	29	9	2	1	14	25	3	0	0	32	3	2	.344	.358
Lyles, Chase	R-R	6-2	206	1-13-87	.241	.275	.229	55	191	34	46	5	3	6	33	24	6	1	0	34	4	5	.393	.344
Maggi, Drew	R-R	6-0	185	5-16-89	.156	.125	.167	18	64	9	10	3	0	0	2	9	0	2	1	15	5	1	.203	.257
Marquez, Jairo	R-R	6-0	170	4-7-88	.167	.000	.333	4	6	0	1	0	0	0	1	1	0	0	0	1	0	0	.167	.286
Mendez, Miguel	R-L	6-1	170	1-8-88	.244	.176	.271	39	119	12	29	3	0	0	10	6	2	2	1	29	7	1	.269	.289
Mort, Kevin	R-R	5-9	170	3-10-88	.222	.500	.143	4	9	1	2	0	0	0	1	3	0	0	0	0	0	0	.222	.417
Ngoepe, Gift	B-R	5-10	165	1-18-90	.205	.283	.178	64	229	30	47	13	5	1	20	36	2	7	3	68	11	7	.319	.315
Rodriguez, Gerlis	R-R	6-2	185	5-29-88	.201	.200	.202	48	159	8	32	8	1	1	24	11	1	3		34	2	1	.283	.253
Rojas Jr., Mel	R-R	6-3	200	5-24-90	.207	.209	.207	43	164	19	34	7	0	0	14	21	3	1	0	42	7	3	.250	.309
Santos, Adalberto	R-R	5-11	185	9-28-87	.319	.200	.364	63	238	45	76	15	7	3	35	33	3	0	2	31	17	7	.479	.406
Saukko, Kyle	L-R	5-11	175	12-21-88	.138	.103	.154	34	94	6	13	3	0	0	8	7	2	3	3	27	1	1	.170	.208
Skirving, Matt	L-R	6-2	215	12-12-89	.217	.231	.213	43	120	15	26	7	1	0	10	12	0	3	1	21	0	0	.292	.286
Vasquez, Andy	L-R	6-1	168	1-0-88	.222	.083	.276	16	41	6	9	1	0	2	6	0	1	1	1	11	0	0	.390	.214
White, Cole	R-R	6-4	205	4-3-85	.250	.268	.243	42	144	14	36	8	2	3	19	15	3	0	3	34	3	1	.396	.327

Pitching	B-T	HT	WT	DOB	W	L	ERA	G	GS	CG	SV	IP	H	R	ER	HR	BB	SO	AVG	vLH	vRH	K/9	BB/9
Beckman, Ryan	R-R	6-4	185	1-2-90	0	2	4.68	21	0	0	3	42	40	25	22	3	16	21	.247	.224	.263	4.46	3.40
Cain, Colton	L-L	6-3	225	2-5-91	1	1	5.03	11	9	0	0	34	23	19	19	2	14	32	.189	.133	.207	8.47	3.71
Cumpton, Brandon	R-R	6-2	198	11-16-88	0	1	2.53	4	3	0	0	11	8	3	3	0	5	6	.200	.278	.136	5.06	4.22
Decker, Kevin	R-R	6-1	185	2-24-88	0	1	3.75	15	4	0	0	58	52	24	24	1	13	30	.243	.330	.183	4.68	2.03
Dodson, Zack	L-L	6-2	190	7-23-90	2	6	4.84	15	13	0	0	58	57	34	31	2	27	41	.265	.221	.286	6.40	4.21
Ennis, Justin	L-L	6-1	210	4-20-88	2	0	5.53	19	0	0	0	28	36	19	17	1	4	22	.316	.350	.297	7.16	1.30
Fallon, Teddy	R-R	6-2	190	10-29-86	0	0	5.06	4	0	0	0	5	2	3	3	0	10	3	.133	.000	.200	5.06	16.88
Fienemann, Mitchell	R-R	6-4	186	5-28-90	3	3	3.62	17	0	0	0	37	39	21	15	3	7	25	.267	.291	.253	6.03	1.69
Fuesser, Zac	L-L	6-2	190	7-19-90	0	4	3.64	15	10	0	1	54	54	25	22	3	27	47	.257	.208	.272	7.79	4.47
Miller, Quinton	R-R	6-1	185	11-28-89	0	1	2.70	4	4	0	0	17	12	7	5	1	2	7	.200	.189	.217	3.78	1.08
Navarro, Eliecer	L-L	5-9	177	10-26-87	1	0	1.04	3	0	0	0	9	6	1	1	1	1	11	.194	.143	.208	11.42	1.04
Payne, Vince	R-R	6-4	175	12-19-90	0	0	1.80	7	0	0	0	5	1	1	1	0	2	3	.063	.000	.111	5.40	3.60
Pounders, Brooks	R-R	6-4	270	9-26-90	3	3	4.46	16	4	0	1	42	40	26	21	5	15	29	.253	.253	.253	6.17	3.19
Ramos, Jhonatan	L-L	5-8	156	8-7-89	3	1	1.62	16	0	0	2	33	22	6	6	0	4	28	.193	.176	.200	7.56	1.08
Rodriguez, Joely	L-L	6-1	175	11-14-91	0	0	6.75	2	0	0	0	4	6	4	3	0	2	2	.333	.500	.286	4.50	4.50
Sadler, Casey	R-R	6-4	200	7-13-90	1	0	3.00	12	1	0	0	24	30	10	8	1	6	21	.309	.267	.346	7.88	2.25
Septimo, Sandobal	R-R	6-0	175	11-24-89	1	1	9.49	10	0	0	0	12	21	13	13	0	5	9	.375	.455	.324	6.57	3.65
Singh, Rinku	L-L	6-2	190	8-8-88	0	0	0.00	1	0	0	0	1	0	0	0	0	1	0	.143	.000	.143	4.50	0.00
Stevenson, Trent	L-R	6-6	175	6-1-90	0	2	4.43	15	0	0	0	41	44	26	20	2	15	23	.286	.237	.316	5.09	3.32
Sullivan, Jarryd	R-R	6-0	181	1-10-90	0	0	8.10	3	0	0	0	3	4	5	3	0	4	1	.267	.167	.333	2.70	10.80
Townsend, Jason	R-R	6-3	190	9-17-88	1	1	3.60	20	0	0	8	20	26	12	8	0	12	16	.313	.378	.261	8.10	5.40
Von Rosenberg, Zack	R-R	6-5	205	9-24-90	1	6	3.20	13	13	0	0	59	60	24	21	4	13	39	.267	.243	.289	5.95	1.98
Waldron, Tyler	R-R	6-2	185	5-1-89	4	7	3.90	14	14	0	0	65	66	33	28	2	11	39	.264	.306	.232	5.43	1.53

Fielding

Catcher	PCT	G	PO	A	E	DP	PB
Irvine	.955	4	20	1	1	0	0
Marquez	.889	4	8	0	1	0	1
Mendez	.987	39	205	23	3	2	2
Skirving	.980	42	228	23	5	0	17

First Base	PCT	G	PO	A	E	DP
Acevedo	1.000	1	10	2	0	1

	PCT	G	PO	A	E	DP
Curry	.990	52	481	33	5	44
Rodriguez	.978	26	252	13	6	22

Second Base	PCT	G	PO	A	E	DP
Brown	1.000	11	21	37	0	6
Gourley	.936	32	56	75	9	20
Mort	1.000	3	4	7	0	1
Ngoepe	.969	28	59	98	5	19

	PCT	G	PO	A	E	DP
Vasquez	.952	5	9	11	1	6

Third Base	PCT	G	PO	A	E	DP
Acevedo	—	1	0	0	0	0
Brown	.976	40	27	96	3	12
Gourley	.885	9	3	20	3	0
Lyles	.922	22	14	45	5	3
Vasquez	.913	6	4	17	2	2

PITTSBURGH PIRATES

Shortstop	PCT	G	PO	A	E	DP
Brown	1.000	3	5	16	0	2
Gourley	.979	21	31	62	2	18
Lyles	—	1	0	0	0	0
Maggi	.905	18	26	50	8	7
Ngoepe	.954	37	67	121	9	22

Outfield	PCT	G	PO	A	E	DP
Acevedo	1.000	7	13	2	0	0
Bencskn	.971	19	31	2	1	1
De La Cruz	.600	2	3	0	2	0
Irvine	1.000	33	57	1	0	0
Rodriguez	—	1	0	0	0	0

Rojas Jr.	.989	43	88	3	1	2
Santos	.992	61	116	6	1	1
Saukko	.984	31	61	1	1	1
Vasquez	—	1	0	0	0	0
White	.984	36	61	2	1	1

GCL PIRATES   ROOKIE
GULF COAST LEAGUE

Batting	B-T	HT	WT	DOB	AVG	vLH	vRH	G	AB	R	H	2B	3B	HR	RBI	BB	HBP	SH	SF	SO	SB	CS	SLG	OBP
Avila, Eric	R-R	6-1	165	6-9-90	.277	.315	.262	54	195	34	54	15	1	7	29	12	4	0	3	33	9	3	.472	.327
Bishop, Jorge	R-R	5-10	152	3-12-91	.257	.321	.228	50	183	27	47	10	4	4	30	11	2	4	1	32	12	4	.421	.305
Cayonez, Exicardo	L-L	6-0	183	10-9-91	.263	.200	.290	46	152	25	40	11	2	0	26	15	11	2	1	34	7	5	.362	.369
Chi, Ping-Hung	L-R	5-7	145	7-1-91	.138	.190	.108	21	58	10	8	0	1	0	3	15	2	1	0	23	4	3	.172	.333
Child, Dylan	R-R	6-1	181	2-21-91	.180	.192	.171	24	61	7	11	1	0	0	2	5	2	2	0	11	1	0	.197	.265
Cornelissen, Daan	L-R	6-2	194	7-6-91	.120	.154	.105	32	83	9	10	4	0	0	5	10	0	1	1	38	3	0	.169	.213
Diaz, Elias	R-R	6-1	175	11-17-90	.218	.333	.170	41	142	20	31	5	1	2	20	10	3	0	2	28	0	2	.310	.280
Farrell, Jeremy	R-R	6-3	200	11-11-86	.357	.000	.385	4	14	4	5	1	0	1	2	2	0	0	0	2	0	0	.643	.438
Freeman, Wes	R-R	6-4	215	1-29-90	.187	.278	.158	21	75	7	14	3	0	1	11	6	2	0	0	35	3	0	.267	.265
Friday, Brian	R-R	5-11	190	12-16-85	.353	.333	.357	5	17	4	6	1	0	1	3	1	0	0	0	0	1	0	.588	.476
Fryer, Eric	R-R	6-2	215	8-26-85	.143	.000	.250	3	7	1	1	0	0	0	0	5	0	0	0	1	0	0	.143	.500
Grovatt, Dan	L-L	6-1	195	10-29-88	.182	.000	.222	3	11	1	2	2	0	0	2	3	0	0	0	3	0	0	.364	.357
Howard, Justin	L-L	6-0	205	8-28-87	.341	.308	.355	15	44	3	15	6	0	0	3	6	0	0	0	12	1	0	.477	.420
Hsu, Chih-Wei	L-L	6-0	200	12-24-91	.154	.188	.130	16	39	6	6	2	0	0	3	0	1	0	0	16	0	0	.205	.214
Lakind, Jared	L-L	6-2	195	3-9-92	.214	.000	.273	4	14	2	3	1	0	1	2	1	0	0	0	7	0	1	.500	.267
Marte, Starling	R-R	6-1	170	10-9-88	.346	.500	.278	8	26	6	9	3	0	2	5	1	1	0	0	6	4	1	.692	.393
Mort, Kevin	R-R	5-9	170	3-10-88	.284	.327	.264	55	176	28	50	7	2	0	20	20	3	3	2	16	6	1	.347	.363
Nivar, Gavi	R-R	6-4	185	9-16-89	.308	.500	.222	4	13	2	4	0	0	0	1	2	1	0	0	2	0	1	.308	.438
Picart, Greg	B-R	5-11	175	9-25-85	.429	.000	.500	2	7	1	3	1	0	0	0	0	0	0	0	1	0	0	.571	.429
Polanco, Gregory	L-L	6-4	170	9-14-91	.202	.167	.216	53	188	21	38	5	1	3	23	9	2	0	1	41	19	2	.287	.245
Schoenfeld, Joey	R-R	6-2	187	6-11-91	.281	.308	.275	23	64	3	18	2	1	0	3	10	1	0	0	21	3	2	.344	.387
Solano, Luis	R-R	6-0	184	7-16-87	.213	.158	.250	31	94	11	20	4	1	1	14	7	4	0	0	19	4	2	.309	.295
Sosa, Junior	L-L	5-10	190	10-3-90	.296	.209	.333	44	142	29	42	3	0	1	11	18	1	3	0	20	20	6	.338	.379
Trinidad, Michaelangel	L-L	5-11	232	8-23-88	.244	.190	.262	27	86	9	21	6	2	4	13	9	4	1	0	14	1	0	.500	.283

Pitching	B-T	HT	WT	DOB	W	L	ERA	G	GS	CG	SV	IP	H	R	ER	HR	BB	SO	AVG	vLH	vRH	K/9	BB/9
Archibald, Cliff	L-R	6-1	190	5-23-90	0	3	5.40	11	8	0	0	35	49	22	21	4	5	17	.329	.377	.295	4.37	1.29
Ascanio, Jose	R-R	5-11	200	5-2-85	0	0	0.00	1	1	0	0	1	0	0	0	0	1	3	.000	.000	.000	27.00	9.00
Cain, Colton	L-L	6-3	225	2-5-91	0	1	3.77	4	4	0	0	14	12	6	6	1	5	15	.214	.231	.209	9.42	3.14
Campos, Fraylin	R-R	5-11	170	1-3-90	2	1	4.01	12	2	0	0	25	26	12	11	2	9	26	.257	.333	.215	9.49	3.28
De Leon, Emmanuel	B-R	6-1	175	12-25-90	1	0	3.86	5	2	0	0	7	11	3	3	0	5	10	.367	.333	.400	12.86	6.43
Hafner, Ryan	R-R	6-6	205	11-22-91	0	1	9.00	2	0	0	0	2	3	2	2	0	1	2	.375	.333	.400	9.00	4.50
Hong, Sheng-Cin	R-R	6-0	160	11-15-90	1	0	14.18	10	0	0	0	13	26	23	21	4	3	10	.406	.391	.415	6.75	2.03
Jakubauskas, Chris	R-R	6-2	215	12-22-78	0	2	7.50	2	2	0	0	6	9	5	5	1	3	6	.346	.400	.273	9.00	4.50
Kingham, Nick	R-R	6-5	220	11-8-91	0	0	0.00	3	3	0	0	3	0	0	0	0	2	2	.273	.000	.375	6.00	0.00
Kleis, Kevin	R-R	6-8	225	8-31-91	0	1	2.78	9	4	0	0	23	25	11	7	1	5	15	.266	.265	.267	5.96	1.99
Lorin, Brett	L-R	6-7	245	3-31-87	0	0	1.29	3	3	0	0	7	1	2	1	1	3	10	.043	.125	.000	12.86	3.86
Miller, Quinton	R-R	6-1	185	11-28-89	0	0	0.00	1	0	0	0	2	0	0	0	0	0	1	.000	.000	.000	4.50	0.00
Montero, Joan	R-R	6-0	186	10-26-88	1	3	3.13	17	1	0	3	37	27	20	13	1	31	36	.206	.163	.232	8.68	7.47
Neverauskas, Dovydas	R-R	6-3	175	1-14-93	1	0	5.40	6	0	0	0	10	14	6	6	0	5	5	.333	.385	.310	5.40	4.50
Pacheco, Yomar	R-R	6-3	200	10-4-89	1	3	4.85	13	0	0	3	30	30	17	16	7	7	23	.259	.239	.239	6.98	2.12
Patel, Dinesh	R-R	5-11	185	5-8-89	0	0	8.59	9	0	0	1	7	14	7	7	1	3	7	.400	.538	.318	8.59	3.68
Payne, Vince	R-R	6-4	175	12-19-90	2	2	2.43	11	10	0	0	37	30	11	10	4	9	21	.222	.167	.242	5.11	2.19
Pevny, Logan	R-R	6-3	190	1-13-92	0	0	5.79	3	0	0	0	5	4	3	3	1	3	3	.222	.500	.143	5.79	5.79
Phillips, Barrett	R-L	6-0	175	6-25-90	5	1	2.63	17	0	0	3	38	33	17	11	2	8	31	.223	.176	.237	7.41	1.91
Rodriguez, Joely	L-L	6-1	175	11-14-91	2	2	3.99	12	9	0	1	47	44	25	21	0	7	26	.240	.278	.231	4.94	1.33
Sanchez, Yeyber	R-R	6-4	198	6-18-90	4	1	5.56	18	0	0	0	34	30	27	21	3	29	24	.236	.220	.250	6.35	7.68
Singh, Rinku	L-L	6-2	190	8-8-88	0	2	2.61	13	0	0	1	21	20	6	6	0	8	20	.253	.227	.263	8.71	3.48
Stevenson, Trent	L-R	6-6	175	6-1-90	1	0	1.80	1	0	0	0	5	2	1	1	0	0	3	.118	.000	.222	5.40	0.00
Sullivan, Jarryd	R-R	6-0	181	1-10-90	3	4	4.11	12	5	0	0	35	40	20	16	3	3	15	.290	.283	.293	3.86	0.77
Taveras, Yerfi	R-R	6-2	160	11-7-88	2	1	3.64	9	4	0	1	30	29	15	12	3	6	19	.256	.256	.247	5.76	1.82
Trepagnier, Bryton	R-R	6-5	180	9-18-91	1	2	4.74	11	0	0	0	19	23	11	10	1	7	15	.311	.300	.318	7.11	3.32
Verdugo, Oscar	R-R	6-1	172	1-21-90	0	1	40.50	1	0	0	0	1	2	3	3	0	1	0	.667	1.000	.500	0.00	13.50
Weidman, Bryce	R-R	6-4	210	12-28-90	0	1	5.63	4	3	0	0	8	6	5	5	0	3	4	.222	.154	.286	4.50	3.38

Fielding

Catcher	PCT	G	PO	A	E	DP	PB
Child	1.000	8	52	5	0	1	2
Diaz	.985	38	234	31	4	2	7
Fryer	1.000	2	5	1	0	0	0
Schoenfeld	1.000	17	86	6	0	4	4

First Base	PCT	G	PO	A	E	DP
Child	.984	14	116	5	2	8
Cornelissen	.993	16	144	6	1	10

Howard	.974	6	34	4	1	5
Hsu	.955	6	21	0	1	3
Lakind	1.000	4	23	4	0	3
Trinidad	1.000	25	176	18	0	13

Second Base	PCT	G	PO	A	E	DP
Avila	1.000	1	6	5	0	3
Bishop	.960	25	36	84	5	10
Friday	1.000	1	0	3	0	0

Mort	1.000	11	19	34	0	8
Solano	.936	24	38	65	7	15

Third Base	PCT	G	PO	A	E	DP
Avila	.928	52	38	116	12	13
Child	—	2	0	0	0	0
Farrell	1.000	2	0	3	0	0
Mort	.800	10	3	13	4	1

Shortstop	PCT	G	PO	A	E	DP
Avila	1.000	1	0	1	0	0
Bishop	.931	23	38	56	7	16
Friday	.750	2	1	2	1	0
Mort	.970	34	44	87	4	13
Picart	.900	2	4	5	1	0

	PCT	G	PO	A	E	DP
Solano	.667	2	1	1	1	0
Outfield	**PCT**	**G**	**PO**	**A**	**E**	**DP**
Cayonez	.985	42	63	1	1	1
Chi	1.000	20	32	0	0	0
Cornelissen	1.000	16	22	1	0	1

	PCT	G	PO	A	E	DP
Freeman	.969	19	29	2	1	1
Marte	.941	7	16	0	1	0
Nivar	.800	2	3	1	1	0
Polanco	.965	48	106	4	4	4
Sosa	.976	38	81	2	2	1

DSL PIRATES   ROOKIE
DOMINICAN SUMMER LEAGUE

Batting	B-T	HT	WT	DOB	AVG	vLH	vRH	G	AB	R	H	2B	3B	HR	RBI	BB	HBP	SH	SF	SO	SB	CS	SLG	OBP
Carvajal, Jodaneli	R-R	5-9	145	4-20-92	.304	.206	.320	64	237	58	72	8	4	1	24	26	6	3	3	41	23	11	.384	.382
Figueroa, Heriberto	R-R	5-11	180	1-25-89	.375	.500	.350	10	24	2	9	1	0	0	4	0	1	1	0	4	2	0	.417	.400
Fortunato, Raul	R-R	6-2	190	9-5-90	.209	.139	.223	67	220	29	46	6	3	1	18	19	5	3	0	48	22	4	.277	.287
Garcia, Willy	R-R	6-3	177	9-4-92	.250	.310	.237	51	168	27	42	11	0	1	22	14	9	3	4	29	8	5	.333	.333
Gonzalez, Samuel	R-R	6-0	180	2-24-89	.349	.350	.349	65	235	33	82	17	5	3	45	14	13	1	1	19	5	5	.502	.414
Goris, Diego	R-R	6-2	165	12-8-90	.310	.296	.313	49	171	31	53	7	1	5	29	9	0	1	1	19	6	6	.450	.343
Hanson, Alen	B-R	5-11	152	10-22-92	.324	.353	.316	68	244	48	79	10	7	2	28	22	2	7	1	37	20	8	.447	.383
Jaquez, Yeffrey	R-R	6-0	180	10-8-90	.293	.333	.287	32	99	6	29	6	0	2	10	8	2	0	0	30	1	1	.414	.358
Jimenez, Jhoanel	B-R	5-11	185	6-19-90	.214	.211	.216	32	70	7	15	3	0	0	6	13	1	0	2	11	0	0	.257	.337
Mejia, Leandro	R-R	6-0	195	6-4-90	.309	.424	.284	59	188	25	58	15	5	0	18	13	4	5	3	35	3	3	.394	.361
Pena, Ramses	B-R	5-10	152	10-9-92	.224	.227	.224	44	98	23	22	5	3	0	5	27	1	4	0	36	14	4	.337	.397
Rivera, Maximo	R-R	5-11	182	12-22-92	.202	.235	.195	37	99	17	20	2	0	0	8	10	3	3	1	27	5	3	.222	.292
Urena, Luis	R-R	6-5	198	8-21-92	.202	.233	.196	50	178	20	36	6	0	0	14	5	6	1	2	63	6	3	.236	.246
Valdemora, Alberto	R-R	6-4	190	12-7-89	.120	.143	.111	21	25	5	3	0	0	1	3	1	0	1	1	11	1	1	.120	.241
Valdez, Robertson	R-R	6-0	204	10-6-92	.203	.000	.241	28	64	8	13	0	0	0	3	7	1	1	1	16	3	2	.203	.288
Vasquez, Jesus	R-R	6-2	180	12-10-91	.265	.355	.245	48	170	24	45	13	0	5	40	10	6	3	2	36	11	4	.429	.324

Pitching	B-T	HT	WT	DOB	W	L	ERA	G	GS	CG	SV	IP	H	R	ER	HR	BB	SO	AVG	vLH	vRH	K/9	BB/9
Aldwey, Darling	L-L	5-10	175	7-27-92	0	0	6.43	9	0	0	0	14	13	13	10	1	17	14	.255	.000	.265	9.00	10.93
Almonte, Brayan	R-R	6-7	188	10-9-91	3	1	5.18	14	0	0	0	24	14	17	14	0	26	16	.165	.103	.196	5.92	9.62
Cadet, Martires	L-L	6-2	170	5-9-91	3	3	2.31	14	14	1	0	70	56	19	18	2	21	47	.220	.261	.216	6.04	2.70
Corporan, Jona	R-R	6-1	195	11-25-91	0	1	7.24	8	2	0	0	14	6	11	11	0	20	17	.133	.000	.176	11.20	13.17
De Leon, Christopher	R-R	6-0	158	8-2-92	0	1	2.29	6	6	0	0	22	12	8	7	0	5	12	.179	.063	.216	4.58	5.49
Ferreras, Miguel	R-R	6-5	221	9-19-91	1	2	15.07	11	1	0	1	14	20	30	24	0	26	12	.328	.333	.326	7.53	16.33
Gonzalez, Yoan	L-L	6-0	165	12-14-89	4	3	3.29	18	0	0	1	52	50	29	19	4	16	34	.249	.077	.261	5.88	2.77
Hernandez, Jimy	R-R	6-2	209	5-22-92	2	4	4.43	15	8	0	1	43	46	29	21	1	20	35	.260	.204	.281	7.38	4.22
Herrand, Yhonatan	R-R	6-5	230	9-11-91	2	3	5.40	13	6	0	0	37	38	26	22	1	24	42	.270	.295	.258	6.14	6.87
Lopez, Porfirio	L-L	5-10	160	3-24-90	3	1	1.53	13	13	0	0	59	36	14	10	1	25	44	.178	.444	.166	6.71	3.81
Lorenzo, Arquimedes	R-R	6-2	187	5-29-91	2	4	6.56	13	13	0	0	48	45	37	35	1	30	26	.257	.362	.205	4.88	5.63
Merejo, Aneudy	R-R	5-10	155	11-9-90	4	2	2.95	22	0	0	8	43	38	18	14	1	16	29	.244	.150	.276	6.12	3.38
Perez, Clario	R-R	6-1	185	8-30-92	1	1	4.56	10	1	0	1	26	31	16	13	0	7	13	.310	.432	.238	4.56	2.45
Perez, Ricky	R-R	6-3	205	5-31-90	1	1	4.58	7	6	0	0	22	12	9	9	0	8	11	.293	.313	.288	5.60	4.08
Richardson, Cristopher	R-R	6-0	184	5-8-92	4	4	5.68	16	0	0	0	38	41	28	24	3	18	47	.231	.279	.113	11.13	4.26
Sanchez, Angel	L-L	6-7	190	3-2-93	4	0	4.02	13	1	0	0	31	25	18	14	1	24	23	.219	.000	.225	6.61	6.89
Sanchez, Isaac	R-R	6-0	170	10-14-92	1	0	1.04	9	0	0	0	9	3	1	1	0	4	9	.107	.143	.095	9.35	4.15
Taveras, Yerfi	R-R	6-2	160	11-7-88	0	3	15.58	7	0	0	2	9	19	17	15	0	8	11	.452	.778	.364	11.42	8.31
Valdez, Luis	R-R	6-0	215	9-27-91	1	0	3.20	11	0	0	0	25	24	14	9	0	13	14	.245	.207	.261	4.97	4.62

Fielding

Catcher	PCT	G	PO	A	E	DP	PB
Figueroa	.964	9	27	0	1	0	2
Gonzalez	.971	32	201	32	7	1	2
Jaquez	.972	14	61	9	2	1	3
Jimenez	.982	32	142	25	3	1	3
Mejia	1.000	1	2	0	0	0	0

First Base	PCT	G	PO	A	E	DP
Gonzalez	1.000	1	3	0	0	0
Goris	1.00+0	6	19	0	0	0
Jaquez	1.000	8	53	2	0	5
Mejia	.985	56	431	32	7	23
Valdez	.978	16	86	1	2	8

Second Base	PCT	G	PO	A	E	DP
Carvajal	1.000	14	25	31	0	6
Goris	.944	8	5	12	1	1
Hanson	.980	40	77	72	3	8
Pena	.958	23	40	29	3	3
Rivera	.923	3	4	8	1	0

Third Base	PCT	G	PO	A	E	DP
Goris	.956	39	46	85	6	6
Hanson	.841	21	14	44	11	3
Rivera	.815	23	10	43	12	1
Valdez	.500	5	1	2	3	1

Shortstop	PCT	G	PO	A	E	DP
Carvajal	.914	47	66	115	17	12
Goris	1.000	8	12	10	0	2
Pena	.912	18	27	35	6	4
Rivera	.929	5	7	19	2	4

Outfield	PCT	G	PO	A	E	DP
Fortunato	.973	67	166	13	5	3
Garcia	.937	47	63	11	5	3
Hanson	1.000	11	11	2	0	0
Jaquez	—	1	0	0	0	0
Mejia	—	1	0	0	0	0
Urena	.974	49	74	2	2	2
Valdemora	1.000	4	5	0	0	0
Vasquez	.971	47	63	3	2	0

VSL PIRATES   ROOKIE
VENEZUELAN SUMMER LEAGUE

Batting	B-T	HT	WT	DOB	AVG	vLH	vRH	G	AB	R	H	2B	3B	HR	RBI	BB	HBP	SH	SF	SO	SB	CS	SLG	OBP
Apomte, Carlos	B-R	5-11	135	2-9-91	.311	.235	.329	63	180	45	56	9	0	0	20	40	3	2	3	24	28	5	.361	.438
Aponte, Kelly	L-R	6-5	220	6-4-91	.241	.200	.250	50	166	18	40	12	0	4	26	16	0	0	2	58	1	0	.386	.304
Avila, Javier	R-R	5-9	162	8-12-91	.133	.143	.131	36	75	9	10	2	0	0	4	4	1	5	0	14	3	1	.160	.188
Cardona, Luis	B-R	5-10	152	7-29-88	.259	.306	.250	63	216	49	56	12	1	2	38	27	7	6	6	29	17	6	.352	.352
Elenes, Norman	L-R	5-11	172	10-7-92	.100	.167	.088	23	40	4	4	0	0	0	6	2	0	0	1	10	1	1	.100	.250
Esqueda, Carlos	R-R	5-8	135	12-6-91	.342	.333	.344	50	152	26	52	8	0	0	16	8	7	2	0	20	9	7	.395	.401

PITTSBURGH PIRATES

	B-T	HT	WT	DOB	AVG	vLH	vRH	G	AB	R	H	2B	3B	HR	RBI	BB	SO	SB	CS				OBP	SLG
Galvez, Jordan	R-R	5-11	157	4-23-92	.309	.231	.325	53	149	20	46	5	2	0	21	9	3	2	0	23	8	7	.369	.360
Marquez, Carlos	L-R	6-2	180	4-29-93	.114	.000	.143	17	35	1	4	1	0	0	2	7	0	0	0	10	0	0	.143	.262
Montilla, Ulises	R-R	5-11	170	5-12-92	.276	.400	.245	45	127	16	35	9	0	0	15	27	3	2	1	11	5	6	.346	.411
Moreno, Manuel	R-R	6-0	165	2-18-92	.286	.429	.238	19	56	10	16	2	3	0	3	13	1	1	1	12	2	0	.429	.423
Ortiz, Jose	R-R	6-0	180	9-15-89	.220	.318	.202	54	141	19	31	8	2	3	15	20	5	0	0	30	3	2	.369	.337
Ozuna, Jose	R-R	6-2	213	12-12-92	.251	.176	.265	64	215	33	54	16	0	10	43	19	5	1	1	35	2	4	.465	.325
Pino, David	R-R	5-11	150	4-28-91	.313	.333	.308	45	160	37	50	15	4	2	33	16	13	0	2	19	12	3	.494	.414
Ponce, Dimas	R-R	5-11	140	1-22-91	.268	.379	.242	41	157	30	42	7	0	0	7	18	2	4	0	17	10	5	.312	.350
Roman, Jose	L-L	6-1	200	12-27-90	.278	.333	.266	58	187	18	52	16	0	3	40	30	0	0	3	41	2	1	.412	.373

Pitching	B-T	HT	WT	DOB	W	L	ERA	G	GS	CG	SV	IP	H	R	ER	HR	BB	SO	AVG	vLH	vRH	K/9	BB/9
Acosta, Jose	R-R	6-2	185	8-12-91	0	0	0.00	1	0	0	0	2	2	0	0	0	1	2	.286	.000	.333	7.71	3.86
Barraza, Jesus	R-R	5-10	150	11-3-90	4	0	0.54	15	0	0	0	33	20	3	2	1	5	15	.172	.080	.198	4.05	1.35
Calderin, Oscar	L-L	6-4	175	2-22-91	0	0	14.73	7	0	0	1	7	14	13	12	1	10	7	.424	.500	.419	8.59	12.27
Campos, Luis	R-R	6-0	188	8-28-90	3	0	1.24	9	5	0	0	29	19	10	4	1	5	15	.178	.200	.172	4.66	1.55
Castro, Orlando	L-L	5-11	194	3-17-92	6	0	1.17	13	11	0	0	54	35	8	7	0	14	34	.191	.333	.173	5.67	2.33
Espinoza, Roberto	R-R	6-1	189	5-7-92	1	1	3.46	14	10	0	0	55	61	28	21	1	17	25	.288	.372	.266	4.12	2.80
Figuera, Luis	R-R	6-1	178	11-11-90	3	2	1.78	23	0	0	8	30	29	10	6	0	11	24	.252	.214	.264	7.12	3.26
Goatache, Deivis	L-L	6-0	160	6-23-88	0	2	6.21	13	3	0	0	29	35	25	20	3	9	22	.289	.143	.298	6.83	2.79
Lopez, Jovany	L-L	5-10	155	3-11-91	5	0	3.90	18	0	0	0	28	30	13	12	1	5	21	.283	.250	.286	6.83	1.63
Marquez, Erick	L-L	5-11	151	2-9-91	3	1	6.26	11	3	0	0	23	34	19	16	2	7	18	.340	.250	.352	7.04	2.74
Marrujo, Jose	R-R	5-10	189	9-21-92	3	0	3.79	15	0	0	1	36	34	18	15	2	14	21	.256	.258	.255	5.30	3.53
Montilla, Richard	R-R	6-0	143	1-10-91	0	1	10.29	13	1	0	0	21	37	28	24	3	27	10	.374	.278	.395	4.29	11.57
Ortiz, Luis	R-R	6-2	170	12-20-91	6	4	4.35	13	12	0	0	52	57	25	25	5	14	24	.281	.256	.287	4.18	2.44
Rocha, Oderman	R-R	6-3	165	11-7-92	0	0	6.30	8	0	0	0	10	13	14	7	0	10	8	.289	.250	.303	7.20	9.00
Rodriguez, Rafael	L-L	5-9	165	7-13-90	1	3	3.54	14	11	0	0	48	54	22	19	4	20	34	.286	.313	.283	6.33	3.72
Romo, Remberto	R-R	5-9	168	10-10-91	6	3	4.55	15	0	0	0	30	30	17	15	2	12	23	.259	.190	.274	6.98	3.64
Ruiz, Carlos	R-R	6-2	169	4-13-91	0	0	0.00	2	0	0	0	2	1	0	0	0	2	2	.143	.500	.000	7.71	7.71
Ruiz, Raul	L-L	5-10	158	12-4-90	1	1	1.63	25	0	0	15	28	19	6	5	0	4	15	.196	.500	.176	4.88	1.30
Vilchez, Francisco	R-R	6-0	183	12-28-90	6	2	2.52	15	12	0	0	64	54	23	18	0	15	39	.224	.258	.212	5.46	2.10

Fielding

Catcher	PCT	G	PO	A	E	DP	PB
Avila	.989	16	77	9	1	1	2
Elenes	.975	18	69	10	2	1	2
Galvez	1.000	1	1	0	0	0	0
Marquez	.872	9	33	1	5	0	5
Ortiz	.982	44	194	25	4	1	11

First Base	PCT	G	PO	A	E	DP
Apomte	.979	14	81	11	2	7
Aponte	.990	26	190	9	2	26
Avila	1.000	2	8	1	0	1
Elenes	1.000	2	6	0	0	0
Galvez	1.000	1	3	0	0	0
Marquez	1.000	3	2	0	0	1
Ortiz	1.000	2	1	1	0	1
Pino	1.000	4	27	1	0	0
Roman	.990	33	274	13	3	21

Second Base	PCT	G	PO	A	E	DP
Apomte	.975	18	40	39	2	11
Esqueda	1.000	2	3	2	0	2
Galvez	.971	25	51	49	3	10
Montilla	1.000	2	2	0	0	0
Pino	.974	32	68	82	4	21

Third Base	PCT	G	PO	A	E	DP
Apomte	.909	8	7	13	2	3
Avila	.917	10	5	6	1	1
Esqueda	.912	36	20	73	9	4
Galvez	.875	21	17	46	9	2
Montilla	.917	5	1	10	1	0
Pino	.882	9	10	20	4	4

Shortstop	PCT	G	PO	A	E	DP
Apomte	.922	20	24	71	8	11
Esqueda	.829	12	12	22	7	2

	PCT	G	PO	A	E	DP
Galvez	.900	4	5	4	1	1
Pino	—	1	0	0	0	0
Ponce	.930	41	69	116	14	25

Outfield	PCT	G	PO	A	E	DP
Apomte	1.000	7	14	0	0	0
Avila	—	1	0	0	0	0
Cardona	.970	63	159	5	5	4
Esqueda	—	1	0	0	0	0
Galvez	1.000	1	1	0	0	0
Montilla	1.000	38	50	5	0	1
Moreno	.933	18	26	2	2	0
Ozuna	.960	53	91	6	4	3
Pino	1.000	4	11	0	0	0
Roman	1.000	9	9	0	0	0
Sucre	.912	50	50	2	5	0

St. Louis Cardinals

SEASON IN A SENTENCE: The Cardinals had star turns from the top players on their roster—Albert Pujols and Matt Holliday in the lineup, Chris Carpenter and Adam Wainwright in the rotation—but they didn't get enough consistent help elsewhere and wilted in August and September to finish second in the National League Central behind the Reds.

HIGH POINT: The Cardinals entered an Aug. 9-11 series against the homestanding Reds trailing by a game in the Central. During a heated series that included the season's biggest brawl—a seven-minute fracas that started with Yadier Molina and Cincinnati's Brandon Phillips jawing and ended with Jason LaRue getting kicked in the head—the Redbirds dominated, sweeping all three games to take a one-game lead into the season's final 49 games.

LOW POINT: St. Louis won its next game against the Cubs, then lost five straight to fall out of first place and never return to the lead. The Cardinals lost 25 of 37 games after the Cubs victory, costing them a playoff spot.

NOTABLE ROOKIES: Lefthander Jaime Garcia may have been the best supporting cast member on the Cardinals, going 13-8, 2.70 in 28 starts and yielding just nine home runs all season. Another rookie, outfielder Jon Jay, struggled down the stretch, but his hot start prompted the Cardinals to trade Ryan Ludwick; Jay took his starting spot and hit a cumulative .300/.359/.422 as the primary right fielder. Third baseman David Freese opened as the regular at the hot corner, and his injury after 70 games hurt the lineup.

KEY TRANSACTIONS: Ludwick was traded to the Padres in a three-team trade that brought Jake Westbrook to St. Louis in an attempt to deepen the rotation. The Cardinals were never able to fill their hole at third after Freese's injury, as Pedro Feliz (acquired from Houston) hit just .208.

DOWN ON THE FARM: St. Louis had a strong year in the minors, with a cumulative .569 winning percentage for affiliates, best in baseball. Rookie-level Johnson City won the Appalachian League, and three other teams made the playoffs. More significantly, the organization took away Jeff Luhnow's responsibilities as farm director and moved John Vuch into that position. Luhnow continues to oversee scouting, and the team signed first-round pick Zach Cox to a major league contract right before the signing deadline.

OPENING DAY PAYROLL: $93.5 million (12th)

2010 PERFORMANCE

General Manager: John Mozeliak. **Farm Director:** John Vuch. **Scouting Director:** Jeff Luhnow.

Class	Team	League	W	L	PCT	Finish*	Manager(s)
Majors	St. Louis Cardinals	National	86	76	.531	6th (16)	Tony La Russa
Triple-A	Memphis Redbirds	Pacific Coast	82	62	.569	t-1st (16)	Chris Maloney
Double-A	Springfield Cardinals	Texas	76	64	.543	2nd (8)	Ron Warner
High A	Palm Beach Cardinals	Florida State	75	65	.536	5th (12)	Luis Aguayo
Low A	Quad Cities River Bandits	Midwest	83	55	.601	2nd (16)	Johnny Rodriguez
Short-season	Batavia Muckdogs	New York-Penn	45	29	.608	2nd (14)	Dann Bilardello
Rookie	Johnson City Cardinals	Appalachian	42	24	.636	†1st (10)	Mike Shildt
Rookie	GCL Cardinals	Gulf Coast	28	28	.500	8th (15)	Steve Turco
Overall 2010 Minor League Record			431	327	.569	1st (30)	

*Finish in overall standings (No. of teams in league). †League champion.

ORGANIZATION STATISTICS

ST. LOUIS CARDINALS

NATIONAL LEAGUE

Batting	B-T	HT	WT	DOB	AVG	vLH	vRH	G	AB	R	H	2B	3B	HR	RBI	BB	HBP	SH	SF	SO	SB	CS	SLG	OBP
Anderson, Bryan	L-R	6-1	200	12-16-86	.281	.500	.250	15	32	1	9	2	0	0	4	1	1	0	1	7	0	0	.344	.314
Craig, Allen	R-R	6-2	210	7-18-84	.246	.208	.273	44	114	12	28	7	0	4	18	9	0	0	1	26	0	1	.412	.298
Descalso, Daniel	L-R	5-10	190	10-19-86	.265	.429	.222	11	34	6	9	2	0	0	4	2	1	0	0	6	1	0	.324	.324
Feliz, Pedro	R-R	6-1	210	4-27-75	.208	.191	.219	40	120	14	25	0	1	1	9	4	0	0	1	10	0	0	.250	.232
2-team total (97 Houston)					.218	—		137	409	36	89	12	2	5	40	13	1	0	6	41	1	1	.293	.240
Freese, David	R-R	6-2	220	4-28-83	.296	.357	.271	70	240	28	71	12	1	4	36	21	4	4	1	59	1	1	.404	.361
Greene, Tyler	R-R	6-2	190	8-17-83	.221	.208	.232	44	104	14	23	3	1	2	10	13	4	0	1	24	2	0	.327	.328
Hamilton, Mark	L-L	6-4	220	7-29-84	.143	.000	.143	9	14	0	2	0	0	0	1	0	0	0	0	5	0	0	.143	.200
Hill, Steven	R-R	5-11	200	3-14-85	.333	.000	.333	1	3	1	1	0	0	1	1	0	0	0	1	0	1	0	.333	.333
Holliday, Matt	R-R	6-4	235	1-15-80	.312	.344	.301	158	596	95	186	45	1	28	103	69	8	0	2	93	9	5	.532	.390
Jay, Jon	L-L	5-11	200	3-15-85	.300	.308	.297	105	287	47	86	19	2	4	27	24	3	8	1	50	2	4	.422	.359
LaRue, Jason	R-R	5-11	205	3-19-74	.196	.250	.182	29	56	3	11	1	0	2	5	5	1	1	0	7	0	0	.321	.274
Lopez, Felipe	B-R	6-0	205	5-12-80	.231	.256	.219	109	376	50	87	18	1	7	36	43	1	3	2	77	8	2	.340	.310
Ludwick, Ryan	R-L	6-3	220	7-13-78	.281	.224	.302	77	281	44	79	20	2	11	43	24	4	0	3	64	0	3	.484	.343
2-team total (59 San Diego)					.251	—		136	490	63	123	27	2	17	69	48	8	0	5	121	0	4	.418	.325
Mather, Joe	R-R	6-4	215	7-23-82	.217	.219	.214	36	60	7	13	4	0	0	3	2	0	2	0	11	1	1	.283	.242
Miles, Aaron	B-R	5-8	180	12-15-76	.281	.281	.280	79	139	14	39	5	0	0	9	6	1	3	2	14	0	1	.317	.311
Molina, Yadier	R-R	5-11	230	7-13-82	.262	.217	.281	136	465	34	122	19	0	6	62	42	7	2	5	51	8	4	.342	.329
Pagnozzi, Matt	R-R	6-2	205	11-10-82	.359	.286	.400	15	39	4	14	2	0	1	2	1	2	0	0	8	0	0	.487	.405
Pujols, Albert	R-R	6-3	230	1-16-80	.312	.306	.314	159	587	115	183	39	1	42	118	103	4	0	6	76	14	4	.596	.414
Rasmus, Colby	L-L	6-2	200	8-11-86	.276	.270	.278	144	464	85	128	28	3	23	66	63	1	2	4	148	12	8	.498	.361
Ryan, Brendan	R-R	6-2	195	3-26-82	.223	.224	.223	139	439	50	98	19	3	2	36	33	2	9	3	60	11	4	.294	.279
Schumaker, Skip	L-R	5-10	195	2-3-80	.265	.211	.275	137	476	66	126	18	1	5	42	43	4	2	4	64	5	3	.338	.328
Stavinoha, Nick	R-R	6-2	240	5-3-82	.256	.262	.250	79	121	11	31	4	0	2	9	4	1	0	0	28	0	0	.339	.286
Winn, Randy	B-R	6-2	195	6-9-74	.250	.237	.255	87	144	16	36	8	1	3	17	13	1	1	3	22	5	0	.382	.311

Pitching	B-T	HT	WT	DOB	W	L	ERA	G	GS	CG	SV	IP	H	R	ER	HR	BB	SO	AVG	vLH	vRH	K/9	BB/9
Boggs, Mitchell	R-R	6-4	215	2-15-84	2	3	3.61	61	0	0	0	67	60	29	27	5	27	52	.243	.253	.238	6.95	3.61
Carpenter, Chris	R-R	6-6	230	4-27-75	16	9	3.22	35	35	1	0	235	214	99	84	21	63	179	.244	.239	.248	6.86	2.41
Franklin, Ryan	R-R	6-3	190	3-5-73	6	2	3.46	59	0	0	27	65	57	25	25	7	10	42	.230	.250	.215	5.82	1.38
Garcia, Jaime	L-L	6-2	215	7-8-86	13	8	2.70	28	28	1	0	163	151	64	49	9	64	132	.243	.211	.251	7.27	3.53
Hawksworth, Blake	R-R	6-3	195	3-1-83	4	8	4.98	45	8	0	0	90	113	56	50	15	35	61	.310	.304	.315	6.08	3.49
Lohse, Kyle	R-R	6-2	210	10-4-78	4	8	6.55	18	18	0	0	92	129	75	67	9	35	54	.336	.344	.330	5.28	3.42
MacDougal, Mike	B-R	6-4	190	3-5-77	1	1	7.23	17	0	0	0	19	23	15	15	1	12	14	.295	.433	.208	6.75	5.79
MacLane, Evan	L-L	6-2	185	11-4-82	0	1	9.00	2	0	0	0	1	1	1	1	1	1	1	.333	.000	.333	0.00	9.00
McClellan, Kyle	R-R	6-2	215	6-19-84	1	4	2.27	68	0	0	2	75	58	20	19	9	23	60	.210	.204	.214	7.17	2.75
Miller, Trever	R-L	6-3	200	5-29-73	0	1	4.00	57	0	0	0	36	30	17	16	2	16	22	.233	.203	.273	5.50	4.00
Motte, Jason	R-R	6-0	200	6-22-82	4	2	2.74	56	0	0	2	52	41	13	13	5	18	54	.220	.267	.198	9.29	3.10
Ottavino, Adam	L-R	6-5	230	11-22-85	0	2	8.46	5	3	0	0	22	37	21	21	5	9	12	.370	.390	.356	4.84	3.63
Penny, Brad	R-R	6-4	230	5-24-78	3	4	3.23	9	9	0	0	56	63	25	20	4	9	35	.293	.360	.248	5.66	1.46
Reyes, Dennys	R-L	6-3	250	4-19-77	3	1	3.55	59	0	0	1	38	34	15	15	2	21	25	.248	.307	.177	5.92	4.97
Salas, Fernando	R-R	6-2	200	5-30-85	0	0	3.52	27	0	0	0	31	28	13	12	4	15	29	.241	.250	.235	8.51	4.40
Suppan, Jeff	R-R	6-2	230	1-2-75	3	8	3.84	15	13	0	0	70	80	32	30	8	25	34	.294	.240	.327	4.22	3.20
2-team total (15 Milwaukee)					3	8	5.06	30	15	0	0	101	130	61	57	13	37	51	—			4.53	3.29
Wainwright, Adam	R-R	6-7	230	8-30-81	20	11	2.42	33	33	5	0	230	186	68	62	15	56	213	.224	.226	.222	8.32	2.19
Walters, P.J.	R-R	6-4	200	3-12-85	2	0	6.00	7	3	0	0	30	32	20	20	5	10	22	.276	.264	.286	6.60	3.00
Westbrook, Jake	R-R	6-3	215	9-29-77	4	4	3.48	12	12	0	0	75	70	31	29	5	24	55	.242	.284	.214	6.60	2.88

Fielding

Catcher	PCT	G	PO	A	E	DP	PB
Anderson	.978	8	40	4	1	0	0
Hill	1.000	1	2	0	0	0	0
LaRue	1.000	28	96	6	0	2	2

	PCT	G	PO	A	E	DP	PB
Molina	.995	135	895	79	5	10	7
Pagnozzi	.988	15	77	4	1	1	1
Stavinoha	1.000	1	1	0	0	0	0

First Base	PCT	G	PO	A	E	DP
Craig	1.000	5	16	1	0	2
Freese	1.000	1	3	0	0	0
Hamilton	1.000	4	23	1	0	3

	PCT	G	PO	A	E	DP
LaRue	1.000	1	1	0	0	0
Lopez	1.000	2	11	0	0	0
Mather	1.000	3	14	0	0	3
Molina	1.000	7	7	0	0	2
Pujols	.998	157	1458	157	4	146
Stavinoha	1.000	3	3	1	0	1

Second Base	PCT	G	PO	A	E	DP
Craig	—	1	0	0	0	0
Greene	.935	15	7	22	2	6
Lopez	1.000	24	35	51	0	14
Miles	.984	50	38	83	2	12
Schumaker	.973	123	210	359	16	76

Third Base	PCT	G	PO	A	E	DP
Craig	.000	2	0	0	1	0
Descalso	1.000	9	2	15	0	4
Feliz	.978	39	18	70	2	4
Freese	.950	66	31	139	9	22
Greene	.929	11	1	12	1	0
Lopez	.926	58	24	102	10	9
Mather	1.000	1	1	0	0	0
Miles	.778	5	3	4	2	0

Shortstop	PCT	G	PO	A	E	DP
Descalso	1.000	1	0	1	0	0
Greene	.934	22	22	49	5	12
Lopez	.969	24	20	43	2	5
Miles	1.000	6	9	5	0	3

Ryan	.974	139	197	430	17	102

Outfield	PCT	G	PO	A	E	DP
Craig	1.000	34	39	1	0	0
Holliday	.989	155	261	8	3	0
Jay	.993	88	137	5	1	1
Lohse	1.000	1	2	0	0	0
Lopez	—	1	0	0	0	0
Ludwick	1.000	68	143	2	0	0
Mather	1.000	25	16	0	0	0
Rasmus	.981	134	260	1	5	0
Schumaker	1.000	17	18	4	0	1
Stavinoha	1.000	27	26	1	0	0
Winn	.983	46	58	0	1	0

MEMPHIS REDBIRDS   TRIPLE-A
PACIFIC COAST LEAGUE

Batting	B-T	HT	WT	DOB	AVG	vLH	vRH	G	AB	R	H	2B	3B	HR	RBI	BB	HBP	SH	SF	SO	SB	CS	SLG	OBP
Anderson, Bryan	L-R	6-1	200	12-16-86	.270	.160	.295	82	270	39	73	12	0	12	42	27	3	0	2	54	0	0	.448	.341
Cazana, Amaury	R-R	6-1	212	9-2-74	.305	.318	.295	78	256	35	78	10	0	13	54	19	0	0	0	51	0	0	.496	.353
Chambers, Adron	L-L	5-10	185	10-8-86	.290	.300	.288	37	69	11	20	0	1	1	8	9	3	1	1	18	6	1	.362	.390
Craig, Allen	R-R	6-2	210	7-18-84	.320	.286	.338	83	306	57	98	24	2	14	81	34	4	0	6	59	1	0	.549	.389
Cruz, Tony	R-R	5-11	205	8-18-86	.214	.000	.250	4	14	2	3	0	0	1	1	1	0	0	0	1	0	0	.429	.267
Derba, Nick	R-R	5-10	190	9-9-85	.000	.000	.000	3	4	0	0	0	0	0	0	0	0	0	0	2	0	0	.000	.000
Descalso, Daniel	L-R	5-10	190	10-19-86	.282	.275	.285	116	468	86	132	32	3	9	71	47	5	5	6	48	8	4	.421	.350
Folli, Mike	B-R	5-10	175	7-17-85	.200	.400	.150	13	25	2	5	1	0	0	2	1	0	1	0	3	0	0	.240	.231
Gotay, Ruben	B-R	5-11	175	12-25-82	.285	.263	.297	139	473	84	135	30	1	13	70	95	6	1	2	116	0	5	.436	.410
Greene, Tyler	R-R	6-2	190	8-17-83	.284	.272	.289	82	338	67	96	21	5	9	34	32	6	8	1	89	12	5	.456	.355
Hamilton, Mark	L-L	6-4	220	7-29-84	.298	.325	.326	72	258	53	77	20	0	18	60	35	7	0	6	70	0	0	.585	.389
Henley, Tyler	L-L	5-10	200	6-10-85	.205	.143	.224	26	88	8	18	6	1	0	7	5	1	0	0	18	0	0	.295	.255
Hill, Steven	R-T	5-11	200	3-14-85	.176	.167	.179	9	34	2	6	1	0	2	6	3	1	0	0	10	0	0	.382	.263
Howard, Kevin	L-R	6-2	190	6-25-81	.242	.227	.246	97	273	30	66	11	1	6	26	19	1	2	0	42	1	1	.355	.294
Jay, Jon	L-L	5-11	200	3-15-85	.321	.180	.404	42	165	31	53	16	0	4	32	17	4	3	2	22	13	0	.491	.394
Ludwick, Ryan	R-L	6-3	220	7-13-78	.333	.000	.333	3	9	2	3	1	0	2	5	0	0	0	2	3	0	0	1.111	.273
Luna, Aaron	R-R	5-11	190	3-28-87	.205	.250	.167	17	44	10	9	1	1	1	5	3	0	0	0	10	0	2	.341	.327
Mather, Joe	R-R	6-4	205	7-23-82	.275	.311	.259	91	335	55	92	18	4	10	46	37	2	0	2	74	6	4	.442	.348
Pagnozzi, Matt	R-R	6-2	205	11-10-82	.242	.257	.226	68	207	20	50	11	0	1	21	27	3	5	0	49	0	0	.309	.338
Rapoport, Jim	L-L	5-11	160	6-25-85	.267	.234	.282	112	408	61	109	12	4	2	34	44	3	7	2	57	8	5	.331	.341
Robinson, Shane	R-R	5-9	160	10-30-84	.279	.458	.210	26	86	9	24	5	0	2	13	7	0	3	1	13	3	3	.407	.330
Shorey, Mark	L-L	6-0	230	8-13-84	.263	.263	.263	63	156	21	41	7	0	3	19	8	1	0	1	37	2	0	.365	.301
Solano, Donovan	R-R	5-10	185	12-17-87	.255	.240	.263	102	330	41	84	12	1	4	27	11	2	1	0	35	2	1	.333	.283
Stavinoha, Nick	R-R	6-2	240	5-3-82	.390	.480	.360	23	100	19	39	9	1	6	28	5	2	0	0	16	0	0	.680	.411

Pitching	B-T	HT	WT	DOB	W	L	ERA	G	GS	CG	SV	IP	H	R	ER	HR	BB	SO	AVG	vLH	vRH	K/9	BB/9
Brown, Andrew	R-R	6-6	230	2-17-81	2	0	6.75	18	0	0	0	24	25	19	18	2	17	18	.269	.412	.186	6.75	4.38
Dickson, Brandon	R-R	6-5	190	11-3-84	11	8	3.23	28	27	0	0	167	180	77	60	11	53	137	.276	.314	.246	7.38	2.86
Fick, Chuck	R-R	6-5	187	11-20-85	3	1	4.78	21	3	0	0	49	51	26	26	7	18	31	.279	.275	.282	5.69	3.31
Hearne, Trey	R-R	6-1	195	8-19-83	0	0	13.03	7	1	0	0	10	17	14	14	2	10	5	.395	.333	.500	4.66	9.31
Hill, Rich	L-L	6-4	185	3-11-80	4	3	4.30	23	4	0	0	46	35	26	22	5	30	47	.217	.196	.227	9.20	5.87
Kinney, Josh	R-R	6-1	215	3-31-79	3	4	1.80	56	0	0	17	60	42	15	12	4	17	51	.200	.167	.225	7.65	2.55
Kopp, David	R-R	6-3	205	10-22-85	0	5	8.63	5	5	0	0	24	38	28	23	4	11	12	.365	.320	.407	4.50	4.13
Kulik, Ryan	L-L	5-11	205	12-3-85	1	4	5.31	10	8	0	0	39	44	37	23	6	30	17	.286	.209	.315	3.92	6.92
Lohse, Kyle	R-R	6-2	210	10-4-78	1	0	3.21	3	3	0	0	14	9	6	5	3	2	14	.170	.182	.161	9.00	1.29
Lynn, Lance	R-R	6-5	250	5-12-87	13	10	4.77	29	29	0	0	164	164	96	87	21	62	141	.259	.262	.257	7.74	3.40
MacDougal, Mike	B-R	6-4	190	3-5-77	2	0	3.86	8	0	0	1	9	4	4	4	1	3	6	.250	.429	.111	5.79	2.89
MacLane, Evan	L-L	6-2	185	11-4-82	7	7	4.45	24	23	1	0	148	163	78	73	21	21	82	.286	.222	.313	5.00	1.28
Motte, Jason	R-R	6-0	200	6-22-82	0	0	3.38	2	0	0	0	3	2	1	1	0	1	2	.200	.000	.250	6.75	3.38
Norrick, Tyler	L-L	6-3	195	9-27-83	3	1	6.60	10	0	0	0	15	16	11	11	1	15	16	.276	.222	.323	9.60	9.00
Ottavino, Adam	L-R	6-5	230	11-22-85	5	3	3.97	9	9	0	0	48	43	23	21	5	12	43	.239	.241	.237	8.12	2.27
Parise, Pete	R-R	6-1	180	12-5-84	0	0	8.50	16	0	0	2	18	28	19	17	5	7	7	.337	.444	.255	3.50	3.50
Perez, Oneli	R-R	6-2	200	5-26-83	2	7	5.09	46	11	0	4	99	100	61	56	11	52	96	.260	.329	.216	8.73	4.73
Pinto, Renyel	L-L	6-4	280	7-8-82	0	0	4.78	18	0	0	0	26	24	17	14	1	22	31	.242	.393	.183	10.59	7.52
Reifer, Adam	R-R	6-2	195	6-3-86	1	0	0.00	1	0	0	0	1	0	0	0	0	1	1	.000	.000	.000	9.00	9.00
Robertson, Nate	R-L	6-2	225	9-3-77	2	1	9.45	6	3	0	0	20	32	22	21	5	6	12	.360	.400	.348	5.40	2.70
Rundles, Rich	L-L	6-5	210	6-3-81	7	1	3.23	56	0	0	0	56	56	24	20	4	18	35	.268	.156	.353	5.66	2.91
Salas, Fernando	R-R	6-2	200	5-30-85	1	0	3.79	34	0	0	19	36	26	15	15	2	9	44	.208	.181	.147	11.10	2.27
Samuel, Francisco	R-R	6-2	185	12-20-86	1	0	4.63	13	0	0	0	12	8	6	6	0	18	10	.190	.250	.136	7.71	13.89
Sanchez, Eduardo	R-R	5-11	155	2-16-89	0	0	1.67	26	0	0	3	27	17	5	5	2	12	31	.200	.262	.151	10.33	4.00
Scherer, Matt	R-R	6-5	260	1-20-83	4	2	3.99	33	0	0	0	47	44	23	21	7	12	30	.244	.291	.208	6.85	2.28
Walters, P.J.	R-R	6-4	200	3-12-85	8	5	3.81	19	18	0	0	109	106	51	46	12	30	106	.254	.296	.219	8.78	2.48

Fielding

Catcher	PCT	G	PO	A	E	DP	PB
Anderson	.991	75	497	41	5	3	4
Cruz	.921	4	31	4	3	0	1
Derba	1.000	3	10	2	0	0	0
Hill	1.000	8	67	4	0	1	0
Pagnozzi	.989	66	423	45	5	4	12

First Base	PCT	G	PO	A	E	DP
Craig	.990	33	286	20	3	29
Descalso	1.000	6	46	0	0	6
Gotay	1.000	6	44	6	0	9
Hamilton	.992	66	554	32	5	68
Howard	.993	32	258	17	2	28
Jay	1.000	1	1	0	0	0
Mather	1.000	1	6	0	0	0
Stavinoha	.985	8	60	4	1	9

Second Base	PCT	G	PO	A	E	DP
Descalso	.973	110	227	311	15	82
Folli	1.000	1	2	2	0	2
Gotay	.982	27	45	62	2	15
Solano	.965	14	23	32	2	8

Third Base	PCT	G	PO	A	E	DP
Folli	1.000	2	3	4	0	1
Gotay	.938	103	68	188	17	16
Howard	.944	35	22	62	5	11
Solano	.973	13	9	27	1	0

Shortstop	PCT	G	PO	A	E	DP
Folli	.917	5	3	8	1	3
Greene	.963	82	128	234	14	62
Solano	.949	63	100	178	15	45

Outfield	PCT	G	PO	A	E	DP
Cazana	.987	48	69	5	1	1
Chambers	.964	21	26	1	1	0
Craig	.974	47	73	3	2	0

	PCT	G	PO	A	E	DP
Dickson	1.000	1	1	0	0	0
Hamilton	1.000	5	3	1	0	0
Henley	.935	23	26	3	2	0
Howard	—	1	0	0	0	0
Jay	.989	41	88	1	1	1
Ludwick	1.000	3	4	0	0	0
Luna	.955	12	21	0	1	0
Mather	.967	85	140	6	5	0
Rapoport	.985	110	255	9	4	2
Robinson	.985	26	64	1	1	0
Shorey	.970	43	65	0	2	0
Stavinoha	1.000	8	14	0	0	0

SPRINGFIELD CARDINALS   DOUBLE-A

TEXAS LEAGUE

Batting	B-T	HT	WT	DOB	AVG	vLH	vRH	G	AB	R	H	2B	3B	HR	RBI	BB	HBP	SH	SF	SO	SB	CS	SLG	OBP
Brown, Andrew	R-R	6-0	185	9-10-84	.291	.340	.258	98	361	65	105	17	1	22	63	41	5	0	0	98	1	2	.526	.371
Carpenter, Matt	L-R	6-3	200	11-26-85	.316	.318	.314	105	396	76	125	26	3	12	53	64	4	4	4	88	11	2	.487	.412
Chambers, Adron	L-L	5-10	185	10-8-86	.282	.252	.302	75	252	52	71	9	5	6	27	31	7	2	0	50	8	4	.417	.376
Cruz, Tony	R-R	5-11	205	8-18-86	.289	.277	.298	40	149	26	43	10	0	6	20	12	1	1	1	30	0	1	.477	.353
Curtis, Jermaine	R-R	5-11	190	7-10-87	.236	.345	.115	23	55	6	13	3	0	0	3	7	2	1	0	10	0	0	.291	.344
Cutler, Charlie	L-R	6-0	200	7-29-86	.218	.244	.205	38	119	11	26	4	0	0	8	15	5	0	1	16	0	0	.252	.329
De La Cruz, Luis	R-R	5-10	165	5-6-89	.143	.000	.143	2	7	0	1	0	0	0	1	0	0	0	0	2	0	0	.143	.143
DeJesus, Antonio	L-L	5-11	185	1-25-86	.206	.218	.201	84	189	31	39	9	5	2	21	26	12	0	2	45	8	0	.339	.336
Derba, Nick	R-R	5-10	190	9-9-85	.240	.208	.269	15	50	7	12	5	0	2	7	3	0	0	0	15	0	0	.460	.283
Folli, Mike	B-R	5-10	175	7-17-85	.214	.114	.268	44	126	10	27	5	2	3	9	15	0	1	0	23	0	3	.357	.298
Freese, David	R-R	6-2	220	4-28-83	.500	.500	.000	1	2	0	1	1	0	0	1	0	0	0	0	1	0	0	1.000	.667
Garcia, Jose	R-R	5-11	170	2-11-88	.259	.202	.296	77	263	35	68	8	1	5	27	19	4	3	2	48	9	3	.354	.316
Henley, Tyler	L-L	5-10	200	6-10-85	.302	.367	.364	16	60	11	22	5	0	3	12	3	0	0	9	0	1	.600	.397
Hill, Steven	R-R	5-11	200	3-14-85	.280	.325	.245	93	361	60	101	27	1	22	86	38	4	0	3	90	1	0	.543	.352
Jones, Daryl	L-L	6-0	180	6-25-87	.244	.275	.225	121	451	67	110	17	6	8	48	52	11	1	3	95	15	9	.361	.335
Kozma, Pete	R-R	6-0	170	4-11-88	.243	.278	.220	132	503	69	122	28	2	13	72	56	1	7	3	111	13	2	.384	.318
Luna, Aaron	R-R	5-11	200	3-28-87	.270	.301	.246	103	319	60	86	13	3	15	54	63	25	0	1	73	5	1	.470	.426
Miles, Aaron	B-R	5-8	180	12-15-76	.279	.200	.355	16	61	11	17	4	0	0	13	7	1	2	0	8	0	1	.344	.362
Pham, Tommy	R-R	6-1	175	3-8-88	.339	.377	.309	38	121	19	41	13	1	3	18	18	1	0	0	28	4	2	.537	.429
Rapoport, Jim	L-L	5-11	160	6-25-85	.321	.286	.347	25	84	13	27	6	0	2	12	10	0	1	1	12	0	0	.464	.389
Scruggs, Xavier	R-R	6-1	210	3-23-87	.245	.250	.242	33	110	16	27	6	0	8	21	10	2	0	0	36	0	0	.518	.320
Sedbrook, Colt	R-R	5-11	180	7-28-85	.165	.136	.191	28	91	10	15	5	0	0	8	12	6	1	0	22	1	0	.220	.303
Smith, Curt	R-R	5-10	210	9-9-86	.279	.238	.314	84	319	39	89	19	2	9	46	15	2	0	4	62	2	1	.436	.312
Swauger, Chris	L-L	6-0	195	8-11-86	.266	.333	.236	47	154	18	41	4	2	5	14	13	2	0	4	40	2	1	.416	.315

Pitching	B-T	HT	WT	DOB	W	L	ERA	G	GS	CG	SV	IP	H	R	ER	HR	BB	SO	AVG	vLH	vRH	K/9	BB/9
Additon, Nick	L-L	6-5	215	12-16-87	9	6	4.43	28	27	0	0	150	155	75	74	22	53	109	.270	.270	.269	6.53	3.17
Broderick, Brian	R-R	6-6	205	9-1-86	11	2	2.77	17	15	2	0	101	96	42	31	6	14	55	.249	.236	.262	4.92	1.25
Buursma, Jason	R-R	6-3	200	9-9-85	2	1	2.50	37	0	0	0	58	39	16	16	5	10	26	.191	.223	.164	4.06	1.56
Daley, Gary	R-R	6-3	200	11-1-85	3	11	6.70	20	18	0	0	89	117	81	66	10	53	62	.322	.321	.323	6.29	5.38
2-team total (2 Midland)					3	11	7.02	22	18	0	0	91	122	86	71	10	58	63	—	—	—	6.23	5.74
Delgado, Ramon	R-R	6-3	195	9-3-86	1	0	1.10	13	0	0	0	16	9	2	2	2	3	17	.164	.130	.188	9.37	1.65
Diapoules, Mark	R-R	6-2	200	5-31-85	1	0	10.13	2	2	0	0	5	4	7	6	0	7	6	.235	.286	.200	10.13	11.81
Eager, Thomas	R-R	6-2	200	8-12-85	2	4	4.15	54	0	0	0	74	62	35	34	6	44	56	.231	.225	.236	6.84	5.38
Fick, Chuck	R-R	6-5	187	11-20-85	2	0	2.00	11	0	0	0	27	19	8	6	0	6	32	.202	.227	.180	10.67	2.00
Garceau, Shaun	R-R	6-1	185	8-28-87	0	6	5.45	7	7	0	0	33	40	26	20	2	19	25	.303	.362	.257	6.82	5.18
Gorgen, Scott	R-R	5-10	190	1-27-87	5	1	1.26	12	8	0	0	50	34	11	7	4	19	46	.188	.169	.200	8.28	3.42
Hearne, Trey	R-R	6-1	195	8-19-83	4	4	4.43	7	7	0	0	43	40	24	21	10	23	31	.255	.294	.225	6.54	4.85
King, Blake	R-R	6-1	195	4-11-87	4	3	2.91	53	0	0	0	68	40	23	22	5	48	84	.173	.200	.153	11.12	6.35
Kopp, David	R-R	6-3	205	10-22-85	12	4	3.05	21	21	1	0	121	126	47	41	9	39	78	.279	.324	.238	5.80	2.90
Kulik, Ryan	L-L	5-11	205	12-3-85	7	5	4.08	23	12	1	1	90	85	46	41	8	29	52	.257	.232	.269	5.18	2.89
Lohse, Kyle	R-R	6-2	210	10-4-78	0	1	9.00	1	1	0	0	5	12	5	5	0	0	4	.500	.556	.333	7.20	0.00
McGregor, Scott	R-R	6-2	193	12-19-86	1	5	3.46	15	12	0	0	81	82	38	31	7	9	49	.264	.293	.229	5.47	1.00
Meyer, Matt	L-L	6-4	220	1-17-85	0	2	6.64	21	0	0	0	26	25	19	15	4	14	20	.294	.281	.302	8.85	6.20
Mulligan, Casey	R-R	6-2	190	10-5-87	0	1	6.00	15	0	0	1	18	22	15	12	1	11	23	.286	.289	.282	11.50	5.50
Mura, Kyle	R-R	6-4	215	11-24-84	0	2	13.50	2	1	0	0	4	5	6	6	2	5	2	.333	.556	.000	4.50	11.25
Nieto, Arquimedes	R-R	6-0	175	4-28-84	1	3	5.30	7	6	0	1	36	36	21	16	9	19	30	.262	.275	.257	7.57	4.79
Norrick, Tyler	L-L	6-3	195	9-27-83	0	1	5.57	22	0	0	0	21	19	13	13	1	18	18	.244	.320	.208	7.71	10.71
Reifer, Adam	R-R	6-2	195	6-3-86	3	1	3.00	51	0	0	17	54	53	18	18	2	15	52	.252	.289	.221	8.67	2.50
Samuel, Francisco	R-R	6-2	185	12-20-86	2	0	3.63	22	0	0	6	22	18	12	9	3	16	27	.217	.184	.244	10.88	6.45
Sanchez, Eduardo	R-R	5-11	155	2-16-89	2	0	3.12	24	0	0	11	26	21	9	9	1	8	27	.232	.325	.164	9.35	2.77

Fielding

Catcher	PCT	G	PO	A	E	DP	PB
Cruz	.986	30	183	32	3	8	3
Cutler	.982	28	199	19	4	1	3

	PCT	G	PO	A	E	DP	PB
De La Cruz	1.000	2	10	1	0	0	1
Derba	.967	15	88	1	3	0	1
Hill	.991	69	476	51	5	4	19

First Base	PCT	G	PO	A	E	DP
Brown	.986	33	261	17	4	27
Folli	1.000	3	5	1	0	0

Hill	.969	6	29	2	1	2
Scruggs	.989	29	248	14	3	27
Smith	.987	80	686	60	10	75
Swauger	1.000	2	13	0	0	1

Second Base	PCT	G	PO	A	E	DP
Curtis	.983	15	22	35	1	15
Folli	.979	21	35	59	2	13
Garcia	.975	69	134	182	8	48
Luna	.950	6	10	9	1	1
Miles	.981	12	21	30	1	11
Sedbrook	.977	28	53	76	3	18

Third Base	PCT	G	PO	A	E	DP
Brown	.946	21	11	42	3	4
Carpenter	.973	104	63	222	8	18
Cruz	1.000	2	2	4	0	1
Curtis	—	1	0	0	0	0
Folli	.939	13	3	28	2	1
Miles	.667	1	1	1	1	0

Shortstop	PCT	G	PO	A	E	DP
Garcia	1.000	7	14	18	0	2
Kozma	.948	132	201	420	34	100
Miles	1.000	3	4	3	0	0

Outfield	PCT	G	PO	A	E	DP
Brown	.981	33	52	1	1	0
Chambers	.969	65	118	8	4	3
DeJesus	.963	71	122	8	5	2
Folli	1.000	1	5	0	0	0
Henley	.938	8	15	0	1	0
Jones	.973	116	207	6	6	1
Luna	.992	76	123	3	1	0
Pham	.927	34	49	2	4	0
Rapoport	.978	23	42	2	1	1
Swauger	.968	31	59	1	2	0

PALM BEACH CARDINALS
HIGH CLASS A
FLORIDA STATE LEAGUE

Batting	B-T	HT	WT	DOB	AVG	vLH	vRH	G	AB	R	H	2B	3B	HR	RBI	BB	HBP	SH	SF	SO	SB	CS	SLG	OBP
Beatty, C.J.	B-R	5-10	190	9-28-88	.245	.143	.262	14	49	11	12	3	0	2	8	6	0	1	0	15	1	0	.429	.327
Bogany, Jarred	R-R	6-3	200	1-4-87	.245	.262	.240	81	265	33	65	8	5	5	38	21	1	6	3	86	19	5	.370	.300
Bolivar, Domnit	R-R	5-11	165	5-12-89	.197	.214	.190	109	366	42	72	12	3	9	33	22	3	10	1	110	9	2	.320	.247
Carpenter, Matt	L-R	6-3	200	11-26-85	.283	.292	.280	28	99	17	28	5	2	1	16	26	2	1	0	14	0	1	.404	.441
Castellanos, Alex	R-R	5-11	180	8-4-86	.270	.264	.272	129	459	62	124	35	7	13	58	38	12	4	4	112	19	9	.462	.339
Cruz, Tony	R-R	5-11	205	8-18-86	.282	.356	.257	46	181	21	51	16	1	1	25	19	0	1	1	33	0	2	.398	.348
Curtis, Jermaine	R-R	5-11	190	7-10-87	.267	.258	.271	56	191	34	51	10	0	0	24	28	13	2	4	25	5	1	.319	.390
Cutler, Charlie	L-R	6-0	200	7-29-86	.292	.200	.330	41	154	23	45	11	2	1	18	17	2	0	1	17	0	0	.409	.368
De La Cruz, Luis	R-R	5-10	165	5-6-89	.194	.292	.159	27	93	11	18	5	3	1	8	3	1	4	0	19	0	1	.344	.227
Derba, Nick	R-R	5-10	190	9-9-85	.202	.167	.216	33	104	13	21	6	0	3	11	14	3	5	1	35	1	0	.346	.311
Espinoza, Roberto	R-R	5-10	165	3-8-89	.158	.250	.133	7	19	2	3	0	0	0	0	4	1	0	0	5	0	0	.158	.333
Garcia, Jose	R-R	5-11	170	2-11-88	.252	.197	.276	49	206	26	52	7	0	1	16	16	1	0	0	35	16	3	.301	.309
Goodwin, Devin	R-R	5-11	185	10-2-86	.200	.000	.200	2	5	0	1	0	0	0	0	0	0	0	0	3	0	0	.200	.200
Greene, Tyler	R-R	6-2	190	8-17-83	.000	.000	.000	2	7	0	0	0	0	0	0	1	0	0	0	4	0	0	.000	.125
Ingram, D'Marcus	R-R	5-9	170	3-30-88	.269	.151	.314	51	193	21	52	10	1	1	20	14	7	1	1	38	11	4	.347	.340
Jackson, Ryan	R-R	6-3	180	5-10-88	.291	.375	.267	41	148	14	43	10	1	1	8	11	1	6	1	21	3	2	.392	.342
Klein, Geoff	B-R	6-3	200	3-27-88	.000	.000	.000	1	5	0	0	0	0	0	1	0	0	1	0	1	0	0	.000	.000
Marmol, Oliver	R-R	5-10	165	7-2-86	.221	.244	.203	33	104	19	23	9	0	2	12	12	7	1	2	33	4	2	.365	.336
Morales, Osvaldo	R-R	6-2	217	7-4-87	.116	.143	.104	17	69	6	8	3	0	0	2	3	0	0	0	26	3	0	.159	.153
Moscatel, Kevin	R-R	6-1	175	5-16-91	.083	.000	.100	5	12	1	1	0	0	0	2	0	0	0	3	0	0	.083	.214
Obregon, Ted	B-R	5-11	170	5-4-90	.174	.250	.143	22	69	11	12	3	0	0	5	3	0	3	0	17	6	1	.217	.208
Pham, Tommy	R-R	6-1	175	3-8-88	.262	.299	.247	68	237	42	62	14	4	3	27	42	3	1	2	59	13	4	.392	.377
Racobaldo, Rich	R-R	6-1	220	7-10-85	.262	.345	.232	118	423	49	111	27	0	4	50	45	4	3	6	100	8	7	.355	.335
Rivera, Francisco	L-L	5-11	170	12-3-88	.250	.286	.243	11	44	4	11	4	1	0	8	2	0	0	1	1	0	.386	.283
Rodriguez, Ryde	B-R	6-3	232	2-2-88	.266	.185	.293	32	109	6	29	6	0	0	11	7	0	1	0	16	0	1	.321	.310
Scruggs, Xavier	R-R	6-1	210	9-23-87	.269	.267	.270	87	316	42	85	18	1	13	53	30	8	0	3	107	5	4	.456	.345
Sedbrook, Colt	R-R	5-11	180	7-28-85	.221	.195	.229	58	181	25	40	4	1	1	13	20	13	3	3	29	9	6	.271	.363
Shepherd, Devin	R-R	6-3	225	9-9-87	.171	.300	.120	9	35	3	6	1	1	0	4	1	0	0	0	14	0	0	.257	.194
Smith, Ross	R-R	6-2	190	10-6-87	.077	.143	.000	4	13	0	1	0	0	0	0	1	0	2	0	7	0	1	.077	.143
Swauger, Chris	L-L	6-0	195	8-11-86	.294	.342	.279	39	160	22	47	13	1	4	26	13	3	1	3	24	5	5	.463	.352
Tartamella, Travis	R-R	5-11	200	12-17-87	.333	.000	.333	1	3	1	0	0	0	0	0	0	0	0	1	0	0	.333	.333
Vasquez, Niko	R-R	5-11	175	2-26-89	.262	.302	.248	59	206	26	54	15	2	3	28	27	1	1	1	49	0	1	.398	.349

Pitching	B-T	HT	WT	DOB	W	L	ERA	G	GS	CG	SV	IP	H	R	ER	HR	BB	SO	AVG	vLH	vRH	K/9	BB/9
Blazek, Michael	R-R	6-0	180	3-16-89	0	1	12.46	1	1	0	0	4	9	6	6	0	5	2	.450	.500	.438	4.15	10.38
Bradford, Jared	R-R	6-1	177	4-3-86	3	6	5.15	33	12	0	1	101	117	61	58	3	25	52	.289	.278	.297	4.62	2.22
Broderick, Brian	R-R	6-6	205	9-1-86	3	5	5.47	9	9	0	0	49	63	32	30	3	11	37	.309	.333	.286	6.75	2.01
Brown, George	L-L	6-1	195	6-18-86	0	0	20.25	2	0	0	0	1	1	3	3	0	2	2	.200	.000	.333	13.50	13.50
Buursma, Jason	R-R	6-3	200	9-9-85	1	0	2.51	7	0	0	0	14	15	4	4	0	3	5	.273	.250	.286	3.14	1.88
Carpenter, David	R-R	6-2	200	7-15-85	5	3	2.36	49	0	0	20	53	45	16	14	3	15	50	.227	.243	.211	8.44	2.53
Castillo, Richard	R-R	5-11	165	10-11-89	7	12	5.20	27	27	1	0	133	169	93	77	10	60	75	.310	.316	.304	5.06	4.05
Delgado, Ramon	R-R	6-3	195	9-3-86	1	2	1.42	38	0	0	2	51	38	9	8	2	10	51	.216	.269	.173	9.06	1.78
Diapoules, Mark	R-R	6-2	200	5-31-88	5	1	2.44	14	9	0	0	55	42	22	15	4	25	38	.220	.223	.216	6.18	4.07
Frevert, Matt	R-R	6-1	190	11-16-86	6	1	2.15	45	0	0	1	54	41	18	13	1	14	66	.210	.204	.216	10.93	2.32
Hearne, Trey	R-R	6-1	195	8-19-83	0	0	0.00	4	0	0	1	8	4	0	0	0	1	11	.148	.167	.133	12.38	1.13
Hooker, Deryk	R-R	6-4	185	6-21-89	3	3	3.27	8	8	0	0	41	39	18	15	0	14	39	.257	.279	.242	8.49	3.05
McGregor, Scott	R-R	6-2	193	12-19-86	4	3	2.68	16	8	1	0	57	69	25	17	1	13	18	.305	.299	.311	2.84	2.05
Mulligan, Casey	R-R	6-2	190	10-5-87	0	0	0.30	25	0	0	12	30	20	1	1	0	8	47	.187	.220	.167	14.26	2.43
Nieto, Arquimedes	R-R	6-0	175	4-28-89	9	7	3.44	20	20	0	0	115	101	49	44	6	39	75	.235	.246	.225	5.87	3.05
Norrick, Tyler	L-L	6-3	195	9-27-83	2	1	3.00	11	0	0	0	12	8	5	4	0	6	16	.205	.200	.207	12.00	4.50
Pichardo, Joel	R-R	5-11	160	2-20-88	3	3	4.52	47	0	0	0	72	88	41	36	7	29	43	.304	.346	.269	5.40	3.64
Rauschenberger, Cory	R-R	6-1	185	7-31-84	1	1	3.23	22	0	0	1	31	24	15	11	0	4	20	.218	.220	.217	5.87	1.17
Samuel, Francisco	R-R	6-2	185	12-20-86	0	0	0.00	3	0	0	1	3	1	0	0	0	1	6	.111	.333	.000	18.00	3.00
Scherer, Matt	R-R	6-5	260	1-20-83	0	0	0.00	2	0	0	0	2	3	0	0	0	0	1	.333	.333	.333	3.86	0.00
Schneider, Scott	R-R	6-1	175	6-7-88	3	7	3.77	13	13	1	0	74	77	31	31	5	22	50	.267	.229	.294	6.08	2.68
Simpson, Jesse	R-R	6-0	180	1-29-87	2	1	4.05	10	0	0	0	13	14	7	6	0	7	11	.286	.500	.200	7.43	4.72
Tapia, Miguel	R-R	6-1	198	2-6-88	0	1	4.50	9	0	0	0	8	5	5	4	1	4	5	12	.237	.235	.238	10.80	4.50
Thomas, Kevin	R-R	6-3	215	7-8-86	10	2	2.27	29	14	0	0	107	93	35	27	0	38	94	.238	.272	.211	7.91	3.20
Zawacki, Brett	R-R	6-1	190	5-2-89	7	5	3.82	21	19	0	0	108	117	52	46	4	32	50	.281	.314	.252	4.15	2.66

Fielding

Catcher	PCT	G	PO	A	E	DP	PB
Cruz	.990	43	264	32	3	4	9
Cutler	.989	26	162	14	2	3	7
De La Cruz	.972	26	156	19	5	1	3
Derba	1.000	32	207	34	0	5	1
Espinoza	1.000	7	52	6	0	1	1
Klein	1.000	1	10	1	0	0	0
Moscatel	.968	5	27	3	1	1	0
Tartamella	1.000	1	4	0	0	0	0

First Base	PCT	G	PO	A	E	DP
Morales	.991	11	99	13	1	9
Racobaldo	.991	51	423	28	4	46
Rivera	1.000	1	1	0	0	0
Scruggs	.991	79	749	50	7	92
Sedbrook	1.000	1	9	0	0	0

Second Base	PCT	G	PO	A	E	DP
Bolivar	.953	107	166	322	24	76
Curtis	.962	22	41	60	4	14
Goodwin	.667	2	1	1	1	0
Marmol	1.000	2	2	1	0	0
Sedbrook	1.000	12	17	26	0	9

Third Base	PCT	G	PO	A	E	DP
Bolivar	1.000	1	0	1	0	0
Carpenter	.987	28	18	57	1	5
Curtis	.952	9	6	14	1	1
Racobaldo	.885	29	19	66	11	6
Sedbrook	.921	18	9	26	3	2
Vasquez	.934	57	31	110	10	8

Shortstop	PCT	G	PO	A	E	DP
Bolivar	1.000	1	1	2	0	0
Garcia	.953	48	79	163	12	38
Greene	1.000	2	0	8	0	0

	PCT	G	PO	A	E	DP
Jackson	.970	41	64	130	6	30
Obregon	.966	22	38	77	4	24
Sedbrook	.942	29	47	82	8	20

Outfield	PCT	G	PO	A	E	DP
Beatty	.857	8	11	1	2	0
Bogany	.994	76	149	8	1	4
Castellanos	.970	126	247	12	8	3
Ingram	.983	49	112	4	2	0
Marmol	.971	22	31	2	1	1
Pham	.983	64	162	8	3	5
Racobaldo	1.000	33	52	4	0	2
Rivera	1.000	1	4	0	0	0
Rodriguez	.870	18	19	1	3	0
Shepherd	1.000	8	13	1	0	0
Smith	1.000	4	8	0	0	0
Swauger	.931	18	25	2	2	0

QUAD CITIES RIVER BANDITS

LOW CLASS A

MIDWEST LEAGUE

Batting	B-T	HT	WT	DOB	AVG	vLH	vRH	G	AB	R	H	2B	3B	HR	RBI	BB	HBP	SH	SF	SO	SB	CS	SLG	OBP
Adams, Matt	L-R	6-3	230	8-31-88	.310	.333	.302	121	464	71	144	41	0	22	88	33	4	0	9	78	5	1	.541	.355
Ahmady, Alan	R-R	5-11	200	12-14-87	.304	.324	.295	41	125	27	38	8	1	1	18	31	1	0	1	31	1	1	.408	.443
Beatty, C.J.	B-R	5-10	190	9-28-88	.259	.267	.257	72	251	40	65	21	3	6	37	31	2	0	1	61	1	2	.438	.344
Castro, Ivan	R-R	6-0	185	11-17-87	.251	.262	.246	62	203	24	51	14	1	3	21	18	1	0	2	54	2	0	.374	.313
Conley, Kyle	R-R	6-4	209	5-7-87	.192	.250	.167	8	26	2	5	0	1	1	2	2	0	0	0	8	0	0	.385	.250
Espinoza, Roberto	R-R	5-10	165	3-8-89	.222	.000	.333	6	18	4	4	0	0	1	2	2	0	0	0	9	0	0	.389	.300
Goodwin, Devin	R-R	5-11	185	10-2-86	.272	.286	.268	62	239	44	65	13	2	7	43	38	1	2	3	39	2	1	.431	.370
Ingram, D'Marcus	R-R	5-9	170	3-30-88	.324	.370	.305	49	185	40	60	11	6	3	28	23	2	1	3	33	11	8	.497	.399
Jackson, Ryan	R-R	6-3	180	5-10-88	.272	.293	.264	84	302	47	82	13	2	2	27	48	0	0	5	63	6	7	.348	.366
Lara, Edgar	R-R	6-3	210	3-2-89	.239	.295	.218	105	352	50	84	20	2	17	73	44	1	0	1	145	2	3	.452	.324
Mateo, Luis	R-R	6-0	160	5-23-90	.249	.247	.249	99	358	60	89	22	5	4	36	39	8	3	1	100	10	3	.372	.335
Obregon, Ted	B-R	5-11	170	5-4-90	.175	.167	.179	44	154	22	27	7	0	2	19	16	1	3	2	40	10	3	.260	.254
Parejo, Frederick	R-R	6-0	165	7-5-90	.216	.233	.210	96	334	59	72	18	2	10	38	52	3	3	1	95	7	2	.371	.326
Rodriguez, Ryde	B-R	6-3	232	2-2-88	.274	.253	.282	72	274	34	75	15	1	5	45	18	3	0	0	61	4	5	.391	.325
Rosario, Rainel	R-R	6-0	188	3-29-89	.263	.167	.290	39	137	27	36	11	3	7	22	26	3	0	2	37	4	2	.540	.387
Shepherd, Devin	R-R	6-3	225	9-9-87	.278	.182	.316	22	79	11	22	5	0	2	15	11	0	0	1	24	3	2	.418	.363
Smith, Ross	R-R	6-2	200	10-6-87	.189	.259	.162	30	95	16	18	5	0	0	4	9	2	0	0	37	2	0	.242	.274
Stanley, Cody	L-R	5-10	190	12-21-88	.250	.000	.250	2	4	1	1	0	0	1	2	0	0	0	1	2	0	0	1.000	.250
Stidham, Jason	L-R	5-11	180	2-26-88	.270	.400	.220	62	233	40	63	18	2	5	42	32	4	0	5	60	4	6	.429	.361
Stock, Robert	L-R	6-0	175	11-21-89	.213	.174	.224	85	310	32	66	17	0	1	31	39	0	1	1	56	2	2	.277	.300
Swinson, Michael	L-R	6-2	185	9-24-89	.222	.149	.250	49	171	27	38	5	4	3	22	19	3	1	0	41	6	3	.351	.311
Vasquez, Niko	R-R	5-11	175	2-26-89	.242	.275	.227	73	252	36	61	17	1	9	42	55	5	1	6	71	1	3	.425	.381
Walsh, Colin	B-R	6-1	202	9-26-89	.214	.200	.218	28	98	15	21	2	2	2	6	20	2	0	0	20	5	1	.337	.358

Pitching	B-T	HT	WT	DOB	W	L	ERA	G	GS	CG	SV	IP	H	R	ER	HR	BB	SO	AVG	vLH	vRH	K/9	BB/9
Bibona, Daniel	L-L	6-0	170	6-19-88	4	0	1.91	8	5	0	0	33	24	9	7	1	14	39	.198	.155	.238	10.64	3.82
Blazek, Michael	R-R	6-0	180	3-16-89	8	4	2.71	32	11	0	3	103	78	41	31	5	31	104	.210	.208	.212	9.09	2.71
Calhoun, Daniel	L-L	6-3	220	9-5-86	10	0	3.75	37	6	0	1	96	109	47	40	9	19	83	.283	.280	.285	7.78	1.78
Corrigan, Chris	R-R	6-2	155	12-24-87	3	0	3.86	13	0	0	0	23	31	15	10	1	8	20	.307	.327	.283	7.71	3.09
Fornataro, Eric	R-R	6-1	195	1-2-88	7	15	5.26	28	28	0	0	140	161	104	82	13	59	100	.290	.298	.280	6.41	3.78
Greenwood, Nick	L-L	6-1	180	9-28-87	1	0	1.16	11	0	0	0	23	20	5	3	0	9	16	.233	.324	.173	6.17	3.47
2-team total (21 Fort Wayne)					5	4	3.56	32	17	0	1	119	129	53	47	4	28	81	—	—	—	6.14	2.12
Hooker, Deryk	R-R	6-4	185	6-21-89	5	4	2.83	18	11	0	1	70	58	26	22	3	22	88	.220	.300	.153	11.31	2.83
Kelly, Joe	R-R	6-1	165	6-9-88	6	8	4.62	26	18	0	1	103	103	66	53	3	45	92	.265	.259	.271	8.01	3.92
Kiekhefer, Dean	L-L	6-0	155	6-7-89	0	0	5.14	14	1	0	1	28	30	17	16	3	9	29	.263	.148	.367	9.32	2.89
Mayes, LaCurtis	R-R	5-11	185	8-2-88	1	0	10.59	12	0	0	0	17	26	20	20	3	11	10	.356	.353	.359	5.29	5.82
Miller, Shelby	R-R	6-3	195	10-10-90	7	5	3.62	24	24	0	0	104	97	51	42	7	33	140	.243	.194	.286	12.08	2.85
Notti, Chris	R-R	6-5	210	9-3-88	1	0	4.60	34	0	0	6	63	78	35	32	4	23	67	.301	.283	.315	9.62	3.30
Novak, Jason	R-R	6-1	205	10-19-87	3	1	3.47	26	0	0	1	36	32	19	14	6	13	45	.229	.258	.205	11.15	3.22
Rada, Jose	R-R	6-1	180	4-13-88	2	0	1.42	14	0	0	7	19	16	3	3	0	9	21	.229	.250	.200	9.95	4.26
Rondon, Jorge	R-R	6-1	175	9-16-88	4	8	5.30	29	19	0	0	109	121	82	64	6	65	76	.287	.320	.256	6.29	5.38
Schneider, Scott	R-R	6-0	175	6-7-88	5	2	3.11	14	8	1	2	64	40	25	22	3	18	65	.175	.172	.176	9.19	2.54
Simpson, Jesse	R-R	6-0	180	1-29-87	3	2	2.87	36	0	0	4	60	44	21	19	3	28	68	.204	.204	.204	10.26	4.22
Smith, Justin	R-R	6-0	190	3-23-88	7	2	3.25	29	7	0	0	80	72	31	29	5	26	102	.238	.266	.214	11.43	2.91
Terry, Aaron	R-R	5-11	185	12-28-86	5	4	3.90	51	0	0	15	55	55	25	24	5	22	55	.256	.211	.292	8.95	3.58

Fielding

Catcher	PCT	G	PO	A	E	DP	PB
Castro	.982	56	438	65	9	2	16
Espinoza	1.000	5	41	8	0	1	1
Stock	.978	82	704	90	18	8	10

First Base	PCT	G	PO	A	E	DP
Adams	.991	110	1016	66	10	81
Ahmady	.989	22	178	6	2	12
Castro	.955	3	21	0	1	1

	PCT	G	PO	A	E	DP
Lara	.957	13	85	5	4	5
Parejo	1.000	1	1	0	0	1
Smith	1.000	2	15	1	0	0
Stidham	.800	1	3	1	1	0

ST. LOUIS CARDINALS

Second Base	PCT	G	PO	A	E	DP
Goodwin	.952	30	45	94	7	17
Mateo	.956	54	77	162	11	28
Obregon	.957	11	13	32	2	5
Stidham	.958	38	54	128	8	21
Walsh	.967	11	21	38	2	8

Third Base	PCT	G	PO	A	E	DP
Ahmady	.829	15	8	26	7	4
Goodwin	1.000	3	2	5	0	0
Mateo	.926	48	18	70	7	3
Vasquez	.945	66	30	107	8	12

Walsh	.902	15	17	29	5	3

Shortstop	PCT	G	PO	A	E	DP
Goodwin	.931	18	36	45	6	7
Jackson	.948	83	124	261	21	42
Obregon	.940	33	56	85	9	22
Vasquez	.968	7	8	22	1	5

Outfield	PCT	G	PO	A	E	DP
Beatty	.957	54	64	3	3	0
Conley	1.000	6	2	1	0	0
Goodwin	1.000	6	6	0	0	0

Ingram	.932	46	67	1	5	0
Kelly	1.000	1	1	0	0	0
Lara	.957	52	86	4	4	0
Parejo	.962	85	122	4	5	0
Rodriguez	.987	64	72	2	1	0
Rosario	.979	32	42	4	1	0
Shepherd	1.000	13	17	5	0	0
Smith	.970	25	31	1	1	0
Stanley	1.000	1	1	0	0	0
Stidham	.900	6	9	0	1	0
Swinson	.967	47	87	2	3	1

BATAVIA MUCKDOGS
NEW YORK-PENN LEAGUE

SHORT-SEASON

Batting	B-T	HT	WT	DOB	AVG	vLH	vRH	G	AB	R	H	2B	3B	HR	RBI	BB	HBP	SH	SF	SO	SB	CS	SLG	OBP
Ahmady, Alan	R-R	5-11	200	12-14-87	.208	.348	.080	13	48	8	10	3	0	0	3	10	1	0	1	11	0	0	.271	.350
Bergman, Joey	L-R	5-10	190	2-7-88	.300	.283	.306	62	210	38	63	12	2	1	31	31	4	3	0	48	5	1	.390	.400
Biserta, Pat	L-R	6-0	185	6-30-89	.281	.257	.288	53	153	18	43	8	0	1	26	15	1	2	5	28	2	3	.353	.339
Castillo, Juan	R-R	5-11	160	12-13-89	.315	.529	.216	16	54	5	17	5	0	0	6	3	1	2	1	7	0	0	.407	.356
Castillo, Yunier	B-R	6-0	160	5-15-89	.262	.173	.295	59	191	28	50	8	0	0	22	6	2	9	4	32	4	3	.304	.286
De La Cruz, Luis	R-R	5-10	165	5-6-89	.231	.222	.235	8	26	6	6	3	0	1	2	2	0	0	4	0	0	0	.462	.286
Edmondson, Chris	L-R	6-0	200	4-7-88	.303	.257	.322	29	122	24	37	9	3	2	20	6	4	0	1	15	0	0	.475	.353
Edwards, Jon	R-R	6-5	230	1-8-88	.180	.171	.185	43	122	12	22	6	1	2	11	14	3	1	0	55	0	3	.295	.281
Espinoza, Roberto	R-R	5-10	165	3-8-91	.172	.250	.143	12	29	3	5	1	0	1	5	6	0	0	1	10	0	0	.310	.306
Klein, Geoff	B-R	6-3	200	3-27-88	.295	.000	.315	30	95	11	28	11	0	0	12	14	0	0	0	26	0	0	.411	.385
Longmire, Nick	R-R	6-3	180	1-5-89	.287	.295	.283	68	265	53	76	11	7	9	55	34	5	0	5	62	12	3	.483	.372
Melker, Adam	L-L	5-11	180	1-31-88	.309	.273	.320	35	97	17	30	4	2	0	11	12	6	3	1	19	4	0	.392	.414
O'Neill, Mike	L-L	5-9	170	2-12-88	.283	.412	.253	40	92	23	26	5	2	0	9	18	0	1	2	13	5	1	.380	.393
Perez, Audry	R-R	5-9	180	12-23-88	.315	.214	.350	45	165	25	52	11	0	4	47	11	5	0	4	33	2	3	.455	.368
Rodriguez, Jonathan	R-R	6-2	205	8-21-89	.258	.268	.254	69	244	46	63	13	5	12	40	28	3	1	4	56	3	2	.500	.337
Rosario, Rainel	R-R	6-0	188	3-29-89	.321	.320	.321	25	78	13	25	4	0	2	9	9	0	0	1	23	0	1	.449	.386
Sanchez, Victor	K-R	6-1	175	12-30-88	.291	.268	.303	57	213	36	62	19	1	3	31	22	8	1	1	42	2	3	.432	.377
Smith, Ross	R-R	6-2	200	10-6-87	.222	.125	.300	10	18	4	4	0	0	1	3	0	0	0	6	0	0	.222	.333
Valaika, Matt	R-R	5-10	180	4-2-88	.186	.161	.198	48	172	19	32	6	1	1	16	14	2	2	1	23	5	2	.250	.254
Walsh, Colin	B-R	6-1	202	9-26-89	.300	.385	.286	24	90	20	27	4	1	2	12	17	3	2	1	14	2	1	.433	.420

Pitching	B-T	HT	WT	DOB	W	L	ERA	G	GS	CG	SV	IP	H	R	ER	HR	BB	SO	AVG	vLH	vRH	K/9	BB/9
Avendano, Javier	R-R	6-3	180	9-6-90	0	0	4.50	1	1	0	0	4	3	2	2	0	4	4	.188	.000	.300	9.00	9.00
Butler, Keith	R-R	6-0	180	1-30-89	0	3	2.93	27	0	0	5	31	29	15	10	1	15	50	.242	.269	.221	14.67	4.40
Corrigan, Chris	R-R	6-2	155	12-24-87	3	1	4.02	13	3	0	1	40	40	22	18	1	14	23	.258	.333	.202	5.13	3.12
Edwards, Justin	L-L	6-2	188	12-3-87	4	5	3.38	15	15	0	0	77	76	42	29	4	22	66	.256	.298	.246	7.68	2.56
Ferrara, Anthony	R-L	6-1	175	9-2-89	1	0	6.00	8	1	0	2	18	23	12	12	2	4	17	.299	.308	.294	8.50	2.00
Gast, John	L-L	6-1	195	2-16-89	6	0	1.54	8	6	0	0	35	27	6	6	1	8	36	.227	.226	.227	9.26	2.06
Kington, David	R-R	6-2	200	12-1-87	1	2	4.34	26	0	0	1	29	22	15	14	3	14	31	.204	.170	.236	9.62	4.34
Lawler, Travis	R-R	6-3	180	6-13-88	1	3	3.86	25	1	0	0	40	36	19	17	4	17	40	.247	.293	.216	9.08	3.86
Mayes, LaCurtis	R-R	5-11	185	8-2-88	2	2	4.55	15	0	0	0	28	31	18	14	3	10	23	.270	.241	.295	7.48	3.25
McCully, Nick	R-R	5-11	195	9-5-88	4	2	4.19	14	13	0	0	69	68	40	32	4	17	44	.264	.252	.275	5.77	2.23
Moss, Andy	R-R	6-1	210	10-8-86	8	2	3.35	14	14	0	0	75	68	32	28	6	23	61	.238	.216	.257	7.29	2.75
North, Matt	R-R	6-5	170	5-23-88	4	3	10.41	19	4	0	0	28	48	37	32	3	20	22	.387	.333	.425	7.16	6.51
Rada, Jose	R-R	6-1	180	4-13-88	4	1	1.13	18	0	0	10	24	11	4	3	0	7	33	.134	.030	.204	12.38	2.63
Reid, Chase	L-R	6-3	212	5-17-88	2	0	2.05	20	0	0	2	31	16	8	7	2	5	43	.151	.159	.145	12.62	1.47
Russell, Zach	R-R	6-2	185	7-27-89	3	3	2.93	14	12	0	0	61	41	22	20	2	31	61	.192	.206	.180	8.95	4.55
Siegrist, Kevin	L-L	6-5	190	7-20-89	0	1	7.29	7	4	0	0	21	24	17	17	1	16	14	.282	.226	.315	6.00	6.86
Summers, Houston	R-R	5-10	180	8-20-87	2	1	4.96	18	0	0	1	33	38	21	18	0	26	20	.295	.280	.304	5.51	7.16
Wright, Justin	L-L	5-9	175	8-18-89	0	0	0.00	5	0	0	1	8	3	0	0	0	2	10	.120	.000	.188	11.74	2.35

Fielding

Catcher	PCT	G	PO	A	E	DP	PB
Castillo	.978	13	79	11	2	1	3
De La Cruz	.976	8	75	6	2	0	4
Espinoza	1.000	12	66	6	0	1	2
Klein	.988	12	74	7	1	0	2
Perez	.997	39	286	34	1	3	10

First Base	PCT	G	PO	A	E	DP
Castillo	1.000	1	8	0	0	1
Klein	1.000	2	13	1	0	4
Rodriguez	1.000	25	237	10	0	15
Sanchez	.995	46	404	25	2	41

Second Base	PCT	G	PO	A	E	DP
Bergman	.956	34	52	79	6	19
Valaika	.968	24	34	56	3	12
Walsh	.969	22	55	70	4	18

Third Base	PCT	G	PO	A	E	DP
Ahmady	.793	11	3	20	6	0
Bergman	1.000	23	16	41	0	4
Rodriguez	.913	39	24	81	10	8
Walsh	1.000	3	2	5	0	0

Shortstop	PCT	G	PO	A	E	DP
Castillo	.934	59	77	163	17	33

Valaika	.987	19	28	48	1	12

Outfield	PCT	G	PO	A	E	DP
Biserta	.932	28	41	0	3	0
Edmondson	.957	27	42	2	2	0
Edwards	.951	33	39	0	2	0
Longmire	.969	64	117	9	4	2
Melker	.961	32	48	1	2	0
O'Neill	.979	38	45	2	1	0
Rosario	1.000	19	23	1	0	1
Smith	.950	8	19	0	1	0
Valaika	1.000	7	11	0	0	0

JOHNSON CITY CARDINALS   ROOKIE
APPALACHIAN LEAGUE

Batting	B-T	HT	WT	DOB	AVG	vLH	vRH	G	AB	R	H	2B	3B	HR	RBI	BB	HBP	SH	SF	SO	SB	CS	SLG	OBP
Castillo, Juan	R-R	5-11	160	12-13-89	.339	.250	.381	16	62	12	21	3	1	4	7	3	1	0	0	4	1	1	.613	.379
Cerreto, Phil	R-R	6-1	195	10-4-87	.425	.429	.423	32	120	26	51	15	2	7	38	7	5	0	5	14	6	0	.758	.460
De La Cruz, Roberto	R-R	6-2	180	11-10-91	.000	.000	.000	2	6	0	0	0	0	0	0	0	0	0	0	4	0	0	.000	.000
Edmondson, Chris	L-R	6-0	200	4-7-88	.283	.185	.316	28	106	20	30	8	1	6	22	8	3	0	0	19	1	0	.547	.350
Elkins, Packy	L-R	5-11	175	11-6-87	.267	.256	.272	46	146	21	39	9	0	2	16	13	6	4	0	35	1	0	.370	.352
Garcia, Anthony	R-R	6-0	180	1-4-92	.333	.000	.500	2	3	1	1	1	0	0	1	1	0	0	1	0	0	0	.667	.400
Garcia, Greg	L-R	6-0	175	8-8-89	.286	.265	.296	58	220	49	63	15	1	4	24	18	9	3	1	36	7	5	.418	.363
Hill, Virgil	R-R	5-11	186	9-9-89	.289	.196	.344	49	152	30	44	11	3	2	16	21	3	0	1	48	7	6	.441	.384
Medina, David	L-L	6-3	162	1-1-89	.365	.278	.400	20	63	13	23	6	1	3	13	7	1	0	0	16	0	0	.635	.437
Ramos, Steve	R-R	6-0	160	7-4-90	.067	.250	.000	8	15	0	1	0	0	0	1	2	0	0	0	8	0	0	.067	.176
Reyes, Roberto	L-L	6-0	185	5-10-89	.249	.186	.270	57	169	22	42	12	2	1	14	15	3	0	3	48	1	2	.361	.316
Rodriguez, Starlin	B-R	5-9	160	12-13-89	.400	.333	.500	2	5	0	2	0	0	0	1	1	0	0	0	0	0	0	.400	.500
Ruiz, Romulo	R-R	6-0	170	11-30-89	.256	.250	.259	60	219	30	56	19	0	3	30	34	2	0	1	45	1	0	.384	.359
Stanley, Cody	L-R	5-10	190	12-21-88	.321	.324	.319	53	209	34	67	12	5	5	39	21	1	0	3	30	8	1	.498	.380
Tartamella, Travis	R-R	5-11	200	12-17-87	.259	.263	.257	30	108	13	28	6	1	3	19	9	0	0	0	25	0	0	.417	.316
Taveras, Oscar	L-L	6-2	180	6-19-92	.322	.258	.352	53	211	39	68	13	3	8	43	12	3	0	3	41	8	5	.526	.362
Teran, Kleininger	L-R	6-1	175	7-23-89	.303	.232	.336	45	178	21	54	14	1	1	23	12	0	0	1	26	1	0	.410	.346
Valera, Cesar	R-R	6-1	180	3-8-92	.214	.200	.220	55	192	32	41	4	0	0	13	17	2	2	2	58	5	2	.234	.282
Walsh, Colin	B-R	6-0	202	9-26-89	.261	.333	.214	6	23	3	6	0	0	0	2	3	0	0	0	3	0	0	.261	.346
Williams Jr., Reggie	B-R	6-4	190	9-15-89	.269	.294	.253	44	134	17	36	0	6	1	18	11	3	0	1	55	3	1	.381	.336

Pitching	B-T	HT	WT	DOB	W	L	ERA	G	GS	CG	SV	IP	H	R	ER	HR	BB	SO	AVG	vLH	vRH	K/9	BB/9
Benes, Drew	R-R	6-2	190	11-4-88	1	0	1.52	18	0	0	0	24	20	8	4	0	6	22	.225	.120	.266	8.37	2.28
Copeland, Ryan	R-L	5-11	180	6-10-88	7	0	1.86	13	6	0	0	53	39	13	11	3	7	48	.202	.185	.205	8.10	1.18
Corpas, Hector	R-R	6-3	170	1-5-90	0	1	2.13	24	0	0	17	25	19	6	6	1	3	27	.209	.154	.231	9.59	1.07
Daugherty, Pat	L-L	6-5	215	8-30-88	2	2	6.00	13	6	0	0	42	52	33	28	5	15	46	.302	.286	.307	9.86	3.21
DeJesus, Angel	R-R	6-6	188	2-3-89	3	1	4.41	13	7	0	0	51	53	27	25	4	14	52	.276	.340	.252	9.18	2.47
Guzman, Francisco	R-R	6-0	180	2-20-88	1	0	4.98	17	0	0	1	22	29	12	12	2	4	19	.330	.367	.310	7.89	1.66
Hernandez, Hector	B-L	6-1	198	2-20-91	0	2	6.85	14	7	0	1	45	56	41	34	7	12	44	.301	.286	.304	8.87	2.42
Jenkins, Tyrell	R-R	6-4	180	7-20-92	0	0	0.00	2	2	0	0	3	2	0	0	0	2	2	.200	.000	.286	6.00	6.00
Jimenez, Charllan	R-R	6-1	180	11-29-89	1	1	4.32	11	5	0	0	33	43	25	16	6	6	25	.305	.310	.301	6.75	1.62
Johnson, Cale	R-R	6-2	200	8-26-87	5	4	3.61	13	10	1	0	62	77	34	25	2	8	36	.301	.264	.327	5.20	1.16
Kiekhefer, Dean	L-L	6-0	155	6-7-89	0	1	6.75	1	0	0	0	3	2	2	2	0	2	2	.182	.000	.182	6.75	0.00
Lucas, Aiden	R-R	6-2	225	4-21-88	2	3	3.32	24	0	0	3	22	19	9	8	1	4	19	.224	.188	.232	7.89	1.66
Nadeau, Jeff	L-L	6-2	185	7-30-89	1	2	2.77	13	3	0	0	39	37	17	12	2	10	28	.239	.192	.248	6.46	2.31
Nazario, Iden	L-L	6-0	190	3-28-89	1	0	4.09	11	0	0	0	11	7	6	5	1	8	15	.189	.200	.185	12.27	6.55
Patterson, Chris	R-R	6-0	200	3-29-88	2	1	5.11	11	0	0	1	12	13	7	7	0	7	16	.271	.455	.216	11.68	5.11
Revesz, Bob	L-L	6-4	195	7-16-88	4	2	4.84	16	0	0	1	22	24	16	12	3	5	17	.276	.304	.266	6.85	2.01
Rosenthal, Trevor	R-R	6-2	190	5-29-90	3	0	2.25	10	6	0	1	32	23	10	8	1	7	30	.200	.054	.269	8.44	1.97
Siegrist, Kevin	L-L	6-5	190	7-20-89	4	3	1.93	7	5	0	0	33	28	12	7	3	6	31	.237	.222	.242	8.54	1.65
Whiting, Boone	R-R	6-1	175	8-20-89	5	3	3.50	13	9	0	0	54	54	28	21	6	5	68	.250	.281	.239	11.33	0.83

Fielding

Catcher	PCT	G	PO	A	E	DP	PB
Castillo	.983	13	105	13	2	1	2
Garcia	1.000	1	6	1	0	1	0
Stanley	.992	28	206	39	2	4	3
Tartamella	.992	28	202	33	2	0	4

First Base	PCT	G	PO	A	E	DP
Cerreto	.970	19	154	8	5	21
Medina	.963	12	96	8	4	9
Ruiz	1.000	3	20	0	0	4
Teran	.986	38	322	22	5	23

Second Base	PCT	G	PO	A	E	DP
Elkins	.979	28	46	47	2	14
Garcia	.985	47	91	103	3	28
Rodriguez	1.000	2	1	4	0	2
Walsh	.944	3	7	10	1	4

Third Base	PCT	G	PO	A	E	DP
De La Cruz	.556	2	3	2	4	1
Elkins	.973	25	18	53	2	4
Ruiz	.866	45	28	108	21	7
Teran	.923	4	3	9	1	1
Walsh	1.000	1	1	1	0	0

Shortstop	PCT	G	PO	A	E	DP
Garcia	.976	16	30	50	2	11
Valera	.921	55	87	157	21	31

Outfield	PCT	G	PO	A	E	DP
Cerreto	.947	15	17	1	1	1
Edmondson	1.000	19	24	3	0	0
Hill	.953	47	59	2	3	0
Ramos	1.000	8	5	0	0	0
Reyes	.986	54	70	3	1	0
Taveras	.930	48	78	2	6	0
Williams Jr.	.957	40	61	5	3	0

GCL CARDINALS   ROOKIE
GULF COAST LEAGUE

Batting	B-T	HT	WT	DOB	AVG	vLH	vRH	G	AB	R	H	2B	3B	HR	RBI	BB	HBP	SH	SF	SO	SB	CS	SLG	OBP
Alcala, Yorbel	B-R	6-0	160	1-17-90	.300	.125	.417	10	20	1	6	0	1	0	3	1	1	0	0	4	0	1	.400	.364
Bryant, Anthony	L-R	6-3	215	1-13-92	.186	.150	.195	35	97	13	18	2	0	2	14	17	2	4	1	41	8	0	.268	.316
Cox, Zack	L-R	6-0	215	5-9-89	.400	.500	.364	4	15	0	6	1	0	0	1	1	0	0	0	3	0	0	.467	.471
De La Cruz, Roberto	R-R	6-2	180	11-10-91	.241	.256	.236	46	162	20	39	6	2	7	21	7	5	0	1	46	0	2	.432	.291
Dodd, Corderious	R-R	6-2	230	2-21-92	.116	.000	.143	19	43	5	5	0	0	0	4	6	5	0	0	22	0	0	.116	.296
Fonseca, Anthony	R-R	6-1	175	2-8-89	.211	.000	.268	39	90	14	19	2	0	0	5	9	6	2	2	28	1	2	.233	.318
Garcia, Anthony	R-R	6-0	180	1-4-92	.284	.389	.265	39	116	20	33	3	1	5	20	19	6	0	2	17	2	0	.457	.406
Garcia, Hector	R-R	6-1	185	5-16-90	.220	.158	.235	33	100	14	22	7	1	0	11	16	2	0	2	17	0	0	.310	.333
Hamilton, Mark	L-L	6-4	220	7-29-84	.296	.125	.368	9	27	2	8	1	0	2	2	4	1	0	0	9	0	0	.556	.406
Martin, Trevor	R-R	6-0	190	8-3-91	.253	.353	.226	23	79	8	20	5	0	0	6	10	3	0	0	29	0	1	.316	.359
Martinez, Jose	R-R	5-11	175	1-24-86	.250		.294	6	20	1	5	2	0	0	1	1	0	0	1	6	0	0	.350	.318

Batting	B-T	HT	WT	DOB	AVG	vLH	vRH	G	AB	R	H	2B	3B	HR	RBI	BB	HBP	SH	SF	SO	SB	CS	SLG	OBP
Montero, Jesus	R-R	5-11	185	6-21-91	.203	.158	.220	24	69	10	14	2	0	0	7	8	5	0	0	16	1	1	.232	.329
Moscatel, Kevin	R-R	6-1	175	5-16-91	.283	.357	.269	28	92	10	26	6	0	1	17	11	3	0	1	19	0	1	.380	.374
Perez, Wader	B-R	5-10	170	6-12-90	.214	.227	.210	29	84	11	18	2	0	0	7	7	2	1	2	10	4	2	.238	.284
Pimentel, Luis	R-R	6-1	180	12-30-88	.301	.290	.303	46	153	23	46	8	0	3	29	10	4	0	3	27	1	1	.412	.353
Ramos, Steve	R-R	6-0	160	7-4-90	.283	.314	.272	40	138	26	39	6	3	1	10	9	4	3	2	26	15	2	.391	.340
Rivero, Alberto	L-L	5-10	155	4-30-89	.250	.250	.250	8	16	2	4	1	1	0	0	0	0	0	0	3	0	0	.438	.250
Rodriguez, Starlin	B-R	5-9	160	12-13-89	.285	.320	.278	47	151	28	43	6	4	0	13	9	8	0	0	32	14	5	.377	.357
Swinson, Michael	L-R	6-2	185	9-24-89	.063	.000	.083	9	16	2	1	0	0	0	1	3	0	0	1	3	2	1	.063	.200
Taveras, Oscar	L-L	6-2	180	6-19-92	.167	.286	.130	7	30	1	5	1	0	0	2	1	0	0	0	5	1	0	.200	.194
Tuivailala, Sam	R-R	6-3	195	10-19-92	.178	.320	.144	42	129	23	23	4	0	2	9	29	2	1	1	35	0	4	.256	.335
Vargas, Ildemaro	R-R	6-0	170	7-16-91	.239	.250	.235	34	88	17	21	7	2	0	15	8	3	3	2	10	2	3	.364	.317
Vivas, Wilfred	R-R	5-11	160	11-8-89	.000	.000	.000	4	4	1	0	0	0	0	0	0	0	0	0	2	0	0	.000	.000
Washington, David	L-L	6-5	200	11-20-90	.284	.500	.247	33	95	10	27	8	0	2	18	12	1	0	0	27	1	1	.432	.370

Pitching	B-T	HT	WT	DOB	W	L	ERA	G	GS	CG	SV	IP	H	R	ER	HR	BB	SO	AVG	vLH	vRH	K/9	BB/9
Aguilar, Cesar	R-R	6-3	250	5-15-92	3	2	3.82	16	4	0	0	31	23	13	13	4	13	25	.211	.286	.185	7.34	3.82
Avendano, Javier	R-R	6-3	180	9-6-90	0	0	1.35	10	8	0	0	40	26	8	6	1	14	52	.179	.194	.175	11.70	3.15
Brand, Cole	R-R	6-2	225	5-19-92	2	3	5.12	22	0	0	1	19	30	19	11	0	5	17	.341	.333	.343	7.91	2.33
Castillo, Amaury	R-R	6-5	210	11-9-90	2	3	6.33	11	4	0	0	21	19	22	15	0	24	22	.244	.217	.255	9.28	10.13
Colorado, Moises	L-L	6-3	170	12-8-89	0	0	5.40	8	0	0	0	13	16	9	8	0	7	12	.314	.375	.302	8.10	4.72
De La Cruz, Manuel	L-L	6-2	225	5-8-90	4	2	1.85	28	0	0	9	34	22	9	7	1	8	43	.182	.167	.184	11.38	2.12
Freeman, Ben	L-L	6-2	150	2-6-92	1	3	3.50	11	9	0	0	44	42	24	17	1	16	37	.263	.129	.295	7.63	3.30
Jimenez, Charllan	R-R	6-1	180	11-29-89	0	1	3.60	1	1	0	0	5	5	2	2	0	1	4	.263	.000	.455	7.20	1.80
Lucas, Josh	R-R	6-6	185	11-5-90	1	2	4.88	14	1	0	0	28	32	22	15	3	9	26	.294	.500	.235	8.46	2.93
Martinez, Bryan	R-R	6-3	172	3-1-91	1	4	1.95	7	6	0	0	37	25	11	8	1	16	31	.197	.243	.178	7.54	3.89
Martinez, Ricky	R-R	6-1	195	4-20-88	3	0	2.25	19	0	0	0	28	23	7	7	2	4	9	.228	.160	.250	2.89	1.29
Mendoza, Richard	B-R	6-1	170	2-25-92	0	1	10.00	14	0	0	0	18	25	26	20	1	17	14	.325	.320	.327	7.00	8.50
Mura, Kyle	R-R	6-4	215	11-24-84	0	0	0.00	2	0	0	0	4	2	0	0	0	1	3	.154	.000	.200	2.45	0.00
Nuernberg, Dyllon	R-R	6-1	220	5-28-91	0	0	5.63	14	0	0	0	16	20	11	10	2	9	20	.313	.412	.277	11.25	5.06
Pasen, Jose	R-R	6-1	180	5-19-90	4	4	3.25	11	11	0	0	55	43	23	20	4	17	52	.211	.224	.206	8.46	2.77
Santana, Michael	R-R	6-0	155	7-1-90	4	0	3.15	12	4	0	0	34	29	13	12	3	4	32	.232	.250	.226	8.39	1.05
Uribe, Adriano	L-L	6-4	200	5-17-89	3	2	3.51	11	8	0	0	49	54	32	19	1	15	37	.274	.077	.288	6.84	2.77

Fielding

Catcher	PCT	G	PO	A	E	DP	PB
Alcala	1.000	7	39	2	0	0	2
Garcia	1.000	10	48	5	0	0	1
Montero	.995	23	159	22	1	3	7
Moscatel	.995	25	184	25	1	0	5
Perez	1.000	1	3	0	0	0	0

First Base	PCT	G	PO	A	E	DP
Garcia	1.000	2	7	0	0	0
Garcia	.991	16	107	7	1	5
Hamilton	.973	9	71	2	2	5
Pimentel	.994	23	170	8	1	13
Washington	.993	19	120	16	1	15

Second Base	PCT	G	PO	A	E	DP
Martin	.891	16	23	26	6	7
Martinez	1.000	3	6	12	0	0
Moscatel	—	1	0	0	0	0
Perez	1.000	12	7	16	0	2
Rodriguez	.947	34	63	62	7	17
Vargas	1.000	5	3	10	0	0
Vivas	.500	2	1	0	1	0

Third Base	PCT	G	PO	A	E	DP
Cox	1.000	3	0	6	0	0
De La Cruz	.858	39	27	64	15	6
Garcia	.875	13	6	22	4	3
Perez	.900	5	5	4	1	1
Rodriguez	—	1	0	0	0	0

Shortstop	PCT	G	PO	A	E	DP
Perez	.925	9	18	31	4	4
Tuivailala	.922	24	36	70	9	10
Vargas	.952	27	37	83	6	15

Outfield	PCT	G	PO	A	E	DP
Alcala	1.000	1	1	0	0	0
Bryant	.865	33	32	0	5	0
Dodd	.900	10	9	0	1	0
Fonseca	.940	37	44	3	3	0
Garcia	1.000	26	38	4	0	2
Garcia	—	2	0	0	0	0
Montero	—	1	0	0	0	0
Perez	1.000	3	1	1	0	0
Ramos	.975	39	73	6	2	2
Rivero	1.000	6	10	1	0	0
Swinson	1.000	8	8	0	0	0
Taveras	.941	7	14	2	1	0
Tuivailala	.929	15	25	1	2	1
Vargas	1.000	1	1	0	0	0
Washington	1.000	12	13	1	0	1

DSL CARDINALS   ROOKIE

DOMINICAN SUMMER LEAGUE

Batting	B-T	HT	WT	DOB	AVG	vLH	vRH	G	AB	R	H	2B	3B	HR	RBI	BB	HBP	SH	SF	SO	SB	CS	SLG	OBP
Agustin, Jose	R-R	6-3	160	2-4-93	.105	.040	.131	33	86	8	9	2	0	0	5	13	4	0	0	38	2	1	.128	.252
Baez, Fernando	R-R	6-1	195	1-2-92	.233	.178	.261	43	133	15	31	6	1	1	19	10	3	0	1	28	5	1	.316	.299
Barbuena, Daniel	R-R	6-0	160	3-23-93	.242	.225	.252	59	186	31	45	8	1	1	25	29	13	2	1	47	12	10	.312	.380
Beras, Andres	R-R	6-2	175	11-30-90	.269	.302	.252	52	156	19	42	6	2	1	27	31	8	1	2	40	11	4	.353	.411
Capellan, Amaury	R-R	5-11	190	9-30-92	.148	.100	.168	49	135	15	20	3	0	0	11	31	7	1	5	33	8	3	.170	.326
Castillo, Ronard	R-R	6-5	200	6-16-92	.255	.244	.262	33	106	10	27	5	3	0	12	20	1	0	0	22	5	1	.358	.378
Celestino, Eduardo	L-R	6-2	175	9-30-92	.206	.265	.185	44	126	16	26	2	0	0	10	19	2	1	1	25	6	2	.222	.318
Diaz, Domingo	R-R	6-2	165	3-8-92	.178	.097	.220	41	90	17	16	4	0	0	7	22	1	3	0	35	6	2	.222	.345
Encanacion, Victor	R-R	6-2	165	3-8-90	.142	.171	.127	48	106	19	15	4	0	0	7	21	8	2	1	36	13	1	.179	.324
Ferreira, Victor	R-R	5-11	180	2-1-91	.161	.156	.164	27	87	8	14	3	0	1	7	15	2	0	1	16	2	1	.230	.295
Lopez, Jorge	R-R	5-11	175	10-28-90	.178	.097	.220	63	185	20	33	5	1	1	19	18	0	1	3	28	7	5	.222	.248
Medina, Rafael	R-R	6-2	170	10-24-93	.234	.270	.213	57	171	28	40	6	0	1	20	34	4	1	1	34	7	5	.287	.371
Pena, Jose	R-R	6-2	190	5-26-92	.156	.100	.186	58	173	15	27	4	2	0	13	23	6	1	1	74	8	2	.202	.276
Perez, Luis	R-R	5-10	160	7-24-91	.302	.270	.319	62	179	41	54	8	3	1	30	29	7	3	5	21	11	5	.397	.409
Reyes, Robelys	B-R	5-9	150	7-25-90	.301	.275	.315	65	226	43	68	8	2	1	20	25	1	4	1	26	21	3	.367	.372

Pitching	B-T	HT	WT	DOB	W	L	ERA	G	GS	CG	SV	IP	H	R	ER	HR	BB	SO	AVG	vLH	vRH	K/9	BB/9
Bautista, Juan	R-R	5-11	195	6-16-93	5	0	1.59	10	2	0	1	34	25	11	6	2	11	37	.205	.235	.200	9.79	2.91
Ceballo, Addelin	R-R	6-0	190	6-29-91	4	2	4.43	11	0	0	1	22	17	17	11	2	13	10	.230	.300	.219	4.03	5.24
Concepcion, Christian	R-R	6-4	198	3-27-90	0	2	7.36	9	1	0	0	9	16	9		0	20	10	.225	.500	.194	8.18	16.36

ST. LOUIS CARDINALS

	B-T	HT	WT	DOB	W	L	ERA	G	GS	CG	SV	IP	H	R	ER	HR	BB	SO	AVG	vLH	vRH	K/9	BB/9
De La Cruz, Anthony	L-L	6-0	170	3-14-93	2	2	6.75	9	3	0	0	23	25	18	17	1	8	14	.278	.200	.282	5.56	3.18
De La Cruz, Jean	R-R	6-1	190	5-8-92	0	0	4.70	7	0	0	0	8	5	8	4	0	19	11	.179	.000	.192	12.91	22.30
De Leon, Victor	R-R	6-2	190	4-19-92	4	3	2.76	14	8	1	0	49	39	20	15	5	26	40	.225	.308	.211	7.35	4.78
De Los Santos, Hansel	R-R	6-3	160	8-7-91	2	1	2.67	12	1	0	3	27	23	8	8	3	11	24	.230	.176	.241	8.00	3.67
Estalis, Eduard	R-R	6-1	170	12-19-88	1	4	2.01	12	4	1	1	45	36	13	10	6	7	45	.220	.200	.224	9.07	1.41
Gonzalez, Ariel	R-R	6-2	170	6-28-90	0	1	3.52	4	0	0	2	8	3	3	3	0	5	7	.130	.286	.063	8.22	5.87
Hiraldo, Eduardo	R-R	6-3	180	8-21-89	1	2	2.70	9	1	0	0	23	14	10	7	0	16	34	.175	.111	.183	13.11	6.17
Lopez, Stalyn	L-L	5-9	160	12-28-91	2	2	7.64	13	7	0	0	33	32	34	28	2	37	30	.269	.200	.272	8.18	10.09
Martinez, Bryan	R-R	6-3	172	3-1-91	2	1	2.97	8	0	0	0	36	20	15	12	0	13	55	.156	.190	.150	13.62	3.22
Mata, Luis	R-R	6-2	190	4-27-91	1	1	3.21	9	0	0	1	14	11	8	5	1	14	12	.216	.100	.244	7.71	9.00
Matias, Carlos	R-R	6-0	165	9-21-91	3	2	0.76	12	12	1	0	59	28	8	5	1	14	78	.144	.213	.122	11.90	2.14
Paulino, Willy	R-R	6-2	190	6-21-90	4	3	2.76	16	10	0	0	62	45	21	19	4	31	55	.207	.188	.211	7.98	4.50
Rodriguez, Delvi	L-L	6-2	170	9-14-90	3	1	3.74	14	3	0	1	34	34	20	14	0	24	41	.270	.400	.259	10.96	6.42
Segundo, Jefferson	R-R	6-3	165	9-30-89	0	1	3.27	4	2	0	0	11	10	11	4	0	13	14	.244	.250	.243	11.45	10.64
Tapia, Angel	R-R	5-11	180	5-21-90	2	0	1.87	10	5	0	0	34	31	12	7	0	15	29	.246	.278	.241	7.75	4.01
Toribio, Arturo	R-R	5-11	185	3-1-92	1	2	2.81	13	4	0	3	42	38	17	13	0	14	41	.248	.333	.235	8.86	3.02

Fielding

Catcher	PCT	G	PO	A	E	DP	PB
Baez	.973	29	202	48	7	0	7
Ferreira	.938	10	79	12	6	0	3
Perez	.989	39	327	23	4	2	7

First Base	PCT	G	PO	A	E	DP
Agustin	1.000	6	12	0	0	2
Baez	.958	12	68	1	3	5
Beras	.993	24	138	10	1	9
Ferreira	.977	7	39	3	1	2
Lopez	1.000	7	54	1	0	5
Medina	1.000	13	53	3	0	2
Perez	1.000	20	124	9	0	7

Second Base	PCT	G	PO	A	E	DP
Barbuena	1.000	8	24	12	0	3
Encanacion	1.000	1	1	1	0	1
Lopez	.972	34	55	51	3	11
Reyes	.985	33	74	61	2	13

Third Base	PCT	G	PO	A	E	DP
Agustin	.787	19	9	28	10	3
Barbuena	1.000	7	10	13	0	1
Lopez	.872	23	17	24	6	2
Medina	.922	36	29	65	8	3
Reyes	.857	4	2	4	1	0

Shortstop	PCT	G	PO	A	E	DP
Barbuena	.921	39	50	102	13	13
Medina	.902	12	17	20	4	0
Reyes	.923	24	33	51	7	7

Outfield	PCT	G	PO	A	E	DP
Beras	.941	28	31	1	2	0
Capellan	1.000	41	57	5	0	1
Castillo	1.000	23	35	1	0	0
Ceballo	—	1	0	0	0	0
Celestino	.974	31	34	3	1	1
Diaz	.957	35	39	5	2	0
Encanacion	.981	38	51	2	1	0
Pena	.950	50	66	10	4	2
Reyes	1.000	3	1	0	0	0

VSL CARDINALS   ROOKIE

VENEZUELAN SUMMER LEAGUE

Batting	B-T	HT	WT	DOB	AVG	vLH	vRH	G	AB	R	H	2B	3B	HR	RBI	BB	HBP	SH	SF	SO	SB	CS	SLG	OBP
Acevedo, Jhohan	R-R	6-1	173	3-28-93	.210	.257	.200	60	200	20	42	6	0	0	18	20	2	5	2	66	6	8	.240	.286
Argenal, Jem	L-L	5-11	180	9-19-91	.243	.265	.238	65	230	28	56	13	2	4	36	20	3	0	4	29	3	3	.370	.307
Bueno, Lainer	R-R	6-1	183	8-12-90	.228	.250	.223	51	184	27	42	2	0	0	9	26	4	2	0	28	3	3	.239	.336
Garcia, Ronnierd	R-R	6-1	185	3-8-90	.223	.225	.223	63	215	20	48	5	1	2	23	19	5	1	1	51	3	1	.284	.300
Gomez, Jose	R-R	5-11	183	1-30-92	.254	.259	.252	42	134	24	34	7	2	2	20	17	4	0	3	31	2	0	.381	.348
Gonzalez, Kevin	R-R	5-11	160	9-18-92	.185	.200	.180	25	81	6	15	1	0	0	5	7	6	1	0	26	2	1	.198	.298
Marquez, Manuel	R-R	6-0	165	12-29-92	.104	.231	.057	15	48	4	5	0	0	0	2	4	2	0	0	12	0	0	.104	.204
Martina, Hayrich	R-R	6-0	170	8-3-90	.207	.211	.206	30	82	10	17	4	0	0	3	4	4	3	1	20	1	0	.256	.275
Martinez, Teharick	R-R	6-2	175	11-19-90	.184	.100	.205	40	103	14	19	2	0	3	13	14	1	4	0	32	1	2	.291	.288
Rivas, Limbert	R-R	6-1	185	2-21-90	.301	.238	.318	62	196	32	59	7	0	1	22	34	4	5	4	21	3	2	.352	.408
Sucre, Marlon	R-R	6-2	160	3-12-90	.269	.255	.273	58	223	35	60	14	0	8	33	11	2	2	0	49	8	2	.439	.309
Valera, Breyvil	B-R	5-11	160	8-1-92	.325	.415	.304	60	212	40	69	16	6	1	22	24	5	4	3	15	10	3	.472	.402
Velasco, Gerwins	R-R	6-1	190	10-7-90	.270	.326	.258	67	233	34	63	14	0	5	38	36	2	2	0	41	1	0	.395	.373

Pitching	B-T	HT	WT	DOB	W	L	ERA	G	GS	CG	SV	IP	H	R	ER	HR	BB	SO	AVG	vLH	vRH	K/9	BB/9
Almeida, Alberth	R-R	6-0	190	11-30-91	1	3	3.77	17	3	0	0	45	41	21	19	3	9	28	.248	.333	.217	5.56	1.79
Bier, Deimer	R-R	6-2	174	1-6-91	4	2	1.68	12	12	0	0	54	34	15	10	0	16	58	.180	.182	.179	9.73	2.68
Brito, Ismael	L-L	5-11	170	3-23-93	1	4	4.82	14	3	0	1	28	24	18	15	0	22	24	.238	.200	.242	7.71	7.07
Canache, Roberto	R-R	6-5	180	5-12-90	2	1	2.01	10	1	0	1	22	17	5	5	2	7	9	.224	.190	.236	3.63	2.82
Cueto, Kevin	R-R	6-0	177	12-4-93	1	1	5.85	15	0	0	0	20	17	19	13	1	19	16	.227	.250	.220	7.20	8.55
Echeverria, Angelo	L-L	6-2	170	1-2-92	0	0	0.00	2	0	0	0	4	2	0	0	0	1	3	.167	.000	.182	6.75	2.25
Escudero, Jhonatan	R-R	6-1	165	7-7-93	0	6	5.24	14	0	0	0	34	34	25	20	0	27	22	.272	.242	.283	5.77	7.08
Garcia, Silfredo	R-R	6-2	170	7-19-91	2	3	4.55	9	6	1	0	28	35	18	14	0	6	15	.321	.480	.274	4.88	1.95
Gerdel, Anderson	R-R	6-4	204	7-19-91	0	2	8.62	15	3	0	2	31	42	32	30	0	12	22	.326	.235	.358	6.32	3.45
Guerra, Geudy	R-R	5-11	179	8-13-93	1	2	4.18	14	0	0	0	24	26	18	11	1	13	10	.277	.179	.318	3.80	4.94
Montanez, Fermin	R-R	6-4	200	1-1-91	1	3	2.72	9	9	0	0	43	40	18	13	3	9	21	.252	.235	.256	4.40	1.88
Perez, Jose	R-R	6-0	178	6-8-93	0	3	6.65	10	3	0	0	22	29	19	16	1	7	11	.326	.412	.306	4.57	2.91
Planchart, Douglas	R-R	6-2	184	12-17-91	2	0	3.57	12	0	0	1	23	20	16	9	0	6	22	.230	.238	.227	8.74	2.38
Polanco, Jhonny	R-R	6-3	191	4-28-92	2	1	3.62	14	0	0	1	27	26	16	11	1	19	19	.252	.185	.276	6.26	6.26
Ramos, Edubray	R-R	6-0	163	12-19-92	1	0	9.53	10	0	0	0	17	26	23	18	1	10	17	.342	.133	.393	9.00	5.29
Solarte, Jackson	R-R	6-0	171	6-14-90	1	2	7.24	7	0	0	0	14	16	11	11	0	8	7	.320	.400	.300	4.51	5.27
Ulacio, Ramon	R-R	6-1	190	3-17-91	2	6	3.86	13	13	0	0	63	64	34	27	3	10	38	.260	.273	.257	5.43	1.43
Villanueva, Dail	L-L	6-3	180	1-23-90	0	4	7.00	12	7	0	0	36	36	33	28	1	32	23	.273	.200	.276	5.75	8.00
Villegas, Kender	R-R	6-2	170	6-8-93	1	0	7.43	13	1	0	1	23	30	24	19	2	16	8	.316	.300	.320	3.13	6.26

Fielding

Catcher	PCT	G	PO	A	E	DP	PB
Gomez	.934	19	109	19	9	1	7
Rivas	1.000	11	48	11	0	0	4
Velasco	.971	42	231	34	8	3	4

First Base	PCT	G	PO	A	E	DP
Argenal	1.000	10	52	4	0	2

	PCT	G	PO	A	E	DP
Garcia	1.000	4	6	1	0	0
Rivas	.984	45	344	30	6	26
Velasco	.988	19	153	8	2	12
Second Base	**PCT**	**G**	**PO**	**A**	**E**	**DP**
Bueno	.980	13	31	17	1	6
Garcia	.909	3	6	4	1	0
Gonzalez	.971	10	17	17	1	8
Marquez	.943	10	18	15	2	2
Martina	.909	7	9	11	2	4

	PCT	G	PO	A	E	DP
Valera	.979	34	73	64	3	17
Third Base	**PCT**	**G**	**PO**	**A**	**E**	**DP**
Garcia	.940	60	59	144	13	12
Gonzalez	1.000	1	1	1	0	0
Rivas	.786	6	3	8	3	0
Valera	.923	7	5	7	1	0
Shortstop	**PCT**	**G**	**PO**	**A**	**E**	**DP**
Bueno	.955	38	49	119	8	15
Gonzalez	.857	12	17	25	7	7

	PCT	G	PO	A	E	DP
Marquez	.786	6	1	10	3	0
Valera	.896	17	20	49	8	4
Outfield	**PCT**	**G**	**PO**	**A**	**E**	**DP**
Acevedo	.967	59	135	11	5	2
Argenal	.951	53	74	3	4	2
Martina	.600	9	6	0	4	0
Martinez	.923	36	56	4	5	1
Sucre	.947	53	105	3	6	1
Valera	.929	7	12	1	1	1

San Diego Padres

SEASON IN A SENTENCE: The Padres led the National League West for all but four days from April 20-Sept. 15, and had a winning record in every month but September, but a 10-game losing streak that straddled the end of August and the start of September vaporized their lead, and San Diego lost the season finale at San Francisco to miss the playoffs.

HIGH POINT: The Padres didn't roll over after their losing streak, and their brightest moment may have come in San Francisco. Needing to sweep the final series to make the playoffs, San Diego won the first two games by scores of 6-4 and 4-2. The six runs in the opener was just the second time the Giants gave up more than four runs in a game in the regular season's final month. Closer Heath Bell picked up saves in both contests, giving him 47 on the season.

LOW POINT: The 10-game losing streak featured a little of everything, but mostly it was the Padres' season-long lack of offense that doomed them. They scored just 23 runs in the streak, which included four losses to last-place Arizona.

NOTABLE ROOKIES: Mat Latos wasn't technically a rookie, but the 22-year-old righthander was San Diego's top starter on the season, going 14-10, 2.92 and striking out 9.2 batters per nine innings. Fellow righty Ryan Webb used his sinker to become a solid contributor in a deep bullpen and was the only rookie to use up his eligibility.

KEY TRANSACTIONS: San Diego tried to improve its offense at the trade deadline, adding Miguel Tejada from the Orioles (for righthander Wynn Pelzer) and Ryan Ludwick from the Cardinals in a three-team trade (that cost them righthander Corey Kluber). While Tejada (.730 OPS) was productive, Ludwich hit just .211 with six homers, not enough to protect Adrian Gonzalez in the lineup. First-year general manager Jed Hoyer brought Jason McLeod with him from Boston to run the team's draft, but the organization's recent run of bad luck in the first round of the draft continued. This time, San Diego couldn't bridge a bonus gap and failed to sign its top pick, Florida prep righthander Karsten Whitson, who headed to Florida to play college ball.

DOWN ON THE FARM: High Class A Lake Elsinore and low Class A Fort Wayne reached their leagues' playoffs, but the organization's overall winning percentage (.485) tied for 23rd with the Tigers.

OPENING DAY PAYROLL: $37.8 million (29th)

PLAYERS OF THE YEAR

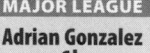

MAJOR LEAGUE	MINOR LEAGUE
Adrian Gonzalez	**Cory Luebke**
1b	**lhp**
.298/.393/.511	(Double-A/Triple-A)
31 HR, 101 RBIs	10-1, 2.68
7th in NL in OPS	Made majors debut

ORGANIZATION LEADERS

BATTING		*Minimum 250 at-bats
MAJORS		
*AVG	Adrian Gonzalez	.298
*OPS	Adrian Gonzalez	.904
HR	Adrian Gonzalez	31
RBI	Adrian Gonzalez	101
MINORS		
*AVG	Cole Figueroa, Lake Elsinore	.303
*OBP	Jason Hagerty, Fort Wayne	.423
*SLG	Mike Baxter, Portland	.517
R	Daniel Robertson, Lake Elsinore	95
H	Daniel Robertson, Lake Elsinore	160
TB	Cody Decker, Lake Elsinore	260
2B	Nathan Freiman, Fort Wayne	43
3B	Mike Baxter, Portland	10
HR	Matt Clark, San Antonio	28
	Cody Decker, Lake Elsinore	28
RBI	Matt Clark, San Antonio	97
BB	Vincent Belnome, Lake Elsinore	102
SO	Matt Clark, San Antonio	146
SB	Danny Payne, Lake Elsinore/Fort Wayne	40

PITCHING		†Minimum 75 innings
MAJORS		
W	Clayton Richard/Jon Garland/Mat Latos	14
†ERA	Tim Stauffer	1.85
SO	Mat Latos	189
MINORS		
W	Erik Davis, Portland/L.E./San Antonio	14
L	Cesar Carrillo, Portland	14
†ERA	Cory Luebke, San Antonio/Portland	2.68
G	Aaron Breit, Lake Elsinore/San Antonio	64
GS	Anthony Bass, Portland/Lake Elsinore	28
	Jeremy Hefner, San Antonio	28
SV	Brad Brach, Lake Elsinore	41
IP	Josh Geer, Portland	171.3
BB	Aaron Poreda, San Antonio/Portland	64
SO	Corey Kluber, San Antonio	136
†AVG	Cory Luebke, San Antonio/Portland	.200

General Manager: Jed Hoyer. **Farm Director:** Randy Smith. **Scouting Director:** Jaron Madison.

Class	Team	League	W	L	PCT	Finish*	Manager(s)
Majors	San Diego Padres	National	90	72	.556	5th (16)	Bud Black
Triple-A	Portland Beavers	Pacific Coast	59	85	.410	15th (16)	Terry Kennedy
Double-A	San Antonio Missions	Texas	68	72	.486	6th (8)	Doug Dascenzo
High A	Lake Elsinore Storm	California	81	59	.579	1st (10)	Carlos Lezcano
Low A	Fort Wayne TinCaps	Midwest	77	63	.550	5th (16)	Jose Flores
Short-season	Eugene Emeralds	Northwest	32	44	.421	6th (8)	Greg Riddoch
Rookie	AZL Padres	Arizona	20	35	.364	12th (12)	Ivan Cruz
Overall 2010 Minor League Record			337	358	.485	t-23rd (30)	

*Finish in overall standings (No. of teams in league). †League champion.

ORGANIZATION STATISTICS

SAN DIEGO PADRES

NATIONAL LEAGUE

Batting	B-T	HT	WT	DOB	AVG	vLH	vRH	G	AB	R	H	2B	3B	HR	RBI	BB	HBP	SH	SF	SO	SB	CS	SLG	OBP
Baxter, Mike	L-R	6-0	190	12-7-84	.125	.000	.125	9	8	0	1	0	0	0	1	0	0	0	1	2	0	0	.125	.111
Blanks, Kyle	R-R	6-6	270	9-11-86	.157	.174	.152	33	102	14	16	6	1	3	15	15	3	0	0	46	1	0	.324	.283
Cabrera, Everth	B-R	5-10	175	11-17-86	.208	.214	.206	76	212	22	44	6	3	1	22	19	2	8	0	54	10	6	.278	.279
Cunningham, Aaron	R-R	5-11	205	4-24-86	.288	.364	.250	53	132	17	38	12	1	1	15	7	3	2	3	28	1	3	.417	.331
Denorfia, Chris	R-R	6-0	205	7-15-80	.271	.295	.257	99	284	41	77	15	2	9	36	27	2	1	3	51	8	4	.433	.335
Durango, Luis	B-R	5-9	160	4-23-86	.250	.182	.270	28	48	8	12	0	0	0	4	4	0	1	0	7	5	0	.250	.308
Eckstein, David	R-R	5-7	175	1-20-75	.267	.265	.268	116	442	49	118	23	0	1	29	27	9	12	2	35	8	1	.326	.321
Gonzalez, Adrian	L-L	6-2	225	5-8-82	.298	.337	.278	160	591	87	176	33	0	31	101	93	2	2	4	114	0	0	.511	.393
Gwynn Jr., Tony	L-R	5-11	195	10-4-82	.204	.325	.185	117	289	30	59	9	3	3	20	41	1	7	1	50	17	4	.287	.304
Hairston Jr., Jerry	R-R	5-10	190	5-29-76	.244	.244	.244	119	430	53	105	13	2	10	50	31	5	4	6	54	9	6	.353	.299
Hairston, Scott	R-R	6-0	195	5-25-80	.210	.233	.198	104	295	34	62	10	0	10	36	31	6	0	4	69	6	1	.346	.295
Headley, Chase	B-R	6 2	210	5-9-84	.264	.217	.285	161	610	77	161	29	3	11	58	56	3	1	4	139	17	5	.375	.327
Hundley, Nick	R-R	6-1	205	9-8-83	.249	.274	.242	85	273	33	68	18	2	8	43	25	1	2	6	66	0	5	.418	.308
Ludwick, Ryan	R-L	6-3	220	7-13-78	.211	.162	.234	59	209	19	44	7	0	6	26	24	4	0	2	57	0	1	.330	.301
2-team total (77 St. Louis)					.251	—	—	136	490	63	123	27	2	17	69	48	8	0	5	121	0	4	.418	.325
Salazar, Oscar	R-R	6-0	195	6-27-78	.237	.235	.238	85	131	19	31	4	0	3	19	16	0	0	1	23	1	2	.336	.318
Stairs, Matt	L-R	5-9	200	2-27-68	.232	.000	.240	78	99	14	23	6	0	6	16	11	0	0	1	32	2	0	.475	.306
Stewart, Chris	R-R	6-4	210	2-19-82	—	.000	.000	2	0	0	0	0	0	0	0	0	0	0	0	0	0	0	—	—
Tejada, Miguel	R-R	5-9	210	5-25-74	.268	.354	.235	59	235	31	63	10	0	8	32	15	2	1	0	28	2	0	.413	.317
Torrealba, Yorvit	R-R	5-11	200	7-19-78	.271	.227	.287	95	325	31	88	14	0	7	37	33	3	1	1	67	7	5	.378	.343
Venable, Will	L-L	6-2	210	10-29-82	.245	.154	.259	131	392	60	96	11	7	13	51	45	3	0	5	128	29	7	.408	.324
Zawadzki, Lance	B-R	5-11	195	5-26-85	.200	.278	.118	20	35	4	7	2	0	1	5	0	2	0	7	1	0	.257	.300

Pitching	B-T	HT	WT	DOB	W	L	ERA	G	GS	CG	SV	IP	H	R	ER	HR	BB	SO	AVG	vLH	vRH	K/9	BB/9
Adams, Mike	R-R	6-5	195	7-29-78	4	1	1.76	70	0	0	0	67	48	14	13	2	23	73	.196	.185	.206	9.85	3.11
Bell, Heath	R-R	6-3	250	9-29-77	6	1	1.93	67	0	0	47	70	56	17	15	1	28	86	.221	.200	.241	11.06	3.60
Correia, Kevin	R-R	6-3	200	8-24-80	10	10	5.40	28	26	0	0	145	152	89	87	20	64	115	.271	.248	.290	7.14	3.97
Frieri, Ernesto	R-R	6-2	200	7-19-85	1	1	1.71	33	0	0	0	32	18	7	6	2	17	41	.162	.176	.156	11.65	4.83
Gallagher, Sean	R-R	6-2	235	12-30-85	0	0	5.40	15	0	0	0	23	24	14	14	5	19	21	.276	.175	.362	8.10	7.33
2-team total (31 Pittsburgh)					2	1	5.77	46	0	0	0	58	62	40	37	7	41	43	—	—	—	6.71	6.40
Garland, Jon	R-R	6-6	210	9-27-79	14	12	3.47	33	33	0	0	200	176	86	77	20	87	136	.240	.254	.228	6.12	3.92
Gregerson, Luke	L-R	6-3	200	5-14-84	4	7	3.22	80	0	0	2	78	47	30	28	8	18	89	.170	.180	.162	10.23	2.07
Latos, Mat	R-R	6-6	225	12-9-87	14	10	2.92	31	31	1	0	185	150	63	60	16	50	189	.217	.220	.214	9.21	2.44
LeBlanc, Wade	L-L	6-3	200	8-7-84	8	12	4.25	26	25	0	0	146	157	69	69	24	51	110	.279	.308	.269	6.78	3.14
Luebke, Cory	R-L	6-4	215	3-4-85	1	1	4.08	4	0	0	0	18	17	8	8	3	6	18	.246	.333	.222	9.17	3.06
Mujica, Edward	R-R	6-2	215	5-10-84	2	1	3.62	59	0	0	0	70	59	29	28	14	6	72	.226	.202	.243	9.30	0.78
Perdomo, Luis	R-R	6-0	170	4-27-84	0	0	9.00	1	0	0	0	1	1	1	1	1	0	0	.250	.000	.500	0.00	0.00
Ramos, Cesar	L-L	6-2	205	6-22-84	0	1	11.88	14	0	0	0	8	18	11	11	1	4	9	.419	.316	.500	9.72	4.32
Richard, Clayton	L-L	6-5	240	9-12-83	14	9	3.75	33	33	1	0	202	206	89	84	16	78	153	.267	.228	.281	6.83	3.48
Russell, Adam	R-R	6-8	255	4-14-83	0	0	4.02	12	0	0	0	16	14	8	7	0	5	18	.255	.143	.324	10.34	2.87
Stauffer, Tim	R-R	6-1	205	6-2-82	7	0	1.85	32	7	0	0	83	65	18	17	3	24	61	.219	.197	.236	6.64	2.61
Thatcher, Joe	L-L	6-2	230	10-4-81	1	0	1.29	65	0	0	0	35	23	5	5	1	7	45	.185	.197	.172	11.57	1.80
Webb, Ryan	R-R	6-6	215	2-5-86	3	1	2.90	54	0	0	0	59	64	21	19	1	19	44	.277	.333	.239	6.71	2.90
Young, Chris	R-R	6-10	280	5-25-79	2	0	0.90	4	4	0	0	20	10	2	2	1	11	15	.143	.167	.130	6.75	4.95

Fielding

Catcher	PCT	G	PO	A	E	DP	PB
Hundley	.994	76	632	28	4	6	6
Stewart	1.000	1	1	0	0	0	0
Torrealba	.996	92	681	45	3	5	7

First Base	PCT	G	PO	A	E	DP
Baxter	1.000	1	1	0	0	0
Blanks	1.000	4	15	1	0	0

	PCT	G	PO	A	E	DP
Gonzalez	.995	159	1324	127	8	125
Salazar	1.000	7	33	1	0	4
Stairs	1.000	3	12	1	0	1
Stewart	1.000	1	2	0	0	0
Venable	1.000	1	1	0	0	0

Second Base	PCT	G	PO	A	E	DP
Cabrera	1.000	6	7	15	0	3

	PCT	G	PO	A	E	DP
Eckstein	1.000	113	191	284	0	71
Hairston Jr.	.995	47	77	112	1	26
Salazar	1.000	6	1	4	0	0
Zawadzki	.931	7	9	18	2	2

Third Base	PCT	G	PO	A	E	DP
Hairston Jr.	1.000	3	1	3	0	0
Headley	.966	158	82	293	13	21

Salazar	1.000	1	0	1	0	0
Tejada	1.000	4	1	3	0	0
Zawadzki	1.000	1	1	4	0	1
Shortstop	**PCT**	**G**	**PO**	**A**	**E**	**DP**
Cabrera	.966	61	63	137	7	30
Hairston Jr.	.976	62	87	162	6	27
Tejada	.987	58	68	162	3	40

Zawadzki	1.000	3	2	5	0	1
Outfield	**PCT**	**G**	**PO**	**A**	**E**	**DP**
Blanks	1.000	30	45	3	0	0
Cunningham	1.000	39	57	0	0	0
Denorfia	.989	92	171	8	2	3
Durango	.950	10	17	2	1	0
Gwynn Jr.	1.000	105	160	5	0	0

Hairston Jr.	1.000	12	16	0	0	0
Hairston	.973	85	141	3	4	1
Ludwick	.983	58	117	2	2	0
Salazar	1.000	24	17	0	0	0
Stairs	1.000	14	13	0	0	0
Venable	.984	121	241	1	4	1

PORTLAND BEAVERS   TRIPLE-A
PACIFIC COAST LEAGUE

Batting	B-T	HT	WT	DOB	AVG	vLH	vRH	G	AB	R	H	2B	3B	HR	RBI	BB	HBP	SH	SF	SO	SB	CS	SLG	OBP
Barfield, Josh	R-R	6-0	190	12-17-82	.294	.300	.291	78	265	33	78	13	0	5	36	13	1	1	4	34	4	1	.400	.325
Baxter, Mike	L-R	6-0	190	12-7-84	.301	.271	.312	136	482	89	145	30	10	18	72	58	8	0	4	78	22	10	.517	.382
Blanks, Kyle	R-R	6-6	270	9-11-86	.333	.000	.500	1	3	0	1	0	0	0	0	1	0	0	0	1	0	0	.333	.500
Cabrera, Everth	B-R	5-10	175	11-17-86	.258	.111	.318	8	31	7	8	1	0	0	3	6	0	0	0	13	3	0	.290	.378
Canham, Mitch	L-R	6-2	205	9-25-84	.320	.091	.500	9	25	2	8	0	1	0	1	2	0	0	0	5	0	2	.400	.370
Chalk, Brad	L-L	6-1	180	1-20-86	.313	.250	.346	27	80	9	25	4	1	0	5	8	0	0	0	10	2	2	.388	.375
Collins, Mike	R-R	6-3	215	7-18-84	.250	.333	.000	3	8	0	2	1	0	0	0	0	0	0	0	0	0	0	.375	.250
Colonel, Christian	R-R	6-2	210	12-25-81	.107	.167	.091	11	28	1	3	0	0	0	1	3	0	0	0	9	0	0	.107	.194
2-team total (13 Las Vegas)					.258	—		24	66	5	17	1	0	0	5	7	0	1	0	16	0	1	.273	.329
Contreras, Anthony	L-R	5-11	185	9-26-83	.273	.194	.296	61	161	19	44	6	0	4	16	8	1	2	1	22	2	1	.385	.310
Cooper, Craig	R-L	6-1	220	10-27-84	.248	.240	.252	102	359	43	89	19	3	9	64	35	2	0	2	79	3	3	.393	.317
Cunningham, Aaron	R-R	5-11	205	4-24-86	.251	.267	.243	80	271	30	68	17	3	7	45	28	6	2	1	68	2	7	.413	.333
Denorfia, Chris	R-R	6-0	205	7-15-80	.306	.367	.286	34	121	17	37	10	4	2	12	12	0	1	0	18	1	1	.504	.368
Durango, Luis	B-R	5-9	160	4-23-86	.300	.266	.318	106	363	42	109	5	2	0	24	45	1	13	1	59	35	16	.325	.378
Gerut, Jody	L-L	6-0	190	9-18-77	.302	.300	.303	14	53	7	16	4	0	1	11	7	1	0	0	5	0	0	.434	.393
Green, Nick	R-R	6-0	190	9-10-78	.264	.250	.270	40	144	17	38	9	1	2	21	13	0	2	0	33	0	4	.382	.325
2-team total (29 Albuquerque)					.240	—		69	242	32	58	18	3	4	31	16	1	4	0	52	1	4	.388	.290
Hunter, Cedric	L-L	6-0	185	3-10-88	.263	.206	.284	65	262	42	69	13	3	3	26	16	0	6	1	22	5	1	.370	.305
Kazmar, Sean	R-R	5-9	160	8-5-84	.275	.318	.252	130	499	70	137	23	3	8	53	37	3	2	4	81	7	2	.381	.326
Munson, Eric	L-R	6-3	220	10-3-77	.201	.143	.212	47	134	14	27	3	0	7	20	26	5	0	0	35	0	1	.381	.352
Pena, Wily Mo	R-R	6-3	270	1-23-82	.324	.440	.261	40	142	28	46	6	0	9	34	15	1	0	1	45	0	1	.556	.390
Phillips, Kyle	L-R	6-1	225	4-3-84	.324	.333	.322	55	176	19	57	6	2	3	28	13	0	3	2	20	0	0	.432	.365
2-team total (19 Las Vegas)					.306	—		74	242	28	74	11	2	3	36	18	0	3	6	30	0	0	.405	.350
Ryan, Dusty	R-R	6-4	220	9-2-84	.199	.163	.217	89	261	29	52	18	0	7	30	50	3	0	1	99	2	1	.349	.333
Stansberry, Craig	R-R	6-0	185	3-8-82	.260	.240	.272	114	346	52	90	19	1	8	32	42	4	4	2	71	6	6	.390	.345
Stewart, Chris	R-R	6-4	210	2-19-82	.248	.280	.229	85	266	31	66	14	2	7	39	30	7	3	3	38	1	0	.395	.337
Zawadzki, Lance	B-R	5-11	195	5-26-85	.231	.264	.216	61	225	34	52	10	1	1	16	21	1	0	1	57	5	5	.298	.298

Pitching	B-T	HT	WT	DOB	W	L	ERA	G	GS	CG	SV	IP	H	R	ER	HR	BB	SO	AVG	vLH	vRH	K/9	BB/9
Bass, Anthony	R-R	6-2	190	11-1-87	0	1	7.94	1	1	0	0	6	7	5	5	1	3	3	.333	.375	.308	4.76	4.76
Berger, Jon	R-R	6-2	215	1-18-87	0	1	27.00	1	0	0	0	2	5	6	6	1	1	1	.455	.000	.625	4.50	4.50
Burke, Greg	R-R	6-4	215	9-21-82	2	2	5.68	53	0	0	0	59	62	42	37	13	21	46	.271	.284	.261	7.06	3.22
Buschmann, Matt	R-R	6-3	210	2-13-84	0	4	9.38	8	4	0	0	24	27	27	25	5	20	20	.290	.302	.280	7.50	7.50
Carrillo, Cesar	R-R	6-3	170	4-29-84	5	14	5.60	27	27	0	0	151	167	103	94	20	57	95	.283	.283	.277	5.66	3.40
Castro, Simon	R-R	6-5	210	4-9-88	0	1	7.84	2	2	0	0	10	16	10	9	1	5	6	.333	.294	.355	5.23	5.23
Culp, Nathan	L-L	6-2	180	10-9-84	0	3	9.95	4	4	0	0	19	29	25	21	4	7	8	.341	.214	.366	3.79	3.32
Davis, Erik	R-R	6-4	200	10-8-86	1	0	3.60	1	1	0	0	5	2	2	2	1	2	7	.176	.286	.100	12.60	3.60
DeMark, Mike	R-R	6-0	198	5-20-83	0	0	4.14	30	0	0	0	41	36	24	19	5	21	37	.234	.262	.215	8.06	4.57
Frieri, Ernesto	R-R	6-2	200	7-19-85	3	1	1.43	34	0	0	17	38	14	6	6	2	18	49	.114	.161	.075	11.71	4.30
Gallagher, Sean	R-R	6-2	235	12-30-85	0	2	4.91	3	3	0	0	11	14	6	6	4	12	9	.298	.296	.300	9.82	3.27
Garrison, Steve	B-L	6-1	185	9-12-86	1	3	8.87	5	5	0	0	22	34	22	22	5	7	17	.354	.222	.385	6.85	2.82
Geer, Josh	R-R	6-3	195	6-2-83	11	11	5.41	29	25	1	0	171	212	111	103	29	32	89	.308	.314	.302	4.68	1.68
Gonzalez, Eric	R-R	6-5	190	9-5-86	0	0	3.00	1	0	0	0	3	3	1	1	0	1	2	.273	.333	.250	6.00	3.00
Inman, Will	R-R	6-0	215	2-6-87	2	4	3.61	11	11	1	0	62	54	31	25	7	27	52	.232	.202	.256	7.51	3.90
Koplove, Mike	R-R	6-0	165	8-30-76	0	0	6.75	10	0	0	0	15	12	11	11	4	8	10	.231	.273	.200	6.14	4.91
2-team total (22 Tacoma)					0	1	5.23	32	0	0	1	43	46	26	25	7	21	31	—	—		6.49	4.40
Lara, Alexis	R-R	6-0	150	3-23-87	0	0	0.00	1	0	0	0	2	0	0	0	0	1	1	.000	.000	.000	5.40	5.40
LeBlanc, Wade	L-L	6-3	200	8-7-84	0	1	7.20	2	2	0	0	10	13	8	8	1	1	15	.302	.250	.323	13.50	0.90
Liz, Radhames	R-R	6-2	185	10-6-83	8	8	4.83	25	22	0	0	123	128	68	66	20	38	109	.269	.264	.273	7.98	2.78
Luebke, Cory	R-L	6-4	215	3-4-85	5	0	2.97	9	9	0	0	58	42	22	19	6	17	44	.201	.221	.189	6.87	2.65
Marona, Chase	R-R	6-1	205	8-18-88	0	0	3.00	2	0	0	0	3	4	1	1	0	1	2	.333	.400	.286	6.00	3.00
Munter, Scott	R-R	6-6	260	3-7-80	4	1	2.66	49	1	0	0	71	57	22	21	3	32	67	.221	.236	.209	8.49	4.06
Ottone, Daniel	R-R	6-4	240	1-26-88	0	0	0.00	1	0	0	0	2	2	0	0	0	2	1	.333	.000	.667	4.50	9.00
Perdomo, Luis	R-R	6-0	170	4-27-84	4	6	3.40	58	3	0	1	82	76	40	31	7	34	49	.248	.250	.246	5.38	3.73
Poreda, Aaron	L-L	6-6	240	10-1-86	1	1	4.97	20	1	0	0	29	13	18	16	0	38	22	.143	.167	.134	6.83	11.79
Ramos, Cesar	L-L	6-2	205	6-22-84	6	7	3.28	30	15	1	0	96	90	37	35	7	43	63	.261	.216	.284	5.91	4.03
Russell, Adam	R-R	6-8	255	4-14-83	4	9	4.88	50	0	0	14	52	58	30	28	5	32	51	.280	.274	.285	8.88	5.57
Stauffer, Tim	R-R	6-1	205	6-2-82	0	0	4.58	6	5	0	0	24	13	13	12	6	10	11	.163	.194	.183	4.08	3.57
Thatcher, Joe	L-L	6-2	230	10-4-81	0	1	3.60	6	0	0	0	5	6	2	2	0	3	3	.316	.500	.267	5.40	5.40
Webb, Ryan	R-R	6-6	215	2-5-86	1	0	0.87	17	0	0	1	21	12	2	2	1	5	23	.169	.240	.130	10.02	2.18
Worrell, Mark	R-R	6-1	215	3-8-83	1	4	5.45	25	0	0	0	33	34	28	20	5	11	34	.254	.293	.224	9.27	3.00
2-team total (4 Tacoma)					2	4	5.84	29	0	0	0	37	41	32	24	5	14	34	—	—		8.27	3.41
Young, Chris	R-R	6-10	280	5-25-79	0	0	1.42	2	2	0	0	6	2	1	1	1	2	4	.095	.111	.083	5.68	2.84

Fielding

Catcher	PCT	G	PO	A	E	DP	PB
Canham	1.000	2	13	2	0	0	0
Phillips	.973	5	34	2	1	0	0
Ryan	.985	68	427	33	7	1	6
Stewart	.991	77	497	40	5	1	1

First Base	PCT	G	PO	A	E	DP
Baxter	.994	46	326	21	2	37
Collins	.952	2	17	3	1	0
Cooper	.986	48	389	28	6	45
Munson	.977	19	156	11	4	13
Pena	.977	14	124	6	3	13
Phillips	.995	22	174	10	1	21
Stewart	.941	7	62	2	4	5

Second Base	PCT	G	PO	A	E	DP
Barfield	.981	32	64	93	3	23
Contreras	1.000	14	29	21	0	7
Green	1.000	11	25	29	0	8
Kazmar	.982	42	94	120	4	33
Stansberry	.986	44	83	129	3	33
Zawadzki	.983	11	23	34	1	5

Third Base	PCT	G	PO	A	E	DP
Barfield	.901	31	19	45	7	10
Baxter	.667	3	1	1	1	0
Colonel	.938	8	5	10	1	0
Contreras	.974	29	17	59	2	8
Green	.923	11	4	20	2	0
Munson	.923	13	10	14	2	1
Phillips	1.000	3	3	4	0	1
Stansberry	.935	52	33	110	10	13
Zawadzki	.957	14	6	16	1	3

Shortstop	PCT	G	PO	A	E	DP
Cabrera	.975	8	15	24	1	7
Contreras	.929	4	6	7	1	1
Green	.985	18	24	43	1	11
Kazmar	.966	83	98	240	12	52
Zawadzki	.952	38	47	93	7	24

Outfield	PCT	G	PO	A	E	DP
Barfield	1.000	11	15	1	0	1
Baxter	.993	80	132	5	1	1
Blanks	—	1	0	0	0	0
Canham	—	3	0	0	0	0
Chalk	.957	24	42	3	2	0
Contreras	1.000	2	1	0	0	0
Cooper	.969	43	92	2	3	1
Cunningham	.961	72	96	3	4	1
Denorfia	1.000	31	61	2	0	1
Durango	.984	99	243	1	4	1
Gerut	1.000	14	17	0	0	0
Hunter	.986	63	141	4	2	2
Kazmar	1.000	2	3	0	0	0
Pena	.929	8	13	0	1	0

SAN ANTONIO MISSIONS

DOUBLE-A

TEXAS LEAGUE

Batting	B-T	HT	WT	DOB	AVG	vLH	vRH	G	AB	R	H	2B	3B	HR	RBI	BB	HBP	SH	SF	SO	SB	CS	SLG	OBP
Berry, Quintin	L-L	6-0	175	11-21-84	.209	.200	.213	33	110	11	23	1	1	1	8	10	3	1	0	28	4	2	.264	.293
Canham, Mitch	L-R	6-2	205	9-25-84	.209	.162	.238	76	263	27	55	10	2	4	26	30	3	3	2	41	1	1	.308	.295
Carroll, Sawyer	L-R	6-4	215	5-9-86	.240	.200	.265	128	458	50	110	21	3	7	55	56	3	0	5	123	1	7	.345	.324
Carvajal, Yefri	R-R	5-11	190	1-22-89	.176	.143	.200	13	34	3	6	1	0	2	6	2	0	0	0	5	0	0	.382	.222
Chalk, Brad	L-L	6-0	180	1-20-86	.214	.226	.204	65	201	23	43	6	2	0	15	15	3	8	0	27	2	4	.264	.279
Clark, Matt	L-R	6-5	215	12-10-86	.269	.251	.278	129	499	62	134	22	1	28	97	47	8	0	4	146	0	0	.485	.339
Collins, Mike	R-R	6-3	215	7-18-84	.260	.314	.232	41	146	24	38	7	3	3	26	14	3	0	0	29	1	0	.411	.337
Colonel, Christian	R-R	6-2	210	12-25-81	.221	.194	.237	39	95	13	21	4	1	1	13	20	1	0	0	17	0	0	.316	.362
Contreras, Anthony	L-R	5-11	185	9-26-83	.250	.375	.208	12	32	4	8	3	0	0	7	0	1	1	0	8	0	0	.344	.242
Cooper, Craig	R-L	6-1	220	10-27-84	.218	.212	.222	25	78	5	17	4	0	0	8	7	0	0	0	18	0	1	.269	.282
Cumberland, Drew	R-R	5-10	175	1-13-89	.278	.190	.333	15	54	5	15	3	0	0	6	1	1	1	1	11	1	2	.333	.298
Darnell, James	R-R	6-2	195	1-19-87	.265	.307	.240	101	373	46	99	21	1	10	50	44	5	1	3	64	2	0	.408	.348
Forsythe, Logan	R-R	6-1	205	1-14-87	.253	.279	.238	107	392	66	99	22	1	3	38	75	4	0	1	95	17	5	.337	.377
Hunter, Cedric	L-L	6-0	185	3-10-88	.308	.299	.315	71	279	34	86	14	3	4	38	31	2	0	5	22	9	7	.423	.375
Kulbacki, Kellen	L-L	5-11	185	11-21-85	.215	.190	.234	39	135	14	29	6	1	2	12	13	1	0	1	26	0	1	.319	.284
Lopez, Jesus	R-R	5-11	165	9-12-87	.193	.122	.233	38	114	13	22	3	0	0	11	11	0	1	2	16	0	0	.219	.260
Martinez, Luis	R-R	6-0	210	4-3-85	.282	.342	.236	106	358	48	101	16	1	3	41	49	1	0	2	59	3	2	.349	.368
Minyeti, Jorge	B-R	5-10	180	11-7-90	.227	.250	.208	22	44	5	10	2	0	0	6	7	0	0	0	11	0	0	.273	.333
Parrino, Andy	B-R	6-0	185	10-31-85	.246	.259	.238	125	410	70	101	28	4	11	49	68	8	4	2	115	4	2	.415	.363
Pozo, Jhonaldo	R-R	6-3	183	3-28-89	.000	.000	.000	1	1	0	0	0	0	0	0	0	0	0	0	0	0	0	.000	.000
Solis, Ali	R-R	5-10	225	9-29-87	.111	.333	.067	10	18	0	2	0	0	0	1	0	1	0	0	5	0	0	.111	.158
Tekotte, Blake	L-R	5-11	175	5-24-87	.250	.240	.256	67	268	44	67	8	7	10	37	26	4	2	1	63	6	9	.444	.324
Venable, Will	L-L	6-2	210	10-29-82	.333	.500	.000	2	6	2	2	0	0	0	1	2	0	0	0	2	2	0	.333	.500
Weems, Beamer	B-R	5-10	175	7-28-87	.149	.152	.146	30	94	10	14	5	1	0	5	18	1	0	1	22	1	2	.223	.289
Zawadzki, Lance	B-R	5-11	195	5-26-85	.216	.222	.214	35	148	21	32	5	1	4	17	13	0	0	0	34	7	1	.345	.280

Pitching	B-T	HT	WT	DOB	W	L	ERA	G	GS	CG	SV	IP	H	R	ER	HR	BB	SO	AVG	vLH	vRH	K/9	BB/9
Adams, Mike	R-R	6-5	195	7-29-78	0	0	0.00	1	0	0	0	1	0	0	0	0	0	0	.000	.000	.000	0.00	0.00
Breit, Aaron	R-R	6-4	205	4-19-86	0	0	9.39	11	0	0	0	15	19	18	16	2	19	11	.297	.240	.333	6.46	11.15
Buschmann, Matt	R-R	6-3	210	2-13-84	2	2	3.46	32	5	0	0	68	59	29	26	2	23	74	.234	.302	.185	9.84	3.06
Castro, Simon	R-R	6-5	210	4-9-88	7	6	2.92	24	23	0	0	130	107	55	42	8	36	107	.223	.248	.197	7.43	2.50
Culp, Nathan	L-L	6-2	180	10-9-84	5	8	4.21	26	18	0	1	118	139	64	55	7	25	69	.297	.306	.293	5.28	1.91
Davis, Erik	R-R	6-4	200	10-8-86	4	0	2.75	7	7	0	0	39	29	13	12	1	12	35	.210	.182	.229	8.01	2.75
DeMark, Mike	R-R	6-0	198	5-20-83	1	0	0.60	12	0	0	0	15	9	1	1	1	3	15	.173	.353	.086	9.00	1.80
Gomes, Brandon	R-R	5-11	175	7-15-84	7	2	1.87	51	0	0	1	72	52	19	15	2	25	93	.198	.242	.161	11.57	3.11
Hardy, Mark	L-L	6-4	195	5-3-88	1	1	5.23	2	2	0	0	10	12	6	6	1	4	10	.293	.278	.304	8.71	3.48
Hefner, Jeremy	R-R	6-4	215	3-11-86	11	8	2.95	28	28	2	0	168	156	63	55	11	51	115	.254	.256	.252	6.17	2.74
Hynes, Colt	L-L	5-11	200	6-28-85	0	1	1.19	24	0	0	0	30	30	5	4	0	10	24	.276	.216	.310	7.12	2.97
Italiano, Craig	R-R	6-4	215	7-22-86	4	6	2.58	47	0	0	17	52	43	25	15	0	27	36	.226	.259	.200	6.19	4.64
Kluber, Corey	R-R	6-4	215	4-10-86	6	6	3.45	22	21	0	0	123	121	59	47	7	40	136	.259	.275	.242	9.98	2.93
Lara, Alexis	R-R	6-0	150	3-23-87	4	5	3.95	44	0	0	0	71	58	35	31	4	33	56	.228	.232	.225	7.13	4.20
Luebke, Cory	R-L	6-4	215	3-4-85	1	5	2.40	10	8	1	0	56	55	18	15	2	12	44	.200	.284	.153	7.03	1.92
Lumsden, Tyler	L-L	6-4	215	5-9-83	1	5	5.36	9	9	0	0	50	59	40	30	3	21	28	.312	.302	.316	5.01	3.75
2-team total (20 Corpus Christi)					5	13	4.51	29	25	1	0	142	151	87	71	7	55	61	—	—		3.88	3.49
Oland, Bryan	R-R	6-3	230	6-5-85	1	4	3.63	33	0	0	2	40	39	19	16	3	15	36	.250	.190	.319	8.17	3.40
Ottone, Daniel	R-R	6-4	240	1-26-88	0	0	1.59	4	0	0	0	6	7	4	1	0	2	3	.304	.286	.313	4.76	3.18
Pelzer, Wynn	R-R	6-1	205	6-23-86	6	9	4.20	22	18	0	0	94	102	57	44	9	56	83	.277	.298	.263	7.92	5.34
Poreda, Aaron	L-L	6-6	240	10-1-86	0	1	2.52	19	0	0	0	25	18	11	7	1	26	25	.212	.292	.180	9.00	9.36
Scribner, Evan	R-R	6-3	190	7-19-85	4	5	2.59	57	0	0	16	66	51	22	19	6	15	81	.213	.206	.217	11.05	2.05
Young, Chris	R-R	6-10	280	5-25-79	0	1	67.50	1	1	0	0	1	2	5	5	0	4	1	.667	1.000	.000	13.50	54.00

Fielding

Catcher	PCT	G	PO	A	E	DP	PB
Canham	.975	24	177	20	5	1	1
Collins	1.000	19	147	11	0	3	2
Martinez	.985	99	743	65	12	9	7
Solis	.977	7	36	6	1	1	0

First Base	PCT	G	PO	A	E	DP
Canham	.991	16	106	8	1	10
Clark	.990	110	897	81	10	74
Collins	1.000	16	136	10	0	11
Cooper	1.000	5	34	1	0	7
Parrino	1.000	2	3	1	0	1

Second Base	PCT	G	PO	A	E	DP
Contreras	1.000	2	3	6	0	0
Cumberland	1.000	3	4	7	0	0
Forsythe	.968	98	188	271	15	61

	PCT	G	PO	A	E	DP
Lopez	.971	6	17	16	1	2
Minyeti	.931	12	21	33	4	10
Parrino	.983	26	49	70	2	11

Third Base	PCT	G	PO	A	E	DP
Canham	.920	12	5	18	2	0
Colonel	.953	17	11	30	2	1
Contreras	.875	4	6	1	1	1
Darnell	.897	95	58	152	24	16
Forsythe	.857	2	1	5	1	0
Parrino	.911	17	10	31	4	5

Shortstop	PCT	G	PO	A	E	DP
Colonel	1.000	1	0	2	0	0
Contreras	.833	2	3	2	1	1
Cumberland	.915	12	17	26	4	5
Lopez	.966	31	36	77	4	8

	PCT	G	PO	A	E	DP
Parrino	.943	44	72	92	10	23
Weems	.933	30	31	80	8	11
Zawadzki	.979	34	46	97	3	26

Outfield	PCT	G	PO	A	E	DP
Berry	.976	28	41	0	1	0
Canham	.946	22	34	1	2	0
Carroll	.976	117	224	18	6	3
Carvajal	.895	11	16	1	2	0
Chalk	.968	55	87	3	3	0
Colonel	1.000	1	0	0	0	0
Cooper	1.000	13	22	2	0	0
Hunter	.994	67	148	6	1	0
Kulbacki	.981	31	47	4	1	0
Parrino	1.000	31	40	3	0	0
Tekotte	.987	63	151	6	2	4
Venable	—	1	0	0	0	0

LAKE ELSINORE STORM

HIGH CLASS A

CALIFORNIA LEAGUE

Batting	B-T	HT	WT	DOB	AVG	vLH	vRH	G	AB	R	H	2B	3B	HR	RBI	BB	HBP	SH	SF	SO	SB	CS	SLG	OBP
Agreste, Joe	L-L	6-4	195	4-10-87	.150	.000	.214	9	20	2	3	0	1	0	2	5	1	0	1	9	0	0	.250	.333
Belnome, Vince	R-L	5-11	205	3-11-88	.273	.276	.272	135	498	81	136	31	1	16	84	102	2	1	3	136	4	1	.436	.397
Blanks, Kyle	R-R	6-6	270	9-11-86	.270	.182	.308	10	37	3	10	3	0	0	4	6	1	0	0	12	0	0	.351	.386
Cabrera, Everth	B-R	5-10	175	11-5-86	.300	.333	.286	3	10	1	3	0	0	0	1	2	0	0	0	4	1	0	.300	.417
Carvajal, Yefri	R-R	5-11	190	1-22-89	.198	.132	.237	56	182	21	36	4	1	3	24	7	1	1	6	35	3	1	.280	.224
Chalk, Brad	L-L	6-1	180	1-20-86	.191	.278	.171	26	94	7	18	2	1	0	10	7	0	2	0	14	1	0	.234	.248
Collins, Mike	R-R	6-3	215	7-18-84	.311	.387	.280	28	106	14	33	11	2	6	19	9	0	0	2	17	2	1	.623	.359
Cumberland, Drew	L-R	5-10	175	1-13-89	.365	.393	.352	60	249	63	91	15	4	7	35	15	3	0	3	34	20	9	.542	.404
Davis, Bo	R-R	6-0	185	8-28-85	.209	.120	.248	61	163	27	34	8	2	4	29	19	5	7	2	48	4	4	.356	.307
Decker, Cody	R-R	5-11	220	1-17-87	.270	.285	.265	130	507	82	137	35	2	28	90	60	8	0	7	135	2	0	.513	.352
Decker, Jaff	L-L	5-10	190	2-23-90	.262	.203	.281	79	290	53	76	14	2	17	58	47	7	0	4	80	5	4	.500	.374
Dykstra, Allan	L-R	6-5	215	5-21-87	.241	.202	.254	113	386	54	93	24	2	16	70	78	3	1	1	122	1	4	.438	.372
Figueroa, Cole	L-R	5-10	180	6-30-87	.303	.277	.313	124	482	88	146	25	3	4	66	81	6	7	2	54	26	9	.392	.408
Hairston, Scott	R-R	6-0	195	5-25-80	.571	1.000	.250	3	7	1	4	1	0	0	1	4	0	0	0	1	0	0	.714	.727
Hansen, Kevin	R-R	5-10	170	11-5-85	.161	.100	.185	67	174	11	28	7	0	0	10	14	2	5	0	35	1	1	.201	.232
Lara, Robert	R-R	6-2	190	11-25-86	.279	.246	.291	75	258	38	72	12	0	8	39	38	1	3	4	55	1	0	.419	.369
Liriano, Rymer	R-R	6-0	211	6-20-91	.220	.222	.220	14	50	3	11	2	0	1	6	5	0	0	0	12	3	0	.320	.291
Lopez, Jesus	R-R	5-11	165	9-12-87	.247	.245	.247	65	231	36	57	17	2	2	24	36	2	2	1	38	3	0	.364	.352
Payne, Danny	L-L	5-10	185	3-28-85	.156	.077	.176	22	64	12	10	1	0	1	8	7	2	0	1	25	2	0	.219	.257
Pozo, Jhonaldo	R-R	6-3	183	3-28-89	.273	1.000	.200	3	11	1	3	1	0	0	0	0	0	0	0	5	0	0	.364	.273
Robertson, Dan	R-R	5-8	175	9-30-85	.300	.270	.311	135	533	95	160	27	9	6	61	59	7	6	4	52	30	9	.418	.375
Salazar, Oscar	R-R	6-0	195	6-27-78	.280	.250	.286	7	25	3	7	1	0	1	4	1	0	0	1	5	0	0	.440	.296
Skube, Ryan	R-R	5-11	175	3-26-91	.412	.500	.385	4	17	4	7	3	0	1	6	2	0	0	0	4	0	0	.765	.474
Solis, Ali	R-R	5-10	225	9-29-87	.270	.300	.259	12	37	6	10	1	0	4	8	2	0	0	0	10	0	0	.622	.308
Tekotte, Blake	L-R	5-11	175	5-24-87	.310	.271	.326	59	203	41	63	17	1	8	27	36	2	0	0	46	22	8	.522	.419
Tremblay, Chris	R-R	5-10	180	11-8-86	.240	.385	.083	10	25	2	6	1	0	0	0	3	0	1	0	6	0	0	.280	.321
Venable, Will	L-L	6-2	210	10-29-82	.071	.000	.077	5	14	0	1	1	0	0	0	4	0	0	0	8	1	0	.143	.278
Zornes, Adam	R-R	6-1	215	4-2-86	.179	.222	.165	30	112	11	20	3	1	3	10	13	4	0	0	51	1	0	.304	.287

Pitching	B-T	HT	WT	DOB	W	L	ERA	G	GS	CG	SV	IP	H	R	ER	HR	BB	SO	AVG	vLH	vRH	K/9	BB/9
Bass, Anthony	R-R	6-2	190	11-1-87	8	7	3.13	27	27	0	0	132	124	59	46	9	20	109	.248	.242	.252	7.41	1.36
Beard, Hayden	R-R	6-1	175	1-22-85	0	1	4.37	20	0	0	0	35	26	20	17	2	20	30	.198	.233	.181	7.71	5.14
Berger, Jon	R-R	6-2	215	1-18-87	1	2	5.29	19	1	0	0	32	42	21	19	4	7	25	.318	.351	.293	6.96	1.95
Brach, Brad	R-R	6-6	210	4-12-86	5	2	2.47	62	0	0	41	66	50	20	18	6	11	74	.207	.171	.234	10.14	1.51
Breit, Aaron	R-R	6-4	205	4-19-86	4	5	3.75	53	0	0	3	66	63	33	25	1	20	50	.275	.308	.254	7.50	3.00
Davis, Erik	R-R	6-4	200	10-8-86	9	3	3.82	19	19	0	0	99	102	49	42	5	34	91	.266	.237	.290	8.27	3.09
Fetter, Chris	R-R	6-8	230	12-23-85	1	1	6.00	4	4	0	0	21	27	16	14	6	9	14	.314	.327	.297	6.00	3.86
Garrison, Steve	B-L	6-1	185	9-12-86	1	1	3.14	9	3	0	0	29	28	13	10	1	10	13	.267	.225	.292	4.08	3.14
Gonzalez, Eric	R-R	6-5	190	9-5-86	6	5	7.26	28	0	0	1	53	75	53	43	5	15	40	.326	.309	.336	6.75	2.53
Hardy, Mark	L-L	6-4	195	5-3-88	0	1	5.79	11	0	0	0	5	6	3	3	0	2	3	.353	.250	.385	5.79	3.86
Herr, Zach	L-L	5-9	185	12-1-86	4	2	3.04	50	4	0	0	71	60	27	24	2	28	53	.230	.196	.249	6.72	3.55
Hynes, Colt	L-L	5-11	200	6-23-85	3	1	2.65	37	0	0	2	51	55	16	15	2	7	38	.281	.282	.280	6.71	1.24
Lara, Alexis	R-R	6-0	150	3-23-87	1	1	22.50	3	0	0	0	4	6	5	5	1	2	4	.400	.400	.400	18.00	9.00
McBryde, Jeremy	R-R	6-2	225	5-1-87	4	4	4.38	13	12	0	0	64	62	37	31	8	17	49	.250	.223	.266	6.93	2.40
Mull, Noah	L-L	5-10	170	11-19-86	1	1	9.95	5	0	0	0	6	11	10	7	1	3	6	.407	.167	.476	8.53	4.26
Musgrave, Rob	L-L	6-1	205	9-26-85	4	4	2.48	51	6	0	0	98	91	37	27	9	27	113	.245	.231	.251	10.38	2.48
Oramas, Juan	L-L	5-10	215	5-11-90	7	3	3.00	24	21	0	0	84	64	34	28	10	26	90	.209	.244	.194	9.64	2.79
Poynter, Gary	R-R	6-2	190	6-12-87	2	0	3.31	22	0	0	0	35	33	19	13	1	20	20	.246	.256	.242	5.09	5.09
Quezada, Jackson	R-R	6-3	215	8-9-86	0	0	18.00	1	0	0	0	2	2	2	2	0	0	0	.500	.667	.333	0.00	0.00
Reyes, Jorge	B-R	6-2	195	12-7-87	8	4	5.00	18	15	0	0	77	93	45	43	4	21	65	.292	.296	.288	7.56	2.44
Schmidt, Nick	L-L	6-5	245	10-10-85	6	9	4.35	24	24	0	0	97	94	54	47	4	43	87	.257	.282	.246	8.04	3.98
Schrader, Adam	R-R	6-3	210	3-10-87	1	1	6.64	4	0	0	0	20	28	18	15	4	9	13	.329	.351	.313	5.75	3.98

SAN DIEGO PADRES

Pitching (cont.)	B-T	HT	WT	DOB	W	L	ERA	G	GS	CG	SV	IP	H	R	ER	HR	BB	SO	AVG	vLH	vRH	K/9	BB/9
Schumacher, Nick	R-R	6-3	195	7-24-85	1	1	7.33	23	0	0	0	27	41	24	22	3	13	19	.360	.380	.344	6.33	4.33
Vincent, Nick	R-R	6-0	175	7-12-86	4	0	1.87	48	1	0	0	82	60	24	17	7	23	76	.201	.208	.196	8.38	2.53

Fielding

Catcher	PCT	G	PO	A	E	DP	PB
Collins	.977	28	194	20	5	2	4
Lara	.990	74	561	59	6	6	10
Pozo	.933	3	13	1	1	0	3
Solis	.980	11	93	3	2	0	0
Zornes	.988	30	221	27	3	2	6
Hansen	.984	26	46	77	2		19
Salazar	.800	1	3	1	1		0
Skube	.955	4	14	7	1		0
Tremblay	1.000	5	3	11	0		3
Tremblay	1.000	3	3	8	0		2

First Base	PCT	G	PO	A	E	DP
Agreste	1.000	1	1	0	0	0
Decker	.992	77	672	61	6	52
Dykstra	.989	62	517	39	6	43
Hansen	1.000	5	19	3	0	1
Salazar	1.000	2	16	2	0	2

Second Base	PCT	G	PO	A	E	DP
Cumberland	1.000	8	20	24	0	3
Figueroa	.993	105	166	276	3	58

Third Base	PCT	G	PO	A	E	DP
Belnome	.913	124	81	255	32	19
Hansen	.946	18	8	27	2	1
Salazar	1.000	1	1	4	0	0
Tremblay	1.000	1	0	2	0	1

Shortstop	PCT	G	PO	A	E	DP
Cabrera	1.000	3	6	6	0	1
Cumberland	.917	48	76	111	17	20
Figueroa	.989	19	32	57	1	12
Hansen	.929	10	7	19	2	5
Lopez	.958	65	118	181	13	37

Outfield	PCT	G	PO	A	E	DP
Agreste	1.000	7	8	0	0	0
Carvajal	.969	50	87	6	3	1
Chalk	.960	26	45	3	2	0
Davis	.957	53	67	0	3	0
Decker	.965	77	129	9	5	1
Hairston	1.000	2	2	0	0	0
Liriano	.885	13	23	0	3	0
Payne	.929	21	38	1	3	0
Robertson	.973	132	273	19	8	2
Salazar	1.000	1	2	0	0	0
Tekotte	.991	58	104	4	1	2
Venable	1.000	4	4	0	0	0

FORT WAYNE TINCAPS

LOW CLASS A

MIDWEST LEAGUE

Batting	B-T	HT	WT	DOB	AVG	vLH	vRH	G	AB	R	H	2B	3B	HR	RBI	BB	HBP	SH	SF	SO	SB	CS	SLG	OBP
Agreste, Joe	L-L	6-4	195	4-10-87	.050	.000	.059	8	20	2	1	0	0	0	3	0	0	0		10	0	0	.050	.174
Alia, Jon	R-R	6-3	230	12-6-85	.278	.286	.275	48	162	25	45	6	0	0	17	18	2	0	2	49	2	2	.315	.353
Anna, Dean	L-R	5-11	180	11-24-86	.271	.297	.266	80	225	42	61	14	2	6	32	39	3	2	3	40	5	1	.431	.381
Basham, Brett	R-R	6-2	205	9-8-86	.000	.000	.000	1	3	0	0	0	0	0	0	0	0	0	0	2	0	0	.000	.000
Benedict, Griffin	L-R	6-0	220	7-4-87	.229	.146	.250	61	201	22	46	8	1	2	21	31	2	1	0	35	2	2	.308	.338
Darnell, James	R-R	6-2	195	1-19-87	.360	.250	.412	7	25	5	9	4	0	1	8	5	2	0	0	4	0	0	.640	.500
Davis, Bo	R-R	6-0	185	8-28-85	.213	.235	.206	24	80	11	17	1	3	0	5	9	0	2	0	20	3	0	.300	.292
Eckstein, David	R-R	5-7	175	1-10-87	.333	.000	.333	3	9	1	3	1	0	0	3	2	1	0	0	0	0	0	.444	.500
Freiman, Nate	R-R	6-7	225	12-31-86	.294	.347	.278	136	523	83	154	43	0	14	84	58	7	0	6	117	0	0	.457	.369
Galvez, Jonathan	R-R	6-2	175	1-18-91	.259	.259	.259	114	398	64	103	19	3	10	49	58	6	2	2	121	18	7	.397	.360
Gyorko, Jedd	R-R	5-10	195	9-23-88	.284	.200	.311	42	162	19	46	11	0	2	19	19	2	0	0	31	1	0	.389	.366
Hagerty, Jason	B-R	6-2	220	9-13-87	.302	.374	.280	122	431	74	130	35	3	14	74	88	8	0	7	104	2	1	.494	.423
Liriano, Rymer	R-R	6-0	211	6-20-91	.191	.343	.157	50	188	21	36	11	1	2	20	10	1	0	2	54	11	6	.293	.234
Meeley, Dan	L-L	6-0	190	7-1-87	.304	.298	.306	58	204	27	62	10	0	3	23	29	4	0	2	46	1	1	.353	.397
Noel, Rico	R-R	5-9	155	1-11-89	.136	.267	.069	12	44	3	6	1	0	1	7	5	3	0	0	8	3	0	.182	.269
Olabisi, Wande	R-R	6-0	212	3-18-88	.256	.196	.278	70	207	36	53	11	2	4	30	24	5	0	0	73	15	4	.386	.347
Payne, Danny	L-L	5-10	185	9-8-85	.246	.226	.252	102	394	74	97	23	8	7	56	74	3	2	4	107	38	6	.398	.366
Rincon, Edinson	R-R	6-1	185	8-11-90	.250	.250	.251	132	511	72	128	35	1	13	69	44	6	0	4	95	1	2	.399	.315
Valdez, Jeudy	R-R	5-11	155	5-5-89	.247	.240	.249	132	527	81	130	34	3	10	76	43	4	1	2	115	34	14	.380	.302
Williams, Everett	L-R	5-10	200	10-1-90	.244	.200	.256	107	390	53	95	25	5	5	59	51	2	2		131	10	5	.372	.333

Pitching	B-T	HT	WT	DOB	W	L	ERA	G	GS	CG	SV	IP	H	R	ER	HR	BB	SO	AVG	vLH	vRH	K/9	BB/9
Adams, Jason	R-R	6-2	185	4-27-85	1	1	10.80	9	0	0	1	12	28	14	14	2	3	7	.467	.478	.459	5.40	2.31
Arias, Rafeal	R-R	6-0	165	1-3-89	0	0	10.38	4	0	0	1	4	5	7	5	0	6	6	.294	.375	.222	12.46	12.46
Beard, Hayden	R-R	6-1	175	1-22-85	4	3	6.19	29	0	0	2	36	37	27	25	1	16	22	.261	.268	.256	5.45	3.96
Berger, Jon	R-R	6-2	215	1-18-87	3	1	4.82	19	1	0	0	37	53	21	20	1	10	26	.338	.271	.367	6.27	2.41
Branham, Matt	R-R	6-5	220	9-28-87	0	0	9.00	1	0	0	0	1	3	1	1	0	0	1	.500	.000	.750	9.00	0.00
Carter, Dexter	R-R	6-6	195	2-5-87	1	1	6.63	11	7	0	0	38	34	31	28	4	28	28	.239	.246	.234	6.63	5.68
De Paula, Jose	L-L	6-1	170	3-4-90	8	5	3.27	20	14	0	0	85	71	33	31	7	20	69	.222	.196	.232	7.28	2.11
Greenwood, Nick	R-L	6-1	180	9-28-87	4	4	4.15	21	17	0	1	95	109	48	44	4	19	65	.288	.223	.313	6.14	1.79
2-team total (11 Quad Cities)					5	4	3.56	32	17	0	1	119	129	53	47	4	28	81				6.14	2.12
Hernandez, Pedro	L-L	5-10	200	4-12-89	4	3	4.04	29	13	0	0	100	122	62	45	6	17	79	.295	.263	.305	7.09	1.52
Hussey, John	R-R	6-3	190	11-22-86	4	3	6.35	12	12	0	0	57	74	48	40	7	16	32	.311	.349	.279	5.08	2.54
Ibarra, Jeff	L-L	6-6	180	8-18-87	1	1	3.96	42	0	0	1	50	56	28	22	3	14	44	.276	.215	.304	7.92	2.52
Irsfeld, Matt	R-R	6-1	185	3-9-87	0	2	19.29	5	0	0	0	5	6	10	10	1	6	2	.353	.429	.300	3.86	11.57
Jackson, Matt	R-R	6-4	175	12-18-87	4	2	5.22	18	3	0	0	50	59	32	29	1	12	33	.296	.378	.248	5.94	2.16
Lollis, Matt	R-R	6-7	230	9-11-90	5	2	1.66	9	0	0	0	54	47	12	10	3	13	45	.234	.171	.277	7.45	2.15
Marona, Chase	R-R	6-1	205	8-18-88	1	2	4.72	9	0	0	0	13	16	10	7	2	8	7	.302	.350	.273	4.72	5.40
McBryde, Jeremy	R-R	6-2	225	5-1-87	0	0	2.25	3	0	0	0	4	2	1	1	0	1	3	.143	.143	.143	6.75	2.25
Mikolas, Miles	R-R	6-5	220	8-23-88	6	3	3.20	60	0	0	13	82	76	27	20	3	15	78	.240	.260	.226	8.60	1.65
Miller, Drew	R-R	6-4	190	2-24-86	0	0	10.80	1	0	0	0	3	5	5	4	0	5	3	.313	.600	.182	13.50	0.00
Mull, Noah	L-L	5-10	170	11-19-86	3	0	3.38	6	0	0	0	8	7	5	3	0	7	7	.233	.231	.235	7.88	7.88
Musgrave, Rob	L-L	6-1	205	9-26-85	2	0	0.00	4	0	0	1	5	2	1	0	0	1	6	.133	.250	.091	11.57	1.93
Oramas, Juan	L-L	5-10	215	5-11-90	0	1	1.20	5	0	0	0	15	9	2	2	0	3	25	.176	.214	.162	15.00	1.80
Osuna, Stiven	R-R	6-3	170	5-5-87	3	3	3.30	37	4	0	1	60	51	25	22	5	26	51	.231	.282	.203	7.65	3.90
Ottone, Daniel	R-R	6-4	240	1-26-88	0	0	0.00	2	0	0	0	2	1	1	0	0	0	1	.143	.000	.200	4.50	0.00
Portillo, Adys	R-R	6-2	185	12-21-91	0	0	4.50	1	0	0	0	2	2	1	1	1	1	2	.286	.500	.000	4.50	4.50
Poutier, Robert	R-R	6-4	190	10-21-85	2	3	2.49	33	0	0	0	51	38	17	14	4	19	40	.207	.200	.210	7.11	3.38
Quezada, Jackson	R-R	6-3	215	8-9-86	0	3	3.72	16	0	0	2	19	15	9	8	2	16	16	.217	.174	.239	7.45	4.65
Sarria, Daniel	R-R	6-1	190	1-31-88	1	2	3.89	11	6	0	0	42	44	18	18	2	11	37	.273	.246	.292	7.99	2.38
Schumacher, Nick	R-R	6-3	195	7-24-85	3	6	3.63	40	0	0	21	40	44	21	16	3	15	31	.273	.292	.260	7.03	3.40

Spence, Josh	L-L	6-1	170	1-22-88	2	2	3.71	7	3	0	0	17	14	7	7	2	6	31	.230	.261	.211	16.41	3.18
Sullivan, Jerry	R-R	6-4	220	1-18-88	7	4	4.03	27	26	0	0	116	119	63	52	9	29	92	.264	.278	.252	7.14	2.25
Watt, Michael	L-L	6-1	185	2-24-89	6	6	3.82	28	25	0	0	125	128	62	53	5	37	105	.263	.322	.238	7.56	2.66

Fielding

Catcher	PCT	G	PO	A	E	DP	PB
Basham	1.000	1	8	1	0	0	0
Benedict	.987	51	338	30	5	6	4
Hagerty	.987	92	682	72	10	8	11

First Base	PCT	G	PO	A	E	DP
Alia	.983	7	58	0	1	4
Freiman	.993	131	1123	86	9	97
Hagerty	1.000	5	44	2	0	3

Second Base	PCT	G	PO	A	E	DP
Anna	1.000	19	38	57	0	10
Eckstein	.917	3	2	9	1	2
Galvez	.889	6	10	14	3	1

	PCT	G	PO	A	E	DP
Gyorko	1.000	1	3	2	0	1
Valdez	.966	116	218	316	19	63

Third Base	PCT	G	PO	A	E	DP
Alia	1.000	5	5	5	0	0
Anna	.833	3	0	5	1	0
Darnell	1.000	4	4	11	0	0
Gyorko	.928	24	14	50	5	4
Rincon	.879	106	75	186	36	15

Shortstop	PCT	G	PO	A	E	DP
Anna	.893	29	39	78	14	21
Galvez	.915	103	149	280	40	51
Valdez	.887	11	16	31	6	3

Outfield	PCT	G	PO	A	E	DP
Agreste	.857	6	6	0	1	0
Anna	.974	19	32	6	1	2
Benedict	1.000	2	5	0	0	0
Davis	.956	23	43	0	2	0
Liriano	.954	50	95	8	5	3
Meeley	.925	58	96	2	8	0
Noel	1.000	12	32	1	0	0
Olabisi	.959	61	91	2	4	0
Payne	.987	98	215	14	3	4
Williams	.984	104	175	7	3	0

EUGENE EMERALDS

SHORT-SEASON

NORTHWEST LEAGUE

Batting	B-T	HT	WT	DOB	AVG	vLH	vRH	G	AB	R	H	2B	3B	HR	RBI	BB	HBP	SH	SF	SO	SB	CS	SLG	OBP
Adamson, Corey	L-R	6-2	185	2-23-92	.119	.167	.100	14	42	4	5	0	0	0	5	6	1	0	1	17	1	2	.119	.240
Basham, Brett	R-R	6-2	205	9-8-86	.245	.000	.364	14	49	4	12	2	0	0	6	3	0	0	0	11	0	0	.286	.288
Bingham, Paul	R-R	6-3	205	3-7-88	.136	.095	.146	30	103	8	14	1	0	0	13	7	3	2	0	34	1	1	.146	.212
Bisson, Chris	L-R	5-11	185	8-14-89	.250	.217	.265	22	72	7	18	3	0	0	4	10	0	1	2	19	5	4	.292	.333
Cunningham, Wes	L-R	6-2	200	12-4-87	.290	.286	.291	60	207	34	60	8	5	5	32	41	4	1	1	50	7	3	.449	.415
D'Amico, Nick	R-R	6-1	180	5-22-87	.059	.200	.000	5	17	0	1	0	0	0	0	2	0	0	0	8	0	0	.059	.158
Domoromo, Luis	L-L	6-1	185	2-4-92	.274	.296	.267	31	113	12	31	5	0	1	8	6	1	0	1	23	0	0	.345	.314
Gale, Rocky	R-R	6-0	180	2-22-88	.292	.310	.288	43	161	16	47	5	0	0	16	7	1	0	0	29	2	2	.323	.325
Garcia, Oscar	L-R	6-1	185	12-5-88	.225	.140	.248	52	200	23	45	6	1	1	22	18	4	1	0	37	4	5	.280	.302
Guinn, Brian	B-R	5-11	165	4-4-89	.162	.182	.154	11	37	3	6	2	0	0	2	4	1	0	0	11	0	0	.216	.262
Gyorko, Jedd	R-R	5-10	195	9-23-88	.330	.250	.359	26	106	16	35	6	0	5	18	9	0	0	0	26	1	1	.528	.383
Liriano, Rymer	R-R	6-0	211	6-20-91	.271	.333	.253	53	203	35	55	13	6	0	12	17	3	1	1	53	17	7	.394	.335
Medica, Tommy	R-R	6-1	205	4-9-88	.176	.235	.147	34	102	7	18	4	0	0	9	18	5	2	4	18	0	2	.216	.318
Meeley, Dan	L-L	6-0	190	7-1-89	.300	.250	.313	5	20	4	6	0	0	1	2	1	0	0	0	7	0	0	.450	.333
Minyeti, Jorge	B-R	5-10	180	11-7-90	.193	.267	.176	26	83	12	16	4	1	0	6	18	0	0	1	24	2	2	.265	.333
Noel, Rico	R-R	5-9	175	1-11-89	.277	.259	.282	32	112	22	31	2	2	1	15	25	4	1	0	24	14	3	.357	.426
Powers, Connor	R-R	6-2	220	12-21-87	.191	.241	.178	40	136	14	26	5	1	2	24	21	1	0	1	43	0	1	.287	.315
Quiles, Emmanuel	R-R	5-11	186	10-26-89	.240	.258	.236	42	154	12	37	7	0	0	18	5	2	2	1	34	0	1	.286	.272
Slemp, Houston	L-R	6-1	200	3-2-88	.136	.105	.143	32	103	6	14	2	0	0	8	6	1	0	1	47	2	1	.155	.189
Stubblefield, Tyler	R-R	5-10	185	11-19-87	.251	.250	.255	58	219	26	55	10	2	1	28	17	6	1	5	47	8	5	.329	.316
Tremblay, Chris	R-R	5-10	180	11-13-86	.308	.400	.282	53	208	22	64	12	0	1	23	9	2	0	3	41	6	2	.380	.338
Tyrell, Cole	R-R	6-0	185	2-8-88	.130	.000	.152	17	54	7	7	1	0	1	3	5	0	2	0	13	1	0	.204	.203
Wright, Ty	R-R	6-1	235	8-10-87	.167	.200	.158	7	24	4	4	0	0	0	2	3	0	0	1	3	0	1	.167	.250

Pitching	B-T	HT	WT	DOB	W	L	ERA	G	GS	CG	SV	IP	H	R	ER	HR	BB	SO	AVG	vLH	vRH	K/9	BB/9
Angelucci, Alessio	R-R	6-2	190	7-28-88	0	1	45.00	1	0	0	0	1	2	5	5	0	5	1	.400	1.000	.000	9.00	45.00
Arias, Rafael	R-R	6-0	165	1-3-89	0	0	0.00	2	0	0	0	2	0	0	0	0	2	4	.000	.000	.000	15.43	7.71
Branham, Matt	R-R	6-5	220	9-28-87	6	3	2.97	14	11	0	0	61	61	23	20	1	15	56	.266	.330	.225	8.31	2.23
Carter, Dexter	R-R	6-6	195	2-5-87	1	2	4.72	18	11	0	0	61	69	34	32	8	18	55	.292	.287	.297	8.11	2.66
Cephas, Josh	R-R	6-0	195	4-17-87	0	0	10.13	5	0	0	0	5	5	7	6	1	3	5	.227	.444	.077	8.44	5.06
Esquivel, Xavier	R-R	5-10	190	9-5-88	0	2	3.35	21	0	0	0	40	40	15	15	3	7	32	.263	.292	.241	7.14	1.56
Everett, Aaron	R-R	6-3	190	1-24-87	5	2	2.76	25	0	0	3	33	31	10	10	1	10	28	.250	.298	.209	7.71	2.76
Franklin, Chris	R-R	6-1	200	11-10-87	1	1	4.01	24	0	0	2	43	44	21	19	2	11	37	.275	.344	.232	7.80	2.32
Gariano, Rob	R-R	5-10	180	5-24-88	0	1	4.50	3	1	0	0	8	10	5	4	1	3	2	.303	.250	.320	10.13	1.13
Hardy, Mark	L-L	6-4	195	5-3-88	2	1	3.00	5	5	0	0	27	28	9	9	2	10	28	.269	.219	.292	9.33	3.33
Hinson, Ryan	L-L	6-3	220	5-12-87	0	1	11.57	8	0	0	0	7	16	10	9	1	7	9	.444	.500	.400	11.57	9.00
Irsfeld, Matt	R-R	6-1	185	3-9-87	0	2	9.00	19	0	0	0	19	32	20	19	2	17	21	.386	.227	.443	9.95	8.05
Jackson, Matt	R-R	6-4	175	12-18-87	0	1	3.00	3	0	0	0	6	5	3	2	0	1	3	.217	.000	.313	4.50	1.50
Lollis, Matt	R-R	6-7	230	9-11-90	2	2	2.86	6	6	0	0	35	21	11	11	0	8	24	.175	.293	.114	6.23	2.08
Marona, Chase	R-R	6-1	205	8-18-88	0	2	1.53	14	0	0	4	18	10	4	3	1	3	26	.167	.235	.140	13.25	1.53
Martinez, Pedro	L-L	6-3	251	9-6-90	2	3	4.94	7	7	0	0	24	21	15	13	2	23	20	.241	.250	.239	7.61	8.75
Ottone, Daniel	R-R	6-4	240	1-26-88	3	2	4.84	18	0	0	0	22	20	12	12	3	5	19	.247	.375	.163	7.66	2.01
Portillo, Adys	R-R	6-2	185	12-21-91	2	6	4.79	14	14	0	0	62	55	41	33	2	40	62	.241	.293	.202	9.00	5.81
Sabo, Robert	R-R	6-2	185	3-3-88	2	2	3.00	8	0	0	3	39	37	14	13	2	13	23	.259	.300	.237	9.46	5.31
Sampson, Keyvius	R-R	6-0	185	1-6-91	3	3	3.56	10	10	0	0	43	35	23	17	4	17	58	.226	.288	.188	12.14	3.56
Sanchez, Deiber	R-R	5-10	170	3-27-89	0	3	4.14	23	0	0	1	50	46	24	23	4	23	42	.253	.200	.294	7.56	4.14
Spence, Josh	L-L	6-1	170	1-22-88	0	0	1.50	2	2	0	0	6	4	1	1	1	1	8	.200	.000	.286	12.00	1.50
Tabachnik, Mauricio	R-R	6-2	198	11-8-89	3	4	3.48	19	6	0	0	62	69	30	24	4	12	42	.279	.330	.243	6.10	1.74

Fielding

Catcher	PCT	G	PO	A	E	DP	PB
Basham	1.000	2	15	0	0	0	0
Gale	.994	37	289	39	2	2	3
Quiles	.992	39	328	42	3	2	7
Tyrell	1.000	1	2	0	0	0	0

First Base	PCT	G	PO	A	E	DP
Basham	.981	6	48	5	1	3
Cunningham	.996	31	229	15	1	23

	PCT	G	PO	A	E	DP
D'Amico	1.000	1	6	1	0	1
Powers	.986	37	342	19	5	31
Tremblay	.938	2	13	2	1	0

Second Base	PCT	G	PO	A	E	DP
Bisson	.963	16	32	46	3	5
D'Amico	1.000	4	2	12	0	1
Guinn	1.000	1	2	3	0	0
Minyeti	.943	23	36	63	6	12
Stubblefield	.956	25	50	58	5	17
Tremblay	1.000	8	14	19	0	4

Third Base	PCT	G	PO	A	E	DP
Bingham	.967	29	20	39	2	7
Gyorko	.939	26	13	49	4	1
Stubblefield	1.000	6	5	7	0	1
Tremblay	.944	5	5	12	1	1
Tyrell	1.000	10	10	15	0	2

Shortstop	PCT	G	PO	A	E	DP
Bisson	.923	4	7	17	2	1
Guinn	.902	10	18	28	5	4
Minyeti	.833	1	1	4	1	1
Stubblefield	.920	25	36	68	9	13

	PCT	G	PO	A	E	DP
Tremblay	.982	37	54	110	3	22
Outfield	**PCT**	**G**	**PO**	**A**	**E**	**DP**
Adamson	.950	13	18	1	1	0
Cunningham	.941	28	30	2	2	0
Domoromo	1.000	27	41	0	0	0
Garcia	1.000	52	101	6	0	1
Liriano	.952	51	93	6	5	1
Meeley	1.000	3	2	0	0	0
Noel	.968	32	85	5	3	1
Slemp	.929	23	25	1	2	0
Wright	.900	6	8	1	1	0

AZL PADRES

ROOKIE

ARIZONA LEAGUE

Batting	B-T	HT	WT	DOB	AVG	vLH	vRH	G	AB	R	H	2B	3B	HR	RBI	BB	HBP	SH	SF	SO	SB	CS	SLG	OBP
Adamson, Corey	L-R	6-2	185	2-23-92	.283	.250	.294	36	138	18	39	7	2	0	19	14	3	1	1	34	2	5	.362	.359
Agreste, Joe	L-L	6-4	195	4-10-87	.240	.306	.215	35	129	25	31	10	5	1	22	18	1	0	2	46	1	1	.419	.333
Altman, Bryan	R-R	6-1	170	8-12-87	.192	.211	.186	27	78	9	15	2	2	1	9	6	1	0	0	20	2	2	.308	.259
Antonelli, Matt	R-R	6-0	205	4-8-85	.000	.000	.000	1	1	1	0	0	0	0	0	1	0	0	0	0	0	0	.000	.500
Bingham, Paul	R-R	6-3	205	3-7-88	.306	.133	.351	20	72	13	22	0	2	0	8	12	0	0	1	20	5	2	.361	.400
Bisson, Chris	L-R	5-11	185	8-14-89	.056	.500	.000	6	18	1	1	0	0	0	4	0	0	1	0	4	0	0	.056	.227
Collins, Mike	R-R	6-3	215	7-18-84	.000	.000	.000	3	9	0	0	0	0	0	0	1	1	0	0	3	0	0	.000	.091
Combs, Matt	R-R	6-0	238	8-7-87	.250	.267	.245	20	64	8	16	7	1	2	9	8	2	1	0	23	0	1	.484	.351
Dore, Jose	L-R	6-1	170	2-9-92	.375	.500	.357	4	16	5	6	1	0	0	2	1	0	0	0	4	0	0	.438	.412
Echevarria, Justin	R-R	6-0	205	9-7-87	.063	.000	.067	4	16	1	1	0	0	0	2	1	0	0	0	7	0	1	.125	.118
Fowler, Brandon	R-R	6-0	185	6-10-89	.231	.333	.217	9	26	2	6	1	0	1	4	2	0	0	0	11	0	0	.385	.286
Garce, Daniel	R-R	6-1	166	6-6-89	.323	.370	.304	26	96	13	31	6	1	1	15	10	0	0	0	27	0	0	.438	.363
Garcia, Carlos	R-R	6-3	165	3-29-89	.263	.333	.243	36	137	23	36	11	1	4	26	13	1	0	0	43	2	1	.445	.331
Guinn, Brian	B-R	5-11	165	4-4-89	.312	.375	.290	31	125	22	39	5	2	0	8	20	0	1	1	28	14	3	.384	.404
Lopez, Yair	R-R	6-3	150	9-9-91	.250	.170	.282	41	164	28	41	7	1	4	26	4	6	1	0	56	5	1	.378	.293
Minyeti, Jorge	B-R	5-10	180	11-7-90	.323	.250	.340	18	62	11	20	3	0	0	7	9	0	0	0	13	2	1	.371	.408
Nuno, Manuel	R-R	6-6	264	1-11-89	.111	.000	.154	6	18	1	2	1	0	0	1	0	0	0	0	4	0	0	.167	.158
Pozo, Jhonaldo	R-R	6-3	183	3-28-89	.328	.263	.356	19	64	6	21	6	0	0	8	2	0	0	3	23	1	1	.422	.333
Skube, Ryan	R-R	5-11	175	3-26-91	.242	.154	.275	27	95	10	23	7	0	1	12	10	1	1	0	20	3	2	.347	.324
Stokes, Mykal	R-R	6-4	170	6-2-90	.230	.288	.209	48	200	24	46	6	0	1	18	6	3	0	1	38	6	1	.275	.262
Tate, Donavan	R-R	6-3	200	9-27-90	.222	.250	.216	25	90	19	20	5	0	2	10	15	1	0	1	41	7	1	.344	.336
Terhune, Gunnar	R-R	5-11	185	10-7-87	.231	.222	.233	24	78	17	18	6	1	0	5	14	3	0	0	19	5	0	.333	.368
Tyrell, Cole	R-R	6-0	185	2-8-88	.190	.100	.208	14	58	8	11	4	0	1	7	2	0	0	1	10	1	1	.310	.242
Velazquez, Adan	R-R	5-10	185	5-19-90	.240	.182	.256	29	100	12	24	7	1	1	12	8	3	1	0	28	3	1	.360	.315

Pitching	B-T	HT	WT	DOB	W	L	ERA	G	GS	CG	SV	IP	H	R	ER	HR	BB	SO	AVG	vLH	vRH	K/9	BB/9
Angelucci, Alessio	R-R	6-2	190	7-28-88	0	0	2.78	14	0	0	0	23	14	12	7	0	22	18	.179	.267	.125	7.15	8.74
Arias, Rafeal	R-R	6-0	165	1-3-89	0	1	3.86	5	0	0	1	5	2	2	2	0	2	6	.118	.200	.083	11.57	3.86
Berroa, Simon	R-R	6-4	165	10-28-87	0	0	1.50	4	0	0	0	6	7	1	1	0	3	6	.269	.250	.286	9.00	4.50
Castillo, Jeury	R-R	6-5	210	1-20-89	0	1	2.96	17	0	0	0	24	15	10	8	1	13	29	.181	.192	.175	10.73	4.81
Cephas, Josh	R-R	6-0	195	4-17-87	1	0	0.00	3	0	0	0	4	0	0	0	0	5	.000	.000	.000	11.25	0.00	
Chavez, Juan	R-R	6-0	200	12-25-89	0	0	7.71	5	0	0	0	5	6	5	4	1	4	5	.286	.364	.200	9.64	7.71
De La Cruz, Luis	R-R	6-6	195	6-15-89	2	3	3.96	16	1	0	0	25	32	17	11	2	13	17	.299	.375	.254	6.12	4.68
Gariano, Rob	R-R	5-10	180	5-24-88	3	3	4.24	13	8	0	0	47	57	33	22	1	13	33	.298	.288	.306	6.36	2.51
Garrison, Steve	B-L	6-1	185	9-12-86	0	0	3.00	3	3	0	0	6	5	2	2	0	1	8	.238	.250	.235	12.00	1.50
Hardy, Mark	L-L	6-4	195	5-3-88	3	2	3.06	6	5	0	0	32	28	14	11	2	4	31	.233	.174	.247	8.63	1.11
Herrera, Juan	R-R	6-0	179	8-21-91	1	4	4.22	11	9	0	0	43	47	31	20	1	30	35	.278	.264	.289	7.38	6.33
Hinson, Ryan	L-L	6-3	210	5-12-87	0	0	6.23	5	0	0	0	4	7	4	3	0	0	3	.368	.000	.368	6.23	0.00
Javier, Esteban	L-L	6-1	155	4-2-89	0	0	7.23	16	0	0	2	19	29	22	15	0	7	15	.341	.438	.319	7.23	3.38
McBryde, Jeremy	R-R	6-2	225	5-1-87	0	0	9.00	1	0	0	0	1	2	1	1	0	0	3	.400	.000	.500	27.00	0.00
Mull, Noah	L-L	5-10	170	11-19-86	0	0	3.86	4	2	0	0	12	7	11	5	0	6	15	.163	.000	.259	11.57	4.63
Nading, Chad	R-R	6-5	205	7-9-87	0	2	14.29	6	0	0	0	6	13	10	9	1	2	3	.448	.538	.375	4.76	3.18
Norwood, Tyler	R-R	6-3	215	2-3-91	1	5	5.68	14	4	0	1	32	37	35	20	2	15	25	.282	.333	.253	7.11	4.26
Ojeda, Erick	R-R	6-5	260	9-18-89	0	0	5.40	16	0	0	0	18	26	20	11	0	15	16	.347	.286	.383	7.85	7.36
Poynter, Gary	R-R	6-2	190	6-12-87	0	0	1.80	4	0	0	0	5	3	1	1	0	0	3	.158	.125	.182	5.40	0.00
Quezada, Jackson	R-R	6-3	215	8-9-86	0	0	1.80	4	0	0	0	5	3	1	1	0	0	3	.158	.222	.100	5.40	0.00
Reyes, Eugenio	R-R	6-3	215	7-13-90	2	6	5.54	14	12	0	0	52	61	44	32	1	26	30	.293	.309	.283	5.19	4.50
Sarria, Daniel	R-R	6-1	190	1-31-88	0	0	9.00	2	0	0	0	3	5	3	3	1	2	1	.417	.800	.143	6.00	6.00
Schrader, Adam	R-R	6-3	210	3-10-87	4	0	2.45	10	8	0	0	51	43	20	14	0	10	48	.229	.255	.202	8.42	1.75
Scott, Will	R-R	6-2	191	9-2-90	1	0	6.35	3	0	0	0	6	8	4	4	1	2	7	.333	.000	.471	11.12	3.18
Spence, Josh	L-L	6-1	170	1-22-88	0	0	0.00	1	0	0	0	1	0	0	0	0	0	3	.200	1.000	.000	27.00	0.00
Valdez, Stalyn	R-R	6-3	185	11-14-89	2	5	3.83	19	2	0	3	42	48	22	18	0	10	23	.293	.295	.291	4.89	2.13
Wilkes, Chris	R-R	6-4	235	9-26-89	0	1	0.00	1	0	0	0	1	1	0	0	0	2	1	.250	.000	.500	9.00	9.00

Fielding

Catcher	PCT	G	PO	A	E	DP	PB
Brayton	.963	10	48	4	2	0	2
Collins	.909	2	10	0	1	0	1
Combs	.958	19	86	28	5	0	10

	PCT	G	PO	A	E	DP
Echevarria	1.000	4	42	6	0	0	1
Fowler	1.000	9	45	5	0	1	2
Pozo	.964	19	145	16	6	1	5

First Base	PCT	G	PO	A	E	DP
Agreste	.965	34	301	28	12	25
Garce	.980	5	46	3	1	7
Garcia	.893	7	61	6	8	5

Nuno	.979	6	45	2	1	7
Tyrell	.977	4	41	2	1	4

Second Base	PCT	G	PO	A	E	DP
Altman	.930	6	12	28	3	9
Antonelli	1.000	1	0	1	0	0
Bisson	1.000	4	6	20	0	4
Guinn	.909	2	5	5	1	0
Minyeti	.867	4	5	8	2	1
Skube	.966	18	27	59	3	12
Velazquez	.964	21	50	58	4	16

Third Base	PCT	G	PO	A	E	DP
Altman	.915	20	15	28	4	4
Bingham	.921	13	9	26	3	2
Garce	.811	21	12	31	10	3
Minyeti	.667	1	1	3	2	1
Skube	.714	2	1	4	2	0
Tyrell	1.000	2	0	9	0	0
Velazquez	.875	3	3	4	1	0

Shortstop	PCT	G	PO	A	E	DP
Altman	1.000	1	1	1	0	0
Bingham	.929	8	11	28	3	2
Guinn	.945	29	47	90	8	21

Minyeti	.873	13	25	44	10	11
Tyrell	.962	4	12	13	1	4
Velazquez	.667	1	0	2	1	0

Outfield	PCT	G	PO	A	E	DP
Adamson	.943	28	50	0	3	1
Dore	1.000	4	4	2	0	0
Garcia	.929	14	21	5	2	2
Lopez	.911	32	37	4	4	1
Stokes	.973	46	103	6	3	2
Tate	.971	23	33	1	1	0
Terhune	.980	22	47	1	1	0

DSL PADRES

ROOKIE

DOMINICAN SUMMER LEAGUE

Batting	B-T	HT	WT	DOB	AVG	vLH	vRH	G	AB	R	H	2B	3B	HR	RBI	BB	HBP	SH	SF	SO	SB	CS	SLG	OBP
Alcantara, Yoan	R-R	6-1	175	11-20-92	.241	.175	.258	66	228	43	55	14	3	5	37	27	5	0	2	40	12	5	.395	.332
Aristy, Alvaro	R-R	6-1	170	12-9-91	.191	.182	.194	39	131	19	25	4	0	3	16	24	2	0	0	37	3	1	.290	.325
Beltre, Jacob	R-R	6-3	234	10-11-92	.148	.143	.154	11	27	2	4	0	0	1	4	4	0	0	1	9	0	0	.259	.250
Brugeura, Reynaldo	B-R	5-10	170	11-5-91	.207	.000	.240	34	87	11	18	3	1	0	5	16	0	0	1	21	3	2	.264	.327
Cabrera, Felix	R-R	6-0	170	7-14-89	.149	.150	.152	35	87	11	13	3	1	0	3	9	3	1	0	24	12	3	.207	.253
Del Castillo, Miguel	R-R	5-10	170	10-14-91	.288	.400	.260	51	125	13	36	9	0	1	18	21	4	0	2	28	4	3	.384	.401
Escarra, Fernando	R-R	6-2	195	1-7-92	.186	.077	.196	31	70	9	13	1	0	0	6	13	0	1	0	18	0	0	.200	.313
Familia, Ariel	R-R	6-3	185	9-29-91	.180	.077	.198	46	133	25	24	5	0	2	8	32	0	1	0	42	3	9	.263	.339
Filpo, Fabel	B-R	6-1	180	9-28-92	.190	.191	.192	65	226	23	43	7	5	0	15	13	0	0	0	51	7	5	.265	.244
Gomez, Jairo	R-R	6-0	170	1-16-92	.261	.185	.277	50	157	25	41	15	0	4	27	23	5	1	3	28	5	3	.433	.367
Jones, Duanel	R-R	6-3	195	5-11-93	.211	.100	.234	20	57	6	12	2	0	0	3	15	1	0	0	16	1	1	.246	.384
Martinez, Alberth	R-R	6-1	170	1-23-91	.272	.290	.264	50	180	27	49	9	2	1	10	18	0	0	2	22	9	4	.361	.337
Martinez, Cristhofer	B-R	6-1	175	11-23-92	.210	.313	.190	54	181	19	38	9	2	2	21	26	3	0	1	36	9	5	.315	.318
Quintana, Gabriel	R-R	6-2	190	9-7-92	.194	.182	.194	61	211	30	41	14	0	1	24	19	7	0	3	56	6	4	.275	.279
Tejada, Luis	R-R	6-3	175	10-12-92	.228	.216	.232	64	189	20	43	10	0	0	24	23	7	0	2	50	3	7	.280	.330
Valenzuela, Ricardo	R-R	6-0	189	8-4-90	.257	.235	.250	29	70	8	18	4	1	0	10	7	1	0	2	13	3	2	.343	.325

Pitching	B-T	HT	WT	DOB	W	L	ERA	G	GS	CG	SV	IP	H	R	ER	HR	BB	SO	AVG	vLH	vRH	K/9	BB/9
Andujar, Rudi	R-R	6-2	190	5-14-91	0	5	8.28	14	2	0	0	29	18	43	27	1	44	14	.180	.200	.169	4.30	13.50
Claveria, Marlon	R-R	6-3	210	8-30-90	2	3	3.63	17	4	0	0	40	39	23	16	1	14	24	.258	.241	.268	5.45	3.18
Cornelio, Andres	R-R	6-1	166	9-12-90	0	8	7.69	13	12	0	0	46	46	52	39	1	56	25	.272	.200	.312	4.93	11.04
Corpas, Jean	R-R	6-2	170	3-9-91	4	4	2.98	15	8	1	0	60	60	34	20	3	15	41	.254	.270	.240	6.12	2.24
Corpas, Juan	R-R	6-0	180	10-28-92	1	4	5.10	13	5	0	0	48	55	36	27	4	21	25	.289	.317	.277	4.72	3.97
De la Cruz, Vladimir	R-R	6-3	174	9-23-90	2	4	2.79	14	6	0	1	39	25	16	12	0	25	39	.184	.200	.177	9.08	5.82
Guerrero, Tayron	R-R	6-7	189	1-9-91	3	2	3.42	16	5	0	1	47	38	21	18	0	32	50	.229	.188	.255	9.51	6.08
Henrique, Freddys	R-R	6-3	218	5-28-90	4	1	2.77	22	0	0	5	26	22	12	8	0	12	27	.222	.222	.222	9.35	4.15
Marcano, Ivan	R-R	6-3	218	6-1-91	0	2	10.46	16	5	0	0	27	17	35	31	0	43	13	.210	.115	.255	4.39	14.51
Mejia, Ruben	R-R	6-1	175	2-23-92	2	3	3.02	36	0	0	36	42	25	19	0	16	31	.288	.379	.227	7.15	4.00
Paulino, Jose	R-R	6-0	182	11-13-88	1	2	5.94	11	1	0	0	17	10	14	11	2	16	10	.175	.211	.158	5.40	8.64
Paz, Uber	R-R	6-4	194	5-4-91	2	1	3.12	17	9	0	0	61	52	32	21	1	24	52	.237	.261	.220	7.71	3.56
Pimentel, Carlos	R-R	6-2	175	10-24-91	0	1	9.64	7	0	0	0	9	13	13	10	1	6	11	.325	.308	.333	10.61	5.79
Rivera, Eddy	R-R	5-11	185	12-18-88	0	1	7.94	8	1	0	2	11	6	10	10	0	11	13	.154	.077	.192	10.32	8.74
Rodriguez, Bryan	R-R	6-5	180	7-6-91	4	1	3.14	10	8	1	0	49	37	23	17	0	23	41	.203	.211	.198	7.58	4.25
Rodriguez, Pedro	R-R	6-0	170	4-12-91	0	0	0.00	4	1	0	0	5	2	0	0	0	3	2	.118	.000	.143	3.38	5.06
Tavarez, Elvin	R-R	6-1	170	9-7-91	0	2	13.50	5	1	0	0	7	7	12	10	0	11	6	.292	.273	.308	8.10	14.85

Fielding

Catcher	PCT	G	PO	A	E	DP	PB
Beltre	.947	8	31	5	2	0	2
Del Castillo	.963	50	245	45	11	1	8
Escarra	.952	31	167	31	10	0	6

First Base	PCT	G	PO	A	E	DP
Beltre	.875	2	14	0	2	1
Familia	.943	16	105	10	7	6
Gomez	—	1	0	0	0	0
Martinez	.983	15	105	14	2	6
Quintana	1.000	2	2	0	0	0
Tejada	.994	20	144	11	1	11
Valenzuela	.981	27	140	13	3	12

Second Base	PCT	G	PO	A	E	DP
Brugeura	.956	10	25	18	2	2
Cabrera	.932	19	46	36	6	6
Gomez	.941	26	41	55	6	14
Martinez	.929	20	30	35	5	5

Third Base	PCT	G	PO	A	E	DP
Cabrera	1.000	2	3	1	0	0
Gomez	.867	10	14	12	4	0
Jones	.765	11	10	16	8	2
Quintana	.808	50	59	84	34	8
Valenzuela	1.000	2	0	4	0	0

Shortstop	PCT	G	PO	A	E	DP
Aristy	.945	39	60	77	8	16
Brugeura	.900	7	7	11	2	3
Cabrera	1.000	2	2	1	0	0
Gomez	.800	7	10	14	6	2
Martinez	.902	25	33	50	9	4

Outfield	PCT	G	PO	A	E	DP
Alcantara	.949	63	83	10	5	6
Cabrera	1.000	1	1	0	0	0
Familia	.977	24	37	5	1	1
Filpo	.916	61	87	11	9	2
Martinez	.984	36	61	2	1	0
Tejada	.969	43	89	4	3	2

SAN DIEGO PADRES

San Francisco Giants

SEASON IN A SENTENCE: The Giants built around young starting pitching, then bolstered their offense on the fly to beat San Diego for the National League West title on the season's final day, beat the Braves and Phillies to win the pennant, then brush aside the Rangers in five games to win the first World Series championship since the franchise moved to San Francisco in 1958.

HIGH POINT: In a championship year, one won't suffice. Jonathan Sanchez's five scoreless innings to start the season finale, closed out by Brian Wilson for his majors-best 48th save, was one. Tim Lincecum provided two more with his playoff opener, a stunning display of power and precision in a 14-strikeout shutout of the Braves, and his valedictory in the World Series clincher, an eight-inning, 10-strikeout gem. In between, waiver pickup Cody Ross became a hero with five postseason home runs, including two off Roy Halladay in the first game of the NL Championship Series.

LOW POINT: Lincecum went through the worst stretch of his career in August, going 0-5, 7.82. The last loss, a 6-0 shutout against Diamondbacks rookie Barry Enright on Aug. 27, left the Giants six games back with 33 to play.

NOTABLE ROOKIES: Few teams got more impact from two rookies than the Giants. Catcher Buster Posey ranked third on the team in homers and RBIs while batting .305/.357/.505 and handling all those electric arms. Lefthander Madison Bumgarner became the team's No. 4 starter behind Lincecum, Matt Cain and Sanchez, saving his best for last with eight scoreless innings in a Game Four World Series victory.

KEY TRANSACTIONS: General manager Brian Sabean never stopped throwing players against the wall to see who would stick in Bruce Bochy's lineup. Adding Posey, Ross, Bay Area native Pat Burrell and outfielder Andres Torres and Cody Ross, gave San Francisco just enough juice to go with its masterful pitching. Relief lefty Javier Lopez, picked up from Pittsburgh in a trade for Joe Martinez and John Bowker, was an invaluable weapon in the playoffs.

DOWN ON THE FARM: The Giants won here, too, posting a .524 winning percentage, and first baseman Brandon Belt won the minor league batting crown, reaching Triple-A in his first full pro season. San Jose won the high Class A California League title, though several prospects stagnated at the team's new Double-A Richmond affiliate.

OPENING DAY PAYROLL: $98.6 million (9th)

PLAYERS OF THE YEAR

MAJOR LEAGUE	MINOR LEAGUE
Matt Cain rhp	**Brandon Belt** 1b
13-11, 3.14	(High A/AA/AAA)
177 SO/61 BB	.352/.455/.620
.221 opponent AVG	Led minors in AVG

ORGANIZATION LEADERS

BATTING	*Minimum 250 at-bats	
MAJORS		
*AVG	Buster Posey	.305
*OPS	Aubrey Huff	.891
HR	Aubrey Huff	26
RBI	Aubrey Huff	86
MINORS		
*AVG	Brandon Belt, San Jose/Richmond/Fresno	.352
*OBP	Brandon Belt, San Jose/Richmond/Fresno	.455
*SLG	Brandon Belt, San Jose/Richmond/Fresno	.620
R	Brandon Belt, San Jose/Richmond/Fresno	99
H	Brandon Belt, San Jose/Richmond/Fresno	173
TB	Brandon Belt, San Jose/Richmond/Fresno	305
2B	Brandon Belt, San Jose/Richmond/Fresno	43
3B	Francisco Peguero, San Jose	16
HR	Brandon Belt, San Jose/Richmond/Fresno	23
RBI	Brandon Belt, San Jose/Richmond/Fresno	112
BB	Brandon Belt, San Jose/Richmond/Fresno	93
SO	Luke Anders, Augusta	147
SB	Jesus Galindo, DSL Giants	43

PITCHING	†Minimum 75 innings	
MAJORS		
W	Tim Lincecum	16
†ERA	Madison Bumgarner	3.00
SO	Tim Lincecum	231
MINORS		
W	Eric Hacker, Fresno	16
L	Christopher Heston, Augusta	13
†ERA	Jorge Bucardo, Augusta/San Jose	2.77
G	Three tied at	53
GS	Eric Hacker, Fresno	29
SV	Jason Stoffel, San Jose	25
IP	Eric Hacker, Fresno	165.7
BB	Clayton Tanner, Richmond	64
SO	Eric Hacker, Fresno	129
†AVG	Jorge Bucardo, Augusta/San Jose	.229

2010 PERFORMANCE

General Manager: Brian Sabean. **Farm Director:** Fred Stanley. **Scouting Director:** John Barr.

Class	Team	League	W	L	PCT	Finish*	Manager(s)
Majors	San Francisco Giants	National	92	70	.568	†2nd (16)	Bruce Bochy
Triple-A	Fresno Grizzlies	Pacific Coast	75	69	.521	6th (16)	Steve Decker
Double-A	Richmond Flying Squirrels	Eastern	68	73	.482	9th (12)	Andy Skeels
High A	San Jose Giants	California	76	64	.543	†3rd (10)	Brian Harper
Low A	Augusta GreenJackets	South Atlantic	79	59	.572	2nd (14)	Dave Machemer
Short-season	Salem-Keizer Volcanoes	Northwest	31	45	.408	7th (8)	Tom Trebelhorn
Rookie	AZL Giants	Arizona	34	20	.630	1st (12)	Mike Goff
Overall 2010 Minor League Record			363	330	.524	7th (30)	

*Finish in overall standings (No. of teams in league). †League champion.

ORGANIZATION STATISTICS

SAN FRANCISCO GIANTS

NATIONAL LEAGUE

Batting	B-T	HT	WT	DOB	AVG	vLH	vRH	G	AB	R	H	2B	3B	HR	RBI	BB	HBP	SH	SF	SO	SB	CS	SLG	OBP
Bowker, John	L-L	6-2	200	7-8-83	.207	.000	.230	41	82	9	17	3	0	3	8	6	0	0	2	23	0	0	.354	.256
2-team total (26 Pittsburgh)					.219	—	—	67	151	16	33	8	0	5	21	14	0	0	2	33	0	1	.371	.281
Burrell, Pat	R-R	6-4	235	10-10-76	.266	.257	.269	96	289	41	77	16	0	18	51	47	0	0	5	77	0	2	.509	.364
Burriss, Emmanuel	B-R	6-0	190	1-17-85	.400	.000	.500	7	5	3	2	0	0	0	0	0	0	0	0	1	0	0	.400	.400
DeRosa, Mark	R-R	6-1	205	2-26-75	.194	.280	.162	26	93	9	18	3	0	1	10	9	2	0	0	16	0	2	.258	.279
Downs, Matt	R-R	6-2	190	3-19-84	.244	.270	.220	29	78	6	19	7	0	1	7	8	1	0	1	18	0	0	.372	.318
2-team total (11 Houston)					.216	—	—	40	97	8	21	7	0	1	9	9	1	0	1	20	0	0	.320	.294
Fontenot, Mike	L-R	5-8	170	6-9-80	.282	.143	.297	28	71	10	20	2	0	0	5	5	0	0	0	13	0	2	.310	.329
2-team total (75 Chicago)					.283	—	—	103	240	24	68	13	3	1	25	15	3	1	2	41	1	4	.375	.331
Ford, Darren	R-R	5-11	195	10-1-85	—	.000	.000	7	0	1	0	0	0	0	0	0	0	0	0	0	2	1	—	—
Guillen, Jose	R-R	6-0	215	5-17-76	.266	.208	.279	42	128	9	34	5	0	3	15	5	5	0	1	29	0	0	.375	.317
Huff, Aubrey	L-R	6-4	230	12-20-76	.290	.296	.287	157	569	100	165	35	5	26	86	83	9	0	7	91	7	0	.506	.385
Ishikawa, Travis	L-L	6-3	225	9-24-83	.266	.111	.286	116	158	18	42	11	0	3	22	13	0	1	1	29	0	0	.392	.320
Molina, Bengie	R-R	5-11	225	7-20-74	.257	.382	.211	61	202	17	52	6	0	3	17	14	3	0	2	19	0	0	.332	.312
Posey, Buster	R-R	6-1	205	3-27-87	.305	.309	.304	108	406	58	124	23	2	18	67	30	4	0	3	55	0	2	.505	.357
Renteria, Edgar	R-R	6-1	200	8-7-75	.276	.286	.272	72	243	26	67	11	2	3	22	21	0	2	1	43	3	0	.374	.332
Rohlinger, Ryan	R-R	6-1	195	10-7-83	.200	.333	.111	12	15	1	3	0	0	0	1	2	0	1	0	5	0	0	.200	.294
Ross, Cody	R-L	5-10	195	12-23-80	.288	.318	.275	33	73	11	21	4	0	3	7	7	1	0	1	21	0	1	.466	.354
2-team total (120 Florida)					.269	—	—	153	525	71	141	28	3	14	65	37	5	0	2	121	9	2	.413	.322
Rowand, Aaron	R-R	6-0	220	8-29-77	.230	.211	.237	105	331	42	76	12	2	11	34	16	8	1	1	74	5	3	.378	.281
Sanchez, Freddy	R-R	5-10	190	12-21-77	.292	.343	.276	111	431	55	126	22	1	7	47	32	3	8	5	68	3	1	.397	.342
Sandoval, Pablo	B-R	5-11	245	8-11-86	.268	.227	.282	152	563	61	151	34	3	13	63	47	1	0	5	81	3	2	.409	.323
Schierholtz, Nate	L-R	6-2	215	2-15-84	.242	.294	.227	137	227	34	55	13	3	3	17	20	3	1	1	38	4	5	.366	.311
Torres, Andres	B-R	5-10	190	1-26-78	.268	.226	.283	139	507	84	136	43	8	16	63	56	2	5	0	128	26	7	.479	.343
Uribe, Juan	R-R	6-0	230	3-22-79	.248	.231	.252	148	521	64	129	24	2	24	85	45	4	0	5	92	1	2	.440	.310
Velez, Eugenio	B-R	6-1	170	5-16-82	.164	.167	.163	29	55	7	9	2	0	2	8	6	0	5	0	9	0	0	.309	.246
Whiteside, Eli	R-R	6-2	215	10-22-79	.238	.172	.258	56	126	19	30	6	1	4	10	8	3	3	0	35	1	2	.397	.299

Pitching	B-T	HT	WT	DOB	W	L	ERA	G	GS	CG	SV	IP	H	R	ER	HR	BB	SO	AVG	vLH	vRH	K/9	BB/9
Affeldt, Jeremy	L-L	6-5	225	6-6-79	4	3	4.14	53	0	0	4	50	56	25	23	4	24	44	.290	.290	7.92	4.32
Bautista, Denny	R-R	6-5	190	8-23-80	2	0	3.74	31	0	0	0	34	25	14	14	4	22	44	.205	.204	.205	11.76	7.22
Bumgarner, Madison	R-L	6-4	215	8-1-89	7	6	3.00	18	18	0	0	111	119	40	37	11	26	86	.272	.243	.283	6.97	2.11
Cain, Matt	R-R	6-3	245	10-1-84	13	11	3.14	33	33	4	0	223	181	84	78	22	61	177	.221	.225	.217	7.13	2.46
Casilla, Santiago	R-R	6-0	200	7-25-80	7	2	1.95	52	0	0	2	55	40	14	12	2	26	56	.208	.203	.211	9.11	4.23
Joaquin, Waldis	R-R	6-2	235	12-25-86	0	0	9.64	4	0	0	0	5	6	5	6	0	7	2	.333	.400	.308	3.86	13.50
Lincecum, Tim	L-R	5-11	170	6-15-84	16	10	3.43	33	33	1	0	212	194	84	81	18	76	231	.242	.254	.229	9.79	3.22
Lopez, Javier	L-L	6-4	225	7-11-77	2	2	1.42	27	0	0	0	19	11	3	3	0	2	16	.164	.111	.273	7.58	0.95
2-team total (50 Pittsburgh)					4	2	2.34	77	0	0	0	58	50	17	15	2	20	38	—	—	—	5.93	3.12
Martinez, Joe	L-R	6-2	195	2-26-83	0	1	4.91	4	1	0	0	11	15	6	6	1	6	3	.333	.176	.429	2.45	4.91
2-team total (5 Pittsburgh)					0	1	4.12	9	1	0	0	20	26	11	9	1	9	9	—	—	4.12	4.12
Medders, Brandon	R-R	6-1	195	1-26-80	0	0	7.20	14	0	0	0	15	26	12	12	3	6	8	.388	.393	.385	4.80	3.60
Mota, Guillermo	R-R	6-5	235	7-25-73	1	3	4.33	56	0	0	1	54	49	29	26	4	22	38	.243	.247	.240	6.33	3.67
Ramirez, Ramon	R-R	5-11	190	8-31-81	1	0	0.67	25	0	0	1	27	13	3	2	1	11	15	.137	.167	.119	5.00	3.67
Ray, Chris	R-R	6-3	210	1-12-82	3	0	4.13	28	0	0	1	24	24	11	11	1	9	15	.276	.333	.241	5.63	3.38
Romo, Sergio	R-R	5-11	190	3-4-83	5	3	2.18	68	0	0	1	62	46	16	15	6	14	70	.204	.241	.185	10.16	2.03
Runzler, Dan	L-L	6-4	230	3-30-85	3	0	3.03	41	0	0	0	33	29	12	11	1	20	37	.244	.260	.232	10.19	5.51
Sanchez, Jonathan	L-L	6-2	190	11-19-82	13	9	3.07	34	33	0	0	193	142	74	66	21	96	205	.204	.181	.219	9.54	4.47
Wellemeyer, Todd	R-R	6-3	225	8-30-78	3	5	5.68	13	11	0	0	59	57	37	37	12	35	41	.259	.316	.216	6.29	5.37
Wilson, Brian	R-R	6-1	195	3-16-82	3	3	1.81	70	0	0	48	75	62	16	15	3	26	93	.220	.206	.231	11.21	3.13
Zito, Barry	L-L	6-4	215	5-13-78	9	14	4.15	34	33	1	0	199	184	97	92	20	84	150	.250	.232	.255	6.77	3.79

Fielding

Catcher	PCT	G	PO	A	E	DP	PB
Molina	.998	58	396	36	1	4	3
Posey	.991	76	615	41	6	4	1
Whiteside	.994	55	334	26	2	3	2

First Base	PCT	G	PO	A	E	DP
Huff	.996	100	756	54	3	54
Ishikawa	1.000	73	263	22	0	22
Posey	.995	30	196	17	1	14
Sandoval	1.000	11	79	0	0	6

Second Base	PCT	G	PO	A	E	DP
Burriss	1.000	5	3	1	0	0
DeRosa	.931	7	13	14	2	3
Downs	.987	19	30	47	1	12
Fontenot	.965	16	23	32	2	5
Sanchez	.991	109	198	256	4	52
Uribe	1.000	24	44	54	0	12
Velez	1.000	1	3	4	0	0

Third Base	PCT	G	PO	A	E	DP
Fontenot	1.000	6	1	5	0	1
Rohlinger	1.000	3	0	2	0	0
Sandoval	.961	143	93	228	13	23
Uribe	.957	26	20	46	3	2

Shortstop	PCT	G	PO	A	E	DP
Fontenot	.917	5	4	7	1	0
Renteria	.983	64	80	149	4	27
Rohlinger	1.000	4	4	3	0	1
Uribe	.984	103	134	233	6	38

Outfield	PCT	G	PO	A	E	DP
Bowker	1.000	24	33	1	0	0
Burrell	.984	87	121	4	2	0
DeRosa	1.000	21	31	0	0	0
Ford	—	1	0	0	0	0
Guillen	.967	38	57	2	2	0
Huff	1.000	63	125	6	0	2
Ross	1.000	33	33	0	0	0
Rowand	1.000	85	192	4	0	2
Schierholtz	.992	109	118	7	1	1
Torres	.997	133	314	7	1	2
Velez	.962	17	25	0	1	0

FRESNO GRIZZLIES
TRIPLE-A

PACIFIC COAST LEAGUE

Batting	B-T	HT	WT	DOB	AVG	vLH	vRH	G	AB	R	H	2B	3B	HR	RBI	BB	HBP	SH	SF	SO	SB	CS	SLG	OBP
Belt, Brandon	L-L	6-5	195	4-20-88	.229	.214	.235	13	48	11	11	4	0	4	10	13	0	0	0	15	2	0	.563	.393
Berroa, Angel	R-R	6-0	195	1-27-77	.205	.176	.222	26	88	3	18	6	0	1	8	4	1	1	0	12	1	0	.307	.247
Bond, Brock	B-R	5-11	185	9-11-85	.285	.346	.264	117	403	62	115	24	4	1	35	66	9	8	1	63	9	4	.372	.397
Borchard, Joe	B-R	6-4	230	11-25-78	.263	.277	.259	125	422	64	111	26	5	17	64	45	5	0	1	105	2	3	.469	.340
Bowker, John	L-L	6-2	200	7-8-83	.310	.224	.338	51	197	36	61	12	1	14	36	23	3	0	1	37	1	2	.594	.388
Boyer, Brad	R-R	6-0	185	10-4-83	.210	.294	.193	46	100	13	21	6	0	0	7	16	2	2	2	19	0	2	.270	.325
Burrell, Pat	R-R	6-4	235	10-10-76	.313	.000	.385	5	16	4	5	1	0	1	6	3	1	0	2	4	0	0	.563	.409
Burriss, Emmanuel	B-R	6-0	190	1-17-85	.282	.306	.274	67	273	32	77	11	2	0	22	19	3	9	1	29	11	5	.337	.334
Ciriaco, Juan	R-R	6-0	160	8-15-83	.250	.176	.304	17	40	7	10	2	0	0	2	5	0	1	0	7	2	1	.300	.333
Copeland, Ben	L-L	6-1	190	12-17-83	.280	.167	.297	127	354	48	99	16	8	4	43	57	0	6	2	67	23	8	.404	.378
DeRosa, Mark	R-R	6-1	205	2-26-75	.364	.500	.200	3	11	1	4	1	0	0	1	1	0	0	0	2	0	0	.455	.417
Downs, Matt	R-R	6-2	190	3-19-84	.254	.295	.242	56	197	37	50	9	1	7	28	25	4	1	1	35	3	4	.416	.348
2-team total (6 Round Rock)					.241	—	—	62	216	37	52	10	1	7	30	26	5	1	1	37	4	5	.394	.335
Graham, Tyler	R-R	6-0	180	1-25-84	.343	.351	.339	109	341	60	117	23	2	2	34	24	6	5	3	54	35	11	.440	.393
Guzman, Jesus	R-R	6-1	215	6-14-84	.321	.344	.312	125	445	66	143	28	1	18	72	38	3	3	3	68	6	4	.510	.376
Holm, Steve	R-R	6-0	205	10-21-79	.246	.241	.247	82	228	34	56	15	2	4	37	29	7	5	4	40	1	3	.382	.343
Lewis, Fred	L-R	6-2	200	12-9-80	.409	.400	.412	7	22	6	9	3	1	1	6	6	0	0	0	2	2	1	.773	.536
Lormand, Ryan	R-R	6-0	165	10-30-85	.125	.333	.056	14	24	2	3	1	0	0	1	0	0	1	0	9	2	1	.167	.160
Martinez-Esteve, Eddy	R-R	6-2	215	7-14-83	.500	1.000	.000	4	4	1	2	0	0	0	1	0	0	0	0	0	0	0	.500	.600
McBryde, Mike	R-R	6-1	215	3-22-85	.243	.190	.264	23	74	11	18	4	0	3	8	1	2	0	0	16	0	2	.419	.273
Monell, Johnny	L-R	5-11	205	3-27-86	.200	1.000	.143	5	15	0	3	1	0	1	2	0	0	0	0	4	0	0	.400	.294
Pill, Brett	R-R	6-4	210	9-9-84	.275	.257	.282	140	520	63	143	34	0	16	84	30	8	0	9	65	7	2	.433	.319
Posey, Buster	R-R	6-1	205	3-27-87	.349	.444	.315	47	172	31	60	13	2	6	32	30	4	0	1	30	1	1	.552	.442
Renteria, Edgar	R-R	6-1	200	8-7-75	.750		.750	4	3	2	3	0	0	0	3	2	0	0	0	0	0	0	.750	.833
Rohlinger, Ryan	R-R	6-1	195	10-7-83	.311	.361	.294	77	283	46	88	23	0	8	48	29	10	1	2	59	3	0	.477	.392
Rojas, Nestor	R-R	6-0	205	11-18-83	.238	.167	.267	15	42	3	10	2	0	1	5	1	0	1	0	5	0	1	.286	.256
Sanchez, Freddy	R-R	5-10	190	12-21-77	.273	.200	.333	4	11	1	3	0	0	0	0	2	0	0	0	3	0	1	.273	.385
Shriner, Jesse	R-R	6-1	195	2-24-85	.000	.000	.000	3	3	0	0	0	0	0	0	0	0	0	0	0	0	0	.000	.000
Velez, Eugenio	B-R	6-1	170	5-16-82	.302	.360	.276	82	321	50	97	13	5	7	35	24	1	6	0	55	31	16	.439	.353
Williams, Jackson	R-R	5-11	195	5-14-86	.224	.185	.235	42	125	16	28	3	0	0	13	15	5	0	2	33	1	1	.352	.327

Pitching	B-T	HT	WT	DOB	W	L	ERA	G	GS	CG	SV	IP	H	R	ER	HR	BB	SO	AVG	vLH	vRH	K/9	BB/9
Bautista, Denny	R-R	6-5	190	8-23-80	3	2	3.18	19	0	0	9	23	14	8	8	1	9	28	.175	.167	.180	11.12	3.57
Bumgarner, Madison	R-L	6-4	215	8-1-89	7	1	3.16	14	14	1	0	83	88	32	29	5	22	59	.275	.194	.298	6.42	2.40
Casilla, Santiago	R-R	6-0	200	7-25-80	0	0	0.00	4	0	0	2	4	2	0	0	0	2	7	.143	.000		15.75	4.50
Edlefsen, Steve	B-R	6-2	180	6-27-85	7	2	2.38	49	0	0	6	64	55	22	17	6	34	50	.239	.250	.232	6.99	4.76
Espineli, Geno	L-L	6-4	195	9-8-82	5	5	3.26	53	0	0	12	61	66	25	22	5	17	38	.286	.217	.324	5.64	2.52
Hacker, Eric	B-R	6-1	210	3-26-83	16	8	4.51	29	29	0	0	166	181	93	83	21	62	129	.280	.257	.298	7.01	3.37
Hinshaw, Alex	L-L	6-4	175	10-31-82	2	4	4.82	50	0	0	0	56	47	35	30	3	40	65	.225	.179	.252	10.45	6.43
Joaquin, Waldis	R-R	6-2	235	12-25-86	1	2	4.93	23	5	0	2	35	44	24	19	4	22	30	.314	.379	.257	8.57	5.71
Kinney, Matt	R-R	6-5	230	12-16-76	0	2	9.64	7	5	0	0	23	37	27	25	9	14		.359	.326	.383	5.40	3.47
Maday, Daryl	R-R	6-2	225	8-12-85	1	4	9.21	7	5	0	0	28	37	29	29	10	13	14	.314	.349	.293	4.45	4.13
Martinez, Joe	L-R	6-2	195	2-26-83	5	3	3.32	14	13	1	0	81	78	35	30	6	26	65	.254	.295	.225	7.19	2.88
Matos, Osiris	R-R	6-1	200	8-6-84	1	4	5.29	38	1	0	3	51	48	30	30	3	25	39	.255	.250	.259	6.88	4.41
Medders, Brandon	R-R	6-1	195	1-26-80	2	1	5.46	22	0	0	1	28	28	17	17	5	10	26	.264	.303	.247	8.36	3.21
Nestor, Scott	R-R	6-2	225	8-20-84	0	2	9.31	8	0	0	0	10	13	10	10	1	7	7	.317	.222	.444	6.52	6.52
Odle, Oliver	R-R	6-0	229	7-11-85	0	0	0.00	5	0	0	0	4	0	0	0	0	0	0	.222	.444	.000	0.00	0.00
Paterson, Joe	R-L	6-1	210	5-19-86	4	3	3.48	46	0	0	2	54	55	28	21	2	24	49	.262	.220	.289	8.12	3.98
Pena Jr., Tony	R-R	6-2	180	3-23-81	0	0	6.60	24	0	0	0	30	39	23	22	3	21	22	.322	.292	.325	6.30	4.20
Pucetas, Kevin	R-R	6-4	215	8-27-84	5	7	5.69	26	26	0	0	136	172	90	86	17	61	95	.316	.322	.311	6.29	4.04
Ramirez, Horacio	L-L	6-1	220	11-24-79	1	1	4.12	6	3	0	0	20	23	9	9	2	2	11	.280	.278	.281	5.03	0.92
Romero, Felix	R-R	6-2	200	6-18-80	1	1	6.52	7	0	0	0	10	11	9	7	3	6	6	.306	.267	.333	5.59	2.79
Romo, Sergio	R-R	6-1	185	3-4-83	0	0	5.73	7	0	0	0	11	14	7	7	1	6	11	.311	.313	.310	4.91	4.91
Runzler, Dan	L-L	6-4	230	3-30-85	0	0	3.86	6	0	0	0	7	4	3	0	4	5		.296	.214	.385	6.43	5.14
Sosa, Henry	R-R	6-2	195	7-28-85	7	8	4.07	36	14	0	0	115	113	61	52	20	55	83	.256	.276	.241	6.50	4.30

	B-T	HT	WT	DOB	W	L	ERA	G	GS	CG	SV	IP	H	R	ER	HR	BB	SO	AVG	vLH	vRH	K/9	BB/9
Wellemeyer, Todd	R-R	6-3	225	8-30-78	1	0	2.25	3	3	0	0	16	9	5	4	1	12	12	.184	.167	.194	6.75	6.75
Whitaker, Craig	R-R	6-4	210	11-19-84	0	1	2.49	14	1	0	0	22	17	6	6	0	16	19	.221	.250	.195	7.89	6.65
Willis, Dontrelle	L-L	6-4	225	1-12-82	0	0	5.06	5	0	0	0	5	2	3	3	1	4	6	.111	.167	.083	10.13	6.75
Yourkin, Matt	R-L	6-3	225	7-4-81	7	8	4.24	29	24	0	0	136	146	67	64	14	39	110	.277	.306	.264	7.28	2.58

Fielding

Catcher	PCT	G	PO	A	E	DP	PB
Holm	.996	68	429	32	2	5	2
Monell	1.000	4	24	5	0	0	0
Posey	1.000	32	219	17	0	0	1
Rojas	.988	14	74	7	1	1	3
Williams	.993	41	262	25	2	2	5

First Base	PCT	G	PO	A	E	DP
Belt	.977	5	39	3	1	1
Bowker	1.000	1	7	0	0	1
Guzman	1.000	5	24	0	0	2
Pill	.996	126	1053	83	5	112
Posey	1.000	12	107	18	0	12

Second Base	PCT	G	PO	A	E	DP
Bond	.979	82	159	219	8	59
Boyer	1.000	2	2	2	0	0
Burriss	.954	33	55	90	7	21
DeRosa	1.000	1	3	0	4	0
Downs	1.000	16	22	46	0	12
Sanchez	1.000	4	7	8	0	4
Velez	.947	22	26	46	4	6

Third Base	PCT	G	PO	A	E	DP
Bond	.923	30	13	35	4	2
Boyer	.922	19	8	39	4	2
Ciriaco	.000	1	0	0	1	0
DeRosa	1.000	1	1	1	0	0
Downs	.941	29	12	36	3	2
Guzman	.926	61	33	79	9	5
Holm	.500	4	0	1	1	0
Lormand	1.000	7	1	5	0	0
Pena Jr.	—	2	0	0	0	0
Pill	—	2	0	0	0	0
Rohlinger	.984	27	13	48	1	4

Shortstop	PCT	G	PO	A	E	DP
Berroa	.964	26	40	66	4	18
Bond	1.000	1	1	4	0	0
Boyer	.975	12	11	28	1	8
Burriss	.953	36	40	81	6	12
Ciriaco	.979	10	16	31	1	9
Downs	.981	14	17	36	1	7
Lormand	.917	4	1	10	1	2
Pena Jr.	1.000	4	5	10	0	3
Renteria	1.000	2	3	6	0	2
Rohlinger	.978	54	110	151	6	45

Outfield	PCT	G	PO	A	E	DP
Belt	1.000	7	9	1	0	0
Borchard	.952	89	135	5	7	0
Bowker	.940	42	78	1	5	0
Boyer	1.000	5	0	0	0	0
Burrell	1.000	3	8	0	0	0
Copeland	.988	122	237	13	3	5
DeRosa	1.000	1	2	0	0	0
Graham	.990	105	198	9	2	2
Guzman	.962	36	48	3	2	1
Holm	—	1	0	0	0	0
Lewis	.909	7	10	0	1	0
Martinez-Esteve	.500	2	1	0	1	0
McBryde	1.000	23	46	2	0	1
Shriner	1.000	2	1	0	0	0
Velez	.951	66	136	1	7	1

RICHMOND FLYING SQUIRRELS

EASTERN LEAGUE

DOUBLE-A

Batting	B-T	HT	WT	DOB	AVG	vLH	vRH	G	AB	R	H	2B	3B	HR	RBI	BB	HBP	SH	SF	SO	SB	CS	SLG	OBP
Ambort, Michael	B-R	6-1	215	4-23-85	.220	.311	.184	47	159	18	35	7	1	3	14	9	1	0	1	34	0	1	.333	.265
Belt, Brandon	L-L	6-5	195	4-20-88	.337	.340	.336	46	175	26	59	11	6	9	40	22	2	0	2	34	2	1	.623	.413
Bond, Brock	B-R	5-11	185	9-11-85	.261	.105	.370	12	46	8	12	3	1	0	4	3	1	0	0	10	0	0	.370	.320
Boyer, Brad	L-R	6-0	185	10-4-83	.232	.303	.213	48	155	24	36	6	2	2	23	25	1	1	1	34	3	2	.335	.341
Ciriaco, Juan	R-R	6-0	160	8-15-83	.263	.366	.217	48	133	14	35	8	3	2	13	8	0	1	3	24	0	4	.414	.299
Crawford, Brandon	L-R	6-2	200	1-21-87	.241	.264	.233	79	291	43	70	12	3	7	22	39	6	1	5	77	4	1	.375	.337
D'Alessio, Andy	L-R	6-4	227	9-23-84	.277	.250	.283	19	65	9	18	5	1	2	10	8	0	0	0	15	0	0	.477	.356
Ford, Darren	R-R	5-11	195	10-1-85	.251	.233	.256	113	463	64	116	20	9	5	40	39	5	8	1	106	37	15	.365	.315
Gillaspie, Conor	L-R	6-1	195	7-18-87	.287	.338	.268	132	491	57	141	25	8	8	67	37	2	2	8	67	0	4	.420	.335
Graham, Tyler	R-R	6-0	180	1-25-84	.125	.000	.500	2	8	0	1	0	0	0	0	0	0	0	0	4	1	0	.125	.125
Kieschnick, Roger	L-R	6-3	215	1-21-87	.251	.185	.272	60	223	21	56	8	3	4	23	18	1	0	4	55	2	3	.368	.305
Klimas, Matt	R-R	5-11	185	7-3-87	.333	.000	.500	2	3	1	1	0	0	0	1	1	0	0	1	0	0	0	.333	.600
La Torre, Tyler	L-R	6-0	219	4-22-83	.204	.111	.229	81	255	27	52	13	1	2	20	36	2	4	1	76	0	3	.286	.306
Lormand, Ryan	R-R	6-0	165	10-30-85	.225	.234	.222	77	253	25	57	14	2	0	24	13	2	3	2	60	5	2	.296	.267
Lowenstein, Aaron	R-R	6-1	195	6-14-85	.130	.125	.133	8	23	2	3	1	0	0	2	1	0	0	0	5	0	0	.174	.167
Martinez-Esteve, Eddy	R-R	6-2	215	7-14-83	.000	.000	.000	6	12	0	0	0	0	0	0	1	1	0	0	5	0	0	.000	.200
Neal, Thomas	R-R	6-1	225	8-17-87	.291	.328	.280	136	525	69	153	40	1	12	69	46	11	0	3	94	11	5	.440	.359
Noonan, Nick	L-R	6-0	180	5-4-89	.237	.172	.260	101	372	43	88	12	2	3	26	22	2	6	4	74	7	3	.304	.280
Rojas, Nestor	R-R	6-0	180	11-18-83	.313	.455	.000	5	16	0	5	0	0	0	0	0	1	1	0	1	0	0	.313	.353
Schoop, Sharlon	R-R	6-2	190	4-15-87	.273	.200	.294	52	183	19	50	9	0	2	25	13	0	1	2	34	1	1	.355	.318
Stromsmoe, Skyler	B-R	5-10	175	3-30-84	.239	.256	.233	47	142	11	34	3	1	2	7	7	2	5	1	34	6	0	.317	.283
Timpner, Clay	L-L	6-2	195	5-13-83	.290	.243	.307	123	417	40	121	18	2	4	51	35	3	2	5	63	6	4	.372	.346
Williams, Jackson	R-R	5-11	200	5-14-86	.192	.204	.188	60	193	17	37	9	1	2	16	29	7	6	1	54	0	1	.280	.317
Zambrano, Eliezer	B-R	5-11	175	9-16-86	.278	.429	.182	5	18	1	5	2	0	0	1	0	0	3	0	3	0	0	.389	.278

Pitching	B-T	HT	WT	DOB	W	L	ERA	G	GS	CG	SV	IP	H	R	ER	HR	BB	SO	AVG	vLH	vRH	K/9	BB/9
Clark, Craig	L-L	6-2	200	7-9-84	2	3	4.01	9	9	0	0	43	42	25	19	4	21	23	.269	.263	.271	4.85	4.43
Cova, Rafael	R-R	6-2	175	3-5-82	0	6	2.35	48	0	0	23	57	31	18	15	3	36	68	.157	.143	.167	10.67	5.65
Lively, Mitch	R-R	6-5	230	9-7-85	2	4	3.90	23	0	0	3	32	32	17	14	1	18	25	.269	.340	.222	6.96	5.01
MacDonald, Mike	R-R	6-1	215	10-29-81	5	8	3.90	27	23	1	0	134	155	63	58	10	31	78	.298	.332	.274	5.24	2.08
Maday, Daryl	R-R	6-2	225	8-12-85	9	8	3.47	25	18	0	1	114	121	48	44	7	33	70	.281	.254	.305	5.53	2.61
Main, Michael	R-R	6-1	170	12-14-88	0	3	13.83	5	4	0	0	14	21	26	21	3	14	7	.362	.355	.370	4.61	9.22
Martin, Adrian	R-R	6-0	165	9-2-84	1	0	0.73	8	0	0	0	12	12	1	1	0	2	12	.255	.286	.242	8.76	1.46
2-team total (29 New Hampshire)					6	1	3.67	37	2	0	1	61	64	26	25	5	25	56	—	—		8.22	3.67
Mixon, David	R-R	6-3	190	9-10-84	11	7	3.50	27	25	1	0	157	149	65	61	12	38	112	.256	.299	.221	6.43	2.18
Pena Jr., Tony	R-R	6-2	180	3-23-81	3	2	2.53	29	0	0	6	46	38	13	13	2	15	41	.228	.328	.160	7.96	2.91
Quinowski, David	L-L	5-10	170	4-23-86	2	0	2.84	12	0	0	1	13	10	5	4	1	5	14	.213	.182	.240	9.95	3.55
Ray, Ronnie	R-R	6-3	215	5-11-84	2	3	3.49	48	5	0	4	80	74	34	31	4	18	69	.246	.305	.208	7.76	2.03
Rodriguez, Wilmin	L-R	6-2	211	5-13-85	0	1	3.51	10	0	0	0	26	24	13	10	1	14	12	.255	.231	.273	4.21	4.91
Romero, Felix	R-R	6-2	200	6-18-80	5	3	3.34	26	14	0	0	100	99	40	37	7	20	73	.257	.255	.259	6.59	1.81
Sisco, Andy	L-L	6-10	270	1-13-83	4	4	4.32	48	0	0	1	67	56	33	32	4	36	75	.226	.261	.205	10.13	4.86
Stevens, Jake	L-L	6-2	215	3-15-85	4	4	2.80	46	3	0	2	64	56	24	20	5	27	45	.238	.159	.286	6.30	3.78
Tanner, Clayton	R-L	6-1	200	12-5-87	9	9	3.68	27	27	0	0	149	150	78	61	10	64	79	.265	.190	.285	4.77	3.87

	B-T	HT	WT	DOB	W	L	ERA	G	GS	CG	SV	IP	H	R	ER	HR	BB	SO			AVG	vLH	vRH	K/9	BB/9
Turpen, Dan	R-R	6-4	230	8-17-86	5	5	4.09	37	0	0	1	51	55	24	23	4	19	42			.278	.261	.287	7.46	3.38
2-team total (12 Portland)					7	6	4.30	49	0	0	4	69	73	35	33	4	28	60			—	—	—	7.83	3.65
Westcott, Craig	L-R	6-4	225	3-1-86	3	3	5.13	13	13	0	0	67	76	42	38	9	28	48			.284	.295	.274	6.48	3.78
Whitaker, Craig	R-R	6-4	210	11-19-84	1	0	4.97	19	0	0	1	25	22	16	14	4	16	21			.234	.233	.235	7.46	5.68

Fielding

Catcher	PCT	G	PO	A	E	DP	PB
Klimas	1.000	1	6	0	0	0	0
La Torre	.990	67	473	28	5	3	7
Lowenstein	1.000	8	27	6	0	0	1
Rojas	1.000	4	18	1	0	0	0
Williams	.998	59	367	43	1	4	6
Zambrano	1.000	5	29	3	0	0	0

First Base	PCT	G	PO	A	E	DP
Ambort	.994	44	443	30	3	63
Belt	.997	36	299	24	1	30
Ciriaco	.979	9	46	1	1	3
D'Alessio	1.000	18	171	10	0	18
La Torre	.980	11	97	3	2	10
Rojas	1.000	1	5	0	0	1
Schoop	.986	25	203	11	3	23
Timpner	.988	9	77	7	1	7

Second Base	PCT	G	PO	A	E	DP
Bond	1.000	2	1	5	0	2
Boyer	1.000	4	8	12	0	2
Ciriaco	.944	5	6	11	1	2
Lormand	.983	23	42	73	2	18
Noonan	.978	99	179	315	11	72
Schoop	1.000	6	4	0	2	
Stromsmoe	.987	13	24	52	1	17

Third Base	PCT	G	PO	A	E	DP
Bond	1.000	2	1	6	0	0
Boyer	.714	3	2	3	2	1
Ciriaco	.923	7	5	7	1	1
Gillaspie	.946	122	66	230	17	26
Schoop	1.000	4	1	6	0	0
Stromsmoe	.889	7	2	6	1	0

Shortstop	PCT	G	PO	A	E	DP
Boyer	.985	14	21	44	1	10
Ciriaco	.944	8	9	25	2	10
Crawford	.977	75	130	286	10	74
Lormand	.936	36	37	109	10	23

	PCT	G	PO	A	E	DP
Schoop	1.000	9	13	33	0	6
Stromsmoe	1.000	3	1	7	0	1

Outfield	PCT	G	PO	A	E	DP
Belt	1.000	7	19	0	0	0
Bond	1.000	7	8	0	0	0
Boyer	1.000	2	4	0	0	0
Ciriaco	1.000	15	25	2	0	1
Ford	.985	110	264	4	4	3
Graham	1.000	1	3	0	0	0
Kieschnick	1.000	52	95	2	0	0
Lormand	1.000	10	16	1	0	0
Martinez-Esteve	—	1	0	0	0	0
Neal	.962	121	216	11	9	1
Schoop	1.000	5	6	0	0	0
Stromsmoe	1.000	16	35	1	0	1
Timpner	.983	87	166	11	3	3

SAN JOSE GIANTS

CALIFORNIA LEAGUE

HIGH CLASS A

Batting	B-T	HT	WT	DOB	AVG	vLH	vRH	G	AB	R	H	2B	3B	HR	RBI	BB	HBP	SH	SF	SO	SB	CS	SLG	OBP
Adrianza, Ehire	B-R	6-1	165	8-21-89	.256	.242	.262	124	445	70	114	22	5	3	35	47	5	10	1	87	33	15	.348	.333
Ambort, Michael	B-R	6-1	215	4-23-85	.167	.222	.143	8	30	3	5	0	0	1	2	4	0	0	1	4	1	1	.267	.257
Belt, Brandon	L-L	6-5	195	4-20-88	.383	.288	.406	77	269	62	103	28	4	10	62	58	3	0	3	50	18	7	.628	.492
Biery, Drew	R-R	6-2	215	5-14-86	.249	.165	.279	115	414	53	103	15	2	14	66	39	9	1	7	99	8	7	.396	.322
Burriss, Emmanuel	B-R	6-0	190	1-17-85	.214	.000	.231	5	14	2	3	0	0	0	1	0	2	1	0	3	1	1	.214	.313
Ciriaco, Juan	R-R	6-0	160	8-15-83	.375	.667	.200	2	8	2	3	0	0	1	1	0	1	0	0	2	0	0	.750	.444
Crawford, Brandon	L-R	6-2	200	1-21-87	.167	.143	.182	5	18	4	3	1	0	0	1	2	0	0	0	5	0	0	.222	.250
Culberson, Charlie	R-R	6-1	185	4-10-89	.290	.268	.299	128	503	80	146	28	4	16	71	33	8	1	6	99	25	7	.457	.340
DeRosa, Mark	R-R	6-1	205	2-26-75	.000	.000	.000	1	4	0	0	0	0	0	0	1	0	0	0	0	0	0	.000	.200
Fairley, Wendell	L-R	6-2	195	3-17-88	.292	.227	.307	115	391	42	114	15	1	1	46	29	15	3	2	86	10	6	.343	.362
Flores, Jose	B-R	5-11	175	8-17-87	.331	.298	.347	96	359	58	119	15	6	6	54	25	4	2	0	41	9	6	.457	.381
Klimas, Matt	R-R	5-11	185	7-3-87	.238	.292	.156	27	80	7	19	1	0	1	13	6	4	0	1	11	0	0	.288	.319
Lormand, Ryan	R-R	6-0	165	10-30-85	.304	.417	.284	23	79	16	24	4	0	1	7	11	0	1	0	14	8	1	.392	.389
Lowenstein, Aaron	R-R	6-1	195	6-9-85	.214	.211	.216	22	70	5	15	4	0	2	4	3	1	0	0	14	0	0	.271	.286
Mazzola, Josh	R-R	6-2	195	4-10-86	.273	.500	.222	3	11	1	3	0	1	0	2	1	0	0	0	2	0	1	.455	.333
Medina, Jose	R-R	6-0	180	11-29-86	.167	.333	.083	10	18	3	3	0	0	2	5	5	0	0	0	8	1	0	.500	.348
Monell, Johnny	L-R	5-11	205	3-27-86	.273	.239	.286	115	421	66	115	25	4	19	70	48	2	0	1	105	12	3	.487	.350
Peguero, Francisco	R-R	6-0	190	6-1-88	.329	.315	.335	122	510	78	168	19	16	10	77	18	6	2	2	88	40	22	.488	.358
Perez, Juan	R-R	5-11	185	11-13-86	.298	.301	.296	131	551	83	164	37	10	13	63	31	5	3	6	116	17	15	.472	.337
Sanchez, Freddy	R-R	5-10	190	12-21-77	.667	.750	.600	3	9	6	6	5	0	0	4	3	1	0	0	0	0	1	1.222	.769
Sandoval, Michael	R-R	5-11	205	7-8-81	.269	.342	.205	44	156	17	42	11	0	3	17	14	2	0	3	44	2	1	.397	.331
Simmons, James	R-R	6-3	190	9-3-85	.252	.261	.247	105	317	56	80	16	5	12	47	37	5	1	1	112	19	7	.448	.339
Weeks, Joel	L-R	5-9	185	11-30-84	.277	.179	.292	69	206	25	57	12	0	4	24	16	2	0	2	32	4	1	.393	.332

Pitching	B-T	HT	WT	DOB	W	L	ERA	G	GS	CG	SV	IP	H	R	ER	HR	BB	SO	AVG	vLH	vRH	K/9	BB/9
Affeldt, Jeremy	L-L	6-5	225	6-6-79	0	0	0.00	2	2	0	0	3	2	0	0	0	1	4	.182	.200	.167	12.00	3.00
Anderson, Brian	R-R	6-3	210	5-25-83	3	1	3.55	33	0	0	1	51	47	28	20	2	20	35	.239	.289	.207	6.22	3.55
Bucardo, Jorge	R-R	6-1	155	10-18-89	2	2	4.42	8	7	0	0	39	46	22	19	3	19	26	.297	.315	.287	6.05	4.42
Fitzgerald, Justin	R-R	6-5	225	3-3-86	10	6	3.45	26	25	0	0	146	140	65	56	11	46	116	.258	.238	.274	7.15	2.84
King, Aaron	L-L	6-4	205	4-27-89	1	2	7.57	7	7	0	0	27	29	25	23	5	16	30	.271	.310	.256	9.88	5.27
Marte, Kelvin	R-R	6-0	180	11-24-87	0	0	14.73	1	1	0	0	4	6	6	6	0	3	6	.462	.500	.444	7.36	12.27
Nestor, Scott	R-R	6-2	185	8-20-84	3	3	5.34	35	0	0	2	57	48	37	34	8	46	57	.238	.211	.259	8.95	7.22
Nicholson, Kyle	R-R	6-0	205	7-31-85	7	9	6.13	22	21	0	0	119	151	94	81	20	19	85	.308	.311	.305	6.43	1.44
Odle, Oliver	R-R	6-0	229	7-11-85	12	7	5.78	30	18	0	0	123	159	82	79	14	15	96	.310	.293	.321	7.02	1.10
Otero, Danny	R-R	6-3	205	2-19-85	3	0	4.05	10	0	0	0	13	11	6	6	2	1	11	.224	.176	.250	7.43	0.68
Paterson, Joe	R-L	6-1	210	5-19-86	1	0	0.82	7	0	0	1	11	9	2	1	0	2	15	.220	.200	.231	12.27	1.64
Quinowski, David	L-L	5-10	170	4-23-86	3	2	2.32	28	0	0	2	43	35	11	11	2	13	51	.217	.281	.183	10.76	2.72
Quirarte, Edwin	R-R	6-2	185	12-20-86	2	3	3.77	41	0	0	6	62	56	31	26	6	22	38	.238	.219	.252	5.52	3.19
Ray, Chris	R-R	6-3	210	1-12-82	0	1	10.80	1	1	0	0	2	7	4	2	0	0	1	.778	.500	.857	5.40	0.00
Reichard, Andy	R-R	6-4	235	12-4-84	2	1	6.57	7	0	0	0	12	17	11	9	0	9	9	.354	.333	.370	5.84	6.57
Romo, Andrew	R-R	6-1	230	6-20-87	0	2	8.22	3	3	0	0	8	7	7	7	1	9	8	.231	.125	.278	9.39	10.57
Ronick, Ari	L-L	6-4	205	3-25-86	0	1	10.80	3	3	0	0	8	14	11	10	4	7	6	.368	.533	.261	6.48	7.56
Runzler, Dan	L-L	6-4	230	3-30-85	0	0	0.00	1	1	0	0	1	0	0	0	0	0	2	.000	.000	.000	18.00	0.00
Stoffel, Jason	R-R	6-2	220	9-15-88	2	4	4.80	52	0	0	25	51	55	33	27	4	24	66	.276	.282	.272	11.72	4.26
Stolp, Eric	R-R	6-3	182	8-18-84	6	8	4.86	31	12	0	0	104	116	65	56	11	37	49	.284	.270	.294	4.23	3.21

	B-T	HT	WT	DOB	W	L	ERA	G	GS	CG	SV	IP	H	R	ER	HR	BB	SO	AVG	vLH	vRH	K/9	BB/9
Surkamp, Eric	L-L	6-4	190	7-16-87	4	2	3.11	17	17	1	0	101	79	39	35	5	22	108	.218	.226	.215	9.59	1.95
Verdugo, Ryan	L-L	6-0	195	4-10-87	4	0	1.47	22	1	0	0	31	15	5	5	3	19	44	.149	.071	.178	12.91	5.58
Westcott, Craig	L-R	6-4	225	3-1-86	6	0	1.83	13	13	0	0	69	63	19	14	3	32	52	.242	.297	.197	6.95	4.19
Whitaker, Craig	R-R	6-4	210	11-19-84	1	0	1.86	7	0	0	0	10	8	2	2	0	6	9	.229	.200	.240	8.38	5.59
Wilshire, Ben	R-R	6-4	200	3-25-85	1	0	4.60	34	0	0	1	59	60	33	30	3	24	47	.273	.255	.286	7.21	3.68
Woodruff, Kyle	R-R	6-6	225	5-2-86	3	3	3.02	25	8	0	1	83	75	35	28	8	23	57	.237	.145	.290	6.16	2.48

Fielding

Catcher	PCT	G	PO	A	E	DP	PB
Klimas	.989	25	166	14	2	0	8
Lowenstein	.980	22	129	21	3	0	4
Monell	.994	87	623	65	4	6	16
Weeks	.970	18	87	9	3	0	5

First Base	PCT	G	PO	A	E	DP
Ambort	1.000	7	56	5	0	5
Belt	.991	71	678	52	7	60
Biery	.994	39	325	18	2	29
Flores	1.000	1	3	1	0	1
Lormand	1.000	1	1	0	0	0
Mazzola	1.000	1	9	3	0	0
Monell	.947	3	16	2	1	0
Sandoval	.996	29	191	32	1	23

Second Base	PCT	G	PO	A	E	DP
Culberson	.975	120	232	342	15	77

	PCT	G	PO	A	E	DP
Flores	.964	14	21	33	2	10
Lormand	1.000	5	13	10	0	3
Sanchez	1.000	3	1	11	0	1
Weeks	1.000	5	6	11	0	2

Third Base	PCT	G	PO	A	E	DP
Biery	.944	75	51	116	10	10
Ciriaco	1.000	2	0	8	0	2
Crawford	1.000	2	1	3	0	2
Flores	.917	29	18	59	7	4
Lormand	.813	7	3	10	3	1
Sandoval	1.000	2	0	2	0	0
Weeks	.927	35	23	66	7	6

Shortstop	PCT	G	PO	A	E	DP
Adrianza	.972	121	164	389	16	70
Burriss	.938	5	3	12	1	3
Crawford	1.000	2	1	3	0	1

	PCT	G	PO	A	E	DP
Flores	.938	12	14	31	3	5
Lormand	1.000	5	5	13	0	1
Weeks	.850	5	5	12	3	2

Outfield	PCT	G	PO	A	E	DP
DeRosa	—	1	0	0	0	0
Fairley	.951	96	133	3	7	0
Flores	1.000	6	5	0	0	0
Mazzola	1.000	1	2	0	0	0
Medina	1.000	8	8	0	0	0
Peguero	.980	104	187	11	4	4
Perez	.982	127	255	17	5	5
Simmons	.984	101	170	11	3	2
Weeks	1.000	1	1	0	0	0

AUGUSTA GREENJACKETS

LOW CLASS A

SOUTH ATLANTIC LEAGUE

Batting	B-T	HT	WT	DOB	AVG	vLH	vRH	G	AB	R	H	2B	3B	HR	RBI	BB	HBP	SH	SF	SO	SB	CS	SLG	OBP
Anders, Luke	L-L	6-6	225	10-2-86	.285	.274	.289	130	501	71	143	29	4	14	62	43	1	2	5	147	1	4	.443	.340
Burg, Alex	R-R	6-0	190	8-9-87	.207	.000	.214	9	29	4	6	2	1	0	1	3	1	0	0	15	0	0	.345	.303
Cavan, Ryan	B-R	5-10	180	6-28-87	.283	.267	.289	136	541	85	153	34	3	17	79	54	6	3	4	93	12	7	.451	.352
Cook, Dan	B-R	6-3	185	6-15-86	.281	.243	.298	97	338	41	95	21	5	1	32	25	3	2	2	78	7	0	.382	.334
Crawford, Evan	R-R	6-2	165	8-5-88	.255	.227	.267	109	432	64	110	12	12	4	29	35	6	3	1	108	24	9	.366	.319
Dominguez, Chris	R-R	6-3	215	11-22-86	.272	.220	.290	137	559	85	152	32	4	21	101	35	11	0	3	133	14	7	.456	.326
Eshleman, John	R-R	6-0	185	4-8-89	.138	.091	.167	9	29	1	4	1	0	0	3	3	0	0	0	11	0	0	.172	.219
Joseph, Tommy	R-R	6-1	215	7-16-91	.236	.276	.224	117	436	46	103	22	1	16	68	26	8	0	3	116	0	0	.401	.290
Liles, Nick	R-R	6-0	165	7-23-87	.316	.260	.334	127	512	86	162	28	4	0	62	36	4	4	8	61	29	11	.387	.361
Lollis, Ryan	L-L	5-10	180	12-16-86	.288	.338	.275	114	389	52	112	9	9	3	36	32	2	2	0	55	8	2	.380	.345
Mach, Kyle	R-R	5-10	190	11-8-86	.250	.333	.000	5	8	1	2	0	0	0	0	1	0	2	0	3	0	1	.250	.333
Martinez, Juan	R-R	5-10	190	12-26-86	.236	.233	.238	63	148	24	35	6	0	1	9	13	6	4	1	33	2	1	.297	.321
Medina, Jose	R-R	6-0	180	11-29-86	.125	.000	.222	6	16	1	2	1	0	0	1	2	0	0	0	6	0	0	.188	.222
Sanchez, Hector	R-R	6-0	185	11-17-89	.274	.290	.267	89	310	29	85	20	1	5	31	28	1	2	0	50	0	2	.394	.336
Schoop, Sharlon	R-R	6-2	190	4-15-87	.281	.310	.267	26	89	10	25	2	1	0	9	7	1	0	1	20	3	2	.326	.337
Shriner, Jesse	R-R	6-1	195	2-24-85	.267	.200	.333	11	30	2	8	0	0	1	2	1	0	0	0	9	0	0	.367	.313
Stromsmoe, Skyler	B-R	5-10	175	3-6-84	.195	.381	.136	25	87	18	17	5	1	0	12	13	4	1	5	16	6	1	.276	.312
Villegas, Ydwin	R-R	5-10	165	9-1-90	.189	.226	.178	79	264	20	50	9	1	1	24	9	0	7	1	55	1	2	.242	.215
Zambrano, Eliezer	B-R	5-11	175	9-16-86	.170	.148	.180	31	88	7	15	2	0	0	7	1	1	2	1	23	1	0	.193	.187

Pitching	B-T	HT	WT	DOB	W	L	ERA	G	GS	CG	SV	IP	H	R	ER	HR	BB	SO	AVG	vLH	vRH	K/9	BB/9
Bucardo, Jorge	R-R	6-1	155	10-18-89	9	4	2.21	19	18	1	0	114	83	36	28	3	31	95	.203	.206	.201	7.50	2.45
Casilla, Jose	R-R	6-1	190	5-21-89	4	1	1.16	46	0	0	14	54	40	9	7	0	17	41	.214	.250	.193	6.79	2.82
Clark, Craig	L-L	6-2	200	7-9-84	3	3	5.21	10	7	0	0	47	53	31	27	4	13	43	.283	.208	.313	8.29	2.51
Correa, Hector	R-R	6-3	165	3-18-88	5	3	4.12	32	0	0	1	44	39	21	20	3	16	58	.239	.263	.226	11.95	3.30
Gloor, Chris	L-L	6-6	255	3-7-87	4	2	2.65	44	0	0	2	68	58	23	20	2	27	73	.227	.219	.233	9.66	3.57
Heston, Chris	R-R	6-4	185	4-10-88	5	13	3.75	26	26	1	0	149	161	83	62	6	33	124	.272	.234	.296	7.51	2.00
Irving, Brian	R-R	6-2	205	4-24-86	7	6	4.42	32	14	0	1	106	119	63	52	6	37	80	.281	.237	.306	6.79	3.14
Jarvis, Jason	R-R	6-2	195	10-1-87	0	1	3.07	13	0	0	7	15	17	8	5	0	2	13	.293	.320	.273	7.98	1.23
Kline, Devan	R-R	6-1	195	10-18-87	1	0	2.59	18	2	0	3	31	26	10	9	3	18	35	.230	.233	.229	10.05	5.17
Lively, Mitch	R-R	6-5	230	9-7-85	4	2	4.89	24	0	0	1	35	37	20	19	2	7	26	.280	.333	.250	6.69	1.80
Marte, Kelvin	R-R	6-0	180	11-24-87	1	0	2.73	7	4	0	0	26	24	8	8	1	7	16	.258	.167	.290	5.47	2.39
Reichard, Andy	R-R	6-4	235	12-4-84	6	1	3.39	16	13	0	0	96	87	40	36	6	22	92	.240	.231	.245	8.66	2.07
Rodriguez, Wilmin	L-L	6-2	211	5-13-85	4	3	3.81	20	1	0	0	28	36	14	12	1	9	20	.298	.271	.315	6.35	2.86
Salsbury, B.J.	R-R	6-2	185	10-22-89	5	3	3.47	11	11	1	0	70	66	32	27	6	10	50	.245	.214	.259	6.43	1.29
Toole, Jeremy	R-R	6-4	235	6-17-88	6	5	3.87	24	17	0	1	98	93	52	42	3	37	75	.251	.265	.239	6.91	3.41
Valdez, Jose	R-R	6-7	150	8-1-88	4	3	3.30	40	0	0	1	60	57	26	22	2	37	68	.263	.300	.245	10.20	5.55
Vazquez, Kyle	R-R	6-3	175	6-29-88	4	3	4.84	17	12	0	0	74	79	45	40	4	28	46	.274	.296	.261	5.57	3.39
Verdugo, Ryan	L-L	6-0	195	4-10-87	4	1	2.25	22	0	0	1	32	26	8	8	0	14	50	.226	.278	.203	14.06	3.94
Wheeler, Zack	R-R	6-3	180	5-30-90	3	3	3.99	21	13	0	0	59	47	27	26	0	38	70	.218	.256	.196	10.74	5.83
Whitaker, Craig	R-R	6-4	210	11-19-84	0	0	2.61	7	0	0	0	10	9	4	3	0	7	18	.237	.167	.269	15.68	6.10
Wilson, Chris	R-R	6-2	205	11-27-86	0	2	2.76	11	0	0	4	16	11	5	5	0	6	18	.190	.150	.231	9.92	3.31

Fielding

Catcher	PCT	G	PO	A	E	DP	PB
Burg	1.000	3	8	2	0	0	0
Joseph	.989	65	479	59	6	1	19
Sanchez	.982	58	427	62	9	5	13
Shriner	1.000	2	6	0	0	0	0
Zambrano	1.000	30	178	17	0	3	4

SAN FRANCISCO GIANTS

First Base	PCT	G	PO	A	E	DP
Anders	.991	127	1184	68	12	107
Joseph	.990	10	93	7	1	6
Liles	1.000	2	18	0	0	2
Shriner	1.000	1	9	1	0	0

Second Base	PCT	G	PO	A	E	DP
Cavan	.963	133	247	422	26	87
Martinez	1.000	8	9	19	0	4

Third Base	PCT	G	PO	A	E	DP
Dominguez	.918	134	85	275	32	29

Mach	1.000	1	0	4	0	0
Martinez	.889	3	1	7	1	0

Shortstop	PCT	G	PO	A	E	DP
Eshleman	.861	8	9	22	5	5
Mach	1.000	2	1	2	0	0
Martinez	.940	36	47	93	9	26
Schoop	.974	26	34	77	3	22
Villegas	.969	77	99	213	10	32

Outfield	PCT	G	PO	A	E	DP
Burg	—	1	0	0	0	0

Cook	.977	91	121	9	3	1
Crawford	.981	108	196	7	4	1
Liles	.993	86	138	3	1	2
Lollis	.984	105	181	7	3	1
Mach	—	1	0	0	0	0
Martinez	—	1	0	0	0	0
Medina	.857	4	6	0	1	0
Shriner	.800	3	4	0	1	0
Stromsmoe	.982	25	55	1	1	0

SALEM-KEIZER VOLCANOES   SHORT-SEASON
NORTHWEST LEAGUE

Batting	B-T	HT	WT	DOB	AVG	vLH	vRH	G	AB	R	H	2B	3B	HR	RBI	BB	HBP	SH	SF	SO	SB	CS	SLG	OBP
Arnold, Jeff	R-R	6-2	205	1-13-88	.241	.182	.256	36	112	11	27	8	1	3	10	6	1	2	0	29	2	1	.411	.286
Brock, Danny	R-R	6-1	210	12-28-87	.239	.372	.203	52	201	20	48	15	0	3	23	17	3	0	0	36	3	2	.358	.308
Brown, Gary	R-R	6-0	170	9-28-88	.136	.000	.136	6	22	2	3	0	1	0	2	2	2	0	1	7	0	1	.227	.259
Burg, Alex	R-R	6-0	190	8-9-87	.242	.188	.261	19	62	7	15	5	0	3	12	7	1	0	1	23	0	0	.468	.324
Burkhart, Dan	L-R	5-11	215	3-6-89	.328	.250	.339	19	64	3	21	3	0	0	11	6	1	0	1	8	0	0	.375	.389
Campbell, Raynor	R-R	5-10	175	7-15-87	.261	.217	.277	45	165	22	43	10	2	3	22	9	2	3	1	41	2	2	.400	.305
Dibbens, Derek	L-R	6-0	200	8-7-87	—	.000	.000	1	0	1	0	0	0	0	0	0	1	0	0	0	0	0	—	1.000
Duvall, Adam	R-R	6-1	205	9-4-88	.245	.304	.226	54	192	30	47	10	1	4	18	14	7	3	1	45	2	3	.370	.318
Eshleman, John	R-R	6-0	185	4-8-89	.250	.100	.274	22	72	4	18	3	0	0	3	8	0	2	0	22	2	2	.292	.325
Harris, Devin	R-R	6-3	225	4-23-88	.273	.308	.267	27	99	8	27	9	1	1	12	4	0	0	1	36	0	3	.414	.298
Izturis, Julio	B-R	5-11	165	8-29-89	.281	.194	.302	51	185	32	52	4	1	0	16	10	1	4	0	29	7	4	.314	.321
Jurica, Carter	R-R	5-11	185	9-23-88	.216	.258	.201	62	236	23	51	7	3	4	31	18	4	3	1	47	10	3	.322	.282
Loberg, Mike	L-R	6-4	225	3-24-85	.333	.500	.267	9	21	2	7	0	0	0	5	7	0	0	0	1	0	1	.333	.500
Lofton, Chris	L-R	6-1	175	5-20-90	.268	.209	.284	52	198	32	53	5	2	2	16	22	3	0	0	41	15	5	.343	.350
Mach, Kyle	R-R	5-10	190	11-8-86	.184	.111	.198	48	158	16	29	7	1	0	11	4	4	2	1	15	3	0	.241	.222
Medina, Jose	R-R	6-0	180	11-29-86	.255	.264	.251	61	220	35	56	12	0	3	28	33	5	2	0	59	4	5	.350	.364
Murray, Mike	L-R	5-11	205	4-24-88	.319	.273	.328	20	69	9	22	3	0	7	8	8	0	0	0	12	0	0	.449	.390
Quintana, Carlos	R-R	6-3	180	6-14-87	.238	.241	.237	53	168	20	40	7	2	2	13	24	1	1	1	56	2	0	.339	.338
Rodriguez, Rafael	R-R	6-5	198	7-13-92	.163	.400	.091	12	43	3	7	0	1	0	4	3	2	0	0	12	1	0	.209	.250
Scoma, Ryan	R-L	6-2	180	9-12-87	.310	.273	.320	68	261	33	81	13	1	3	34	26	2	0	0	38	4	2	.402	.377
Shriner, Jesse	R-R	6-1	195	2-24-85	.247	.259	.243	29	97	17	24	10	0	3	14	16	2	0	1	22	0	1	.443	.362

Pitching	B-T	HT	WT	DOB	W	L	ERA	G	GS	CG	SV	IP	H	R	ER	HR	BB	SO	AVG	vLH	vRH	K/9	BB/9
Concepcion, Edward	R-R	6-3	190	10-3-88	3	7	6.39	16	14	0	0	63	63	54	45	6	46	57	.260	.273	.253	8.10	6.54
Couture, Kevin	R-R	6-0	170	4-20-88	3	4	4.97	11	7	0	0	38	37	23	21	3	8	31	.250	.328	.200	7.34	1.89
Downing, Kaohi	R-R	5-11	180	5-7-86	2	2	1.47	24	0	0	0	43	34	12	7	2	22	34	.224	.231	.220	7.12	4.60
Dunning, Jake	R-R	6-4	188	8-12-88	1	0	2.95	18	0	0	2	37	30	15	12	2	8	46	.221	.246	.203	11.29	1.96
Escobar, Edwin	L-L	6-1	185	4-22-92	2	4	4.86	14	14	0	0	63	64	40	34	6	40	69	.270	.200	.297	9.86	5.71
Flick, Brennan	R-R	6-1	180	9-12-89	1	0	5.11	14	0	0	1	25	32	18	14	4	11	26	.317	.400	.262	9.49	4.01
Graham, Matt	R-R	6-4	225	5-1-90	3	3	6.85	9	3	0	0	22	30	18	17	3	10	19	.323	.325	.321	7.66	4.03
Harrold, Stephen	R-R	6-1	200	3-12-89	1	1	2.78	18	0	0	7	23	17	8	7	2	5	28	.202	.370	.123	11.12	1.99
Kaufman, Shane	R-R	6-0	185	12-11-85	1	5	5.48	15	12	0	0	64	80	42	39	1	26	45	.308	.281	.333	6.33	3.66
King, Aaron	L-L	6-4	205	4-27-89	0	0	3.05	16	0	0	0	21	7	7	7	0	29	31	.111	.048	.143	13.50	12.63
Kline, Devan	R-R	6-1	195	10-15-87	0	1	9.82	5	0	0	1	7	9	8	8	1	3	7	.321	.333	.316	8.59	3.68
Lamb, Cameron	R-R	6-3	195	5-29-89	0	1	9.58	6	2	0	0	10	17	11	11	2	6	8	.395	.471	.346	6.97	5.23
Newton, David	R-R	5-11	195	3-4-86	0	0	11.81	5	0	0	0	5	10	7	7	0	2	7	.400	.571	.182	11.81	3.38
Proszek, A.J.	R-R	6-5	260	4-17-87	1	1	8.85	13	0	0	0	20	26	22	20	4	4	18	.310	.455	.216	7.97	1.77
Rodriguez, Mario	L-L	6-2	190	8-21-88	1	2	5.36	22	0	0	0	44	51	28	26	3	16	42	.302	.255	.322	8.66	3.30
Rogers, Taylor	R-R	6-4	200	6-5-87	6	7	4.46	16	16	0	0	83	98	51	41	6	25	49	.298	.353	.267	5.33	2.72
Romo, Andrew	R-R	6-1	230	6-20-87	2	2	2.19	12	0	0	1	25	20	6	6	1	5	23	.225	.216	.231	8.39	1.82
Rosin, Seth	R-R	6-5	235	11-2-88	1	1	4.91	6	1	0	0	11	9	6	6	0	1	9	.214	.364	.161	7.36	0.82
Sanford, Shawn	R-R	6-0	200	8-28-88	4	3	2.14	22	3	0	4	42	35	12	10	3	14	40	.227	.213	.237	8.57	3.00
Schumer, Justin	R-R	6-0	180	8-2-88	1	0	1.27	6	4	0	0	21	16	6	3	0	9	14	.208	.231	.196	5.91	3.80
Shackleford, Stephen	R-R	6-1	185	5-5-89	1	1	1.23	9	0	0	0	15	13	8	2	0	9	15	.228	.250	.216	9.20	5.52

Fielding

Catcher	PCT	G	PO	A	E	DP	PB
Arnold	.996	36	243	37	1	4	5
Burg	.987	17	133	18	2	0	6
Burkhart	.989	12	84	9	1	1	0
Dibbens	1.000	1	3	0	0	0	0
Murray	.974	10	71	3	2	1	2
Shriner	.968	12	88	4	3	1	7

First Base	PCT	G	PO	A	E	DP
Brock	.990	31	288	22	3	25
Burg	1.000	1	1	0	0	0
Duvall	1.000	1	1	0	0	0
Quintana	.993	50	420	32	3	28
Shriner	1.000	2	5	0	0	1

Second Base	PCT	G	PO	A	E	DP
Campbell	.946	24	52	71	7	17
Duvall	.972	26	53	87	4	10
Izturis	.942	35	71	107	11	14

Third Base	PCT	G	PO	A	E	DP
Campbell	.875	4	2	5	1	0
Duvall	.907	17	8	31	4	1
Eshleman	.885	17	6	40	6	2
Mach	.927	45	20	81	8	5

Shortstop	PCT	G	PO	A	E	DP
Eshleman	1.000	5	6	15	0	3
Izturis	.939	12	6	40	3	4
Jurica	.951	61	82	187	14	33

Mach	1.000	1	1	1	0	1

Outfield	PCT	G	PO	A	E	DP
Brown	1.000	5	13	0	0	0
Campbell	.941	17	13	3	1	0
Harris	1.000	20	35	1	0	0
Loberg	1.000	4	4	1	0	0
Lofton	.990	50	96	2	1	1
Medina	1.000	59	86	4	0	0
Quintana	.714	4	5	0	2	0
Rodriguez	1.000	12	4	0	0	0
Scoma	.978	63	85	5	2	0
Shriner	.941	11	16	0	1	0

SAN FRANCISCO GIANTS

SAN FRANCISCO GIANTS

Batting	B-T	HT	WT	DOB	AVG	vLH	vRH	G	AB	R	H	2B	3B	HR	RBI	BB	HBP	SH	SF	SO	SB	CS	SLG	OBP
Brown, Gary	R-R	6-0	170	9-28-88	.182	.500	.150	6	22	6	4	1	0	0	4	1	0	0	5	2	0	.227	.333
Burg, Alex	R-R	6-0	190	8-9-87	.333	.333	.333	4	15	3	5	3	0	0	2	1	1	0	0	1	0	0	.533	.412
Burkhart, Dan	L-R	5-11	215	3-6-89	.333	.000	.462	5	18	4	6	1	1	1	3	3	1	0	0	6	0	0	.667	.455
Cuevas, Jose	R-R	6-2	190	4-5-88	.206	.267	.188	37	131	22	27	5	0	2	19	7	3	0	0	23	2	5	.290	.262
Cutspec, Brice	L-R	6-4	250	12-7-87	.296	.219	.318	38	142	19	42	9	1	3	21	10	1	1	2	39	0	2	.437	.342
De La Cruz, Jose	R-R	6-3	190	4-28-91	.236	.276	.224	36	127	7	30	5	1	1	12	3	5	0	0	23	2	2	.315	.281
DeBerry, Johnathan	R-R	5-9	210	7-22-88	.255	.462	.190	25	55	14	14	2	0	0	3	6	2	2	0	17	4	1	.291	.349
Dibbens, Derek	L-R	6-0	200	8-7-87	.353	.600	.310	12	34	4	12	1	0	0	1	2	0	1	0	7	0	0	.382	.395
Downs, Matt	R-R	6-2	190	3-19-84	.286	1.000	.167	2	7	1	2	1	0	0	2	1	0	0	0	1	0	0	.429	.375
Eshleman, John	R-R	6-0	185	4-8-89	.220	.294	.190	18	59	7	13	3	1	0	7	6	1	1	2	18	2	1	.305	.294
Haney, Bobby	L-R	6-0	147	8-16-88	.239	.200	.250	20	71	7	17	2	1	0	10	4	1	2	2	11	1	1	.296	.282
Harris, Devin	R-R	6-3	225	4-23-88	.275	.357	.243	14	51	7	14	3	0	1	6	5	1	0	0	14	3	0	.392	.351
Hobson, Wes	L-R	6-0	187	11-12-87	.288	.290	.287	34	139	22	40	6	4	1	17	12	0	1	1	24	4	2	.410	.342
Honeycutt, Ryan	L-R	6-0	195	9-6-88	.213	.333	.195	18	47	6	10	3	0	1	8	6	0	0	2	12	1	1	.340	.291
Jones, Chuckie	R-R	6-3	235	7-28-92	.279	.231	.294	46	165	25	46	7	4	5	17	20	2	1	2	61	6	2	.461	.360
Lopez, Josh	R-R	5-9	170	1-31-89	.204	.235	.197	35	93	20	19	4	4	1	8	9	2	2	1	32	4	3	.366	.286
Murray, Mike	L-R	5-11	205	4-24-88	.400	.385	.412	9	30	4	12	3	0	0	6	0	0	0	0	3	0	0	.500	.400
Navarro, Jesus	R-R	6-0	180	1-3-88	—	.000	.000	1	0	0	0	0	0	0	0	0	0	0	0	0	0	0	—	—
Nordgren, Nick	B-R	6-3	170	1-6-87	.143	.000	.182	9	28	2	4	1	0	0	3	3	1	0	2	7	2	0	.179	.235
Rodriguez, Rafael	R-R	6-5	198	7-13-92	.301	.258	.315	32	123	20	37	6	0	2	14	5	1	0	4	23	4	2	.398	.323
Rohlinger, Ryan	R-R	6-1	195	10-7-83	.444	.333	.500	3	9	5	4	0	0	3	0	0	0	0	0	2	1	0	1.444	.444
Salters, Carlton	R-R	5-11	200	9-15-87	.250	.000	.250	4	8	1	2	0	0	0	0	0	0	0	0	3	0	0	.250	.250
Sim, Eric	R-R	6-2	215	1-3-89	.108	.429	.033	11	37	2	4	0	0	0	1	2	3	1	0	8	0	0	.108	.214
Staley, Joe	R-R	6-3	185	9-29-88	.250	.483	.179	33	124	17	31	9	1	5	25	9	3	0	2	35	2	1	.460	.312
Willoughby, Carlos	B-R	5-10	170	11-12-88	.295	.281	.299	45	176	34	52	9	6	1	24	17	5	6	1	36	23	4	.432	.372
Windster, Sundrendy	R-R	6-3	185	2-23-89	.311	.250	.329	31	106	18	33	11	2	5	19	18	1	0	0	28	3	2	.594	.416

Pitching	B-T	HT	WT	DOB	W	L	ERA	G	GS	CG	SV	IP	H	R	ER	HR	BB	SO	AVG	vLH	vRH	K/9	BB/9
Allen, Brandon	R-R	6-6	190	8-15-91	0	0	7.94	5	0	0	0	6	8	5	5	0	4	6	.308	.500	.143	9.53	6.35
Altemus, Andy	R-R	6-4	180	4-12-88	1	2	4.87	17	1	0	0	20	27	11	11	1	5	10	.321	.432	.234	4.43	2.21
Bean, Ryan	R-R	6-4	225	3-9-90	1	0	1.47	19	0	0	0	18	11	4	3	0	8	25	.175	.150	.186	12.27	3.93
Bradley, Ryan	B-L	6-1	180	7-15-88	3	1	6.62	18	0	0	0	18	27	16	13	1	9	18	.342	.462	.283	9.17	4.58
Dunnington, Jacob	L-R	6-2	160	2-2-91	3	0	0.63	17	0	0	3	29	10	2	2	0	15	45	.109	.139	.089	14.13	4.71
Fleet, Austin	R-R	6-1	175	4-17-87	6	3	2.65	12	11	0	0	51	42	18	15	2	8	65	.222	.221	.223	11.47	1.41
Flick, Brennan	R-R	6-1	180	9-12-89	0	0	2.35	7	0	0	0	8	7	4	2	0	3	10	.241	.154	.313	11.74	3.52
Flores, Kendry	R-R	6-2	175	11-24-91	5	4	3.60	13	11	0	0	55	49	27	22	2	13	56	.241	.278	.221	9.16	2.13
Graham, Matt	R-R	6-4	225	5-1-90	1	0	5.63	6	0	0	0	8	8	5	5	0	5	8	.267	.357	.188	9.00	5.63
Harrold, Stephen	R-R	6-1	200	3-12-89	1	0	0.00	4	0	0	0	7	5	0	0	0	2	6	.200	.250	.176	7.36	2.45
Hembree, Heath	R-R	6-4	210	1-13-89	0	0	0.82	12	0	0	3	11	9	1	1	0	0	22	.220	.417	.138	18.00	0.00
Joaquin, Waldis	R-R	6-2	235	12-25-86	0	0	1.50	4	0	0	0	6	3	1	1	0	3	7	.143	.222	.083	10.50	4.50
Kickham, Mike	R-R	6-4	205	12-12-88	0	0	11.57	3	0	0	0	2	4	3	3	0	2	3	.400	.667	.000	11.57	7.71
Kline, Devan	R-R	6-1	195	10-15-87	0	1	14.54	5	0	0	0	4	10	10	7	1	4	8	.435	.400	.462	16.62	8.31
Marte, Kelvin	R-R	6-0	180	11-24-87	0	0	3.52	6	0	0	0	8	10	5	3	0	2	8	.333	.500	.273	10.57	2.35
Martinez, Rafael	R-R	6-3	185	7-9-88	1	0	4.15	11	0	0	2	13	13	6	6	2	3	11	.260	.471	.152	7.62	2.08
McCulley, Reese	L-R	6-3	210	6-8-88	0	0	8.10	5	0	0	0	3	2	4	3	1	4	7	.167	.000	.222	18.90	10.80
Mendoza, Lorenzo	R-R	5-10	190	8-6-91	0	4	3.50	13	12	0	0	44	53	23	17	2	9	32	.301	.275	.318	6.60	1.85
Montero, Raymundo	R-R	6-2	185	9-20-89	1	1	2.70	18	0	0	1	17	14	5	5	0	6	17	.226	.263	.209	9.18	3.24
Newton, David	R-R	5-11	195	3-4-86	0	0	1.80	5	0	0	0	5	3	1	1	0	2	6	.176	.250	.154	10.80	3.60
Otero, Danny	R-R	6-3	205	2-19-85	2	0	0.00	9	0	0	1	11	7	4	0	0	1	7	.179	.133	.208	5.91	0.84
Paniagua, Armando	R-R	5-11	155	1-11-90	1	1	5.13	10	9	0	0	33	41	20	19	0	15	30	.308	.268	.338	8.10	4.05
Proszek, A.J.	R-R	6-5	260	4-17-87	0	0	4.15	4	0	0	0	4	4	2	2	0	2	6	.250	.167	.300	12.46	4.15
Roibal, Reinier	R-R	6-2	215	1-19-89	2	0	2.08	9	0	0	0	8	9	3	2	0	5	14	.250	.417	.150	14.54	5.19
Runzler, Dan	L-L	6-4	230	3-30-85	0	0	0.00	1	1	0	0	2	0	0	0	0	0	4	.000	.000	.000	18.00	0.00
Santiago, Gaspar	L-L	6-0	200	9-23-89	1	1	3.00	13	2	0	0	15	16	6	5	0	7	15	.262	.294	.250	9.00	4.20
Schumer, Justin	R-R	6-0	180	8-2-88	1	0	0.00	3	1	0	0	6	3	0	0	0	4	4	.150	.125	.167	6.35	6.35
Shackleford, Stephen	R-R	6-1	185	5-5-89	1	1	1.89	12	0	0	1	19	11	4	4	0	5	26	.169	.174	.167	12.32	2.37
Shadle, Jake	R-R	6-2	175	4-25-90	1	0	7.29	15	1	0	1	21	25	18	17	2	13	30	.298	.265	.320	12.86	5.57
Walls, Jason	R-R	6-5	205	2-22-88	2	0	6.75	14	0	0	0	15	14	11	11	1	20	11	.255	.273	.242	6.75	12.27
Wellemeyer, Todd	R-R	6-3	225	8-30-78	0	0	6.75	1	1	0	0	3	3	2	2	1	1	3	.273	.500	.143	10.13	3.38
Willis, Dontrelle	L-L	6-4	225	1-12-82	0	1	9.00	3	0	0	0	2	4	2	2	1	1	1	.400	1.000	.333	4.50	4.50
Wilson, Chris	R-R	6-2	205	11-27-86	0	0	1.42	6	0	0	1	6	2	2	1	1	0	10	.091	.000	.133	14.21	0.00

Fielding

Catcher	PCT	G	PO	A	E	DP	PB
Burg	.973	3	32	4	1	0	0
Burkhart	1.000	2	16	0	0	0	0
Dibbens	1.000	10	66	6	0	0	2
Murray	1.000	3	13	4	0	0	1
Navarro	1.000	1	1	0	0	0	0
Sim	.984	11	113	13	2	0	3
Staley	.991	29	290	32	3	4	2

First Base	PCT	G	PO	A	E	DP
Cuevas	.958	8	42	4	2	3
Cutspec	.986	37	265	23	4	23
Dibbens	1.000	1	1	0	0	0
Hobson	1.000	1	10	1	0	0
Windster	.974	14	103	8	3	13

Second Base	PCT	G	PO	A	E	DP
Hobson	1.000	9	18	27	0	11

Lopez	.833	5	2	8	2	0
Willoughby	.980	42	73	119	4	22

Third Base	PCT	G	PO	A	E	DP
Cuevas	.897	14	5	21	3	0
Downs	1.000	1	2	2	0	0
Eshleman	.909	6	2	8	1	0
Hobson	.925	14	10	27	3	0
Lopez	.915	22	12	31	4	4

Shortstop	PCT	G	PO	A	E	DP
Cuevas	.938	16	24	37	4	8
Downs	1.000	1	1	3	0	1
Eshleman	.933	12	24	32	4	8
Haney	.938	20	31	60	6	10
Lopez	1.000	5	2	7	0	2

Rohlinger	1.000	3	4	4	0	0

Outfield	PCT	G	PO	A	E	DP
Brown	1.000	5	5	1	0	0
De La Cruz	.930	30	37	3	3	1
DeBerry	.947	22	18	0	1	0
Harris	.897	12	26	0	3	0

Honeycutt	.850	16	14	3	3	0
Jones	.923	45	68	4	6	0
Nordgren	1.000	5	7	0	0	0
Rodriguez	.958	32	45	1	2	0
Salters	—	1	0	0	0	0
Windster	1.000	11	20	2	0	0

DSL GIANTS
ROOKIE

DOMINICAN SUMMER LEAGUE

Batting	B-T	HT	WT	DOB	AVG	vLH	vRH	G	AB	R	H	2B	3B	HR	RBI	BB	HBP	SH	SF	SO	SB	CS	SLG	OBP
Cedeno, Jose	R-R	6-0	185	5-30-90	.207	.000	.228	32	87	12	18	2	0	1	5	10	7	2	1	27	1	2	.264	.333
Cornier, Gabriel	B-R	6-0	190	6-10-92	.269	.381	.250	42	130	23	35	6	1	0	16	22	2	1	1	32	6	2	.331	.381
Feliz, Victor	R-R	6-0	185	11-23-90	.301	.289	.294	56	176	36	53	9	3	0	20	25	8	0	4	45	9	4	.386	.404
Fuentes, Leonardo	R-R	6-4	215	11-29-92	.240	.321	.224	61	200	32	48	14	1	4	33	25	7	0	3	73	3	5	.380	.340
Galindo, Jesus	B-R	5-11	175	8-23-90	.246	.185	.257	63	167	46	41	6	0	0	23	35	4	1	2	30	43	7	.281	.385
Lopez, Eduardo	L-L	6-0	185	2-23-91	.256	.200	.269	23	82	18	21	6	0	1	14	8	3	1	1	20	5	2	.366	.340
Lopez, Jorge	R-R	6-2	180	9-9-91	.237	.321	.211	45	152	26	36	6	3	1	24	18	2	1	1	41	7	4	.336	.324
Mercedes, Hector	R-R	6-3	188	10-5-91	.211	.205	.214	53	194	16	41	1	1	1	19	12	2	0	1	68	1	4	.242	.263
Mujica, Shurendell	R-R	6-1	158	0-0-00	.219	.135	.235	60	192	35	42	1	4	0	13	25	8	6	1	47	22	6	.266	.332
Paulino, Cristian	R-R	5-10	168	9-4-91	.251	.222	.255	59	215	33	54	10	0	3	38	20	7	2	6	51	19	6	.340	.327
Pujadas, Fernando	R-R	6-1	179	1-2-92	.289	.353	.271	26	76	12	22	6	0	2	16	8	2	0	0	8	0	2	.447	.372
Robles, Alberto	R-R	5-11	155	9-14-90	.263	.289	.256	69	247	50	65	6	3	0	24	31	10	5	1	23	20	8	.312	.367
Soto, Cesar	B-R	5-11	170	4-17-91	.226	.219	.230	62	168	23	38	3	0	0	19	34	2	9	1	35	0	2	.244	.361
Vasquez, Luis	L-R	5-10	170	3-20-91	.281	.273	.279	35	128	14	36	6	0	2	26	16	1	0	3	26	1	1	.375	.358

Pitching	B-T	HT	WT	DOB	W	L	ERA	G	GS	CG	SV	IP	H	R	ER	HR	BB	SO	AVG	vLH	vRH	K/9	BB/9
Angeles, Luis	R-R	6-0	165	12-15-89	8	3	1.85	14	13	1	0	78	55	25	16	2	16	56	.199	.156	.220	6.49	1.85
Barrios, Marvin	R-R	6-3	145	9-23-92	2	2	1.87	13	2	0	2	34	26	18	7	0	9	30	.210	.214	.207	8.02	2.41
Feliz, Keurin	R-L	6-0	180	8-17-90	7	2	1.75	11	10	0	0	62	52	15	12	2	17	40	.244	.227	.246	5.84	2.48
Fernandez, Ebert	L-L	6-3	192	10-28-90	5	1	3.38	13	0	0	2	27	28	14	10	0	15	15	.269	.273	.269	5.06	5.06
Ferrer, Miguel	R-R	6-3	168	8-7-90	1	3	2.37	20	2	0	10	38	32	13	10	2	17	29	.232	.200	.247	6.87	4.03
Freite, Renzo	R-R	6-1	170	0-0-00	3	0	1.82	10	1	0	1	25	21	7	5	1	7	15	.239	.318	.212	5.47	2.55
Garcia, Alexis	R-R	6-4	170	1-17-92	0	1	10.50	6	0	0	0	6	4	9	7	0	11	0	.174	.000	.235	0.00	16.50
Garcia, Bertoni	R-R	5-11	173	7-8-91	0	0	3.08	9	2	0	2	26	22	15	9	2	14	22	.232	.294	.218	7.52	4.78
Gregorio, Joan	R-R	6-7	180	1-12-92	6	3	2.80	14	14	0	0	74	65	26	23	1	17	41	.242	.313	.202	4.99	2.07
Hernandez, Ariel	R-R	6-3	180	3-2-92	2	0	2.01	9	7	0	0	31	7	11	7	0	33	30	.077	.133	.066	8.62	9.48
Martinez, Yeini	R-R	6-3	186	11-29-90	3	3	2.40	13	4	0	1	45	36	19	12	0	14	24	.213	.286	.189	4.80	2.80
Minier, Gregorio	R-R	6-0	170	2-20-92	0	0	16.71	6	0	0	0	7	7	13	13	1	8	2	.269	.250	.286	2.57	10.29
Noel, Franklin	L-L	6-1	175	12-20-88	3	0	0.64	14	0	0	0	28	21	9	2	0	9	28	.202	.182	.204	9.00	2.89
Nova, Juan	R-R	6-3	190	10-7-91	3	4	3.04	13	12	1	0	56	50	25	19	3	28	45	.246	.238	.250	7.19	4.47
Reyes, Jose	R-R	6-1	184	1-3-91	2	2	3.34	12	4	0	1	35	30	16	13	0	12	19	.240	.235	.242	4.89	3.09
Utria, Luis	L-L	5-11	170	9-9-92	1	1	3.72	9	0	0	2	29	25	13	12	2	19	19	.231	.188	.239	5.90	4.03

Fielding

Catcher	PCT	G	PO	A	E	DP	PB
Cornier	.982	41	233	42	5	0	5
Pujadas	.983	17	96	19	2	1	4
Vasquez	.983	16	101	15	2	4	6

First Base	PCT	G	PO	A	E	DP
Cedeno	.992	29	230	7	2	32
Feliz	.978	25	213	12	5	26
Paulino	1.000	1	2	1	0	0
Pujadas	1.000	1	1	1	0	0
Robles	1.000	2	2	0	0	0
Soto	1.000	26	189	17	0	13

Second Base	PCT	G	PO	A	E	DP
Mujica	.973	8	17	19	1	4
Paulino	.938	36	99	114	14	31
Robles	.991	24	51	56	1	11
Soto	.967	12	25	34	2	7

Third Base	PCT	G	PO	A	E	DP
Paulino	.954	24	17	45	3	4
Robles	.896	25	16	44	7	5
Soto	.971	29	23	43	2	9

Shortstop	PCT	G	PO	A	E	DP
Mujica	.946	52	81	163	14	29

Robles	.894	24	42	85	15	17

Outfield	PCT	G	PO	A	E	DP
Cedeno	—	1	0	0	0	0
Feliz	1.000	1	1	1	0	0
Fuentes	1.000	51	65	10	0	2
Galindo	.983	63	109	8	2	0
Lopez	.938	13	13	2	1	0
Lopez	1.000	43	61	1	0	0
Mercedes	.976	51	75	6	2	1

Seattle Mariners

SEASON IN A SENTENCE: Nothing went right in Seattle in 2010, on the field or off it, as the Mariners scored just 513 runs, fewest of any American League team in the DH era (since 1973) and virtually every Mariners player not named Ichiro Suzuki or Felix Hernandez performed below expectations.

HIGH POINT: With a hit on Sept. 23, Ichiro became the first player in major league history to record 200 hits in 10 consecutive seasons, surpassing Ty Cobb's American League record for 200-hit seasons. Hernandez stated his case for the AL Cy Young Award with consistent excellence, with a two-hit shutout at Yankee Stadium on June 30 standing as his best single-game effort.

LOW POINT: Take your pick. Was it Sleepgate, when a newspaper article alleged that Ken Griffey Jr. was asleep in the clubhouse when manager Don Wakamatsu needed him to pinch-hit? Griffey retired soon thereafter, while Wakamatsu was fired on Aug. 5. For a longer stretch, try July, when the Mariners went 6-22 and wound up trading Cliff Lee late in the month to the Rangers.

NOTABLE ROOKIES: First baseman Justin Smoak, the key player the Rangers sent to Seattle in the Lee trade, righted himself with a solid September after a tepid start and will be a centerpiece to the organization's rebuilding effort. Catcher Adam Moore struggled mightily, while righthander David Pauley, 27, was modestly capable in 15 starts in his first extended look.

KEY TRANSACTIONS: The Lee trade proved to be another low point, as the Mariners endured a public-relations disaster over one of the players they acquired, righthander Josh Lueke. Lueke missed most of the 2009 season after being charged with rape while playing for high Class A Bakersfield. While Lueke pleaded guilty to a lesser charge, the Mariners badly mishandled their explanation of what they knew about Lueke and when. Pro scouting director Carmen Fusco was fired, taking the fall for the Lueke trade and a bevy of moves that didn't work out.

DOWN ON THE FARM: Seattle affiliates posted a .530 winning percentage, and Triple-A Tacoma—featuring prospects such as 2009 first-rounder Dustin Ackley and righthander Michael Pineda—won the Triple-A National Championship. Six of the seven domestic affiliates went to the playoffs, and short-season Everett won the Northwest League crown.

OPENING DAY PAYROLL: $86.5 million (14th)

ORGANIZATION LEADERS

BATTING		*Minimum 250 at-bats
MAJORS		
*AVG	Ichiro Suzuki	.315
*OPS	Ichiro Suzuki	.754
HR	Russell Branyan	15
RBI	Franklin Gutierrez	64
MINORS		
*AVG	Kyle Seager, High Desert	.345
*OBP	Kyle Seager, High Desert	.419
*SLG	Rich Poythress, High Desert	.580
R	Kyle Seager, High Desert	126
H	Kyle Seager, High Desert	192
TB	Johermyn Chavez, High Desert	308
2B	Vincent Catricala, Clinton	41
	Johan Limonta, West Tenn	41
3B	James Jones, Clinton	10
	Nate Tenbrink, High Desert/West Tenn	10
HR	Greg Halman, Tacoma	33
RBI	Rich Poythress, High Desert	130
BB	Dustin Ackley, Jackson/Tacoma	75
SO	Denny Almonte, High Desert	192
SB	Randy Perez, DSL Mariners	31
PITCHING		†Minimum 75 innings
MAJORS		
W	Felix Hernandez	13
†ERA	Felix Hernandez	2.27
SO	Felix Hernandez	232
MINORS		
W	Taylor Stanton, Clinton	12
L	Steve Bray, Tacoma/West Tenn	12
†ERA	Anthony Vasquez, Clinton/H.D./West Tenn	2.46
G	Brandon Josselyn, Clinton	52
GS	James Gillheeney, Clinton/H.D./West Tenn	28
SV	Brandon Josselyn, Clinton	15
IP	Anthony Vasquez, Clinton/H.D./West Tenn	171.7
BB	Mauricio Robles, West Tenn/Tacoma	71
SO	Michael Pineda, West Tenn/Tacoma	154
	Mauricio Robles, West Tenn/Tacoma	154
†AVG	Michael Pineda, West Tenn/Tacoma	.227

2010 PERFORMANCE

General Manager: Jack Zdurienci k. **Farm Director:** Pedro Grifol. **Scouting Director:** Tom McNamara.

Class	Team	League	W	L	PCT	Finish*	Manager(s)
Majors	Seattle Mariners	American	61	101	.377	14th (14)	Don Wakamatsu/Daren Brown
Triple-A	Tacoma Rainiers	Pacific Coast	74	69	.517	†7th (16)	Daren Brown/Jose Castro
Double-A	West Tenn Diamond Jaxx	Southern	73	66	.525	4th (10)	Tim Laker
High A	High Desert Mavericks	California	75	65	.536	4th (10)	Jim Horner/Darrin Garner
Low A	Clinton LumberKings	Midwest	74	65	.532	6th (16)	John Tamargo
Short-season	Everett AquaSox	Northwest	49	27	.645	†1st (8)	Jose Moreno
Rookie	Pulaski Mariners	Appalachian	37	28	.569	3rd (10)	Eddie Menchaca
Rookie	AZL Mariners	Arizona	20	36	.357	11th (12)	Jesus Azuaje
Overall 2010 Minor League Record			402	356	.530	5th (30)	

*Finish in overall standings (No. of teams in league). †League champion.

ORGANIZATION STATISTICS

SEATTLE MARINERS
AMERICAN LEAGUE

Batting	B-T	HT	WT	DOB	AVG	vLH	vRH	G	AB	R	H	2B	3B	HR	RBI	BB	HBP	SH	SF	SO	SB	CS	SLG	OBP
Alfonzo, Eliezer	R-R	5-11	220	2-7-79	.220	.188	.240	13	41	4	9	1	0	1	4	0	0	0	0	10	0	0	.317	.220
Bard, Josh	B-R	6-3	225	3-30-78	.214	.283	.167	39	112	9	24	7	0	3	10	10	0	3	1	27	0	0	.357	.276
Bradley, Milton	B-R	6-0	215	4-15-78	.205	.235	.190	73	244	28	50	9	1	8	29	28	3	1	2	75	8	2	.348	.292
Branyan, Russell	L-R	6-3	230	12-19-75	.215	.180	.229	57	205	23	44	10	0	15	33	30	2	0	1	82	1	0	.483	.319
2-team total (52 Cleveland)					.237	—		109	376	47	89	19	0	25	57	46	3	1	2	131	1	0	.487	.323
Byrnes, Eric	R-R	6-2	205	2-16-76	.094	.000	.158	15	32	1	3	2	0	0	6	4	0	0	0	9	1	0	.156	.237
Carp, Mike	L-R	6-2	215	6-30-86	.189	.222	.179	14	37	1	7	2	0	0	4	4	0	0	0	8	0	0	.243	.268
Figgins, Chone	B-R	5-8	180	1-22-78	.259	.286	.247	161	602	62	156	21	2	1	35	74	3	17	6	114	42	15	.306	.340
Griffey Jr., Ken	L-L	6-2	230	11-21-69	.184	.250	.174	33	98	6	18	2	0	0	7	9	0	0	1	17	0	0	.204	.250
Gutierrez, Franklin	R-R	6-2	190	2-21-83	.245	.248	.744	152	568	61	139	25	3	12	64	50	1	2	8	137	25	3	.363	.303
Halman, Greg	R-R	6-4	200	8-26-87	.138	.286	.000	9	29	1	4	1	0	0	3	1	0	0	0	11	1	0	.172	.167
Johnson, Rob	R-R	6-1	215	7-22-82	.191	.184	.193	61	178	24	34	10	0	2	13	25	2	1	3	46	1	1	.281	.293
Kotchman, Casey	L-L	6-3	215	2-22-83	.217	.179	.231	125	414	37	90	20	1	9	51	35	3	0	5	57	0	0	.336	.280
Langerhans, Ryan	L-L	6-3	220	2-20-80	.196	.091	.243	60	107	16	21	2	1	3	4	24	0	1	0	51	4	1	.318	.344
Lopez, Jose	R-R	6-0	205	11-24-83	.239	.27	.226	150	593	49	142	29	0	10	58	23	3	0	3	66	3	2	.339	.270
Mangini, Matt	L-R	6-4	230	12-21-85	.211	.133	.261	11	38	2	8	0	0	1	2	0	1	0	0	13	0	0	.211	.250
Moore, Adam	R-R	6-3	220	5-8-84	.195	.212	.190	60	205	12	40	6	0	4	15	8	2	1	2	63	0	1	.283	.230
Quiroz, Guillermo	R-R	6-1	215	11-29-81	.286	.333	.250	2	7	1	2	1	0	0	0	0	0	0	0	1	0	0	.429	.286
Saunders, Michael	L-R	6-4	210	11-19-86	.211	.202	.215	100	289	29	61	11	2	10	33	35	0	2	1	84	6	3	.367	.295
Smoak, Justin	B-L	6-4	220	12-5-86	.239	.357	.169	30	113	11	27	4	0	5	14	8	0	0	1	34	0	0	.407	.287
2-team total (70 Texas)					.218	—		100	348	40	76	14	0	13	48	46	0	0	3	91	1	0	.371	.307
Suzuki, Ichiro	L-R	5-11	170	10-22-73	.315	.309	.318	162	680	74	214	30	3	6	43	45	3	3	1	86	42	9	.394	.359
Sweeney, Mike	R-R	6-3	225	7-22-73	.263	.227	.291	30	99	11	26	3	0	6	18	9	1	0	1	14	2	0	.475	.327
Tuiasosopo, Matt	R-R	6-2	225	5-10-86	.173	.133	.195	50	127	12	22	5	0	4	11	9	1	1	0	49	0	0	.307	.234
Wilson, Jack	R-R	6-0	200	12-29-77	.249	.264	.243	61	193	17	48	11	1	0	14	7	3	5	3	35	1	2	.316	.282
Wilson, Josh	R-R	6-0	175	3-26-81	.227	.196	.239	108	361	22	82	14	2	2	25	14	12	0	1	74	5	0	.294	.278
Woodward, Chris	R-R	6-0	190	6-27-76	.158	.333	.077	8	19	0	3	1	0	0	3	0	0	0	0	9	0	0	.211	.273

Pitching	B-T	HT	WT	DOB	W	L	ERA	G	GS	CG	SV	IP	H	R	ER	HR	BB	SO	AVG	vLH	vRH	K/9	BB/9
Aardsma, David	R-R	6-3	205	12-27-81	0	6	3.44	53	0	0	31	50	33	19	19	5	25	49	.198	.244	.148	8.88	4.53
Colome, Jesus	R-R	6-2	240	12-23-77	0	1	5.29	12	0	0	0	17	15	10	10	1	11	16	.242	.294	.179	8.47	5.82
Cordero, Chad	R-R	6-0	220	3-18-82	0	1	6.52	9	0	0	0	10	10	7	7	1	5	6	.313	.294	.333	5.59	4.66
Cortes, Danny	R-R	6-6	230	3-4-87	0	1	3.38	4	0	0	0	5	3	3	2	0	3	6	.158	.222	.100	10.13	5.06
Fister, Doug	L-R	6-8	195	2-4-84	6	14	4.11	28	28	0	0	171	187	85	78	13	32	93	.277	.274	.279	4.89	1.68
French, Luke	L-L	6-4	220	9-13-85	5	7	4.83	16	13	0	0	88	88	47	47	13	29	37	.262	.256	.264	3.80	2.98
Hernandez, Felix	R-R	6-3	225	4-8-86	13	12	2.27	34	34	6	0	250	194	80	63	17	70	232	.212	.213	.212	8.36	2.52
Kelley, Shawn	R-R	6-2	215	4-26-84	3	1	3.96	22	0	0	0	25	26	11	11	5	12	26	.265	.261	.269	9.36	4.32
League, Brandon	R-R	6-2	205	3-16-83	9	7	3.42	70	0	0	6	79	67	38	30	7	27	56	.229	.243	.218	6.38	3.08
Lee, Cliff	L-L	6-3	190	8-30-78	8	3	2.34	13	13	5	0	104	92	31	27	5	6	89	.231	.287	.214	7.73	0.52
2-team total (15 Texas)					12	9	3.18	28	28	7	0	212	195	84	75	16	18	185	—			7.84	0.76
Lowe, Mark	L-R	6-3	210	6-7-83	1	3	3.48	11	0	0	0	10	11	5	4	1	5	7	.282	.400	.208	6.10	4.35
2-team total (3 Texas)					1	3	5.40	14	0	0	0	13	18	9	8	2	6	12	—			8.10	4.05
Olson, Garrett	R-L	6-1	205	10-18-83	0	3	4.54	35	0	0	1	38	42	20	19	6	15	31	.271	.245	.284	7.41	3.58
Pauley, David	R-R	6-2	210	6-17-83	4	9	4.07	19	15	0	0	91	89	44	41	13	30	51	.254	.247	.261	5.06	2.98
Rowland-Smith, Ryan	L-L	6-3	240	1-26-83	1	10	6.75	27	20	0	0	109	141	94	82	25	44	49	.314	.342	.304	4.03	3.62
Seddon, Chris	L-L	6-3	220	10-13-83	0	1	5.64	14	0	0	0	22	21	14	14	4	10	16	.250	.276	.236	6.45	4.03
Snell, Ian	R-R	5-11	200	10-30-81	0	5	6.41	12	8	0	0	46	60	36	33	10	25	26	.308	.302	.313	5.05	4.86
Sweeney, Brian	R-R	6-2	200	6-13-74	1	2	3.16	24	0	0	0	37	33	16	13	5	6	14	.239	.308	.198	3.41	1.46
Texeira, Kanekoa	R-R	6-2	200	2-6-86	0	1	5.30	16	0	0	0	19	22	12	11	0	10	14	.293	.270	.316	6.75	4.82
2-team total (27 Kansas City)					1	1	4.84	43	0	0	0	61	73	36	33	3	25	33	—			4.84	3.67
Vargas, Jason	L-L	6-0	215	2-2-83	9	12	3.78	31	31	0	0	193	187	86	81	18	54	116	.251	.200	.268	5.42	2.52
Varvaro, Anthony	R-R	6-0	195	10-31-84	0	1	11.25	4	0	0	0	4	5	5	5	2	6	5	.333	.200	.385	11.25	13.50
White, Sean	R-R	6-4	215	4-25-81	1	0	5.24	38	0	0	0	34	45	20	20	4	11	15	.336	.357	.321	3.93	2.88

Wright, Jamey	R-R	6-6	230	12-24-74	0	1	3.41	28	0	0	0	37	30	15	14	2	16	19	.231	.153	.296	4.62	3.89
2-team total (18 Cleveland)					1	3	4.17	46	0	0	0	58	55	33	27	3	25	28	—	—	—	4.32	3.86

Fielding

Catcher	PCT	G	PO	A	E	DP	PB
Alfonzo	.966	12	54	2	2	0	0
Bard	.991	39	202	12	2	0	0
Johnson	.990	61	347	35	4	5	9
Moore	.990	59	372	24	4	1	7
Quiroz	.900	2	8	1	1	0	0

First Base	PCT	G	PO	A	E	DP
Branyan	1.000	4	32	1	0	2
Carp	1.000	9	65	4	0	3
Kotchman	.999	116	946	74	1	92
Langerhans	1.000	6	28	2	0	4
Smoak	.996	25	233	15	1	18
Sweeney	1.000	3	28	1	0	1
Tuiasosopo	.985	9	65	2	1	8

	PCT	G	PO	A	E	DP	PB
Wilson	.970	3	30	2	1		4

Second Base	PCT	G	PO	A	E	DP
Figgins	.973	161	274	414	19	110
Tuiasosopo	.500	2	0	1	1	0
Wilson	1.000	2	6	5	0	4

Third Base	PCT	G	PO	A	E	DP
Lopez	.960	142	107	322	18	29
Mangini	1.000	7	4	14	0	3
Tuiasosopo	.941	12	8	24	2	0
Wilson	.909	4	2	8	1	1

Shortstop	PCT	G	PO	A	E	DP
Tuiasosopo	.895	6	6	11	2	2
Wilson	.972	60	88	191	8	36

	PCT	G	PO	A	E	DP
Wilson	.955	98	124	304	20	53
Woodward	.938	7	5	10	1	1

Outfield	PCT	G	PO	A	E	DP
Bradley	.978	40	88	3	2	0
Byrnes	1.000	11	28	0	0	0
Carp	—	1	0	0	0	0
Gutierrez	1.000	146	413	2	0	0
Halman	1.000	9	20	0	0	0
Langerhans	.986	40	67	5	1	0
Saunders	.981	89	197	8	4	4
Suzuki	.989	160	354	7	4	1
Tuiasosopo	.957	14	21	1	1	0

TACOMA RAINIERS — TRIPLE-A
PACIFIC COAST LEAGUE

Batting	B-T	HT	WT	DOB	AVG	vLH	vRH	G	AB	R	H	2B	3B	HR	RBI	BB	HBP	SH	SF	SO	SB	CS	SLG	OBP
Ackley, Dustin	L-R	6-1	185	2-26-88	.274	.192	.300	52	212	37	58	12	4	5	23	20	2	0	3	38	2	1	.439	.338
Alfonzo, Eliezer	R-R	5-11	220	2-7-79	.253	.200	.266	48	174	23	44	9	2	9	23	8	4	0	2	48	0	1	.483	.298
Bard, Josh	B-R	6-3	225	3-30-78	.235	.278	.204	24	85	7	20	6	0	3	15	7	0	0	3	18	0	0	.412	.284
Carp, Mike	L-R	6-2	215	6-30-86	.257	.170	.283	110	409	67	105	17	1	29	76	41	6	0	7	93	1	2	.516	.328
Carrera, Ezequiel	L-L	5-10	185	6-11-87	.268	.302	.253	64	213	24	57	6	2	0	18	20	3	7	0	32	9	5	.315	.339
Denker, Travis	R-R	5-9	205	8-5-85	.176	.333	.143	7	17	1	3	2	0	0	0	3	0	0	0	3	0	1	.294	.300
2-team total (13 Albuquerque)					.222	—		20	54	5	12	3	1	1	6	5	1	0	0	10	1	1	.370	.300
Dominguez, Jeff	B-R	6-2	160	7-31-86	.227	.233	.224	29	88	7	20	2	1	1	2	8	1	1	0	25	1	1	.307	.299
Everidge, Tommy	R-R	6-0	275	4-20-83	.229	.206	.238	65	249	28	57	18	0	7	36	27	1	0	2	62	0	0	.386	.305
3-team total (30 Round Rock, 7 Sacramento)				.249	—		102	390	48	97	22	0	13	57	40	3	0	4	95	0	0	.405	.320
Halman, Greg	R-R	6-4	200	8-26-87	.243	.246	.242	112	424	82	103	21	4	33	80	37	4	0	0	169	15	4	.545	.310
Hannahan, Jack	L-R	6-2	210	3-4-80	.228	.125	.269	63	224	32	51	9	1	5	33	34	2	1	3	55	1	0	.344	.331
Hulett, Tug	L-R	5-10	185	2-28-83	.318	.143	.365	19	66	11	21	6	1	3	12	7	1	1	1	11	0	2	.545	.387
Johnson, Rob	R-R	6-1	215	7-22-82	.297	.353	.277	19	64	9	19	7	0	1	8	10	2	0	1	12	0	0	.453	.403
Langerhans, Ryan	L-L	6-3	220	2-20-80	.282	.500	.270	12	39	8	11	5	0	0	3	7	0	2	0	11	3	1	.410	.391
Mangini, Matt	L-R	6-4	230	12-21-85	.313	.275	.329	117	447	73	140	31	4	18	63	26	2	0	2	96	3	0	.521	.352
Moore, Adam	R-R	6-3	220	5-8-84	.321	.324	.320	36	134	18	43	8	1	3	15	7	1	0	0	24	1	0	.463	.359
Nelson, Brad	L-R	6-2	260	12-23-82	.259	.188	.286	114	409	59	106	26	0	17	60	61	2	0	7	78	2	2	.447	.353
Ochoa, Blake	R-R	6-0	180	9-5-85	.222	.250	.200	3	9	1	2	0	0	0	1	0	0	0	0	5	0	0	.222	.300
Phillips, Anthony	R-R	5-9	160	4-11-90	.250	1.000	.000	4	4	0	1	0	0	0	0	1	0	0	1	1	0	0	.250	.200
Quiroz, Guillermo	R-R	6-1	215	11-29-81	.297	.323	.283	28	91	13	27	5	1	2	11	6	1	0	0	16	0	0	.440	.347
Saunders, Michael	L-R	6-4	210	11-19-86	.200	.286	.182	21	80	6	16	1	0	0	5	11	0	1	1	17	4	0	.213	.293
Smoak, Justin	B-L	6-4	220	12-5-86	.271	.333	.250	35	133	23	36	7	0	7	25	23	1	0	2	32	0	0	.481	.377
2-team total (15 Oklahoma City)					.279	—		50	183	33	51	13	0	9	30	39	1	0	2	40	0	0	.497	.404
Sweeney, Mike	R-R	6-3	225	7-22-73	.366	.500	.333	12	41	7	15	3	0	2	9	8	0	0	1	3	1	0	.585	.460
Tuiasosopo, Matt	R-R	6-2	225	5-10-86	.252	.229	.259	38	143	26	36	6	0	5	21	32	1	0	0	35	2	2	.399	.392
Vazquez, Ramon	L-R	5-11	195	8-21-76	.216	.162	.239	35	125	13	27	8	1	1	10	9	2	2	0	24	0	0	.320	.279
2-team total (16 Round Rock)					.257	—		51	179	19	46	14	1	1	17	18	2	2	1	32	0	0	.363	.330
Wilson, Jack	R-R	6-0	200	12-29-77	.303	.286	.316	9	33	3	10	2	0	1	4	1	0	0	0	2	2	1	.455	.324
Wilson, Josh	R-R	6-0	175	3-26-81	.333	.583	.290	20	81	7	27	11	1	0	11	0	2	1	2	15	0	1	.494	.341
Wilson, Mike	R-R	6-2	245	6-29-83	.273	.253	.283	88	286	52	78	12	1	17	56	38	3	0	0	67	10	4	.500	.364
Winfree, David	R-R	6-3	230	8-5-85	.315	.359	.297	57	219	40	69	16	1	10	42	11	2	0	3	46	4	1	.534	.349
Woodward, Chris	R-R	6-0	190	6-27-76	.232	.195	.248	103	401	49	93	17	2	6	35	40	2	7	3	73	4	1	.329	.303
Yepez, Jose	R-R	6-0	205	6-19-81	.500	.000	.500	1	4	0	2	0	0	0	0	1	0	0	0	0	0	0	.500	.600

Pitching	B-T	HT	WT	DOB	W	L	ERA	G	GS	CG	SV	IP	H	R	ER	HR	BB	SO	AVG	vLH	vRH	K/9	BB/9
Baldwin, Andy	R-R	6-5	215	10-20-82	9	7	4.90	32	15	0	1	118	136	79	64	13	37	87	.288	.311	.269	6.65	2.83
Beavan, Blake	R-R	6-7	250	1-17-89	2	2	6.47	7	7	0	0	40	56	31	29	6	8	22	.331	.274	.375	4.91	1.79
Bedard, Erik	L-L	6-1	200	3-5-79	0	0	0.00	1	1	0	0	4	3	1	0	0	3	3	.200	.200	.200	6.23	6.23
Bray, Steve	R-R	6-1	195	12-22-80	1	1	5.00	5	0	0	0	9	6	6	5	3	4	8	.182	.231	.150	8.00	4.00
Cordero, Chad	R-R	6-0	220	3-18-82	0	1	4.12	17	0	0	6	20	19	11	9	2	4	22	.250	.241	.255	10.07	1.83
Cortes, Danny	R-R	6-6	230	3-4-87	1	2	4.97	9	0	0	1	13	13	8	7	1	4	13	.277	.313	.258	9.24	2.84
Feierabend, Ryan	L-L	6-3	225	8-22-85	4	7	5.30	17	17	1	0	88	122	56	52	8	28	45	.333	.277	.353	4.58	2.85
Fister, Doug	L-R	6-8	195	2-4-84	0	0	4.50	1	1	0	0	4	4	2	2	0	0	3	.267	.000	.571	6.75	0.00
French, Luke	L-L	6-4	220	9-13-85	11	3	2.94	17	17	1	0	113	109	45	37	7	23	63	.259	.262	.258	5.00	1.83
Grube, Jarrett	R-R	6-4	220	11-5-81	0	0	6.23	2	1	0	0	9	10	6	6	2	1	4	.278	.091	.360	4.15	1.04
Kelley, Shawn	R-R	6-2	215	4-26-84	0	0	4.91	3	0	0	1	4	1	2	2	0	1	3	.091	.333	.000	14.73	7.36
Koplove, Mike	R-R	6-0	165	8-30-76	0	1	4.45	22	0	0	1	28	34	15	14	3	13	21	.296	.294	.297	6.67	4.13
2-team total (10 Portland)					0	1	5.23	32	0	0	1	43	46	26	25	7	21	31	—	—	—	6.49	4.40
Lee, Cliff	L-L	6-3	190	8-30-78	0	0	0.00	1	1	0	0	3	0	0	0	0	0	4	.158	.000	.188	6.00	0.00
Littleton, Wes	R-R	6-3	200	9-2-82	0	0	6.00	3	0	0	0	3	5	2	2	0	1	2	.333	.333	.333	6.00	3.00
Lueke, Josh	R-R	6-5	220	12-5-84	1	0	2.08	12	0	0	2	17	14	5	4	0	5	18	.215	.222	.211	9.35	2.60

Medina, Yoervis	R-R	6-3	210	7-27-88	1	0	0.00	1	1	0	0	6	3	0	0	0	4	4	.158	.167	.154	6.35	6.35
Munoz, Luis	R-R	6-2	195	1-10-82	0	0	10.80	3	0	0	0	5	6	6	0	5	4	.286	.222	.333	7.20	9.00
Nelson, Joe	R-R	6-1	205	10-25-74	0	0	6.75	8	0	0	0	8	10	6	6	0	7	8	.303	.300	.304	9.00	7.88
Olson, Garrett	R-L	6-1	205	10-18-83	2	5	3.66	12	6	0	0	47	36	22	19	4	15	50	.216	.135	.238	9.64	2.89
Palazzolo, Steve	R-R	6-10	260	3-31-82	2	1	5.11	9	0	0	0	12	16	7	7	1	5	12	.320	.412	.273	8.76	3.65
Paredes, Edward	L-L	6-0	180	9-30-86	0	2	6.64	19	0	0	0	20	24	17	15	1	15	12	.289	.250	.309	5.31	6.64
Patterson, Scott	R-R	6-7	235	6-20-79	2	1	2.67	29	0	0	6	34	29	11	10	6	9	36	.228	.250	.211	9.62	2.41
Pauley, David	R-R	6-2	210	6-17-83	1	6	3.68	15	14	1	0	86	82	38	35	6	26	56	.254	.228	.275	5.88	2.73
Petit, Yusmeiro	R-R	6-1	255	11-22-84	4	2	4.85	24	6	0	0	59	54	36	32	9	16	55	.237	.269	.208	8.34	2.43
Pineda, Michael	R-R	6-5	180	1-18-89	3	3	4.76	12	12	0	0	62	54	33	33	9	17	76	.227	.265	.190	10.97	2.45
Rivera, Mumba	R-R	6-5	205	12-10-80	0	1	2.45	11	0	0	0	15	12	4	4	1	4	8	.222	.226	.217	4.91	2.45
Robles, Mauricio	L-L	5-10	205	3-5-89	3	1	3.54	5	5	0	0	28	19	12	11	2	20	34	.188	.300	.160	10.93	6.43
Rowland-Smith, Ryan	L-L	6-3	240	1-26-83	2	4	5.11	6	6	0	0	37	45	22	21	4	5	24	.292	.375	.255	5.84	1.22
Seddon, Chris	L-L	6-3	220	10-13-83	10	4	3.39	18	15	2	0	101	95	45	38	7	29	65	.247	.345	.220	5.79	2.58
Shell, Steven	R-R	6-4	215	3-10-83	3	2	3.59	21	9	1	0	73	76	33	29	7	19	51	.268	.213	.312	6.32	2.35
Snell, Ian	R-R	5-11	200	10-30-81	3	4	6.66	9	9	0	0	49	58	37	36	6	22	39	.304	.260	.347	7.21	4.07
Speigner, Levale	R-R	5-11	180	9-24-80	5	7	4.98	45	0	0	10	65	75	43	36	8	21	45	.282	.259	.299	6.23	2.91
Sweeney, Brian	R-R	6-2	200	6-13-74	2	1	2.51	15	0	0	1	29	20	11	8	1	8	32	.192	.125	.234	10.05	2.51
Traber, Billy	L-L	6-5	205	9-18-79	0	1	3.86	7	0	0	0	7	5	4	3	2	2	7	.200	.250	.154	9.00	2.57
Varvaro, Anthony	R-R	6-0	195	10-31-84	0	0	5.26	19	0	0	0	26	24	17	15	1	14	26	.242	.243	.242	9.12	4.91
White, Sean	R-R	6-4	215	4-25-81	1	0	0.00	10	0	0	0	13	7	1	0	0	8	10	.159	.136	.182	6.92	5.54
Worrell, Mark	R-R	6-1	215	3-8-83	1	0	9.00	4	0	0	0	4	7	4	4	0	3	0	.438	.500	.333	0.00	6.75
2-team total (25 Portland)					2	4	5.84	29	0	0	0	37	41	32	24	5	14	34	—	—	—	8.27	3.41

Fielding

Catcher	PCT	G	PO	A	E	DP	PB
Alfonzo	.985	48	373	29	6	4	3
Bard	.994	23	149	7	1	2	0
Johnson	.987	19	131	17	2	1	5
Moore	.987	31	203	18	3	2	1
Ochoa	1.000	3	15	0	0	0	0
Quiroz	.974	28	137	10	4	0	4
Yepez	1.000	1	2	0	0	0	0

First Base	PCT	G	PO	A	E	DP
Carp	.987	53	425	32	6	29
Everidge	.967	3	27	2	1	3
Langerhans	1.000	1	0	1	0	0
Mangini	.972	16	130	8	4	8
Nelson	.994	41	326	25	2	31
Smoak	.988	31	231	19	3	15
Sweeney	1.000	1	9	0	0	1

Second Base	PCT	G	PO	A	E	DP
Ackley	.977	51	104	109	5	24
Denker	1.000	5	4	13	0	4

	PCT	G	PO	A	E	DP	PB
Dominguez	.969	8	14	17	1	4	
Hannahan	.993	34	52	86	1	20	
Tuiasosopo	1.000	2	3	4	0	0	
Vazquez	.990	28	39	62	1	13	
Wilson	1.000	1	6	3	0	2	
Woodward	.962	22	33	43	3	8	

Third Base	PCT	G	PO	A	E	DP
Dominguez	1.000	1	1	1	0	0
Everidge	1.000	1	1	2	0	0
Hannahan	.870	19	17	50	10	4
Hulett	1.000	2	2	2	0	0
Mangini	.918	97	74	194	24	14
Phillips	1.000	1	1	0	0	0
Tuiasosopo	.939	24	24	38	4	1
Vazquez	1.000	3	0	3	0	0
Woodward	1.000	1	0	2	0	0

Shortstop	PCT	G	PO	A	E	DP
Dominguez	.918	12	21	35	5	6
Hannahan	.966	10	10	18	1	6

	PCT	G	PO	A	E	DP
Hulett	.983	16	21	37	1	4
Phillips	1.000	2	2	3	0	1
Tuiasosopo	1.000	2	6	5	0	0
Vazquez	1.000	4	6	11	0	5
Wilson	.975	9	13	26	1	3
Wilson	.971	19	17	51	2	7
Woodward	.955	75	118	182	14	33

Outfield	PCT	G	PO	A	E	DP
Carp	1.000	43	91	5	0	0
Carrera	.980	63	144	6	3	1
Dominguez	1.000	6	13	0	0	0
Halman	.965	112	295	5	11	1
Langerhans	.963	11	25	1	1	0
Nelson	.984	28	58	3	1	2
Saunders	1.000	21	49	2	0	0
Tuiasosopo	1.000	11	16	0	0	0
Wilson	.939	84	146	7	10	0
Winfree	.966	56	110	4	4	1
Woodward	1.000	8	13	0	0	0

WEST TENN DIAMOND JAXX

DOUBLE-A

SOUTHERN LEAGUE

Batting	B-T	HT	WT	DOB	AVG	vLH	vRH	G	AB	R	H	2B	3B	HR	RBI	BB	HBP	SH	SF	SO	SB	CS	SLG	OBP
Ackley, Dustin	L-R	6-1	185	2-26-88	.263	.225	.280	82	289	42	76	21	4	2	28	55	5	0	1	41	8	2	.384	.389
Bantz, Brandon	R-R	6-1	211	1-7-87	.241	.250	.235	24	79	9	19	6	1	1	6	4	2	1	0	17	0	0	.380	.294
Bonilla, Leury	R-R	6-3	170	2-8-85	.268	.305	.253	91	280	40	75	16	1	7	37	25	4	3	4	78	10	3	.407	.332
Britton, Dwight	B-R	6-0	195	7-17-87	.667	.000	.667	1	3	2	2	0	0	1	3	0	0	0	0	0	0	0	1.667	.667
Dominguez, Jeff	B-R	6-2	160	7-31-86	.213	.258	.167	22	61	5	13	2	1	2	4	5	0	4	0	18	0	2	.377	.273
Dunigan, Joe	L-L	6-1	215	3-29-86	.214	.194	.221	81	280	36	60	14	0	10	42	28	2	1	1	110	12	2	.371	.289
Franklin, Nick	B-R	6-1	170	3-2-91	.667	.667	.000	1	3	3	2	0	0	0	1	0	0	0	1	0	0	0	.667	.750
Haveman, Brandon	L-R	5-9	165	6-21-86	.296	.286	.299	62	230	29	68	6	3	1	20	14	3	2	1	28	10	4	.361	.343
Henriquez, Ralph	R-R	6-1	190	4-7-87	.324	.571	.267	11	37	5	12	3	0	1	8	0	0	0	0	5	0	0	.486	.324
Jimenez, Hassiel	R-R	6-0	205	5-8-91	.000	.000	.000	1	2	0	0	0	0	0	0	0	0	0	0	0	0	0	.000	.000
Lawson, Matt	R-R	6-0	195	11-18-85	.319	.340	.311	42	166	27	53	10	2	2	22	11	4	1	0	31	3	1	.440	.376
Liddi, Alex	R-R	6-4	176	8-14-88	.281	.315	.266	134	502	78	141	37	8	15	92	50	7	4	2	145	5	7	.476	.353
Limonta, Johan	L-L	6-0	205	8-4-83	.302	.276	.314	132	486	82	147	41	2	14	83	55	6	2	5	104	3	3	.481	.377
Lo, Kuo Hui	R-R	6-2	188	9-26-85	.237	.208	.255	67	249	28	59	9	1	4	19	21	3	1	2	49	5	3	.329	.302
Martinez-Esteve, Eddy	R-R	6-2	215	7-14-83	.000	.000	.000	1	1	0	0	0	0	0	0	0	0	0	0	0	0	0	.000	.000
Mendez, Maximo	L-L	6-0	150	11-24-86	.250	.000	.333	4	8	0	2	0	0	1	1	1	0	0	0	6	0	0	.250	.333
Oliveros, Luis	R-R	6-1	225	6-18-83	.333	.333	.333	15	42	6	14	3	0	2	7	7	0	1	1	6	0	0	.548	.420
Peguero, Carlos	L-L	6-5	210	2-22-87	.254	.219	.269	130	488	86	124	23	5	23	73	56	8	0	1	178	7	9	.463	.340
Quiroz, Guillermo	R-R	6-1	215	11-29-81	.282	.206	.313	68	234	24	66	17	1	5	35	21	4	1	3	59	0	2	.427	.347
Savastano, Scott	R-R	6-4	190	6-12-86	.287	.358	.250	68	237	39	68	11	1	6	30	30	0	2	0	58	4	2	.426	.367
Scott, Travis	L-R	6-3	220	4-24-85	.091	.000	.143	4	11	0	1	1	0	0	1	2	0	0	0	3	0	0	.182	.231
Shaffer, Jake	L-L	6-1	190	8-16-87	.250	.500	.000	3	8	0	2	0	0	0	2	0	1	0	0	2	0	1	.250	.400
Tanabe, Carlton	R-R	6-0	190	10-28-91	—	.000	.000	1	0	0	0	0	0	0	0	0	0	0	0	0	0	0	—	—
Tenbrink, Nate	L-R	6-2	202	12-21-86	.274	.274	.273	72	234	37	64	11	5	5	28	38	5	3	4	54	12	2	.427	.381
Trlunfel, Carlos	R-R	5-11	175	2-27-90	.257	.285	.245	129	470	51	121	12	1	7	42	13	7	5	3	54	2	8	.332	.286

SEATTLE MARINERS

Batting	B-T	HT	WT	DOB	AVG	vLH	vRH	G	AB	R	H	2B	3B	HR	RBI	BB	HBP	SH	SF	SO	SB	CS	SLG	OBP
Wilson, Jack	R-R	6-0	200	12-29-77	.500	.500	.000	1	2	1	1	0	0	0	0	0	0	0	0	0	0	0	.500	.500
Wilson, Mike	R-R	6-2	245	6-29-83	.292	.269	.300	29	106	25	31	5	1	8	22	20	0	0	1	34	3	1	.585	.402
Yepez, Jose	R-R	6-0	205	6-19-81	.322	.373	.271	34	118	15	38	12	0	0	20	10	4	4	2	20	0	0	.424	.388

Pitching	B-T	HT	WT	DOB	W	L	ERA	G	GS	CG	SV	IP	H	R	ER	HR	BB	SO	AVG	vLH	vRH	K/9	BB/9
Beavan, Blake	R-R	6-7	250	1-17-89	2	1	5.00	3	3	0	0	18	18	11	10	1	1	11	.277	.306	.241	5.50	0.50
Bray, Steve	R-R	6-1	195	12-22-80	7	11	5.50	26	23	1	1	131	161	102	80	15	32	64	.305	.318	.291	4.40	2.20
Cortes, Danny	R-R	6-6	230	3-4-87	6	4	5.27	25	16	0	1	84	77	54	49	4	53	85	.239	.200	.275	9.14	5.70
Feierabend, Ryan	L-L	6-3	225	8-22-85	1	0	2.57	1	1	0	0	7	5	2	2	1	0	3	.217	.000	.217	3.86	0.00
Fields, Josh	R-R	6-0	185	8-19-85	1	1	3.14	21	0	0	6	29	19	12	10	0	18	28	.190	.175	.200	8.79	5.65
Gillheeney, Jimmy	L-L	6-1	200	11-8-87	1	2	6.87	4	4	0	0	18	20	17	14	3	6	22	.267	.200	.311	10.80	2.95
Grube, Jarrett	R-R	6-4	220	11-5-81	5	5	3.23	15	15	0	0	95	85	37	34	5	26	75	.239	.241	.235	7.13	2.47
Hensley, Steven	R-R	6-3	180	12-27-86	7	11	4.62	22	22	0	0	117	118	69	60	7	50	81	.262	.252	.270	6.23	3.85
Hill, Nick	L-L	6-0	190	1-30-85	2	1	4.22	28	2	0	1	43	47	23	20	3	18	37	.270	.239	.290	7.80	3.80
Jensen, Aaron	R-R	6-3	180	11-3-84	1	4	4.40	42	0	0	3	59	84	36	29	1	16	38	.326	.342	.313	5.76	2.43
Jimenez, Cesar	L-L	5-11	220	11-12-84	1	0	1.00	7	1	0	0	9	7	2	1	1	3	9	.212	.143	.263	9.00	3.00
Littleton, Wes	R-R	6-3	200	9-2-82	3	3	6.57	19	0	0	3	25	33	22	18	2	18	20	.330	.275	.388	7.30	6.57
Lueke, Josh	R-R	6-5	220	12-5-84	1	0	0.00	3	0	0	0	3	7	4	0	0	0	14	.148	.063	.273	17.18	0.00
Merry, Jorden	R-R	6-1	190	6-30-87	1	0	0.00	1	0	0	0	2	2	0	0	0	0	2	.286	.500	.000	9.00	0.00
Moran, Brian	L-L	6-3	185	9-30-88	0	0	13.50	2	0	0	0	2	4	3	3	0	1	1	.500	.333	.600	4.50	4.50
Munoz, Luis	R-R	6-2	195	1-10-82	7	6	3.88	35	10	0	1	95	94	48	41	11	31	66	.258	.269	.247	6.25	2.94
Palazzolo, Steve	R-R	6-10	260	3-31-82	0	0	9.00	6	0	0	0	6	15	6	6	1	4	5	.484	.429	.529	7.50	6.00
Paredes, Edward	L-L	6-0	180	9-30-86	2	1	3.63	26	0	0	3	35	35	15	14	1	16	35	.255	.295	.237	9.09	4.15
Pineda, Michael	R-R	6-5	180	1-18-89	8	1	2.22	13	13	0	0	77	67	23	19	1	17	78	.228	.300	.162	9.12	1.99
Richard, Steve	R-R	6-3	240	3-7-85	2	0	4.08	22	0	0	0	29	41	14	13	2	9	23	.331	.369	.288	7.22	2.83
Rivera, Mumba	R-R	6-3	180		0	3	5.65	28	0	0	4	37	31	28	23	4	20	35	.223	.274	.182	8.59	4.91
Robles, Mauricio	L-L	5-10	205	3-5-89	6	6	4.11	22	22	0	0	114	102	58	52	10	51	120	.239	.294	.222	9.47	4.03
Rohrbaugh, Robert	R-L	6-2	195	12-28-83	4	2	3.70	31	0	0	2	73	83	35	30	4	11	62	.284	.357	.247	7.64	1.36
Sorce, Chris	R-R	6-0	190	10-28-87	0	0	19.29	2	0	0	0	2	4	5	5	0	7	0	.400	.400	.400	0.00	27.00
Varvaro, Anthony	R-R	6-0	195	10-31-84	1	3	3.20	31	0	0	9	39	27	15	14	2	21	46	.194	.096	.253	10.53	4.81
Vasquez, Anthony	L-L	6-0	175	9-19-86	2	3	2.61	7	6	0	0	38	44	15	11	2	5	27	.297	.250	.315	6.39	1.18
Wild, Jake	R-R	6-5	195	8-18-84	0	1	9.64	1	1	0	0	5	7	5	5	0	2	3	.368	.455	.250	5.79	3.86

Fielding

Catcher	PCT	G	PO	A	E	DP	PB
Bantz	.984	24	164	20	3	2	4
Bonilla	1.000	4	4	0	0	0	0
Henriquez	1.000	11	73	9	0	0	2
Jimenez	1.000	1	3	0	0	0	0
Oliveros	.983	15	109	7	2	1	4
Quiroz	.991	59	392	29	4	5	7
Scott	1.000	3	29	1	0	1	0
Tanabe	1.000	1	1	0	0	0	0
Yepez	.992	34	239	17	2	2	5

First Base	PCT	G	PO	A	E	DP
Bantz	1.000	2	2	0	0	1
Bonilla	1.000	3	13	1	0	3
Dunigan	1.000	2	5	0	0	1
Liddi	.977	23	148	20	4	4
Limonta	.989	93	708	39	8	59
Savastano	1.000	10	67	4	0	7
Tenbrink	.982	21	148	14	3	9

Second Base	PCT	G	PO	A	E	DP
Ackley	.955	70	119	160	13	34
Bonilla	.987	20	32	43	1	11
Dominguez	1.000	12	19	33	0	6
Franklin	1.000	1	1	0	0	0
Lawson	.988	39	66	93	2	14
Savastano	1.000	8	6	17	0	2
Triunfel	1.000	2	5	3	0	2

Third Base	PCT	G	PO	A	E	DP
Bonilla	1.000	23	10	39	0	0
Dominguez	1.000	2	2	4	0	2
Liddi	.909	117	70	200	27	20
Tenbrink	.909	11	6	14	2	0

Shortstop	PCT	G	PO	A	E	DP
Bonilla	.981	14	16	35	1	7
Dominguez	1.000	1	3	1	0	0
Franklin	1.000	1	1	2	0	1
Lawson	1.000	2	2	6	0	1
Triunfel	.939	126	198	282	31	53

Outfield	PCT	G	PO	A	E	DP
Bonilla	.963	39	74	4	3	1
Britton	1.000	1	1	0	0	0
Dominguez	1.000	5	17	0	0	0
Dunigan	.952	70	108	11	6	4
Haveman	.987	60	147	4	2	1
Limonta	1.000	16	21	0	0	0
Lo	.987	63	152	2	2	1
Mendez	1.000	4	1	0	0	0
Peguero	.953	99	198	6	10	1
Savastano	1.000	29	51	1	0	0
Shaffer	1.000	1	3	0	0	0
Tenbrink	.941	42	64	0	4	0
Wilson	.957	11	20	2	1	0

HIGH DESERT MAVERICKS — HIGH CLASS A

CALIFORNIA LEAGUE

Batting	B-T	HT	WT	DOB	AVG	vLH	vRH	G	AB	R	H	2B	3B	HR	RBI	BB	HBP	SH	SF	SO	SB	CS	SLG	OBP
Almonte, Denny	B-R	6-2	187	9-24-88	.255	.255	.255	127	494	71	126	22	6	22	76	25	2	3	2	192	13	6	.457	.293
Carroll, Dan	R-R	6-1	175	1-6-89	.214	.333	.158	9	28	6	6	3	0	0	2	0	3	0		8	0	0	.429	.267
Chavez, Johermyn	R-R	6-3	220	1-26-89	.315	.333	.308	136	534	109	168	30	7	32	96	52	13	3	3	131	6	9	.577	.387
Choi, Ji-Man	L-R	6-1	195	5-19-91	.302	.231	.333	11	43	7	13	1	1	1	7	6	0	0	1	9	0	0	.442	.380
Coleman, Trevor	R-R	6-1	205	1-19-88	.216	.188	.231	83	282	34	61	14	0	6	34	25	7	3	2	63	1	2	.330	.294
Colina, Edilio	R-R	6-2	175	10-10-88	.290	.268	.298	114	452	90	131	28	1	3	40	33	23	10	3	48	13	6	.376	.366
Diaz, Juan	B-R	6-3	180	12-12-88	.295	.318	.283	70	254	39	75	8	3	7	41	19	1	1	1	45	8	2	.433	.345
Dunigan, Joe	L-L	6-1	215	3-29-86	.091	.000	.111	3	11	1	1	0	0	1	1	1	0	0	0	1	0	0	.364	.167
Gebbers, Hawkins	R-R	6-2	205	7-29-86	.200	.250	.188	8	20	2	4	1	1	0	2	0	0	0	4	0	0		.350	.200
Hansen, Shaver	B-R	6-0	185	12-19-87	.217	.136	.247	69	221	36	48	9	4	6	29	25	2	1	5	78	6	1	.376	.296
Henriquez, Ralph	B-R	6-1	190	4-7-87	.257	.238	.261	31	113	10	29	9	0	1	6	3	0	0		26	0	1	.363	.276
Jimenez, Hassiel	R-R	6-0	205	5-8-91	.400	.500	.286	6	15	2	6	1	0	0	0	1	0	0		2	0	0	.467	.438
Lo, Kuo Hui	R-R	6-2	188	9-26-85	.224	.056	.258	31	107	13	24	7	2	0	16	12	0	2	1	20	6	2	.327	.300
Martinez-Esteve, Eddy	R-R	6-2	215	7-14-83	.325	.375	.310	53	203	30	66	12	0	7	36	24	2	0	1	33	0	0	.488	.400
Mendez, Maximo	L-L	6-2	150	11-24-86	.212	.229	.206	48	132	25	28	2	0	2	10	16	1	3	1	50	11	4	.273	.300
Morban, Julio	L-L	6-1	190	2-13-92	.333	1.000	.000	2	6	0	2	0	0	0	1	0	0	0	0	2	0	0	.333	.333
Nunez, Luis	R-R	6-0	170	12-31-86	.216	.100	.244	18	51	11	11	0	0	0	5	2	0	1	0	11	2	1	.216	.245
Ochoa, Blake	R-R	6-0	180	9-5-85	.333	.200	.368	7	24	4	8	3	0	1	7	1	0	0	1	0	0		.583	.385

	B-T	HT	WT	DOB	AVG	vLH	vRH	G	AB	R	H	2B	3B	HR	RBI	BB	HBP	SH	SF	SO	SB	CS	SLG	OBP
Poythress, Rich	R-R	6-4	235	8-11-87	.315	.336	.308	123	476	88	150	33	0	31	130	52	5	0	11	100	3	2	.580	.381
Raben, Dennis	L-L	6-3	200	7-31-87	.356	.256	.388	40	160	35	57	10	3	12	43	15	2	0	2	47	0	0	.681	.413
Savastano, Scott	R-R	6-4	190	6-12-86	.318	.207	.373	25	88	10	28	6	0	2	13	9	2	2	1	11	2	1	.455	.390
Scott, Travis	L-R	6-3	220	4-24-85	.269	.278	.267	33	119	14	32	6	0	5	22	11	3	0	1	22	1	0	.445	.343
Seager, Kyle	L-R	5-10	175	11-3-87	.345	.371	.334	135	557	126	192	40	3	14	74	71	5	3	7	94	13	12	.503	.419
Shaffer, Jake	L-L	6-1	190	8-16-87	.338	.381	.326	107	391	58	132	31	6	9	78	26	7	4	2	73	4	10	.517	.387
Tanabe, Carlton	R-R	6-0	190	10-28-91	.500	.000	.667	2	4	1	2	0	1	0	0	0	0	1	0	0	0	0	1.000	.500
Tenbrink, Nate	L-R	6-2	202	12-21-86	.377	.358	.385	44	175	38	66	10	5	9	42	22	1	3	0	33	14	1	.646	.449

Pitching	B-T	HT	WT	DOB	W	L	ERA	G	GS	CG	SV	IP	H	R	ER	HR	BB	SO	AVG	vLH	vRH	K/9	BB/9
Carraway, Andrew	R-R	6-2	200	9-4-86	11	8	5.33	27	27	0	0	150	190	100	89	25	31	120	.307	.333	.287	7.18	1.86
Cleto, Maikel	R-R	6-3	220	5-1-89	4	9	6.16	23	21	0	0	102	125	81	70	10	44	83	.305	.282	.319	7.30	3.87
Cooper, Daniel	R-R	6-3	205	11-6-86	1	1	4.50	5	0	0	1	8	6	6	4	1	9	11	.200	.455	.053	12.38	10.13
Czyz, Nick	L-L	6-2	215	4-10-87	2	0	5.34	10	2	0	0	29	35	19	17	2	13	17	.294	.270	.305	5.34	4.08
Diaz, Ogui	R-R	6-2	170	12-1-85	1	0	5.06	2	0	0	0	5	6	3	3	1	2	2	.286	.500	.091	3.38	3.38
Feierabend, Ryan	L-L	6-2	215	8-22-85	0	1	5.27	7	6	0	0	27	31	18	16	5	2	20	.298	.194	.342	6.59	0.66
Gillheeney, Jimmy	L-L	6-1	200	11-8-87	1	1	5.06	3	3	0	0	16	18	11	9	4	7	21	.277	.444	.213	11.81	3.94
Hann, Cheyne	R-R	6-6	235	9-17-84	4	5	6.79	42	1	0	4	64	84	51	48	12	8	42	.323	.245	.373	5.94	1.13
Hesketh, John	L-L	6-0	175	6-3-86	3	4	4.30	12	12	0	0	61	67	38	29	8	31	62	.278	.318	.269	9.20	4.60
Jimenez, Jose	L-L	6-0	180	3-23-87	0	0	2.45	3	0	0	0	4	3	1	1	0	2	3	.214	.500	.100	7.36	4.91
Kasparek, Kenn	R-R	6-8	200	9-23-85	9	5	4.06	24	22	1	0	146	138	73	66	21	37	87	.248	.252	.245	5.35	2.28
Kirkland, Chris	R-R	6-4	220	10-6-85	0	0	12.38	5	0	0	0	8	19	13	11	3	2	6	.400	.273	.571	11.25	2.25
LaFromboise, Bobby	L-L	6-4	190	6-25-86	10	5	4.51	33	14	0	1	114	138	63	57	15	38	92	.301	.293	.305	7.28	3.01
Littleton, Wes	R-R	6-3	200	9-2-82	0	1	3.86	15	0	0	5	16	22	7	7	2	8	15	.319	.235	.346	8.27	4.41
Martinez, Fray	R-R	6-3	170	5-20-89	0	0	0.00	1	0	0	0	3	2	0	0	0	0	3	.182	.125	.333	9.00	0.00
Moorer, Ryan	R-R	6-3	208	3-2-86	1	1	7.07	19	0	0	0	28	34	23	22	2	25	7	.321	.356	.295	2.25	8.04
Moran, Brian	L-L	6-3	185	9-30-88	2	0	1.42	17	0	0	1	25	22	4	4	0	2	29	.232	.227	.233	10.30	0.71
Mortimore, Travis	L-L	6-5	225	8-1-84	0	2	8.36	8	1	0	0	14	16	14	13	1	3	15	.281	.304	.265	9.64	1.93
Munoz, Luis	R-R	6-2	195	1-10-82	1	0	0.00	1	0	0	0	3	0	0	0	0	1	2	.333	.750	.000	9.00	4.50
Nation, Blake	R-R	6-8	218	5-16-87	4	4	4.72	47	0	0	6	80	100	50	42	7	28	58	.306	.339	.287	6.53	3.15
Penney, Stephen	R-R	6-7	240	8-14-86	5	3	3.53	49	0	0	6	66	66	31	26	8	9	64	.261	.208	.299	8.68	1.22
Reed, Nate	R-R	6-3	180	12-1-87	1	1	8.25	3	0	0	0	12	18	12	11	1	8	8	.340	.353	.333	6.00	6.00
Richard, Steve	R-R	6-3	240	3-7-85	2	3	3.78	27	0	0	8	33	38	16	14	2	10	30	.281	.304	.266	8.10	2.70
Vasquez, Anthony	L-L	6-0	175	9-19-86	7	4	3.07	13	11	2	0	85	87	38	29	6	12	53	.263	.177	.298	5.61	1.27
Vega, Marwin	R-R	6-0	175	10-27-86	0	2	11.97	24	0	0	0	29	55	46	39	8	13	18	.385	.368	.395	5.52	3.99
Wild, Jake	R-R	6-5	195	8-18-84	6	5	5.35	29	17	0	0	113	136	74	67	19	36	92	.303	.306	.300	7.35	2.88

Fielding

Catcher	PCT	G	PO	A	E	DP	PB
Coleman	.990	81	524	52	6	3	14
Henriquez	.990	30	192	16	2	0	7
Jimenez	.976	6	37	3	1	0	0
Ochoa	.976	7	37	3	1	0	4
Scott	.975	27	178	16	5	1	2
Tanabe	1.000	2	9	0	0	0	0

First Base	PCT	G	PO	A	E	DP
Choi	.976	5	36	5	1	9
Coleman	1.000	1	12	1	0	1
Dunigan	.958	2	23	0	1	1
Hansen	1.000	8	64	2	0	3
Martinez-Esteve	.971	17	125	7	4	14
Poythress	.989	93	764	59	9	73
Raben	.982	7	53	3	1	5
Savastano	.989	10	81	8	1	6
Scott	1.000	1	9	0	0	0
Tenbrink	.955	4	21	0	1	3

Second Base	PCT	G	PO	A	E	DP
Colina	1.000	16	26	42	0	10
Gebbers	.947	8	7	11	1	3
Hansen	.944	16	22	45	4	7
Nunez	.947	9	13	23	2	3
Seager	.971	100	163	272	13	68

Third Base	PCT	G	PO	A	E	DP
Coleman	1.000	1	0	2	0	0
Colina	.907	44	45	62	11	7
Hansen	.925	38	25	73	8	9
Henriquez	1.000	1	0	1	0	0
Martinez-Esteve	.970	14	9	23	1	1
Poythress	.900	14	6	21	3	2
Seager	.951	22	17	41	3	5
Tenbrink	.942	21	25	24	3	3

Shortstop	PCT	G	PO	A	E	DP
Colina	.967	55	98	166	9	36
Diaz	.948	69	110	197	17	45

	PCT	G	PO	A	E	DP
Hansen	.750	1	0	3	1	2
Seager	.946	17	24	46	4	8

Outfield	PCT	G	PO	A	E	DP
Almonte	.982	127	317	14	6	2
Carroll	.889	5	8	0	1	0
Chavez	.973	136	284	9	8	0
Hansen	.875	4	7	0	1	0
Lo	1.000	19	35	2	0	0
Martinez-Esteve	1.000	3	2	0	0	0
Mendez	.953	45	79	3	4	0
Morban	.667	2	2	0	1	0
Nunez	1.000	4	4	0	0	0
Raben	1.000	7	10	0	0	0
Savastano	1.000	2	3	1	0	0
Shaffer	.992	73	124	3	1	0
Tenbrink	.966	13	27	1	1	1

CLINTON LUMBERKINGS
LOW CLASS A
MIDWEST LEAGUE

Batting	B-T	HT	WT	DOB	AVG	vLH	vRH	G	AB	R	H	2B	3B	HR	RBI	BB	HBP	SH	SF	SO	SB	CS	SLG	OBP
Bantz, Brandon	R-R	6-1	211	1-7-87	.228	.148	.253	32	114	15	26	6	1	1	18	7	3	0	2	27	0	0	.325	.286
Baron, Steve	R-R	6-0	200	12-7-90	.182	.114	.209	45	154	10	28	3	0	1	14	10	0	1	2	47	1	1	.221	.229
Carroll, Dan	R-R	6-1	175	1-6-89	.282	.323	.261	81	277	44	78	9	5	9	34	19	13	7	0	86	25	6	.448	.356
Catricala, Vinnie	R-R	6-2	210	10-31-88	.302	.355	.282	135	496	90	150	41	0	17	79	56	17	0	8	112	7	3	.488	.386
Cerione, Matt	L-L	6-2	192	1-4-88	.287	.270	.292	87	275	54	79	15	4	12	42	37	11	1	2	101	11	3	.502	.391
Contreras, Henry	R-R	5-11	208	5-5-86	.333	.355	.325	33	108	25	36	8	0	2	17	16	5	0	2	24	0	0	.463	.435
Dotel, Welington	R-R	6-1	180	10-2-85	.241	.233	.244	34	108	16	26	5	4	1	17	6	2	0	1	24	4	2	.389	.291
Franklin, Nick	B-R	6-1	170	3-2-91	.281	.174	.318	129	513	89	144	22	7	23	65	50	7	2	2	123	25	10	.485	.351
Gebbers, Hawkins	R-R	6-2	205	7-29-86	.255	.211	.278	19	55	6	14	2	0	2	5	4	3	0	0	4	3	0	.400	.339
Hansen, Shaver	B-R	6-0	185	12-19-87	.167	.200	.158	16	48	2	8	3	0	0	4	3	0	0	0	16	0	0	.229	.216
Jones, James	R-R	6-4	195	9-24-88	.269	.256	.273	132	491	87	132	24	10	12	65	62	5	1	1	122	24	10	.432	.356
Martinez, Mario	R-R	6-1	208	11-13-89	.239	.262	.231	118	440	51	105	22	3	12	66	17	4	2	6	114	4	1	.384	.270
Morris, Tim	L-L	6-3	220	12-11-87	.250	.243	.252	83	308	41	77	14	3	5	46	34	8	1	7	87	2	1	.364	.333

	B-T	HT	WT	DOB	AVG	vLH	vRH	G	AB	R	H	2B	3B	HR	RBI	BB	HBP	SH	SF	SO	SB	CS	SLG	OBP
Noriega, Gabriel	R-R	6-2	170	9-13-90	.227	.224	.228	112	374	47	85	15	0	2	28	20	8	6	2	108	6	4	.283	.280
Nunez, Luis	R-R	6-0	170	12-31-86	.289	.294	.287	42	173	18	50	2	0	0	13	5	2	2	1	37	12	6	.301	.315
Ochoa, Blake	R-R	6-0	180	9-5-85	.279	.250	.288	33	104	20	29	5	1	8	25	23	0	4	4	23	2	0	.577	.397
Raben, Dennis	L-L	6-3	200	7-31-87	.221	.129	.246	42	149	26	33	8	1	8	23	15	8	0	3	49	0	1	.450	.320
Ramirez, Carlos	B-R	5-11	145	12-2-88	.000	.000	.000	1	4	0	0	0	0	0	0	0	0	0	0	0	1	0	0	.000	.000
Royster, Ryan	L-L	6-1	170	10-13-85	.238	.000	.313	10	21	5	5	1	1	0	3	4	0	0	0	6	0	1	.381	.360
Sams, Kalian	R-R	6-3	220	8-25-86	.180	.208	.169	79	266	41	48	11	3	15	46	24	8	1	3	132	5	4	.414	.266
Wiswall, Mickey	L-R	6-1	200	11-25-88	.301	.243	.323	33	136	13	41	14	0	4	18	6	1	0	2	29	1	0	.493	.331

Pitching	B-T	HT	WT	DOB	W	L	ERA	G	GS	CG	SV	IP	H	R	ER	HR	BB	SO	AVG	vLH	vRH	K/9	BB/9
Arias, Jonathan	R-R	6-3	190	2-8-88	0	1	4.09	4	2	0	0	11	8	5	5	2	6	6	.222	.238	.200	4.91	4.91
Blandford, Tyler	R-R	6-3	165	1-25-88	1	2	3.67	7	7	0	0	27	24	16	11	3	25	26	.247	.250	.245	8.67	8.33
Cooper, Daniel	R-R	6-3	205	11-6-86	4	2	3.81	40	0	0	1	57	56	26	24	1	21	37	.260	.292	.238	5.88	3.34
Czyz, Nick	L-L	6-2	215	4-10-87	4	5	4.48	17	13	0	0	74	75	44	37	10	18	57	.265	.281	.257	6.90	2.18
Gallagher, Nolan	R-R	6-3	190	12-20-85	0	4	6.32	9	5	0	0	31	41	25	22	3	14	18	.318	.271	.357	5.17	4.02
Gillheeney, Jimmy	L-L	6-1	200	11-8-87	8	8	2.83	21	21	0	0	118	97	45	37	7	44	102	.229	.222	.232	7.80	3.37
Hesketh, John	L-L	6-0	175	6-3-86	3	5	4.43	14	14	0	0	67	66	39	33	5	25	82	.253	.224	.265	11.01	3.36
Housey, John	R-R	6-4	180	6-4-88	5	4	4.35	25	3	0	0	50	50	36	24	4	26	42	.260	.247	.269	7.61	4.71
Jimenez, Jose	L-L	6-0	180	3-23-87	3	4	3.08	42	0	0	3	61	61	33	21	3	27	51	.257	.276	.248	7.48	3.96
Josselyn, Brandon	L-R	6-3	200	8-22-86	3	6	4.53	52	0	0	15	56	63	34	28	2	18	50	.286	.247	.317	8.08	2.91
Kirkland, Chris	R-R	6-4	220	10-6-85	1	1	2.19	19	0	0	2	37	27	15	9	2	10	41	.196	.137	.230	9.97	2.43
Lewis, Taylor	R-R	6-4	190	6-2-88	3	2	6.06	20	5	0	0	49	60	40	33	8	27	18	.314	.382	.270	3.31	4.96
Markovitz, Jason	L-L	6-3	195	8-27-88	0	0	4.50	9	2	0	0	20	20	10	10	2	5	15	.278	.281	.275	6.75	2.25
Martinez, Fray	R-R	6-3	170	5-20-89	0	1	9.00	12	0	0	0	14	20	14	14	1	11	9	.333	.393	.281	5.79	7.07
Maurer, Brandon	R-R	6-5	200	7-3-90	0	1	2.08	2	0	0	0	4	5	2	1	1	0	6	.294	.200	.429	12.46	0.00
Medina, Yoervis	R-R	6-3	210	7-24-88	5	0	2.50	6	6	0	0	36	30	10	10	3	12	42	.221	.191	.277	10.50	3.00
Merry, Jorden	R-R	6-1	190	6-30-87	0	0	4.91	13	0	0	1	18	17	10	10	1	9	23	.246	.261	.239	11.29	4.42
Moorer, Ryan	R-R	6-3	208	3-2-86	0	1	10.00	8	0	0	0	9	11	12	10	0	6	1	.333	.385	.300	1.00	6.00
Moran, Brian	L-L	6-3	185	9-30-88	4	1	1.34	22	0	0	3	40	34	8	6	0	6	48	.230	.214	.239	11.01	1.34
Pryor, Stephen	R-R	6-6	225	7-23-89	0	2	3.71	12	0	0	1	17	17	12	7	0	6	29	.250	.349	.080	15.35	3.18
Ramirez, Erasmo	R-R	5-11	180	5-2-90	10	4	2.97	26	23	1	1	152	142	63	50	13	21	117	.248	.274	.224	6.94	1.25
Snow, Forrest	R-R	6-6	195	12-30-88	0	1	1.35	15	0	0	6	20	9	3	3	1	7	26	.132	.111	.156	11.70	3.15
Stanton, Taylor	R-R	6-2	230	1-15-88	12	7	4.30	27	24	0	1	138	155	74	66	13	35	111	.285	.313	.262	7.24	2.28
Vasquez, Anthony	L-L	6-0	175	9-19-86	2	2	1.29	8	8	1	0	49	31	11	7	2	7	45	.181	.154	.198	8.32	1.29
Wilhelmsen, Tom	R-R	6-6	197	12-16-83	6	1	2.23	7	6	1	0	44	33	16	11	1	15	37	.198	.204	.188	7.51	3.05

Fielding

Catcher	PCT	G	PO	A	E	DP	PB
Bantz	.985	31	233	34	4	1	2
Baron	.972	45	359	28	11	3	11
Contreras	.992	32	202	32	2	2	3
Ochoa	.986	33	255	19	4	1	4

First Base	PCT	G	PO	A	E	DP
Catricala	.992	54	436	35	4	33
Jones	1.000	2	5	0	0	0
Morris	.995	47	381	32	2	32
Raben	.977	24	198	13	5	17
Wiswall	.982	17	147	16	3	12

Second Base	PCT	G	PO	A	E	DP
Franklin	.983	28	37	76	2	14

	PCT	G	PO	A	E	DP
Gebbers	.889	11	9	15	3	1
Hansen	.939	13	25	37	4	6
Noriega	.973	69	105	185	8	37
Nunez	.948	24	34	58	5	12
Ramirez	1.000	1	3	6	0	2

Third Base	PCT	G	PO	A	E	DP
Catricala	.940	26	22	41	4	4
Gebbers	.750	1	1	2	1	0
Hansen	1.000	1	1	1	0	0
Martinez	.944	114	103	215	19	14

Shortstop	PCT	G	PO	A	E	DP
Franklin	.947	98	149	241	22	47
Noriega	.954	45	61	125	9	21

Outfield	PCT	G	PO	A	E	DP
Carroll	.947	80	152	9	9	0
Catricala	.963	27	49	3	2	0
Cerione	1.000	86	170	7	0	2
Dotel	1.000	27	40	1	0	0
Gebbers	1.000	1	1	0	0	0
Hansen	1.000	2	1	0	0	0
Jones	.955	131	224	12	11	1
Nunez	.909	9	10	0	1	0
Royster	1.000	9	11	1	0	0
Sams	.952	68	95	4	5	1

EVERETT AQUASOX   SHORT-SEASON

NORTHWEST LEAGUE

Batting	B-T	HT	WT	DOB	AVG	vLH	vRH	G	AB	R	H	2B	3B	HR	RBI	BB	HBP	SH	SF	SO	SB	CS	SLG	OBP
Anston, Robbie	L-L	5-11	190	4-13-88	.292	.189	.318	65	264	41	77	13	1	2	24	23	4	4	1	47	15	8	.371	.356
Baron, Steve	R-R	6-0	200	12-7-90	.253	.200	.266	53	198	18	50	12	3	2	22	6	2	3	0	60	1	0	.379	.282
Bello, Fred	R-R	5-10	165	10-6-87	.189	.227	.179	36	106	11	20	2	4	3	13	14	1	2	1	33	1	5	.368	.287
Britton, Dwight	B-R	6-0	195	7-17-87	.216	.250	.207	42	148	20	32	7	0	4	10	9	6	0	0	50	9	1	.345	.288
Burgess, Jarrett	R-R	6-2	180	8-10-90	.000	.000	.000	1	1	0	0	0	0	0	0	0	0	0	0	1	0	0	.000	.000
Gebbers, Hawkins	R-R	6-2	205	7-29-86	.240	.333	.213	49	183	25	44	16	1	3	22	11	8	1	1	20	5	2	.388	.310
Jacquot, Jimmy	R-R	6-1	195	6-15-88	.208	.250	.198	37	120	11	25	8	0	4	19	10	4	1	1	37	0	1	.375	.289
Mailloux, Kevin	R-R	6-0	200	3-5-86	.296	.288	.298	65	250	63	74	19	3	15	52	28	2	1	3	51	7	4	.576	.367
Marcoe, Billy	R-R	5-10	195	6-5-87	.153	.231	.130	22	59	5	9	0	0	0	3	1	5	1	0	15	0	1	.153	.231
Morban, Julio	L-L	6-1	190	2-13-92	.250	.000	.250	1	4	0	1	0	0	0	0	0	0	0	0	2	0	0	.250	.250
Phillips, Anthony	R-R	5-9	160	4-11-90	.204	.074	.229	55	167	21	34	11	0	2	12	24	5	8	0	49	5	1	.305	.321
Rivero, Jose	R-R	6-2	180	1-8-90	.189	.083	.220	17	53	8	10	2	1	0	6	7	2	0	0	20	2	1	.264	.306
Rivers, Kevin	L-R	6-2	210	8-24-88	.332	.320	.335	71	241	48	80	13	4	11	48	60	4	0	4	62	5	3	.556	.466
Royster, Ryan	L-L	6-1	170	10-13-85	.237	.207	.245	35	135	11	32	12	4	2	12	12	4	1	0	35	8	2	.430	.318
Sams, Kalian	R-R	6-3	220	8-25-86	.193	.286	.161	26	83	11	16	4	1	5	12	12	1	0	1	34	1	0	.446	.299
Serrano, Terry	B-R	6-1	165	2-6-87	.307	.239	.325	62	212	39	65	11	2	1	19	29	0	13	1	61	16	13	.392	.388
Sharpley, Evan	L-R	6-2	205	11-4-86	.231	.216	.234	71	242	27	56	14	3	6	42	30	3	0	5	92	4	2	.388	.318
Wiswall, Mickey	L-R	6-1	200	11-25-88	.271	.125	.300	12	48	7	13	3	0	5	17	2	2	0	0	16	0	0	.646	.327

Pitching	B-T	HT	WT	DOB	W	L	ERA	G	GS	CG	SV	IP	H	R	ER	HR	BB	SO	AVG	vLH	vRH	K/9	BB/9
Arias, Jonathan	R-R	6-3	190	2-8-88	2	0	2.19	12	0	0	3	25	16	6	6	0	13	22	.190	.382	.060	8.03	4.74
Attard, Jarett	R-R	6-0	185	1-16-87	0	1	24.55	3	0	0	0	4	11	10	10	0	2	2	.579	.400	.643	4.91	4.91
Burgoon, Tyler	R-R	5-10	160	4-25-89	1	1	4.40	8	0	0	1	14	10	7	7	2	4	15	.200	.154	.216	9.42	2.51
Diaz, Ogui	R-R	6-2	170	12-1-85	4	3	5.12	17	4	0	0	39	36	24	22	5	15	31	.242	.327	.200	7.22	3.49
Fernandez, Anthony	L-L	6-4	180	6-8-90	8	3	2.59	15	15	0	0	83	75	29	24	1	18	69	.245	.261	.241	7.45	1.94
Housey, John	L-R	6-4	180	6-4-88	1	1	2.29	9	1	0	1	20	19	5	5	2	3	15	.264	.095	.333	6.86	1.37
Hudson, Austin	R-R	6-4	185	1-6-88	4	2	2.92	20	7	0	3	52	50	29	17	1	21	31	.255	.246	.260	5.33	3.61
Kesler, Willy	R-R	6-0	225	8-11-87	3	2	1.47	19	0	0	4	31	23	8	5	0	10	33	.213	.156	.237	9.68	2.93
Kessinger, Chris	R-R	6-0	195	6-5-86	2	0	5.71	9	0	0	2	17	16	11	11	1	12	15	.258	.273	.250	7.79	6.23
Kurowski, Kody	L-L	6-4	270	12-23-86	0	0	0.00	1	0	0	0	1	0	0	0	0	1	0	.000	.000	.000	9.00	0.00
Lewis, Taylor	R-R	6-4	190	6-2-88	0	1	22.09	3	0	0	0	4	6	11	9	0	7	2	.429	.500	.375	4.91	17.18
Markovitz, Jason	L-L	6-3	195	8-27-88	2	2	3.20	11	0	0	4	20	17	8	7	0	4	25	.230	.182	.250	11.44	1.83
Martinez, Fray	R-R	6-3	170	5-20-89	2	0	2.25	12	0	0	2	20	18	7	5	1	7	25	.234	.233	.234	11.25	3.15
Medina, Yoervis	R-R	6-3	210	7-27-88	3	2	4.20	8	8	0	0	41	49	30	19	4	15	48	.297	.338	.264	10.62	3.32
Merry, Jorden	R-R	6-1	190	6-30-87	2	0	3.93	10	0	0	1	18	10	11	8	1	12	26	.154	.150	.156	12.76	5.89
Pryor, Stephen	R-R	6-2	225	7-23-89	0	0	0.49	11	0	0	4	18	7	1	1	0	7	26	.119	.097	.143	12.76	3.44
Seco, Edlando	L-L	6-2	178	7-23-88	3	3	2.48	14	14	0	0	69	40	28	19	2	43	73	.169	.229	.154	9.52	5.61
Sena, Jandy	L-R	6-6	245	8-10-89	0	1	1.80	1	0	0	0	5	3	1	1	0	1	6	.176	.000	.200	10.80	1.80
Snow, Forrest	R-R	6-6	195	12-30-88	0	0	0.00	10	0	0	3	25	8	0	0	0	9	26	.104	.111	.098	9.24	3.20
Sorce, Chris	R-R	6-0	190	10-28-87	8	2	3.64	15	15	0	0	82	81	38	33	5	24	70	.261	.282	.250	7.71	2.64
Thomas, Eric	R-R	5-11	170	10-8-86	2	2	4.22	15	8	0	0	53	57	38	25	2	29	35	.270	.287	.258	5.91	4.89
Valdez, Eric	R-R	6-1	195	5-4-87	0	0	0.64	7	0	0	1	14	10	2	1	1	4	16	.192	.188	.194	10.29	2.57
Whitmore, Ben	L-L	6-4	215	4-17-88	0	1	3.68	6	0	0	0	7	9	4	3	1	5	5	.310	.333	.304	6.14	6.14
Wilhelmsen, Tom	R-R	6-6	197	12-16-83	1	0	3.68	3	3	0	0	15	14	6	6	1	2	14	.255	.400	.171	8.59	1.23

Fielding

Catcher	PCT	G	PO	A	E	DP	PB
Baron	.994	50	420	47	3	6	7
Jacquot	.988	18	144	23	2	1	3
Marcoe	1.000	11	71	6	0	0	2

First Base	PCT	G	PO	A	E	DP
Gebbers	1.000	5	39	3	0	1
Mailloux	1.000	9	70	7	0	5
Sharpley	.985	64	535	37	9	51

Second Base	PCT	G	PO	A	E	DP
Bello	.989	20	36	50	1	11
Gebbers	.948	33	55	91	8	26
Mailloux	1.000	3	6	3	0	3

	PCT	G	PO	A	E	DP
Phillips	1.000	3	3	5	0	2
Serrano	.940	25	41	53	6	10

Third Base	PCT	G	PO	A	E	DP
Bello	.833	4	1	4	1	1
Gebbers	1.000	2	0	2	0	0
Mailloux	.933	48	34	92	9	7
Serrano	.938	16	11	49	4	5
Sharpley	.900	2	2	1	0	0
Wiswall	.955	8	6	15	1	0

Shortstop	PCT	G	PO	A	E	DP
Bello	.667	2	3	3	3	2
Mailloux	1.000	1	2	2	0	0

	PCT	G	PO	A	E	DP
Phillips	.979	51	78	158	5	29
Serrano	.938	25	48	57	7	18

Outfield	PCT	G	PO	A	E	DP
Anston	.971	63	130	3	4	1
Bello	1.000	3	6	0	0	0
Britton	.965	34	53	2	2	1
Burgess	—	1	0	0	0	0
Rivero	1.000	15	27	0	0	0
Rivers	.980	63	94	5	2	1
Royster	.938	28	28	2	2	0
Sams	.929	26	50	2	4	1

PULASKI MARINERS

ROOKIE

APPALACHIAN LEAGUE

Batting	B-T	HT	WT	DOB	AVG	vLH	vRH	G	AB	R	H	2B	3B	HR	RBI	BB	HBP	SH	SF	SO	SB	CS	SLG	OBP
Agudelo, Jorge	R-R	6-0	175	5-30-89	.287	.290	.286	59	223	41	64	16	7	2	41	17	8	3	0	46	24	7	.448	.359
Blash, Jabari	R-R	6-4	195	7-4-89	.266	.242	.276	32	109	21	29	6	1	5	20	13	4	0	1	44	1	1	.477	.362
Browning, Matt	R-R	6-0	210	1-7-88	.330	.308	.338	34	106	21	35	7	0	4	24	17	4	0	1	19	6	4	.509	.438
Burgess, Jarrett	R-R	6-2	180	8-10-90	.150	.000	.188	5	20	3	3	0	0	2	5	2	0	0	0	11	0	0	.450	.227
Contreras, Henry	R-R	5-11	208	5-5-86	.321	.167	.364	7	28	5	9	0	0	2	8	4	2	0	0	3	0	0	.536	.441
Extrano, Jetsy	B-R	6-1	175	8-13-88	.230	.191	.244	49	178	29	41	8	1	2	24	17	6	3	0	48	7	2	.320	.318
Giobbi, Andrew	R-R	6-2	194	10-25-86	.291	.280	.295	32	103	16	30	6	0	2	12	8	3	3	1	28	1	1	.408	.357
Gonzalez, Larry	R-R	5-11	170	2-1-88	.267	.294	.254	31	101	12	27	7	0	1	17	7	3	1	0	22	0	2	.366	.333
Jimenez, Hassiel	R-R	6-0	205	5-8-91	.229	.143	.258	25	83	9	19	4	0	0	8	4	2	0	0	27	1	1	.277	.264
Morban, Julio	L-L	6-1	190	2-13-92	.100	.000	.125	4	10	1	1	0	0	0	0	4	0	0	0	3	0	0	.100	.357
Morla, Ramon	R-R	6-1	175	11-20-89	.323	.347	.313	62	251	60	81	17	2	17	49	15	3	0	3	65	13	4	.610	.364
Paquette, Ethan	R-R	6-3	220	3-12-88	.236	.194	.250	46	140	17	33	4	0	3	19	12	4	0	0	31	4	2	.329	.314
Poppert, Derek	R-R	6-1	190	7-27-88	.242	.271	.228	48	149	23	36	8	0	1	11	10	9	5	0	23	14	1	.315	.327
Rivero, Jose	R-R	6-2	180	1-8-90	.295	.211	.303	46	190	39	56	7	3	7	35	13	1	0	0	54	11	4	.474	.343
Schlander, Jake	R-R	6-2	195	8-4-88	.259	.352	.222	54	189	26	49	7	1	1	25	23	4	3	2	43	6	5	.323	.349
Wood, James	L-L	6-2	200	12-19-87	.291	.292	.291	28	103	18	30	7	1	1	8	12	4	1	0	28	8	2	.408	.387
Yepez, Mario	B-R	6-2	160	6-15-88	.231	.294	.207	60	242	36	56	12	1	6	27	13	7	5	2	47	3	2	.364	.288

Pitching	B-T	HT	WT	DOB	W	L	ERA	G	GS	CG	SV	IP	H	R	ER	HR	BB	SO	AVG	vLH	vRH	K/9	BB/9
Abbott, Lance	R-R	6-2	205	9-22-86	0	0	2.25	10	1	0	1	24	24	7	6	2	7	17	.258	.333	.236	6.38	2.63
Bischoff, Matt	R-R	6-0	190	5-21-87	4	3	3.30	17	0	0	5	30	22	12	11	2	8	45	.204	.242	.187	13.50	2.40
Boyce, Tim	R-R	6-2	193	2-6-87	9	3	2.98	13	8	0	0	57	48	28	19	3	11	55	.221	.247	.206	8.63	1.73
Chang, Yao Wen	R-R	6-2	202	10-31-90	0	0	10.07	11	0	0	1	20	32	23	22	4	6	20	.360	.344	.368	9.15	2.75
Diaz, Nolan	R-R	6-1	175	3-28-91	3	3	6.39	12	8	0	1	49	67	40	35	7	13	36	.324	.333	.319	6.57	2.37
Griffin, Tim	B-R	6-1	200	3-1-88	1	0	4.67	13	0	0	2	27	27	16	14	2	5	31	.252	.308	.221	10.33	1.67
Kiel, Ryan	L-L	6-4	230	6-26-87	1	1	3.97	13	0	0	0	23	21	12	10	4	11	27	.247	.267	.243	10.72	4.37
Kim, Seon Gi	R-R	6-2	185	9-1-91	0	0	0.00	1	0	0	0	3	1	0	0	0	1	7	.091	.000	.100	21.00	3.00
Kohlscheen, Stephen	R-R	6-6	200	9-20-88	3	0	2.51	7	5	0	0	29	30	8	8	1	5	28	.268	.250	.276	8.79	1.57
Krist, Josh	R-R	6-1	187	10-10-87	0	0	13.50	2	0	0	0	2	4	4	3	0	2	0	.400	.000	.500	0.00	9.00
Leigh, Bryan	L-R	6-0	200	2-11-88	2	0	1.71	12	0	0	3	21	16	8	4	2	6	19	.203	.207	.200	8.14	2.57

	B-T	HT	WT	DOB	W	L	ERA	G	GS	CG	SV	IP	H	R	ER	HR	BB	SO	AVG	vLH	vRH	K/9	BB/9
Mieses, George	R-R	6-2	180	5-3-91	4	4	3.45	13	13	0	0	76	80	39	29	5	10	48	.266	.261	.269	5.71	1.19
Nava, Jessie	R-R	6-3	165	9-18-87	4	3	4.36	13	13	0	0	66	78	42	32	8	25	54	.285	.288	.284	7.36	3.41
Olivero, Yovanny	R-R	6-2	176	3-5-88	3	5	5.01	13	6	1	1	50	63	31	28	1	11	34	.304	.313	.299	6.08	1.97
Rodriguez, Leonardo	R-R	6-2	185	4-15-88	0	0	3.60	1	1	0	0	5	3	3	2	1	1	5	.188	.000	.250	9.00	1.80
Vancil, Preston	R-R	6-4	250	11-15-86	2	1	2.84	9	0	0	0	19	19	7	6	2	3	20	.257	.174	.294	9.47	1.42
Vargas, Richard	R-R	6-3	170	4-19-91	1	2	4.54	9	7	0	0	34	36	24	17	0	14	28	.283	.340	.250	7.49	3.74
Versnik, Ben	R-R	6-3	240	12-5-88	0	0	3.38	6	0	0	0	8	4	3	3	1	4	13	.154	.000	.211	14.63	4.50
Vitale, Michael	L-L	6-2	195	11-26-87	0	2	5.91	9	3	0	0	21	28	19	14	1	3	9	.308	.174	.353	3.80	1.27
Whitmore, Ben	L-L	6-4	215	4-17-88	0	0	6.75	7	0	0	0	15	23	15	11	1	4	14	.343	.167	.382	8.59	2.45

Fielding

Catcher	PCT	G	PO	A	E	DP	PB
Giobbi	.991	15	103	10	1	1	2
Gonzalez	.984	31	225	28	4	0	5
Jimenez	.966	25	187	11	7	1	9

First Base	PCT	G	PO	A	E	DP
Browning	.984	32	235	16	4	23
Contreras	1.000	1	11	1	0	2
Giobbi	1.000	6	61	5	0	2
Morla	1.000	2	13	0	0	0
Paquette	.971	32	259	9	8	22

Second Base	PCT	G	PO	A	E	DP
Agudelo	.959	31	48	70	5	16

	PCT	G	PO	A	E	DP
Extrano	.962	12	10	40	2	5
Poppert	.963	20	38	40	3	13
Schlander	1.000	6	14	12	0	3
Wood	1.000	1	0	2	0	1

Third Base	PCT	G	PO	A	E	DP
Agudelo	.947	8	5	13	1	1
Browning	1.000	1	2	3	0	0
Extrano	1.000	6	3	10	0	2
Morla	.879	51	33	120	21	6

Shortstop	PCT	G	PO	A	E	DP
Extrano	.974	18	24	51	2	14
Poppert	.800	3	2	6	2	2

	PCT	G	PO	A	E	DP
Schlander	.919	45	63	108	15	21

Outfield	PCT	G	PO	A	E	DP
Agudelo	.944	14	17	0	1	0
Blash	.986	32	67	2	1	0
Burgess	.846	5	11	0	2	0
Extrano	.500	1	1	0	1	0
Paquette	1.000	5	7	0	0	0
Poppert	.875	11	14	0	2	0
Rivero	.989	46	92	2	1	0
Wood	1.000	27	50	1	0	0
Yepez	.991	59	105	6	1	0

AZL MARINERS

ROOKIE

ARIZONA LEAGUE

Batting	B-T	HT	WT	DOB	AVG	vLH	vRH	G	AB	R	H	2B	3B	HR	RBI	BB	HBP	SH	SF	SO	SB	CS	SLG	OBP
Acevedo, Michael	R-R	6-0	185	12-5-90	.329	.280	.338	40	155	19	51	8	2	0	14	6	1	0	0	31	7	4	.406	.358
Brady, Patrick	R-R	5-10	175	2-5-88	.143	.143	.143	21	56	5	8	2	0	1	1	2	1	0	0	6	1	2	.232	.186
Brito, Bryan	R-R	6-2	170	2-16-92	.157	.219	.139	44	140	13	22	1	1	0	6	10	0	3	1	69	9	6	.179	.212
Browning, Matt	R-R	6-0	210	1-7-88	.267	.333	.250	13	45	7	12	3	1	0	8	6	2	0	0	7	1	1	.378	.377
Burgess, Jarrett	R-R	6-2	180	8-10-90	.278	.500	.250	7	18	2	5	2	0	0	1	2	0	0	0	10	1	0	.389	.350
Carmichael, Christian	R-R	5-11	200	4-25-92	.100	.000	.103	11	30	1	3	0	0	0	1	2	2	1	0	8	1	0	.100	.206
Choi, Ji-Man	L-R	6-1	195	5-19-91	.378	.348	.384	39	135	23	51	15	2	1	23	21	1	0	2	30	10	1	.541	.459
Christian, Frankie	L-L	6-1	192	6-6-91	.196	.333	.186	15	46	8	9	1	0	0	3	2	0	0	0	15	3	0	.217	.229
Dunigan, Joe	L-L	6-1	215	3-29-86	.364	.429	.346	9	33	2	12	5	1	0	4	2	1	0	0	12	3	0	.576	.417
Flores, Mario	R-R	6-3	195	10-9-87	.228	.172	.245	38	127	17	29	10	0	3	21	14	5	0	3	45	1	2	.378	.322
Hernandez, Jose	R-R	6-1	165	1-12-88	.157	.125	.167	22	70	3	11	5	0	0	3	2	0	0	2	20	0	0	.229	.213
Lopez, Danny	R-R	5-11	180	1-21-88	.236	.150	.269	22	72	16	17	1	0	3	11	9	2	1	1	14	9	1	.375	.333
Martinez, Jose	R-R	6-1	180	7-22-92	.150	.185	.140	40	120	7	18	4	0	1	9	15	0	4	0	48	2	1	.208	.261
Morales, Alfredo	R-R	6-2	190	11-6-92	.224	.128	.252	48	174	25	39	17	2	1	14	14	1	1	2	59	6	3	.362	.283
Morban, Julio	L-L	6-1	190	2-13-92	.400	1.000	.250	3	5	0	2	0	0	1	0	0	0	0	0	1	0	0	.400	.400
Pimentel, Guillermo	R-L	6-1	180	10-5-92	.250	.182	.265	51	184	20	46	7	6	6	31	5	2	0	1	58	5	1	.451	.276
Ramirez, Carlos	B-R	5-11	145	12-2-88	.234	.194	.245	40	141	25	33	10	1	0	22	6	0	3	4	30	3	4	.319	.341
Rangel, Rigoberto	R-R	6-1	167	6-21-89	.240	.235	.241	32	100	6	24	2	1	0	10	8	1	0	2	31	4	0	.280	.297
Rodriguez, Robert	R-R	6-4	180	7-22-90	.239	.105	.274	33	92	9	22	3	0	1	6	1	2	1	0	34	3	2	.304	.263
Royster, Ryan	L-L	6-1	170	10-13-85	.444	.750	.391	8	27	8	12	6	0	0	3	5	1	0	0	5	2	0	.667	.545
Tanabe, Carlton	R-R	6-0	190	10-28-91	.107	.050	.127	21	75	5	8	2	0	0	2	3	2	1	0	20	2	1	.133	.163

Pitching	B-T	HT	WT	DOB	W	L	ERA	G	GS	CG	SV	IP	H	R	ER	HR	BB	SO	AVG	vLH	vRH	K/9	BB/9
Attard, Jarett	R-R	6-0	185	1-16-87	0	0	4.15	8	0	0	1	13	22	6	6	0	2	16	.379	.348	.400	11.08	1.38
Aviles, Mike	R-R	6-1	200	10-21-89	0	1	6.98	14	0	0	1	19	22	17	15	1	10	21	.293	.269	.306	9.78	4.66
Bedard, Erik	L-L	6-1	200	3-5-79	0	0	2.70	2	2	0	0	7	7	2	2	0	0	11	.250	.300	.222	14.85	0.00
Cruz, Danny	R-R	6-0	180	4-20-89	1	0	4.05	8	0	0	3	13	13	6	6	1	3	23	.255	.278	.242	15.52	2.03
de Haas, Jeroen	R-R	6-5	175	1-1-91	3	3	4.18	15	1	0	0	28	33	21	13	2	6	23	.280	.340	.239	7.39	1.93
Gallagher, Nolan	R-R	6-3	190	12-20-85	1	1	5.40	2	2	0	0	10	12	8	6	2	3	7	.286	.000	.300	6.30	2.70
Jimenez, Cesar	L-L	5-11	220	11-12-84	0	0	0.00	3	3	0	0	9	4	0	0	0	0	8	.182	.000	.211	12.00	0.00
Kaalekahi, Charles	B-R	6-2	175	5-13-92	1	1	5.21	8	0	0	0	19	24	13	11	1	4	18	.304	.333	.288	8.53	1.89
Kim, Seon Gi	R-R	6-1	185	9-1-91	6	2	5.14	13	7	0	0	61	76	37	35	3	12	71	.302	.283	.315	10.42	1.76
Kurowski, Kody	L-L	6-4	270	12-23-86	1	3	4.30	15	0	0	5	23	34	20	11	0	8	17	.370	.357	.372	6.65	3.13
Landazuri, Steve	R-R	6-0	175	1-6-92	1	2	3.60	9	0	0	0	20	20	9	8	0	7	11	.274	.200	.326	4.95	3.15
Maurer, Brandon	R-R	6-5	200	7-3-90	0	1	1.64	4	4	0	0	11	8	4	2	0	2	14	.205	.154	.231	11.45	1.64
Petiton, Matt	L-L	6-1	170	1-2-88	0	3	5.17	8	0	0	0	16	20	11	9	2	1	19	.313	.133	.367	10.91	0.57
Reed, Nate	R-R	6-3	180	12-1-87	1	5	4.13	11	9	0	0	48	51	22	22	3	10	46	.279	.215	.314	8.63	1.88
Ronnenbergh, Scott	L-L	6-2	175	1-11-92	0	1	2.13	9	0	0	0	13	12	7	3	2	11	8	.255	.143	.275	5.68	7.82
Saito, Derrick	L-L	5-9	155	12-26-87	0	0	5.14	3	3	0	0	7	7	4	4	0	5	4	.280	.286	.238	11.57	5.14
Sena, Jandy	L-R	6-6	245	8-10-89	4	2	4.01	13	4	0	1	43	43	22	19	0	14	35	.262	.290	.245	7.38	2.95
Taylor, Luke	R-R	6-6	200	7-14-92	0	3	5.24	10	0	0	0	22	25	22	13	1	17	14	.287	.308	.279	5.64	6.85
Unsworth, Dylan	R-R	6-1	170	9-23-92	2	5	3.93	11	10	0	0	50	71	27	22	1	1	44	.340	.359	.328	7.87	0.18
Valdez, Eric	R-R	6-1	195	5-4-87	0	2	4.95	5	4	0	0	20	21	12	11	1	11	26	.269	.281	.261	11.70	4.95
Vancil, Preston	R-R	6-4	250	11-15-86	0	0	0.00	3	0	0	0	8	5	0	0	0	0	9	.167	.083	.222	9.72	0.00
Walker, Taijuan	R-R	6-4	195	8-13-92	1	1	1.29	6	0	0	0	7	3	1	1	0	3	9	.087	.143	.063	11.57	3.86
Wilhelmsen, Tom	R-R	6-6	197	12-16-83	0	0	0.60	5	3	0	0	15	4	1	1	0	2	22	.078	.000	.118	13.20	1.20

Fielding

Catcher	PCT	G	PO	A	E	DP	PB
Carmichael	.962	10	69	7	3	0	1
Choi	1.000	10	88	12	0	1	0
Hernandez	.984	18	164	17	3	0	4
Tanabe	.983	21	153	19	3	3	9

First Base	PCT	G	PO	A	E	DP
Acevedo	.977	5	42	1	1	4
Browning	1.000	1	4	0	0	0
Choi	.996	29	202	22	1	29
Dunigan	1.000	1	9	1	0	2
Flores	.990	22	194	10	2	16
Hernandez	.923	3	11	1	1	0

Second Base	PCT	G	PO	A	E	DP
Acevedo	.889	10	17	23	5	4
Brady	.957	18	26	41	3	10
Lopez	.852	7	7	16	4	4
Ramirez	.993	28	57	83	1	24

Third Base	PCT	G	PO	A	E	DP
Acevedo	.850	12	7	10	3	1
Browning	.882	8	4	11	2	2
Martinez	.871	38	20	68	13	10
Ramirez	1.000	3	0	2	0	0

Shortstop	PCT	G	PO	A	E	DP
Brady	1.000	2	2	1	0	0
Brito	.957	44	62	115	8	28

Lopez	.941	5	4	12	1	1
Ramirez	.953	9	9	32	2	6

Outfield	PCT	G	PO	A	E	DP
Acevedo	1.000	12	13	0	0	0
Burgess	1.000	6	5	0	0	0
Christian	.917	10	11	0	1	0
Dunigan	1.000	4	6	1	0	0
Morales	.941	47	90	6	6	1
Morban	1.000	2	2	0	0	0
Pimentel	.938	44	55	6	4	2
Rangel	.930	28	38	2	3	1
Rodriguez	.915	28	41	2	4	1
Royster	.909	6	8	2	1	0

DSL MARINERS   ROOKIE
DOMINICAN SUMMER LEAGUE

Batting	B-T	HT	WT	DOB	AVG	vLH	vRH	G	AB	R	H	2B	3B	HR	RBI	BB	HBP	SH	SF	SO	SB	CS	SLG	OBP
Batista, David	R-R	5-11	170	8-10-93	.200	.125	.219	21	40	2	8	2	0	0	5	7	2	3	1	15	1	0	.250	.340
Beltre, Marbin	B-R	6-3	180	3-30-90	.000	.000	.000	8	10	1	0	0	0	0	0	3	1	0	0	3	5	2	.000	.286
Berro, Noe	L-R	6-3	180	8-21-93	.200	.214	.198	50	120	12	24	5	1	1	9	23	1	3	0	47	5	3	.283	.333
Brea, Ivan	R-R	6-2	190	7-5-88	.192	.143	.202	47	120	13	23	4	1	0	13	8	1	0	0	28	1	1	.242	.248
Drullard, George	R-R	6-3	180	9-27-91	.231	.250	.228	51	121	25	28	3	1	1	11	33	5	2	2	35	9	5	.298	.410
Lara, Jordy	R-R	6-3	180	5-21-91	.191	.342	.158	61	209	35	40	12	0	7	46	44	4	0	6	69	4	4	.349	.335
Marcelino, Westlonder	R-R	6-4	200	3-2-91	.188	.235	.173	33	69	9	13	2	0	0	7	13	2	4	0	16	1	1	.217	.333
Matias, Luis	R-R	6-2	180	8-27-90	.224	.424	.171	56	156	30	35	4	0	0	15	23	4	5	0	34	9	6	.250	.339
Morales, Estarlyn	R-R	6-3	180	10-28-92	.167	.333	.139	38	84	13	14	3	1	1	9	13	3	2	0	27	3	2	.262	.300
Nunez, Efrain	B-R	6-3	190	2-17-91	.205	.217	.203	55	151	27	31	2	2	3	17	34	6	3	2	55	11	11	.305	.368
Perez, Randy	R-R	6-3	180	2-23-89	.272	.379	.246	57	147	34	40	3	3	0	14	34	7	3	1	32	31	9	.333	.429
Sanchez, Miguel	R-R	6 2	180	9-27-91	.186	.294	.163	42	97	12	18	3	0	1	13	22	3	0	2	34	0	1	.247	.347
Sanon, Bertin	R-R	5-10	180	7-14-89	.212	.222	.211	38	113	17	24	5	0	1	13	11	4	4	1	35	3	4	.283	.302
Soto, George	R R	6-2	190	11-19-89	.203	.500	.158	50	153	16	31	3	2	3	20	26	6	4	2	37	5	4	.307	.337
van Heydoorn, Rudy	R-R	6-3	180	4-17-89	.305	.276	.311	61	177	31	54	15	0	7	26	42	4	0	5	51	2	8	.508	.439
Wel, Axel	L-L	6-4	180	4-10-91	.179	.250	.168	44	123	22	22	5	0	1	18	20	3	2	2	19	1	1	.244	.304
Zorrilla, Janelfry	R-R	6-2	180	9-2-90	.286	.212	.301	63	196	34	56	12	2	4	36	26	4	2	3	37	12	5	.429	.376

Pitching	B-T	HT	WT	DOB	W	L	ERA	G	GS	CG	SV	IP	H	R	ER	HR	BB	SO	AVG	vLH	vRH	K/9	BB/9
Abad, Martin	L-L	6-2	170	0-0-00	2	3	1.29	16	0	0	5	35	22	7	5	0	7	28	.190	.444	.168	7.20	1.80
Aquino, Gregorio	R-R	6-5	175	3-5-90	3	1	3.03	14	1	0	0	33	27	16	11	2	18	26	.231	.235	.230	7.16	4.96
Brazoban, Domingo	R-R	6-2	175	8-8-89	1	2	3.51	10	4	0	0	33	24	16	13	1	11	24	.203	.400	.185	6.48	2.97
Cortoreal, Leonel	L-L	6-5	175	9-6-92	2	0	5.14	11	11	0	0	42	30	28	24	4	35	28	.201	.250	.200	6.00	7.50
De La Cruz, Noel	R-R	6-3	180	12-17-91	1	1	2.01	10	0	0	1	22	18	9	5	1	11	14	.220	.231	.217	5.64	4.43
DeJesus, Yunior	R-R	6-2	180	9-22-88	2	1	2.57	19	0	0	8	35	34	15	10	1	12	36	.254	.308	.248	9.26	3.09
Gonzalez, Yeuri	R-R	6-2	170	12-22-92	0	0	5.40	1	0	0	0	2	2	1	1	0	1	0	.286	.500	.000	0.00	5.40
Hidalgo, Ambioris	R-R	6-2	196	2-4-91	5	3	3.95	14	10	0	0	57	52	28	25	1	30	48	.242	.324	.227	7.58	4.74
Marte, Wander	L-L	6-2	180	6-30-92	0	0	2.66	9	5	0	0	20	11	9	6	0	19	28	.155	.000	.164	12.39	8.41
Munoz, Leoncio	L-L	6-4	170	8-18-90	2	1	3.82	15	1	0	1	31	25	16	13	1	16	24	.221	.750	.202	7.04	4.70
Nunez, Junior	R-R	6-3	210	3-1-92	3	2	1.60	15	0	0	0	34	25	7	6	0	18	27	.212	.417	.189	7.22	4.81
Ogando, Jochi	R-R	6-5	210	5-27-93	2	2	3.99	12	9	0	1	38	28	25	17	2	27	32	.200	.227	.195	7.51	6.34
Perez, Brandol	R-L	6-4	175	8-10-93	7	0	0.19	11	6	1	1	48	20	3	1	0	14	68	.125	.143	.124	12.66	2.61
Perez, Henry	L-L	6-2	170	10-18-89	7	1	0.86	11	11	3	0	73	49	7	7	0	10	76	.187	.444	.178	9.37	1.23
Rosario, Enrique	R-R	6-1	180	6-23-91	2	3	4.97	16	1	0	0	29	33	28	16	3	16	37	.282	.353	.270	11.48	4.97
Vizcaino, Joan	R-R	6-6	195	4-25-89	3	2	3.06	10	7	0	0	35	31	20	12	0	15	26	.231	.316	.217	6.62	3.82

Fielding

Catcher	PCT	G	PO	A	E	DP	PB
Batista	1.000	2	10	2	0	1	1
Brea	.985	46	295	34	5	1	3
Sanchez	1.000	27	168	28	0	0	4
van Heydoorn	.971	16	91	8	3	3	7

First Base	PCT	G	PO	A	E	DP
Brea	1.000	1	7	0	0	1
Lara	.960	6	46	2	2	4
Marcelino	.994	28	168	2	1	12
Matias	1.000	3	18	1	0	2
Sanchez	1.000	4	20	3	0	1
Sanon	.984	9	59	2	1	4
van Heydoorn	.986	34	213	5	3	24

Wel	1.000	3	14	1	0	3

Second Base	PCT	G	PO	A	E	DP
Batista	1.000	5	3	4	0	1
Lara	1.000	2	0	2	0	0
Matias	.981	3	4	56	2	17
Sanon	1.000	5	5	7	0	5
Soto	.948	42	83	82	9	15

Third Base	PCT	G	PO	A	E	DP
Batista	.864	8	2	17	3	2
Lara	.909	53	44	105	15	10
Matias	.800	7	3	9	3	2
Sanon	.818	8	6	12	4	0
van Heydoorn	.889	4	2	6	1	1

Shortstop	PCT	G	PO	A	E	DP
Berro	.900	46	48	105	17	15
Matias	.959	19	26	45	3	12
Perez	1.000	1	1	1	0	0
Sanon	.892	20	20	38	7	7

Outfield	PCT	G	PO	A	E	DP
Beltre	.909	5	10	0	1	0
Drullard	.945	48	66	3	4	1
Marcelino	.750	1	3	0	1	0
Morales	.977	33	40	2	1	1
Nunez	.959	47	70	0	3	0
Perez	1.000	53	88	3	0	0
Zorrilla	.938	54	101	4	7	0

VENEZUELAN SUMMER LEAGUE

Batting	B-T	HT	WT	DOB	AVG	vLH	vRH	G	AB	R	H	2B	3B	HR	RBI	BB	HBP	SH	SF	SO	SB	CS	SLG	OBP
Acevedo, Michael	R-R	6-0	185	12-5-90	.304	.185	.354	28	92	14	28	5	1	4	23	12	2	1	1	7	3	0	.511	.393
Batista, Yidid	R-R	6-0	150	10-13-89	.274	.231	.290	62	190	24	52	4	0	1	31	7	5	8	1	10	13	5	.311	.315
Brito, Miguel	R-R	6-3	228	9-11-92	.283	.234	.298	60	198	24	56	12	1	2	44	13	4	0	2	23	1	2	.384	.336
Burin, Felipe	B-R	5-10	160	2-10-92	.335	.370	.324	58	182	41	61	13	0	2	22	40	5	3	1	18	4	1	.440	.465
Coronel, Ramon	R-R	5-11	155	2-2-92	.265	.200	.289	46	113	27	30	3	1	0	7	12	1	7	0	15	4	1	.310	.341
Diaz, Franklin	B-R	6-1	170	7-20-90	.281	.211	.300	34	89	19	25	5	0	0	6	14	1	0	0	10	2	0	.337	.385
Gonzalez, Ricardo	R-R	6-0	206	3-25-92	.185	.211	.174	27	65	7	12	3	0	1	7	10	1	1	2	22	0	0	.277	.295
Hart, Kenny	R-R	6-3	180	3-21-90	.288	.286	.289	36	104	21	30	4	1	2	13	13	9	5	0	24	8	5	.404	.413
Kalbakgi, Jose	R-R	6-1	200	9-16-92	.153	.192	.130	29	72	5	11	3	0	0	5	8	1	0	0	14	1	0	.194	.247
Lampe, Reginald	R-R	6-3	170	3-1-90	.292	.341	.266	44	120	16	35	11	0	2	16	14	4	1	0	21	2	5	.433	.384
Michel, Rashynol	B-R	6-2	175	11-30-92	.218	.256	.200	44	119	12	26	1	0	0	6	7	0	4	2	32	9	3	.227	.258
Mina, Diego	R-R	5-11	181	10-13-92	.216	.208	.220	33	74	13	16	3	0	0	10	7	3	0	0	18	2	1	.257	.310
Okuda, Pedro	L-R	5-10	160	4-20-90	.220	.125	.242	21	41	7	9	1	0	0	6	6	1	2	1	7	0	0	.244	.327
Palma, Alexy	R-R	6-3	195	12-24-92	.276	.269	.278	61	185	35	51	11	1	3	29	27	8	1	2	28	7	5	.395	.387
Posso, Carlos	R-R	6-0	186	8-20-93	.214	.100	.278	17	28	3	6	0	0	0	2	9	2	0	2	12	0	0	.214	.415
Ramirez, Ivan	R-R	6-1	190	7-25-92	.330	.296	.346	65	227	32	75	14	0	0	29	27	1	0	4	23	0	0	.392	.398
Ugueto, Jesus	R-R	6-0	170	5-30-91	.291	.250	.304	55	196	30	57	12	2	3	26	17	1	1	4	36	4	2	.418	.344
Velasquez, Roberto	B-R	5-11	160	2-14-90	.301	.320	.293	63	166	26	50	10	0	0	21	16	7	7	1	14	4	3	.361	.384

Pitching	B-T	HT	WT	DOB	W	L	ERA	G	GS	CG	SV	IP	H	R	ER	HR	BB	SO	AVG	vLH	vRH	K/9	BB/9
Alvarez, Waldy	R-R	6-3	178	7-27-92	0	0	9.00	1	0	0	0	1	2	1	1	0	0	0	.400	.000	.400	0.00	0.00
Bravo, Oscar	L-L	6-0	210	4-19-92	2	0	3.38	11	3	0	1	19	18	11	7	0	9	8	.247	.333	.234	3.86	4.34
Campos, Jose	R-R	6-4	195	7-27-92	8	2	3.16	13	12	1	0	57	49	22	20	0	19	59	.231	.167	.247	9.32	3.00
Carrera, Rafael	R-R	6-0	190	10-29-92	0	0	5.52	6	1	0	0	15	17	10	9	0	6	9	.293	.176	.341	5.52	3.68
Flores, Jose	R-R	6-2	190	12-31-92	1	1	3.16	7	4	0	1	26	23	14	9	0	5	18	.240	.208	.250	6.31	1.75
Gonzalez, Isliexel	R-R	6-3	185	5-10-91	3	2	3.40	16	3	0	4	50	49	25	19	2	19	40	.251	.239	.255	7.15	3.40
Guaipe, Mayckol	R-R	6-3	175	8-11-90	4	2	2.77	18	1	0	4	49	47	22	15	0	13	41	.257	.260	.256	7.58	2.40
Julio, Ivan	R-R	6-3	175	8-19-91	3	1	2.13	9	6	1	0	38	37	15	9	1	18	26	.268	.261	.270	6.16	4.26
Mata, Daniel	R-R	6-2	180	7-3-93	2	3	4.85	15	8	0	2	43	57	30	23	0	19	34	.333	.317	.338	7.17	4.01
Mendoza, Jose	R-R	6-2	193	9-29-92	1	0	4.32	6	0	0	1	8	6	4	4	2	1	4	.200	.286	.174	4.32	1.08
Morales, Osmel	R-R	6-3	196	10-30-92	0	0	0.00	2	0	0	1	6	3	1	0	0	0	6	.136	.200	.118	8.53	0.00
Pereira, Cruz	L-L	5-10	175	12-18-90	5	1	3.48	13	5	0	1	41	36	18	16	1	22	21	.237	.250	.236	4.57	4.79
Pereira, Ricardo	R-R	6-3	150	4-18-91	3	4	3.69	21	6	0	7	46	46	25	19	5	19	25	.274	.241	.291	4.86	3.69
Pirela, Jesus	R-R	6-3	190	9-17-91	0	1	10.64	8	2	0	0	11	11	14	13	0	18	10	.289	.167	.313	8.18	14.73
Quintanilla, Kevin	R-R	6-0	174	5-21-92	1	2	5.06	10	2	0	1	27	30	17	15	0	11	18	.297	.409	.266	6.07	3.71
Raga, Angel	R-R	6-1	168	7-25-89	4	2	2.76	13	8	0	1	59	56	19	18	3	15	51	.253	.327	.233	7.82	2.30
Sabala, Reynaldo	R-R	6-3	187	8-16-90	4	3	2.66	14	4	0	1	47	41	23	14	0	18	40	.237	.231	.240	7.61	3.42
Ynfantes, Maykel	R-R	6-0	190	12-6-90	4	2	3.44	15	6	0	1	52	61	27	20	1	9	33	.293	.304	.290	5.68	1.55

Fielding

Catcher	PCT	G	PO	A	E	DP	PB
Diaz	.973	30	146	33	5	1	3
Gonzalez	.984	24	109	13	2	0	5
Ramirez	.991	31	196	22	2	2	4

First Base	PCT	G	PO	A	E	DP
Acevedo	1.000	2	10	0	0	0
Batista	.988	16	83	2	1	5
Brito	.975	15	106	9	3	15
Coronel	1.000	1	2	0	0	0
Diaz	1.000	2	14	1	0	0
Gonzalez	1.000	1	7	0	0	1
Kalbakgi	.971	22	159	6	5	20
Lampe	.966	5	28	0	1	3
Ramirez	.997	29	275	11	1	34

Second Base	PCT	G	PO	A	E	DP
Acevedo	.946	18	28	42	4	6
Batista	.982	27	49	60	2	27
Burin	.902	15	34	40	8	15
Coronel	1.000	10	8	8	0	3
Mina	1.000	17	9	17	0	2
Okuda	.894	9	16	26	5	8

Third Base	PCT	G	PO	A	E	DP
Acevedo	—	1	0	0	0	0
Batista	.904	22	9	38	5	5
Brito	.821	30	12	52	14	4
Burin	.917	21	8	25	3	0
Coronel	.935	24	10	33	3	2
Ramirez	1.000	1	0	3	0	0

	PCT	G	PO	A	E	DP
Ugueto	—	1	0	0	0	0

Shortstop	PCT	G	PO	A	E	DP
Burin	.892	7	9	24	4	1
Coronel	.938	19	26	50	5	10
Okuda	.500	2	1	1	2	0
Velasquez	.936	62	83	197	19	52

Outfield	PCT	G	PO	A	E	DP
Acevedo	1.000	5	5	0	0	0
Hart	.898	35	49	4	6	1
Lampe	.955	36	40	2	2	1
Michel	.955	41	59	5	3	1
Palma	.981	59	99	4	2	1
Posso	1.000	13	8	0	0	0
Ugueto	.920	53	62	7	6	1

Tampa Bay Rays

SEASON IN A SENTENCE: The Rays bolted out to a 30-11 start and finished with the best record in the American League, but after overcoming the Yankees to win the AL East, the Rays lost all three of their home games in the AL Division Series, including Game Five to Cliff Lee and the Rangers.

HIGH POINT: The last game of the regular season was a tough, 12-inning 3-2 victory at Kansas City, clinching the second division championship in three years for a franchise that was a perennial doormat for its first decade.

LOW POINT: The Rays' offense was productive, ranking third in the AL in runs despite a .247 average that ranked 13th. But it also was inconsistent, which was most evident in the Rangers series. It also showed when the Athletics' Dallas Braden (May 9) and Diamondbacks' Edwin Jackson (June 25) no-hit Tampa Bay. The Rays narrowly avoided becoming the first team to be no-hit three times in a season against the Blue Jays on Aug. 8, when Evan Longoria singled with two outs to break up Brandon Morrow's no-hitter. Morrow struck out 17 in the Rays' 1-0 loss.

NOTABLE ROOKIES: The Rays broke in a trio of rookies in the middle of the field. John Jaso surprisingly emerged as their top catcher, ranking among rookie leaders with a .372 on-base percentage; Sean Rodriguez slugged nine homers as the team's most regular second baseman while seeing time at six other positions; and Reid Brignac hit eight more while playing mostly shortstop and second.

KEY TRANSACTIONS: The Rays stayed in-house and didn't pull off a significant deal at the trade deadline. They released expensive bust Pat Burrell after 84 unproductive at-bats, then saw Burrell win a World Series ring after rejuvenating himself with the Giants.

DOWN ON THE FARM: The Rays produced their second Minor League Player of the Year in righthander Jeremy Hellickson (joining 2002 winner Rocco Baldelli), who helped pitch Triple-A Durham to another International League playoff berth. Lefthander Matt Moore, pitching at high Class A Charlotte, led the minors in strikeouts for a second straight season, while veteran Dan Johnson earned MVP honors in the IL before making the Rays' postseason roster. Only Rookie-level Princeton failed to post a winning record among Rays affiliates.

OPENING DAY PAYROLL: $71.9 million (19th)

2010 PERFORMANCE

General Manager: Andrew Friedman. **Farm Director:** Mitch Lukevics. **Scouting Director:** R.J. Harrison.

Class	Team	League	W	L	PCT	Finish*	Manager(s)
Majors	Tampa Bay Rays	American	96	66	.593	1st (14)	Joe Maddon
Triple-A	Durham Bulls	International	88	55	.615	1st (14)	Charlie Montoyo
Double-A	Montgomery Biscuits	Southern	72	66	.522	5th (10)	Billy Gardner
High A	Charlotte Stone Crabs	Florida State	80	59	.576	2nd (12)	Jim Morrison
Low A	Bowling Green Hot Rods	Midwest	61	78	.439	12th (16)	Brady Williams
Short-season	Hudson Valley Renegades	New York-Penn	39	36	.520	5th (14)	Jared Sandberg
Rookie	Princeton Rays	Appalachian	33	35	.485	6th (10)	Mike Johns
Rookie	GCL Rays	Gulf Coast	34	26	.567	2nd (15)	Joe Alvarez
Overall 2010 Minor League Record			407	355	.534	4th (30)	

*Finish in overall standings (No. of teams in league). †League champion.

ORGANIZATION STATISTICS

TAMPA BAY RAYS

AMERICAN LEAGUE

Batting	B-T	HT	WT	DOB	AVG	vLH	vRH	G	AB	R	H	2B	3B	HR	RBI	BB	HBP	SH	SF	SO	SB	CS	SLG	OBP
Aybar, Willy	B-R	5-11	205	3-9-83	.230	.246	.212	100	270	22	62	13	0	6	43	30	3	2	4	61	0	0	.344	.309
Baldelli, Rocco	R-R	6-4	200	9-25-81	.208	.278	.000	10	24	3	5	1	0	1	5	1	0	0	0	5	1	0	.375	.240
Bartlett, Jason	R-R	6-0	190	10-30-79	.254	.273	.244	135	468	71	119	27	3	4	47	45	5	11	3	83	11	6	.350	.324
Blalock, Hank	L-R	6-1	200	11-21-80	.254	.143	.268	26	63	8	16	3	0	1	7	6	0	0	0	15	1	1	.349	.319
Brignac, Reid	L-R	6-3	195	1-16-86	.256	.227	.261	113	301	39	77	13	1	8	45	20	3	0	2	77	3	3	.385	.307
Burrell, Pat	R-R	6-4	235	10-10-76	.202	.053	.246	24	84	9	17	5	0	2	13	10	1	0	1	28	0	0	.333	.292
Crawford, Carl	L-L	6-2	215	8-5-81	.307	.256	.332	154	600	110	184	30	13	19	90	46	3	3	5	104	47	10	.495	.356
Hawpe, Brad	L-L	6-3	210	6-22-79	.179	.273	.143	15	39	7	7	0	0	2	7	6	1	0	0	17	0	0	.333	.304
Jaso, John	L-R	6-2	205	9-19-83	.263	.191	.274	109	339	57	89	18	3	5	44	59	2	1	3	39	4	0	.378	.372
Jennings, Desmond	R-R	6-2	200	10-30-86	.190	.273	.100	17	21	5	4	1	1	0	2	1	0	0	0	4	2	2	.333	.292
Johnson, Dan	L-R	6-2	215	8-10-79	.198	.235	.191	40	111	15	22	3	0	7	23	25	1	0	3	27	1	0	.414	.343
Joyce, Matt	L-R	6-2	205	8-3-84	.241	.080	.262	77	216	30	52	15	3	10	40	40	2	0	3	55	2	2	.477	.360
Kapler, Gabe	R-R	6-2	205	7-31-75	.210	.206	.222	59	124	19	26	4	0	2	14	11	3	1	1	24	1	1	.290	.288
Longoria, Evan	R-R	6-2	210	10-7-85	.294	.324	.281	151	574	96	169	46	5	22	104	72	5	0	10	124	15	5	.507	.372
Navarro, Dioner	B-R	5-9	205	2-9-84	.194	.184	.200	48	124	11	24	5	0	1	7	12	1	5	0	20	0	1	.258	.270
Pena, Carlos	L-L	6-2	225	5-17-78	.196	.179	.204	144	484	64	95	18	0	28	84	87	7	0	4	158	5	1	.407	.325
Rodriguez, Sean	R-R	6-1	215	4-26-85	.251	.292	.229	118	343	53	86	19	2	9	40	21	8	5	1	97	13	3	.397	.308
Shoppach, Kelly	R-R	6-0	220	4-29-80	.196	.261	.114	63	158	17	31	8	0	5	17	20	6	2	1	71	0	0	.342	.308
Upton, B.J.	R-R	6-3	185	8-21-84	.237	.278	.218	154	536	89	127	38	4	18	62	67	2	1	4	164	42	9	.424	.322
Zobrist, Ben	B-R	6-3	200	5-26-81	.238	.247	.235	151	541	77	129	28	2	10	75	92	3	7	12	107	24	3	.353	.346

Pitching	B-T	HT	WT	DOB	W	L	ERA	G	GS	CG	SV	IP	H	R	ER	HR	BB	SO	AVG	vLH	vRH	K/9	BB/9
Balfour, Grant	R-R	6-2	195	12-30-77	2	1	2.28	57	0	0	0	55	43	16	14	3	17	56	.216	.267	.174	9.11	2.77
Benoit, Joaquin	R-R	6-3	220	7-26-77	1	1	1.34	63	0	0	1	60	30	10	9	6	11	75	.147	.144	.150	11.19	1.64
Choate, Randy	L-L	6-1	200	9-5-75	4	3	4.23	85	0	0	0	45	41	23	21	3	17	40	.252	.202	.410	8.06	3.43
Cormier, Lance	R-R	6-1	200	8-19-80	4	3	3.92	60	0	0	0	62	68	28	27	7	34	30	.281	.252	.320	4.35	4.94
Davis, Wade	R-R	6-5	220	9-7-85	12	10	4.07	29	29	0	0	168	165	77	76	24	62	113	.255	.260	.250	6.05	3.32
Ekstrom, Mike	R-R	5-11	190	8-30-83	0	1	3.31	15	0	0	0	16	12	6	6	0	9	10	.214	.185	.241	5.51	4.96
Garza, Matt	R-R	6-4	215	11-26-83	15	10	3.91	33	32	3	1	205	193	94	89	28	63	150	.248	.241	.255	6.60	2.77
Hellickson, Jeremy	R-R	6-1	185	4-8-87	4	0	3.47	10	4	0	0	36	32	14	14	5	8	33	.232	.301	.154	8.17	1.98
McGee, Jake	L-L	6-3	190	8-6-86	0	0	1.80	8	0	0	0	5	2	1	1	0	3	6	.118	.222	.000	10.80	5.40
Niemann, Jeff	R-R	6-9	260	2-28-83	12	8	4.39	30	29	1	0	174	159	86	85	25	61	131	.242	.244	.239	6.76	3.15
Price, David	L-L	6-6	225	8-26-85	19	6	2.72	32	31	2	0	209	170	71	63	15	79	188	.221	.211	.224	8.11	3.41
Qualls, Chad	R-R	6-5	220	8-17-78	2	0	5.57	27	0	0	0	21	24	15	13	5	6	15	.293	.415	.171	6.43	2.57
Shields, James	R-R	6-4	220	12-20-81	13	15	5.18	34	33	0	0	203	246	128	117	34	51	187	.294	.286	.304	8.28	2.26
Sonnanstine, Andy	L-R	6-3	190	3-18-83	3	1	4.44	41	4	0	1	81	83	40	40	11	27	50	.259	.267	.253	5.56	3.00
Soriano, Rafael	R-R	6-1	220	12-19-79	3	2	1.73	64	0	0	45	62	36	14	12	4	14	57	.163	.196	.132	8.23	2.02
Thayer, Dale	R-R	6-0	195	12-17-80	0	0	27.00	1	0	0	0	2	7	6	6	1	0	2	.500	.500	.556	9.00	0.00
Wheeler, Dan	R-R	6-3	220	12-10-77	2	4	3.35	64	0	0	3	48	36	20	18	7	16	46	.207	.154	.222	8.57	2.98

Fielding

Catcher	PCT	G	PO	A	E	DP	PB
Jaso	.992	96	611	30	5	5	7
Navarro	.986	46	272	20	4	2	0
Shoppach	.994	56	324	18	2	1	2

First Base	PCT	G	PO	A	E	DP
Aybar	1.000	3	13	1	0	1
Blalock	1.000	1	6	0	0	1
Hawpe	1.000	3	12	0	0	1
Jaso	1.000	1	4	0	0	0
Johnson	1.000	13	82	3	0	11
Pena	.995	142	1074	83	6	95
Rodriguez	1.000	3	23	1	0	2

	PCT	G	PO	A	E	DP
Zobrist	1.000	14	77	8	0	6

Second Base	PCT	G	PO	A	E	DP
Aybar	1.000	9	2	5	0	0
Brignac	.976	68	77	129	5	19
Rodriguez	.984	92	138	222	6	56
Zobrist	.984	55	74	116	3	27

Third Base	PCT	G	PO	A	E	DP
Aybar	.857	7	0	6	1	0
Blalock	.800	2	1	3	1	0
Johnson	.846	6	5	6	2	0
Longoria	.966	151	127	276	14	46
Rodriguez	1.000	7	7	5	0	2

	PCT	G	PO	A	E	DP
Zobrist	.500	2	1	0	1	0

Shortstop	PCT	G	PO	A	E	DP
Bartlett	.977	131	152	309	11	58
Brignac	.976	50	56	108	4	20
Rodriguez	1.000	5	5	3	0	0

Outfield	PCT	G	PO	A	E	DP
Baldelli	1.000	4	6	0	0	0
Blalock	1.000	2	1	0	0	0
Brignac	1.000	3	1	0	0	0
Crawford	.994	147	306	7	2	0
Hawpe	1.000	3	1	0	0	0
Jennings	1.000	10	18	0	0	0

Johnson	1.000	3	1	0	0	0				
Joyce	.975	63	115	4	3	0				
Kapler	1.000	50	58	1	0	0				
Rodriguez	1.000	21	22	0	0	0				
Upton	.988	154	397	3	5	0				
Zobrist	1.000	110	204	6	0	3				

DURHAM BULLS   TRIPLE-A
INTERNATIONAL LEAGUE

TAMPA BAY RAYS

Batting	B-T	HT	WT	DOB	AVG	vLH	vRH	G	AB	R	H	2B	3B	HR	RBI	BB	HBP	SH	SF	SO	SB	CS	SLG	OBP
Albernaz, Craig	R-R	5-8	195	10-30-82	.250	.000	.333	1	4	1	1	0	0	0	0	0	0	0	0	1	0	0	.250	.250
Anderson, Leslie	R-R	6-1	205	3-30-82	.328	.276	.344	30	122	14	40	5	0	2	13	5	1	1	0	20	0	0	.418	.359
Ashley, Nevin	R-R	6-1	215	8-14-84	.167	.250	.150	7	24	2	4	0	0	1	2	1	0	1	0	7	1	0	.292	.200
Baldelli, Rocco	R-R	6-4	200	9-25-81	.273	.267	.276	11	44	7	12	3	0	2	8	1	1	0	2	11	0	0	.477	.292
Bartlett, Jason	R-R	6-0	190	10-30-79	.667	.000	.667	1	3	0	2	1	0	0	1	0	0	0	0	1	0	0	1.000	.750
Blalock, Hank	L-R	6-1	200	11-21-80	.349	.500	.306	26	109	18	38	5	0	4	24	10	1	0	1	19	2	0	.505	.405
Chavez, Angel	R-R	6-0	185	7-22-81	.275	.275	.275	113	411	46	113	17	1	9	55	32	3	0	4	68	5	3	.387	.329
Colina, Alvin	R-R	6-3	210	12-26-81	.231	.175	.247	51	186	19	43	9	1	0	7	28	10	3	0	2	51	1	1	.398	.279
Dillon, Joe	R-R	6-2	215	8-2-75	.262	.299	.248	96	351	58	92	23	0	9	57	34	7	2	6	56	5	0	.405	.334
Eldridge, Rashad	R-L	6-1	185	10-16-81	.215	.182	.224	34	107	20	23	5	1	1	3	13	2	1	1	25	4	1	.308	.309
Furmaniak, J.J.	R-R	6-0	190	7-31-79	.264	.186	.290	77	284	51	75	16	3	1	22	41	5	3	1	53	9	4	.352	.366
Holloway, Kyle	R-R	6-0	204	6-13-88	.154	.000	.167	4	13	2	2	0	0	0	1	0	0	0	1	8	0	0	.308	.143
Jaso, John	L-R	6-2	205	9-19-83	.364	.250	.429	3	11	1	4	1	0	0	2	0	0	0	1	2	0	0	.455	.333
Jennings, Desmond	R-R	6-2	200	10-30-86	.278	.198	.300	109	399	82	111	25	6	3	36	47	6	5	1	67	37	4	.393	.362
Johnson, Dan	L-R	6-2	215	8-10-79	.303	.229	.332	98	340	66	103	19	0	30	95	75	5	0	6	71	0	0	.624	.430
Johnson, Elliot	B-R	6-0	190	3-9-84	.319	.347	.310	109	427	72	136	24	5	11	56	37	3	12	2	92	30	6	.475	.375
Joyce, Matt	L-R	6-2	205	8-3-84	.293	.323	.279	25	92	18	27	8	0	3	12	22	1	0	0	21	1	3	.478	.435
Lobaton, Jose	B-R	6-0	195	10-21-84	.261	.329	.232	72	241	26	63	11	0	7	33	27	1	1	1	52	1	0	.394	.337
Luna, Omar	R-R	5-11	165	12-13-86	.291	.286	.293	40	141	16	41	6	1	1	9	2	1	5	0	28	3	2	.369	.306
Navarro, Dioner	B-R	5-9	205	2-9-84	.284	.209	.316	43	141	19	40	9	0	2	21	23	2	1	2	25	3	0	.390	.387
Perez, Fernando	R-R	6-1	195	4-23-83	.223	.235	.219	116	385	46	86	11	3	4	32	29	2	8	2	97	24	7	.299	.280
Richard, Chris	L-L	6-2	210	6-7-74	.300	.192	.332	117	430	68	129	39	1	20	79	60	5	0	2	96	0	0	.535	.390
Ruggiano, Justin	R-R	6-2	205	4-12-82	.287	.282	.288	117	457	77	131	31	0	15	70	42	8	0	0	129	24	6	.453	.357
Salem, Emeel	L-L	6-0	180	2-11-85	.182	.000	.250	3	11	1	2	2	0	0	1	0	0	0	0	3	0	0	.364	.182
Shealy, Ryan	R-R	6-5	240	8-29-79	.238	.250	.250	48	172	27	41	15	1	10	38	29	3	0	2	48	0	0	.512	.354
2-team total (32 Pawtucket)					.231	—	—	80	286	41	66	22	1	15	55	46	5	0	2	82	0	0	.472	.345
Shoppach, Kelly	R-R	6-0	220	4-29-80	.308	.000	.333	4	13	0	4	0	0	0	2	0	0	0	0	3	0	0	.308	.308

Pitching	B-T	HT	WT	DOB	W	L	ERA	G	GS	CG	SV	IP	H	R	ER	HR	BB	SO	AVG	vLH	vRH	K/9	BB/9
Abreu, Winston	R-R	6-2	170	4-5-77		4	2.28	51	0	0	23	55	35	15	14	1	21	82	.177	.235	.137	13.34	3.42
Baker, Brian	R-R	6-5	190	1-10-83	9	5	3.86	37	12	0	0	105	100	50	45	10	43	72	.253	.288	.217	6.17	3.69
Bateman, Joe	R-R	6-1	185	5-6-80	7	0	1.66	54	0	0	4	76	57	16	14	3	25	66	.206	.233	.181	7.82	2.96
Bennett, Jeff	R-R	6-3	200	6-10-80	0	3	10.97	3	3	0	0	11	13	13	13	0	10	7	.302	.261	.350	5.91	8.44
Benoit, Joaquin	R-R	6-3	225	7-26-77	0	1	2.79	8	0	0	2	10	8	3	3	2	3	17	.216	.067	.318	15.83	2.79
Cromer, Jason	R-L	6-4	225	12-11-80	0	1	2.25	4	0	0	0	8	9	5	2	1	7	1	.310	.100	.421	1.13	7.88
De Los Santos, Richard	R-R	6-1	170	6-1-84	14	5	3.52	28	23	0	0	148	154	63	58	6	48	90	.275	.277	.273	5.46	2.91
Downs, Darin	R-L	6-3	190	12-26-84	6	2	4.46	23	1	0	0	40	44	21	20	4	17	45	.277	.282	.273	10.04	3.79
Ekstrom, Mike	R-R	5-11	190	8-30-83	6	1	2.79	39	1	0	1	58	55	21	18	5	19	48	.252	.278	.227	7.45	2.95
Garcia, Justin	R-R	6-1	195	12-14-86	0	0	5.79	2	0	0	0	5	4	3	3	0	2	5	.222	.091	.429	9.64	3.86
Hellickson, Jeremy	R-R	6-1	185	4-8-87	12	3	2.45	21	21	0	0	118	103	35	32	5	35	123	.238	.208	.269	9.41	2.68
Hernandez, Carlos	B-L	5-11	205	4-22-80	6	5	4.17	18	17	0	0	91	88	52	42	8	38	78	.250	.261	.245	7.74	3.77
Livingston, Bobby	L-L	6-3	205	9-3-82	0	0	5.20	5	5	0	0	28	34	17	16	4	5	15	.301	.340	.267	4.88	1.63
2-team total (22 Buffalo)					3	8	5.31	27	20	0	0	120	142	81	71	12	44	73	—	—		5.46	3.29
McGee, Jake	L-L	6-3	190	8-6-86	1	1	0.52	11	1	0	1	17	9	1	1	0	3	27	.148	.097	.200	14.02	1.56
Ortiz, Ramon	R-R	6-0	175	5-23-73	0	1	6.35	4	4	0	0	17	23	13	12	2	6	12	.315	.375	.268	6.35	3.18
2-team total (8 Buffalo)					2	4	4.57	12	12	1	0	65	66	35	33	3	14	44	—	—		6.09	1.94
Phillips, Heath	L-L	6-3	275	3-24-82	8	7	4.07	24	24	1	0	139	131	70	63	21	40	81	.249	.286	.226	5.23	2.58
Phillips, Paul	R-L	6-1	211	1-26-84	1	0	1.69	3	0	0	0	11	14	3	2	1	6	19	.269	.389		10.97	0.00
Rodriguez, Aneury	R-R	6-3	180	12-13-87	6	5	3.80	27	17	0	0	114	104	52	48	10	49	94	.240	.251	.228	7.44	3.88
Rollins, Heath	R-R	6-1	185	5-25-85	0	2	5.40	13	1	0	0	23	25	15	14	2	14	15	.284	.359	.224	5.79	5.40
Shouse, Brian	L-L	5-10	190	9-26-68	0	2	7.11	10	1	0	0	13	19	10	10	1	8	9	.358	.333	.385	6.39	5.63
Swindle, R.J.	L-L	6-3	190	7-7-83	2	4	2.45	40	0	0	2	55	45	17	15	6	10	55	.223	.233	.214	9.00	1.64
Thayer, Dale	R-R	6-0	195	12-17-80	4	1	3.45	46	0	0	3	60	68	28	23	3	25	55	.283	.267	.298	8.25	3.75
Vasquez, Virgil	R-R	6-3	205	6-7-82	6	2	4.88	12	12	1	0	66	74	39	36	9	16	40	.281	.303	.252	5.43	2.17

Fielding

Catcher	PCT	G	PO	A	E	DP	PB
Albernaz	1.000	1	7	0	0	0	0
Ashley	1.000	6	40	4	0	0	1
Colina	.989	37	254	26	3	1	4
Dillon	1.000	1	3	2	0	1	0
Holloway	1.000	2	16	1	0	0	0
Jaso	1.000	3	25	3	0	0	0
Lobaton	.996	62	440	28	2	0	5
Navarro	1.000	35	271	24	0	2	3
Shoppach	1.000	2	7	0	0	0	0

First Base	PCT	G	PO	A	E	DP
Anderson	.988	9	71	8	1	8
Chavez	—	1	0	0	0	0
Dillon	.979	12	87	5	2	7
Johnson	1.000	14	98	5	0	10
Richard	.995	82	711	32	4	59
Shealy	1.000	29	251	16	0	22

Second Base	PCT	G	PO	A	E	DP
Chavez	.882	4	5	10	2	1
Dillon	.979	75	136	195	7	43
Furmaniak	.994	42	59	101	1	16
Johnson	.987	16	25	52	1	15
Luna	.962	12	19	31	2	7

Third Base	PCT	G	PO	A	E	DP
Blalock	1.000	24	18	38	0	6
Chavez	.960	73	69	125	8	8
Dillon	.889	5	9	7	2	1
Furmaniak	1.000	14	7	16	0	2
Johnson	.990	36	28	70	1	5
Ruggiano	1.000	1	0	1	0	0

Shortstop	PCT	G	PO	A	E	DP
Bartlett	1.000	1	4	1	0	1
Chavez	.970	39	43	88	4	20
Furmaniak	.967	21	31	56	3	14
Johnson	.954	64	77	150	11	23

Luna	.962	26	39	87	5	20
Outfield	**PCT**	**G**	**PO**	**A**	**E**	**DP**
Anderson	.933	17	24	4	2	0
Baldelli	—	1	0	0	0	0

Eldridge	.977	30	41	1	1	0
Furmaniak	1.000	2	3	0	0	0
Jennings	.988	106	249	4	3	0
Johnson	1.000	22	30	1	0	0
Johnson	.981	32	49	2	1	0

Joyce	1.000	15	29	0	0	0
Perez	.978	111	215	3	5	1
Richard	.941	11	15	1	1	1
Ruggiano	.981	114	243	10	5	2
Salem	1.000	3	7	0	0	0

MONTGOMERY BISCUITS DOUBLE-A

SOUTHERN LEAGUE

Batting	B-T	HT	WT	DOB	AVG	vLH	vRH	G	AB	R	H	2B	3B	HR	RBI	BB	HBP	SH	SF	SO	SB	CS	SLG	OBP
Albernaz, Craig	R-R	5-8	195	10-30-82	.250	.298	.229	53	156	20	39	5	0	2	15	18	2	5	0	35	2	1	.321	.335
Anderson, Drew M.	B-R	5-9	170	2-2-83	.259	.298	.244	107	374	61	97	12	11	7	37	38	1	3	3	56	5	3	.406	.327
Anderson, Leslie	R-R	6-1	205	3-30-82	.304	.212	.357	48	181	24	55	11	1	6	25	18	5	0	0	28	3	1	.475	.382
Ashley, Nevin	R-R	6-1	215	8-14-84	.255	.304	.237	92	341	49	87	14	3	7	45	34	9	1	6	76	4	2	.375	.333
Cipriano, Cody	R-R	6-0	200	1-7-85	.275	.278	.273	71	233	36	64	11	3	4	24	32	5	1	2	60	4	1	.399	.371
De La Cruz, Chris	B-R	6-0	175	5-3-82	.270	.291	.260	94	330	32	89	12	4	4	26	27	0	9	1	44	0	4	.367	.324
Eldridge, Rashad	B-R	6-1	185	10-16-81	.253	.238	.260	84	316	42	80	12	1	1	32	55	2	3	5	50	10	5	.307	.362
Fields, Matt	R-R	6-5	235	7-8-85	.220	.210	.224	87	309	33	68	14	0	12	50	29	4	0	5	119	0	0	.382	.291
Folli, Mike	B-R	5-10	175	7-17-85	.174	.111	.183	22	69	7	12	2	0	1	10	8	1	2	0	11	2	0	.246	.269
Furmaniak, J.J.	R-R	6-0	190	7-31-79	.310	.000	.351	11	42	4	13	3	0	0	5	2	0	1	0	8	1	0	.381	.341
Lobaton, Jose	B-R	6-0	195	10-21-84	.250	.250	.250	7	24	3	6	1	0	0	2	4	0	0	0	5	0	0	.292	.357
Luna, Omar	R-R	5-11	165	12-13-86	.250	.250	.250	4	8	1	2	0	0	0	0	0	0	0	0	1	0	0	.250	.250
Matulia, John	L-L	6-0	175	8-19-86	.269	.304	.257	132	475	54	128	23	8	9	59	34	7	2	6	119	4	4	.408	.324
Nowak, Chris	R-R	6-5	225	2-21-83	.248	.213	.261	64	222	33	55	9	1	7	33	40	1	0	3	51	8	1	.392	.361
2-team total (49 Huntsville)					.243	—	—	113	404	60	98	17	2	12	61	59	4	0	6	99	12	2	.384	.340
O'Malley, Shawn	R-R	5-11	160	12-28-87	.181	.146	.194	44	144	18	26	1	3	0	7	16	6	3	0	32	9	1	.229	.289
Paxton, Ian	R-R	6-1	210	9-4-83	.286	.667	.000	3	7	0	2	2	0	0	3	0	0	1	0	0	0	0	.571	.286
Royster, Ryan	R-R	6-2	210	7-25-86	.108	.000	.148	10	37	5	4	2	0	1	5	3	1	1	0	12	0	0	.243	.195
Ruiz, Jose	L-R	6-3	235	3-24-85	.272	.250	.276	23	92	12	25	2	1	1	11	13	0	0	1	19	0	1	.348	.358
Salem, Emeel	L-L	6-0	180	2-11-85	.262	.230	.275	128	519	72	136	22	7	4	42	49	8	9	1	65	23	11	.355	.334
Sexton, Greg	R-R	6-2	205	2-8-85	.212	.344	.160	33	113	11	24	6	0	1	13	19	2	0	0	21	0	2	.310	.336
Spring, Matt	R-R	6-2	215	11-7-84	.182	.158	.191	19	66	10	12	5	0	3	15	4	2	0	2	20	1	0	.394	.243
Strait, Cody	R-R	6-1	180	5-28-83	.195	.207	.192	39	133	14	26	11	0	0	10	10	3	4	0	29	8	2	.278	.267
Sweeney, Matt	L-R	6-3	215	4-4-88	.196	.175	.203	46	163	13	32	7	0	2	25	12	3	0	1	52	1	0	.276	.263
Wrigley, Henry	R-R	6-3	180	8-9-86	.248	.275	.236	62	254	31	63	12	1	9	37	12	1	0	4	54	1	1	.409	.280

Pitching	B-T	HT	WT	DOB	W	L	ERA	G	GS	CG	SV	IP	H	R	ER	HR	BB	SO	AVG	vLH	vRH	K/9	BB/9
Cobb, Alex	R-R	6-1	180	10-7-87	7	5	2.71	23	22	0	0	120	120	47	36	7	35	128	.262	.293	.230	9.63	2.63
De La Rosa, Dane	R-R	6-6	220	2-1-83	9	3	1.97	47	0	0	4	73	66	20	16	3	26	75	.249	.238	.256	9.25	3.21
De Los Santos, Richard	R-R	6-1	170	6-1-84	0	0	4.50	1	0	0	0	2	2	1	1	1	0	1	.250	.200	.333	4.50	0.00
Dowdy, Justin	L-L	6-1	175	8-13-83	0	0	2.04	11	0	0	0	18	13	4	4	2	6	17	.194	.192	.195	8.66	3.06
Downs, Darin	R-L	6-3	190	12-26-84	6	2	1.69	18	3	0	0	48	40	16	9	2	15	57	.231	.261	.212	10.69	2.81
Espinosa, Sergio	L-L	5-10	175	1-2-86	3	3	4.83	30	0	0	0	50	50	29	27	4	16	29	.260	.277	.248	5.19	2.86
Garcia, Justin	R-R	6-1	195	12-14-86	3	3	5.20	18	2	0	0	45	55	26	26	8	14	36	.306	.330	.283	7.20	2.80
Gorgen, Matt	R-R	6-0	210	1-27-87	3	2	1.65	42	0	0	22	49	34	11	9	2	21	47	.191	.244	.150	8.63	3.86
Hall, Jeremy	R-R	6-3	200	9-16-83	6	9	3.52	27	27	0	0	148	134	71	58	11	61	94	.241	.245	.236	5.70	3.70
McGee, Jake	L-L	6-3	200	8-6-86	3	7	3.57	19	19	0	0	88	81	42	35	3	33	100	.245	.218	.258	10.19	3.36
Morlan, Eduardo	R-R	6-2	220	3-1-86	1	0	5.24	12	0	0	0	22	32	13	13	4	9	16	.344	.442	.260	6.45	3.63
2-team total (32 Huntsville)					3	2	3.52	44	0	0	3	72	78	30	28	7	21	60	—	—	—	7.53	2.64
Newmann, David	R-L	6-2	200	6-24-85	3	9	4.50	23	23	0	0	114	136	64	57	7	45	80	.302	.297	.304	6.32	3.55
Oliveros, Rayner	R-R	6-2	180	9-23-85	2	7	7.59	21	6	0	1	51	67	46	43	9	17	22	.309	.333	.287	3.88	3.00
Phillips, Paul	R-R	6-1	211	1-26-84	5	2	3.98	38	3	0	7	61	67	28	27	6	16	55	.277	.318	.244	8.11	2.36
Reid, Ryan	L-R	5-11	215	4-24-85	3	3	3.98	43	0	0	2	72	70	38	32	2	39	61	.258	.305	.222	7.59	4.85
Rodriguez, Aneury	R-R	6-3	180	12-13-87	1	0	2.70	2	2	0	0	10	9	6	3	0	2	6	.243	.111	.368	5.40	1.80
Rollins, Heath	R-R	6-1	185	5-25-85	5	1	5.22	31	2	0	0	59	59	37	34	5	26	39	.268	.263	.272	5.98	3.99
Satow, Josh	L-L	5-10	155	12-18-85	1	4	6.85	23	2	0	1	45	55	36	34	2	28	32	.313	.270	.343	6.45	5.64
Torres, Alex	L-L	5-10	175	12-8-87	11	6	3.47	27	27	0	0	143	136	63	55	9	70	150	.256	.250	.258	9.46	4.42

Fielding

Catcher	PCT	G	PO	A	E	DP	PB
Albernaz	.992	50	322	63	3	4	4
Ashley	.992	75	586	68	5	6	3
Lobaton	.983	6	50	8	1	1	0
Paxton	1.000	3	10	1	0	0	0
Spring	.976	9	74	7	2	1	1

First Base	PCT	G	PO	A	E	DP
Anderson	.986	24	200	17	3	14
Fields	.986	55	462	31	7	38
Nowak	.989	23	161	17	2	13
Ruiz	.982	19	148	15	3	17
Sexton	1.000	2	15	0	0	0
Wrigley	.994	17	149	13	1	13

Second Base	PCT	G	PO	A	E	DP
Albernaz	.667	3	0	4	2	0
Anderson	.959	43	72	93	7	24
Cipriano	.977	65	109	145	6	35

	PCT	G	PO	A	E	DP
De La Cruz	1.000	2	4	3	0	1
Folli	.958	5	10	13	1	2
Furmaniak	1.000	7	12	22	0	4
Luna	.500	1	0	1	1	0
O'Malley	.989	22	41	51	1	9

Third Base	PCT	G	PO	A	E	DP
Anderson	.789	11	2	13	4	0
De La Cruz	1.000	5	5	6	0	0
Folli	1.000	5	5	9	0	2
Furmaniak	—	1	0	0	0	0
Nowak	.958	15	14	32	2	6
Sexton	.953	26	33	48	4	3
Sweeney	.844	42	22	54	14	4
Wrigley	.964	40	32	75	4	6

Shortstop	PCT	G	PO	A	E	DP
Anderson	.925	24	34	65	8	13
De La Cruz	.968	86	123	208	11	35

	PCT	G	PO	A	E	DP
Folli	.977	12	16	27	1	5
Furmaniak	1.000	3	4	7	0	4
Luna	1.000	2	2	5	0	1
O'Malley	1.000	15	24	45	0	11

Outfield	PCT	G	PO	A	E	DP
Anderson	.980	28	48	2	1	0
Anderson	.963	18	24	2	1	0
Eldridge	.996	83	221	3	1	1
Matulia	.983	122	217	21	4	3
Nowak	1.000	4	8	0	0	0
Royster	.944	5	14	3	1	1
Ruiz	1.000	2	3	0	0	0
Salem	.992	118	237	10	2	1
Strait	.976	37	78	3	2	0
Wrigley	1.000	4	1	0	0	0

CHARLOTTE STONE CRABS
FLORIDA STATE LEAGUE

Batting	B-T	HT	WT	DOB	AVG	vLH	vRH	G	AB	R	H	2B	3B	HR	RBI	BB	HBP	SH	SF	SO	SB	CS	SLG	OBP
Anderson, Leslie	R-R	6-1	205	3-30-82	.262	.150	.297	21	84	13	22	3	0	3	11	4	1	0	0	6	0	1	.405	.303
Baldelli, Rocco	R-R	6-4	200	9-25-81	.283	.385	.242	12	46	6	13	4	0	0	6	1	0	0	0	11	0	0	.370	.298
Beckham, Tim	R-R	6-0	190	1-27-90	.256	.245	.259	123	465	68	119	23	5	5	57	62	4	7	4	119	22	14	.359	.346
Bortnick, Tyler	R-R	5-11	185	7-3-87	.206	.333	.194	12	34	4	7	3	0	1	9	5	0	1	1	10	2	0	.382	.300
Fields, Matt	R-R	6-5	235	7-8-85	.188	.188	.000	6	16	2	3	0	0	1	2	0	0	0	0	11	0	0	.375	.278
Fronk, Reid	L-R	6-2	200	7-21-86	.267	.243	.273	115	382	49	102	30	5	4	49	61	12	5	3	76	10	2	.403	.382
Hall, Matt	R-R	6-2	180	3-10-87	.181	.177	.182	91	277	32	50	10	3	3	20	15	4	11	1	69	5	0	.271	.232
Hawpe, Brad	L-L	6-3	210	6-22-79	.167	.000	.333	3	6	0	1	0	0	0	3	0	0	0	0	1	0	0	.167	.444
Jefferies, Jake	L-R	6-2	200	10-30-87	.215	.247	.207	102	363	31	78	15	2	1	30	31	9	4	4	41	1	1	.275	.290
Joyce, Matt	L-R	6-2	205	8-3-84	.379	.250	.400	10	29	6	11	5	0	2	8	10	0	0	1	8	1	0	.759	.525
Kang, K.D.	L-L	6-2	200	2-6-88	.241	.232	.243	86	270	32	65	15	1	1	22	34	2	0	2	75	2	4	.315	.328
Kapler, Gabe	R-R	6-2	205	7-31-75	.077	.000	.083	4	13	0	1	0	0	0	1	1	0	0	0	3	0	0	.077	.143
Luna, Omar	R-R	5-11	165	12-13-86	.083	.000	.133	10	24	3	2	1	0	0	3	1	0	1	0	3	0	0	.125	.120
Murrill, Chris	L-L	6-2	190	6-5-88	.226	.156	.243	45	168	18	38	2	0	0	11	11	0	4	2	45	9	3	.238	.271
O'Malley, Shawn	R-R	5-11	160	12-28-87	.320	.500	.304	8	25	8	8	2	2	0	3	4	3	2	0	2	4	0	.560	.469
Pena, Carlos	L-L	6-2	225	5-17-78	.667	.000	.667	1	3	1	2	0	0	0	1	0	0	0	0	0	0	0	.667	.667
Royster, Ryan	R-R	6-2	210	7-25-86	.206	.000	.233	12	34	3	7	2	0	0	2	3	0	0	0	9	1	0	.265	.270
Scelfo, Anthony	L-R	5-10	195	9-19-86	.240	.263	.236	82	271	33	65	15	4	4	30	25	1	3	68	3	3	.369	.303	
Sexton, Greg	R-R	6-2	205	2-8-85	.272	.253	.279	93	356	37	97	14	1	2	38	34	7	2	3	62	5	4	.334	.345
Sheridan, Mike	L-L	6-2	205	8-8-87	.250	.238	.253	112	408	39	102	17	3	3	42	38	4	7	4	39	3	2	.328	.317
Spring, Matt	R-R	6-2	215	11-7-84	.252	.244	.258	29	103	14	26	4	0	4	12	8	0	2	1	25	0	0	.408	.304
Sweeney, Matt	R-R	6-3	215	4-4-88	.264	.200	.281	34	121	20	32	9	0	6	16	16	0	1	2	34	0	0	.488	.345
Thomas, Mark	R-R	6-1	180	5-5-88	.000	.000	.000	1	4	0	0	0	0	0	0	1	0	0	0	0	0	0	.000	.200
Velasquez, Isaias	R-R	5-11	155	5-7-88	.289	.333	.275	127	457	46	132	17	4	2	36	45	4	6	2	68	41	13	.357	.356
Vogt, Stephen	L-R	6-3	215	11-1-84	.345	.377	.338	106	368	56	127	31	3	8	47	31	6	3	6	46	3	1	.511	.399
Williams, Shawn	B-R	6-2	190	9-18-83	.294	.500	.231	6	17	2	5	0	0	0	2	1	1	0	0	3	0	0	.294	.368
Wrigley, Henry	R-R	6-3	180	8-9-86	.292	.250	.304	68	260	35	76	13	3	12	46	19	2	1	2	37	5	2	.504	.343

Pitching	B-T	HT	WT	DOB	W	L	ERA	G	GS	CG	SV	IP	H	R	FR	HR	BB	SO	AVG	vLH	vRH	K/9	BB/9
Andujar, Chris	R-R	6-2	180	8-24-87	9	6	4.11	25	18	0	0	103	105	59	47	2	39	55	.257	.264	.252	4.81	3.41
Balfour, Grant	R-R	6-2	195	12-30-77	0	1	10.80	2	2	0	0	2	3	2	3	2	0	3	2	.286	.000	.500	10.80	16.20
Barnese, Nick	R-R	6-2	170	1-11-89	8	4	3.02	21	20	1	0	122	114	46	41	5	26	100	.246	.214	.267	7.36	1.91
Bush, Matt	R-R	5-10	185	2-8-86	0	0	4.32	6	0	0	1	8	7	4	4	1	2	12	.219	.182	.238	12.96	2.16
Chavez, Kevin	R-R	6-3	206	6-24-89	0	0	0.00	2	0	0	0	4	3	0	0	0	3	.200	.250	.143	6.75	0.00	
Colome, Alexander	R-R	6-2	184	12-31-88	0	0	2.25	1	0	0	0	4	5	1	1	0	0	8	.333	.714	.000	18.00	0.00
Cruz, Joe	R-R	6-4	190	7-20-88	13	6	2.85	25	25	1	0	142	137	53	45	6	39	131	.258	.257	.259	8.30	2.47
De La Rosa, Dane	R-R	6-6	220	2-1-83	0	0	3.00	2	0	0	0	3	4	1	1	0	0	5	.308	.250	.333	15.00	0.00
De Los Santos, Frank	L-L	6-0	165	11-17-87	10	9	4.33	25	24	1	0	150	181	90	72	8	37	105	.306	.282	.313	6.31	2.22
Dyer, Shane	R-R	6-3	185	3-9-88	5	8	3.17	17	16	1	0	94	91	38	33	4	24	75	.252	.244	.259	7.21	2.31
Espinosa, Sergio	L-L	5-10	175	1-2-86	0	0	1.17	3	0	0	0	8	6	1	1	0	3	5	.200	.333	.333	5.87	1.17
Fleming, Marquis	R-R	6-1	181	9-11-86	5	2	2.49	42	0	0	5	72	45	24	20	3	30	96	.179	.200	.167	11.94	3.73
Garcia, Justin	R-R	6-1	195	12-14-86	0	0	2.63	7	0	0	1	14	9	4	4	1	1	14	.180	.095	.241	9.22	0.66
Hellickson, Jeremy	R-R	6-1	185	4-8-87	0	0	21.60	1	0	0	0	2	4	4	4	0	2	4	.444	.500	.429	21.60	10.80
Jarman, Michael	L-L	6-1	195	6-6-85	4	4	3.04	45	1	0	3	77	65	36	26	2	38	72	.223	.179	.239	8.42	4.44
Mavares, Deivis	R-R	5-11	156	9-19-86	1	1	1.42	8	2	0	1	19	10	3	3	1	11	17	.161	.190	.146	8.05	5.21
Moore, Matt	L-L	6-2	205	6-18-89	6	11	3.36	26	26	0	0	145	109	62	54	7	61	208	.210	.234	.204	12.94	3.79
Oliveros, Rayner	R-R	6-2	180	9-23-85	2	1	2.53	10	0	0	1	21	18	6	3	6	16	.195	.192	.675	2.53	
Quate, Zach	R-R	6-1	200	9-12-87	2	2	1.49	49	0	0	25	72	51	12	12	2	18	90	.199	.277	.154	11.20	2.24
Rafferty, Tommy	R-R	6-1	165	2-5-85	3	1	2.14	13	0	0	0	21	10	5	5	2	9	14	.147	.200	.116	6.00	3.86
Satow, Josh	L-L	5-10	155	12-18-85	4	1	1.76	22	0	0	9	31	18	6	6	1	9	42	.165	.120	.179	12.33	2.64
Schenk, Neil	L-L	6-3	220	6-17-86	5	2	2.79	44	0	0	0	68	67	24	21	2	25	86	.262	.228	.271	11.44	3.33
Shouse, Brian	L-L	5-10	190	9-26-68	0	0	1.54	7	0	0	3	12	9	2	2	0	1	7	.225	.333	.179	5.40	0.77
Shuman, Scott	R-R	6-3	205	3-28-88	0	0	0.00	1	0	0	0	2	0	0	0	0	2	3	.000	.000	.000	11.57	7.71
Sonnanstine, Andy	R-R	6-3	190	3-18-83	0	0	6.75	1	0	0	0	1	2	1	1	0	1	4	.333	.333	.333	27.00	6.75
Thompson, Jake	R-R	6-3	225	8-8-89	2	0	0.00	2	2	0	0	11	2	0	0	0	2	6	.059	.000	.100	4.91	1.64
Yates, Kirby	R-R	5-10	170	3-25-87	0	0	5.06	1	1	0	0	5	7	3	3	0	2	3	.368	.222	.500	5.06	3.38

Fielding

Catcher	PCT	G	PO	A	E	DP	PB
Jefferies	.993	98	817	70	6	3	6
Spring	.988	19	145	15	2	1	4
Thomas	1.000	1	7	0	0	0	0
Vogt	.983	27	221	17	4	1	2

First Base	PCT	G	PO	A	E	DP
Anderson	1.000	9	74	2	0	4
Sheridan	.994	106	929	37	6	80
Vogt	.979	15	127	11	3	17
Wrigley	.989	10	79	7	1	10

Second Base	PCT	G	PO	A	E	DP
Bortnick	.976	11	17	24	1	3
Hall	.970	69	108	186	9	37
Luna	1.000	2	1	3	0	0

	PCT	G	PO	A	E	DP
O'Malley	.963	5	11	15	1	4
Scelfo	.955	60	112	141	12	43
Williams	.889	3	1	7	1	1

Third Base	PCT	G	PO	A	E	DP
Hall	1.000	4	3	4	0	2
Sexton	.931	91	50	221	20	22
Sweeney	.882	23	15	45	8	5
Wrigley	.926	22	8	42	4	3

Shortstop	PCT	G	PO	A	E	DP
Beckham	.949	121	167	296	25	62
Hall	.983	19	17	42	1	11
Luna	1.000	3	3	8	0	1
O'Malley	.500	1	0	1	1	0

Outfield	PCT	G	PO	A	E	DP
Anderson	1.000	9	5	1	0	1
Fronk	.976	104	157	6	4	2
Joyce	1.000	4	6	0	0	0
Kang	.963	69	102	3	4	1
Kapler	1.000	3	3	0	0	0
Luna	1.000	5	6	0	0	0
Murrill	.989	42	82	4	1	1
Royster	1.000	2	1	0	0	0
Scelfo	.941	18	32	0	2	0
Velasquez	.984	127	234	15	4	0
Vogt	1.000	26	38	2	0	0
Wrigley	1.000	23	29	2	0	0

MIDWEST LEAGUE

Batting	B-T	HT	WT	DOB	AVG	vLH	vRH	G	AB	R	H	2B	3B	HR	RBI	BB	HBP	SH	SF	SO	SB	CS	SLG	OBP
Acosta, Mayobanex	R-R	6-1	205	11-20-87	.237	—	—	32	118	10	28	4	1	0	14	7	0	2	1	20	1	1	.288	.278
Biell, Dustin	L-R	6-0	175	3-19-89	.247	—	—	97	364	45	90	14	2	6	32	28	5	5	2	91	13	9	.346	.308
Bortnick, Tyler	R-R	5-11	185	7-3-87	.303	—	—	113	406	72	123	32	2	8	45	63	11	2	3	67	39	14	.451	.408
Cedeno, Julio	R-R	6-2	185	8-25-89	.261	—	—	104	371	34	97	22	2	3	40	30	2	2	4	75	5	3	.356	.317
Cohen, Gabe	R-R	6-2	205	11-7-87	.293	—	—	43	157	19	46	14	0	1	18	8	1	0	1	45	3	2	.401	.329
Davis, Bennett	R-R	5-10	185	2-9-86	.244	—	—	40	127	23	31	4	0	3	16	22	5	1	2	38	7	2	.346	.372
Estrada, Robi	B-R	5-10	170	10-8-88	.240	—	—	103	317	36	76	13	0	0	27	50	1	8	4	62	14	4	.281	.341
Francisco, Tomas	R-R	6-0	210	4-4-88	.247	—	—	50	162	22	40	8	0	0	17	12	4	1	1	33	2	0	.296	.313
Luis, Diogenes	B-R	5-10	169	5-7-87	.179	—	—	39	106	12	19	1	0	0	3	9	3	7	0	34	3	5	.189	.263
Morrison, Ty	L-R	6-2	170	7-22-90	.250	—	—	131	452	65	113	21	13	6	56	43	7	9	1	133	58	10	.394	.324
Murrill, Chris	L-L	6-2	190	6-5-88	.292	—	—	70	277	47	81	11	3	2	22	21	5	6	2	59	28	7	.375	.351
Nommensen, Brett	L-L	5-11	190	10-6-86	.263	—	—	109	395	55	104	19	4	10	68	53	8	0	2	65	35	10	.408	.360
Reynolds, Burt	R-R	6-1	190	9-13-88	.212	—	—	12	33	4	7	0	0	1	6	4	0	0	2	15	5	0	.303	.282
Rogers, Cody	L-R	6-2	175	9-13-88	.196	—	—	34	138	25	27	2	2	7	20	17	4	1	1	39	8	2	.391	.300
Sonoqui, Eli	L-L	6-2	195	1-20-88	.238	—	—	24	80	6	19	4	1	0	6	6	1	0	0	21	1	0	.325	.299
Spraker, Kyle	R-R	5-11	170	1-10-86	.212	—	—	86	278	36	59	10	0	5	32	38	6	4	3	61	10	4	.302	.317
Thomas, Mark	R-R	6-1	180	5-5-88	.264	—	—	95	348	37	92	21	1	6	44	33	2	0	2	79	10	1	.382	.330
Wendt, David	R-R	6-5	205	1-2-87	.220	—	—	13	50	4	11	1	0	0	8	1	2	0	1	8	2	0	.240	.259
Wiegand, Ryan	R-R	6-4	225	12-30-86	.250	—	—	118	428	55	107	20	3	9	67	55	5	0	4	85	5	3	.374	.339

Pitching	B-T	HT	WT	DOB	W	L	ERA	G	GS	CG	SV	IP	H	R	ER	HR	BB	SO	AVG	vLH	vRH	K/9	BB/9
Colome, Alexander	R-R	6-2	184	12-31-88	6	6	3.95	22	22	1	0	114	98	59	50	14	45	118	—	—	—	9.32	3.55
De La Rosa, Jairo	R-R	6-2	170	9-8-85	0	2	8.88	16	0	0	0	25	28	25	3	13	22	—	—	—	7.82	4.62
Dott, Aaron	R-L	6-4	215	5-17-88	4	4	4.17	23	9	0	1	78	86	44	36	4	38	76	—	—	—	8.81	4.40
Dyer, Shane	R-R	6-3	185	3-9-88	2	3	1.71	7	7	2	0	42	34	12	8	1	4	34	—	—	—	7.29	0.86
Hayes, Tyree	R-R	6-0	175	8-8-88	4	1	3.79	12	0	0	2	36	35	20	15	4	14	25	—	—	—	6.31	3.53
Kelly, Merrill	R-R	6-1	170	10-14-88	0	1	7.16	5	2	0	0	16	15	15	13	1	8	10	—	—	—	5.51	4.41
Koronis, Alex	R-R	6-2	187	1-4-88	8	4	4.24	43	1	0	5	85	69	50	40	8	40	100	—	—	—	10.59	4.24
Lobstein, Kyle	L-L	6-3	200	8-12-89	9	8	4.14	27	27	1	0	148	140	76	68	14	54	128	—	—	—	7.78	3.28
Mavares, Deivis	R-R	5-11	156	9-19-86	1	5	3.63	39	0	0	3	74	56	36	30	5	37	69	—	—	—	8.35	4.48
Mayora, Yorman	R-R	5-11	199	4-20-87	1	3	5.93	11	3	0	0	27	33	22	18	2	15	21	—	—	—	6.91	4.94
McEachern, Jason	R-R	6-2	160	10-12-90	4	11	5.68	27	24	0	0	120	143	88	76	20	60	95	—	—	—	7.11	4.49
Minks, Shane	R-R	6-3	205	4-25-88	1	0	0.00	2	0	0	0	5	5	1	0	1	5	5	—	—	—	9.00	1.80
Riefenhauser, C.J.	L-L	6-0	180	1-30-90	1	0	1.00	2	2	0	0	9	7	1	1	0	1	4	—	—	—	4.00	1.00
Rodriguez, Wilking	R-R	6-1	160	3-2-90	4	10	4.23	22	19	0	0	106	109	66	50	11	28	93	—	—	—	7.87	2.37
Shuman, Scott	R-R	6-3	205	3-28-88	4	5	3.01	46	0	0	14	72	50	29	24	5	38	111	—	—	—	13.94	4.77
Stabelfeld, Matt	L-L	5-10	185	8-21-86	4	1	4.75	37	0	0	0	61	61	35	32	6	26	42	—	—	—	6.23	3.86
Suarez, Albert	R-R	6-2	186	10-8-89	2	5	3.89	12	11	0	0	42	38	24	18	5	16	30	—	—	—	6.48	3.46
Sullivan, Jake	L-L	6-5	210	11-15-86	3	3	4.31	39	0	0	4	63	62	45	30	4	33	53	—	—	—	7.61	4.74
Yates, Kirby	R-R	5-10	170	3-25-87	3	6	3.30	27	12	0	5	90	73	41	33	9	41	97	—	—	—	9.70	4.10

Fielding

Catcher	PCT	G	PO	A	E	DP	PB
Acosta	.992	27	225	15	2	2	2
Francisco	.996	26	214	17	1	1	1
Thomas	.986	85	694	75	11	6	12
Wendt	.939	5	29	2	2	0	1

First Base	PCT	G	PO	A	E	DP
Davis	1.000	2	14	0	0	3
Francisco	.993	19	119	15	1	13
Sonoqui	.986	16	126	10	2	10
Spraker	—	1	0	0	0	0
Wiegand	.988	107	789	39	10	64

Second Base	PCT	G	PO	A	E	DP
Bortnick	.968	97	163	231	13	51

	PCT	G	PO	A	E	DP
Davis	.969	20	22	41	2	6
Estrada	.981	10	19	33	1	8
Luis	.958	8	9	14	1	3
Spraker	.961	15	22	27	2	7

Third Base	PCT	G	PO	A	E	DP
Cedeno	.923	91	67	162	19	14
Davis	.864	8	5	14	3	0
Luis	.000	2	0	1	0	0
Spraker	.961	45	29	93	5	7

Shortstop	PCT	G	PO	A	E	DP
Bortnick	.971	8	14	19	1	4
Estrada	.944	85	119	187	18	41
Luis	.956	26	43	65	5	9

	PCT	G	PO	A	E	DP
Spraker	.976	21	32	49	2	9

Outfield	PCT	G	PO	A	E	DP
Biell	.976	85	198	5	5	2
Cohen	.983	33	55	3	1	0
Davis	1.000	3	4	0	0	0
Luis	—	1	0	0	0	0
Morrison	.967	122	252	12	9	1
Murrill	.954	63	80	3	4	1
Nommensen	.985	88	187	4	3	1
Reynolds	.818	9	9	0	2	0
Rogers	1.000	23	42	0	0	0

HUDSON VALLEY RENEGADES   SHORT-SEASON

NEW YORK-PENN LEAGUE

Batting	B-T	HT	WT	DOB	AVG	vLH	vRH	G	AB	R	H	2B	3B	HR	RBI	BB	HBP	SH	SF	SO	SB	CS	SLG	OBP
Acosta, Mayobanex	R-R	6-1	205	11-20-87	.271	.333	.253	51	188	29	51	12	0	7	27	18	0	0	0	30	0	2	.447	.335
Bryles, Brian	R-R	6-1	170	11-4-89	.249	.188	.262	54	173	29	43	9	3	0	18	19	3	3	2	56	12	5	.335	.330
Davis, Bennett	R-R	5-10	185	2-9-86	.000	.000	.000	3	10	0	0	0	0	0	1	2	0	0	0	4	2	0	.000	.167
Dietrich, Derek	L-R	6-1	200	7-18-89	.279	.226	.302	45	179	33	50	12	2	3	20	11	6	1	1	42	2	2	.419	.340
Glynn, Geno	R-R	6-1	190	10-27-86	.161	.167	.160	11	31	0	5	0	0	0	2	3	0	1	0	10	0	0	.161	.235
Gonzalez, Felix	B-R	5-10	165	4-4-90	.286	1.000	.167	2	7	4	2	0	1	0	1	0	0	0	0	2	0	0	.571	.375
Guillen, Cesar	R-R	6-1	175	3-15-89	.083	.000	.143	4	12	0	1	1	0	0	0	2	0	0	0	4	0	0	.167	.214
Holloway, Kyle	R-R	6-0	204	6-13-88	.300	.500	.167	12	30	6	9	4	0	0	1	6	0	0	0	9	0	0	.433	.417
Lawson, Scott	L-R	5-10	185	8-12-87	.316	.667	.250	5	19	3	6	1	0	0	2	0	0	0	0	2	0	1	.368	.350
Luis, Diogenes	B-R	5-10	169	5-7-87	.258	.345	.221	54	198	26	51	6	3	1	27	15	5	9	2	58	10	3	.333	.323

	B-T	HT	WT	DOB	AVG	vLH	vRH	G	AB	R	H	2B	3B	HR	RBI	BB	HBP	SH	SF	SO	SB	CS	SLG	OBP
Lusson, Kyle	R-R	5-11	190	1-19-88	.161	.250	.105	10	31	0	5	0	1	0	4	2	0	3	0	14	0	0	.226	.212
Lyerly, Craige	R-R	5-11	175	8-24-88	.091	.077	.100	11	33	1	3	1	0	0	2	4	0	1	0	12	1	0	.121	.189
Otero, Elias	B-R	6-2	166	12-19-87	.214	.225	.211	53	192	23	41	12	2	1	17	18	0	0	0	51	2	0	.313	.281
Price, Robby	L-R	5-10	188	4-20-88	.294	.300	.292	57	194	36	57	17	1	2	23	36	15	3	2	25	13	1	.423	.437
Reynolds, Burt	R-R	6-1	190	9-13-88	.223	.089	.271	56	211	22	47	17	4	2	28	12	8	1	0	65	12	2	.370	.290
Rodriguez, Junior	R-R	6-3	215	1-24-88	.208	.000	.238	12	24	4	5	1	0	1	4	4	0	0	0	11	0	0	.375	.321
Schwaner, Nick	L-R	6-1	215	2-27-88	.280	.298	.272	68	268	36	75	16	1	7	53	19	1	0	6	57	14	5	.425	.323
Tinoco, Steve	R-R	6-0	200	4-11-88	.274	.293	.266	68	259	35	71	10	1	1	35	30	11	0	3	34	8	7	.332	.370
Torres, Alejandro	R-R	6-1	178	9-30-88	.250	.216	.268	30	108	11	27	5	0	0	10	6	0	2	1	22	1	0	.296	.287
Wendt, David	R-R	6-5	205	1-2-87	.400	.000	.667	1	5	2	2	0	1	0	0	0	0	0	0	0	0	0	.800	.400
Winder, Chris	R-R	5-10	157	9-28-89	.225	.208	.232	55	173	27	39	4	2	0	7	13	7	3	0	59	13	1	.272	.306
Wunderlich, Phil	L-R	6-0	225	11-4-88	.330	.339	.327	52	209	31	69	19	0	4	36	9	6	0	2	40	0	1	.478	.372

Pitching

	B-T	HT	WT	DOB	W	L	ERA	G	GS	CG	SV	IP	H	R	ER	HR	BB	SO	AVG	vLH	vRH	K/9	BB/9
Almonte, Wilmer	R-R	5-11	164	8-19-89	4	3	2.77	15	14	0	0	78	67	32	24	4	15	73	.232	.185	.265	8.42	1.73
Ayers, Kyle	R-R	6-4	220	9-6-89	0	1	6.32	8	0	0	0	16	24	15	11	1	6	13	.369	.333	.395	7.47	3.45
Bencomo, Omar	R-R	6-1	168	2-10-89	1	3	4.60	15	3	0	0	47	42	29	24	4	7	41	.228	.226	.230	7.85	1.34
Broyles, Wade	R-R	6-3	200	11-9-86	0	0	3.38	6	0	0	1	11	5	5	4	0	9	12	.143	.083	.174	10.13	7.59
Chavez, Kevin	R-R	6-3	206	6-24-89	0	1	9.88	7	0	0	0	14	22	15	15	2	10	13	.379	.333	.400	8.56	6.59
Dettrich, Joey	L-L	6-4	175	9-23-88	1	4	6.35	6	3	0	0	23	26	19	16	0	14	9	.310	.421	.277	3.57	5.56
Dickmann, Robert	L-L	5-11	200	12-25-86	4	2	2.41	16	2	0	1	41	38	15	11	2	16	31	.247	.288	.225	6.80	3.51
Fuller, Devin	R-R	6-2	225	12-15-88	2	3	5.34	15	10	0	0	57	64	35	34	6	15	34	.287	.273	.298	5.34	2.35
Garcia, Nate	R-R	6-1	190	5-9-88	3	2	2.88	16	6	0	2	50	37	18	16	5	18	45	.208	.143	.243	8.10	3.24
Hill, Hunter	R-R	5-11	185	11-30-88	2	1	4.87	14	0	0	1	20	19	11	11	1	7	19	.244	.325	.158	8.41	3.10
Hiscock, Stephen	R-R	6-2	153	1-23-88	3	3	2.95	19	0	0	3	37	32	12	12	1	12	38	.241	.211	.263	9.33	2.95
Hubbard, Austin	R-R	6-2	206	6-14-88	3	1	0.39	19	0	0	12	23	16	2	1	1	9	25	.198	.229	.174	9.64	3.47
Kelly, Merrill	R-R	6-1	170	10-14-88	1	1	2.11	7	1	0	0	21	16	7	5	0	5	19	.200	.256	.146	8.02	2.11
Liberatore, Adam	L-L	6-3	239	5-12-87	2	1	2.63	17	0	0	2	27	32	12	8	1	12	33	.276	.289	.269	10.87	3.95
Patterson, Jimmy	R-L	6-0	190	2-9-89	3	3	2.55	9	6	0	0	35	25	10	10	2	8	28	.205	.185	.211	7.13	2.04
Robinson, J.R.	L-L	5-10	185	2-16-88	1	1	1.38	10	0	0	0	13	13	5	2	0	4	19	.236	.235	.237	13.15	2.77
Romero, Enny	L-L	6-3	165	1-24-91	1	0	1.80	1	1	0	0	5	1	1	1	0	5	4	.071	.000	.091	7.20	9.00
Rosscup, Zach	R-L	6-2	205	6-9-88	3	1	3.03	9	7	0	1	36	27	16	12	0	7	35	.205	.237	.191	8.83	1.77
Sierra, Miguel	R-R	6-5	170	7-28-88	3	4	4.35	16	15	0	0	70	84	43	34	6	19	42	.293	.281	.302	5.37	2.43
Thompson, Jake	R-R	6-3	225	8-8-89	2	1	1.35	10	7	0	0	40	28	10	6	0	6	33	.200	.217	.188	7.43	1.35

Fielding

Catcher	PCT	G	PO	A	E	DP	PB
Acosta	.990	50	373	44	4	3	3
Glynn	1.000	1	7	1	0	0	0
Holloway	.938	4	13	2	1	0	2
Rodriguez	—	2	0	0	0	0	0
Torres	.965	24	177	17	7	2	2
Wendt	1.000	1	6	3	0	0	0

First Base	PCT	G	PO	A	E	DP
Glynn	.986	8	68	5	1	5
Tinoco	.985	30	242	13	4	20
Torres	1.000	4	21	1	0	1
Wunderlich	.987	38	286	22	4	34

Second Base	PCT	G	PO	A	E	DP
Luis	.966	6	13	15	1	5

	PCT	G	PO	A	E	DP
Otero	.961	22	38	60	4	8
Price	.974	51	90	133	6	32

Third Base	PCT	G	PO	A	E	DP
Davis	1.000	2	1	8	0	1
Glynn	1.000	1	0	1	0	0
Lawson	.800	5	3	9	3	0
Lusson	.750	1	1	2	1	0
Otero	.873	31	11	51	9	5
Rodriguez	1.000	1	1	4	0	0
Schwaner	.907	40	29	78	11	9

Shortstop	PCT	G	PO	A	E	DP
Davis	.714	1	2	3	2	0
Dietrich	.942	32	42	71	7	18
Gonzalez	.889	2	3	5	1	3

	PCT	G	PO	A	E	DP
Luis	.887	41	62	95	20	19
Otero	1.000	1	2	1	0	1

Outfield	PCT	G	PO	A	E	DP
Bryles	1.000	52	118	2	0	0
Guillen	1.000	3	5	0	0	0
Luis	1.000	6	8	0	0	0
Lusson	1.000	8	19	1	0	1
Lyerly	1.000	10	19	1	0	1
Reynolds	.931	55	90	4	7	0
Rodriguez	1.000	3	2	1	0	0
Schwaner	1.000	11	20	0	0	0
Tinoco	.985	35	63	4	1	2
Winder	.962	53	125	1	5	0

PRINCETON RAYS   ROOKIE
APPALACHIAN LEAGUE

Batting	B-T	HT	WT	DOB	AVG	vLH	vRH	G	AB	R	H	2B	3B	HR	RBI	BB	HBP	SH	SF	SO	SB	CS	SLG	OBP
Contreras, Ruben	B-R	6-2	190	8-18-87	.250	.214	.264	58	200	29	50	14	2	5	23	17	2	1	3	49	4	6	.415	.311
Fogle, Bryan	R-R	6-2	225	1-14-88	.260	.250	.263	48	181	22	47	16	0	5	35	11	1	0	1	61	1	0	.431	.304
Glaesmann, Todd	R-R	6-4	220	10-24-90	.233	.205	.245	62	236	41	55	17	5	4	24	13	9	2	1	70	13	6	.398	.297
Glynn, Geno	R-R	6-1	190	10-27-86	.139	.154	.130	15	36	0	5	1	0	0	2	2	0	0	0	10	0	1	.167	.184
Gonzalez, Felix	B-R	5-10	165	4-4-90	.253	.206	.267	47	150	15	38	7	1	1	12	4	0	3	0	33	6	3	.333	.273
Guevara, Hector	R-R	5-11	170	10-7-91	.251	.329	.216	64	223	24	56	13	3	2	26	15	5	1	4	31	9	3	.363	.308
Guillen, Cesar	R-R	6-1	175	3-15-89	.297	.220	.333	45	155	24	46	8	3	4	19	21	1	1	2	30	5	5	.465	.380
Harris, Brian	R-R	5-9	180	11-10-87	.178	.100	.211	39	101	14	18	1	0	1	5	13	5	2	1	19	2	3	.218	.300
Holloway, Kyle	R-R	6-0	204	6-13-88	.279	.364	.190	13	43	4	12	3	0	1	6	3	2	0	1	12	0	0	.419	.347
Kiermaier, Kevin	L-R	6-1	200	4-22-90	.303	.288	.307	57	218	44	66	8	7	2	16	24	3	1	0	54	17	5	.431	.380
Lawson, Scott	L-R	5-10	185	8-12-87	.257	.214	.273	60	210	34	54	11	3	4	34	32	5	2	2	31	16	4	.395	.365
Malm, Jeff	L-L	6-3	225	10-31-90	.220	.170	.238	61	200	20	44	9	0	3	25	17	5	0	1	46	2	1	.310	.296
Olivares, Gerardo	R-R	6-0	187	8-14-88	.215	.185	.225	33	107	10	23	7	0	2	9	7	1	2	0	23	1	0	.336	.270
Reginatto, Leonardo	R-R	6-2	180	4-10-90	.279	.200	.304	16	61	4	17	4	0	0	4	0	0	0	0	8	2	2	.344	.323
Segovia, Alejandro	R-R	6-0	181	4-27-90	.268	.294	.256	34	112	10	30	7	0	0	10	6	1	0	1	19	1	0	.330	.278
Williams, Zane	R-R	5-10	190	8-19-87	.063	.000	.080	17	32	2	2	0	0	0	6	0	0	0	13	0	0	.063	.211

Pitching	B-T	HT	WT	DOB	W	L	ERA	G	GS	CG	SV	IP	H	R	ER	HR	BB	SO	AVG	vLH	vRH	K/9	BB/9
Bellatti, Andrew	R-R	6-1	170	8-5-91	2	5	4.04	13	13	0	0	65	56	35	29	4	16	63	.237	.233	.241	8.77	2.23
Broyles, Wade	R-R	6-3	200	11-9-86	0	2	2.16	6	0	0	1	17	11	5	4	0	5	18	.186	.273	.135	9.72	2.70

Name	B-T	HT	WT	DOB	W	L	ERA	G	GS	CG	SV	IP	H	R	ER	HR	BB	SO	AVG	vLH	vRH	K/9	BB/9
Carruth, Garret	R-R	6-5	220	11-12-87	0	1	3.52	13	0	0	0	15	18	9	6	2	4	13	.286	.263	.295	7.63	2.35
Furdal, Brad	R-R	6-2	185	10-21-90	0	2	8.22	6	0	0	0	8	8	8	7	2	4	3	.286	.250	.300	3.52	4.70
Gilson, Matt	L-L	6-4	215	12-15-86	4	1	1.53	16	0	0	3	35	26	7	6	3	4	28	.197	.250	.183	7.13	1.02
Hall, Justin	R-R	6-0	205	6-14-88	1	0	3.93	6	0	0	0	18	19	11	8	5	1	17	.260	.194	.310	8.35	0.49
Jannis, Mickey	R-R	6-0	190	12-16-87	3	1	2.52	14	0	0	3	36	48	26	10	1	11	29	.310	.214	.364	7.32	2.78
Jensen, George	R-R	6-4	215	4-12-90	1	2	2.97	12	1	0	1	36	38	14	12	5	6	30	.260	.350	.226	7.43	1.49
Lara, Braulio	L-L	6-1	180	12-20-88	6	4	2.18	13	13	1	0	66	49	26	16	2	25	58	.200	.152	.208	7.91	3.41
Mateo, Victor	R-R	6-5	180	7-27-89	2	5	4.89	15	5	0	0	46	52	33	25	2	19	36	.277	.365	.243	7.04	3.72
Minks, Shane	R-R	6-3	205	4-25-88	1	1	2.53	6	0	0	0	11	9	5	3	0	7	14	.225	.182	.241	11.81	5.91
Partridge, Jacob	L-L	6-3	200	12-21-90	4	3	3.23	13	9	0	0	53	56	24	19	6	19	42	.277	.231	.284	7.13	3.23
Rearick, Chris	L-L	6-3	190	12-5-87	3	1	4.72	13	1	0	0	40	59	25	21	0	7	29	.331	.421	.307	6.53	1.58
Riefenhauser, C.J.	L-L	6-0	180	1-30-90	1	0	2.84	11	0	0	1	19	14	6	6	1	6	26	.203	.111	.235	7.58	2.84
Robinson, J.R.	L-L	5-10	185	2-16-88	0	0	0.00	2	0	0	0	3	5	0	0	0	1	2	.417	.667	.333	6.75	3.38
Romero, Enny	L-L	6-3	165	1-24-91	4	1	1.95	13	13	0	0	69	51	15	15	2	14	72	.204	.171	.211	9.35	1.82
Suero, Eliazer	R-R	6-4	170	6-7-89	1	6	4.03	13	13	0	0	60	60	31	27	5	18	52	.264	.196	.315	7.76	2.69

Fielding

Catcher	PCT	G	PO	A	E	DP	PB
Holloway	.977	10	77	8	2	0	0
Olivares	.970	33	220	38	8	1	5
Segovia	.969	28	191	27	7	2	5
Williams	.969	10	30	1	1	0	4

First Base	PCT	G	PO	A	E	DP
Glynn	.984	6	59	4	1	5
Lawson	.977	5	41	2	1	3
Malm	.984	59	522	36	9	39

Second Base	PCT	G	PO	A	E	DP
Gonzalez	.913	4	9	12	2	2
Guevara	.950	62	109	159	14	32
Harris	1.000	7	13	16	0	2

Third Base	PCT	G	PO	A	E	DP
Glynn	1.000	8	1	10	0	1
Gonzalez	.765	3	5	8	4	0
Harris	1.000	11	9	14	0	0
Lawson	.916	55	23	118	13	9

Shortstop	PCT	G	PO	A	E	DP
Gonzalez	.903	36	53	96	16	16
Harris	.956	23	26	61	4	9
Reginatto	.918	16	38	52	8	9

Outfield	PCT	G	PO	A	E	DP
Contreras	.986	45	70	1	1	1
Fogle	.886	26	31	0	4	0
Glaesmann	.967	54	84	3	3	0
Guillen	.965	40	52	3	2	1
Kiermaier	.971	48	94	8	3	2

GCL RAYS   ROOKIE
GULF COAST LEAGUE

Batting	B-T	HT	WT	DOB	AVG	vLH	vRH	G	AB	R	H	2B	3B	HR	RBI	BB	HBP	SH	SF	SO	SB	CS	SLG	OBP
Bailey, Luke	R-R	6-0	198	3-11-91	.182	.150	.196	42	137	18	25	8	0	5	14	17	6	0	1	47	0	0	.350	.298
Biagini, Tanner	R-R	6-2	200	8-6-88	.235	.211	.245	20	68	8	16	5	0	0	11	7	0	0	2	16	0	0	.309	.299
Brett, Ryan	B-R	5-9	180	10-9-91	.303	.300	.304	27	89	8	27	5	2	0	9	8	1	0	1	17	12	3	.404	.364
Caminero, Leandro	R-R	6-1	185	10-24-89	.251	.190	.279	52	187	17	47	8	4	0	20	10	0	3	1	41	2	5	.337	.288
DePew, Jake	R-R	6-1	220	3-1-92	.273	.333	.250	4	11	0	3	0	0	0	1	0	0	0	0	1	0	0	.273	.273
Diaz, Alex	R-R	6-1	180	11-15-91	.304	.273	.314	42	135	16	41	8	2	0	11	17	2	0	0	39	1	2	.393	.390
Dixon, Deshun	R-L	6-0	190	9-20-91	.220	.188	.235	16	50	9	11	1	1	1	3	3	0	1	1	13	4	0	.340	.259
Dorville, Edward	B-R	6-1	185	11-5-88	.197	.260	.168	52	157	25	31	4	4	2	14	12	5	2	3	63	7	5	.312	.271
Fields, Matt	R-R	6-5	235	7-8-85	.227	.000	.313	6	22	3	5	0	0	2	5	3	1	0	0	9	3	0	.500	.346
Flores, Travis	R-R	6-1	215	7-12-92	.182	.000	.250	6	11	1	2	0	0	0	0	3	0	0	1	1	0	0	.182	.357
Gomez, Jhonatan	R-R	6-1	180	11-13-88	.152	.111	.160	36	99	10	15	5	1	1	5	6	1	0	0	28	0	0	.253	.208
Henry, Seth	R-R	5-9	178	3-23-87	.220	.286	.206	21	41	8	9	2	0	1	6	7	1	3	0	12	5	0	.341	.347
Lusson, Kyle	R-R	5-11	190	1-19-88	.158	.143	.161	18	38	7	6	2	0	0	11	5	0	0	0	12	4	1	.211	.407
Lyerly, Craige	R-R	5-11	175	8-24-88	.225	.083	.269	32	102	22	23	3	1	2	11	11	5	2	0	28	9	2	.333	.331
McCrann, Ryan	L-R	6-3	195	5-15-86	.285	.286	.284	45	137	14	39	4	0	1	12	9	3	2	1	27	7	2	.336	.340
Morillo, Julian	B-R	5-11	167	12-10-91	.218	.257	.202	41	124	16	27	2	0	0	16	17	2	1	0	17	4	2	.234	.322
O'Conner, Justin	R-R	6-0	190	3-31-92	.211	.222	.207	48	161	18	34	13	0	3	29	18	4	1	3	46	1	0	.348	.301
O'Malley, Shawn	R-R	5-11	160	12-28-87	.375	.000	.429	2	8	1	3	0	0	1	0	1	0	1	0	2	0	0	.375	.400
Perez, Cesar	R-R	6-2	190	3-8-93	.174	.282	.133	43	144	15	25	4	0	1	11	17	1	2	2	33	0	2	.222	.262
Querecuto, Juniel	B-R	5-9	155	9-19-92	.251	.203	.278	46	167	20	42	4	1	0	11	13	3	4	1	26	11	2	.287	.315
Rogers, Cody	L-R	6-2	175	9-13-88	.250	.167	.278	9	24	3	6	1	1	1	5	4	2	0	0	1	1	0	.500	.400
Royster, Ryan	R-R	6-2	210	7-25-86	.381	.400	.375	7	21	2	8	1	1	0	5	1	0	0	0	4	0	0	.524	.409
Torres, Marcos	R-R	6-1	215	11-8-87	.000	.000	.000	4	4	0	0	0	0	0	0	0	0	0	0	2	0	0	.000	.000
Vasquez, Cristian	R-R	6-1	155	3-9-90	.133	.000	.192	11	30	1	4	0	0	2	2	2	0	0	0	2	0	0	.133	.188

Pitching	B-T	HT	WT	DOB	W	L	ERA	G	GS	CG	SV	IP	H	R	ER	HR	BB	SO	AVG	vLH	vRH	K/9	BB/9
Bush, Matt	R-R	5-10	185	2-8-86	1	0	1.69	4	1	0	0	5	2	1	1	0	1	8	.100	.083	.125	13.50	1.69
Cromer, Jason	R-L	6-4	225	12-11-80	0	0	1.80	3	3	0	0	5	3	1	1	0	1	7	.176	.200	.167	12.60	1.80
Fleckenstein, Ryan	R-L	5-11	200	12-14-85	3	0	2.57	20	0	0	9	28	19	8	8	0	4	31	.183	.154	.192	9.96	1.29
Galan, Genaro	L-L	6-2	196	1-20-88	0	0	12.46	3	0	0	0	4	9	6	6	5	4	5	.500	.333	.583	8.31	10.38
Hall, Justin	R-R	6-0	205	6-14-88	0	0	5.25	9	0	0	0	12	21	13	7	0	1	14	.375	.395	.333	10.50	0.75
Havlicek, Stepan	R-L	6-1	160	2-25-93	0	0	0.00	3	0	0	0	4	1	0	0	0	1	2	.071	.000	.100	4.50	2.25
Hayes, Tyree	R-R	6-0	175	8-8-88	0	0	2.35	3	3	0	0	8	5	2	2	1	2	3	.192	.125	.300	3.52	2.35
Henderson, Brandon	L-L	6-3	175	4-19-92	0	1	1.59	9	2	0	1	23	13	4	4	2	3	28	.167	.095	.193	11.12	1.19
James, Kevin	L-L	6-4	190	10-1-90	0	1	7.27	4	2	0	0	9	9	7	7	1	6	9	.281	.455	.190	9.35	6.23
Johnson, D.J.	L-R	6-4	235	8-30-89	0	0	2.05	14	0	0	2	22	24	7	5	0	3	16	.276	.273	.279	6.55	1.23
Kendall, Ian	R-R	6-0	205	11-11-91	0	1	12.46	4	0	0	0	4	9	6	6	1	2	2	.409	.545	.273	6.23	4.15
Lopez, Reinaldo	R-R	6-2	221	4-27-91	5	1	2.98	13	8	0	1	57	56	24	19	3	14	35	.263	.277	.245	5.49	2.20
Markel, Parker	R-R	6-4	220	9-15-90	2	0	1.74	7	0	0	0	10	8	2	2	0	3	13	.222	.263	.176	11.32	2.61
Minks, Shane	R-R	6-3	205	4-25-88	0	0	0.00	6	0	0	0	4	8	5	0	0	2	8	.194	.111	.308	7.04	4.70
Molina, Jose	L-L	5-11	160	6-26-91	5	4	3.88	15	2	0	0	51	45	25	22	3	19	37	.237	.271	.225	6.53	3.35
Proctor, Marcus	R-R	6-3	170	8-21-91	2	3	2.91	12	8	0	0	53	42	24	17	2	17	35	.207	.269	.137	5.98	2.91
Quinonez, Eduar	R-R	6-3	182	8-9-89	2	4	3.99	12	9	0	0	50	58	24	22	2	15	43	.304	.283	.333	7.79	2.72

Name	B-T	HT	WT	DOB	W	L	ERA	G	GS	CG	SV	IP	H	R	ER	HR	BB	SO	AVG	vLH	vRH	K/9	BB/9
Reyes, Robinson	L-L	6-4	200	11-15-88	0	3	17.69	8	0	0	0	10	14	24	19	0	21	7	.341	.333	.344	6.52	19.55
Rosscup, Zach	R-L	6-2	205	6-9-88	0	0	1.04	3	1	0	0	9	5	3	1	0	2	6	.161	.143	.167	6.23	2.08
Shouse, Brian	L-L	5-10	190	9-26-68	1	3	3.00	6	6	0	0	6	5	2	2	0	0	3	.208	.125	.250	4.50	0.00
Silvestre, Pedro	R-R	6-2	185	10-23-89	6	0	2.29	13	5	0	1	51	49	16	13	2	15	32	.250	.234	.270	5.65	2.65
Spann, Matt	L-L	6-7	185	2-17-91	1	1	1.48	10	1	0	0	24	22	4	4	1	4	22	.244	.240	.246	8.14	1.48
Suarez, Albert	R-R	6-2	186	10-8-89	0	0	1.00	3	3	0	0	9	4	1	1	0	1	8	.129	.045	.333	8.00	1.00
Swilley, Matt	R-R	6-2	175	12-19-90	2	4	6.17	13	5	0	1	42	47	33	29	2	26	22	.283	.290	.274	4.68	5.53
Vasquez, Virgil	R-R	6-3	205	6-7-82	1	0	0.00	1	1	0	0	5	4	0	0	0	0	6	.211	.231	.167	10.80	0.00
Woodworth, Pete	R-R	6-2	190	7-29-88	1	1	2.42	17	0	0	1	26	19	7	7	1	9	26	.204	.208	.200	9.00	3.12

Fielding

Catcher	PCT	G	PO	A	E	DP	PB
Bailey	.967	26	143	31	6	1	3
DePew	1.000	1	3	2	0	0	0
Gomez	1.000	22	83	8	0	0	5
O'Conner	.981	27	185	23	4	3	8
Torres	1.000	4	9	1	0	0	0

First Base	PCT	G	PO	A	E	DP
Biagini	.980	4	49	0	1	5
Fields	.971	6	63	5	2	5
Flores	1.000	6	38	0	0	1
Gomez	.979	15	133	5	3	12
McCrann	.968	41	328	31	12	18

Second Base	PCT	G	PO	A	E	DP
Brett	.935	24	27	60	6	9

	PCT	G	PO	A	E	DP
Henry	1.000	13	20	44	0	7
Morillo	.961	30	51	96	6	16
O'Malley	1.000	1	0	6	0	0

Third Base	PCT	G	PO	A	E	DP
Biagini	.907	14	15	24	4	1
Henry	—	1	0	0	0	0
Lusson	.600	2	1	2	2	0
McCrann	.750	4	5	4	3	0
Perez	.930	42	29	90	9	1
Rogers	1.000	1	0	2	0	0
Vasquez	—	1	0	0	0	0

Shortstop	PCT	G	PO	A	E	DP
Brett	1.000	1	1	0	0	0
Lusson	1.000	1	2	2	0	0

	PCT	G	PO	A	E	DP
Morillo	.904	11	15	32	5	7
O'Malley	1.000	1	2	2	0	1
Querecuto	.942	46	71	141	13	23
Vasquez	1.000	5	6	8	0	4

Outfield	PCT	G	PO	A	E	DP
Caminero	.982	52	109	3	2	1
Diaz	.981	41	49	3	1	1
Dixon	1.000	15	18	3	0	1
Dorville	.985	45	61	4	1	0
Lusson	.938	14	15	0	1	0
Lyerly	1.000	28	25	1	0	0
Rogers	.900	5	9	0	1	0
Royster	1.000	3	4	0	0	0
Vasquez	1.000	7	4	0	0	0

DSL RAYS   ROOKIE

DOMINICAN SUMMER LEAGUE

Batting	B-T	HT	WT	DOB	AVG	vLH	vRH	G	AB	R	H	2B	3B	HR	RBI	BB	HBP	SH	SF	SO	SB	CS	SLG	OBP
Aguero, Ismael	R-R	6-0	185	6-19-93	.300	.375	.278	26	70	10	21	4	0	0	7	5	4	2	0	12	3	0	.357	.380
Araiza, Jesus	R-R	5-11	185	6-19-93	.230	.208	.234	50	152	26	35	10	3	0	20	36	2	2	4	46	4	1	.336	.376
Cabrera, Jose	R-R	6-3	185	2-17-91	.000	.000	.000	2	1	0	0	0	0	0	0	1	0	0	0	1	0	0	.000	.500
De Castro, Raynill	R-R	6-3	175	12-11-89	.000	.000	.000	4	6	1	0	0	0	0	0	1	0	0	0	3	0	0	.000	.250
Eder, Federico	L-R	5-9	165	9-5-90	.198	.143	.215	35	86	12	17	0	0	0	7	24	4	2	0	32	3	4	.198	.395
Guillen, Cesar	R-R	6-1	175	3-15-89	.183	.231	.175	23	93	15	17	4	0	2	14	5	2	0	2	10	1	0	.290	.235
Infante, Jhancarlos	R-R	6-0	180	10-12-89	.267	.286	.263	21	45	9	12	5	0	0	3	5	0	1	1	12	2	1	.378	.333
Lafontaines, Jose	B-R	5-9	185	10-6-88	.285	.281	.286	58	172	24	49	5	0	0	9	14	12	4	2	40	13	7	.314	.375
Maldonado, Darwin	R-R	6-0	160	7-10-89	.250	.000	.250	6	16	1	4	0	0	0	0	2	1	0	0	8	2	1	.250	.368
Marte, Luis	R-R	6-3	180	2-23-91	.223	.063	.244	47	139	19	31	7	2	3	13	15	6	0	0	50	8	1	.367	.325
Martin, Juan	R-R	6-1	200	5-12-90	.192	.167	.197	28	73	6	14	2	0	0	8	10	3	1	1	25	0	0	.219	.310
Medina, Julio	R-R	5-10	188	12-26-90	.282	.250	.287	61	195	26	55	12	0	2	28	19	5	4	3	34	11	7	.374	.356
Natera, Jesus	R-R	6-0	180	4-10-92	.229	.200	.234	72	249	35	57	13	7	2	34	36	3	1	0	67	14	4	.361	.333
Rodriguez, Hector	R-R	6-2	210	11-5-89	.273	.333	.263	67	238	28	65	14	2	2	38	23	7	0	3	40	1	2	.374	.351
Rosa, Adderly	B-R	6-0	167	7-4-91	.236	.324	.220	66	225	38	53	4	2	0	19	44	10	6	2	45	15	8	.271	.381
Rosario, Francisco	R-R	6-1	175	1-26-91	.226	.286	.218	25	62	6	14	3	0	0	7	6	0	0	2	11	0	1	.274	.286
Rosario, Waldo	R-R	6-2	185	10-13-89	.200	.000	.214	6	15	3	3	0	0	0	0	7	1	0	0	4	2	2	.200	.478
Ruiz, Jose	L-R	6-3	235	3-24-85	.447	.333	.474	13	47	13	21	7	1	1	9	8	0	0	0	6	0	0	.702	.527
Soriano, Ariel	R-R	5-11	160	11-24-90	.273	.256	.276	64	231	32	63	10	3	2	33	20	6	4	5	35	9	5	.368	.340
Tapia, Juan	R-R	6-0	156	3-1-92	.118	.095	.125	41	93	11	11	0	0	0	3	9	2	6	1	35	6	1	.118	.210

Pitching	B-T	HT	WT	DOB	W	L	ERA	G	GS	CG	SV	IP	H	R	ER	HR	BB	SO	AVG	vLH	vRH	K/9	BB/9
Alonzo, Jose	R-R	6-4	191	2-24-93	2	1	1.17	16	0	0	0	23	19	5	3	0	18	16	.229	.211	.234	6.26	7.04
Canturiano, Miguel	R-R	6-4	185	4-10-93	0	0	0.00	2	0	0	0	2	1	0	0	0	2	2	.143	.000	.200	9.00	9.00
Cedeno, Carlos	R-R	6-2	180	7-19-90	2	2	3.23	20	0	0	0	31	27	23	11	1	27	23	.225	.194	.236	6.75	7.92
Colon, Roque	R-R	5-10	152	4-23-88	2	1	0.94	22	0	0	16	29	17	5	3	0	6	26	.175	.103	.206	8.16	1.88
De La Cruz, Geisel	L-L	6-0	139	4-11-93	2	3	4.25	17	2	0	0	30	39	25	14	4	10	20	.320	.250	.325	6.07	3.03
Gomez, Roberto E	R-R	6-5	178	8-3-89	4	0	1.85	8	8	0	0	39	32	12	8	0	9	28	.218	.300	.187	6.46	2.08
Guerrero, Joan	L-L	6-2	170	1-22-91	1	3	3.12	14	13	1	0	66	67	29	23	1	15	48	.261	.250	.261	6.51	2.04
Hernandez, Wilmer	R-R	6-3	175	8-29-91	4	2	2.48	16	2	0	0	36	29	12	10	0	13	25	.220	.111	.248	6.19	3.22
Mercedes, Aneuris	R-R	6-0	180	5-1-87	4	6	3.62	16	9	1	0	50	45	26	20	3	18	43	.245	.245	.244	7.79	3.26
Mercedes, Luis	L-L	5-11	170	3-30-92	0	1	3.00	4	0	0	1	6	4	3	2	0	3	5	.200	.000	.200	7.50	4.50
Monegro, Jose	R-R	6-2	180	3-24-92	6	1	2.53	23	1	0	4	43	37	16	12	0	12	35	.231	.245	.224	7.38	2.53
Rodriguez, Junior	R-R	6-0	189	2-8-89	1	0	1.50	6	0	0	0	6	4	2	1	0	3	7	.182	.000	.235	10.50	4.50
Serrano, Ronald	R-R	6-1	186	2-21-91	0	0	4.70	12	0	0	0	15	15	10	8	0	15	12	.254	.063	.326	7.04	8.80
Soriano, Dauris	L-L	6-1	156	12-16-89	0	0	6.10	9	0	0	0	10	15	13	7	2	7	9	.313	1.000	.167	7.84	6.10
Suero, Bruedlin	L-L	6-4	170	2-28-90	4	1	2.61	13	12	0	0	59	59	23	17	2	21	41	.255	.294	.252	6.29	3.22
Thomas, Yamal	R-R	6-7	225	11-4-89	0	0	21.60	3	0	0	0	2	5	6	4	0	3	1	.556	.667	.500	5.40	16.20
Torres, Jose	R-R	6-2	180	4-18-91	2	5	3.92	16	7	0	0	41	37	25	18	3	23	20	.239	.265	.231	4.35	5.01
Vizcaino, Francisco	L-L	6-0	160	7-26-88	2	0	2.35	12	0	0	1	15	19	6	4	1	10	10	.311	.333	.310	5.87	5.87
Wilsino, Juan	R-R	6-3	190	3-22-89	3	3	3.27	16	6	1	1	44	41	19	16	0	12	22	.265	.244	.271	4.50	2.45

Fielding

Catcher	PCT	G	PO	A	E	DP	PB
Araiza	.982	23	134	27	3	2	6

	PCT	G	PO	A	E	DP
Infante	.944	20	76	8	5	1	3
Martin	.983	21	106	12	2	0	3
Rosario	.969	25	134	20	5	0	2

TAMPA BAY RAYS

First Base	PCT	G	PO	A	E	DP
Araiza	1.000	10	55	6	0	8
De Castro	.667	1	2	0	1	0
Guillen	1.000	1	2	0	0	0
Infante	1.000	1	6	1	0	1
Martin	1.000	7	50	2	0	4
Rodriguez	.984	53	464	25	8	35
Rosa	1.000	1	1	0	0	0
Ruiz	.976	4	40	1	1	5
Tapia	1.000	1	2	0	0	0

Second Base	PCT	G	PO	A	E	DP
Aguero	1.000	2	1	0	0	0
Eder	.968	9	14	16	1	5
Lafontaines	.969	48	84	103	6	19

Medina	.750	2	1	2	1	1
Rosa	.921	20	38	44	7	13
Soriano	.913	7	13	8	2	4
Tapia	.667	1	1	1	1	0

Third Base	PCT	G	PO	A	E	DP
Aguero	.840	16	13	29	8	3
Araiza	—	1	0	0	0	0
De Castro	1.000	2	1	0	0	0
Eder	1.000	1	0	1	0	0
Medina	.899	57	50	146	22	11
Rosa	1.000	4	6	7	0	0
Soriano	1.000	4	2	2	0	0

Shortstop	PCT	G	PO	A	E	DP
Rosa	.959	44	76	113	8	23
Soriano	.769	3	3	7	3	1
Tapia	.880	31	34	91	17	11

Outfield	PCT	G	PO	A	E	DP
Eder	1.000	25	30	1	0	0
Guillen	.955	21	40	2	2	0
Lafontaines	—	1	0	0	0	0
Marte	.963	45	71	7	3	0
Natera	.938	71	129	6	9	2
Rosario	1.000	3	3	0	0	0
Ruiz	1.000	3	3	0	0	0
Soriano	.989	55	84	5	1	0
Tapia	.667	4	2	0	1	0

VSL RAYS

ROOKIE

VENEZUELAN SUMMER LEAGUE

Batting	B-T	HT	WT	DOB	AVG	vLH	vRH	G	AB	R	H	2B	3B	HR	RBI	BB	HBP	SH	SF	SO	SB	CS	SLG	OBP
Acosta, Ronald	R-R	5-11	170	3-16-91	.241	.250	.239	61	203	27	49	5	0	3	23	21	7	2	0	31	11	1	.310	.333
Alcala, Franklin	L-L	6-2	200	3-9-91	.162	.074	.192	35	105	14	17	5	0	2	14	17	2	0	1	35	1	0	.267	.288
Antunez, Ismel	L-R	5-7	166	6-17-91	.269	.295	.260	48	171	36	46	7	1	1	13	29	6	2	0	45	26	10	.339	.393
Bellorin, Jose	R-R	6-0	160	12-14-90	.242	.241	.242	43	124	16	30	4	1	2	17	15	3	4	0	20	5	4	.339	.338
Correa, Leopoldo	L-R	6-0	186	12-3-91	.251	.341	.228	59	203	33	51	13	2	0	19	22	5	0	3	29	1	3	.335	.335
Dominguez, Wilmer	R-R	5-10	182	6-19-90	.271	.158	.291	41	129	13	35	8	0	3	20	13	0	2	0	20	3	0	.403	.338
Epifano, Erick	R-R	6-1	160	3-31-90	.200	.333	.143	7	20	3	4	0	0	0	4	3	0	0	0	3	0	0	.200	.304
Hernandez, Nahum	R-R	6-0	180	9-20-89	.380	.410	.370	50	166	35	63	14	2	4	26	28	8	0	0	27	11	5	.560	.490
Hernandez, Oscar	R-R	6-0	196	7-9-93	.223	.207	.230	34	103	17	23	6	0	4	14	11	4	0	1	19	0	0	.398	.319
Narvaez, Omar	B-R	5-10	172	2-10-92	.308	.263	.324	46	143	29	44	4	1	1	20	27	2	1	2	11	3	0	.371	.420
Paez, Jose	B-R	6-0	165	8-11-93	.174	.103	.190	45	155	25	27	1	3	0	11	21	3	1	0	42	14	8	.219	.285
Paz, Franklin	R-R	6-1	166	5-7-91	.286	.185	.319	62	220	42	63	14	5	4	47	29	5	1	0	45	16	4	.450	.382
Quinonez, Jonathan	R-R	6-1	187	11-27-90	.290	.383	.264	62	210	38	61	8	4	6	41	20	10	2	4	19	7	3	.452	.373
Reyes, Keiverson	R-R	5-9	152	2-7-91	.194	.000	.231	18	31	6	6	0	0	1	4	7	1	0	1	4	2	3	.290	.350
Salas, Roan	R-R	5-11	175	6-9-90	.345	.422	.326	60	220	35	76	16	2	5	42	23	6	1	4	24	3	1	.505	.415
Silva, Wester	R-L	6-0	170	1-10-92	.123	.071	.140	25	57	9	7	0	0	0	2	9	1	0	0	12	1	0	.123	.254

Pitching	B-T	HT	WT	DOB	W	L	ERA	G	GS	CG	SV	IP	H	R	ER	HR	BB	SO	AVG	vLH	vRH	K/9	BB/9
Aguilera, Hector	R-R	6-3	185	3-26-90	1	5	4.46	17	0	0	1	42	48	24	21	2	24	29	.314	.333	.308	6.17	5.10
Cabrera, Orlando	R-R	5-11	165	10-25-89	3	2	2.74	20	0	0	4	46	35	14	14	3	10	19	.213	.289	.190	3.72	1.96
Crespo, Ali	R-R	6-4	209	2-1-90	1	0	3.72	5	0	0	0	10	8	4	4	1	3	5	.211	.444	.138	4.66	2.79
Duarte, Hugo	R-R	6-1	169	1-7-90	4	3	4.91	16	5	0	0	48	45	29	26	10	23	47	.253	.282	.245	8.87	4.34
Echarry, Eli	R-R	6-1	150	7-1-92	4	2	3.13	10	0	0	0	59	45	24	21	3	19	59	.211	.226	.206	9.00	2.90
Gonzalez, Joynerd	R-R	6-1	150	7-22-92	1	1	2.84	14	0	0	1	25	19	9	8	0	13	13	.216	.278	.200	4.62	4.62
Hurtado, Jhefferson	R-R	6-0	181	12-19-91	0	3	6.00	12	7	0	0	24	25	24	16	0	25	5	.272	.391	.232	1.88	9.38
Mayora, Yorman	R-R	5-11	199	4-20-87	0	0	8.64	5	5	0	0	8	13	8	8	0	10	8	.361	.625	.286	10.80	4.32
Moya, Dennis	R-R	6-3	180	8-16-91	0	0	6.75	2	0	0	0	3	2	5	2	0	4	1	.222	.667	.000	3.38	13.50
Orasmo, Carlos	L-L	5-9	154	12-13-91	2	2	4.20	14	5	0	1	49	50	28	23	7	24	32	.262	.333	.251	5.84	4.38
Rivero, Felipe	L-L	6-0	151	7-5-91	3	3	2.09	14	9	0	2	52	46	20	12	1	10	44	.243	.200	.247	7.66	1.74
Rosal, Gregory	R-R	6-1	207	9-24-92	0	0	3.86	3	1	0	0	7	4	3	3	1	1	6	.160	.125	.176	1.29	1.29
Sabala, Wilmer	R-R	6-2	184	12-22-91	0	1	10.97	3	0	0	0	11	17	13	13	1	5	13	.370	.333	.382	10.97	4.22
Salazar, Danmar	L-L	6-1	172	7-23-92	2	3	2.50	12	7	0	0	36	34	20	10	1	16	16	.264	.286	.262	4.00	4.00
Salinas, Guillermo	R-R	6-1	180	10-28-88	2	2	2.10	17	0	0	4	26	25	12	6	0	6	36	.240	.259	.234	12.62	2.10
Sanchez, Daniel	R-R	6-2	180	5-29-89	0	1	14.29	3	0	0	0	6	6	9	9	1	9	4	.316	.333	.313	6.35	14.29
Sanchez, Yerwin	R-R	6-1	258	5-5-93	5	0	3.38	14	2	0	0	29	27	16	11	3	14	15	.239	.200	.253	4.60	4.30
Wilches, Luis	L-L	6-1	200	10-1-91	6	2	1.19	13	5	0	1	45	37	10	6	2	6	35	.224	.133	.233	6.95	1.19
Yendis, Luis	R-R	6-3	178	7-19-89	3	3	4.11	14	10	0	1	61	71	34	28	2	17	23	.296	.354	.281	3.38	2.49

Fielding

Catcher	PCT	G	PO	A	E	DP	PB
Dominguez	.944	21	95	23	7	2	3
Hernandez	.970	19	112	18	4	1	4
Narvaez	.975	35	202	31	6	0	2

First Base	PCT	G	PO	A	E	DP
Alcala	.987	32	279	15	4	20
Dominguez	.962	12	98	3	4	7
Narvaez	1.000	7	56	5	0	3
Quinonez	1.000	7	80	4	0	8
Salas	.988	17	154	10	2	13

Second Base	PCT	G	PO	A	E	DP
Acosta	.972	5	13	22	1	3

Bellorin	.966	12	25	31	2	10
Epifano	1.000	2	4	3	0	1
Quinonez	1.000	23	53	59	0	17
Salas	.951	30	71	64	7	18

Third Base	PCT	G	PO	A	E	DP
Bellorin	.864	10	10	9	3	1
Correa	.927	57	40	163	16	7
Quinonez	.864	14	17	21	6	1
Salas	—	1	0	0	0	0

Shortstop	PCT	G	PO	A	E	DP
Acosta	.924	55	72	158	19	32
Bellorin	.833	13	13	32	9	10

Epifano	.875	5	5	9	2	1

Outfield	PCT	G	PO	A	E	DP
Antunez	.953	42	78	4	4	2
Bellorin	.889	4	8	0	1	0
Hernandez	1.000	46	77	1	0	1
Paez	.941	39	75	5	5	1
Paz	.982	52	50	4	1	0
Quinonez	1.000	20	33	5	0	1
Silva	.931	21	23	4	2	1

Texas Rangers

SEASON IN A SENTENCE: The Rangers had the best year in franchise history, taking control of the American League West early on and clinching the division on Sept. 25, then winning the American League pennant for the first time before losing in the World Series.

HIGH POINT: When the Rangers beat the Rays in the AL Division Series, they got the franchise's first postseason win and first postseason series victory. But that was only the first part of Texas' two-step, as Josh Hamilton slugged four homers during the AL Championship Series against the Yankees. Righthander Colby Lewis tossed eight dominant innings in the Game Six clincher. Eight days later, in the first World Series game in Arlington, Lewis got the Rangers' only World Series victory in a 4-2 victory in front of 52,419 fans.

LOW POINT: Former owner Tom Hicks' finances forced him to put the Rangers up for sale, and Major League Baseball even helped the team cover its payroll, making it possible for the team to add players such as Cliff Lee, Bengie Molina and Jorge Cantu at the trade deadline. Dallas Mavericks owner Mark Cuban made a strong run to buy the team out of bankruptcy before team president Nolan Ryan and partner Chuck Greenberg won the franchise for a bid of $593 million on Aug. 5.

NOTABLE ROOKIES: The Rangers tried several first basemen, including top prospect Justin Smoak, but settled on 2008 17th-rounder Mitch Moreland, who wound up as their hottest hitter in the World Series. Former minor league Rule 5 pick Alexi Ogando posted a 1.30 ERA out of the bullpen and was reliable in the postseason, giving up one run in six innings.

KEY TRANSACTIONS: General manager Jon Daniels was aggressive, giving up modest minor leaguers for the likes of Molina, Cantu and Cristian Guzman, and most crucially was willing to part with Smoak and three other minor leaguers to pry Lee away from the Mariners in July.

DOWN ON THE FARM: The system has been thinned by prospect graduations and trades, and a tighter budget brought on by ownership issues prompted less aggressiveness on the international front. The Rangers still have talent, though, led by lefthander Martin Perez and shortstop Jurickson Profar. Only one club, high Class A Bakersfield, had a losing season, and the Rangers shuffled affiliates in the offseason, moving from Bakersfield to a Greenberg-owned club in Myrtle Beach.

OPENING DAY PAYROLL: $55.3 million (27th)

PLAYERS OF THE YEAR

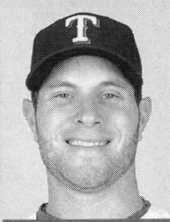

MAJOR LEAGUE	MINOR LEAGUE
Josh Hamilton of	**Michael Kirkman** lhp
.359/.411/.633	(Triple-A)
Led AL in AVG, SLG	13-3, 3.09
and OPS (1.044)	PCL pitcher of year

ORGANIZATION LEADERS

BATTING		*Minimum 250 at-bats
MAJORS		
*AVG	Josh Hamilton	.359
*OPS	Josh Hamilton	1.044
HR	Josh Hamilton	32
RBI	Vladimir Guerrero	115
MINORS		
*AVG	Chris Davis, Oklahoma City	.327
*OBP	Brandon Boggs, Oklahoma City	.406
*SLG	Chris Davis, Oklahoma City	.520
R	Esteban German, Oklahoma City	79
H	David Paisano, Bakersfield	148
TB	Davis Stonebunner, AZL/Frisco/Bake./Okla.	219
2B	Chris Davis, Oklahoma City	31
3B	Engel Beltre, Bakersfield/Frisco	8
HR	Michael Bianucci, Bakersfield	18
RBI	Chris Davis, Oklahoma City	80
BB	Brandon Boggs, Oklahoma City	72
SO	Tommy Mendonca, Bakersfield	126
SB	Leury Garcia, AZL Rangers/Hickory	51

PITCHING		†Minimum 75 innings
MAJORS		
W	C.J. Wilson	15
†ERA	C.J. Wilson	3.35
SO	Colby Lewis	196
MINORS		
W	Michael Kirkman, Oklahoma City	13
L	Wilfredo Boscan, Bakersfield	14
†ERA	Robert Erlin, Hickory	2.12
G	Cody Eppley, Bakersfield/Frisco/Okla. City	51
GS	Richard Bleier, Frisco	28
SV	Mark Hamburger, Bakersfield/Frisco	21
IP	Richard Bleier, Frisco	164.3
BB	Michael Kirkman, Oklahoma City	68
SO	Neil Ramirez, Hickory	142
†AVG	Robert Erlin, Hickory	.213

2010 PERFORMANCE

General Manager: Jon Daniels. **Farm Director:** Scott Servais. **Scouting Director:** Ron Hopkins.

Class	Team	League	W	L	PCT	Finish*	Manager(s)
Majors	Texas Rangers	American	90	72	.556	†4th (14)	Ron Washington
Triple-A	Oklahoma City RedHawks	Pacific Coast	73	70	.510	8th (16)	Bobby Jones
Double-A	Frisco RoughRiders	Texas	72	67	.518'	3rd (8)	Steve Buechele
High A	Bakersfield Blaze	California	67	73	.479	8th (10)	Bill Haselman
Low A	Hickory Crawdads	South Atlantic	75	64	.540	t-4th (14)	Bill Richardson
Short-season	Spokane Indians	Northwest	43	33	.566	t-2nd (8)	Tim Hulett
Rookie	AZL Rangers	Arizona	31	24	.564	t-3rd (12)	Jayce Tingler
Overall 2010 Minor League Record			361	331	.522	8th (30)	

*Finish in overall standings (No. of teams in league). †League champion.

ORGANIZATION STATISTICS

TEXAS RANGERS

AMERICAN LEAGUE

Batting	B-T	HT	WT	DOB	AVG	vLH	vRH	G	AB	R	H	2B	3B	HR	RBI	BB	HBP	SH	SF	SO	SB	CS	SLG	OBP
Andrus, Elvis	R-R	6-0	200	8-26-88	.265	.268	.264	148	588	88	156	15	3	0	35	64	5	17	0	96	32	15	.301	.342
Arias, Joaquin	R-R	6-1	170	9-21-84	.276	.320	.260	50	98	18	27	5	1	0	9	2	0	1	0	17	1	0	.347	.290
Blanco, Andres	B-R	5-10	190	4-11-84	.277	.220	.302	68	166	17	46	10	1	0	13	11	3	3	2	24	0	2	.349	.330
Boggs, Brandon	B-R	5-10	210	1-9-83	.000	.000	.000	4	7	0	0	0	0	0	0	1	0	0	0	4	0	0	.000	.125
Borbon, Julio	L-L	6-0	195	2-20-86	.276	.247	.284	137	438	60	121	11	4	3	42	19	2	8	1	59	15	7	.340	.309
Cantu, Jorge	R-R	6-3	210	1-30-82	.235	.196	.277	30	98	9	23	4	1	1	2	6	0	1	0	19	0	0	.327	.279
Cora, Alex	L-R	6-0	200	10-18-75	.286	.167	1.000	4	7	0	2	0	0	0	0	0	0	0	0	0	0	0	.286	.286
Cruz, Nelson	R-R	6-2	240	7-1-80	.318	.330	.314	108	399	60	127	31	3	22	78	38	1	1	6	81	17	4	.576	.374
Davis, Chris	L-R	6-3	230	3-17-86	.192	.148	.204	45	120	7	23	9	0	1	4	15	0	0	1	40	3	0	.292	.279
Francoeur, Jeff	R-R	6-5	220	1-8-84	.340	.400	.303	15	53	9	18	2	0	2	11	1	1	0	1	5	0	1	.491	.357
Garko, Ryan	R-R	6-2	225	1-2-81	.091	.095	.083	15	33	0	3	0	0	0	3	3	0	2	0	4	0	0	.091	.167
Gentry, Craig	R-R	6-2	190	11-29-83	.212	.174	.300	20	33	4	7	0	0	0	3	1	0	0	1	11	1	0	.212	.229
German, Esteban	R-R	5-9	195	1-26-78	.231	.500	.182	13	13	5	3	0	0	0	1	3	0	0	0	2	4	1	.231	.375
Guerrero, Vladimir	R-R	6-3	235	2-9-75	.300	.338	.287	152	593	83	178	27	1	29	115	35	9	0	6	60	4	5	.496	.345
Guzman, Cristian	B-R	6-0	210	3-21-78	.152	.182	.143	15	46	4	7	1	0	1	3	0	0	1	0	10	0	0	.174	.204
Hamilton, Josh	L-L	6-4	240	5-21-81	.359	.271	.401	133	518	95	186	40	3	32	100	43	5	1	4	95	8	1	.633	.411
Kinsler, Ian	R-R	6-0	200	6-22-82	.286	.376	.258	103	391	73	112	20	1	9	45	56	7	2	4	57	15	5	.412	.382
Molina, Bengie	R-R	5-11	225	7-20-74	.240	.311	.215	57	175	10	42	6	1	2	19	10	1	5	4	15	0	0	.320	.279
Moreland, Mitch	L-L	6-2	230	9-6-85	.255	.200	.264	47	145	20	37	4	0	9	25	25	1	0	2	36	3	1	.469	.364
Murphy, David	L-L	6-4	205	10-18-81	.291	.272	.298	138	419	54	122	26	2	12	65	45	0	0	3	71	14	2	.449	.358
Ramirez, Max	R-R	5-11	175	10-11-84	.217	.158	.240	28	69	8	15	3	0	2	8	12	2	0	2	22	0	0	.348	.341
Saltalamacchia, Jarrod	B-R	6-4	235	5-2-85	.200	.000	.200	2	5	0	1	0	0	0	1	0	0	0	0	1	0	0	.200	.200
2-team total (10 Boston)					.167	—	—	12	24	2	4	3	0	0	2	6	0	0	0	5	0	0	.292	.333
Smoak, Justin	B-L	6-4	220	12-5-86	.209	.139	.244	70	235	29	49	10	0	8	34	38	0	0	2	57	1	0	.353	.316
2-team total (30 Seattle)					.218	—	—	100	348	40	76	14	0	13	48	46	0	0	3	91	1	0	.371	.307
Teagarden, Taylor	R-R	6-0	200	12-21-83	.155	.185	.136	28	71	10	11	1	0	4	6	8	2	4	0	34	0	0	.338	.259
Treanor, Matt	R-R	6-0	205	3-3-76	.211	.137	.244	82	237	22	50	6	1	5	27	22	5	4	4	43	1	2	.308	.287
Young, Michael	R-R	6-1	200	10-19-76	.284	.322	.270	157	656	99	186	36	3	21	91	50	1	0	11	115	4	2	.444	.330

Pitching	B-T	HT	WT	DOB	W	L	ERA	G	GS	CG	SV	IP	H	R	ER	HR	BB	SO	AVG	vLH	vRH	K/9	BB/9
Beltre, Omar	R-R	6-3	190	8-24-81	0	1	9.00	2	2	0	0	7	9	7	7	3	7	9	.321	.333	.308	11.57	9.00
Feldman, Scott	L-R	6-6	230	2-7-83	7	11	5.48	29	22	0	0	141	181	98	86	18	45	71	.313	.302	.323	4.78	2.87
Feliz, Neftali	R-R	6-3	215	5-2-88	4	3	2.73	70	0	0	40	69	43	21	21	5	18	71	.176	.127	.220	9.22	2.34
Francisco, Frank	R-R	6-2	250	9-11-79	6	4	3.76	56	0	0	2	53	49	23	22	5	18	60	.247	.205	.275	10.25	3.08
Harden, Rich	L-R	6-1	195	11-30-81	5	5	5.58	20	18	0	0	92	91	61	57	18	62	75	.256	.273	.238	7.34	6.07
Harrison, Matt	L-L	6-4	240	9-16-85	3	2	4.71	37	6	0	2	78	80	45	41	10	39	46	.262	.235	.273	5.29	4.48
Holland, Derek	B-L	6-2	195	10-9-86	3	4	4.08	14	10	0	0	57	55	30	26	6	24	54	.247	.130	.277	8.48	3.77
Hunter, Tommy	R-R	6-3	280	7-3-86	13	4	3.73	23	22	1	0	128	126	55	53	21	33	68	.255	.272	.231	4.78	2.32
Kirkman, Michael	L-L	6-4	195	9-8-86	0	0	1.65	14	0	0	0	16	9	3	3	0	10	16	.161	.214	.107	8.82	5.51
Lee, Cliff	L-L	6-3	190	8-30-78	4	6	3.98	15	15	2	0	109	103	53	48	11	12	96	.248	.276	.240	7.95	0.99
2-team total (13 Seattle)					12	9	3.18	28	28	7	0	212	195	84	75	16	18	185	—	—	—	7.84	0.76
Lewis, Colby	R-R	6-4	230	8-2-79	12	13	3.72	32	32	1	0	201	174	90	83	21	65	196	.227	.239	.216	8.78	2.91
Lowe, Mark	L-R	6-3	210	6-7-83	0	0	12.00	3	0	0	0	3	7	4	4	1	1	5	.467	.500	.400	15.00	3.00
2-team total (11 Seattle)					1	3	5.40	14	0	0	0	13	18	9	8	2	6	12	—	—	—	8.10	4.05
Mathis, Doug	R-R	6-3	220	6-7-83	1	1	6.04	13	0	0	0	22	30	15	15	7	11	10	.337	.293	.375	4.03	4.43
Moscoso, Guillermo	R-R	6-1	200	11-14-83	0	0	27.00	1	0	0	0	1	2	2	2	0	2	2	.500	.000	.500	27.00	27.00
Nippert, Dustin	R-R	6-8	225	5-6-81	4	5	4.29	38	2	0	0	57	61	28	27	7	34	47	.277	.305	.261	7.46	5.40
O'Day, Darren	R-R	6-4	220	10-22-82	6	2	2.03	72	0	0	0	62	43	15	14	5	12	45	.196	.229	.181	6.53	1.74
Ogando, Alexi	R-R	6-4	185	10-5-83	4	1	1.30	44	0	0	0	42	31	6	6	2	16	39	.208	.229	.198	8.42	3.46
Oliver, Darren	R-L	6-2	200	10-6-70	1	2	2.48	64	0	0	1	62	53	20	17	4	15	65	.242	.200	.281	9.49	2.19
Rapada, Clay	R-L	6-5	200	3-9-81	0	0	4.00	13	0	0	0	9	6	4	4	2	7	5	.188	.053	.385	5.00	7.00
Ray, Chris	R-R	6-3	210	1-12-82	2	0	3.41	35	0	0	1	32	24	12	12	4	16	16	.205	.245	.172	4.55	4.55
Strop, Pedro	R-R	6-0	175	6-13-85	0	0	10.13	15	0	0	0	11	17	12	12	2	11	11	.362	.368	.357	9.28	9.28
Wilson, C.J.	L-L	6-1	210	11-18-80	15	8	3.35	33	33	3	0	204	161	83	76	10	93	170	.217	.144	.236	7.50	4.10

Fielding

Catcher	PCT	G	PO	A	E	DP	PB
Molina	.987	55	355	24	5	1	1
Ramirez	.988	26	154	7	2	0	2
Saltalamacchia	1.000	1	8	0	0	0	0
Teagarden	.989	28	171	9	2	2	3
Treanor	.994	81	512	21	3	1	2

First Base	PCT	G	PO	A	E	DP
Arias	.973	5	34	2	1	4
Cantu	1.000	23	158	11	0	20
Davis	.993	41	269	22	2	27
Garko	1.000	6	17	6	0	3
Moreland	.993	40	289	16	2	18
Smoak	.993	69	545	35	4	53

Second Base	PCT	G	PO	A	E	DP
Arias	.986	25	27	45	1	13

	PCT	G	PO	A	E	DP
Blanco	.972	40	48	92	4	19
Cantu	—	1	0	0	0	0
Cora	1.000	2	2	3	0	2
German	1.000	3	5	6	0	2
Guzman	.971	9	12	21	1	3
Kinsler	.985	103	190	278	7	64

Third Base	PCT	G	PO	A	E	DP
Blanco	.857	9	1	5	1	0
Cantu	1.000	8	2	6	0	0
Cora	1.000	1	1	0	0	
Davis	1.000	1	0	1	0	0
Young	.950	155	95	265	19	26

Shortstop	PCT	G	PO	A	E	DP
Andrus	.976	148	242	401	16	89
Arias	1.000	3	5	6	0	2

	PCT	G	PO	A	E	DP
Blanco	.964	16	16	37	2	8
German	—	1	0	0	0	0
Guzman	.889	3	4	4	1	0

Outfield	PCT	G	PO	A	E	DP
Boggs	1.000	4	5	0	0	0
Borbon	.988	133	337	2	4	0
Cruz	.981	101	250	3	5	1
Francoeur	.952	14	20	0	1	0
Gentry	1.000	15	16	1	0	0
German	—	1	0	0	0	0
Guerrero	.935	18	28	1	2	0
Hamilton	.985	119	254	9	4	2
Moreland	.909	7	10	0	1	0
Murphy	.995	125	206	9	1	1

OKLAHOMA CITY REDHAWKS   TRIPLE-A
PACIFIC COAST LEAGUE

Batting	B-T	HT	WT	DOB	AVG	vLH	vRH	G	AB	R	H	2B	3B	HR	RBI	BB	HBP	SH	SF	SO	SB	CS	SLG	OBP
Bankston, Wes	R-R	6-4	215	11-27-83	.308	.286	.316	7	26	3	8	2	0	2	5	2	1	0	0	4	0	0	.615	.379
Boggs, Brandon	B-R	5-10	210	1-9-83	.290	.308	.285	103	362	72	105	25	5	10	50	72	1	1	3	93	3	6	.470	.406
Brown, Matt	R-R	6-0	200	8-8-82	.249	.210	.264	79	301	40	75	18	5	10	32	25	3	2	2	83	2	0	.442	.311
Chavez, Endy	L-L	6-0	170	2-7-78	.200	.000	.200	1	5	2	1	1	0	0	0	0	0	0	0	2	0	0	.400	.200
Cora, Alex	L-R	6-0	200	10-18-75	.182	.000	.182	6	22	5	4	1	0	1	2	3	0	0	0	2	1	0	.364	.280
Cruz, Nelson	R-R	6-2	240	7-1-80	.211	.200	.222	5	19	1	4	1	0	0	4	2	0	0	1	5	0	0	.263	.273
Davis, Chris	L-R	6-3	230	3-17-86	.327	.353	.319	103	398	67	130	31	2	14	80	37	3	0	6	105	3	2	.520	.383
Frostad, Emerson	L-L	6-1	210	1-13-83	.281	.250	.286	19	64	5	18	5	2	0	6	2	0	0	1	9	0	1	.422	.299
Garko, Ryan	R-R	6-2	225	1-2-81	.235	.254	.230	93	340	42	80	11	1	12	48	41	5	0	1	62	1	1	.379	.326
Gentry, Craig	R-R	6-2	190	11-29-83	.309	.317	.307	69	259	43	80	7	4	4	35	29	8	3	2	47	12	5	.413	.393
German, Esteban	R-R	5-9	195	1-26-78	.280	.291	.277	126	485	79	136	27	5	5	55	64	9	4	5	77	50	7	.388	.371
Gradoville, Chris	R-R	6-1	220	7-10-84	.000	.000	.000	2	3	0	0	0	0	0	0	1	0	0	0	2	0	0	.000	.250
Iribarren, Hernan	L-R	6-1	195	6-29-84	.275	.237	.285	128	463	62	128	23	2	8	70	41	2	9	6	79	10	5	.385	.333
Jenkins, Andy	R-R	6-0	205	7-23-83	.266	.414	.180	23	79	12	21	1	2	0	7	7	1	0	0	18	2	0	.329	.333
Moreland, Mitch	L-L	6-2	230	9-6-85	.289	.272	.294	95	353	52	102	29	2	12	65	47	3	2	7	63	2	1	.484	.371
Petit, Gregorio	R-R	5-10	195	12-10-84	.251	.170	.274	130	471	59	118	20	1	7	53	40	6	6	2	96	12	3	.342	.316
Ramirez, Max	R-R	5-11	175	10-11-84	.286	.264	.294	56	189	24	54	9	0	3	29	27	3	1	6	51	4	0	.381	.373
Richardson, Kevin	R-R	6-3	230	9-12-80	.235	.412	.173	41	132	17	31	6	0	8	22	5	1	2	0	44	2	0	.462	.268
Rodriguez, Guilder	B-R	6-1	160	7-24-83	.254	.188	.275	21	67	17	17	3	0	0	8	9	0	0	1	7	4	1	.299	.342
Saltalamacchia, Jarrod	B-R	6-4	235	5-2-85	.244	.208	.254	63	238	37	58	11	2	11	33	25	5	0	2	60	1	0	.445	.326
Smoak, Justin	B-L	6-4	220	12-5-86	.300	.273	.321	15	50	10	15	6	0	2	5	16	0	0	0	8	0	0	.540	.470
2-team total (35 Tacoma)					.279	—	—	50	183	33	51	13	0	9	30	39	1	0	2	40	0	0	.497	.404
Stoneburner, Davis	R-R	6-0	175	1-14-85	.167	.000	.200	2	6	0	1	1	0	0	0	0	0	0	0	2	0	0	.333	.167
Taveras, Willy	R-R	6-0	180	12-25-81	.275	.250	.277	23	91	12	25	3	1	2	10	6	1	1	1	9	2	2	.396	.323
Teagarden, Taylor	R-R	6-1	200	12-21-83	.167	.333	.152	11	36	6	6	0	0	2	2	2	0	1	0	15	0	0	.333	.211
Tomlin, James	R-R	6-0	183	8-12-82	.143	.000	.167	15	42	7	6	1	0	2	2	4	1	0	0	15	0	0	.310	.234
Tracy, Chad	R-R	6-3	210	7-4-85	.263	.236	.270	78	281	51	74	14	1	17	55	35	4	0	4	52	5	2	.502	.349
Treanor, Matt	R-R	6-0	205	3-3-76	.200	.000	.200	5	15	2	3	0	0	0	2	1	1	0	0	3	0	0	.200	.294

Pitching	B-T	HT	WT	DOB	W	L	ERA	G	GS	CG	SV	IP	H	R	ER	HR	BB	SO	AVG	vLH	vRH	K/9	BB/9
Ballard, Michael	R-L	6-2	180	2-6-84	6	8	5.09	29	18	1	0	111	142	72	63	13	33	73	.311	.350	.290	5.90	2.67
Beltre, Omar	R-R	6-3	190	8-24-81	3	9	2.65	24	14	0	2	85	69	35	25	2	38	85	.229	.211	.242	9.00	4.02
Colome, Jesus	R-R	6-2	240	12-23-77	0	0	8.10	4	0	0	0	3	3	3	3	0	1	2	.214	.500	.100	5.40	2.70
2-team total (3 Albuquerque)					0	0	15.43	7	0	0	0	5	7	10	8	0	3	3	—			5.79	5.79
Eppley, Cody	R-R	6-5	205	10-8-85	2	1	4.08	18	0	0	1	29	32	13	13	3	13	31	.278	.375	.209	9.73	4.08
Eyre, Willie	R-R	6-0	225	7-21-78	5	4	3.50	49	0	0	2	72	74	36	28	2	25	59	.264	.254	.272	7.38	3.13
Feldman, Scott	L-R	6-4	230	2-7-83	0	0	4.50	1	0	0	0	4	5	2	2	2	0	3	.313	.250	.375	6.75	0.00
Garr, Brennan	R-R	6-2	190	2-22-84	0	0	0.00	1	1	0	0	3	2	0	0	0	2	6	.182	.200	.167	6.00	0.00
Geary, Geoff	R-R	6-0	180	8-26-76	4	5	5.37	23	6	0	0	59	83	43	35	7	21	32	.337	.308	.365	4.91	3.22
2-team total (8 Albuquerque)					4	6	5.32	31	6	0	0	69	96	49	41	7	25	48	—			6.23	3.25
Harden, Rich	L-R	6-1	195	11-30-81	0	2	3.86	5	5	0	0	23	21	13	10	3	8	34	.236	.275	.184	13.11	3.09
Harrison, Matt	L-L	6-4	240	9-16-85	0	1	6.23	1	1	0	0	4	9	4	3	1	1	4	.450	.400	.467	8.31	2.08
Holland, Derek	B-L	6-2	195	10-9-86	6	2	1.87	11	11	0	0	63	50	17	13	5	18	51	.216	.148	.241	7.32	2.59
Hunter, Tommy	R-R	6-3	240	7-3-86	1	2	4.05	6	6	0	0	27	28	12	12	2	11	14	.282	.250	.333	4.72	3.71
Kirkman, Michael	L-L	6-4	195	9-18-86	13	3	3.09	24	22	0	0	131	115	52	45	8	68	130	.235	.213	.246	8.93	4.67
Madrigal, Warner	R-R	6-1	265	3-21-84	4	2	3.73	27	0	0	2	41	33	17	17	5	7	33	.214	.194	.228	7.24	1.54
Mathis, Doug	R-R	6-3	220	6-7-83	5	7	5.66	18	15	1	0	89	116	61	56	7	31	54	.317	.292	.338	5.46	3.13
McCarthy, Brandon	R-R	6-7	200	7-7-83	4	2	3.36	11	9	0	0	56	51	22	21	8	11	44	.234	.227	.240	7.03	1.76
Moscoso, Guillermo	R-R	6-1	200	11-14-83	7	7	5.18	23	22	1	0	123	142	82	71	17	49	107	.283	.295	.274	7.81	3.58
Nippert, Dustin	R-R	6-8	225	5-6-81	0	0	0.00	1	1	0	0	3	1	0	0	0	0	3	.111	.200	.000	9.00	0.00
Ogando, Alexi	R-R	6-4	185	10-5-83	0	0	3.00	11	0	0	1	15	10	7	5	0	6	16	.175	.222	.133	12.60	3.60
Peguero, Jailen	R-R	6-0	185	1-4-81	2	1	4.09	13	0	0	0	22	18	11	10	1	16	23	.222	.222	.222	9.41	6.55
Phillips, Zach	L-L	6-1	200	9-21-86	3	2	3.22	33	1	0	1	50	50	22	18	1	29	40	.267	.241	.279	7.15	5.19

Prior, Mark	R-R	6-5	225	9-7-80	0	0	0.00	1	0	0	0	1	2	0	0	1	2	.400	.000	.500	18.00	9.00
Ramirez, Elizardo	B-R	6-0	180	1-28-83	4	4	5.13	26	3	0	0	53	68	36	30	8	10	26	.306	.323	.295	4.44	1.71
Rapada, Clay	R-L	6-5	200	3-9-81	1	2	1.82	50	0	0	2	59	32	16	12	1	21	61	.158	.120	.191	9.25	3.19
Reed, Evan	R-R	6-4	225	12-31-85	1	0	4.50	1	0	0	0	2	1	1	1	1	0	2	.143	.500	.000	9.00	0.00
Scheppers, Tanner	R-R	6-4	200	1-17-87	1	3	5.48	30	7	0	4	69	82	45	42	5	30	71	.297	.254	.336	9.26	3.91
Snyder, Ben	L-L	6-2	225	7-20-85	0	1	17.61	2	1	0	0	8	17	17	15	4	2	6	.405	.455	.387	7.04	2.35
Strop, Pedro	R-R	6-0	175	6-13-85	1	2	1.91	39	0	0	13	42	32	12	9	1	14	57	.203	.235	.178	12.12	2.98

Fielding

Catcher	PCT	G	PO	A	E	DP	PB
Frostad	1.000	6	35	2	0	0	1
Gradoville	.909	1	9	1	1	0	1
Ramirez	.986	34	256	17	4	0	2
Richardson	.987	38	289	18	4	4	2
Saltalamacchia	.988	55	408	20	5	2	4
Teagarden	1.000	10	69	7	0	4	1
Treanor	.964	4	27	0	1	0	0

First Base	PCT	G	PO	A	E	DP
Brown	.994	21	156	21	1	11
Davis	.982	37	300	25	6	32
Garko	.995	46	336	30	2	40
Moreland	.989	12	87	7	1	9
Smoak	.980	14	135	9	3	7
Tracy	.968	19	141	8	5	16

Second Base	PCT	G	PO	A	E	DP
Cora	.952	4	8	12	1	1
German	.978	54	82	139	5	29
Iribarren	.989	71	132	224	4	54
Rodriguez	1.000	20	29	50	0	11
Stoneburner	.500	2	1	1	2	0

Third Base	PCT	G	PO	A	E	DP
Brown	.861	34	18	44	10	6
Davis	.939	56	41	83	8	10
Frostad	.714	2	3	2	2	0
German	.898	51	21	67	10	7
Jenkins	.900	4	0	9	1	1

Shortstop	PCT	G	PO	A	E	DP
Cora	1.000	2	4	5	0	2
German	.927	11	9	29	3	6
Petit	.969	130	191	369	18	80

	PCT	G	PO	A	E	DP
Rodriguez	1.000	1	0	3	0	1

Outfield	PCT	G	PO	A	E	DP
Bankston	1.000	7	16	0	0	0
Boggs	.986	102	209	6	3	1
Brown	.980	26	47	3	1	1
Chavez	1.000	1	1	0	0	0
Cruz	1.000	4	8	0	0	0
Davis	1.000	4	3	0	0	0
Gentry	.994	68	170	3	1	2
German	1.000	15	16	1	0	0
Iribarren	1.000	60	103	5	0	2
Jenkins	1.000	19	24	2	0	0
Moreland	.989	83	170	11	2	4
Taveras	.984	23	59	1	1	0
Tomlin	.964	14	25	2	1	0
Tracy	1.000	15	19	0	0	0

FRISCO ROUGHRIDERS

DOUBLE-A

TEXAS LEAGUE

Batting	B-T	HT	WT	DOB	AVG	vLH	vRH	G	AB	R	H	2B	3B	HR	RBI	BB	HBP	SH	SF	SO	SB	CS	SLG	OBP
Arias, Joaquin	R-R	6-1	170	9-21-84	.194	.250	.133	8	31	4	6	0	0	0	1	3	0	0	1	7	0	0	.194	.257
Bankston, Wes	R-R	6-4	215	11-27-83	.218	.253	.199	55	220	21	48	17	0	3	27	15	2	1	2	44	2	0	.336	.272
Beltre, Engel	L-L	6-2	180	11-1-89	.254	.304	.223	47	181	14	46	4	4	1	14	10	3	2	2	24	8	2	.337	.301
Butler, Joey	R-R	6-2	210	3-12-86	.277	.272	.280	132	516	67	143	26	6	10	58	47	5	0	5	120	8	6	.409	.340
Chavez, Endy	L-L	6-0	170	2-7-78	.333	.429	.250	4	15	3	5	0	0	0	1	2	0	1	0	2	0	0	.333	.412
Cruz, Nelson	R-R	6-2	240	7-1-80	.364	.000	.444	3	11	1	4	1	0	0	1	1	0	0	1	0	1	0	.455	.385
Felix, Jose	R-R	5-10	198	6-28-88	.267	.267	.267	27	105	7	28	3	0	1	6	1	0	1	0	6	0	1	.324	.274
Frostad, Emerson	L-R	6-1	210	11-23-83	.264	.303	.237	78	299	39	79	8	5	5	39	37	0	0	4	54	2	2	.375	.341
Greene, Jonathan	R-R	6-0	200	9-16-85	.194	.211	.184	42	144	17	28	6	0	5	15	8	5	0	3	51	0	0	.340	.256
Guzman, Cristian	B-R	6-0	210	3-21-78	.308	.200	.375	4	13	1	4	0	0	0	3	3	0	0	0	1	1	0	.308	.438
Hilligoss, Mitch	L-R	6-1	195	6-17-85	.304	.259	.327	24	79	11	24	4	0	1	10	12	0	1	1	14	0	2	.380	.391
Jenkins, Andy	R-R	6-0	205	7-23-83	.239	.211	.254	97	360	41	86	21	0	10	50	33	3	2	3	76	3	4	.381	.306
Kaase, Jake	L-R	6-1	185	4-14-86	.281	.294	.275	21	57	11	16	2	1	0	4	7	1	0	2	12	2	0	.351	.358
Kinsler, Ian	R-R	6-0	200	6-22-82	.263	.167	.308	6	19	3	5	0	1	0	2	1	0	1	2	3	2	0	.368	.348
Lawson, Matt	R-R	6-1	195	11-18-85	.277	.351	.232	76	292	48	81	16	5	7	34	37	8	5	3	64	3	3	.438	.371
Lemon, Marcus	L-R	5-11	173	6-3-88	.271	.306	.253	111	468	55	127	22	4	3	40	36	3	5	4	82	7	7	.355	.325
Osuna, Renny	R-R	6-0	172	4-24-85	.293	.303	.287	119	450	59	132	21	5	4	49	28	5	13	2	77	20	10	.389	.340
Richardson, Kevin	R-R	6-3	230	9-12-80	.265	.364	.230	22	83	9	22	7	0	4	9	5	1	0	1	32	0	0	.494	.311
Rodriguez, Guilder	R-R	6-1	160	7-24-83	.266	.275	.262	96	323	44	86	4	3	2	31	41	4	14	3	42	15	5	.297	.335
Sarmiento, Elio	R-R	5-11	200	6-20-86	.191	.273	.142	59	204	20	39	8	3	2	21	17	4	3	1	43	2	0	.289	.265
Stoneburner, Davis	R-R	6-0	175	1-14-85	.297	.250	.333	10	37	4	11	1	0	0	2	3	1	0	0	8	2	0	.324	.366
Teagarden, Taylor	R-R	6-1	200	12-21-83	.242	.250	.237	52	190	24	46	10	1	3	32	25	3	0	2	75	0	0	.353	.336
Tomlin, James	R-R	6-0	183	8-12-82	.270	.292	.258	107	397	46	107	20	1	5	35	35	2	3	6	67	10	0	.363	.327
Whittleman, Johnny	L-R	6-2	195	2-11-87	.201	.237	.186	74	259	24	52	14	1	5	30	42	0	0	0	72	1	2	.320	.312

Pitching	B-T	HT	WT	DOB	W	L	ERA	G	GS	CG	SV	IP	H	R	ER	HR	BB	SO	AVG	vLH	vRH	K/9	BB/9
Beavan, Blake	R-R	6-7	250	1-17-89	10	5	2.78	17	17	0	0	110	100	37	34	6	12	68	.242	.237	.247	5.56	0.98
Bleier, Richard	L-L	6-3	195	4-16-87	7	11	5.04	28	28	2	0	164	191	98	92	13	28	82	.291	.255	.314	4.49	1.53
Castillo, Fabio	R-R	6-1	235	2-19-89	0	0	4.91	3	0	0	0	4	3	2	2	0	4	2	.214	.125	.333	4.91	9.82
Chick, Travis	R-R	6-3	220	6-10-84	2	2	6.53	5	5	0	0	21	16	15	15	1	11	18	.303	.340	.262	7.84	4.79
Eppley, Cody	R-R	6-5	205	10-8-85	1	1	1.19	19	0	0	9	23	12	3	3	0	9	27	.154	.257	.070	10.72	3.57
Falcon, Ryan	R-L	6-0	195	8-27-84	0	0	17.36	4	0	0	0	5	6	9	9	2	6	3	.286	.250	.308	5.79	11.57
Flores, Adalberto	R-R	6-7	225	11-4-86	3	4	4.33	38	0	0	4	60	61	30	29	3	20	61	.258	.213	.307	9.10	2.98
Garr, Brennan	R-R	6-2	190	2-22-84	8	5	5.37	42	0	0	0	62	74	39	37	7	25	62	.297	.276	.316	9.00	3.63
Gutierrez, Danny	R-R	6-1	180	3-8-87	1	0	0.00	1	1	0	0	6	2	0	0	0	2	7	.105	.000	.133	10.50	3.00
Hamburger, Mark	R-R	6-4	195	2-5-87	1	0	3.20	13	0	0	3	20	20	7	7	1	8	20	.270	.311	.207	9.15	3.66
Hamilton, Clayton	R-R	6-5	205	6-15-82	1	1	2.25	4	4	0	0	20	21	5	5	1	1	13	.273	.233	.324	5.85	0.45
Harrison, Matt	L-L	6-4	240	9-16-85	0	0	3.00	2	0	0	0	3	3	1	1	0	0	4	.250	.000	.429	12.00	0.00
Jones, Beau	L-L	6-1	195	8-25-86	3	2	2.91	34	2	0	3	53	34	19	17	0	30	62	.197	.315	.122	10.59	5.13
Kiker, Kasey	L-L	5-10	185	11-19-87	1	4	7.65	14	7	0	0	40	28	34	34	1	46	42	.209	.163	.235	9.45	10.35
Laughter, Andrew	R-R	6-4	227	2-24-85	1	0	8.10	4	0	0	0	3	4	3	3	0	3	3	.286	.429	.143	8.10	8.10
Lueke, Josh	R-R	6-5	220	12-5-84	1	1	3.86	15	0	0	2	19	18	9	8	2	5	26	.254	.286	.212	12.54	2.41
Madrigal, Warner	R-R	6-1	265	3-21-84	1	0	3.72	8	0	0	1	10	8	4	4	1	7	9	.216	.353	.100	8.38	6.52
Mobley, Chris	R-R	5-11	170	8-16-83	2	2	3.49	14	0	0	0	28	25	13	11	1	14	26	.238	.236	.240	8.26	4.45
Murphy, Tim	L-L	6-2	190	5-7-87	0	1	1.59	17	0	0	0	23	19	8	4	3	4	23	.229	.326	.125	9.13	1.59

Name	B-T	HT	WT	DOB	W	L	ERA	G	GS	CG	SV	IP	H	R	ER	HR	BB	SO	AVG	vLH	vRH	K/9	BB/9
Nippert, Dustin	R-R	6-8	225	5-6-81	0	0	0.00	2	2	0	0	3	1	0	0	0	1	7	.091	.111	.000	18.90	2.70
Ogando, Alexi	R-R	6-4	185	10-5-83	0	0	1.15	7	3	0	0	16	4	2	2	1	5	21	.078	.091	.069	12.06	2.87
Perez, Martin	L-L	6-0	178	4-4-91	5	8	5.96	24	23	0	0	100	117	73	66	12	50	101	.290	.267	.301	9.12	4.52
Phillips, Zach	L-L	6-1	200	9-21-86	0	0	1.08	12	0	0	4	17	9	2	2	0	5	23	.155	.148	.161	12.42	2.70
Pimentel, Carlos	R-R	6-3	180	12-1-89	0	1	11.25	1	1	0	0	4	5	7	5	3	1	2	.278	.375	.200	4.50	2.25
Ramirez, Elizardo	R-R	6-0	180	1-28-83	0	1	3.65	3	3	0	0	12	17	6	5	1	4	7	.340	.417	.143	5.11	2.92
Reed, Evan	R-R	6-4	225	12-31-85	1	1	1.62	30	0	0	5	39	35	7	7	0	13	34	.238	.221	.253	7.85	3.00
Roark, Tanner	R-R	6-2	220	10-5-86	10	5	4.20	22	17	0	0	105	113	57	49	8	33	75	.276	.324	.221	6.43	2.83
Scheppers, Tanner	R-R	6-4	200	1-17-87	0	0	0.82	6	0	0	2	11	3	1	1	0	1	19	.079	.095	.059	15.55	0.00
Schlact, Michael	R-R	6-7	205	12-9-85	1	5	7.09	12	8	0	0	53	73	45	42	6	20	25	.327	.336	.318	4.22	3.38
Snyder, Ben	L-L	6-2	225	7-20-85	3	5	3.28	38	5	0	1	96	78	38	35	9	31	86	.227	.235	.220	8.06	2.91
Tatusko, Ryan	R-R	6-5	200	3-27-85	9	2	2.97	24	13	1	0	100	94	34	33	2	40	58	.254	.257	.251	5.22	3.60
Tufts, Tyler	R-R	6-3	195	12-5-86	0	2	2.50	14	0	0	2	18	14	5	5	0	4	12	.226	.241	.212	6.00	2.00
Young, Corey	L-L	6-2	185	12-30-86	0	0	11.25	3	0	0	0	4	6	5	5	0	2	6	.333	.333	.333	13.50	4.50

Fielding

Catcher	PCT	G	PO	A	E	DP	PB
Felix	.996	27	201	21	1	5	3
Richardson	.995	22	185	20	1	3	1
Sarmiento	.982	48	340	44	7	3	5
Teagarden	.994	44	313	27	2	3	2

First Base	PCT	G	PO	A	E	DP
Arias	1.000	4	32	0	0	5
Bankston	1.000	23	200	18	0	20
Frostad	.994	54	441	44	3	42
Hilligoss	1.000	1	1	0	0	0
Jenkins	1.000	9	89	2	0	6
Kaase	1.000	2	16	0	0	1
Whittleman	.986	48	413	24	6	33

Second Base	PCT	G	PO	A	E	DP
Arias	1.000	1	3	2	0	1
Guzman	1.000	1	2	1	0	0
Kaase	1.000	6	16	22	0	1

	PCT	G	PO	A	E	DP
Kinsler	.958	6	8	15	1	3
Lawson	.980	60	125	164	6	36
Lemon	.949	34	58	92	8	13
Osuna	.987	31	57	92	2	22
Stoneburner	.955	4	10	11	1	4

Third Base	PCT	G	PO	A	E	DP
Arias	1.000	1	1	2	0	0
Greene	.861	16	9	22	5	0
Guzman	—	1	0	0	0	0
Hilligoss	.944	16	9	25	2	3
Jenkins	.973	61	39	104	4	15
Kaase	1.000	4	1	4	0	0
Osuna	.982	44	24	84	2	8

Shortstop	PCT	G	PO	A	E	DP
Arias	1.000	2	3	5	0	1
Guzman	1.000	2	4	8	0	0
Kaase	.895	4	6	11	2	3

	PCT	G	PO	A	E	DP
Osuna	1.000	32	46	71	0	9
Rodriguez	.967	96	167	302	16	59
Stoneburner	.931	6	11	16	2	4

Outfield	PCT	G	PO	A	E	DP
Bankston	1.000	18	32	3	0	1
Beltre	.986	45	133	3	2	0
Butler	.970	129	253	6	8	1
Chavez	1.000	3	6	1	0	0
Cruz	.750	2	3	0	1	0
Greene	.975	19	38	1	1	0
Hilligoss	1.000	2	3	1	0	0
Jenkins	1.000	17	33	3	0	1
Kaase	—	1	0	0	0	0
Lawson	1.000	14	26	1	0	0
Lemon	.959	60	89	4	4	0
Sarmiento	1.000	10	12	0	0	0
Tomlin	.988	104	232	7	3	3

BAKERSFIELD BLAZE

HIGH CLASS A

CALIFORNIA LEAGUE

Batting	B-T	HT	WT	DOB	AVG	vLH	vRH	G	AB	R	H	2B	3B	HR	RBI	BB	HBP	SH	SF	SO	SB	CS	SLG	OBP
Beltre, Engel	L-L	6-2	180	11-1-89	.331	.377	.312	68	263	38	87	11	4	5	35	11	10	3	3	34	10	7	.460	.376
Bianucci, Mike	R-R	6-1	225	6-26-86	.258	.290	.246	120	462	66	119	23	2	18	72	31	5	5	4	114	0	3	.433	.309
Bolden, Jared	L-L	6-2	190	3-17-87	.219	.353	.185	62	169	21	37	5	1	1	15	14	0	1	1	41	4	3	.278	.277
Bonadonna, Joe	R-R	5-8	170	9-6-85	.129	.250	.053	12	31	5	4	3	0	0	1	4	1	2	0	11	2	0	.226	.202
DiFazio, Vin	R-R	6-0	215	5-15-86	.216	.067	.278	16	51	8	11	5	0	2	4	11	0	0	0	10	1	0	.431	.355
Felix, Jose	R-R	5-10	198	6-28-88	.282	.236	.295	73	248	27	70	13	1	2	31	17	1	7	4	25	2	0	.367	.326
Fry, Eric	L-R	5-10	204	8-9-87	.111	.000	.125	5	9	1	1	1	0	0	0	1	0	0	0	4	0	0	.222	.200
Gradoville, Chris	R-R	6-1	220	7-10-84	.280	.247	.292	73	282	35	79	24	2	4	27	15	10	0	1	61	2	0	.422	.338
Greene, Jonathan	R-R	6-0	200	9-16-85	.262	.188	.286	18	65	11	17	3	2	4	14	5	4	0	2	22	0	1	.554	.342
Hilligoss, Mitch	L-R	6-1	195	6-17-85	.293	.244	.309	45	164	16	48	6	0	2	19	15	1	0	2	17	2	1	.366	.352
Hogan, Doug	R-R	6-3	210	9-29-84	.240	.236	.242	67	221	24	53	13	0	5	28	13	3	2	1	69	0	0	.367	.290
James, Andres	B-R	5-9	150	11-25-87	.280	.290	.276	106	353	48	99	17	1	1	26	10	0	8	2	75	16	4	.343	.299
Kaase, Jake	L-R	6-1	185	4-14-86	.241	.200	.250	75	245	29	59	12	0	6	30	21	3	6	1	51	2	0	.363	.307
Lima, Daniel	R-R	6-1	175	2-21-87	.000	.000	.000	2	3	0	0	0	0	0	0	0	0	0	0	1	0	0	.000	.000
McGuiness, Chris	L-L	6-1	210	4-11-88	.250	.263	.244	34	120	19	30	3	0	7	22	24	2	0	1	32	1	1	.450	.381
Mendonca, Tommy	L-R	6-1	200	4-12-88	.248	.253	.247	120	419	62	104	26	2	10	47	36	17	2	3	126	1	4	.391	.331
Morrison, Erik	R-R	6-0	190	10-23-85	.242	.274	.225	83	297	37	72	14	0	13	45	13	4	2	3	58	2	4	.421	.281
Paisano, David	R-R	6-1	165	11-26-87	.278	.284	.276	131	532	71	148	23	5	6	49	37	6	1	0	113	19	5	.374	.332
Podraza, Cody	R-R	5-8	185	11-6-87	.295	.160	.327	37	129	23	38	9	1	2	8	9	1	1	4	27	5	0	.426	.331
Stoneburner, Davis	R-R	6-0	175	1-14-85	.290	.284	.292	103	403	68	117	28	4	16	57	39	9	3	4	83	15	5	.499	.363
Vail, Taylor	R-L	6-2	200	9-5-86	.000	.000	.000	2	5	0	0	0	0	0	1	0	0	0	0	1	0	0	.000	.000
Velazquez, Miguel	R-R	6-1	205	5-15-88	.270	.195	.291	48	189	27	51	6	1	5	25	12	6	0	0	38	3	1	.392	.333
Whittleman, Johnny	L-R	6-2	195	2-11-87	.248	.261	.244	33	113	21	28	6	0	7	23	25	0	0	2	32	0	1	.487	.379

Pitching	B-T	HT	WT	DOB	W	L	ERA	G	GS	CG	SV	IP	H	R	ER	HR	BB	SO	AVG	vLH	vRH	K/9	BB/9
Boscan, Wilfredo	R-R	6-2	187	10-26-89	9	14	4.67	27	27	1	0	164	189	93	85	17	40	130	.291	.299	.286	7.15	2.20
Brigham, Jake	R-R	6-3	210	2-10-88	1	5	6.93	11	10	0	0	49	67	46	38	5	26	39	.333	.368	.295	7.11	4.74
Castillo, Fabio	R-R	6-1	235	2-19-89	1	3	1.92	36	0	0	6	52	41	15	11	2	26	65	.219	.284	.183	11.32	4.53
Doyle, Andrew	R-R	6-3	200	11-12-87	1	0	5.91	7	4	0	0	21	25	15	14	4	10	15	.305	.233	.346	6.33	4.22
Eppley, Cody	R-R	6-5	205	10-8-85	2	0	0.00	14	0	0	6	18	9	0	0	0	1	24	.143	.174	.125	12.00	0.50
Flores, Adalberto	R-R	6-2	225	11-4-86	1	1	4.70	7	0	0	2	8	5	4	4	2	6	9	.185	.091	.250	10.57	7.04
Font, Wilmer	R-R	6-4	210	5-24-90	1	2	3.86	9	9	0	0	49	38	26	21	5	32	52	.217	.230	.205	9.55	5.88
Gomez, Kennil	R-R	6-3	170	4-8-88	5	9	6.47	24	14	1	1	97	127	79	70	14	48	53	.321	.337	.308	4.90	4.44
Grullon, Geuris	L-L	6-5	185	12-20-89	0	0	3.00	1	0	0	0	3	1	0	1	0	1	3	.308	.200	.375	9.00	3.00
Gunter, Jason	R-R	6-4	200	3-10-88	0	0	4.50	1	0	0	0	2	3	1	1	0	4	3	.333	.667	.167	13.50	18.00
Gutierrez, Danny	R-R	6-1	180	3-8-87	1	4	5.17	6	6	0	0	31	37	23	18	4	12	30	.306	.400	.239	8.62	3.45
Hamburger, Mark	R-R	6-4	195	2-5-87	3	2	1.77	37	0	0	18	46	38	12	9	3	18	49	.221	.263	.188	9.66	3.55

Name	B-T	HT	WT	DOB	W	L	ERA	G	GS	CG	SV	IP	H	R	ER	HR	BB	SO	AVG	vLH	vRH	K/9	BB/9
Hurley, Trevor	R-R	6-3	215	7-28-87	2	2	2.22	19	0	0	4	28	17	10	7	5	16	34	.170	.171	.169	10.80	5.08
Laughter, Andrew	R-R	6-4	227	2-24-85	0	1	8.10	10	0	0	1	10	16	9	9	1	4	8	.340	.348	.333	7.20	3.60
Main, Michael	R-R	6-1	170	12-14-88	5	3	3.45	15	15	1	0	91	87	47	35	14	21	72	.250	.285	.221	7.09	2.07
Miller, Justin	R-R	6-3	190	6-13-87	4	3	3.06	32	0	0	0	47	35	18	16	3	21	52	.205	.238	.185	9.96	4.02
Murphy, Tim	L-L	6-2	190	5-7-87	2	1	3.25	19	1	0	0	36	27	15	13	2	24	23	.225	.297	.193	5.75	6.00
Nam, Yoon-Hee	L-L	6-2	190	8-4-87	4	2	4.25	22	3	0	0	55	52	29	26	12	18	56	.242	.213	.253	9.16	2.95
Nelo, Hector	R-R	6-1	200	11-5-86	0	1	5.93	20	0	0	0	27	25	21	18	5	19	32	.250	.333	.203	10.54	6.26
Ortiz, Joseph	L-L	5-7	175	8-13-90	0	0	3.86	2	0	0	0	2	3	1	1	0	1	4	.333	.250	.400	15.43	3.86
Pimentel, Carlos	R-R	6-3	180	12-1-89	7	7	4.96	23	23	0	0	123	140	83	68	15	56	97	.292	.308	.280	7.08	4.09
Rijo, Ezequiel	R-R	6-4	190	9-12-90	0	1	45.00	1	1	0	0	1	4	5	5	1	2	1	.571	.500	.600	9.00	18.00
Ross, Robbie	L-L	5-11	185	6-24-89	4	4	5.37	11	11	0	0	52	67	38	31	4	17	49	.305	.469	.257	8.48	2.94
Schlact, Michael	R-R	6-7	205	12-9-85	3	0	4.50	6	6	1	0	34	33	20	17	6	8	18	.254	.296	.224	4.76	2.12
Tufts, Tyler	R-R	6-3	195	12-5-86	2	1	4.50	12	0	0	0	18	20	10	9	6	6	12	.286	.222	.326	6.00	3.00
Wieland, Joe	R-R	6-3	175	1-21-90	4	3	5.19	11	10	0	0	59	67	36	34	6	10	62	.283	.298	.275	9.46	1.53
Young, Corey	L-L	6-2	185	12-30-86	3	3	3.27	47	0	0	1	52	45	25	19	2	25	53	.233	.176	.264	9.11	4.30
Zegarac, Shane	L-L	6-2	185	8-15-85	2	1	2.79	34	0	0	0	39	34	13	12	3	15	33	.252	.205	.275	7.68	3.49

Fielding

Catcher	PCT	G	PO	A	E	DP	PB
DiFazio	.989	11	84	6	1	0	3
Felix	.989	70	496	66	6	13	10
Gradoville	1.000	7	51	3	0	0	4
Hogan	.992	59	475	46	4	5	9

First Base	PCT	G	PO	A	E	DP
Bolden	1.000	38	292	23	0	24
Gradoville	.983	8	54	5	1	4
Greene	.980	14	134	11	3	16
Hilligoss	.989	12	84	4	1	5
McGuiness	.997	34	270	22	1	31
Morrison	.960	10	65	7	3	2
Whittleman	.988	31	229	17	3	21

Second Base	PCT	G	PO	A	E	DP
Bonadonna	1.000	3	5	9	0	2
James	.949	13	19	37	3	5
Kaase	.979	38	78	109	4	24

	PCT	G	PO	A	E	DP
Mendonca	1.000	1	0	3	0	0
Morrison	.960	34	70	100	7	15
Stoneburner	.956	59	106	154	12	40

Third Base	PCT	G	PO	A	E	DP
Gradoville	1.000	1	1	0	0	0
Greene	1.000	1	2	2	0	0
Hilligoss	1.000	7	2	10	0	1
Kaase	1.000	5	5	6	0	1
Mendonca	.904	114	89	176	28	20
Morrison	.976	15	10	30	1	2

Shortstop	PCT	G	PO	A	E	DP
Bonadonna	1.000	2	3	3	0	0
James	.930	88	121	237	27	53
Kaase	.980	12	17	32	1	6
Morrison	—	2	0	0	0	0
Stoneburner	.923	44	62	93	13	15

Outfield	PCT	G	PO	A	E	DP
Beltre	.981	68	151	7	3	4
Bianucci	.915	80	99	9	10	2
Bolden	.939	22	28	3	2	0
Bonadonna	1.000	6	17	2	0	0
Felix	.000	1	0	0	1	0
Fry	—	1	0	0	0	0
Greene	1.000	3	7	0	0	0
Hilligoss	.963	15	24	2	1	1
Hogan	1.000	2	1	0	0	0
Kaase	1.000	20	26	2	0	0
Lima	—	1	0	0	0	0
Morrison	1.000	23	40	0	0	0
Murphy	1.000	1	1	0	0	0
Paisano	.970	125	243	13	8	3
Podraza	1.000	33	38	0	0	0
Vail	—	2	0	0	0	0
Velazquez	.941	46	75	5	5	1

HICKORY CRAWDADS

SOUTH ATLANTIC LEAGUE

LOW CLASS A

Batting	B-T	HT	WT	DOB	AVG	vLH	vRH	G	AB	R	H	2B	3B	HR	RBI	BB	HBP	SH	SF	SO	SB	CS	SLG	OBP
Adair, Travis	L-R	5-10	180	12-23-87	.319	.286	.328	83	320	44	102	15	3	2	23	24	3	4	2	44	13	5	.403	.370
Bolden, Jared	L-L	6-2	190	3-17-87	.294	.289	.295	58	218	34	64	12	2	7	37	18	2	3	3	45	4	8	.463	.349
Bonadonna, Joe	R-R	5-8	170	9-6-85	.297	.333	.283	69	202	29	60	15	2	3	24	33	2	5	2	45	10	4	.436	.397
Castillo, Yefry	R-R	5-11	175	4-22-90	.232	.333	.197	26	95	4	22	7	0	0	12	1	2	0	0	13	0	0	.305	.255
De Los Santos, Leonel	R-R	5-10	170	10-2-89	.206	.229	.197	55	180	21	37	8	0	1	8	2	2	4	0	33	4	4	.267	.223
DiFazio, Vin	R-R	6-0	215	5-15-86	.283	.212	.305	38	138	25	39	8	0	9	31	23	3	0	2	30	1	0	.536	.392
Garcia, Edwin	B-R	6-0	150	3-1-91	.229	.293	.209	94	314	32	72	11	0	2	25	28	0	3	2	56	3	1	.283	.291
Garcia, Leury	B-R	5-7	153	3-18-91	.262	.299	.248	89	359	51	94	5	4	3	22	23	1	8	1	57	47	9	.323	.307
Koncel, Ed	R-R	6-3	195	7-29-88	.178	.232	.159	86	264	37	47	14	3	9	37	38	4	0	0	106	6	2	.356	.291
Ortiz, Mike	L-L	6-2	200	5-2-89	.223	.238	.219	103	358	38	80	15	3	6	35	29	1	1	3	100	2	5	.332	.281
Pimentel, Guillermo	R-R	6-1	190	11-12-90	.228	.138	.250	45	149	20	34	4	1	3	14	13	2	0	1	53	1	2	.329	.297
Podraza, Cody	R-R	5-8	185	11-6-87	.261	.296	.243	42	157	21	41	10	2	1	13	13	4	3	1	26	3	3	.369	.331
Prince, Jared	R-R	6-3	200	5-25-86	.270	.275	.269	122	444	66	120	29	0	8	75	57	16	3	5	60	3	4	.390	.370
Roof, Jonathan	R-R	6-1	165	1-23-89	.256	.345	.229	38	125	15	32	4	0	0	11	13	2	2	1	14	4	5	.288	.333
Santana, Cristian	R-R	6-0	175	6-18-89	.260	.222	.276	75	273	41	71	22	1	11	46	23	5	3	0	87	6	3	.469	.329
Vail, Taylor	R-L	6-2	200	9-5-86	.000	.000	.000	4	10	1	0	0	0	0	0	3	0	0	0	3	0	1	.000	.231
Velazquez, Miguel	R-R	6-2	205	5-15-88	.270	.279	.266	71	274	46	74	17	1	10	53	26	6	0	4	47	12	4	.449	.342
West, Matt	R-R	6-1	215	11-21-88	.223	.260	.209	115	391	52	87	25	2	13	48	38	24	0	4	125	7	2	.390	.326
Zaneski, Zach	R-R	6-2	215	6-27-86	.310	.431	.273	85	303	50	94	27	0	9	52	31	5	0	3	67	1	0	.488	.380

Pitching	B-T	HT	WT	DOB	W	L	ERA	G	GS	CG	SV	IP	H	R	ER	HR	BB	SO	AVG	vLH	vRH	K/9	BB/9
Bell, Chad	R-L	6-3	200	2-28-89	3	3	2.98	26	4	1	0	60	51	29	20	5	18	50	.225	.219	.227	7.46	2.69
Brigham, Jake	R-R	6-3	210	2-10-88	6	5	3.36	14	13	2	0	83	66	37	31	5	24	67	.214	.176	.243	7.27	2.60
Brown, Sam	R-R	6-5	215	6-10-87	0	1	6.75	19	0	0	0	24	31	25	18	0	15	25	.304	.298	.309	9.38	5.63
De Los Santos, Miguel	L-L	6-1	170	7-10-88	2	2	3.99	12	6	0	0	38	27	21	17	3	24	62	.199	.226	.190	14.56	5.63
De Los Santos, Ovispo	R-R	6-1	180	11-19-87	1	3	3.48	20	0	0	3	21	17	12	8	2	6	25	.213	.250	.192	10.89	2.61
Doyle, Andrew	R-R	6-3	200	11-12-87	2	0	3.04	13	1	0	0	24	21	8	8	1	7	16	.241	.257	.231	6.08	2.66
Erlin, Robbie	L-L	6-0	175	10-8-90	6	3	2.12	28	17	0	1	115	89	37	27	9	17	125	.213	.309	.179	9.81	1.33
Font, Wilmer	R-R	6-4	210	5-24-90	4	1	5.16	7	7	0	0	30	35	18	17	3	13	33	.294	.327	.269	10.01	3.94
Gunter, Johnny	R-R	6-4	230	3-10-88	0	1	9.00	11	0	0	0	13	17	14	13	0	6	6	.321	.296	.346	4.15	6.92
Gutierrez, Danny	R-R	6-1	180	3-8-87	1	0	1.93	8	1	0	0	14	17	12	3	1	5	5	.298	.417	.232	3.21	3.21
Hurley, Trevor	R-R	6-3	215	7-28-87	1	0	1.43	26	0	0	0	38	18	10	6	0	10	50	.136	.091	.169	11.95	2.39
Lueke, Josh	R-R	6-5	220	12-5-84	2	1	0.46	17	0	0	10	20	12	4	1	0	5	36	.167	.161	.171	16.47	2.29
Melo, Carlos	R-R	6-3	180	2-27-91	0	0	5.40	1	0	0	0	2	2	1	1	0	1	2	.286	.200	.500	10.80	5.40

Name	B-T	HT	WT	DOB	W	L	ERA	G	GS	CG	SV	IP	H	R	ER	HR	BB	SO	AVG	vLH	vRH	K/9	BB/9
Nelo, Hector	R-R	6-1	200	11-5-86	1	2	6.82	19	0	0	1	32	40	26	24	3	11	31	.313	.310	.314	8.81	3.13
Ocampo, Kyle	R-R	6-3	195	9-9-88	2	2	4.43	26	0	0	2	41	46	32	20	5	21	38	.274	.324	.237	8.41	4.65
Ortiz, Joseph	L-L	5-7	175	8-13-90	4	1	1.50	26	0	0	5	42	30	9	7	2	5	59	.190	.170	.198	12.64	1.07
Ramirez, Neil	R-R	6-3	185	5-25-89	10	8	4.43	28	26	1	0	140	150	79	69	14	37	142	.281	.290	.274	9.11	2.37
Ross, Robbie	L-L	5-11	185	6-24-89	8	7	2.59	16	16	0	0	94	89	38	27	2	20	62	.245	.254	.242	5.94	1.91
Thompson, Matt	R-R	6-3	210	2-10-90	9	9	4.66	28	21	0	1	129	167	78	67	14	23	130	.310	.270	.334	9.05	1.60
Tufts, Tyler	R-R	6-3	195	12-5-86	1	5	3.33	19	0	0	7	24	22	14	9	1	5	20	.232	.281	.206	7.40	1.85
Tullis, Braden	R-R	6-2	200	1-23-90	6	3	4.21	32	12	0	3	92	106	60	43	9	26	78	.291	.295	.289	7.63	2.54
Van Meter, Joe	R-R	6-2	195	10-18-88	0	0	0.00	2	0	0	0	2	2	1	0	0	0	2	.200	.400	.000	7.71	0.00
Wieland, Joe	R-R	6-3	175	1-21-90	7	4	3.34	15	15	2	0	89	84	36	33	4	15	71	.251	.230	.268	7.18	1.52
Yan, Johan	R-R	6-3	185	9-27-88	0	2	2.70	22	0	0	2	40	28	14	12	2	12	36	.193	.200	.188	8.10	2.70

Fielding

Catcher	PCT	G	PO	A	E	DP	PB
Castillo	.967	3	25	4	1	0	4
De Los Santos	.990	53	423	68	5	4	9
DiFazio	.995	22	202	14	1	0	1
Zaneski	.987	64	474	60	7	2	8

First Base	PCT	G	PO	A	E	DP
Bolden	.986	24	208	4	3	20
Koncel	.969	27	204	15	7	16
Ortiz	.980	95	814	56	18	58
Zaneski	1.000	1	2	0	0	1

Second Base	PCT	G	PO	A	E	DP
Adair	.982	50	98	117	4	31
Bonadonna	.981	15	20	31	1	8

	PCT	G	PO	A	E	DP
Castillo	1.000	1	1	3	0	0
Garcia	.968	63	95	147	8	27
Roof	.956	16	23	42	3	10

Third Base	PCT	G	PO	A	E	DP
Adair	.778	4	2	5	2	0
Bonadonna	.897	16	6	29	4	3
Koncel	.867	9	1	12	2	1
Roof	1.000	2	4	2	0	0
West	.922	113	58	249	26	17

Shortstop	PCT	G	PO	A	E	DP
Bonadonna	1.000	4	5	8	0	3
Garcia	.958	32	34	79	5	9
Garcia	.929	89	131	263	30	45

	PCT	G	PO	A	E	DP
Roof	.907	19	30	58	9	7

Outfield	PCT	G	PO	A	E	DP
Adair	.905	17	16	3	2	0
Bolden	.968	35	59	1	2	0
Bonadonna	1.000	32	52	2	0	0
Castillo	.941	12	15	1	1	1
Koncel	.954	44	59	3	3	1
Pimentel	.987	45	75	2	1	0
Podraza	.950	24	38	0	2	0
Prince	.994	109	169	5	1	2
Santana	.986	49	64	9	1	2
Vail	1.000	2	2	0	0	0
Velazquez	.966	64	142	1	5	1

SPOKANE INDIANS   SHORT-SEASON

NORTHWEST LEAGUE

Batting	B-T	HT	WT	DOB	AVG	vLH	vRH	G	AB	R	H	2B	3B	HR	RBI	BB	HBP	SH	SF	SO	SB	CS	SLG	OBP
Castillo, Yefry	R-R	5-11	175	4-22-90	.284	.429	.245	17	67	8	19	6	0	1	10	5	0	2	0	9	1	0	.418	.333
Chirino, Santiago	R-R	5-10	154	2-11-91	.288	.346	.275	39	146	21	42	6	2	0	20	13	2	2	3	16	2	1	.356	.348
Clark, Andrew	L-L	6-2	220	8-12-87	.295	.224	.315	63	217	32	64	9	0	1	41	37	4	0	4	36	2	1	.350	.401
Deglan, Kellin	L-R	6-2	195	5-3-92	.159	.167	.156	22	82	7	13	2	0	1	4	7	0	0	1	21	0	0	.220	.222
Gomez, Jhonny	R-R	5-11	190	12-21-89	.125	.167	.000	3	8	0	1	0	0	0	1	0	0	0	0	2	0	0	.125	.125
Herrera, David	L-R	5-11	165	12-29-91	.222	.286	.000	4	9	0	2	1	0	0	0	0	0	0	0	1	0	0	.333	.222
Hoying, Jared	L-R	6-3	190	5-18-89	.325	.321	.326	62	243	47	79	13	5	10	51	19	3	0	2	70	20	9	.543	.378
Kudlock, Jason	R-R	6-3	200	9-16-87	.213	.333	.195	12	47	4	10	6	0	1	6	0	1	0	0	18	0	1	.404	.229
Lima, Daniel	R-R	6-1	175	2-21-87	.345	.250	.362	15	55	9	19	3	1	0	7	3	2	0	0	14	3	0	.436	.400
Murphy, Clark	L-L	6-2	190	12-18-89	.319	.278	.325	46	144	23	46	8	1	1	27	31	3	1	4	24	2	0	.410	.440
Nicholas, Brett	L-L	6-2	210	7-18-88	.245	.250	.243	51	192	24	47	10	0	3	32	20	2	0	2	49	2	0	.344	.319
Olt, Mike	R-R	6-2	215	8-27-88	.293	.309	.288	69	263	57	77	16	1	9	43	40	4	0	3	77	6	0	.464	.390
Pimentel, Guillermo	R-R	6-1	190	11-12-89	.344	.750	.286	9	32	3	11	1	0	1	6	1	1	0	1	10	1	2	.469	.371
Profar, Jurickson	B-R	5-11	165	2-20-93	.250	.222	.258	63	252	42	63	19	0	4	23	28	0	6	2	46	8	3	.373	.323
Richmond, Josh	R-R	6-3	205	6-14-89	.297	.357	.278	35	118	23	35	8	1	3	19	16	9	0	1	23	4	3	.458	.417
Rodland, Kevin	R-R	6-0	185	9-13-87	.211	.208	.211	38	114	16	24	4	1	3	13	12	8	3	1	34	6	2	.342	.326
Selen, Alejandro	R-R	5-10	175	3-20-89	.330	.214	.377	31	97	15	32	6	2	2	11	9	2	0	3	28	0	1	.495	.387
Skole, Jake	L-R	6-1	190	1-17-92	.254	.105	.288	57	201	29	51	9	2	2	27	23	0	2	2	52	6	4	.348	.327
Strausborger, Ryan	R-R	6-0	180	3-4-88	.255	.327	.235	64	231	42	59	9	4	2	15	23	6	2	2	59	21	4	.355	.336
Torres, Kevin	R-L	6-0	195	2-24-90	.188	.286	.175	21	64	8	12	2	1	0	8	6	0	1	1	21	1	0	.250	.254
Vitale, Carson	R-R	6-1	195	8-25-88	.000	.000	.000	2	8	0	0	0	0	0	0	0	0	0	0	6	0	0	.000	.000

Pitching	B-T	HT	WT	DOB	W	L	ERA	G	GS	CG	SV	IP	H	R	ER	HR	BB	SO	AVG	vLH	vRH	K/9	BB/9
Bell, Chad	R-L	6-3	200	2-28-89	2	0	3.25	8	8	0	0	44	35	16	16	3	12	47	.213	.290	.195	9.54	2.44
Brown, Sam	R-R	6-5	215	6-10-87	0	0	2.25	2	0	0	0	6	6	2	1	0	1	6	.353	.500	.333	13.50	2.25
De Los Santos, Miguel	L-L	6-1	170	7-10-88	2	0	1.69	7	7	0	0	32	13	8	6	0	20	50	.116	.227	.089	14.06	5.63
De Los Santos, Ovispo	R-R	6-1	180	11-19-87	0	0	0.00	4	0	0	3	5	2	0	0	0	2	9	.118	.000	.143	15.19	3.38
Doyle, Andrew	R-R	6-3	200	11-12-87	0	0	2.08	3	2	0	0	9	7	5	2	1	4	8	.206	.333	.160	8.31	4.15
Earls, Justin	R-L	6-3	190	12-4-87	1	3	5.29	20	1	0	2	32	34	20	19	2	16	20	.279	.243	.294	5.57	4.45
Grullon, Geuris	L-L	6-5	185	12-20-89	1	0	4.26	6	0	0	0	6	9	6	3	0	5	4	.321	.444	.263	5.68	7.11
Grullon, Juan	L-L	6-0	185	3-4-90	0	3	4.26	7	0	0	0	25	28	14	12	2	9	22	.275	.345	.247	7.82	3.20
Hanna, Chris	R-L	6-1	180	3-7-92	0	0	0.00	1	0	0	0	1	1	0	0	0	0	2	.000		.333	18.00	0.00
Henry, Ben	R-R	6-4	190	4-9-89	4	4	5.88	16	8	0	0	52	64	37	34	6	20	49	.309	.391	.243	8.48	3.46
Johnson, Kevin	L-L	6-5	215	12-3-87	2	2	1.24	18	0	0	0	29	22	7	4	2	19	24	.222	.240	.216	7.45	5.90
Killian, Colby	R-R	6-0	192	6-5-88	1	1	2.22	20	0	0	7	24	19	9	6	1	16	22	.224	.282	.174	8.14	5.92
Marban, Jorge	R-R	6-1	215	12-5-88	0	0	0.00	5	0	0	0	8	5	0	0	0	4	10	.179	.250	.125	11.25	4.50
McBride, Nick	R-R	6-4	180	5-13-91	2	5	4.24	15	15	0	0	70	76	42	33	9	20	51	.279	.328	.242	6.56	2.57
Melo, Carlos	R-R	6-3	180	2-27-91	1	0	1.80	1	1	0	0	5	1	1	1	0	4	3	.063	.000	.071	5.40	7.20
Mendez, Roman	R-R	6-2	180	7-25-90	1	1	2.31	3	3	0	0	12	19	11	3	2	3	13	.391	.481	.250	10.03	2.31
Mendoza, Francisco	R-R	6-0	175	12-7-87	2	1	4.18	19	0	0	0	28	34	16	13	1	17	35	.296	.304	.290	11.25	5.46
Osborne, Zach	R-R	6-5	205	5-9-88	1	3	3.92	10	3	0	1	21	17	9	9	0	5	21	.224	.222	.224	9.15	2.18
Peralta, Denny	R-R	6-4	170	12-11-89	0	1	16.88	2	0	0	0	3	6	5	5	1	0	2	.462	.667	.400	6.75	0.00
Reyes, Jimmy	L-L	5-10	195	3-7-89	2	0	2.36	18	0	0	0	27	16	10	7	1	3	35	.168	.143	.179	11.81	1.01

	B-T	HT	WT	DOB	W	L	ERA	G	GS	CG	SV	IP	H	R	ER	BB	SO	SB	CS	AVG	vLH	vRH	K/9	BB/9
Rodebaugh, Ryan	L-R	6-0	165	3-30-89	4	1	3.33	19	0	0	2	24	18	10	9	1	9	34		.200	.280	.169	12.58	3.33
Rojas, Randol	R-R	6-0	160	9-28-90	5	4	2.79	15	15	0	0	77	77	29	24	2	20	40		.265	.276	.256	4.66	2.33
Rowen, Ben	R-R	6-3	190	11-15-88	2	0	1.09	21	0	0	1	33	18	4	4	0	14	30		.155	.167	.149	8.18	3.82
Stanford, Tim	R-R	6-0	191	5-7-89	6	0	1.66	16	6	0	0	54	43	11	10	3	11	42		.222	.224	.220	6.96	1.82
Steggall, Tim	R-R	6-1	200	8-18-88	3	2	6.61	12	0	0	0	16	21	17	12	2	9	15		.304	.269	.326	8.27	4.96
Weibley, Brett	R-R	6-3	195	1-3-89	1	1	8.36	19	0	0	0	28	40	28	26	3	14	30		.331	.317	.338	9.64	4.50
Yan, Johan	R-R	6-3	185	9-27-88	0	1	2.70	2	0	0	0	3	5	2	1	0	1	2		.385	.667	.300	5.40	2.70

Fielding

Catcher	PCT	G	PO	A	E	DP	PB
Castillo	1.000	5	24	1	0	0	0
Deglan	.993	17	125	15	1	2	4
Nicholas	1.000	37	310	34	0	3	7
Torres	.983	19	155	21	3	0	4
Vitale	1.000	1	3	1	0	0	0

First Base	PCT	G	PO	A	E	DP
Clark	.991	44	426	17	4	42
Gomez	1.000	1	5	1	0	1
Hoying	1.000	1	1	0	0	0
Lima	1.000	1	5	0	0	0
Murphy	.988	33	311	17	4	30
Rodland	1.000	1	1	0	0	0

Second Base	PCT	G	PO	A	E	DP
Chirino	.976	34	68	94	4	22

Herrera	1.000	4	9	9	0	4
Lima	.950	4	9	10	1	4
Rodland	.946	16	32	55	5	13
Selen	.897	21	38	58	11	12

Third Base	PCT	G	PO	A	E	DP
Chirino	1.000	1	1	1	0	0
Lima	.909	4	1	9	1	1
Olt	.942	64	37	124	10	12
Rodland	.938	6	4	11	1	3
Selen	1.000	2	0	1	0	1

Shortstop	PCT	G	PO	A	E	DP
Chirino	1.000	6	13	14	0	2
Profar	.953	63	90	232	16	49
Rodland	.881	9	6	31	5	5

Outfield	PCT	G	PO	A	E	DP
Castillo	.941	10	15	1	1	0
Gomez	1.000	1	1	0	0	0
Hoying	.932	60	65	3	5	1
Kudlock	1.000	9	15	1	0	0
Lima	.500	1	1	0	1	0
Murphy	—	1	0	0	0	0
Pimentel	1.000	9	18	2	0	1
Richmond	.962	31	46	4	2	0
Rodland	1.000	2	3	0	0	0
Selen	1.000	7	5	0	0	0
Skole	.957	55	88	2	4	1
Strausborger	.971	55	66	1	2	1

AZL RANGERS   ROOKIE
ARIZONA LEAGUE

Batting	B-T	HT	WT	DOB	AVG	vLH	vRH	G	AB	R	H	2B	3B	HR	RBI	BB	HBP	SH	SF	SO	SB	CS	SLG	OBP
Akins, Jordan	R-R	6-3	192	4-19-92	.187	.182	.188	36	107	14	20	3	2	0	8	5	3	0	1	35	5	1	.252	.241
Alfonzo, Edward	R-R	6-1	185	10-29-89	—	.000	.000	1	0	0	0	0	0	0	0	0	0	0	0	0	0	0	—	—
Brown, Matt	R-R	6-0	200	8-8-82	.200	.333	.143	3	10	1	2	1	0	0	2	1	0	0	1	3	0	1	.300	.250
Chavez, Endy	L-L	6-0	170	2-7-78	.545	.500	.571	3	11	3	6	0	0	0	1	2	0	0	0	0	3	0	.545	.615
Chirino, Santiago	R-R	5-10	154	2-11-91	.316	.375	.293	17	57	13	18	2	1	0	8	3	4	2	0	5	3	2	.386	.391
Deglan, Kellin	L-R	6-2	195	5-3-92	.286	.333	.273	10	28	5	8	0	1	0	5	2	1	0	0	7	0	0	.357	.355
DiFazio, Vin	R-R	6-0	215	5-15-86	.400	.333	.417	5	15	4	6	1	0	1	2	2	3	0	0	6	0	0	.667	.550
Garcia, Leury	B-R	5-7	153	3-18-91	.500	.333	.533	6	18	5	9	2	0	0	2	4	0	0	0	4	4	2	.611	.591
Gomez, Jhonny	R-R	5-11	190	12-21-89	.369	.353	.374	40	141	17	52	7	2	0	14	0	3	2	28	3	4		.447	.420
Gradoville, Chris	R-R	6-1	220	7-10-84	.600	.000	.600	2	5	2	3	2	0	0	1	1	1	0	0	2	0	0	1.000	.714
Greene, Jonathan	R-R	6-0	200	9-16-85	.280	.300	.300	7	25	4	7	0	0	0	6	3	0	2	0	6	0	0	.280	.333
Hall, Toby	R-R	6-2	255	10-21-75	.000	.000	.000	1	2	0	0	0	0	0	1	0	0	0	0	0	0	0	.000	.000
Herrera, David	L-R	5-11	165	12-29-91	.337	.310	.346	48	178	33	60	7	4	0	31	16	2	2	2	27	8	5	.421	.394
Lane, Braxton	B-R	5-10	190	12-30-90	.239	.333	.206	34	92	17	22	5	1	0	9	11	0	1	2	39	6	4	.315	.314
Martinez, Teodoro	R-R	5-11	155	3-16-92	.313	.260	.329	53	211	43	66	14	3	1	22	9	7	3	3	25	20	7	.422	.357
Meiners, Travis	R-R	6-0	205	6-7-88	.279	.281	.278	38	111	26	31	5	0	3	15	14	4	1	0	16	6	1	.405	.380
Moore, Johnathan	R-R	6-0	180	3-24-88	.364	.333	.375	13	33	3	12	2	0	0	3	2	0	0	0	8	1	0	.424	.432
Nicholas, Brett	L-L	6-2	210	7-18-88	.167	.000	.250	3	6	1	1	1	0	0	3	0	1	0	0	1	0	0	.333	.286
Payano, Junior	B-R	6-1	175	2-20-90	.154	.000	.194	22	39	5	6	0	2	0	2	4	1	0	0	17	0	1	.256	.250
Perez, Alison	R-R	5-11	190	9-3-89	.212	.333	.156	28	66	5	14	0	0	0	8	3	1	0	1	18	2	0	.212	.254
Podraza, Cody	R-R	5-8	185	11-6-87	.667	1.000	.600	3	6	2	4	2	0	0	2	1	2	0	0	1	1	0	1.000	.778
Puello, Alberto	R-R	6-2	180	10-20-87	.147	.111	.160	11	34	2	5	1	0	0	3	2	0	0	0	4	0	0	.176	.194
Robinson, Drew	L-R	6-1	185	4-20-92	.286	.313	.278	44	140	26	40	6	2	0	11	26	3	0	1	41	6	3	.357	.406
Roof, Jonathan	R-R	6-1	165	1-20-88	.357	.000	.385	6	14	4	5	1	0	0	2	1	0	0	0	3	0	0	.429	.400
Sardinas, Luis	B-R	6-0	150	5-16-93	.311	.250	.329	26	103	22	32	4	0	0	8	7	2	6	1	15	8	2	.350	.363
Sierra Jr., Ruben	L-L	6-2	172	3-10-91	.302	.222	.324	14	43	7	13	4	0	2	10	3	1	0	0	14	0	1	.535	.362
Skole, Jake	L-R	6-1	190	1-17-92	.286	.143	.333	8	28	7	8	2	0	0	5	5	0	0	0	6	3	0	.357	.394
Stoneburner, Davis	R-R	6-0	175	1-14-85	.286	.000	.400	2	7	2	2	1	0	1	1	1	0	0	0	2	0	0	.571	.444
Telis, Tomas	B-R	5-8	175	6-18-91	.326	.256	.352	37	144	22	47	7	1	2	35	6	1	4	3	16	4	1	.431	.351
Tracy, Chad	R-R	6-3	210	7-4-85	.000	.000	.000	1	3	0	0	0	0	0	0	0	0	0	0	1	0	0	.000	.000
Villanueva, Christian	R-R	5-11	160	6-19-91	.314	.333	.308	51	188	30	59	14	1	2	35	13	4	2	3	42	6	2	.431	.365
Vitale, Carson	R-R	6-1	195	8-25-88	.290	.182	.310	28	69	9	20	4	1	0	11	11	1	0	0	10	1	0	.420	.395

Pitching	B-T	HT	WT	DOB	W	L	ERA	G	GS	CG	SV	IP	H	R	ER	HR	BB	SO	AVG	vLH	vRH	K/9	BB/9
Ahn, Tae Kyung	R-R	6-3	185	5-25-90	0	0	18.69	9	0	0	0	4	5	12	9	1	13	5	.263	.000	.417	10.38	27.00
Alvarez, Richard	R-R	6-2	180	8-14-92	0	3	6.48	11	8	0	0	25	33	21	18	3	12	32	.308	.395	.261	11.52	4.32
Blackwell, Shawn	R-R	6-5	195	11-15-90	6	3	4.10	13	13	0	0	59	63	35	27	7	9	42	.269	.264	.273	6.37	1.37
Buckel, Cody	R-R	6-1	170	6-18-92	0	0	0.00	4	0	0	0	5	2	0	0	1	9	.125	.333	.000	16.20	1.80
Claudio, Alexander	L-L	6-3	160	1-31-92	0	1	6.60	12	1	0	0	15	19	11	11	1	6	13	.311	.727	.220	7.80	3.60
Doyle, Andrew	R-R	6-3	200	11-12-87	0	0	0.00	2	0	0	0	1	3	3	0	0	0	3	.429	.500	.333	0.00	0.00
Grullon, Geuris	L-L	6-5	185	12-20-89	0	0	2.03	14	0	0	0	13	13	7	3	0	7	21	.241	.300	.227	14.18	4.72
Grullon, Juan	L-L	6-0	185	3-4-90	1	0	0.00	2	0	0	0	9	6	1	0	0	1	8	.188	.091	.238	8.00	1.00
Gunter, Johnny	R-R	6-4	230	3-10-88	0	0	4.50	3	0	0	0	4	4	2	1	1	6	2	.235	.143	.300	13.50	2.25
Haase, Anthony	R-R	6-3	190	3-1-90	4	0	4.98	13	0	0	0	22	20	12	12	1	10	28	.235	.412	.118	11.63	4.15
Hanna, Chris	R-L	6-1	180	3-7-92	1	1	0.98	11	1	0	0	28	20	6	3	0	4	38	.194	.278	.176	12.36	1.30

Pitching	B-T	HT	WT	DOB	W	L	ERA	G	GS	CG	SV	IP	H	R	ER	HR	BB	SO	AVG	vLH	vRH	K/9	BB/9
Hill, Matt	R-L	6-1	180	2-5-89	0	0	12.96	10	0	0	0	8	17	13	12	0	2	7	.415	.556	.375	7.56	2.16
Holland, Derek	B-L	6-2	195	10-9-86	0	0	0.00	1	1	0	0	3	0	0	0	0	0	6	.000	.000	.000	18.00	0.00
Kukuruda, John	R-R	6-4	180	6-9-92	0	0	18.00	4	0	0	0	3	8	6	6	2	2	3	.500	.250	.583	9.00	6.00
Marban, Jorge	R-R	6-1	215	12-5-88	1	0	0.00	3	0	0	1	5	1	0	0	0	2	10	.067	.000	.111	18.00	3.60
Mavare, Jose	R-R	6-0	175	2-19-90	4	1	3.29	17	0	0	2	27	23	13	10	0	11	34	.230	.056	.328	11.20	3.62
Melo, Carlos	R-R	6-3	180	2-27-91	3	4	3.83	12	12	0	0	52	41	28	22	0	26	65	.212	.237	.201	11.32	4.53
Monegro, Jose	R-R	6-3	200	9-19-89	1	0	4.70	17	0	0	1	23	24	14	12	1	5	29	.270	.393	.213	11.35	1.96
Ocampo, Kyle	R-R	6-3	195	9-9-88	0	0	0.00	2	0	0	0	3	3	0	0	0	1	2	.231	.250	.222	5.40	2.70
Peralta, Denny	R-R	6-4	170	12-11-89	1	3	4.26	8	4	0	0	25	33	18	12	0	0	25	.311	.357	.281	8.88	0.00
Perez-Lobo, Andres	R-R	5-11	184	3-3-92	1	1	5.95	11	0	0	0	20	25	18	13	0	11	14	.316	.355	.292	6.41	5.03
Rijo, Ezequiel	R-R	6-4	190	9-12-90	4	3	4.39	13	13	0	0	55	53	34	27	5	18	44	.251	.253	.250	7.16	2.93
Rojas, Jonathan	R-R	6-2	205	3-22-88	1	0	5.50	13	0	0	0	18	23	15	11	2	6	16	.307	.364	.283	8.00	3.00
Steggall, Tim	R-R	6-1	200	8-18-88	1	0	2.45	4	0	0	0	4	4	2	1	0	2		.250	.143	.333	4.91	0.00
Strong, Paul	L-L	6-2	195	8-18-90	2	2	2.73	15	0	0	0	26	21	14	8	0	15	25	.219	.150	.237	8.54	5.13
Thompson, Aaron	R-R	6-0	205	1-11-91	0	1	7.30	9	0	0	0	12	16	11	10	0	7	11	.308	.273	.333	8.03	5.11
Van Meter, Joe	R-R	6-2	195	10-18-88	0	1	2.79	8	0	0	1	10	9	4	3	1	1	11	.237	.091	.296	10.24	0.93

Fielding

Catcher	PCT	G	PO	A	E	DP	PB
Deglan	1.000	7	29	6	0	1	1
DiFazio	1.000	4	25	3	0	0	0
Gradoville	1.000	1	4	1	0	0	0
Hall	1.000	1	6	1	0	0	0
Moore	.971	5	29	4	1	0	2
Nicholas	1.000	1	5	0	0	0	2
Perez	.986	23	121	19	2	1	2
Puello	.961	10	91	8	4	0	3
Vitale	1.000	27	171	13	0	0	6

First Base	PCT	G	PO	A	E	DP
Brown	1.000	2	21	0	0	2
Gomez	.990	40	294	13	3	25
Greene	1.000	3	28	1	0	0
Meiners	1.000	5	35	4	0	2
Moore	1.000	4	16	2	0	0
Perez	1.000	2	10	0	0	0
Puello	1.000	1	2	0	0	0
Robinson	1.000	5	47	1	0	3

Second Base	PCT	G	PO	A	E	DP
Chirino	.964	17	32	49	3	8
Garcia	1.000	1	0	2	0	0
Herrera	.959	29	58	60	5	15
Meiners	1.000	1	0	1	0	0
Payano	1.000	1	2	1	0	0
Robinson	1.000	12	19	27	0	4
Roof	.667	1	1	1	1	0
Stoneburner	1.000	1	0	5	0	0

Third Base	PCT	G	PO	A	E	DP
Brown	1.000	1	1	1	0	0
Greene	1.000	2	1	3	0	0
Meiners	1.000	5	0	4	0	0
Robinson	.750	2	0	3	1	0
Roof	—	1	0	0	0	0
Villanueva	.917	50	31	91	11	6

Shortstop	PCT	G	PO	A	E	DP
Garcia	.818	2	3	6	2	2

	PCT	G	PO	A	E	DP
Herrera	.963	18	24	53	3	5
Robinson	.783	13	12	24	10	3
Roof	.900	3	1	8	1	1
Sardinas	.920	25	19	62	7	11
Stoneburner	1.000	1	0	3	0	0

Outfield	PCT	G	PO	A	E	DP
Akins	.920	35	45	1	4	0
Chavez	1.000	3	9	0	0	0
Greene	1.000	1	4	0	0	0
Lane	.932	32	37	4	3	1
Martinez	.980	51	95	5	2	1
Meiners	.976	28	37	3	1	0
Payano	.923	18	24	0	2	0
Podraza	1.000	3	2	0	0	0
Robinson	1.000	12	11	1	0	0
Sierra Jr.	1.000	13	13	1	0	0
Skole	1.000	7	10	0	0	0

DSL RANGERS   ROOKIE

DOMINICAN SUMMER LEAGUE

Batting	B-T	HT	WT	DOB	AVG	vLH	vRH	G	AB	R	H	2B	3B	HR	RBI	BB	HBP	SH	SF	SO	SB	CS	SLG	OBP
Abreu, Esdras	R-R	6-3	185	3-21-92	.236	.200	.246	50	161	23	38	7	1	4	25	8	6	2	0	61	5	4	.366	.297
Alberto, Hanser	R-R	5-11	175	10-17-92	.358	.389	.350	50	179	25	64	15	2	0	24	6	2	5	4	9	16	3	.464	.377
Alfaro, Jorge	R-R	6-2	185	6-11-93	.221	.256	.209	48	172	18	38	5	2	1	23	5	9	0	1	48	1	4	.291	.278
Campos, Belarmino	B-R	5-10	165	6-19-93	.225	.214	.227	34	80	9	18	7	1	0	5	11	3	0	0	17	2	4	.338	.340
Ceballo, Edward	L-R	5-11	180	10-8-90	.269	.333	.261	9	26	4	7	0	2	0	3	0	0	0	0	4	1	0	.423	.269
Cedeno, Diego	L-L	5-11	160	5-19-92	.217	.385	.170	42	60	12	13	1	1	0	4	7	2	2	1	11	4	6	.267	.310
Edmonds, Guy	R-R	6-2	180	0-0-00	.186	.167	.190	34	102	11	19	2	0	0	9	11	6	0	0	31	2	0	.206	.303
Frias, Andres	R-R	6-2	185	2-18-90	.250	.000	.286	4	8	0	2	0	0	0	2	0	0	0	0	2	0	0	.250	.250
Garia, Christopher	R-R	6-0	165	12-16-92	.205	.237	.197	60	190	44	39	3	2	1	10	22	5	4	0	40	22	7	.258	.304
Gonzalez, Alex	R-R	5-11	165	7-7-91	.280	.343	.258	42	132	22	37	6	1	0	18	16	1	4	1	24	12	2	.341	.360
Lugo, Francisco	R-R	6-0	180	10-22-91	.254	.242	.257	58	185	21	47	9	4	0	29	21	4	4	1	20	8	3	.346	.341
Martinez, Hector	L-L	6-1	185	9-17-91	.217	.348	.189	39	129	16	28	5	0	0	7	10	2	0	0	50	3	2	.256	.284
Mendez, Luis	B-R	5-9	155	1-1-93	.256	.300	.250	28	90	20	23	3	1	0	12	14	4	1	1	13	3	2	.311	.376
Morillo, Robert	R-R	6-1	188	6-21-91	.273	.292	.267	37	99	10	27	5	1	1	15	11	5	0	1	12	2	1	.374	.371
Obispo, Christefer	R-R	6-3	180	6-21-92	.230	.133	.252	58	161	27	37	5	3	2	15	23	4	2	1	47	7	4	.335	.339
Oropeza, Carlos	B-R	6-0	180	7-7-92	.243	.286	.236	37	103	16	25	4	0	0	9	20	6	0	2	29	2	0	.282	.389
Pirela, Oswaldo	R-R	5-10	165	10-13-91	.190	.500	.118	25	42	2	8	3	0	0	2	1	2	0	0	8	0	0	.262	.244
Santa, Johan	R-R	5-11	178	3-27-92	.247	.200	.262	39	85	12	21	6	1	1	8	9	3	0	0	16	1	1	.376	.340
Sierra Jr., Ruben	L-L	6-2	172	3-10-91	.244	.071	.278	24	86	10	21	1	2	1	9	8	0	0	1	27	3	1	.337	.305
Villegas, Luis	R-R	5-10	175	5-24-92	.133	.000	.143	7	15	3	2	0	0	0	2	0	0	3	0	2	0	0	.133	.133

Pitching	B-T	HT	WT	DOB	W	L	ERA	G	GS	CG	SV	IP	H	R	ER	HR	BB	SO	AVG	vLH	vRH	K/9	BB/9
Baez, Luis	R-R	6-2	185	11-29-89	0	0	20.25	1	0	0	0	1	3	3	0		4	1	.000	.000	.000	6.75	27.00
Beltre, Dario	R-R	6-3	170	11-19-92	1	1	3.21	16	0	0	0	14	13	8	5	1	6	15	.236	.091	.273	9.64	3.86
De Jesus, Jorge	R-R	6-0	205	1-17-92	1	2	2.36	24	0	0	8	34	21	16	9	0	23	49	.168	.152	.174	12.84	6.03
De Los Santos, Abel	R-R	6-2	180	11-21-92	3	3	1.85	14	13	0	0	58	46	19	12	1	21	56	.214	.234	.205	8.64	3.24
Diaz, Jesus	R-R	6-1	170	10-16-92	5	0	2.08	11	1	0	0	26	28	8	6		6	15	.283	.148	.333	5.19	2.08
Gil, Leonel	L-L	6-0	160	2-5-91	4	1	0.25	18	0	0	1	36	21	1	1	0	7	38	.168	.000	.172	9.50	1.75
Grullon, Juan	L-L	6-0	185	3-4-90	2	0	0.79	5	1	0	1	11	10	4	1	1	0	14	.227	.000	.233	11.12	0.00
Herrera, Hector	R-R	6-4	195	10-28-90	0	1	13.50	2	0	0	0	2	4	4	3	0	2	4	.400	.250	.500	9.00	13.50
Jimenez, Jose	R-R	6-5	195	5-16-91	2	2	1.39	18	0	0	5	39	28	9	5	0	6	39	.228	.296	.208	10.86	1.39
Leclerc, Angelo	R-R	6-0	170	10-9-91	0	0	—	1	0	0	0	0	1	0	0	0	0	0	1.000	1.000	.000	—	—
Mavare, Jose	R-R	6-0	175	2-19-90	1	0	0.00	6	0	0	0	16	5	1	0		4	27	.100	.083	.105	15.19	2.25

Medina, Emiliano	R-R	6-3	175	7-18-90	2	2	0.57	20	0	0	8	32	18	3	2	0	7	31	.162	.174	.159	8.81	1.99
Montero, Dennys	R-R	6-0	170	11-20-89	0	0	0.00	1	0	0	0	1	0	0	0	0	1	2	.000	.000	.000	18.00	9.00
Moreno, Luis	R-R	6-0	170	6-18-92	6	0	0.96	16	1	0	0	38	13	6	4	0	9	25	.102	.172	.082	5.97	2.15
Oviedo, Jose	R-R	6-5	190	1-29-93	1	0	1.00	7	0	0	0	9	3	2	1	0	4	7	.111	.000	.136	7.00	4.00
Parra, Luis	L-L	6-2	160	11-21-91	1	3	3.12	14	9	1	0	52	41	22	18	1	30	55	.216	.200	.217	9.52	5.19
Payano, Victor	L-L	6-5	185	10-17-92	3	1	3.40	17	12	0	0	50	44	25	19	3	24	52	.234	.143	.238	9.30	4.29
Perez, David	R-R	6-5	200	12-20-92	4	4	1.41	14	14	0	0	70	50	20	11	0	8	68	.201	.215	.196	8.74	1.03
Perez, Roberto	R-R	6-4	150	1-8-92	0	0	0.00	1	0	0	0	3	4	4	0	0	0	3	.286	.000	.333	9.00	0.00
Perez, Santo	R-R	6-5	200	11-22-88	5	2	2.59	12	11	0	0	59	47	24	17	0	9	41	.210	.245	.199	6.25	1.37
Tirado, Pedro	L-L	6-2	180	12-18-90	1	1	3.45	7	2	0	0	16	13	6	6	1	8	22	.232	.400	.216	12.64	4.60

Fielding

Catcher	PCT	G	PO	A	E	DP	PB
Alfaro	.976	26	192	14	5	1	9
Edmonds	.975	23	175	18	5	0	1
Obispo	1.000	1	2	1	0	0	0
Oropeza	1.000	14	93	9	0	0	3
Pirela	1.000	20	92	10	0	1	1

First Base	PCT	G	PO	A	E	DP
Frias	.941	3	16	0	1	1
Lugo	1.000	1	1	0	0	1
Morillo	1.000	4	19	3	0	3
Obispo	.978	56	412	32	10	26
Oropeza	1.000	15	129	5	0	10
Pirela	1.000	3	6	1	0	0
Santa	1.000	1	3	0	0	0

Second Base	PCT	G	PO	A	E	DP
Alberto	.938	8	18	12	2	3
Campos	.967	12	15	14	1	0
Garia	—	1	0	0	0	0
Gonzalez	1.000	16	24	31	0	6
Mendez	.976	13	14	26	1	4
Santa	.974	30	36	38	2	8
Villegas	.875	6	9	12	3	2

Third Base	PCT	G	PO	A	E	DP
Alberto	1.000	1	0	3	0	0
Campos	—	1	0	0	0	0
Gonzalez	.846	10	5	17	4	0
Lugo	.917	41	22	88	10	5
Mendez	—	1	0	0	0	0
Morillo	.864	22	14	37	8	5
Santa	1.000	1	1	0	0	0

Shortstop	PCT	G	PO	A	E	DP
Alberto	.945	40	49	105	9	17
Campos	.973	21	19	52	2	5
Gonzalez	1.000	2	0	1	0	0
Mendez	.915	14	10	44	5	3
Morillo	.500	1	0	1	1	0
Villegas	—	1	0	0	0	0

Outfield	PCT	G	PO	A	E	DP
Abreu	.906	44	43	5	5	0
Ceballo	1.000	3	6	1	0	0
Cedeno	.929	35	26	0	2	0
Edmonds	—	1	0	0	0	0
Garia	1.000	55	83	2	0	1
Gonzalez	1.000	17	13	0	0	0
Lugo	1.000	17	13	0	0	0
Martinez	.927	36	46	5	4	3
Obispo	1.000	2	1	0	0	0
Oropeza	1.000	1	1	0	0	0
Pirela	1.000	1	5	0	0	0
Sierra Jr.	.938	21	29	1	2	1

Toronto Blue Jays

SEASON IN A SENTENCE: The Blue Jays sent out manager Cito Gaston with a younger team posting an 85-77 record, a third straight fourth-place finish, as the offense came through for the ace-less pitching staff with a franchise-record 257 home runs, best in the majors.

HIGH POINT: Amid all the home runs, Brandon Morrow produced the best single performance on Aug. 8. He struck out 17 in a one-hitter against the Rays, missing a no-hitter when Evan Longoria reached on an infield hit with two outs in the ninth. Also, Jose Bautista clubbed a franchise-record 54 homers to best (by seven) George Bell's mark set in his MVP season of 1987, breaking the record Sept. 17 at Boston.

LOW POINT: The Jays had boosted attendance back over the 2 million mark from 2005-2008, but dropped to 1.625 million in 2010, with a season-low 10,314 fans witnessing a game against the Royals on April 19. It was the worst season attendance ever at Rogers Centre, and you have to go back to 1982 at Exhibition Stadium to find a season when fewer fans attended Jays games.

NOTABLE ROOKIES: No Jays broke in full-time as rookies, but catcher J.P. Arencibia made a dramatic debut. He went 4-for-5 with a pair of home runs on Aug. 7 in a 17-11 victory against the Rays. He went just 1-for-30 after that, though. Righthanders Josh Roenicke (acquired from the Reds in the Scott Rolen trade) and Kyle Drabek (the key piece of the Roy Halladay trade with the Phillies) reached the majors in September.

KEY TRANSACTIONS: First-year general manager Alex Anthopoulos made some bold moves, such as trading ace Roy Halladay for prospects after the 2009 season. The Jays got younger and potentially better at shortstop when they traded veteran Alex Gonzalez to the Braves for 27-year-old Yunel Escobar. Toronto worked itself into the three-team Roy Oswalt deal in July, picking up speedy outfielder Anthony Gose for slugging corner infielder Brett Wallace. Toronto also signed its first 13 draft picks, after failing to sign three of its first four selections in 2009.

DOWN ON THE FARM: High Class A Dunedin and Double-A New Hampshire both reached the playoffs. Dunedin first baseman Michael McDade led the Florida State League with 21 homers. For the Fisher Cats, Drabek led the Eastern League in wins and was the league's pitcher of the year and top prospect.

OPENING DAY PAYROLL: $62.2 million (22nd)

PLAYERS OF THE YEAR

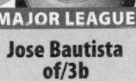

MAJOR LEAGUE	MINOR LEAGUE
Jose Bautista	**Kyle Drabek**
of/3b	rhp
.260/.378/.617	(Double-A)
124 RBIs, 54 HRs led	14-9, 2.94
major leagues	EL pitcher of the year

ORGANIZATION LEADERS

BATTING		*Minimum 250 at-bats
MAJORS		
*AVG	John Buck	.281
*OPS	Jose Bautista	.995
HR	Jose Bautista	54
RBI	Jose Bautista	124
MINORS		
*AVG	Manny Mayorson, Las Vegas/New Hamp.	.324
*OBP	Brad Emaus, New Hampshire/Las Vegas	.397
*SLG	J.P. Arencibia, Las Vegas	.626
R	Darin Mastroianni, New Hampshire	101
H	Darin Mastroianni, New Hampshire	158
TB	Eric Thames, New Hampshire	261
2B	Sean Ochinko, Lansing	37
3B	Ryan Schimpf, Lansing/Dunedin	11
HR	J.P. Arencibia, Las Vegas	32
RBI	Eric Thames, New Hampshire	104
BB	Brad Emaus, New Hampshire/Las Vegas	81
SO	Adam Loewen, New Hampshire	142
SB	Darin Mastroianni, New Hampshire	46

PITCHING		†Minimum 75 innings
MAJORS		
W	Brett Cecil	15
†ERA	Shaun Marcum	3.64
SO	Brandon Morrow	178
MINORS		
W	Kyle Drabek, New Hampshire	14
L	Ryan Shopshire, Lansing/Dunedin	12
†ERA	Kyle Drabek, New Hampshire	2.94
G	Matt Daly, Dunedin	56
GS	Ryan Shopshire, Lansing/Dunedin	28
SV	Matt Daly, Dunedin	31
IP	Kyle Drabek, New Hampshire	162
BB	Luis Perez, New Hampshire/Las Vegas	84
SO	Joel Carreno, Dunedin	173
†AVG	Kyle Drabek, New Hampshire	.215

2010 PERFORMANCE

General Manager: Alex Anthopoulos. **Farm Director:** Charlie Wilson. **Scouting Director:** Andrew Tinnish.

Class	Team	League	W	L	PCT	Finish*	Manager(s)
Majors	Toronto Blue Jays	American	85	77	.525	7th (14)	Cito Gaston
Triple-A	Las Vegas 51s	Pacific Coast	66	78	.458	12th (16)	Dan Rohn
Double-A	New Hampshire Fisher Cats	Eastern	79	62	.560	3rd (12)	Luis Rivera
High A	Dunedin Blue Jays	Florida State	72	67	.518	6th (12)	Clayton McCullough
Low A	Lansing Lugnuts	Midwest	70	69	.504	10th (16)	Sal Fasano
Short-season	Auburn Doubledays	New York-Penn	35	40	.467	9th (14)	Dennis Holmberg
Rookie	GCL Blue Jays	Gulf Coast	31	28	.525	t-5th (15)	John Schneider
Overall 2010 Minor League Record			353	344	.506	14th (30)	

*Finish in overall standings (No. of teams in league). †League champion.

ORGANIZATION STATISTICS

TORONTO BLUE JAYS

AMERICAN LEAGUE

Batting	B-T	HT	WT	DOB	AVG	vLH	vRH	G	AB	R	H	2B	3B	HR	RBI	BB	HBP	SH	SF	SO	SB	CS	SLG	OBP
Arencibia, J.P.	R-R	6-1	210	1-5-86	.143	.000	.217	11	35	3	5	1	0	2	4	2	0	0	0	11	0	0	.343	.189
Bautista, Jose	R-R	6-0	195	10-19-80	.260	.222	.269	161	569	109	148	35	3	54	124	100	10	0	4	116	9	2	.617	.378
Buck, John	R-R	6-3	230	7-7-80	.281	.248	.288	118	409	53	115	25	0	20	66	16	6	0	6	111	0	0	.489	.314
Encarnacion, Edwin	R-R	6-2	230	1-7-83	.244	.234	.246	96	332	47	81	16	0	21	51	29	2	0	4	60	1	0	.482	.305
Escobar, Yunel	R-R	6-2	200	11-2-82	.275	.275	.276	60	236	32	65	7	0	4	16	19	4	7	0	26	1	1	.356	.340
Gonzalez, Alex	R-R	5-11	215	2-15-77	.259	.213	.273	85	328	47	85	25	1	17	50	17	1	0	2	65	1	0	.497	.296
Green, Nick	R-R	6-0	180	9-10-78	.154	.200	.125	9	13	2	2	0	0	1	1	0	0	0	0	3	0	0	.154	.214
Hill, Aaron	R-R	5-11	205	3-21-82	.205	.125	.228	138	528	70	108	22	0	26	68	41	8	1	2	85	2	2	.394	.271
Hoffpauir, Jarrett	R-R	5-9	190	6-18-83	.206	.308	.143	13	34	1	7	1	0	0	2	0	1	0	0	5	0	0	.235	.250
Lewis, Fred	L-R	6-0	200	12-9-80	.262	.247	.266	110	428	70	112	31	5	8	36	38	9	1	4	104	17	6	.414	.332
Lind, Adam	L-L	6-1	215	7-17-83	.237	.117	.275	150	569	57	135	32	3	23	72	38	3	0	3	144	0	0	.425	.287
McCoy, Mike	R-R	5-9	175	4-2-81	.195	.276	.151	46	82	9	16	4	0	0	3	8	0	0	0	20	5	1	.244	.267
McDonald, John	R-R	5-10	175	9-24-74	.250	.250	.250	63	152	27	38	9	2	6	23	6	0	2	3	26	2	1	.454	.273
Molina, Jose	R-R	6-2	235	6-3-75	.246	.174	.273	57	167	13	41	4	0	6	12	9	5	2	0	36	1	0	.377	.304
Overbay, Lyle	L-L	6-2	235	1-28-77	.243	.222	.250	154	534	75	130	37	2	20	67	67	3	0	3	131	1	0	.433	.329
Reed, Jeremy	L-L	6-0	195	6-15-81	.143	.000	.150	14	21	1	3	0	0	1	3	2	0	0	0	8	1	0	.286	.217
Ruiz, Randy	R-R	6-3	250	10-19-77	.150	.176	.130	13	40	3	6	2	0	1	1	0	0	0	0	11	1	0	.275	.150
Snider, Travis	L-L	6-0	235	2-2-88	.255	.254	.255	82	298	36	76	20	0	14	32	21	0	0	0	79	6	3	.463	.304
Wells, Vernon	R-R	6-1	230	12-8-78	.273	.195	.291	157	590	79	161	44	3	31	88	50	3	0	3	84	6	4	.515	.331
Wise, Dewayne	L-L	5-11	195	2-24-78	.250	.231	.253	52	112	20	28	3	2	3	14	4	1	1	0	29	4	0	.393	.282

Pitching	B-T	HT	WT	DOB	W	L	ERA	G	GS	CG	SV	IP	H	R	ER	HR	BB	SO	AVG	vLH	vRH	K/9	BB/9
Accardo, Jeremy	R-R	6-1	190	12-8-81	0	1	8.10	5	0	0	0	7	12	6	6	0	3	3	.400	.462	.353	4.05	4.05
Buchholz, Taylor	R-R	6-4	220	10-13-81	0	0	0.00	2	0	0	0	2	0	0	0	0	0	0	.000	.000	.000	0.00	0.00
Camp, Shawn	R-R	6-0	205	11-18-75	4	3	2.99	70	0	0	2	72	71	26	24	8	18	46	.259	.299	.234	5.72	2.24
Carlson, Jesse	L-L	6-1	160	12-31-80	0	0	4.61	20	0	0	1	14	13	7	7	3	5	8	.250	.158	.303	5.27	3.29
Cecil, Brett	R-L	6-1	235	7-2-86	15	7	4.22	28	28	0	0	173	175	87	81	18	54	117	.264	.224	.275	6.10	2.81
Downs, Scott	L-L	6-2	210	3-17-76	5	5	2.64	67	0	0	6	61	47	19	18	3	14	48	.211	.152	.243	7.04	2.05
Drabek, Kyle	R-R	6-1	190	12-8-87	0	3	4.76	3	3	0	0	17	18	9	9	2	5	12	.295	.292	.308	6.35	2.65
Eveland, Dana	L-L	6-1	235	10-29-83	3	4	6.45	9	9	0	0	45	57	35	32	4	27	21	.313	.317	.312	4.23	5.44
Frasor, Jason	R-R	5-10	175	8-9-77	3	4	3.68	69	0	0	4	64	61	30	26	4	27	65	.247	.248	.247	9.19	3.82
Gregg, Kevin	R-R	6-6	240	6-20-78	2	6	3.51	59	0	0	37	59	52	24	23	4	30	58	.237	.225	.248	8.85	4.58
Hill, Shawn	R-R	6-2	225	4-28-81	1	2	2.61	4	4	0	0	21	24	8	6	1	4	14	.282	.302	.262	6.10	1.74
Janssen, Casey	R-R	6-3	225	9-17-81	5	2	3.67	56	0	0	0	69	74	29	28	8	21	63	.272	.283	.264	8.26	2.75
Lewis, Rommie	L-L	6-5	230	9-2-82	0	0	6.75	14	0	0	0	19	20	14	14	4	8	15	.270	.233	.295	7.23	3.86
Litsch, Jesse	R-R	6-1	215	3-9-85	1	5	5.79	9	9	0	0	47	53	30	30	7	15	16	.286	.276	.300	3.09	2.89
Marcum, Shaun	R-R	6-0	195	12-14-81	13	8	3.64	31	31	1	0	195	181	84	79	24	43	165	.242	.190	.298	7.60	1.98
Mills, Brad	L-L	5-11	185	3-5-85	1	0	5.64	7	3	0	0	22	20	14	14	2	13	18	.241	.273	.220	7.25	5.24
Morrow, Brandon	R-R	6-3	195	7-26-84	10	7	4.49	26	26	1	0	146	136	76	73	11	66	178	.248	.245	.253	10.95	4.06
Purcey, David	L-L	6-4	240	4-22-82	1	1	3.71	33	0	0	1	34	26	16	14	3	15	32	.210	.163	.235	8.47	3.97
Ray, Robert	R-R	6-5	195	1-21-84	0	0	2.45	3	0	0	0	4	2	1	1	0	5	3	.154	.333	.100	7.36	12.27
Roenicke, Josh	R-R	6-3	195	8-4-82	1	0	5.68	16	0	0	0	19	18	15	12	1	13	18	.237	.219	.250	8.53	6.16
Romero, Ricky	R-L	6-0	210	11-6-84	14	9	3.73	32	32	3	0	210	189	98	87	15	82	174	.242	.276	.231	7.46	3.51
Rzepczynski, Marc	L-L	6-1	205	8-29-85	4	4	4.95	14	12	0	0	64	72	37	35	8	30	57	.289	.262	.298	8.06	4.24
Tallet, Brian	L-L	6-6	220	9-21-77	2	6	6.40	34	5	0	0	77	84	60	55	20	38	53	.273	.176	.320	6.17	4.42
Valdez, Merkin	R-R	6-5	230	11-10-81	0	0	20.25	2	0	0	0	1	2	3	3	0	3	0	.333	.333	.333	0.00	20.25

Fielding

Catcher	PCT	G	PO	A	E	DP	PB
Arencibia	1.000	8	48	3	0	0	1
Buck	.994	112	733	40	5	6	4
Molina	.996	56	417	37	2	3	5

First Base	PCT	G	PO	A	E	DP
Bautista	1.000	4	26	0	0	0
Lind	1.000	11	70	9	0	7
Overbay	.996	153	1310	101	6	150
Reed	1.000	2	2	0	0	0

	PCT	G	PO	A	E	DP
Ruiz	1.000	3	25	2	0	2
Second Base	**PCT**	**G**	**PO**	**A**	**E**	**DP**
Green	1.000	3	3	8	0	0
Hill	.984	137	235	383	10	89

	1.000	2	1	5	0	0			Lind	1.000	16	22	0	0	0
Hoffpauir	1.000	2	1	5	0	0			Lind	1.000	16	22	0	0	0
McCoy	1.000	14	10	31	0	7			McCoy	.962	15	25	0	1	0
McDonald	.988	23	32	50	1	20			McDonald	1.000	2	2	0	0	0

Third Base	PCT	G	PO	A	E	DP			Reed	1.000	9	11	0	0	0
Bautista	.969	48	26	100	4	7			Snider	.979	80	135	3	3	0
Encarnacion	.932	95	71	174	18	16			Wells	1.000	151	354	5	0	2
Hoffpauir	1.000	11	6	25	0	3			Wise	1.000	44	60	3	0	1
McCoy	1.000	4	0	2	0	0									
McDonald	.925	19	11	26	3	3									

Shortstop	PCT	G	PO	A	E	DP
Escobar	.969	60	105	173	9	48
Gonzalez	.972	85	104	272	11	67
Green	1.000	3	3	2	0	0
McCoy	.952	7	10	10	1	1
McDonald	.985	19	24	42	1	13

Outfield	PCT	G	PO	A	E	DP
Bautista	.985	113	180	12	3	5
Lewis	.983	99	169	1	3	0

LAS VEGAS 51S

PACIFIC COAST LEAGUE

TORONTO BLUE JAYS

TRIPLE-A

Batting	B-T	HT	WT	DOB	AVG	vLH	vRH	G	AB	R	H	2B	3B	HR	RBI	BB	HBP	SH	SF	SO	SB	CS	SLG	OBP
Aguila, Chris	R-R	5-11	200	2-23-79	.275	.180	.318	44	160	30	44	13	2	4	21	18	1	0	3	38	3	1	.456	.346
2-team total (10 New Orleans)					.274	—	—	54	186	35	51	14	2	6	26	19	1	0	4	41	3	1	.468	.338
Arencibia, J.P.	R-R	6-1	210	1-5-86	.301	.228	.322	104	412	76	124	36	1	32	85	38	3	0	6	85	0	0	.626	.359
Calderone, Adam	L-R	6-2	205	3-17-84	.227	.159	.253	64	229	32	52	11	5	10	34	18	4	1	3	68	4	2	.450	.291
Chavez, Raul	R-R	5-11	225	3-18-73	.210	.158	.222	55	200	18	42	13	0	3	24	11	3	2	1	22	0	0	.320	.260
Colonel, Christian	R-R	6-2	210	12-25-81	.368	.400	.357	13	38	4	14	1	0	0	4	4	0	1	0	7	0	1	.395	.429
2-team total (11 Portland)					.258	—	—	24	66	5	17	1	0	0	5	7	0	1	0	16	0	1	.273	.329
Crabbe, Callix	B-R	5-7	185	2-14-83	.200	.308	.118	10	30	8	6	0	0	3	6	6	0	0	0	9	1	0	.200	.333
Diaz, Jonathan	R-R	5-8	155	4-10-85	.266	.348	.239	28	94	20	25	3	0	2	10	8	0	10	1	18	1	0	.362	.320
Dopirak, Brian	R-R	6-4	225	12-20-83	.274	.218	.294	86	339	43	93	26	1	11	53	15	4	0	5	57	0	1	.454	.309
Emaus, Brad	R-R	6-0	200	3-28-86	.298	.206	.321	87	309	58	92	25	3	10	49	50	1	2	2	50	8	2	.495	.395
Encarnacion, Edwin	R-R	6-2	230	1-7-83	.438	.429	.440	7	32	9	14	2	0	3	13	2	1	0	0	2	0	0	.781	.486
Figueroa, Luis	B-R	5-9	165	2-16-74	.326	.369	.310	62	239	26	78	15	3	2	35	12	0	2	1	7	1	1	.439	.357
2-team total (53 Salt Lake)					.319	—	—	115	457	51	146	27	4	5	71	25	2	5	5	19	3	2	.429	.354
Hoffpauir, Jarrett	R-R	5-9	190	6-18-83	.295	.252	.308	107	431	73	127	26	6	16	73	58	2	3	6	34	8	3	.494	.376
Jacobs, Mike	L-R	6-3	215	10-30-80	.308	.167	.362	34	130	26	40	6	0	6	34	21	0	0	6	31	0	0	.492	.389
Jeroloman, Brian	L-R	6-0	200	5-10-85	.316	.500	.231	7	19	8	6	3	0	2	5	8	0	1	0	10	0	0	.789	.519
Lane, Jason	R-L	6-2	225	12-22-76	.323	.229	.349	42	164	28	53	15	0	6	35	27	1	0	0	26	3	2	.524	.422
2-team total (47 New Orleans)					.275	—	—	89	334	50	92	21	0	9	44	44	3	0	3	46	4	3	.419	.362
Lubanski, Chris	L-L	6-3	210	3-24-85	.293	.234	.306	100	355	72	104	24	6	17	57	40	1	0	6	94	4	1	.538	.361
Mathews, Aaron	R-R	5-10	215	5-10-82	.330	.286	.344	88	327	48	108	26	2	11	48	25	1	0	0	53	3	0	.523	.380
Mayorson, Manny	R-R	5-9	195	3-30-83	.333	.258	.351	43	165	31	55	15	0	1	19	7	1	2	1	9	11	0	.442	.362
McCoy, Mike	R-R	5-9	175	4-2-81	.310	.333	.304	53	213	48	66	14	1	6	26	37	1	6	2	31	17	2	.469	.411
Merchan, Jesus	R-R	5-11	180	3-26-81	.315	.306	.319	39	149	18	47	14	1	1	12	11	2	3	1	10	0	2	.443	.368
Padilla, Jorge	R-R	6-2	205	8-11-79	.330	.340	.326	50	185	32	61	12	0	4	27	17	7	0	1	26	7	2	.459	.405
Perales, Daniel	L-L	6-0	195	3-18-85	.255	.152	.287	52	196	30	50	14	1	5	30	13	2	1	1	36	4	1	.413	.307
Phillips, Kyle	L-R	6-1	225	4-3-84	.258	.500	.233	19	66	9	17	5	0	0	8	5	0	0	0	8	0	0	.333	.310
2-team total (55 Portland)					.306	—	—	74	242	28	74	11	2	3	36	18	0	0	3	36	0	0	.405	.350
Quintana, Al	R-R	5-11	205	11-9-82	.174	.091	.250	8	23	1	4	2	0	0	2	0	0	0	0	6	0	0	.261	.174
Reed, Jeremy	L-L	6-0	195	6-15-81	.271	.216	.288	41	155	25	42	7	0	2	14	21	0	0	1	21	3	3	.355	.356
Wallace, Brett	L-R	6-2	235	8-26-86	.301	.384	.267	95	385	64	116	24	1	18	61	27	9	0	2	83	1	1	.509	.359

Pitching	B-T	HT	WT	DOB	W	L	ERA	G	GS	CG	SV	IP	H	R	ER	HR	BB	SO	AVG	vLH	vRH	K/9	BB/9
Accardo, Jeremy	R-R	6-1	190	12-8-81	3	2	3.48	42	0	0	24	44	52	22	17	1	15	26	.306	.341	.273	5.32	3.07
Broadway, Lance	R-R	6-3	195	8-20-83	3	11	7.66	29	20	0	0	141	195	127	120	16	76	89	.333	.337	.330	5.68	4.85
Buzachero, Bubbie	R-R	5-11	180	6-13-81	1	0	16.88	6	0	0	0	8	20	15	15	4	3	4	.476	.357	.536	4.50	3.38
Carlson, Jesse	L-L	6-1	160	12-31-80	3	1	4.24	45	0	0	4	51	56	32	24	6	11	43	.275	.242	.290	7.59	1.94
Cecil, Brett	R-L	6-1	235	7-2-86	2	0	2.45	2	2	0	0	11	13	4	3	0	2	11	.302	.444	.265	9.00	1.64
Collazo, Willie	L-L	5-8	180	11-7-79	0	0	4.70	4	0	0	0	8	11	7	4	0	1	6	.324	.000	.440	7.04	1.17
Gonzalez, Rei	R-R	5-9	215	11-1-85	6	6	9.18	16	16	0	0	82	138	90	84	16	36	55	.374	.399	.352	6.01	3.94
Henn, Sean	R-L	6-3	235	4-23-81	3	4	4.73	38	9	0	2	97	110	57	51	7	53	65	.289	.341	.272	6.03	4.92
Hill, Shawn	R-R	6-2	225	4-28-81	2	2	3.00	5	5	0	0	21	16	8	7	2	5	9	.216	.229	.205	3.86	2.14
Jackson, Zach	L-L	6-5	220	5-13-83	2	3	5.64	35	5	0	0	81	103	55	51	10	46	49	.319	.286	.333	5.42	5.09
LaMura, B.J.	R-R	6-1	200	1-1-81	0	0	0.00	1	0	0	0	1	0	1	0	0	1	0	.000	.000	.000	0.00	9.00
Lewis, Rommie	L-L	6-5	230	9-2-82	1	5	7.59	24	8	0	5	53	72	51	45	7	22	41	.323	.404	.301	6.92	3.71
Litsch, Jesse	R-R	6-1	215	3-9-85	0	3	8.18	4	4	0	0	22	34	26	20	4	3	13	.375	.295	.389	5.32	1.23
McLeary, Marty	R-R	6-4	225	10-26-74	0	5	12.21	9	5	0	0	28	61	49	38	7	18	23	.418	.465	.373	7.39	5.79
2-team total (14 Nashville)					7	9	7.00	23	19	1	0	107	165	101	83	20	45	79	—	—	—	6.67	3.80
Mills, Brad	L-L	5-11	185	3-5-85	8	6	4.97	20	20	0	0	112	118	66	62	15	43	100	.268	.217	.284	8.01	3.45
Perez, Luis	L-L	6-0	160	1-20-85	5	15	6.13	15	15	1	0	87	107	66	59	5	47	56	.305	.257	.318	5.82	4.88
Purcey, David	L-L	6-4	240	4-22-82	2	1	3.38	17	0	0	0	19	14	9	7	2	15	23	.209	.188	.216	11.09	7.23
Ray, Robert	R-R	6-5	195	1-21-84	6	6	5.51	18	18	1	0	96	118	66	59	13	45	75	.309	.344	.274	7.01	4.20
Register, Steven	R-R	6-1	170	5-16-83	1	4	5.27	48	1	0	1	82	98	65	48	9	25	58	.288	.287	.289	6.37	2.74
Richmond, Scott	R-R	6-5	215	8-30-79	1	1	2.70	2	2	0	0	10	8	6	3	1	6	9	.205	.200	.211	8.10	5.40
Roenicke, Josh	R-R	6-3	195	8-4-82	9	1	3.64	36	0	0	1	59	61	29	24	7	25	54	.269	.372	.195	8.19	3.79
Rzepczynski, Marc	L-L	6-1	205	8-29-85	5	5	6.04	12	12	0	0	67	81	49	45	10	27	61	.301	.308	.300	8.19	3.63
Tallet, Brian	L-L	6-6	220	9-21-77	0	1	54.00	1	1	0	0	1	9	8	8	2	1	1	.692	.500	.778	6.75	6.75
Valdez, Merkin	R-R	6-5	230	11-10-81	3	5	7.91	39	0	0	1	58	92	59	51	6	26	35	.358	.388	.331	5.43	4.03
Vermilyea, Jamie	R-R	6-4	190	2-10-82	0	1	5.40	4	0	0	1	7	9	4	4	1	4	5	.333	.250	.455	6.75	5.40

Fielding

Catcher	PCT	G	PO	A	E	DP	PB
Arencibia	.991	94	605	51	6	6	13
Chavez	.987	43	266	32	4	0	2
Jeroloman	1.000	7	45	0	0	0	0
Quintana	.923	6	22	2	2	0	0

First Base	PCT	G	PO	A	E	DP
Dopirak	.992	28	235	19	2	31
Jacobs	.997	31	279	17	1	27
Lane	1.000	9	74	5	0	8
Phillips	1.000	1	9	0	0	1
Wallace	.992	76	685	50	6	90

Second Base	PCT	G	PO	A	E	DP
Crabbe	1.000	1	4	6	0	2
Emaus	1.000	10	24	24	0	8
Figueroa	.969	32	78	79	5	23
Hoffpauir	.968	79	164	261	14	74

	PCT	G	PO	A	E	DP
Mayorson	.971	20	39	63	3	17
Merchan	.953	8	16	25	2	6

Third Base	PCT	G	PO	A	E	DP
Chavez	.333	1	0	1	2	0
Colonel	.735	13	5	20	9	1
Dopirak	.667	1	0	2	1	1
Emaus	.917	76	54	167	20	22
Encarnacion	.737	7	3	11	5	0
Figueroa	1.000	6	2	12	0	0
Hoffpauir	.947	27	15	56	4	6
Phillips	.950	15	8	30	2	6
Quintana	—	1	0	0	0	0

Shortstop	PCT	G	PO	A	E	DP
Diaz	.976	28	42	82	3	17
Figueroa	.934	23	30	84	8	25
Mayorson	.949	19	22	53	4	16

	PCT	G	PO	A	E	DP
McCoy	.964	47	71	172	9	32
Merchan	.947	31	51	75	7	24

Outfield	PCT	G	PO	A	E	DP
Aguila	.923	44	70	2	6	0
Calderone	.993	62	132	5	1	3
Crabbe	1.000	9	13	0	0	0
Dopirak	.000	1	0	0	1	0
Lane	.912	15	30	1	3	0
Lubanski	.985	92	129	3	2	0
Mathews	.966	81	161	9	6	0
McCoy	.929	5	12	1	1	1
Padilla	.960	50	92	5	4	1
Perales	.957	51	104	6	5	1
Quintana	—	1	0	0	0	0
Reed	.988	39	77	3	1	0

NEW HAMPSHIRE FISHER CATS

DOUBLE-A

EASTERN LEAGUE

Batting	B-T	HT	WT	DOB	AVG	vLH	vRH	G	AB	R	H	2B	3B	HR	RBI	BB	HBP	SH	SF	SO	SB	CS	SLG	OBP
Bowman, Shawn	R-R	6-3	225	12-9-84	.263	.282	.256	106	411	66	108	25	0	22	69	37	5	0	2	96	2	2	.484	.330
Buck, John	R-R	6-3	230	7-7-80	.273	.250	.286	3	11	2	3	0	0	0	3	0	0	0	0	3	0	0	.818	.333
Calderone, Adam	L-R	6-2	205	3-17-84	.266	.275	.264	69	267	38	71	20	2	9	42	16	5	0	8	64	6	4	.457	.311
Cooper, David	L-L	6-0	200	2-12-87	.257	.281	.249	132	498	59	128	30	1	20	78	52	1	0	2	74	0	0	.442	.327
Crabbe, Callix	B-R	5-7	185	2-14-83	.225	.250	.216	81	285	45	64	16	1	4	27	31	5	6	2	57	19	6	.330	.310
Diaz, Jonathan	R-R	5-8	155	4-10-85	.231	.288	.213	99	312	48	72	20	1	0	33	53	9	8	3	48	4	2	.301	.355
Dominguez, Oliver	B-R	5-9	156	4-23-89	.000	.000	.000	2	2	0	0	0	0	0	0	0	0	0	0	2	0	0	.000	.000
Emaus, Brad	R-R	6-0	200	3-28-86	.272	.316	.265	38	136	21	37	7	0	5	26	31	0	1	2	19	5	0	.434	.402
Hechavarria, Adeiny	R-R	5-11	180	4-15-89	.273	.269	.274	61	253	36	69	11	1	3	34	12	2	1	5	40	6	3	.360	.305
Jaspe, Jonathan	B-R	5-9	205	4-11-85	.238	.259	.230	61	206	19	49	13	1	3	17	12	2	2	1	33	1	0	.354	.285
Jeroloman, Brian	L-R	6-0	200	5-10-85	.261	.200	.283	81	245	37	64	16	0	7	33	69	4	0	1	91	0	1	.412	.429
Liuzza, Matt	R-R	6-0	215	2-3-84	.250	.242	.253	37	120	11	30	8	0	4	11	18	1	0	0	34	0	2	.417	.353
Loewen, Adam	L-L	6-6	235	4-9-84	.246	.236	.250	129	459	70	113	31	3	13	70	66	9	1	2	142	17	6	.412	.351
Mastroianni, Darin	R-R	5-11	190	8-26-85	.301	.319	.295	132	525	101	158	25	7	4	46	77	3	7	5	96	46	10	.398	.390
Mayorson, Manny	R-R	5-9	195	3-10-83	.316	.353	.297	54	196	30	62	12	0	0	23	19	0	3	2	14	8	0	.378	.373
Nanita, Ricardo	L-L	6-0	205	6-12-81	.238	.167	.267	6	21	2	5	3	0	0	3	2	0	0	1	3	0	0	.381	.227
Perales, Daniel	L-L	6-0	195	3-18-85	.280	.286	.278	21	75	16	21	4	1	5	9	4	3	2	1	15	2	0	.560	.337
Quintana, Al	R-R	5-11	205	11-9-82	.200	.280	.120	16	50	5	10	4	0	1	3	1	0	1	0	16	0	0	.340	.255
Rodriguez, Concepcion	R-R	6-2	205	9-19-86	.240	.167	.263	6	25	0	6	0	0	0	5	0	0	0	1	6	1	0	.240	.231
Sanchez, Luis	B-R	5-11	180	5-27-87	.184	.258	.149	38	98	8	18	3	0	0	10	8	1	2	3	25	1	0	.214	.245
Snider, Travis	L-L	6-0	235	2-2-88	.296	.280	.304	20	81	14	24	5	0	5	17	2	0	0	2	21	3	1	.543	.306
Thames, Eric	L-R	6-0	205	11-10-86	.288	.252	.303	130	496	95	143	25	6	27	104	50	18	2	7	121	8	5	.526	.370

Pitching	B-T	HT	WT	DOB	W	L	ERA	G	GS	CG	SV	IP	H	R	ER	HR	BB	SO	AVG	vLH	vRH	K/9	BB/9
Bell, Bobby	R-R	6-4	200	8-26-85	3	2	6.24	10	10	0	0	49	63	38	34	11	12	34	.315	.290	.340	6.24	2.20
Bongiovanni, Vince	R-R	6-5	215	1-11-83	6	7	5.13	35	0	0	2	60	57	39	34	5	38	42	.260	.274	.250	6.34	5.73
Boone, Randy	R-R	6-0	200	8-6-84	5	10	3.98	24	22	2	0	133	128	68	59	8	39	96	.252	.280	.223	6.48	2.63
Buzachero, Bubbie	R-R	5-11	180	6-13-81	6	0	5.62	25	0	0	1	58	66	41	36	9	23	37	.287	.325	.245	5.77	3.59
Collins, Tim	L-L	5-7	155	8-21-89	1	0	2.51	35	0	0	9	43	27	12	12	4	16	73	.174	.204	.158	15.28	3.35
Dials, Zach	R-R	6-0	200	7-22-85	0	0	5.68	5	0	0	0	6	8	4	4	0	5	1	.308	.231	.385	1.42	7.11
2-team total (5 Harrisburg)					0	0	5.84	10	0	0	0	12	18	8	8	0	8	8	—	—		5.84	5.84
Drabek, Kyle	R-R	6-1	190	12-8-87	14	9	2.94	27	27	1	0	162	126	67	53	12	68	132	.215	.227	.202	7.33	3.78
Everts, Clint	B-R	6-2	195	8-10-84	1	0	4.38	15	3	0	0	39	36	19	19	3	27	30	.254	.246	.260	6.92	6.23
2-team total (26 Binghamton)					4	1	5.59	41	3	0	2	74	82	47	46	6	48	67	—	—		8.15	5.84
Farina, Alan	R-R	5-11	190	9-8-86	1	0	1.40	17	0	0	4	19	6	3	3	0	9	28	.092	.040	.125	13.03	4.19
Farquhar, Danny	R-R	5-11	180	2-17-87	4	3	3.52	53	0	0	17	77	50	32	30	7	42	79	.189	.229	.156	9.27	4.93
Garcia, Dumas	R-R	6-2	165	7-7-83	0	0	10.38	6	0	0	0	9	11	10	10	2	11	7	.324	.294	.353	7.27	11.42
Gonzalez, Rei	R-R	5-9	215	11-1-85	2	4	6.93	9	9	0	0	51	79	44	39	3	20	27	.357	.350	.364	4.80	3.55
Hill, Shawn	R-R	6-2	225	4-28-81	1	0	0.00	1	1	0	0	7	3	0	0	0	2	4	.125	.100	.143	5.14	2.57
Huggins, Chuck	L-L	6-0	185	5-6-86	0	2	9.58	2	2	0	0	10	13	12	11	4	3	6	.317	.333	.310	5.23	2.61
LaMura, B.J.	R-R	6-1	200	1-1-81	5	6	3.73	30	15	0	0	94	60	42	39	9	48	83	.182	.204	.163	7.95	4.60
Magnuson, Trystan	L-R	6-7	210	6-6-85	3	0	2.58	46	0	0	5	73	70	22	21	1	10	63	.256	.281	.237	7.73	1.23
Martin, Adrian	R-R	6-0	165	9-2-84	5	1	4.41	29	2	0	1	49	52	25	24	5	23	44	.274	.337	.207	8.08	4.22
2-team total (8 Richmond)					6	1	3.67	37	2	0	1	61	64	26	25	5	25	56	—	—		8.22	3.67
McCleary, Marty	R-R	6-4	225	10-26-74	1	1	6.75	3	3	0	0	9	15	7	7	0	5	7	.349	.400	.304	4.82	4.82
Page, Ryan	L-L	6-1	205	9-16-85	0	1	27.00	1	0	0	0	2	5	6	6	1	3	1	.556	.500	.600	4.50	13.50
Perez, Luis	L-L	6-0	160	1-20-85	5	6	4.54	13	12	1	0	73	67	43	37	6	37	49	.246	.220	.258	6.01	4.54
Potts, Jared	L-L	6-3	210	7-4-85	2	2	7.78	15	0	0	0	20	28	18	17	3	12	22	.333	.278	.375	10.07	5.49
Purcey, David	L-L	6-4	240	4-22-82	0	1	13.50	3	0	0	0	3	4	4	4	1	5	2	.273	.400	.167	16.88	8.38
Reyes, Jo-Jo	L-L	6-2	230	11-20-84	1	1	2.57	2	2	0	0	14	7	4	4	0	4	10	.143	.095	.179	6.43	2.57
Richmond, Scott	R-R	6-5	215	8-30-79	0	0	2.70	2	2	0	0	10	7	3	3	2	0	14	.189	.143	.217	12.60	0.00
Stewart, Zach	R-R	6-2	205	9-28-86	8	3	3.63	26	26	0	0	136	131	59	55	13	54	106	.255	.253	.258	7.00	3.56

	B-T	HT	WT	DOB	W	L	ERA	G	GS	CG	SV	IP	H	R	ER	HR	BB	SO	AVG	vLH	vRH	K/9	BB/9
Uviedo, Ronald	R-R	6-1	160	10-7-86	5	3	5.31	25	5	0	1	58	56	41	34	12	27	65	.241	.236	.246	10.14	4.21
2-team total (16 Altoona)					5	5	4.72	41	5	0	1	80	69	49	42	15	39	93	—	—	—	10.46	4.39

Fielding

Catcher	PCT	G	PO	A	E	DP	PB
Buck	1.000	1	3	1	0	0	0
Jaspe	1.000	35	241	33	0	5	3
Jeroloman	.997	80	573	43	2	4	2
Liuzza	.983	29	208	18	4	2	5
Quintana	.938	5	29	1	2	0	0

First Base	PCT	G	PO	A	E	DP
Cooper	.993	128	1084	94	8	121
Jaspe	.978	6	45	0	1	7
Mayorson	1.000	7	48	7	0	4
Quintana	1.000	5	34	2	0	6

Second Base	PCT	G	PO	A	E	DP
Crabbe	.973	62	121	172	8	45
Diaz	.984	45	106	143	4	39
Dominguez	1.000	1	0	1	0	0

	PCT	G	PO	A	E	DP
Emaus	1.000	22	44	78	0	23
Mayorson	1.000	10	9	20	0	5
Sanchez	.895	6	5	12	2	5

Third Base	PCT	G	PO	A	E	DP
Bowman	.952	100	62	174	12	22
Crabbe	1.000	7	6	12	0	1
Diaz	.857	1	1	5	1	0
Dominguez	.000	1	0	0	1	0
Emaus	1.000	11	6	22	0	1
Jaspe	.750	1	1	2	1	0
Mayorson	.939	12	8	23	2	2
Quintana	1.000	2	0	3	0	2
Sanchez	.973	15	8	28	1	7

Shortstop	PCT	G	PO	A	E	DP
Diaz	.983	51	89	146	4	36

	PCT	G	PO	A	E	DP
Hechavarria	.962	61	86	192	11	43
Mayorson	.938	20	20	55	5	10
Sanchez	.957	16	17	28	2	5

Outfield	PCT	G	PO	A	E	DP
Calderone	.990	57	96	4	1	0
Crabbe	1.000	7	13	0	0	0
Loewen	.981	102	191	13	4	5
Mastroianni	.990	124	281	7	3	1
Nanita	1.000	2	3	0	0	0
Perales	1.000	18	40	1	0	0
Rodriguez	.917	5	10	1	1	0
Sanchez	—	1	0	0	0	0
Snider	1.000	15	26	0	0	0
Thames	.968	98	174	6	6	1

DUNEDIN BLUE JAYS — HIGH CLASS A

FLORIDA STATE LEAGUE

Batting	B-T	HT	WT	DOB	AVG	vLH	vRH	G	AB	R	H	2B	3B	HR	RBI	BB	HBP	SH	SF	SO	SB	CS	SLG	OBP
Ahrens, Kevin	B-R	6-1	195	4-26-89	.187	.296	.150	28	107	12	20	6	1	1	8	7	1	2	1	20	1	0	.290	.241
Barron, Raul	R-R	5-10	180	4-4-86	.254	.261	.253	33	122	13	31	6	0	2	12	9	1	3	2	19	9	3	.352	.306
Bowman, Shawn	R-R	6-3	225	12-9-84	.462	.500	.455	4	13	3	6	4	0	0	1	0	0	0	0	4	0	1	.769	.462
d'Arnaud, Travis	R-R	6-2	195	2-10-89	.259	.353	.226	71	263	36	68	20	1	6	38	20	4	0	5	63	3	1	.411	.315
Del Campo, Jon	R-R	5-11	195	5-18-88	.258	.318	.239	28	89	10	23	5	0	2	7	4	0	0	0	22	3	1	.382	.290
Encarnacion, Edwin	R-R	6-2	230	1-7-83	.100	.000	.143	3	10	2	1	0	0	1	1	2	1	0	0	3	0	0	.400	.308
Goins, Ryan	L-R	5-10	170	2-13-88	.205	.237	.195	47	166	8	34	9	0	0	18	11	0	3	2	33	1	1	.259	.251
Gomes, Yan	R-R	6-2	215	7-19-87	.275	.164	.309	66	233	37	64	21	1	9	40	9	4	0	1	64	0	0	.489	.312
Gose, Anthony	L-L	6-1	190	8-10-90	.255	.259	.254	27	94	21	24	3	2	3	6	13	3	2	1	29	9	5	.426	.360
2-team total (103 Clearwater)					.262	—	—	130	512	88	134	20	13	7	27	45	9	7	1	132	45	32	.393	.332
Hechavarria, Adeiny	R-R	5-11	180	4-15-89	.193	.250	.178	41	161	21	31	7	3	1	7	5	0	1	0	25	7	0	.292	.217
Hopkins, Chris	R-R	5-11	175	9-10-87	.147	.250	.115	12	34	5	5	1	0	1	5	3	1	1	0	7	3	2	.265	.237
Jackson, Justin	R-R	6-1	186	12-11-88	.200	.200	.200	10	30	2	6	1	0	0	0	5	0	0	0	8	1	0	.233	.314
Jimenez, A.J.	R-R	5-11	200	5-1-90	.111	.000	.167	2	9	1	1	0	0	1	0	0	0	0	0	5	0	0	.444	.111
Liuzza, Matt	R-R	6-0	215	2-3-84	.000	.000	.000	4	14	0	0	0	0	0	1	0	0	0	0	3	1	0	.000	.067
McClanahan, Justin	R-R	5-11	210	8-22-85	.261	.246	.266	71	211	30	55	13	3	5	26	14	7	0	3	60	3	3	.422	.323
McDade, Mike	B-R	6-1	260	5-8-89	.267	.250	.272	128	480	60	128	22	1	21	64	27	8	0	2	141	2	4	.448	.315
McElroy, Brad	L-R	5-11	195	4-24-86	.210	.162	.221	58	200	25	42	10	0	3	18	17	2	4	0	47	8	1	.305	.279
Merchan, Jesus	R-R	5-11	180	3-26-81	.263	.333	.231	5	19	0	5	1	0	0	4	0	0	0	0	4	0	0	.316	.263
Pastornicky, Tyler	R-R	5-11	170	12-13-89	.258	.344	.233	77	287	50	74	16	0	6	35	39	1	3	1	49	24	7	.376	.348
Perales, Daniel	L-L	6-0	195	3-18-85	.257	.368	.240	40	148	15	38	6	2	6	16	6	1	0	1	26	6	0	.446	.288
Quintana, Al	R-R	5-11	205	11-9-82	.255	.429	.227	15	51	7	13	4	0	1	7	5	1	1	0	12	0	0	.392	.333
Ramirez, Welinton	R-R	6-2	205	4-13-87	.237	.256	.231	119	397	40	94	25	1	9	49	14	6	4	4	131	12	6	.373	.271
Rodriguez, Concepcion	R-R	6-2	205	9-19-86	.250	.182	.273	15	44	4	11	3	0	0	5	7	1	0	0	9	1	2	.318	.365
Sanchez, Luis	B-R	5-11	180	5-27-87	.000	.000	.000	2	5	0	0	0	0	0	0	2	0	0	1	0	0	0	.000	.286
Schimpf, Ryan	L-R	5-9	181	3-11-88	.221	.091	.246	18	68	10	15	3	1	2	7	4	1	1	0	27	3	0	.382	.274
Shoffit, Sean	L-R	6-2	195	6-9-85	.233	.200	.242	31	116	12	27	4	3	2	11	8	0	1	0	34	9	0	.371	.282
Sierra, Moises	R-R	6-0	225	9-24-88	.162	.100	.185	10	37	4	6	1	0	1	5	1	0	0	2	11	0	1	.270	.175
Snider, Travis	L-L	6-0	235	2-2-88	.000	.000	.000	1	4	0	0	0	0	0	0	0	0	0	0	2	0	0	.000	.000
Sobolewski, Mark	R-R	6-0	190	12-24-86	.262	.239	.271	70	248	26	65	19	0	6	35	19	2	1	2	68	2	1	.411	.317
Talley, Jon	L-R	6-3	200	2-18-89	.231	.207	.235	72	242	34	56	19	0	6	36	19	3	0	0	87	0	1	.384	.295
Tolisano, John	B-R	5-11	190	10-7-88	.252	.167	.280	61	218	39	55	12	3	5	21	29	0	1	2	65	4	3	.404	.337
Van Kirk, James	R-R	5-11	210	8-10-85	.241	.274	.230	117	399	48	96	14	2	10	47	44	5	0	5	97	1	0	.361	.320
Wilson, Kenny	R-R	5-10	185	1-30-90	.138	.048	.189	18	58	5	8	1	0	0	4	8	0	2	0	15	5	0	.155	.242

Pitching	B-T	HT	WT	DOB	W	L	ERA	G	GS	CG	SV	IP	H	R	ER	HR	BB	SO	AVG	vLH	vRH	K/9	BB/9
Alvarez, Henderson	R-R	6-0	190	4-18-90	8	7	4.33	23	21	0	0	112	137	65	54	10	27	78	.300	.332	.275	6.25	2.16
Beck, Chad	R-R	6-4	245	1-17-85	3	6	3.72	41	11	0	0	102	97	44	42	5	31	79	.244	.243	.246	6.99	2.74
Bell, Bobby	B-R	6-4	200	8-26-85	0	1	9.82	2	1	0	0	4	9	4	4	3	5	3	.500	.333	.583	7.36	7.36
Buckwalter, Ross	L-R	6-0	195	1-27-85	2	4	2.64	34	0	0	0	44	40	14	13	1	12	34	.250	.241	.255	6.90	2.44
Carreno, Joel	R-R	6-0	190	3-7-87	9	6	3.73	27	25	1	0	138	147	65	57	8	30	173	.275	.295	.257	11.31	1.96
Crawford, Evan	R-L	6-1	175	9-2-86	1	2	2.04	23	0	0	3	35	31	11	8	0	14	33	.237	.189	.255	8.41	3.57
Daly, Matt	R-R	5-8	180	8-14-86	2	2	2.50	56	0	0	31	58	45	19	16	2	23	63	.214	.241	.197	9.83	3.59
DeLucia, Dan	L-L	6-4	220	6-1-85	4	2	3.38	29	1	0	0	48	58	23	18	2	17	44	.299	.317	.290	8.25	3.19
Farina, Alan	R-R	5-11	190	8-9-86	2	1	1.24	32	0	0	2	36	19	7	5	0	11	46	.156	.154	.157	11.39	2.72
Gailey, Frank	L-L	5-9	190	11-18-85	6	4	2.55	45	1	0	0	92	87	28	26	2	10	99	.246	.226	.255	9.72	0.98
Garcia, Dumas	R-R	6-2	165	7-7-83	3	5	3.58	30	1	0	1	50	55	25	20	2	21	38	.275	.317	.255	6.79	3.75
Griffith, Shawn	R-R	5-10	180	5-24-87	0	0	2.25	4	0	0	0	3	1	1	1		1	4	.231	.200	.250	9.00	2.25
Hernandez, Juan	L-L	6-0	180	10-25-87	0	0	6.00	2	0	0	0	3	3	2	2	0	3	3	.273	.250	.286	9.00	9.00
Hill, Shawn	R-R	6-2	225	4-28-81	0	0	3.00	1	1	0	0	6	7	2	2	0	0	5	.304	.300	.308	7.50	0.00

TORONTO BLUE JAYS

Name	B-T	HT	WT	DOB	W	L	ERA	G	GS	CG	SV	IP	H	R	ER	HR	BB	SO	AVG	vLH	vRH	K/9	BB/9
Huggins, Chuck	L-L	6-0	185	5-6-86	11	4	3.47	23	23	0	0	127	114	56	49	6	43	91	.239	.252	.235	6.45	3.05
Jenkins, Chad	R-R	6-4	235	12-22-87	2	6	4.33	13	13	1	0	62	73	37	30	6	18	42	.281	.280	.281	6.06	2.60
LaMura, B.J.	R-R	6-1	200	1-1-81	0	0	3.48	9	0	0	0	10	8	4	4	0	9	13	.216	.267	.182	11.32	7.84
Liebel, Andrew	R-R	6-0	195	3-22-86	5	5	5.86	13	13	0	0	63	75	48	41	4	31	41	.299	.353	.252	5.86	4.43
Litsch, Jesse	R-R	6-1	215	3-9-85	1	1	1.80	2	2	0	0	15	9	3	3	1	4	10	.170	.182	.167	6.00	2.40
Longpre, Bryan	R-R	6-2	195	7-13-87	1	0	3.18	3	0	0	0	6	6	2	2	0	2	8	.273	.231	.333	12.71	3.18
Molina, Nestor	R-R	6-1	179	1-9-89	0	0	2.08	2	0	0	0	4	7	4	1	0	0	3	.350	.300	.400	6.23	0.00
Page, Ryan	L-L	6-0	205	9-16-85	3	8	5.00	19	14	0	0	85	96	52	47	8	26	43	.285	.296	.281	4.57	2.76
Potts, Jared	L-L	6-3	210	7-4-85	3	1	3.16	33	0	0	1	43	39	15	15	0	20	38	.250	.231	.260	8.02	4.22
Richmond, Scott	R-R	6-5	215	8-30-79	3	0	1.29	5	4	0	0	21	14	4	3	0	6	13	.177	.125	.258	5.57	2.57
Rodriguez, Kenny	R-R	6-2	190	3-17-85	3	1	8.57	6	3	0	0	21	34	22	20	4	11	18	.370	.450	.308	7.71	4.71
Shopshire, Ryan	R-R	6-5	200	11-8-85	0	1	3.86	4	4	0	0	21	23	11	9	3	5	18	.277	.278	.277	7.71	2.14
Tallet, Brian	L-L	6-6	220	9-21-77	0	0	0.00	1	1	0	0	4	2	0	0	0	1	3	.154	.000	.200	6.75	2.25

Fielding

Catcher	PCT	G	PO	A	E	DP	PB
d'Arnaud	.996	58	427	38	2	3	2
Gomes	.995	53	377	30	2	6	3
Jimenez	1.000	2	17	1	0	1	0
Liuzza	1.000	3	25	2	0	0	2
Quintana	1.000	11	91	6	0	1	0
Talley	.985	23	126	8	2	0	1

First Base	PCT	G	PO	A	E	DP
McClanahan	1.000	6	43	2	0	6
McDade	.992	116	969	77	8	74
Schimpf	.500	1	2	0	2	1
Talley	.989	24	164	11	2	13

Second Base	PCT	G	PO	A	E	DP
Barron	.975	24	48	71	3	17
Del Campo	.975	19	35	42	2	7
Jackson	.973	7	11	25	1	5
McClanahan	.971	40	60	108	5	21
Merchan	1.000	3	4	4	0	3
Pastornicky	.970	30	43	53	3	8
Sanchez	1.000	2	5	4	0	1
Schimpf	.906	16	23	35	6	7
Sobolewski	—	1	0	0	0	0
Tolisano	.930	10	18	22	3	6

Third Base	PCT	G	PO	A	E	DP
Ahrens	.947	25	20	52	4	7
Barron	.857	5	3	9	2	1
Bowman	.667	2	0	2	1	0
Del Campo	.750	3	1	5	2	1
Encarnacion	1.000	2	0	5	0	0
McClanahan	.818	10	7	20	6	2
McDade	—	1	0	0	0	0
Merchan	1.000	1	1	0	0	0
Quintana	.800	2	0	4	1	0
Sobolewski	.933	65	37	116	11	8
Tolisano	.848	29	12	44	10	6

Shortstop	PCT	G	PO	A	E	DP
Barron	1.000	5	7	10	0	3
Goins	.954	47	56	130	9	21
Hechavarria	.955	40	65	126	9	20
Jackson	1.000	3	1	5	0	0
McClanahan	.500	1	0	2	2	0
Merchan	1.000	1	1	4	0	1
Pastornicky	.966	46	58	143	7	23

Outfield	PCT	G	PO	A	E	DP
Barron	.000	1	0	0	1	0
Gose	.983	25	58	1	1	0
Hopkins	1.000	9	25	0	0	0
McClanahan	1.000	15	20	0	0	0
McElroy	.992	56	127	1	1	0
Perales	.986	40	67	4	1	2
Ramirez	.968	119	228	17	8	5
Rodriguez	.963	12	26	0	1	0
Shoffit	.986	30	67	1	1	0
Sierra	.941	9	16	0	1	0
Tolisano	1.000	16	28	0	0	0
Van Kirk	.976	80	112	8	3	0
Wilson	1.000	18	32	0	0	0

LANSING LUGNUTS

LOW CLASS A

MIDWEST LEAGUE

Batting	B-T	HT	WT	DOB	AVG	vLH	vRH	G	AB	R	H	2B	3B	HR	RBI	BB	HBP	SH	SF	SO	SB	CS	SLG	OBP
Ahrens, Kevin	B-R	6-1	195	4-26-89	.265	.329	.239	66	253	30	67	12	2	8	35	21	0	0	2	51	2	4	.423	.319
Brisker, Markus	R-R	6-3	210	8-21-90	.167	.000	.231	6	18	0	3	0	0	0	3	0	0	0	0	5	0	1	.167	.286
Crouse, Michael	R-R	6-4	215	11-22-90	.216	.120	.254	28	88	11	19	5	2	2	9	14	1	1	1	35	5	2	.386	.327
Del Campo, Jon	B-R	5-11	195	5-18-88	.300	.222	.327	17	70	8	21	6	0	1	11	3	0	1	1	13	3	1	.429	.324
Dominguez, Oliver	B-R	5-9	156	4-23-89	.264	.189	.301	41	110	22	29	6	0	3	14	21	1	2	1	19	11	4	.400	.383
Eiland, Eric	L-L	6-2	220	9-16-88	.232	.239	.230	99	323	42	75	13	5	0	31	44	4	3	3	71	20	10	.303	.329
Fuenmayor, Balbino	R-R	6-3	235	11-26-89	.220	.215	.221	100	346	32	76	20	3	9	46	20	3	0	3	123	0	0	.373	.266
Glenn, Brad	R-R	6-2	220	4-2-87	.271	.355	.240	109	398	63	108	21	5	17	69	41	4	0	4	100	14	5	.477	.342
Goins, Ryan	L-R	5-10	170	2-13-88	.308	.204	.332	77	295	49	91	19	2	3	35	35	1	4	3	60	6	7	.417	.380
Gomes, Yan	R-R	6-2	215	7-19-87	.231	.000	.250	7	26	2	6	2	0	0	2	1	0	0	2	11	0	0	.308	.290
Hobson, K.C.	L-L	6-2	205	8-22-90	.261	.231	.266	23	92	14	24	4	1	2	9	4	0	0	2	17	0	0	.391	.286
Hopkins, Chris	R-R	5-11	175	9-10-87	.268	.310	.250	50	138	20	37	6	0	0	13	20	1	2	1	22	15	4	.312	.363
Jackson, Justin	R-R	6-1	186	12-11-88	.249	.282	.234	61	229	27	57	3	3	1	17	26	1	1	0	67	13	4	.301	.328
Jimenez, A.J.	R-R	5-11	200	5-1-90	.305	.304	.306	70	262	35	80	22	0	4	54	18	3	1	8	56	17	4	.435	.347
Marisnick, Jake	R-R	6-4	200	3-30-91	.220	.263	.202	34	127	16	28	8	2	1	12	9	5	2	0	37	9	2	.339	.298
McElroy, Brad	L-R	5-11	195	4-24-86	.330	.286	.340	52	194	37	64	14	3	4	22	21	3	0	0	34	12	1	.495	.404
Murphy, Jack	B-R	6-4	235	4-6-88	.000	.000	.000	2	2	0	0	0	0	0	0	1	1	0	0	1	0	0	.000	.250
Nolan, Kevin	R-R	6-2	200	12-13-87	.295	.344	.275	83	285	42	84	25	2	0	30	31	5	3	2	34	11	10	.396	.372
Ochinko, Sean	R-R	5-11	205	10-21-87	.311	.392	.277	109	412	57	128	37	0	8	65	30	5	0	6	58	1	0	.459	.360
Schimpf, Ryan	L-R	5-9	181	3-11-88	.240	.173	.262	92	337	46	81	23	10	6	45	39	10	4	5	96	11	7	.421	.332
Schwartz, Randy	R-R	6-4	235	1-25-86	.191	.167	.195	14	47	3	9	1	0	1	5	3	0	0	1	13	1	0	.255	.235
Sobolewski, Mark	R-R	6-0	190	12-24-86	.313	.325	.310	44	166	22	52	15	1	4	24	9	0	0	3	32	0	2	.488	.343
Talley, Jon	L-R	6-3	220	2-18-89	.273	.400	.235	7	22	2	6	2	0	0	3	3	0	0	0	5	0	1	.364	.360
Turkamani, Karim	R-R	5-9	215	1-20-87	.252	.105	.284	38	107	8	27	2	0	1	9	8	1	1	1	32	0	1	.299	.308
Wilson, Kenny	R-R	5-10	185	1-30-90	.216	.252	.200	95	361	54	78	10	4	0	22	51	8	6	0	112	35	11	.296	.309

Pitching	B-T	HT	WT	DOB	W	L	ERA	G	GS	CG	SV	IP	H	R	ER	HR	BB	SO	AVG	vLH	vRH	K/9	BB/9
Antolin, Dustin	R-R	6-2	195	8-9-89	2	2	2.93	18	0	0	0	21	10	9	9	0	9	24	.206	.029	.299	7.81	2.93
Barnes, Dan	L-R	6-1	195	10-21-89	0	0	5.91	8	0	0	0	11	17	8	7	0	8	16	.354	.435	.280	13.50	6.75
Beck, Casey	R-R	6-1	215	3-28-87	1	3	3.74	38	0	0	6	43	31	19	18	4	23	54	.199	.218	.188	11.22	4.78
Crawford, Evan	R-L	6-1	175	9-2-86	3	2	4.01	16	7	0	0	49	51	24	22	2	20	29	.273	.268	.275	7.11	3.65
Fields, Matt	R-R	6-3	190	7-10-86	5	7	4.14	19	19	0	0	100	120	59	46	5	19	61	.297	.314	.281	5.49	1.71
Gracey, Scott	R-R	6-2	190	10-15-86	0	0	5.28	31	1	0	0	60	75	42	35	2	21	41	.307	.297	.315	6.18	3.17
Hernandez, Juan	L-L	6-0	180	10-25-87	0	0	40.50	1	0	0	0	1	2	3	3	0	2	1	.500	.500	.500	13.50	27.00
Hutchison, Drew	L-R	6-2	165	8-22-90	1	2	1.52	5	5	0	0	24	17	7	4	1	7	19	.191	.211	.176	7.23	2.66

Name	B-T	HT	WT	DOB	W	L	ERA	G	GS	CG	SV	IP	H	R	ER	HR	BB	SO	AVG	vLH	vRH	K/9	BB/9
Jenkins, Chad	R-R	6-4	235	12-22-87	5	4	3.63	13	13	1	0	79	87	35	32	5	13	64	.277	.258	.290	7.26	1.47
Lawrence, Casey	R-R	6-2	170	10-28-87	1	1	3.98	4	3	0	1	20	21	9	9	1	3	13	.273	.419	.174	5.75	1.33
Loup, Aaron	L-L	5-11	180	12-19-87	3	2	4.54	35	5	0	2	73	79	37	37	4	22	73	.283	.348	.251	8.96	2.70
Molina, Nestor	R-R	6-1	179	1-9-89	8	2	3.17	37	2	0	4	77	64	31	27	4	20	61	.224	.224	.224	7.16	2.35
Sever, Dave	R-R	6-4	195	8-29-86	6	9	4.41	24	22	0	0	118	126	73	58	10	43	74	.272	.248	.294	5.63	3.27
Shopshire, Ryan	R-R	6-5	200	11-8-85	7	11	5.28	24	24	1	0	138	161	89	81	19	44	104	.295	.291	.298	6.78	2.87
Slover, Brian	R-R	6-3	230	6-10-88	3	8	5.52	38	0	0	0	59	60	42	36	2	25	37	.265	.217	.308	5.68	3.84
Smith, Egan	L-L	6-5	200	3-16-89	7	4	4.54	15	14	0	0	81	100	47	41	4	22	65	.303	.319	.297	7.19	2.43
Tepera, Ryan	R-R	6-1	180	11-3-87	9	6	3.98	24	22	0	0	120	113	61	53	7	44	79	.251	.229	.267	5.93	3.30
Turnbull, Steve	R-R	6-3	215	11-25-86	3	3	3.86	52	0	0	21	63	63	35	27	4	19	69	.256	.298	.225	9.86	2.71
Webb, Daniel	R-R	6-3	210	8-18-89	1	1	2.31	2	2	0	0	12	8	7	3	0	6	4	.195	.286	.100	3.09	4.63
Wright, Matt	L-L	5-10	170	5-7-87	5	2	2.53	38	0	0	1	68	50	25	19	2	22	82	.201	.209	.196	10.91	2.93

Fielding

Catcher	PCT	G	PO	A	E	DP	PB
Gomes	1.000	5	40	5	0	1	0
Jimenez	.990	59	428	56	5	2	8
Murphy	1.000	2	13	0	0	0	0
Ochinko	.997	45	298	21	1	3	6
Turkamani	.981	38	231	27	5	4	6

First Base	PCT	G	PO	A	E	DP
Fuenmayor	.990	82	708	53	8	53
Glenn	1.000	1	2	0	0	0
Hobson	.984	21	173	13	3	14
Nolan	.989	25	182	5	2	19
Ochinko	.985	16	128	6	2	15
Schwartz	1.000	4	32	3	0	2
Talley	1.000	2	21	1	0	3

Second Base	PCT	G	PO	A	E	DP
Del Campo	1.000	13	16	42	0	7

	PCT	G	PO	A	E	DP
Dominguez	.959	17	25	45	3	9
Jackson	.978	9	19	25	1	3
Nolan	.987	20	23	53	1	8
Schimpf	.960	83	141	247	16	52

Third Base	PCT	G	PO	A	E	DP
Ahrens	.932	61	29	108	10	9
Del Campo	1.000	2	1	6	0	0
Dominguez	.875	9	1	6	1	0
Jackson	.833	3	1	4	1	0
Nolan	.800	6	3	5	2	0
Ochinko	.926	22	14	49	5	8
Schwartz	1.000	6	4	8	0	1
Sobolewski	.916	39	28	70	9	4

Shortstop	PCT	G	PO	A	E	DP
Dominguez	.938	7	7	23	2	3
Goins	.964	71	104	216	12	43

	PCT	G	PO	A	E	DP
Jackson	.927	44	71	131	16	27
Nolan	.917	20	34	54	8	11

Outfield	PCT	G	PO	A	E	DP
Brisker	1.000	6	8	0	0	0
Crouse	.955	27	60	4	3	1
Eiland	.961	93	166	6	7	2
Glenn	.993	81	130	7	1	0
Hopkins	1.000	40	72	2	0	1
Jackson	1.000	1	1	0	0	0
Marisnick	.963	33	100	4	4	1
McElroy	.989	45	83	3	1	1
Nolan	1.000	4	4	0	0	0
Wilson	.991	93	203	7	2	2

AUBURN DOUBLEDAYS

NEW YORK-PENN LEAGUE

SHORT-SEASON

Batting	B-T	HT	WT	DOB	AVG	vLH	vRH	G	AB	R	H	2B	3B	HR	RBI	BB	HBP	SH	SF	SO	SB	CS	SLG	OBP
Aponte, Yeico	L-L	6-2	190	12-17-88	.250	.316	.240	52	144	12	36	4	3	0	11	14	2	1	0	45	8	1	.319	.325
Bowen, Joe	B-R	6-1	190	9-25-87	.176	.176	.176	21	51	2	9	3	0	1	5	5	0	0	1	13	0	0	.294	.246
Brisker, Markus	R-R	6-3	210	8-21-90	.184	.193	.180	56	185	26	34	9	1	1	17	17	3	2	0	66	7	2	.259	.263
Dominguez, Oliver	B-R	5-9	156	4-23-89	.241	.259	.234	57	199	39	48	12	1	3	21	32	2	5	1	48	14	2	.357	.350
Durham, Lance	L-R	5-11	210	2-20-88	.256	.195	.272	62	203	34	52	14	1	9	35	35	2	0	0	72	1	1	.468	.371
Fermin, Andy	L-R	6-0	180	7-27-89	.273	.158	.290	45	150	13	41	9	0	1	20	15	2	1	1	28	0	0	.353	.345
Fernandez, Jonathan	B-R	6-0	175	9-17-87	.189	.143	.205	25	53	8	10	3	0	0	3	3	0	2	0	20	0	1	.245	.232
Hernandez, Yudelmis	R-R	6-4	205	5-18-87	.186	.154	.205	22	70	10	13	2	0	6	14	5	2	0	0	34	1	0	.471	.260
Hurtado, Luis	R-R	5-11	175	11-4-88	.125	.000	.125	5	8	2	1	0	0	0	1	0	0	0	0	2	0	1	.125	.222
Johnson, Matt	R-R	6-3	210	5-26-88	.205	.250	.190	29	78	11	16	1	1	1	7	8	2	2	0	23	4	1	.282	.295
Jones, Jonathan	R-R	6-0	190	8-2-89	.237	.259	.229	52	194	35	46	9	2	0	16	29	9	3	0	25	10	4	.304	.362
Knecht, Marcus	R-R	6-1	200	6-21-90	.268	.278	.266	61	231	32	62	18	3	5	34	26	1	0	0	48	7	1	.437	.345
McQuail, Steve	R-R	6-2	225	6-10-89	.272	.273	.272	50	147	19	40	7	1	6	26	15	2	0	3	38	1	0	.456	.341
Murphy, Jack	B-R	6-4	235	4-6-88	.224	.200	.233	35	116	8	26	9	0	3	12	8	1	0	0	29	0	0	.379	.280
Nuzzo, Matt	R-R	6-0	205	3-18-87	.250	.295	.219	39	108	23	27	2	4	1	14	13	2	1	1	35	2	0	.370	.339
Perez, Carlos	R-R	6-0	193	10-27-90	.298	.259	.309	66	235	44	70	11	8	2	41	34	6	0	3	41	7	3	.438	.396
Pierre, Gustavo	R-R	6-2	183	12-28-91	.236	.172	.258	66	250	29	59	12	3	3	22	17	1	3	4	64	8	4	.344	.283
Roberts, Johnny	L-L	6-1	215	7-24-86	.250	.154	.277	19	60	9	15	3	2	0	11	5	0	0	1	17	0	0	.367	.303
Schwartz, Randy	R-R	6-4	235	1-25-86	.200	.182	.207	10	40	2	8	4	0	0	2	2	0	0	0	9	0	0	.300	.238

Pitching	B-T	HT	WT	DOB	W	L	ERA	G	GS	CG	SV	IP	H	R	ER	HR	BB	SO	AVG	vLH	vRH	K/9	BB/9
Anderson, Zach	R-R	6-0	195	10-20-86	3	1	3.27	26	0	0	2	33	34	16	12	1	18	27	.272	.213	.308	7.36	4.91
Berl, Brandon	R-R	6-0	185	4-9-88	1	1	4.41	19	0	0	0	35	40	23	17	3	10	34	.284	.269	.297	8.83	2.60
Diaz, Misual	R-R	6-2	180	12-20-89	1	1	2.78	5	5	0	0	23	20	8	7	0	4	23	.227	.139	.288	9.13	1.59
Garrett, Travis	R-R	5-11	205	10-27-89	4	3	4.05	20	0	0	0	27	29	17	12	0	13	31	.279	.327	.133	10.46	4.39
Gracey, Scott	R-R	6-2	190	10-15-86	1	0	0.00	2	0	0	0	5	1	0	0	0	1	6	.059	.143	.000	10.80	1.80
Griffith, Shawn	R-R	5-10	180	5-24-87	2	4	4.91	20	1	0	1	37	25	22	20	4	23	47	.195	.259	.143	11.54	5.65
Hernandez, Jesse	R-R	6-1	200	8-23-88	3	4	3.73	14	11	0	0	51	60	37	21	2	16	60	.287	.383	.209	10.66	2.84
Hernandez, Juan	L-L	6-0	180	10-25-87	2	0	3.22	19	0	0	0	36	37	18	13	3	17	45	.253	.362	.182	11.15	4.21
Hutchison, Drew	L-R	6-2	165	8-22-90	1	1	3.00	10	10	0	0	45	34	18	15	1	12	44	.201	.210	.193	8.80	2.40
Kelly, Michael	L-L	6-5	195	12-4-86	1	2	2.66	17	0	0	1	24	21	14	7	1	3	25	.228	.219	.233	9.51	1.14
Lawrence, Casey	R-R	6-2	170	10-28-87	6	1	1.74	12	10	0	0	57	41	13	11	2	9	48	.202	.261	.153	7.58	1.42
Marze, Dayton	R-R	6-2	185	1-1-89	2	1	2.73	21	0	0	8	26	25	14	8	0	6	20	.250	.159	.321	6.84	2.05
Mella, Leandro	L-L	6-4	190	5-5-90	0	3	13.50	6	0	0	0	8					5		.294	.250	.308	9.64	15.43
Nolin, Sean	L-L	6-5	235	12-26-89	0	2	6.05	6	6	0	0	19	25	13	13	0	9	22	.313	.273	.328	10.24	4.19
Outman, Zach	R-R	6-4	190	12-29-87	0	1	5.27	23	0	0	0	27	27	22	16	0	27	28	.252	.238	.262	9.22	8.89
Permison, Drew	R-R	5-10	170	2-24-89	1	1	2.31	27	0	0	7	39	23	15	10	0	19	59	.164	.210	.128	13.62	4.38
Powell, Tyler	R-R	6-4	210	2-16-89	2	0	10.13	9	0	0	0	16	23	18	18	3	9	16	.348	.269	.400	9.00	5.06
Sanchez, Aaron	R-R	6-4	190	7-1-92	0	1	4.50	2	2	0	0	6	4	5	3	0	5	9	.182	.000	.286	13.50	7.50

Pitching	B-T	HT	WT	DOB	W	L	ERA	G	GS	CG	SV	IP	H	R	ER	HR	BB	SO	AVG	vLH	vRH	K/9	BB/9
Smith, Egan	L-L	6-5	200	3-16-89	2	0	0.00	2	2	0	0	11	9	3	0	0	2	11	.205	.333	.171	9.00	1.64
Strickland, Sam	L-L	6-5	210	6-9-87	3	6	4.02	14	12	0	0	65	73	40	29	5	22	45	.280	.250	.291	6.23	3.05
Webb, Daniel	R-R	6-3	210	8-18-89	0	6	5.24	13	13	0	0	57	69	43	33	4	26	39	.299	.350	.258	6.19	4.13
Wojciechowski, Asher	R-R	6-4	235	12-21-88	0	0	0.75	3	3	0	0	12	6	1	1	0	4	11	.146	.143	.150	8.25	3.00

Fielding

Catcher	PCT	G	PO	A	E	DP	PB
Bowen	.974	10	35	3	1	1	1
Hurtado	1.000	4	17	1	0	1	0
Murphy	.996	29	251	25	1	3	7
Perez	.987	44	344	45	5	3	13

First Base	PCT	G	PO	A	E	DP
Bowen	.867	3	13	0	2	0
Durham	.979	55	447	30	10	27
Hernandez	.973	19	138	6	4	9
Nuzzo	1.000	3	17	0	0	3
Schwartz	1.000	2	21	2	0	1

Second Base	PCT	G	PO	A	E	DP
Dominguez	.959	55	103	152	11	29
Fermin	1.000	3	3	10	0	3
Fernandez	1.000	17	23	28	0	6
Johnson	.914	8	13	19	3	1
Nuzzo	—	1	0	0	0	0

Third Base	PCT	G	PO	A	E	DP
Dominguez	.500	2	0	1	1	0
Fermin	.935	41	24	77	7	6
Fernandez	1.000	3	1	6	0	0
Johnson	.941	7	4	12	1	2
Nuzzo	.868	29	16	50	10	0

	PCT	G	PO	A	E	DP
Schwartz	.950	8	3	16	1	1
Shortstop						
Dominguez	1.000	1	1	1	0	0
Johnson	.936	14	17	27	3	9
Pierre	.895	66	78	170	29	26
Outfield						
Aponte	.875	40	48	1	7	1
Brisker	.926	55	97	3	8	1
Jones	.971	52	95	6	3	3
Knecht	1.000	41	56	6	0	0
McQuail	.982	41	50	5	1	0
Roberts	.857	15	17	1	3	0

GCL BLUE JAYS   ROOKIE
GULF COAST LEAGUE

Batting	B-T	HT	WT	DOB	AVG	vLH	vRH	G	AB	R	H	2B	3B	HR	RBI	BB	HBP	SH	SF	SO	SB	CS	SLG	OBP
Abraham, Matt	R-R	5-8	165	1-27-87	.193	.154	.200	33	83	9	16	0	0	0	4	6	1	0	0	19	0	1	.193	.256
Arcila, Daniel	R-L	6-1	170	7-4-90	.181	.053	.213	29	94	7	17	2	2	3	9	5	1	2	0	21	1	0	.340	.230
Crouse, Michael	R-R	6-4	215	11-22-90	.333	.333	.333	28	96	17	32	7	3	4	20	9	2	0	0	32	9	6	.594	.402
Falcon, Manuel	R-R	5-11	165	1-31-90	.077	.000	.100	9	13	0	1	0	0	0	0	0	0	0	0	6	0	0	.077	.077
Fermin, Andy	L-R	6-0	180	7-27-89	.462	.333	.529	7	26	4	12	3	0	0	5	4	1	0	0	2	0	0	.577	.548
Frias, Christian	R-R	5-10	170	7-19-89	.000	.000	.000	3	3	1	0	0	0	0	0	1	0	0	1	0	0	0	.000	.000
Garcia, Melvin	R-R	6-0	170	9-17-91	.209	.154	.233	19	43	5	9	3	1	0	5	5	1	0	0	17	0	1	.326	.306
Gomez, Angel	B-R	6-2	180	1-12-92	.074	.000	.100	15	27	1	2	0	0	0	1	1	2	0	0	7	0	1	.074	.167
Hawkins, Christopher	L-R	6-2	195	8-17-91	.255	.250	.256	46	157	29	40	9	3	0	15	15	1	1	0	37	8	3	.350	.324
Hobson, K.C.	L-L	6-2	205	8-22-90	.279	.200	.303	35	129	17	36	5	0	4	17	7	0	0	0	17	1	5	.411	.316
Jones, Jonathan	R-R	6-0	190	8-2-89	.000	.000	.000	4	6	0	0	0	0	0	0	2	1	0	0	6	0	0	.000	.143
Lassley, Cody	R-R	5-11	205	5-17-87	.192	.333	.174	9	26	2	5	1	1	0	2	0	2	0	0	8	0	0	.308	.250
Maines, Garrett	R-R	5-11	195	2-7-87	.167	.111	.185	15	36	2	6	2	0	0	1	3	1	1	0	13	0	0	.222	.225
Marisnick, Jake	R-R	6-4	200	3-30-91	.287	.306	.279	35	122	17	35	12	0	3	14	13	5	0	2	18	14	1	.459	.373
Melendez, Ronnie	R-R	5-10	170	9-29-89	.259	.250	.261	36	112	18	29	8	3	0	5	11	2	6	1	23	11	5	.384	.333
Mims, Brandon	B-R	5-11	180	6-18-92	.500	1.000	.000	1	2	0	1	0	0	0	0	0	0	0	0	1	0	0	.500	.500
Namba, Bryson	R-R	6-2	210	1-31-91	.205	.080	.239	35	117	9	24	5	2	4	15	5	1	0	1	53	0	1	.385	.242
Opitz, Shane	L-R	6-1	180	1-10-92	.303	.222	.333	10	33	3	10	3	1	0	3	2	1	0	0	5	1	0	.455	.361
Pena, Gary	R-R	5-11	178	3-10-92	.204	.154	.222	44	147	12	30	4	0	2	15	6	3	0	0	40	1	1	.272	.245
Pompey, Dalton	B-R	6-1	170	12-11-92	.191	.125	.205	11	47	4	9	0	0	2	5	3	1	0	0	10	4	1	.319	.255
Ramirez, Carlos	R-R	6-3	172	4-24-91	.205	.241	.197	47	151	14	31	4	1	2	12	16	5	0	1	48	2	1	.285	.301
Rankin, Pierce	R-R	6-0	190	4-26-89	.265	.273	.262	41	136	17	36	11	4	2	22	15	7	1	1	33	2	1	.449	.365
Sierra, Moises	R-R	6-0	225	9-24-88	.265	.000	.321	10	34	4	9	2	0	1	3	4	0	0	0	8	0	0	.412	.342
Snider, Travis	L-L	6-0	235	2-2-88	.286	.000	.333	4	14	2	4	0	0	0	1	0	0	0	1	1	1	1	.286	.267
Suero, Edward	R-R	6-2	200	9-30-89	.400	.000	.500	3	5	1	2	1	0	0	1	2	0	0	0	0	0	0	.600	.571
Sweeney, Kellen	L-R	6-0	180	9-14-91	.267	.000	.324	16	45	7	12	3	1	1	7	15	0	1	0	12	0	1	.444	.450
Valdez, Jonnathan	L-R	6-3	230	9-5-90	.150	.167	.147	17	40	4	6	1	0	0	2	8	0	0	0	13	0	0	.175	.292

Pitching	B-T	HT	WT	DOB	W	L	ERA	G	GS	CG	SV	IP	H	R	ER	HR	BB	SO	AVG	vLH	vRH	K/9	BB/9
Barnes, Dan	L-R	6-1	195	10-21-89	1	1	0.67	14	0	0	1	27	17	2	2	1	5	37	.173	.175	.172	12.33	1.67
Bell, Bobby	B-R	6-4	200	8-26-85	0	0	0.00	2	0	0	0	5	1	0	0	0	4	.167	.143	.182	7.20	1.80
Berl, Brandon	R-R	6-0	185	4-9-88	0	0	0.00	3	0	0	0	3	2	0	0	0	0	3	.200	.500	.125	9.00	0.00
Diaz, Misual	R-R	6-2	180	12-20-89	0	4	2.52	8	8	0	0	36	27	11	10	0	7	33	.208	.174	.226	8.33	1.77
Elliott, Drew	L-R	6-3	215	8-2-88	0	0	3.24	14	0	0	1	17	16	6	6	4	8	22	.258	.150	.310	11.88	4.32
Enourato, Chris	R-R	6-1	210	12-7-87	2	0	6.50	13	0	0	0	18	23	13	13	2	7	17	.307	.409	.264	8.50	3.50
Escalante, Alesone	B-R	6-4	180	8-29-88	6	1	1.77	20	0	0	1	36	26	13	7	2	14	27	.203	.190	.209	6.81	3.53
Estrada, Deivy	R-R	5-11	178	8-22-92	4	3	3.02	12	8	0	0	54	55	23	18	4	21	42	.259	.266	.257	7.04	3.52
Hernandez, Jesse	R-R	6-1	200	8-23-88	0	1	27.00	1	0	0	0	1	4	3	3	0	1	1	.571	.000	.667	9.00	3.00
Hill, Shawn	R-R	6-2	225	4-28-81	3	0	0.41	4	4	0	0	22	18	1	1	0	1	21	.214	.308	.172	8.59	0.41
Kelly, Michael	L-R	6-5	195	12-4-86	0	1	2.84	5	0	0	0	6	6	2	2	0	1	6	.250	.333	.222	8.53	1.42
Longpre, Bryan	R-R	6-2	195	7-13-87	1	1	3.10	17	0	0	0	20	21	11	7	2	8	20	.256	.130	.305	8.85	3.54
Mella, Leandro	L-L	6-4	190	5-5-90	0	0	5.87	8	0	0	0	8	7	5	5	0	4	4	.269	.200	.286	4.70	4.70
Morgal, Matt	R-R	6-5	220	9-18-86	3	0	2.35	18	0	0	1	23	16	8	6	1	12	12	.200	.233	.180	5.09	4.70
Nolin, Sean	L-L	6-5	235	12-26-89	0	0	0.00	1	1	0	0	1	0	0	0	0	1	2	.000	.000	.167	18.00	4.50
Pepe, Alex	L-L	6-2	190	4-14-87	1	0	10.50	13	0	0	0	12	14	19	14	1	9	11	.286	.556	.225	8.25	6.75
Powell, Tyler	R-R	6-4	210	2-16-89	3	2	2.86	9	0	0	1	22	20	8	7	0	3	14	.244	.278	.234	5.73	1.23
Purdy, Nick	R-R	6-5	205	10-2-89	3	4	3.76	12	10	0	0	55	48	26	23	6	16	50	.241	.264	.228	8.18	2.62
Sanchez, Aaron	R-R	6-4	190	7-1-92	0	2	1.42	8	8	0	0	19	10	3	3	0	12	28	.271	.269	.273	13.26	5.68
Santana, Kenllie	L-L	6-0	192	7-13-89	0	0	0.00	1	0	0	0	1	0	0	0	0	2	1	.333	.000	.333	13.50	27.00
Santana, Milciades	R-R	6-5	214	1-20-89	1	2	2.70	22	0	0	1	30	19	9	9	0	11	35	.179	.244	.138	10.50	3.30
Syndergaard, Noah	R-R	6-5	200	8-29-92	0	1	2.70	5	5	0	0	43	43	15	13	4	13	46	.229	.125	.250	4.05	2.70
Vargas, Jose	L-L	6-0	166	7-19-90	1	2	4.18	10	10	0	0	47	56	24	22	0	11	27	.301	.275	.331	5.23	2.09

Fielding

Catcher	PCT	G	PO	A	E	DP	PB
Lassley	.988	9	79	2	1	0	2
Maines	1.000	14	81	3	0	0	0
Rankin	.994	41	297	29	2	1	14

First Base	PCT	G	PO	A	E	DP
Charles	.974	23	177	10	5	22
Hawkins	1.000	1	0	0	0	0
Hobson	.979	27	214	17	5	11
Namba	1.000	1	10	1	0	1
Valdez	1.000	11	59	5	0	3

Second Base	PCT	G	PO	A	E	DP
Abraham	.962	27	32	43	3	12
Arcila	.973	26	40	68	3	12

	PCT	G	PO	A	E	DP
Falcon	.818	7	5	4	2	0
Fermin	.958	7	9	14	1	2
Frias	1.000	3	2	4	0	3
Mims	—	1	0	0	0	0

Third Base	PCT	G	PO	A	E	DP
Hawkins	.917	29	21	67	8	3
Namba	.930	18	16	24	3	3
Sweeney	.977	14	16	26	1	3

Shortstop	PCT	G	PO	A	E	DP
Abraham	.909	6	3	17	2	0
Arcila	1.000	2	2	2	0	0
Opitz	1.000	9	13	21	0	6
Pena	.973	44	73	110	5	21

Outfield	PCT	G	PO	A	E	DP
Crouse	.983	27	55	2	1	0
Garcia	.957	16	19	3	1	0
Gomez	1.000	15	10	0	0	0
Hawkins	1.000	8	12	0	0	0
Jones	—	1	0	0	0	0
Marisnick	.987	34	70	4	1	1
Melendez	.964	30	50	3	2	1
Pompey	.889	9	8	0	1	0
Ramirez	.971	44	62	4	2	2
Sierra	.909	8	18	2	2	0
Snider	1.000	3	4	0	0	0
Suero	.667	3	2	0	1	0
Sweeney	—	1	0	0	0	0

DSL BLUE JAYS   ROOKIE

DOMINICAN SUMMER LEAGUE

Batting	B-T	HT	WT	DOB	AVG	vLH	vRH	G	AB	R	H	2B	3B	HR	RBI	BB	HBP	SH	SF	SO	SB	CS	SLG	OBP
Barazarte, Cesar	R-R	6-1	195	4-19-93	.193	.120	.223	54	171	14	33	6	0	1	14	20	4	1	2	33	8	8	.246	.289
Blanco, Alvaro	R-R	5-10	185	4-29-92	.210	.267	.187	40	105	15	22	0	0	1	5	14	4	1	1	26	7	0	.238	.323
De La Cruz, Maydawin	L-L	6-1	200	7-16-93	.092	.125	.082	23	65	2	6	0	0	0	1	6	3	0	0	29	1	0	.092	.203
Delgado, John	L-R	6-4	255	9-10-90	.292	.407	.262	42	130	12	38	8	0	1	17	8	2	0	0	11	1	1	.377	.343
Feliz, Angel	R-R	6-1	200	8-21-91	.180	.182	.179	37	111	8	20	2	1	0	11	16	3	0	3	37	0	3	.216	.293
Ferrini, Leonardo	B-R	5-11	175	4-17-89	.274	.240	.286	36	95	19	26	2	0	0	6	25	0	2	0	29	13	2	.295	.425
Gonzalez, Gonzalo	R-R	5-9	190	7-10-89	.241	.304	.212	48	145	15	35	5	3	0	13	18	2	1	0	18	4	5	.317	.333
Hernandez, Leonardo	R-R	5-10	195	2-22-90	.207	.275	.173	41	121	5	25	5	0	0	14	8	1	0	2	17	0	0	.248	.258
Javier, Sony	R-R	6-0	195	6-15-91	.264	.216	.287	41	159	19	42	10	0	1	13	11	3	0	0	20	1	3	.327	.324
Monge, Manuel	R-R	6-1	200	2-10-90	.226	.250	.217	26	62	5	14	3	0	0	3	0	1	0	0	21	2	0	.274	.238
Natera, Fausto	B-R	6-1	180	8-15-88	.238	.274	.244	59	227	25	54	9	2	0	12	15	7	2	1	37	17	6	.295	.304
Nessy, Santiago	R-R	6-2	230	12-8-92	.248	.138	.277	44	141	15	35	12	0	2	17	14	4	0	3	44	4	0	.376	.327
Perez, Tonguard	R-R	5-9	210	0-0-00	.221	.281	.200	40	122	7	27	4	1	0	12	8	3	1	1	35	0	0	.270	.284
Pumarol, Jonathan	R-R	5-9	194	0-0-00	.132	.091	.148	15	38	2	5	0	0	0	1	6	0	0	0	13	1	1	.132	.250
Quintana, Gabriel	R-R	5-9	155	10-17-92	.207	.276	.172	34	87	8	18	2	0	0	4	2	2	0	0	24	6	2	.230	.258
Rodriguez, Alexys	R-R	5-10	200	11-23-88	.226	.500	.185	12	31	3	7	1	0	0	4	4	1	0	2	6	0	1	.258	.316
Rojas, Angel	R-R	5-11	160	4-7-93	.169	.154	.176	43	130	11	22	3	0	0	3	6	1	2	0	38	7	3	.192	.212
Santiago, Kervin	R-R	5-11	185	4-5-93	.220	.357	.148	16	41	3	9	0	0	1	1	1	1	1	0	10	0	0	.220	.256

Pitching	B-T	HT	WT	DOB	W	L	ERA	G	GS	CG	SV	IP	H	R	ER	HR	BB	SO	AVG	vLH	vRH	K/9	BB/9
Avila, Jose	L-L	6-2	210	9-14-90	0	4	5.26	14	5	0	0	39	41	31	23	0	17	19	.273	.375	.268	4.35	3.89
Calatayud, Edgar	R-R	6-1	185	6-10-92	0	1	0.00	2	2	0	0	6	2	2	0	0	0	4	.095	.200	.063	6.00	0.00
Carmona, Julio	R-R	6-1	205	10-10-90	1	3	3.26	16	14	0	0	58	38	28	21	0	33	67	.189	.213	.179	10.40	5.12
German, Victor	R-R	5-11	220	5-26-89	3	3	1.82	18	0	0	1	59	52	19	12	2	9	35	.227	.270	.206	5.31	1.37
Guerrero, Eyerys	R-R	6-3	208	10-14-92	1	2	3.23	13	9	0	0	39	40	16	14	1	6	11	.267	.194	.289	2.54	1.38
Jerez, Nelson	R-R	6-2	171	3-9-90	0	2	3.60	11	1	0	4	20	20	11	8	0	7	10	.267	.263	.268	4.50	3.15
Lopez, Manuel	R-R	6-2	182	3-2-91	1	4	4.81	17	4	0	1	34	39	28	18	1	16	24	.296	.287	.642	4.28
Mendez, Luis	R-R	6-7	250	10-14-89	2	2	3.06	19	0	0	0	47	39	19	16	0	17	27	.234	.091	.269	5.17	3.26
Ramirez, Alex	R-R	6-2	200	2-11-90	4	5	2.01	17	8	0	0	54	42	17	12	0	14	48	.216	.170	.231	8.05	2.35
Rodriguez, Richard	R-R	6-0	205	8-31-88	3	4	2.25	15	11	2	2	64	57	27	16	0	14	44	.238	.265	.227	6.19	1.97
Romero, Steven	R-R	6-0	190	8-2-90	3	4	4.15	16	0	0	1	43	38	22	20	1	15	37	.238	.225	.242	7.68	3.12
Sanchez, Cesar	R-R	6-2	210	8-29-91	2	5	3.69	14	7	0	0	54	42	28	22	0	20	35	.219	.157	.241	5.87	3.35
Zerpa, Luis	R-R	6-1	190	9-28-92	3	1	3.60	16	4	0	0	50	49	23	20	2	10	41	.255	.240	.261	7.38	1.80

Fielding

Catcher	PCT	G	PO	A	E	DP	PB
Hernandez	.959	14	63	8	3	1	2
Nessy	.987	31	196	29	3	1	10
Perez	.974	18	97	16	3	1	3
Pumarol	.900	3	7	2	1	0	1
Rodriguez	1.000	6	30	4	0	1	0
Santiago	1.000	4	24	4	0	0	4

First Base	PCT	G	PO	A	E	DP
Delgado	.994	41	340	12	2	23
Gonzalez	1.000	8	71	3	0	4
Hernandez	.996	30	215	12	1	21
Rodriguez	.933	1	12	2	1	1

	PCT	G	PO	A	E	DP
Rojas	1.000	1	1	0	0	0
Santiago	1.000	1	0	1	0	0

Second Base	PCT	G	PO	A	E	DP
Blanco	.968	33	80	71	5	19
Ferrini	.973	25	32	76	3	9
Natera	.960	14	34	38	3	7
Quintana	1.000	1	1	0	0	0
Rojas	1.000	1	1	1	0	1

Third Base	PCT	G	PO	A	E	DP
Ferrini	.750	6	4	5	3	0
Gonzalez	.947	20	23	48	4	5
Natera	.927	46	51	115	13	10

Shortstop	PCT	G	PO	A	E	DP
Ferrini	1.000	1	1	8	0	3
Quintana	.896	28	31	90	14	10
Rojas	.957	39	45	133	8	12

Outfield	PCT	G	PO	A	E	DP
Barazarte	.957	52	84	5	4	2
De La Cruz	1.000	16	24	1	0	0
Feliz	.960	34	45	3	2	1
Gonzalez	.927	26	47	4	4	0
Gonzalez	1.000	17	22	3	0	1
Javier	1.000	41	73	5	0	2
Monge	.957	23	21	1	1	0

Washington Nationals

SEASON IN A SENTENCE: The Nationals had an older roster and posted a winning record in April, but had a losing record every other month and finished 69-93—still their best record since 2007.

HIGH POINT: For both the season and the history of the franchise, it's June 8, when righthander Stephen Strasburg made one of baseball's great debuts. He struck out 14, walked none and yielded two runs on four hits en route to a 5-2 Nats victory. The 2009 No. 1 overall pick tore up the minors in a fast rise to Washington, and a capacity crowd of 40,315 was on hand at Nationals Park for his debut, not to mention hordes of national media.

LOW POINT: Strasburg spent time on the disabled list in July and August, and then grimaced after throwing a changeup in the fifth inning of an Aug. 21 game against the Phillies. He had Tommy John surgery in September, likely sidelining him for all of 2011.

NOTABLE ROOKIES: Strasburg went 5-3, 2.91 with 92 strikeouts in 68 innings, and set a major league record with 41 strikeouts in his first four starts. Fellow 2009 first-rounder Drew Storen took over as closer after Matt Capps was traded to the Twins and went 4-4, 3.58 with five saves. Shortstop Ian Desmond batted .269/.308/.392 with 17 stolen bases and led NL shortstops in both putouts (221) and errors (34). Outfielder Roger Bernadina became a regular, spending most of his time in right and hitting .246/.307/.384 with 11 homers and 16 stolen bases.

KEY TRANSACTIONS: The Nats signed Capps as a free agent, got 26 saves out of him, then traded him to the Twins for catcher-of-the-future Wilson Ramos. But the most important transaction once again came in August as the Nats signed No. 1 overall pick Bryce Harper, giving him a $6.25 million bonus as part of a $9.9 million contract. It's the largest guarantee ever given to a position player in the draft.

DOWN ON THE FARM: The minor league affiliates posted a 348-346 record, and high Class A Potomac won the Carolina League title. Double-A Harrisburg had strong pitching, starting with Strasburg and getting a consistent season from lefthander Tommy Milone (12-5, 2.85). They also had shortstop Danny Espinosa for much of the season, and he hit 22 homers en route to the big leagues. First basemen Tyler Moore earned Carolina League player of the year honors and led the organization with 31 homers and 111 RBIs.

OPENING DAY PAYROLL: $61.4 million (23rd)

PLAYERS OF THE YEAR

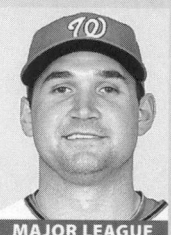

MAJOR LEAGUE	MINOR LEAGUE
Ryan Zimmerman 3b	**Danny Espinosa** ss
.307/.388/.510	(Double-A/Triple-A)
8th in NL in AVG	.268/.337/.464
and OPS (.898)	22 HR, 25 SB

ORGANIZATION LEADERS

BATTING		*Minimum 250 at-bats
MAJORS		
*AVG	Ryan Zimmerman	.307
*OPS	Ryan Zimmerman	.899
HR	Adam Dunn	38
RBI	Adam Dunn	103
MINORS		
*AVG	Justin Bloxom, Hagerstown	.309
*OBP	Derek Norris, Potomac	.419
*SLG	Tyler Moore, Potomac	.552
R	Steve Lombardozzi, Potomac/Harrisburg	90
H	Steve Lombardozzi, Potomac/Harrisburg	160
TB	Tyler Moore, Potomac	277
2B	Tyler Moore, Potomac	43
3B	Steve Lombardozzi, Potomac/Harrisburg	11
HR	Tyler Moore, Potomac	31
RBI	Tyler Moore, Potomac	111
BB	Derek Norris, Potomac	89
SO	Tyler Moore, Potomac	125
SB	Eury Perez, Hagerstown	64

PITCHING		†Minimum 75 innings
MAJORS		
W	Tyler Clippard	11
†ERA	Tyler Clippard	3.07
SO	Livan Hernandez	114
MINORS		
W	Tom Milone, Harrisburg	12
L	Aaron Thompson, Syracuse/Harrisburg	13
†ERA	Daniel Rosenbaum, Hagerstown/Potomac	2.25
G	Cole Kimball, Potomac/Harrisburg	57
GS	Four players tied at	27
SV	Joel Peralta, Syracuse	20
IP	Tom Milone, Harrisburg	158
BB	Shairon Martis, Syracuse	60
SO	Tom Milone, Harrisburg	155
†AVG	Adrian Alaniz, Potomac/Harrisburg	.227

General Manager: Mike Rizzo. **Farm Director:** Doug Harris. **Scouting Director:** Kris Kline.

Class	Team	League	W	L	PCT	Finish*	Manager(s)
Majors	Washington Nationals	National	69	93	.426	14th (16)	Jim Riggleman
Triple-A	Syracuse Chiefs	International	76	67	.531	6th (14)	Trent Jewett
Double-A	Harrisburg Senators	Eastern	77	65	.542	4th (12)	Randy Knorr
High A	Potomac Nationals	Carolina	70	69	.504	†5th (8)	Gary Cathcart
Low A	Hagerstown Suns	South Atlantic	65	75	.464	12th (14)	Matthew LeCroy
Short-season	Vermont Lake Monsters	New York-Penn	36	38	.486	8th (14)	Jeff Garber
Rookie	GCL Nationals	Gulf Coast	24	32	.429	t-12th (15)	Bobby Williams
Overall 2010 Minor League Record			348	346	.501	16th (30)	

*Finish in overall standings (No. of teams in league). †League champion.

ORGANIZATION STATISTICS

WASHINGTON NATIONALS

NATIONAL LEAGUE

Batting	B-T	HT	WT	DOB	AVG	vLH	vRH	G	AB	R	H	2B	3B	HR	RBI	BB	HBP	SH	SF	SO	SB	CS	SLG	OBP
Bernadina, Roger	L-L	6-2	200	6-12-84	.246	.250	.246	134	414	52	102	18	3	11	47	35	4	2	6	93	16	2	.384	.307
Burke, Jamie	R-R	6-0	225	9-74-71	—	.000	.000	1	0	0	0	0	0	0	0	0	0	0	0	0	0	0	—	—
Desmond, Ian	R-R	6-2	210	9-20-85	.269	.300	.257	154	525	59	141	27	4	10	65	28	5	9	7	109	17	5	.392	.308
Dunn, Adam	L-R	6-6	285	11-9-79	.260	.199	.286	158	558	85	145	36	2	38	103	77	9	0	4	199	0	1	.536	.356
Espinosa, Danny	B-R	6-0	190	4-25-87	.214	.200	.218	28	103	16	22	4	1	6	15	9	0	0	0	30	0	2	.447	.277
Gonzalez, Alberto	R-R	5-10	195	4-18-83	.247	.254	.244	114	186	19	46	8	1	0	5	7	1	3	1	30	0	0	.301	.277
Guzman, Cristian	B-R	6-0	210	3-21-78	.282	.330	.257	89	319	44	90	11	4	2	25	17	5	3	2	53	4	2	.361	.327
Harris, Willie	L-R	5-9	190	6-22-78	.183	.222	.180	132	224	25	41	6	2	10	32	33	2	1	2	60	5	2	.362	.291
Kennedy, Adam	L-R	6-1	195	1-10-76	.249	.316	.240	135	342	43	85	16	1	3	31	37	5	1	4	44	14	2	.327	.327
Maldonado, Carlos	R-R	6-2	250	1-3-79	.273	.000	.429	4	11	1	3	0	0	1	3	1	0	0	0	2	0	0	.545	.333
Maxwell, Justin	R-R	6-5	235	11-6-83	.144	.155	.130	67	104	16	15	6	0	3	12	25	0	0	2	43	5	1	.288	.305
Mench, Kevin	R-R	6-0	215	1-7-78	.111	.111	.111	27	27	2	3	0	0	1	2	0	0	0	0	6	0	0	.111	.172
Morgan, Nyjer	L-L	6-0	175	7-2-80	.253	.200	.273	136	509	60	129	17	7	0	24	40	10	15	3	88	34	17	.314	.319
Morse, Mike	R-R	6-5	230	3-22-82	.289	.295	.287	98	266	36	77	12	2	15	41	22	4	0	1	64	0	1	.519	.352
Nieves, Wil	R-R	5-10	180	9-25-77	.203	.212	.200	59	158	10	32	8	0	3	16	8	1	4	1	29	0	0	.310	.244
Ramos, Wilson	R-R	6-0	220	8-10-87	.269	.571	.222	15	52	3	14	4	0	1	4	2	0	0	0	9	0	0	.404	.296
Rodriguez, Ivan	R-R	5-9	205	11-30-71	.266	.292	.258	111	398	32	106	18	1	4	49	16	1	2	4	66	2	3	.347	.294
Taveras, Willy	R-R	6-0	180	12-25-81	.200	.389	.000	27	35	7	7	0	1	0	4	2	0	0	0	6	1	2	.257	.243
Willingham, Josh	R-R	6-2	215	2-17-79	.268	.277	.264	114	370	54	99	19	2	16	56	67	9	0	4	85	8	0	.459	.389
Zimmerman, Ryan	R-R	6-3	230	9-28-84	.307	.331	.300	142	525	85	161	32	0	25	85	69	4	0	5	98	4	1	.510	.388

Pitching	B-T	HT	WT	DOB	W	L	ERA	G	GS	CG	SV	IP	H	R	ER	HR	BB	SO	AVG	vLH	vRH	K/9	BB/9
Atilano, Luis	R-R	6-2	220	5-10-85	6	7	5.15	16	16	0	0	86	96	56	49	11	32	40	.282	.275	.286	4.20	3.36
Balester, Collin	R-R	6-5	200	6-6-86	0	1	2.57	17	0	0	0	21	15	6	6	2	11	28	.203	.257	.154	12.00	4.71
Batista, Miguel	R-R	6-1	210	2-19-71	1	2	3.70	58	1	0	2	83	71	36	34	9	39	55	.234	.243	.229	5.99	4.25
Bergmann, Jason	R-R	6-3	220	9-25-81	0	1	15.43	4	0	0	0	2	3	4	4	2	1	2	.300	.200	.400	7.71	3.86
Bisenius, Joe	R-R	6-4	205	9-18-82	0	0	9.64	5	0	0	0	5	6	5	5	1	6	5	.300	.167	.357	9.64	11.57
Bruney, Brian	R-R	6-3	235	2-17-82	1	2	7.64	19	0	0	0	18	21	18	15	1	20	16	.309	.219	.389	8.15	10.19
Burnett, Sean	L-L	6-1	200	9-17-82	1	7	2.14	73	0	0	3	63	52	17	15	3	20	62	.220	.273	.182	8.86	2.86
Capps, Matt	R-R	6-2	245	9-3-83	3	3	2.74	47	0	0	26	46	51	20	14	5	9	38	.274	.244	.300	7.43	1.76
Chico, Matt	L-L	5-11	220	6-10-83	0	0	3.60	1	1	0	0	5	6	2	2	0	4	2	.286	.500	.263	5.40	0.00
Clippard, Tyler	R-R	6-3	200	2-14-85	11	8	3.07	78	0	0	1	91	69	33	31	8	41	112	.212	.242	.188	11.08	4.05
Detwiler, Ross	R-L	6-5	185	3-6-86	1	3	4.25	8	5	0	0	30	34	22	14	5	14	17	.288	.381	.268	5.16	4.25
English, Jesse	L-L	6-3	220	9-13-84	0	0	3.86	7	0	0	0	7	10	3	3	2	4	4	.323	.188	.467	5.14	2.57
Hernandez, Livan	R-R	6-2	245	2-20-75	10	12	3.66	33	33	2	0	212	216	93	86	16	64	114	.270	.295	.248	4.85	2.72
Lannan, John	L-L	6-4	215	9-27-84	8	8	4.65	25	25	0	0	143	175	82	74	14	49	71	.302	.287	.307	4.46	3.08
Marquis, Jason	L-R	6-1	210	8-21-78	2	9	6.60	13	13	0	0	59	76	47	43	9	24	31	.315	.336	.296	4.76	3.68
Martin, J.D.	R-R	6-4	200	1-2-83	1	5	4.13	9	9	0	0	48	56	30	22	9	11	30	.287	.337	.245	5.81	2.06
Maya, Yunesky	R-R	5-11	170	8-28-81	0	3	5.88	5	5	0	0	26	30	18	17	3	11	12	.294	.333	.250	4.15	3.81
Mock, Garrett	R-R	6-4	230	4-25-83	0	0	5.40	1	1	0	0	3	4	2	2	2	5	3	.286	.000	.400	8.10	13.50
Olsen, Scott	L-L	6-4	210	1-12-84	4	8	5.56	17	15	0	0	81	93	54	50	10	27	53	.289	.289	.289	5.89	3.00
Peralta, Joel	R-R	5-11	195	3-23-76	1	0	2.02	39	0	0	0	49	30	12	11	5	9	49	.170	.212	.145	9.00	1.65
Slaten, Doug	L-L	6-5	215	2-4-80	1	1	3.10	49	0	0	0	41	34	18	14	2	19	36	.225	.151	.295	7.97	4.20
Stammen, Craig	R-R	6-3	200	3-9-84	4	4	5.13	35	19	0	0	128	151	78	73	13	41	85	.297	.291	.301	5.98	2.88
Storen, Drew	B-R	6-2	180	8-11-87	4	4	3.58	54	0	0	5	55	48	24	22	3	22	52	.241	.247	.238	8.46	3.58
Strasburg, Stephen	R-R	6-4	220	7-20-88	5	3	2.91	12	12	0	0	68	56	25	22	5	17	92	.221	.241	.207	12.18	2.25
Walker, Tyler	R-R	6-3	260	5-15-76	1	0	3.57	24	0	0	0	35	35	16	14	5	8	30	.265	.245	.277	7.64	2.04
Zimmermann, Jordan	R-R	6-2	220	5-23-86	1	2	4.94	7	7	0	0	31	31	20	17	8	10	27	.256	.276	.238	7.84	2.90

Fielding

Catcher	PCT	G	PO	A	E	DP	PB
Burke	1.000	1	1	0	0	0	0
Maldonado	1.000	4	10	2	0	0	1
Nieves	.984	51	290	20	5	4	1
Ramos	1.000	15	96	9	0	0	1
Rodriguez	.995	102	709	55	4	5	2

First Base	PCT	G	PO	A	E	DP
Dunn	.990	153	1203	93	13	118
Gonzalez	1.000	3	15	0	0	3

	PCT	G	PO	A	E	DP
Kennedy	.991	51	105	7	1	11
Morse	1.000	19	58	5	0	4
Second Base	**PCT**	**G**	**PO**	**A**	**E**	**DP**
Espinosa	1.000	25	57	74	0	20
Gonzalez	.987	38	35	42	1	16
Guzman	.980	63	122	165	6	29
Kennedy	.980	86	143	207	7	44
Third Base	**PCT**	**G**	**PO**	**A**	**E**	**DP**
Gonzalez	.955	27	16	47	3	3
Harris	.900	6	1	8	1	0

	PCT	G	PO	A	E	DP
Kennedy	.889	8	2	6	1	0
Zimmerman	.951	137	85	242	17	23
Shortstop	**PCT**	**G**	**PO**	**A**	**E**	**DP**
Desmond	.947	149	221	382	34	87
Espinosa	.917	2	2	9	1	1
Gonzalez	.972	16	9	26	1	6
Guzman	.974	20	23	52	2	5
Outfield	**PCT**	**G**	**PO**	**A**	**E**	**DP**
Bernadina	.982	130	207	9	4	4
Desmond	—	1	0	0	0	0

Gonzalez	—	1	0	0	0	0
Guzman	.889	8	8	0	1	0
Harris	.980	80	98	0	2	0
Maxwell	.975	51	73	4	2	1
Mench	—	1	0	0	0	0
Morgan	.986	134	339	2	5	0
Morse	1.000	72	123	2	0	0
Taveras	1.000	22	17	1	0	1
Willingham	.994	108	164	7	1	2

SYRACUSE CHIEFS   TRIPLE-A
INTERNATIONAL LEAGUE

Batting	B-T	HT	WT	DOB	AVG	vLH	vRH	G	AB	R	H	2B	3B	HR	RBI	BB	HBP	SH	SF	SO	SB	CS	SLG	OBP
Bernadina, Roger	L-L	6-2	200	6-12-84	.377	.300	.415	14	61	8	23	2	1	2	6	4	0	1	1	5	7	2	.541	.426
Bixler, Brian	R-R	6-1	195	10-22-82	.340	.296	.355	27	103	12	35	5	2	1	19	9	2	1	1	25	6	3	.456	.400
3-team total (64 Columbus, 11 Indianapolis)					.285	—	—	102	368	45	105	18	4	4	47	30	7	2	4	82	18	7	.389	.347
Botts, Jason	R-R	6-5	250	7-26-80	.279	.319	.265	80	276	34	77	20	0	8	48	30	0	0	4	46	0	1	.438	.345
Bruntlett, Eric	R-R	6-2	200	3-29-78	.210	.196	.216	44	162	26	34	10	1	1	11	21	2	0	2	35	4	2	.302	.308
2-team total (70 Scranton/W-B)					.243	—	—	114	415	61	101	24	1	10	49	37	6	2	2	94	8	2	.378	.313
Burke, Jamie	R-R	6-0	225	9-24-71	.234	.333	.196	47	128	12	30	8	0	1	9	13	3	0	1	25	1	0	.320	.317
Bynum, Seth	R-R	6-0	185	12-19-80	.233	.211	.243	88	305	42	71	20	0	14	52	35	0	0	4	94	13	1	.436	.308
Daniel, Mike	L-R	6-3	180	8-17-84	.000	.000	.000	1	1	0	0	0	0	0	0	0	0	0	0	1	0	0	.000	.000
Davis, Leonard	L-R	5-10	215	12-24-83	.254	.283	.243	96	327	44	83	13	3	15	58	26	5	2	1	85	7	3	.450	.318
Duncan, Chris	L-R	6-5	230	5-5-81	.191	.138	.214	82	262	25	50	8	0	7	27	31	0	0	3	68	4	5	.302	.274
Espinosa, Danny	B-R	6-0	190	4-25-87	.295	.357	.269	24	95	14	28	2	1	4	15	8	1	2	2	22	5	3	.463	.349
Ivany, Devin	R-R	6-2	185	7-27-82	.197	.146	.219	44	137	15	27	7	2	1	13	15	0	1	4	36	5	2	.299	.269
Lambin, Chase	B-R	6-2	195	7-7-79	.252	.278	.240	136	488	53	123	28	3	15	58	45	10	3	2	124	8	3	.414	.327
Lopez, Pedro	R-R	6-1	190	4-28-84	.216	.224	.211	58	148	16	32	10	0	1	11	17	0	3	2	23	5	4	.304	.293
Lowrance, Marvin	L-L	6-0	215	7-16-84	.234	.150	.273	20	64	7	15	1	0	1	2	5	0	0	3	13	1	2	.297	.290
Maldonado, Carlos	R-R	6-2	250	1-3-79	.223	.258	.206	63	188	16	42	8	0	3	27	19	2	3	6	45	2	1	.314	.293
Martinez, Michael	R-R	5-9	145	9-16-82	.325	.324	.326	33	126	16	41	7	0	3	19	3	3	2	1	20	8	3	.452	.353
Maxwell, Justin	R-R	6-5	235	11-6-83	.287	.348	.262	66	230	34	66	17	0	8	35	35	4	0	3	75	16	7	.439	.390
Mench, Kevin	R-R	6-0	215	1-7-78	.249	.241	.252	86	281	27	70	16	0	3	40	35	3	0	7	30	3	1	.338	.331
Morse, Mike	R-R	6-3	230	3-22-82	.255	.250	.256	15	51	12	13	2	0	3	8	8	1	0	0	10	0	0	.471	.347
Ordaz, Luis	R-R	5-11	170	8-12-75	.265	.294	.258	29	83	10	22	4	1	1	12	2	0	2	0	17	4	0	.373	.284
Orr, Pete	L-R	6-1	195	6-8-79	.264	.244	.271	137	489	63	129	32	8	12	45	33	12	2	0	90	25	9	.436	.326
Ramos, Wilson	R-R	6-0	220	8-10-87	.316	.316	.317	20	79	14	25	3	1	3	8	3	0	0	0	12	0	0	.494	.341
2-team total (71 Rochester)					.258	—	—	91	357	39	92	17	1	8	38	15	3	2	0	61	1	2	.378	.293
Rhinehart, Bill	L-L	6-0	202	11-22-84	.222	.000	.286	5	9	4	2	1	0	1	2	4	0	0	0	3	0	0	.667	.462
Rooney, Sean	B-R	5-10	205	4-12-86	.200	.333	.143	4	10	1	2	1	0	0	1	0	0	0	0	2	0	0	.300	.200
Whitesell, Josh	L-L	6-3	220	4-14-82	.304	.295	.309	54	184	23	56	12	1	4	34	30	3	0	2	61	0	0	.446	.406
Whiting, Boomer	R-R	5-10	170	11-5-83	.255	.309	.230	88	310	54	79	12	3	0	16	51	7	7	0	86	36	12	.313	.372

Pitching	B-T	HT	WT	DOB	W	L	ERA	G	GS	CG	SV	IP	H	R	ER	HR	BB	SO	AVG	vLH	vRH	K/9	BB/9
Arnesen, Erik	R-R	6-3	260	3-19-84	6	8	3.95	21	18	1	0	107	107	53	47	12	31	70	.260	.296	.229	5.89	2.61
Atilano, Luis	R-R	6-2	220	5-10-85	2	1	4.72	3	3	0	0	13	17	7	7	1	5	9	.333	.379	.273	6.07	3.38
Balester, Collin	R-R	6-5	200	6-6-86	3	3	5.87	35	5	0	0	69	74	47	45	8	32	52	.276	.286	.268	6.78	4.17
Bergmann, Jason	R-R	6-3	220	9-25-81	6	4	2.84	43	0	0	0	51	42	26	16	6	19	56	.221	.233	.210	9.95	3.38
Bisenius, Joe	R-R	6-4	205	9-18-82	1	0	2.70	14	0	0	0	17	14	6	5	1	6	19	.226	.150	.262	10.80	3.24
Brown, Andrew	R-R	6-6	230	2-17-81	1	0	2.45	4	0	0	0	7	3	3	2	0	3	10	.125	.250	.063	12.27	3.68
Carr, Adam	R-R	6-2	220	4-1-84	0	1	2.08	17	0	0	0	22	16	5	5	1	10	22	.203	.235	.178	7.89	4.15
Chico, Matt	L-L	5-11	220	6-10-83	6	7	3.73	21	21	0	0	116	120	53	48	12	34	69	.268	.268	.269	5.37	2.65
Detwiler, Ross	R-L	6-5	185	3-6-86	1	0	1.80	1	1	0	0	5	5	3	1	0	1	2	.294	.167	.364	3.60	1.80
English, Jesse	L-L	6-3	220	9-13-84	2	1	5.03	16	0	0	0	20	18	11	11	1	10	14	.250	.207	.279	6.41	4.58
Garate, Victor	L-L	6-2	210	9-25-84	1	1	4.91	23	0	1	0	26	20	14	14	4	15	26	.208	.189	.220	11.92	5.26
James, Chuck	L-L	6-0	190	11-9-81	2	1	3.92	5	5	0	0	21	23	11	9	3	4	19	.277	.321	.255	8.27	1.74
Jones, Jason	R-R	6-5	225	11-20-82	1	6	8.81	4	2	0	0	32	42	33	31	9	10	14	.309	.353	.265	3.98	2.84
Kown, Andrew	R-R	6-7	210	10-7-82	2	4	3.48	15	11	0	1	62	67	25	24	5	16	41	.273	.261	.286	5.95	2.32
Leatherman, Dan	R-R	6-2	210	7-12-85	0	0	8.10	5	0	0	0	7	12	6	6	1	3	7	.429	.333	.474	9.45	4.05
MacDougal, Mike	B-R	6-4	190	3-5-77	2	0	3.29	10	0	0	1	14	13	5	5	2	6	9	.265	.158	.333	5.93	3.95
Mandel, Jeff	B-R	6-3	190	4-30-85	5	6	4.75	25	15	0	0	95	120	62	50	8	33	60	.308	.356	.253	5.70	3.14
Marquis, Jason	L-R	6-1	210	8-21-78	0	0	4.09	2	2	0	0	11	6	5	5	2	3	11	.189	.286	.130	9.00	2.45
Martin, J.D.	R-R	6-4	200	1-2-83	2	2	3.51	7	7	0	0	41	40	18	16	3	8	25	.260	.247	.273	5.49	1.76
Martis, Shairon	R-R	6-1	225	3-30-87	8	7	4.09	27	27	2	0	152	156	73	69	14	60	99	.270	.291	.252	5.86	3.55
Maya, Yunesky	R-R	5-11	170	8-28-81	1	1	0.87	2	2	0	0	10	8	2	1	0	5	9	.211	.273	.125	7.84	4.35
Mock, Garrett	R-R	6-4	230	4-25-83	1	1	4.09	2	2	0	0	11	11	5	5	0	3	6	.256	.269	.235	4.91	2.45
Olsen, Scott	L-L	6-4	210	1-12-84	0	0	5.68	1	1	0	0	6	6	4	4	1	1	4	.308	.300	.313	5.68	1.42
Peralta, Joel	R-R	6-0	180	3-23-76	2	0	1.08	28	0	0	20	33	24	5	4	1	7	38	.200	.135	.250	10.26	1.89
Severino, Atahualpa	L-L	5-9	170	11-6-84	6	3	3.34	54	0	0	1	67	60	27	25	5	29	46	.237	.275	.212	6.15	3.88
Slaten, Doug	L-L	6-5	215	2-4-80	0	0	0.00	11	0	0	0	7	12	0	0	0	3	17	.200	.227	.184	9.00	0.53
Spradlin, Jack	R-L	6-2	170	9-23-84	0	0	6.30	8	0	0	0	10	15	7	7	1	7	4	.341	.267	.379	3.60	6.30
Stammen, Craig	R-R	6-3	200	3-9-84	2	0	2.25	3	3	0	0	20	18	5	5	2	3	10	.237	.286	.195	4.50	1.35

Name	B-T	HT	WT	DOB	W	L	ERA	G	GS	CG	SV	IP	H	R	ER	HR	BB	SO	AVG	vLH	vRH	K/9	BB/9
Storen, Drew	B-R	6-2	180	8-11-87	0	0	1.23	6	0	0	0	7	7	1	1	0	2	4	.259	.308	.214	4.91	2.45
Strasburg, Stephen	R-R	6-4	220	7-20-88	4	1	1.08	6	6	0	0	33	18	5	4	1	7	38	.154	.148	.159	10.26	1.89
Thompson, Aaron	L-L	6-2	190	2-28-87	1	0	1.80	1	1	0	0	5	5	1	1	0	3	4	.250	.000	.313	7.20	5.40
Villone, Ron	L-L	6-3	245	1-16-70	2	5	6.59	41	1	0	1	42	50	33	31	7	30	25	.309	.264	.330	5.31	6.38
Walker, Tyler	R-R	6-3	260	5-15-76	0	0	16.20	2	0	0	0	2	2	3	3	2	2	1	.286	.333	.250	5.40	10.80
Wilkie, Josh	R-R	6-2	190	7-22-84	4	4	2.45	53	1	0	8	70	57	22	19	2	22	62	.228	.225	.230	8.01	2.84
Zimmermann, Jordan	R-R	6-2	220	5-23-86	1	0	0.53	4	4	0	0	17	8	1	1	0	3	12	.140	.129	.154	6.35	1.59
Zinicola, Zech	R-R	6-1	220	3-2-85	0	0	4.30	11	0	0	1	15	15	7	7	0	5	11	.273	.158	.333	6.75	3.07

Fielding

Catcher	PCT	G	PO	A	E	DP	PB
Burke	.991	35	208	11	2	1	5
Ivany	.992	40	243	14	2	0	3
Maldonado	1.000	54	370	28	0	4	1
Ramos	1.000	18	122	12	0	1	2
Rooney	1.000	2	17	0	0	0	1

First Base	PCT	G	PO	A	E	DP
Botts	.983	46	378	33	7	27
Bruntlett	1.000	2	1	0	0	0
Duncan	.988	37	291	26	4	42
Lambin	.989	19	166	9	2	14
Morse	1.000	6	59	5	0	6
Rhinehart	1.000	4	24	0	0	1
Whitesell	.991	42	320	25	3	28

Second Base	PCT	G	PO	A	E	DP
Bixler	1.000	1	1	3	0	0
Bruntlett	.951	14	28	30	3	8
Bynum	.983	53	92	140	4	31
Davis	1.000	8	18	18	0	5
Espinosa	1.000	7	18	21	0	5
Lambin	.987	48	92	143	3	29

	PCT	G	PO	A	E	DP
Lopez	1.000	7	9	3	0	1
Martinez	1.000	1	3	3	0	1
Ordaz	1.000	10	17	24	0	7
Orr	.968	14	20	41	2	3

Third Base	PCT	G	PO	A	E	DP
Bixler	.962	9	6	19	1	3
Bruntlett	.958	10	5	18	1	4
Bynum	.971	19	11	56	2	3
Davis	.893	13	8	17	3	3
Lambin	.910	51	30	91	12	3
Lopez	1.000	4	1	7	0	0
Martinez	—	1	0	0	0	0
Morse	1.000	3	1	2	0	1
Ordaz	.957	10	6	16	1	1
Orr	.971	39	29	72	3	5

Shortstop	PCT	G	PO	A	E	DP
Bixler	.933	7	15	13	2	4
Bruntlett	1.000	15	18	37	0	7
Bynum	.926	16	19	31	4	9
Espinosa	.965	17	16	39	2	4
Lopez	.955	43	53	117	8	27

	PCT	G	PO	A	E	DP
Martinez	.948	11	13	42	3	7
Orr	.968	39	45	104	5	23

Outfield	PCT	G	PO	A	E	DP
Bernadina	1.000	14	40	1	0	0
Bixler	1.000	9	16	2	0	0
Botts	.952	15	20	0	1	0
Bruntlett	.952	8	20	0	1	0
Daniel	—	1	0	0	0	0
Davis	.993	76	137	7	1	1
Duncan	1.000	28	54	2	0	0
Lambin	1.000	10	15	0	0	0
Lowrance	1.000	15	19	0	0	0
Martinez	.973	19	36	0	1	0
Maxwell	.966	64	164	5	6	1
Mench	.992	69	116	5	1	0
Morse	1.000	5	8	0	0	0
Orr	1.000	47	106	3	0	1
Rhinehart	1.000	1	1	0	0	0
Whiting	1.000	88	149	1	0	0

HARRISBURG SENATORS

EASTERN LEAGUE

DOUBLE-A

Batting	B-T	HT	WT	DOB	AVG	vLH	vRH	G	AB	R	H	2B	3B	HR	RBI	BB	HBP	SH	SF	SO	SB	CS	SLG	OBP
Baez, Edgardo	R-R	6-2	190	7-12-85	.259	.333	.229	82	270	26	70	12	1	3	28	27	2	0	1	73	7	3	.344	.330
Burgess, Michael	L-L	5-11	195	10-20-88	.284	.200	.305	21	74	11	21	5	2	6	15	10	3	0	0	27	0	0	.649	.391
Castro, Ofilio	R-R	6-0	160	8-18-83	.209	.183	.221	69	196	20	41	5	2	1	16	21	2	2	4	26	1	0	.270	.287
Coon, Brad	L-L	6-0	175	12-11-82	.250	.253	.249	108	368	49	92	12	4	6	37	37	1	5	2	80	10	7	.353	.319
Daniel, Mike	L-R	6-3	180	8-17-84	.182	.000	.213	19	55	4	10	1	1	0	2	4	2	0	0	13	3	1	.236	.262
Davis, Leonard	L-R	5-10	215	12-24-83	.252	.219	.265	33	115	17	29	5	3	5	18	4	0	3	1	27	3	0	.478	.275
Espinosa, Danny	B-R	6-0	190	4-25-87	.262	.293	.251	99	386	66	101	16	4	18	54	33	10	3	2	94	20	8	.464	.334
Fox, Adam	R-R	5-11	200	11-23-81	.160	.059	.212	55	150	18	24	8	1	2	15	15	2	1	3	35	1	1	.267	.241
Ivany, Devin	R-R	6-2	185	7-27-82	.289	.333	.277	28	83	14	24	3	0	4	12	12	2	2	1	27	1	1	.470	.388
Jacobsen, Robby	R-R	6-1	205	8-30-84	—	.000	.000	1	0	0	0	0	0	0	0	0	0	0	0	0	0	0	—	—
Johnson, Josh R.	B-R	5-11	170	1-11-86	.287	.270	.294	74	223	43	64	16	2	5	31	29	3	2	1	37	5	5	.444	.375
Lombardozzi, Steve	B-R	6-0	170	9-20-88	.295	.150	.329	27	105	19	31	5	2	1	12	11	2	1	0	15	4	2	.524	.373
Lopez, Pedro	R-R	6-1	190	4-28-84	.174	.316	.120	24	69	3	12	2	0	0	4	3	0	0	1	13	0	0	.203	.205
Lowrance, Marvin	L-L	6-0	215	7-16-84	.283	.274	.286	87	311	48	88	13	2	13	33	39	5	1	1	62	5	4	.463	.371
Marrero, Chris	R-R	6-3	210	7-2-88	.294	.348	.275	141	524	73	154	28	0	18	82	43	5	0	5	102	1	3	.450	.350
Martinez, Michael	B-R	5-9	145	9-16-82	.253	.230	.261	100	359	41	91	14	6	8	37	20	3	4	1	54	15	9	.393	.298
Nelson, Dan	B-R	5-11	180	2-12-84	.250	.000	.333	5	12	0	3	0	0	0	0	1	0	0	0	3	0	0	.250	.308
Pahuta, Tim	L-R	6-4	225	5-3-81	.212	.167	.221	81	283	35	60	14	1	10	37	16	1	0	3	68	4	0	.375	.254
Rhinehart, Bill	L-L	6-0	202	11-22-84	.196	.240	.179	28	92	6	18	0	2	0	8	10	0	1	1	22	1	1	.348	.227
Rooney, Sean	B-R	5-10	205	4-12-86	.165	.182	.160	31	97	6	16	6	0	0	5	10	0	1	1	17	0	0	.227	.241
Solano, Jhonatan	R-R	6-0	180	8-12-85	.252	.259	.250	90	317	28	80	15	0	4	32	21	3	1	3	28	1	1	.356	.302
Valdez, Jesus	R-R	6-2	170	11-24-83	.273	.319	.258	139	527	61	144	31	4	9	65	28	8	1	5	83	2	2	.398	.317

Pitching	B-T	HT	WT	DOB	W	L	ERA	G	GS	CG	SV	IP	H	R	ER	HR	BB	SO	AVG	vLH	vRH	K/9	BB/9
Alaniz, Adrian	R-R	6-2	200	3-12-84	1	0	1.64	2	2	0	0	11	6	2	2	0	4	7	.158	.263	.053	5.73	3.27
Arnesen, Erik	R-R	6-3	260	3-19-84	2	2	2.81	13	5	0	2	42	36	15	13	2	7	35	.234	.238	.231	7.56	1.51
Bisenius, Joe	R-R	6-4	205	9-18-82	3	0	4.40	14	0	0	0	14	10	7	7	1	8	17	.192	.278	.147	10.67	5.02
Carr, Adam	R-R	6-2	220	4-1-84	5	1	3.04	36	0	0	5	50	43	17	17	2	14	48	.231	.214	.241	8.58	2.50
Chico, Matt	L-L	5-11	220	6-10-83	1	2	3.12	5	5	0	0	26	26	14	9	2	7	17	.257	.235	.262	5.88	2.42
Detwiler, Ross	R-L	6-5	185	3-6-86	2	2	2.48	7	7	0	0	33	38	10	9	1	7	31	.292	.226	.313	8.54	1.93
Dials, Zach	R-R	6-0	200	7-22-85	0	0	6.00	5	0	0	0	6	10	4	4	0	3	7	.370	.400	.353	10.50	4.50
2-team total (5 New Hampshire)					0	0	5.84	10	0	0	0	12	18	8	8	0	8	8	—			5.84	5.84
Garate, Victor	L-L	6-2	210	9-25-84	0	1	0.87	17	0	0	4	21	8	2	2	0	6	25	.116	.087	.130	10.89	2.61
Hernandez, Orlando	R-R	6-2	220	10-11-69	1	1	1.86	6	0	0	0	10	5	2	2	1	5	12	.147	.176	.118	11.17	4.66
James, Chuck	L-L	6-0	190	11-9-81	3	0	1.59	21	2	0	2	45	28	8	8	2	7	50	.181	.219	.154	9.93	1.39
Jones, Jason	R-R	6-5	225	11-20-82	1	2	4.37	6	4	0	0	23	25	13	11	3	6	15	.272	.324	.236	5.96	2.38
Kimball, Cole	R-R	6-3	225	8-1-85	5	1	2.33	38	0	0	12	54	33	21	14	4	31	74	.171	.145	.188	12.33	5.17
Kown, Andrew	L-R	6-7	210	10-7-82	6	4	3.83	15	15	0	0	85	83	40	36	13	19	47	.254	.252	.256	5.00	2.02

Pitching (cont.)	B-T	HT	WT	DOB	W	L	ERA	G	GS	CG	SV	IP	H	R	ER	HR	BB	SO	AVG	vLH	vRH	K/9	BB/9
Lannan, John	L-L	6-4	215	9-27-84	1	4	4.20	7	7	0	0	41	49	25	19	3	10	28	.306	.314	.303	6.20	2.21
Leatherman, Dan	R-R	6-2	210	7-12-85	1	0	5.40	2	0	0	0	3	2	2	2	1	1	5	.200	.167	.250	13.50	2.70
MacDougal, Mike	B-R	6-4	190	3-5-77	2	1	7.36	8	0	0	1	7	11	6	6	0	5	4	.355	.214	.471	4.91	6.14
Mandel, Jeff	B-R	6-3	190	4-30-85	1	4	3.83	7	7	0	0	40	37	21	17	1	13	27	.248	.324	.173	6.08	2.93
Marquis, Jason	L-R	6-1	210	8-21-78	0	0	8.10	1	1	0	0	3	5	3	3	0	1	3	.357	.286	.429	8.10	2.70
Martin, Rafael	R-R	6-2	195	5-16-84	5	4	3.61	47	0	0	0	67	55	31	27	5	26	58	.222	.224	.220	7.75	3.48
Meyers, Brad	R-R	6-6	195	9-13-85	1	0	1.47	6	6	0	0	31	23	7	5	3	7	35	.205	.268	.143	10.27	2.05
Milone, Tom	L-L	6-1	205	2-16-87	12	5	2.85	27	27	2	0	158	161	57	50	10	23	155	.261	.322	.237	8.83	1.31
Mock, Garrett	R-R	6-4	230	4-25-83	0	1	7.20	1	1	0	0	5	6	4	4	1	2	0	.353	.167	.455	0.00	3.60
Novoa, Yunior	L-L	6-4	180	9-11-84	0	5	5.57	23	1	0	1	32	34	20	20	2	17	26	.283	.303	.276	7.24	4.73
Peacock, Brad	R-R	6-1	175	2-2-88	2	2	4.66	7	7	0	0	39	33	21	20	5	22	30	.234	.254	.214	6.98	5.12
Pena, Hassan	R-R	6-2	210	3-25-85	2	2	4.29	48	0	0	1	71	73	39	34	5	30	64	.265	.250	.275	8.07	3.79
Roark, Tanner	R-R	6-2	220	10-5-86	1	1	2.50	6	6	0	0	36	35	13	10	5	9	33	.254	.229	.279	8.25	2.25
Spradlin, Jack	R-L	6-2	170	9-23-84	1	1	4.09	39	1	0	1	51	51	26	23	5	18	49	.264	.163	.336	8.70	3.20
Storen, Drew	B-R	6-2	180	8-11-87	0	0	0.96	7	0	0	4	9	5	1	1	1	1	11	.161	.286	.059	10.61	0.96
Strasburg, Stephen	R-R	6-4	220	7-20-88	3	1	1.64	5	5	0	0	22	13	9	4	0	6	27	.165	.132	.195	11.05	2.45
Tatusko, Ryan	R-R	6-5	200	3-27-85	1	1	1.72	6	0	0	0	37	30	8	7	2	13	36	.222	.208	.241	8.84	3.19
Thompson, Aaron	L-L	6-2	190	2-28-87	4	13	5.80	26	26	0	0	137	164	96	88	16	53	95	.299	.272	.311	6.26	3.49
VanAllen, Cory	L-L	6-3	180	12-24-84	0	1	3.24	8	0	0	0	8	7	3	3	2	4	6	.233	.143	.313	6.48	4.32
Walker, Tyler	R-R	6-3	260	5-15-76	0	0	0.00	1	0	0	0	2	0	0	0	0	0	2	.000	.000	.000	9.00	0.00
Zimmermann, Jordan	R-R	6-2	220	5-23-86	0	0	0.00	1	1	0	0	5	1	0	0	0	2	3	.071	.000	.125	5.79	3.86
Zinicola, Zech	R-R	6-1	220	3-2-85	2	3	2.57	26	0	0	11	28	21	9	8	3	13	26	.206	.243	.185	8.36	4.18

Fielding

Catcher	PCT	G	PO	A	E	DP	PB
Ivany	.987	24	220	12	3	0	5
Rooney	.982	30	195	20	4	2	5
Solano	.993	89	688	61	5	9	4

First Base	PCT	G	PO	A	E	DP
Ivany	1.000	1	6	1	0	1
Marrero	.984	129	1067	62	18	93
Pahuta	.980	12	91	6	2	7
Rhinehart	.980	9	47	2	1	3

Second Base	PCT	G	PO	A	E	DP
Castro	1.000	10	11	19	0	3
Davis	1.000	3	8	2	0	0
Fox	1.000	5	4	2	0	0
Johnson	.977	19	33	51	2	11
Lombardozzi	.971	27	41	59	3	14
Lopez	.943	8	11	22	2	5
Martinez	.964	83	169	211	14	44

Third Base	PCT	G	PO	A	E	DP
Castro	.977	57	30	97	3	6
Davis	.917	5	1	10	1	1
Fox	.867	36	21	64	13	5
Johnson	.950	17	14	24	2	6
Lopez	.750	2	0	3	1	1
Pahuta	.934	50	28	71	7	7

Shortstop	PCT	G	PO	A	E	DP
Espinosa	.964	98	138	269	15	47
Johnson	.985	35	45	89	2	23
Lopez	1.000	12	12	34	0	2
Martinez	1.000	3	7	9	0	1

Outfield	PCT	G	PO	A	E	DP
Baez	.983	76	159	11	3	4
Burgess	1.000	19	20	0	0	0
Coon	.996	107	222	3	1	1
Daniel	1.000	16	25	2	0	1
Davis	.941	25	48	0	3	0
Fox	—	1	0	0	0	0
Lowrance	.978	61	88	1	2	0
Martinez	1.000	17	33	2	0	0
Rhinehart	1.000	18	29	0	0	0
Valdez	.990	118	189	12	2	1

POTOMAC NATIONALS

HIGH CLASS A

CAROLINA LEAGUE

Batting	B-T	HT	WT	DOB	AVG	vLH	vRH	G	AB	R	H	2B	3B	HR	RBI	BB	HBP	SH	SF	SO	SB	CS	SLG	OBP
Arata, Nick	R-R	5-10	175	10-13-86	.133	.400	.000	5	15	0	2	0	0	0	2	1	0	0	0	8	0	0	.133	.188
Baez, Edgardo	R-R	6-2	190	7-12-85	.263	.200	.286	18	57	10	15	4	0	0	6	18	1	0	1	18	1	3	.333	.442
Burgess, Michael	L-L	5-11	195	10-20-88	.262	.281	.252	101	386	57	101	21	4	12	70	47	7	0	2	89	5	2	.430	.351
Curran, Chris	L-R	5-9	170	12-21-87	.226	.038	.249	74	239	31	54	8	4	1	17	17	8	8	3	42	10	8	.305	.296
Guerrero, Michael	R-R	6-0	175	10-16-86	.167	.500	.000	2	6	0	1	0	0	0	0	0	0	0	0	0	0	0	.167	.286
Jacobsen, Robby	R-R	6-1	205	8-30-84	.223	.231	.218	93	332	37	74	13	6	6	37	34	2	3	4	90	9	8	.352	.296
Johnson, Josh R.	B-R	5-11	170	1-11-86	.309	.423	.265	26	94	18	29	8	0	2	11	17	0	0	2	17	3	1	.457	.407
Jones, Marcus	R-R	6-2	190	9-9-86	.000	.000	.000	2	4	0	0	0	0	0	0	0	0	0	0	2	0	0	.000	.000
Lombardozzi, Steve	B-R	6-0	170	9-20-88	.293	.245	.316	110	440	71	129	30	9	1	38	49	6	10	2	60	20	10	.409	.370
Lozada, Jose	B-R	6-0	170	12-29-85	.256	.218	.274	104	344	45	88	18	5	6	34	21	8	4	8	63	1	9	.390	.307
Lyons, Dan	R-R	5-10	185	8-21-84	.221	.139	.260	67	222	40	49	14	1	0	14	6	4	2		57	8	2	.306	.352
Moore, Tyler	R-R	6-2	185	1-30-87	.269	.294	.257	129	502	78	135	43	3	31	111	40	2	2	7	125	0	0	.552	.321
Moresi, Nick	R-R	6-4	180	11-22-84	.236	.238	.235	85	301	25	71	25	2	1	24	15	5	3	1	86	2	3	.342	.283
Morgan, Nyjer	L-L	6-0	175	7-2-80	.000	.000	.000	1	3	0	0	0	0	0	0	0	0	0	0	0	0	0	.000	.000
Nelson, Dan	B-R	5-11	180	2-12-84	.262	.333	.216	17	61	12	16	2	0	2	16	12	2	0	1	13	2	0	.393	.370
2-team total (72 Myrtle Beach)					.278	—	—	89	331	59	92	20	0	11	56	40	3	2	4	55	6	4	.438	.357
Nicol, Sean	R-R	5-10	175	9-25-86	.288	.227	.324	16	59	10	17	2	2	0	9	5	0	0		15	0	0	.390	.344
Norris, Derek	R-R	6-0	210	2-14-89	.235	.253	.227	94	298	67	70	19	0	12	49	89	8	0	4	94	6	3	.419	.419
Ortiz, Wilberto	R-R	5-10	180	1-30-85	.253	.233	.264	47	170	21	43	9	0	2	18	13	0	0	4	40	0	0	.341	.306
Pahuta, Tim	L-R	6-4	225	5-3-83	.283	.211	.308	39	145	19	41	9	3	10	28	10	0	0	0	28	1	2	.593	.329
Peacock, Brian	R-R	6-1	185	8-26-84	.251	.280	.235	60	207	23	52	17	1	2	19	22	1	2	0	62	8	1	.372	.329
Pena, Wilfri	R-R	6-0	180	5-2-87	.095	.000	.118	8	21	3	2	1	0	1	2	2	0	0	0	8	0	0	.286	.174
Plasencia, Francisco	L-L	6-1	192	6-19-84	.114	.154	.097	13	44	5	5	0	0	0	3	8	0	0	1	10	1	0	.114	.245
Rhinehart, Bill	L-L	6-0	202	11-22-84	.254	.197	.271	85	307	37	78	19	2	14	51	33	2	1	3	57	1	2	.466	.328
Rodriguez, Ivan	R-R	5-9	205	11-30-71	.000	.000	.000	1	3	0	0	0	0	0	0	0	0	0	0	1	0	0	.000	.000
Rooney, Sean	B-R	5-10	205	4-12-86	.258	.255	.260	40	155	22	40	13	0	3	22	14	0	1	0	35	1	0	.400	.320
Soriano, Francisco	B-R	5-11	169	6-16-87	.198	.125	.222	29	96	15	19	3	2	1	10	18	0	1	2	24	5	1	.302	.319
Walton, Jamar	R-R	6-4	195	1-5-86	.204	.250	.306	16	53	6	16	3	1	1	11	10	0	1	0	15	0	0	.453	.309
2-team total (59 Wilmington)					.220	—	—	75	268	28	59	8	4	4	35	9	4	1	4	72	4	4	.325	.253
Weeden, Ty	R-R	6-2	220	9-26-87	.500	1.000	.400	2	6	1	3	0	0	0	2	0	0	0	0	3	0	0	.500	.625
Whiting, Boomer	R-R	5-10	170	11-5-83	.225	.258	.200	20	71	12	16	2	0	0	2	13	1	5	2	16	12	5	.254	.345

Pitching

Pitching	B-T	HT	WT	DOB	W	L	ERA	G	GS	CG	SV	IP	H	R	ER	HR	BB	SO	AVG	vLH	vRH	K/9	BB/9
Alaniz, Adrian	R-R	6-2	200	3-12-84	8	4	2.61	24	12	0	1	107	93	38	31	3	26	101	.233	.241	.228	8.50	2.19
Barthmaier, Jimmy	R-R	6-5	205	1-6-84	4	1	3.62	9	5	0	0	32	36	14	13	1	7	26	.295	.282	.301	7.24	1.95
Beno, Marty	R-R	6-0	180	8-24-86	2	3	3.99	16	0	0	2	29	17	14	13	2	11	36	.165	.170	.161	11.05	3.38
Bisenius, Joe	R-R	6-4	205	9-18-82	0	0	1.23	6	0	0	1	7	6	4	1	0	2	9	.207	.375	.143	11.05	2.45
Bronson, Evan	L-L	6-3	195	2-13-87	4	7	3.88	21	16	0	0	95	107	50	41	3	17	59	.284	.232	.301	5.59	1.61
Detwiler, Ross	R-L	6-5	185	3-6-86	0	0	1.50	2	2	0	0	6	6	1	1	0	1	6	.250	.182	.308	9.00	1.50
Dials, Zach	R-R	6-0	200	7-22-85	1	1	3.00	20	0	0	1	30	31	11	10	3	6	34	.263	.286	.253	10.20	1.80
Dill, Clayton	R-L	5-11	190	1-3-86	6	7	4.41	40	0	0	1	51	50	28	25	3	33	48	.263	.298	.252	8.47	5.82
Estrada, Jesse	R-R	6-8	260	10-27-83	3	2	5.11	22	4	0	1	56	73	38	32	8	20	39	.320	.318	.321	6.23	3.20
Fabian, Robinson	R-R	6-3	208	2-10-86	2	1	4.02	8	6	0	0	31	36	15	14	1	14	23	.298	.228	.359	6.61	4.02
Frias, Marcos	R-R	6-2	190	12-19-88	7	5	5.69	20	17	0	0	92	105	63	58	17	35	59	.285	.300	.273	5.79	3.44
Garcia, Luis	R-R	6-2	212	1-30-87	0	0	10.38	6	0	0	0	9	21	17	10	0	10	3	.488	.304	.700	3.12	10.38
Holder, Trevor	R-R	6-2	185	1-8-87	3	3	4.09	15	14	0	0	70	76	40	32	11	22	52	.277	.275	.279	6.65	2.82
Jones, Jason	R-R	6-5	225	11-20-82	0	1	0.00	1	1	0	0	4	7	3	0	0	1	1	.412	.400	.417	2.25	2.25
Kimball, Cole	R-R	6-3	225	8-1-85	3	0	1.82	19	0	0	6	25	17	5	5	0	8	27	.210	.158	.256	9.85	2.92
Leatherman, Dan	R-R	6-2	210	7-12-85	3	2	2.12	31	0	0	11	47	31	14	11	4	12	57	.191	.169	.200	10.99	2.31
Lehman, Pat	R-R	6-3	210	10-18-86	5	4	4.84	21	14	0	0	87	87	52	47	14	28	88	.258	.235	.281	9.07	2.89
Marquis, Jason	L-R	6-1	210	8-21-78	0	0	7.36	1	1	0	0	4	6	3	3	0	1	3	.375	.286	.444	7.36	2.45
Martinez, Carlos	R-R	6-4	180	3-30-84	0	0	2.57	18	1	0	1	35	35	11	10	1	6	14	.267	.352	.208	3.60	1.54
Maya, Yunesky	R-R	5-11	170	8-28-81	0	1	13.50	1	1	0	0	4	7	6	6	1	3	4	.389	.571	.273	9.00	6.75
McCoy, Patrick	L-L	6-4	200	8-3-88	2	1	2.93	30	0	0	6	46	52	20	15	3	12	44	.287	.286	.288	8.61	2.35
Mock, Garrett	R-R	6-4	230	4-25-83	0	1	4.50	2	2	0	0	8	12	4	4	1	0	9	.364	.222	.417	10.13	0.00
Morris, A.J.	R-R	6-2	185	12-1-86	5	3	3.88	23	12	0	2	72	67	43	31	4	27	61	.240	.269	.214	7.63	3.38
Olsen, Scott	L-L	6-4	210	1-12-84	0	0	5.40	1	1	0	0	5	6	4	3	1	0	4	.286	.000	.353	7.20	0.00
Peacock, Brad	R-R	6-1	175	2-2-88	4	9	4.44	19	18	1	0	103	109	59	51	11	25	118	.268	.299	.245	10.28	2.18
Pecina, Ricardo	L-L	5-11	180	7-1-87	0	0	15.43	4	0	0	0	5	8	8	8	0	3	3	.400	.375	.417	5.79	15.43
Phillabaum, Justin	R-R	6-2	180	4-18-86	0	6	6.87	29	0	0	3	37	50	33	28	1	15	28	.327	.431	.275	6.87	3.68
Rosenbaum, Danny	R-L	6-1	210	10-10-87	3	2	2.09	8	7	0	0	43	35	12	10	2	13	31	.230	.280	.220	6.49	2.72
Testa, Joe	L-L	5-10	175	12-18-85	1	1	2.79	11	0	0	0	19	15	6	6	3	8	19	.211	.294	.185	8.84	3.72
VanAllen, Cory	L-L	6-3	180	12-24-84	2	3	4.14	36	0	0	1	41	49	21	19	2	8	48	.302	.292	.311	10.45	1.74
Walker, Tyler	R-R	6-3	260	5-15-76	0	0	40.50	1	1	0	0	1	3	3	0	4	2	1	.333	.500	.000	9.00	27.00	54.00
Wort, Rob	R-R	6-2	170	2-7-89	1	0	1.08	8	0	0	0	8	4	1	1	0	8	11	.148	.143	.150	11.88	8.64
Zimmermann, Jordan	R-R	6-2	220	5-23-86	0	1	0.00	4	4	0	0	13	11	1	0	0	0	13	.244	.250	.240	9.00	0.00

Fielding

Catcher	PCT	G	PO	A	E	DP	PB
Jacobsen	1.000	10	56	9	0	1	1
Norris	.988	69	526	46	7	4	6
Peacock	.994	41	302	38	2	3	4
Pena	1.000	8	49	4	0	1	0
Rodriguez	1.000	1	9	2	0	0	0
Rooney	1.000	19	129	13	0	1	1
Weeden	1.000	2	16	2	0	1	1

First Base	PCT	G	PO	A	E	DP
Jacobsen	1.000	2	10	1	0	1
Lozada	1.000	3	18	3	0	4
Moore	.990	116	965	109	11	98
Pahuta	1.000	4	39	5	0	3
Rhinehart	1.000	17	114	15	0	8

Second Base	PCT	G	PO	A	E	DP
Johnson	—	1	0	0	0	0
Lombardozzi	.989	107	241	282	6	61
Lozada	1.000	1	2	4	0	0

	PCT	G	PO	A	E	DP
Lyons	1.000	5	4	6	0	2
Nicol	1.000	3	5	9	0	5
Ortiz	1.000	1	2	0	0	0
Soriano	.939	21	44	64	7	22

Third Base	PCT	G	PO	A	E	DP
Arata	1.000	2	0	1	0	0
Jacobsen	.892	26	15	43	7	2
Johnson	.964	12	10	17	1	5
Lyons	.956	53	38	113	7	15
Nicol	.947	6	5	13	1	1
Ortiz	.951	25	20	58	4	4
Pahuta	.890	22	18	47	8	4
Peacock	1.000	2	2	2	0	1

Shortstop	PCT	G	PO	A	E	DP
Arata	.875	3	4	10	2	3
Johnson	.966	12	27	30	2	11
Lozada	.934	95	139	243	27	49
Lyons	1.000	1	1	1	0	0

	PCT	G	PO	A	E	DP
Nicol	.968	7	9	21	1	3
Ortiz	.911	19	30	52	8	7
Soriano	.906	7	10	19	3	3

Outfield	PCT	G	PO	A	E	DP
Baez	1.000	18	32	1	0	0
Burgess	.981	100	143	8	3	0
Curran	.981	70	143	10	3	5
Guerrero	.833	2	4	1	1	0
Jacobsen	.988	59	78	3	1	1
Jones	—	1	0	0	0	0
Lozada	—	2	0	0	0	0
Moresi	.978	76	127	7	3	0
Nelson	1.000	3	5	0	0	0
Peacock	1.000	4	6	1	0	0
Plasencia	.957	11	21	1	1	0
Rhinehart	.950	55	89	7	5	0
Walton	.950	15	19	0	1	0
Whiting	1.000	20	37	1	0	0

HAGERSTOWN SUNS
LOW CLASS A

SOUTH ATLANTIC LEAGUE

Batting	B-T	HT	WT	DOB	AVG	vLH	vRH	G	AB	R	H	2B	3B	HR	RBI	BB	HBP	SH	SF	SO	SB	CS	SLG	OBP
Bloxom, Justin	R-B	6-1	205	4-29-88	.309	.306	.310	104	418	66	129	29	4	11	70	27	5	0	4	77	10	5	.476	.355
Cuevas, Justino	R-R	5-10	160	11-30-88	.266	.200	.288	65	203	25	54	13	1	3	26	8	0	2	3	29	6	3	.384	.290
Hague, Rick	R-R	6-2	190	9-18-88	.327	.442	.284	39	159	26	52	12	5	3	27	14	2	0	1	34	3	2	.522	.386
Higley, J.R.	R-R	6-3	210	6-21-88	.233	.048	.274	35	116	22	27	8	0	2	16	13	0	1	3	46	1	3	.353	.303
Hood, Destin	R-R	6-1	225	4-3-90	.285	.266	.291	129	492	56	140	30	3	5	65	33	6	0	6	119	5	7	.388	.333
Jones, Marcus	R-R	6-2	190	9-9-86	.204	.196	.225	56	186	21	38	6	2	4	13	8	2	1	0	71	2	0	.323	.245
King, Stephen	R-R	6-2	195	10-2-87	.184	.143	.200	30	98	11	18	4	0	2	13	15	6	0	0	27	0	2	.286	.328
Kobernus, Jeff	R-R	6-2	210	6-30-88	.279	.282	.278	74	312	40	87	18	0	1	42	17	3	4	7	58	21	10	.346	.316
Leon, Sandy	B-R	5-11	175	3-13-89	.249	.321	.227	98	325	48	81	10	6	2	36	50	0	5	5	79	3	5	.335	.345
Lyons, Dan	R-R	5-10	185	8-21-84	.231	.286	.205	20	65	9	15	2	0	0	8	11	3	0	2	11	2	0	.262	.358
Morgan, Nyjer	L-L	6-0	175	7-2-80	.000	.000	.000	1	3	0	0	0	0	0	0	1	0	0	0	1	0	0	.000	.250
Newsome, Brett	L-L	6-2	210	8-24-86	.273	.308	.264	97	315	43	86	20	4	2	38	43	8	0	0	77	2	4	.381	.374
Nicol, Sean	R-R	5-10	175	9-25-86	.259	.333	.234	26	85	16	22	7	0	0	17	13	0	5	2	15	0	0	.341	.350
Nieto, Adrian	B-R	6-0	200	11-12-89	.195	.225	.187	60	174	23	34	4	0	2	14	23	1	4	1	44	1	0	.253	.291
Oduber, Randolph	R-L	6-3	186	3-18-89	.077	.000	.100	8	26	0	2	1	0	0	1	0	0	0	0	10	0	0	.115	.077

Name	B-T	HT	WT	DOB	AVG	vLH	vRH	G	AB	R	H	2B	3B	HR	RBI	BB	HBP	SH	SF	SO	SB	CS	SLG	OBP
Perez, Eury	R-R	6-0	180	5-30-90	.299	.294	.301	131	438	88	131	17	5	3	42	23	8	21	1	74	64	13	.381	.345
Ramirez, J.P.	L-L	5-10	185	9-29-89	.296	.287	.299	132	506	74	150	32	4	16	75	25	13	0	7	83	3	6	.470	.341
Rogers, Mills	R-R	6-1	195	6-8-88	.286	.389	.237	18	56	10	16	1	1	2	9	5	2	1	0	15	0	1	.446	.365
Sanchez, Adrian	B-R	6-0	160	8-16-90	.317	.333	.313	25	104	15	33	1	0	1	15	0	2	1	0	18	0	2	.356	.330
Soriano, Francisco	B-R	5-11	169	6-16-87	.274	.344	.249	91	361	66	99	19	7	2	38	41	2	5	5	73	20	10	.382	.347
Souza, Steven	R-R	6-3	205	4-24-89	.231	.221	.235	81	303	49	70	16	6	11	56	27	8	1	5	85	18	4	.432	.306
Taveras, Hector	R-R	6-2	192	1-22-89	.667	1.000	.500	1	3	2	2	0	1	0	0	0	0	0	0	0	0	0	1.333	.667
Taylor, Michael	R-R	6-2	190	3-26-91	.231	.400	.125	5	13	0	3	1	0	0	1	1	1	0	0	2	0	0	.308	.333

Pitching	B-T	HT	WT	DOB	W	L	ERA	G	GS	CG	SV	IP	H	R	ER	HR	BB	SO	AVG	vLH	vRH	K/9	BB/9
Applebee, Paul	L-L	6-3	195	5-17-88	6	6	4.10	29	11	0	1	108	119	57	49	12	27	67	.281	.290	.278	5.60	2.26
Arnold, Patrick	B-L	6-1	190	10-31-88	2	3	4.27	26	0	0	1	46	56	28	22	4	16	33	.299	.254	.323	6.41	3.11
Bronson, Evan	L-L	6-3	195	2-13-87	4	2	5.40	8	8	0	0	43	59	32	26	3	6	24	.326	.314	.329	4.98	1.25
Clegg, Mitchell	R-L	6-5	225	12-22-86	9	3	3.48	20	13	0	2	93	95	40	36	6	22	55	.273	.333	.255	5.32	2.13
Demny, Paul	R-R	6-2	200	8-3-89	6	10	4.23	27	27	1	0	130	128	78	61	10	47	106	.253	.256	.252	7.36	3.26
Erb, Shane	R-R	6-5	180	5-3-87	2	2	6.19	39	0	0	1	48	53	41	33	0	37	30	.276	.300	.265	5.63	6.94
Garcia, Luis	R-R	6-2	212	1-30-87	4	4	3.88	26	0	0	0	51	48	25	22	3	17	43	.250	.254	.248	7.59	3.00
Gibson, Glenn	L-L	6-4	195	9-21-87	2	1	8.06	16	0	0	0	26	37	26	23	2	11	28	.339	.444	.319	9.82	3.86
Graham, Ben	R-R	6-4	195	11-23-87	3	1	4.13	17	0	0	0	33	34	18	15	4	5	26	.270	.323	.253	7.16	1.38
Hicks, Graham	L-L	6-5	170	2-9-90	1	6	5.27	15	15	0	0	67	84	42	39	5	25	58	.303	.304	.303	7.83	3.37
Holder, Trevor	R-R	6-2	185	1-8-87	4	3	3.15	12	12	0	0	66	68	30	23	3	7	50	.262	.279	.250	6.85	0.96
Jordan, Taylor	R-R	6-3	190	1-17-89	0	1	13.50	1	0	0	0	3	4	5	5	0	3	5	.308	.250	.333	13.50	8.10
McCatty, Shane	R-R	6-3	205	5-18-87	1	1	3.28	9	2	0	0	25	24	11	9	1	7	22	.250	.313	.219	8.03	2.55
McGeary, Jack	L-L	6-3	195	3-19-89	4	1	4.62	8	8	0	0	39	38	22	20	4	15	32	.252	.042	.291	7.38	3.46
Mock, Garrett	R-R	6-4	230	4-25-83	0	0	0.00	1	1	0	0	3	1	0	0	0	1	3	.100	.200	.000	9.00	3.00
Morrison, Kyle	R-R	6-1	190	12-22-87	3	6	5.30	37	0	0	2	73	86	53	43	7	29	88	.292	.330	.270	10.85	3.58
Olsen, Scott	L-L	6-4	210	1-12-84	0	0	2.25	1	1	0	0	4	2	1	1	0	0	4	.154	.000	.154	9.00	0.00
Ott, Billy	R-R	6-4	200	2-20-88	1	1	6.75	2	2	0	0	8	8	7	6	0	2	5	.258	.267	.250	5.63	2.25
Rosenbaum, Danny	R-L	6-1	210	10-10-87	2	5	2.32	18	18	0	0	101	95	40	26	5	28	84	.253	.390	.227	7.49	2.50
Smoker, Josh	R-L	6-2	195	11-26-88	3	10	6.50	30	19	0	3	91	106	73	66	15	56	92	.300	.333	.290	9.07	5.52
Solis, Sammy	R-L	6-5	230	8-10-88	0	0	0.00	2	2	0	0	4	2	0	0	0	0	3	.143	.000	.182	6.75	0.00
Vasquez, Wanel	R-R	6-3	190	1-15-87	2	4	7.00	38	0	0	3	54	66	48	42	7	25	32	.304	.391	.264	5.33	4.17
Weaver, Dean	R-R	6-4	207	5-17-88	1	3	3.04	42	0	0	16	50	49	22	17	1	18	36	.262	.295	.246	6.44	3.22
Willems, Colton	R-R	6-4	175	7-30-88	0	1	9.49	5	0	0	0	12	18	13	13	2	9	16	.346	.154	.410	11.68	6.57
Wort, Rob	R-R	6-2	170	2-7-89	5	0	2.08	33	0	0	8	43	28	12	10	2	9	53	.185	.203	.174	11.01	1.87
Zimmermann, Jordan	R-R	6-2	220	5-23-86	0	1	10.80	1	1	0	0	5	7	7	6	2	1	3	.292	.200	.357	5.40	1.80

Fielding

Catcher	PCT	G	PO	A	E	DP	PB
Leon	.975	91	634	115	19	17	9
Nieto	.967	50	335	47	13	2	15
Taveras	1.000	1	7	1	0	0	0

First Base	PCT	G	PO	A	E	DP
Bloxom	.992	81	712	41	6	54
Cuevas	1.000	1	2	0	0	0
Newsome	.994	64	481	34	3	39
Nieto	—	1	0	0	0	0
Rogers	1.000	2	19	0	0	1
Taylor	.952	3	18	2	1	3

Second Base	PCT	G	PO	A	E	DP
Cuevas	1.000	3	8	10	0	1
Kobernus	.959	71	141	137	12	31
Lyons	1.000	17	34	45	0	11

	PCT	G	PO	A	E	DP
Rogers	.968	9	13	17	1	4
Sanchez	.940	24	57	68	8	15
Soriano	.911	24	42	50	9	14

Third Base	PCT	G	PO	A	E	DP
Bloxom	.774	13	6	18	7	2
Cuevas	.924	31	33	64	8	8
King	.878	29	12	53	9	4
Rogers	1.000	4	2	9	0	2
Sanchez	1.000	1	1	0	0	0
Souza	.889	75	53	163	27	8

Shortstop	PCT	G	PO	A	E	DP
Cuevas	.932	25	25	57	6	8
Hague	.879	29	35	88	17	16
Nicol	.954	25	49	96	7	19
Soriano	.929	68	109	193	23	37

	PCT	G	PO	A	E	DP
Souza	1.000	2	0	2	0	0

Outfield	PCT	G	PO	A	E	DP
Bloxom	.966	18	27	1	1	0
Cuevas	—	2	0	0	0	0
Higley	1.000	34	73	8	0	1
Hood	.959	124	199	14	9	2
Jones	.948	45	68	5	4	2
Lyons	—	1	0	0	0	0
Morgan	1.000	1	2	0	0	0
Oduber	.917	8	10	1	1	0
Perez	.981	130	298	15	6	4
Ramirez	.922	73	116	3	10	1
Rogers	—	1	0	0	0	0
Souza	—	1	0	0	0	0

VERMONT LAKE MONSTERS   SHORT-SEASON
NEW YORK-PENN LEAGUE

Batting	B-T	HT	WT	DOB	AVG	vLH	vRH	G	AB	R	H	2B	3B	HR	RBI	BB	HBP	SH	SF	SO	SB	CS	SLG	OBP
Freitas, David	R-R	6-2	225	3-18-89	.307	.377	.280	62	218	32	67	19	0	4	40	34	5	1	3	47	2	0	.450	.408
Hughes, Rick	R-R	6-3	225	5-25-90	.000	.000	.000	3	7	1	0	0	0	0	1	4	0	0	0	1	0	0	.000	.364
Jimenez, Hendry	B-R	5-10	160	12-30-89	.218	.140	.248	51	179	20	39	7	2	0	9	16	3	7	1	30	5	4	.279	.291
Jones, Marcus	R-R	6-2	190	9-9-86	.217	.154	.234	16	60	5	13	4	0	2	10	5	1	2	0	20	0	0	.383	.288
Kelso, Blake	R-R	5-10	170	3-28-89	.309	.338	.297	61	236	29	73	10	1	1	21	20	1	14	3	21	10	2	.373	.362
Keyes, Kevin	R-R	6-3	225	3-15-89	.175	.143	.187	39	126	13	22	4	0	3	23	24	5	1	4	36	1	2	.278	.321
King, Stephen	R-R	6-2	195	10-2-87	.242	.294	.230	22	91	15	22	6	0	2	11	9	1	1	1	29	0	0	.374	.314
Labrie, Ronnie	R-R	6-3	205	10-22-86	.260	.348	.221	67	223	33	58	11	5	3	35	44	7	3	3	71	6	3	.395	.394
Leonida, Cole	R-R	6-2	220	12-25-88	.146	.161	.139	31	103	13	15	4	0	0	3	11	2	4	0	34	0	0	.184	.241
Martinson, Jason	R-R	6-1	190	10-15-88	.241	.250	.237	70	253	38	61	8	6	2	36	38	3	11	1	74	4	2	.344	.346
Miller, Justin	R-R	6-0	180	11-28-88	.231	.308	.198	50	130	26	30	8	2	2	18	13	10	2	0	33	2	1	.369	.346
Moldenhauer, Russ	R-R	6-0	200	9-24-87	.262	.306	.255	38	138	30	37	8	0	8	32	22	2	0	0	28	2	0	.500	.377
Moore, Wade	L-R	6-1	215	12-27-87	.287	.269	.293	63	209	36	60	7	3	3	29	37	2	7	3	47	17	2	.392	.394
Mozingo, Chad	L-L	5-11	190	9-3-88	.253	.242	.257	60	229	42	58	7	3	0	17	38	2	5	4	36	7	5	.310	.359
Pena, Wilfri	R-R	6-0	180	5-2-87	.238	.333	.212	16	42	6	10	4	0	1	9	4	0	1	0	14	0	0	.405	.304
Rowe, Connor	R-R	6-0	175	8-16-88	.202	.100	.247	39	129	13	26	5	2	3	16	6	1	4	0	44	1	2	.341	.243
Walker, Jack	R-R	6-3	220	2-12-87	.105	.143	.100	20	57	13	6	0	0	0	5	15	3	0	2	26	1	0	.105	.320

Pitching	B-T	HT	WT	DOB	W	L	ERA	G	GS	CG	SV	IP	H	R	ER	HR	BB	SO	AVG	vLH	vRH	K/9	BB/9
Barrett, Aaron	R-R	6-4	175	1-2-88	0	5	9.43	10	4	0	0	21	26	25	22	3	22	25	.299	.372	.227	10.71	9.43
Bates, Colin	R-R	6-1	175	3-10-88	3	3	5.40	15	5	0	2	48	55	31	29	4	8	45	.293	.309	.286	8.38	1.49
Cahill, Kevin	R-R	6-2	205	10-20-87	0	1	3.54	12	0	0	0	20	19	8	8	0	9	25	.247	.206	.279	11.07	3.98
Cole, A.J.	R-R	6-4	180	1-5-92	0	0	0.00	1	0	0	0	1	1	0	0	0	1	1	.333	.000	.500	9.00	9.00
Crane, Dustin	R-R	6-2	195	8-13-86	2	2	4.60	19	0	0	2	29	23	16	15	3	18	20	.213	.270	.183	6.14	5.52
Demmin, Ryan	L-L	6-1	210	4-5-88	2	1	1.45	14	1	0	2	31	25	6	5	1	10	32	.223	.235	.218	9.29	2.90
Eusebio, Wilson	R-R	6-0	170	8-20-88	2	1	4.26	16	0	0	0	44	44	27	21	4	26	32	.260	.333	.229	6.50	5.28
Garrett, Austin	L-L	6-0	190	3-26-87	0	0	0.00	2	0	0	0	1	1	0	0	0	2	0	.333	.000	.333	0.00	27.00
Gibson, Glenn	L-L	6-4	195	9-21-87	1	1	4.15	8	0	0	0	17	16	13	8	2	4	12	.239	.350	.191	6.23	2.08
Grace, Matt	L-L	6-3	190	12-14-88	0	1	6.75	2	2	0	0	8	8	10	6	1	3	4	.250	.333	.231	4.50	3.38
Graham, Ben	R-R	6-4	195	11-23-87	1	0	0.00	4	0	0	0	8	4	0	0	0	6	6	.154	.125	.167	6.75	4.50
Hansen, Bobby	L-L	6-5	220	12-17-89	3	2	4.79	13	12	0	0	56	72	35	30	5	19	51	.317	.375	.294	8.15	3.04
Herrera, Mark	R-R	6-3	230	3-11-90	2	1	2.88	14	0	0	1	25	20	10	8	0	8	31	.220	.188	.237	11.16	2.88
Hicks, Graham	L-L	6-5	170	2-9-90	1	0	1.80	1	1	0	0	5	3	3	1	1	0	8	.158	.182	.125	14.40	0.00
Holland, Neil	R-R	6-0	190	8-14-88	3	1	2.20	19	0	0	3	33	25	10	8	2	9	37	.212	.286	.171	10.19	2.48
Jenkins, Chad	L-L	6-4	195	3-12-88	2	7	4.67	15	12	0	0	54	40	32	28	3	34	52	.211	.214	.209	8.67	5.67
Jordan, Taylor	R-R	6-3	190	1-17-89	2	3	4.94	13	13	0	0	62	73	40	34	6	17	54	.296	.316	.282	7.84	2.47
Mattheus, Ryan	R-R	6-3	215	11-10-83	1	0	0.00	4	1	0	0	5	3	1	0	0	2	5	.150	.167	.143	8.44	3.38
McCatty, Shane	R-R	6-3	205	5-18-87	2	2	4.30	7	2	0	0	23	20	11	11	1	8	15	.247	.343	.174	5.87	3.13
McKenzie, Chris	R-R	6-3	185	12-6-89	1	2	8.54	8	6	0	0	26	40	29	25	2	12	22	.357	.397	.315	7.52	4.10
Meza, Christian	L-L	6-0	185	8-3-90	1	1	36.00	2	0	0	0	1	3	4	4	0	0	2	.500	.667	.333	18.00	0.00
Ott, Billy	R-R	6-4	200	2-20-88	0	2	3.68	4	3	0	0	15	13	7	6	0	9	15	.241	.263	.229	9.20	5.52
Ray, Robbie	L-L	6-2	170	10-1-91	0	0	0.00	1	0	0	0	1	0	0	0	0	0	0	.000	.000	.000	18.00	0.00
Selik, Cameron	R-R	6-2	245	8-25-87	1	0	2.54	15	0	0	1	28	22	10	8	1	13	32	.210	.273	.146	10.16	4.13
Swynenberg, Matt	R-R	6-5	185	2-16-89	5	2	4.60	14	12	0	0	63	65	33	32	1	17	43	.272	.341	.232	6.18	2.44
Zellers, Shane	R-R	6-3	185	7-14-88	1	0	5.24	17	0	0	0	22	27	14	13	3	11	16	.297	.297	.296	6.45	4.43

Fielding

Catcher	PCT	G	PO	A	E	DP	PB
Freitas	.994	35	295	35	2	4	
Leonida	.988	31	211	29	3	3	
Peña	.989	14	75	15	1	2	3

First Base	PCT	G	PO	A	E	DP
Labrie	.990	67	561	35	6	39
Moldenhauer	1.000	1	6	1	0	0
Walker	.985	6	57	7	1	5

Second Base	PCT	G	PO	A	E	DP
Jimenez	.973	45	98	122	6	25

Kelso	.973	27	48	61	3	9
Miller	.875	2	4	3	1	2

Third Base	PCT	G	PO	A	E	DP
Kelso	.928	30	15	49	5	7
King	.917	17	9	46	5	0
Miller	.848	15	11	28	7	1
Walker	.917	14	11	22	3	1

Shortstop	PCT	G	PO	A	E	DP
Kelso	.846	3	2	9	2	1
King	.926	4	5	20	2	3

Martinson	.944	68	101	188	17	28

Outfield	PCT	G	PO	A	E	DP
Hughes	1.000	3	5	0	0	0
Jones	.947	16	35	1	2	1
Keyes	.895	37	49	2	6	2
Miller	1.000	19	26	1	0	0
Moore	.969	60	115	9	4	3
Mozingo	.975	59	113	4	3	1
Rowe	.955	38	59	5	3	3

GCL NATIONALS
ROOKIE
GULF COAST LEAGUE

Batting	B-T	HT	WT	DOB	AVG	vLH	vRH	G	AB	R	H	2B	3B	HR	RBI	BB	HBP	SH	SF	SO	SB	CS	SLG	OBP
Brannon, Nolan	L-R	6-0	185	7-5-85	.222	.250	.200	4	9	1	2	1	0	0	0	2	0	0	0	2	0	0	.333	.364
Hague, Rick	R-R	6-2	190	9-18-88	.275	.300	.267	10	40	7	11	1	0	0	6	8	0	0	2	9	3	0	.300	.380
Hatcher, Rashad	R-R	6-2	190	6-17-90	.200	.188	.205	32	55	8	11	1	0	0	6	6	3	1	0	20	2	2	.218	.241
Hughes, Rick	R-R	6-3	205	5-25-90	.293	.077	.356	17	58	12	17	4	1	1	8	5	1	1	0	9	0	0	.448	.359
Killian, Dan	L-R	6-4	195	1-14-89	.000	.000	.000	2	6	1	0	0	0	0	0	2	0	0	0	2	0	0	.000	.250
Maldonado, Carlos	R-R	6-2	250	1-3-79	.222	.333	.167	3	9	1	2	0	0	0	2	1	0	0	0	2	0	0	.222	.300
Martinez, Estarlin	R-R	6-1	185	3-8-92	.239	.172	.270	32	92	13	22	8	1	0	14	10	2	0	2	22	1	1	.348	.321
Mayo, Jeremy	R-R	5-10	194	6-17-88	.284	.233	.304	35	109	20	31	10	1	3	19	20	1	2	1	33	1	1	.477	.397
Montilla, Angelberth	R-R	6-1	180	4-11-89	.285	.238	.298	51	193	33	55	10	3	1	24	20	1	5	3	36	17	4	.383	.350
Morales, Jesus	R-R	6-1	165	12-4-90	.167	.000	.200	2	6	0	1	1	0	0	1	0	0	0	0	2	1	0	.333	.167
Nicol, Sean	R-R	5-10	175	9-25-86	.167	.000	.200	5	18	3	3	0	0	0	1	3	1	0	0	1	0	0	.167	.318
Nunez, Wander	R-R	5-11	174	6-27-90	.232	.286	.211	40	125	15	29	3	5	0	13	8	5	0	1	25	6	3	.336	.302
Oduber, Randolph	R-L	6-3	186	3-18-89	.366	.326	.383	39	153	38	56	13	3	4	30	13	6	2	1	38	18	1	.569	.434
Oliver, Tyler	R-R	6-0	230	11-3-88	.204	.240	.193	37	113	13	23	6	0	2	15	15	4	0	1	28	1	0	.310	.316
Perez, Roberto	R-R	6-1	180	4-4-91	.310	.400	.284	36	113	20	35	6	0	2	11	13	3	7	1	19	11	1	.416	.392
Phillips, Derrick	R-R	6-3	220	9-21-90	.280	.400	.240	9	25	2	7	4	0	0	4	2	1	0	0	8	0	1	.440	.357
Ramirez, Andruth	R-R	5-11	180	3-10-89	.197	.231	.189	22	66	8	13	2	0	1	8	1	1	0	0	15	0	1	.273	.293
Ramos, Wander	R-R	6-3	192	4-26-90	.253	.211	.264	25	91	12	23	5	0	0	11	6	1	0	1	24	2	1	.308	.303
Rodriguez, Johan	R-R	6-0	165	11-8-90	.231	.292	.213	32	104	12	24	2	0	0	3	7	1	2	0	12	1	1	.250	.286
Rogers, Mills	R-R	6-1	195	6-8-88	.254	.306	.234	37	130	22	33	8	1	0	22	23	1	0	0	25	3	1	.331	.370
Romero, Alexander	R-R	6-1	180	1-3-90	.000	.000	.000	1	1	0	0	0	0	0	0	0	0	0	0	0	0	0	.000	.000
Rosa, Gianison	L-R	6-0	205	10-15-89	.000	.000	.000	2	5	0	0	0	0	0	0	1	0	1	0	4	0	0	.000	.167
Sanchez, Adrian	B-R	6-0	160	8-16-90	.318	.412	.265	29	119	23	45	10	0	3	21	2	2	3	1	15	4	2	.538	.395
Taveras, Hector	R-R	6-2	192	1-22-89	.291	.317	.279	39	127	14	37	7	0	0	24	8	6	1	3	12	1	1	.346	.354
Taylor, Michael	R-R	6-2	190	3-26-91	.195	.207	.192	38	128	14	25	4	3	1	12	14	1	1	5	31	1	2	.297	.270

Pitching	B-T	HT	WT	DOB	W	L	ERA	G	GS	CG	SV	IP	H	R	ER	HR	BB	SO	AVG	vLH	vRH	K/9	BB/9
Baez, Gregory	L-L	6-3	185	5-5-92	1	2	5.92	11	6	0	0	38	44	27	25	2	23	40	.306	.259	.316	9.47	5.45
Barthmaier, Jimmy	R-R	6-5	205	1-6-84	0	0	3.60	4	2	0	0	10	8	5	4	1	3	6	.211	.500	.194	5.40	2.70
Clegg, Mitchell	R-L	6-2	225	12-22-86	0	1	1.29	4	3	0	0	14	15	6	2	1	3	8	.254	.250	.255	5.14	1.93
Dupuis, Tim	R-R	6-2	220	8-2-88	3	1	4.79	16	0	0	3	21	23	11	11	0	5	21	.288	.348	.263	9.15	2.18

Name	B-T	HT	WT	DOB	W	L	ERA	G	GS	CG	SV	IP	H	R	ER	HR	BB	SO	AVG	vLH	vRH	K/9	BB/9
Encarnacion, Pedro	R-R	6-4	175	6-26-91	0	3	6.48	8	6	0	0	25	28	24	18	3	12	15	.280	.323	.261	5.40	4.32
English, Jesse	L-L	6-3	220	9-13-84	0	0	0.00	3	0	0	0	4	1	1	0	0	0	6	.071	.000	.071	13.50	0.00
Frias, Marcos	R-R	6-2	190	12-19-88	0	1	5.40	1	0	0	0	5	6	3	3	0	0	6	.273	.000	.273	10.80	0.00
Gallo, Mike	R-R	6-3	230	4-28-87	0	2	8.38	12	0	0	0	19	25	23	18	5	11	11	.291	.370	.254	5.12	5.12
Gerler, Zachary	R-R	6-3	190	8-22-87	0	1	6.19	11	0	0	0	16	16	13	11	0	6	11	.258	.300	.238	6.19	3.38
Grace, Matt	L-L	6-3	190	12-14-88	1	1	6.27	8	5	0	0	19	23	17	13	0	3	14	.303	.231	.317	6.75	1.45
Hanks, Tyler	R-R	6-2	186	3-19-90	4	1	3.51	10	4	0	1	33	37	17	13	2	6	25	.285	.375	.244	6.75	1.62
Hernandez, Orlando	R-R	6-2	220	10-11-69	1	0	1.50	5	0	0	0	6	5	2	1	0	0	9	.217	.222	.214	13.50	0.00
King, Brandon	R-R	6-4	235	11-14-90	0	2	10.32	6	4	0	0	11	20	16	13	2	7	12	.364	.438	.333	9.53	5.56
Lehman, Pat	R-R	6-3	210	10-18-86	1	0	1.80	4	1	0	0	10	8	4	2	0	0	10	.200	.167	.206	9.00	0.00
Lopez, Kelvin	R-R	6-1	150	1-22-90	4	4	4.44	11	8	1	0	47	54	31	23	6	12	26	.289	.171	.316	5.01	2.31
Manno, Chris	L-L	6-3	170	11-4-88	1	1	2.50	12	0	1	0	18	12	6	5	0	10	29	.190	.250	.170	14.50	5.00
Marquis, Jason	L-R	6-1	210	8-21-78	0	0	0.00	1	1	0	0	3	2	0	0	0	0	4	.200	.333	.143	12.00	0.00
Martinez, Carlos	R-R	6-4	180	3-30-84	1	0	0.00	1	0	0	0	3	2	0	0	0	0	5	.182	.333	.125	15.00	0.00
Mattheus, Ryan	R-R	6-3	215	11-10-83	0	1	1.50	6	3	0	0	6	5	2	1	0	1	6	.227	.400	.176	9.00	1.50
Maya, Yunesky	R-R	5-11	177	8-28-81	0	0	1.29	2	2	0	0	7	3	2	1	0	2	5	.125	.143	.118	6.43	2.57
Meister, Brandon	R-R	6-0	195	12-31-87	0	0	1.86	8	0	0	0	10	7	2	2	0	0	11	.200	.214	.190	10.24	0.00
Meza, Christian	L-L	6-0	185	8-3-90	1	2	1.52	9	2	0	0	24	16	7	4	1	10	23	.188	.222	.179	8.75	3.80
Morris, A.J.	R-R	6-2	185	12-1-86	0	0	3.21	4	4	0	0	14	9	5	5	1	1	10	.176	.176	.176	6.43	0.64
Mower, Randy	L-L	6-2	190	10-29-87	0	2	7.20	7	0	0	0	10	19	11	8	3	2	7	.404	.556	.368	6.30	1.80
Navarro, Miguel	R-R	6-2	180	3-4-93	1	1	8.10	14	1	0	0	20	19	19	18	0	21	11	.257	.286	.239	4.95	9.45
Olsen, Scott	L-L	6-4	210	1-12-84	0	0	1.80	2	2	0	0	5	3	1	1	0	1	3	.176	.000	.176	5.40	1.80
Ott, Billy	R-R	6-4	200	2-20-88	1	0	1.17	7	0	0	1	23	16	3	3	0	3	19	.203	.200	.203	7.43	1.17
Rivera, Manuel	R-R	6-2	170	7-2-87	2	2	2.61	13	0	0	0	21	15	11	6	0	12	21	.208	.136	.240	9.15	5.23
Santiago, John	R-R	6-0	185	10-10-88	0	2	5.51	15	0	0	1	16	21	16	10	1	8	13	.296	.238	.320	7.16	4.41
Serino, Nick	R-L	5-10	205	10-25-88	2	2	3.16	14	1	0	0	26	21	10	9	2	5	25	.219	.385	.193	8.77	1.75

Fielding

Catcher	PCT	G	PO	A	E	DP	PB
Brannon	1.000	3	28	2	0	0	2
Maldonado	1.000	2	6	1	0	0	0
Martinez	1.000	1	1	0	0	0	0
Mayo	.980	27	177	16	4	2	12
Ramirez	.971	20	118	18	4	0	8
Rosa	.875	1	6	1	1	0	0
Taveras	.978	12	84	7	2	2	2

First Base	PCT	G	PO	A	E	DP
Brannon	—	1	0	0	0	0
Killian	1.000	1	10	0	0	0
Martinez	1.000	4	24	1	0	3
Mayo	1.000	3	27	0	0	2
Oliver	.995	25	204	8	1	14
Ramos	1.000	5	42	2	0	4
Rogers	1.000	26	201	15	0	16

	PCT	G	PO	A	E	DP
Romero	1.000	1	3	0	0	0

Second Base	PCT	G	PO	A	E	DP
Martinez	.917	1	5	6	1	2
Perez	.952	31	58	82	7	19
Rodriguez	.925	11	16	21	3	8
Sanchez	1.000	8	15	21	0	5
Taylor	.878	9	13	23	5	2

Third Base	PCT	G	PO	A	E	DP
Martinez	.806	24	13	41	13	3
Perez	1.000	4	3	7	0	1
Rogers	.921	13	8	27	3	1
Sanchez	.929	14	6	33	3	4
Taylor	.879	9	11	18	4	2

Shortstop	PCT	G	PO	A	E	DP
Hague	.912	9	6	25	3	2
Nicol	.960	5	7	17	1	2

	PCT	G	PO	A	E	DP
Rodriguez	.831	18	21	43	13	8
Rogers	.875	2	1	6	1	2
Sanchez	.844	7	10	17	5	3
Taylor	.876	19	33	59	13	12

Outfield	PCT	G	PO	A	E	DP
Hatcher	.958	20	23	0	1	0
Hughes	1.000	13	22	0	0	0
Montilla	.953	51	75	6	4	2
Morales	1.000	2	1	0	0	0
Nunez	1.000	36	55	5	0	0
Oduber	.986	36	66	2	1	0
Phillips	.818	8	9	0	2	0
Ramos	.958	17	19	4	1	0

DSL NATIONALS ROOKIE

DOMINICAN SUMMER LEAGUE

Batting	B-T	HT	WT	DOB	AVG	vLH	vRH	G	AB	R	H	2B	3B	HR	RBI	BB	HBP	SH	SF	SO	SB	CS	SLG	OBP
Alvarez, Carlos	B-R	5-11	175	11-25-85	.307	.359	.281	55	176	37	54	8	4	2	19	47	8	2	1	26	10	5	.432	.470
Arismendy, jose	L-L	5-11	165	8-12-92	.190	.059	.203	51	137	13	26	3	0	0	12	14	5	0	0	20	0	3	.212	.288
Caseres, Emilio	R-R	6-1	175	7-10-92	.123	.000	.149	26	57	5	7	0	0	0	4	2	1	0	0	15	0	2	.123	.167
Chacin, Paul	R-R	6-0	180	2-27-91	.281	.192	.305	50	146	15	41	4	2	0	20	14	4	1	2	29	2	2	.336	.355
Chavez, Victor	R-R	6-0	196	12-24-90	.309	.321	.306	46	136	27	42	3	1	3	24	16	10	0	0	26	11	3	.412	.420
Difo, Wilmer	R-R	6-0	175	4-2-92	.209	.160	.220	45	148	18	31	2	4	0	11	16	2	2	1	27	12	4	.277	.293
Gonzalez, Edgar	B-R	5-11	160	0-0-00	.253	.233	.248	59	174	35	44	6	1	0	10	39	6	2	2	28	8	11	.299	.403
Mesa, Narciso	R-R	5-11	175	0-0-00	.224	.175	.240	58	196	21	44	8	2	0	15	8	5	3	1	41	12	7	.286	.271
Norberto, Jose	L-R	6-0	160	8-23-90	.182	.333	.125	10	11	4	2	0	0	0	1	6	1	0	1	6	2	3	.182	.474
Ortega, Nelalexfred	R-R	5-11	155	8-1-92	.218	.229	.213	63	229	43	50	3	0	0	18	28	9	5	1	34	29	7	.231	.326
Pena, Bill	R-R	6-0	180	4-14-92	.293	.286	.294	16	41	6	12	0	1	0	2	1	0	0	0	10	3	0	.341	.310
Pena, Jose	R-R	6-2	171	9-17-90	.182	.125	.194	19	44	2	8	1	2	0	6	0	0	1	0	17	0	1	.295	.250
Reyes, Aladin	R-R	6-4	180	8-1-90	.260	.278	.256	33	104	12	27	4	1	0	9	4	1	0	2	30	7	0	.317	.319
Rodriguez, Elvin	R-R	6-0	186	4-17-89	.143	.000	.143	2	7	1	1	0	0	0	0	0	0	0	0	4	0	0	.143	.143
Rodriguez, Kelvin	R-R	6-0	190	11-6-91	.200	.500	.125	9	10	1	2	1	0	0	1	2	1	0	0	5	0	0	.300	.385
Ruiz, Adderling	R-R	6-1	175	5-3-91	.218	.290	.198	49	133	12	29	4	0	1	15	11	3	3	3	32	3	2	.271	.287
Tejeda, Yamaicol	R-R	6-3	190	4-27-89	.042	.000	.057	32	48	5	2	0	0	0	6	0	0	3	1	23	5	0	.042	.148
Urdaneta, Juan	L-L	6-4	185	5-20-89	.205	.000	.258	14	39	4	8	2	0	0	6	1	0	0	0	6	0	0	.256	.326
Valdez, Bienvenido	R-R	6-0	188	11-25-90	.259	.136	.295	62	201	25	52	13	1	4	21	33	5	2	1	40	9	5	.393	.392

Pitching	B-T	HT	WT	DOB	W	L	ERA	G	GS	CG	SV	IP	H	R	ER	HR	BB	SO	AVG	vLH	vRH	K/9	BB/9
Becerra, Yordith	R-R	6-2	175	5-20-91	1	1	8.25	9	1	0	0	12	12	13	11	0	13	11	.293	.000	.400	6.00	9.75
Burgos, Karin	R-R	6-4	195	12-26-90	0	1	3.60	13	0	0	0	15	14	7	6	1	11	10	.250	.450	.139	6.00	6.60
De La Cruz, Jorge	R-R	6-4	205	4-25-89	0	0	9.88	11	0	0	0	14	16	16	15	0	15	7	.314	.316	.313	4.61	9.88
De La Rosa, Yunior	R-R	5-10	182	6-7-89	0	0	9.00	1	0	0	0	3	1	3	3	0	2	4	.100	.250	.000	12.00	6.00

Name	B-T	Ht	Wt	DOB	W	L	ERA	G	GS	CG	SV	IP	H	R	ER	HR	BB	SO	AVG	vLH	vRH	K/9	BB/9
Diaz, Juan	R-R	5-3	197	3-2-91	2	4	5.74	7	6	1	0	27	25	19	17	0	10	28	.243	.200	.260	9.45	3.38
Estevez, Wirkin	R-R	6-1	170	3-15-92	6	7	2.61	15	14	3	0	83	74	41	24	1	12	95	.233	.274	.209	10.34	1.31
Guzman, Antonio	R-R	6-1	145	12-15-87	4	5	3.36	14	13	0	1	83	74	41	31	0	27	81	.239	.270	.221	8.78	2.93
Guzman, Jesus	L-L	6-3	175	1-2-91	1	1	3.43	18	0	0	0	21	18	9	8	0	18	23	.247	.625	.200	9.86	7.71
Heredia, Inocencio	R-R	5-11	172	0-0-00	3	3	1.69	26	0	0	10	37	24	8	7	0	11	34	.190	.191	.190	8.20	2.65
Hernandez, Jorge	R-R	6-0	170	4-27-90	2	1	2.05	13	0	0	4	31	21	8	7	0	9	38	.194	.276	.165	11.15	2.64
Herrera, Saskuel	R-R	6-1	185	11-15-89	1	0	4.32	13	0	0	1	17	19	14	8	0	11	13	.284	.167	.327	7.02	5.94
Lellis, Dennis	R-R	6-2	175	10-17-92	1	0	10.50	9	2	0	0	12	24	20	14	2	12	9	.393	.611	.302	6.75	9.00
Matos, Luis	L-L	6-0	165	12-26-90	0	0	4.50	11	0	0	0	12	12	10	6	0	12	15	.261	.333	.250	11.25	9.00
Medina, Silvio	R-R	6-1	190	6-3-90	5	4	3.06	13	11	2	0	68	68	34	23	3	19	46	.260	.271	.255	6.12	2.53
Mieses, Adalberto	R-R	6-3	190	1-1-90	3	3	2.98	13	12	0	1	63	57	31	21	5	33	40	.243	.286	.222	5.68	4.69
Santana, Andy	R-R	6-2	187	12-5-90	5	0	1.27	13	1	0	0	28	19	4	4	2	14	24	.192	.250	.169	7.62	4.45
Suero, Wander	R-R	6-3	175	9-15-91	2	3	4.72	15	4	0	0	34	35	22	18	2	23	39	.269	.243	.280	10.22	6.03

Fielding

Catcher	PCT	G	PO	A	E	DP	PB
Chacin	.974	21	127	21	4	1	5
Pena	.922	13	60	11	6	2	2
Rodriguez	1.000	2	11	1	0	0	1
Rodriguez	.964	9	23	4	1	1	0
Ruiz	.978	46	298	65	8	3	11
Urdaneta	1.000	1	2	0	0	0	0

First Base	PCT	G	PO	A	E	DP
Alvarez	.992	14	119	8	1	8
Arismendy	.988	11	75	4	1	4
Caseres	1.000	10	49	4	0	5
Chacin	1.000	13	72	7	0	7
Chavez	.800	3	4	0	1	1
Urdaneta	1.000	12	87	5	0	4

	PCT	G	PO	A	E	DP
Valdez	1.000	1	8	1	0	2
Valdez	.978	25	211	8	5	15

Second Base	PCT	G	PO	A	E	DP
Alvarez	1.000	4	9	10	0	1
Caseres	.923	4	7	5	1	0
Difo	1.000	1	0	1	0	0
Ortega	.964	63	126	144	10	29
Valdez	1.000	6	8	1	0	0

Third Base	PCT	G	PO	A	E	DP
Caseres	.880	10	7	15	3	2
Valdez	.893	38	29	71	12	2
Valdez	.876	31	28	57	12	4

Shortstop	PCT	G	PO	A	E	DP
Alvarez	.930	24	29	78	8	8

	PCT	G	PO	A	E	DP
Difo	.911	44	75	130	20	32
Valdez	.853	9	9	20	5	1

Outfield	PCT	G	PO	A	E	DP
Arismendy	.980	41	47	3	1	0
Chavez	.882	22	13	2	2	1
Gonzalez	.977	54	82	2	2	1
Mesa	.961	57	69	4	3	3
Norberto	.933	6	11	3	1	0
Pena	1.000	18	27	4	0	1
Reyes	.949	33	35	2	2	1
Tejeda	.920	30	22	1	2	0
Urdaneta	—	1	0	0	0	0
Valdez	—	1	0	0	0	0

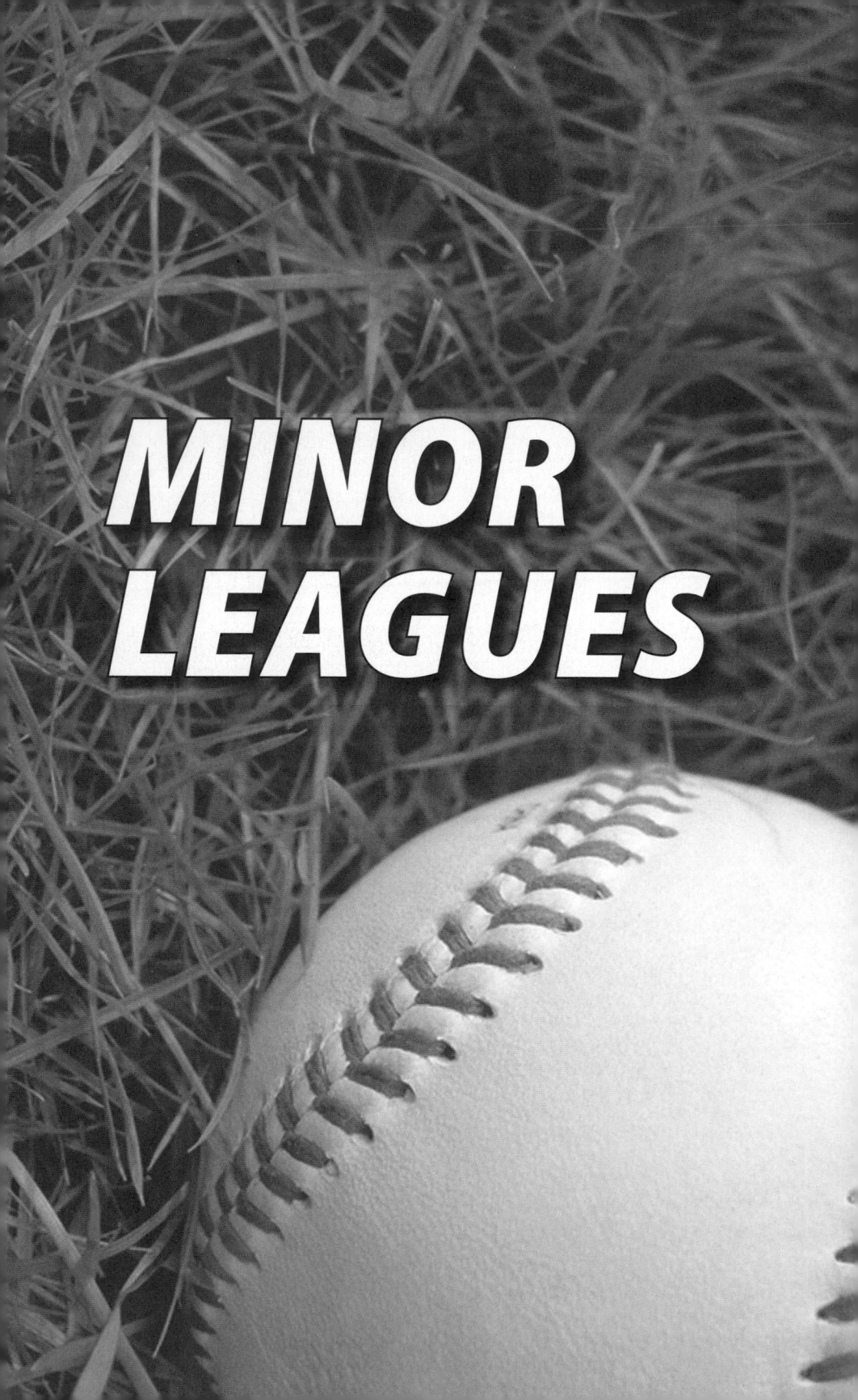

MINOR
LEAGUES

Stephen Strasburg attracted sellout crowds during his 11-game swing through the minors

MIKE JANES

Stars shine in minors before promotions

Some things never change in minor league baseball.

The sport's family-friendly business model proved yet again in 2010 that it can weather a tough economy. As it has in past years, the minors continue to serve as a testing ground for major league baseball—this time in further advances for drug testing. And a pair of pitching phenoms took the minors by storm in 2010 before becoming the talk of major league baseball.

Yet there was plenty of change as well. The sale of the Texas Rangers kicked off a minor league affiliate shuffle that ultimately ended a couple of long-term partnerships. A handful of new ballparks and new teams took the field this season, resulting in significant attendance jumps that helped boost the minors' overall attendance. And the Royals (that's right, those Royals) might very well boast the best farm system in baseball after several players enjoyed breakout seasons.

Since baseball is considered a game of numbers, let's wrap up the 2010 minor league season in by-the-numbers style.

102,713

Total number of fans who turned out to see Nationals phenom Stephen Strasburg's 11 minor league starts (one of which was the first-half of a

double-header and did not have an official gate).

Stephen Strasburg did not give up many hits on the field this year, but he sure was a hit off of it. Strasburg's spring tour of the Double-A Eastern League and Triple-A International League resulted in sellouts nearly everywhere he went. Strasburg's starts set attendance records three times—including when 13,766 filled Syracuse's Alliance Bank Stadium, breaking a record that had stood since 1876.

Strasburg, who finished 7-2, 1.30 with 65 strikeouts in 55 innings, was easily the best pitcher in the minors this season but didn't stick around long enough to be included on a Minor League Top 10 Prospects list. However, Strasburg was not the only pitcher to generate headlines in the minors . . .

105 mph

Top speed reliever Aroldis Chapman's fastball was clocked during his final minor league start for Triple-A Louisville before his promotion to the big leagues.

It's a special moment anytime a pitcher hits triple digits on the radar gun. There are few pitchers in baseball who can run it up to 100 mph. But what Chapman did in a three-up, three-down, three-strikeout inning against Columbus enters into Sidd Finch territory.

Consider this: That kind of velocity almost breaks the 20-80 scouting scale. If grading purely on velocity, many clubs' scouting scales regard a 97 mph fastball as an 80, or the upper end of the scale. Subtract eight miles per hour from that down to 89 and you are looking at a 40-45 on the scouting scale. There's nothing in the scouting scale to account for a pitch 8 mph faster than what's already considered an 80.

53

Number of games Mike Stanton played with Double-A Jacksonville before earning a promotion to the major leagues.

The brief stay didn't keep the 20-year-old from making a mark in the Southern League. Despite not taking a swing in the minors after June 5, Stanton still tied for second in the Southern League at the end of the season with 21 home runs.

Equally impressive was that Stanton tied for first in all of minor league baseball with 10 intentional walks. He shared the lead with Mike Moustakas and Konrad Schmidt—each of whom had at least 200 more at-bats than Stanton.

1995

The year the Rockies drafted John Lindsey in the 13th round out of a Mississippi high school.

The Rockies also drafted another first baseman that year, Todd Helton. Until 2007, the only times the 33-year-old Lindsey had hit .300 were in indy ball and at Triple-A Las Vegas. In 2009, Lindsey hit .251/.331/.433 at Triple-A New Orleans.

In other words, nothing indicated he was set for a year like he had, batting .353/.400/.657 for Triple-A Colorado Springs and earning his first big league promotion. Lindsey wound up ranking second behind 2009 fifth-round pick Brandon Belt for the minor league's top average thanks to an 0-for-3 rehab stint in the Rookie-level Arizona League. Belt, a Giants' first baseman, shot from high Class A to Triple-A in his first full season and hit .352.

1.73

Speaking of unheralded players, that's the overall ERA posted by Braves righthander Brandon Beachy.

A nondrafted free agent out of Indiana Wesleyan in 2008, the 23-year-old Beachy shot from Double-A Mississippi to the big leagues this season. The Braves moved Beachy from the bullpen to the rotation in mid-June, and the 23-year-old went 2-0, 0.72 with 31 strikeouts, five walks and just 13 hits allowed in his first four starts over 25 innings.

1-7, 6.08/5-4, 1.39

The first- and second-half season splits for Rays

Which teams changed affiliations this offseason

PACIFIC COAST LEAGUE		TRIPLE-A
Team	New Affiliate	Old Affiliate
Oklahoma City	Astros	Rangers
Round Rock	Rangers	Astros

CALIFORNIA LEAGUE		HIGH CLASS A
Team	New Affiliate	Old Affiliate
Bakersfield	Reds	Rangers
Inland Empire	Angels	Dodgers
Rancho Cucamonga	Dodgers	Angels

CAROLINA LEAGUE		HIGH CLASS A
Team	New Affiliate	Old Affiliate
Lynchburg	Braves	Reds
Myrtle Beach	Rangers	Braves

MIDWEST LEAGUE		LOW CLASS A
Team	New Affiliate	Old Affiliate
Burlington	Athletics	Royals
Kane County	Royals	Athletics

NEW YORK-PENN LEAGUE		SHORT-SEASON
Team	New Affiliate	Old Affiliate
Auburn	Nationals	Blue Jays
Vermont	Athletics	Nationals

NORTHWEST LEAGUE		SHORT-SEASON
Team	New Affiliate	Old Affiliate
Vancouver	Blue Jays	Athletics

APPALACHIAN LEAGUE		ROOKIE
Team	New Affiliate	Old Affiliate
Bluefield	Blue Jays	Orioles

lefthander Matt Moore.

It was certainly a tale of two seasons at high Class A Charlotte for Moore, who posted double-digit strikeout totals in nine of his final 13 starts en route to topping the minors in strikeouts for a second straight season.

Moore changed his fastball grip (he had been holding the ball too tightly) and altered his windup as midseason approached. The results were remarkable. Moore's walks dipped from 37 in 61 first-half innings to 24 in 84 innings in the second half. Additionally, his strikeouts spiked from 78 to 130.

Moore became the first minor leaguer since Francisco Liriano in 2005 to amass at least 200 strikeouts in a season.

0

The number of games the Lehigh Valley IronPigs have been above .500 in its three-year history.

That's right, Lehigh Valley has never posted a winning record—not even 1-0. However, the Phillies Triple-A affiliate's onfield misery (including a 58-86 mark in 2010) has hardly translated to their off-field success.

The IronPigs—whose many pig-themed mottos includes "Laugh. Cheer. Oink."—were the minors'

MINOR LEAGUES

best draw this season with a 9,227 per-game average. Lehigh Valley has increased its attendance in each of its three seasons, and general manager Kurt Landes was named the International League's executive of the year for a second straight season.

"If our team was competitive in August, it would be such an incredible environment, to be involved in a playoff chase," Landes said.

41,432,456

Overall attendance in minor league baseball.

If flat is indeed the new up, then minor league baseball had another good season.

The days of setting attendance records annually may be gone, but the industry did an admirable job of weathering a difficult economy in 2010. The 15 leagues tracked by Minor League Baseball (which includes the Mexican League) drew 41,452,436 fans this season, a 0.5 percent decrease from last year's total of 41,644,518. "Once again, Minor League Baseball is showing its resiliency in the current economic conditions," Minor League Baseball president Pat O'Conner said.

The minors remain well behind the attendance numbers of their pre-recession glory days. That's when two decades of growth driven by new markets and a ballpark building boom peaked with overall attendance records being established for five consecutive seasons-culminating in 2008 with 43,263,740. But things are at least heading in the right direction. More teams saw an increase at the gate this season than last, with 63 of 160 teams averaging more fans. In 2009, just 58 of 160 teams increased average attendance.

13

Minor league teams that will have a new big league affiliate in 2011.

The minor league landscape typically changes every two years during the affiliation shuffle. It was no different this past offseason, which also included the end of a few long-standing relationships.

The sale of the Texas Rangers to Nolan Ryan and Chuck Greenberg spurred these moves, as the Rangers pulled its Triple-A club out of Oklahoma City (where it has been an affiliate since 1983) to Ryan-owned Round Rock, which had been an Astros affiliate since its inception in 2000.

The Rangers also switched their high Class A affiliate from Bakersfield in the California League across the country to the Greenberg-owned Myrtle Beach, which had been the Braves Carolina League affiliate since 1999.

1,449

Miles the Triple-A Portland Beavers are moving in

ORGANIZATION STANDINGS

Cumulative farm club records for the 30 major league organizations, with winning percentages going back five years. Most organizations have six affiliates.

		2010 W	L	PCT	2009	2008	2007	2006
1.	St. Louis	431	327	.569	.498	.525	.478	.483
2.	Chi. Cubs	374	316	.542	.487	.488	.499	.525
3.	N.Y. Yankees	371	318	.538	.554	.586	.597	.551
4.	Tampa Bay	407	355	.534	.502	.475	.527	.526
5.	Seattle	402	356	.530	.528	.472	.443	.474
6.	Oakland	366	328	.527	.494	.520	.492	.499
7.	San Francisco	363	330	.524	.603	.553	.562	.557
8.	Texas	361	331	.522	.495	.556	.489	.495
9.	N.Y. Mets	389	372	.511	.466	.453	.461	.465
10.	Pittsburgh	356	341	.511	.499	.430	.480	.456
11.	L.A. Dodgers	351	340	.508	.498	.484	.506	.530
12.	Philadelphia	353	342	.508	.507	.462	.488	.426
13.	L.A. Angels	351	341	.507	.514	.542	.490	.534
14.	Toronto	353	344	.506	.467	.511	.523	.504
15.	Cleveland	351	346	.504	.501	.506	.535	.524
16.	Washington	348	346	.501	.501	.481	.443	.481
17.	Milwaukee	341	351	.493	.488	.469	.565	.491
18.	Kansas City	373	385	.492	.482	.442	.497	.477
19.	Boston	341	354	.491	.505	.518	.501	.490
20.	Florida	339	353	.490	.502	.530	.465	.537
21.	Chi. White Sox	345	360	.489	.551	.503	.475	.496
22.	Arizona	346	362	.489	.476	.426	.494	.440
23.	San Diego	337	358	.485	.501	.517	.465	.519
24.	Detroit	337	358	.485	.492	.448	.531	.513
25.	Colorado	342	371	.480	.513	.499	.496	.487
26.	Cincinnati	320	366	.466	.453	.476	.519	.423
27.	Baltimore	355	412	.463	.475	.468	.490	.499
28.	Atlanta	313	372	.457	.503	.506	.486	.506
29.	Houston	334	432	.436	.426	.376	.441	.557
30.	Minnesota	298	388	.434	.535	.532	.534	.537

POSTSEASON RESULTS

League	Champion	Runner-Up
International	Columbus	Durham
Pacific Coast	Tacoma	Memphis
Eastern	Altoona	Trenton
Southern	Jacksonville	Tennessee
Texas	Northwest Arkansas	Midland
California	San Jose	Rancho Cucamonga
Carolina	Potomac	Winston-Salem
Florida State	Tampa	Charlotte
Midwest	Lake County	Clinton
South Atlantic	Lakewood	Greenville
New York-Penn	Tri-City	Brooklyn
Northwest	Everett	Spokane
Appalachian	Johnson City	Elizabethton
Pioneer	Helena	Ogden
Arizona	Brewers	Reds
Gulf Coast	Rays	Myrtle Beach

its relocation to Tucson in 2011.

The Beavers are headed to Tucson, at least temporarily, after Portland owner Merritt Paulson decided to convert PGE Park into a soccer-only facility and his three proposals for a new ballpark were rejected by voters or local officials.

Paulson is selling the team to an ownership group headed by Jeff Moorad, who would like to relocate the team to the San Diego suburb of Escondido. Moorad was awaiting the Escondido city council to decide on a $50 million ballpark proposal. The Padres were hoping to begin play in

Escondido in the 2012 season.

28

The unofficial tally of domestic minor leaguers suspended in 2010 under Minor League Baseball's drug prevention and treatment program (through October).

The most notable player to fail a drug test in 2010 was Dodgers farmhand Andrew Lambo, who entered the season as the Dodgers' No. 7 prospect. The 22-year-old outfielder was hit with a 50-game suspension on May 1 after a second positive test for a drug of abuse. He returned to the field on June 25 with Double-A Chattanooga but was included in a trade to the Pirates for Octavio Dotel a month later.

"I am working on making better choices and moving forward in a positive way," Lambo told the Ventura County (Calif.) Star after his return to Chattanooga. " I want this to just die out and show people by my actions what I came here to do and why I got drafted."

Other notable domestic suspensions included several players testing positive for the stimulant Methylhexaneamine. No player had tested positive for it before July 28, but little more than two weeks later eight minor leaguers from four levels of the minors had tested positive for the drug and received 50-game suspensions. The pre-workout supplement that baseball recently banned contained stimulants that proved to be the culprit.

Marlins Double-A lefty Daniel Jennings was the first player to have his failed test announced on July 28. Seven others followed in rapid succession, including former big league utility infielder Omar Quintanilla.

The supplement at the root of a number of these positive tests is "Jack3d", a supplement made by USP Labs that can be bought over the counter.

The supplement is designed to help give the user more energy before they work out, and the ingredient that plays a big part in that is Methylhexaneamine. Don Catlin, the former director of the UCLA Olympic Analytical Lab, likened the drug's effects to those of amphetamines and ephedrine, both of which are banned by baseball.

1st

Minor League Baseball became the first domestic professional sport to implement blood testing for human growth hormone (HGH).

Minor league players will be subject to random blood testing for the detection of human growth hormone. The sport's minor league drug prevention and treatment program will manage the testing and assess penalties.

The National Center for Drug Free Sport, the organization that currently performs all urine sample collections under the minor league drug program, will perform all blood sample collections. All blood samples will be collected post-game from the non-dominant arms of randomly selected players (among those not on 40-man rosters). Blood samples will be shipped to the Sports Medicine Research and Testing Laboratory in Salt Lake City for analysis.

The sport also adopted a ban on many maple bats and introduced new helmets designed to resist fastballs up to 100 mph.

$4.25 million/9 innings

Latin American bonus record the Athletics gave Michael Ynoa in 2008 compared to his performance on the mound this season (which also matches his career totals).

In this space last year, we noted that Dominican righthander Michael Ynoa created plenty of buzz but no results. Well, Ynoa did get on the mound this season in the Rookie-level Arizona League, but lasted just nine innings before requiring Tommy John surgery on his elbow.

Ynoa was scheduled to make his pro debut in 2009, but he missed the entire season with elbow tendinitis. The 18-year-old made three starts this year in the AZL, yielding five runs in nine innings with four walks and 11 strikeouts, and reports were that he had been clocked up to 95 mph before getting hurt.

The injury could also make for an interesting decision in a couple of years. Ynoa won't pitch next year, but the A's will have to decide whether to protect him from the Rule 5 draft after the 2012 season.

4

The number of minor league teams that repeated as league champions.

Double-A Jacksonville (Southern), low Class A Lakewood (South Atlantic), high Class A San Jose (California) and high Class A Tampa (Florida State) each won a second straight league title. Three other teams finished as runners-up this season after winning it all a year ago: Triple-A Durham (International), Triple-A Memphis (Pacific Coast) and Double-A Midland (Texas).

37

Consecutive-game hit streak for high Class A Clearwater second baseman Harold Garcia, a Florida

CONTINUED ON PAGE 348

Hellickson proves his worth

BY J.J. COOPER

Like any precocious student, Jeremy Hellickson was ready to graduate.

He'd been a gifted kid who stood out wherever he went. He earned praise from instructors for thinking two steps ahead of the rest of the students. He'd gotten good grades year after year, and aced his final exam.

So it should have been a shock to find out that he was being held back. But it wasn't that much of a surprise for Hellickson. It's just the way the Tampa Bay Rays operate.

"Around here, you don't graduate to the big leagues. You earn your way," Triple-A Durham pitching coach Xavier Hernandez said.

In almost any other organization, going 6-1, 2.59 in nine Triple-A starts—capping off a 57-20, 2.73 record in five minor league seasons—would have been enough to lock down a job in the big league rotation. But the Rays do things a little differently.

David Price returned to Durham in 2009 after dominating hitters in the 2008 World Series. Jeff Niemann, the fourth pick in the 2004 draft, spent two seasons in Triple-A learning how to succeed on days when he lacked his best stuff. Wade Davis spent six years in the minors before the Rays deemed him ready.

"Triple-A is very important at finishing the development process," farm director Mitch Lukevics said. "There are a lot of players who (played) in the big leagues in Triple-A. For a young guy it's a great training ground."

Hellickson added plenty of polish. He went 12-3, 2.45 for Durham this year, earning a late-August promotion to the big leagues and our Minor League Player of the Year award.

Hellickson was given a to-do list when he reported to Durham. Hellickson could toy with International League hitters with his above-average changeup. And his big-breaking curveball would be more than enough to handle the Charlotte Knights. But against Mark Teixeira or Derek Jeter, the same curveball wouldn't work.

"The big breaker was obvious when it left his hand," Hernandez said. "A major leaguer could recognize it right away."

Hellickson and Hernandez worked on adding a slider to see if it would be a better pitch for him than his curveball. The slider didn't really take, but along the way he did tighten up and learn to camouflage his curveball—now big league hitters aren't as likely to lay off it. And in trying to develop the slider, he learned to throw a cutter.

Once the cutter was mastered, Hellickson and Hernandez continued to tinker. He added a two-seam fastball to go with his four-seamer. With a 91-92 mph straight fastball that touches 94, Hellickson could succeed because he can paint the corners with it. But adding a two-seamer with movement gave him a chance to dominate.

Hellickson may have had to wait to make it to the big leagues, but it has ensured he's better equipped to succeed for

Jeremy Hellickson

the long haul.

And because he had plenty of time to perfect his craft, he had no problems making the jump to the big leagues. In his first four starts, he went 3-0, 2.05.

"What we can do with the type of patience we have is, they can experience almost everything that will come up in baseball in the minor leagues," Lukevics said. "We can't duplicate size of crowd and speed of the game, but we can duplicate most everything else."

PREVIOUS WINNERS

2000: Jon Rauch, rhp, Winston-Salem/Birmingham (White Sox)
2001: Josh Beckett, rhp, Brevard County/Portland (Marlins)
2002: Rocco Baldelli, of, Bakersfield/Orlando/Durham (Devil Rays)
2003: Joe Mauer, c, Fort Myers/New Britain (Twins)
2004: Jeff Francis, lhp, Tulsa/Colorado Springs (Rockies)
2005: Delmon Young, of, Montgomery/Durham (Devil Rays)
2006: Alex Gordon, 3b, Wichita (Royals)
2007: Jay Bruce, of, Sarasota/Chattanooga/Louisville (Reds)
2008: Matt Wieters, c, Frederick/Bowie (Orioles)
2009: Jason Heyward, Braves
Full list: BaseballAmerica.com/awards

Hoppel thrives in Midland

Monty Hoppel may have to build an addition to that shiny ballpark he works so hard to maintain to house all of the awards he has earned during a 22-year career as Double-A Midland's general manager.

Hoppel has been named Texas League executive of the year four times, most recently in 2009, and led Midland to Texas League team of the year honors three times. He guided the Rockhounds to the John H. Johnson award as the minors' top franchise in 2007 and a Bob Freitas Award in 1995. And, fittingly, Hoppel earned a plaque last year in the Midland Rockhounds hall of fame.

Now Baseball America has wised to Hoppel's game and named him the 2010 Executive of the Year. It's an honor well-earned by Hoppel, who since arriving to Midland in 1989 has made the Rockhounds arguably the Texas League's steadiest affiliate despite playing in the circuit's smallest market.

Opening a brand new ballpark in 2002 may have been the culmination of years of work

EXECUTIVE OF THE YEAR

PREVIOUS WINNERS

2002: Randy Mobley, International League
2003: Chuck Domino, Reading (Eastern)
2004: Chris Kemple, Wilmington Blue Rocks (Carolina)
2005: Jay Miller, Round Rock Express (Pacific Coast)
2006: Alan Ledford, Sacramento River Cats (Pacific Coast)
2007: Mike Moore, Minor League Baseball
2008: Naomi Silver, Rochester Red Wings (International)
2009: Ken Young, Norfolk Tides (International)

for Hoppel and his staff, but it was only the beginning of great things for Midland. Nine seasons later and the Rockhounds are still drawing new fans to the ballpark, as overall attendance increased to 285,188—almost 3,000 more than last year and better than the 276,380 when Citibank Ballpark debuted in 2002. The feat is particularly impresive considering the Midland-Odessa market has a combined population of less than 200,000.

CONTINUED FROM PAGE 346

State League record.

Clearwater second baseman Harold Garcia swung his way into Florida State League record books in his first at-bat against Daytona on July 4, driving a single up the middle to extend his hitting streak to 37 games.

Garcia's feat snaps a 59-year-old record set by Joe Altobelli when he was an 18-year-old with the Indians' Class D Daytona Beach Islanders affiliate. Garcia, a 23-year-old out of Venezuela, joined Clearwater on May 15 and recorded at least one hit in 43 of his 45 games, with a batting line that sat at .341/.400/.500 to go along with 17 steals in 22 attempts. Garcia's hit streak came to an end the following day.

Altobelli, a former big league player and manager, acknowledged Garcia's success.

"(The record hitting streak's) been up there for a long time and I've had my day in the sun," Altobelli told the Rochester Democrat and Chronicle. "I've enjoyed the run."

48⅓

Consecutive scoreless innings streak by high Class A Charlotte's bullpen.

What started on May 26 when high Class A Charlotte reliever Sergio Espinosa got Palm Beach's Tony Cruz to ground into a seemingly innocent inning-ending 4-6 force out quickly became one of the most impressive pitching streaks in the history of the Florida State League.

When Charlotte reliever Chris Andujar allowed an RBI triple in the seventh inning of the June 16 meeting between the Stone Crabs and Jupiter, it was the first run yielded by the Charlotte bullpen in three weeks—a streak of 18 games and 48 ⅓ innings.

"For as long as I have been playing baseball, I have never seen anything even close to a streak like that," said closer Zach Quate, who contributed nine scoreless innings and six saves during the streak. "Our bullpen has been so good it's almost like it's expected. We didn't really think about it."

4 inches

Amount of snow that fell and postponed Opening Day for the low Class A Wisconsin Timber Rattlers

Our photo of the year comes from Appleton, Wis., where the Timber Rattlers had grand plans for Opening Day before Mother Nature dictated otherwise. A sudden spring storm forced the team to postpone the game (and its bobblehead promo-

Sarbaugh stands out

BY STEPHANIE STORM

When Mike Sarbaugh found out that he had been named Minor League Manager of the Year, his first thought was that it must be a mistake.

"You sure they got the right guy?" he asked. Sarbaugh was only half-joking.

As a humble servant of the Cleveland Indians for 21 years—first as a player, then as a hitting coach and the last seven as a manager—Sarbaugh can no longer go about his job in relative obscurity. Not after leading Triple-A Columbus to the International League title and Triple-A National Championship in 2010.

In his first season with Columbus, Sarbaugh led the Clippers to a 79-65 regular season record and disposed of the Durham Bulls in four games in the Governors' Cup Championship.

A few days later, the Clippers were off to Oklahoma City to face Pacific Coast League champion Tacoma in the Triple-A National Championship game. Sarbaugh's Clippers easily disposed of the Rainiers 12-6.

MANAGER OF THE YEAR

PREVIOUS 10 WINNERS

2000: Joel Skinner, Buffalo (Indians)
2001: Jackie Moore, Round Rock (Astros)
2002: John Russell, Edmonton (Twins)
2003: Dave Brundage, San Antonio (Mariners)
2004: Marty Brown, Buffalo (Indians)
2005: Ken Oberkfell, Norfolk (Mets)
2006: Todd Claus, Portland (Red Sox)
2007: Matt Wallbeck, Erie (Tigers)
2008: Rocket Wheeler, Myrtle Beach (Braves)
2009: Charlie Montoyo, Durham Bulls (Rays)
Full list: BaseballAmerica.com/awards

"It was such a fun year," Sarbaugh said. "We started well, but were struggling at the end of the regular season having lost so many players to the big league club. But the young kids came in and really helped. And to the players' credit, they all kept fighting."

Sarbaugh's teams always do. Only one—his 2005 low Class A Lake County squad—did not reach the playoffs with him at the helm.

tion), but players like infielder Scooter Gennett still took the field to get in a few swings—at a snowman.

12

The number of weeks Royals lefthander Danny Duffy missed this season after announcing his retirement in spring training.

Duffy walked away from the game in mid-March, telling team officials he had lost the desire to play and wanted to return home to California. The 2007 third-round pick didn't stay on the sidelines for long, announcing in early June his return to baseball, which officially resumed with Kansas City's Rookie-level Arizona League club on June 28.

Duffy, 21, finished the season 5-3, 2.74 while working his way up to Double-A Northwest Arkansas.

16

Years between games the Durham Bulls played at the Durham Athletic Park before returning this season for a game at their old home.

The Bulls returned to the park made famous in the movie Bull Durham for a May 10 game against the Toledo Mud Hens. Nearly 4,000 spectators

Scooter Gennett's only swings on Opening Day in Wisconsin were at a snow man

TRIPLE-A

Pos	Player, Team (Organization)	League	AVG	OBP	SLG	AB	R	H	2B	3B	HR	RBI	BB	SO	SB	CS
C	J.P. Arencibia, Las Vegas (Blue Jays)	PCL	.301	.359	.626	412	76	124	36	1	32	85	38	85	0	0
1B	Mark Trumbo, Salt Lake (Angels)	PCL	.301	.368	.577	532	103	160	29	5	36	122	58	126	3	4
2B#	Cord Phelps, Columbus (Indians)	IL	.317	.386	.506	243	41	77	20	4	6	31	24	39	3	2
3B	* Mat Gamel, Nashville (Brewers)	PCL	.309	.387	.511	311	54	96	24	0	13	67	38	64	3	1
SS	Zack Cozart, Louisville (Reds)	IL	.255	.310	.416	553	91	141	30	4	17	67	40	107	30	4
CF	Peter Bourjos, Salt Lake (Angels)	PCL	.314	.364	.498	414	85	130	13	12	13	52	24	78	27	5
OF	* Lucas Duda, Buffalo (Mets)	IL	.314	.389	.610	264	44	83	23	2	17	53	31	57	0	0
OF	Brendan Katin, Nashville (Brewers)	PCL	.286	.382	.580	336	65	96	19	1	26	76	39	91	1	0
DH	*Kila Ka'aihue, Omaha (Royals)	PCL	.319	.463	.598	323	67	103	16	1	24	78	88	69	2	0

Pos	Pitcher, Team (Organization)	League	W	L	ERA	G	GS	SV	IP	H	HR	BB	SO	G/F	WHIP	AVG
SP	Jeremy Hellickson, Durham (Rays)	IL	12	3	2.45	21	21	0	118	103	5	35	123	0.82	1.17	.238
SP	Dan Hudson, Charlotte (White Sox)	IL	11	4	3.47	17	17	0	93	81	13	31	108	1.05	1.20	.228
SP	*Michael Kirkman, Oklahoma City (Rangers)	PCL	13	3	3.09	24	22	0	131	115	8	68	130	0.80	1.40	.235
SP	Ivan Nova, Scranton/W-B (Yankees)	IL	12	3	2.86	23	23	0	145	135	10	48	115	1.66	1.26	.250
RP	Jonathan Albaladejo, Scranton/WB (Yankees)	IL	4	2	1.42	57	0	43	63	38	3	18	82	0.81	0.88	.170

Player of the Year: Jeremy Hellickson, rhp, Durham (Rays). **Manager of the Year:** Rick Sweet, Louisville (Reds). **Team of the Year:** Columbus (Indians).

DOUBLE-A

Pos	Player, Team (Organization)	League	AVG	OBP	SLG	AB	R	H	2B	3B	HR	RBI	BB	SO	SB	CS
C	Robinson Chirinos, Tennessee (Cubs)	SL	.318	.412	.580	264	53	84	24	0	15	64	42	35	1	5
1B	* Matt Rizzotti, Reading (Phillies)	EL	.361	.452	.635	266	48	96	25	0	16	62	40	56	1	1
2B	*Jason Kipnis, Akron (Indians)	EL	.311	.385	.502	315	63	98	20	5	10	43	31	61	7	1
3B	* Mike Moustakas, NW Arkansas (Royals)	TL	.347	.413	.687	259	58	90	25	0	21	76	26	42	0	1
SS	#Danny Espinosa, Harrisburg (Nationals)	EL	.262	.334	.464	386	66	101	16	4	18	54	33	94	20	8
CF	Dave Sappelt, Carolina (Reds)	SL	.361	.416	.548	330	53	119	19	8	9	62	31	46	15	13
OF	*Domonic Brown, Reading (Phillies)	EL	.318	.391	.602	236	50	75	16	3	15	47	29	51	12	6
OF	Mike Stanton, Jacksonville (Marlins)	SL	.313	.442	.729	192	42	60	13	2	21	52	44	53	1	0
DH	* Eric Thames, New Hampshire (Blue Jays)	EL	.288	.370	.526	496	95	143	25	6	27	104	50	121	8	5

Pos	Pitcher, Team (Organization)	League	W	L	ERA	G	GS	SV	IP	H	HR	BB	SO	G/F	WHIP	AVG
SP	Chris Archer, Tennessee (Cubs)	SL	8	2	1.80	13	13	0	70	48	2	39	67	1.50	1.24	.198
SP	Alex Cobb, Montgomery (Rays)	SL	7	5	2.71	23	22	0	120	120	7	35	128	1.55	1.30	.262
SP	Kyle Drabek, New Hampshire (Blue Jays)	EL	14	9	2.94	27	27	0	162	126	12	68	132	1.59	1.20	.215
SP	Michael Pineda, West Tenn (Mariners)	SL	8	1	2.22	13	13	0	77	67	1	17	78	0.90	1.09	.228
RP	*Tim Collins, New Hamp./Mississippi (TOR/ATL)	EL/SL	1	0	2.29	41	0	11	51	31	5	19	87	0.78	0.98	.171

Player of the Year: Domonic Brown, Reading (Phillies). **Manager of the Year:** Bill Dancy, Tennessee (Cubs). **Team of the Year:** Northwest Arkansas (Royals).

HIGH CLASS A

Pos	Player, Team (Organization)	League	AVG	OBP	SLG	AB	R	H	2B	3B	HR	RBI	BB	SO	SB	CS
C	*Steve Vogt, Charlotte (Rays)	FSL	.345	.399	.511	368	56	127	31	3	8	47	31	46	3	1
1B	* Eric Hosmer, Wilmington (Royals)	CAR	.354	.429	.545	325	48	115	29	6	7	51	44	39	11	1
2B	*Kyle Seager, High Desert (Mariners)	CAL	.345	.419	.503	557	126	192	40	3	14	74	71	94	13	12
3B	* Steve Parker, Stockton (Athletics)	CAL	.296	.392	.508	524	102	155	38	5	21	98	84	105	3	1
SS	Grant Green, Stockton (Athletics)	CAL	.318	.363	.520	548	107	174	39	6	20	87	38	117	9	5
CF	* Brett Jackson, Daytona (Cubs)	FSL	.316	.420	.517	263	56	83	19	8	6	38	43	63	12	7
OF	Johermyn Chavez, High Desert (Mariners)	CAL	.315	.387	.577	534	109	168	30	7	32	96	52	131	6	9
OF	* Marc Krauss, Visalia (Diamondbacks)	CAL	.302	.371	.509	530	107	160	27	4	25	87	57	141	1	3
DH	*Brandon Belt, San Jose (Giants)	CAL	.383	.492	.628	269	62	103	28	4	10	62	58	50	18	7

Pos	Pitcher, Team (Organization)	League	W	L	ERA	G	GS	SV	IP	H	HR	BB	SO	G/F	WHIP	AVG
SP	Dellin Betances, Tampa (Yankees)	FSL	8	1	1.77	14	14	0	71	43	1	19	88	1.00	0.87	.169
SP	Joe Gardner, Kinston (Indians)	CAR	12	6	2.65	22	22	0	122	85	4	51	104	2.95	1.11	.199
SP	*John Lamb, Wilmington (Royals)	CAR	6	3	1.45	13	13	0	75	59	1	15	90	1.40	0.99	.219
SP	*Matt Moore, Charlotte (Rays)	FSL	6	11	3.36	26	26	0	145	109	7	61	208	1.11	1.18	.210
RP	Diego Moreno, Bradenton (Pirates)	FSL	4	1	1.17	28	0	1	38	14	3	5	57	0.73	0.50	.105

Player of the Year: Matt Moore, Charlotte (Rays). **Manager of the Year:** Joe McEwing, Winston-Salem (White Sox). **Team of the Year:** Tampa (Yankees).

MINOR LEAGUES

turned out for the game that proved such a hit the Bulls have scheduled another one for next season.

53

Years the Orioles had an affiliate in Bluefield before the team decided to pull out of the Rookie-level Appalachian League after this season.

The Orioles played more than 3,600 games in Bluefield since they affiliated in 1958. Baltimore sent over 1,400 players to the small West Virginia town, with roughly 150 becoming major leaguers—including Eddie Murray and Cal Ripken, Jr.

LOW CLASS A

Pos	Player, Team (Organization)	League	AVG	OBP	SLG	AB	R	H	2B	3B	HR	RBI	BB	SO	SB	CS
C	Wil Myers, Burlington (Royals)	MWL	.289	.408	.500	242	42	70	19	1	10	45	48	55	10	3
1B	* Jonathan Singleton, Lakewood (Phillies)	SAL	.290	.393	.479	376	64	109	25	2	14	77	62	74	9	7
2B	Jean Segura, Cedar Rapids (Angels)	MWL	.313	.365	.464	515	89	161	24	12	10	79	45	72	50	10
3B	Nolan Arenado, Asheville (Rockies)	SAL	.308	.338	.520	373	45	115	41	1	12	65	19	52	1	3
SS	#Nick Franklin, Clinton (Mariners)	MWL	.281	.351	.485	513	89	144	22	7	23	65	50	123	25	10
CF	Mike Trout, Cedar Rapids (Angels)	MWL	.362	.454	.526	312	76	113	19	7	6	39	46	52	45	9
OF	Brian Cavazos-Galvez, Great Lakes (Dodgers)	MWL	.318	.343	.520	490	76	156	43	4	16	77	12	60	43	13
OF	J.D. Martinez, Lexington (Astros)	SAL	.362	.433	.598	348	83	126	31	3	15	64	33	55	3	0
DH	Jerry Sands, Great Lakes (Dodgers)	MWL	.333	.432	.646	243	48	81	16	3	18	46	40	61	14	2

Pos	Pitcher, Team (Organization)	League	W	L	ERA	G	GS	SV	IP	H	HR	BB	SO	G/F	WHIP	AVG
SP	Chris Balcom-Miller, Ashe./Green. (COL/BOS)	SAL	7	7	3.30	20	20	0	115	91	4	19	120	2.21	0.96	.215
SP	*Robbie Erlin, Hickory (Rangers)	SAL	6	3	2.12	28	17	1	115	89	9	17	125	0.79	0.92	.213
SP	*Ian Krol, Kane County (Athletics)	MWL	9	4	2.65	24	23	0	119	98	5	19	91	1.28	0.99	.223
SP	Jake Odorizzi, Wisconsin (Brewers)	MWL	7	3	3.43	23	20	1	121	99	7	40	135	0.98	1.15	.220
RP	Scott Shuman, Bowling Green (Rays)	MWL	4	5	3.01	46	0	14	72	50	5	38	111	1.22	1.23	.195

Player of the Year: Mike Trout, Cedar Rapids (Angels). **Manager of the Year:** Mark Parent, Lakewood (Phillies). **Team of the Year:** Great Lakes (Dodgers).

SHORT-SEASON

Pos	Player, Team (Organization)	League	AVG	OBP	SLG	AB	R	H	2B	3B	HR	RBI	BB	SO	SB	CS
C	Carlos Perez, Auburn (Blue Jays)	NYP	.298	.396	.438	235	44	70	11	8	2	41	34	41	7	3
1B	* Yazy Arbelo, Yakima (Diamondbacks)	NWL	.285	.377	.521	242	38	69	13	1	14	55	36	62	4	1
2B	#Cesar Hernandez, Williamsport (Phillies)	NYP	.325	.390	.392	255	36	83	13	2	0	23	26	27	32	6
3B	Mike Olt, Spokane (Rangers)	NWL	.293	.390	.464	263	57	77	16	1	9	43	40	77	6	0
SS	#Zach Walters, Yakima (Diamondbacks)	NWL	.302	.338	.440	275	44	83	18	4	4	43	16	59	14	4
CF	* Darrell Ceciliani, Brooklyn (Mets)	NYP	.351	.410	.531	271	56	95	19	12	2	35	24	56	21	14
OF	*Jared Hoying, Spokane (Rangers)	NWL	.325	.378	.543	243	47	79	13	5	10	51	19	70	20	9
OF	Cory Vaughn, Brooklyn (Mets)	NYP	.307	.396	.557	264	45	81	14	5	14	56	34	63	12	5
DH	Marcell Ozuna, Jamestown (Marlins)	NYP	.267	.314	.556	270	53	72	11	2	21	60	17	94	3	1

Pos	Pitcher, Team (Organization)	League	W	L	ERA	G	GS	SV	IP	H	HR	BB	SO	G/F	WHIP	AVG
SP	Chad Bettis, Tri-City (Rockies)	NWL	4	1	1.12	10	9	0	48	44	0	10	39	1.91	1.12	.227
SP	Drew Hutchison, Auburn (Blue Jays)	NYP	1	1	3.00	10	10	0	45	34	1	12	44	2.30	1.02	.201
SP	Jake Thompson, Hudson Valley (Rays)	NYP	2	1	1.35	10	7	0	40	28	0	6	33	1.10	0.85	.200
SP	Matt Thomson, Vancouver (Athletics)	NWL	3	2	2.15	12	9	0	46	35	0	8	61	0.87	0.93	.202
RP	Aaron Kurcz, Boise (Cubs)	NWL	2	1	2.05	25	0	9	26	15	2	11	46	0.60	0.99	.161

Player of the Year: Cory Vaughn, Brooklyn (Mets). **Manager of the Year:** Wally Backman, Brooklyn (Mets). **Team of the Year:** Everett (Mariners).

ROOKIE

Pos	Player, Team (Organization)	League	AVG	OBP	SLG	AB	R	H	2B	3B	HR	RBI	BB	SO	SB	CS
C	*Cody Stanley, Johnson City (Cardinals)	APP	.321	.380	.498	209	34	67	12	5	5	39	21	30	8	1
1B	* Cody Hawn, Helena (Brewers)	PIO	.308	.407	.542	253	36	78	20	0	13	61	35	58	0	0
2B	#Billy Hamilton, Billings (Reds)	PIO	.318	.383	.456	283	61	90	13	10	2	24	28	56	48	9
3B	Ramon Morla, Pulaski (Mariners)	APP	.323	.364	.610	251	60	81	17	2	17	49	15	65	13	4
SS	Jake Lemmerman, Ogden (Dodgers)	PIO	.363	.434	.610	259	69	94	24	2	12	47	31	56	5	4
CF	* Rafael Ortega, Casper (Rockies)	PIO	.358	.416	.510	288	69	103	17	3	7	45	28	42	23	9
OF	*Oswaldo Arcia, Elizabethton (Twins)	APP	.375	.424	.672	259	47	97	21	7	14	51	19	67	4	4
OF	* Ramon Flores, GCL Yankees (Yankees)	GCL	.329	.436	.481	158	33	52	10	4	2	22	28	22	4	1
DH	*Corey Dickerson, Casper (Rockies)	PIO	.348	.412	.634	276	54	96	22	9	13	61	28	51	12	6

Pos	Pitcher, Team (Organization)	League	W	L	ERA	G	GS	SV	IP	H	HR	BB	SO	G/F	WHIP	AVG
SP	Albert Campos, Casper (Rockies)	PIO	4	4	2.05	15	15	0	88	80	5	17	68	1.24	1.10	.244
SP	*Braulio Lara, Princeton (Rays)	APP	6	4	2.18	13	13	0	66	49	2	25	58	1.52	1.12	.200
SP	*Enny Romero, Princeton (Rays)	APP	4	1	1.95	13	13	0	69	51	2	14	72	1.78	0.94	.204
SP	Manuel Soliman, Elizabethton (Twins)	APP	5	2	3.48	12	12	0	65	47	5	21	74	0.82	1.05	.201
RP	Hector Corpas, Johnson City (Cardinals)	APP	0	1	2.13	24	0	17	25	19	1	3	27	1.04	0.87	.209

Player of the Year: Oswaldo Arcia, Elizabethton (Twins). **Manager of the Year:** Chris Cron, Great Falls (White Sox). **Team of the Year:** Johnson City (Cardinals).

The Orioles cited the renovation of their new spring training facility in Sarasota, Fla., the construction of a complex they share with two teams in the Dominican Republic and their short-season New York-Penn League affiliate in Aberdeen, Md., as reasons to end their relationship with Bluefield.

"Personally, I've been devastated," veteran Bluefield general manager George McGonagle said before the team's finale. "There are many people who are sad this could happen. There are so many people here that have grown up with the black and orange."

CLIFF WELCH

Domonic Brown tallied 20 home runs before earning a big league promotion

ROBERT GURGANUS

Braves righthander Julio Teheran had a 2.59 ERA over three classifications

FIRST TEAM

Pos	Player, Level (Organization)	Age	AVG	OBP	SLG	G	AB	R	H	2B	3B	HR	RBI	BB	SO	SB
C	Wil Myers, LoA/HiA (Royals)	19	.315	.429	.506	126	447	70	141	37	3	14	83	85	94	12
1B	Eric Hosmer, HiA/AA (Royals)	20	.338	.406	.571	137	520	87	176	43	9	20	86	59	66	14
2B	Jason Kipnis, AA/HiA (Indians)	23	.307	.386	.492	133	518	96	159	32	8	16	74	55	107	9
3B	Mike Moustakas, AA/AAA (Royals)	21	.322	.369	.630	118	484	94	156	41	0	36	124	34	67	2
SS	Nick Franklin, LoA/AA (Mariners)	19	.283	.354	.486	130	516	92	146	22	7	23	65	51	124	25
CF	Mike Trout, LoA/HiA (Angels)	19	.341	.428	.490	131	508	106	173	28	9	10	58	73	85	56
OF	Jerry Sands, AA/LoA (Dodgers)	22	.301	.395	.586	137	502	102	151	28	5	35	93	73	123	18
OF	Domonic Brown, AA/AAA (Phillies)	23	.327	.391	.589	93	343	65	112	22	4	20	68	37	74	17
DH	Brandon Belt, HiA/AA/AAA (Giants)	22	.352	.455	.620	136	492	99	173	43	10	23	112	93	99	22

Pos	Pitcher, Level (Organization)	Age	W	L	ERA	G	GS	SV	IP	H	HR	BB	SO	G/F	AVG	WHIP
SP	Chris Archer, HiA/AA (Cubs)	21	15	3	2.34	28	27	0	142	102	6	65	149	1.42	.200	1.17
SP	Jeremy Hellickson, AAA (Rays)	23	12	3	2.72	22	21	0	119	107	5	37	127	0.81	.242	1.21
SP	John Lamb, HiA/LoA/AA (Royals)	20	10	7	2.38	28	28	0	148	122	5	45	159	0.97	.226	1.13
SP	Matt Moore, HiA (Rays)	21	6	11	3.36	26	26	0	145	109	7	61	208	1.11	.210	1.18
SP	Julio Teheran, HiA/AA/LoA (Braves)	19	9	8	2.59	24	24	0	143	108	9	40	159	0.93	.208	1.04
RP	Tim Collins, AA/AAA (Royals)	21	3	1	2.02	56	0	15	71	40	5	27	108	0.76	.159	0.94

SECOND TEAM

Pos	Player, Level (Organization)	Age	AVG	OBP	SLG	G	AB	R	H	2B	3B	HR	RBI	BB	SO	SB
C	Devin Mesoraco, AA/HiA/AAA (Reds)	22	.302	.377	.587	113	397	71	120	25	5	26	75	43	80	3
1B	Freddie Freeman, AAA (Braves)	20	.319	.378	.521	124	461	73	147	35	2	18	87	43	84	6
2B	Brett Lawrie, AA (Brewers)	20	.285	.346	.451	135	554	90	158	36	16	8	63	47	118	30
3B	Steve Parker, HiA (Athletics)	23	.296	.392	.508	139	524	102	155	38	5	21	98	84	105	3
SS	Grant Green, HiA (Athletics)	22	.318	.363	.520	131	548	107	174	39	6	20	87	38	117	9
CF	Brett Jackson, AA (Cubs)	22	.297	.395	.493	128	491	103	146	32	14	12	66	73	126	30
OF	Eric Thames, AA (Blue Jays)	23	.288	.370	.526	130	496	95	143	25	6	27	104	50	121	8
OF	Mike Stanton, AA (Marlins)	20	.313	.442	.729	53	192	42	60	13	2	21	52	44	53	1
DH	Jesus Montero, AAA (Yankees)	20	.289	.353	.517	123	453	66	131	34	3	21	75	46	91	0

Pos	Pitcher, Level (Organization)	Age	W	L	ERA	G	GS	SV	IP	H	HR	BB	SO	G/F	AVG	WHIP
SP	Brandon Beachy, AAA (Braves)	24	5	1	1.73	35	13	2	119	93	5	28	148	0.85	.211	1.01
SP	Zach Britton, AA/AAA (Orioles)	22	10	7	2.70	27	26	0	153	139	7	51	124	2.80	.237	1.24
SP	Robbie Erlin, LoA (Rangers)	19	6	3	2.12	28	17	1	115	89	9	17	125	0.79	.213	0.92
SP	Trey McNutt, LoA/HiA/AA (Cubs)	21	10	1	2.48	25	25	0	116	93	5	37	132	1.05	.217	1.12
SP	Michael Pineda, AA/AAA (Mariners)	21	11	4	3.36	25	25	0	139	121	10	34	154	0.97	.227	1.11
RP	Kenley Jansen, AA/HiA (Dodgers)	22	5	1	1.60	33	0	8	45	29	0	23	78	0.74	.184	1.16

MINOR LEAGUES

A Natural winner

BY J.J. COOPER

When Mike Moustakas first stepped to the plate for Northwest Arkansas, the team realized that they may have something special brewing.

The third-base prospect had missed the first two weeks of the season with a minor injury, but in his first swing as a Natural, he lined a home run. In his next swing, he crushed another home run. Two swings, two home runs and the start of a pretty impressive run.

"He came in and his first two swings were home runs. We had seen a little bit of what he could do in spring training, but we hadn't seen him a whole lot (because of injuries)," Northwest Arkansas manager Brian Poldberg said. "Other guys saw that and saw that they didn't have to press. It took the pressure off the other guys."

Before the first half of the season was over, the Naturals had bashed their way to the best record in the Texas League and a first-half title. Moustakas moved on up to Triple-A Omaha after hitting .347/.413/.687 with 21 home runs and 76 RBIs in only 65 games, but was replaced by a new wave of prospects, including first baseman Eric Hosmer and lefthanders Mike Montgomery, Danny Duffy, John Lamb and Chris Dwyer.

The Naturals wrapped up the second-half title as well, then won the league title with playoff wins over Springfield and Midland.

Very rarely in minor league baseball does having great prospects equate with winning. Northwest Arkansas managed to do both.

The Naturals had one of the most prospect-laden lineups and rotations in the minors and they managed to win 92 games. For that combination of success and future stars, the Naturals are the 2010 Minor League Team of the Year.

"I knew we had some good players, but I didn't sense that we could have a chance to be as good as we would become," Poldberg said. "I didn't expect to end up winning 92 games when we left spring training."

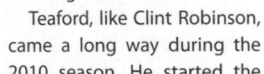

The Naturals got contributions from a variety of sources. Moustakas and Hosmer (who hit .313/.365/.615 with 13 home runs and 35 RBIs in 50 games) were the big names of the lineup, but first baseman Clint Robinson was just as vital. The 25th-round pick out of Troy in 2007 won the Texas League triple crown by hitting .335 with 29 homers and 98 RBIs. And second baseman Johnny Giavotella and outfielders Paulo Orlando and Derrick Robinson each had the best seasons of their careers.

And when the playoffs rolled around, it was the Naturals pitching that provided a needed boost. In the Naturals three wins in the championship series against Midland, the Rockhounds scored just three runs. Starters Everett Teaford and Duffy had ERA's under 2.00 during the playoffs while Will Smith finished off the series by shutting out Midland.

Teaford, like Clint Robinson, came a long way during the 2010 season. He started the season in the rotation, moved into the bullpen when the more highly regarded prospects arrived from high Class A Wilmington, then moved back into the rotation to fill in when injuries struck. Along the way he succeeded in either role, and actually helped his own status as a prospect by showing improved velocity to go with his excellent command.

"He didn't allow the bouncing around affect him. He took advantage of it every chance he had to pitch," Poldberg said.

Mike Moustakas

BRIAN FLEMING

PREVIOUS 10 WINNERS

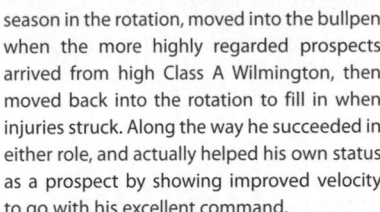

2000: Round Rock/Texas (Astros)
2001: Lake Elsinore/California (Padres)
2002: Akron/Eastern (Indians)
2003: Sacramento/Pacific Coast (Athletics)
2004: Lancaster/California (Diamondbacks)
2005: Jacksonville/Southern (Dodgers)
2006: Tucson/Pacific Coast (Diamondbacks)
2007: San Antonio/Texas (Padres)
2008: Frisco/Texas (Rangers)
2009: Akron/Eastern (Indians)
Full list: BaseballAmerica.com/awards

MINOR LEAGUES

ANAHEIM

In the biggest offensive explosion in Futures Game history, the United States thumped the World 9-1 at Angel Stadium. Hometown heroes provided much of the offense, as Angels catcher Hank Conger drilled a three-run homer in the fifth inning and Angels center fielder Mike Trout hit the first of three consecutive U.S. doubles with two out in the eighth.

Conger became the first player to win the Futures Game MVP award while playing in his parent club's ballpark. His blast came on a 96-mph fastball from Blue Jays righthander Henderson Alvarez.

"This, to be honest, does not feel real," Conger said. "It's just so much adrenaline. It's an unbelievable feeling. I'll never forget this in my life."

The youngest player in the game at age 18, Trout electrified the crowd with his speed. He reached twice on errors, beat out an infield hit and turned what would have been a single into the right-center gap for most players into a double in the eighth.

Scouts clocked him in 3.9 seconds from the right side of the plate to first base on his infield hit and he also covered ground effortlessly in center field. Royals first baseman Eric Hosmer also helped power the U.S. attack, going 4-for-5 with a double, two runs and an RBI.

The U.S. pitching was nearly as impressive as its offense. The World had 10 hits, but just twice did it string together multiple hits in an inning and it advanced only five runners into scoring position.

Rays righthander Jeremy Hellickson set the tone by working the first two innings for the win. Though he gave up a run in the second, he required just 25 pitches to get six outs, worked at 92-95 mph with his fastball and struck out Yonder Alonso on a changeup.

Nine U.S. pitchers combined to blank the World for seven innings after Hellickson departed, with Zach Britton (Orioles) and Mike Minor (Braves) among the most impressive. Britton has the best sinker in the minors, and he also showed a 95-96 mph four-seam fastball. Minor worked a perfect fourth, touching 94 mph with his fastball and using his slider and changeup to record all three outs.

Tanner Scheppers (Rangers) got the final two outs of the game, hitting 99 mph four times and never dipping under 97 with his fastball.

FUTURES GAME BOX SCORE

JULY 11 IN ANAHEIM
UNITED STATES 9, WORLD 1

WORLD	AB	R	H	BI	U.S.	AB	R	H	BI
Lawrie, 2b	3	0	0	0	Jennings, lf	3	3	0	0
Ciriaco, 2b	1	0	0	0	Gordon, ss	2	1	1	0
Martinez, ss	2	0	0	0	Green, ss/2b	2	0	1	1
Lee, ss	2	0	1	0	Moustakas, 3b	3	0	0	0
Alonso, 1b	4	0	1	0	Chisenhall, 3b	1	0	0	1
Liddi, 3b	2	0	0	0	Brown, rf	1	0	1	1
Baez, 3b	2	0	1	0	Trout, cf	4	2	2	0
Peguero C, lf	4	1	2	0	Hosmer, dh	5	2	4	2
Ramirez, rf	2	0	1	0	Conger, c	3	1	1	3
Perez, rf	2	0	2	0	Romine, c	2	0	1	1
Rosario, c	2	0	0	1	Jackson, cf/rf	1	0	0	0
Chen, c	2	0	0	0	Revere, rf	3	0	0	0
Hernandez, cf	3	0	0	0	Morrison, 1b	2	0	1	0
Peguero F, dh	2	0	1	0	Cumberland, 2b	2	0	0	0
Jimenez, dh/3b	2	0	1	0	Espinosa, 2b/ss	2	0	0	0
Totals	**35**	**1**	**10**	**1**	**Totals**	**36**	**9**	**12**	**9**

WORLD		010	000	000	1 10 4
U.S.		200	031	03X	9 12 0

E: Rosario, Martinez, Liddi, Lee. **LOB:** World 8, U.S. 10. **2B:** C Peguero, Trout, Hosmer, Romine. **HR:** Conger. **GIDP:** Ciriaco, Moustakas. **SB:** Jennings. **CS:** Trout.

WORLD	IP	H	R	ER	BB	SO	U.S.	IP	H	R	ER	BB	SO
Castro L	1	2	2	1	1	Hellickson W	2	2	1	1	0	1
Noesi	1	1	0	0	0	0	Britton	1	0	0	0	0	1
Torres	1	1	0	0	0	0	Wheeler	1	1	0	0	0	0
Teheran	1	0	0	0	2	1	Minor	1	0	0	0	0	0
Alvarez	1	3	3	0	0	0	Lyles	1	1	0	0	0	1
Pimentel	⅔	0	0	0	0	0	Miller	⅔	1	0	0	0	0
Magnuson	⅔	2	1	1	2	0	Morris	⅓	0	0	0	0	0
Valiquette	⅔	0	0	0	1	0	Slama	1	3	0	0	0	1
Sanchez	⅓	0	1	0	0	0	Friedrich	⅓	0	0	0	0	0
Familia	⅓	3	2	2	0	0	Scheppers	⅔	1	0	0	1	0
Totals	**8**	**12**	**9**	**3**	**6**	**2**	**Totals**	**9**	**10**	**1**	**1**	**1**	**4**

Umpires: HP: Adam Hamari. **1B:** Brett Robson. **2B:** Gerard Ascani. **3B:** Dan Oliver.

The World team played a sloppy game, committing four errors that led to six unearned runs. But they did provide a few highlights.

Outfielders Carlos Peguero (Mariners) and Eury Perez (Nationals) had two hits each. Catcher Wilin Rosario (Rockies) threw out Trout trying to steal second, but he also picked Brett Jackson (Cubs) off first base.

On the mound, Yankees righthander Hector Noesi threw harder than advertised (92-94 mph) without sacrificing his trademark command. Braves righthander Julio Teheran didn't throw a fastball under 95 mph, used his changeup for strikes and froze Desmond Jennings (Rays) with a 96-mph heater for a strikeout.

The U.S. victory was the most lopsided in Futures Game history.

TRIPLE-A: The International League bullpen shut out the Pacific Coast League over the final four innings of the Triple-A all-star game, preserving a 2-1 victory at Coca Cola Park, home of the Lehigh Valley IronPigs.

Working one inning apiece, the IL's parade of closers, from Rochester's Anthony Slama (Twins) to Toledo's Jay Sborz (Tigers) to Gwinnett's Mike Dunn (Braves) to Scranton/Wilkes-Barre's Jonathan Albaladejo (Phillies), struck out five while allowing only one hit.

Durham shortstop Elliot Johnson (Rays) delivered a pinch-hit double that drove in Syracuse's Chase Lambin (Nationals) with the decisive run. Lambin, who spent last year in Japan, was 1-for-3 with a walk and an RBI, earning the game's MVP award. He drove in Chris Valaika (Reds) to tie the game at 1-1 in the sixth.

EASTERN LEAGUE: On the strength of a six-run seventh inning, the Western Division trounced the Eastern by a 10-3 score in Harrisburg.

Elliot Johnson

Altoona shortstop Chase d'Arnaud (Pirates) was named MVP after he launched a grand slam to deep left field to break a 2-2 tie. Akron left fielder John Drennen (Indians) chipped in with a two-run shot in the eighth.

SOUTHERN LEAGUE: Jacksonville third baseman Matt Dominguez (Marlins) secured game MVP honors by going 3-for-4 with a pair of solo home runs in a losing effort for the Southern Division in Huntsville.

The Northern Division prevailed 3-2 and set the pitching tone, completing four scoreless innings to begin the contest. Mobile righty Josh Collmenter started and allowed two hits and one walk in two innings, striking out one and receiving credit for the win. Mississippi righthander Brandon Beachy followed with a perfect third inning in which he struck out two of the three batters he faced.

TEXAS LEAGUE: San Antonio catcher Luis Martinez snagged MVP honors for his part in the Southern Division's three-run fourth inning during it's 5-4 win over the Northern Division at Midland. He delivered two runs with a single to left field and then scored the decisive fifth run on a sacrifice fly later in the frame.

CALIFORNIA-CAROLINA LEAGUE: San Jose center fielder Juan Perez (Giants) won MVP honors by going 2-for-4 with a home run, a double, two runs scored and two RBIs during the Cal League's 4-3 win over the Carolina League in Myrtle Beach.

Myrtle Beach righthander Julio Teheran hit a game-high 98 mph on the radar gun while striking out two in two innings of work.

Perez put on a show in the pre-game home derby, doubled to start the game then scored by aggressively tagging on a fly ball and scoring on the subsequent throwing error. He hit a two-run home run to left in his next at-bat.

FLORIDA STATE LEAGUE: St. Lucie second baseman Josh Satin drove in the tying and winning runs in the Southern Division's 5-4, extra-inning victory at Space Coast Stadium, home of the Brevard County Manatees. He stated his MVP case loudly and clearly.

Satin, who started the game and went 3-for-5, drilled a two-run, opposite-field home run in the eighth inning against Daytona righty Aaron Shafer to tie the game. Two innings later, Satin singled to right field to plate Bradenton's Quincy Latimore, who singled to lead off the 10th and then stole second base.

MIDWEST LEAGUE: The East opened up a five-run lead through two innings and cruised to a 6-2 win at Fort Wayne. Great Lakes first baseman Jerry Sands, the MWL home run leader, took Peoria righty Trey McNutt deep in the first inning, clubbing a two-run shot. The game featured plenty of prospects, as West shortstops Hak-Ju Lee and Nick Franklin each went 1-for-2, while West catcher Wil Myers went 0-for-1 with a walk.

SOUTH ATLANTIC LEAGUE: The Northern and Southern divisions played to a 5-5 tie in 10 innings at Greenville. Asheville outfielder Eliezer Mesa earned MVP honors after going 3-for-5 with a double, two RBIs and a steal for the Southern Division.

Greensboro catcher Kyle Skipworth (Marlins) homered in the first inning for the North and went on to finish 1-for-3. Savannah shortstop Wilmer Flores (Mets) went just 1-for-5 for the South, but drove in two runs with a second-inning double.

(*Full-season teams only)

MINOR LEAGUES

WINS

Great Lakes (Midwest)	90
Durham (International)	88
Scranton/WB (International)	87
NW Arkansas (Texas)	86
Tennessee (Southern)	86

LONGEST WINNING STREAK*

Daytona (Florida State)	14
Stockton (California)	14
Akron (Eastern)	12
West Michigan (Midwest)	12
Durham (International)	11
Louisville (International)	11

LOSSES

New Britain (Eastern)	98
Rochester (International)	95
Jupiter (Florida State)	92
Burlington (Midwest)	90
Inland Empire (California)	90

LONGEST LOSING STREAK*

Corpus Christi (Texas)	16
Jupiter (Florida State)	15
Rochester (International)	12
Carolina (Southern)	11
Dayton (Midwest)	11
Erie (Eastern)	11
Inland Empire (California)	11
Lancaster (California)	11
Toledo (International)	11

BATTING AVERAGE*

Albuquerque (Pacific Coast)	.302
High Desert (California)	.296
Las Vegas (Pacific Coast)	.293
NW Arkansas (Texas)	.291
San Jose (California)	.289

RUNS

Albuquerque (Pacific Coast)	871
High Desert (California)	860
Las Vegas (Pacific Coast)	838
Sacramento (Pacific Coast)	827
Iowa (Pacific Coast)	796

HOME RUNS

Tacoma (Pacific Coast)	185
High Desert (California)	172
Las Vegas (Pacific Coast)	172
Albuquerque (Pacific Coast)	163
Louisville Bats (International)	160

STOLEN BASES

Bowling Green (Midwest)	249
Greenville (South Atlantic)	241
San Jose (California)	208
Rancho Cucamonga (California)	197
Lansing (Midwest)	186

EARNED RUN AVERAGE*

Lakewood (South Atlantic)	3.04
Charlotte (Florida State)	3.06
Savannah (South Atlantic)	3.08
Tampa (Florida State)	3.30
Lakeland (Florida State)	3.30

STRIKEOUTS

Quad Cities (Midwest)	1220
Lakewood (South Atlantic)	1207
Charlotte (Florida State)	1189
Savannah (South Atlantic)	1187
Great Lakes (Midwest)	1177

INDIVIDUAL BATTING

BATTING AVERAGE*

Brandon Belt (San Jose, Richmond, Fresno)	.352
John Lindsey (Albuquerque)	.350
Stephen Vogt (Charlotte)	.345
Kyle Seager (High Desert)	.345
Brandon Guyer (Tennessee)	.344

RUNS

Kyle Seager (High Desert)	126
Johermyn Chavez (High Desert)	109
Grant Green (Stockton)	107
Marc Krauss (Visalia)	107
J.D. Martinez (Lexington, Corpus Christi)	107

HITS

Kyle Seager (High Desert)	192
J.D. Martinez (Lexington, Corpus Christi)	183
Jon Gilmore (Winston-Salem Dash)	177
Eric Hosmer (Wilmington, NW Arkansas)	176
Grant Green (Stockton)	174
DJ LeMahieu (Daytona)	174
Dave Sappelt (Lynchburg, Carolina, Louisville)	174

TOP HITTING STREAKS

Harold Garcia (Clearwater)	37
Kyle Seager (High Desert)	32
Brandon Short (Winston-Salem)	26
Roberto Lopez (Rancho Cucamonga)	25
Brian Cavazos-Galvez (Great Lakes)	24
Jiwan James (Lakewood)	24

MOST HITS (ONE GAME)

Tim Ferguson (Idaho Falls)	6
Jim Gallagher (Birmingham)	6
Gregory Hopkins (Helena)	6
Brett Tanos (Casper)	6
Justin Turner (Buffalo)	6

TOTAL BASES

Paul Goldschmidt (Visalia)	318
Johermyn Chavez (High Desert)	308
Mark Trumbo (Salt Lake)	307
Brandon Belt (San Jose, Richmond, Fresno)	305
Mike Moustakas (NW Arkansas, Omaha)	305

EXTRA-BASE HITS

Paul Goldschmidt (Visalia)	80
Tyler Moore (Potomac)	77
Mike Moustakas (NW Arkansas, Omaha)	77
Brandon Belt (San Jose, Richmond, Fresno)	76
Clint Robinson (NW Arkansas)	75

DOUBLES

Jacob Goebbert (Lexington)	48
Luis Jimenez (Cedar Rapids, R. Cucamonga)	46
Nick Evans (Binghamton, Buffalo)	44
Tyler Moore (Potomac)	43
Ryan Adams (Bowie)	43
Brandon Belt (San Jose, Richmond, Fresno)	43
Brian Cavazos-Galvez (Great Lakes)	43
Nathan Freiman (Fort Wayne)	43
Eric Hosmer (Wilmington, NW Arkansas)	43
Kirk Nieuwenhuis (Binghamton, Buffalo)	43
Steve Singleton (New Britain)	43

TRIPLES

Keon Broxton (South Bend)	19
Brett Lawrie (Huntsville)	16
Francisco Peguero (San Jose)	16
Albert Cartwright (Lancaster, Corpus Christi)	14
Evan Crawford (Augusta, Daytona)	14
Brett Jackson (Daytona, Tennessee)	14
Carlo Testa (Burlington)	14

HOME RUNS

Mike Moustakas (NW Arkansas, Omaha)	36
Mark Trumbo (Salt Lake)	36
Jerry Sands (Great Lakes, Chattanooga)	35
Paul Goldschmidt (Visalia)	35
Joel Guzman (Bowie)	33
Greg Halman (Tacoma)	33

RUNS BATTED IN

Rich Poythress (High Desert)	130
Mike Moustakas (NW Arkansas, Omaha)	124
Mark Trumbo (Salt Lake)	122
Brandon Belt (San Jose, Richmond, Fresno)	112
Tyler Moore (Potomac)	111

MOST RBIS, ONE GAME

Mike Moustakas (Omaha)	11
JR Murphy (Charleston)	9
Jeff Bailey (Reno)	8
Matt Clark (San Antonio)	8
Devin Goodwin (Quad Cities)	8
Dan Johnson (Durham)	8
Gregorio Petit (Oklahoma City)	8
Alex Presley (Altoona)	8
David Vidal (AZL Reds)	8

WALKS

Conner Crumbliss (Kane County)	126
Vincent Belnome (Lake Elsinore)	102

Jamie Johnson (West Michigan)	98
Tyreace House (Kane County)	96
Ruben Gotay (Memphis)	95

STRIKEOUTS

Denny Almonte (High Desert)	192
Brandon Waring (Bowie)	179
Carlos Peguero (Jackson)	178
Kyle Russell (Inland Empire, Chattanooga)	177
Brock Kjeldgaard (Brevard County)	175

STOLEN BASES

Delvi Cid (Lake County)	71
Eury Perez (Hagerstown)	64
Jeremy Hazelbaker (Greenville)	63
Ty Morrison (Bowling Green)	58
Mike Trout (Cedar Rapids, Rancho Cucamonga)	56
Corey Wimberly (Sacramento)	56

CAUGHT STEALING

Anthony Gose (Clearwater, Dunedin)	32
Kyle Rose (GCL Braves, Rome)	23
Francisco Peguero (San Jose)	22
Tyson Auer (R. Cucamonga, Arkansas, Salt Lake)	20
Jay Austin (Lancaster)	20
Tony Campana (Tennessee)	20
Dee Gordon (Chattanooga)	20
Jiwan James (Lakewood)	20

ON BASE PERCENTAGE*

Kila Ka'aihue (Omaha)	.463
Brandon Belt (San Jose, Richmond, Fresno)	.455
Matt Rizzotti (Clearwater, Reading, Lehigh Valley)	.430
Dan Johnson (Durham)	.430
William Myers (Burlington, Wilmington)	.429

SLUGGING PERCENTAGE*

John Lindsey (Albuquerque)	.657
Tagg Bozied (Reading)	.631
Mike Moustakas (NW Arkansas, Omaha)	.630
J.P. Arencibia (Las Vegas)	.626
Clint Robinson (NW Arkansas)	.625

ON BASE PLUS SLUGGING (OPS)*

Brandon Belt (San Jose, Richmond, Fresno)	1.075
Kila Ka'aihue (Omaha)	1.060
John Lindsey (Albuquerque)	1.057
Dan Johnson (Durham)	1.053
Clint Robinson (NW Arkansas)	1.035

HIT BY PITCH

Seth Loman (Winston-Salem)	30
Aaron Luna (Memphis, Springfield)	28
Matthew West (Hickory)	24
Edilio Colina (High Desert)	23
Cesar Puello (Savannah)	22

SACRIFICE BUNTS

Eury Perez (Hagerstown)	21
Michael Marseco (Wisconsin)	21
Adrian Ortiz (Wilmington)	20
David Lough (Omaha)	19
Jonathan Diaz (New Hampshire, Las Vegas)	18
Logan Watkins (Peoria)	18

SACRIFICE FLIES

Sergio Miranda (Brevard County)	14
Roberto Lopez (Rancho Cucamonga, Arkansas)	13
Jeudy Valdez (Fort Wayne)	12
Stephen Parker (Stockton)	12
Wladimir Balentien (Louisville)	11
Jeremy Barfield (Stockton)	11
Adam Calderone (Las Vegas, New Hampshire)	11
Ryan Flaherty (Tennessee, Daytona)	11
Rich Poythress (High Desert)	11

BATTING AVERAGE*
BY POSITION

CATCHERS

Robinson Chirinos (Tennessee, Iowa)	.326
Jordan Pacheco (Modesto, Tulsa)	.323
William Myers (Burlington, Wilmington)	.315
Chun-Hsiu Chen (Lake County, Kinston)	.315
Konrad Schmidt (Mobile)	.315

FIRST BASEMEN

Brandon Belt (San Jose, Richmond, Fresno)	.352
John Lindsey (Albuquerque)	.350

Matt Rizzotti (Clearwater, Reading, Lehigh Valley) .343
Eric Hosmer (Wilmington, NW Arkansas) .338
Clint Robinson (NW Arkansas) .335

SECOND BASEMEN
Kyle Seager (High Desert) .345
Johnny Giavotella (NW Arkansas) .322
Luis Figueroa (Las Vegas, Salt Lake) .319
Justin Turner (Norfolk, Buffalo) .316
Danny Richar (New Orleans) .315

THIRD BASEMEN
Brent Morel (Birmingham, Charlotte) .322
Mike Moustakas (NW Arkansas, Omaha) .322
Jesus Guzman (Fresno) .321
Tagg Bozied (Reading) .315
Russ Mitchell (Albuquerque) .315

SHORTSTOPS
Manny Mayorson (New Hampshire, Las Vegas) .324
Elliot Johnson (Durham) .319
Grant Green (Stockton) .318
Chris Gutierrez (Inland Empire) .312
Osvaldo Martinez (Jacksonville) .302

OUTFIELDERS
Brandon Guyer (Tennessee) .344
Dave Sappelt (Lynchburg, Carolina, Louisville).342
J.D. Martinez (Lexington, Corpus Christi) .341
Mike Trout (Cedar Rapids, Rancho Cucamonga) .341
Tyler Graham (Richmond, Fresno) .338

DESIGNATED HITTERS
Stephen Vogt (Charlotte) .345
Barbaro Canizares (Gwinnett) .341
Jose Flores (San Jose) .331
Nick Liles (Augusta) .316
James Cesario (Modesto) .316

INDIVIDUAL PITCHING
EARNED RUN AVERAGE*
Brandon Beachy (Mississippi, Gwinnett) 1.73
Matt Packer (Lake County, Akron) 2.04
Robert Erlin (Hickory) 2.12
James Fuller (Savannah, St. Lucie) 2.19
Daniel Rosenbaum (Hagerstown, Potomac) 2.25

WORST ERA*
Rey Gonzalez (Las Vegas, New Hampshire) 8.32
Lance Broadway (Las Vegas) 7.66
Marty McLeary (New Hampshire, Las Vegas, Nashville) 6.98
Ross Seaton (Lancaster) 6.64
Heitor Correa (Clearwater) 6.62

WINS
Eric Hacker (Fresno) 16
Tom Koehler (Jacksonville) 16
Christopher Archer (Daytona, Tennessee) 15
Blake Beavan (Frisco, West Tenn, Tacoma) 14
Brian Broderick (Palm Beach, Springfield) 14
Josh Collmenter (Visalia, Reno, Mobile) 14
Erik Davis (Portland, Lake Elsinore, San Antonio) 14
Richard De Los Santos (Montgomery, Durham) 14
Kyle Drabek (New Hampshire) 14
J.J. Hoover (Myrtle Beach, Mississippi) 14
Charles Leesman (Winston-Salem, Birmingham) 14
Hector Noesi (Tampa, Trenton, Scranton/WB) 14
Everett Teaford (Omaha, NW Arkansas) 14
Elih Villanueva (Jacksonville) 14

LOSSES
Jesus A. Castillo (Albuquerque, Chattanooga) 15
Eric Fornataro (Quad Cities) 15
Jose Ortegano (Myrtle Beach, Gwinnett) 15
Wilfredo Boscan (Bakersfield) 14
Cesar Carrillo (Portland) 14
Heitor Correa (Clearwater) 14
Brandon Durden (Colorado Springs, Tulsa) 14
Manuel Flores (Rancho Cucamonga, Arkansas) 14
Bradley Holt (Binghamton, St. Lucie) 14
Dallas Keuchel (Lancaster, Corpus Christi) 14
Ethan Martin (Inland Empire) 14
Tyler Robertson (Rochester, New Britain) 14

GAMES
Aaron Breit (Lake Elsinore, San Antonio) 64
Roy Merritt (Buffalo, Binghamton) 64
Noah Krol (Bradenton) 63
Nick Schumacher (Fort Wayne, Lake Elsinore) 63
Brad Brach (Lake Elsinore) 62

GAMES STARTED
Michael Antonini (Binghamton, Buffalo) 29
Aaron Crow (NW Arkansas, Wilmington) 29
Trevor Feeney (West Michigan) 29
Eric Hacker (Fresno) 29
Lance Lynn (Memphis) 29

COMPLETE GAMES
Brooks Brown (Erie) 4
Mark Cohoon (Savannah, Binghamton) 4
Elih Villanueva (Jacksonville) 4
Josh Banks (Round Rock) 3
Justin Collop (Kannapolis) 3
Shane Dyer (Bowling Green, Charlotte) 3
Wirkin Estevez (DSL Nationals) 3
Dallas Keuchel (Lancaster, Corpus Christi) 3
Tom Layne (Mobile) 3
Scott McGregor (Palm Beach, Springfield) 3
Drew Naylor (Reading) 3
Hector Noesi (Tampa, Trenton, Scranton/WB) 3
Henry Perez (DSL Mariners) 3
Ramon Reyes (DSL Cubs2) 3
Jeffrey Saba (DSL Brewers) 3
Jose Urena (DSL Marlins) 3
Anthony Vasquez (Clinton, High Desert, West Tenn) 3

SHUTOUTS
Mark Cohoon (Savannah, Binghamton) 3
Elih Villanueva (Jacksonville) 3
Jayson Aquino (DSL Rockies) 2
Richard Bleier (Frisco) 2
Brooks Brown (Erie) 2
Nathan Eovaldi (Inland Empire, AZL Dodgers, Ogden) 2
Jeff Ferrell (GCL Tigers, Connecticut) 2
Brad Hand (Jupiter, Jacksonville) 2
Drew Naylor (Reading) 2
Andre Rienzo (Kannapolis) 2
Jared Rogers (GCL Marlins, Jamestown) 2
Chris Seddon (Tacoma) 2
Giovanni Soto (West Michigan, Lake County) 2
Chris Tillman (Norfolk) 2
Jose Urena (DSL Marlins) 2

SAVES
Jonathan Albaladejo (Scranton/WB) 43
Cory Burns (Lake County, Kinston) 42
Brad Brach (Lake Elsinore) 41
Noah Krol (Bradenton) 34
Yonata Ortega (South Bend, Visalia) 33

INNINGS PITCHED
Thad Weber (Erie, Toledo) 189.2
Trevor Feeney (West Michigan) 184.2
Matt Torra (Mobile, Reno) 183.0
Elih Villanueva (Jacksonville) 179.0
Juan Nicasio (Modesto) 177.1
Andy Van Hekken (Round Rock) 177.1

WALKS
Tyler Sample (Burlington) 95
Anthony Capra (Midland) 89
Trey Haley (Lake County) 86
Trevor Reckling (Salt Lake, Arkansas) 85
Shooter Hunt (Fort Myers) 84
Luis Perez (New Hampshire, Las Vegas) 84

STRIKEOUTS
Matthew Moore (Charlotte) 208
Charles Furbush (Lakeland, Erie, Toledo) 183
Trevor May (Clearwater, Lakewood) 182
Austin Hyatt (Clearwater, Reading) 181
Joel Carreno (Clearwater, Reading) 173

HITS ALLOWED
Matt Torra (Mobile, Reno) 230
Rey Gonzalez (Las Vegas, New Hampshire) 217
Trevor Feeney (West Michigan) 216
Tim Kiely (Salt Lake, Arkansas) 216
Josh Geer (Portland) 212

HOME RUNS ALLOWED
Gaby Hernandez (Omaha) 31
Josh Geer (Portland) 29
Ryan Brasier (Arkansas) 28
Josh Banks (Round Rock) 25
Andrew Carraway (High Desert) 25
Yohan Pino (Columbus) 25

STRIKEOUTS PER NINE INNINGS
(STARTERS)*
Matthew Moore (Charlotte) 12.94
Trevor May (Clearwater, Lakewood) 12.27

Austin Hyatt (Clearwater, Reading) 11.29
Joel Carreno (Dunedin) 11.23
Mike Minor (Mississippi, Gwinnett) 10.92

STRIKEOUTS PER NINE INNINGS
(RELIEVERS)*
Donnie Joseph (Dayton, Lynchburg, Carolina) 14.26
Bryce Stowell (Kinston, Akron, Columbus) 13.99
Scott Shuman (Bowling Green, Charlotte) 13.86
Tim Collins (New Hampshire, Mississippi, Omaha)13.63
Ryan Verdugo (Augusta, San Jose) 13.58

OPPONENT AVERAGE (STARTERS)*
Matt Magill (Great Lakes) .194
Joseph Gardner (Lake County, Kinston) .197
Christopher Archer (Daytona, Tennessee) .198
Julio Teheran (Rome, Myrtle Beach, Mississippi) .208
Graham Stoneburner (Charleston, Tampa) .209

OPPONENT AVERAGE (RELIEVERS)*
Trevor Hurley (Bakersfield, Hickory) .151
Rafael Cova (Richmond) .157
Clay Rapada (Oklahoma City) .158
Tim Collins (New Hampshire, Mississippi, Omaha) .159
Blaine Hardy (NW Arkansas, Omaha) .162

MOST STRIKEOUTS, ONE GAME
Joel Carreno (Dunedin) 15
Adam Warren (Trenton) 15
Terry Doyle (Kannapolis) 14
Austin Hyatt (Clearwater) 14
Trevor May (Lakewood) 14
Pat McAnaney (Visalia) 14
Taylor Stanton (Clinton) 14
Eric Surkamp (San Jose) 14
Julio Teheran (Myrtle Beach) 14
Joseph Wieland (Bakersfield) 14

WILD PITCHES
Eric Beaulac (St. Lucie, Binghamton) 29
Evan Frederickson (Brevard County, Helena) 29
Jeurys Familia (St. Lucie) 25
Ivan Marcano (DSL Padres) 25
Bradley Holt (Binghamton, St. Lucie) 23
Ben Hornbeck (Midland, Stockton) 23
Rolando Pascual (DSL Brewers) 23

BALKS
Bubbie Buzachero (Las Vegas, New Hampshire, Corpus Christi) 7
Paul Demny (Hagerstown) 6
Zael Honora (VSL Phillies) 6
Anvioris Ramirez (Stockton, Kane County, Vancouver) 6
Eric Basurto (Wilmington) 5
Yinio Calderon (DSL Tigers) 5
Juan Espinoza (VSL Tigers) 5
Ryan Feierabend (High Desert, West Tenn, Tacoma) 5
Pedro Figueroa (Savannah) 5
Armando Rodriguez (Savannah) 5
Adriano Uribe (GCL Cardinals) 5

HIT BATTERS
Juan Minaya (Lexington) 21
Brad Dydalewicz (Lancaster, Lexington) 20
Joseph Gardner (Lake County, Kinston) 19
Nick Barnese (Charlotte) 18
Gary Daley (Springfield, Midland) 18

INDIVIDUAL FIELDING
MOST ERRORS
Jonathan Villar (Lakewood, Lancaster) 56
Garabez Rosa (Delmarva) 46
Jimmy Paredes (Charleston, Lexington) 45
Jonathan Galvez (Fort Wayne) 43
Mycal Jones (Rome, Myrtle Beach, Mississippi) 4

MINOR LEAGUES

MINOR LEAGUES

	INTERNATIONAL LEAGUE	PACIFIC COAST LEAGUE	EASTERN LEAGUE	SOUTHERN LEAGUE	TEXAS LEAGUE	CALIFORNIA LEAGUE	CAROLINA LEAGUE	FLORIDA STATE LEAGUE	MIDWEST LEAGUE	SOUTH ATLANTIC LEAGUE
Best Batting Prospect	Carlos Santana, Columbus	Buster Posey, Fresno	Domonic Brown, Reading	Mike Stanton, Jacksonville	Mike Moustakas, Northwest Arkansas	Brandon Belt, San Jose	Eric Hosmer, Wilmington	Brett Jackson, Daytona	Mike Trout, Cedar Rapids	J.D. Martinez, Lexington
Best Power Prospect	Carlos Santana, Columbus	J.P. Arencibia, Las Vegas	Brandon Laird, Trenton	Mike Stanton, Jacksonville	Mike Moustakas, Northwest Arkansas	Paul Goldschmidt, Visalia	Eric Hosmer, Wilmington	Michael McDade, Dunedin	Jerry Sands, Great Lakes	Chris Dominguez, Augusta
Best Strike-Zone Judgment	Michael Brantley, Columbus	Kila Ka'aihue, Omaha	Nate Spears, Portland	Dustin Ackley, West Tenn	Logan Forsythe, San Antonio	Cole Figueroa, Lake Elsinore	Eric Hosmer, Wilmington	Brett Jackson, Daytona	Conner Chambliss, Kane County	Brian Conley, Delmarva
Best Baserunner	Desmond Jennings, Durham	Peter Bourjos, Salt Lake	Darin Mastroianni, New Hampshire	Dee Gordon, Chattanooga	Paulo Orlando, Northwest Arkansas	Tyson Auer, Rancho Cucamonga	Kyle Hudson, Frederick	Josh Prince, Brevard County	Mike Trout, Cedar Rapids	Leury Garcia, Hickory
Fastest Baserunner	Jose Constanza, Columbus	Peter Bourjos, Salt Lake	Ben Revere, New Britain	Dee Gordon, Chattanooga	Derrick Anderson, Northwest Arkansas	Francisco Peguero, San Jose	Xavier Avery, Frederick	Anthony Gose, Clearwater	Mike Trout, Cedar Rapids	Jeremy Hazelbaker, Lakewood
Best Pitching Prospect	Jeremy Hellickson, Durham	Madison Bumgarner, Fresno	Kyle Drabek, New Hampshire	Michael Pineda, West Tenn	Blake Beavan, Frisco	Tyler Chatwood, Rancho Cucamonga	John Lamb, Wilmington	Matt Moore, Charlotte	Shelby Miller, Quad Cities	Arody Vizcaino, Rome
Best Fastball	Aroldis Chapman, Louisville	Henry Rodriguez, Sacramento	Zach Britton, Bowie	Michael Pineda, West Tenn	Jordan Walden, Arkansas	Tyler Chatwood, Rancho Cucamonga	Julio Teheran, Myrtle Beach	Jhan Marinez, Jupiter	Rubby de la Rosa, Great Lakes	Jarred Cosart, Lakewood
Best Breaking Pitch	Aroldis Chapman, Louisville	Michael Kirkman, Oklahoma City	Kyle Drabek, New Hampshire	Josh Fields, West Tenn	Evan Scribner, San Antonio	Eric Surkamp, San Jose	John Lamb, Wilmington	Matt Moore, Charlotte	Trey McNutt, Peoria	Chad James, Greensboro
Best Changeup	Jeremy Hellickson, Durham	Luke French, Tacoma	Rudy Owens, Altoona	Alex Torres, Montgomery	Edgar Osuna, Northwest Arkansas	Dallas Keuchel, Lancaster	John Lamb, Wilmington	Henderson Alvarez, Brevard County	Kyle Heckathorn, Wisconsin	Jose Ramirez, Charleston
Best Control	Dan Hudson, Charlotte	Luke French, Tacoma	Rudy Owens, Altoona	Barry Enright, Mobile	Blake Beavan, Frisco	Anthony Bass, Lake Elsinore	Caleb Clay, Salem	Adam Wilk, Lakeland	Erasmo Ramirez, Clinton	Mark Cohoon, Savannah
Best Reliever	Jonathan Albaladejo, Scranton/Wilkes-Barre	Ernesto Frieri, Portland	Daniel Moskos, Altoona	Kenley Jansen, Chattanooga	Craig Italiano, Midland	Brad Brach, Lake Elsinore	Cory Burns, Kinston	Zach Quate, Charlotte	Steve Turnbull, Lansing	Trevor Hurley, Hickory
Best Defensive Catcher	Lou Marson, Columbus	Jackson Williams, Fresno	Tuffy Gosewisch, Reading	Robinson Chirinos, Tennessee	Wilian Rosario, Tulsa	Matt Wallach, Inland Empire	Salvador Perez, Wilmington	Travis D'Arnaud, Dunedin	A.J. Jimenez, Lansing	Miguel Gonzalez, Kannapolis
Best Defensive First Baseman	Freddie Freeman, Gwinnett	Chris Davis, Oklahoma City	Anthony Rizzo, Portland	Jimmy Gallagher, Birmingham	Efren Navarro, Arkansas	Brandon Belt, San Jose	Eric Hosmer, Wilmington	Michael Sheridan, Charlotte	Jerry Sands, Great Lakes	Jonathan Singleton, Lakewood
Best Defensive Second Baseman	Chris Valaika, Louisville	Ivan De Jesus, Albuquerque	Michael Martinez, Harrisburg	Ryan Curry, Jacksonville	Alexi Amarista, Arkansas	Alexi Amarista, Rancho Cucamonga	Andrew Garcia, Winston-Salem	Corban Joseph, Tampa	Jean Segura, Cedar Rapids	Jose Altuve, Lexington
Best Defensive Third Baseman	Brent Morel, Charlotte	Travis Metcalf, Colorado Springs	Ray Chang, Portland	Matt Dominguez, Jacksonville	Mike Moustakas, Northwest Arkansas	Ryan Wheeler, Visalia	Will Middlebrooks, Salem	Matt Cline, Brevard County	Mario Martinez, Clinton	Chris Dominguez, Augusta
Best Defensive Shortstop	Eduardo Nunez, Scranton/Wilkes-Barre	Luis Cruz, Nashville	Jose Iglesias, Portland	Kris Negron, Carolina	Andrew Romine, Arkansas	Ehire Adrianza, San Jose	Eduardo Escobar, Winston-Salem	Gustavo Nunez, Lakeland	Hak-Ju Lee, Peoria	Leury Garcia, Hickory
Best Infield Arm	Eduardo Nunez, Scranton/Wilkes-Barre	Gregorio Petit, Oklahoma City	Danny Espinosa, Harrisburg	Carlos Triunfel, West Tenn	Jhon Florentino, Corpus Christi	Pedro Baez, Inland Empire	Will Middlebrooks, Salem	Junior Lake, Daytona	Marielkson Gregorus, Dayton	Jonathan Villar, Lakewood
Best Defensive Outfielder	Desmond Jennings, Durham	Peter Bourjos, Salt Lake	Che-Hsuan Lin, Portland	Lorenzo Cain, Huntsville	Antone Delesus, Springfield	Juan Perez, San Jose	Brandon Short, Winston-Salem	Anthony Gose, Clearwater	Mike Trout, Cedar Rapids	Reymond Fuentes, Greenville
Best Outfield Arm	Wladimir Balentien, Louisville	Michael Taylor, Sacramento	Gorkys Hernandez, Altoona	Sal Sanchez, Birmingham	Sawyer Carroll, San Antonio	Johermyn Chavez, High Desert	Michael Burgess, Potomac	Melky Mesa, Tampa	Aaron Hicks, Beloit	Leandro Castro, Lakewood
Most Exciting Player	Desmond Jennings, Durham	Peter Bourjos, Salt Lake	Domonic Brown, Reading	Dee Gordon, Chattanooga	Mike Moustakas, Northwest Arkansas	Francisco Peguero, San Jose	Eric Hosmer, Myrtle Beach	Anthony Gose, Clearwater	Mike Trout, Cedar Rapids	Jonathan Singleton, Lakewood
Best Manager Prospect	Mike Sarbaugh, Columbus	Ryne Sandberg, Iowa	Arnie Beyeler, Portland	Billy Gardner, Montgomery	Billy Gardner, Montgomery	Brian Harper, San Jose	Joe McEwing, Winston-Salem	Jim Morrison, Charlotte	Juan Bustabad, Great Lakes	Andy Haines, Greensboro

Honoring excellence

MINOR LEAGUES

TRIPLE-A: LOUISVILLE BATS

The debut of Louisville Slugger Park in 2000 certainly ushered in a new era for the International League affiliate. Louisville saw attendance nearly double from 361,419 (5,020 average) in 1999 to 685,863 (9,526) average when the shiny new ballpark along the shores of the Mississippi River replaced aging Cardinal Stadium.

The team has continued to fill the park in the 11 years since it's opening, as baseball fans and casual observers alike are attracted to the facility that offers scenic views from a variety of group-seating areas and helped spur over $150 million of private investment in the area surrounding the facility.

Louisville has led the IL in attendance five times since 2000 and remains one of the circuits best and most consistent draws. The club drew 8,634 fans in 2010—good for third in the IL.

In addition to a wonderful facility, the Bats boast an experienced front office, that includes minor league veterans Gary Ulmer, Dale Owens and assistant GM Gary Galiette.

DOUBLE-A: CORPUS CHRISTI HOOKS

Corpus Christi Hooks president Ken Schrom believes being a part of the community is one of the highest priorities of the team.

"We are, for six months of the year, asking people to spend their hard-earned dollars to come and watch baseball and buy our concessions and buy our souvenirs," Schrom said. "I think to be a good community partner you have to give something back and that's what we try to do."

The Hooks provide one of the most scenic venues in the minors, as Whataburger Field sits on land right on the shipping channel, with the Harbor Bridge towering over the field. The location's heritage surrounds the park, with the remaining roof from an old warehouse, antique cotton presses, and a permanently docked USS Lexington aircraft carrier beyond the outfield.

The Hooks' goal of positively impacting the community has been realized through programs like Field of Dreams, in which they have helped rebuild ball fields, and the Miracle League, which gives children with disabilities a safe place to play baseball.

CLASS A: LYNCHBURG HILLCATS

Few teams can claim to be a part of the community quite like this high Class A Carolina League affiliate. The club's stockholders are each local leaders and they have never declared a dividend—all the proceeds are re-invested in the team.

The team has been owned by the Lynchburg Baseball Corporation since 1966 with Calvin Falwell presiding as chairman of the board each season since. City Stadium, which was christened by an exhibition between the Brooklyn Dodgers and New York Yankees in 1940, underwent a $6.5 million renovation in 2002 that included a new concourse, group-seating areas and luxury suites.

SHORT-SEASON: IDAHO FALLS CHUKARS

Idaho Falls general manager Kevin Greene had to be creative to attract fans to the ballpark before the team built a new facility in 2007. So he went after something near and dear to the fans' hearts, or perhaps their stomachs: barbecue. The Chukars offered some of the best 'cue in town, and through a variety of other methods, became entrenched in the community. They've reaped the rewards since debuting a completely renovated ballpark in 2007—which includes better facilities for serving barbecue—with increased attendance.

"Back in the old days, when he had lesser stadium, (Greene) made good use of the space. He really provided what the local population wanted and enjoyed," Pioneer League president Jim McCurdy said.

PREVIOUS WINNERS

TRIPLE-A	DOUBLE-A	CLASS A	SHORT-SEASON
2000: Edmonton (Pacific Coast)	2000: Reading (Eastern)	2000: Charleston, S.C. (South Atlantic)	2000: Lowell (New York-Penn)
2001: Buffalo (International)	2001: Mobile (Southern)	2001: Delmarva (South Atlantic)	2001: Salem-Keizer (Northwest)
2002: Memphis (Pacific Coast)	2002: Chattanooga (Southern)	2002: Fort Myers (Florida State)	2002: Ogden (Pioneer)
2003: Pawtucket (International)	2003: New Britain (Eastern)	2003: Modesto (California)	2003: Spokane (Northwest)
2004: Sacramento (Pacific Coast)	2004: Round Rock (Texas)	2004: Dayton (Midwest)	2004: Burlington (Appalachian)
2005: Toledo (International)	2005: Tulsa (Texas)	2005: Lakewood (South Atlantic)	2005: Brooklyn (New York-Penn)
2006: Durham (International)	2006: Altoona (Eastern)	2006: Daytona (Florida State)	2006: Aberdeen (New York-Penn)
2007: Albuquerque (Pacific Coast)	2007: Frisco (Texas)	2007: Lake Elsinore (California)	2007: Missoula (Pioneer)
2008: Columbus (International)	2008: Birmingham (Southern)	2008: Greensboro (South Atlantic)	2008: Greeneville (Appalachian)
2009: Iowa (Pacific Coast)	2009: New Hamshire (Eastern)	2009: San Jose (California)	2009: Tri-City (New York-Penn)

MINOR LEAGUES

BY JOHN WAGNER

The relationship between Columbus and Cleveland got off to a rocky start in 2009, as the Clippers struggled to just 57 wins in their first season as the Indians top affiliate. But things were much rosier for Columbus last season as the Clippers won their first Governors' Cup since 1996, then tacked on a victory over Tacoma in the Triple-A National Championship Game.

Cleveland sought to give the Clippers a better team in 2010 and stocked it with prospects like catcher Carlos Santana and veterans like Shelley Duncan. Columbus went 49-32 over the season's first three months, then found enough offense to compensate when Santana and Duncan were promoted to the big leagues.

And once the Clippers reached the playoffs, they cruised to the Governors' Cup by toppling Scranton/Wilkes-Barre and Durham.

While Columbus was making its first playoff appearance since 2004—and just the second since 1999—the rest of the IL's playoff roster was filled with familiar faces. Durham (Rays) cruised to the South Division crown by 16 games to earn its fourth straight division title and sixth playoff berth in the past eight seasons; Louisville (Reds) posted a 43-20 record after July 1 to overtake Columbus and win the West Division title for the second straight season; and Scranton/Wilkes-Barre (Yankees) went 42-21 after July 1 to pull away from the North Division field and claim its fifth straight division crown.

Stephen Strasburg, the 2009 No. 1 overall draft pick, spent a month with Syracuse (Nationals) and went 4-1, 1.08 with 38 strikeouts in 33 innings.

Gwinnett's Freddy Freeman (Braves), 20, hit .319/.378/.521 in 124 games, finishing second in

the batting race and third with 87 RBIs. Another highly regarded 20-year-old was Scranton catcher Jesus Montero, who hit .289/.353/.517.

On the mound, Montero's batterymate Jonathan Albaladejo broke the IL record with 45 saves.

Durham's Jeremy Hellickson earned pitcher of the year honors. The 23-year-old righthander led the league with a 2.45 ERA. Hellickson's teammate Dan Johnson was voted player of the year after leading the IL in home runs (30), finishing second in RBIs (95) and eighth in batting average.

Norfolk's Chris Tillman no-hit the Braves, working around a walk and an error in the fifth inning on April 28. Exactly one month later Gwinnett's Todd Redmond (Braves) allowed just two sixth-inning walks in a no-hitter at Louisville.

Sadly, the league also lost two of long-time leaders when Pawtucket owner Ben Mondor and former IL president Harold Cooper both passed away in early October.

TOP 20 PROSPECTS

1. Carlos Santana, c, Columbus Clippers (Indians)
2. Jeremy Hellickson, rhp, Durham Bulls (Rays)
3. Aroldis Chapman, lhp, Louisville Bats (Reds)
4. Jesus Montero, c, Scranton/Wilkes-Barre Yankees
5. Freddie Freeman, 1b, Gwinnett Braves
6. Zach Britton, lhp, Norfolk Tides (Orioles)
7. Desmond Jennings, of, Durham Bulls (Rays)
8. Pedro Alvarez, 3b, Indianapolis Indians (Pirates)
9. Ivan Nova, rhp, Scranton/Wilkes-Barre Yankees
10. Daniel Hudson, rhp, Charlotte Knights (White Sox)
11. Brent Morel, 3b/ss, Charlotte Knights (White Sox)
12. Yonder Alonso, 1b/of, Louisville Bats (Reds)
13. Eduardo Nunez, ss/3b, Scranton/Wilkes-Barre Yankees
14. Jake Arrieta, rhp, Norfolk Tides (Orioles)
15. Brad Lincoln, rhp, Indianapolis Indians (Pirates)
16. Jose Tabata, of, Indianapolis Indians (Pirates)
17. Ryan Kalish, of, Pawtucket Red Sox
18. Wilson Ramos, c, Rochester (Twins)/Syracuse (Nationals)
19. Andy Oliver, lhp, Toledo Mud Hens (Tigers)
20. Carlos Carrasco, rhp, Columbus Clippers (Indians)

STANDINGS

North (Organization)	W	L	PCT	GB	Manager(s)	Attendance	Average	Last Penn.
Scranton/Wilkes-Barre (Yankees)	87	56	.608	—	Dave Miley	338,731	4,981	2008
Syracuse Chiefs (Nationals)	76	67	.531	11	Trent Jewett	416,382	6,123	1976
Buffalo Bisons (Mets)	76	68	.528	11 ½	Ken Oberkfell	575,296	8,219	2004
Pawtucket (Red Sox)	66	78	.458	21 ½	Torey Lovullo	592,326	8,343	1984
Lehigh Valley IronPigs (Phillies)	58	86	.403	29 ½	Dave Huppert	645,905	9,227	1995
Rochester Red Wings (Twins)	49	95	.340	38 ½	Tom Nieto	462,004	6,600	1997
South (Organization)	**W**	**L**	**PCT**	**GB**	**Manager(s)**	**Attendance**	**Average**	**Last Penn.**
Durham Bulls (Rays)	88	55	.615	—	Charlie Montoyo	500,073	7,043	2009
Gwinnett Braves (Braves)	72	71	.503	16	Dave Brundage	337,240	4,818	2007
Charlotte Knights (White Sox)	67	77	.465	21 ½	Chris Chambliss	305,842	4,248	1999
Norfolk Tides (Orioles)	67	77	.465	21 ½	G. Allenson/B. Dickerson	392,752	5,455	1985
East (Organization)	**W**	**L**	**PCT**	**GB**	**Manager(s)**	**Attendance**	**Average**	**Last Penn.**
Louisville Bats (Reds)	79	64	.552	—	Rick Sweet	613,020	8,634	2001
Columbus Clippers (Indians)	79	65	.549	½	Mike Sarbaugh	635,141	8,946	2010
Indianapolis Indians (Pirates)	71	73	.493	8 ½	Frank Kremblas	569,969	8,028	2000
Toledo Mud Hens (Tigers)	70	73	.490	9	Larry Parrish	558,059	7,972	2006

PLAYOFFS—Semifinals: Columbus defeated Scranton/WB 3-1 and Durham defeated Louisville 3-2 in best-of-five series. **Finals:** Columbus defeated Durham 3-1 in best-of-five series.

CLUB BATTING

	AVG	G	AB	R	H	2B	3B	HR	RBI	BB	SO	SB	OBP	SLG
Columbus	.285	144	4945	731	1407	304	33	139	699	526	895	120	.356	.444
Durham	.277	143	4921	757	1363	288	22	142	699	542	1056	150	.353	.431
Buffalo	.273	144	4979	701	1359	330	21	153	651	414	937	41	.334	.440
Louisville	.272	143	4926	708	1338	314	34	160	667	397	1072	124	.330	.447
Scranton/Wilkes-Barre	.267	143	4827	630	1291	286	26	118	591	408	957	83	.330	.411
Toledo	.264	143	4851	645	1280	279	42	131	609	413	1133	122	.328	.420
Gwinnett	.263	143	4760	627	1253	238	21	111	568	450	896	142	.333	.392
Indianapolis	.262	144	4790	672	1254	295	41	118	613	544	1102	132	.340	.414
Charlotte	.255	144	4856	627	1236	254	27	149	583	397	1063	93	.315	.410
Pawtucket	.253	144	4742	588	1202	269	21	116	567	487	990	80	.327	.392
Rochester	.252	144	4863	592	1227	269	30	102	559	434	1094	64	.319	.383
Syracuse	.252	143	4715	595	1190	250	28	110	549	487	1089	161	.327	.387
Lehigh Valley	.251	144	4798	563	1202	228	32	106	525	422	1068	112	.315	.378
Norfolk	.251	144	4895	629	1231	239	24	122	578	454	986	129	.318	.385

CLUB PITCHING

	ERA	G	CG	SHO	SV	IP	H	R	ER	HR	BB	SO	AVG
Durham	3.56	143	2	14	36	1269	1216	562	502	104	445	1051	.252
Louisville	3.76	143	2	13	42	1271	1223	583	531	109	416	1034	.255
Scranton/Wilkes-Barre	3.78	143	3	7	58	1248	1235	565	524	114	409	1046	.258
Lehigh Valley	3.83	144	1	6	36	1268	1253	618	539	117	470	1051	.259
Syracuse	3.84	143	4	11	43	1256	1239	597	536	115	440	932	.259
Gwinnett	3.93	143	3	9	41	1249	1209	624	546	107	491	1115	.256
Toledo	4.13	143	3	7	33	1247	1299	643	572	139	436	985	.270
Norfolk	4.16	144	2	7	34	1280	1318	673	592	119	449	1017	.264
Columbus	4.25	144	4	9	33	1273	1281	658	601	142	455	1051	.261
Buffalo	4.40	144	6	8	31	1268	1343	689	620	130	393	1063	.273
Indianapolis	4.44	144	1	8	42	1265	1296	677	624	126	445	996	.266
Charlotte	4.52	144	1	3	36	1269	1243	719	637	162	541	990	.257
Pawtucket	4.54	144	2	14	41	1247	1264	677	629	136	524	1000	.264
Rochester	4.93	144	1	5	26	1255	1414	840	687	157	461	1007	.284

CLUB FIELDING

	PCT	PO	A	E	DP		PCT	PO	A	E	DP
Durham	.984	3807	1364	85	111	Lehigh Valley	.980	3804	1372	105	118
Louisville	.982	3812	1494	96	151	Syracuse	.980	3767	1488	105	123
Pawtucket	.982	3741	1251	93	127	Columbus	.979	3820	1389	112	129
Scranton/Wilkes-Barre	.982	3744	1364	93	125	Toledo	.979	3740	1360	112	146
Buffalo	.980	3804	1478	107	130	Gwinnett	.978	3747	1394	116	125
Charlotte	.980	3807	1481	108	153	Rochester	.978	3764	1364	118	125
Indianapolis	.980	3795	1591	112	153	Norfolk	.973	3840	1455	147	155

INDIVIDUAL BATTING LEADERS (MINIMUM 3.1 PA/TEAM GAME)

	AVG	G	AB	R	H	2B	3B	HR	RBI	BB	SO	SB
Canizares, Barbaro, Gwinnett	.341	126	425	58	145	28	1	13	77	40	54	2
Constanza, Jose, Columbus	.319	113	404	69	129	11	8	1	32	35	54	34
Freeman, Freddie, Gwinnett	.319	124	461	73	147	35	2	18	87	43	84	6
Johnson, Elliot, Durham	.319	109	427	72	136	24	5	11	56	37	92	30
Turner, Justin, Norfolk, Buffalo	.316	101	396	69	125	30	1	12	43	33	51	7
Rhymes, Will, Toledo	.305	95	364	59	111	20	7	2	35	36	35	22
Valaika, Chris, Louisville	.304	118	424	49	129	28	2	4	53	19	72	3
Johnson, Dan, Durham	.303	98	340	66	103	19	0	30	95	75	71	0
Richard, Chris, Durham	.300	117	430	68	129	39	1	20	79	60	96	0
Young, Matt, Gwinnett	.300	134	487	88	146	33	5	3	35	57	53	39

INDIVIDUAL PITCHING LEADERS (MINIMUM 1 IP/TEAM GAME)

	W	L	ERA	G	GS	CG	SV	IP	H	R	ER	BB	SO
Hellickson, Jeremy, Durham	12	3	2.46	21	21	0	0	118	103	35	32	35	123
Nova, Ivan, Scranton/WB	12	3	2.86	23	23	0	0	145	135	50	46	48	115
Misch, Pat, Buffalo	11	4	3.24	23	23	2	0	151	150	61	54	24	99
Tillman, Chris, Norfolk	11	7	3.34	21	21	2	0	121	120	50	45	30	94
Maloney, Matt, Louisville	10	7	3.35	24	23	0	0	135	132	65	50	28	104
Torres, Carlos, Charlotte	9	9	3.43	27	25	0	0	160	125	65	61	71	140
Gagnier, L.J., Toledo	7	7	3.52	21	20	1	0	121	111	60	47	44	94
De Los Santos, Richard, Durham	14	5	3.52	28	23	0	0	148	154	63	58	48	90
Carrasco, Carlos, Columbus	10	6	3.66	25	25	0	0	150	139	69	61	46	133
Chico, Matt, Syracuse	6	7	3.75	21	21	0	0	116	120	53	48	34	69

ALL-STAR TEAM

C: Jesus Montero, Scranton/Wilkes-Barre. **1B:** Freddie Freeman, Gwinnett. **2B:** Chris Valaika, Louisville. **3B:** Dan Johnson, Durham. **SS:** Eduardo Nunez, Scranton/Wilkes-Barre. **OF:** Wladimir Balentien, Louisville; Jose Constanza, Columbus; Jeff Frazier, Toledo. **DH:** Barbaro Canizares, Gwinnett. **UTIL:** Elliot Johnson, Durham. **SP:** Jeremy Hellickson, Durham. **RP:** Jonathan Albaladejo, Scranton/Wilkes-Barre. **Most Valuable Player:** Dan Johnson, Durham. **Most Valuable Pitcher:** Jeremy Hellickson, Durham. **Rookie of the Year:** Freddie Freeman, Gwinnett. **Manager of the Year:** Charlie Montoyo, Durham.

DEPARTMENT LEADERS

BATTING

OBP	Johnson, Dan, Durham	.430
SLG	Johnson, Dan, Durham	.624
OPS	Johnson, Dan, Durham	1.053
R	Cozart, Zack, Louisville	91
H	Freeman, Freddie, Gwinnett	147
TB	Freeman, Freddie, Gwinnett	240
XBH	Frazier, Jeff, Toledo	61
2B	Richard, Chris, Durham	39
3B	Constanza, Jose, Columbus	8
	Orr, Pete, Syracuse	8
HR	Johnson, Dan, Durham	30
RBI	Moss, Brandon, Indianapolis	96
SAC	Rhymes, Will, Toledo	13
BB	Johnson, Dan, Durham	75
HBP	Orr, Pete, Syracuse	12
SO	Gartrell, Stefan, Charlotte	152
SB	Young, Matt, Gwinnett	39
CS	Whiting, Boomer, Syracuse	12
AB/SO	Timmons, Wes, Gwinnett	11.7

PITCHING

G	Delaney, Rob, Rochester	61
GS	Three tied at	28
GF	Albaladejo, Jonathan, Scranton/WB	54
SV	Albaladejo, Jonathan, Scranton/WB	43
W	De Los Santos, Richard, Durham	14
L	Johnson, Kris, Pawtucket	13
	Mazone, Brian, Lehigh Valley	13
IP	Mazone, Brian, Lehigh Valley	165
H	McAllister, Zach, Scranton/WB, Columbus	185
R	Pino, Yohan, Columbus	101
ER	Pino, Yohan, Columbus	93
HB	Gee, Dillon, Buffalo	13
BB	Torres, Carlos, Charlotte	71
SO	Gee, Dillon, Buffalo	165
SO/9	Hellickson, Jeremy, Durham	9.45
SO/9 (RP)	Albaladejo, Jonathan, Scranton/WB	11.7
BB/9	Misch, Pat, Buffalo	1.44
WP	Chapman, Aroldis, Louisville	14
BK	De Los Santos, Richard, Durham	3
	Phillips, Heath, Durham	3
HR	Pino, Yohan, Columbus	25
AVG	Torres, Carlos, Charlotte	.217

FIELDING

C	FPCT	Sammons, Clint, Gwinnett	.998
	PO	Montero, Jesus, Scranton/WB	703
	A	Montero, Jesus, Scranton/WB	76
	E	Hoover, Paul, Lehigh Valley	7
		Kratz, Erik, Indianapolis	7
	DP	Three tied at	8
	PB	Montero, Jesus, Scranton/WB	15
1B	FPCT	Freeman, Freddie, Gwinnett	.994
	PO	Peterson, Brock, Rochester	1000
	A	Peterson, Brock, Rochester	86
	E	Three tied at	11
	DP	Peterson, Brock, Rochester	99
2B	FPCT	Valaika, Chris, Louisville	.984
	PO	Valaika, Chris, Louisville	173
	A	Corona, Reegie, Scranton/WB	282
	E	Cortez, Fernando, Charlotte	10
	DP	Figueroa, Paco, Norfolk	63
3B	FPCT	Timmons, Wes, Gwinnett	.966
	PO	Chavez, Angel, Durham	69
		Jimenez, Jorge, Pawtucket	69
	A	Timmons, Wes, Gwinnett	156
	E	Ransom, Cody, Lehigh Valley	19
	DP	Goedert, Jared, Columbus	19
SS	FPCT	Cozart, Zack, Louisville	.977
	PO	Cozart, Zack, Louisville	228
	A	Cozart, Zack, Louisville	411
	E	Andino, Robert, Norfolk	29
	DP	Cozart, Zack, Louisville	109
OF	FPCT	Mayberry, John, Lehigh Valley	.996
	PO	Martin, Dustin, Rochester	288
	A	Wells, Casper, Toledo	12
	E	Martin, Dustin, Rochester	9
	DP	Wells, Casper, Toledo	6

MINOR LEAGUES

BY JIM SHONERD

In some ways, the Tacoma Rainiers (Mariners) were a long shot to win the Pacific Coast League championship. The Rainiers' 74-69 regular season record was only seventh best in the league, but they got hot when it mattered most, knocking off Sacramento (Athletics) and Memphis (Cardinals) on their way to their first PCL title since 2001.

The Rainiers didn't clinch their division title until the next-to-last day of the regular season, then nearly lost a 2-0 series lead in the semifinals against Sacramento. Tacoma rallied to win Game Five, but then had to face defending champ Memphis in the final. Further complicating matters was the fact that ongoing renovations at the Rainiers' home field meant that the entire series would have to be played in Memphis, where the Redbirds were the league's most dominant home team, going 48-26 during the regular season.

None of that fazed the Rainiers, who went on the road and swept Memphis in three straight. It didn't hurt that the Rainiers had received reinforcements during the second half of the season. First baseman Justin Smoak came over from the Rangers when the Mariners dealt ace Cliff Lee and hit .423/.595/.538 in the postseason. Also joining in was second baseman Dustin Ackley, the second overall pick in the 2009 draft.

Salt Lake first baseman Mark Trumbo (Angels) tied for the minor league home run lead with 36 and also captured the PCL's RBI title. Trumbo shared the minors' home run crown with Royals third baseman Mike Moustakas, who hit the last

TOP 20 PROSPECTS

1. Buster Posey, c/1b, Fresno Grizzlies (Giants)
2. Mike Moustakas, 3b, Omaha Royals
3. Michael Pineda, rhp, Tacoma Rainiers (Mariners)
4. Madison Bumgarner, lhp, Fresno Grizzlies (Giants)
5. Dustin Ackley, 2b, Tacoma Rainiers (Mariners)
6. Logan Morrison, 1b/of, New Orleans Zephyrs (Marlins)
7. Tanner Scheppers, rhp, Oklahoma City RedHawks (Rangers)
8. J.P. Arencibia, c, Las Vegas 51s (Blue Jays)
9. Justin Smoak, 1b, Oklahoma City (Rangers)/Tacoma (Mariners)
10. Brett Wallace, 1b, Las Vegas 51s (Blue Jays)
11. Jason Castro, c, Round Rock Express (Astros)
12. Mat Gamel, 3b, Nashville Sounds (Brewers)
13. Michael Kirkman, lhp, Oklahoma City RedHawks (Rangers)
14. Chris Carter, 1b/of, Sacramento River Cats (Athletics)
15. Peter Bourjos, of, Salt Lake Bees (Angels)
16. Mitch Moreland, 1b/of, Oklahoma City RedHawks (Rangers)
17. Henry Rodriguez, rhp, Sacramento River Cats (Athletics)
18. Greg Halman, of, Tacoma Rainiers (Mariners)
19. Cory Luebke, lhp, Portland Beavers (Padres)
20. Mark Trumbo, 1b/of, Salt Lake Bees (Angels)

15 of his 36 homers in an Omaha uniform. One of Trumbo's teammates with the Bees, outfielder Peter Bourjos, set a modern-era PCL record for hits in a month when he collected 56 in July.

Las Vegas catcher J.P. Arencibia (Blue Jays) won MVP honors after hitting .301 with 32 homers. Oklahoma City lefthander Michael Kirkman (Rangers) went 13-3, 3.09 and won the league's pitcher of the year award.

Omaha played its final game at Rosenblatt Stadium, which had been home to minor league baseball since 1949. The O-Royals are moving a new park in nearby Sarpy County. Portland was left without a home when its park was scheduled to be converted into a soccer-only facility. The Beavers wll seek temporary shelter in Tucson.

STANDINGS

AMERICAN CONFERENCE

North (Organization)	W	L	PCT	GB	Manager(s)	Attendance	Average	Last Penn.
Memphis Redbirds (Cardinals)	82	62	.569	—	Chris Maloney	462,041	6,508	2009
Iowa Cubs (Cubs)	82	62	.569	—	Ryne Sandberg	521,669	7,672	Never
Omaha Royals (Royals)	81	63	.563	1	Mike Jirschele	406,276	5,888	Never
Nashville Sounds (Brewers)	77	67	.535	5	Don Money	319,235	4,765	2005
South (Organization)	**W**	**L**	**PCT**	**GB**	**Manager(s)**	**Attendance**	**Average**	**Last Penn.**
Oklahoma City RedHawks (Rangers)	73	70	.510	—	Bobby Jones	367,082	5,479	1965
Albuquerque Isotopes (Dodgers)	72	71	.503	1	Tim Wallach	571,100	8,159	1994
New Orleans Zephyrs (Marlins)	66	77	.462	7	E. Rodriguez/G. Norton	380,538	5,596	2001
Round Rock Express (Astros)	57	87	.396	16 ½	Marc Bombard	596,985	8,408	Never

PACIFIC CONFERENCE

North (Organization)	W	L	PCT	GB	Manager(s)	Attendance	Average	Last Penn.
Tacoma Rainiers (Mariners)	74	69	.517	—	Daren Brown	351,095	5,163	2010
Salt Lake Bees (Angels)	73	71	.507	1 ½	Bobby Mitchell	510,484	7,293	1979
Colorado Springs Sky Sox (Rockies)	64	79	.448	10	Stu Cole	328,003	4,824	1995
Portland Beavers (Padres)	59	85	.410	15 ½	Terry Kennedy	294,332	4,266	1983
South (Organization)	**W**	**L**	**PCT**	**GB**	**Manager(s)**	**Attendance**	**Average**	**Last Penn.**
Sacramento River Cats (Athletics)	79	65	.549	—	Tony DeFrancesco	657,910	9,138	2008
Fresno Grizzlies (Giants)	75	69	.521	4	Steve Decker	481,606	6,783	Never
Reno Aces (Diamondbacks)	69	74	.483	9 ½	Brett Butler	447,701	6,218	2006
Las Vegas 51s (Blue Jays)	66	78	.458	13	Dan Rohn	336,488	4,739	1988

PLAYOFFS—Semifinals: Memphis defeated Oklahoma City 3-0 and Tacoma defeated Sacramento 3-2 in best-of-five series. **Finals:** Tacoma defeated Memphis 3-0 in best-of-five series.

MINOR LEAGUES

CLUB BATTING

	AVG	G	AB	R	H	2B	3B	HR	RBI	BB	SO	SB	OBP	SLG
Albuquerque	.302	143	5080	871	1533	341	37	163	816	403	910	80	.357	.480
Las Vegas	.293	144	5045	838	1480	352	33	172	782	499	831	79	.359	.478
Colorado Springs	.285	143	4934	776	1407	296	52	116	719	480	972	76	.352	.437
Fresno	.283	144	4954	725	1401	291	37	118	661	519	894	143	.357	.428
Salt Lake	.282	144	4941	770	1391	256	55	124	707	462	981	85	.345	.431
Iowa	.281	144	4904	796	1378	293	33	156	745	514	929	105	.354	.450
Reno	.277	143	4895	793	1357	292	62	130	733	577	990	116	.359	.442
Nashville	.275	144	4822	687	1328	252	24	124	647	439	972	94	.342	.415
Omaha	.275	144	4991	744	1371	270	40	154	699	546	903	87	.351	.437
Memphis	.272	144	4907	754	1337	268	25	133	703	495	978	62	.344	.419
Sacramento	.272	144	4916	827	1337	266	39	159	783	588	1053	133	.356	.439
New Orleans	.271	143	4799	670	1302	247	25	128	613	452	1031	69	.337	.413
Oklahoma City	.271	143	4799	727	1300	256	35	132	680	542	1011	112	.349	.421
Portland	.265	144	4835	646	1283	233	37	101	596	466	960	106	.337	.392
Tacoma	.264	143	4904	726	1297	273	27	185	697	504	1111	65	.336	.444
Round Rock	.259	144	4951	638	1284	247	25	108	593	444	991	99	.325	.385

CLUB PITCHING

	ERA	G	CG	SHO	SV	IP	H	R	ER	HR	BB	SO	AVG
Omaha	4.01	144	3	11	31	1289	1276	639	574	150	436	899	.259
Oklahoma City	4.03	143	3	7	28	1249	1289	653	559	107	464	1070	.265
Nashville	4.27	144	3	6	42	1251	1265	662	594	135	490	938	.265
Tacoma	4.29	143	6	9	29	1261	1292	678	601	120	408	975	.264
Sacramento	4.31	144	1	5	36	1278	1307	725	612	118	565	1065	.266
Memphis	4.42	144	1	8	46	1274	1287	713	625	143	495	1032	.264
Fresno	4.45	144	2	7	37	1280	1351	697	633	141	540	997	.274
Iowa	4.45	144	2	7	38	1262	1223	688	624	144	502	971	.254
Portland	4.67	144	3	5	33	1252	1261	728	650	154	502	950	.263
Round Rock	4.68	144	7	6	22	1267	1428	742	658	142	385	812	.286
New Orleans	4.72	143	5	10	33	1230	1344	725	645	131	522	954	.277
Salt Lake	5.19	144	1	3	38	1252	1443	792	722	130	534	944	.293
Reno	5.44	143	1	4	34	1264	1435	833	764	135	548	966	.288
Colorado Springs	5.68	143	4	5	22	1240	1467	853	783	141	516	992	.298
Albuquerque	5.78	143	1	6	32	1257	1517	887	807	161	494	1038	.299
Las Vegas	6.10	144	2	5	38	1252	1601	973	849	151	559	914	.312

CLUB FIELDING

	PCT	PO	A	E	DP		PCT	PO	A	E	DP
Iowa	.982	3786	1439	97	109	Portland	.978	3756	1452	118	145
Omaha	.981	3867	1524	107	154	Salt Lake	.978	3756	1469	120	154
Colorado Springs	.979	3720	1498	112	164	New Orleans	.977	3689	1238	114	104
Fresno	.979	3840	1486	117	142	Oklahoma City	.977	3747	1389	121	132
Nashville	.979	3753	1642	118	168	Memphis	.976	3822	1454	128	160
Reno	.979	3793	1555	114	169	Sacramento	.975	3833	1436	137	125
Round Rock	.979	3800	1548	117	139	Tacoma	.972	3782	1330	148	99
Albuquerque	.978	3772	1401	116	125	Las Vegas	.970	3755	1605	167	165

INDIVIDUAL BATTING LEADERS (MINIMUM 3.1 PA/TEAM GAME)

	AVG	G	AB	R	H	2B	3B	HR	RBI	BB	SO	SB
Lindsey, John, Albuquerque	.353	107	408	74	144	41	4	25	97	19	78	0
Davis, Chris, Okla. City	.327	103	398	67	130	31	2	14	80	37	105	3
Miller, Matt, Colorado Springs	.325	136	507	90	165	22	2	10	81	66	93	2
Payton, Jay, Colorado Springs	.323	116	439	62	142	36	5	6	74	25	47	13
Guzman, Jesus, Fresno	.321	125	445	66	143	28	1	18	72	38	68	6
Oeltjen, Trent, Nashville, Albuquerque	.320	119	465	87	149	42	7	13	71	44	102	27
Figueroa, Luis, Las Vegas, Salt Lake	.319	115	457	51	146	27	4	5	71	25	19	3
Ka'aihue, Kila, Omaha	.319	94	323	67	103	16	1	24	78	88	69	2
Mitchell, Russ, Albuquerque	.315	127	505	97	159	38	2	23	87	38	78	1
Richar, Danny, New Orleans	.315	128	467	57	147	29	0	7	50	19	74	7

INDIVIDUAL PITCHING LEADERS (MINIMUM 1 IP/TEAM GAME)

	W	L	ERA	G	GS	CG	SV	IP	H	R	ER	BB	SO
Lerew, Anthony, Omaha	9	4	2.56	22	19	1	0	124	121	43	35	44	74
Kirkman, Michael, Okla. City	13	3	3.09	24	22	0	0	131	115	52	45	68	130
Dickson, Brandon, Memphis	11	8	3.23	28	27	0	0	167	180	77	60	53	137
Banks, Josh, Round Rock	9	12	4.05	27	27	3	0	172	177	88	77	37	72
Sosa, Henry, Fresno	7	8	4.07	36	14	0	0	115	113	61	52	55	83
Coleman, Casey, Iowa	10	7	4.07	20	20	2	0	117	106	58	53	35	59
Mendoza, Luis, Omaha	10	9	4.12	24	22	0	0	132	145	66	60	32	59
Yourkin, Matt, Fresno	7	8	4.24	29	24	0	0	136	146	67	64	39	110
Mortensen, Clay, Sacramento	13	6	4.25	26	26	0	0	165	161	91	78	53	112
Van Hekken, Andy, Round Rock	8	8	4.37	29	27	2	0	177	184	92	86	50	114

ALL-STAR TEAM

C: J.P. Arencibia, Las Vegas. **1B:** Mark Trumbo, Salt Lake. **2B:** Daniel Descalso, Memphis. **3B:** Russ Mitchell, Albuquerque. **SS:** Darwin Barney, Iowa. **OF:** Peter Bourjos, Salt Lake; Chris Carter, Sacramento; Brad Snyder, Iowa. **DH:** John Lindsey, Albuquerque. **RHP:** Eric Hacker, Fresno. **LHP:** Michael Kirkman, Oklahoma City. **RP:** Jeremy Accardo, Las Vegas.

Most Valuable Player: J.P. Arencibia, Las Vegas. **Pitcher of the Year:** Michael Kirkman, Oklahoma City. **Rookie of the Year:** Peter Bourjos, Salt Lake. **Manager of the Year:** Ryne Sandberg, Iowa.

DEPARTMENT LEADERS

BATTING

OBP	Ka'aihue, Kila, Omaha	.463
SLG	Lindsey, John, Albuquerque	.657
OPS	Ka'aihue, Kila, Omaha	1.060
R	Trumbo, Mark, Salt Lake	103
H	Hoffmann, Jamie, Albuquerque	169
TB	Trumbo, Mark, Salt Lake	307
XBH	Trumbo, Mark, Salt Lake	70
2B	Oeltjen, Trent, Nashville, Albuquerque	42
3B	Bourjos, Peter, Salt Lake	12
	Lough, David, Omaha	12
HR	Trumbo, Mark, Salt Lake	36
RBI	Trumbo, Mark, Salt Lake	122
SAC	Lough, David, Omaha	19
BB	Gotay, Ruben, Memphis	95
HBP	Parraz, Jordan, Omaha	19
SO	Halman, Greg, Tacoma	169
SB	Wimberly, Corey, Sacramento	56
CS	Wimberly, Corey, Sacramento	18
AB/SO	Figueroa, Luis, Las Vegas, Salt Lake	24.05

PITCHING

G	Perdomo, Luis, Portland	58
	Sinkbeil, Brett, New Orleans	58
GS	Hacker, Eric, Fresno	29
	Lynn, Lance, Memphis	29
GF	Smith, Chris, Nashville	43
SV	Smith, Chris, Nashville	26
W	Hacker, Eric, Fresno	16
L	Carrillo, Cesar, Portland	14
IP	Torra, Matt, Reno	178
H	Torra, Matt, Reno	224
R	Broadway, Lance, Las Vegas	127
ER	Broadway, Lance, Las Vegas	120
HB	Dillard, Tim, Nashville	16
BB	Broadway, Lance, Las Vegas	76
SO	Lynn, Lance, Memphis	141
SO/9	Kirkman, Michael, Okla. City	8.93
SO/9 (RP)	Escalona, Edgmer, Colorado Springs	9.7
BB/9	MacLane, Evan, Memphis	1.28
WP	Marte, Jose, Reno	16
BK	Four tied at	4
HR	Hernandez, Gaby, Omaha	31
AVG	Kirkman, Michael, Okla. City	.235

FIELDING

C	FPCT	Clark, Cody, Omaha	.996
	PO	McKenry, Michael, Colo. Springs	624
	A	McKenry, Michael, Colo. Springs	60
	E	Conger, Hank, Salt Lake	13
	DP	Conger, Hank, Salt Lake	9
	PB	May, Lucas, Albuquerque, Omaha	14
1B	FPCT	Pill, Brett, Fresno	.996
	PO	Pill, Brett, Fresno	1053
	A	Koshansky, Joe, Nashville	90
	E	Trumbo, Mark, Salt Lake	12
	DP	Koshansky, Joe, Nashville	125
2B	FPCT	Richar, Danny, New Orleans	.985
	PO	Descalso, Daniel, Memphis	227
	A	Descalso, Daniel, Memphis	311
	E	Descalso, Daniel, Memphis	15
	DP	Descalso, Daniel, Memphis	82
3B	FPCT	Mitchell, Russ, Albuquerque	.958
	PO	Mangini, Matt, Tacoma	74
	A	Metcalf, Travis, Colorado Springs	208
	E	Mangini, Matt, Tacoma	24
	DP	Metcalf, Travis, Colorado Springs	25
SS	FPCT	Barney, Darwin, Iowa	.970
	PO	Cruz, Luis, Nashville	214
	A	Cruz, Luis, Nashville	405
	E	Cruz, Luis, Nashville	21
	DP	Cruz, Luis, Nashville	104
OF	FPCT	Adduci, James, Iowa	1.000
	PO	Hoffmann, Jamie, Albuquerque	297
	A	Copeland, Ben, Fresno	13
		Evans, Terry, Salt Lake	13
	E	Halman, Greg, Tacoma	11
	DP	Three tied at	5

MINOR LEAGUES

BY JOHN MANUEL

Scouts who did pro coverage in the Eastern League agreed with managers who asserted that the Altoona Curve (Pirates) fielded as many prospects as any club in the league.

The Curve was not a team long on stars, the consensus went, but it was a team with plenty of good players.

That collection of talent, ably managed by Matt Walbeck, led the Curve to the Eastern League championship. Altoona won the West Division, beat Harrisburg in four games in the first round of the playoffs, then won the championship series against the Trenton Thunder (Yankees).

The Thunder had the league's best regular-season record, one game better than Altoona. Trenton also had the league's MVP in third baseman Brandon Laird, though he moved up to Triple-A in August and wasn't around for playoffs. But in the postseason, the Thunder had plenty of big names, such as rehabbing major leaguer Andy Pettitte, hard-throwing Yankees prospects Manny Banuelos, Dellin Betances, Andrew Brackman and Adam Warren, and catcher Austin Romine.

Altoona won anyway, as lefthander Justin Wilson won both of his playoff starts, throwing 13 scoreless innings, to earn playoff MVP honors. It was the second postseason hero turn in three years for Wilson, who helped lead Fresno State to the 2008 College World Series championship.

Nevertheless, when the season was over, the parent Pirates let Walbeck go. Walbeck was BA's Minor League Manager of the Year in 2007 with Erie, and has won three championships in six years as a minor league manager.

"We appreciate Matt's efforts and wish him the best in his future endeavors but felt that it was best that we allow him to pursue other opportunities," the Pirates stated in a release.

TOP 20 PROSPECTS

1. Domonic Brown, of, Reading Phillies
2. Zach Britton, lhp, Bowie Baysox (Orioles)
3. Kyle Drabek, rhp, New Hampshire Fisher Cats (Blue Jays)
4. Brandon Belt, Richmond Flying Squirrels (Giants)
5. Andrew Brackman, Trenton Thunder (Yankees)
6. Lonnie Chisenhall, 3b, Akron Aeros (Indians)
7. Kyle Gibson, rhp, New Britain Rock Cats (Twins)
8. Alex White, rhp, Akron Aeros (Indians)
9. Jason Kipnis, 2b, Akron Aeros (Indians)
10. Casey Kelly, rhp, Portland Sea Dogs (Red Sox)
11. Brandon Laird, 3b, Trenton Thunder (Yankees)
12. Danny Espinosa, ss, Harrisburg Senators (Nationals)
13. Andy Oliver, Erie SeaWolves (Tigers)
14. Bryan Morris, rhp, Altoona Curve (Pirates)
15. Rudy Owens, lhp, Altoona Curve (Pirates)
16. Hector Noesi, rhp, Trenton Thunder (Yankees)
17. Jose Iglesias, ss, Portland Sea Dogs (Red Sox)
18. Anthony Rizzo, 1b, Portland Sea Dogs (Red Sox)
19. Kirk Nieuwenhuis, of, Binghamton Mets
20. Austin Romine, c, Trenton Thunder (Yankees)

Outfielder Domonic Brown (Phillies) needed just a month at Reading in 2009 to rank No. 6 on our Eastern League prospects list. His tools were even more apparent this season when he spent the first two months with Reading and he vaulted to the No. 1 spot on the list on his way to Philadelphia.

Brown's Reading teammate, 31-year-old Tagg Bozied, won the "modern" triple crown by leading the league in batting, on-base and slugging, hitting .315/.402/.631. Another minor league veteran, former Dodgers top prospect Joel Guzman, led the EL with 33 homers with the Bowie Baysox.

However, youth was served a bit more on the mound, where New Hampshire righthander Kyle Drabek (Blue Jays)—son of Doug Drabek, the former Cy Young Award winner—led the league with 14 victories and ranked third with 132 strikeouts.

Baseball returned to Richmond when the Connecticut Defenders moved there before the season. The newly-named Richmond Flying Squirrels led the EL in attendance.

STANDINGS

East (Organization)	W	L	PCT	GB	Manager(s)	Attendance	Average	Last Penn.
Trenton Thunder (Yankees)	83	59	.585	—	Tony Franklin	384,028	5,409	2008
New Hampshire Fisher Cats (Blue Jays)	79	62	.560	3 ½	Luis Rivera	386,102	5,516	2004
Portland Sea Dogs (Red Sox)	70	71	.496	12 ½	Arnie Beyeler	390,772	5,832	2006
Reading Phillies (Phillies)	69	72	.489	13 ½	Steve Roadcap	456,466	6,615	2001
Binghamton Mets (Mets)	66	76	.465	17	Tim Teufel	203,823	3,088	1994
New Britain Rock Cats (Twins)	44	98	.310	39	Jeff Smith	368,523	5,500	2001
West (Organization)	**W**	**L**	**PCT**	**GB**	**Manager(s)**	**Attendance**	**Average**	**Last Penn.**
Altoona Curve (Pirates)	82	60	.577	—	Matt Walbeck	286,321	4,150	2010
Harrisburg Senators (Nationals)	77	65	.542	5	Randy Knorr	294,325	4,205	1999
Bowie Baysox (Orioles)	75	67	.528	7	Brad Komminsk	251,728	3,545	Never
Akron Aeros (Indians)	71	71	.500	11	Joel Skinner	261,563	3,791	2009
Richmond Flying Squirrels (Giants)	68	73	.482	13 ½	Andy Skeels	463,842	6,626	2002
Erie SeaWolves (Tigers)	66	76	.465	16	Phil Nevin	218,748	3,217	Never

PLAYOFFS—Semifinals: Trenton defeated New Hampshire 3-0 and Altoona defeated Harrisburg 3-1 in best-of-five series. **Finals:** Altoona defeated Trenton 3-1 in best-of-five series.

CLUB BATTING

	AVG	G	AB	R	H	2B	3B	HR	RBI	BB	SO	SB	OBP	SLG
Akron	.273	142	4784	682	1305	249	32	111	625	461	856	53	.341	.408
Altoona	.268	142	4835	688	1294	268	38	80	627	475	960	120	.339	.388
Binghamton	.268	142	4805	718	1288	312	19	150	668	470	1104	48	.339	.435
Portland	.265	141	4782	706	1267	288	29	112	656	554	931	103	.347	.408
Reading	.264	141	4695	671	1239	229	24	128	621	472	994	130	.337	.405
New Hampshire	.263	141	4772	723	1255	278	24	134	672	561	1020	129	.346	.416
Trenton	.259	142	4665	704	1208	256	39	106	660	511	981	107	.337	.399
Bowie	.256	142	4786	647	1223	251	20	126	599	457	1133	85	.328	.395
Richmond	.253	141	4764	547	1207	230	47	71	513	423	1035	87	.318	.366
Harrisburg	.251	142	4726	598	1188	222	35	121	561	398	948	86	.314	.390
Erie	.247	142	4747	630	1172	247	33	129	590	454	1175	124	.320	.394
New Britain	.246	142	4693	553	1156	226	33	86	503	409	961	94	.313	.364

CLUB PITCHING

	ERA	G	CG	SHO	SV	IP	H	R	ER	HR	BB	SO	AVG
Harrisburg	3.51	142	2	10	44	1252	1171	559	488	102	400	1108	.247
Altoona	3.55	142	1	7	47	1268	1158	560	500	99	399	1094	.244
Trenton	3.66	142	2	12	41	1240	1118	576	504	94	480	1125	.241
Richmond	3.71	141	2	11	43	1254	1227	586	517	92	456	915	.260
Bowie	3.97	142	0	6	37	1255	1266	643	554	121	457	937	.262
Akron	4.08	142	1	12	36	1230	1176	652	557	100	535	1118	.251
New Hampshire	4.23	141	4	10	40	1265	1170	643	595	121	539	1063	.247
Erie	4.42	142	6	6	34	1252	1261	701	615	139	445	980	.262
Portland	4.60	141	0	7	33	1239	1278	689	633	122	492	1007	.268
Reading	4.63	141	7	7	36	1224	1276	681	630	120	400	925	.269
Binghamton	4.99	142	4	8	31	1231	1282	753	682	122	542	970	.270
New Britain	5.17	142	4	3	26	1218	1415	804	700	122	500	856	.292

CLUB FIELDING

	PCT	PO	A	E	DP		PCT	PO	A	E	DP
Reading	.981	3673	1353	96	107	Binghamton	.977	3692	1356	120	127
Trenton	.981	3720	1369	97	130	Harrisburg	.977	3756	1388	123	119
New Hampshire	.980	3794	1504	108	155	Bowie	.974	3764	1544	142	121
Richmond	.980	3761	1588	107	167	Akron	.973	3689	1437	141	178
Portland	.979	3718	1476	109	135	New Britain	.973	3654	1569	146	150
Altoona	.977	3804	1443	125	124	Erie	.972	3757	1507	153	169

INDIVIDUAL BATTING LEADERS (MINIMUM 3.1 PA/TEAM GAME)

	AVG	G	AB	R	H	2B	3B	HR	RBI	BB	SO	SB
Bozied, Tagg, Reading	.315	104	355	65	112	29	1	27	92	47	85	1
Gimenez, Hector, Altoona	.305	94	338	49	103	29	0	16	72	46	72	6
Revere, Ben, New Britain	.305	94	361	44	110	10	4	1	23	32	41	36
Spidale, Michael, Reading	.303	131	479	74	145	21	3	5	50	35	64	31
Mastroianni, Darin, New Hampshire	.301	132	525	101	158	25	7	4	46	77	96	46
Harrison, Josh, Altoona	.300	135	520	74	156	33	5	4	75	32	52	19
Drennen, John, Akron	.300	119	440	44	132	26	6	7	58	33	56	2
Adams, Ryan, Bowie	.298	134	530	81	158	43	0	15	68	47	121	2
Chang, Ray, Portland	.298	116	440	57	131	30	2	9	55	51	64	0
Christian, Justin, Trenton	.297	87	343	65	102	21	6	9	51	40	47	20

INDIVIDUAL PITCHING LEADERS (MINIMUM 1 IP/TEAM GAME)

	W	L	ERA	G	GS	CG	SV	IP	H	R	ER	BB	SO
Owens, Rudy, Altoona	12	6	2.46	26	26	0	0	150	124	46	41	23	132
Milone, Tom, Harrisburg	12	5	2.85	27	27	2	0	158	161	57	50	23	155
Drabek, Kyle, New Hampshire	14	9	2.94	27	27	1	0	162	126	67	53	68	132
Wilson, Justin, Altoona	11	8	3.10	27	26	0	0	143	109	59	49	71	134
Pendleton, Lance, Trenton	10	4	3.44	23	22	0	0	121	95	50	46	45	111
Maday, Daryl, Richmond	9	8	3.47	25	18	0	1	114	121	48	44	33	70
Mixon, David, Richmond	11	7	3.51	27	25	1	0	157	149	65	61	38	112
Stewart, Zach, New Hampshire	8	3	3.64	26	26	0	0	136	131	59	55	54	106
Tanner, Clayton, Richmond	9	9	3.68	27	27	0	0	149	150	78	61	64	79
MacDonald, Mike, Richmond	5	8	3.90	27	23	1	0	134	155	63	58	31	78

ALL-STAR TEAM

C: Hector Gimenez, Altoona. **1B:** Matthew Rizzotti, Reading. **2B:** Ryan Adams, Bowie. **3B:** Brandon Laird, Trenton. **SS:** Danny Espinosa, Harrisburg. **DH:** Joel Guzman, Bowie. **OF:** Darin Mastroianni, New Hampshire; Ben Revere, New Britain; Eric Thames, New Hampshire. **UTIL:** Ray Chang, Portland. **RHP:** Kyle Drabek, New Hampshire. **LHP:** Rudy Owens, Altoona. **RP:** Rafael Cova, Richmond.
Most Valuable Player: Brandon Laird, Trenton. **Pitcher of the Year:** Kyle Drabek, New Hampshire.
Manager of the Year: Matt Walbeck, Erie.

DEPARTMENT LEADERS

BATTING

OBP	Bozied, Tagg, Reading	.402
SLG	Bozied, Tagg, Reading	.631
OPS	Bozied, Tagg, Reading	1.033
R	Spears, Nate, Portland	104
H	Adams, Ryan, Bowie	158
	Mastroianni, Darin, New Hampshire	158
TB	Adams, Ryan, Bowie	246
	Guzman, Joel, Bowie	264
TB	Thames, Eric, New Hampshire	261
XBH	Adams, Ryan, Bowie	58
	Thames, Eric, New Hampshire	58
2B	Adams, Ryan, Bowie	43
	Singleton, Steve, New Britain	43
3B	D'Arnaud, Chase, Altoona	9
	Ford, Darren, Richmond	9
HR	Guzman, Joel, Bowie	33
RBI	Thames, Eric, New Hampshire	104
SAC	Harrison, Josh, Altoona	14
BB	Spears, Nate, Portland	84
HBP	Thames, Eric, New Hampshire	18
SO	Waring, Brandon, Bowie	179
SB	Mastroianni, Darin, New Hampshire	46
CS	Ford, Darren, Richmond	15
AB/SO	Harrison, Josh, Altoona	10

PITCHING

G	Merritt, Roy, Binghamton	60
GS	Below, Duane, Erie	28
	Johnson, Steve, Bowie	28
GF	Rice, Jason, Portland	44
SV	Cova, Rafael, Richmond	23
W	Drabek, Kyle, New Hampshire	14
L	Three tied at	13
IP	Weber, Thad, Erie	167.2
H	Robertson, Tyler, New Britain	181
R	Robertson, Tyler, New Britain	100
ER	McCardell, Mike, New Britain	88
	Thompson, Aaron, Harrisburg	88
HB	Weiland, Kyle, Portland	16
BB	Spoone, Chorye, Bowie	79
SO	Milone, Tom, Harrisburg	155
SO/9	Milone, Tom, Harrisburg	8.83
SO/9 (RP)	Uviedo, Ronald, Altoona, New Hampshire	12
BB/9	Milone, Tom, Harrisburg	1.31
WP	Hughes, Jared, Altoona	15
BK	Three tied at	4
HR	Johnson, Steve, Bowie	24
AVG	Drabek, Kyle, New Hampshire	.215

FIELDING

C	FPCT	Gosewisch, Tuffy, Reading	.997
	PO	Romine, Austin, Trenton	787
	A	Exposito, Luis, Portland	95
	E	Gimenez, Hector, Altoona	10
	DP	Solano, Jhonatan, Harrisburg	9
	PB	Exposito, Luis, Portland	14
1B	FPCT	Cooper, David, New Hampshire	.993
	PO	Hague, Matt, Altoona	1211
	A	Cooper, David, New Hampshire	94
	E	Marrero, Chris, Harrisburg	18
	DP	Cooper, David, New Hampshire	121
2B	FPCT	Spears, Nate, Portland	.982
	PO	Spears, Nate, Portland	201
	A	Spears, Nate, Portland	389
	E	Adams, Ryan, Bowie	20
	DP	Spears, Nate, Portland	96
3B	FPCT	Bowman, Shawn, New Hampshire	.952
	PO	Harrison, Josh, Altoona	70
	A	Gillaspie, Conor, Richmond	230
	E	Laird, Brandon, Trenton	20
	DP	Gillaspie, Conor, Richmond	26
SS	FPCT	Galvis, Freddy, Reading	.982
	PO	Galvis, Freddy, Reading	220
	A	Galvis, Freddy, Reading	393
	E	D'Arnaud, Chase, Altoona	28
		Rivero, Carlos, Akron	28
	DP	Nunez, Luis, Trenton	92
OF	FPCT	Coon, Brad, Harrisburg	.996
	PO	Lin, Che-Hsuan, Portland	320
	A	Dirks, Andy, Erie	16
	E	Neal, Thomas, Richmond	9
	DP	Dirks, Andy, Erie	5
		Loewen, Adam, New Hampshire	5

MINOR LEAGUES

BY BEN BADLER

From beginning to end, the Tennessee Smokies and Jacksonville Suns were the two powerhouses of the Southern League.

Both teams finished first in their divisions in the first and second halves of the season, but Jacksonville (Marlins) leaned on its strong pitching staff to beat Tennessee (Cubs) in four games for the league title.

Tennessee won the first game of the series 5-0 behind six shutout innings from young righthander Chris Archer before the Suns evened the series with a 7-6 victory in Game Two. The Suns closed out with a pair of shutouts, from lefthander Brad Hand and righthander Jose Rosario.

Pitching was Jacksonville's strength all season, as the Suns finished second in the league with 557 runs allowed, edged only by Mobile (538). Righthander Elih Villanueva's 2.26 ERA led the league, while fellow Suns righthander Tom Kohler posted the second-best mark (2.61 ERA). The Suns managed to win the championship despite losing right fielder Mike Stanton to a big league promotion in early June. Despite playing just 53 games, Stanton finished the year tied for second in the league with 21 home runs, two behind West Tenn's Carlos Peguero (Mariners).

With Archer and righthanders Chris Carpenter and Trey McNutt, the Cubs sent three of their top pitching prospects to Tennessee, but it was the Smokies offense that carried them. Tennessee led the Southern League in runs with 749, surpassing the second-highest scoring team (West Tenn) by 79 runs. Smokies outfielder Brandon Guyer led the league in slugging, while third baseman Russ Canzler (second) and second baseman Tony Thomas (fourth) both were among the league leaders in slugging. Center fielder Brett Jackson hit .276/.366/.465 after joining the team in June.

Last-place Carolina (Reds) got strong production from league MVP Dave Sappelt, who finished first with a .361 average. The Mudcats got a midseason boost from Devin Mesoraco, 22, who

arrived in late May and hit .294/.363/.594 while throwing out 41 percent of basestealers.

Dodgers shortstop Dee Gordon skipped high Class A Inland Empire to join Chattanooga, where he led the league with 53 steals. Dustin Ackley, the 2009 No. 2 overall pick, made his pro debut with West Tenn and hit .263/.389/.384 before getting promoted to Triple-A. Ackley and righthander Michael Pineda formed the best prospect duo in the league before Pineda also went to Tacoma in June after posting a 2.22 ERA over 77 innings.

TOP 20 PROSPECTS

1. Mike Stanton, of, Jacksonville Suns (Marlins)
2. Dustin Ackley, 2b, West Tenn Diamond Jaxx (Mariners)
3. Michael Pineda, rhp, West Tenn Diamond Jaxx (Mariners)
4. Mike Minor, lhp, Mississippi Braves
5. Brett Lawrie, 2b, Huntsville Stars (Brewers)
6. Dee Gordon, ss, Chattanooga Lookouts (Dodgers)
7. Devin Mesoraco, c, Carolina Mudcats (Reds)
8. Brett Jackson, of, Tennessee Smokies (Cubs)
9. Chris Archer, rhp, Tennessee Smokies (Cubs)
10. Matt Dominguez, 3b, Jacksonville Suns (Marlins)
11. Chris Withrow, rhp, Chattanooga Lookouts (Dodgers)
12. Alex Torres, lhp, Montgomery Biscuits (Rays)
13. Trayvon Robinson, of, Chattanooga Lookouts (Dodgers)
14. Brandon Guyer, of, Tennessee Smokies (Cubs)
15. David Sappelt, of, Carolina Mudcats (Reds)
16. Alex Liddi, 3b/1b, West Tenn Diamond Jaxx (Mariners)
17. Brandon Beachy, rhp, Mississippi Braves
18. Brent Morel, 3b, Birmingham Barons (White Sox)
19. Alex Cobb, rhp, Montgomery Biscuits (Rays)
20. Jerry Sands, of/1b, Chattanooga Lookouts (Dodgers)

STANDINGS: SPLIT SEASON

FIRST HALF

NORTH	W	L	PCT	GB
Tennessee	42	27	.609	—
West Tenn	39	30	.565	3
Chattanooga	33	36	.478	9
Huntsville	33	37	.471	9½
Carolina	30	39	.435	12

SOUTH	W	L	PCT	GB
Jacksonville	40	30	.571	—
Montgomery	38	30	.559	1
Mobile	36	32	.529	3
Mississippi	30	38	.441	9
Birmingham	24	46	.343	16

SECOND HALF

NORTH	W	L	PCT	GB
Tennessee	44	26	.629	—
Huntsville	34	36	.486	10
West Tenn	34	36	.486	10
Chattanooga	32	38	.457	12
Carolina	28	40	.412	15

SOUTH	W	L	PCT	GB
Jacksonville	41	29	.586	—
Mobile	39	30	.565	1½
Montgomery	34	36	.486	7
Mississippi	33	36	.478	7½
Birmingham	29	41	.414	12

PLAYOFFS—Semifinals: Jacksonville defeated Mobile 3-1 and Tennessee defeated West Tenn 3-1 in best-of-five series. **Finals:** Jacksonville defeated Tennessee 3-1 in best-of-five series.

OVERALL STANDINGS

Team (Organization)	W	L	PCT	GB	Manager(s)	Attendance	Average	Last Penn.
Tennessee Smokies (Cubs)	86	53	.619	—	Bill Dancy	262,415	3,859	2004
Jacksonville Suns (Marlins)	81	59	.579	5 ½	Tim Leiper	354,725	5,141	2010
Mobile BayBears (Diamondbacks)	75	62	.547	10	Rico Brogna	186,256	3,053	2004
West Tenn Diamond Jaxx (Mariners)	73	66	.525	13	Tim Laker	118,503	1,823	2000
Montgomery Biscuits (Rays)	72	66	.522	13 ½	Billy Gardner	269,840	4,027	2007
Huntsville Stars (Brewers)	67	73	.479	19 ½	Mike Guerrero	91,237	1,404	2001
Chattanooga Lookouts (Dodgers)	65	74	.468	21	Carlos Subero	217,469	3,246	1988
Mississippi Braves (Braves)	63	74	.460	22	Phillip Wellman	178,138	2,620	2008
Carolina Mudcats (Reds)	58	79	.423	27	David Bell	255,360	3,811	2003
Birmingham Barons (White Sox)	53	87	.379	33 ½	Ever Magallanes	275,887	4,180	2002

CLUB BATTING

	AVG	G	AB	R	H	2B	3B	HR	RBI	BB	SO	SB	OBP	SLG
Tennessee	.285	139	4768	749	1358	293	45	120	689	462	887	147	.353	.441
West Tenn	.272	139	4626	670	1259	262	37	116	623	469	1101	84	.345	.420
Mobile	.266	137	4428	592	1177	222	26	69	536	533	928	141	.350	.374
Carolina	.265	137	4651	604	1231	246	31	92	541	401	955	128	.330	.390
Birmingham	.261	140	4631	570	1207	233	32	77	528	435	973	99	.327	.375
Chattanooga	.261	139	4632	641	1209	248	40	88	570	509	1095	183	.339	.389
Huntsville	.258	140	4630	620	1196	261	43	78	566	478	1089	103	.334	.384
Jacksonville	.258	140	4672	653	1204	262	35	104	601	525	1090	84	.339	.396
Mississippi	.257	137	4532	585	1164	230	23	72	525	449	930	108	.331	.365
Montgomery	.248	138	4608	585	1145	201	44	81	531	477	970	86	.325	.364

CLUB PITCHING

	ERA	G	CG	SHO	SV	IP	H	R	ER	HR	BB	SO	AVG
Mobile	3.41	137	8	9	32	1189	1148	538	450	84	423	993	.256
Jacksonville	3.43	140	4	14	38	1234	1133	557	470	94	463	984	.247
Tennessee	3.71	139	1	10	49	1228	1251	605	506	86	432	996	.266
Montgomery	3.84	138	0	16	40	1221	1231	600	521	89	480	1047	.264
Mississippi	3.98	137	0	9	34	1195	1162	617	529	71	505	1147	.256
Huntsville	4.07	140	4	6	33	1205	1192	661	545	101	477	1015	.258
West Tenn	4.25	139	1	8	37	1198	1241	662	566	83	437	994	.266
Birmingham	4.28	140	2	4	33	1211	1249	658	576	93	462	905	.270
Carolina	4.42	137	3	6	30	1207	1227	662	593	102	508	915	.269
Chattanooga	4.54	139	3	4	38	1220	1316	709	615	94	551	1042	.278

CLUB FIELDING

	PCT	PO	A	E	DP		PCT	PO	A	E	DP
Birmingham	.976	3632	1499	126	132	Mississippi	.972	3586	1369	141	119
Montgomery	.976	3663	1365	125	108	Tennessee	.971	3684	1485	157	154
Carolina	.975	3621	1501	134	134	West Tenn	.971	3593	1277	147	104
Jacksonville	.975	3702	1337	127	109	Chattanooga	.970	3660	1431	157	126
Mobile	.975	3568	1415	130	123	Huntsville	.969	3616	1469	164	153

INDIVIDUAL BATTING LEADERS (MINIMUM 3.1 PA/TEAM GAME)

	AVG	G	AB	R	H	2B	3B	HR	RBI	BB	SO	SB
Sappelt, Dave, Carolina	.361	89	330	53	119	19	8	9	62	31	46	15
Guyer, Brandon, Tennessee	.344	102	369	76	127	39	6	13	58	27	51	30
Campana, Tony, Tennessee	.319	131	489	76	156	22	5	0	39	44	82	48
Schmidt, Konrad, Mobile	.315	107	394	48	124	30	3	11	65	32	63	7
Lalli, Blake, Tennessee	.311	130	453	63	141	23	0	4	52	68	53	0
Rottino, Vinny, Jacksonville	.307	116	433	67	133	27	1	8	69	53	51	22
Cabrera, Willie, Mississippi	.306	99	366	48	112	37	1	5	56	29	36	13
Linton, Ollie, Mobile	.304	125	398	60	121	12	5	3	38	63	100	22
Limonta, Johan, West Tenn	.302	132	486	82	147	41	2	14	83	55	104	3
Martinez, Osvaldo, Jacksonville	.302	130	516	90	156	28	4	5	54	49	64	13

INDIVIDUAL PITCHING LEADERS (MINIMUM 1 IP/TEAM GAME)

	W	L	ERA	G	GS	CG	SV	IP	H	R	ER	BB	SO
Villanueva, Elih, Jacksonville	14	4	2.26	28	28	4	0	179	137	56	45	34	115
Koehler, Tom, Jacksonville	16	2	2.62	28	28	0	0	159	140	57	46	46	145
Cochran, Tom, Carolina	8	5	2.69	25	25	0	0	137	117	52	41	53	99
Cobb, Alex, Montgomery	7	5	2.72	23	22	0	0	120	120	47	36	35	128
Carpenter, Chris, Tennessee	8	6	3.17	23	23	0	0	120	118	56	42	48	100
Rivas, Amaury, Huntsville	11	6	3.38	25	25	2	0	142	130	59	53	55	114
Torres, Alexander, Montgomery	11	6	3.48	27	27	0	0	143	136	63	55	70	150
Hall, Jeremy, Montgomery	6	9	3.52	27	27	0	0	148	134	71	58	61	94
Carroll, Scott, Carolina	3	9	3.69	20	20	2	0	117	120	58	48	30	66
Cordier, Erik, Mississippi	11	7	3.73	25	21	0	0	136	116	61	56	69	113

ALL-STAR TEAM

C: Robinson Chirinos, Tennessee. **1B:** Johan Limonta, West Tenn. **2B:** Brett Lawrie, Huntsville. **3B:** Matt Dominguez, Jacksonville. **SS:** Osvaldo Martinez, Jacksonville. **OF:** Tony Campana, Tennessee; Collin Cowgill, Mobile; Brandon Guyer, Tennessee; Dave Sappelt, Carolina. **DH:** Corey Smith, Chattanooga. **UTIL:** Vinny Rottino, Jacksonville. **RHP:** Elih Villanueva, Jacksonville. **LHP:** Tom Cochran, Carolina. **RP:** Matt Gorgen, Montgomery.
Most Valuable Player: Dave Sappelt, Carolina. **Most Outstanding Pitcher:** Tom Koehler, Jacksonville. **Manager of the Year:** Bill Dancy, Tennessee.

DEPARTMENT LEADERS

BATTING

OBP	Linton, Ollie, Mobile	.411
SLG	Guyer, Brandon, Tennessee	.588
OPS	Guyer, Brandon, Tennessee	.986
R	Lawrie, Brett, Huntsville	90
	Martinez, Osvaldo, Jacksonville	90
H	Lawrie, Brett, Huntsville	158
TB	Lawrie, Brett, Huntsville	250
XBH	Lawrie, Brett, Huntsville	60
2B	Gomez, Mauro, Mississippi	42
3B	Lawrie, Brett, Huntsville	16
HR	Peguero, Carlos, West Tenn	23
RBI	Liddi, Alex, West Tenn	92
SAC	Curry, Ryan, Jacksonville	12
	Herrera, Elian, Chattanooga	12
BB	Byrne, Bryan, Mobile	81
HBP	Tripp, Brandon, Jacksonville	18
SO	Peguero, Carlos, West Tenn	178
SB	Gordon, Dee, Chattanooga	53
CS	Campana, Tony, Tennessee	20
	Gordon, Dee, Chattanooga	20
AB/SO	Curry, Ryan, Jacksonville	10.75

PITCHING

G	Parcell, Garrett, Jacksonville	53
GS	Koehler, Tom, Jacksonville	28
	Villanueva, Elih, Jacksonville	28
GF	Gorgen, Matt, Montgomery	37
SV	Carter, Anthony, Birmingham	22
	Gorgen, Matt, Montgomery	22
W	Koehler, Tom, Jacksonville	16
L	Bowman, Michael, Huntsville	13
IP	Villanueva, Elih, Jacksonville	179
H	Thompson, Jacob, Mississippi	163
R	Bray, Steve, Jackson	102
ER	Withrow, Chris, Chattanooga	86
IIB	Three tied at	12
BB	Torres, Alexander, Montgomery	70
SO	Torres, Alexander, Montgomery	150
SO/9	Cobb, Alex, Montgomery	9.66
SO/9 (RP)	Heath, Deunte, Birmingham	13.1
BB/9	Muschko, Craig, Tennessee	1.7
WP	Cortes, Dan, Jackson	19
BK	Heath, Deunte, Birmingham	3
	Miley, Wade, Mobile	3
HR	Edwards, Justin, Birmingham	20
AVG	Villanueva, Elih, Jacksonville	.212

FIELDING

C	FPCT	Ashley, Nevin, Montgomery	.992
	PO	Schmidt, Konrad, Mobile	627
	A	Hatcher, Chris, Jacksonville	81
		Mercado, Orlando, Mississippi	81
	E	Schmidt, Konrad, Mobile	14
	DP	Rivera, Mike, Chattanooga	10
	PB	Mercado, Orlando, Mississippi	12
1B	FPCT	Byrne, Bryan, Mobile	.995
	PO	Gomez, Mauro, Mississippi	1038
	A	Byrne, Bryan, Mobile	75
	E	Gomez, Mauro, Mississippi	13
	DP	Lalli, Blake, Tennessee	95
2B	FPCT	Thomas, Tony, Tennessee	.973
	PO	Lawrie, Brett, Huntsville	226
	A	Lawrie, Brett, Huntsville	385
	E	Lawrie, Brett, Huntsville	25
	DP	Lawrie, Brett, Huntsville	89
3B	FPCT	Dominguez, Matt, Jacksonville	.955
	PO	Dominguez, Matt, Jacksonville	119
	A	Dominguez, Matt, Jacksonville	246
	E	Liddi, Alex, Jackson	27
	DP	Dominguez, Matt, Jacksonville	30
SS	FPCT	Negron, Kris, Carolina	.965
	PO	Gordon, Dee, Chattanooga	199
	A	Negron, Kris, Carolina	346
	E	Gordon, Dee, Chattanooga	37
	DP	Gordon, Dee, Chattanooga	73
OF	FPCT	Salem, Emeel, Jacksonville	.992
	PO	Campana, Tony, Tennessee	268
	A	Cowgill, Collin, Mobile	23
	E	Peguero, Carlos, Jackson	10
		Phipps, Denis, Carolina	10
	DP	Wright, Ty, Tennessee	5

MINOR LEAGUES

BY WILL LINGO

Scouting the Double-A Texas League was relatively easy this season: Head to Northwest Arkansas and watch the parade of talent come through. The Naturals (Royals) not only won their first league title, but also dominated the league's prospect list, grabbing the top three spots.

Northwest Arkansas had a premium hitter in the middle of its lineup all season, with No. 1 prospect Mike Moustakas holding the job through mid-July and Eric Hosmer taking over when Moustakas moved on to Triple-A. The Naturals had plenty of pitching talent as well, led by Mike Montgomery and Aaron Crow. Danny Duffy and John Lamb also would have found spots on the prospect list if they had enough innings to qualify.

Northwest Arkansas first baseman/DH Clint Robinson won the triple crown, batting .335/.410/.625 with 29 home runs and 98 RBIs. He missed the Top 20 because scouts don't like his defense and see him as an extra bat at the big league level. He also benefited from an extremely hitter-friendly home park, as well as the opportunity to hit in the middle of a stacked lineup.

The Naturals dominated the league in just about every way imaginable, winning both halves in the Northern Division and finishing with the best record in the league by 13½ games. Northwest Arkansas' 86 wins were not only a franchise record, but also the most by any Double-A affiliate in the history of the Royals organization.

Moustakas was the league's player of the year, but he was gone by the time the playoffs rolled around, leaving Hosmer to anchor the lineup. He was up to the task, hitting six home runs and 12 RBIs in nine playoff games. Northwest Arkansas' biggest challenge actually came in the first round, when it fell down in the series 2-1 to the Springfield Cardinals before rallying to win the series in five games. Hosmer hit two two-run home runs in a dramatic 6-5 win in Game Four that sent the series to a decisive game. Springfield was led by third baseman Matt Carpenter, who batted .312 with 12 home runs.

The Naturals met Midland, the defending TL champion, in the finals, after the RockHounds defeated Frisco in the semifinals and took that series 3-1. Lefthander Will Smith pitched the clincher, finishing the season with Northwest Arkansas after starting it with Arkansas as a member of the Angels organization. Smith came to the Royals in the July trade that sent Alberto Callaspo to the Angels.

Smith threw 6⅔ scoreless innings as the Naturals won Game Four 2-0, with Henry Barrera and Patrick Keating finishing out the shutout. Hosmer drove in one of Northwest Arkansas' runs, and Anthony Seratelli had the other RBI as well as three hits.

TOP 20 PROSPECTS

1. Mike Moustakas, 3b, Northwest Arkansas Naturals (Royals)
2. Eric Hosmer, 1b, Northwest Arkansas Naturals (Royals)
3. Mike Montgomery, lhp, Northwest Arkansas Naturals (Royals)
4. Wilin Rosario, c, Tulsa Drillers (Rockies)
5. Martin Perez, lhp, Frisco Roughriders (Rangers)
6. Aaron Crow, rhp, Northwest Arkansas Naturals (Royals)
7. Jordan Lyles, rhp, Corpus Christi Hooks (Astros)
8. Simon Castro, rhp, San Antonio Missions (Padres)
9. Blake Beaven, rhp, Frisco Roughriders (Rangers)
10. Christian Friedrich, lhp, Tulsa Drillers (Rockies)
11. Cory Luebke, lhp, San Antonio Missions (Padres)
12. Jordan Walden, rhp, Arkansas Travelers (Angels)
13. James Darnell, 3b, San Antonio Missions (Padres)
14. Eduardo Sanchez, rhp, Springfield Cardinals
15. Rex Brothers, lhp, Tulsa Drillers (Rockies)
16. Louis Coleman, rhp, Northwest Arkansas Naturals (Royals)
17. Charlie Blackmon, of, Tulsa Drillers (Rockies)
18. Engel Beltre, of, Frisco Roughriders (Rangers)
19. Wynn Pelzer, rhp, San Antonio Missions (Padres)
20. Trevor Reckling, lhp, Arkansas Travelers (Angels)

STANDINGS: SPLIT SEASON

FIRST HALF

NORTH	W	L	PCT	GB	NORTH	W	L	PCT	GB
NW Arkansas	42	28	.600	—	NW Arkansas	44	26	.629	—
Springfield	38	32	.543	4	Tulsa	40	30	.571	4
Tulsa	29	40	.420	12½	Springfield	38	32	.543	6
Arkansas	26	44	.371	16	Arkansas	29	41	.414	15

SOUTH	W	L	PCT	GB	SOUTH	W	L	PCT	GB
Frisco	38	31	.551	—	Midland	35	35	.500	—
Corpus Christi	36	34	.514	2½	Frisco	34	36	.486	1
Midland	35	35	.500	3½	San Antonio	33	37	.471	2
San Antonio	35	35	.500	3½	Corpus Christi	27	43	.386	8

PLAYOFFS—Semifinals: Northwest Arkansas defeated Springfield 3-2 and Midland defeated Frisco 3-1 in best-of-five series. **Finals:** Northwest Arkansas defeated Midland 3-1 in best-of-five series.

OVERALL STANDINGS

Team (Organization)	W	L	PCT	GB	Manager(s)	Attendance	Average	Last Penn.
Northwest Arkansas Naturals (Royals)	86	54	.614	0	Brian Poldberg	320,523	4,856	2010
Springfield Cardinals (Cardinals)	76	64	.543	10	Ron Warner	357,336	5,333	1994
Frisco RoughRiders (Rangers)	72	67	.518	13 ½	Steve Buechele	544,152	7,886	2004
Midland RockHounds (Athletics)	70	70	.500	16	Darren Bush	285,188	4,194	2009
Tulsa Drillers (Rockies)	69	70	.496	16 ½	Ron Gideon	408,183	6,185	1998
San Antonio Missions (Padres)	68	72	.486	18	Doug Dascenzo	289,113	4,190	2007
Corpus Christi Hooks (Astros)	63	77	.450	23	Wes Clements	412,369	5,976	2006
Arkansas Travelers (Angels)	55	85	.393	31	Bobby Magallanes	326,066	4,940	2008

CLUB BATTING

	AVG	G	AB	R	H	2B	3B	HR	RBI	BB	SO	SB	OBP	SLG
Northwest Arkansas	.291	140	4697	770	1368	291	37	132	712	486	817	152	.364	.453
Midland	.264	140	4719	646	1247	239	42	74	593	525	1022	126	.341	.380
Springfield	.264	140	4717	721	1245	248	34	146	660	544	1065	78	.350	.424
Frisco	.258	139	4753	573	1225	215	41	68	510	440	977	91	.324	.363
Tulsa	.256	139	4619	611	1182	245	28	105	566	455	960	104	.329	.389
Corpus Christi	.254	140	4700	548	1195	194	31	89	508	441	1030	96	.321	.366
Arkansas	.248	140	4534	535	1124	167	36	84	476	399	952	123	.313	.356
San Antonio	.245	140	4695	605	1150	212	33	93	566	566	1006	62	.331	.364

CLUB PITCHING

	ERA	G	CG	SHO	SV	IP	H	R	ER	HR	BB	SO	AVG
San Antonio	3.33	140	3	13	37	1252	1158	574	463	70	460	1085	.247
Corpus Christi	3.65	140	5	8	27	1235	1238	581	501	89	498	949	.262
Northwest Arkansas	3.84	140	2	14	37	1213	1195	600	517	97	452	1017	.259
Springfield	3.88	140	6	7	37	1212	1160	606	523	117	489	931	.255
Midland	4.10	140	0	4	38	1236	1269	645	563	76	534	997	.266
Frisco	4.11	139	3	10	36	1230	1229	619	571	85	445	1036	.257
Tulsa	4.13	139	2	5	41	1226	1247	625	562	134	396	906	.265
Arkansas	4.82	140	6	7	29	1209	1240	750	648	123	582	908	.269

CLUB FIELDING

	PCT	PO	A	E	DP		PCT	PO	A	E	DP
Frisco	.981	3754	1440	98	120	Northwest Arkansas	.974	3639	1477	139	144
Midland	.978	3708	1494	118	125	Springfield	.974	3635	1511	137	146
Tulsa	.976	3678	1611	130	126	Arkansas	.973	3627	1455	139	123
Corpus Christi	.975	3704	1461	133	153	San Antonio	.970	3756	1465	160	119

INDIVIDUAL BATTING LEADERS (MINIMUM 3.1 PA/TEAM GAME)

	AVG	G	AB	R	H	2B	3B	HR	RBI	BB	SO	SB
Robinson, Clint, NW Arkansas	.335	129	477	90	160	41	5	29	98	58	86	4
Giavotella, Johnny, NW Arkansas	.322	134	522	92	168	35	5	9	65	61	67	13
Brown, Corey, Midland	.320	90	331	63	106	14	8	10	49	52	93	19
Carpenter, Matt, Springfield	.316	105	396	76	125	26	3	13	72	56	57	3
Orlando, Paulo, NW Arkansas	.305	121	419	84	128	22	6	13	64	24	62	25
Moore, Jeremy, Arkansas	.303	128	456	72	138	14	10	13	61	39	122	24
Shuck, Jack, Corpus Christi	.298	101	389	52	116	14	2	2	38	46	56	9
Blackmon, Charles, Tulsa	.297	86	337	53	100	22	4	11	55	32	43	19
Osuna, Renny, Frisco	.293	119	450	59	132	21	5	4	49	28	77	20
Brown, Andrew, Springfield	.291	98	361	65	105	17	1	22	63	41	98	1

INDIVIDUAL PITCHING LEADERS (MINIMUM 1 IP/TEAM GAME)

	W	L	ERA	G	GS	CG	SV	IP	H	R	ER	BB	SO
Arguello, Douglas, Corpus Christi	7	5	2.55	22	22	2	0	127	120	50	36	47	100
Castro, Simon, San Antonio	7	6	2.93	24	23	0	0	130	107	55	42	36	107
Hefner, Jeremy, San Antonio	11	8	2.96	28	28	2	0	168	156	63	55	51	115
Kopp, David, Springfield	12	4	3.05	21	21	1	0	121	126	47	41	39	78
Lyles, Jordan, Corpus Christi	7	9	3.12	21	20	1	0	127	133	54	44	35	115
Edell, Ryan, Midland	10	4	3.17	21	20	0	0	125	136	47	44	20	92
Kluber, Corey, San Antonio	6	6	3.46	22	21	0	0	123	121	59	47	40	136
Riordan, Cory, Tulsa	8	5	4.02	27	24	0	0	162	168	75	72	38	135
Paulino, Eduardo, NW Arkansas	8	5	4.05	28	21	0	0	114	118	62	51	63	85
Weiser, Keith, Tulsa	10	8	4.18	26	26	1	0	157	182	88	73	33	84

ALL-STAR TEAM

C: Steven Hill, Springfield; Wilin Rosario, Tulsa. **1B:** Clint Robinson, Northwest Arkansas. **2B:** Johnny Giavotella, Northwest Arkansas. **3B:** Mike Moustakas, Northwest Arkansas. **SS:** Andrew Romine, Arkansas. **OF:** Corey Brown, Midland; Jeremy Moore, Arkansas; Paulo Orlando, Northwest Arkansas; Derrick Robinson, Northwest Arkansas. **DH:** Matt Carpenter, Springfield. **UTIL:** Josh Horton, Midland.
P: Douglas Arguello, Corpus Christi; Blake Beavan, Frisco; Simon Castro, San Antonio; Jeremy Hefner, San Antonio; David Kopp, Springfield; Jordan Lyles, Corpus Christi; Ryan Tatusko, Frisco.
Player of the Year: Mike Moustakas, Northwest Arkansas. **Pitcher of the Year:** Blake Beavan, Frisco. **Manager of the Year:** Brian Poldberg, Northwest Arkansas. Mike Coolbaugh **Coach of the Year:** Webster Garrison, Midland.

DEPARTMENT LEADERS

BATTING

OBP	Luna, Aaron, Springfield	.426
SLG	Robinson, Clint, NW Arkansas	.625
OPS	Robinson, Clint, NW Arkansas	1.035
R	Giavotella, Johnny, NW Arkansas	92
H	Giavotella, Johnny, NW Arkansas	168
TB	Robinson, Clint, NW Arkansas	298
XBH	Robinson, Clint, NW Arkansas	75
2B	Robinson, Clint, NW Arkansas	41
3B	Moore, Jeremy, Arkansas	10
HR	Robinson, Clint, NW Arkansas	29
RBI	Robinson, Clint, NW Arkansas	98
SAC	Rodriguez, Guilder, Frisco	14
BB	Forsythe, Logan, San Antonio	75
HBP	Luna, Aaron, Springfield	25
SO	Clark, Matt, San Antonio	146
SB	Robinson, Derrick, NW Arkansas	50
CS	Robinson, Derrick, NW Arkansas	17
AB/SO	Navarro, Efren, Arkansas	9.64

PITCHING

G	Scribner, Evan, San Antonio	57
GS	Three tied at	28
GF	Scribner, Evan, San Antonio	36
SV	Pomeranz, Stuart, Tulsa	18
W	Teaford, Everett, NW Arkansas	14
L	Capra, Anthony, Midland	13
	Lumsden, Tyler, Corpus Christi, San Antonio	13
IP	Hefner, Jeremy, San Antonio	167.2
H	Bleier, Richard, Frisco	191
R	Bleier, Richard, Frisco	98
ER	Bleier, Richard, Frisco	92
HB	Daley, Gary, Springfield, Midland	18
BB	Capra, Anthony, Midland	89
SO	Kluber, Corey, San Antonio	136
SO/9	Kluber, Corey, San Antonio	10.02
SO/9 (RP)	Gomes, Brandon, San Antonio	11.6
BB/9	Edell, Ryan, Midland	1.44
WP	Capra, Anthony, Midland	15
BK	Figueroa, Pedro, Midland	5
HR	Brasier, Ryan, Arkansas	28
AVG	Castro, Simon, San Antonio	.223

FIELDING

C	FPCT	Santangelo, Lou, Corpus Christi	.989
	PO	Martinez, Luis, San Antonio	743
	A	Martinez, Luis, San Antonio	65
	E	Martinez, Luis, San Antonio	12
		Pina, Manuel, San Antonio	12
	DP	Martinez, Luis, San Antonio	9
	PB	Hill, Steven, Springfield	19
1B	FPCT	Navarro, Efren, Arkansas	.995
	PO	Navarro, Efren, Arkansas	1007
	A	Navarro, Efren, Arkansas	96
	E	Robinson, Clint, NW Arkansas	14
	DP	Clemens, Koby, Corpus Christi	113
2B	FPCT	Giavotella, Johnny, NW Arkansas	.978
	PO	Van Kooten, Jason, Tulsa	214
	A	Giavotella, Johnny, NW Arkansas	364
	E	Forsythe, Logan, San Antonio	15
	DP	Giavotella, Johnny, NW Arkansas	81
3B	FPCT	Carpenter, Matt, Springfield	.973
	PO	Valdez, Alex, Midland	74
	A	Carpenter, Matt, Springfield	222
	E	Darnell, James, San Antonio	24
	DP	Moustakas, Mike, NW Arkansas	21
SS	FPCT	Romine, Andrew, Arkansas	.974
	PO	Kozma, Peter, Springfield	201
	A	Kozma, Peter, Springfield	420
	E	Kozma, Peter, Springfield	34
	DP	Kozma, Peter, Springfield	100
OF	FPCT	Gaston, Jonathan, Corpus Christi	.993
	PO	Robinson, Derrick, NW Arkansas	274
	A	Carroll, Sawyer, San Antonio	18
	E	Moore, Jeremy, Arkansas	13
		Orlando, Paulo, NW Arkansas	13
	DP	Van Stratten, Nick, NW Arkansas	6

MINOR LEAGUES

BY JOSH LEVENTHAL

Tearing up the low Class A Midwest League and starring in the Futures Game wasn't enough for Mike Trout. The 2009 first-round pick moved up to the high Class A California League a month before he turned 19, and his five-tool talent jumped out against older competition.

"It's just rare to see a kid that young have such a good feel for the game," said Keith Johnson, his manager at Rancho Cucamonga. "Obviously there are some things that need to be ironed out through experience and at-bats, but his ability to take instruction and put it into a game is plus. You take that aptitude and his skill set and you'll have a guy who will do what he did this year: run through an organization and force someone to try and find a reason that he is not ready for the next level."

Trout made a case for himself as the minors' best prospect. He ranked No. 1 on our Top 20 Prospects lists in both the California and Midwest leagues, the only player this year to earn top billing in multiple circuits.

Last season, San Jose loaded its roster with seven of the Giants' top 10 prospects (including Madison Bumgarner and Buster Posey) and rolled through the regular season en route to winning its third league title in five years. The Giants didn't exactly repeat that formula in 2010, but behind the slugging of first baseman Brandon Belt, San Jose won a first-half title before grinding through the postseason to become the league's first repeat champion since the San Bernardino Stampede did it in 1999-2000.

Lake Elsinore reliever Brad Brach (Padres) earned pitcher of the year honors after setting the league's saves record, breaking the previous mark of 37 by former San Jose reliever Brian Anderson before finishing with 41. High Desert second baseman Kyle Seager (Mariners) compiled the minors' second-longest hit streak this season at 32—falling short of the league record 45 set by Mavericks' outfielder Jamie McOwen last season.

Visalia first baseman Paul Goldschmidt earned

player of the year honors after topping the circuit with 35 home runs and finishing second with 108 RBIs—he also placed second with 161 strikeouts.

The Cal League will have a new look next season as several teams changed affiliates. The Rangers left Bakersfield for Myrtle Beach in the Carolina League. Rancho Cucamonga and Inland Empire will swap affiliates, as the Quakes cut ties with the Angels after 10 seasons in favor of the Dodgers.

TOP 20 PROSPECTS

1. Mike Trout, of, Rancho Cucamonga Quakes (Angels)
2. Brandon Belt, 1b, San Jose Giants
3. Grant Green, ss, Stockton Ports (Athletics)
4. Tyler Chatwood, rhp, Rancho Cucamonga Quakes (Angels)
5. Engel Beltre, of, Bakersfield Blaze (Rangers)
6. Jonathan Villar, ss, Lancaster JetHawks (Astros)
7. Jaff Decker, of, Lake Elsinore Storm (Padres)
8. Aaron Miller, lhp, Inland Empire 66ers (Dodgers)
9. Juan Nicasio, rhp, Modesto Nuts (Rockies)
10. Pat Corbin, lhp, Rancho Cucamonga (Angels)/Visalia (Diamondbacks)
11. Francisco Peguero, of, San Jose Giants
12. Rex Brothers, lhp, Modesto Nuts (Rockies)
13. Ehire Adrianza, ss, San Jose Giants
14. Marc Krauss, of, Visalia Rawhide (Diamondbacks)
15. Ethan Martin, rhp, Inland Empire 66ers (Dodgers)
16. Kyle Russell, of, Inland Empire 66ers (Dodgers)
17. Paul Goldschmidt, 1b, Visalia Rawhide (Diamondbacks)
18. Johermyn Chavez, of, High Desert Mavericks (Mariners)
19. Eric Surkamp, lhp, San Jose Giants
20. Drew Cumberland, ss, Lake Elsinore Storm (Padres)

STANDINGS: SPLIT SEASON

FIRST HALF					SECOND HALF				
NORTH	W	L	PCT	GB	**NORTH**	W	L	PCT	GB
San Jose	45	25	.643	—	Stockton	43	27	.614	—
Modesto	37	33	.529	8	Bakersfield	38	32	.543	5
Visalia	37	33	.529	8	Modesto	36	34	.514	7
Stockton	31	39	.443	14	Visalia	35	35	.500	8
Bakersfield	29	41	.414	16	San Jose	31	39	.443	12
SOUTH	W	L	PCT	GB	**SOUTH**	W	L	PCT	GB
Lake Elsinore	46	24	.657	—	Rancho Cucamonga	39	31	.557	—
Rancho Cucamonga	39	31	.557	7	High Desert	38	32	.543	1
High Desert	37	33	.529	9	Lake Elsinore	35	35	.500	4
Inland Empire	26	44	.371	20	Lancaster	31	39	.443	8
Lancaster	23	47	.329	23	Inland Empire	24	46	.343	15

PLAYOFFS—Division Series: Rancho Cucamonga defeated High Desert 2-0 and Modesto defeated Stockton 2-0 in best-of-three series. **Semifinals:** Rancho Cucamonga defeated Lake Elsinore 3-1 and San Jose defeated Modesto 3-0 in best-of-five series. **Finals:** San Jose defeated Rancho Cucamonga 3-2 in best-of-five series.

OVERALL STANDINGS

Team (Organization)	W	L	PCT	GB	Manager(s)	Attendance	Average	Last Penn.
Lake Elsinore Storm (Padres)	81	59	.579	—	Carlos Lezcano	217,826	3,203	2001
Rancho Cucamonga Quakes (Angels)	78	62	.557	3	Keith Johnson	150,687	2,153	1994
San Jose Giants (Giants)	76	64	.543	5	Brian Harper	201,123	2,873	2010
High Desert Mavericks (Mariners)	75	65	.536	6	Jim Horner/Darrin Garner	109,368	1,585	1997
Stockton Ports (Athletics)	74	66	.529	7	Steve Scarsone	198,016	2,829	2008
Modesto Nuts (Rockies)	73	67	.521	8	Jerry Weinstein	180,344	2,692	2004
Visalia Rawhide (Diamondbacks)	72	68	.514	9	Audo Vicente	108,681	1,598	1978
Bakersfield Blaze (Rangers)	67	73	.479	14	Bill Haselman	64,321	932	1989
Lancaster JetHawks (Astros)	54	86	.386	27	Tom Lawless	156,840	2,241	Never
Inland Empire 66ers (Dodgers)	50	90	.357	31	Jeff Carter	179,295	2,561	2006

CLUB BATTING

	AVG	G	AB	R	H	2B	3B	HR	RBI	BB	SO	SB	OBP	SLG
High Desert	.296	140	4960	860	1466	286	43	172	813	452	1104	103	.361	.475
San Jose	.289	140	4883	739	1409	258	58	117	670	432	1023	208	.353	.437
Lancaster	.278	140	4883	721	1358	258	52	124	663	363	1000	138	.334	.428
Rancho Cucamonga	.278	140	4808	738	1339	252	54	117	662	377	1067	197	.338	.426
Inland Empire	.277	140	4892	665	1355	260	40	95	618	434	1007	98	.341	.405
Modesto	.270	140	4794	714	1296	266	56	84	651	458	1112	170	.342	.402
Stockton	.269	140	4788	755	1286	277	38	143	701	563	1109	86	.350	.432
Bakersfield	.266	140	4775	657	1272	251	26	116	594	362	1045	87	.327	.403
Lake Elsinore	.266	140	4785	760	1275	267	34	136	696	662	1053	133	.360	.422
Visalia	.263	140	4793	689	1262	247	19	124	626	462	1177	56	.335	.400

CLUB PITCHING

	ERA	G	CG	SHO	SV	IP	H	R	ER	HR	BB	SO	AVG
Lake Elsinore	3.83	140	0	6	47	1252	1243	640	533	97	387	1086	.259
Rancho Cucamonga	4.26	140	2	10	36	1252	1262	657	593	124	426	1116	.262
San Jose	4.27	140	1	4	39	1235	1254	673	586	115	437	1025	.264
Bakersfield	4.36	140	4	7	39	1218	1257	696	590	135	487	1079	.268
Visalia	4.49	140	1	6	43	1238	1333	706	618	101	454	1149	.275
Modesto	4.50	140	2	3	38	1242	1330	720	621	108	438	1130	.274
Stockton	4.60	140	1	2	42	1240	1333	763	634	140	516	1163	.274
High Desert	5.01	140	3	3	26	1241	1459	793	691	163	381	964	.293
Inland Empire	5.03	140	3	5	25	1239	1372	797	693	104	564	1057	.283
Lancaster	5.33	140	4	3	21	1230	1475	853	728	141	475	928	.299

CLUB FIELDING

	PCT	PO	A	E	DP		PCT	PO	A	E	DP
Rancho Cuca.	.980	3757	1526	107	123	Lake Elsinore	.971	3755	1502	155	114
San Jose	.976	3706	1557	128	134	Lancaster	.971	3691	1604	158	136
Visalia	.973	3715	1560	144	113	Modesto	.971	3725	1404	155	119
High Desert	.972	3724	1418	150	124	Bakersfield	.968	3653	1429	170	124
Inland Empire	.972	3717	1501	149	137	Stockton	.965	3721	1424	185	129

INDIVIDUAL BATTING LEADERS (MINIMUM 3.1 PA/TEAM GAME)

	AVG	G	AB	R	H	2B	3B	HR	RBI	BB	SO	SB
Seager, Kyle, High Desert	.345	135	557	126	192	40	3	14	74	71	94	13
Shaffer, Jake, High Desert	.338	107	391	58	132	31	6	9	78	26	73	4
Flores, Jose, San Jose	.331	96	359	58	119	15	6	6	54	25	41	9
Peguero, Francisco, San Jose	.329	122	510	78	168	19	16	10	77	18	88	40
Pacheco, Jordan, Modesto	.321	104	390	59	125	27	3	5	70	54	36	5
Cartwright, Albert, Lancaster	.319	92	354	72	113	26	13	10	48	33	80	24
Green, Grant, Stockton	.318	131	548	107	174	39	6	20	87	38	117	9
Cesario, James, Modesto	.316	128	475	78	150	30	10	6	71	29	76	16
Poythress, Rich, High Desert	.315	123	476	88	150	33	0	31	130	52	100	3
Chavez, Johermyn, High Desert	.315	136	534	109	168	30	7	32	96	52	131	6

INDIVIDUAL PITCHING LEADERS (MINIMUM 1 IP/TEAM GAME)

	W	L	ERA	G	GS	CG	SV	IP	H	R	ER	BB	SO
Bass, Anthony, Lake Elsinore	8	7	3.13	27	27	0	0	132	124	59	46	20	109
Hollingsworth, Ethan, Modesto	12	8	3.32	25	25	0	0	160	161	79	59	34	153
Keuchel, Dallas, Lancaster	5	8	3.37	19	18	3	0	121	129	58	45	25	97
Fitzgerald, Justin, San Jose	10	6	3.45	26	25	0	0	146	140	65	56	46	116
Haviland, Shawn, Stockton	9	6	3.66	27	27	0	0	150	156	77	61	40	166
Murray, Justin, Stockton	10	4	3.69	26	18	1	1	118	133	59	48	54	83
Nicasio, Juan, Modesto	12	10	3.91	28	28	1	0	177	186	91	77	31	171
Kasparek, Kenn, High Desert	9	5	4.07	24	22	1	0	146	138	73	66	37	87
LaFromboise, Bobby, High Desert	10	5	4.53	33	14	0	1	114	138	63	57	38	92
Boscan, Wilfredo, Bakersfield	9	14	4.69	27	27	1	0	164	189	93	85	40	130

ALL-STAR TEAM

C: Jordan Pacheco, Modesto. **1B:** Paul Goldschmidt, Visalia. **2B:** Kyle Seager, High Desert. **3B:** Stephen Parker, Stockton. **SS:** Grant Green, Stockton. **OF:** Johermyn Chavez, High Desert; Francisco Peguero, San Jose; Marc Krauss, Visalia. **DH:** Rich Poythress, San Jose. **SP:** Eric Surkamp, San Jose; Anthony Bass, Lake Elsinore; Shawn Haviland, Stockton. **RP:** Brad Brach, Lake Elsinore.
Most Valuable Player: Paul Goldschmidt, Visalia. **Most Valuable Pitcher:** Brad Brach, Lake Elsinore. **Manager of the Year:** Carlos Lezcano, Lake Elsinore.

DEPARTMENT LEADERS

BATTING

OBP	Belt, Brandon, San Jose	.492
SLG	Goldschmidt, Paul, Visalia	.606
OPS	Goldschmidt, Paul, Visalia	.990
R	Seager, Kyle, High Desert	126
H	Seager, Kyle, High Desert	192
TB	Goldschmidt, Paul, Visalia	318
XBH	Goldschmidt, Paul, Visalia	80
2B	Goldschmidt, Paul, Visalia	42
3B	Peguero, Francisco, San Jose	16
HR	Goldschmidt, Paul, Visalia	35
RBI	Poythress, Rich, High Desert	130
SAC	Wikoff, Brandon, Lancaster	17
BB	Belnome, Vincent, Lake Elsinore	102
HBP	Colina, Edilio, High Desert	23
SO	Almonte, Denny, High Desert	192
SB	Austin, Jay, Lancaster	54
CS	Peguero, Francisco, San Jose	22
AB/SO	Pacheco, Jordan, Modesto	10.83

PITCHING

G	Brach, Brad, Lake Elsinore	62
GS	Nicasio, Juan, Modesto	28
	Seaton, Ross, Lancaster	28
GF	Brach, Brad, Lake Elsinore	60
SV	Brach, Brad, Lake Elsinore	41
W	Hollingsworth, Ethan, Modesto	12
	Nicasio, Juan, Modesto	12
	Odle, Oliver, San Jose	12
L	Boscan, Wilfredo, Bakersfield	14
	Martin, Ethan, Inland Empire	14
IP	Nicasio, Juan, Modesto	177.1
H	Seaton, Ross, Lancaster	198
R	Seaton, Ross, Lancaster	126
ER	Seaton, Ross, Lancaster	108
HB	Haviland, Shawn, Stockton	17
BB	Martin, Ethan, Inland Empire	81
SO	Nicasio, Juan, Modesto	171
SO/9	Haviland, Shawn, Stockton	9.95
SO/9 (RP)	Smyth, Paul, Stockton	10.9
BB/9	Odle, Oliver, San Jose	1.1
WP	Pimentel, Carlos, Bakersfield	20
BK	Three tied at	4
HR	Carraway, Andrew, High Desert	25
AVG	Bass, Anthony, Lake Elsinore	.248

FIELDING

C	FPCT	Monell, Johnny, San Jose	.994
	PO	Perez, Rossmel, Visalia	685
	A	Perez, Rossmel, Visalia	88
	E	Ortiz, Ryan, Stockton	8
	DP	Felix, Jose, Bakersfield	13
	PB	Carter, Yusuf, Stockton	21
1B	FPCT	Jacobo, Gabriel, Rancho Cucamonga	.998
	PO	Goldschmidt, Paul, Visalia	1162
	A	Goldschmidt, Paul, Visalia	90
	E	Spina, Michael, Stockton	17
	DP	Ori, Mark, Lancaster	96
2B	FPCT	Figueroa, Cole, Lake Elsinore	.993
	PO	Culberson, Charlie, San Jose	232
	A	Culberson, Charlie, San Jose	342
	E	Cartwright, Albert, Lancaster	20
	DP	Culberson, Charlie, San Jose	77
3B	FPCT	Wheeler, Ryan, Visalia	.947
	PO	Parker, Stephen, Stockton	94
	A	Belnome, Vincent, Lake Elsinore	255
	E	Parker, Stephen, Stockton	33
	DP	Parker, Stephen, Stockton	35
SS	FPCT	Wikoff, Brandon, Lancaster	.979
	PO	Adrianza, Ehire, San Jose	164
	A	Adrianza, Ehire, San Jose	389
	E	Green, Grant, Stockton	37
	DP	Adrianza, Ehire, San Jose	70
OF	FPCT	Christensen, David, Modesto	.994
	PO	Almonte, Denny, High Desert	317
	A	Barfield, Jeremy, Stockton	24
	E	Barfield, Jeremy, Stockton	11
	DP	Barfield, Jeremy, Stockton	5
		Perez, Juan, San Jose	5

MINOR LEAGUES

BY LACY LUSK

After a first half of the season they would have liked to have forgotten, first baseman Tyler Moore and the Potomac Nationals still managed to put together an unforgettable year.

Moore, a 16th-round pick out of Mississippi State in 2008, was hitting .184 with 10 home runs at the end of June—and that was an improvement on an April in which he hit .173 with two homers. His team had gone 31-39 and finished the first half in third place, 10 games behind Frederick.

That all changed with a torrid summer in which Potomac went 39-30 to take the second-half title in the Northern Division as Moore slugged his way to an MVP award. The Nationals then beat Frederick (Orioles) and Winston-Salem (White Sox) to capture their second Mills Cup championship in the past three years.

Moore finished with league bests of 43 doubles, 31 home runs and 111 RBIs. He was the league's hitter of the week four times in a six-week stretch.

"He had made things too complicated, but then he went up there with the single thought of being aggressive," Potomac manager Gary Cathcart said. "I've seen a lot of streaks over the years, but none for six weeks like that."

Potomac had gone 19 years with five parent clubs before winning its first championship since 1989 as the Prince William Cannons. The wait was much shorter this time for a franchise that found stability since the Nationals began play in Washington in 2005.

Winston-Salem fell short of a championship, but it was a successful season for the Dash in its long-awaited first year at BB&T Ballpark. The club drew a high Class A-best 312,313 fans after straggling through one more year than expected at Ernie Shore Field. In 2009, the Dash was last in the league with a total attendance of 57,665.

Wilmington (Royals) missed the playoffs but impressed scouts and managers with its talent. First baseman Eric Hosmer was the highest-rated of those farmhands, placing second to Myrtle Beach righthander Julio Teheran (Braves) in the league's

prospect rankings. Lynchburg (Reds) righthander Jordan Hotchkiss was the league's pitcher of the year after winning 10 games and the ERA title.

Lynchburg's affiliation with the Reds lasted only one year. After the season, the club signed a four-year affiliation with the Braves. Atlanta had been with Myrtle Beach since 1999 but switched to the Rangers with a four-year arrangement. Pelicans owner Chuck Greenberg is also a co-owner of the American League champion Rangers, who will visit Myrtle Beach for an exhibition game in March. The two new player development contracts forced the Reds to Bakersfield (California League).

TOP 20 PROSPECTS

1. Julio Teheran, rhp, Myrtle Beach Pelicans (Braves)
2. Eric Hosmer, 1b, Wilmington Blue Rocks (Royals)
3. John Lamb, lhp, Wilmington Blue Rocks (Royals)
4. Wil Myers, c, Wilmington Blue Rocks (Royals)
5. Devin Mesoraco, c, Lynchburg Hillcats (Reds)
6. Randall Delgado, rhp, Myrtle Beach Pelicans (Braves)
7. Chris Dwyer, lhp, Wilmington Blue Rocks (Royals)
8. Oscar Tejeda, 2b, Salem Red Sox
9. Christian Colon, ss, Wilmington Blue Rocks (Royals)
10. Jason Kipnis, 2b, Kinston Indians
11. Derek Norris, c, Potomac Nationals
12. Xavier Avery, of, Frederick Keys (Orioles)
13. Will Middlebrooks, 3b, Salem Red Sox
14. Michael Burgess, of, Potomac Nationals
15. Gregory Infante, rhp, Winston-Salem Dash (White Sox)
16. J.J. Hoover, rhp, Myrtle Beach Pelicans (Braves)
17. Ryan Lavarnway, c, Salem Red Sox
18. Tyler Moore, 1b, Potomac Nationals
19. Jordan Henry, 1b, Kinston Indians
20. Santos Rodriguez, lhp, Winston-Salem Dash (White Sox)

STANDINGS: SPLIT SEASON

FIRST HALF					SECOND HALF				
NORTH	**W**	**L**	**PCT**	**GB**	**NORTH**	**W**	**L**	**PCT**	**GB**
Frederick	41	29	.586	—	Potomac	39	30	.565	—
Wilmington	32	38	.457	9	Wilmington	36	32	.529	2½
Potomac	31	39	.443	10	Lynchburg	32	36	.471	6½
Lynchburg	29	41	.414	12	Frederick	31	39	.443	8½
SOUTH	**W**	**L**	**PCT**	**GB**	**SOUTH**	**W**	**L**	**PCT**	**GB**
W-S	43	27	.614	—	W-S	38	31	.551	—
Salem	42	28	.600	1	Kinston	37	33	.529	1½
Kinston	36	34	.514	7	Myrtle Beach	32	38	.457	6½
Myrtle Beach	26	44	.371	17	Salem	31	37	.456	6½

PLAYOFFS—Semifinals: Potomac defeated Frederick 3-1 and Winston-Salem defeated Kinston 3-0 in best-of-five series. **Finals:** Potomac defeated Winston-Salem 3-1 in best-of-five series.

OVERALL STANDINGS

Team (Organization)	W	L	PCT	GB	Manager(s)	Attendance	Average	Last Penn.
Winston-Salem Dash (White Sox)	81	58	.583	—	Joe McEwing	312,313	4,593	2003
Salem Red Sox (Red Sox)	73	65	.529	7 ½	Kevin Boles	211,527	3,205	2001
Kinston Indians (Indians)	73	67	.521	8 ½	Aaron Holbert	118,741	1,799	2006
Frederick Keys (Orioles)	72	68	.514	9 ½	Orlando Gomez	291,299	4,222	2007
Potomac Nationals (Nationals)	70	69	.504	11	Gary Cathcart	205,279	3,064	2010
Wilmington Blue Rocks (Royals)	68	70	.493	12 ½	Brian Rupp	296,041	4,554	1999
Lynchburg Hillcats (Pirates)	61	77	.442	19 ½	Pat Kelly	152,161	2,341	2009
Myrtle Beach Pelicans (Braves)	58	82	.414	231/2	Rocket Wheeler	223,176	3,282	2000

CLUB BATTING

	AVG	G	AB	R	H	2B	3B	HR	RBI	BB	SO	SB	OBP	SLG
Winston-Salem	.288	139	4805	738	1384	282	44	112	690	387	1024	54	.350	.435
Frederick	.267	140	4729	691	1263	242	27	87	632	475	1122	157	.343	.385
Lynchburg	.262	138	4654	555	1219	274	19	98	495	329	977	95	.318	.392
Wilmington	.262	138	4605	602	1205	250	53	74	550	361	884	130	.319	.387
Salem	.259	138	4580	638	1188	277	32	75	577	466	1041	89	.334	.383
Kinston	.252	140	4568	570	1150	209	32	73	524	507	1107	112	.334	.359
Potomac	.251	139	4641	665	1166	283	45	109	597	539	1081	96	.334	.402
Myrtle Beach	.238	140	4733	575	1126	207	36	95	511	416	1070	104	.303	.357

CLUB PITCHING

	ERA	G	CG	SHO	SV	IP	H	R	ER	HR	BB	SO	AVG
Kinston	3.31	140	1	13	48	1222	1097	535	449	91	479	1109	.241
Wilmington	3.89	138	1	10	34	1216	1192	629	526	86	416	1145	.257
Salem	3.91	138	2	9	34	1205	1177	611	523	74	377	893	.257
Potomac	3.95	139	1	9	37	1227	1268	642	539	101	393	1082	.268
Myrtle Beach	4.00	140	2	5	28	1249	1261	664	555	83	449	1104	.262
Winston-Salem	4.04	139	2	5	34	1224	1271	640	550	64	488	974	.271
Frederick	4.06	140	2	4	35	1227	1241	670	553	122	484	1013	.263
Lynchburg	4.07	138	0	12	32	1199	1194	643	543	102	394	986	.260

CLUB FIELDING

	PCT	PO	A	E	DP		PCT	PO	A	E	DP
Salem	.978	3614	1549	116	126	Wilmington	.974	3648	1344	135	105
Kinston	.975	3666	1538	131	131	Lynchburg	.972	3598	1454	147	128
Winston-Salem	.975	3673	1602	137	157	Myrtle Beach	.971	3747	1458	154	123
Potomac	.974	3681	1503	138	125	Frederick	.966	3681	1565	183	141

INDIVIDUAL BATTING LEADERS (MINIMUM 3.1 PA/TEAM GAME)

	AVG	G	AB	R	H	2B	3B	HR	RBI	BB	SO	SB
Hosmer, Eric, Wilmington	.354	87	325	48	115	29	6	7	51	44	39	11
Short, Brandon, Winston-Salem	.316	116	491	77	155	31	5	15	79	28	107	7
Gilmore, Jon, Winston-Salem	.312	135	568	79	177	24	4	5	80	34	89	1
Tejeda, Oscar, Salem	.307	126	508	76	156	32	5	11	69	32	96	17
Lewis, Ozzie, Winston-Salem	.300	108	414	62	124	26	1	10	56	33	92	2
Lombardozzi, Steve, Potomac	.293	110	440	71	129	30	9	1	38	49	60	20
Loman, Seth, Winston-Salem	.292	133	514	88	150	33	3	25	88	43	127	0
Perez, Salvador, Wilmington	.290	99	365	35	106	21	1	7	53	18	38	1
Ortiz, Adrian, Wilmington	.289	106	436	59	126	17	8	2	34	22	71	32
Hassan, Alex, Salem	.287	104	342	46	98	28	3	8	48	57	69	6

INDIVIDUAL PITCHING LEADERS (MINIMUM 1 IP/TEAM GAME)

	W	L	ERA	G	GS	CG	SV	IP	H	R	ER	BB	SO
Hotchkiss, Jordan, Lynchburg	10	4	2.31	31	15	0	0	114	86	33	29	31	90
Gardner, Joseph, Kinston	12	6	2.65	22	22	0	0	122	85	44	36	51	104
Delgado, Randall, Myrtle Beach	4	7	2.77	20	20	0	0	117	89	46	36	32	120
McFarland, T.J., Kinston	11	5	3.14	24	19	1	0	127	121	50	44	40	92
Hoover, J.J., Myrtle Beach	11	6	3.27	24	24	0	0	133	126	56	48	35	118
Doyle, Terry, Winston-Salem	8	8	3.72	20	20	0	0	121	115	60	50	34	99
O'Shea, Ryan, Frederick	7	8	3.85	28	28	0	0	141	148	73	60	64	105
House, T.J., Kinston	6	10	3.93	27	26	0	0	136	135	74	59	61	106
Pimentel, Stolmy, Salem	9	11	4.07	26	26	0	0	129	120	65	58	42	102
Jones, Nathan, Winston-Salem	11	6	4.08	28	28	1	0	152	176	77	69	56	109

ALL-STAR TEAM

C: Ryan Lavarnway, Salem. **1B:** Eric Hosmer, Wilmington. **2B:** Oscar Tejeda, Salem. **3B:** Will Middlebrooks, Salem. **SS:** Eduardo Escobar, Winston-Salem. **OF:** Brandon Short, Winston-Salem; Xavier Avery, Frederick; Ronnie Welty, Frederick. **DH:** Tyler Moore, Potomac. **UTIL INF:** Jon Gilmore, Winston-Salem. **UTIL OF:** Justin Greene, Winston-Salem; Adrian Ortiz, Wilmington. **Most Valuable Player:** Tyler Moore, Potomac. **Pitcher of the Year:** Jordan Hotchkiss, Lynchburg. **Manager of the Year:** Joe McEwing, Winston-Salem.

DEPARTMENT LEADERS

BATTING

OBP	Hosmer, Eric, Wilmington	.429
SLG	Moore, Tyler, Potomac	.552
OPS	Loman, Seth, Winston-Salem	.893
R	Loman, Seth, Winston-Salem	88
H	Gilmore, Jon, Winston-Salem	177
TB	Moore, Tyler, Potomac	277
XBH	Moore, Tyler, Potomac	77
2B	Moore, Tyler, Potomac	43
3B	Three tied at	9
HR	Moore, Tyler, Potomac	31
RBI	Moore, Tyler, Potomac	111
SAC	Ortiz, Adrian, Wilmington	20
BB	Norris, Derek, Potomac	89
HBP	Loman, Seth, Winston-Salem	30
SO	Welty, Ronnie, Frederick	159
SB	Hudson, Kyle, Frederick	40
CS	Norris, Patrick, Wilmington	17
AB/SO	Perez, Salvador, Wilmington	9.61

PITCHING

G	Bowman, Andrew, Lynchburg	45
	Freeman, Justin, Lynchburg	45
	Langwell, Matthew, Kinston	45
GS	Jones, Nathan, Winston-Salem	28
	O'Shea, Ryan, Frederick	28
GF	Burns, Cory, Kinston	39
SV	Burns, Cory, Kinston	30
W	Gardner, Joseph, Kinston	12
L	Clay, Caleb, Salem	13
IP	Jones, Nathan, Winston-Salem	152.1
H	Sauer, Stephen, Winston-Salem	193
R	Crim, Matthew, Myrtle Beach	101
ER	Sauer, Stephen, Winston-Salem	82
HB	Gardner, Joseph, Kinston	18
RR	O'Shea, Ryan, Frederick	64
SO	Delgado, Randall, Myrtle Beach	120
SO/9	Delgado, Randall, Myrtle Beach	9.22
SO/9 (RP)	Langwell, Matthew, Kinston	9.3
BB/9	Oberholtzer, Brett, Myrtle Beach	1.44
WP	Partch, Curtis, Lynchburg	14
BK	Basurto, Eric, Wilmington	5
HR	Drake, Oliver, Frederick	19
AVG	Gardner, Joseph, Kinston	.199

FIELDING

C	FPCT	Perez, Salvador, Wilmington	.993
	PO	Perez, Salvador, Wilmington	732
	A	Perez, Salvador, Wilmington	77
	E	Ward, Brian, Frederick	12
	DP	Ward, Brian, Frederick	8
	PB	Sierra, Luis, Winston-Salem	15
1B	FPCT	Loman, Seth, Winston-Salem	.992
	PO	Loman, Seth, Winston-Salem	1061
	A	Moore, Tyler, Potomac	109
	E	Moore, Tyler, Potomac	11
	DP	Loman, Seth, Winston-Salem	118
2B	FPCT	Lombardozzi, Steve, Potomac	.989
	PO	Garcia, Andrew, Winston-Salem	254
	A	Garcia, Andrew, Winston-Salem	377
	E	Tejeda, Oscar, Salem	24
	DP	Garcia, Andrew, Winston-Salem	97
3B	FPCT	Bellows, Kyle, Kinston	.978
	PO	Bellows, Kyle, Kinston	77
	A	Bellows, Kyle, Kinston	286
	E	Gilmore, Jon, Winston-Salem	38
	DP	Bellows, Kyle, Kinston	30
SS	FPCT	Dent, Ryan, Salem	.965
	PO	Dent, Ryan, Salem	165
	A	Dent, Ryan, Salem	331
	E	Lozada, Jose, Potomac	27
	DP	Dent, Ryan, Salem	61
OF	FPCT	Ortiz, Adrian, Wilmington	1.000
	PO	Hissey, Peter, Salem	269
	A	Fellhauer, Josh, Lynchburg	13
	A	Ortiz, Adrian, Wilmington	13
	E	Norris, Patrick, Wilmington	9
	DP	Curran, Chris, Potomac	5

MINOR LEAGUES

MINOR LEAGUES

BY J.J. COOPER

No team had repeated as Florida State League champions in 35 years. The Tampa Yankees made it look easy.

A year after a club led by Jesus Montero, Austin Romine and D.J. Mitchell knocked off Charlotte (Rays) in the championship series for the team's first title since 2001, Tampa once again beat Charlotte in the championship series.

Tampa didn't have a prospect as impressive as Montero, but depth may have made this team even better. Tampa featured Dellin Betances, Hector Noesi, Adam Warren and Andrew Brackman in the rotation to start the season. Manny Banuelos and Graham Stoneburner joined the rotation during its push for the second-half title.

League MVP Melky Mesa and second baseman Corban Joseph provided much of Tampa's offense during the regular season, but Brad Suttle provided the big bat in the playoffs. He hit .304 with three home runs and nine RBIs in six games as Tampa swept Dunedin in the first round and beat Charlotte three games to one in the final.

Charlotte didn't win the title, but it did boast the league's most impressive prospect. Matt Moore (6-11, 3.36) overcame a rough start to become the minors' most dominant pitcher. He went 5-4, 1.39 with 130 strikeouts in 84 innings over the second half of the season. Overall, he finished with 208 strikeouts to become the first minor league pitcher to top 200 strikeouts since 2005.

As usual, it was a pitching dominated league. Pitchers claimed the first four spots on our FSL Top 20 Prospects list, led by Moore. Daytona's Chris Archer (Cubs), Lakeland's Jacob Turner (Tigers) and Tampa's Dellin Betances also showed frontline-starter stuff.

Several other pitchers, most notably Fort Myers' Kyle Gibson (Twins), Bradenton's Bryan Morris (Pirates), Daytona's Trey McNutt and Tampa's Banuelos and Noesi would have made the Top 20

if they had enough innings to qualify.

Clearwater's Austin Hyatt was named the league's pitcher of the year.

Daytona's Brett Jackson was one of the league's most impressive hitters, and the outfielder made his mark by hitting for the cycle in mid-June. He earned a midseason promotion to Double-A.

TOP 20 PROSPECTS

1. Matt Moore, lhp, Charlotte Stone Crabs (Rays)
2. Chris Archer, rhp, Daytona Cubs
3. Jacob Turner, rhp, Lakeland Flying Tigers
4. Dellin Betances, rhp, Tampa Yankees
5. Travis D'Arnaud, c, Dunedin Blue Jays
6. Tony Sanchez, c, Bradenton Pirates
7. Brett Jackson, of, Daytona Cubs
8. Anthony Gose, of, Clearwater (Phillies)/Dunedin Blue Jays
9. Trevor May, rhp, Clearwater Threshers (Phillies)
10. Wilmer Flores, ss, St. Lucie Mets
11. Adieny Hechavarria, ss, Dunedin Blue Jays
12. Henderson Alvarez, rhp, Dunedin Blue Jays
13. Adam Warren, rhp, Tampa Yankees
14. Liam Hendriks, rhp, Fort Myers Miracle (Twins)
15. Joe Cruz, rhp, Charlotte Stone Crabs (Rays)
16. Diego Moreno, rhp, Bradenton Marauders (Pirates)
17. Francisco Martinez, 3b, Lakeland Tigers
18. Jhan Marinez, rhp, Jupiter Hammerheads (Marlins)
19. Melky Mesa, of, Tampa Yankees
20. Andrew Brackman, rhp, Tampa Yankees

STANDINGS: SPLIT SEASON

FIRST HALF

NORTH	W	L	PCT	GB
Dunedin	41	29	.586	—
Tampa	36	32	.529	4
Clearwater	37	33	.529	4
Lakeland	37	33	.529	4
Daytona	34	36	.486	7
Brevard Co.	27	42	.391	13½

SOUTH	W	L	PCT	GB
Charlotte	43	26	.623	—
Bradenton	39	31	.557	4½
Palm Beach	39	31	.557	4½
St. Lucie	33	35	.485	9½
Fort Myers	28	42	.400	15½
Jupiter	22	46	.324	20½

SECOND HALF

NORTH	W	L	PCT	GB
Tampa	42	25	.627	—
Daytona	41	28	.594	2
Brevard Co.	37	33	.529	6½
Lakeland	34	34	.500	8½
Dunedin	31	38	.449	12
Clearwater	30	39	.435	13

SOUTH	W	L	PCT	GB
Bradenton	37	31	.544	—
Fort Myers	36	32	.529	1
Charlotte	37	33	.529	1
Palm Beach	36	34	.514	2
St. Lucie	29	41	.414	9
Jupiter	24	46	.343	14

PLAYOFFS—Semifinals: Tampa defeated Dunedin 2-0 and Charlotte defeated Bradenton 2-1 in best-of-three series. **Finals:** Tampa defeated Charlotte 3-1 in best-of-five series.

OVERALL STANDINGS

Team (Organization)	W	L	PCT	GB	Manager(s)	Attendance	Average	Last Penn.
Tampa Yankees (Yankees)	78	57	.578	—	Torre Tyson	99,736	1,534	2010
Charlotte Stone Crabs (Rays)	80	59	.576	00	Jim Morrison	171,450	2,679	1990
Bradenton Marauders (Pirates)	76	62	.551	3 ½	P.J. Forbes	51,856	823	1963
Daytona Cubs (Cubs)	75	64	.540	5	Buddy Bailey	150,157	2,241	2008
Palm Beach Cardinals (Cardinals)	75	65	.536	5 ½	Luis Aguayo	64,767	967	2005
Dunedin Blue Jays (Blue Jays)	72	67	.518	8	Clayton McCullough	36,892	576	Never
Lakeland Flying Tigers (Tigers)	71	67	.514	8 ½	Andy Barkett	64,010	1,016	1992
Clearwater Threshers (Phillies)	67	72	.482	13	Dusty Wathan	172,716	2,540	2007
Fort Myers Miracle (Twins)	64	74	.464	15 ½	Jake Mauer	112,733	1,708	1985
Brevard County Manatees (Brewers)	64	75	.460	16	Bob Miscik	89,729	1,339	2001
St. Lucie Mets (Mets)	62	76	.449	17 ½	Edgar Alfonzo	100,921	1,506	2006
Jupiter Hammerheads (Marlins)	46	92	.333	33 ½	Ron Hassey	67,614	994	1991

CLUB BATTING

	AVG	G	AB	R	H	2B	3B	HR	RBI	BB	SO	SB	OBP	SLG
Bradenton	.265	138	4596	681	1218	248	24	65	606	468	1030	133	.343	.372
Clearwater	.264	139	4656	602	1231	249	32	70	551	377	1027	129	.327	.377
Tampa	.263	135	4544	609	1196	235	43	72	569	455	1034	166	.333	.381
Brevard County	.261	139	4712	597	1232	217	29	59	560	426	1014	145	.332	.357
Daytona	.261	139	4739	607	1236	248	40	69	545	366	946	98	.319	.374
St. Lucie	.261	138	4666	590	1217	235	33	80	532	337	1117	99	.318	.377
Charlotte	.259	139	4604	558	1191	235	36	62	503	466	871	117	.332	.366
Lakeland	.253	138	4628	543	1172	190	32	68	489	486	1072	138	.332	.352
Palm Beach	.250	140	4525	586	1129	255	36	69	522	457	1065	136	.328	.368
Fort Myers	.249	138	4532	517	1127	219	29	52	467	483	1010	76	.327	.344
Dunedin	.241	139	4577	580	1102	256	24	110	534	352	1191	118	.300	.379
Jupiter	.229	138	4492	465	1030	214	32	51	426	348	1022	116	.294	.325

CLUB PITCHING

	ERA	G	CG	SHO	SV	IP	H	R	ER	HR	BB	SO	AVG
Charlotte	3.06	139	4	12	49	1219	1088	495	414	50	389	1189	.239
Lakeland	3.30	138	4	14	37	1218	1141	509	447	76	307	989	.249
Tampa	3.30	135	3	19	34	1189	1141	536	436	63	299	1127	.250
Bradenton	3.43	138	0	12	40	1185	1112	559	451	80	362	943	.246
Palm Beach	3.52	140	3	12	39	1203	1213	549	470	50	389	873	.264
Daytona	3.54	139	1	6	38	1235	1143	572	486	82	441	1087	.244
Dunedin	3.64	139	2	11	38	1215	1239	568	492	65	379	1043	.263
Brevard County	3.84	139	2	8	30	1230	1197	597	525	64	500	1046	.256
Fort Myers	3.89	138	4	12	39	1200	1197	621	519	69	443	994	.260
Jupiter	4.01	138	6	10	26	1196	1263	615	533	58	426	965	.271
Clearwater	4.04	139	3	7	33	1208	1151	622	542	99	476	1083	.252
St. Lucie	4.42	138	0	3	34	1205	1196	692	592	71	610	1060	.261

CLUB FIELDING

	PCT	PO	A	E	DP		PCT	PO	A	E	DP
Lakeland	.978	3655	1473	118	138	Dunedin	.972	3645	1438	144	107
Brevard County	.976	3689	1482	129	122	Daytona	.971	3704	1511	156	108
Clearwater	.975	3625	1300	124	101	Jupiter	.970	3587	1453	154	141
Tampa	.975	3568	1331	125	111	St. Lucie	.970	3616	1344	151	124
Charlotte	.973	3656	1408	143	124	Fort Myers	.969	3600	1393	159	122
Palm Beach	.973	3609	1522	143	168	Bradenton	.967	3555	1506	171	117

INDIVIDUAL BATTING LEADERS *(MINIMUM 3.1 PA/TEAM GAME)*

	AVG	G	AB	R	H	2B	3B	HR	RBI	BB	SO	SB
Vogt, Stephen, Charlotte	.345	106	368	56	127	31	3	8	47	31	46	3
Komatsu, Erik, Brevard County	.323	130	486	90	157	31	6	5	63	68	61	28
LeMahieu, DJ, Daytona	.314	135	554	63	174	24	5	2	73	29	61	15
Joseph, Corban, Tampa	.302	98	381	52	115	27	3	6	52	43	74	5
Cline, Matt, Brevard County	.298	112	406	61	121	19	2	0	39	50	53	14
Miranda, Sergio, Brevard County	.294	126	486	52	143	18	3	3	71	28	45	14
Halton, Sean, Brevard County	.292	104	397	42	116	17	1	10	77	28	88	2
Velasquez, Isaias, Charlotte	.289	127	457	46	132	17	4	2	36	45	68	41
Flaherty, Ryan, Daytona	.286	108	420	65	120	34	3	9	63	41	74	6
Susdorf, Steve, Clearwater	.278	128	489	60	136	28	2	11	77	46	109	6

INDIVIDUAL PITCHING LEADERS *(MINIMUM 1 IP/TEAM GAME)*

	W	L	ERA	G	GS	CG	SV	IP	H	R	ER	BB	SO
Osterbrock, Daniel, Fort Myers	7	8	2.73	20	18	0	0	112	103	43	34	23	79
Cruz, Joseph, Charlotte	13	6	2.85	25	25	1	0	142	137	53	45	39	131
Sanchez, Jesus, Clearwater	9	7	3.00	23	22	1	0	129	109	47	43	33	84
Wilk, Adam, Lakeland	9	5	3.02	24	24	1	0	144	139	58	48	19	100
Barnese, Nick, Charlotte	8	4	3.02	21	20	1	0	122	114	46	41	26	100
Hyatt, Austin, Clearwater	11	5	3.05	23	21	0	0	124	100	47	42	35	156
Putkonen, Luke, Lakeland	9	7	3.19	27	26	1	0	153	144	55	54	44	87
Pribanic, Aaron, Bradenton	7	6	3.33	27	27	0	0	154	157	74	57	33	71
Hand, Brad, Jupiter	8	8	3.34	26	26	2	0	141	153	68	52	49	134
Moore, Matthew, Charlotte	6	11	3.37	26	26	0	0	145	109	62	54	61	208

ALL-STAR TEAM

C: Michael Brenly, Daytona/Travis d'Arnaud, Dunedin. 1B: Rebel Ridling, Daytona. 2B: D.J. LeMahieu, Daytona. 3B: Brian Dozier, Fort Myers. SS: Brad Suttle, Tampa. UTIL INF: Sergio Miranda, Brevard County. LF: Quincy Latimore, Bradenton. CF: Melky Mesa, Tampa. RF: Erik Komatsu, Brevard County. UTIL OF: Anthony Gose, Dunedin. DH: Stephen Vogt, Charlotte. SP: Joe Cruz, Charlotte; Austin Hyatt, Clearwater; Matt Moore, Charlotte; Adam Wilk, Lakeland. RP: Noah Krol, Bradenton; Zach Quate, Charlotte.

Player of the Year: Melky Mesa, Tampa. Pitcher of the Year: Austin Hyatt, Clearwater. Manager of the Year: Jim Morrison, Charlotte.

DEPARTMENT LEADERS

BATTING

OBP	Komatsu, Erik, Brevard County	.413
SLG	Vogt, Stephen, Charlotte	.511
OPS	Vogt, Stephen, Charlotte	.910
R	Komatsu, Erik, Brevard County	90
H	LeMahieu, DJ, Daytona	174
TB	Latimore, Quincy, Bradenton	230
XBH	Castellanos, Alex, Palm Beach	55
2B	Castellanos, Alex, Palm Beach	35
3B	Gose, Anthony, Clearwater, Dunedin	13
	Pirela, Jose, Tampa	13
HR	McDade, Michael, Dunedin	21
RBI	Latimore, Quincy, Bradenton	100
SAC	Nunez, Gustavo, Lakeland	16
BB	Komatsu, Erik, Brevard County	68
HBP	Cline, Matt, Brevard County	20
SO	Kjeldgaard, Brock, Brevard County	175
SB	Gose, Anthony, Clearwater, Dunedin	45
CS	Gose, Anthony, Clearwater, Dunedin	32
AB/SO	Miranda, Sergio, Brevard County	10.8

PITCHING

G	Krol, Noah, Bradenton	63
GS	Five tied at	27
GF	Krol, Noah, Bradenton	61
SV	Krol, Noah, Bradenton	34
W	Cruz, Joseph, Charlotte	13
L	Correa, Heitor, Clearwater	14
IP	Pribanic, Aaron, Bradenton	154
H	Bono, Robert, Jupiter	187
R	Correa, Heitor, Clearwater	116
ER	Correa, Heitor, Clearwater	101
HB	Barnese, Nick, Charlotte	18
BB	Hunt, Shooter, Fort Myers	84
SO	Moore, Matthew, Charlotte	208
SO/9	Moore, Matthew, Charlotte	12.98
SO/9 (RP)	Fleming, Marquis, Charlotte	11.9
BB/9	Wilk, Adam, Lakeland	1.19
WP	Beaulac, Eric, St. Lucie	26
BK	Correa, Heitor, Clearwater	5
HR	Correa, Heitor, Clearwater	18
AVG	Moore, Matthew, Charlotte	.210

FIELDING

C	FPCT	Brenly, Michael, Daytona	.995
	PO	Jefferies, Jake, Charlotte	817
	A	Jefferies, Jake, Charlotte	70
	E	Kennelly, Tim, Clearwater	8
		Sanchez, Tony, Bradenton	8
	DP	Gomes, Yan, Dunedin	6
		Zarraga, Shawn, Brevard County	6
	PB	Blaquiere, Jean Luc, St. Lucie	13
1B	FPCT	Sheridan, Michael, Charlotte	.994
	PO	Anderson, Calvin, Bradenton	1023
	A	Hanson, Nathan, Fort Myers	78
	E	Anderson, Calvin, Bradenton	23
	DP	Lasater, Ben, Jupiter	95
2B	FPCT	Pertusati, Daniel, Jupiter	.954
	PO	Pertusati, Daniel, Jupiter	194
	A	Bolivar, Domnit, Palm Beach	322
	E	Bolivar, Domnit, Palm Beach	24
	DP	Bolivar, Domnit, Palm Beach	76
3B	FPCT	Suttle, Bradley, Tampa	.951
	PO	Suttle, Bradley, Tampa	64
	A	Lucas, Richard, St. Lucie	225
	E	Lucas, Richard, St. Lucie	21
	DP	Sexton, Greg, Charlotte	22
SS	FPCT	Hanzawa, Troy, Clearwater	.960
	PO	Nunez, Gustavo, Lakeland	214
	A	Nunez, Gustavo, Lakeland	388
	E	Lake, Junior, Daytona	35
	DP	Nunez, Gustavo, Lakeland	76
OF	FPCT	Fields, Daniel, Lakeland	.996
	PO	Gose, Anthony, Clear., Dunedin	310
	A	Wyatt, Brent, Lakeland	20
	E	Castellanos, Alex, Palm Beach	8
		Ramirez, Welinton, Dunedin	8
	DP	McClune, Austin, Bradenton	6

MINOR LEAGUES

BY JIM SHONERD

The Midwest League was perhaps the minors' most prospect-laden circuit in 2010. And while Cedar Rapids outfielder Mike Trout (Angels) wasn't the lone attraction, he was undoubtedly the name at the top of the marquee.

In his first full season, Trout won the league batting title and was named MVP despite being promoted to high Class A in July. By the end of the season, Trout was widely regarded as the best prospect in the minor leagues. Trout had company in the form of fellow teenagers like Quad Cities righthander Shelby Miller (Cardinals), Burlington catcher Wil Myers (Royals) and Clinton shortstop Nick Franklin (Mariners)—who broke the franchise's 49-year-old home run record on his way to claiming the league's home run title with 23. The ERA title also went to a teenager, Kane County lefthander Ian Krol (Athletics) at 2.65.

Great Lakes (Dodgers) was the only team in the minors to win 90 games and was led by Jerry Sands, who hit 18 first-half home runs before earning a promotion.

The Loons were ousted from the playoffs by one of the league's newcomers. The MWL expanded to 16 teams in 2010, as Bowling Green and Lake County shifted from the South Atlantic League. The Captains finished 13 games behind Great Lakes in the regular season, but got the better of the Loons when the two met in the league semifinals.

Lake County needed five games to knock off Clinton for the title in a series best remembered for a marathon Game Two. Clinton won in 18 innings in a game that saw the teams combine to use 13 pitchers and required 5 hours, 37 minutes to complete.

TOP 20 PROSPECTS

1. Mike Trout, of, Cedar Rapids Kernels (Angels)
2. Shelby Miller, rhp, Quad Cities River Bandits (Cardinals)
3. Wil Myers, c, Burlington Bees (Royals)
4. Jacob Turner, rhp, West Michigan Whitecaps (Tigers)
5. Aaron Hicks, of, Beloit Snappers (Twins)
6. Nick Franklin, ss/2b, Clinton LumberKings (Mariners)
7. Trey McNutt, rhp, Peoria Chiefs (Cubs)
8. Jake Odorizzi, rhp, Wisconsin Timber Rattlers (Brewers)
9. Matt Davidson, 3b, South Bend Silver Hawks (Diamondbacks)
10. Tyler Skaggs, lhp, Cedar Rapids (Angels)/South Bend (Diamondbacks)
11. Allen Webster, rhp, Great Lakes Loons (Dodgers)
12. Jean Segura, 2b, Cedar Rapids Kernels (Angels)
13. Hak-Ju Lee, ss, Peoria Chiefs (Cubs)
14. Fabio Martinez, rhp, Cedar Rapids Kernels (Angels)
15. Rubby de la Rosa, rhp, Great Lakes Loons (Dodgers)
16. Alex Colome, rhp, Bowling Green Hot Rods (Rays)
17. Chris Owings, ss, South Bend Silver Hawks (Diamondbacks)
18. Jerry Sands, 1b/of, Great Lakes Loons (Dodgers)
19. Matt Lollis, rhp, Fort Wayne TinCaps (Padres)
20. Chad Jenkins, rhp, Lansing Lugnuts (Blue Jays)

STANDINGS: SPLIT SEASON

FIRST HALF

EAST	W	L	PCT	GB
Lake County	44	25	.638	—
Great Lakes	43	26	.623	1
Lansing	36	33	.522	8
Fort Wayne	36	34	.514	8½
B. Green	31	38	.449	13
South Bend	30	38	.441	13½
Dayton	30	39	.435	14
W. Michigan	26	43	.377	18

WEST	W	L	PCT	GB
Cedar Rapids	43	25	.632	—
Quad Cities	40	29	.580	3½
Peoria	38	31	.551	5½
Beloit	37	32	.536	6½
Clinton	37	32	.536	6½
Kane County	32	37	.464	11½
Wisconsin	26	42	.382	17
Burlington	22	47	.319	21½

SECOND HALF

EAST	W	L	PCT	GB
Great Lakes	47	23	.671	—
Fort Wayne	41	29	.586	6
W. Michigan	36	34	.514	11
Lansing	34	36	.486	13
Lake County	33	37	.471	14
B. Green	30	40	.429	17
South Bend	29	40	.420	17½
Dayton	23	46	.333	23½

WEST	W	L	PCT	GB
Quad Cities	43	26	.623	—
Kane County	39	30	.565	4
Cedar Rapids	39	31	.557	4½
Clinton	37	33	.529	6½
Beloit	34	33	.507	8
Peoria	33	35	.485	9½
Wisconsin	32	38	.457	11½
Burlington	24	43	.358	18

PLAYOFFS—Division Series: Clinton defeated Cedar Rapids 2-1, Great Lakes defeated Fort Wayne 2-1, Kane County defeated Quad Cities 2-1 and Lake County defeated West Michigan 2-1 in best-of-three series. **Semifinals:** Clinton defeated Kane County 2-1 and Lake County defeated Great Lakes 2-1 in best-of-three series. **Finals:** Lake County defeated Clinton 3-2 in best-of-five series.

OVERALL STANDINGS

Team (Organization)	W	L	PCT	GB	Manager(s)	Attendance	Average	Last Penn.
Great Lakes Loons (Dodgers)	90	49	.647	—	Juan Bustabad	263,878	4,060	2000
Quad Cities River Bandits (Cardinals)	83	55	.601	6 ½	Johnny Rodriguez	224,128	3,502	1990
Cedar Rapids Kernels (Angels)	82	56	.594	7 ½	Bill Mosiello	173,210	2,585	1994
Lake County Captains (Indians)	77	62	.554	13	Ted Kubiak	287,935	4,234	2010
Fort Wayne TinCaps (Padres)	77	63	.550	13 ½	Jose Flores	404,942	5,785	2009
Clinton LumberKings (Mariners)	74	65	.532	16	John Tamargo	123,553	1,817	1991
Beloit Snappers (Twins)	71	65	.522	17 ½	Nelson Prada	73,440	1,096	1995
Peoria Chiefs (Cubs)	71	66	.518	18	Casey Kopitzke	203,558	3,132	2002
Kane County Cougars (Athletics)	71	67	.514	18 ½	Aaron Nieckula	430,831	6,244	2001
Lansing Lugnuts (Blue Jays)	70	69	.504	20	Sal Fasano	360,510	5,302	2003
West Michigan Whitecaps (Tigers)	62	77	.446	28	Joe DePastino	371,575	5,385	2007
Bowling Green Hot Rods (Rays)	61	78	.439	29	Brady Williams	235,412	3,514	Never
South Bend Silver Hawks (Diamondbacks)	59	78	.431	30	Mark Haley	129,599	2,025	2005
Wisconsin Timber Rattlers (Brewers)	58	80	.420	31 ½	Jeff Isom	244,331	3,759	1984
Dayton Dragons (Reds)	53	85	.384	36 ½	Todd Benzinger	597,433	8,535	Never
Burlington Bees (Royals)	46	90	.338	42 ½	Jim Gabella	60,508	917	2008

CLUB BATTING

	AVG	G	AB	R	H	2B	3B	HR	RBI	BB	SO	SB	OBP	SLG
Cedar Rapids	.278	138	4613	763	1284	252	64	89	670	467	871	181	.350	.419
Great Lakes	.272	139	4675	705	1272	277	43	127	642	412	957	165	.336	.431
Lansing	.266	139	4708	642	1250	275	45	75	589	478	1103	186	.337	.391
Peoria	.266	137	4606	635	1224	214	39	61	574	438	947	108	.334	.369
West Michigan	.262	139	4718	609	1235	243	41	53	540	444	1049	81	.333	.364
Fort Wayne	.260	140	4707	715	1223	292	33	90	656	610	1162	146	.349	.393
Clinton	.259	139	4614	700	1194	230	43	134	628	418	1272	132	.331	.414
Wisconsin	.256	138	4565	663	1167	256	58	81	591	475	1082	130	.334	.390
Kane County	.255	138	4650	669	1184	248	30	66	593	612	1184	144	.347	.363
Quad Cities	.255	138	4664	729	1187	283	38	114	663	606	1165	88	.343	.405
Beloit	.254	136	4496	663	1144	253	34	81	591	504	1041	116	.336	.380
Bowling Green	.254	139	4607	607	1170	221	33	68	545	500	1030	249	.334	.361
Dayton	.252	138	4760	605	1198	240	36	101	555	321	1047	135	.310	.381
Lake County	.247	139	4568	611	1130	226	36	87	538	442	1091	154	.323	.370
South Bend	.245	137	4562	538	1118	233	50	71	487	405	1129	58	.314	.365
Burlington	.238	136	4489	577	1069	220	45	65	514	465	1077	145	.313	.351

CLUB PITCHING

	ERA	G	CG	SHO	SV	IP	H	R	ER	HR	BB	SO	AVG
Great Lakes	3.44	139	3	13	58	1220	1068	531	466	70	500	1177	.235
Clinton	3.66	139	3	10	34	1199	1152	603	488	88	401	1039	.253
Lake County	3.72	139	2	10	43	1213	1116	564	501	102	382	1176	.246
Cedar Rapids	3.83	138	5	10	40	1203	1096	594	512	75	516	1126	.243
Kane County	3.89	138	0	6	27	1224	1137	618	529	81	447	1161	.247
Quad Cities	3.91	138	1	11	36	1228	1195	642	533	80	466	1220	.254
Peoria	4.02	137	1	11	37	1185	1124	630	529	92	477	1078	.252
Fort Wayne	4.03	140	0	6	45	1230	1178	649	551	82	366	996	.266
West Michigan	4.05	139	4	9	29	1217	1261	625	548	74	484	974	.268
Lansing	4.17	139	2	6	35	1223	1266	663	567	76	392	980	.267
Bowling Green	4.20	139	4	8	34	1214	1142	692	567	116	512	1133	.249
Beloit	4.22	136	3	11	35	1196	1213	673	561	77	541	1095	.262
Dayton	4.29	138	0	5	32	1235	1275	718	588	92	507	1015	.266
South Bend	4.37	137	3	6	35	1186	1197	684	576	72	427	1046	.277
Wisconsin	4.78	138	1	6	35	1200	1215	735	637	85	534	1021	.262
Burlington	5.35	136	2	3	21	1173	1214	810	698	101	645	970	.269

CLUB FIELDING

	PCT	PO	A	E	DP		PCT	PO	A	E	DP
Great Lakes	.976	3659	1353	122	108	Kane County	.968	3671	1444	167	112
Lake County	.975	3640	1395	127	128	Peoria	.968	3556	1397	164	122
Cedar Rapids	.974	3610	1482	138	131	South Bend	.968	3559	1352	162	91
West Michigan	.973	3650	1417	139	109	Quad Cities	.967	3685	1547	177	112
Lansing	.972	3670	1487	148	120	Wisconsin	.965	3599	1404	184	115
Bowling Green	.971	3642	1274	146	103	Beloit	.964	3588	1299	180	106
Clinton	.969	3598	1433	162	105	Dayton	.964	3704	1435	194	128
Burlington	.968	3520	1398	164	137	Fort Wayne	.964	3690	1467	192	121

INDIVIDUAL BATTING LEADERS (MINIMUM 3.1 PA/TEAM GAME)

	AVG	G	AB	R	H	2B	3B	HR	RBI	BB	SO	SB
Trout, Mike, Cedar Rapids	.362	81	312	76	113	19	7	6	39	46	52	45
Cavazos-Galvez, Brian, Great Lakes	.318	121	490	76	156	43	4	16	77	12	60	43
Segura, Jean, Cedar Rapids	.313	130	515	89	161	24	12	10	79	43	72	50
Dykstra, Cutter, Wisconsin	.312	100	353	66	110	10	5	5	39	55	72	27
Ochinko, Sean, Lansing	.311	109	412	57	128	37	0	8	65	30	58	1
Adams, Matthew, Quad Cities	.310	121	464	71	144	41	0	22	88	33	78	5
Gennett, Ryan, Wisconsin	.309	118	482	87	149	39	4	9	55	31	91	14
Rodriguez, Henry, Dayton	.307	124	514	76	158	37	3	14	78	22	70	33
Haerther, Casey, Cedar Rapids	.307	113	433	54	133	26	2	8	74	29	72	10
Long, Matt, Cedar Rapids	.305	125	466	87	142	30	12	4	74	59	67	23

INDIVIDUAL PITCHING LEADERS (MINIMUM 1 IP/TEAM GAME)

	W	L	ERA	G	GS	CG	SV	IP	H	R	ER	BB	SO
Krol, Ian, Kane County	9	4	2.66	24	23	0	0	119	98	42	35	19	91
Gillheeney, James, Clinton	8	8	2.84	21	21	0	0	118	97	45	37	44	102
Webster, Allen, Great Lakes	12	9	2.88	26	23	0	0	131	119	55	42	53	114
Soto, Giovanni, W. Mich./Lake County	9	8	2.94	22	22	2	0	114	97	42	37	36	107
Ramirez, Erasmo, Clinton	10	4	2.98	26	23	1	1	152	142	63	50	21	117
Struck, Nicholas, Peoria	8	8	3.23	25	18	1	0	115	93	50	41	40	84
Magill, Matt, Great Lakes	7	4	3.28	24	20	1	2	126	87	50	46	52	135
Cook, Clayton, Lake County	6	7	3.35	23	23	0	0	118	109	49	44	37	83
Odorizzi, Jake, Wisconsin	7	3	3.44	23	20	0	1	121	99	52	46	40	135
Brach, Brett, Lake County	5	8	3.46	22	22	1	0	120	115	49	46	28	90

ALL-STAR TEAM

C: Jason Hagerty, Fort Wayne. 1B: Matt Adams, Quad Cities. 2B: Scooter Gennett, Wisconsin. 3B: Matt Davidson, South Bend. SS: Nick Franklin, Clinton. OF: Brian Cavazos-Galvez, Great Lakes; Khris Davis, Wisconsin; Blake Smith, Great Lakes; Mike Trout, Cedar Rapids. DH: Matt Davidson, South Bend. RHP: Erasmo Ramirez, Clinton. LHP: Ian Krol, Kane County. RHRP: Yonata Ortega, South Bend. LHRP: Jon Pokorny, Wisconsin.
Most Valuable Player: Mike Trout, Cedar Rapids. **Manager of the Year:** Juan Bustabad, Great Lakes.

DEPARTMENT LEADERS

BATTING

OBP	Trout, Mike, Cedar Rapids	.454
SLG	Adams, Matthew, Quad Cities	.541
OPS	Hagerty, Jason, Fort Wayne	.917
R	Crumbliss, Conner, Kane County	95
H	Segura, Jean, Cedar Rapids	161
TB	Cavazos-Galvez, Brian, Great Lakes	255
XBH	Cavazos-Galvez, Brian, Great Lakes	63
2B	Cavazos-Galvez, Brian, Great Lakes	43
	Freiman, Nathan, Fort Wayne	43
3B	Broxton, Keon, South Bend	19
HR	Franklin, Nick, Clinton	23
RBI	Adams, Matthew, Quad Cities	88
SAC	Marseco, Michael, Wisconsin	21
BB	Crumbliss, Conner, Kane County	126
HBP	Catricala, Vincent, Clinton	17
SO	Broxton, Keon, South Bend	172
SB	Cid, Delvi, Lake County	71
CS	Cid, Delvi, Lake County	16
AB/SO	Beresford, James, Beloit	8.77

PITCHING

G	Mikolas, Miles, Fort Wayne	60
GS	Feeney, Trevor, West Michigan	29
GF	Turnbull, Steve, Lansing	48
SV	Ortega, Yonata, South Bend	22
W	Four tied at	12
L	Fornataro, Eric, Quad Cities	15
IP	Feeney, Trevor, West Michigan	184.2
H	Feeney, Trevor, West Michigan	216
R	Fornataro, Eric, Quad Cities	104
ER	Fornataro, Eric, Quad Cities	82
HB	Johnson, Jacob, Dayton	15
BB	Sample, Tyler, Burlington	95
SO	Wall, Josh, Great Lakes	151
SO/9	Odorizzi, Jake, Wisconsin	10.11
SO/9 (RP)	Shuman, Scott, Bowling Green	13.9
BB/9	Feeney, Trevor, West Michigan	1.07
WP	Wall, Josh, Great Lakes	20
BK	Three tied at	4
HR	McEachern, Jason, Bowling Green	20
AVG	Magill, Matt, Great Lakes	.194

FIELDING

C	FPCT	Perez, Roberto, Lake County	.997
	PO	Perez, Roberto, Lake County	850
	A	Perez, Roberto, Lake County	109
	E	Stock, Robert, Quad Cities	18
	DP	Ramirez, Carlos, Cedar Rapids	11
	PB	Myers, William, Burlington	17
1B	FPCT	Freiman, Nathan, Fort Wayne	.993
	PO	Freiman, Nathan, Fort Wayne	1123
	A	Aliotti, Anthony, Kane County	96
	E	Bour, Justin, Peoria	15
	DP	Freiman, Nathan, Fort Wayne	97
2B	FPCT	Ynoa, Rafael, Great Lakes	.988
	PO	Rodriguez, Henry, Dayton	219
	A	Segura, Jean, Cedar Rapids	396
	E	Gennett, Ryan, Wisconsin	21
	DP	Rodriguez, Henry, Dayton	77
		Segura, Jean, Cedar Rapids	77
3B	FPCT	Gil, Leonardo, Kane County	.951
	PO	Martinez, Mario, Clinton	103
	A	Pfister, Frank, Dayton	241
	E	Rincon, Edinson, Fort Wayne	36
	DP	Gil, Leonardo, Kane County	20
SS	FPCT	Marseco, Michael, Wisconsin	.978
	PO	Perez, Hernan, West Michigan	200
	A	Perez, Hernan, West Michigan	380
	E	Galvez, Jonathan, Fort Wayne	40
	DP	Lee, Hak-Ju, Peoria	73
OF	FPCT	Folgia, Greg, Lake County	.994
	PO	Broxton, Keon, South Bend	282
	A	Richardson, D'Vontrey, Wisconsin	18
	E	Richardson, D'Vontrey, Wisconsin	17
	DP	Long, Matt, Cedar Rapids	6
		Testa, Carlo, Burlington	6

MINOR LEAGUES

BY BILL BALLEW

Winning is becoming a perennial event in Lakewood. For the second straight season and third time since 2006, the BlueClaws (Phillies) won the South Atlantic League championship behind a team filled with six players placing among the circuit's top 20 prospects.

Lakewood first baseman Jonathan Singleton, 18, was a near-unanimous choice for top prospect recognition after tying for third in the league with a .393 on-base percentage and slugging at a .479 clip, good for fourth on the circuit. Catcher Sebastian Valle led the team with 16 big flies while hitting the game-winning home run in the clinching contest in the SAL championship series.

As strong as those prospects may have been, the BlueClaws were led by their pitching staff. The staff was headlined by righthander Brody Colvin, who allowed one earned run in 10 playoff innings, ranked eighth in the league with a 3.39 ERA but owned a 2.00 norm after May 14.

Lexington outfielder J.D. Martinez (Astros) won the Triple Crown in the slash categories by hitting .362/.433/.598 despite being promoted to Double-A Corpus Christi on July 16. Augusta third baseman Chris Dominguez (Giants), led the league with 255 total bases while ranking second with 21 homers and 57 extra-base hits. Asheville first baseman Jared Clark (Rockies) topped the league with 24 homers and was a Triple Crown contender prior to suffering a late-season injury.

Youth, however, was served on the mound, particularly in Rome, which finished with the league's second-worst winning percentage. The problem centered on the fact that the pitching didn't stay in place, with Julio Teheran, Brett Oberholtzer and Arodys Vizcaino dominating during their stints in the first half before receiving promotions. Hickory also had its share of young arms, with Robbie Ross and Joe Wieland, both 20, posting impressive first halves before moving up. Fortunately for the Crawdads, 19-year-old Robbie Erlin remained with the team throughout the campaign and led the SAL with a 2.12 ERA despite being slated for the short-season ranks during spring training.

TOP 20 PROSPECTS

1. Jonathan Singleton, 1b, Lakewood Blueclaws
2. Nolan Arenado, 3b, Asheville Tourists (Rockies)
3. Tyler Matzek, lhp, Asheville Tourists (Rockies)
4. Brody Colvin, rhp, Lakewood Blueclaws (Phillies)
5. Robbie Erlin, lhp, Hickory Crawdads (Rangers)
6. Arodys Vizcaino, rhp, Rome Braves
7. Jarred Cosart, rhp, Lakewood Blueclaws (Phillies)
8. Jonathan Villar, ss, Lakewood Blueclaws (Phillies)
9. Reymond Fuentes, of, Greenville Drive (Red Sox)
10. Chad James, lhp, Greensboro Grasshoppers (Marlins)
11. Trevor May, rhp, Lakewood Blueclaws (Phillies)
12. Zack Wheeler, rhp, Augusta Greenjackets (Giants)
13. Cesar Puello, of, Savannah Sand Gnats (Mets)
14. Christian Bethancourt, C, Rome Braves
15. Robbie Ross, lhp, Hickory Crawdads (Rangers)
16. Drake Britton, lhp, Greenville Drive (Red Sox)
17. J.D. Martinez, of, Lexington Legends (Astros)
18. Slade Heathcott, of, Charleston Riverdogs (Yankees)
19. Sebastian Valle, C, Lakewood Blueclaws (Phillies)
20. Chris Dominguez, 3b, Augusta Greenjackets (Giants)

STANDINGS: SPLIT SEASON

FIRST HALF

NORTH	W	L	PCT	GB
Lakewood	42	28	.600	—
Hickory	40	30	.571	2
Hagerstown	36	34	.514	6
Delmarva	32	38	.457	10
Greensboro	32	38	.457	10
Kannapolis	31	38	.449	10½
West Virginia	31	39	.443	11

SOUTH	W	L	PCT	GB
Savannah	42	28	.600	—
Augusta	41	29	.586	1
Greenville	36	34	.514	6
Lexington	35	35	.500	7
Charleston	31	38	.449	10½
Rome	30	39	.435	11½
Asheville	29	40	.420	12½

SECOND HALF

NORTH	W	L	PCT	GB
Lakewood	42	27	.609	—
Hickory	35	34	.507	7
West Virginia	34	35	.493	8
Greensboro	34	36	.486	8½
Kannapolis	34	36	.486	8½
Hagerstown	29	41	.414	13½
Delmarva	27	43	.386	15½

SOUTH	W	L	PCT	GB
Greenville	41	28	.594	—
Asheville	40	30	.571	1½
Augusta	38	30	.559	2½
Lexington	36	33	.522	5
Charleston	34	36	.486	7½
Savannah	33	36	.478	8
Rome	29	41	.414	12½

PLAYOFFS—Semifinals: Lakewood defeated Hickory 2-1 and Greenville defeated Savannah 2-0 in best-of-three series. **Finals:** Lakewood defeated Greenville 3-1 in best-of-five series.

OVERALL STANDINGS

Team (Organization)	W	L	PCT	GB	Manager(s)	Attendance	Average	Last Penn.
Lakewood BlueClaws (Phillies)	84	55	.604	—	Mark Parent	431,954	6,171	2010
Augusta GreenJackets (Giants)	79	59	.572	4½	Dave Machemer	201,760	3,011	2008
Greenville Drive (Red Sox)	77	62	.554	7	Billy McMillon	337,918	4,969	1998
Hickory Crawdads (Rangers)	75	64	.540	9	Bill Richardson	140,789	2,070	2004
Savannah Sand Gnats (Mets)	75	64	.540	9	Pedro Lopez	120,426	1,825	1996
Lexington Legends (Astros)	71	68	.511	13	Rodney Linares	336,168	4,872	2001
Asheville Tourists (Rockies)	69	70	.496	15	Joe Mikulik	160,023	2,353	1984
Greensboro Grasshoppers (Marlins)	66	74	.471	18½	Andy Haines	379,511	5,500	1982
Charleston RiverDogs (Yankees)	65	74	.468	19	Greg Colbrunn	269,023	3,899	Never
Kannapolis Intimidators (White Sox)	65	74	.468	19	Ernie Young	123,828	2,030	2005
West Virginia Power (Pirates)	65	74	.468	19	Gary Green	172,344	2,572	1990
Hagerstown Suns (Nationals)	65	75	.464	19½	Matthew LeCroy	135,799	2,058	Never
Rome Braves (Braves)	59	80	.424	25	Randy Ingle	193,061	2,839	2003
Delmarva Shorebirds (Orioles)	59	81	.421	25½	Ryan Minor	221,051	3,251	2001

CLUB BATTING

	AVG	G	AB	R	H	2B	3B	HR	RBI	BB	SO	SB	OBP	SLG
Hagerstown	.271	140	4764	710	1289	251	49	72	622	398	1052	161	.333	.389
Lexington	.268	139	4781	700	1279	265	23	75	630	469	913	161	.341	.380
Asheville	.266	139	4724	640	1257	272	36	84	582	399	1127	167	.328	.392
Augusta	.266	138	4806	647	1279	235	47	84	568	367	1032	108	.323	.387
Lakewood	.259	140	4817	694	1249	285	46	83	620	432	1196	183	.327	.389
Charleston	.258	139	4663	602	1201	257	30	84	547	427	1116	133	.324	.380
Kannapolis	.258	139	4660	617	1203	247	37	90	559	354	1089	116	.317	.385
Hickory	.256	139	4574	633	1170	248	24	97	566	436	1011	127	.330	.384
Greenville	.254	140	4670	652	1184	254	41	82	564	485	1079	241	.332	.378
Savannah	.253	139	4798	629	1216	229	40	58	548	377	1020	158	.317	.354
Rome	.248	139	4619	520	1144	221	39	40	471	311	995	137	.305	.338
West Virginia	.247	139	4572	624	1127	255	43	105	570	446	1173	130	.321	.390
Delmarva	.243	140	4743	578	1154	249	42	63	507	439	1160	118	.316	.353
Greensboro	.239	140	4634	600	1109	220	14	123	549	430	1074	109	.312	.372

CLUB PITCHING

	ERA	G	CG	SHO	SV	IP	H	R	ER	HR	BB	SO	AVG
Lakewood	3.04	140	2	10	37	1277	1112	539	432	72	394	1207	.234
Savannah	3.08	139	5	15	35	1258	1141	535	430	60	418	1187	.241
Charleston	3.43	139	2	12	30	1221	1150	597	465	54	377	1002	.246
Augusta	3.52	138	3	12	36	1236	1175	570	483	53	417	1114	.251
Hickory	3.57	139	6	14	46	1206	1167	615	479	87	330	1171	.252
Rome	3.66	139	1	10	32	1216	1176	649	495	65	468	989	.253
Greenville	3.68	140	2	8	40	1226	1245	592	501	91	346	1120	.263
Kannapolis	3.80	139	7	12	35	1208	1220	619	510	64	397	1047	.264
Delmarva	4.07	140	1	6	29	1250	1265	689	565	89	441	1043	.263
Greensboro	4.11	140	0	7	38	1228	1212	661	560	89	478	1163	.258
Lexington	4.26	139	1	3	41	1225	1183	686	580	112	506	1010	.256
Asheville	4.33	139	1	9	39	1224	1250	669	589	93	428	1031	.267
West Virginia	4.39	139	1	8	30	1212	1249	693	591	113	346	955	.264
Hagerstown	4.50	140	1	6	37	1227	1316	732	614	98	424	998	.275

CLUB FIELDING

	PCT	PO	A	E	DP		PCT	PO	A	E	DP
Augusta	.972	3707	1552	149	125	Hickory	.967	3618	1459	175	103
Asheville	.971	3671	1501	156	134	West Virginia	.967	3635	1456	175	119
Lakewood	.971	3832	1522	159	110	Kannapolis	.964	3623	1558	196	134
Greenville	.970	3678	1481	162	112	Charleston	.963	3664	1562	203	103
Savannah	.969	3774	1348	165	117	Delmarva	.963	3749	1560	205	140
Greensboro	.968	3683	1475	172	111	Hagerstown	.961	3682	1533	214	122
Lexington	.968	3674	1448	168	132	Rome	.956	3648	1452	236	110

INDIVIDUAL BATTING LEADERS (MINIMUM 3.1 PA/TEAM GAME)

	AVG	G	AB	R	H	2B	3B	HR	RBI	BB	SO	SB
Martinez, J.D., Lexington	.362	88	348	83	126	31	3	15	64	33	55	3
Liles, Nick, Augusta	.316	127	512	86	162	28	4	0	62	36	61	29
Lyerly, Robert, Charleston	.312	131	503	72	157	36	0	7	71	34	129	9
Bloxom, Justin, Hagerstown	.309	104	418	66	129	29	4	11	70	27	77	10
Arenado, Nolan, Asheville	.308	92	373	45	115	41	1	12	65	19	52	1
Altuve, Jose, Lexington	.308	94	393	75	121	15	3	11	45	33	49	39
Mesa, Eliezer, Asheville	.302	117	483	83	146	33	9	2	42	39	91	29
Clark, Jared, Asheville	.299	110	381	62	114	20	0	24	82	76	113	10
Perez, Eury, Hagerstown	.299	131	438	88	131	17	5	3	42	23	74	64
Ramirez, J.P., Hagerstown	.296	132	506	74	150	32	4	16	75	25	83	3

INDIVIDUAL PITCHING LEADERS (MINIMUM 1 IP/TEAM GAME)

	W	L	ERA	G	GS	CG	SV	IP	H	R	ER	BB	SO
Erlin, Robert, Hickory	6	3	2.13	28	17	0	1	115	89	37	27	17	125
Bucardo, Jorge, Augusta	9	4	2.21	19	18	1	0	114	83	36	28	31	95
Rodriguez, Armando, Savannah	8	9	3.08	27	27	0	0	146	116	61	50	46	152
Montgomery, Matthew, Greensboro	11	12	3.23	27	27	0	0	159	162	68	57	28	135
Balcom-Miller, Chris, Avl/Greenville	7	7	3.31	20	20	1	0	115	91	44	42	19	120
McHugh, Collin, Savannah	7	8	3.34	28	20	0	1	132	139	65	49	38	129
Irwin, Phillip, West Virginia	6	3	3.35	23	20	0	0	113	99	46	42	20	111
Colvin, Brody, Lakewood	6	8	3.39	27	27	0	0	138	138	73	52	42	120
Pettibone, Jonathan, Lakewood	8	6	3.50	24	23	1	0	131	114	63	51	41	84
Bayne, Cameron, Kannapolis	12	9	3.60	27	26	2	0	165	174	87	66	35	101
Ramirez, Jose A., Charleston	6	5	3.60	22	21	0	0	115	106	56	46	42	105

ALL-STAR TEAM

C: Sebastian Valle, Lakewood. **1B:** Jared Clark, Asheville. **2B:** Jose Altuve, Lexington. **3B:** Chris Dominguez, Augusta. **SS:** Jonathan Villar, Lakewood. **UTIL IF:** Rob Lyerly, Charleston. **OF:** Jeremy Hazelbaker, Greenville; J.D. Martinez, Lexington; Eliezer Mesa, Asheville. **DH:** Justin Bloxom, Hagerstown. **UTIL OF:** Destin Hood, Hagerstown. **RHP:** Jorge Bucardo, Augusta. **LHP:** James Fuller, Savannah.
Most Valuable Player: J.D. Martinez, Lexington. Most Outstanding Pitcher: James Fuller, Savannah.
Manager of the Year: Mark Parent, Lakewood. **Coach of the Year:** Marc Valdes, Savannah.

DEPARTMENT LEADERS

BATTING

OBP	Martinez, J.D., Lexington	.433
SLG	Martinez, J.D., Lexington	.598
OPS	Martinez, J.D., Lexington	1.030
R	Goebbert, Jacob, Lexington	91
H	Liles, Nick, Augusta	162
TB	Dominguez, Christopher, Augusta	255
XBH	Goebbert, Jacob, Lexington	59
2B	Goebbert, Jacob, Lexington	48
3B	Crawford, Evan, Augusta	12
HR	Clark, Jared, Asheville	24
RBI	Dominguez, Christopher, Augusta	101
SAC	Perez, Eury, Hagerstown	21
BB	Chambers, Evan, West Virginia	92
HBP	West, Matthew, Hickory	24
SO	Hewitt, Anthony, Lakewood	158
SB	Perez, Eury, Hagerstown	64
CS	Rose, Kyle, Rome	23
AB/SO	Gentile, Zach, Greenville	8.92

PITCHING

G	Bargas, Paul, Asheville	58
GS	Four tied at	27
GF	Ramos, Alejandro, Greensboro	45
SV	Clark, Kirk, Lexington	29
W	Bayne, Cameron, Kannapolis	12
L	Heston, Christopher, Augusta	13
IP	Bayne, Cameron, Kannapolis	165
H	Bayne, Cameron, Kannapolis	174
R	Hopps, Matthew, Kannapolis	92
ER	Hopps, Matthew, Kannapolis	78
	Schnaitmann, Nicholas, Asheville	78
HB	Minaya, Juan, Lexington	21
BB	Minaya, Juan, Lexington	73
SO	Rodriguez, Armando, Savannah	152
SO/9	Erlin, Robert, Hickory	9.85
SO/9 (RP)	Rosario, Sandy, Greensboro	12.2
BB/9	Volz, Kendal, Greenville	1.09
WP	Minaya, Juan, Lexington	22
BK	Demny, Paul, Hagerstown	6
HR	Bushue, Tanner, Lexington	18
AVG	Bucardo, Jorge, Augusta	.203

FIELDING

C	FPCT	Cabrera, Ramon, West Virginia	.990
	PO	Valle, Sebastian, Lakewood	823
	A	Leon, Sandy, Hagerstown	115
	E	Leon, Sandy, Hagerstown	19
	DP	Leon, Sandy, Hagerstown	17
	PB	Joseph, Thomas, Augusta	19
1B	FPCT	Singleton, Jonathan, Lakewood	.995
	PO	Anders, Luke, Augusta	1184
	A	Gac, Ian, Kannapolis	81
	E	Baker, Aaron, West Virginia	19
	DP	Anders, Luke, Augusta	107
2B	FPCT	Wagner, Daniel, Kannapolis	.973
	PO	Cavan, Ryan, Augusta	247
	A	Cavan, Ryan, Augusta	422
	E	Paredes, Jimmy, Char., Lexington	32
	DP	Cavan, Ryan, Augusta	87
3B	FPCT	Austin, Chase, Greensboro	.926
	PO	Meyer, Jonathan, Lexington	89
	A	Dominguez, Christopher, Augusta	275
	E	Almanzar, Michael, Greenville	36
	DP	Dominguez, Christopher, Augusta	29
SS	FPCT	Gibson, Derrik, Greenville	.960
	PO	Rosa, Garabez, Delmarva	202
	A	Castro, Kelvin, Charleston	378
	E	Rosa, Garabez, Delmarva	46
	DP	Mier, Jiovanni, Asheville	80
		Rosa, Garabez, Delmarva	80
OF	FPCT	Prince, Jared, Hickory	.994
	PO	Perez, Eury, Hagerstown	298
	A	Planeta, Michael, Delmarva	17
	E	Ramirez, J.P., Hagerstown	10
	DP	Ciolli, Nick, Kannapolis	5
		Mesa, Eliezer, Asheville	5

MINOR LEAGUES

BY AARON FITT

Tri-City (Astros) won the New York-Penn League title after sweeping Brooklyn (Mets) in the best-of-three championship series. Carlos Quevedo pitched seven strong innings in Tri-City's 5-1 win in the clincher. The franchise previously won a title in 1997 as the Pittsfield Mets, but this was its first championship since moving in 2002 to Troy, N.Y.

It was a remarkable turnaround for the ValleyCats, who were 9½ games out of first place in the Stedler Division in mid-July but rallied to win the division by a half-game over Connecticut (Tigers). After beating Batavia (Cardinals) in the semifinals, Tri-City advanced to face Brooklyn, which won the McNamara Division by 12 games.

Tri-City pitchers allowed just eight hits in the two-game sweep of the Cyclones.

"I can't say enough about this pitching staff," Tri-City manager Jim Pankovits told The (Saratoga Springs, N.Y.) Saratogian. "Carlos Quevedo, Jake Buchanan, David Martinez, Mike Ness down the stretch, Jorge DeLeon, all those guys who rose to occasion that last six weeks (of the season) and especially in the playoffs."

Tri-City featured some of the best players in the league—most notably second baseman Ben Orloff—but no top-flight prospects.

"Everyone on their staff could throw strikes and throw breaking balls for strikes," Connecticut manager Howard Bushong said.

The league featured plenty of young, raw prospects with significant upside, but very few sure things. There was no clear-cut No. 1 prospect in the league like Ryan Westmoreland, Jason Castro and Brett Cecil in each of the last three years. There was only one 2010 first-round pick who

spent any meaningful time in the league—Lowell's Kolbrin Vitek—and many of the biggest-name college products struggled.

"The New York-Penn League wasn't as good as it was last year," Bushong said. "Especially the pitching—it wasn't even close. And there wasn't a position player who blew you away like Westmoreland last year, and no (Alex) Colome like last year that made you go, 'wow.' I saw some good players, but I didn't see the 'wow' factor we saw last year."

Connecticut moved from Oneonta before the season and played its games in the former home of the Double-A Connecticut Defenders. The league saw even more changes after the 2010 season, as the Blue Jays left their long-time short-season home in Auburn. The Nationals moved from Vermont to Auburn, and the Athletics moved into the NY-P at Vermont.

TOP 20 PROSPECTS

1. Carlos Perez, c, Auburn Doubledays (Blue Jays)
2. Jake Thompson, rhp, Hudson Valley Renegades (Rays)
3. Cory Vaughn, of, Brooklyn Mets
4. Marcell Ozuna, of, Jamestown Jammers (Marlins)
5. Roman Mendez, rhp, Lowell Spinners (Red Sox)
6. Zack Von Rosenberg, rhp, State College Spikes (Pirates)
7. Kolbrin Vitek, 3b, Lowell Spinners (Red Sox)
8. Nick Longmire, of, Batavia Muckdogs (Cardinals)
9. Cesar Hernandez, 2b, Williamsport Crosscutters (Phillies)
10. Colton Cain, lhp, State College Spikes (Pirates)
11. Darrell Ceciliani, of, Brooklyn Mets
12. Domingo Santana, of, Williamsport Crosscutters (Phillies)
13. Bryce Brentz, of, Lowell Spinners (Red Sox)
14. Mike Kvasnicka, of/3b/c, Tri-City Valley Cats (Astros)
15. Aaron Altherr, of, Williamsport Crosscutters (Phillies)
16. Drew Hutchison, rhp, Auburn Doubledays (Blue Jays)
17. Zack Dodson, lhp, State College Spikes (Pirates)
18. Daniel Webb, rhp, Auburn Doubledays (Blue Jays)
19. Josue Carreno, rhp, Connecticut Tigers
20. Madison Younginer, rhp, Lowell Spinners (Red Sox)

STANDINGS

McNAMARA DIVISION (Organization)	W	L	PCT	GB	Manager(s)	Attendance	Average	Last Penn.
Brooklyn Cyclones (Mets)	51	24	.680	—	Wally Backman	155,315	4,314	2001
Hudson Valley Renegades (Rays)	39	36	.520	12	Jared Sandberg	65,639	1,774	1999
Aberdeen Ironbirds (Orioles)	34	40	.459	16 ½	Gary Kendall	114,556	3,015	1983
Staten Island Yankees (Yankees)	34	40	.459	16 ½	Jody Reed/Josh Paul	175,287	4,737	2009
PINCKNEY DIVISION (Organization)	**W**	**L**	**PCT**	**GB**	**Manager(s)**	**Attendance**	**Average**	**Last Penn.**
Batavia Muckdogs (Cardinals)	45	29	.608	—	Dann Bilardello	209,018	5,806	2008
Jamestown Jammers (Marlins)	43	32	.573	2 ½	Dave Berg	105,671	2,781	1991
Williamsport Crosscutters (Phillies)	43	33	.566	3	Chris Truby	70,695	1,860	2003
Auburn Doubledays (Blue Jays)	35	40	.467	10 ½	Dennis Holmberg	140,927	3,709	2007
State College Spikes (Pirates)	33	42	.440	12 ½	Gary Robinson	96,219	2,532	1994
Mahoning Valley Scrappers (Indians)	30	46	.395	16	Travis Fryman	90,079	2,502	2004
STEDLER DIVISION (Organization)	**W**	**L**	**PCT**	**GB**	**Manager(s)**	**Attendance**	**Average**	**Last Penn.**
Tri-City ValleyCats (Astros)	38	36	.514	—	Jim Pankovits	84,921	2,235	2010
Connecticut Tigers (Tigers)	38	37	.507	½	Howie Bushong	88,340	2,524	1998
Vermont Lake Monsters (Nationals)	36	38	.486	2	Jeff Garber	154,592	4,068	1996
Lowell Spinners (Red Sox)	24	50	.324	14	Bruce Crabbe	107,561	2,831	Never

PLAYOFFS—Semifinals: Tri-City defeated Batavia 2-1 and Brooklyn defeated Jamestown 2-1 in best-of-three series. **Finals:** Tri-City defeated Brooklyn 2-0 in best-of-three series.

CLUB BATTING

	AVG	G	AB	R	H	2B	3B	HR	RBI	BB	SO	SB	OBP	SLG
Brooklyn	.283	75	2522	405	713	144	37	64	363	227	562	84	.348	.445
Batavia	.273	74	2485	410	678	143	25	41	369	276	526	46	.352	.400
Jamestown	.264	75	2501	402	661	134	35	45	367	260	579	58	.339	.400
Hudson Valley	.258	75	2554	358	659	147	22	29	321	230	607	90	.332	.367
Williamsport	.255	76	2506	317	639	151	16	27	276	200	507	84	.316	.360
Aberdeen	.249	74	2493	301	620	115	23	32	270	264	557	37	.328	.353
Vermont	.246	74	2430	365	597	112	24	34	315	340	591	58	.347	.353
Tri-City	.244	74	2546	340	621	115	16	50	299	258	542	73	.321	.361
Auburn	.243	75	2522	358	613	132	30	42	311	284	653	70	.327	.369
Staten Island	.239	74	2429	290	581	120	13	37	266	239	550	51	.320	.345
Connecticut	.238	75	2450	271	583	110	21	23	232	185	579	88	.297	.328
Lowell	.235	74	2426	285	570	121	18	28	255	253	625	81	.312	.334
State College	.232	75	2469	316	572	118	27	25	279	283	569	77	.317	.332
Mahoning Valley	.231	76	2505	275	578	108	18	30	236	250	541	53	.307	.324

CLUB PITCHING

	ERA	G	CG	SHO	SV	IP	H	R	ER	HR	BB	SO	AVG
Brooklyn	3.05	75	1	4	26	672	604	289	228	31	221	578	.239
Jamestown	3.38	75	0	7	24	644	576	311	242	34	257	511	.237
Tri-City	3.43	74	0	5	13	673	665	300	256	49	208	604	.262
Hudson Valley	3.44	75	0	3	23	664	618	312	254	36	204	566	.246
Connecticut	3.59	75	2	3	21	655	611	315	261	37	298	575	.247
Williamsport	3.63	76	1	6	31	666	574	311	269	33	286	611	.232
Auburn	3.70	75	0	12	19	659	634	370	271	29	265	657	.249
Batavia	3.85	74	0	3	21	651	604	332	278	37	255	598	.245
Staten Island	3.86	74	1	6	21	643	605	340	276	24	258	624	.250
Aberdeen	3.96	74	0	7	15	659	611	331	290	35	245	553	.249
State College	3.96	75	0	6	16	663	650	346	292	31	215	458	.258
Mahoning Valley	4.14	76	0	5	18	667	644	363	307	48	281	549	.255
Vermont	4.47	74	0	4	11	649	648	375	322	43	266	587	.262
Lowell	4.53	74	0	1	15	641	641	398	323	40	790	517	.259

CLUB FIELDING

	PCT	PO	A	E	DP		PCT	PO	A	E	DP
Aberdeen	.974	1978	891	77	63	Mahoning Valley	.967	2000	853	97	67
Tri-City	.973	2018	833	80	80	Vermont	.965	1947	791	99	54
Batavia	.972	1952	771	78	65	Staten Island	.964	1930	760	101	63
State College	.971	1989	855	85	76	Hudson Valley	.960	1993	730	114	66
Williamsport	.970	1999	749	84	56	Auburn	.959	1977	789	117	53
Brooklyn	.969	2017	774	89	64	Jamestown	.958	1931	822	120	66
Connecticut	.969	1964	731	86	54	Lowell	.958	1924	767	118	65

INDIVIDUAL BATTING LEADERS (MINIMUM 3.1 PA/TEAM GAME)

	AVG	G	AB	R	H	2B	3B	HR	RBI	BB	SO	SB
Ceciliani, Darrell, Brooklyn	.351	68	271	56	95	19	12	2	35	24	56	21
Wunderlich, Phillip, Hudson Valley	.330	52	209	31	69	19	0	4	36	9	40	0
Sandoval, Rylan, Brooklyn	.330	47	185	34	61	13	0	9	29	16	35	8
Alvarez, Miguel, Williamsport	.329	68	258	42	85	21	4	1	34	11	48	13
Bonfe, Joe, Brooklyn	.326	72	270	41	88	13	1	4	28	26	56	8
Hernandez, Cesar, Williamsport	.325	65	255	36	83	13	2	0	23	26	27	32
Sanchez, Felix, Lowell	.323	57	220	45	71	6	2	0	9	26	59	38
Santos, Adalberto, State College	.319	63	238	45	76	15	7	3	35	33	31	17
Schutz, Kipp, Aberdeen	.313	68	265	32	83	11	5	4	42	18	50	1
Kelso, Blake, Vermont	.309	61	236	29	73	10	1	1	21	20	21	10

INDIVIDUAL PITCHING LEADERS (MINIMUM 1 IP/TEAM GAME)

	W	L	ERA	G	GS	CG	SV	IP	H	R	ER	BB	SO
Almonte, Yohan, Brooklyn	8	4	1.92	15	15	1	0	90	68	28	19	15	60
Cuan, Angel, Brooklyn	5	1	2.05	14	14	0	0	80	68	26	18	17	64
Pinera, A. J., Brooklyn	2	3	2.46	16	11	0	0	63	62	24	17	12	54
Kaminsky, Alex, Mahoning Valley	6	5	2.48	14	14	0	0	69	55	20	19	18	58
Almonte, Wilmer, Hudson Valley	4	3	2.77	15	14	0	0	78	67	32	24	15	73
Rayl, Mike, Mahoning Valley	2	4	2.82	14	14	0	0	67	57	26	21	21	56
Copeland, Scott, Aberdeen	2	5	2.91	12	12	0	0	65	45	22	21	23	49
Russell, Zach, Batavia	3	3	2.95	14	12	0	0	61	41	22	20	31	61
Sprague, Holden, Jamestown	5	4	2.99	18	9	0	0	64	55	30	21	29	34
Martinez, David, Tri-City	5	2	3.04	17	10	0	0	66	72	29	22	11	57

DEPARTMENT LEADERS

BATTING

OBP	Price, Robby, Hudson Valley	.437
SLG	Vaughn, Cory, Brooklyn	.557
OPS	Vaughn, Cory, Brooklyn	.953
R	Ceciliani, Darrell, Brooklyn	56
H	Ceciliani, Darrell, Brooklyn	95
TB	Ozuna, Marcell, Jamestown	150
XBH	Fisher, Ryan, Jamestown	41
2B	Fisher, Ryan, Jamestown	24
3B	Ceciliani, Darrell, Brooklyn	12
HR	Ozuna, Marcell, Jamestown	21
RBI	Ozuna, Marcell, Jamestown	60
SAC	Kelso, Blake, Vermont	14
BB	Heere, Brian, Mahoning Valley	49
HBP	Price, Robby, Hudson Valley	15
SO	Ozuna, Marcell, Jamestown	94
SB	Sanchez, Felix, Lowell	38
CS	Ceciliani, Darrell, Brooklyn	14
AB/SO	Orloff, Ben, Tri-City	12.53

PITCHING

G	Conley, Jordan, Jamestown	30
GS	Seven tied at	15
GF	Conley, Jordan, Jamestown	30
SV	Conley, Jordan, Jamestown	16
W	Hilliard, Chris, Brooklyn	9
L	Five tied at	7
IP	Almonte, Yohan, Brooklyn	89.2
H	Mendoza, Clemente, Connecticut	86
R	Sexton, Tyler, Aberdeen	49
ER	Sexton, Tyler, Aberdeen	45
HB	Jenkins, Chad, Vermont	13
BB	Cervenka, Hunter, Lowell	42
SO	Varce, Zachary, Staten Island	74
SO/9	Varce, Zachary, Staten Island	9.37
SO/9 (RP)	Rutler, Keith, Brooklyn	14.7
BB/9	Quevedo, Carlos, Tri-City	0.85
WP	Eusebio, Wilson, Vermont	11
BK	Fuesser, Zachary, State College	3
HR	Cooper, Jordan, Mahoning Valley	9
AVG	Russell, Zach, Batavia	.192

FIELDING

C	FPCT	Perez, Audry, Batavia	.997
	PO	Rodriguez, Julio, Connecticut	391
	A	Rodriguez, Julio, Connecticut	53
	E	Rupp, Cameron, Williamsport	7
		Torres, Alejandro, Hudson Valley	7
	DP	Hord, Dallas, Lowell	4
	PB	Skirving, Matthew, State College	17
1B	FPCT	Flagg, Jeff, Brooklyn	.997
	PO	Flagg, Jeff, Brooklyn	659
	A	Head, Miles, Lowell	38
	E	Durham, Lance, Auburn	10
		Senne, Aaron, Jamestown	10
	DP	Flagg, Jeff, Brooklyn	56
2B	FPCT	Hernandez, Cesar, Williamsport	.978
	PO	Hernandez, Cesar, Williamsport	135
	A	Hernandez, Cesar, Williamsport	179
	E	Dominguez, Oliver, Auburn	11
	DP	Hernandez, Cesar, Williamsport	40
3B	FPCT	Gaylord, Adam, Aberdeen	.970
	PO	Urshela, Giovanny, M. V.	52
	A	Gaylord, Adam, Aberdeen	164
	E	Renfroe, David, Lowell	15
	DP	Brown, Kelson, State College	12
SS	FPCT	Rooney, Michael, Aberdeen	.967
	PO	Martinson, Jason, Vermont	101
	A	Martinson, Jason, Vermont	188
	E	Pierre, Gustavo, Auburn	29
	DP	Duran, Edga-r, Williamsport	36
OF	FPCT	Bailey, Adam, Tri-City	1.000
		Bryles, Brian, Hudson Valley	1.000
	PO	Ceciliani, Darrell, Brooklyn	154
	A	Heere, Brian, Mahoning Valley	11
	E	Brisker, Markus, Auburn	8
	DP	Brentz, Bryce, Lowell	5

MINOR LEAGUES

BY CONOR GLASSEY

Neither team won the championship, but Spokane (Rangers) and Eugene (Padres) featured the best of collection of individual talent in the Northwest League.

Spokane won the Eastern Division with a 43-33 record and advanced to the finals, led by shortstop Jurickson Profar, the NWL's No. 1 prospect.

This summer in Spokane was Profar's first exposure to professional baseball. But it wasn't his first time playing in front of large crowds. He was on the Curacao team that made it to the final game of the 2005 Little League World Series. If Profar grew up in the United States, he'd be spending the summer on the showcase circuit, preparing for his senior year of high school. Instead, he signed in 2009 for $1.55 million and held his own this summer as a 17-year-old in a league where most players were four to five years older.

Profar was joined by five other members of the league's Top 20 Prospects list. Eugene didn't have as much success on the field, but also claimed a half-dozen spots on the Top 20 with a mix of draftees from 2009 and 2010.

Everett (Mariners) opened the season with a seven-game winning streak and never looked back tying a franchise record for wins (49) and claiming the club's first title in 25 years.

Everett dropped the first game of the best-of-three to Spokane behind five shutout innings from Indians starter Nicholas McBride. The Aqua Sox rallied for a one-run win in Game Two before Anthony Fernandez tossed seven shutout innings in the decisive Game Three.

Spokane outfielder Jared Hoying, the Rangers' 10th-round pick out of Toledo in 2010, was named the league's MVP after hitting .325/.378/.543, ranking fifth in the NWL in average and third in RBIs (51). Fernandez and Tri-City righthander Chad Bettis split the pitcher of the year honors. Fernandez finished tied for first in victories (8) and third in ERA (2.59). Bettis went 10-1, 1.12 before earning a promotion to low Class A Asheville.

The biggest changes going into the 2011 Northwest League season are that the Vancouver Canadians will now be a Blue Jays affiliate. The Athletics were affiliated with Vancouver since 2000, but will be leaving the Northwest League in 2011 and moving to the New York-Penn League.

Short-season managerial changes aren't often big news, but the Eugene Emeralds will have a new skipper next season with a long history of success. Former Arizona State head coach Pat Murphy will be handed the reins of the team, taking over for Greg Riddoch, who retired after managing the Emeralds the past four seasons.

TOP 20 PROSPECTS

1. Jurickson Profar, ss, Spokane Indians (Rangers)
2. Michael Choice, of, Vancouver Canadians (Athletics)
3. Jedd Gyorko, 3b, Eugene Emeralds (Padres)
4. Mike Olt, 3b, Spokane Indians (Rangers)
5. Chad Bettis, rhp, Tri-City Dust Devils (Rockies)
6. Matt Lollis, rhp, Eugene Emeralds (Padres)
7. Erik Stavert, rhp, Tri-City Dust Devils (Rockies)
8. Rymer Liriano, of, Eugene Emeralds (Padres)
9. Adys Portillo, rhp, Eugene Emeralds (Padres)
10. Miguel de los Santos, lhp, Spokane Indians (Rangers)
11. Kellin Deglan, c, Spokane Indians (Rangers)
12. Keyvius Sampson, rhp, Eugene Emeralds (Padres)
13. Jake Skole, of, Spokane Indians (Rangers)
14. Zach Walters, ss, Yakima Bears (Diamondbacks)
15. Yoervis Medina, rhp, Everett AquaSox (Mariners)
16. Jared Hoying, of, Spokane Indians (Rangers)
17. Stephen Pryor, rhp, Everett AquaSox (Mariners)
18. Josh Slaats, rhp, Tri-City Dust Devils (Rockies)
19. Rico Noel, of, Eugene Emeralds (Padres)
20. Jake Dunning, rhp, Salem-Keizer Volcanoes (Giants)

STANDINGS: SPLIT SEASON

FIRST HALF					SECOND HALF				
EAST	W	L	PCT	GB	EAST	W	L	PCT	GB
Spokane	22	16	.579	—	Yakima	25	13	.658	—
Boise	19	19	.500	3	Spokane	21	17	.553	4
Yakima	18	20	.474	4	Boise	15	23	.395	10
Tri-City	17	21	.447	5	Tri-City	13	25	.342	12
WEST	W	L	PCT	GB	WEST	W	L	PCT	GB
Everett	27	11	.711	—	Vancouver	25	13	.658	—
Salem-Keizer	17	21	.447	10	Everett	22	16	.579	3
Vancouver	17	21	.447	10	Eugene	17	21	.447	8
Eugene	15	23	.395	12	Salem-Keizer	14	24	.368	11

PLAYOFFS—Semifinals: Spokane defeated Yakima 2-0 and Everett defeated Vancouver 2-0 in best-of-three series. **Finals:** Everett defeated Spokane 2-1 in best-of-three series.

OVERALL STANDINGS

Team (Organization)	W	L	PCT	GB	Manager(s)	Attendance	Average	Last Penn.
Everett AquaSox (Mariners)	49	27	.645	—	Jose Moreno	36,601	1,017	2010
Spokane Indians (Rangers)	43	33	.566	6	Tim Hulett	50,511	1,486	2008
Yakima Bears (Diamondbacks)	43	33	.566	6	Bob Didier	201,512	5,446	2000
Vancouver Canadians (Athletics)	42	34	.553	7	Rick Magnante	44,895	1,213	Never
Boise Hawks (Cubs)	34	42	.447	15	Jody Davis	242,258	6,548	2004
Eugene Emeralds (Padres)	32	44	.421	17	Greg Riddoch	56,810	1,535	1980
Salem-Keizer Volcanoes (Giants)	31	45	.408	18	Tom Trebelhorn	264,441	7,147	2009
Tri-City Dust Devils (Rockies)	30	46	.395	19	Fred Ocasio	158,932	4,415	Never

CLUB BATTING

	AVG	G	AB	R	H	2B	3B	HR	RBI	BB	SO	SB	OBP	SLG
Spokane	.273	76	2590	410	706	138	21	44	364	293	616	85	.353	.393
Boise	.261	76	2572	319	671	128	23	22	281	174	540	53	.315	.354
Yakima	.255	76	2586	370	660	126	17	39	320	298	642	156	.339	.362
Everett	.254	76	2514	376	638	147	26	66	333	278	685	79	.338	.412
Salem-Keizer	.254	76	2645	330	671	131	17	36	293	245	579	57	.326	.357
Vancouver	.250	76	2537	317	635	124	12	34	285	273	592	43	.330	.349
Eugene	.240	76	2525	298	607	98	18	19	261	261	619	72	.318	.316
Tri-City	.231	76	2505	290	579	109	21	42	252	242	678	64	.310	.342

CLUB PITCHING

	ERA	G	CG	SHO	SV	IP	H	R	ER	HR	BB	SO	AVG
Everett	3.22	76	0	4	29	677	585	314	242	30	267	631	.235
Vancouver	3.27	76	0	3	24	681	686	316	247	25	207	613	.261
Yakima	3.30	76	0	4	23	684	607	314	251	24	296	598	.234
Tri-City	3.38	76	0	6	16	671	623	319	252	31	221	671	.242
Spokane	3.47	76	0	5	16	674	636	319	260	42	258	626	.249
Eugene	4.00	76	0	3	16	673	661	337	299	47	262	630	.261
Boise	4.43	76	0	4	21	663	690	389	326	54	254	564	.268
Salem-Keizer	4.52	76	0	3	16	682	698	402	342	49	299	618	.267

CLUB FIELDING

	PCT	PO	A	E	DP		PCT	PO	A	E	DP
Eugene	.975	2020	807	73	63	Spokane	.967	2022	881	100	82
Everett	.972	2030	838	82	71	Boise	.965	1989	859	102	76
Yakima	.969	2053	896	95	90	Tri-City	.963	2012	816	109	54
Salem-Keizer	.968	2045	895	96	60	Vancouver	.961	2042	813	117	74

INDIVIDUAL BATTING LEADERS (MINIMUM 3.1 PA/TEAM GAME)

	AVG	G	AB	R	H	2B	3B	HR	RBI	BB	SO	SB
Ramirez, Alvaro, Boise	.350	62	246	40	86	11	4	4	29	8	35	10
Freeman, Michael, Yakima	.333	53	189	39	63	9	1	1	23	24	29	20
Rivers, Kevin, Everett	.332	71	241	48	80	13	4	11	48	60	62	5
LePage, Pierre, Boise	.331	65	254	39	84	20	4	1	38	11	26	9
Hoying, Jared, Spokane	.325	62	243	47	79	13	5	10	51	19	70	20
Scoma, Ryan, Salem-Keizer	.310	68	261	33	81	13	1	3	34	26	38	4
Tremblay, Chris, Eugene	.308	53	208	22	64	12	0	1	23	9	41	6
Serrano, Terry, Everett	.307	62	212	39	65	11	2	1	19	29	61	16
Walters, Zachary, Yakima	.302	69	275	44	83	18	4	4	43	16	59	14
Mailloux, Kevin, Everett	.296	65	250	63	74	19	3	15	52	28	51	7

INDIVIDUAL PITCHING LEADERS (MINIMUM 1 IP/TEAM GAME)

	W	L	ERA	G	GS	CG	SV	IP	H	R	ER	BB	SO
Hungerman, Josh, Tri-City	5	4	2.18	14	11	0	0	66	47	20	16	22	77
Seco, Edlando, Everett	3	3	2.48	14	14	0	0	69	40	28	19	43	73
Fernandez, Anthony, Everett	8	3	2.60	15	15	0	0	83	75	29	24	18	69
Rojas, Randol, Spokane	5	4	2.80	15	15	0	0	77	77	29	24	20	40
Stavert, Erik, Tri-City	3	4	2.91	13	13	0	0	68	57	28	22	26	61
Cabrera, Edwar, Tri-City	1	8	3.08	14	14	0	0	73	71	34	25	24	87
Long, Nathan, Vancouver	8	2	3.10	15	15	0	0	87	95	34	30	19	47
Ramirez, Anvioris, Vancouver	2	6	3.42	14	14	0	0	63	63	31	24	17	55
Pena, Miguel, Yakima	4	6	3.47	15	15	0	0	76	87	44	29	32	47
Tabachnik, Mauricio, Eugene	3	4	3.48	19	6	0	0	62	69	30	24	12	42

ALL-STAR TEAM

C: Steve Baron, Everett; Emmanuel Quiles, Eugene. **1B:** Yazy Abelo, Yakima. **2B:** Pierre LePage, Boise. **3B:** Kevin Mailloux, Everett. **SS:** Zachary Walter, Yakima. **DH:** A.J. Kirby Jones, Vancouver. **OF:** Jared Hoying, Spokane; Alvaro Ramirez, Spokane; Ryan Scoma, Salem-Keizer. **LHSP:** Anthony Fernandez, Everett. **RHSP:** Chad Bettis, Tri-City. **LHRP:** Eury De La Rosa, Yakima. **RHSP:** A.J. Griffin, Vancouver. **Most Valuable Player:** Jared Hoying, Spokane. **Manager of the Year:** Tim Hulett, Spokane.

DEPARTMENT LEADERS

BATTING

OBP	Rivers, Kevin, Everett	.466
SLG	Mailloux, Kevin, Everett	.576
OPS	Rivers, Kevin, Everett	1.022
R	Mailloux, Kevin, Everett	63
H	Ramirez, Alvaro, Boise	86
TB	Mailloux, Kevin, Everett	144
XBH	Mailloux, Kevin, Everett	37
2B	LePage, Pierre, Boise	20
3B	Alcantara, Arismendy, Boise	6
	Liriano, Rymer, Eugene	6
HR	Mailloux, Kevin, Everett	15
RBI	Arbelo, Yazy, Yakima	55
SAC	Serrano, Terry, Everett	13
BB	Kirby-Jones, A.J., Vancouver	61
HBP	Ortiz, Roberto, Yakima	13
SO	Hilt, Justin, Yakima	92
	Sharpley, Evan, Everett	92
SB	Ortiz, Roberto, Yakima	23
CS	Serrano, Terry, Everett	13
AB/SO	LePage, Pierre, Boise	9.77

PITCHING

G	Cantwell, Keith, Yakima	30
GS	Rogers, Taylor, Salem-Keizer	16
GF	Hogben, Kable, Yakima	19
	Kurcz, Aaron, Boise	19
SV	Griffin, A.J., Vancouver	15
W	Three tied at	8
L	Cabrera, Edwar, Tri-City	8
IP	Long, Nathan, Vancouver	87
H	Rogers, Taylor, Salem-Keizer	98
R	Concepcion, Edward, Salem-Keizer	54
ER	Concepcion, Edward, Salem-Keizer	45
HB	Reagan, Miles, Yakima	11
BB	Burgos, Enrique, Yakima	54
SO	Cabrera, Edwar, Tri-City	87
SO/9	Cabrera, Edwar, Tri-City	10.71
SO/9 (RP)	Dunning, Jake, Salem-Keizer	11.3
BB/9	Tabachnik, Mauricio, Eugene	1.74
WP	Three tied at	12
BK	Ramirez, Anvioris, Vancouver	5
HR	McBride, Nicholas, Spokane	9
AVG	Seco, Edlando, Everett	.169

FIELDING

C	FPCT	Emsley-Pai, Kawika, Yakima	.996
	PO	Baron, Steven, Everett	420
	A	Baron, Steven, Everett	47
	E	Massanari, Bryce, Tri-City	7
	DP	Baron, Steven, Everett	6
	PB	Emsley-Pai, Kawika, Yakima	8
		Garneau, Dustin, Tri-City	8
1B	FPCT	Tracy, Mark, Everett	.988
	PO	Arbelo, Yazy, Yakima	607
	A	Kirby-Jones, A.J., Vancouver	37
		Sharpley, Evan, Everett	37
	E	Arbelo, Yazy, Yakima	12
		Kirby-Jones, A.J., Vancouver	12
	DP	Arbelo, Yazy, Yakima	59
2B	PO	LePage, Pierre, Boise	104
	A	LePage, Pierre, Boise	163
	E	Izturis, Julio, Salem-Keizer	11
		Selen, Alejandro, Spokane	11
	DP	Freeman, Michael, Yakima	37
3B	FPCT	Olt, Michael, Spokane	.942
	PO	Olt, Michael, Spokane	37
	A	Olt, Michael, Spokane	124
	E	Thompson, Tony, Vancouver	21
	DP	Olt, Michael, Spokane	12
SS	FPCT	Phillips, Anthony, Everett	.979
	PO	Kirkland, Wade, Vancouver	111
	A	Profar, Jurickson, Spokane	232
	E	Kirkland, Wade, Vancouver	24
	DP	Profar, Jurickson, Spokane	49
OF	FPCT	Garcia, Oscar, Eugene	1.000
		Medina, Jose, Salem-Keizer	1.000
	PO	Anston, Robert, Everett	130
	A	Four tied at	9
	E	Ramirez, Alvaro, Boise	8
	DP	Bercume, Jeff, Vancouver	3

MINOR LEAGUES

BY MATT EDDY

The Johnson City Cardinals hit .287/.355/.438 as a team, leading the Appalachian League in average, on-base percentage and slugging as well as with 383 runs scored. They won a league-best 42 games and excelled in all facets in their four-game sweep through the playoffs, which culminated with the franchise's first league title since 1976.

Johnson City outfielder Virgil Hill homered in both championship games over Elizabethton (Twins), going 3-for-8 with four RBIs. Led by center fielder Oscar Taveras, who went 8-for-16 with five RBIs, the Cardinals hit .342 as a team with eight home runs in their four playoff games. The pitching staff was even more dominant in compiling a 2.00 ERA and 37-to-4 strikeout-to-walk ratio. The rotation—lefties Ryan Copeland (the league's pitcher of the year) and Kevin Siegrist and righthanders Cale Johnson and Boone Whiting—combined to allow five runs in 24 ⅓ innings.

The Appy League introduced the wild card for 2010 to ostensibly lessen the advantage enjoyed by Danville (Braves) and Elizabethton, the two clubs that won the league title six out of seven seasons from 2003-09 with older, more experienced rosters. But in an ironic twist, neither the Braves nor the Twins would have qualified for the playoffs in '10 had the league's old format been preserved.

The results confirm that the Twins were, in fact, the top pitching club in the league. They led in ERA (2.98), WHIP (1.13), strikeouts per nine innings (9.8) and strikeout-to-walk ratio (4.44). But Elizabethton featured plenty of offensive firepower as well, leading the circuit with 59 home runs.

Center fielder Oswaldo Arcia paced the Twins' attack and was an easy choice as the league's player of the year. The 19-year-old Venezuelan led the loop in seven key categories: average (.375), on-base percentage (.424), slugging (.672), hits (97), RBIs (51), extra-base hits (42) and total bases

TOP 20 PROSPECTS

1. Carlos Perez, lhp, Danville Braves
2. Enny Romero, lhp, Princeton Rays
3. Oswaldo Arcia, of, Elizabethton Twins
4. Oscar Taveras, of, Johnson City Cardinals
5. Delino Deshields, of, Greeneville Astros
6. Ramon Morla, 3b, Pulaski Mariners
7. Mike Foltynewicz, rhp, Greeneville Astros
8. Adrian Salcedo, rhp, Elizabethton Twins
9. Aderlin Rodriguez, 3b, Kingsport Mets
10. Manuel Soliman, rhp, Elizabethton Twins
11. Vincent Velasquez, rhp, Greeneville Astros
12. Andrelton Simmons, ss, Danville Braves
13. Braulio Lara, lhp, Princeton Rays
14. Cody Stanley, c, Johnson City Cardinals
15. Todd Glaesmann, of, Princeton Rays
16. Pat Dean, lhp, Elizabethton Twins
17. Matt Heidenreich, rhp, Bristol White Sox
18. Richard Vargas, rhp, Pulaski Mariners
19. Jacob Petricka, rhp, Bristol White Sox
20. Hector Guevara, 2b, Princeton Rays

(174). With 14 home runs, Arcia trailed Pulaski's Ramon Morla (Mariners) by three to fall just short of the triple crown.

Regardless, Arcia set a high water mark for slugging percentage bettered only once in the league in 14 seasons—by Greeneville's Mitch Einertson, who slugged .692 in 2004.

With players such as Arcia, Morla, Salcedo, Solliman and Taveras leading the way, young players from Latin America claimed eight of the top 10 spots on our postseason prospect list. This has become more rule than exception in recent years because most organizations prefer to send their just-drafted high school players to complex-based Rookie-level affiliates in the Arizona or Gulf Coast leagues.

The Astros, however, sent three of their top four draft choices (outfielder Delino DeShields and righthanders Mike Foltynewicz and Vincent Velasquez) to the Appy League in an effort to expedite their development. Similarly, Houston sent past premium picks Jordan Lyles and Jay Austin (2008) and Jiovanni Mier and Jonathan Meyer (2009) to Greeneville to launch their careers.

STANDINGS

EASTERN DIVISION (Organization)	W	L	PCT	GB	Manager(s)	Attendance	Average	Last Penn.
Pulaski Mariners (Mariners)	37	28	.569	—	Eddie Menchaca	32,348	980	Never
Burlington Royals (Royals)	34	34	.500	4 ½	Nelson Liriano	30,273	917	1993
Danville Braves (Braves)	34	34	.500	4 ½	Paul Runge	30,615	928	2009
Princeton Rays (Rays)	33	35	.485	5 ½	Mike Johns	26,946	869	1994
Bluefield Orioles (Orioles)	23	45	.338	15 ½	Einar Diaz	22,868	715	2001
WESTERN DIVISION (Organization)	W	L	PCT	GB	Manager(s)	Attendance	Average	Last Penn.
Johnson City Cardinals (Cardinals)	42	24	.636	—	Mike Shildt	24,049	752	2010
Elizabethton Twins (Twins)	41	25	.621	1	Ray Smith	24,668	796	2008
Bristol White Sox (White Sox)	32	36	.471	11	Ryan Newman	22,019	667	2002
Greeneville Astros (Astros)	31	35	.470	11	Ed Romero	47,321	1,392	2004
Kingsport Mets (Mets)	28	39	.418	14 ½	Mike DiFelice	28,822	901	1995

PLAYOFFS—Semifinals: Elizabethton defeated Pulaski 2-0 and Johnson City defeated Burlington 2-0 in best-of-three series. **Finals:** Johnson City defeated Elizabethton 2-0 in best-of-three series.

CLUB BATTING

	AVG	G	AB	R	H	2B	3B	HR	RBI	BB	SO	SB	OBP	SLG
Johnson City	.287	66	2341	383	673	148	27	50	340	215	516	50	.355	.438
Danville	.277	68	2380	337	660	133	21	37	297	140	386	58	.332	.397
Pulaski	.269	65	2225	377	599	116	17	56	333	187	542	99	.342	.412
Elizabethton	.266	66	2301	334	611	144	16	59	301	161	583	33	.323	.419
Kingsport	.265	67	2341	326	620	130	14	45	286	175	472	54	.323	.390
Greeneville	.251	66	2213	297	555	111	23	53	252	171	589	62	.316	.394
Princeton	.249	68	2265	297	563	126	24	34	250	190	509	79	.316	.370
Bristol	.246	68	2221	256	546	123	9	35	225	174	549	32	.313	.357
Burlington	.237	68	2275	265	540	104	16	31	228	150	532	85	.297	.338
Bluefield	.227	68	2273	276	516	93	30	24	227	194	629	30	.296	.326

CLUB PITCHING

	ERA	G	CG	SHO	SV	IP	H	R	ER	HR	BB	SO	AVG
Elizabethton	2.89	66	0	10	18	589	520	234	189	38	145	644	.236
Princeton	3.23	68	1	6	9	597	579	280	214	40	167	522	.251
Bristol	3.37	68	1	5	19	588	512	277	220	27	168	514	.233
Burlington	3.40	68	0	6	19	616	578	282	233	47	182	533	.247
Johnson City	3.72	66	1	2	25	588	597	306	243	47	129	547	.261
Danville	3.88	68	0	3	19	605	569	315	261	36	208	532	.250
Pulaski	4.23	65	1	2	15	578	626	341	272	47	150	510	.272
Kingsport	4.40	67	0	1	14	593	624	372	290	55	221	578	.269
Bluefield	4.44	68	1	5	10	588	608	378	290	39	225	468	.265
Greeneville	4.54	66	0	4	18	577	670	363	291	48	162	459	.290

CLUB FIELDING

	PCT	PO	A	E	DP		PCT	PO	A	E	DP
Danville	.976	1816	846	66	72	Kingsport	.962	1778	749	101	73
Elizabethton	.968	1766	671	80	51	Johnson City	.961	1764	757	103	64
Burlington	.965	1848	774	96	71	Pulaski	.961	1735	659	96	52
Bristol	.963	1765	793	98	70	Princeton	.958	1791	766	113	52
Greeneville	.962	1730	727	97	67	Bluefield	.950	1765	789	134	75

INDIVIDUAL BATTING LEADERS (MINIMUM 3.1 PA/TEAM GAME)

	AVG	G	AB	R	H	2B	3B	HR	RBI	BB	SO	SB
Arcia, Oswaldo, Elizabethton	.375	64	259	47	97	21	7	14	51	19	67	4
Morla, Ramon, Pulaski	.323	62	251	60	81	17	2	17	49	15	65	13
Taveras, Oscar, Johnson City	.322	53	211	39	68	13	3	8	43	12	41	8
Stanley, Cody, Johnson City	.321	53	209	34	67	12	5	5	39	21	30	8
Rodriguez, Aderlin, Kingsport	.312	61	250	44	78	22	0	13	48	15	43	3
Wallace, Chris, Greeneville	.310	47	171	29	53	6	3	8	32	17	44	3
Teran, Kleininger, Johnson City	.303	45	178	21	54	14	1	1	23	12	26	1
Nidiffer, Marcus, Greeneville	.303	48	165	27	50	10	2	11	34	13	48	6
Stovall, Ryan, Burlington	.303	61	241	33	73	15	5	4	24	20	41	12
Kiermaier, Kevin, Princeton	.303	57	218	44	66	8	7	2	16	24	54	17

INDIVIDUAL PITCHING LEADERS (MINIMUM 1 IP/TEAM GAME)

	W	L	ERA	G	GS	CG	SV	IP	H	R	ER	BB	SO
Romero, Enny, Princeton	4	1	1.95	13	13	0	0	69	51	15	15	14	72
Lara, Braulio, Princeton	6	4	2.18	13	13	1	0	66	49	26	16	25	58
Arroyo, Spencer, Bristol	7	2	2.49	13	13	1	0	76	57	22	21	14	75
Heidenreich, Matthew, Bristol	6	2	2.49	13	11	0	0	76	73	30	21	11	58
Avinazar, Willian, Burlington	6	3	2.63	13	13	0	0	72	67	27	21	11	67
Pettit, Jacob, Bluefield	3	5	2.68	11	11	1	0	57	57	26	17	4	50
Simmons, Crawford, Burlington	6	2	2.77	14	14	0	0	78	62	27	24	19	70
Santiago, Leonel, Burlington	6	3	2.78	14	14	0	0	81	73	29	25	17	66
Young, Robert, Bristol	4	3	2.80	14	12	0	0	65	53	28	20	14	44
Boyce, Timothy, Pulaski	9	3	2.99	13	8	0	0	57	48	28	19	11	55

ALL-STAR TEAM

C: Cody Stanley, Johnson City. **1B:** Marcus Nidiffer, Greeneville. **2B:** Drew Lee, Bristol. **3B:** Ramon Morla, Pulaski. **SS:** Andrelton Simmons, Danville. **UTIL IF:** Jorge Agudelo, Pulaski. **OF:** Oswaldo Arcia, Elizabethton; Javier Rodriguez, Kingsport; Oscar Taveras, Johnson City. **UTIL OF:** Jose Rivero, Pulaski. **DH:** Chris Wallace, Greeneville. **RHP:** Tim Boyce, Pulaski. **LHP:** Ryan Copeland, Johnson City. **RP:** Hector Corpas, Johnson City.

Player of the Year: Oswaldo Arcia, Elizabethton. **Pitcher of the Year:** Ryan Copeland, Johnson City. **Manager of the Year:** Mike Shildt, Johnson City.

DEPARTMENT LEADERS

BATTING

OBP	Arcia, Oswaldo, Elizabethton	.424
SLG	Arcia, Oswaldo, Elizabethton	.672
OPS	Arcia, Oswaldo, Elizabethton	1.096
R	Morla, Ramon, Pulaski	60
H	Arcia, Oswaldo, Elizabethton	97
TB	Arcia, Oswaldo, Elizabethton	174
XBH	Arcia, Oswaldo, Elizabethton	42
2B	Lee, Drew, Bristol	24
3B	Webb, Brenden, Bluefield	8
HR	Morla, Ramon, Pulaski	17
RBI	Arcia, Oswaldo, Elizabethton	51
SAC	Millender, Qualon, Bristol	8
	Rodriguez, Derek, Burlington	8
BB	Ruiz, Romulo, Johnson City	34
HBP	MacDougall, Gabe, Burlington	15
SO	Thomas, Corey, Bluefield	81
SB	Agudelo, Jorge, Pulaski	24
CS	Piterson, Luis, Burlington	9
AB/SO	Simmons, Andrelton, Danville	17.07

PITCHING

G	Corpas, Hector, Johnson City	24
	Lucas, Aidan, Johnson City	24
GS	Santiago, Leonel, Burlington	14
	Simmons, Crawford, Burlington	14
GF	Corpas, Hector, Johnson City	21
SV	Corpas, Hector, Johnson City	17
W	Boyce, Timothy, Pulaski	9
L	Casey, Jarrett, Bristol	7
	Hebert, Michael, Kingsport	7
IP	Santiago, Leonel, Burlington	81
H	Cespedes, Angel, Bluefield	84
R	Batista, Ricardo, Greeneville	46
ER	Quezada, Euris, Greeneville	41
HB	Mieses, George, Pulaski	11
BB	Martin, Jarret, Bluefield	46
SO	Arroyo, Spencer, Bristol	75
SO/9	Whiting, Boone, Johnson City	11.33
SO/9 (RP)	Torres, Jhonathan, Kingsport	13.7
BB/9	Pettit, Jacob, Bluefield	0.63
WP	Martin, Jarret, Bluefield	18
BK	Pacheco, Ronan, Danville	4
HR	Nava, Jessie, Pulaski	8
	Quezada, Euris, Greeneville	8
AVG	Lara, Braulio, Princeton	.200

FIELDING

C	FPCT	Gattis, Evan, Danville	.986
	PO	Blackwood, Chase, Bristol	331
	A	Cordero, Albert, Kingsport	51
	E	Olivares, Gerardo, Princeton	8
	DP	Zapata, Nelfi, Kingsport	5
	PB	Zapata, Nelfi, Kingsport	16
1B	FPCT	Burke, Brian, Elizabethton	.994
	PO	Malm, Jeff, Princeton	522
	A	Thomas, Corey, Bluefield	45
	E	Baldwin, Geoffrey, Burlington	16
	DP	Stewart, Lucas, Kingsport	56
2B	FPCT	Garcia, Greg, Johnson City	.985
	PO	Piterson, Luis, Burlington	140
	A	Piterson, Luis, Burlington	179
	E	Guevara, Hector, Princeton	14
	DP	Piterson, Luis, Burlington	43
3B	FPCT	Leer, Andy, Elizabethton	.937
	PO	Rodriguez, Aderlin, Kingsport	47
	A	Leer, Andy, Elizabethton	123
	E	Morla, Ramon, Pulaski	21
		Ruiz, Romulo, Johnson City	21
	DP	Rodriguez, Aderlin, Kingsport	15
SS	FPCT	Simmons, Andrelton, Danville	.974
	PO	Simmons, Andrelton, Danville	101
	A	Simmons, Andrelton, Danville	231
	E	Merritt, Jonathan, Greeneville	21
		Valera, Cesar, Johnson City	21
	DP	Simmons, Andrelton, Danville	47
OF	FPCT	Four tied at	1.000
	PO	King, Emilio, Greeneville	132
	A	King, Emilio, Greeneville	14
	E	Hoppy, Kyle, Bluefield	7
		Nash, Telvin, Greeneville	7
	DP	King, Emilio, Greeneville	5

MINOR LEAGUES

BY MATT EDDY

The four Pioneer League clubs with the oldest rosters—Great Falls (White Sox), Helena (Brewers), Orem (Angels) and Ogden (Dodgers)—qualified for the playoffs, marking a departure from last season when inexperienced Orem and Missoula (Diamondbacks) teams advanced to the finals.

This year's Pioneer League showdown, Helena versus Ogden, also pitted two clubs rich with talent from the most recent draft.

Helena captured its first PL championship since 1996, winning four of five playoff games and sweeping Ogden in two games to take the crown. The Brewers received key contributions from a bushel of 2010 draft picks, most notably college righthanders Jimmy Nelson (second round, Alabama), Tyler Thornburg (third, Charleston Southern), Matt Miller (fifth, Michigan) and Austin Ross (eighth, Louisiana State).

That quartet accounted for just over half of the Helena's postseason innings, with Miller leading the way with two wins and 11 innings. Helena first baseman Cody Hawn (sixth round, Tennessee) slugged two home runs and drove in eight runs in the decisive game.

Despite coming up short in the finals, Ogden paced the league in average (.298), on-base percentage (.365), slugging (.469) and runs (494), while scoring a full run per game more than No. 2 Casper. The Dodgers affiliate narrowly missed leading the PL in home runs, finishing two behind Orem.

A pair of college draft picks paced the offense: third-round center fielder Leon Landry (LSU) and fifth-round shortstop Jake Lemmerman (Duke), the league's player of the year.

Lemmerman drew praise from opposing managers as the best overall shortstop in the circuit. He led the PL in doubles (24) and runs scored (69), finished runner-up in average (.363) and extra-base hits (38) and ranked third in on-base percentage (.434) and slugging (.610).

Landry helped LSU win the 2009 College World Series in a part-time role before roaring back to win a starting gig one year later as a junior,

hitting a career best .338/.418/.513 with 16 steals. His gains carried over to pro ball, where he finished fifth in the PL batting race at .349.

Playing supporting roles for Ogden were right fielder Jonathan Garcia and 23-year-old left fielder Nick Akins, who led the league with 15 homers and a .650 slugging percentage.

In a similar vein, the White Sox used college picks to help propel Great Falls to a PL best 47 victories. The key contributors: righthanders Addison Reed (third round) and Thomas Royse (third round supplemental), third baseman Andy Wilkins (fifth), second baseman Ross Wilson (10th) and catcher Mike Blanke (14th).

TOP 20 PROSPECTS

1. Billy Hamilton, 2b/ss, Billings (Reds)
2. Albert Campos, rhp, Casper (Rockies)
3. Daniel Tillman, rhp, Orem (Angels)
4. Leon Landry, of, Ogden (Dodgers)
5. Yorman Rodriguez, of, Billings (Reds)
6. Jake Lemmerman, ss, Ogden (Dodgers)
7. Mike Blanke, c, Great Falls (White Sox)
8. Addison Reed, rhp, Great Falls (White Sox)
9. Matt Miller, rhp, Helena (Brewers)
10. Will Swanner, c, Casper (Rockies)
11. Daniel Corcino, rhp, Billings (Reds)
12. Cristhian Adames, ss, Casper (Rockies)
13. Garrett Gould, rhp, Ogden (Dodgers)
14. Jimmy Nelson, rhp, Helena (Brewers)
15. David Holmberg, lhp, Great Falls (White Sox)/ Missoula (Diamondbacks)
16. Robby Rowland, rhp, Missoula (Diamondbacks)
17. Travis Witherspoon, of, Orem (Angels)
18. Rafael Ortega, of, Casper (Rockies)
19. Thomas Royse, rhp, Great Falls (White Sox)
20. Kevin Eichhorn, rhp, Missoula (Diamondbacks)

STANDINGS: SPLIT SEASON

FIRST HALF

NORTH	W	L	PCT	GB
Great Falls	23	15	.605	—
Billings	21	17	.553	2
Helena	19	19	.500	4
Missoula	14	24	.368	9

SOUTH	W	L	PCT	GB
Ogden	23	15	.605	—
Orem	19	19	.500	4
Casper	17	21	.447	6
Idaho Falls	16	22	.421	7

SECOND HALF

NORTH	W	L	PCT	GB
Great Falls	24	13	.649	—
Helena	22	15	.595	2
Billings	17	20	.459	7
Missoula	14	23	.378	10

SOUTH	W	L	PCT	GB
Ogden	21	16	.568	—
Orem	20	17	.541	1
Casper	20	18	.526	1½
Idaho Falls	11	27	.289	10½

PLAYOFFS—Semifinals: Ogden defeated Orem 2-1 and Helena defeated Great Falls 2-1 in best-of-three series. **Finals:** Helena defeated Ogden 2-0 in best-of-three series.

OVERALL STANDINGS

Team (Organization)	W	L	PCT	GB	Manager(s)	Attendance	Average	Last Penn.
Great Falls Voyagers (White Sox)	47	28	.627	—	Chris Cron	66,106	1,836	2008
Ogden Raptors (Dodgers)	44	31	.587	3	Damon Berryhill	132,799	3,495	Never
Helena Brewers (Brewers)	41	34	.547	6	Joe Ayrault	32,723	884	2010
Orem Owlz (Angels)	39	36	.520	8	Tom Kotchman	81,229	2,195	2009
Billings Mustangs (Reds)	38	37	.507	9	Delino DeShields	101,516	2,744	2001
Casper Ghosts (Rockies)	37	39	.487	10½	Tony Diaz	57,120	1,503	Never
Missoula Osprey (Diamondbacks)	28	47	.373	19	Hector De La Cruz	87,345	2,361	2006
Idaho Falls Chukars (Royals)	27	49	.355	20½	Brian Buchanan	91,551	2,409	2000

CLUB BATTING

	AVG	G	AB	R	H	2B	3B	HR	RBI	BB	SO	SB	OBP	SLG
Ogden	.298	75	2695	494	803	178	21	79	451	237	562	82	.365	.468
Casper	.283	76	2678	423	759	130	26	56	361	201	604	81	.338	.414
Great Falls	.278	75	2623	451	729	151	19	43	383	313	564	71	.361	.399
Helena	.275	75	2681	418	738	140	18	63	372	264	636	55	.353	.411
Orem	.275	75	2672	454	735	127	29	81	398	244	695	57	.345	.435
Missoula	.272	75	2573	369	700	126	25	56	329	226	640	63	.341	.406
Billings	.264	75	2544	374	672	117	31	32	320	250	597	135	.336	.372
Idaho Falls	.260	76	2612	376	679	123	20	38	313	266	677	106	.333	.366

CLUB PITCHING

	ERA	G	CG	SHO	SV	IP	H	R	ER	HR	BB	SO	AVG
Billings	3.83	75	1	9	17	663	636	341	282	46	268	616	.253
Great Falls	4.02	75	0	4	16	676	704	369	302	57	216	608	.267
Casper	4.47	76	1	2	18	672	799	438	334	58	212	547	.293
Orem	4.50	75	1	3	15	674	727	406	337	48	270	613	.275
Helena	4.54	75	0	2	19	682	652	398	344	51	310	677	.252
Ogden	4.67	75	0	1	26	668	752	436	347	63	218	669	.283
Missoula	4.98	75	1	1	15	647	723	473	358	65	270	578	.280
Idaho Falls	5.30	76	0	3	11	669	822	498	394	60	237	667	.301

CLUB FIELDING

	PCT	PO	A	E	DP		PCT	PO	A	E	DP
Great Falls	.969	2029	833	91	55	Ogden	.959	2005	795	120	67
Helena	.966	2047	818	102	48	Casper	.956	2016	852	133	59
Orem	.963	2022	866	111	80	Idaho Falls	.952	2006	845	145	66
Billings	.962	1988	804	109	69	Missoula	.952	1942	774	138	71

INDIVIDUAL BATTING LEADERS (MINIMUM 3.1 PA/TEAM GAME)

	AVG	G	AB	R	H	2B	3B	HR	RBI	BB	SO	SB
Eaton, Adam, Missoula	.385	68	226	48	87	14	4	7	37	35	44	20
Lemmerman, Jake, Ogden	.363	66	259	69	94	24	2	12	47	31	56	5
Heid, Andrew, Orem	.362	68	287	62	104	12	1	9	34	35	40	9
Ortega, Rafael, Casper	.358	71	288	69	103	17	3	7	45	28	42	23
Landry, Leon, Ogden	.349	57	249	46	87	20	4	4	38	20	36	13
Dickerson, Corey, Casper	.348	69	276	54	96	22	9	13	61	28	51	12
Henderson, Chris, Ogden	.341	47	176	36	60	12	1	1	24	21	22	2
Blanke, Michael, Great Falls	.329	62	240	35	79	20	1	7	43	23	33	0
McDade, Blake, Casper	.327	58	220	36	72	14	1	3	40	22	31	1
George, Carlos, Helena	.324	59	241	34	78	9	2	1	25	6	38	8

INDIVIDUAL PITCHING LEADERS (MINIMUM 1 IP/TEAM GAME)

	W	L	ERA	G	GS	CG	SV	IP	H	R	ER	BB	SO
Campos, Albert, Casper	4	4	2.05	15	15	1	0	88	80	29	20	17	68
Patterson, Red, Ogden	6	1	3.35	14	14	0	0	68	70	37	25	17	66
Schuster, Patrick, Missoula	5	4	3.78	15	15	0	0	77	76	50	32	34	60
Upchurch, Steven, Great Falls	4	2	3.80	15	15	0	0	86	82	48	36	18	47
Gagnon, Tyler, Casper	5	3	3.90	15	15	0	0	76	94	41	33	17	63
Jang, Pil Joon, Orem	2	3	3.96	15	15	0	0	75	88	49	33	16	39
Miller, Matthew, Helena	7	2	4.06	14	14	0	0	71	63	35	32	28	53
Burnside, Paul, Great Falls	7	3	4.17	17	13	0	1	72	69	42	33	20	77
Holmberg, David, GF/Missoula	2	5	4.20	15	15	0	0	78	99	49	36	16	76
Gerson, Stalin, Billings	3	4	4.91	15	15	0	0	76	89	46	41	18	52

ALL-STAR TEAM

C: Mike Blanke, Great Falls. **1B:** Cody Hawn, Helena. **2B:** Billy Hamilton, Billings. **3B:** Andy Wilkins, Great Falls. **SS:** Jake Lemmerman, Ogden. **OF:** Corey Dickerson, Casper; Adam Eaton, Missoula; Rafael Ortega, Casper. **DH:** Murray Watts, Idaho Falls. **P:** Albert Campos, Casper; Matt Miller, Helena; Red Patterson, Ogden; Tanner Robles, Billings; Shawn Tolleson, Ogden.
Most Valuable Player: Jake Lemmerman, Ogden. **Pitcher of the Year:** Albert Campos, Casper. **Manager of the Year:** Joe Ayrault, Helena; Chris Cron, Great Falls.

DEPARTMENT LEADERS

BATTING

OBP	Eaton, Adam, Missoula		.500
SLG	Akins, Nick, Ogden		.650
OPS	Eaton, Adam, Missoula		1.075
R	Lemmerman, Jake, Ogden		69
	Ortega, Rafael, Casper		69
H	Heid, Andrew, Orem		104
TB	Dickerson, Corey, Casper		175
XBH	Dickerson, Corey, Casper		44
2B	Lemmerman, Jake, Ogden		24
3B	Hamilton, Billy, Billings		10
HR	Akins, Nick, Ogden		15
RBI	Dickerson, Corey, Casper		61
	Hawn, Cody, Helena		61
SAC	Trapp, Justin, Idaho Falls		13
BB	Walker, Michael, Helena		60
HBP	Eaton, Adam, Missoula		19
SO	Dishon, John, Helena		105
SB	Hamilton, Billy, Billings		48
CS	Four tied at		9
AB/SO	Dean, Blake, Ogden		15.47

PITCHING

G	Tolleson, Shawn, Ogden		26
GS	Delk, Charles, Great Falls		16
GF	Tolleson, Shawn, Ogden		25
SV	Tolleson, Shawn, Ogden		17
W	Burnside, Paul, Great Falls		7
	Delk, Charles, Great Falls		7
	Miller, Matthew, Helena		7
L	Billo, Gregory, Idaho Falls		8
IP	Campos, Albert, Casper		88
H	Delk, Charles, Great Falls		107
	Mejias, Alving, Casper		107
R	Mejias, Alving, Casper		66
ER	Mejias, Alving, Casper		57
HB	Tuttle, Daniel, Billings		11
BB	Frederickson, Evan, Helena		48
SO	Delk, Charles, Great Falls		81
SO/9	Perez, Leondy, Idaho Falls		10.21
SO/9 (RP)	Tillman, Daniel, Orem		13.9
BB/9	Mejias, Alving, Casper		1.68
WP	Frederickson, Evan, Helena		20
BK	Barraza, Alejandro, Casper		3
	Gerson, Stalin, Billings		3
HR	Eichhorn, Kevin, Missoula		12
AVG	Campos, Albert, Casper		.244

FIELDING

C	FPCT	Kim, Jae Yun, Missoula	.985
	PO	Blanke, Michael, Great Falls	380
	A	Barnhart, Tucker, Billings	56
	E	Blanke, Michael, Great Falls	10
		Dean, Brent, Helena	10
	DP	Five tied at	4
	PB	Pericht, Michael, Ogden	14
1B	FPCT	Dean, Blake, Ogden	.991
	PO	Stone, Bobby, Missoula	613
	A	McDade, Blake, Casper	64
	E	McDade, Blake, Casper	9
		Stone, Bobby, Missoula	9
	DP	Stone, Bobby, Missoula	65
2B	FPCT	Hamilton, Billy, Billings	.979
	PO	Hamilton, Billy, Billings	106
	A	Hatton, Wes, Orem	203
	E	Espinal, Yowill, Idaho Falls	22
	DP	Hamilton, Billy, Billings	43
3B	FPCT	Santos, Oliver, Billings	.960
	PO	Santos, Oliver, Billings	41
	A	Nichols, Thomas, Orem	111
	E	Bosnik, Jesse, Ogden	16
	DP	Three tied at	11
SS	FPCT	Davis, Kyle, Great Falls	.948
	PO	Davis, Kyle, Great Falls	115
		Navarro, Raul, Missoula	115
	A	Davis, Kyle, Great Falls	193
	E	Trapp, Justin, Idaho Falls	33
	DP	Navarro, Raul, Missoula	46
OF	FPCT	Landry, Leon, Ogden	0.99
	PO	Ortega, Rafael, Casper	160
	A	Garcia, Jonathan, Ogden	12
		Heid, Andrew, Orem	12
	E	Garcia, Jonathan, Ogden	9
	DP	Heid, Andrew, Orem	4

MINOR LEAGUES

MINOR LEAGUES

BY BILL MITCHELL

The Brewers, winners of the first three Arizona League championships during the league's formative years, ended a 20-year drought in 2010, defeating the Reds for their first title since 1990.

Jason Rogers drove in five runs with a home run, double and single to pace the Brewers offense, with 25th-rounder Nick Shaw going 4-4 and scoring four times.

The league expanded for the second straight year, adding a 12th team after the relocation of the Reds' training facility from Florida to a new complex in the Phoenix suburb of Goodyear.

Mariners international prospect Ji-Man Choi, a 19-year-old Korean native, led the league in batting with a .378 average and was named MVP. Reds outfielder Robert Maddox topped all hitters with 46 RBIs and tied with four other players for the home run lead with seven. Royals outfielder Darian Sandford led the league with 30 stolen bases. Royals righthander Robinson Yambati recorded the most wins with eight; Brewers southpaw Charly Bashara posted a league-leading 2.37 ERA.

Bonus babies Michael Ynoa and Donavan Tate were the preseason favorites to rank as the Arizona League's top prospect. Instead, Mariners outfielder Guillermo Pimentel and lesser-known Royals righthanders Yordano Ventura and Yambati headlined our Top 20 Prospects in a year when there was no clear choice for No. 1.

Pimentel received one of the top bonuses during the 2009 international signing period when the Mariners signed the Dominican Republic native for $2 million. He struggled in the early part of his first professional season, especially with pitch selection and curveballs, but finished strongly with a .293/.318/.537 line in August. The 17-year-

TOP 20 PROSPECTS

1. Guillermo Pimentel, of, Mariners
2. Yordano Ventura, rhp, Royals
3. Robinson Yambati, rhp, Royals
4. Tyler Roberts, c, Brewers
5. Junior Arias, ss, Reds
6. Donavan Tate, of, Padres
7. Cheslor Cuthbert, 3b, Royals
8. Luis Sardinas, ss, Rangers
9. Ismael Guillon, lhp, Reds
10. James Baldwin, of, Dodgers
11. Austin Reed, rhp, Cubs
12. Jonathan Correa, rhp, Reds
13. Chuckie Jones, of, Giants
14. Christian Villanueva, 3b, Rangers
15. Carlos Melo, rhp, Rangers
16. Heath Hembree, rhp, Giants
17. Chevez Clarke, of, Angels
18. Ji-Man Choi, 1b/c, Mariners
19. Teodoro Martinez, of, Rangers
20. Ralston Cash, rhp, Dodgers

old lefthanded hitter drew raves for his plus-plus power and five-tool potential.

Ventura, a slight 19-year-old Dominican native, regularly operated in the mid-90s with his fastball and hit triple digits multiple times late in the season.

Meanwhile, Ynoa and Tate were disappointments. Ynoa, who signed for a Dominican-record $4.25 million in 2008, made his first pro appearance after missing all of 2009 with elbow tendinitis. He hit 95 mph while throwing three scoreless innings on Opening Day, but he pitched only twice more before being shut down again with elbow soreness. He had Tommy John surgery in late August.

The third overall pick in the 2009 draft, Tate saw his progress stymied by an ongoing stomach ailment that sidelined him for large portions of the season. When he did play, he showed much more athleticism than hitting aptitude, striking out 41 times in 90 at-bats.

STANDINGS

EASTERN DIVISION	Complex	W	L	PCT	GB	Manager(s)	Last Penn.
Giants	Scottsdale	34	20	.630	—	Mike Goff	2008
Athletics	Phoenix	30	26	.536	5	Marcus Jensen	2001
Cubs	Mesa	26	29	.473	8 ½	Juan Cabreja	2002
Angels	Tempe	24	31	.436	10 ½	Tyrone Boykin	Never
CENTRAL DIVISION	**Complex**	**W**	**L**	**PCT**	**GB**	**Manager(s)**	**Last Penn.**
Brewers	Phoenix	34	22	.607	—	Tony Diggs	2010
Reds	Goodyear	31	24	.564	2 ½	Julio Garcia	Never
Dodgers	Phoenix	30	25	.545	3 ½	Lorenzo Bundy	Never
Indians	Goodyear	21	35	.375	13	Chris Tremie	Never
WESTERN DIVISION	**Complex**	**W**	**L**	**PCT**	**GB**	**Manager(s)**	**Last Penn.**
Rangers	Surprise	31	24	.564	—	Jayce Tingler	Never
Royals	Surprise	31	25	.554	½	Darryl Kennedy	2003
Padres	Peoria	20	35	.364	11	Ivan Cruz	2006
Mariners	Peoria	20	36	.357	11 ½	Jesus Azuaje	2009

PLAYOFFS—Semifinals: Brewers defeated Rangers and Reds defeated Giants in one-game playoffs. **Finals:** Brewers defeated Reds in one-game playoff.

CLUB BATTING

	AVG	G	AB	R	H	2B	3B	HR	RBI	BB	SO	SB	OBP	SLG
Rangers	.299	55	1934	334	578	97	22	12	275	169	401	90	.366	.390
Reds	.287	55	1971	331	566	112	29	34	292	169	408	32	.352	.425
Cubs	.266	55	1897	278	504	75	20	14	236	188	453	87	.337	.348
Brewers	.265	56	1934	328	512	111	26	20	275	182	513	94	.337	.380
Giants	.264	54	1817	277	480	95	26	32	236	152	439	66	.330	.398
Dodgers	.255	55	1863	278	475	82	24	24	247	182	521	65	.328	.363
Padres	.253	55	1881	282	476	104	19	21	238	182	532	59	.326	.362
Athletics	.245	56	1945	276	477	100	21	17	226	177	541	54	.315	.344
Royals	.241	56	1870	253	450	92	42	16	212	165	514	96	.309	.360
Angels	.238	55	1897	247	452	69	40	15	208	172	577	62	.310	.341
Mariners	.235	56	1845	221	434	104	17	17	191	152	555	73	.302	.338
Indians	.232	56	1948	233	452	78	23	25	204	168	533	57	.299	.334

CLUB PITCHING

	ERA	G	CG	SHO	SV	IP	H	R	ER	HR	BB	SO	AVG
Royals	3.38	56	0	2	21	500	473	255	188	17	146	530	.245
Athletics	3.49	56	0	1	10	497	447	263	193	18	167	533	.234
Giants	3.56	54	0	7	13	478	453	225	189	18	181	532	.249
Reds	3.63	55	0	6	12	486	443	260	196	23	192	535	.240
Dodgers	4.01	55	0	6	10	487	516	288	217	21	169	452	.268
Angels	4.02	55	0	3	13	499	543	281	223	23	152	484	.276
Brewers	4.13	56	1	3	16	499	471	266	229	28	194	501	.250
Mariners	4.13	56	0	2	13	480	536	275	220	21	131	481	.283
Cubs	4.19	55	0	5	14	492	502	285	229	22	152	505	.262
Indians	4.24	56	0	2	9	507	473	311	239	17	201	534	.244
Padres	4.25	55	0	2	7	477	507	326	225	14	199	392	.270
Rangers	4.34	55	0	3	5	484	492	303	233	25	174	508	.259

CLUB FIELDING

	PCT	PO	A	E	DP		PCT	PO	A	E	DP
Brewers	.975	1497	606	55	56	Athletics	.955	1492	614	100	42
Giants	.965	1434	551	71	43	Reds	.954	1457	536	96	35
Rangers	.963	1451	551	77	36	Indians	.952	1521	603	108	47
Cubs	.960	1476	604	87	47	Royals	.949	1500	582	111	36
Mariners	.959	1439	574	87	57	Dodgers	.947	1460	632	117	42
Angels	.956	1498	631	99	44	Padres	.946	1430	647	118	57

INDIVIDUAL BATTING LEADERS (MINIMUM 3.1 PA/TEAM GAME)

	AVG	G	AB	R	H	2B	3B	HR	RBI	BB	SO	SB
Choi, Ji-Man, Mariners	.378	39	135	23	51	15	2	1	23	21	30	10
Gomez, Jhonny, Rangers	.369	40	141	17	52	7	2	0	20	14	28	3
Consigli, Royce, Athletics	.340	41	156	25	53	12	4	1	31	20	33	4
Shaw, Nick, Brewers	.339	48	165	34	56	13	5	0	19	37	31	14
Herrera, Odubel, Rangers	.337	48	178	33	60	7	4	0	31	16	27	8
Pan, Zhi Fang, Athletics	.331	43	157	31	52	9	4	0	11	13	24	3
Acevedo, Jean, Mariners	.329	40	155	19	51	8	2	0	14	6	31	7
Moreno, Henry, Royals	.327	45	162	32	53	22	5	4	32	16	39	0
Telis, Tomas, Rangers	.326	37	144	22	47	7	1	2	35	6	16	4
Muller, Kurtis, Reds	.317	49	189	28	60	6	2	0	22	16	24	7

INDIVIDUAL PITCHING LEADERS (MINIMUM 1 IP/TEAM GAME)

	W	L	ERA	G	GS	CG	SV	IP	H	R	ER	BB	SO
Bashara, Charly, Brewers	5	2	2.37	13	2	0	0	57	45	17	15	15	64
Liria, Luis, Cubs	2	2	2.40	12	7	0	0	45	36	16	12	12	46
Schrader, Adam, Padres	4	0	2.47	10	8	0	0	51	43	20	14	10	48
Fleet, Austin, Giants	6	3	2.65	12	11	0	0	51	42	18	15	8	65
Baez, Suammy, Angels	4	4	2.68	13	13	0	0	74	78	31	22	17	70
Yambati, Robinson, Royals	8	2	2.72	14	6	0	0	66	65	28	20	12	64
Sterling, Felix, Indians	2	3	3.17	12	11	0	0	51	40	21	18	20	57
Paez, Argenis, Athletics	6	3	3.17	14	10	0	0	66	69	29	23	17	53
Ventura, Yordano, Royals	4	2	3.28	14	6	0	0	53	49	28	19	17	58
Guillon, Ismael, Reds	3	3	3.32	12	10	0	0	57	39	26	21	23	73

ALL-STAR TEAM

C: Ji-Man Choi, Mariners. **1B:** Henry Moreno, Royals. **2B:** Nick Shaw, Brewers. **3B:** Christian Villanueva, Rangers. **SS:** Oduber Herrera, Rangers. **OF:** Royce Consigli, Athletics; Teodoro Martinez, Rangers; Kurtis Muller, Reds. **DH:** Robert Maddox, Reds. **P:** Charly Bashara, Brewers; Omar Duran, Athletics; Tyler Gatrell, Royals; Robinson Yambati, Royals.

Most Valuable Player: Ji-Man Choi, Mariners. **Manager of the Year:** Tony Diggs, Brewers.

DEPARTMENT LEADERS

BATTING

OBP	Shaw, Nick, Brewers	.471
SLG	Moreno, Henry, Royals	.599
OPS	Choi, Ji-Man, Mariners	1
R	Arias, Junior, Reds	44
H	Martinez, Teodoro, Rangers	66
TB	Maddox, Robert, Reds	104
XBH	Moreno, Henry, Royals	31
2B	Moreno, Henry, Royals	22
3B	Clarke, Chevez, Angels	7
HR	Five tied at	7
RBI	Maddox, Robert, Reds	46
SAC	Three tied at	6
BB	Shaw, Nick, Brewers	37
HBP	Muller, Kurtis, Reds	9
SO	Marte, Miguel, Athletics	73
SB	Sandford, Darian, Royals	30
CS	Four tied at	7
AB/SO	Telis, Tomas, Rangers	9

PITCHING

G	Gardner, Ryan, Indians	22
GS	Four tied at	13
GF	Gardner, Ryan, Indians	19
SV	Gatrell, Tyler, Royals	12
W	Yambati, Robinson, Royals	8
L	Morales, Alexander, Indians	8
IP	Baez, Suammy, Angels	74
H	Baez, Suammy, Angels	78
R	Morales, Alexander, Indians	45
ER	Morales, Alexander, Indians	36
HB	Reyes, Eugenio, Padres	9
BB	Herrera, Juan, Padres	30
SO	Guillon, Ismael, Reds	73
SO/9	Guillon, Ismael, Reds	11.53
SO/9 (RP)	Dunnington, Jacob, Giants	14.1
BB/9	Unsworth, Dylan, Mariners	0.18
WP	Encarnacion, Luis, Indians	14
	Morales, Alexander, Indians	14
BK	Reyes, Eugenio, Padres	3
HR	Contreras, Carlos, Reds	8
AVG	Guillon, Ismael, Reds	.193

FIELDING

C	FPCT	Staley, Joseph, Giants	.991
	PO	Monsalve, Alex, Indians	363
	A	Gonzalez, Yovan, Reds	50
	E	Monsalve, Alex, Indians	12
	DP	Staley, Joseph, Giants	4
	PB	Marquez, Alexander, Royals	16
1B	FPCT	Gomez, Jhonny, Rangers	.990
	PO	Marte, Miguel, Athletics	421
	A	Yakubik, Jerod, Angels	35
	E	Agreste, Joe, Padres	12
	DP	Marte, Miguel, Athletics	31
2B	FPCT	Willoughby, Carlos, Giants	.980
	PO	Willoughby, Carlos, Giants	73
	A	Lindsey, Taylor, Angels	136
	E	Clime, Neudy, Athletics	11
	DP	Shaw, Nick, Brewers	28
3B	FPCT	Villanueva, Christian, Rangers	.917
	PO	Villanueva, Christian, Rangers	31
	A	Villanueva, Christian, Rangers	91
	E	Bolaski, Michael, Angels	15
	DP	Geiger, Dustin, Cubs	10
		Martinez, Jose, Mariners	10
SS	FPCT	Brito, Bryan, Mariners	.957
	PO	Rivera, Yadiel, Brewers	83
	A	Rivera, Yadiel, Brewers	164
	E	Arias, Junior, Reds	25
	DP	Rivera, Yadiel, Brewers	40
OF	FPCT	Three tied at	1.000
	PO	Stokes, Mykal, Padres	103
	A	Mitchell, Gary, Angels	8
	E	Four tied at	6
	DP	Muller, Kurtis, Reds	4

MINOR LEAGUES

BY NATHAN RODE

For the second time in three years, the Phillies captured the Gulf Coast League title.

In the first round, the Phillies beat the Mets 8-4 to advance to the championship, best-of-three series. On the other side of the bracket, the Rays defeated the Marlins 1-0.

The Rays took the first game of the championships series 4-1, but the Phillies bounced back to win the next two contests, 6-3 and 10-4, to win the 2010 title.

A Nationals outfielder won the batting title in 2009—Eury Perez hit .381—and in 2010 the batting title once again went to an outfielder in Washington's system. Randolph Oduber hit .366 in 153 at-bats, besting Yankees outfielder Ramon Flores (.329) by 27 points.

Third basemen Erica Avila (Pirates) and Roberto De La Cruz (Cardinals) tied for the home run lead with seven.

Talented position players ran deep in the GCL in 2010. Just three pitchers made the Top 20 Prospects list, including none in the top five. Mets lefthander Juan Urbina checked in as the top arm at No. 6. While 2009 was heavy with international signees, the 2010 edition was more balanced with several draft picks making their mark.

The Blue Jays led all teams with four players on the list, two from the 2009 draft who earned a promotion partway through the summer—outfielder Jake Marisnick and first baseman K.C. Hobson—while 2010 draftees Kellen Sweeney and Christopher Hawkins accrued enough playing time to qualify. Toronto could have easily had six make it as righthanders Noah Syndergaard and Aaron Sanchez, taken in the first and supplemen-

tal first-round this year, performed well and have upside, but fell just short of the minimum innings requirement.

Competition for a spot on this list also proves difficult because there are 15 teams in the league. Good prospects and high-profile signings can be left out because they struggled and didn't live up to expectations.

Niko Goodrum has a plus-plus arm and is an above-average runner, helping him become a second-round pick of the Twins this year. But he didn't play his way onto the list after hitting .161/.219/.195 in 118 at-bats.

Cardinals third baseman Roberto de la Cruz, who signed for $1.1 million in 2008, experienced similar struggles. He showed impressive power in his second GCL stint, but still doesn't make enough contact. He batted .241/.291/.432 and barely missed the cut.

TOP 20 PROSPECTS

1. Gary Sanchez, c, Yankees
2. Miguel Sano, 3b/ss, Twins
3. Justin O'Conner, c, Rays
4. Jake Marisnick, of, Blue Jays
5. Matt Lipka, ss, Braves
6. Juan Urbina, lhp, Mets
7. Jesse Biddle, lhp, Phillies
8. Aaron Altherr, of, Phillies
9. Max Kepler, of, Twins
10. Cito Culver, ss, Yankees
11. Luke Bailey, c, Rays
12. Kellen Sweeney, 3b, Blue Jays
13. Ramon Flores, 1b/of, Yankees
14. K.C. Hobson, 1b, Blue Jays
15. Bruce Rondon, rhp, Tigers
16. Keury de la Cruz, of, Red Sox
17. Christopher Hawkins, 3b, Blue Jays
18. Ryan Brett, 2b, Rays
19. Henry Ramos, of, Red Sox
20. Dixon Machado, ss, Tigers

STANDINGS

NORTHERN DIVISION	Organization	W	L	PCT	GB	Manager(s)	Last Penn.
Phillies	Clearwater	32	24	.571	—	Rolando de Armas	2010
Blue Jays	Dunedin	31	28	.525	2 ½	John Schneider	Never
Tigers	Lakeland	30	28	.517	3	Basilio Cabrera	Never
Pirates	Bradenton	29	30	.492	4 ½	Tom Prince	Never
Braves	Kissimmee	27	31	.466	6	Luis Ortiz	2003
Yankees	Tampa	24	32	.429	8	Tom Slater	2007
EASTERN DIVISION	Organization	W	L	PCT	GB	Manager(s)	Last Penn.
Marlins	Jupiter	37	19	.661	—	Jorge Hernandez	Never
Mets	Port St. Lucie	31	25	.554	6	Sandy Alomar	Never
Cardinals	Jupiter	28	28	.500	9	Steve Turco	Never
Nationals	Viera	24	32	.429	13	Bobby Williams	2009
Astros	Kissimmee	20	36	.357	17	Omar Lopez	Never
SOUTHERN DIVISION	Organization	W	L	PCT	GB	Manager(s)	Last Penn.
Rays	Port Charlotte	34	26	.567	—	Joe Alvarez	Never
Red Sox	Fort Myers	31	28	.525	2 ½	Dave Tomlin	2006
Twins	Fort Myers	29	31	.483	5	C. Heintz/R. Borrego	Never
Orioles	Sarasota	25	34	.424	8 ½	Ramon Sambo	Never

PLAYOFFS—Semifinals: Phillies defeated Mets and Rays defeated Marlins in one-game playoffs. **Finals:** Phillies defeated Rays 2-1 in best-of-three series.

CLUB BATTING

	AVG	G	AB	R	H	2B	3B	HR	RBI	BB	SO	SB	OBP	SLG
Nationals	.266	56	1895	292	505	106	18	18	257	194	404	76	.343	.370
Phillies	.262	56	1883	269	494	110	17	23	245	172	373	57	.337	.375
Yankees	.258	56	1876	275	484	88	15	36	242	184	446	69	.332	.378
Red Sox	.254	59	1939	295	492	92	24	38	250	193	482	89	.333	.385
Marlins	.253	56	1768	264	447	79	16	14	227	180	367	43	.331	.339
Mets	.248	56	1810	248	448	94	17	25	195	151	400	51	.321	.360
Braves	.247	58	1891	262	467	78	19	33	228	164	394	74	.319	.361
Twins	.247	60	1983	248	490	108	9	17	201	173	441	67	.312	.336
Cardinals	.244	56	1834	262	448	80	15	25	219	198	432	52	.336	.345
Tigers	.243	58	1858	197	452	78	17	17	177	132	498	46	.301	.331
Pirates	.242	59	1891	270	458	93	16	28	230	178	416	98	.319	.353
Blue Jays	.238	59	1867	224	444	97	19	34	200	171	490	60	.313	.365
Orioles	.238	59	1967	225	469	85	12	12	199	161	405	43	.306	.312
Astros	.232	56	1876	216	436	74	20	11	188	162	437	55	.305	.311
Rays	.228	60	1967	242	449	80	18	20	203	196	493	74	.309	.318

CLUB PITCHING

	ERA	G	CG	SHO	SV	IP	H	R	ER	HR	BB	SO	AVG
Marlins	2.50	56	2	11	15	476	386	172	132	5	162	417	.220
Blue Jays	3.14	59	0	5	14	495	450	215	173	22	163	449	.242
Orioles	3.14	59	0	5	11	517	441	244	180	20	214	500	.229
Tigers	3.17	58	3	11	19	499	422	209	176	19	140	487	.228
Twins	3.41	60	3	3	11	515	472	245	195	24	181	456	.244
Red Sox	3.42	59	0	2	19	510	487	272	194	22	148	439	.249
Phillies	3.44	56	2	4	16	486	448	219	186	23	171	445	.244
Rays	3.44	60	0	6	20	536	500	249	205	21	180	426	.246
Mets	3.51	56	1	2	19	477	445	236	186	15	169	360	.247
Cardinals	3.73	56	0	5	10	478	443	259	198	25	183	436	.246
Yankees	4.03	56	0	1	8	485	442	301	217	24	214	470	.237
Pirates	4.26	59	0	1	13	501	513	280	237	51	170	370	.262
Nationals	4.29	56	1	1	7	483	483	295	230	30	167	412	.258
Braves	4.36	58	0	6	9	489	524	273	237	32	143	396	.276
Astros	4.38	56	2	1	15	491	527	320	239	18	204	415	.270

CLUB FIELDING

	PCT	PO	A	E	DP		PCT	PO	A	E	DP
Blue Jays	.973	1486	564	57	44	Cardinals	.961	1434	584	82	45
Phillies	.971	1458	598	61	44	Mets	.960	1431	568	84	49
Marlins	.970	1427	613	64	44	Rays	.956	1609	725	107	49
Braves	.968	1468	584	67	38	Red Sox	.951	1531	598	109	51
Tigers	.968	1498	551	68	37	Nationals	.950	1449	613	108	47
Pirates	.967	1503	618	73	53	Astros	.940	1474	643	135	50
Twins	.963	1546	606	82	50	Yankees	.938	1455	556	132	41
Orioles	.962	1550	618	85	43						

INDIVIDUAL BATTING LEADERS *(MINIMUM 3.1 PA/TEAM GAME)*

	AVG	G	AB	R	H	2B	3B	HR	RBI	BB	SO	SB
Oduber, Randolph, Nationals	.366	39	153	38	56	13	3	4	30	13	38	18
Flores, Ramon, Yankees	.329	43	158	33	52	10	4	2	22	28	22	4
Murray, Patrick, Phillies	.313	52	192	27	60	15	0	2	26	17	33	4
McConkey, Brian, Marlins	.304	53	181	24	55	14	2	1	30	21	25	1
Lipka, Matt, Braves	.302	48	192	33	58	8	4	1	24	14	22	20
Scott, Jordan, Astros	.301	42	146	19	44	6	2	0	10	14	33	6
Pimentel, Luis, Cardinals	.301	46	153	23	46	8	0	3	29	10	27	1
Sosa, Junior, Pirates	.296	44	142	29	42	3	0	1	11	18	20	20
Serrata, Martin, Orioles	.295	42	156	19	46	5	1	0	10	10	24	7
Rosario, Eddie, Twins	.294	51	194	34	57	9	2	5	26	16	28	22

INDIVIDUAL PITCHING LEADERS *(MINIMUM 1 IP/TEAM GAME)*

	W	L	ERA	G	GS	CG	SV	IP	H	R	ER	BB	SO
Ferguson, Douglas, Orioles	4	3	1.09	12	8	0	1	58	40	13	7	14	44
Alfonso, Orlando, Orioles	6	1	1.58	12	8	0	0	52	48	13	9	11	34
Perdomo, Jose, Astros	4	3	1.68	11	11	0	0	59	38	19	11	20	69
Adrian, Yancorix, Orioles	3	2	2.14	12	7	0	0	59	44	25	14	21	52
Parker, Justin, Twins	6	2	2.24	12	12	0	0	61	63	19	15	16	42
Silvestre, Pedro, Rays	6	0	2.29	13	5	0	1	51	49	16	13	15	32
Velette, Raynel, Red Sox	5	2	2.56	12	2	0	1	50	34	21	14	11	45
Jimenez, Enrico, Orioles	2	2	2.68	12	8	0	0	57	45	24	17	25	72
Deminsky, David, Twins	3	3	2.71	10	8	1	0	53	45	19	16	8	51
Palacios, Wilsen, Tigers	4	4	2.80	11	11	1	0	61	52	20	19	11	58

ALL-STAR TEAM

C: Gary Sanchez, Yankees. **1B:** Kenny Vargas, Twins. **2B:** Anderson Feliz, Yankees. **3B:** Eric Avila, Pirates. **SS:** Matt Lipka, Braves. **OF:** Ramon Flores, Yankees; Geancarlo Mendez, Phillies; Randolph Oduber, Nationals. **DH:** Chris Duffy, Phillies. **SP:** Jose Perdomo, Astros. **RP:** Bruce Rondon, Tigers. **Most Valuable Player:** Randolph Oduber, Nationals. **Manager of the Year:** Jorge Hernandez, Marlins.

DEPARTMENT LEADERS

BATTING

OBP	Flores, Ramon, Yankees	.436
SLG	Oduber, Randolph, Nationals	.569
OPS	Oduber, Randolph, Nationals	1.002
R	Yoder, Luke, Red Sox	43
H	Murray, Patrick, Phillies	60
TB	De La Cruz, Keury, Red Sox	94
XBH	Mendez, Geancarlo, Phillies	25
2B	Sanchez, Alexander, Mets	16
3B	De La Cruz, Keury, Red Sox	7
HR	Avila, Eric, Pirates	7
	De La Cruz, Roberto, Cardinals	7
RBI	Mendez, Geancarlo, Phillies	40
SAC	Mendoza, Pedro, Marlins	7
	Perez, Roberto, Nationals	7
BB	Duffy, Christopher, Phillies	29
	Tuivailala, Samuel, Cardinals	29
HBP	Yoder, Luke, Red Sox	12
SO	Aguasvivas, Juaner, Tigers	66
SB	Rosario, Eddie, Twins	22
CS	Feliz, Anderson, Yankees	7
AB/SO	Mendoza, Pedro, Marlins	11.35

PITCHING

G	De La Cruz, Manuel, Cardinals	28
GS	Four tied at	12
GF	De La Cruz, Manuel, Cardinals	22
	Rondon, Bruce, Tigers	22
SV	Rondon, Bruce, Tigers	15
W	Five tied at	6
L	Three tied at	7
IP	Ciurcina, Cesar, Twins	65
H	Del Rio, Danilo, Astros	72
R	Del Rio, Danilo, Astros	46
ER	Del Rio, Danilo, Astros	36
HB	Manzueta, Jheyson, Marlins	13
BB	Montero, Joan, Pirates	31
SO	Jimenez, Enrico, Orioles	72
SO/9	Jimenez, Enrico, Orioles	11.37
SO/9 (RP)	Barnes, Daniel, Blue Jays	12.3
BB/9	Ciurcina, Cesar, Twins	1.11
WP	Reyes, Robinson, Rays	14
BK	Uribe, Adriano, Cardinals	5
HR	Rodriguez, Joely, Pirates	10
AVG	Perdomo, Jose, Astros	.172

FIELDING

C	FPCT	Rankin, Pierce, Blue Jays	.994
	PO	Rankin, Pierce, Blue Jays	297
	A	Five tied at	31
	E	Liccien, Jhorge, Yankees	7
		Sanchez, Gary, Yankees	7
	DP	Perez, Oscar, Red Sox	5
	PB	Rankin, Pierce, Blue Jays	14
		Sanchez, Gary, Yankees	14
1B	FPCT	Sanchez, Alexander, Mets	.995
	PO	Aguasvivas, Juaner, Tigers	387
	A	McCrann, Ryan, Rays	31
	E	McCrann, Ryan, Rays	12
	DP	Sanchez, Alexander, Mets	33
2B	FPCT	Payton, Matthew, Phillies	.977
	PO	Magee, Joshua, Astros	89
	A	Thompson, Jason, Red Sox	114
	E	Thompson, Jason, Red Sox	12
	DP	Thompson, Jason, Red Sox	25
3B	FPCT	Meneses, Heiker, Red Sox	.949
	PO	Franco, Maikel, Phillies	50
	A	Avila, Eric, Pirates	116
	E	Kuo, Fu-Lin, Yankees	16
	DP	Avila, Eric, Pirates	13
SS	FPCT	Pena, Gari, Blue Jays	.973
	PO	Fernandez, Jose, Astros	87
	A	Fernandez, Jose, Astros	146
	E	Fernandez, Jose, Astros	32
	DP	Fernandez, Jose, Astros	28
OF	FPCT	Four tied at	1.000
	PO	Gomez, Gilbert, Mets	112
	A	Montilla, Angelberth, Nationals	6
		Ramos, Steven, Cardinals	6
	E	Vargas, Jose, Astros	10
	DP	Polanco, Gregory, Pirates	4

MINOR LEAGUES

BY BEN BADLER
DOMINICAN SUMMER LEAGUE

In a matchup that featured two of the Dominican Summer League's best offenses, the Giants defeated the Reds 3-1 in the championship series.

While the Reds ranked fourth in the DSL in runs scored, the Giants' balance of offense and defense (they ranked second in runs scored and eighth in runs allowed) propelled them to 7-0, 8-5, and 3-1 victories in the championship round. The Cubs finished with the regular season's best record but fell to the Reds in the semifinals.

Cardinals righthander Carlos Martinez used his mid-90s fastball to lead the league in ERA (0.76) and strikeouts per nine innings (11.9). Nationals shortstop Carlos Alvarez, formerly known as Esmailyn Gonzalez when he lied about his age to sign for $1.4 million with the Nationals in 2006, hit .307/.432/.470 to lead the league in on-base percentage, while Yankees outfielder Yeicok Calderon hit .339/.439/.551 to lead the league in slugging.

DSL STANDINGS

BOCA CHICA NORTH	W	L	PCT	GB
Mets2	43	29	.597	—
Rays	42	30	.583	1
Dodgers	40	31	.563	2½
Pirates	37	34	.521	5½
Indians	37	35	.514	6
Red Sox	37	35	.514	6
Royals	35	35	.500	7
Yankees2	28	44	.389	15
Astros	26	43	.377	15½

BOCA CHICA SOUTH	W	L	PCT	GB
Giants	46	25	.648	—
Yankees1	44	27	.620	2
Phillies	43	29	.597	3½
Mets1	39	32	.549	7
Nationals	36	35	.507	10
Marlins	28	41	.406	17
Orioles2	28	42	.400	17½
Cubs2	19	52	.268	27

VENEZUELAN SUMMER LEAGUE

The Pirates allowed fewer runs than any other team in the Venezuelan Summer League, but it was their lineup that made the loudest noise in the league's final game.

After finishing the regular season with the league's best record, the Pirates blasted the Mariners 21-2 in the decisive third game of the championship series.

Reds infielder Ronald Torreyes, 17, hit .390/.468/.606 to lead the league in average and slugging while ranking second in on-base percentage and third in stolen bases (23). The Reds also had the league's leader in ERA, as 17-year-old lefthander Luis Gonzalez had a 2.49 mark in 65 innings while ranking second in strikeouts per nine innings (6.1) and walks per nine (1.9).

SANTO DOMINGO

NORTH	W	L	PCT	GB
Mariners	43	28	.606	—
Cardinals	39	32	.549	4
Athletics	32	39	.451	11
Brewers	28	43	.394	15

BOCA CHICA

BASEBALL CITY	W	L	PCT	GB
Cubs1	51	21	.708	—
Reds	45	27	.625	6
White Sox	40	32	.556	11
Rockies	37	35	.514	14
Diamondbacks	34	38	.472	17
Twins	29	42	.408	21½
Padres	25	45	.357	25
Orioles1	25	46	.352	25½

SAN PEDRO DE MACORIS

DE MACORIS	W	L	PCT	GB
Rangers	42	23	.646	—
Angels	37	28	.569	5
Braves	36	29	.554	6
Blue Jays	23	42	.354	19
Tigers	20	45	.308	22

INDIVIDUAL BATTING LEADERS
(Minimum 2.7 Plate Appearances Per League Game)

	AVG	G	AB	R	H	2B	3B	HR	RHI	BB	SO	SB
Alberto, Hanser, Rangers	.358	50	179	25	64	15	2	0	24	6	9	16
Gonzalez, Samuel, Pirates	.349	65	235	33	82	17	5	3	45	14	19	5
Sanchez, Carlos, Reds	.348	71	244	40	85	13	4	3	44	35	21	14
Gonzalez, Erik, Indians	.346	64	240	38	83	18	1	1	27	14	19	9
Calderon, Yeicok, Yankees1	.339	69	245	40	83	16	6	8	44	43	56	5
Bonifacio, Jorge, Royals	.335	48	164	22	55	16	2	1	28	26	27	13
Puentes, Jerry, White Sox	.330	56	188	31	62	6	1	0	22	18	31	8
Hanson, Alen, Pirates	.324	68	244	48	79	10	7	2	28	22	37	20
Polo, Rafael, Yankees2	.323	63	248	43	80	17	9	1	30	12	29	6
Santana, Ravel, Yankees2	.322	63	199	46	64	10	1	10	38	35	38	22

INDIVIDUAL PITCHING LEADERS
(Minimum 0.8 Innings Per League Game)

	W	L	ERA	G	GS	CG	SV	IP	H	R	BB	SO
Matias, Carlos, Cardinals	3	2	0.76	12	12	1	0	59	28	8	14	78
Perez, Henry, Mariners	7	1	0.86	11	11	3	0	73	49	7	10	76
Aquino, Jayson, Rockies	4	3	1.03	12	12	2	0	62	35	10	9	59
Duque, Jean, White Sox	3	3	1.21	14	13	1	0	74	50	23	27	82
Arias, Gabirel, Phillies	4	2	1.23	14	10	2	0	74	62	19	6	67
Sierra, Adrian, Phillies	3	4	1.24	15	13	1	0	88	65	16	25	66
Brazoban, Jose, Royals	4	1	1.3	14	14	0	0	69	45	15	26	49
Garcia, Elvin, Braves	5	1	1.35	23	4	0	2	61	57	11	5	27
Bonilla, Sterling, Twins	4	2	1.36	14	13	2	0	66	43	19	14	40
Espinosa, Abraham, Braves	5	3	1.41	14	12	1	0	70	60	21	11	54
Perez, David, Rangers	4	4	1.41	14	14	0	0	70	50	20	8	68

	W	L	PCT	GB			W	L	PCT	GB
Pirates	48	20	.706	—		Phillies	32	36	.471	16
Mariners	45	26	.634	4½		Cardinals	22	45	.328	25½
Rays	37	33	.529	12		Tigers	20	46	.303	27
Reds	35	33	.515	13						

INDIVIDUAL BATTING LEADERS
(Minimum 2.7 Plate Appearances Per League Game)

	AVG	G	AB	R	H	2B	3B	HR	RHI	BB	SO	SB
Torreyes, Ronald, Reds	.390	67	241	56	94	20	10	4	33	23	11	23
Hernandez, Nahum, Rays	.380	50	166	35	63	14	2	4	26	28	27	11
Salas, Roan, Rays	.345	60	220	35	76	16	2	5	42	23	24	3
Burin, Felipe, Mariners	.335	58	182	41	61	13	0	2	22	40	18	4
Ramirez, Ivan, Mariners	.330	65	227	32	75	14	0	0	29	27	23	0
Valera, Breyvil, Cardinals	.325	60	212	40	69	16	6	1	22	24	15	10
Astudillo, Willians, Phillies	.312	56	186	24	58	14	1	0	24	13	4	9
Aponte, Francisco, Pirates	.311	63	180	45	56	9	0	0	20	40	24	28
Suarez, Eugenio, Tigers	.311	61	225	32	70	12	2	1	18	23	44	8
Velasquez, Roberto, Mariners	.301	63	166	26	50	10	0	0	21	16	14	4

INDIVIDUAL PITCHING LEADERS
(Minimum 0.8 Innings Per League Game)

	W	L	ERA	G	GS	CG	SV	IP	H	R	BB	SO
Gonzalez, Luis, Reds	3	2	2.49	12	12	1	0	65	49	23	14	44
Vilchez, Francisco, Pirates	6	2	2.53	15	12	0	0	64	54	23	15	39
Romero, Franderlin, Reds	3	6	2.65	13	12	1	0	68	68	40	23	43
Raga, Angel, Mariners	4	2	2.78	13	8	0	1	59	56	19	15	51
Echarry, Eli, Rays	4	3	3.20	13	10	0	0	59	45	24	19	59
Bastidas, Leonel, Phillies	4	4	3.82	14	9	0	0	66	69	40	16	45
Ulacio, Ramon, Cardinals	2	6	3.86	13	13	0	0	63	64	34	10	38
Mieres, Oswaldo, Reds	7	2	3.86	14	14	0	0	73	60	37	23	61
Yendis, Luis, Rays	3	3	4.12	14	14	0	0	61	71	34	17	23

BY BILL MITCHELL

PHOENIX

As usual, the bulk of the better prospects in the Arizona Fall League were hitters, as most major league organizations shut down their best pitchers after a full regular season.

To qualify for the AFL Top 10 Prospects list, a player must have had a minimum of 32 plate appearances or pitched 10⅔ innings.

1. BRYCE HARPER, OF, NATIONALS: Joining the Scottsdale Scorpions just after his 18th birthday, the 2010 No. 1 overall draft pick quickly proved that he was not overmatched by older competition. Harper hit .343/.410/.629 with six of his 12 hits going for extra bases. He showed plus-plus power in batting practice and in games, with an ability to hit to the opposite field.

He was susceptible to good curveballs but showed an ability to make adjustments. He attacks the ball and at times his swing was overly aggressive. Harper showed good routes to fly balls and a plus arm in the outfield

2. DUSTIN ACKLEY, 2B, MARINERS: Ackley put together one of the best seasons in AFL history, batting .424/.581/.758 and breaking the single season on-base percentage record of .537 set by Ken Harvey in 2002. The power that many observers were waiting to see since his pro debut in the AFL in 2009 was on display this fall.

His second-base defense is still a work in progress but improving as he completes his first season at the position.

3. ERIC HOSMER, 1B, ROYALS: Hosmer was late arriving in Arizona due to his time with Team USA in the Pan Am Games qualifying tournament in Puerto Rico. His disappointing batting line (.203/.284/.291) in the AFL was due mostly to fatigue from the long season. Hosmer was making consistent contact but not driving the ball as well as in the regular season. However, he still controlled the strike zone, and there were no problems with his defense.

4. BRANDON BELT, 1B, GIANTS: Belt's surprising performance in his first pro season continued in the AFL as the lefthanded hitter batted .372/.427/.616 for Scottsdale. He showed impressive power to all fields and plus defense. His makeup and approach are off the charts, and one scout praised Belt for his even-keeled personality.

5. MIKE MONTGOMERY, LHP, ROYALS: Montgomery, 21, was making up for time lost to a sore elbow during the 2010 season. His fastball was generally in the 91-95 mph range with downhill

plane, and he used a sharp-breaking curveball and solid changeup. While his numbers weren't anything special (6.10 ERA, .310 OBA), he struck out 11 and walked just two.

6. MANNY BANUELOS, LHP, YANKEES: Banuelos, 19, was limited to 15 starts in 2010 due to an early season appendectomy, but was impressive in seven AFL games. He gave up one run in his last nine innings, and ended with a 3.60 ERA. Despite his 5-foot-10, 155-pound size, the lefty from Mexico has a fastball up to 95 mph as well as a plus changeup and a good curveball.

7. DEREK NORRIS, C, NATIONALS: Norris, 21, spent 2010 at high Class A Potomac but wasn't intimidated by more experienced pitchers in Arizona. He hit .278/.403/.667 with four homers and 19 RBIs. He drew 11 walks in 54 at-bats.

Most of the questions on Norris' future revolve around his abilities behind the plate. His defense in Arizona was better than advertised, as he showed soft hands and a strong arm; he primarily needs to improve his release times on throws to second base.

8. CASEY KELLY, RHP, RED SOX: Kelly was in the AFL last year as a shortstop after spending the 2009 season after splitting time between the mound and infield. He was strictly a pitcher in 2010 and returned to Arizona in that role.

Kelly pitched just four times in the AFL before the Red Sox shut him down for the year. He yielded only one earned run in nine innings over his first two starts before a bad third outing inflated his ERA. He finished the season 1-0, 6.75.

His fastball was in the 93-94 mph range and he mixed in a good changeup and curveball with a compact delivery.

9. DEVIN MESORACO, C, REDS: Mesoraco, 22, finally showed the promise expected of a first-round choice in his fourth pro season, batting .302/.377/.587 at three levels during the 2010 season. While his numbers in Arizona (.242/.250/.455) were only fair, he at times flashed his offensive potential and raw power.

Mesoraco's defense drew mixed reviews from scouts, and his deficiencies in catching may have been due to fatigue that often affects AFL catchers.

10. JASON KIPNIS, 2B, INDIANS: Scouts described the lefthanded-hitting Kipnis as "hard-nosed" and "blue collar." He shows a natural feel for second base in his first season at the position. He's an aggressive contact hitter with gap power and the ability to also drive the ball out of the park. He tied for the AFL lead in doubles (11).

MINOR LEAGUES

STANDINGS

EAST	W	L	PCT	GB	WEST	W	L	PCT	GB
Scottsdale Scorpions	20	12	.625	—	Peoria Javelinas	20	10	.667	—
Mesa Solar Sox	13	17	.433	6	Surprise Rafters	17	12	.586	2½
Phoenix Desert Dogs	11	17	.393	7	Peoria Saguaros	9	22	.290	11½

INDIVIDUAL BATTING LEADERS
(MINIMUM 2.0 PA/LEAGUE GAMES)

BATTER	AVG	G	AB	R	H	HR	RBI
Ackley, Dustin, Javelinas	.424	20	66	28	28	4	19
Linares, Juan Carlos, Javelinas	.397	17	68	17	27	3	14
McDade, Mike, Javelinas	.375	22	88	22	33	1	12
Belt, Brandon, Scottsdale	.372	22	86	16	32	1	16
Phelps, Cord, Javelinas	.367	19	79	16	29	3	10
Culberson, Charlie, Scottsdale	.366	21	93	21	34	2	16
Valdespin, Jordany, Mesa	.355	19	76	19	27	1	11
Farris, Eric, Surprise	.351	17	74	16	26	0	8
Parrino, Andy, Saguaros	.349	20	63	12	22	0	4
Moore, Jeremy, Mesa	.343	17	70	15	24	2	15

INDIVIDUAL PITCHING LEADERS
(MINIMUM 0.4 IP/LEAGUE GAMES)

PITCHER	W	L	ERA	IP	H	BB	SO
Rzepczynski, Marc, Javelinas	4	0	1.16	31	24	9	27
Schenk, Neil, Saguaros	1	0	1.72	16	14	6	5
Hurley, Eric, Surprise	3	0	1.82	25	16	9	14
Pribanic, Aaron, Mesa	0	1	2.00	18	18	6	9
Carr, Adam, Scottsdale	1	0	2.08	13	6	3	8
Egan, pat, Scottsdale	0	1	2.13	13	11	3	7
Greenwalt, Kyle, Javelinas	2	0	2.35	15	15	3	10
Verdugo, Ryan, Scottsdale	4	1	2.45	22	20	16	26
Heyer, Craig, Phoenix	1	2	2.50	18	16	3	7
Sisk, Brandon, Surprise	0	0	2.51	14	9	3	11

MESA SOLAR SOX

BATTERS	AVG	AB	R	H	2B	3B	HR	RBI	BB	SO	SB
* Flaherty, Ryan, of	.268	82	13	22	3	0	0	5	12	14	1
Gronauer, Kai, c	.222	45	3	10	3	1	0	8	4	5	0
Harrison, Josh, 2b	.330	91	19	30	10	2	1	8	10	12	6
* Jackson, Brett, of	.250	12	3	3	1	0	0	5	1	5	1
Kennelly, Tim, of	.293	41	8	12	4	0	0	4	3	7	0
* Lambo, Andrew, of	.274	106	19	29	8	0	4	23	7	22	0
Mayberry, John, of	.000	2	0	0	0	0	0	0	0	0	0
Mercer, Jordy, ss	.267	75	10	20	4	0	1	13	6	14	1
* Moore, Jeremy, of	.343	70	15	24	4	2	2	15	8	14	8
* Nieuwenhuis, Kirk, of	.256	90	14	23	6	1	1	12	12	25	2
* Rizzotti, Matt, 1b	.333	63	7	21	2	0	0	12	12	15	0
# Romine, Andrew, ss	.233	86	15	20	3	0	0	3	9	17	5
Sanchez, Tony, c	.206	68	11	14	1	0	4	9	7	21	0
Satin, Josh, 1b	.390	41	4	16	2	0	1	6	6	13	0
# Tolisano, John, of	.417	24	4	10	2	0	1	9	8	3	1
* Valdespin, Jordany, 2b	.355	76	19	27	3	1	1	11	4	12	7
Vitters, Josh, 3b	.253	83	14	21	6	0	2	13	7	12	5
Wood, Brandon, 3b	.341	88	15	30	5	1	2	20	7	16	0

PITCHERS	W	L	ERA	G	GS	SV	IP	H	BB	SO	AVG
Brasier, Ryan	0	0	3.95	10	1	0	14	13	6	14	.241
Brummett, Tyson	1	1	3.79	10	3	0	19	21	2	13	.276
Cales, David	0	1	1.80	9	0	0	10	9	4	8	.231
Carpenter, Chris	0	1	5.52	10	0	0	15	16	9	14	.281
Carr, Nicholas	0	1	5.06	10	0	0	16	18	12	10	.265
* Carson, Robert	1	2	7.71	6	6	0	19	27	5	14	.351
De Fratus, Justin	0	0	0.00	7	0	1	7	3	3	11	.125
* Diekman, Jacob	0	0	29.45	5	0	0	4	14	4	3	.583
* Fish, Robert	0	2	10.45	11	0	1	10	17	5	11	.378
Geltz, Steven	0	0	3.86	11	0	0	12	11	5	15	.239
Holt, Brad	2	1	2.92	5	4	0	12	10	9	13	.222
Kissock, Chris	1	0	2.38	10	1	1	11	11	2	5	.268
Leach, Brian	0	0	0.00	10	0	0	11	7	7	7	.268
McKiernan, Eddie	0	1	5.23	10	0	1	10	11	6	9	.256
Muyco, Jake	0	3	10.48	7	7	0	22	39	11	11	.406
* Niesen, Eric	1	0	5.40	11	0	0	12	17	4	8	.309
Pribanic, Aaron	0	1	2.00	11	0	0	18	18	6	9	.254
Rosenberg, B.J.	1	0	8.53	10	0	0	13	18	8	10	.333
Smit, Kyle	3	2	4.05	10	0	0	13	13	8	8	.255

BATTERS	AVG	AB	R	H	2B	3B	HR	RBI	BB	SO	SB
* Wilson, Justin	0	1	4.41	6	6	0	16	19	8	16	.279
Zeid, Josh	3	0	3.86	4	4	0	14	11	1	12	.204

PEORIA JAVELINAS

BATTERS	AVG	AB	R	H	2B	3B	HR	RBI	BB	SO	SB
Abraham, Adam, c	.222	36	7	8	1	1	0	3	9	8	0
* Ackley, Dustin, 2b	.424	66	28	28	10	0	4	19	26	11	5
* Austin, Jay, of	.156	45	3	7	0	0	0	7	7	9	2
Barnes, Brandon, of	.250	80	14	20	2	2	4	18	4	21	2
Clemens, Koby, 1b	.288	80	17	23	6	1	2	13	6	23	1
Hechavarria, Adeiny, ss	.000	4	0	0	0	0	0	1	0	1	0
Iglesias, Jose, ss	.269	67	7	18	1	0	0	8	2	7	4
* Kipnis, Jason, 2b	.295	78	13	23	11	3	3	19	5	9	2
Lavarnway, Ryan, c	.268	82	15	22	3	0	3	12	16	16	0
Lawson, Matt, ss	.286	63	10	18	1	0	1	7	6	21	1
Linares, Juan Carlos, of	.397	68	17	27	7	1	3	14	1	7	2
* Loewen, Adam, of	.333	54	15	18	3	0	5	19	10	13	2
# McDade, Mike, 1b	.375	88	22	33	11	1	1	12	11	13	0
Perez, Roberto, c	.159	44	3	7	2	0	0	5	3	11	0
# Phelps, Cord, 3b	.367	79	16	29	4	1	3	10	16	14	4
* Shuck, J.B., of	.350	20	7	7	1	0	1	3	1	2	2
* Tenbrink, Nate, of	.298	84	16	25	8	0	2	16	11	15	4
* Thames, Eric, of	.264	87	15	23	7	0	3	16	14	24	3

PITCHERS	W	L	ERA	G	GS	SV	IP	H	BB	SO	AVG
* Barnes, Scott	4	1	3.65	7	7	0	25	23	7	28	.250
* Berger, Eric	0	0	0.82	9	0	0	11	7	8	12	.171
Carpenter, David	0	0	5.14	6	0	1	7	10	4	10	.323
Cleto, Maikel	2	1	7.91	6	6	0	19	31	13	14	.365
Daly, Matt	0	1	8.74	10	0	1	11	12	8	5	.279
Farina, Alan	0	0	0.87	10	0	1	10	8	1	8	.216
Farquhar, Danny	1	0	4.50	9	0	0	18	12	6	12	.211
Fields, Josh	1	1	3.09	9	0	0	12	11	5	8	.239
Garrison, Seth	0	1	6.23	10	1	0	13	18	11	15	.333
Greenwalt, Kyle	2	0	2.35	5	5	0	15	10	3	10	.259
Kelly, Casey	1	0	6.75	4	4	0	16	19	4	11	.260
Lee, Chen	0	1	9.00	6	0	0	6	7	3	7	.280
Lueke, Josh	0	0	0.79	10	0	2	11	7	3	12	.175
Nevarez, Matt	0	0	8.10	7	0	1	7	11	2	3	.355
Portice, Eammon	3	1	6.57	6	3	0	12	11	6	8	.239
Price, Bryan	0	0	5.40	9	0	0	12	13	6	3	.277
Rice, Jason	0	0	3.86	9	0	0	12	17	3	13	.321
* Rzepczynski, Marc	4	0	1.16	9	9	0	31	24	9	27	.214
Turek, Travis	0	0	5.40	7	0	0	8	10	3	3	.294
Turpen, Daniel	0	1	5.40	10	0	1	12	15	6	10	.326
* Urckfitz, Pat	1	0	3.86	9	0	0	12	10	4	8	.227
Wilhelmsen, Tom	1	1	5.25	10	0	1	12	11	6	15	.229

PEORIA SAGUAROS

BATTERS	AVG	AB	R	H	2B	3B	HR	RBI	BB	SO	SB
* Anderson, Leslie, of	.255	94	13	24	4	0	2	15	4	14	1
Benson, Joe, of	.236	55	9	13	6	0	1	5	3	16	1
Bour, Jason, c	.273	22	3	6	4	0	0	1	1	5	0
# Escobar, Eduardo, ss	.300	110	22	33	4	5	4	15	9	14	2
* Figueroa, Cole, 2b	.290	31	3	9	1	0	0	2	7	4	0
Martinez, Luis, c	.361	36	7	13	0	1	0	3	3	6	0
Mesoraco, Devin, c	.242	66	7	16	6	1	2	11	1	15	0
* Mitchell, Jared, of	.163	80	5	13	1	1	0	2	8	27	2
Negron, Kris, 2b	.296	81	14	24	4	4	4	16	8	24	0
* Parmelee, Chris, 1b	.339	109	16	37	11	2	0	13	12	17	0
# Parrino, Andy, 3b	.349	63	12	22	7	0	0	4	9	21	0
* Revere, Ben, of	.295	112	20	33	2	1	0	9	11	12	13
Ruiz, Jose, ss	.323	96	7	31	3	1	0	11	5	24	0
Sappelt, Dave, of	.292	72	9	21	2	0	0	10	3	11	0
Wrigley, Henry, 3b	.183	82	7	15	4	0	3	19	3	24	0

PITCHERS	W	L	ERA	G	GS	SV	IP	H	BB	SO	AVG
Avery, James	0	0	7.04	9	2	0	15	21	7	10	.318
Brach, Brad	1	1	2.84	11	0	1	13	8	3	4	.174
Bromberg, David	0	2	6.75	6	6	0	23	34	7	25	.347
Carter, Anthony	0	0	3.60	10	0	3	10	9	0	16	.237
Cobb, Alex	1	3	6.12	7	7	0	25	31	14	30	.304
Davis, Erik	1	3	6.48	6	6	0	17	28	9	14	.368
Espinosa, Sergio	1	1	7.71	11	0	0	12	19	5	6	.388
Gutierrez, Carlos	1	0	6.55	12	0	0	11	13	9	10	.295
Hall, Jeremy	0	0	7.71	2	0	0	2	5	3	1	.385
* Horst, Jeremy	0	0	3.46	11	0	0	13	12	6	9	.250

	W	L	ERA	G	GS	SV	IP	H	BB	SO	AVG
* Hynes, Colt	1	1	6.14	12	0	0	15	15	5	4	.246
Lara, Alexis	0	2	12.46	10	0	0	9	14	8	10	.350
* Leesman, Charles	0	1	11.81	11	0	0	11	23	9	12	.418
Lowe, Johnnie	0	4	14.58	6	6	0	17	38	11	9	.447
Mabee, Henry	0	0	6.92	9	0	0	13	15	9	5	.278
* Robertson, Tyler	0	1	4.50	12	0	0	14	18	6	9	.327
* Schenk, Neil	1	0	1.72	12	0	0	16	14	6	5	.246
Thompson, Daryl	2	2	4.50	6	5	0	18	18	8	16	.269
* Valiquette, Philippe	0	1	14.14	6	0	0	7	14	5	5	.412
Waldrop, Kyle	1	0	16.05	10	0	0	12	24	6	5	.414

PHOENIX DESERT DOGS

BATTERS	AVG	AB	R	H	2B	3B	HR	RBI	BB	SO	SB
Curry, Ryan, ss	.206	63	6	13	3	0	2	6	3	5	2
De Jesus, Ivan, 3b	.321	78	13	25	6	0	1	10	10	16	0
* Freeman, Freddie, 1b	.125	16	3	2	1	1	0	1	2	3	0
Green, Grant, ss	.200	45	4	9	0	1	0	3	2	14	0
Harrilchak, Cory, of	.333	75	14	25	3	1	3	11	12	17	2
Laird, Brandon, of	.236	110	12	26	10	0	4	22	6	27	0
Martinez, Osvaldo, ss	.160	25	4	4	1	0	1	0	4	0	1
Parker, Stephen, 3b	.327	98	14	32	10	1	1	8	13	18	1
Pastornicky, Tyler, ss	.278	54	10	15	1	1	0	6	1	7	1
Pirela, Jose, 2b	.180	89	8	16	3	0	1	5	6	20	2
# Robinson, Trayvon, of	.250	72	10	18	4	0	1	7	16	22	6
Romine, Austin, c	.279	61	2	17	3	0	0	7	3	13	1
Sands, Jerry, 1b	.299	87	13	26	8	0	3	13	16	19	2
Skipworth, Kyle, c	.267	60	8	16	4	0	3	12	5	15	0
Taylor, Michael, of	.278	108	20	30	8	0	2	15	16	17	6
* Wallach, Matt, c	.235	34	3	8	2	0	1	5	9	7	0

PITCHERS	W	L	ERA	G	GS	SV	IP	H	BB	SO	AVG
Ames, Steven	0	0	148.50	2	0	0	1	9	3	1	.818
Andrelczyk, Peter	0	0	2.81	9	1	0	16	12	7	16	.200
* Banuelos, Manny	0	2	3.60	7	7	0	25	31	10	16	.298
Banwart, Travis	4	1	3.76	7	7	0	26	30	8	21	.297
Benacka, Michael	0	0	5.14	5	0	0	7	6	9	10	.231
Broadway, Michael	0	1	10.13	4	0	0	5	10	1	5	.400
Cishek, Steve	0	0	4.05	11	0	1	13	15	4	18	.278
Cofield, Kyle	0	0	9.00	1	0	0	1	1	0	0	.250
Cordier, Erik	0	1	9.00	2	2	0	5	7	6	6	.318
* Elbert, Scott	1	0	3.09	10	0	0	12	8	4	15	.195
Evans, Bryan	1	2	5.40	3	3	0	10	13	2	10	.310
Gearrin, Cory	1	0	3.93	10	0	0	18	16	6	14	.232
Guerra, Javy	0	0	1.80	8	0	2	10	10	6	9	.263
Hartsock, Aaron	0	0	3.00	3	0	0	3	4	1	2	.286
Harvey, Kris	1	0	6.75	3	0	0	4	5	2	2	.333
# Hernandez, Carlos	0	0	7.11	5	0	0	6	4	5	4	.174
Heyer, Craig	1	2	2.50	7	3	0	18	16	3	7	.242
* Horst, Jeremy	0	0	3.46	11	0	0	13	12	6	9	.250
James, Justin	0	0	5.59	9	0	2	10	12	4	12	.293
Kontos, George	1	2	12.08	10	0	0	13	21	10	11	.362
Link, Jon	0	2	4.43	5	5	0	20	24	4	15	.300
* Luetge, Lucas	0	0	8.68	8	0	0	9	14	4	3	.350
* Merklinger, Dan	1	1	3.77	6	5	0	14	16	6	16	.276
Miller, Justin	0	0	8.03	8	0	0	12	20	10	6	.351
* Paterson, Joe	0	0	2.25	10	0	0	12	6	2	15	.154
Pope, Ryan	0	1	3.18	9	0	1	11	14	4	10	.292
Pruneda, Benino	0	0	14.21	5	0	0	6	15	7	9	.484
* Sewell, Lance	0	0	7.88	6	0	0	8	11	6	5	.297
* West, Sean	1	0	13.50	1	1	0	2	4	2	2	.364

SCOTTSDALE SCORPIONS

BATTERS	AVG	AB	R	H	2B	3B	HR	RBI	BB	SO	SB
Adams, Ryan, 3b	.265	68	10	18	3	0	1	14	5	10	0
* Avery, Xavier, of	.188	69	10	13	2	2	0	5	9	16	6
* Belt, Brandon, 1b	.372	86	16	32	8	5	1	16	9	24	1
* Blackmon, Charles, of	.264	72	18	19	2	0	3	11	13	6	2
* Burgess, Michael, of	.246	65	8	16	3	3	2	12	4	20	1
* Culberson, Charlie, 2b	.366	93	21	34	11	2	2	16	5	22	1
Easley, Ed, c	.238	21	3	5	0	0	0	2	4	1	0
Field, Thomas, ss	.209	67	9	14	3	0	1	5	5	22	2
* Gillaspie, Conor, 3b	.306	72	10	22	6	0	5	16	4	5	1
* Harper, Bryce, of	.343	35	6	12	3	2	1	7	4	11	1
Joseph, Caleb, c	.390	41	13	16	2	0	1	7	4	6	0
* Krauss, Marc, of	.289	84	20	25	5	1	4	23	15	22	0
# Lombardozzi, Steve, 2b	.293	82	16	24	8	2	0	4	10	8	2

	AVG	AB	R	H	2B	3B	HR	RBI	BB	SO	SB
# Miclat, Greg, ss	.308	52	3	16	4	0	0	4	7	13	1
Norris, Derek, c	.278	54	10	15	5	2	4	19	11	18	2
Pacheco, Jordan, c	.317	63	16	20	5	2	0	11	9	14	2
Pollock, A.J., of	.313	64	10	20	6	0	0	9	6	10	7
Schmidt, Konrad, c	.250	4	1	1	0	0	0	1	0	1	0
Townsend, Tyler, 1b	.250	4	0	1	0	0	0	2	0	1	0

PITCHERS	W	L	ERA	G	GS	SV	IP	H	BB	SO	AVG
Billings, Bruce	2	1	3.27	8	0	0	11	9	0	10	.214
* Brothers, Rex	1	0	4.09	9	0	0	11	14	3	16	.318
Carr, Adam	1	0	2.08	10	0	1	13	6	3	8	.130
Collmenter, Josh	4	0	3.04	7	7	0	27	26	7	30	.248
Drake, Oliver	1	3	8.38	6	6	0	19	26	8	19	.325
Egan, Pat	0	1	2.13	10	0	0	13	11	3	7	.229
Jorgenson, Adam	0	0	1.93	10	0	1	9	10	5	4	.286
Kimball, Cole	0	0	0.75	11	0	1	12	8	2	15	.186
Mickolio, Kam	0	0	0.75	8	0	0	12	9	2	18	.205
* Paterson, Joe	0	0	2.25	10	0	0	12	6	2	15	.154
Peacock, Brad	0	0	4.50	9	0	0	12	10	3	17	.222
Pelzer, Wynn	0	0	2.45	10	0	0	11	8	12	9	.211
Reynolds, Greg	1	5	4.13	7	7	0	24	33	7	19	.324
* Runzler, Dan	1	0	0.00	3	0	0	3	0	1	3	.000
Shaw, Bryan	0	0	3.48	9	0	2	10	13	2	6	.317
* Solis, Sammy	1	0	3.80	6	5	0	24	22	7	12	.247
Stange, Daniel	2	0	7.71	9	0	0	12	16	4	8	.333
Stoffel, Jason	1	0	5.27	9	0	0	14	14	4	11	.269
* Verdugo, Ryan	4	1	2.45	7	7	0	22	20	16	26	.241
Woodall, Bryan	1	0	5.40	5	0	0	7	9	1	4	.310

SURPRISE RAFTERS

BATTERS	AVG	AB	R	H	2B	3B	HR	RBI	BB	SO	SB
* Beltre, Engel, of	.245	53	9	13	2	1	1	7	6	8	6
* Bolden, Jared, of	.143	21	5	3	0	1	0	2	3	7	1
Butler, Joey, of	.228	57	9	13	2	1	2	8	4	13	4
* Chambers, Adron, of	.333	66	13	22	5	0	1	10	5	14	10
* Cox, Zack, 3b	.262	65	8	17	4	1	2	14	8	21	0
Cruz, Tony, c	.342	76	13	26	3	0	3	17	7	14	0
Farris, Eric, 2b	.351	74	16	26	4	1	0	8	7	11	9
Felix, Jose, c	.347	49	6	17	4	0	0	4	1	3	2
Giavotella, Johnny, 2b	.262	64	11	21	10	0	2	13	4	6	0
* Gindl, Caleb, of	.259	58	11	15	5	1	2	6	9	20	0
Guez, Ben, of	.228	57	8	13	2	1	3	6	5	21	4
* Hosmer, Eric, 1b	.203	79	12	16	5	1	0	14	9	10	0
Iorg, Cale, ss	.304	56	11	17	1	2	2	9	6	16	5
Kozma, Peter, ss	.269	67	13	18	7	2	0	4	6	18	1
Martinez, Francisco, 3b	.278	54	6	15	4	1	0	8	2	13	2
* Morris, Hunter, 3b	.242	66	7	16	2	1	1	11	5	8	0
Perez, Salvador, c	.211	38	4	8	2	0	1	10	2	4	0
# Robinson, Derrick, of	.260	50	11	13	1	0	0	7	8	15	0
* Schafer, Logan, of	.323	31	6	10	0	0	0	3	7	4	2
Stoneburner, Davis, 2b	.231	52	13	12	2	1	1	9	3	14	2

PITCHERS	W	L	ERA	G	GS	SV	IP	H	BB	SO	AVG
Broderick, Brian	3	1	4.39	6	6	0	27	30	7	11	.297
Brown, Brooks	1	3	12.05	7	7	0	19	37	11	13	.416
Castillo, Fabio	1	2	2.79	9	2	0	10	7	3	6	.189
Delgado, Ramon	0	0	3.65	10	0	0	12	12	3	6	.261
* Duffy, Danny	1	1	8.04	7	3	1	16	17	9	18	.258
Fiers, Michael	2	1	4.82	5	5	0	19	16	3	17	.222
Flores, Adalberto	0	1	6.97	9	0	0	10	15	12	7	.341
Gutierrez, Danny	0	0	0.00	1	0	0	1	1	1	1	.250
Hoffman, Matt	0	0	7.27	9	0	1	9	15	5	9	.395
Hurley, Eric	3	0	1.82	6	6	0	25	16	9	14	.198
Jeffress, Jeremy	0	0	3.09	10	0	0	12	9	12	14	.200
Keating, Patrick	2	0	3.27	10	0	0	11	9	5	12	.220
King, Blake	1	0	6.30	10	0	0	10	11	8	10	.282
* Kintzler, Brandon	1	0	3.14	11	0	2	14	16	2	15	.286
* Luetge, Lucas	0	0	8.68	8	0	0	9	14	4	3	.350
McClendon, Mike	0	0	3.38	11	0	0	16	14	4	13	.233
* Montgomery, Mike	2	1	6.10	3	3	0	10	13	2	11	.310
Ruffin, Chance	1	1	3.86	10	0	4	9	3	5	8	.107
* Sisk, Brandon	0	0	2.51	10	0	0	14	9	3	11	.167
Swagerty, Jordan	1	0	3.60	4	0	0	5	7	0	3	.318
Wise, Brendan	0	1	6.57	11	0	0	12	13	7	7	.271
* Young, Corey	0	0	2.08	8	0	0	9	8	2	3	.258

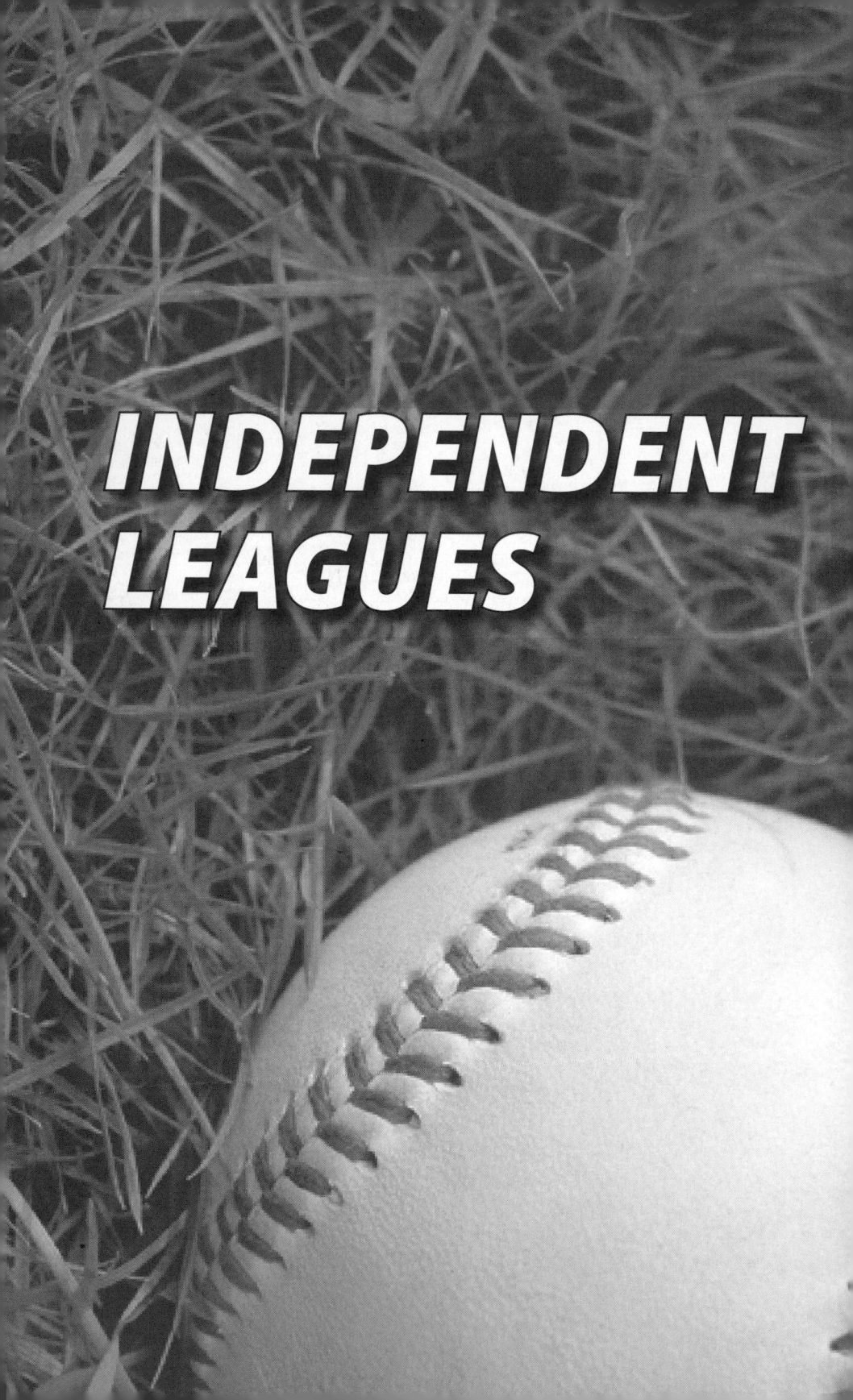

INDEPENDENT LEAGUES

Economic downturn takes toll on independent leagues

The 2010 season is one several independent leagues would rather forget.

It proved to be the final year of the Northern League in its current form—as four teams left for the American Association soon after the season ended. The Golden League had to deal with the dissolution of three different ownership groups in a two-month stretch, forcing the league to take over all three teams. Another team, Victoria, announced after the season that it would not return in 2011, while the league was working to sign new leases for other key franchises.

And the Continental League, which had skirted the boundaries between semipro and independent baseball for a couple of years, announced in mid-summer that it was calling it quits at the end of the season, then shut its season down early.

The economic downturn had forced independent league teams to tighten their belts for a couple of seasons, but 2010 proved to be the point when some teams, and some owners, found scrimping and saving could only do so much.

That's not to say there weren't highlights. The seven biggest leagues drew more than eight million fans in 2010, led the the Atlantic League's 2.15 million fans and nearly 4,000 fans per game. Four different leagues drew more than 2,500 fans per game and all seven significant leagues drew more than 1,800 fans per game.

On the field, the product was still quite good, and success stories like the promotions of Bobby Cramer and Justin James (Athletics) and Brandon Kintzler (Brewers) to the big leagues helped remind people that players do make it from the independent leagues to the majors.

But no one was a better sales pitch for what independent baseball can do for a player than Red Sox outfielder Daniel Nava. Nava went undrafted out of college before signing with the Golden League's Chico Outlaws. Nava was the league's rookie of the year and MVP before signing with the Red Sox in 2007. Three years later, he was promoted to the major leagues, and he hit a grand slam in his first big league at-bat. He ended up spending much of the season on the Red Sox major league roster.

The economic troubles in 2010 guarantee that the face of independent baseball will be different in 2011. Where there have been more and more leagues popping up over the past decade, indepen-

Former indy league star Daniel Nava hit a grand slam in his first major league at-bat

MIKE JANES

INDEPENDENT ATTENDANCE, 2010		
	TOTAL	AVG
Atlantic	2,151,416	3,992
Northern	1,478,694	3,841
American Association	1,227,518	2,677
Frontier	1,498,061	2,568
Can-Am	523,894	1,959
Golden	742,394	1,827
United	483,069	1,823
OVERALL	**8,105,046**	**2,853.89**

dent baseball appears headed toward consolidation in the new decade with fewer, but larger leagues filling out the independent roster.

The addition of four Northern League clubs to the American Association was a prime example of that change. The American Association formed in large part because several teams were unhappy with the direction of the Northern League.

There was plenty of animosity on both sides of the issue. But in the end, the possibility of better travel arrangements and improved rivalries helped to cool off any of the residual anger between the two sides.

Steady Torbert keeps on hitting

When Beau Torbert played for the Astros, he was a self-described worrier. He pressed, he replayed at-bats in his heads, always wondering what he could do better or differently.

In a way, you could say that being released by the Astros has given him some freedom.

"Before I was let go by Houston I put a lot of stress on myself to perform," Torbert said. "When I got to independent ball, I took a mindset that I'm in indy ball now, I can get back to basic baseball and having fun. Ever since I took that approach I try to not let too much good stuff or bad stuff go to my head."

It's hard to argue with the results. In the three seasons since he was released by Houston, Torbert, an outfielder for the Sioux Falls Pheasants, has won two American Association MVP awards. His first came when he hit .324 with 19 home runs, 71 RBIs and 14 steals in 2008. This year, he earned his second MVP award by blowing those numbers away. Torbert flirted with hitting .400 but settled for a league leading .394 average to go with .435 on-base percentage and .684 slugging percentage. Led by Torbert, Sioux Falls finished with the best record in the American Association before losing in the championship series to Shreveport-Bossier. For all that, Torbert is the 2010 Independent League Player of the Year.

Beau Torbert

"He was a highlight film all year," Sioux Falls manager Steve Shirley said. "He was phenomenal for the entire season. It wasn't like he had one stretch where he was unbelievable. He was that good all year. It was something to stand back and watch him perform."

As a 27-year-old, Torbert had the season of his life. He hit for average with the Astros (.286/.338/.404 career numbers that saw him reach Triple-A Round Rock in 2007), but he was a leadoff hitter who rarely hit for power. When Sioux Falls signed him, Shirley and the rest of the coaching staff looked at his build (now 6-foot-4, 235 pounds) and his swing and saw that he could do more than set the table. Torbert quickly became a run producer in the middle of the lineup. After hitting 14 home runs in four seasons in affiliated ball, Torbert has hit 55 in three years in Sioux Falls.

"The thing with Beau that has to be maddening for the opposition is that he'll hit anything," Shirley said. "He's a very difficult guy to pitch to. He'll expand his strike zone because he knows he's up there to drive in a run. I know there are times in the other dugout where they had to wonder how he hit that, because we're wondering it. And he didn't just hit it but rocketed it off the scoreboard."

The last time Torbert won the MVP award, the Tigers signed him. He hit well in spring training, but as many independent league stars find, there are many more players than roster spots. He was back in Sioux Falls for the start of the 2009 season.

Torbert is hopeful of another shot, but he's not pressing when he sees a scout in the stands at a Pheasants game. As he sees it, he's done what he can do already.

"At this point in my career, it's not a deal where I prove myself to get a shot; it's more of will a team give me that shot," Torbert said. "It goes back to relaxing and have fun. If there's a scout there, good, but if not, it's OK."

The approach has worked for Torbert for three years, so he's not about to change it.

PREVIOUS WINNERS

1996: Darryl Motley, of, Fargo-Moorhead (Northern)
1997: Mike Meggers, of, Winnipeg/Duluth (Northern)
1998: Morgan Burkhart, 1b, Richmond (Frontier)
1999: Carmine Cappucio, of, New Jersey (Northeast)
2000: Anthony Lewis, 1b, Duluth-Superior (Northern)
2001: Mike Warner, of, Somerset (Atlantic)
2002: Bobby Madritsch, lhp, Winnipeg (Northern)

2003: Jason Shelley, rhp, Rockford (Frontier)
2004: Victor Rodriguez, ss, Somerset (Atlantic)
2005: Eddie Lantigua, 3b, Quebec (Can-Am)
2006: Ian Church, of, Kalamazoo (Frontier)
2007: Darryl Brinkley, of, Calgary (Northern)
2008: Patrick Breen, of, Orange County (Golden)
2009: Greg Porter, of, Wichita (American Association)

AMERICAN ASSOCIATION

For three months, the Sioux Falls Pheasants were the dominant team in the American Association. But the Shreveport-Bossier Captains proved that in the playoffs, there are no rewards for having the best regular season record.

Sioux Falls' lineup, with Beau Torbert, Reggie Abercrombie and Brandon Sing, was the league's best all year, but in the championship series Ryan DiPetro, Osvaldo Rodriguez and Richard Salazar shut down the Captains. The three Captains starters held Sioux Falls to one run in 21 innings, leading the Captains to a surprisingly easy sweep.

FIRST HALF

NORTH DIVISION	W	L	PCT	GB
Sioux Falls Pheasants	32	16	.667	—
Lincoln Saltdogs	29	19	.604	3
Sioux City Explorers	25	23	.521	7
St Paul Saints	21	27	.438	11
Wichita Wingnuts	20	28	.417	12

SOUTH DIVISION	W	L	PCT	GB
Shreveport-Bossier Captains	29	18	.617	—
Grand Prairie AirHogs	24	23	.511	5
Pensacola Pelicans	20	28	.417	9.5
El Paso Diablos	19	27	.413	9.5
Fort Worth Cats	18	28	.391	10.5

SECOND HALF

NORTH DIVISION	W	L	PCT	GB
Sioux Falls Pheasants	31	17	.646	—
Wichita Wingnuts	30	18	.625	1
Sioux City Explorers	24	24	.500	7
St Paul Saints	24	24	.500	7
Lincoln Saltdogs	22	26	.458	9

SOUTH DIVISION	W	L	PCT	GB
Pensacola Pelicans *	29	18	.617	—
Shreveport-Bossier Captains	29	19	.604	0.5
Fort Worth Cats	19	28	.404	10
Grand Prairie AirHogs	19	29	.396	10.5
El Paso Diablos	12	36	.250	17.5

Playoffs—Semifinals: Shreveport-Bossier defeated Pensacola 3-2 and Sioux Falls defeated Lincoln 3-0 in best-of-five series. **Finals:** Shreveport-Bossier defeated Sioux Falls 3-0 in best-of-five series.

ATTENDANCE: St Paul Saints 237,994; El Paso Diablos 179,452; Lincoln Saltdogs 163,676; Wichita Wingnuts 134,773; Fort Worth Cats 122,062; Grand Prairie AirHogs 124,539; Sioux Falls Pheasants 86,518; Shreveport-Bossier Captains 71,468; Sioux City Explorers 56,428; Pensacola Pelicans 50,608.

MANAGERS: El Paso—Butch Henry; **Fort Worth**—Chad Tredaway; **Grand Prairie**—Pete Incaviglia; **Lincoln**—Marty Scott; **Pensacola**—Talmadge Nunnari; **St. Paul**—George Tsamis; **Shreveport-Bossier**—Ricky VanAsselberg; **Sioux City**—Les Lancaster; **Sioux Falls**—Steve Shirley; **Wichita**—Kevin Hooper.

ALL-STAR TEAM: C—Lou Palmisano, Pensacola ; **1B**—Brandon Sing, Sioux Falls; **2B**—Hector Bernal, El Paso/St. Paul; **3B**—Trevor Lawhorn, Sioux Falls ; **SS**—David Espinosa, Grand Prairie; **OFs**—Beau Torbert, Sioux Falls; Reggie Abercrombie, Sioux Falls; Greg Porter, Grand Prairie; **DH**—Christopher Garcia, Shreveport-Bossier.
LHP—Chris Salberg, Sioux Falls; **RHP**—Ben Moore, Sioux Falls; **RP**—Aaron Cotter, Sioux Falls.

Player of the Year: Beau Torbert, of, Sioux Falls. **Manager of the Year:** Steve Shirley, Sioux Falls.

INDIVIDUAL BATTING LEADERS

PLAYER, TEAM	AVG	G	AB	R	H	HR	RBI
Torbert, Beau, Sioux Falls	.394	95	393	79	155	24	100
Garcia , Chris, S-B	.383	94	350	71	134	14	90
Porter, Greg, Grand Prairie	.379	93	380	79	144	20	87
Espinosa, David, Grand Prairie	.351	95	362	86	127	9	59
Sing, Brandon, Sioux Falls	.349	95	332	87	116	27	73
Serrano, Ray, Sioux City	.349	88	344	54	120	6	66
Palmisano , Lou, Pensacola	.347	84	294	65	102	16	64
Allen, John, Fort Worth	.339	93	348	57	118	14	92
Alvarez , Rafael, Lincoln	.337	93	350	78	118	9	53
Perry, Robert, Shreveport-Bossier	.336	87	339	62	114	4	43

INDIVIDUAL PITCHING LEADERS

PLAYER, TEAM	W	L	ERA	IP	H	BB	SO
Singleton, Nick, Wichita	7	3	2.36	88	73	40	73
Moore, Ben, Sioux Falls	11	8	3.10	134	132	22	126
Salberg, Chris, Sioux Falls	11	1	3.26	127	117	55	81
Rodriguez , Osvaldo, Shreveport-Bossier	11	3	3.50	121	108	56	101
Welch, David, Sioux City	8	6	3.59	108	121	32	94
Peterson , Zach, St. Paul	7	6	3.65	101	106	25	77
Salazar , Richard, Shreveport-Bossier	10	4	3.78	121	127	39	83
Medina, Gabe, Wichita	5	7	3.82	130	124	52	116
Cowart, Adam, Wichita	7	7	3.93	110	142	28	78
Pollok, Dwayne, Fort Worth	10	5	4.00	124	130	36	90

EL PASO DIABLOS

PLAYER	AVG	AB	R	H	2B	3B	HR	RBI	SB
Bernal, Hector	.343	312	48	107	18	7	4	48	6
Deleo, Adam	.243	148	12	36	9	0	1	22	0
Hulett, Jeff	.236	55	5	13	1	0	0	4	2
Imwalle, Matt	.224	76	12	17	3	0	2	10	1
Johnson, Benji	.305	190	41	58	16	0	10	35	1
Medina, Juan	.194	31	3	6	0	0	0	3	1
Nichols, Kyle	.305	279	42	85	22	0	14	66	0
Ponce, Arnoldo	.295	386	73	114	9	7	4	45	4
Provencher, Mike	.300	287	43	86	19	3	0	39	5
Reininger, J.D.	.268	325	58	87	24	1	11	57	3
Reynoso, Jonathan	.258	306	47	79	13	5	3	34	9
Santana, Rico	.307	225	36	69	16	3	3	38	4
Smith, Bryon	.296	375	67	111	22	0	4	60	5
Vincent, Jeff	.269	316	58	85	21	4	2	39	27
Washington, David	.212	33	3	7	3	1	0	5	4

PLAYER	W	L	ERA	G	SV	IP	H	BB	SO
Baca, Noel	0	2	5.72	16	0	22	34	7	15
Birosak, Dustin	0	8	8.22	10	0	23	41	16	15
Buzhardt, William	2	4	7.83	14	1	56	89	33	43
Ellis, Shaun	9	4	4.61	20	0	121	129	82	69
Estrada, Jesse	1	3	7.28	8	0	30	41	19	17
Fowler, Barry	0	5	5.97	22	1	35	60	13	18
Jiggitts, Kris	0	2	5.87	23	0	23	29	15	18
Kalb, Aaron	2	5	5.28	14	0	77	96	56	36
Landeros, Leonard	0	3	8.75	5	0	24	34	16	15
Lawler, Patrick	0	1	8.99	14	0	14	27	12	5
Mattox, D.J.	8	6	4.55	16	0	97	88	70	75
Oakes, Earl	0	1	6.27	16	0	19	28	16	19
Patterson, Lonnie	1	0	11.12	5	0	11	21	12	6
Pena, Eddie	0	0	13.00	12	0	10	18	9	3
Renault, Nick	1	3	4.74	24	5	25	24	19	19
Staehely, Christian	0	5	5.63	27	0	32	44	21	32
Stephens, Amad	5	10	5.77	24	0	106	133	38	67
Whigham, David	2	8	6.45	24	2	52	66	23	31

FORT WORTH CATS

PLAYER	AVG	AB	R	H	2B	3B	HR	RBI	SB
Allen, John	.339	348	57	118	28	4	14	92	11
Avila, Gerardo	.344	96	12	33	6	1	4	23	1
Bell, Mike	.215	135	9	29	6	0	1	11	1
Bibbs, Kennard	.289	235	48	68	8	3	0	17	12
Bistagne, Brian	.135	37	2	5	2	0	0	2	1
Dennis, Spenser	.095	21	4	2	1	0	0	0	0
Duran, Jose	.311	106	11	33	4	2	1	16	1
Fortenberry, Seth	.354	48	10	17	5	0	1	9	4
Fryer, Brian	.289	367	68	106	10	2	3	50	30
Gulledge, Kelley	.319	304	32	97	21	0	10	52	0
Herrera, Brenan	.197	117	9	23	4	0	0	12	0
Holloway, Justin	.217	46	2	10	1	0	0	4	0
McCoola, Nick	.282	301	57	85	13	1	0	24	9
Morales, Cory	.250	208	19	52	5	0	1	16	4
Recuenco, Rob	.283	127	27	36	11	3	0	13	5
Santana, Rico	.212	33	2	7	3	0	0	2	0
Sauceda, Jeremy	.271	292	42	79	19	4	4	32	14
Smith, Stantrel	.246	57	3	14	2	2	0	4	3

PLAYER	AVG	AB	R	H	2B	3B	HR	RBI	SB
Suarez, Cesar	.273	77	12	21	4	0	0	9	3
Thompson, Kevin	.389	108	29	42	12	0	4	27	13
Underkofler, B.J.	.100	20	0	2	0	0	0	0	0

PLAYER	W	L	ERA	G	SV	IP	H	BB	SO
Allen, Colin	3	10	4.98	20	0	108	121	63	49
Bittner, Tim	2	6	6.02	8	0	43	47	30	35
Cameron, Dustin	3	5	3.35	40	16	40	40	18	36
Fernandez, Jason	5	9	4.69	20	0	121	144	56	81
Hurn, Doug	1	2	6.29	15	0	24	23	17	16
Kirsten, Joel	3	8	4.30	22	0	132	148	49	94
Lee, Gary	3	3	7.34	41	0	54	78	25	42
Migl, Scott	1	3	5.45	25	0	36	52	20	17
Pollok, Dwayne	10	5	4.00	20	0	124	130	36	90
Romero, Robert	1	0	4.21	15	0	15	16	11	21
Vaclavik, Justin	2	3	6.00	31	1	27	27	20	24
Vander Weg, Scott	2	1	3.92	38	1	39	44	12	36

GRAND PRAIRIE AIRHOGS

PLAYER	AVG	AB	R	H	2B	3B	HR	RBI	SB
Banks, Ernie	.358	53	6	19	5	0	2	14	0
Berg, Daniel	.377	154	33	58	11	1	2	21	4
Brown, Chris	.167	36	1	6	2	0	0	4	0
Camacho, Juan	.309	178	25	55	8	2	4	29	0
Carrillo, Steve	.264	91	7	24	2	1	1	10	0
Caves, Chris	.174	23	2	4	1	0	0	1	0
Duran, Jose	.234	124	19	29	5	1	0	5	7
Espinosa, David	.351	362	86	127	22	6	9	59	13
Gabriel, Chad	.277	173	23	48	7	0	0	20	0
Garza, Aaron	.266	265	41	71	18	3	5	32	13
Gray, Antoin	.340	153	32	52	10	0	7	28	2
Hollimon, Michael	.256	211	33	54	15	2	6	36	10
Incaviglia, Thomas	.206	63	5	13	1	0	0	5	4
Jordan, Danny	.178	73	10	13	6	0	0	6	0
Logan, Nook	.273	55	7	15	0	0	0	1	7
Perry, Robert	.320	303	53	97	13	5	4	41	16
Petralli, Ben	.232	198	23	46	12	0	0	24	1
Porter, Greg	.379	380	79	144	28	0	20	87	4
Spiers, Joe	.274	179	30	49	7	2	1	22	19
Stokes, Jason	.247	85	12	21	3	1	4	13	0
Wipke, Flint	.323	93	11	30	10	2	4	17	1

PLAYER	W	L	ERA	G	SV	IP	H	BB	SO
Bille, Mike	0	1	4.85	24	1	30	30	11	33
Estanga, Edgar	3	0	6.84	16	0	26	31	18	19
Garcia, Geivy	4	5	3.47	39	11	49	41	29	45
Green, Matt	3	2	6.11	8	0	35	40	22	26
Griffin, Dan	0	0	3.29	7	1	14	11	4	20
Krause, Greg	4	6	5.36	20	1	86	115	31	46
Maertz, Santo	0	1	6.75	10	0	17	13	18	14
Martin, Chris	4	0	1.96	13	0	37	34	9	36
Morrison, James	0	1	4.66	15	0	19	25	12	9
Morrison, Wade	0	1	7.41	5	0	17	24	12	14
Paxton, Ben	2	3	6.03	22	1	31	35	19	18
Paxton, James	1	2	4.08	4	0	18	15	7	18
Plummer, Jared	2	3	6.08	7	0	40	49	8	31
Prihoda, Luke	6	6	5.02	23	0	100	128	20	71
Salmon, Marcus	1	1	9.88	5	0	14	21	6	13
Schmidt, Daniel	3	6	5.67	21	0	81	109	25	34
Scurry, Rod	1	2	5.33	22	0	27	38	9	21
Stanley, Patrick	0	2	5.12	5	0	19	15	14	11
Tacker, Ryne	8	5	4.20	26	0	114	114	58	94

LINCOLN SALTDOGS

PLAYER	AVG	AB	R	H	2B	3B	HR	RBI	SB
Albitz, Vance	.288	52	10	15	1	0	0	1	2
Alvarez, Rafael	.337	350	78	118	29	1	9	53	15
Alvarez, Roberto	.283	219	31	62	12	0	5	25	7
Brown, Chris	.281	96	15	27	6	0	2	5	3
Camacho, Juan	.304	207	27	63	12	0	9	34	2
Dickey, Gavin	.299	394	74	118	17	5	17	55	20
Gillan, Jeremy	.275	51	11	14	2	1	1	3	0
Hawke, Phil	.229	245	43	56	14	1	11	50	2
Jadlowski, Jake	.118	34	1	4	0	0	0	3	0
Jones, Brandon	.239	318	44	76	18	0	15	53	1

PLAYER	AVG	AB	R	H	2B	3B	HR	RBI	SB
Machado, Albenis	.252	337	51	85	13	1	4	42	7
McGill, Shawn	.347	147	29	51	6	0	8	35	4
Nunez, Argelis	.308	360	64	111	15	0	22	82	4
PoVey, Tycen	.143	35	4	5	2	0	0	4	0
Richardson, Juan	.313	336	61	105	17	0	14	63	0
Trettel, Pat	.277	141	29	39	9	0	11	26	1

PLAYER	W	L	ERA	G	SV	IP	H	BB	SO
Baca, Noel	0	3	6.96	5	0	22	32	10	18
Britton, Chris	4	4	7.58	10	0	57	89	8	34
Brown, Tim	7	5	4.52	13	0	78	92	20	43
Castro, Angel	3	3	3.16	6	0	31	30	13	21
Chestnut, Nolan	2	1	4.05	34	0	53	53	25	34
Cullen, Chris	5	6	4.74	24	0	106	122	39	53
Daniels, Adam	6	5	5.37	43	3	50	27	36	68
Furrow, Donald	0	0	7.57	15	0	27	45	10	28
James, John	6	2	4.99	10	0	58	56	28	45
Lane, Greg	2	0	4.50	13	0	20	26	3	14
Marceaux, Jacob	0	2	9.79	5	0	23	37	13	18
Paduch, Jim	9	6	4.65	23	0	120	143	63	118
Paxton, Ben	0	0	7.92	15	1	19	31	7	11
PoVey, Tycen	0	1	3.35	26	1	38	32	14	33
Smith, Brendon	3	0	5.79	20	2	33	39	19	10
Thompson, Chris	2	2	5.12	38	21	39	32	42	28
Tyson, Nick	0	1	5.96	6	0	23	31	13	8
Walden, Cody	0	1	8.10	2	0	10	16	6	6
Weitzman, Billy	2	3	5.18	6	0	24	37	5	16

PENSACOLA PELICANS

PLAYER	AVG	AB	R	H	2B	3B	HR	RBI	SB
Alonso, John	.335	322	56	108	22	2	11	50	0
Brito, Javier	.324	383	74	124	20	2	21	69	2
Brown, Kyle	.250	180	27	45	2	1	0	15	6
Chiarappa, Chris	.192	78	14	15	4	0	0	5	0
Christison, Dallas	.228	272	38	62	6	0	2	34	10
Gonzalez, Adolfo	.294	330	48	97	15	2	5	41	2
Gray, Antoin	.321	187	27	60	15	0	1	26	2
Leandro, Francisco	.293	362	74	106	24	4	6	61	18
Leon, Carlos	.234	137	29	32	2	1	0	14	13
Palmisano, Lou	.347	294	65	102	22	0	16	64	0
Porch, Chase	.286	283	38	81	14	0	4	40	9
Rodriguez, Marcos	.303	350	30	106	15	0	1	48	11
Side, Joey	.364	44	9	16	3	0	0	4	1

PLAYER	W	L	ERA	G	SV	IP	H	BB	SO
Baumgardner, Tommy	1	0	0.50	17	3	18	12	2	13
Chambliss, Austin	4	1	4.15	21	3	26	23	13	24
Cooper, Kevin	1	2	6.00	3	0	18	31	7	7
De Valk, Dane	7	9	5.38	20	0	104	123	49	67
Franzblau, Jason	2	0	5.44	27	1	45	49	25	41
Gothreaux, Jared	9	8	5.02	20	0	131	186	30	93
Henry, Lee	1	0	2.89	20	3	44	39	22	44
Hill, Ron	4	3	2.44	35	6	52	52	12	37
Jackson, Aaron	1	2	10.88	10	0	24	38	14	14
Jones, Jason	1	0	0.66	2	0	14	14	4	8
Nathanson, David	8	5	4.56	19	0	118	128	31	70
Overbey, Seth	0	3	3.09	29	9	32	27	21	30
Quinn, Austin	4	4	6.91	11	0	59	84	17	22
Rembisz, Bryan	4	5	5.58	15	0	90	112	25	60
Wedner, Joey	0	2	7.79	8	0	17	26	4	9
Wilson, Tyler	1	0	4.15	13	1	22	24	9	23

SHREVEPORT-BOSSIER CAPTAINS

PLAYER	AVG	AB	R	H	2B	3B	HR	RBI	SB
Alvarez, Jorge	.319	254	31	81	15	0	4	44	1
Cooksey, Bryan	.225	40	4	9	1	0	0	10	1
Frichter, Bryan	.324	219	45	71	12	2	3	22	3
Garcia, Christopher	.383	350	71	134	31	1	14	90	2
Hulett, Jeff	.229	35	4	8	1	0	0	3	1
Karr Jr, Palmer	.317	328	53	104	20	2	13	67	7
Marquez, Uriak	.260	296	42	77	16	0	9	56	28
Marshall, Andre	.184	38	4	7	4	0	0	3	0
Nichols, Brian	.250	28	4	7	3	0	0	2	0
Perry, Robert	.472	36	9	17	2	2	0	2	4
Peterson, Brian	.277	303	42	84	17	0	3	36	11

PLAYER	AVG	AB	R	H	2B	3B	HR	RBI	SB
Provencher, Mike	.231	39	5	9	2	2	0	4	2
Rodriguez, Andres	.327	349	51	114	20	0	1	51	2
Rosario, Jovanny	.290	393	64	114	6	5	2	43	57
Sabatella, Bryan	.334	353	86	118	25	1	3	40	41
Urtuzuastegui, Joe	.257	144	25	37	7	0	3	16	2
Welch, Zach	.100	20	2	2	0	0	0	1	0
Wilson, Glenn	.300	60	6	18	4	0	0	6	0

PLAYER	W	L	ERA	G	SV	IP	H	BB	SO
Barnard, Chandler	1	2	7.94	4	0	17	27	8	11
Carrasco, Hector	2	4	3.83	41	22	42	32	9	29
Carter, Matt	1	0	6.56	8	0	12	14	5	8
Cunningham, Aaron	1	2	7.03	13	0	24	35	7	19
DiPietro, Ryan	8	3	4.04	16	0	100	123	33	76
Haynes, Mark	0	0	7.05	16	1	15	17	17	14
Kelley, Cody	2	2	6.97	10	0	50	73	23	35
Linder, Chad	0	5	9.07	10	0	42	72	23	20
Maj, Jameson	5	0	2.68	50	1	54	57	11	45
Prihoda, Luke	1	0	6.36	2	0	11	15	3	10
Railsback, Cody	3	0	1.29	19	1	21	14	6	22
Rodriguez, Osvaldo	11	3	3.50	19	0	121	108	56	101
Salazar, Richard	10	4	3.78	19	0	121	127	39	83
Salmon, Marcus	1	0	5.06	26	0	32	41	13	28
Tucker, Cardoza	3	4	4.99	7	0	40	47	16	30
Young, Justin	5	4	4.75	36	1	85	109	32	61

SIOUX CITY EXPLORERS

PLAYER	AVG	AB	R	H	2B	3B	HR	RBI	SB
Alberts, Tim	.338	148	27	50	8	1	3	29	1
Banks, Ernie	.338	77	8	26	6	0	1	8	0
Bohn, TJ	.270	355	69	96	19	2	15	65	14
Bridenbaugh, Paul	.118	34	5	4	0	0	0	0	0
Brown, Javier	.385	91	13	35	4	0	1	9	1
Cruz, Jacob	.400	80	16	32	7	0	4	26	0
Garza, Aaron	.075	40	3	3	1	0	1	2	1
Gray, Antoin	.185	27	4	5	1	0	0	2	0
Hale, Darrick	.274	310	49	85	15	2	1	26	9
Jones, Dustin	.296	304	47	90	17	0	4	32	17
Keel, Jared	.204	147	21	30	7	0	5	16	3
Kramer, Matt	.346	52	11	18	5	0	3	7	0
Mieras, Brett	.221	113	12	25	2	1	0	7	0
Owings, Jon	.235	183	27	43	13	1	6	27	1
Pearson, Steve	.259	81	14	21	2	2	2	16	0
Sakamoto, Kent	.315	356	61	112	29	5	9	67	9
Schermerhorn, Derek	.310	336	54	104	18	5	2	38	27
Serrano, Ray	.349	344	54	120	34	0	6	66	1
Smith, Stantrel	.271	59	9	16	1	0	0	7	6
Williams, Eric	.242	91	22	22	2	1	0	9	11

PLAYER	W	L	ERA	G	SV	IP	H	BB	SO
Arneson, Jamie	0	0	3.32	17	0	19	8	21	28
Bille, Mike	1	1	3.93	16	1	18	19	8	16
Delacruz, Eddie	5	2	2.77	53	9	65	49	20	65
Jones, Chris	1	2	5.79	3	0	14	21	2	8
Jung, Jae	5	7	4.44	13	0	81	103	20	21
Leonard, John	0	2	2.25	7	0	24	21	14	12
Marotz, Ty	6	7	5.38	24	0	100	132	33	72
Miller, Jayson	1	2	9.23	3	0	13	27	6	10
Phelps, Mike	2	2	4.74	23	0	38	35	19	24
Povich, Chad	5	2	5.17	26	0	94	96	57	83
Reid, Brett	0	0	0.00	13	10	14	8	5	22
Ryder, Mikael	10	7	4.78	20	0	124	162	26	57
Trahan, David	4	4	5.69	31	2	81	85	56	86
Welch, David	8	6	3.59	18	0	108	121	32	94

SIOUX FALLS EXPLORERS

PLAYER	AVG	AB	R	H	2B	3B	HR	RBI	SB
Abercrombie, Reggie	.328	360	89	118	19	4	22	90	34
Anthonsen, Joe	.327	382	81	125	13	2	0	34	13
Carby, Kevin	.278	216	39	60	12	3	3	34	16
Hutting, Tim	.307	358	59	110	12	2	5	36	1
Jobes, Hunter	.279	290	47	81	24	5	6	48	5
Lawhorn, Trevor	.292	349	54	102	20	2	16	65	3
Milner, Gus	.261	276	53	72	16	5	6	39	15
Richards, Will	.319	72	11	23	9	0	0	15	0

PLAYER	AVG	AB	R	H	2B	3B	HR	RBI	SB
Rodriguez, Eddy	.259	290	44	75	20	1	13	55	1
Sing, Brandon	.349	332	87	116	32	2	27	73	7
Torbert, Beau	.394	393	79	155	38	2	24	100	6

PLAYER	W	L	ERA	G	SV	IP	H	BB	SO
Cotter, Aaron	2	0	3.16	37	25	37	36	8	44
Flores, Brian	1	3	7.71	9	0	35	46	15	18
Grant, Ryan	3	3	4.12	28	0	44	41	14	40
Kane, Travis	5	6	6.48	20	0	83	94	30	46
Moore, Ben	11	8	3.10	20	0	134	132	22	126
Pluta, Andrew	4	3	4.04	35	0	36	40	15	17
Rapoza, Brandon	2	1	2.65	36	3	37	39	9	22
Rodriguez, Ryan	12	4	5.23	22	0	126	149	51	49
Rosen, Ben	2	0	2.08	14	0	26	17	13	21
Salberg, Chris	11	1	3.26	20	0	127	117	55	81
Shaver, Ryan	8	3	4.96	20	0	107	119	64	55
Zachary, Matt	2	1	6.60	26	0	30	47	11	19

ST. PAUL SAINTS

PLAYER	AVG	AB	R	H	2B	3B	HR	RBI	SB
Alley, Josh	.321	346	74	111	24	5	8	49	30
Bernal, Hector	.207	29	4	6	1	1	0	5	1
Burrus, Josh	.309	81	16	25	3	1	8	27	8
Butler, Steve	.272	180	24	49	4	1	1	8	0
Carter, Brandon	.243	333	48	81	22	2	4	38	14
Clemente, Edgard	.333	84	9	28	4	0	1	9	0
Cooper, Jason	.322	366	71	118	38	2	12	58	0
Estrella, Hector	.192	52	5	10	3	1	0	1	0
Gabriel, Chad	.247	93	13	23	3	2	3	16	1
Haran, Gerard	.245	261	33	64	21	1	12	54	0
Krause, Brent	.311	347	62	108	29	4	6	55	13
Mays, Steve	.219	260	28	57	7	0	1	20	0
Millar, Kevin	.208	24	1	5	0	0	0	2	0
Miller, Brad	.077	26	2	2	0	0	0	0	0
Petersen, Josh	.237	118	15	28	5	0	1	21	1
Schmiesing, Andrew	.140	43	3	6	0	0	0	6	0
Sheldon, Ole	.280	368	67	103	25	0	22	79	0
Smith, Coby	.178	118	17	21	7	1	0	6	11
Wipke, Flint	.226	115	15	26	5	1	3	14	3

PLAYER	W	L	ERA	G	SV	IP	H	BB	SO
DAlessandro, Joe	3	3	3.99	36	3	50	47	30	45
Davis, Hunter	0	3	5.54	14	6	13.0	15	6	5
Foster, Kyle	2	7	4.71	30	1	86.0	115	32	76
Godin, Jason	7	7	5.57	18	0	97.0	120	54	75
Mathison, Todd	2	2	6.83	10	0	53	82	18	16
McKenzie, Marcus	0	1	10.50	5	0	12.0	20	4	7
Meyer, Matt	3	0	0.00	18	9	21	6	8	42
Morse, Ryan	5	5	5.26	22	0	116	160	47	65
Peterson, Zach	7	6	3.65	26	1	101.0	106	25	77
Plefka, Jon	6	1	2.65	43	1	58	54	30	55
Schmidt, Jacob	8	7	5.46	22	0	114	129	48	101
Tweddale, Payton	0	1	6.24	27	0	22	29	13	21
Viola, Frank	1	2	4.58	21	0	37	39	23	20
Woerman, Joe	1	5	7.78	10	0	39	35	53	41

WICHITA WINGNUTS

PLAYER	AVG	AB	R	H	2B	3B	HR	RBI	SB
Bell, Mike	.337	163	29	55	15	1	3	31	0
Bradshaw, Jake	.209	43	5	9	3	0	1	7	1
Brooks, Patrick	.212	66	4	14	4	0	0	6	0
Christy, Jeff	.289	284	40	82	12	1	1	39	1
Colton, Chris	.270	100	20	27	4	0	2	8	6
Cortes, Jorge	.320	200	38	64	20	1	5	46	6
Delgado, Jorge	.391	115	24	45	6	0	3	26	2
Delgado, Mario	.288	271	25	78	16	0	11	54	2
Gonzalez, Raul	.286	84	14	24	3	0	0	4	0
Horn, Josh	.331	287	44	95	15	3	3	27	11
Mansolino, Tony	.174	46	3	8	0	0	0	4	0
Melian, Jackson	.238	63	11	15	3	1	0	9	2
Patterson, Ryan	.296	406	63	120	24	3	15	72	8
Pearson, Steve	.306	265	36	81	15	2	3	33	5
Rivera, Carlos	.372	121	23	45	8	0	6	16	0
Rothford, Chad	.244	45	7	11	2	0	1	5	0
Ruiz, Rene	.308	39	8	12	0	0	0	4	1

INDEPENDENT LEAGUES

Sharp, Mike	.204	54	3	11	0	0	0	9	0
Spiers, Joe	.317	82	18	26	2	0	2	8	11
Suarez, Cesar	.278	115	18	32	2	0	1	14	7
Thompson, Michael	.298	181	24	54	5	0	2	19	1
Williams, Eric	.296	142	21	42	2	0	0	6	8

PLAYER	W	L	ERA	G	SV	IP	H	BB	SO
Angelle, Kevin	3	1	3.18	4	0	23	20	12	22
Cowart, Adam	7	7	3.93	19	0	110	142	28	78
Dowdy, Justin	2	1	1.08	26	17	25	12	10	40
Graham, Ben	1	0	5.06	2	0	11	11	3	4
Howard, Cephas	3	3	4.17	35	4	37	23	13	39
Hurn, Doug	2	4	5.70	19	1	30	40	8	30
Massetti, Luke	4	7	4.94	23	0	98	117	14	73
Mathes, Brandon	3	3	4.35	33	1	52	49	25	46
Medina, Gabe	5	7	3.82	20	0	130	124	52	116
ODonnell, Bubba	3	2	8.55	5	0	26	35	10	19
Pease, Dustin	6	1	2.46	54	0	55	45	20	64
Petty, Matt	0	1	8.31	13	0	13	22	8	4
Singleton, Nick	7	3	2.36	16	0	88	73	40	73
Teague, Sean	3	4	3.51	14	0	67	74	41	48
Wiley, Jacob	0	1	6.63	14	0	19	29	10	12

ATLANTIC LEAGUE

It had been 41 years since a York baseball team won a title. And these days, you'd be hard-pressed to find many who remember the York Pirates 1969 Eastern League title—that year rainouts and lackluster attendance forced the league to declare a champion.

But York has another trophy to celebrate, as the Revolution swept the Bridgeport Bluefish in the Atlantic League championship series. In the deciding Game Three, York rallied from three runs down in the ninth inning to tie it before winning in the 10th. Ian Bladergroen's two-run double and a run-scoring error tied it up off of all-star closer Jorge Julio in the ninth while Scott Grimes singled and eventually scored on playoff MVP Ramon Castro's sacrifice fly with the winning run in the 10th.

It was an impressive playoff run for York after a disappointing second half of the season. Led by Atlantic League co-player of the year Scott Grimes, York finished in first place in the Freedom Division in the first half of the season, but slumped badly in the second half, going 29-41 to finish the year with a below .500 record.

FIRST HALF

FREEDOM DIVISION	W	L	PCT
York Revolution	40	30	.571
Somerset Patriots	36	34	.514
Lancaster Barnstormers	31	39	.443
Newark Bears	21	49	.300
LIBERTY DIVISION	W	L	PCT
Southern Maryland Blue Crabs	41	29	.586
Camden Riversharks	39	31	.557
Bridgeport Bluefish	36	34	.514
Long Island Ducks	36	34	.514

SECOND HALF

FREEDOM DIVISION	W	L	PCT
Somerset Patriots	39	31	.557
Lancaster Barnstormers	32	37	.464
Newark Bears	32	37	.464
York Revolution	29	41	.414
LIBERTY DIVISION	W	L	PCT
Bridgeport Bluefish	47	23	.671
Southern Maryland Blue Crabs	41	28	.594
Long Island Ducks	34	34	.500
Camden Riversharks	23	46	.333

PLAYOFFS—Semifinals: York defeated Somerset 3-2 and Bridgeport defeated Southern Maryland 3-1 in best-of-five series. Finals: York defeated Bridgeport 3-0 in best-of-five series.

ATTENDANCE: Long Island Ducks 410,619; Somerset Patriots 369,466; Lancaster Barnstormers 327,467; York Revolution 278,410; Camden Riversharks 246,039; Southern Maryland Blue Crabs 240,777; Bridgeport Bluefish 160,653; Newark Bears 117,985.

ALL-STAR TEAM: C—Christian Lopez, Southern Maryland. 1B—Ian Bladergroen, York. 2B—Casey Benjamin, Southern Maryland. 3B—Aaron Herr, Lancaster. SS—Bryant Nelson, Lancaster. UTIL—Ramon Castro, York. OF—Scott Grimes, York; Brian Barton, Newark; Steve Moss, Bridgeport; James Shanks, York. DH—Jose Herrera, York. RHSP—Dan Reichert, Southern Maryland. LHSP—Randy Leek, Long Island. RP—Jim Ed Warden, Southern Maryland. Closer—Jorge Julio, Bridgeport.

Player of the Year: Scott Grimes, York; Aaron Herr, Lancaster. Manager of the Year: Willie Upshaw, Bridgeport. Pitcher of the Year: Dan Reichert, Southern Maryland.

INDIVIDUAL BATTING LEADERS

PLAYER,TEAM	AVG	G	AB	R	H	HR	RBI	SB
Barton, Brian, Newark	.348	102	368	86	128	19	72	20
Castro, Ramon, York	.339	109	416	81	141	8	85	2
Herrera, Jose, York	.337	115	472	61	159	10	87	0
Jiannetti, Joe, Bridgeport	.326	108	383	52	125	13	64	8
Shanks, James, York	.325	131	530	91	172	19	86	14
Craig, Matt, Southern Maryland	.323	104	378	60	122	15	62	0
Herr, Aaron, Lancaster	.321	127	508	91	163	23	103	4
Moss, Steve, Bridgeport	.321	115	446	88	143	22	83	5
Grimes, Scott, York	.312	132	520	138	162	17	59	28
Phelps, Josh, Bridgeport	.310	100	390	71	121	10	67	15

INDIVIDUAL PITCHING LEADERS

PLAYER,TEAM	W	L	ERA	IP	H	BB	SO
Newby, Joe, Southern Maryland	6	5	2.48	113	85	53	80
Miller, Josh, Somerset	12	9	3.65	187	200	27	101
Fritz, Ben, Lancaster	3	7	3.72	126	118	52	119
Reichert, Dan, Southern Maryland	18	9	3.95	189	191	43	148
Pike, Matt, Bridgeport	12	5	4.15	167	186	51	85
Leek, Randy, Long Island	12	9	4.21	169	189	32	106
Mannix, Kevin, Bridgeport	11	6	4.36	136	142	57	89
Knox, Brad, Camden	4	9	4.36	130	154	48	60
Youman, Shane, Newark	6	5	4.54	127	135	48	94
Thurman, Corey, York	10	8	4.56	132	128	45	100

BRIDGEPORT BLUEFISH

PLAYER	AVG	AB	R	H	2B	3B	HR	RBI	SB
Barton, Brian	.264	91	12	24	1	0	3	7	2
Bocachica, Hiram	.282	252	43	71	21	1	8	34	8
Chaves, Brandon	.258	431	74	111	23	4	7	47	20
Greenberg, Adam	.258	384	67	99	9	6	4	39	44
Jennings, Todd	.301	83	9	25	2	0	0	11	2
Jiannetti, Joe	.326	383	52	125	24	3	13	64	8
Jimerson, Charlton	.346	182	40	63	17	2	10	43	12
Johnson, Tim	.203	222	26	45	5	0	3	18	6
Lopez, Luis	.281	416	49	117	18	0	8	58	0
Mercedes, Victor	.439	66	15	29	4	0	4	16	1
Moss, Steve	.321	446	88	143	24	8	22	83	5
Pena, Wily Mo	.310	155	27	48	6	1	8	34	3
Pennino, Tom	.260	100	19	26	9	0	4	16	1
Phelps, Josh	.310	390	71	121	24	0	10	67	15
Putnam, Danny	.272	364	62	99	21	5	11	56	12
Redman, Tike	.239	213	39	51	4	0	2	27	2
Roberson, Colin	.285	214	29	61	16	5	8	29	12
Rodriguez, Luis	.225	373	36	84	16	4	6	42	0

PLAYER	W	L	ERA	G	SV	IP	H	BB	SO
Alfonseca, Antonio	2	3	4.13	59	2	65	64	23	46
Arroyo, Luis	3	3	5.89	27	0	55	63	32	26
Fortunato, Bartolome	3	2	4.41	13	0	16	21	8	9
Gonzalez, Luis	9	4	3.56	16	0	96	93	65	88
Jackson, Kyle	2	7	6.67	13	0	58	78	35	47
Julio, Jorge	0	1	1.15	55	28	55	39	22	57
Kaiser, Marc	2	4	8.88	6	0	25	40	14	16
Mannix, Kevin	11	6	4.36	26	0	136	142	57	89
Oseguera, Paul	4	5	3.82	14	0	78	84	24	64
Perez, Jorge	5	2	3.30	36	0	60	55	16	47
Pike, Matt	12	5	4.15	27	0	167	186	51	85
Rivera, Chris	7	3	3.54	62	1	86	87	26	51
Ryan, Patrick	5	1	1.39	19	2	58	38	24	65
Saladin, Miguel	2	0	0.00	18	1	24	6	9	18
Serafini, Dan	4	1	3.42	11	0	50	51	19	39
Shuckerow, Riley	0	3	9.92	7	0	16	27	7	12
Stark, Denny	8	4	4.68	37	1	135	140	65	86
Yan, Esteban	3	1	3.57	6	0	35	46	9	22

CAMDEN RIVERSHARKS

PLAYER	AVG	AB	R	H	2B	3B	HR	RBI	SB
Bonvechio, Brett	.330	112	17	37	7	0	3	18	1
Botts, Jason	.342	149	30	51	13	3	3	20	2
Burgamy, Brian	.307	424	68	130	27	0	15	85	14
Ceriani, Matt	.219	128	12	28	5	0	0	6	0
Chiaravalloti, Vito	.233	43	5	10	4	0	0	9	0
Costanzo, Mike	.278	54	8	15	3	0	4	10	0
Francia, Juan	.279	183	20	51	8	1	0	8	21
Guzman, Garrett	.283	424	58	120	20	5	10	74	4
Haines, Kyle	.254	358	45	91	14	0	1	23	6
Harris, Estee	.195	149	17	29	7	0	4	15	5
Harris, Shea	.130	123	8	16	5	0	0	12	1
Horn, Gabriel	.244	41	1	10	1	0	0	4	2
Malec, Chris	.270	485	70	131	38	1	7	65	6
Olivares, Teuris	.230	287	36	66	12	1	7	34	3
Padron, Raul	.255	321	32	82	18	0	13	52	0
Pascucci, Valentino	.275	51	8	14	3	0	3	9	0
Piedra, Jorge	.231	78	9	18	4	0	1	10	0
Rivera, Rene	.280	82	10	23	6	0	7	19	0
Robnett, Richie	.275	491	73	135	26	6	13	67	20
Smith, Sean	.257	109	26	28	8	3	3	14	2
Suarez, Cesar	.171	70	5	12	4	0	1	6	1

PLAYER	W	L	ERA	G	SV	IP	H	BB	SO
Alfaro, Gabriel	3	6	7.29	32	1	67	78	43	51
Bittner, Tim	1	3	5.33	32	2	27	33	14	17
Camacho, Eddy	6	1	2.68	54	2	97	96	26	64
Chick, Travis	5	4	4.40	14	1	59	62	33	47
Davis, Ben	5	11	4.61	28	0	137	164	36	84
Hammond, Steve	7	5	2.71	15	0	86	72	43	83
Knox, Brad	4	9	4.36	23	0	130	154	48	60
Loop, Derrick	0	1	1.72	33	2	31	22	17	40
Madsen, Mike	2	3	4.65	10	0	50	41	33	52
Mattison, Kieran	1	1	7.30	16	0	25	26	21	25
McCall, Derell	1	7	7.14	10	0	47	56	21	21
McKeller, Ryan	4	7	3.64	67	2	89	68	39	82
Muldowney, Bill	0	0	4.77	9	0	11	14	4	7
Narron, Sam	4	2	1.61	7	0	50	46	5	31
Neal, Blaine	6	1	5.06	42	4	43	47	26	44
Sharpe, Steve	3	2	3.74	9	0	43	44	17	24
Thorpe, Tracy	1	3	5.40	36	10	35	36	19	36
Vaughan, William	1	1	3.80	14	0	21	16	10	16

LANCASTER BARNSTORMERS

PLAYER	AVG	AB	R	H	2B	3B	HR	RBI	SB
Biernbaum, L.J.	.225	89	16	20	2	0	1	8	1
Flowers, Brett	.143	42	3	6	0	0	0	1	0
Gaetti, Joe	.218	385	56	84	14	0	14	46	3
Gutierrez, Vic	.286	266	31	76	10	1	1	23	7
Harper, Brett	.372	78	14	29	9	0	6	14	0
Herr, Aaron	.321	508	91	163	35	0	23	103	4
Johnson, Josh	.237	139	16	33	5	0	1	8	3
Martinez, Octavio	.296	189	24	56	9	1	2	29	0
Morris, Jed	.224	210	26	47	10	0	7	27	1
Mulhern, Ryan	.322	298	49	96	19	1	14	59	4
Nelson, Bryant	.288	549	84	158	28	0	22	91	4
Nishi, Toshihisa	.208	106	9	22	2	0	1	3	2
Perry, Jason	.295	370	75	109	22	2	22	72	13
Taylor, Reggie	.308	393	66	121	20	1	23	69	11
Turner, Lloyd	.240	521	76	125	29	4	8	52	19
Watson, Matt	.317	101	22	32	7	2	4	14	1
Witter, Adam	.275	222	41	61	12	1	17	48	1
Woods, Michael	.229	297	41	68	13	3	3	26	11

PLAYER	W	L	ERA	G	SV	IP	H	BB	SO
Ackerman, Eric	2	0	8.81	16	0	16	27	8	13
Bauer, Rick	0	4	8.00	14	0	36	57	28	26
Franklin, Wayne	2	5	8.72	9	0	43	62	27	34
Fritz, Ben	3	7	3.72	23	0	126	118	52	119
Hall, Josh	13	7	4.90	28	0	167	181	65	111
Hamulack, Tim	6	5	2.35	55	11	65	54	17	92
Heuser, James	1	0	4.05	21	0	27	23	13	33
Hinkle, Austin	0	2	5.76	29	0	45	62	24	33
Junge, Eric	2	1	3.08	4	0	26	25	8	36

PLAYER	W	L	ERA	G	SV	IP	H	BB	SO
Maness, Nick	0	3	7.99	8	0	24	32	20	15
Muller, John	1	1	1.45	15	0	19	11	7	23
Musser, Neal	1	1	5.94	4	0	17	22	4	7
Overholt, Pat	4	4	7.12	37	1	43	54	24	41
Patterson, Scott	1	1	2.81	17	8	16	14	3	18
Peeples, Ross	4	1	3.28	41	1	69	71	15	49
Sanchez, Jose	7	11	5.45	28	0	154	198	65	102
Simontacchi, Jason	5	7	5.78	26	0	100	136	16	69
Thompson, Sean	4	8	5.64	30	0	97	102	67	81
Weatherby, Charlie	1	5	6.36	23	2	28	40	14	21

LONG ISLAND DUCKS

PLAYER	AVG	AB	R	H	2B	3B	HR	RBI	SB
Cancel, Robinson	.304	388	64	118	23	2	14	81	13
Cavagnaro, Matt	.280	443	71	124	17	4	9	67	14
Colina, Javier	.266	267	44	71	19	1	7	37	4
Esquivel, Matt	.281	469	85	132	28	3	17	78	11
Francia, Juan	.247	267	36	66	9	2	0	21	18
Gathright, Joey	.269	160	31	43	5	2	3	19	4
Hernandez, Johnny	.254	311	41	79	11	0	5	34	8
Hunt, Bridger	.259	116	16	30	6	1	1	13	7
Kovatch, Billy	.239	213	28	51	10	0	0	11	4
Mohr, Dustan	.270	263	45	71	16	1	9	41	1
Monaghan, Brendan	.291	237	33	69	18	2	2	24	4
Monzon, Erick	.267	374	42	100	17	1	11	56	17
Navarrete, Ray	.275	338	55	93	25	0	13	54	2
Otanez, Willis	.393	84	14	33	3	0	2	15	1
Padgett, Matt	.275	287	41	79	20	1	5	43	1
Pavkovich, Adam	.205	83	14	17	6	0	1	10	3
Rodriguez, John	.304	329	50	100	21	0	10	43	4
Suarez, Gabe	.259	54	5	14	2	1	0	5	0

PLAYER	W	L	ERA	G	SV	IP	H	BB	SO
Bauer, Rick	3	9	5.49	15	0	84	90	54	56
Davis, Kane	0	1	1.69	31	14	32	22	12	43
Diaz, Joselo	5	2	2.52	13	0	61	41	34	39
Dittler, Jake	11	11	5.56	29	0	159	205	61	108
Drese, Ryan	1	1	1.59	4	0	17	16	6	13
Esposito, Joe	3	4	2.98	25	3	48	51	23	53
Gamble, Jerome	2	0	2.46	24	0	44	39	16	38
Gomez, Ricardo	3	3	3.15	43	9	46	38	21	64
Guerrero, Julio	0	1	5.76	18	0	30	44	5	13
Harang, Daryl	4	4	7.77	15	0	73	100	35	35
Jackson, Kyle	2	3	5.47	19	0	74	84	34	50
Keisler, Randy	5	0	3.65	8	0	49	43	18	43
Leek, Randy	12	9	4.21	26	0	169	189	32	106
Maldonado, Ivan	4	4	4.53	39	2	48	48	18	37
McCoy, Chris	3	0	4.64	19	1	43	42	16	31
Norderum, Jason	1	1	5.16	31	0	30	31	24	34
Ponson, Sidney	4	5	5.64	11	0	67	85	20	29
Simas, Bill	2	1	3.30	29	4	30	25	12	28
Spurling, Chris	3	3	4.01	33	0	43	47	12	35
Valentine, Joe	0	1	4.91	11	2	11	10	5	10
Wells, Kip	2	2	4.00	5	0	27	26	15	23
White, Bill	0	1	8.81	19	0	14	7	21	21

NEWARK BEARS

PLAYER	AVG	AB	R	H	2B	3B	HR	RBI	SB
Alfonzo, Edgardo	.154	78	6	12	2	0	1	7	0
Barton, Brian	.375	277	74	104	24	4	16	65	18
Cooper, James	.299	311	62	93	12	2	4	37	15
Cortez, Fernando	.313	128	17	40	4	0	3	14	5
Dukes, Elijah	.366	101	19	37	7	0	5	19	2
Everett, Carl	.279	340	37	95	17	0	16	69	1
Gress, Randy	.218	238	33	52	8	3	3	20	5
Griffin, John Ford	.235	166	13	39	8	1	4	20	2
House, J.R.	.345	58	13	20	4	0	0	8	0
Jennings, Todd	.108	37	4	4	0	0	0	2	1
Jones, Kennard	.296	517	80	153	28	12	5	51	40
Kaaihue, Isaiah	.216	185	19	40	7	0	5	21	1
Logan, Nook	.217	161	18	35	3	2	2	11	6
Madera, Sandy	.292	89	13	26	5	1	4	16	1
Manuel, Anthony	.231	52	7	12	3	0	0	4	1
Matera, Paddy	.200	125	19	25	3	1	7	8	1

PLAYER	AVG	AB	R	H	2B	3B	HR	RBI	SB
Mejia, Manny	.275	178	29	49	5	1	9	33	1
Munson, Eric	.261	161	22	42	6	0	8	27	0
Ozuna, Pablo	.294	119	24	35	8	0	1	13	3
Pennino, Tom	.208	101	5	21	3	0	2	10	1
Raines Jr., Tim	.367	158	43	58	9	2	5	22	20
Rodriguez, Victor	.217	60	4	13	6	0	0	6	1
Seguignol, Fernando	.337	101	17	34	4	0	3	16	1
Shults, Stephen	.232	56	8	13	2	0	1	6	0
Spiezio, Scott	.279	179	24	50	13	0	3	35	0
Suarez, Gabe	.271	140	16	38	2	1	0	9	5
Ward, Daryle	.286	399	54	114	22	1	14	79	0
Williams, Shawn	.253	79	10	20	5	1	0	3	0

PLAYER	W	L	ERA	G	SV	IP	H	BB	SO
Banks, Willie	1	3	9.21	12	0	28	47	17	22
Benitez, Armando	2	1	2.86	33	12	35	22	12	52
Blacksher, Derek	2	6	7.03	17	0	65	78	24	48
Carrasco, Hector	1	4	8.88	5	0	24	35	25	19
Coffey, Drew	1	1	4.60	22	0	31	32	19	20
Cunnane, Will	1	1	3.24	12	1	17	18	10	18
De la Cruz, Maximo	0	1	10.33	7	0	11	25	6	12
Fagan, Paul	3	8	5.38	17	0	85	109	42	52
Glynn, Ryan	2	2	6.11	6	1	28	31	10	27
Holliday, Brian	2	0	4.32	9	0	33	34	16	17
Loree, Mike	6	9	6.09	26	0	130	170	43	119
Mehlich, Michael	1	2	6.30	23	0	30	37	27	30
Melody, Matt	1	1	6.23	20	0	26	29	11	24
Nix, Michael	4	2	2.15	42	5	50	48	16	55
ODonnell, Bubba	4	5	4.36	20	0	76	82	29	48
Perkins, Vince	0	6	4.93	14	0	53	58	33	42
Reinhard, Greg	3	4	2.74	42	0	62	51	16	67
Renault, Nick	0	1	5.02	12	0	23	25	12	15
Smith, Matt	9	11	5.86	29	2	124	153	73	77
Vasami, Chris	0	0	7.65	14	0	20	27	14	14
Villa, Kelvin	3	10	7.01	19	1	89	120	48	93
Youman, Shane	4	1	3.66	13	1	66	64	29	49
Zimmermann, Bob	2	5	4.80	10	0	60	54	20	69

SOMERSET PATRIOTS

PLAYER	AVG	AB	R	H	2B	3B	HR	RBI	SB
Ayala, Elliott	.284	366	60	104	16	7	2	35	8
Belcher, Jason	.269	342	32	92	15	0	7	54	0
Burke, Joe	.295	441	70	130	18	2	10	66	25
Freel, Ryan	.265	34	3	9	0	0	0	4	1
Hagen, Matt	.281	417	67	117	27	1	9	57	11
Hall, Noah	.281	423	81	119	26	3	10	68	25
Hernandez, Michael	.303	307	41	93	18	2	15	56	2
Holden, Joe	.252	159	25	40	6	1	2	17	6
Hopf, J.R.	.265	155	20	41	7	0	5	19	0
Housel, David	.228	149	12	34	7	2	1	18	2
LaForest, Pete	.269	156	19	42	11	0	8	41	0
Lydon, Wayne	.296	540	108	160	19	10	9	53	66
Nettles, Jeff	.299	324	47	97	17	0	12	52	0
Pressley, Josh	.274	339	54	93	17	1	22	75	1
Raines Jr., Tim	.241	323	46	78	8	6	6	27	22
Suarez, Iggy	.266	297	40	79	15	1	2	30	3

PLAYER	W	L	ERA	G	SV	IP	H	BB	SO
Adams, Brian	4	4	3.24	10	0	58	62	23	55
Cahill, Casey	5	4	6.30	47	0	94	120	39	44
Darcy, Jesse	1	9	6.19	14	0	68	103	12	40
Dobies, Andrew	3	2	1.54	23	1	23	17	7	29
Dunn, Jerry	3	2	3.30	39	0	44	45	12	37
Ellis, Jonathon	3	2	3.88	15	0	53	43	39	25
Grezlovski, Ben	9	3	3.18	46	3	65	62	26	48
Henderson, Brian	4	3	4.23	33	1	38	37	13	40
Hines, Carlos	2	2	4.67	45	0	52	53	36	39
Houston, Ryan	2	2	4.18	30	18	28	24	12	37
Jones, Justin	4	6	5.38	18	0	95	122	39	76
Kennard, Jeff	3	2	4.24	51	3	57	53	27	58
Kirsten, Joel	1	0	2.84	2	0	13	10	0	9
Lavigne, Tim	0	2	4.97	9	0	25	24	18	21
Mastny, Tom	3	1	3.32	7	0	38	32	18	18
Miller, Josh	12	9	3.65	29	0	187	200	27	101
Monti, Jason	5	6	3.77	43	0	107	108	42	86

PLAYER	W	L	ERA	G	SV	IP	H	BB	SO
Pulsipher, Bill	5	1	3.18	11	0	62	65	17	50
Reilly, Matt	1	0	7.20	17	0	20	19	21	8
Thompson, Mike	4	3	4.29	11	0	63	74	15	35
Williamson, Scott	1	1	3.94	15	11	16	11	9	21

SOUTHERN MARYLAND BLUE CRABS

PLAYER	AVG	AB	R	H	2B	3B	HR	RBI	SB
Armiger, Justin	.247	73	7	18	5	1	2	4	0
Benjamin, Casey	.304	454	61	138	19	7	20	66	5
Craig, Matt	.323	378	60	122	30	0	15	62	0
Crozier, Eric	.269	427	68	115	23	9	21	69	9
Cumberland, Shaun	.296	324	65	96	16	2	12	48	7
Espinosa, David	.340	50	9	17	4	2	1	7	1
Garcia, Travis	.262	489	68	128	16	2	17	71	7
Giannotti, Richard	.188	304	30	57	10	0	5	29	6
Harrison, Ben	.207	92	11	19	5	0	3	12	2
Hill, Jamar	.278	309	44	86	16	7	11	36	8
Howell, Travis	.154	65	3	10	2	0	1	2	0
Kirkland, Kody	.303	234	38	71	15	6	11	39	10
Lane, Jason	.231	65	10	15	2	0	3	11	0
Lopez, Christian	.274	325	38	89	13	0	7	41	7
Martinez, Octavio	.164	110	12	18	1	0	1	11	0
McFall, Brian	.247	93	12	23	7	0	3	15	0
Osborn, Patrick	.298	446	72	133	16	3	8	48	1
Owens, Jeremy	.230	453	81	104	25	5	18	64	18
Porter, Greg	.324	34	4	11	1	0	3	8	0

PLAYER	W	L	ERA	G	SV	IP	H	BB	SO
Anderson, Craig	9	3	4.31	19	0	104	123	26	64
Dumesnil, Bryan	2	3	5.03	50	1	43	43	20	48
Grube, Jarrett	3	3	2.06	8	0	48	42	15	36
Halama, John	2	3	1.90	7	0	43	34	6	27
Hayes, Chris	3	0	2.17	17	1	50	48	10	32
Koronka, John	0	4	11.74	6	0	15	15	33	14
Mann, Brandon	1	2	5.14	5	0	28	32	14	22
Mobley, Chris	4	3	2.53	40	0	46	41	15	50
Palazzolo, Steve	3	0	2.67	25	1	30	24	8	34
Petrusek, Matt	0	0	9.00	13	0	12	21	7	3
Reichert, Dan	18	9	3.95	29	0	189	191	43	148
Ridgway, Jeff	0	0	3.95	39	0	43	49	31	47
Robertson, Connor	6	4	3.64	29	1	96	92	30	71
Santos, Jarrett	5	2	2.82	14	0	83	87	15	50
Speier, Ryan	3	4	3.36	56	0	56	46	22	49
Waddell, Jason	1	1	2.89	37	0	44	40	25	42
Warden, Jim Ed	6	4	2.61	58	30	59	46	32	57

YORK REVOLUTION

PLAYER	AVG	AB	R	H	2B	3B	HR	RBI	SB
Andrus, Erold	.289	342	55	99	21	0	8	48	3
Bladergroen, Ian	.280	483	79	135	30	3	17	86	3
Castro, Ramon	.339	416	81	141	37	2	8	85	2
DeLeon, Sandy	.237	59	3	14	1	0	0	1	0
Grimes, Scott	.312	520	138	162	32	8	17	59	28
Haake, Steve	.261	249	42	65	12	1	12	50	2
Harrison, Vince	.362	47	12	17	3	0	1	7	0
Herrera, Jose	.337	472	61	159	30	1	10	87	0
Hill, Jamar	.261	92	14	24	6	0	2	15	1
Jeroloman, Chuck	.249	485	77	121	35	2	14	66	1
Lisk, Charlie	.158	57	5	9	2	1	2	8	0
Majewski, Val	.328	119	22	39	10	1	2	24	4
Manriquez, Salomon	.327	101	13	33	8	1	3	15	0
Pachot, John	.322	338	39	109	28	0	4	45	5
Polanco, Enohel	.139	36	4	5	0	0	1	0	0
Rodriguez, Liu	.296	460	71	136	31	2	3	57	3
Rodriguez, Victor	.323	130	20	42	9	0	6	19	0
Shanks, James	.325	530	91	172	29	4	19	86	14

PLAYER	W	L	ERA	G	SV	IP	H	BB	SO
Ackerman, Eric	3	3	4.18	17	0	19	15	5	19
Angelle, Kevin	0	2	5.04	4	0	20	24	7	15
Basner, Ryan	2	2	4.41	52	0	53	50	28	39
Beltran, Francis	0	3	2.81	16	3	16	13	6	14
DeSalvo, Matt	5	2	4.67	12	0	52	53	22	52
Hampson, Justin	1	0	4.96	11	1	16	16	9	11
Harikkala, Tim	1	2	7.46	25	0	25	43	7	14

Name									
Heuser, James	1	2	6.18	34	0	28	29	12	29
Lewis, Jeremy	0	1	11.46	3	0	11	22	3	5
Manon, Julio	0	3	11.71	5	0	20	33	13	20
Marceaux, Jacob	0	1	5.06	4	0	11	11	14	9
McCall, Derell	7	3	4.46	21	0	81	89	27	54
McCurdy, Nick	1	0	8.48	11	0	12	23	5	11
Morrison, James	1	1	4.39	14	0	14	17	3	11
Moss, Damian	1	0	4.32	5	0	17	23	10	8
Muller, John	1	1	5.96	21	7	23	23	9	22
Murray, A.J.	0	1	7.79	14	0	17	26	5	8
Perkins, Vince	0	2	8.18	13	0	22	27	29	18
Plummer, Jarod	3	3	7.13	10	0	48	70	17	39
Polanco, Celson	1	1	6.26	20	0	46	55	19	36
Richardson, Jason	3	4	4.61	61	1	70	75	33	63
Riley, Matt	4	1	5.87	38	1	46	47	37	56
Rodriguez, R.J.	2	3	2.51	41	8	47	33	18	49
Ruhlman, Jayson	1	3	7.36	11	0	18	26	6	10
Sanchez, Jesus	7	6	3.65	16	0	86	77	35	73
Starner, Nate	1	1	6.58	13	0	14	21	7	5
Stidfole, Sean	2	3	1.90	68	11	71	74	22	51
Thurman, Corey	10	8	4.56	26	0	132	128	45	100
Youman, Shane	2	4	5.49	14	0	61	71	19	45
Zimmermann, Bob	7	1	4.43	21	0	85	101	53	53

CAN-AM LEAGUE

When he was playing at Lousiana State, Ivan Naccarrata got a taste of life in a pressure cooker as the Tigers made a pair of trips to the College World Series.

LSU didn't win a game in Omaha during Naccarrata's two trips. It may not have happened in Omaha, but Naccarrata has now had the chance to celebrate a season-ending dogpile. The Quebec shortstop had three hits in a Game Two win, a triple and a run in Game Three and another three hits in Game Four as Quebec rallied after a series-opening loss to beat Pittsfield three straight games for the Can-Am League title.

Quebec got plenty of pitching along the way as well. Karl Gelinas brought Quebec to the clinching game by shutting out Pittsfield with a five-hitter in Game Three. In the clincher, Michel Simard allowed one run in seven innings before handing it over to the bullpen.

It was a fitting title for Les Capitales. Quebec has finished first in both halves of the regular season.

FIRST HALF

	W	L	PCT	GB
Quebec Les Capitales	30	17	.638	-
Brockton Rox	27	20	.574	3
Sussex Skyhawks	25	21	.543	4.5
Pittsfield Colonials	20	27	.426	10
New Jersey Jackals	19	27	.413	10.5
Worcester Tornadoes	19	28	.404	11

SECOND HALF

	W	L	PCT	GB
Pittsfield Colonials	28	18	.609	—
Brockton Rox	27	19	.587	1
Quebec Les Capitales	27	20	.574	1.5
Worcester Tornadoes	23	23	.500	5
New Jersey Jackals	23	23	.500	5
Sussex Skyhawks	10	35	.222	17.5

PLAYOFFS-Semifinals: Quebec defeated New Jersey 3-0 and Pittsfield defeated Brockton 3-1 in best-of-five series. **Finals:** Quebec defeated Pittsfield 3-1 in best-of-five series.
ATTENDANCE: Quebec 147,978; Brockton 100,092; Worcester 88,499; New Jersey 86,014; Sussex 71,826; Pittsfield 29,485.
MANAGERS: Brockton—Chris Carminucci. **Pittsfield**—Brian Daubach. **New Jersey**—Joe Calfapietra. **Quebec**—Michel Laplante. **Sussex**—Ed Ott. **Worcester**—Rich Gedman.
ALL-STARS: C—Chris Grossman, Brockton. **1B**—Melvin Falu, Brockton. **2B**—Danny Bomback, Pittsfield. **3B**—Mark Minicozzi, Worcester. **SS**—Matt Nandin, Pittsfield. **OF**—Daniel Carte, Pittsfield; Carl Loadenthal, Sussex; Sebastien Boucher, Quebec. **DH**—Caleb Stewart, Sussex. **LHP**—Mike Wlodarczyk, Brockton. **RHP**—Mike Smith, Brockton. **RP**—Andrew Albers, Quebec.
Player of the Year: Melvin Falu, Brockton. **Manager of the Year:** Brian Daubach, Pittsfield.

INDIVIDUAL BATTING LEADERS

PLAYER, TEAM	AVG	G	AB	R	H	2B	3B	HR	RBI
Carte, Daniel, Pittsfield	.347	88	346	59	120	18	3	12	67
Boucher, Sebastian, Quebec	.336	68	259	58	87	16	1	11	75
Bomback, Danny, Pittsfield	.324	93	364	64	118	22	3	7	62
Nandin, Matt, Pittsfield	.321	93	368	68	118	25	0	8	48
Minicozzi, Mark, Worcester	.317	86	325	54	103	14	2	12	54
Naccarata, Ivan, Quebec	.316	90	392	68	124	17	3	4	56
Loadenthal, Carl, Sussex	.315	84	336	67	106	17	7	3	59
Falu, Melvin, Brockton	.314	90	366	72	115	15	2	20	66
Grossman, Chris, Brockton	.313	86	297	50	93	24	0	9	57
Stewart, Caleb, Sussex	.313	91	342	59	107	23	4	15	88

INDIVIDUAL PITCHING LEADERS

PLAYER, TEAM	W	L	ERA	IP	H	BB	SO
Smith, Mike, Brockton	12	3	2.87	125	126	45	108
Gelinas, Karl, Quebec	4	3	3.07	88	87	24	64
Sausville, Dan, Quebec	7	6	3.11	116	121	43	80
Wlodarczyk, Mike, Brockton	10	3	3.25	130	123	50	115
Flores, Freddy, Brockton	10	2	3.29	120	117	19	87
Rusch, Matthew, Quebec	11	2	3.29	107	96	20	107
Kelly, John, Worcester	9	5	3.61	107	91	38	109
Flores, Miguel, Pittsfield	10	4	3.63	112	125	58	89
Pavlik, Issac, New Jersey	7	6	3.73	104	115	16	78
Zaleski, Kyle, Pittsfield	8	6	3.88	107	99	35	79

BROCKTON ROX

PLAYER	AVG	AB	R	H	2B	3B	HR	RBI	SB
Brachold, Keith	.279	359	71	100	19	3	15	67	5
Conroy, Mike	.256	308	48	79	9	2	5	43	4
Cuadrado, Phillip	.308	234	44	72	9	1	13	63	3
Falu, Melvin	.314	366	72	115	15	2	20	66	3
Grossman, Chris	.313	297	50	93	24	0	9	57	2
Kinzler, Derek	.210	167	16	35	4	0	0	17	1
Parke, John	.250	36	6	9	0	0	0	2	0
Ramos, Dominic	.288	330	46	95	19	3	1	35	9
Valencia, Chris	.280	378	61	106	24	4	2	46	10
Wearne, Scott	.300	297	49	89	21	3	2	35	10
Williams, Clyde	.207	184	23	38	7	0	5	22	2
Williams, Shawn	.368	155	33	57	10	0	5	24	0

PLAYER	W	L	ERA	IP	G	SV	H	BB	SO
Aquino, Jose	1	3	7.53	35	10	0	43	20	15
Davis, Hunter	1	2	4.30	23	22	11	24	11	12
Flores, Freddy	10	2	3.29	120	19	1	117	19	87
Hertzler, Brad	3	1	5.01	47	36	2	55	8	40
Kennedy, Jimmer	1	2	4.27	13	5	0	11	4	14
Lundgren, Wayne	7	6	4.69	113	20	0	130	33	69
Lussier, Buster	1	5	5.09	58	20	1	69	15	43
Lynch, Colin	6	4	4.11	46	41	4	46	16	35
Ortiz, Francisco	0	1	6.42	14	6	0	21	6	10
Papelbon, Josh	1	0	4.55	30	22	7	37	10	17
Smith, Mike	12	3	2.87	125	19	0	126	45	108
Tyson, Nick	0	1	4.24	17	3	0	19	2	7
Williamson, Logan	0	1	6.89	16	3	0	16	7	9
Wlodarczyk, Mike	10	3	3.25	130	19	0	123	50	115

NEW JERSEY JACKALS

PLAYER	AVG	AB	R	H	2B	3B	HR	RBI	SB
Bergeron, Jabe	.297	279	52	83	10	2	19	63	0
Betteridge, Dan	.206	68	8	14	2	0	0	6	1
Butler, Jacob	.290	293	50	85	15	0	16	55	0
Clark, Kevin	.283	357	62	101	13	3	9	38	27
Davis, Quentin	.257	35	5	9	0	1	0	3	3
DeJesus, Mike	.293	283	35	83	17	0	2	32	3
Flores, Angel	.248	105	15	26	5	0	1	15	0
Forthun, Dean	.143	56	6	8	2	0	1	6	0
Godwin, Adam	.345	206	37	71	9	5	4	32	17
Grose, Jeff	.239	205	25	49	6	0	0	19	10
Jones, Travis A.	.243	177	15	43	11	0	3	23	6
Knazek, Scott	.316	38	4	12	1	0	1	3	0
Newton, Jordan	.364	99	22	36	9	2	2	20	3
Nunez, Abraham O.	.307	309	44	95	11	1	2	29	15
Reyes, Argenis	.279	129	22	36	6	1	2	15	5

Riggans, Shawn .328 122 19 40 6 1 4 26 1
Rosa, Jovan .178 135 9 24 5 0 2 11 3
Sosa, Carlos .336 140 25 47 7 3 1 22 2

PLAYER	W	L	ERA	IP	G	SV	H	BB	SO
Allen, Chris	0	3	6.17	23	4	0	33	10	11
Asselin, Nick	1	7	8.05	57	10	0	77	20	27
Estanga, Edgar	3	7	4.29	50	39	2	46	21	51
Fagan, Paul	0	1	9.00	16	3	0	29	6	6
Fernandez, Luis	2	0	6.46	46	30	0	59	23	27
Griffin, Dan	2	1	7.11	51	14	0	63	21	46
Hicks, Romas	1	3	6.27	37	38	18	47	19	42
Jones, Justin W.	0	2	7.83	23	4	0	27	10	19
Lobban, Ryan	5	3	5.56	104	19	0	129	34	73
Miller, Jayson	4	4	4.33	60	11	0	76	7	38
Pavlik, Isaac	7	6	3.73	104	25	0	115	16	78
Pontius, Mike	3	3	5.81	48	42	2	44	38	55
Rodriguez, Edward R.	7	4	3.26	50	39	0	42	21	40
Vasami, Chris	3	1	4.63	45	8	0	47	19	26
Wideman, A.J.	4	5	4.88	59	11	0	78	18	41

PITTSFIELD COLONIALS

PLAYER	AVG	AB	R	H	2B	3B	HR	RBI	SB
Baez, Welinson	.173	52	3	9	0	0	0	3	1
Bomback, Danny	.324	364	64	118	22	3	7	62	41
Cabreja, Rafael	.307	274	41	84	17	3	13	55	5
Carte, Daniel	.347	346	59	120	18	3	12	67	8
Chavez, Zane	.192	52	4	10	4	0	0	2	0
Davis, Quentin	.232	220	36	51	10	4	7	22	15
Edmondson, Jerod	.244	377	62	92	21	2	9	48	23
Fink, Wes	.244	45	9	11	1	2	0	6	2
Knazek, Scott	.256	219	27	56	13	1	1	17	4
Leon, Donny	.259	166	23	43	6	0	6	26	0
Manuel, Anthony	.222	36	3	8	0	0	0	3	1
Molina, Angel	.350	203	35	71	21	0	7	35	14
Nandin, Matt	.321	368	68	118	25	0	8	48	25
Taylor, Jason	.306	258	47	79	20	0	12	45	16
Torres, Chris	.262	126	10	33	4	0	3	17	1

PLAYER	W	L	ERA	IP	G	SV	H	BB	SO
Bradley, Kyle	0	0	6.23	17	10	1	21	12	14
Bresnahan, Pat	3	2	5.51	16	13	0	16	8	9
Corgan, Chance	0	1	5.75	16	4	0	16	12	7
Cruz, Reymond	1	2	5.03	34	29	3	30	17	38
Flores, Miguel A.	10	4	3.63	112	20	0	125	58	89
Granitto, Giuseppe	1	1	4.43	22	21	1	25	16	12
Lluberes, Rafael	2	1	4.10	22	26	0	17	22	23
Lyons, Matt	1	0	3.22	22	18	0	11	15	32
Marcotte, Trevor	4	4	4.93	49	9	0	61	20	25
Moran, Patrick	5	2	4.12	68	18	1	70	26	42
Padilla, Juan	2	0	2.86	28	25	17	24	9	27
Paradoski, Matthew	1	3	9.29	20	5	0	31	16	14
Qualben, David	6	7	5.42	115	20	0	136	39	75
Rollins, Chris	1	1	5.54	13	12	0	12	10	14
Shepherd, Cory	0	0	7.80	15	11	0	19	9	11
Sprouse, Shannon	0	2	5.40	22	18	0	20	17	19
Venters, Jon	2	4	5.76	45	9	0	54	24	31
Wasylak, David	0	1	5.32	22	14	1	18	11	15
White, Matt	1	3	4.70	23	4	0	20	13	10
Zaleski, Kyle	8	6	3.88	107	20	1	99	35	79

QUEBEC CAPITALES

PLAYER	AVG	AB	R	H	2B	3B	HR	RBI	SB
Boucher, Sebastien	.336	259	58	87	16	1	11	75	15
Colafemina, Josh	.261	299	62	78	17	3	1	29	25
Cros, Anthony	.234	184	33	43	6	0	0	22	6
DAoust, Patrick	.238	210	43	50	17	0	3	22	2
Deschenes, Patrick	.288	52	10	15	1	0	2	9	1
Hunt, Jeremy	.268	209	36	56	10	0	4	33	3
LaForest, Pete	.256	125	18	32	6	0	9	28	3
Lemieux, Jared	.228	101	16	23	7	0	3	18	0
Leveret, Rene	.309	175	23	54	11	0	4	40	1
Mimeault, Marc	.246	195	30	48	9	0	4	24	0
Naccarata, Ivan	.316	392	68	124	17	3	4	56	17
Nunez, AleA.	.298	339	55	101	13	3	4	33	29

Thompson, Michael L. .284 197 26 56 17 0 6 33 0
Tomlinson, Goefrey .285 249 52 71 7 1 5 37 10
Wagner, Robert .319 185 26 59 17 2 8 34 4

PLAYER	W	L	ERA	IP	G	SV	H	BB	SO
Albers, Andrew	3	0	1.41	58	40	17	41	16	59
Arnold, Adam	3	3	7.76	27	26	1	32	27	27
Cate, Troy	5	3	3.39	74	12	0	80	24	41
Gelinas, Karl	4	3	3.07	88	16	0	87	24	64
Gregory, Sean	4	2	5.83	42	29	4	42	22	36
Hunt, Jeremy	1	3	4.96	33	25	0	35	18	24
Kukucka, James	2	2	6.37	30	16	0	39	20	22
Malkowski, Brendon	3	2	4.28	27	11	0	36	11	20
Rusch, Matthew	11	2	3.29	107	23	1	96	20	107
Sausville, Dan	7	6	3.11	116	22	1	121	43	80
Schon, Andy	3	2	5.10	55	27	0	69	19	57
Simard, Michel	9	6	5.23	114	20	0	127	42	98

SUSSEX SKYHAWKS

PLAYER	AVG	AB	R	H	2B	3B	HR	RBI	SB
Binick, Kraig	.289	381	75	110	18	3	4	25	45
Blue, Vincent	.218	133	14	29	4	1	0	6	8
Boelsen, Ryan	.257	214	20	55	15	0	1	31	2
Fontaine, Chase	.293	273	58	80	19	1	4	33	18
Giarraputo, Nick	.243	280	31	68	12	1	7	41	5
Gossard, Jonathan	.258	97	10	25	4	0	3	8	0
Keowen, Kade	.217	129	25	28	9	0	2	11	2
Loadenthal, Carl	.315	336	67	106	17	7	3	59	32
Megale, Mike	.243	74	9	18	4	1	0	4	2
Persichina, Joe	.259	347	42	90	13	5	3	36	10
Ruiz, Rene	.069	58	2	4	1	0	0	3	0
Sanchez, Kris	.281	352	47	99	21	1	19	74	0
Sosnoskie, Anthony	.243	37	4	9	0	0	0	3	0
Stewart, Caleb	.313	342	59	107	23	4	15	88	2

PLAYER	W	L	ERA	IP	G	SV	H	BB	SO
Berlind, Dan	2	3	4.38	64	14	0	73	45	43
Frias, Jusef	1	5	7.10	65	12	0	90	31	58
Gunter, Kevin	3	2	3.39	66	35	0	61	27	44
Hassett, Will	0	2	6.32	16	3	0	22	15	10
Icenogle, Jeff	5	7	5.62	107	19	0	111	53	99
Jordat, Donald	3	5	4.89	42	28	0	38	25	45
Locke, Jared	6	8	3.93	53	49	2	51	24	50
Marcotte, Trevor	0	2	7.83	23	5	0	34	10	15
McGuire, Mike	3	4	5.29	48	8	0	50	22	41
Roque, Ulysses	0	0	3.97	11	8	0	11	5	8
Salvato, Matt	1	0	4.01	34	25	2	33	19	20
Sanchez, Duaner	2	2	3.76	26	28	17	25	9	20
Streaman, Michael	0	0	5.19	17	10	0	20	7	10
Stringer, Tim	3	7	6.09	86	19	1	96	56	54
Vicaro, Mike	6	5	4.70	84	14	0	74	35	67

WORCESTER TORNADOES

PLAYER	AVG	AB	R	H	2B	3B	HR	RBI	SB
Asadoorian, Rick	.210	119	14	25	3	1	3	13	1
Baillargeon, Mike	.172	87	12	15	2	1	1	6	1
Billingslea, Courtney	.224	49	4	11	2	0	2	5	1
Blanchard, Boomer	.273	128	20	35	6	0	0	9	4
Cather, Billy	.302	215	31	65	14	3	3	22	3
Colabello, Chris	.301	316	53	95	16	1	13	59	3
Contreras, Lester	.361	36	5	13	2	0	2	3	0
Crespi, Ryan	.295	251	46	74	12	1	8	26	7
Gronkowski, Gordon	.291	103	15	30	9	1	2	12	1
Maddox, Craig	.210	105	14	22	6	1	3	10	1
Minicozzi, Mark	.317	325	54	103	14	2	12	54	1
Pena, Omar	.285	260	46	74	12	0	4	30	10
Pennell, Vinny	.188	48	10	9	1	0	1	3	3
Salotti, Nick	.265	313	37	83	22	1	10	48	0
Santiesteban, Danny	.246	228	39	56	12	1	14	42	6
Smith, Stantrel	.281	192	26	54	10	3	4	33	14
Trezza, Alex	.256	324	41	83	22	0	12	54	4

PLAYER	W	L	ERA	IP	G	SV	H	BB	SO
Asadoorian, Rick	2	2	1.99	23	22	8	17	11	27
Ayala, Albert	4	3	3.30	44	35	3	32	28	56
Farley, Chris	7	7	4.69	111	18	0	106	67	86

Gilblair, Shawn	1	1	2.68	54	36	0	53	12	47
Giusti, Matt	2	8	7.83	77	17	2	123	31	48
Hollis, Jon	1	3	4.67	35	10	0	38	20	20
Kelly, John	9	5	3.61	107	19	0	91	38	109
Knoff, Justin	3	4	4.74	70	11	0	80	23	55
McDonald, Matt	2	5	6.50	64	18	0	81	35	51
Santiesteban, Danny	0	0	4.08	18	12	0	23	8	18
Short, Baron	0	6	6.07	40	11	0	59	19	24
Slusarz, John	4	5	3.50	54	25	5	57	25	57
Taylor, Dustin	0	0	6.52	19	12	0	32	11	21
Zuercher, Zach	7	2	3.89	83	14	0	78	44	67

FRONTIER LEAGUE

The year of the pitcher stretched beyond just the big leagues. Pitching dominated the Frontier League in 2010, so it was fitting that the championship series ended up being decided by a shutout.

River City's Zack Sterner, Kirkland Rivers and Derrick Miramontes combined to hold Traverse City to three hits in the deciding Game Four of the championship series. After losing the opening game of the series, River City won the final three to claim its first Frontier League title.

"We don't have the most talent in the league, but we always find ways to win," Rascals manager Steve Brook said. "That's what makes this team so special."

River City truly earned its way to the title. The Rascals were matched up against Southern Illinois in the first round of the playoffs. The Miners had the best record in the league during the regular season and jumped out to a 2-0 lead in the best-of-five series, but River City rallied to win the final three games to advance to the championship series.

River City had lost its ace reliever Jason Lowey during the season, as the Braves signed him, but Lowey still got to celebrate the title. Jason's twin brother Josh picked up a complete game win over Traverse City in the championship series.

EAST	W	L	PCT	GB
Windy City ThunderBolts	56	38	.596	—
Traverse City Beach Bums	55	41	.573	2
Oakland County Cruisers	53	43	.552	4
Lake Erie Crushers	50	46	.521	7
Washington Wild Things	38	57	.400	18.5
Kalamazoo Kings	28	68	.292	29

WEST	W	L	PCT	GB
Southern Illinois Miners	64	32	.667	—
River City Rascals	57	38	.600	6.5
Gateway Grizzlies	54	40	.574	9
Normal CornBelters	44	52	.458	20
Florence Freedom	38	58	.396	26
Evansville Otters	35	59	.372	28

PLAYOFFS—Semifinals: River City defeated Southern Illinois 3-2 and Traverse City defeated Windy City 3-1 in best-of-five series. **Finals:** Lake Erie defeated River City 3-2 in best-of-five series.

ATTENDANCE: Southern Illinois 204,181; Gateway 186,147; Traverse City 204,440; Lake Erie 159,580; Normal 132,309; Washington 116,722; River City 113,431; Florence 112,844; Evansville 110,711; Windy City 92,240; Kalamazoo 56,342; Oakland County 9,114.

MANAGERS: Evansville—Wayne Krenchicki/Andy McCauley. **Florence**—Toby Rumfield. **Gateway**—Phil Warren. **Kalamazoo**—Jamie Keefe/Matt Maloney. **Lake Erie**—John Massarelli. **Normal**—Hal Lanier. **Oakland County**—Gera Alvarez. **River City**—Steve Brook. **Southern Illinois**—Mike Pinto. **Traverse City**—Gregg Langbehn. **Washington**—Darin Everson. **Windy City**—Mike Kashirsky.

ALL-STARS: C—Charlie Lisk, Gateway. **1B**—Joash Brodin, Oakland County . **2B**—Gilberto Mejia, Windy City. **3B**—Daniel Cox, Normal. **SS**—Stephen Shults, Florence. **DH**—Chase Burch, Traverse City. **OF**—Stephen Holdren, River City; Jereme Milons, Southern Illinois; Jason Patton, Gateway.

SP—Joe Augustine, Southern Illinois. **RP**—P.J. Zocchi, Oakland County. **Most Valuable Player:** Charlie Lisk, Gateway. **Pitcher of the Year:** Joe Augustine, Southern Illinois. **Manager of the Year:** Gera Alvarez, Oakland County.

INDIVIDUAL BATTING LEADERS

PLAYER, TEAM	AVG	G	AB	R	H	HR	RBI
Aakhus, Zach, Windy City	.330	79	267	49	88	4	40
Cox, Daniel, Normal	.323	96	350	61	113	15	78
Hall, Nate, Southern Illinois	.318	89	336	62	107	9	50
Shah, Asif, Normal	.316	89	316	44	100	4	34
Curry, Caleb, River City	.315	65	235	55	74	0	24
Brown, Matt, Traverse City	.313	92	345	71	108	2	43
Maddox, Chad, River City	.311	92	331	55	103	7	55
Shults, Stephen, Florence	.309	80	314	59	97	23	65
Torres, Mike, Windy City	.307	91	303	44	93	0	30
Holdren, Stephen, River City	.305	95	334	68	102	16	72

INDIVIDUAL PITCHING LEADERS

PLAYER, TEAM	W	L	ERA	IP	H	BB	SO
Augustine, Joe, Southern Illinois	10	3	1.97	114	86	30	121
Shelton, Ryan, Normal	9	5	2.21	126	92	26	121
Cinadr, Jeff, Lake Erie	4	3	2.21	77	48	27	52
Williams, Dustin, Windy City	7	3	2.39	102	73	47	90
Roberts, Josh, Lake Erie	10	5	2.62	137	112	36	78
Rolon, Alberto, Lake Erie	3	4	2.65	95	66	32	90
Moran, Gary, River City	10	4	2.68	111	107	22	98
Risser, Travis, Lake Erie	8	4	2.7	113	98	30	58
Kitchens, Wayde, Oakland County	5	7	2.77	97	75	67	91
Solich, Brent, Windy City	8	6	2.84	130	124	34	89

EVANSVILLE OTTERS

PLAYER	AVG	AB	R	H	2B	3B	HR	RBI	SB
Alexander, Gregory	.284	278	49	79	13	0	7	41	12
Alvarado, Andre	.189	74	5	14	0	0	0	8	2
Ball, Jarred	.197	71	7	14	2	0	0	5	3
Champagnie, Marcel	.276	105	14	29	5	1	1	5	2
Cohen, Brandon	.219	178	24	39	11	0	9	46	1
DAmico, Nick	.233	116	14	27	2	0	0	10	6
Davis, Toby	.225	111	11	25	1	1	2	8	0
Hanson, Jeff	.263	76	8	20	4	0	2	9	0
Harris, Estee	.270	196	31	53	12	0	3	28	5
Killian, Billy	.240	242	24	58	6	1	0	21	3
Kolb, Brian	.229	144	21	33	3	0	1	9	8
McCoy, Ross	.163	49	5	8	1	0	0	4	1
Meade, Frank	.298	94	18	28	5	0	4	22	1
Rogers, Jake	.227	264	36	60	12	0	7	28	5
Rose, Patrick	.279	201	35	56	9	0	1	16	4
Scarduzio, Vinnie	.238	227	39	54	13	2	15	44	4
Smyth, Ryan	.143	56	4	8	0	0	0	1	0
Stanton, Zach	.200	105	8	21	1	0	1	6	6
Waltenbury, Jonathan	.306	160	19	49	10	0	3	29	0
Wiley, Derek	.247	223	35	55	13	0	9	40	0

PLAYER	W	L	ERA	G	SV	IP	H	BB	SO
Aspaas, Cameron	1	2	6.90	3	0	16	21	5	11
Barry, Kyle	2	7	4.78	22	0	75	78	41	61
Crider, Patrick	1	1	3.79	32	1	38	33	19	34
Edwards, Chad	4	7	3.45	14	0	86	78	21	48
LaMar, Travis	2	1	6.48	24	0	25	30	11	20
Lugo, Jorge	4	2	5.47	11	0	52	61	26	41
Maxwell, James	1	1	4.91	8	1	11	11	7	11
Morales, Angelo	0	6	6.00	7	0	36	45	15	18
Perez, Eduardo	4	6	6.71	15	0	58	67	25	41
Peters, Chris	2	11	5.51	20	0	101	96	64	99
Roenicke, Jason	3	3	4.76	29	0	70	81	18	33
Rollins, Chris	0	0	4.13	24	0	28	30	19	36
Romero, Robert	0	1	4.29	15	2	15	15	8	14
Simon, Jared	2	0	1.90	37	7	38	29	14	34
Sottung, Nick	6	4	4.81	28	3	86	94	34	66
Tweddale, Payton	1	1	4.63	12	0	11.2	13	3	9
Werner, Andrew	1	1	2.46	3	0	18	14	5	24
Worthington, Kent	1	1	3.60	9	0	20	14	15	23

FLORENCE FREEDOM

PLAYER	AVG	AB	R	H	2B	3B	HR	RBI	SB
Baker, Jimmy	.325	237	45	77	16	2	13	50	5
Campbell, Michael	.317	180	25	57	15	2	5	30	8
Cohen, Brandon	.256	125	13	32	4	0	5	16	3
Grogan, Tim	.280	357	64	100	25	3	12	48	1
Holloway, Justin	.237	59	11	14	1	0	2	9	2
Jacobs, Justin	.255	141	20	36	9	0	4	13	3
Jones, Daryl	.136	44	5	6	0	0	3	5	3
Koca, Dustin	.158	38	2	6	3	0	0	2	0
Manning, Beau	.189	106	18	20	1	0	1	6	15

INDEPENDENT LEAGUES

PLAYER	AVG	AB	R	H	2B	3B	HR	RBI	SB
Marshall, Curt	.161	31	4	5	3	0	0	1	0
Mottram, Billy	.260	393	59	102	18	3	8	37	22
Pickett, Justin	.231	364	37	84	21	0	13	49	2
Rose, Patrick	.289	97	13	28	2	3	1	7	2
Shults, Stephen	.309	314	59	97	13	1	23	65	5
Welch, Johnny	.303	307	55	93	13	1	14	46	7
Wheeler, Michael	.265	249	23	66	11	1	4	34	1
Wine, Cory	.226	84	7	19	2	0	1	7	2

PLAYER	W	L	ERA	G	SV	IP	H	BB	SO
Arballo, Julian	4	7	4.99	27	0	58	51	34	39
Aspaas, Cameron	2	0	5.14	6	0	35	36	17	30
Banes, Bryan	3	4	6.11	14	0	53	67	29	39
Bridges, Austin	0	0	5.66	14	0	14	10	12	8
Chambliss, Austin	0	3	6.66	7	0	26	29	15	22
Clark, Andy	9	4	3.41	19	0	116	114	35	93
Flanagan, John	1	2	9.49	5	0	25	40	12	21
Gonell, Jacinto	2	2	2.88	25	5	25	20	18	21
Guilin, Mario	1	2	8.18	3	0	11	16	10	5
Holguin, Chris	0	3	3.86	13	1	32	36	10	25
Holmes, Tim	3	9	5.08	21	0	117	134	53	63
Lydon, Sean	0	3	8.74	11	0	22	32	14	9
Mehlich, Michael	1	1	5.69	13	0	25	29	14	20
Moore, Ryan	1	4	6.20	8	0	41	49	21	19
Ohlmann, Liam	2	3	2.97	54	6	58	43	28	78
Palmer, Will	2	0	3.03	46	1	41.2	44	21	32
Saul, Everett	1	2	5.50	6	0	36	47	11	33
Shivers, Ben	6	2	3.63	42	4	69	62	30	72
Whittaker, Kevin	0	3	8.87	11	0	21	31	14	5

GATEWAY GRIZZLIES

PLAYER	AVG	AB	R	H	2B	3B	HR	RBI	SB
Baum, Justin	.270	100	17	27	6	0	6	24	0
Burk, Bobby	.265	211	37	56	11	0	8	30	2
Davis, Toby	.212	85	11	18	7	1	2	13	2
Draper, Breck	.241	266	48	64	10	1	13	48	5
Ecker, Donnie	.264	87	17	23	1	0	4	23	6
Eggemeyer, Adam	.197	71	9	14	0	0	1	4	1
Gronkowski, Gordon	.319	182	46	58	12	1	16	50	0
Heil, Tyler	.283	244	48	69	13	0	3	33	15
Hernandez, Landon	.246	142	20	35	9	1	2	12	1
Johnson, Matty	.313	182	43	57	6	3	0	19	24
Lisk, Charlie	.303	373	63	113	23	2	21	88	9
Mantle, Ryan	.139	36	3	5	1	0	0	1	0
Miraldi, Matt	.224	58	9	13	1	0	0	3	2
Parker, Logan	.305	348	67	106	28	1	13	77	16
Patton, Jason	.304	329	54	100	19	1	10	57	22
Peters, Brandon	.301	246	59	74	11	1	10	34	4
Sanders, Matt	.171	70	8	12	3	0	0	3	1
West, Jareck	.271	181	40	49	7	1	12	39	9

PLAYER	W	L	ERA	G	SV	IP	H	BB	SO
Barrett, Richard	2	2	2.08	13	1	30	26	11	26
Blackwell, Eric	2	1	5.18	22	1	33	31	21	40
Brackman, Mark	13	4	3.18	21	0	152	136	39	118
Clubb, Tim	8	6	3.42	19	0	118	104	54	77
Dail, B.J.	7	7	5.04	19	0	105	94	67	95
Flanagan, John	5	5	4.94	13	0	75	85	30	49
Garza, Adrian	2	0	3.78	4	0	17	12	8	15
Gilliland, Eric	5	1	3.46	33	0	52	41	19	52
Gonell, Jacinto	0	0	1.59	12	0	17	10	9	17
Goodenough, David	0	4	4.91	8	0	29	34	12	18
Meinhold, Ricky	1	2	8.19	9	0	30	39	10	20
Miller, David	1	2	2.92	35	4	37	28	22	35
Shafer, Jake	1	3	2.38	33	11	34	25	20	48
Toler, Sean	0	0	2.30	11	0	16	15	9	17
Walters, Nick	5	0	1.14	41	3	47	18	33	71
Whitlock, Josh	2	0	4.82	3	0	19	18	10	14

KALAMAZOO KINGS

PLAYER	AVG	AB	R	H	2B	3B	HR	RBI	SB
Alvarez, Leo	.191	47	2	9	4	0	0	5	1
Fon, Diallo	.135	37	4	5	0	0	0	1	3
Greener, Matt	.300	180	29	54	10	0	3	31	0
Helps, Jeff	.247	227	32	56	10	0	0	19	10

PLAYER	AVG	AB	R	H	2B	3B	HR	RBI	SB
Makonnen, Destan	.221	235	30	52	11	0	5	28	1
Maloney, Matt	.261	329	54	86	22	2	9	43	9
Malvagna, Steve	.256	86	9	22	6	0	2	12	0
Marquez, Bryan	.222	257	25	57	8	0	0	22	5
Miller, Kris	.280	161	23	45	9	1	8	31	0
Murphy, Brendan	.218	252	25	55	15	0	8	46	0
Poulter, Joseph	.176	176	24	31	4	0	2	14	6
Riddick, Andrew	.250	40	3	10	2	1	0	3	2
Robinson, Brooks	.230	113	13	26	0	1	1	10	7
Rubin, Lee	.266	154	23	41	7	0	4	14	0
Ruiz, Jett	.126	135	13	17	5	1	3	9	0
Sferra, JJ	.294	377	40	111	10	1	2	33	18
Suttle, Eric	.272	279	44	76	9	5	2	25	39
Yost, Jordon	.170	47	5	8	3	0	0	4	1

PLAYER	W	L	ERA	G	SV	IP	H	BB	SO
DiPietro, Joe	6	11	6.26	21	0	125	165	35	85
Dixon, Curt	1	3	7.45	6	0	29	36	17	14
Fonseca Jr., Guido	4	8	6.54	35	3	76	93	39	80
Gomez, Javier	1	1	10.24	5	0	19	25	8	17
Goodenough, David	0	4	4.50	9	0	28	31	8	18
Herron, Tyler	1	3	3.50	14	3	36	30	15	26
Hyde, Tyler	2	0	6.90	9	0	16	24	11	15
Miller, Justin	1	2	4.18	14	0	24	20	10	21
Parillo, Brandon	0	0	4.77	3	0	11	14	4	4
Reid, Scott	4	0	3.12	44	7	49	48	9	37
Robert, Bernard	2	6	3.81	14	0	73	62	28	63
Spencer, Micah	0	1	6.36	5	0	11	21	11	10
Stanley, Jimmy	1	5	4.41	38	1	65	58	26	63
Stolzenburg, Greg	0	1	5.56	7	1	11	7	8	15
Szymanski, Alex	1	2	3.18	8	0	51	43	15	37
Whitlock, Josh	1	10	4.65	17	0	93	91	60	62
Wilkins, Bobby	1	3	8.61	30	1	39	59	16	39
Wolfe, Ryan	0	1	7.11	15	0	12	19	9	8
Yost, Jordon	0	0	4.50	8	0	12	17	8	10
Zenko, Mike	2	3	5.04	15	0	30	31	11	26

LAKE ERIE CRUSHERS

PLAYER	AVG	AB	R	H	2B	3B	HR	RBI	SB
Bond, Wayne	.229	236	36	54	7	4	4	24	6
Collins, Joel	.257	222	20	57	13	0	2	17	2
Davis, Andrew	.285	347	44	99	16	2	10	61	5
Duggan, Dom	.231	360	54	83	12	5	4	33	48
Gore, Trae	.167	36	5	6	1	0	0	1	3
Huggins, Lee	.244	234	29	57	10	2	7	33	3
McGrew, Casey	.194	72	9	14	3	1	0	4	1
McWilliams, Arden	.192	229	31	44	5	3	8	24	2
Rivera, Jodam	.249	349	36	87	13	2	1	35	15
Rivera, Julio	.181	105	10	19	3	0	3	15	3
Saylor, Andrew	.215	275	28	59	9	2	4	28	1
Sutton, Matt	.173	81	8	14	2	0	1	10	1
Tisdale, Eddie	.253	221	24	56	17	1	2	22	3
Turner, Raphael	.193	114	20	22	9	1	0	15	13
Vetters, Travis	.194	170	20	33	5	1	3	14	3

PLAYER	W	L	ERA	G	SV	IP	H	BB	SO
Cinadr, Jeff	4	3	2.21	41	8	77	48	27	52
Durket, Jon	1	3	5.87	11	0	15	15	10	10
Jimenez, Esmelvin	6	4	4.33	22	0	69	64	28	46
Mata, Cristobal	0	0	1.77	13	0	20	17	10	11
Morales, Ronnie	4	2	2.57	48	0	63	36	35	50
Orosco, Jesse	0	1	13.95	8	0	10	19	7	5
Pacella, J.J.	2	2	3.62	28	9	32	25	26	44
Raymond, Michael	0	3	9.19	7	0	16	20	15	12
Risser, Travis	8	4	2.70	20	0	113	98	30	58
Roberts, Josh	10	5	2.62	21	0	137	112	36	78
Rolon, Alberto	3	4	2.65	32	7	95	66	32	90
Rummel, Phil	2	7	5.85	24	1	75	80	35	54
Smith, Matthew	10	7	3.66	23	1	121	108	50	90

NORMAL CORNBELTERS

PLAYER	AVG	AB	R	H	2B	3B	HR	RBI	SB
Agustin, Brad	.228	224	30	51	7	1	1	17	4
Alexander, Steven	.249	281	41	70	6	0	13	44	0
Alvarado, Andre	.292	48	4	14	4	2	0	5	3

Amar, Adam	.216	51	2	11	2	0	0	6	0
Barbaro, Andrew	.237	207	27	49	7	0	2	24	4
Bass, Garret	.240	75	12	18	4	0	1	5	5
Bralver, Steve	.225	40	0	9	2	0	0	4	0
Brown, Eric	.214	192	22	41	5	2	0	11	26
Cowan, Jeff	.238	328	49	78	15	1	5	30	7
Cox, Daniel	.323	350	61	113	23	2	15	78	6
Dufek, Mike	.251	207	22	52	8	0	5	29	2
Garcia, Mike	.240	100	15	24	4	0	4	19	0
Hicks, Joe	.229	105	13	24	6	0	1	7	11
Hughes, Mike	.239	71	9	17	3	0	3	13	0
Laurent, Phil	.164	61	6	10	2	1	1	8	0
McCoy, Ross	.317	249	48	79	19	1	14	48	8
Nolan, Partick	.159	63	8	10	1	0	0	2	2
Petralli, Ben	.204	49	8	10	2	1	0	5	0
Rebecca, Chad	.256	43	9	11	3	0	1	3	1
Ross, Jonathon	.309	110	10	34	2	1	1	8	2
Shah, Asif	.316	316	44	100	19	1	4	34	6

PLAYER	W	L	ERA	G	SV	IP	H	BB	SO
Bennet, Chris	0	2	5.21	15	2	19	24	9	24
Blewett, Dan	6	7	3.90	19	0	113	101	53	82
Coburn, Matt	0	2	6.47	14	1	40	58	25	33
Coker, Jarret	0	2	11.25	4	0	12	20	8	5
Furrow, Donald	3	3	2.56	14	2	31.2	26	10	38
Furrow, Jason	0	2	6.29	21	1	59	73	28	45
Guarrasi, Andrew	2	3	5.83	12	0	41.2	42	24	35
Kreier, Kevin	3	6	7.28	11	0	56	74	28	37
LaLuna, Mike	4	5	3.42	33	9	47	40	34	60
Lane, Greg	0	4	3.99	23	1	29	35	8	13
Lavigne, Tyler	7	2	1.38	10	0	71.2	48	29	55
Lester, Brett	7	7	4.42	16	0	90	82	44	76
Pritchett, Bobby	2	2	2.86	13	0	72	45	29	79
Raburn, Steve	0	0	1.29	8	2	14	8	4	13
Shelton, Ryan	9	5	2.21	20	0	126	92	26	121

OAKLAND COUNTY CRUSHERS

PLAYER	AVG	AB	R	H	2B	3B	HR	RBI	SB
Andrews, Bobby	.254	224	37	57	10	1	1	15	31
Baker, Jimmy	.219	73	16	16	1	0	4	10	0
Barrone, Ben	.205	176	16	36	8	0	5	16	2
Brodin, Joash	.301	355	55	107	25	1	9	62	29
Burk, Bobby	.097	31	1	3	2	0	0	0	0
Epping, Mike	.254	126	24	32	9	2	1	11	10
Fernandez, Luis	.238	281	24	67	15	2	2	22	4
Jones, Jeremy	.280	347	49	97	23	3	9	62	10
Kasarjian, Kris	.205	44	6	9	1	1	0	4	0
Killian, Dan	.322	90	8	29	6	1	1	12	1
Maunus, Kyle	.250	252	34	63	14	1	4	39	7
Pace, Zachary	.268	355	58	95	13	1	1	27	30
Parra, Martin	.207	232	32	48	5	2	6	31	12
Rogers, Tyler	.237	38	4	9	1	0	0	2	5
Rubin, Lee	.295	95	13	28	5	1	0	7	2
Shay, Ryan	.213	47	7	10	0	0	1	1	4
Taylor, Jacob	.097	31	1	3	0	0	0	0	1
Tolan, Robbie	.245	233	19	57	8	3	3	30	3

PLAYER	W	L	ERA	G	SV	IP	H	BB	SO
Albury, James	6	5	4.73	15	0	67	62	28	40
Asselin, Kevin	9	3	3.28	23	0	134	127	51	89
Dominick, Adam	3	7	3.17	43	0	60	44	26	73
Esquibel, Andres	6	6	4.49	18	0	108	100	40	76
Frymier, Kurt	1	0	1.17	12	2	15	9	5	14
Kitchens, Wayde	5	7	2.77	19	0	97	75	67	91
Maffei, C.J.	2	0	5.55	10	0	24	27	19	21
Reid, Brad	4	1	3.18	33	0	45	43	16	30
Robert, Bernard	3	3	4.39	7	0	39	44	16	30
Rodriguez, Joe	1	3	5.15	15	0	37	38	25	35
Shaffer, Nolan	4	6	5.21	19	0	85	88	32	67
Wulf, Taylor	1	1	2.66	18	1	24	16	12	21
Zocchi, P.J.	3	0	2.96	45	26	46	28	23	39

RIVER CITY RASCALS

PLAYER	AVG	AB	R	H	2B	3B	HR	RBI	SB
Banda, Josh	.270	326	49	88	15	1	14	52	5

Burk, Bobby	.259	54	11	14	3	0	4	10	2
Chavarria, Joe	.120	50	6	6	1	0	0	0	1
Curry, Caleb	.315	235	55	74	11	2	0	24	28
Gutierrez, Jorge	.222	270	25	60	11	0	1	19	13
Holdren, Stephen	.305	334	68	102	23	2	16	72	11
Maddox, Chad	.311	331	55	103	25	4	7	55	3
McClendon, Chris	.279	290	64	81	13	2	4	24	33
Robinson, Scott	.261	372	61	97	18	0	10	64	11
Sanders, Doug	.298	319	48	95	15	2	5	57	5
Sawyer, Danny	.263	270	35	71	20	3	4	43	2
Stewart, Cooper	.167	54	5	9	2	0	0	6	0
Ubbenga, Jon	.224	98	7	22	2	0	0	10	5
Wehrle, Ryan	.230	61	5	14	2	0	0	8	0
Wiley, Keenan	.308	39	5	12	1	2	0	6	1

PLAYER	W	L	ERA	G	SV	IP	H	BB	SO
Krout, Will	7	1	2.46	29	0	59	57	14	49
Lowey, Jason	1	3	2.90	31	21	31	24	14	48
Lowey, Josh	8	5	3.55	18	0	111.2	126	49	96
Marsala, Tony	10	8	4.20	21	0	109	114	48	81
Miramontes, Derrick	3	3	2.19	44	5	53	37	25	58
Moran, Gary	10	4	2.68	19	0	111	107	22	98
Patterson, Paul David	0	1	7.00	6	0	27	38	7	18
Phillips, Nick	0	0	4.95	17	0	20	24	4	25
Rivers, Kirkland	1	1	2.84	30	0	31.2	29	11	32
Rose, Josh	0	1	4.80	4	0	15	17	4	8
Soto, Diego	0	0	7.14	10	0	11	11	9	17
Sterner, Zack	5	1	3.61	12	0	57	57	29	38
Woodward, Tim	4	2	4.34	18	1	64	74	11	26
Zablan, Kelii	2	1	3.15	28	0	40	29	14	29
Zink, Ryan	6	5	3.62	13	0	75	79	17	54

SOUTHERN ILLINOIS MINERS

PLAYER	AVG	AB	R	H	2B	3B	HR	RBI	SB
Akashian, Brendan	.292	274	50	80	16	2	4	36	22
Banks, Ernie	.246	114	21	28	7	0	4	23	2
Block, Will	.269	283	47	76	21	5	4	37	10
Brown, Javier	.227	97	14	22	2	0	0	11	4
Bullock, Tyler	.323	130	12	42	12	0	1	24	0
Gerst, Kent	.230	139	24	32	3	1	1	13	16
Hall, Nate	.318	336	62	107	20	4	9	50	5
Head, Stephen	.265	366	65	97	19	5	13	68	2
Hood, Jordin	.213	47	5	10	0	0	1	3	1
Martin, Todd	.291	175	28	51	14	0	7	37	0
Metropoulos, Joey	.241	166	29	40	12	2	10	28	0
Miller, Brad	.256	133	21	34	5	0	7	24	1
Milons, Jereme	.283	385	78	109	12	4	11	60	41
Netzel, Brad	.222	162	16	36	3	3	0	20	7
Randall, Justin	.373	83	18	31	5	0	0	16	7
Stalter, Michael	.210	167	23	35	6	0	0	18	9
Wight, Jesse	.217	115	19	25	2	0	1	19	11

PLAYER	W	L	ERA	G	SV	IP	H	BB	SO
Allen, Chris	3	1	3.74	15	0	46	51	16	31
Augustine, Joe	10	3	1.97	17	0	114	86	30	121
Bird, Ryan	6	2	3.00	10	0	60	52	23	59
Brader, Dustin	5	1	2.55	9	0	49	45	25	32
Damchuk, Mike	5	2	1.25	30	9	36	27	14	25
DeFoor, Brent	3	1	3.90	28	5	28	25	14	21
Draxton, Erik	1	0	0.00	10	5	10	5	3	9
Fussell, Eric	5	4	5.35	14	0	69	81	31	55
Hedrick, Robert	1	0	4.34	29	0	48	52	26	26
Johnson, Randy	0	3	7.29	5	0	21	31	4	10
Joy, Shawn	4	0	3.36	32	0	56	57	12	33
Kussmaul, Ryan	3	1	2.68	9	0	50	34	13	49
McMurran, Jake	5	1	1.89	38	3	48	29	10	44
Scarpetta, Brett	8	5	3.60	20	0	128	122	37	80
Sommerville, Erik	1	1	5.04	5	0	25	29	14	13
Thieroff, Alex	1	4	3.00	23	1	24	22	15	27

TRAVERSE CITY BEACH BUMS

PLAYER	AVG	AB	R	H	2B	3B	HR	RBI	SB
Alia, Jonathan	.263	95	15	25	0	2	3	14	0
Brown, Matt	.313	345	71	108	19	6	2	43	30
Burch, Chase	.299	335	70	100	21	2	19	88	1

INDEPENDENT LEAGUES

	AVG	AB	R	H	2B	3B	HR	RBI	SB
Codiroli, Jason	.222	293	51	65	11	4	1	22	11
Cruz, Paul	.210	100	11	21	3	1	0	8	4
Diaz, Michael	.270	366	60	99	11	2	3	43	9
Engell, Chris	.268	168	26	45	7	1	0	15	5
Eveland, Kyle	.239	138	21	33	10	0	1	14	2
Franco, Andrew	.228	123	18	28	5	0	1	13	1
Hall, JT	.253	371	58	94	15	5	8	48	10
Howard, Brandon	.232	69	9	16	3	0	2	12	2
Johnson, Tommy	.176	108	9	19	5	1	0	11	0
Marshall, Andrew	.200	120	16	24	2	2	1	8	0
Miller, Brad	.316	95	10	30	7	0	1	19	0
Spain, Bobby	.195	154	10	30	4	0	3	19	1
Ziegler, CJ	.226	336	39	76	19	0	13	53	0

PLAYER	W	L	ERA	G	SV	IP	H	BB	SO
Adams, Jack	1	1	6.75	9	1	15	19	7	15
Banes, Bryan	1	0	2.70	8	0	13	12	5	5
Bravo, Jonny	5	2	3.29	22	0	90	80	52	59
DeLazzer, Trent	0	0	3.47	10	0	23	25	4	8
Dunn, Scott	1	2	2.20	29	6	57	44	18	52
Folmer, Richard	3	2	3.94	22	0	34	33	21	33
Lechuga, Enrique	10	3	2.88	20	0	125	114	46	83
Moore, Michael	9	6	3.28	18	0	99	85	48	56
Mueller, Scott	4	4	2.04	38	14	53	41	11	51
Paulauskas, Andrew	1	2	6.87	6	0	18	21	13	11
Platt, Ryan	8	3	2.92	18	0	108	96	56	117
Reese, Kevin	10	9	4.47	22	0	139	161	32	79
Slovak, David	2	5	3.76	37	3	55	59	19	28

WASHINGTON WILD THINGS

PLAYER	AVG	AB	R	H	2B	3B	HR	RBI	SB
Amar, Adam	.255	149	15	38	7	1	2	26	3
Delaney, John	.235	234	27	55	10	0	2	21	7
Dempsey, Jacob	.229	218	27	50	9	1	9	38	0
Duron, Denny	.230	278	27	64	8	2	4	31	2
Dyer, Jared	.226	53	4	12	2	0	0	3	1
Hartman, Joel	.225	71	13	16	3	0	2	9	3
Kourie, Jon	.301	156	19	47	5	1	3	25	7
Matos, Wilson	.292	113	16	33	6	0	0	13	2
McGonigle, Mark	.252	326	42	82	22	4	1	35	8
O Conner, Billy	.201	189	17	38	3	0	0	13	3
Parker, Michael	.258	349	50	90	15	2	3	43	18
Raniere, Chris	.258	62	8	16	2	0	1	10	2
Rivera, Luis	.260	265	33	69	13	2	6	29	12
Robbins, Alan	.224	107	15	24	4	0	1	8	1
Sidick, Chris	.300	250	46	75	13	5	4	21	32
Stephens, Eric	.241	187	27	45	4	0	6	22	5
Suprenant, Kyle	.133	30	1	4	1	0	0	2	0

PLAYER	W	L	ERA	G	SV	IP	H	BB	SO
Bennet, Chris	0	1	5.57	17	1	21	23	16	19
Bright, Quinn	0	1	10.50	8	1	18	31	7	13
Edwards, Justin	5	2	3.79	27	1	78	65	31	71
Groh, Zach	4	5	5.18	11	0	57	60	21	51
Hammons, Kevin	5	4	2.62	38	2	55	37	26	72
Houck, Kurt	0	1	6.17	9	0	12	10	15	10
Hylander, Spencer	1	2	7.55	8	0	39	45	21	18
Keeler, Sean	0	0	4.63	8	0	12	12	9	16
Macfarland, Steve	3	2	5.45	7	0	36	37	19	45
McConnell, Eryk	3	6	3.07	38	15	44	39	9	33
Muldowney, Billy	1	4	1.80	12	0	70	51	13	62
Rodewald, Ben	2	2	5.74	23	1	38	41	28	18
Rosenbaum, Zach	1	9	4.61	17	0	94	92	53	54
Rossignol, Matt	0	4	6.11	4	0	17.2	23	10	7
Smith, Tim	5	4	6.51	26	0	73	93	34	47
Sonnenberg, Jeff	6	7	2.97	16	0	103	87	18	67
Vieira, Matt	0	2	5.52	19	1	31	47	12	29

WINDY CITY THUNDERBOLTS

PLAYER	AVG	AB	R	H	2B	3B	HR	RBI	SB
Aakhus, Zach	.330	267	49	88	18	1	4	40	5
Alberts, Tim	.236	106	14	25	5	1	3	15	0
Anderson, Brandon	.275	178	39	49	7	5	3	31	23
Basham, Ryan	.302	252	34	76	19	1	3	39	10
Calderone, Jim	.200	45	11	9	3	0	0	3	0

	AVG	AB	R	H	2B	3B	HR	RBI	SB
Ecker, Donnie	.318	85	15	27	2	2	0	7	7
Gerst, Kent	.278	158	26	44	9	2	0	15	13
Hamilton, Jeremy	.238	160	27	38	5	1	2	16	1
Jobe, Tim	.188	48	3	9	0	0	0	5	0
Jordan, Dan	.194	98	9	19	1	1	1	12	2
Kuroczko, Nick	.261	161	30	42	6	2	3	22	2
Martinez, Guillermo	.247	146	18	36	7	0	1	15	8
Mejia, Gilberto	.294	333	50	98	16	7	1	38	35
Mooney, Mike	.283	92	11	26	6	1	0	11	5
Paris, Pete	.283	60	12	17	0	0	0	5	0
Restko, J.T.	.303	294	34	89	13	3	10	58	0
Sullivan, Mike	.256	78	12	20	3	1	0	14	5
Torres, Mike	.307	303	44	93	11	0	0	30	22
White, Ryne	.274	212	34	58	15	0	5	30	2

PLAYER	W	L	ERA	G	SV	IP	H	BB	SO
Barrett, Richard	6	1	3.54	10	0	53	63	17	40
Blanks, Bradley	1	2	2.74	19	1	26	15	5	28
Garner, Brandon	0	3	3.19	40	3	37	26	28	35
Hall, Nick	5	4	3.44	34	15	34	27	23	39
Jernstad, Matt	4	2	2.23	6	0	40	31	9	43
Johnson, Greg	2	0	2.32	47	3	50	42	10	36
Meinhold, Ricky	0	2	5.56	16	0	34	34	19	28
Mueller, Thomas	0	0	5.51	25	0	34	33	10	24
Quigley, Ryan	3	4	4.74	33	1	62	69	42	77
Rowe, Ryan	1	0	6.36	8	0	11	13	5	9
Scumaci, Joe	1	4	8.44	9	0	21	33	12	19
Solich, Brent	8	6	2.84	21	0	130	124	34	89
Toler, Sean	8	1	2.97	9	0	58	45	23	44
Werner, Andrew	10	4	3.51	16	0	100	96	42	73
Williams, Dustin	7	3	2.39	16	0	101.2	73	47	90

GOLDEN LEAGUE

Blake Gailen proved he'd run into walls to win a title.

The Chico outfielder missed a month after a collision with the outfield wall gave him whiplash. He returned in time for the playoffs, where he went 7-for-10 in the championship series to be named the playoff MVP as Chico swept through two series with no troubles. The Chico center fielder got plenty of help. Righthander Garret Holleran went 2-0, 0.68 during the playoffs for the Outlaws.

FIRST HALF

NORTH	W	L	PCT	GB
Chico Outlaws	33	12	.733	—
Edmonton Capitals	29	16	.644	4
Calgary Vipers	23	20	.535	9
Victoria Seals	22	23	.489	11
St. George Roadrunners	15	30	.333	18
SOUTH	**W**	**L**	**PCT**	**GB**
Maui Na Koa Ikaika	26	17	.605	—
Yuma Scorpions	27	18	.600	—
Orange County Flyers	22	23	.489	5
Tucson Toros	20	25	.444	7
Tijuana Cimarrones	6	39	.133	21

SECOND HALF

NORTH	W	L	PCT	GB
Calgary Vipers	30	15	.667	—
Chico Outlaws	22	18	.550	5.5
Victoria Seals	23	20	.535	6
Edmonton Capitals	22	22	.500	7.5
St. George Roadrunners	8	28	.222	17.5
SOUTH	**W**	**L**	**PCT**	**GB**
Maui Na Koa Ikaika	30	9	.769	—
Orange County Flyers	29	12	.707	2
Tucson Toros	26	18	.591	6.5
Yuma Scorpions	14	31	.311	18
Tijuana Cimarrones	4	35	.103	26

PLAYOFFS: Semifinals—Chico defeated Calgary 3-0 and Maui defeated Orange County 3-2 in best-of-five series. **Finals:** Chico defeated Maui 3-0 in best-of-five series.

ATTENDANCE: Tucson Toros 117,068; Victoria Seals 116,872; Chico Outlaws 113,819; Edmonton Capitals 92,126; Calgary Vipers 66,518; Yuma Scorpions 58,083; Maui Na Koa Ikaika 50,343; Orange County Flyers 49,064; Tijuana Cimarrones 46,748; St. George Roadrunners 31,753.

MANAGERS: Calgary—Morgan Burkhart. **Chico**—Garry Templeton. **Edmonton**—Brent Bowers/Gordan Gerlach. **Maui**—Cory Snyder. **Orange County**—Paul Abbott. **Tucson**—Tim Johnson. **St. George**—Darrell Evans. **Tijuana**—Enrique Brito. **Victoria**—Darrell Evans. **Yuma**—Darryl Brinkley.

ALL-STAR TEAM:
C—Josh Arhart, Victoria. **1B**—Cliff Brumbaugh, Edmonton. **2B**—Jimmy Rohan, Orange County. **3B**—Santo DeLeon, Chico. **SS**—Ryan Priddy, Tucson. **Utility**—Wilver Perez, Victoria. **OFs**—Blake Gailen, Chico; Drew Miller, Calgary; Larry Bigbie, Edmonton.
SPs—Donald Brandt, Maui; Manny Ayala, Orange County; Lew Pote, Edmonton; Wes Etheridge, Maui; Demetrius Banks, Chico; **RPs**—Emiliano Fruto, Tucson; Justin Segal, Chico; Jamie Vermilyea, Maui; Brandon Villafuerte, Victoria.
Player of the Year: Cliff Brumbaugh, Edmonton. **Pitcher of the Year:** Donald Brandt, Maui.

INDIVIDUAL BATTING LEADERS

PLAYER, TEAM	AVG	G	AB	R	H	HR	RBI
Bigbie, Larry, Edmonton	.403	69	231	54	93	16	74
Gailen, Blake, Chico	.387	55	204	61	79	7	31
Mochizuki, Gered, Maui	.384	78	263	60	101	1	36
Brumbaugh, Cliff, Edmonton	.383	76	298	55	114	23	90
Cruz, Enrique, Edmonton	.381	60	252	53	96	6	34
Samuelson, Mark, Chico	.376	67	205	29	77	3	50
Acey, Jermy, Maui	.367	80	275	55	101	10	65
Rohan, Jimmy, Orange County	.364	84	343	70	125	4	67
Santana, Cristobal, Tucson	.359	79	320	50	115	6	61
Almario, Yosvany, St. George	.357	55	213	45	76	8	52

INDIVIDUAL PITCHING LEADERS

PLAYER, TEAM	W	L	ERA	IP	H	BB	SO
Ethridge, Wes, Maui	10	0	1.76	92	72	18	86
Brandt, Donald, Maui	15	0	2.58	101	84	40	100
Ayala, Manny, Orange County	14	0	2.86	91	79	27	77
Francisco, Alexander, Edmonton	8	3	3.22	106	110	31	78
Bodishbaugh, Chris, Victoria	1	3	3.3	71	86	32	65
Cline, Zac, Orange County	6	3	3.31	90	85	30	62
Diaz, Raymar, St. George	5	6	3.49	85	88	23	66
Banks, Demetrius, Chico	10	3	3.52	84	96	25	69
Smith, Jesse, Orange County	6	5	3.59	93	94	35	83
Honel, Kris, Chico	8	3	3.61	92	74	63	89

CALGARY VIPERS

PLAYER	AVG	AB	R	H	2B	3B	HR	RBI	BB	SO	SB
Cosme, Caonabo	.254	280	46	71	11	3	6	39	37	68	2
Edgecombe, Matt	.321	106	17	34	6	1	2	17	9	20	0
Kaplan, Jonny	.342	322	85	110	26	6	8	41	49	42	28
Mejia, Jorge	.300	313	61	94	16	3	6	47	29	62	15
Metheny, Brent	.313	265	65	83	26	0	13	56	42	33	20
Miller, Drew	.353	329	64	116	28	2	21	94	37	53	1
O Krane, Dillon	.273	77	10	21	4	0	3	13	3	12	0
Perez, Isidro	.278	36	4	10	1	0	0	3	7	5	0
Price, Kevin	.320	200	59	64	20	0	8	45	53	39	1
Ramirez, Julio	.322	283	69	91	18	0	18	73	41	60	12
Reyes, Guillermo	.286	297	57	85	15	1	3	31	32	23	14
Taveras, Luis	.273	271	32	74	13	0	8	60	21	40	2

PLAYER	W	L	ERA	G	SV	IP	H	BB	SO
Broughton, Jay	2	2	4.01	5	0	25	17	14	23
Chaffardet, Daniel	1	1	8.44	15	0	16	20	14	15
Dessau, Erik	4	3	6.15	18	0	79	108	27	57
Fasking, Berek	2	2	5.65	13	0	14	21	5	7
Galva, Claudio	2	4	5.11	13	19	37	44	15	41
Gober, Dusty	10	1	4.78	22	0	117	141	35	88
Mansfield, Monte	1	0	3.18	11	1	11	9	7	8
Martinez, Anastacio	2	4	7.74	10	0	43	54	25	28
McKenzie, Marcus	0	2	9.42	4	0	14	24	5	8
Michael, Mark	3	5	5.22	13	0	59	65	24	56
Miniel, Rene	2	3	6.86	19	3	21	25	13	16
Morari, Daniel	3	0	3.62	24	0	27	39	6	18
Muir, Jordan	1	1	3.37	20	0	19	20	7	14
Naegele, Rob	2	0	1.64	12	0	11	13	6	7
Rivard, Reggie	5	1	3.97	10	0	57	52	19	46
Serqent, Joe	3	2	8.47	14	0	34	51	21	36
Stickel, Brant	0	1	6.00	15	0	27	33	24	16

Suzuki, Mac	2	2	5.72	6	0	28	28	16	14
Vasquez, Jorge	3	1	3.06	35	0	35	32	19	42
Watson, Scott	3	0	5.59	27	0	39	54	14	36

CHICO OUTLAWS

PLAYER	AVG	AB	R	H	2B	3B	HR	RBI	BB	SO	SB
Alcombrack, Robby	.309	136	23	42	6	1	10	29	21	38	2
Castro, Ismael	.331	151	22	50	13	0	2	22	3	9	5
Del Real, Pascual	.274	197	29	54	7	0	2	22	20	31	1
Deleon, Santo	.319	163	27	52	10	0	5	28	15	27	3
Einertson, Mitch	.325	246	57	80	19	1	9	47	26	36	5
Gailen, Blake	.387	204	61	79	15	4	7	31	35	26	18
Hill, Bobby	.307	293	53	90	13	0	4	36	50	53	9
Janeway, Rich	.348	92	27	32	9	0	5	24	22	21	5
Jova, Maikel	.321	321	54	103	16	0	6	65	11	26	1
Lopez, Carlos	.289	38	4	11	1	1	1	5	6	10	0
Manuel, Anthony	.283	99	17	28	5	2	0	10	3	20	3
Prieto, Alex	.324	74	15	24	6	0	0	10	10	10	0
Rose, Mike	.320	178	29	57	8	1	10	36	23	34	2
Samuelson, Mark	.375	80	17	30	6	0	1	20	12	23	0
Sherrill, JJ	.310	306	78	95	21	1	16	67	41	53	12
Urick, John	.307	176	30	54	10	2	10	35	27	30	1

PLAYER	W	L	ERA	G	SV	IP	H	BB	SO
Banks, Demetrius	10	3	3.52	16	0	84	96	25	69
Dew, Josh	4	1	2.68	36	1	47	37	11	49
Dickert, Reed	1	1	5.92	5	0	24	28	8	25
Dinelli, David	2	1	5.82	27	2	34	42	33	47
Franklin, Wayne	4	2	3.79	10	0	40	44	14	30
Holleran, Garret	9	2	3.86	18	0	98	110	36	70
Honel, Kris	8	3	3.61	17	0	92	74	63	89
Jones, Rusty	2	3	2.95	32	0	43	43	21	34
McLemore, Mark	7	5	4.33	16	0	96	92	32	82
Ortiz, Javier	1	2	3.47	8	0	49	51	11	33
Oster, Jesse	1	0	2.70	9	0	17	18	4	13
Perisho, Matt	3	1	2.55	32	8	35	34	11	43
Segal, Justin	3	2	0.92	40	5	49	34	12	48
Yoshida, Eri	0	4	12.28	8	0	26	34	21	4

EDMONTON CAPITALS

PLAYER	AVG	AB	R	H	2B	3B	HR	RBI	BB	SO	SB
Battle, Tim	.204	54	6	11	1	1	3	6	3	18	5
Bigbie, Larry	.403	231	54	93	26	4	16	74	49	30	1
Brown, Steve	.268	183	38	49	8	0	4	30	17	42	17
Brumbaugh, Cliff	.383	298	55	114	21	1	23	90	32	47	5
Chavez, Alex	.262	103	18	27	4	1	2	13	11	12	6
Collaro, Tom	.294	340	60	100	25	1	15	74	35	63	2
Cortes, Jorge	.245	94	21	23	8	0	0	2	19	8	4
Cruz, Enrique	.381	252	53	96	18	1	6	34	20	41	9
Farina, Pete	.200	65	5	13	2	0	0	4	3	10	0
House, Kevin	.273	33	6	9	1	0	1	5	4	8	4
McNamee, Eric	.234	94	10	22	4	1	0	7	15	17	1
Pote, Lou	.191	47	4	9	1	0	0	0	0	9	0
Prieto, Alex	.288	208	36	60	15	0	5	29	36	45	4
Rogelstad, Matt	.309	282	39	87	25	2	5	38	25	33	6
Rose, Mike	.238	42	3	10	3	0	0	5	7	12	0
Scriven, Eric	.158	38	3	6	0	0	0	2	2	11	1
Stevenson, Ryan	.301	286	75	86	11	4	4	26	43	54	6
Tarnow, Josh	.245	110	15	27	5	0	4	16	20	29	0
Valdez, Nick	.225	102	13	23	6	1	1	15	13	26	1

PLAYER	W	L	ERA	G	SV	IP	H	BB	SO
Arreola, Daryl	3	3	6.45	10	0	53	67	23	39
Blackwell, Chad	4	6	3.40	44	19	50	52	9	36
Francisco, Alexander	8	3	3.22	18	0	106	110	31	78
Hrynio, Mike	5	2	4.03	30	0	74	91	25	72
Ibanez, Yosandy	3	1	2.74	17	0	23	22	5	33
Johnson, Mike	2	1	0.45	13	0	20	12	4	27
Kelly, Scott	1	2	5.05	31	0	41	48	19	41
Little, Chris	6	5	5.93	18	0	85	109	34	67
Nageotte, Clinton	4	2	5.65	12	0	37	39	24	27
Oster, Jesse	1	1	3.31	22	0	33	35	14	25
Paul, Ryan	2	1	5.32	39	0	22	26	19	26
Pote, Lou	9	3	3.68	22	0	120	120	51	123
White, Evan	3	5	4.46	17	0	73	92	22	50

MAUI NA KOA IKAIKA

PLAYER	AVG	AB	R	H	2B	3B	HR	RBI	BB	SO	SB
Acey, Jermy	.345	58	11	20	4	0	2	16	17	8	2
Avlas, Phil	.325	243	37	79	12	0	7	40	23	29	9
Battle, Tim	.279	122	20	34	5	2	4	15	7	48	10
Farina, Pete	.229	35	4	8	3	0	1	9	4	5	2
Higa, Michael	.325	200	28	65	9	3	0	30	28	35	10
Jackson, Travon	.398	88	15	35	4	1	1	15	10	8	12
Lentini, Fehlandt	.299	288	70	86	24	4	13	30	28	53	36
Mochizuki, Gered	.384	263	60	101	27	1	1	36	38	48	22
Murray-Thornton, J.	.220	118	22	26	5	0	2	17	7	25	3
Nash, Chris	.233	73	8	17	3	0	2	8	7	12	2
Nishimura, Paul	.288	212	23	61	9	3	1	25	18	52	12
Okano, Mark	.246	228	39	56	7	2	10	45	32	64	11
Rundgren, Rex	.280	232	24	65	13	4	2	29	24	36	3
Ruth, Keoni	.299	194	32	58	7	3	3	30	13	15	13
Wilson, Chester	.267	60	13	16	1	0	2	14	9	11	3

PLAYER	W	L	ERA	G	SV	IP	H	BB	SO
Brandt, Donald	15	0	2.58	18	0	101	84	40	100
Ethridge, Wes	10	0	1.76	15	0	92	72	18	86
Mackintosh, Jason	5	0	1.22	9	0	37	33	4	22
Macy, TJ	1	3	2.46	30	4	37	24	13	46
Martinez, Gregorio	3	7	3.96	21	0	89	86	20	67
Mead, Kaimi	4	3	3.74	28	0	55	53	26	43
Seccombe, David	4	3	5.82	13	0	60	71	19	40
Spradlin, Jerry	3	6	4.47	32	0	52	65	12	36
Spurgeon, Steven	0	0	5.27	5	0	14	19	4	13
Tsujimoto, Kent	3	2	2.88	32	2	34	33	15	48
Uyechi, Clayton	1	0	1.05	14	1	26	12	7	35
Vermilyea, Jamie	1	2	1.64	31	20	38	31	9	28
Williams, Harold	5	0	2.17	18	0	46	33	29	39

ORANGE COUNTY FLYERS

PLAYER	AVG	AB	R	H	2B	3B	HR	RBI	BB	SO	SB
Ayala, Manny	.225	40	7	9	0	0	0	6	4	12	0
Benavidez, Julian	.296	186	41	55	16	0	14	50	21	46	3
Boggs, Steve	.284	349	68	99	11	1	1	36	34	50	15
Ginter, Keith	.282	227	40	64	15	0	5	39	53	44	8
Goethals, Jim	.274	175	30	48	14	1	4	34	31	54	0
Harris, David	.330	264	56	87	12	3	8	49	43	53	17
Jamieson, Alex	.240	96	23	23	4	1	1	13	21	22	1
Johnson, Ben	.405	42	12	17	1	0	4	17	15	8	4
Keeble, Tyler	.302	344	79	104	19	7	9	60	26	66	18
Mandelblatt, Zach	.263	80	18	21	4	0	0	5	21	19	9
Pedroza, Sergio	.332	205	48	68	16	1	14	65	56	54	6
Perren, Derek	.288	285	53	82	16	1	6	46	34	45	7
Pringle, Eric	.338	71	14	24	5	1	0	9	8	11	5
Rohan, Jimmy	.364	343	70	125	22	1	2	46	26	32	6

PLAYER	W	L	ERA	G	SV	IP	H	BB	SO
Altman, Kevin	7	5	4.84	22	0	87	103	35	59
Ayala, Manny	14	0	2.86	17	0	91	79	27	77
Baek, Cha-Seung	0	1	7.72	9	0	19	26	7	21
Cline, Zac	4	1	2.02	10	0	49	36	16	34
Durkin, Matt	1	3	6.95	15	0	67	85	33	51
Harris, Bryan	3	6	3.31	41	1	52	49	4	40
Kim, Byung Hyun	3	1	2.56	10	0	46	39	24	48
Koons, Mike	4	1	3.50	28	0	36	30	21	36
Prior, Mark	0	0	0.00	9	0	11	5	5	22
Renshaw, Jake	3	4	2.39	16	0	53	46	17	31
Simpson, Andre	3	4	3.09	41	14	47	32	28	54
Smith, Brett	0	3	10.08	6	0	25	36	17	17
Smith, Jesse	6	5	3.59	19	0	93	94	35	83

ST. GEORGE ROADRUNNERS

PLAYER	AVG	AB	R	H	2B	3B	HR	RBI	BB	SO	SB
Acey, Jermy	.373	217	44	81	16	2	8	49	37	36	2
Almario, Yosvany	.357	213	45	76	16	1	8	52	18	29	12
Brown, Chris	.211	57	7	12	2	0	2	7	6	16	0
Buttler, Victor	.353	190	40	67	10	1	3	24	27	28	17
Calderon, Henry	.308	234	44	72	19	0	4	25	18	34	12
Castellano, Mike	.350	40	4	14	3	0	0	4	1	4	3
Clement, Scott	.301	146	21	44	14	0	2	25	27	41	0

PLAYER	AVG	AB	R	H	2B	3B	HR	RBI	BB	SO	SB
Cramer, Jason	.236	55	8	13	0	0	1	5	5	11	4
Demarco, Gabe	.281	32	3	9	2	0	0	4	2	5	0
Fitzgerald, Nick	.230	100	10	23	4	0	3	10	8	36	0
Flowers, Brett	.270	185	29	50	14	0	6	34	20	31	1
Huggins, Matt	.282	78	9	22	3	3	0	9	4	19	2
Juarez, Chris	.211	38	5	8	1	0	0	1	3	7	2
Lang, C.J.	.274	215	40	59	15	0	1	33	22	20	5
Long, Keenan	.361	36	1	13	0	0	0	5	3	8	1
McMorris, Cody	.238	63	12	15	2	1	0	4	6	13	14
Nastasi, Chris	.153	59	7	9	3	0	0	7	7	23	4
Raisbeck, Casey	.243	103	18	25	5	0	1	12	16	32	1
Ramirez, David	.239	92	12	22	6	0	3	15	3	23	0
Rotola, Tim	.226	53	5	12	0	0	0	4	2	12	2
Sosa, Carlos	.278	108	18	30	5	0	5	23	17	21	0
Sumner, Alex	.265	34	2	9	1	0	0	2	3	7	1
Yan, Ruddy	.288	66	15	19	3	0	0	5	8	4	7

PLAYER	W	L	ERA	G	SV	IP	H	BB	SO
Arnold, Mitch	1	1	7.53	25	0	29	38	24	32
Boggio, Kyle	1	1	7.05	18	0	23	39	21	18
Brito, Eude	0	2	10.13	12	0	13	21	9	8
Diaz, Raymar	5	6	3.49	13	0	85	88	23	66
Dickert, Reed	3	4	5.66	13	0	76	92	27	64
Dutton, Jon	4	6	6.96	13	0	76	102	23	44
Foltz, Alex	0	2	4.80	3	0	15	20	2	11
Guinard, Sean	0	2	5.06	5	0	11	12	10	4
Hildreth, Ben	0	1	4.76	5	0	17	16	7	4
Holliday, Brian	1	7	7.87	13	0	56	86	27	27
Lauver, Loren	0	3	7.92	5	0	19	29	8	6
Liffers, Dave	0	1	14.73	6	0	11	27	7	2
Mansfield, Monte	3	3	3.21	28	0	34	30	23	34
McGee, Todd	1	1	8.51	4	0	18	32	9	7
Naegele, Rob	0	1	3.31	22	0	33	31	7	21
Rossignol, Matt	0	4	9.68	15	0	53	92	34	37
Roth, Mike	0	2	9.49	9	1	12	16	17	6
Tiffany, Chuck	1	3	8.10	5	0	20	22	16	13
Weatherby, Charlie	2	1	4.00	16	2	18	21	6	17

TIJUANA CIMARRONES

PLAYER	AVG	AB	R	H	2B	3B	HR	RBI	BB	SO	SB
Burris, Kenny	.343	70	9	24	7	0	0	3	7	13	2
Chavez, Marco	.186	59	3	11	2	0	0	3	9	13	1
Corolla, Michael	.250	112	8	28	2	0	0	8	3	19	3
Davis, Odie	.377	61	8	23	2	0	0	1	5	12	3
Dominguez, Carlos	.226	168	6	38	5	0	1	20	7	29	1
Fullman, Chris	.273	77	6	21	4	0	1	7	3	29	0
Garcia, Bubba	.257	35	4	9	4	0	1	5	3	9	2
Kokubo, Youhei	.254	59	6	15	3	1	2	7	7	19	0
Lara, Hebert	.324	37	2	12	0	1	0	3	2	7	1
Lopez, Carlos	.279	68	7	19	4	0	4	12	8	14	0
Lopez, Jose	.189	53	4	10	2	0	1	5	3	12	0
Luick, Chris	.315	89	13	28	7	0	0	5	6	13	2
Madueno, Jerry	.220	50	4	11	0	0	0	1	2	9	2
McGraw, Jaime	.297	74	12	22	2	1	1	8	9	12	1
Melian, Jackson	.329	85	11	28	4	0	2	9	5	18	3
Melo, Juan	.236	89	15	21	6	0	3	7	7	11	0
Montero, Gabriel	.286	49	7	14	3	2	0	4	1	13	0
Ochoa, Jon	.222	72	10	16	1	0	1	6	10	13	0
Ochoa, Joannes	.215	65	5	14	0	0	1	6	2	10	0
Pellow, Kit	.300	160	23	48	5	0	7	34	7	19	0
Rivas, David	.184	38	7	7	1	0	0	3	4	8	2
Samuelson, Mark	.370	81	7	30	6	0	2	22	7	25	1
Scriven, Eric	.309	55	13	17	0	0	3	15	11	4	
Starkey, Zach	.108	93	8	10	1	1	0	2	2	21	0
Surina, Michael	.211	71	8	15	4	0	0	2	5	11	1
Torres, Leonel	.256	39	3	10	1	0	0	3	10	3	0
Velasquez, Juan	.304	79	8	24	3	0	4	16	4	16	2
Villescusa, Ivan	.239	46	11	11	6	0	1	7	9	13	2
Wright, Steve	.128	47	3	6	0	0	1		3	16	0

PLAYER	W	L	ERA	G	SV	IP	H	BB	SO
Bourguillos, Davis	0	2	11.05	16	2	22	34	22	24
Chaffardet, Daniel	0	3	12.27	4	0	15	25	7	4
Chaput, Brian	1	5	7.20	8	0	35	47	18	25
Corbin, Kyle	0	6	12.75	6	0	24	47	14	16

INDEPENDENT LEAGUES

PLAYER	W	L	ERA	G	SV	IP	H	BB	SO
DeMott, Andrew	1	1	3.12	12	1	17	21	3	10
Enriquez, Robert	0	2	13.86	5	0	12	23	9	10
Estrada, Paul	0	1	8.05	13	0	19	24	12	16
Fasking, Berek	0	2	5.61	6	0	26	37	7	9
Fraijo, Alberto	0	1	4.01	4	0	25	25	13	22
Kendall, Jordan	1	3	9.93	12	0	23	42	21	17
Kuzniak, James	0	7	9.62	7	0	29	47	33	15
Martinez, Cesar	1	0	2.31	2	0	12	9	6	7
Martinez, Peter	0	2	15.71	11	0	22	49	22	18
Martinez, Yoffri	0	2	7.29	6	0	21	33	11	17
Nieto, Jose	0	3	14.09	9	0	15	28	12	6
Oliver, Brian	1	0	3.54	14	0	20	28	6	16
Oseguera, Jordan	0	1	16.46	14	0	14	31	17	4
Paulino, Ricardo	1	2	7.83	4	0	23	30	14	8
Rios, Jose	1	3	8.74	5	0	23	40	9	8
Rivas, David	0	1	20.02	5	0	10	26	12	7
Rodriguez, Pedro	0	2	6.92	7	0	26	32	7	20
Santana, Julio	0	2	3.24	12	2	17	15	11	11
Serra, Jorge	0	5	16.20	16	0	27	42	44	10
Serrano, Elio	1	1	11.49	13	0	16	28	6	7
Stone, Matt	0	2	8.87	10	0	23	35	21	19

TUCSON TOROS

PLAYER	AVG	AB	R	H	2B	3B	HR	RBI	BB	SO	SB
Apodaca, Luis	.337	246	39	83	10	2	0	42	23	40	0
Backman Jr., Wally	.279	340	51	95	12	4	4	54	46	74	16
Bannister, John	.194	36	5	7	0	0	0	4	2	13	0
Bistagne, Brian	.297	64	9	19	3	1	1	9	3	13	6
Blakely, Darren	.295	61	10	18	5	1	3	10	5	11	1
Courcha, Adam	.192	52	7	10	3	0	0	4	7	15	1
Davis, Vince	.244	41	6	10	0	0	1	4	4	15	1
Ferrante, Victor	.250	104	15	26	2	0	3	17	4	21	1
Garcia, James	.204	49	4	10	4	1	1	5	3	19	0
Garcia, Lino	.357	305	62	109	19	0	8	51	49	48	25
Lopez, Albie	.182	33	2	6	1	0	0	4	0	13	0
Perodin, Ron	.329	158	43	52	8	1	0	20	29	22	19
Plasencia, Francisco	.313	195	33	61	9	1	2	25	24	36	1
Priddy, Ryan	.330	361	77	119	18	7	4	48	18	65	13
Santana, Cristobal	.359	320	50	115	19	0	6	61	13	37	2
Valadez, Mike	.190	58	4	11	3	0	1	4	5	13	0
Valdez, Jose	.251	307	48	77	13	8	3	44	46	57	5
Womack, Josh	.286	269	53	77	16	12	7	41	21	52	19

PLAYER	W	L	ERA	G	SV	IP	H	BB	SO
Bannister, John	7	3	3.65	16	0	99	98	38	69
Bello, Cibney	0	2	11.40	13	0	15	29	7	14
Daly, Brian	1	0	6.06	17	0	33	43	19	16
Davis, Vince	5	7	4.95	19	0	116	133	48	86
Fruto, Emiliano	5	4	2.15	41	17	50	43	21	72
Garcia, James	7	4	3.81	18	0	113	117	44	74
Hanna, Jason	0	3	6.07	21	0	30	48	19	21
Lincoln, Matt	1	5	7.53	9	0	43	58	21	32
Lopez, Albie	7	5	3.93	16	0	92	111	18	52
Nordman, Toby	1	3	3.99	20	0	20	25	9	13
Orosco Jr., Jesse	3	3	6.20	17	0	20	36	12	13
Price, Reid	3	1	1.80	19	0	25	21	9	24
Snowdon, Andrew	2	2	2.97	22	0	39	38	11	34
Walden, Cody	4	1	3.44	17	0	65	72	13	41

VICTORIA SEALS

PLAYER	AVG	AB	R	H	2B	3B	HR	RBI	BB	SO	SB
Arhart, Josh	.352	230	43	81	12	0	17	55	30	25	0
Calderon, Henry	.211	71	8	15	1	0	3	12	4	14	0
Cronin, Shane	.274	62	8	17	3	0	4	13	6	12	1
Edgecombe, Matt	.262	145	15	38	3	0	0	13	13	27	0
Gonzalez, Jino	.270	37	4	10	0	0	0	4	1	7	1
Hess, Isaac	.364	33	6	12	5	0	1	8	1	7	0
Kavanaugh, Matt	.315	235	36	74	21	1	7	38	31	41	2
Maddueno, Jerry	.177	62	7	11	1	0	0	5	2	12	1
McClain, Terrance	.330	339	63	112	23	1	14	63	30	67	19
Mooney, Mike	.243	37	9	9	0	1	2	6	3	8	2
Moro, Colin	.294	293	66	86	13	0	6	50	50	50	4
Perez, Wilver	.317	338	83	107	25	4	8	48	48	38	64
Pluta, Anthony	.313	32	10	10	0	1	0	7	2	6	0

PLAYER	AVG	AB	R	H	2B	3B	HR	RBI	BB	SO	SB
Rios, Brian	.337	288	53	97	21	0	9	40	24	25	9
Rodriguez, Tim	.230	148	28	34	9	1	6	23	9	47	13
Smith, Sean	.131	61	12	8	2	0	0	3	7	14	12
Strandlund, Charlie	.204	49	4	10	2	0	1	10	4	17	1
Swinford, Dale	.283	191	22	54	6	0	0	16	9	26	9
Van Rossum, Chris	.184	136	14	25	4	0	5	14	8	37	5

PLAYER	W	L	ERA	G	SV	IP	H	BB	SO
Arreola, Andrew	6	7	4.78	27	0	75	93	26	43
Bevis, P.J.	0	2	6.59	26	2	27	36	16	31
Bodishbaugh, Chris	1	3	3.30	40	1	71	86	32	65
Duda, Jeff	4	3	3.90	21	0	65	81	14	63
Easton, Aaron	4	4	3.38	44	1	45	45	17	45
Gonzalez, Jino	7	6	4.05	19	0	107	121	29	80
Hess, Isaac	5	4	3.91	12	0	74	71	26	80
Kershner, Jason	6	6	5.77	22	0	83	101	37	53
Koons, Mike	0	0	7.51	13	0	12	19	10	10
Pluta, Anthony	6	4	4.56	22	0	77	83	42	81
Trolia, Aaron	0	2	5.95	4	0	20	24	13	25
Villafuerte, Brandon	6	0	2.74	39	12	43	48	17	43
Wilson, Kyle	0	1	9.69	9	0	26	35	21	23

YUMA SCORPIONS

PLAYER	AVG	AB	R	H	2B	3B	HR	RBI	BB	SO	SB
Albornoz, Henry	.270	115	18	31	7	0	0	14	16	26	6
Celis, Johny	.296	230	42	68	14	1	6	38	31	42	6
Ceriani, Matt	.295	44	6	13	5	0	0	7	8	11	1
Church, Eric	.265	151	34	40	6	1	1	18	23	37	12
Correa, Walter	.292	120	17	35	5	2	1	12	11	24	9
Cruz, Lee	.433	67	20	29	5	3	3	26	1	3	1
DAlfonso, Anthony	.290	31	5	9	3	1	1	7	1	9	0
Davis, Odie	.235	68	11	16	1	0	0	7	9	16	3
Deleon, Santo	.350	180	32	63	11	2	4	41	10	27	7
Dominguez, Carlos	.210	62	7	13	1	0	0	2	6	15	1
Garcia, Bubba	.258	120	17	31	7	0	3	21	16	43	2
Gordon, Adam	.280	82	15	23	1	1	1	10	13	41	4
Grable, AC	.375	32	4	12	1	0	0	8	3	9	0
Herrera, Javier	.368	57	17	21	7	0	2	14	7	10	3
Lara, Herbert	.294	102	12	30	3	1	1	17	9	17	5
Lopez, Franklen	.265	151	22	40	6	0	1	13	13	23	2
Murillo, Francisco	.255	110	17	28	1	1	2	20	10	25	2
Muse, JJ	.287	115	17	33	6	1	3	18	17	25	0
Pacheco, Jonel	.349	109	28	38	11	1	2	21	15	16	4
Perodin, Ron	.256	90	24	23	5	1	0	8	16	15	5
Ramos, Peeter	.297	148	29	44	6	2	1	14	19	29	8
Rodriguez, Jose	.121	33	2	4	0	0	0	1	2	8	0
Rodriguez, Tim	.349	149	34	52	9	3	6	51	13	35	7
Samuelson, Mark	.386	44	5	17	4	0	0	8	3	12	0
Sanchez, Ruben	.294	85	13	25	6	2	1	15	11	16	1
Scriven, Eric	.368	57	21	21	1	0	1	3	14	14	11
Surina, Michael	.246	65	13	16	4	0	1	11	8	16	3

PLAYER	W	L	ERA	G	SV	IP	H	BB	SO
Alvarez, Wilner	1	2	6.32	10	0	16	18	13	9
Arreola, Daryl	7	1	2.59	10	0	59	59	26	49
Aucoin, Tim	2	1	3.68	9	0	22	21	10	11
Azocar, Luis	0	1	7.60	9	0	11	13	14	7
Baek, Cha-Seung	2	1	3.37	4	0	19	17	2	13
Bello, Cibney	1	2	3.65	12	4	12	19	2	8
Cline, Zac	2	2	4.87	14	0	41	49	14	28
Coffey, Drew	0	0	5.68	4	0	13	14	13	9
De La Vara, Gilbert	5	1	2.70	9	1	57	41	18	43
DeMott, Andrew	0	1	6.75	20	2	25	33	7	24
Fraijo, Alberto	0	2	8.48	9	1	12	19	6	7
Giulin, Mario	1	2	6.08	3	0	13	14	7	9
Gomez, Jesus	1	0	6.75	8	0	13	14	14	9
Guilin, Mario	0	0	4.77	2	0	11	10	7	11
LoPresti, Jim	0	1	3.65	5	0	12	10	8	8
Malave, Ronny	1	3	6.45	14	0	38	54	11	21
Moreno, Adam	1	1	11.40	11	0	15	24	17	8
Muir, Jordan	2	0	3.74	24	3	34	30	19	25
Oliver, Brian	2	0	6.38	14	1	24	27	10	17
Pulsipher, Bill	3	5	4.98	10	0	56	71	14	38
Ramos-Dominko, Dan	2	0	4.74	18	0	25	28	16	17
Robertson, Shelby	0	2	8.10	5	0	17	25	5	9

Rojas, Jose	1	1	6.27	16	1	19	27	13 23
Screener, Ryan	3	4	4.91	13	0	33	42	15 19
Stone, Matt	2	2	6.46	21	0	31	44	21 20
Wheatley, Grant	0	2	4.19	8	0	19	23	5 23
Wortham, Jacob	2	4	5.67	7	0	27	36	15 17

NORTHERN LEAGUE

In their final season in the league, Fargo-Moorhead left with a fine parting gift. The RedHawks won their second straight title and their fifth overall, before announcing that they were leaving along with three other teams to join the American Association. RedHawks pitcher T.J. Stanton threw a one-hitter to finish off the sweep of Kansas City in the championship series. Fargo first baseman Hoorelbeke hit .500 (6-for-12) with two home runs, eight RBI and scored three runs to earn the championship MVP award.

	W	L	PCT	GB
Fargo-Moorhead RedHawks	61	39	.610	-
Kansas City T-Bones	58	42	.580	3
Joliet JackHammers	53	47	.530	8
Gary SouthShore RailCats	52	48	.520	9
Rockford RiverHawks	47	52	.475	13.5
Winnipeg Goldeyes	46	53	.465	14.5
Schaumburg Flyers	41	59	.410	20
Lake County Fielders	41	59	.410	20

PLAYOFFS—Semifinals: Kansas City defeats Joliet 3-2 and Fargo-Moorhead defeats Gary 3-0 in best-of-five semifinals. **Finals:** Fargo-Moorhead defeated Kansas City 3-0 in best-of-five series.
ATTENDANCE: Winnipeg 271,399, Kansas City 264,368, Fargo-Moorhead 183,145, Schaumburg 172,732, Gary SouthShore 166,366, Joliet 165,396, Lake County 128,856, Rockford 126,432.
MANAGERS: Fargo-Moorhead—Doug Simunic. **Gary**—Greg Tagert. **Joliet**—Chad Parker. **Kansas City**—Andy McCauley. **Lake County**—Fran Riordan. **Rockford**—Bob Koopman. **Schaumburg**—Mike Busch. **Winnipeg**—Rick Forney.
ALL-STAR TEAM: C—Richard Mercado, Joliet. **1B**—Jesse Hoorelbeke, Fargo-Moorhead. **2B**—Jacob Blackwood, Kansas City. **3B**—Eric Campbell, Fargo-Moorhead. **SS**—Travis Brown, Schaumburg. **OF**—Kevin West, Winnipeg; Keanon Simon, Kansas City; Ray Sadler, Kansas City. **DH**—Josh Short, Lake County. **RHP**—Willie Glen, Gary SouthShore. **LHP**—Scott Fogelson, Fargo-Moorhead.
Most Valuable Player: Jacob Blackwood, Kansas City. **Pitcher of the Year:** Willie Glen, Gary SouthShore. **Manager of the Year:** Chad Parker, Joliet.

INDIVIDUAL BATTING LEADERS

PLAYER, TEAM	AVG	G	AB	R	H	HR	RBI
West, Kevin, Winnipeg	.337	99	383	62	129	9	70
Diaz, Juan, Winnipeg	.335	97	373	68	125	24	75
Blackwood, Jacob, Kansas City	.331	99	426	82	141	31	86
Short, Josh, Lake County	.326	100	374	66	122	26	84
Wyatt, Jonathan, Joliet	.324	98	392	70	127	10	56
Long, Wes, Winnipeg	.323	69	285	47	92	7	41
Fasano, Jim, Kansas City	.319	98	364	69	116	20	76
Sadler, Ray, Kansas City	.318	97	390	82	124	23	83
Correll, Brad, Joliet	.317	92	344	59	109	13	59
Ramon, Amos, Lake County	.316	92	370	53	117	8	57

INDIVIDUAL PITCHING LEADERS

PLAYER, TEAM	W	L	ERA	IP	H	BB	SO
Hoorelbeke, Casey, Fargo-Moorhead	10	5	1.84	83	56	31	75
Glen, Willie, Gary	11	2	2.39	135	118	42	110
Fogelson, Scott, Fargo-Moorhead	8	3	3.08	105	90	42	91
Bay, Ronald, Joliet	10	5	3.08	143	139	28	116
Cruse, Andrew, Kansas City	11	6	3.28	132	124	24	102
Wright, Kyle, Rochester	10	3	3.41	124	132	22	83
Glant, Dustin, Schaumburg	10	6	3.52	133	154	44	69
Quijano, Alain, Schaumburg	5	10	3.77	115	110	59	99
Halsey, Brad, Gary	7	7	3.82	123	126	38	81
Laber, Jake, Fargo-Moorhead	11	4	3.90	132	140	32	75

FARGO-MOORHEAD REDHAWKS

PLAYER	AVG	AB	R	H	2B	3B	HR	RBI	SB
Campbell, Eric	.311	302	72	94	19	0	22	80	4
Coles, Michael	.312	420	78	131	27	0	3	45	25

	AVG	AB	R	H	2B	3B	HR	RBI	SB
Cota, Carlos	.284	328	56	93	26	0	12	44	15
Cox, Jay	.296	348	53	103	30	1	10	58	7
Hoorelbeke, Jesse	.273	363	61	99	22	0	29	75	0
Jackson, Nic	.305	400	75	122	30	0	14	71	19
Krause, Jake	.290	93	17	27	5	0	8		3
Patton, Cory	.279	208	26	58	17	0	2	29	2
Penprase, Zach	.236	335	62	79	16	1	4	39	41
Piepkorn, Jeremiah	.295	122	17	36	7	1	3	23	0
Rick, Alan	.253	288	34	73	13	1	11	49	0
Zimmerman, Kole	.280	182	32	51	8	1	6	26	11

PLAYER	W	L	ERA	G	SV	IP	H	BB	SO
Byrd, Darren	0	2	4.58	4	0	20	20	10	18
Fogelson, Scott	8	3	3.08	18	0	105	90	42	91
Gregory, Sean	0	1	5.90	5	0	11	12	7	7
Hauer, Jeremy	0	2	6.61	20	0	48	55	34	40
Hoorelbeke, Casey	10	5	1.84	52	7	83	56	31	75
Kent, Alex	2	0	2.84	10	0	19	22	3	13
Laber, Jake	11	4	3.90	21	0	132	140	32	75
Mossey, Matt	7	5	4.88	22	1	94	96	39	49
Patton, Cory	1	1	3.64	18	4	17	12	9	9
Petrusek, Matt	4	2	5.85	22	0	48	53	15	31
Rhoades, Chad	3	2	2.68	9	0	40	41	10	21
Seaman, Tyler	1	1	5.75	8	0	31	37	20	12
Smith, Donnie	4	1	4.03	39	8	38	30	27	41
Stanton, T.J.	4	5	4.17	25	2	91	84	49	64
Tollefson, Adam	4	1	3.29	41	3	38	34	11	38
Zoltak, Matt	1	2	7.02	4	0	17	16	8	15

GARY SOUTHSHORE RAILCATS

PLAYER	AVG	AB	R	H	2B	3B	HR	RBI	SB
Beachum, Jeff	.278	234	28	65	7	1	5	30	8
Carrara, Chris	.275	229	37	63	8	1	1	20	7
Dulaney, Todd	.273	33	5	9	0	0	0	3	0
Guerrero, Cristian	.297	310	56	92	11	2	19	62	7
Klein, Adam	.299	398	59	119	18	5	0	54	29
Massaro, Mike	.312	382	55	119	18	3	3	43	7
Matsumoto, Yuki	.180	50	6	9	1	0	0	3	0
Ott, Louis	.301	312	43	94	26	6	6	53	9
Parham, John	.239	176	24	42	6	1	3	25	0
Pecci, Jay	.216	287	36	62	11	0	6	39	1
Reese, Mike	.271	192	26	52	9	1	4	21	2
Rodeghero, Zach	.209	43	7	9	2	0	0	5	0
Rohde, Mike	.285	312	45	89	20	1	3	39	2
Simon, Randall	.333	120	19	40	9	0	3	19	2
Townsend, Tanner	.278	288	49	80	17	5	6	36	2
Valadez, Mike	.265	83	10	22	4	0	1	9	2

PLAYER	W	L	ERA	G	SV	IP	H	BB	SO
Baker, James	3	5	4.91	39	0	48	43	21	39
Chavez, Chris	0	0	3.46	8	0	13	21	4	12
Cook, Aaron	4	2	5.79	43	0	51	62	26	34
Engle, Zeb	5	2	3.72	32	0	56	56	19	46
Furnish, Brad	4	0	3.28	39	2	49	45	22	49
Glen, Willie	11	2	2.39	21	0	135	118	42	110
Halsey, Brad	7	7	3.82	20	0	123	126	38	81
Magee, Brandon	3	2	3.25	7	0	36	36	10	26
McClellan, Zach	1	2	4.16	4	0	17	21	6	18
Nicholson, Nolan	5	6	4.87	16	0	85	99	43	46
Shipman, Andy	4	2	2.94	43	21	46	42	12	43
Thornton, Tom	1	9	5.33	17	0	78	99	27	48
Weeks, Andy	1	2	5.83	12	0	46	56	23	52
Williams, Jeff	2	3	2.96	37	1	46	37	19	35
Zink, Ryan	1	3	7.08	6	0	34	38	16	21

JOLIET JACKHAMMERS

PLAYER	AVG	AB	R	H	2B	3B	HR	RBI	SB
Basham, Ryan	.200	90	10	18	4	0	2	13	3
Billick, Joe	.196	219	26	43	7	0	2	10	0
Colton, Chris	.273	249	40	68	14	1	7	33	12
Correll, Brad	.317	344	59	109	27	2	13	59	10
Flores, Josh	.309	139	32	43	9	2	1	22	23
Justice, Justin	.242	62	9	15	5	0	1	3	1
Mena, Roberto	.279	330	44	92	17	1	4	33	11
Mendez, Rafael	.236	123	11	29	1	1	2	11	1

PLAYER	AVG	AB	R	H	2B	3B	HR	RBI	SB
Mercado, Richard	.429	42	10	18	1	0	2	10	4
Nelson, Jon	.307	381	66	117	18	0	27	68	14
Rios, Kevin	.265	374	59	99	25	1	7	53	7
Rodriguez, Jorge	.200	55	10	11	3	1	0	4	2
Thon, Freddie	.298	392	45	117	19	1	11	76	9
Wehrle, Ryan	.277	155	16	43	8	0	1	17	4
Wyatt, Jonathan	.324	392	70	127	29	1	10	56	16

PLAYER	W	L	ERA	G	SV	IP	H	BB	SO
Alsup, Wes	0	0	2.05	22	0	26	15	19	21
Anderson, Devin	7	5	4.10	21	0	108	131	27	67
Bailey, Griffin	4	4	3.86	45	15	47	49	12	37
Bay, Ronald	10	5	3.08	22	0	143	139	28	116
Dahman, Kyle	2	1	6.93	19	0	25	35	11	23
Fagan, Paul	1	0	5.19	6	0	26	30	15	13
Gartley, Brian	4	0	6.12	34	0	43	57	17	32
Hamren, Erik	0	1	0.84	7	1	11	11	5	16
Jackel, William	5	4	3.25	46	2	55	60	30	44
Privett, Todd	9	5	4.06	20	0	113	110	38	101
Rocco, Mike	2	2	6.23	31	1	43	54	16	38
Shetrone, Drew	0	3	6.18	13	5	12	11	5	14
Shortell, Rory	4	9	5.51	22	0	113	146	33	65
Stout, Ross	5	8	5.83	14	0	80	106	17	59

KANSAS CITY T-BONES

PLAYER	AVG	AB	R	H	2B	3B	HR	RBI	SB
Blackwood, Jacob	.331	426	82	141	27	5	31	86	16
Fasano, Jim	.319	364	69	116	15	1	20	76	1
Fox, Ryan	.239	197	33	47	11	0	17	41	3
Hernandez, Keith	.237	207	29	49	18	0	5	35	0
Joynt, Brian	.283	339	58	96	17	2	15	43	2
Martinez, Gabriel	.415	53	18	22	3	0	10	22	0
Mojica, Jimmy	.281	334	56	94	15	3	8	43	24
Rodriguez, Eladio	.223	139	15	31	7	0	3	13	3
Sadler, Ray	.318	390	82	124	27	1	23	83	21
Simon, Keanon	.309	382	75	118	17	6	6	41	31
Washington, Rico	.268	343	63	92	16	1	9	48	18
White, Dwayne	.313	284	47	89	17	1	15	54	5

PLAYER	W	L	ERA	G	SV	IP	H	BB	SO
Cruse, Andrew	11	6	3.28	20	0	132	124	24	102
Dahman, Kyle	0	1	5.25	8	1	12	16	5	9
Davis, Brett	2	2	7.53	10	0	35	43	14	20
Graham, Drew	2	2	4.85	25	0	26	28	15	27
Hamren, Erik	0	1	3.94	37	2	50	47	21	35
Heim, Kyle	1	1	6.36	17	0	23	36	15	12
Hodges, Casey	2	1	3.04	18	0	24	25	8	18
James, Justin	0	0	1.69	11	6	11	6	1	10
Knippschild, Ryan	10	8	5.87	20	0	120	142	39	94
Light, Kevin	3	2	4.86	26	0	54	55	26	37
McAllister, Cody	11	7	5.07	21	0	124	130	37	79
Moser, Todd	1	0	0.87	6	0	10	8	6	10
Perez, Franklin	0	1	0.87	11	6	10	9	5	6
Rocco, Mike	1	0	2.19	4	0	12	9	5	11
Santos, Reid	7	5	5.10	20	0	113	133	37	65
Shetrone, Drew	1	1	7.54	13	5	14	20	11	12
Stewart, Steven	5	3	5.23	33	0	62	69	24	52

LAKE COUNTY FIELDERS

PLAYER	AVG	AB	R	H	2B	3B	HR	RBI	SB
Anderson, Brandon	.216	97	12	21	3	1	0	7	8
Cone, Aaron	.205	83	8	17	2	0	0	10	0
Dunbar, Jeff	.230	356	40	82	16	1	16	49	1
Esquer, Anthony	.292	284	38	83	19	2	1	30	0
Gomes, Joey	.200	45	4	9	2	0	1	8	0
Haas, Kevin	.203	79	17	16	6	0	0	6	3
Hale, Adam	.202	109	13	22	5	1	4	12	0
Higgins, Kyle	.279	341	43	95	20	2	2	30	13
Larson, Zach	.260	77	10	20	5	0	3	6	0
Martinez, Guillermo	.301	153	31	46	10	1	1	15	9
McFall, Brian	.269	268	40	72	21	0	16	42	0
Petersen, Josh	.278	97	9	27	7	1	0	6	1
Ramon, Amos	.316	370	53	117	27	6	8	57	4
Ramos, Joseph	.229	153	18	35	7	0	1	13	8
Short, Joshua	.326	374	66	122	22	0	26	84	0

PLAYER	AVG	AB	R	H	2B	3B	HR	RBI	SB
Strait, Cody	.227	194	28	44	11	1	6	22	7
Suttle, Eric	.225	40	5	9	1	0	0	1	6
Valdes, Juan	.292	185	31	54	14	1	4	32	3

PLAYER	W	L	ERA	G	SV	IP	H	BB	SO
Bakker, Garry	5	10	5.52	20	0	106	109	89	88
Bass, Corey	2	3	6.35	14	1	34	36	12	19
Bicondoa, Ryan	3	9	5.15	18	0	121	164	24	83
Brownell, John	4	9	5.31	21	0	124	132	43	104
Falcon, Ryan	4	3	7.58	32	0	46	56	13	39
Feliciano, Roberto	1	1	7.14	5	0	11	11	10	8
Gonzalez, Marco	4	4	5.09	37	5	41	45	19	30
Homer, Chris	1	0	2.08	27	11	26	20	9	24
Jordan, Justin	0	0	2.32	3	0	12	15	2	15
Lewis, Alec	1	4	5.52	17	0	62	82	14	51
Long, Jeff	0	2	8.76	3	0	12	18	4	6
Lundahl, Chad	1	2	4.34	20	0	19	16	12	17
Ruckle, Jake	0	1	5.71	10	0	17	22	9	13
Schweitzer, Matt	2	2	8.48	22	0	35	54	7	38
Sherrill, Garrett	6	2	3.96	30	0	36	32	17	30
Smith, Alex	0	0	5.79	12	0	14	17	7	7
Ward, Zach	7	5	3.95	15	0	98	90	41	85
Wasylak, David	0	0	5.40	11	0	13	9	11	7

ROCKFORD RIVERHAWKS

PLAYER	AVG	AB	R	H	2B	3B	HR	RBI	SB
Austin, Rich	.296	321	59	95	23	0	9	55	10
Brooks, Jono	.225	315	40	71	14	4	7	35	22
Buttler, Victor	.286	70	12	20	1	1	2	7	11
Church, Ian	.202	94	10	19	4	1	1	9	0
Cooper, David	.297	101	26	30	0	0	0	7	12
Diaz, Victor	.339	59	12	20	2	0	6	11	0
Eigsti, Jake	.253	340	54	86	18	1	11	52	21
House, Kevin	.262	282	45	74	15	5	7	35	18
James, Jason	.283	385	47	109	24	2	10	57	3
Long, Bud	.323	62	13	20	4	0	2	8	4
McArthur, Evan	.286	304	38	87	18	0	6	49	5
Millan Jr., Elvin	.214	42	4	9	2	0	0	3	0
OSullivan, Patrick	.287	293	43	84	22	0	13	50	1
Scott, Travis	.300	243	41	73	18	2	5	29	3
Shorsher, Adam	.211	57	5	12	2	0	2	6	0
Simon, Randall	.250	104	13	26	6	0	7	19	2
Valdes, Franco	.186	86	7	16	2	0	4	13	0
Wagle, John	.326	178	28	58	13	2	2	15	4

PLAYER	W	L	ERA	G	SV	IP	H	BB	SO
Diaz, Raymar	1	1	5.00	5	0	27	29	8	14
Durand, Brett	8	8	4.94	21	0	113	122	26	106
Huizinga, Jon	3	1	3.64	43	2	47	46	19	30
Johnson, Jimmy	0	0	6.01	12	0	12	15	5	11
Knoff, Justin	0	1	9.01	8	1	16	18	7	10
Lincoln, Roger	6	8	5.88	22	0	109	145	26	52
McTamney, Mike	2	2	3.84	35	0	61	65	16	51
Muller, John	0	1	10.02	11	0	12	13	10	12
Olivares, Manuel	2	0	5.73	9	0	11	19	8	8
Pfalzgraf, Chris	0	2	5.65	9	0	14	19	10	7
Roehl, Scott	5	2	4.05	30	18	33	26	12	35
Ruwe, Kyle	6	9	6.64	20	0	121	160	35	54
Todd, Brandon	0	4	8.17	21	0	25	25	19	18
Wagner, David	0	1	8.71	9	0	10	17	8	5
Wood, Mike	3	7	5.53	17	0	85	109	31	39
Wright, Kyle	10	3	3.41	19	0	124	132	22	83

SCHAUMBURG FLYERS

PLAYER	AVG	AB	R	H	2B	3B	HR	RBI	SB
Borquin, Ron	.307	228	36	70	14	0	5	24	6
Brown, Travis	.274	379	60	104	14	5	3	36	7
Burrus, Josh	.252	103	21	26	7	1	3	10	6
Delgado, Mario	.355	141	14	50	8	0	8	28	0
Fitzgerald, Tom	.239	280	27	67	10	1	0	16	1
Gomes, Joey	.301	342	39	103	18	0	8	45	2
Marshall, Andre	.219	128	12	28	4	4	5	13	3
Mercado, Richard	.288	288	31	83	17	3	7	44	1
Mermer, Terry	.220	50	7	11	4	0	2	8	0
Mooney, Mike	.244	86	10	21	2	1	3	8	3

INDEPENDENT LEAGUES

PLAYER	AVG	AB	R	H	2B	3B	HR	RBI	SB
Newton, Brandon	.298	326	46	97	15	1	2	27	23
Nowicki, Joe	.279	197	22	55	15	2	4	22	0
Parzyk, Dylan	.210	100	16	21	1	0	1	6	1
Pauley, Joe	.191	94	8	18	2	1	0	11	0
Pellow, Kit	.320	147	18	47	8	0	4	32	0
Schultz, Chris	.257	241	29	62	10	3	4	27	1
Yan, Ruddy	.319	204	31	65	7	3	1	19	4

PLAYER	W	L	ERA	G	SV	IP	H	BB	SO
Elliott, Matt	4	1	4.22	24	2	43	38	23	42
Evans, Cody	3	6	5.07	30	4	66	71	27	44
Gehring, Ryan	3	11	5.13	20	0	98	143	18	47
Giles, Joshua	0	1	4.08	32	4	46	43	29	57
Glant, Dustin	10	6	3.52	21	0	133	154	44	69
Guinn, Aaron	0	2	7.11	8	0	25	32	7	11
Harker, Brett	8	9	5.09	19	0	117	130	37	67
Lyons, Tom	1	1	3.81	31	2	52	57	15	46
McCullough, Brian	5	2	2.66	33	6	61	50	19	35
Moser, Todd	2	7	6.54	15	0	65	82	32	35
Price, Reid	0	3	5.66	14	0	21	22	8	15
Quijano, Alain	5	10	3.77	22	0	115	110	59	99
Reeser, Ben	0	0	5.46	14	0	30	36	17	16

WINNIPEG GOLDEYES

PLAYER	AVG	AB	R	H	2B	3B	HR	RBI	SB
Alen, Luis	.290	331	50	96	22	1	11	56	1
Asanovich, Josh	.171	111	17	19	4	0	3	12	1
Brown, Dee	.284	349	43	99	26	2	8	40	5
Diaz, Juan C.	.335	373	68	125	11	0	24	75	0
Dowdy, Brett	.061	33	3	2	0	0	0	2	1
Eggleston, Aharon	.311	354	64	110	19	3	3	31	9
Hamilton, Jeremy	.244	90	15	22	7	0	0	6	0
Harrison, Vince	.268	370	42	99	17	0	7	58	5
Justice, Justin	.296	250	46	74	10	7	14	51	7
Kendall, Price	.302	182	31	55	5	0	3	20	5
Long, Wes	.323	285	47	92	18	0	7	41	6
McDonald, Donzell	.304	56	12	17	5	0	1	9	4
Wallace, Brett	.233	172	22	40	7	1	2	20	0
West, Kevin	.337	383	62	129	28	3	9	70	20
Williams, Zach	.170	47	4	8	2	0	0	1	0

PLAYER	W	L	ERA	G	SV	IP	H	BB	SO
Baldwin, Zach	5	3	3.21	36	2	76	72	23	52
Bass, Corey	1	0	9.39	10	0	15	24	4	11
Bello, Anthony	4	7	4.91	21	0	77	95	31	49
Benefield, Chad	1	3	4.29	23	0	29	32	12	27
Flake, Stephen	5	5	4.89	25	0	101	101	55	89
Graham, Drew A.	0	0	11.43	9	0	11	19	9	11
Hodges, Casey	0	1	6.10	8	0	10	19	7	11
Holliman, Mark	4	1	2.02	8	0	49	42	18	47
Kniginyzky, Matt	1	0	6.97	3	0	10	16	5	9
Korecky, Bobby	0	2	5.32	23	10	22	20	4	21
Mackintosh, Jason	1	6	5.52	10	0	60	71	17	32
Roque, Ulysses	0	1	6.08	12	0	13	20	4	12
Roy, Philip	2	2	7.32	19	6	20	29	13	24
Salamida, Chris	10	9	5.31	21	0	125	152	30	111
Shetrone, Drew	0	3	7.71	11	2	12	16	3	11
Thomas, Ian	5	1	1.64	34	4	55	36	20	60
Walker, Andrew	7	6	4.85	22	0	141	164	24	87

UNITED LEAGUE

When Brady Bogart was named the Amarillo Dillas' manager, he heard from people wondering if he was up to the job. You won't hear anyone questioning it anymore. Bogart's Dillas won their third consecutive United League title by beating Edinburg in the league's championship series.

	W	L	PCT	GB
Amarillo Dillas	52	39	.571	—
Edinburg Roadrunners	50	39	.561	1
Rio Grande Valley WhiteWings	47	45	.511	5.5
Laredo Broncos	47	45	.511	5.5
San Angelo Colts	46	45	.505	6
Coastal Bend Thunder	31	60	.342	21

PLAYOFFS: Semifinals—Amarillo Dillas defeated Rio Grande Valley WhiteWings 2-0 and Edinburg Roadrunners defeated Laredo Broncos 2-1 in best-of-three series. **Finals**—Amarillo Dillas defeated Edinburg Roadrunners 3-1 in best-of-five series.

ATTENDANCE: Amarillo 139,790; San Angelo 112,164; Edinburg 101,620; Laredo 66,194; Rio Grande Valley 51,427; Coastal Bend 11,874.

MANAGERS: Amarillo—Brady Bogart. **Coastal Bend**—Al Gallagher. **Edinburg**—Vince Moore. **Laredo**—Dan Firova. **Rio Grande Valley**—Eddie Dennis. **San Angelo**—Doc Edwards.

AMARILLO DILLAS

PLAYER	AVG	AB	R	H	2B	3B	HR	RBI	SB
Bueno, Brian	.209	148	18	31	4	0	1	24	0
Butler, Kevin	.351	37	2	13	1	0	0	10	0
Ceriani, Matt	.262	61	11	16	1	0	2	14	0
Cisneros, Jonathan	.406	32	7	13	2	0	2	10	0
Cruz, Alberto	.299	328	70	98	19	1	14	78	3
De La Garza, Adam	.305	367	73	112	20	2	7	55	9
Douglas, Stephen	.316	348	83	110	24	6	8	56	35
Figueroa, Carlos	.332	346	72	115	27	3	4	59	1
Jones, Daryl	.307	215	46	66	16	0	9	45	11
Lomack, Jermel	.300	243	56	73	7	4	1	25	30
Martinez, Julio	.326	129	26	42	4	1	5	31	6
Palace, Sam	.255	102	16	26	13	0	0	24	1
Recuenco, Rob	.391	179	44	70	18	3	0	41	11
Rodriguez, Joaquin	.372	363	76	135	30	10	6	63	19
Warren, TJ	.294	153	37	45	9	3	2	29	8
Wine, Cory	.391	46	8	18	5	0	1	12	1
Wong, Andrew	.351	97	20	34	4	0	2	15	1

PLAYER	W	L	ERA	G	SV	IP	H	BB	SO
Allen, Taylor	3	3	8.61	11	0	54	77	25	24
Brasher, Turner	2	2	6.75	13	1	36	45	17	33
Buffa, Brent	2	1	9.00	8	0	13	21	6	5
Cole, Zachary	0	0	6.38	9	0	18	28	4	9
Corolla IV, Frank	1	5	7.62	18	0	28	43	11	25
Geronimo, Ramon	4	1	3.11	37	21	38	29	11	36
Ingoglia, Chris	4	3	6.98	29	1	59	82	26	60
Jessup, Richard	3	5	8.12	19	0	75	119	37	39
Little, Dane	0	0	1.54	8	0	12	10	7	13
Lowe, Ronald	7	4	4.34	18	0	110	127	49	114
Mitchell, Ryan	5	3	4.29	17	0	107	114	41	103
Nyman, Chris	3	3	6.64	22	0	41	67	22	38
Pearson, Tyler	6	1	2.85	35	3	41	30	15	55
Roberts, Ralph	6	5	6.99	18	0	95	132	50	84
Van Buren, Jermaine	1	1	5.90	4	0	21	27	9	20

COASTAL BEND THUNDER

PLAYER	AVG	AB	R	H	2B	3B	HR	RBI	SB
Butler, Kevin	.242	161	19	39	9	0	1	13	1
Cabrera, Juan	.281	57	7	16	3	0	2	7	0
Contreras, Lester	.292	65	6	19	5	0	0	9	3
Fenwick, Ron	.317	309	59	98	15	1	0	35	0
Fernandez, Alex	.305	246	25	75	21	1	4	40	1
Gonzales, Albert	.277	141	20	39	9	4	0	17	1
Goss, Mike	.342	243	44	83	11	2	2	36	12
Griffin, Kevin	.200	40	5	8	2	0	0	3	1
Guy, Lamar	.270	211	39	57	10	1	8	33	11
Johnson, Carl	.233	116	16	27	4	2	1	11	7
Lewis, Mike	.275	313	58	86	9	2	3	21	20
Matera, Patty	.298	124	16	37	6	1	3	17	2
Meija, Manny	.228	79	15	18	2	0	5	22	0
Nichols, Brian	.353	255	51	90	14	3	17	56	1
Rosa, Gianican	.272	114	21	31	9	1	6	21	0
Smith, Dustin	.241	315	51	76	8	3	2	38	30
Ventura, Leivi	.297	286	54	85	16	2	16	64	2

PLAYER	W	L	ERA	G	SV	IP	H	BB	SO
Brandt, Doug	5	7	5.04	24	0	89	100	57	73
Fernandez, Alex	1	1	6.00	17	0	36	35	23	17
Foss, Ryan	1	2	5.67	9	0	27	31	16	16
Fries, Tyler	1	0	6.15	21	0	34	43	14	24
Haggerty, Hunter	1	2	5.23	19	0	41	55	19	34
James, Frank	4	8	6.43	19	1	77	107	39	62
Liedka, Jacob	1	5	9.00	13	0	39	71	22	23
Lugo, Jorge	0	2	4.91	4	0	18	25	7	8

Lundahl, Chad	3	2	2.45	15	1	18	12	7	22
Martinez, Luis	1	2	4.91	4	0	22	31	8	15
Polanco, Celson	0	0	2.61	12	3	21	20	6	17
Rangel, Carlos	5	6	6.36	14	1	69	86	25	47
Sutton, Jared	0	3	9.00	13	0	33	42	21	36
Trevino, Raul	0	1	5.18	8	1	24	31	8	16
Trevino, Toro	3	8	8.59	18	0	87	131	33	53
Trujillo, J.J.	5	8	4.70	24	5	82	104	35	61

EDINBURG ROADRUNNERS

PLAYER	AVG	AB	R	H	2B	3B	HR	RBI	SB
Batista, Wilson	.294	309	46	91	22	2	7	52	15
Blue, Vincent	.236	174	35	41	7	5	2	28	4
Concepcion, Ambiorix	.297	316	66	94	19	1	10	60	23
Flores, Osiel	.289	228	35	66	12	1	4	21	4
Gonzalez, Albert	.231	78	11	18	2	0	1	8	2
Hereaud, Carlos	.313	297	58	93	13	5	11	58	11
Hernandez, Alexis	.311	254	36	79	7	0	10	43	3
Jones, Daryl	.418	55	13	23	10	0	2	9	5
Matlock, Robert	.299	298	52	89	17	2	1	37	10
Matos, Adam	.208	72	16	15	0	0	0	6	9
Molina, Felix	.333	324	67	108	21	4	7	47	15
Perez, Melvin	.230	74	12	17	3	0	0	8	0
Pino, Wilmer	.325	348	70	113	21	1	7	54	50
Teilon, Nelson	.304	138	23	42	7	0	8	27	3
Wilson, Eddie	.250	64	8	16	4	0	0	10	0

PLAYER	W	L	ERA	G	SV	IP	H	BB	SO
Castro, Julio	2	0	1.46	34	22	37	9	9	59
Cunningham, Evan	1	1	8.37	12	0	24	39	8	25
DiBernardo, Mark	9	5	5.04	19	0	109	144	33	64
Guerra, Aaron	6	1	4.91	40	0	77	115	17	51
Haines, Tim	3	11	5.76	18	0	100	130	58	59
Montoya, Eric	9	6	5.18	18	0	99	137	37	66
Nelson, Robbie	1	2	9.95	13	0	19	27	22	11
PabloOyervidez, Jose	2	2	3.69	5	0	32	28	18	32
Reeves, Mike	4	4	7.01	11	0	53	74	38	42
Serrano, Ricardo	3	2	3.43	38	1	63	61	28	46
Silva, Raymond	2	2	2.12	30	0	30	25	17	25
Starling, Wardell	8	4	3.19	18	0	104	108	23	90

LAREDO BRONCOS

PLAYER	AVG	AB	R	H	2B	3B	HR	RBI	SB
Arroyo, Carlos	.308	224	52	69	14	1	11	40	10
Canseco, Jose	.385	39	14	15	3	0	4	13	0
Cisneros, Jonathan	.379	211	45	80	16	0	4	37	1
Diaz, Jason	.326	347	82	113	18	3	0	31	40
Dixon, D.J	.395	215	29	85	11	0	5	49	0
Flynn, Ryan	.278	270	35	75	15	1	0	40	7
Fowler, David	.244	119	21	29	5	0	3	10	7
Gilbert, Kenneth	.363	212	43	77	16	3	4	55	10
Goldsmith, Bradley	.279	43	3	12	2	2	0	4	2
Loyola, Maiko	.272	81	19	22	5	2	1	11	5
Mahin, Nick	.305	305	56	93	11	3	11	53	2
Memmert, Gabe	.228	79	11	18	2	0	1	8	0
Murphy, Michael	.303	132	21	40	6	0	1	16	1
Pacheco, Jonel	.350	117	32	41	8	1	6	26	3
Paniagua, Salvador	.301	209	46	63	6	0	14	48	0
Sanchez, Luany	.208	77	13	16	4	0	1	6	0
Spruill, Dustin	.278	54	8	15	3	0	3	12	0
Thennis, Doug	.283	219	45	62	8	3	10	39	5
Wolgamot, Ben	.240	104	25	25	5	0	0	7	4

PLAYER	W	L	ERA	G	SV	IP	H	BB	SO
Buchanan, Brian	6	5	7.76	29	0	63	97	44	53
Camareno, Dimitri	1	4	5.59	7	0	29	38	11	20
De La Cruz, Maximinio	1	3	3.42	31	4	50	55	19	44
DeChristofaro, Vinnie	0	4	6.59	19	3	14	12	6	13
Dorado, Reyes	2	0	2.87	14	8	16	14	2	21
Eden, Eric	1	2	5.80	17	0	59	72	44	40
Gibbs, Matt	7	4	4.19	18	0	73	67	22	51
Hernandez, Santo	8	3	5.01	18	0	111	98	53	124
Jamnik, Jeff	5	4	4.61	23	0	84	96	24	72
Lucas, Michael	2	3	5.26	12	1	26	31	9	20
Maxwell, James	1	0	7.36	26	0	29	36	18	14
Peralta, Juan	10	2	4.22	18	0	96	103	61	80

Roth, Robert	2	5	7.83	12	0	44	55	36	38
Vessella, Thomas	0	1	8.00	31	0	24	40	9	18

RIO GRANDE VALLEY WHITEWINGS

PLAYER	AVG	AB	R	H	2B	3B	HR	RBI	SB
Baez, Welinson	.310	174	36	54	9	0	11	37	2
Cabrera, Juan	.250	40	4	10	2	0	0	1	0
Di Ricco, Domenic	.269	160	28	43	7	0	0	22	4
Diaz, Javis	.342	371	72	127	25	6	7	45	36
Dietrich, Kevin	.275	69	7	19	2	0	0	4	1
Dotel, Welington	.357	171	32	61	10	5	2	23	14
Fulgencio, Jose	.136	66	3	9	0	0	0	1	2
Gonzalez, Eric	.315	286	41	90	14	0	4	52	3
Griffin, Kevin	.277	220	35	61	13	2	4	27	0
Paniagua, Salvador	.324	136	27	44	6	1	9	34	0
Quiroz, Arlon	.294	326	71	96	15	10	14	58	35
Roa, Joel	.225	178	24	40	14	0	7	25	0
Rodriguez, Roberto	.272	232	38	63	8	1	2	32	9
Sanchez, Jose	.278	54	10	15	1	0	3	11	0
Sanchez, Luany	.354	209	38	74	16	0	5	40	3
Tejeda, Yeurys	.324	287	61	93	19	2	16	56	13
Ventura, Leivi	.424	85	22	36	4	0	8	20	6

PLAYER	W	L	ERA	G	SV	IP	H	BB	SO
Ballestas, Freddy	4	0	1.21	13	0	30	25	10	38
Barbosa, Michael	1	1	4.36	16	5	21	26	7	20
Cassidy, Mickey	2	0	2.70	18	8	23	19	9	22
Conrad, Greg	0	1	7.33	6	0	20	32	9	9
Cross, David	7	5	4.14	18	0	122	132	45	77
De La Rosa, Ruben	2	1	5.83	15	3	29	37	18	30
DeJesus, Misael	9	5	4.01	18	0	101	79	58	122
Garcia, Anderson	2	2	5.02	15	4	14	18	6	11
Kelly, Tate	0	1	9.00	12	0	22	29	19	14
Martinez, Luis	0	0	5.59	9	1	19	24	10	17
Matos, Miguel	4	4	6.24	23	1	62	76	35	56
Montano, Luis	7	6	6.88	19	1	89	123	41	78
Montoya, Johnny	1	1	7.87	5	0	16	22	13	6
Moody, Jason	0	1	3.99	14	0	29	32	16	15
Raburn, Steve	4	2	2.97	8	0	36	38	15	36
Rosales, Andres	4	4	5.94	18	0	77	95	38	73
Whalen, Stephen	0	2	3.86	4	0	19	28	8	21

SAN ANGELO COLTS

PLAYER	AVG	AB	R	H	2B	3B	HR	RBI	SB
Ballez, Butch	.324	290	53	94	13	0	7	42	2
Camp, Landon	.355	262	59	93	22	0	24	68	0
Cardona, David	.253	158	16	40	7	0	3	12	0
Carter, Trey	.317	164	31	52	14	0	5	23	0
Collazzo, Joshua	.361	371	73	134	29	0	17	83	0
Crosland, Jason	.290	331	74	96	19	2	25	82	1
Fernandez, Alex	.342	79	12	27	9	0	1	13	0
Gaines, Ronnie	.330	394	85	130	34	3	10	71	21
Garcia, Isaac	.265	147	28	39	2	2	5	18	6
Goodro, Tyler	.242	120	15	29	5	0	1	15	0
Hale, Adam	.264	159	32	42	9	1	6	28	5
Horn, Mike	.219	32	1	7	0	0	0	3	0
Landreth, Jason	.355	172	52	61	19	0	13	55	2
Pettibone, Michael	.258	93	9	24	2	2	3	14	2
Ramos, Mark	.310	303	59	94	12	8	1	30	5
Wagle, John	.256	82	16	21	2	3	0	9	2

PLAYER	W	L	ERA	G	SV	IP	H	BB	SO
Astacio, Ezequiel	6	8	5.85	21	0	115	137	37	125
Barnard, Chandler	8	3	2.99	16	0	102	105	27	82
Bukvich, Brett	0	2	5.40	9	0	22	26	16	14
Chutchian, Matt	3	0	5.14	21	2	28	27	15	22
Cunningham, Aaron	4	5	5.71	11	0	58	73	19	35
Gaines, Tristan	1	3	6.30	28	0	40	53	30	24
Hacker, Michael	0	2	3.68	21	9	22	24	7	26
Heaston, Bryan	3	4	6.93	23	0	62	90	28	35
Henschel, Brian	6	8	6.17	18	0	127	184	28	49
Morales, Alex	0	1	7.65	8	0	20	27	15	19
Rodgers, Caleb	1	3	9.87	10	0	17	34	4	14
Romero, Gorman	7	0	3.43	25	1	58	64	16	48
Vacek, Chace	3	3	4.95	29	4	36	45	19	30
Williamson, Logan	4	2	3.69	12	0	46	53	31	33

INTERNATIONAL

Cuba, Dominican claim top-level tournaments

BY JOHN MANUEL

Parity came to international baseball in 2010.

Name a prominent international baseball power, and it probably had a success story in the calendar year. With no single tournament dominating the calendar—no Olympics, or World Baseball Classic or even World Cup to point to—several events had strong fields, leading to upsets and some surprise winners.

USA Baseball fielded teams in six different events: the women's World Cup; a professional team of minor leaguers at the Pan Am Qualifier; a college national team in the FISU World University Championships; and teams at the 18U, 16U and 14U levels.

The Americans wound up with a championship at the 16U level, beating host Mexico 11-4 in the COPABE Pan Am Youth Championships. But the U.S. didn't win any other tournaments during the year, despite fielding strong teams and performing well.

Cuba won two tournaments—the FISU World University Games and the Intercontinental Cup. However, Cuba was denied a trio of gold medals when the Dominican Republic beat the Cubans 5-2 to win the gold medal at the Pan Am Qualifier, a tournament in Puerto Rico that earned nations spots in the 2011 Pan American Games and World Cup.

On the amateur level, Taiwan won the 18U World Championships, held in Thunder Bay, Ontario, Canada, while Venezuela won the 14U tournament on its home turf, beating Mexico.

The light international schedule pointed out a transition period for the International Baseball Federation, which was under the direction of first-year president Riccardo Fraccari. The Federation announced this would be the last Intercontinental Cup, and Fraccari put its entire schedule up for review. Major League Baseball proposed replacing the World Cup—IBAF's current top tournament, held every two years—with the World Baseball Classic and a series of qualifying tournaments for the WBC. However, IBAF made no move on the future schedule yet and still plans a 2011 World Cup, with Panama a possible host.

"We have done a lot of work together with president Riccardo Fraccari," MLB representative

Mike Trout paced USA Baseball's pro team with three home runs in Puerto Rico

James Pearce told reporters in Taiwan during the Intercontinental Cup. "And I am confident we will soon have an agreement."

American Exploits

USA Baseball's top club was its professional team it sent to Puerto Rico for the Pan Am Qualifier. Team USA tabbed Ernie Young—a hero on the 2000 gold-medal Olympic team and a manager in the White Sox organization the previous two seasons—to manage a team of non-40-man roster players.

The result was a young, talented team that blitzed opponents in the first two rounds, only to be upset by the Dominican Republic 7-2 in the one-and-done medal round.

Dodgers lefthander Mario Alvarez. 26, got the best of Team USA on the mound. Alvarez went 6-6, 4.94 at Double-A Chattanooga during the regular season and has arm strength, with reports that his fastball can reach 94 mph, but scouts generally pan his secondary stuff. He was on in Puerto Rico, though, and gave up just five hits and one run in five innings to get the victory. Ex-big leaguers Juan

Perez (Dodgers) and 37-year-old Dario Veras, who still is active in the Mexican League, closed out the U.S. and gave up just one hit and one run in the last four innings.

Team USA was limited to six hits and racked up 13 strikeouts, while big league veterans such as ex-all-star Tony Batista (two-run single) and Willis Otanez (two-run homer) powered the offense.

Team USA had dominated pool play, winning nine straight games to qualify for both future tournaments. The highlight was a 4-1 victory against Cuba, spearheaded by righthander Chris Archer (Cubs). The 2007 fifth-round pick went six scoreless, two-hit inning and struck out 10.

"I don't know how hard I was throwing my fastball, but I was nicking it, and I had the fastball, slider and change all working," Archer said. "Early counts, I was throwing my slider for strikes, and when I got ahead, I was burying it, and because they had to respect the fastball, I got them to chase."

With a mix of veterans and young talent, this was an excellent USA Baseball professional roster, one that featured six Royals farmhands. Prospects Eric Hosmer (.389), Mike Moustakas (team-best eight RBIs) and lefty Mike Montgomery (2-0, 1.80, 14 SO/10 IP) all shined and should establish themselves in the majors by 2012 at the latest. And 19-year-old Mike Trout (Angels) continued his amazing season, batting .350 with a team-best three homers out of the U.S. leadoff spot.

"His transformation from the time we reported to Cary (to USA Baseball headquarters) to the time we got to San Juan was remarkable," Young said. "In Cary, he seemed tight, like he was trying to do too much. When we came to San Juan, he just matured at such a fast pace. He was unbelievable; he definitely played older than 19. Mentally, he was prepared to play every day."

A rainout in the bronze-medal matchup with Venezuela left the U.S. tied for third. Cuba and the Dominican played for gold, though, with Cuba using ageless veteran Norge Vera. The Dominicans chased him with a five-run first and held on for a 5-2 win behind former White Sox righthander Lorenzo Barcelo, who pitched five innings for the victory. Former Tigers outfielder Alexis Gomez had a three-run triple to provide the big offensive blow for the Dominicans.

Cuba beat the U.S. earlier in the summer in the FISU Games in Tokyo when Alfredo Despaigne—currently the single-season record holder in Cuba for home runs—hit a game-winning homer in extra innings off Nick Ramirez (Cal State Fullerton). Despaigne hit two homers and drove in all four Cuba runs in the game. The

24-year-old isn't technically a college student, but the tournament is open to players 27-and-under. The U.S. had won the last FISU gold medals since losing to Cuba in Italy in 2002.

Cuba also claimed the Intercontinental Cup, beating the Netherlands 4-1 in the championship game behind starter Miguel Gonzalez, who tossed a two-hitter to best veteran Dutch ace Rob Cordemans. Alexei Bell hit a two-run homer in the eighth inning to put away the victory. Italy had its best finish in an international tournament by beating host Taiwan to win the bronze medal, with Cubs farmhand Alessandro Maestri recording the save.

High Schoolers Perform

USA Baseball's 16U National Team ran its winning streak to 40 games over the last five years by winning the gold medal in the COPABE Youth Championships, beating Mexico 11-4 in the final.

"I was really proud of everyone involved with the program this year, from the staff down to all of the players who participated in our trials," said Jeff Singer, director of the 16U program. "It was a particularly challenging year in regards to how late in the calendar the event fell and the fact that two weeks before trials started we didn't officially know

Team USA's Philip Pfeifer tags out Cuba's Lazaro Hernandez at home plate in the quarterfinal

if we'd be able to compete due to safety concerns in Mexico. In the end everyone put all of that aside, we came together as an incredibly close team and we kept our focus day after day and proved that we were the best team in the tournament. We really hit the ball incredibly well."

Infielders Alex Bregman and Corey Seager led the squad on offense. Bregman, a junior at Albuquerque Academy, hit .564/.596/.846 in 39 at-bats with two home runs, 17 runs and 17 RBIs. He also stole five bases. Seager hit .514/.622/.829 in 35 at-bats with 16 runs scored and 12 RBIs. He proved to be the team's most patient hitter, drawing 10 walks in nine games. While Bregman and Seager did plenty of damage on their own, Team USA destroyed opposing pitching as a whole. In nine games the squad hit .437/.500/.749 with 15 home runs and outscored opponents 127-23.

Four pitchers sported a 0.00 ERA, but the two with the most innings were righthanders Carson Kelly and Felipe Perez. Kelly hurled 13 innings, going 2-0, 3.46 with nine strikeouts and one walk. Perez hurled one-third of an inning more and went 2-0, 3.38, allowing just nine hits and three walks while striking out 15.

The 18U National Team finished fifth at the COPABE Pan Am 'AAA' 18U Youth Championships in Thunder Bay, Ont. this summer. At a glance, fifth place seems uncharacteristic and unacceptable for a U.S. team, but in the first game of the medal round, Team USA was matched up with Cuba—a contest typically more fit for a championship final. Even so, Team USA was disappointed in the finish and questioned its own process and selections this year.

"I think it's natural to do that," said Rick Riccobono, the former 18U director, after the tournament. "I wholeheartedly believe we were the best team in Thunder Bay. The reality is we were playing in a championship tournament and we didn't win the tournament. And there's no excuses for that."

After being eliminated from winning a medal, Team USA bounced back in its next two games to beat Korea and the Netherlands to capture fifth place.

"I credit the kids for bouncing back," Riccobono said. "There's a lot of pride in the way we finished."

Outfielder Michael Lorenzen, a 2010 seventh-rounder who is now at Cal State Fullerton, led the team in the tournament in hitting with a .565/.630/.870 line in 23 at-bats. Righthander A.J. Vanegas, also a seventh round-pick and now at Stanford, hurled 14 innings, striking out 21. He was 1-0, 1.93.

The 18U gold medal game was an intriguing one with Taiwan beating upstart Australia 8-4.

"What helped us get to the gold game was our overall execution whether it had been offensive or defensive, including some outstanding individual pitching efforts together with some timely offense and perfect defense," Australia head coach Tony Harris said. "One thing we as a country realize is, to be a contender and compete with the best in the world we have to be defensively perfect and not allow more than three outs per inning. We were able to achieve that in those lead up games."

USA Baseball's 14U team had been rolling through the COPABE Pan Am 'A' 14U Championships before running into Venezuela in the semifinals. Team USA lost 11-1, but bounced back to win the bronze medal by defeating Brazil 6-0.

Contributing: Aaron Fitt, Nathan Rode

INTERNATIONAL BASEBALL

Sarape Makers rally to repeat championship

BY BRUCE BASKIN

The Saltillo Saraperos were on the brink of playoff elimination in the first round before mounting a furious comeback and winning 11 of their next 14 games to cop their second consecutive Mexican League pennant in 2010.

The Sarape Makers trailed Mexico City three games to one before reeling off three straight victories (including two on the road) to win that series. Saltillo then dispatched Monterrey in six games and Puebla in five to complete the repeat, ending the season with a resounding 21-2 win against the Parrots on Aug. 16. Refugio "Cuco" Cervantes clubbed two homers to support a solid complete-game effort from former major league pitcher José Mercedes. Mercedes registered 90 strikes out of 120 pitches while walking no Puebla batters.

Pitcher Danny Rodriguez was named playoff MVP after going 5-0, 0.66 for Saltillo, which was also fueled by Cervantes' nine postseason homers in just 18 contests for manager Orlando Sanchez' club.

Puebla reached the finals despite losing batting champion Willis Otañez for their first two series due to a foot injury. Sub Valentin Gámez picked up the slack by batting .365 in Otañez's place while pitcher Andrés Meza posted a 4-0 postseason record.

Saltillo barely qualified for the playoffs after a tepid second half landed the team in a three-way tie with Chihuahua and Reynosa for the final two playoff berths in the northern Madera Zone point chase. All three teams ended with 12 points apiece—points in the Mexican League are based on a team's finish in the standings for each half of the regular season—but Reynosa was eliminated because its 56-51 overall record was the worst of the three teams.

In the first half, Monterrey's 32-21 record held off Saltillo (30-23) and both Mexico City and Reynosa (29-24) for first place and the eight accompanying points. Monterrey and Saltillo each had indifferent second halves as Mexico City (35-16) beat out surprising Monclova (33-19) for first. Mexico City dominated the league offensively, winning the triple crown of team batting by hitting .322 with 110 homers and 617 RBIs.

OVERALL STANDINGS

MADERA ZONE (NORTH)

	W	L	PCT	GB
†Mexico	64	40	.615	—
Chihuahua	59	48	.551	6½
*Monterrey	58	48	.547	7
Saltillo	55	49	.529	9
Reynosa	56	51	.523	9½
Monclova	53	52	.505	11½
Laguna	45	62	.421	20½
Nuevo Laredo	32	72	.308	32

HIDALGO ZONE (SOUTH)

	W	L	PCT	GB
*Puebla	66	39	.629	—
Oaxaca	60	45	.571	6
Quintana Roo	56	47	.544	9
Yucatan	54	50	.519	11½
†Campeche	52	50	.510	12½
Tabasco	46	60	.434	20½
Minatitlan	44	60	.423	21½
Veracruz	39	66	.371	27

*First-half division winner. †Second-half division winner.

Division Series: Monterrey defeated Chihuahua 4-1, Saltillo defeated Mexico 4-3, Puebla defeated Yucatan 4-2 and Oaxaca defeated Quintana Roo 4-3 in best-of-seven series. **Semifinals:** Saltillo defeated Monterrey 4-2 and Puebla defeated Oaxaca 4-2 in best-of-seven series. Finals: Saltillo defeated Puebla 4-1 in best-of-seven series.

ATTENDANCE—Monterrey, 356755; Monclova, 265222; Mexico, 246568; Saltillo, 237435; Laguna, 211825; Reynosa, 187614; Puebla, 170252; Yucatan, 170226; Oaxaca, 166393; Chihuahua, 143658; Quintana Roo, 123086; Tabasco, 105379; Veracruz, 98780; Campeche, 91636; Minatitlan, 74529; Nuevo Laredo, 65597.

INDIVIDUAL BATTING LEADERS

PLAYER, TEAM	AVG	AB	R	H	2B	3B	HR	RBI	BB	SO	2B
Otanez, Willis, Puebla	.393	338	71	133	26	1	12	76	49	37	0
Madera, S., Sal./Yuc.	.383	381	86	146	30	5	18	70	33	43	10
Rivera, Carlos, Min.	.373	367	59	137	17	0	16	82	55	37	1
Terrazas, Ivan, Mex.	.368	323	61	119	22	2	11	68	20	39	14
Amador, Japhet, Mex.	.366	273	50	100	26	0	14	63	36	45	2
Cabrera, Jolbert, Oax.	.364	330	63	120	23	4	10	63	40	55	9
Suarez, Luis, Puebla	.361	338	71	122	23	1	8	63	39	36	2
Rivera, Ruben, Cam.	.360	344	80	124	17	3	21	73	57	48	16
Arredondo, E., Mex.	.356	278	58	99	14	5	2	29	26	15	15
Jimenez, D. Yuc.	.355	273	61	97	22	1	9	60	63	42	4

INDIVIDUAL PITCHING LEADERS

PLAYER, TEAM	W	L	ERA	G	GS	IP	H	R	ER	BB	SO
Suzuki, Mac, Chi.	9	4	2.89	20	20	131	119	54	42	74	88
Velazquez, Hector, Cam.	6	4	2.93	29	14	92	84	33	30	39	50
Cramer, Bobby, QR	13	3	2.95	22	20	128	116	47	42	27	123
Tovar, Marco, Rey.	8	4	3.25	24	16	94	98	37	34	46	56
Martinez, J., Yuc./Mex.	11	3	3.32	19	18	101	112	43	37	41	64
Garcia, Rosman, NL	6	8	3.33	18	16	100	100	41	37	30	59
Armenta, Alejandro, Cam.	6	8	3.33	17	17	108	93	45	40	55	74
Cordoba, Francisco, QR	7	5	3.34	20	19	116	115	46	43	36	57
Garrido, Alejandro, Sal.	5	3	3.39	23	19	99	107	43	37	32	79
Barcelo, Lorenzo, Pueb.	11	5	3.66	21	21	136	156	62	55	30	76

Murton record highlights NPB year

BY WAYNE GRACZYK

The Pacific League Chiba Lotte Marines, after finishing in third place during the regular season, won the 2010 Japan Series to emerge as champions of Japan professional baseball. The Marines defeated the Central League pennant-winning Chunichi Dragons four games to two in the best-of-seven series that almost went to an eighth game.

Chiba Lotte, managed by Norifumi Nishimura, clinched the Japan Series title with a thrilling 12-inning, 8-7 victory over the Dragons, managed by Hiromitsu Ochiai, in Game Seven at Nagoya Dome. In Game Six, the teams played to a 2-2 tie in 15 innings, the limit for Japan Series games. Had Chunichi won in Game Seven—or had that contest also ended in a deadlock—an eighth game would have been played.

The Marines qualified for the Japan Series after barely finishing third in the six-team Pacific League during the regular season. The top three teams in each league qualify for the postseason Climax Series of playoffs, and Lotte beat the regular season second place Saitama Seibu Lions and the first place Fukuoka SoftBank Hawks for the right to meet Chunichi.

The Dragons were the Central League regular-season winner and clinched a Japan Series berth after beating the Yomiuri Giants in the C.L. Climax Series finals. The Giants had finished third during the regular year and beat the second place Hanshin Tigers in the CLCS first stage.

A total of 71 foreigners played in Japanese pro baseball in 2010, including players from the United States, Canada, Australia, Korea, Taiwan, Puerto Rico, Venezuela, Panama and the Dominican Republic.

The top performers among the foreign hitters were Hanshin Tigers outfielder Matt Murton and first baseman Craig Brazell, Yomiuri Giants cleanup hitter Alex Ramirez and Orix Buffaloes first baseman Alex Cabrera.

Murton, playing his first year in Japan, made headlines Oct. 5 when he broke the Japanese baseball record for most hits in a season. He surpassed the mark of 210 set by Ichiro Suzuki of the Orix BlueWave in 1994. Murton ended the year with 214 hits, averaged .349 and was third in the Central League in batting.

Brazell slammed 47 home runs and drove in 117 while batting .296. He was runner-up in the power categories to Ramirez, who won titles with 49 homers and 129 RBIs, both career highs, while hitting .304. Cabrera batted .331, the fourth highest average in the Pacific League.

Chiba Lotte shortstop Tsuyoshi Nishioka was the Pacific League batting leader with a .346 average. He was posted in November by the Marines; the winning bid had not been determined as the Almanac went to press. Rakuten Eagles righthander Hisashi Iwakuma (10-9, 2.82 in 2010) also was posted for major league service, and his rights were won by the Oakland Athletics, who had an exclusive window to try to sign him to a major league contract.

The Fighters' touted Japanese-Iranian right-hander Yu Darvish (12-8) posted the best ERA in the P.L. at 1.78 and led with 222 strikeouts. Southpaw Tsuyoshi Wada of SoftBank and righty Chihiro Kaneko tied for the most wins with 17 apiece, while ex-big leaguer Brian Sikorski led the way with 33 saves for Seibu. Fellow American Brian Falkenborg shined for Fukuoka with 39 holds and a 1.02 ERA.

There were two all-star games played in Japanese baseball in 2010, with the Central League winning at Fukuoka Dome, and a game ending in a tie at Hard-Off Eco Stadium in Niigata. The Pacific League continues to lead the all-star series 75-70 with nine ties in games played since 1950.

The so-called era of American managers in Japan came to an end following the 2010 season when skipper Marty Brown was fired by the Tohoku Rakuten Golden Eagles. In 2007, there were four U.S. field bosses with Brown leading the Hiroshima Carp, Bobby Valentine at the helm of the Chiba Lotte Marines, Trey Hillman directing the Nippon Ham club and Terry Collins guiding the Orix team. All are now gone from Japan.

CENTRAL LEAGUE

	W	L	T	PCT.	GB
Chunichi Dragons	79	62	3	.560	—
Hanshin Tigers	78	63	3	.553	1
Yomiuri Giants	79	64	1	.552	1
Tokyo Yakult Swallows	72	68	4	.514	6½
Hiroshima Carp	58	84	2	.408	21½
Yokohama BayStars	48	95	1	.336	32

CLIMAX SERIES PLAYOFFS—Stage One: Yomiuri defeated Hanshin 2-0 in best-of-three series. **Stage Two:** Chunichi defeated Yomiuri 4-1 in best-of-seven series.

INDIVIDUAL BATTING LEADERS
(Minimum 446 Plate Appearances)

	AVG	AB	R	H	2B	3B	HR	RBI	SB
Aoki, Norichika, Swallows	.358	583	92	209	44	1	14	63	19
Hirano, Keiichi, Tigers	.350	492	77	172	22	5	1	24	6

	AVG	AB	R	H	2B	3B	HR	RBI	SB
Murton, Matt, Tigers	.349	613	105	214	35	3	17	91	11
Wada, Kazuhiro, Dragons	.339	505	94	171	29	2	37	93	5
Morino, Masahiko, Dragons	.327	547	85	179	45	2	22	84	2
Uchikawa, Seiichi, BayStars	.315	577	75	182	36	4	9	66	1
Arai, Takahiro, Tigers	.311	570	96	177	42	0	19	112	7
Hirose, Jun, Carp	.309	482	65	149	32	3	12	57	3
Ogasawara, Michihiro, Giants	.308	510	83	157	24	1	34	90	1
Soyogi, Eishin, Carp	.306	562	82	172	34	3	13	56	43
Ramirez, Alex, Giants	.304	566	93	172	28	0	49	129	1
Johjima, Kenji, Tigers	.303	554	76	168	29	0	28	91	9
Toritani, Takashi, Tigers	.301	575	98	173	31	6	19	104	13
Tanaka, Hiroyasu, Swallows	.300	516	64	155	16	2	4	54	4
Brazell, Craig, Tigers	.296	564	82	167	15	0	47	117	1
Kurihara, Kenta, Carp	.295	386	62	114	22	0	15	65	3
Ishikawa, Takehiro, BayStars	.294	521	69	153	23	6	0	18	36
Araki, Masahiro, Dragons	.294	579	65	170	29	5	3	39	20
Aikawa, Ryoji, Swallows	.293	427	44	125	17	2	11	65	2
Chono, Hisayoshi, Giants	.288	430	66	124	24	3	19	52	12
Shimozono, Tatsuya, BayStars	.286	402	41	115	21	3	3	28	1

REMAINING NORTH AMERICAN, AUSTRALIAN AND LATIN PLAYERS

	AVG	AB	R	H	2B	3B	HR	RBI	SB
Harper, Brett, BayStars	.316	225	27	71	6	0	19	56	0
Whitesell, Josh, Swallows	.309	230	44	71	16	2	15	53	0
Gonzalez, Edgar, Giants	.263	289	26	76	18	1	12	44	2
Fiorentino, Jeff, Carp	.246	126	13	31	4	0	2	15	2
D'Antona, Jamie, Swallows	.245	294	33	72	17	0	15	50	0
Huber, Justin, Carp	.220	177	20	29	7	0	7	17	0
Cesar, Dionys, Dragons	.215	186	16	40	7	0	1	10	2
Guiel, Aaron, Swallows	.199	251	33	50	7	0	16	41	0

INDIVIDUAL PITCHING LEADERS
(Minimum 144 Innings)

	W	L	ERA	G	SV	IP	H	BB	SO
Maeda, Kenta, Carp	15	8	2.21	28	0	216	166	46	174
Chen, Wei Yin, Dragons	13	10	2.87	29	0	188	166	49	153
Tateyama, Shohei, Swallows	12	7	2.93	21	0	148	147	24	112
Kubo, Yasutomo, Tigers	14	5	3.25	29	0	202	183	45	158
Tono, Shun, Giants	13	8	3.27	27	0	157	152	55	140
Muranaka, Kyohei, Swallows	11	10	3.44	20	0	178	176	69	163
Yoshimi, Kazuki, Dragons	12	9	3.50	25	0	157	159	25	115
Ishikawa, Masanori, Swallows	13	8	3.53	28	0	186	209	27	98
Sato, Yoshinori, Swallows	12	9	3.60	25	0	168	158	74	149
Kaga, Shigeru, BayStars	3	12	3.66	27	0	145	165	28	83

REMAINING U.S. AND LATIN PLAYERS

	W	L	ERA	G	SV	IP	H	BB	SO
Romero, Levi, Giants	1	0	0.00	6	0	8	7	0	9
Nelson, Maximo, Dragons	4	3	3.16	15	0	68	65	37	38
Schultz, Mike, Carp	0	1	3.48	11	7	10	10	2	8
Standridge, Jason, Tigers	11	5	3.49	23	0	126	121	37	98
Alvarado, Giancarlo, Carp	8	8	4.07	20	0	119	110	37	97
Randolph, Stephen, BayStars	2	9	4.25	16	0	91	77	52	83
Kroon, Marc, Giants	4	3	4.26	52	25	51	35	29	73
Soriano, Dioni, Carp	2	3	4.30	10	0	46	45	18	27
Bootcheck, Chris, BayStars	1	0	4.62	15	0	25	38	7	25
Valdez, Edward, Dragons	1	3	4.91	8	0	33	36	14	13
Messenger, Randy, Tigers	5	6	4.93	26	0	80	88	31	48
Stults, Eric, Carp	6	10	5.07	21	0	124	149	46	87
Obispo, Wirfin, Giants	2	3	5.21	14	0	48	60	18	22
Gonzalez, Dicky, Giants	5	13	5.29	25	0	133	161	32	88
Greisinger, Seth, Giants	0	2	5.48	6	0	21	31	1	16
Fossum, Casey, Tigers	2	5	5.72	12	0	57	65	24	48
Chulk, Vinnie, Carp	2	0	5.79	16	1	19	24	7	12
Barnette, Tony, Swallows	4	5	5.99	16	0	80	99	41	70
Bale, John, Carp	0	3	7.09	30	1	27	29	15	21
De La Cruz, Eulo, Swallows	0	0	7.84	9	0	10	14	1	4

PACIFIC LEAGUE

	W	L	T	PCT.	GB
Fukuoka SoftBank Hawks	76	63	5	.547	—
Saitama Seibu Lions	78	65	1	.545	—
Chiba Lotte Marines	75	67	2	.528	2½
Hokkaido Nippon Ham Fighters	74	67	6	.525	3
Orix Buffaloes	69	71	4	.493	7½
Tohoku Rakuten Golden Eagles	62	79	3	.440	15

CLIMAX SERIES PLAYOFFS—State One: Lotte defeated Seibu 2-0 in best-of-three series. **Stage Two:** Lotte defeated SoftBank 4-3 in best-of-seven series.

INDIVIDUAL BATTING LEADERS
(Minimum 446 Plate Appearances)

	AVG	AB	R	H	2B	3B	HR	RBI	SB
Nishioka, Tsuyoshi, Marines	.346	596	121	206	32	8	11	59	22
Tanaka, Kensuke, Fighters	.335	576	88	193	24	4	5	54	34
Imae, Toshiaki, Marines	.331	531	74	176	37	1	10	77	8
Cabrera, Alex, Buffaloes	.331	408	66	135	21	2	24	82	1
Tamura, Hitoshi, Hawks	.324	513	74	166	33	1	27	89	2
Tsuchiya, Teppei, Eagles	.318	481	86	153	29	7	9	64	13
Kawasaki, Munenori, Hawks	.316	602	74	190	27	5	4	53	30
Shima, Motohiro, Eagles	.315	422	33	133	17	0	3	43	9
Nakajima, Hiroyuki, Lions	.314	503	80	158	33	3	20	93	15
Koyano, Eiichi, Fighters	.311	569	73	177	41	0	16	109	8
Kuriyama, Takumi, Lions	.310	554	77	172	35	2	4	74	14
Itoi, Yoshio, Fighters	.309	488	86	151	33	3	15	64	26
Sakaguchi, Tomotaka, Buffaloes	.308	558	84	172	31	10	5	50	12
Honda, Yuichi, Hawks	.296	564	88	167	21	10	3	39	59
Kataoka, Yasuyuki, Lions	.295	576	100	170	31	5	13	54	59
Goto, Mitsutaka, Buffaloes	.295	590	82	174	32	3	16	73	2
Iguchi, Tadahito, Marines	.294	531	88	156	44	1	17	103	2
Hijirisawa, Ryo, Eagles	.290	517	72	150	25	4	6	43	24
Inaba, Atsunori, Fighters	.287	530	68	152	36	4	16	79	3
Okada, Takahiro, Buffaloes	.284	461	70	131	31	2	33	96	0
Kokubo, Hiroki, Hawks	.279	427	60	119	22	0	15	68	1

REMAINING U.S. AND LATIN PLAYERS

	AVG	AB	R	H	2B	3B	HR	RBI	SB
Fernandez, Jose, Lions	.339	221	28	75	11	0	11	45	1
Baldiris, Aarom, Buffaloes	.301	385	44	116	20	0	14	50	1
Ruiz, Randy, Eagles	.266	282	35	75	16	0	12	38	0
Petagine, Roberto, Hawks	.261	264	34	69	12	0	10	41	0
Caraballo, Francisco, Buffaloes	.257	113	12	29	4	0	7	18	0
LaRocca, Greg, Buffaloes	.256	133	16	34	8	0	7	21	0
Phillips, Andy, Eagles	.198	81	11	16	2	0	2	12	0
Seguignol, Fernando, Buffaloes	.189	37	1	7	3	0	0	3	0
Linden, Todd, Eagles	.185	162	18	30	5	0	5	18	1
Bynum, Freddie, Buffaloes	.138	29	5	4	2	0	0	1	0
Muniz, Juan, Marines	.136	22	1	3	1	0	0	1	1

INDIVIDUAL PITCHING LEADERS
(Minimum 144 Innings)

	W	L	ERA	G	SV	IP	H	BB	SO
Darvish, Yu, Fighters	12	8	1.78	26	0	202	158	47	222
Takeda, Masaru, Fighters	14	7	2.41	26	0	168	161	19	106
Tanaka, Masahiro, Eagles	11	6	2.50	20	0	155	159	32	119
Iwakuma, Hisashi, Eagles	10	9	2.82	28	0	201	184	36	153
Wada, Tsuyoshi, Hawks	17	8	3.14	26	0	169	145	55	169
Kaneko, Chihiro, Buffaloes	17	8	3.30	30	0	184	184	60	190
Naruse, Yoshihisa, Marines	13	11	3.31	28	0	204	173	34	192
Keppel, Bobby, Fighters	12	8	3.35	25	0	159	156	53	85
Sugiuchi, Toshiya, Hawks	16	7	3.55	27	0	183	169	60	218
Wakui, Hideaki, Lions	14	8	3.67	27	0	196	191	54	154
Hoashi, Kazuyuki, Lions	11	8	3.69	27	0	163	173	35	104
Nagai, Satoshi, Eagles	10	10	3.74	27	0	183	173	69	125
Murphy, Bill, Marines	12	6	3.75	38	0	144	127	84	125
Kisanuki, Hiroshi, Buffaloes	10	12	3.98	28	0	174	174	71	140
Rasner, Darrell, Eagles	5	11	4.48	26	0	153	154	58	118
Watanabe, Shunsuke, Marines	8	8	4.49	26	0	148	171	45	63

REMAINING U.S. AND LATIN PLAYERS

	W	L	ERA	G	SV	IP	H	BB	SO
Falkenborg, Brian, Hawks	3	2	1.02	60	1	62	39	8	83
Sikorski, Brian, Lions	2	5	2.57	58	33	63	50	19	48
Morillo, Juan, Eagles	0	0	2.70	7	0	7	3	5	9
Wolfe, Brian, Fighters	4	3	3.03	42	3	62	66	13	24
Penn, Hayden, Marines	1	3	3.69	8	0	46	45	16	27
Leicester, Jon, Buffaloes	2	2	4.78	35	10	38	45	16	33
Corey, Bryan, Marines	4	4	4.87	14	0	44	48	17	30
Carlyle, Buddy, Fighters	0	3	4.88	7	0	28	35	11	14
Houlton, D.J., Hawks	8	6	5.70	16	0	79	97	25	69
Durbin, J.D., Hawks	0	2	6.75	3	0	16	16	10	11
Graman, Alex, Lions	0	0	17.36	7	0	5	15	4	2

Wyverns sweep past Samsung

The SK Wyverns dominated the Korean Baseball Organization in the regular season, then swept past the Samsung Lions to win the league championship series. The Wyverns then went on to split two games with Brother Elephants, Taiwan's CPBL champion, in a two-game set and also played a series in mid-November against Japan's champion.

The Inchon-based team won the fourth and final game 4-2 and won its third title in the last four seasons. Park Jung-kwon was named the series MVP thanks to hitting .294 with a homer and six RBIs, including a three-run double in the clinching fourth game. Lefthander Kim Kwang-hyun won 17 games to lead the league, with ex-big leaguer Gary Glover contributing in the Wyverns' rotation.

Lotte corner infielder Lee Dae-ho, playing for manager Jerry Royster, was named league MVP after winning the triple crown, batting .364/.444/.667 with 44 home runs and 133 RBIs. Royster was let go after three seasons, even though the team made the playoffs all three years.

Four teams made the playoffs, but the Wyverns didn't play games that ounted until two weeks of five-game series involving three other teams wrapped up. Doosan beat Lotte in a five-game first-round series, then Samsung beat Doosan in five games for the right to face the Wyverns

STANDINGS

	W	L	PCT	GB
SK Wyverns	84	47	.632	—
Samsung Lions	79	52	.594	5
Doosan Bears	73	57	.549	10½
Lotte Giants	69	61	.519	14½
KIA Tigers	59	74	.444	26
LG Twins	57	71	.429	26½
Nexen Heroes	52	78	.391	31½
Hanwha Eagles	49	82	.368	35

INDIVIDUAL BATTING LEADERS

PLAYER, TEAM	AVG	AB	R	R	2B	3B	HR	RBI
Lee Dae-Ho, Lotte	.364	479	99	174	13	0	44	133
Hong Sung-hoon, Lotte	.350	431	88	151	28	1	26	116
Cho Seong-hwan, Lotte	.336	414	83	139	31	0	8	52
Lee Jin-young, LG	.331	378	56	125	28	0	7	50
Cho Jun-suk, Doosan	.321	424	63	136	26	1	22	82

INDIVIDUAL PITCHING LEADERS

Player, Team	W	L	ERA	G	IP	H	SO
Ryu Jin-hyeon, Hanwha	16	4	1.82	25	193	149	187
Kim Kwayng-hyun, SK	17	7	2.37	31	194	153	183
Ken Kadokura, SK	14	7	3.22	30	154	146	143
Kelvin Jimenez, Doosan	14	5	3.32	27	152	139	87
Seo Jae-Weong	9	7	3.34	24	140	134	68

Elephants choose wisely

Heading into the Chinese Professional Baseball League playoffs, Brother Elephants rookie manager Chen Rei-Chen faced an unpalatable decision.

His rotation of Jim Magrane, Carlos Castillo and Orlando Roman was considered one of the league's best. And his closer Ryan Cullen had set the league record with 34 saves.

But league rules only allow three foreign players on the playoff roster. So Rei-Chen faced a choice-- he could have his rotation built the way he wanted or he could feel confident that any late-inning lead was safe. But he couldn't have both.

He chose wisely. Rei-Chen left Cullen off the playoff roster. He ended up not really needing him as the three starters won their four starts to sweep the Sinon Bulls. Magrane pitched a complete game in the deciding fourth game to pick up second win. He was named the MVP of the series.

Elephants first baseman Peng Cheng-Min was named the league's regular season MVP as he won his fifth batting title and a gold glove. Teammate Castillo led the league in wins (14) and ERA (2.17) while Roman led the league with 142 strikeouts. Rei-Chen was named the manager of the year.

The Elephants didn't sweep the awards, as Uni-President pitcher Wang Jing-Ming was named the league's rookie of the year. La New Bears' Lin Chih-Sheng was named the league's silver slugger after leading the league in home runs (21) and RBIs (79).

STANDINGS

TEAM	W	L	PCT	GB
Sinon	65	53	.551	—
Elephants	61	57	.517	4
La New	55	62	.470	9½
Unity	54	63	.462	10½

INDIVIDUAL BATTING LEADERS

PLAYER, TEAM	AVG	AB	R	H	2B	3B	HR	RBI	SB
Peng Cheng Min, Eleph	.357	387	59	138	22	1	8	72	20
Lin Yi-Chuan, Unity	.330	406	61	134	22	2	8	30	4
Chang Tai-Shan, Sinon	.313	453	73	142	23	0	16	47	7
Lin Zhi-sheng, La New	.312	443	71	138	23	2	21	51	12
Lin Wang Yu, La New	.303	380	40	115	22	2	8	22	1

INDIVIDUAL PITCHING LEADERS

Player, Team	W	L	ERA	G	SV	CG	IP
Carlos Castillo, Eleph.	14	5	2.17	19	2	2	166
Jim Magrane, Eleph.	11	9	2.25	28	0	4	192
Ken Ray, La New	7	8	2.32	25	0	1	163
Yang Chien-Fu, Unity	11	5	2.33	30	0	1	143
Chris Mason, La New	10	7	2.63	24	0	2	154

Parma, Bologna earn victories

Parma defeated Bologna in the Italy Series to win their 10th league title. The champs lost the first two games of the series at home, then won two straight in Bologna. The host club then prevailed in each of the last three games, giving Parma their first title since 1997.

Longtime Expos/Nationals farmhand Marco Yepez batted .464 for Parma and was voted Italy Series MVP. The 28-year old shortstop knocked in both runs in Parma's 2-1 Game Seven victory. Yepez was even better in the Italian Baseball League's round robin semifinal series, hitting .500 in nine games. In 16 postseason contests, he amassed eight doubles and 18 RBIs.

Righthander Marco Grifantini was a workhorse out of the Parma bullpen in the playoffs, making eight appearances and logging more than 30 innings. The UC Davis alumnus was 4-1, 0.89, in the postseason and had a save in Game Seven of the Italy Series, tossing four shutout innings.

Former big leaguer Jim Brower threw a no-hitter for Rimini at Grosseto on Opening Day. Brower faced one batter over the minimum, striking out ten batters and walking two. Rimini won the game 5-0. In his second outing, Brower took a no-hitter into the eighth inning in a 2-0 victory over Godo.

San Marino outfielder Carlos Duran won the first Italian triple crown since 1981. A native of Venezuela and former Atlanta and Baltimore farmhand, Duran batted .349, knocked in 39 runs and tied for the league lead with six homers.

Nettuno loaded up on major league alumni but lost seven in a row during the first month of the season. They rebounded and won 19 of their last 28 games, but it wasn't enough to qualify for the playoffs. Newcomer Kris Wilson, who pitched for the Royals and the Yankees, joined returnees Manny Alexander and Jeff Farnsworth. Alexander, 39, led the IBL in stolen bases with 22.

Bologna won the European Cup for the first time since 1985. At the Final Four in suburban Barcelona, it defeated San Marino 3-2 in their semifinal. In the final, Bologna beat Heidenheim of Germany's Bundesliga 2-1 in 10 innings. After the ninth frame, each half-inning automatically began with runners on first and second. It was the first time in 43 years that a German team finished as high as second in the continental club championship.

KEVIN PATAKY

Marco Yepez

STANDINGS

	G	W	L	GB
Parma	42	30	12	—
San Marino	42	28	14	2
Rimini	42	27	15	3
Bologna	42	25	17	5
Nettuno	42	23	19	7
Grosseto	42	20	22	10
Paterno	42	8	34	22
Godo	42	7	35	23

PLAYOFFS—Semifinal Round Robin: Bologna and Parma went 6-3 to advance to finals. San Marino went 4-5, Rimini went 2-7. **Finals:** Parma defeated Bologna 4-3 in best-of-seven series.

INDIVIDUAL BATTING LEADERS

PLAYER, TEAM	AVG	G	AB	R	H	2B	3B	HR	RBI	BB
Duran, Carlos, SM	.349	42	175	37	61	17	4	6	39	8
Munoz, Orlando, Par	.339	35	109	24	37	10	0	1	27	24
De Biase, Maximiliano, SM	.336	42	146	23	49	8	0	3	31	24
Sandoval, Danny, Gro	.333	41	153	26	51	9	0	1	24	22
Burnham, Gary, GodO	.329	41	143	18	47	11	0	4	24	21
Infante, Juan Carlos, Bol	.327	42	156	27	51	6	3	2	28	34
Camilo, Juan, Par	.325	41	160	30	52	9	3	3	34	17
Ramos, Gizzi Jario, Bol	.325	42	151	25	49	11	1	1	32	31
Chapelli, Laidel, Rim	.322	41	149	28	48	7	3	0	22	28
Connel, Lino, Net	.320	32	122	20	39	8	0	2	17	18

INDIVIDUAL PITCHING LEADERS

PLAYER, TEAM	W	L	ERA	G	SV	IP	H	R	BB	SO
Matos, Jesus, Bol	10	4	1.44	14	0	88	69	22	20	77
Di Roma, Christopher, Rim	1	1	1.64	17	8	44	32	11	27	37
Grifantini, Marco, Par	5	0	1.85	15	4	49	33	13	25	46
Orta, Pedro, Par	3	0	1.87	16	4	34	30	9	8	18
Patrone, Sandy, Rim	6	3	1.99	14	0	77	68	20	20	76
Da Silva, Tiago, SM	8	4	2.23	14	0	93	70	28	24	60
Bonilla, Vincente, SM	8	3	2.28	14	0	87	49	25	29	52
Marquez, Enorbel, Rim	9	2	2.37	14	0	80	63	22	35	65
Brower, Jim, Rim	8	4	2.38	14	0	83	59	29	25	68
Cooper, Christopher, Gro	4	4	2.38	13	0	76	72	30	27	49

Neptunus finds twice is nice

BY HARVEY SAHKER

Neptunus dominated the Dutch Major League and won its second straight title by defeating the Amsterdam Pirates four games to two in the Holland Series. The Rotterdam club has now won a record thirteen Dutch championships. Neptunus started the regular season with 10 consecutive victories. After their first defeat, they proceeded to win 23in a row.

Former Blue Jay farmhand Diegomar Markwell clinched the Holland Series by throwing a one-hitter in Game Six. It was a fitting end for what could easily be called the Year of the Pitcher in the Netherlands. The eight DML clubs had a combined 3.47 ERA. The Neptunus staff had a 1.39 ERA, allowed only one home run and logged thirteen shutouts in the regular season.

Heading into the playoffs, Neptunus hurlers had white-washed their opponents in four straight games. They then reeled off three more shutouts in the semifinals, sweeping the Hoofddorp Pioniers and holding them to a .099 batting average in the process.

CLIFF WELCH
Dushan Ruzic

Australian righthander Dushan Ruzic was named Holland Series MVP. The 6-foot-8, 28-year-old former Marlins and Reds farmhand won two Series games for Neptunus, saved one and allowed no earned runs in nine innings as a long reliever. Ruzic worked out of the bullpen and started during the regular season. On April 30, he threw a seven-inning no-hitter as Neptunus defeated Almere 11-0. The game was halted after seven frames because of the DML's 10-run "mercy rule".

The next day, Dutch-Canadian Leon Boyd and two Neptunus relievers held Almere to one hit in a 7-0 victory. Batters hit just .152 overall against Boyd, who rejoined Neptunus in 2010 after spending the previous season in the Toronto organization. He led the DML with a microscopic 0.39 ERA.

On Aug. 19, Joey Eijpe of HCAW threw a no-hitter against Almere. HCAW won the game 3-1. Almere's run was the result of a pair of walks, a sacrifice bunt and a groundout. The same day, Markwell and Ruzic tossed a combined 11-inning one hitter in a 1-0 Neptunus win over the Pioniers.

At the bottom of the standings and on the wrong end of the season's two no-hitters, Almere batted just .196 as a team and failed to score in nine games. They withdrew from the DML at the end of the season. UVV will take their place in 2011.

STANDINGS

	G	W	L	T	GB
Neptunus	42	39	3	0	—
Kinheim	41	30	11	0	8 ½
Amsterdam Pirates	42	25	17	0	14
Hoofddorp Pioniers	42	22	20	0	17
HCAW	42	19	23	0	20
Sparta/Feyenoord	42	13	28	1	25 ½
ADO	41	9	31	1	29
Almere Magpies	42	9	33	0	30

PLAYOFFS—Semifinals: Neptunus defeated Hoofddorp 3-0, Amsterdam Pirates defeated Kinheim 3-1 in best-of-five series. **Finals:** Neptunus defeated Amsterdam 4-2 in best-of-seven series.

INDIVIDUAL BATTING LEADERS

PLAYER, TEAM	AVG	AB	R	H	HR	RBI	BB	SO	SB
Van't Klooster, Dirk, Kin	.400	140	30	56	1	18	13	11	1
Vasquez, Wuillians M, HCAW	.376	117	23	44	1	28	23	12	6
Engelhardt, Bryan, Kin	.373	153	37	57	6	36	16	19	16
Koster Lennart, Pio	.344	96	16	33	0	15	18	12	1
Legito, Raily, Nep	.340	144	30	49	3	35	23	9	11
De Jong, Sidney, Ams	.333	144	26	48	1	20	25	13	1
Gabriels, Bart, HCAW	.326	132	21	43	1	15	23	24	8
De Jong, Bas, Ams	.324	136	24	44	3	30	8	12	2
Arends, Jeffrey, Nep	.323	133	24	43	0	22	25	14	4
Gario, Mervin, Pio	.323	127	25	41	1	17	21	19	6

INDIVIDUAL PITCHING LEADERS

PLAYER, TEAM	W	L	ERA	G	SV	IP	H	R	BB	SO
Boyd, Leon, Nep	9	0	0.39	15	0	69	36	5	25	83
Cordemans, Rob, Ams	7	2	0.81	13	0	77	44	10	15	76
Markwell, Diegomar, Nep	9	1	1.32	12	0	75	60	20	19	54
Bergman, David, Kin	12	1	1.38	15	0	98	70	18	19	100
Veltkamp, Nick, Kin	5	3	1.42	17	0	44	37	15	19	38
Ruzic, Dushan, Nep	9	0	1.56	18	2	81	45	16	26	78
Asjes, Arshwin, Pio	2	3	1.66	15	2	38	40	13	15	35
Aucoin, Eddie, Pio	7	5	1.72	14	0	94	66	25	19	67
Carrington, Bobby, Ado	3	3	1.82	14	0	79	48	26	37	77
Grover, Ben, Ams	5	1	1.93	14	0	84	58	25	41	42

INTERNATIONAL BASEBALL

Industriales win 12th league title

BY JOHN MANUEL

Cuba's 49th National Series saw Granma outfielder Alfredo Despaigne continue to emerge as the island's best player, while Industriales added to their legend with their 12th league championship.

Industriales had stumbled to a 37-53 record the year before and improved by 10 games in the regular season, finishing fourth in the West Division with a 47-43 record. However, the Blue Lions caught fire in the postseason, winning five-game series romps against Sancti Spiritus and La Habana to represent the West in the championship series.

There, Industriales played Villa Clara, the 2008-2009 runner-up and the East's regular-season and playoff champion. The series went the full seven games, and Game Seven went into extra innings, tied at 5-5. Raiko Olivares (sacrifice fly) and Carlos Tabares (single) drove in runs in the top of the 10th, and Yoan Socarras got the victory on the mound. Socarras got the final seven outs for Industriales, five of them via strikeout, after Villa Clara had tied the game in the eighth with a three-run homer by second baseman Yandrys Canto Ramirez.

Despaigne did his best work again with Granma, which went 45-43 and failed to make the postseason. The 24-year-old outfielder had a monster season, nearly winning the triple crown, and becoming the third back-to-back MVP winner in league history, joining Wilfredo Sanchez and Yulieski Gourriel. He won the batting title, hitting .404, and his 31 homers led the league by one over Jose Abreu and Gourriel. It was his second straight home run title. Gourriel, runner up for MVP, kept Despaigne from winning the triple crown with 105 RBIs, eight better than the Granma outfielder.

Alexei Bell, who set the league home run record with 31 in the 47th National Series in '07-'08 and was the top player in the '08 Olympics, bounced back from an eye injury to become a force again, hitting .268 with 20 home runs for Santiago de Cuba. Eight of his homers were grand slams.

Two of Bell's fellow Olympians and veterans of the Cuban National Team retired in 2010. Catcher Ariel Pestano helped Villa Clara get to the finals again and had a game-winning homer in Game Five of the championship series but called it a career after the series. Also retiring was 37-year-old Pedro Luis Lazo, one of the best pitchers in Cuban history and a veteran of international play, where he was Cuba's closer. He finished 257 victories, best in National Series history, and ranks second all-time in strikeouts and innings pitched.

STANDINGS

WEST	W	L	PCT	GB
Sancti Spiritus Roosters	63	27	.700	—
Cienfuegos Elephants	51	39	.567	12
Habana Province Cowboys	49	40	.551	13½
Industriales Blue Lions	47	43	.522	16
Pinar del Rio Foresters	46	43	.511	16½
Matanzas Crocodiles	33	57	.367	30
Isla de la Juventud Pine Cutters	26	64	.289	37
Metropolitanos Warriors	22	68	.244	41

EAST	W	L	PCT	GB
Villa Clara Orangemen	56	32	.629	—
Guantanamo Indians	52	37	.584	4½
Ciego de Avila Tigers	49	40	.551	7½
Santiago de Cuba Wasps	48	41	.539	8½
Las Tunas Woodcutters	47	43	.522	10
Granma Stallions	45	43	.506	11
Holguin Dogs	45	44	.506	11½
Camaguey Potters	35	53	.393	21

Records do not include ties

POSTSEASON ALL-STARS: C—Yosvani Alarcon, Las Tunas. **1B**—Jose Dariel Abreu, Cienfuegos. **2B**—Danel Castro, Las Tunas. **3B**—Yulieski Gourriel, Sancti Spiritus. **SS**—Alexander Guerrero, Las Tunas. **OF**—Alexei Bell, Santiago de Cuba; Friederich Cepeda, Sancti Spiritus; Alfredo Despaigne, Granma. **DH**—Rolando Merino, Santiago de Cuba. **UT**—Raul Gonzalez, Ciego de Avila. **RHP**—Vladimir Garcia, Ciego de Avila. **LHP**—Yulieski Gonzalez, Habana Province. **RP**—Dunier Ibarra, Cienfuegos.

INDIVIDUAL BATTING LEADERS
(Minimum 235 plate appearances)

PLAYER, TEAM	AVG	AB	R	H	2B	3B	HR	RBI
Alfredo Despaigne, Gran	.404	317	79	128	37	0	31	97
Jose Abreu, Cien	.399	286	82	114	25	3	30	76
Henry Urrutia, LT	.397	305	55	121	23	1	12	76
Kenen Bailly, Guan	.377	260	52	98	15	1	11	65
Yunier Mendoza, SS	.377	355	71	134	16	1	6	51
Alexei Bell, SdC	.368	261	65	96	17	4	20	80
Jorge Jhonson, LT	.365	285	59	104	15	5	2	29
Yulieski Gourriel, SS	.363	344	90	125	17	2	30	105
Yordanis Samon, Gran	.356	329	50	117	24	1	14	78
Rolando Merino, SdC	.355	313	74	111	19	2	17	72
Danel Castro, LT	.354	347	84	123	24	4	11	79
Ramon Lunar, VC	.350	329	76	115	14	2	18	75
Lazaro Herrera, Matz	.348	359	55	125	23	0	14	68
Luis Nava, SdC	.347	340	55	105	21	0	8	48
Jose Fernandez, Matz	.346	382	55	132	19	2	8	57

INDIVIDUAL PITCHING LEADERS
(Minimum 87 innings pitched)

PLAYER, TEAM	W	L	ERA	G	IP	BB	SO
Angel Pena, SS	10	2	2.14	16	109	33	60
Yulieski Gonzalez, Habana	11	7	2.22	19	142	29	101
Jonder Martinez, Habana	8	4	2.48	17	127	32	80
Vladimir Garcia, CdA	11	4	2.68	27	114	43	115
Pedro Lazo, PdR	8	4	2.77	17	114	31	78
Osmel Cintra, SdC	7	4	2.80	17	106	22	63
Miguel Gonzalez, Habana	6	6	2.98	16	100	16	77
Norberto Gonzalez, Cien	11	4	3.10	20	125	37	76
Robelio Carrillo, VC	7	3	3.11	17	104	36	70
Yosvani Torres, PdR	7	5	3.13	19	127	26	85
Arley Sanchez, Ind	8	6	3.21	19	118	38	70
Maikel Folch, CdA	11	5	3.30	19	128	59	66
Yosvani Perez, VC	8	2	3.32	14	89	18	23
Yunier Colon, Guan	10	4	3.47	21	106	44	42
Frank Navarro, Guan	8	4	3.66	26	106	30	29

Dominican brings home Caribbean crown again

The Caribbean Series proved to be a letdown for host Venezuela, which finished last. Given one last chance to play spoiler, the host nation couldn't even do that against the Dominican Republic.

The Dominicans were represented by Dominican League champ Escogido, which had to survive a nine-game slog in its league finals. Escogido lost the first game of the series against Gigantes, then tied the series or trailed up until the ninth and final game, when lefthander Francisco Liriano capped a strong winter performance by beating Victor Zambrano in the ninth-game clincher.

In the Caribbean Series, Escogido didn't have Liriano but got a pair of strong starts from Cuban native Raul Valdes, including five innings in the finale against Venezuela. That was enough as the Dominican put up four runs in the first inning off Ramon A. Ramirez, then held on the rest of the way to beat Venezuela 7-4 and clinch the Series championship. It was the second title in three seasons for the Dominican representative and the first for Escogido since 1990.

That 1990 team was managed by Felipe Alou. His son, ex-big leaguer Moises, was general manager of the 2009-2010 club and put together a roster that mixed veterans such as Kevin Barker and closer Dario Veras with prospects such as Juan Francisco (Reds) and Fernando Martinez (Mets). Martinez, who hit .348 with two homers in six Series games, had two hits and an RBI in the clincher against Venezuela, while Francisco batted third and had an RBI double in the fifth, when the Dominicans put the game away and took a commanding 6-1 lead.

"This is very emotional," Martinez, the Series MVP, told MLB.com. "To be able to contribute to the Dominican Republic team is something you dream about as a child. This is a wonderful feeling. I don't have the words.

"We won as a team. That's the most important part of this experience. We did it together."

It was a bitter ending for Venezuela, which was represented by league champion Caracas. The Lions got a boost when Pablo Sandoval (Giants) flew in from San Francisco to help them win Game Seven of the Venezuelan League playoffs against Magallanes. But Sandoval didn't play in the Caribbean Series, and the home team struggled

Mets prospect Fernando Martinez hit two homers to earn Caribbean Series MVP

ED WOLFSTEIN

offensively, batting just .195 as a team.

The Lions also missed Wilson Ramos, who played for the Tigers during the VWL season but who went 12-for-50 with a pair of home runs in the playoffs after being added to Caracas' roster. The parent Twins—who traded Ramos during the 2010 season—didn't want Ramos to play in the Caribbean Series, and he complied. Ramos' effort (.332/.397/.582, 12 home runs, 49 RBIs) made him Baseball America's Winter Player of the Year.

Puerto Rico finished second as its representative, Mayaguez, matched its best Series finish of the last six years. Puerto Rico had gone just 9-21 since 2004 and didn't participate in 2008, when its winter league went on hiatus.

DOMINICAN LEAGUE

TEAM	W	L	PCT	GB
Escogido	30	19	.612	—
Licey	28	22	.560	2½
Gigantes	27	22	.551	3
Toros	27	23	.540	3½
Aguilas	25	25	.500	5½
Estrellas	15	35	.300	15½

ROUND ROBIN

Gigantes	12	6	.667	—
Escogido	10	8	.556	2
Licey	8	10	.444	4
Toros	6	12	.333	6

FINALS: Escogido defeated Gigantes 5-4.

INDIVIDUAL BATTING LEADERS

PLAYER, TEAM	AVG	G	AB	R	H	2B	3B	HR	RBI	SB
Perez, Timo, Licey	.356	38	132	20	47	8	2	3	26	9
Diaz, Robinzon, Est	.333	38	141	18	47	7	1	1	20	0
Almonte, Erick, Gig	.325	49	157	18	51	8	0	4	26	0
Barker, Kevin, Agu	.324	45	170	30	55	13	1	6	31	0
Valdez, Alex, Esc	.308	40	156	25	48	10	6	1	13	5
Mercedes, Victor, Tor	.306	45	157	21	48	5	3	1	21	5
Francisco, Juan, Gig	.302	46	182	29	55	11	2	11	42	0
Mayorson, Manny, Tor	.302	37	139	19	42	9	0	1	19	5
Betemit, Wilson, Gig	.301	47	166	19	50	11	2	8	36	2
Cesar, Dionys, Agu	.297	42	155	20	46	9	0	4	19	5

INDIVIDUAL PITCHING LEADERS

PITCHER, TEAM	W	L	ERA	G	SV	IP	H	BB	SO
Capellan, Jose, Gig	7	3	2.15	12	0	63	67	12	41
Halama, John, Agu	4	3	2.45	9	0	55	56	3	30
Castro, Fabio, Gig	0	1	2.47	9	0	44	41	16	36
Jukich, Ben, Agu	4	3	2.86	11	0	57	61	15	42
MacLane, Evan, Est	5	2	2.87	11	0	63	55	11	41
Stoner, Tobi, Esc	4	2	3.10	9	0	52	44	15	31
Valdez, Edward, Esc	2	3	3.17	11	0	54	54	14	33
Abad, Fernando, Tor	3	1	3.42	10	0	47	42	15	32
Sosa, Jorge, Licey	4	2	3.83	9	0	40	45	12	20
Narron, Sam, Gig	0	2	4.10	14	0	42	44	14	14

MEXICAN PACIFIC LEAGUE

TEAM	W	L	PCT	GB
Mazatlan	40	28	.588	—
Hermosillo	38	29	.567	1½
Obregon	37	30	.552	2½
Mexicali	34	34	.500	6
Navojoa	32	36	.471	8
Culiacan	30	35	.462	8½
Guasave	29	37	.439	10
Los Mochis	28	39	.418	11½

FINALS: Hermosillo defeated Mazatlan 4-3.

INDIVIDUAL BATTING LEADERS

PLAYER, TEAM	AVG	G	AB	R	H	2B	3B	HR	RBI	SB
Madera, Sandy, Moc	.413	60	208	47	86	8	0	14	28	2
Snyder, Brad, Mxc	.379	55	211	46	80	16	2	9	48	18
Cervenak, Mike, Cul	.330	67	276	39	91	13	0	11	48	0
Camp, Matt, Mxc	.329	59	252	45	83	18	3	2	29	14
Lindsey, John, Maz	.325	65	243	31	79	16	0	11	37	0
Pena, Roman, Mxc	.323	66	229	41	74	18	7	6	34	5
Morejon, Oswaldo, Mxc	.318	66	283	35	90	18	2	0	33	7
Young, Matt, Nav	.315	66	241	54	76	18	4	8	32	21
Cruz, Luis, Cul	.314	53	204	26	64	15	1	4	22	3
Cota, Humberto, Her	.313	65	224	42	70	16	0	9	30	1

INDIVIDUAL PITCHING LEADERS

PITCHER, TEAM	W	L	ERA	G	SV	IP	H	BB	SO
Ortega, Pablo, Maz	8	2	2.43	14	0	85	85	11	35
Mendoza, Luis, Obr	7	4	2.89	14	0	90	84	27	82
Delgadillo, Juan, Her	6	4	3.31	15	0	87	92	30	33
Campos, Francisco, Her	3	6	3.71	14	0	78	82	22	42
Magrane, Jim, Gsv	6	4	3.98	15	0	84	101	28	57
Cordoba, Francisco, Gsv	7	4	4.14	15	0	76	79	21	42
Sanchez, Alfonso, Maz	5	5	4.52	14	0	70	77	22	27

PUERTO RICAN LEAGUE

TEAM	W	L	PCT	GB
Arecibo	25	14	.641	—
Carolina	21	20	.512	5
Caguas	20	20	.500	5½

Mayaguez	18	24	.429	8½
Ponce	15	27	.357	11½

FINALS: Mayaguez defeated Caguas 4-1

INDIVIDUAL BATTING LEADERS

PLAYER, TEAM	AVG	G	AB	R	H	2B	3B	HR	RBI	SB
Rios, Armando, Car	.367	32	98	14	36	8	0	0	16	5
Rodriguez, Victor, Car	.362	29	105	11	38	8	0	0	17	0
Feliciano, Jesus, Are	.352	39	159	27	56	12	2	0	14	4
Abreu, Michel, Are	.351	36	131	28	46	12	0	12	42	0
Valdes, Pedro, Car	.346	37	136	16	47	10	0	3	26	0
Ruiz, Randy, May	.344	26	96	21	33	3	0	7	27	1
Mercado, Orlando, Car	.337	28	92	12	31	10	0	1	12	0
Baez, Edgardo, Cag	.329	39	140	27	46	9	2	3	23	2
Cuadrado, Phillip, Are	.326	29	95	18	31	7	0	4	20	1
Montanez, Lou, Cag	.324	28	111	15	36	10	1	3	13	1

INDIVIDUAL PITCHING LEADERS

PITCHER, TEAM	W	L	ERA	G	SV	IP	H	BB	SO
Speigner, Levale, Are	7	0	2.03	18	1	40	33	9	21
Lawrence, Brian, Car	3	3	2.23	8	0	40	46	7	33
Burgos, Hiram, May	3	2	2.27	10	0	48	41	10	37
Rainwater, Josh, Pon	1	1	2.45	14	1	40	36	19	23
Santiago, Mario, Car	3	2	2.49	11	0	47	45	8	33
Maroth, Mike, May	3	0	2.60	8	0	35	33	13	15
Pulsipher, Bill, Are	2	4	2.78	9	0	45	53	11	25
Padilla, Juan, Pon	5	3	2.91	14	1	53	46	10	35
Byrd, Darren, May	4	3	3.04	10	0	50	41	17	30
Kershner, Jason, Are	3	1	3.09	9	0	47	51	14	19

VENEZUELAN LEAGUE

TEAM	W	L	PCT	GB
Caracas	41	22	.651	—
Magallanes	41	22	.651	—
La Guaira	32	31	.508	9
Margarita	30	33	.476	11
Zulia	30	34	.469	11½
Lara	29	35	.453	12½
Aragua	28	35	.444	13
Anzoategui	22	41	.349	19

ROUND ROBIN

Magallanes	11	5	.688	—
Caracas	10	6	.625	1
La Guaira	7	9	.438	4
Zulia	7	9	.438	4
Margarita	5	11	.313	6

FINALS: Caracas defeated Magallanes 4-3.

INDIVIDUAL BATTING LEADERS

PLAYER, TEAM	AVG	G	AB	R	H	2B	3B	HR	RBI	SB
Escobar, Alcides, Lara	.393	45	173	30	68	9	1	2	19	16
Thole, Josh, Car	.381	44	155	33	59	16	2	3	28	0
Chirinos, Robinson, Mag	.366	48	153	24	56	10	1	10	34	0
Yepez, Jose, Lara	.359	49	142	25	51	10	0	4	25	0
Evans, Tom, Lara	.349	59	209	53	73	16	0	9	43	7
Romero, Alex, Ara	.345	48	171	22	59	12	0	0	14	4
Castillo, Jose, Car	.344	51	186	38	64	9	2	7	34	17
Amarista, Alexi, Ori	.339	47	192	33	65	7	10	2	17	8
Suarez, Cesar, Lag	.337	50	193	39	65	14	4	6	34	6
Ramos, Wilson, Ara	.332	54	208	38	69	14	1	12	49	0

INDIVIDUAL PITCHING LEADERS

PITCHER, TEAM	W	L	ERA	G	SV	IP	H	BB	SO
Bastardo, Alberto, Mar	4	0	2.77	11	0	52	45	15	38
Rivero, Raul, Lara	3	2	2.91	9	0	53	50	17	39
Etherton, Seth, Ara	2	3	3.04	11	0	53	47	12	47
Sanchez, Jose, Mag	4	0	3.24	14	0	58	61	14	48
Schmidt, Josh, Zul	2	5	3.58	16	0	75	61	31	71
Pino, Yohan, Ara	3	3	3.65	14	0	57	64	9	40
Totten, Heath, Zul	4	7	3.68	15	0	86	99	25	53
Shell, Steven, Lara	4	1	4.17	12	0	69	72	10	39
Monasterios, Carlos, Mar	7	4	4.35	13	0	62	60	19	46
Pollok, Dwayne, Zul	3	3	4.84	12	0	58	68	13	47

COLLEGE

South Carolina teammates swarm Scott Wingo as he scores the championship-winning run

South Carolina sends out Rosenblatt in style

BY AARON FITT

Ray Tanner stood by himself, a few paces off the dirt surrounding home plate, where his players were being introduced one-by-one. He looked around, trying to process what he was seeing, trying to catch his breath. He shook his head. "It's beautiful, isn't it?" he said. "Just a blue-collar team . . . "

He trailed off, and shook his head again.

Tanner's blue-collar team will be remembered as the final College World Series champion in Rosenblatt Stadium history. South Carolina won its first national title in dramatic fashion, as Whit Merrifield's walk-off RBI single in the 11th gave the Gamecocks a 2-1 win against UCLA. It was the first CWS-ending walk-off hit since 2000.

"This is what everyone dreams about. This," Merrifield said, nodding toward the celebration continuing on the field around him. "It hasn't sunk in yet what actually just happened. Growing up as a little kid, you dream about getting the big hit to win the World Series. I just can't believe that happened."

It was a storybook ending for the Gamecocks

(54-16) and for Rosenblatt Stadium, which hosted its 61st and final College World Series. The final CWS game in the venerable ballpark was a true classic.

"The game was special," UCLA coach John Savage said. "The game was as good as it gets at this level . . . You know, a national championship's supposed to be played like that."

Rob Rasmussen battled his way through six scoreless innings for the Bruins, working around six hits and four walks thanks in part to five strikeouts. He left with a 1-0 lead, as the Bruins (51-17) managed to scratch out a run against South Carolina starter Michael Roth in the fifth.

In college baseball's modern 64-team era, which dates back to 1999, only one team—Oregon State in 2006—has run through the losers' bracket to win the College World Series. It's not easy to do, and heroic performances are required to pull it off. South Carolina's magical ride was chock full of heroes.

There was Roth, the lefthanded specialist who threw a complete-game three-hitter in his first start of the season in the CWS bracket finals against Clemson. Roth threw 108 pitches in that one,

COACHING CAROUSEL

SCHOOL	NEW COACH (PREVIOUS SCHOOL/JOB)	FORMER COACH (REASON FOR DEPARTURE)
Air Force	* Mike Kazlausky (Air Force assistant)	Mike Hutcheon (resigned)
Alabama A&M	Ed McCann (Centenary head coach)	Demetrius Mitchell (resigned)
Ball State	Alex Marconi (Ball State assistant)	Greg Beals (Ohio State head coach)
Boston College	Mike Gambino (Virginia Tech assistant)	Mik Aoki (Notre Dame head coach)
Bryant	Steve Owens (Le Moyne head coach)	Jamie Pinzino (resigned)
Cal State Northridge	Matt Curtis (Fresno State assistant)	Steve Rousey (fired)
Centenary	Mike Diaz (Centenary associate head coach)	Ed McCann (Alabama A&M head coach)
Central Arkansas	Allen Gum (Southern Arkansas head coach)	Doug Clark (resigned)
Coppin State	Sherman Reed (former Coppin State assistant)	Mike Scolinos (resigned)
Fairleigh Dickinson	Gary Puccio (Briarcliff, N.Y., head coach)	Jerry DiFabbia (resigned)
Houston	Todd Whitting (Texas Christian assistant)	Rayner Noble (fired)
Le Moyne	Scott Cassidy (Le Moyne assistant)	Steve Owens (Bryant head coach)
Long Beach State	Troy Buckley (Long Beach assistant)	Mike Weathers (retired)
New Jersey Tech	Mike Cole (Maine assistant)	Brian Callahan (resigned)
Nicholls State	Seth Thibodeaux (Nicholls State associate head coach)	Chip Durham (resigned)
North Florida	Smoke Laval (North Florida assistant)	Dusty Rhodes (retired)
Northern Colorado	Carl Iwasaki (Austin, Texas, College head coach)	Kevin Smallcomb (fired)
Notre Dame	Mik Aoki (Boston College head coach)	Dave Schrage (fired)
Ohio State	Greg Beals (Ball State head coach)	Bob Todd (retired)
Old Dominion	* Nate Goulet (Old Dominion assistant)	Jerry Meyers (South Carolina pitching coach)
Nevada-Las Vegas	Tim Chambers (CC of Southern Nevada head coach)	Buddy Gouldsmith (fired)
Southern California	* Frank Cruz (USC assistant)	Chad Kreuter (fired)
Western Michigan	Billy Gernon (Michigan State assistant)	Randy Ford (fired)
Winthrop	Tom Riginos (Clemson assistant)	Joe Hudak (fired)

*Interim

then came back on three days' rest and gave South Carolina five strong innings in the clincher against UCLA.

"I was planning on going nine innings again," quipped Roth, a relative unknown-turned-CWS media darling. "You know, never would I have ever thought that I was going to start a game here in Omaha. But it's been great . . . It's a wonderful feeling to be a starting pitcher of the final game."

There was closer Matt Price, the flame-throwing redshirt freshman righthander who threw 130 pitches over three dominating relief outings earlier in the World Series. Three days after he worked 2⅓ strong innings to earn the win against Clemson that propelled the Gamecocks to the Finals, Price worked 2⅔ scoreless innings to earn the final win against the Bruins, allowing one hit and a walk while striking out three. The Bruins loaded the bases against him in the top of the ninth, but he saved the game by striking out Niko Gallego on a slider low and away, stranding three. Price went 2-0, 0.93 with 15 strikeouts and one walk in 9⅔ innings over 10 appearances in Omaha.

"Matt Price and the entire bullpen have been very special for us the entire year, and toward the latter part, he's been sort of the guy that we get on his back there at the end and say, 'Either keep us alive or win it for us or save it for us,' " Tanner said.

"And he came up huge again tonight."

There was Blake Cooper, who carried a one-hit shutout into the ninth inning in the CWS Finals opener—in his second consecutive start on three days' rest.

There was Jackie Bradley Jr., the CWS Most Outstanding Player, who kept South Carolina's season alive with a two-out, two-strike, game-tying RBI single in the 12th inning against Oklahoma in the Gamecocks' second elimination game.

There was Brady Thomas, who delivered the game-winning hit in that 12th inning against Oklahoma. Thomas came up big again in the finale against UCLA, delivering a pinch-hit single to lead off the eighth against hard-throwing reliever Erik Goeddel. Robert Beary pinch-ran for him and scored the tying run on an error by first baseman Dean Espy.

There was second baseman Scott Wingo, a defensive specialist who drew a walk leading off the 11th against UCLA closer Dan Klein, advanced to second on a passed ball, advanced to third on Evan Marzilli's sacrifice bunt, then scored the winning run on Merrifield's sharp single to right.

There was Bayler Teal, the avid 7-year-old Gamecock fan who lost his two-year battle with cancer during the CWS. The Gamecocks had visited him in the hospital, and in March he threw out the first pitch of a game in Columbia. The team dedicated its CWS run to Teal, even writing his initials on their hats.

Tanner got emotional when asked about Teal in the postgame news conference, pausing for 15 or so seconds before answering with glassy eyes. Moments earlier, on the field, he had invoked Teal's name when speaking to the remaining crowd at the end of the championship celebration.

"He's in a better place now," Tanner told the crowd. "But I am assured that he's watching down on us, smiling."

Teal's favorite player was Merrifield—the man who delivered the final indelible image in the rich history of Rosenblatt Stadium.

Fans had been waiting for that moment since the ninth inning, as the stadium was illuminated with flashbulbs on every pitch when the Gamecocks were up. Every pitch had a chance to be the last at Rosenblatt.

"You don't notice it until you're in the dugout," Merrifield said of the flashbulbs. "I came back in and guys were like, 'Did you not get blinded up there?' I looked around and saw all the flashbulbs going off. It's unbelievable."

Merrifield gave Rosenblatt the picture-perfect ending all those fans were dreaming of. And he gave Rosenblatt the ideal champion for its last hurrah—a gritty, blue-collar bunch that lost its CWS opener to Oklahoma and went on to become the first team in history to win six straight games in a single College World Series, including the final two against a favored UCLA team.

"I was sitting out by the third-base line for opening ceremonies with the other teams thinking, 'What a venue, what an atmosphere, what a history,' " Tanner said. "And it dawned on me—it would be wonderful to go deep into this thing and be around at the end. And to be able to survive and win the last game is really incredible.

"I know the new stadium will be very special and a great facility. But this is history. And we'll be a part of the College World Series and Rosenblatt for a long, long time.

"It's an incredible journey and an incredible ending."

UCLA, TCU Raise Bar

UCLA got close enough to the national championship trophy to touch it.

That's exactly what sophomore righthander Trevor Bauer did during the postgame handshake line, giving the trophy a wistful pat after he congratulated South Carolina catcher Kyle Enders, who was carrying it.

STANDINGS

BRACKET ONE	W	L
South Carolina	6	1
Clemson	2	2
Oklahoma	1	2
Arizona State	0	2

BRACKET TWO	W	L
UCLA	3	3
Texas Christian	3	2
Florida State	1	2
Florida	0	2

CWS FINALS (BEST OF THREE)

June 28: South Carolina 7, UCLA 1
June 29: South Carolina 2, UCLA 1 (11)

ALL-TOURNAMENT TEAM

C: Bryan Holaday, TCU. **1B:** Christian Walker, South Carolina. **2B:** Cody Regis, UCLA. **3B:** John Hinson, Clemson. **SS:** Taylor Featherston, TCU. **OF:** Beau Amaral, UCLA; *Jackie Bradley Jr., South Carolina; Evan Marzilli, South Carolina. **DH:** Brady Thomas, South Carolina. **P:** Trevor Bauer, UCLA; Matt Purke, TCU.
*Named Most Outstanding Player.

BATTING
(Minimum 10 PA)

PLAYER	AVG	AB	R	H	2B	3B	HR	RBI	SB
Tyler Ogle, OU	.455	11	3	5	1	0	2	4	0
Sherman Johnson, FSU	.455	11	4	5	0	0	1	1	0
John Hinson, Clem	.438	16	3	7	0	1	0	3	2
Tyler Holt, FSU	.417	12	5	5	0	0	1	2	0
Stephen Cardullo, FSU	.417	12	1	5	0	0	1	3	1
Christian Walker, SC	.414	29	3	12	0	0	2	5	0
Bryan Holaday, TCU	.409	22	8	9	1	0	4	5	0
Brady Thomas, SC	.381	21	4	8	1	0	0	2	0
Beau Amaral, UCLA	.375	24	4	9	3	0	0	2	1
Jantzen Witte, TCU	.375	16	5	6	1	0	1	2	0

PITCHING
(Minimum 6 IP)

PITCHER	W-L	ERA	G	SV	IP	H	BB	SO
Matt Price, SC	2-0	0.93	4	0	10	7	1	15
Michael Roth, SC	1-0	1.10	2	0	16	9	3	9
Jeremy Erben, OU	0-0	1.29	3	0	7	6	3	4
Zach Neal, OU	0-0	1.29	1	0	7	5	1	7
Matt Purke, TCU	2-0	1.35	2	0	13	7	6	9
Blake Cooper, SC	1-1	2.41	3	0	19	13	4	21
Rob Rasmussen, UCLA	0-1	2.61	2	0	10	12	7	11
Trevor Bauer, UCLA	2-0	3.00	2	0	15	10	4	24
Sam Dyson, SC	1-0	3.86	2	0	14	13	4	8
Gerrit Cole, UCLA	1-1	4.20	2	0	15	16	3	15

UCLA's long journey ended in disappointment as it was swept in the College World Series Finals. That journey began with a 22-0 streak at the start of the season and continued with a dominating run through the Los Angeles Regional. The Bruins were one out away from elimination in the second game of their super regional against Cal State Fullerton, but a ninth-inning comeback kept their season alive, and lefthander Rob Rasmussen overpowered the Titans the next day to send UCLA to Omaha for the first time since 1997. The Bruins had never won a CWS game before this year, when

they won three games to reach the Finals.

"This team can say that they have been the best team in UCLA history, which is a long and rich

COLLEGE WORLD SERIES CHAMPIONS: 1947—2010

*Undefeated

YEAR	CHAMPION	COACH	RECORD	RUNNER-UP	MVP
1947	California*	Clint Evans	31-10	Yale	None selected
1948	Southern California	Sam Barry	40-12	Yale	None selected
1949	Texas*	Bibb Falk	23-7	Wake Forest	Charles Teague, 2b, Wake Forest
1950	Texas	Bibb Falk	27-6	Washington State	Ray VanCleef, of, Rutgers
1951	Oklahoma*	Jack Baer	19-9	Tennessee	Sid Hatfield, 1b-p, Tennessee
1952	Holy Cross	Jack Barry	21-3	Missouri	Jim O'Neill, p, Holy Cross
1953	Michigan	Ray Fisher	21-9	Texas	J.L. Smith, p, Texas
1954	Missouri	Hi Simmons	22-4	Rollins	Tom Yewcic, c, Michigan State
1955	Wake Forest	Taylor Sanford	29-7	Western Michigan	Tom Borland, p, Oklahoma State
1956	Minnesota	Dick Siebert	33-9	Arizona	Jerry Thomas, p, Minnesota
1957	California*	George Wolfman	35-10	Penn State	Cal Emery, 1b-p, Penn State
1958	Southern California	Rod Dedeaux	35-7	Missouri	Bill Thom, p, Southern California
1959	Oklahoma State	Toby Greene	27-5	Arizona	Jim Dobson, 3b, Oklahoma State
1960	Minnesota	Dick Siebert	34-7	Southern California	John Erickson, 2b, Minnesota
1961	Southern California*	Rod Dedeaux	43-9	Oklahoma State	Littleton Fowler, p, Oklahoma State
1962	Michigan	Don Lund	31-13	Santa Clara	Bob Garibaldi, p, Santa Clara
1963	Southern California	Rod Dedeaux	37-16	Arizona	Bud Hollowell, c, Southern California
1964	Minnesota	Dick Siebert	31-12	Missouri	Joe Ferris, p, Maine
1965	Arizona State	Bobby Winkles	54-8	Ohio State	Sal Bando, 3b, Arizona State
1966	Ohio State	Marty Karow	27-6	Oklahoma State	Steve Arlin, p, Ohio State
1967	Arizona State	Bobby Winkles	53-12	Houston	Ron Davini, c, Arizona State
1968	Southern California*	Rod Dedeaux	45-14	Southern Illinois	Bill Seinsoth, 1b, Southern California
1969	Arizona State	Bobby Winkles	56-11	Tulsa	John Dolinsek, of, Arizona State
1970	Southern California	Rod Dedeaux	51-13	Florida State	Gene Ammann, p, Florida State
1971	Southern California	Rod Dedeaux	53-13	Southern Illinois	Jerry Tabb, 1b, Tulsa
1972	Southern California	Rod Dedeaux	50-13	Arizona State	Russ McQueen, p, Southern California
1973	Southern California*	Rod Dedeaux	51-11	Arizona State	Dave Winfield, of-p, Minnesota
1974	Southern California	Rod Dedeaux	50-20	Miami	George Milke, p, Southern California
1975	Texas	Cliff Gustafson	56-6	South Carolina	Mickey Reichenbach, 1b, Texas
1976	Arizona	Jerry Kindall	56-17	Eastern Michigan	Steve Powers, dh-p, Arizona
1977	Arizona State	Jim Brock	57-12	South Carolina	Bob Horner, 3b, Arizona State
1978	Southern California*	Rod Dedeaux	54-9	Arizona State	Rod Boxberger, p, Southern California
1979	Cal State Fullerton	Augie Garrido	60-14	Arkansas	Tony Hudson, p, Cal State Fullerton
1980	Arizona	Jerry Kindall	45-21	Hawaii	Terry Francona, of, Arizona
1981	Arizona State	Jim Brock	55-13	Oklahoma State	Stan Holmes, of, Arizona State
1982	Miami	Ron Fraser	57-18	Wichita State	Dan Smith, p, Miami
1983	Texas	Cliff Gustafson	66-14	Alabama	Calvin Schiraldi, p, Texas
1984	Cal State Fullerton	Augie Garrido	66-20	Texas	John Fishel, of, Cal State Fullerton
1985	Miami*	Ron Fraser	64-16	Texas	Greg Ellena, dh, Miami
1986	Arizona	Jerry Kindall	49-19	Florida State	Mike Senne, of, Arizona
1987	Stanford	Mark Marquess	53-17	Oklahoma State	Paul Carey, of, Stanford
1988	Stanford	Mark Marquess	46-23	Arizona State	Lee Plemel, p, Stanford
1989	Wichita State	Gene Stephenson	68-16	Texas	Greg Brummett, p, Wichita State
1990	Georgia	Steve Webber	52-19	Oklahoma State	Mike Rebhan, p, Georgia
1991	Louisiana State*	Skip Bertman	55-18	Wichita State	Gary Hymel, c, Louisiana State
1992	Pepperdine*	Andy Lopez	48-11	Cal State Fullerton	Phil Nevin, 3b, Cal State Fullerton
1993	Louisiana State	Skip Bertman	53-17	Wichita State	Todd Walker, 2b, Louisiana State
1994	Oklahoma*	Larry Cochell	50-17	Georgia Tech	Chip Glass, of, Oklahoma
1995	Cal State Fullerton*	Augie Garrido	57-9	Southern California	Mark Kotsay, of-p, Cal State Fullerton
1996	Louisiana State*	Skip Bertman	52-15	Miami	Pat Burrell, 3b, Miami
1997	Louisiana State*	Skip Bertman	57-13	Alabama	Brandon Larson, ss, Louisiana State
1998	Southern California	Mike Gillespie	49-17	Arizona State	Wes Rachels, 2b, Southern California
1999	Miami*	Jim Morris	50-13	Florida State	Marshall McDougall, 2b, Florida State
2000	Louisiana State*	Skip Bertman	52-17	Stanford	Trey Hodges, rhp, Louisiana State
2001	Miami*	Jim Morris	53-12	Stanford	Charlton Jimerson, of, Miami
2002	Texas*	Augie Garrido	57-15	South Carolina	Huston Street, rhp, Texas
2003	Rice	Wayne Graham	58-12	Stanford	John Hudgins, rhp, Stanford
2004	Cal State Fullerton	George Horton	47-22	Texas	Jason Windsor, rhp, Cal State Fullerton
2005	Texas*	Augie Garrido	56-16	Florida	David Maroul, 3b, Texas
2006	Oregon State	Pat Casey	50-16	North Carolina	Jonah Nickerson, rhp, Oregon State
2007	Oregon State*	Pat Casey	49-18	North Carolina	Jorge Reyes, rhp, Oregon State
2008	Fresno State	Mike Batesole	47-31	Georgia	Tommy Mendonca, 3b, Fresno State
2009	Louisiana State	Paul Mainieri	56-17	Texas	Jared Mitchell, of, Louisiana State
2010	South Carolina	Ray Tanner	54-16	UCLA	Jackie Bradley Jr., of, South Carolina

tradition," coach John Savage said after the Finals. "And I just can't say how proud I am about every single person that's been part of our program."

Rasmussen, who gave the Bruins six shutout innings in the final game, said the UCLA locker room was understandably emotional after the loss, but he tried to put the season into perspective.

"To get so close and to fall short hurts," he said. "But . . . as it all kind of sinks in and as we look back on it, we're all going to be proud of what we did. We were under .500 last year at 27-29. And we really were, like Coach, said, the best team that this school has ever seen."

The good news for UCLA is that the future is bright. Rasmussen and closer Dan Klein will head to professional ball, but co-aces Gerrit Cole and Bauer will be back to anchor what should again be one of the nation's best pitching staffs. The lineup was young this year and could return every starter. And now that the Bruins know how to get to Omaha, getting back should be easier.

"They've experienced the rigors of the regionals and super regionals and the bracket of coming out and playing for a national championship," Savage said. "So now every player in that locker room knows what it feels like, all the hard work and all the sacrifice to get to where they are. And we can sit there and be very proud of our entire program. Now the bar has been raised, and we look to be back as soon as possible."

While its players were new to Omaha, UCLA wasn't making its first CWS appearance. Before this year, eight schools had made their first appearance in the CWS since the new 64-team format was established in 1999. Five of them went home winless. Louisiana-Lafayette (2-2) was the only one to win more than one game.

TCU, the only newcomer in this year's eight-team field, proved to be an exception. And it took another exceptional pitching performance from UCLA's Trevor Bauer to make the Horned Frogs pack up their gear. TCU's three victories were the most by a team making its Omaha debut since 1994, when Georgia Tech won three games and finished runner-up to Oklahoma.

"I think there's a lot of people that expected us to keep our video cameras out and take a lot of pictures during the games and go home in two games. And we didn't do that," said TCU coach Jim Schlossnagle. "I am really proud of them to come out here and not just show up and feel good about it, but to compete within one game of the championship series is amazing."

TCU had shown it could dominate the

RPI RANKINGS

The Ratings Percentage Index is an important tool used by the NCAA in selecting at-large teams for the 64-team Division I regional tournament. The NCAA now releases its RPI rankings during the season. These were the top 100 finishers for 2010. A team's rank in the final Baseball America Top 25 is indicated in parentheses, and College World Series teams are in bold.

1. **Arizona State** (4) 52-10	51. Southeastern Louisiana 40-19
2. **Coastal Carolina** (12) 55-10	52. Western Carolina 37-21
3. Virginia (8) 51-14	53. Florida International 36-25
4. **Florida** (7) 47-17	54. North Carolina State 38-24
5. **UCLA** (2) 51-17	54. Appalachian State 38-18
6. Texas (9) 50-13	56. Rutgers 30-26
7. **South Carolina** (1) 54-16	57. Wichita State 41-19
8. Louisville (17) 50-14	58. Pittsburgh 38-18
9. **Texas Christian** (3) 54-14	59. Kansas 31-27
10. Vanderbilt (14) 46-20	60. Texas Tech 28-29
11. Alabama (16) 42-25	61. Southern Mississippi 36-24
12. Cal State Fullerton (11) 46-18	62. Southern California 28-32
13. Miami (15) 43-20	63. Troy 36-25
14. Arkansas (13) 43-21	64. Northwestern State 36-21
15. **Oklahoma** (5) 50-18	65. Nebraska 27-27
16. **Clemson** (10) 45-25	66. Georgia Southern 34-24
17. Georgia Tech (18) 47-15	67. Middle Tenn. State 35-23
18. **Florida State** (6) 48-20	68. Washington 28-28
19. Auburn (19) 43-21	69. Hawaii 35-28
20. Texas A&M (23) 43-21	70. Michigan 35-22
21. College of Charleston 44-19	71. Mississippi State 23-33
22. Louisiana State 41-22	72. Samford 31-25
23. Oregon (25) 40-24	73. South Alabama 32-27
24. North Carolina 38-22	74. UC Riverside 32-23
25. Washington State (24) 37-22	75. Missouri 29-26
26. Connecticut 48-16	76. James Madison 30-23
27. Mississippi 39-24	77. Fresno State 38-25
28. Oregon State 32-24	78. Central Florida 33-22
29. Arizona 34-24	79. East Carolina 32-27
30. Rice (21) 40-23	80. Michigan State 34-19
31. Citadel 43-22	81. Charlotte 39-17
32. Kentucky 31-25	82. Illinois State 32-24
33. San Diego 37-22	83. Duke 29-27
34. Baylor 36-24	84. Houston 25-32
35. Virginia Tech (20) 40-22	85. Radford 29-26
36. Florida Atlantic 37-24	86. Jacksonville State 32-26
37. Stanford 31-25	87. Manhattan 31-20
38. Western Kentucky 35-23	88. Tulane 32-24
39. UC Irvine (22) 39-21	89. Minnesota 32-30
40. Louisiana-Lafayette 38-22	90. VMI 33-22
41. Kansas State 37-22	91. Stephen F. Austin 34-20
42. Florida Gulf Coast 38-20	92. Evansville 32-27
43. California 29-25	93. South Florida 26-32
44. St. John's 43-20	94. Portland 34-18
45. Tennessee 30-26	95. Long Beach State 23-32
46. Boston College 30-28	96. Oklahoma State 29-26
47. Elon 38-24	97. Arkansas State 30-28
48. Liberty 42-19	98. Winthrop 27-30
49. Texas State 38-22	99. Ohio State 28-23
50. New Mexico 38-22	100. UNC Wilmington 33-27

Mountain West Conference, winning the conference championship all five years it has been a member. But before this spring, the Frogs had yet to prove themselves as bona fide contenders for the national title, having never broken through to the CWS. The Frogs had a breakthrough this year with a hard-fought super regional victory at Texas that sent them to Omaha. And they stuck around longer than most people would have expected.

ALL-AMERICA TEAM

FIRST TEAM

POS.	NAME	YEAR	AVG	OBP	SLG	AB	R	H	HR	RBI	BB	SO	SB
C	Yasmani Grandal, Miami	Jr.	.401	.527	.721	222	56	89	15	60	57	35	1
1B	Hunter Morris, Auburn	Jr.	.386	.455	.743	272	66	105	23	76	26	50	6
2B	Zack MacPhee, Arizona State	So.	.394	.491	.679	221	66	87	9	64	40	38	19
3B	Anthony Rendon, Rice	So.	.394	.530	.801	226	83	89	26	85	65	22	14
SS	Christian Colon, Cal State Fullerton	Jr.	.358	.447	.631	268	73	96	17	68	34	18	13
OF	Jeremy Baltz, St. John's	Fr.	.396	.479	.771	240	64	95	24	85	28	44	6
OF	Michael Choice, Texas-Arlington	Jr.	.383	.568	.704	196	67	75	16	59	76	54	12
OF	Taylor Dugas, Alabama	So.	.395	.525	.523	243	70	96	2	37	59	21	19
DH	Chris Duffy, Central Florida	Sr.	.447	.539	.850	246	54	92	21	81	33	35	3
UT	Mike McGee, Florida State	Jr.	.328	.443	.584	238	58	78	15	68	44	50	5

POS.	NAME	YEAR	W	L	ERA	G	CG	SV	IP	H	BB	SO	AVG
SP	Seth Blair, Arizona State	Jr.	12	0	3.35	17	0	0	102	105	24	104	.269
SP	Barret Loux, Texas A&M	Jr.	11	2	2.83	17	1	0	105	78	34	136	.202
SP	Drew Pomeranz, Mississippi	Jr.	9	2	2.24	16	0	0	101	71	49	139	.195
SP	Chris Sale, Florida Gulf Coast	Jr.	11	0	2.01	17	2	2	103	83	14	146	.218
RP	Chance Ruffin, Texas	Jr.	6	1	1.11	37	0	14	63	42	19	97	.180
UT	Mike McGee, Florida State	Jr.	4	0	1.37	18	0	12	26	11	16	33	.125

SECOND TEAM

POS.	NAME	YEAR	AVG	OBP	SLG	AB	R	H	HR	RBI	BB	SO	SB
C	Micah Gibbs, Louisiana State	Jr.	.388	.458	.592	245	47	95	10	60	29	31	7
1B	Ricky Oropesa, Southern California	So.	.353	.434	.711	235	53	83	20	67	33	51	7
2B	Ryan Wright, Louisville	So.	.366	.413	.638	254	61	93	16	80	20	26	10
3B	Garrett Buechele, Oklahoma	So.	.371	.452	.645	248	54	92	16	64	19	45	3
SS	Jedd Gyorko, West Virginia	Jr.	.381	.472	.750	236	71	90	19	57	43	24	1
OF	Gary Brown, Cal State Fullerton	Jr.	.438	.485	.695	210	63	92	6	41	9	12	32
OF	Tyler Holt, Florida State	Jr.	.352	.468	.628	247	82	87	12	46	56	47	30
OF	Kyle Parker, Clemson	Jr.	.353	.481	.672	235	82	83	20	64	53	55	4
DH	Zack Cox, Arkansas	Jr.	.429	.505	.609	238	67	102	9	48	34	37	11
UT	Kolbrin Vitek, Ball State	Jr.	.361	.445	.691	233	73	84	17	68	33	36	16

POS.	NAME	YEAR	W	L	ERA	G	CG	SV	IP	H	BB	SO	AVG
SP	Trevor Bauer, UCLA	So.	10	3	3.02	16	1	0	116	111	37	141	.252
SP	Danny Hultzen, Virginia	So.	10	1	2.83	15	1	0	99	69	23	114	.192
SP	Taylor Jungmann, Texas	So.	8	3	2.03	17	1	0	120	88	41	129	.209
SP	Matt Purke, Texas Christian	Fr.	14	0	3.23	18	1	0	103	84	28	133	.219
RP	John Stilson, Texas A&M	So.	9	1	0.80	33	0	10	79	51	23	114	.181
UT	Kolbrin Vitek, Ball State	Jr.	3	4	3.28	13	1	3	80	76	20	60	.252

THIRD TEAM

POS.	NAME	YEAR	AVG	OBP	SLG	AB	R	H	HR	RBI	BB	SO	SB
C	C.J. Cron, Utah	So.	.431	.487	.817	197	55	85	20	81	17	23	0
1B	Paul Hoilman, East Tenn. State	Jr.	.421	.526	.860	235	79	99	25	84	51	41	1
2B	Garrett Wittels, Florida International	So.	.413	.463	.541	242	47	100	2	60	22	19	4
3B	Phil Wunderlich, Louisville	Jr.	.355	.434	.691	256	54	91	21	62	21	18	12
SS	Derek Dietrich, Georgia Tech	Jr.	.350	.457	.650	240	68	84	17	61	28	37	8
OF	Alex Dickerson, Indiana	So.	.419	.472	.805	236	62	99	24	75	20	35	3
OF	Rico Noel, Coastal Carolina	Jr.	.349	.466	.592	238	83	83	12	63	41	43	56
OF	Nate Roberts, High Point	Jr.	.416	.573	.746	209	88	87	19	69	53	35	36
DH	A.J. Kirby-Jones, Tennessee Tech	Jr.	.388	.531	.859	206	64	80	26	71	58	53	0
UT	Brett Eibner, Arkansas	Jr.	.333	.446	.718	216	66	72	22	71	39	55	3

POS.	NAME	YEAR	W	L	ERA	G	CG	SV	IP	H	BB	SO	AVG
SP	Kyle Blair, San Diego	Jr.	8	4	2.84	15	2	0	98	79	28	126	.218
SP	Gerrit Cole, UCLA	So.	10	3	3.25	17	0	0	108	76	49	138	.195
SP	Noe Ramirez, Cal State Fullerton	So.	12	1	2.54	16	2	0	106	92	19	119	.229
SP	Asher Wojciechowski, The Citadel	Jr.	12	3	3.58	17	3	0	126	111	32	155	.233
RP	Neil Holland, Louisville	Jr.	8	1	2.08	29	0	17	56	30	16	59	.160
UT	Brett Eibner, Arkansas	Jr.	3	5	4.34	15	0	1	58	65	11	56	.273

"It elevates our program in every fashion," Schlossnagle said. "To host a regional again, you win a conference championship, regular-season tournament, regional at home, and then go to the University of Texas in that environment and win. We've been talking for seven years about what we're going to do at TCU, what we can do, and now we've proven that we can do that. We still have something to strive for, which is to win the whole thing."

CWS NOTES

■ South Carolina's championship formula was defense and pitching. The Gamecocks led all teams with a .979 fielding percentage in Omaha and seven double plays. And South Carolina's pitching staff posted a 2.15 ERA with 57 strikeouts and 12 walks while holding opponents to a .191 batting average. The Gamecocks allowed four runs or fewer in all seven of their CWS games. Their team ERA is the lowest by a national champion since Texas posted a 1.40 ERA in 2005, and it is the second-lowest since 1996. And South Carolina's bullpen went 3-0, 1.33 with 21 strikeouts and one walk over 20 exceptional innings.

■ The final game of the CWS drew the biggest crowd of the event: 24,390. The total attendance (330,922) ranks second all-time, but the average attendance was down markedly from a year ago—from 22,405 to 20,683. Weather played a part in the dip; storms forced Game Four to be postponed as part of the first CWS tripleheader in 30 years. That game drew just 14,198 fans, but that was still better than both "if necessary" games to decide the bracket championships the following Saturday. The UCLA-TCU game that day drew 10,907—the smallest CWS crowd since 1991—and the Clemson-South Carolina game drew just 12,593.

■ South Carolina center fielder **Jackie Bradley Jr.** was named the Most Outstanding Player of the 2010 CWS. Though his 22-game hitting streak was snapped in the final game against UCLA, Bradley hit .345 in Omaha with a Series-high nine RBIs. He also kept South Carolina's season alive with a two-out, two-strike, game-tying RBI single in the 12th inning of an elimination game against Oklahoma."

OTHER TOP STORIES FROM 2010

■ Florida International infielder **Garrett Wittels** entered the season as a virtual unknown, having hit .246 in 118 at-bats as a freshman in 2009. By the end of the spring, he was arguably the best-known player in college baseball. Wittels captured the nation's imagination by hitting safely in 56 consecutive games, the second-longest streak in Division I history. His streak was still active when FIU's season came to an end in the Coral Gables Regional, so Wittels will continue his pursuit of former Oklahoma State star **Robin Ventura's** record 58-game hitting streak in 2011. Ventura set his mark in 1987; the overall NCAA record is 60 straight games by Damian Costantino of Division III Salve Regina (R.I.).

■ Perhaps the only college player with more mainstream name recognition than Wittels in 2010 was **Bryce Harper**, the phenom who appeared as a 15-year-old on the cover of Sports Illustrated. Harper lived up to the gargantuan hype in his only season in college baseball. After taking his GED and forgoing his final two years of high school eligiblity, Harper enrolled at JC of Southern Nevada and proceeded to obliterate the wood-bat Scenic West Athletic Conference's single-season home run record. He finished with 31 long balls, 98 RBIs and a .443 average, on his way to the Golden Spikes Award. The Nationals drafted him No. 1 overall in June.

■ The struggling economy took a toll on college baseball. A year after Vermont and Northern Iowa folded their programs, Duquesne followed suit after the 2010 season. But the college

Jackie Bradley Jr. took the CWS MOP award

ANDREW WOOLLEY

baseball world was shocked in September when California announced that it will eliminate its 108-year-old baseball program after the 2011 season.

"It's shocking—that's the perfect word for it. It is shocking," Cal coach **David Esquer** said the day of the announcement. "It's a big statement—it's a Pac-10 school that decided not to have baseball. That's saying something. We think we're the strongest conference in America as far as baseball, and our track record with national championships would probably prove that."

Though they play the worst facility in the Pac-10—a stadium without lights—the Golden Bears went to regionals in 2008 and 2010, and they return a strong core of talent for 2011, bolstered by the nation's NO. 11 recruiting class.

■ Fans can expect games to take much less time in 2011. In July, the NCAA Baseball Rules Committee voted to mandate the use of a timing device and enforce a 20-second limit between pitches and a 90-second limit between innings in all regular-season and postseason games in every conference.

The previous summer, the rules committee voted to change bat standards in an effort to make the metal bats more "wood-like." That change will also go into effect in 2011, but coaches got a taste of the new bats in fall ball. Almost across the board, they reported the bats to be much less potent, and many intrasquad scrimmages were far quicker than usual. Coaches expect offense to be down dramatically in 2011, and the pace of play figures to quicken accordingly.

■ For the second straight year, the NCAA's "no agent" rule made headlines. Former Oklahoma State lefty **Andy Oliver** successfully challenged the rule in court in 2009, but when he settled the case that fall, the rule remained intact. Over the winter, Kentucky lefthander **James Paxton**—an unsigned supplemental first-round pick as a junior in 2009—refused to meet with NCAA investigators regarding a possible violation of the "no agent" rule during his negotiations with the Blue Jays. Paxton chose to leave Kentucky and play in an independent league rather than surrender his due process rights (as attorney **Richard Johnson** framed it) and meet with the NCAA.

REGIONALS

JUNE 4-7
64 teams, 16 four-team, double-elimination tournaments. Winners advance to super regionals.

TEMPE, ARIZ.
Host: Arizona State (No. 1 national seed).
Participants: No. 1 Arizona State (47-8), No. 2 San Diego (36-20), No. 3 Hawaii (33-26), No. 4 Wisconsin-Milwaukee (33-24).
Champion: Arizona State (3-0).
Runner-Up: Hawaii (2-2).
Outstanding Player: Kole Calhoun, 1b, Arizona State.

FAYETTEVILLE, ARK.
Host: Arkansas
Participants: No. 1 Arkansas (40-18), No. 2 Washington State (34-20), No. 3 Kansas State (36-20), No. 4 Grambling State (22-30).
Champion: Arkansas (3-1).
Runner-Up: Washington State (3-2).
Outstanding Player: Collin Kuhn, of, Arkansas.

AUBURN, ALA.
Host: Auburn
Participants: No. 1 Auburn (40-19), No. 2 Clemson (38-21), No. 3 Southern Mississippi (35-22), No. 4 Jacksonville State (32-24)
Champion: Clemson (3-1).
Runner-Up: Auburn (3-2).
Outstanding Player: John Hinson, 3b, Clemson.

ATLANTA
Host: Georgia Tech (No. 8 national seed).
Participants: No. 1 Georgia Tech (45-13), No. 2 Alabama (37-22), No. 3 Elon (38-22), No. 4 Mercer (37-22).
Champion: Alabama (4-1).
Runner-Up: Georgia Tech (2-2).
Outstanding Player: Nathan Kilcrease, rhp, Alabama.

CHARLOTTESVILLE, VA.
Host: Virginia (No. 5 national seed).
Participants: No. 1 Virginia (47-11), No. 2 Mississippi (38-22), No. 3 St. John's (40-18), No. 4 Virginia Commonwealth (34-24-1).
Champion: Virginia (3-1).
Runner-Up: St. John's (3-2).
Outstanding Player: Jeremy Baltz, of, St. John's.

NORMAN, OKLA.
Host: Oklahoma.
Participants: No. 1 Oklahoma (44-15), No. 2 California (29-23), No. 3 North Carolina (36-20), No. 4 Oral Roberts (35-25).
Champion: Oklahoma (3-0).
Runner-Up: North Carolina (2-2).
Outstanding Player: Bobby Shore, rhp, Oklahoma.

COLUMBIA, S.C.
Host: South Carolina.
Participants: No. 1 South Carolina (43-15), No. 2 Virginia Tech (38-20), No. 3 The

LARRY GOREN

Trevor Bauer

Citadel (42-20), No. 4 Bucknell (25-33).
Champion: South Carolina (3-0).
Runner-Up: Virginia Tech (2-2).
Outstanding Player: Adrian Morales, 3b, South Carolina.

MYRTLE BEACH, S.C.
Host: North Carolina (No. 4 national seed).
Participants: No. 1 Coastal Carolina (51-7), No. 2 College of Charleston (42-17), No. 3 North Carolina State (38-22), No. 4 Stony Brook (29-25).
Champion: Coastal Carolina (4-1).
Runner-Up: College of Charleston (2-2).
Outstanding Player: Rico Noel, of, Coastal Carolina.

AUSTIN
Host: Texas (No. 2 national seed).
Participants: No. 1 Texas (46-11), No. 2 Rice (38-21), No. 3 Louisiana-Lafayette (37-20), No. 4 Rider (36-21).
Champion: Texas (3-0).
Runner-Up: Rice (2-2).
Outstanding Player: Anthony Rendon, 3b, Rice.

FORT WORTH
Host: Texas Christian.
Participants: No. 1 Texas Christian (46-11), No. 2 Baylor (34-22), No. 3 Arizona (33-22), No. 4 Lamar (35-24).
Champion: Texas Christian (3-0).
Runner-Up: Baylor (2-2).
Outstanding Player: Taylor Featherston, ss, Texas Christian.

NORWICH, CONN.
Host: Connecticut.
Participants: No. 1 Florida State (42-17), No. 2 Connecticut (47-14), No. 3 Oregon (38-22), No. 4 Central Connecticut State (33-21).
Champion: Florida State (3-0).
Runner-Up: Oregon (2-2).
Outstanding Player: Sherman Johnson, 3b, Florida State.

LOUISVILLE
Host: Louisville (No. 7 national seed).
Participants: No. 1 Louisville (48-12), No. 2 Vanderbilt (41-17), No. 3 Illinois State (31-22), No. 4 Saint Louis (33-27)
Champion: Vanderbilt (4-1).
Runner-Up: Louisville (2-2).
Outstanding Player: Richie Goodenow, lhp, Vanderbilt.

LOS ANGELES
Host: UCLA (No. 6 national seed).

Participants: No. 1 UCLA (43-13), No. 2 Louisiana State (40-20), No. 3 UC Irvine (37-19), No. 4 Kent State (39-23)
Champion: UCLA (3-0).
Runner-Up: UC Irvine (2-2).
Outstanding Player: Trevor Bauer, rhp, UCLA.

FULLERTON, CALIF.
Host: Cal State Fullerton.
Participants: No. 1 Cal State Fullerton (41-15), No. 2 Stanford (31-23), No. 3 New Mexico (37-20), No. 4 Minnesota (30-28).
Champion: Cal State Fullerton (4-1).
Runner-Up: Minnesota (2-2).
Outstanding Player: Corey Jones, 2b, Cal State Fullerton.

CORAL GABLES, FLA.
Host: Miami.
Participants: No. 1 Miami (40-17), No. 2 Texas A&M (40-19-1), No. 3 Florida International (36-23), No. 4 Dartmouth (26-17)
Champion: Miami (3-1).
Runner-Up: Texas A&M (3-2)
Outstanding Player: Scott Lawson, 1b, Miami.

GAINESVILLE, FLA.
Host: Florida (No. 3 national seed).
Participants: No. 1 Florida (42-15), No. 2 Florida Atlantic (35-22), No. 3 Oregon State (31-22), Bethune-Cookman (35-20).
Champion: Florida (3-0).
Runner-Up: Florida Atlantic (2-2).
Outstanding Player: Brian Johnson, lhp/dh, Florida.

SUPER REGIONALS

JUNE 11-14
16 teams, eight best-of-three series. Winners advance to College World Series.

ARKANSAS AT ARIZONA STATE
Site: Tempe, Ariz.
Arizona State wins 2-0, advances to CWS.

ALABAMA AT CLEMSON
Site: Clemson, S.C.
Clemson wins 2-1, advances to CWS.

OKLAHOMA AT VIRGINIA
Site: Charlottesville, Va.
Oklahoma wins 2-1, advances to CWS.

SOUTH CAROLINA AT COASTAL CAROLINA
Site: Myrtle Beach, S.C.
South Carolina wins 2-0, advances to CWS.

TEXAS CHRISTIAN AT TEXAS
Site: Austin.
Texas Christian wins 2-1, advances to CWS.

VANDERBILT AT FLORIDA STATE
Site: Tallahassee, Fla.
Florida State wins 2-1, advances to CWS.

CAL STATE FULLERTON AT UCLA
Site: Los Angeles.
UCLA wins 2-1, advances to CWS.

MIAMI AT FLORIDA
Site: Gainesville, Fla.
Florida wins 2-0, advances to CWS.

Rendon rakes his way to top honor

BY AARON FITT

For the first time in a decade, Baseball America's College Player of the Year is an underclassman. In the 30-year history of the award, underclassmen won just three times before this year, and all three were special talents who went on to long, successful big league careers: sophomores Robin Ventura of Oklahoma State (1987), John Olerud of Washington State (1988) and Mark Teixeira of Georgia Tech (2000).

Rice sophomore third baseman Anthony Rendon fits the same mold. The early favorite to be drafted No. 1 overall in 2011, Rendon put up numbers that match his prodigious talent, hitting .394/.530/.801 with 26 home runs and 85 RBIs. That power output is even more impressive given how seldom he got good pitches to hit, as evidenced by his 65 walks and 22 strikeouts in 226 at-bats. If that weren't enough, Rendon also stole 14 bases in 18 tries and posted a .973 fielding percentage at the hot corner, where he committed just five errors all season.

ANDREW WOOLLEY

Anthony Rendon

We asked those who coached with and against Rendon, as well as Rendon himself, to try to put his season and his talent into perspective.

Rice coach Wayne Graham: "I think you get a little comfortable sometimes with how good a guy is; you expect him to do it every time. He does some phenomenal things. The thing that in my mind stood out is this year, defensively, he was absolutely wonderful. He had five errors the whole year, and that doesn't tell the whole story—he made a lot of sensational plays. And the bat is obvious.

"He's got remarkable wrist action. I remember the first time he hit on our field, I'd seen him hit a little in high school and knew he could hit. He started the second round of batting practice, I said to our coaches, 'You want to see Hank Aaron's wrists? There they are.' I said, 'Don't mess with him.' And we haven't. Him and Teixeira are the two best hitters I've seen in college baseball. (Lance) Berkman is right up there too, but the bat was different in those days.

"I've got to get him to Omaha next year. People in Omaha deserve to see him play."

East Carolina coach Billy Godwin: "He's a baseball player, No. 1. If you look at him, you're not going to be overwhelmingly impressed physically, but he plays the game with as much feel as anybody I've ever seen. Just his confidence at the plate . . . I've been as impressed with him defensively as I have been offensively. He made two plays against us that were as good as I've seen in college baseball.

Anthony Rendon: "I didn't think I'd be able to do it back-to-back years—even better improve my numbers from last year. Last year everything just clicked, and this year it felt like everything clicked again. I got in that groove and kept seeing the ball well the last month of the season.

PREVIOUS WINNERS

1981: Mike Sodders, 3b, Arizona State
1982: Jeff Ledbetter, of/lhp, Florida State
1983: Dave Magadan, 1b, Alabama
1984: Oddibe McDowell, of, Arizona State
1985: Pete Incaviglia, of, Oklahoma State
1986: Casey Close, of, Michigan
1987: Robin Ventura, 3b, Oklahoma State
1988: John Olerund, 1b/lhp, Washington St.
1989: Ben McDonald, rhp, Louisiana State
1990: Mike Kelly, of, Arizona State

1991: David McCarthy, 1b, Stanford
1992: Phil Nevin, 3b, Cal State Fullerton
1993: Brooks Kieschnick, dh/rhp, Texas
1994: Jason Varitek, c, Georgia Tech
1995: Todd Helton, 1b/lhp, Tennessee
1996: Kris Benson, rhp, Clemson
1997: J.D. Drew, of, Florida State
1998: Jeff Austin, rhp, Stanford
1999: Jason Jennings, rhp, Baylor
2000: Mark Teixeira, 3b, Georgia Tech

2001: Mark Prior, rhp, Southern California
2002: Khalil Greene, ss, Clemson
2003: Rickie Weeks, 2b, Southern
2004: Jered Weaver, rhp, Long Beach State
2005: Alex Gordon, 3b, Nebraska
2006: Andrew Miller, lhp, North Carolina
2007: David Price, lhp, Vanderbilt
2008: Buster Posey, c/rhp, Florida State
2009: Stephen Strasburg, rhp, San Diego State

Tanner's trail leads to first CWS title

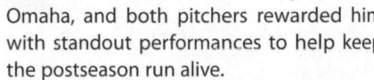

COACH OF THE YEAR

Even at the end, as Ray Tanner and his players sat draped in national championship hats and T-shirts answering questions from media, Tanner insisted that his scrappy bunch was not a juggernaut.

"Even after tonight we're not a great team," the South Carolina's coach said an hour or so after his Gamecocks had been crowned national champions, "but we've been a really, really special baseball team that approached it the right way and found a way to win and never gave in, never gave up. And it was real. It wasn't just talk. And when we did have some adversity, they flushed it rather quickly and got back up."

South Carolina's even keel starts at the top. Tanner's steadying, calming presence as well as his magic touch with lineup decisions were integral to his team's title run. It's no surprise, then, that Tanner is Baseball America's 2010 College Coach of the Year. Tanner, who also won the award in 2000, joins Augie Garrido, Gene Stephenson, Skip Bertman and Dave Snow as two-time winners.

Ray Tanner

TONY FARLOW

"We know we're good, but we're never really thinking, 'Oh, we're so good,' " said South Carolina outfielder Jackie Bradley Jr., the Most Outstanding Player of the College World Series. "Then when we get down in certain games, we're like, 'We're not that bad.' We're kind of a happy medium team, and I think (Tanner's) presence in the dugout just means a lot. He's kind of steady."

Scoring runs was a challenge at times for South Carolina in 2010, but Tanner found ways to motivate his hitters. Bradley said he can't help but chuckle sometimes when his coach starts reading players the riot act, but Tanner's style gets players' attention without creating too much tension.

"He really gets everything out of you," Bradley said.

During South Carolina's remarkable run to the title, Tanner showed a masterful ability to put his players in position to succeed. He heeded the advice of pitching coach Scott Calvi and rode the hot hand of lefthanded specialist Michael Roth in Omaha. Roth yielded just one run over 14 innings in his first two starts of the season. He installed freshman Evan Marzilli atop the lineup down the stretch. Marzilli quickly emerged as a catalyst and wound up earning all-CWS honors.

He trusted that ace Blake Cooper (twice) and No. 2 starter Sam Dyson were conditioned enough to bounce back on three days' rest in Omaha, and both pitchers rewarded him with standout performances to help keep the postseason run alive.

He mixed and matched in the bullpen all season, and his bullpen was one of the nation's best. And when his Gamecocks faced adversity, Tanner made sure they were ready for it.

"It doesn't work out for you all the time," Tanner said. "I tell the players all the time, it's a game of percentages. But if you play it the right way and have a good approach, you're going to get yours, too."

PREVIOUS WINNERS

1981: Ron Fraser, Miami	**1990:** Steve Webber, Georgia	**2000:** Ray Tanner, South Carolina
1982: Gene Stephenson, Wichita State	**1991:** Jim Hendry, Creighton	**2001:** Dave Van Horn, Nebraska
1983: Barry Shollenberger, Alabama	**1992:** Andy Lopez, Pepperdine	**2002:** Augie Garrido, Texas
1984: Augie Garrido, Cal State Fullerton	**1993:** Gene Stephenson, Wichita State	**2003:** George Horton, Cal State Fullerton
1985: Ron Polk, Mississippi State	**1994:** Jim Morris, Miami	**2004:** David Perno, Georgia
1986: Skip Bertman, Louisiana State	**1995:** Pat Murphy, Arizona State	**2005:** Rick Jones, Tulane
Dave Snow, Loyola Marymount	**1996:** Skip Bertman, Louisiana State	**2006:** Pat Casey, Oregon State
1987: Mark Marquess, Stanford	**1997:** Jim Wells, Alabama	**2007:** Dave Serrano, UC Irvine
1988: Jim Brock, Arizona State	**1998:** Pat Murphy, Arizona State	**2008:** Mike Fox, North Carolina
1989: Dave Snow, Long Beach State	**1999:** Wayne Graham, Rice	**2009:** Paul Mainieri, Louisiana State

TCU's Purke lives up to top billing

BY AARON FITT

Jim Schlossnagle still remembers the moment his program changed forever: Aug. 17, 2009. It was the deadline for major league teams to sign their drafted players or lose their rights, and the Texas Christian coach was nervously awaiting word from his prized recruit, Matt Purke—the No. 14 overall pick by the Rangers.

"It was 11:04—I'll never forget it," Schlossnagle recalled. "I was waiting on my phone, and then he called and it said 'Purke' on there, and I said, 'All right, here it goes, he signed five minutes ago.'

"He was pretty emotional, because it was a tough thing for him. He said, 'Coach, I just want to know, do you have a roster spot for me? I didn't sign.' I said, 'We'll find one.'

"I called (TCU recruiting coordinator)

Matt Purke

ANDREW WOOLLEY

FRESHMAN OF THE YEAR

Todd Whitting right after—he's the first person I called. He said, 'All right, what'd he sign for?' I said, 'Dude, he's coming to school.'"

Purke is exactly the kind of player who can help a strong program like TCU make the leap to elite status, and that's exactly what he did. The lefthander emerged early on as TCU's ace, and he finished 16-0, 3.02 with 132 strikeouts and 34 walks in 116 innings. He dominated against Texas in the Austin Super Regional to help the Horned Frogs reach the College World Series for the first time, and he shut down Florida State and UCLA to lead TCU to a pair of victories in Omaha.

His 16 wins are tied for the most by a Division I pitcher since 2004 (Arizona State's Mike Leake also did it last year). For meeting or exceeding lofty expectations that accompanied him to TCU, Purke is the 2010 Freshman of the Year.

PREVIOUS WINNERS

1982: Cory Snyder, 3b, Brigham Young
1983: Rafael Palmeiro, of, Mississippi State
1984: Greg Swindell, lhp, Texas
1985: Jack McDowell, rhp, Stanford
1986: Robin Ventura, 3b, Oklahoma State
1987: Paul Carey, of, Stanford
1988: Kirk Dressendorfer, rhp, Texas
1989: Alex Fernandez, rhp, Miami
1990: Jeffrey Hammonds, of, Stanford
1991: Brooks Kieschnick, rhp-dh, Texas
1992: Todd Walker, 2b, Louisiana State
1993: Brett Laxton, rhp, Louisiana State
1994: R.A. Dickey, rhp, Tennessee
1995: Kyle Peterson, rhp, Stanford
1996: Pat Burrell, 3b, Miami
1997: Brian Roberts, ss, North Carolina
1998: Xavier Nady, 2b, California
1999: James Jurries, 2b, Tulane
2000: Kevin Howard, 3b, Miami
2001: Michael Aubrey, of/lhp, Texas
2002: Stephen Drew, ss, Florida State
2003: Ryan Braun, ss, Miami
2004: Wade LeBlanc, lhp, Alabama
2005: Joe Savery, lhp, Rice
2006: Pedro Alvarez, 3b, Vanderbilt
2007: Dustin Ackley, 1b, North Carolina
2008: Chris Hernandez, lhp, Miami
2009: Anthony Rendon, 3b, Rice

FRESHMAN ALL-AMERICA TEAMS

FIRST TEAM

POS. PLAYER, SCHOOL	AVG	OBP	SLG	AB	R	H	HR	RBI	SB
C Mike Zunino, Florida	.269	.317	.480	171	31	46	9	41	8
1B Barrett Barnes, Texas Tech	.341	.465	.641	217	71	74	14	53	12
2B Anthony Gomez, Vanderbilt	.379	.418	.453	214	41	81	2	30	9
3B Kenny Diekroeger, Stanford	.356	.391	.491	216	42	77	5	41	1
SS Nolan Fontana, Florida	.283	.434	.415	212	54	60	3	23	11
OF Jeremy Baltz, St. John's	.396	.479	.771	240	64	95	24	85	6
OF Logan Vick, Baylor	.329	.473	.553	228	59	75	10	27	11
OF Max White, Oklahoma	.307	.360	.604	202	48	62	15	43	7
DH Austin Maddox, Florida	.332	.362	.591	259	48	86	17	71	0
UT Brian Johnson, Florida	.405	.458	.631	84	13	34	4	21	0

	W	L	ERA	G	SV	IP	H	BB	SO	AVG
SP Kurt Heyer, Arizona	7	4	3.26	17	0	102	97	29	109	.255
SP Matt Purke, Texas Christian	15	0	3.03	19	0	110	88	32	140	.216
SP Hudson Randall, Florida	8	3	2.95	19	0	94.2	98	19	68	.266
SP Michael Wacha, Texas A&M	9	2	2.90	25	1	106	86	22	97	.218
RP Matt Price, South Carolina	3	1	2.54	27	10	46	30	18	68	.182
UT Brian Johnson, Florida	6	4	3.97	15	0	70	82	14	48	.289

SECOND TEAM

C-Kevin Plawecki, Purdue (.337-8-53). **1B-**Christian Walker, South Carolina (.320-8-47). **2B-**Corey Spangenberg, VMI (.370-11-49). **3B-**Ryan Dalton, Texas-San Antonio (.305-17-51). **SS-**Deven Marrero, Arizona State (.388-6-41). **OF-**Beau Amaral, UCLA (.360-4-30); Jabari Henry, Florida International (.315-12-51); Cohl Walla, Texas (.316-8-40, 14 SB). **DH-**Dan Gulbransen, Jacksonville (.391-8-46). **UT-**Marcus Stroman, Duke (.265-2-20; 6-4, 5.31, 3 SV). **SP-**Dylan Floro, Cal State Fullerton (7-2, 3.26, 91 IP/69 SO); Kyle Hansen, St. John's (8-3, 3.71, 95 IP/85 SO); Justin Jones, California (10-6, 4.22, 98 IP/74 SO); Corey Roberts, Charlotte (6-3, 3.48, 85 IP/75 SO). **RP-**Brett Huber, Mississippi (2-0, 3.54, 12 SV, 48 IP/54 SO).

Minimum 120 plate appearances, 3.0 plate appearances per team game

BATTING

BATTING AVERAGE

RANK. NAME, TEAM	YEAR	G	AB	H	AVG
1. Justin Howard, New Mexico	Sr.	59	261	119	.456
2. Jace Brinkerhoff, Utah Valley	Sr.	59	259	118	.456
3. Chad Oberacker, Tennessee Tech	Jr.	56	239	108	.452
4. Chris Duffy, Central Florida	Sr.	55	206	92	.447
5. Matt Szczur, Villanova	Jr.	39	174	77	.443
6. Effrey Valdez, New York Tech	Sr.	57	219	96	.438
7. Ryan Soares, George Mason	Sr.	48	194	85	.438
8. Gary Brown, Cal State Fullerton	Jr.	50	210	92	.438
9. Rob Segedin, Tulane	So.	55	212	92	.434
10. Joe Van Meter, Va. Commonwealth	Jr.	61	249	108	.434
11. Joe Leonard, Pittsburgh	Jr.	55	240	104	.433
12. D.J. Leonard, Bethune-Cookman	Jr.	45	155	67	.432
13. J.D. Ashbrook, Morehead State	Sr.	49	190	82	.432
14. C.J. Cron, Utah	So.	49	197	85	.431
15. Matt Prokopowicz, Hofstra	Sr.	43	174	75	.431
16. Tom Zebroski, George Washington	Sr.	54	240	103	.429
17. Zack Cox, Arkansas	So.	59	238	102	.429
18. Shane Brown, Central Florida	Sr.	52	208	89	.428
19. Garrett Bivone, Texas-Pan American	Sr.	53	201	86	.428
20. Sean Allaire, Central Connecticut State	Sr.	56	235	100	.426
21. Jason Summers, Western Illinois	Sr.	48	182	77	.423
22. Jon Berti, Bowling Green State	So.	54	220	93	.423
23. Paul Hoilman, East Tennessee State	Jr.	60	235	99	.421
24. Alex Dickerson, Indiana	So.	55	236	99	.419
25. Tom Coulombe, Rhode Island	Jr.	57	208	87	.418
26. Pat Epps, Central Connecticut State	Jr.	56	220	92	.418
27. Chris Bangi, Campbell	Sr.	52	187	78	.417
28. Nate Roberts, High Point	Jr.	59	209	87	.416
29. Johnathan Ross, Savannah State	Sr.	47	178	74	.416
30. Nick Martini, Kansas State	So.	59	231	96	.416
31. Keith Werman, Virginia	So.	51	152	63	.414
32. Phil Cerreto, Longwood	Sr.	48	186	77	.414
Mark Hill, George Mason	Sr.	50	186	77	.414
34. Garrett Wittels, Florida International	So.	56	242	100	.413
35. Kevin Quaranto, Siena	Jr.	54	206	85	.413
36. Tom Clayton, Youngstown State	Sr.	50	170	70	.412
Drew Lee, Morehead State	Sr.	50	204	84	.412
Kevin Tokarski, Illinois State	So.	53	204	84	.412
39. Chris Engell, San Diego	Sr.	54	197	81	.411
40. Derrick Shaw, Florida A&M	So.	42	163	67	.411
41. Casey Havers, Longwood	Sr.	48	190	78	.411
42. Steve Nyisztor, Rutgers	Fr.	56	229	94	.410
43. Matt Fenster, Lafayette	Jr.	36	122	50	.410
44. Kevin Medrano, Missouri State	So.	55	210	86	.410
45. Mikel Alvarez, Florida Gulf Coast	Jr.	58	242	99	.409
Matt Perry, Holy Cross	Sr.	52	198	81	.409
47. Cotez Cole, Jackson State	Sr.	50	164	67	.409
48. Chris Benson, Utah Valley	Jr.	59	262	107	.408
49. Andrew Heck, Duquesne	Jr.	54	223	91	.408
Brandon Williams, Georgia State	So.	57	223	91	.408
51. Wes Cunningham, Murray State	Sr.	57	233	95	.408
52. John Shultz, Pittsburgh	Jr.	56	225	91	.404
53. Wes Hobson, Appalachian State	Sr.	57	235	95	.404
54. James Teas, Central Michigan	Sr.	52	193	78	.404
55. Curtis Wagner, Santa Clara	Jr.	44	161	65	.404
56. Dan Williams, Pennsylvania	Jr.	41	159	64	.403
57. Brant Jones, Longwood	Jr.	47	184	74	.402
58. Rob Lind, Georgia State	Jr.	56	194	78	.402
59. Chris Juarez, New Mexico	Sr.	58	204	82	.402
60. Robert Griffith, Sacred Heart	So.	48	167	67	.401
61. Yasmani Grandal, Miami	Jr.	62	222	89	.401
62. Brendan Norton, La Salle	So.	52	200	80	.400
Aaron Senne, Missouri	Jr.	55	210	84	.400
64. John Lee, South Dakota State	Sr.	59	228	91	.399
65. Blake McDade, Middle Tenn. State	Sr.	58	223	89	.399
66. Tom Grandieri, Pennsylvania	Sr.	41	178	71	.399
67. Casey Jones, Southeast Missouri State	Jr.	50	206	82	.398
68. Gaunlett Eldemire, Ohio	Jr.	50	201	80	.398
69. Jeff Simpson, Stetson	Jr.	53	181	72	.398
70. Ryan Enos, Dallas Baptist	Sr.	55	234	93	.397
71. Steve McQuail, Canisius	Jr.	60	224	89	.397
72. Ty Nelson, Tennessee-Martin	Sr.	55	212	84	.396
Cameron Nelson, Campbell	Jr.	51	159	63	.396
74. Jeremy Baltz, St. John's	Fr.	63	240	95	.396
75. Chad Zurcher, Memphis	So.	55	230	91	.396
76. Taylor Dugas, Alabama	So.	67	243	96	.395
77. Brodie Greene, Texas A&M	Sr.	65	266	105	.395
78. Cory Brownsten, Pittsburgh	Sr.	49	185	73	.395
79. Ben Yoder, Bucknell	Sr.	49	180	71	.394
80. Jerrud Sabourin, Indiana	Jr.	55	241	95	.394
81. Anthony Rendon, Rice	So.	63	226	89	.394
82. Brian Heere, Kansas	Jr.	59	234	92	.393
Riccio Torrez, Arizona State	So.	59	234	92	.393
84. Mark Micowski, Georgia State	Jr.	54	232	91	.392
85. Billy Stitz, South Dakota State	Jr.	60	283	111	.392
86. Rodney Warren, Alcorn State	Jr.	49	176	69	.392
87. Jarod Berggren, Northern Colorado	So.	54	222	87	.392
88. Michael Langley, Mercer	Jr.	62	263	103	.392
89. Joel Blake, South Dakota State	Jr.	60	253	99	.391
Chris Dudics, Toledo	Jr.	56	253	99	.391
91. Dan Gulbransen, Jacksonville	Fr.	54	202	79	.391
Mark Onorati, Manhattan	Jr.	49	202	79	.391
93. Joe Goldenberg, Southern Utah	Fr.	45	156	61	.391
94. T.J. Berge, Northern Colorado	Jr.	58	220	86	.391
95. Preston Hale, North Florida	Sr.	58	238	93	.391
96. Richard Gonzalez, Va. Commonwealth	Sr.	60	233	91	.391
97. Nick Baligod, Oral Roberts	Jr.	54	210	82	.390
98. Jake Rickenbach, Utah Valley	Jr.	57	251	98	.390
99. Justin Shultz, UC Riverside	Jr.	52	187	73	.390
100. Drew Heid, Gonzaga	Sr.	56	236	92	.390

RICK BATTLE

Villanova two-sport star Matt Szczur

ON-BASE PERCENTAGE

RANK. NAME, TEAM	OBP
1. Nate Roberts, High Point	.573
2. Michael Choice, Texas-Arlington	.568
3. Chris Bangi, Campbell	.548
4. Shane Brown, Central Florida	.541
5. J.D. Ashbrook, Morehead State	.540
6. Chris Duffy, Central Florida	.539
7. Kevin Tokarski, Illinois State	.538
8. Effrey Valdez, New York Tech	.536
9. Curtis Wagner, Santa Clara	.533
10. A.J. Kirby-Jones, Tennessee Tech	.531
11. Anthony Rendon, Rice	.530
12. Kyle Roller, East Carolina	.529
13. Chad Oberacker, Tennessee Tech	.527
14. Mark Hill, George Mason	.527
15. Yasmani Grandal, Miami	.527
16. Paul Hoilman, East Tenn. State	.526
17. Taylor Dugas, Alabama	.525
18. John Shultz, Pittsburgh	.521
19. Matt Prokopowicz, Hofstra	.519
20. Cotez Cole, Jackson State	.519
21. Chad Salem, Manhattan	.519
22. Jace Brinkerhoff, Utah Valley	.518
23. Rob Segedin, Tulane	.516
24. Blake McDade, Middle Tenn. State	.511
25. Jason Summers, Western Illinois	.509
26. Nick Martini, Kansas State	.509
27. Justin Howard, New Mexico	.508
28. Kevin Quaranto, Siena	.508
29. Garrett Bivone, Texas-Pan American	.506
30. Thomas Nichols, Georgia Tech	.506
31. Pat Epps, Central Conn. State	.506
32. Zack Cox, Arkansas	.505
33. Jeff Simpson, Stetson	.504
34. Nick Melino, Nevada	.503
35. Justyn Carter, St. Peter's	.502
36. Frazier Hall, Southern	.500
Dexter Kelley, Savannah State	.500
Jesse Sawyer, South Dakota State	.500
39. Aaron Senne, Missouri	.498
40. Dan Gulbransen, Jacksonville	.498
41. Brendan Norton, La Salle	.498
42. Matt Perry, Holy Cross	.498
43. Kyle Wilson, North Carolina State	.498
44. Johnathan Ross, Savannah State	.498
45. Rich Mascheri, Western Illinois	.497
46. Lynn Lewis, Jackson State	.497
47. Ian Choy, Canisius	.496
48. Gaunlett Eldemire, Ohio	.496
49. Packy Elkins, Belmont	.495
50. Scott Woodward, Coastal Carolina	.495

SLUGGING PERCENTAGE

RANK. NAME, TEAM	SLG
1. Paul Hoilman, East Tenn. State	.860
2. A.J. Kirby-Jones, Tennessee Tech	.859
3. Chris Duffy, Central Florida	.850
4. Wes Cunningham, Murray State	.824
5. C.J. Cron, Utah	.817
6. Dan Paolini, Siena	.816
7. Ryan Soares, George Mason	.809
8. Alex Dickerson, Indiana	.805
9. Anthony Rendon, Rice	.801
10. J.D. Ashbrook, Morehead State	.795
11. Rob Segedin, Tulane	.788
12. Kevin Patterson, Auburn	.782
13. Pat Epps, Central Conn. State	.773
14. Jeremy Baltz, St. John's	.771
15. Steve McQuail, Canisius	.768
16. Drew Lee, Morehead State	.765
17. Jordan Ribera, Fresno State	.761
18. Mac Doyle, Wofford	.755
19. Jedd Gyorko, West Virginia	.750

RANK. NAME, TEAM	
20. Ben Heath, Penn State	.747
21. Nate Roberts, High Point	.746
22. Chace Perkins, New Mexico State	.746
23. Chris Benson, Utah Valley	.744
24. Adam Bryant, Troy	.744
25. Peter O'Brien, Bethune-Cookman	.744
26. Hunter Morris, Auburn	.743
27. Dario Pizzano, Columbia	.741
28. Doug Shribman, Bucknell	.737
29. Robert Maddox, Ohio	.737
30. Sean Allaire, Central Conn. State	.736
31. Jacob Tanis, Mercer	.735
32. Aaron Senne, Missouri	.733
Tom Zebroski, George Washington	.733
34. Kevin Quaranto, Siena	.733
35. Johnathan Ross, Savannah State	.730
36. Seth Furmanek, Oral Roberts	.730
37. B.A. Vollmuth, Southern Miss.	.729
38. Ryan Enos, Dallas Baptist	.726
39. Gaunlett Eldemire, Ohio	.726
40. D.J. Leonard, Bethune-Cookman	.723
41. Yasmani Grandal, Miami	.721
42. Brett Eibner, Arkansas	.718
43. Chad Salem, Manhattan	.717
44. Phil Cerreto, Longwood	.715
45. Ricky Oropesa, Southern California	.711
46. Jace Brinkerhoff, Utah Valley	.710
47. Adam Eaton, Miami (Ohio)	.709
48. Justin Howard, New Mexico	.709
49. Ryan Durrence, Bethune-Cookman	.708
50. Carlos Alonso, Delaware	.708

HOME RUNS

RANK. NAME, TEAM	HR
1. Jordan Ribera, Fresno State	27
2. A.J. Kirby-Jones, Tennessee Tech	26
Dan Paolini, Siena	26
Anthony Rendon, Rice	26
5. Seth Furmanek, Oral Roberts	25
Paul Hoilman, East Tenn. State	25
7. Jeremy Baltz, St. John's	24
Alex Dickerson, Indiana	24
9. Adam Bryant, Troy	23
Hunter Morris, Auburn	23
Mike Olt, Connecticut	23
12. Wes Cunningham, Murray State	22
Brett Eibner, Arkansas	22
Brian Fletcher, Auburn	22
Jacob Tanis, Mercer	22
16. Chris Duffy, Central Florida	21
Matt Leeds, College of Charleston	21
Robert Maddox, Ohio	21
Harold Martinez, Miami	21
John Moreland, Mercer	21
Tony Plagman, Georgia Tech	21
Doug Shribman, Bucknell	21
Luke Stewart, Alabama-Birmingham	21
Phil Wunderlich, Louisville	21
25. C.J. Cron, Utah	20
Steve McQuail, Canisius	20
Justin Miller, Middle Tenn. State	20
Robbie Monday, UNC Wilmington	20
Peter O'Brien, Bethune-Cookman	20
Ricky Oropesa, Southern California	20
Kyle Parker, Clemson	20
Bo Reeder, East Tenn. State	20
Matt Skole, Georgia Tech	20
B.A. Vollmuth, Southern Miss.	20
Nate Woods, Belmont	20
36. Cody Fick, Evansville	19
Matt Gaudet, Louisiana State	19
Jedd Gyorko, West Virginia	19
Ben Heath, Penn State	19
Nate Roberts, High Point	19

Jesse Sawyer, South Dakota State	19
Mickey Wiswall, Boston College	19
43. J.D. Ashbrook, Morehead State	18
Adam Bailey, Nebraska	18
Jordan Ballard, VMI	18
Brian Barnett, Nevada	18
Pat Biserta, Rutgers	18
Danny Brock, Saint Louis	18
Matt Curry, Texas Christian	18
Ryan Ditthardt, Troy	18
Ryan Durrence, Bethune-Cookman	18
Ryan Enos, Dallas Baptist	18
Pat Epps, Central Conn. State	18
Kyle Hardman, Northern Colorado	18
Sean McNaughton, Brigham Young	18
Jordan Owen, Tennessee-Martin	18
Tyler Saladino, Oral Roberts	18
George Springer, Connecticut	18
Shaun VanDriessche, IPFW	18
Tom Zebroski, George Washington	18

RUNS BATTED IN

RANK. NAME, TEAM	RBI
1. Chris Benson, Utah Valley	89
2. Matt Leeds, College of Charleston	88
Jacob Tanis, Mercer	88
4. Jeff Schaus, Clemson	87
5. Wes Cunningham, Murray State	86
6. Jeremy Baltz, St. John's	85
Jace Brinkerhoff, Utah Valley	85
Anthony Rendon, Rice	85
9. Paul Hoilman, East Tenn. State	84
Mike Nemeth, Connecticut	84
11. Eric Cain, South Dakota State	83
12. C.J. Cron, Utah	81
Chris Duffy, Central Florida	81
Anthony Gallas, Kent State	81
Steve McQuail, Canisius	81
16. Jose Iglesias, Coastal Carolina	80
Ryan Wright, Louisville	80
18. Robert Maddox, Ohio	78
Tony Plagman, Georgia Tech	78
Nate Woods, Belmont	78
21. Andrew Ciencin, North Carolina State	77
22. Kyle Blackburn, Georgia Southern	76
Hunter Morris, Auburn	76
Mike Olt, Connecticut	76
Tyler Saladino, Oral Roberts	76
Joe Van Meter, Va. Commonwealth	76
B.A. Vollmuth, Southern Miss.	76
28. Danny Brock, Saint Louis	75
Alex Dickerson, Indiana	75
Mac Doyle, Wofford	75
Brian Fletcher, Auburn	75
John Hinson, Clemson	75
Nick Ramirez, Cal State Fullerton	75
Greg Wallace, Evansville	75
35. Justin Miller, Middle Tenn. State	74
Jake Overstreet, South Alabama	74
37. Sean Allaire, Central Conn. State	73
Pat Epps, Central Conn. State	73
Mike McGee, Florida State	73
Drew Poulk, North Carolina State	73
Jesse Sawyer, South Dakota State	73
Brandon Williams, Georgia State	73
43. Ryan Durrence, Bethune-Cookman	72
Justin Howard, New Mexico	72
Austin Maddox, Florida	72
Jon Myers, Saint Louis	72
47. Brian Barnett, Nevada	71
Brett Eibner, Arkansas	71
Matt Gantner, High Point	71
A.J. Kirby-Jones, Tennessee Tech	71
Joe Leonard, Pittsburgh	71

Ryan Soares, George Mason   71

DOUBLES

RANK. NAME, TEAM	2B
1. Joel Blake, South Dakota State	33
2. Justin Howard, New Mexico	32
3. Ellis Lowe, Campbell	31
4. Chad Oberacker, Tennessee Tech	29
Rob Segedin, Tulane	29
Ryan Soares, George Mason	29
7. Jedd Gyorko, West Virginia	28
Scott Lejeune, Texas Tech	28
Nick Ramirez, Cal State Fullerton	28
10. Steve Domecus, Virginia Tech	27
Adam Duvall, Louisville	27
Jeff Harkensee, Southeastern La.	27
Ben Klafczynski, Kent State	27
Riccio Torrez, Arizona State	27
15. Matt Curry, Texas Christian	26
Tyler Holt, Florida State	26
Cole Rakar, College of Charleston	26
Billy Stitz, South Dakota State	26
19. Shane Brown, Central Florida	25
Jason Esposito, Vanderbilt	25
Max Fulginiti, High Point	25
Matt Gantner, High Point	25
Andrew Heck, Duquesne	25
Goose Kallunki, Utah Valley	25
Mike Kvasnicka, Minnesota	25
Michael Langley, Mercer	25
Barry McDonley, Ark.-Pine Bluff	25
Jacob Tanis, Mercer	25
Kevin Tokarski, Illinois State	25
Chris Walker, Fordham	25
31. Chris Benson, Utah Valley	24
Phil Cerreto, Longwood	24
Mike Dufek, Michigan	24
Mike Freeman, Clemson	24
Anthony Gallas, Kent State	24
Yasmani Grandal, Miami	24
Derek Hamblen, Belmont	24
Paul Hoilman, East Tenn. State	24
Bryan Holaday, Texas Christian	24
Shaun Kort, Nevada	24
Kevin Quaranto, Siena	24
42. Michael Adamson, Southeast Missouri State	23
Jett Bandy, Arizona	23
Garrett Bivone, Texas-Pan American	23
Jace Brinkerhoff, Utah Valley	23
Matt Browning, James Madison	23
Thomas Carroll, Mercer	23
Jason Coats, Texas Christian	23
Kerry Doane, East Tenn. State	23
Mac Doyle, Wofford	23
Chris Joyce, Norfolk State	23
Matt Leeds, College of Charleston	23
Joe Leonard, Pittsburgh	23
Chris Luick, George Washington	23
Kyle Muhlsteff, Valparaiso	23
Dallas Poulk, North Carolina State	23

TRIPLES

RANK. NAME, TEAM	3B
1. Zack MacPhee, Arizona State	14
2. Taylor Lewis, Maine	13
Greg Wallace, Evansville	13
4. Chris Benson, Utah Valley	11
Nathan Carter, Air Force	11
6. Matt Payton, Western Kentucky	10
7. Adam Eaton, Miami (Ohio)	9
Jonathan Johnson, Loyola Marymount	9
Steve McGuigan, Illinois-Chicago	9
10. Jarod Berggren, Northern Colorado	8
Gary Brown, Cal State Fullerton	8

Rico Noel ignited Coastal Carolina's offense with 56 steals

ROBERT GURGANUS

Kyle Gaedele, Valparaiso	8
Brian Goodwin, North Carolina	8
Jarrett Parker, Virginia	8
Ryan Strausborger, Indiana State	8
16. Joel Ansley, Houston	7
C.J. Belanger, Cal State Northridge	7
Jonathan Cluff, Brigham Young	7
Zach Cone, Georgia	7
Tony DiCesare, Northeastern	7
Taylor Featherston, Texas Christian	7
Brodie Greene, Texas A&M	7
Cass Hargis, Southeastern La.	7
Riley Henricks, Portland	7
Kurt Lipton, Marshall	7
Jeff Rowland, Georgia Tech	7
Johnny Ruettiger, Arizona State	7
Tyler Spillner, Purdue	7
Matt Szczur, Villanova	7
Joe Van Meter, Va. Commonwealth	7

STOLEN BASES

RANK. NAME, TEAM	SB	CS
1. Rico Noel, Coastal Carolina	56	13
2. Scott Woodward, Coastal Carolina	55	8
3. Willie Wesley, Jackson State	52	5
4. Dexter Kelley, Savannah State	44	10
5. Shawn Payne, Georgia Southern	43	2
Eric Stamets, Evansville	43	8
7. Willie Argo, Illinois	41	4
Damian Csakai, Wagner	41	5
Ryan Strausborger, Indiana State	41	5
10. Tyler Wilson, Lipscomb	40	10
11. Jerry Hildredth, Miss. Valley State	38	8
Braneric Holmes, Jackson State	38	3
13. Drew Maggi, Arizona State	36	9
Nate Roberts, High Point	36	3
Bert Smith, Jacksonville State	36	4
16. Jace Peterson, McNeese State	35	5
17. Nick Ahmed, Connecticut	34	8
Chase Lyles, Northwestern State	34	9
19. Justyn Carter, St. Peter's	33	7
Cotez Cole, Jackson State	33	0
Derick Daniel, Texas Southern	33	9
Mike Drowne, Sacred Heart	33	2
Billy Ferriter, Connecticut	33	6
Tyren Rivers, Radford	33	3
George Springer, Connecticut	33	2
Kevin Tokarski, Illinois State	33	6

27. Chris Bisson, Kentucky	32	7
Gary Brown, Cal State Fullerton	32	5
29. Hector Crespo, Appalachian State	31	4
Jason Esposito, Vanderbilt	31	4
Adam Heisler, South Alabama	31	4
George Hines, N.C. A&T	31	8
Reggie Keen, Radford	31	7
34. Billy Burns, Mercer	30	4
Dylan De Graaf, Western Carolina	30	2
Adam Eaton, Miami (Ohio)	30	4
Tyler Holt, Florida State	30	3
Trey Karlen, Tennessee-Martin	30	5
Kurtis Muller, Iowa	30	8
40. Jon Berti, Bowling Green State	29	6
Patrick Biondi, Michigan	29	6
Jon Clinard, Austin Peay State	29	4
Davis Duren, Oklahoma State	29	5
John Kenny, Hofstra	29	6
Pierre LePage, Connecticut	29	6
Tommy Lee, Georgetown	29	3
47. Jamal Austin, Alabama-Birmingham	28	5
J.D. Dunn, Saint Louis	28	6
Phil Vaughn, Md.-Eastern Shore	28	8
50. Niko Gallego, UCLA	27	2
John Lynch, Norfolk State	27	1
Kellon McFarlin, Chicago State	27	6
Daniel Merck, Gardner-Webb	27	6
Craig Richmond, Coppin State	27	5
Kenneth Rowan, Alcorn State	27	3
Cory Tilton, Charlotte	27	6
Taylor White, South Alabama	27	2
Chris Wolfe, Grambling	27	8

RUNS

RANK. NAME, TEAM	R
1. Jace Brinkerhoff, Utah Valley	88
Nate Roberts, High Point	88
3. Tyler Holt, Florida State	87
4. Jake Rickenbach, Utah Valley	86
5. Kyle Parker, Clemson	85
6. George Springer, Connecticut	84
7. Anthony Rendon, Rice	83
8. Rico Noel, Coastal Carolina	82
9. Dallas Poulk, North Carolina State	80
10. Paul Hoilman, East Tenn. State	79
11. Wes Cunningham, Murray State	77
Justin Howard, New Mexico	77
13. Ryan Aguayo, New Mexico State	76

	Levi Michael, North Carolina	76
	Cole Rakar, College of Charleston	76
	John Shultz, Pittsburgh	76
17.	Jeff Rowland, Georgia Tech	75
	Tyler Saladino, Oral Roberts	75
	Billy Stitz, South Dakota State	75
	Scott Woodward, Coastal Carolina	75
	Tom Zebroski, George Washington	75
22.	Brodie Greene, Texas A&M	74
	John Lee, South Dakota State	74
	Perry Silverman, Canisius	74
25.	Billy Burns, Mercer	73
	Christian Colon, Cal State Fullerton	73
	Kolbrin Vitek, Ball State	73
28.	Bryan Holaday, Texas Christian	72
	Whit Merrifield, South Carolina	72
	Jesse Sawyer, South Dakota State	72
	B.A. Vollmuth, Southern Miss.	72
32.	Barrett Barnes, Texas Tech	71
	Jedd Gyorko, West Virginia	71
	Rick Hague, Rice	71
	Jared Humphreys, Kent State	71
	Brad Miller, Clemson	71
37.	Adam Bryant, Troy	70
	Taylor Dugas, Alabama	70
	Steve McQuail, Canisius	70
	Bo Reeder, East Tenn. State	70
	Kevin Tokarski, Illinois State	70
42.	J.D. Ashbrook, Morehead State	69
	Pablo Bermudez, Fla. Intl.	69
	Patrick Biondi, Michigan	69
	Stephen Cardullo, Florida State	69
	Joe Corfman, Toledo	69
	Steven Felix, Troy	69
	Wes Hobson, Appalachian State	69
	Mark Micowski, Georgia State	69
	Chad Salem, Manhattan	69
	Jeff Schaus, Clemson	69
	Jacob Tanis, Mercer	69

HITS

RANK. NAME, TEAM		H
1.	Justin Howard, New Mexico	119
2.	Jace Brinkerhoff, Utah Valley	118
3.	Billy Stitz, South Dakota State	111
4.	Chad Oberacker, Tennessee Tech	108
	Joe Van Meter, Va. Commonwealth	108
6.	Chris Benson, Utah Valley	107
	Josh Rutledge, Alabama	107
8.	Brodie Greene, Texas A&M	105
	Hunter Morris, Auburn	105
10.	Joe Leonard, Pittsburgh	104
	Jacob Tanis, Mercer	104
12.	Michael Langley, Mercer	103
	Tom Zebroski, George Washington	103
14.	Zack Cox, Arkansas	102
	Cole Rakar, College of Charleston	102
16.	Sean Allaire, Central Conn. State	100
	Phil Gosselin, Virginia	100
	Garrett Wittels, Florida International	100
19.	Mikel Alvarez, Florida Gulf Coast	99
	Joel Blake, South Dakota State	99
	Jason Coats, Texas Christian	99
	Alex Dickerson, Indiana	99
	Chris Dudics, Toledo	99
	Mike Freeman, Clemson	99
	Anthony Gallas, Kent State	99
	Paul Hoilman, East Tenn. State	99
	Bryan Holaday, Texas Christian	99
	Andy Mee, Florida Atlantic	99
29.	Drew Martinez, Memphis	98
	Mike Nemeth, Connecticut	98
	Jimmy Parque, St. John's	98
	Jake Rickenbach, Utah Valley	98

DANNY PARKER

Slugger Hunter Morris led Auburn back to regional play

33.	Eric Cain, South Dakota State	97
34.	Tyler Bream, Liberty	96
	Christian Colon, Cal State Fullerton	96
	Bobby Coyle, Fresno State	96
	Taylor Dugas, Alabama	96
	Nick Martini, Kansas State	96
	Tyler Saladino, Oral Roberts	96
	Effrey Valdez, New York Tech	96
41.	Jeremy Baltz, St. John's	95
	Wes Cunningham, Murray State	95
	Micah Gibbs, Louisiana State	95
	Justin Guidry, Middle Tenn. State	95
	Wes Hobson, Appalachian State	95
	Whit Merrifield, South Carolina	95
	Jon Myers, Saint Louis	95
	Jimmy Rider, Kent State	95
	Jerrud Sabourin, Indiana	95
	Drew Turocy, Akron	95
51.	Garrett Buechele, Oklahoma	94
	Jason Esposito, Vanderbilt	94
	Ben Klafczynski, Kent State	94
	Adam Muenster, Kansas State	94
	Steve Nyisztor, Rutgers	94
	Dallas Poulk, North Carolina State	94
	Garrett Weber, Fresno State	94

TOTAL BASES

RANK. NAME, TEAM		TB
1.	Paul Hoilman, East Tenn. State	202
	Hunter Morris, Auburn	202
3.	Jacob Tanis, Mercer	197
4.	Chris Benson, Utah Valley	195
5.	Wes Cunningham, Murray State	192
6.	Jordan Ribera, Fresno State	191
7.	Alex Dickerson, Indiana	190
8.	Adam Bryant, Troy	186
9.	Jeremy Baltz, St. John's	185
	Justin Howard, New Mexico	185
11.	Jace Brinkerhoff, Utah Valley	184
12.	Anthony Rendon, Rice	181
13.	Brodie Greene, Texas A&M	179
14.	Jedd Gyorko, West Virginia	177
	A.J. Kirby-Jones, Tennessee Tech	177
	Phil Wunderlich, Louisville	177
17.	Anthony Gallas, Kent State	176
	Bryan Holaday, Texas Christian	176
	Tom Zebroski, George Washington	176

20.	Chris Duffy, Central Florida	175
	Brian Fletcher, Auburn	175
22.	Robert Maddox, Ohio	174
	Mike Olt, Connecticut	174
24.	Sean Allaire, Central Conn. State	173
	Dan Paolini, Siena	173
26.	Steve McQuail, Canisius	172
	B.A. Vollmuth, Southern Miss.	172
28.	Ryan Enos, Dallas Baptist	170
	Pat Epps, Central Conn. State	170
	Tyler Saladino, Oral Roberts	170
31.	Jason Coats, Texas Christian	169
	Christian Colon, Cal State Fullerton	169
	Tony Plagman, Georgia Tech	169
34.	Matt Curry, Texas Christian	168
	Nick Ramirez, Cal State Fullerton	168
36.	Chase Burnette, Georgia Tech	167
	Matt Leeds, College of Charleston	167
	Jon Myers, Saint Louis	167
	Ricky Oropesa, Southern California	167
	Rob Segedin, Tulane	167
41.	Mac Doyle, Wofford	166
	Greg Wallace, Evansville	166
43.	Garrett Buechele, Oklahoma	165
	Mike Nemeth, Connecticut	165
	Chad Oberacker, Tennessee Tech	165
	Bo Reeder, East Tenn. State	165
	Joe Van Meter, Va. Commonwealth	165
48.	Phil Gosselin, Virginia	163
	Tyler Holt, Florida State	163
	Billy Stitz, South Dakota State	163
51.	Kyle Parker, Clemson	162
	Ryan Wright, Louisville	162

WALKS

RANK. NAME, TEAM		BB
1.	Michael Choice, Texas-Arlington	76
2.	Anthony Rendon, Rice	65
3.	Kole Calhoun, Arizona State	64
	Pratt Maynard, North Carolina State	64
5.	Kyle Roller, East Carolina	61
6.	George Springer, Connecticut	60
7.	Taylor Dugas, Alabama	59
	Tyler Holt, Florida State	59
	Logan Vick, Baylor	59
10.	A.J. Kirby-Jones, Tennessee Tech	58
	Rob Kral, College of Charleston	58

12.	Matt Curry, Texas Christian	57
	Yasmani Grandal, Miami	57
	Corbin Smith, Texas Southern	57
15.	Ryan Adams, Elon	56
	Kyle Parker, Clemson	56
	John Shultz, Pittsburgh	56
18.	Brian Harris, Vanderbilt	55
19.	Nolan Fontana, Florida	53
	Nate Roberts, High Point	53
	Kevin Tokarski, Illinois State	53
22.	Paul Hoilman, East Tenn. State	51
23.	Brad Miller, Clemson	50
	James Ramsey, Florida State	50
	Jesse Sawyer, South Dakota State	50
26.	Travis Shaw, Kent State	49
27.	Donnie Corsner, Old Dominion	48
	Zach Maxfield, Florida Gulf Coast	48
	Danny Muno, Fresno State	48
30.	Ryan Brown, William & Mary	47
	Stephen Cardullo, Florida State	47
	Jerod Faggart, Appalachian State	47
	Sherman Johnson, Florida State	47
	Zak Presley, Houston	47
	Zane Williams, Charlotte	47
	Scott Woodward, Coastal Carolina	47
37.	Packy Elkins, Belmont	46
	Chris Epps, Clemson	46
	Keith Hernandez, Delaware State	46
	Mike Kvasnicka, Minnesota	46
	Michael Ratterree, Rice	46
	Matt Townsend, James Madison	46
43.	Kyle Blackburn, Georgia Southern	45
	Raymond Church, Florida Atlantic	45
	Brian Goodwin, North Carolina	45
	Robbie Monday, UNC Wilmington	45
	Nate Shaver, New Mexico State	45
	Matt Skole, Georgia Tech	45
	Murray Watts, Arkansas State	45
50.	Bear Comer, Nicholls State	44
	Scott Lawson, Miami	44
	Mike McGee, Florida State	44
	Tate McMillan, Tennessee Tech	44
	Vincent Mejia, Texas-Pan American	44
	Levi Michael, North Carolina	44
	Thomas Nichols, Georgia Tech	44
	Andy Wilkins, Arkansas	44

TOUGHEST TO STRIKE OUT

RANK. NAME, TEAM	AB/SO
1. Pierre LePage, Connecticut	82.7
2. Marquis Riley, N.C. A&T	42.4
3. Michael Bottoms, Morehead State	33.0
4. Alex Azor, Navy	30.8
5. Kevin Bowles, Georgia Southern	25.4
6. Mark Onorati, Manhattan	25.3
7. Anthony Gomez, Vanderbilt	23.8
8. Jeff Cusick, UC Irvine	23.2
9. Greg Gilroy, New York Tech	22.3
10. Jerry Hildredth, Miss. Valley State	21.1
11. Matt Holsman, Fairleigh Dickinson	20.7
12. Caleb Clowers, Louisiana-Monroe	20.1
13. Rob Elliott, Bradley	19.9
14. Curran Redal, Liberty	19.6
15. Oscar Garcia, Northwestern State	19.3
Matt Szczur, Villanova	19.3
17. Jim Klocke, Southeast Missouri State	19.2
18. Max Casper, North Dakota State	19.1
19. Zack Osborne, Tennessee	18.7
20. Eric Phillips, Georgia Southern	18.7
21. Kevin Plawecki, Purdue	18.5
22. Dane Nielsen, Brigham Young	18.4
23. Ray Hernandez, Texas Southern	17.8
24. Gary Brown, Cal State Fullerton	17.5
25. Steve Gable, Pennsylvania	17.3

Brian Harris set a Division I single-season mark with 37 HBPs

HIT BY PITCH

RANK. NAME, TEAM	HBP
1. Brian Harris, Vanderbilt	37
2. Cotez Cole, Jackson State	29
3. Daniel Dellasega, Kansas State	27
4. Chris Barker, UNC Greensboro	26
5. Cameron Dullnig, Western Carolina	25
Steven Felix, Troy	25
Matt Fritz, Bradley	25
Collin Kuhn, Arkansas	25
Nate Roberts, High Point	25
Riccio Torrez, Arizona State	25
Scott Woodward, Coastal Carolina	25
12. Ian Choy, Canisius	24
Steve McGuiggan, Illinois-Chicago	24
Pablo Rosario, High Point	24
15. Alex Acheson, Evansville	23
Tyler Grimes, Wichita State	23
Cam Stykemain, Niagara	23
18. Chris Bangi, Campbell	22
Shane Brown, Central Florida	22
Josh Cryer, Southeastern La.	22
Scott Davis, Delaware State	22
Michael Gallic, Marist	22
Dexter Kelley, Savannah State	22
Matt Leeds, College of Charleston	22
Casey Lytle, Kansas	22
Ryan McCurdy, Duke	22
Kyle Murphy, Manhattan	22
Anthony Ottrando, Eastern Kentucky	22
Neal Pritchard, Elon	22
Kyle Roller, East Carolina	22

SACRIFICE BUNTS

RANK. NAME, TEAM	SH
1. Mike Albaladejo, Florida Atlantic	20
Matt Hamlet, Boston College	20
3. Scott Woodward, Coastal Carolina	19
4. Bret Atwood, Texas State	17
Drew Haynes, Louisville	17
Brandon Loy, Texas	17
7. Ryan Ford, Middle Tenn. State	16
8. Brandon Brown, South Alabama	15

Nick Crawford, Alabama-Birmingham	15
Colin Durborow, West Virginia	15
Chris Ellison, Oklahoma	15
Keith Jennette, Oregon State	15
Whit Merrifield, South Carolina	15
Kyle Olasin, La.-Lafayette	15
K.J. Randhawa, Air Force	15
Keith Werman, Virginia	15
17. Jake Brown, Kansas State	14
Marlon Calbi, Villanova	14
Doug Cherry, Washington	14
Derick Daniel, Texas Southern	14
R.J. Gundolff, Wright State	14
Mike Mercurio, High Point	14
Joey Winiecki, Oral Roberts	14

SACRIFICE FLIES

RANK. NAME, TEAM	SF
1. Ryan Soares, George Mason	13
2. Dan Grovatt, Virginia	10
Steven Proscia, Virginia	10
4. Chris Benson, Utah Valley	9
Jerry Hildredth, Miss. Valley State	9
Bradley Logan, Georgia State	9
Jake Overstreet, South Alabama	9
Ricky Pacione, Marist	9
9. Ryan Adams, Elon	8
John Andreoli, Connecticut	8
Eric Charles, Purdue	8
Kevin David, Oklahoma State	8
David Freitas, Hawaii	8
Matt Gaudet, Louisiana State	8
Andrew Heck, Duquesne	8
Mason Heyne, Rider	8
Chad Keefer, La.-Lafayette	8
Quentin Luquette, Lamar	8
Xavier Macklin, N.C. A&T	8
Rico Noel, Coastal Carolina	8
Tony Plagman, Georgia Tech	8
Shon Roc, Loyola Marymount	8
Chase Whitley, Troy	8
Matt Zeblo, Belmont	8

PITCHING

Minimum 50 IP, 1 IP per team game

EARNED RUN AVERAGE

RANK. NAME, TEAM, YEAR	G	IP	R	ER	ERA
1. John Stilson, Texas A&M, So.	33	79	12	7	0.80
2. Chance Ruffin, Texas, Jr.	37	65	10	8	1.11
3. Kenny Long, Illinois State, So.	31	65	16	10	1.38
4. Trever Vermeulen, South Dakota State, Jr.	35	68	17	11	1.45
5. Alex Wimmers, Ohio State, Jr.	10	73	14	13	1.60
6. Kevin Munson, James Madison, Jr.	28	55	13	10	1.64
7. Matt Davenport, William & Mary, So.	20	96	25	21	1.96
8. Chris Sale, Florida Gulf Coast, Jr.	17	103	28	23	2.01
9. Jordan Cooper, Wichita State, So.	15	107	30	24	2.01
10. Taylor Jungmann, Texas, So.	17	120	32	27	2.03
11. Brady Rodgers, Arizona State, Fr.	22	73	23	17	2.10
12. Dietrich Enns, Central Michigan, Fr.	20	59	25	14	2.12
13. James Giulietti, Binghamton, Jr.	14	88	25	21	2.15
14. Mitchell Lambson, Arizona State, So.	39	75	18	18	2.16
15. Drew Pomeranz, Mississippi, Jr.	16	101	27	25	2.23
16. Garrett Claypool, UCLA, Sr.	21	83	24	21	2.29
17. Ben Nelson, Navy, Fr.	14	62	21	16	2.33
18. Zach Osborne, La.-Lafayette, Sr.	16	122	43	32	2.37
19. Chris Kaminski, Jacksonville, Jr.	24	68	27	18	2.38
20. Matt Bywater, Pepperdine, Jr.	13	98	34	26	2.40
21. Andrew Barbosa, South Florida, Jr.	14	86	33	23	2.40
22. Nick Tropeano, Stony Brook, So.	14	100	36	27	2.44
23. Shawn Teufel, Liberty, Sr.	15	103	31	28	2.44
24. Daniel Bibona, UC Irvine, Sr.	13	94	34	26	2.48
25. Addison Reed, San Diego State, Jr.	11	79	30	22	2.50
26. Jonathan Watson, Va. Commonwealth, Jr.	31	61	19	17	2.51
27. Noe Ramirez, Cal State Fullerton, So.	16	106	34	30	2.54
28. Owen Jones, Portland, So.	16	56	20	16	2.56
29. Anthony Meo, Coastal Carolina, So.	18	97	39	28	2.61
30. Chris Hernandez, Miami, Jr.	19	106	45	31	2.64
31. Lee Henry, Tennessee Tech, Sr.	16	80	29	24	2.69
32. Steven Maxwell, Texas Christian, Jr.	18	103	38	31	2.70
33. Rob Rasmussen, UCLA, Jr.	19	109	36	33	2.72
34. Cole Green, Texas, Jr.	17	112	38	34	2.74
35. Blake Cooper, South Carolina, Sr.	20	137	52	42	2.76
36. Danny Hultzen, Virginia, So.	16	107	37	33	2.78
37. Kyle Hald, Old Dominion, Jr.	13	100	41	31	2.79
38. Drew Smyly, Arkansas, So.	18	103	38	32	2.80
39. Barret Loux, Texas A&M, Jr.	17	105	42	33	2.83
40. John Soldinger, Manhattan, Fr.	21	60	28	19	2.84
41. Kyle Blair, San Diego, Jr.	15	98	44	31	2.84
42. Nathan Kilcrease, Alabama, Jr.	34	98	33	31	2.85
43. Thomas Royse, Louisville, Jr.	16	104	37	33	2.85
44. Tyler Herriage, Stephen F. Austin, Jr.	15	93	33	30	2.89
45. Michael Wacha, Texas A&M, Fr.	25	106	38	34	2.89
46. Luke Irvine, Northwestern State, Jr.	16	93	41	30	2.91
47. Cole Cook, Pepperdine, Jr.	14	104	44	34	2.93
48. Kent Worthington, Mount St. Mary's, Sr.	14	76	35	25	2.95
49. Deck McGuire, Georgia Tech, Jr.	16	113	44	37	2.95
50. Cameron Roth, UNC Wilmington, Jr.	16	94	44	31	2.98
51. Tyler Anderson, Oregon, Jr.	17	103	41	34	2.98
52. Elliot Glynn, Connecticut, Jr.	15	87	40	29	2.99
53. Matt Ridings, Western Kentucky, Sr.	14	93	38	31	3.01
54. Steven Evans, Liberty, Jr.	15	90	35	30	3.01
55. Trevor Bauer, UCLA, So.	18	131	64	44	3.02
56. Kevin Crimmel, Villanova, Sr.	24	54	22	18	3.02
57. Matt Purke, Texas Christian, Fr.	20	116	48	39	3.02
58. Willie Kempf, Baylor, So.	22	83	33	28	3.03
59. David Lutz, Penn State, Sr.	36	71	32	24	3.04
60. Stephen McCray, Tennessee, Sr.	14	92	32	31	3.04
61. Joe Sawicki, Northern Colorado, Sr.	14	97	44	33	3.06
62. Matt Harvey, North Carolina, Jr.	14	96	42	33	3.09
63. Carson Smith, Texas State, So.	24	105	45	36	3.09
64. Matt Benedict, Western Carolina, Jr.	18	93	48	32	3.11
65. Ty Blach, Creighton, Fr.	14	75	34	26	3.11
66. Lance Harting, Longwood, Sr.	22	81	35	28	3.11
67. Adam Champion, Arkansas-Little Rock, Sr.	14	98	38	34	3.11
68. Andrew Leenhouts, Northeastern, So.	12	71	30	25	3.16
69. Casey Henn, Wright State, So.	15	85	37	30	3.19
70. Evan Brock, UC Irvine, Fr.	19	62	24	22	3.19
71. Boone Whiting, Centenary, Jr.	14	84	38	30	3.21
72. Matt Bischoff, Purdue, Sr.	13	95	39	34	3.22
73. Hudson Randall, Florida, Fr.	20	97	39	35	3.24
74. Dylan Floro, Cal State Fullerton, Fr.	27	91	39	33	3.26
75. Kurt Heyer, Arizona, Fr.	17	102	42	37	3.26
76. Esterlin Paulino, N.C. A&T, So.	17	88	46	32	3.27
77. Logan Verrett, Baylor, So.	16	91	40	33	3.27
78. Kolbrin Vitek, Ball State, Jr.	17	80	33	29	3.27
79. Andrew Gagnon, Long Beach State, So.	15	93	50	34	3.28
80. Nathan Forer, Southern Illinois, Sr.	14	74	37	27	3.28
81. Zach Varce, Portland, Jr.	14	93	40	34	3.29
82. Kyle Kraus, Portland, So.	15	109	46	40	3.30
83. Todd McInnis, Southern Miss., Jr.	16	95	41	35	3.31
84. Adam Conley, Washington State, Jr.	29	68	32	25	3.32
85. Jeff Tardiff, Le Moyne, Jr.	14	81	41	30	3.33
86. Brandon Workman, Texas, Jr.	17	105	42	39	3.35
87. Andrew Berger, Lehigh, Sr.	9	62	28	23	3.35
88. Gerrit Cole, UCLA, So.	19	123	51	46	3.37
89. Kyle Winkler, Texas Christian, So.	19	117	49	44	3.39
90. Zack Thornton, Oregon, Sr.	17	90	36	34	3.40
91. Sammy Solis, San Diego, Sr.	15	92	45	35	3.42
92. Brock Stassi, Nevada, Jr.	13	79	36	30	3.43
93. Jeremy Erben, Oklahoma, Sr.	34	76	31	29	3.43
Tanner Robles, Oregon State, Jr.	14	76	39	29	3.43
95. Chase Reid, Vanderbilt, Jr.	28	68	37	26	3.46
96. Pat Lowery, Columbia, So.	11	65	32	25	3.46
97. Seth Cutler-Voltz, Va. Commonwealth, So.	17	119	68	46	3.47
98. Sonny Gray, Vanderbilt, So.	19	109	48	42	3.48
99. Corey Roberts, Charlotte, Fr.	15	85	44	33	3.48
100. Kyle Hunter, Dartmouth, Fr.	12	62	27	24	3.48

JOHN WILLIAMSON

Aggies closer John Silson led D-I in ERA

WINS

RANK. NAME, TEAM	W	L
1. Matt Purke, Texas Christian	16	0
2. Blake Cooper, South Carolina	13	2
Anthony Meo, Coastal Carolina	13	2
Quintavious Drains, Jackson State	13	4
5. Cody Wheeler, Coastal Carolina	12	0
Seth Blair, Arizona State	12	1
Noe Ramirez, Cal State Fullerton	12	1
Daniel Renken, CS Fullerton	12	2
Brandon Workman, Texas	12	2
Trevor Bauer, UCLA	12	3
Kyle Winkler, Texas Christian	12	3
Asher Wojciechowski, Citadel	12	3
13. Chris Sale, Florida Gulf Coast	11	0
Jake Borup, Arizona State	11	1
Scott Copeland, Southern Miss.	11	1
Danny Hultzen, Virginia	11	1

Cole Green, Texas	11	2
Matt Iannazzo, Pittsburgh	11	2
Tim Kelley, Wichita State	11	2
Barret Loux, Texas A&M	11	2
Steven Maxwell, Texas Christian	11	2
Corey Baker, Pittsburgh	11	3
Alex Panteliodis, Florida	11	3
Rob Rasmussen, UCLA	11	3
Gerrit Cole, UCLA	11	4
26. Lance Harting, Longwood	10	0
Matt Bischoff, Purdue	10	2
Jordan Cooper, Wichita State	10	3
Chris Hernandez, Miami	10	3
Tyler Johnson, Stony Brook	10	3
Merrill Kelly, Arizona State	10	3
Kyle Kraus, Portland	10	3
Seth Maness, East Carolina	10	3
Nick Rogers, N.C. A&T	10	3
Jimmy Reyes, Elon	10	4
Carson Smith, Texas State	10	4
Matison Smith, Lamar	10	4
Shawn Teufel, Liberty	10	4
Sonny Gray, Vanderbilt	10	5
Cortney Nelson, Jackson State	10	5
Bobby Shore, Oklahoma	10	5
D.D. Hanks, South Alabama	10	6
Justin Jones, California	10	6

SAVES

RANK. NAME, TEAM	SV
1. Kevin Arico, Virginia	18
2. Neil Holland, Louisville	17
3. Andrew Burkett, Cincinnati	14
Chris Dennis, Portland	14
Jordan Swagerty, Arizona State	14
Chance Ruffin, Texas	14
7. Kevin McKague, Army	13
Mike McGee, Florida State	13
Kevin Lee, Iowa	13
Chris Patterson, Appalachian State	13
11. Brooks Pinckard, Baylor	12
Ryan Duke, Oklahoma	12
Paul Snieder, Northwestern	12
Austin Coan, Marshall	12
Tyler Gebler, Rutgers	12
Adam Conley, Washington State	12
Lenny Linsky, Hawaii	12
Daniel Burawa, St. John's	12
Brett Huber, Mississippi	12
Ryne Purcell, Eastern Kentucky	12
Andy Deain, Northern Illinois	12
22. Andy Mee, Florida Atlantic	11
Nick Ramirez, Cal State Fullerton	11
Pat Christensen, La Salle	11
Matty Ott, Louisiana State	11
Kevin Chapman, Florida	11
Lex Rutledge, Samford	11
28. Tyler Burgoon, Michigan	10
Tyler Graham, Nevada	10
Tom Heithoff, Evansville	10
Juan Perez, Bethune-Cookman	10
Chad Bettis, Texas Tech	10
Jordan Jankowski, Miami (Ohio)	10
Austin Hubbard, Auburn	10
Chad Sheppard, Northwestern State	10
Jon Ivie, Belmont	10
Dexter Bobo, Georgia Southern	10
Kevin Munson, James Madison	10
Tyler Browning, Indiana State	10
Matt Price, South Carolina	10
John Stilson, Texas A&M	10
Zach Gerler, Austin Peay State	10
Trever Vermeulen, South Dakota State	10
Dan Klein, UCLA	10
45. Cory Kent, Lehigh	9

Bryan Roberts, Illinois	9
Gardner Leaver, Rhode Island	9
Cameron Amsrud, Milwaukee	9
Mike Roth, New York Tech	9
Matt Click, McNeese State	9
Collin Cargill, Southern Miss.	9
James Allen, Kansas State	9
Seth Simmons, East Carolina	9
Jason West, Stephen F. Austin	9
Robbie Andrews, Va. Commonwealth	9
Matt Brazis, Boston College	9
Kenny Long, Illinois State	9
Tyler Smith, Rider	9
Chris Squires, Indiana	9
Rye Davis, Western Kentucky	9
Eric Berkowitz, Florida International	9

STRIKEOUTS

RANK. NAME, TEAM	SO
1. Trevor Bauer, UCLA	165
2. Asher Wojciechowski, Citadel	155
3. Gerrit Cole, UCLA	153
4. Chris Sale, Florida Gulf Coast	146
5. Matt Purke, Texas Christian	142
6. Drew Pomeranz, Mississippi	139
7. Barret Loux, Texas A&M	136
8. Taylor Jungmann, Texas	129
9. Rob Rasmussen, UCLA	128
10. Kyle Blair, San Diego	126
Blake Cooper, South Carolina	126
12. Josh Smith, Lipscomb	124
13. Danny Hultzen, Virginia	123
14. Bryce Shafer, Valparaiso	121
15. Boone Whiting, Centenary	120
16. Noe Ramirez, Cal State Fullerton	119
17. Deck McGuire, Georgia Tech	118
18. Eric Cantrell, George Washington	114
Jonathan Dziedzic, Lamar	114
Drew Smyly, Arkansas	114
John Stilson, Texas A&M	114
22. Sonny Gray, Vanderbilt	113
A.J. Griffin, San Diego	113
Jason Mitchell, Texas-Arlington	113
Jacob Petricka, Indiana State	113
Cody Wheeler, Coastal Carolina	113
27. Nate Garcia, Santa Clara	112
Zach Osborne, La.-Lafayette	112
29. Zach Varce, Portland	111
30. Chris Hernandez, Miami	110
Tanner Peters, UNLV	110
32. Kurt Heyer, Arizona	109
33. Seth Blair, Arizona State	108
Sean Gilmartin, Florida State	108
35. Nick Tropeano, Stony Brook	106
36. Tyler Anderson, Oregon	105
Randy Fontanez, South Florida	105
Casey Harman, Clemson	105
39. Luke Irvine, Northwestern State	104
40. Clint Dempster, Nicholls State	103
Mike Kickham, Missouri State	103
Zach Woods, East Carolina	103
43. Chad Bettis, Texas Tech	102
Daniel Bibona, UC Irvine	102
Matt Harvey, North Carolina	102
46. Sam Dyson, South Carolina	101
Brandon Workman, Texas	101

STRIKEOUTS PER NINE INNINGS

RANK. NAME, TEAM	SO/9
1. Chance Ruffin, Texas	13.49
2. John Stilson, Texas A&M	12.99
3. Thomas Keeling, Oklahoma State	12.88
4. Boone Whiting, Centenary	12.86
5. Chris Sale, Florida Gulf Coast	12.76
6. Drew Pomeranz, Mississippi	12.42

7. Grant Gordon, Missouri State	11.89
8. Barret Loux, Texas A&M	11.66
9. Kyle Blair, San Diego	11.54
10. Mitchell Lambson, Arizona State	11.52
11. Kevin Munson, James Madison	11.45
12. Trevor Bauer, UCLA	11.31
13. Gerrit Cole, UCLA	11.20
14. Adam Lopez, VMI	11.13
15. Andrew Leenhouts, Northeastern	11.11
16. Asher Wojciechowski, Citadel	11.10
17. Matt Purke, Texas Christian	10.99
18. Jonathan Dziedzic, Lamar	10.91
19. Nate Garcia, Santa Clara	10.87
20. Zach Varce, Portland	10.74
21. Nick Serino, Massachusetts	10.72
22. Chad Bettis, Texas Tech	10.71
23. Chris Squires, Indiana	10.71
24. Josh Smith, Lipscomb	10.70
25. Tanner Peters, UNLV	10.68

FEWEST HITS PER NINE INNINGS

RANK. NAME, TEAM	H/9
1. Mitchell Lambson, Arizona State	4.92
2. Evan Brock, UC Irvine	4.94
3. Dietrich Enns, Central Michigan	5.16
4. Garrett Claypool, UCLA	5.33
5. Kevin Munson, James Madison	5.40
6. John Stilson, Texas A&M	5.81
7. Chance Ruffin, Texas	5.84
8. Kenny Long, Illinois State	6.06
9. Danny Hultzen, Virginia	6.33
10. Drew Pomeranz, Mississippi	6.35
11. Chase Whitley, Troy	6.55
12. Brady Rodgers, Arizona State	6.56
13. Taylor Jungmann, Texas	6.60
14. Barret Loux, Texas A&M	6.69
15. Gerrit Cole, UCLA	6.73
16. Tyler Johnson, Stony Brook	6.75
17. Nick Tropeano, Stony Brook	6.86
18. Matt Suschak, Toledo	6.93
19. Matt Purke, Texas Christian	7.04
20. Jonathan Watson, Va. Commonwealth	7.08
21. Cole Green, Texas	7.09
22. Brian Busch, Florida State	7.11
23. Jacob Clem, Washington	7.12
24. Tyler Thornburg, Charleston So.	7.13
25. Alex Wimmers, Ohio State	7.15

FEWEST WALKS PER NINE INNINGS

RANK. NAME, TEAM	BB/9
1. Mike Hoekstra, Eastern Illinois	0.67
2. Francis Brooke, Northwestern	0.71
3. Lindsey Caughel, Stetson	0.84
4. Damon McCormick, Valparaiso	0.94
5. Seth Rosin, Minnesota	1.05
6. Dylan Floro, Cal State Fullerton	1.09
7. Doug Murray, San Francisco	1.11
8. Brandon Smith, Old Dominion	1.13
9. Kyle Hunter, Dartmouth	1.16
10. Chris Sale, Florida Gulf Coast	1.22
11. Ryan Copeland, Illinois State	1.29
12. Matt Bischoff, Purdue	1.33
13. Ryan Dull, UNC Asheville	1.33
14. Andrew Heck, Duquesne	1.34
15. Brady Rodgers, Arizona State	1.36
16. Alex Kaminsky, Wright State	1.38
17. Justin Braddock, Stephen F. Austin	1.39
18. Christian Bergman, UC Irvine	1.42
19. Seth Maness, East Carolina	1.42
20. Daniel Bibona, UC Irvine	1.43
21. James Giulietti, Binghamton	1.43
22. Jared Rogers, Rice	1.45
23. Dane Beakler, Liberty	1.48
Bobby Bolling, Radford	1.48
25. Kyle Kraus, Portland	1.49

BATTING

SCORING

RANK. SCHOOL	G	R	R/G
1. Georgia State	58	608	10.5
2. Utah Valley	59	611	10.4
3. New Mexico State	60	613	10.2
4. South Dakota State	60	578	9.6
5. Pittsburgh	56	531	9.5
6. North Carolina State	62	571	9.2
7. College of Charleston	63	576	9.1
8. Coastal Carolina	66	603	9.1
9. Auburn	64	584	9.1
10. Georgia Tech	62	563	9.1
11. Canisius	60	544	9.1
12. Rice	63	564	9.0
13. Morehead State	50	445	8.9
14. Northern Colorado	58	510	8.8
15. High Point	60	526	8.8
16. Campbell	55	482	8.8
17. Southern Miss.	60	516	8.6
18. Charlotte	56	481	8.6
19. Clemson	70	600	8.6
20. Troy	61	521	8.5
21. Jackson State	53	451	8.5
22. George Mason	50	425	8.5
23. Louisiana Tech	57	484	8.5
24. Connecticut	64	542	8.5
25. Texas Christian	68	574	8.4

BATTING AVERAGE

RANK, SCHOOL	AVG
1. Utah Valley	.372
2. Pittsburgh	.365
3. Georgia State	.355
4. South Dakota State	.350
5. New Mexico State	.349
6. Auburn	.348
7. Southeast Missouri State	.346
8. New Mexico	.346
9. Campbell	.345
10. Northern Colorado	.345

HOME RUNS

RANK. SCHOOL	HR
1. Auburn	131
2. Georgia Tech	122
3. Coastal Carolina	111
4. Miami	106
5. College of Charleston	105
Oklahoma	105
Oral Roberts	105
8. New Mexico State	104
9. Texas Christian	101
10. Troy	100

DOUBLES

RANK. SCHOOL	2B
1. Utah Valley	188
2. Kent State	181
3. Texas Christian	178
4. Mercer	173
5. South Dakota State	163
Louisville	163
7. Texas Tech	162
8. New Mexico	161
9. Vanderbilt	160
College of Charleston	160
Virginia	160

TRIPLES

RANK. SCHOOL	3B
1. Arizona State	37
2. Air Force	36
3. Virginia	32
4. Maine	30
5. Utah Valley	29
6. Wright State	28
7. Arizona	27
Villanova	27
Cal State Fullerton	27
Brigham Young	27

SLUGGING PERCENTAGE

RANK. SCHOOL	SLG
1. Auburn	.591
2. Utah Valley	.586
3. Georgia Tech	.575
4. New Mexico State	.572
5. Morehead State	.569
6. Bethune-Cookman	.561
7. Georgia State	.558
8. South Dakota State	.553
9. Coastal Carolina	.553
10. Texas Christian	.551

STOLEN BASES

RANK. SCHOOL	SB	CS
1. Jackson State	216	25
2. Connecticut	171	33
3. Coastal Carolina	161	37
4. Savannah State	147	47
5. Radford	143	31
6. Grambling	142	27
7. Mississippi Valley State	140	43
8. Arizona State	136	42
9. Alabama A&M	132	26
10. Citadel	127	34

WALKS

RANK. SCHOOL	BB
1. Florida State	402
2. New Mexico State	382
3. Clemson	375
4. North Carolina State	333
5. Arizona State	320
Rice	320
7. Georgia Tech	313
8. Georgia State	311
9. Coastal Carolina	310
10. Elon	302

PITCHING

EARNED RUN AVERAGE

RANK. SCHOOL	ERA
1. Texas	2.45
2. UCLA	3.00
3. Oregon	3.29
4. Arizona State	3.32
5. Portland	3.42
6. Louisiana-Lafayette	3.43
7. South Carolina	3.45
8. Coastal Carolina	3.53
9. Texas Christian	3.55
10. Miami	3.68
11. Louisville	3.69
12. Vanderbilt	3.69
13. Texas A&M	3.70
14. Oklahoma	3.76
15. Cal State Fullerton	3.78
16. Virginia	3.89
17. Connecticut	3.91
18. Arkansas	3.93
19. Northwestern State	3.94
20. Baylor	3.95
21. UC Irvine	3.96
22. Georgia Tech	4.02
23. Florida	4.13
24. Oregon State	4.19
25. North Carolina	4.19

STRIKEOUTS PER NINE INNINGS

RANK. SCHOOL	SO/9
1. UCLA	10.2
2. Texas A&M	9.3
3. San Diego	9.3
4. Arizona State	8.9
5. Oklahoma State	8.9
6. South Carolina	8.9
7. Mississippi	8.9
8. Miami	8.8
9. North Carolina	8.7
10. Virginia Tech	8.7

FEWEST HITS PER NINE INNINGS

RANK. SCHOOL	H/9
1. Texas	7.13
2. UCLA	7.31
3. South Carolina	7.48
4. Virginia	7.99
5. Arizona State	8.19
6. Miami	8.32
7. Coastal Carolina	8.37
8. Louisiana-Lafayette	8.46
9. Texas Christian	8.52
10. Texas A&M	8.63

FEWEST WALKS PER NINE INNINGS

RANK. SCHOOL	BB/9
1. Dartmouth	1.95
2. Florida	2.15
3. Oregon	2.41
4. Cal State Fullerton	2.46
5. UC Irvine	2.56
6. Louisville	2.57
7. Louisiana-Lafayette	2.65
8. Arizona State	2.69
9. Columbia	2.73
10. Texas	2.77

FIELDING

FIELDING PERCENTAGE

RANK. SCHOOL	PCT
1. Texas	.980
2. Creighton	.980
3. Boston College	.979
4. San Francisco	.978
5. Oklahoma State	.978
6. Florida	.978
7. Virginia	.977
8. Alabama	.977
9. Pittsburgh	.977
10. Indiana State	.976
11. Oklahoma	.976
12. Arizona State	.976
13. South Carolina	.975
14. Troy	.975
15. Evansville	.975
16. Villanova	.975
17. Duke	.975
18. Louisiana State	.975
19. Michigan State	.975
20. Vanderbilt	.975
21. Dartmouth	.975
22. Mississippi	.974
23. UC Irvine	.974
24. Tennessee	.974
25. Rice	.974

DOUBLE PLAYS PER GAME

RANK. SCHOOL	PG
1. Southern Mississippi	1.40
2. Washington State	1.32
3. Maine	1.20
4. California	1.19
5. Evansville	1.17

Batters: 10 or more at-bats. Pitchers: 5 or more innings.

1. SOUTH CAROLINA

Coach: Ray Tanner. **Record:** 54-16.

PLAYER, POS., YEAR	AVG	AB	R	H	2B	3B	HR	RBI	SB
Evan Marzilli, lf, Fr.	.385	91	30	35	8	0	3	12	8
Jackie Bradley Jr., of, So.	.368	242	56	89	12	1	13	60	7
Brady Thomas, dh, Sr.	.331	139	37	46	13	1	8	30	3
Christian Walker, 1b, Fr.	.327	226	35	74	12	2	9	51	2
Whit Merrifield, of, Jr.	.321	296	72	95	12	1	13	42	12
Adam Matthews, of, So.	.307	189	30	58	12	2	7	31	7
Jeffery Jones, if, Sr.	.300	110	21	33	7	0	8	29	0
Kyle Enders, c, Sr.	.281	185	26	52	9	1	3	32	2
Robert Beary, c, Jr.	.276	98	18	27	3	1	1	14	3
Adrian Morales, 3b, Jr.	.273	245	50	67	15	0	9	56	5
Nick Ebert, 1b, Sr.	.272	125	27	34	7	1	7	31	0
Parker Bangs, dh, Jr.	.267	60	10	16	6	0	3	18	1
Bobby Haney, ss, Sr.	.263	217	30	57	8	1	3	24	1
Scott Wingo, 2b, Jr.	.247	198	52	49	8	3	9	31	2

PLAYER, POS., YEAR	W	L	ERA	G	SV	IP	H	BB	SO
Michael Roth, lhp, So.	2	1	1.34	37	3	40	27	10	35
Patrick Sullivan, rhp, Jr.	0	0	1.50	7	0	6	7	4	7
Matt Price, rhp, Fr.	4	1	2.26	31	10	56	37	19	83
Jose Mata, rhp, Jr.	7	1	2.40	33	0	45	35	10	37
Nolan Belcher, lhp, So.	3	1	2.43	11	0	30	18	18	32
Blake Cooper, rhp, Sr.	13	2	2.76	20	0	137	111	39	126
John Taylor, rhp, Jr.	3	2	3.38	28	1	29	27	5	21
Tyler Webb, lhp, Fr.	3	2	3.96	17	0	36	29	13	36
Steven Neff, rhp, So.	2	1	4.11	17	0	15	16	8	16
Sam Dyson, rhp, Jr.	6	5	4.28	18	0	103	98	24	101
Jay Brown, rhp, Sr.	3	0	4.44	17	0	51	46	21	34
Jimmy Revan, lhp, So.	1	0	4.85	9	0	13	8	13	20
Parker Bangs, rhp, Jr.	1	0	5.27	14	0	14	7	9	21
Colby Holmes, rhp, Fr.	2	0	5.33	11	0	27	29	16	27
Ethan Carter, rhp, Fr.	3	0	5.46	24	0	28	25	9	30

2. UCLA

Coach: John Savage. **Record:** 51-17.

PLAYER, POS., YEAR	AVG	AB	R	H	2B	3B	HR	RBI	SB
Dennis Holt, of, Fr.	.600	10	2	6	0	0	0	3	0
Beau Amaral, of, Fr.	.354	223	45	79	12	0	4	31	9
Dean Espy, 1b, So.	.345	174	38	60	7	3	9	52	8
Tyler Rahmatulla, 2b, So.	.328	232	52	76	19	1	7	45	13
Jeff Gelalich, of, Fr.	.321	78	17	25	4	1	2	13	7
Cody Keefer, of, Fr.	.318	148	29	47	9	0	2	31	1
Blair Dunlap, dh, Sr.	.314	242	45	76	20	2	6	28	7
Cody Regis, 3b, Fr.	.312	189	41	59	17	1	9	47	7
Justin Uribe, ss, Fr.	.308	172	20	53	6	0	3	27	3
Trevor Brown, c, Fr.	.300	60	8	18	1	0	1	9	3
Brett Krill, of, Jr.	.289	201	44	58	14	1	7	38	7
Adrian Williams, ss, Jr.	.286	21	4	6	0	0	0	1	0
Niko Gallego, ss, Fr.	.267	232	51	62	14	2	3	33	27
Chris Giovinazzo, of, Jr.	.264	144	30	38	4	2	3	16	8
Steve Rodriguez, c, So.	.249	181	35	45	8	1	8	37	1

PLAYER, POS., YEAR	W	L	ERA	G	SV	IP	H	BB	SO
Dan Klein, rhp, So.	6	1	1.90	39	10	52	39	11	55
Garett Claypool, rhp, Sr.	8	3	2.29	21	0	83	49	21	74
Rob Rasmussen, lhp, Jr.	11	3	2.72	19	0	109	88	35	128
Trevor Bauer, rhp, So.	12	3	3.02	18	0	131	121	41	165
Erik Goeddel, rhp, So.	2	0	3.06	36	1	50	44	23	59
Matt Grace, lhp, Jr.	0	1	3.18	33	1	28	26	8	23
Gerrit Cole, rhp, So.	11	4	3.37	19	0	123	92	52	153
Mitchell Beacom, lhp, So.	1	1	4.58	14	0	18	13	3	22
Brandon Lodge, rhp, So.	0	0	5.06	7	0	5	11	0	3
Matt Drummond, lhp, Jr.	0	1	5.23	11	0	10	12	8	8

3. TEXAS CHRISTIAN

Coach: Jim Schlossnagle. **Record:** 54-14.

PLAYER, POS., YEAR	AVG	AB	R	H	2B	3B	HR	RBI	SB
Jantzen Witte, 3b, Fr.	.374	163	32	61	15	1	4	39	2

PLAYER, POS., YEAR	AVG	AB	R	H	2B	3B	HR	RBI	SB
Jimmie Pharr, c, Jr.	.363	91	26	33	9	0	7	21	0
Jason Coats, of, So.	.361	274	68	99	23	4	13	69	8
Joe Weik, dh, Jr.	.357	112	23	40	7	0	6	29	0
Josh Elander, of, Fr.	.356	194	41	69	16	4	2	33	11
Bryan Holaday, c, Sr.	.355	279	72	99	24	1	17	53	3
Brance Rivera of, So.	.342	187	46	64	8	0	6	28	9
Matt Curry, 1b, Sr.	.339	248	65	84	26	2	18	65	12
Taylor Featherston, ss, So.	.338	231	59	78	16	7	8	52	6
Jerome Pena, 2b, Jr.	.313	243	55	76	13	1	11	52	7
Aaron Schultz, of, So.	.293	222	46	65	13	1	9	53	11
Zac Jordan, of, So.	.273	44	10	12	3	0	0	4	0
Kyle Von Tungeln, of, Fr.	.236	89	25	21	4	2	0	16	3
Davy Wright, ss, Fr.	.195	41	5	8	1	0	0	3	0

PLAYER, POS., YEAR	W	L	ERA	G	SV	IP	H	BB	SO
Kaleb Merck, rhp, So.	2	1	1.47	22	3	31	21	6	23
Tyler Lockwood, rhp, Sr.	6	2	2.19	28	8	66	58	21	41
Steven Maxwell, rhp, Jr.	11	2	2.70	18	0	103	89	34	93
Matt Purke, lhp, Fr.	16	0	3.02	20	0	116	91	34	142
Kyle Winkler, rhp, So.	12	3	3.39	19	0	117	111	36	92
Trent Appleby, rhp, Jr.	3	1	4.39	23	1	41	49	12	24
Paul Gerrish, rhp, Sr.	1	3	4.65	19	0	50	67	17	42
Erik Miller, rhp, So.	1	1	4.67	19	0	27	28	12	30
Walker Kelly, lhp, Sr.	0	0	5.87	6	0	8	5	11	13
Eric Marshall, rhp, Sr.	0	0	6.28	14	0	14	13	9	15
Greg Holle, rhp, Sr.	2	1	7.79	16	1	35	43	10	38

4. ARIZONA STATE

Coach: Tim Esmay. **Record:** 52-10.

PLAYER, POS., YEAR	AVG	AB	R	H	2B	3B	HR	RBI	SB
Deven Marrero, ss, Fr.	.397	156	31	62	12	3	6	42	11
Riccio Torrez, 1b, So.	.393	234	65	92	27	1	10	54	20
Zack MacPhee, 2b, So.	.389	229	67	89	8	14	9	64	20
Xorge Carrillo, c, Jr.	.353	34	10	12	3	0	2	7	1
Jordan Swagerty, c, So.	.352	54	13	19	6	0	0	7	1
Johnny Ruettiger, of, So.	.351	191	49	67	7	7	4	35	10
Zach Wilson, dh, So.	.349	186	38	65	17	2	8	45	4
Andrew Aplin, of, Fr.	.337	89	25	30	3	2	0	14	7
Jimmy Patterson, of, Jr.	.333	15	6	5	3	0	1	4	1
Drew Maggi, ss/of, Jr.	.326	261	54	85	10	3	5	41	36
Kole Calhoun, of, Sr.	.321	224	61	72	11	2	17	59	7
Austin Barnes, c, So.	.272	147	31	40	12	1	1	24	5
Raoul Torrez, 3b, Jr.	.268	190	35	51	12	1	3	45	9
Matt Newman, of, So.	.265	155	32	41	15	1	2	28	4

PLAYER, POS., YEAR	W	L	ERA	G	SV	IP	H	BB	SO
Josh Moody, lhp, Jr.	2	0	0.75	7	0	12	9	2	11
Brady Rodgers, rhp, Fr.	4	3	2.11	22	3	73	53	11	67
Mitchell Lambson, lhp, So.	8	2	2.16	39	3	75	41	20	96
Jordan Swagerty, rhp, So.	2	0	2.19	34	14	37	34	10	48
Jake Barrett, rhp, Fr.	2	0	3.41	28	2	29	26	10	43
Seth Blair, rhp, Jr.	12	1	3.64	18	0	106	112	29	108
Jake Borup, rhp, So.	11	1	4.08	16	0	82	79	26	63
Merrill Kelly, rhp, Jr.	10	3	4.23	18	0	100	99	37	78
Alex Blackford, rhp, Fr.	0	0	4.50	6	1	12	13	8	12
Jimmy Patterson, lhp, Jr.	1	0	4.73	16	0	32	42	14	27

5. OKLAHOMA

Coach: Sunny Golloway. **Record:** 50-18.

PLAYER, POS., YEAR	AVG	AB	R	H	2B	3B	HR	RBI	SB
Cale Ellis, ss, Jr.	.429	21	9	9	0	1	1	14	1
Elliott Blair, of, Jr.	.414	29	13	12	1	1	3	7	2
Garrett Buechele, 3b, Jr.	.359	262	55	94	16	2	17	65	3
Cody Reine, of, So.	.340	144	35	49	7	1	10	42	4
Tyler Ogle, c, So.	.331	163	39	54	11	0	11	46	4
Kaleb Herren, of, Jr.	.329	73	13	24	7	0	2	10	3
Chris Ellison, of, So.	.326	193	55	63	10	3	4	32	24
Danny Black, 2b, Jr.	.320	206	38	66	11	6	5	48	14
Ross Hubbard, c, Sr.	.318	88	24	28	1	1	4	11	0
Cameron Seitzer, 1b, So.	.305	220	49	67	15	1	16	53	2
Max White, of, Fr.	.293	215	48	63	13	1	15	43	7
Ricky Eisenberg, dh, Jr.	.275	120	22	33	5	2	3	12	3

PLAYER, POS., YEAR	AVG	AB	R	H	2B	3B	HR	RBI	SB
Casey Johnson, of, Jr.	.267	105	16	28	3	0	2	10	2
Drew Harrison, if, Fr.	.243	70	14	17	5	0	3	14	0
Jack Mayfield, if, Fr.	.235	34	5	8	2	0	0	6	1
Erik Ross, of, Jr.	.194	67	26	13	2	0	0	8	12

PLAYER, POS., YEAR	W	L	ERA	G	SV	IP	H	BB	SO
Jason Chowning, rhp, Sr.	1	0	2.11	13	0	21	16	10	30
Jack Mayfield, rhp, Fr.	5	0	2.47	17	0	44	43	13	29
Jarrett Semler, rhp, Sr.	0	0	3.14	12	0	14	13	6	20
Drew Verhagen, rhp, Fr.	0	0	3.38	6	0	13	14	6	13
Jeremy Erben, rhp, Sr.	7	1	3.43	34	5	76	70	29	79
Michael Rocha, rhp, Jr.	8	2	3.53	20	0	74	67	22	55
Ryan Duke, rhp, Jr.	3	2	3.75	25	12	36	33	16	39
Ryan Gibson, lhp, Fr.	5	2	3.76	12	0	41	40	23	40
Anthony Collazo, lhp, Jr.	1	0	3.92	24	0	21	18	9	27
Brandon Bargas, lhp, Fr.	0	0	3.97	12	0	11	13	6	13
Bobby Shore, rhp, Jr.	10	5	4.12	17	0	94	90	36	77
J.R. Robinson, lhp, Sr.	2	3	4.31	18	0	56	64	24	65
Zach Neal, rhp, Jr.	8	3	4.43	18	0	106	112	24	95

6. FLORIDA STATE

Coach: Mike Martin. Record: 48-20.

PLAYER, POS., YEAR	AVG	AB	R	H	2B	3B	HR	RBI	SB
Sean Gilmartin, of/1b, So.	.383	47	11	18	6	1	0	11	0
Tyler Holt, of, Jr.	.355	259	87	92	26	3	13	48	30
Sherman Johnson, 3b, Jr.	.337	249	55	84	15	1	10	58	7
Stephen McGee, c, Fr.	.333	12	1	4	4	0	0	2	0
Mike McGee, of, Jr.	.328	250	61	82	15	1	17	73	5
Jayce Boyd, 1b, Fr.	.326	227	49	74	15	1	8	39	4
James Ramsey, of, So.	.287	230	57	66	14	6	9	63	11
Justin Gonzalez, if, Fr.	.287	94	24	27	4	2	2	21	2
Stephen Cardullo, ss, Sr.	.283	258	69	73	15	1	11	53	21
Rafael Lopez, c, Jr.	.278	151	30	42	10	1	2	24	0
Devon Travis, 2b, Fr.	.276	156	29	43	8	4	3	22	5
Stuart Tapley, dh, Jr.	.272	195	42	53	11	0	7	38	7
Ohmed Danesh, of, Jr.	.238	42	8	10	1	0	1	11	4
Parker Brunelle, c, Jr.	.207	82	16	17	3	1	3	19	0
Taiwan Easterling, of, So.	.130	23	1	3	0	0	0	2	1

PLAYER, POS., YEAR	W	L	ERA	G	SV	IP	H	BB	SO
Tye Buckley, lhp, Jr.	0	0	2.70	19	0	13	9	14	8
Mike McGee, rhp, Jr.	4	1	2.96	20	13	27	15	18	33
Daniel Bennett, rhp, Jr.	5	1	3.51	35	3	41	41	16	46
Scott Sitz, rhp, Fr.	5	0	3.76	17	0	41	30	15	27
Tyler Everett, rhp, Jr.	3	1	3.77	23	1	45	49	22	39
Brian Busch, lhp, So.	6	2	3.94	21	0	82	65	37	73
Hunter Scantling, rhp, So.	3	2	4.47	19	0	46	46	13	42
Geoff Parker, rhp, Jr.	4	1	4.69	32	3	81	84	40	72
Sean Gilmartin, lhp, So.	9	8	5.24	20	0	112	134	34	108
John Gast, lhp, Jr.	7	3	5.30	21	0	71	83	28	64
Robert Benincasa, rhp, Fr.	2	0	5.32	13	0	22	24	18	16
Robby Scott, lhp, Jr.	0	0	5.40	8	0	5	1	4	6
Andrew Durden, rhp, Jr.	0	1	7.71	11	0	9	12	5	8

7. FLORIDA

Coach: Kevin O'Sullivan. Record: 41-17.

PLAYER, POS., YEAR	AVG	AB	R	H	2B	3B	HR	RBI	SB
Brian Johnson, dh, Fr.	.405	84	13	34	5	1	4	21	0
Matt den Dekker, of, Sr.	.352	247	65	87	7	3	13	49	23
Austin Maddox, 3b, Fr.	.333	264	48	88	16	0	17	72	0
Preston Tucker, 1b, So.	.331	245	50	81	17	2	11	49	8
Ben McMahan, c, So.	.325	77	12	25	3	0	2	11	4
Kamm Washington, of, Fr.	.308	65	15	20	3	0	1	6	8
Tyler Thompson, of, So.	.301	146	26	44	4	3	6	28	6
Nolan Fontana, ss, Fr.	.287	216	56	62	15	2	3	23	11
Daniel Pigott, of, So.	.268	149	25	40	10	2	1	22	4
Mike Zunino, c, Fr.	.267	176	31	47	7	1	9	41	8
Jerico Weitzel, if, So.	.262	42	10	11	3	0	1	4	4
Jonathan Pigott, of, Sr.	.260	96	18	25	5	1	3	13	3
Bryson Smith, 3b, Jr.	.255	106	17	27	2	0	3	22	7
Cody Dent, if, Fr.	.233	30	4	7	0	0	0	2	2
Josh Adams, 2b, Jr.	.224	232	43	52	12	0	9	42	6
Hampton Tignor, c, Sr.	.125	16	3	2	1	0	0	3	0

PLAYER, POS., YEAR	W	L	ERA	G	SV	IP	H	BB	SO
Kevin Chapman, lhp, Jr.	3	0	1.65	31	11	44	30	7	44
Steven Rodriguez, lhp, Fr.	2	0	2.57	20	1	28	28	5	26
Hudson Randall, rhp, Fr.	8	4	3.24	20	0	97	102	21	69
Jeff Barfield, rhp, Sr.	4	0	3.38	25	2	37	31	2	24
Alex Panteliodis, lhp, So.	11	3	3.51	18	0	100	86	23	82
Chas Spottswood, rhp, Sr.	1	0	3.95	8	0	14	15	4	7
Brian Johnson, lhp, Fr.	6	4	4.03	16	0	74	88	14	51
Tommy Toledo, rhp, So.	3	2	4.39	11	0	27	32	8	27
Greg Larson, rhp, So.	3	1	5.70	25	3	36	46	4	31
Nick Maronde, lhp, So.	2	0	6.15	22	1	26	22	24	37
Anthony DeSclafani, rhp, So.	2	3	7.08	19	0	41	60	8	29
Justin Poovey, rhp, So.	1	0	7.20	14	0	20	33	10	16
Matt Campbell, rhp, Jr.	0	0	9.53	8	0	11	23	0	8

8. VIRGINIA

Coach: Brian O'Connor. Record: 51-14.

PLAYER, POS., YEAR	AVG	AB	R	H	2B	3B	HR	RBI	SB
Keith Werman, 2b, So.	.414	152	32	63	5	4	0	23	10
Stephen Bruno, if, Fr.	.388	98	30	38	9	1	3	30	5
Phil Gosselin, of, Jr.	.382	262	67	100	22	4	11	61	18
John Barr, dh, Jr.	.373	142	34	53	11	2	1	22	7
Reed Gragnani, if, Fr.	.365	63	12	23	3	0	0	18	3
Jarrett Parker, of, Jr.	.333	243	56	81	17	8	10	56	12
Tyler Cannon, ss, Sr.	.330	227	49	75	19	3	3	38	10
Kenny Swab, c/1b/of, Jr.	.328	122	30	40	7	0	4	28	2
Steven Proscia, 3b, So.	.314	255	52	80	18	4	10	65	8
John Hicks, 1b, So.	.307	244	59	75	20	0	8	48	9
Chris Taylor, if, Fr.	.305	59	19	18	3	1	0	7	0
Dan Grovatt, of, Jr.	.291	234	47	68	10	4	9	60	6
Danny Hultzen, 1b, Jr.	.281	57	16	16	0	0	0	10	3
David Coleman, of, Jr.	.217	23	6	5	1	0	1	4	0
Franco Valdes, c, Jr.	.217	106	14	23	5	1	1	13	0

PLAYER, POS., YEAR	W	L	ERA	G	SV	IP	H	BB	SO
Chad O'Connor, rhp, Fr.	0	0	1.35	10	0	13	10	4	16
Shane Halley, rhp, So.	2	0	1.98	8	0	14	10	9	16
Danny Hultzen, lhp, Jr.	11	1	2.78	16	0	107	75	24	123
Kevin Arico, rhp, Jr.	1	1	2.88	29	18	34	32	8	44
Tyler Wilson, rhp, Jr.	8	4	3.41	31	3	63	45	25	67
Branden Kline, rhp, Fr.	5	1	3.62	22	3	65	54	20	56
Will Roberts, rhp, So.	3	0	3.82	10	1	31	32	20	26
Robert Morey, rhp, Jr.	9	4	4.20	16	0	99	84	41	77
Cody Winiarski, rhp, Jr.	5	0	4.68	17	0	75	82	27	44
Justin Thompson, rhp, So.	3	0	4.79	13	0	21	16	8	27
Corey Hunt, rhp, Jr.	0	0	6.00	11	0	12	16	7	10
Whit Mayberry, rhp, Fr.	1	2	6.29	13	0	24	30	11	24
Neal Davis, lhp, Sr.	2	1	6.43	21	0	21	26	8	14

9. TEXAS

Coach: Augie Garrido. Record: 50-13.

PLAYER, POS., YEAR	AVG	AB	R	H	2B	3B	HR	RBI	SB
Tant Shepherd, 1b, Jr.	.337	246	64	83	19	2	8	37	14
Jordan Weymouth, if, Jr.	.333	33	10	11	2	2	0	4	0
Russell Moldenhauer, dh, Sr.	.326	178	41	58	14	1	9	41	0
Cohl Walla, of, Fr.	.316	228	41	72	12	2	8	40	14
Paul Montalbano, of, Jr.	.316	19	4	6	1	1	0	7	0
Kevin Keyes, of, Jr.	.311	238	49	74	12	0	15	59	14
Cameron Rupp, c, Jr.	.304	240	50	73	13	0	10	54	0
Jonathan Walsh, c/of, Fr.	.273	77	15	21	7	0	3	20	1
Kyle Lusson, of, Sr.	.264	53	15	14	1	1	2	8	6
Kevin Lusson, 3b, So.	.263	205	41	54	11	0	14	48	6
Brandon Loy, ss, So.	.252	214	43	54	10	2	1	24	12
Connor Rowe, of, Jr.	.237	169	21	40	9	3	2	17	6
Jordan Etier, 2b, So.	.224	205	31	46	8	2	9	33	14
Tim Maitland, of, So.	.071	14	1	1	0	1	0	2	0

PLAYER, POS., YEAR	W	L	ERA	G	SV	IP	H	BB	SO
Chance Ruffin, rhp, Jr.	6	1	1.11	37	14	65	42	19	97
Keifer Nuncio, rhp, Fr.	2	0	1.35	5	0	7	5	3	2
Kendal Carrillo, rhp, Jr.	3	0	1.45	11	0	19	10	2	16
Hoby Milner, lhp, Fr.	3	1	1.97	18	0	32	29	12	31
Taylor Jungmann, rhp, So.	8	3	2.03	17	0	120	88	41	129
Sam Stafford, lhp, So.	0	0	2.61	8	0	21	11	13	29
Cole Green, rhp, Jr.	11	2	2.74	17	0	112	88	27	75
Andrew McKirahan, lhp, So.	2	1	2.78	23	0	23	15	7	17
Stayton Thomas, rhp, Jr.	3	0	2.92	29	1	37	37	14	28

Brandon Workman, rhp, Jr.	12	2	3.35	17	0	105	98	23	101
Austin Dicharry, rhp, So.	0	3	3.62	7	0	27	25	12	20

10. CLEMSON

Coach: Jack Leggett. **Record:** 45-25.

PLAYER, POS., YEAR	AVG	AB	R	H	2B	3B	HR	RBI	SB
Brad Miller, ss, So.	.357	252	71	90	19	4	8	49	9
John Hinson, 3b, So.	.351	251	60	88	9	1	17	75	25
Kyle Parker, of, Jr.	.344	247	86	85	15	1	20	64	4
Mike Freeman, 2b, Sr.	.331	299	68	99	24	1	8	57	11
Richie Shaffer, 1b, Fr.	.323	158	45	51	11	0	7	36	2
Jeff Schaus, of, Jr.	.320	284	69	91	14	2	15	87	9
Wilson Boyd, of, Jr.	.301	229	47	69	14	0	5	46	2
Will Lamb, dh, So.	.289	173	42	50	6	2	4	36	14
Spencer Kieboom, c, Fr.	.263	57	10	15	5	0	0	10	0
Addison Johnson, of, Jr.	.256	82	16	21	1	2	2	14	8
John Nester, c, Jr.	.245	143	20	35	9	0	2	24	2
Jason Stolz, if, So.	.222	81	10	18	3	0	1	14	4
Chris Epps, of, Jr.	.221	172	45	38	8	1	3	16	16
Phil Pohl, c, So.	.212	66	12	14	7	1	1	19	0

PLAYER, POS., YEAR	W	L	ERA	G	SV	IP	H	BB	SO
Kevin Kyle, lhp, Fr.	0	1	3.00	13	0	12	10	5	5
Scott Firth, rhp, Fr.	2	1	3.58	16	0	33	43	12	25
Alex Frederick, rhp, Jr.	7	2	3.75	33	4	62	63	28	54
Casey Harman, lhp, Jr.	8	4	3.79	19	0	121	115	34	105
Kevin Brady, rhp, Fr.	1	0	4.58	22	1	37	47	8	45
David Haselden, rhp, So.	4	4	4.61	22	2	41	47	13	29
Josh Thrailkill, rhp, Jr.	0	0	4.63	10	0	12	12	1	12
Dominic Leone, rhp, Fr.	3	2	4.78	22	0	58	69	22	40
Scott Weisman, rhp, So.	9	2	4.90	19	0	97	102	34	73
Will Lamb, lhp, So.	4	4	5.02	18	2	52	57	25	30
Tomas Cruz, rhp, Sr.	3	3	5.36	24	3	40	48	18	27
Jonathan Meyer, rhp, Fr.	2	1	5.90	20	2	29	34	8	23
Mike Kent, rhp, Fr.	1	1	7.80	6	0	15	15	10	8
Justin Sarratt, rhp, Sr.	1	0	11.12	6	0	11	17	7	6

11. CAL STATE FULLERTON

Coach: Dave Serrano. **Record:** 46-18.

PLAYER, POS., YEAR	AVG	AB	R	H	2B	3B	HR	RBI	SB
Gary Brown, of, Jr.	.438	210	63	92	20	8	6	41	32
Corey Jones, 2b, Jr.	.374	222	50	83	13	6	9	56	6
Christian Colon, ss, Jr.	.358	268	73	96	18	2	17	68	13
Carlos Lopez, dh, Fr.	.354	237	44	84	16	3	7	51	5
Tyler Pill, of, So.	.354	198	43	70	13	1	7	42	10
Casey Watkins, if, Fr.	.347	49	17	17	7	1	0	10	2
Nick Ramirez, 1b, So.	.346	260	62	90	28	1	16	75	6
Billy Marcoe, c, Sr.	.333	207	33	69	11	1	3	32	6
Richie Pedroza, if, Fr.	.331	124	30	41	5	1	0	22	4
Joey Siddons, of, Sr.	.303	175	32	53	6	0	0	15	5
Austin Kingsolver, of, Fr.	.247	85	13	21	3	2	0	12	10
Walker Moore, if, Jr.	.227	75	8	17	3	0	0	11	5
Zach Tanida, c, Jr.	.212	33	6	7	3	0	0	4	0
Anthony Hutting, of, Fr.	.208	48	7	10	4	0	0	13	0
Geno Escalante, c, Fr.	.154	13	1	2	0	0	0	1	0
Matt Orloff, if, Jr.	.139	36	5	5	1	0	0	3	3
Ivory Thomas, of, Fr.	.118	17	3	2	0	1	0	2	5

PLAYER, POS., YEAR	W	L	ERA	G	SV	IP	H	BB	SO
Noe Ramirez, rhp, So.	12	1	2.54	16	0	106	92	19	119
Dylan Floro, rhp, Fr.	7	2	3.26	27	2	91	102	11	69
Tyler Pill, rhp, So.	4	4	3.36	10	0	62	54	13	58
Nick Ramirez, lhp, So.	1	3	3.50	27	11	44	41	8	38
Collin O'Connell, rhp, So.	1	1	3.65	17	1	44	42	9	35
Daniel Renken rhp, Jr.	12	2	3.96	20	0	105	104	40	91
Derrick Dingeman, rhp, So.	1	0	4.58	16	0	18	19	4	13
Raymond Hernandez, rhp, Jr.	1	0	4.70	4	0	8	7	2	8
Kyle Mertins, rhp, Sr.	3	2	4.75	20	0	47	61	16	31
Kevin Rath, lhp, Jr.	2	3	4.94	20	1	31	25	28	23
David Hurlbut, lhp, Sr.	2	0	9.92	17	0	16	20	6	19

12. COASTAL CAROLINA

Coach: Gary Gilmore. **Record:** 46-18.

PLAYER, POS., YEAR	AVG	AB	R	H	2B	3B	HR	RBI	SB
Tommy LaStella, 2b, So.	.378	246	63	93	14	2	14	66	6

PLAYER, POS., YEAR	AVG	AB	R	H	2B	3B	HR	RBI	SB
Keith Hardwick, c, Jr.	.364	11	5	4	2	0	0	5	0
Rico Noel, of, Jr.	.349	238	82	83	18	2	12	63	56
Jose Iglesias, c, Sr.	.344	224	55	77	16	0	16	80	2
Taylor Motter, ss, So.	.336	214	55	72	22	1	12	49	11
Chance Gilmore, of, Sr.	.336	226	63	76	21	1	12	55	10
Scott Woodward, 3b, Jr.	.324	210	75	68	7	4	5	35	55
Steve Davis, if, So.	.322	146	36	47	8	4	4	28	4
Rich Witten, if, So.	.312	77	22	24	9	0	4	22	0
Adam Rice, 1b, Sr.	.308	237	43	73	13	2	9	50	3
Hayes Orton, of, Jr.	.280	25	10	7	0	0	1	6	0
Daniel Bowman, of, So.	.279	262	53	73	13	2	15	53	8
Josh Conway, of, Jr.	.274	62	18	17	1	0	3	16	6
Luke Schlechte, of, Jr.	.217	23	6	5	1	0	0	6	0
Tucker Frawley, c, Sr.	.209	43	10	9	2	0	3	7	0

PLAYER, POS., YEAR	W	L	ERA	G	SV	IP	H	BB	SO
Jackson Geary, rhp, Fr.	1	0	2.12	13	0	17	14	5	11
Ryan Connolly, rhp, Fr.	3	0	2.15	40	0	50	45	11	48
Anthony Meo, rhp, So.	13	2	2.61	18	0	97	82	34	94
Austin Fleet, rhp, Sr.	6	2	2.85	31	8	60	55	19	57
Matt Rein, lhp, Jr.	7	1	2.97	24	2	58	50	23	43
Josh Conway, rhp, So.	2	0	3.30	19	1	46	39	15	33
Cody Wheeler, lhp, Jr.	12	0	3.64	18	0	111	106	41	113
Keith Hessler, lhp, So.	2	2	3.82	16	1	31	32	13	26
Jim Birmingham, lhp, Jr.	6	2	4.82	14	0	52	46	28	29
Matt Laney, lhp, Jr.	3	1	4.93	34	2	42	43	24	44
Mike Hughes, rhp, Fr.	0	0	7.20	5	0	10	13	7	16
Brad Goldberg, rhp, So.	0	0	7.94	5	0	6	9	3	6

13. ARKANSAS

Coach: Dave Van Horn. **Record:** 46-21.

PLAYER, POS., YEAR	AVG	AB	R	H	2B	3B	HR	RBI	SB
Zack Cox, 3b, So.	.429	238	67	102	14	1	9	48	11
Tom Hauskey, c, Sr.	.357	28	5	10	3	0	1	8	0
Kyle Robinson, of, Jr.	.353	17	9	6	2	0	0	5	0
Collin Kuhn, of, So.	.336	259	66	87	18	4	16	52	17
Brett Eibner, of, Jr.	.333	216	66	72	17	0	22	71	3
Travis Sample, of, Jr.	.321	137	18	44	8	1	3	21	1
Bo Bigham, 2b, So.	.316	228	43	72	15	1	3	30	14
James McCann, c, So.	.286	213	32	61	6	0	9	34	3
Monk Kreder, dh, Jr.	.284	222	28	63	14	0	4	45	1
Andy Wilkins, 1b, Jr.	.281	235	49	66	14	1	15	69	4
Tim Carver, ss, Fr.	.267	232	33	62	11	1	4	36	9
Derrick Bleeker, if, Fr.	.267	15	6	4	0	0	1	3	1
Kyle Atkins, of, Fr.	.214	14	7	3	0	0	0	2	5
Matt Vinson, of, Fr.	.204	93	24	19	3	2	3	15	2
Matt Reynolds, if, Fr.	.203	64	13	13	3	0	1	5	0
Jarrod McKinney, of, So.	.190	63	14	12	2	0	1	5	2

PLAYER, POS., YEAR	W	L	ERA	G	SV	IP	H	BB	SO
Christian Kowalchuk, lhp, Sr.	3	0	2.11	13	0	21	19	3	21
Drew Smyly, lhp, So.	9	1	2.80	18	0	103	85	36	114
T.J. Forrest, rhp, Sr.	8	1	3.38	20	1	53	57	11	41
D.J. Baxendale, rhp, Fr.	0	2	3.58	29	7	60	62	18	44
Geoffrey Davenport, lhp, So.	2	2	3.63	26	0	40	40	17	46
Jordan Pratt, rhp, Fr.	3	1	3.76	24	2	41	37	18	50
Jeremy Heatley, rhp, So.	5	0	4.01	23	2	43	37	16	47
Brett Eibner, rhp, Jr.	3	5	4.34	15	1	58	65	11	56
Randall Fant, lhp, Fr.	3	2	4.37	10	0	35	29	10	25
Jason Fuqua, rhp, Jr.	0	0	4.50	10	0	12	16	4	10
Mike Bolsinger, rhp, Sr.	6	5	4.81	23	0	86	85	27	79
Sam Murphy, rhp, So.	1	2	6.87	7	0	18	19	13	14

14. VANDERBILT

Coach: Tim Corbin. **Record:** 46-20.

PLAYER, POS., YEAR	AVG	AB	R	H	2B	3B	HR	RBI	SB
Anthony Gomez, 2b, Fr.	.379	214	41	81	10	0	2	30	9
Jordan Wormsley, of, Jr.	.375	16	3	6	3	0	0	2	0
Bryan Johns, if, Jr.	.370	135	31	50	13	2	1	22	3
Jason Esposito, 3b, So.	.359	262	65	94	25	1	12	64	31
Drew Fann, c, So.	.358	53	9	19	6	0	0	7	0
Curt Casali, c, Jr.	.309	175	37	54	13	0	8	42	3
Aaron Westlake, 1b/c, Jr.	.308	260	66	80	16	1	14	61	6
Connor Harrell, of, Fr.	.300	210	33	63	15	0	3	39	5
Regan Flaherty, 1b/of, Fr.	.292	24	4	7	5	0	0	8	0

PLAYER, POS., YEAR	AVG	AB	R	H	2B	3B	HR	RBI	SB
Brian Harris, ss, Sr.	.286	227	58	65	12	1	5	34	4
Andrew Giobbi, c, Sr.	.284	275	46	78	16	0	7	57	8
Joe Loftus, of, So.	.277	235	46	65	15	1	8	39	4
Mike Yastrzemski, of, Fr.	.260	131	18	34	7	1	3	18	5
Andrew Harris, if	.214	14	2	3	1	0	0	5	0
Riley Reynolds, if, So.	.209	86	20	18	3	0	0	7	2

PLAYER, POS., YEAR	W	L	ERA	G	SV	IP	H	BB	SO
Grayson Garvin, lhp, So.	1	1	1.25	13	1	36	32	10	38
Richie Goodenow, lhp, Jr.	3	1	2.23	31	1	44	31	12	47
Corey Williams, lhp, Fr.	1	0	2.65	12	1	17	14	6	17
Will Clinard, rhp, Fr.	4	0	2.68	21	1	44	43	17	38
Russell Brewer, rhp, Jr.	2	2	3.07	19	6	29	30	8	39
Chase Reid, rhp, Jr.	4	2	3.46	28	3	68	63	14	66
Sonny Gray, rhp, So.	10	5	3.48	19	1	109	101	48	113
Drew Hayes, rhp, Sr.	6	0	3.91	24	0	53	44	26	49
Taylor Hill, rhp, Jr.	6	5	4.46	20	0	107	118	27	74
Jack Armstrong, rhp, So.	7	4	4.71	16	0	78	90	39	50
Sam Selman, lhp, Fr.	0	0	9.00	4	0	6	10	4	8
Navery Moore, rhp, Jr.	2	0	9.24	10	0	13	15	12	16

15. MIAMI

Coach: Jim Morris. **Record:** 43-20.

PLAYER, POS., YEAR	AVG	AB	R	H	2B	3B	HR	RBI	SB
Yasmandi Grandal, c, Jr.	.367	245	56	90	18	1	18	78	4
Chris Pelaez, of, Jr.	.350	254	82	89	21	2	9	55	1
Scott Lawson, 1b, Sr.	.345	258	80	89	12	2	25	82	19
Nathan Melendres, of, So.	.335	257	43	86	16	2	5	66	12
Harold Martinez, 3b, So.	.328	268	83	88	21	2	11	51	12
Frankie Ratcliff, 2b, Fr.	.307	238	54	73	14	4	7	31	5
Stephen Perez, ss, Fr.	.297	128	17	38	5	3	3	25	1
Zeke DeVoss, of, Fr.	.246	187	37	46	6	1	3	32	13
Michael Broad, of, Jr.	.245	200	17	49	8	2	0	22	3
David Villasuso, c, So.	.209	67	17	14	0	0	4	14	3
Rony Rodriguez, if, So.	.208	144	26	30	1	0	0	13	17
Chantz Mack, of, Fr.	.179	39	6	7	1	0	0	0	0
Ryan Perry, of/1b, Sr.	.172	29	4	5	1	0	0	1	0

PLAYER, POS., YEAR	W	L	ERA	G	SV	IP	H	BB	SO
E.J. Encinosa, rhp, Fr.	6	2	3.25	21	2	44	38	10	31
Eric Erickson, lhp, Jr.	0	0	3.38	7	0	5	7	1	4
Chris Hernandez, lhp, Jr.	3	2	3.48	12	2	41	35	10	48
Daniel Miranda, lhp, So.	2	0	3.52	8	1	38	34	12	28
Eric Whaley, rhp, Fr.	3	1	3.73	29	3	51	46	12	47
David Gutierrez, rhp, Sr.	11	3	3.77	18	1	105	86	35	129
Jason Santana, rhp, Sr.	0	0	3.80	16	1	24	27	11	27
Sam Robinson, lhp, So.	1	0	3.86	3	0	9	12	3	10
Taylor Wulf, rhp, Sr.	7	0	3.88	22	1	46	47	14	34
Travis Miller, rhp, So.	2	0	4.00	29	1	36	39	11	30
Jerad Grundy, lhp, Fr.	4	2	4.40	23	1	61	74	12	28
Steven Ewing, lhp, Fr.	6	5	5.00	18	0	77	96	21	63
Joe Lovecchio, rhp, Fr.	1	3	6.00	14	0	30	26	13	28
Iden Nazario, lhp, Jr.	1	0	9.26	11	0	23	21	14	27

16. ALABAMA

Coach: Mitch Gaspard. **Record:** 42-25.

PLAYER, POS., YEAR	AVG	AB	R	H	2B	3B	HR	RBI	SB
Taylor Dugas, of, So.	.395	243	70	96	15	5	2	37	19
Josh Rutledge, ss, Jr.	.360	297	65	107	16	2	10	69	15
David Kindred, of, Jr.	.314	102	17	32	10	0	3	18	0
Clay Jones, 1b, Sr.	.313	249	53	78	14	1	17	66	3
John David Smelser, if, Jr.	.306	49	12	15	4	0	0	7	6
Jon Kelton, of/if, So.	.286	203	39	58	14	1	2	33	6
Brock Bennett, c, Jr.	.283	159	32	45	6	0	2	17	3
Ross Wilson, 2b, Jr.	.277	231	44	64	8	2	9	47	10
Brett Whitaker, dh, Fr.	.263	19	5	5	0	0	1	3	0
Cal Tinsley, if, Sr.	.262	61	11	16	6	0	0	8	0
Jake Smith, 3b, Sr.	.260	250	43	65	9	0	15	57	2
Brett Booth, c, Sr.	.255	106	16	27	4	1	2	15	1
Brandt Hendricks, of, Fr.	.250	52	5	13	1	0	0	3	0
Andrew Miller, of, Fr.	.247	178	27	44	8	1	1	27	0
Cody Trotter, c, Sr.	.210	81	17	17	6	0	2	13	0
Chris Smelley, c, Jr.	.152	33	5	5	0	0	0	2	0

PLAYER, POS., YEAR	W	L	ERA	G	SV	IP	H	BB	SO
Nathan Kilcrease, rhp, Jr.	8	3	2.85	34	4	98	81	21	82

Jimmy Nelson, rhp, Jr.	9	3	4.01	18	0	110	110	33	98
Tucker Hawley, rhp, Fr.	2	1	4.20	16	1	41	47	4	31
Brett Whitaker, rhp, Jr.	2	3	4.65	23	3	31	33	10	27
Jonathan Smart, lhp, Jr.	2	1	5.56	17	0	44	56	10	25
Jason Townsend, rhp, Jr.	2	1	5.77	22	0	39	47	25	38
Taylor Wolfe, lhp, Fr.	3	2	6.13	14	0	40	50	22	44
Adam Morgan, lhp, So.	7	5	6.18	18	0	90	113	32	72
Tyler White, rhp, So.	3	3	6.89	22	1	31	43	16	34
Jake Smith, rhp, Sr.	1	2	0.89	13	6	20	14	11	22
David Head, lhp, So.	1	0	6.14	20	1	22	26	14	15
Adam Windsor, lhp, Jr.	1	0	8.64	6	0	8	15	4	3
Matt Taylor, lhp, Fr.	0	0	12.79	11	0	13	20	8	16

17. LOUISVILLE

Coach: Dan McDonnell. **Record:** 50-14.

PLAYER, POS., YEAR	AVG	AB	R	H	2B	3B	HR	RBI	SB
Andrew Clark, 1b, Sr.	.370	189	52	70	15	1	13	61	1
Ryan Wright, 2b/ss, So.	.366	254	61	93	17	2	16	80	10
Phil Wunderlich, 3b, Jr.	.355	256	54	91	21	1	21	62	12
Adam Duvall, ss/2b, Sr.	.327	263	68	86	27	1	12	47	10
Stewart Ijames, of, So.	.324	244	47	79	18	0	14	63	7
Zak Wasserman, 1b, Fr.	.324	74	9	24	7	0	0	11	0
Jeff Arnold, c, Sr.	.306	242	64	74	20	2	3	32	16
J.J. Ethel, c, Jr.	.303	109	15	33	9	1	2	15	0
Drew Haynes, of, So.	.291	203	39	59	5	0	0	21	15
Josh Richmond, of, So.	.262	84	17	22	6	0	1	10	4
Cade Stallings, 3b, Jr.	.257	113	8	29	6	0	4	24	0
Mike Morrison, 1b/of, So.	.250	36	2	9	2	0	1	6	0
Kyle Grieshaber, if/of, Fr.	.239	155	24	37	9	1	1	15	7
Jarred Clarkson, of, Jr.	.125	16	6	2	1	0	0	0	0
Drew Fitzpatrick, of, Fr.	.045	22	5	1	0	0	0	1	0

PLAYER, POS., YEAR	W	L	ERA	G	SV	IP	H	BB	SO
Tyler Mathis, rhp, Sr.	2	0	1.89	12	1	19	17	11	19
Neil Holland, rhp, Jr.	8	1	2.08	29	17	56	30	16	59
Bob Revesz, lhp, Jr.	1	1	2.38	22	0	34	34	14	20
Thomas Royse, rhp, Jr.	9	1	2.85	16	0	104	100	26	99
Matt Koch, rhp, Fr.	3	0	3.27	11	0	44	37	9	31
Gabriel Shaw, rhp, So.	5	2	3.88	28	3	46	55	8	41
Justin Amlung, rhp, Fr.	5	2	4.27	20	0	65	72	14	55
Dean Kiekhefer, lhp, Jr.	3	4	4.31	19	0	63	65	19	39
Andy Flett, rhp, Fr.	0	1	4.32	5	0	8	6	2	3
Derek Self, rhp, So.	7	0	4.52	27	0	62	77	11	50
Matt Lea, rhp, Sr.	2	0	4.61	10	0	14	11	7	11
Tony Zych, rhp, So.	5	2	5.13	22	0	60	63	19	50

18. GEORGIA TECH

Coach: Danny Hall. **Record:** 47-15.

PLAYER, POS., YEAR	AVG	AB	R	H	2B	3B	HR	RBI	SB
Thomas Nichols, if, Jr.	.376	189	53	71	16	0	10	41	2
Tony Plagman, 1b, Sr.	.360	239	66	86	16	2	21	78	8
Chase Burnette, of, Jr.	.356	250	61	89	19	4	17	66	7
Derek Dietrich, ss, Jr.	.350	240	68	84	15	3	17	61	8
Jay Dantzler, of, Sr.	.336	113	33	38	4	1	8	33	6
Matt Skole, 3b, So.	.335	233	62	78	15	3	20	63	1
Jason Garofalo, 2b, Sr.	.333	27	7	9	1	1	1	9	0
Jeff Rowland, of, Jr.	.322	245	75	79	11	7	10	42	13
Sam Dove, if, Fr.	.300	10	4	3	1	0	0	0	0
Cole Leonida, c, Jr.	.296	240	52	71	14	1	11	56	4
Connor Winn, ss/2b, So.	.294	17	3	5	2	0	2	7	0
Jacob Esch, 2b, So.	.284	211	43	60	6	0	3	38	2
Brandon Thomas, of, Fr.	.262	84	18	22	4	3	0	13	5
Evan Martin, of/if, So.	.227	44	11	10	3	0	0	5	1
Jake Davies, 1b, So.	.200	25	2	5	1	0	0	3	0

PLAYER, POS., YEAR	W	L	ERA	G	SV	IP	H	BB	SO
Clay Dalton, rhp, Fr.	0	0	0.00	5	0	6	4	5	5
Taylor Wood, lhp, Jr.	0	0	2.03	13	0	13	6	6	17
Andrew Robinson, rhp, Sr.	4	0	2.43	26	8	33	35	8	25
Deck McGuire, rhp, Jr.	9	4	2.96	16	0	113	94	33	118
Patrick Long, rhp, Sr.	0	0	3.12	21	0	17	12	7	21
Jake Davies, lhp, So.	2	0	3.52	17	0	15	15	6	10
Zach Brewster, lhp, Jr.	1	0	3.60	15	0	10	9	11	9
Buck Farmer, rhp, Fr.	5	1	3.63	19	0	52	39	18	44
Mark Pope, rhp, So.	8	1	3.78	13	1	79	90	13	73

PLAYER, POS., YEAR	W	L	ERA	G	SV	IP	H	BB	SO
Ben McKinney, rhp, Fr.	0	1	4.82	11	0	9	11	3	7
Jed Bradley, lhp, So.	9	5	4.83	16	0	91	107	25	99
Kevin Jacob, rhp, Jr.	0	0	5.23	10	2	10	11	6	13
Brandon Cumpton, rhp, Jr.	9	3	5.50	15	0	74	86	32	53
Luke Bard, rhp, Fr.	0	0	7.43	19	2	27	30	14	25

19. AUBURN

Coach: John Pawlowski. **Record:** 43-21.

PLAYER, POS., YEAR	AVG	AB	R	H	2B	3B	HR	RBI	SB
Caleb Bowen, c, So.	.529	17	3	9	0	0	1	5	0
Hunter Morris, 1b, Jr.	.386	272	66	105	18	5	23	76	6
Trent Mummey, of, Jr.	.366	153	46	56	15	0	17	54	8
Ryan Jenkins, c, Sr.	.365	178	36	65	14	0	7	38	2
Dan Gamache, 3b, So.	.365	189	51	69	15	1	8	37	7
Justin Fradejas, of, Jr.	.358	193	52	69	8	1	3	33	14
Brian Fletcher, of, Jr.	.357	252	62	90	17	1	22	75	4
Tony Caldwell, c, Jr.	.349	189	42	66	8	0	10	41	6
Wes Gilmer, if/c, Jr.	.341	82	22	28	3	0	2	13	1
Casey McElroy, ss, So.	.325	209	47	68	11	0	9	43	1
Justin Bryant, 2b, Jr.	.323	99	27	32	4	1	5	32	0
Justin Hargett, if, Jr.	.316	209	46	66	15	1	2	32	6
Kevin Patterson, of/if, Jr.	.315	124	34	39	6	2	16	33	0
Creede Simspon, of/if, So.	.308	159	42	49	11	2	5	31	6

PLAYER, POS., YEAR	W	L	ERA	G	SV	IP	H	BB	SO
Austin Hubbard, rhp, Sr.	6	2	2.44	26	10	48	44	23	60
Sean Ray, lhp, Jr.	2	3	3.72	26	0	36	29	21	33
Michael Hurst, rhp, Sr.	2	1	4.20	18	2	30	30	13	30
Grant Dayton, lhp, Jr.	8	3	4.36	16	0	95	101	19	69
Dexter Price, rhp, So.	3	0	4.39	5	0	27	33	9	14
Slade Smith, rhp, Fr.	4	0	4.65	18	0	60	73	14	42
Bradley Hendrix, rhp, Jr.	4	2	5.35	22	1	34	48	14	28
Zach Blatt, rhp, So.	1	0	5.40	20	1	33	42	11	24
Cole Nelson, lhp, Jr.	6	3	5.64	18	0	69	76	30	67
Cory Luckie, lhp, So.	6	4	5.91	19	0	70	81	23	57
Stephen Kohlscheen, rhp, Jr.	1	0	6.49	17	2	26	25	15	23
Jon Luke Jacobs, rhp, So.	0	3	7.22	10	0	34	42	23	24

20. VIRGINIA TECH

Coach: Pete Hughes. **Record:** 40-22.

PLAYER, POS., YEAR	AVG	AB	R	H	2B	3B	HR	RBI	SB
Austin Wates, of/1b, Jr.	.382	225	61	86	16	5	8	54	18
Steve Domecus, c/of, Sr.	.365	252	62	92	27	1	13	60	12
Tim Smalling, ss, Jr.	.349	209	51	73	14	4	7	37	5
Buddy Sosnoskie, of, So.	.347	202	46	70	10	2	13	48	5
Andrew Rash, of, Fr.	.344	90	18	31	6	1	6	16	0
Luke Padgett, if/of, Sr.	.333	12	8	4	0	0	1	1	1
Brent Zimmerman, if, Fr.	.333	36	12	12	0	2	1	10	0
Sean Ryan, of, Sr.	.317	249	50	79	15	2	2	30	5
Michael Seaborn, 2b, Jr.	.283	230	43	65	12	1	7	44	2
Mike Kaminski, of, Sr.	.253	83	12	21	5	0	2	12	3
Anthony Sosnoskie, c, Sr.	.252	159	29	40	11	0	5	28	0
Matt Blow, 1b/3b, Jr.	.245	94	15	23	6	0	4	19	1
Tony Balisteri, if, Jr.	.217	115	20	25	3	1	3	13	8
Chris Kay, c, Jr.	.200	25	3	5	2	0	1	5	0

PLAYER, POS., YEAR	W	L	ERA	G	SV	IP	H	BB	SO
Ben Rowen, rhp, Sr.	5	2	2.67	38	6	54	44	10	63
Ronnie Shaban, rhp, So.	0	0	2.84	6	0	6	4	5	7
Jesse Hahn, rhp, Jr.	5	4	3.70	13	0	73	71	20	76
Justin Wright, lhp, Jr.	8	5	3.95	16	0	98	89	33	100
Brandon Fisher, rhp, Jr.	2	0	4.01	17	0	25	27	7	20
Sean McDermott, lhp, Jr.	1	1	4.66	14	0	19	23	5	12
Marc Zecchino, rhp, So.	1	1	4.74	14	0	44	37	15	26
Mathew Price, rhp, So.	7	4	4.95	17	0	91	100	26	85
Joe Mantiply, lhp, Fr.	4	1	5.62	22	0	58	67	18	59
Jake Joyce, rhp, Fr.	1	0	5.68	15	0	19	24	9	21
Manny Martir, rhp, So.	4	3	7.97	12	0	35	36	21	39
Patrick Scoggin, rhp, Fr.	1	1	9.00	8	0	19	28	12	18
Joe Parsons, rhp, Jr.	1	0	10.13	6	0	5	6	5	4

DAVID STONER

Virginia Tech's top hitter, Austin Wates

21. RICE

Coach: Wayne Graham. **Record:** 40-23.

PLAYER, POS., YEAR	AVG	AB	R	H	2B	3B	HR	RBI	SB
Anthony Rendon, 3b, So.	.394	226	83	89	12	1	26	85	14
Diego Seastrunk, c, Sr.	.369	179	47	66	17	1	9	52	3
Michael Fuda, of, So.	.346	231	59	80	7	6	7	45	6
Rick Hague, ss, Jr.	.340	259	71	88	20	0	15	55	10
Jimmy Comerota, 1b, Sr.	.329	216	61	71	7	3	6	47	8
Chad Mozingo, of, Jr.	.322	258	53	83	13	4	3	39	14
Jeremy Rathjen, of, So.	.317	221	52	70	20	0	13	69	0
Steven Sultzbaugh, of, Sr.	.317	180	46	57	11	2	6	39	2
Craig Manuel, c, So.	.288	118	12	34	5	1	1	17	0
Michael Ratterree, 2b, Fr.	.281	224	60	63	9	1	10	64	3
Abe Gonzales, if, Jr.	.231	26	4	6	2	0	0	8	0
Chase McDowell, of, Fr.	.222	45	4	10	1	1	0	12	0
Geoff Perrott, c, Fr.	.200	20	0	4	0	0	0	0	1

PLAYER, POS., YEAR	W	L	ERA	G	SV	IP	H	BB	SO
Doug Simmons, lhp, Jr.	4	0	2.66	20	0	20	12	17	14
Abe Gonzales, lhp, Jr.	4	3	3.13	28	3	55	57	15	33
J.T. Chargois, rhp, Fr.	3	2	3.29	15	0	27	33	4	14
Mike Ojala, rhp, Sr.	6	2	3.36	12	0	56	40	20	60
Jared Rogers, rhp, Sr.	8	2	3.83	18	1	87	96	14	49
Holt McNair, lhp, Fr.	1	0	3.93	15	0	18	21	7	11
Mark Haynes, rhp, Sr.	1	0	3.99	17	2	29	30	7	22
Anthony Fazio, rhp, Fr.	1	1	4.00	11	0	18	17	13	8
Boogie Anagnostou, rhp, Jr.	3	5	4.11	19	0	66	68	22	28
Taylor Wall, rhp, So.	5	5	4.45	17	0	85	75	30	61
Tyler Duffey, rhp, Fr.	2	2	5.27	26	4	41	43	16	45
Matthew Reckling, rhp, So.	1	1	6.32	10	1	16	14	11	13
Tony Cingrani, lhp, Jr.	1	0	8.59	6	0	22	27	16	13

22. UC IRVINE

Coach: Mike Gillespie. **Record:** 39-21.

PLAYER, POS., YEAR	AVG	AB	R	H	2B	3B	HR	RBI	SB
Jeff Cusick, 1b, Sr.	.379	232	43	88	21	0	8	62	1
Drew Hillman, of/if, Jr.	.352	91	24	32	7	1	4	19	0
Matt Summers, of, So.	.343	35	7	12	4	0	0	8	1
Jonathan Hurst, of/c, Jr.	.342	79	11	27	4	1	0	12	0

Baseball America 2011 Almanac • **455**

PLAYER, POS., YEAR	AVG	AB	R	H	2B	3B	HR	RBI	SB
Casey Stevenson, 2b, Sr.	.324	238	63	77	16	4	4	41	8
Brian Hernandez, 3b, Jr.	.322	236	44	76	19	2	4	44	5
Ronnie Shaeffer, c/dh, So.	.318	173	22	55	10	1	3	31	1
Ryan Fisher, of/if, Jr.	.308	130	24	40	11	0	4	20	3
Francis Larson, c, Sr.	.303	211	37	64	12	2	8	42	0
Jordan Leyland, if, So.	.301	83	9	25	6	2	2	13	2
D.J. Crumlich, ss, So.	.284	116	20	33	7	1	1	16	2
Sean Madigan, of, Jr.	.280	193	41	54	11	0	1	29	1
Jordan Fox, if, So.	.275	69	9	19	3	0	0	9	6
Dillon Bell, of, Sr.	.234	64	11	15	3	0	0	8	4
Tommy Reyes, if, So.	.229	105	20	24	3	0	0	9	4
Cory Olson, of, Sr.	.114	44	9	5	1	0	1	5	2

PLAYER, POS., YEAR	W	L	ERA	G	SV	IP	H	BB	SO
Daniel Bibona, lhp, Sr.	9	2	2.48	13	0	94	75	15	102
Nick Hoover, rhp, So.	2	0	2.48	20	1	29	18	14	34
Evan Brock, rhp, Fr.	6	4	3.14	20	1	63	34	30	62
Eric Pettis, rhp, Sr.	9	5	3.62	24	6	124	142	27	89
Christian Bergman, rhp, Sr.	9	3	3.72	20	1	102	109	16	78
Kyle Necke, rhp, Sr.	1	4	4.50	5	7	42	51	9	41
Matt Whitehouse, lhp, Fr.	0	0	4.50	10	0	6	8	7	10
Ruben Orosco, lhp, Fr.	0	0	5.40	14	0	12	14	3	6
Kyle Hooper, rhp, Fr.	0	0	7.61	18	0	24	45	4	14
Andy Lines, lhp, Fr.	1	1	8.44	20	1	11	11	11	13
Matt Summers, rhp, So.	2	2	8.51	21	0	31	40	18	32

23. TEXAS A&M

Coach: Rob Childress. **Record:** 43-21.

PLAYER, POS., YEAR	AVG	AB	R	H	2B	3B	HR	RBI	SB
Gregg Alcazar, c, Jr.	.418	55	11	23	4	0	2	11	0
Brodie Greene, of/if, Sr.	.395	266	74	105	18	7	14	55	23
Matt Juengel, if, So.	.359	167	30	60	10	1	11	39	2
Joe Patterson, 1b/c, Sr.	.348	253	47	88	16	0	9	48	9
Caleb Shofner, 3b, Jr.	.331	160	23	53	9	1	6	35	2
Kevin Gonzalez, c, Jr.	.318	192	24	61	10	0	9	38	5
Joaquin Hinojosa, of, Jr.	.270	148	22	40	6	2	1	20	3
Adam Smith, ss/2b, So.	.268	194	40	52	11	2	10	42	11
Kenny Jackson, if, Jr.	.263	114	21	30	4	0	0	9	3
John Stilson, if, So.	.250	36	5	9	4	1	0	3	4
Andrew Collazo, if/of, Jr.	.245	204	28	50	4	1	3	22	12
Tyler Naquin, of, Fr.	.244	172	29	42	8	0	2	19	6
Scott Arthur, if/of, So.	.218	170	31	37	9	1	0	8	20
Brandon Wood, of, Jr.	.206	68	13	14	5	1	0	8	5
Brett Parsons, of/1b, Jr.	.133	30	2	4	2	0	0	3	1

PLAYER, POS., YEAR	W	L	ERA	G	SV	IP	H	BB	SO
John Stilson, rhp, So.	9	1	0.80	33	10	79	51	23	114
Barret Loux, rhp, Jr.	11	2	2.83	17	0	105	78	34	136
Michael Wacha, rhp, Fr.	9	2	2.90	25	1	106	86	22	97
Ross Stripling, rhp, So.	6	5	4.50	17	0	88	100	29	89
Clayton Ehlert, rhp, Sr.	4	6	4.87	19	0	81	88	25	66
Shane Minks, rhp, Sr.	2	2	3.52	25	0	38	37	20	34
Nick Fleece, rhp, Jr.	1	2	3.76	17	1	38	50	7	23
Jake Feckley, rhp, Fr.	0	1	4.24	13	0	17	24	4	15
Dylan Mendoza, lhp, Fr.	0	0	6.75	9	0	7	8	9	2
Estevan Uriegas, lhp, So.	1	0	10.47	24	0	16	21	11	17
Kyle Martin, rhp, Fr.	0	0	13.50	6	0	5	9	6	10

24. WASHINGTON STATE

Coach: Donnie Marbut. **Record:** 37-22.

PLAYER, POS., YEAR	AVG	AB	R	H	2B	3B	HR	RBI	SB
Brett Jacobs, if, Fr.	.340	156	14	53	9	0	0	22	5
Cody Bartlett, 2b, Jr.	.323	189	46	61	16	1	7	34	8
Matt Fanelli, dh, Sr.	.318	195	40	62	15	2	7	47	6
Brady Steiger, if, Fr.	.318	22	5	7	0	0	0	2	0
Michael Weber, 1b, Sr.	.313	176	40	55	17	1	8	44	4
Derek Jones, of, So.	.309	191	44	59	12	2	12	49	10
J.K. Dykes, if, Fr.	.308	13	4	4	0	0	0	4	0
Tommy Richards, if, So.	.300	30	5	9	1	0	0	5	0
Paul Clingan, c, Fr.	.292	24	4	7	1	0	0	2	1
Kyle Buchanan, c, So.	.292	24	3	7	1	0	0	4	0
Garry Kuykendall, of, Sr.	.284	222	39	63	8	2	1	25	13
Patrick Claussen, of, So.	.282	85	18	24	2	0	1	17	2
Kyle Johnson, of, So.	.282	71	17	20	1	0	0	8	3
Matt Argyropoulos, 3b, Jr.	.272	195	33	53	15	1	3	39	3

Tyler Anderson was Oregon's top starter

KEETON GALE

PLAYER, POS., YEAR	AVG	AB	R	H	2B	3B	HR	RBI	SB
Shea Vucinich, ss, Jr.	.262	202	45	53	11	4	4	32	7
Ryan Peterson, 1b, Jr.	.257	74	12	19	4	1	1	11	0
Jay Ponciano, c, Jr.	.225	151	28	34	5	1	1	11	3

PLAYER, POS., YEAR	W	L	ERA	G	SV	IP	H	BB	SO
Adam Conley, lhp, So.	5	4	3.33	29	12	68	67	20	47
Chad Arnold, rhp, Jr.	5	3	3.74	17	1	108	94	49	80
Paris Shewey, lhp, Jr.	7	3	3.47	30	2	57	48	28	49
Connor Lambert, rhp, Sr.	5	1	3.53	25	2	43	45	13	36
Seth Harvey, rhp, Sr.	3	1	4.88	26	3	31	39	14	26
Spencer Jackson, lhp, So.	3	1	5.00	9	0	36	46	11	14
James Wise, rhp, Jr.	4	1	5.18	15	0	57	57	28	46
Richie Ochoa, lhp, Fr.	2	2	6.21	15	0	29	28	12	20
Travis Cook, rhp, Fr.	1	3	6.33	11	0	27	32	13	11
David Stilley, lhp, So.	2	2	6.75	7	0	24	37	6	8
Rusty Shellhorn, lhp, So.	0	1	6.75	5	1	15	21	5	12
Michael Ratigan, rhp, Sr.	0	0	7.80	13	0	15	26	5	10
Bret DeRooy, lhp, Fr.	0	0	12.38	3	0	8	18	0	2

25. OREGON

Coach: George Horton. **Record:** 40-24.

PLAYER, POS., YEAR	AVG	AB	R	H	2B	3B	HR	RBI	SB
Shawn Peterson, 1b, Sr.	.350	120	16	42	10	0	0	19	0
K.C. Serna, ss, So.	.348	233	45	81	13	1	5	37	14
Steven Packard, of, Fr.	.333	159	23	53	11	0	2	18	0
Eddie Rodriguez, c, Fr.	.329	228	38	75	12	1	7	45	2
Andrew Mendenhall, of, Fr.	.318	44	6	14	4	0	0	5	4
Dylan Gavin, if, So.	.302	43	11	13	0	1	1	7	2
Danny Pulfer, 2b, So.	.300	247	47	74	14	0	3	38	6
Mitch Karraker, c, Jr.	.300	40	10	12	5	0	0	8	0
Curtis Raulinaitis, of, Sr.	.278	151	30	42	6	2	2	32	13
J.J. Altobelli, 3b, Fr.	.275	200	31	55	8	1	1	33	3
Marcus Piazzisi, of, Jr.	.269	186	39	50	13	3	3	34	12
Jack Marder, of, Fr.	.249	197	38	49	11	1	5	33	7
Paul Eshleman, c, So.	.250	88	11	22	8	0	3	8	0
Jett Hart, of, Sr.	.236	72	13	17	2	2	0	3	9
Ryan Hambright, if, Fr.	.224	67	15	15	1	0	0	4	0
Nick Wagner, of, Fr.	.185	27	2	5	1	0	0	6	0
Stephen Kaupang, 1b, Jr.	.040	25	0	1	0	0	0	1	0

PLAYER, POS., YEAR	W	L	ERA	G	SV	IP	H	BB	SO
Kellen Moen, rhp, Jr.	3	0	1.69	3	0	5	4	2	6
Joey Housey, rhp, So.	3	2	1.88	23	1	29	24	4	28
Madison Boer, rhp, Jr.	3	1	2.44	23	5	52	51	9	48
Scott McGough, rhp, So.	5	2	2.45	25	4	59	59	14	56
Tyler Anderson, lhp, Jr.	7	5	2.98	17	0	103	84	33	105
Drew Gagnier, rhp, Jr.	0	2	3.18	23	4	23	20	12	25
Zach Thornton, rhp, Sr.	9	0	3.40	17	0	90	92	16	73
Justin LaTempa, rhp, Sr.	6	3	3.65	15	0	89	85	21	68
Christian Jones, lhp, Fr.	2	2	3.71	20	0	27	25	12	21
Alex Keudell, rhp, So.	5	6	4.14	23	0	78	91	25	78
Ryan Fleckenstein, lhp, Sr.	0	1	4.76	8	0	6	5	1	2

NCAA regional teams in bold.
*Won automatic bid.
Conference category leaders in bold.
#Conference department leader who is a non-qualifier for batting or pitching title.

AMERICA EAST CONFERENCE

	Conference		Overall	
	W	L	W	L
Binghamton	21	3	31	20
Maine	17	7	34	22
*Stony Brook	15	9	30	27
Albany	10	14	13	40
Hartford	5	19	11	37
Maryland-Baltimore County	4	20	9	39

ALL-CONFERENCE TEAM: C—Joe Mercurio, Sr., Maine **1B**—Dave Ciocchi, So., Binghamton **2B**—Jim Calderone, Sr., Binghamton. **3B**—Stephen Marino, Jr., Stony Brook. **SS**—Tony Patane, Sr., Maine. **OF**— Henry Dunn, Jr., Binghamton; Taylor Lewis, So., Maine; Corey Taylor, Jr., Binghamton. **DH**—William Carmona, Fr., Stony Brook. **SP**—James Giulietti, Jr., Binghamton; Tyler Johnson, So., Stony Brook; Dave Kubiak, Jr., Albany; Nick Tropeano, So., Stony Brook. **RP**—Justin Latta, Sr., Maine.
Player of the Year: Corey Taylor, Binghamton. **Co-Pitchers of the Year:** James Giulietti, Binghamton; Nick Tropeano, Stony Brook. **Rookie of the Year:** William Carmona, Stony Brook. **Coach of the Year:** Tim Sinicki, Binghamton.

INDIVIDUAL BATTING LEADERS
(Minimum 125 At-Bats)

	AVG	AB	R	H	2B	3B	HR	RBI	SB
Carmona, William, Stony Brook	.387	191	33	74	12	2	6	48	0
Calderone, Jim, Binghamton	.373	201	53	75	13	1	3	21	11
Taylor, Corey, Binghamton	.370	184	54	68	15	0	**14**	**66**	20
Lewis, Taylor, Maine	.369	214	53	**79**	14	**13**	5	52	21
Ciocchi, Dave, Binghamton	.366	202	57	74	14	3	7	57	8
Mercurio, Joe, Maine	.363	190	48	69	**19**	1	12	58	1
Cantwell, Pat, Stony Brook	.361	205	46	74	15	2	3	36	2
Tissenbaum, Maxx, Stony Brook	.344	183	38	63	10	1	4	21	1
Dunn, Henry, Binghamton	.344	195	**64**	67	17	4	10	51	13
Bregartner, Peter, Binghamton	.342	146	40	50	8	2	5	34	7
Marino, Stephen, Stony Brook	.339	230	44	78	**19**	2	2	39	1
Martin, Joey, Maine	.332	196	42	65	15	1	3	46	8
Patane, Tony, Maine	.330	206	40	68	18	0	4	47	4
Rowland, Brendan, Albany	.330	188	42	62	11	2	7	39	24
Bullard, Brian, Albany	.326	178	37	58	9	0	4	32	8
Stephan, Michael, Stony Brook	.325	191	50	62	17	0	10	51	0
Gaige, Nolan, Albany	.323	192	40	62	7	0	3	19	6
Patzalek, Tyler, Maine	.323	189	32	61	11	0	2	31	1
Charron, Joe, Binghamton	.319	166	32	53	8	3	1	35	6
Siano, Andrew, Hartford	.319	135	29	43	3	3	2	13	12
Himmelstein, Max, UMBC	.316	155	20	49	10	2	4	27	0
Dyer, Robert, Stony Brook	.314	223	44	70	13	1	6	44	3
Aldrich, Mike, Hartford	.314	137	16	43	8	0	2	29	0
Fransoso, Michael, Maine	.300	220	57	66	14	6	3	30	16
Drexel, Andy, Hartford	.300	160	37	48	15	1	12	36	5
Marshall, Chad, Stony Brook	.299	197	43	59	14	0	7	32	6
Amendola, Mike, Hartford	.294	163	28	48	10	0	4	25	2
Nivins, Tanner, Stony Brook	.292	178	37	52	12	2	9	48	2
Echevarria, Justin, Stony Brook	.291	148	18	43	7	0	2	23	0
Klukowicz, Brian, UMBC	.286	154	26	44	4	1	4	17	2

INDIVIDUAL PITCHING LEADERS
(Minimum 50 Innings)

	W	L	ERA	G	SV	IP	H	BB	SO
Giulietti, James, Binghamton	8	2	**2.15**	14	0	88	79	14	74
Tropeano, Nick, Stony Brook	8	4	2.44	14	0	**100**	76	29	106
#Latta, Justin, Maine	4	2	3.13	**30**	**5**	46	41	17	38
Gibbs, Jeffrey, Maine	5	4	3.44	14	0	75	80	39	72
Johnson, Tyler, Stony Brook	**10**	3	3.95	14	0	93	70	35	81
Kubiak, Dave, Albany	3	5	4.57	11	0	65	79	23	66
Augliera, Mike, Binghamton	6	2	4.77	16	0	77	87	22	63

	W	L	ERA	G	SV	IP	H	BB	SO
Bazdanes, A.J., Maine	7	5	5.05	17	0	66	59	52	66
Jebb, Matt, Maine	3	3	5.14	15	1	70	86	21	38
Lynch, Jay, Binghamton	5	4	5.33	14	0	74	76	21	44
Brown, Adam, Stony Brook	5	6	5.69	14	0	74	88	29	55
Perakslis, Steve, Maine	4	4	6.33	13	1	58	71	28	53
Graham, Kasceim, Albany	1	6	6.50	12	0	54	71	24	27
Thatcher, Mike, Hartford	3	5	6.68	15	0	62	80	38	33
Bach, Ed, UMBC	4	9	6.89	18	1	64	93	17	44
Greiner, Chris, Hartford	2	4	7.32	12	1	55	72	40	42
White, Ryan, Albany	2	5	7.47	12	0	53	71	29	29

ATLANTIC COAST CONFERENCE

	Conference		Overall	
ATLANTIC	W	L	W	L
*Florida State	18	12	48	19
Clemson	18	12	44	23
North Carolina State	15	15	38	24
Boston College	14	16	30	28
Wake Forest	8	22	18	37
Maryland	5	25	17	39
COASTAL	W	L	W	L
Virginia	23	7	51	14
Georgia Tech	21	9	47	15
Miami	20	10	43	20
Virginia Tech	16	14	40	22
North Carolina	14	16	38	22
Duke	8	22	29	27

ALL-CONFERENCE TEAM: C—Yasmani Grandal, Jr., Miami. **1B**—Tony Plagman, Sr., Georgia Tech; Mickey Wiswall, Jr., Boston College. **2B**—Dallas Poulk, Sr., North Carolina State. **3B**—Matt Skole, So., Georgia Tech. **SS**—Derek Dietrich, Jr., Georgia Tech. **OF**—Phil Gosselin, Jr., Virginia; Tyler Holt, Jr., Florida State; Kyle Parker, Jr., Virginia; Austin Wates, Jr., Virginia Tech. **UTIL**—Mike McGee, Jr., Florida State. **SP**—Matt Harvey, Jr., North Carolina; Chris Hernandez, Jr., Miami; Danny Hultzen, So., Virginia; Deck McGuire, Jr., Georgia Tech. **RP**—Kevin Arico, Jr., Virginia.
Player of the Year: Yasmani Grandal, Miami. **Pitcher of the Year:** Danny Hultzen, Virginia. **Freshman of the Year:** Marcus Stroman, Duke. **Coach of the Year:** Brian O'Connor, Virginia.

INDIVIDUAL BATTING LEADERS
(Minimum 125 At-Bats)

	AVG	AB	R	H	2B	3B	HR	RBI	SB
Grandal, Yasmani, Miami	.401	222	56	89	24	1	15	60	1
Wates, Austin, Virginia Tech	.382	225	61	86	16	5	8	54	18
Gosselin, Phil, Virginia	.382	262	67	**100**	22	4	11	61	18
Conway, Matt, Wake Forest	.382	152	27	58	18	0	6	32	2
Nichols, Thomas, Georgia Tech	.376	189	53	71	16	0	10	41	2
Wilson, Kyle, N.C. State	.368	185	61	68	9	1	7	34	12
Domecus, Steve, Virginia Tech	.365	252	62	92	**27**	1	13	60	12
Poulk, Dallas, N.C. State	.360	261	80	94	23	3	11	60	6
Plagman, Tony, Georgia Tech	.360	239	66	86	16	2	**21**	78	8
Melchionda, Anthony, Boston College	.358	218	39	78	12	1	7	41	4
Miller, Brad, Clemson	.357	252	71	90	19	4	8	49	9
Burnette, Chase, Georgia Tech	.356	250	61	89	19	4	17	66	7
Holt, Tyler, Florida State	.355	259	**87**	92	26	3	13	48	30
Poulk, Drew, N.C. State	.354	263	50	93	21	1	14	73	1
Hinson, John, Clemson	.351	251	60	88	9	1	17	75	25
Dietrich, Derek, Georgia Tech	.350	240	68	84	15	3	17	61	8
Brooks, Steven, Wake Forest	.349	209	55	73	20	1	6	39	23
Smalling, Tim, Virginia Tech	.349	209	51	73	14	4	7	38	5
Sosnoskie, Buddy, Virginia Tech	.347	202	46	70	10	2	13	48	5
Shaban, Ronnie, Virginia Tech	.346	237	54	82	20	3	8	67	8
Michael, Levi, North Carolina	.346	214	76	74	14	4	9	54	20
Murray, Mike, Wake Forest	.345	200	33	69	14	0	6	53	3
Parker, Kyle, Clemson	.344	247	85	85	15	1	20	64	4
Johnson, Sherman, Florida State	.337	249	55	84	15	1	10	58	7
Lemmerman, Jake, Duke	.335	218	47	73	12	3	11	45	9
Skole, Matt, Georgia Tech	.335	233	62	78	15	3	20	63	1
Parker, Jarrett, Virginia	.333	243	56	81	17	**8**	10	56	13
Padula, Brandon, Maryland	.333	189	24	63	11	0	5	33	8
Riggins, Harold, N.C. State	.331	166	43	55	11	2	12	44	1

COLLEGE BASEBALL

	AVG	AB	R	H	2B	3B	HR	RBI	SB
Freeman, Mike, Clemson	.331	**299**	68	99	24	1	8	57	11
#Schaus, Jeff, Clemson	.320	284	69	91	14	2	15	**87**	9

INDIVIDUAL PITCHING LEADERS
(Minimum 50 Innings)

	W	L	ERA	G	SV	IP	H	BB	SO
Erickson, Eric, Miami	4	1	2.52	11	0	54	48	6	47
Hernandez, Chris, Miami	10	3	**2.64**	19	0	106	87	35	110
Rowen, Ben, Virginia Tech	5	2	2.67	38	6	54	44	10	63
Hultzen, Danny, Virginia	**11**	1	2.78	16	0	107	75	24	123
#Arico, Kevin, Virginia	1	1	2.88	29	**18**	34	32	8	44
McGuire, Deck Georgia Tech	9	4	2.96	16	0	113	94	33	118
Harvey, Matt, North Carolina	8	3	3.09	14	0	96	80	35	102
Wilson, Tyler, Virginia	8	4	3.41	31	3	63	45	25	67
Kline, Branden, Virginia	5	1	3.62	22	3	65	54	20	56
Hahn, Jesse, Virginia Tech	5	4	3.70	13	0	73	71	20	76
Johnson, Patrick, North Carolina	6	3	3.71	14	0	78	86	30	67
Frederick, Alex, Clemson	7	2	3.75	33	4	62	63	28	54
Bates, Colin, North Carolina	6	2	3.76	21	1	67	64	26	69
Pope, Mark, Georgia Tech	8	1	3.78	13	1	79	90	13	73
Harman, Casey, Clemson	8	4	3.79	19	0	**121**	115	34	105
Busch, Brian, Florida State	6	2	3.94	21	0	82	65	37	73
Buchanan, Jake, N.C. State	8	6	3.94	18	0	105	112	27	96
Wright, Justin, Virginia Tech	8	5	3.95	16	0	98	89	33	100
Morey, Robert, Virginia	9	4	4.20	16	0	99	84	41	77
Harman, Brett, Maryland	5	8	4.50	14	0	86	91	25	91

ATLANTIC SUN CONFERENCE

	Conference		Overall	
	W	L	W	L
Florida Gulf Coast	25	5	38	20
*Mercer	16	11	38	24
East Tennessee State	15	12	32	28
North Florida	14	12	30	28
Jacksonville	14	12	27	29
Stetson	14	13	27	31
Belmont	13	13	27	27
Kennesaw State	12	15	23	32
Lipscomb	9	17	19	36
Campbell	8	18	28	27
South Carolina-Upstate	8	19	19	37

ALL-CONFERENCE TEAM: C—Derek Trent, Jr., East Tennessee State. **1B**—Paul Hoilman, Jr., East Tennessee State. **2B**—Mikel Alvarez, Jr., Florida Gulf Coast. **3B**—Jacob Tanis, So., Mercer. **SS**—Stephen Wickens, Jr., Florida Gulf Coast. **OF**—Sean Emory, Jr., Stetson; Dan Gulbransen, Fr., Jacksonville; Preston Hale, Sr., North Florida. **DH**—Nate Woods, Jr., Belmont **SP**—Chris Sale, Jr., Florida Gulf Coast; Josh Smith, Sr., Lipscomb; Pete Woodworth, Sr., Florida Gulf Coast. **RP**—Jon Ivie, Jr., Belmont.
Player of the Year: Paul Hoilman, East Tennessee State. **Pitcher of the Year:** Chris Sale, Florida Gulf Coast. **Freshman of the Year:** Dan Gulbransen, Jacksonville. **Coach of the Year:** Dave Tollet, Florida Gulf Coast.

INDIVIDUAL BATTING LEADERS
(Minimum 125 At-Bats)

	AVG	AB	R	H	2B	3B	HR	RBI	SB
Hoilman, Paul, ETSU	**.421**	235	79	99	24	2	**25**	84	1
Bangi, Chris, Campbell	.417	187	58	78	15	3	0	32	26
Alvarez, Mikel, Fla. Gulf Coast	.409	242	63	99	15	2	5	39	11
Simpson, Jeff, Stetson	.398	181	42	72	9	2	0	28	18
Nelson, Cameron, Campbell	.396	159	40	63	12	2	6	29	15
Langley, Michael, Mercer	.392	263	52	103	25	1	6	49	5
Gulbransen, Dan, Jacksonville	.391	202	53	79	14	2	8	46	5
Hale, Preston, North Florida	.391	238	59	93	20	2	12	63	6
Tanis, Jacob, Mercer	.388	268	69	104	25	1	22	**88**	7
Craig, Dylan, Belmont	.382	233	63	89	9	5	3	36	9
Lowe, Ellis, Campbell	.382	241	59	92	**31**	2	3	47	7
Karmeris, Andrew, North Florida	.382	207	52	79	14	0	10	47	1
Burns, Billy, Mercer	.381	210	73	80	15	4	2	25	30
Theisen, Spencer, Stetson	.373	233	51	87	13	3	3	43	24
Hamblen, Derek, Belmont	.370	238	61	88	24	3	7	42	4
Maxfield, Zach, Fla. Gulf Coast	.366	213	54	78	10	0	11	59	0
Freeman, Ronnie, Kennesaw State	.365	211	27	77	8	0	9	47	2
Tanner, Jimmy, S.C.-Upstate	.364	217	32	79	12	0	6	38	0

	AVG	AB	R	H	2B	3B	HR	RBI	SB
Wickens, Stephen, Fla. Gulf Coast	.359	256	62	92	17	2	1	34	18
Emory, Sean, Stetson	.359	192	33	69	6	1	3	32	8
Reeder, Bo, ETSU	.357	**249**	70	89	10	3	20	61	2
Holskey, Josh, Campbell	.356	118	29	42	9	1	6	37	1
McCarty, Tyler, Mercer	.356	239	54	85	19	0	4	36	8
Jones, Mark, Stetson	.352	159	33	56	10	**6**	4	38	12
Johnson, Zach, Campbell	.352	216	50	76	20	2	10	61	13
Byrne, Chas, ETSU	.351	171	32	60	13	2	1	31	12
Preckajlo, Justin, North Florida	.350	197	59	69	13	2	17	41	6
Trent, Derek, ETSU	.348	247	54	86	17	0	13	66	0
Denman, Alan, Campbell	.348	161	40	56	16	1	4	33	12
Chester, Josh, Fla. Gulf Coast	.344	212	36	73	13	1	3	57	0
#Wilson, Tyler, Lipscomb	.331	245	50	81	12	2	6	39	40

INDIVIDUAL PITCHING LEADERS
(Minimum 50 Innings)

	W	L	ERA	G	SV	IP	H	BB	SO
Sale, Chris, Fla. Gulf Coast	**11**	0	**2.01**	17	2	103	83	14	**146**
Kaminski, Chris, Jacksonville	5	5	2.38	24	7	68	60	23	56
#Ivie, Jon, Belmont	3	1	4.04	27	**10**	36	35	9	27
Branham, Matt, S.C.-Upstate	6	3	4.20	15	0	84	104	23	86
Burton, Bo, ETSU	9	6	4.22	31	5	75	73	17	54
Erath, Richie, Fla. Gulf Coast	7	4	4.42	16	1	98	101	28	79
Long, Brad, Kennesaw State	4	4	4.45	25	3	65	67	23	63
DeGrom, Jacob, Stetson	4	6	4.48	17	2	82	104	16	56
Rydman, Jeff, Campbell	3	3	4.59	16	0	69	88	13	51
Kelly, Michael, North Florida	5	8	4.65	16	0	91	120	28	79
Smith, Josh, Lipscomb	8	4	4.66	14	0	**104**	103	40	124
Teasley, David, Mercer	6	1	4.67	**43**	5	71	66	28	64
Rodebaugh, Ryan, Kennesaw State	4	6	4.67	13	0	79	91	35	86
Atteo, John, North Florida	4	4	4.78	16	0	64	82	21	38
McCall, Matt, Mercer	7	2	4.79	18	0	73	72	34	44
Lott, George, North Florida	7	3	4.96	17	0	85	95	37	65
Tomshaw, Matt, Jacksonville	8	2	4.99	14	0	92	123	24	44
Brannon, Philip, S.C.-Upstate	4	7	5.16	15	1	75	98	29	49
Nathanson, Patrick, Fla. Gulf Coast	5	4	5.29	20	2	68	68	38	66
Woodworth, Pete, Fla. Gulf Coast	8	2	5.31	17	0	85	101	36	67
Davis, Logan, Campbell	6	3	5.50	14	0	90	119	21	64

ATLANTIC 10 CONFERENCE

	Conference		Overall	
	W	L	W	L
Charlotte	20	7	39	17
Xavier	18	9	26	32
Rhode Island	17	10	31	26
*Saint Louis	15	12	33	29
Fordham	15	12	21	35
George Washington	14	13	26	28
La Salle	14	13	22	32
Massachusetts	13	14	19	27
St. Joseph's	13	14	18	29
Dayton	12	15	23	32
Richmond	10	17	24	28
Duquesne	10	17	16	40
Temple	10	17	14	37
St. Bonaventure	8	19	17	31

ALL-CONFERENCE TEAM: C—Chris Walker, Jr., Fordham. **1B**—Ben Thomas, Jr., Xavier. **2B**—Corey Shaylor, Jr., Charlotte. **3B**—Jon Myers, Jr., Saint Louis. **SS**—Tom Zebroski, Sr., George Washington. **OF**—Bobby Freking, Sr., Xavier; Andrew Heck, Jr., Duquesne; Justin Wilson, Jr., Charlotte. **SP**—Tim Boyce, Sr., Rhode Island; Eric Cantrell, Jr., George Washington. **RP**—Patrick Lawson, Sr., Charlotte.
Player of the Year: Tom Zebroski, George Washington. **Pitcher of the Year:** Tim Boyce, Rhode Island. **Rookie of the Year:** Alex Alemann, Saint Louis. **Coach of the Year:** Mike Lake, La Salle.

INDIVIDUAL BATTING LEADERS
(Minimum 125 At-Bats)

	AVG	AB	R	H	2B	3B	HR	RBI	SB
Zebroski, Tom, GW	**.429**	240	**75**	**103**	15	2	**18**	58	13
Coulombe, Tom, Rhode Island	.418	208	56	87	15	1	3	41	23
Heck, Andrew, Duquesne	.408	223	55	91	**25**	2	10	49	15
Norton, Brendan, La Salle	.400	200	51	80	11	4	2	33	16
Shaylor, Corey, Charlotte	.388	183	45	71	14	1	3	49	7

	AVG	AB	R	H	2B	3B	HR	RBI	SB
Bosnik, Jesse, St. Bonaventure	.387	204	50	79	20	5	11	62	12
Fredette, Eric, Massachusetts	.384	185	32	71	11	1	4	31	0
Kelliher, Brendon, GW	.381	189	44	72	13	0	15	56	8
Barber, Billy, Richmond	.372	199	52	74	17	1	11	49	17
Walker, Chris, Fordham	.370	219	37	81	25	0	6	61	2
Luick, Chris, GW	.367	210	59	77	23	1	11	53	13
Myers, Jon, Saint Louis	.365	260	52	95	18	3	16	72	5
Thomas, Ben, Xavier	.359	220	42	79	9	0	13	69	1
Wilson, Justin, Charlotte	.358	229	58	82	7	2	1	35	20
Negrin, Tony, La Salle	.357	154	29	55	1	0	0	13	10
Rivers, Ryan, Charlotte	.356	216	54	77	16	2	13	63	3
Brown, Shane, Charlotte	.356	177	58	63	8	1	1	32	15
Brock, Danny, Saint Louis	.356	239	64	85	15	0	18	75	15
McCrann, Ryan, Fordham	.355	220	44	78	13	2	5	34	16
Blasik, Brian, Delaware	.346	217	45	75	18	1	8	37	6
Brown, Cameron, Richmond	.345	197	48	68	15	0	6	44	6
Gyles, Jon, La Salle	.343	207	35	71	21	3	2	47	2
Perkins, Mike, Charlotte	.340	156	27	53	9	2	1	32	1
Oriente, Dewey, Saint Joseph's	.339	189	36	64	10	5	4	35	3
LeBel, Mike, Rhode Island	.338	237	65	80	14	4	9	34	19
Urban, Billy, St. Bonaventure	.337	178	30	60	9	1	3	44	0
Donato, Mike, Massachusetts	.337	181	42	61	13	0	4	26	1
Angulo, Zoey, Rhode Island	.337	202	34	68	8	2	1	41	15
Borden, Kyle, Rhode Island	.333	195	36	65	11	0	5	39	4
Freking, Bobby, Xavier	.332	241	39	80	15	2	12	44	2
#Dunn, J.D., Saint Louis	.296	243	54	72	16	4	5	30	28

INDIVIDUAL PITCHING LEADERS
(Minimum 50 Innings)

	W	L	ERA	G	SV	IP	H	BB	SO
Roberts, Corey, Charlotte	6	3	3.48	15	0	85	81	23	75
Boyce, Tim, Rhode Island	6	3	3.55	15	0	101	89	21	90
Cantrell, Eric, GW	8	4	3.67	14	0	101	102	27	114
Christensen, Pat, La Salle	4	4	3.99	28	11	56	61	19	55
Shirley, Tommy, Xavier	4	3	4.03	15	0	96	100	25	98
Marshall, Ian, Richmond	4	4	4.04	19	0	78	82	17	59
Krakowiak, Max, Fordham	7	4	4.10	15	0	99	93	40	69
Rothlin, Chad, Charlotte	5	3	4.22	15	0	60	61	20	33
Cotton, Bryant, Saint Louis	9	5	4.35	18	1	124	142	29	99
Rossignol, Dan, Rhode Island	8	2	4.48	22	0	74	79	19	52
Alemann, Alex, Saint Louis	9	6	4.71	17	0	117	146	27	72
Leigh, Bryan, Massachusetts	6	5	4.80	12	0	69	76	20	55
Pilkington, Tyler, Charlotte	5	2	4.82	16	0	71	69	37	49
Graveline, Ken, Rhode Island	6	3	4.86	15	0	80	98	22	46
Richard, Jon, Xavier	7	3	4.95	14	0	80	89	43	40
Hauschild, Mike, Delaware	4	7	5.01	20	0	65	82	18	53
Richardson, Joe, GW	7	4	5.09	14	0	74	93	17	39
#Nalepa, Robert, St. Bonaventure	2	2	5.21	14	0	48	58	21	22
White, Ben, Temple	4	6	5.32	14	0	91	106	40	94
Mower, Randy, Saint Joseph's	3	5	5.47	14	0	76	107	21	42

BIG EAST CONFERENCE

	Conference		Overall	
	W	L	W	L
Louisville	21	6	50	14
Connecticut	20	6	48	16
Pittsburgh	18	8	38	18
*St. John's	16	11	43	20
South Florida	16	11	26	32
Rutgers	15	12	30	26
Cincinnati	13	14	29	29
West Virginia	10	17	27	30
Notre Dame	10	17	22	32
Villanova	9	18	29	23
Seton Hall	8	19	19	30
Georgetown	5	22	24	31

ALL-CONFERENCE TEAM: C—Cory Brownsten, Sr., Pittsburgh. **1B**—Andrew Clark, Sr., Louisville. **2B**—Ryan Wright, So., Louisville. **3B**—Joe Leonard, Jr., Pittsburgh. **SS**—Jedd Gyorko, Jr., West Virginia. **OF**—Jeremy Baltz, Fr., St. John's; Pat Biserta, Jr., Rutgers; Matt Szcur, Jr., Villanova. **DH**—Kevan Smith, Jr., Pittsburgh. **P**—Corey Baker, Jr., Pittsburgh; Matt Barnes, So., Connecticut; Neil Holland, Jr., Louisville; Thomas Royse, Jr., Louisville.
Players of the Year: Joe Leonard, Pittsburgh. **Pitcher of the Year:** Thomas

Royse, Louisville. **Rookie of the Year:** Jeremy Baltz, St. John's. **Coach of the Year:** Jim Penders, Connecticut.

INDIVIDUAL BATTING LEADERS
(Minimum 125 At-Bats)

	AVG	AB	R	H	2B	3B	HR	RBI	SB
Szczur, Matt, Villanova	.443	174	40	77	13	7	4	38	10
Leonard, Joe, Pittsburgh	.433	240	62	104	23	4	8	71	6
Nyisztor, Steve, Rutgers	.410	229	52	94	17	3	4	51	11
Schultz, John, Pittsburgh	.404	225	76	91	20	1	4	48	7
Baltz, Jeremy, St. John's	.396	240	64	95	16	1	24	85	6
Brownsten, Cory, Pittsburgh	.395	185	41	73	12	2	3	46	3
Nemeth, Mike, Connecticut	.386	254	63	98	20	1	15	84	1
Gyorko, Jedd, West Virginia	.381	236	71	90	28	1	19	57	1
Panik, Joe, St. John's	.374	227	66	85	18	4	10	53	6
Clark, Andrew, Louisville	.370	189	52	70	15	1	13	61	1
Whitmore, Travis, Pittsburgh	.369	214	45	79	14	6	3	46	11
Biserta, Pat, Rutgers	.368	234	60	86	17	2	18	56	5
Wright, Ryan, Louisville	.366	254	61	93	17	2	16	80	10
Buckner, Grant, West Virginia	.363	201	37	73	17	0	8	50	5
Ferriter, Billy, Connecticut	.363	223	57	81	15	5	0	30	33
Andreoli, John, Connecticut	.362	196	43	71	11	2	1	37	24
Smith, Kevan, Pittsburgh	.361	233	59	84	18	1	5	46	3
Hopkins, Greg, St. John's	.358	257	65	92	21	0	7	59	5
Parque, Jimmy, St. John's	.358	274	54	98	21	2	4	47	8
Bencsko, Justin, Villanova	.356	194	55	69	10	5	2	31	24
Wunderlich, Phil, Louisville	.355	256	54	91	21	1	21	62	12
Hayes, Dom, West Virginia	.352	236	39	83	22	2	0	25	5
Lopez, Danny, Pittsburgh	.349	209	67	73	16	2	3	44	24
O'Hare, Sean, St. John's	.347	216	28	75	16	3	1	30	5
Ravnaas, Rand, Georgetown	.347	190	40	66	16	2	11	35	12
Duggan, Zach, Pittsburgh	.346	217	49	75	12	5	2	52	25
Springer, George, Connecticut	.337	243	84	82	16	4	18	62	33
Connolly, Ryan, Notre Dame	.335	197	47	66	15	2	11	38	7
Desico, Frank, Notre Dame	.333	189	29	63	6	0	1	25	4
Hopkins, Russ, St. John's	.333	150	20	50	11	1	1	25	3

INDIVIDUAL PITCHING LEADERS
(Minimum 50 Innings)

	W	L	ERA	G	SV	IP	H	BB	SO
Holland, Neil, Louisville	8	1	2.08	29	17	56	30	16	59
Barbosa, Andrew, South Florida	8	2	2.40	14	0	86	72	22	95
Royse, Thomas, Louisville	9	1	2.85	16	0	104	100	26	99
Glynn, Elliot, Connecticut	7	3	2.99	15	0	87	97	34	46
Crimmel, Kevin, Villanova	6	2	3.02	24	3	54	59	16	44
Fontanez, Randy, South Florida	5	7	3.59	15	0	110	98	28	105
Hansen, Kyle, St. John's	8	3	3.71	18	0	95	77	38	85
Iannazzo, Matt, Pittsburgh	11	2	3.76	13	0	93	111	22	58
Garman, Brian, Cincinnati	4	4	3.79	17	0	59	65	19	65
Smith, Tyler, Cincinnati	1	7	3.84	14	0	61	70	13	26
Barnes, Matt, Connecticut	8	3	3.92	15	0	83	79	25	75
Jensen, Dan, Cincinnati	4	2	4.02	11	0	54	50	18	42
Prosinski, Jon, Seton Hall	3	3	4.04	14	0	76	79	27	45
Streilein, Brian, Villanova	6	3	4.20	13	0	90	105	29	78
Helisek, Kyle, Villanova	3	7	4.23	13	0	77	87	27	40
Amlung, Justin, Louisville	5	2	4.27	20	0	65	72	14	55
Kiekhefer, Dean, Louisville	3	4	4.31	19	0	63	65	19	39
Nappo, Greg, Connecticut	8	5	4.44	15	0	97	99	36	72
Hood, Nathan, Pittsburgh	4	1	4.48	11	0	60	61	18	48
Self, Derek, Louisville	7	0	4.52	21	0	62	77	11	50

BIG SOUTH CONFERENCE

	Conference		Overall	
	W	L	W	L
*Coastal Carolina	25	0	55	10
Liberty	19	8	42	19
Radford	15	11	29	26
High Point	15	12	31	29
Virginia Military Institute	13	14	33	22
Winthrop	13	14	27	30
Gardner-Webb	10	17	25	30
UNC Asheville	10	17	17	35
Presbyterian	7	20	15	39
Charleston Southern	6	20	17	38

ALL-CONFERENCE TEAM: C—Jose Iglesias, Sr., Coastal Carolina. **1B**—Jordan Ballard, Sr., VMI. **2B**—Tommy La Stella, So., Coastal Carolina. **3B**—Scott Woodward, Jr., Coastal Carolina. **SS**—Taylor Motter, So., Coastal Carolina. **DH**—Matt Hillsinger, So., Radford. **OF**—Matt Gantner, Sr., High Point; Rico Noel, Jr., Coastal Carolina; Nate Roberts, Jr., High Point. **SP**—Anthony Meo, So., Coastal Carolina; Shawn Teufel, Sr., Liberty; Cody Wheeler, Jr., Coastal Carolina. **RP**—Matt Rein, Jr., Coastal Carolina. **Player of the Year:** Nate Roberts, High Point. **Pitcher of the Year:** Anthony Meo, Coastal Carolina. **Freshman of the Year:** Cory Spangenberg, VMI. **Coach of the Year:** Gary Gilmore, Coastal Carolina.

INDIVIDUAL BATTING LEADERS
(Minimum 125 At-Bats)

	AVG	AB	R	H	2B	3B	HR	RBI	SB
Roberts, Nate, High Point	.416	209	88	87	10	1	19	69	36
Chinners, Nick, Charleston Southern	.385	205	26	79	15	1	7	43	1
Schumer, Justin, UNC Asheville	.384	190	39	73	16	1	9	37	1
Gantner, Matt, High Point	.379	232	59	88	25	1	8	71	9
Meier, Brantley, Charleston Southern	.378	222	41	84	13	1	2	33	25
La Stella, Tommy, Coastal Carolina	.378	246	63	93	14	2	14	66	6
Jimenez, P.J., Liberty	.377	244	61	92	14	2	3	41	9
Merck, Daniel, Gardner-Webb	.372	218	48	81	21	4	2	38	27
Spangenberg, Cory, VMI	.370	235	62	87	14	3	11	49	24
Fulginiti, Max, High Point	.365	230	47	84	25	1	1	41	6
Turner, Raphael, Radford	.363	193	48	70	14	1	10	51	22
Watts, Jake, Gardner-Webb	.362	174	30	63	8	1	4	27	4
Cook, Tyler, Wofford	.361	205	43	74	16	0	1	37	1
Williams, Matt, Liberty	.360	236	52	85	22	2	4	30	10
Sullivan, Graham, VMI	.358	226	44	81	19	2	10	55	5
Bream, Tyler, Liberty	.357	269	56	96	22	1	9	57	1
White IV, Murray, High Point	.353	232	55	82	11	1	6	40	9
Keen, Reggie, Radford	.353	201	51	71	16	1	6	49	31
Redal, Curran, Liberty	.353	255	55	90	13	0	3	42	13
Noel, Rico, Coastal Carolina	.349	238	82	83	18	2	12	63	56
Haitsuka, Alex, VMI	.348	161	34	56	7	2	7	29	5
Hillsinger, Matt, Radford	.348	187	40	65	13	6	2	36	15
Iglesias, Jose, Coastal Carolina	.344	224	55	77	16	0	16	80	2
Gliebe, Adam, Wofford	.343	204	34	70	10	3	3	42	3
Miller, Aaron, Gardner-Webb	.339	242	48	82	15	3	4	46	11
Robertson, Michael, Liberty	.337	178	39	60	13	4	4	43	4
Crane, Chas, Wofford	.337	208	49	70	18	1	14	45	4
Roberts, Sam, VMI	.336	211	56	71	16	2	9	52	9
Motter, Taylor, Coastal Carolina	.336	214	55	72	22	1	12	49	11
Gilmore, Chance, Coastal Carolina	.336	226	63	76	21	1	12	55	10

INDIVIDUAL PITCHING LEADERS
(Minimum 50 Innings)

	W	L	ERA	G	SV	IP	H	BB	SO
Connolly, Ryan, Coastal Carolina	3	0	2.15	40	0	50	45	11	48
Teufel, Shawn, Liberty	10	4	2.44	15	0	103	85	40	92
Meo, Anthony, Coastal Carolina	13	2	2.61	18	0	97	82	34	94
Fleet, Austin, Coastal Carolina	6	2	2.85	31	8	60	55	19	57
Rein, Matt, Coastal Carolina	7	1	2.97	24	2	58	50	23	43
Evans, Steven, Liberty	9	2	3.01	15	0	90	91	25	85
Wheeler, Cody, Coastal Carolina	12	0	3.64	18	0	111	106	41	113
Beakler, Dane, Liberty	4	2	3.84	26	2	61	60	10	56
D'Angelo, Matteo, Wofford	8	5	4.01	15	0	94	100	18	76
Izokovic, Adam, Gardner-Webb	5	4	4.04	25	6	56	55	21	43
Farley, Jason, VMI	4	5	4.12	15	0	74	75	17	42
Wimmer, Brad, Radford	3	4	4.33	13	0	52	61	10	40
Thornburg, Tyler, Charleston Southern	5	4	4.14	12	0	78	62	34	88
Dull, Ryan, UNC Asheville	6	4	4.40	16	1	88	101	13	45
Schumer, Justin, UNC Asheville	2	6	4.50	15	1	72	72	28	49
Birmingham, Jim, Coastal Carolina	6	2	4.82	14	0	52	46	29	33
Schultz, Jaime, High Point	5	0	4.84	20	0	58	51	43	68
Foushee, Andrew, Presbyterian	2	4	4.93	26	0	66	85	9	48
Lake, Robert, Wofford	6	5	5.07	15	0	94	105	23	72
Taylor, Aerik, Radford	6	1	5.13	15	0	88	113	25	54
#Rodenberg, Mikel, High Point	1	2	6.75	23	8	23	21	14	19

BIG TEN CONFERENCE

	Conference		Overall	
	W	L	W	L
*Minnesota	15	9	32	30
Michigan	14	10	35	22
Iowa	13	11	30	28
Northwestern	13	11	24	32
Purdue	12	12	33	24
Indiana	12	12	28	27
Michigan State	11	13	34	19
Ohio State	11	13	28	23
Illinois	10	14	26	26
Penn State	9	15	22	30

ALL-CONFERENCE TEAM: C—Ben Heath, Jr., Penn State. **1B**—Nick O'Shea, So., Minnesota. **2B**—Zach Morton, So., Northwestern. **3B**—Chris Lashmet, Jr., Northwestern. **SS**—Jonathan Roof, Jr., Michigan State. **OF**— Alex Dickerson, So., Indiana; Zach Hurley, Sr., Ohio State; Ryan LaMarre, Jr., Michigan. **DH**—Josh Lyon, So., Indiana. **SP**—Matt Bischoff, Sr., Purdue; Eric Jokisch, Jr., Northwestern; Alex Wimmers, Jr., Ohio State. **RP**—Jake Hale, Sr., Ohio State.

Player of the Year: Alex Dickerson, Indiana. **Pitcher of the Year:** Alex Wimmers, Ohio State. **Freshman of the Year:** Ryan Jones, Michigan State. **Coach of the Year:** John Anderson, Minnesota.

INDIVIDUAL BATTING LEADERS
(Minimum 125 At-Bats)

	AVG	AB	R	H	2B	3B	HR	RBI	SB
Dickerson, Alex, Indiana	.419	236	62	99	19	0	24	75	3
Sabourin, Jerrud, Indiana	.394	241	54	95	16	1	7	45	0
Hurley, Zach, Ohio State	.385	221	51	85	19	4	7	39	6
Boike, Eli, Michigan State	.384	203	47	78	14	4	8	48	5
Muller, Kurtis, Iowa	.381	218	57	83	15	6	3	36	30
Jones, Ryan, Michigan State	.380	192	33	73	12	4	1	37	9
Rogers, Tyler, Indiana	.377	162	30	61	10	5	3	37	10
Berset, Chris, Michigan	.373	217	54	81	15	1	7	50	1
Lyon, Josh, Indiana	.371	178	41	66	21	2	11	39	1
Heath, Ben, Penn State	.369	198	53	73	16	1	19	57	3
Morton, Zach, Northwestern	.363	193	31	70	11	0	1	23	6
Eckerle, Brandon, Michigan State	.362	224	57	81	7	1	1	28	22
Stephens, Michael, Ohio State	.360	189	39	68	7	0	10	43	5
Rupert, Cory Ohio State	.356	149	30	53	5	1	2	22	1
Snyder, Steve, Penn State	.355	166	31	59	4	4	0	37	12
Kvasnicka, Michael, Minnesota	.355	245	51	87	25	2	8	50	4
Noble, Chad, Northwestern	.355	203	42	72	11	4	2	24	4
DeBernardis, Joey, Penn State	.354	212	41	75	14	3	2	33	1
Snieder, Paul, Northwestern	.353	215	34	76	15	2	7	36	1
Burkhart, Dan Ohio State	.353	190	37	67	15	3	1	29	0
Earley, Michael, Indiana	.351	194	50	68	8	2	13	40	15
Holm, Jeff, Michigan State	.350	206	54	72	21	5	3	50	23
Dew, Ryan, Ohio State	.348	201	38	70	7	1	7	46	1
McMurray, Casey, Illinois	.348	187	41	65	14	4	6	39	9
Knudson, Kyle Minnesota	.346	234	37	81	17	2	6	48	1
Kovanda, Cory, Ohio State	.346	185	42	64	9	2	2	28	5
McQuillan, Mike, Iowa	.344	212	38	73	7	2	3	39	8
Plawecki, Kevin, Purdue	.343	204	36	70	12	1	8	53	2
McCool, Zach, Iowa	.343	181	34	62	12	3	2	36	12
Boss, Torsten, Michigan State	.341	164	37	56	10	0	6	41	5
#Spillner, Tyler, Purdue	.319	220	46	72	13	7	1	28	19
#Argo, Willie, Illinois	.318	198	46	63	11	6	4	33	41
#Biondi, Patrick, Michigan	.313	230	69	72	11	6	2	30	29

INDIVIDUAL PITCHING LEADERS
(Minimum 50 Innings)

	W	L	ERA	G	SV	IP	H	BB	SO
Wimmers, Alex, Ohio State	9	0	1.60	10	0	73	58	23	86
Lutz, David, Penn State	4	3	3.04	36	1	71	70	15	50
Bischoff, Matt, Purdue	10	2	3.22	13	0	95	98	14	95
Oakes, T.J., Minnesota	4	3	3.62	16	0	87	93	22	57
Burgoon, Tyler, Michigan	6	4	3.71	23	10	61	59	19	72
Hippen, Jarred, Iowa	6	4	3.71	16	0	99	115	22	71
Phil Isaksson, Minnesota	6	2	3.72	18	0	85	78	28	57
Oaks, Alan, Michigan	6	5	3.82	15	0	92	82	42	71
Leininger, Drew, Indiana	9	3	4.04	15	0	98	101	28	67
Achter, A.J., Michigan State	4	4	4.20	14	0	99	106	36	74
Wunderlich, Kurt, Michigan State	8	3	4.28	13	0	88	102	28	48
Squires, Chris, Indiana	5	3	4.31	31	9	56	69	40	27
Brooke, Francis, Northwestern	5	5	4.33	16	0	89	105	7	48
Brosnahan, Bobby, Michigan	5	4	4.38	16	0	72	77	37	61
Jokisch, Eric, Northwestern	5	7	4.39	15	0	92	107	37	62

	W	L	ERA	G	SV	IP	H	BB	SO
Seth Rosin, Minnesota	9	4	4.72	16	0	103	99	12	95
#Lee, Kevin, Iowa	2	0	4.87	21	**13**	20	27	10	14
Miller, Matt, Michigan	3	3	5.06	17	0	64	83	28	51
Bucciferro, Tony, Michigan State	7	5	5.08	14	0	89	105	17	52
Manson, Kevin, Illinois	3	3	5.23	15	0	53	70	12	17
Johnson, Kevin, Illinois	5	2	5.23	13	0	76	82	28	53

BIG 12 CONFERENCE

	Conference		Overall	
	W	L	W	L
Texas	24	3	50	13
Oklahoma	15	10	50	16
*Texas A&M	14	12	43	21
Kansas State	14	12	37	22
Baylor	12	13	36	24
Texas Tech	13	14	28	29
Kansas	11	15	29	26
Missouri	10	16	29	26
Nebraska	10	17	27	27
Oklahoma State	8	19	29	26

ALL-CONFERENCE TEAM: C—Cameron Rupp, Jr., Texas. **IF**—Garrett Buechele, So., Oklahoma; Carter Jurica, Jr., Kansas State; Adam Muenster, Sr., Kansas State; Robby Price, Sr., Kansas; Aaron Senne, Sr., Missouri. **OF**—Adam Bailey, Sr., Nebraska; Brian Heere, Jr., Kansas; Nick Martini, So., Kansas State. **DH**—Russell Moldenhauer, Sr., Texas. **UTIL**—Brett Nicholas, Jr., Missouri; Brooks Pinckard, So., Baylor. **SP**—Cole Green, Jr., Texas; Barret Loux, Jr., Texas A&M; Brandon Workman, Jr., Texas. **RP**—Chance Ruffin, Jr., Texas; John Stilson, So., Texas A&M.
Players of the Year: Nick Martini, Kansas State; Aaron Senne, Missouri. **Pitcher of the Year:** Cole Green, Texas. **Newcomer of the Year:** John Stilson, Texas A&M. **Freshman of the Year:** Barrett Barnes, Texas Tech. **Coach of the Year:** Augie Garrido, Texas.

INDIVIDUAL BATTING LEADERS
(Minimum 125 At-Bats)

	AVG	AB	R	H	2B	3B	HR	RBI	SB
Martini, Nick, Kansas State	.416	231	49	96	17	4	4	59	19
Senne, Aaron, Missouri	.400	210	61	84	22	0	16	59	1
Greene, Brodie, Texas A&M	.395	**266**	74	105	18	**7**	14	55	23
Heere, Brian Kansas	.393	234	59	92	13	3	6	51	7
Duren, Davis, Oklahoma State	.383	230	46	88	17	1	6	55	29
Muenster, Adam Kansas State	.381	247	65	94	21	1	3	33	26
Belfonte, D.J., Nebraska	.376	218	49	82	13	3	7	37	13
Bailey, Adam, Nebraska	.368	223	57	82	16	1	**18**	**69**	3
Jurica, Carter, Kansas State	.363	237	61	86	17	3	13	**69**	18
Juengel, Matt, Texas A&M	.359	167	30	60	10	1	11	39	2
Buechele, Garrett, Oklahoma	.359	262	55	94	16	2	17	65	3
Uribe, Luis, Oklahoma State	.355	166	41	59	11	0	9	35	2
Nicholas, Brett, Missouri	.351	211	51	74	15	0	12	64	2
Price, Robby, Kansas	.351	231	67	81	19	5	6	49	1
Patterson, Joe, Texas A&M	.348	253	47	88	16	0	9	48	9
Kiser, Kale, Nebraska	.345	168	49	58	14	1	2	27	5
Barnes, Barrett, Texas Tech	.341	217	71	74	19	2	14	53	12
DeBord, Blair, Kansas State	.340	156	23	53	13	0	2	22	3
Reed, Michael, Texas Tech	.340	209	46	71	21	3	4	39	3
Hainsfurther, Joey, Baylor	.339	236	37	80	12	3	2	48	4
Thompson, Tony, Kansas	.338	148	25	50	10	1	6	38	0
Shepherd, Tant, Texas	.338	246	64	83	19	2	8	37	14
Phillips, Dane, Oklahoma State	.337	193	33	65	14	2	3	34	1
Campbell, Raynor, Baylor	.335	224	39	75	15	0	7	41	12
Dellasega, Daniel, Kansas State	.330	209	44	69	19	0	0	48	3
Vick, Logan, Baylor	.329	228	59	75	17	2	10	27	11
Bushyhead, Caleb, Oklahoma	.327	257	49	84	16	3	6	40	13
Moldenhauer, Russell, Texas	.326	178	41	58	14	1	9	41	0
Ellison, Chris, Oklahoma	.326	193	55	63	10	3	4	32	24
Black, Danny, Oklahoma	.320	206	38	66	11	6	5	48	14
#LeJeune, Scott, Texas Tech	.323	229	36	74	**28**	2	4	58	4

INDIVIDUAL PITCHING LEADERS
(Minimum 50 Innings)

	W	L	ERA	G	SV	IP	H	BB	SO
Stilson, John, Texas A&M	9	1	**0.80**	33	10	79	51	23	114
Ruffin, Chance, Texas	6	1	1.11	**37**	**14**	65	42	19	97
Jungmann, Taylor, Texas	8	3	2.03	17	0	**120**	88	41	129

	W	L	ERA	G	SV	IP	H	BB	SO
Green, Cole, Texas	11	2	2.74	17	0	112	88	27	75
Loux, Barret, Texas A&M	11	2	2.83	17	0	105	78	34	136
Wacha, Michael, Texas A&M	9	2	2.90	25	1	106	86	22	97
Kempf, Willie, Baylor	9	2	3.02	22	1	83	83	28	80
Verrett, Logan, Baylor	5	3	3.28	16	1	91	88	23	97
Workman, Brandon, Texas	**12**	2	3.35	17	0	105	98	23	101
Erben, Jeremy, Oklahoma	7	1	3.43	34	5	76	70	29	79
Rocha, Michael, Oklahoma	8	2	3.53	20	0	74	67	22	55
Fritsch, Craig, Baylor	2	4	3.68	19	2	71	72	24	64
Marshall, Evan, Kansas State	5	5	3.90	27	1	83	79	20	51
Shore, Bobby, Oklahoma	10	5	4.12	17	0	94	90	36	77
Tepesch, Nick, Missouri	6	6	4.20	15	0	99	108	27	75
Hauptman, Casey, Nebraska	2	5	4.28	23	3	74	79	21	58
Neal, Zach, Oklahoma	8	3	4.43	18	0	106	112	24	95
Strong, Mike, Oklahoma State	4	3	4.48	16	0	64	61	36	66
Stripling, Ross, Texas Tech	5	4	4.50	17	0	88	100	29	89
Hunter, Kyle, Kansas State	9	2	4.59	17	0	84	88	32	58

BIG WEST CONFERENCE

	Conference		Overall	
	W	L	W	L
*Cal State Fullerton	21	3	46	18
UC Irvine	17	7	39	21
UC Riverside	13	11	32	23
Pacific	12	12	31	23
UC Santa Barbara	10	14	24	30
Cal Poly	10	14	23	32
Cal State Northridge	9	15	29	27
UC Davis	9	15	26	29
Long Beach State	7	17	23	32

ALL-CONFERENCE TEAM: C—Rob Brantly, So., UC Riverside. **1B**—Nick Ramirez, So., Cal State Fullerton. **2B**—Ryan Pineda, Jr., Cal State Northridge. **3B**—Brian Hernandez, Jr., UC Irvine. **SS**—Christian Colon, Jr., Cal State Fullerton; Francis Larson, Sr., UC Irvine. **OF**—Gary Brown, Jr., Cal State Fullerton; Tony Nix, Jr., UC Riverside; Luke Yoder, Sr., Cal Poly. **DH**—Justin Shults, Jr., UC Riverside. **UTIL**—David Popkins, So., UC Davis. **SP**—Daniel Bibona, Sr., UC Irvine; Noe Ramirez, So., Cal State Fullerton; Daniel Renken, Jr., Cal State Fullerton. **RP**—Hunter Carnevale, Sr., Pacific. **CP**—Eric Pettis, Sr., UC Irvine
Player of the Year: Gary Brown, Cal State Fullerton. **Pitcher of the Year:** Daniel Bibona, UC Irvine. **Freshman Player of the Year:** Mitch Haniger, Cal Poly. **Freshman Pitcher of the Year:** Dylan Floro, Cal State Fullerton. **Coach of the Year:** Dave Serrano, Cal State Fullerton

INDIVIDUAL BATTING LEADERS
(Minimum 125 At-Bats)

	AVG	AB	R	H	2B	3B	HR	RBI	SB
Brown, Gary, CS Fullerton	.438	210	63	92	20	**8**	6	41	32
Lohman, Devin, Long Beach State	.404	151	31	61	17	1	1	24	7
Shults, Justin, UC Riverside	.390	187	44	73	20	2	11	62	0
Popkins, David, UC Davis	.388	188	40	73	15	3	5	43	2
Cusick, Jeff, UC Irvine	.379	232	43	88	21	0	8	62	1
Brown, J.B., Pacific	.376	221	43	83	10	0	6	31	4
Jones, Corey, CS Fullerton	.374	222	50	83	13	6	9	56	6
Brantly, Robert, UC Riverside	.373	209	50	78	18	1	7	39	0
Martin, Brian, Pacific	.364	228	37	83	15	1	0	38	0
Nix, Tony, UC Riverside	.361	166	45	60	19	2	11	43	5
Colon, Christian, CS Fullerton	.358	**268**	73	96	18	2	17	**68**	13
Belanger, C.J., CS Northridge	.357	213	41	76	16	7	4	43	6
Lyman, Scott, UC Davis	.356	202	39	72	19	0	5	40	1
Pill, Tyler, CS Fullerton	.354	198	43	70	13	1	7	42	10
Lopez, Carlos, CS Fullerton	.353	238	44	84	16	3	7	51	5
Crocker, Bobby, Cal Poly	.351	222	42	78	15	5	3	49	18
Tinoco, Steve, Long Beach State	.348	210	30	73	11	1	1	45	2
Yoder, Luke, Cal Poly	.347	222	61	77	21	5	15	46	17
Ramirez, Nick, CS Fullerton	.346	260	62	90	**28**	1	16	75	6
Johnson, Eric, UC Davis	.343	201	30	69	10	1	1	39	4
D'Anna, Dominic, CS Northridge	.338	213	41	72	17	0	8	47	2
Melker, Adam, Cal Poly	.337	199	52	67	18	1	6	33	4
Marcoe, Billy, CS Fullerton	.333	207	33	69	11	1	3	32	6
Oliveira, Joe, Pacific	.332	187	46	62	8	3	5	29	12
Mittelstaedt, T.J., Long Beach State	.332	187	28	62	14	5	1	29	8
Hur, Michael, UC Riverside	.329	216	50	71	13	3	8	43	3
Walker, Mike, Pacific	.327	223	49	73	12	1	12	52	4

	AVG	AB	R	H	2B	3B	HR	RBI	SB
Longmire, Nick, Pacific	.327	202	49	66	18	1	5	35	9
Terdoslavich, Joey, Long Beach State	.326	224	34	73	12	2	7	46	3
Haniger, Mitch, Cal Poly	.326	178	38	58	15	1	7	45	7

INDIVIDUAL PITCHING LEADERS
(Minimum 50 Innings)

	W	L	ERA	G	SV	IP	H	BB	SO
Bibona, Daniel, UC Irvine	9	2	2.48	13	0	94	75	15	102
Ramirez, Noe, CS Fullerton	12	1	2.54	16	0	106	92	19	119
Brock, Evan, UC Irvine	6	4	3.14	20	1	63	34	30	62
Floro, Dylan, CS Fullerton	7	2	3.26	27	2	91	102	11	69
Gagnon, Andrew, Long Beach State	5	7	3.28	15	0	93	87	27	65
Pill, Tyler, CS Fullerton	4	4	3.36	10	0	62	54	13	58
#Ramirez, Nick, CS Fullerton	1	3	3.50	27	11	44	41	8	38
Carnevale, Hunter, Pacific	5	4	3.53	24	5	74	79	21	66
Pettis, Eric, UC Irvine	9	5	3.62	24	6	124	142	27	89
Jolicoeur, Jimmy, CS Northridge	5	1	3.70	29	4	56	50	21	39
Bergman, Christian, UC Irvine	9	3	3.72	20	1	102	109	16	78
Hollands, Mario, UC Santa Barbara	5	5	3.77	14	0	98	111	28	80
Renken, Daniel, CS Fullerton	12	2	3.96	20	0	105	104	40	91
Emmons, Dustin, UC Riverside	9	4	3.99	16	0	90	114	24	51
Meaux, Jesse, UC Santa Barbara	8	3	4.41	18	3	98	123	18	39
Pointer, Marcus, Pacific	7	5	4.58	15	0	106	105	45	65
Hummel, Jake, Pacific	7	4	4.65	22	3	93	111	25	57
Pinder, Branden, Long Beach State	4	7	4.85	17	0	85	106	22	45
Davis, Greg, UC Santa Barbara	2	2	4.91	20	0	55	66	14	47
Andriese, Matt, UC Riverside	5	5	4.95	15	0	104	130	18	69
Leonard, Matt, Cal Poly	2	7	4.97	15	0	96	124	20	49

COLONIAL ATHLETIC ASSOCIATION

	Conference		Overall	
	W	L	W	L
James Madison	18	6	30	23
Georgia State	17	6	34	23
*Virginia Commonwealth	16	7	34	26
UNC Wilmington	13	11	33	27
George Mason	11	13	28	22
Old Dominion	11	13	24	30
Towson	11	13	19	36
William & Mary	10	14	27	24
Hofstra	10	14	20	28
Delaware	9	15	27	24
Northeastern	5	19	13	31

ALL-CONFERENCE TEAM: C—Cody Stanley, Jr., UNC Wilmington. 1B—Trevor Knight, Jr., James Madison. 2B—Matt Prokopowicz, Sr., Hofstra. 3B—Joe Van Meter, Jr., Virginia Commonwealth. SS—Ryan Soares, Sr., George Mason. OF—Matt Browning, Sr., James Madison; Pat Dameron, Jr., Delaware; Mark Micowski, Jr., Georgia State. UTIL—Ethan Paquette, Sr., Hofstra. DH—Steve Ulaky, Jr., Delaware. SP—Matt Davenport, So., William & Mary; Kyle Hald, Jr., Old Dominion; Andrew Leenhouts, Jr., Northeastern. RP—Kevin Munson, Jr., James Madison
Player of the Year: Ryan Soares, George Mason. **Pitcher of the Year:** Kevin Munson, James Madison. **Defensive Player of the Year:** Mike Rooney, UNC Wilmington. **Rookie of the Year:** Anthony Montefusco, George Mason. Co-Coaches of the Year: Paul Keyes, Virginia Commonwealth; Spanky McFarland, James Madison

INDIVIDUAL BATTING LEADERS
(Minimum 125 At-Bats)

	AVG	AB	R	H	2B	3B	HR	RBI	SB
Soares, Ryan, George Mason	.438	194	57	85	29	2	13	71	4
Van Meter, Joe, VCU	.434	249	60	108	13	7	10	76	14
Prokopowicz, Matt, Hofstra	.431	174	47	75	18	0	6	41	4
Hill, Mark, George Mason	.414	186	49	77	19	0	6	47	8
Williams, Brandon, Georgia State	.408	223	59	91	20	2	10	73	8
Lind, Rob, Georgia State	.402	194	59	78	8	2	9	56	6
Micowski, Mark, Georgia State	.392	232	69	91	17	2	5	40	17
Gonzalez, Richard VCU	.391	233	67	91	19	0	0	37	20
Alonso, Carlos, Delaware	.389	226	62	88	20	2	16	47	8
Wood, Joey, Georgia State	.386	153	49	59	12	1	9	39	8
Browning, Matt, James Madison	.378	209	58	79	23	1	10	41	6
Fleming, Ryan, Georgia State	.375	176	59	66	12	2	13	59	3
Ulaky, Steve, Delaware	.374	182	36	68	19	0	7	43	3
Paquette, Ethan, Hofstra	.371	205	44	76	19	0	14	70	3

	AVG	AB	R	H	2B	3B	HR	RBI	SB
Baker, Chris, Old Dominion	.369	160	39	59	18	1	8	51	0
Moniz, Carl, Georgia State	.369	217	58	80	13	4	10	63	12
Tison, Brig, George Mason	.367	199	45	73	10	2	3	33	15
Logan, Bradley, Georgia State	.364	217	66	79	19	0	11	60	15
Palumbo, Dan, George Mason	.364	154	39	56	13	1	2	29	4
Knight, Trevor, James Madison	.360	222	61	80	17	4	13	45	15
Dameron, Pat, Delaware	.353	204	48	72	19	1	14	59	2
Cuneo, Ryan, Delaware	.350	217	54	76	17	3	16	65	0
Long, D.J., Delaware	.350	203	34	71	16	0	2	35	3
Ridge, Hunter, UNC Wilmington	.348	221	32	77	17	0	5	49	1
A'Hara, Scott, Hofstra	.346	153	35	53	9	1	3	23	8
Collins, Kevin, Towson	.346	214	49	74	15	4	8	47	26
Yarsinsky, Steve, Towson	.344	186	37	64	14	0	10	40	4
Winter, Ben, Towson	.343	230	55	79	18	6	3	25	4
Mikionis, Brent, VCU	.343	207	40	71	13	0	11	54	1
Wychock, Chris, Towson	.343	213	44	73	20	2	13	52	8
#Monday, Robbie, UNC Wilmington	.317	205	50	65	14	1	20	66	2

INDIVIDUAL PITCHING LEADERS
(Minimum 50 Innings)

	W	L	ERA	G	SV	IP	H	BB	SO
Munson, Kevin, James Madison	8	1	1.64	28	10	55	33	24	70
Davenport, Matt, William & Mary	8	2	1.96	20	1	96	85	33	88
Watson, Jonathan, VCU	4	2	2.51	31	0	61	48	22	53
#Booth, Bryan, UNC Wilmington	3	3	2.70	32	3	30	23	15	25
Hald, Kyle, Old Dominion	8	4	2.79	13	0	100	100	29	95
Roth, Cameron, UNC Wilmington	7	4	2.98	16	0	94	87	52	74
Leenhouts, Andrew, Northeastern	3	4	3.15	12	1	71	64	30	88
Cutler-Voltz, Seth, VCU	8	4	3.47	17	0	119	118	30	67
Williams, Les, Northeastern	3	4	3.77	11	0	74	66	22	50
McSwain, Tyler, UNC Wilmington	6	3	4.02	14	0	81	82	27	65
O'Grady, Chris, George Mason	3	1	4.06	12	0	62	63	19	47
Bradley, Justin, UNC Wilmington	3	2	4.40	15	0	74	75	40	73
Cropper, Daniel, UNC Wilmington	3	4	4.69	16	0	63	69	11	49
Buchanan, David, Georgia State	4	2	4.72	11	0	55	62	25	53
Bashara, Charly, Northeastern	1	4	4.74	15	2	57	65	18	53
Crum, Kevin, George Mason	5	4	4.81	13	0	64	75	15	44
Frankoff, Seth, UNC Wilmington	5	1	4.95	26	1	56	54	27	68
Francis, Aidan, Georgia State	6	3	4.96	19	0	78	97	22	75
Olson, Charley, Georgia State	5	4	5.09	18	0	94	102	38	75
Billbrough, Logan, William & Mary	5	5	5.34	14	0	62	72	36	64
Rorick, Brian, Delaware	6	2	5.51	19	2	98	102	42	90

CONFERENCE USA

	Conference		Overall	
	W	L	W	L
Rice	17	7	40	23
*Southern Mississippi	14	10	36	24
Memphis	12	12	28	30
Marshall	12	12	27	31
East Carolina	11	13	32	27
Alabama-Birmingham	11	13	28	25
Houston	11	13	25	32
Central Florida	10	14	33	22
Tulane	10	14	32	24

ALL-CONFERENCE TEAM: C—Victor Gomez, Jr., Marshall. IF—Anthony Rendon, So., Rice; Rob Segedin, So., Tulane; Luke Stewart, Sr., Alabama-Birmingham; B.A. Vollmuth, So., Southern Mississippi. OF—Shane Brown, Sr., Central Florida; Chris Duffy, Sr., Central Florida; Kurt Lipton, Sr., Marshall. DH—Kyle Roller, Sr., East Carolina. P—Scott Copeland, Sr., Southern Mississippi; Seth Maness, Jr., East Carolina; Todd McInnis, Jr., Southern Mississippi; Arik Sikula, Jr., Marshall. RP—Collin Cargill, Jr., Southern Mississippi.
Player of the Year: Anthony Rendon, Rice. **Pitcher of the Year:** Seth Maness, East Carolina. **Freshman of the Year:** Chris Taladay, Central Florida. **Newcomer of the Year:** Zach Woods, East Carolina. **Coach of the Year:** Wayne Graham, Rice.

INDIVIDUAL BATTING LEADERS
(Minimum 150 At-Bats)

	AVG	AB	R	H	2B	3B	HR	RBI	SB
Duffy, Chris, UCF	.447	206	54	92	18	1	21	81	3
Segedin, Rob, Tulane	.434	212	55	92	29	2	14	54	4
Brown, Shane, UCF	.428	208	58	89	25	0	10	43	4

	AVG	AB	R	H	2B	3B	HR	RBI	SB
Zurcher, Chad, Memphis	.396	230	51	91	13	3	6	41	20
Rendon, Anthony, Rice	.394	226	**83**	89	12	1	**26**	**85**	14
Vollmuth, B.A., Southern Miss	.386	236	72	91	17	2	20	76	4
Thompson, Corey, East Carolina	.377	228	61	86	16	3	8	54	1
Martinez, Drew, Memphis	.377	**260**	62	**98**	10	5	0	41	19
Lipton, Kurt, Marshall	.375	192	42	72	11	**7**	10	41	1
Seastrunk, Diego, Rice	.369	179	47	66	17	1	9	52	3
Walker, Taylor, Southern Miss	.365	244	64	89	11	0	8	57	10
Gomez, Victor, Marshall	.364	220	39	80	15	0	17	63	7
Austin, Jamal, UAB	.364	209	41	76	13	3	2	29	28
Sweeney, Darnell, UCF	.358	232	51	83	14	1	2	38	17
Taylor, Beau, UCF	.354	198	45	70	16	2	7	35	1
Taladay, Chris, UCF	.352	210	49	74	19	0	8	47	3
Doleac, Adam, Southern Miss	.352	162	38	57	11	2	7	57	4
Breen, Ryan, UCF	.348	164	46	57	7	0	5	29	11
Fuda, Michael, Rice	.346	231	59	80	7	6	7	45	6
Presley, Zak, Houston	.344	180	46	62	5	1	3	29	21
Huelsing, Tyler, Memphis	.343	242	54	83	16	2	12	67	8
Ramsey, Caleb, Houston	.341	205	33	70	14	3	3	40	10
Wilson, Jacob, Memphis	.341	214	41	73	19	0	4	41	5
Hague, Rick, Rice	.340	259	71	88	20	0	15	55	10
Crohan, Blake, Tulane	.340	215	53	73	14	0	8	42	2
Frost, John, UAB	.338	210	37	71	14	1	5	50	2
Kelso, Blake, Houston	.338	237	45	80	10	5	3	32	17
Ansley, Joel, Houston	.333	222	45	74	10	**7**	5	43	17
Koelling, Tyler, Southern Miss	.333	183	40	61	13	4	4	39	5
Whitehead, Trent, East Carolina	.331	245	51	81	15	0	4	31	15

INDIVIDUAL PITCHING LEADERS
(Minimum 1 Inning Per Team Game)

	W	L	ERA	G	SV	IP	H	BB	SO
McInnis, Todd, Southern Miss	6	5	**3.30**	16	0	95	85	34	87
Copeland, Scott, Southern Miss	**11**	1	3.75	15	0	96	95	25	64
Rogers, Jared, Rice	8	2	3.83	18	1	87	96	14	49
Sikula, Arik, Marshall	6	5	3.88	17	0	70	69	33	57
Anagnostou, Boogie, Rice	3	5	4.11	19	0	66	68	28	28
Maness, Seth, East Carolina	10	3	4.17	17	1	**101**	123	16	90
Martin, Brennon, Memphis	6	6	4.35	16	0	93	115	29	70
Wall, Taylor, Rice	5	5	4.45	17	0	85	75	30	61
Woods, Zach, East Carolina	8	4	4.50	20	1	90	97	25	103
Kloskowski, Mitch, UAB	5	5	4.50	12	0	68	64	23	47
Flynn, Conrad, Tulane	3	7	4.57	14	0	85	95	14	60
Brandt, Kevin, East Carolina	3	7	5.21	19	0	76	73	33	69
Petiton, Matt, Tulane	4	4	5.27	17	0	68	83	24	40
Goodnight, Michael, Houston	7	7	5.36	16	0	86	90	54	90
Broach, Robby, Tulane	7	3	5.40	14	0	77	88	26	76
Cicio, Nick, UCF	4	5	5.64	18	0	59	58	31	56
Fraser, Ryan, Memphis	7	4	5.77	16	1	92	116	46	96
Dew, Owen, UCF	5	3	5.89	13	0	73	96	22	48
Sedlock, Johnny, UCF	3	4	5.95	16	1	56	75	19	41
Pender, Beau, UAB	6	5	6.75	14	0	75	85	37	57
#Blank, Marshall	1	1	7.52	**35**	0	20	23	14	14
#Coan, Austin, Marshall	0	1	7.62	27	**12**	28	34	20	21

GREAT WEST CONFERENCE

	Conference		Overall	
	W	L	W	L
Utah Valley	26	2	42	17
Northern Colorado	22	6	34	24
Houston Baptist	15	13	28	31
New York Tech	15	13	26	29
North Dakota	13	15	19	35
Texas-Pan American	9	18	22	33
New Jersey Tech	9	18	13	44
Chicago State	2	26	4	52

ALL-CONFERENCE TEAM: C—Kevin Arendse, Sr., Utah Valley. **1B**—Jake Magner, Jr., North Dakota. **2B**—T.J. Berge, Jr., Northern Colorado. **3B**—Jace Brinkerhoff, Sr., Utah Valley. **SS**—Jake Rickenbach, Jr., Utah Valley. **OF**—Chris Benson, Jr., Utah Valley; Jarod Berggren, Fr., Northern Colorado; Jason Zundel, So., Utah Valley. **DH**—Robbie Buller, So., Houston Baptist. **UT**—Chase Hernandez, Jr., Houston Baptist. **P**—Andrew Guarrasi, Sr., New York Tech; Joe Sawicki, So., Northern Colorado; Mark Shannon, Fr., Northern Colorado. **RP**—Brian Whatcott, So., Utah Valley.
Player of the Year: Jace Brinkerhoff, Utah Valley. **Pitcher of the Year:** Joe Sawicki, Northern Colorado. **Newcomer of the Year:** Mark Shannon, Northern Colorado. **Coach of the Year:** Eric Madsen, Utah Valley.

INDIVIDUAL BATTING LEADERS
(Minimum 2.5 At-Bats Per Team Game)

	AVG	AB	R	H	2B	3B	HR	RBI	SB
Brinkerhoff, Jace, Utah Valley	**.456**	259	**88**	**118**	23	2	13	85	5
Valdez, Effrey, New York Tech	.438	219	58	96	21	1	11	46	9
Bivone, Garrett, UT Pan American	.428	201	39	86	23	0	4	46	3
Benson, Chris, Utah Valley	.408	**262**	68	107	24	**11**	14	**89**	15
Berggren, Jarod, Northern Colorado	.392	222	61	87	14	8	11	54	15
Berge, T.J., Northern Colorado	.391	220	54	86	18	3	10	59	3
Rickenbach, Jake, Utah Valley	.390	251	86	98	19	4	6	39	2
Thorpe, Sage, Utah Valley	.388	147	41	57	11	1	4	30	0
Prestera, Paul, Houston Baptist	.384	229	60	88	24	3	1	41	11
Mejia, Vincent, UT Pan American	.380	208	64	79	15	1	8	51	0
Smith, Jerry, New York Tech	.374	195	48	73	15	0	8	59	11
Zundel, Jason, Utah Valley	.372	188	58	70	9	2	6	41	9
Kallunki, Goose, Utah Valley	.370	246	47	91	**25**	1	0	66	1
Raudenbush, Northern Colorado	.362	174	40	63	9	2	5	37	5
Buller, Robbie, Houston Baptist	.353	221	39	78	20	1	10	57	0
Crudo, Tony, Northern Colorado	.352	210	52	74	21	1	7	52	9
Macinnes, Stuart, UT Pan American	.352	193	42	68	17	3	4	42	4
Hardman, Kyle, Northern Colorado	.350	223	59	78	15	3	18	53	4
Nelson, Josh, North Dakota	.350	163	20	57	12	1	0	30	6
Moore, Jonathan, Houston Baptist	.349	218	51	76	11	2	6	51	4
Ray, Josh, North Dakota	.347	173	42	60	15	3	5	36	3
Magner, Jake, North Dakota	.346	211	49	73	10	0	**21**	59	1
Budde, Seth, New York Tech	.342	187	36	64	11	0	7	49	0
Smith, Brian, New York Tech	.342	243	61	83	8	4	12	44	15
Heaps, Austin, Utah Valley	.338	195	45	66	17	2	3	35	2
Arendse, Kevin, Utah Valley	.338	216	54	73	21	0	7	48	6
Wallace, Tyler, Northern Colorado	.333	183	34	61	13	0	7	37	2
Zikeli, Zeke, Houston Baptist	.330	230	56	76	10	7	0	43	13
Smith, Derek, Houston Baptist	.330	182	41	60	9	5	1	24	4
Ibanez, Angel, UT Pan America	.328	201	43	66	7	3	5	35	6
#Mcfarlin, Kellon, Chicago State	.320	169	33	54	4	2	1	18	27

INDIVIDUAL PITCHING LEADERS
(Minimum 1.0 IP Per Team Game)

	W	L	ERA	G	SV	IP	H	BB	SO
#Roth, Mike, New York Tech	2	3	2.16	25	**9**	50	39	23	28
Sawicki, Joe, Northern Colorado	**9**	2	**3.06**	14	0	97	90	29	67
Nikonchik, Stephen, Houston Baptist	4	2	4.27	**28**	3	65	59	34	48
Kotchie, Kyle, UT Pan American	4	6	4.28	15	0	55	35	48	68
Guarrasi, Andrew, New York Tech	8	3	4.34	17	1	87	90	33	91
Shannon, Mark, Northern Colorado	6	3	4.52	14	0	84	95	33	64
Willman, Joe, Northern Colorado	7	5	4.55	14	0	87	113	26	50
Anderson, Sam, North Dakota	4	5	4.92	11	0	57	65	31	31
Plunk, Cody, UT Pan America	3	3	5.04	10	0	50	48	37	41
Schafer, Dalton, Houston Baptist	5	5	5.06	16	0	**100**	133	27	50
Flores, Luis, UT Pan America	4	2	5.06	15	0	64	71	23	26
Krahenbuhl, Blake, Utah Valley	**9**	1	5.22	17	0	79	83	15	57
Wingo, Scott, UT Pan America	2	2	5.22	15	0	71	96	25	64
Lind, David, North Dakota	4	4	5.50	11	0	74	107	14	31
Storey, Jamie, Houston Baptist	4	6	5.71	18	0	82	111	30	33
Wasmund, Preston, New York Tech	6	3	5.99	16	1	77	94	30	35
Gray, Zane, Utah Valley	6	6	6.06	16	0	88	106	36	42
Biermaier, Derek, North Dakota	4	7	6.16	13	0	73	87	41	54
Campbell, Justin, Utah Valley	5	0	6.27	14	1	60	84	34	30
Beecher, Kyle, Utah Valley	4	2	6.32	15	0	63	85	21	19

HORIZON LEAGUE

	Conference		Overall	
	W	L	W	L
Wright State	17	6	31	25
*Wisconsin-Milwaukee	17	8	33	26
Illinois-Chicago	15	9	24	30
Valparaiso	9	10	24	32
Butler	11	13	21	29
Youngstown State	9	17	22	34
Cleveland State	5	20	12	43

ALL-CONFERENCE TEAM: C—Gerald Ogrinc, Sr., Wright State. **1B**—Jake Hibberd, So., Wright State. **2B**—Matt Serna, Jr., Illinois-Chicago. **3B**—

Quentin Cate, Sr., Wright State. **SS**—Jacke Healey, Sr., Youngstown State. **OF**—Tom Clayton, Sr., Youngstown State; Casey McGrew, Sr., Wright State; Tim Patzman, Sr., Milwaukee. **DH**—Garrett Gray, So., Wright State. **UT**—Paul Hoenecke, So., Milwaukee. **P**—Casey Henn, So., Wright State; Bryce Shafer, Jr., Valparaiso.

Player of the Year: Tom Clayton, Youngstown State. **Pitcher of the Year:** Bryce Shafer, Valparaiso. **Relief Pitcher of the Year:** Cameron Amsrud, Milwaukee. **Co-Newcomers of the Year:** Chad Pierce, Milwaukee; Matt Serna, Illinois-Chicago. **Coach of the Year:** Rob Cooper, Wright State.

INDIVIDUAL BATTING LEADERS
(Minimum 2.0 At-Bats Per Team Game)

	AVG	AB	R	H	2B	3B	HR	RBI	SB
Patzman, Tim, UWM	.417	156	37	65	12	4	5	34	9
Clayton, Tom, Youngstown State	.412	170	45	70	17	1	10	47	6
McGrew, Casey, Wright State	.383	230	58	88	19	3	5	48	8
Serna, Matt, UIC	.379	211	49	80	17	4	2	49	11
Gaedele, Kyle, Valparaiso	.373	236	61	88	19	8	7	63	17
Iacobucci, Joe, Youngstown State	.369	214	46	79	18	1	10	52	3
Moylan, Corey, Butler	.369	187	43	69	15	2	3	37	6
Hibberd, Jake, Wright State	.368	223	41	82	16	2	1	54	2
Cate, Quentin, Wright State	.367	229	44	84	22	1	8	67	5
Frane, Justin, Valparaiso	.361	194	43	70	9	4	2	35	4
Gray, Garrett, Wright State	.360	214	44	77	15	2	10	47	2
McGuiggan, Steve, UIC	.355	217	66	77	19	9	6	35	19
Healey, Jacke, Youngstown State	.355	234	63	83	13	2	12	59	14
Moore, Tristan, Wright State	.353	167	51	59	7	5	7	33	7
Rutta, Chris, UIC	.353	190	38	67	19	3	13	62	2
Sivilotti, Sam, UWM	.352	176	28	62	10	2	1	37	8
Kraft, Cole, UWM	.350	223	48	78	21	1	5	35	6
Duncan, Luke, Butler	.342	187	35	64	11	3	0	26	4
Long, Ben, UWM	.342	228	43	78	16	1	8	55	3
Ganek, Jason, UIC	.342	202	54	69	16	3	5	45	7
Muhlsteff, Kyle, Valparaiso	.339	245	59	83	23	1	6	29	8
Marzec, Eric, Youngstown State	.338	130	27	44	7	1	6	28	6
Ogrinc, Gerald, Wright State	.337	193	40	65	14	2	4	31	6
Shaffer, Kyle, Cleveland State	.336	232	44	78	16	3	10	59	9
Schultz, Kyle, Butler	.333	159	23	53	12	1	2	24	1
Buchholz, Dan, UWM	.332	226	50	75	13	2	9	49	3
Robinson, Robbie, Valparaiso	.327	205	45	67	10	1	2	43	3
Fields, Aaron, Wright State	.325	169	38	55	10	3	4	36	2
Fillipitch, Grant, Butler	.322	202	40	65	12	1	6	40	2
Scoby, Steven, Valparaiso	.322	143	25	46	6	1	2	24	7

INDIVIDUAL PITCHING LEADERS
(Minimum 1.0 Innings Per Team Game)

	W	L	ERA	G	SV	IP	H	BB	SO
Henn, Casey, Wright State	7	0	3.19	15	0	85	76	20	82
Pierce, Chad, UWM	7	5	4.03	16	0	103	103	43	64
Shafer, Bryce, Valparaiso	7	4	4.10	19	1	105	108	51	121
Gulbransen, Jon, Valparaiso	4	6	4.67	15	0	94	117	23	75
McCulloh, Kevin, Youngstown State	1	5	4.96	28	0	53	73	24	40
McCormick, Damon, Valparaiso	7	1	5.35	11	0	67	80	7	49
Kaminsky, Alex, Wright State	5	5	5.53	15	0	98	104	15	88
Swenson, Aaron, Youngstown State	8	1	5.60	14	0	100	114	38	94
Ochs, Joe, Butler	3	5	5.65	11	0	51	58	15	41
Schmidt, Kyle, UWM	4	3	5.67	15	0	86	100	27	43
Heesch, Michael, UIC	6	6	5.68	20	1	84	112	19	42
Hernandez, Mike, Butler	5	5	5.72	15	0	79	107	21	57
Sambula, Anthony, Cleveland State	4	6	5.90	12	0	61	65	42	56
Deetjen, Tyler, Valparaiso	4	6	6.02	16	0	52	65	15	42
Klein, Phil, Youngstown State	2	4	6.51	17	0	65	86	26	57
Blankemeyer, Nate, Cleveland State	1	5	6.63	16	0	56	72	25	19
#Michael Schum, Wright State	0	5	7.23	28	2	37	58	4	31
Riegler, Brad, UIC	3	3	7.48	25	3	65	88	25	30
Bates, Coty, Cleveland State	0	6	7.82	12	0	59	84	35	44
Aquadro, Blake, Youngstown State	2	6	7.87	17	0	58	69	26	31

IVY LEAGUE

GEHRIG

	Conference		Overall	
	W	L	W	L
Columbia	14	6	26	21
Pennsylvania	10	10	21	20
Cornell	9	11	18	20
Princeton	6	14	12	30

ROLFE

	Conference		Overall	
*Dartmouth	13	7	27	19
Harvard	10	10	17	26
Brown	10	10	13	31
Yale	8	12	21	22

ALL-CONFERENCE TEAM: C—Matt Colantonio, Jr., Brown; Dean Forthun, Sr., Columbia. **1B**—Trygg Larsson-Danforth, Sr., Yale. **2B**—Chris Tanabe, Sr. Brown. **3B**—Dan Williams, Jr., Penn. **SS**—Sean O'Hara, Jr., Harvard. **OF**—Tom Grandieri, Sr., Penn; Jeremy Mass, Jr., Penn.; Dario Pizzano, Fr., Columbia. **UT**—Mickey Brodsky, Jr., Cornell; Pete Greskoff, Jr., Brown. **DH**— Alex Aurrichio, So., Columbia; Michael DiBiase, So., Brown. **P**—Pat Lowery, So., Columbia; Brent Suter, So., Harvard. **RP**—David Rochefort, Sr., Cornell.

Player of the Year: Tom Grandieri, Penn. **Pitcher of the Year:** Pat Lowery, Columbia. **Co-Rookies of the Year:** Chris O'Dowd, Dartmouth; Dario Pizzano, Columbia.

INDIVIDUAL BATTING LEADERS
(Minimum 125 At-Bats)

	AVG	AB	R	H	2B	3B	HR	RBI	SB
Williams, Dan, Pennsylvania	.403	159	51	64	14	2	4	26	5
Grandieri, Tom, Pennsylvania	.399	178	45	71	22	1	7	46	9
O'Dowd, Chris, Dartmouth	.384	125	32	48	12	1	6	26	2
Eisen, Jon, Columbia	.383	167	39	64	8	2	1	22	10
Rallis, Trey, Yale	.377	138	33	52	20	0	5	31	2
Pizzano, Dario, Columbia	.374	147	38	55	12	3	12	36	2
Larsson-Danforth, Trygg, Yale	.373	161	39	60	16	1	11	44	12
Josh, Feit, Brown	.361	155	33	56	9	2	4	27	7
Vigoa, Derek, Pennsylvania	.361	144	28	52	7	1	1	25	6
Reynolds, Jeff, Harvard	.359	156	21	56	9	1	3	25	5
Zrenda, Ryan, Brown	.357	171	35	61	13	1	11	30	0
Brooks, Jason, Dartmouth	.355	155	26	55	8	5	7	48	2
Colantonio, Matt, Brown	.346	156	33	54	6	2	4	30	5
Tanabe, Chris, Brown	.343	134	24	46	11	0	3	18	2
O'Hara, Sean, Harvard	.342	149	36	51	16	3	1	26	5
Elmore, Gant, Yale	.339	171	35	58	9	0	0	23	7
Forthun, Dean, Columbia	.333	138	26	46	11	0	2	21	5
Aurrichio, Alexander, Columbia	.329	152	32	50	9	1	13	40	2
DiBiase, Mike, Brown	.326	138	27	45	12	0	8	34	0
Sclafani, Joe, Dartmouth	.325	166	35	54	9	2	3	23	11
Albright, Tyler, Harvard	.321	134	28	43	9	0	2	30	2
Bellenger, Zack, Dartmouth	.320	150	27	48	12	0	7	33	1
Carlson, Jake, Dartmouth	.313	163	27	51	7	1	2	22	4
Megee, Andy, Yale	.310	171	38	53	15	2	8	43	11
Gordon, Will, Pennsylvania	.309	152	39	47	16	2	4	37	4
Mishu, John, Princeton	.304	138	21	42	7	2	5	23	1
Gonzales-Lun, Noel, Princeton	.304	135	19	41	5	1	1	23	0
Banos, Jason, Columbia	.301	156	35	47	11	0	5	34	3
Zailskas, Dan, Harvard	.301	133	19	40	6	0	0	18	3
Mulroy, Sam, Princeton	.300	160	36	48	8	2	8	31	2
#Greskoff, Pete, Brown	.294	170	43	50	9	0	17	54	0
#O'Neill, Dillon, Harvard	.241	162	25	39	5	3	0	16	16

INDIVIDUAL PITCHING LEADERS
(Minimum 40 Innings)

	W	L	ERA	G	SV	IP	H	BB	SO
#Terry, Reid, Pennsylvania	4	4	1.60	23	0	34	29	11	31
Bertucci, Tony, Cornell	3	2	2.62	8	0	45	51	4	36
Pappel, Corey, Cornell	2	2	3.26	8	0	47	50	17	46
Lowery, Pat, Columbia	5	3	3.46	11	0	65	56	12	45
Hunter, Kyle, Dartmouth	2	0	3.48	12	0	62	75	8	46
Sulser, Cole, Dartmouth	8	0	3.70	19	4	58	53	10	60
McNulty, Chris, Pennsylvania	5	1	4.25	12	0	55	56	16	33
Bracey, Dan, Columbia	4	4	4.55	10	0	59	59	11	53
Lally, Vinny, Yale	7	2	4.71	9	0	57	59	37	51
#Smith, Ryan, Dartmouth	3	2	4.81	18	6	24	24	4	21
Voiro, Vince, Pennsylvania	3	2	5.04	12	0	61	59	19	47
Barnes, Dan, Princeton	1	3	5.14	9	0	49	57	19	40
Carlow, Kevin, Brown	4	3	5.25	10	0	48	56	27	42
Suter, Brent, Harvard	4	2	5.26	10	1	49	62	14	47
Roth, Todd, Pennsylvania	3	2	5.26	11	0	50	56	25	30
Ludwig, Pat, Yale	3	6	5.29	10	0	48	59	17	48
O'Hare, Christopher, Yale	2	0	5.36	10	0	44	54	17	34
Olson, Stefan, Columbia	2	2	5.47	10	0	49	63	20	40
Eadington, Eric, Harvard	4	3	5.63	9	0	46	57	14	30

Hulse, Conner, Harvard	1	3	6.14	11	1	44	49	21	36	
Hart, Brook, Yale	3	3	6.26	12	1	42	53	14	38	
Kimball, Matthew, Brown	2	5	6.35	14	1	45	66	23	38	

METRO ATLANTIC ATHLETIC CONFERENCE

	Conference		Overall	
	W	L	W	L
Canisius	19	5	39	21
Marist	16	8	33	22
*Rider	15	9	36	23
Manhattan	15	9	31	20
Siena	13	11	27	27
Niagara	13	11	17	36
Fairfield	8	16	18	32
St. Peter's	6	18	18	34
Iona	3	21	9	40

ALL-CONFERENCE TEAM: C—Bryce Nugent, Jr., Marist. **1B**—Kevin Quaranto, Jr., Siena. **2B**—Dan Paolini, So., Siena. **3B**—Chad Salem, Jr., Manhattan. **SS**—Sean Jamieson, Jr., Canisius. **OF**—Kevin Nieto, Sr., Manhattan; Mark Onorati, Jr., Manhattan; Andrew Passerelle, Sr., Iona. **UT**—Anthony Giansanti, Sr., Siena. **DH**—Ian Choy, Sr., Canisius. **P**—Shane Davis, R-Jr., Canisius; Mike Thomas, Jr., Rider. **Player of the Year:** Dan Paolini, Siena. **Pitcher of the Year:** Mike Thomas, Rider. **Relief Pitcher of the Year:** John Soldinger, Manhattan. **Rookie of the Year:** Anthony Hajjar, Fairfield. **Coach of the Year:** Mike McRae, Canisius.

INDIVIDUAL BATTING LEADERS
(Minimum 1.0 At-Bats Per Team Game)

	AVG	AB	R	H	2B	3B	HR	RBI	SB
Quaranto, Kevin, Siena	.413	206	53	85	24	3	12	54	9
McQual, Steve, Canisius	.397	224	70	89	21	1	20	81	9
Onorati, Mark, Manhattan	.391	202	59	79	19	0	7	51	14
Wojnowski, Nick, Rider	.388	196	45	76	14	1	9	46	3
Salem, Chad, Manhattan	.383	180	69	69	13	1	15	68	5
Hajjar, Anthony, Fairfield	.380	200	37	76	14	2	7	46	0
Gauck, Ryan, Marist	.380	187	51	71	17	2	3	38	9
Choy, Ian, Canisius	.377	220	59	83	13	0	7	57	3
Burton, Brian, Canisius	.373	212	57	79	11	1	17	68	2
Jamieson, Sean, Canisius	.371	210	66	78	15	1	7	52	15
Nieto, Kevin, Manhattan	.368	190	51	70	12	1	10	43	12
Paolini, Dan, Siena	.368	212	62	78	13	2	26	64	12
Albee, A.J., Rider	.360	239	63	86	15	3	9	60	14
Carter, Justyn, St. Peter's	.359	167	49	60	10	1	3	27	33
Nathans, Tucker, Fairfield	.357	210	46	75	22	2	7	50	10
Galella, Steve, Rider	.352	179	42	63	10	0	2	30	1
Cotten, Brandon, Rider	.351	194	56	68	9	1	1	32	12
Prano, John, Marist	.350	137	32	48	5	1	0	30	4
Schwind, Jon, Marist	.346	217	39	75	20	1	4	42	10
McCann, Mike, Manhattan	.340	200	57	68	17	2	10	56	4
Wilson, Shayne, Canisius	.338	210	40	71	12	1	10	56	12
Rossetti, Nick, Iona	.337	187	40	63	11	5	1	34	12
Giansanti, Anthony, Siena	.336	232	56	78	11	1	10	47	25
Wietlispach, Matt, Niagara	.333	219	48	73	10	1	1	9	19
Orefice, Mike, Marist	.331	154	36	51	8	3	2	36	1
Pacione, Ricky, Marist	.330	203	49	67	14	4	3	51	11
Shroeder, Brian, St. Peter's	.326	193	26	63	8	1	5	39	1
Sheffield, Austin, Manhattan	.326	172	28	56	16	0	6	52	2
Nugent, Bryce, Marist	.325	206	43	67	13	1	4	48	1
Passarelle, Andrew, Iona	.325	197	50	64	15	0	13	43	15
#Silverman, Perry, Canisius	.315	238	74	75	19	3	6	47	14

INDIVIDUAL PITCHING LEADERS
(Minimum 1.0 IP Per Team Game)

	W	L	ERA	G	SV	IP	H	BB	SO
Soldinger, John, Manhattan	5	3	2.83	21	7	60	61	23	48
Smith, Tyler, Rider	6	4	3.38	31	9	51	54	12	41
Chapin, Brendan, Marist	6	5	3.69	23	1	54	65	20	43
Thomas, Mike, Rider	9	3	4.14	15	0	104	102	32	98
Poplawski, Ryan, Siena	6	1	4.18	21	1	56	75	17	38
Gariano, Rob, Fairfield	4	5	4.29	13	0	94	117	31	74
Davis, Shane, Canisius	9	3	4.58	15	0	98	124	26	70
Gallagher, Chad, Marist	4	4	4.58	14	0	75	96	20	38
Maculuso, Dom, St. Peter's	5	8	4.90	15	0	86	105	26	60
Morari, Dan, Niagara	4	7	5.15	13	0	86	94	32	62

Luksis, Eric, Manhattan	5	6	5.27	14	0	70	86	35	44
Costigan, Tom, Manhattan	6	3	5.29	12	0	66	66	21	45
Devlin, Patrick, Rider	7	3	5.37	14	0	69	79	35	55
Calogero, Joe, Rider	3	0	5.56	15	0	55	72	17	22
Schaaf, Mike, St. Peter's	3	4	5.58	16	0	50	53	37	49
Putnam, Kyle, Marist	4	4	5.84	14	0	82	110	21	55
Goemans, Mike, Canisius	5	5	5.85	15	0	88	102	28	38
Giordano, Mike, Manhattan	6	3	5.87	22	3	69	90	23	43
Murphy, Mike, Rider	4	5	6.05	22	1	58	67	29	39
Cox, Chris, Canisius	5	4	6.07	17	0	70	69	51	67

MID-AMERICAN CONFERENCE

	Conference		Overall	
EAST	W	L	W	L
*Kent State	18	9	39	25
Bowling Green State	18	9	31	23
Miami (Ohio)	13	14	28	28
Ohio	13	14	20	35
Buffalo	9	18	23	29
Akron	3	24	21	34
WEST	W	L	W	L
Central Michigan	20	7	36	22
Toledo	19	8	34	22
Ball State	19	8	29	29
Eastern Michigan	13	14	27	32
Northern Illinois	12	15	24	31
Western Michigan	5	22	12	42

ALL-CONFERENCE TEAM: C—Zach Dygert, Sr., Ball State. **1B**—Nate Theunissen, So., Central Michigan. **2B**—Brad Agustin, Jr., Buffalo. **3B**—Joe Corfman, So., Toledo. **SS**—Jon Berti, So., Bowling Green. **OF**—Anthony Gallas, Sr., Kent State; Gauntlett Eldemire, Jr., Ohio; Robert Maddox, Jr., Ohio. **DH**—Matt Delewski, So., Toledo. **UT**—Kolbrin Vitek, Jr., Ball State. **SP**—Perci Garner, So., Ball State; Jesse Hernandez, Sr., Central Michigan; Kevin Leady, Sr., Bowling Green; Kendall Lewis, So., Eastern Michigan. **RP**—Dietrich Enns, Fr., Central Michigan. **Player of the Year:** Kolbrin Vitek, Ball State. **Pitcher of the Year:** Jesse Hernandez, Central Michigan. **Freshman of the Year:** Dietrich Enns, Central Michigan. **Coach of the Year:** Cory Mee, Toledo.

INDIVIDUAL BATTING LEADERS
(Minimum 125 At-Bats)

	AVG	AB	R	H	2B	3B	HR	RBI	SB
Berti, Jon, Bowling Green	.423	220	62	93	10	6	4	33	29
Teas, James, Central Michigan	.404	193	45	78	14	1	3	44	3
Eldemire, Gauntlett, Ohio	.398	201	59	80	16	1	16	55	16
Dudics, Chris, Toledo	.391	253	57	99	16	3	2	33	14
Theunissen, Nate, Central Michigan	.384	216	44	83	20	0	7	54	1
Corfman, Joe, Toledo	.383	230	69	88	20	1	7	61	15
Delewski, Matt, Toledo	.377	167	30	63	11	1	2	35	1
Maddox, Robert, Ohio	.377	236	54	89	20	1	21	78	3
Blanton, T.J., Bowling Green	.374	214	64	80	15	2	15	54	16
Skonieczki, Adam, Buffalo	.370	200	44	74	13	2	6	42	13
Gallas, Anthony, Kent State	.369	268	68	99	24	1	17	81	3
Eaton, Adam, Miami (Ohio)	.368	220	64	81	18	9	13	55	30
Klafczynski, Ben, Kent State	.367	256	66	94	27	3	10	62	2
Vitek, Kolbrin, Ball State	.361	233	73	84	20	3	17	68	16
Turocy, Drew, Akron	.358	265	62	95	15	5	6	57	10
Lewis, Chris, Western Michigan	.357	213	39	76	18	0	7	42	3
McMillen, Kyle, Kent State	.354	198	51	70	15	0	6	46	2
Barnes, Bryan, Ohio	.353	215	43	76	12	1	7	39	2
Pitzulo, Matthew, Bowling Green	.352	145	31	51	13	0	4	28	0
Turk, John, Akron	.350	203	26	71	13	0	1	26	1
Rider, Jimmy, Kent State	.344	276	46	95	21	2	1	44	6
Pizzuto, Bobby, Buffalo	.344	157	32	54	9	0	1	32	15
Agustin, Brad, Buffalo	.343	201	59	69	17	1	8	39	18
Dudley, Aaron, Toledo	.342	225	40	77	15	1	6	42	8
Vaughn, Dennis, Bowling Green	.340	194	42	66	13	1	10	58	3
Baumet, T.J., Ball State	.337	246	58	83	12	1	9	40	26
Galvin, Mark, Bowling Green	.337	190	45	64	10	2	2	25	7
Campbell, Evan, Kent State	.335	182	38	61	12	4	2	34	2
Kaup, Ryan, Miami (Ohio)	.333	171	32	57	6	1	1	21	4
Magsig, Ben, Eastern Michigan	.331	133	33	44	9	0	3	24	3

INDIVIDUAL PITCHING LEADERS
(Minimum 50 Innings)

	W	L	ERA	G	SV	IP	H	BB	SO
Enns, Dietrich, Central Michigan	7	0	2.12	20	0	59	34	27	64
Vitek, Kolbrin, Ball State	3	4	3.28	17	3	80	76	20	60
Howard, Trent, Central Michigan	4	3	3.58	17	5	60	57	20	65
Suschak, Matt, Toledo	5	1	3.84	21	3	61	47	22	60
Shaw, Kyle, Toledo	5	4	3.84	19	1	73	76	21	47
Morrow, Bryce, Central Michigan	4	2	4.00	16	1	63	74	19	43
Hamann, Michael, Toledo	6	3	4.12	14	0	79	82	26	56
Lewis, Kendall, Eastern Michigan	7	4	4.21	14	0	83	81	37	62
Gonzales, Jeremy, Northern Illinois	4	4	4.30	15	0	88	76	48	59
Bossenberry, Chris, Western Michigan	2	5	4.35	16	0	50	49	21	22
Brown, Andrew, Akron	4	6	4.50	17	0	98	124	31	65
Hernandez, Jesse, Central Michigan	8	3	4.58	15	0	98	108	28	72
Garner, Perci, Ball State	5	3	4.62	17	0	74	74	37	83
Sabo, Robert, Kent State	6	5	4.65	16	0	93	86	39	72
Moulton, Jason, Ohio	3	5	4.76	12	0	59	69	22	54
Grabner, Derek, Ball State	5	3	4.77	25	1	55	64	16	40
Rassi, Lincoln, Toledo	5	3	4.85	14	0	69	74	33	35
Loftin, Alex, Akron	4	8	4.86	16	0	96	126	35	63
Leady, Kevin, Bowling Green	8	3	4.96	14	0	94	105	25	68
Thoreson, Mac, Miami (Ohio)	5	6	5.08	16	1	73	83	18	48
#Dean, Andy, Northern Illinois	3	3	5.35	33	12	37	43	21	34

MID-EASTERN ATHLETIC CONFERENCE

	Conference		Overall	
	W	L	W	L
*Bethune-Cookman	18	6	35	22
North Carolina A&T	15	3	31	26
Norfolk State	9	9	21	29
Delaware State	8	10	13	36
Coppin State	7	11	14	33
Florida A&M	3	15	10	31
Maryland-Eastern Shore	3	15	8	43

ALL-CONFERENCE TEAM: C—Peter O'Brien, So., Bethune-Cookman. **IF**—Ryan Durrence, Jr., Bethune-Cookman; Chris Joyce, Jr., Norfolk State; Nick Rogers, Sr., North Carolina A&T; Derrick Shaw, So., Florida A&M. **OF**—D.J. Leonard, Jr., Bethune-Cookman; John Lynch, Jr., Norfolk State; Xavier Macklin, Jr., North Carolina A&T. **DH**—Jeremy Davis, Sr., Bethune-Cookman. **SP**—Esterlin Paulino, So., North Carolina A&T; Ali Simpson, So., Bethune-Cookman. **RP**—Juan Perez, Jr., Bethune-Cookman.
Player of the Year: Peter O'Brien, Bethune-Cookman. **Pitcher of the Year:** Esterlin Paulino, North Carolina A&T. **Rookie of the Year:** Kelvin Freeman, North Carolina A&T. **Coach of the Year:** Mervyl Melendez, Bethune-Cookman.

INDIVIDUAL BATTING LEADERS
(Minimum 125 At-Bats)

	AVG	AB	R	H	2B	3B	HR	RBI	SB
Leonard, D.J., B-CU	.432	155	36	67	13	1	10	45	2
Shaw, Derrick, Florida A&M	.411	163	45	67	11	3	6	36	21
O'Brien, Peter, B-CU	.384	203	51	78	13	0	20	56	0
Davis, Jeremy, B-CU	.382	152	40	58	10	1	5	34	3
Joyce, Chris, Norfolk State	.380	200	41	76	23	0	4	42	1
Riley, Marquis, N.C. A&T	.373	212	58	79	14	0	8	56	11
Freeman, Kelvin, N.C. A&T	.369	149	30	55	6	0	6	43	1
Williams, Harry, Coppin State	.364	162	31	59	14	1	2	32	1
Durrence, Ryan, B-CU	.364	209	57	76	16	1	18	72	1
Rogers, Nick, N.C. A&T	.364	198	57	72	10	0	15	64	11
Lynch, John, Norfolk State	.364	198	46	72	10	5	5	34	27
Davis, Scott, Delaware State	.353	153	47	54	15	1	3	23	3
Macklin, Xavier, N.C. A&T	.351	208	61	73	14	4	15	65	14
Eubank, Abe, Delaware State	.349	172	45	60	20	0	13	50	0
Vaughn, Phil, UMES	.347	176	31	61	8	2	0	17	28
Perez, Juan, B-CU	.347	176	47	61	13	1	1	34	10
Robinson, Dwight, Coppin State	.339	165	31	56	12	1	2	27	7
Nales, Mark, N.C. A&T	.339	174	36	59	5	0	2	19	12
Gleiberman, Dan, Coppin State	.337	172	32	58	10	1	2	28	1
Sanchez, Alejandro, B-CU	.335	188	38	63	14	2	6	36	7
Hairston, Brandon, Nor. State	.326	181	37	59	5	2	8	36	10
Richards, Derek, Coppin State	.320	169	33	54	15	3	2	26	2
Evans, Darryl, Florida A&M	.317	145	27	46	6	6	5	22	20
Gatto, Tony, Delaware State	.317	161	32	51	7	0	4	33	1

Hoyte, Justin, B-CU	.317	126	33	40	11	1	5	24	13
Howard, James, N.C. A&T	.315	127	26	40	8	0	1	29	6
Hines, George, N.C. A&T	.307	218	64	67	11	4	7	38	31
Rasberry, John, Norfolk State	.307	192	44	59	11	0	3	31	17
Johnson, Tre-von, UMES	.302	162	31	49	5	6	3	26	15
Kashangaki, Chris, Coppin State	.301	153	25	46	0	4	1	23	23

INDIVIDUAL PITCHING LEADERS
(Minimum 50 Innings)

	W	L	ERA	G	SV	IP	H	BB	SO
Paulino, Easterling, N.C. A&T	9	2	3.27	17	0	88	90	23	75
Moore, Brent, N.C. A&T	6	4	4.16	16	0	71	86	33	32
Simpson, Ali, B-CU	6	2	4.93	14	0	69	82	37	65
Barker, Jason, Norfolk State	4	5	4.99	16	0	79	92	26	41
Rogers, Nick, N.C. A&T	10	3	5.09	15	0	87	90	35	93
Lancara, Roman, B-CU	4	3	5.35	16	0	71	84	32	50
#Perez, Juan, B-CU	1	3	5.40	23	10	33	36	20	40
Pomierski, Tim, Coppin State	4	7	5.50	12	0	74	99	33	59
Dollar, Steven, Florida A&M	3	7	5.68	19	1	70	98	30	45
Vagnier, Jim, Coppin State	4	8	5.80	14	0	81	83	57	55
Davenport, Chase, Norfolk State	4	6	5.87	19	0	80	95	40	51
Smith, Jonathan, N.C. A&T	0	4	5.90	24	0	58	74	28	30
Goelz, Patrick, B-CU	5	2	6.39	17	0	51	67	14	40
Gardner, Elliot, Delaware State	4	5	6.88	15	0	72	91	36	51
Gonzales, Tony, UMES	0	6	6.90	20	0	74	123	16	41
Oelker, Nick, N.C. A&T	5	6	6.92	15	0	68	88	30	46
Deschamps, John, UMES	2	8	7.01	20	0	77	106	25	49
Blackburn, Heath, Florida A&M	2	7	7.18	14	0	84	132	40	45
Gonzalez, Karim, UMES	1	9	7.34	16	0	69	101	32	36
Haas, Ryan, Delaware State	0	8	8.21	16	0	72	102	41	49
Adkins, Zach, Delaware State	2	6	8.36	16	0	66	95	40	51

MISSOURI VALLEY CONFERENCE

	Conference		Overall	
	W	L	W	L
Wichita State	15	6	41	19
*Illinois State	15	6	32	24
Indiana State	10	10	35	19
Southern Illinois	10	10	28	29
Evansville	10	11	32	27
Creighton	9	12	27	25
Bradley	8	13	20	32
Missouri State	6	15	21	34

ALL-CONFERENCE TEAM: C—Cody Lassley, Sr. Wichita State. **1B**—Chris Serritella, So., Southern Illinois. **2B**—Kevin Tokarski, So., Illinois State. **3B**—Cody Fick, Jr., Evansville. **SS**—Eric Stamets, Fr., Evansville. **OF**—Bret Bascue, Sr., Wichita State; Ryan Strausborger, Sr., Indiana State; Greg Wallace, Jr., Evansville. **DH**—Preston Springer, Jr. Wichita State. **UT**—Kevin Medrano, So., Missouri State. **SP**—Jordan Cooper, So., Wichita State; Tim Kelley, Jr., Wichita State; Jake Petricka, Jr., Indiana State. **RP**—Kenny Long, So., Illinois State; Ryan Copeland, Sr., Illinois State.
Player of the Year: Kevin Tokarski, Illinois State. **Pitcher of the Year:** Jordan Cooper, Wichita State. **Newcomer of the Year:** Preston Springer, Wichita State. **Coach of the Year:** Eric Stamets, Evansville.

INDIVIDUAL BATTING LEADERS
(Minimum 125 At-Bats)

	AVG	AB	R	H	2B	3B	HR	RBI	SB
Tokarski, Kevin, Illinois State	.412	204	70	84	25	3	8	53	33
Madrano, Kevin, Missouri State	.410	210	44	86	18	2	4	29	16
Serritella, Chirs, So. Illinois	.374	222	51	83	19	1	13	64	0
Wallace, Greg, Evansville	.371	245	55	91	22	13	9	75	9
Lassley, Cody, Wichita State	.366	202	51	74	11	4	11	46	9
Martin, Brian, Bradley	.364	206	35	75	12	4	3	39	24
Fieser, Luke, Indiana State	.362	218	43	79	14	1	2	42	7
Adams, Trever, Creighton	.356	208	41	74	15	3	12	58	6
Ort, Robby, Indiana State	.353	207	44	73	10	2	5	50	9
McMillan, Mike, Bradley	.352	145	17	51	8	3	2	21	1
Fick, Cody, Evansville	.351	225	50	79	15	0	19	65	12
Strausborger, Ryan, Ind. State	.344	241	63	83	19	8	3	40	41
Elliott, Rob, Bradley	.341	179	45	61	9	2	3	27	15
Burnam, Kyle, Indiana State	.340	215	45	73	14	1	1	40	7
Pinnon, Blake, Southern Illinois	.333	210	49	70	16	0	8	45	1
Coy, Johnny, Wichita State	.331	139	34	46	13	1	7	32	2
Lucas, Jeremy, Indiana State	.326	175	40	57	13	0	1	24	9

	AVG	AB	R	H	2B	3B	HR	RBI	SB
Fritz, Matt, Bradley	.326	175	58	57	12	3	7	31	14
Springer, Preston, Wichita State	.324	219	54	71	20	1	11	59	1
Mirabel, Matt, Illinois State	.323	195	36	63	14	0	4	42	9
Leblebijian, Jason, Bradley	.323	155	26	50	8	2	0	20	5
Copeland, Trentt, Evansville	.322	239	44	77	20	1	4	36	19
Acheson, Alex, Evansville	.321	193	54	62	15	1	1	26	8
Stamets, Eric, Evansville	.321	234	57	75	15	0	4	27	43
Murphy, Chris, Southern Illinois	.320	225	47	72	16	2	1	31	11
Montgomery, Austin, So. Illinois	.319	135	22	43	5	0	3	27	1
Johnson, Nick, Southern Illinois	.309	191	37	59	8	2	2	22	4
Bullock, Tyler, Southern Illinois	.306	186	34	57	10	0	14	44	0
Ruffolo, Anthony, Illinois State	.305	203	42	62	14	3	8	48	12
Ferrell, Ben, Indiana State	.303	175	28	53	6	1	1	37	7

INDIVIDUAL PITCHING LEADERS
(Minimum 50 Innings)

	W	L	ERA	G	SV	IP	H	BB	SO
Long, Kenny, Illinois State	4	4	**1.38**	31	9	65	44	22	74
Cooper, Jordan, Wichita State	10	3	2.01	15	0	**107**	102	20	95
Blach, Ty, Creighton	3	3	3.11	14	0	75	63	18	58
Forer, Nathan, Southern Illinois	3	4	3.28	14	0	74	76	29	42
#Heithoff, Tom, Evansville	3	5	3.65	23	**10**	44	42	17	39
Kelley, Tim, Wichita State	**11**	3	3.94	16	0	96	108	26	80
Koenigstein, Brandon, Creighton	5	2	3.95	18	0	93	96	20	43
Davisson, Corey, Evansville	9	1	3.95	**33**	1	66	61	22	38
Cooper, Patrick, Bradley	4	5	3.99	18	2	70	64	26	61
Dennis, Keegan, Evansville	4	3	4.10	16	0	83	74	55	76
Petricka, Jake, Indiana State	7	4	4.11	20	0	101	100	47	113
Meade, Aaron, Missouri State	2	4	4.18	15	0	75	77	40	72
Doyle, Pat, Missouri State	5	9	4.18	16	0	95	112	33	71
Maines, Corey, Illinois State	6	3	4.60	17	0	86	97	42	67
Copeland, Ryan, Illinois State	4	5	4.63	31	5	84	83	12	78
Gordon, Grant, Missouri State	4	2	4.66	23	7	56	56	21	74
Van Skike, Jason, Indiana State	3	3	4.70	14	0	75	68	39	58
Dufek, Jonas, Creighton	8	3	4.92	16	0	82	95	19	65
Smith, Josh, Wichita State	4	3	5.02	14	0	61	73	23	37
Rodriguez, Joe, Indiana State	7	2	5.03	16	0	91	101	41	76
Kickham, Mike, Missouri State	4	9	5.25	15	0	96	101	30	103
#Browning, Tyler, Indiana State	1	2	5.90	30	**10**	29	33	16	37

MOUNTAIN WEST CONFERENCE

	Conference		Overall	
	W	L	W	L
*Texas Christian	19	5	52	13
New Mexico	14	8	38	22
San Diego State	13	11	28	28
Brigham Young	12	12	27	31
Nevada-Las Vegas	11	13	29	29
Utah	10	13	23	28
Air Force	3	20	13	42

ALL-CONFERENCE TEAM: C—Bryan Holaday, Sr., Texas Christian. **1B**—Matt Curry, Sr., Texas Christian. **2B**—Jerome Pena, Jr., Texas Christian. **3B**—Nick Kuroczko, Sr., Utah. **SS**—Taylor Featherston, So., Texas Christian. **OF**—Jason Coats, So., Texas Christian; Brandon Meredith, So., San Diego State; Brance Rivera, So., Texas Christian. **DH**—C.J. Cron, So., Utah. **P**—Matt Purke, Sr., New Mexico; Steven Maxwell, Jr., Texas Christian; Matt Purke, Fr., Texas Christian. **RP**—Tyler Lockwood, Sr., Texas Christian.

Player of the Year: C.J. Cron, Utah. **Pitcher of the Year:** Steven Maxwell, Texas Christian. **Freshman of the Year:** Matt Purke, Texas Christian. **Coach of the Year:** Jim Schlossnagle, Texas Christian.

INDIVIDUAL BATTING LEADERS
(Minimum 125 At-Bats)

	AVG	AB	R	H	2B	3B	HR	RBI	SB
Howard, Justin, New Mexico	.456	261	77	119	32	2	10	72	6
Cron, C.J., Utah	.431	197	55	85	16	0	**20**	**81**	0
Juarez, Chris, New Mexico	.402	204	46	82	11	0	2	33	9
Meredith, Brandon, San Diego State	.383	201	53	77	11	0	7	54	9
Vaughn, Cory, San Diego State	.378	188	42	71	14	1	9	55	15
Witte, Jansen, TCU	.374	163	32	61	15	1	4	39	2
Blackburn, Mitch, San Diego State	.372	234	63	87	12	2	4	36	6
Kretchmer, Kyle, UNLV	.366	131	25	48	9	0	9	40	0
Neda, Rafael, New Mexico	.362	232	47	84	22	0	11	64	1
Coats, Jason, TCU	.361	274	68	99	23	4	13	69	8

	AVG	AB	R	H	2B	3B	HR	RBI	SB
Frierson, Jarred, UNLV	.359	234	53	84	15	6	6	53	6
Relf, Brandon, BYU	.358	254	66	91	18	4	4	30	7
Cluff, Jonathan, BYU	.358	246	54	88	20	7	5	51	12
Elander, Josh, TCU	.356	194	41	69	16	4	2	33	11
Beuerlein, Drew, UNLV	.355	228	54	81	19	1	10	60	1
Holaday, Bryan, TCU	.355	**279**	72	99	24	1	17	53	3
Wolfe, Alex, BYU	.355	234	52	83	18	0	11	63	2
Honeycutt, Ryan, New Mexico	.353	221	43	78	11	2	6	55	2
Bayardi, Brandon, UNLV	.350	243	58	85	22	4	9	57	5
Nielsen, Dane, BYU	.347	202	40	70	13	2	3	39	3
Gentry, Addison, Air Force	.346	185	38	64	14	4	13	61	1
Alexander, Matt, Air Force	.345	232	45	80	14	3	7	46	2
Rivera, Brance, TCU	.342	187	46	64	8	0	6	28	9
Wells, Stephen, BYU	.340	203	47	69	9	4	6	46	2
McNaughton, Sean, BYU	.339	233	58	79	17	2	18	60	10
Curry, Matt, TCU	.339	248	65	84	26	2	18	65	12
Beltran, Michael, Utah	.338	145	33	49	7	1	0	20	16
Featherston, Taylor, TCU	.338	231	59	78	16	7	8	52	6
Ayoso, Bryce, BYU	.337	184	33	62	15	1	6	28	1
Gonzalez, Daniel, New Mexico	.332	214	47	71	9	5	0	43	3
#Carter, Nathan, Air Force	.309	204	51	63	8	**11**	9	28	13

INDIVIDUAL PITCHING LEADERS
(Minimum 50 Innings)

	W	L	ERA	G	SV	IP	H	BB	SO
Lockwood, Tyler, TCU	6	2	**2.19**	28	**8**	66	58	21	41
Reed, Addison, San Diego State	8	2	2.50	11	0	79	65	16	90
Maxwell, Steven, TCU	11	2	2.70	18	0	103	89	34	93
Purke, Matt, TCU	**16**	0	3.02	20	0	116	91	34	142
Sloan, Kevin, BYU	9	2	3.15	**29**	0	54	57	17	37
Winkler, Kyle, TCU	12	3	3.39	19	0	**117**	111	36	92
Crabb, Bryan, San Diego State	4	5	3.89	13	0	72	73	35	58
Kesler, Willy, New Mexico	6	3	3.92	16	0	101	98	25	97
Olson, Richard, New Mexico	4	3	4.19	19	1	54	69	29	48
Hutchinson, Matt, UNLV	6	4	4.46	23	4	79	95	28	62
Card, Bryn, Utah	2	4	4.55	14	0	63	68	17	40
Toves, Kenny, New Mexico	5	2	4.59	21	0	69	86	33	46
Gerrish, Paul, TCU	1	3	4.65	19	0	50	67	17	42
Capper, Chris, BYU	4	2	4.80	21	1	81	107	20	45
Anton, Rick, Utah	7	3	5.13	14	0	88	101	26	64
Peters, Tanner, UNLV	7	5	5.54	18	0	93	110	35	110
Jaramillo, Rudy, New Mexico	4	2	5.83	16	0	66	84	15	30
Neil, Matthew, BYU	4	4	5.94	14	0	67	102	18	46
Anderson, Mark, BYU	3	1	6.14	15	0	51	57	41	35
Wilding, Andrew, Utah	4	3	6.29	15	0	59	90	25	40

NORTHEAST CONFERENCE

	Conference		Overall	
	W	L	W	L
Bryant	25	7	34	22
Sacred Heart	20	12	31	27
*Central Connecticut State	18	14	33	23
Wagner	17	15	26	31
Monmouth	15	17	22	27
Mount St. Mary's	14	18	20	31
Quinnipiac	13	19	14	39
Fairleigh Dickinson	11	21	16	38
Long Island	11	21	14	42

ALL-CONFERENCE TEAM: C—Jeff Heppner, Sr., Sacred Heart. **1B**—Tommy Meade, Sr. Central Connecticut State. **2B**—Ryan Terry, Jr., Monmouth. **3B**—Mitch Wells, So., Central Connecticut State. **SS**—Brian Martutartus, Jr., Wagner. **OF**—Nick Campbell, Sr., Bryant; Patt Epps, Jr., Central Connecticut State; Richie Tri, Sr., Central Connecticut State. **DH**—Jon Lucas, Jr., Wagner. **UT**—Sean Allaire, Sr., Central Connecticut State. **SP**—Brent Almeida, Sr., Bryant; Jared Balbach, Sr., Sacred Heart. **RP**—Mark Andrews, Jr., Bryant.

Player of the Year: Sean Allaire, Central Connecticut State. **Pitcher of the Year:** Brent Almeida, Bryant. **Rookie of the Year:** Kevin Brown, Bryant. **Coach of the Year:** Jamie Pinzino, Bryant.

INDIVIDUAL BATTING LEADERS
(Minimum 125 At-Bats)

	AVG	AB	R	H	2B	3B	HR	RBI	SB
Allaire, Sean, CCSU	.426	235	65	100	22	6	13	73	10
Epps, Pat, CCSU	.418	220	66	92	14	5	18	73	2
Griffith, Robert, Sacred Heart	.401	167	28	67	10	1	5	39	1
Campbell, Nick, Bryant	.391	215	43	84	12	0	2	45	4
Tri, Ritchie, CCSU	.381	194	46	74	15	2	6	39	2
Wells, Mitch, CCSU	.369	217	55	80	21	2	8	45	2
Meade, Tommy, CCSU	.366	216	48	79	13	4	10	56	4
Murphy, John, Sacred Heart	.358	179	27	64	14	1	4	44	1
Brown, Kevin, Bryant	.355	231	52	82	23	7	6	40	6
Casale, Mike, Monmouth	.354	161	47	57	12	2	3	24	3
Rosenkranz, Jamie, Monmouth	.346	162	30	56	9	2	7	36	10
Farina, Ben, Quinnipiac	.344	209	42	72	16	0	2	26	6
Kane, Kyle, Mount St. Mary's	.339	174	34	59	12	0	3	30	4
Robinson, D.J., Farleigh Dickinson	.339	183	32	62	15	0	8	49	4
Terry, Ryan, Monmouth	.337	196	49	66	20	2	9	33	15
Laforge, Steven, Fair. Dickinson	.336	211	40	71	15	1	3	36	7
Nisson, Kyle, Quinnipiac	.335	161	13	54	7	2	0	24	1
English, Jordan, Bryant	.335	167	36	56	11	0	1	21	8
Vigurs, Jeff, Bryant	.333	222	35	74	13	1	4	41	5
Dombrowski, Bobby, Monmouth	.327	162	22	53	6	0	7	39	0
Avella, Vin, Wagner	.327	208	52	68	16	0	17	60	2
Martutartus, Brian, Wagner	.327	196	35	64	18	2	2	24	15
Eyler, Shane, Mount St. Mary's	.326	178	31	58	9	0	6	31	8
Tedesco, Steve, Sacred Heart	.325	203	53	66	7	2	5	36	17
Cianciolo, Zakary, Bryant	.324	176	33	57	18	4	3	32	2
Boyd, Seth, Wagner	.321	184	42	59	9	2	4	30	15
Heppner, Jeff, Sacred Heart	.321	209	51	67	12	2	13	56	1
Poletsky, Joe, Quinnipiac	.318	195	31	62	14	0	2	38	2
Zarotney, Kyle, CCSU	.318	151	34	48	6	0	4	32	1
Tingos, Gerard, Long Island	.318	192	38	61	15	0	5	36	2
#Csakai, Damian, Wagner	.313	198	39	62	7	1	0	18	41

INDIVIDUAL PITCHING LEADERS
(Minimum 50 Innings)

	W	L	ERA	G	SV	IP	H	BB	SO
Almeida, Brent, Bryant	6	0	1.94	10	0	65	52	24	33
#Rees, David, Wagner	2	3	2.37	30	6	38	37	23	36
#Andrews, Mark, Bryant	3	1	2.73	23	12	33	31	6	27
Worthington, Kent, Mount St. Mary's	4	2	2.95	14	0	76	65	28	72
Polvani, Eric, Bryant	6	6	3.43	14	0	97	85	26	89
Balbach, Jared, Sacred Heart	9	3	3.63	15	0	92	97	30	72
Meyers, Nick, Monmouth	6	3	3.93	12	0	76	74	31	51
Matta, Mike, Mount St. Mary's	4	6	3.98	26	6	61	71	23	39
Kelich, Peter, Bryant	9	1	4.23	14	0	72	88	13	52
Scribner, Troy, Sacred Heart	5	4	4.50	15	2	78	77	13	59
Zaccherio, Chris, Sacred Heart	7	5	4.61	15	0	98	112	22	81
Topa, Justin, Long Island	6	6	4.67	16	1	71	78	15	66
Birdsall, Kyle, Quinnipiac	4	5	4.83	11	0	63	67	21	41
Krasnowiecki, Dave, CCSU	7	3	4.84	14	0	80	90	29	57
Breese, Kyle, Monmouth	3	4	4.91	11	0	70	83	15	49
Sauter, Adam, Long Island	2	7	5.53	14	0	73	94	24	51
Cinelli, Anthony, Quinnipiac	3	5	5.34	13	0	57	84	13	16
Lucas, Jon, Wagner	4	5	5.91	12	0	56	70	19	45
Light, Pat, Monmouth	2	6	6.12	11	1	57	74	19	33
Corcoran, Corey, Sacred Heart	1	7	6.39	12	0	62	75	16	31
Van Spronsen, Ryan, Wagner	2	7	6.41	18	0	59	79	24	43
Smith, Dan, Monmouth	2	5	6.46	17	2	70	92	14	31

OHIO VALLEY CONFERENCE

	Conference		Overall	
	W	L	W	L
Tennesee Tech	14	6	31	25
*Jacksonville State	15	8	32	26
Southeast Missouri State	13	9	30	25
Murray State	12	8	28	28
Eastern Illinois	11	12	18	35
Eastern Kentucky	9	12	28	27
Austin Peay State	8	13	28	25
Morehead State	6	12	24	25
Tennessee-Martin	8	16	24	31

ALL-CONFERENCE TEAM
C—Jim Klocke, Sr., Southeast Missouri State. **1B**—Wes Cunningham, Sr., Murray State. **2B**—Bert Smith, Sr., Jacksonville State. **3B**—Jayson Langfels, Jr., Eastern Kentucky. **SS**—Drew Lee, Sr., Morehead State. **OF**—J.D. Ashbrook, Sr., Morehead State; Todd Cunningham, Jr., Jacksonville State; Chad Oberacker, Jr., Tennessee Tech. **DH**—A.J. Kirby-Jones, Jr., Tennessee Tech. **UT**—Casey Jones, Jr., Southeast Missouri State. **SP**—Lee Henry, Sr., Tennessee Tech; Mike Recchia, Jr., Eastern Illinois. **RP**—Shae Simmons, Fr., Southeast Missouri State.

Player of the Year: Wes Cunningham, Murray State. **Pitcher of the Year:** Lee Henry, Tennessee Tech. **Freshman of the Year:** Shae Simmons, Southeast Missouri State. **Coach of the Year:** Matt Bragga, Tennessee Tech.

INDIVIDUAL BATTING LEADERS
(Minimum 125 At-Bats)

	AVG	AB	R	H	2B	3B	HR	RBI	SB
Oberacker, Chad, Tenn. Tech	.452	239	67	108	29	5	6	70	14
Ashbrook, J.D., Morehead State	.432	190	69	82	15	0	18	55	14
Lee, Drew, Morehead State	.412	204	60	84	19	1	17	66	13
Cunningham, Wes, Murray State	.408	233	77	95	19	6	22	86	10
Jones, Casey, Southeast Mo.	.398	206	41	82	15	1	10	66	0
Nelson, Ty, Tennessee-Martin	.396	212	53	84	20	4	8	45	19
Kirby-Jones, A.J., Tennessee Tech	.388	206	64	80	19	0	26	71	0
Adamson, Michael, Southeast Mo.	.388	237	63	92	23	3	6	49	4
Parmley, Kenton, Southeast Mo.	.380	237	67	90	10	1	11	42	12
Smith, Bert, Jacksonville State	.371	240	58	89	11	2	0	40	36
Klocke, Jim, Southeast Mo.	.370	230	59	85	22	0	13	66	0
Propst, Bryan, Murray State	.366	205	57	75	19	2	14	56	4
Cunningham, Todd, JSU	.359	237	61	85	17	4	11	42	21
Rodriguez, Richie, Eastern Ky.	.357	244	55	87	11	4	5	37	21
Karlen, Trey, Tennessee-Martin	.356	216	61	77	22	2	14	45	30
Lucas, Trey, Austin Peay State	.356	160	38	57	16	0	6	42	2
Langfels, Jayson, Eastern Kentucky	.353	204	61	72	14	4	16	52	12
Borenstein, Zach, Eastern Illinois	.353	207	50	73	13	0	11	47	12
Davis, Taylor, Morehead State	.350	183	40	64	8	2	11	57	0
Adamson, Daniel, JSU	.349	218	60	76	11	5	13	53	12
Elliott, Brandon, Murray State	.347	170	41	59	13	5	1	25	4
Rupp, Tim, Southeast Mo.	.344	189	36	65	15	0	3	36	8
Patterson, Wes, Tennessee-Martin	.344	192	44	66	15	0	16	64	1
Browett, Adam, Austin Peay State	.342	193	53	66	18	4	6	51	16
Fear, Michael, Morehead State	.341	167	33	57	10	1	4	35	0
Wulf, Austin, Tennessee Tech	.340	156	36	53	8	2	2	33	4
Morris, Brent, Tennessee-Martin	.339	171	30	58	12	0	3	25	10
Pugh, Daniel, Morehead State	.335	161	45	54	4	1	4	32	2
Ottrando, Anthony, Eastern Ky.	.335	200	47	67	15	2	17	67	11
Donaldson, Casanova, Tenn. Tech	.333	201	40	67	16	0	7	37	13

INDIVIDUAL PITCHING LEADERS
(Minimum 50 Innings)

	W	L	ERA	G	SV	IP	H	BB	SO
Lee, Henry, Tennessee Tech	7	3	2.69	16	0	80	66	37	85
Jones, Alex, JSU	1	6	3.53	28	6	51	38	38	61
Tobik, Dan, Tennessee-Martin	3	2	3.63	22	2	67	72	22	59
McGaha, Matt, Murray State	5	3	3.90	27	3	67	80	13	52
Underwood, Jordan, Southeast Mo.	6	5	4.11	17	0	72	86	39	56
Hoekstra, Mike, Eastern Illinois	4	4	4.16	15	0	67	87	5	39
Recchia, Mike, Eastern Illinois	6	6	4.29	22	2	86	86	39	87
Mueller Josh, Eastern Illinois	3	2	4.35	12	0	69	70	30	78
Craycraft, Chris, Murray State	6	4	5.05	16	1	93	108	35	72
Marshall, Ricky, Austin Peay State	7	6	5.19	14	0	78	89	42	52
Liberatore, Adam, Tennessee Tech	6	4	5.30	13	0	75	91	24	74
Lucas, Austin, JSU	6	0	5.31	14	0	63	62	26	46
Bazzani, Anthony, Eastern Kentucky	5	5	5.47	19	1	77	84	30	41
Gumieny, Kyle, Southeast Mo.	8	1	5.50	19	0	75	90	21	48
Love, Alex, Murray State	8	1	5.63	19	0	70	90	23	35
McNeil, Brent, Eastern Illinois	2	4	5.64	24	0	53	60	32	31
Terry, Greg, Eastern Kentucky	3	3	5.76	22	1	50	84	10	24
Donze, Jake, Murray State	6	6	5.92	16	0	84	92	56	71
Freshour, Tanner, JSU	6	1	6.02	29	1	52	58	24	27
Purcell, Ryne, Eastern Kentucky	2	1	6.03	30	12	55	61	25	29
#Green, Cory, Tennessee-Martin	9	4	7.38	17	0	88	130	17	64

PACIFIC-10 CONFERENCE

	Conference		Overall	
	W	L	W	L
*Arizona State	20	7	52	9
UCLA	18	9	50	14
Washington State	15	12	37	22
Stanford	14	13	31	25
Oregon	13	14	40	24
California	13	14	29	25
Arizona	12	15	34	24
Oregon State	12	15	32	24
Washington	11	16	28	28
Southern California	7	20	28	32

ALL-CONFERENCE TEAM: C—Jeff Brandy, So., Arizona; Chadd Krist, So., California **1B**—Mark Canha, Jr., California; Ricky Oropesa, So., USC; Riccio Torrez, So., Arizona State. **2B**—Zack MacPhee, So., Arizona State; Tyler Rahmatulla, So., UCLA. **3B**—Kenny Diekroeger, Fr., Stanford; Stefen Romero, Jr., Oregon State. **SS**—Drew Maggi, So., Arizona State. **OF**—Kole Calhoun, Sr., Arizona State; Adalberto Santos, Sr., Oregon State; Steve Selsky, So., Arizona. **DH**—Tony Renda, Fr., California. **P**—Tyler Anderson, So., Oregon; Chad Arnold, Jr., Washington State; Trevor Bauer, So., UCLA; Seth Blair, Jr., Arizona State; Gerrit Cole, So., UCLA; Adam Conley, So., Washington State; Kurt Heyer, Fr., Arizona; Justin Jones, Fr., California, Dan Klein, So., UCLA; Mitchell Lambson, So., Arizona State; Rob Rasmussen, Jr., UCLA; Jordan Swagerty, So., Arizona State. **Player of the Year:** Zack MacPhee, Arizona State. **Pitcher of the Year:** Seth Blair, Arizona State. **Defensive Player of the Year:** Brian Guinn, California. **Freshman of the Year:** Kenny Diekroeger, Stanford. **Coach of the Year:** Tim Esmay, Arizona State.

INDIVIDUAL BATTING LEADERS
(Minimum 125 At-Bats)

	AVG	AB	R	H	2B	3B	HR	RBI	SB
Torrez, Riccio, Arizona State	.399	228	65	91	27	1	10	53	20
MacPhee, Zack, Arizona State	.394	228	66	87	8	14	9	64	19
Renda, Tony, California	.373	217	55	81	21	4	3	37	13
Selsky, Steve, Arizona	.370	235	57	87	17	6	9	52	11
Diekroeger, Kenny, Stanford	.356	216	42	77	12	1	5	41	1
Bandy, Jett, Arizona	.354	223	53	79	23	0	6	42	4
Oropesa, Ricky, USC	.353	235	53	83	22	1	20	67	7
Amaral, Beau, UCLA	.352	199	41	70	9	0	4	29	8
Ruettiger, Johnny, Arizona State	.352	182	47	64	7	7	4	35	10
Wilson, Zach, Arizona State	.352	182	38	64	17	2	8	45	4
Serna, KC, Oregon	.348	233	45	81	13	1	5	37	14
Lamb, Jacob, Washington	.347	202	33	70	14	0	4	32	1
O'Neill, Mike, USC	.344	186	40	64	14	0	3	25	5
Refanyder, Robert, Arizona	.344	218	38	75	9	3	2	40	6
Krist, Chadd, California	.344	192	43	66	15	3	10	44	2
Cherry, Doug, Washington	.340	191	30	65	14	0	2	22	9
Santos, Adalberto, Oregon State	.336	217	48	73	15	4	10	36	20
Maggi, Drew, Arizona State	.335	251	54	84	10	3	5	39	35
Uribe, Justin, UCLA	.329	155	17	51	5	0	3	27	3
Rodriguez, Eddie, Oregon	.329	228	38	75	12	1	7	45	2
Kaskow, Jonathan, Stanford	.328	134	20	44	9	1	1	28	0
Gaffney, Tyler, Stanford	.328	198	42	65	13	3	3	24	2
Semien, Marcus, California	.328	195	40	64	17	2	4	34	5
Rahmatulla, Tyler, UCLA	.328	195	40	64	17	2	4	34	5
Guinn, Brian, California	.327	223	47	73	12	4	2	30	15
Calhoun, Kole, Arizona State	.327	217	60	71	11	2	17	59	7
Romero, Stefen, Oregon State	.326	184	39	60	10	1	13	41	5
Piscotty, Stephen, Stanford	.326	227	45	74	17	0	4	36	8
Bartlett, Cody Washington State	.323	189	46	61	16	1	7	34	8
Dunlap, Blair, UCLA	.323	220	42	71	20	2	5	23	7
#Canha, Mark, California	.319	204	48	65	11	0	10	69	9
#De Pinto, Joe, USC	.286	252	50	72	15	2	2	23	4

INDIVIDUAL PITCHING LEADERS
(Minimum 50 Innings)

	W	L	ERA	G	SV	IP	H	BB	SO
Rodgers, Brady, Arizona State	4	3	2.03	17	3	71	49	11	66
#Jordan, Swagerty, Arizona State	2	0	2.06	33	14	35	32	10	46
Claypool, Garett, UCLA	8	3	2.05	20	0	79	46	19	72
Lambson, Mitchell, Arizona State	8	2	2.10	37	3	69	38	18	90
Rasmussen, Rob, UCLA	11	2	2.73	17	0	99	76	28	117

Anderson, Tyler, Oregon	7	5	2.98	17	0	103	84	33	105
Bauer, Trevor, UCLA	10	3	3.02	16	0	116	111	37	141
Cole, Gerrit, UCLA	10	3	3.25	17	0	108	76	49	138
Heyer, Kurt, Arizona	4	3	3.26	17	0	102	97	29	109
Conley, Adam, Washington State	5	4	3.33	29	12	68	67	20	47
Blair, Seth, Arizona State	12	0	3.35	17	0	102	105	24	104
Thornton, Zack, Oregon	9	0	3.40	17	0	90	92	16	73
Robles, Tanner, Oregon State	5	4	3.43	14	0	76	73	28	75
Kelly, Merrill, Arizona State	10	2	3.57	17	0	98	89	37	75
Peavey, Greg, Oregon State	6	3	3.64	15	0	99	97	29	72
LaTempa, Justin, Oregon	6	3	3.65	15	0	89	85	21	68
Clem, Jacob, Washington	4	4	3.70	30	6	66	52	19	49
Arnold, Chad, Washington State	5	3	3.74	17	1	108	94	49	80
Triggs, Andrew, USC	2	7	3.95	11	0	71	71	21	62
Pries, Jordan, Stanford	4	4	4.07	15	0	97	97	42	65
Bandilla, Bryce, Arizona	6	4	4.07	29	1	77	90	34	70

PATRIOT LEAGUE

	Conference		Overall	
	W	L	W	L
Army	16	4	28	17
Lehigh	12	8	23	27
Holy Cross	10	10	26	26
*Bucknell	8	12	25	35
Navy	7	13	30	21
Lafayette	7	13	15	30

ALL-CONFERENCE TEAM: C—B.J. LaRosa, Sr., Bucknell. **1B**—Doug Shribman, Jr., Bucknell. **2B**—Ben Yoder, Sr., Bucknell. **3B**—Matt Perry, Sr., Holy Cross. **SS**—Clint Moore, Jr., Army. **OF**—Alex Azor, So. Navy; Andrew Brouse, Sr., Bucknell; Ben Koenigsfeld, Jr., Army; Jack Laurendeau, Jr., Holy Cross. **DH**—Matt Fenster, Jr., Lafayette. **SP**—Andrew Berger, Sr., Lehigh; Matt Fouch, Sr., Army. **RP**—Kevin McKague, Jr., Army. **Player of the Year:** Andrew Brouse, Bucknell. **Pitcher of the Year:** Matt Fouch, Army. **Rookie of the Year:** Stephen Wadsworth, Holy Cross. **Coach of the Year:** Sean Leary, Lehigh.

INDIVIDUAL BATTING LEADERS
(Minimum 2.5 At-Bats Per Team Game)

	AVG	AB	R	H	2B	3B	HR	RBI	SB
Fenster, Matt, Lafayette	.410	122	20	50	10	2	1	22	2
Perry, Matt, Holy Cross	.409	198	54	81	16	2	5	36	2
Yoder, Ben, Bucknell	.394	180	49	71	16	0	11	48	2
Speciale, Michael, Navy	.381	189	40	71	12	3	8	44	9
LaRosa, B.J., Bucknell	.371	202	43	75	8	1	5	36	0
Ciardiello, Nick, Holy Cross	.368	185	39	68	20	0	10	57	1
Brouse, Andrew, Bucknell	.365	211	60	77	13	1	17	52	17
May, Steve, Army	.364	121	22	44	4	0	1	16	6
Azor, Alex, Navy	.362	185	31	67	10	3	0	34	6
Henshaw, Joey, Army	.361	119	29	43	11	2	4	25	3
Shribman, Doug, Bucknell	.359	217	45	78	17	1	21	62	1
Koenigsfeld, Ben, Army	.359	142	24	51	10	1	5	33	3
Laurendeau, Jack, Holy Cross	.355	183	46	65	12	4	7	25	18
Wadsworth, Stephen, Holy Cross	.354	147	25	52	8	2	3	37	0
Curley, Matthew, Navy	.342	196	41	67	5	1	1	33	7
Pisarri, A.J., Lafayette	.335	164	29	55	5	1	1	15	8
Tkowski, Steven, Holy Cross	.333	192	37	64	21	2	7	44	1
McKague, Kevin, Army	.331	151	34	50	9	1	8	36	3
Watkins, J.T., Army	.320	153	30	49	5	1	1	18	5
Mihalik, Kevin, Lehigh	.319	144	20	46	6	0	2	24	6
#Allen, Ben, Bucknell	.317	249	50	79	13	6	1	25	2
#Froio, Rob, Lafayette	.281	167	33	47	12	1	2	20	19

INDIVIDUAL PITCHING LEADERS
(Minimum 1 IP Per Team Game)

	W	L	ERA	G	SV	IP	H	BB	SO
#McKague, Kevin, Army	0	0	1.33	17	13	20	19	7	26
Nelson, Ben, Navy	5	3	2.34	14	1	62	55	15	37
Berger, Andrew, Lehigh	5	2	3.36	9	0	62	51	14	42
Fouch, Matt, Army	6	2	3.49	11	1	67	66	20	44
Koneski, Nate, Holy Cross	6	2	3.74	13	1	77	72	15	51
Lee, Logan, Army	4	1	3.80	14	1	45	52	22	25
Longernecker, Ken, Lehigh	7	2	3.86	14	0	61	67	21	41
Seeley, Dylan, Bucknell	5	3	4.08	14	0	88	102	22	50
#Snell, Jeff, Lafayette	3	1	4.19	23	5	39	32	11	29
Olson, Wes, Navy	4	4	4.40	13	0	59	70	20	31

	W	L	ERA	G	SV	IP	H	BB	SO
Long, Sam, Navy	4	4	4.52	11	0	62	67	11	57
Cummings, Steve, Army	6	2	4.64	13	0	54	73	12	47
Lebo, Mike, Lehigh	4	4	4.73	13	0	59	72	12	37
Shapiro, Matt, Holy Cross	4	3	5.37	11	0	54	67	20	39
Sipe, Zach, Navy	5	2	5.46	11	0	61	63	26	34
Frahler, Trey, Bucknell	4	7	7.23	14	0	75	108	37	55
Shea, Corey, Lafayette	4	2	8.47	9	0	46	73	15	30
Fritz, Zach, Lafayette	2	7	8.80	10	0	46	63	21	33
Atkins, Jeremy, Lafayette	1	3	9.29	18	0	51	86	15	41

SOUTHEASTERN CONFERENCE

	Conference		Overall	
EAST	W	L	W	L
Florida	22	8	47	17
South Carolina	21	9	50	16
Vanderbilt	16	12	46	20
Kentucky	13	17	31	25
Tennessee	12	18	30	26
Georgia	5	23	16	37
WEST				
Auburn	20	10	43	21
Arkansas	18	12	43	21
Mississippi	16	14	39	24
Alabama	15	15	42	25
*Louisiana State	14	16	41	22
Mississippi State	6	24	23	33

ALL-CONFERENCE TEAM: C—Micah Gibbs, Jr., LSU. **1B**—Hunter Morris, Jr., Auburn. **2B**—Anthony Gomez Fr., Vanderbilt. **3B**—Zack Cox, So., Arkansas. **SS**—Josh Rutledge, Jr., Alabama. **OF**—Taylor Dugas, So., Alabama; Brian Fletcher, Jr., Auburn; Trent Mummey, Jr., Auburn. **DH**—Kevin Patterson, Jr., Auburn. **SP**—Blake Cooper, Sr., South Carolina; Drew Pomeranz, Jr., Mississippi. **RP**—Kevin Chapman, Sr., Florida.
Player of the Year: Hunter Morris, Auburn. **Pitcher of the Year:** Drew Pomeranz, Mississippi. **Freshman of the Year:** Austin Maddox, Florida. **Coach of the Year:** Kevin O'Sullivan, Florida.

INDIVIDUAL BATTING LEADERS
(Minimum 125 At-Bats)

	AVG	AB	R	H	2B	3B	HR	RBI	SB
Cox, Zack, Arkansas	.429	238	67	102	14	1	9	48	11
Dugas, Taylor, Alabama	.395	243	70	96	15	5	2	37	19
Gibbs, Micah, LSU	.388	245	47	95	14	3	10	60	7
Morris, Hunter, Auburn	.386	272	66	105	18	5	23	76	6
Powers, Connor, Miss. State	.379	214	55	81	18	1	16	68	3
Gomez, Anthony, Vanderbilt	.379	214	41	81	10	0	2	30	9
Bradley Jr., Jackie, So. Carolina	.371	213	51	79	11	1	11	51	7
Jenkins, Ryan, Auburn	.365	178	36	65	14	0	7	38	2
Gamache, Dan, Auburn	.365	189	51	69	15	1	8	37	7
Cone, Zach, Georgia	.363	212	45	77	12	7	10	53	13
Rutledge, Josh, Auburn	.360	297	65	107	16	2	10	69	15
Esposito, Jason, Vanderbilt	.359	262	65	94	25	1	12	64	31
den Dekker, Matt, Florida	.358	240	64	86	7	3	13	49	23
Fradejas, Justin, Auburn	.358	193	52	69	8	3	3	33	14
Fletcher, Brian, Auburn	.357	252	62	90	17	1	22	75	4
Polk, P.J., Tennessee	.352	216	56	76	11	2	12	51	25
Caldwell, Tony, Auburn	.349	189	42	66	8	0	10	41	6
Smith, Matt, Mississippi	.348	224	63	78	14	0	12	54	3
Dean, Blake, LSU	.341	255	64	87	15	0	12	70	2
Farmer, Kyle, Georgia	.340	153	27	52	16	2	3	25	5
Tucker, Preston, Florida	.339	236	50	80	16	2	11	46	8
Landry, Leon, LSU	.338	240	55	81	12	6	6	45	17
Taylor, Jonathan, Georgia	.337	199	29	67	6	3	0	29	13
Glad, Gunner, Kentucky	.336	214	49	72	11	1	12	45	3
Kuhn, Collin, Arkansas	.336	259	66	87	18	4	16	52	17
Mahtook, Mikie, LSU	.335	239	68	80	19	4	14	50	22
Maddox, Austin, Florida	.333	255	48	85	16	0	17	71	0
Eibner, Brett, Arkansas	.333	216	66	72	17	0	22	71	3
Hyams, Levi, Georgia	.333	162	33	54	13	0	4	32	3
Hanover, Tyler, LSU	.332	247	49	82	16	1	2	35	4
#Bisson, Chris, Kentucky	.329	210	43	69	12	1	5	35	32
#Merrifield, Whit, So. Carolina	.327	263	70	86	11	0	12	38	12

INDIVIDUAL PITCHING LEADERS
(Minimum 50 Innings)

	W	L	ERA	G	SV	IP	H	BB	SO
Pomeranz, Drew, Mississippi	9	2	2.24	16	0	101	71	49	139
Smyly, Drew, Arkansas	9	1	2.80	14	0	103	85	36	114
Cooper, Blake, South Carolina	12	1	2.81	17	0	118	98	35	105
Kilcrease, Nathan, Auburn	8	3	2.85	34	4	98	81	21	82
Randall, Hudson, Florida	8	3	2.95	19	0	95	98	19	68
McCray, Stephen, Tennessee	6	4	3.04	14	0	92	73	30	64
Panteliodis, Alex, Florida	11	2	3.26	17	0	97	81	22	80
Reid, Chase, Vanderbilt	4	2	3.46	28	3	68	63	14	66
Gray, Sunny, Vanderbilt	10	5	3.48	19	1	109	101	48	113
#Huber, Brett, Mississippi	2	0	3.54	30	12	48	38	19	54
Johnson, Brian, Florida	6	4	3.97	15	0	70	82	14	48
Nelson, Jimmy, Alabama	9	3	4.01	18	0	110	110	33	98
Aaron, Barrett, Mississippi	7	5	4.34	16	0	91	83	49	98
Dyson, Sam, South Carolina	5	5	4.35	16	0	89	85	20	93
Dayton, Grant, Auburn	8	3	4.36	16	0	95	101	19	69
Hill, Taylor, Vanderbilt	6	5	4.46	20	0	107	118	27	74
Armstrong, Jack, Vanderbilt	7	4	4.71	16	0	78	90	39	50
Bolsinger, Mike, Arkansas	6	5	4.81	23	0	86	85	27	79
Ross, Austin, LSU	5	4	5.22	21	1	88	90	19	98
Stratton, Chris, Mississippi State	5	3	5.29	14	0	78	84	42	76
Grimm, Justin, Georgia	3	7	5.49	15	0	77	82	35	73
Darnell, Logan, Kentucky	5	3	5.50	14	1	74	92	28	55
Crnkovich, Steve, Tennessee	6	2	5.58	25	1	71	84	22	39

SOUTHERN CONFERENCE

	Conference		Overall	
	W	L	W	L
*The Citadel	24	6	43	22
College of Charleston	22	8	44	19
Elon	19	11	38	24
Georgia Southern	19	11	38	24
Samford	17	12	31	25
Western Carolina	16	13	37	21
Appalachian State	14	14	38	18
Furman	11	19	19	37
Wofford	9	21	17	38
UNC Greensboro	7	23	20	33
Davidson	5	25	19	32

ALL-CONFERENCE TEAM: C—Rob Kral, So., College of Charleston. **1B**—Kyle Blackburn, Sr., Georgia Southern. **2B**—Wes Hobson, Sr., Appalachian State. **3B**—Matt Leeds, So., College of Charleston. **SS**—Neal Pritchard, Jr., Elon. **OF**—Cole Rakar, Jr., College of Charleston; Jose Rodriguez, So., College of Charleston; David Schulze, Sr., Samford. **DH**—Mac Doyle, So., Wofford. **SP**—Jimmy Reyes, Jr., Elon; Asher Wojciechowski, Jr., The Citadel. **RP**—Chris Patterson, Sr., Appalachian State.
Player of the Year: Matt Leeds, College of Charleston. **Pitcher of the Year:** Asher Wojciechowski, The Citadel. **Freshman of the Year:** Will Muzika, Furman. **Coach of the Year:** Fred Jordan, The Citadel.

INDIVIDUAL BATTING LEADERS
(Minimum 125 At-Bats)

	AVG	AB	R	H	2B	3B	HR	RBI	SB
Hobson, Wes, App. State	.404	235	69	95	22	2	11	54	17
Foster, James, Wofford	.387	230	57	89	18	1	0	35	18
Rakar, Cole, Charleston	.378	270	76	102	26	2	8	54	20
Doyle, Mac, Wofford	.377	220	46	83	23	6	16	75	8
Schulze, David, Samford	.377	191	39	72	13	0	12	56	6
Behrendt, Kyle, Wofford	.374	227	60	85	19	4	6	48	20
Weiss, Danny, Davidson	.368	144	42	53	11	2	6	35	6
Meredeth, Mason, Samford	.365	219	59	80	12	2	12	58	11
Heffley, Ross, Western Carolina	.361	238	37	86	15	0	11	63	2
Hayes, Trey, Samford	.358	218	49	78	14	1	11	46	5
Rodriguez, Jose, Charleston	.355	245	63	87	18	1	16	69	4
Blackburn, Kyle, George So.	.353	224	60	79	18	0	17	76	0
Owens, Will, Furman	.351	205	48	72	9	3	8	38	11
Johns, Matt, Western Carolina	.346	228	65	79	19	2	11	40	23
Gadaire, Drew, Davidson	.346	214	54	74	14	3	1	30	18
Payne, Shawn, Georgia So.	.345	206	68	71	15	1	5	33	43
Miller, Wayne, Samford	.344	244	60	84	14	2	8	42	10
Kral, Rob, Charleston	.344	215	66	74	11	1	15	57	4
Altman, Bryan, Citadel	.343	248	61	85	17	0	14	70	15

Thompkins, Aaron, Furman	.342	196	38	67	9	1	3	30	9
Phillips, Eric, Georgia Southern	.342	243	44	83	15	0	7	56	15
Pritchard, Neal, Elon	.340	235	53	80	15	1	12	47	6
Stetson, Ryan, App. State	.339	180	32	61	7	2	4	33	11
Dowdy, Jeremy, App. State	.338	222	43	75	13	0	6	48	4
Bergman, Joey, Charleston	.335	197	60	66	16	2	5	40	16
Crespo, Hector, App. State	.335	215	55	72	9	3	3	31	31
Mackert, Justin, Citadel	.335	239	49	80	12	1	5	38	24
Orvin, Nick, Citadel	.335	263	66	88	11	3	7	30	22
Bennett, Landon, Wofford	.333	189	39	63	15	1	4	35	7
Kirkpatrick, Tyler, W. Carolina	.332	229	54	76	16	0	13	56	5
#Leeds, Matt, Charleston	.326	242	61	79	23	1	21	88	1

INDIVIDUAL PITCHING LEADERS
(Minimum 50 Innings)

	W	L	ERA	G	SV	IP	H	BB	SO
#Patterson, Chris, App. State	4	4	1.67	29	13	43	34	13	60
Johnson, Brandon, W. Carolina	9	1	2.89	33	2	53	44	29	50
Benedict, Matt, Western Carolina	9	2	3.11	18	0	93	104	33	66
Wojciechowski, Asher, Citadel	12	3	3.58	17	0	126	111	32	155
Talley, Matt, Citadel	8	3	3.71	16	0	104	103	32	85
Decker, Kevin, Charleston	8	0	3.78	17	0	81	75	36	67
Reifsnider, Matt, Citadel	2	1	4.09	29	1	55	68	6	40
Schiller, Tom, Charleston	5	1	4.26	30	2	51	49	23	56
Hyatt, Colby, UNC Greensboro	7	4	4.29	22	1	94	108	25	57
Brown, Jake, Georgia Southern	7	6	4.32	17	0	102	109	19	79
Frongello, Mike, Davidson	2	4	4.50	31	2	52	61	13	36
Parry, Ian, Furman	5	7	4.51	15	0	102	105	20	89
Reyes, Jimmy, Elon	10	4	4.56	16	0	99	100	24	96
Slack, Warren, UNC Greensboro	3	10	4.75	20	1	89	104	40	75
Britt, Daniel, Elon	5	2	4.99	15	0	79	94	25	54
Stallsmith, Daniel, Furman	5	3	5.08	23	1	73	85	37	29
Clevinger, Michael, Citadel	5	3	5.15	16	0	93	115	35	77
Sandefur, Taylor, Western Carolina	1	2	5.19	12	0	50	58	30	24
Jones, Andrew, Samford	5	3	5.19	32	1	61	76	16	54
Peterson, David, Charleston	8	3	5.30	15	0	87	100	21	68
Jackson, Tyler, Appalachian State	2	4	5.34	15	0	64	69	39	43
Kernodle, Jared, Elon	6	3	5.40	18	0	68	78	19	52
Middour, Thomas, Davidson	4	5	5.42	18	0	78	97	25	71
#Chilcoat, Andrew, W. Carolina	1	1	7.32	34	1	39	45	19	26

SOUTHLAND CONFERENCE

	Conference		Overall	
	W	L	W	L
Texas State	23	10	38	22
Northwestern State	22	10	36	21
Southeastern Louisiana	21	12	40	19
Stephen F. Austin State	20	12	34	20
Texas-Arlington	19	14	29	31
*Lamar	16	17	35	26
McNeese State	16	17	31	27
Nicholls State	15	18	27	29
Texas-San Antonio	13	20	22	28
Sam Houston State	11	22	19	36
Texas A&M-Corpus Christi	10	22	20	33
Central Arkansas	10	22	19	35

ALL-CONFERENCE TEAM: C—Aaron Munoz, Jr., Northwestern State. **1B**—Kyle Livingstone, Sr. Texas State. **2B**—Ryan Hutson, Jr., UTSA. **3B**—Kyle Kubitza, So., Texas State. **SS**—Jace Peterson, So., McNeese State. **OF**—Michael Choice, Jr., Texas-Arlington; Eric DeBlanc, Sr., Northwestern State; Oscar Garcia, Jr., Northwestern State. **DH**—Chris Andreas, Jr., Sam Houston State. **P**—Chris Franklin, Sr., Southeastern Louisiana; Luke Irvine, Jr., Northwestern State; Carson Smith, So., Texas State. **Player of the Year:** Michael, Choice, Texas-Arlington. **Hitter of the Year:** Michael Choice, Texas-Arlington. **Pitcher of the Year:** Carson Smith, Texas State. **Freshman of the Year:** Ryan Dalton, UTSA. **Newcomer of the Year:** Carson Smith, Texas State. **Relief Pitcher of the Year:** Chad Sheppard, Northwestern State. **Coach of the Year:** Johnny Cardenas, Stephen F. Austin

INDIVIDUAL BATTING LEADERS
(Minimum 125 At-Bats)

	AVG	AB	R	H	2B	3B	HR	RBI	SB
Choice, Michael, Texas-Arlington	.383	196	67	75	11	2	16	59	12
DeBlanc, Eric, NW State	.382	217	57	83	15	4	6	39	10
Garcia, Oscar, NW State	.375	232	61	87	9	4	6	48	13
Andreas, Chris, Sam Houston State	.373	212	32	79	15	1	7	41	0
Comer, Bear, Nicholls State	.372	207	51	77	9	0	0	30	16
Livingstone, Kyle, Texas State	.369	244	56	90	14	1	11	63	10
Smith, Garrett, Stephen F. Austin	.368	212	50	78	17	1	3	29	14
Hernandez, Trey, Texas A&M-CC	.361	191	44	69	11	2	17	63	2
Riley, Braeden, Sam Houston State	.361	252	43	91	18	2	0	36	5
Faulk, Beau, Nicholls State	.358	159	25	57	8	1	5	49	3
Kubitza, Kyle, Texas State	.358	229	59	82	20	2	11	58	7
Mooney, Ryan, Sam Houston State	.357	213	38	76	11	0	3	26	11
Holland, Matt, Texas A&M-CC	.357	129	22	46	7	2	3	22	5
Loveless, Bobby, Stephen F. Austin	.355	200	39	71	18	0	8	50	1
Peterson, Jace, McNeese State	.353	232	68	82	14	3	4	49	35
Beck, Preston, Texas-Arlington	.352	233	37	82	10	3	2	44	1
McVaney, Jeff, Texas State	.350	177	46	62	16	2	10	44	1
Lyles, Chase, NW State	.350	220	54	77	13	1	7	56	34
Irvine, Steven, McNeese State	.350	243	63	85	15	1	12	64	12
Baisley, Tyler, NW State	.349	215	39	75	12	2	9	44	11
Buchanan, Aaron, Lamar	.349	238	65	83	21	3	1	37	13
Hutson, Ryan, UTSA	.348	184	42	64	10	1	14	43	3
Mena, Andy, Lamar	.347	170	27	59	11	1	2	41	6
Atwood, Bret, Texas State	.345	255	46	88	13	1	0	36	13
Riche', Andy, McNeese	.344	218	49	75	14	2	4	37	5
Marx, Caleb, Texas A&M-CC	.343	134	28	46	11	0	1	19	9
Roberts, Blake, Central Arkansas	.341	205	41	70	5	1	6	38	3
Hines, Tanner, Stephen F. Austin	.338	216	43	73	14	3	0	24	21
Gougler, Cody, Southeastern La.	.337	208	64	70	14	0	4	41	4
Priest, Ryan, Stephen F. Austin	.335	170	31	57	10	0	8	40	6
#Boudreaux, Justin, Southeastern La.	.313	230	66	72	13	1	13	66	17
#Harkensee, Jeff, Southeastern La.	.325	240	43	78	27	2	6	47	0
#Hargis, Cass, Southeastern La.	.303	261	56	79	16	7	1	42	1

INDIVIDUAL PITCHING LEADERS
(Minimum 50 Innings)

	W	L	ERA	G	SV	IP	H	BB	SO
Herriage, Tyler, Stephen F. Austin	8	4	2.89	15	0	93	81	52	73
Irvine, Luke, Northwestern State	7	4	2.91	16	0	93	92	36	104
Janway, Josh, Southeastern La.	4	2	3.07	27	6	59	64	19	49
Smith, Carson, Texas State	10	4	3.10	24	3	105	93	24	94
Varner, Rett, Texas-Arlington	8	5	3.56	15	0	104	110	24	95
#Sheppard, Chad, NW State	2	0	3.60	26	10	40	36	20	49
Borski, Brian, Texas State	7	3	3.71	15	0	85	100	36	49
Zimmerman, Ryan, NW State	6	5	3.74	16	0	87	82	29	77
Watkins, Tyler, Southeastern La.	6	3	3.80	19	1	90	103	24	59
Logan, Bawcom, Texas-Arlington	5	4	3.87	20	5	91	102	26	87
Franklin, Chris, Southeastern La.	8	7	3.87	26	7	88	85	30	82
Dempster, Clint, Nicholls State	6	6	3.92	16	0	99	92	38	103
Minto, Tyler, Nicholls State	5	4	3.94	13	0	80	84	19	56
Pritchett, Bobby, Central Arkansas	5	2	3.94	16	2	75	81	27	67
Hennigan, Heath, NW State	1	3	3.95	25	2	55	67	12	66
#Carruth, Garret, Texas State	5	3	4.08	30	5	40	39	15	41
Efferson, Brandon, Southeastern La.	8		44.10	14	0	90	98	24	50
Russo, Michael, Texas State	5	2	4.22	15	0	96	117	33	59
Wild, Michael, Central Arkansas	7	8	4.23	27	3	100	62	25	75
Cooper, Ryan, Nicholls State	4	6	4.52	18	0	70	84	14	40
Dillon, Jaden, McNeese State	8	0	4.61	20	1	82	77	34	43
Pitts, Mitchell, Texas State	6	1	4.61	20	1	55	77	10	39
Mitchell, Jason, Texas-Arlington	7	6	4.66	19	0	112	124	30	113
Selsor, Casey, UTSA	5	6	4.71	14	0	86	112	38	60
#Smith, Matison, Lamar	10	4	4.76	18	0	117	146	34	64
#Jonathan, Dziedzic, Lamar	5	6	4.88	19	2	94	104	44	114

SOUTHWESTERN ATHLETIC CONFERENCE

EAST	Conference		Overall	
	W	L	W	L
Jackson State	19	6	36	17
Mississippi Valley State	16	8	23	30
Alcorn State	15	8	27	28
Alabama State	6	18	13	28
Alabama A&M	3	20	17	32
WEST				
Texas Southern	18	6	30	26
Southern	17	6	25	22
*Grambling State	11	14	22	32
Arkansas-Pine Bluff	8	16	19	34
Prairie View A&M	6	17	12	35

ALL-CONFERENCE TEAM: C—Cortez Cole, Sr., Jackson State. **1B**—Frazier Hall, Jr., Southern. **2B**—Lynn Lewis, So., Jackson State. **3B**—Rodney Warren, Jr., Alcorn State. **SS**—Jerry Hildredth, Jr., Mississippi State. **OF**—Donquarius Farmer, Fr., Mississippi Valley State; LeDale Hayes, Sr., Alabama A&M; Jeremy Shelby, Sr. Grambling State. **DH**—Kilby Perdomo, Jr., Alcorn State **P**—Quintavious Drains, So., Jackson State; Steve Easter, So., Alcorn State; Bryan Smith, Jr., Texas Southern.
Player of the Year: Frazier Hall, Southern. **Pitcher of the Year:** Quintavious Drains, Jackson State. **Hitter of the Year:** Cortez Cole, Jackson State. **Freshman of the Year:** Malcolm Tate, Jackson State. **Newcomer of the Year:** Kilby Perdomo, Alcorn State.

INDIVIDUAL BATTING LEADERS
(Minimum 100 At-Bats)

	AVG	AB	R	H	2B	3B	HR	RBI	SB
Cole, Cortez, Jackson State	**.409**	164	51	67	10	6	3	39	33
Warren, Rodney, Alcorn State	.393	173	39	68	14	2	6	47	3
Hall, Frazier, Southern	.382	173	49	66	16	1	8	50	1
Hildreth, Jerry, Mississippi Valley	.368	190	52	70	10	5	2	42	38
McDonley, Barry, Ark.-Pine Bluff	.368	174	31	64	25	2	7	59	1
Hernandez, Ray, Texas State	.362	213	48	77	15	6	1	58	18
Worthington, David, Southern	.361	133	33	48	11	2	6	37	5
Shelby, Jeremy, Grambling State	.360	189	51	68	15	2	6	42	21
Olson, Paul, Mississippi Valley	.359	181	39	65	15	6	4	49	11
Jones, Terrel, Texas Southern	.357	199	43	71	11	3	6	52	8
Perdomo, Kilby, Alcorn State	.355	203	61	72	13	1	10	54	12
Wilson, Curtis, Southern	.352	122	44	43	14	0	5	32	2
Wolfe, Chris, Grambling State	.351	188	50	66	9	2	0	42	27
Gonzalez, Eduardo, Alcorn State	.350	217	48	76	16	4	6	53	4
Wesley, Willie, Jackson State	.345	203	66	70	7	4	3	38	52
Thomas, Jason, Prairie View	.336	122	22	41	8	1	0	27	4
Prater, Sean, Ark.-Pine Bluff	.335	164	35	55	8	3	1	21	4
Hall, Chad, Jackson State	.331	181	63	60	18	2	1	42	23
Hayes, LaDale, Alabama A&M	.331	169	38	56	13	3	4	37	22
Reed, David, Alcorn State	.330	191	35	63	18	0	4	39	5
Vicars, Cole, Alcorn State	.321	165	39	53	7	4	0	32	13
Mikell, Brandon, Texas Southern	.314	175	37	55	11	3	5	47	17
Lamis, Ozzie, Southern	.314	185	51	58	2	3	1	36	17
White, Kerry, Texas Southern	.313	150	36	47	6	2	7	27	8
Oliver, Andre, Prairie View	.310	184	36	57	9	2	0	31	16
Rowan, Kenneth, Alcorn State	.309	207	60	64	13	3	3	36	27
Duarte, Kency, Alabama A&M	.308	143	23	44	3	1	1	23	17
Solis, Frank, Jackson State	.307	179	40	55	8	0	1	33	17
Pace, Matthew, Ark.-Pine Bluff	.307	176	35	54	15	3	4	34	1
Angel, Giovan, Prairie View	.306	173	20	53	7	0	0	20	0
#Kletke, Steve, Grambling State	.300	150	39	45	11	0	11	42	0

INDIVIDUAL PITCHING LEADERS
(Minimum 40 Innings)

	W	L	ERA	G	SV	IP	H	BB	SO
#Laufenberg, Dakota, Texas Southern	7	3	3.10	28	4	52	52	23	59
Nelson, Cortney, Jackson State	10	5	**3.65**	25	2	118	107	35	69
#Cody Parker, Mississippi Valley	1	1	4.20	**40**	2	41	31	18	43
Campbell, Anderson, Alabama A&M	4	5	4.78	10	0	53	65	16	25
Drains, Quintavious, Jackson State	13	4	4.85	19	1	117	127	43	93
Aleman, Jesus, Mississippi Valley	3	5	4.99	28	1	61	63	36	62
Smith, Bryan, Texas Southern	7	2	5.07	14	0	87	94	37	71
Hernandez, Chris, Alabama A&M	2	9	5.09	16	0	74	84	49	43

Easter, Steve Alcorn State	6	4	5.34	15	0	93	99	24	75
Arnold, Collin, Alcorn State	7	5	5.40	16	1	110	146	25	49
Ricciardi, Anthony, Alabama State	3	6	5.40	12	0	70	78	46	50
Pomerlee, Cedric, Alcorn State	5	7	5.45	15	0	76	85	48	79
Gray, Jeremy, Jackson State	5	1	5.54	21	2	67	68	38	37
Rodriguez, Esteban, Ark.-Pine Bluff	0	5	5.59	16	0	76	88	29	54
Losoya, Adrian, Texas Southern	3	8	5.59	14	0	74	87	28	68
Wahl, Kyle, Southern	4	5	5.67	17	1	60	71	22	40
Blackburn, Ben, Prairie View	3	8	5.67	17	0	86	104	28	67
Dominguez, Devin, Alabama State	3	3	5.68	16	**4**	57	63	34	41
Meintie, Mathias, Texas Southern	4	2	5.77	16	0	58	53	29	56
Simmons, Kellen, Prairie View	3	5	5.87	14	0	61	86	26	31
Cook, Joe, Ark.-Pine Bluff	5	7	5.90	16	0	76	90	32	48
Goodman, Britt, Mississippi Valley	3	5	6.03	17	0	63	72	23	47

SUMMIT LEAGUE

	Conference		Overall	
	W	L	W	L
South Dakota State	19	9	39	21
*Oral Roberts	19	9	36	27
Centenary	17	9	28	26
Oakland	13	14	23	34
IPWF	13	15	17	38
North Dakota State	11	16	22	30
Southern Utah	11	16	18	36
Western Illinois	6	21	14	39

ALL-CONFERENCE TEAM: C—Taylor Shaw, Fr., Southern Utah. **1B**—Joel Blake, Jr., South Dakota State. **2B**—Bo Cuthbertson, So., Southern Utah. **3B**—Jesse Sawyer, Jr., South Dakota State. **SS**—Tyler Saladino, Jr., Oral Roberts. **OF**—Nick Baligod, Jr., Oral Roberts; John Lee, Sr., South Dakota State; Billy Stitz, Jr., South Dakota State. **DH**—Seth Furmanek, Sr., Oral Roberts. **Util**—Joe Goldenberg, Fr., Southern Utah. **SP**—Bryce Smolen, Jr., Oral Roberts; Blake Trienen, Jr., South Dakota State; Boone Whiting, Jr., Centenary. **RP**—Trever Vermeulen, Jr. South Dakota State.
Player of the Year: Tyler Saladino, Oral Roberts. **Pitcher of the Year:** Boone Whiting, Centenary. **Newcomer of the Year:** Tyler Saladino, Oral Roberts. **Coach of the Year:** Richie Price, South Dakota State.

INDIVIDUAL BATTING LEADERS
(Minimum 125 At-Bats)

	AVG	AB	R	H	2B	3B	HR	RBI	SB
Summers, Jason, Western Illinois	.423	182	41	77	15	0	6	46	1
Lee, John, S. Dakota State	.399	228	74	91	21	2	9	61	5
Stitz, Billy, S. Dakota State	.392	**283**	75	111	26	4	6	67	9
Blake, Joel, San Diego State	.391	253	63	99	**33**	0	8	66	1
Goldenberg, Joe, Southern Utah	.391	156	35	61	13	0	10	48	1
Baligod, Nick, Oral Roberts	.390	210	61	82	17	1	11	54	7
Wentz, Zach, N. Dakota State	.389	193	41	75	17	0	7	42	4
Cain, Eric, S. Dakota State	.385	252	61	97	10	2	16	**83**	1
Saladino, Tyler, Oral Roberts	.379	253	**75**	96	16	2	18	76	16
Shaw, Taylor, Southern Utah	.364	154	30	56	12	0	4	28	4
Jablonski, Tommy, Oakland	.362	174	21	63	9	1	0	24	5
Shepard, Cliff, Centenary	.359	206	38	74	20	2	6	48	4
Sawyer, Jesse, S. Dakota State	.359	223	72	80	17	1	19	73	3
Koszulinski, John, Western Illinois	.354	164	32	58	4	1	6	49	1
Romero, Marcus, Southern Utah	.352	179	35	63	14	0	1	29	6
Rhodes, Zach, S. Dakota State	.350	177	48	62	14	1	8	38	4
Cuthbertson, Bo, Southern Utah	.344	224	50	77	21	**6**	4	29	3
Acker, Keegen, Centenary	.341	164	45	56	7	0	1	8	17
Clark, Brett, IPFW	.340	159	29	54	15	2	3	25	1
Hanowski, Beau, S. Dakota State	.337	163	41	55	10	3	0	27	8
Ryan, Tim, Oakland	.336	211	46	71	9	3	1	21	23
Elder, Chris, Oral Roberts	.331	175	41	58	11	0	11	59	7
Briggs, Zach, S. Dakota State	.330	179	38	59	9	0	9	45	0
Winiecki, Joey, Oral Roberts	.329	213	51	70	8	1	0	23	14
Furmanek, Seth, Oral Roberts	.326	215	57	70	12	0	**25**	70	1
Christensen, A.J., IPFW	.325	206	28	67	15	0	9	41	0
Aona, Bucky, Southern Utah	.323	164	29	53	12	0	7	32	1
Lilja, Tom, Western Illinois	.319	204	37	65	13	1	2	32	3
Waldhart, Ryan, Oakland	.318	198	32	63	13	0	4	37	5
Sowers, Brett, Oral Roberts	.318	192	33	61	14	0	8	38	1

INDIVIDUAL PITCHING LEADERS
(Minimum 50 Innings)

	W	L	ERA	G	SV	IP	H	BB	SO
Vermeulen, Trever, S. Dakota State	9	1	1.45	35	10	68	59	19	62
Whiting, Boone, Centenary	6	2	3.21	14	1	84	70	37	120
Hermes, Mark, N. Dakota State	1	3	4.10	13	0	53	55	32	46
Guest, Mark, Oral Roberts	3	4	4.35	23	0	79	96	55	50
Smolen, Bryce, Oral Roberts	9	3	4.41	23	1	98	98	29	86
Benson, David, Centenary	4	3	4.85	14	0	65	78	30	46
Neubauer, Justin, Southern Utah	4	4	4.99	12	0	61	75	28	39
Teague, Kyle, Oakland	5	6	5.11	16	0	81	98	29	73
LaMothe, Matt, Oakland	3	5	5.25	17	1	70	68	41	65
Treinen, Blake, S. Dakota State	7	1	6.09	12	0	75	85	33	82
Burleson, Jeff, Oral Roberts	8	4	6.14	24	3	73	87	31	72
Oberle, Alex, S. Dakota State	8	5	6.16	23	0	64	82	23	30
Maristuen, McHale, N. Dakota State	1	8	6.23	13	0	56	79	22	39
Kesterson, Lucas, IPFW	1	9	6.35	14	0	72	103	24	48
Antos, Matt, IPFW	4	6	6.35	16	0	68	76	34	66
Lingle, Randon, Western Illinois	3	7	6.38	15	0	72	92	27	43
Opitz, Nick, IPFW	5	4	6.39	13	0	75	99	17	27
Kraft, Justin, Centenary	4	5	6.82	18	0	61	90	19	47
Mielock, Connor, Oakland	4	6	6.96	13	0	63	87	30	38
Furmanek, Seth, Oral Roberts	5	2	7.29	16	0	67	91	22	45

SUN BELT CONFERENCE

	Conference		Overall	
	W	L	W	L
Louisiana-Lafayette	21	9	38	22
Florida Atlantic	21	9	37	24
Middle Tennessee State	18	12	35	23
*Florida International	17	13	36	25
South Alabama	17	13	32	27
Western Kentucky	16	14	35	23
Troy	16	14	36	25
Arkansas State	16	14	30	28
Arkansas-Little Rock	12	16	29	25
Louisiana-Monroe	7	23	17	38
New Orleans	2	26	13	39

ALL-CONFERENCE TEAM: C—Matt Rice, Jr., Western Kentucky. **1B**—Dan Scheffler, Jr., Florida Atlantic. **2B**—Justin Miller, Jr., Middle Tennessee State. **3B** — Garrett Wittels, So., Florida International. **SS**—Adam Bryant, Jr., Troy. **OF**—Bryce Brentz, Jr., Middle Tennessee State; Kes Carter, So., Western Kentucky; Andy Mee, Jr., Florida Atlantic. **DH**—Justin Guidry, So., Middle Tennessee State. **SP**—Zach Osborne, Sr., Louisiana-Lafayette; Matt Ridings, Sr. Western Kentucky. **RP**—Rye Davis, So., Western Kentucky.

Player of the Year: Garrett Wittels, Florida International. **Pitcher of the Year:** Matt Ridings, Western Kentucky. **Freshman of the Year:** Jabari Henry, Florida International. **Newcomer of the Year:** Boomer Blanchard, Louisiana-Monroe. **Coach of the Year:** John McCormack, Florida Atlantic.

INDIVIDUAL BATTING LEADERS
(Minimum 125 At-Bats)

	AVG	AB	R	H	2B	3B	HR	RBI	SB
Wittels, Garrett, FIU	.413	242	47	100	21	2	2	60	4
McDade, Blake, MTSU	.399	223	63	89	19	3	6	47	4
Guidry, Justin, MTSU	.389	244	48	95	15	0	7	51	7
Martinez, Mike, FIU	.378	238	47	90	19	1	9	55	4
Mee, Andy, Florida Atlantic	.378	262	58	99	17	5	8	55	4
Watts, Murray, Arkansas State	.374	222	45	83	13	1	13	65	3
Scheffler, Dan, Florida Atlantic	.371	224	67	83	22	3	15	65	0
Rice, Matt, Western Kentucky	.369	241	51	89	16	3	10	65	1
Whitley, Chase, Troy	.364	236	60	86	11	3	10	56	1
Patton, Jeremy, FIU	.364	231	50	84	19	2	8	45	8
Castaldo, Jordan, Arkansas State	.363	204	30	74	20	1	2	39	0
Clowers, Caleb, Louisiana-Monroe	.357	221	39	79	15	1	4	36	2
Bryant, Adam, Troy	.356	250	70	89	16	6	23	65	4
Payton, Matt, Western Kentucky	.354	237	63	84	14	10	7	55	6
Burnett, Tyler, MTSU	.351	245	56	86	17	2	12	46	9
Laird, Sean, South Alabama	.350	217	51	76	11	1	9	54	2
Brentz, Bryce, MTSU	.348	184	51	64	8	0	15	49	4
Overstreet, Jake, South Alabama	.346	237	51	82	10	1	11	74	5
White, Taylor, South Alabama	.346	217	55	75	12	1	0	34	27
Carter, Kes, Western Kentucky	.343	236	38	81	12	1	7	53	13

Andreoli, Jared, Western Kentucky	.341	246	61	84	12	4	5	49	14
Baumgartner, Todd, Arkansas State	.336	220	49	74	14	1	3	42	10
Faulkner, Michael, Arkansas State	.336	241	55	81	12	2	0	25	23
Wilson, Landis, Ark.-Little Rock	.335	176	40	59	11	0	3	37	5
Ditthardt, Ryan, Troy	.333	258	65	86	19	0	18	61	2
Edwards, Judd, Louisiana-Monroe	.333	210	33	70	11	0	2	20	5
Bermudez, Pablo, FIU	.332	256	69	85	15	4	8	52	21
Cassidy, Eddie, Florida Atlantic	.329	173	20	57	7	0	10	42	0
Church, Raymond, Florida Atlantic	.329	240	54	79	15	1	10	46	9

INDIVIDUAL PITCHING LEADERS
(Minimum 50 Innings)

	W	L	ERA	G	SV	IP	H	BB	SO
Osborne, Zach, Louisiana-Lafayette	9	4	2.37	16	0	122	100	21	112
#Mee, Andy, Florida Atlantic	1	2	2.96	21	11	24	26	12	22
Ridings, Matt, Western Kentucky	9	1	3.01	14	0	93	77	17	90
Champion, Adam, Ark.-Little Rock	7	4	3.11	14	0	98	93	33	74
Whitley, Chase, Troy	7	3	3.68	32	7	66	48	24	65
Gipson, Mike, Florida Atlantic	8	2	3.70	16	0	112	98	43	96
Lee, Jacob, Arkansas State	8	3	3.80	15	0	92	85	35	83
Humes, Ross, Arkansas State	5	4	4.11	22	2	72	87	14	41
Dickinson, Andrew, Troy	7	5	4.15	8	0	113	114	23	71
Edwards, Chad, MTSU	8	2	4.21	13	0	83	89	17	51
Hanks, D.D., South Alabama	10	6	4.28	16	0	97	120	22	86
Gilley, Eric, MTSU	6	2	4.32	16	0	75	76	36	41
Geith, T.J., Louisiana-Lafayette	6	2	4.67	15	0	91	96	22	64
Rembisz, Scott, FIU	9	4	4.70	18	0	92	101	28	79
Fondon, R.J., FIU	5	4	4.70	19	0	92	102	24	77
Fergusons, Andy, Arkansas State	5	5	4.71	16	0	102	118	30	74
Baxter, Lance, South Alabama	6	4	4.81	21	5	88	100	34	65
Cameron, Shane, Western Kentucky	4	2	4.84	19	0	87	86	26	80
Garton, Ryan, Florida Atlantic	7	3	4.87	17	0	81	93	27	70
Harris, Garrett, South Alabama	5	4	4.89	18	1	81	107	26	64
#Berkowitz, Eric, FIU	2	2	5.24	37	3	46	61	18	41
Arboleya, Aaron, FIU	5	2	5.27	17	0	80	81	31	64

WEST COAST CONFERENCE

	Conference		Overall	
	W	L	W	L
*San Diego	19	2	37	22
Portland	14	7	34	18
Pepperdine	12	9	24	30
San Francisco	10	11	28	28
Santa Clara	8	13	23	31
St. Mary's	8	13	19	32
Gonzaga	8	13	20	36
Loyola Marymount	5	16	23	33

ALL-CONFERENCE TEAM: C—Rocky Gale, Sr., Portland; Nick McCoy, Sr., San Diego. **IF**—Nik Balog, So., San Francisco; Troy Channing, So., St. Mary's; Chris Engell, Sr., San Diego; Riley Henricks, Jr., Portland; Geoff Klein, Sr., Santa Clara; Colin Rooney, Sr., Pepperdine; Stephen Yarrow, Jr., San Francisco. **OF**—Connor Bernatz, Jr., San Francisco; Mark Castellitto, Sr., Gonzaga; Brian Humphries, So., Pepperdine; James Meador, of, San Diego; Tommy Medica, Jr., Santa Clara; Kevin Muno, Jr., San Diego. **P**—Kyle Blair, Jr., San Diego; Matt Bywater, Jr., Pepperdine; Cole Cook, Jr., Pepperdine; Chris Dennis, rhp, Portland; A.J. Griffin, Sr., San Diego; Kyle Kraus, So., Portland; Sammy Solis, So., San Diego; Matt Thomson, Sr., San Diego.

Player of the Year: James Meador, San Diego. **Pitcher of the Year:** Kyle Blair, San Diego. **Defensive Player of the Year:** Rocky Gale, Portland. **Freshman of the Year:** Matt Lowenstein, Loyola Marymount. **Coach of the Year:** Rich Hill, San Diego.

INDIVIDUAL BATTING LEADERS
(Minimum 2.0 At-Bats Per Team Game)

	AVG	AB	R	H	2B	3B	HR	RBI	SB
Engell, Chris, San Diego	.411	197	48	81	7	4	1	35	10
Wagner, Curtis, Santa Clara	.404	161	46	65	16	0	3	32	1
Heid, Drew, Gonzaga	.390	236	54	92	18	4	8	28	8
Meador, James, San Diego	.389	216	43	84	22	1	7	61	8
Medica, Tommy, Santa Clara	.386	228	60	88	21	2	13	67	15
Hawthorne, Ryan, LMU	.364	214	30	78	17	1	2	44	4
Ferraro, Mike, San Diego	.364	143	22	52	13	0	4	34	3
Gale, Rocky, Portland	.347	144	20	50	11	0	2	16	1

	AVG	AB	R	H	2B	3B	HR	RBI	SB
Klein, Geoff, Santa Clara	.346	217	36	75	19	1	6	47	2
Lowenstein, Matt, LMU	.344	163	32	56	15	4	1	30	5
Rieger, Ryan, Santa Clara	.339	109	13	37	13	1	0	22	2
Cullen, C.J., Portland	.335	191	38	64	8	1	4	34	3
Castellitto, Mark, Gonzaga	.335	218	50	73	17	1	11	50	3
Terry, Patrick, Santa Clara	.328	131	18	43	7	1	4	22	4
Fazio, Justin, St. Mary's	.327	153	23	50	10	1	5	20	2
Peters, Evan, Santa Clara	.320	206	34	66	18	0	2	21	2
Barmasse, Jason, LMU	.318	173	38	55	12	0	4	28	3
Fraser, Beau, Portland	.316	177	29	56	7	1	7	45	0
Johnson, Jonathan, LMU	.315	222	59	70	14	**9**	1	24	10
McCoy, Nick, San Diego	.315	184	39	58	9	0	4	35	3
Lipkin, Ryan, San Francisco	.313	208	30	65	19	2	7	37	2
Yarrow, Stephen, San Francisco	.310	203	48	63	12	3	**16**	47	2
Sever, Joe, Pepperdine	.310	213	37	66	7	3	1	19	9
Channing, Troy, St. Mary's	.310	184	37	57	9	0	15	54	6
Poppert, Derek, San Francisco	.308	201	34	62	19	1	3	30	11
Given, Floyd, Pepperdine	.308	130	21	40	7	0	3	23	1
Denham, Jared, San Francisco	.305	128	18	39	12	2	0	15	1
Humphries, Brian, Pepperdine	.305	220	35	67	17	2	2	32	5
Strazzara, Tony, San Diego	.304	204	36	62	10	0	1	36	3
Bernatz, Connor, San Francisco	.303	178	32	54	15	0	4	25	5
#Muno, Kevin, San Diego	.289	218	**64**	63	14	2	3	18	25

INDIVIDUAL PITCHING LEADERS
(Minimum 1.0 IP Per Team Game)

	W	L	ERA	G	SV	IP	H	BB	SO
#Dennis, Chris, Portland	5	1	1.88	**30**	**14**	43	31	11	51
Bywater, Matt, Pepperdine	6	5	**2.40**	13	0	98	88	30	83
Jones, Owen, Portland	4	2	2.56	16	0	56	47	29	42
Blair, Kyle, San Diego	8	4	2.84	15	0	98	79	24	126
Cook, Cole, Pepperdine	5	6	2.93	14	1	104	103	24	87
Varce, Zach, Portland	6	2	3.29	14	0	93	96	25	111
Kraus, Kyle, Portland	**10**	3	3.30	15	0	**109**	111	18	89
Solis, Sammy, San Diego	9	2	3.42	15	0	92	82	29	92
Murray, Doug, San Francisco	8	6	3.60	18	1	105	104	13	70
Anderson, Mark, St. Mary's	5	5	4.19	14	0	103	118	23	55
Lujan, Matt, San Francisco	6	5	4.26	17	0	82	91	34	58
Dickmann, Robert, Pepperdine	8	4	4.44	15	0	99	117	23	75
Griffin, A.J., San Diego	8	3	4.47	16	0	99	94	28	113
Rivers, Alex, Santa Clara	5	9	4.50	17	0	100	124	34	78
Inman, Kevin, Pepperdine	1	1	4.80	19	1	54	60	23	20
Gillingham, Alex, LMU	2	4	5.28	17	1	77	101	22	63
Agosta, Martin, St. Mary's	3	6	5.40	17	1	70	78	30	52
Barraclough, Kyle, St. Mary's	6	6	5.42	18	0	89	101	47	81
Carpenter, Ryan, Gonzaga	4	4	5.67	12	0	60	65	29	53
Baron, Liam, Gonzaga	0	7	5.79	26	2	79	103	22	36
Mendoza, Chris, Santa Clara	4	6	5.83	16	0	66	91	23	33

WESTERN ATHLETIC CONFERENCE

	Conference		Overall	
	W	L	W	L
Fresno State	16	8	38	25
Nevada	14	9	36	22
New Mexico State	14	9	36	23
*Hawaii	12	12	35	28
Louisiana Tech	11	13	27	30
San Jose State	9	15	23	37
Sacramento State	7	17	18	35

ALL-CONFERENCE TEAM: 1B—Leo Aguirre, Sr., New Mexico State; Shaun Kort, Sr., Nevada; Jordan Ribera, Jr., Fresno State. **2B**—Kolten Wong, So., Hawaii. **3B**—Mark Threlkeld, So., Louisiana Tech; Corey Valine, Sr., San Jose State. **SS**—Greg Garcia, Jr., Hawaii. **OF**—Devon Dageford, Sr., Louisiana Tech; Dusty Robinson, Jr., Fresno State. **DH**—Bobby Coyle, Jr., Fresno State; Jeffrey Van Doornum, Jr., Hawaii. **SP**—Greg Gonzalez, Jr., Fresno State; Blake McFarland, Jr., San Jose State; Brock Stassi, Jr., Nevada. **RP**—Lenny Linsky, So., Hawaii.
Player of the Year: Jordan Ribera, Fresno State. **Pitcher of the Year:** Brock Stassi, Nevada. **Freshman of the Year:** Zack Jones, San Jose State. **Coach of the Year:** Mike Batesole, Fresno State.

INDIVIDUAL BATTING LEADERS
(Minimum 125 At-Bats)

	AVG	AB	R	H	2B	3B	HR	RBI	SB
Aguirre, Leo, New Mexico State	**.388**	224	60	87	19	1	11	58	0
Melino, Nick, Nevada	.388	152	41	59	15	0	7	35	5
Weber, Garrett, Fresno State	.387	243	45	94	14	0	1	38	9
Paine, Trevor, Sacramento State	.381	176	30	67	10	0	10	44	0
Sodders, Mike, New Mexico State	.380	150	50	57	8	0	15	46	2
Martin, Jason, San Jose State	.373	236	46	88	13	1	2	23	7
Dageford, Devon, Louisiana Tech	.371	229	63	85	21	0	17	56	7
Ford, Joey, Louisiana Tech	.371	213	38	79	14	0	3	48	2
Shaver, Nate, New Mexico State	.367	221	66	81	19	4	5	52	2
Aguayo, Ryan, New Mexico State	.365	252	**76**	92	14	3	12	66	5
Kort, Shaun, Nevada	.365	211	64	77	**24**	1	9	55	9
Starkes, Wesley, New Mexico State	.364	184	46	67	8	**5**	1	39	9
Stassi, Brock, Nevada	.364	176	45	64	16	5	**9**	42	2
Perkins, Chance, New Mexico State	.363	193	55	70	17	3	17	70	5
Coyle, Bobby, Fresno State	.360	**267**	53	**96**	21	1	11	68	5
Gowens, Brennan, Fresno State	.359	248	54	89	19	3	4	35	11
Garcia, Greg, Hawaii	.358	218	45	78	13	**5**	3	40	5
Wong, Kolton, Hawaii	.357	249	57	89	15	4	7	40	19
Ewing, Clint, Louisiana Tech	.350	177	48	62	12	0	11	49	2
Hipp, Parker, New Mexico State	.349	166	44	58	10	1	1	37	5
Barnett, Brian, Nevada	.348	224	52	78	21	2	18	**71**	9
Quiery, Tim, San Jose State	.344	157	26	54	7	0	1	25	3
Ribera, Jordan, Fresno State	.343	251	65	86	20	2	**27**	69	1
Williams, Alex, Louisiana Tech	.343	216	43	74	17	1	11	46	1
Garrison, Trent, Fresno State	.339	189	32	64	11	0	5	46	2
Threlkeld, Mark, Louisiana Tech	.335	239	62	80	14	0	14	62	5
Van Doornum, Jeffrey, Hawaii	.330	212	45	70	8	2	14	38	6
Roliard, Kyle, Louisiana Tech	.330	230	59	76	16	2	5	30	6
Muno, Danny, Fresno State	.329	246	68	81	17	2	7	33	10
Bennett, Collin, Hawaii	.323	229	41	74	19	2	5	49	4
#Moss, Westley, Nevada	.282	212	42	60	6	2	2	21	21

INDIVIDUAL PITCHING LEADERS
(Minimum 50 Innings)

	W	L	ERA	G	SV	IP	H	BB	SO
#Linsky, Lenny, Hawaii	4	0	1.64	29	**12**	44	40	12	58
Slaats, Josh, Hawaii	5	4	**3.77**	17	0	74	72	33	75
Stassi, Brock, Nevada	7	4	3.43	13	0	79	71	25	69
McFarland, Blake, San Jose State	7	4	3.62	15	0	**99**	109	27	71
Jameson, Tom, Nevada	6	1	3.84	15	2	66	74	18	30
Spangler, Sam, Hawaii	5	6	4.42	15	0	73	80	33	62
Cole, Jeremy, Nevada	4	3	4.95	17	2	73	77	18	30
Darrah, Jesse, Sacramento State	3	6	5.07	14	0	82	83	32	55
Garcia, Chris, Nevada	6	3	5.07	13	0	60	56	37	47
Martin, Sean, San Jose State	2	3	5.12	15	0	70	83	26	35
Sisto, Matt, Hawaii	5	5	5.27	15	0	72	86	16	48
Robertson, Charlie, Fresno State	5	3	5.47	17	0	74	97	29	41
Jefferson, Mike, Louisiana Tech	4	4	5.60	19	0	72	64	59	69
Capaul, Alex, Hawaii	4	2	5.65	21	0	72	91	14	44
Bradshaw, Jamey, Louisiana Tech	4	2	5.77	14	0	73	86	30	64
Poytress, Josh, Fresno State	6	6	5.87	21	0	77	97	36	60
Morse, Matt, Fresno State	4	5	6.21	18	2	75	111	25	47
Reid, Dan, New Mexico State	6	3	6.38	14	0	73	118	13	50
Gonzales, Greg, Fresno State	**8**	2	6.54	21	1	63	70	35	73
Petersen, Trevor, Louisiana Tech	5	8	6.81	19	0	73	94	28	42
#Harlan, Tom, Fresno State	0	0	6.84	**29**	1	26	31	11	25
Cooper, Justin, New Mexico State	4	2	7.82	16	1	63	84	43	47

INDEPENDENTS

	Overall	
	W	L
Longwood	28	20
Dallas Baptist	28	27
Le Moyne	28	27
Savannah State	24	26
Cal State Bakersfield	26	30
Southern Illinois-Edwardsville	14	38
Seattle	11	39
North Carolina Central	3	44

INDIVIDUAL BATTING LEADERS
(Minimum 125 At-Bats)

	AVG	AB	R	H	2B	3B	HR	RBI	SB
Ross, Jonathan, Savannah State	**.416**	178	64	74	13	5	11	43	20
Cerreto, Phil, Longwood	.414	186	42	77	**24**	1	10	**60**	6
Havers, Casey, Longwood	.411	190	33	78	17	2	3	49	1

	AVG	AB	R	H	2B	3B	HR	RBI	SB
Jones, Brant, Longwood	.402	184	60	74	10	4	7	38	10
Rodriguez, Jeremy, CS Bakersfield	.400	195	51	78	16	0	4	38	0
Enos, Ryan, Dallas Baptist	.397	234	66	93	19	2	18	59	4
Boren, Brandon, CS Bakersfield	.397	247	53	98	18	2	2	43	0
Kelley, Dexter, Savannah State	.386	176	55	68	16	2	5	60	44
Kimble, Scott, Longwood	.383	183	47	70	11	2	4	27	12
Younger, Kevin, CS Bakersfield	.379	140	35	53	10	1	0	19	1
McCrary, Joseph, Savannah State	.378	148	29	56	10	3	1	33	13
Robbins, Tyler, Dallas Baptist	.373	220	58	82	18	0	6	45	4
Kudlock, Jason, CS Bakersfield	.364	220	40	80	17	6	8	51	0
Krizan, Jason, Dallas Baptist	.356	222	52	79	20	2	11	57	2
Wiley, Zach, Le Moyne	.356	202	47	72	14	0	5	27	9
Lee, Blake, Savannah State	.349	166	43	58	13	2	3	43	10
Edmondson, Chris, Le Moyne	.348	201	41	70	13	2	12	50	14
Bailey, Robbie, Longwood	.345	177	44	61	8	2	5	23	14
Brooks, Dustin, SIU-Edwardsville	.342	161	27	55	15	1	5	32	4
Meiners, Travis, Dallas Baptist	.342	196	50	67	11	3	7	41	5
Elkins, Austin, Dallas Baptist	.341	176	38	60	15	1	8	39	5
Eggemeyer, Adam, SIU-Edwardsville	.335	197	40	66	18	4	9	41	10
Behmanesh, Ryan, Dallas Baptist	.333	201	41	67	13	2	7	41	2
Marra, Matt, Le Moyne	.320	203	37	65	13	2	3	51	6
Barkley, Emory, Savannah State	.320	125	16	40	9	0	1	18	1
Medina, Martin, CS Bakersfield	.311	238	44	74	16	2	12	52	1
Hood, Akeem, N.C. Central	.309	178	25	55	6	2	0	10	8
Knight, Austin, Dallas Baptist	.307	215	48	66	17	0	7	36	1
Vazquez, James, SIU-Edwardsville	.305	174	34	53	10	3	2	19	3
Matecki, Mitch, SIU-Edwardsville	.298	198	36	59	10	3	1	33	11
Smith, Nate, N.C. Central	.283	152	25	43	7	7	1	18	18

INDIVIDUAL PITCHING LEADERS
(Minimum 50 Innings)

	W	L	ERA	G	SV	IP	H	BB	SO
Lambe, Erik, Le Moyne	7	1	2.82	17	1	54	45	20	43
#Montgomery, Mark, Longwood	3	1	3.09	22	6	35	26	10	45
Harting, Lance, Longwood	10	0	3.11	22	0	81	76	23	59
Tardiff, Jeff, Le Moyne	6	3	3.33	14	1	81	76	44	52
Reyes, Matt, CS Bakersfield	4	3	3.79	14	0	57	69	26	35
Whieldon, Max, Seattle	2	7	3.81	25	0	85	83	20	45
Gilbreath, Aaron, Dallas Baptist	2	4	4.33	19	2	62	63	32	57
Kizer, Brandon, Seattle	1	5	4.71	18	1	80	84	38	40
Jannis, Mickey, CS Bakersfield	4	5	4.74	15	0	99	112	35	65
Nelson, Cory, Le Moyne	2	6	5.15	13	0	65	69	41	50
Kuzma, Mark, Le Moyne	3	4	5.19	13	0	68	80	24	50
Allegretti, Michael, Savannah State	6	6	5.25	18	2	86	107	37	62
Evasick, Arlo, Seattle	2	9	5.34	19	1	89	104	26	60
Millard, Ryan, Dallas Baptist	4	2	5.46	16	0	61	75	24	32
McCarthy, Mike, CS Bakersfield	5	6	5.47	15	0	104	133	30	82
Williamso, Brandon, Dallas Baptist	7	5	5.51	15	0	101	116	41	71
Montoya, Jonathan, CS Bakersfield	4	5	5.83	16	0	66	78	35	58
Lane, Will, Dallas Baptist	3	5	6.14	14	0	59	78	21	47
Jackson, Joseph, Savannah State	5	2	6.57	14	0	51	68	16	18
Briere, Chris, Longwood	6	5	6.63	14	0	77	102	28	57
Sherrod, Mark, Savannah State	4	4	7.14	15	0	69	97	63	50

SMALL COLLEGES

NCAA DIVISION II

Southern Indiana held off a late rally by top-ranked UC San Diego to capture the Division II College World Series title, 6-4, at the USA Baseball National Training Complex in Cary, N.C.

UC San Diego entered the CWS as the top seed and rallied from a 6-2 deficit in the eighth, plating two runs. But Southern Indiana reliever Dan Marcacci got out of the jam by retiring Vance Albitz on a fielder's choice grounder to third baseman Wes Fink, stranding two runners. Marcacci, who finished the year 6-3, 4.33 while normally serving as the third starter, finished the job in the ninth to preserve Southern Indiana's first Division II national title.

Marcacci and teammate Trevor Leach were fresh for the final, after having been suspended for four games after hitting batters in the regional tournament final. In their first game back, Leach earned the win while Marcacci got the save.

Leach, who finished 12-1, 3.05, was solid in the victory, going seven innings while limiting UC San Diego to three runs on seven hits. "This is a dream come true," Leach said. "Growing up, everyone dreams about winning a national championship, and I was just fortunate enough to pitch in it."

UC San Diego (54-8) got to Leach in the early going, however, as Kyle Saul hit a solo homer in the first, which was followed later in the inning by a run-scoring double off the bat of Evan Kehoe.

The Southern Indiana offense got some help by UC San Diego's defensive lapses in the second to erase the deficit. After Southern Indiana used two San Diego errors to put runners on second and third with one run already in, Todd Martin doubled down the left-field line off of UC San Diego starter Tim Shibuya to give his team a lead it wouldn't relinquish.

DIVISION II WORLD SERIES

Site: Cary, N.C.
Participants: Central Missouri (51-9); Tampa (46-9); UC San Diego (51-7); Georgia College (39-15); Kutztown, Pa. (41-13); Franklin Pierce, N.H. (41-15-1); Minnesota State Mankato (44-14); Southern Indiana (48-13).
Champion: Southern Indiana.
Runner-up: UC San Diego.
Outstanding Player: Taylor Dennis, Southern Indiana.
PRELIMINARIES
Central Missouri 3, Tampa 0
UC San Diego 3, Georgia College 2
Kutztown 2, Franklin Pierce 1
Southern Indiana 8, Minnesota State Mankato 6
UC San Diego 2, Central Missouri 1
Georgia College 2, Tampa 1 (Tampa eliminated)
Southern Indiana 7, Kutztown 1
Franklin Pierce 6, Minnesota State Mankato 2 (Mankato eliminated)
Georgia College 9, Central Missouri 4 (Central Missouri eliminated)

Franklin Pierce 6, Kutztown 2 (Kutztown eliminated)
SEMIFINALS
UC San Diego 6, Franklin Pierce 3 (Franklin Pierce eliminated)
Georgia College 3, Southern Indiana 0
Southern Indiana 3, Georgia College 2 (Georgia College eliminated)
CHAMPIONSHIP
Southern Indiana 6, UC San Diego 4 (UC San Diego eliminated)

NCAA DIVISION III

Illinois Wesleyan capped off its remarkable run through the postseason with a 17-5 win over Cortland State (N.Y.) in Grand Chute, Wis., to win the Division III World Series.

After finishing the regular season at just 19-19, Illinois Wesleyan raced through the College Conference of Illinois and Wisconsin tournament, in which it was the bottom seed, to earn a birth in the regionals, then won 11 of its last 12 games to capture the title.

"It's unbelievable," Illinois Wesleyan coach Dennis Martel said. "Where we were three weeks ago, this is a real Cinderella story to get here and accomplish what we have done. What an unbelievable 19 days since our conference tournament started."

In the final, Cortland jumped out to a lead in the first inning on a two-run homer by Steve Nickel off Illinois Wesleyan starter Jason Pankau. From there, it was all Illinois Wesleyan, which scored its 17 runs in the next four innings.

Jeff Grodecki homered in the second inning off Cortland pitcher Mike Assman to start Illinois Wesleyan's scoring. Illinois Wesleyan added three more in the third, highlighted by a two-run triple by Kevin Sullivan, and tacked on another four runs in the fourth with the help of Grodecki's second homer of the day.

Illinois Wesleyan starter Pankau, who went 11-2, 2.60 on the season, worked 7 1/3 innings in the title game, allowing three runs—two unearned—on six hits while fanning nine.

DIVISION III WORLD SERIES

Site: Appleton, Wis.
Participants: Cortland State, N.Y. (36-8-1); Wisconsin-Stevens Point (33-16); Massachusetts-Boston (32-15); Linfield, Ore. (34-11); Heidelberg, Ohio (40-6); Johns Hopkins, Md. (43-5); Shenandoah, Va. (38-8); Illinois Wesleyan (27-20).
Champion: Illinois Wesleyan.
Runner-up: Cortland State.
Outstanding Player: Jeff Grodecki, Illinois Wesleyan
PRELIMINARIES
Cortland State 9, Wisconsin-Stevens Point 8
Linfield 12, UMass-Boston 0
Heidelberg 3, Johns Hopkins 2
Illinois Wesleyan 7, Shenandoah 5
Wisconsin-Stevens Point 13, UMass-Boston 3 (UMass Boston eliminated)
Johns Hopkins 7, Shenandoah 5 (Shenandoah eliminated)
Linfield 25, Cortland State 11
Illinois Wesleyan 4, Heidelberg 3
Cortland State 23, Johns Hopkins 8 (Johns Hopkins eliminated)

Heidelberg 8, Wisconsin-Stevens Point 3 (Stevens Point eliminated)
SEMIFINALS
Illinois Wesleyan 4, Linfield 3
Linfield 6, Heidelberg 4 (Heidelberg eliminated)
Cortland State 11, Illinois Wesleyan 10
Cortland State 12, Linfield 9 (Linfield eliminated)
CHAMPIONSHIP
Illinois Wesleyan 17, Cortland State 5 (Cortland State eliminated)

NAIA

In an all-Tennessee final played at Harris Field in Lewiston, Idaho, second-seeded Cumberland (Tenn.) rode the arm of junior righthander Aaron Wilkerson to the NAIA World Series title over fourth-seeded Lee in a 4-3 victory.

The win gives Cumberland, located in Lebanon in the central part of the state, its second national title, and its first since 2004..

Wilkerson (14-1, 2.13 overall with 125 strikeouts in 101 innings) tossed a complete game while giving up three runs on seven hits to earn the win. In the ninth, Wilkerson gave up a three-run homer to Michael Brown, cutting Cumberland's lead to one run. The next batter, Seth Walker, singled on a chopper over the shortstop, putting the tying run on base, but Wilkerson got Taylor Comford to hit into a game-ending double play.

The game was scoreless heading into the fourth inning when Troy Frazier led off with a single for Cumberland, followed by a two-run homer by David Fanshawe off Lee starter Matthew Gilson. Cumberland added two more runs in the fifth, which was all Wilkinson needed.

NAIA WORLD SERIES

Site: Lewiston, Idaho.
Participants: Belhaven, Miss. (43-16); California Baptist (48-14); Cumberland, Tenn. (53-9); Embry-Riddle, Fla. (45-17); Lee, Tenn. (50-11); Lewis-Clark State, Idaho (47-3); Lubbock Christian, Texas (46-15); Oklahoma City (50-14); Point Loma Nazarene, Calif. (39-18-1); Tennessee Wesleyan (46-17).
Champion: Cumberland.
Runner-Up: Lee.
Outstanding Player: Kris Miller, Cumberland.

JUNIOR COLLEGES

NJCAA DIVISION I

Iowa Western CC scored two runs in the bottom of the eighth to overcome top-seeded San Jacinto (Texas) JC to clinch the school's first Division I title, 5-4, in Grand Junction, Colo. It's the first championship for a Northern program, as the Reivers were the first team from the Northern District to even reach Grand Junction.
Site: Grand Junction, Colo.
Participants: Chattanooga State, Tenn. (37-13); Crowder, Mo. (42-22); Faulkner State, Ala. (37-19); Hutchinson, Kan. (37-22); Iowa Western (46-12); Pitt, N.C. (42-10); San Jacinto, Texas (48-10); Southern Nevada (49-14); State College of Florida (37-13); Temple, Texas (37-23).
Champion: Iowa Western.

Runner-Up: San Jacinto.
Outstanding player: Ivan Hartle, Iowa Western.

NJCAA DIVISION II

Louisiana State-Eunice held onto an early lead to defeat Connecticut-Avery Point 10-2 at David Allen Memorial Ballpark in Enid, Okla. LSU-Eunice scored three in the third inning and two in the fourth to build a 5-0 lead. Chance Mistric earned the win with 6⅓ innings of two-run, four-hit ball.
Site: Enid, Okla.
Participants: Connecticut-Avery Point (37-8); Frederick, Mc. (52-5); Iowa Central (48-15); Louisiana State-Eunice (47-12); Lenoir, N.C. (34-13); Madison, Wis. (44-13); Paradise Valley, Ariz. (40-19); Parkland, Ill. (48-11); Vincennes, Ind. (28-19); Western Oklahoma State (53-5).
Champion: LSU-Eunice.
Runner-Up: UConn-Avery Point.
Outstanding Player: Gabriel Thibodeaux, LSU-Eunice.

NJCAA DIVISION III

Top-ranked Gloucester County (N.J.) JC beat Tyler (Texas) JC 5-4 at Mike Carter Field in Tyler to win its sixth national title. Logan Morello's RBI double in the top of the 10th inning broke a 4-4 tie.
Site: Tyler, Texas.
Participants: Gloucester County, N.J. (39-2); Herkimer County, N.Y. (34-12); Manchester, Conn. (28-21); Montgomery, Md. (31-21); Nassau, N.Y. (37-11); Riverland, Minn. (36-10); Tyler, Texas (43-12); Waubonsee, Ill. (35-26).
Champion: Gloucester County.
Runner-Up: Tyler.
Outstanding Player: Logan Morello, Gloucester County.

CALIFORNIA CC ATHLETIC ASSOCIATION

Ohlone JC defeated JC of San Mateo 16-10 to earn its first California junior college championship at John Euless Ballpark in Fresno. Tournament MVP Jeff Johnson was the star of the game, hitting a three-run homer and a grand slam.
Site: Fresno, Calif.
Participants: El Camino (32-9); Ohlone (34-10); Rio Hondo (31-10); San Mateo (32-8-1).
Champion: Ohlone.
Runner-Up: San Mateo.
Outstanding Player: Jeff Johnson.

NORTHWEST ATHLETIC ASSOCIATION OF CCS

Lower Columbia (Wash.) JC shut out Lane (Ore.) CC 6-0 at David Story Field in Longview, Wash., to win its 10th NWAACC title. Alex Phillips, a Kentucky signee who was the tournament MVP, threw eight innings of shutout ball while giving up six hits and striking out seven to earn the win.
Site: Longview, Wash.
Participants: Bellevue, Wash. (29-18); Chemeketa, Ore. (32-10); Columbia Basin, Wash. (33-13); Edmonds, Wash. (32-12); Lane, Ore. (29-15); Lower Columbia, Wash. (36-4); Tacoma, Wash. (24-15); Treasure Valley, Ore. (33-11).
Champion: Lower Columbia.
Runner-Up: Lane.
Outstanding Player: Alex Phillips, Lower Columbia.

USA Baseball's collegiate national team fell just short of its fourth straight FISU World University Championships title in Tokyo, as Cuba overcame a pair of late deficits in the gold-medal game to stun the Americans, 4-3, in 10 innings.

"It was one of the greatest games I've ever watched, I think," Team USA coach Bill Kinneberg said. "The intensity of both teams, the play of both teams, just the way it unfolded was really something. It was just too bad somebody had to lose, and it was really too bad we came out on the losing end of it. I don't know if I've ever seen a team of mine play with that emotion and that intensity for 10 innings."

After Drew Maggi (Arizona State) broke a scoreless tie with a solo homer in the top of the eighth, Cuban star Alfredo Despaigne answered with a game-tying solo homer of his own in the bottom of the frame against USA closer Noe Ramirez (Cal State Fullerton), who had entered in relief of starter Gerrit Cole (UCLA). Cole had scattered 10 hits over seven shutout innings.

Lefthander Nick Ramirez (Cal State Fullerton) rescued his Titans teammate from a bases-loaded, no-outs jam in the ninth to force extra innings. International tie-breaker rules allowed each team to start its 10th inning with runners on first and second and no outs. Team USA finally got to Cuban starter Miguel Gonzalez (who struck out

14 over 9 2/3 innings, throwing 151 pitches) for two runs in the top of the 10th, but Despaigne answered again in the bottom of the inning.

With one out, Despaigne cranked his second homer of the game—a walk-off, three-run shot against Nick Ramirez. It came on an 0-and-1 changeup.

There's no shame in losing to Despaigne, who is the best player in Cuban baseball right now. The 24-year-old outfielder is a veteran of the 2008 Olympics (when he homered against Stephen Strasburg in a Cuban rout of the USA in the semifinals) and 2009 World Baseball Classic. In 2008-09, he hit 32 home runs in Cuba's Serie Nacional, breaking the league record. He nearly won the league's triple crown this past season, when he became the third player to repeat as MVP.

So Team USA had to settle for the silver medal, but it took a heroic performance from Cuba's best player to keep the Americans from the gold.

Team USA finished its summer tour with a 16-3 record, including two losses against Chinese Taipei immediately after the Americans landed in Asia. The team rebounded from those losses, splitting the four-game series against the Taiwanese and then outscoring its five opponents 46-10 to reach the FISU finals. That run included quality wins against Canada in pool play and Japan in the semifinals.

As usual, pitching was Team USA's greatest

COLLEGIATE NATIONAL TEAM STATS

Year indicates 2010-11 class standing

PLAYER, POS.	YEAR	SCHOOL	AVG	OBP	SLG	G	AB	R	H	2B	3B	HR	RBI	BB	SO	SB
Brad Miller, 3b/ss	Jr.	Clemson	.441	.525	.647	14	34	11	15	4	0	1	6	6	7	1
Ryan Wright, 3b/1b	Jr.	Louisville	.361	.451	.541	19	61	18	22	3	1	2	12	5	8	3
Jackie Bradley Jr., of	Jr.	South Carolina	.318	.395	.394	18	66	13	21	2	0	1	11	8	17	2
Peter O'Brien, c	Jr.	Bethune-Cookman	.306	.350	.694	13	36	9	11	2	0	4	10	2	11	0
George Springer, of	Jr.	Connecticut	.292	.342	.472	18	72	12	21	7	0	2	18	4	14	2
Nick Ramirez, 1b	Jr.	Cal State Fullerton	.290	.371	.403	16	62	8	18	1	0	2	14	5	10	0
Jason Esposito, 3b	Jr.	Vanderbilt	.273	.347	.386	14	44	6	12	2	0	1	6	1	8	2
Mikie Mahtook, of	Jr.	Louisiana State	.271	.368	.390	19	59	11	16	2	1	1	6	7	15	10
Drew Maggi, 2b/of	Jr.	Arizona State	.262	.387	.410	19	61	18	16	4	1	1	7	12	19	14
Nolan Fontana, ss	So.	Florida	.250	.459	.273	17	44	8	11	1	0	0	3	16	11	2
Alex Dickerson, of/1b	Jr.	Indiana	.250	.349	.389	14	36	5	9	2	0	1	8	5	5	2
Steve Rodriguez, c	Jr.	UCLA	.080	.281	.080	11	25	2	2	0	0	0	0	5	8	1
Anthony Rendon, 3b	Jr.	Rice	.500	.500	.500	2	4	0	2	0	0	0	1	1	0	1
Sean Gilmartin, dh	Jr.	Florida State	.000	.000	.000	3	3	0	0	0	0	0	0	0	0	0
Brian Johnson, dh	So.	Florida	.000	.000	.000	2	2	1	0	0	0	0	1	1	1	0

PITCHER, POS.	YEAR	SCHOOL	W	L	ERA	G	GS	CG	SV	IP	H	R	ER	BB	SO	AVG
Tyler Anderson, lhp	Jr.	Oregon	1	0	0.00	3	3	0	0	16	6	0	0	3	14	.120
Sonny Gray, rhp	Jr.	Vanderbilt	3	0	0.38	5	4	1	0	24	8	2	1	4	37	.103
Brian Johnson, lhp	So.	Florida	1	0	0.63	7	1	0	1	14	6	2	1	5	16	.128
Gerrit Cole, rhp	Jr.	UCLA	2	0	0.72	5	4	0	1	25	24	4	2	4	23	.267
Scott McGough, rhp	Jr.	Oregon	1	1	0.82	5	0	0	0	11	4	3	1	5	13	.108
Brett Mooneyham, lhp	Jr.	Stanford	2	0	0.82	4	3	0	0	11	6	3	1	2	8	.158
Matt Barnes, rhp	Jr.	Connecticut	3	0	1.42	4	3	0	0	19	8	3	3	5	26	.129
Nick Ramirez, lhp	Jr.	Cal State Fullerton	0	1	1.59	4	0	0	1	6	2	3	1	1	6	.111
Kyle Winkler, rhp	Jr.	Texas Christian	1	0	2.13	6	0	0	0	13	9	4	3	3	14	.196
Noe Ramirez, rhp	Jr.	Cal State Fullerton	0	0	2.70	9	0	0	5	13	11	4	4	4	17	.234
Sean Gilmartin, lhp	Jr.	Florida State	2	1	4.35	4	1	0	0	10	12	7	5	5	14	.286

strength. The team's 11-man pitching staff posted a 1.22 combined ERA with 188 strikeouts and 41 walks in 162 innings. Six different pitchers posted sub-1.00 ERAs in 11 or more innings, led by lefthander Tyler Anderson (1-0, 0.00 in 16 innings over three starts) and righty Sonny Gray (3-0, 0.38 in 24 innings over five appearances, including the semifinal win against Japan). Gray and Cole (2-0, 0.72) turned in their second straight dominant summers with Team USA.

"Our pitching was really good throughout the summer," Kinneberg said. "Our pitching and defense were really good. I think we struggled at times offensively, and mainly because of the type of pitching we were seeing . . . Offensively I thought we were a little bit shy, and without Anthony (Rendon), that probably hurt us a little bit."

Still, the Americans rebounded after Rendon—BA's 2010 College Player of the Year—suffered a major ankle injury in the second game of the summer. Team USA brought in Jason Esposito (Vanderbilt) to play third base, and he provided superb defense as well as extra energy and intensity. Team USA was plenty athletic—the outfield alone contained a trio of legitimate five-tool center fielders in George Springer (Connecticut), Jackie Bradley Jr. (South Carolina) and Mikie Mahtook (Louisiana State)—and had a bit of power (most notably from Bethune-Cookman's Peter O'Brien and Springer, two of the summer's biggest breakout players). A third breakout star—versatile infielder Ryan Wright (Louisville)—might have been the team's MVP. Wright led all regulars with a .361 average and delivered clutch hit after clutch hit.

The infield defense was strong; Team USA posted a solid .976 fielding percentage. It was a well-constructed club, though it fell just short of its No. 1 goal. But Kinneberg praised the character and toughness of his team and said he regarded the summer as a success.

Cotuit Captures Cape Title

The Cotuit Kettleers won their first Cape Cod League title since 1999 with a 6-0 win against Yarmouth-Dennis in the decisive third game of the championship series. Cotuit capitalized on four Y-D errors and got a brilliant relief outing from righthander Nick Tropeano (Stony Brook) after starter Brady Rodgers (Arizona State) left with a back strain in the third inning. Tropeano, the top prospect in the Atlantic Collegiate League in 2009, retired the first nine batters he faced and finished with seven strikeouts over 6 2/3 hitless innings of relief.

"There was no doubt in my mind that if

Nick Tropeano finished that ballgame, the Cotuit Kettleers were going to win," Cotuit coach Mike Roberts told the Cape Cod Times. "(He) is one of the greatest competitors I've ever seen in collegiate baseball in my 30-plus years of coaching. "

Cotuit stifled Y-D's previously red-hot offense in the finals, allowing just two runs in three games. Righty Matt Andriese (UC Riverside) threw a complete-game shutout in the opener.

SUMMER LEAGUE ROUNDUP

■ Behind two home runs and four RBIs from outfielder Steve McGuiggan (Illinois-Chicago), Eau Claire cruised to a 9-1 win against Rochester in the decisive third game of the Northwoods League championship series. Lefthander Felix Cardenas (Texas-Permian Basin) shut down the Honkers in the winner-take-all game, allowing just five hits over seven scoreless innings. The Honkers, who won the title in 2009, fell just short of their sixth championship.

■ In the Coastal Plain League, the Forest City Owls defeated the Edenton Steamers 2-1 in a best-of-three championship series, giving them their second consecutive Pettit Cup. With a 94-30 record over the past two seasons, Forest City became the fifth team in CPL history to win back-to-back titles. The Owls won 5 0 in the decisive game of the series. Brian Burton (Canisius) hit a two-run homer in the second inning to put the Owls ahead for good. Starter Jeremy Fant (Rice) and reliever Andrew Brown (Akron) combined on a five-hit shutout, allowing just one walk while striking out four.

■ The North Shore Navigators won their first-ever NECBL title with a come-from-behind 5-4 win over Danbury in the deciding game of the best-of-three championship series. The Navigators won the first game 2-0 behind a dominant performance from righthander Kevin Kyle (Clemson), who struck out 12 while pitching into the eighth inning. Danbury slugged its way to a 9-3 victory in the second game and was leading 4-3 heading into the bottom of the seventh of the deciding game. But with the bases loaded, Navigators catcher Garret Smith (Boston College) became the hero, doubling home two runs to give North Shore the lead for good.

■ In the NBC World Series, the Liberal BeeJays of the Jayhawk League won their fifth title—and first since 2000—with a 9-6 win against the Seattle Studs in the championship game. Liberal finished with a 7-1 record in the tournament and avenged a quarterfinals loss to the Studs in the championship. Joe Vaskas (Concordia, N.Y., College) went 4-for-5 with three runs and three RBIs to lead Liberal's 15-hit attack in the finale.

■ For the second year in a row, the Mat-Su Miners won the Alaska League title, with a record of 31-14. The Alaska Goldpanners of Fairbanks finished second at 30-15 and the Peninsula Oilers were a close third, at 29-15. The Oilers represented the league in the NBC World Series, where they were knocked out in the first round.

■ The Luray Wranglers swept the Front Royal Cardinals in the best-of-three Valley League championship series by a combined

Gray continues Team USA tradition

In his first start of the summer, Sonny Gray struck out nine over six scoreless innings as part of a combined no-hitter against Korea.

In his final start of the summer in front of a boisterous crowd in Tokyo, Gray limited Japan to two runs (one earned) over seven strong innings to lead USA Baseball's collegiate national team to the gold-medal game of the FISU World University Championship.

But Gray's signature outing of the summer came a week before the Japan game, in Team USA's FISU opener—a 15-0 blowout win against a severely over-matched Sri Lanka team. In a five-inning complete game, Gray needed just 69 pitches to strike out 14. He did not issue a walk and allowed just one hit.

"Forty pitches into his outing," USA pitching coach Dave Serrano said, "I turned to the dugout and said, 'Sonny Gray is taking a professional approach to this.' If he missed his spot, it may have been one pitch. It didn't matter who he was pitching against, how good or bad they were, he was pitching at a major league level. Then he started pitching in the stretch on his own just to get work pitching out of the stretch for his next outing.

"That told me everything I needed to know about Sonny Gray. It was quality work at the highest level. He was pitching like it was the gold-medal game, against a team that had no shot at all to beat him."

SUMMER PLAYER OF THE YEAR

SPORTS ON FILM
Sonny Gray

That mature, professional approach is a big part of what makes Gray special, but it's just a part. Gray is a 5-foot-11, 180-pound pit bull on the mound, but he has a gregarious, fun-loving, slightly mischievous personality off the field, and he emerged as a true clubhouse leader in his second tour with Team USA.

And, of course, Gray's electric right arm makes him special. With a lively 93-96 mph two-seam fastball and a power curveball in the 82-85 range, Gray has some of the best pure stuff in college baseball, and he used it to go 3-0, 0.38 with an eye-popping 37-4 strikeout-walk ratio in 24 innings this summer.

The total package—the leadership, the absurd numbers and the strong performance in Team USA's biggest win of the summer against Japan—makes Gray Baseball America's 2010 Summer Player of the Year. A rising junior righthander at Vanderbilt, Gray is the third Commodore to win the award in the last five years. He's in good company; his two Vandy predecessors—former Team USA star lefthanders David Price and Mike Minor—have already tasted big league success.

"I love Sonny Gray," Serrano said. "I think he was one of the best guys to be around this summer—you talk about leadership, competitiveness, an ambassador for USA baseball, as a teammate."

PREVIOUS WINNERS

1984: Will Clark, 1b, Team USA; Rafael Palmeiro, of, Hutchinson (Jayhawk)
1985: Jeff King, 3b, Team USA; Bob Zupcic, of, Liberal (Jayhawk)
1986: Jack Armstrong, rhp, Wareham (Cape Cod); Mike Harkey, rhp, Fairbanks (Alaska)
1987: Cris Carpenter, rhp, Team USA
1988: Robin Ventura, 3b, Team USA; Ty Griffin, 2b, Team USA
1989: John Olerud, 1b-lhp, Palouse (Alaska)
1990: Calvin Murray, of, Anchorage

Bucs (Alaska)
1991: Chris Roberts, of, Team USA
1992: Jeffrey Hammonds, of, Team USA
1993: Geoff Jenkins, of, Team USA
1994: Steve Carver, 1b, Anchorage Glacier Pilots (Alaska)
1995: Travis Lee, 1b, Team USA
1996: Seth Greisinger, rhp, Team USA
1997: Pat Burrell, 3b, Team USA
1998: Bobby Kielty, of, Bourne (Cape Cod)
1999: Xavier Nady, 3b, Team USA
2000: Mark Teixeira, 3b, Team USA

2001: Bobby Brownlie, rhp, Team USA
2002: Brad Sullivan, rhp, Team USA
2003: Jered Weaver, rhp, Team USA
2004: Daniel Carte, of, Falmouth (Cape Cod)
2005: Andrew Miller, lhp, Chatham (Cape Cod)
2006: David Price, lhp, Team USA
2007: Luke Greinke, of/rhp, Winchester (Valley)
2008: Mike Minor, lhp, Team USA
2009: Christian Colon, ss, Team USA

COLLEGE *SUMMER LEAGUES*

For players who played for multiple teams:
1: Stats with first team 2: Stats with second team
3: Stats with third team T: combined stats

COLLEGE BASEBALL

CAPE COD LEAGUE

EAST	W	L	T	PCT	PTS
Yarmouth-Dennis	27	17	0	.614	54
Brewster	26	17	1	.591	53
Orleans	23	19	2	.523	48
Harwich	22	21	1	.500	45
Chatham	20	22	2	.455	42

WEST	W	L	T	PCT	PTS
Bourne	24	20	0	.545	48
Falmouth	21	22	1	.477	43
Cotuit	19	23	2	.432	40
Wareham	19	24	1	.432	39
Hyannis	14	30	0	.318	28

PLAYOFFS— Semifinals: Cotuit defeated Wareham 2-0 and Yarmouth-Dennis defeated Orleans 2-0 in best-of-three series. **Finals:** Cotuit defeated Yarmouth-Dennis 2-1 in best-of-three series.

TOP 30 PROSPECTS: 1. Anthony Ranaudo, rhp, Brewster (SIGNED: Red Sox). 2. George Springer, of, Wareham (Jr., Connecticut). 3. Matt Barnes, rhp, Wareham (Jr., Connecticut). 4. Jed Bradley, lhp, Wareham (Jr., Georgia Tech). 5. Andrew Susac, c, Falmouth (So., Oregon State). 6. Brian Goodwin, of, Harwich (So., North Carolina). 7. Deven Marrero, ss, Cotuit (So., Arizona State). 8. Austin Wood, rhp, Cotuit (Jr., Southern California). 9. Jason Coats, of, Bourne (Jr., Texas Christian). 10. Lex Rutledge, lhp, Harwich (So., Samford). 11. Anthony Meo, rhp, Bourne (Jr., Coastal Carolina). 12. John Ruettiger, of, Hyannis (Jr., Arizona State). 13. Kolten Wong, 2b, Orleans (Jr., Hawaii). 14. Marcus Stroman, rhp, Orleans (So., Duke). 15. Zach Wilson, of/3b, Wareham (Jr., Arizona State). 16. Jason Esposito, 3b, Orleans (Jr., Vanderbilt). 17. Tony Zych, rhp, Bourne (Jr., Louisville). 18. Levi Michael, if, Harwich (Jr., North Carolina). 19. Logan Verrett, rhp, Chatham (Jr., Baylor). 20. Andrew Gagnon, rhp, Brewster (Jr., Long Beach State). 21. Brady Rodgers, rhp, Cotuit (So., Arizona State). 22. Ryan Carpenter, lhp, Orleans (Jr., Gonzaga). 23. Jack Armstrong, rhp, Wareham (Jr., Vanderbilt). 24. Joe Panik, ss, Yarmouth-Dennis (Jr., St. John's). 25. Aaron Westlake, 1b, Chatham (Jr., Vanderbilt). 26. R.J. Alvarez, rhp, Bourne (So., Florida Atlantic). 27. Ricky Oropesa, 1b/3b, Chatham (Jr., Southern California). 28. Grayson Garvin, lhp, Bourne (Jr., Vanderbilt). 29. Kevin Medrano, 2b, Falmouth (Jr., Missouri State). 30. Andy Burns, 3b, Brewster (Jr., Arizona).

INDIVIDUAL BATTING LEADERS
(MINIMUM 2.7 PLATE APPEARANCES PER TEAM GAME)

	AVG	G	AB	R	H	HR	RBI
Ruettiger, John, Hyannis	.369	27	111	16	41	0	5
Martinez, Drew, Brewster	.359	41	145	25	52	1	18
Wong, Kolten, Orleans	.341	38	135	19	46	3	11
Medrano, Kevin, Falmouth	.321	35	137	17	44	1	16
Ramsey, Caleb, Yarmouth-Dennis	.311	42	151	29	47	1	1
Oh, Danny, Brewster	.299	34	97	17	29	1	16
Wilson, Zach, Wareham	.294	28	109	19	32	5	15
Susac, Andrew, Falmouth	.290	29	100	17	29	5	15
Wright, Chad, Cotuit	.290	40	138	18	40	0	7
Hanover, Tyler, Yarmouth-Dennis	.286	38	140	18	40	0	12

INDIVIDUAL PITCHING LEADERS
(MINIMUM 0.8 INNINGS PITCHED PER TEAM GAME)

	W	L	ERA	IP	H	BB	SO
Garvin, Grayson, Bourne	5	0	0.74	37	18	12	37
Wood, Austin, Cotuit	3	0	0.74	36	18	19	25
Verrett, Logan, Chatham	2	1	0.87	41	22	5	34
Simon, Kyle, Orleans	1	2	0.92	39	21	8	19
Achter, A.J., Cotuit	2	2	1.42	38	40	14	31
Hendricks, Kyle, Brewster	2	0	1.73	36	28	12	33
Dennhardt, Mike, Chatham	2	3	1.80	45	32	12	38
Sisto, Matt, Orleans	2	2	1.88	38	33	2	20
Lubinsky, Austin, Brewster	3	1	1.91	42	34	4	17
Perlman, Max, Wareham	3	2	1.92	52	37	6	42

BOURNE

BATTING	AVG	AB	R	H	2B	3B	HR	RBI	SB
Ahmed, Nick	.212	146	24	31	6	0	0	10	17
1 Besinger, Billy	.000	1	0	0	0	0	0	0	0
Blaser, Tyson	.111	27	1	3	1	0	0	1	0
Bowers, Brett	.111	9	0	1	0	0	0	0	0
Bowman, Daniel	.202	119	13	24	4	0	5	19	4
Brunelle, Parker	.143	7	1	1	0	0	0	0	0
Brunty, Kameron	.200	5	1	1	0	0	0	0	0
Coats, Jason	.314	86	11	27	9	0	2	15	2
Elander, Josh	.186	59	1	11	2	0	0	5	0
Jankowski, Travis	.346	26	5	9	1	0	0	0	6
Lalli, Andy	.103	29	3	3	0	0	0	1	1
LaStella, Tommy	.262	122	14	32	6	0	1	15	4
MacPhee, Zack	.247	73	12	18	2	1	1	6	5
Martin, Cody	.250	4	1	1	0	0	0	0	0
Mende, Sam	.133	15	1	2	0	0	0	0	0
Nemeth, Mike	.221	131	9	29	2	0	0	13	2
O'Brien, Peter	.300	40	3	12	1	0	0	2	1
Shaw, Travis	.260	127	19	33	7	1	3	17	0
Simpson, Creede	.244	135	12	33	3	1	2	14	4
Sossamon, Chance	.000	1	1	0	0	0	0	0	0
Theisen, Spencer	.000	14	0	0	0	0	0	1	1
Travis, Devon	.133	15	0	2	0	0	0	0	0
Woodward, Scott	.308	78	18	24	4	0	0	3	20
Wrenn, Taylor	.250	4	0	1	1	0	0	0	0
Wright, Ryan	.239	71	10	17	3	0	0	12	3
Wunderlich, Phil	.063	16	0	1	0	0	0	2	0

PITCHING	W	L	ERA	G	SV	IP	H	BB	SO
Alvarez, R.J.	3	2	0.79	15	0	23	12	8	29
Billbrough, Logan	1	1	3.32	15	0	19	14	9	24
Brady, Kevin	4	0	0.97	6	0	9	5	3	12
Busch, Brian	0	0	9.00	1	0	2	3	2	2
Bush, Garrett	0	1	9.84	2	0	4	5	2	4
Dimock, Michael	0	1	2.49	8	0	22	20	7	27
Garvin, Grayson	5	0	0.74	6	0	37	18	12	37
Heller, Michael	0	0	6.75	3	0	4	5	6	0
Jolin, Will	1	4	2.60	9	0	35	30	15	30
Jones, Devin	2	2	5.60	8	0	27	32	11	22
1 Kahnle, Tommy	0	1	3.38	7	0	5	1	6	8
Loftin, Alex	0	0	0.00	1	0	2	0	3	0
McMyne, Kyle	1	1	6.46	14	0	15	13	11	24
Meo, Anthony	2	1	3.12	5	0	26	17	12	19
Morin, Mike	1	3	3.29	8	0	38	27	13	38
Orlan, R.C.	0	0	1.62	13	0	17	9	6	15
Roberts, Will	1	0	2.25	7	0	16	16	3	11
Sossamon, Chance	1	1	2.08	10	0	17	7	8	17
Stadler, Austin	2	2	2.75	7	0	36	20	14	33
Zych, Tony	0	0	0.89	17	12	20	17	4	29

BREWSTER

BATTING	AVG	AB	R	H	2B	3B	HR	RBI	SB
1 Andreoli, John	.240	25	4	6	3	0	0	2	5
Ard, Taylor	.263	118	13	31	9	0	1	14	6
Barrett, Jake	.500	2	1	1	1	0	0	0	0
Berti, Jon	.225	102	15	23	5	0	0	9	13
Botsford, Brett	.000	3	2	0	0	0	0	0	0
Burns, Andy	.211	152	19	32	6	1	1	18	25
Channing, Troy	.130	77	7	10	2	0	2	7	0
Dowd, Mike	.244	41	2	10	1	0	0	2	0
Ellison, Chris	.163	49	4	8	1	0	2	4	5
Etier, Jordan	.143	14	1	2	1	0	0	2	0
Featherston, Taylor	.267	30	2	8	2	0	0	3	1
Jones, Derek	.211	90	9	19	5	1	0	12	3
Maguire, Ryan	.000	5	1	0	0	0	0	0	0
Martinez, Drew	.359	145	25	52	2	0	1	18	22
Melendres, Nathan	.225	71	7	16	3	1	1	5	13
Norfork, Khayyan	.258	31	7	8	2	0	0	2	6
Ogle, Tyler	.087	23	1	2	0	0	0	1	1
Oh, Danny	.299	97	17	29	7	0	1	16	3

	AVG	AB	R	H	2B	3B	HR	RBI	SB
Schaffer, Jeremy	.175	97	4	17	4	0	0	10	0
Singer, Kirk	.206	107	12	22	2	1	1	7	3
Walla, Cohl	.259	85	9	22	5	0	0	7	6

PITCHING	W	L	ERA	G	SV	IP	H	BB	SO
Bard, Luke	0	2	4.44	12	0	24	25	16	19
Barrett, Jake	0	2	1.35	10	0	13	15	9	15
Buchanan, David	0	1	2.25	1	0	4	3	3	3
Carillo, Kendall	0	1	3.97	6	0	11	9	3	5
Crouse, Matt	4	0	2.28	7	0	28	21	6	18
Floethe, Jake	2	3	3.22	10	0	36	34	15	24
Gagnon, Andrew	5	1	2.10	8	0	39	31	17	43
Hendricks, Kyle	2	0	1.73	14	3	36	28	12	33
2 Kahnle, Tommy	0	0	7.36	6	3	4	6	4	6
T Kahnle, Tommy	0	1	5.00	13	3	9	7	10	14
Larkins, Matt	2	1	4.32	13	0	25	26	15	22
Lubinsky, Austin	3	1	1.91	8	0	42	34	4	17
Monroe, Brad	1	0	20.30	2	0	1	2	2	2
Murray, Colton	1	1	0.47	18	8	19	14	8	25
Palazzone, Mike	1	1	1.67	6	0	32	24	4	31
Ranaudo, Anthony	3	0	0.00	5	0	30	10	8	31
Renken, Daniel	1	2	4.34	8	2	19	14	9	19
Smith, Chad	0	1	9.00	3	0	4	5	4	4
Soule, Billy	1	0	3.68	5	0	7	7	2	3
Walla, Cohl	0	0	0.00	1	0	1	0	1	0
Walters, Eric	0	0	27.27	1	0	0	2	0	0
Wright, Austin	0	0	0.00	1	0	0	2	0	1

CHATHAM

BATTING	AVG	AB	R	H	2B	3B	HR	RBI	SB
Amaral, Beau	.232	69	5	16	1	0	0	4	5
2 Besinger, Billy	.200	15	0	3	0	0	0	1	0
Carroll, George	.167	6	0	1	1	0	0	0	0
DePinto, Joe	.129	70	2	9	0	0	0	3	0
Gates, Aaron	.000	1	0	0	0	0	0	0	0
Ginther, Mark	.215	130	13	28	6	1	2	10	0
Humphries, Brian	.253	158	17	40	12	0	1	12	2
Jones, Zack	.267	15	0	4	0	0	0	0	1
Martin, Jason	.209	134	12	28	1	0	0	5	8
Oropesa, Rick	.222	153	13	34	5	0	7	19	0
Paolini, Dan	.200	110	13	22	4	1	1	5	1
Pavone, Joe	.290	100	3	29	2	0	0	8	1
Perez, Stephen	.162	68	5	11	4	0	0	0	1
Pohl, Philip	.250	28	2	7	2	0	0	3	1
Reynolds, Riley	.235	68	4	16	0	0	0	7	0
Smith, Garret	.250	12	1	3	1	0	0	1	0
Stallings, Jacob	.157	51	4	8	1	0	0	1	0
Vance, Kevin	.162	37	5	6	2	0	1	3	0
Verdin, Peter	.232	95	11	22	1	0	0	3	5
Westlake, Aaron	.292	106	13	31	5	0	5	10	1

PITCHING	W	L	ERA	G	SV	IP	H	BB	SO
Berry, Kevin	1	4	5.64	11	0	22	20	9	23
Brazis, Matt	3	0	1.32	12	3	14	5	4	15
Davis, Garrett	0	0	9.74	9	0	8	12	17	3
Dennhardt, Mike	2	3	1.80	8	0	45	32	12	38
Gates, Aaron	0	4	5.74	9	0	16	14	21	9
Jones, Zack	2	0	2.33	11	1	19	18	6	12
Larson, Greg	1	3	2.19	7	0	25	26	4	20
LeBarron, Zach	0	0	13.53	2	0	1	3	0	1
Miller, Joe	0	0	10.11	2	0	3	6	0	2
Monteith, Ken	0	0	1.59	10	0	17	13	6	15
Munnelly, Chris	0	1	1.71	7	0	32	25	9	22
Scanlan, Kevin	0	0	6.75	2	0	4	5	1	3
Schreiber, Phil	1	2	3.47	15	0	23	17	11	20
Self, Derek	3	0	2.36	8	0	42	35	3	17
Vance, Kevin	3	1	0.50	13	4	18	9	5	19
Verrett, Logan	2	1	0.87	6	0	41	22	5	34
Zecchino, Marc	2	1	2.08	8	0	35	28	10	28
Zimmermann, Joe	0	2	6.55	7	0	22	26	12	14

COTUIT

BATTING	AVG	AB	R	H	2B	3B	HR	RBI	SB
Black, Taylor	.125	24	1	3	0	0	0	1	2
Bushyhead, Caleb	.053	19	0	1	0	0	0	1	1

	AVG	AB	R	H	2B	3B	HR	RBI	SB
Casali, Curtis	.292	24	6	7	0	0	1	7	1
Cone, Zach	.187	75	8	14	3	0	0	7	7
Cron, C.J.	.275	69	9	19	8	0	3	13	2
Faulkner, Michael	.254	63	9	16	1	0	0	6	8
Foster, James	.179	28	2	5	0	0	0	0	1
Hainsfurther, Joey	.250	84	6	21	2	0	0	11	2
Hinson, John	.246	69	8	17	3	0	1	8	6
Hoilman, Paul	.206	102	8	21	8	0	2	8	4
Hyams, Levi	.217	138	9	30	0	0	1	14	3
Johnson, Jonathan	.000	1	0	0	0	0	0	0	0
Leyland, Jordan	.264	125	17	33	6	0	2	14	7
Marrero, Deven	.306	98	17	30	4	0	1	7	7
McCann, James	.105	76	6	8	2	0	1	6	2
McMillen, Kyle	.083	12	1	1	0	0	0	0	0
Patterson, Kevin	.233	30	5	7	2	0	1	2	0
Pinckard, Brooks	.239	67	9	16	4	0	1	4	9
Taylor, Jonathan	.000	21	2	0	0	0	0	0	3
Tropeano, Nick	1.000	1	1	1	0	0	0	0	0
Wright, Chad	.290	138	18	40	4	0	0	7	6
Yastrzemski, Michael	.235	102	15	24	1	1	2	17	14

PITCHING	W	L	ERA	G	SV	IP	H	BB	SO
Achter, AJ	2	2	1.42	14	3	38	40	14	31
Andriese, Matt	1	2	3.52	11	1	38	49	7	25
Colvin, David	3	1	1.93	12	2	23	24	6	19
Devine, Michael	0	1	6.36	5	0	6	8	2	4
Dicharry, Austin	0	1	9.00	3	0	3	4	2	0
Duke, Ryan	0	1	1.69	6	3	11	7	5	15
Eadington, Eric	0	0	0.00	1	0	2	0	2	0
Frongello, Michael	0	1	5.63	11	0	16	18	10	6
Healy, John	0	1	0.00	1	0	0	1	0	0
Keeling, Thomas	0	1	27.07	1	0	1	2	5	2
Kolinsky, Keenan	0	0	3.00	1	0	3	3	1	0
McMillen, Kyle	1	3	5.87	10	1	15	21	13	10
Murray, Matt	2	1	2.89	8	0	37	36	11	38
Pinckard, Brooks	0	1	4.27	12	1	19	18	7	12
Robinson, Joe	0	1	6.14	2	0	7	11	4	6
Rodgers, Brady	2	2	2.87	6	1	31	26	5	38
Shore, Bobby	2	0	1.93	4	0	23	17	6	19
Spence, Josh	1	0	0.90	3	0	10	7	5	11
Tropeano, Nick	2	4	3.76	9	0	55	56	19	44
Wood, Austin	3	0	0.74	7	0	36	18	19	25

FALMOUTH

BATTING	AVG	AB	R	H	2B	3B	HR	RBI	SB
Barnes, Barrett	.223	121	18	27	9	1	3	24	7
3 Besinger, Billy	.286	35	4	10	0	0	0	2	1
T Besinger, Billy	.255	51	4	13	0	0	0	3	1
Bluestein, Kyle	.220	82	9	18	3	0	2	7	0
Capeless, Dan	.211	19	3	4	1	0	0	1	0
Craig, Dylan	.143	21	7	3	1	0	0	0	1
Gomez, Victor	.000	4	0	0	0	0	0	0	0
Jones, Christian	.000	2	0	0	0	0	0	0	0
Lowe, Derek	.250	16	1	4	0	0	0	0	0
Martini, Nick	.257	140	20	36	6	2	2	21	10
Medrano, Kevin	.321	137	17	44	9	1	1	16	9
Mortimer, Kevin	.000	1	0	0	0	0	0	0	0
O'Brien, Chris	.197	137	15	27	3	0	0	8	1
Serna, K.C.	.250	176	20	44	7	1	0	16	7
Skole, Matt	.245	143	15	35	11	0	3	21	3
Summers, Matt	.286	28	4	8	0	0	0	3	0
Susac, Andrew	.290	100	17	29	6	0	5	15	1
Taylor, Zach	.000	9	0	0	0	0	0	0	0
Vollmuth, B.A.	.175	126	5	22	4	1	1	7	1
Von Tungeln, Kyle	.250	72	11	18	3	1	0	7	3
Wright, Zach	.127	55	8	7	0	1	2	5	3

PITCHING	W	L	ERA	G	SV	IP	H	BB	SO
Brown, Nick	0	1	2.84	7	1	13	10	6	22
Catapano, Max	0	0	1.50	1	0	6	3	3	6
Chamra, Rob	2	2	3.45	12	0	31	27	12	19
Gruver, Steven	1	0	5.13	11	1	26	35	8	31
Harris, Will	0	0	4.50	2	0	2	1	0	2
Hegarty, Matthew	0	0	0.00	1	0	0	0	0	0
Hippen, Jarred	0	1	4.50	5	0	14	18	5	9

PITCHING	W	L	ERA	G	SV	IP	H	BB	SO
Jones, Christian	3	3	2.36	7	0	34	22	12	26
Koneski, Nate	2	0	1.04	8	1	17	10	5	18
Maronde, Nick	2	0	2.29	10	0	20	12	5	27
Merck, Kaleb	1	0	1.08	9	2	17	12	5	18
Pena, Miguel	0	0	3.24	3	0	17	16	2	21
Pope, Mark	2	2	3.22	9	0	45	42	16	42
Simmons, Doug	2	1	4.41	11	1	16	13	9	11
Stites, Matthew	2	2	4.18	10	0	32	32	16	28
Summers, Matt	2	3	3.04	16	4	27	24	13	29
Tanner, Cecil	2	2	5.48	9	0	23	18	26	17
Wall, Taylor	0	2	7.17	9	0	21	21	16	8
Weismann, Scott	0	3	3.96	5	0	25	33	5	24

HARWICH

BATTING	AVG	AB	R	H	2B	3B	HR	RBI	SB
Ciencin, Andrew	.105	19	1	2	0	0	0	0	0
Conway, Aaron	.221	68	9	15	1	1	0	5	16
Dugas, Taylor	.159	44	7	7	1	0	0	2	4
Goodwin, Brian	.281	114	18	32	4	1	1	9	15
Hicks, John	.222	99	10	22	1	0	1	9	6
1 Ijames, Stewart	.188	16	0	3	1	0	0	1	1
Kapyten, Braden	.176	17	3	3	0	0	0	1	0
Mahtook, Mikie	.182	33	3	6	0	0	1	1	9
Manuel, Craig	.204	54	4	11	3	1	0	7	0
Maynard, Pratt	.241	108	18	26	7	0	2	20	1
Michael, Levi	.252	119	15	30	6	1	2	16	4
Moore, Clint	.270	100	16	27	4	1	2	17	4
Motter, Taylor	.154	65	9	10	4	0	0	5	2
Nola, Austin	.221	113	6	25	2	0	0	4	2
Pill, Tyler	.245	98	8	24	8	0	1	13	0
Proscia, Steven	.160	100	3	16	2	1	1	11	0
Ramsey, Matt	.118	17	0	2	0	0	0	0	0
Richardson, Ronnie	.267	116	19	31	4	2	1	9	13
Wooten, John	.217	92	8	20	4	0	1	4	2

PITCHING	W	L	ERA	G	SV	IP	H	BB	SO
Burawa, Daniel	1	2	5.70	19	2	24	24	17	25
Eliopoulos, Alex	1	0	0.00	1	0	2	1	1	1
Holtmeyer, Joe	1	3	3.18	7	0	40	26	13	37
Johnson, Pierce	3	1	2.11	7	0	43	40	12	41
Kapteyn, Braden	3	1	0.64	15	1	28	9	11	29
Leenhouts, Andrew	4	2	2.02	8	0	45	37	13	25
Locante, Will	2	2	10.19	17	0	18	18	19	19
McKenzie, Kyle	0	2	14.80	8	0	14	33	11	7
Moore, Clint	0	1	2.25	5	0	12	6	4	10
Morgan, Adam	1	0	1.44	4	0	25	18	5	21
Ott, Matty	2	0	0.44	15	7	20	9	4	19
Peavey, Greg	0	1	1.93	3	0	19	15	6	13
Ramsey, Matt	4	1	3.22	11	0	22	17	5	22
Rutledge, Lex	0	0	1.84	4	0	15	9	7	14
Sharpley, Ryan	0	1	2.25	3	0	4	3	4	3
Shepard, Brenden	0	0	0.00	1	0	3	3	2	2
Williams, Les	0	1	4.05	2	0	7	8	3	4
Wright, Mike	0	2	2.52	11	1	39	28	10	34
Yerina, Ryan	0	1	0.00	1	0	6	5	3	4

HYANNIS

BATTING	AVG	AB	R	H	2B	3B	HR	RBI	SB
Crespo, Hector	.088	34	1	3	0	0	0	2	0
Gianis, John	.158	19	2	3	0	0	0	0	1
Lusardi, Jeff	.226	84	6	19	2	0	0	4	2
McElroy, Casey	.269	160	17	43	5	0	3	25	4
Micowski, Mark	.232	125	7	29	3	0	0	7	11
Nappi, Jason	.200	95	7	19	3	0	1	10	4
Osborne, Zach	.209	129	9	27	2	0	0	5	3
Pettersen, A.J.	.236	140	22	33	3	0	0	5	7
Phillips, Dane	.152	105	9	16	2	0	2	4	4
Ruettiger, John	.369	111	16	41	5	0	0	5	11
Seitzer, Cam	.253	75	5	19	6	0	1	16	1
Sheppard, Dan	.194	93	8	18	2	0	0	10	3
Stubbs, Cody	.167	72	4	12	3	0	1	8	2
Thompson, Tyler	.118	34	1	4	0	0	0	1	0
Thurber, Charley	.268	97	12	26	7	1	3	7	4
Williams, Matt	.208	53	3	11	1	0	0	1	5

PITCHING	W	L	ERA	G	SV	IP	H	BB	SO
Brandt, Kevin	1	4	3.62	6	0	32	31	6	25
Cook, Cole	2	1	4.50	3	0	18	14	6	17
D'Angelo, Matteo	0	2	3.06	9	0	32	36	4	14
Dermody, Matt	0	0	5.50	7	0	18	16	11	13
Dupra, Brian	0	4	3.76	7	0	41	44	11	37
Gallant, Dallas	2	2	3.06	14	8	18	14	9	27
Howard, Trent	1	4	4.13	6	0	33	31	8	36
Mata, Jose	1	1	1.98	9	0	14	10	4	6
Messer, Jimmy	0	3	4.26	10	0	25	28	15	21
Mizenko, Tyler	2	0	1.62	14	0	17	19	5	14
Moran, Kevin	0	0	0.00	1	0	3	1	0	2
Pettersen, A.J.	0	0	0.00	1	0	2	1	2	2
Ray, Tyler	3	4	3.86	8	0	47	51	6	35
Rea, Colin	1	0	2.25	2	0	8	5	3	7
Ruettiger, John	0	0	3.00	1	0	3	3	0	2
Stiles, Cody	0	2	4.09	9	0	22	27	15	16
Verhagen, Drew	0	1	1.66	11	1	22	18	6	18
Williams, Matt	0	0	0.00	1	0	1	0	0	1
Wright, Justin	1	2	4.13	7	0	28	29	5	32

ORLEANS

BATTING	AVG	AB	R	H	2B	3B	HR	RBI	SB
Boyd, Jayce	.236	89	12	21	3	1	2	16	3
Cleary, Sean	.000	1	0	0	0	0	0	0	0
Doyle, Mick	.154	26	0	4	1	0	0	2	0
Esposito, Jason	.246	65	2	16	0	0	1	4	8
Glynn, Elliot	.000	0	1	0	0	0	0	0	0
Gowens, Brennan	.050	20	1	1	0	0	0	0	0
Kneeland, Cam	.083	12	2	1	1	0	0	1	1
Koch, Matt	.258	93	8	24	2	0	1	13	1
Loftus, Joe	.186	70	6	13	2	0	2	6	1
1 Muno, Danny	.256	43	7	11	2	0	1	3	1
Muno, Kevin	.243	144	18	35	3	0	1	9	13
Newman, Matt	.233	103	6	24	4	0	0	8	4
O'Grady, Dennis	.056	18	0	1	1	0	0	0	1
Piwnica-Worms, Will	.200	110	12	22	2	0	0	10	8
Roe, Shon	.299	107	8	32	4	1	0	8	6
Selsky, Steve	.273	121	14	33	6	0	4	18	5
Shaeffer, Ronnie	.190	63	4	12	3	0	0	4	1
Stroman, Marcus	.118	17	0	2	0	0	0	2	0
Tissenbaum, Maxx	.182	11	1	2	0	0	0	0	0
Torrez , Riccio	.155	97	12	15	4	0	1	5	6
Tucker, Preston	.113	80	7	9	3	0	0	6	0
Wong, Kolten	.341	135	19	46	6	0	3	11	22

PITCHING	W	L	ERA	G	SV	IP	H	BB	SO
Belcher, Nolan	1	0	1.93	7	0	9	0	3	15
Brebbia, John	1	1	2.65	13	1	17	14	4	14
Carpenter, Ryan	3	0	2.56	7	0	39	32	10	39
Clinard, Will	1	1	3.70	16	1	17	18	5	14
Glynn, Elliot	0	2	7.88	3	0	8	11	6	2
Hobson, Cameron	1	1	2.44	9	0	44	30	17	27
Kittredge, Andrew	2	2	3.99	7	0	29	32	7	26
Lambson, Mitchell	1	1	0.96	12	1	19	10	3	21
Leathersich, Jack	0	1	1.71	17	1	21	14	9	31
Loftus, Joe	0	0	5.39	2	0	2	2	0	0
Long, Kenny	4	3	1.13	21	1	32	21	11	36
Mitchem, Burny	3	1	2.41	18	1	19	13	11	21
O'Grady, Dennis	0	1	9.00	3	0	4	6	3	4
Sisto, Matt	2	2	1.88	8	0	38	33	2	20
Stroman, Marcus	1	0	0.00	15	10	25	10	3	32
Viramontes, Martin	2	1	2.15	6	0	29	19	18	19

WAREHAM

BATTING	AVG	AB	R	H	2B	3B	HR	RBI	SB
2 Andreoli, John	.244	45	6	11	2	0	0	4	6
T Andreoli, John	.243	70	10	17	5	0	0	6	11
Armstrong, Jack	.000	3	0	0	0	0	0	0	0
Bream, Tyler	.260	146	11	38	8	1	2	26	3
Caldwell, Tony	.297	91	9	27	3	0	1	8	2
Davies, Jake	.192	26	3	5	2	0	0	4	0
Dennis, Derek	.178	107	4	19	1	1	0	6	0
Dickerson, Alex	.500	34	6	17	4	0	1	7	0

	AVG	AB	R	H	2B	3B	HR	RBI	SB
Kral, Robert	.000	6	0	0	0	0	0	0	0
Ludy, Josh	.160	50	2	8	4	0	0	6	0
Mazzilli, L.J.	.207	92	11	19	1	0	1	1	11
McClain, Adam	.213	94	7	20	2	0	0	5	4
Muncy, Max	.244	135	17	33	9	2	3	25	2
Rosthenhausler, Nico	.250	84	8	21	4	0	0	7	4
Sabourin, Jerrud	.189	90	7	17	4	0	1	5	1
Smith, Jonathan	.250	148	31	37	4	0	1	11	14
Springer, George	.288	52	12	15	0	1	3	7	7
Toth, Anthony	.211	71	6	15	1	0	0	1	3
Walker, Chris	.270	63	5	17	3	0	0	7	0
Wilson, Zach	.294	109	19	32	5	0	5	15	2

PITCHING	W	L	ERA	G	SV	IP	H	BB	SO
Armstrong, Jack	4	3	2.96	7	0	46	36	19	41
Barnes, Matt	1	2	2.18	3	0	21	12	7	20
Bilodeau, Keith	1	2	3.12	14	4	17	16	9	21
Bodjiak, Brian	0	0	0.00	2	0	2	0	1	3
Bradley, Jed	2	3	1.98	6	0	41	33	6	44
Burke, Devin	1	4	5.23	11	0	31	37	8	25
Davies, Jake	1	0	2.38	12	0	11	10	7	7
DiRocco, Joe	0	0	13.50	1	0	2	3	1	3
Ferrer, Ken	1	0	1.93	15	4	19	12	17	23
Flynn, Joseph	1	1	2.13	11	1	25	22	10	19
McKirahan, Andrew	0	0	3.09	12	1	12	14	2	13
Miller, Erik	0	0	13.50	7	0	8	11	4	5
Perlman, Max	3	2	1.92	7	0	52	37	6	42
Pfisterer, Eric	3	2	3.06	9	0	53	44	26	43
Urban, Josh	1	4	5.26	7	0	39	43	17	24
1 Yarusi, Brett	0	0	3.00	1	0	3	3	0	1
Young, Matthew	0	1	13.43	1	0	1	2	0	1

YARMOUTH-DENNIS

BATTING	AVG	AB	R	H	2B	3B	HR	RBI	SB
Bandy, Jett	.200	5	1	1	0	0	0	0	0
Crocker, Bobby	.258	93	17	24	4	0	0	7	4
Hamlet, Matt	.167	36	5	6	1	0	0	0	1
Hanover, Tyler	.286	140	18	40	10	0	0	12	6
2 Ijames, Stewart	.231	104	16	24	6	0	2	12	1
T Ijames, Stewart	.225	120	16	27	7	0	2	13	2
Jensen, Matt	.216	102	13	22	3	0	1	14	1
Law, Andrew	.071	14	2	1	0	0	0	1	0
McMahan, Ben	.323	65	13	21	6	0	2	10	1
2 Muno, Danny	.254	67	7	17	0	0	3	10	5
T Muno, Danny	.255	110	14	28	2	0	4	13	6
Panik, Joe	.276	145	23	40	8	0	2	19	11
Ramsey, Caleb	.311	151	29	47	7	1	1	18	22
Ribera, Jordan	.259	147	19	38	9	1	7	26	3
Robinson, Dusty	.195	87	13	17	1	2	0	11	3
Rodriguez, Alfredo	1.000	1	0	1	0	0	0	0	0
Shaban, Ronnie	.282	39	6	11	2	0	1	2	2
Snodgress, Scott	.000	0	0	0	0	0	0	0	0
Taylor, Beau	.170	53	7	9	1	0	0	4	0
Vinson, Matt	.239	67	10	16	2	1	1	11	3
Watson, Matt	.239	92	14	22	1	0	4	21	1

PITCHING	W	L	ERA	G	SV	IP	H	BB	SO
Baxendale, D.J.	2	3	2.57	17	9	21	14	3	14
Benny, Derek	2	1	6.41	11	0	20	25	6	14
Blanc, Rob	0	1	9.00	2	0	3	5	1	0
DeSclafani, Anthony	3	0	2.12	9	2	17	13	8	18
Emmons, Dustin	0	1	3.68	3	1	7	7	1	4
Fontanez, Randy	2	0	2.95	7	0	37	41	12	25
Gibson, Ryan	0	0	21.91	4	0	5	13	10	9
Goodnight, Michael	3	1	2.89	6	0	37	25	10	27
Iannazzo, Matt	1	0	4.57	13	1	22	24	9	17
Leonard, John	3	3	1.96	6	0	37	29	11	33
Meaux, Jesse	0	0	3.38	2	0	5	5	1	8
Mooneyham, Brett	3	0	3.18	4	0	23	20	8	22
Poppe, Tanner	3	1	4.01	11	0	34	25	25	27
Pries, Jordan	2	0	1.23	3	0	15	7	7	9
Rush, Matt	0	0	1.00	2	0	9	7	2	2
Shaban, Ronnie	0	0	0.00	4	1	4	3	1	1
Shafer, Bryce	0	1	0.00	1	0	1	2	0	0
Shaw, Gabriel	2	1	2.75	6	1	20	22	2	15

	W	L	ERA	G	SV	IP	H	BB	SO
Simpson, Ali	0	0	2.79	5	0	10	8	7	15
Snodgress, Scott	0	2	3.97	13	0	23	21	17	15
Toledo, Tommy	1	2	6.36	5	0	23	27	10	22
2 Yarusi, Brett	0	0	6.24	1	0	4	5	3	2
T Yarusi, Brett	0	0	5.14	2	0	7	8	3	3

ALASKA LEAGUE

	W	L	PCT	GB
Mat-Su Miners	31	14	.689	—
Alaska Goldpanners of Fairbanks	30	15	.667	1
Kenai Peninsula Oilers	29	15	.659	1½
Anchorage Bucs	17	27	.386	13½
Fairbanks AIA Fire	15	30	.333	16
Anchorage Glacier Pilots	12	33	.267	19

TOP 10 PROSPECTS: 1. Jake Stewart, of, Fairbanks (So., Stanford). 2. Jarod Berggren, of, Fairbanks (Jr., Northern Colorado). 3. Stephen Piscotty, of, Peninsula (So., Stanford). 4. Kyle Richter, lhp, Fairbanks (Fr., Southern California). 5. Tyler Grimes, ss, Peninsula (Jr., Wichita State). 6. Chase McDowell, rhp, Fairbanks (So., Rice). 7. Chad Smith, rhp, Peninsula (Jr., Southern California). 8. D.J. Crumlich, ss, Fairbanks (Jr., UC Irvine). 9. Geoffrey Davenport, lhp, Mat-Su (Jr., Arkansas). 10. Jeff Popick, of, Peninsula (Jr., Mesa State, Colo.).

INDIVIDUAL BATTING LEADERS
(MINIMUM 3 PLATE APPEARANCES PER TEAM GAME)

	AVG	AB	R	H	2B	3B	HR	RBI	SB
Schwartz, Bret, Mat-Su	.420	157	34	66	11	0	1	0	13	6
Mee, Andy, Mat-Su	.353	173	32	61	18	4	1	37	0
Bermudez, Pablo, Mat-Su	.351	131	21	46	10	4	1	25	0
DeBiasse, Nick, Mat-Su	.325	163	24	53	15	0	0	32	2
Ruch, Tyler, Mat-Su	.323	127	29	41	9	0	0	12	10
Watson, Will, Fairbanks AIA	.322	149	16	48	2	1	0	11	8
Tauchman, Mike, Goldpanners	.313	131	23	41	2	3	0	18	5
Schoch, Mark, Fairbanks AIA	.311	135	16	42	6	0	1	26	1
Thigpen, Wesley, Mat-Su	.307	140	27	43	12	1	2	17	2
Serritella, Chris, Bucs	.304	148	17	45	7	1	3	15	1
Hairgrove, Trevor, Glacier Pilots	.304	138	16	42	11	2	3	18	6

INDIVIDUAL PITCHING LEADERS
(MINIMUM 0.9 INNINGS PITCHED PER TEAM GAME)

	W	L	ERA	G	SV	IP	BB	SO
Bircher, Joe, Mat-Su	6	1	1.29	8	0	49	11	34
Orozco, Eddie, Kenai	4	2	1.52	10	1	41	18	22
Sabol, Jake, Kenai	4	1	2.36	8	0	46	13	23
Bersano, Tyler, Fairbanks AIA	7	0	2.47	9	0	51	24	37
Hauptman, Casey, Bucs	3	3	2.57	7	0	42	3	18
Cabral, Ryan, Goldpanners	5	0	2.59	9	0	49	18	34
McDowell, Chase, Goldpanners	3	2	2.63	7	0	41	12	33
White, Zach, Bucs	2	3	2.83	10	0	41	15	23
Applegate, Matt, Mat-Su	4	2	2.86	7	0	44	10	19
Jameson, Thomas, Glacier Pilots	2	7	3.40	8	0	48	11	21

ATLANTIC COLLEGIATE LEAGUE

WOLFF	W	L	PCT	GB
Quakertown Blazers	23	15	.605	—
Lehigh Valley Catz	19	17	.528	3
Jersey Pilots	18	20	.474	5
Lackawanna Lumberjacks	16	22	.421	7

KAISER	W	L	PCT	GB
Long Island Collegians	22	15	.595	—
Staten Island Tide	21	18	.538	2
Torrington Titans	21	18	.538	2
North Jersey Eagles	12	26	.316	10½

HAMPTON	W	L	PCT	GB
North Fork Ospreys	27	14	.659	—
Westhampton Aviators	22	19	.537	5
Riverhead Tomcats	19	22	.463	8
Southampton Breakers	18	23	.439	9
Sag Harbor Whalers	16	25	.390	11

PLAYOFFS—North Fork defeated Quakertown in a one-game championship.
TOP 10 PROSPECTS: 1. Chris Reed, lhp, Torrington (Jr., Stanford). 2. Chase Fowler, c, Riverhead (So., Southern Mississippi). 3. Eric Smith,

3b, Torrington (So., Stanford). 4. Billy Ferriter, of, North Fork (So., Connecticut). 5. Zack Godley, rhp, Southampton (So., Tennessee). 6. Mike Russo, rhp, Jersey (Jr., Kean, N.J.). 7. Brandon Kuter, rhp, Westhampton (So., George Mason). 8. Kevin Grove, of, Sag Harbor (R-Fr., St. John's). 9. Matt Soren, rhp, Long Island (So., Delaware). 10. David Bartuska, rhp, Lackawanna, (Jr., Dominican, N.Y.).

INDIVIDUAL BATTING LEADERS
(MINIMUM 74 PLATE APPEARANCES)

	AVG	AB	R	H	2B	3B	HR	RBI	SB
Gregory, Ken, Jersey	.473	110	19	52	10	2	1	25	6
Bamford, Joseph, Lehigh Valley	.397	73	15	29	3	0	0	9	3
Ferriter, Billy, North Fork	.373	126	32	47	8	0	2	15	17
Quigley, James, Quakertown	.352	88	25	31	11	3	1	25	4
Roeske, Brett, Long Island	.352	108	22	38	5	0	0	11	25
Citro, Matt, Jersey	.338	133	27	45	4	4	3	19	20
Kammler, Eric, Quakertown	.336	116	25	39	11	2	1	21	5
Graczyk, Zack, Torrington	.336	140	26	47	4	1	2	25	11
Kalamar, Scott, Quakertown	.331	148	29	49	10	0	0	22	16
Cornelia, Larry, Long Island	.330	91	17	30	2	0	0	14	12

INDIVIDUAL PITCHING LEADERS
(MINIMUM 35 INNINGS)

	W	L	ERA	G	SV	IP	H	BB	SO
Scudero, Michael, Long Island	6	0	0.62	8	1	43	24	10	37
Mandarino, Mike, Southampton	4	3	0.83	8	0	54	41	17	41
Shimo, Brandon, Lackawanna	3	2	1.04	12	1	35	31	15	31
Drinks, David, Quakertown	5	1	1.09	10	0	49	46	9	34
Macaluso, Dom, Riverhead	3	1	1.21	11	2	45	27	9	30
Lamacchia, Derek, North Fork	5	1	1.37	8	0	46	23	23	40
Cardona, Tom, Sag Harbor	3	3	1.62	10	0	44	34	17	39
Glynne, Harry, Torrington	3	1	1.80	7	0	40	29	7	17
Monteagudo, Victor, N. Jersey	4	2	2.14	7	0	46	33	15	45
Bartuska, Dave, Lackawanna	1	3	2.33	10	2	39	30	5	37

CAL RIPKEN COLLEGIATE LEAGUE

	W	L	PCT	GB
Youse's Orioles	29	13	.690	—
Baltimore Redbirds	28	14	.667	1
Bethesda Big Train	26	16	.619	3
Herndon Braves	22	20	.524	7
Rockville Express	19	22	.463	9½
Alexandria Aces	17	25	.405	12
Southern Maryland Nationals	14	28	.333	15
Silver Spring-Takoma T-Bolts	12	29	.293	16½

PLAYOFFS— Bethesda defeated Baltimore in the championship of a four-team, double-elimination tournament.
TOP 10 PROSPECTS: 1. Glynn Davis, of/1b, Youse's Orioles (SIGNED: Orioles). 2. Blake Hauser, rhp, Youse's Orioles (So., Virginia Commonwealth). 3. Keenan Kish, rhp, Youse's Orioles (Fr., Florida). 4. Josh Conway, rhp/if, Baltimore (So., Coastal Carolina). 5. Cody Allen, rhp, Bethesda (Jr., High Point). 6. Ben Carhart, rhp/3b, Youse's Orioles (Jr., Stetson). 7. Johnny Bladel, of, Herndon (So., James Madison). 8. Patrick Scoggin, rhp, Baltimore (So., Virginia Tech). 9. Rand Ravnaas, of, Alexandria (Jr., Georgetown). 10. Bryan Hamilton, rhp, Bethesda (Sr., Charlotte).

INDIVIDUAL BATTING LEADERS
(MINIMUM 2.7 PLATE APPEARANCES PER TEAM GAME)

	AVG	AB	R	H	2B	3B	HR	RBI	SB
Culverson, Kasey, Rockville	.360	100	12	36	6	1	0	7	12
Blair, Patrick, Youse's	.348	115	19	40	9	1	2	18	5
Kime, Nick, Herndon	.333	117	22	39	6	2	2	12	7
Rhine, Mark, Baltimore	.333	141	22	47	7	0	0	13	7
Bladel, Johnny, Herndon	.317	123	21	39	6	3	1	23	29
Stienstra, Danny, Bethesda	.315	149	27	47	6	0	0	18	5
Whitten, Fran, T-Bolts	.315	143	14	45	8	0	1	15	3
Davis, Will, Alexandria	.315	149	16	47	9	1	4	25	0
Ravnaas, Rand, Alexandria	.313	131	19	41	8	4	3	26	15
Maas, Jeremy, Herndon	.311	161	25	50	12	0	2	15	8

INDIVIDUAL PITCHING LEADERS
(MINIMUM 0.8 INNINGS PITCHED PER TEAM GAME)

	W	L	ERA	G	SV	IP	H	BB	SO
Geiger, Blake, Youse's	4	1	0.63	8	0	43	24	12	42
Knowles, Max, Alexandria	6	2	1.23	10	0	66	52	14	60

Zimmer, Kyle, Alexandria	2	2	1.57	10	1	46	46	11	32
O'Grady, Christopher, Youse's	2	2	1.64	8	0	49	30	18	31
Tobik, Dan, T-Bolts	1	3	1.93	13	0	42	36	12	44
Austin, Tyler, Baltimore	4	1	2.16	7	0	42	21	18	41
Haynes, Kyle, Baltimore	4	2	2.29	7	0	35	31	17	17
Love, Cameron, Bethesda	5	2	2.57	8	0	49	50	9	31
Cooney, Tim, Baltimore	4	1	2.60	8	0	45	38	10	39
Rothschild, Brooks, T-Bolts	2	2	2.68	8	0	44	33	27	27

CALIFORNIA COLLEGIATE LEAGUE

	W	L	PCT	GB
Santa Barbara Foresters	29	7	.806	—
San Luis Obispo Blues	24	12	.667	5
MLB Academy Barons	17	19	.472	12
Santa Maria Packers	16	20	.444	13
Team Vegas Baseball Club	16	20	.444	13
Conejo Oaks	13	23	.361	16
San Luis Obispo Rattlers	11	25	.306	18

TOP 10 PROSPECTS: 1. Ryon Healy, 3b, Conejo Oaks (Fr., Oregon). 2. Hoby Milner, lhp, Santa Barbara (So., Texas). 3. Kevin Gausman, rhp, Team Vegas (Fr., Louisiana State). 4. Sam Stafford, lhp, Santa Barbara (Jr., Texas). 5. Carson Smith, rhp, Santa Barbara (Jr., Texas State). 6. Chris Joyce, lhp, Santa Barbara (So., Santa Barbara CC). 7. Jordan Shipers, lhp, Team Vegas (SIGNED: Mariners). 8. Kris Bryant, 3b, Team Vegas (Fr., San Diego). 9. Sean Yost, rhp, SLO Blues (Jr., Nebraska). 10. Michael Ratterree, 2b, Santa Barbara (So., Rice).

INDIVIDUAL BATTING LEADERS
(MINIMUM 2.5 PLATE AT-BATS PER TEAM GAME)

	AVG	AB	R	H	2B	3B	HR	RBI	SB
Juengel, Matt, Blues	.378	143	37	54	10	1	2	23	22
Mallory, Chris, Santa Maria	.373	166	33	62	9	3	5	29	19
Melino, Nick, Santa Barbara	.365	156	36	57	9	3	5	28	10
Healy, Ryon, Conejo	.360	178	29	64	17	0	4	38	2
Hannick, Chris, Conejo	.333	165	33	55	13	0	5	34	1
McVaney, Jeff, Santa Barbara	.329	158	30	52	14	6	0	30	13
Aguayo, Ryan, Blues	.321	156	27	50	12	0	3	25	4
Rathjen, Jeremy, Santa Barbara	.320	125	29	40	6	2	3	26	21
Kindel, Mike, Blues	.307	140	23	43	8	3	0	19	20
Brooks, James, Santa Maria	.303	119	17	36	10	0	2	20	13

INDIVIDUAL PITCHING LEADERS
(MINIMUM 0.8 INNINGS PITCHED PER TEAM GAME)

	W	L	ERA	SV	IP	H	BB	SO
Mirowski, Richie, Rattlers	3	2	1.64	0	44	38	10	53
Joyce, Chris, Santa Barbara	5	0	1.69	0	48	24	30	62
Nielbeck, Michael, Rattlers	2	1	1.71	0	42	33	7	28
Shipers, Jordan, Team Vegas	2	2	1.80	0	30	24	22	25
Morris, Matt, Santa Maria	3	2	2.10	0	51	46	13	20
Duke, Brock, Blues	4	1	2.47	1	40	31	21	47
Walters, Blair, Conejo	4	3	2.61	0	62	57	12	64
Plum, Ryan, Santa Maria	4	3	2.87	0	63	64	19	51
Salles, J.D., Rattlers	4	0	3.10	0	41	31	17	30
Lindsey, Sam, Team Vegas	3	1	3.55	0	33	42	14	24

COASTAL PLAIN LEAGUE

NORTH	W	L	PCT	GB
Wilson Tobs	37	19	.661	—
Edenton Steamers	32	23	.582	4 ½
Peninsula Pilots	32	24	.571	5
Outer Banks Daredevils	23	31	.426	13
Petersburg Generals	13	43	.232	24

SOUTH	W	L	PCT	GB
Morehead City Marlins	34	20	.630	—
Florence RedWolves	32	23	.582	2 ½
Wilmington Sharks	27	29	.482	8
Columbia Blowfish	24	31	.436	10 ½
Fayetteville SwampDogs	21	32	.396	12 ½

WEST	W	L	PCT	GB
Forest City Owls	37	19	.661	—
Gastonia Grizzlies	35	21	.625	2
Asheboro Copperheads	27	28	.491	9 ½

Martinsville Mustangs	22	33	.400	14 ½
Thomasville HiToms	17	37	.315	19

PLAYOFFS— Forest City defeated Edenton 2-1 in a best-of-three championship series of an eight-team tournament.

TOP 10 PROSPECTS: 1. Carter Capps, rhp, Fayetteville (So., Mount Olive, N.C.). 2. Buck Farmer, rhp, Peninsula (So., Georgia Tech). 3. Will Lamb, lhp/of, Peninsula (Jr., Clemson). 4. Peter Mooney, ss, Florence (Jr., South Carolina). 5. Brian Billigen, of, Edenton (Jr., Cornell). 6. Jordan Jankowski, rhp, Thomasville (Jr., Miami, Ohio). 7. Chas Crane, 3b, Peninsula (Jr., Winthrop). 8. Mark Montgomery, rhp, Edenton (Jr., Longwood). 9. Chase Boruff, rhp, Forest City (SIGNED: Royals). 10. Kramer Sneed, lhp, Wilson (SIGNED: Yankees).

INDIVIDUAL BATTING LEADERS
(MINIMUM 149 PLATE APPEARANCES)

	AVG	AB	R	H	2B	3B	HR	RBI	SB
Rusbarsky, A.J., Edenton	.345	200	29	69	10	1	0	23	15
Crane, Chas, Peninsula	.344	180	37	62	15	2	9	48	11
Hargis, Cass, Thomasville	.326	193	30	63	9	3	3	23	15
Billigen, Brian, Edenton	.325	194	31	63	9	5	6	34	19
Grabe, Eric, Fayetteville	.316	193	23	61	12	1	3	33	8
Boyd, Seth, Gastonia	.315	184	36	58	8	0	1	23	13
Ridge, Hunter, Asheboro	.315	178	34	56	9	1	4	24	3
Frederick, Tyler, Thomasville	.310	142	13	44	9	0	0	17	7
Hernandez, Trey, Florence	.309	175	28	54	12	0	5	40	0
Skinner, Will, Forest City	.307	202	32	62	23	2	5	30	3

INDIVIDUAL PITCHING LEADERS
(MINIMUM 44 INNINGS)

	W	L	ERA	G	SV	IP	H	BB	SO
Saranthus, Coty, Edenton	7	0	0.68	30	1	53	18	9	59
Holmes, Colby, Florence	3	3	1.18	8	1	46	27	22	40
Cornelius, Jonathan, Martinsville	5	1	1.23	10	0	73	39	10	91
Capps, Carter, Fayetteville	3	1	1.60	11	4	45	35	10	47
Nikorak, Steve, Wilson	6	2	1.76	11	2	51	39	21	36
Underwood, Jordan, Gastonia	4	2	1.77	9	0	56	51	19	44
Powers, Brent, Morehead City	7	2	1.86	9	0	53	36	15	70
Taylor, Zach, Wilmington	4	2	1.91	11	0	47	31	12	32
Fant, Jeremy, Forest City	3	2	1.91	11	0	47	37	12	40
Arrowood, Ryan, Forest City	2	4	1.99	8	0	50	35	13	53

FLORIDA COLLEGIATE SUMMER LEAGUE

	W	L	PCT	GB
Winter Park Diamond Dawgs	28	11	.718	—
Sanford River Rats	28	13	.683	1
Leesburg Lightning	19	23	.452	10 ½
Orlando Mavericks	15	25	.375	13 ½
DeLand Suns	11	29	.275	17 ½

PLAYOFFS— Winter Park defeated Leesburg in the championship of a five-team playoff.

TOP 10 PROSPECTS: 1. Brandon Thomas, of, Sanford (So., Georgia Tech). 2. Jabari Blash, of, Sanford (SIGNED: Mariners). 3. Robert Beary, c/if/of, Leesburg (Sr., South Carolina). 4. Nick Goody, rhp, Winter Park (So., State JC of Florida). 5. Spencer Theisen, of, Winter Park (Jr., Stetson). 6. Joe Lovecchio, rhp, Orlando (So., Seminole State, Fla., JC). 7. D.J. Hicks, 1b/rhp, Orlando (So., Central Florida). 8. Spencer Medick, lhp, Sanford (So., Hampden-Sydney, Va.). 9. Hunter Scantling, rhp, DeLand (Jr., Florida State). 10. Trey Pilkington, rhp, Sanford (So., Alabama).

INDIVIDUAL BATTING LEADERS
(MINIMUM 2.0 PLATE APPEARANCES PER TEAM GAME)

	AVG	AB	R	H	2B	3B	HR	RBI	SB
Kimmel, Samuel, W. Park	.378	135	21	51	7	0	1	23	9
Dantzler, Brad, W. Park	.375	96	26	36	7	2	3	29	4
Clark, Kelvin, Sanford	.333	144	31	48	13	1	1	21	2
Benzel, Tyler, Sanford	.321	165	32	53	8	0	3	26	6
Kelley, Dexter, DeLand	.314	105	20	33	7	3	1	12	17
Thomas, Brandon, Sanford	.312	138	28	43	3	1	3	21	17
Brennan, Mitchel, W. Park	.311	106	21	33	8	1	3	24	1
Coronia, Anthony, Orlando	.307	127	15	39	4	0	0	6	6
Adametz, Bryan, DeLand	.306	144	12	44	7	1	1	20	9
Blash, Jabari, Sanford	.303	66	16	20	2	1	3	17	1

INDIVIDUAL PITCHING LEADERS
(MINIMUM 0.8 INNINGS PITCHED PER TEAM GAME)

	W	L	ERA	G	SV	IP	H	BB	SO
Bolling, Bobby, Winter Park	4	0	1.42	6	0	38	30	13	25
Strawn, Josh, Sanford	4	1	1.75	9	0	46	39	11	22
Goody, Nick, Winter Park	4	2	1.84	9	2	34	17	9	40
Wahl, Kyle, Leesburg	2	2	2.16	9	0	42	40	19	41
Kovacs, Nic, Leesburg	2	4	2.33	9	0	46	44	10	24
Rowe, Kyle, DeLand	1	2	2.38	9	0	34	35	20	23
Renner, Brad, Sanford	3	2	2.57	12	1	42	31	15	29
Starbird, Steven, Orlando	5	1	2.63	9	0	55	46	14	42
Lovecchio, Joe, Orlando	2	1	2.73	6	0	33	31	7	19
Madden, Corben, Orlando	2	2	2.81	8	0	32	23	28	21

GREAT LAKES LEAGUE

	W	L	PCT	GB
Licking County Settlers	29	11	.725	—
Hamilton Joes	25	15	.625	4
Southern Ohio Copperheads	23	14	.622	4 ½
Stark County Terriers	21	19	.525	8
Delaware Cows	19	19	.500	9
Cincinnati Steam	17	19	.472	10
Lima Locos	18	21	.462	10 ½
Grand Lake Mariners	18	22	.450	11
Lake Erie Monarchs	17	22	.436	11 ½
Xenia Scouts	15	25	.375	14
Lexington Hustlers	12	27	.308	16 ½

PLAYOFFS—Hamilton defeated Licking County in the championship of a six-team, double-elimination tournament.

TOP 10 PROSPECTS: 1. Adam Brett Walker, of, Licking County (So., Jacksonville). 2. Brent Suter, lhp, Hamilton (Jr., Harvard). 3. Ryan Rua, ss, Hamilton (Jr., Lake Erie, Ohio, College). 4. Ryan Jones, 2b, Southern Ohio (So., Michigan State). 5. John McCambridge, of, Licking County (Sr., Xavier). 6. Brennen Glass, rhp, Grand Lake (Sr., Kent State). 7. Seth Streich, rhp, Southern Ohio (So., Ohio). 8. Zach Isler, rhp, Cincinnati (So., Cincinnati). 9. Justin Riddell, of, Lexington (Sr., Cincinnati). 10. J.T. Odom, rhp, Lima (Sr., Mercer).

INDIVIDUAL BATTING LEADERS
(MINIMUM 2.0 PLATE APPEARANCES PER TEAM GAME)

	AVG	AB	R	H	2B	3B	HR	RBI	SB
Austin, Jamal, Lima	.463	82	18	38	7	1	0	11	13
McCambridge, John, LC	.444	153	32	68	8	1	0	22	0
Jones, Ryan, Southern Ohio	.385	109	31	42	3	3	1	16	22
Riddell, Justin, Lexington	.385	148	28	57	17	0	5	28	1
Thomas, Ben, Cincinnati	.354	113	25	40	9	2	2	29	3
Douglas, Andrew, Xenia	.347	121	19	42	8	2	3	23	7
Shaw, Evan, Delaware	.346	133	32	46	4	0	0	10	17
Brenner, Ryan, Grand Lake	.345	87	24	30	5	1	0	3	28
Walker II, Adam, LC	.344	131	29	45	9	3	8	35	6
Redmon, Travis, Lexington	.343	137	18	47	13	1	1	14	7

INDIVIDUAL PITCHING LEADERS
(MINIMUM 0.8 INNINGS PITCHED PER TEAM GAME)

	W	L	ERA	G	SV	IP	H	BB	SO
Odom, J.T., Lima	3	1	0.82	21	6	33	14	7	47
Suter, Brent, Hamilton	5	0	1.27	8	0	50	32	9	47
Hayes, David, Delaware	4	1	1.64	9	0	44	40	17	27
Mace, Ryan, Licking County	3	0	1.64	7	0	38	32	9	24
Gerdeman, Ross, Grand Lake	5	2	2.27	17	0	32	29	12	19
Gulbransen, Jon, LC	4	1	2.39	7	0	38	37	7	26
Radon, Alex, Lake Erie	2	3	2.57	9	0	42	31	16	20
Newhart, Tyler, Stark County	3	0	3.00	8	0	39	43	14	20
Glass, Brennan, Grand Lake	0	4	3.05	11	2	38	31	11	26
Johnson, Michael, Xenia	2	4	3.09	14	1	35	31	14	23

HAWAII COLLEGIATE LEAGUE

	W	L	PCT	GB
Oahu Paddlers	22	13	.629	—
Waikiki Surfers	20	15	.571	2
Waimea Waves	18	17	.513	4
Kamuela Paniolos	17	18	.486	5
Kauai Menehunes	14	21	.400	8
Hawaii Aliis	14	21	.400	8

PLAYOFFS—Waikiki defeated Kauai in a six-team, double-elimination tournament.

TOP 10 PROSPECTS: 1. Joc Pederson, of, Waimea (SIGNED: Dodgers). 2. Kai'ana Eldredge, c/ss, Oahu (Fr., Kansas). 3. Jimmy Roberts, ss, Kamuela (Fr., Southern California). 4. Ridge Carpenter, of, Kauai (Sr., Cal State Northridge). 5. Daniel Rockett, of, Waikiki (So., Texas-San Antonio). 6. Paul Snieder, 1b/rhp, Kauai (Jr., Northwestern). 7. Jonathan Meyer, rhp, Oahu (So., Clemson). 8. Ben McQuown, of, Waikiki (So., Lower Columbia Basin JC). 9. Robert Rogers, rhp, Hawaii (So., Binghamton). 10. Tyler Kuresa, 1b, Oahu (Fr., Oregon).

INDIVIDUAL BATTING LEADERS
(MINIMUM 3.1 PLATE APPEARANCES PER TEAM GAME)

	AVG	AB	R	H	2B	3B	HR	RBI	SB
Rockett, Daniel, Waikiki	.345	116	33	40	8	4	2	22	13
Laurendeau, Jack, Oahu	.343	140	24	48	6	3	0	23	21
Hendrickson, Cullen, Kauai	.333	147	25	49	6	1	0	33	5
Wells, Mitch, Kamuela	.328	122	14	40	11	2	0	26	5
Harrison, Matt, Waimea	.327	104	9	34	8	0	0	20	4
Aurricih, Alexander, Kamuela	.324	105	18	34	7	2	0	14	10
McQuown, Ben, Waikiki	.322	121	30	39	8	0	2	15	29
Pederson, Joc, Waimea	.319	116	23	37	10	2	0	19	6
Vogelsang, Cal, Waimea	.305	105	26	32	11	1	2	21	9
Eldredge, Ka'iana, Oahu	.305	105	28	32	6	1	1	16	14

INDIVIDUAL PITCHING LEADERS
(MINIMUM 0.8 INNINGS PITCHED PER TEAM GAME)

	W	L	ERA	G	SV	IP	H	BB	SO
Meyer, Jonathan, Oahu	4	1	1.22	7	0	37	30	11	40
Rogers, Robert, Hawaii	3	0	1.25	8	0	36	24	15	29
Ibanez, Peter, Oahu	7	2	1.93	15	1	33	22	3	20
Dyer, Kyle, Waikiki	4	0	1.99	10	1	59	41	14	38
Mark, Ricks, Kamuela	4	1	2.06	9	2	44	33	16	42
Greenhouse, Jack, Waimea	2	2	2.20	8	0	33	24	14	14
Gailey, Matt, Kauai	3	2	2.90	10	0	50	51	26	23
Duffie, Tyler, Kamuela	4	2	2.92	8	0	37	26	23	36
Tolmachoff, Alex, Oahu	4	1	3.19	9	0	54	54	8	28
Smith, Morgan, Oahu	3	0	3.57	8	0	45	47	13	17

JAYHAWK LEAGUE

	W	L	PCT	GB
Haysville Heat	23	8	.742	—
Liberal BeeJays	22	12	.647	2 ½
Hays Larks	17	15	.531	6 ½
El Dorado Broncos	11	18	.379	11
Derby Twins	11	21	.344	12 ½
Dodge City A's	11	21	.344	12 ½

TOP 10 PROSPECTS: 1. Charlie Lowell, lhp, El Dorado (Jr., Wichita State). 2. Brian Flynn, lhp, El Dorado (So., Wichita State). 3. Kelby Tomlinson, ss, Liberal (Jr., Texas Tech). 4. Brock Green, 3b/1b, Dodge City/Haysville (Jr., Ouachita Baptist, Ark.). 5. Ben Kline, ss, Haysville (Jr., Creighton). 6. Connor Sinclair, rhp, El Dorado (Jr., Lipscomb). 7. Garrett Bayliff, of, Derby (So., Wichita State). 8. Brian Martin, of, Hays (Sr., Bradley). 9. Kirk Walker, 3b, El Dorado (Sr., Oklahoma City). 10. Andrew Heck, rhp/of, Hays (Sr., Oklahoma State).

INDIVIDUAL BATTING LEADERS
(MINIMUM 80 PLATE APPEARANCES)

	AVG	AB	H	2B	3B	HR	RBI
Owens, Gary, Haysville	.391	110	43	7	1	6	24
Martin, Brian, Hays	.386	127	49	11	2	2	22
Walker, Kirk, El Dorado	.375	96	36	7	0	3	23
Tomlinson, Kelby, Liberal	.363	135	49	11	2	0	18
Noonan, Zach, El Dorado	.359	92	33	8	0	0	8
Pfister, K.C., Haysville	.359	128	46	8	1	6	31
Kline, Ben, Haysville	.359	103	37	10	1	5	26
Gomez, Mark, Liberal	.342	117	40	12	1	4	33
Miller, Justin, Haysville	.341	126	43	9	1	6	19
Green, Brock, Dodge City	.336	110	37	13	0	3	26

INDIVIDUAL PITCHING LEADERS
(MINIMUM 20 INNINGS)

	W	L	ERA	IP	H	SO
McBride, Mike, Liberal	3	0	2.10	34	28	18
Anderson, Jon, Derby	3	4	2.32	44	35	37

Heck, Andrew, Hays	5	0	2.50	50	58	31
Rea, Robbie, El Dorado	0	0	2.61	22	17	17
Harden, David, Haysville	6	0	2.66	47	41	30
Parker, Travis, Liberal	2	2	2.66	25	26	18
Zinkovich, Justin, Haysville	3	3	2.70	38	32	35
Gonzalez, Paul, Liberal	4	0	3.12	36	35	30
Stone, Tucker, Haysville	4	1	3.30	45	38	31
Markel, Parker, Liberal	3	2	3.31	34	25	36

MINK LEAGUE

NORTH	W	L	PCT	GB
St. Joseph Mustangs	26	15	.634	—
Chillicothe Mudcats	26	16	.619	½
Clarinda A's	22	17	.564	3
Excelsior Springs Cougars	17	22	.436	8
Omaha Diamond Spirit	12	30	.286	14 ½

SOUTH	W	L	PCT	GB
Sedalia Bombers	35	8	.814	—
Nevada Griffons	22	19	.537	12
Joplin Outlaws	12	21	.364	18
Ozark Generals	13	23	.361	18 ½
Mac-N-Seitz A's	8	22	.267	20 ½

PLAYOFFS—Sedalia defeated Chillicothe 2-0 in best-of-three championship series.

TOP 10 PROSPECTS: 1. Mike Kickham, lhp, Sedalia (SIGNED: Giants). 2. Johnny Coy, 1b, St. Joseph (So., Wichita State). 3. Jeremy Patton, 2b, Sedalia (Jr., Florida International). 4. Matt Skipper, 1b, Mac-N-Seitz (Jr., San Diego State). 5. Jose Behar, c, Sedalia (Sr., Florida International). 6. Luke Voit, c, Sedalia (So., Missouri State). 7. Dan Kickham, rhp, Sedalia (Jr., Missouri State). 8. Mark Robinette, rhp, Chillicothe (So., Northeast Texas CC). 9. Jake Johansen, rhp, Omaha (So., Dallas Baptist). 10. Jon Wegener, of, Sedalia (Sr., Central Missouri).

INDIVIDUAL BATTING LEADERS
(MINIMUM 2.7 PLATE APPEARANCES PER TEAM GAME)

	AVG	AB	R	H	2B	3B	HR	RBI	SB
Behar, Jose, Sedalia	.433	120	19	52	10	0	0	26	2
Skipper, Matt, Mac-N-Seitz	.367	79	17	29	10	0	4	15	1
Carter, Zach, Nevada	.362	138	24	50	16	0	4	30	3
Robinette, Mark, Chillicothe	.355	124	14	44	10	1	2	26	4
Templeton, Louie, Chillicothe	.352	108	25	38	11	1	1	12	21
Peterson, Ryan, Clarinda	.346	130	27	45	17	2	0	19	12
Coy, Johnny, St. Joseph	.340	141	29	48	9	1	12	49	7
McComack, Travis, Sedalia	.336	131	25	44	11	1	0	19	3
Quinn, Cody, Nevada	.328	116	26	38	11	3	5	25	2
Collins, Matt, Clarinda	.326	89	17	29	1	0	1	21	5

INDIVIDUAL PITCHING LEADERS
(MINIMUM 0.8 INNINGS PITCHED PER TEAM GAME)

	W	L	ERA	G	SV	IP	H	BB	SO
Potje, Danny, Sedalia	5	0	1.50	8	0	42	30	17	48
Potter, Sean, Chillicothe	4	3	1.62	9	0	48	37	16	38
Trudell, Cory, Chillicothe	5	1	1.68	10	0	50	36	29	61
Alva, Austin, Clarinda	4	2	1.91	8	0	44	32	21	35
Robinette, Mark, Chillicothe	2	2	2.08	9	1	37	22	17	49
Wallmeyer, Gabriel, Clarinda	3	2	2.15	6	0	39	36	7	14
Parson, Ryan, Nevada	4	0	2.22	8	0	35	31	6	25
Powers, Jake, Sedalia	6	2	2.23	16	1	38	34	20	43
Schaeffer, Tony, Excelsior Springs	2	2	2.28	11	0	40	37	15	21
Trentacosta, Mark, Clarinda	5	2	2.33	10	0	54	44	25	49

NEW ENGLAND COLLEGIATE LEAGUE

EAST	W	L	PCT	GB
Newport Gulls	27	15	.643	—
North Shore Navigators	25	17	.595	2
Sanford Mainers	23	19	.548	4
Laconia Muskrats	20	22	.476	7
New Bedford Bay Sox	18	24	.429	9
Lowell All-Americans	15	27	.357	12

WEST	W	L	PCT	GB
North Adams SteepleCats	26	16	.619	—
Danbury Westerners	24	18	.571	2
Bristol Collegiate	23	19	.548	3

Keene Swamp Bats	20	22	.476	6
Holyoke Blue Sox	16	26	.381	10
Vermont Mountaineers	15	27	.357	11

PLAYOFFS—Quarterfinals: North Shore defeated Sanford 2-1, Danbury defeated Bristol 2-1, North Adams defeated Keene 2-1, Newport defeated Laconia 2-0. **Semifinals:** North Shore defeated Newport 2-1, Danbury defeated North Adams 2-1. **Finals:** North Shore defeated Danbury 2-1 in best-of-three championship series.

TOP 10 PROSPECTS: 1. Kenny Diekroeger, ss, Newport (So., Stanford). 2. Mark Appel, rhp, Newport (So., Stanford). 3. Jeremy Baltz, of, Keene (So., St. John's). 4. Mike Williams, c, Danbury (Jr., Kentucky). 5. Evan Marzilli, of, Laconia (So., South Carolina). 6. Matt Carasiti, rhp, Bristol (So., St. John's). 7. Alex Wood, lhp, Keene (So. Georgia). 8. Ian Gardeck, rhp, Danbury (So., Angelina, Texas, JC). 9. William Carmona, 3b/of, Vermont (So., Stony Brook). 10. Jarett Miller, rhp, Laconia (Jr., UNC Greensboro).

INDIVIDUAL BATTING LEADERS
(MINIMUM 2.7 PLATE APPEARANCES PER TEAM GAME)

	AVG	AB	R	H	2B	3B	HR	RBI	SB
Chavez, Matt, New Bedford	.355	141	20	50	11	0	4	22	1
Petty, Matt, North Adams	.352	128	27	45	13	0	4	20	9
Banos, Jason, North Shore	.348	132	21	46	5	2	1	15	8
Valdez, Effrey, Lowell	.337	163	25	55	16	3	4	42	1
Schult, Jim, Sanford	.333	105	17	35	6	1	2	14	3
Diekroeger, Kenny, Newport	.324	139	17	45	9	1	2	19	5
Gallic, Michael, Bristol	.324	145	22	47	7	1	0	15	12
Miller, Matt, Lowell	.315	162	30	51	7	0	1	13	10
Wendle, Joe, Sanford	.311	164	31	51	4	2	1	15	11
Baltz, Jeremy, Keene	.301	113	25	34	6	0	2	15	2

INDIVIDUAL PITCHING LEADERS
(MINIMUM 0.8 INNINGS PITCHED PER TEAM GAME)

	W	L	ERA	G	SV	IP	H	BB	SO
Bucciferro, Tony, Newport	4	1	0.82	8	0	44	27	8	42
Hauschild, Mike, Danbury	6	2	1.24	9	0	58	36	17	50
Parker, Ryland, North Adams	3	0	1.53	7	0	35	24	10	30
Nixon, Robert, North Adams	2	3	1.80	8	0	50	44	6	39
Ramey, Dustin, Sanford	3	2	1.82	7	0	35	23	16	18
Appel, Mark, Newport	6	1	1.87	8	0	43	33	16	24
Brown, Geoff, Newport	3	0	1.96	8	0	37	29	10	25
Joyner, Tyler, Laconia	2	2	1.97	9	0	46	33	22	53
Bare, Crayton, North Shore	3	1	1.98	9	0	41	27	12	25
Wood, Taylor, Holyoke	2	4	2.06	8	0	48	47	11	43

NEW YORK COLLEGIATE LEAGUE

WEST	W	L	PCT	GB
Elmira Pioneers	27	15	.643	—
Allegany County Nitros	22	17	.564	3 ½
Webster Yankees	22	19	.537	4 ½
Alfred Thunder	20	22	.476	7
Geneva Red Wings	19	23	.463	7 ½
Hornell Dodgers	19	23	.452	8
Niagara Power	15	26	.366	11 ½

EAST	W	L	PCT	GB
Amsterdam Mohawks	27	15	.643	—
Oneonta Outlaws	26	16	.619	1
Glens Falls Golden Eagles	22	20	.524	5
Cooperstown Hawkeyes	21	21	.500	6
Mohawk Valley DiamondDawgs	17	22	.436	8 ½
Watertown Wizards	15	24	.385	10 ½
Albany Dutchmen	16	26	.381	11

PLAYOFFS—Quarterfinals: Amsterdam defeated Cooperstown 2-0, Elmira defeated Alfred 2-0, Allegany County defeated Webster 2-1, Glens Falls defeated Oneonta 2-0. **Semifinals:** Amsterdam defeated Glens Falls 2-0, Elmira defeated Allegany County 2-0. **Championship:** Amsterdam defeated Elmira 2-0 in best-of-three championship series.

TOP 10 PROSPECTS: 1. Mel Rojas Jr., of, Amsterdam (SIGNED: Pirates). 2. Jon Schwind, if, Amsterdam (Jr., Marist). 3. Cody Kulp, of, Amsterdam (Jr., Amsterdam). 4. Kyle Hunter, lhp, Amsterdam (So., Dartmouth). 5. Dan Zlotnick, lhp, Amsterdam (So., Marist). 6. Vincent Mejia, if, Glens Falls (Jr., Texas-Pan American). 7. Matt Conway, 1b/lhp, Amsterdam (So., Wake Forest). 8. John Colella, rhp, Elmira (So., Holy Cross). 9. Alex Todd, ss, Cooperstown (Sr., Sonoma, Calif., State). 10. Shae Simmons, rhp, Watertown (So., Southeast Missouri State).

INDIVIDUAL BATTING LEADERS
(MINIMUM 3.0 PLATE APPEARANCES PER TEAM GAME)

	AVG	AB	R	H	2B	3B	HR	RBI	SB
Simone, Jason, Mohawk Valley	.372	145	24	54	6	0	0	17	17
Fisher, Tyler, Allegany County	.366	142	30	52	15	0	5	25	4
Richardson, Kyle, Mohawk Valley	.366	134	28	49	3	0	2	16	15
Gilot, Dan, Geneva	.344	125	19	43	10	2	1	25	11
Snyder, John, Elmira	.338	145	32	49	7	2	1	26	13
Ferguson, Ryan, Elmira	.333	153	26	51	14	1	1	29	2
Boulter, Matt, Webster	.331	145	29	48	8	2	1	20	6
Mejia, Vincent, Glens Falls	.329	155	21	51	16	0	4	34	3
Keller, Corey, Elmira	.329	140	22	46	5	3	1	16	4
Rickenbach, Jake, Elmira	.327	162	34	53	8	1	1	15	3

INDIVIDUAL PITCHING LEADERS
(MINIMUM 1.0 INNINGS PITCHED PER TEAM GAME)

	W	L	ERA	G	SV	IP	H	BB	SO
Hicks, Isaac, Allegany County	3	4	1.38	8	0	52	41	8	27
Mayberry, Whit, Oneonta	3	0	1.52	8	0	53	47	9	34
Zlotnick, Dan, Amsterdam	4	0	1.57	10	0	46	39	15	43
Martin, Beau, Allegany County	2	0	1.92	9	0	56	45	16	32
Shore, Tyler, Niagara	3	2	2.05	18	1	61	56	18	27
Wiley, Justin, Watertown	2	2	2.23	7	1	40	33	18	33
Koehler, Brett, Glens Falls	2	1	2.28	8	0	51	46	9	29
James, Justin, Allegany County	5	2	2.28	9	0	47	35	23	51
Sumple, Kyle, Glens Falls	3	1	2.44	11	0	52	43	29	38
Dooley, Kevin, Geneva	2	3	2.45	8	0	48	44	16	29

NORTHWOODS LEAGUE

NORTH	W	L	PCT	GB
St. Cloud River Bats	40	28	.588	—
Willmar Stingers	39	31	.557	2
Rochester Honkers	36	29	.554	2 ½
Duluth Huskies	34	32	.515	5
Brainerd Lakes Area Lunkers	32	36	.471	8
Alexandria Beetles	32	38	.457	9
Thunder Bay Border Cats	31	38	.449	9 ½
Mankato MoonDogs	29	41	.414	12

SOUTH	W	L	PCT	GB
Eau Claire Express	48	22	.686	—
Wisconsin Woodchucks	42	28	.600	6
Madison Mallards	41	29	.586	7
Green Bay Bullfrogs	39	31	.557	9
La Crosse Loggers	39	31	.557	9
Waterloo Bucks	31	39	.443	17
Wisconsin Rapids Rafters	20	50	.286	28
Battle Creek Bombers	20	50	.286	28

PLAYOFFS—Semifinals: Eau Claire defeated Wisconsin 2-1, Rochester defeated St. Cloud 2-0. **Championship:** Eau Claire defeated Rochester 2-1 in best-of-three championship series.

TOP 20 PROSPECTS: 1. Steve Nyisztor, ss, St. Cloud (So., Rutgers). 2. Kyle Gaedele, of, Madison (Jr., Valparaiso). 3. Sam Selman, lhp, Mankato (So., Vanderbilt). 4. Cody Asche, 3b/1b, Duluth (Jr., Nebraska). 5. Harold Riggins, 1b/of, Madison (Jr., North Carolina State). 6. Scott Schebler, of, Green Bay (SIGNED: Dodgers). 7. Andrew Aplin, of, St. Cloud (So., Arizona State). 8. Marcus Semien, ss, Alexandria (Jr., California). 9. Sean Dwyer, of/1b, Willmar (Fr., Florida Gulf Coast). 10. Madison Boer, rhp, La Crosse (Jr., Oregon). 11. Brad Schreiber, rhp, Green Bay (So., Purdue). 12. Mike Strong, lhp, Rochester (Sr., Oklahoma State). 13. Jason Wheeler, lhp, St. Cloud (Jr., Loyola Marymount). 14. Ray Black, rhp, Brainerd Lakes Area (So., Pittsburgh). 15. Jordan Smith, of, Willmar (So., St. Cloud State, Minn.). 16. Mark Threlkeld, 3b, Duluth (Jr., Louisiana Tech). 17. Isaac Ballou, of, Willmar (So., Marshall). 18. Zeke DeVoss, of, Duluth (So., Miami). 19. J.R. Graham, rhp, Madison (Jr., Santa Clara). 20. Ben Hughes, rhp, Duluth (Jr., St. Olaf, Minn.).

INDIVIDUAL BATTING LEADERS
(MINIMUM 2.7 PLATE APPEARANCES PER TEAM GAME)

	AVG	AB	R	H	2B	3B	HR	RBI	SB
Heithoff, Drew, Eau Claire	.389	157	33	61	9	1	1	17	17
Smith, Jordan, Willmar	.374	254	45	95	8	5	5	56	11
Hutter, Joel, Green Bay	.350	183	30	64	10	0	2	31	5
Riggins, Harold, Madison	.337	166	36	56	10	0	8	32	2
Dittman, Matt, Rochester	.332	202	44	67	17	0	5	40	0
Davis, Adam, Madison	.328	204	44	67	19	3	6	44	14

Reynolds, Jeff, Duluth	.326	221	25	72	20	3	0	30	0	
Leyva, Carlos, Willmar	.323	217	44	70	3	2	0	24	29	
Rieger, Ryan, Waterloo	.322	174	23	56	12	1	7	40	1	
Coyle, Tommy, St. Cloud	.320	178	39	57	8	1	1	14	15	
Lind, Rob, Wisconsin	.320	231	49	74	15	0	4	25	15	
Schultz, John, St. Cloud	.320	175	40	56	9	8	1	20	8	

INDIVIDUAL PITCHING LEADERS
(MINIMUM 0.8 INNINGS PITCHED PER TEAM GAME)

	W	L	ERA	G	SV	IP	H	BB	SO
Wheeler, Jason, St. Cloud	8	1	1.35	15	0	67	47	15	74
Campbell, Ian, Eau Claire	7	1	1.36	10	0	60	47	25	35
Beck, Sander, Alexandria	5	3	1.41	12	0	64	31	28	58
Hurlbut, David, Rochester	3	0	1.52	12	1	53	47	21	42
Strong, Mike, Rochester	5	2	1.83	12	0	59	47	33	72
Massey, Taylor, Waterloo	5	3	1.99	12	0	72	66	28	46
Flemer, Matt, La Crosse	8	2	2.05	12	0	70	57	13	62
Collier, Robbie, Duluth	7	2	2.31	12	0	58	40	27	63
Odom, Logan, Mankato	5	3	2.35	19	1	69	52	24	66
Shellhorn, Rusty, Madison	3	3	2.40	17	1	64	49	36	58

PROSPECT LEAGUE

CENTRAL
	W	L	PCT	GB
Danville Dans	32	24	.570	—
Nashville Outlaws	30	24	.555	1
Richmond River Rats	30	26	.536	2
Terre Haute Rex	29	26	.527	2 ½
Dubois County Bombers	21	33	.389	10

EAST
	W	L	PCT	GB
Chillicothe Paints	39	17	.696	—
West Virginia Miners	26	30	.464	13
Butler Blue Sox	24	30	.444	14
Slippery Rock Sliders	21	33	.389	17
Lorain County Ironmen	21	35	.375	18

WEST
	W	L	PCT	GB
Springfield Sliders	35	19	.648	—
Quincy Gems	29	24	.547	5 ½
DeKalb County Liners	27	25	.519	7
Hannibal Cavemen	27	28	.491	8 ½
DuPage Dragons	17	34	.333	16 ½

PLAYOFFS—Chillicothe defeated Danville in a six-team playoff.
TOP 10 PROSPECTS: 1. Navery Moore, rhp, Nashville (Jr., Vanderbilt). 2. Zach Kometani, c, Quincy (Jr., San Diego). 3. Kevin Plawecki, c, Richmond (So., Purdue). 4. Chris Marlowe, lhp, West Virginia (Jr., Oklahoma State). 5. Chuck Ghysels, rhp, Richmond (Jr., Maryland). 6. Jeff Holm, of, Chillicothe (Sr., Michigan State). 7. Kenton Parmley, ss, DeKalb (Jr., Southeast Missouri State). 8. Kevan Smith, c/1b, Butler (Sr., Pittsburgh). 9. Corey Kimes, lhp, Springfield (Jr., Illinois). 10. Jon Ivie, rhp, Nashville (Sr., Belmont).

INDIVIDUAL BATTING LEADERS
(MINIMUM 2.7 PLATE APPEARANCES PER TEAM GAME)

	AVG	AB	R	H	2B	3B	HR	RBI	SB
Smith, Kevin, Nashville	.366	142	31	52	11	4	1	23	6
Holm, Jeff, Chillicothe	.359	217	56	78	18	3	11	60	38
Tierney, Jesse, Danville	.353	156	26	55	10	2	0	22	8
Smith, Kevan, Butler	.347	170	35	59	10	2	1	30	5
Fayard, Vinnie, Quincy	.344	209	35	72	6	0	4	36	7
McPike, Rob, Richmond	.329	161	30	53	6	2	1	17	4
Corrigan, Michael, Dubois County	.324	148	19	48	3	0	2	23	1
Judkins, Nick, Springfield	.324	170	24	55	11	4	2	28	9
Porter, Ryan, Hannibal	.323	192	29	62	8	2	4	37	0
Van Horn, Greg, Chillicothe	.317	164	33	52	14	5	4	33	13

INDIVIDUAL PITCHING LEADERS
(MINIMUM 0.8 INNINGS PITCHED PER TEAM GAME)

	W	L	ERA	G	SV	IP	H	BB	SO
Wolosiansky, Dean, West Virginia	5	1	1.19	9	0	68	44	25	54
McGhee, Justin, Hannibal	4	1	1.40	9	0	58	39	17	42
Brua, Phil, Lorain County	4	2	1.46	30	10	49	30	10	30
Henn, Casey, Quincy	4	1	1.49	8	0	48	24	15	46
Cabrera, Freddie, Richmond	2	3	1.74	27	4	47	40	11	41
Daniels, Gage, Dubois County	4	4	1.82	9	1	59	52	14	54

Wynveen, Ryan, DuPage	6	1	1.86	10	0	58	47	18	45
Giel, Tim, Butler	6	3	2.05	10	0	66	42	22	41
Painter, Adam, Richmond	5	3	2.37	23	0	49	41	9	49
Brandt, Aaron, Danville	6	0	2.47	10	0	66	61	12	43

TEXAS COLLEGIATE LEAGUE

	W	L	PCT	GB
Victoria Generals	30	16	.652	—
East Texas PumpJacks	32	18	.640	—
Brazos Valley Bombers	32	20	.615	1
Texas Tomcats	23	23	.500	7
Alexandria Aces	18	26	.409	11
McKinney Marshals	17	30	.362	13 ½
North Texas Copperheads	11	30	.268	16 ½

PLAYOFFS—Semifinals: Victoria defeated Texas 2-1, East Texas defeated Brazos Valley 2-1. **Championship:** Victoria defeated East Texas 2-0 in best-of-three championship series.
TOP 10 PROSPECTS: 1. Lee Orr, of, East Texas (Jr., McNeese State). 2. Miguel Pena, lhp, East Texas (So., San Jacinto JC). 3. Nick Fleece, rhp, Brazos Valley (Sr., Texas A&M). 4. Zach Nuding, rhp, North Texas (SIGNED: Yankees). 5. Zac Fisher, c, East Texas (So., New Mexico State). 6. Joe Leftridge, of, North Texas (Jr., Angelo, Texas, State). 7. Bryson Myles, of, McKinney (Jr., Stephen F. Austin State). 8. Brock Hebert, ss/2b, Texas (So., Southeastern Louisiana). 9. Mark Hudson, of, Victoria (Sr., Sam Houston State). 10. Kolt Browder, rhp, Victoria (So., Baylor).

INDIVIDUAL BATTING LEADERS
(MINIMUM 50 PLATE APPEARANCES)

	AVG	AB	R	H	2B	3B	HR	RBI	SB
Peters, Bryan, East Texas	.356	59	10	21	6	0	1	7	3
Carvutto, Matt, East Texas	.338	157	22	53	16	1	1	30	3
Hudson, Mark, Victoria	.330	103	20	34	10	1	1	20	1
Myles, Bryson, McKinney	.328	116	77	38	5	1	6	18	20
Marek, Jeramie, Victoria	.328	119	23	39	2	1	0	18	4
Grayson, Casey, Texas	.327	101	18	33	9	0	3	19	3
Fisher, Zac, East Texas	.327	165	30	54	17	1	4	34	2
White, Troy, Texas	.323	130	22	42	6	3	0	21	11
Ragsdale, Zach, McKinney	.311	74	13	23	7	0	3	10	6
Fuselier, Alex, East Texas	.303	66	13	20	2	0	2	12	12

INDIVIDUAL PITCHING LEADERS
(MINIMUM 25 INNINGS)

	W	L	ERA	G	SV	IP	H	BB	SO
Browder, Kolt, Victoria	4	1	0.65	13	4	28	7	16	47
Kottman, Brad, East Texas	4	1	1.06	11	2	51	31	18	59
Tromblee, Stephen, Texas	0	1	1.08	22	9	25	11	21	30
West, Jason, Texas	4	1	1.73	16	1	57	45	32	61
Stennett, Trevor, Alexandria	3	2	1.82	21	6	40	22	18	49
Gonzales, Abel, East Texas	5	2	1.87	9	0	43	33	15	36
Madrid, Roman, Victoria	4	1	1.88	15	3	29	15	18	32
Branstetter, Josh, Alexandria	4	1	2.12	9	0	51	33	20	48
Manville, Tony, Texas	4	4	2.17	12	0	62	51	25	46
Oros, Michael, Victoria	4	1	2.19	10	0	53	39	17	49
Parrent, Brandon, North Texas	0	2	2.19	4	0	25	15	20	14

VALLEY LEAGUE

	W	L	PCT	GB
Haymarket Senators	30	14	.682	—
Luray Wranglers	27	17	.614	3
Winchester Royals	26	18	.521	4
Front Royal Cardinals	23	21	.591	7
Harrisonburg Turks	22	22	.500	8
Waynesboro Generals	22	22	.500	8
Covington Lumberjacks	20	24	.454	10
New Market Rebels	19	25	.431	11
Rockbridge Rapids	18	26	.409	12
Staunton Braves	18	26	.409	12
Woodstock River Bandits	17	17	.386	13

PLAYOFFS—Quarterfinals: Luray defeated Convington 2-0, Front Royal defeated Waynesboro 2-1, Winchester defeated Harrisonburg 2-1, Haymarket defeated New Market 2-0. **Semifinals:** Luray defeated Winchester 2-1, Front Royal defeated Haymarket 2-1. **Championship:** Luray defeated Front Royal 2-0 in best-of-three championship series.
TOP 10 PROSPECTS: 1. Jerome Werniuk, rhp, Haymarket (So., Le Moyne).

2. Taylor Sandefur, rhp, Waynesboro (So., Western Carolina). 3. Corey Spangenberg, ss, Winchester (So., Indian River State, Fla., JC). 4. Nick Rickles, c, Luray (Jr., Stetson). 5. Rudy Flores, 1b, Haymarket (So., Florida International). 6. Vince Voiro, rhp, Woodstock (Jr., Pennsylvania). 7. Cody Weiss, rhp, Luray (Jr., La Salle). 8. Yoandy Barroso, of, Haymarket (Sr., Florida International). 9. Greg Nappo, lhp, Haymarket (Sr., Connecticut). 10. Drew Granier, rhp, Harrisonburg (Sr., Louisiana-Monroe).

INDIVIDUAL BATTING LEADERS
(MINIMUM 2.5 PLATE APPEARANCES PER TEAM GAME)

	AVG	AB	R	H	2B	3B	HR	RBI	SB
Spangenberg, Cory, Winchester	.399	203	46	37	15	1	3	81	21
Garza, Mike, Woodstock	.388	170	35	30	13	4	3	66	23
Turocy, Andrew, Waynesboro	.370	192	33	31	9	1	1	71	8
Jones, Brant, Haymarket	.352	145	29	38	7	2	5	51	7
Owen, Jordan, New Market	.345	174	31	22	8	1	3	60	9
Martinez, Mike, Covington	.336	125	24	36	3	0	10	42	2
Griffin, Jonathan, Luray	.333	189	31	44	15	0	13	63	1
Gaskill, Cody, Winchester	.323	186	33	41	10	0	9	60	3
White, Tyler, Haymarket	.315	149	28	21	7	0	2	47	5
Church, Raymond, Winchester	.314	156	31	34	9	2	4	49	5

INDIVIDUAL PITCHING LEADERS
(MINIMUM 1.0 INNINGS PITCHED PER TEAM GAME)

	W	L	ERA	G	SV	IP	H	BB	SO
Nappo, Greg, Haymarket	5	1	1.64	9	2	49	33	18	68
Jensen, Tucker, Luray	6	1	1.71	12	0	63	51	21	60
Sandefur, Taylor, Waynesboro	7	0	2.26	13	0	60	46	21	60
Rusinski, Drew, Luray	6	1	2.36	15	2	53	50	9	48
Dickson, Ian, Rockbridge	3	1	2.37	10	0	49	32	19	55
Ford, Blake, Front Royal	3	4	2.38	9	0	57	54	18	41
Mejia, Benny, Covington	1	2	2.47	8	2	47	35	17	52
Greiner, Chris, Rockbridge	2	2	2.50	10	0	58	55	22	52
Weiss, Cody, Luray	4	3	2.51	13	2	68	51	24	87
Benedict, Matthew, Haymarket	7	3	2.52	10	0	54	46	18	37

WEST COAST LEAGUE

EAST

	W	L	PCT	GB
Wenatchee AppleSox	29	19	.604	—
Kelowna Falcons	22	26	.458	7
Moses Lake Pirates	21	27	.438	8
Walla Walla Sweets	18	30	.375	11

WEST

	W	L	PCT	GB
Corvallis Knights	31	17	.646	—
Bend Elks	27	21	.563	4
Bellingham Bells	25	22	.532	5 ½
Kitsap BlueJackets	24	23	.511	6 ½
Cowlitz Black Bears	18	30	.375	13

PLAYOFFS—Semifinals: Wenatchee defeated Kelowna 2-0, Bend defeated Corvallis 2-1. **Championship:** Wenatchee defeated Bend 2-1 in best-of-three championship series.

TOP 10 PROSPECTS: 1. Stefan Sabol, c/3b/of, Cowlitz (Fr., Oregon). 2. Chase Anselment, c, Kitsap (So., Washington). 3. Jeff Ames, rhp, Wenatchee (So., Washington). 4. Scott Griggs, rhp, Bellingham (So., UCLA). 5. Mitch Haniger, of, Corvallis (So., Cal Poly). 6. Marco Gonzales, lhp, Wenatchee (Fr., Gonzaga). 7. Royce Bolinger, of, Kelowna (Jr., Gonzaga). 8. Kerry Jenkins, of, Bend (Sr., San Jose State). 9. Collin Bennett, of, Wenatchee (Jr., Hawaii). 10. Dayne Quist, lhp, Kelowna (Jr., UC Davis).

INDIVIDUAL BATTING LEADERS
(MINIMUM 2.7 PLATE APPEARANCES PER TEAM GAME)

	AVG	AB	R	H	2B	3B	HR	RBI	SB
Richards, Tommy, Bend	.364	165	28	60	10	3	2	33	4
Edelstein, Ben, Kelowna	.347	124	25	43	6	3	0	11	7
Blake, Michael, Corvallis	.344	163	19	56	6	0	1	19	10
Peterson, Eric, Wenatchee	.342	149	25	51	10	0	5	33	2
Jones, Dylan, Corvallis	.336	134	24	45	10	3	2	21	9
Roberts, Nate, Moses Lake	.335	161	23	54	9	0	1	35	5
Eslick, Clayton, Wenatchee	.333	147	28	49	6	0	0	15	9
Fox, Jordan, Cowlitz	.331	142	26	47	6	3	0	13	14
Miller, Braxton, Cowlitz	.329	146	22	48	6	1	2	25	10
Stewart, Elliot, Walla Walla	.321	131	18	42	9	1	3	24	2

INDIVIDUAL PITCHING LEADERS
(MINIMUM 0.8 INNINGS PER TEAM GAME)

	W	L	ERA	G	SV	IP	H	BB	SO
Quist, Dayne, Kelowna	6	1	1.40	9	0	51	33	18	50
Kraus, Kyle, Corvallis	5	1	1.75	8	0	46	37	8	40
Fassold, Cody, Bellingham	4	1	1.75	9	1	62	39	27	55
Garcia, Mark, Cowlitz	2	2	1.83	19	2	39	24	11	40
Dennis, Chris, Cowlitz	2	3	1.98	11	0	41	31	8	41
Mascheri, Richie, Kitsap	6	1	2.01	11	0	54	37	18	31
Davis, Greg, Bend	3	1	2.06	7	0	39	32	10	29
Guidos, Ben, Bend	3	2	2.09	8	0	52	44	7	35
Nygren, James, Bend	4	0	2.25	8	0	44	35	16	26
McIver, Michael, Wenatchee	6	2	2.42	12	0	67	67	9	50

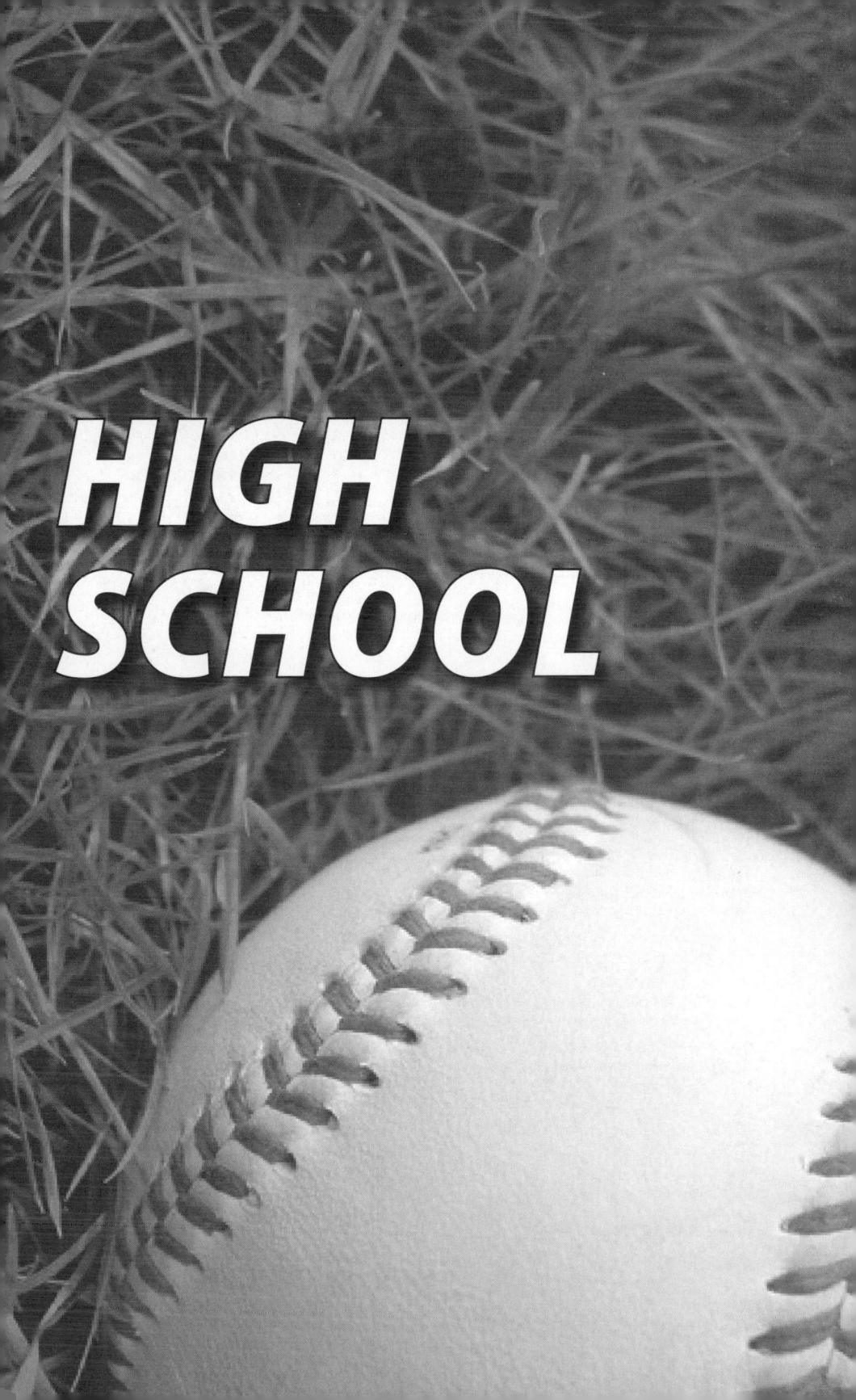

HIGH SCHOOL

Flanagan benefits from Texas state final

BY NATHAN RODE

Flanagan's Florida title also gave the school a national crown

PHIL SEARS

When Flanagan High players rushed the center of the diamond to dogpile in late May, the jubilation was for winning the Florida 6-A state title—the third in six years for the Pembroke Pines school.

A few weeks later head coach Ray Evans was pacing in a restaurant parking lot while on the phone with his second baseman Collin Martindale, who was giving the play-by-play of the seventh inning of the Texas 5-A state championship. The game was being broadcast live online, and Klein High (Spring, Texas) was down 5-2 with the tying run at the plate against Corpus Christi's Carroll High. As Carroll center fielder Mark Blackmar made a spectacular diving catch to end the game, Martindale delivered the news.

"Coach, Klein lost! We're national champs!" he said on the phone.

The loss dropped the Bearkats from the No. 1 national ranking and allowed Flanagan to claim the title of Baseball America Team of the Year in 2010. The Falcons couldn't dogpile, but there was plenty of excitement.

"I still can't believe it," Evans said. "It was really emotional, high intensity."

The Falcons put together an incredible season, going 25-2 in Florida's largest classification. After winning the state title, they jumped to No. 4 in the country, and then watched the scoreboard. In the next poll, two teams were upset in the playoffs—Bishop Amat High of La Puente, Calif. and Rockwall-Heath High of Heath, Texas—and Flanagan climbed to No. 2. Evans and his players were well aware of the possible outcomes and kept track of the other teams' performances.

Challenging Road

But Flanagan's rise to the top was certainly well earned. Losing just two games in a season is a tough task in any state, and Flanagan's losses were to quality opponents. The first came in February to American Heritage High (Plantation, Fla.)—the 2008 national champs and a perennial power. The 1-0 loss came in Flanagan's own tournament championship, with the decisive run coming in the first inning.

"When we lost that game, I told them I think they're a special team," Evans said. "These guys were a true family. There were no groups or cliques. The umpires told us after the game they were spoiled and would never see another game like that."

The Falcons won their next 11 games before meeting national No. 1 Farragut High of Knoxville. It was another tournament championship game, this time in the Orlando National Classic. Farragut's junior tandem of lefthander Philip Pfeifer and shortstop Nicky Delmonico—both first-team All-Americans and premium draft prospects for 2011—paced the Admirals' 2-0 win. Pfeifer struck out 16 and allowed just four hits in a complete game shutout while Delmonico hit a two-run double in the third inning.

"He's one of the best pitchers I've seen in high school," Evans said of Pfeifer. "We just didn't get the hits we needed."

While the Farragut game would be Flanagan's last loss, it wouldn't be the last speed bump. Senior righthander Justin Machado, the team's No. 1 starter, was taking longer to recover from starts

HIGH SCHOOL TOP 50

Flanagan High (Pembroke Pines, Fla.) took over the top spot in the final poll to be crowned national champions. Flanagan's title marks the seventh time a Florida team has finished atop the rankings. The staffs of Baseball America and the National High School Baseball Coaches Association compile the rankings. Records indicated do not include ties.

Rk.	School	Record	Previous	Season conclusion
1	Flanagan HS, Pembroke Pines, Fla.	25-2	2	State 6-A Champion
2	Bishop Gorman HS, Las Vegas	36-4	3	State 4-A Champion
3	The Bolles School, Jacksonville	29-3	4	State 3-A Champion
4	Sumrall (Miss.) HS	36-1	5	State 3-A Champion
5	Archbishop Mitty HS, San Jose, Calif.	31-3	6	CIF Central Coast Section Champion
6	Rocky Mountain HS, Fort Collins, Colo.	26-2	7	State 5-A Champion
7	Pace (Fla.) HS	29-2	8	State 5-A Champion
8	Farragut HS, Knoxville	42-6	9	State 3-A Champion
9	Columbus (Ga.) HS	32-5	10	State 3-A Champion
10	Archbishop McCarthy HS, Southwest Ranches, Fla.	27-5	11	State 4-A Champion
11	Brenham (Texas) HS	37-5	12	State 4-A Champion
12	Mater Dei HS, Santa Ana, Calif.	20-10	13	CIF Southern Section D-I Champion
13	Petal (Miss.) HS	30-4	14	State 6-A Champion
14	Germantown Academy, Fort Washington, Pa.	29-3	15	State Independent School Champion
15	Desert Ridge HS, Mesa, Ariz.	31-4	16	State 5-A I Champion
16	La Cueva HS, Albuquerque	28-2	17	State 5-A Champion
17	St. Edward HS, Lakewood, Ohio	28-3	18	State D-I Champion
18	Carroll HS, Corpus Christi, Texas	38-7	25	State 5-A Champion
19	Alder HS, Plain City, Ohio	34-0	19	State D-II Champion
20	Buchanan HS, Clovis, Calif.	29-5	20	CIF Central Section Champion
21	Harrison HS, Kennesaw, Ga.	29-9	21	State 5-A Champion
22	Klein HS, Spring, Texas	34-7	1	State 5-A Runner-Up
23	Rancho Bernardo HS, San Diego	26-8	23	CIF San Diego Section Champion
24	West Springfield HS, Springfield, Va.	24-4	NR	State 3-A Champion
25	Spanish Fork (Utah) HS	25-1	NR	State 4-A Champion
26	Calhoun (Ga.) HS	35-1	NR	State 1-A Champion
27	Blue Valley HS, Stillwell, Kan.	20-5	NR	State 6-A Champion
28	Marist School, Atlanta	30-8	NR	State 4-A Champion
29	Glendora (Calif.) HS	26-2	NR	CIF Southern Section D-II Champion
30	Calallen HS, Corpus Christi, Texas	38-5	NR	State 4-A Runner-Up
31	Owasso (Okla.) HS	32-7	NR	State 6-A Runner-Up
32	Woodbridge (Va.) HS	28-1	24	State 3-A Runner-Up
33	Walsh Jesuit HS, Cuyahoga Falls, Ohio	30-2	NR	State D-II Runner-Up
34	Poquoson (Va.) HS	28-1	NR	State 2-A Champion
35	Naperville (Ill.) Central HS	38-4	NR	State 4-A Champion
36	Harrisburg (Ill.) HS	40-1	NR	State 2-A Champion
37	Madison (Miss.) Central HS	31-4	NR	State 6-A Runner-Up
38	Canyon del Oro HS, Del Oro, Ariz.	28-3	NR	State 4-A I Runner-Up
39	White Knoll HS, Lexington, S.C.	32-2	NR	State 5-A Champion
40	St. Mary's HS, Stockton, Calif.	26-7	NR	CIF Sac-Joaquin Champion
41	Eden Prairie (Minn.) HS	25-1	NR	State 3-A Champion
42	Tottenville HS, New York	25-1	NR	PSAL Champion
43	Westminster Chrisitan School, Miami	25-7	NR	State 3-A Champion
44	Bishop Amat HS, La Puente, Calif.	27-4	NR	CIF Southern Section D-IV Quarterfinalist
45	Memorial HS, Houston	35-9	NR	State 5-A Semi-finalist
46	Christian Brothers College HS, St. Louis	26-7	NR	State Class 4 Champion
47	Nitro (W.Va.) HS	38-6	NR	State 3-A Champion
48	Clovis West HS, Fresno, Calif.	29-4	NR	CIF Central Section Runner-Up
49	Pappillion-La Vista HS, Pappillion, Neb.	19-5	NR	State Class A Champion
50	Elk Grove (Calif.) HS	26-6	NR	CIF Sac-Joaquin Runner-Up

and in the seventh inning of a 1-0 game against Douglas High (Parkland, Fla.) something wasn't quite right. Evans pulled Machado from the game and called on senior outfielder/righthander Juan "Pichi" Torres to close it out. He shut the door, but found himself thrust into the ace's role as Machado would be shut down with arm trouble after the game.

"We had some guys step up and do really well for us," Evans said. "You've got to have a horse and that ended up being Pichi."

Pitching Pichi

Torres twirled several gems as the Falcons marched through the playoffs. In the region semifinal, Flanagan met with West Broward High—another Pembroke Pines school. Torres said that was his toughest outing during the title run. He gave up seven runs (five earned) on eight hits while striking out four. Down 7-5 in the bottom of the seventh, Martindale reached on a hit by pitch and junior shortstop Ricky Santiago collected his second hit of the game. That brought Torres to the plate as the winning run. He wasted no time in lifting his team to victory again as he deposited the first pitch over the center-field fence for a walk-off home run.

"It was amazing," Torres said. "I've never hit (a walk-off) before. I couldn't wait to get to home plate."

Torres continued to dominate on the mound the following week and pitched Flanagan into the state final four. Against Coral Springs (Fla.) High he pitched with efficiency, throwing just 82 pitches over nine innings, allowing one run on seven hits. The Falcons tied the game 1-1 in the top of the seventh before a scoreless eighth and plated the winning run in the ninth.

After the Coral Springs win, things actually got easier for the Falcons and there were no more stressful victories. They exploded for 14 hits in the semifinal against Orlando's Timber Creek High and advanced to the state final with an 8-4 win, where they met Miami's American High. Flanagan scored 10 runs in the first frame and easily held on for a 12-3 win and the state title.

Then the Falcons went into wait-and-see mode. Evans knew a state title would give them a good boost in the poll and that several teams were still playing. The same scenario played out in 2009, with a Texas team sitting atop the rankings as it headed into the state championship game. Last season, it was Moody High of Corpus Christi. The Trojans fell in the 4-A title game to Texarkana's Texas High, allowing Bishop Gorman High of Las Vegas to celebrate for a second time after winning a fourth straight 4-A championship in Nevada.

However, Klein made it a little more tense. The Bearkats broke a 3-3 tie with a walk-off, two-out single in the bottom of the seventh against Plano (Texas) West High in the state semifinal.

But as much help was provided by teams losing late, Flanagan put itself in a position to move up.

"Every time we had a close game, someone pulled something out of their hat," Evans said. "Sure enough, we won it. I told them, 'You guys earned it. We are done and we can't go down. We can only go up. Things can happen.'"

And sure enough, things happened.

Torres finished the season 10-1, 1.96 in 75 innings with 58 strikeouts and just 12 walks. Junior first baseman Mike Melendez led the team in hitting with a .459/.515/.800 line in 85 at-bats with six home runs and 32 RBIs.

"We had a refuse to lose mentality," Evans said. "It was all about getting back to the final four for the seniors. They were phenomenal, relentless all year long. When it was all over it was like a dream."

Marlette's Blast Nets Aflac Win

BY KIRK KENNEY

SAN DIEGO There's an old notion that a professional should act like he's been there before when he's on the field. Apparently, it applies to high school players now, too.

In the case of the 2010 Aflac All-American High School Baseball Classic, won by the East team 5-3, virtually all of the participants had been here before. Not on the field at the Padres' Petco Park necessarily—although West shortstop Phillip Evans and first baseman/pitcher Daniel Camarena are locals who had played here with their high school teams—but a big league ballfield nonetheless.

Now, about Petco's reputation as a pitcher's park. Tell that to righthander Ricky Jacquez, who pitched the fourth inning for the West. Jacquez allowed back-to-back triples to shortstop Francisco Lindor and third baseman Javier Baez leading off the inning. The spaciousness of the outfield allowed Lindor to drive a ball through the gap in left-center. Baez did likewise in right-center. One out later, East catcher Tyler Marlette didn't bother going to the gap. Marlette pounded a Jacquez pitch into the left-field seats some 375 feet away for a two-run homer that earned him MVP honors.

While this wasn't Marlette's first game at a big league park—he has also played at Tropicana Field and the Twins' Metrodome—Petco did provide the backdrop for another first.

"My first pro field bomb," said Marlette, holding his award while wearing an ear-to-ear grin after the game. "It was amazing. This was probably my favorite game ever. Ever."

Marlette was surrounded by players from both teams and their coaches in front of home plate as he answered postgame questions. At one point, some of the players standing toward the back noticed the interview was televised live on the scoreboard beyond the left field wall. They started jumping up and down, simultaneously turning to see themselves on the scoreboard. Kids. They acted like they've never been on a major league scoreboard before.

Local Product Shines At Wrigley

BY NATHAN RODE

CHICAGO For the third consecutive year the Under Armour All-America Game powered by Baseball Factory was played at Wrigley Field, a fitting conclusion to a multi-day event that provided some of the best high school players in the country with a unique and unforgettable experience.

The fanfare climaxed when the weather cleared up and the got under way in the early afternoon, with MLB Network broadcasting live. Things got off to a hot start with local prospect Nick Burdi, playing for the National team, striking out the side in the top of the first. Burdi, a righthander, attends Downer's Grove High, about 25 miles west of Chicago.

"I felt pretty good," Burdi said. "Everything was working pretty well and then the slider came around after the first two outs. So, it was pretty good."

Burdi couldn't have asked for a better experience, starting the game and performing the way he did, especially considering the venue.

"I had my entire family here and it was just a special moment," Burdi said. "I'm honored to have this privilege of playing in the Under Armour All-America game. This is my first time playing at Wrigley, so it was pretty special. I've always dreamed about playing here."

The American team put a two-spot up in the second inning when outfielder Mason Robbins reached on a single, stole second, advanced to third on a throwing error and finally scored when outfielder Brandon Nimmo doubled to the left-field corner and advanced to third when the relay throw got away from the cut-off man. Nimmo scored moments later on a wild pitch to make it 2-0, American. The American team eventually won 7-0 after going up 3-0 in the third and adding a four-run seventh.

There were plenty of raw tools on display, but a lot of crooked numbers in undesirable stat categories. While both teams combined to strike out 29, there were also 11 walks and eight hit batters.

Nimmo and Burdi were the MVPs. Nimmo went 2-for-4 with two RBIs and two runs scored. Burdi struck out all three batters, using a 91-94 mph fastball, changeup and slider.

Looking Up

North Carolina's impact on the draft has grown in the last decade as the state has grown. It will be hard for the state to surpass the level of talent it produced in 2006—when the college ranks produced first-rounders Andrew Miller and Daniel Bard, while the prep ranks included Dustin Ackley, Alex White and Lonnie Chisenhall.

The 2010 draft class in the state's prep ranks was strong with three players—outfielder Ty Linton, infielder Connor Narron and catcher Matt Roberts—ranked among the top 200 draft prospects. However, 2011 is shaping up as the best prep class in the state since '06 and '07, a year when a half-dozen Tar Heel State prep products got popped in the first 10 rounds.

Leading the 2011 class are three righthanders, all verbally committed to play their college ball at North Carolina. They are: Dillon Maples of Pinecrest High, in Southern Pines; Benton Moss of Rocky Mount High and Adam Griffin of Forsyth Country Day School in Lewisville. It's still far too early to tell whether these young athletes will end up at school or where a team may elect to take them in the draft, but all three are certainly large spots on the prospect radar.

Maples, the top prospect in the state for 2011, has a slender frame and broad shoulders. He is not an imposing figure on the mound, but don't be fooled. He has a strong lower half that helps him double as a standout kicker on the Pinecrest football team. His delivery is easy and generates a fastball that has reached the mid 90s. . At the Impact Invitational in Cary, N.C., Maples impressed spectators in what was his first start of the 2010 season. He touched several 92-93s in the first inning and settled in at 88-91, inducing bad contact with a lively heater while mixing in a good, yet inconsistent, curveball. He also showed off his strength by crushing an opposite-field home run that easily cleared 350 feet. Maples finished the season at 8-2, 0.95 with 117 strikeouts in 59 innings.

Jeff Hewitt has been the head coach at Pinecrest for 12 years. Each year, the coaching staff and players head to the local Little League for their opening day to help out. Several years ago Hewitt saw a kid throwing in the bullpen and was hoping that the 6-foot-4 gentleman next to him was his father. The kid was Maples and the man was in fact his father, Tim, a second round pick of the Orioles in 1979.

"You could tell he had it," Hewitt said. "As a high school coach you have those guys you can't wait until they get there. You can tell he's played a lot of baseball at a young age."

Cowart dominates both sides

BY NATHAN RODE

Kaleb Cowart can't be blamed for being a little overwhelmed this summer.

The third baseman/righthander from Cook High in Adel, Ga. was the 18th overall pick in the 2010 draft by the Angels after a stellar finish to his high school career and had until Aug. 16 to decide if he is going to sign a pro contract—which he eventually did.

On top of all that, while attending orientation for Florida State in Tallahassee, Cowart learned he was named Baseball America's 2010 High School Player of the Year.

"We had a great season," Cowart said. "The team did really well. We all played great. I just went out every day and thanked God for another day out there and left everything on the field."

Cowart is the second player out of Georgia to win the award in the past three years. His credentials are similar to those of 2008 POY-winner Ethan Martin, also a Peach State product.

Like Martin, Cowart dominated on both sides of the ball and was named a first-team All-American utility player. In 107 at-bats, Cowart hit .654 with 11 home runs, 55 runs, 16 doubles, 59 RBIs and 36 stolen bases. On the mound he went 10-1, 1.05 with one save. In 73 innings he allowed just 35 hits and 24 walks while striking out 116. His lone loss came against Calhoun (Ga.) High, a frequent state title contender.

It wasn't the first time Coward faced the Yellow Jackets.

"He started as a freshman and every year we've been deep in the playoffs," Cook head coach Bob Owsley said. "Calhoun had some guys that year and he shut them down. Right then and there I knew if he progressed, good things would happen. He's paid his dues and gotten better every year."

Owsley has known Cowart for several years and remembers how much he stood out from his peers when he started switch-hitting as a 12-year-old.

Cowart's growing talent can be attributed to his dedication to baseball all year. He's a prominent member of the East Cobb Baseball program and has traveled all over the country facing top, including the No. 2 overall pick this year, righthander Jameson Taillon.

"He's something else," Cowart laughed. "I got a hit off of him at the Metrodome (at the Perfect

PLAYER OF THE YEAR

PREVIOUS WINNERS

1992: Preston Wilson, of/rhp, Bamberg-Ehrhardt (S.C.) HS
1993: Trot Nixon, of/lhp, New Hanover HS, Wilmington, N.C.
1994: Doug Million, lhp, Sarasota (Fla.) HS
1995: Ben Davis, c, Malvern (Pa.) Prep
1996: Matt White, rhp, Waynesboro Area (Pa.) HS
1997: Darnell McDonald, of, Cherry Creek HS, Englewood, Colo.
1998: Drew Henson, 3b/rhp, Brighton (Mich.) HS
1999: Josh Hamilton, of/lhp, Athens Drive HS, Raleigh, N.C.
2000: Matt Harrington, rhp, Palmdale (Calif.) HS
2001: Joe Mauer, c, Cretin-Derham Hall HS, St. Paul, Minn.
2002: Scott Kazmir, lhp, Cypress Falls HS, Houston
2003: Jeff Allison, rhp, Veterans Memorial HS, Peabody, Mass.
2004: Homer Bailey, rhp, LaGrange (Texas) HS
2005: Justin Upton, ss, Great Bridge HS, Chesapeake, Va.
2006: Adrian Cardenas, ss/2b, Mons. Pace HS, Opa Locka, Fla.
2007: Mike Moustakas, ss, Chatsworth (Calif.) HS
2008: Ethan Martin, rhp/3b, Stephens County HS, Toccoa, Ga.
2009: Bryce Harper, c, Las Vegas HS

Game National Showcase) and he struck me out. I took the first pitch to see what it was like. That was the best pitch I saw. He threw a disgusting curveball and made me look dumb and then I chased a fastball out of the zone."

Cowart also scores high marks from his head coach for how he plays the game. "He has a competitive nature," Owsley said. "We started six sophomores. All of them fed off him, how he attacked the competition, the intensity he played with and his love of the game."

Training has been instrumental to Cowart's success. During the season, Cowart avoids getting overworked. He lifts weights to keep his core strong and stay in shape. He also throws and hits every day, taking 50 cuts off the tee, works on hitting opposite field in batting practice before doing infield drills.

In the offseason, Cowart steps up his routine with heavy lifting that helps increase his lower body strength. Since it doesn't get too cold in South Georgia, he throws long toss three or four times a week on the football field. His goal each time out is to throw through both goal posts, a distance of at least 330 feet.

Cowart says he does all of this to keep his talent growing.

"When you quit getting better, you need to stop playing," he said.

2010 HIGH SCHOOL ALL-AMERICA TEAM

Kalab Cowart

RYAN GIBSON

Philip Pfeifer

DANNY PARKER

FIRST TEAM

Pos., Name , School	B/T	Ht.	Wt.	Yr.	AVG	AB	R	H	2B	3B	HR	RBI	SB	DRAFTED
C Ethan Bennett, Farragut HS, Knoxville	R/R	6-1	215	Sr.	.407	140	57	57	9	0	27	73	0	Undrafted
IF Sean Coyle, Germantown Academy, Fort Washington, Pa.	R/R	5-8	175	Sr.	.562	89	45	50	14	4	13	55	22	Red Sox (3)
IF Nick Delmonico, Farragut HS, Knoxville	L/R	6-3	190	Jr.	.485	136	66	66	12	4	18	75	30	Not eligible
IF Christopher Hawkins, North Gwinnett HS, Suwanee, Ga.	L/R	6-2	195	Sr.	.520	123	49	64	21	1	15	44	7	Blue Jays (3)
IF Manny Machado, Brito Private HS, Hialeah, Fla.	R/R	6-3	190	Sr.	.639	86	43	55	27	5	12	56	17	Orioles (1)
OF Josh Sale, Bishop Blanchet HS, Seattle	L/R	6-0	215	Sr.	.520	50	27	26	6	2	5	20	6	Rays (1)
OF Austin Wilson, Harvard-Westlake School, Los Angeles	R/R	6-4	210	Sr.	.485	101	52	49	13	2	5	23	27	Cardinals (12)
OF Ryan Wilson, Owasso (Okla.) HS	R/L	6-0	175	Sr.	.419	136	63	57	9	5	19	58	19	Undrafted
DH Kris Bryant, Bonanza HS, Las Vegas	R/R	6-5	205	Sr.	.469	96	48	45	5	3	22	51	2	Blue Jays (18)
UT Kaleb Cowart, Cook HS, Adel, Ga.	B/R	6-3	190	Sr.	.654	107	55	70	16	5	11	59	36	Angels (1)

Pos., Name , School	B/T	Ht.	Wt.	Yr.	W	L	ERA	G	SV	IP	H	BB	K	DRAFTED
RHP Dylan Covey, Maranatha HS, Pasadena, Calif.	R/R	6-2	200	Sr.	7	1	0.40	14	3	71	32	20	138	Brewers (1)
LHP Philip Pfeifer, Farragut HS, Knoxville	L/L	6-0	190	Jr.	16	0	1.23	18	1	96	66	26	165	Not eligible
RHP Jameson Taillon, The Woodlands (Texas) HS	R/R	6-6	225	Sr.	8	1	1.78	11	0	62	42	21	114	Pirates (1)
RHP A.J. Vanegas, Redwood Christian HS, San Lorenzo, Calif.	R/R	6-2	205	Sr.	11	0	0.67	15	3	73	23	24	141	Padres (7)
RHP Karsten Whitson, Chipley (Fla.) HS	R/R	6-3	185	Sr.	7	3	0.62	10	0	56	16	15	122	Padres (1)
UT Kaleb Cowart, Cook HS, Adel, Ga.	B/R	6-3	190	Sr.	10	1	1.05	13	1	73	35	24	116	Angels (1)

SECOND TEAM

Pos., Name, School	B/T	Ht.	Wt.	Yr.	AVG	AB	R	H	2B	3B	HR	RBI	SB	DRAFTED
C Justin O'Conner, Cowan HS, Muncie, Ind.	R/R	6-1	190	Sr.	.494	77	53	38	13	1	11	49	16	Rays (1)
IF Nick Castellanos, Archbishop McCarthy HS, SW Ranches, Fla.	R/R	6-4	210	Sr.	.542	72	34	39	8	3	6	41	22	Tigers (1s)
IF Gavin Cecchini, Barbe HS, Lake Charles, La.	L/R	6-3	195	So.	.430	135	56	58	24	1	10	54	21	Not eligible
IF David Thompson, Westminster Christian Academy, Miami	R/R	6-1	195	So.	.486	105	47	51	10	2	19	54	6	Not eligible
IF Christian Yelich, Westlake HS, Westlake Village, Calif.	L/R	6-3	190	Sr.	.455	77	39	35	14	2	9	25	27	Marlins (1)
OF Aaron Shipman, Brooks County HS, Quitman, Ga.	L/L	6-1	185	Sr.	.525	59	40	31	6	5	5	22	38	A's (3)
OF Josh Alexander, Mountain Pointe HS, Phoenix	R/R	6-2	185	Sr.	.518	114	39	59	9	1	14	45	9	Reds (19)
OF Kyle Waldrop, Riverdale HS, Fort Myers, Fla.	L/L	6-1	185	Sr.	.506	79	46	40	7	2	8	34	21	Reds (12)
DH Hommy Rosado, Barbe HS, Lake Charles, La.	R/R	6-0	215	Sr.	.475	118	45	56	8	0	26	62	8	Rockies (11)
UT Dylan Bundy, Owasso (Okla.) HS	B/R	6-1	200	Jr.	.442	129	50	57	16	2	7	51	3	Not eligible

Pos., Name, School	B/T	Ht.	Wt.	Yr.	W	L	ERA	G	SV	IP	H	BB	K	DRAFTED
LHP Jesse Biddle, Germantown Friends HS, Philadelphia	L/L	6-4	225	Sr.	9	2	1.06	12	1	59	21	29	140	Phillies (1)
RHP Cody Buckel, Royal HS, Simi Valley, Calif.	R/R	6-0	170	Sr.	12	1	0.61	14	0	80	37	17	123	Rangers (2)
LHP Daniel Gibson, Jesuit HS, Tampa	L/L	6-4	210	Sr.	14	1	1.64	17	0	90	66	31	129	Brewers (26)
RHP Robby Rowland, Cloverdale (Calif.) HS	R/R	6-6	210	Sr.	7	1	0.32	11	0	65	26	11	117	D'backs (3)
RHP John Simms, College Park HS, The Woodlands, Texas	R/R	6-3	190	Sr.	8	1	1.07	12	0	65	31	15	123	Nationals (39)
UT Dylan Bundy, Owasso (Okla.) HS	B/R	6-1	200	Jr.	11	1	1.58	14	1	80	41	20	164	Not eligible

Team USA 16U Continues Streak

USA Baseball's 2010 season for high school-aged teams came to a close in October with the 16U National Team capturing a gold medal by beating Mexico 11-4 in the COPABE Pan Am 'AA' 16U Youth Championships. The 16U program is now unbeaten in the last five years, running the streak to 40 games.

"I was really proud of everyone involved with the program this year, from the staff down to all of the players who participated in our trials," said Jeff Singer, director of the 16U program.

Infielders Alex Bregman and Corey Seager led the squad on offense. Bregman, a junior at Albuquerque Academy, hit .564/.596/.846 in 39 at-bats with two home runs, 17 runs and 17 RBIs. He also stole five bases. Seager hit .514/.622/.829 in 35 at-bats with 16 runs scored and 12 RBIs. He proved to be the team's most patient hitter, drawing 10 walks in nine games. While Bregman and Seager did plenty of damage on their own, Team USA destroyed opposing pitching as a whole. In nine games the squad hit .437/.500/.749 with 15 home runs and outscored opponents 127-23.

The 16U team was the last to wrap up its season. The 18U National Team finished fifth at the COPABE Pan Am 'AAA' 18U Youth Championships in Thunder Bay, Ont. this summer after losing in the first medal round to Cuba.

USA Baseball's 14U team had been rolling through the COPABE Pan Am 'A' 14U Championships before running into Venezuela in the semifinals. Team USA lost 11-1, but bounced back to win the bronze medal by defeating Brazil 6-0.

AMATEUR/YOUTH CHAMPIONS 2010

USA BASEBALL

Event	Site	Champion	Runner-up
18U/Tournament of Stars	Cary, N.C.	Babe Ruth	American Legion
16U/USA Junior Olympics—East	Palm Beach County, Fla.	CCB	Team Worth Florida
16U/USA Junior Olympics—West	Peoria & Surprise, Ariz.	Conejo Oaks	Team Rawlings Elite
14U/USA Junior Olympics—East	Palm Beach County, Fla.	Lamorinda National	Team Strikezone
14U/USA Junior Olympics—West	Peoria & Surprise, Ariz.	Team Rawlings Elite	San Diego Show

ALL-AMERICAN AMATEUR BASEBALL ASSOCIATION

Event	Site	Champion	Runner-up
World Series (21-and-Under)	Johnstown, Pa.	Baltimore	Johnstown, Pa.

AMATEUR ATHLETIC UNION (AAU)

Event	Site	Champion	Runner-up
10-and-Under Diamond (60-foot)	Lake Buena Vista, Fla.	Team Florida	Houston Wranglers
10-and-Under Gold (60-foot)	Lake Buena Vista, Fla.	Pinellas Park	Wesley Chapel Wildcats
11-and-Under Diamond (70-foot)	Lake Buena Vista, Fla.	MBA Pride	Team Anderson
11-and-Under Gold (70-foot)	Lake Buena Vista, Fla.	Wellington Colts	Capital Diamond Rats
12-and-Under Diamond (70-foot)	Richmond, Va.	Lamorinda Monarchs	Team Rawlings
12-and-Under Gold (70-foot)	Richmond, Va.	Clap Bat	World of Baseball
13-and-Under (90-foot)	Virginia Beach, Va.	Md. Baseball Acad.	Bullets Grey
13-and-Under (90-foot)	Virginia Beach, Va.	Miami Outlaws	ATL Blue Jays
14-and-Under (90-foot)	Sarasota, Fla.	Jax Royals White	Jax Royals Blue
15-and-Under	Salem, Va.	Virginia Diamonds	Carrollwood Gators
16-and-Under	Detroit, Mich.	NE Hurricanes	Rockledge Baseball Club
18/19-and-Under Diamond	Lake Buena Vista, Fla.	Brazos Valley	Tallahassee Bb Club
18/19-and-Under Gold	Lake Buena Vista, Fla.	Louisiana Warriors	Georgia Eagles

AMERICAN AMATEUR BASEBALL CONGRESS (AABC)

Event	Site	Champion	Runner-up
Gil Hodges	Brooklyn, N.Y.	Wolcott, Conn.	Unavailable
Pee Wee Reese (12 & U)	Toa Baja, Puerto Rico	D-Bat Mustangs	Unavailable
Sandy Koufax (13 & U)	Battle Creek, Mich.	The Gravel	Unavailable
Sandy Koufax (14 & U)	Surprise, Ariz.	Arizona All Star Academy	Unavailable
Mickey Mantle (15 & U)	Owasso, Okla.	D-Bat Mustangs	Unavailable
Mickey Mantle (16 & U)	McKinney, Texas	San Gabriel Valley Arsenal	Unavailable
Connie Mack (18 & U)	Farmington, N.M.	Midland Redskins	Unavailable
Stan Musial (open)	Huntsville, Texas	Canton Stallions	Unavailable

AMERICAN LEGION BASEBALL

Event	Site	Champion	Runner-up
World Series (19 & U)	Shelby, N.C.	Midwest City, Okla.	Eden Prairie, Minn.

BABE RUTH BASEBALL

Event	Site	Champion	Runner-up
Cal Ripken (10 & U)	Ocala, Fla.	Scott County, Ky.	Middletown, N.J.
Cal Ripken 12-year-old (60 feet)	Wilson County, N.C.	Nassau, Bahamas	Visalia, Calif.
13-year-old	Levelland, Texas	Torrance, Calif.	College Point, N.Y.
14-year-old	Loudoun County, Va.	Tri Valley, Calif.	Tallahassee, Fla.
13-15-year-olds	Monticello, Ark.	North Syracuse, N.Y.	Saginaw Valley, Mich.
16-18-year-old	Newark, Ohio	Mobile	Portland

CONTINENTAL AMATEUR BASEBALL ASSOCIATION (CABA)

Event	Site	Champion	Runner-up
9-and-Under	Woodstock, Ill.	Lincoln Way Prospects	Tri-County Drillers
10-and-Under	Westfield/Carmel, Ind.	Mac-N-Seitz	Lincoln Way Prospects
11-and-Under	Northern Illinois	Ohio Glaciers	Lou Collier Baseball (STARS)
12-and-Under	Cincinnati, Ohio	Technique Tigers	Ohio XStreme
13-and-Under	Westfield/Carmel, Ind.	Georgia Roadrunners	East Cobb Astros
14-and-Under (60x90)	Lebanon, Tenn.	Bergan Beach	Ohio Force
15-and-Under	Charleston, S.C.	Diamond Devils Blue	Diamond Devils Black
16-and-Under	Marietta, Ga.	East Cobb Astros	Atlanta Braves Baseball
High school age	Euclid, Ohio	Top Tier Americans	Midwest Stallions
18-and-Under (wood)	Charleston, S.C.	Midland Indians	Diamond Devils
18-and-Under (aluminum)	Youngstown, Ohio	Dayton Dodgers	Summit City Sluggers

LITTLE LEAGUE BASEBALL

Event	Site	Champion	Runner-up
Little League (11-12)	Williamsport, Pa.	Japan	Waipahu, Hawaii
Junior League (13-14)	Taylor, Mich.	Taiwan	Tyler, Texas
Senior League (15-16)	Bangor, Maine	Aruba	Bangor, Maine
Big League (17-18)	Easley, S.C.	Puerto Rico	Thousand Oaks, Calif.

NATIONAL AMATEUR BASEBALL FEDERATION (NABF)

Event	Site	Champion	Runner-up
Freshman (12 & U)	Southaven, Miss.	Banditus Black	Chet Lemon's Juice
Sophomore (14 & U)	Altavista, Va.	Liberty Christian Acad	Long Island Titans
Junior (16 & U)	Northville, Mich.	Rotterdam Rangers	West Islip Lions
High School (17 & U)	Knoxville	Va Barnstormers	Huntington Hounds
Senior (18 & U)	Jackson, Miss.	Houston Raiders	Maryland Monarchs

PERFECT GAME/BCS FINALS

Event	Site	Champion	Runner-up
14-and-Under	Fort Myers, Fla.	So Cal National	Dulin Dodgers
15-and-Under	Fort Myers, Fla.	Indiana Prospects	St. Pete Hurricanes Elite
16-and-Under	Fort Myers, Fla.	Palm Beach PAL	South Florida Elite Black
17-and-Under	Fort Myers, Fla.	East Cobb Astros	Orl Scorpions Purple
18-and-Under	Fort Myers, Fla.	East Cobb Braves	SWFL Baseball

PERFECT GAME/WORLD WOOD BAT ASSOCIATION

Event	Site	Champion	Runner-up
14-and-Under	Marietta, Ga.	East Cobb Astros	Dulin Dodgers
15-and-Under	Marietta, Ga.	6-4-3 DP Cougars	Dulin Dodgers
16-and-Under	Marietta, Ga.	Canes Green	Carolina Cubs Blue
17-and-Under	Marietta, Ga.	Diamond Devils	Blue, FTB Mizuno
18-and-Under	Marietta, Ga.	Florida Bombers	East Cobb Braves

PONY BASEBALL

Event	Site	Champion	Runner-up
Mustang (9-10)	Irving, Texas	Santa Clarita, Calif.	Caguas, P.R.
Bronco (11)	Chesterfield, Va.	Tijuana, Mexico	Torrance, Calif.
Bronco (11-12)	Monterey, Calif.	Ewa Beach, Hi.	Miami
Pony (13)	Chino Hills, Calif.	Chula Vista, Calif.	Simi Valley, Calif.
Pony (13-14)	Washington, Pa.	Chesterfield, Va.	Japan
Colt (15-16)	Lafayette, Ind.	Gurabo, P.R.	Greensboro, N.C.
Palomino (17-18)	San Jose, Calif.	Tijuana, Mexico	Torrance, Calif.

REVIVING BASEBALL IN INNER CITIES (RBI)

Event	Site	Champion	Runner-up
Junior (13-15)	Jupiter, Fla.	Santo Domingo, D.R.	Washington, D.C.
Senior (16-18)	Los Angeles	Houston	Los Angeles

U.S. SPECIALTY SPORTS ASSOCIATION (USSSA)

Event	Site	Champion	Runner-up
10-and-Under/Majors Elite	Lake Buena Vista, Fla.	Miami Brawlers	Piranaz
11-and-Under/Majors Elite	Lake Buena Vista, Fla.	MBA Pride	San Diego Stars
12-and-Under/Majors Elite	Lake Buena Vista, Fla.	Tomateros de Calif	San Diego Show
13-and-Under/Majors Elite	Lake Buena Vista, Fla.	TABU (Can.)	Meteors Baseball
14-and-Under/Majors Elite	Lake Buena Vista, Fla.	East Cobb Astros	CBC Storm Black

DRAFT

After entering the draft early, Harper impressed wire-to-wire

BY CONOR GLASSEY

If 2009 was known as the Stephen Strasburg draft, then 2010 will certainly go down as the Bryce Harper draft.

And the Nationals couldn't be happier that they had the No. 1 overall pick in both drafts.

The 17-year-old phenom Harper was Baseball America's High School Player of the Year as a sophomore, after hitting .626/.723/1.339 for his Las Vegas high school in 2009. With nothing left to prove at the high school level, and in an effort to get into the draft a year earlier than he would have otherwise, he left high school two years early by getting his GED diploma and enrolling at the JC of Southern Nevada.

From hitting 500-foot home runs to scoring from second base on a passed ball, Harper's high school exploits have become the stuff of legend. Still, there were questions about how he would perform after making the jump from high school baseball to a competitive junior college conference that uses wood bats. After all, Harper was coming off a strenuous summer on the showcase circuit and with Team USA when he lost 25 pounds.

Harper was off limits to the media for most of the year, focusing on baseball and school. While we don't know his grades from the classroom, he earned straight A's on the baseball field. Over his 180 regular season at-bats, Harper hit .417/.509/.917 with 17 doubles, two triples and 23 home runs. He also had 33 walks, 33 strikeouts and was 16-for-20 in stolen base attempts.

"Certainly, I expected him to have success, but I never saw this coming," Southern Nevada head coach Tim Chambers said.

Harper led his league in batting, slugging, hits, runs, RBIs and home runs. Harper's home runs gave him more than half the teams in the league and broke the previous Southern Nevada single-season for home runs of 12, set by Joe Wagner in 2001, when the Scenic West Athletic Conference still used aluminum bats. Some of Harper's shots were epic.

"We're 400 (feet) to center field with a 25-foot fence," Chambers said. "I've personally seen every game here since this program's existence, which is 11 years, and I've seen six balls go over the scoreboard in center field and five of them were with aluminum and one of them was with wood, and that was Bryce's this year."

Bryce Harper crushed the competition in junior college, hitting .417/.509/.917

JESSE SOLL

Nationals general manager Mike Rizzo said the team had decided by the beginning of May to take Harper with the No. 1 overall pick, after watching him one weekend at Southern Nevada. He talked over the decision with scouting director Kris Kline and assistant GM Roy Clark, and it was unanimous.

"On the plane home from Vegas, we kind of cemented that he was the guy we were going to take," Rizzo said.

Although Harper played catcher in high school and at Southern Nevada, the Nationals drafted him as a right fielder, which will allow him to focus on hitting and not worry about the mechanical tweaks he would have had to make behind the plate.

"We've made the early decision that we're going to take the rigors and the pressure of learning the difficult position of catcher away from him, and (we will) really let him concentrate on the offensive part of the game and let his athleticism take over as an outfielder," Rizzo said. "He's got above-average speed and a plus-plus throwing arm.

We just think it will accelerate his development in the minor leagues and also extend his career as a major leaguer."

Harper did not play all summer and agreed to a major league deal just minutes before the signing deadline on Aug. 16. The deal was worth $9.9 million and included a $6.25 million signing bonus—breaking Mark Teixeira's previous record for the largest guarantee ever given to a position player from the draft.

Another Busy Signing Deadline

At the end of the press conference to celebrate the Nationals' signing of No. 1 overall draft pick Bryce Harper, team president Stan Kasten celebrated by giving general manager Mike Rizzo a whipped-cream pie to the face. It was the perfect capper to a typically zany signing deadline.

On a deadline day when teams left more deals unfinished until the final 24 hours and finished shelling out more money on a single draft than ever before, Washington finalized the terms of Harper's $9.9 million major league contract with agent Scott Boras with less than a minute to spare.

Seventeen first-round choices and 79 total players in the first 10 rounds were unsigned as Aug. 16 began. By the time the deadline struck at midnight, 54 of them had signed for bonuses totaling $83.8 million, pushing total spending on the draft to $194.8 million, up from a record $189.3 million a year earlier. Add in major league salaries guaranteed to Harper and fellow first-round picks Yasmani Grandal (Reds) and Zack Cox (Cardinals), and teams committed $200.9 million to draftees.

Harper's $6.25 million bonus, part of the largest guarantee ever given to a drafted position player, pushed the Nationals' bonus total to $11,927,200, eclipsing the record $11,511,500 they in 2009 with Strasburg's help. The Pirates ($11,900,400) and Blue Jays ($11,594,400) also beat Washington's 2009 mark. The Red Sox ($10,664,400) were the fourth team to top $10 million, matching the combined total from 45 previous drafts.

Twenty-eight of the 30 clubs exceeded MLB's bonus guidelines to sign at least one player, led by Toronto with 13. The only teams not to participate in the over-slot frenzy were the Braves and Twins.

The commissioner's office worked as hard as ever to keep spending down, pressuring teams into adhering to the slotting system and delaying the approval and announcement of deals. While overall spending reached record highs, first-round bonuses dipped slightly to an average $2,220,966—a 9

DRAFT EXPENDITURES BY CLUB

Teams broke the industry record for draft spending for the third straight year, handing out a combined $194.8 million in bonuses. Including guaranteed salaries given as part of major league contracts to first-round picks Bryce Harper (Nationals), Yasmani Grandal (Reds) and Zack Cox (Cardinals), the 30 clubs combined to spend $200.9 million. The Nationals ($11,927,000), Pirates ($11,900,400) and Blue Jays ($11,594,400) all eclipsed the previous record for single-club bonus spending, set by Washington in 2009 at $11,511,500. The Red Sox ($10,664,400) were the fourth team to top $10 million, matching the combined total from 45 previous drafts.

TEAM	2010	2009	2008
Nationals	$11,927,200	$11,511,500	$4,761,500
Pirates	$11,900,400	$8,918,900	$9,780,500
Blue Jays	$11,594,400	$4,895,200	$4,359,500
Red Sox	$10,664,400	$7,095,400	$10,515,000
Indians	$9,381,500	$4,943,000	$6,984,500
Orioles	$9,159,900	$8,730,200	$6,916,500
Rangers	$8,487,800	$4,684,200	$7,388,300
Angels	$8,095,300	$6,792,900	$2,728,500
Dodgers	$7,992,900	$4,037,100	$4,442,500
Tigers	$7,301,400	$9,395,100	$3,742,000
Astros	$7,275,530	$4,212,800	$6,544,500
Rays	$7,150,800	$4,004,500	$9,921,000
Royals	$6,697,000	$6,657,000	$11,148,000
Cardinals	$6,692,200	$5,388,500	$5,542,000
Yankees	$6,652,500	$7,564,500	$5,122,000
Reds	$5,739,300	$5,855,400	$4,801,000
Athletics	$5,022,400	$6,439,400	$6,522,000
Rockies	$4,785,700	$7,924,300	$4,157,000
Cubs	$4,727,100	$4,044,200	$5,545,000
Mets	$4,721,200	$3,134,300	$6,460,000
Diamondbacks	$4,399,300	$9,328,200	$4,493,500
Marlins	$4,380,500	$4,142,800	$5,377,000
Padres	$4,262,000	$9,139,000	$5,449,000
Giants	$4,102,900	$6,289,000	$9,080,000
Mariners	$4,000,000	$10,945,600	$4,295,000
White Sox	$3,930,200	$4,178,600	$4,663,500
Phillies	$3,927,900	$3,229,500	$6,740,500
Braves	$3,925,100	$4,400,500	$5,091,500
Twins	$3,511,300	$4,694,100	$7,330,498
Brewers	$2,432,200	$6,759,500	$8,395,800
Total	**$194,840,330**	**$189,335,200**	**$188,297,598**
Average	**$6,494,678**	**$6,311,173**	**$6,276,587**

percent decrease from $2,434,800 a year ago and the lowest since 2007.

That decline came in part because no club gave a major league contract to a college pitcher after 12 had received big league deals in the six previous drafts. Three of the consensus top four college arms (the Indians' Drew Pomeranz, the Mets' Matt Harvey and the Jays' Deck McGuire) held out until deadline day, yet received bonuses that averaged just $228,667 above MLB's recommendations.

Still, the commissioner's office expressed its displeasure with what it considers profligate spending, rebuking teams and threatening fines when it believed protocol for over-slot deals was breached. Bringing draft expenses more under control was a main topic at the owners' meetings the week before the deadline, and will be a focal point of negotiations for a new collective bargaining agreement. The current deal expires in December 2011.

The owners will push for hard slotting, which could drive high school players to college baseball or other sports each year. While it remains to be seen if mandated bonuses will be part of the 2012 draft, teams are preparing as if they will be.

"If you thought we were aggressive this year, wait until you see next year," an American League scouting director said. "It may be our last chance to sign a lot of the high school players, and we're going to take advantage. A lot of other teams will, too."

More Big Fish Get Away

Three first-round picks did not sign in 2010: Texas A&M righthander Barret Loux, California high school righthander Dylan Covey and Florida high school righthander Karsten Whitson. The three unsigned picks were the most since Charles Johnson, Calvin Murray and Scott Burrell declined to turn pro in 1989.

The Diamondbacks used their first-round pick (sixth overall) on Loux. But when he took a physical, the Diamondbacks were concerned with the wear and tear in his shoulder (where he had tenderness as a high school senior) and elbow (from which he had bone chips removed after his sophomore season at Texas A&M in 2009). Though he was healthy all spring, Arizona worried about how long he'd hold up and decided it would be better off not signing Loux and taking the No. 7 pick in

HIGHEST BONUSES EVER

Four draftees received bonuses of $5 million or more in 2010, matching 2008 for the most ever in one draft. Jameson Taillon (No. 2 overall pick, Pirates) set a new record for high schoolers by signing for $6.5 million, while Bryce Harper (No. 1, Nationals) matched the mark for position players at $6.25 million.

PLAYER, POS.	TEAM, YEAR (PICK)	BONUS
Stephen Strasburg, rhp	Nationals, 2009 (No. 1)	*$7,500,000
Jameson Taillon, rhp	Pirates, 2010 (No. 2)	$6,500,000
Donavan Tate, of	Padres, 2009 (No. 3)	+$6,250,000
Bryce Harper, of	Nationals, 2010 (No. 1)	*$6,250,000
Buster Posey, c	Giants, 2008 (No. 5)	$6,200,000
Tim Beckham, ss	Rays, 2008 (No. 1)	+$6,150,000
Justin Upton, ss	D'backs, 2005 (No. 1)	+$6,100,000
Matt Wieters, c	Orioles, 2007 (No. 5)	$6,000,000
Pedro Alvarez, 3b	Pirates, 2008 (No. 2)	*$6,000,000
Eric Hosmer, 1b	Royals, 2008 (No. 3)	$6,000,000
Dustin Ackley, of	Mariners, 2009 (No. 2)	*$6,000,000
David Price, lhp	Devil Rays, 2007 (No. 1)	*$5,600,000
Joe Borchard, of	White Sox, 2000 (No. 12)	+$5,300,000
Manny Machado, ss	Orioles, 2010 (No. 3)	$5,250,000
Zach Lee, rhp	Dodgers, 2010 (No. 28)	+$5,250,000
Joe Mauer, c	Twins, 2001 (No. 1)	+$5,150,000

*Part of major league contract.
+Bonus spread over multiple years under MLB provisions for two-sport athletes.

a deeper 2011 draft as compensation. Rather than leave Loux in a tough situation, MLB declared the day after the signing deadline that he'd become a free agent. He has yet to sign in mid-November.

Most teams considered Loux a sandwich-round talent, and he was chosen in part because of his willingness to accept a below-slot $2 million bonus. Tracy Ringolsby of Fox Sports and Baseball America reported that Allison wanted to choose lefthander Chris Sale, who ended the season in the majors with the White Sox, but was overruled by former GM Josh Byrnes.

In perhaps the most shocking development on deadline day, it was revealed that Covey had been diagnosed with Type 1 diabetes following his physical with the Brewers. Milwaukee didn't consider Covey's $2 million asking price out of line, but he and his family decided it would be best if he learned to adjust to his condition while attending college close to home at San Diego. After failing to sign Covey, the Brewers spent just $2,432,200 on the 2010 draft, the lowest total in baseball.

While the other two had medical concerns, Whitson simply failed to come to terms with San Diego after the two sides disagreed on

LARGEST BIG LEAGUE CONTRACTS

The draft started in 1965, but no player received a multiyear major league contract until the Royals gave Heisman Trophy winner Bo Jackson a $1.066 million deal as a fourth-round pick in 1986 to lure him away from the NFL. Including Jackson, 46 draftees have received multiyear big league pacts, including three in 2010: Bryce Harper ($9.9 million from the Nationals as the No. 1 overall pick), Yasmani Grandal ($3.2 million from the Reds at No. 12) and Zack Cox ($3.2 million from the Cardinals at No. 25).

Harper's deal was the third-largest guaranteed contract in draft history and the highest ever for a position player. Below are the 15 biggest major league contracts given to draftees:

PLAYER, POS.	TEAM, YEAR (PICK)	BONUS	GUARANTEE
Stephen Strasburg, rhp	Nationals, 2009 (No. 1)	$7,500,000	$15,107,104
Mark Prior, rhp	Cubs, 2001 (No. 2)	$4,000,000	$10,500,000
Bryce Harper, of	Nationals, 2010 (No. 1)	$6,250,000	$9,900,000
Mark Teixeira, 3b	Rangers, 2001 (No. 5)	$4,500,000	$9,500,000
David Price, lhp	Devil Rays, 2007 (No. 1)	$5,600,000	$8,500,000
Pat Burrell, 1b/of	Phillies, 1998 (No. 1)	$3,150,000	$8,000,000
Dustin Ackley, of	Mariners, 2009 (No. 2)	$6,000,000	$7,500,000
J.D. Drew, of	Cardinals, 1998 (No. 5)	$3,000,000	$7,000,000
Josh Beckett, rhp	Marlins, 1999 (No. 2)	$3,625,000	$7,000,000
Rick Porcello, rhp	Tigers, 2007 (No. 27)	$3,580,000	$7,000,000
Eric Munson, c	Tigers, 1999 (No. 3)	$3,500,000	$6,750,000
Pedro Alvarez, 3b	Pirates, 2008 (No. 2)	$6,000,000	$6,335,000
Delmon Young, of	Devil Rays, 2003 (No. 1)	$3,700,000	$5,800,000
Stephen Drew, ss	Diamondbacks, 2004 (No. 15)	$4,000,000	$5,500,000
Jacob Turner, rhp	Tigers, 2009 (No. 9)	$4,700,000	$5,500,000

what parameters they had agreed to before the draft. The Padres upped their offer to $2.75 million, matching what the Royals paid No. 4 overall choice Christian Colon, but the consensus second-best prep pitching prospect in the draft opted to attend Florida.

Draft Data

■ In 2009, Kentucky lefthander James Paxton was one of three Blue Jays picks in the first three rounds not to agree to terms. Toronto offered him $1 million, while Paxton sought $1.35 million. Afterward, Jays officials let slip to a Toronto newspaper that they had negotiated directly with agent Scott Boras, a violation of NCAA rules. Kentucky wouldn't allow Paxton to return to its team until he submitted to an NCAA interview, and when he couldn't get a temporary injunction in Kentucky courts, he went to pitch in the independent American Association. His stuff wasn't as sharp in 2010, as he worked mostly with an 88-93 mph fastball and a decent curve, rather than the 93-97 mph fastball and plus curve he showed with the Wildcats. The Mariners took him in the fourth round in 2010. Paxton continued to negotiate because the signing deadline doesn't apply to players who were drafted after their junior year of college; didn't sign with the team that selected him before the deadline; signed a professional

DAVID STONER

Righthander Jameson Taillon received the largest bonus in the 2010 draft class

contact with a non-MLB-affiliated team after he was drafted; and didn't play college baseball again between the two drafts.

■ The Rays used two of their top three picks on the two best hitters in the Northwest, both high school hitters from Washington. They selected outfielder Josh Sale at No. 17 and outfielder Drew Vettleson as the 42nd overall pick in the supplemental first round.

"It feels great," Sale said. "To say the least, it's been an emotional day. I'm as happy as can be right now."

Sale, whose name is pronounced sah-lay, said he had a small family get-together to watch the event. He talked about hearing his name called as

FIRST-ROUND TRENDS

Year	College	HS	Hitters	Pitchers	Average Bonus	Change
2000	12	18	13	17	$1,872,586	+3.5%
2001	18	12	10	*20	$2,154,280	+15.0%
2002	14	16	14	16	$2,106,793	-2.2%
2003	18	12	*20	10	$1,765,667	*-16.2%
2004	17	13	11	19	$1,958,448	+10.9%
2005	19	10	17	13	$2,018,000	+3.0%
2006	16	13	12	18	$1,933,333	-4.2%
2007	13	17	13	17	$2,098,083	+8.5%
2008	*21	9	11	19	*$2,458,714	+17.2%
2009	15	16	16	16	$2,434,800	-1.0%
2010	15	17	18	14	$2,220,966	-8.8%

*Draft record.

DRAFT RECORDS BY ROUND

ROUND	PLAYER, POS, TEAM	YEAR	BONUS
1st	Stephen Strasburg, rhp, Nationals	2009	$7,500,000
Supp. 1st	Nick Castellanos, 3b, Tigers	2010	$3,450,000
2nd	Jason Young, rhp, Rockies	2000	$2,750,000
3rd	Matt Tuiasosopo, ss, Mariners	2004	$2,290,000
4th	A.J. Cole, rhp, Nationals	2010	$2,000,000
5th	Ryan Westmoreland, of, Red Sox	2008	$2,000,000
6th	Jack McGeary, lhp, Nationals	2007	$1,800,000
7th	Brett Hunter, rhp, Athletics	2008	$1,100,000
8th	Colton Cain, lhp, Pirates	2009	$1,125,000
9th	Jason Middlebrook, rhp, Padres	1996	$750,000
10th	Luis Cota, rhp, Royals*	2003	$1,050,000
11th	Chris Huseby, rhp, Cubs	2006	$1,300,000
12th	Mike Rozier, lhp, Red Sox	2004	$1,575,000
13th	Jimmy Barthmaier, rhp, Astros	2003	$750,000
14th	Ty Linton, of, Diamondbacks	2010	$1,250,000
15th	J.P. Ramirez, of, Nationals	2008	$1,000,000
Post-15th	Sean Henn, lhp, Yankees*	2000	$1,701,000

*Signed following year as draft-and-follow.

THE BONUS RECORD

Rick Monday, the No. 1 overall pick in baseball's first draft in 1965, signed with the Athletics for $100,000—a figure that no draftee bettered for a decade. The record has been broken several times since, most recently in 2009. No. 3 overall choice Donavan Tate signed with the Padres for $6.25 million on Aug. 16 and was topped a few hours later by No. 1 pick Stephen Strasburg, who agreed to a big league contract that included a $7.5 million bonus minutes before the midnight deadline. The list below represents only cash bonuses and doesn't include guaranteed money from major league deals, college scholarship plans or incentives. It also considers only players who signed with the clubs that drafted them and doesn't include draft picks who signed after being granted free agency, such as Bill Bordley ($200,000 from the Giants after the Reds selected him in the January 1979 draft) and Matt White ($10.2 million from the Devil Rays after the Giants chose him in the 1996 draft).

YEAR	PLAYER, POS., CLUB (ROUND)	BONUS
1965	Rick Monday, of, Athletics (1)	$100,000
1975	Danny Goodwin, c, Angels (1)	$125,000
1978	Kirk Gibson, of, Tigers (1)	$150,000
	*Bob Horner, 3b, Braves (1)	$162,000
1979	Todd Demeter, 1b, Yankees (2)	$208,000
1988	Andy Benes, rhp, Padres (1)	$235,000
1989	Tyler Houston, c, Braves (1)	$241,500
	*Ben McDonald, rhp, Orioles (1)	$350,000
	*John Olerud, 1b, Blue Jays (3)	$575,000
1991	Mike Kelly, of, Braves (1)	$575,000
	Brien Taylor, lhp, Yankees (1)	$1,550,000
1994	Paul Wilson, rhp, Mets (1)	$1,550,000
	Josh Booty, 3b, Marlins (1)	$1,600,000
1996	Kris Benson, rhp, Pirates (1)	$2,000,000
1997	Rick Ankiel, lhp, Cardinals (2)	$2,500,000
	Matt Anderson, rhp, Tigers (1)	$2,505,000
1998	*J.D. Drew, of, Cardinals (1)	$3,000,000
	*Pat Burrell, 3b, Phillies (1)	$3,150,000
	Mark Mulder, lhp, Athletics (1)	$3,200,000
	Corey Patterson, of, Cubs (1)	$3,700,000
1999	Josh Hamilton, of, Devil Rays (1)	$3,960,000
2000	Joe Borchard, of, White Sox (1)	$5,300,000
2005	Justin Upton, ss, Diamondbacks (1)	$6,100,000
2008	Tim Beckham, ss, Rays (1)	$6,150,000
	Buster Posey, c, Giants (1)	$6,200,000
2009	Donavan Tate, cf, Padres (1)	$6,250,000
	*Stephen Strasburg, rhp, Nationals (1)	$7,500,000

*Part of major league contract.

a first-rounder. "I heard my first name and stood up, then I heard the mispronunciation of my last name and I gave a little fist pump, ran out the door and ran up the block, down the block and back up the block again. I was ecstatic, to say the least," he said. "It was actually amazing. As soon as I heard (Vettleson's) name called, I bolted out the front door to run up and down the street again!"

The Rays continued to make picks on the recommendation of Paul Kirsch, their Northwest area scout. In the first five rounds, they also got Washington high school second baseman Ryan Brett and Oregon high school righthander Ian Kendall.

■ Teams potentially signed three quarterbacks away from football. The biggest signing came when the Dodgers inked Louisiana State recruit Zack Lee with their first-round pick, giving him a $5.25 million bonus spread over five years thanks to MLB's provisions for players who show prowess in two sports. Lee was considered such a tough sign that some people thought the Dodgers intended to punt the pick and would take the compensation selection in the next draft.

The Rockies also signed two notable Atlantic Coast Conference quarterbacks, though they signed contracts that allowed them to continue their college football careers. Clemson's Kyle Parker, the 26th overall pick, signed for a $1.4 million bonus, after he and the Rockies could not agree to a price earlier in the summer that would have compelled him to give up football. North Carolina State's Russell Wilson, a fourth-round pick, signed for a $200,000 bonus.

■ The Pirates spent big on high school righthanders. First-rounder Jameson Taillon, the No. 2

overall pick, signed for a $6.5 million bonus, the biggest bonus any player received in 2010, while second-rounder Stetson Allie got $2.25 million. The Pirates' total draft expenditure was nearly $12 million.

■ The Tigers set a record by giving Miami prep infielder Nick Castellanos the largest bonus in supplemental first-round history, at $3.45 million. The Yankees gave fourth-round pick Mason Williams a $1.45 million bonus, but that wasn't a fourth-round record, because the Nationals gave Florida prep righty A.J. Cole a $2 million bonus a couple of days earlier.

■ Loux signed as a free agent with the Rangers on Nov. 19 for a $312,000 bonus, meaning they had five of the first 49 selections in the 2010 draft under contract..

CLIFF WELCH

David Price went from No. 1 pick to Cy Young contender in just three years

DRAFT

YEAR	NO. 1 PICK	SCHOOL	HOMETOWN	BONUS	HIGHEST LEVEL	LARGEST BONUS (PICK NUMBER)	AMOUNT
1965	Rick Monday, of, Athletics	Arizona State	Santa Monica, Calif.	$100,000	Majors	same	
1966	Steve Chilcott, c, Mets	Antelope Valley HS	Lancaster, Calif.	75,000	Triple-A	Reggie Jackson, of, Athletics (2)	$80,000
1967	Ron Blomberg, 1b, Yankees	Druid Hills HS	Atlanta	65,000	Majors	#Mike Adamson, rhp, Orioles	75,000
1968	Tim Foli, ss, Mets	Notre Dame HS	Sherman Oaks, Calif.	74,000	Majors	Lloyd Allen, rhp, Angels (12)	75,000
1969	Jeff Burroughs, of, Senators	Wilson HS	Long Beach, Calif.	88,000	Majors	same	
1970	Mike Ivie, c, Padres	Walker HS	Decatur, Ga.	75,000	Majors	#Dave Kingman, 1b, Giants	80,000
1971	Danny Goodwin, c, White Sox	Central HS	Peoria, Ill.	DNS	Majors	Ed Kurpiel, 1b, Cardinals (8)	83,750
1972	Dave Roberts, 3b, Padres	Oregon	Corvallis, Ore.	70,000	Majors	Jamie Quirk, ss, Royals (18)	78,000
1973	*David Clyde, lhp, Rangers	Westchester HS	Houston	65,000	Majors	^Alan Bannister, ss, Phillies	85,000
1974	*Bill Almon, ss, Padres	Brown	Warwick, R.I.	90,000	Majors	Willie Wilson, of, Royals (18)	90,000
1975	*Danny Goodwin, c, Angels	Southern	Peoria, Ill.	125,000	Majors	same	
1976	Floyd Bannister, lhp, Astros	Arizona State	Seattle	100,000	Majors	same	
1977	Harold Baines, of, White Sox	St. Michaels HS	St. Michaels, Md.	32,000	Majors	Paul Molitor, ss, Twins (3)	77,500
1978	*Bob Horner, 3b, Braves	Arizona State	Glendale, Ariz.	162,000	Majors	same	
1979	Al Chambers, 1b, Mariners	Harris HS	Harrisburg, Pa.	60,000	Majors	Todd Demeter, 1b, Yankees (51)	208,000
1980	Darryl Strawberry, of, Mets	Crenshaw HS	Los Angeles	152,500	Majors	same	
1981	Mike Moore, rhp, Mariners	Oral Roberts	Eakly, Okla.	100,000	Majors	Terry Blocker, of, Mets (4)	127,500
1982	Shawon Dunston, ss, Cubs	Jefferson HS	New York	135,000	Majors	Kenny Williams, of, White Sox (78)	160,000
1983	Tim Belcher, rhp, Twins	Mt. Vernon Nazarene	Sparta, Ohio	DNS	Majors	Kurt Stillwell, ss, Reds (2)	135,000
1984	Shawn Abner, of, Mets	Mechanicsburg HS	Mechanicsburg, Pa.	150,500	Majors	same	
1985	B.J. Surhoff, c, Brewers	North Carolina	Rye, N.Y.	150,000	Majors	Bobby Witt, rhp, Rangers (3)	179,000
1986	Jeff King, 3b, Pirates	Arkansas	Colorado Springs	180,000	Majors	same	
1987	Ken Griffey Jr., of, Mariners	Moeller HS	Cincinnati	160,000	Majors	Mark Merchant, of, Pirates (2)	165,000
						Jack McDowell, rhp, White Sox (5)	165,000
1988	Andy Benes, rhp, Padres	Evansville	Evansville, Ind.	235,000	Majors	same	
1989	*Ben McDonald, rhp, Orioles	Louisiana State	Denham Springs, La.	350,000	Majors	John Olerud, 1b, Blue Jays (79)	575,000
1990	Chipper Jones, ss, Braves	The Bolles School	Jacksonville	275,000	Majors	*Todd Van Poppel, rhp, As (14)	500,000
1991	Brien Taylor, lhp, Yankees	East Carteret HS	Beaufort, N.C.	1,550,000	Double-A	Tony Clark, 1b, Tigers (2)	500,000
1992	Phil Nevin, 3b, Astros	Cal State Fullerton	Placentia, Calif.	700,000	Majors	same	
1993	*Alex Rodriguez, ss, Mariners	Westminster Christian HS	Miami	1,000,000	Majors	Jeffrey Hammonds, of, Orioles (4)	975,000
1994	Paul Wilson, rhp, Mets	Florida State	Orlando, Fla.	1,550,000	Majors	Darren Dreifort, rhp, Dodgers (2)	1,300,000
1995	Darin Erstad, of, Angels	Nebraska	Jamestown, N.D.	1,575,000	Majors	Josh Booty, ss, Marlins (5)	1,600,000
1996	*Kris Benson, rhp, Pirates	Clemson	Kennesaw, Ga.	2,000,000	Majors	same	
1997	Matt Anderson, rhp, Tigers	Rice	Louisville	2,505,000	Majors	Matt White, rhp, Giants (7)	10,200,000
1998	*Pat Burrell, 3b, Phillies	Miami	Boulder Creek, Calif.	3,150,000	Majors	same	
1999	Josh Hamilton, of, Devil Rays	Athens Drive HS	Raleigh, N.C.	3,960,000	Majors	Corey Patterson, of, Cubs (3)	3,700,000
2000	Adrian Gonzalez, 1b, Marlins	Eastside HS	Chula Vista, Calif.	3,000,000	Majors	same	
2001	Joe Mauer, c, Twins	Cretin-Derham Hall	St. Paul, Minn.	5,150,000	Majors	Joe Borchard, of, White Sox (12)	5,300,000
2002	Bryan Bullington, rhp, Pirates	Ball State	Fishers, Ind.	4,000,000	Majors	B.J. Upton, ss, Devil Rays (2)	4,600,000
2003	*Delmon Young, of, Devil Rays	Camarillo HS	Camarillo, Calif.	3,700,000	Majors	same	
2004	Matt Bush, ss, Padres	Mission Bay HS	El Cajon, Calif.	3,150,000	Class A	Jered Weaver (12)/Stephen Drew (15)	4,000,000
2005	Justin Upton, ss, D'backs	Great Bridge HS	Chesapeake, Va.	6,100,000	Majors	same	
2006	*Luke Hochevar, rhp, Royals	No School	Fowler, Colo.	3,500,000	Majors	Andrew Miller, lhp, Tigers (6)	3,550,000
2007	*David Price, lhp, Devil Rays	Vanderbilt	Murfreesboro, Tenn.	5,600,000	Majors	Matt Wieters, c, Orioles (5)	6,000,000
2008	Tim Beckham, ss, Rays	Griffin HS	Griffin, Ga.	6,150,000	Short-season	Buster Posey, c, Giants (5)	6,200,000
2009	*Stephen Strasburg, rhp, Nationals	San Diego State	San Diego	7,500,000	Did not play	same	
2010	*Bryce Harper, of, Nationals	JC of Southern Nevada	Las Vegas	6,250,000	Did not play	Jameson Taillon, rhp, Pirates (2)	6,500,000

*Signed major league contract. #Selected in June secondary phase. ^Selected in January draft. †Includes four loophole free agents; White signed with Devil Rays.

RON VESELY

After 11 minor league games, Chris Sale was the first 2010 pick to get to the big leagues

TEAM, PLAYER, POS., SCHOOL	BONUS
1. Nationals. Bryce Harper, of, JC of Southern Nevada	$6,250,000
2. Pirates. Jameson Taillon, rhp, HS—Woodlands, Texas	$6,500,000
3. Orioles. Manny Machado, ss, HS—Miami	$5,250,000
4. Royals. Christian Colon, ss, Cal State Fullerton	$2,750,000
5. Indians. Drew Pomeranz, lhp, Mississippi	$2,650,000
6. Diamondbacks. Barret Loux, rhp, Texas A&M	Did not sign
7. Mets. Matt Harvey, rhp, North Carolina	$2,525,000
8. Astros. Delino DeShields, 2b, HS—College Park, Ga.	$2,150,000
9. Padres. Karsten Whitson, rhp, HS—Chipley, Fla.	Did not sign
10. Athletics. Michael Choice, of, Texas-Arlington	$2,000,000
11. Blue Jays. Deck McGuire, rhp, Georgia Tech	$2,000,000
12. Reds. Yasmani Grandal, c, Miami	$2,000,000
13. White Sox. Chris Sale, lhp, Florida Gulf Coast	$1,656,000
14. Brewers. Dylan Covey, rhp, HS—Pasadena, Calif.	Did not sign
15. Rangers. Jake Skole, of, HS—Roswell, Ga.	$1,557,000
16. Cubs. Hayden Simpson, rhp, Southern Arkansas	$1,060,000
17. Rays. Josh Sale, of, HS—Seattle	$1,620,000
18. Angels. Kaleb Cowart, 3b/rhp, HS—Adel, Ga.	$2,300,000
19. Astros. Mike Foltynewicz, rhp, HS—Minooka, Ill.	$1,305,000
20. Red Sox. Kolbrin Vitek, 2b/of, Ball State	$1,359,000
21. Twins. Alex Wimmers, rhp, Ohio State	$1,332,000
22. Rangers. Kellin Deglan, c, HS—Langley, B.C.	$1,000,000
23. Marlins. Christian Yelich, of, HS—Westlake Village, Calif.	$1,700,000
24. Giants. Gary Brown, of, Cal State Fullerton	$1,450,000
25. Cardinals. Zack Cox, 3b, Arkansas	$2,000,000
26. Rockies. Kyle Parker, of, Clemson	$1,400,000
27. Phillies. Jesse Biddle, lhp, HS—Philadelphia	$1,160,000
28. Dodgers. Zach Lee, rhp, HS—McKinney, Texas	$5,250,000
29. Angels. Cam Bedrosian, rhp, HS—Sharpsburg, Ga.	$1,116,000
30. Angels. Chevez Clarke, of, HS—Marietta, Ga.	$1,089,000
31. Rays. Justin O'Conner, c, HS—Muncie, Ind.	$1,025,000
32. Yankees. Cito Culver, ss, HS—Rochester, N.Y.	$954,000
33. Astros. Mike Kvasnicka, 3b/c, Minnesota	$936,000
34. Blue Jays. Aaron Sanchez, rhp, HS—Barstow, Calif.	$775,000
35. Braves. Matt Lipka, ss, HS—McKinney, Texas	$800,000
36. Red Sox. Bryce Brentz, of, Middle Tennessee State	$889,200
37. Angels. Taylor Lindsey, ss, HS—Scottsdale, Ariz.	$873,000
38. Blue Jays. Noah Syndergaard, rhp, HS—Mansfield, Texas	$600,000
39. Red Sox. Anthony Ranaudo, rhp, Louisiana State	$2,550,000
40. Angels. Ryan Bolden, of, HS—Madison, Miss.	$829,800
41. Blue Jays. Asher Wojciechowski, rhp, The Citadel	$815,400
42. Rays. Drew Vettleson, of, HS—Silverdale, Wash.	$845,000
43. Mariners. Taijuan Walker, rhp, HS—Yucaipa, Calif.	$800,000
44. Tigers. Nick Castellanos, 3b, HS—SW Ranches, Fla.	$3,450,000
45. Rangers. Luke Jackson, rhp, HS—Fort Lauderdale, Fla.	$1,545,000
46. Cardinals. Seth Blair, rhp, Arizona State	$751,500
47. Rockies. Peter Tago, rhp, HS—Dana Point, Calif.	$982,500
48. Tigers. Chance Ruffin, rhp, Texas	$1,150,000
49. Rangers. Mike Olt, 3b, Connecticut	$717,300
50. Cardinals. Tyrell Jenkins, rhp, HS—Henderson, Texas	$1,300,000

TEAM, PLAYER, POS., SCHOOL	BONUS
51. Nationals. Sammy Solis, lhp, San Diego	$1,000,000
52. Pirates. Stetson Allie, rhp, HS—Lakewood, Ohio	$2,250,000
53. Braves. Todd Cunningham, of, Jacksonville State	$674,100
54. Royals. Brett Eibner, of/rhp, Arkansas	$1,250,000
55. Indians. LeVon Washington, of, Chipola (Fla.) JC	$1,200,000
56. Diamondbacks. J.R. Bradley, rhp, HS—Nitro, W.Va.	$643,500
57. Red Sox. Brandon Workman, rhp, Texas	$800,000
58. Astros. Vincent Velasquez, rhp, HS—Garey, Calif.	$655,830
59. Padres. Jedd Gyorko, 2b, West Virginia	$614,700
60. Athletics. Yordy Cabrera, 3b, HS—Lakeland, Fla.	$1,250,000
61. Blue Jays. Griffin Murphy, lhp, HS—Redlands, Calif.	$800,000
62. Reds. Ryan LaMarre, of, Michigan	$587,700
63. White Sox. Jacob Petricka, rhp, Indiana State	$540,000
64. Brewers. Jimmy Nelson, rhp, Alabama	$570,600
65. Cubs. Reggie Golden, of, HS—Wetumpka, Ala.	$720,000
66. Rays. Jake Thompson, rhp, Long Beach State	$555,000
67. Mariners. Marcus Littlewood, ss, HS—St. George, Utah	$900,000
68. Tigers. Drew Smyly, lhp, Arkansas	$1,100,000
69. Blue Jays. Kellen Sweeney, 3b, HS—Cedar Rapids, Iowa	$600,000
70. Braves. Andrelton Simmons, ss, Western Okla. State JC	$522,000
71. Twins. Niko Goodrum, ss, HS—Fayetteville, Ga.	$514,800
72. Rangers. Cody Buckel, rhp, HS—Simi Valley, Calif.	$590,000
73. Marlins. Rob Rasmussen, lhp, UCLA	$499,500
74. Giants. Jarrett Parker, of, Virginia	$700,000
75. Cardinals. Jordan Swagerty, rhp, Arizona State	$625,000
76. Rockies. Chad Bettis, rhp, Texas Tech	$477,000
77. Phillies. Perci Garner, rhp, Ball State	$470,700
78. Dodgers. Ralston Cash, rhp, HS—Cornelia, Ga.	$463,500
79. Rays. Derek Dietrich, 3b, Georgia Tech	$457,200
80. Blue Jays. Justin Nicolino, lhp, HS—Orlando Fla.	$615,000
81. Angels. Daniel Tillman, rhp, Florida Southern	$443,700
82. Yankees. Angelo Gumbs, of, HS—Torrance, Calif.	$750,000
83. Nationals. Rick Hague, ss, Rice	$430,200
84. Pirates. Mel Rojas Jr., of, Wabash Valley (Ill.) CC	$423,900
85. Orioles. Dan Klein, rhp, UCLA	$499,900
86. Royals. Mike Antonio, ss, HS—New York	$411,000
87. Indians. Tony Wolters, ss, HS—Vista, Calif.	$1,350,000
88. D'backs. Robby Rowland, rhp, HS—Cloverdale, Calif.	$395,000
89. Mets. Blake Forsythe, c, Tennessee	$392,400
90. Astros. Austin Wates, of, Virginia Tech	$550,000
91. Padres. Zach Cates, rhp, Northeast Texas CC	$765,000
92. Athletics. Aaron Shipman, of, HS—Quitman, Ga.	$500,000
93. Blue Jays. Christopher Hawkins, 3b, HS—Suwanee, Ga.	$350,000
94. Reds. Devin Lohman, ss, Long Beach State	$363,600
95. White Sox. Addison Reed, rhp, San Diego State	$358,200
96. Brewers. Tyler Thornburg, rhp, Charleston Southern	$351,900
97. Cubs. Micah Gibbs, c, Louisiana State	$350,000
98. Rays. Ryan Brett, 2b, HS—Burien, Wash.	$341,100
99. Mariners. Ryne Stanek, rhp, HS—Stilwell, Kan.	Did not sign
100. Tigers. Rob Brantly, c, UC Riverside	$330,300

DRAFT

ORDER OF SELECTION IN PARENTHESES PLAYERS SIGNED IN BOLD

ARIZONA DIAMONDBACKS (6)

1. Barret Loux, rhp, Texas A&M
2. **J.R. Bradley, rhp, Nitro (W.Va.) HS**
3. **Robby Rowland, rhp, Cloverdale (Calif.) HS**
4. **Kevin Munson, rhp, James Madison**
5. **Cody Wheeler, lhp, Coastal Carolina**
6. **Blake Perry, rhp, Pendleton School, Bradenton, Fla.**
7. **Jeff Shields, rhp, Chattahoochee Valley (Ala.) CC**
8. **Tyler Green, rhp, Brazoswood HS, Clute, Texas**
9. **Zach Walters, ss, San Diego**
10. **Kawika Emsley-Pai, c, Lewis-Clark State (Idaho)**
11. **Mike Freeman, ss, Clemson**
12. **Blake Cooper, rhp, South Carolina**
13. Kevin Ziomek, lhp, Amherst (Mass.) Regional HS
14. **Tyler Linton, of, Charlotte (N.C.) Christian HS**
15. **Mike Bolsinger, rhp, Arkansas**
16. **Westley Moss, of, Nevada**
17. **Derek Eitel, rhp, Rose-Hulman (Ind.)**
18. **Jimmy Comerota, 1b, Rice**
19. **Adam Eaton, of, Miami (Ohio)**
20. Michael Hur, of, UC Riverside (Contract voided)
21. **Raoul Torrez, 2b, Arizona State**
22. **Jeremy Erben, rhp, Oklahoma**
23. Roberto Padilla, lhp, Ohlone (Calif.) JC
24. **Stephen Cardullo, 3b, Florida State**
25. Matt Talley, lhp, The Citadel
26. **Yazy Arbelo, 1b, Keystone (Pa.)**
27. **Niko Gallego, 2b, UCLA**
28. Keith Hessler, lhp, Coastal Carolina
29. Chris Floethe, rhp, Cal State Fullerton
30. Ryan Zimmerman, rhp, Northwestern State
31. Steven Sultzbaugh, of, Rice
32. **Greg Robinson, rhp, Wright State**
33. Andrew Whittington, c, Southern Arkansas (Contract voided)
34. **Victor Lara, rhp, Keystone (Pa.)**
35. Konner Wade, rhp, Chaparral HS, Scottsdale, Ariz.
36. **Justin Hilt, of, Elon**
37. **Michael Weber, 2b, Washington State**
38. Matt Roberts, c, Graham (N.C.) HS
39. Garrett Nash, 3b, Oregon State
40. Ryan Casillas, 1b, Hamilton HS, Chandler, Ariz.
41. Mike McGee, rhp, Florida State
42. **Chris Jarrett, of, Anderson (Ind.)**
43. **Tom Belza, 2b, Oklahoma State**
44. **Eric Groff, 3b, Keystone (Pa.)**
45. **Javan Williams, of, Contra Costa (Calif.) JC**
46. Jorge Flores, ss, Hamilton HS, Chandler, Ariz.
47. **Casey Upperman, rhp, Yavapai (Ariz.) JC**
48. Kenny Sigman, rhp, South Mountain (Ariz.) CC
49. Tad Barton, rhp, Muhlenberg HS, Laureldale, Pa.
50. Trey Ford, 3b, South Mountain (Ariz.) CC

ATLANTA BRAVES (35)

1. (Pick to Red Sox as compensation for Type A free agent Billy Wagner)
1s. **Matt Lipka, ss, McKinney (Texas) HS** (Supplemental pick—35th—for loss of Type A free agent Mike Gonzalez)
2. **Todd Cunningham, of, Jacksonville State** (Pick from Orioles as compensation for Gonzalez)
2. **Andrelton Simmons, ss, Western Oklahoma State JC**
3. **Joe Leonard, 3b, Pittsburgh**
4. **Dave Filak, rhp, Oneonta State (N.Y.)**
5. **Phil Gosselin, 2b, Virginia**
6. **Joey Terdoslavich, 3b, Long Beach State**
7. **Matt Suschak, rhp, Toledo**
8. **Kurt Fleming, of, St. Christopher's HS, Richmond**
9. **David Rohm, 1b, Fresno CC**
10. **Matt Lewis, rhp, UC Davis**
11. **Chase Shreve, lhp, JC of Southern Nevada**
12. **Barrett Kleinknecht, ss, Francis Marion (S.C.)**
13. **Brandon Drury, ss, Grants Pass (Ore.) HS**

14. **Richie Tate, rhp, Market Tree (Ark.) HS**
15. **Cory Brownsten, c, Pittsburgh**
16. **Dan Winnie, rhp, Lackawanna (Pa.) JC**
17. Stefan Sabol, c, Aliso Niguel HS, Aliso Viejo, Calif.
18. Zach Alvord, 2b, South Forsyth HS, Cumming, Ga.
19. **Tyler Hess, rhp, Sonoma State (Calif.)**
20. **Jason Mowry, of, St. Petersburg (Fla.) JC**
21. **William Beckwith, 1b, George Wallace (Ala.) CC**
22. Jordan Buckley, of, New Mexico JC
23. **Evan Gattis, c, Texas-Permian Basin**
24. **Evan Danieli, rhp, Notre Dame**
25. **Dan Jurik, rhp, St. John Fisher (N.Y.)**
26. **Jonathan Burns, rhp, St. Edward's (Texas)**
27. **Willie Kempf, rhp, Baylor**
28. **Kyle Mertins, rhp, Cal State Fullerton**
29. Reid Roper, ss, Harrisburg (Ill.) HS
30. **Kenny Fleming, of, Shelton State (Ala.) CC**
31. Jack Reinheimer, ss, Kell HS, Charlotte, N.C.
32. **Ryan Delgado, rhp, Azusa Pacific (Calif.)**
33. Albert Minnis, lhp, Lawrence (Kan.) HS
34. **Matt Fouch, lhp, Army**
35. Kenny Swab, c, Virginia
36. **Jarred Frierson, 2b, Nevada-Las Vegas**
37. Kollin Dowdy, of, Harrisburg (Ill.) HS
38. Jake Wark, 1b, Jesuit HS, Beaverton, Ore.
39. **Stephen Foster, rhp, Lewis-Clark State (Idaho)**
40. **Ian Marshall, rhp, Richmond**
41. Spencer Jordan, rhp, Florence-Darlington Tech (S.C.) JC
42. Ben Waldrip, 1b, Cypress (Calif.) JC
43. LeJon Baker, of, Crenshaw HS, Los Angeles
44. Ryan Morrow, c, St. Mary's (Texas)
45. **Joe Lucas, ss, Dakota County Tech (Minn.) JC**
46. Kendall Logan, of, Copiah-Lincoln (Miss.) JC
47. **Frank LaFreniere, rhp, St. Petersburg (Fla.) JC**
48. James Mahler, rhp, Salt Lake (Utah) CC
49. Ryan Turner, rhp, McLennan (Texas) CC
50. Cody Gabella, ss, Notre Dame HS, Burlington, Iowa

BALTIMORE ORIOLES (3)

1. **Manny Machado, ss, Brito Miami Private HS**
2. (Pick to Braves as compensation for Type A free agent Mike Gonzalez)
3. **Dan Klein, rhp, UCLA**
4. **Trent Mummey, of, Auburn**
5. **Connor Narron, ss, Aycock HS, Pikeville, N.C.**
6. Dixon Anderson, rhp, California
7. **Matt Bywater, lhp, Pepperdine**
8. **Wynston Sawyer, c, Scripps Ranch HS, San Diego**
9. **Parker Bridwell, rhp, Hereford (Texas) HS**
10. **Clay Schrader, rhp, San Jacinto (Texas) JC**
11. Alex Gonzalez, rhp, Boca Raton (Fla.) Community HS
12. **Riley Hornback, of, San Jacinto (Texas) JC**
13. **Jeremy Nowak, of, Mount Olive (N.C.)**
14. **Michael Mosby, 3b, Wabash Valley (Ill.) CC**
15. **Joe Oliveira, c, Pacific**
16. Brandon King, of, Fresno (Calif.) CC
17. **David Richardson, of, Hillsborough (Fla.) CC**
18. **Sebastian Vader, rhp, San Marcos (Calif.) HS**
19. **Ken Wise, rhp, Santa Fe (Fla.) CC**
20. **Matt Drummond, lhp, UCLA**
21. **Scott Copeland, rhp, Southern Mississippi**
22. **Tanner Murphy, c, Mountain Ridge HS, Glendale, Ariz.**
23. **Chris Clinton, of, Eckerd (Fla.)**
24. **Tim Adleman, rhp, Georgetown**
25. **Vinny Zazueta, ss, Arizona Western JC**
26. **Austin Goolsby, c, Embry-Riddle (Fla.)**
27. Austin Urban, rhp, Richland HS, Johnstown, Pa.
28. **Jaime Esquivel, rhp, South Houston (Texas) HS**
29. **Cameron Roth, rhp, UNC Wilmington**
30. **Michael Rooney, lhp, UNC Wilmington**
31. **Adam Gaylord, 3b, Stanford**
32. Joe Robinson, rhp, JC of Southern Nevada

33. Steven Mazur, rhp, Notre Dame
34. Sammie Starr, ss, British Columbia
35. Auburn Donaldson, ss, Southeastern (Fla.)
36. Brad Decater, ss, Cal State Northridge
37. Austin Knight, 2b, Palm Beach (Fla.) CC
38. Jeremy Shelby, of, Grambling State
39. Travis Strong, rhp, Wildomar, Calif. (No school)
40. Joe Velleggia, c, Old Dominion
41. Coty Blanchard, ss, Cherokee County HS, Centre, Ala.
42. Jacob Pettit, lhp, Western Oregon
43. Blair Dunlap, of, UCLA
44. Preston Hale, of, North Florida
45. Nathan Williams, rhp, Scripps Ranch HS, San Diego
46. Dan Torres, c, Countryside HS, Clearwater, Fla.
47. Cody Young, of, Anderson (Ind.)
48. Alex Schmarzo, rhp, St. Mary's
49. Hayden Jordan, rhp, Whitewater HS, Fayetteville, Ga.
50. Philip Walby, rhp, Scripps Ranch HS, San Diego

BOSTON RED SOX (20)

1. Kolbrin Vitek, 2b/of, Ball State (Pick from Braves as compensation for Type A free agent Billy Wagner)
1. (Pick to Angels as compensation for Type A free agent John Lackey)
1s. Bryce Brentz, of, Middle Tennessee State (Supplemental pick—36th—for loss of Type A free agent Jason Bay)
1s. Anthony Ranaudo, rhp, Louisiana State (Supplemental pick—39th—for loss of Wagner)
2. Brandon Workman, rhp, Texas (Pick from Mets as compensation for Bay)
2. (Pick to Blue Jays as compensation for Type A free agent Marco Scutaro)
3. Sean Coyle, ss, Germantown Acad., Fort Washington, Pa.
4. Garin Cecchini, ss, Barbe HS, Lake Charles, La.
5. Henry Ramos, of, Alfonso Casta Martinez HS, Maunabo, P.R.
6. Kendrick Perkins, of, La Porte (Texas) HS
7. Chris Hernandez, lhp, Miami
8. Mathew Price, rhp, Virginia Tech
9. Tyler Barnette, rhp, Hickory (N.C.) HS
10. Jacob Dahlstrand, rhp, Memorial HS, Houston
11. Lucas LeBlanc, of, Delgado (La.) JC
12. Garrett Rau, rhp, California Baptist
13. Keith Couch, rhp, Adelphi (N.Y.)
14. Mike Hollenbeck, c, Joliet Township (Ill.) HS
15. Steve Wilkerson, ss, Pope HS, Marietta, Ga.
16. Adam Duke, rhp, Spanish Fork (Utah) HS
17. Jason Garcia, rhp, Land O'Lakes (Fla.) HS
18. Dallas Chadwick, rhp, Shasta HS, Redding, Calif.
19. Eric Jaffe, rhp, Bishop O'Dowd HS, Oakland
20. Roderick Shoulders, c, Brandon (Fla.) HS
21. Mason Justice, rhp, Holland Hall, Tulsa, Okla.
22. Trace Tam Sing, 2b, Newport HS, Bellevue, Wash.
23. Austin Wright, lhp, Chipola (Fla.) JC
24. Sean Yost, rhp, Nebraska
25. Tyler Lockwood, rhp, Texas Christian
26. Dillon Overton, lhp, Weatherford (Okla.) HS
27. Jay Gonzalez, of, Freedom HS, Orlando
28. Mike Wagner, rhp, Centennial HS, Las Vegas
29. Paul Davis, rhp, Pensacola (Fla.) JC
30. DeSean Anderson, of, Ragsdale HS, Jamestown, N.C.
31. Hunter Renfroe, c, Copiah Academy, Gallman, Miss.
32. Jordan Alexander, of, Vista (Calif.) HS
33. Mark Donham, rhp, Jupiter (Fla.) Community HS
34. Mike Gleason, rhp, Chico State (Calif.)
35. J.T. Riddle, ss, Western Hills HS, Frankfort, Ky.
36. Shane Rowland, c, Tampa Catholic HS
37. Aaron Jones, c, San Clemente (Calif.) HS
38. Tom Bourdon, of, Northwest Catholic HS, West Hartford, Conn.
39. Nick Robinson, ss, North Central (Ill.)
40. Luke Yoder, of, Cal Poly
41. Jayson Hernandez, c, Rutgers
42. Dan Slania, rhp, Salpointe Catholic HS, Tucson, Ariz.
43. Patrick Smith, of, Redan HS, Stone Mountain, Ga.
44. Zach Kapstein, c, Tiverton (R.I.) HS
45. James Kang, ss, Pomona-Pitzer (Calif.)
46. Drake Thomason, rhp, Eastside HS, Taylors, S.C.

47. David Roseboom, lhp, LaSalle Institute, Troy, N.Y.
48. J.T. Autrey, rhp, Stephenville (Texas) HS
49. Trygg Larsson-Danforth, 1b, Yale
50. Weston Hoekel, rhp, Bishop Kenny HS, Jacksonville, Fla.

CHICAGO CUBS (16)

1. Hayden Simpson, rhp, Southern Arkansas
2. Reggie Golden, of, Wetumpka (Ala.) HS
3. Micah Gibbs, c, Louisiana State
4. Hunter Ackerman, lhp, Louisburg (N.C.) JC
5. Matt Szczur, of, Villanova
6. Ivan DeJesus, of, Cupeyville School, San Juan, P.R.
7. Ben Wells, rhp, Bryant (Ark.) HS
8. Cam Greathouse, lhp, Gulf Coast (Fla.) CC
9. Kevin Rhoderick, rhp, Oregon State
10. Aaron Kurcz, rhp, JC of Southern Nevada
11. Eric Jokisch, lhp, Northwestern
12. Austin Reed, rhp, Rancho Cucamonga (Calif.) HS
13. Pierre LePage, 2b, Connecticut
14. Colin Richardson, rhp, Winter Haven (Fla.) HS
15. Elliot Soto, ss, Creighton
16. Ryan Hartman, rhp, Mount Zion (Ill.) HS
17. Steven Brooks, of, Wake Forest
18. Brooks Pinckard, of/rhp, Baylor
19. Dustin Fitzgerald, rhp, Hill (Texas) JC
20. Ryan Cuneo, 1b, Delaware
21. Cody Cox, rhp, Grassfield HS, Chesapeake, Va.
22. Jeff Vigurs, c, Bryant (R.I.)
23. Matt Loosen, rhp, Jacksonville
24. Dustin Geiger, of, Merritt Island (Fla.) HS
25. Eric Rice, rhp, Palm Beach (Fla.) CC
26. Danny Muno, ss, Fresno State
27. Bryan Harper, lhp, JC of Southern Nevada
28. Joe Zeller, rhp, The Master's (Calif.)
29. Casey Harman, lhp, Clemson
30. Karsten Strieby, 1b, Arizona Western JC
31. Benito Santiago, 1b, Lon Morris (Texas) JC
32. Brent Ebinger, lhp, Lambuth (Tenn.)
33. Matt Stites, rhp, Jefferson (Mo.) JC
34. Dustin Harrington, 3b, East Carolina
35. Chris Anderson, rhp, Centennial HS, Blaine, Minn.
36. Tyler Bremer, rhp, Yavapai (Ariz.) JC
37. Chad Noble, c, Northwestern
38. Jeremy Fitzgerald, rhp, Patrick Henry (Va.) CC
39. Casey Lucchese, rhp, College of Charleston
40. Brian Smith, lhp, St. Mary Catholic SS, Pickering, Ont.
41. Dallas Beeler, rhp, Oral Roberts
42. Trey Nielsen, rhp, Skyline HS, Salt Lake City
43. Danny Winkler, rhp, Parkland (Ill.) JC
44. Jake Rogers, 1b, St. Petersburg (Fla.) JC
45. Devon Austin, c, Coeur d'Alene (Idaho) HS
46. Jerad Eickhoff, rhp, Olney Central (Ill.) JC
47. Clayton Crum, rhp, Klein HS, Spring, Texas
48. Eric Paulson, 3b, Fremd HS, Palatine, Ill.
49. Bryce Shafer, rhp, Valparaiso
50. Eric Jagielo, ss, Downers Grove (Ill.) North HS

CHICAGO WHITE SOX (13)

1. Chris Sale, lhp, Florida Gulf Coast
2. Jacob Petricka, rhp, Indiana State
3. Addison Reed, rhp, San Diego State
3s. Thomas Royse, rhp, Louisville (Supplemental pick—114th—for failure to sign 2009 third-round pick Bryan Morgado)
4. Matthew Grimes, rhp, Mill Creek HS, Hoschton, Ga.
5. Andy Wilkins, 1b, Arkansas
6. Rangel Ravelo, 3b, Hialeah (Fla.) HS
7. Tyler Saladino, ss, Oral Roberts
8. Josef Terry, 2b, Cerritos (Calif.) JC
9. Kevin Moran, rhp, Boston College
10. Ross Wilson, 2b, Alabama
11. James McDonald, ss, Chaparral HS, Phoenix
12. Drew Lee, ss, Morehead State
13. Ethan Icard, rhp, Wilkes (N.C.) CC
14. Mike Blanke, c, Tampa

15. Sean O'Connell, c, Chatsworth (Calif.) HS
16. Stephen McCray, rhp, Tennessee
17. Mike Schwartz, 1b, Tampa
18. Randall Thorpe, of, San Jacinto (Texas) JC
19. Doug Murray, rhp, San Francisco
20. Jose Ramos, c, Western Oklahoma State JC
21. Tyler Jones, rhp, Madison (Wis.) JC
22. Ozney Guillen, of, Pace HS, Opa Locka, Fla.
23. Austin Evans, rhp, Tampa
24. Jordan Keegan, of, JC of Southern Nevada
25. Ethan Wilson, ss, Indiana
26. Kevin Rath, lhp, Cal State Fullerton
27. Pete Gehle, lhp, Azusa Pacific (Calif.)
28. Thomas Windle, lhp, Osseo (Minn.) HS
29. Michael Earley, of, Indiana
30. Kylin Turnbull, lhp, Santa Barbara (Calif.) CC
31. Robert Young, lhp, Dartmouth
32. Jarrett Casey, lhp, Northern Kentucky
33. Jamaal Hollis, rhp, Miami (Ohio)
34. Dusty Harvard, of, Oklahoma State
35. John Spatola, of, Boston College
36. Ben Griset, lhp, Gustine (Calif.) HS
37. Chris Lee, lhp, Robinson HS, Tampa
38. Brad Salgado, ss, Great Oak HS, Temecula, Calif.
39. Levi Schlick, lhp, Barton County (Kan.) CC
40. Conrad Gregor, of, Carmel (Ind.) HS
41. Sam Phippen, rhp, UC Santa Barbara
42. Brett Bruening, rhp, Texas Tech
43. Luke Irvine, rhp, Northwestern State
44. Matt Chavez, rhp, San Francisco
45. Ronald Cotton, of, Boone County HS, Florence, Ky.
46. Ronzelle Fort, lhp, Harlan HS, Chicago
47. Matt Reida, 2b, Western HS, Russiaville, Ind.
48. Audry Santana, 2b, Mariner HS, Cape Coral, Fla.
49. Pat Schatz, rhp, Iowa
50. David Vazquez, 2b, Archbishop McCarthy HS, SW Ranches, Fla.

CINCINNATI REDS (12)

1. Yasmani Grandal, c, Miami
2. Ryan LaMarre, of, Michigan
3. Devin Lohman, ss, Long Beach State
4. Brodie Greene, 2b, Texas A&M
5. Wes Mugarian, rhp, Pensacola (Fla.) Catholic HS
6. Drew Cisco, rhp, Wando HS, Mt. Pleasant, S.C.
7. Tony Amezcua, rhp, Bellflower (Calif.) HS
8. David Vidal, 3b, Miami Dade CC
9. Tanner Robles, lhp, Oregon State
10. Kevin Arico, rhp, Virginia
11. Drew Hayes, rhp, Vanderbilt
12. Kyle Waldrop, of, Riverdale HS, Fort Myers, Fla.
13. Lucas O'Rear, rhp, Northern Iowa
14. Dan Wolford, rhp, California
15. Stephen Hunt, lhp, South Florida
16. Rob Kral, c, College of Charleston
17. Brent Peterson, ss, Liberty HS, Bakersfield, Calif.
18. Robert Maddox, of, Ohio
19. Josh Alexander, of, Mountain Pointe HS, Phoenix
20. Chris Berset, c, Michigan
21. Josh Smith, rhp, Lipscomb
22. Kurt Muller, of, Iowa
23. Randy Fontanez, rhp, South Florida
24. Pat Doyle, rhp, Missouri State
25. Daniel Renken, rhp, Cal State Fullerton
26. Ty Stuckey, lhp, Houston
27. Joel Bender, lhp, Oak Hills HS, Cincinnati
28. Chad Rogers, rhp, Galveston (Texas) CC
29. Adam Muenster, 3b, Kansas State
30. Brad Hendrix, rhp, Auburn
31. Dominic D'Anna, 1b, Cal State Northridge
32. Jaren Matthews, 1b, Rutgers
33. David Garner, rhp, Niles (Mich.) HS
34. Brandon Dailey, ss, Pauline Johnson SS, Brantford, Ont.
35. Tyler Wilson, rhp, Virginia
36. Chuck Ghysels, rhp, Lincoln Trail (Ill.) CC
37. Nick Sawyer, rhp, Hebron HS, Carrollton, Texas

38. Matt Leonard, lhp, Cal Poly
39. Jacob May, ss, Lakota West HS, West Chester, Ohio
40. Lee Orr, of, McNeese State
41. Jonathan Kaskow, 1b, Stanford
42. Mitchell Hopkins, lhp, Louisiana State-Eunice JC
43. Matt Campbell, rhp, Florida
44. Eddie Campbell, lhp, Bridgewater Raynham HS, Bridgewater, Mass.
45. Will Harford, c, Notre Dame
46. Pat Quinn, rhp, St. Petersburg (Fla.) JC
47. Tant Shepherd, 1b, Texas
48. Kaiana Eldredge, c, Punahou HS, Honolulu
49. El'Hajj Muhammad, rhp, CC of Morris (N.J.)
50. Dexter Kjerstad, of, Randall HS, Amarillo, Texas

CLEVELAND INDIANS (5)

1. Drew Pomeranz, lhp, Mississippi
2. LeVon Washington, of, Chipola (Fla.) JC
3. Tony Wolters, ss, Rancho Buena Vista HS, Vista, Calif.
4. Kyle Blair, rhp, San Diego
5. Cole Cook, rhp, Pepperdine
6. Nick Bartolone, ss, Chabot (Calif.) JC
7. Robbie Aviles, rhp, Suffern (N.Y.) HS
8. Alex Lavisky, c, St. Edward HS, Lakewood, Ohio
9. Jordan Cooper, rhp, Wichita State
10. Tyler Holt, of, Florida State
11. Hunter Jones, of, Lakewood (Calif.) HS
12. Tyler Cannon, 3b, Virginia
13. Michael Goodnight, rhp, Houston
14. Diego Seastrunk, c, Rice
15. Ben Wetzler, lhp, Clackamas (Ore.) HS
16. Cody Allen, rhp, St. Petersburg (Fla.) JC
17. Aaron Siliga, of, Oceanside (Calif.) HS
18. Chase Burnette, 1b, Georgia Tech
19. Mark Brown, of, King HS, Detroit
20. Burch Smith, rhp, Howard (Texas) JC
21. Owen Dew, rhp, Central Florida
22. Nate Striz, rhp, North Carolina
23. Tony Dischler, rhp, Louisiana State-Eunice JC
24. Andrew Triggs, rhp, Southern California
25. Jay Gause, rhp, West Brunswick HS, Shallotte, N.C.
26. Ben Lively, rhp, Gulf Breeze (Fla.) HS
27. Jeff Schaus, of, Clemson
28. DeMarcus Tidwell, rhp, Yavapai (Ariz.) JC
29. Kirby Bellow, lhp, Nederland (Texas) HS
30. Taylor Hill, rhp, Vanderbilt
31. David Goforth, rhp, Mississippi
32. Michael Palazzone, rhp, Georgia
33. Logan Thompson, 2b, Palm Beach (Fla.) CC
34. Kyle Petter, lhp, El Camino (Calif.) JC
35. Ken Ferrer, rhp, Elon
36. Rye Davis, rhp, Western Kentucky
37. Trey Griffin, of, King HS, Lithonia, Ga.
38. Tyler Pearson, c, Monterey HS, Lubbock, Texas
39. Bobby Wahl, rhp, West Springfield HS, Springfield, Va.
40. Jordan Casas, of, Long Beach State
41. Brian Heere, of, Kansas
42. Aaron Fields, 2b, Wright State
43. Chris Waylock, ss, Cary-Grove HS, Cary, Ill.
44. Brock Stassi, lhp, Nevada
45. Frank DeJiulio, rhp, Daytona Beach (Fla.) CC
46. Justin Haley, rhp, Sierra (Calif.) JC
47. Luke Malloy, rhp, Alamo Heights HS, San Antonio
48. C.T. Bradford, of, Pace (Fla.) HS
49. Marcus Bradley, of, Central Arizona JC
50. Henry Dunn, of, Binghamton

COLORADO ROCKIES (26)

1. Kyle Parker, of, Clemson
1s. Peter Tago, rhp, Dana Hills HS, Dana Point, Calif. (Supplemental pick—47th—for loss of Type B free agent Jason Marquis)
2. Chad Bettis, rhp, Texas Tech
3. Josh Rutledge, ss, Alabama
4. Russell Wilson, of, North Carolina State
5. Josh Slaats, rhp, Hawaii

6. Jared Simon, of, Tampa
7. Kraig Sitton, lhp, Oregon State
8. Corey Dickerson, of, Meridian (Miss.) CC
9. Geoff Parker, rhp, Florida State
10. Brett Tanos, 2b, Santa Ana (Calif.) JC
11. Hommy Rosado, 1b, Barbe HS, Lake Charles, La.
12. Matt Crocker, lhp, Texas-San Antonio
13. Josh Mueller, rhp, Eastern Illinois
14. Taylor Reid, rhp, St. Mary's
15. Will Swanner, c, La Costa Canyon HS, Carlsbad, Calif.
16. Jayson Langfels, 3b, Eastern Kentucky
17. Ryan Casteel, c, Cleveland State (Tenn.) JC
18. Juan Perez, rhp, Bethune-Cookman
19. Ryan Eades, rhp, Northshore HS, Slidell, La.
20. Blake McDade, 1b, Middle Tennessee State
21. Chris Giovinazzo, of, UCLA
22. Mark Tracy, c, Duquesne
23. Bruce Kern, rhp, St. John's
24. Christian Bergman, rhp, UC Irvine
25. Kenny Roberts, lhp, Middle Tennessee State
26. Jacob Tanis, 3b, Mercer
27. Blake Keitzman, lhp, Western Oregon
28. Tony Rizzotti, rhp, Martin HS, Arlington, Texas
29. Marco Gonzales, lhp, Rocky Mountain HS, Fort Collins, Colo.
30. Jeff Ames, rhp, Lower Columbia (Wash.) JC
31. Russell Brewer, rhp, Vanderbilt
32. Jason Monda, of, Capital HS, Olympia, Wash.
33. Jordan Ballard, 1b, Virginia Military Institute
34. Steve Selsky, of, Arizona
35. Justin Fradejas, of, Auburn
36. Jimmie Koch, of, Sarasota (Fla.) HS
37. Dan Kickham, rhp, Crowder (Mo.) CC
38. Logan Davis, ss, Cactus Shadows HS, Cave Creek, Ariz.
39. Joel McKeithan, ss, Roberson HS, Asheville, N.C.
40. Brandon Brennan, rhp, Capistrano Valley HS, Mission Viejo, Calif.
41. Ben Mordini, rhp, Cherry Creek HS, Greenwood Village, Colo.
42. Thomas Pereira, rhp, Indian Hills (Iowa) CC
43. Kaleb Barlow, 3b, Jackson (Miss.) Prep
44. Kyle Richter, lhp, Santa Margarita HS, Rancho Santa Margarita, Calif.
45. Mike Benjamin, ss, Basha HS, Gilbert, Ariz.
46. Mitch Horacek, lhp, Thunder Ridge HS, Littleton, Colo.
47. Landon Appling, of, El Campo (Texas) HS
48. Hunter Greenwood, rhp, Franklin HS, Elk Grove, Calif.
49. Brett Thomas, rhp, Poway (Calif.) HS
50. Jimmy Dykstra, rhp, Yavapai (Ariz.) JC

DETROIT TIGERS (44)

1. (Pick to Astros as compensation for Type A free agent Jose Valverde)
1s. Nick Castellanos, 3b, Archbishop McCarthy HS, SW Ranches, Fla. (Supplemental pick—44th—for loss of Type B free agent Brandon Lyon)
1s. Chance Ruffin, rhp, Texas (Supplemental pick—48th—for loss of Type B free agent Fernando Rodney)
2. Drew Smyly, lhp, Arkansas
3. Rob Brantly, c, UC Riverside
4. Cole Green, rhp, Texas
5. Alex Burgos, lhp, State JC of Florida
6. Bryan Holaday, c, Texas Christian
7. Corey Jones, 2b, Cal State Fullerton
8. Patrick Leyland, c, Bishop Canevin HS, Pittsburgh
9. Tony Plagman, 1b, Georgia Tech
10. Cole Nelson, lhp, Auburn
11. Brian Dupra, rhp, Notre Dame
12. Kyle Ryan, lhp, Auburndale (Fla.) HS
13. P.J. Polk, of, Tennessee
14. Patrick Cooper, rhp, Bradley
15. Collin Kuhn, of, Arkansas
16. Jordan Pratt, rhp, Arkansas
17. Drew Gagnier, rhp, Oregon
18. Josh Ashenbrenner, 2b, Lewis-Clark State (Idaho)
19. Jeff Rowland, of, Georgia Tech
20. Tyler White, rhp, Alabama
21. James Meador, 1b, San Diego
22. Jake Hernandez, c, Los Osos HS, Rancho Cucamonga, Calif.
23. Dominic Ficociello, ss, Fullerton (Calif.) Union HS

24. Tyler Clark, rhp, Missouri
25. Shawn Teufel, lhp, Liberty
26. Jeff Ferrell, rhp, Pitt (N.C.) CC
27. Les Smith, of, Meramec (Mo.) CC
28. Jack Duffey, lhp, Heritage HS, Newnan, Ga.
29. Chris Joyce, lhp, Central Arizona JC
30. Logan Hoch, lhp, Wichita State
31. Matt Little, rhp, Kentucky
32. Clay Jones, 1b, Alabama
33. Brennan Smith, rhp, Bowling Green State
34. Nolan Sanburn, of, Kokomo (Ind.) HS
35. Cody Hall, rhp, Southern
36. Ryan Soares, ss, George Mason
37. Carlos Lopez, 1b, Cal State Fullerton
38. Jake Dziubczynski, lhp, Central Arizona JC
39. Bo McClendon, of, Valparaiso
40. Pete Miller, ss, Trinity International (Ill.)
41. Matt Perry, 3b, Holy Cross
42. Kevin Grant, of, Millard West HS, Omaha
43. Blake Bell, rhp, Bishop Carroll Catholic HS, Wichita
44. Ricky Knapp, rhp, Port Charlotte (Fla.) HS
45. Jake Morton, of, Hudsonville (Mich.) HS
46. Ben Verlander, rhp, Goochland (Va.) HS
47. Chris Triplett, ss, Sandy Creek HS, Fayetteville, Ga.
48. Tyler Marincov, of, Timber Creek HS, Orlando
49. Tyson Kendrick, c, Tabor (Kan.)
50. Jake Ross, lhp, Wor-Wic (Md.) CC

FLORIDA MARLINS (23)

1. Christian Yelich, of, Westlake HS, Westlake Village, Calif.
2. Rob Rasmussen, lhp, UCLA
3. J.T. Realmuto, ss, Albert HS, Midwest City, Okla.
4. Andrew Toles, of, Sandy Creek HS, Tyrone, Ga.
5. Robert Morey, rhp, Virginia
6. Rett Varner, rhp, Texas-Arlington
7. Mark Canha, of, California
8. Alan Oaks, rhp, Michigan
9. Austin Brice, rhp, Northwood HS, Pittsboro, N.C.
10. Aaron Senne, 1b, Missouri
11. Grant Dayton, lhp, Auburn
12. James Wooster, of, Alvin (Texas) CC
13. Kentrell Dewitt, of, Southeastern (N.C.) CC
14. Danny Black, 2b, Oklahoma
15. Ryan Fisher, of, UC Irvine
16. Randy LeBlanc, rhp, Covington (La.) HS
17. Zach Neal, rhp, Oklahoma
18. Corey Goudeau, rhp, Frank Phillips (Texas) JC
19. Dallas Poulk, 2b, North Carolina State
20. Alfredo Lopez, ss, Compton (Calif.) CC
21. Ken Toves, lhp, New Mexico
22. Jeremy Heatley, rhp, Arkansas
23. Blake Treinen, rhp, South Dakota State
24. Gregg Glime, c, Baylor
25. Mike Ojala, rhp, Rice
26. Todd Muecklisch, ss, Lewis-Clark State (Idaho)
27. Brandon Cunniff, rhp, Cal State San Bernardino
28. Chad Keefer, c, Louisiana-Lafayette
29. Viosergy Rosa, 1b, Odessa (Texas) JC
30. Zach Robertson, lhp, Iowa
31. Taiwan Easterling, of, Florida State
32. Eddie Rodriguez, c, Oregon
33. D'Andre Toney, of, Hardaway HS, Columbus, Ga.
34. Steve Dennison, lhp, Wheaton (Ill.)
35. Taylor Ard, 1b, Mount Hood (Ore.) CC
36. Jared Rogers, rhp, Rice
37. Chris Squires, rhp, Indiana
38. Forrest Moore, lhp, Mississippi State
39. Sam Bates, 1b, Crowder (Mo.) JC
40. Dustin Emmons, rhp, UC Riverside
41. Seth Maness, rhp, East Carolina
42. Jonathon Crawford, rhp, Okeechobee (Fla.) HS
43. Matt Tracy, lhp, Mississippi
44. Tyler Abbott, lhp, Royal HS, Simi Valley, Calif.
45. Jeremy Weber, rhp, Chaffey (Calif.) JC
46. Daniel Johnston, of, Canada (Calif.) JC

47. Travis Huber, rhp, JC of Southern Idaho
48. **Beau Wright, lhp, Orange Coast (Calif.) CC**
49. Cody Lavalli, rhp, Granite Hills HS, Porterville, Calif.
50. Dan Carney, 1b, Notre Dame HS, East Stroudsburg, Pa.

HOUSTON ASTROS (8)

1. **Delino DeShields, 2b, Woodward Academy, College Park, Ga.**
1. **Mike Foltynewicz, rhp, Minooka (Ill.) Community HS** (Pick from Tigers as compensation for Type A free agent Jose Valverde)
1s. **Mike Kvasnicka, 3b/c, Minnesota** (Supplemental pick—33rd—for loss of Valverde)
2. **Vincent Velasquez, rhp, Garey (Calif.) HS**
3. **Austin Wates, 2b, Virginia Tech**
4. **Bobby Doran, rhp, Texas Tech**
5. **Ben Heath, c, Penn State**
6. **Adam Plutko, rhp, Glendora (Calif.) HS**
7. **Roberto Pena, c, Eloisa Pascual HS, Caguas, P.R.**
8. **Jake Buchanan, rhp, North Carolina State**
9. **Tommy Shirley, lhp, Xavier**
10. **Evan Grills, lhp, Sinclair SS, Whitby, Ont.**
11. **Kyle Redinger, 3b, Cedar Crest HS, Lebanon, Pa.**
12. **Andrew Robinson, rhp, Georgia Tech**
13. Davis Duren, 2b, Oklahoma State
14. **Jordan Scott, of, Riverside HS, Greer, S.C.**
15. **Jamaine Cotton, rhp, Western Oklahoma State JC**
16. **Chris Wallace, c, Houston**
17. **Tyler Burnett, 3b, Middle Tennessee State**
18. **Josh Magee, of, Hoover (Ala.) HS**
19. Jacoby Jones, ss, Richton (Miss.) HS
20. **Daniel Adamson, of, Jacksonville State**
21. Aaron Blair, rhp, Spring Valley HS, Las Vegas
22. Zach Dygert, c, Ball State
23. **Adam Bailey, of, Nebraska**
24. **Adam Champion, lhp, Arkansas-Little Rock**
25. **Rodney Quintero, rhp, Chipola (Fla.) JC**
26. **Alex Sogard, lhp, North Carolina State**
27. **Jacke Healey, ss, Youngstown State**
28. **Jason Chowning, rhp, Oklahoma**
29. Broughan Jantz, of, Nevada Union HS, Nevada City, Calif.
30. **Kellen Kiilsgaard, of, Stanford**
31. **Travis Blankenship, lhp, Kansas**
32. Austin Chrismon, rhp, Menchville HS, Newport News, Va.
33. **Michael Ness, rhp, Duke**
34. **Ryan Cole, rhp, St. John's**
35. Esteban Gomez, 1b, Bishop Ford Central Catholic HS, Brooklyn
36. Ryan Halstead, rhp, Los Osos HS, Rancho Cucamonga, Calif.
37. **Brian Streilein, rhp, Villanova**
38. Ryan Ford, 1b, Plano (Texas) West HS
39. **Krishawn Holley, rhp, Mid-Carolina HS, Prosperity, S.C.**
40. **Jeremiah Meiners, lhp, Francis Marion (S.C.)**
41. **Bryce Lane, of, Gulf Coast (Fla.) CC**
42. **Paul Gerrish, rhp, Texas Christian**
43. DeMarcus Henderson, ss, Wayne County HS, Waynesboro, Miss.
44. Alexis Garza, rhp, McAllen (Texas) HS
45. Ian Vazquez, ss, Perkiomen HS, Pennsburg, Pa.
46. Larry Pardo, lhp, Columbus HS, Miami
47. Joe Carcone, ss, New Hartford (N.Y.) HS
48. T.J. Pecoraro, rhp, Half Hollow Hills West HS, Dix Hills, N.Y.
49. **Kenny Diaz, c, Colegio Angel David HS, Toa Alta, P.R.**
50. David Donald, of, Mann HS, Greenville, S.C.

KANSAS CITY ROYALS (4)

1. **Christian Colon, ss, Cal State Fullerton**
2. **Brett Eibner, of/rhp, Arkansas**
3. **Mike Antonio, ss, Washington HS, New York**
4. **Kevin Chapman, lhp, Florida**
5. **Jason Adam, rhp, Blue Valley NW HS, Overland Park, Kan.**
6. **Scott Alexander, lhp, Sonoma State (Calif.)**
7. **Eric Cantrell, rhp, George Washington**
8. **Michael Mariot, rhp, Nebraska**
9. **Whit Merrifield, of, South Carolina**
10. **Tim Ferguson, of, Mississippi**
11. **Alex McClure, ss, Middle Tennessee State**
12. **Danny Hernandez, rhp, Miami Dade CC**

13. Jon Gray, rhp, Chandler (Okla.) HS
14. **Mike Giovenco, rhp, North Park (Ill.)**
15. **Jason Mitchell, rhp, Texas-Arlington**
16. **Chas Byrne, rhp, East Tennessee State**
17. **Ryan Jenkins, c, Auburn**
18. **Brian Fletcher, of, Auburn**
19. **Kevin David, c, Oklahoma State**
20. **Cameron Conner, of, Indiana Southeast**
21. **Michael Liberto, ss, Missouri**
22. **Tyler Graham, rhp, Nevada**
23. Steven Neff, lhp, South Carolina
24. Brandon Glazer, ss, Clear Spring (Md.) HS
25. Buddy Sosnoskie, of, Virginia Tech
26. **Gates Dooley, rhp, Henderson State (Ark.)**
27. **Jose Rodriguez, of, Miami Dade CC**
28. **Murray Watts, 1b, Arkansas State**
29. **Alexander Marquez, c, Martinez HS, Manaubo, P.R.**
30. **Chad Blauer, rhp, Point Loma Nazarene (Calif.)**
31. **Parker Bangs, rhp, South Carolina**
32. Justin Hageman, rhp, Hopkinsville (Ky.) HS
33. **Cole Lohden, rhp, Southern Arkansas**
34. Mark Blackmar, rhp, Carroll HS, Southlake, Texas
35. Kris Carlson, rhp, Wenatchee Valley (Wash.) CC
36. Mitchell Beacom, lhp, UCLA
37. **Robbie Penny, rhp, Pitt (N.C.) CC**
38. **Nick Graffeo, rhp, Alabama-Birmingham**
39. **Alex Rivers, rhp, Santa Clara**
40. **Dale Cornstubble, c, Central Michigan**
41. **Matt Ridings, rhp, Western Kentucky**
42. Mike Botelho, c, Chabot (Calif.) JC
43. Dillon Wilson, lhp, Western Oklahoma State JC
44. Shawn Payne, 2b, Georgia Southern
45. **Tom Zebroski, ss, George Washington**
46. **Drew Robertson, c, Middle Tennessee State**
47. **Darian Sandford, of, Park (Mo.)**
48. Jacob Hannemann, of, Lone Peak HS, Highland, Utah
49. **Jordan Propst, rhp, South Carolina**
50. Joe Jackson, c, Mauldin HS, Greenville, S.C.

LOS ANGELES ANGELS (18)

1. **Kaleb Cowart, 3b/rhp, Cook HS, Adel, Ga.** (Pick from Mariners as compensation for Type A free agent Chone Figgins)
1. **Cam Bedrosian, rhp, East Coweta HS, Sharpsburg, Ga.**
1. **Chevez Clarke, of, Marietta (Ga.) HS** (Pick from Red Sox as compensation for Type A free agent John Lackey)
1s. **Taylor Lindsey, ss, Desert Mountain HS, Scottsdale, Ariz.** (Supplemental pick—37th—for loss of Lackey)
1s. **Ryan Bolden, of, Madison (Miss.) Central HS** (Supplemental pick—40th—for loss of Figgins)
2. **Daniel Tillman, rhp, Florida Southern**
3. **Wendell Soto, ss, Riverview HS, Sarasota, Fla.**
3s. **Donn Roach, rhp, JC of Southern Nevada** (Supplemental pick—115th—for failure to sign 2009 third-round pick Josh Spence)
4. **Max Russell, lhp, Florida Southern**
5. Jesus Valdez, rhp, Hueneme HS, Oxnard, Calif.
6. **Brian Diemer, rhp, California**
7. Josh Osich, lhp, Oregon State
8. **Kole Calhoun, of, Arizona State**
9. **Drew Heid, of, Gonzaga**
10. **Aaron Meade, lhp, Missouri State**
11. Jake Rodriguez, ss, Elk Grove (Calif.) HS
12. **Justin LaTempa, rhp, Oregon**
13. **Bryant George, rhp, Southern Illinois**
14. **James Sneed, of, St. Croix Educ. Complex HS, Christiansted, V.I.**
15. **Carmine Giardina, lhp, Tampa**
16. **Thomas Nichols, 3b, Georgia Tech**
17. **Kevin Moesquit, ss, Highlands Chris. HS, Pompano Beach, Fla.**
18. **Ryan Broussard, ss, Louisiana State-Eunice JC**
19. Jonathan Bobea, rhp, Lewis HS, Flushing, N.Y.
20. **Kevin Johnson, rhp, West Florida**
21. **Gary Mitchell, of, Neumann (Pa.)**
22. Francis Larson, c, UC Irvine
23. **Michael Bolaski, 3b, Hanks HS, El Paso**
24. **Jesus Campos, ss, Cal State Los Angeles**
25. **A.J. Schugel, 3b, Central Arizona JC**

26. **Dakota Robinson, lhp, Centenary**
27. **Brandon Decker, of, Valdosta State (Ga.)**
28. Tim Helton, c, Upland (Calif.) HS
29. Taylor Brennan, 2b, Meadowdale HS, Lynnwood, Wash.
30. **Steven Irvine, 2b, McNeese State**
31. **Mike Sodders, 2b, New Mexico State**
32. **Drew Beuerlein, c, Nevada-Las Vegas**
33. **Eric Cendejas, rhp, Cal State Stanislaus**
34. **Jerod Yakubik, 1b, Ohio**
35. **Ryan Rivers, of, Charlotte**
36. **Hampton Tignor, c, Florida**
37. Tagen Struhs, of, Snohomish, Wash. (No school)
38. Jace Brinkerhoff, 3b, Utah Valley
39. Jimmy Allen, 2b, Rancho Buena Vista HS, Vista, Calif.
40. **Drew Oldfield, c, Dixie State (Utah)**
41. Justin Poovey, rhp, Florida
42. **Chance Mistric, rhp, Louisiana State-Eunice JC**
43. **George Barber, of, Broward (Fla.) CC**
44. **Mike Turner, of, Chesapeake (Md.) JC**
45. **Vinnie St. John, rhp, Southern California**
46. Darren Fischer, lhp, Cumberland Regional HS, Bridgeton, N.J.
47. Kenny Hatcher, 3b, Chandler-Gilbert (Ariz.) CC
48. **Chad Yinger, rhp, Southern Arkansas**
49. **Alex Burkard, lhp, Georgia College and State**
50. **John Wiedenbauer, lhp, Tampa**

LOS ANGELES DODGERS (28)

1. **Zach Lee, rhp, McKinney (Texas) HS**
2. **Ralston Cash, rhp, Lakeview Academy, Cornelia, Ga.**
3. **Leon Landry, of, Louisiana State**
4. **James Baldwin III, of, Pinecrest HS, Southern Pines, N.C.**
5. **Jake Lemmerman, ss, Duke**
6. Kevin Gausman, rhp, Grandview HS, Centennial, Colo.
7. **Ryan Christenson, lhp, South Mountain (Ariz.) CC**
8. **Blake Dean, of, Louisiana State**
9. **Steve Domecus, c, Virginia Tech**
10. **Bobby Coyle, of, Fresno State**
11. **Joc Pederson, of, Palo Alto (Calif.) HS**
12. **Matt Kirkland, 3b, South Doyle HS, Knoxville**
13. **Jesse Bosnik, 3b, St. Bonaventure**
14. **Alex McRee, lhp, Georgia**
15. Jake Eliopoulos, lhp, Chipola (Fla.) JC
16. **Andrew Pevsner, lhp, Johns Hopkins (Md.)**
17. **Logan Bawcom, rhp, Texas-Arlington**
18. Chad Arnold, rhp, Washington State
19. Ben Carhart, 3b, Palm Beach (Fla.) CC
20. Shane Henderson, rhp, Flower Mound (Texas) HS
21. **Noel Cuevas, of, Universidad Interamericana (P.R.) JC**
22. Andre Wheeler, of, Anderson HS, Austin
23. **B.J. LaRosa, c, Bucknell**
24. **Andrew Edge, c, Jacksonville State**
25. **Chance Gilmore, of, Coastal Carolina**
26. **Scott Schebler, of, Des Moines Area CC**
27. **Yimy Rodriguez, rhp, Peru State (Neb.)**
28. **Mike Drowne, of, Sacred Heart (Conn.)**
29. **Red Patterson, rhp, Southwestern Oklahoma State**
30. **Shawn Tolleson, rhp, Baylor**
31. **Derek Cone, rhp, Mesa (Ariz.) CC**
32. **Devon Ethier, of, Gateway (Ariz.) CC**
33. Brett Lee, lhp, Bishop State (Ala.) CC
34. **Joe Lincoln, c, Missouri Southern**
35. **Beau Brett, 1b, Southern California**
36. Johnny Fasola, rhp, Walsh Jesuit HS, Cuyahoga Falls, Ohio
37. Cal Vogelsang, 2b, JC of the Canyons (Calif.)
38. Lucas Witt, of, Lexington (Ky.) Christian HS
39. **Steve Matre, rhp, Mount St. Joseph (Ohio)**
40. Kaleb Clark, rhp, Riverton (Kan.) HS
41. Kevin Williams, ss, Crespi Carmelite HS, Encino, Calif.
42. Miles Williams, 3b, Windsor (Calif.) HS
43. Chad Wallach, rhp, Calvary Chapel HS, Pacific Grove, Calif.
44. Nick Baker, rhp, Palm Desert (Calif.) HS
45. Logan Gallagher, ss, Louisburg (N.C.) JC
46. **Bret Montgomery, rhp, Cal State Dominguez Hills**
47. Cody Martin, 1b, Chipola (Fla.) JC
48. Anthony Garcia, 2b, Chavez HS, Laveen, Ariz.

49. Robby Shultz, rhp, Eastside Catholic HS, Sammamish, Wash.
50. Taylor Kaczmarek, rhp, Desert Ridge HS, Mesa, Ariz.

MILWAUKEE BREWERS (14)

1. **Dylan Covey, rhp, Maranatha HS, Pasadena, Calif.**
2. **Jimmy Nelson, rhp, Alabama**
3. **Tyler Thornburg, rhp, Charleston Southern**
4. **Hunter Morris, 1b, Auburn**
5. **Matt Miller, rhp, Michigan**
6. **Cody Hawn, 3b, Tennessee**
7. **Joel Pierce, rhp, Massey SS, Windsor, Ont.**
8. **Austin Ross, rhp, Louisiana State**
9. **Yadiel Rivera, ss, Manuela Toro HS, Caguas, P.R.**
10. **Rafael Neda, c, New Mexico**
11. **Greg Holle, rhp, Texas Christian**
12. **John Bivens, of, Virginia State**
13. **Michael White, rhp, Walters State (Tenn.) CC**
14. **Mike Walker, 3b, Pacific**
15. Chris Bates, lhp, Regis HS, New York
16. Andrew Morris, rhp, Gulf Coast (Fla.) CC
17. **Brian Garman, lhp, Cincinnati**
18. **Thomas Keeling, lhp, Oklahoma State**
19. Rowan Wick, of, Graham SS, North Vancouver, B.C.
20. **Shea Vucinich, ss, Washington State**
21. **Kevin Shackelford, rhp, Marshall**
22. **Kevin Berard, c, Barbe HS, Lake Charles, La.**
23. **Ryan Bernal, rhp, Florida Atlantic**
24. **Greg Hopkins, 3b, St. John's**
25. **Nick Shaw, ss, Barry (Fla.)**
26. Daniel Gibson, lhp, Jesuit HS, Tampa
27. **Alex Jones, rhp, Jacksonville State**
28. **Dane Amedee, lhp, Louisiana State-Eunice JC**
29. **Dan Britt, rhp, Elon**
30. **Eric Marzec, rhp, Youngstown State**
31. **Mike Melillo, c, Elon**
32. **Jason Rogers, 1b, Columbus State (Ga.)**
33. William Kankel, lhp, Houston
34. Conor Fisk, rhp, Grafton (Wis.) HS
35. T.C. Mark, c, Pinnacle HS, Phoenix
36. **R.J. Johnson, rhp, Starkville (Miss.) HS**
37. **Seth Harvey, rhp, Washington State**
38. **Michael Schaub, rhp, Loara HS, Anaheim**
39. **Kenny Allison, of, Angelina (Texas) JC**
40. Scott Matyas, rhp, Minnesota
41. **Derrick Shaw, of, Florida A&M**
42. **Johnny Dishon, of, Louisiana State**
43. Steven Okert, lhp, Grayson County (Texas) CC
44. **T.J. Mittelstaedt, of, Long Beach State**
45. Lucas Moran, rhp, Lutheran HS North, Houston
46. Derek Goodwin, c, Diamond Ranch HS, Pomona, Calif.
47. Billy Schroeder, c, Grand Canyon (Ariz.)
48. **Marques Kyles, lhp, Limestone (S.C.)**
49. Alexander Simone, of, Christian Brothers Academy, Syracuse, N.Y.
50. Chad Jones, of, Louisiana State

MINNESOTA TWINS (21)

1. **Alex Wimmers, rhp, Ohio State**
2. **Niko Goodrum, ss, Fayette County HS, Fayetteville, Ga.**
3. **Pat Dean, lhp, Boston College**
4. **Eddie Rosario, of, Rafael Lopez Landron HS, Guayama, P.R.**
5. **Nate Roberts, of, High Point**
6. **Logan Darnell, lhp, Kentucky**
7. **Matt Hauser, rhp, San Diego**
8. **Lance Ray, of, Kentucky**
9. **Kyle Knudson, c, Minnesota**
10. **J.D. Williams, ss, Brooks-DeBartolo HS, Tampa**
11. Tyler Kuresa, 1b, Oakmont HS, Roseville, Calif.
12. Steven Maxwell, rhp, Texas Christian
13. **Ryan O'Rourke, lhp, Merrimack (Mass.)**
14. DeAndre Smelter, rhp, Tattnall Square Academy, Macon, Ga.
15. Thomas Girdwood, rhp, Elon
16. **Clint Dempster, lhp, Nicholls State**
17. Devin Grigg, rhp, Cal State East Bay
18. **David Gutierrez, rhp, Miami**

DRAFT

19. Matt Arguello, lhp, Davidson HS, Mobile, Ala.
20. Cody Martin, rhp, Gonzaga
21. **Nathan Fawbush, rhp, Georgia Perimeter JC**
22. Dillon Moyer, ss, Pendleton School, Bradenton, Fla.
23. **Dallas Gallant, rhp, Sam Houston State**
24. **Michael Quesada, c, Sierra (Calif.) JC**
25. Andy Leer, ss, Mary (N.D.)
26. **Kelly Cross, c, Pearland (Texas) HS**
27. **Brandon Henderson, of, Fresno (Calif.) CC**
28. **Jamaal Hawkins, ss, Jacksonville**
29. **Brian Burke, 3b, Lewis-Clark State (Idaho)**
30. Sergio Perez (Dernal), ss, Palmetto Ridge HS, Orangetree, Fla.
31. Mark Payton, of, St. Rita HS, Orland Park, Ill.
32. Tommy Toledo, rhp, Florida
33. **Justin Parker, lhp, Consumnes River (Calif.) JC**
34. **Kyle Necke, rhp, UC Irvine**
35. **Nick Alloway, rhp, Gloucester (N.J.) CC**
36. **Kelvin Mention, of, Brooks-DeBartolo HS, Tampa**
37. Grant Muncrief, rhp, Wichita State
38. Jared Ray, rhp, Houston
39. **Bart Carter, lhp, Western Kentucky**
40. Vance Woodruff, rhp, Grayson County (Texas) CC
41. **Sam Spangler, lhp, Hawaii**
42. **Brett Carroll, lhp, William Paterson (N.J.)**
43. **Derek Christensen, rhp, Salt Lake CC**
44. **David Deminsky, lhp, St. Cloud State (Minn.)**
45. James Buckelew, lhp, Collins Hills HS, Suwanee, Ga.
46. **A.J. Achter, rhp, Michigan State**
47. Collin Reynolds, rhp, McLennan (Texas) CC
48. Troy Scott, 1b, Washington
49. LeAndre Davis, ss, Georgia Perimeter JC
50. James Harris, 3b, Etowah HS, Woodstock, Ga.

NEW YORK METS (7)

1. **Matt Harvey, rhp, North Carolina**
2. (Pick to Red Sox as compensation for Type A free agent Jason Bay)
3. **Blake Forsythe, c, Tennessee**
4. **Cory Vaughn, of, San Diego State**
5. **Matt den Dekker, of, Florida**
6. **Greg Peavey, rhp, Oregon State**
7. **Jeff Walters, rhp, Georgia**
8. **Kenny McDowall, rhp, JC of Southern Nevada**
9. **Jacob deGrom, rhp, Stetson**
10. **Akeel Morris, rhp, Charlotte Amaile HS, St. Thomas, V.I.**
11. **Adam Kolarek, lhp, Maryland**
12. **Bret Mitchell, rhp, Minnesota State-Mankato**
13. **Brian Harrison, 3b, Furman**
14. **J.B. Brown, 2b, Pacific**
15. **Tillman Pugh, of, Sonoma State (Calif.)**
16. **Ryan Fraser, rhp, Memphis**
17. **Chad Sheppard, rhp, Northwestern State**
18. **A.J. Pinera, rhp, Tampa**
19. **Jonathan Kountis, rhp, Embry-Riddle (Fla.)**
20. **Luke Stewart, 1b, Alabama-Birmingham**
21. Dabias Johnson, 2b, Cook HS, Adel, Ga.
22. **Brandon Brown, ss, South Alabama**
23. Drew Martinez, of, Memphis
24. **Erik Goeddel, rhp, UCLA**
25. **Peter Birdwell, rhp, Vanguard (Calif.)**
26. **Jet Butler, ss, Mississippi State**
27. **Todd Weldon, rhp, Wayland Baptist (Texas)**
28. **Jeremy Gould, lhp, Duke**
29. **Hamilton Bennett, lhp, Tennessee Wesleyan CC**
30. **Josh Edgin, lhp, Francis Marion (S.C.)**
31. **Steve Winnick, rhp, Point Loma Nazarene (Calif.)**
32. **Patrick Farrell, c, Regis (Colo.)**
33. **Hunter Carnevale, rhp, Pacific**
34. **Justin Schafer, 2b, UC Davis**
35. Josh Easley, rhp, Weatherford (Texas) JC
36. Jesen Dygestile-Therrien, rhp, Edouard Montpetit HS, Montreal
37. **Dylan Brown, of, Tampa**
38. Peter Miller, rhp, Cambridge Christian HS, Tampa
39. Brian Cruz, ss, Varela HS, Miami
40. Brock Stewart, ss, Normal (Ill.) West HS
41. Taylor Christian, rhp, Weatherford (Texas) JC

42. John Franco, ss, Poly Prep, Brooklyn, N.Y.
43. **Donnie Tabb, ss, East Central (Miss.) CC**
44. Kevin Gelinas, lhp, UC Santa Barbara
45. Terrance Jackson, lhp, Oklahoma City
46. Mike Jefferson, lhp, Louisiana Tech
47. Sean O'Connor, rhp, Carroll HS, Southlake, Texas
48. Austin Smith, 1b, Pensacola (Fla.) Catholic HS
49. Dillon Newman, rhp, Belton (Texas) HS
50. Mark Eveld, c, Tampa Jesuit HS

NEW YORK YANKEES (32)

1. **Cito Culver, ss, Irondequoit HS, Rochester, N.Y.**
2. **Angelo Gumbs, of, Torrance (Calif.) HS**
3. **Rob Segedin, 3b, Tulane**
4. **Mason Williams, of, West Orange HS, Winter Garden, Fla.**
5. **Tommy Kahnle, rhp, Lynn (Fla.)**
6. **Gabe Encinas, rhp, St. Paul HS, Santa Fe Springs, Calif.**
7. **Jake Anderson, of, Woodlawn HS, Baton Rouge**
8. **Kyle Roller, 1b, East Carolina**
9. **Taylor Morton, rhp, Bartlett (Tenn.) HS**
10. **Ben Gamel, of, Bishop Kenny HS, Jacksonville**
11. **Zach Varce, rhp, Portland**
12. **Daniel Burawa, rhp, St. John's**
13. **Tyler Austin, c, Heritage HS, Conyers, Ga.**
14. Travis Dean, rhp, Newton (Mass.) South HS
15. **Chase Whitley, rhp, Troy**
16. **Evan Rutckyj, lhp, St. Joseph's HS, St. Thomas, Ont.**
17. **Preston Claiborne, rhp, Tulane**
18. Kevin Jacob, rhp, Georgia Tech
19. Kevin Jordan, of, Northside HS, Columbus, Ga.
20. **Mike Ferraro, of, San Diego**
21. **Dustin Hobbs, rhp, Yavapai (Ariz.) JC**
22. **Trevor Johnson, lhp, JC of the Desert (Calif.)**
23. **Shane Brown, c, Central Florida**
24. **Conor Mullee, rhp, Saint Peter's (N.J.)**
25. **Casey Stevenson, 2b, UC Irvine**
26. R.J. Hively, rhp, Santa Ana (Calif.) JC
27. Martin Viramontes, rhp, Loyola Marymount
28. Josh Dezse, rhp, Olentangy Liberty HS, Powell, Ohio
29. Stewart Ijames, of, Louisville
30. **Zach Nuding, rhp, Weatherford (Texas) JC**
31. **Mike Gipson, rhp, Florida Atlantic**
32. **Kramer Sneed, lhp, Barton (N.C.)**
33. Michael Hachadorian, rhp, San Diego Mesa JC
34. Keenan Kish, rhp, Germantown Academy, Fort Washington, Pa.
35. **Will Oliver, rhp, Palomar (Calif.) JC**
36. **Nick McCoy, c, San Diego**
37. Cameron Hobson, lhp, Dayton
38. James Ramsay, of, Brandon (Fla.) HS
39. Jaycob Brugman, of, Desert Vista HS, Phoenix
40. Mike Gerber, of, Neuqua Valley HS, Naperville, Ill.
41. Tym Pearson, of, Columbia Basin (Wash.) JC
42. Mike O'Neill, of, Olentangy Liberty HS, Powell, Ohio
43. Kyle Hunter, lhp, Kansas State
44. David Middendorf, lhp, Northern Kentucky
45. Tyler Johnson, of, Penn State
46. **Nathan Forer, rhp, Southern Illinois**
47. **Freddy Lewis, lhp, Tennessee Wesleyan**
48. Alex Brown, rhp, Amphitheater HS, Tucson
49. Will Arthur, of, Abbotsford (B.C.) SS
50. Matt Rice, c, Western Kentucky

OAKLAND ATHLETICS (10)

1. **Michael Choice, of, Texas-Arlington**
2. **Yordy Cabrera, 3b, Lakeland (Fla.) HS**
3. **Aaron Shipman, of, Brooks County HS, Quitman, Ga.**
4. **Chad Lewis, 3b, Marina HS, Huntington Beach, Calif.**
5. **Tyler Vail, rhp, Notre Dame HS, Easton, Pa.**
6. **Tony Thompson, 3b, Kansas**
7. **Jordan Tripp, of, Golden West (Calif.) JC**
8. **Blake Hassebrock, rhp, UNC Greensboro**
9. **A.J. Kirby-Jones, 1b, Tennessee Tech**
10. **Josh Bowman, rhp, Tampa**
11. **Wade Kirkland, ss, Florida Southern**

12. Matt Thomson, rhp, San Diego
13. A.J. Griffin, rhp, San Diego
14. J.C. Menna, rhp, Brookdale (N.J.) CC
15. Scott Woodward, 3b, Coastal Carolina
16. Ryan Hughes, lhp, Nebraska
17. Drew Tyson, rhp, Reinhardt (Ga.)
18. Jose Macias, rhp, Franklin Pierce (N.H.)
19. Logan Chitwood, rhp, Texas-Tyler
20. Rashad Ramsey, of, Chattooga HS, Summerville, Ga.
21. Michael Anarumo, lhp, LeMoyne
22. Mike Strong, lhp, Oklahoma State
23. Zack Thornton, rhp, Oregon
24. Ryan Lipkin, c, San Francisco
25. Josh Whitaker, 3b, Kennesaw State
26. Jake Brown, lhp, Georgia Southern
27. Seth Frankoff, rhp, UNC Wilmington
28. Ryan Pineda, 2b, Cal State Northridge
29. Zach Hurley, of, Ohio State
30. Jeff Urlaub, lhp, Grand Canyon (Ariz.)
31. Aaron Judge, 1b, Linden (Calif.) HS
32. Todd McInnis, rhp, Southern Mississippi
33. Sean Murphy, rhp, Keystone (Pa.)
34. Aaron Larsen, rhp, Bethany (Kan.)
35. Andrew Bailey, rhp, Concord (W.Va.)
36. Bobby Geren, 3b, San Ramon Valley HS, Danville, Calif.
37. Daniel Petitti, c, North Georgia College and State
38. Michael Fabiaschi, 2b, James Madison
39. John Nester, c, Clemson
40. Andrew Smith, rhp, Roswell (Ga.) HS
41. Andrew Knapp, c, Granite Bay (Calif.) HS
42. Louie Lechich, lhp, St. Mary's HS, Stockton, Calif.
43. Spencer Haynes, ss, Brandon (Fla.) HS
44. Lonnie Kauppila, ss, Burbank (Calif.) HS
45. Krey Bratsen, of, Bryan (Texas) HS
46. Tyler Skulina, rhp, Walsh Jesuit HS, Cuyahoga Falls, Ohio
47. Tony McClendon, of, Fullerton (Calif.) JC
48. Zach Johnson, 1b, Ohlone (Calif.) JC
49. Nick Rosso, of, Lincoln HS, Stockton, Calif.
50. T.J. Walz, rhp, Kansas

PHILADELPHIA PHILLIES (27)

1. Jesse Biddle, lhp, Germantown Friends HS, Philadelphia
2. Perci Garner, rhp, Ball State
3. Cameron Rupp, c, Texas
4. Bryan Morgado, lhp, Tennessee
5. Scott Frazier, rhp, Upland (Calif.) HS
6. Gauntlett Eldemire, of, Ohio
7. David Buchanan, rhp, Georgia State
8. Stephen Malcolm, ss, San Joaquin Delta (Calif.) JC
9. Brenton Allen, of, Gahr HS, Cerritos, Calif.
10. Mario Hollands, lhp, UC Santa Barbara
11. Garett Claypool, rhp, UCLA
12. Tyler Knigge, rhp, Lewis-Clark State (Idaho)
13. John Hinson, 3b, Clemson
14. Chace Numata, c, Pearl City (Hawaii) HS
15. Jake Smith, 3b, Alabama
16. Craig Fritsch, rhp, Baylor
17. Mike Nesseth, rhp, Nebraska
18. Jeff Cusick, 1b, UC Irvine
19. Daniel Palka, 1b, Greer (S.C.) HS
20. Kevin Walter, rhp, Legacy HS, Westminster, Colo.
21. Jonathan Musser, rhp, Dowling Catholic HS, West Des Moines, Iowa
22. Jonathan Paquet, rhp, St. Lawrence (Quebec) JC
23. Jake Borup, rhp, Arizona State
24. Chad Thompson, rhp, Orange Coast (Calif.) CC
25. Matt Hutchison, rhp, Nevada-Las Vegas
26. Chris Duffy, of, Central Florida
27. Matt Payton, 2b, Western Kentucky
28. Brian Pointer, of, Galena HS, Reno, Nev.
29. Patrick Lala, rhp, Kirkwood (Iowa) CC
30. Nick Gonzalez, lhp, Leto HS, Tampa
31. Jim Klocke, c, Southeast Missouri State
32. Carlos Alonso, 3b, Delaware
33. Bob Stumpo, c, West Chester (Pa.)

34. Pat Murray, 1b, Lewis-Clark State (Idaho)
35. Eric Pettis, rhp, UC Irvine
36. Neal Davis, lhp, Virginia
37. Marshall Schuler, rhp, Colorado School of Mines
38. Keenyn Walker, of, Central Arizona JC
39. Justin Cummings, of, Santa Fe (Fla.) CC
40. Jeff Harvill, lhp, Evangel Christian Academy, Shreveport, La.
41. Taylor Zeutenhorst, of, Sheldon (Iowa) HS
42. Tim Chadd, 1b, Bishop Carroll Catholic HS, Wichita
43. Jimmy Hodgskin, lhp, Bishop Moore HS, Orlando
44. Jesse Meaux, rhp, UC Santa Barbara
45. Mike Francisco, lhp, Villanova
46. Tyler Ross, c, Collier HS, Naples, Fla.
47. Ethan Stewart, lhp, New Mexico JC
48. Kyle Ottoson, lhp, South Mountain (Ariz.) CC
49. Kyle Hallock, lhp, Kent State
50. Damek Tomscha, 3b, Sioux City (Iowa) North HS

PITTSBURGH PIRATES (2)

1. Jameson Taillon, rhp, The Woodlands (Texas) HS
2. Stetson Allie, rhp, St. Edward HS, Lakewood, Ohio
3. Mel Rojas Jr., of, Wabash Valley (Ill.) CC
4. Nick Kingham, rhp, Sierra Vista HS, Las Vegas
5. Tyler Waldron, rhp, Oregon State
6. Jason Hursh, rhp, Trinity Christian HS, Addison, Texas
7. Austin Kubitza, rhp, Heritage HS, Colleyville, Texas
8. Dace Kime, rhp, Defiance (Ohio) HS
9. Brandon Cumpton, rhp, Georgia Tech
10. Zach Weiss, rhp, Northwood HS, Irvine, Calif.
11. Dan Grovatt, of, Virginia
12. Vince Payne, ss, Cypress (Calif.) JC
13. Chris Kirsch, lhp, Marple Newtown HS, Newtown Square, Pa.
14. Bryce Weidman, rhp, Southwestern Oregon CC
15. Drew Maggi, ss, Arizona State
16. Matt Curry, 1b, Texas Christian
17. Ryan Hafner, rhp, Lee's Summit (Mo.) West HS
18. Chase Wentz, of, Louisiana State-Shreveport
19. Kent Emanuel, lhp, Woodstock (Ga.) HS
20. Justin Bencsko, of, Villanova
21. Dale Carey, of, Wheeler HS, Marietta, Ga.
22. Adalberto Santos, 2b, Oregon State
23. Jared Lakind, 1b, Cypress Woods HS, Cypress, Texas
24. Justin Howard, 1b, New Mexico
25. Casey Sadler, rhp, Western Oklahoma State JC
26. Brandon Pierce, rhp, Gunter (Texas) HS
27. Kevin Kleis, rhp, Grossmont (Calif.) JC
28. Zack Powers, ss, Armwood HS, Seffner, Fla.
29. Garret Levsen, rhp, Sonora HS, La Habra, Calif.
30. Matt Skirving, c, Eastern Michigan
31. Jason Townsend, rhp, Alabama
32. Chase Lyles, 3b, Northwestern State
33. Justin Ennis, lhp, Louisiana State-Shreveport
34. Kelson Brown, ss, Linfield (Ore.)
35. Drew Muren, of, Cal State Northridge
36. Cliff Archibald, rhp, McLennan (Texas) CC
37. Will Allen, c, Buchholz HS, Gainesville, Fla.
38. Alex Cox, rhp, Santiago HS, Corona, Calif.
39. Kevin Decker, rhp, College of Charleston
40. Harrison Cooney, rhp, Vero Beach (Fla.) HS
41. Bryton Trepagnier, rhp, East St. John HS, Reserve, La.
42. Stephen Lumpkins, lhp, American (D.C.)
43. Garrett Hicks, rhp, Yucaipa (Calif.) HS
44. Cory McGinnis, rhp, Shelton State (Ala.) CC
45. Connor Sadzeck, rhp, Crystal Lake (Ill.) Central HS
46. Ryan Wiggins, c, West Seattle HS, Seattle
47. Nathan Sorenson, of, Texas HS, Texarkana, Texas
48. Dillon Haviland, lhp, South Fayette HS, McDonald, Pa.
49. Logan Pevny, rhp, West Milford (N.J.) HS
50. Dusty Isaacs, rhp, Lebanon (Ohio) HS

ST. LOUIS CARDINALS (25)

1. Zack Cox, 3b, Arkansas
1s. Seth Blair, rhp, Arizona State (Supplemental pick—46th—for loss of Type B free agent Mark DeRosa)

1s. **Tyrell Jenkins, rhp, Henderson (Texas) HS** (Supplemental pick—50th—for loss of Type B free agent Joel Pineiro)
2. **Jordan Swagerty, rhp, Arizona State**
3. **Sam Tuivailala, ss, Aragon HS, San Mateo, Calif.**
4. **Cody Stanley, c, UNC Wilmington**
5. **Nick Longmire, of, Pacific**
6. **John Gast, lhp, Florida State**
7. **Greg Garcia, ss, Hawaii**
8. **Daniel Bibona, lhp, UC Irvine**
9. **Tyler Lyons, lhp, Oklahoma State**
10. **Reggie Williams Jr., of, Middle Georgia JC**
11. **Ben Freeman, lhp, Lake Gibson HS, Lakeland, Fla.**
12. Austin Wilson, of, Harvard-Westlake HS, Los Angeles
13. **Colin Walsh, 2b, Stanford**
14. **Cesar Aguilar, rhp, Miller HS, Fontana, Calif.**
15. **Geoff Klein, c, Santa Clara**
16. **Anthony Bryant, of, Connally HS, Austin**
17. **Corderious Dodd, of, North Side HS, Jackson, Tenn.**
18. **Boone Whiting, rhp, Centenary**
19. Chad Oberacker, of, Tennessee Tech
20. **Trevor Martin, ss, West Seattle HS**
21. **Josh Lucas, rhp, State JC of Florida**
22. **Steve Ramos, of, Ohlone (Calif.) JC**
23. **Dyllon Nuernberg, rhp, Western Nevada CC**
24. **Pat Biserta, of, Rutgers**
25. **Richard Mendoza, rhp, Isabel Flores HS, Juncos, P.R.**
26. **Victor Sanchez, 1b, San Diego**
27. **Aiden Lucas, rhp, Denison (Ohio)**
28. Taylor Black, ss, Kentucky
29. **Chris Patterson, rhp, Appalachian State**
30. **Iden Nazario, lhp, Miami**
31. **Mike O'Neill, of, Southern California**
32. **Ryan Copeland, lhp, Illinois State**
33. **Joey Bergman, 2b, College of Charleston**
34. **Matt Valaika, 2b, UC Santa Barbara**
35. **Drew Benes, 3b, Arkansas State**
36. **Dean Kiekhefer, lhp, Louisville**
37. **Packy Elkins, ss, Belmont**
38. **Jeff Nadeau, lhp, Louisiana State-Shreveport**
39. Ian Parry, rhp, Furman
40. **Phil Cerreto, 3b, Longwood**
41. **Chase Reid, rhp, Vanderbilt**
42. **Cole Brand, rhp, Bradley Central HS, Cleveland, Tenn.**
43. **Chris Edmondson, of, Le Moyne**
44. **Adam Melker, of, Cal Poly**
45. Robert Hansen, rhp, Beech HS, Hendersonville, Tenn.
46. Peter Mooney, ss, Palm Beach (Fla.) CC
47. **Justin Wright, lhp, Virginia Tech**
48. Hector Acosta, c, Coffeyville (Kan.) CC
49. **Bob Revesz, lhp, Louisville**
50. Andy Moye, rhp, Georgia Southern

SAN DIEGO PADRES (9)

1. Karsten Whitson, rhp, Chipley (Fla.) HS
2. **Jedd Gyorko, 2b, West Virginia**
3. **Zach Cates, rhp, Northeast Texas CC**
4. **Chris Bisson, 2b, Kentucky**
5. **Rico Noel, of, Coastal Carolina**
6. **John Barbato, rhp, Varela HS, Miami**
7. A.J. Vanegas, rhp, Redwood Christian HS, San Lorenzo, Calif.
8. **Jose Dore, of, The First Academy, Orlando**
9. **Josh Spence, lhp, Arizona State**
10. **Houston Slemp, of, Eastern Oklahoma State JC**
11. **Brian Guinn, ss, California**
12. **Chris Franklin, rhp, Southeastern Louisiana**
13. Miguel Pena, lhp, San Jacinto (Texas) JC
14. **Tommy Medica, c, Santa Clara**
15. Sean Dwyer, 1b, Tavares (Fla.) HS
16. Conor Hofmann, of, St. Augustine HS, San Diego
17. **Wes Cunningham, 1b, Murray State**
18. **Dan Meeley, of, Connors State (Okla.) JC**
19. **Tyler Norwood, rhp, Southern Union State (Ala.) CC**
20. **Paul Bingham, ss, Indiana (Pa.)**
21. **Connor Powers, 1b, Mississippi State**
22. **Tyler Stubblefield, 2b, Kennesaw State**

23. Xorge Carrillo, c, Arizona State
24. **Rocky Gale, c, Portland**
25. Josue Montanez, lhp, Ramon Vila Mayo HS, San Juan, P.R.
26. Cory Hahn, of, Mater Dei HS, Santa Ana, Calif.
27. **Matt Branham, rhp, South Carolina-Upstate**
28. Jacoby Almaraz, 3b, Johnson HS, San Antonio
29. **Mykal Stokes, of, Orange Coast (Calif.) CC**
30. D.J. Snelten, lhp, Lakes Community HS, Lake Villa, Ill.
31. **Oscar Garcia, of, Northwestern State**
32. **Will Scott, rhp, Walters State (Tenn.) CC**
33. **Daniel Ottone, rhp, Western Carolina**
34. **Xavier Esquivel, rhp, Loyola Marymount**
35. Mike Ellis, rhp, Fleetwood Park SS, Surrey, B.C.
36. **Rob Gariano, rhp, Fairfield**
37. **Chase Marona, rhp, Northwest-Shoals (Ala.) CC**
38. **Noah Mull, lhp, Wheeling Jesuit (W.Va.)**
39. **Adam Schrader, rhp, Southwest Minnesota State**
40. **Justin Echevarria, c, Stony Brook**
41. **Bryan Altman, 2b, The Citadel**
42. **Cole Tyrell, ss, Dayton**
43. **Mark Hardy, lhp, British Columbia**
44. **Robert Sabo, rhp, Kent State**
45. Michael Fagen, lhp, San Diego Jewish Academy
46. Dominick Francia, of, St. Paul's Episcopal HS, Mobile, Ala.
47. Kraig Kelly, 3b, Collinsville (Okla.) HS
48. Dan Child, rhp, Jesuit HS, Sacramento
49. Elliot Glynn, lhp, Connecticut
50. **Gunnar Terhune, of, UC Santa Barbara**

SAN FRANCISCO GIANTS (24)

1. **Gary Brown, of, Cal State Fullerton**
2. **Jarrett Parker, of, Virginia**
3. **Carter Jurica, ss, Kansas State**
4. **Seth Rosin, rhp, Minnesota**
5. **Heath Hembree, rhp, College of Charleston**
6. **Mike Kickham, lhp, Missouri State**
7. **Chuckie Jones, of, Boonville (Mo.) HS**
8. **Joe Staley, c, Lubbock Christian (Texas)**
9. **Chris Lofton, of, Jones County (Miss.) JC**
10. **Dan Burkhart, c, Ohio State**
11. **Adam Duvall, 2b, Louisville**
12. **Stephen Harrold, rhp, UNC Wilmington**
13. **Tyler Christman, rhp, South Carolina-Sumter JC**
14. **Raynor Campbell, 2b, Baylor**
15. Andrew Barbosa, lhp, South Florida
16. **Austin Fleet, rhp, Coastal Carolina**
17. **Ryan Bean, rhp, Edmonds (Wash.) CC**
18. **Brandon Allen, rhp, Milton (Fla.) HS**
19. Austin Southall, of, University HS, Baton Rouge
20. **Brett Bochy, rhp, Kansas**
21. Zach Arneson, rhp, Cal State Bakersfield
22. **Bobby Haney, ss, South Carolina**
23. Alec Asher, rhp, Lakeland (Fla.) HS
24. Kyle Wilson, 3b, North Carolina State
25. **Brett Krill, of, UCLA**
26. **Jeff Arnold, c, Louisville**
27. **Eric Sim, c, South Florida**
28. **Gaspar Santiago, lhp, Ranger (Texas) JC**
29. **Jose Cuevas, ss, Lee (Tenn.)**
30. **Ryan Bradley, lhp, Southern Illinois**
31. Kyle Hardy, 3b, Crowder (Mo.) JC
32. **Kevin Couture, rhp, Southern California**
33. Jimmy Birmingham, lhp, Coastal Carolina
34. **Johnathan DeBerry, of, Bethel (Tenn.)**
35. **Stephen Shackleford, rhp, Savannah College Art & Design (Ga.)**
36. John Leonard, rhp, Boston College
37. Eric Sisco, rhp, Davis HS, Modesto, Calif.
38. Jake McCasland, rhp, Piedra Vista HS, Farmington, N.M.
39. Tommy Tremblay, c, Edouard Montpetit (Quebec) JC
40. **Wes Hobson, 2b, Appalachian State**
41. **Ryan Honeycutt, of, New Mexico**
42. James Roberts, rhp, Archbishop Mitty HS. San Jose, Calif.
43. Raymond Ruggles, rhp, Tusculum (Tenn.)
44. **Jake Shadle, rhp, Green River (Wash.) CC**
45. Greg Greve, rhp, Walsh Jesuit HS, Cuyahoga Falls, Ohio

46. Caleb Hougesen, 3b, Lutheran HS, Indianapolis
47. Ray Hanson, rhp, Cypress (Calif.) JC
48. Devin Harris, of, East Carolina
49. Dan Pellegrino, c, UC Riverside
50. Golden Tate, of, Notre Dame

SEATTLE MARINERS (43)

1. (Pick to Angels as compensation for Type A free agent Chone Figgins)
1s. Taijuan Walker, rhp, Yucaipa (Calif.) HS (Supplemental pick—43rd—for loss of Type B free agent Adrian Beltre)
2. Marcus Littlewood, ss, Pine View HS, St. George, Utah
3. Ryne Stanek, rhp, Blue Valley HS, Stilwell, Kan.
4. James Paxton, lhp, Grand Prairie (American Association)
5. Stephen Pryor, rhp, Tennessee Tech
6. Christian Carmichael, c, Mililani (Hawaii) HS
7. Mickey Wiswall, 1b, Boston College
8. Jabari Blash, of, Miami Dade CC
9. Luke Taylor, rhp, Woodinville (Wash.) HS
10. Tyler Burgoon, rhp, Michigan
11. Jon Keller, rhp, Xavier HS, Cedar Rapids, Iowa
12. Stefen Romero, 3b, Oregon State
13. Jason Markovitz, lhp, Long Beach State
14. Tyler Linehan, lhp, Sheldon HS, Sacramento
15. Charles Kaalekahi, rhp, Campbell HS, Ewa Beach, Hawaii
16. Jordan Shipers, lhp, South Harrison HS, Bethany, Mo.
17. Danny Lopez, ss, Pittsburgh
18. Willy Kesler, rhp, New Mexico
19. Frankie Christian, of, Upland (Calif.) HS
20. Matt Bischoff, rhp, Purdue
21. Luke Guarnaccia, c, St. Thomas Aquinas HS, Fort Lauderdale
22. Steve Landazuri, rhp, Carter HS, Rialto, Calif.
23. Jandy Sena, rhp, Miami (No school)
24. Ben Whitmore, lhp, Concordia (Calif.)
25. Ernesto Zaragoza, rhp, Kaiser HS, Fontana, Calif.
26. Robbie Anston, of, Boston College
27. Nick Fleece, rhp, Texas A&M
28. Tim Griffin, rhp, Rollins (Fla.)
29. Jon McGibbon, 1b, Lindenhurst (N.Y.) HS
30. Derek Poppert, ss, San Francisco
31. Jake Schlander, ss, Stanford
32. Andrew Giobbi, c, Vanderbilt
33. D.J. Peterson, 3b, Gilbert (Ariz.) HS
34. Tyler Whitney, lhp, Mississippi State (Contract voided)
35. Ethan Paquette, 1b, Hofstra
36. Forrest Snow, rhp, Washington
37. Ryan Kiel, lhp, Marshall
38. Ben Versnik, rhp, Wisconsin-Whitewater
39. Josh Krist, rhp, Cal Poly Pomona
40. Nate Reed, lhp, Kutztown (Pa.)
41. Billy Marcoe, c, Cal State Fullerton
42. Mike Aviles, rhp, St. Thomas Aquinas (N.Y.)
43. Matt Browning, 3b, James Madison
44. Tim Boyce, rhp, Rhode Island
45. Stephen Kohlscheen, rhp, Auburn
46. David Rollins, lhp, San Jacinto (Texas) JC
47. James Wood, of, Trinity (Conn.)
48. Patrick Brady, 2b, Bellarmine (Ky.)
49. Colton Keough, of, Tesoro HS, Las Flores, Calif.
50. David Holman, rhp, Hutchinson (Kan.) CC

TAMPA BAY RAYS (17)

1. Josh Sale, of, Bishop Blanchet HS, Seattle
1. Justin O'Conner, c, Cowan HS, Muncie, Ind. (Supplemental pick—31st—for failure to sign 2009 first-round pick LeVon Washington)
1s. Drew Vettleson, of, Central Kitsap HS, Silverdale, Wash. (Supplemental pick—42nd—for loss of Type B free agent Gregg Zaun)
2. Jake Thompson, rhp, Long Beach State
2. Derek Dietrich, 3b, Georgia Tech (Supplemental pick—79th—for failure to sign 2009 second-round pick Kenny Diekroeger)
3. Ryan Brett, 2b, Highline HS, Burien, Wash.
4. Austin Wood, rhp, St. Petersburg (Fla.) JC
5. Ian Kendall, rhp, Ashland (Ore.) HS

6. Jesse Hahn, rhp, Virginia Tech
7. Michael Lorenzen, of, Fullerton (Calif.) Union HS
8. Merrill Kelly, rhp, Arizona State
9. Jake DePew, c, Granite City (Ill.) HS
10. Deshun Dixon, of, Terry HS, Jackson, Miss.
11. Travis Flores, 1b, Desert Ridge HS, Mesa, Ariz.
12. Phil Wunderlich, 1b, Louisville
13. Robby Price, 2b, Kansas
14. Austin Hubbard, rhp, Auburn
15. Brandon Henderson, lhp, Chesnee (S.C.) HS
16. Nate Garcia, rhp, Santa Clara
17. Cody Anderson, rhp, Feather River (Calif.) JC
18. Jimmy Patterson, lhp, Arizona State
19. Craige Lyerly, 2b, Catawba (N.C.)
20. C.J. Riefenhauser, lhp, Chipola (Fla.) JC
21. Adam Liberatore, lhp, Tennessee Tech
22. Matt Koch, c, Loyola Marymount
23. Kevin Patterson, 1b, Auburn
24. Daniel Ponce de Leon, rhp, La Mirada (Calif.) HS
25. Matt Spann, lhp, Columbia (Tenn.) Central HS
26. Justin Woodall, lhp, Alabama
27. Chris Winder, of, Odessa (Texas) JC
28. Julio Espinoza, ss, Rialto (Calif.) HS
29. Scott Lawson, 2b, Miami
30. Nick Schwaner, 3b, New Orleans
31. Kevin Kiermaier, of, Parkland (Ill.) JC
32. Bryan Fogle, of, Erskine (S.C.)
33. Scott Simon, rhp, Central Valley HS, Spokane, Wash.
34. Steve Tinoco, 1b, Long Beach State
35. Spencer Davis, rhp, The Woodlands (Texas) HS
36. Robert Dickmann, lhp, Pepperdine
37. DeMondre Arnold, rhp, Creekside HS, Fairburn, Ga.
38. Will Anderson, rhp, Foothill HS, Pleasanton, Calif.
39. Parker Markel, rhp, Yavapai (Ariz.) JC
40. Wade Broyles, rhp, Belhaven (Miss.)
41. Chris Rearick, lhp, North Georgia College and State
42. Preston Overbey, 3b, University School HS, Jackson, Tenn.
43. Ryan Hornback, c, San Jacinto (Texas) JC
44. Mickey Jannis, rhp, Cal State Bakersfield
45. Blake Freeman, lhp, Sunnyslope HS, Phoenix
46. George Jensen, rhp, Des Moines Area CC
47. Hector Montes, 1b, Bonita Vista HS, Chula Vista, Calif.
48. Blake Barnes, rhp, Howard (Texas) JC
49. Danny Hoilman, 1b, East Tennessee State
50. Cory Maltz, rhp, Weatherford (Texas) JC

TEXAS RANGERS (15)

1. Jake Skole, of, Blessed Trinity HS, Roswell, Ga. (Supplemental pick—15th—for failure to sign 2009 first-round pick Matt Purke)
1. Kellin Deglan, c, Mountain SS, Langley, B.C.
1s. Luke Jackson, rhp, Calvary Christian HS, Fort Lauderdale, Fla. (Supplemental pick—45th—for loss of Type B free agent Marlon Byrd)
1s. Mike Olt, 3b, Connecticut (Supplemental pick—49th—for loss of Type B free agent Ivan Rodriguez)
2. Cody Buckel, rhp, Royal HS, Simi Valley, Calif.
3. Jordan Akins, of, Union Grove HS, McDonough, Ga.
4. Drew Robinson, ss, Silverado HS, Las Vegas
5. Justin Grimm, rhp, Georgia
6. Brett Nicholas, c, Missouri
7. Jimmy Reyes, lhp, Elon
8. Jonathan Roof, ss, Michigan State
9. Zach Osborne, rhp, Louisiana-Lafayette
10. Jared Hoying, ss, Toledo
11. Chris Hanna, lhp, Stratford HS, Goose Creek, S.C.
12. Josh Richmond, of, Louisville
13. Andrew Clark, 1b, Louisville
14. Nick Tepesch, rhp, Missouri
15. Ryan Rodebaugh, rhp, Kennesaw State
16. Ryan Strausborger, of, Indiana State
17. Anthony Haase, rhp, Cochise (Ariz.) JC
18. Garrett Buechele, 3b, Oklahoma
19. Brett Weibley, rhp, Kent State
20. Sam Wilson, lhp, Eldorado HS, Albuquerque
21. Joe Van Meter, rhp, Virginia Commonwealth

DRAFT

22. **Ben Rowen, rhp, Virginia Tech**
23. **Andres Perez-Lobo, rhp, Columbus HS, Miami**
24. Jake Cole, rhp, Sahuaro HS, Tucson, Ariz.
25. **Kendall Radcliffe, of, Morgan Park HS, Chicago**
26. Chase Johnson, rhp, Fallbrook (Calif.) HS
27. **Alexander Claudio, lhp, Isabel Flores HS, Juncos, P.R.**
28. **John Kukuruda, rhp, East Nicolaus HS, Nicolaus, Calif.**
29. Trae Davis, rhp, Mexia (Texas) HS
30. Brian Ragira, of, Martin HS, Arlington, Texas
31. **Justin Earls, lhp, Georgia**
32. **Steve McKinnon, rhp, Cowichan SS, Duncan, B.C.**
33. **Matt Hill, lhp, Georgia Perimeter JC**
34. **Kevin Rodland, ss, Nevada**
35. John Lieske, rhp, Harlem HS, Machesney Park, Ill.
36. **Jason Kudlock, of, Cal State Bakersfield**
37. John Pustay, of, Pine Creek HS, Colorado Springs
38. **Carson Vitale, c, Creighton**
39. Ryan Woolley, rhp, Alabama-Birmingham
40. **Travis Meiners, of, Dallas Baptist**
41. **Colby Killian, rhp, Emporia State (Kan.)**
42. **Kevin Johnson, lhp, Cincinnati**
43. Chris Roglen, of, Rocky Mountain HS, Fort Collins, Colo.
44. Shawn Stuart, rhp, Merced (Calif.) JC
45. **Johnathan Moore, c, Houston Baptist**
46. Darryl Norris, rhp, Fairhope (Ala.) HS
47. Daniel Ward, rhp, Garfield Heights (Ohio) HS
48. Forrest Koumas, rhp, Lugoff-Elgin HS, Lugoff, S.C.
49. Juan Gomes, c, Miami Southridge HS
50. Trevor Teykl, rhp, Kempner HS, Sugar Land, Texas

TORONTO BLUE JAYS (11)

1. **Deck McGuire, rhp, Georgia Tech**
1s. **Aaron Sanchez, rhp, Barstow (Calif.) HS** (Supplemental pick—34th—for loss of Type A free agent Marco Scutaro)
1s. **Noah Syndergaard, rhp, Legacy HS, Mansfield, Texas** (Supplemental pick—38th—for failure to sign 2009 supplemental first-round pick James Paxton)
1s. **Asher Wojciechowski, rhp, The Citadel** (Supplemental pick—41st—for loss of Type B free agent Rod Barajas)
2. **Griffin Murphy, lhp, Redlands (Calif.) East Valley HS**
2. **Kellen Sweeney, 3b, Jefferson HS, Cedar Rapids, Iowa** (Supplemental pick—69th—for failure to sign 2009 second-round pick Jake Eliopoulos)
2. **Justin Nicolino, lhp, University HS, Orlando** (Pick from Red Sox as compensation for Scutaro)
3. **Christopher Hawkins, 3b, North Gwinnett HS, Suwanee, Ga.**
3s. **Marcus Knecht, of, Connors State (Okla.) JC** (Supplemental pick—113th—for failure to sign 2009 third-round pick Jake Barrett)
4. **Sam Dyson, rhp, South Carolina**
5. **Dickie Joe Thon, ss, Academia Perpetio Socorro, San Juan, P.R.**
6. **Sean Nolin, lhp, San Jacinto (Texas) JC**
7. **Mitchell Taylor, lhp, Spring (Texas) HS**
8. Logan Ehlers, lhp, Nebraska City (Neb.) HS
9. **Brandon Mims, ss, Smith HS, Carrollton, Texas**
10. Tyler Shreve, rhp, Phelps County HS, Redlands, Calif.
11. **Shane Opitz, ss, Heritage HS, Centennial, Colo.**
12. Omar Cotto, of, Bonneville School, San Juan, P.R.
13. Tyler Painton, lhp, Centennial HS, Bakersfield, Calif.
14. **Dayton Marze, rhp, Louisiana-Lafayette**
15. **Zak Adams, lhp, Flower Mound (Texas) HS**
16. **Dalton Pompey, of, Fraser SS, Mississauga, Ont.**
17. **Myles Jaye, rhp, Starrs Mill HS, Fayetteville, Ga.**
18. Kris Bryant, 3b, Bonanza HS, Las Vegas
19. **Travis Garrett, rhp, Cypress (Calif.) JC**
20. **Art Charles, lhp, Bakersfield (Calif.) JC**
21. Chris Marlowe, rhp, Navarro (Texas) JC
22. Aaron Westlake, of, Vanderbilt
23. **Angel Gomez, of, Maria Cruz Buitrago HS, San Lorenzo, P.R.**
24. **Ronnie Melendez, of, Cowley County (Kan.) CC**
25. Brando Tessar, rhp, Chaminade HS, West Hills, Calif.
26. Jay Johnson, lhp, Texas Tech (Contract voided)
27. Eric Arce, c, Lakeland (Fla.) HS
28. **Adaric Kelly, rhp, Trinity Christian Academy, Lake Worth, Fla.**
29. **Jonathan Jones, of, Long Beach State**
30. **Steve McQuail, 2b, Canisius**

31. Luis Benitez, rhp, Ashworth HS, Carolina, P.R.
32. **Andy Fermin, 2b, Chipola (Fla.) JC**
33. **Melvin Garcia, of, Monroe HS, New York**
34. **Tyler Powell, rhp, Belmont-Abbey (N.C.)**
35. **Dan Barnes, rhp, Princeton**
36. David Whitehead, rhp, Moeller HS, Cincinnati
37. Chad Green, rhp, Effingham (Ill.) HS
38. **Pierce Rankin, c, Washington**
39. Nick Vander Tuig, rhp, Oakdale (Calif.) HS
40. **Brandon Berl, rhp, St. Mary's**
41. **Seth Conner, 3b, Logan-Rogersville HS, Rogersville, Mo.**
42. **Drew Permison, rhp, Towson**
43. Ronald Schreurs, lhp, Freedom HS, Orlando
44. Mott Hyde, 2b, Calhoun (Ga.) HS
45. Phil Diedrick, of, Pickering HS, Ajax, Ont.
46. Connor Smith, rhp, Blessed Trinity SS, Grimsby, Ont.
47. Gabriel Romero, rhp, Roosevelt HS, Los Angeles
48. Nick Studer, c, St. Michael's College HS, Toronto
49. **Matt Abraham, 2b, Eckerd (Fla.)**
50. Kelly Norris-Jones, c, Lambrick Park SS, Victoria, B.C.

WASHINGTON NATIONALS (1)

1. **Bryce Harper, of, JC of Southern Nevada**
2. **Sammy Solis, lhp, San Diego**
3. **Rick Hague, ss, Rice**
4. **A.J. Cole, rhp, Oviedo (Fla.) HS**
5. **Jason Martinson, ss, Texas State**
6. **Cole Leonida, c, Georgia Tech**
7. **Kevin Keyes, of, Texas**
8. **Matt Grace, lhp, UCLA**
9. **Aaron Barrett, rhp, Mississippi**
10. **Blake Kelso, ss, Houston**
11. **Neil Holland, rhp, Louisville**
12. **Robbie Ray, lhp, Brentwood (Tenn.) HS**
13. **Chris McKenzie, rhp, San Jacinto (Texas) JC**
14. Tim Smalling, ss, Virginia Tech
15. **David Freitas, c, Hawaii**
16. **Mark Herrera, rhp, San Jacinto (Texas) JC**
17. **Tyler Hanks, rhp, JC of Southern Nevada**
18. **Justin Miller, 2b, Middle Tennessee State**
19. **Wade Moore, of, Catawba (N.C.)**
20. **Chad Mozingo, of, Rice**
21. **Connor Rowe, of, Texas**
22. **Cameron Selik, rhp, Kansas**
23. **Colin Bates, rhp, North Carolina**
24. **Russ Moldenhauer, 1b, Texas**
25. **Christian Meza, lhp, Santa Ana (Calif.) JC**
26. **Chris Manno, lhp, Duke**
27. Sean Hoelscher, rhp, Texas A&M-Corpus Christi
28. Joey Rapp, 1b, Chipola (Fla.) JC
29. **Rick Hughes, of, Marin (Calif.) CC**
30. Tim Kiene, 1b, Avon Old Farms HS, Avon, Conn.
31. **Jeremy Mayo, c, Texas Tech**
32. **Randolph Oduber, of, Western Oklahoma State JC**
33. Ryan Sherriff, lhp, West Los Angeles JC
34. Rolando Botello, rhp, Jay HS, San Antonio, Texas
35. **Tyler Oliver, 1b, Wabash Valley (Ill.) CC**
36. **Wander Nunez, of, Western Oklahoma State JC**
37. **Nick Serino, lhp, Massachusetts**
38. Nick Lee, lhp, Weatherford (Texas) JC
39. John Simms, rhp, College Park HS, The Woodlands, Texas
40. Alejandro Diaz, ss, Ferguson HS, Miami
41. **Kevin Cahill, rhp, Purdue**
42. Taylor Stark, 2b, Northwest Rankin HS, Brandon, Miss.
43. Corey Littrell, lhp, Trinity HS, Louisville
44. Bryce Hines, rhp, Hanahan (S.C.) HS
45. Jeff Bouton, of, Hoggard HS, Wilmington, N.C.
46. Erick Fernandez, c, Georgetown
47. Lance Jarreld, of, Goodpasture HS, Madison, Tenn.
48. Brandon Miller, c, Northwest Florida State JC
49. **Rashad Hatcher, rhp, Patrick Henry (Va.) CC**
50. Harrison Fanaroff, lhp, Churchill HS, Potomac, Md.

APPENDIX

■ **Oscar Azocar**, an outfielder who played in three big league seasons, died June 14 in Valencia, Venezuela. He was 45.

Azocar hit .291 with five homers for Triple-A Columbus (International) in 1990 and was called up to the Yankees that July. Azocar got into 65 games his rookie year, batting .248 with eight doubles and five homers. The Yankees traded Azocar to the Padres after the 1990 season. The Padres kept him in the majors throughout the 1992 season, but Azocar, a noted free-swinger, struggled with the bat, hitting just .190 in 168 at-bats.

■ **Frank Baker**, an outfielder who played in parts of two seasons with the Indians, died Jan. 28 in Raleigh, N.C. He was 66.

Baker appeared in 52 games for the Indians in 1969, batting .258 with three home runs. He was called up again in 1971 and saw action at all three outfield positions while batting .210 in 181 at-bats.

■ **Stan Benjamin**, an outfielder who played in parts of five big league seasons, died Dec. 24, 2009, in Harwich, Mass. He was 95.

In his only full sesaon in the majors, Benjamin served as one of the Phillies' primary outfielders in 1941. He hit .235 with three home runs that season. He joined the Astros as a scout in 1965 and remained with the organization for nearly 40 years.

■ **Frank Bertaina**, a lefthander who pitched seven seasons in the majors, died March 3 in Santa Rosa, Calif. He was 65.

Bertaina started his big league career with the Orioles, and he later became a regular in the Washington Senators' rotation starting in 1967, going 6-5, 2.92 in 17 starts. Bertaina tossed 127 innings for the Senators in 1968 but went just 7-13, 4.68.

■ **Jim Bibby**, a righthander who pitched in the major leagues for 12 seasons for four teams, died Feb. 16 in Lynchburg, Va. He was 65.

Bibby opened the 1973 season with the Cardinals but was traded that June to the Rangers, where he had his first extended success at the big league level. He made 23 starts for Texas and posted a 9-10, 3.25 record. Included in that mark was a no-hitter he threw against the defending World Series-champion Athletics in Oakland on July 30th.

Bibby signed with the Pirates as a free agent heading into 1978 and would go on to have his greatest success in Pittsburgh. He went 8-7, 3.53 for the Pirates in '78, splitting his time between the rotation and the bullpen. Bibby had his best big league season for the Pirates' World Series winners in 1979, going 12-4, 2.80 in 138 innings. Bibby made his first and only trip to the All-Star Game in

1980 during a season in which he went on to win 19 games and put up a 3.33 ERA in 238 innings.

■ **Joe Brown**, who was the Pirates' general manager for 21 years, died Aug. 15 in Albuquerque. He was 91.

Brown took the helm in 1956 and the Pirates went on to win two World Series titles, in 1960 and 1971, under his stewardship.

■ **Freddie Burdette**, a righthander who pitched in parts of three seasons with the Cubs, died June 1 in Albany, Ga. He was 73.

Burdette played professionally for 13 seasons, all of them in the Cubs organization, making a total of 30 big league appearances. He saw his most extensive big league action in 1964, appearing in 18 games for the Cubs and putting up a 3.15 ERA.

■ **Bill Burich**, a second baseman who played in two big league seasons with the Phillies, died Dec. 25, 2009, in Apple Valley, Calif. He was 92.

Burich saw most of his big league action in 1942, when he appeared in 25 games for the Phillies and hit .288 with seven RBIs in 80 at-bats.

■ **Pete Castiglione**, a third baseman who played eight seasons in the major leagues, died April 22 in Pompano Beach, Fla. He was 89.

Castiglione served in a utility role for the Pirates over four seasons from 1949-52, playing primarily at third base but also seeing some action at shortstop. His offensive production remained fairly steady, as he hit at least .255 in each of his four full years in Pittsburgh.

■ **Bob Chakales**, a righthander who pitched in the major leagues for seven seasons, died Feb. 18 in Richmond. He was 82.

Chakales made his big league debut with the Indians in 1951 and went on to pitch for five different teams in his seven big league seasons. He saw the most action with the Washington Senators, going 6-8, 4.58 in 169 innings there from 1955-57.

■ **George Cisar**, an outfielder who played one season with the Brooklyn Dodgers, died Feb. 19 in Elmhurst, Ill. He was 99.

Cisar appeared in 20 big league games late in the 1937 season and went 6-for-29 at the plate with four RBIs.

■ **Mike Cuellar**, a lefthander who was a four-time all-star and pitched 15 seasons in the majors, died April 2 in Orlando. He was 72.

Traded from the Astros to the Orioles after the 1968 season, Cuellar blossomed in Baltimore. He won 23 games with a 2.38 ERA in his first season and was co-winner of the 1969 American League Cy Young Award. Cuellar helped pitch the Orioles to the 1970 World Series title and didn't slow down over the next four seasons, winning at least 18 games in each of them, ending with his 22-10, 3.11 season as a 37-year-old in 1974. He was a four-time 20-game winner and had a 4-4, 2.85 record in 12 career postseason starts.

Willie Davis, an outfielder who was a three-time all-star for the Dodgers, died March 9 in Burbank, Calif. He was 69.

Davis took over as the Dodgers' everyday center fielder in 1961. An exceptional defender and base-stealer, he held the job for 13 years. The Dodgers made three World Series appearances during Davis' tenure there, winning twice. Davis hit .294 with 12 homers in 1964, beginning a stretch of three consecutive seasons in which he hit at least 10 homers. He hit a career-high .311 in 1969 and added 11 homers and 24 steals. He would bat over .300 in each of the next two seasons as well.

Davis earned his first All-Star Game appearance and Gold Glove in 1971, when he hit .309 and hit 10 homers. He added two more Gold Gloves the next two years, and he returned to the All-Star Game in 1973. Davis ended his big league career in 1979 with 2,561 hits, good enough for a .279 career average along with 182 home runs and 398 steals.

■ **Bob Dillinger**, a third baseman who played six seasons in the majors, died Nov. 7, 2009, in Santa Clarita, Calif. He was 91.

Dillinger was one of the few bright spots for the St. Louis Browns from 1947-49. He batted .324 in '49 and earning his only all-star invite. The struggling Browns traded Dillinger to the Philadelphia Athletics after the '49 season, and he was sold to the Pirates in July 1950. Dillinger still hit .301 with 50 RBIs between his two stops, but he would stay only one more season in the big leagues.

■ **Sammy Drake**, a second baseman who saw action in three major league seasons, died Jan. 27 in Los Angeles. He was 75.

The Mets picked Drake up from the Cubs in the expansion draft after the 1961 season and he saw his most extensive big league time in their inaugural season. Drake appeared in 25 games for the Mets' historically woeful first squad, batting .192 with seven RBIs in 52 at-bats.

■ **Keith Drumright**, a second baseman who played in parts of two seasons in the majors, died Aug. 7 in Springfield, Mo. He was 55.

Drumright got into 17 games for the Astros in 1978 and hit .164. He got his second crack at the majors with Oakland in 1981, appearing in 31 games for the A's, batting .291.

■ **Jerry Fahr**, a righthander who pitched in one season for the Indians as part of a 10-year pro career, died Feb. 12 in Duluth, Ga. He was 85.

Fahr made five appearances for the Indians early in the 1951 season and didn't record any decisions while posting a 4.50 ERA in six innings of work.

■ **Van Fletcher**, a righthander who pitched in one major league season, died March 17 in Yadkinville, N.C. He was 85.

Fletcher's pro career spanned eight seasons, but he only made it to the big leagues once, making nine appearances for the 1955 Tigers.

■ **Joe Gates**, a second baseman who played two seasons with the White Sox, died March 28 in Gary, Ind. He was 55.

Gates caught fire in 1978, his first season in Chicago's system, earning his first big league callup that September. He got into eight games for the White Sox and went 6-for-24. Gates went back to the minors for most of the 1979 season but did make 16 appearances for the White Sox.

■ **Bob Hartman**, a lefthander who pitched in two major league seasons as part of a nine-year pro career, died June 16 in Kenosha, Wis. He was 72.

Hartman pitched in three games for the Milwaukee Braves in 1959. After two more years back in the minors, Hartman was traded to the Indians in 1962 and got into eight games there, going 0-1, 3.18 in 17 innings.

■ **Clint Hartung**, a righthander and outfielder who played in the majors for six seasons, died July 8 in Sinton, Texas. He was 87.

Hartung's major league debut in 1947 was highly anticipated, as he'd achieved a good deal of notoriety for his success pitching against big leaguers while he was in the armed forces during World War II. The New York Giants signed him after the war and he went 9-7, 4.57 in his rookie season at the age of 24. That would be his best season as a big leaguer though, and he converted to the outfield full-time in 1951, extending his big league career by a couple of seasons.

■ **Ernie Harwell**, who was a broadcaster for the Tigers for 42 seasons, died May 4 in Novi, Mich. He was 92.

Harwell made his big league broadcasting debut with the Brooklyn Dodgers in August 1948. He also called games for the New York Giants and the Orioles before landing with the Tigers in 1960. Harwell became one of the most renowned announcers in the sport and was a pillar of Michigan sports culture. Harwell received the Ford Frick Award in 1981 He retired from broadcasting in 2002.

APPENDIX

■ **Tommy Henrich**, an outfielder who was a five-time all-star with the Yankees, died Dec. 1, 2009, in Dayton, Ohio. He was 96.

Henrich's career took off after he returned from World War II. He slugged 19 home runs in 1946, his first season back, then began a streak of four straight all-star seasons in 1947. Henrich set career highs for average (.308), home runs (25) and RBIs (100) in 1948, while also leading the AL in both triples (14) and runs (138). He didn't tail off in 1949 either, batting .287 with 24 long balls and 85 runs driven in as the Yankees went on to capture their sixth World Series during Henrich's career. Henrich's career came to a close with him sporting a .282 career average with 183 home runs.

■ **Gene Hermanski**, an outfielder who played in nine big league seasons, died Aug. 9 in Homosassa Springs, Fla. He was 89.

Hermanski was a productive player for the Dodgers in the late 1940s, peaking when he hit .290 with 15 home runs and 15 steals in 1948. His power production dropped off over the next two years, but he continued hitting for a high average. Hermanski was traded to the Cubs in June 1951 and finished his career with the Pirates in 1953.

■ **Billy Hoeft**, a lefthander who pitched in the majors for 15 seasons, died March 16 in Canadian Lakes, Mich. He was 77.

Hoeft worked mostly out of Detroit's bullpen as a 20-year-old rookie in 1952, but also made 10 starts and went 2-7, 4.32 in 125 innings overall. He transitioned to the Tigers' rotation full-time in 1953 and had his breakout season in 1955, going 16-7, 2.99 in 220 innings and making the all-star team. Despite pitching for a fifth-place team, he posted a career-best 20 wins in 1956, though his ERA slipped to 4.06 in 248 innings.

Hoeft was traded to the Red Sox in May 1959, then was dealt again a month later to the Orioles. He went 2-5, 5.56 between his three stops that season, and would spend most of the remainder of his career pitching out of the bullpen for the Orioles, Giants, Cubs and the Milwaukee Braves.

■ **Ken Holcombe**, a righthander who pitched six seasons in the major leagues, died March 15 in Weaverville, N.C. He was 91.

Holcombe spent two seasons as a regular in the White Sox's rotation. He went just 3-10, 4.59 in 1950, but was much better in '51, winning 11 games and posting a 3.79 ERA in 159 innings. That would be the high point of his big league career though, as the White Sox waived him in June 1952.

■ **Dick Kenworthy**, a third baseman who played in parts of six seasons for the White Sox, died April 22 in Kansas City, Mo. He was 69.

Kenworthy logged less than 10 games in four of his six seasons. He saw his first meaningful action with the White Sox in 1967, getting into 50 games and batting .227 with four homers. He continued his part-time role in 1968, batting .221 in 122 at-bats.

■ **Nellie King**, a righthander who pitched in four seasons for the Pirates, died Aug. 11 in Lebanon, Pa. He was 82.

King was a regular in the Pirates' bullpen for two seasons, making 38 appearances in 1956 and 36 in 1957. Arm injuries ended King's career after the 1957 season. He returned to the Pirates as a commentator on the club's radio broadcasts from 1967-75.

■ **Bill Kirk**, a lefthander who made one major league appearance as part of a nine-year pro career, died Oct. 26, 2009, in Lititz, Pa. He was 74.

Kirk's lone big league appearance came Sept. 23, 1961, for the Kansas City Athletics against the Indians, but he was hit hard and allowed four runs over three innings of work.

■ **Ron Klimkowski**, a righthander who pitched four seasons in the majors, died Nov. 13, 2009, in Plainview, N.Y. He was 65.

Klimkowski was a valuable contributor on the Yankees' 1970 team finished second in the American League East. Klimkowski made 45 appearances that season and posted a 2.66 ERA, but that was his only full season in the majors.

■ **Ken Kuhn**, a shortstop who played in parts of three big league seasons with the Indians, died July 16 in Layton, Utah. He was 73.

The Indians signed Kuhn, a promising young infielder, as an 18-year-old bonus baby in 1955. Kuhn appeared in four games for Cleveland in '55 and 67 over the next two years, batting a combined .210 in 81 at-bats. Unfortunately, Kuhn's lack of playing time didn't help his development, and he never made it back to the majors after the '57 season.

■ **Al LaMacchia**, a righthander who pitched in parts of three big league seasons before going on to a successful scouting career, died Sept. 15 in San Antonio. He was 89.

LaMacchia's playing career spanned 15 seasons from 1940-54. He saw most of his big league time with the St. Louis Browns, making 14 appearances there over three seasons from 1943-46 and going a combined 2-1, 5.46 in 28 innings.

As a scout, LaMacchia made an impact on several organizations, working with the Braves from 1961-76 and being involved in the drafting and signing of Dale Murphy and Bruce Benedict. He went on to work for the Blue Jays and helped lay the foundation for their back-to-back World Series titles in 1992 and 1993, as he's credited with helping bring in Dave Stieb and George Bell.

■ **Paul LaPalme**, a lefthander who pitched seven seasons in the majors in the 1950s, died Feb. 7 in Leominster, Mass. He was 86.

LaPalme, a knuckleballer, joined the Pirates' rotation in 1953 but went 8-16, 4.60 in his first extended look as a big league starter. The Pirates traded LaPalme to the Cardinals after the 1954 season and he had his best year in a big league uniform in his first season in St. Louis, working exclusively out of the bullpen and posting a 2.74 ERA in 92 innings to go with a 4-3 record.

■ **Hillis Layne**, a third baseman who played three seasons for the Washington Senators, died Jan. 12 in Signal Mountain, Tenn. He was 91.

Layne earned his first big league callup in September 1941, appearing in 13 games for the Senators. Layne put his baseball career on hold after the '41 season however, entering the military and losing the next two seasons to serve in World War II. Layne returned to the game in 1944, rejoining the Senators, and rediscovered his stroke in 1945. He upped his average to .299 with 14 RBIs in 147 at-bats, but that would be his last big league action.

■ **Jose Lima**, a righthander who pitched 13 seasons in the majors and was an all-star in 1999, died May 23 in Pasadena, Calif. He was 37.

Lima was well known for his vibrant personality just as much as for his pitching ability. He had his finest season in 1999, when he went 21-10, 3.58 for Houston, made the National League all-star team and finished fourth in NL Cy Young Award voting. But Lima was never able to sustain that success, and he last pitched in the majors in 2006 with the Mets.

■ **Billy Loes**, a righthander who pitched in the majors for 11 seasons, died July 16 in Tucson, Ariz. He was 80.

Loes was a mainstay in the Brooklyn Dodgers' rotation for four seasons, from 1952-55. Loes' best major league season came in 1952, when he went 13-8, 2.69 in 187 innings. He won at least 10 games in each of his four full seasons in Brooklyn and helped the Dodgers reach three World Series, winning it all in 1955.

■ **Hal Manders**, a righthander who pitched in the major leagues for parts of three seasons, died Jan. 21 in Waukee, Iowa. He was 92.

Manders earned his first big league callup in August 1941 when the Tigers summoned him to the majors and he made eight appearances, all in relief, for Detroit down the stretch. He remained a part of the Tigers' bullpen during the 1942 season, making 18 appearances and going 2-0, 4.09. His only other big league time came in brief stints with the Tigers and Cubs in 1946.

■ **Morrie Martin**, a righthander who pitched in the majors for 10 seasons, died March 25 in Washington, Mo. He was 87.

Martin didn't get a full season in the majors until age 28 in 1951 with the Philadelphia Athletics, who had picked him up in the Rule 5 draft. Martin made the most of his first season with the A's, going 11-4, 3.78 in 138 innings, seeing time as both a starter and reliever. He wasn't able to build on that momentum in 1952 though, as his pitching hand was struck by a line drive in his fifth start, injuring it badly enough that he couldn't pitch again that season. He shuffled between a handful of organizations over the rest of his career, with his last big league stop coming with the Cubs in 1959.

■ **Rogelio Martinez**, a righthander who pitched in two major league games, died May 24 in Waterford, Conn. He was 91.

A native of Cuba, Martinez received his only big league callup in July 1950, working in two games for the Washington Senators.

■ **Keli McGregor**, who was president of the Rockies organization at the time of his passing, died April 20 in Salt Lake City. He was 47.

A former college football player at Colorado State, McGregor joined the Rockies as assistant director of operations in 1993 and rose up the organization to become team president in 2001.

■ **Bill Moisan**, a righthander who pitched in three major league games, died April 9 in Brentwood, N.H. He was 84.

Moisan pitched eight seasons in the minors before getting his only big league callup with the Cubs at the tail end of the 1953 season. Moisan worked in three games, all in relief.

■ **Curt Motton**, an outfielder who played in eight major league seasons, died Jan. 21 in Parkton, Md. He was 69.

Motton broke into the majors with the Orioles in 1967 after four seasons in the minors and was a useful contributor off the bench during Baltimore's run as one of the American League's dominant teams in the late 1960s and early '70s. He hit .303 in 89 at-bats for the 1969 club and his most memorable contribution was his walk-off single in the 11th inning of Game 2 of the '69 AL Championship Series against the Twins. Although Motton never received much playing time, he was known as a positive force in the clubhouse.

■ **Jim Pagliaroni**, a catcher who played parts of 11 seasons in the major leagues, died April 3 in Grass Valley, Calif. He was 72.

Pagliaroni was a productive offensive catcher throughout his career by the standards of his era. After hitting 14 homers and batting .258 for the Red Sox in 1962, Pagliaroni was traded to the Pirates and was their starting catcher for the next four seasons. He hit a career best .295 in 302 at-bats for the Pirates in 1964. Pagliaroni hit double-digit home runs in each of his four years as Pittsburgh's regular, highlighted by his 17 homers in 1965.

■ **Ed Palmquist**, a righthander who pitched in two big league seasons, died July 10 in Santa Maria, Calif. He was 77.

Palmquist reached the majors in 1960 at age 27 and got into 22 games for the Dodgers, all in relief, and went 0-1, 2.54. He made just five appearances for Los Angeles in 1961 before being traded to the Twins, where he got into nine games and went 1-1, 9.43.

■ **John Purdin**, a righthander who pitched for the Dodgers for four seasons, died March 28 in Charleston, S.C. He was 67.

The Dodgers signed Purdin in 1964 and he quickly made his way to the big leagues. The Dodgers called him up that September and he threw a two-hit shutout against the Pirates on Sept. 30 in his first career start. Purdin saw his most extensive action as a big leaguer in 1968, pitching in 35 games and going 2-3, 3.05 in 56 innings.

■ **Herman Reich**, a first baseman who played one season in the big leagues, died Oct. 22, 2009, in Fallbrook, Calif. He was 91.

As a 31-year-old rookie, Reich was the Cubs' regular first baseman for most of the 1949 season, appearing in 108 games and batting .280 with three home runs and 34 RBIs.

■ **Tommy Reis**, a righthander who pitched one season in the majors as part of a 20-year pro career, died Nov. 6, 2009, in Ocala, Fla. He was 95.

Reis made his only trip to the big leagues in 1938, pitching in four games for the Phillies, all in relief, before being sold to the Boston Bees in late April. He made four more relief appearances for Boston before being sent back to the minors.

■ **Robin Roberts**, a Hall of Fame righthander who pitched 19 seasons in the majors, died May 6 in Temple Terrace, Fla. He was 83.

The ace of the Phillies' 1950 National League champion Whiz Kids, Roberts was one of the pre-eminent pitchers of his generation. He broke into the majors in 1948 then won 15 games for the Phillies in 1949. Roberts then reeled off a string on dominant seasons beginning in 1950, when he went 20-11, 3.02. He won at least 20 games in six consecutive seasons from 1950-55. He made the all-star team in each of those seasons and again in 1956. The best of those seasons came in 1952, when Roberts went 28-7, 2.59 and finished second in NL MVP voting. Roberts ended his career in 1966 with a 286-245, 3.41 lifetime record and was inducted into the Hall of Fame in 1976.

■ **Jeriome Robertson**, a lefthander who pitched in the majors for three seasons, died May 29 in Exeter, Calif.. He was 33.

The 2003 season was Robertson's only full year in the majors, as he went 15-9, 5.10 as a full-time member of the Astros' rotation. He was traded to Cleveland after that season but made only eight appearances there in 2004.

■ **Jim Roland**, a lefthander who spent 10 seasons in the major leagues, died March 6 in Shelby, N.C. He was 67.

Roland spent his first full year in the majors in 1964, making 30 appearances, including 13 starts, for the Twins as a 21-year-old and going 2-6, 4.12. He was sent back to the minors for most of the next two seasons before getting back to the majors as a full-time reliever in 1967. Roland was sold to the Athletics before the 1969 season and had a successful three-year run with the A's. He went 5-1, 2.20 in 86 innings in his first season with Oakland in 1969 and was nearly as outstanding the next year, posting a 3-3, 2.72 mark in 43 innings. He was still effective in 1971 but was sold to the Yankees early in the 1972 season, his last in the majors.

■ **Bob Roselli**, a catcher who played parts of five seasons in the major leagues, died Nov. 5, 2009, in Roseville, Calif. He was 77.

Roselli reached the big leagues for the first time with the Milwaukee Braves in 1955. He saw his most meaningful big league action with the White Sox, making 22 appearances in 1961 and hitting .263 with four RBIs in 38 at-bats. He got into 35 games the next year but hit just .188 in 64 at-bats.

■ **Jay Schlueter**, an outfielder who played briefly for the Astros in 1971, died May 13 in Phoenix. He was 60.

■ **Howie Schultz**, a first baseman who played six seasons in the majors in the 1940s, died Oct. 30, 2009, in Clarksa, Minn. He was 87.

Schultz was the Brooklyn Dodgers' everyday first baseman in 1944 and hit .255 with 11 long balls, but he would spend most of the 1945 season back in the minors. Schultz got back to the big leagues full-time in 1946 and hit .253 over 249 at-bats. Schultz became expendable when the Dodgers brought Jackie Robinson on board in 1947. He left baseball and pursued a career in the National Basketball Association, where he played three seasons.

■ **George Steinbrenner**, who had owned the Yankees franchise since 1973, died July 13 in Tampa. He was 80.

When Steinbrenner bought the Yankees, they were in the midst of a decade of decline. They hadn't won a World Series since 1962 and hadn't been to one since 1964, with five losing seasons in the eight prior to Steinbrenner's arrival. After going 80-82 in 1973, New York had a losing record just four more times in the Steinbrenner era, while winning seven World Series.

While Steinbrenner will be well remembered for his free spending and his revolving door of managers, there was far more to his ownership. Under Steinbrenner, the Yankees developed their own television network and their own ballpark food business, innovative ideas that other sports teams have copied. They went from a franchise that Steinbrenner and his partners bought for $8.7 million to a franchise that Forbes valued at $1.6 billion after the 2009 season.

■ **Jerry Stephenson**, a righthander who pitched in seven big league seasons, died June 6 in Anaheim. He was 66.

Stephenson mostly saw limited action as both a starter and reliever during his career with the Red Sox, Dodgers and the Seattle Pilots. Only 19 when he made his big league debut with Boston in 1963, Stephenson's most active big league season came in 1968, when he went 2-8, 5.64 in 69 innings for the Red Sox. Stephenson went on to a long career as a scout for the Dodgers and Red Sox.

■ **George Strickland**, a shortstop who played 10 seasons in the big leagues, died Feb. 21 in New Orleans. He was 84.

A glove-first shortstop, Strickland took over the Pirates' everyday job at the position in 1951. He was splitting time between short and second base in 1952 when the Pirates dealt him to the Indians that August. Strickland had easily his best offensive season in his first full year in an Indians uniform in 1953, batting .284 with five homers and 47 RBIs. He hit .213 as the regular shortstop for Cleveland's pennant-winning 1954 squad, although he broke his jaw that July and missed over a month of the season. Strickland spent one more season as Cleveland's everyday shortstop, batting .209 in

1955, before he was reduced to more of a utility role in 1956. After his playing career ended in 1960, Strickland served two separate stints as the Indians' manager, in 1964 and 1966.

■ **George Susce**, a righthander who pitched for five seasons in the majors, died May 8 in Matlacha, Fla. He was 78.

Susce made 29 appearances, including 15 starts, for the Red Sox as a rookie in 1955, going 9-7, 3.06 in 144 innings. He pitched mostly out of the bullpen over the next two years, then was placed on waivers early in the 1958 season. Susce made nine appearances for the Tigers in 1959 but called it a career after that season.

■ **Bobby Thomson**, the outfielder who hit "The Shot Heard 'Round The World" in 1951, died Aug. 16 in Savannah, Ga. He was 86.

Thomson's big league career spanned 15 seasons, but his place in the sport's history was solidified with one swing of the bat, when he went deep off Brooklyn's Ralph Branca to win the third game of the National League playoff between the Dodgers and his Giants. Although Thomson will always be remembered for the homer off Branca, he was by no means a one hit wonder. Thomson was a three-time all-star who hit over 20 home runs seven times in his 15-year career. The '51 season was finest year, as he hit a career-high 32 homers and drove in 108 runs. He finished his career with 1,705 hits, a .270 lifetime average and 264 home runs.

■ **Ken Walters**, an outfielder who played three seasons in the majors in the 1960s, died Jan. 26 in San Ramon, Calif. He was 76.

Walters earned a spot on the Phillies' Opening Day roster in 1960, and he would be a regular in the club's outfield that season, batting .239 with eight home runs over 426 at-bats. His playing time decreased in 1961 and he was sold to the Reds after the season.

■ **Jim Waugh**, a righthander who pitched two seasons for the Pirates, died Feb. 16 in Rock Hill, S.C. He was 76.

All of Waugh's big league experience came before his 20th birthday. He made 17 appearances for the Pirates in 1952 and 29 in 1953, going a combined 5-11, 6.43.

APPENDIX